Encyclopedia of the American Constitution

Editorial Board

Encyclopedia of the American Constitution

LEONARD W. LEVY, Editor-in-Chief
Claremont Graduate School, Claremont, California

KENNETH L. KARST, Associate Editor
University of California, Los Angeles

DENNIS J. MAHONEY, Assistant Editor
Claremont Graduate School, Claremont, California

MACMILLAN PUBLISHING COMPANY
A Division of Macmillan, Inc.
NEW YORK
Collier Macmillan Publishers
LONDON

Macmillan Publishing Company
A Division of Macmillan, Inc.
866 Third Avenue, New York, NY 10022

Collier Macmillan Canada, Inc.

Printed in the United States of America

printing number
1 2 3 4 5 6 7 8 9 10

Library of Congress Catalog in Publication Data

Encyclopedia of the American Constitution.

Includes index.
1. United States—Constitutional Law—Dictionaries.
I. Levy, Leonard Williams, 1923– II. Karst, Kenneth L. III. Mahoney, Dennis J.
KF4548.E53 1986 342.73'023'03 86–3038
ISBN 0–02–918610–2 347.3022303
ISBN (this edition) 0-02-918695-1

STAFF:

Charles E. Smith, *Publisher*
Elly Dickason, *Project Editor*
Morton I. Rosenberg, *Production Manager*
Joan Greenfield, *Designer*

Complete and unabridged edition 1990

Contents

Preface

In the summer of 1787 delegates from the various states met in Philadelphia; because they succeeded in their task, we now call their assembly the Constitutional Convention. By September 17 the delegates had completed the framing of the Constitution of the United States. The year 1987 marks the bicentennial of the Constitutional Convention. This Encyclopedia is intended as a scholarly and patriotic enterprise to commemorate the bicentennial. No encyclopedia on the Constitution has heretofore existed. This work seeks to fill the need for a single comprehensive reference work treating the subject in a multidisciplinary way.

The Constitution is a legal document, but it is also an institution: a charter for government, a framework for building a nation, an aspect of the American civic culture. Even in its most limited sense as a body of law, the Constitution includes, in today's understanding, nearly two centuries' worth of court decisions interpreting the charter. Charles Evans Hughes, then governor of New York, made this point pungently in a 1907 speech: "We are under a Constitution, but the Constitution is what the judges say it is." Hughes's remark was, if anything, understated. If the Constitution sometimes seems to be chiefly the product of judicial decisions, it is also what Presidents say it is—and legislators, and police officers, and ordinary citizens, too. In the final analysis today's Constitution is the product of the whole political system and the whole history of the many peoples who have become a nation. "Constitutional law is history," wrote Professor Felix Frankfurter in 1937, "But equally true is it that American history is constitutional law."

Thus an Encyclopedia of the American Constitution would be incomplete if it did not seek to bridge the disciplines of history, law, and political science. Both in identifying subjects and in selecting authors we have sought to build those bridges. The subjects fall into five general categories: doctrinal concepts of constitutional law (about fifty-five percent of the total words); people (about fifteen percent); judicial decisions, mostly of the Supreme Court of the United States (about fifteen percent); public acts, such as statutes, treaties, and executive orders (about five percent); and historical periods (about ten percent). (These percentages are exclusive of the appendices—printed at the end of the final volume—and bibliographies.) The articles vary in length, from brief definitions of terms to treatments of major subjects of constitutional doctrine, which may be as long as 6,000 words, and articles on periods of constitutional history, which may be even longer. A fundamental concept like "due process of law" is the subject of three 6,000-word articles: Procedural Due Process of Law (Civil), Procedural Due Process of Law (Criminal), and Substantive Due Process of Law. In addition, there is a 1,500-word article on the historical background of due process of law. The standard length of an article on a major topic, such as the First Amendment, is 6,000 words; but each principal component of the amendment—Freedom of Speech, Freedom of the Press, Religious Liberty, Separation of Church and State—is also the subject of a 6,000-word article. There are also other, shorter articles on other aspects of the amendment.

The reader will find an article on almost any topic reasonably conceivable. At the beginning of the first volume there is a list of all entries, to spare the reader from paging through the volumes to determine whether particular entries exist. This list, like many another efficiency device, may be a mixed blessing; we commend to our readers the joys of encyclopedia-browsing.

The Encyclopedia's articles are arranged alphabetically and are liberally cross-referenced by the use of small capital letters indicating the titles of related articles. A reader may thus begin with an article focused on one feature of his or her field of inquiry, and move easily to other articles on other aspects of the subject. For example, one who wished to read about the civil rights movement of the 1950s and 1960s might begin with the large-scale subject of Civil Rights itself; or with a particular doctrinal topic (Desegregation, or Miscegenation), or an article focused on a narrower factual setting (Public Accommodations, or Sit-Ins). Alternatively, the reader might start with an important public act (Civil Rights Act of 1964), or with a biographical entry on a particular person (Martin Luther King, Jr., or Earl Warren). Other places to start would be articles on the events in particular eras (Warren Court or Constitutional History, 1945–1961 and 1961–1977). The reader can use any of these articles to find all the others, simply by following the network of cross-references. A Subject Index and a Name Index, at the end of the last volume, list all the pages on which the reader can find, for example, references to the freedom of the press or to Abraham Lincoln. Full citations to all the judicial decisions mentioned in the Encyclopedia are set out in the Case Index, also at the end of the final volume.

The Encyclopedia's approximately 2,100 articles have been written by 262 authors. Most of the authors fall into three groups: 41 historians, 164 lawyers (including academics, practitioners, and judges), and 53 political scientists. The others are identified with the fields of economics and journalism. Our lawyer-authors, who represent about three-fifths of all our writers, have produced about half the words in the Encyclopedia. Historian-authors, although constituting only about sixteen percent of all authors, produced about one-third of the words; political scientists, although responsible for only one-sixth of the words, wrote more than a quarter of the articles. Whether this information is an occasion for surprise may depend on the reader's occupation.

In addition to the interdisciplinary balance, the reader will find geographical balance. Although a large number of contributors is drawn from the School of Law of the University of California, Los Angeles, the Claremont Colleges, and other institutions in California, most come from the Northeast, including twelve from Harvard University, thirteen from Yale University, and nine from Columbia University. Every region of the United States is represented, however, and there are many contributors from the South (Duke University, University of Virginia, University of North Carolina, University of Texas, etc.), from the Midwest (University of Chicago, University of Notre Dame, University of Wisconsin, University of Michigan, etc.), and from the Northwest (University of Oregon, Portland State University, University of Washington, etc.). There are several contributors from foreign countries, including Austria, Canada, and Great Britain.

Every type of academic environment is represented among the eighty-six colleges and universities at which the authors work. The contributors include scholars based at large public universities, smaller state colleges, Ivy League universities, private liberal arts colleges, and religiously affiliated institutions. Not all of the authors are drawn from academia; one is a member of Congress and nine are federal judges. In addition, other government offices, research institutions, libraries, newspaper staffs, and law firms are represented.

Each article is signed by its author; we have encouraged the authors to write commentaries, in essay form, not merely describing and analyzing their subjects but expressing their own views. On the subject of the Constitution, specialists and citizens alike will hold divergent viewpoints. In inviting authors to contribute to the Encyclopedia, we have sought to include a range of views. The reader should be alert to the possibility that a cross-referenced article may discuss similar issues from a different perspective—especially if those issues have been the subject of recent controversy. We hope this awareness will encourage readers to read more widely and to expand the range of their interests concerning the Constitution.

Planning of the Encyclopedia began in 1978, and production began in 1979; nearly all articles were written by 1985. Articles on decisions of the Supreme Court include cases decided during the Court's October 1984 Term, which ended in July 1985. Given the ways in which American constitutional law develops, some of the subjects treated here are moving targets. In a project like this one, some risk of obsolescence is necessarily present; at this writing we can predict with confidence that some of our authors will wish they had one last chance to modify their articles to take account of decisions in the 1985 Term. To minimize these concerns we have asked the authors of articles on doctrinal subjects to concentrate on questions that are fundamental and of enduring significance.

We have insisted that the authors keep to the constitutional aspects of their various topics. There is much to be said about abortion or antitrust law, or about foreign affairs or mental illness, that is not comprehended within the fields of constitutional law and history. In effect, the title of every article might be extended by the phrase ". . . and the Constitution." This statement is emphatically true of the biographical entries; every author was admonished to avoid writing a conventional biography and, instead, to write an appreciation of the subject's significance in American constitutional law and history.

We have also asked authors to remember that the Encyclopedia will be used by readers whose interests and training vary widely, from the specialist in constitutional law or history to the high school student who is writing a paper. Not every article will be within the grasp of that student, but the vast majority of articles are accessible to the general reader who is neither historian nor lawyer not political scientist. Although a constitutional specialist on a particular subject will probably find the articles on that specialty too general, the same specialist may profit from reading articles in other fields. A commerce clause expert may not be an expert on the First Amendment; and First Amendment scholars may know little about criminal justice. The deluge of cases, problems, and information flowing from courts, other agencies of government, law reviews, and scholarly monographs has forced constitutional scholarship to become specialized, like all branches of the liberal arts. Few, if any, can keep in command of it all and remain up to date. The Encyclopedia organizes in readable form an epitome of all that is known and understood on the subject of the Constitution by the nation's specialist scholars.

Because space is limited, no encyclopedia article can pretend to exhaust its subject. Moreover, an encyclopedia is not the same kind of contribution to knowledge as a monograph based on original research in the primary sources is. An encyclopedia is a compendium of knowledge, a reference work addressed to a wide variety of interested audiences: students in secondary school, college, graduate school, and law school; scholars and teachers of constitutional law and history; lawyers; legislators; jurists; government officials; journalists; and educated citizens who care about their Constitution and its history. Typically, an article in this Encyclopedia contains not only cross-references to other articles but also a bibliography that will aid the reader in pursuing his or her own study of the subject.

In addition to the articles, the Encyclopedia comprises several appendices. There is a copy of the complete text of the Constitution as well as of George Washington's Letter of Transmittal. A glossary defines legal terms that may be unfamiliar to readers who are not lawyers. Two chronologies will help put topics in historical perspective; one is a detailed chronology of the framing and ratification of the Constitution and the Bill of Rights, and the other is a more general chronology of American constitutional history. Finally, there are three indices: the first is an index of court cases, with the complete citation to every case mentioned in the Encyclopedia (to which is attached a brief guide to the use of legal citations); the second is an index of names; and the third is a general topical index.

For some readers an encyclopedia article will be a stopping-point, but the articles in this Encyclopedia are intended to be doorways leading to ideas and to additional reading, and perhaps to the reader's development of independent judgment about the Constitution. After all, when the American Constitution's tricentennial is celebrated in 2087, what the Constitution has become will depend less on the views of specialists than on the beliefs and behavior of the nation's citizens.

June 1986

Leonard W. Levy
Kenneth L. Karst
Dennis J. Mahoney

Acknowledgments

The editors are grateful to our authors, to our editorial board, and to our advisory committee (all listed in the early pages of the Encyclopedia) for their labors and advice during these seven years.

The editors acknowledge with utmost appreciation the financial support given to this project by four institutions. The National Endowment for the Humanities made a major grant which the Weingart Foundation of Los Angeles matched. The Macmillan Publishing Company and The Claremont Graduate School also handsomely underwrote this encyclopedia. The earliest private funds came from a small group of southern California attorneys and foundations: The Times Mirror Foundation; James Greene, Judge Dyson William Cox and Janice T. Cox, Robert P. Hastings, James E. Ludlam, and J. Patrick Waley; Musick, Peeler & Garrett; and The Ralph B. Lloyd Foundation.

The Claremont Graduate School and University Center also provided facilities and logistical support for the Encyclopedia. Former President Joseph B. Platt gave the project his encouragement. Executive Vice-President Paul A. Albrecht significantly assisted our grant applications from the outset and remained helpful throughout the project. Associate Dean Christopher N. Oberg has seen to the efficient management of administrative aspects of the project. Sandra Glass, now of the Keck Foundation, provided invaluable aid while she was associated with The Claremont Graduate School. We are also grateful for the unflagging support of the School of Law of the University of California, Los Angeles, and its deans, William D. Warren and Susan Westerberg Prager.

A succession of graduate students at The Claremont Graduate School worked on the project as editorial assistants, research assistants, typists, and proofreaders. First was Dr. David Gordon, who also acted as assistant editor for one year, and who wrote over one hundred of the articles before going on to law school. Dr. Michael E. DeGolyer and Susan Marie Meyer served ably as editorial assistants. Others who worked on the project were Michael Walker, Kenneth V. Benesh, Susan

Orr, Suzanne Kovacs, Dr. Steven Varvis, Dr. Patrick Delana, and Paul R. Huard.

The secretaries in the History Department of The Claremont Graduate School have typed thousands of letters and hundreds of articles, in addition to performing numerous other small tasks to keep the project going; particular thanks are due to Lelah Mullican. The Claremont Graduate School Academic Computing Center and its director, Gunther Freehill, showed us how to automate our record keeping and provided facilities for that purpose.

Most important, we gratefully acknowledge the support of Charles E. Smith, Vice-President and Publisher, Professional Books Division, Macmillan Publishing Company, and of Elly Dickason, our editor at Macmillan. Mr. Smith actively and continuously supported the project from its early days and by his prodding kept us on a Stakhanovite schedule. Ms. Dickason performed arduous labors with supreme professional skill and unfailing good humor.

Finally, we thank Elyse Levy and Smiley Karst for their own indispensable contributions to this project. A personal dedication page seems inappropriate for a reference work, otherwise this Encyclopedia would have been dedicated to them. Natalie Glucklich, Renee Karst, Aaron Harris, and Adam Harris, the grandchildren of the senior editors, entered the world without realizing that the Encyclopedia project was underway. They assisted not a whit, but we acknowledge our pleasure in seeing their names in print.

List of Articles

Advisory Opinion	*Jonathan Varat*
Affected with a Public Interest	*Harry N. Scheiber*
Affirmative Action	*Henry J. Abraham*
Afroyim v. Rusk	*Michael E. Parrish*
Age Discrimination	*Theodore Eisenberg*
Age Discrimination Act	*Theodore Eisenberg*
Agnello v. United States	*Jacob W. Landynski*
Agricultural Adjustment Act of 1933	*David Gordon*
Agricultural Adjustment Act of 1938	*David Gordon*
Agricultural Marketing Agreement Act	*David Gordon*
Aguilar v. Felton	*Leonard W. Levy*
Aguilar v. Texas	*Jacob W. Landynski*
Ake v. Oklahoma	*Kenneth L. Karst*
Albertson v. Subversive Activities Control Board	*Leonard W. Levy*
Alderman v. United States	*Herman Schwartz*
Alexander v. Holmes County Board of Education	*Kenneth L. Karst*
Alien	*Kenneth L. Karst*
Alien and Sedition Acts	*Merrill D. Peterson*
Alien Registration Act	*Paul L. Murphy*
All Deliberate Speed	*Kenneth L. Karst*
Allen v. Wright	*Kenneth L. Karst*
Allen-Bradley Local v. Wisconsin Employee Relations Board	*David Gordon*
Allgeyer v. Louisiana	*David Gordon*
Allied Structural Steel Co. v. Spannaus	*Kenneth L. Karst*
Almeida-Sanchez v. United States	*Jacob W. Landynski*
Ambach v. Norwick	*Kenneth L. Karst*
Amending Process	*Walter Dellinger*
American Civil Liberties Union	*Norman Dorsen*
American Communications Association v. Douds	*Martin Shapiro*
American Indians and the Constitution	*Carole E. Goldberg-Ambrose*
American Insurance Company v. Canter	*Leonard W. Levy*
American Jewish Congress	*Leo Pfeffer*
American System	*Merrill D. Peterson*
Ames, Fisher	*David Gordon*
Amicus Curiae	*Samuel Krislov*
Amnesty	*Dennis J. Mahoney*
Ancillary Jurisdiction	*Kenneth L. Karst*
Annexation of Texas	*William M. Wiecek*
Antidiscrimination Legislation	*Theodore Eisenberg*
Antifederalist Constitutional Thought	*Murray Dry*
Antitrust Law and the Constitution	*Arthur I. Rosett*
Apex Hosiery Company v. Leader	*David Gordon*
Appalachian Electric Power Company, United States v.	*David Gordon*

Norris-LaGuardia Act	*David Gordon*
North Atlantic Treaty	*Burns H. Weston*
Northern Pipeline Co. v. Marathon Pipe Line Co.	*Kenneth L. Karst*
Northern Securities Co. v. United States	*David Gordon*
Northwestern Fertilizer Co. v. Hyde Park	*Leonard W. Levy*
Northwest Ordinance	*Leonard W. Levy*
Notice	*Stephen C. Yeazell*
Noxious Products Doctrine	*Dennis J. Mahoney*
Nullification	*William M. Wiecek*
Obiter Dictum	*David Gordon*
Obligation of Contracts	*Dennis J. Mahoney*
O'Brien, United States v.	*Kenneth L. Karst*
O'Brien v. Brown	*Ward E. Y. Elliott*
Obscenity	*Steven H. Shiffrin*
O'Connor, Sandra Day	*Edward J. Erler*
O'Connor v. Donaldson	*Kenneth L. Karst*
Office of Management and Budget	*Harold H. Bruff*
Ogden v. Saunders	*Leonard W. Levy*
Oliver, In Re	*Leonard W. Levy*
Oliver v. United States	*Leonard W. Levy*
Olmstead v. United States	*Herman Schwartz*
Olney, Richard	*David Gordon*
Olsen v. Nebraska ex rel. Reference & Bond Association	*David Gordon*
Omnibus Act	*William M. Wiecek*
Omnibus Crime Control and Safe Streets Act	*Paul L. Murphy*
One Person, One Vote	*Ward E. Y. Elliott*
On Lee v. United States	*Herman Schwartz*
Open Housing Laws	*Theodore Eisenberg*
Opinion of the Court	*Dennis J. Mahoney*
Oral Argument	*Kenneth L. Karst*
Ordered Liberty	*Henry J. Abraham*
Ordinance of 1784	*Dennis J. Mahoney*
Oregon v. Elstad	*Leonard W. Levy*
Oregon v. Mitchell	*Theodore Eisenberg*
Organized Crime Control Act	*Paul L. Murphy*
Original Jurisdiction	*Kenneth L. Karst*
Original Package Doctrine	*Edward L. Barrett*
Orozco v. Texas	*Leonard W. Levy*
Osborn v. Bank of the United States	*Leonard W. Levy* *Kenneth L. Karst*
O'Shea v. Littleton	*Kenneth L. Karst*
Otis, James, Jr.	*William J. Cuddihy*
Overbreadth	*Jonathan Varat*
Overruling	*James R. Asperger*
Overt Acts Test	*Leonard W. Levy*

LIST OF ARTICLES

Wheaton, Henry	*Paul Finkelman*
Wheeler, Burton K.	*Leonard W. Levy*
Whiskey Rebellion	*Merrill D. Peterson*
White, Byron R.	*Jonathan Varat*
White, Edward D.	*Michael E. Parrish*
White, United States v.	*Herman Schwartz*
White Court	*Benno C. Schmidt, Jr.*
Whitney v. California	*Martin Shaprio*
Whittaker, Charles	*Michael E. Parrish*
Wickard v. Filburn	*Leonard W. Levy*
Wickersham, George	*David Gordon*
Widmar v. Vincent	*Kenneth L. Karst*
Wieman v. Updegraff	*Michael E. Parrish*
Wigmore, John Henry	*Richard B. Bernstein*
Wilkes Cases	*William J. Cuddihy*
Williams, Roger	*Thomas Curry*
Williams v. Florida	*Leonard W. Levy*
Williams v. Mississippi	*Leonard W. Levy*
Williams v. Vermont	*Kenneth L. Karst*
Williamson, Hugh	*Dennis J. Mahoney*
Williamson v. Lee Optical Company	*Dennis J. Mahoney*
Willoughby, Westel W.	*Dennis J. Mahoney*
Willson v. Black Bird Creek Marsh Company	*Leonard W. Levy*
Wilmot Proviso	*Paul Finkelman*
Wilson, James	*Ralph Rossum*
Wilson, Woodrow	*Dennis J. Mahoney*
Wilson v. New	*David Gordon*
Winship, In Re	*David Gordon*
Wiretapping	*Herman Schwartz*
Wirt, William	*Paul Finkelman*
Wisconsin v. Yoder	*Richard E. Morgan*
Wolf v. Colorado	*Jacob W. Landynski*
Wolff Packing Company v. Court of Industrial Relations	*David Gordon*
Wolman v. Walter	*Richard E. Morgan*
Wong Kim Ark, United States v.	*Leonard W. Levy*
Wong Sun v. United States	*Jacob W. Landynski*
Wood v. Strickland	*Theodore Eisenberg*
Woodbury, Levi	*Paul Finkelman*
Woodruff v. Parham	*Leonard W. Levy*
Woods, William B.	*Charles W. McCurdy*
Woods v. Cloyd W. Miller Company	*David Gordon*
Workers' Compensation Legislation	*William B. Gould*
Wortman, Tunis	*Leonard W. Levy*
Wright v. Vinton Branch of Mountain Trust Bank of Roanoke	*Leonard W. Levy*

List of Contributors

Benjamin Aaron
Professor of Law, Emeritus
University of California, Los Angeles

LABOR AND THE ANTITRUST LAWS

Henry J. Abraham
James Hart Professor of Government and Foreign Affairs
University of Virginia

AFFIRMATIVE ACTION
APPOINTMENT OF SUPREME COURT JUSTICES
BIDDLE, FRANCIS
FUNDAMENTAL RIGHTS
HARLAN, JOHN MARSHALL (1833–1911)
ORDERED LIBERTY

Norman Abrams
Professor of Law
University of California, Los Angeles

BALLEW V. GEORGIA
BURCH V. LOUISIANA
JURY SIZE
JURY UNANIMITY
LAW ENFORCEMENT AND FEDERAL-STATE RELATIONS

David Adamany
Professor of Law and Political Science, and President
Wayne State University

CAMPAIGN FINANCING
ELECTIONS, REGULATION OF
POLITICAL PARTIES IN CONSTITUTIONAL LAW
PRIMARY ELECTIONS

Lee A. Albert
Professor of Law
State University of New York, Buffalo

FEDERAL GRANTS-IN-AID

Francis A. Allen
Edson R. Sunderland Professor of Law
University of Michigan

RIGHT TO COUNSEL

Reginald Alleyne
Professor of Law
University of California, Los Angeles

EMPLOYMENT DISCRIMINATION

George Anastaplo
Professor of Law
Loyola University of Chicago Law School
Lecturer in the Liberal Arts
The University of Chicago

POLITICAL PHILOSOPHY OF THE CONSTITUTION

Alison Grey Anderson
Professor of Law
University of California, Los Angeles

SECURITIES LAW AND THE CONSTITUTION

* Deceased.

David A. Anderson
Rosenberg Centennial Professor of Law
The University of Texas at Austin

GAG ORDER
NEW YORK TIMES CO. V. SULLIVAN
SEDITIOUS LIBEL

Michael R. Asimow
Professor of Law
University of California, Los Angeles

NATIONAL POLICE POWER
SIXTEENTH AMENDMENT

James R. Asperger
United States Attorney
Los Angeles

ARREST WARRANT
OVERRULING
SEARCH WARRANT
VAGRANCY LAWS

Carl A. Auerbach
Professor of Law
University of Minnesota, Twin Cities

SUBVERSIVE ADVOCACY

Barbara Allen Babcock
Ernest W. McFarland Professor of Law
Stanford Law School

ARGERSINGER V. HAMLIN
ASH, UNITED STATES V.
BETTS V. BRADY
ESCOBEDO V. ILLINOIS
FARETTA V. CALIFORNIA
FRUIT OF THE POISONOUS TREE
JOHNSON V. ZERBST
KIRBY V. ILLINOIS
LINEUP
MASSIAH V. UNITED STATES
POWELL V. ALABAMA
PRETRIAL DISCLOSURE
WADE, UNITED STATES V.

Stewart Abercrombie Baker
Attorney
Steptoe & Johnson, Washington, D.C.

STEVENS, JOHN PAUL

Lance Banning
Professor of History
University of Kentucky

MADISON, JAMES

Sotirios A. Barber
Professor of Government
University of Notre Dame

CHECKS AND BALANCES
DELEGATION OF POWER
ENUMERATED POWERS
GENERAL WELFARE CLAUSE
INHERENT POWERS
INTERGOVERNMENTAL IMMUNITIES
INTERPOSITION
LIMITED GOVERNMENT
NECESSARY AND PROPER CLAUSE
TENTH AMENDMENT
UNWRITTEN CONSTITUTION

Edward L. Barrett, Jr.
Professor of Law
University of California, Davis

DIRECT AND INDIRECT TAXES
EXCISE TAX
FOREIGN COMMERCE
IMPORT-EXPORT CLAUSE
IMPORTS
JURISDICTION TO TAX
ORIGINAL PACKAGE DOCTRINE
STATE REGULATION OF COMMERCE
STATE TAXATION OF COMMERCE
TAKING AND SPENDING POWERS

Paul M. Bator
John P. Wilson Professor of Law
The University of Chicago

JUDICIAL SYSTEM
JUDICIARY ACT OF 1789

Maurice G. Baxter
Professor of History
Indiana University

WEBSTER, DANIEL

Derrick A. Bell, Jr.
Professor of Law
Harvard Law School

DESEGREGATION

Herman Belz
Professor of History
University of Maryland

CONSTITUTIONAL HISTORY, 1861–1865
CONSTITUTIONALISM AND THE AMERICAN FOUNDING
THEORIES OF THE UNION
WAITE, MORRISON R.

Paul Bender
Dean and Professor of Law
Arizona State University

RETROACTIVITY OF JUDICIAL DECISIONS

Michael Les Benedict
Professor of History
The Ohio State University

CONSTITUTIONAL HISTORY, 1865–1877

Raoul Berger
Professor of Law, Emeritus
Harvard Law School

IMPEACHMENT

Walter Berns
John M. Olin Distinguished Scholar in Constitutional and Legal Studies
American Enterprise Institute
Professorial Lecturer
Georgetown University

CAPITAL PUNISHMENT CASES (1972)
CAPITAL PUNISHMENT CASES (1976)
NATURAL RIGHTS

Richard B. Bernstein
Research Curator, U.S. Constitution Exhibition
The New York Public Library

BALDWIN, ROGER
BOUDIN, LOUIS
BRANT, IRVING
CARR, ROBERT
COHEN, MORRIS R.
CRIMINAL SYNDICALISM LAWS
CROSSKEY, WILLIAM W.
CUSHMAN, ROBERT E.
HAMILTON, WALTER H.
HOWE, MARK DEWOLFE
JENSEN, MERRILL
KELLY, ALFRED H.
MINTON, SHERMAN
ROSSITER, CLINTON
STORY, JOSEPH
SWISHER, CARL BRENT
TEN BROEK, JACOBUS
TUGWELL, REXFORD G.
WIGMORE, JOHN HENRY

Scott H. Bice
Professor of Law and Dean of the Law Center
University of Southern California

LEGISLATIVE INTENT

*Joseph W. Bishop, Jr.
Richard Ely Professor of Law
Yale Law School

DECLARATION OF WAR
MILITARY JUSTICE AND THE CONSTITUTION
POLICE ACTION
STATE OF WAR

Charles L. Black, Jr.
Sterling Professor of Law, Emeritus
Yale Law School
Professor of Law
Columbia University

ADMIRALTY AND MARITIME JURISDICTION
EQUITY
STATE ACTION

Vincent Blasi
Corliss Lamont Professor of Civil Liberties
Columbia University

DEMONSTRATION
PUBLIC FORUM

Albert P. Blaustein
Professor of Law
Rutgers-Camden School of Law

INFLUENCE OF THE AMERICAN CONSTITUTION ABROAD

Maxwell Bloomfield
Professor of History and Law
The Catholic University of America

COMMENTATORS ON THE CONSTITUTION

Grace Ganz Blumberg
Professor of Law
University of California, Los Angeles

HELVERING V. DAVIS
SOCIAL SECURITY ACT
STEWARD MACHINE COMPANY V. DAVIS

Lee C. Bollinger
Professor of Law
University of Michigan

BURGER, WARREN E.

Robert H. Bork
Judge

* Deceased

United States Court of Appeals for the District of Columbia Circuit

JUDICIAL REVIEW AND DEMOCRACY

Paul Brest
Kenneth and Harle Montgomery Professor of Clinical Legal Education
Stanford Law School

CONSTITUTIONAL INTERPRETATION
LEGISLATION

Ralph S. Brown
Simeon E. Baldwin Professor of Law, Emeritus
Yale Law School

LOYALTY OATH
LOYALTY-SECURITY PROGRAMS

Barbara Brudno
Attorney
Former Professor of Law
University of California, Los Angeles

WEALTH DISCRIMINATION

Harold H. Bruff
John S. Redditt Professor of Law
The University of Texas at Austin

OFFICE OF MANAGEMENT AND BUDGET

Robert A. Burt
Southmayd Professor of Law
Yale University

FAMILY AND THE CONSTITUTION
MENTAL ILLNESS AND THE CONSTITUTION
MENTAL RETARDATION AND THE CONSTITUTION

Paul D. Carrington
Professor of Law and Dean of the Law School
Duke University

TRIAL BY JURY

Robert L. Carter
Judge
United States District Court, Southern District of New York

UNITED STATES DISTRICT COURTS

Gerhard Casper
William B. Graham Professor of Law and Dean of the Law School
The University of Chicago

CONSTITUTIONALISM

Donald S. Chisum
Professor of Law
University of Washington, Seattle

PATENTS

Jesse H. Choper
Dean and Professor of Law
University of California, Berkeley

SEPARATION OF CHURCH AND STATE

William Cohen
C. Wendell and Edith M. Carlsmith Professor of Law
Stanford Law School

CLERKS
DOUGLAS, WILLIAM O.
PREEMPTION

Henry Steele Commager
Professor of History, Emeritus
Amherst College

STORY, JOSEPH

Richard C. Cortner
Professor of Political Science
University of Arizona

CONSTITUTIONAL HISTORY, 1961–1977

*Robert M. Cover
Chancellor Kent Professor of Law
Yale Law School

TAFT COURT

Archibald Cox
Carl M. Loeb University Professor, Emeritus
Harvard University
Visiting Professor of Law
Boston University

FIRST AMENDMENT
HUGHES COURT
STONE COURT

William J. Cuddihy
Claremont, California

ASSISTANCE, WRIT OF
BONHAM'S CASE
CALVIN'S CASE
FOURTH AMENDMENT (ORIGINS)
GENERAL WARRANT

OTIS, JAMES
PAXTON'S CASE
WILKES CASES

David P. Currie
Harry N. Wyatt Professor of Law
The University of Chicago

JUDICIAL POWER OF THE UNITED STATES

Thomas Curry
Vicar for Priests
Archdiocese of Los Angeles

BACKUS, ISAAC
HOOKER, THOMAS
LELAND, JOHN
WILLIAMS, ROGER

Richard Danzig
Attorney
Latham, Watkins & Hills, Washington, D.C.

CONSCRIPTION

Robert Dawidoff
Associate Professor of History
The Claremont Graduate School

ADAMS, HENRY
RANDOLPH, JOHN

Howard E. Dean
Professor of Political Science
Portland State University

JUDICIAL POLICYMAKING
MECHANICAL JURISPRUDENCE
THAYER, JAMES BRADLEY

Walter Dellinger
Professor of Law
Duke University

AMENDING PROCESS

John P. Diggins
Professor of History
University of California, Irvine

PROGRESSIVE CONSTITUTIONAL THOUGHT

Norman Dorsen
Stokes Professor of Law
New York University
President
American Civil Liberties Union

AMERICAN CIVIL LIBERTIES UNION
CIVIL LIBERTIES
DRAFT CARD BURNING
FLAG DESECRATION

Robert F. Drinan, S. J.
Professor of Law
Georgetown University
Former Member of Congress (1971–1981)

CIVIL DISOBEDIENCE AND THE CONSTITUTION

Murray Dry
Professor of Political Science
Middlebury College

ANTI-FEDERALIST CONSTITUTIONAL THOUGHT
STORING, HERBERT J.

Patrick Dutton
Attorney
Vinnedge, Lance & Glenn, Ontario, California

NEW JERSEY V. T.L.O.

Frank H. Easterbrook
Judge
United States Court of Appeals for the Seventh Circuit
Former Lee and Brena Freeman Professor of Law
The University of Chicago

REHNQUIST, WILLIAM H.

Theodore Eisenberg
Professor of Law
Cornell University

AGE DISCRIMINATION
AGE DISCRIMINATION ACT
ANTIDISCRIMINATION LEGISLATION
ARLINGTON HEIGHTS V. METROPOLITAN HOUSING DEVELOPMENT CORP.
BANKRUPTCY ACT
BANKRUPTCY POWER
BANKRUPTCY REFORM ACT
BIVENS V. SIX UNKNOWN NAMED AGENTS
BUTZ V. ECONOMOU
CIVIL RIGHTS ACT OF 1866 (JUDICIAL INTERPRETATION)
CIVIL RIGHTS ACT OF 1957
CIVIL RIGHTS ACT OF 1960
CIVIL RIGHTS ACT OF 1964
CIVIL RIGHTS ACT OF 1968
CIVIL RIGHTS COMMISSION
CIVIL RIGHTS DIVISION
CIVIL RIGHTS REMOVAL

CIVIL RIGHTS REPEAL ACT
CLASSIC, UNITED STATES V.
COLOR OF LAW
DAMAGES
DAVIS V. PASSMAN
DEVELOPMENTALLY DISABLED ACT
DOMBROWSKI V. PFISTER
EDELMAN V. JORDAN
EDUCATION AMENDMENTS
EDUCATION OF HANDICAPPED CHILDREN ACT
EXECUTIVE IMMUNITY
EXECUTIVE ORDER
EXECUTIVE ORDER 11246
EXECUTIVE ORDERS 9980 AND 9981: INTEGRATION OF THE FEDERAL GOVERNMENT
EXHAUSTION OF REMEDIES
FEDERAL PROTECTION OF CIVIL RIGHTS
FEDERAL TORT CLAIMS ACT
FITZPATRICK V. BITZER
GRAVEL V. UNITED STATES
GRIFFIN V. BRECKINRIDGE
GRIGGS V. DUKE POWER COMPANY
GUEST, UNITED STATES V.
HAGUE V. C.I.O.
HODGES V. UNITED STATES
HUTCHINSON V. PROXMIRE
IMBLER V. PACHTMAN
IMPLIED CONSTITUTIONAL RIGHTS OF ACTION
INSTITUTIONAL LITIGATION (WITH STEPHEN C. YEAZELL)
JONES V. ALFRED H. MAYER CO.
JUDICIAL IMMUNITY
KATZENBACH V. MORGAN
LAKE COUNTRY ESTATES V. TAHOE REGIONAL PLANNING AGENCY
LARSON V. DOMESTIC AND FOREIGN COMMERCE CORP.
LAU V. NICHOLS
LEGISLATIVE IMMUNITY
MITCHUM V. FOSTER
MONELL V. DEPARTMENT OF SOCIAL SERVICES OF NEW YORK CITY
MONROE V. PAPE
MUNICIPAL IMMUNITY
OPEN HOUSING LAWS
OREGON V. MITCHELL
OWEN V. CITY OF INDEPENDENCE
PALMER V. THOMPSON
PIERSON V. RAY
QUERN V. JORDAN
REHABILITATION ACT
REVISED STATUTES
SCHEUER V. RHODES
SCREWS V. UNITED STATES
SECTION 1983, TITLE 42, U.S. CODE (JUDICIAL INTERPRETATION)
SOUTH CAROLINA V. KATZENBACH
SPEECH OR DEBATE CLAUSE
STRICT CONSTRUCTION
STUMP V. SPARKMAN
TENNEY V. BRANDHOVE
UNITED STEELWORKERS OF AMERICA V. WEBER
VOTING RIGHTS ACT OF 1965
WAIVER OF CONSTITUTIONAL RIGHTS
WASHINGTON V. DAVIS
WOOD V. STRICKLAND

Daniel J. Elazar
President, Center for the Study of Federalism and Professor of Political Science
Temple University

FEDERALISM (THEORY)

Ward E. Y. Elliott
Professor of Government
Claremont McKenna College

AVERY V. MIDLAND COUNTY
BAKER V. CARR
COLEGROVE V. GREEN
COLEMAN V. MILLER
DIRECT ELECTIONS
ELECTORAL COLLEGE
FIFTEENTH AMENDMENT (JUDICIAL INTERPRETATION)
GERRYMANDER
MULTIMEMBER DISTRICT
O'BRIEN V. BROWN
ONE PERSON, ONE VOTE
REPRESENTATION

Richard E. Ellis
Professor of History
State University of New York, Buffalo

CHASE, SAMUEL J.
CUSHING, WILLIAM
DUVALL, GABRIEL
ELLSWORTH, OLIVER
IREDELL, JAMES
JAY, JOHN
PATERSON, WILLIAM
TODD, THOMAS
WASHINGTON, BUSHROD

Thomas I. Emerson
Augustus E. Lines Professor of Law, Emeritus
Yale Law School

FREEDOM OF SPEECH
FREEDOM OF THE PRESS

David F. Epstein
Analyst
United States Department of Defense, Washington, D.C.

THE FEDERALIST

Edward J. Erler
Professor of Political Science
California State University, San Bernardino

CONCURRENT POWERS
DISCRETE AND INSULAR MINORITY
EX POST FACTO
FIREFIGHTERS' LOCAL NO. 1784 v. STOTTS
JUDICIAL LEGISLATION
O'CONNOR, SANDRA DAY
RODGERS v. LODGE

Robert K. Faulkner
Professor of Political Science
Boston College

BICKEL, ALEXANDER M.
LOCKE, JOHN
MARSHALL, JOHN

John D. Feerick
Professor of Law and Dean of the Law School
Fordham University

PRESIDENTIAL SUCCESSION

Don E. Fehrenbacher
Professor of History
Stanford University

CONSTITUTIONAL HISTORY, 1848–1861
DRED SCOTT v. SANDFORD

David Fellman
Vilas Professor of Political Science, Emeritus
University of Wisconsin, Madison

CRIMINAL PROCEDURE
FREEDOM OF ASSEMBLY AND ASSOCIATION

Martha A. Field
Professor of Law
Harvard Law School

ABSTENTION DOCTRINE
FORTAS, ABE

Paul Finkelman
Professor of History
State University of New York, Binghamton

ARTHUR, CHESTER A.
BATES, EDWARD
BENTON, THOMAS HART
BINGHAM, JOHN A.
BINNEY, HORACE
BIRNEY, JAMES
BLACK, JEREMIAH S.
BRECKINRIDGE, JOHN C.
BUCHANAN, JAMES
BUTLER, BENJAMIN F.
CARPENTER, MATTHEW
COMMONWEALTH v. JENNISON
CONKLING, ROSCOE
CRITTENDEN, JOHN J.
CURTIS, GEORGE T.
DAVIS, JEFFERSON
DOUGLAS, STEPHEN A.
FEDERAL TEST ACTS
FESSENDEN, WILLIAM PITT
FILLMORE, MILLARD
GARFIELD, JAMES A.
GARRISON, WILLIAM LLOYD
GRANT, ULYSSES S.
HAYES, RUTHERFORD B.
HAYNE, ROBERT YOUNG
JACKSON'S PROCLAMATION TO THE PEOPLE OF SOUTH CAROLINA
JACKSON'S VETO OF THE BANK BILL
JOHNSON, REVERDY
JULIAN, GEORGE
PIERCE, FRANKLIN
PINKNEY, WILLIAM
PRIGG v. PENNSYLVANIA
SEWARD, WILLIAM
STANBERY, HENRY
STANTON, EDWIN M.
STEPHENS, ALEXANDER H.
STEVENS, THADDEUS
SUMNER, CHARLES
TARIFF ACT OF 1828
TAYLOR, ZACHARY
TOOMBS, ROBERT A.
TRUMBULL, LYMAN
TYLER, JOHN
WHEATON, HENRY
WILMOT PROVISO
WIRT, WILLIAM
WOODBURY, LEVI

Louis Fisher
Specialist in American National Government
Congressional Research Service, The Library of Congress

CARTER, JIMMY
EMERGENCY POWERS
EXECUTIVE ORDER 10340

LEGISLATIVE VETO
PRESIDENTIAL ORDINANCE-MAKING POWER
PRESIDENTIAL SPENDING POWER
TRUMAN, HARRY S.
VETO POWER
YOUNGSTOWN SHEET & TUBE COMPANY V. SAWYER

Owen M. Fiss
Alexander M. Bickel Professor of Public Law
Yale Law School

FULLER COURT
RACIAL DISCRIMINATION

David H. Flaherty
Professor of History
University of Western Ontario

FUNDAMENTAL LAW (HISTORY)

Caleb Foote
Elizabeth Josselyn Boalt Professor of Law
University of California, Berkeley

BAIL

George Forsyth
Claremont, California

ADAMS, JOHN QUINCY

Marvin E. Frankel
Attorney
Kramer, Levin, Nessen, Kamen & Frankel
Former Judge
United States District Court, Eastern District of New York

GRAND JURY

John Hope Franklin
James B. Duke Professor of History, Emeritus
Duke University

SLAVERY AND THE CONSTITUTION

Paul A. Freund
Carl M. Loeb University Professor, Emeritus
Harvard Law School

SUPREME COURT (HISTORY)

Gerald E. Frug
Professor of Law
Harvard Law School

CITIES AND THE CONSTITUTION

Jaime B. Fuster
Member of Congress (Puerto Rico)
Professor of Law
University of Puerto Rico

PUERTO RICO, CONSTITUTIONAL STATUS OF

David J. Garrow
Associate Professor of Political Science
City College of New York and City University Graduate School

KING, MARTIN LUTHER, JR.

William Gillette
Professor of History
Rutgers University

FIFTEENTH AMENDMENT (FRAMING)

Ruth Bader Ginsburg
Judge
United States Court of Appeals for the District of Columbia Circuit

REPRODUCTIVE AUTONOMY
SEX DISCRIMINATION

Robert Jerome Glennon
Professor of Law
University of Arizona

BROWN, HENRY BILLINGS
FRANK, JEROME

Carole E. Goldberg-Ambrose
Professor of Law
University of California, Los Angeles

AMERICAN INDIANS AND THE CONSTITUTION
CONCURRENT JURISDICTION
DECLARATORY JUDGMENT
DIVERSITY JURISDICTION
FEDERAL QUESTION JURISDICTION
FEDERAL RULES OF CIVIL PROCEDURE
REMOVAL OF CASES

Abraham S. Goldstein
Sterling Professor of Law
Yale Law School

RIGHT TO BE INFORMED OF ACCUSATION

Joel K. Goldstein
Attorney
Goldstein & Price, St. Louis

VICE-PRESIDENCY

David Gordon
Attorney
D'Ancona & Pflaum, Chicago

ACT OF STATE DOCTRINE
ADAMS v. TANNER
ADAMSON EIGHT-HOUR ACT
AGRICULTURAL ADJUSTMENT ACT OF 1933
AGRICULTURAL ADJUSTMENT ACT OF 1938
AGRICULTURAL MARKETING AGREEMENT ACT
ALLEN-BRADLEY LOCAL v. WISCONSIN EMPLOYEE RELATIONS BOARD
ALLGEYER v. LOUISIANA
AMES, FISHER
APEX HOSIERY CO. v. LEADER
APPALACHIAN ELECTRIC POWER, UNITED STATES v.
ARNOLD, THURMAN W.
BARTKUS v. ILLINOIS
BATES v. STATE BAR OF ARIZONA
BENTON v. MARYLAND
BIBB v. NAVAJO FREIGHT LINES
BITUMINOUS COAL ACT
BOB-LO EXCURSION COMPANY v. MICHIGAN
BREWSTER v. UNITED STATES
BURBANK v. LOCKHEED AIR TERMINAL
BURNS BAKING COMPANY v. BRYAN
BUSHELL'S CASE
CARTER, JAMES COOLIDGE
CHAE CHAN PING v. UNITED STATES
CHAMPION v. AMES
CHAPMAN v. HOUSTON WELFARE RIGHTS ORGANIZATION
CHICAGO, BURLINGTON & QUINCY RAILWAY v. CHICAGO
CHICAGO, MILWAUKEE & ST. PAUL RAILWAY v. MINNESOTA
CHILD LABOR TAX ACT
CHINESE EXCLUSION ACT
CHOATE, JOSEPH H.
CIRCUIT COURTS OF APPEALS ACT
CLARK DISTILLING CO. v. WESTERN MARYLAND RAILWAY CO.
CLAYTON ACT
CLEVELAND, GROVER
CODISPOTI v. PENNSYLVANIA
COPPAGE v. KANSAS
CORRIGAN v. BUCKLEY
COYLE v. SMITH
CUMMINGS, HOMER S.
DAVIS, JOHN W.
DAYTON-GOOSE CREEK RAILWAY CO. v. UNITED STATES
DEAN MILK COMPANY v. MADISON
DE MINIMIS NON CURAT LEX
DILLON, JOHN F.
DIONISIO, UNITED STATES v.
DISANTO v. PENNSYLVANIA
DISTRICT OF COLUMBIA MINIMUM WAGE LAW
DOREMUS, UNITED STATES v.
DUNCAN v. KAHANAMOKU
DUNCAN v. LOUISIANA
DUPLEX PRINTING PRESS COMPANY v. DEERING
EISNER v. MACOMBER
ELKINS ACT
EMERGENCY BANK ACT
EMPLOYERS' LIABILITY ACTS
EMPLOYERS' LIABILITY CASES
EN BANC
ERDMAN ACT
ERNST, MORRIS L.
ESCH-CUMMINGS TRANSPORTATION ACT
ESTES v. TEXAS
EXECUTIVE ORDER 9066 AND PUBLIC LAW 503
FEDERAL POWER COMMISSION v. HOPE NATURAL GAS COMPANY
FEDERAL TRADE COMMISSION v. GRATZ
FEDERAL TRADE COMMISSION ACT
FIELD, DAVID DUDLEY
FOOD, DRUG, AND COSMETIC ACT
FRANK v. MANGUM
FRAZIER-LEMKE ACTS
FREEMAN v. HEWITT
FREUND, ERNST
FROTHINGHAM v. MELLON
GALLOWAY, JOSEPH
GERRY, ELBRIDGE
GOLD CLAUSE CASES
GOLD RESERVE ACT
GOLDFARB v. VIRGINIA STATE BAR
GOMPERS v. BUCKS' STOVE AND RANGE COMPANY
GONG LUM v. RICE
GRIMAUD, UNITED STATES v.
GROSSMAN, EX PARTE
GUTHRIE, WILLIAM
HABEAS CORPUS ACT
HALL v. DECUIR
HARPER, ROBERT G.
HARRIS v. NEW YORK
HARRISON ACT
HARRISON, BENJAMIN
HAYS, ARTHUR GARFIELD
HEPBURN ACT
HILDRETH, RICHARD
HIPOLITE EGG COMPANY v. UNITED STATES
HITCHMAN COAL AND COKE CO. v. MITCHELL
HOKE v. UNITED STATES
HOUSTON, EAST & WEST TEXAS RAILWAY COMPANY v. UNITED STATES
HURON PORTLAND CEMENT CO. v. DETROIT
INTERSTATE COMMERCE COMMISSION v. CINCINNATI, NEW ORLEANS & TEXAS PACIFIC RAILWAY
INTERSTATE COMMERCE COMMISSION v. ILLINOIS CENTRAL RAILROAD
INTERSTATE COMMERCE
INTERSTATE COMMERCE ACT
INTRASTATE COMMERCE

JAMES V. BOWMAN
JUDICIARY ACT OF 1925
JUDICIARY REFORM ACT
KNIGHT CO., E. C., UNITED STATES V.
KNOX, PHILANDER C.
LAMAR, JOSEPH R.
LANDIS, JAMES M.
LANZA, UNITED STATES V.
LEVER FOOD AND DRUG CONTROL ACT
LONG HAUL/SHORT HAUL RATE DISCRIMINATION
LOUISVILLE, NEW ORLEANS & TEXAS RAILWAY V. MISSISSIPPI
LURTON, HORACE H.
MANN ACT
MANN-ELKINS ACT
MARTIN, LUTHER
MASSACHUSETTS BODY OF LIBERTIES
MASSACHUSETTS GENERAL LAWS AND LIBERTIES
MCCRAY V. UNITED STATES
MCKINLEY, WILLIAM
MICHELIN TIRE COMPANY V. WAGES
MIDDENDORF V. HENRY
MINNESOTA RATE CASES
MOODY, WILLIAM H.
MOORE, ALFRED
MUGLER V. KANSAS
MUNICIPAL BANKRUPTCY ACT
MUSKRAT V. UNITED STATES
MYERS V. UNITED STATES
NATIONAL INDUSTRIAL RECOVERY ACT
NEW STATE ICE COMPANY V. LIEBMANN
NEW YORK CENTRAL RAILROAD V. WHITE
NOLO CONTENDERE
NORRIS-LAGUARDIA ACT
NORTHERN SECURITIES CO. V. UNITED STATES
OBITER DICTUM
OLNEY, RICHARD
OLSEN V. NEBRASKA EX REL. REFERENCE & BOND ASSOCIATION
PACKERS AND STOCKYARDS ACT
PALMER, A. MITCHELL
PARKER V. BROWN
PATTON V. UNITED STATES
PAUL V. VIRGINIA
PELL V. PROCUNIER
PER CURIAM
PHELPS, EDWARD J.
POLLAK, WALTER H.
POLLOCK V. WILLIAMS
PRUDENTIAL INSURANCE COMPANY V. BENJAMIN
PURE FOOD AND DRUG ACT
RAILROAD CONTROL ACT
RAILROAD RETIREMENT ACT
RAYMOND MOTOR TRANSPORTATION V. RICE
RIBNIK V. MCBRIDE
ROBINSON-PATMAN ACT
SELDEN, JOHN
SHERMAN ANTITRUST ACT
SHREVEPORT DOCTRINE
SIMON V. EASTERN KENTUCKY WELFARE RIGHTS ORGANIZATION
SMYTH V. AMES
SOUTH-EASTERN UNDERWRITERS ASSOCIATION, UNITED STATES V.
STAFFORD V. WALLACE
STANDARD OIL COMPANY V. UNITED STATES
STETTLER V. O'HARA
STREAM OF COMMERCE DOCTRINE
SWIFT & COMPANY V. UNITED STATES
TENNESSEE VALLEY AUTHORITY ACT
TRANS-MISSOURI FREIGHT ASSOCIATION, UNITED STATES V.
TYSON & BROTHER V. BANTON
ULTRA VIRES
UNITED MINE WORKERS V. CORONADO COAL COMPANY
UNITED MINE WORKERS, UNITED STATES V.
VICINAGE
WABASH, ST. LOUIS, PACIFIC RAILWAY V. ILLINOIS
WAGNER ACT
WALZ V. TAX COMMISSION
WATER POWER ACT
WEBB-KENYON ACT
WICKERSHAM, GEORGE W.
WILSON V. NEW
WINSHIP, IN RE
WOLFF PACKING CO. V. COURT OF INDUSTRIAL RELATIONS
WOODS V. CLOYD W. MILLER CO.
WYTHE, GEORGE
YAKUS V. UNITED STATES
YAMASHITA, IN RE

William B. Gould
Charles A. Beardsley Professor of Law
Stanford Law School

LOCHNER V. NEW YORK
WORKERS' COMPENSATION

Henry F. Graff
Professor of History
Columbia University

NIXON, RICHARD M.

Kent Greenawalt
Cardozo Professor of Jurisprudence
Columbia University

CONSCIENTIOUS OBJECTION
INCITEMENT TO UNLAWFUL CONDUCT

Jack Greenberg
Professor of Law
Columbia University
Former General Counsel
NAACP Legal Defense & Educational Fund

CIVIL RIGHTS
NAACP LEGAL DEFENSE AND EDUCATIONAL FUND

Linda Greenhouse
Staff writer
The New York Times

GOLDBERG, ARTHUR J.

Eugene Gressman
William Rand Kenan, Jr. Professor of Law
The University of North Carolina at Chapel Hill

JUDICIAL CODE
MURPHY, FRANK
STAY OF EXECUTION
SUPREME COURT PRACTICE

Thomas C. Grey
Professor of Law
Stanford Law School

HIGHER LAW

Erwin N. Griswold
Partner
Jones, Day, Reavis & Pogue, Washington, D.C.
Former Solicitor General of the United States
Former Dean
Harvard Law School

SOLICITOR GENERAL

Gerald Gunther
William Nelson Cromwell Professor of Law
Stanford Law School

DOWLING, NOEL T.
HAND, LEARNED
JUDICIAL REVIEW

Nathan Hakman
Professor of Political Science
State University of New York, Binghamton

INTEREST GROUP LITIGATION

Kermit L. Hall
Professor of History and Law
University of Florida

BOND, HUGH LENNOX
BREWER, DAVID J.
CAMPBELL, JOHN A.
CIRCUIT COURTS
CRANCH, WILLIAM
GRIER, ROBERT C.
GROSSCUP, PETER
HASTIE, WILLIAM
MORROW, WILLIAM
NELSON, SAMUEL
PARDEE, DON ALBERT
PETERS, RICHARD
POLK, JAMES K.
SAWYER, LORENZO

Catherine Hancock
Associate Professor of Law
Tulane University

CRIMINAL CONSPIRACY
FAY V. NOIA
NO-KNOCK ENTRY
PORNOGRAPHY
TOWNSEND V. SAIN

Louis Henkin
University Professor
Columbia University

FOREIGN AFFAIRS AND THE CONSTITUTION

Harold W. Horowitz
Vice Chancellor for Faculty Relations and Professor of Law
University of California, Los Angeles

CHOICE OF LAW

A. E. Dick Howard
White Burkett Miller Professor of Law and Public Affairs
University of Virginia

BURGER COURT
MAGNA CARTA

Samuel P. Huntington
Director, Center for International Affairs
Eaton Professor of the Science of Government
Harvard University

CIVIL-MILITARY RELATIONS AND THE CONSTITUTION

James Willard Hurst
Vilas Professor of Law, Emeritus
University of Wisconsin, Madison

FREEDOM OF CONTRACT
TREASON

Harold M. Hyman
William P. Hobby Professor of History
Rice University

CHASE, SALMON P.
CIVIL RIGHTS ACT OF 1866 (FRAMING)
EMANCIPATION PROCLAMATION
HABEAS CORPUS ACT
JOHNSON, ANDREW
MILLIGAN, EX PARTE
SLAUGHTERHOUSE CASES
TEXAS V. WHITE
THIRTEENTH AMENDMENT (FRAMING)
VALLANDIGHAM, EX PARTE
WADE-DAVIS BILL

Clyde E. Jacobs
Professor of Political Science, Emeritus
University of California, Davis

ELEVENTH AMENDMENT
SOVEREIGN IMMUNITY

Henry V. Jaffa
Henry Salvatori Research Professor of Political Philosophy
Claremont McKenna College and The Claremont Graduate School

LINCOLN, ABRAHAM

Alan R. Jones
Professor of History
Grinnell College

COOLEY, THOMAS M.

Sanford H. Kadish
Morrison Professor of Law
University of California, Berkeley

PROCEDURAL DUE PROCESS OF LAW, CRIMINAL

Yale Kamisar
Henry K. Ransom Professor of Law
University of Michigan

POLICE INTERROGATION AND CONFESSIONS

John Kaplan
Jackson Eli Reynolds Professor of Law
Stanford Law School

CLARK, TOM C.
DRUG REGULATION AND THE CONSTITUTION
EVIDENCE
HARMLESS ERROR

Kenneth L. Karst
Professor of Law
University of California, Los Angeles

ABSOLUTISM
ACCESS TO THE COURTS
ADEQUATE STATE GROUNDS
AKE V. OKLAHOMA
ALEXANDER V. HOLMES COUNTY BOARD OF EDUCATION
ALIEN
ALL DELIBERATE SPEED
ALLEN V. WRIGHT
ALLIED STRUCTURAL STEEL CO. V. SPANNAUS
AMBACH V. NORWICK
ANCILLARY JURISDICTION
APPEAL
APPELLATE JURISDICTION
ARNETT V. KENNEDY
ASHWANDER V. TENNESSEE VALLEY AUTHORITY
ATASCADERO STATE HOSPITAL V. SCANLON
BADGES OF SERVITUDE
BALDWIN V. FISH & GAME COMMISSION
BARROWS V. JACKSON
BELL V. MARYLAND
BEREA COLLEGE V. KENTUCKY
BIRTH CONTROL
BISHOP V. WOOD
BLUM V. YARETZKY
BOARD OF CURATORS OF UNIVERSITY OF MISSOURI V. HOROWITZ
BOARD OF EDUCATION V. PICO
BOARD OF REGENTS V. ROTH
BODDIE V. CONNECTICUT
BOLLING V. SHARPE
BOUNDS V. SMITH
BRANDEIS BRIEF
BREEDLOVE V. SUTTLES
BRIEF
BROADRICK V. OKLAHOMA
BROCKETT V. SPOKANE ARCADES, INC.
BROWN, UNITED STATES V.
BROWN V. BOARD OF EDUCATION
BROWN V. SOCIALIST WORKERS '74 CAMPAIGN COMMITTEE
BUCHANAN V. WARLEY
BUCK V. BELL
BURTON V. WILMINGTON PARKING AUTHORITY
CALIFANO V. GOLDFARB
CALIFANO V. WESTCOTT
CAREY V. POPULATION SERVICES INTERNATIONAL
CARROLL V. PRESIDENT AND COMMISSIONERS OF PRINCESS ANNE
CBS, INC. V. FEDERAL COMMUNICATIONS COMMISSION

Central Hudson Gas Co. v. Public Service Commission
Certification
Certiorari, Writ of
Chilling Effect
City of Los Angeles v. Taxpayers for Vincent
Claims Court of the United States
Cleveland Board of Education v. LaFleur
Columbus Board of Education v. Penick
Comity
Commerce Court
Companion Case
Compelling State Interest
Conference
Consent Decree
Constitutional Courts
Cooper v. Aaron
Cornelius v. NAACP Legal Defense & Educational Fund
Court of Customs and Patent Appeals
Court of International Trade
Court of Military Appeals
Craig v. Boren
Crawford v. Board of Education
Dandridge v. Williams
De Facto/De Jure
DeFunis v. Odegaard
Department of Agriculture v. Murry
Divorce and the Constitution
Doctrine
Douglas v. California
Dun & Bradstreet v. Greenmoss Builders, Inc.
Dunn v. Blumstein
Edwards v. California
Effects on Commerce
Eisenstadt v. Baird
Emergency Court of Appeals
Equal Employment Opportunity Commission v. Wyoming
Equal Protection of the Laws
Error, Writ of
Euthanasia
Evans v. Abney
Evitts v. Lucey
Federal Courts Improvement Act
Ferguson v. Skrupa
Final Judgment Rule
Flagg Brothers, Inc. v. Brooks
Foley v. Connelie
Freedman v. Maryland
Freedom of Intimate Association
Frontiero v. Richardson
Fullilove v. Klutznick
Fundamental Interests
Garcia v. San Antonio Metropolitan Transit Authority
Goesaert v. Cleary
Goldberg v. Kelly
Goldwater v. Carter
Gomillion v. Lightfoot
Goss v. Lopez
Grace, United States v.
Graham v. Richardson
Grandfather Clause
Gray v. Sanders
Great Atlantic & Pacific Tea Company v. Cottrell
Green v. New Kent County School Board
Griffin v. Illinois
Griffin v. School Board of Prince Edward County
Griswold v. Connecticut
Grovey v. Townsend
Gulf of Tonkin Resolution
Hampton v. Mow Sun Wong
Harper v. Virginia State Board of Elections
Harris v. McCrae
Hart, Henry M.
Hawaii Housing Authority v. Midkiff
Heart of Atlanta Motel v. United States
Heffron v. International Society for Krishna Consciousness
Hills v. Gautreaux
Hines v. Davidowitz
Hodel v. Virginia Surface Mining and Reclamation Association
Hodgson and Thompson v. Bowerbank
Hostile Audience
Hyde Amendment
Illegitimacy
Immigration (with Gerald P. López)
Indigent
Ingraham v. Wright
Interlocutory
Invidious Discrimination
Irrebuttable Presumptions
Jackson v. Metropolitan Edison Company
James v. Valtierra
Japanese American Cases
Judiciary Act of 1875
Kalven, Harry, Jr.
Keyes v. School District No. 1 of Denver
Kramer v. Union Free School District
Lalli v. Lalli
Larson v. Valente
Leary v. United States
Least Restrictive Means Test
Lee, United States v.
Legislative Courts
Legislative Facts
Levy v. Louisiana
Literacy Test
Loretto v. Teleprompter Manhattan CATV Co.
Loving v. Virginia

MAHAN V. HOWELL
MAHER V. ROE
MARRIAGE AND THE CONSTITUTION
MASSACHUSETTS BOARD OF RETIREMENT V. MURGIA
MATHEWS V. ELDRIDGE
MEMORANDUM ORDER
MEMPHIS V. GREENE
METROPOLITAN LIFE INSURANCE COMPANY V. WARD
MEYER V. NEBRASKA
MICHAEL M. V. SUPERIOR COURT
MILLIKEN V. BRADLEY
MISCEGENATION
MISSISSIPPI UNIVERSITY FOR WOMEN V. HOGAN
MISSOURI EX REL. GAINES V. CANADA
MOBILE V. BOLDEN
MOORE V. CITY OF EAST CLEVELAND
MOORE V. DEMPSEY
MOOSE LODGE NO. 107 V. IRVIS
MORGAN V. VIRGINIA
NAACP V. ALABAMA
NEW HAMPSHIRE SUPREME COURT V. PIPER
NEW ORLEANS V. DUKES
NEW YORK V. FERBER
NIXON, UNITED STATES V.
NIXON V. CONDON
NIXON V. FITZGERALD
NIXON V. HERNDON
NORTHERN PIPELINE CONSTRUCTION COMPANY V. MARATHON PIPE LINE CO.
O'BRIEN, UNITED STATES V.
O'CONNOR V. DONALDSON
O'SHEA V. LITTLETON
ORAL ARGUMENT
ORIGINAL JURISDICTION
OSBORN V. BANK OF THE UNITED STATES (with Leonard W. Levy)
OYAMA V. CALIFORNIA
PALMORE V. SIDOTI
PARHAM V. J. R.
PAUL V. DAVIS
PENDENT JURISDICTION
PENN CENTRAL TRANSPORTATION CO. V. NEW YORK CITY
PENNHURST STATE SCHOOL AND HOSPITAL V. HALDERMAN
PENUMBRA THEORY
PERRY EDUCATION ASSOCIATION V. PERRY LOCAL EDUCATORS' ASSOCIATION
PERSON
PERSONNEL ADMINISTRATOR OF MASSACHUSETTS V. FEENEY
PIERCE V. SOCIETY OF SISTERS
PLANNED PARENTHOOD OF CENTRAL MISSOURI V. DANFORTH
PLYLER V. DOE
POLICE DEPARTMENT OF CHICAGO V. MOSLEY
POLL TAX
POLYGAMY
PRECEDENT
PRIVILEGES AND IMMUNITIES
PROHIBITION, WRIT OF
PRUNEYARD SHOPPING CENTER V. ROBINS
PUBLIC ACCOMMODATIONS
PUBLIC UTILITY HOLDING COMPANY ACT
RACIAL BALANCE
RACIAL QUOTAS
RAILWAY EXPRESS AGENCY V. NEW YORK
RATIONAL BASIS
REAL EVIDENCE
REGAN V. WALD
REGENTS OF UNIVERSITY OF CALIFORNIA V. BAKKE
REHEARING
REITMAN V. MULKEY
REMAND
RESIDENCE REQUIREMENTS
RES JUDICATA
RESTRICTIVE COVENANT
REYNOLDS V. SIMS
RIGHT OF PRIVACY
RIGHT–PRIVILEGE DISTINCTION (with Dennis J. Mahoney)
RIGHT TO TRAVEL
RIZZO V. GOODE
ROE V. WADE
ROSS V. MOFFITT
ROSTKER V. GOLDBERG
RULE OF FOUR
RUNYON V. MCCRARY
SAN ANTONIO INDEPENDENT SCHOOL DISTRICT V. RODRIGUEZ
SCHAD V. VILLAGE OF MT. EPHRAIM
SCHOOL BUSING
SEGREGATION
SEPARATE BUT EQUAL DOCTRINE
SERRANO V. PRIEST
SEVERABILITY
SEXUAL PREFERENCE AND THE CONSTITUTION
SHAPIRO V. THOMPSON
SHELLEY V. KRAEMER
SHOPPING CENTERS
SIPUEL V. BOARD OF REGENTS OF UNIVERSITY OF OKLAHOMA
SIT-INS
SKINNER V. OKLAHOMA EX REL. WILLIAMSON
SMITH V. ALLWRIGHT
SOSNA V. IOWA
SOUTHERN PACIFIC CO. V. ARIZONA EX REL. SULLIVAN
SPECIAL MASTER
STANDARDS OF REVIEW
STATE ACTION—BEYOND RACE
STERILIZATION
STRICT SCRUTINY
SUGARMAN V. DOUGALL

SUSPECT CLASSIFICATION
SWANN V. CHARLOTTE-MECKLENBURG BOARD OF EDUCATION
SWEATT V. PAINTER
TAKAHASHI V. FISH AND GAME COMMISSION
TAX COURT OF THE UNITED STATES
TAYLOR V. LOUISIANA
TERM (SUPREME COURT)
TERRITORIAL COURTS
TERRY V. ADAMS
THIRTEENTH AMENDMENT (JUDICIAL INTERPRETATION)
THOMAS V. INDIANA REVIEW BOARD
THOMAS V. UNION CARBIDE AGRICULTURAL PRODUCTS COMPANY
THREE-JUDGE COURTS
TINKER V. DES MOINES SCHOOL DISTRICT
TOOMER V. WITSELL
TOTH, UNITED STATES EX REL., V. QUARLES
TREATY OF GUADALUPE HIDALGO (with Gerald P. López)
TRIMBLE V. GORDON
TUCKER ACT
TUITION GRANT
UNCONSTITUTIONALITY
UNITED JEWISH ORGANIZATIONS OF WILLIAMSBURGH V. CAREY
UNITED STATES COURT OF APPEALS FOR THE FEDERAL CIRCUIT
UNITED STATES TRUST CO. OF NEW YORK V. NEW JERSEY
VACCINATION
VALLEY FORGE CHRISTIAN COLLEGE V. AMERICANS UNITED FOR SEPARATION OF CHURCH AND STATE
VENUE
VLANDIS V. KLINE
WAINWRIGHT V. SYKES
WALKER V. BIRMINGHAM
WARD V. ILLINOIS
WATKINS V. UNITED STATES
WAYTE V. UNITED STATES
WENGLER V. DRUGGISTS' MUTUAL INSURANCE CO.
WESBERRY V. SANDERS
WHALEN V. ROE
WIDMAR V. VINCENT
WILLIAMS V. VERMONT
YOUNGER V. HARRIS
ZABLOCKI V. REDHAIL

Don B. Kates, Jr.
Attorney
Benenson & Kates, San Francisco

SECOND AMENDMENT

Andrew L. Kaufman
Charles Stebbins Fairchild Professor of Law
Harvard Law School

CARDOZO, BENJAMIN N.

David Kaye
Professor of Law
Arizona State University

SOCIAL SCIENCE RESEARCH AND CONSTITUTIONAL LAW (with Hans Zeisel)

Morton Keller
Spector Professor of History
Brandeis University

CONSTITUTIONAL HISTORY, 1877–1901
CONSTITUTIONAL HISTORY, 1901–1921

James H. Kettner
Professor of History
University of California, Berkeley

CITIZENSHIP (HISTORICAL DEVELOPMENT)

Edward Keynes
Professor of Political Science
Pennsylvania State University

VIETNAM WAR

Louis W. Koenig
Professor of Political Science
New York University

CABINET

Donald P. Kommers
Professor of Government and International Studies
University of Notre Dame

REGULATORY AGENCIES
SUBJECTS OF COMMERCE
SUPREMACY CLAUSE

Sheldon Krantz
Professor of Law and Dean of the School of Law
University of San Diego

CRUEL AND UNUSUAL PUNISHMENT

James E. Krier
Professor of Law
University of Michigan

ENVIRONMENTAL REGULATION AND THE CONSTITUTION

Samuel Krislov
Professor of Political Science
University of Minnesota, Twin Cities

AMICUS CURIAE
ULYSSES, A BOOK NAMED, UNITED STATES V.

Philip B. Kurland
William R. Kenan Distinguished Service Professor
The University of Chicago

APPOINTING AND REMOVAL POWER, PRESIDENTIAL
EXECUTIVE PRIVILEGE
IMPOUNDMENT OF FUNDS
PARDONING POWER
PRESIDENTIAL POWERS

Stanley I. Kutler
Fox Professor of American Institutions
University of Wisconsin, Madison

BAILEY V. DREXEL FURNITURE COMPANY
BRADLEY, JOSEPH P.
BUNTING V. OREGON
BUTLER, PIERCE
CATRON, JOHN
CHARLES RIVER BRIDGE V. WARREN BRIDGE COMPANY
CHILD LABOR AMENDMENT
CLIFFORD, NATHAN
CURTIS, BENJAMIN R.
DAVIS, DAVID
DAY, WILLIAM R.
EAKIN V. RAUB
EXECUTIVE ORDERS 9835 AND 10450
GIBSON, JOHN BANNISTER
HAMMER V. DAGENHART
HUNT, WARD
KEATING-OWEN CHILD LABOR ACT
KENT V. DULLES
LEGAL TENDER CASES
MATTHEWS, STANLEY
MCREYNOLDS, JAMES C.
MISSISSIPPI V. JOHNSON
MULLER V. OREGON
PITNEY, MAHLON
SANFORD, EDWARD T.
STRONG, WILLIAM
SWAYNE, NOAH H.
TRUAX V. CORRIGAN
VAN DEVANTER, WILLIS
WEST COAST HOTEL CO. V. PARRISH

Wayne R. LaFave
David C. Baum Professor of Law
Professor in the Center for Advanced Study, University of Illinois

SEARCH AND SEIZURE
ADMINISTRATIVE SEARCH
AGNELLO V. UNITED STATES
AGUILAR V. TEXAS
ALMEIDA-SANCHEZ V. UNITED STATES
AUTOMOBILE SEARCH
BORDER SEARCH
BRINEGAR V. UNITED STATES
CALANDRA, UNITED STATES V.
CAMARA V. MUNICIPAL COURT
CARROLL V. UNITED STATES
CHIMEL V. CALIFORNIA
CONSENT SEARCH
DRAPER V. UNITED STATES
ELKINS V. UNITED STATES
EXIGENT CIRCUMSTANCES SEARCH
INFORMANT'S TIP
KER V. CALIFORNIA
MAPP V. OHIO
MARSHALL V. BARLOW'S INC.
PLAIN VIEW DOCTRINE
ROBINSON, UNITED STATES V.
SCHNECKLOTH V. BUSTAMONTE
SEARCH INCIDENT TO ARREST
SILVER PLATTER DOCTRINE
SILVERTHORNE LUMBER COMPANY V. UNITED STATES
SPINELLI V. UNITED STATES
STONE V. POWELL
TERRY V. OHIO
UNREASONABLE SEARCH
WEEKS V. UNITED STATES
WOLF V. COLORADO
WONG SUN V. UNITED STATES
WYMAN V. JAMES

Jacob W. Landynski
Professor of Political Science
New School for Social Research

Leon Letwin
Professor of Law
University of California, Los Angeles

EVIDENTIARY PRIVILEGES

William Letwin
Professor of Economics
London School of Economics and Political Science

ECONOMIC REGULATION AND THE CONSTITUTION

Betsy Levin
Professor of Law and Dean of the Law School
University of Colorado

EDUCATION AND THE CONSTITUTION

Leonard W. Levy
Andrew W. Mellon All-Claremont Professor of the Humanities
Chairman, Graduate Faculty of History
The Claremont Graduate School

ADAIR V. UNITED STATES
ADAMSON V. CALIFORNIA
ADKINS V. CHILDREN'S HOSPITAL
AGUILAR V. FELTON
ALBERTSON V. SUBVERSIVE ACTIVITIES CONTROL BOARD
AMERICAN INSURANCE COMPANY V. CANTER
ARTICLES OF CONFEDERATION
ASHTON V. CAMERON COUNTY WATER IMPROVEMENT DISTRICT
BALDWIN V. NEW YORK
BANCROFT, GEORGE
BANK OF AUGUSTA V. EARLE
BARRON V. BALTIMORE
BAYARD V. SINGLETON
BEDFORD CUT STONE CO. V. JOURNEYMEN STONECUTTERS
BILL OF RIGHTS (ENGLISH)
BILL OF RIGHTS (UNITED STATES)
BLASPHEMY
BOLLMAN AND SWARTWOUT, EX PARTE
BOSTON BEER COMPANY V. MASSACHUSETTS
BOWMAN V. CHICAGO & NORTHWESTERN RAILWAY COMPANY
BOYD V. UNITED STATES
BRADWELL V. ILLINOIS
BREITHAUPT V. ABRAM
BREWER V. WILLIAMS
BRISCOE V. BANK OF KENTUCKY
BRONSON V. KINZIE
BROWN V. MARYLAND
BROWN V. MISSISSIPPI
BROWN V. WALKER
BURSTYN, JOSEPH, INC. V. WILSON
BUTCHERS UNION SLAUGHTERHOUSE CO. V. CRESCENT CITY CO.
BUTLER V. MICHIGAN
BUTLER V. UNITED STATES
CALDER V. BULL
CARTER V. CARTER COAL COMPANY
CATO'S LETTERS
CHAMBERS V. FLORIDA
CHAMBERS V. MARONEY
CHAMPION AND DICKASON V. CASEY
CHANDLER V. FLORIDA
CHEROKEE INDIAN CASES
CHISHOLM V. GEORGIA
CIVIL RIGHTS ACT OF 1875
CIVIL RIGHTS CASES
CLARK, CHARLES E.
COHENS V. VIRGINIA
COLGATE V. HARVEY
COLLECTOR V. DAY
COMMITTEE FOR PUBLIC EDUCATION AND RELIGIOUS LIBERTY V. NYQUIST
COMMONWEALTH V. AVES
COMMONWEALTH V. CATON
CONCORD RESOLUTIONS
CONFIRMATIO CARTARUM
CONNALLY, THOMAS T. (TOM)
CONSTITUTION
CONSTITUTIONAL CONVENTION
CONSTITUTIONAL HISTORY, 1776–1789
CONTINENTAL CONGRESS
COOLEY V. BOARD OF WARDENS OF PORT OF PHILADELPHIA
COOPER, THOMAS
CORFIELD V. CORYELL
COUNSELMAN V. HITCHCOCK
CRAIG V. MISSOURI
CRUIKSHANK, UNITED STATES V.
DANE, NATHAN
DARTMOUTH COLLEGE V. WOODWARD
DEBS, IN RE
DI FRANCESCO, UNITED STATES V.
DIRKSEN, EVERETT M.
DODGE V. WOOLSEY
DUE PROCESS OF LAW
DU PONCEAU, PETER S.
EDWARDS V. ARIZONA
EMBARGO ACTS
EDMUND V. FLORIDA
ENTRAPMENT DEFENSE
ERVIN, SAMUEL J.
ESTABLISHMENT OF RELIGION
ESTELLE V. SMITH
EUCLID V. AMBLER REALTY
EVARTS, WILLIAM
EXCLUSIONARY RULE
FAIR RETURN ON FAIR VALUE
FEDERAL COMMON LAW OF CRIMES
FIELD V. CLARK
FIRST CONTINENTAL CONGRESS, DECLARATIONS AND RESOLVES OF
FISKE, JOHN
FLETCHER V. PECK
FUNDAMENTAL ORDERS OF CONNECTICUT
FURNEAUX, PHILIP
GARRITY V. NEW JERSEY
GELPCKE V. DUBUQUE
GERTZ V. ROBERT WELCH, INC.
GIBBONS V. OGDEN
GLOBE NEWSPAPER V. SUPERIOR COURT
GODFREY V. GEORGIA
GOOD FAITH EXCEPTION
GOUDY, WILLIAM
GRAVES V. NEW YORK EX REL. O'KEEFE
GREAT COMPROMISE
GREEN V. BIDDLE
GRIFFIN V. CALIFORNIA
GROSJEAN V. AMERICAN PRESS COMPANY
HABEAS CORPUS ACT OF 1679
HAIG V. AGEE
HAINES, CHARLES G.

HAND, AUGUSTUS N.
HARRIS, UNITED STATES V.
HARTFORD CONVENTION
HAYBURN'S CASE
HAYNES V. WASHINGTON
HOFFA V. UNITED STATES
HOLDEN V. HARDY
HOLMES V. WALTON
HOME BUILDING & LOAN ASSOCIATION V. BLAISDELL
HOUSTON, CHARLES H.
HOWARD, JACOB M.
HUMPHREY, HUBERT H.
HUMPHREY'S EXECUTOR V. UNITED STATES
HURTADO V. CALIFORNIA
HYLTON V. UNITED STATES
ILLINOIS V. GATES
IMMUNITY GRANT
INALIENABLE POLICE POWER
INCORPORATION DOCTRINE
JACOBS, IN RE
JENKINS V. ANDERSON
JOHNS, UNITED STATES V.
JOHNSON V. LOUISIANA
JONES V. SECURITIES AND EXCHANGE COMMISSION
JUDGE PETERS, UNITED STATES V.
JUDICIARY ACT OF 1801
JUDICIARY ACTS OF 1802
KASTIGAR V. UNITED STATES
KEMMLER, IN RE
KIDD V. PEARSON
KILBOURN V. THOMPSON
KIRSCHBAUM V. WALLING
KOLENDER V. LAWSON
LA FOLLETTE, ROBERT M.
LAMONT V. POSTMASTER GENERAL
LARKIN V. GRENDEL'S DEN
LEISY V. HARDIN
LICENSE CASES
LILBURNE, JOHN
LOAN ASSOCIATION V. TOPEKA
LOEWE V. LAWLOR
LOUISVILLE JOINT STOCK LAND BANK V. RADFORD
LYNCH V. DONNELLY
MACDONALD V. UNITED STATES
MADDEN V. KENTUCKY
MADISON'S "MEMORIAL AND REMONSTRANCE"
MADISON'S NOTES OF THE DEBATE
MALLOY V. HOGAN
MANDAMUS, WRIT OF
MARBURY V. MADISON
MARCHETTI V. UNITED STATES
MARSH V. CHAMBERS
MARSHALL COURT
MARTIN V. HUNTER'S LESSEE
MARTIN V. MOTT
MARYLAND TOLERATION ACT
MASSACHUSETTS BAY, CHARTERS OF
MASSACHUSETTS CIRCULAR LETTER
MASSACHUSETTS CONSTITUTION
MAXWELL V. DOW
MAYOR OF NEW YORK V. MILN
MCCULLOCH V. MARYLAND
MCKEIVER V. PENNSYLVANIA
MCLAUGHLIN, ANDREW C.
MEIKLEJOHN, ALEXANDER
MICHIGAN V. SUMMERS
MILLETT V. PEOPLE
MINNESOTA V. BARBER
MINOR V. HAPPERSETT
MIRANDA V. ARIZONA
MISSOURI PACIFIC RAILROAD V. HUMES
MOREHEAD, NEW YORK EX REL., V. TIPALDO
MUELLER V. ALLEN
MURRAY'S LESSEE V. HOBOKEN LAND & IMPROVEMENT CO.
NEAL V. DELAWARE
NEW JERSEY, COLONIAL CHARTERS OF
NEW JERSEY V. WILSON
NEW JERSEY PLAN
NEW YORK V. QUARLES
NEW YORK CHARTER OF LIBERTIES AND PRIVILEGES
NIX V. WILLIAMS
NORRIS V. ALABAMA
NORTHWESTERN FERTILIZING COMPANY V. HYDE PARK
NORTHWEST ORDINANCE
OGDEN V. SAUNDERS
OLIVER, IN RE
OLIVER V. UNITED STATES
OREGON V. ELSTAD
OROZCO V. TEXAS
OSBORN V. BANK OF THE UNITED STATES (with Kenneth L. Karst)
OVERT ACTS TEST
PACE V. ALABAMA
PALKO V. CONNECTICUT
PANAMA REFINING COMPANY V. RYAN
PARLIAMENTARY PRIVILEGE
PASSENGER CASES
PAYTON V. NEW YORK
PENNSYLVANIA COLONIAL CHARTERS
PENNSYLVANIA CONSTITUTION AND BILL OF RIGHTS
PENSACOLA TELEGRAPH CO. V. WESTERN UNION TELEGRAPH COMPANY
PEOPLE V. CROSWELL
PETITION OF RIGHT
PHILADELPHIA & READING RAILROAD V. PENNSYLVANIA
PIQUA BRANCH BANK V. KNOOP
PLESSY V. FERGUSON
POINTER V. TEXAS
POLLOCK V. FARMERS' LOAN AND TRUST CO.
PREFERRED FREEDOMS
PRICE, UNITED STATES V.

PRODUCTION
PROPELLER GENESEE CHIEF V. FITZHUGH
PROVIDENCE BANK V. BILLINGS
PUBLIC FIGURES
RAILROAD RETIREMENT BOARD V. ALTON RAILWAY COMPANY
RAWLE, WILLIAM
REAGAN V. FARMERS' LOAN & TRUST COMPANY
REESE, UNITED STATES V.
RESERVED POLICE POWER
REYNOLDS V. UNITED STATES
RHODE ISLAND, CHARTER OF
RHODE ISLAND V. INNES
RIGHT AGAINST SELF-INCRIMINATION
ROANE, SPENCER
ROBERTS V. CITY OF BOSTON
ROCHIN V. CALIFORNIA
ROGERS V. RICHMOND
ROSS, UNITED STATES V.
RULE OF REASON
RUMMEL V. ESTELLE
RUTGERS V. WADDINGTON
SCHALL V. MARTIN
SCHECHTER POULTRY CORP. V. UNITED STATES
SCHMERBER V. CALIFORNIA
SCHROEDER, THEODORE
SELECTIVE EXCLUSIVENESS
SHAW, LEMUEL
SIMS' CASE
SINKING FUND CASES
SOCIAL COMPACT THEORY
SOLEM V. HELM
SONZINSKY V. UNITED STATES
SOUTH DAKOTA V. NEVILLE
SPRINGER V. UNITED STATES
STAMP ACT CONGRESS, RESOLUTIONS OF
STEAGALD V. UNITED STATES
STONE V. FARMERS' LOAN AND TRUST COMPANY
STONE V. MISSISSIPPI
STRAUDER V. WEST VIRGINIA
STUART V. LAIRD
STURGES V. CROWNINSHIELD
SULLIVAN, UNITED STATES V.
SUPREME COURT, 1789–1801
TAXATION WITHOUT REPRESENTATION
TENNESSEE V. GARNER
TEN POUND ACT CASES
TERRETT V. TAYLOR
TESTIMONIAL AND NONTESTIMONIAL COMPULSION
TEST OATH CASES
TEXAS V. BROWN
THORNTON V. CALDOR, INC.
TIEDEMAN, CHRISTOPHER G.
TOLERATION ACT
TREVETT V. WEEDEN
TUCKER, ST. GEORGE
TWINING V. NEW JERSEY
TWO SOVEREIGNTIES RULE
ULLMAN V. UNITED STATES
UNITED RAILWAYS & ELECTRIC COMPANY V. West
VAN HORNE'S LESSEE V. DORRANCE
VEAZIE BANK V. FENNO
VERMONT, CONSTITUTION OF
VIRGINIA, CHARTER OF
VIRGINIA CONSTITUTION AND DECLARATION OF RIGHTS
VIRGINIA PLAN
VIRGINIA STATUTE OF RELIGIOUS LIBERTY
VON HOLST, HERMANN
WALKER, TIMOTHY
WALKER V. SAUVINET
WALLACE V. JAFFREE
WARE V. HYLTON
WARREN, CHARLES
WELSH V. WISCONSIN
WESTON V. CITY COUNCIL OF CHARLESTON
WHEELER, BURTON K.
WICKARD V. FILBURN
WILLIAMS V. FLORIDA
WILLIAMS V. MISSISSIPPI
WILLSON V. BLACK BIRD CREEK MARSH COMPANY
WONG KIM ARK, UNITED STATES V.
WOODRUFF V. PARHAM
WORTMAN, TUNIS
WRIGHT V. VINTON BRANCH OF MOUNTAIN TRUST COMPANY
WRIGHTWOOD DAIRY, UNITED STATES V.
WYNEHAMER V. NEW YORK
YARBROUGH, EX PARTE
YBARRA V. ILLINOIS
YELLOW DOG CONTRACT
YICK WO V. HOPKINS
ZENGER'S CASE

Wendy E. Levy
Deputy District Attorney
Los Angeles County

BARKER V. WINGO
KLOPFER V. NORTH CAROLINA
MCNABB-MALLORY RULE

Anthony Lewis
Columnist
The New York Times
Lecturer on Law
Harvard Law School

GIDEON V. WAINWRIGHT
PUBLIC TRIAL
WARREN, EARL

Hans A. Linde
Justice
Supreme Court of Oregon

STATE CONSTITUTIONAL LAW

Charles Lister
Attorney
Covington & Burling, Washington, D.C.

HARLAN, JOHN MARSHALL (1899–1971)

Charles A. Lofgren
Crocker Professor of American Politics and History
Claremont McKenna College

CURTISS-WRIGHT EXPORT CORP., UNITED STATES V.
KOREAN WAR
MISSOURI V. HOLLAND
NATIONAL LEAGUE OF CITIES V. USERY
WAR POWERS

Gerald P. López
Professor of Law
Stanford Law School

CITIZENSHIP (THEORY)
IMMIGRATION (with Kenneth L. Karst)
TREATY OF GUADALUPE HIDALGO (with Kenneth L. Karst)
TREATY ON EXECUTION OF PENAL SENTENCES

Richard Loss
Evanston, Illinois

CORWIN, EDWARD S.

Daniel H. Lowenstein
Professor of Law
University of California, Los Angeles

HATCH ACTS

Theodore J. Lowi
John L. Senior Professor of American Institutions
Cornell University

POLITICAL PARTIES AND THE CONSTITUTION

Dennis J. Mahoney
Assistant Professor of Political Science
California State University, San Bernardino

ADAMS, SAMUEL
ADVICE AND CONSENT
AMNESTY
APTHEKER V. SECRETARY OF STATE
ARTICLES OF IMPEACHMENT (JOHNSON)
ARTICLES OF IMPEACHMENT (NIXON)
ASSOCIATION, THE
ATTAINDER OF TREASON
BAILEY V. ALABAMA
BALDWIN, ABRAHAM
BAREFOOT V. ESTELLE
BASSETT, RICHARD
BEACON THEATRES, INC. V. WESTOVER
BEARD, CHARLES A.
BECKER AMENDMENT
BEDFORD, GUNNING, JR.
BENIGN RACIAL CLASSIFICATIONS
BEVERIDGE, ALBERT J.
BICAMERALISM
BILL OF ATTAINDER
BILL OF CREDIT
BLAINE AMENDMENT
BLAIR, JOHN
BLOUNT, WILLIAM
BLUE RIBBON JURY
BOB JONES UNIVERSITY V. UNITED STATES
BORROWING POWER
BREARLY, DAVID
BRICKER AMENDMENT
BROAD CONSTRUCTION
BROOM, JACOB
BROWN V. ALLEN
BRYCE, JAMES
BUDGET
BUDGET AND ACCOUNTING ACT
BURGESS, JOHN W.
BURR, AARON
BUTLER, PIERCE
CAPITATION TAXES
CARROLL, DANIEL
CARY, JOHN W.
CEASE-AND-DESIST ORDER
CHIPMAN, NATHANIEL
CLOSED SHOP
CLOTURE
CLYMER, GEORGE
COKER V. GEORGIA
COLLECTIVE BARGAINING
COMMONWEALTH STATUS
COMMUNICATIONS ACT
CONCURRENT RESOLUTION
CONCURRING OPINION
CONFEDERATE CONSTITUTION
CONGRESSIONAL PRIVILEGES AND IMMUNITIES
CONSTITUTIONAL HISTORY, 1977–1985
CORWIN AMENDMENT
CRAMER V. UNITED STATES
CRIMINAL JUSTICE ACT OF 1964
CROLY, HERBERT
DAIRY QUEEN, INC. V. WOOD
DALLAS, ALEXANDER J.
DAYTON, JONATHAN
DECISION

Declaration of Independence
Dickinson, John
Dies, Martin
Dissenting Opinion
District of Columbia
Duane, James
Dulany, Daniel
Economic Opportunity Act
Eighteenth Amendment
Eisenhower, Dwight D.
Ex Parte
Exposition and Protest
Farrand, Max
Federal Election Campaign Acts
Federal Energy Agency v. Algonquin SNG, Inc.
Few, William
FitzSimons, Thomas
Ford, Gerald L.
Fraenkel, Osmond K.
Franklin, Benjamin
Freeport Doctrine
Fries' Rebellion
Fugitive from Justice
Gallatin, Albert
Garland, Augustus H.
Giles, William B.
Gilman, Nicholas
Good Behavior
Goodnow, Frank J.
Gorham, Nathaniel
Government Instrumentality
Gramm-Rudman-Hollings Act
Ground of Opinion
Guinn v. United States
Hampton & Co. v. United States
Haupt v. United States
Henry, Patrick
Hicklin v. Orbeck
Holding
Homestead Act
Hoover, Herbert
Hoover, J. Edgar
Hunter v. Erickson
Hutchinson, Thomas
Immigration and Naturalization Service v. Chadha
In Forma Pauperis
In Personam
In Re
In Rem
Incorporation of Territories
Infamy
Ingersoll, Jared
Initiative
Insular Cases
Interstate Compact
Jay's Treaty
Jenifer, Daniel of St. Thomas
Johnson v. Avery
Johnson, Thomas
Johnson, William Samuel
Joint Resolution
Judgment
Jus Dare
Jus Dicere
Kennedy, Robert F.
King, Rufus
Kunz v. New York
Lsngdon, John
Lansing, John, Jr.
Laski, Harold J.
Lee, Richard Henry
Legislative Contempt Power
Letters of Marque and Reprisal
Lincoln, Levi
Livingston, Robert
Livingston, William
Lodge, Henry Cabot
Macon, Nathaniel
Mason, George
Massachusetts v. Laird
McHenry, James
McIlwain, Charles H.
Mifflin, Thomas
Ministerial Act
Monroe, James
Monroe Doctrine
Montesquieu
Morris, Gouverneur
Morris, Robert
Murphy v. Florida
Murphy v. Ford
Murray, William
National Security Act
Nixon v. Administrator of General Services
Norris, George W.
Noxious Products Doctrine
Obligation of Contracts
Opinion of the Court
Ordinance of 1784
Paine, Thomas
Palmer Raids
Panama Canal Treaties
Pendleton, Edmund
Pendleton Act
Penn, William
Perez v. United States
Petit Jury
Philadelphia v. New Jersey
Pickering, John
Pierce, William
Pinckney, Charles
Pinckney, Charles Cotesworth
Pinckney Plan
Pitt, William
Plurality Opinion

POCKET VETO
POCKET VETO CASE
POLICE POWER
POSSE COMITATUS ACT
POWELL v. MCCORMACK
POWELL, THOMAS REED
PRATT, CHARLES
PREAMBLE
PRIVACY ACT
PRIVILEGE FROM ARREST
PRIVY COUNCIL
PROHIBITION
QUIRIN, EX PARTE
RANDOLPH, EDMUND
RATIFICATION OF CONSTITUTIONAL AMENDMENTS
RATIO DECIDENDI
READ, GEORGE
RECALL
REFERENDUM
REID v. COVERT
RETROACTIVITY OF LEGISLATION
REVENUE SHARING
RIGHT-PRIVILEGE DISTINCTION (with Kenneth L. Karst)
RODNEY, CAESAR AUGUSTUS
ROOSEVELT, THEODORE
RUTLEDGE, JOHN
SCHICK v. REED
SCHNELL v. DAVIS
SCHOULER, JAMES
SEDITION
SELECTIVE DRAFT LAW CASES
SELECTIVE SERVICE ACTS
SERIATIM
SEVENTEENTH AMENDMENT
SEVENTH AMENDMENT
SHAYS' REBELLION
SHERMAN, ROGER
SMITH, J. ALLEN
SOUNDTRUCKS AND AMPLIFIERS
SOVEREIGNTY
SPAIGHT, RICHARD DOBBS
SPOT RESOLUTIONS
STARE DECISIS
STATE
STATES' RIGHTS
SUBVERSIVE ACTIVITY
SWAIN v. ALABAMA
TAFT, ROBERT A.
TAYLOR, JOHN
TERRITORIES
THIRD AMENDMENT
THORPE, FRANCIS NEWTON
TITLES OF NOBILITY
TOCQUEVILLE, ALEXIS DE
TOWNSHEND ACTS
TROP v. DULLES
TUCKER, HENRY ST. GEORGE
TUCKER, JOHN RANDOLPH
TUCKER, N. BEVERLEY
TWELFTH AMENDMENT
TWENTIETH AMENDMENT
TWENTY-FIFTH AMENDMENT
TWENTY-FIRST AMENDMENT
TWENTY-FOURTH AMENDMENT
TWENTY-SECOND AMENDMENT
TWENTY-SIXTH AMENDMENT
TWENTY-THIRD AMENDMENT
VATTEL, EMERICH DE
VOLSTEAD ACT
WAR POWERS ACTS
WASHINGTON, GEORGE
WASHINGTON'S FAREWELL ADDRESS
WEEMS v. UNITED STATES
WELFARE BENEFITS
WILLIAMSON, HUGH
WILLIAMSON v. LEE OPTICAL COMPANY
WILLOUGHBY, WESTEL W.
WILSON, WOODROW
YATES, ROBERT
YOUNG, EX PARTE
ZEMEL v. RUSK

Daniel R. Mandelker
Stamper Professor of Law
Washington University, St. Louis

ZONING (with Barbara Ross)

Everett E. Mann, Jr.
Associate Professor of Public Policy and Administration
California State College, Bakersfield

FREEDOM OF INFORMATION ACT

Burke Marshall
Nicholas deB. Katzenbach Professor of Law
Yale Law School
Former Solicitor General of the United States

ATTORNEY GENERAL AND DEPARTMENT OF JUSTICE

Alpheus Thomas Mason
McCormick Professor of Jurisprudence, Emeritus
Princeton University

ROBERTS, OWEN J.
STONE, HARLAN F.
TAFT, WILLIAM HOWARD

Charles W. McCurdy
Associate Professor of History and Law
University of Virginia

BLATCHFORD, SAMUEL
FIELD, STEPHEN J.
FULLER, MELVILLE W.
GRAY, HORACE
JACKSON, HOWELL E.
LAMAR, L. Q. C.
MILLER, SAMUEL F.
MONETARY POWER
PECKHAM, RUFUS W.
SHIRAS, GEORGE, JR.
WAITE COURT
WOODS, WILLIAM B.

Gary L. McDowell
Associate Professor of Political Science
Newcomb College of Tulane University

CONGRESS AND THE SUPREME COURT

Carl McGowan
Senior Judge
United States Court of Appeals for the District of Columbia Circuit

UNITED STATES COURTS OF APPEALS

Robert B. McKay
Professor of Law
New York University

REAPPORTIONMENT

Daniel J. Meador
James Monroe Professor of Law
University of Virginia

COKE, EDWARD

Bernard D. Meltzer
Distinguished Service Professor of Law, Emeritus
The University of Chicago

RIGHT TO WORK LAWS

Wallace Mendelson
Professor of Government
The University of Texas at Austin

CONTRACT CLAUSE

Frank I. Michelman
Professor of Law
Harvard Law School

PROCEDURAL DUE PROCESS OF LAW, CIVIL

Abner J. Mikva
Judge
U.S. Court of Appeals for the District of Columbia Circuit

PREVENTIVE DETENTION

Arthur S. Miller
Professor of Law, Emeritus
The George Washington University

CONSTITUTIONAL REASON OF STATE
CORPORATIONS AND THE CONSTITUTION

Paul J. Mishkin
Emanuel S. Heller Professor of Law
University of California, Berkeley

HABEAS CORPUS

Robert H. Mnookin
Professor of Law
Stanford Law School

CHILDREN'S RIGHTS
GAULT, IN RE
GINSBURG V. NEW YORK
JUVENILE PROCEEDINGS

Henry P. Monaghan
Thomas Macioce Professor of Law
Columbia University

CONSTITUTIONAL COMMON LAW

*Donald G. Morgan
Professor of Politics
Mount Holyoke College

JOHNSON, WILLIAM

Edmund S. Morgan
Sterling Professor of History
Yale University

CONSTITUTIONAL HISTORY BEFORE 1776

Richard E. Morgan
William Nelson Cromwell Professor of Constitutional Law and Government
Bowdoin College

ABINGTON TOWNSHIP SCHOOL DISTRICT V. SCHEMPP
BOARD OF EDUCATION V. ALLEN

* Deceased.

CANTWELL V. CONNECTICUT
CHURCH OF JESUS CHRIST OF LATTER-DAY SAINTS V. UNITED STATES
COCHRAN V. LOUISIANA BOARD OF EDUCATION
COMMITTEE FOR PUBLIC EDUCATION & RELIGIOUS LIBERTY V. REGAN
DAVIS V. BEASON
DOREMUS V. BOARD OF EDUCATION OF HAWTHORNE
ENGEL V. VITALE
EPPERSON V. ARKANSAS
EVERSON V. BOARD OF EDUCATION OF EWING TOWNSHIP
FLAG SALUTE CASES
GIROUARD V. UNITED STATES
HAMILTON V. REGENTS OF UNIVERSITY OF CALIFORNIA
JACOBSON V. MASSACHUSETTS
LEMON V. KURTZMAN
LOVELL V. GRIFFIN
MCCOLLUM, ILLINOIS EX REL., V. BOARD OF EDUCATION
MURDOCK V. PENNSYLVANIA
PRINCE V. MASSACHUSETTS
SCHWIMMER, UNITED STATES V.
SEEGER, UNITED STATES V.
SHERBERT V. VERNER
TORCASO V. WATKINS
WISCONSIN V. YODER
WOLMAN V. WALTER
ZORACH V. CLAUSEN

Paul L. Murphy
Professor of History and American Studies
University of Minnesota

ALIEN REGISTRATION ACT
ATOMIC ENERGY ACT
ATTORNEY GENERAL'S LIST
CHAFEE, ZECHERIAH, JR.
COMMUNIST CONTROL ACT
CONGRESSIONAL BUDGET AND IMPOUNDMENT CONTROL ACT
CONSTITUTIONAL HISTORY, 1921–1933
CONSTITUTIONAL HISTORY, 1945–1961
DISTRICT OF COLUMBIA REPRESENTATION AMENDMENT
DISTRICT OF COLUMBIA SELF-GOVERNING AND GOVERNMENT REORGANIZATION ACT
ECONOMIC STABILIZATION ACT
ELEMENTARY AND SECONDARY EDUCATION ACT
EMERGENCY PRICE CONTROL ACT
ESPIONAGE ACT
FEDERAL IMMUNITY ACT
FULL EMPLOYMENT ACT
HEALTH INSURANCE FOR THE AGED ACT
HOUSE COMMITTEE ON UN-AMERICAN ACTIVITIES
INTERNAL SECURITY ACT
JENCKS ACT
LANDRUM-GRIFFIN ACT
MUNDT-NIXON BILL
OMNIBUS CRIME CONTROL AND SAFE STREETS ACT
ORGANIZED CRIME CONTROL ACT
PENNSYLVANIA V. NELSON
REPORT OF THE STATE CHIEF JUSTICES
SEDITION ACT
SELECTIVE SERVICE ACT
SHEPPARD-TOWNER MATERNITY ACT
SOUTHERN MANIFESTO
STEEL SEIZURE CONTROVERSY
SUBVERSIVE ACTIVITIES CONTROL BOARD
TAFT-HARTLEY LABOR MANAGEMENT RELATIONS ACT
WATERGATE AND THE CONSTITUTION
YATES V. UNITED STATES

Walter F. Murphy
McCormick Professor of Jurisprudence
Princeton University

JUDICIAL STRATEGY
JUDICIAL SUPREMACY

William P. Murphy
Paul B. Eaton Professor of Law
The University of North Carolina at Chapel Hill

FAIR LABOR STANDARDS ACT
MAXIMUM HOURS AND MINIMUM WAGES LEGISLATION

John M. Murrin
Professor of History
Princeton University

BRITISH CONSTITUTION

William E. Nelson
Professor of Law
New York University

FOURTEENTH AMENDMENT (FRAMING)

Ira Nerken
Attorney
Latham, Watkins & Hills, Washington, D.C.

CONSCRIPTION (with Richard Danzig)

Burt Neuborne
Professor of Law
New York University
Director of Litigation
American Civil Liberties Union

BLACKMUN, HARRY A.
LITIGATION STRATEGY

Roger K. Newman
Attorney
New York

BLACK, HUGO L.
CAHN, EDMOND

R. Kent Newmyer
Professor of History
University of Connecticut

BALDWIN, HENRY
BARBOUR, PHILIP P.
MCKINLEY, JOHN
MCLEAN, JOHN
TANEY COURT
TRIMBLE, ROBERT

*Melville B. Nimmer
Professor of Law
University of California, Los Angeles

COPYRIGHT
PRIVACY AND THE FIRST AMENDMENT
SYMBOLIC SPEECH

W. John Niven
Professor of History
The Claremont Graduate School

VAN BUREN, MARTIN

John T. Noonan, Jr.
Judge
United States Court of Appeals for the Ninth Circuit
Former Professor of Law
University of California, Berkeley

REAGAN, RONALD W.

John E. Nowak
Professor of Law
University of Illinois

BREACH OF THE PEACE
FELONY
SUBPOENA
TRESPASS

David M. Oshinsky
Professor of History
Rutgers University

MCCARTHYISM

Lewis J. Paper
Attorney
Washington, D.C.

BRANDEIS, LOUIS D.

* Deceased.

Michael E. Parrish
Professor of History
University of California, San Diego

AFROYIM V. RUSK
BRIDGES V. CALIFORNIA
BURTON, HAROLD H.
BYRNES, JAMES F.
CLARKE, JOHN H.
COMMONWEALTH V. SACCO AND VANZETTI
CONSTITUTIONAL HISTORY, 1933–1945
DEBS V. UNITED STATES
ELFBRANDT V. RUSSELL
FRANKFURTER, FELIX
FROHWERK V. UNITED STATES
GERENDE V. BOARD OF SUPERVISORS OF ELECTIONS OF BALTIMORE
GIBONEY V. EMPIRE STORAGE AND ICE COMPANY
HUGHES, CHARLES EVANS
IRVIN V. DOWD
JACKSON, ROBERT H.
JOINT ANTI-FASCIST REFUGEE COMMITTEE V. MCGRATH
KENNEDY, JOHN F.
LINMARK ASSOCIATES V. WILLINGBORO
LOVETT, UNITED STATES V.
MCKENNA, JOSEPH
NIEMOTKO V. MARYLAND
PARKER V. LEVY
PROCUNIER V. MARTINEZ
ROBEL, UNITED STATES V.
ROSENBERG V. UNITED STATES
RUTLEDGE, WILEY B.
SHAUGHNESSY, UNITED STATES EX REL. MEZEI V.
STATE OF TENNESSEE V. SCOPES
STROMBERG V. CALIFORNIA
WHITE, EDWARD D.
WHITTAKER, CHARLES E.
WIEMAN V. UPDEGRAFF

J. Francis Paschal
Professor of Law
Duke University

SUTHERLAND, GEORGE H.

Michael J. Perry
Professor of Law
Northwestern University

ABORTION AND THE CONSTITUTION

Merrill D. Peterson
Thomas Jefferson Professor of History and Former Dean of Faculty
University of Virginia

ADAMS, JOHN
ALIEN AND SEDITION ACTS

AMERICAN SYSTEM
BANK OF THE UNITED STATES ACTS
CALHOUN, JOHN C.
CLAY, HENRY
CONSTITUTIONAL HISTORY, 1789–1801
CONSTITUTIONAL HISTORY, 1801–1829
INTERNAL IMPROVEMENTS
JACKSON, ANDREW
JEFFERSON, THOMAS
LOUISIANA PURCHASE TREATY
PROCLAMATION OF NEUTRALITY
VIRGINIA AND KENTUCKY RESOLUTIONS
WHISKEY REBELLION

Leo Pfeffer
Professor of Constitutional Law
Long Island University
Former General Counsel
American Jewish Congress

AMERICAN JEWISH CONGRESS
CHILD BENEFIT THEORY
CULTS (RELIGIOUS) AND THE CONSTITUTION
GOVERNMENT AID TO RELIGIOUS INSTITUTIONS
RELEASED TIME
RELIGION AND FRAUD
RELIGION IN PUBLIC SCHOOLS
RELIGIOUS LIBERTY
RELIGIOUS TEST FOR PUBLIC OFFICE
RELIGIOUS USE OF STATE PROPERTY
SUNDAY CLOSING LAWS

Louis H. Pollak
Judge
United States District Court, Eastern District of Pennsylvania

VOTING RIGHTS

Robert Post
Professor of Law
University of California, Berkeley

BRENNAN, WILLIAM J.

Monroe E. Price
Professor of Law and Dean
Cardozo School of Law
Yeshiva University of New York

BROADCASTING
FAIRNESS DOCTRINE
PRISONERS' RIGHTS
STEWART, POTTER

C. Herman Pritchett
Professor of Political Science, Emeritus
University of California, Santa Barbara

CONGRESSIONAL MEMBERSHIP
VINSON COURT

A. Kenneth Pye
Samuel Fox Mordecai Professor of Law
Duke University

SPEEDY TRIAL

David M. Rabban
Professor of Law
The University of Texas at Austin

ACADEMIC FREEDOM

Jeremy Rabkin
Professor of Political Science
Cornell University

LEGISLATIVE POWER

Norman Redlich
Dean and Judge Edward Weinfeld Professor of Law
New York University

NINTH AMENDMENT

Willis L. M. Reese
Charles Evans Hughes Professor of Law, Emeritus and Special Service Professor
Columbia University

FULL FAITH AND CREDIT

Donald H. Regan
Professor of Law and Professor of Philosophy
University of Michigan

PHILOSOPHY AND THE CONSTITUTION

John Phillip Reid
Professor of Law
New York University

COLONIAL CHARTERS
DOE, CHARLES

Deborah L. Rhode
Professor of Law
Stanford Law School

EQUAL RIGHTS AMENDMENT
NINETEENTH AMENDMENT

Charles E. Rice
Professor of Law
University of Notre Dame

FREEDOM OF PETITION

Kenneth F. Ripple
Judge
United States Court of Appeals for the Seventh Circuit
Professor of Law
University of Notre Dame

CHIEF JUSTICE, ROLE OF

John P. Roche
Professor of Civilization and Foreign Affairs and Former Dean of the Fletcher School of Law and Diplomacy
Tufts University

CONSTITUTIONAL CONVENTION OF 1787

Donald M. Roper
Professor of History
State University of New York, New Paltz

KENT, JAMES
LIVINGSTON, HENRY BROCKHOLST
THOMPSON, SMITH

Arthur Rosett
Professor of Law
University of California, Los Angeles

ANTITRUST LAW AND THE CONSTITUTION
PLEA BARGAINING
REED, STANLEY F.
UNCONSTITUTIONAL CONDITIONS

Barbara Ross
Attorney
Ross & Hardies, Chicago

ZONING (with Daniel R. Mandelker)

Ralph A. Rossum
Alice Tweed Tuohy Professor of Government
Claremont McKenna College

DENATURALIZATION
DEPORTATION
EXPATRIATION
NATURALIZATION
WILSON, JAMES

Eugene V. Rostow
Sterling Professor of Law, Emeritus
Yale Law School
Distinguished Visiting Research Professor of Law and Diplomacy
National Defense University

COMMANDER-IN-CHIEF
WAR, FOREIGN AFFAIRS, AND THE CONSTITUTION

W. W. Rostow
Professor of Economics and History
The University of Texas at Austin

JOHNSON, LYNDON BAINES

Wilfrid E. Rumble
Professor of Political Science
Vassar College

LEGAL REALISM
POUND, ROSCOE
SOCIOLOGICAL JURISPRUDENCE

Robert A. Rutland
Editor-in-Chief, Papers of James Madison
University of Virginia

RATIFICATION OF THE CONSTITUTION

Stephen A. Saltzburg
Professor of Law
University of Virginia

REASONABLE DOUBT

Joseph L. Sax
Philip A. Hart Distinguished University Professor of Law
University of Michigan

TAKING OF PROPERTY

Frederick F. Schauer
Professor of Law
University of Michigan

NEW YORK TIMES COMPANY v. UNITED STATES

Harry N. Scheiber
Professor of Law
University of California, Berkeley

AFFECTED WITH A PUBLIC INTEREST
COMPETITIVE FEDERALISM
COOPERATIVE FEDERALISM
DUAL FEDERALISM
EMINENT DOMAIN
FEDERALISM (HISTORY)
GRANGER CASES
NEBBIA v. NEW YORK
PUBLIC PURPOSE DOCTRINE
STATE POLICE POWER
VESTED RIGHTS DOCTRINE
WEST RIVER BRIDGE COMPANY v. DIX

Arthur Schlesinger, Jr.
Schweitzer Professor in the Humanities
City University of New York

ROOSEVELT, FRANKLIN D.

Benno C. Schmidt, Jr.
President
Yale University

COMMERCIAL SPEECH
FREE PRESS/FAIR TRIAL
LIBEL AND THE FIRST AMENDMENT
PRIOR RESTRAINT AND CENSORSHIP
REPORTER'S PRIVILEGE
SHIELD LAWS
WHITE COURT

Gary T. Schwartz
Professor of Law
University of California, Los Angeles

ECONOMIC ANALYSIS

Herman Schwartz
Professor of Law
Washington College of Law, American University

ALDERMAN V. UNITED STATES
BERGER V. NEW YORK
ELECTRONIC EAVESDROPPING
GELBARD V. UNITED STATES
IRVINE V. CALIFORNIA
KATZ V. UNITED STATES
LOPEZ V. UNITED STATES
NARDONE V. UNITED STATES
NATIONAL SECURITY AND THE FOURTH AMENDMENT
OLMSTEAD V. UNITED STATES
ON LEE V. UNITED STATES
SILVERMAN V. UNITED STATES
UNITED STATES DISTRICT COURT, UNITED STATES V.
WHITE, UNITED STATES V.
WIRETAPPING

Murray L. Schwartz
Professor of Law
University of California, Los Angeles

VINSON, FRED M.

David L. Shapiro
William Nelson Cromwell Professor of Law
Harvard Law School

ERIE RAILROAD V. TOMPKINS
FEDERAL COMMON LAW, CIVIL
SWIFT V. TYSON

Martin Shapiro
Professor of Law
University of California, Berkeley

ABOOD V. DETROIT BOARD OF EDUCATION
ABRAMS V. UNITED STATES
ADDERLEY V. FLORIDA
ADLER V. BOARD OF EDUCATION OF CITY OF NEW YORK
AMERICAN COMMUNICATIONS ASSOCIATION V. DOWDS
BAD TENDENCY TEST
BALANCING TEST
BARENBLATT V. UNITED STATES
BEAUHARNAIS V. ILLINOIS
BRANDENBURG V. OHIO
BUCKLEY V. VALEO
CAPTIVE AUDIENCE
CHAPLINSKY V. NEW HAMPSHIRE
CLEAR AND PRESENT DANGER
COHEN V. CALIFORNIA
COMMUNIST PARTY V. SUBVERSIVE ACTIVITY CONTROL BOARD
COX V. LOUISIANA
COX V. NEW HAMPSHIRE
DE JONGE V. OREGON
DENNIS V. UNITED STATES
FEINER V. NEW YORK
FIGHTING WORDS
FIRST NATIONAL BANK OF BOSTON V. BELLOTTI
GIBSON V. FLORIDA LEGISLATIVE INVESTIGATION COMMISSION
GITLOW V. NEW YORK
HERNDON V. LOWRY
HUDGENS V. N.L.R.B.
KEYISHIAN V. BOARD OF REGENTS
KONIGSBERG V. STATE BAR OF CALIFORNIA
KOVACS V. COOPER
LAIRD V. TATUM
MARSH V. ALABAMA
MASSES PUBLISHING COMPANY V. PATTEN
MCCLOSKEY, ROBERT G.
MCGRAIN V. DAUGHERTY
MIAMI HERALD PUBLISHING COMPANY V. TORNILLO
NAACP V. BUTTON
NEAR V. MINNESOTA EX REL. OLSON
RED LION BROADCASTING CO. V. F.C.C.
SCALES V. UNITED STATES
SCHENCK V. UNITED STATES
SCHWARE V. NEW MEXICO BOARD OF BAR EXAMINERS
SPEISER V. RANDALL
TERMINIELLO V. CHICAGO
THORNHILL V. ALABAMA
UPHAUS V. WYMAN
VIRGINIA STATE BOARD OF PHARMACY V. VIRGINIA CITIZENS CONSUMER COUNCIL
WHITNEY V. CALIFORNIA

Steven H. Shiffrin
Professor of Law
University of California, Los Angeles

BRANZBURG V. HAYES
COLUMBIA BROADCASTING SYSTEM V. DEMOCRATIC NATIONAL COMMITTEE
COOLIDGE V. NEW HAMPSHIRE
COX BROADCASTING CORP. V. COHN
FEDERAL COMMUNICATIONS COMMISSION V. PACIFICA FOUNDATION
GOVERNMENT SPEECH
GROUP LIBEL
KINGSLEY INTERNATIONAL PICTURES CORP. V. REGENTS
LISTENERS' RIGHTS
MARKETPLACE OF IDEAS
OBSCENITY
RIGHT TO KNOW
TWO-LEVEL THEORY

Bernard H. Siegan
Distinguished Professor of Law
University of San Diego

ECONOMIC LIBERTIES AND THE CONSTITUTION

Stanley Siegel
Professor of Law
University of California, Los Angeles

POSTAL POWER

Jay A. Sigler
Distinguished Professor of Political Science
Rutgers University

DOUBLE JEOPARDY

Thomas B. Silver
President
Public Research Syndicated

COOLIDGE, CALVIN
HARDING, WARREN G.

Aviam Soifer
Professor of Law
Boston University

BRANTI V. FINKEL
CAROLENE PRODUCTS CO., UNITED STATES V.
GUILT BY ASSOCIATION
RICHMOND NEWSPAPERS, INC. V. VIRGINIA

Theodore J. St. Antoine
James E. and Sarah A. Degan Professor of Law
University of Michigan

BOYCOTT
PICKETING

Robert L. Stern
Attorney
Mayer, Brown & Platt, Chicago

COMMERCE CLAUSE
DARBY LUMBER COMPANY, UNITED STATES V.
WAGNER ACT CASES

Gerald Stourzh
Professor of History
University of Vienna

HAMILTON, ALEXANDER

Frank R. Strong
Cary C. Boshamer University Distinguished Professor of Law, Emeritus
University of North Carolina

FUNDAMENTAL LAW AND THE SUPREME COURT
LAW OF THE LAND

Philippa Strum
Professor of Political Science
City University of New York (Brooklyn College and the Graduate Center)

POLITICAL QUESTIONS

*William F. Swindler
John Marshall Professor of Law
Marshall-Wythe School of Law
College of William and Mary

BLACKSTONE, WILLIAM

Nathan Tarcov
Associate Professor of Political Science
University of Chicago

POPULAR SOVEREIGNTY (IN DEMOCRATIC POLITICAL THEORY)

Telford Taylor
Nash Professor of Law, Emeritus
Columbia University
Dr. Herman George and Kate Kaiser Professor of Constitutional Law
Cardozo College of Law
Yeshiva University of New York

LEGISLATIVE INVESTIGATIONS

Glen E. Thurow

* Deceased.

Associate Professor of Politics
University of Dallas

DORMANT POWERS
EXCLUSIVE POWERS

Laurence H. Tribe
Tyler Professor of Constitutional Law
Harvard Law School

SUBSTANTIVE DUE PROCESS OF LAW

Phillip R. Trimble
Professor of Law
University of California, Los Angeles

DAMES & MOORE V. REGAN
EXTRATERRITORIALITY

Mark V. Tushnet
Professor of Law
Georgetown University

MARSHALL, THURGOOD

*Arvo Van Alstyne
Professor of Law
University of Utah
Commissioner of Higher Education
State of Utah

INVERSE CONDEMNATION
JUST COMPENSATION
PUBLIC USE

William Van Alstyne
Perkins Professor of Law
Duke University

IMPLIED POWERS
JUDICIAL ACTIVISM AND JUDICIAL RESTRAINT
SUPREME COURT (ROLE IN AMERICAN GOVERNMENT)

Jonathan D. Varat
Professor of Law
University of California, Los Angeles

ADVISORY OPINION
CASES AND CONTROVERSIES
COLLUSIVE SUIT
FLAST V. COHEN
INVALID ON ITS FACE
JUSTICIABILITY
MOOTNESS
OVERBREADTH
PUBLIC EMPLOYEES
RIPENESS
SIERRA CLUB V. MORTON
STANDING
STOCKHOLDER'S SUIT
STUDENTS CHALLENGING REGULATORY AGENCY PROCEDURES (SCRAP), UNITED STATES V.
TAXPAYERS' AND CITIZENS' SUITS
VAGUENESS
WHITE, BYRON R.

Maurice J. C. Vile
Professor of History
University of Kent at Canterbury

SEPARATION OF POWERS

*Clement Ellery Vose
John E. Andrus Professor of Government
Wesleyan University

TEST CASE

Kim McLane Wardlaw
Attorney
O'Melveny & Myers, Los Angeles

BANTAM BOOKS V. SULLIVAN
ERZNOZNIK V. JACKSONVILLE
GANNETT V. DEPASQUALE
HERBERT V. LANDO
JACOBELLIS V. OHIO
KINGSLEY BOOKS, INC. V. BROWN
MEMOIRS V. MASSACHUSETTS
MILLER V. CALIFORNIA
NEBRASKA PRESS ASSOCIATION V. STUART
ROTH V. UNITED STATES
SNEPP V. UNITED STATES
STANLEY V. GEORGIA

Stephen L. Wasby
Professor of Political Science
State University of New York, Albany

IMPACT OF SUPREME COURT DECISIONS

Lloyd L. Weinreb
Professor of Law
Harvard Law School

FAIR TRIAL
WARRANTLESS SEARCH

Robert Weisberg
Professor of Law
Stanford Law School

CAPITAL PUNISHMENT

* Deceased.

Harry H. Wellington
Sterling Professor of Law
Yale Law School

LABOR AND THE CONSTITUTION

Peter Westen
Professor of Law
University of Michigan

COMPULSORY PROCESS
CONFRONTATION, RIGHT OF
HEARSAY RULES

Burns H. Weston
Bessie Dutton Murray Professor of Law
University of Iowa

BELMONT, UNITED STATES v.
EXECUTIVE AGREEMENTS
INTERNATIONAL EMERGENCY ECONOMIC POWERS ACT
MARSHALL PLAN
NORTH ATLANTIC TREATY
PINK, UNITED STATES v.
STATUS OF FORCES AGREEMENT
TREATY POWER
UNITED NATIONS CHARTER

G. Edward White
Professor of Law
University of Virginia

HOLMES, OLIVER WENDELL
WARREN COURT

James Boyd White
L. Hart Wright Professor of Law and Professor of English Language and Literature
University of Michigan

ARREST
BURDEN OF PROOF
FEDERAL RULES OF CRIMINAL PROCEDURE
JURY DISCRIMINATION

Charles H. Whitebread
George T. Pfleger Professor of Law
University of Southern California

DISCOVERY
INDICTMENT
INFORMATION
MERE EVIDENCE RULE
MIRANDA RULES
MISDEMEANOR
PRESENTMENT
PROBABLE CAUSE
STOP AND FRISK
VOIR DIRE

William M. Wiecek
Congdon Professor of Public Law and Legislation
Syracuse University

ABLEMAN v. BOOTH
ABOLITIONIST CONSTITUTIONAL THEORY
ANNEXATION OF TEXAS
BLACK CODES
CHASE COURT
CIVIL LIBERTIES AND THE ANTISLAVERY CONTROVERSY
COMPROMISE OF 1850
CONFISCATION ACTS
CONQUERED PROVINCES THEORY
CONSTITUTIONAL HISTORY, 1829–1848
DANIEL, PETER V.
FORCE ACT
FORCE ACTS
FREEDMEN'S BUREAU
FUGITIVE SLAVERY
GROVES v. SLAUGHTER
GUARANTEE CLAUSE
JOINT COMMITTEE ON RECONSTRUCTION
KANSAS-NEBRASKA ACT
LECOMPTON CONSTITUTION
LINCOLN'S PLAN OF RECONSTRUCTION
LINCOLN-DOUGLAS DEBATES
LUTHER v. BORDEN
MAYSVILLE ROAD BILL
MCCARDLE, EX PARTE
MILITARY RECONSTRUCTION ACTS
MISSOURI COMPROMISE
MORRILL ACT
NASHVILLE CONVENTION RESOLUTIONS
NULLIFICATION
OMNIBUS ACT
PEONAGE
PERSONAL LIBERTY LAWS
POPULAR SOVEREIGNTY AND SLAVERY IN THE TERRITORIES
PRIZE CASES
PROHIBITION OF SLAVE TRADE ACT
REPUBLICAN FORM OF GOVERNMENT
SECESSION
SLAVERY IN THE TERRITORIES
SOMERSET'S CASE
SOUTH CAROLINA ORDINANCE OF NULLIFICATION
SOUTH CAROLINA ORDINANCE OF SECESSION
STATE SUICIDE THEORY
STRADER v. GRAHAM
TANEY, ROGER B.
TENURE OF OFFICE ACT
THREE-FIFTHS CLAUSE
WAYNE, JAMES M.

J. Harvie Wilkinson III
Judge
United States Court of Appeals for the Fourth Circuit

POWELL, LEWIS F., JR.

Peter Woll
Professor of Politics
Brandeis University

BUREAUCRACY

C. Vann Woodward
Sterling Professor of History, Emeritus
Yale University

COMPROMISE OF 1877

L. Kinvin Wroth
Professor of Law and Dean of the School of Law
University of Maine

COMMON LAW
RULE OF LAW

Stephen C. Yeazell
Professor of Law
University of California, Los Angeles

ADMINISTRATIVE LAW
CLASS ACTION
COLLATERAL ATTACK
CONTEMPT POWER
FAIR HEARING
INJUNCTION
INSTITUTIONAL LITIGATION (with Theodore Eisenberg)
JURISDICTION
NOTICE

Hans Zeisel
Professor of Law, Emeritus
The University of Chicago

SOCIAL SCIENCE RESEARCH AND CONSTITUTIONAL LAW (with David Kaye)

John Zvesper
Professor of Politics
University of East Anglia at Norwich

RIGHT OF REVOLUTION

A

ABBATE v. UNITED STATES

See: *Bartkus v. Illinois*

ABINGTON TOWNSHIP SCHOOL DISTRICT v. SCHEMPP
374 U.S. 203 (1963)

A Pennsylvania statute required that at least ten verses from the Holy Bible be read, without comment, at the opening of each public school day. A child might be excused from this exercise upon the written request of his parents or guardian.

In ENGEL V. VITALE (1962) the school prayer held unconstitutional had been written by state officials. The question in *Schempp* was whether this made a difference—there being no claim that Pennsylvania was implicated in the authorship of the holy scripture.

Justice TOM C. CLARK concluded that the Pennsylvania exercise suffered from an establishment-clause infirmity every bit as grave as that afflicting New York's prayer. Clark's opinion in *Schempp* was the first strict separationist opinion of the Court not written by Justice HUGO L. BLACK, and Clark formulated a test for establishment clause validity with a precision that had eluded Black. A state program touching upon religion or religious institutions must have a valid secular purpose and must not have the primary effect of advancing or inhibiting religion. The Pennsylvania Bible reading program failed the test on both counts.

Justices WILLIAM O. DOUGLAS and WILLIAM J. BRENNAN concurred separately in opinions reflecting an even stricter separationism than Clark's. Justice ARTHUR J. GOLDBERG also filed a brief concurring opinion.

Justice POTTER STEWART dissented, as he had in *Engel,* arguing that religious exercises as part of public ceremonies were permissible so long as children were not coerced to participate.

Schempp, along with *Murray v. Curlett* (decided the same day), settled whatever lingering question there may have been about the constitutionality of RELIGION IN PUBLIC SCHOOLS.

RICHARD E. MORGAN

ABLEMAN v. BOOTH
21 Howard 506 (1859)

Ableman v. Booth, Chief Justice ROGER B. TANEY's last major opinion, was part of the dramatic confrontation between the Wisconsin Supreme Court, intent on judicial nullification of the FUGITIVE SLAVE ACTS, and the Supreme Court of the United States, seeking to protect the reach of that statute into the free states.

For his role in organizing a mob that freed Joshua Glover, an alleged fugitive, Sherman Booth was charged with violation of the Fugitive Slave Act of 1850. After trial and conviction, he was released by a writ of habeas corpus from the Wisconsin Supreme Court, which held the Fugitive Slave Act unconstitutional, the first instance in which a state court did so. The Wisconsin court instructed its clerk to make no return to a WRIT OF ERROR from the United States Supreme Court and no entry on the records of the court concerning that writ, thus defying the United States Supreme Court.

The Court took JURISDICTION despite the procedural irregularity. In a magisterial opinion for a unanimous Court, Taney condemned the obstruction of the Wisconsin court and reaffirmed federal JUDICIAL SUPREMACY under section 25 of the JUDICIARY ACT OF 1789. Because the state's sovereignty "is limited and restricted by the Constitution of the United States," no state court process, including habeas corpus, could interfere with the enforcement of federal law. Taney also delivered two significant dicta. He anticipated the later doctrine of DUAL SOVEREIGNTY, which was to hamper state and federal regulatory authority in the early twentieth century, when he wrote that though the powers of the state and federal governments are exercised within the same territorial limits, they "are yet separate and distinct sovereignties, acting separately and independently of each other, within their respective spheres." Taney concluded his opinion by declaring the Fugitive Slave Act of 1850 to be "in all of its provisions, fully authorized by the Constitution."

A reconstituted Wisconsin Supreme Court later conceded the validity of Taney's interpretation of section 25 and apologized to the United States Supreme Court, conceding that its earlier actions were "a breach of that comity, or good behavior, which should be maintained between the courts of the two governments."

WILLIAM M. WIECEK

ABOLITIONIST CONSTITUTIONAL THEORY

American abolitionists developed comprehensive but conflicting theories about the place of slavery in the American constitution. Though these ideas did not positively influence political and legal debate until the 1850s, they exercised profound influence over subsequent constitutional development, merging with constitutional aspirations of nonabolitionist Republicans after the Civil War to provide the basis for what one writer has called the "Third Constitution": the THIRTEENTH through FIFTEENTH AMENDMENTS. From abolitionist constitutional ideals embedded in section 1 of the FOURTEENTH AMENDMENT, there emerged some principal trends of constitutional development in the century after the Civil War: SUBSTANTIVE DUE PROCESS, equality before the law, protection for the privileges of national and state CITIZENSHIP.

By the time abolitionists began systematically to expound constitutional ideas in the 1830s, the constitutional aspects of the controversy over slavery were well developed. Even before American independence, Quakers in the Middle Colonies and some Puritan ministers in New England had attacked slavery on religio-ethical grounds. In SOMERSET'S CASE (1772) WILLIAM MURRAY (Lord Mansfield), Chief Justice of King's Bench, suggested that slavery could be established only by positive law and that, as a legal institution, it was "odious." The American Revolution witnessed the total abolition, exclusion, or disappearance of slavery in some northern jurisdictions (Vermont, Massachusetts and Maine, New Hampshire, the Northwest Territory) and its gradual abolition in the rest (Pennsylvania, New York, New Jersey, Connecticut, Rhode Island). Early antislavery groups, federated as the American Convention of Abolition Societies, worked in legal and paternalistic ways to protect freed blacks and provide them jobs and education. Yet these Revolutionary-era inhibitions on slavery were offset by gains slavery made in the drafting of the United States Constitution, in which ten clauses promoted slavery's security, most notably in the federal number clause (Article I, section 2, clause 3), the slave trade clause (Article I, section 9, clause 1), and the fugitive slave clause (Article IV, section 2, clause 3).

Constitutional controversy flared over slavery in several early episodes: the federal abolition of the international slave trade and its incidents, the Missouri crisis (1819–1821), the disputes over federal aid to colonization of free blacks, Denmark Vesey's slave revolt (Charleston, 1822), and the Negro Seamen's Acts of the southern coastal states (1822–1830). But not until the ideas of immediate abolition rejuvenated the antislavery movement did abolitionists begin a systematic constitutional assault on slavery. When they organized the American Anti-Slavery Society (AASS) in 1833, abolitionists, in a document drafted by WILLIAM LLOYD GARRISON, pledged themselves to tolerate the continued existence of slavery in the states and rejected the possibility that the federal government could abolish it there. But they insisted that slavery should be abolished immediately, that blacks should not suffer legal discrimination because of race, and that Congress should abolish the interstate slave trade, ban slavery in the DISTRICT OF COLUMBIA and the TERRITORIES, and refuse to admit new slave states.

The newly reorganized movement promptly encountered resistance that directed its thinking into constitutional modes. Federal efforts to suppress abolitionist mailings and to gag abolitionists' FREEDOM OF PETITION, together with mobbings throughout the northern states, diverted abolitionists briefly from the pursuit of freedom for blacks to a defense of CIVIL LIBERTIES of whites. At the same time, they assaulted slavery's incidents piecemeal, attempting to protect fugitive slaves from rendition, and seeking repeal of statutes that permitted sojourning masters to keep their slaves with them for limited periods of time in northern states. They secured enactment of PERSONAL LIBERTY LAWS: statutes that protected the freedom of black people in the northern states by providing them HABEAS CORPUS relief when seized as fugitives and by prohibiting state officials or public facilities from being used in the recapture of fugitives.

In 1839–1840, the unified antislavery movement split apart into three factions. Ironically, this organizational disaster stimulated abolitionists' systematic constitutional theorizing and broadcast their ideas widely outside the movement. Because of theological and tactical disagreements, the movement first broke into Garrisonian and political action wings, the Garrisonians condemning conventional electoral politics and the activists organizing a third party, the Liberty party, which ran its own presidential candidate in 1840 and 1844. The political action group subsequently split into those who believed slavery to be everywhere illegitimate and who therefore sought to have the federal government abolish slavery in the states, and those who continued to maintain the position of the original AASS Constitution, namely, that Congress lacked constitutional power to abolish slavery in the states. The Garrisonians, meanwhile, had concluded that the United States Constitution supported slavery and therefore called on northern states to secede from the Union and on individuals to disavow their allegiance to the Constitution.

Those who always maintained slavery's universal illegitimacy relied first on the DUE PROCESS clause of the Fifth Amendment, arguing that slaves were deprived of life, liberty, and property without legal justification, but they soon broadened their attack, ingeniously interpreting nearly a third of the Constitution's clauses, from the PREAMBLE to the TENTH AMENDMENT, to support their untenable thesis that slavery had usurped its preferred constitutional status. The 1840 publication of JAMES MADISON's notes of proceedings at the CONSTITUTIONAL CONVENTION OF 1787 was an embarrassment to them, disclosing as it did the concessions the Framers willingly made to the political power of slavery. Exponents of the universal-illegitimacy theory included Alvan Stewart, G. W. F. Mellen, Lysander Spooner, Joel Tiffany, and later, Gerrit Smith, JAMES G. BIRNEY, Lewis Tappan, and Frederick Douglass. Their principal contributions to later constitutional development included: their insistence on equality before the law irrespective of race; their vision of national citizenship protecting individuals' rights throughout the Union; their reliance on the PRIVILEGES AND IMMUNITIES clause (Article IV, section 2, clause 1) as a protection for persons of both races; and their uncompromising egalitarianism, which led them to condemn all forms of RACIAL DISCRIMINATION. They were scorned as extremists in their own time, even by fellow abolitionists, and modern scholars such as Robert Cover dismiss their ideas as "utopian."

Political action abolitionists who conceded the legality of slavery in the states remained closest to the mainstream of American politics and established a political alliance with like-minded men outside the abolitionist movement to create the Free Soil party in 1848. Their insistence that, as the federal government could not abolish slavery, neither could it establish it, led them to proclaim the doctrines of "divorce" and "freedom national." "Divorce" called for an immediate and absolute separation of the federal government from the support of slavery (for example, by abolishing the interstate slave trade and repealing the Fugitive Slave Act of 1793), coupled with an aggressive attack on the political bases of slavery's strength (repeal of the federal number clause, refusal to appoint slaveholders to federal posts). "Divorce" provided the doctrinal basis of the three-way Free Soil coalition of 1848, comprised of Conscience Whigs, Barnburner Democrats, and former Libertymen. Liberty leaders in the Free Soil group included SALMON P. CHASE (later Chief Justice of the United States), Gamaliel Bailey, STANLEY MATTHEWS (a future justice of the United States Supreme Court), Representative Owen Lovejoy, and Joshua Leavitt.

Stimulated by the widespread popularity of the WILMOT PROVISO (1846) in the north, which would have excluded slavery from all territories acquired as a result of the Mexican War, the abolitionist Free Soilers demanded "non-extension": the refusal to permit slavery in any American territories, and the nonadmission of new slave states. This became transformed into "freedom national," a constitutional doctrine holding that, under *Somerset,* freedom is the universal condition of humans, and slavery a local aberration created and continued only by local positive law. These ideas were cordially received by Whigs who formed a nucleus of the Republican party after the demise of the Free Soilers and the fragmentation of the regular parties as a result of the KANSAS-NEBRASKA ACT (1854): Joshua Giddings, CHARLES SUMNER, Charles Francis Adams, and Horace Mann. Other Republicans such as ABRAHAM LINCOLN and WILLIAM SEWARD refused to accept "divorce" but made nonextension the cornerstone of Republican policy. "Freedom national" even influenced anti-abolitionists such as Lewis Cass and then STEPHEN A. DOUGLAS, who promoted a modified version of it as the FREEPORT DOCTRINE of 1858.

Garrisonians dismissed the United States Constitution as the "covenant with death and agreement with hell" denounced by Isaiah, but they too influenced later constitutional development, principally through their insistence that the proslavery clauses of the Constitution would have to be repealed or nullified, and the federal government fumigated of its contamination with support of slavery. Though they included competent lawyers (Wendell Phillips, William I. Bowditch), the Garrisonians were distinguished chiefly by literary and polemical talent (Edmund Quincy, Lydia Maria Child) and consequently made little contribution to systematic constitutional exposition.

The crises of the union in the 1850s, beginning with enactment of the Fugitive Slave Act in 1850, leading through the dramatic fugitive recaptures and rescues, the Kansas-Nebraska Act (1854) and "Bleeding Kansas," and culminating, constitutionally, in DRED SCOTT V. SANDFORD (1857), ABLEMAN V. BOOTH (1859), and the pending appeal of *People v. Lemmon* (1860), together with legislative activity (chiefly enactment of ever broader personal liberty laws, including Vermont's Freedom Act of 1858), enabled abolitionists to work together toward common goals, and to overcome or survive their sectarian quarrels of the 1840s. Though fragmented as a distinct movement, abolitionists permeated the press, parties, and the churches, diffusing their ideas widely among persons who had not been theretofore involved in the antislavery movement. Thus egalitarians like Sumner and THADDEUS STEVENS, conservative lawyers like JOHN BINGHAM and William Lawrence, and political leaders like WILLIAM PITT FESSENDEN and ROSCOE CONKLING were influenced by abolitionist constitutional ideas, appropriating them after the war and injecting them into the Constitution and its interpretation, both in cases and in statutes.

WILLIAM M. WIECEK

Bibliography

DUMOND, DWIGHT L. 1961 *Antislavery.* Ann Arbor: University of Michigan Press.

FEHRENBACHER, DON 1978 *The Dred Scott Case: Its Significance in American Law and Politics.* New York: Oxford University Press.

GRAHAM, HOWARD J. 1968 *Everyman's Constitution.* Madison: State Historical Society of Wisconsin.

TEN BROEK, JACOBUS 1965 *Equal under Law.* New York: Collier Books.

WIECEK, WILLIAM M. 1977 *The Sources of Antislavery Constitutionalism in America, 1760–1848.* Ithaca, N.Y.: Cornell University Press.

ABOLITION OF SLAVERY

See: Slavery and the Constitution; Thirteenth Amendment

ABOOD v. DETROIT BOARD OF EDUCATION
431 U.S. 209 (1977)

Abood is one of the cases where union or agency shop agreements create speech and association problems, because individuals must join unions in order to hold jobs and then must pay dues to support union activities with which the individuals may not agree. Here the union represented public employees. The Supreme Court has consistently held that there is no right *not* to associate in a labor union for the purposes of COLLECTIVE BARGAINING but that a union must develop methods of relieving a member of those portions of union dues devoted to union ideological activities to which he objects.

MARTIN SHAPIRO

(SEE ALSO: *Labor and the Constitution; Freedom of Speech; Freedom of Assembly and Association.*)

ABORTION AND THE CONSTITUTION

The story of abortion and the Constitution is in part an episode in the saga of SUBSTANTIVE DUE PROCESS. During the period from the early 1900s to the mid-1930s, the Supreme Court employed the principle of substantive due process—the principle that governmental action abridging a person's life, liberty, or property interests must serve a legitimate governmental policy—to invalidate much state and federal legislation that offended the Court's views of legitimate policy, particularly socioeconomic policy. In the late 1930s and early 1940s, the Court, with a new majority composed in part of Justices appointed by

President FRANKLIN D. ROOSEVELT, reacted to the perceived judicial excesses of the preceding generation by refusing to employ substantive due process to invalidate any state or federal legislation. During the next quarter century—the period between the demise of the "old" substantive due process and the birth of the "new"—the Court did not formally reject the principle of substantive due process; from time to time the Court inquired whether challenged legislation was consistent with the principle. But the Court's substantive due process review was so deferential to the legislation in question as to be largely inconsequential, as, for example, in WILLIAMSON v. LEE OPTICAL CO. (1955).

Then, in the mid-1960s, the Court changed direction. In GRISWOLD v. CONNECTICUT (1965) the Court relied on a constitutional RIGHT OF PRIVACY to rule that a state could not ban the use of contraceptives by married persons. In *Eisenstadt v. Baird* (1972), on EQUAL PROTECTION grounds, it ruled that a state may not ban the distribution of contraceptives to unmarried persons. Despite the rhetoric of the Court's opinions, there is no doubt that both were substantive due process decisions in the methodological (if not the rhetorical) sense: in each case the Court invalidated legislation that offended not any specific prohibition of the Constitution but simply the Court's views of the governmental policies asserted in justification of the states' regulations.

If any doubt remained about whether the Court had returned to substantive due process, that doubt could not survive the Court's decision in ROE v. WADE (1973), which employed substantive due process in both the rhetorical and the methodological senses. The Court ruled in *Roe* that the due process clause of the FOURTEENTH AMENDMENT prohibited a state from forbidding a woman to obtain an abortion in the period of pregnancy prior to the fetus's viability. Indeed, in *Roe* the Court applied a particularly strong version of the substantive-due-process requirement: because the criminal ban on abortion challenged in *Roe* abridged a "fundamental" liberty interest of the woman—specifically, her "privacy" interest in deciding whether to terminate her pregnancy—the Court insisted that the legislation not merely serve a legitimate governmental policy but that it be *necessary* to serve a COMPELLING STATE INTEREST. The Court concluded that only after viability was government's interest in protecting the life of the fetus sufficiently strong to permit it to ban abortion.

Obviously the written Constitution says nothing about abortion, and no plausible "interpretation" or "application" of any determinate value judgment fairly attributable to the framers of the Fourteenth Amendment prohibits state government from forbidding a woman to obtain an abortion. In that sense, the Supreme Court's decision in *Roe v. Wade* is an exemplar of JUDICIAL ACTIVISM. Thus, it was not surprising that the decision—the Court's constitutionalization of the matter of abortion—ignited one of those periodic explosions about the legitimacy of judicial activism in a democracy. (Earlier such explosions attended the Court's activism in the period from *Lochner v. New York* (1905) to the late 1930s and, more recently, the Court's decision in *Brown v. Board of Education* (1954) outlawing racially segregated public schooling.)

Many critics of the Court's decision in *Roe* complained about the judicial activism underlying the decision. In the view of most such critics, *Roe v. Wade* is simply a contemporary analogue of the almost universally discredited *Lochner v. New York* (1905), and no one who opposes the activist mode of judicial review exemplified by *Lochner* can consistently support the activist mode exemplified by *Roe.* Of course, the force of this argument depends on one's perception of what is wrong with *Lochner:* the activist mode of review exemplified by it or simply the Court's answer in *Lochner* to the question of economic liberty addressed there. There is no inconsistency in opposing *Lochner's* doctrinal conclusions and supporting the activist mode of review exemplified by *Roe* (and by *Lochner*). Indeed, one might support the activist mode of review exemplified by *Roe* and at the same time oppose *Roe*'s reasoning and result.

A second, distinct criticism of the Court's decision in *Roe* concerns not the legitimacy of judicial activism but the soundness of the Court's answer to the political-moral question it addressed. Because many persons believe, often on religious grounds, that the Court gave the wrong answer to the question whether state government should be permitted to ban abortion, there was, in the decade following *Roe,* a vigorous political movement to overrule *Roe* legislatively—either by taking away the Court's JURISDICTION to review state abortion laws, or by constitutional amendment or even simple congressional legislation to the effect that a fetus is a person within the meaning of the Fourteenth Amendment and that therefore state government may ban abortion to protect the life of the fetus. The proposals to limit the jurisdiction of the Court and to overrule *Roe* by simple congressional legislation, as opposed to constitutional amendment, became subjects of vigorous political and constitutional controversy.

The vigor of the political controversy over abortion

cannot be fully comprehended—indeed, the Court's decision to constitutionalize the matter of abortion cannot be fully comprehended—without reference to an important development in American society that gained momentum in the 1970s and 1980s: a fundamental shift in attitudes toward the role of women in society. Many of those who opposed abortion and the "liberalization" of public policy regarding abortion did so as part of a larger agenda based on a "traditional" vision of woman's place and of the family. Many of those on the other side of the issue were seeking to implement a different vision—a feminist vision in which women are free to determine for themselves what shapes their lives will take, and therefore free to determine whether, and when, they will bear children.

Not surprisingly, this basic shift in attitudes toward women—from patriarchal to feminist—has been an occasion for deep division in American society. "Abortion politics" was merely one manifestation of that division (although an important one, to be sure). Thus, a controversy that sometimes seemed on the surface to consist mainly of a philosophical-theological dispute over the question, "When does 'life' begin?," actually involved much more. The complexity of the abortion controversy was dramatically evidenced by the fact that even within the Roman Catholic Church in the United States, which was the most powerful institutional opponent of abortion, attitudes toward abortion were deeply divided precisely because attitudes toward women were deeply divided.

As a consequence of its decision in *Roe v. Wade,* the Court has had to resolve many troublesome, controversial issues regarding abortion. For example, in PLANNED PARENTHOOD OF MISSOURI V. DANFORTH (1976) the Court ruled that a state may not require a woman to obtain the consent of her spouse before she terminates her pregnancy. The Court's rulings with respect to parental-consent and parental-notification requirements have not been a model of clarity, in part because the rulings have been fragmented. In *Bellotti v. Baird* (1979), for example, an 8–1 decision striking down the parental consent requirement, the majority split 4–4 as to the proper rationale. This much, however, is clear: state government may not require *every* minor, whatever her level of independence or maturity, to obtain parental consent before she terminates her pregnancy.

Undoubtedly the most controversial issue concerning abortion that the Court has addressed since *Roe v. Wade* involved abortion funding. In MAHER V. ROE (1977), the Court ruled that a state government that spends welfare funds to subsidize medical expenses incident to pregnancy and childbirth may decline to subsidize medical expenses incident to nontherapeutic abortion even if its sole reason for doing so is to discourage abortion. In a companion case, *Poelker v. Doe* (1977), the Court ruled that a public hospital that provides medical services relating to pregnancy and childbirth may decline to provide nontherapeutic abortions even if its sole reason for doing so is to discourage abortion. Three years later, in HARRIS V. MCRAE (1980), the Court sustained the HYDE AMENDMENT (to appropriations for the Medicaid program), which prohibited federal funding of abortion, including therapeutic abortion, even though the sole purpose of the amendment was to discourage abortion.

Some commentators have claimed that, notwithstanding the Court's arguments to the contrary, these abortion-funding cases cannot be reconciled with *Roe v. Wade.* They reason that the Court's decision in *Roe* can be satisfactorily explained only on the ground that government may not take action predicated on the view that abortion (in the pre-viability period) is morally objectionable, but that the governmental policies sustained in *Maher, Poelker,* and *McRae* were all manifestly predicated on just that view. There is probably no final explanation of the Court's decisions in the abortion-funding cases except in terms of judicial *Realpolitik*—that is, as an effort to retrench in the face of vigorous, often bitter, and widespread criticism of its decision in *Roe v. Wade* and threats to overrule *Roe* legislatively.

Its decision, in *Roe v. Wade,* to constitutionalize the deeply controversial issue of abortion represents one of the Supreme Court's most problematic ventures in recent times. Other moves by the Court were as controversial when initially taken—for example, the Court's choice in *Brown v. Board of Education* (1954) to begin to disestablish racially segregated public schooling—but few have been so persistently controversial. Whatever their eventual fate, *Roe* and its progeny have served as an occasion for some of the most fruitful thinking in this century on the proper role of the Supreme Court in American government.

MICHAEL J. PERRY

(SEE ALSO: *Reproductive Autonomy.*)

Bibliography

ELY, JOHN HART 1973 The Wages of Crying Wolf: A Comment on *Roe v. Wade. Yale Law Journal* 82:920.

PERRY, MICHAEL 1980 Why the Supreme Court was

Plainly Wrong in the Hyde Amendment Case: A Brief Comment on *Harris v. McRae. Stanford Law Review* 32:1113–1128.

REGAN, DONALD 1979 Rewriting *Roe v. Wade. Michigan Law Review* 77:1569–1646.

TRIBE, LAURENCE H. 1978 *American Constitutional Law.* Pages 921–934. Mineola, N.Y.: Foundation Press.

ABRAMS v. UNITED STATES
250 U.S. 616 (1919)

In SCHENCK V. UNITED STATES (1919) Justice OLIVER WENDELL HOLMES introduced the CLEAR AND PRESENT DANGER test in upholding the conviction under the ESPIONAGE ACT of a defendant who had mailed circulars opposing military CONSCRIPTION. Only nine months later, in very similar circumstances, the Supreme Court upheld an Espionage Act conviction and Holmes and LOUIS D. BRANDEIS offered the danger test in dissent. *Abrams* is famous for Holmes's dissent which became a classic libertarian pronouncement.

Abrams and three others distributed revolutionary circulars that included calls for a general strike, special appeals to workers in ammunitions factories, and language suggesting armed disturbances as the best means of protecting the Russian revolution against American intervention. These circulars had appeared while the United States was still engaged against the Germans in World War I. Their immediate occasion was the dispatch of an American expeditionary force to Russia at the time of the Russian revolution. The majority reasoned that, whatever their particular occasion, the circulars' purpose was that of hampering the general war effort. Having concluded that "the language of these circulars was obviously intended to provoke and to encourage resistance to the United States in the war" and that they urged munitions workers to strike for the purpose of curtailing the production of war materials, the opinion upheld the convictions without actually addressing any constitutional question. The majority obviously believed that the Espionage Act might constitutionally be applied to speech intended to obstruct the war effort.

Justice Holmes mixed a number of elements in his dissent, and the mixture has bedeviled subsequent commentary. Although it is not clear whether Holmes was focusing on the specific language of the Espionage Act or arguing a more general constitutional standard, his central argument was that speech may not be punished unless it constitutes an attempt at some unlawful act; an essential element in such an attempt must be a specific intent on the part of the speaker to bring about the unlawful act. He did not read the circulars in evidence or the actions of their publishers as showing the specific intent to interfere with the war effort against Germany that would be required to constitute a violation of the Espionage Act.

His *Abrams* opinion shows the extent to which Holmes's invention of the danger rule was a derivation of his thinking about the role of specific intent and surrounding circumstances in the law of attempts. For in the midst of his discussion of specific intent he wrote, "I do not doubt . . . that by the same reasoning that would justify punishing persuasion to murder, the United States constitutionally may punish speech that produces or is intended to produce a clear and imminent danger that it will bring about forthwith certain substantive evils that the United States constitutionally may seek to prevent. . . . It is only the present danger of immediate evil or an intent to bring it about that warrants Congress in setting a limit to the expression of opinion . . . ."

Over time, however, what has survived from Holmes's opinion is not so much the specific intent argument as the more general impression that the "poor and puny anonymities" of the circulars could not possibly have constituted a clear and present danger to the war effort. At least in contexts such as that presented in *Abrams*, the clear and present danger test seems to be a good means of unmasking and constitutionally invalidating prosecutions because of the ideas we hate, when the precautions are undertaken not because the ideas constitute any real danger to our security but simply because we hate them. Although the specific intent aspect of the *Abrams* opinion has subsequently been invoked in a number of cases, particularly those involving membership in the Communist party, the *Abrams* dissent has typically been cited along with *Schenck* as the basic authority for the more general version of the clear and present danger standard that became the dominant FREEDOM OF SPEECH doctrine during the 1940s and has since led a checkered career.

Justice Holmes also argued in *Abrams* that the common law of SEDITIOUS LIBEL has not survived in the United States; the Supreme Court finally adopted that position in NEW YORK TIMES V. SULLIVAN (1964).

The concluding paragraph of the *Abrams* dissent has often been invoked by those who wish to make of Holmes a patron saint of the libertarian movement.

> Persecution for the expression of opinions seems to me perfectly logical . . . but when men have realized that time has upset many fighting faiths, they may come to believe

even more the very foundations of their own conduct that the ultimate good desired is better reached by free trade in ideas—that the best test of truth is the power of the thought to get itself accepted in the competition of the market, and that truth is the only ground upon which their wishes safely can be carried out. That at any rate is the theory of our Constitution. It is an experiment, as all life is an experiment. Every year if not every day we have to wager our salvation upon some prophecy based upon imperfect knowledge. While that experiment is part of our system I think that we should be eternally vigilant against attempts to check the expression of opinions that we loathe and believe to be fraught with death, unless they so imminently threaten immediate interference with the lawful and pressing purposes of the law that an immediate check is required to save the country. . . . Only the emergency that makes it immediately dangerous to leave the correction of evil counsels to time warrants making any exception to the sweeping command, "Congress shall make no law . . . abridging the freedom of speech."

Sensitized by the destructive powers of such "fighting faiths" as Fascism and communism, subsequent commentators have criticized the muscular, relativistic pragmatism of this pronouncement as at best an inadequate philosophic basis for the libertarian position and at worst an invitation to totalitarianism. The ultimate problem is, of course, what is to be done if a political faith that proposes the termination of freedom of speech momentarily wins the competition in the marketplace of ideas and then shuts down the market. Alternatively it has been argued that Holmes's clear and present danger approach in *Abrams* was basically conditioned by his perception of the ineffectualness of leftist revolutionary rhetoric in the American context of his day. In this view, he was saying no more than that deviant ideas must be tolerated until there is a substantial risk that a large number of Americans will listen to them. The clear and present danger test is often criticized for withdrawing protection of political speech at just the point when the speech threatens to become effective. Other commentators have argued that no matter how persuasive Holmes's comments may be in context, the clear and present danger approach ought not to be uncritically accepted as the single freedom of speech test, uniformly applied to speech situations quite different from those in *Abrams.* Perhaps the most telling criticism of the Holmes approach is that it vests enormous discretion in the judge, for ultimately it depends on the judge's prediction of what will happen rather than on findings of what has happened. Subsequent decisions such as that in FEINER V. NEW YORK (1951) showed that judges less brave than Holmes or less contemptuously tolerant of dissident ideas, might be quicker to imagine danger.

MARTIN SHAPIRO

Bibliography

CHAFEE, ZECHARIAH 1941 *Free Speech in the United States.* Cambridge, Mass.: Harvard University Press.

ABSOLUTISM (Freedom of Speech and Press)

In the 1950s and 1960s, some Justices of the Supreme Court and some commentators on the Court's work debated an abstract issue of constitutional theory pressed on it by Justice HUGO L. BLACK: Is the FIRST AMENDMENT an "absolute," totally forbidding government restrictions on speech and the press that fall within the Amendment's scope, or is the FREEDOM OF SPEECH properly subject to BALANCING TESTS that weigh restrictions on speech against governmental interests asserted to justify them? With Black's retirement in 1971, the whole airy question simply collapsed.

The argument that the First Amendment "absolutely" guaranteed speech and press freedoms was first raised in the debate over the Sedition Act (1798) but did not become the focus of debate in Supreme Court opinions for another century and a half. The occasion was presented when the Court confronted a series of cases involving governmental restrictions on SUBVERSIVE ACTIVITIES. For ALEXANDER MEIKLEJOHN, First Amendment absolutism was built into the structure of a self-governing democracy. For Justice Black, it was grounded in the constitutional text.

Black argued that "the Constitution guarantees absolute freedom of speech"—he used the modern locution, including the press when he said "speech"—and, characteristically, he drew support from the First Amendment's words: "Congress shall make no law . . . abridging the freedom of speech, or of the press." He viewed all OBSCENITY and libel laws as unconstitutional; he argued, often supported by Justice WILLIAM O. DOUGLAS, that government could not constitutionally punish discussions of public affairs, even if they incited to illegal action. But Black never claimed that the First Amendment protected all communications, irrespective of context. He distinguished between speech, which was absolutely protected, and conduct, which was subject to reasonable regulation. So it was that the First Amendment absolutist, toward the end of his life, often voted to send marchers and other demonstrators to jail for expressing themselves in places where he said they had no right to be.

First Amendment absolutism fails more fundamentally, on its own terms. A witness who lies under oath surely has no constitutional immunity from prosecution, and yet her perjury is pure speech. Most observers, conceding the force of similar examples, have concluded that even Justice Black, a sophisticated analyst, must have viewed his absolutism as a debating point, not a rigid rule for decision. In the Cold War atmosphere of the 1950s, a debating point was sorely needed; there was truth to Black's charge that the Court was "balancing away the First Amendment." As Judge LEARNED HAND had argued many years previously, in times of stress judges need "a qualitative formula, hard, conventional, difficult to evade," if they are to protect unpopular political expression against hostile majorities. A "definitional" technique has its libertarian advantages. Yet it is also possible to "define away" the First Amendment, as the Court has demonstrated in its dealings with obscenity, FIGHTING WORDS, and some forms of libel and COMMERCIAL SPEECH.

Even when the Court is defining a category of speech out of the First Amendment's scope, it states its reasons. Thus, just as "balancers" must define what it is that they are balancing, "definers" must weigh interests in order to define the boundaries of protected speech. Since Justice Black's departure from the Court, First Amendment inquiry has blended definitional and interest-balancing techniques, focusing—as virtually all constitutional inquiry must ultimately focus—on the justifications asserted for governmental restrictions. Justice Black's enduring legacy to this process is not the theory of First Amendment absolutes, but his lively concern for the values of an open society.

KENNETH L. KARST

Bibliography

KALVEN, HARRY, JR. 1967 Upon Rereading Mr. Justice Black on the First Amendment. *UCLA Law Review* 14:422–453.

ABSTENTION DOCTRINE

All the abstention doctrines refer to circumstances in which federal courts, having JURISDICTION over a case under a congressional enactment, nonetheless may defer to state tribunals as decision makers. Federal courts may not abstain simply because they believe that particular cases, on their facts, would more appropriately be heard in state courts; they have a general obligation to exercise jurisdiction in cases Congress has placed before them. Abstention is justified only in exceptional circumstances, and then only when it falls within a particular abstention doctrine.

There are several abstention doctrines; they differ in their consequences and in their requirements. *Colorado River Water Conservation District v. United States* (1976) suggests a general doctrine that federal courts have power to defer in favor of ongoing state proceedings raising the same or closely related issues. This type of deference to ongoing proceedings often is not identified as abstention at all, and courts have not spelled out its requirements other than general discretion.

When a federal court does defer under this doctrine, it stays federal proceedings pending completion of the state proceedings. If the state does not proceed expeditiously, or if issues remain for decision, the federal court can reenter the case. When it does not abstain and both state and federal forums exercise their CONCURRENT JURISDICTION over a dispute, the JUDGMENT that controls is the first to become final. Federal courts deferring in favor of ongoing state proceedings avoid this wasteful race to judgment, but the price paid is that the federal plaintiff may lose the federal forum she has chosen and to which federal law entitles her.

In reconciling the competing interests, federal courts are much more likely to defer to prior state proceedings, in which the state plaintiff has won the race to the courthouse, than they are when the federal suit was first filed.

Deference, even to previously commenced state proceedings involving the same parties as the federal suit, is by no means automatic; it is discretionary—justified by the court's INHERENT POWER to control its docket in the interests of efficiency and fairness—and the Supreme Court has said that it is to be invoked sparingly. In *Colorado River Water Conservation District v. United States* the Court stated that the inherent problems in duplicative proceedings are not sufficient to justify deference to the state courts because of "the virtually unflagging obligation of the federal courts to exercise the jurisdiction given them."

This doctrine permitting deference serves as a backdrop to other doctrines that the Supreme Court more consistently calls "abstention." The most important of these today is the doctrine of YOUNGER V. HARRIS (1971). The doctrine started as a principle against enjoining state criminal prosecutions, but it has grown enormously. It has been expanded to bar not only suits for federal injunction but also suits for federal declaratory judgment concerning the constitutionality of an enactment involved in a pending prosecution; and today some believe it goes so far as to bar a federal damage action against state officials that might decide issues that would interfere with a state prosecution. Moreover, the doctrine has grown to protect state civil proceedings as well as criminal ones. Most remarkably, as the Court held in *Hicks v. Miranda* (1975), the doctrine now allows abstention even if the federal action is first filed, so long as the state commences prosecution "before any proceedings of substance on the merits" have occurred in federal court. That rule effectively deters federal suit; a federal plaintiff who wins the race to the courthouse may simply provoke his own criminal prosecution. These developments together have turned *Younger* into a doctrine that permits federal courts to dismiss federal constitutional challenges to state criminal prosecution (or quasi-criminal) enactments whenever a state criminal prosecution (or other enforcement proceeding) provides a forum for the federal constitutional issue. The state forum in theory must be an adequate one, but courts applying the doctrine often overlook this aspect of the inquiry.

Courts abstaining under the *Younger* doctrine generally dismiss the federal suit rather than retaining jurisdiction. Federal plaintiffs who are left to defend state proceedings generally cannot return to federal court for adjudication of the federal or any other issues, and the state court's decision on the constitutional issue and others may control future litigation through collateral estoppel. Litigants do, of course, retain the possibility of Supreme Court review of the federal issues they raise in state court, but the chances that the Supreme Court will hear such cases are slim.

The *Younger* doctrine therefore often deprives the federal plaintiff of any federal forum—prior, concurrent, or subsequent to the state proceeding against him—for his CIVIL RIGHTS action against state officials. This contradicts the apparent purpose of SECTION 1983, TITLE 42, UNITED STATES CODE and its jurisdictional counterpart (section 1343, Title 28) that such a forum be available. Some of those convicted in state criminal prosecutions may later raise federal issues in federal HABEAS CORPUS proceedings, but ACCESS to habeas corpus is itself increasingly limited. (See STONE V. POWELL, 1976; WAINWRIGHT V. SYKES, 1977.)

The *Younger* doctrine does have exceptions. If the federal court finds state courts inadequate on the facts of the particular case (because of what the Court in *Younger* termed "bad faith, harassment, or any other unusual circumstance that would call for equitable relief"), it will exercise its jurisdiction. But this approach turns around the usual rule that it takes exceptional circumstances to decline jurisdiction, not to justify its exercise. To avoid this conflict with the usual rules allowing Congress, not the courts, to determine the appropriate cases for federal jurisdiction, *Younger* abstention should be cut back, at least by limiting it to cases in which state proceedings began before the federal one. Such an approach would assimilate *Younger* abstention to the general doctrine of deference to ongoing state proceedings, discussed above.

In the meantime the expanded version of the *Younger* doctrine has largely displaced what had been the key form of abstention, formulated in RAILROAD COMMISSION OF TEXAS V. PULLMAN COMPANY (1941). *Pullman* abstention applies to cases involving federal constitutional challenges to state law. It allows (but does not require) federal judges to refrain from deciding highly uncertain questions of state law when resolution of the questions may avoid or affect the federal constitutional issue.

Pullman today is the only abstention doctrine in which deference to state courts is limited to state law issues. When the federal court abstains under the *Pullman* doctrine, it holds the case while the parties seek declaratory relief on the state law issues in state court. Unless the parties voluntarily submit federal along with state issues to the state court, they have a right to return to federal court after the state adjudication is completed, for decision of the federal issues and for federal factfinding. In this respect *Pullman* abstention is a narrower intrusion on federal court jurisdiction than the *Younger* doctrine is, although the cost of shuttling back and forth from state to federal court dissuades many federal plaintiffs from retaining their federal forum. *Pullman* also differs from *Younger* because the federal plaintiff generally initiates the proceedings in state court, and they are declaratory judgment proceedings rather than criminal prosecutions or civil enforcement proceedings.

As *Younger* has expanded to include some civil enforcement proceedings and to allow abstention in favor of later-filed state proceedings, it has reduced the area for *Pullman* abstention. Both doctrines typically apply to constitutional litigation against state officials. In many cases where *Pullman* abstention could be at issue, *Younger* is operative because a state enforcement proceeding against the federal plaintiff is a possibility as long as the federal plaintiff has violated the law she challenges. If, however, the federal plaintiff has not violated the enactment she challenges, *Youn-*

ger abstention cannot apply, for the state is unable to bring a prosecution or civil enforcement proceeding against her and thereby displace the federal forum. *Pullman,* therefore, is the applicable doctrine for pre-violation suits and for challenges to state enactments that do not involve state enforcement proceedings. Many of those cases, however, will be dismissed before abstention is considered; where the plaintiff has not violated the enactment she complains of, she may have trouble showing that her controversy is justiciable. (See RIPENESS.)

While *Pullman* abstention has therefore become less and less important, a new area has recently been created for a *Pullman*-like abstention. PENNHURST STATE SCHOOL V. HALDERMAN (1984), restricting federal courts' pendent jurisdiction, requires federal litigants in suits against state governments to use state courts to pursue any related state causes of action they do not wish to forfeit. *Pennhurst* thus creates the equivalent of a mandatory *Pullman* abstention category—where state courts must be given certain state law questions to adjudicate even while a federal court exercises jurisdiction over the rest of the case. This new category is not, however, dependent upon uncertainty in state law.

Another abstention doctrine, administrative abstention, was first articulated in *Burford v. Sun Oil Company* (1943). The *Burford* doctrine allows a federal court with jurisdiction of a case to dismiss in favor of state court adjudication, ongoing or not. Like *Younger* abstention, *Burford* abstention displaces federal jurisdiction; if abstention is ordered, state courts adjudicate all issues, subject only to Supreme Court review. The Court has never clearly explained which cases are eligible for administrative abstention. The doctrine is typically employed when a state administrative process has dealt with a controversy in the first instance and the litigant then asks a federal district court to exercise either its federal question or diversity jurisdiction to review that administrative interpretation. The federal court's ability to abstain under this doctrine may be limited to situations in which state statutes concentrate JUDICIAL REVIEW of the administrative process in a particular state court so that it becomes "an integral part of the regulatory process," as the Court said in *Alabama Public Service Commission v. Southern Railway* (1951), or to situations involving complex factual issues. There is no requirement that legal issues, state or federal, be unclear for this abstention to be ordered, or that the case contain any federal issues.

Burford abstention does not apply when state administrative remedies have been skipped altogether and the litigant has sued first in federal court. The only issue then is whether state administrative remedies must be exhausted. There is no overlap between *Burford* and the *Younger* or *Pullman* abstention doctrines, because exhaustion of administrative remedies has not been required in suits under section 1983, which today includes all constitutional litigation. The Court recently affirmed this exception to the exhaustion requirement in Patsy v. Board of Regents (1982). If the Court were to modify the section 1983 exception to the exhaustion requirement, retreat from the *Burford* doctrine would seem to follow. Otherwise, *Burford* would mandate state judicial review after deference to state administrative proceedings, so federal jurisdiction would be altogether unavailable in section 1983 cases whenever an administrative agency was available.

A final minor category of abstention, which seems to have been limited to EMINENT DOMAIN cases involving unclear state issues, is reflected in *Louisiana Light & Power Company v. Thibodaux* (1959). In contexts other than eminent domain, abstention is not proper simply to clarify difficult state law issues. (In states that provide for certification, however, a federal court without more can certify difficult state issues to the state supreme court.)

All these theories of abstention are judge-made rules, without any statutory authority; they avoid jurisdiction in cases where Congress has given it. By contrast, Congress itself has provided for deference to state processes in narrow categories of cases, most notably cases involving INJUNCTIONS against state rate orders and tax collections. And in the Anti-Injunction Act, Congress has generally prohibited federal injunctions against state proceedings. This prohibition is limited by explicit statutory exceptions, however, and by some judge-made exceptions, and since the area outside the prohibition also is limited, by the judge-made abstention doctrines, the statute apparently has little effect.

MARTHA A. FIELD

Bibliography

FIELD, MARTHA A. 1974 Abstention in Constitutional Cases: The Scope of the Pullman Abstention Doctrine. *University of Pennsylvania Law Review* 122:1071–1087.

——— 1981 The Uncertain Nature of Federal Jurisdiction. *William & Mary Law Review* 22:683–724.

FISS, OWEN 1977 Dombrowksi. *Yale Law Journal* 86:1103–1164.

LAYCOCK, DOUGLAS 1977 Federal Interference with State Prosecutions: The Need for Prospective Relief. *Supreme Court Review* 1977:193–238.

ACADEMIC FREEDOM

Although academic freedom has become a FIRST AMENDMENT principle of special importance, its content and theoretical underpinnings have barely been defined. Most alleged violations of academic freedom can be sorted into three catagories: claims of individual professors against the state, claims of individual professors against the university administration or governing board, and claims of universities against the state. Judicial decisions have upheld claims in all three contexts.

The Supreme Court, however, has not developed a comprehensive theory of academic freedom comparable to its recent elaboration of freedom of association as a distinctive First Amendment DOCTRINE. The relationship between "individual" and "institutional" academic freedom has not been clarified. Nor has the Supreme Court decided whether academic freedom is a separate principle, with its own constitutional contours justified by the unique roles of professors and universities in society, or whether it highlights but is essentially coextensive with the general First Amendment rights of all citizens. Similarly unsettled is the applicability, if any, of academic freedom in primary and secondary schools. While acknowledging that teachers, unlike university professors, are expected to inculcate societal values in their students, the Supreme Court in BOARD OF EDUCATION V. PICO (1982) expressed concern about laws that "cast a pall of orthodoxy" over school as well as university classrooms. Student claims of academic freedom also remain unresolved.

This uncertainty about the constitutional definition of academic freedom contrasts with the internal understanding of the university community, which had elaborated its meaning before any court addressed its legal or constitutional significance. The modern American conception of academic freedom arose during the late nineteenth and early twentieth centuries, when the emerging research university eclipsed the religious college as the model institution of higher education. This structural change reflected an equally profound transformation of educational goals from conserving to searching for truth.

Academic freedom became associated with the search for truth and began to define the very idea of the university. Its content developed under the influence of Darwinism and the German university. The followers of Charles Darwin maintained that all beliefs are subject to the tests of inquiry and that apparent errors must be tolerated, and even expected, in the continuous search for truth. The German academic influence reinforced the growing secular tendencies in the United States. Many attributed the international preeminence of German universities to their traditions of academic freedom. As universities in the United States strove for similar excellence, they adapted these traditions.

This adaptation produced several major changes. The clear German differentiation between great freedom for faculty members within the university and little protection for any citizen outside it did not take hold in America. The ideal of FREEDOM OF SPEECH, including its constitutional expression in the First Amendment, and the philosophy of pragmatism, which encouraged the participation of all citizens in social and political life, prompted American professors to view academic freedom as an aspect of more general CIVIL LIBERTIES. The traditions of powerful administrators and lay boards of governors in American universities posed threats to academic freedom that did not exist in Germany, where universities were largely governed by their faculties. As a result, American professors sought freedom from university authorities as well as from external interference. And academic freedom, which in Germany encompassed freedom for both students and professors, became limited to professors in the United States.

The first major codification of the American conception of academic freedom was produced in 1915 by a committee of the nascent American Association of University Professors (AAUP). Subsequent revisions culminated in the 1940 *Statement of Principles on Academic Freedom and Tenure,* jointly sponsored by the AAUP and the Association of American Colleges, and currently endorsed by over 100 educational organizations. The 1940 *Statement* defines three aspects of academic freedom: freedom in research and publication, freedom in the classroom, and freedom from institutional censorship or discipline when a professor speaks or writes as a citizen. Many colleges and universities have incorporated the 1940 *Statement* into their governing documents. In cases involving the contractual relationship between professors and universities, courts have recently begun to cite it as the COMMON LAW of the academic profession. This contractual theory has provided substantial legal protection for academic freedom without the support of the First Amendment, whose applicability to private universities is limited by the doctrine of STATE ACTION.

The emergence of academic freedom as a constitutional principle did not begin until the McCarthy era of the 1950s, when public and university officials throughout the country challenged and investigated the loyalty of professors. Although earlier decisions had imposed some limitations on governmental intrusions into universities and schools, no Supreme Court opinion explicitly referred to academic freedom until Justice WILLIAM O. DOUGLAS, dissenting in ADLER v. BOARD OF EDUCATION (1952), claimed that it is contained within the First Amendment.

The Supreme Court endorsed this identification of academic freedom with the First Amendment in SWEEZY v. NEW HAMPSHIRE (1957), which reversed the contempt conviction of a Marxist scholar who had refused to answer questions from the state attorney general regarding his political opinions and the contents of his university lecture. A plurality of the Justices concluded that the state had invaded the lecturer's "liberties in the areas of academic freedom and political expression." Both the plurality and concurring opinions in *Sweezy* emphasized the importance to a free society of the search for knowledge within free universities and warned against governmental interference in university life. Justice FELIX FRANKFURTER's concurrence included a particularly influential reference to academic freedom that has often been cited in subsequent decisions. Quoting from a plea by South African scholars for open universities, Frankfurter identified " 'the four essential freedoms of a university'—to determine for itself on academic grounds who may teach, what may be taught, how it shall be taught, and who may be admitted to study."

The opinions in *Sweezy* indicated that academic freedom and political expression are distinct yet related liberties, and that society benefits from the academic freedom of professors as individuals and of universities as institutions. Yet neither in *Sweezy* nor in subsequent decisions did the Supreme Court untangle and clarify these complex relationships. Throughout the 1950s, it alluded only intermittently to academic freedom in cases involving investigations of university professors, and reference to this term did not necessarily lead to protective results. Even the votes and reasoning of individual Justices fluctuated unpredictably. During this period, many within the academic community resisted the advocacy of academic freedom as a constitutional principle, fearing that a judicial definition might both weaken and preempt the one contained in the 1940 *Statement* and widely accepted throughout American universities.

Supreme Court opinions since the 1950s have emphasized that academic freedom is a "transcendent value" and "a special concern of the First Amendment," as the majority observed in KEYISHIAN v. BOARD OF REGENTS (1967). Justice LEWIS F. POWELL's opinion in REGENTS OF THE UNIVERSITY OF CALIFORNIA v. BAKKE (1978) reiterated the university's academic freedom to select its student body, but the Court has held in MINNESOTA STATE BOARD FOR COMMUNITY COLLEGES v. KNIGHT (1984) that academic freedom does not include the right of individual faculty members to participate in institutional governance. By eliminating the RIGHT-PRIVILEGE DISTINCTION, which had allowed dismissal of PUBLIC EMPLOYEES for speech otherwise protected by the First Amendment, the Supreme Court during the 1960s and 1970s dramatically expanded the rights of all public employees, including university professors, to speak in ways that criticize or offend their employers. Yet none of these decisions has refined the relationships between "individual" and "institutional" academic freedom or between "academic freedom" and "political expression," issues posed but not resolved in *Sweezy.* The Supreme Court's continuing reluctance even to recognize issues of academic freedom in cases decided on other grounds underlines the primitive constitutional definition of this term.

Cases since the early 1970s have raised novel issues of academic freedom. University administrators and governing boards have asserted the academic freedom of the university as an institution to resist JUDICIAL REVIEW of their internal policies and practices, which have been challenged by government agencies seeking to enforce CIVIL RIGHTS laws and other statutes of general applicability, by citizens claiming rights to freedom of expression on university property, and by professors maintaining that the university violated their own academic freedom or their statutory protection against employment discrimination. Faculty members have even begun to make contradictory claims of academic freedom against each other. Professors have relied on academic freedom to seek a constitutionally based privilege against compelled disclosure of their deliberations and votes on faculty committees to junior colleagues who want this information to determine whether they were denied reappointment or tenure for impermissible reasons, including reasons that might violate their academic freedom. These difficult issues may force the courts to address more directly the meaning and scope of academic freedom and to resolve many of the lingering ambiguities of previous decisions.

DAVID M. RABBAN

Bibliography

HOFSTADTER, RICHARD and METZGER, WALTER 1955 *The Development of Academic Freedom in the United States.* New York: Columbia University Press.

LOVEJOY, ARTHUR 1937 Academic Freedom. In E. Seligman, ed., *Encyclopedia of the Social Sciences,* Vol. 1, pages 384–388. New York: Macmillan.

SYMPOSIUM 1963 Academic Freedom. *Law & Contemporary Problems* 28:429–671.

VAN ALSTYNE, WILLIAM 1972 The Specific Theory of Academic Freedom and the General Issue of Civil Liberty, In E. Pincoffs, ed., *The Concept of Academic Freedom,* pages 59–85. Austin: University of Texas Press.

ACCESS TO THE COURTS

Writing for the Supreme Court in BOUNDS V. SMITH (1977), Justice THURGOOD MARSHALL spoke confidently of "the fundamental constitutional right of access to the courts." In one sense, such a right has been a traditional and noncontroversial part of our constitutional law; barring unusual circumstances, anyone can bring a lawsuit, or be heard in his or her own defense. Justice Marshall, however, was referring to another kind of access. "Meaningful" access to the courts, *Bounds* held, gave state prisoners a right to legal assistance; the state must provide them either with law libraries or with law-trained persons to help them prepare petitions for HABEAS CORPUS or other legal papers. The modern constitutional law of access to the courts, in other words, is focused on the affirmative obligations of government to provide services to people who cannot afford to pay their costs. In this perspective, Justice Marshall's sweeping characterization goes far beyond the results of the decided cases.

The development began in the WARREN COURT era, with GRIFFIN V. ILLINOIS (1957) (state must provide free transcripts to convicted indigents when transcripts are required for effective APPEAL of their convictions) and DOUGLAS V. CALIFORNIA (1963) (state must provide appellate counsel for convicted indigents). GIDEON V. WAINWRIGHT (1963) interpreted the RIGHT TO COUNSEL to require state-appointed trial counsel in FELONY cases. The *Griffin* plurality had rested on both DUE PROCESS and EQUAL PROTECTION grounds, but by the time of *Douglas* equal protection had become the Court's preferred doctrine: the state, by refusing to pay for appellate counsel for some indigent defendants, had drawn "an unconstitutional line . . . between rich and poor." By the close of the Warren years, the Court seemed well on the way to a broad equal protection principle demanding strict judicial scrutiny of WEALTH DISCRIMINATIONS in the criminal justice system, including simple cases of inability to pay the costs of services needed for effective defense.

The Court remained sharply divided, however; the dissenters in *Griffin* and *Douglas* argued in forceful language that nothing in the Constitution required the states to take affirmative steps to relieve people from the effects of poverty. They saw no principled stopping-place for the majority's equality principle, and they objected to judicial intrusion into state budgetary processes. Even so, the same Justices found no difficulty in joining the 8–1 decision in BODDIE V. CONNECTICUT (1971), holding that a state could not constitutionally bar an indigent plaintiff from its divorce court for failure to pay a $60 filing fee. The *Boddie* majority, however, rested on a due process ground. The marriage relationship was "basic," and the state had monopolized the means for its dissolution; thus fundamental procedural fairness demanded access to the divorce court irrespective of ability to pay the fee.

From *Boddie* forward, the Court has dealt with constitutional claims of access to justice by emphasizing due process considerations of minimal fairness, and deemphasizing the equal protection notion that animated the Warren Court's decisions. At the same time, the Court has virtually ended the expansion of access rights. Thus ROSS V. MOFFITT (1974) pounced on language in *Douglas* about the "first appeal as of right," and refused to require state-appointed counsel to pursue discretionary appeals or Supreme Court review. And in *United States v. Kras* (1971) and *Ortwein v. Schwab* (1971) the Court, emphasizing the "monopoly" aspects of *Boddie,* upheld the application of filing fees to deny indigents access to a bankruptcy court and to judicial review of the denial of WELFARE BENEFITS. A similarly artificial line was drawn in the BURGER COURT's decisions on the right to counsel. The *Gideon* principle was extended, in ARGERSINGER V. HAMLIN (1972), to all prosecutions resulting in imprisonment. Yet in LASSITER V. DEPARTMENT OF SOCIAL SERVICES (1981) a 5–4 Court refused to hold that due process required a state to provide counsel for an indigent mother in a proceeding to terminate her parental rights, absent a showing of complexity or other special circumstances. Behind all these flimsy distinctions surely lay the same considerations urged from the beginning by the *Griffin* and *Douglas* dissenters: keep the "floodgates" closed; keep judges' hands off the allocation of public funds.

An access principle of minimal fairness is better than nothing. Yet in a great many contexts the essence of the access claim is an interest in equality itself. To have one's effective say is to be treated as a respected, participating member of the society. An effective hearing in court is more than a chance to influence a judge's decision; it is a vivid symbol of equal citizenship.

KENNETH L. KARST

Bibliography

GOODPASTER, GARY 1970 The Integration of Equal Protection, Due Process Standards, and the Indigent's Right of Free Access to the Courts. *Iowa Law Review* 56:223–266.

MICHELMAN, FRANK I. 1973, 1974 The Supreme Court and Litigation Access Fees. Part 1, *Duke Law Journal* 1973:1153–1215; Part 2, *Duke Law Journal* 1974:527–570.

ACT OF STATE DOCTRINE

Recognized by English courts as early as 1674, the act of state DOCTRINE prohibits United States courts from examining the validity of foreign acts of state. Chief Justice JOHN MARSHALL mentioned a doctrine of noninvolvement in 1808, but the Supreme Court did not accord it formal recognition until *Underhill v. Hernandez* (1897). Initially, the doctrine strongly resembled the doctrine of SOVEREIGN IMMUNITY which protects the person or acts of a sovereign. In fact, the act of state doctrine may have been invented to deal with technical deficiencies in sovereign immunity.

The act of state doctrine received renewed attention in *Banco Nacional de Cuba v. Sabbatino* (1964) where an 8–1 Supreme Court held that it applied even when the foreign state's sovereign act violated international law. Justice JOHN MARSHALL HARLAN's majority opinion rejected earlier assertions that the "inherent nature of sovereign authority" underlay the doctrine; instead it arose out of the SEPARATION OF POWERS. Justice BYRON R. WHITE, dissenting, read Harlan's opinion to declare "exclusive absolute [executive] control" of foreign relations. Acknowledging executive control, White claimed that "this is far from saying . . . that the validity of a foreign act of state is necessarily a POLITICAL QUESTION." The Court had, in fact, dismissed a specific executive branch request, contending that it need not be bound by executive determinations; the Court repeated this position in *Zschernig v. Miller* (1968) and unequivocally denied such executive control in *First National City Bank v. Banco Nacional de Cuba* (1972) (where two majority Justices joined four dissenters to so argue).

In an effort to harmonize the act of state doctrine with that of sovereign immunity, Justice White tried to create a commercial act exception to the act of state doctrine in *Alfred Dunhill of London, Inc. v. Cuba* (1976), but he failed to convince a majority on this issue. Because the case had involved no formal governmental decree, White would not have allowed the act of state defense. Even had an act of state been shown, White opposed the doctrine's extension to "purely commercial" acts of a sovereign or its commercial instrumentalities. He relied on the notion, accepted ever since *Bank of the United States v. Planters' Bank of Georgia* (1824), that a government's partnership in a commercial business does not confer sovereign status on that business.

Also in 1976, Congress passed the Foreign Sovereign Immunities Act which authorized American courts to determine foreign claims of sovereign immunity, thus approving judicial—as opposed to executive—decisions on the validity of such claims. Although the act established a general rule of immunity of foreign states from the jurisdiction of American courts, its "exceptions" were wide-ranging. Immunity is denied, for example, when the foreign state engages in commercial activity, or takes certain property rights in violation of international law, or is sued for damages for certain kinds of injury to person or property.

DAVID GORDON

Bibliography

GORDON, DAVID 1977 The Origin and Development of the Act of State Doctrine. *Rutgers Law Journal* 8:595–616.

ADAIR v. UNITED STATES
208 U.S. 161 (1908)

After the Pullman strike, which paralyzed the nation's railroads, a federal commission blamed the antiunion activities of the railroads and recommended legislation which Congress enacted in 1898. The ERDMAN ACT sought to free INTERSTATE COMMERCE from railroad strikes by establishing a railroad labor board with arbitration powers and by protecting the right of railroad workers to organize in unions. This second objective was the subject of section ten of the act, which prohibited YELLOW DOG CONTRACTS, blacklisting union members, and discharging employees solely for belonging to a union. The act applied to carriers engaged in interstate commerce. Adair, a manager of a carrier, fired an employee solely because of his union membership; a federal court found Adair guilty of violating section ten. On appeal the Supreme Court, by a vote of 6–2, found section ten unconstitutional for violating the Fifth Amendment's DUE PROCESS clause and for exceeding the powers of Congress under the COMMERCE CLAUSE.

Justice JOHN MARSHALL HARLAN, who spoke for the Court, usually wrote broad commerce clause opinions, but this one was constricted. He could see "no legal or logical connection" between an employee's membership in a labor organization and the carrying on of interstate commerce. The Pullman strike, the federal commission, and Congress's finding that such a connection existed meant nothing to the Court. A week later the Court held, in LOEWE V. LAWLOR (1908), that members of a labor organization who boycotted a manufacturing firm, whose products were intended for interstate commerce, had restrained interstate commerce in violation of the SHERMAN ANTITRUST ACT. In *Adair,* however, the Court found no constitutional authority for Congress to legislate on the labor affairs of interstate railroads.

Most of Harlan's opinion dealt with the due process issue. He found section ten to be "an invasion of the personal liberty, as well as the right to property," guaranteed by the Fifth Amendment. It embraced the right of employers to contract for labor and the right of labor to contract for its services without government intervention. In his exposition of FREEDOM OF CONTRACT, which is a doctrine derived from SUBSTANTIVE DUE PROCESS, Harlan contended that "it is not within the functions of government . . . to compel any person, in the course of his business and against his will, to accept or retain the personal services of another. . . ." The right of the employee to quit, said Harlan, "is the same as the right of the employer, for whatever reason, to dispense with the services of such employee." The Court forgot the more realistic view it had expressed in HOLDEN V. HARDY (1898), and held that "any legislation" disturbing the "equality of right" arbitrarily interferes with "the liberty of contract which no government can legally justify in a free land." Justice JOSEPH MCKENNA dissented mainly on the ground that the Court "stretched to its extreme" the liberty of contract doctrine. The Court overruled *Adair* in 1949.

LEONARD W. LEVY

Bibliography

LIEBERMAN, ELIAS 1950 *Unions Before the Bar.* Pages 44–55. New York: Harper & Row.

ADAMS, HENRY
(1838–1918)

Born to a family whose service to the Constitution was matched by a reverence for it "this side of idolatry," Henry Brooks Adams served the Constitution as a historian of the nation it established. His great *History of the United States during the Administrations of Jefferson and Madison* as well as his biographies of JOHN RANDOLPH and ALBERT GALLATIN and his *Documents Relating to New England Federalism* remain standard sources for the events and characters of the early republican years during which the Constitution was being worked out in practice. Among the highlights of these works are Adams's ironic account of THOMAS JEFFERSON's exercise of his constitutional powers in the face of his particularist scruples, the Republican hostility to the federal judiciary, and the fate of STATES' RIGHTS views. In reply to HERMANN VON HOLST's criticism of the Constitution, Adams wrote in 1876, "the Constitution has done its work. It has made a nation." Adams's own disillusion with this nation affected his writings. Like others of his generation, he became more determinist as he became less sanguine, and the *History* shows this shift in his view as the Constitution is described becoming an engine of American nationalism, democracy, expansion, and centralization. In his novels, historical theory, letters, and *The Education of Henry Adams,* he came to regard the Constitution as almost a figment of human intention in a modern age—an age in which the kind of person it once was possible for an Adams to be has no role.

ROBERT DAWIDOFF

Bibliography

SAMUELS, ERNEST 1948–1964 *Henry Adams.* 3 Vols. Cambridge, Mass: Harvard University Press.

ADAMS, JOHN
(1735–1826)

Massachusetts lawyer and revolutionary leader, first vice-president and second President of the United States, John Adams was also a distinguished political and constitutional theorist. Born in 1735, the descendant of three generations of hardy independent farmers in Braintree, Massachusetts, near Boston, he attended Harvard College and after graduation studied law for several years, gaining admission to the bar in 1758. The practice of a country lawyer held no charms for him. He took delight in the study of law and government, however, and this scholarly pursuit merged imperceptibly with the polemics of the revolutionary controversy, which probed the nature and history of the English CONSTITUTION. Adams made his political debut in 1765 as the author of Braintree's protest against the Stamp Act. Increasingly, from the pressures of politics as well as of business, he was drawn to Boston, moving there with his young family in 1768. Unlike his cousin SAMUEL ADAMS, he was not an ardent revolutionist. He worried about the "mischievous democratic principles" churned up by the agitation; he braved the popular torrent to defend Captain Thomas Preston and the British soldiers accused of murder in the Boston Massacre. For several years he was torn between Boston and Braintree, and the different worlds they represented. Only in 1773 did he commit himself fully to the Revolution.

The next year, during the crisis produced by the Intolerable Acts, Adams was elected one of the Massachusetts delegates to the FIRST CONTINENTAL CONGRESS, in Philadelphia. Events had shaken his lawyer-like stance on the issues, and he championed the patriots' appeal to "the law of nature," as well as to the English constitution and COLONIAL CHARTERS, in defense of American liberties. He wrote the crucial fourth article of the congress's declaration of rights denying the authority of Parliament to legislate for the colonies, though acquiescing in imperial regulation of trade as a matter of convenience. Back in Boston he expounded his views at length in the series of *Novanglus* letters in the press. TREASON and rebellion, he argued, were on the other side—the advocates of parliamentary supremacy abroad and the Tory oligarchy at home. He had no quarrel with George III, and he lauded the English constitution with its nice balance between king, lords, and commons and its distinctly republican character. Unfortunately, the constitution was not made for colonies. Denied REPRESENTATION in Parliament, they were deprived of the constitution's best feature. The proper relationship between the colonies and the mother country, Adams said, was the same as Scotland's before the Act of Union, that is, as an independent government owing allegiance to a common king. Had America been conquered, like Ireland, imperial rule would be warranted; but America was a discovered, not a conquered, country, and so the people possessed the NATURAL RIGHT to make their own laws as far as compatible with allegiance to the king.

In the Second Continental Congress Adams lost all hope of reconciliation on these terms, and he became a leading advocate of American independence. Although a member of the committee to draft the DECLARATION OF INDEPENDENCE, he made his greatest contribution when it came to the floor for debate. Before this he co-authored and championed the resolution—"a machine to fabricate independence" in opposition eyes—calling upon the colonies to form new governments. Nothing was more important to Adams than the making of new constitutions and the restoration of legitimate authority. He had read all the political theorists from Plato to Rousseau; now he reread them with a view to incorporating their best principles into the foundations of the polity. Government was "the divine science"—"the first in importance"—and American independence opened, in his eyes, a grand "age of political experiments." It was, he declared, "a time when the greatest lawgivers of antiquity would have wished to live. How few of the human race have ever enjoyed an opportunity of making an election of government—more than of air, soil, or climate—for themselves or their children!" To aid this work Adams sketched his ideas in an epistolary essay, *Thoughts on Government*, which was destined to have wide influence. Years later, in his autobiography, Adams said that he wrote to counteract the plan of government advanced by that "disastrous meteor" THOMAS PAINE in *Common Sense*. Paine's ideas, which gave shape to the new PENNSYLVANIA CONSTITUTION OF 1776, were "too democratical," mainly because they concentrated all power in a single representative assembly without mixture or balance. Adams, by contrast, proposed a "complex" government of representative assembly, council (or senate), and governor, each endowed with a negative on the others. The people would glide easily into such a government because of its close resemblance to the colonial governments they had known. It possessed additional merit for Adams as a thoroughly republican adaptation of the idealized balance of the English constitution. Even as he challenged the work of constitution-making, however, Adams was assailed by doubts. The new governments might be too free to survive. The essence of republics was *virtue*, that is, selfless devotion to the common weal, but Adams, still a Puritan under his republican skin, clung to a theory of human nature that emphasized man's capacity for selfishness, ignorance, and vice. The POPULAR SOVEREIGNTY that was the basis of republican government possessed the power to destroy it.

In 1779, after returning to the United States from the first of two diplomatic missions abroad, Adams had the opportunity to amplify his constitutional theory, indeed to become the Solon of his native state. Massachusetts continued to be governed by a revolutionary body, the provincial congress, without legitimate constitutional authority. Only in the previous year the citizenry had rejected a constitution framed by the congress. Now they elected a CONSTITUTIONAL CONVENTION for the specific purpose of framing a FUNDAMENTAL LAW, which would then be referred back to them for approval. (When the process was completed in 1780, the MASSACHUSETTS CONSTITUTION exhibited, for the first time anywhere, all the means by which the theory of "constituent sovereignty," one of the foundations of the American republic, was put into practice.) Elected Braintree's delegate, Adams was assigned the task of preparing a draft constitution for consideration by the convention, and this became, after comparatively few changes, its final product. The preamble reiterated the contractual and consensual basis of government. It was followed by a declaration of rights, derivative of the Virginia model but much more elaborate. Adams was not responsible for Article III—the most disputed provision—making it the duty of the legislature, and thus in turn of the various towns and parishes, to support religion; yet this was consistent with the aim of the constitution as a whole to keep Massachusetts a Christian commonwealth. For Adams religion was as essential to virtue as virtue was to republicanism. Thus he proposed a RELIGIOUS TEST for all elected officials. (The delegates voted to confine the test to the office of governor.) The strength and independence of the executive was an unusual feature of the constitution. Reacting against monarchy, most of the new state constitutions weakened and shackled the governors; but Adams believed that a kingly executive was necessary to control the conflicting passions and interests in the legislature. Accordingly, he proposed to vest the Massachusetts governor with an absolute negative on legislation. The convention declined to follow him, however, conferring a suspensive veto only. Adams ever after felt that the trimming of the governor's legislative power was the one serious error of the convention. Otherwise, with respect to the legislature, his principles were fully embodied in the constitution. Representation in the lower house was based upon population, while representation in the upper house, being proportioned to the taxable wealth of the several senatorial districts, was based upon property. This system of giving representation to property as well as numbers had its principal source in the philosophy of James Harrington, whose axiom "power always follows property," Adams said, "is as infallible a maxim in politics as that action and reaction are equal in mechanics." Property was further joined to office by requiring wealth on an ascending scale of value to make representatives, senators, and governors eligible for their offices. Finally, the constitution retained the freehold qualification for the franchise. In these features it was a distinctly conservative document, and it would, Adams later complained, give him "the reputation of a man of high principles and strong notions in government, scarcely compatible with republicanism."

Adams was in France when the Massachusetts Constitution was ratified in 1780. After helping negotiate the treaty of peace, he was named by Congress the first minister of the United States to Great Britain. He did not return home until 1788. He had, therefore, no direct part in the formation of the United States Constitution. Of course, he took a keen interest in that event. Observing it from his station abroad, he was inevitably influenced by Europe's perception of the terrible weakness of the American confederation and by the tide of democratic revolution that, in his own perception, threatened to inundate the European continent.

Like many of the Americans who would attend the CONSTITUTIONAL CONVENTION OF 1787, Adams was alarmed by SHAYS' REBELLION in Massachusetts, and he took up his pen once again to show the way to constitutional salvation. His three-volume work, *Defence of the American Constitutions* (1787) was devoted to the classical proposition that the *"unum necessarium"* of republican government is the tripartite division of the legislative power, each of the branches embodying a distinctive principle and power—the one, the few, and the many, or monarchy, aristocracy, democracy—and the dynamics of the balance between them securing the equilibrium of the whole. The book's title was misleading. It was not actually a defense of the state constitutions, most of which Adams thought indefensible, but rather a defense of the true republican theory against the criticism of those constitutions by the French *philosophe* Robert Jacques Turgot and his school, who held that instead of collecting all authority at one center, as the logic of equality and popular sovereignty dictated, the American constitutions erred in dividing power among different social orders and principles of government in pale imitation of the English king, lords, and commons. Adams sought to demonstrate, of course, that this balanced government was founded in the law of reason and nature. He ransacked European history, carving huge chunks from the writings of philosophers and historians—about eighty percent of the text—and adding his own argumentative comments to prove his point. All societies are divided between the few and the many, the rich and the poor, aristocrats and commoners; and these two orders, actuated by passion and ambition, are constantly at war with each other. The only escape, the only security, is through the tripartite balance. It involves, primarily, erecting a third power, a monarchical executive, to serve as a balance wheel and umpire between the democracy and the aristocracy. It involves also constituting these two great orders in insulated chambers, wherein each may flourish but neither may dominate or subvert the other. Vice, interest, and ambition are rendered useful when these two orders are made to control each other and a monarchical executive is installed as the presiding genius over the whole.

With the publication of the *Defence,* Adams's political thought hardened into a system that placed him at odds with democratic forces and opinion in both Europe and the United States. In 1789 the French National Assembly rejected his doctrine. At home he was alienated from many former political friends. The subject of his apostasy from republicanism became, it was said, "a kind of political phenomenon." He denied any apostasy, of course, and his use of such galvanizing abstractions as "monarchy" and "aristocracy" undoubtedly opened him to misrepresentation. Nevertheless, the character of his thought had changed. During his sojourn abroad Adams became the captive of Old World political fears, which he then transferred to the United States, where they did not belong. Here, as he sometimes recognized, all men were of one order. Yet for several years after his return to the United States, Adams did not disguise his belief that hereditary monarchy and aristocracy must eventually prove as necessary to the American republic as they had to every other. They were, he said, the only institutions that could preserve the laws and liberties of the people against discord, sedition, and civil war.

These beliefs did not prevent Adams's election as vice-president in 1788. Long a friend of a national government, he approved of the Constitution and even imagined the *Defence* had influenced it. He wished the executive were stronger and feared the recurrent shocks to the system from frequent elections and the factions, turbulence, and intrigue they bred. For a time he toyed with the idea of a second convention to overcome these weaknesses. His concern for the authority and dignity of the government led him to propose in the First Congress a high-sounding title ("His Most Benign Highness") for the President and splendid ceremonies of state in order to awe the people. He reiterated those views and continued the argument of the *Defence* in a series of articles (*Discourses on Davila*) in the *Gazette of the United States,* in Philadelphia. Since the articles also denounced the French Revolution, they were an American parallel to Edmund Burke's *Reflections on the Revolution in France.* When the doctrines were publicly labeled "political heresies" by Adams's old friend, THOMAS JEFFERSON, the secretary of state, the ideological division between them entered into the emerging party conflict. In this conflict Adams proved himself a loyal Federalist. Not wishing to cause further embarrassment to GEORGE WASHINGTON's administration, which the Republicans assailed as Anglican and monarchical, Adams put away his pen in 1791 and withdrew into the recesses of the vice-presidency.

Elected President in 1797, Adams at first sought political reconciliation with his Republican rival, Jefferson, but the effort foundered amidst intense partisanship and foreign crisis. The issue of war and peace with France absorbed his administration. Working to resolve it, Adams was handicapped both by the Republican opposition and by the High Federalists in his cabinet who took their orders from ALEXANDER HAMILTON. The collapse of negotiations with France was followed by frantic preparations for war in the spring of 1798. Adams favored naval defense—and the Navy Department was created. He distrusted Hamilton, who favored a large army, seeing in him a potential Caesar. When General Washington, called out of retirement to command the new army, demanded that the second place be given to Hamilton, Adams resisted, citing his prerogative as COMMANDER-IN-CHIEF, he but was finally forced to yield. He did not recommend and had no direct responsibility for the ALIEN AND SEDITION ACTS passed by Congress in July. Yet he contributed as much as anyone to the war hysteria that provoked this repressive legislation. In his public answers to the addresses of loyalty that poured into Philadelphia, Adams repeatedly condemned "the wild philosophy," "domestic treachery," and "spirit of party, which scruples not to go all lengths of profligacy, falsehood, and malignity in defaming our government." Thus branded disloyal by a President whose philosophy made no place for organized POLITICAL PARTIES, the Republican leaders became easy targets. Moreover, Adams cooperated in the enforcement of these laws. The Alien Law was not fully executed in a single instance, but Adams deserves little credit for this. He apparently approved the numerous prosecutions under the Sedition Law, and showed no mercy for its victims. In retrospect, when the impolicy of the laws was generally conceded, Adams still never doubted their constitutionality.

Despite the prescriptions of his political theory, Adams was not a strong President. Indeed, because of that theory, he continued to consider the office above party and politics, though the conception was already unworkable. In the end he asserted his authority and in one glorious act of statesmanship broke with the High Federalists and made peace with France. The domestic consequences were as important as the foreign. Adams sometimes said he made peace in order to squelch Hamilton and his designs for the army. Standing army, foreign adventurism, mounting debt and taxes—these dangers recalled to Adams the Whig doctrines of his youth. "All the declarations . . . of Trenchard and Gordon [see CATO'S LETTERS], Bolingbroke, Barnard and Walpole, Hume, Burgh, and Burke, rush upon my memory and frighten me out of my wits," he confessed. Patriotic, courageous, and wise, Adams's actions nevertheless split the Federalist party and paved the way for Jefferson's triumph in the election of 1800. Before he left office, Adams signed into law the JUDICIARY ACT OF 1801, creating many new federal courts and judgeships, which he proceeded to fill with faithful partisans. In the Republican view the Federalists retreated to the judiciary as a fortress from which to defeat every popular reform. Less noticed at the time but more important for the nation's constitutional development was the nomination and appointment of JOHN MARSHALL as Chief Justice of the United States.

In retirement at Quincy, Adams slowly made peace with Jeffersonian Republicanism and watched his son JOHN QUINCY ADAMS, who broke with the Federalists in 1808, rise to become the sixth President of the United States. A compulsive and contentious reader, Adams never lost his enthusiasm for political speculation; and although he grew more and more hopeful about the American experiment, he continued to the end to warn the people against their own suicidal tendencies. In 1820 he attended the convention to revise the Massachusetts constitution he had drafted forty years before. When the reformers attacked the "aristocratical principle" of a senate bottomed on property, Adams spoke spiritedly in its defense. And, with most of the original constitution, it survived. The finest literary product of these years—one of the intellectual monuments of the age—was his correspondence with Thomas Jefferson, with whom he was reconciled in friendship in 1812. The correspondence traversed an immense field. In politics, the two men discoursed brilliantly on "natural aristocracy," further defining a fundamental issue of principle between them. Interestingly, Adams's political anxieties, unlike Jefferson's, never fixed upon the Constitution. He did not turn political questions into constitutional questions. He was a nationalist, of course, and spoke highly of the Union; but for all his work on constitutional government, Adams rarely uttered a complete thought on the United States Constitution. The amiability and learning, the candor and humor, with the occasional banter and abandon of his letters were all perfectly in character. In the often quoted observation of BENJAMIN FRANKLIN, John Adams was "always an honest man, often a wise one, but sometimes, and in some things, absolutely out of his senses." He died, as did Jefferson, on the fiftieth anniversary of American independence, July 4, 1826.

MERRILL D. PETERSON

Bibliography

ADAMS, CHARLES FRANCIS, ED. 1850–1856 *The Works of John Adams.* 10 Vols. Boston: Little, Brown.

BUTTERFIELD, LYMAN C., ED. 1961 *The Diary and Autobiography of John Adams.* 4 Vols. Cambridge, Mass.: Harvard University Press.

HARASZTI, ZOLTAN 1952 *John Adams and the Prophets of Progress.* Cambridge, Mass.: Harvard University Press.

HOWE, JOHN R., JR. 1966 *The Changing Political Thought of John Adams.* Princeton, N.J.: Princeton University Press.

KURTZ, STEPHEN G. 1957 *The Presidency of John Adams.* Philadelphia: University of Pennsylvania Press.

SMITH, PAGE 1962 *John Adams.* 2 Vols. Garden City, N.Y.: Doubleday.

ADAMS, JOHN QUINCY
(1767–1848)

John Quincy Adams served the nation in its earliest days, contributing as diplomat, secretary of state, President, and congressman to the development of constitutional government in America. Throughout his career he sought to be a "man of the whole nation," an ambition that earned him enemies in his native New England and in the South during a period of political sectionalism. As congressman from Massachusetts between 1831 and 1848, he played a decisive role in the development of the Whig theory of the United States Constitution. His speeches in this period inspired a whole generation of Americans to resist the expansion of SLAVERY and to defend the Union.

Adams's political career began at the age of fifteen, when he went as private secretary to his father, JOHN ADAMS, on the diplomatic mission that negotiated the Treaty of Paris (1783). In 1801 he was elected United States senator. He angered Federalists by his support of THOMAS JEFFERON's acquisition of Louisiana and by his cooperation with the administration's policy of countering English and French attacks on American shipping by economic means. This policy resulted in the Embargo (1807) and gave rise to a SECESSION movement in New England (culminating in the HARTFORD CONVENTION of 1814–1815). Eighteen months before his term ended, the legislature elected a replacement and Adams resigned his Senate seat. He returned to private practice of the law, supporting the Yazoo claimants before the Supreme Court in FLETCHER V. PECK (1809). In the same year, President JAMES MADISON appointed him minister to Russia. As secretary of state under JAMES MONROE (1816–1824), Adams secured American territorial claims to the Pacific Northwest and defended ANDREW JACKSON's conduct in Florida during the Seminole Wars. Adams was the principal author of the MONROE DOCTRINE, defending the Latin American republics from fresh incursions by European imperialism.

In 1824 Adams was elected President by the House of Representatives, none of the major candidates (Adams, Jackson, William Crawford, and HENRY CLAY) having achieved a majority in the ELECTORAL COLLEGE. The 1824 election created a political enmity between Adams and Jackson that seriously undermined Adams's presidency. Jackson had received a large plurality of popular votes, and the general's supporters portrayed Adams's election as an antidemocratic "corrupt bargain" between Adams and Clay, whom Adams appointed as secretary of state. In spite of Adams's strong disapproval of partisan politics, his administration gave rise to the second party system: Jacksonian Democrats versus Whigs.

In addition to the conflict between "plain republicans" and "aristocrats"—a popular division recalling the rhetoric of the Jeffersonians—another conflict arising from Adams's presidency was that between partisans of "BROAD CONSTRUCTION" and of "STRICT CONSTRUCTION" of the constitutional powers of the federal government. This division arose from Adams's call for a vigorous program of nationally funded INTERNAL IMPROVEMENTS—roads, canals, harbors, naval facilities, etcetera—a program that Henry Clay named the AMERICAN SYSTEM. But at bottom the division resulted from fundamental disagreements about the character of the Union.

Defeated for reelection in 1828, Adams seemed at the end of his career. In 1829 he wrote the least prudent, if most interesting, of his many essays and pamphlets, an account of the events leading up to the convening of the Hartford Convention, implicating many of New England's most famous men in TREASON. In writing this long essay (published posthumously as *Documents Relating to New England Federalism, 1801–1815*) he developed a THEORY OF THE UNION that constituted the burden of his speeches and public writings until his death in 1848, and that became the political gospel of the new Republican party and its greatest leader, ABRAHAM LINCOLN.

According to Adams, the Constitution was not a compact between sovereign states but was the organic law of the American nation, given by the American people to themselves in the exercise of their inalienable right to consent to the form of government over them. The state governments derived their existence from the same act of consent that created the federal government. They did not exist before the federal government, therefore, and could not have created it themselves by compact. What is more, the state governments, like the federal government, depended decisively on the truth of those first principles of politics enunciated in the DECLARATION OF INDEPENDENCE for their own legitimacy.

This Whig theory of the Constitution was politically provocative. By it slavery was a clear moral evil. Adams, like Lincoln after him, justified the compromise with slavery as necessary in the circumstances to the existence of a constitutional union in America, but Adams vehemently maintained the duty to prevent the spread of what was at best a necessary evil. While he advocated a scrupulous care for the legal rights of slavery where it was established, he insisted that the government of the United States must always speak as a free state in world affairs. He believed it to be a duty of the whole nation to set slavery, as Lincoln would later say, on the course of ultimate extinction.

This theory guided his words and deeds in the House of Representatives from 1831 until his death. For fourteen years he waged an almost single-handed war against the dominant Jacksonian Democratic majority in the House, a struggle focused on the GAG RULE. The gag rule was actually a series of standing rules adopted at every session of Congress from 1836 on. In its final form it read: "No petition, memorial, resolution, or other paper praying the abolition of slavery in the DISTRICT OF COLUMBIA or any State or Territory, or the slave trade between the States or Territories in which it now exists, shall be received by this House, or entertained in any way whatever."

The gag rule was part of a policy followed by the Democratic party in this period, on the advice of JOHN C. CALHOUN, among others, never in the least thing to admit the authority of Congress over slavery. Adams argued that the gag was a patent abrogation of the FIRST AMENDMENT's guarantee of FREEDOM

OF PETITION. His speeches against the gag became a rallying point for the growing free-soil and abolition movements in the North, though Adams himself was cautious about endorsing the program of the radicals.

Through a long and varied career, Adams's statesmanship was guided by the twin principles of liberty and union. As a diplomat and architect of American foreign policy, Adams played a large part in the creation of a continental Republic. He believed that the westward expansion of the country was necessary if the United States was to minimize foreign interference in its domestic politics. Yet expansion brought the most powerful internal forces of disruption of the Union into play and prepared the way for the Civil War.

GEORGE FORSYTH

Bibliography

BEMIS, SAMUEL F. 1949 *John Quincy Adams and the Foundations of American Foreign Policy.* New York: Knopf.

_____ 1956 *John Quincy Adams and the Union.* New York: Knopf.

LIPSKY, GEORGE A. 1950 *John Quincy Adams: His Theories and Ideas.* New York: Crowell.

ADAMS, SAMUEL (1722–1803)

Samuel Adams was one of the greatest leaders of the American Revolution whose career flourished during the long struggle with Great Britain. His strength was in Massachusetts state politics; he was less successful as a national politician. His speeches and writings influenced the shape of American constitutional thought.

Adams's political career began in 1764 when he wrote the instructions of the Boston town meeting to Boston's representatives in the legislature. These included the first formal denial of the right of Parliament to tax the colonists: "If taxes are laid upon us in any shape without our having a legal representation where they are laid, are we not reduced from the character of free subjects to the miserable state of tributary slaves?"

The next year he was elected to the legislature and assumed leadership of the radical popular opposition to the governing clique headed by THOMAS HUTCHINSON. Adams maintained that he was defending not only the rights of British colonists but also the NATURAL RIGHTS of all men: "The leading principles of the British Constitution have their foundation in the Laws of Nature and universal Reason. . . . British rights are in great measure the Rights of the Colonists, and of all men else." Adams led the opposition to the Stamp Act and the TOWNSHEND ACTS. He denounced these acts as unconstitutional, since they involved TAXATION WITHOUT REPRESENTATION.

In the MASSACHUSETTS CIRCULAR LETTER of 1768 Adams wrote of constitutions in general that they should be fixed and unalterable by ordinary legislation, and that under no constitution could subjects be deprived of their property except by their consent, given in person or by elected representatives. Of the British Constitution in particular he argued that, although Parliament might legislate on imperial matters, only the colonial assemblies could legislate on local matters or impose special taxes.

When the British government landed troops at Boston, Adams published a series of letters denouncing as unconstitutional the keeping of a standing army in peacetime without the consent of the people of the colony. "The Americans," he wrote, "as they were not and could not be represented in Parliament, were therefore suffering under military tyranny over which they were allowed to exercise no control."

In the early 1770s, Adams worked to create a network of committees of correspondence. In November 1772, on behalf of the Boston Committee of Correspondence, he drafted a declaration of the rights of the colonists. In three sections it proclaimed the rights of Americans as men, as Christians, and as British subjects. A list of infringements of those rights followed, including the assumption by Parliament of the power to legislate for the colonies in all cases whatsoever and the grant of a royal salary to Governor Thomas Hutchinson and the judges in Massachusetts.

In January 1773 Hutchinson, addressing the legislature, argued for acceptance of the absolute supremacy of the British Parliament and asserted that there was no middle ground between unqualified submission and independence. Samuel Adams, along with JOHN ADAMS, drafted the reply of the Assembly, arguing anew that under the British Constitution the colonial legislature shared power with Parliament.

Samuel Adams was an early proponent of a Continental Congress, and in June 1774 he was elected to the First Continental Congress. There he played a key role in the adoption of the ASSOCIATION. In the Second Continental Congress he moved, in January 1776, for immediate independence and for a federation of the colonies. In July 1776, he signed the DECLARATION OF INDEPENDENCE.

Adams remained a member of the Continental

Congress until 1781. He was a member of the original committee to draft the ARTICLES OF CONFEDERATION. Suspicious of any concentration of power, he opposed creation of the executive departments of finance, war, and foreign affairs. In 1779–1780 he was a delegate to the Massachusetts CONSTITUTIONAL CONVENTION, which produced the first of the Revolutionary state constitutions to be ratified by popular vote.

Throughout the Revolutionary period Adams was a staunch supporter of unified action. When, in 1783, a Massachusetts convention was held to plan resistance to congressional enactment of a pension for army officers, Adams, who had opposed the pension, defended Congress's right to pass it and spoke out against those who would dishonor the state's commitment to pay continental debts.

In 1787, after SHAYS' REBELLION had broken out, Adams, then president of the state senate, proposed to invoke the assistance of the United States as provided in the Articles of Confederation, but his motion failed in the lower house. Later, opposing the pardon of the rebels, he argued that there is a crucial difference between monarchy and self-government and that any "man who dares to rebel against the laws of a republic ought to suffer death."

Adams was not named a delegate to the CONSTITUTIONAL CONVENTION OF 1787, but he was influential at the Massachusetts ratifying convention: "I stumble at the threshold," he wrote to RICHARD HENRY LEE, "I meet with a national government, instead of a federal union of sovereign states." He was troubled by the division of powers in the proposed federal system, which constituted "*Imperia in Imperio* [supreme powers within a supreme power] justly deemed a Solecism in Politicks, highly dangerous, and destructive of the Peace Union and Safety of the Nation." Ironically, he echoed the argument of his old enemy Hutchinson that SOVEREIGNTY was indivisible. But, after a meeting of his constituents passed a resolution that "any vote of a delegate from Boston against adopting it would be contrary to the interests, feelings, and wishes of the tradesmen of the town," Adams altered his position. In the end he supported a plan whereby Massachusetts ratified the Constitution unconditionally but also proposed a series of amendments, including a BILL OF RIGHTS.

Adams was defeated by FISHER AMES for election to the first Congress. Thereafter, although he remained active in state politics as a legislator and governor (1794–1797), he never again sought or held national office under the Constitution.

DENNIS J. MAHONEY

Bibliography

MAIER, PAULINE 1980 *The Old Revolutionaries: Political Lives in the Age of Samuel Adams.* New York: Knopf.

MILLER, JOHN C. 1936 *Sam Adams: Pioneer in Propaganda.* Boston: Little, Brown.

WELLS, WILLIAM V. 1865 *Life and Public Services of Samuel Adams . . . With Extracts from His Correspondence, State Papers, and Political Essays.* Boston: Little, Brown.

ADAMS v. TANNER
244 U.S. 590 (1917)

In a 5–4 decision, the Supreme Court declared unconstitutional a Washington state statute prohibiting individuals from paying employment agencies for their services. Although a loophole allowed prospective employers to pay the agencies' fees, Justice JAMES C. MCREYNOLDS nevertheless voided the law as a prohibition, not a regulation, of business. Citing ALLGEYER V. LOUISIANA (1897), McReynolds also declared the statute a violation of DUE PROCESS OF LAW. Justice LOUIS D. BRANDEIS dissented, joined by Justices OLIVER WENDELL HOLMES and JOHN H. CLARKE, demonstrating the "vast evils" that justified the legislature under STATE POLICE POWERS.

DAVID GORDON

(SEE ALSO: *Ribnik v. McBride,* 1928; *Tyson & Brother v. Banton,* 1927; and *Olsen v. Nebraska ex rel. Reference & Bond Association,* 1941.)

ADAMSON v. CALIFORNIA
332 U.S. 46 (1947)

By a 5–4 vote the Supreme Court, speaking through Justice STANLEY F. REED, sustained the constitutionality of provisions of California laws permitting the trial court and prosecutor to call the jury's attention to the accused's failure to explain or deny evidence against him. Adamson argued that the Fifth Amendment's RIGHT AGAINST SELF-INCRIMINATION is a fundamental national privilege protected against state abridgment by the FOURTEENTH AMENDMENT and that the same amendment's DUE PROCESS clause prevented comment on the accused's silence. Reed, relying on TWINING V. NEW JERSEY (1908) and PALKO V. CONNECTICUT (1937), ruled that the Fifth Amendment does not apply to the states and that even adverse comment on the right to silence does not deny due process.

The case is notable less for Reed's opinion, which GRIFFIN V. CALIFORNIA (1965) overruled, than for the classic debate between Justices FELIX FRANKFURTER, concurring, and HUGO L. BLACK, in dissent, on the INCORPORATION DOCTRINE. Joined by Justice WILLIAM O. DOUGLAS, Black read the history of the origins of the Fourteenth Amendment to mean that its framers and ratifiers intended to make the entire BILL OF RIGHTS applicable to the states, a position that Justice FRANK MURPHY, joined by Justice WILEY RUTLEDGE, surpassed by adding that the Fourteenth Amendment also protected unenumerated rights. Frankfurter, seeking to expose the inconsistency of the dissenters, suggested that they did not mean what they said. They would not fasten on the states the requirement of the SEVENTH AMENDMENT that civil cases involving more than $20 require a TRIAL BY JURY. They really intended only a "selective incorporation," Frankfurter declared, and consequently they offered "a merely subjective test." Black, in turn, purporting to be quite literal in his interpretation, ridiculed Frankfurter's subjective reliance on "civilized decency" to explain due process. History probably supports Frankfurter's argument on the original intent of the Fourteenth Amendment, but the Justices on both sides mangled the little historical evidence they knew to make it support preconceived positions.

LEONARD W. LEVY

ADAMSON EIGHT-HOUR ACT
39 Stat. 721 (1916)

In 1916 major railway unions demanded an eight-hour working day and extra pay for overtime work. The railroads' refusal prompted a union call for a nationwide general strike. President WOODROW WILSON, fearing disastrous consequences, appealed to Congress for legislation to avert the strike and to protect "the life and interests of the nation." The Adamson Act mandated an eight-hour day for railroad workers engaged in INTERSTATE COMMERCE. The act also established a commission to report on the law's operation. Pending that report, the act prohibited reduction in pay rates for the shorter workday. Overtime would be recompensed at regular wages, not time and a half. Congress effectively constituted itself a labor arbitrator and vested its award with the force of law. The Supreme Court rejected the argument that Congress exceeded its constitutional authority in WILSON V. NEW (1917), sustaining the act. The Court distinguished LOCHNER V. NEW YORK (1905) by asserting that the Adamson Act did no more than supplement the rights of the contracting parties; the act did not interfere with the FREEDOM OF CONTRACT.

DAVID GORDON

ADDERLEY v. FLORIDA
385 U.S. 39 (1966)

A 5–4 Supreme Court, speaking through Justice HUGO L. BLACK, upheld TRESPASS convictions of CIVIL RIGHTS advocates demonstrating in a jail driveway, holding that where public property is devoted to a special use, FREEDOM OF SPEECH constitutionally may be limited in order to "preserve the property . . . for the use to which it is lawfully dedicated." This case signaled a new attention to the extent to which speakers have a right to carry their expressive activity onto private property and non-PUBLIC FORUM public property. It was also one of the first cases in which Justice Black exhibited the increasingly critical attitude toward demonstrations and other nontraditional forms of speech that marked his last years.

MARTIN SHAPIRO

ADEQUATE STATE GROUNDS

Although most decisions of state courts falling within the Supreme Court's APPELLATE JURISDICTION involve questions of both state and federal law, the Supreme Court limits its review of such cases to the FEDERAL QUESTIONS. Moreover, the Court will not even decide the federal questions raised by such a case if the decision below rests on a ground of state law that is adequate to support the judgment and is independent of any federal issue. This rule applies to grounds based on both state substantive law and state procedures.

In its substantive-ground aspect, the rule not only protects the state courts' authority as the final arbiters of state law but also bolsters the principle forbidding federal courts to give ADVISORY OPINIONS. If the Supreme Court were to review the federal issues presented by a decision resting independently on an adequate state ground, the Court's pronouncements on the federal issues would be advisory only, having no effect on the resolution of the case. It has been assumed that ordinarily no federal policy dictates Supreme Court review of a decision resting on an independent state substantive ground; the winner in the state court typically is the same party who has asserted the federal claim. The point is exemplified by a state court decision invalidating a state statute on both state and federal constitutional grounds. This assumption, however, is a hindrance to Justices bent on contracting the reach of particular constitutional guarantees. In *Michigan v. Long* (1983) the BURGER COURT announced that when the independence of a state court's judgment from federal law is in doubt, the Court will assume that the judgment does not rest independently on state law. To insulate a decision from Supreme Court review now requires a plain statement by the state court of the independence of its state law ground.

Obviously, the highest state court retains considerable control over the reviewability of many of its decisions in the Supreme Court. If the state court chooses to rest decision only on grounds of federal law, as the California court did in REGENTS OF THE UNIVERSITY OF CALIFORNIA V. BAKKE (1978), the case is reviewable by the Supreme Court. Correspondingly, the state court can avoid review by the Supreme Court by resting solely on a state-law ground, or by explicitly resting on *both* a state and a federal ground. In the latter case, the state court's pronouncements on federal law are unreviewable. Recently, several state supreme courts (Alaska, California, Massachusetts, New Jersey, and Oregon) have used these devices to make important contributions to the development of both state and federal constitutional law.

When the state court's decision rests on a procedural ground, the usual effect is to cut off a party's right to claim a federal right, because of some procedural default. The Supreme Court generally insists that federal questions be raised in the state courts according to the dictates of state procedure. However, when the state procedural ground itself violates the federal Constitution (and thus is not "independent" of a federal claim), the Supreme Court will consider the federal issues in the case even though state procedure was not precisely followed. Another exception is exemplified in NAACP V. ALABAMA (1964). There the Court reviewed the NAACP's federal claims although the state court had refused to hear them on the transparently phony ground that they had been presented in a brief that departed from the prescribed format. The adequate state ground rule protects judicial federalism, not shamming designed to defeat the claims of federal right.

A similar rule limits the availability of federal HABEAS CORPUS relief for state prisoners. (See FAY V. NOIA, 1963; WAINWRIGHT V. SYKES, 1977.)

KENNETH L. KARST

Bibliography

FALK, JEROME B., JR. 1973 The Supreme Court of California, 1971–1972—Foreword: The State Constitution: A More Than "Adequate" Nonfederal Ground. *California Law Review* 61:273–286.

ADKINS v. CHILDREN'S HOSPITAL
261 U.S. 525 (1923)

The *Adkins* case climaxed the assimilation of laissez-faire economics into constitutional law. At issue was the constitutionality of a congressional minimum wage law for women and children in the District of Columbia. (See DISTRICT OF COLUMBIA MINIMUM WAGE ACT.) The impact of the case was nationwide, affecting all similar state legislation. In the exercise of its police power over the District, Congress in 1918 established an administrative board with investigatory powers over wages and living standards for underprivileged, unorganized workers. After notice and hearing, the board could order wage increases by fixing minima for women and minors. The board followed a general standard set by the legislature: wages had to be reasonably sufficient to keep workers "in good health" and "protect their morals." A corporation maintaining a hospital in the District and a woman who had lost a job paying $35 a month and two meals daily claimed that the statute violated the Fifth Amendment's DUE PROCESS clause which protected their FREEDOM OF CONTRACT on terms mutually desirable.

The constitutionality of minimum wage legislation had come before the Court in STETTLER V. O'HARA (1917) but because Justice LOUIS D. BRANDEIS had disqualified himself, the Court had split evenly, settling nothing. In the same year, however, Professor FELIX FRANKFURTER won from the Court a decision sustaining the constitutionality of a state maximum hours law in BUNTING V. OREGON (1917). Although the Court sustained that law for men as well as for women and children, it neglected to overrule LOCHNER V. NEW YORK (1905). In that case the Court had held that minimum wage laws for bakers violated the freedom of contract protected by due process of law. Nevertheless, *Bunting* seemed to supersede *Lochner* and followed Justice OLIVER WENDELL HOLMES'S *Lochner* dissent. The Court in *Bunting* presumed the constitutionality of the statute, disavowed examination of the legislature's wisdom in exercising its POLICE POWER, and asserted that the reasonableness of the legislation need not be proved;

the burden of proving unreasonableness fell upon those opposed to the social measure.

Because *Bunting* superseded *Lochner* without overruling it, Frankfurter, who again defended the constitutionality of the statute, took no chances in *Adkins.* He relied on the principles of *Bunting,* the plenary powers of Congress over the District, and the overwhelmingly favorable state court precedents. In the main, however, he sought to show the reasonableness of the minimum wage law for women and children in order to rebut the freedom of contract DOCTRINE. In a BRANDEIS BRIEF, he proved the relation between the very low wages that had prevailed before the statute and the high incidences of child neglect, disease, broken homes, prostitution, and death.

A recent appointee, Justice GEORGE SUTHERLAND, spoke for the *Adkins* majority. Chief Justice WILLIAM HOWARD TAFT, joined by Justice EDWARD SANFORD, dissented also, separately. The vote was 5–3. Brandeis disqualified himself from participating because his daughter worked for the minimum wage board. Sutherland dismissed Frankfurter's brief with the comment that his facts were "interesting but only mildly persuasive." Such facts, said Sutherland, were "proper enough for the consideration of lawmaking bodies, since their tendency is to establish the desirability or undesirability of the legislation; but they reflect no legitimate light upon the question of its validity, and that is what we are called upon to decide." The Court then found, on the basis of its own consideration of policy, that the statute was unwise and undesirable. Sutherland assumed that prostitution among the poor was unrelated to income. He claimed that the recently acquired right of women to vote had elevated them to the same status as men, stripping them of any legal protection based on sexual differences. That disposed of the 1908 ruling in MULLER V. OREGON. Consequently, women had the same right of freedom of contract as men, no more or less.

That freedom was not an absolute, Sutherland conceded, but this case did not fall into any of the exceptional categories of cases in which the government might reasonably restrict that freedom. Female elevator operators, scrubwomen, and dishwashers had a constitutional right to work for whatever they pleased, even if for less than a minimum prescribed by an administrative board. Employers had an equal right to pay what they pleased. If the board could fix minimum wages, employers might be forced to pay more than the value of the services rendered and might have to operate at a loss or even go out of business. By comparing the selling of labor with the selling of goods, Sutherland, ironically, supported the claim that capitalism regarded labor as a commodity on the open market. On such reasoning the Court found that the statute conflicted with the freedom of contract incorporated within the Fifth Amendment's due process clause. Paradoxically the Court distinguished away *Muller* and *Bunting* because they were maximum hours cases irrelevant to a case involving minimum wages, yet it relied heavily on *Lochner* as controlling, though it too was a maximum hours case. (See MAXIMUM HOURS AND MINIMUM WAGES.)

All this was too much for even that stalwart conservative, Chief Justice Taft, who felt bound by precedent to support the statute. Like Holmes, Taft perceived no difference in principle between a maximum hours law, which was valid, and a minimum wages law, which was not. Holmes went further. In addition to showing that both kinds of legislation interfered with freedom of contract to the same extent, he repudiated the freedom of conduct doctrine as he had in his famous *Lochner* dissent. He criticized the Court for expanding an unpretentious assertion of the liberty to follow one's calling into a far-reaching, rigid dogma. Like Taft, Holmes thought that *Bunting* had silently overruled *Lochner.* Both Taft and Holmes took notice of Frankfurter's evidence to make the point that the statute was not unreasonable. Holmes observed that it "does not compel anybody to pay anything. It simply forbids employment at rates below those fixed as the minimum requirement of health and right living." Holmes also remarked that more than a women's suffrage amendment would be required to make him believe that "there are no differences between men and women, or that legislation cannot take those differences into account." Yet, the most caustic line in the dissenting opinions was Taft's: "it is not the function of this court to hold congressional acts invalid simply because they are passed to carry out economic views which the court believes to be unwise or unsound."

By this decision, the Court voided minimum wage laws throughout the country. Per curiam opinions based on *Adkins* disposed of state statutes whose supporters futilely sought to distinguish their administrative standards from the one before the Court in *Adkins.* Samuel Gompers, the leader of American trade unionism, bitterly remarked, "To buy the labor of a woman is not like buying pigs' feet in a butcher shop." A cartoon in the New York *World* showed Sutherland handing a copy of his opinion to a woman wage earner, saying, "This decision affirms your constitutional right to starve." By preventing minimum wage laws, the Court kept labor unprotected when the Depression struck. *Adkins* remained the law of the land controlling decisions as late as 1936; the Court did not overrule it until 1937. (See WEST COAST HOTEL v. PARRISH.)

LEONARD W. LEVY

Bibliography

BERMAN, EDWARD The Supreme Court and the Minimum Wage. *Journal of Political Economy* 31:852–856.

POWELL, THOMAS REED 1924 The Judiciality of Minimum Wage Legislation. *Harvard Law Review* 37:545–573.

ADLER v. BOARD OF EDUCATION OF CITY OF NEW YORK
342 U.S. 485 (1952)

Adler was one of the cases in which state statutes barring members of "subversive" organizations from public school and other public employment were upheld against FIRST AMENDMENT attack on the basis that public employment is a privilege not a right. Most of these decisions were effectively overruled by KEYISHIAN v. BOARD OF REGENTS (1967).

MARTIN SHAPIRO

(SEE ALSO: *Subversive Activities and the Constitution.*)

ADMINISTRATIVE LAW

"Administrative law" describes the legal structure of much of the executive branch of government, particularly the quasi-independent agencies, and the procedural constraints under which they operate. Most of these constraints are statutory; those that do involve the Constitution flow chiefly from the doctrine of SEPARATION OF POWERS and the DUE PROCESS clause. To comprehend the effects of either of these on administrative law one must understand the growth of the administrative agency in the modern American state.

The early years of the twentieth century saw both a growth in the executive branch of the federal government and, perhaps more important, increased expectations about tasks it should perform. Some have seen these changes as a natural concomitant of industrialization; some as a growth in the power of a new professional class claiming to possess a nonpolitical expertise; some as the result of political pressure developed by farmers and small-town residents who looked to government to contain corporate juggernauts; some as the consequence of the desire of those very juggernauts to gain government sanction shielding them from the competitive forces of the marketplace. Whatever the causes, federal, state, and municipal governments took on new tasks in the closing decades of the nineteenth and the opening ones of the twentieth centuries.

Agencies such as the Interstate Commerce Commission, the Federal Trade Commission, the Food and Drug Administration, and the Federal Reserve Board bore witness to national perceptions that the existing economic and social mechanisms left something to be desired and that increased government intervention was the solution. At the local level the rise of social welfare agencies and zoning boards bespoke similar concerns.

With the coming of the Great Depression the federal government sought to revive the economy through numerous public programs designed both to coordinate sectors of the nation's industrial and commercial life (the WAGNER NATIONAL LABOR RELATIONS ACT, the AGRICULTURAL ADJUSTMENT ACT, the NATIONAL INDUSTRIAL RECOVERY ACT) and to create public jobs to reduce unemployment and increase consumer demand (the Civilian Conservation Corps, the Works Progress Administration, the Public Works Administration). Such agencies, generating regulations under the statutory umbrella of broad enabling legislation, came to be a standard feature on the American scene.

In a parallel development state governments created a number of agencies to coordinate and regulate everything from barbers to new car dealers, from avocado marketing to the licensing of physicians. Some of these boards appear to function chiefly as means of controlling entry into occupations and thereby shielding current practitioners from competition, but all function as branches of the government armed with at least some forms of regulatory power.

In some respects such state and national agencies represent not a new form of governmental power but a transfer to state and national levels of what had once been tasks of city government. The functioning of such municipal bureaucracies was, however, largely idiosyncratic and local—defined by the terms of the cities' charters and thus beyond the reach of national law. The migration of regulatory control from city to state and nation both enabled and necessitated the development of a new "administrative" law, which in America is almost entirely a creature of the twentieth century.

Most of that law is statutory, a function of the legislation that creates the board, agency, or commission and defines its tasks and powers. Citizens and enterprises wishing either to invoke or to challenge such powers use the statutorily specified procedures, which often involve both internal agency and external JUDICIAL REVIEW of administrative actions. At two points, however, the Constitution does speak to the structure and conduct of the agencies. In the formative years of the administrative state the Supreme Court expressed doubt about the place of the agency in the divided federal system of government. Since the New Deal the constitutional focus has turned to the processes employed by administrative agencies, and the courts have regularly required agencies' procedures to conform to the due process clause.

The Constitution establishes three branches of the national government, and the courts early decided that no branch should exceed its own powers or intrude on areas designated as the province of another branch. This principle, known as the separation of powers, applies to numerous activities of the federal government, but it impinges particularly on the operation of administrative agencies charged with the formation and enforcement of broad federal policy.

Congress could not possibly specify just what tasks it wishes federal agencies to accomplish and also exactly how to perform them. At the opposite extreme it would just as obviously violate the separation of powers if Congress were to throw up its hands at the task of forming policy and instead direct the President to hit on whatever combination of revenue collection and expenditure he deemed best to fulfill the needs of the country. The concern is that Congress, if it asks an administrative agency not just to carry out defined tasks but also to participate in the formation of policy, has impermissibly given—delegated—its legislative power to the agency (a part of the executive branch).

That concern surfaced in a pair of Supreme Court decisions invalidating New Deal legislation. PANAMA REFINING CO. V. RYAN (1935) struck down a portion of the National Industrial Recovery Act that permitted the President to ban the interstate shipment of petroleum; the Court's ground was that Congress had provided no guidance as to when the President should do so or what aims were to justify the ban. A few months later, in SCHECHTER POULTRY CORP. V. UNITED STATES, the Court held unconstitutional another section of the same act; its DELEGATION OF POWER permitted the President to create codes of fair competition for various industries. Congress had defined neither the content of such codes nor the conditions for their proclamation, and some members of the Court evinced concern that the absence of standards could pave the way for what amounted to a governmentally sanctioned system of industrial cartels.

Since these two cases the Court has not invalidated a congressional delegation of power, but some have argued that the memory of these cases has induced the legislature to indicate more clearly the goals it intends the agency to accomplish, the means by which they are to be accomplished, and the processes that should accompany their implementation.

Even though an administrative agency does not perform tasks that constitutionally belong only to Congress, it might nevertheless violate the constitutional structure of government by performing tasks belonging to the courts. The problem has several guises.

In some instances Congress in creating the agency has given it JURISDICTION that might otherwise have been exercised by the courts (for example, over maritime accidents). Did such congressional action, which could be viewed as a transfer of federal judicial jurisdiction to an agency, violate the constitutional structure of government or the rights of the parties? In *Crowell v. Benson* (1932) the Court concluded that if Congress established fair administrative procedures, the agency could hear and determine cases that might otherwise have been heard by the courts—with the saving proviso that the federal courts might review the agency's determination of questions of law.

That proviso pointed to another difficult question: the extent to which the courts might review agency decisions. Summarizing the history of this question, Louis Jaffe has said that we have moved from a nineteenth-century presumption of unreviewability to a twentieth-century presumption of reviewability. Such reviewability, however, flows from statutory interpretation rather than from constitutional compulsion: if Congress is sufficiently explicit, it can make an agency determination final and unreviewable—either because the statute explicitly says so or because it so clearly makes the decision in question a matter of agency discretion that there is no law to apply. For the most part, however, courts routinely scrutinize agency action for legality and at least minimal rationality and are prepared to give the agencies fairly great leeway in performing their tasks.

One measure of this leeway the agencies enjoy is the set of requirements imposed on litigants seeking to invoke federal judicial review of agency action. Such parties must satisfy the courts that they have STANDING (that is, actual injury caused by the agency action), that the dispute is ripe for judicial review (that is, that the case comes to the courts when it has sufficiently developed to render a judicial decision not merely abstract or hypothetical), and that they have exhausted their administrative remedies (that is, that they have sought such administrative redress as is available). Only the first two of these requirements—standing and RIPENESS—stem from the Constitution; all of them, however, condition the federal courts' exercise of judicial review.

Courts are prepared to grant such leeway, however, only to the extent that they are assured that the agency has complied with the requirements of due process in making its decisions. Due process plays two roles in administrative law. To the extent that agencies make rules only after extensive public participation in their deliberations, they address some of the concerns lying at the base of the delegation doctrine—ill-considered and hasty action. Due process also plays a second, more traditional role of assuring adjudicatory fairness. To the extent that agencies take action against those violating their rules, courts have often required that the agencies afford the violators various procedural protections.

Because an increasing number of Americans, from defensc contractors and television broadcasters to mothers of dependent children and disabled veterans, depend on state and federal government for their livelihood, such protections have become increasingly important. In the second half of the twentieth century the courts have held many of those interests to be property, thus giving their holders the right to due process—sometimes including a FAIR HEARING—before suffering their deprivation. Thus state and federal agencies must give welfare recipients an opportunity to know and to contest factual findings before ending benefits; public schools and colleges have to supply students some form of NOTICE and process before suspending or expelling them; and public employers must grant tenured employees an opportunity to contest their dismissal. Courts have left the agencies some discretion as to the form of such procedures, which need not, for example, always include a hearing, but the process must suit the circumstances.

Because such protections flow from the due process clauses, they apply equally to state and to federal government; indeed, an important consequence of the constitutionalization of administrative process is that it has penetrated to state bureaucracies, some of which were perhaps less than exemplary in their concern for those affected by their actions. As a result both state courts and state legislatures have directed attention to the procedures of their agencies.

In a large sense, to understand the relationship of the administrative state to the Constitution, one has to spell constitution with a small "c," for the difficulties have been less with specific constitutional provisions than with the general picture of how executive action—especially action in new spheres—fits into received understandings of the world. That question is still debatable, but the debates, at least in the last half of the twentieth century, have taken place at the level of desirable policy, not of constitutional legality: so long as the agencies operate fairly, that much, apparently, is assured.

STEPHEN C. YEAZELL

Bibliography

DAVIS, KENNETH C. 1978 *Administrative Law Treatise.* San Diego, Calif.: Davis.

JAFFE, LOUIS 1965 *Judicial Control of Administrative Action.* Boston: Little, Brown.

KOLKO, GABRIEL 1963 *The Triumph of Conservatism: A Reinterpretation of American History, 1900–1916.* New York: Free Press.

WIEBE, ROBERT 1967 *The Search for Order, 1877–1920.* New York: Hill & Wang.

ADMINISTRATIVE SEARCH

Safety inspections of dwellings by government officials, unlike police searches, are conducted to correct hazardous conditions rather than to secure EVIDENCE. Initially, therefore, the Supreme Court regarded such inspection as merely touching interests that were peripheral to the FOURTH AMENDMENT; the RIGHT OF PRIVACY of the householder must give way, even in the absence of a SEARCH WARRANT, to the interest in preserving a safe urban environment. *Frank v. Maryland* (1959) paradoxically granted greater protection under the Fourth Amendment to suspected criminals than to law-abiding citizens.

Later, the Court reversed itself in CAMARA V. MUNICIPAL COURT (1967), holding that the amendment was designed "to safeguard the privacy and security of individuals against arbitrary invasions by government officials," regardless of their purpose. However, because inspections would be crippled if the standard of proof needed for a warrant were the same as that required in a criminal case, the traditional PROBABLE CAUSE standard was discarded in favor of a flexible test based on the condition of the area and the time elapsed since the last inspection, rather than specific knowledge of the condition of the particular dwelling. After WYMAN V. JAMES (1971) WELFARE BENEFITS for support of a dependent child may be made conditional upon periodic visits to the home by a caseworker; a warrant is not required for such a visit.

The requirement of a warrant for inspections generally applies to business premises, as the Court held in *See v. City of Seattle* (1967). But in *Donovan v. Dewey* (1981) the Court held that coal mines, establishments dealing in guns and liquor, and other commercial properties that are comprehensively regulated by government may be inspected without a warrant, because an owner is obviously aware that his property will be subject to inspection.

JACOB W. LANDYNSKI

Bibliography

LAFAVE, WAYNE R. 1967 Administrative Searches and the Fourth Amendment: The *Camara* and *See* Cases. *Supreme Court Review* 1967:2–38.

ADMIRALTY AND MARITIME JURISDICTION

In Article III of the Constitution, the JUDICIAL POWER OF THE UNITED STATES is made to extend "to all cases of admiralty and maritime jurisdiction." ALEXANDER HAMILTON says, in THE FEDERALIST #80, that "the most bigotted idolizers of State authority have not thus far shown a disposition to deny the national judiciary the cognizance of maritime causes." There is no reason not to believe him. The First Congress, in the JUDICIARY ACT OF 1789, gave this JURISDICTION to the UNITED STATES DISTRICT COURTS, which were to have "exclusive original cognizance of all civil causes of admiralty and maritime jurisdiction, saving to suitors, in all cases, the right of a COMMON LAW remedy, where the common law is competent to give it."

This language was verbally changed in the JUDICIAL CODE of 1948, but the change has had no effect, and was pretty surely not meant to have any, so that one may organize the subject (as it has, indeed, organized itself) around the two questions suggested by the original formula: (1) What is the content of the "exclusive cognizance" given the District Court? and (2) What is "saved" to suitors in the saving clause?

There is an admiralty jurisdiction in "prize"—a jurisdiction to condemn and sell, as lawful prize of war, enemy vessels and cargo. This jurisdiction was employed to effect a few condemnations after World War II, but it has on the whole been very little used in this century. There is an admiralty jurisdiction over crime, but the admiralty clause serves in these cases solely as a firm theoretical foundation for American jurisdiction over certain crimes committed outside the country but on navigable waters; these cases are rarely thought of as "admiralty" cases, because INDICTMENT and trial are "according to the course of the common law," with such statutory and rule-based changes as affect all federal criminal proceedings. Normally, then, "admiralty jurisdiction" refers to jurisdiction over certain private-law concerns affecting the shipping industry—contracts to carry goods, charters of ships, marine insurance, ship collisions, seamen's or passengers' personal injuries, salvage, and so on.

The courts early followed the English rule limiting the jurisdiction to tidal waters, but a rather tortuous development around the middle of the nineteenth century extended this base to include first, the Great Lakes, then the Mississippi River, and at last all interior waters navigable in INTERSTATE or FOREIGN COMMERCE.

There was an early effort, moreover, to limit the jurisdiction to causes very strictly "arising" on these waters. Suits in marine insurance, for example, were thought to be outside the jurisdiction, because the contracts were made on land, and were to be performed (by payment) on land. On the other hand, some quite late cases extended the admiralty jurisdiction to events having no maritime flavor (e.g., an injury to a bather by a surfboard), on the basis of this same "locality" test. This "test," productive of ludicrous results, has often been abjured by the courts, but has a way of popping up again and again, in context after context.

The "saving clause" has been given an interpretation not at all of obvious correctness. The "common-law remedy" saved to suitors was held to comprise all IN PERSONAM causes of action. Thus, if a shipowner's ship is lost, and he claims indemnity from the insurance company, he is free to sue either in admiralty court or in a regular land-based court—and so on through the whole range of admiralty matters. What is *not* "saved to suitors," and is therefore really "exclusive" to the District Courts, is the suit IN REM, wherein a vessel, or other maritime property, is treated as the defendant party, and sued directly under its own name. In practice, this means that the plaintiff (or "libellant," as he used to be called) enjoys a high-priority security interest in the vessel, an interest called a "maritime lien."

The intricacies of admiralty procedure have been simplified in recent years. But one dominating peculiarity remains. Like EQUITY, admiralty (usually) does not use the jury. This fact is normally determinative of the plaintiff's choice, made under the "saving clause," between the admiralty forum and the land-bound court of law.

CHARLES L. BLACK, JR.

Bibliography

GILMORE, GRANT and BLACK, CHARLES L., JR. 1975 *Admiralty*, 2nd ed. Mineola, N.Y.: Foundation Press.

ROBERTSON, DAVID W. 1970 *Admiralty and Federalism*. Mineola, N.Y.: Foundation Press.

ADVICE AND CONSENT

Under Article II, section 2, of the Constitution, the President's powers to make treaties and to appoint important public officials are to be exercised "by and with the advice and consent of the Senate."

The formula "advice and consent" is an ancient one. It was used in British and American state papers and documents for over a thousand years prior to 1787. The use of these words in the Constitution was proposed by the CONSTITUTIONAL CONVENTION'S Committee on Remaining Matters, to which both the TREATY POWER and the APPOINTING POWER had been referred. The first proposal to associate the President and the Senate in the exercise of those powers was made by ALEXANDER HAMILTON, who wanted the Senate to act as a kind of PRIVY COUNCIL. In the debates over RATIFICATION OF THE CONSTITUTION opponents charged that the provision violated the principle of SEPARATION OF POWERS. But in THE FEDERALIST the practice was defended as an instance of CHECKS AND BALANCES and a means of involving the states in the making of important national policy.

In practice, the phrase "advice and consent" has come to have different meanings with respect to the two powers to which it is applied.

In the making of treaties, the advisory function has virtually disappeared. In August 1789, President GEORGE WASHINGTON sought to honor the letter of the Constitution by appearing in person before the Senate to ask its advice prior to negotiating an Indian treaty. When the Senate referred the matter to a committee, Washington walked out, and since that incident, no President has made such a formal request for advice in advance. The common modern practices by which Presidents include senators among American negotiators and consult with influential senators, the party leadership, and members of the Senate Foreign Relations Committee are better understood as political devices to improve the chances of obtaining consent than as deference to the constitutional mandate to obtain advice. In giving its consent to the President's making—or ratification—of a treaty, the Senate is not bound to accept or reject the whole document as submitted. The Senate may amend a treaty or attach reservations to it. Since either of these actions may compel renegotiation, they might be considered perverse forms of giving advice.

In the appointment of officers, the advisory function has become far more important. Nominees to the Supreme Court and to the most important executive and diplomatic posts are normally approved (or rejected) by the Senate on grounds of merit, integrity, and policy. In the case of other executive and judicial appointments, a practice known as "senatorial courtesy" has transformed the requirement for "advice and consent" into an instrument of senatorial control. Nominees cannot expect the Senate's consent to their appointment if it is not supported by senators of the President's party from their home states. If a federal appointee is to serve in a particular state, the senior senator of the President's party from that state (if there is one) customarily makes the actual selection.

DENNIS J. MAHONEY

ADVISORY OPINION

Article III of the Constitution extends the JUDICIAL POWER OF THE UNITED STATES only to the decision of CASES OR CONTROVERSIES. Since 1793, when the Supreme Court declined, in the absence of a concrete dispute, to give legal advice to President GEORGE WASHINGTON on the correct interpretation of treaties with France and Britain, the Court has refused steadfastly to issue advisory opinions, finding them inconsistent with Article III. This refusal is required whether the request seeks advice on interpretation of existing law or on the constitutionality of pending LEGISLATION or anticipated action. The Justices' view is that the federal courts function not as lawyers giving advice but as judges limited to deciding cases presented by adverse parties with a real, not a hypothetical, dispute, one that is subject to judicial resolution and the granting of meaningful relief. The Court held in *Aetna Life Insurance Co. v. Haworth* (1937) that the prohibition against advisory opinions does not preclude declaratory relief, but there must be a concrete controversy between parties of adverse legal positions which a DECLARATORY JUDGMENT can settle.

If doubts exist about the constitutionality of a proposed government policy or the legality of a contemplated application of current law, an advisory opinion could prevent the interim harm that adoption and application of law subsequently found invalid would cause. Moreover, advisory opinions could save time, money, and effort in deliberation and enforcement by clarifying legal limitations before invalid action is taken. Clearing away unlawful options could also contribute to the quality and focus of public debate and accountability.

The rule against advisory opinions responds to different considerations, however. It limits workload, but the dominant concerns involve judicial competence to decide issues in an advisory context and the place of the federal judiciary in a regime characterized by SEPARATION OF POWERS. Fear that decision before a dispute arises would be premature and unwise, that is, made without relevant facts stemming from application of law or other experience and without the benefit of perspectives presented by already affected parties, combined with concern that the advisory opinion may prejudge unfairly the decision of later concrete cases raising the same questions, induces judges to avoid making nonessential and potentially vulnerable decisions that might weaken judicial legitimacy. In addition, the prevailing belief views advisory opinions as likely to stifle rather than clarify the deliberative process, to distort the obligations of legislative or executive officials to evaluate legal questions independently, thereby blurring accountability, and to deprive experimental proposals of an opportunity to prove themselves before being reviewed for the legality of their actual effects.

JONATHAN D. VARAT

Bibliography

FRANKFURTER, FELIX 1924 Note on Advisory Opinions. *Harvard Law Review* 37:1002–1009.

AFFECTED WITH A PUBLIC INTEREST

The phrase "affected with a public interest," first used by the Supreme Court in *Munn v. Illinois* (1877), had a long and distinguished doctrinal lineage in the English COMMON LAW. The fountainhead of the modern development of that phrase was its formulation by Lord Chief Justice Matthew Hale, in his treatise *De Jure Maris,* written about 1670 and first published in 1787. In this work, Lord Hale discussed the basis for distinguishing property that was strictly private, property that was public in ownership, and an intermediate category of property (such as in navigable waters) that was private in ownership but subject to public use and hence a large measure of public control. In cases of business under a servitude to the public, such as wharves and cranes and ferries, according to Hale, it was legitimate for government to regulate in order to assure that the facilities would be available for "the common use" at rates that would be "reasonable and moderate." Once the public was invited to use such facilities, Hale wrote, "the wharf and the crane and other conveniences are affected with a publick interest, and they cease to be *juris privati* [a matter of private law] only." (See GRANGER CASES.)

When Chief Justice MORRISON R. WAITE, writing for the majority in *Munn,* cited Lord Hale, it was for the purpose of upholding rate regulation of grain elevators against a FOURTEENTH AMENDMENT defense that claimed that the elevator operator's vested property rights were being taken without JUST COMPENSATION. Explaining the *Munn* rule a year later, in his *Sinking Fund Cases* opinion, Justice JOSEPH P. BRADLEY pinned the "affectation" doctrine squarely to the concept of monopoly. The question in *Munn,* Bradley contended, was "the extent of the POLICE POWER in cases where the public interest is affected"; and the Court had concluded that regulation was valid when "an employment or business becomes a matter of such public interest and importance as to create a common charge or burden upon the citizens; in other words, when it becomes a practical monopoly, to which the citizen is compelled to resort. . . ."

In the period immediately following the decision in *Munn,* the Court erected a series of new doctrinal bulwarks for property interests. Among them were the concept of FREEDOM OF CONTRACT, the requirement that regulation must be "reasonable" as judged by the Court, and the notion of PUBLIC PURPOSE as a test for the validity of tax measures. As a result, the concept "affectation with a public interest" was pushed into the background, placing in abeyance such questions as whether only "monopoly" business came within its reach or whether instead it could be invoked to cover regulation of businesses that were not of this character.

In the decade of the 1920s, state legislation directly regulating prices and charges for service was challenged in federal courts and led to revitalization of the "affectation" doctrine by the Supreme Court. The issue, as the Court confronted it, had been set forth succinctly by Justice DAVID J. BREWER in an earlier opinion (*Cotting v. Kansas City Stockyards Co.,* 1901), upholding a state's regulation of stockyard charges on the ground that the business was affected with a public interest no less than a grain elevator or railroad or wharf. Yet the question must be posed, Brewer insisted, "To what extent may this regulation go?" Did any limits pertain, even in clear cases such as a stockyard's operation? Were the yards' owners left in a position, constitutionally, that they could be deprived "altogether of the ordinary privileges of others in mercantile business?"

In the hands of a property-minded, conservative Court the case-by-case development of the principle at issue, responding to Brewer's challenge, resulted in the creation of a closed legal category: only a business "affected with a public interest" might have prices or charges for service regulated; other, "ordinary," businesses were outside that closed category and therefore *not* subject to price or rate regulation. Chief Justice WILLIAM H. TAFT took on the challenge of defining more precisely the closed legal category in his opinion for the Court in WOLFF PACKING CO. V. COURT OF INDUSTRIAL RELATIONS OF KANSAS. Price and rate regulation were constitutional, Taft asserted, in regard to businesses that were public utilities (under an affirmative duty to render service to the public), businesses that historically had been subject to price regulation, and, finally, a rather baffling category, businesses that "though not public at their inception [historically] may be said to have risen to be such." Over strong objections of dissenters—most consistently Justices OLIVER WENDELL HOLMES and LOUIS D. BRANDEIS—the Court in subsequent years relied on this refined "affectation" doctrine to rule that even businesses subject to regulation in other respects could not be regulated as to rates of charge unless they met the criteria set down by Taft in *Wolff.* Mandated price minima or maxima were found unconstitutional with respect to theater ticket agencies, dairy vendors, gasoline retailers, and manufacturers and sellers of ice.

Dissenting Justices objected that the phrase "affected with a public interest" was so "vague and illusory" (as Justice HARLAN F. STONE charged in his dissent in *Tyson v. Banton,* 1927) as to amount to *carte blanche* for the Court to impose arbitrarily its policy preferences. Holmes was more direct: the concept, he stated in his own dissent in *Tyson,* was "little more than a fiction intended to beautify what is disagreeable to the sufferers." In Holmes's view, Lord Hale's language had been misapplied and had become a contrived limitation on the state's legitimate police power. "Subject to compensation when compensation is due," Holmes declared, "the legislature may forbid or restrict any business when it has a force of public opinion behind it."

Along with freedom of contract, the VESTED RIGHTS concept, the public purpose concept, and the doctrine of DUAL FEDERALISM, the "affectation" concept became emblematic of doctrinaire formalism mobilized by practitioners of JUDICIAL ACTIVISM. Such doctrines could undermine entirely, critics argued, the capacity of government to respond to changing objective social conditions or to emergency situations that required sweeping legislative intervention. Building on Justice Holmes's views, for example, the legal scholar WALTON H. HAMILTON wrote a widely noticed, wholesale attack on the Court in 1930. Although Hamilton was wrong in his view of the alleged novelty and obscurity of Lord Hale's treatise when Waite used it in *Munn,* he provided an eloquent argument for abandoning the notion of a closed category of businesses immune from price regulation. It was imperative, he argued, for the law to recognize the transformation of industrial structure and the competitive order in the previous half-century; the "affectation" doctrine was a conceptual straitjacket.

The advent of the Great Depression, along with the enactment of extraordinary legislation to deal with a great variety of emergency situations in a stricken society, lent additional weight to the realist argument that Holmes and commentators such as Hamilton and FELIX FRANKFURTER had set forth. Ruling on the constitutionality of an emergency milk price control law, enacted by New York State at the depth of the Depression spiral, the Supreme Court dramatically terminated the use of the "affectation" doctrine as a defense against price regulation: In NEBBIA V. NEW YORK (1934), the Court concluded that the phrase from Lord Hale meant simply "subject to the exercise of the police power." After *Nebbia,* so long as the procedural requirements of DUE PROCESS were met, the legislature was left "free to adopt whatever economic policy may reasonably be deemed to promote public welfare."

HARRY N. SCHEIBER

Bibliography

HAMILTON, WALTON 1930 Affectation with a Public Interest. *Yale Law Journal* 34:1089–1112.

SCHEIBER, HARRY N. 1971 The Road to *Munn:* Eminent Domain and the Concept of Public Purpose in the State Courts. *Perspectives in American History* 5:327–402.

AFFIRMATIVE ACTION

The Supreme Court's momentous decisions in BROWN V. BOARD OF EDUCATION and BOLLING V. SHARPE (1954), and its subsequent implementation decision in *Brown II* (1955), were followed by a long string of rulings designed to render meaningful and effective the egalitarian promise inherent in the FOURTEENTH AMENDMENT. Compulsory racial SEGREGATION was at last no longer constitutionally permissible; the Fourteenth Amendment's guarantee of the EQUAL PROTECTION OF THE LAWS had become the effective law of the land for all levels of the public sector.

But in the judgment of a good many Americans, equality *qua* equality, even when conscientiously enforced with an even hand, would neither suffice to enable those previously deprived on racial grounds to realize the promises of equality of opportunity, nor would it atone, and provide redress, for the ravages wrought by two centuries of past discrimination. Consequently, as strongly urged by President LYNDON B. JOHNSON, programs were established in both the public and the private realms that were designed to go well beyond "mere" equality of opportunity and provide not only remedial but preferential compensatory action, especially in the worlds of EDUCATION and employment. Labeled "affirmative action"—as distinguished from "neutrality"—these programs were instituted to bring about increased minority employment opportunities, job promotions, and admissions to colleges and universities, among others. Understandably, affirmative action programs quickly became controversial because of their resort to RACIAL QUOTAS, also called euphemistically "goals" or "guidelines." Their proponents' justification has been that to provide an absolute measure of full equality of opportunity based upon individual merit does not suffice; that, given the injustices of the past, both preferential and compensatory treatment must be accorded through "affirmative action" that all but guarantees numerically targeted slots or posts based upon membership in racial groups or upon gender. Most critics of the policy's underlying philosophy have not necessarily objected to "affirmative action" policies such as aggressive recruiting, remedial training (no matter what the expense), and perhaps not even to what Justice LEWIS F. POWELL in REGENTS OF THE UNIVERSITY OF CALIFORNIA V. BAKKE (1978) termed a justifiable "plus" consideration of race along with other equitable factors. They do, however, object strenuously to policies that represent, or may be regarded as sanctioning, "reverse discrimination," generally characterized by the resort to such devices as the *numerus clausus,* that is, rigid quotas set aside to benefit identifiable racial groups, as in the controversial case of UNITED STEELWORKERS OF AMERICA V. WEBER (1979); to double standards in grading, ranking, and similar requirements on the employment, educational, and other relevant fronts of opportunity; and to "set aside" laws that guarantee specified percentages of contracts to minority groups, as in FULLILOVE V. KLUTZNICK (1980).

The basic issue, while philosophically replete with moral and ethical considerations, was ultimately bound to be fought out on the legal and constitutional front, thus engendering judicial decisions. Several provisions of the CIVIL RIGHTS ACT OF 1964, as amended—for example, Titles IV, VI, VII, and IX—seemed quite specifically not only to forbid racial, sexual, and other discrimination per se but also to proscribe the use of racial and related quotas. The Supreme Court rapidly confronted five major opportunities to address the issue; in each instance it found itself seriously divided. Each of the five decisions involved "affirmative action" and/or "reverse discrimination."

The first and second, DEFUNIS V. ODEGAARD (1974) and *Regents v. Bakke* (1978), dealt with preferential racial admissions quotas that by design advantaged nonwhite applicants and thereby ipso facto disadvantaged whites. In *De Funis* a five-member majority rendered a nondecision on the merits by ruling the case moot, because whatever the outcome of the case, Marco De Funis would be graduated by the University of Washington Law School. Justice WILLIAM O. DOUGLAS, dissenting from the MOOTNESS determination, warned that "the equal protection clause commands the elimination of racial barriers, not their creation in order to satisfy our theory as to how society ought to be organized." In *Bakke* the Court did reach the merits of the racial quota established by the University of California (Davis) medical school, ruling 5–4 (in two diverse lineups, each headed by Justice Powell) that whereas the latter's rigid quota violated Allan Bakke's rights under the Constitution and the Civil Rights Act of 1964, the use of race as a "plus" along with other relevant considerations in admissions decisions did not. The third case, *United Steelworkers v. Weber,* concerned an employer–union craft-training plan that, on its face, directly violated Title VII of the Civil Rights Act of 1964, which clearly, indeed literally, interdicts racial quotas in employment. However, with Justices Powell and JOHN PAUL STEVENS disqualifying themselves from sitting in the cases, Justice WILLIAM J. BRENNAN, speaking for a majority of five, ruled that although the letter of the law appeared to forbid the arrangement, its purpose, as reflected in the legislative history, did not. The fourth case, *Fullilove v. Klutznick,* raised the fundamental question whether Congress, notwithstanding the Fourteenth Amendment's equal protection clause, could constitutionally legislate a ten percent set-aside plan for minority-owned construction companies desirous of obtaining government contracts. "Yes," held a 6–3 plurality—actually, the Court split 3–3–3—finding such legislation to be within the federal legislature's spending and regulatory powers under Article I of the Constitution. In his scathing DISSENTING OPINION, which he read in full from the bench on the day of the decision, Justice Stevens charged that the law represented a "perverse form of reparation," a "slapdash" law that rewards some who may not need rewarding and hurts others who may not deserve hurting. Suggesting that such a law could be used simply as a patronage tool by its authors—it had, in fact, been written on the floor of the House of Representatives without having gone to committee for hearings—he warned that it could breed more resentment and prejudice than it corrected. Echoing the first Justice JOHN MARSHALL HARLAN's memorable phrase in dissent in PLESSY V. FERGUSON (1896), namely, that "our Constitution is color-blind and neither knows nor tolerates classes among citizens," Stevens asked what percentage of "oriental blood or what degree of Spanish-speaking skill is required for membership in the preferred class?" With deep feelings, he suggested sarcastically that now the government must devise its version of the Nazi laws that defined who is a Jew, musing that "our statute books will once again have to contain laws that reflect the odious practice of delineating the qualities that make one person a Negro and make another white." The fifth case, *Memphis Fire Department v. Stotts,* seemed to draw a line (although only by the narrowest of margins, 5–4) when the Justice White-authored majority opinion held that duly established bona fide nondiscriminatory seniority systems supersede affirmative action plans.

Depending upon interpretation, one person's "affirmative action" may well constitute another's "reverse discrimination". Nonetheless, it is possible to essay distinctions. Thus, "affirmative action" may be regarded as encompassing the following five phenomena, all of which would appear to be both legal and constitutional: (1) both governmentally and privately sponsored activity designed to remedy the absence of needed educational preparation by special, even if costly, primary, and/or secondary school level preparatory programs or occupational skill development, always provided that access to these programs is not bottomed upon race or related group criteria or characteristics, but upon educational or economic need; (2) special classes or supplemental training, regardless of costs, on any level of education or training from the prenursery school bottom to the very top of the professional training ladder; (3) scrupulous enforcement of absolute standards of nondiscrimination on the basis of race, sex, religion, nationality, and age; (4) above-the-table special recruiting efforts to reach out to those members of heretofore underused, deprived, or discriminated-against segments of the citizenry; (5) provided the presence of explicit or implicit merit, of bona fide demonstrated or potential ability, the taking into account of an individual's race, gender, religion as an equitable consideration—the "plus" of which Justice Powell spoke in *Bakke*—but *only* if "all other things are equal."

"Reverse discrimination," on the other hand, which is acceptable neither legally nor constitutionally, would constitute the following quartet: (1) adoption of a *numerus clausus,* the setting aside of quotas, be they rigid or semirigid, on behalf of the admission, recruitment, employment, or promotion of individuals and groups identified and classified by racial, religious, sexual, age, or nationality characteristics; such characteristics are *non sequiturs* on the fronts of individual merit and ability and may well be regarded as an insult to the dignity and intelligence of the quota beneficiaries; (2) slanting of what should be neutral qualification examinations or requirements; double standards in grading and rating; double standards in attendance, retention, and disciplinary requirements; (3) those "goals" and "guidelines" that allegedly differ from rigid quotas, and thus presumably pass legal and constitutional muster, but that, in application, are all but synonymous with enforced quotas; (4) legislative or executive "set aside" programs, such as the one at issue in the *Fullilove* case, that mandate percentage-quotas of awards and activities based upon racial, gender, and related classifications.

"Reverse discrimination" purports to justify itself as atonement for past discrimination. It sanctions the call to children to pay for the sins of their forebears; it embraces a policy that two wrongs make one right, that "temporary" discrimination is "benign" rather than "invidious" when it is designed to remedy past wrongs. Since the "temporary" all too often becomes the "permanent," temporary suspensions of fundamental rights are fraught with permanent dangers and represent prima facie denials of the equal protection of the laws guaranteed by the Fourteenth Amendment and the DUE PROCESS OF LAW guaranteed by the Fifth.

The line between "affirmative action" and "reverse discrimination" may be thin and vexatious, but it does not lie beyond recognition and establishment in our constitutional constellation.

HENRY J. ABRAHAM

Bibliography

DWORKIN, RONALD 1977 *Taking Rights Seriously.* Cambridge, Mass.: Harvard University Press.

GLAZER, NATHAN 1976 *Affirmative Discrimination.* New York: Basic Books.

O'NEILL, ROBERT M. 1975 *Discriminating against Discrimination.* Bloomington: Indiana University Press.

ROCHE, GEORGE C., III 1974 *The Balancing Act: Quota Hiring in Higher Education.* La Salle, Ill.: Open Court.

ROSSUM, RALPH A. 1980 *Reverse Discrimination: The Constitutional Debate.* New York: Marcel Dekker.

SOWELL, THOMAS 1975 *Affirmative Action Reconsidered: Was It Necessary in Academia?* Washington, D.C.: American Enterprise Institute.

AFROYIM v. RUSK
387 U.S. 253 (1967)

A section of the Nationality Act of 1940 stripped Americans of their CITIZENSHIP if they voted in a foreign political election. In PEREZ V. BROWNELL (1957) the Supreme Court upheld the constitutionality of this provision, 5–4. On the authority of *Perez,* the State Department refused a passport to Afroyim, a naturalized citizen, who had voted in an Israeli election. In *Afroyim,* however, a new five-Justice majority, speaking through Justice HUGO L. BLACK, overruled *Perez* and declared that the FOURTEENTH AMENDMENT's citizenship clause denied Congress authority to strip Americans of their citizenship without their consent. "Citizenship in this Nation is a part of a cooperative affair," Black wrote. "Its citizenry is the country and the country is its citizenry."

MICHAEL E. PARRISH

AGE DISCRIMINATION

The racial CIVIL RIGHTS revolution of the 1950s and 1960s generated interest in constitutional protection for groups other than racial and religious minorities. Enhanced constitutional scrutiny of SEX DISCRIMINATION may be a consequence of the civil rights struggle.

Discrimination on the basis of age, however, has not become constitutionally suspect. In MASSACHUSETTS BOARD OF RETIREMENT V. MURGIA (1976) the Supreme Court held that some forms of age classification are not suspect and sustained against EQUAL PROTECTION attack a state statute requiring uniformed state police officers to retire at age fifty. In a PER CURIAM opinion, the Court concluded that the retirement did not affect a FUNDAMENTAL RIGHT, and characterized the affected class as uniformed police officers over age fifty. Perhaps intending to leave open heightened scrutiny of some age classifications, the Court stated that the requirement in *Murgia* did not discriminate against the elderly. In light of its findings with respect to the nature of the right and the relevant class, the Court held that mere rationality, rather than STRICT SCRUTINY, was the proper STANDARD OF REVIEW in determining whether the statute violated the equal protection clause. It found that the age classification was rationally related to furthering the state's interest of protecting the public by assuring physical preparedness of its uniformed state police.

In *Vance v. Bradley* (1979) the Court, in an opinion by Justice BYRON R. WHITE, again applied the RATIONAL BASIS test and held that Congress may require retirement at age sixty of federal employees covered by the Foreign Service retirement and disability system, even though it imposes no such limit on employees covered by the Civil Service retirement and disability system. In sustaining the mandatory retirement age, the Court emphasized Congress's special consideration of the needs of the Foreign Service. "Congress has legislated separately for the Foreign Service and has gone to great lengths to assure that those conducting our foreign relations will be sufficiently competent and reliable in all respects. If Congress attached special importance to high performance in these positions . . . it was quite rational to avoid the risks connected with having older employees in the Foreign Service but to tolerate those risks in the Civil Service."

But in the legislative arena, age discrimination did feel the effects of the constitutional egalitarian revolution. Section 715 of the CIVIL RIGHTS ACT OF 1964 required the secretary of labor to report to Congress on age discrimination in employment. In 1965 the secretary reported persistent arbitrary discrimination against older Americans. In 1967, upon the recommendation of President LYNDON B. JOHNSON, and relying on its powers under the COMMERCE CLAUSE, Congress passed the Age Discrimination in Employment Act (ADEA). The act, which has been amended several times, prohibits employment discrimination against persons between the ages of forty and seventy.

In EQUAL EMPLOYMENT OPPORTUNITY COMMISSION V. WYOMING (1983), prior to its OVERRULING of NATIONAL LEAGUE OF CITIES V. USERY (1976) in GARCIA V. SAN ANTONIO METROPOLITAN TRANSIT AUTHORITY (1985), the Court sustained against a TENTH AMENDMENT attack the constitutionality of

Congress's 1974 extension of the ADEA to state and local governments. In a 5–4 decision, the Court found that applying the act's prohibition to a Wyoming mandatory retirement age for game wardens would not interfere with integral state functions because the state remained free to apply reasonable standards of fitness to game wardens.

Building on a provision in Title VII of the Civil Rights Act of 1964, the ADEA allows employers to take otherwise prohibited age-based action when age is a "bona fide occupational qualification reasonably necessary to the normal operation of the particular business." In its early interpretations of this provision, the Court has not given the defense an expansive reading. In *Western Air Lines, Inc. v. Criswell* (1985), in an opinion by Justice JOHN PAUL STEVENS, the Court held that Congress's "reasonably necessary" standard requires something more than a showing that an age-based requirement is rationally connected to the employer's business. Relying on the heightened standard, the Court therefore rejected an airline's defense of its requirement that flight engineers retire at age sixty. In *Johnson v. Mayor & City Council of Baltimore* (1985) the Court held that a federal statute generally requiring federal fire fighters to retire at age fifty-five does not establish that being under fifty-five is a bona fide occupational qualification under the ADEA for nonfederal fire fighters.

In the Age Discrimination Act of 1975 (ADA), following the racial antidiscrimination model of Title VI of the Civil Rights Act of 1964, Congress prohibited discrimination on the basis of age in programs or activities receiving federal financial assistance. The ADA thus joins Title IX of the EDUCATION AMENDMENTS OF 1972 and section 504 of the REHABILITATION ACT OF 1973, which prohibit, respectively, sex discrimination and discrimination against the handicapped in federally assisted programs. The ADA vests broad authority in the secretary of health and human services to promulgate regulations to effectuate the statute's antidiscrimination mandate. Like the ADEA, the ADA contains exceptions allowing discrimination on the basis of age when age is reasonably related to the program or activity. Other specific federal spending programs contain their own statutory prohibitions on age discrimination.

THEODORE EISENBERG

Bibliography

SCHUCK, PETER H. 1979 The Graying of Civil Rights Law: The Age Discrimination Act of 1975. *Yale Law Journal* 89:27–93.

UNITED STATES DEPARTMENT OF LABOR 1965 *Report to the Congress on Age Discrimination in Employment under Section 715 of the Civil Rights Act of 1964.* Washington D.C.: Government Printing Office.

AGE DISCRIMINATION ACT

89 Stat. 728 (1975)

Enacted as Title III of the Older Americans Amendments of 1975, the Age Discrimination Act of 1975, like Title VI of the CIVIL RIGHTS ACT OF 1964 and other laws, links ANTIDISCRIMINATION LEGISLATION to Congress's spending power. Subject to important but ambiguous exceptions, the act prohibits exclusion on the basis of age from federally financed programs. In covered programs, the act affords greater protection against AGE DISCRIMINATION than the Supreme Court has held to be required under the EQUAL PROTECTION clause. In MASSACHUSETTS BOARD OF RETIREMENT V. MURGIA (1976), in upholding a statute requiring police officers to retire at age fifty, the Court found age not to be a SUSPECT CLASSIFICATION. The Age Discrimination in Employment Act, as well as some state laws, protect against age discrimination in employment.

THEODORE EISENBERG

Bibliography

SCHUCK, PETER H. 1979 The Graying of Civil Rights Laws: The Age Discrimination Act of 1975. *Yale Law Journal* 89:27–93.

AGNELLO v. UNITED STATES

269 U.S. 20 (1925)

In *Agnello* the Supreme Court extended the scope of SEARCH INCIDENT TO ARREST from the person of the arrestee, previously authorized in WEEKS V. UNITED STATES (1914), to the premises on which the arrest was made. The precise extent of the allowable search was, however, not delineated; it became a matter of great judicial contention in later cases.

JACOB W. LANDYNSKI

AGRICULTURAL ADJUSTMENT ACT OF 1933

48 Stat. 31

This act, the set piece of the New Deal for agriculture, emphasized PRODUCTION controls in an effort to revive farming from its 1920s torpor. Stressing collective action, the act sought to boost farm prices. After World War I ended, American farmers had found stiff new competition in the world market for the tremendously expanded U.S. farm output. As a result, surpluses ballooned and prices deflated. A modest recovery by 1923 had not taken firm hold, and the Depression in 1929 struck hard at farmers. Agricultural prices had dropped four times as far as industrial prices between 1929 and 1933. Shortly after FRANKLIN D. ROOSEVELT's inauguration in March 1933, his secretary of agriculture, Henry Wallace, met with farm leaders to formulate a relief plan. The resulting bill, drafted in part by JEROME FRANK, was ready in five days. To secure wide support, REXFORD TUGWELL and others recommended that this "farm relief" measure comprise elements of plans already proposed. As a result, it established parity prices—a price level that would allow the purchasing power of income from a commodity to equal its purchasing power in the base period, 1909–1914.

The act's avowed purpose, "to relieve the existing national economic emergency by increasing agricultural purchasing power," would be accomplished primarily by raising prices of seven basic commodities to parity levels. Control of production would be the means of achieving this goal. The secretary of agriculture could exert control by regulating benefit payments to farmers who voluntarily reduced production, by imposing marketing quotas, and by providing for government purchase of surpluses. The government would fund these efforts by imposing on the primary processors of agricultural goods an EXCISE TAX based on the difference between farm and parity prices. Benefit payments were designed to entice cooperation although participation was theoretically voluntary.

Senate opposition gave way to substantial public pressure for action and a lack of workable alternatives. The act also granted the secretary of agriculture power to make regulations to enforce the act (subject to presidential approval), assess penalties, and (with the secretary of the treasury) to have ultimate say in issues of payments to farmers. By late 1935 the act and a drought had provided much relief (net farm income rose 250 per cent), forecasting a profitable recovery for American agriculture. In January 1936, however, a 6–3 Supreme Court invalidated the statute in UNITED STATES V. BUTLER. A determined Congress passed a second AGRICULTURAL ADJUSTMENT ACT in 1938.

DAVID GORDON

AGRICULTURAL ADJUSTMENT ACT OF 1938

50 Stat. 246

After the Supreme Court invalidated the AGRICULTURAL ADJUSTMENT ACT (AAA) OF 1933 in UNITED STATES V. BUTLER (1936), Congress passed a second AAA in 1938, citing the effect of farm PRODUCTION on INTERSTATE COMMERCE as the act's basis. Congress once again sought to achieve parity levels for principal commodities and maintain earlier soil conservation payments as well. The act retained voluntary participation and, acknowledging *Butler,* Congress now levied no processing taxes nor did it set up production quotas; instead the act inaugurated a system of marketing quotas. Such a quota applied only when two-thirds of a commodity's producers approved. Once a general quota was authorized, the secretary of agriculture could set specific quotas for individual farms and assess a penalty tax on violators. Moreover, approval of quotas made available special loans to help store surplus production. The 1938 act also provided means of increasing consumption to help alleviate surpluses, and created a Commodity Credit Corporation to make loans when income fell because of low prices, and a Federal Crop Insurance Corporation. The Supreme Court sustained the act in *Mulford v. Smith* (1939) and WICKARD V. FILBURN (1942).

DAVID GORDON

AGRICULTURAL MARKETING AGREEMENT ACT

50 Stat. 246 (1937)

In 1933 the first AGRICULTURAL ADJUSTMENT ACT (AAA) developed programs for marketing various commodities. Congress strengthened that act two years later and, in 1937, reenacted many of the AAA provisions and amended others. The Agricultural Marketing Agreement Act stressed regulation of marketing, not of PRODUCTION. Responding to Supreme Court decisions that cast doubt on the marketing agreement provisions of the AAA, Congress now emphasized the separability of those sections. The act authorized the secretary of agriculture to set marketing quotas and price schedules and to sign voluntary agreements with producers. If fifty percent of the handlers and two-thirds of the producers of a commodity approved, the secretary could issue marketing orders. All such agreements were exempted from federal antitrust laws. The AAA's earlier effort to achieve parity prices (a level providing income with buying power equivalent to that for 1909–1914) by balancing production with consumption was now replaced by maintenance of "orderly marketing conditions for agricultural commodities in INTERSTATE COMMERCE." In addition, the 1937 act contained a broader definition of interstate and FOREIGN COMMERCE, declaring it to include any part of the "current" that is usual in the handling of a commodity. (See STREAM OF COMMERCE DOCTRINE.) The Supreme Court sustained the act in *United States v. Rock Royal Co-operative* (1939), finding that even a local transaction was "inextricably mingled with and directly affect[ed]" marketing in interstate commerce. The Court took similar action in WRIGHTWOOD DAIRY V. UNITED STATES (1942), even though that case involved purely INTRASTATE COMMERCE.

DAVID GORDON

AGRICULTURE

See: *Butler, United States v.;* Subjects of Commerce; *Wickard v. Filburn*

AGUILAR v. FELTON
473 U.S. (1985)
GRAND RAPIDS SCHOOL DISTRICT v. BALL
473 U.S. (1985)

In COMPANION CASES a 5–4 Supreme Court held unconstitutional the assignment of public school teachers to parochial schools for special auxiliary services. In the Grand Rapids "shared time" case, Justice WILLIAM J. BRENNAN for the majority concerned himself only with the possibility that the teachers might advance religion by conforming their instruction to the environment of the private sectarian schools. The evidence did not validate his fear. In *Aguilar*, Brennan expressed the same fear but focused on the "excessive entanglement of church and state" which he asserted was present in New York City's program to implement the ELEMENTARY AND SECONDARY EDUCATION ACT passed by Congress in 1965. Advancing religion and excessive entanglement show violations of the FIRST AMENDMENT'S SEPARATION OF CHURCH AND STATE as construed by the Court in LEMON V. KURTZMAN (1971), where it devised a test to determine whether government has passed a law respecting an ESTABLISHMENT OF RELIGION.

The New York City program employed guidance counselors, psychologists, psychiatrists, social workers, and other specialists to teach remedial reading, mathematics, and English as a second language, and to provide guidance services. They worked part-time on parochial school premises, using only materials and equipment supplied by secular authorities; and, they acted under a ban against participation in religious activities. They worked under supervision similar to that which prevailed in public schools; the city monitored instruction by having supervisory personnel make unannounced "monthly" and "occasional" visits. Almost three-fourths of the educators in the program did not share the religious affiliation of any school in which they taught.

Brennan for the majority traveled a far path to find infirmities in the city's program. He expressed concern that the program might infringe the RELIGIOUS LIBERTY of its intended beneficiaries. He saw government "intrusion into sacred matters" and the necessity of an "ongoing inspection" to ensure the absence of inculcation of religion in the instruction. The need for "a permanent and pervasive State presence in the sectarian schools receiving aid" infringed values protected by the establishment clause.

Thus, if government fails to provide for surveillance to ward off inculcation, its aid unconstitutionally advances the religious mission of the church schools; if government does provide for monitoring, even if only periodically, it gets excessively entangled with religion. Justice SANDRA DAY O'CONNOR, dissenting, declared that the conclusion that the religious mission of the schools would be advanced by auxiliary services provided by the public was "not supported by the facts of this case." The nineteen-year record of the program showed not a single allegation of an attempt to indoctrinate religiously at public expense. The decision adversely affected disadvantaged parochial school children who needed special auxiliary services not provided by their parochial schools.

LEONARD W. LEVY

AGUILAR v. TEXAS
378 U.S. 108 (1964)

The rule that an officer's affidavit supporting an application for a SEARCH WARRANT must contain more than the officer's "mere affirmation of suspicion" was established in *Nathanson v. United States* (1933). Probable cause requires a statement of "facts or circumstances" explaining the affiant's belief that criminal activity is afoot, thus allowing the magistrate to make an independent judgment. In *Aguilar* the same rule was applied to an affidavit based on information supplied by an informant.

The *Aguilar* affidavit stated that the officers "had received reliable information from a credible person" that narcotics were kept on the premises. Nothing in the affidavit allowed the magistrate to determine the accuracy of the informant's conclusion. Though hearsay information can satisfy PROBABLE CAUSE, said the Court, the affidavit must give EVIDENCE that the informant spoke from personal knowledge, and explain the circumstances that led the officer to conclude that he "was 'credible' or his information 'reliable.'" The *Aguilar* rule was discarded in ILLINOIS v. GATES (1983).

JACOB W. LANDYNSKI

AKE v. OKLAHOMA
470 U.S. (1985)

Following the PRECEDENTS of decisions holding that the RIGHT TO COUNSEL requires a state to provide a lawyer to an INDIGENT defendant, the Supreme Court held, 8–1, that the FOURTEENTH AMENDMENT's guarantee of PROCEDURAL DUE PROCESS requires a state to provide an indigent defendant access to such psychiatric examination and assistance necessary to prepare an effective defense based on the claim of insanity. Justice THURGOOD MARSHALL wrote the OPINION OF THE COURT. Chief Justice WARREN E. BURGER, in a CONCURRING OPINION, said that the decision was limited to capital cases. Justice WILLIAM H. REHNQUIST, dissenting, agreed that some such cases might require the state to provide psychiatric assistance, but argued that in this case, where the burden of proving insanity was on the defendant, the state had no such obligation.

KENNETH L. KARST

AKRON v. AKRON CENTER FOR REPRODUCTIVE CHOICE

See: Reproductive Autonomy

A. L. A. SCHECHTER POULTRY CORP. v. UNITED STATES

See: *Schechter v. United States*

ALBANY PLAN

See: Franklin, Benjamin

ALBERTS v. CALIFORNIA

See: *Roth v. United States*

ALBERTSON v. SUBVERSIVE ACTIVITIES CONTROL BOARD
382 U.S. 70 (1965)

This was one of several cases in which the WARREN COURT, on self-incrimination grounds, struck down compulsory registration provisions aimed at individuals who were members of inherently suspect groups. (See MARCHETTI V. UNITED STATES, 1968.) The Communist party failed to register with the government as required by the SUBVERSIVE ACTIVITIES CONTROL BOARD. The Board's order obligated all members of the party to register. By refusing, Albertson made himself liable to criminal penalties; he offered numerous constitutional objections. The Supreme Court decided only his claim that the order violated his RIGHT AGAINST SELF-INCRIMINATION.

Justice WILLIAM J. BRENNAN for an 8–0 Court observed, "Such an admission of membership may be used to prosecute the registrant under the membership clause of the SMITH ACT . . . or under . . . the Subversive Activities Control Act. . . ." The government relied on an old decision requiring all taxpayers to file returns, but Brennan answered that tax regulations applied to the public, not to "a highly selective group inherently suspect of criminal activities." The government also argued that a grant of immunity from prosecution for registrants supplanted the right against self-incrimination. Relying on COUNSELMAN V. HITCHCOCK (1892), Brennan ruled that unless the government provided "absolute immunity" for all transactions relating to coerced admissions, it failed to supplant the right. In KASTIGAR V. UNITED STATES (1972) the Court switched from transactional to use immunity. (See IMMUNITY GRANTS.)

LEONARD W. LEVY

ALDERMAN v. UNITED STATES
394 U.S. 165 (1969)

During the 1960s, the government admitted it had engaged in illegal electronic surveillance. Criminal defendants overheard in such surveillance sought the transcripts of the conversations to determine whether their convictions had been based on illegal surveillance and were therefore reversible. The government tried to limit the right to challenge electronic surveillance to persons actually overheard and to restrict disclosure of the transcripts to the judge.

The Supreme Court ruled that (1) anyone overheard, or anyone on whose premises conversations were overheard, could challenge the legality of the surveillance, but no one else; and (2) a person found to have been illegally overheard was entitled to see the transcripts to determine whether his conviction was based on illegal surveillance.

HERMAN SCHWARTZ

ALEXANDER, JAMES

See: Zenger's Case

ALEXANDER v. HOLMES COUNTY BOARD OF EDUCATION 396 U.S. 19 (1969)

Part of the "southern strategy" that helped elect President RICHARD M. NIXON had been an assertion that the Supreme Court had been too rigid in its treatment of school SEGREGATION. Thus it was no surprise when, on the eve of the opening of the fall 1969 school year, the Justice Department proposed that thirty-three Mississippi school boards be given an extension until December 1 to present DESEGREGATION plans. The UNITED STATES COURT OF APPEALS agreed, and the next day the plaintiffs sought an order from Justice HUGO L. BLACK staying this decision. Justice Black refused the stay but suggested that the case be brought to the whole Supreme Court for an early decision. The Court promptly granted CERTIORARI, heard the case in late October, and before month's end issued its order. The time for ALL DELIBERATE SPEED in school desegregation had run out; the school boards had an obligation "to terminate dual school systems at once." The BURGER COURT would not be a "Nixon Court" on this issue.

KENNETH L. KARST

ALIEN

The status of aliens—persons who are not citizens of the United States—presented perplexing constitutional problems in this country only after the great waves of IMMIGRATION began in the nineteenth century. The question seems not to have troubled the Framers of the Constitution. JAMES MADISON, in THE FEDERALIST #42, defended the power of Congress to set a uniform rule of NATURALIZATION as a means for easing interstate friction. Absent such a congressional law, he argued, State A might grant CITIZENSHIP to an alien who, on moving to State B, would become entitled to most of the PRIVILEGES AND IMMUNITIES granted by State B to its citizens. Evidently it was assumed from the beginning that aliens were not protected by Article IV's privileges and immunities clause, and it is still the conventional wisdom—although not unchallenged—that aliens cannot claim "the privileges and immunities of citizens of the United States" guaranteed by the FOURTEENTH AMENDMENT.

Alienage has sometimes been treated as synonymous with dissent, or even disloyalty. The ALIEN AND SEDITION ACTS (1798), for example, were aimed not only at American citizens who opposed President JOHN ADAMS but also at their supporters among French and Irish immigrants. The PALMER RAIDS of 1919–1920 culminated in the DEPORTATION of hundreds of alien anarchists and others suspected of SUBVERSIVE ACTIVITIES. At the outbreak of World War II, Attorney General FRANCIS BIDDLE was determined to avoid the mass internment of aliens; in the event, however, Biddle deferred to War Department pressure, and more than 100,000 persons of Japanese ancestry, alien and citizen alike, were removed from their West Coast homes and taken to camps in the interior. (See JAPANESE AMERICAN CASES, 1943–1944.)

When the KENTUCKY RESOLUTIONS (1798) protested against the Alien and Sedition Acts, they defended not so much the rights of aliens as STATES' RIGHTS. Indeed, the *rights* of aliens were not a major concern in the nation's early years. Even the federal courts' DIVERSITY JURISDICTION could be invoked in a case involving aliens only when citizens of a state were on the other side, as HODGSON V. BOWERBANK (1809) held. For this jurisdictional purpose, a "citizen" of a state still means a United States citizen who is also a state citizen. (An alien can sue another alien in a state court.) Thus, while a state can grant "state citizenship"—can allow aliens to vote, hold public office, or receive state benefits—that state citizenship does not qualify a person as a "citizen" within the meaning of the Constitution. Some states have previously allowed aliens to vote; even today, some states allow aliens to hold public office.

Most individual rights protected by the Constitution are not limited to "citizens" but extend to "people" or "persons," including aliens. An exception is the right to vote, protected by the FIFTEENTH, NINETEENTH, and TWENTY-SIXTH AMENDMENTS, which is limited to citizens. Aliens do not, of course, have the constitutional freedom of entry into the country that citizens have; aliens' stay here can be conditioned on conduct—for example, the retention of student status—that could not constitutionally be required of citizens. An alien, but not a citizen, can be deported for certain violations of law. In wartime, the property of enemy aliens can be confiscated. Yet aliens are subject to many of the obligations fastened on citizens: they pay taxes along with the rest of us, and, if Congress so disposes, they are as susceptible as citizens to CONSCRIPTION into the armed forces.

Congress, by authorizing the admission of some aliens for permanent residence, accepts those admittees as at least limited members of the national community. The CIVIL RIGHTS ACT OF 1866, for example, protects a resident alien against state legislation that interferes with the alien's earning a livelihood. The vitality of the PREEMPTION DOCTRINE in such cases no doubt rests on two assumptions: that the national government, not the states, has the primary responsibility for the nation's dealings with foreign countries, and that the regulation of another country's nationals is likely to affect those dealings.

Throughout our history, state laws have discriminated against aliens by disqualifying them from various forms of public and private employment, and from receiving public assistance benefits. Early decisions of the Supreme Court mostly upheld these laws, ignoring their evident tensions with congressional policy and rejecting claims based on the Fourteenth Amendment's EQUAL PROTECTION clause. Two decisions in 1948, OYAMA V. CALIFORNIA and TAKAHASHI V. FISH & GAME COMMISSION, undermined the earlier precedents, and in the 1970s the Court made a frontal assault on state discriminations against aliens.

A legislative classification based on the status of alienage, the Court announced in GRAHAM V. RICHARDSON (1971), was a SUSPECT CLASSIFICATION, analogous to a racial classification. Thus, justifications offered to support the classification must pass the test of STRICT SCRUTINY. State restrictions of WELFARE BENEFITS, on the basis of alienage, were accordingly invalidated. Two years later, this reasoning was extended to invalidate a law disqualifying aliens from a state's civil service, SUGARMAN V. DOUGALL (1973), and a law barring aliens from the practice of law, IN RE GRIFFITHS (1973). The string of invalidations of state laws continued with *Examining Board v. Flores de Otero* (1976) (disqualification to be a civil engineer) and *Nyquist v. Mauclet* (1977) (limiting eligibility for state scholarship aid).

In the *Sugarman* opinion, the Court had remarked that some state discriminations against aliens would not have to pass strict judicial scrutiny. The right to vote in state elections, or to hold high public office, might be limited to United States citizens on the theory that such rights are closely connected with the idea of membership in a political community. By the end of the decade, these words had become the foundation for a large exception to the principle of strict scrutiny of alienage classifications. The "political community" notion was extended to a broad category of public employees performing "government functions" requiring the exercise of discretion and responsibility. Disqualification of aliens from such jobs would be upheld if it was supported by a RATIONAL BASIS. FOLEY V. CONNELIE (1978) thus upheld a law disqualifying aliens to serve as state troopers, and AMBACH V. NORWICK (1979) upheld a law barring aliens from teaching in public schools unless they had shown an intent to become U.S. citizens. *Cabell v. Chavez-Salido* (1982) extended the same reasoning to state probation officers.

At the same time, the Court made clear that when Congress discriminated against aliens, nothing like strict judicial scrutiny was appropriate. *Mathews v. Diaz* (1976) announced an extremely deferential standard of review for such congressional laws, saying that the strong federal interest in regulating foreign affairs provided a close analogy to the doctrine of POLITICAL QUESTIONS—which suggests, of course, essentially no judicial scrutiny at all.

It was argued for a time that the preemption doctrine provides the most complete explanation of the Court's results in alienage cases. The early 1970s decisions, grounded on equal protection theory, instead might have been rested on congressional laws such as the 1866 act. The decisions on "governmental functions," seen in this light, would amount to a recognition that Congress has not admitted resident aliens to the "political community." On this theory, because Congress has not admitted "undocumented" aliens for any purpose at all, state laws regulating them would be viewed favorably. In PLYLER V. DOE (1982), the Supreme Court rejected this line of reasoning and held, 5–4, that Texas had denied equal protection by refusing free public education to children not lawfully admitted to the country while providing it for all other children. The majority, conceding that Congress might authorize some forms of state discrimination, discerned no such authorization in Congress's silence.

The preemption analysis, no less than an equal protection analysis, leaves the key term ("political community") for manipulation; on either theory, for example, the school teacher case seems wrongly decided. And the equal protection approach has one advantage that is undeniable: it focuses the judiciary on questions that bear some relation to life—substantive questions about degrees of discrimination and proffered justifications—rather than on the metaphysics of preemption.

KENNETH L. KARST

Bibliography

NOTE 1975 Aliens' Right to Teach: Political Socialization and the Public Schools. *Yale Law Journal* 85:90–111.

NOTE 1979 A Dual Standard for State Discrimination Against Aliens. *Harvard Law Review* 92:1516–1537.

NOTE 1979 The Equal Treatment of Aliens: Preemption or Equal Protection? *Stanford Law Review* 31:1069–1091.

NOTE 1980 State Burdens on Resident Aliens: A New Preemption Analysis. *Yale Law Journal* 89:940–961.

PRESTON, WILLIAM, JR. 1963 *Aliens and Dissenters: Federal Suppression of Radicals, 1903–1933.* Cambridge, Mass.: Harvard University Press.

ROSBERG, GERALD M. 1977 The Protection of Aliens from Discriminatory Treatment by the National Government. *Supreme Court Review* 1977:275–339.

ALIEN AND SEDITION ACTS

Naturalization Act
1 Stat. 566 (1798)
Alien Act
1 Stat. 570 (1798)
Alien Enemies Act
1 Stat. 577 (1798)
Sedition Act
1 Stat. 596 (1798)

These acts were provoked by the war crisis with France in 1798. Three of the four acts concerned ALIENS. Federalist leaders feared the French and Irish, in particular, as a potentially subversive force and as an element of strength in the Republican party. The Naturalization Act increased the period of residence required for admission to CITIZENSHIP from five to fourteen years. The Alien Act authorized the President to deport any alien deemed dangerous to the peace and safety of the United States. The Alien Enemies Act authorized incarceration and banishment of aliens in time of war. The Sedition Act, aimed at "domestic traitors," made it a federal crime for anyone to conspire to impede governmental operations or to write or publish "any false, scandalous, and malicious writing" against the government, the Congress, or the President.

While Republicans conceded the constitutionality, though not the necessity, of the Naturalization and Alien Enemies acts, they assailed the others, not only as unnecessary and unconstitutional but as politically designed to cripple or destroy the opposition party under the pretense of foreign menace. The constitutional argument received authoritative statement in the VIRGINIA AND KENTUCKY RESOLUTIONS. In defense of the Alien Act, with its summary procedures, Federalists appealed to the inherent right of the government to protect itself. The same appeal was made for the Sedition Act. Federalists denied, further, that the act violated FIRST AMENDMENT guarantees of FREEDOM OF SPEECH and PRESS, which they interpreted as prohibitions of PRIOR RESTRAINT only. They also claimed that the federal government had JURISDICTION over COMMON LAW crimes, such as SEDITIOUS LIBEL, and so could prosecute without benefit of statute. The statute, they said, liberalized the common law by admitting truth as a defense and authorizing juries to return a general verdict.

Despite the zeal of President JOHN ADAMS's administration, no one was actually deported under the Alien Act. (War not having been declared, the Alien Enemies Act never came into operation.) The Sedition Act, on the other hand, was widely enforced. Twenty-five persons were arrested, fourteen indicted (plus three under common law), ten tried and convicted, all of them Republican printers and publicists. The most celebrated trials were those of Matthew Lyon, Republican congressman and newspaper editor in Vermont; Dr. Thomas Cooper, an English-born scientist and political refugee, in Philadelphia; and James T. Callender, another English refugee, who possessed a vitriolic pen, in Richmond. All were fined upward to $1,000 and imprisoned for as long as nine months. Before partisan judges and juries, in a climate of fear and suspicion, the boasted safeguards of the law proved of no value to the defendants, and all constitutional safeguards were rejected.

The repressive laws recoiled on their sponsors, contributing to the Republican victory in the election of 1800. The Sedition Act expired the day THOMAS JEFFERSON became President. He immediately voided actions pending under it and pardoned the victims. In 1802 the Alien Act expired and Congress returned the NATURALIZATION law to its old footing.

Only the Alien Enemies Act remained on the statute book. Nothing like this legislation would be enacted again until the two world wars of the twentieth century.

MERRILL D. PETERSON

Bibliography

SMITH, JAMES MORTON 1956 *Freedom's Fetters: The Alien and Sedition Laws and American Civil Liberties.* Ithaca, N.Y.: Cornell University Press.

ALIEN REGISTRATION ACT
54 Stat. 670 (1940)

This measure, popularly known as the Smith Act, was destined to become the most famous of the anticommunist measures of the Cold War, McCarthy period. The act required all ALIENS living in the United States to register with the government, be fingerprinted, carry identification cards, and report annually. Persons found to have ties to "subversive organizations" could be deported. The registration requirement was rescinded in 1982.

Such alien registration was only one of the various purposes of the act. It was directed primarily at SUBVERSIVE ACTIVITIES which were causing growing concerns on the eve of war, particularly communist-inspired strikes intended to injure American defense production. As the first federal peacetime SEDITION statute since 1798, the Smith Act in its most significant section made it a crime to "knowingly, or willfully, advocate, abet, advise, or teach the duty, necessity, desirability, or propriety of overthrowing or destroying any government in the United States by force and violence. . . ." Any attempts forcibly to overthrow the government of the United States by publication or display of printed matters, to teach, or to organize any group, or to become a "knowing" member of such an organization were forbidden. Section 3 forbade conspiracy to accomplish any of these ends. The act carried maximum criminal penalties of a $10,000 fine or ten years in prison or both; no one convicted under the law was to be eligible for federal employment during the five years following conviction.

The act, which did not mention the Communist party, attracted little attention at the time of its passage, and initial enforcement was spotty. Although five million aliens were registered and fingerprinted shortly following its passage, its antisubversive sections were not used until 1943, when a small group of Minneapolis Trotskyites were convicted. When the Cold War intensified, following 1947, the HARRY S. TRUMAN administration began a series of dramatic prosecutions of Communist party leaders. These and subsequent prosecutions eventually forced the Supreme Court to clarify the act's terms, starting with DENNIS V. UNITED STATES (1951), and extending through YATES V. UNITED STATES (1957), SCALES V. UNITED STATES (1961), and *Noto v. United States* (1961). As a result of these rulings, the measure's advocacy, organizing, and membership provisions were limited and made more precise.

PAUL L. MURPHY

Bibliography

BELKNAP, MICHAEL R. 1977 *Cold War Political Justice: The Smith Act, the Communist Party, and American Civil Liberties.* Westport, Conn.: Greenwood Press.

ALL DELIBERATE SPEED

Chief Justice EARL WARREN achieved a unanimous decision in BROWN V. BOARD OF EDUCATION (1954) by assuring that enforcement of school DESEGREGATION would be gradual. Ordinarily, state officials found to be violating the Constitution are simply ordered to stop. *Brown II* (1955), however, instructed lower courts to insist only that offending school boards make "a prompt and reasonable start," proceeding toward full desegregation with "all deliberate speed."

This calculatedly elusive phrase was contributed by Justice FELIX FRANKFURTER, who had borrowed it from an old opinion by Justice OLIVER WENDELL HOLMES. Holmes attributed it to English EQUITY practice, but he may also have seen it in Francis Thompson's poem, "The Hound of Heaven." Whatever the phrase's origins, it was a thin cover for compromise. The objective presumably was to allow time for the white South to become accustomed to the end of SEGREGATION, in the hope of avoiding defiance of the courts and even violence. Robert Penn Warren, a southern man of letters who had not studied quantum mechanics, even tried to make gradualism in desegregation a historical necessity: "History, like nature, knows no jumps."

The South responded not with accommodation but with politically orchestrated defiance. A full decade after *Brown I,* two percent of southern black children were attending integrated schools. By 1969, the Supreme Court explicitly abandoned "all deliberate speed"; in ALEXANDER V. HOLMES COUNTY BOARD

OF EDUCATION school boards were told to desegregate "at once."

No one pretends that the Supreme Court could have ended Jim Crow overnight, certainly not without support from Congress or the President. Yet the Court's decisions can command respect only when they are understood to rest on principle. *Brown II*, widely seen to be precisely the political accommodation it was intended to be, did not merely consign a generation of southern black school children to segregated schools. The decision weakened the Court's own moral authority in the very process gradualism was designed to aid.

KENNETH L. KARST

Bibliography

WILKINSON, J. HARVIE, III 1979 *From Brown to Bakke.* New York: Oxford University Press.

ALLEN v. WRIGHT
468 U.S. 737 (1984)

The parents of black school children in districts that were undergoing DESEGREGATION brought suit against officials of the Internal Revenue Service (IRS). Alleging that the IRS had not adopted standards and procedures that would fulfill the agency's obligation to deny tax-exempt status to racially discriminatory private schools, the plaintiffs argued that the IRS in effect subsidized unconstitutional school SEGREGATION. The Supreme Court, 5–3, held that the plaintiffs lacked STANDING to raise this claim.

Justice SANDRA DAY O'CONNOR, for the majority, said that the plaintiffs' claim that they had been stigmatized by the IRS conduct was insufficient as a specification of injury, amounting to little more than a general claim that government must behave according to law. The parents' second claim of injury was that they had been denied the right to have their children attend school in a system that was not segregated. Here the asserted injury was sufficient, Justice O'Connor said, but the injury was not fairly traceable to IRS conduct. The Court thus reinforced the "causation" requirement for standing established in *Warth v. Seldin* (1975). The three dissenters made the familiar charge that the "causation" line of inquiry disguised a rejection of the plaintiffs' claim without really addressing the constitutional issue. As in *Warth,* the Court rejected the plaintiffs' claim of injury without giving them the chance to prove their case.

KENNETH L. KARST

ALLEN-BRADLEY COMPANY v. LOCAL UNION #3
325 U.S. 797 (1945)

An 8–1 Supreme Court, dominated by appointees of FRANKLIN D. ROOSEVELT, held here that union actions that prompted nonlabor market control and business profits violated the SHERMAN ANTITRUST ACT. The union had obtained CLOSED SHOP agreements with New York City manufacturers of electrical equipment in return for a promise to strike or boycott any contractor who did not use the local manufacturers' equipment. Because out-of-city materials were cheaper, these agreements effectively restrained competition. Justice HUGO L. BLACK, for the Court, found that such action could be enjoined under the Sherman Act because neither the CLAYTON ACT nor the NORRIS-LAGUARDIA ACT protected union action not solely in its own interests.

DAVID GORDON

ALLGEYER v. LOUISIANA
165 U.S. 578 (1897)

The Louisiana legislature sought to encourage local business by forbidding state citizens from buying marine insurance from out-of-state companies. Justice RUFUS PECKHAM, building on a long line of dissents by Justice STEPHEN J. FIELD, expounded a broad concept of "liberty" including the idea of FREEDOM OF CONTRACT. Liberty, said the Court, "is deemed to embrace the right of the citizen to be free in the enjoyment of all his faculties." In thus circumscribing state authority over interstate business, *Allgeyer* represents the first invalidation of a state act as a deprivation of freedom of contract without violating the FOURTEENTH AMENDMENT guarantee of DUE PROCESS OF LAW.

DAVID GORDON

ALLIED STRUCTURAL STEEL COMPANY v. SPANNAUS
438 U.S. 234 (1978)

The modern revival of the CONTRACT CLAUSE began with UNITED STATES TRUST COMPANY V. NEW JERSEY (1977), a case in which the Supreme Court showed its willingness to make states live up to their own obligations as contracting parties. *Spannaus* carried the new doctrine further, imposing the contract clause as a significant limitation on the power of a state to regulate relations between private contracting parties.

Minnesota law required certain large employers, when they terminated pension plans or left the state, to provide for the funding of pensions for employees with ten years' service. Allied, in its pension plan, had reserved the right to terminate the plan and distribute the fund's assets to retired and current employees. On closing its Minnesota office, under the law Allied had to provide about $185,000 to fund pensions for its ten-year employees. The Supreme Court, 5–3, held the law unconstitutional as an impairment of the OBLIGATION OF CONTRACTS.

Justice POTTER STEWART wrote for the Court. Much of his opinion was devoted to distinguishing HOME BUILDING & LOAN ASSOCIATION V. BLAISDELL (1934). Here the law did not deal with a "broad, generalized economic or social problem" but focused narrowly, not on all employers or even all who left the state, but on those who previously had voluntarily established pension plans. The law did not merely temporarily alter contractual relationships but "worked a severe, permanent and immediate change in those relationships—irrevocably and retroactively." The law also "invaded an area never before subject to regulation by the State," thus invading reliance interests to a greater degree than would result from a more common (and hence foreseeable) type of regulation.

Justice WILLIAM J. BRENNAN, for the dissenters, correctly noted that the Court's opinion amounted to a major change in the judicial role in supervising state economic regulation, demanding STRICT SCRUTINY under the contract clause to protect contract-based expectations.

Spannaus seemed to invite businesses to challenge all manner of ECONOMIC REGULATIONS on the ground of excessive interference with contractual expectations. In EXXON CORP. V. EAGERTON (1983), however, the Court sought to exorcise the ghost of FREEDOM OF CONTRACT. *Exxon* sharply limited the *Spannaus* principle to laws whose "sole effect" is "to alter contractual duties."

KENNETH L. KARST

ALMEIDA-SANCHEZ v. UNITED STATES
413 U.S. 266 (1973)

A roving United States border patrol, without warrant or PROBABLE CAUSE, stopped and searched an automobile for illegal aliens twenty-five miles from the Mexican border. The Court ruled that while routine searches of persons and vehicles at the border are permissible, this search was conducted too far from the border to be reasonable under the FOURTH AMENDMENT.

JACOB W. LANDYNSKI

AMALGAMATED FOOD EMPLOYEES UNION v. LOGAN VALLEY PLAZA

See: Shopping Centers

AMBACH v. NORWICK
441 U.S. 68 (1979)

Ambach completed the process, begun in FOLEY V. CONNELIE (1978), of carving out a major exception to the principle that discrimination against ALIENS amounts to a SUSPECT CLASSIFICATION, triggering STRICT SCRUTINY of its justifications. New York forbade employment as public school teachers of aliens who had not shown an intention to seek U.S. CITIZENSHIP. The Supreme Court held, 5–4, that this discrimination did not deny its victims the EQUAL PROTECTION OF THE LAWS.

Justice LEWIS F. POWELL, for the majority, concluded that *Foley*, following OBITER DICTA in SUGARMAN V. DOUGALL (1973), implied the exception in question. Where "governmental functions" were involved, the state need show only that the exclusion of aliens had a RATIONAL BASIS. Public school teachers, like police officers, have great individual responsibility and discretion; part of a teacher's function is to transmit our society's values and prepare children to be participating citizens. Under the RATIONAL BASIS standard, the state need not show a close fit between its classification and its objectives; the standard is met if it is rational to conclude that citizens generally would be better able than aliens to transmit citizenship values.

Justice HARRY A. BLACKMUN, author of the *Sugarman* opinion, led the dissenters, pointing out the indiscriminate sweep of the disqualification of aliens, and its tenuous connection with educational goals. (Private schools, for example, were permitted to use alien teachers, even though they were charged with transmitting citizenship values to eighteen percent of New York's children.)

KENNETH L. KARST

AMENDING PROCESS

Article V, which stipulates the methods by which the Constitution may be amended, reflects the Framers' attempt to reconcile the principles of the Revolution with their desire for stable government in the future. Early in the CONSTITUTIONAL CONVENTION OF 1787, GEORGE MASON of Virginia suggested that inclusion in the Constitution of a specified mechanism for future amendments would help channel zeal for change into settled constitutional processes. "Amendments therefore will be necessary," he said, "and it will be better to provide for them, in an easy, regular and constitutional way than to trust to chance and violence." So viewed, the Article V amendment process is a somewhat conservative rendering of the revolutionary spirit that had claimed for the people an inalienable right to alter or abolish an inadequate government.

The Constitution sets out alternative methods both for proposing and for ratifying amendments. Amendments may be proposed by a two-thirds vote of both houses of Congress, or by a national constitutional convention. All of the amendments proposed thus far in our history have emanated from Congress. To become part of the Constitution, proposed amendments must gain the assent of three-fourths of the states. Article V gives Congress the power to choose whether proposed amendments (including any proposed by a constitutional convention) should be submitted to state legislatures or to state conventions for RATIFICATION. Congress has submitted every proposed amendment but one to the state legislatures.

Since 1789, over 5,000 bills proposing amendments to the Constitution have been introduced in Congress. Of these, only thirty-three received the necessary two-thirds vote of both houses of Congress and proceeded to the states for ratification. Twenty-six have been adopted; the remaining seven failed to be ratified. With only a few exceptions, the amendments proposed by Congress have come in clusters; virtually all of them arose during four brief periods.

The first of these periods ran from 1789 to 1804 and produced what may loosely be called the "Anti-Federalist amendments"—the BILL OF RIGHTS, the ELEVENTH AMENDMENT, and the TWELFTH AMENDMENT—each of which was, in part, a concession to Anti-Federalist or Jeffersonian interests. More than half a century passed before the Constitution was again amended. In 1865, sixty-one years after adoption of the Twelfth Amendment, Congress proposed and the states ratified the THIRTEENTH AMENDMENT, the first of the three Reconstruction amendments. The adoption of the FOURTEENTH AMENDMENT and the FIFTEENTH AMENDMENT followed in 1868 and 1870. A gap of almost another half-century intervened between the Reconstruction amendments and the next four amendments. These last grew out of the Populist and Progressive movements and provided for federal income taxation (the SIXTEENTH AMENDMENT, ratified in 1913), DIRECT ELECTION of senators (the SEVENTEENTH AMENDMENT, ratified in 1913), PROHIBITION (the EIGHTEENTH AMENDMENT, ratified in 1919), and women's suffrage (the NINETEENTH AMENDMENT, ratified in 1920). A fifth Progressive amendment, the CHILD LABOR AMENDMENT, was proposed in 1924 but was not ratified.

Together, the first three periods accounted for all but three of the amendments adopted before 1960. (The only amendments that did not fall into one of these clusters were the TWENTIETH AMENDMENT, which limits the lameduck session of Congress and was adopted in 1933; the TWENTY-FIRST AMENDMENT, which repealed prohibition and was adopted in 1933; and the TWENTY-SECOND AMENDMENT, which limits the President to two terms in office and was adopted in 1951). A fourth period of amendment activity lasted from 1961 to 1978. During these years, Congress proposed six amendments, four of which were adopted. The TWENTY-THIRD AMENDMENT gave the DISTRICT OF COLUMBIA three electoral votes in presidential elections. The TWENTY-FOURTH AMENDMENT abolished the POLL TAX for federal elections. The TWENTY-FIFTH AMENDMENT provided rules for presidential disability and PRESIDENTIAL SUCCESSION. The TWENTY-SIXTH AMENDMENT lowered the voting age to eighteen for both state and federal elections.

The fights over adoption of these twenty-six amendments, as well as battles over the proposed amendments that failed to be ratified, have produced conflicts over the proper procedures to be followed under the amendment article. The spare language of Article V leaves a number of questions unanswered. Between 1791 and 1931 the Supreme Court had occasion to address some of these issues. Arguments that there are implicit limits on the kind of amendments that may be adopted have not been accepted. In the *National Prohibition Cases* (1920) the Court rejected the argument that the Eighteenth Amendment (prohibition) was improper because of its interference with the states' exercise of their POLICE POWER. And in *Leser v. Garnett* (1922) the Court held that the Nineteenth Amendment's conferral of VOTING RIGHTS upon women was an appropriate exercise of the amendment power, rejecting the contention that "so great an addition to the electorate if made without the State's consent, destroys its autonomy as a political body."

In several decisions, the Court has given a broad reading to the power of Congress to propose amendments. In *Hollingsworth v. Virginia* (1798) the Court, sustaining the validity of the Eleventh Amendment, held that in spite of the veto clause of Article I, amendments proposed by Congress do not have to be submitted to the President for his signature. In the *National Prohibition Cases* (1920) the Court held that a two-thirds vote of a quorum of each house (rather than two-thirds of the entire membership) is sufficient to propose an amendment. In *Dillon v. Gloss* (1921) the Court held that Congress, when it proposes an amendment, has the power to set a reasonable time limit on ratification, and that seven years is a reasonable limit. The Court also rejected in *United States v. Sprague* (1931) the claim that amendments granting the federal government new, direct powers over the people may properly be ratified only by the people themselves acting through state conventions, and held that the mode of ratification is completely dependent upon congressional discretion. And when Congress does choose to submit an amendment to state legislatures, those legislatures are exercising a federal function under Article V and are not subject to the control of state law. Thus, in *Hawke v. Smith* (1919) the Court held that a state may not make the legislature's ratification of an amendment dependent upon subsequent approval by a voter REFERENDUM.

From 1798 to 1931 the Supreme Court assumed in decisions such as *Hollingsworth*, *Hawke*, and *Dillon* that issues of constitutional law arising under Article V were to be determined by the Court in the ordinary course of JUDICIAL REVIEW. In COLEMAN V. MILLER (1939), however, the Court refused to address several challenges to Kansas's ratification of the proposed Child Labor Amendment. Issues such as the timeliness of a ratification and the effect of a state's prior rejection of the validity of its ratification were held to be nonjusticiable questions committed to "the ultimate authority in the Congress of its control over the promulgation of the amendment." The *Coleman* decision suggests that judicial review is precluded for all issues that might be considered and resolved by Congress when, at the end of the state ratification process, Congress decides whether or not to "promulgate" the amendment.

Critics of the *Coleman* decision have disputed the Court's conclusion that "congressional promulgation" should preclude the judiciary from resolving challenges to the constitutional validity of an amendment. Critics even question the very notion of "congressional promulgation" as final, necessary step in the amendment process. The text of Article V notes only two stages for the adoption of an amendment: proposal by Congress (or a convention) and ratification by the states. There is no mention of any further action for an amendment to become valid. The Court had expressly held in *Dillon v. Gloss* (1921) what the language of Article V implies: that a proposed amendment becomes part of the Constitution immediately upon ratification by the last necessary state legislature. No further "promulgation" by Congress (or anyone else) appears to be necessary under Article V.

The only occasion upon which Congress ever undertook, at the end of a ratification process, to "promulgate" the adoption of an amendment was during Reconstruction when Congress passed a resolution declaring the Fourteenth Amendment to have been validly adopted despite disputed ratifications from two states that had attempted to rescind. In deciding *Coleman*, the Supreme Court treated the isolated Reconstruction precedent as a settled feature of the amendment process and held that congressional promulgation of an amendment would be binding on the Courts. *Coleman* remains the Court's last word on how disputed amendment process issues are to be resolved. Unless *Coleman* is reconsidered, any challenges to the validity of the procedures used for amendment will be conclusively determined by the Congress sitting when the required number of ratifications are reported to have been received.

It is difficult to predict how unresolved questions concerning the amendment process might be answered. Among the more warmly disputed issues has been the question of whether a state that has ratified an amendment may validly rescind its ratification. The text of Article V is inconclusive; while it does not mention any right of rescission, such a right might be inferred from the right to ratify. However, most treatise writers and scholars of the nineteenth and twentieth centuries have assumed that ratification was final and rescission ineffective. OBITER DICTUM in *Coleman*, moreover, suggests that the Court might have affirmatively approved the decision of the Reconstruction Congress to ignore purported rescissions.

Arguments that rescission by a subsequent legislature ought to nullify a state's earlier ratification, or that ratifications should be considered valid only if they are sufficiently close in time to reflect a "contemporaneous consensus" among ratifying states, may reflect, in part, an unstated assumption that it ought to be very difficult to amend the Constitution. But even without a requirement that ratifications must remain unrescinded or must come within a confined period of time, an amendment will not become part of the Constitution as long as one chamber in thirteen of the fifty state legislatures simply does nothing. An amendment proposed by a supermajority of the national Congress, and formally accepted at some time by the legislatures of three-fourths of the states (even if some state legislatures also pass resolutions of "rescission"), has passed the tests Article V expressly requires. As JAMES MADISON noted in THE FEDERALIST #43, the amendment article was designed to guard "equally against that extreme facility, which would render the constitution too mutable; and that extreme difficulty which might perpetuate its discovered faults."

To insure that the full range of future constitutional changes would be a viable possibility, the Framers sought to provide some means of constitutional change free of the control of existing governmental institutions. The Framers therefore included alternative mechanisms both for proposing and for ratifying amendments. From the earliest days of the Constitutional Convention, the delegates sought to avoid giving Congress the sole authority to propose amendments. If the proposal of all amendments ultimately depended upon Congress, George Mason argued, "no amendments of the proper kind would ever be obtained by the people, if the Government should become oppressive, as he verily believed would be the case." Other delegates, however, were apprehensive about the threat to national authority if state legislatures could effectively propose and ratify amendments without the involvement of some institution reflecting the national interest.

The solution to this dilemma was the "convention of the people." In addition to providing that amendments could be proposed by Congress, the final version of Article V provides that Congress must call "a Convention for proposing Amendments" whenever two-thirds of the state legislatures apply for one. Such a convention would be, like Congress, a deliberative body capable of assessing from a national perspective the need for constitutional change and capable of drafting proposed amendments for submission to the states for ratification. At the same time it would not be Congress itself, and therefore would not pose the threat of legislative self-interest's blocking needed reform of Congress.

No national convention for proposing amendments has ever been called. In recent years, however, a number of state legislatures have petitioned Congress to call a convention limited to proposing a particular amendment specified by the applying state legislatures. Some scholars consider these applications to be valid and argue that if similar applications are received from two-thirds of the state legislatures Congress should call the convention and seek to limit the convention to the particular amendment (or subject) specified in the state legislative applications. Others argue that such state applications are invalid because they erroneously assume that the agenda of the convention can properly be controlled by the applying state legislatures. These scholars argue that the only valid applications are those that recognize that a convention for proposing amendments is to be free to determine for itself what amendments should be proposed.

In addition to providing the alternative of a national convention for proposing amendments, Article V also provides an alternative method of ratifying amendments. For each amendment (whether proposed by Congress or by a national convention) Congress is free to choose whether to submit the amendment for ratification to state legislatures or to "conventions" in each state. By giving Congress this authority, Article V preserves the possibility of reforms restricting the power of state legislatures. The Constitution itself was submitted to ratifying conventions in each state, rather than to state legislatures. For thirty-two of the thirty-three proposed amendments Congress chose to submit its proposal to state legislatures. But the use of the convention method of ratification is not unprecedented: The Twenty-First Amendment repealing prohibition was submitted by Congress in 1933 to state conventions. Virtually every state chose to have delegates to its ratifying convention elected, and in every state the election of delegates was, for all practical purposes, a dispositive referendum on whether or not to ratify the amendment. In every state the voters' wishes were expeditiously carried out by the slate that had won election. In less than ten months from the time it was proposed by Congress, the amendment was ratified by elected conventions in three-fourths of the states.

The "convention of the people" was a familiar device in the eighteenth century. It now seems archaic, and the use of either a national convention for proposing amendments or state conventions for ratification are at present fraught with uncertainties. The convention device was nonetheless an imaginative effort to address a universal problem of constitution drafting: how to provide the means for future reform of governmental institutions when the only institutions readily available for proposing and approving changes are those already in existence, and possibly in need of reform themselves.

WALTER DELLINGER

Bibliography

DELLINGER, WALTER 1984 The Legitimacy of Constitutional Change: Rethinking the Amendment Process. *Harvard Law Review* 97:386–432.

GRIMES, ALLEN P. 1978 *Democracy and the Amendments to the Constitution.* Lexington, Mass.: Lexington Books.

GUNTHER, GERALD 1979 The Convention Method of Amending the United States Constitution. *Georgia Law Review* 14:1–25.

ORFIELD, LESTER BERNHARDT 1942 *The Amending of the Federal Constitution.* Ann Arbor: University of Michigan Press; Chicago: Callaghan & Co.

TRIBE, LAURENCE H. 1984 A *Constitution* We Are Amending: In Defense of a Restrained Judicial Role. *Harvard Law Review* 97:433–445.

AMERICAN CIVIL LIBERTIES UNION

The American Civil Liberties Union (ACLU) is the most important national organization dedicated to the protection of individual liberty. It was founded in 1920 by a distinguished group that included ROGER BALDWIN, Jane Addams, FELIX FRANKFURTER, Helen Keller, Scott Nearing, and Norman Thomas.

The principles of the ACLU are contained in the BILL OF RIGHTS: the right to free expression, above all, the freedom to dissent from the official view and majority opinion; the right to equal treatment regardless of race, sex, religion, national origin, or physical handicap; the right to DUE PROCESS in encounters with government institutions—courts, schools, police, bureaucracy—and with the repositories of great private power; the right to be let alone—to be secure from spying, from the unwarranted collection of personal information, and from interference in private lives.

The ACLU has participated in many controversial cases. It represented John Scopes when he was fired for teaching evolution; it fought for the rights of Sacco and Vanzetti; it defended the Scottsboro Boys, who were denied a FAIR TRIAL for alleged rape (see POWELL V. ALABAMA, 1932; NORRIS V. ALABAMA, 1935); it fought the Customs Bureau when it banned James Joyce's *Ulysses* (see UNITED STATES V. "ULYSSES," (1934); it opposed the censorship of the Pentagon Papers (see NEW YORK TIMES V. UNITED STATES, 1971) and religious exercises in schools.

The ACLU has supported racial and religious minorities, the right of LABOR to organize, and equal treatment for women, and it has opposed arbitrary treatment of persons in closed institutions such as mental patients, prisoners, military personnel, and students.

The concept of CIVIL LIBERTIES, as understood by the ACLU, has developed over the years. For example, in the 1960s it declared that CAPITAL PUNISHMENT violated civil liberties because of the finality and randomness of executions; that military conscription, which substantially restricts individual autonomy, violated civil liberties except during war or national emergency; and that the undeclared VIETNAM WAR was illegal because of failure to abide by constitutional procedures for committing the country to hostilities.

On the other hand, while endorsing many legal protections for poor people, the ACLU has never held that poverty itself violated civil liberties. In addition, since a cardinal precept of the ACLU is political nonpartisanship, it does not endorse or oppose judicial nominees or candidates for public office.

The ACLU has been frequently attacked as subversive, communistic, and even a "criminals' lobby." Its detractors have not recognized that by representing radicals and despised minorities the ACLU does not endorse their causes but rather the primacy and indivisibility of the Bill of Rights. This confusion cost the ACLU many members when in 1977 it secured the right of American Nazis to demonstrate peacefully in Skokie, Illinois.

The ACLU's national headquarters are in New York City; it maintains a legislative office in Washington, D.C., and regional offices in Atlanta and Denver. Its 250,000 members are organized in branches in all fifty states, which are tied to the national organization through revenue-sharing, participation in policy decisions, and united action on common goals. Each affiliate has its own board of directors and hires its own staff. The ACLU participates annually in thousands of court cases and administrative actions, legislative lobbying, and public education.

NORMAN DORSEN

Bibliography

DORSEN, NORMAN 1984 The American Civil Liberties Union: An Institutional Analysis. *Tulane Lawyer* (Spring) 1984:6–14.

AMERICAN COMMUNICATIONS ASSOCIATION v. DOUDS
339 U.S. 382 (1950)

In one of the first cases in which the Supreme Court gave constitutional approval to the anticommunist crusade, Chief Justice FRED VINSON upheld provisions of the TAFT-HARTLEY ACT denying National Labor Relations Board services to unions whose officers had not filed affidavits stating they were not members of the Communist party and that they did "not believe in . . . the overthrow of the . . . Government by force or by any illegal or unconstitutional methods." The opinion of the Court became a model for denying FIRST AMENDMENT protections to alleged subversives through the use of a balancing technique. The Court argued that the statute touched only a few persons and that the only effect even upon them was that they must relinquish their union offices, not their beliefs. It argued that banning communists from NLRB-supported labor negotiations was reasonably related to the legitimate congressional end of protecting INTERSTATE COMMERCE, given the nature of the Communist party and the threat of political strikes. The Court concluded that "Considering the circumstances . . . the statute . . . did not unduly infringe freedoms protected by the First Amendment."

MARTIN SHAPIRO

AMERICAN INDIANS AND THE CONSTITUTION

Indians are mentioned only three times in the Constitution. Yet the Supreme Court has developed a vast body of law defining the status of Indians and tribes in our federal system. This law makes use of constitutional sources but also draws heavily on the history between Indians and the federal government, including wars, conquest, treaties, and the assumption by the government of a protectorate relationship toward the tribes. It reveals that our government is not only, as is popularly believed, one of dual sovereigns, federal and state. There is also a third sovereign, consisting of Indian tribes, operating within a limited but distinct sphere.

The three references to Indians in the Constitution presage this body of law. Two of the three are found in Article I and the FOURTEENTH AMENDMENT, which exclude "Indians not taxed" from the counts for apportioning DIRECT TAXES and representatives to Congress among the states. The third reference is a grant of power to Congress in the COMMERCE CLAUSE of Article I to "regulate Commerce with . . . the Indian Tribes."

The phrase "Indians not taxed" was not a grant of tax exemption. Rather, it described the status of Indians at the time the Constitution was written. Indians were not taxed because generally they were treated as outside the American body politic. They were not United States citizens, and they were not governed by ordinary federal and state legislation. Tribal laws, treaties with the United States, and special federal Indian legislation governed their affairs. Only the few Indians who had severed their tribal relations and come to live in non-Indian communities were treated as appropriate for counting in the constitutionally mandated apportionment.

The phrase probably was chosen because the apportionment served partly to allocate tax burdens. That aspect of the apportionment has lost significance, however, since the SIXTEENTH AMENDMENT made it unnecessary for the federal government to apportion income taxes.

The exclusion of "Indians not taxed" from all aspects of apportionment has, in fact, been mooted by changes in the status of American Indians since ratification of the Fourteenth Amendment in 1868. Treaty-making with Indian tribes ended in 1871, and in 1924 all native-born Indians who had not already been made citizens by federal statute were naturalized. Indians were held subject to federal statutes, including tax laws, except where special Indian legislation or treaties offered exemptions. By 1940 the Department of the Interior officially recognized that there no longer were Indians who can properly be considered "Indians not taxed."

The commerce clause reference to Indians, by contrast, continues to have real force. Since the abandonment of federal treaty-making with Indian tribes in 1871, it has been the primary constitutional provision supporting exercises of federal power over Indians as such. Notwithstanding its reference to commerce "with the Indian Tribes," the clause also applies to transactions with individual tribal Indians, including some off-reservation transactions, and to non-Indians doing business on reservations. Congress's Article I power to regulate "the Territory or other Property belonging to the United States" supplements the treaty and Indian commerce clause powers. Most Indian lands are held in fee by the United States, subject to a beneficial tribal interest in reservations set aside by treaty or EXECUTIVE ORDER, and to the Indians' right of occupancy. Congress's power to make war was also invoked in the early years of dealing with the Indians.

This combination of powers, read together with the NECESSARY AND PROPER CLAUSE of Article I and the SUPREMACY CLAUSE of Article VI, has been the foundation of a complex structure of federal, state, and tribal relations. The federal government's power over Indian affairs is extensive and preemptive of state power. (See CHEROKEE INDIAN CASES, 1831–1832.) In the nineteenth century the courts called the federal power "plenary," and challenges to its exercise were labeled POLITICAL QUESTIONS. In fact this federal authority is a general POLICE POWER, comparable to Congress's power over the DISTRICT OF COLUMBIA and the TERRITORIES. In *Delaware Tribal Business Committee v. Weeks* (1977), the Court held that ordinary constitutional strictures apply to federal Indian legislation, and that, under the Fifth Amendment's DUE PROCESS CLAUSE in particular, such legislation must be reviewed to determine whether it is "tied rationally to the fulfillment of Congress's unique obligation toward the Indians." Even though this trust obligation has not prevented Congress from enacting laws contrary to the best interests of Indians, the Supreme Court now insists upon some determination that Indians will be protected when disadvantageous laws are passed. Thus, for example, Congress may not take Indian property for a non-Indian use without paying JUST COMPENSATION, and it may not arbitrarily give tribal assets to some tribal members but not others.

A law that satisfies the "tied rationally" test is not constitutionally defective under the EQUAL PROTECTION requirement of the Fifth Amendment's due process clause simply because it singles out Indians for special treatment. For example, Congress may establish a preference for employment of tribal Indians with the Bureau of Indian Affairs, or may subject Indians to harsher punishments than non-Indians would suffer in state court for doing the same acts. Such legislation is held not to constitute an otherwise forbidden racial classification, because of the separate status of Indians under the Constitution (*i.e.*, their subjection to federal and tribal rather than state jurisdiction).

Although Congress has enacted laws governing a wide variety of activities on Indian reservations, there is no detailed code comparable to the District of Columbia's. In the absence of such federal legislation, states and Indian tribes have competed for control. The Supreme Court has repeatedly upheld tribal independence from state jurisdiction, basing its decisions on preemptive federal power over Indian affairs and the broad federal policy of setting aside lands for tribal self-government. Although in cases outside Indian law the Supreme Court has refused to apply the PREEMPTION DOCTRINE to exclude the operation of state law where congressional intent was doubtful, in Indian cases it has inferred preemptive intent from the general purposes of treaties and statutes to protect tribal resources and promote tribal sovereignty. Thus, absent clear and express congressional consent, states may not regulate non-Indian activities that affect tribal self-government. Despite their lack of authority over reservation Indians, states are prohibited by the Fourteenth Amendment from denying Indians rights available under state law.

Within their realm of authority, Indian tribes exercise powers of self-government, not because of any DELEGATION OF POWERS, but rather because of their original, unrelinquished tribal sovereignty. The Supreme Court recognized this sovereign status of Indian tribes in *United States v. Wheeler* (1978), which held that it would not constitute DOUBLE JEOPARDY to try an Indian in federal court after he had been convicted in tribal court because the court systems belong to separate sovereigns. The Constitution has never been invoked successfully to prevent Congress from abolishing tribal authority in whole or in part; but the Supreme Court has required a clear and specific expression of congressional intent before recognizing the termination of tribal powers. This canon of construction was established to implement the federal government's obligation to protect the Indian tribes. Some tribal powers were necessarily relinquished when the United States incorporated the tribes, such as the power to carry on foreign relations, the power to transfer Indian land without consent of the United States, and the power to prosecute non-Indians for crimes. These relinquished powers are few, however, and Congress could restore them if it chose.

Because the BILL OF RIGHTS limits only the federal government and the Fourteenth Amendment limits only the states, Indian tribes need not follow their dictates. However, in 1968, Congress enacted the Indian Civil Rights Act, which conferred some but not all protections of the Bill of Rights on individuals subject to tribal authority.

CAROLE E. GOLDBERG-AMBROSE

Bibliography

COHEN, F. 1982 *Handbook of Federal Indian Law.* Indianapolis: Bobbs-Merrill.

GETCHES, D.; ROSENFELT, D.; and WILKINSON, C. 1979 *Federal Indian Law: Cases and Materials.* St. Paul, Minn.: West Publishing Co.

PRICE, M. 1973 *Law and the American Indian: Readings, Notes and Cases.* Indianapolis: Bobbs-Merrill.

AMERICAN INSURANCE COMPANY v. CANTER

1 Peters 511 (1828)

Although the Constitution authorizes Congress to govern the TERRITORIES of the United States, it does not authorize the acquisition of territories. Consequently

THOMAS JEFFERSON had constitutional qualms when he acquired the Louisiana Territory by treaty. This case settled the authority of the United States to acquire territory by the WAR POWERS or TREATY POWER, and sustained the power of Congress to establish LEGISLATIVE COURTS with JURISDICTION extending beyond the JUDICIAL POWER OF THE UNITED STATES as defined by Article III, section 2.

LEONARD W. LEVY

AMERICAN JEWISH CONGRESS

Formed originally in 1918 as a temporary confederation of Jewish organizations to propose a postwar program by the Jewish people for presentation at the Versailles Peace Conference, the American Jewish Congress continued in existence and became fully organized under the chairmanship of Rabbi Stephen S. Wise in 1928. In the 1930s it emerged as a leading force in the anti-Nazi movement and in efforts to aid the victims of Hitlerism.

A new and still continuing chapter in its history was initiated in 1945 when, under the leadership of three socially minded lawyers, Alexander H. Pekelis, Will Maslow, and Leo Pfeffer, it established a Commission on Law and Social Action. The commission was based on two premises: that the security of American Jews is interdependent with that of all religions, races, and other national minorities, and that the security of all is dependent upon the integrity of the BILL OF RIGHTS and the EQUAL PROTECTION clause of the FOURTEENTH AMENDMENT.

Accordingly, the organization's legal staff have instituted litigation or submitted briefs AMICUS CURIAE in a wide variety of constitutional law cases, acquiring a status parallel to that of the AMERICAN CIVIL LIBERTIES UNION and the National Association for the Advancement of Colored People. Typical of these are suits challenging the constitutionality of the death penalty under the Eighth Amendment, racial SEGREGATION in public schools, anti-abortion legislation, racially RESTRICTIVE COVENANTS, LITERACY TESTS for voters, disinheritance of illegitimate children, and denial of tax exemption to organizations advocating overthrow of government.

However, by far the majority of suits in which the organization has participated, either as amicus or as party, have involved either the establishment clause or the free exercise clause of the FIRST AMENDMENT, or the ban in Article VI of RELIGIOUS TESTS for public office. The commission's primacy in this arena is generally recognized among jurists, organizations, and scholars.

LEO PFEFFER

Bibliography

PEKELIS, ALEXANDER H. 1950 *Law and Social Action.* Ithaca, N.Y.: Cornell University Press.

AMERICAN SYSTEM

"American System" was the name given by HENRY CLAY (in the House of Representatives, March 30–31, 1824) to the national program of economic policy that centered on the protective tariff for the encouragement of domestic manufactures. It assigned the general government a positive role in promoting balanced economic development within the "home market." Each of the great sections would concentrate on the productions for which it was best suited: the South on staples like cotton, the West on grains and livestock, the Northeast on manufacturing. The tariff would protect the market; INTERNAL IMPROVEMENTS would facilitate exchanges and bind the parts together; the national bank would furnish commercial credit and ensure a stable and uniform currency. These measures were implemented in varying degrees, but the system was overtaken by the disintegrating sectionalism of the 1820s and finally buried by Jacksonian Democracy. Constitutionally, the American System posited a broad view of federal powers. It was attacked as dangerously consolidating, indeed unconstitutional in all its leading measures. Although the opposition had other and deeper sources, it tended to become a constitutional opposition, culminating in South Carolina's NULLIFICATION of the tariff in 1832.

MERRILL D. PETERSON

Bibliography

GOODRICH, CARTER, ED. 1967 *The Government and the Economy, 1783–1861.* Indianapolis: Bobbs-Merrill.

AMERICAN TOBACCO COMPANY, UNITED STATES v.

See: *Standard Oil Co. v. United States*

AMES, FISHER (1758–1808)

An extreme Federalist, Fisher Ames published his "Camillus" essays to promote the idea of the CONSTITUTIONAL CONVENTION OF 1787. The French Revolution inspired his suspicion of democracy—"only the dismal passport to a more dismal hereafter"—and led him to call for a government run by an "aristocracy of talent." Ames also opposed the BILL OF RIGHTS as unnecessary and unwise. Representing Massachusetts in Congress from 1789 to 1797, he vigorously defended JAY'S TREATY and the ALIEN AND SEDITION ACTS, but, by 1802, his radical partisanship left him an embittered STATES' RIGHTS advocate.

DAVID GORDON

AMICUS CURIAE

(Latin: Friend of the Court.) The amicus curiae originally was a lawyer aiding the court. Today in American practice, the lawyers represent an organization, which is the amicus; the group's "friendship" to the court has become an artifice slightly disguising the fact that it is as much an advocate as any party. Although economic interests early employed the amicus brief, CIVIL LIBERTIES groups did not lag far behind. As early as 1904, a group representing Chinese immigrants participated in a Supreme Court case. By the 1940s, the activities of amici were extensive, well coordinated among sister organizations, and highly publicized. In the aftermath of several antisegregation decisions of the mid-1950s, southern legislators and other spokesmen criticized that participation as nonjudicial.

Prior to 1937 the Supreme Court had no formal rule governing amicus briefs. It was standard procedure first to seek consent of the parties to the filing of an amicus brief, but the Court almost invariably accepted an amicus brief irrespective of party consent. The 1937 rule required a request for party consent, but the same easy acceptance of participation continued. In 1949, in the face of criticism, the Court noted that consent of the parties would be expected; without such consent "such motions are not favored." For a decade thereafter denials exceeded granting of motions by a wide margin.

The rule has been retained in subsequent revisions. In practice, however, such motions are now virtually (though not quite) automatically granted, with or without party consent. It is rare for any amicus curiae other than the United States to be given leave to make an ORAL ARGUMENT.

The excitement over use of amicus briefs has died down. Most such presentations are well-coordinated with the main brief, serving chiefly to announce the positions of certain groups. The Court, however, seems well-served by broader sources of information, and some amicus briefs are more cogent or influential than the parties' briefs. Many potential amici curiae qualify for participation through intervention or CLASS ACTIONS. Critics of wider participation, therefore, concentrate their guns on those more significant targets.

SAMUEL KRISLOV

AMNESTY

Amnesty is the blanket forgiveness of a group of people for some offense, usually of a political nature. Although there is a technical distinction between an amnesty, which "forgets" the offense, and a pardon, which remits the penalty, historical practice and common usage have made the terms virtually interchangeable. In the United States, amnesty may be granted by the President (under the PARDONING POWER) or by Congress (as NECESSARY AND PROPER to the carrying out of any of several powers). Amnesty may be granted before or after conviction, and may be conditional or unconditional. But neither Congress nor the President may grant amnesty for offenses against state law.

The first instance of amnesty under the Constitution was extended in 1801 by President THOMAS JEFFERSON to persons convicted or charged under the ALIEN AND SEDITION ACTS. Between 1862 and 1868, Presidents ABRAHAM LINCOLN and ANDREW JOHNSON issued a series of six proclamations of conditional amnesty for southern rebels. Congress specifically authorized the first three but repealed the authorizing statute in 1867; President Johnson issued the last three on his own authority alone. In the TEST OATH CASES (1867), the Supreme Court struck down, as an unconstitutional interference with the pardoning power, an attempt by Congress to limit the effect of Johnson's amnesty. In 1872, exercising its power under section 3 of the FOURTEENTH AMENDMENT, Congress passed the Amnesty Act restoring the CIVIL RIGHTS of most rebels.

President GERALD R. FORD granted conditional amnesty in 1974 to military deserters and draft evaders of the VIETNAM WAR period. The terms of the amnesty required case-by-case determination by a special Presidential Clemency Board empowered to direct performance by applicants of alternative public service. Ford acted on his own authority after Congress failed to approve any of several amnesty proposals.

DENNIS J. MAHONEY

ANCILLARY JURISDICTION

In some cases federal courts hear claims over which no statute confers federal JURISDICTION. Typically, this ancillary jurisdiction has been exercised in cases brought under the federal courts' DIVERSITY JURISDICTION. Suppose a California citizen sues an Arizona citizen in federal court, claiming a right to property. If another Californian claims the same property interest, no state court can take jurisdiction over the property under the federal court's control. It is thus necessary for the federal court to be able to hear that claim, even though the case of one Californian against another would not initially be within its jurisdiction. Similarly, a defendant sued in federal court can file a third-party claim against a co-citizen, which will be heard under the federal court's ancillary jurisdiction.

Ancillary jurisdiction is sometimes confused with PENDENT JURISDICTION, which permits a state *claim* to be heard in federal court along with a closely related FEDERAL QUESTION. Ancillary jurisdiction results in the addition of a *party* who otherwise would not fall within the federal court's jurisdiction. The Supreme Court has not been hospitable to the suggestion that a federal court in a federal question case should take "pendent" jurisdiction over a closely related state law claim against a new party.

KENNETH L. KARST

Bibliography

WRIGHT, CHARLES ALAN 1983 *The Law of Federal Courts,* 4th ed. Pages 28–32. St. Paul, Minn.: West Publishing Co.

ANNEXATION OF TEXAS

American settlers in the Mexican province of Texas revolted against the central government and established the independence of the Lone Star Republic in 1836. President ANDREW JACKSON was unable to effect annexation, however, because many feared war with Mexico and because abolitionists suspected a slaveholders' plot to increase the number of slave states. In 1842, President John Tyler revived annexationist efforts, abetted by a clique of proslavery expansionists, but an annexation treaty failed once again, due in part to the argument that the territories clause (Article IV, section 3) permitted annexation only of dependent TERRITORIES of other nations, not of independent nations themselves. Tyler then recommended annexation by JOINT RESOLUTION of Congress to obviate the constitutional requirement of a two-thirds Senate vote to ratify a treaty. This aroused further opposition, now including influential southern Whigs, who insisted that the issue involved grave foreign policy risks and hence was precisely the sort of question for which the Framers had required a supermajority. Despite this argument, congressional Democrats enacted a joint resolution in February 1845 declaring the Republic of Texas to be the twenty-eighth state.

WILLIAM M. WIECEK

Bibliography

MERK, FREDERICK 1972 *Slavery and the Annexation of Texas.* New York: Knopf.

ANTIDISCRIMINATION LEGISLATION

From its inception, antidiscrimination legislation has shaped and been shaped by the Constitution. Antidiscrimination legislation's very existence is attributable to developments in constitutional law. Enactment of such legislation usually reflects a relatively favorable atmosphere for the promise of equality embodied in the THIRTEENTH, FOURTEENTH, and FIFTEENTH AMENDMENTS. When the values underlying these amendments are in decline, antidiscrimination legislation is not enacted, and often is not enforced.

Federal antidiscrimination laws have been enacted during two time periods. During the first period, which commenced near the end of the Civil War, Congress enacted the CIVIL RIGHTS ACT OF 1866, the Civil Rights Act of 1870, the FORCE ACT OF 1871, the Civil Rights Act of 1871, and the CIVIL RIGHTS ACT OF 1875. These early provisions, portions of which survive, exemplify two basic forms of antidiscrimination legislation. Some provisions, such as section 1 of the 1871 act (now section 1983) and section 3 of the 1866 act were purely remedial. They provided remedies for violations of federal rights but created no new substantive rights. Other provisions, such as section 1 of the 1866 act and section 16 of the 1870 act (now sections 1981 and 1982), were express efforts to change substantive law by fostering greater equality between black and white Americans.

The COMPROMISE OF 1877 marks the end of the first era during which antidiscrimination legislation flourished. Afterward, congressional and judicial developments favored neither enactment nor enforcement of antidiscrimination legislation. In the CIVIL RIGHTS REPEAL ACT of 1894 the first Democratic Congress since the Civil War repealed the few effective remnants of post-Civil War antidiscrimination legislation. A favorable climate for legislative implementation of the post-Civil War constitutional amendments did not reemerge until the late 1950s and early 1960s. There were no significant antidiscrimination statutes in the intervening years.

As the constitutional amendments were given new vigor by the WARREN COURT, however, antidiscrimination legislation experienced a renaissance. Modern statutes, including the CIVIL RIGHTS ACTS OF 1957, 1960, 1964, and 1968, protect against discrimination in voting, employment, education, and housing. They represent a second era of federal antidiscrimination legislation, sometimes called part of the second reconstruction.

As in the case of earlier antidiscrimination statutes, the primary reason for enactment was to protect blacks from RACIAL DISCRIMINATION. Again, two kinds of provisions were enacted. Some provisions, such as the 1957 and 1960 Acts and Title VI of the 1964 act, are remedial in tone (though not always so interpreted) and do not purport to create new substantive rights. Others, such as Title VII of the 1964 act, which prohibits private discrimination in employment, confer new substantive rights.

Modern antidiscrimination legislation contains a recognizable subcategory that has been the fastest growing area of antidiscrimination law. Until about 1960 or 1970, antidiscrimination legislation could be equated with laws prohibiting one or more forms of racial discrimination. Subsequently, however, legislation prohibiting discrimination surfaced in many areas. For example, the AGE DISCRIMINATION ACT OF 1975, the Age Discrimination in Employment Act, the REHABILITATION ACT OF 1973, the DEVELOPMENTALLY DISABLED AND BILL OF RIGHTS ACT, the Education of Handicapped Children Acts, the Equal Pay Act, and the EDUCATION AMENDMENTS OF 1972 provide substantial protection to the aged, to the handicapped, and to women. Building on a technique first employed in Title VI of the 1964 act, most of these provisions apply only to programs or entities receiving federal financial assistance.

Although constitutional values can be viewed as the raison d'être of antidiscrimination legislation, the relationship between the Constitution and antidiscrimination laws runs much deeper. Their more complex relationship may be divided into two parts. First, antidiscrimination legislation has been the setting for judicial and congressional decisions concerning the scope of congressional power. One of the few universally agreed upon facts about the history of the Fourteenth Amendment is that it was meant to place the first major antidiscrimination statute, the Civil Rights Act of 1866, on firm constitutional footing. Before ratification of the Fourteenth Amendment, doubts were expressed about Congress's power under the Thirteenth Amendment to ban racially discriminatory state laws. Many believe that the Fourteenth Amendment was meant primarily to constitutionalize the 1866 Act's prohibitions. With the Fourteenth Amendment in place by 1868, Congress reaffirmed the 1866 Act's bans by reenacting them as part of the Civil Rights Act of 1870. Some claim that the 1866 Act is so akin to a constitutional provision that its surviving remnants should be interpreted more like constitutional provisions than statutory ones.

Soon after this initial interplay between the Constitution and antidiscrimination laws, a foundation of constitutional interpretation grew out of litigation under antidiscrimination statutes. In a line of cases commencing with UNITED STATES v. CRUIKSHANK (1876) and culminating in UNITED STATES v. HARRIS (1883) and the CIVIL RIGHTS CASES (1883), the Court relied on what has come to be known as the STATE ACTION doctrine to invalidate antidiscrimination measures. The *Civil Rights Cases* invalidated the last piece of nineteenth-century civil rights legislation, the Civil Rights Act of 1875. In so doing the Court not only limited the Fourteenth Amendment to prohibiting state action but also rendered a narrow interpretation of the Thirteenth Amendment as a possible source of congressional power to enact antidiscrimination statutes.

The state action doctrine was not the only early limit on antidiscrimination legislation. In UNITED STATES v. REESE (1876) the Court found sections 3 and 4 of the Civil Rights Act of 1870, which prohibited certain interferences with voting, to be beyond Congress's power to enforce the Fifteenth Amendment because the sections were not limited to prohibiting racial discrimination. These limitations on antidiscrimination legislation carried over into the early twentieth century.

But some early antidiscrimination legislation survived constitutional attack and shifting political stances in Congress. For example, in EX PARTE YARBROUGH (1884) the Court sustained use of section 6 of the 1870 act (now section 241) to impose criminal sanctions against private individuals who used force to prevent blacks from voting in federal elections. And in *Ex parte Virginia* (1880), the Court sustained the federal prosecution of a state judge for excluding blacks from juries in violation of section 4 of the 1875 act. (See STRAUDER v. WEST VIRGINIA, 1880.)

The two lines of early constitutional interpretation

of antidiscrimination laws have never been fully reconciled. As a result of the early limits on congressional power to enact antidiscrimination legislation, modern civil rights statutes have been drafted to reduce potential constitutional attacks. Thus, much of the Civil Rights Act of 1964 operates only on individuals and entities engaged in some form of INTERSTATE COMMERCE. Other portions of the 1964 act, and many other modern antidiscrimination laws, are based on Congress's TAXING AND SPENDING POWERS. By tying antidiscrimination legislation to the COMMERCE CLAUSE or the spending power, Congress hoped to avoid some of the constitutional problems that plagued early legislation enacted under the Thirteenth, Fourteenth, and Fifteenth Amendments.

A potential clash between the Court and Congress over the constitutionality of modern antidiscrimination legislation has not surfaced. The modern Court sustains antidiscrimination legislation even in the face of troublesome nineteenth-century precedents. In a landmark holding barely reconcilable with portions of the *Civil Rights Cases,* the Court in JONES v. ALFRED H. MAYER COMPANY (1968) found that Congress has power under the Thirteenth Amendment to ban private racial discrimination in housing. Later, in RUNYON v. MCCRARY (1976), the Court acknowledged Congress's power to outlaw racial discrimination in private contractual relations, including those relations involved in a child's attendance at a private segregated school. In GRIFFIN v. BRECKENRIDGE (1971) the Court relied on the Thirteenth Amendment to sustain a remnant of the 1871 act allowing for causes of action against private conspiracies to violate federal rights. The case undermined *United States v. Harris* and overruled an earlier contrary decision, *Collins v. Hardyman* (1948). Another antidiscrimination statute, the VOTING RIGHTS ACT OF 1965, provided the setting for important decisions in KATZENBACH v. MORGAN (1966) and SOUTH CAROLINA v. KATZENBACH (1966), which found Congress to have broad discretion to interpret and extend Fourteenth Amendment protection to situations which the judiciary had not found violative of the Fourteenth Amendment.

There is a second respect in which constitutional provisions and antidiscrimination legislation influence each other. From the beginning, their relationship has gone beyond one of merely testing the constitutionality of a particular antidiscrimination statute. Interpretation of one set of provisions has shaped the other. This interplay began with the Civil Rights Act of 1866. Soon after ratification of the Fourteenth Amendment, the question arose as to what constituted "the PRIVILEGES AND IMMUNITIES of citizens of the United States" referred to in the Fourteenth Amendment. In the SLAUGHTERHOUSE CASES (1873) the Court's first decision construing the Fourteenth Amendment, Justice STEPHEN J. FIELD argued in dissent that section 1 of the 1866 act provided Congress's interpretation of at least some of the privileges or immunities of United States citizens. Although Field's view did not prevail—the Court limited the privileges or immunities clause to a narrow class of rights—even the majority view of the privileges or immunities clause may have had a profound effect on subsequent development of antidiscrimination legislation.

This effect stems from the strong linguistic parallel between the Fourteenth Amendment's privileges or immunities clause and the rights listed as protected by many antidiscrimination laws. Sections 1983 and 242 protect persons against deprivations of their federal "rights, privileges or immunities." Section 1985(3) refers in part to "equal privileges and immunities." Section 241 refers to any federal "right or privilege." In subsequent cases brought under antidiscrimination statutes, federal courts, relying on the *Slaughterhouse Cases'* narrow interpretation of the Fourteenth Amendment's privileges or immunities clause, plausibly could render a similar narrow interpretation of the antidiscrimination statute. Not until MONROE v. PAPE (1961) did the Court settle that the rights, privileges, and immunities protected by section 1983 include at least all rights secured by the Fourteenth Amendment.

Just as CONSTITUTIONAL INTERPRETATION influenced early antidiscrimination laws and vice versa, modern antidiscrimination legislation influences constitutional interpretation. In GRIGGS v. DUKE POWER COMPANY (1971) the Court found that an employer's selection criteria with unintentional disparate effect on a minority could lead to a violation of Title VII of the Civil Rights Act of 1964. This and earlier Supreme Court cases generated pressure to find violative of the Fourteenth Amendment government action with uneven adverse effects on minorities. Not until WASHINGTON v. DAVIS (1976) and ARLINGTON HEIGHTS v. METROPOLITAN HOUSING DEVELOPMENT CORPORATION (1977) did the Court expressly reject the *Griggs* standard as a basis for constitutional interpretation. And in REGENTS OF THE UNIVERSITY OF CALIFORNIA v. BAKKE (1978), a major theme of the opinions is the relationship between the antidiscrimination standards embodied in Title VI of the Civil Rights Act of 1964 and those of the Fourteenth Amendment.

Judicial hostility to the Reconstruction CIVIL

RIGHTS program and subsequent congressional inaction left much of the civil rights field to the states. Early Massachusetts legislation covered school desegregation and PUBLIC ACCOMMODATIONS, but few other states enacted protective laws prior to 1883 and some laws that had been enacted by southern Reconstruction legislatures were repealed.

The *Civil Rights Cases'* invalidation of the Civil Rights Act of 1875 triggered the first major group of state antidiscrimination laws. Within two years of the decision, eleven states outlawed discrimination in public accommodations. Modest further legislative developments occurred before World War II, including legislation aimed at violence generated by the Ku Klux Klan, some northern prohibitions on school segregation, and some categories of employment discrimination.

The next widespread state civil rights initiative, which covered employment discrimination, drew upon experience under the wartime Committee on Fair Employment Practices. New York's 1945 Law Against Discrimination, the first modern comprehensive fair employment law, established a commission to investigate and adjudicate complaints and became a model for other states' laws. Resort to administrative agencies, now possible in the vast majority of states, remains the primary state method of dealing with many categories of discrimination.

THEODORE EISENBERG

Bibliography

BARDOLPH, RICHARD 1970 *The Civil Rights Record.* New York: Crowell.

KONVITZ, MILTON R. 1961 *A Century of Civil Rights.* New York: Columbia University Press.

MURRAY, PAULI 1961 *States' Laws on Race and Color.* New York: Woman's Division of Christian Service, The Methodist Church.

U.S. COMMISSION ON CIVIL RIGHTS 1970 *Federal Civil Rights Enforcement Effort.* Washington, D.C.: U.S. Government Printing Office.

ANTI-FEDERALIST CONSTITUTIONAL THOUGHT

The men who opposed the Constitution's unconditional RATIFICATION in 1787–1788 were called Anti-Federalists, although they claimed to be the true federalists and the true republicans. Contrary to common opinion, their major contribution to the American founding lies more in their critical examination of the new form of FEDERALISM and the new form of republican government than in their successful argument for a BILL OF RIGHTS.

The federalism issue was complicated by an ambiguity in usage during the Confederation period and by changes in both the Federalist and Anti-Federalist conceptions of federalism during the ratification debates. HERBERT J. STORING has explained the ambiguity by showing how "federal" referred to measures designed to strengthen the national authority, as opposed to state authority, but also to the principle of state supremacy. In the CONSTITUTIONAL CONVENTION, the federal principle meant congressional reliance on state requisitions for armies and taxes, in contrast to the national principle of direct governmental authority over individuals. The Anti-Federalists argued that the Constitution, which strengthened the national authority, went beyond the federal principle by moving away from requisitions and state equality in representation. Supporters of the Constitution were able to take, and keep, the name Federalists by treating any recognition of the state governments in the Constitution (for example, election, apportionment, ratification, amendment) as evidence of federalism, thereby redefining the term. JAMES MADISON, in THE FEDERALIST #39, consequently called the Constitution partly federal, partly national. For their part, the authors of the two best Anti-Federalist writings, who wrote under the pseudonyms Brutus and Federal Farmer, conceded the need for some direct governmental authority over individuals, thereby acknowledging the inadequacy of traditional federalism.

The Anti-Federalists emphasized the need to restrict the national power to what was absolutely necessary to preserve the union. They proposed limiting the national taxing power to imported goods, relying on requisitions if that source was insufficient. Moreover, Brutus proposed limiting standing armies in time of peace to what was necessary for defending the frontiers. If it became necessary to raise an army to repel an attack, he favored a two-thirds vote by both houses of Congress.

As part of their argument that a consolidation of power in the general government was incompatible with republicanism, the Anti-Federalists frequently cited MONTESQUIEU for the proposition that republics must be small, lest the public good be sacrificed. But they agreed with the Federalists, against Montesquieu, that the first principle of republican government was the regulation and protection of individual rights, not the promotion of civic virtue. They also, with rare exceptions, assumed the necessity of representation, while Montesquieu mentioned it only in his discussion of England, not in his discussion of republics.

Defining republican government somewhere between a selfless dedication to the common good, on the one hand, and individualism plus the elective principle, on the other, the Anti-Federalists emphasized mildness in government as essential for public confidence. This mildness required a similarity "in manners, sentiments, and interests" between citizens and officials and among citizens themselves. This, in turn, made possible a genuine REPRESENTATION of the people. Federal Farmer called such representation and local jury trials "the essential parts of a free and good government."

When the Anti-Federalists examined the representation in Congress, they saw an emerging aristocracy. They claimed that the democratic class, especially the middle class or the yeomanry, would have little chance of gaining election against the aristocracy, the men of wealth and of political and professional prominence. Since the middle class was substantially represented in the state governments, the Anti-Federalists argued that the powers of Congress had to be restricted to produce a proper balance between the nation and the states.

The Anti-Federalist objections to the structure of the proposed government related either to federalism or to republicanism. As examples of the former, the Senate, despite state equality, did not satisfy federalism because the legislatures did not pay the senators and could not recall them, and because the voting was by individuals, not by state delegations. And Brutus, who viewed the JUDICIAL POWER as the vehicle of consolidation, objected to Congress's power to ordain and establish lower federal courts. He thought the state courts were adequate to handle every case arising under the Constitution in the first instance, and he favored a limited right of APPEAL to the Supreme Court. As examples of their republicanism, the Anti-Federalists feared the Senate, with its six-year term, plus reeligibility, and its substantial powers, especially regarding appointments and treaty-making, as a special source of aristocracy. The Anti-Federalists were only somewhat less critical of the executive. They favored the proposed mode of election but opposed reeligibility; they generally favored unity but wanted a separately elected council to participate in appointments; some supported and others opposed the qualified executive VETO POWER; and some expressed apprehension about the pardoning power and the COMMANDER-IN-CHIEF power. As for the judiciary, Brutus argued that the combination of tenure for GOOD BEHAVIOR plus a judicial power that extends to "all cases in law and EQUITY, arising under this Constitution," meant not only JUDICIAL REVIEW but JUDICIAL SUPREMACY. He preferred that the legislature interpret the Constitution, since the people could easily correct the errors of their lawmakers.

Finally, the Bill of Rights was as much a Federalist as an Anti-Federalist victory. The Anti-Federalists wanted a bill of rights to curb governmental power. When the Federalists denied the necessity of a federal bill of rights, on the ground that whatever power was not enumerated could not be claimed, the Anti-Federalists pointed to the Constitution's SUPREMACY CLAUSE and to the extensiveness of the enumeration of powers. Paradoxically, this decisive argument resulted in a bill of rights that confirmed the new federalism, with its extended republic. Neither the Anti-Federalist proposals to restrict the tax and WAR POWERS nor their proposal to restrict IMPLIED POWERS was accepted. Nevertheless, the Anti-Federalist concern about "big government" has continued to find occasional constitutional expression in the restrictive interpretation of the ENUMERATED POWERS, along with the TENTH AMENDMENT.

MURRAY DRY

Bibliography

KENYON, CECELIA 1966 *The Antifederalists.* Indianapolis: Bobbs-Merrill.

STORING, HERBERT J. 1981 *The Complete Anti-Federalist.* 7 Vols. Chicago: University of Chicago Press. (Volume 1 separately published in paperback as *What the Anti-Federalists Were For.*)

_____ 1978 The Constitution and the Bill of Rights. Pages 32–48 in M. Judd Harmon, ed., *Essays on the Constitution of the United States.* Port Washington, N.Y.: Kennikat Press Corp.

ANTIPEONAGE ACT OF 1867

See: Peonage

ANTITRUST LAW

Federal antitrust law comprises a set of acts of Congress, administrative regulations, and court decisions that attempt to regulate market structure and competitive behavior in the national economy. The substance of this law is found in the first two sections of the SHERMAN ACT (1890), which forbid concerted action in "restraint of trade" and acts that seek to "monopolize" any part of commerce. The COMMERCE CLAUSE is the nexus between antitrust law and constitutional law.

There are several persistent uncertainties concerning the proper meaning of these prohibitions: the extent to which they embody a particular concept of economic efficiency as a primary value; the degree to which they are designed to protect competition by valuing a market composed of a large number of small competitors rather than a few large units; and the extent to which they embody specific notions of consumer protection. Despite these disagreements, there is general consensus that the antitrust laws express a preference for free and open markets in which prices and production are set by competitive forces and in which neither restraint of trade nor monopolization determines important market conditions. The three most common forms of restraint of trade are competitor agreements to fix prices, to allocate customers and markets, and to exclude parties from the market by a boycott or group refusal to deal. Monopolization is behavior by a dominant firm in the relevant market designed to give the firm power to fix prices, set market conditions, and exclude potential competitors.

The antitrust laws have ancient roots in the English and American COMMON LAW. Most states have comparable laws which complement the congressional scheme with varying degrees of effectiveness. In addition, Congress has amended the original acts, most notably to deal with corporate mergers and consolidations and with price discrimination in the distribution of goods. After a generation of judicial interpretation of the Sherman Act's general prohibitions, Congress in 1914 adopted the CLAYTON ACT and FEDERAL TRADE COMMISSION ACT to supplement the Sherman Act with more specific prohibitions and to supplement judicial interpretation and enforcement with administrative agency rule-making and enforcement. Nonetheless, these additions are largely derivative; the Sherman Act's prohibitions of "restraints of trade" and "monopolization" remain the core of federal antitrust law.

Antitrust law bears a strong resemblance to constitutional law, both in the broad intentions and organic implications of its substantive law and in the methodology of its enforcement and interpretive growth. These laws have long been seen as more than simple statutes. The delphic demands of the Sherman Act are considered a structural imperative with social and political, as well as economic, implications. Justice HUGO L. BLACK summed up this perspective in *Northern Pacific Railroad v. United States* (1958): "The Sherman Act was designed to be a comprehensive charter of economic liberty aimed at preserving free and unfettered competition as the rule of trade. It rests on the premise that the unrestrained interaction of competitive forces will yield the best allocation of our economic resources, the lowest prices, the highest quality and the greatest material progress, while at the same time providing an environment conducive to the preservation of our democratic political and social institutions."

The Sherman Act was a political response to the threats presented by economic power associated with the industrial revolution in the late nineteenth century. Certainly farmers, industrial workers, and tradespersons suffered from the concentrated economic power of the new order. From their beginning, however, these laws also identified threats presented by concentrated economic power to the social and political fabric. The specifics of the Sherman Act are not demanded by the constitutional text, but they can be seen as the economic corollaries of a constitutional commitment to individual autonomy, free association, and the separation and division of power within society. The antitrust laws seek to prevent economic power from becoming so highly concentrated that political freedom is unworkable.

As units of economic organization have grown in size and markets have become more concentrated over the past century, the antitrust laws have provided one alternative to extensive and detailed governmental ECONOMIC REGULATION. In most of the world's political systems, industrialization has been matched by growing control of the economy by bureaucratic *dirigisme*. Although the American economy has hardly been free from governmental intervention, this involvement has been more modest as a result of the emphasis on private planning and control over enterprises through a competitive market regime. In this perspective, excessive bureaucratic control is seen as the enemy of both economic efficiency and individual liberty.

Not only do antitrust law and constitutional law share comparable legislative approaches; their interpretive processes also show strong similarities—a tendency reinforced by the degree to which the Supreme Court is given broad powers to articulate basic norms in both areas.

The antitrust laws present a uniquely varied set of enforcement procedures. In addition to the sanctions available under state law, the basic federal antitrust norms may be enforced by the Department of Justice in federal court either by criminal prosecution or by civil suit for INJUNCTION relief or DAMAGES. The Federal Trade Commission enforces the same basic norms by administrative CEASE AND DESIST ORDERS backed up by civil penalties. A third level of enforcement is available to any private party aggrieved through a damage action in federal court in which treble damages may be awarded. Finally, legislation enacted in 1976 permits state officials to bring damage actions in federal court on behalf of their citizens.

Antitrust cases may be instituted in any one of the federal district courts and be appealed to a court of appeals. Administrative proceedings may also be reviewed in any one of the courts of appeals. Thus, no single agency has policy control over the bringing of antitrust suits, nor is there any coordination of the often contradictory decisions by local courts and agencies below the level of the Supreme Court. To a degree familiar to constitutional lawyers but atypical in other areas of federal law, a question of antitrust law is not considered settled until the Supreme Court decides it. The Court accepts only a few antitrust cases each year for decision, and the doctrinal impact of these decisions is profound.

Both constitutional and antitrust law generate the "big case," that peculiarly American form of political controversy in the form of litigation. Although there is reason to doubt the actual influence of antitrust law on the grand issues of national economic structure, the bringing of a major case is properly seen as an important political event. The investment of personnel and resources needed to accumulate the economic data necessary to prove a claim under these laws has long presented a major constraint to full enforcement. A big case is likely to exceed the natural lifespan of the national administration that institutes the suit, and may extend beyond the professional career span of government attorneys. As a consequence, charges of monopolization and other abuses of dominant market position are relatively rare. Cases charging specific acts in restraint of trade—particularly price fixing, production limits, and other cartelization—are more common because they are more susceptible to proof within the limits of a judicial trial.

The constraint of the big case produce two kinds of attempts to avoid full trial of cases. First, the great majority of antitrust cases are settled by consent decrees in which the government or private plaintiff is granted substantial relief. Concerned about the consistency of this practice with public interest, Congress in 1976 amended the law to require fuller judicial examination and public scrutiny of proposed settlements. Second, the problems of the big case have promoted the development of other enforcement techniques. The Federal Trade Commission Act of 1914 and the short-lived COMMERCE COURT represent two efforts to move both legislation and enforcement out of court and into specialized forums. The Federal Trade Commission (FTC) has broad power to proscribe unfair and anticompetitive behavior by rule, but the full potential of this technique has never been realized. Recently a hostile Congress has suspended many of the more important FTC trade rules.

The FTC and the Justice Department have also issued guidelines stating when the government will bring antitrust suits against proposed mergers or other changes in industry structure perceived to threaten overconcentration or monopoly. Because the confidence of securities markets is normally crucial to a successful merger, the threat of a suit often forecloses such a transaction.

The Constitution and the Sherman Act both use language drawn primarily from English common law sources to respond to dimly perceived new social needs that were expected to extend far into the future. In both cases the choice of operative terms served effectively to delegate to the Supreme Court power to pour meaning into common law terms. As few would suggest today that the full meaning of DUE PROCESS OF LAW is found in eighteenth-century common law sources, few would suggest that the meaning of "restraint of trade" is to be found in congressional understanding (actually, misunderstanding) of that common law term at the time the Sherman Act was enacted.

This protean aspect of the Sherman Act has always engendered the complaint that the act provides inadequate guidance to the economic decision makers who are subject to the law's commands. Despite three generations of attempts to contain the law in more specific statutory prohibitions and to delegate its enforcement to administrative experts, antitrust law retains its strong similarity to the process of constitutional adjudication by judicial decision. Even in those few areas of antitrust enforcement marked by heavy reliance on the specifics of the Clayton Act or administrative rules, the Sherman Act's general concepts of restraint of trade and monopolization retain their influence, broadening and reshaping the narrower rules.

As in constitutional litigation, the shifting tides of antitrust interpretation follow major changes in American economic and social thought. The conception of "restraint of trade," for example, has been modified by a RULE OF REASON, which exempts reasonable restraints of trade from the antitrust laws. Most contracts of any duration restrain the freedom of the parties to enter the market by obligating the parties to deal with each other. By the middle of the eighteenth century, the common law prohibition on contracts in restraint of trade had been made into a rule prohibiting only unreasonable restraints. This rule, of course, vastly expanded the potential power of judges, who decide what is reasonable.

When Congress enacted the Sherman Act it certainly had in mind this common law doctrine—although perhaps not the doctrine's specifics. The text declares all contracts in restraint of trade illegal. A persistent interpretive theme from the beginning has been the extent to which the Sherman Act incorporates a rule of reason. During periods when the dominant political thought is permissive of consolidations or economic power, the rule of reason tends to enlarge, thus increasing the power of the lower federal judiciary, who typically have been sympathetic to business interests. This development complicates the trial of cases, for defendants are permitted to enlarge the inquiry with evidence that their behavior, while generally of a prohibited sort, was reasonable under the circumstances. In contrast, during periods of vigorous antitrust enforcement the rule of reason recedes in favor of a per se rule of violation.

The earliest period of interpretation of the Sherman Act was marked by the dominance of a per se approach: competitor agreements fixing prices or allocating markets were per se offenses and could not be justified by evidence that the prices fixed were reasonable, or that conditions in the industry demanded efforts to stabilize market prices. The tone of majority opinions began to change with STANDARD OIL COMPANY V. UNITED STATES (1911), in which a general rule of reason standard was announced. Opposition to this vague standard during WOODROW WILSON's Democratic administration contributed to the enactment of the Clayton Act and the Federal Trade Commission Act. With the arrival of "normalcy" under President WARREN C. HARDING, a permissive rule of reason again flowered, and remained dominant for two decades.

Not until the late 1930s, when a new Supreme Court was in place and the New Deal administration had turned away from unhappy experience with the *dirigisme* of the NATIONAL INDUSTRIAL RECOVERY ACT, did vigorous challenges to anticompetitive private market behavior again become popular. Per se rules forbidding a wide range of competitor collaboration and group refusals to deal were announced by the Court for the first time, or brought down from the attic in which they had lain since the Wilson era. This period lasted for a generation; toward its close in the late 1960s per se rules were extended beyond price fixing and competitor agreements to nonprice market allocations between manufacturers and distributors. The early 1970s brought changes in political climate and in the personnel of the Court, and again the course of antitrust doctrine changed. The new mood was apparent in a more restricted interpretation of merger policy, greater receptivity to distribution agreements, and the reassertion of the rule of reason in peripheral areas. As of the mid-1980s, however, the Court had not adopted the more radical shifts toward permissiveness urged by critics of the antitrust laws.

The Supreme Court's restrictive view of Congress's power under the commerce clause in the years following adoption of the Sherman Act produced an extremely narrow interpretation of the act in UNITED STATES V. E. C. KNIGHT COMPANY (1895). Manufacturing, said the Court, was not commerce; thus the act did not reach the stock transactions that gave one company almost complete control over sugar refining in the United States. Only "direct" restraints of interstate commerce itself were subject to the act, as the Court held in *Addyston Pipe & Steel Company v. United States* (1899). The "constitutional revolution" of the 1930s broadened not only the Court's conception of the commerce power but also its interpretation of the reach of the antitrust laws. By the time of SOUTH-EASTERN UNDERWRITERS ASSOCIATION V. UNITED STATES (1944), both changes were complete.

More recently, courts and commentators have noted a potential conflict between state authority to control alcoholic beverages under the TWENTY-FIRST AMENDMENT and claims that state regulatory authorities have participated in price fixing. This issue illustrates a more basic question: does the Sherman Act decree a national free market, or may the states depart from competitive structures for economic activity otherwise within their regulatory power? The issue has arisen in connection with state utility regulation, control of the legal and medical professions, and agricultural marketing programs, all of which operate on a franchise or monopoly regulation model rather than a free market model. In general, the Supreme Court has held that state action regulating a market does not violate federal law and those complying with state law are not in violation of federal law.

The antitrust laws raise other constitutional questions. The vague language of the Sherman Act has given rise to claims of unconstitutionality when that act is the basis of a felony prosecution. The "big case" raises a variety of due process concerns, for it presses the judicial model to the outer limits of its capacity. The meaning of the right to TRIAL BY JURY, for example, requires clarification in cases presenting the complexity and gargantuan size found in many antitrust suits.

Perhaps the most puzzling set of constitutional concerns involves the connections between the Sherman Act's prohibitions on collective behavior (which it describes as contracts, combinations, and conspiracies in restraint of trade) and the associational rights protected by the FIRST AMENDMENT. An agreement among competitors seeking to exclude other potential competitors from the market is a conspiracy under the Sherman Act, even if the competitors enlist government agencies in their effort. On the other hand, an agreement among members of an industry to petition the government for legal relief from the economic threat of their competitors is constitutionally protected political activity. Supreme Court opinions "distinguishing" between these two kinds of activity have resorted to a pejorative label to explain their results, finding the political activity immune from antitrust claims unless it is a sham.

Comparable tensions exist between the Sherman Act's prohibitions of economic boycotts—which are seen as concerted refusals to deal—and political boycotts. To maintain this distinction requires a worldview in which economics and politics are unconnected spheres. Yet boycotts are per se offenses under the Sherman Act and some courts have held that political boycotts are a protected form of political protest.

A third tension is found in the case of permissible "natural monopolies"—for example, the owners of the railway terminal at the only point on a wide river suitable for a railway crossing. For three quarters of a century the Court has held that such holders of monopoly power are obligated to share it fairly with others. Several of these decisions treat this obligation as one resembling governmental power which carries along with it an obligation of "due process" procedural fairness. These decisions might be said to impose the constitutional obligation of government on those private accumulations of power that are found not to be prohibited outright by the Sherman Act. Together, the Constitution and the Sherman Act thus represent a total response to the problems of concentrated power in modern society: the Constitution controls governmental power, and the antitrust law controls concentrations of private economic power. At the seam between public and private organizations, the two bodies of law combine to limit the excesses of concentrated power.

ARTHUR ROSETT

Bibliography

AREEDA, P. and TURNER, D. 1978–1980 *Antitrust Law: An Analysis of Antitrust Principles and their Application,* 5 vols. Boston: Little, Brown.

NEALE, A. D. and GOYDER, D. G. 1980 *The Antitrust Laws of the USA,* 3rd ed. Cambridge: At the University Press.

SULLIVAN, L. 1977 *Antitrust.* St. Paul, Minn.: West Publishing Co.

APEX HOSIERY COMPANY v. LEADER

310 U.S. 469 (1940)

Destroying the effect of CORONADO COAL COMPANY V. UNITED MINE WORKERS (1925), although not overruling it, this opinion marked the shift toward a prolabor sentiment in the Supreme Court. The Court reaffirmed the application of the SHERMAN ANTITRUST ACT to unions but held that even a strike that effected a reduction of goods in INTERSTATE COMMERCE was no Sherman Act violation if it furthered legitimate union objectives. (See ALLEN-BRADLEY COMPANY V. LOCAL #3, 1945.) A particularly violent sit-down strike at the Apex plant reduced the volume of goods in commerce and resulted in extensive physical damage. Did the act forbid the union's actions? Justice HARLAN FISKE STONE, for a 6–3 Court, condemned the union's conduct, declaring that the company had a remedy under state law, but held that restraints not outlawed by the Sherman Act when accomplished peacefully could not be brought within the law's scope because they were accompanied by violence. The Court also denied that the resulting restraint of trade fell under the act. The union was not proceeding illegally by acting to eliminate nonunion or commercial competition in the market, even though a production halt must accompany a strike and lead to a temporary restraint. Only if the restraint led to a monopoly, price control, or discrimination among consumers would a violation occur. The Court thus substituted a test of restraint in the marketplace for the test of intent previously announced in BEDFORD CUT STONE V. JOURNEYMEN STONECUTTERS (1927). In dissent, Chief

Justice CHARLES EVANS HUGHES, joined by Justices OWEN ROBERTS and JAMES C. MCREYNOLDS, insisted that the earlier decisions governed and that they had not confined the test of restraint to market control. The Court had abandoned its earlier approach; the next year it would supplement *Apex*, excluding both jurisdictional strikes and SECONDARY BOYCOTTS from Sherman Act coverage in *United States v. Hutcheson* (1941).

DAVID GORDON

(SEE ALSO: *Antitrust Law and the Constitution.*)

APODACA v. OREGON

See: *Johnson v. Louisiana*

APPALACHIAN ELECTRIC POWER COMPANY v. UNITED STATES
311 U.S. 377 (1940)

Until this decision, federal authority over waterways extended only to those that were navigable. In this case the Supreme Court agreed to review the scope of federal power over completely nonnavigable waters. The Appalachian Electric Company asserted that the WATER POWER ACT of 1920 did not apply to the New River because its waters were not navigable; moreover, the act imposed conditions dealing with neither navigation nor its protection. Justice STANLEY F. REED, for a 6–2 Court, concluded that it was sufficient that the river might eventually be made navigable, thus broadening the earlier definition of federal authority. The COMMERCE CLAUSE was the constitutional provision involved and navigation was merely one of its parts. "Flood control, watershed development, recovery of the cost of improvements through utilization of power [also renders navigable waters subject] to national planning and control in the broad regulation of commerce granted the Federal Government." Justice OWEN ROBERTS, joined by Justice JAMES C. MCREYNOLDS, dissented from Reed's expansion of the test for navigability: "No authority is cited and I think none can be cited which countenances any such test."

DAVID GORDON

APPEAL

An appeal is the invocation of the JURISDICTION of a higher court to reverse or modify a lower court's decision. Appeal from the decision of a federal district court, for example, is normally taken to a federal court of appeals. In earlier federal practice, an appeal was taken by way of a WRIT OF ERROR; today, the term "appeal" has replaced references to the former writ. In the Supreme Court, "appeal" is a term of art, referring to the Court's obligatory APPELLATE JURISDICTION. In this sense, filing an appeal is distinguished from petitioning for a WRIT OF CERTIORARI, which is the method of invoking the Court's discretionary jurisdiction.

In a case coming to the Supreme Court from a state court, appeal is the appropriate remedy when the highest state court has rejected one of two types of claims based on federal law: either the state court has upheld a state law, rejecting the claim that the law violates the federal Constitution or a federal statute or treaty, or it has held invalid a federal statute or treaty. In those two kinds of cases, the Supreme Court is, in theory, obliged to review state court decisions; in all other cases, only the discretionary remedy of certiorari is available. A similarly obligatory review, by way of appeal, is appropriate when a federal court of appeals holds a state statute invalid. However, the overwhelming majority of court of appeals decisions reviewed by the Supreme Court lie within the Court's discretionary review, on writ of certiorari.

Whether a case is or is not an appropriate case for an appeal lies to some extent within the control of counsel, who may be able to cast the case as a challenge to the constitutionality of a state law as applied to particular facts. Yet some cases lie outside counsel's power to characterize; thus, a claim that a valid statute is being applied in a discriminatory manner, in violation of the equal protection clause, is reviewable only on certiorari.

With each passing year the practical distinction between appeal and certiorari has lessened. The Supreme Court often dismisses an appeal "for want of a substantial federal question" under circumstances strongly indicating the Court's determination, on a discretionary basis, that the appeal is not worthy of being heard. Furthermore, the Court has had the power since 1925 to treat improperly filed appeal papers as if they were a petition for certiorari. The same "RULE OF FOUR" applies to both appeal and certiorari: the vote of four Justices is necessary for a case to be heard. With these factors in mind, commentators have persistently urged Congress to abolish the Supreme Court's appeal jurisdiction entirely, leaving the Court in full discretionary control over the cases it will hear.

KENNETH L. KARST

Bibliography

STERN, ROBERT L. and GRESSMAN, EUGENE 1978 *Supreme Court Practice,* 5th ed. Chaps. 2–5. Washington, D.C.: Bureau of National Affairs.

APPELLATE JURISDICTION

A court's appellate jurisdiction is its power to review the actions of another body, usually a lower court. The appellate jurisdiction of our federal courts lies within the control of Congress. Article III of the Constitution, after establishing the Supreme Court's ORIGINAL JURISDICTION over certain cases, gives the Court appellate jurisdiction over all other types of cases within "the JUDICIAL POWER OF THE UNITED STATES," but empowers Congress to make "exceptions and regulations" governing that jurisdiction. In the JUDICIARY ACT OF 1789 Congress did not, formally, make exceptions to the Supreme Court's appellate jurisdiction; rather it purported to *grant* the Court jurisdiction to hear various types of cases on WRIT OF ERROR. The assumption has been that such an affirmative grant of appellate jurisdiction over specified types of cases is, by implication, an "exception," excluding the Court from taking appellate jurisdiction over cases not mentioned.

The Supreme Court itself accepted this line of reasoning in EX PARTE MCCARDLE (1869), stating that without a statutory grant of appellate jurisdiction it had no power to hear a case. Read broadly, this holding empowers Congress to undermine JUDICIAL REVIEW by withdrawing the Supreme Court's most important functions. Some commentators argue that Congress, in controlling the Supreme Court's appellate jurisdiction, is constitutionally bound to respect the Court's essential role in a system of SEPARATION OF POWERS. Other writers, however, reject this view, and the Supreme Court has been presented with no modern occasion to face the issue. (See JUDICIAL SYSTEM.)

Whatever the Constitution may ultimately require, Congress has acted on the assumption that it need not extend the Supreme Court's appellate jurisdiction to occupy the whole of the judicial power established by Article III. Until 1925, for example, the Court's appellate review of civil cases was limited by a requirement of a certain dollar amount in controversy. For the first century of the Court's existence, it had no general appellate jurisdiction over federal criminal cases, but reviewed such a case only on writ of HABEAS CORPUS or upon a lower court's certification of a division of opinion on an issue of law. Until 1914, the Supreme Court could review state court decisions only when they *denied* claims of federal right, not when they validated those claims. Although all these major limitations on the Court's appellate jurisdiction have now been eliminated, the halls of Congress perennially ring with calls for removing the Court's power over cases involving such emotion-charged subjects as SUBVERSIVE ACTIVITIES, school prayers, or ABORTION.

From the beginning the Supreme Court has reviewed cases coming from the lower federal courts and the state courts. The latter jurisdiction has been the source of political controversy, not only in its exercise but in its very existence. In a doctrinal sense, the power of Congress to establish the Court's appellate jurisdiction over state court decisions was settled early, in MARTIN V. HUNTER'S LESSEE (1816). In the realm of practical politics, the issue was settled when any serious thoughts of INTERPOSITION or NULLIFICATION were laid to rest by the outcome of the Civil War. (Ironically, the CONFEDERATE CONSTITUTION had provided a similar appellate jurisdiction for the Confederacy's own supreme court.) By the late 1950s, when the Court confronted intense opposition to school DESEGREGATION, its appellate jurisdiction was firmly entrenched; southern efforts to curb the Court failed miserably.

The Supreme Court's review of state court decisions is limited to issues of federal law. Even federal questions will not be decided by the Court if the state court's judgment rests on an ADEQUATE STATE GROUND. By congressional statute the Court is instructed to review only FINAL JUDGMENTS of state courts, but this limitation is now riddled with judge-made exceptions. The Court does, however, obey strictly its statutory instruction to review the decision of only the highest state court in which judgment is available in a given case. As THOMPSON V. LOUISVILLE (1960) shows, even a justice of the peace may constitute that "highest court" if state law provides no APPEAL from the justice's decision.

When the Supreme Court reviews a state court decision, all the jurisdictional limitations on the federal courts come into play. For example, although a state court may routinely confer STANDING on any state taxpayer to challenge state governmental action, the Supreme Court can take appellate jurisdiction only if the taxpayer satisfies the federal standards for standing.

Of the 4,000 cases brought to the Court in a typical year, only about 150 will be decided with full opinion. A large number of state criminal convictions raise substantial issues of federal constitutional law, but they largely go unreviewed in the Supreme Court. The WARREN COURT sought to provide a substitute federal remedy, facilitating access for state prisoners to federal habeas corpus. In the 1970s, however, the BURGER COURT drastically limited that access; in practical terms, a great many state convictions now escape review of their federal constitutional issues in any federal forum.

Final judgments of the federal district courts are normally reviewed in the courts of appeals, although direct appeal to the Supreme Court is available in a very few categories of cases. Usually, then, a case brought to the Supreme Court has already been the subject of one appeal. The Court thus can husband its resources for its main appellate functions: nourishing the development of a coherent body of federal law, and promoting that law's uniformity and supremacy.

For the Supreme Court's first century, its appellate jurisdiction was mostly obligatory; when Congress authorized a writ of error, the Court had no discretion to decline. The Court's second century has seen a progressive increase in the use of the discretionary WRIT OF CERTIORARI as a means of invoking Supreme Court review, with a corresponding decline in statutory entitlements to review on appeal. Today the Court has a high degree of discretion to choose which cases it will decide. Some observers think this discretion weakens the theoretical foundation of judicial review, expressed in MARBURY V. MADISON (1803). The Court there based its power to hold an act of Congress unconstitutional on the necessity to decide a case. If the Court has discretion whether to decide, the necessity disappears, and thus (so the argument goes) judicial review's legitimacy. Ultimately, that legitimacy may come to depend, both theoretically and politically, on the very power of congressional control so often seen as a threat to the Supreme Court's appellate jurisdiction.

KENNETH L. KARST

Bibliography

BATOR, PAUL M., MISHKIN, PAUL J., SHAPIRO, DAVID L., and WECHSLER, HERBERT, EDS. 1973 *The Federal Courts and the Federal System,* 2nd ed. Chaps. 5, 11. Mineola, N.Y.: Foundation Press.

APPOINTING AND REMOVAL POWER, PRESIDENTIAL

Article II, section 2, clause 2, of the Constitution provides in part that the President "shall nominate, and by and with the ADVICE AND CONSENT of the Senate, he shall appoint, Ambassadors, other public Ministers and Consuls, Judges of the Supreme Court, and all other Officers of the United States, whose appointments are not herein otherwise provided for, and which shall be established by Law." It goes on to authorize Congress to provide for the appointment of "inferior officers" by the President, the courts, or the heads of departments. The only patent ambiguity is in the distinction between the appointment of "inferior officers" and those presidential appointments requiring advice and consent of the Senate. This problem has given little cause for concern, perhaps because Congress has erred on the side of requiring advice and consent appointments, so that even every officer in the armed forces receives such a presidential appointment.

The processes of the appointment power were canvassed by JOHN MARSHALL in MARBURY V. MADISON (1803), where he also addressed the question that has plagued the construction of Article II, section 2, clause 2, not the meaning of the appointment provisions but what meaning they have for the removal power. The language of the Constitution is silent about removal, except for impeachment and the life tenure it gives to judges. Marshall said:

> Where an officer is removable at the will of the executive, the circumstance which completes his appointment is of no concern; because the act is at any time revocable; and the commission may be arrested, if still in the office. But when the officer is not removable at the will of the executive, the appointment is not revocable, and cannot be annulled. It has conferred legal rights which cannot be resumed.
>
> The discretion of the executive is to be exercised until the appointment has been made. But having once made the appointment, his power over the office is terminated in all cases, where by law the officer is not removable by him. The right to the office is *then* in the person appointed, and he has the absolute, and unconditional power of accepting or rejecting it.
>
> Mr. Marbury, then, since his commission was signed by the president, and sealed by the secretary of state, was appointed; and as the law creating the office, gave the officer a right to hold for five years, independent of the executive, the appointment was not revocable, but vested in the officer legal rights, which are protected by the laws of his country.

Obviously, it was to Congress that Marshall ascribed the power to determine the length of the term, and the conditions for removal, except that all officers of the United States were removable by the process of IMPEACHMENT.

The question whether an appointment made by the President with the advice and consent of the Senate could be terminated by the executive without such senatorial approval was soon mooted. ALEXANDER HAMILTON had answered the question in THE FEDERALIST #77:

It has been mentioned as one of the advantages to be expected from the cooperation of the Senate, in the business of appointments, that it would contribute to the stability of the administration. The consent of that body would be necessary to displace as well as to appoint. A change of the Chief Magistrate, therefore, would not occasion so violent or so general a revolution in the officers of the government as might be expected, if he were the sole disposer of offices. Where a man in any station had given satisfactory evidence of his fitness for it, a new President would be restrained from attempting a change in favor of a person more agreeable to him, by the apprehension that a discountenance of the Senate might frustrate the attempt, and bring some discredit upon himself. Those who can best estimate the value of a steady administration, will be most disposed to prize a provision which connects the official existence of public men with the approbation or disapprobation of that body, which from the greater permanence of its own composition, will in all probability be less subject to inconsistency than any other member of the government.

Thus spake the founding father most given to support a strong presidency.

In the very first Congress, however, when it was concerned with the creation of the office of secretary of state, there was extensive debate about whether the removal power was inherently an executive function and therefore not to be encumbered by the necessity for senatorial approval. It was conceded that the appointment power, too, was intrinsically an executive power and, but for constitutional provision to the contrary, would have remained untrammeled by legislative authority. JAMES MADISON thus construed the provision in his lengthy argument in the House of Representatives: the President did not need the acquiescence of the Senate to remove an official who had been appointed with its consent. The impasse that developed in the House was resolved not by choosing one side or the other of the controversial question but rather by omission of any provision concerning the power of removal. Madison's position at the CONSTITUTIONAL CONVENTION OF 1787 had been that the President, like the king, should have the appointment power without condition. He failed to carry the Convention on that point. He sought in the legislature to protect the President's exclusive power of removal. He failed there, too, although the point was not taken definitively against him as it had been at the Convention. But if he failed in 1789, he was nevertheless to be vindicated in MYERS V. UNITED STATES (1926).

The issue had not remained moribund in the interim. In 1833, when ANDREW JACKSON removed two secretaries of the treasury for refusing to withdraw government deposits from the BANK OF THE UNITED STATES and put ROGER B. TANEY in their place, motions of censure were moved and passed in the Senate, supported by DANIEL WEBSTER, HENRY CLAY, and JOHN C. CALHOUN. But Jackson had his way, as he usually did. The issue reached proportions of a constitutional crisis in 1867, when President ANDREW JOHNSON was impeached, largely on the ground that he had violated the TENURE OF OFFICE ACT which forbade the removal of a cabinet officer before his successor had been nominated and approved by the Senate. Johnson escaped a guilty verdict in the Senate because the vote fell one shy of the two-thirds necessary for conviction. There were other instances in which the courts were called upon for construction of the removal power, and for the most part the decisions sided with the President, but usually by statutory rather than constitutional construction.

The controlling Supreme Court decision came in the *Myers* case in 1926, which arose out of the removal by the President of a local postmaster. Here Chief Justice WILLIAM HOWARD TAFT, after his experience as chief magistrate, was not prepared to tolerate the suggestion that a President could have foisted on his administration aides that he did not want, even if the aide were only a lowly postmaster. Perhaps Taft's first concern was that Congress would take over the execution of the laws by the creation of independent agencies over whose members the President would have no control at all if he could not exercise the power of removal. That was not the issue in *Myers*, but Taft wished to forestall future problems of independent agencies as well as to lay to rest the canard that the President could not remove those in the direct chain of command, such as a postmaster. He read the debates in the first Congress as establishing Madison's position rather than bypassing it. It took seventy pages of abuse of history to make Taft's point. The presidential power of removal thus became plenary. Justice OLIVER WENDELL HOLMES, in dissent, disposed of the Taft position in less than a page:

We have to deal with an office that owes its existence to Congress and that Congress may abolish tomorrow. Its duration and the pay attached to it while it lasts depend on Congress alone. Congress alone confers on the President the power to appoint to it and at any time may transfer that power to other hands. With such power over its own creation, I have no more trouble in believing that Congress has power to prescribe a term of life for it free from any interference than I have in accepting the undoubted power of Congress to decree its end. I have equally little trouble in accepting its power to prolong the tenure of an incumbent until Congress or the Senate shall have assented to his removal. The duty of the President to see that the laws be executed is a duty that does not go beyond the laws or require him to achieve more than Congress sees fit to leave within his power.

History, however, has been on the side of Taft and Madison rather than on that of Hamilton, Marshall, and Holmes. An exception has been carved by the Court from the President's power of removal where the incumbent is charged with duties that may be called judicial, even if mixed with legislative and executive discretion, such as those involved in HUMPHREY'S EXECUTOR V. UNITED STATES (1935). Thus, Taft's championing of the presidential removal power has been sustained, except in the situation that bothered him most, the independent administrative agencies where legislative, executive, and judicial powers are all exercised by the incumbent.

PHILIP B. KURLAND

Bibliography

CORWIN, EDWARD S. 1927 Tenure of Office and the Removal Power under the Constitution. *Columbia Law Review* 27:353–399.

KURLAND, PHILIP B. 1978 *Watergate and the Constitution,* chap. 5. Chicago: University of Chicago Press.

MILLER, CHARLES A. 1969 *The Supreme Court and the Uses of History.* Chap. 4. Cambridge, Mass.: Harvard University Press.

APPOINTMENT OF SUPREME COURT JUSTICES

Under Article II, section 2, of the Constitution, Supreme Court Justices, like all other federal judges, are nominated and, with the ADVICE AND CONSENT of the Senate, appointed by the President. No other textual mandate, either procedural or substantive, governs the Chief Executive's selection. However, section 1 of Article III—which deals exclusively with the judicial branch of the government—provides GOOD BEHAVIOR tenure for all federal judges; in effect, that means appointment for life. As additional security, that provision of the Constitution provides that the compensation of federal judges "shall not be diminished during their Continuance in Office." But neither the Constitution nor any federal statute provides any clue as to qualifications for office; neither a law degree nor any other proof of professional capability is formally required. But in practice none other than lawyers are appointable to the federal judiciary, in general, and the Supreme Court, in particular. All of the 102 individuals who sat on that highest tribunal through 1985 held degrees from a school of law or had been admitted to the bar via examination. Indeed, although all the Justices were members of the professional bar in good standing at the time of their appointment, it was not until 1922 that a majority of sitting Justices was composed of law school graduates, and not until 1957 that every Justice was a law school graduate. Once confirmed by the Senate, a Justice is removable only via IMPEACHMENT (by simple majority vote by the House of Representatives) and subsequent conviction (by two-thirds vote of the Senate, there being a quorum on the floor). Only one Justice of the Supreme Court has been impeached by the House—Justice SAMUEL CHASE, by a 72–32 vote in 1804—but he was acquitted on all eight charges by the Senate in 1805. To all intents and purposes, once appointed, a Supreme Court Justice serves as long as he or she wishes—typically until illness or death intervenes.

Theoretically, the President has *carte blanche* in selecting his nominees to the Court. In practice, three facts of political life inform and limit his choices. The first is that it is not realistically feasible for the Chief Executive to designate a Justice and obtain confirmation by the Senate without the at least grudging approval by the two home state senators concerned, especially if the latter are members of the President's own political party. The time-honored practice of "Senatorial courtesy" is an omnipresent phenomenon, because of senatorial camaraderie and the "blue slip" approval system, under which the Judiciary Committee normally will not favorably report a nominee to the floor if an objecting home-state senator has failed to return that slip. (Senator Edward Kennedy, during his two-year tenure as head of the Committee, abandoned the system in 1979, but it was partly restored by his successor, Senator Strom Thurmond, in 1981.) Although nominations to the Supreme Court are regarded as a personal province of presidential choice far more than the appointment of other judges, the Senate's "advice and consent" is neither routine nor perfunctory, to which recent history amply attests. In 1968, despite a favorable Judiciary Committee vote, the Senate refused to consent to President Johnson's promotion of Justice ABE FORTAS to the Chief Justiceship; in 1969 it rejected President RICHARD M. NIXON's nomination of Judge Clement Haynsworth, Jr., by 55 to 45; and in 1970 it turned down that same President's selection of Judge G. Harrold Carswell by 51 to 45. Indeed, to date the Senate, for a variety of reasons, has refused to confirm twenty-seven Supreme Court nominees out of the total of 139 sent to it for its "advice and consent" (twenty-one of these during the nineteenth century).

The second major factor to be taken into account by the President is the evaluative role played by the American Bar Association's fourteen-member Committee on the Federal Judiciary, which has been an unofficial part of the judicial appointments process since 1946. The committee scrutinizes the qualifications of all nominees to the federal bench and normally assigns one of four "grades": Exceptionally Well Qualified, Well Qualified, Qualified, and Not Qualified. In the rare instances of a vacancy on the Supreme Court, however, the committee has in recent years adopted a different, threefold, categorization: "High Standards of Integrity, Judicial Temperament, and Professional Competence"; "Not Opposed"; and "Not Qualified."

The third consideration incumbent upon the Chief Executive is the subtle but demonstrable one of the influence, however *sub rosa* and *sotto voce,* of sitting and retired jurists. Recent research points convincingly to that phenomenon, personified most prominently by Chief Justice WILLIAM HOWARD TAFT. If Taft did not exactly "appoint" colleagues to vacancies that occurred during his nine-year tenure (1921–1930), he assuredly vetoed those unacceptable to him. Among others also involved in advisory or lobbying roles, although on a lesser scale than Taft, were Chief Justices CHARLES EVANS HUGHES, HARLAN F. STONE, FRED VINSON, EARL WARREN, and WARREN E. BURGER and Associate Justices JOHN MARSHALL HARLAN I, SAMUEL F. MILLER, WILLIS VAN DEVANTER, LOUIS D. BRANDEIS, and FELIX FRANKFURTER.

A composite portrait of the 101 men and one woman who have been Justices of the Supreme Court provides the following cross-section: native-born: 96; male: 101 (the first woman, SANDRA DAY O'CONNOR, was appointed by President RONALD REAGAN in the summer of 1981); white: 101 (the first black Justice, THURGOOD MARSHALL, was appointed by President LYNDON B. JOHNSON in 1967); predominantly Protestant: 91 (there have been six Roman Catholic and five Jewish Justices—the first in each category were ANDREW JACKSON's appointment of Chief Justice ROGER B. TANEY in 1836 and WOODROW WILSON's of Louis D. Brandeis in 1916, respectively); 50–55 years of age at time of appointment (the two youngest have been JOSEPH STORY, 33, in 1812 and WILLIAM O. DOUGLAS, 41, in 1939); of Anglo-Saxon ethnic stock (all except fifteen); from an upper middle to high social status (all except a handful); reared in a nonrural but not necessarily urban environment; member of a civic-minded, politically aware, economically comfortable family (all except a handful); holders of B.A. and, in this century, LL.B. or J.D. degrees (with one-third from "Ivy League" institutions); and a background of at least some type of public or community service (all except Justice GEORGE SHIRAS). Contemporary recognition of egalitarianism and "representativeness" may alter this profile, but it is not likely to change radically.

Only the President and his close advisers know the actual motivations for the choice of a particular Supreme Court appointee. But a perusal of the records of the thirty-five Presidents who nominated Justices (four—W. H. Harrison, ZACHARY TAYLOR, ANDREW JOHNSON, and JIMMY CARTER—had no opportunity to do so) points to several predominating criteria, most apparent of which have been: (1) objective merit; (2) personal friendship; (3) considerations of "representativeness"; (4) political ideological compatibility, what THEODORE ROOSEVELT referred to as a selectee's "real politics"; and (5) past judicial experience. Appropriate examples of (1) would be BENJAMIN N. CARDOZO (HERBERT HOOVER) and JOHN MARSHALL HARLAN (DWIGHT D. EISENHOWER); of (2) HAROLD H. BURTON (HARRY S. TRUMAN) and Abe Fortas (Lyndon Johnson); of (4) HUGO BLACK (FRANKLIN D. ROOSEVELT) and William Howard Taft (WARREN G. HARDING); of (5) OLIVER WENDELL HOLMES (Theodore Roosevelt) and DAVID J. BREWER (BENJAMIN HARRISON). Deservedly most contentious is motivation (3), under which Presidents have been moved to weigh such "equitable" factors as geography, religion, gender, race, and perhaps even age in order to provide a "representative" profile of the Court. Of uncertain justification, it is nonetheless a fact of life of the appointive process. Thus geography proved decisive in Franklin D. Roosevelt's selection of WILEY RUTLEDGE of Iowa ("Wiley, you have geography," Roosevelt told him) and ABRAHAM LINCOLN's selection of STEPHEN J. FIELD of California. But given the superb qualifications of Judge Cardozo, despite the presence of two other New Yorkers (Hughes and Stone), the former's selection was all but forced upon Hoover. The notion that there should be a "Roman Catholic" and "Jewish" seat has been present ever since the appointments of Taney and Brandeis. Although there have been periods without such "reserved" seats (for example, 1949–1956 in the former case and since 1965 in the latter), Presidents are aware of the insistent pressures for such "representation." These pressures have increased since the "establishment" of a "black" seat (Marshall in 1967, by Johnson) and a "woman's seat" (O'Connor, by Reagan, in 1981). It has become all but unthinkable that future Supreme Court lineups will not henceforth have "representatives" from such categories. That the Founding Fathers neither considered nor addressed any of these "representative" factors does not gainsay their presence and significance in the political process.

Whatever may be the merits of other criteria motivating presidential Supreme Court appointments, the key factor is the Chief Executive's perception of a candidate's "real" politics—for it is the nominee's likely voting pattern as a Justice that matters most to an incumbent President. To a greater or lesser extent, all Presidents have thus attempted to "pack" the bench. Court-packing has been most closely associated with Franklin D. Roosevelt. Failing a single opportunity to fill a Court vacancy during his first term (and five months of his second), and seeing his domestic programs consistently battered by "the Nine Old Men," Roosevelt moved to get his way in one fell swoop with his "Court Packing Bill" of 1937; however, it was reported unfavorably by the Senate Judiciary Committee and was interred by a decisive recommittal vote. Ultimately, the passage of time enabled him to fill nine vacancies between 1937 and 1943. Yet GEORGE WASHINGTON was able to nominate fourteen, of whom ten chose to serve, and his selectees were measured against a sextet of criteria: (1) support and advocacy of the Constitution; (2) distinguished service in the revolution; (3) active participation in the political life of the new nation; (4) prior judicial experience on lower tribunals; (5) either a "favorable reputation with his fellows" or personal ties with Washington himself; and (6) geographic "suitability." Whatever the specific predispositions may be, concern with a nominee's "real" politics has been and will continue to be crucial in presidential motivations. It even prompted Republican President Taft to award half of his six nominations to the Court to Democrats, who were kindred "real politics" souls (HORACE H. LURTON, EDWARD D. WHITE's promotion to Chief Justice, and JOSEPH R. LAMAR). In ten other instances the appointee came from a formal political affiliation other than that of the appointer, ranging from Whig President JOHN TYLER's appointment of Democrat SAMUEL NELSON in 1845 to Republican Richard M. Nixon's selection of Democrat LEWIS F. POWELL, JR., in 1971.

But to predict the ultimate voting pattern or behavior of a nominee is to lean upon a slender reed. In the characteristically blunt words of President Truman: "Packing the Supreme Court simply can't be done. . . . I've tried and it won't work. . . . Whenever you put a man on the Supreme Court he ceases to be your friend. I'm sure of that." There is indeed a considerable element of unpredictability in the judicial appointment process. To the question whether a judicial robe makes a person any different, Justice Frankfurter's sharp retort was always, "If he is any good, he does!" In ALEXANDER M. BICKEL's words, "You shoot an arrow into a far-distant future when you appoint a Justice and not the man himself can tell you what he will think about some of the problems that he will face." And late in 1969, reflecting upon his sixteen years as Chief Justice of the United States, Earl Warren pointed out that he, for one, did not "see how a man could be on the Court and not change his views substantially over a period of years . . . for change you must if you are to do your duty on the Supreme Court." It is clear beyond doubt that the Supreme Court appointment process is fraught with imponderables and guesswork, notwithstanding the carefully composed constitutional obligations of President and Senate.

HENRY J. ABRAHAM

Bibliography

ABRAHAM, HENRY J. 1985 *Justices and Presidents: A Political History of Appointments to the Supreme Court,* 2nd ed. New York: Oxford University Press.

______ 1986 *The Judicial Process: An Introductory Analysis of the Courts of the United States, England and France,* 5th ed. New York: Oxford University Press.

DANELSKI, DAVID J. 1964 *A Supreme Court Justice Is Appointed.* New York: Random House.

SCHMIDHAUSER, JOHN R. 1960 *The Supreme Court: Its Politics, Personalities and Procedures.* New York: Holt, Rinehart & Winston.

______ 1979 *Judges and Justices: The Federal Appellate Judiciary.* Boston: Little, Brown.

APPORTIONMENT

See: Reapportionment

APTHEKER v. SECRETARY OF STATE

378 U.S. 500 (1959)

Two top leaders of the Communist party appealed the revocation of their passports under section 6 of the Subversive Activities Control Act of 1950.

Justice ARTHUR J. GOLDBERG, in a plurality opinion for a 6–3 Supreme Court, held that that section "too broadly and indiscriminately restrict[ed] the RIGHT TO TRAVEL" and therefore abridged the liberty protected by the Fifth Amendment. The section was overly broad on its face because it did not discriminate between active and inactive members of subversive groups or among the various possible purposes for foreign travel.

Justices HUGO L. BLACK and WILLIAM O. DOUGLAS, concurring, would have held the entire act unconstitutional.

DENNIS J. MAHONEY

ARGERSINGER v. HAMLIN
407 U.S. 25 (1972)

Argersinger culminated four decades of progression in RIGHT TO COUNSEL doctrine: from a DUE PROCESS requirement in CAPITAL PUNISHMENT cases, to application of the Sixth Amendment to the states in serious FELONIES, and finally, in *Argersinger,* to extension of the requirement to any case in which there is a sentence of imprisonment.

Argersinger, unrepresented by counsel, was convicted of a MISDEMEANOR and sentenced by a state court to ninety days in jail. The arguments in the Supreme Court were of an unusually practical rather than doctrinal nature. Much was made of the burden on state criminal justice systems that the extension of the right to counsel would cause. The state also argued that many misdemeanors, though carrying potential jail sentences, are exceedingly straightforward cases that a layperson could handle by him- or herself. Moreover, it was argued that people who can afford lawyers often do not hire them for such simple cases because the cost is not worth what a lawyer could accomplish. The Court rejected all these contentions and established imprisonment as a clear test for requiring the appointment of counsel.

Seven years later, in *Scott v. Illinois* (1979), the Court held that the appointment of counsel was not required for a trial when imprisonment was a possibility but was not actually imposed. The anomalous result is that a judge must predict before the trial whether he will impose imprisonment in order to know whether to appoint counsel.

BARBARA ALLEN BABCOCK

ARLINGTON HEIGHTS v. METROPOLITAN HOUSING DEVELOPMENT CORP.
429 U.S. 252 (1977)

This decision confirmed in another context the previous term's holding in WASHINGTON v. DAVIS (1976) that discriminatory purpose must be shown to establish race-based violations of the EQUAL PROTECTION clause. The Supreme Court declined to strike down a village's refusal to rezone land to allow multiple-family dwellings despite the refusal's racially discriminatory adverse effects. Writing for the Court, Justice LEWIS F. POWELL elaborated on the nature of the showing that must be made to satisfy the purpose requirement announced in *Washington v. Davis.* A plaintiff need not prove that challenged action rested solely on racially discriminatory purposes. Instead, proof that a discriminatory purpose was a motivating factor would require the offending party to prove that it would have taken the challenged action even in the absence of a discriminatory purpose. Powell noted the types of evidence that might lead to a finding of discriminatory purpose: egregious discriminatory effects, the historical background of the governmental action, departures from normal procedure, legislative and administrative history, and, in some instances, testimony by the decision makers themselves.

THEODORE EISENBERG

ARNETT v. KENNEDY
416 U.S. 134 (1974)

A fragmented Supreme Court held, 6–3, that a federal civil service employee had no PROCEDURAL DUE PROCESS right to a full hearing before being dismissed. Justice WILLIAM H. REHNQUIST, for three Justices, concluded that because the governing statute had provided for removal of an employee to "promote the efficiency of the service," the employee's "property" interest was conditioned by this limitation. Thus due process required no predismissal hearing. The other six Justices rejected this view, concluding that the Constitution itself defined the protection required, once the guarantee of procedural due process attached. However, three of the six found no right to a predismissal hearing in the protection defined by the Constitution. The dissenters, led by Justice WILLIAM J. BRENNAN, argued that GOLDBERG v. KELLY (1970) demanded a predismissal hearing, and commented that Justice Rehnquist's view would revive the "right–privilege" distinction that *Goldberg* had rejected. In BISHOP v. WOOD (1976) the Rehnquist position came to command a majority of the Court.

KENNETH L. KARST

ARNOLD, THURMAN
(1891–1969)

Law professor, assistant attorney general, and federal judge, Thurman Arnold of Wyoming was a vigorous champion of both CIVIL LIBERTIES and ANTITRUST regulation. In 1930, when Arnold joined the Yale Law School faculty, which included WILLIAM O. DOUGLAS and WALTON HAMILTON, he had already developed a social and psychological approach to law. He had an extraordinary commitment to the concept of FAIR TRIAL in which he saw ritual significance, and, in *The Symbols of Government* (1935), Arnold described law as a mode of symbolic thinking that conditioned behavior. A witty and sarcastic writer, he described the interplay between CORPORATIONS and antitrust law in *The Folklore of Capitalism* (1937). The following year President FRANKLIN D. ROOSEVELT chose him to head the Antitrust Division of the Justice Department. Arnold was a zealous enforcer of antitrust legislation; he launched over 200 major investigations and saw his budget and personnel quadruple before his departure in 1943 to become a federal judge. Naturally unsuited for judicial office, he resigned within two years to enter private practice where ABE FORTAS soon joined him. Arnold welcomed controversial issues and represented defendants in loyalty cases of the late 1940s and the McCarthy era. Arnold was a spirited libertarian, and his career reflected his belief in the need to erase traditional intellectual boundaries and integrate disciplines and approaches.

DAVID GORDON

Bibliography

KEARNY, EDWARD N. 1970 *Thurman Arnold, Social Critic.* Albuquerque: University of New Mexico Press.

ARREST

The constitutional law of arrest governs every occasion on which a government officer interferes with an individual's freedom, from full-scale custodial arrests at one end of the spectrum to momentary detentions at the other. Its essential principle is that a court, not a police officer or other executive official, shall ultimately decide whether a particular interference with the liberty of an individual is justified. The court may make this judgment either before an arrest, when the police seek a judicial warrant authorizing it, or shortly after an arrest without a warrant, in a hearing held expressly for that purpose. The law of arrest gives practical meaning to the ideal of the liberty of the individual, by defining the circumstances in which, and the degree to which, that liberty may be curtailed by the police or other officers of the government; it is thus a basic part of what we mean by the RULE OF LAW in the United States.

The principal constitutional standard governing arrest is the FOURTH AMENDMENT. This amendment is one article of the original BILL OF RIGHTS, which was held in BARRON V. BALTIMORE (1833) to apply only to the federal government. But in MAPP V. OHIO (1961) the Fourth Amendment was held to be among those provisions of the Bill of Rights that are "incorporated" in the FOURTEENTH AMENDMENT and is thus applicable to arrests by state as well as federal officers. (See INCORPORATION DOCTRINE.) Even without such a holding, of course, the Fourteenth Amendment, which regulates state interference with individual liberty, would have required the development of a body of law governing state arrests. The law so made might have been no less protective of the individual than the law actually made under the Fourth Amendment. As things are, however, the "unreasonableness" standard of the Fourth Amendment has been the basis of the constitutional law governing arrests by both federal and state officers.

What seizures are "unreasonable"? One obvious possibility is that seizures of the person should be held subject to the warrant clause, as searches are, and should accordingly be found "unreasonable" unless a proper warrant has been obtained or, by reason of emergency, excused. For many years the court flirted with such a rule, as in *Trupiano v. United States* (1948) and TERRY V. OHIO (1968), but it never flatly required a warrant for arrests, and in UNITED STATES V. WATSON (1976) it rejected that rule at least for FELONIES. This decision rested partly upon a historical English COMMON LAW rule excusing the warrant for felonies, but despite the similarities of language the analogy is not precise. In English law the term "felony" was reserved for offenses punishable by death and forfeiture, which give rise to a high probability of an attempt to flee; with us "felony" is usually defined by statute as an offense for which the possible punishment exceeds one year's imprisonment. The other basis for *Watson* was a combination of convenience and probability: because a warrant will in fact be excused on emergency grounds in a large class of cases, it is wise to dispense with the requirement entirely, and thus avoid the costs—improper arrests without warrants, delays to obtain unnecessary warrants—necessarily associated with close cases. The Court left open the possibility that arrest warrants may be required for MISDEMEANORS, at least (as at common law) for those not involving a BREACH OF THE PEACE nor committed in the presence of the arresting officer. This question is at present unresolved.

Somewhat more stable as a standard of reasonableness has been the substantive requirement that an arrest must be based upon PROBABLE CAUSE. This is not a term of scientific precision. It means essentially that an officer must demonstrate to a magistrate, before or after the arrest, that he has sufficient reason to believe in the guilt of the suspect to justify his arrest. Although probable cause is not susceptible of precise definition, the cases decided by the Court have gradually given it some content, especially where, as in SPINELLI V. UNITED STATES (1969), an officer's judgment rests on information received from another. In such cases the basic rule is that the officer must give the magistrate reason to trust the honesty of his informant, and reveal the grounds upon which the informant's charge rests—for example, that the informant saw a crime committed, or the suspect told him he had done it.

Probable cause is of course required only when there has been a "seizure" to which the Fourth Amendment speaks. The courts have found that term difficult to define as well, and difficult in ways that make the meaning of "probable cause" itself more uncertain. The world presents a wide range of police interferences with individual liberty, from minor detentions to full-scale incarceration, and it is widely agreed that some of these intrusions, at every level on the scale, are reasonable and appropriate and that others—again at every level—are inappropriate. Were every interference with liberty regarded as a "seizure" requiring demonstration of "probable cause," the Court would thus face a serious delemma: to hold minor intrusions invalid without a showing of traditional probable cause would outlaw an obviously important and generally accepted method of police work; but to permit them on probable cause grounds would water down the probable cause standard, greatly reducing the justification required to support a full-scale arrest. On the other hand, to hold that such intrusions were not "seizures" would seem to say that they are not regulated by the Fourth Amendment at all—nor under present doctrine, by the Fourteenth—and could therefore be inflicted upon a citizen at an officer's whim. In *Terry v. Ohio* the Court tried to deal with this problem by regarding some "seizures" (less than full-scale arrests) as not requiring "probable cause" but as nonetheless subject to the "reasonableness" requirement of the Fourth Amendment. *Terry* involved the detention of persons an officer reasonably suspected to be planning an armed robbery, during which he asked them their identity and frisked them for weapons. The Court took great pains to make clear that it was not establishing a general right to detain on less than probable cause, and that the "reasonableness" of the seizure validated there was closely tied to the protective nature of the officer's measures and to his realistic apprehension of danger. The Court intimated that no detention beyond that necessarily involved in the frisk would be valid. But cases since *Terry* have undercut that position deeply. In *Adams v. Williams* (1972), for example, the Court explicitly talked about a right to detain on suspicion, and in *United States v. Mendenhall* (1980) a plurality of the Court held that there is no seizure when officers merely approach a person and ask him questions, even if they intend to arrest him, unless he can establish "objective grounds" upon which a reasonable person in his position would have believed he was not free to go. On the other hand, *Dunaway v. New York* (1979) expressly refused to adopt the view that increasingly lengthy detentions were permissible on increasingly good justification (which would effectively eliminate the idea that probable cause is required before "arrest," except in the technical sense of full-custody arrest); and *Delaware v. Prouse* (1979) held that a person driving a car may be stopped upon less than probable cause, but only if there is reasonable suspicion of a violation of law.

The precedents come to this: some confrontations between officers and citizens are not seizures at all; others are seizures that must be justified by a "reasonableness" requirement; still others are "arrests" for which probable cause is required. But there are no clear lines between the categories, and the Supreme Court has not given adequate attention to the ways in which a "seizure" can grow into an "arrest," thus defeating the basic aim of the probable cause requirement.

JAMES BOYD WHITE

Bibliography

HALE, MATTHEW (1685)1972 *The Pleas of the Crown.* London: Professional Books.

LAFAVE, WAYNE R. 1978 *Search and Seizure: A Treatise on the Fourth Amendment.* Mineola, N.Y.: Foundation Press.

ARREST WARRANT

Under the FOURTH AMENDMENT, arrest warrants, like SEARCH WARRANTS, may be issued only upon PROBABLE CAUSE, supported by oath or affirmation, and particularly describing the person to be seized. Much of the constitutional doctrine governing search warrants is therefore applicable by analogy to arrest warrants.

At English COMMON LAW, a law enforcement officer was authorized to make a warrantless arrest when he had reasonable grounds to believe that a FELONY had been committed and that the person to be arrested was the perpetrator. A warrantless misdemeanor arrest, however, was permitted only when the misdemeanor was committed in the officer's presence. Consistent with this rule, Congress and almost all states have permitted warrantless arrests in public places since the beginning of the nation.

In view of this history, the Supreme Court held in UNITED STATES V. WATSON (1976) that the Fourth Amendment does not require a law enforcement officer to obtain a warrant for a felony arrest made in a public place even though there may be ample opportunity to obtain the warrant. Although recognizing that the preference for a neutral and detached magistrate applies to the issuance of arrest warrants, the Court reasoned that this judicial preference was insufficient to justify a departure from the common law at the time of the adoption of the Fourth Amendment and from the judgment of Congress and the states.

It may be argued that the preference for a warrant for searches should apply with equal, if not greater, force to arrests because of the significant infringement of personal liberty involved. Unless history is to be regarded as irrelevant in constitutional interpretation, however, the result in *Watson* is correct in view of the unambiguous history relating to warrantless arrests in public places. Moreover, the Court in *Gerstein v. Pugh* (1975) recognized that after a warrantless arrest a timely judicial determination of probable cause is a prerequisite to detention.

The Court has distinguished between arrests made in public places and those made in private homes. Because of, among other things, the historical importance attached to one's privacy at home and the uncertainty in the common law over warrantless arrests in private homes, a law enforcement officer may not enter a person's home to make an arrest without first obtaining a warrant. The distinction has been made in such cases as PAYTON V. NEW YORK (1980) and STEAGALD V. UNITED STATES (1981).

Probable cause in the context of arrest warrants means probable cause to believe that a crime was committed and that the person to be arrested committed it. Unlike a search warrant, an arrest warrant may be issued on the basis of a grand jury INDICTMENT, provided that the GRAND JURY is "properly constituted" and the indictment is "fair upon its face." The Court's willingness to let a grand jury's judgment substitute for that of a neutral and detached magistrate is attributable to that grand jury's relationship to the courts and its historical role in protecting individuals from unjust prosecution. An INFORMATION filed by a prosecutor, by contrast, will not justify the issuance of an arrest warrant, for the prosecutor's role is inconsistent with that of a neutral and detached magistrate.

The particularity requirement, expressly applied to arrest warrants by the warrant clause, mandates that the warrant contain sufficient information to identify the person to be arrested. It is intended to preclude the use of a general or "dragnet" arrest warrant.

If a person is illegally arrested without a warrant, such an arrest will not prevent the person from being tried or invalidate his conviction. Any EVIDENCE obtained as a result of the arrest, however, including statements made by the person arrested, may be excluded under the FRUIT OF THE POISONOUS TREE DOCTRINE as applied in WONG SUN V. UNITED STATES (1963).

JAMES R. ASPERGER

Bibliography

LAFAVE, WAYNE R. 1978 *Search and Seizure: A Treatise on the Fourth Amendment.* Vol. 2:215–260. St. Paul, Minn.: West Publishing Co.

ARTHUR, CHESTER A. (1830–1886)

A New York lawyer and politician, Chester Alan Arthur was nominated for vice-president in 1880 to placate the ULYSSES S. GRANT or "stalwart" branch of the Republican party. In September 1881 Arthur became President when President JAMES GARFIELD was assassinated. Although his previous political activities had revolved around the New York customs house and the distribution of Republican patronage, as President Arthur supported civil service reform and opposed unnecessary federal expenditures. He was denied the Republican nomination in 1884 by a combination of reformers, who did not trust him, and by party members opposed to any reforms.

PAUL FINKELMAN

Bibliography

DUENECKE, JUSTIN D. 1981 *The Presidencies of James A. Garfield and Chester A. Arthur.* Lawrence: Regents Press of Kansas.

ARTICLE III

See: Judicial Power of the United States

ARTICLE III COURTS

See: Constitutional Courts

ARTICLES OF CONFEDERATION

On March 1, 1781, Congress proclaimed ratification of the constitution for a confederation named "the United States of America." People celebrated with fireworks and toasts, and a Philadelphia newspaper predicted that the day would forever be memorialized "in the annals of America. . . ." Another newspaper gave thanks because the states had at last made perpetual a union begun by the necessities of war.

The war was only three months old when BENJAMIN FRANKLIN proposed the first continental constitution. He called it "Articles of Confederation and Perpetual Union," a name that stuck. Because the war was then being fought to achieve a reconciliation with England on American terms, Congress would not even consider Franklin's plan. But a year later, when Congress appointed a committee to frame a DECLARATION OF INDEPENDENCE, it also appointed a committee, consisting of one member from each state, to prepare "the form of a confederation to be entered into by these colonies." JOHN DICKINSON of Pennsylvania, whom the committee entrusted to draft the document, borrowed heavily from Franklin's plan and seems not to have been influenced by other committee members. One complained that Dickinson's plan involved "the Idea of destroying all Provincial Distinctions and making every thing of the most minute kind bend to what they call the good of the whole."

Dickinson was a "nationalist" in the sense that he believed that a strong central government was needed to build a union that could effectively manage its own affairs and compete with other nations. Congress, which was directing the war, became the hub of the Confederation. It was a unicameral house in which each state delegation had a single vote, making the states equal, and Dickinson proposed no change. Franklin, by contrast, had recommended that REPRESENTATION in Congress be apportioned on the basis of population, with each delegate having one vote. Dickinson carried over Franklin's generous allocation of powers to Congress, except for a power over "general commerce." Neither Franklin nor Dickinson recommended a general tax power. Congress requisitioned monies from each state for a common treasury, leaving each state to raise its share by taxation. Congress had exclusive powers over war and peace, armies and navies, foreign affairs, the decision of disputes between states, admiralty and prize courts, the coinage of money and its value, borrowing money on the credit of the United States, Indian affairs, the western boundaries of the states claiming lands to the Pacific, the acquisition of new territory and the creation of new states, standards of weights and measures, and the post office. Dickinson also recommended a "council of state" or permanent executive agency that would enforce congressional measures and administer financial, diplomatic, and military matters. Dickinson proposed many limitations on state power, mainly to secure effective control over matters delegated to Congress. The states could not, for example, levy IMPOSTS or duties that violated treaties of the United States. Even the sovereign power of the states over their internal concerns was limited by the qualification in Article III, the crux of the Dickinson draft: "Each colony [Dickinson always referred to "colony" and not "state"] shall retain and enjoy as much of its present Laws, Rights and Customs, as it may think fit, and reserves to itself the sole and exclusive Regulation and Government of its internal police, in all matters that shall not interfere with the Articles of Confederation." Clearly Dickinson envisioned a confederation in which the states did not master the central government.

Nationalists who supported the Dickinson draft in Congress argued, as did JOHN ADAMS, that the purpose of the confederation was to meld the states into "one common mass. We shall no longer retain our separate individuality" on matters delegated to Congress. The four New England states had the same relation to Congress that "four counties bore to a single state," Adams declared. The states could build roads and enact poor laws but "they have no right to touch upon continental subjects." JAMES WILSON, another centralist, contended that the Congress should represent all the people, not the states, because "As to those matters which are referred to Congress, we are not so many states, we are one large state." Few Congressmen were nationalists, however, and few nationalists were consistent. Congressmen from Virginia, the largest state, rejected state equality in favor of proportional representation in Congress with each delegate voting; but because Virginia claimed a western boundary on the Pacific, it rejected the nationalist contention that Congress had succeeded to British SOVER-

EIGNTY with respect to the West and should govern it for the benefit of all. Congressmen from Maryland, a small state without western claims, adamantly held to that nationalist position but argued for state equality—one state, one vote—on the issue of representation. How requisitions should be determined also provoked dissension based on little principle other than self-interest.

The disputes over representation, western lands, and the basis for requisitions deadlocked the Congress in 1776. The next year, however, state supremacists who feared centralization won a series of victories that decisively altered the character of the confederation proposed by Dickinson and championed by Franklin, Adams, and Wilson. Dickinson's Article III was replaced by a declaration that "Each State retains its sovereignty, freedom, and independence, and every power, jurisdiction, and right, which is not by this confederation expressly delegated to the United States, in Congress assembled." Thus, colonial control over internal police became state sovereignty over all reserved powers, and the central government received only "expressly delegated" powers rather than implied powers to control even internal police involving matters of continental concern. State supremacists also restricted the power of Congress to make commercial treaties: no treaty could prohibit imports or exports, and no treaty could prevent a state from imposing retaliatory imposts. The revised Articles also scrapped Dickinson's executive branch, accepted the state sovereignty principle that each state cast an equal vote, modified Congress's judicial authority to decide all intercolonial disputes, and denied the power of Congress to fix the western boundaries of states.

Maryland, however, refused to accept the decision on the boundary issue. Although Congress completed the Articles in November 1777, unanimous ratification by state legislatures came hard. By the beginning of 1779, however, Maryland stood alone, the only state that had not ratified, and Maryland was unmovable. As unanimity was necessary, Maryland had the advantage as well as a great cause, the creation of a national domain. In 1780 New York and Connecticut ceded their western lands to the United States. Congress then adopted a report recommending the cession of western claims by other states, and in October 1780, Congress yielded to Maryland by resolving that ceded lands should be disposed of for the common benefit of the United States and be formed into "republican states, which shall become members of the federal union" on equal terms with the original states. Virginia's acceptance in January 1781 was decisive. Maryland ratified.

When Congress had submitted the Articles for ratification its accompanying letter accurately stated that its plan was the best possible under the circumstances; combining "in one general system" the conflicting interests of "a continent divided into so many sovereign . . . communities" was a "difficulty." The Articles were the product of the American Revolution and constituted an extraordinary achievement. Congress had framed the first written constitution that established a federal system of government in which the sovereign powers were distributed between the central and local governments. Those powers that unquestionably belonged to Parliament were delegated to the United States. Under the Articles Congress possessed neither tax nor commerce powers, the two powers that Americans in the final stages of the controversy with Britain refused to recognize in Parliament. Americans were fighting largely because a central government claimed those powers, which Americans demanded for their provincial legislatures. Given the widespread identification of liberty with local autonomy, the commitment to limited government, and the hostility to centralization, the states yielded as much as could be expected at the time. Because Congress represented the states and the people of the states, to deny Congress the power to tax was not logical, but the opposition to centralized powers of taxation was so fierce that even nationalists supported the requisition system. "It takes time," as JOHN JAY remarked, "to make sovereigns of subjects."

The sovereignty claimed by the states existed—within a limited sphere of authority. The Articles made the United States sovereign, too, within its sphere of authority: it possessed "sole and exclusive" power over fundamental matters such as foreign affairs, war and peace, western lands, and Indian affairs. The reservation of some sovereign powers in the states meant the surrender of other sovereign powers to the central government. Americans believed that sovereignty was divisible and divided it. In part, FEDERALISM is a system of divided sovereign powers. The Articles had many defects, the greatest of which was that the United States acted on the states rather than the people and had no way of making the states or anyone but soldiers obey. The failure to create executive and judicial branches, the requirement for unanimity for amendments, and the refusal to concede to Congress what had been denied to Parliament resulted in the eventual breakdown of the Articles. They were, nevertheless, a necessary stage in the evolution of the Constitution of 1787 and contained many provisions that were carried over into that document. (See CONSTITUTIONAL HISTORY, 1776–1789.)

LEONARD W. LEVY

Bibliography

HENDERSON, H. JAMES 1974 *Party Politics in the Continental Congress.* New York: McGraw-Hill.

JENSEN, MERRILL 1963(1940) *Articles of Confederation: An Interpretation of the Social-Constitutional History of the American Revolution.* Madison: University of Wisconsin Press.

RAKOVE, JACK N. 1979 *The Beginnings of National Politics: An Interpretive History of the Continental Congress.* New York: Knopf.

ARTICLES OF IMPEACHMENT OF ANDREW JOHNSON (1868)

Eleven articles of IMPEACHMENT of President ANDREW JOHNSON were voted by the House of Representatives in March 1868. The impeachment was largely a product of partisan dissatisfaction with Johnson's approach to reconstruction of the South.

Nine of the articles concerned Johnson's attempt to remove Secretary of War EDWIN M. STANTON, supposedly in defiance of the TENURE OF OFFICE ACT of 1867—although, by its letter, the act did not apply to Stanton, who had been appointed by ABRAHAM LINCOLN. The charges ranged from simple violation of the act to conspiracy to seize the property of the War Department and to gain control over its expenditures. However far-fetched, each of the nine articles alleged a specific illegal or criminal act.

The last two articles were overtly political and reflected a different notion of the concept of impeachable offense. Based on accounts of Johnson's speeches, the articles charged that he ridiculed and abused Congress and had questioned the constitutional legitimacy of the Thirty-Ninth Congress.

The impeachment was tried to the Senate which, in May 1868, failed by one vote to give a two-thirds vote for conviction of any of the articles, and so acquitted Johnson.

DENNIS J. MAHONEY

Bibliography

BENEDICT, MICHAEL LES 1973 *The Impeachment and Trial of Andrew Johnson.* New York: W. W. Norton.

ARTICLES OF IMPEACHMENT OF RICHARD M. NIXON (1974)

Three articles of IMPEACHMENT of President RICHARD M. NIXON were voted by the Committee on the Judiciary of the House of Representatives between July 27 and July 30, 1974. The vote on the articles followed an extended investigation of the so-called WATERGATE affair, the President's knowledge of an involvement in that affair, and a prolonged controversy concerning what constitutes an "impeachable offense." All three articles, as voted, had reference to Watergate, and all charged breach of the oath of office.

The first article charged Nixon with having "prevented, obstructed, and impeded the administration of justice" by withholding evidence and participating in the "cover-up" of the Watergate affair. The nine specifications included making false statements to investigators, approving of others giving false testimony, condoning the payment of "hush money" to potential witnesses, and interfering with the conduct of the investigation.

The second article charged Nixon with misusing the powers of his office and with "repeated conduct violating the constitutional rights of citizens." Five specifications included misusing the Internal Revenue Service, Federal Bureau of Investigation, and Central Intelligence Agency; attempting to prejudice the right to a FAIR TRIAL (of one Daniel Ellsberg); and failing to act against subordinates who engaged in illegal activities.

The third article charged Nixon with disobeying subpoenas issued by the committee itself in the course of its investigation. This article was approved only narrowly since some committee members argued that a good faith assertion of EXECUTIVE PRIVILEGE was not a constitutionally impeachable offense. Two other articles were defeated in the committee vote.

The articles of impeachment never came to a vote in the full House of Representatives. On August 9, 1974, facing the virtual certainty of impeachment and of conviction by the Senate, Richard M. Nixon became the first president ever to resign.

DENNIS J. MAHONEY

Bibliography

UNITED STATES HOUSE OF REPRESENTATIVES, COMMITTEE ON THE JUDICIARY 1974 *Impeachment of Richard Nixon, President of the United States.* Washington, D.C.: Government Printing Office.

ARVER v. UNITED STATES

See: Selective Draft Cases

ASH, UNITED STATES v.
413 U.S. 300 (1973)

The RIGHT TO COUNSEL did not apply when the prosecutor showed eyewitnesses to a crime an array of photographs, including that of the indicted accused. The photographic showing was merely a part of the prosecutor's trial preparation (that is, done in order to refresh recollection) and neither the defendant's nor his lawyer's presence was constitutionally required.

BARBARA ALLEN BABCOCK

ASHTON v. CAMERON COUNTY WATER IMPROVEMENT DISTRICT
298 U.S. 513 (1936)

This is one of the several cases of the period whose decision gave the impression that the United States was constitutionally incapable of combating the Great Depression. Over 2,000 governmental units ranging from big cities to small school districts had defaulted, and the CONTRACT CLAUSE prevented the states from relieving their subdivisions. Congress, responding to pressure from states and creditors, passed the Municipal Bankruptcy Act of 1934, authorizing state subdivisions to apply to federal bankruptcy courts to get their debts scaled down. In accordance with the statute, a Texas water district, supported by state law, applied for a bankruptcy plan that would make possible a final settlement of fifty cents on the dollar, the payment financed by a federal loan. The federal bankruptcy court controlled the bankruptcy plan, which could not be enforced unless approved by creditors holding at least two-thirds of the debt, as required by the statute.

The Supreme Court held the Municipal Bankruptcy Act to be an unconstitutional exercise of Congress's delegated BANKRUPTCY POWER. For a five-member majority, Justice JAMES C. MCREYNOLDS declared that that power was subject to state sovereignty, which cannot be surrendered or impaired by legislation. Congress had violated the TENTH AMENDMENT by infringing on state control over the fiscal affairs of state subdivisions. That the act required state consent, here eagerly given, was irrelevant to the Court. Thus the Court protected the states and even creditors against their will. Justice BENJAMIN N. CARDOZO, for the dissenters, characterizing the majority opinion as "divorced from the realities of life," argued that Congress had framed the statute with sedulous regard for state sovereignty and the structure of the federal system. The Court retreated in *United States v. Bekins* (1938).

LEONARD W. LEVY

ASHWANDER v. TENNESSEE VALLEY AUTHORITY
297 U.S. 288 (1936)

Ashwander was part of a protracted litigation over the constitutionality of the Tennessee Valley Authority (TVA), a government development corporation established by the New Deal. (See CONSTITUTIONAL HISTORY, 1933–1945; TENNESSEE VALLEY AUTHORITY ACT.) TVA was organized to develop the economy of a river valley by improving navigation and flood control and especially by generating cheap electric power for homes, farms, and industry. In *Ashwander* preferred shareholders in an existing power company sued in federal court to enjoin the company and TVA from carrying out a contract under which TVA would purchase much of the company's property and equipment, and TVA would allocate areas for the sale of power. The plaintiffs attacked the whole TVA program as exceeding the scope of congressional power. The district court granted the INJUNCTION, but the court of appeals reversed, upholding the contract. The Supreme Court, 8–1, affirmed the court of appeals.

Chief Justice CHARLES EVANS HUGHES, for the majority, concluded that Wilson Dam, where TVA was generating power, had been built in 1916 to provide power for national defense needs, including the operation of nitrate plants used in the making of munitions, and to improve navigation—both objectives concededly within the powers of Congress. If excess electricity were generated at the dam, Hughes said, Congress had the power to sell it, as it might sell any other property owned by the United States. Justice JAMES C. MCREYNOLDS, dissenting alone on the constitutional merits, pointed out the transparency of the majority's doctrinal clothing: TVA was in the power-generating business for its own sake, not as an adjunct to some military program long since abandoned.

Justice LOUIS D. BRANDEIS, dissenting in part, agreed with the majority's views on congressional power but argued that the plaintiffs' complaint should have been dismissed for want of STANDING. As preferred shareholders, they could show no injury to themselves from the contract. Brandeis went on, in *Ashwander*'s most famous passages, to discuss a series of "rules" under which the Supreme Court had "avoided passing upon a large part of all the constitutional questions pressed upon it for decision." Some of the "rules" flow from Article III of the Constitution, including the standing requirement Brandeis sought to effectuate in *Ashwander* itself. Others, however, express policies of preference for nonconstitutional grounds for decision, for formulating the narrowest possible constitutional grounds, for construing federal statutes to avoid constitutional questions, and the like.

Some modern commentators have read the Brandeis opinion in *Ashwander* to stand for a broad policy of judicial discretion to avoid deciding cases that might place the Court in awkward political positions. Brandeis himself, a stickler for principled application of the Court's jurisdictional requirements, surely had no such generalized discretion in mind. Nonetheless, some of his successors have found it convenient to cite his comments in *Ashwander* in support of far less principled avoidance techniques. (See POE V. ULLMAN, 1961.)

KENNETH L. KARST

ASSISTANCE, WRIT OF

The term "writ of assistance" is applied to several distinct types of legal documents. Of greatest significance to American constitutional history was the writ of assistance issued to customs inspectors by the English Court of the Exchequer authorizing the search of all houses suspected of containing contraband. Such writs were first used no later than 1621, and their form was codified in 1662. They are still used regularly in Britain and in many nations of the British Commonwealth.

In colonial America, writs of assistance were used as GENERAL SEARCH WARRANTS and were authorized by a statute of the British Parliament. In a famous Massachusetts case, PAXTON'S CASE (1761), JAMES OTIS argued that the statute authorizing writs of assistance should be held invalid because it was contrary to MAGNA CARTA and the COMMON LAW; but his argument was rejected. The colonial experience with writs of assistance led to the requirement in the FOURTH AMENDMENT that SEARCH WARRANTS particularly describe the place to be searched and the object of the search.

WILLIAM J. CUDDIHY

Bibliography

SMITH, M. H. 1978 *The Writs of Assistance Case.* Berkeley: University of California Press.

ASSOCIATED PRESS v. N.L.R.B.

See: Wagner Act Cases

ASSOCIATION, THE

The Continental Association was created by the First Continental Congress on October 18, 1774. It was "a non-importation, non-consumption, and non-exportation agreement" undertaken to obtain redress of American grievances against the British Crown and Parliament. The Articles of Association were signed on October 20 by the representatives of twelve colonies, solemnly binding themselves and their constituents to its terms.

The articles listed the most pressing American grievances (TAXATION WITHOUT REPRESENTATION, extension of admiralty court jurisdiction, denial of TRIAL BY JURY in tax cases), enumerated the measures to be taken (cessation of commercial ties to Britain), prescribed the penalty for noncompliance (a total breaking off of communication with offenders), and established the machinery for enforcement (through committees of correspondence).

The Association was a major step toward the creation of a federal union of American states. It was the first prescriptive act of a national Congress to be binding directly on individuals, and the efforts at enforcement of or compliance with its terms certainly contributed to the formation of a national identity. With but little exaggeration the historian RICHARD HILDRETH wrote: "The signature of the Association may be considered as the commencement of the American union."

DENNIS J. MAHONEY

ATASCADERO STATE HOSPITAL v. SCANLON
473 U.S. (1985)

The opinions in this case made clear that PENNHURST STATE SCHOOL AND HOSPITAL V. HALDERMAN (1984) was a watershed in the Supreme Court's modern treatment of the ELEVENTH AMENDMENT. By the same 5–4 division as in *Pennhurst,* the Court here held that an individual could not obtain relief against a state agency in federal court for harm caused by the agency's violation of the federal REHABILITATION ACT of 1973. In an opinion by Justice LEWIS F. POWELL, the majority concluded that California had not waived its SOVEREIGN IMMUNITY under that amendment, and that Congress, in the act, had not lifted the state's immunity to suit by individual plaintiffs. The latter point carried the Court's restrictive reading of the Eleventh Amendment a step beyond even the *Pennhurst* opinion: a congressional purpose to lift state immunity, the majority said, cannot be found by implication from a statute's purposes, but only in an explicit statement in the statute itself.

The four dissenters, speaking primarily through Justice WILLIAM J. BRENNAN, made a vigorous and broad-ranging attack on the majority's recent approach to Eleventh Amendment issues. Justice Brennan, as before, accused the majority of misconceiving the purposes of the Framers in writing Article III, misreading the text and the purposes of the Eleventh Amendment, and generally twisting the fundamental premises of American FEDERALISM to "put the federal judiciary in the unseemly position of exempting the states from compliance with laws that bind every other legal actor in our nation."

It seems clear that the shock of *Pennhurst* persuaded some of the *Scanlon* dissenters to join Justice Brennan's campaign for a fundamental reorientation of Eleventh Amendment jurisprudence. Four Justices agreed that the recent majority's doctrine "intrudes on the ideal of liberty under law by protecting the States from the consequences of their illegal conduct."

KENNETH L. KARST

ATOMIC ENERGY ACT
68 Stat 919 (1954)

The initial Atomic Energy Act (1946) had created an independent five-person Atomic Energy Commission (AEC) to exercise complete civilian control over the production of atomic energy and associated research programs. By the early 1950s, criticism of the statute mounted because it limited the role of private enterprise in the atomic energy field, overemphasized military phases, and created unwarranted secrecy, precluding the dissemination of technical information to other nations.

The 1954 Amendment addressed these concerns. Its overriding policy objective, strongly supported by President DWIGHT D. EISENHOWER, was to facilitate the commercial development and exploitation of nuclear power by private industry. The key provisions were: private ownership of nuclear facilities; private use of fissionable material (though the AEC still retained title, until revision in 1964); liberalized patenting rights; industrial access to needed technical information; and a program for international cooperation in developing peaceful applications of nuclear energy, particularly nuclear power. The principal focus of the act was to make the nuclear industry economically independent and internally competitive.

Regulatory provisions of the 1954 act authorized the AEC to license facilities and operators producing or using radioactive materials. This licensing process, subject to judicial review by the terms of the act, was to protect the public health, safety, life, and property. Little guidance or standards for licensure was provided, and the question of safety hazards from nuclear technology was not considered. Thus the AEC's administration of the act was slowly hammered out through the regulatory process; that situation continued after the Commission was folded into the Department of Energy in 1974.

PAUL L. MURPHY

Bibliography

ROLPH, ELIZABETH S. 1979 *Nuclear Power and the Public Safety.* Lexington, Mass.: Lexington Books.

ATTAINDER, BILL OF

See: Bill of Attainder

ATTAINDER OF TREASON

Upon conviction of and sentencing for TREASON, a person is attainted: he loses all claim to the protection of the law. Under English law attainder of treason worked "corruption of blood," depriving the traitor's descendants of the right to inherit property from or through him. The second clause of Article III, section 2, of the Constitution virtually abolishes attainder of treason. Because of that clause, ABRAHAM LINCOLN insisted that the forfeiture of ex-Confederates' property under the CONFISCATION ACT of 1862 be only for the lifetime of the owner. Construing the act and the constitutional provision in *Wallach v. Van Riswick* (1872), the Supreme Court held that the limitation on attainder of treason was solely for the benefit of the heirs.

DENNIS J. MAHONEY

ATTORNEY GENERAL AND DEPARTMENT OF JUSTICE

The job of attorney general for the United States, as it was then called, was created by the JUDICIARY ACT OF 1789. The last sentence of that remarkable statute called for the appointment (presumably by the President) of "a meet person, learned in the law, . . . whose duty it shall be to prosecute and conduct all suits in the Supreme Court in which the United States shall be concerned, and to give his advice and opinion upon questions of law when required by the President of the United States, or when requested by the heads of any of the departments, touching any matters that may concern their departments, and [who] shall receive such compensation for his services as shall by law be provided." The first attorney general was EDMUND RANDOLPH, and his salary was $1,500. He had no office or staff provided by his government.

There have been seventy-three attorneys general between Randolph's tenure and that of William French Smith (1981–1985), counting JOHN J. CRITTENDEN twice. From the beginning they have been members of the President's cabinet—fourth in rank after the secretaries of state, treasury, and war (now defense). Since 1870 the attorney general has also been head of the Department of Justice. For the most part, the attorneys general have been citizens of outstanding achievement and public service, although not necessarily of extraordinary professional and intellectual ability; the latter qualities have traditionally been associated with the SOLICITOR GENERAL. Nine attorneys general subsequently sat on the Supreme Court of the United States, two as Chief Justice (ROGER B. TANEY, 1831–1833, and HARLAN F. STONE, 1924–1925); three were nominated to that bench but never confirmed; one was confirmed but never took his seat (EDWIN M. STANTON, 1860–1861); and at least two turned down nominations to the Court (Charles Lee, 1795–1801, as Chief Justice, and LEVI LINCOLN, 1801–1805). Only three attorneys general have had their careers seriously eroded by personal and professional misconduct (Harry M. Daugherty, 1921–1924; John N. Mitchell, 1969–1972; and Richard G. Kleindienst, 1972–1974). Of these, Daugherty was acquitted of charges of attempting to defraud the United States in the Teapot Dome scandal, Mitchell served a prison term for a conspiracy to obstruct justice in connection with the WATERGATE affair, and Kleindienst entered a plea bargain of guilty to a MISDEMEANOR involving his veracity in congressional testimony.

The Department of Justice grew with government after 1870, but at an increasingly accelerated rate, expanding enormously in the 1970s and early 1980s. The budget of the Department for fiscal year 1984 was over three billion dollars; it had increased by almost fifty percent since the beginning of 1981. In addition to the attorney general, top officials now include one deputy attorney general, five deputy associate attorneys general, one associate attorney general, five deputy associate attorneys general, the solicitor general, ten assistant attorneys general, and ninety-four United States attorneys (with coordinate United States marshals), all appointed by the President and all bearing responsibility of some sort in the litigation and advice-giving functions of the Department. These officers are backed by the vast investigative resources of the Federal Bureau of Investigation (FBI). In addition, the Department runs the Immigration and Naturalization Service, the Federal Bureau of Prisons, the Drug Enforcement Agency, and various research and public policy arms.

Public perception of the department as a major instrument of public policy, with a significant effect on the quality of American society, started roughly with the JOHN F. KENNEDY administration in the 1960s, when ROBERT F. KENNEDY (1961–1964) was appointed attorney general by his brother. Before that, the department mostly functioned as a professional law office charged with enforcing the few federal criminal statutes that existed, representing the government in other litigation, and giving advice to the President, especially on questions requiring construction of the Constitution. There had been sporadic periods, however, during which the department temporarily emerged as an important arm of federal government.

The department was established by Congress primarily as the instrument of government to work with the FREEDMEN'S BUREAU in implementing the CIVIL RIGHTS statutes that accompanied the passage of the Civil War amendments. The first attorneys general to run the Department—Amos T. Akerman (1870–1872) and George Henry Williams (1872–1875)—were accordingly deeply engaged in the temporary and unsuccessful efforts then to protect the ideal of racial equality through law. Charles J. Bonaparte (1906–1909), both under President THEODORE ROOSEVELT and in his professional life after that, was also active in the cause of racial justice, using in part the technique of AMICUS CURIAE briefs. Bonaparte also actively enforced the SHERMAN ANTITRUST ACT of 1890, following the traditions of his immediate predecessors, PHILANDER C. KNOX (1901–1904) and WILLIAM H. MOODY (1904–1906). On the darker side, A. MITCH-

ELL PALMER (1919–1921) brought the department into public controversy in the stunning PALMER RAIDS of 1919, in which more than 5,000 persons were taken into custody, their names apparently culled from lists of over 60,000 put together by the agency that became the FBI. No federal criminal charges were lodged against any of them, proposals for federal laws against peacetime SEDITION having failed to pass Congress, and the affair remains a moment of disgrace in the department's history.

The inescapable intertwining of law enforcement priorities and public policy has caused debate over the qualifications that attorneys general should meet. On the one hand, there is the tradition of the even-handed, objective, nonpolitical rule of law, implemented by an impartial Department of Justice. The department's own slogan exemplifies this strand of its work: "The United States wins its case whenever justice is done one of its citizens in the courts." Yet it is not possible to run the department without making choices that have wide public impact; not surprisingly, those choices reflect the political goals of the President. Since the mid-1950s the department's political role has been especially visible in civil rights matters, but it has been marked in antitrust policy, for example, since the passage of the Sherman Act of 1890. Even the work of the Lands Division, which is now also responsible for laws affecting ENVIRONMENTAL REGULATION and the use of natural resources, has strong political effects. The Criminal Division has devoted major energies to the control of organized crime as the result of new policy initiatives of the Kennedy administration in the early 1960s. The FBI, since the death of J. EDGAR HOOVER, has changed not only its direction—away from a concentration on perceived threats to internal security, for one part, and automobile thefts, for another—but also its techniques and training programs, by the initiation of elaborate undercover investigations called "scams."

In the mid-1970s, White House manipulation of the department during the Watergate scandal led Senator Sam J. Ervin of North Carolina seriously to examine, in a series of hearings, the possibility of separating the Department of Justice from presidential control. There were substantial constitutional objections to his plan, stemming from the undoubted constitutional power of the President to run the executive branch with people of his own choosing, at least in policymaking positions. The proposed legislation failed, partly for that reason, and partly because of principled opposition from many lawyers and former government officials who believed it not only inevitable but also appropriate that law enforcement priorities and policies be part of a presidential candidate's platform and a presidential program. No one, however, supported a presidential right to corruption, and Congress did create the office of a special prosecutor to be filled from time to time by appointment triggered by nonfrivolous charges against any presidential appointee or personal staff member. Such a special prosecutor is, by law, immunized against political accountability to the attorney general or the White House.

The creation of a statutory special prosecutor, in place of the ad hoc use of such a position at the time of Teapot Dome and Watergate, did not, of course, end discussion of the qualifications required of an attorney general. Robert F. Kennedy (1961–1964), John N. Mitchell (1969–1972), and Edwin Meese (1985–) had been campaign managers for the Presidents who appointed them, and Herbert Brownell (1953–1957), Griffin B. Bell (1977–1979), and William French Smith (1981–1985) were closely associated with their Presidents' political careers. The argument that close political associates should be disqualified from appointment as the nation's chief law enforcement officer is not borne out by the public careers of these men. Only one, Mitchell, was connected with corruption or scandal. Robert Kennedy, professionally the least qualified of all at the time of his appointment, was a spectacularly successful leader of the department; his tenure was marked by policy innovation and attention to career professionals, and scrupulously devoid of political favoritism. In short, it is difficult to generalize, from the record, on what background is best. A full commitment to the rule of law, an ability to command professional respect, the administrative skill to run a large and diverse bureaucracy, a constitutional regard for an independent judiciary, and the political habit of appropriate deference to the place of Congress in the constitutional scheme are the traits that the Senate must look for in giving its advice and consent. None of these qualifications is necessarily associated with any particular background.

There is implicit in the periodic debate about what qualifications are needed for an attorney general an ambivalence about the identification of his (or her) client. The legal profession has come to realize that the client–lawyer relationship imagined in lawyers' codes of professional responsibility does not fit the corporate-bureaucratic world. Lawyers who are used to concern about whether they represent the managers of a corporation, or some abstract corporate entity, or other financial interests find the problem even more acute in government service. The attorney general is the lawyer for the President, but he is also the lawyer for the United States, which includes the

Congress, and which is governed by a Constitution. The conflicts inherent in this multifaceted responsibility have been reflected, for example, in the department's use of WIRETAPPING and electronic surveillance. Both originated with ambiguous presidential approval, though neither was authorized by Congress nor controlled by explicit legislation. When the Supreme Court applied the exclusionary rule to surveillance by TRESPASS, and then to the product of taps, the response of the department was to confine the use of those devices to investigative work; they were not to be used as EVIDENCE in court. The combining of constitutional constraints on law enforcement behavior, legislative policy, and presidential direction did not take place until decades after the process started. Similar problems of ambiguity of duty are reflected whenever the Congress enacts legislation, or the Supreme Court announces constitutional rules, that the President wants to avoid.

The emergence, in the years since mid-century, of the federal role in ending racial discrimination is largely a product of Justice Department policymaking, mostly with, but sometimes ahead of, the approval of the President. Until recently, the department was consistently in advance of congressional policy. In 1939, without any statutory authority, Attorney General FRANK MURPHY (1939–1940) set up a Civil Rights Section in the Criminal Division to enforce the criminal code's civil rights provisions, which had not been used for years. For the first time, the FBI was thereby drawn, against its will, into the investigation of civil rights violations, particularly in police brutality cases. The section had no authority in civil matters, but its creation immediately created a focus inside the executive branch for the emerging civil rights constituency. The resulting tie between Justice Department policy and the civil rights movement lasted, with some erosion in the early 1970s, until 1981.

In 1948, under TOM C. CLARK (1945–1949), the department initiated a consistent practice of supporting civil rights groups through amicus curiae briefs in private litigation in the Supreme Court. The case was SHELLEY V. KRAEMER (1948), which held racially RESTRICTIVE COVENANTS to be unenforceable in state courts. The solicitor general filed important briefs thereafter in BROWN V. BOARD OF EDUCATION (1954) and its progeny, even though it was far from clear that President DWIGHT D. EISENHOWER supported the positions taken, and it was certain that a majority of Congress did not. In 1960 the department went a step further, although in a technically ambiguous fashion, when it urged reversal in one of the first SIT-IN cases to reach the Court, BOYNTON V. VIRGINIA (1960). A total of twenty-five amicus curiae briefs were filed between 1955 and 1961. In the meantime, the department took the lead in persuading Congress to give it limited litigation authority in VOTING RIGHTS cases, through the CIVIL RIGHTS ACTS of 1957 and 1960. It seems clear that the 1957 statute at least was drafted and steered through the Congress without the participation, and perhaps without the full understanding, of the President.

Under Robert Kennedy (1961–1964), the department increased its activity in the civil rights field, filing nine amicus curiae briefs in the Supreme Court in 1961, nineteen in 1962, and twenty-eight in 1963. The department at the same time drastically increased not only its own litigation in the lower federal courts in voting rights cases but also its intervention as a party in private suits. In one unusual case, despite the general duty of the attorney general to defend federal legislation, the department attacked the constitutionality of a federal statute that contemplated racially separate hospitals. Civil Rights Division lawyers effectively took over the litigation in crucial cases involving schools in New Orleans, Birmingham, and Montgomery; the University of Mississippi at Oxford in 1962; and the University of Alabama in Huntsville and Tuscaloosa in 1963. They also initiated an INJUNCTION suit to protect the Freedom Riders in 1961, and, following that incident, sought to persuade the Interstate Commerce Commission to require the immediate DESEGREGATION of all interstate bus and rail facilities. All these actions were taken with the approval of the President, but despite congressional refusal to authorize Department of Justice initiatives outside the voting area.

The comprehensive CIVIL RIGHTS ACT OF 1964 finally legitimated the kind of litigating activism the department had undertaken, and the VOTING RIGHTS ACT OF 1965 authorized massive federal intervention, outside the judicial system, into areas where racial discrimination in registration or voting persisted. In the meantime, the department was forced, on its own, to seek to protect the physical security of civil rights workers operating in severely hostile territories. The problem was never quite solved. United States marshals and special temporary deputies volunteering from other branches of the department, especially the Immigration and Naturalization Service, and on one occasion the Bureau of Prisons, served at the direction of the attorney general as ad hoc peace-keeping forces. The FBI, a natural source of manpower for such purposes, never let its people be used for police duty. Several times, starting with Little Rock in 1957, troops were required, with the authorization of the President. At such moments, the department was converted from a law office to a crisis-management center, with consequences for its public responsibility that still persist.

If the Department of Justice is free to participate actively in promoting one direction in the formulation of government policy, and of constitutional rule-making in the courts, it can also undertake to move in the opposite direction. Starting in 1981, the department did just that. In the area of civil rights, it opposed positions previously advocated by the government in school, employment, and voting rights matters, both in its own litigation and through amicus curiae briefs. The civil rights organizations thus found themselves in legal combat with their national government. Further, the department moved far outside the scope of its mandated law enforcement function, filing briefs in constitutional litigation opposing assertions by private citizens of their RIGHT OF PRIVACY in abortion decisions in one line of cases, for example, and their rights under the religion clause of the FIRST AMENDMENT in another. The department's earlier role in civil rights matters had been different, because it had reflected not only the policies of several administrations but also the will of the nation as expressed in the RULE OF LAW, under the Reconstruction amendments, especially the EQUAL PROTECTION clause.

The department's new social mission, announced as official policy by Attorney General Smith in a speech in 1981, fortified the Senate in its questioning of what kind of attorney general is appropriate for a Department of Justice possessing the enormous power it now does. Whether the department should be confined to a traditional role of impartial law enforcement or should continue to press for shifts in social and legal policy is an issue that may never be cleanly and finally resolved. Yet the issue is important in a nation where, in the oft-quoted words of ALEXIS DE TOCQUEVILLE, "scarcely any political question arises . . . that is not resolved, sooner or later, into a judicial question."

BURKE MARSHALL

Bibliography

BIDDLE, FRANCIS BEVERLEY 1962 *In Brief Authority.* Garden City, N.Y.: Doubleday.

CARR, ROBERT K. (1947)1964 *Federal Protection of Civil Rights.* Ithaca, N.Y.: Cornell University Press.

CUMMINGS, HOMER STILLE and MCFARLAND, CARL 1937 *Federal Justice.* New York: Macmillan.

DEPARTMENT OF JUSTICE 1980 *Attorney General of the United States.* Washington, D.C.: Department of Justice.

HUSTON, LUTHER A. 1968 *The Department of Justice.* New York: Praeger.

HUSTON, LUTHER A., MILLER, ARTHUR SELWYN, KRISLOV, SAMUEL, and DIXON, ROBERT G., JR. 1968 *Roles of the Attorney General of the United States.* Washington, D.C.: American Enterprise Institute for Public Policy Research.

NAVASKY, VICTOR S. 1971 *Kennedy Justice.* New York: Atheneum.

ATTORNEY GENERAL'S LIST

President HARRY S. TRUMAN's Executive Order 9835 inaugurated a comprehensive investigation of all federal employees and made any negative information a potential basis for a security dismissal. A list of subversive organizations was to be prepared by the attorney general, and membership in any listed group was a ground for REASONABLE DOUBT as to an employee's loyalty. The only guidelines the order provided were that any designated organization must be "totalitarian, Fascist, Communist, or subversive," or one "approving the commission of acts of force or violence to deny to others their constitutional rights." During the first year under the order, the attorney general so designated 123 organizations. Over time, and frequently as a result of protests, certain organizations were deleted; new ones were also added. By November 1950, 197 organizations had been so listed, eleven of which were labeled subversive, twelve as seeking to overthrow the government by unconstitutional means, and 132 as communist or communist front.

Critics questioned the constitutionality of the list's compilation and use, on FIRST AMENDMENT grounds, as an "executive BILL OF ATTAINDER" and as involving unfair procedures violating the DUE PROCESS CLAUSE of the Fifth Amendment. The Supreme Court in JOINT ANTI-FASCIST REFUGEE COMMITTEE V. MCGRATH (1951) raised serious questions regarding the fairness of the compilation procedure, and demands grew for suitable hearings to be granted organizations before their inclusion. No procedural changes were instituted in the Truman years, however, and the list continued to be used under the Eisenhower loyalty program. (See LOYALTY-SECURITY PROGRAMS.)

PAUL L. MURPHY

Bibliography

BONTECOU, ELEANOR 1953 *The Federal Loyalty-Security Program.* Ithaca, N.Y.: Cornell University Press.

AUTOMOBILE SEARCH

Automobile searches constitute a recognized exception to the FOURTH AMENDMENT's requirement of a SEARCH WARRANT. When police have PROBABLE

CAUSE to believe an automobile is transporting contraband, they may, under CARROLL V. UNITED STATES (1925) and BRINEGAR V. UNITED STATES (1941), conduct a WARRANTLESS SEARCH of the vehicle lest it disappear before a warrant can be obtained. Under CHAMBERS V. MARONEY (1970) the search may be delayed until the vehicle has been removed to a police station, though the emergency that attends a search on the road has dissipated. The rules governing automobile searches apply also to mobile homes, according to *California v. Carney* (1985).

Early cases stressed the vehicle's mobility as justification for a warrantless search, but most recent cases have also emphasized an individual's reduced expectation of privacy in an automobile. In contrast to a dwelling, an automobile usually does not serve as a repository of one's belongings; its interior is plainly visible from the outside; and it is commonly stopped by police enforcing inspection and licensing laws. Nonetheless, as the court held in COOLIDGE V. NEW HAMPSHIRE (1971), a car parked on private property may not be searched without a warrant.

Systematic stopping of automobiles at checkpoints for license and registration checks is permitted, but under the Court's decision in *Delaware v. Prouse* (1979), their random stopping is forbidden absent suspicious circumstances. And under *Opperman v. South Dakota* (1976) a lawfully impounded vehicle may be subjected to a warrantless inventory search to safeguard the owner's possessions and protect police from false property claims.

The scope of the warrantless automobile search is as broad as one a magistrate could authorize with a warrant. As the Court held in UNITED STATES V. ROSS (1982), the search may encompass "every part of the vehicle that might contain the object of the search," including the trunk, glove compartment, and closed containers. Furthermore, the Court has applied lenient standards in automobile search cases as to the EVIDENCE needed to establish probable cause. Justice JOHN MARSHALL HARLAN, dissenting in UNITED STATES V. HARRIS (1971), accurately remarked that the problem of automobile searches "has typically been treated as *sui generis* by this Court."

JACOB W. LANDYNSKI

Bibliography

LAFAVE, WAYNE R. 1978 *Search and Seizure: A Treatise on the Fourth Amendment,* Vol. 2:508–544, 565–581. St. Paul, Minn.: West Publishing Co.

LANDYNSKI, JACOB W. 1971 The Supreme Court's Search for Fourth Amendment Standards: The Warrantless Search. *Connecticut Bar Journal* 45:30–39.

AVERY v. MIDLAND COUNTY
390 U.S. 474 (1968)

In this case, the Supreme Court held that the ONE PERSON, ONE VOTE rule required equal districts in a Texas county commissioners' court election. The decision, in effect, extended the rule's sway from the fifty states to such of the 81,304 units of government as possessed "general responsibility and power for local affairs." Justices JOHN M. HARLAN, ABE FORTAS, and POTTER STEWART dissented, arguing that the Court had overreached its APPELLATE JURISDICTION; that a rigidly uniform one person, one vote rule ignored the special needs functions of most local governments; and that it would discourage joint activity by metropolitan units, thereby undermining the practical benefits of state-level reapportionment.

WARD E. Y. ELLIOTT

B

BACKUS, ISAAC (1724–1806)

A Baptist minister in Massachusetts from 1756, Isaac Backus gained increasing recognition as an agent, chief spokesman, and campaigner for RELIGIOUS LIBERTY for his New England co-religionists, who were harassed by hostile local officials' narrow interpretation and restrictive implementation of laws exempting Baptists from contributing to the support of Congregational churches. In pamphlets and newspapers, in an appearance before the Massachusetts delegation to the First Continental Congress, and in promoting civil disobedience by encouraging Baptists not to comply with statutes dealing with support of churches, he struggled unsuccessfully to abolish public tax support for religion.

More pietist than civil libertarian, Backus sought religious freedom primarily to prevent state interference with the church. He supported his arguments by citing the Massachusetts Charter's grant of religious liberty to all Protestants and by pointing up the contrast between local oppression of Baptists and New Englanders' charges of English tyranny. By 1780, however, he had come to affirm religious liberty as a NATURAL RIGHT.

As a delegate to the Massachusetts ratifying convention, Backus supported the federal Constitution, convinced that its prohibition against tests precluded any ESTABLISHMENT OF RELIGION. He showed little or no interest in the passage of the FIRST AMENDMENT. Backus equated religious liberty almost entirely with voluntary choice of churches and voluntary support of ministers. He perceived America as a Christian country, did not object to Sabbath laws or to public days of prayer, and approved a Massachusetts law requiring legislators to profess Christianity. Such views typified contemporary evangelical opinion.

THOMAS CURRY

Bibliography

MCLAUGHLIN, WILLIAM G. 1967 *Isaac Backus and the American Pietistic Tradition.* Boston: Little, Brown.

———, ed. 1968 *Isaac Backus on Church, State, and Calvinism—Pamphlets, 1754–1789.* Cambridge, Mass.: Harvard University Press.

BADGES OF SERVITUDE

There was truth in the claim of slavery's defenders that many a northern "wage slave" worked under conditions less favorable than those of his enslaved counterpart down South. The evil of slavery was not primarily its imposition of hard work but its treatment of a person as if he or she were a thing. The laws governing slaves carried out this basic theme by systematically imposing a wide range of legal disabilities on slaves, preventing them not only from entering into the public life of the community (by voting, being members of juries, or speaking in public meetings) but also from owning property, making contracts, or even learning to read and write. All these disabilities were designed not merely to preserve a system of bondage to service, but to serve as badges of servitude, symbolizing the slaves' degraded status. In a moment of racist candor, Chief Justice ROGER B. TANEY extended this view of the stigmatized status of slaves to all black persons, slave or free. His opinion for the Supreme Court in DRED SCOTT V. SANDFORD (1857) spoke of blacks as "a subordinate and inferior class of beings," upon whom had been impressed "deep and enduring marks of inferiority and degradation."

Although slaves were often physically branded, the "marks" of which Taney spoke were metaphorical; they were the aggregate of legal restrictions imposed on slaves. When slavery was abolished by the THIRTEENTH AMENDMENT (1865), those marks did not disappear. The amendment, however, did not stop with the abolition of slavery and involuntary servitude; it also empowered Congress to enforce the abolition. From an early time it was argued that the amendment authorized Congress to enact laws to eradicate not only slavery itself but the "badges of servitude" as well. This view was at first accepted in principle by the Supreme Court, and then rejected in the early twentieth century. However, in JONES V. ALFRED H. MAYER CO. (1968), the Court reverted to the earlier interpretation, concluding that RACIAL DISCRIMINATION was the sort of "badge of servitude" that Congress could prohibit.

In the meanwhile, a parallel doctrinal development has become apparent. The CIVIL RIGHTS ACT OF 1866 and the FOURTEENTH AMENDMENT both recognized the CITIZENSHIP of the freed slaves. Both were designed to end the notion of superior and inferior classes of persons and to replace a system of sociopolitical subordination with the status of equal citizenship. (See EQUAL PROTECTION OF THE LAWS.) Because the principle of equal citizenship protects against the imposition of stigma, it often operates in the same symbolic universe that produced badges of servitude. To give full effect to the symbol and substance of equal citizenship is one of the major challenges of the nation's third century.

KENNETH L. KARST

Bibliography

KINOY, ARTHUR 1967 The Constitutional Right of Negro Freedom. *Rutgers Law Review* 21:387–441.

BAD TENDENCY TEST

In 1920 New York convicted Benjamin Gitlow of violating its statute prohibiting "advocating, advising or teaching the doctrine that organized government should be overthrown by force." Gitlow had published in the journal *Revolutionary Age* a "Left Wing Manifesto," thirty-four pages of Marxist rhetoric calling for class struggle leading to revolution and the dictatorship of the proletariat.

In GITLOW V. NEW YORK (1925) Gitlow's counsel argued in the Supreme Court that since the manifesto contained no direct INCITEMENT to criminal action, Gitlow must have been convicted under the "bad tendency test." That test was borrowed from the eighteenth-century English law of SEDITIOUS LIBEL which made criticism of government criminal because such criticism might tend to contribute to government's eventual collapse.

This bad tendency test ran counter to the CLEAR AND PRESENT DANGER test of SCHENCK V. UNITED STATES (1919). In *Gitlow* Justice EDWARD SANFORD virtually adopted the bad tendency test for instances in which a legislature had decided that a particular variety of speech created a sufficient danger. Even though there was no evidence of any effect resulting from the Manifesto's publication, the Court stressed that its language constituted advocacy of

> mass action which shall progressively foment industrial disturbances, and, through . . . mass action, overthrow . . . government. . . . The immediate danger is none the less real and substantial because the effect of a given utterance cannot be accurately foreseen. . . . A single revolutionary spark may kindle a fire that, smoldering for a time, may burst into a sweeping and destructive conflagration. . . . [The State] cannot reasonably be required to defer the adoption of measures for its own peace and safety until the revolutionary utterances lead to . . . imminent and immediate danger of its own destruction.

Justices OLIVER WENDELL HOLMES and LOUIS D. BRANDEIS dissented in *Gitlow,* invoking the clear and present danger test. When that test came to dominate the Court's FIRST AMENDMENT opinions in the 1930s and early 1940s, the bad tendency test seemed to be overthrown.

Nevertheless much of Sanford's approach survived. Judge LEARNED HAND's "discounting formula" as adopted in DENNIS V. UNITED STATES (1951) allows speech to be suppressed "where the gravity of the evil, discounted by its improbability" justifies suppression. As *Dennis* itself illustrates, if the danger is painted as sufficiently grave, speech may be suppressed even if there is a very low probability that the evil will occur or that the particular speech in question will contribute to that occurrence. In *Dennis* the Court replaced the present danger test with the requirement that where an organized subversive group exists, the group intends to bring about overthrow "as speedily as the circumstances would permit." Such an approach echoed Sanford's plea that the government need not wait until the danger of revolution is imminent.

MARTIN SHAPIRO

(SEE ALSO: *Subversive Activities and the Constitution; Freedom of Speech.*)

Bibliography

CHAFEE, ZECHARIAH, JR. (1941)1969 *Free Speech in the United States.* New York: Atheneum.

LINDE, HANS 1970 "Clear and Present Danger" Reexamined: Dissonance in the Brandenburg Concerto. *Stanford Law Review* 22:1163–1186.

BAIL

Bail is the prevailing method by which American law has dealt with a puzzling problem: what to do with a person accused of crime during the time between arrest and trial? Imprisonment imposed before trial subjects one who has not been and may never be convicted to disabilities that have all the attributes of punishment, disrupts employment and family ties, hampers the preparation of a defense, increases pressures to plead guilty, and, compared with bailed defendants, may prejudice trial outcomes and lead to more severe sentences. The development of the institution of bail over centuries of English history and its acceptance and liberalization in colonial America was an attempt to mitigate these handicaps and, by affording an opportunity for pretrial release, to emphasize the values underlying the presumption of innocence while also minimizing the risk that an accused who was not jailed would flee and evade justice. Thus bail makes possible pretrial release if the accused can provide financial security, which is subject to forfeiture if the conditions of the bond are violated.

Traditionally, the amount of security is set in an amount deemed by the court to be sufficient to deter flight and enforce compliance with the court's orders. The defendant's own money or property may be put up for this purpose, but in modern times the prevalent method of providing the required security is the purchase by the defendant of a commercial bail bond for a premium, usually about ten percent of the prescribed security. Conditional release on bail may also be available at later stages of the criminal process, for example, pending APPEAL after conviction or pending a hearing on parole or probation revocation, but the predominant use of bail and the most difficult questions raised by its administration relate to the pretrial period.

A "right to bail" is not a right to pretrial release but merely a right to have a court set the amount of the security to be required. A majority of criminal defendants have little or no financial ability to provide security. Furthermore, bondsmen can and often do refuse to bond those they regard as poor risks even if the amount of the premium is tendered. Thus a high rate of pretrial detention of those unable to provide bail has long been a characteristic feature of American criminal justice. Since the early 1960s a widespread bail reform movement has introduced procedures designed to reduce the dependence of the traditional system on the requirement of financial security, but these changes have supplemented rather than replaced money bail, which remains a dominant feature of the system.

The only direct reference to bail in the Constitution is the brief clause in the Eighth Amendment that "excessive bail shall not be required." There are serious problems in the interpretation of the scope of this limited clause and its application under modern conditions. On its face the language is only a restriction of the amount of security which a judge can require, and poses no constitutional barrier to legislative or judicial denial of bail. Alternatively, the clause has been read as necessarily implying a right to bail, as otherwise the clause is left with little significance.

There is no easy resolution of this problem. To infer from the clause a right to bail that is protected from legislative abrogation reads into it words that are not there and necessarily leaves the scope of such a right uncertain. But a literal interpretation renders the clause superfluous, as PROCEDURAL DUE PROCESS OF LAW would protect against judicial abuse of a legislatively granted right to bail. A narrow reading also takes no account of the long history of what the Supreme court in *Stack v. Boyle* (1951) called the "traditional right to freedom before conviction . . . secured only after centuries of struggle," and leaves in a constitutional vacuum a critical stage of the criminal process which has significant impact on the implementation of other constitutionally protected rights of defendants. For nearly two centuries the question has remained unresolved, for two main reasons. First, the transitory nature of detention and the poverty of most defendants unable to raise bail pose barriers to appellate review. Second, until 1984 federal statutory law and the constitutions or laws of most states guaranteed a pretrial right to bail in all but some capital cases, thereby rendering it unnecessary to reach the constitutional issue. Little direct evidence of what was intended by the framers of the clause can be found in the sparse and inconclusive legislative history of the

Eighth Amendment's proposal by the First Congress. At the same time that Representative JAMES MADISON introduced the amendment in the House, a Senate committee was preparing the JUDICIARY ACT OF 1789, which included a right to bail in all but capital cases. Both bail provisions were uncontroversial and undebated, and both went their separate ways to enactment. There is no indication that anyone in Congress recognized the anomaly of incorporating the basic right governing pretrial practice in a statute while enshrining in the Constitution the derivative protection against judicial abuse of that right. The anomaly is compounded by Madison's insistence, in the House debates on the BILL OF RIGHTS, that whereas England's Bill of Rights raised a barrier only against the power of the Crown, "a different opinion prevails in the United States," where protection against abuse "must be levelled against the Legislative" branch. What we do know, however, about the origin of the clause and the context in which it arose sheds some light relevant to its interpretation.

The words of the bail clause were taken verbatim from the revolutionary VIRGINIA DECLARATION OF RIGHTS of 1776, drafted by GEORGE MASON, and by him taken, with the substitution of "shall" for "ought," from the 1689 English Bill of Rights. Mason states that his purpose in drafting the Virginia Declaration was to provide effectual securities for the essential rights of CIVIL LIBERTY, and it is difficult to believe that he intended to deal with the issue of pretrial liberty by words that, literally construed, offer no security against its denial. Although steeped in English constitutional history, Mason was not a lawyer, may not have understood the complexity of the English law, and may have thought that the clause encapsulated the whole subject. In its English context, however, the excessive bail clause in the 1689 Bill of Rights was the culmination of a chain of events that went back to MAGNA CARTA and of a long succession of detailed statutes that established the scope of the right to bail.

This development was climaxed in the seventeenth century by three important acts of Parliament which had been provoked by abuses in the administration of bail law. In 1628, by the PETITION OF RIGHT, the provision of Magna Carta that "no freeman shall be . . . detained in prison . . . unless by the law of the land" was made applicable to pretrial detention and thus was not limited, as the Crown had maintained in *Darnell's Case* (1627), to imprisonment only after conviction. Next, the HABEAS CORPUS ACT OF 1679, after referring to prolonged detentions caused by the inability of detainees to get any judge to set and take bail, mandated a speedy procedure for this purpose. Finally, the Bill of Rights of 1689 sought to curb the judicial abuse of requiring excessive bail. Thus the English structure was tripartite, and protection against denial of pretrial release through the prohibition of excessive bail must be read in the context not only of the extraordinary procedure provided by HABEAS CORPUS but also with reference to the long history of parliamentary bail statutes. Habeas corpus, of course, was included in the body of the American constitution, but the substantive right to bail was omitted. The argument that this omission seems to have been inadvertent at a time when the Framers were preoccupied with other, more immediately pressing issues, and that such a substantive right must have been the intent of the clause, is the core of the historical case for a broad interpretation.

Beginning with the MASSACHUSETTS BODY OF LIBERTIES in 1641, most of the American colonies reduced the number of capital offenses and otherwise liberalized the English law of bail, and in 1682 Pennsylvania extended the right to bail to those charged with all offenses except those capital cases "where the proof is evident or the presumption great," language that was widely copied in state constitutions after Independence. Besides the Judiciary Act of 1789, the closest contemporary record reflecting what seems to have been a widespread political approach to the right to bail, at the time that the Bill of Rights was before the First Congress, was the enactment two years earlier by the CONTINENTAL CONGRESS of the NORTHWEST ORDINANCE for the governance of the territories beyond the Appalachians. In substantially the same language as that used in Pennsylvania nearly a century earlier, the ordinance made bailable as of right those charged with any except capital offenses.

Given the widespread right to bail that had been provided by federal statute and state law, it is not surprising that until recent years there has been a dearth of litigation asserting an Eighth Amendment constitutional right to pretrial bail. The few occasions on which the Supreme Court has dealt with the subject have not required a resolution of the issue, but there are inconclusive and inconsistent OBITER DICTA in some of the cases. On the one hand, in *Schilb v. Kuebel* (1971), which upheld a bail reform statute, the Court said that "Bail, of course, is basic to our system of law," and earlier a unanimous Court in *Stack v. Boyle* had stressed the importance of providing for pretrial release lest "the presumption of innocence, secured only after centuries of struggle, would lose its meaning." But in *Carlson v. Landon,* decided in the same term as *Stack,* a 5–4 Court held that alien communists were not entitled to bail pending adjudication of DEPORTATION charges against them. Most of the *Carlson* majority's long opinion concerned the limited rights of ALIENS, the classification of deportation as a noncriminal proceeding, and the validity and exercise of the attorney general's discretionary delegated power to bail aliens; but it also included six sentences implying that even in criminal proceedings the Eighth Amendment does not afford a right to bail. Although frequently cited, considering the noncriminal emphasis in the case and the brevity and superficiality of the Eighth Amendment analysis, the *Carlson* obiter dictum warrants little weight. Probably more significant is SCHALL V. MARTIN (1984), upholding PREVENTIVE DETENTION for an accused juvenile delinquent pending a family court fact-finding hearing. The case was decided under the due process clause. The Court stressed the noncriminal classification of the proceeding; it noted the limited rights of juveniles compared with adults and the detention's very limited duration; and it observed that there is no historical tradition of a right to juvenile pretrial release and that the detention practice that was upheld has existed throughout the country. Despite all these distinguishing characteristics, the weight given to the importance of preventing pretrial crime and to the possibility of its prediction is suggestive of how the Court might deal with parallel questions in an adult denial-of-bail criminal case.

A number of other controversial issues in pretrial bail law will remain whether or not the Supreme Court infers some form of a right to bail from the Eighth Amendment. The 1984 federal Bail Reform Act and some state constitutional or statutory amendments permit preventive detention of those charged with noncapital offenses if a court finds that pretrial release would pose a danger of future criminal activity. Besides extending the traditional practice which has denied the right to bail only in some capital cases, these enactments also breach long-standing PRECEDENT that only the risk of failure to appear for trial or other limited conduct directly impairing the court's processes, such as threats against witnesses, is relevant to the bail decision. Although the change is in some sense more theoretical than real, direct authorization for judges to explore the uncharted waters of predictions of future dangerousness will in practice undermine the values that gave rise to bail and result in further increases in the proportion of defendants jailed pending trial.

Bail is not constitutionally excessive if the amount does not exceed that normally required for the charged offense. These normal amounts are sufficient to result in very high rates of detention and to mask the existence of de facto preventive detention for those unable to post bond. It was a concern for more equal justice in criminal law administration and a reaction against this discrimination against the poor that gave rise to the bail reform movement of the 1960s and the widespread introduction of other incentives and sanctions as substitute deterrents for money bail. Although this reform, unevenly and incompletely implemented, has had some success, the number of those detained has remained high and is growing. The issue of blatant WEALTH DISCRIMINATION in bail law administration remains to be resolved.

CALEB FOOTE

Bibliography

FLEMMING, ROY B. 1982 *Punishment before Trial: An Organizational Perspective of Felony Bail Processes.* New York: Longman's.

FOOTE, CALEB 1985 The Coming Constitutional Crisis in Bail. *University of Pennsylvania Law Review* 113:959–999, 1125–1185.

FREED, DANIEL J. and WALD, PATRICIA M. 1964 *Bail in the United States, 1964.* Washington, D.C.: U.S. Department of Justice.

TRIBE, LAURENCE H. 1970 An Ounce of Detention: Preventive Justice in the World of John Mitchell. *Virginia Law Review* 56:371–407.

BAILEY v. ALABAMA
219 U.S. 219 (1911)

After the demise of the BLACK CODES some southern states resorted to other devices to insure a steady supply of labor. One Alabama statute effectively converted civil breach of contract into the crime of fraud by making it *prima facie* EVIDENCE of intent to defraud that a worker accept an advance on wages and then neither repay the advance nor perform the work contracted for.

In *Bailey* the Supreme Court held (7–2) that the Alabama law constituted a system of PEONAGE in violation of the THIRTEENTH AMENDMENT's prohibition of involuntary servitude. Justice CHARLES EVANS HUGHES, for the majority, argued that involuntary servitude was a broader concept than SLAVERY and included schemes for enforced labor.

Justice OLIVER WENDELL HOLMES, dissenting, argued that Alabama was acting within its power to define crimes and their punishments.

DENNIS J. MAHONEY

BAILEY v. DREXEL FURNITURE CO.

(Child Labor Tax Case)
259 U.S. 20 (1922)

Following the decision invalidating the KEATING-OWEN CHILD LABOR ACT in HAMMER V. DAGENHART (1918), Congress passed a new law in 1919, this time based on its TAXING POWER. The statute levied a ten percent tax on the net profits of mines or factories that employed underage children. Congress had previously used the tax power for social and economic purposes, and the Supreme Court consistently had upheld such enactments, notably in VEAZIE BANK V. FENNO (1869) and MCCRAY V. UNITED STATES (1904).

When the Child Labor Tax Case was decided in 1922, only Justice JOHN H. CLARKE dissented, without opinion, from Chief Justice WILLIAM HOWARD TAFT's opinion for the Court. Taft concluded that the obvious regulatory effect of the law infringed on state JURISDICTION over PRODUCTION and that *Hammer v. Dagenhart* was controlling. Congress, he said, had imposed a tax that was really a penalty for the purpose of reaching a local subject. Like the Justices in *Hammer,* Taft feared the destruction of federalism. "To give such magic to the word 'tax,' " he said, would remove all constitutional limitations upon Congress and abolish "the sovereignty of the States." He distinguished the Court's earlier rulings upholding federal taxes on state bank notes, oleomargarine, and narcotics by insisting that they had involved regulations or prohibitions that were "reasonably adapted to the collection of the tax." Taft, in fact, advanced the unhistorical proposition that the regulatory purposes of the taxes in those cases were only "incidental" to a primary motive of raising revenue.

The Child Labor Tax Case was favorably cited in UNITED STATES V. BUTLER (1936), but a year later, in SONZINSKY V. UNITED STATES, the Court upheld a federal licensing tax on firearms dealers. Justice HARLAN FISKE STONE's opinion sharply repudiated Taft's, contending that the incidental effect of regulation was irrelevant. Courts, he said, were incompetent to question congressional motives; specifically, they should not measure a tax's regulatory effect and use it to argue that Congress had exercised another power denied by the Constitution. Similar arguments were registered in UNITED STATES V. KAHRIGER (1953) when the Court sustained a federal tax on gambling businesses.

STANLEY I. KUTLER

Bibliography

WOOD, STEPHEN 1968 *Constitutional Politics in the Progressive Era: Child Labor and the Law.* Chicago: University of Chicago Press.

BAKER v. CARR

369 U.S. 186 (1962)

Chief Justice EARL WARREN considered *Baker v. Carr* the most important case decided by the Warren Court. Its holding was cryptic: "the right [to equal districts in the Tennessee legislature] is within the reach of judicial protection under the FOURTEENTH AMENDMENT." Many people expected REAPPORTIONMENT under *Baker* to vitalize American democracy. Others feared that it would snare the judiciary in unresolvable questions of political REPRESENTATION, outside the proper bounds of its constitutional authority.

Tennesseans, like others, had moved from countryside to urban and suburban districts, but no redistricting had taken place since 1901. Supporters of reapportionment claimed that the resulting swollen districts made "second-class citizens" of city voters; they blamed "malapportionment" for urban woes and legislative apathy. Finding little legislative sympathy for these claims, they turned to the courts.

But they had several hurdles to clear. The framers of the Fourteenth Amendment had repeatedly denied that it protected the right to vote. Perhaps it protected rights of representation, but the Court had found such rights too cloudy, too sensitive, and too "political" to settle judicially. (See POLITICAL QUESTIONS.)

The central hurdle was the "standards problem" expounded by Justice FELIX FRANKFURTER in COLEGROVE V. GREEN (1946) and in his *Baker* dissent. How could the Court tell lower courts and legislatures the difference between good representation and bad, lacking clear constitutional guidance? The Constitution was a complex blend of competing and countervailing principles, not a mandate for equal districts. "What is actually asked of the Court . . . is to choose among competing bases of representation—ultimately, really, among competing theories of philosophy—in order to establish an appropriate form of government for . . . the states. . . ." Frankfurter accused the Court of sending the lower courts into a "mathematical quagmire."

Writing for the majority, Justice WILLIAM J. BRENNAN argued that the *Colegrove* court had not found apportionment a political question but had declined to hear it using EQUITY discretion. But he did not answer Frankfurter's challenge to lay down workable standards, nor Justice JOHN MARSHALL HARLAN's objection, later reasserted in REYNOLDS V. SIMS (1964), that nothing in the Constitution conveyed a right to equal districts. Brennan merely claimed that "judicial standards under the EQUAL PROTECTION CLAUSE are well developed and familiar," and that "the right asserted is within the reach of judicial protection under the Fourteenth Amendment."

The concurring Justices, WILLIAM O. DOUGLAS and TOM C. CLARK, were not so cautious. Clark felt that "rational" departures from equal districts, such as districts approved by popular referendum, should be permitted. Douglas emphasized that the standards would be flexible (though he would later vote for rigid standards).

These opinions, and *Baker*'s place in history, make sense only in the context of Solicitor General Archibald Cox's AMICUS CURIAE brief supporting intervention. To take on a cause that could, and later did, jeopardize the seats of most of the legislators in the country, and invite formidable political reprisals, the Justices had to move with caution. Cox's brief reassured them that the JOHN F. KENNEDY administration, like its predecessor, favored intervention. The executive support probably swayed the votes of at least two Justices, Clark and POTTER STEWART. Had these voted against intervention, the Court would have divided 4–4, leaving intact the lower court's decision not to hear the case.

Moreover, Cox's brief did address Harlan's and Frankfurter's challenges. As with BROWN V. BOARD OF EDUCATION (1954), he argued, constitutional authority could be demonstrated from social need, as perceived by social scientists, incorporated into a spacious reading of the Fourteenth Amendment. As for standards, there were two possibilities: an absolute, individual right to vote, perhaps grounded on the equal protection clause, and a loose, group right to equal representation, perhaps grounded on the DUE PROCESS CLAUSE. Of the two, Cox seemed to favor the looser one, forbidding "egregious cases" of "gross discrimination." He even showed how such a standard might be drawn on a map of Tennessee. Because he was explicit, Brennan could afford to be cryptic and let the Cox brief draw most of Frankfurter's and Harlan's fire.

Within two years the Court announced in *Reynolds v. Sims* that equal representation for equal numbers was the "fundamental goal" of the Constitution and laid down standards so strict that every state but one, Oregon, was compelled to reapportion. Compliance with *Baker* was widespread and quick. Opposition was strong but late. By 1967 the states had come within a few votes of the two-thirds needed to call a CONSTITUTIONAL CONVENTION to strip courts of redistricting power, but by then reapportionment was largely completed, and the movement died.

Reapportionment added many urban and suburban seats to legislatures, replacing rural ones, but there is little evidence that it produced any of the liberalizing, vitalizing policies its proponents had predicted. What it did bring was a plague of GERRYMANDERING, renewed after each census, because it forced legislators to redistrict without forcing them to be nonpartisan. The Court since *Baker* has been powerless to control gerrymanders. Packing or diluting a group in a district can strengthen or weaken the group, or do both at once. There is no way short of commanding PROPORTIONAL REPRESENTATION to equalize everyone's representation. Nor is there a workable way to equalize representation in the ELECTORAL COLLEGE, the Senate, the national party conventions, party committees, runoff elections, executive appointments, or MULTIMEMBER DISTRICTS. The Court opened these doors when it announced that representation was the fundamental goal of the Constitution, but it closed them when it found that they raised the standards problem too plainly to permit intervention, exactly as Frankfurter had warned.

Baker has left us two legacies. The good one is equalizing district size. The bad one is rhetorical indirection, constitutional fabrication, and a penchant for overriding the wishes of people and their representatives, as for example, in *Lucas v. Forty-fourth General Assembly* (1964). Whether the good legacy is worth the bad, and whether it even added on balance to equal representation, can be told only with reference to the full breadth of representation which was too complicated for the Court to touch.

WARD E. Y. ELLIOTT

Bibliography

COX, ARCHIBALD 1967 *The Warren Court: Constitutional Decision as an Instrument of Reform.* Cambridge, Mass.: Harvard University Press.

DIXON, ROBERT G., JR. 1968 *Democratic Representation: Reapportionment in Law and Politics.* New York: Oxford University Press.

ELLIOTT, WARD E. Y. 1975 *The Rise of Guardian Democracy: The Supreme Court's Role in Voting Rights Dis-*

putes, 1845–1969. Cambridge, Mass.: Harvard University Press.

NAVASKY, VICTOR 1971 *Kennedy Justice.* New York: Atheneum.

BALANCING TEST

Although the intellectual origins of the balancing of interests formula lie in ROSCOE POUND's sociological jurisprudence, the formula was introduced into constitutional law as a means of implementing the Supreme Court's oft-repeated announcement that FIRST AMENDMENT rights are not absolute. In determining when infringement on speech may be justified constitutionally, the Court may balance the interest in FREEDOM OF SPEECH against the interest that the infringing statute seeks to protect. Thus the Court may conclude that the interests in NATIONAL SECURITY protected by the Smith Act outweigh the interests in speech of those who advocate forcible overthrow of the government, or that the free speech interests of pamphleteers outweigh the interest in clean streets protected by an antilittering ordinance forbidding the distribution of handbills.

The 1950s campaign against alleged subversives brought two interlocking problems to the Supreme Court. The dominant free speech DOCTRINES of the Court were PREFERRED FREEDOMS and the CLEAR AND PRESENT DANGER TEST. Because alleged subversives were exercising preferred speech rights and the government was unprepared to offer evidence that their speech did constitute a present danger of violent overthrow of the government, the Court found it difficult under the existing formulas to uphold government anticommunist action. Because established First Amendment doctrine appeared to be on a collision course with an anticommunist crusade that appeared to enjoy overwhelming popular support, free speech provided the crucial arena for the penultimate crisis of the judicial self-restraint movement. (The ultimate crisis came in BROWN V. BOARD OF EDUCATION, 1954.) Although the logical implication of that movement suggested that the Court ought never declare an act of Congress unconstitutional as a violation of the BILL OF RIGHTS, the Court was not prepared to go so far. The Justices' dilemma was that they were the inheritors of pro-freedom of speech doctrines but wished to uphold infringements upon speech without openly abdicating their constitutional authority.

The way out of this dilemma was the balancing formula. It allowed the Court to vindicate legislative and executive anticommunist measures case by case without ever flatly announcing that the Court had gone out of the business of enforcing the First Amendment. LEARNED HAND's "clear and probable" or "discounting" formula adopted by the Supreme Court in DENNIS V. UNITED STATES (1951) was the vital bridge in moving from a clear and present danger test that impels judicial action to a balancing test that veils judicial withdrawal. For Hand's test permits conversion of the danger test from an exception to freedom of speech invoked when speech creates an immediate danger of violent crime to a general formula for outweighing speech claims whenever the goals espoused in the speech are sufficiently antithetical to those of the majority. Justice FELIX FRANKFURTER's concurrence in *Dennis* and the majority opinion in BARENBLATT V. UNITED STATES (1959) not only made the antispeech potential of the balancing doctrine clear but also exhibited its great potential for absolute judicial deference to coordinate branches. For if constitutional judgments are ultimately a matter of balancing interests, in a democratic society who is the ultimate balancer? Necessarily, it is the Congress in which all the competing interests are represented. Thus the Court deferred to Congress's judgment that the needs of national security outweighed the speech rights of the enemies of that security.

Proponents of the balancing doctrine argue that no one is really willing to give any constitutional right absolute sway and that the act of judging always involves a weighing of competing claims. Certainly when constitutional rights such as free speech and FAIR TRIAL come into conflict, balancing of the two appears inevitable. The opponents of balancing argue for "principled" versus "ad hoc" or case-by-case balancing. If judges are left free to balance the particular interests in each particular case, they are always free to decide any case for or against the rights claimed by the way they state the interests. Opponents of ad hoc balancing insist that whatever balancing must be done should be done in the course of creating constitutional rules that will then be applied even-handedly in all cases. Thus, if fair trial and free speech values conflict, we may want a rule that upholds the constitutionality of banning prosecutors from pretrial release of confessions, but we do not want the kind of ad hoc balancing in which judges are free to find that in some cases such bans are constitutional and in others they are not.

Balancing has remained a principal doctrine in the freedom of speech area and has spread to other constitutional areas such as PRIVACY. Its capacity as a vehicle for judicial discretion is illustrated by BUCKLEY V. VALEO (1976), in which the Court used the balancing doctrine to march through the complex CAMPAIGN FINANCE ACT, striking down some provisions and upholding others in what was effectively a total legislative redrafting, and by the ABORTION cases (see ROE V. WADE, 1973) in which the Court used the balancing doctrine to invest with constitutional authority the "trimester" scheme it invented.

In GIBSON V. FLORIDA LEGISLATIVE INVESTIGATING COMMITTEE (1963) the Court held that government might infringe upon a First Amendment right only when it could show a COMPELLING STATE INTEREST. This formula may be viewed as weighting the balance of interests in favor of constitutional rights, but any government interests can be stated in such a way as to appear compelling. The Court's employment of the balancing test always leaves us uncertain whether any legislative infringement of free speech or other rights, no matter how direct or how open, will be declared unconstitutional, for the Court may always be prepared to find some state interest sufficiently weighty to justify the infringement.

MARTIN SHAPIRO

(SEE ALSO: *Absolutism; Judicial Activism and Restraint.*)

Bibliography

FRANTZ, LAURENT B. 1963 Is the First Amendment Law? *California Law Review* 51:729–754.

HAND, LEARNED 1958 *The Bill of Rights.* Cambridge, Mass.: Harvard University Press.

MENDELSON, WALLACE 1962 On the Meaning of the First Amendment: Absolutes in the Balance. *California Law Review* 50:821–828.

BALDWIN, ABRAHAM (1754–1807)

Abraham Baldwin represented Georgia at the CONSTITUTIONAL CONVENTION OF 1787 and signed the Constitution. He served on the Committee on Representation, and, although personally opposed to equal representation of states in the Senate, the Connecticut-born Baldwin played a key role in securing the GREAT COMPROMISE. He later spent eighteen years in Congress.

DENNIS J. MAHONEY

BALDWIN, HENRY (1780–1844)

Henry Baldwin of Pittsburgh was appointed to the Supreme Court on January 4, 1830, by ANDREW JACKSON. After graduating from Yale College in 1797, he studied law with ALEXANDER J. DALLAS and began his practice in Pittsburgh where he joined the bar in 1801. Law spilled over naturally into politics for Baldwin, and from 1816 to 1822 he served in Congress, where he gained a reputation as an economic nationalist. He also defended Andrew Jackson from charges of misconduct in Spanish Florida and later supported him for President—efforts that won him a seat on the Supreme Court.

Though an unknown judicial quantity, Baldwin was acceptable to the still-dominant JOSEPH STORY-JOHN MARSHALL wing of the Court because of his reputation as a "sound" man and talented lawyer—and because he was not JOHN BANNISTER GIBSON, whom conservatives feared would get the appointment. Baldwin's supporters were soon disappointed, then shocked. Almost immediately the new Justice was out of phase with the Court's nationalism and at odds with several of its members, especially Story, whose scholarly, didactic style Baldwin found offensive and threatening. After serving less than a year on the Court, he wanted off. Worse still, his collapse in 1833 (which caused him to miss that term of the Court) signaled the onset of a mental condition that progressively incapacitated him. Occasionally he rose to the level of his early promise, as for example in *United States v. Arredondo* (1832) where the principle was established that land claims resting on acts of foreign governments (which in the Spanish and Mexican cessions amounted to millions of acres) were presumed valid unless the United States could prove otherwise. Another solid effort was *Holmes v. Jennison* (1840) where he upheld the right of a state to surrender fugitives to a foreign country even though such a power cut into the policymaking authority of the national government in FOREIGN AFFAIRS. His circuit efforts were also well received at first and deservedly so, judging from such opinions as *McGill v. Brown* (1833) where he handled a complicated question of charitable bequests with considerable sophistication.

Baldwin's constitutional philosophy, so far as it can be detected, was set forth in his *General View of the Origin and Nature of the Constitution and Government of the United States,* a rambling, unconvincing treatise published in 1837 (mainly, it would seem, to rescue him from pressing debts). Baldwin presumed to stake out a middle constitutional ground for himself between extreme STATES' RIGHTS constitutional doctrine and the broad nationalism of Marshall and Story which he explicitly condemned as unfounded and usurpatory. He took particular pains to refute the thesis in Story's *Commentaries on the Constitution* (1833) that SOVEREIGNTY devolved on the whole people after 1776. Baldwin's final position on the matter appeared to be little more than a reductionist version of JOHN C. CALHOUN's theories.

The states' rights theory set forth in *General View* was consistent with Baldwin's *Jennison* opinion and his preference for STATE POLICE POWER as stated in the slavery case of GROVES V. SLAUGHTER (1841). On the other hand, in *McCracken v. Hayward* (1844), he did not hesitate to strike down an Illinois stay law that impaired contractual rights. His unpublished opinion in BANK OF AUGUSTA V. EARLE (1839) took the extremely nationalist position that a foreign corporation's right to do business in a state was protected by the PRIVILEGES AND IMMUNITIES clause of Article IV, section 2, of the Constitution.

To say where Baldwin really stood is difficult. He wrote less than forty majority opinions during his fourteen years on the Court. Of those, few were important and fewer still were coherent expositions of constitutional DOCTRINE. He withdrew more and more into paranoiac isolation, carping at his colleagues, criticizing reporter Richard Peters, and pondering his rapidly deteriorating financial situation. He dissented more and more (thirty-some times counting unwritten dissents) and with less and less purpose. That a number of his separate opinions were delivered too late to be included in the reports suggests that his impact in the Court's CONFERENCE was peripheral at best. His effectiveness on the circuit declined, too, if one credits the growing complaints of district judge Joseph Hopkinson who sat with him in Pennsylvania. Baldwin died in 1844, deeply in debt, without friends and with no prospect of being remembered favorably. Illness had taken a heavy toll. His influence on American law was negligible and his presence on the Supreme Court was probably counterproductive.

R. KENT NEWMYER

Bibliography

BALDWIN, HENRY 1837 *A General View of the Origin and Nature of the Constitution and Government of the United States. . . .* Philadelphia: John C. Clark.

GATELL, FRANK O. 1969 Henry Baldwin. In Leon Friedman and Fred L. Israel (eds.), *The Justices of the United States Supreme Court, 1789–1969,* Vol. 1, pages 571–598. New York: Chelsea House.

BALDWIN, ROGER N.
(1884–1981)

Until the United States entered World War I, Roger Nash Baldwin was a social worker and a leading expert on juvenile courts. A pacifist who feared that the war might cause repression of individual rights, Baldwin helped to found the National Civil Liberties Bureau in 1917. The Bureau defended CONSCIENTIOUS OBJECTORS and those prosecuted for allegedly antiwar speeches and publications. Reorganized in 1920 by Baldwin and others as the AMERICAN CIVIL LIBERTIES UNION, it expanded its efforts to include among its many clients leaders of the International Workers of the World and other labor organizations; John T. Scopes, who violated Tennessee's anti-evolution law in 1925 and was prosecuted in the infamous "monkey trial"; the Jehovah's Witnesses; and even those, such as the Ku Klux Klan and the German-American Bund, who opposed FREEDOM OF SPEECH for all but themselves. Baldwin was also committed to efforts on behalf of human rights abroad; despite his sympathy for radical causes, his investigation of the Soviet Union led him to oppose communism. In 1940, at his urging, the ACLU adopted a loyalty resolution barring supporters of totalitarian dictatorships from membership, only to find later that the government LOYALTY OATHS, which it fought in court, were based on its own resolution. Baldwin served as director of the ACLU until 1950, as its chairman from 1950 to 1955, and as its international work adviser until his death. After World War II, Baldwin was counselor on CIVIL LIBERTIES in the reconstruction of the governments of Japan, Korea, and Germany.

RICHARD B. BERNSTEIN

Bibliography

LAMSON, PEGGY 1976 *Roger Baldwin, Founder of the American Civil Liberties Union: A Portrait.* Boston: Houghton Mifflin.

BALDWIN v. FISH & GAME COMMISSION
436 U.S. 371 (1978)

The Supreme Court, 6–3, sustained Montana's exaction of a substantially higher elk-hunting license fee for nonresidents than for residents. Temporarily abandoning the approach of TOOMER V. WITSELL (1948), the Court said that the PRIVILEGES AND IMMUNITIES clause of Article IV of the Constitution protected citizens of other states only as to fundamental rights, a category that did not include the "sport" of killing elk. *Toomer*'s approach returned four weeks later in HICKLIN V. ORBECK (1978), but the Court in Hicklin neither overruled nor distinguished *Baldwin.* (See RESIDENCE REQUIREMENTS.)

KENNETH L. KARST

BALDWIN v. NEW YORK
399 U.S. 66 (1970)

When DUNCAN V. LOUISIANA extended the SIXTH AMENDMENT'S TRIAL BY JURY provision to the states in 1968, the Court said that MISDEMEANORS, crimes punishable by imprisonment for less than six months, may be tried without a jury. Petty offenses have always been exempt from the amendment's guarantee of trial by jury in "all criminal prosecutions." Baldwin, having been sentenced to a year in jail for pickpocketing, claimed on APPEAL that New York City had deprived him of his right to a trial by jury. The Court held that the Constitution requires a trial by jury if an offense can be punished by imprisonment for more than six months. Justice BYRON R. WHITE, for a plurality, found decisive the fact that one city alone in the nation denied trial by jury when the possible punishment exceeded six months. Justices HUGO L. BLACK and WILLIAM O. DOUGLAS, concurring separately, would have ruled that the Constitution requires a jury for all accused persons without exception.

LEONARD W. LEVY

BALLARD, UNITED STATES v.

See: Postal Power; Religion and Fraud

BALLEW v. GEORGIA
435 U.S. 223 (1978)

In *Ballew v. Georgia,* the Supreme Court unanimously held that a five-person jury in a nonpetty criminal case does not satisfy the right to TRIAL BY JURY under the Sixth Amendment as applied to the states through the FOURTEENTH AMENDMENT. *Ballew* involved a misdemeanor conviction for exhibiting an obscene motion picture.

Although all the Justices agreed upon the result, four separate opinions were written on the five-person jury issue. Justice HARRY A. BLACKMUN joined by Justice JOHN PAUL STEVENS relied heavily on SOCIAL SCIENCE RESEARCH in concluding that there was substantial doubt that a five-person jury functioned effectively, was likely to reach accurate results, or truly represented the community. Justice BYRON R. WHITE concluded that a jury of less than six would fail to represent the sense of the community. Justice LEWIS F. POWELL joined by Chief Justice WARREN E. Burger and Justice WILLIAM H. REHNQUIST agreed that five-person juries raised "grave questions of fairness" indicating that "a line has to be drawn somewhere if the substance of jury trial is to be preserved." Since an earlier case, WILLIAMS V. FLORIDA (1970), had upheld the constitutionality of six-person juries, the effect of *Ballew* was to draw the constitutional line between five and six.

NORMAN ABRAMS

(SEE ALSO: *Jury Size.*)

BANCROFT, GEORGE
(1800–1891)

A liberal Democrat from Massachusetts, Bancroft served as JAMES POLK's secretary of the navy and acting secretary of war, as ANDREW JOHNSON's adviser, and as minister to Great Britain and to Germany. He was also the most popular, influential, and respected American historian of the nineteenth century. His twelve-volume epic on American liberty, the *History of the United States from the Discovery of the Continent,* written over half a century, contains 1,700,000 words. The last two volumes, a *History of the Formation of the Constitution of the United States* (1882), covered 1782–1789. The work benefited from Bancroft's notes of his interview with JAMES MADISON in 1836; Madison also opened his private archives to him. Bancroft was an indefatigable researcher. His chronological narrative of the origins, framing, and RATIFICATION OF THE CONSTITUTION was based on manuscript letters as well as public records. He included over 300 pages of letters, many printed for the first time.

Bancroft wrote in a grand style that is today considered florid. His essentially political interpretation remained the standard work of its kind until superseded in 1928 by CHARLES WARREN's *The Making of the Constitution,* although ANDREW C. MCLAUGHLIN's *Confederation and Constitution* (1908) exceeded both in judicious analysis. Bancroft's work is remarkably fair, although Madisonian in approach. He viewed the Constitution as a bundle of compromises between nationalists and states' rightists, North and South, large states and small ones. The epigraph to his work was William Gladstone's judgment that "the American Constitution is the most wonderful work ever struck off at a given time by the brain and purpose of man." CHARLES BEARD made Bancroft one of his prime targets because of Bancroft's belief that the Framers were principled patriots who gave their loyalty to a concept of national interest that transcended purse and status without compromising republican ideals.

LEONARD W. LEVY

Bibliography

NYE, RUSSELL 1964 *George Bancroft.* New York: Washington Square Press.

BANK HOLIDAY OF 1933

See: Emergency Bank Act

BANK OF AUGUSTA v. EARLE
13 Peters 519 (1839)

This case was vitally important to CORPORATIONS because it raised the question whether a corporation chartered in one state could do business in another. Justice JOHN MCKINLEY on circuit duty ruled against corporations, provoking Justice JOSEPH STORY to say that McKinley's opinion frightened "all the corporations of the country out of their proprieties. He has held that a corporation created in one State has no power to contract or even to act in any other State. . . . So, banks, insurance companies, manufacturing companies, etc. have no capacity to take or discount notes in another State, or to underwrite policies, or to buy or sell goods." McKinley's decision seemed a death sentence to all interstate corporate business. On APPEAL, DANIEL WEBSTER, representing corporate interests, argued that corporations were citizens entitled to the same rights, under the COMITY CLAUSE in Article IV, section 2, of the Constitution, as natural persons to do business. With only McKinley dissenting, Chief Justice ROGER B. TANEY for the Court steered a middle way between the extremes of McKinley and Webster. He ruled that a corporation, acting through its agents, could do business in other states if they did not expressly prohibit it from doing so. In the absence of such a state prohibition, the Court would presume, from the principle of comity, that out-of-state corporations were invited to transact business. Thus a state might exclude such corporations or admit them conditionally; but the Court overruled McKinley's decision, and corporations as well as Whigs, like Webster and Story, rejoiced.

LEONARD W. LEVY

(SEE ALSO: *Citizenship; Privileges and Immunities.*)

BANK OF THE UNITED STATES ACTS
1 Stat. 191 (1791)
3 Stat. 266 (1816)

The first Bank of the United States (1791–1811) was chartered by Congress on a plan submitted by Secretary of the Treasury ALEXANDER HAMILTON as part of his financial system. Modeled on the century-old Bank of England, the national bank harnessed private interest and profit for public purposes. It received an exclusive twenty-year charter. It was capitalized at $10,000,000, of which the government subscribed one-fifth and private investors the remainder, one-fourth in specie and three-fourths in government stock. Located at Philadelphia and authorized to establish branches, it was to be the financial arm of government (a ready lender, a keeper and tranferrer of funds); through its powers to mount a large paper circulation and advance commercial credit, the bank would also augment the active capital of the country and stimulate enterprise. JAMES MADISON had opposed the bank bill in Congress entirely on constitutional grounds. His arguments, turning on the absence of congressional power and invasion of the reserved rights of the states, were repeated in opinions submitted to President GEORGE WASHINGTON by Attorney General EDMUND RANDOLPH and Secretary of State THOMAS JEFFERSON. They were answered, convincingly in Washington's mind, by Hamilton's argument on the doctrine of IMPLIED POWERS.

The Second Bank of the United States (1816–1836) was an enlarged and revised version of the first. Republican constitutional objections had finally prevailed when Congress refused to recharter the first bank in 1811. But the disorganization of the country's finances during the War of 1812 led the Madison administration to propose a national bank. After several false starts, a plan was agreed upon by Congress in 1816. In 1791, there had been three state-chartered banks; in 1816 there were 260, and Congress acted to recover its abandoned power to regulate the currency. As the constitutional issue receded, controversy shifted to practical and technical questions of banking policy. Inept management, state bank jealousy, and severe financial pressure in 1818–1819 produced demands for revocation of the bank's charter. Aided by the Supreme Court's decision in MCCULLOCH V. MARYLAND (1819), the bank weathered this storm and under the efficient direction of Nicholas Biddle not only prospered but gained widespread public support in the 1820s. Nevertheless, President ANDREW JACK-

SON attacked the bank on financial, political, and constitutional grounds. Biddle and his political friends decided to make the bank the leading issue in the 1832 presidential election by seeking immediate renewal of the charter not due to expire until 1836. Congress obliged, and Jackson vetoed the recharter bill with a powerful indictment of the bank as a privileged moneyed institution that trampled on the Constitution. (See JACKSON'S VETO OF THE BANK BILL.) Asserting the independence of the three branches of government in the interpretation of the Constitution, he declared, "The opinion of the judges has no more authority over Congress than the opinion of Congress has over the judges, and on that point the President is independent of both." After Jackson's reelection, the ties between the government and the bank were quickly severed.

MERRILL D. PETERSON

Bibliography

HAMMOND, BRAY 1957 *Banks and Politics in America from the Revolution to the Civil War.* Princeton, N.J.: Princeton University Press.

BANKRUPTCY (CHANDLER) ACT
52 Stat. 883 (1938)

The Bankruptcy Act of 1938, known as the Chandler Act, represented Congress's first comprehensive revision of the Bankruptcy Act of 1898. (See BANKRUPTCY POWER.) Under the financial strain caused by the Depression, the nation needed supplementary bankruptcy legislation. In a series of measures from 1933 through 1937, Congress sought to foster rehabilitation and reorganization of financially distressed debtors' nonexempt assets. The measures covered individual workers, railroads, farmers, nonrailroad CORPORATIONS, and municipalities. The Chandler Act both revised the basic bankruptcy provisions of the 1898 act and restructured and refined the Depression-era amendments. It segregated the rehabilitation and reorganization provisions into separate chapters, a structure adhered to in the Bankruptcy Reform Act of 1978. But the 1938 act neither sought nor achieved organic changes in bankruptcy law.

THEODORE EISENBERG

Bibliography

WARREN, CHARLES 1935 *Bankruptcy in United States History.* Cambridge, Mass.: Harvard University Press.

BANKRUPTCY POWER

Article I, section 8, of the Constitution authorizes Congress to establish "uniform Laws on the subject of Bankruptcies throughout the United States." As interpreted in the CIRCUIT COURT decision in *In re Klein* (1843), this clause empowers Congress to enact laws covering all aspects of the distribution of a debtor's property and the discharge of his debts. Contrary to some early arguments, Congress's bankruptcy power is not limited to legislating only for the trader class. Commencing in 1800, Congress repeatedly exercised its bankruptcy power during periods of depression or financial unrest, but all early bankruptcy laws were repealed whenever unrest subsided. Since 1898, however, the United States continuously has had a comprehensive bankruptcy law, one completely revised by the BANKRUPTCY REFORM ACT of 1978.

Article I expressly requires bankruptcy legislation to be uniform. As interpreted in *Hanover National Bank v. Moyses* (1902), the uniformity limitation does not prevent incorporation of state law into federal bankruptcy provisions. Bankruptcy law, the Court held in that case, is uniform "when the trustee takes in each state whatever would have been available to the creditor if the bankrupt law had not been passed. The general operation of the law is uniform although it may result in certain particulars differently in different states." And under the *Regional Rail Reorganization Act Cases* (1974) a bankruptcy statute may confine its operations to a single region where all covered bankrupt entities happen to be located. *Railway Executives' Association v. Gibbons* (1982), the only Supreme Court case to invalidate a bankruptcy law for lack of uniformity, struck down the Rock Island Transition and Employee Assistance Act because it covered only one of several railroads then in reorganization.

However many other theoretical limitations restrict Congress's bankruptcy power, only a few have led to invalidation of bankruptcy legislation. As interpreted in reorganization cases, the Fifth Amendment's DUE PROCESS CLAUSE limits Congress's bankruptcy power to alter or interfere with the rights of secured creditors. In LOUISVILLE JOINT STOCK LAND BANK V. RADFORD (1934) the Court found the original FRAZIER-LEMKE ACT unconstitutional because it too drastically interfered with a mortgagee's interest in property. But within months Congress enacted the second Frazier-Lemke Act, with scaled down interference, which the Court upheld in WRIGHT V. VINTON BRANCH OF MOUNTAIN TRUST BANK OF ROANOKE (1937). And in *Continental Illinois National Bank and Trust Co. v. Chicago, Rock Island and Pacific Railway*

Company (1935) the Court held that secured creditors could at least temporarily be enjoined from selling their security. *Van Huffel v. Harkelrode* (1931) allows property to be sold free of a mortage holder's encumbrance where his or her rights are transferred to the proceeds of the sale. The *Regional Rail Reorganization Act Cases* found no constitutional flaw in the government's refusal to permit liquidation of an unsuccessful business where the Tucker Act permitted a suit for damages in the COURT OF CLAIMS.

For a brief period, there was doubt about Congress's authority to regulate municipal bankruptcies. In ASHTON V. CAMERON COUNTY WATER IMPROVEMENT DISTRICT (1937) the Supreme Court invalidated, as an interference with state sovereignty, a 1934 municipal bankruptcy law. But in *United States v. Bekins* (1938), in a shift that may be attributable to changes in Court personnel, the Court sustained a similar law. The Bankruptcy Reform Act of 1978 contains an updated municipal bankruptcy law.

Under STURGES V. CROWNINSHIELD (1819), when no national bankruptcy laws are in effect, states may regulate insolvency. Their effectiveness in doing so is limited by the requirement that states not impair the OBLIGATION OF CONTRACTS. When national bankruptcy legislation is in effect, *Stellwagen v. Clum* (1918) and other cases indicate that state laws are abrogated only to the extent that they undermine federal law.

THEODORE EISENBERG

Bibliography

WARREN, CHARLES 1935 *Bankruptcy in United States History.* Cambridge, Mass.: Harvard University Press.

BANKRUPTCY REFORM ACT
92 Stat. 2549 (1978)

The Bankruptcy Reform Act of 1978 was the first comprehensive revision of federal bankruptcy law since 1938 and the first completely new bankruptcy law since 1898. (See BANKRUPTCY POWER.) Although the 1978 act made many substantive changes in bankruptcy law, its most controversial changes concern the organization of the bankruptcy system. The act expanded the bankruptcy court's authority to include JURISDICTION over virtually all matters relating to the bankrupt and the bankrupt's assets. This expansion, combined with Congress's failure to staff the new bankruptcy courts with life-tenured judges, led the Supreme Court in NORTHERN PIPELINE CONSTRUCTION CO. V. MARATHON PIPE LINE CO. (1982) to invalidate portions of the act's jurisdictional scheme. (See JUDICIAL POWER OF THE UNITED STATES.) In an effort to upgrade the bankruptcy courts, the act, in selected pilot districts, creates a system of United States trustees to administer and supervise bankruptcy cases, leaving courts free to perform more traditional adjudicatory functions. One of the statute's most significant changes is to consolidate into a single reorganization proceeding what had been three different methods for reorganizing financially distressed CORPORATIONS.

THEODORE EISENBERG

Bibliography

Selected Articles on the Bankruptcy Reform Act of 1978 1979 *St. Mary's Law Journal* 11:247–501.

BANTAM BOOKS, INC. v. SULLIVAN
372 U.S. 58 (1963)

In *Bantam Books v. Sullivan* the Supreme Court struck down a state system of informal censorship, holding that the regulation of OBSCENITY must meet rigorous procedural safeguards to guard against the repression of constitutionally protected FREEDOM OF SPEECH. Rhode Island had created a commission to educate the public concerning books unsuitable to youths. The commission informed book and magazine distributors that certain publications were "objectionable" for distribution to youths under eighteen years of age and threatened legal sanctions should a distributor fail to "cooperate." Distributors, rather than risk prosecution, had removed books from public circulation, resulting in the suppression of publications the state conceded were not obscene.

KIM MCLANE WARDLAW

BARBOUR, PHILIP P.
(1783–1841)

Philip P. Barbour was appointed to the Supreme Court by ANDREW JACKSON in December 1835 to fill the seat vacated by GABRIEL DUVALL. Born into Virginia's slaveholding plantation elite, Barbour held constitutional values that promoted the interest of that class. His law was largely self-taught, though he attended the College of William and Mary briefly in

1802 before beginning full-time practice in Orange County, Virginia. Beginning in 1812, Barbour served two years in the Virginia Assembly, following which he was elected to Congress where he served until 1825 and then again for two years beginning in 1827. For a brief time he was a Judge of the General Court of Virginia, and in 1830 he was appointed to the federal district court for Eastern Virginia, where he remained until assuming his Supreme Court duties in 1836.

Barbour's views on the Constitution were essentially those of the Richmond Junto of which he was a member. As a STATES' RIGHTS constitutionalist, he was opposed to federally sponsored INTERNAL IMPROVEMENTS, the protective tariff, and the second BANK OF THE UNITED STATES, an institution he viewed as a private CORPORATION whose stock the government should not own. He defended SLAVERY vigorously during the Missouri debates and, at the Virginia Constitutional Convention of 1829–1830, voted consistently with tidewater slaveholders against the democratic forces of the West. Barbour also supported the court-curbing plan of Senator Richard Johnson of Kentucky, prompted by the Court's decision in COHENS V. VIRGINIA (1821), and in 1827 he himself sponsored a measure that would have required a majority of five of seven Justices to hold a law unconstitutional.

Four years on the Court gave Barbour little chance to translate his states' rights philosophy and theory of judicial power into law. He wrote only a handful of opinions, and only in MAYOR OF NEW YORK V. MILN (1837) did he speak for the majority in an important case. There he upheld a New York regulation of immigrants as a STATE POLICE POWER measure, but his exposition of doctrine was inchoate at best and did little to influence future decisions. States' rights thinking also informed his vote in CHARLES RIVER BRIDGE V. WARREN BRIDGE (1837) (where he joined the new Jacksonian majority in refusing to extend by implication the 1819 ruling in DARTMOUTH COLLEGE V. WOODWARD) and in BRISCOE V. BANK OF KENTUCKY, also in 1837 (where the new majority refused to invalidate state bank notes on the ground that they were not BILLS OF CREDIT prohibited by Article I, section 10, of the Constitution).

Although he was a consistent advocate of states' rights, Barbour was not, as JOHN QUINCY ADAMS charged, a "shallow-pated wild-cat" bent on destroying the Union. Indeed, compared to the states' rights views of PETER DANIEL who succeeded him, Barbour's appear moderate and restrained. Even DANIEL WEBSTER conceded that he was "honest and conscientious," and Justice JOSEPH STORY, for all his objection to Barbour's constitutional notions, thought him a "perspicacious" and "vigorous" judge.

R. KENT NEWMYER

Bibliography

CYNN, P. P. 1913 Philip Pendleton Barbour. *The John P. Branch Historical Papers* (Randolph Macon College) 4:67–77.

GATELL, FRANK O. 1969 Philip Pendleton Barbour. In Leon Friedman and Fred L. Israel (eds.), *The Justices of the United States Supreme Court, 1789–1969,* Vol. 1, pages 717–734. New York: Chelsea House.

BAREFOOT v. ESTELLE
463 U.S. 880 (1983)

In *Barefoot v. Estelle* the Supreme Court gave its approval to expedited federal collateral review of CAPITAL PUNISHMENT cases. In a 6–3 decision the Court approved the consolidation of hearings on procedural and substantive motions, the separate arguing of which had frustrated imposition of the death penalty even when the claims supporting the appeal were without merit. The opinion by Justice BYRON R. WHITE declared that no constitutional right of the convict was impaired by the one-step appeals process.

DENNIS J. MAHONEY

BARENBLATT v. UNITED STATES
360 U.S. 109 (1959)

In a 5–4 decision, Justice JOHN MARSHALL HARLAN writing for the majority, the Supreme Court upheld Barenblatt's conviction for contempt of Congress based on his refusal to answer questions of the House Committee on Un-American Activities about his membership in the Communist party. He argued that such questions violated his rights of FREEDOM OF SPEECH and association by publically exposing his political beliefs. In an earlier decision, WATKINS V. UNITED STATES (1957), the Court had offered some procedural protections to witnesses before such committees and held out hope that it would offer even greater protections in the future. *Barenblatt* ended that hope.

The Court did follow the *Watkins* approach of denouncing "exposure for the exposure's sake" and requiring that Congress have a legislative purpose for its investigations. But it presumed that Congress did have such a purpose, refusing to look at the actual congressional motives behind the investigation.

Barenblatt is the classic case of a FIRST AMENDMENT ad hoc BALANCING TEST. The Court held that the First Amendment protected individuals from compelled disclosure of their political associations. But Justice Harlan went on to say, "Where First Amendment rights are asserted to bar governmental interrogation, resolution of the issue always involved a balancing by the Courts of the competing private and public interest at stake in the circumstances shown." Then he balanced Barenblatt's interest in not answering questions about his communist associations against Congress's interest in frustrating the international communist conspiracy to overthrow the United States government. The interests thus defined, the Court had no trouble striking the balance in favor of the government. More than any other decision, *Barenblatt* establishes that the freedom of speech may be restricted by government if, in the Court's view, the government's interest in committing the infringement is sufficiently compelling.

MARTIN SHAPIRO

BARKER v. WINGO
407 U.S. 514 (1972)

The SPEEDY TRIAL right protects a defendant from undue delay between the time charges are filed and trial. When a defendant is deprived of that right, the only remedy is dismissal with prejudice of the charges pending against him. In *Barker,* the leading speedy trial decision, the Supreme Court discussed the criteria by which the speedy trial right is to be judged. The Court adopted a BALANCING TEST involving four factors to be weighed in each case where the issue arises. They are: (1) the length of the delay; (2) the reasons for the delay; (3) the defendant's assertion of his right; and (4) prejudice to the defendant, such as pretrial incarceration and inability to prepare a defense. In reaching its decision the Court noted that the speedy trial right is unique inasmuch as it protects societal rights as well as those of the accused. In many instances, delayed trials benefit a defendant because witnesses disappear or memories fade. The balancing takes into consideration the varied interests protected by that right.

WENDY E. LEVY

BARRON v. CITY OF BALTIMORE
7 Peters 243 (1833)

When JAMES MADISON proposed to the First Congress the amendments that became the BILL OF RIGHTS, he included a provision that no state shall violate FREEDOM OF RELIGION, FREEDOM OF PRESS, or TRIAL BY JURY in criminal cases; the proposal to restrict the states was defeated. The amendments constituting a Bill of Rights were understood to be a bill of restraints upon the United States only. In *Barron,* Chief Justice JOHN MARSHALL for a unanimous Supreme Court ruled in conformance with the clear history of the matter. *Barron* invoked against Baltimore the clause of the Fifth Amendment prohibiting the taking of private property without JUST COMPENSATION. The "fifth amendment," the Court held, "must be understood as restraining the power of the general government, not as applicable to the states."

LEONARD W. LEVY

BARROWS v. JACKSON
346 U.S. 249 (1953)

Following the decision in SHELLEY V. KRAEMER (1948), state courts could no longer constitutionally enforce racially RESTRICTIVE COVENANTS by INJUNCTION. The question remained whether the covenants could be enforced indirectly, in actions for damages. In *Barrows,* white neighbors sued for damages against co-covenantors who had sold a home to black buyers in disregard of a racial covenant. The Supreme Court held that the sellers had STANDING to raise the EQUAL PROTECTION claims on behalf of the black buyers, who were not in court, and went on to hold that the FOURTEENTH AMENDMENT barred damages as well as injunctive relief to enforce racial covenants. Chief Justice FRED M. VINSON, who had written the *Shelley* opinion, dissented, saying the covenant itself, "standing alone," was valid, in the absence of judicial ejectment of black occupants.

KENNETH L. KARST

BARTKUS v. ILLINOIS
359 U.S. 121 (1959)
ABBATE v. UNITED STATES
359 U.S. 187 (1959)

A 5–4 Supreme Court held in *Bartkus v. Illinois* that close cooperation between state and federal officials did not violate the DOUBLE JEOPARDY clause when

Illinois tried (and convicted) Bartkus for a robbery of which a federal court had acquitted him. Justice FELIX FRANKFURTER's majority opinion de-emphasized the connection between the prosecutions. Despite "substantially identical" INDICTMENTS and although the Federal Bureau of Investigation had given all its EVIDENCE to state authorities, Frankfurter could find no basis for the claim that Illinois was "merely a tool of the federal authorities" or that the Illinois prosecution violated the DUE PROCESS CLAUSE of the FOURTEENTH AMENDMENT. He rejected the assertion that the Fourteenth Amendment was a "short-hand incorporation" of the BILL OF RIGHTS and also cited the test of PALKO v. CONNECTICUT (1937) with approval.

Justice HUGO L. BLACK, joined by Chief Justice EARL WARREN and Justice WILLIAM O. DOUGLAS, dissented. Black found such prosecutions "so contrary to the spirit of our free country that they violate even the prevailing view of the Fourteenth Amendment." Justice WILLIAM J. BRENNAN, dissenting separately, presented convincing evidence that federal officers solicited, instigated, guided, and prepared the Illinois case, amounting to a second federal prosecution "in the guise of a state prosecution."

Justice Brennan joined the *Bartkus* majority in *Abbate v. United States,* decided the same day. The defendants here were indicted and convicted in both state and federal courts for the same act, the federal prosecution following the state conviction. Brennan, for the majority, relied squarely on UNITED STATES v. LANZA (1922), concluding that "the efficiency of federal law enforcement must suffer if the Double Jeopardy Clause prevents successive state and federal prosecutions." Black, for the same minority, relied on his *Bartkus* dissent and the distinction "that a State and the Nation can [not] be considered two wholly separate sovereignties for the purpose of allowing them to do together what, generally, neither can do separately."

DAVID GORDON

BASSETT, RICHARD
(1745–1815)

Richard Bassett represented Delaware at the CONSTITUTIONAL CONVENTION OF 1787 and signed the Constitution. Although there is no record of his speaking at the Convention, he was a leader in securing Delaware's ratification. He went on to become governor and chief justice of Delaware, and a United States senator.

DENNIS J. MAHONEY

BATES, EDWARD
(1793–1869)

A St. Louis attorney and Whig leader, Edward Bates, a moderate on slavery, opposed the LECOMPTON Constitution and repeal of the MISSOURI COMPROMISE. In 1860 he sought the Republican presidential nomination, and from 1861 to 1864 he was President ABRAHAM LINCOLN'S ATTORNEY GENERAL and most conservative adviser. In response to EX PARTE MERRYMAN (1861) he defended Lincoln's suspension of HABEAS CORPUS on the weak rationale that the three branches of government were co-equal and that Chief Justice ROGER B. TANEY therefore could not order Lincoln to act. Bates personally disliked the suspension but thought it preferable to martial law. The CONFISCATION ACTS undermined Bates's sense of property rights, and his department rarely supported these acts. Bates strongly supported the EMANCIPATION PROCLAMATION, but he insisted it be limited to areas still under rebel control. He believed that free blacks could be United States citizens because he narrowly construed DRED SCOTT v. SANDFORD (1857) to apply only to Negroes "of *African* descent" suing in Missouri. Bates supplied legal opinions to support the legal tender statutes, but he opposed the admission of West Virginia on constitutional grounds. He also opposed the use of black troops and retaliation for atrocities by Confederates committed on black prisoners of war. Nevertheless, he urged Lincoln to give Negro soldiers equal pay once they were enlisted. Bates consistently urged Lincoln to assert his constitutional role as COMMANDER-IN-CHIEF when Union generalship was poor. Bates had a broad view of his office and exerted a greater control over the United States district attorneys than his predecessors.

PAUL FINKELMAN

Bibliography

CAIN, MARVIN E. 1965 *Lincoln's Attorney General: Edward Bates of Missouri.* Columbia: University of Missouri Press.

BATES v. STATE BAR OF ARIZONA
433 U.S. 350 (1977)

In 1976 two Phoenix lawyers ran newspaper advertisements offering "routine" legal services for "very reasonable" prices. A 5–4 Supreme Court declared here that the FIRST AMENDMENT protected this form of COMMERCIAL SPEECH. The majority rejected a number of "countervailing state interests" urged against the FREEDOM OF SPEECH protection, relying on VIRGINIA STATE BOARD OF PHARMACY V. VIRGINIA CITIZENS' CONSUMER COUNCIL (1976). The dissenters strenuously objected to the majority's equating intangible services—which they found impossible to standardize and rarely "routine"—with "prepackaged prescription drugs." The Court rejected, 9–0, a contention that the SHERMAN ANTITRUST ACT barred any restraint on such advertising.

DAVID GORDON

BAYARD v. SINGLETON
1 Martin (N. Car.) 42 (1787)

This was the first reported American state case in which a court held a legislative enactment unconstitutional. This and the TEN POUND ACT CASES are the only authentic examples of the exercise of JUDICIAL REVIEW carried to its furthest limit before the circuit work of the Justices of the Supreme Court of the United States in the 1790s. During the Revolution, North Carolina had confiscated and sold Tory estates; to protect the new owners, the legislature enacted that in any action to recover confiscated land, the courts must grant a motion to dismiss the suit. Bayard brought such a suit, and Singleton made a motion for dismissal. Instead of granting the motion, the high court of the state delayed decision and recommended a jury trial to settle the issue of ownership. The court seemed to be seeking a way to avoid holding the act unconstitutional and hoped that the legislature might revise it. The legislature summoned the judges before it to determine whether they were guilty of malpractice in office by disregarding a statute. The legislature found no basis for IMPEACHMENT but refused to revise the statute. On a renewed motion to dismiss, the court held the act void, on the ground that "by the constitution every citizen had undoubtedly a right to a decision of his property by TRIAL BY JURY." In defense of judicial review, the court reasoned that no statute could alter or repeal the state constitution, which was FUNDAMENTAL LAW. The court then submitted the case to a jury. The committee of the legislature that had heard the charges against the judges included RICHARD DOBBS SPAIGHT, a vehement antagonist of judicial review, and WILLIAM R. DAVIE, co-counsel for Bayard; shortly after, both men represented North Carolina at the CONSTITUTIONAL CONVENTION OF 1787. JAMES IREDELL, later one of the first Justices of the Supreme Court of the United States, also represented Bayard. Iredell published an address, "To the Public," in 1786, anticipating the doctrine of *Bayard v. Singleton,* and his correspondence with Spaight on judicial review best reflects the arguments at that time for and against the power of courts to hold enactments unconstitutional. Spaight's position, that such a power was a "usurpation" by the judiciary, accorded with the then prevailing theory and practice of legislative supremacy.

LEONARD W. LEVY

BEACON THEATRES, INC. v. WESTOVER
359 U.S. 500 (1964)

Fox West Coast Theatres, Inc., contending that it was being harassed and that its business was being impeded by the threats of a competitor, Beacon Theatres, Inc., to bring an ANTITRUST suit, brought an action for DECLARATORY JUDGMENT in the U.S. District Court. Beacon, in a countersuit, alleged conspiracy in restraint of trade, and asked treble damages under the SHERMAN ANTITRUST ACT.

Judge Westover, exercising his discretion under the Declaratory Judgment Act and the FEDERAL RULES OF CIVIL PROCEDURE, decided to hear first the declaratory judgment suit, which, as an action in EQUITY did not require a jury. Only if that suit were decided in favor of Beacon would the antitrust suit be tried.

The Supreme Court, in an opinion by Justice HUGO L. BLACK, held (5–3) that Westover's decision deprived Beacon of its right to TRIAL BY JURY in a civil case. Because trial by jury is a constitutional right, judicial discretion must be used to preserve it unless there is a showing that irreparable harm would result from the delay. "Only under the most imperative circumstances," Black wrote, ". . . can the right to a jury trial of legal issues be lost through prior determination of equitable claims."

DENNIS J. MAHONEY

BEARD, CHARLES A.
(1874–1948)

Charles Austin Beard, more than any other historian, shaped the way twentieth-century Americans look at the framing of the Constitution. He thus occupied, as he said a historian should, "the position of a statesman dealing with public affairs."

After being graduated at de Pauw and Columbia Universities, Beard continued his studies in Europe. His early writings reflect a theory of strict economic determinism; in *The Rise of American Civilization* (1927) he argued that the Civil War was less a struggle between SLAVERY and freedom than an epiphenomenon of emerging industrialism. Throughout his career as a teacher at Columbia University and the New School for Social Research and as a writer he maintained that historians cannot discover or describe the past as it actually was, but must instead reinterpret the past in order to shape their own times and the future.

Beard's most influential work was his *Economic Interpretation of the Constitution.* First published in 1913, the book was part of the Progressive movement's assault on such "undemocratic" constitutional obstacles to reform as the SEPARATION OF POWERS, CHECKS AND BALANCES, and FEDERALISM. The work was republished, with a new introduction, in 1935, when the forms of CONSTITUTIONALISM again seemed to frustrate attempts at reform legislation. The thesis of the book is that the Constitution was framed by large holders of personal property and capital (especially government securities) in order to further their own economic interests and to frustrate the majority will. The effect of the book at the time of each publication was to undermine the legitimacy of the Constitution in the public mind by ascribing base motives to its authors. Beard's assumptions about the amounts and types of property owned by the Framers have been thoroughly discredited; yet his thesis about the origin of the Constitution became the standard version taught in universities and public schools. Even his opponents have adopted Beard's analytical framework.

Besides the *Economic Interpretation,* Beard, alone or with his wife, Mary Ritter Beard, was author of some two dozen books on politics and history. He was also president both of the American Historical Association and of the American Political Science Association.

DENNIS J. MAHONEY

Bibliography

BROWN, ROBERT E. 1956 *Charles Beard and the Constitution.* Princeton, N.J.: Princeton University Press.

BEAUHARNAIS v. ILLINOIS
343 U.S. 250 (1952)

The Supreme Court upheld, 5–4, an Illinois GROUP LIBEL statute that forbade publications depicting a racial or religious group as depraved or lacking in virtue. Justice FELIX FRANKFURTER first argued that certain categories of speech including LIBEL had traditionally been excluded from FIRST AMENDMENT protection, and he then deferred to the legislative judgment redefining libel to include defamation of groups as well as individuals. By mixing excluded-categories arguments with arguments for judicial deference to legislative judgments for which there is a RATIONAL BASIS, the opinion moves toward a position in which the relative merits of a particular speech are weighed against the social interests protected by the statute, with the ultimate constitutional balance heavily weighted in favor of whatever balance the legislature has struck. Although *Beauharnais* has not been overruled, its continued validity is doubtful after NEW YORK TIMES V. SULLIVAN (1964).

MARTIN SHAPIRO

(SEE ALSO: *Freedom of Speech.*)

BECKER AMENDMENT
(1964)

The public indignation aroused by the Supreme Court's decisions on school prayer and Bible reading (ENGEL V. VITALE, 1962; ABINGTON TOWNSHIP V. SCHEMPP, 1963) provoked the introduction in Congress of over 160 proposals to amend the Constitution. When Chairman Emmanuel Celler, who opposed the amendments, bottled them up in his House Judiciary Committee, the proponents united behind a compromise measure drafted by Representative Frank J. Becker of New York.

The Becker Amendment was worded as a guide to interpretation of existing constitutional provisions rather than as new law. It had three parts. The first two provided that nothing in the Constitution should be deemed to prohibit voluntary prayer or scripture reading in schools or public institutions or the invocation of divine assistance in government documents or ceremonies or on coins or currency. The third part declared: "Nothing in this article shall constitute an ESTABLISHMENT OF RELIGION."

Under pressure of parliamentary maneuvering, Celler conducted hearings in 1964—at which many denominational leaders and constitutional scholars expressed opposition to the Becker Amendment—but his committee never reported any proposal to the House. Amendments similar to Becker's have been introduced in subsequent Congresses, but none has come close to the majority votes needed for submission to the states.

DENNIS J. MAHONEY

BEDFORD, GUNNING, JR.
(1747–1812)

Gunning Bedford, Jr., represented Delaware at the CONSTITUTIONAL CONVENTION OF 1787 and signed the Constitution. A spokesman for small-state positions, he vigorously advocated equal representation of the states in Congress; he also argued for easy removal of the president and against the VETO POWER. He was a delegate to Delaware's ratifying convention.

DENNIS J. MAHONEY

BEDFORD CUT STONE COMPANY v. JOURNEYMEN STONE CUTTERS ASSOCIATION
273 U.S. 37 (1927)

The company sought to destroy the union. The union's national membership of 5,000 men then refused to work on buildings made of the stone quarried by the company, which sought an INJUNCTION on the ground that the union's activities restrained INTERSTATE COMMERCE in violation of the ANTITRUST laws. Lower federal courts refused to enjoin the union. The Supreme Court commanded the injunction. The dissenting opinion of Justices LOUIS D. BRANDEIS and OLIVER WENDELL HOLMES revealed the significance of the case. When, Brandeis observed, capitalists combined to control major industries, the Court ruled that their restraints on commerce were "reasonable" and not violations of the antitrust acts. When, however, a small union, as its only means of self-protection, refused to work on products of an antiunion company, the Court forgot its RULE OF REASON and discovered unreasonable restraint. Brandeis might have added that the Court had made "antitrust" a synonym for "antilabor."

LEONARD W. LEVY

BELL v. MARYLAND
378 U.S. 226 (1964)

This case was the last SIT-IN case decided before the PUBLIC ACCOMMODATIONS provisions of the CIVIL RIGHTS ACT OF 1964 took effect. Twelve black students were convicted of criminal trespass for their participation in a sit-in demonstration in Baltimore. The Supreme Court reversed their conviction and remanded to the Maryland courts for clarification of state law. Six Justices, however, addressed the larger constitutional question that had been presented to the Court in case after case in the early 1960s: whether the FOURTEENTH AMENDMENT, in the absence of congressional legislation, provided a right to service in places of public accommodation. These six Justices divided 3–3.

Justices WILLIAM O. DOUGLAS and ARTHUR J. GOLDBERG, concurring in the reversal of the convictions, argued that racial SEGREGATION in public accommodations imposed a caste system that was inconsistent with the abolition of slavery and with the Fourteenth Amendment's establishment of CITIZENSHIP. The refusal to serve blacks, Douglas said, did not reflect any interest in the proprietor's associational RIGHT OF PRIVACY, but rather was aimed at promoting business. Because the restaurant was "property that is serving the public," it had a constitutional obligation not to exclude a portion of the public on racial grounds. Chief Justice EARL WARREN joined Goldberg's opinion, which focused on the rights of citizenship.

Justice HUGO L. BLACK dissented, joined by Justices JOHN MARSHALL HARLAN and BYRON R. WHITE. He indicated strongly his view that Congress, in enforcing the Fourteenth Amendment, could provide a right of access to public accommodations. In the absence of such a law, however, Black was unwilling to find in the Fourteenth Amendment a right to enter on the property of another against the owner's will. (At the ORAL ARGUMENT of the *Bell* case, Justice Black had observed, "But this was *private* property.") The state was entitled to protect the owner's decision by the ordinary processes of law without converting the owner's personal prejudices into state policy, and thus STATE ACTION.

KENNETH L. KARST

BELL v. WOLFISH

See: Right of Privacy

BELMONT, UNITED STATES v.
301 U.S. 324 (1937)

Belmont arose in the wake of President FRANKLIN D. ROOSEVELT's formal recognition of the Soviet Union in 1933 pursuant to an EXECUTIVE AGREEMENT between the two countries. In conjunction with this act of recognition, Soviet claims to assets located in the United States and nationalized by the Soviet Union in 1918 were assigned to the United States under a collateral agreement known as the "Litvinov Assignment." When the federal government sought to enforce these claims in the state of New York, however, the New York courts dismissed the suit, holding that to allow the federal government to enforce the assignment would contradict New York public policy against confiscation of private property.

The Supreme Court unanimously reversed, holding that the Litvinov Assignment, as part of the process of recognition, not only created international obligations but also superseded any conflicting state law or policy. In so holding, the Court affirmed the President's constitutional authority to speak "as the sole organ" of the national government in formally recognizing another nation and to take all steps necessary to effect such recognition. The Court stated that all acts of recognition unite as one transaction (here, in an "international compact" or executive agreement) which, unlike a formal TREATY, becomes a part of the "supreme Law of the Land" without requiring the ADVICE AND CONSENT of the Senate.

BURNS H. WESTON

(SEE ALSO: *Foreign Affairs and the Constitution; Pink, United States v.*)

Bibliography

HENKIN, LOUIS 1972 *Foreign Affairs and the Constitution.* Mineola, N.Y.: Foundation Press.

BENIGN RACIAL CLASSIFICATION

Although race must always be regarded as a SUSPECT CLASSIFICATION, there are circumstances in which official RACIAL DISCRIMINATION may be constitutionally permissible because the purpose is "benign and ameliorative." In *United States v. Montgomery County Board of Education* (1969), for example, the Supreme Court upheld a system of RACIAL QUOTAS for teachers imposed by a federal judge as part of a desegregation program. In REGENTS OF UNIVERSITY OF CALIFORNIA V. BAKKE (1978) the Court invalidated quotas but indicated that preferential treatment of minority applicants would be acceptable. The question remains whether the government can sponsor AFFIRMATIVE ACTION without denying any person EQUAL PROTECTION OF THE LAWS.

DENNIS J. MAHONEY

BENTON, THOMAS HART (1782–1858)

A Missouri attorney, senator (1821–1851), and congressman (1853–1855), Thomas Hart Benton was an avid Jacksonian Democrat who led the opposition, on constitutional and economic grounds, to rechartering the second BANK OF THE UNITED STATES. A hard-money man, nicknamed "Old Bullion," Benton supported President ANDREW JACKSON's "specie circular" despite its adverse effects on his cherished goal of westward expansion. Benton opposed NULLIFICATION, and was ever after an enemy of JOHN C. CALHOUN and state sovereignty, allegedly saying in 1850 that Calhoun "died with TREASON in his heart and on his lips." Benton opposed extension of and agitation over SLAVERY, and he personally favored gradual emancipation. Thus, Benton opposed the ANNEXATION OF TEXAS, bellicose agitation over Oregon, war with Mexico (although he ultimately voted for the war), the WILMONT PROVISO, and HENRY CLAY's "Omnibus Bill" because all of these issues would impede western expansion and California statehood by involving them with slavery extension. Benton ultimately voted for some of the compromise measures in 1850, including the extension of slavery into some of the territories, but he opposed the new fugitive slave law. His opposition led to proslavery backlash and his defeat for reelection in 1850. In 1854 Benton published his senatorial memoirs, *Thirty Years View,* and in 1856–1857 *An Abridgement of the Debates of Congress.* While on his death bed, Benton wrote a long tract on DRED SCOTT V. SANDFORD in which he argued for the constitutionality of the MISSOURI COMPROMISE and savaged Chief Justice ROGER B. TANEY's opinion, which Benton believed was legally, historically, and constitutionally invalid, blatantly proslavery, and antiunion.

PAUL FINKELMAN

Bibliography

CHAMBERS, WILLIAM W. 1956 *Old Bullion Benton: Senator from the New West.* Boston: Little, Brown.

BENTON v. MARYLAND 395 U.S. 784 (1969)

This decision, one of the last of the WARREN COURT, extended the DOUBLE JEOPARDY provision of the Fifth Amendment to the states. (See INCORPORATION DOCTRINE.) A Maryland prisoner, having been acquitted on a larceny charge, successfully appealed his burglary conviction, only to be reindicted and convicted on both counts. A 7–2 Supreme Court, speaking through Justice THURGOOD MARSHALL, overruled PALKO V. CONNECTICUT (1937) and, relying on DUNCAN V. LOUISIANA (1968), declared that the Fifth Amendment guarantee "represents a fundamental ideal" which must be applied. Dissenting, Justices JOHN MARSHALL HARLAN and POTTER STEWART reiterated their opposition to incorporation, concluding that the WRIT OF CERTIORARI had been improvidently granted. In OBITER DICTUM they added that retrial here violated even the *Palko* standards.

DAVID GORDON

BEREA COLLEGE v. KENTUCKY
211 U.S. 45 (1908)

Berea College, founded half a century earlier by abolitionists, was fined $1,000 under a Kentucky statute forbidding the operation of racially integrated schools. The Supreme Court affirmed the conviction, 7–2, sustaining the law as an exercise of state power to govern CORPORATIONS. Justice JOHN MARSHALL HARLAN, a Kentuckian personally acquainted with the college, dissented, arguing that the law unconstitutionally deprived the school of liberty and property without DUE PROCESS OF LAW. His denunciation of state-enforced SEGREGATION also echoed his dissent in PLESSY V. FERGUSON (1896). The majority addressed neither issue.

KENNETH L. KARST

BERGER v. NEW YORK
388 U.S. 41 (1967)

A New York statute authorized electronic surveillance by police under certain circumstances. A conviction for conspiring to bribe a state official based on such surveillance was set aside because the statute did not meet FOURTH AMENDMENT requirements: (1) it did not require the police to describe in detail the place to be searched or the conversation to be seized, or to specify the particular crime being investigated; (2) it did not adequately limit the period of the intrusion; (3) it did not provide for adequate notice of the eavesdropping to the people overheard. These requirements were later incorporated in the OMNIBUS CRIME CONTROL AND SAFE STREETS ACT (1968).

HERMAN SCHWARTZ

BERMAN v. PARKER

See: Eminent Domain; Public Use; Taking of Property

BETTS v. BRADY
316 U.S. 455 (1942)

In *Betts* an INDIGENT defendant was convicted of robbery after his request for appointed counsel was denied. The Court held that the DUE PROCESS clause of the FOURTEENTH AMENDMENT required states to furnish counsel only when special circumstances showed that otherwise the trial would be fundamentally unfair. Here, because the defendant was of "ordinary intelligence" and not "wholly unfamiliar" with CRIMINAL PROCEDURE, the Court found no special circumstances.

Over the next two decades, *Betts* was consistently undermined by expansion of the "special circumstances" exception, resulting in the appointment of counsel in most FELONY cases, until it was finally overruled in GIDEON V. WAINWRIGHT (1963).

BARBARA ALLEN BABCOCK

(SEE ALSO: *Right to Counsel.*)

BEVERIDGE, ALBERT J.
(1862–1927)

Albert Jeremiah Beveridge of Indiana, a lawyer and orator of extraordinary talent and overweening ambition, served two terms in the United States Senate (1899–1911) as a Republican. He advocated imperialism to open new markets for American industry and favored permanent annexation of the insular TERRITORIES gained in the Spanish-American War, without extension of constitutional protections and self-government, for which their non-Anglo-Saxon inhabitants were unfit. An economic nationalist, Beveridge favored repeal of the SHERMAN ANTITRUST ACT, believing that trusts should not be broken up but regulated in the national interest. Defeated for reelection, Beveridge joined THEODORE ROOSEVELT's Progressive Party and was its candidate for governor in 1912. Defeated again, he turned to writing a long-planned biography of Chief Justice JOHN MARSHALL. The four-volume work, completed in 1919, won a Pulitzer Prize for biography. In the book Beveridge presents Marshall as the statesman who molded the Constitution to meet the needs of a vigorous, commercial nation, over the objections of petty agrarians and disunionists like THOMAS JEFFERSON.

DENNIS J. MAHONEY

Bibliography

BOWERS, CLAUDE G. 1932 *Beveridge and the Progressive Era.* New York: Literary Guild.

BIBB v. NAVAJO FREIGHT LINES, INC.
359 U.S. 520 (1959)

A unanimous Supreme Court here voided a state highway safety regulation because the state failed to demonstrate sufficient justification to balance the burden it imposed on INTERSTATE COMMERCE. An Illinois statute required trucks using its highways to employ a particular mudguard, outlawed in Arkansas and distinct from those allowed elsewhere. The Court said that cost and safety problems alone were insufficient reason for invalidation, given the "strong presumption of validity" owing to the statute. But, by creating a conflicting standard, the Illinois statute had seriously interfered with and imposed a "massive" burden on interstate commerce.

DAVID GORDON

(SEE ALSO: *State Regulation of Commerce.*)

BIBLE READING

See: Religion in Public Schools

BICAMERALISM

Bicameralism, the principle of CONSTITUTIONALISM that requires the legislature to be composed of two chambers (or houses), is a feature of the United States Constitution and of the constitution of every state except Nebraska. Bicameralism is supposed to guarantee deliberation in the exercise of the LEGISLATIVE POWER, by requiring that measures be debated in and approved by two different bodies before becoming law. It is also one of those "auxiliary precautions" by which constitutional democracy is protected from the mischiefs latent in popular self-government.

Bicameralism is not distinctively American; there were bicameral legislatures in the ancient republics of Greece and Rome, and there are bicameral legislatures in most countries of the world today. Bicameralism is found in the constitutions of nondemocratic countries (such as the Soviet Union) as well as of democratic countries. And, despite historical association with disparities of social class, both legislative chambers in democratic countries—emphatically including the United States—are typically chosen in popular elections; in countries where one house is chosen other than by election, that house is significantly less powerful than the elective house. Moreover, although it is the practice of most federal nations (such as Australia, Switzerland, and the Federal Republic of Germany) to reflect the constituent SOVEREIGNTY of the states in one house of the legislature, there are bicameral legislatures in countries where FEDERALISM is unknown.

The American colonists came originally from Britain and were familiar with the BRITISH CONSTITUTION. In Parliament, as the Framers knew it, there were two houses with equal power, reflecting two orders of society: the House of Lords comprising the hereditary aristocracy of England (together with representatives of the Scots nobility and the ecclesiastical hierarchy), and the House of Commons representing the freeholders of the counties and the chartered cities. Seats in the House of Commons were apportioned according to the status of the constituency (five seats per county, two per city), not according to population.

The local lawmaking bodies in the colonies were originally unicameral. Bicameralism was introduced in Massachusetts in 1644, in Maryland in 1650, and (in a unique form) in Pennsylvania in 1682; but in each case the "upper house" was identical with the governor's council, and so performed both legislative and executive functions. In the eighteenth century, all of the colonial legislatures but one were bicameral, with a lower house elected by the freeholders and an upper house generally comprising representatives of the wealthier classes. At the same time the upper houses (although retaining the name "council") became distinctly legislative bodies.

When the newly independent states began constructing constitutions after 1776, all but Pennsylvania and Georgia provided for bicameral legislatures. Typically, the upper house was elected separately from the lower and had higher qualifications for membership, but it was elected from districts apportioned on the same basis and by electorates with the same qualifications. In two states, Maryland and South Carolina, the upper houses were elected indirectly.

The CONTINENTAL CONGRESS, although it conducted a war, negotiated a peace, and directed the collective business of the United States, was never in form a national legislature. Even after its status was regularized by the ARTICLES OF CONFEDERATION, the Congress was a body composed of delegates selected by the state governments and responsible to them. A bicameral Congress was neither desirable nor feasible until Congress became the legislative branch of a national government.

The delegates to the CONSTITUTIONAL CONVENTION OF 1787 agreed at the outset on a bicameral national legislature. In the VIRGINIA PLAN, membership in the first house of Congress would have been apportioned according to the population of the states, and the second house would have been elected by the first. The GREAT COMPROMISE produced the Congress as we know it, with the House of Representatives apportioned by population (described by JAMES MADISON in THE FEDERALIST #39 as a "national" feature of the Constitution) and with equal REPRESENTATION of the states in the Senate (a "federal" feature), so that Congress itself reflects the compound character of American government.

The two principles of apportionment serve to insure that different points of view are brought to bear on deliberations in the two houses. That consideration is also advanced by having different terms for members of the two houses; a shorter term bringing legislators into more frequent contact with public opinion, a longer term permitting legislators to take a more extended view of the public interest. The priority of the House of Representatives with respect to revenue (taxing) measures and the association of the Senate with the executive in the exercise of the TREATY POWER and the APPOINTING POWER also tend to introduce different points of view into legislative deliberations. Until abolished by the SEVENTEENTH AMENDMENT, the election of senators by the state legislatures also contributed to the formation of different viewpoints.

The principal justification for bicameralism is that it increases and improves the deliberation on public measures. But bicameralism is also a device to protect constitutional government against the peculiar evils inherent in democratic government. One must guard against equating democracy, or even majority rule, with the immediate satisfaction of the short-term demands of transient majorities. As *The Federalist* #10 points out, a faction—a group whose aims are at odds with the rights of other citizens or with permanent and aggregate interests of the whole country—may at any given time amount to a majority of the population. Although no mechanical device can guarantee that a majority faction will not prevail, the bicameral structure of Congress operates to make such a result less likely than it might otherwise be.

The Supreme Court cited the importance of bicameralism in the American constitutional system as one reason for striking down the LEGISLATIVE VETO in IMMIGRATION AND NATURALIZATION SERVICE V. CHADHA (1983). According to Chief Justice WARREN E. BURGER, that device permitted public policy to be altered by either house of Congress, contravening the belief of the Framers "that legislation should not be enacted unless it has been carefully and fully considered" lest special interests "be favored at the expense of public needs."

Bicameralism is also a principle of American constitutionalism at the state level. At one time representation of the lesser political units, typically the counties, was the rule for state upper houses. In REYNOLDS V. SIMS (1964), however, the Supreme Court held that such schemes of representation resulted in the overvaluation of the votes of rural citizens relative to those of urban and suburban citizens and that they therefore denied the latter the EQUAL PROTECTION OF THE LAWS in violation of the FOURTEENTH AMENDMENT. Some commentators, both scholars and politicians, predicted that imposition of the ONE PERSON, ONE VOTE standard would spell the doom of bicameralism at the state level. However, no state has changed to a unicameral system since the *Reynolds* decision.

Even more than to the innate reluctance of politicians to abolish any public office, this fact is testimony to the independent vitality of bicameralism as a constitutional principle. Even when territoriality is removed as a rationale, the desirability of having a second opinion on proposals before they become law cannot be gainsaid. Hence there is a tendency in the states to find ways of giving their upper houses a distinct perspective. The ordinary differentiation is by the size of the chambers and the length of the terms of office. Some states have tried, with the Supreme Court's approval, to preserve the territorial basis of the upper house by creating MULTIMEMBER DISTRICTS in the more populous territorial units.

The meaning of constitutionalism in a democratic polity is that the short-term interests of the majority will not be allowed to prevail if they are contrary to the rights of the minority or to the permanent and aggregate interests of the whole. The permanent and aggregate interests are not represented by any person or group of people, but they are protected by a constitutional system that requires prudent deliberation in the conduct of lawmaking. Bicameralism is an important constitutional principle because, and to the extent that, it institutionalizes such deliberation.

DENNIS J. MAHONEY

Bibliography

EIDELBERG, PAUL 1968 *The Political Philosophy of the American Constitution.* New York: Free Press.

WHEARE, KENNETH C. 1963 *Legislatures.* New York: Oxford University Press.

BICKEL, ALEXANDER M. (1925–1974)

Alexander Bickel was a professor at Yale Law School from 1956 to 1974 and a prolific writer on law and politics. He became the most influential academic critic of the progressive liberal jurisprudence of his time, although he at first made only sympathetic refinements of that doctrine. Having served as a clerk for Justice FELIX FRANKFURTER and edited some unpublished judicial opinions of Justice LOUIS D. BRANDEIS, he, like they, rejected the old CONSTITUTIONALISM of private rights and unchanging FUNDAMENTAL LAW in favor of a living law, evolving with social conditions and with a progressive consciousness. His first important book, *The Least Dangerous Branch* (1962), advanced a variation of Frankfurter's prescription of judicial restraint. Bickel elaborated ways, such as avoiding a constitutional question, by which the SUPREME COURT might accommodate political democracy while enforcing the "principled goals" of a more open, humane, and free society.

In *The Supreme Court and the Idea of Progress* (1970), however, Bickel departed sharply from his role of political tactician for the rule of Supreme Court principle. He attacked the WARREN COURT's principles as themselves impolitic. In Bickel's view, the Court, confident that progress required nationalizing and leveling constitutional limits on the electoral process and an extension of desegregation to racial balancing, had imposed an egalitarianism that was subjective and arbitrary. As a result, Bickel argued, the Court had bred a legalistic authoritarianism and threatened the quality of public schools and distinctive communities.

The Morality of Consent (1975) was published posthumously. It examined the turmoil attending the VIETNAM WAR, student revolt, and WATERGATE, extended Bickel's critique, and attempted a reconstruction. Bickel portrayed the entire American order as under siege and ill-defended. He saw universities as well as governments and corporations endangered by two extremes of theory—a committed moralism, which tended to a dictatorship of the self-righteous, and a permissive relativism, which would defend nothing and eroded the moral and social fabric. Bickel recurred to Edmund Burke's critique of the French Declaration of the Rights of Man, and then painstakingly set forth his own morality of consent, a morality to sustain not individual claims but the social process of communicating and governing.

ROBERT K. FAULKNER

Bibliography

FAULKNER, ROBERT K. 1978 Bickel's Constitution: The Problem of Moderate Liberalism. *American Political Science Review* 72:925–940.

BIDDLE, FRANCIS (1886–1968)

Born to wealth and social position, Francis Biddle of Pennsylvania was graduated from Harvard College and Harvard Law School and became a law CLERK to Justice OLIVER WENDELL HOLMES. He entered public service in 1934 as FRANKLIN D. ROOSEVELT's chairman of the National Labor Relations Board. He also served as counsel for the congressional investigation of the Tennessee Valley Authority (1938); as a judge on the United States Court of Appeals for the Third Circuit (1939–1940); as solicitor general (1940–1941); and as attorney general (1941–1945). Biddle stoutly championed CIVIL LIBERTIES and, albeit unsuccessfully, opposed the evacuation of Japanese-Americans from the West Coast. He also served on the International Military Tribunal at Nuremberg, which tried the major German war criminals (1945–1946). Thereafter, Biddle retired to a life of writing and leisure. His chief books were *Fear of Freedom* (1951), an assault on McCarthyism; *Justice Holmes, Natural Law, and the Supreme Court* (1961); and *In Brief Authority* (1962), a record of his public service.

HENRY J. ABRAHAM

Bibliography

BIDDLE, FRANCIS 1962 *In Brief Authority: From the Years with Roosevelt to the Nürnberg Trial.* Garden City, N.Y.: Doubleday.

BILL OF ATTAINDER

In American constitutional law, a bill of attainder is any legislative act that inflicts punishment on designated individuals without a judicial trial. The term includes both the original English bill of attainder, which condemned a person to death for treason or felony and confiscated his property, and the bill of pains and penalties, used for lesser offenses and punishments. The first bill of attainder was passed by Parliament in 1459. They were common during the Tudor and Stuart reigns, and Cromwell's and William and Mary's parliaments also resorted to them. During the Revolutionary period, several state legislatures used bills of attainder to condemn Tories and to confiscate their property. THOMAS JEFFERSON in 1778 drafted, and the Virginia legislature passed, a bill of attainder against Josiah Philips, a notorious Tory brigand. The abuse of the procedure in English and American history foreshadowed the possibility of even greater abuse in the future. The bill of attainder, with its disregard of DUE PROCESS OF LAW, could be a potent weapon for the vengeful and covetous.

At the CONSTITUTIONAL CONVENTION OF 1787, ELBRIDGE GERRY proposed a prohibition against bills of attainder. The measure passed unanimously; it appears in Article I, section 9, as a limitation on Congress, and in Article I, section 10, as a limitation on the states. That the prohibition was meant to extend to all legislative punishments may be seen from a congressional debate in 1794. When Federalist Representative THOMAS FITZSIMONS introduced a resolution to censure the Jeffersonian Democratic Societies and to accuse them of fomenting the WHISKEY REBELLION, JAMES MADISON denounced it as a bill of attainder.

The Supreme Court first spoke to the question in the TEST OATH CASES (1867). The Court held unconstitutional both a Missouri requirement that practitioners of certain professions swear that they had not aided the Confederate cause and a federal requirement that lawyers take such an oath to practice before federal courts. Since former rebels could not take the oaths, they were effectively deprived of their livelihoods. The Missouri legislature and the Congress had therefore passed bills imposing punishment on the ex-Confederates without judicial trial or conviction of any crime.

No other federal law was held to violate the ban on bills of attainder until UNITED STATES V. LOVETT (1946). In that case the Court held unconstitutional a rider to an appropriations bill which prohibited any payment to three named PUBLIC EMPLOYEES, previously identified as subversives before a congressional committee, unless they were first discharged and reappointed. In *Lovett* the Court expanded on the definition it had given in the *Test Oath Cases,* making clear that all legislative acts were covered, "no matter what their form."

In recent judicial interpretation of the bills-of-attainder clause a law prohibiting Communist party members from holding labor union office was declared unconstitutional (see UNITED STATES V. BROWN, 1965); but a law requiring subversive organizations to register with a government agency, and another commandeering the records of a disgraced ex-President were upheld.

DENNIS J. MAHONEY

(SEE ALSO: *Communist Party v. S.A.C.B., 1961; Nixon v. Administrator of General Services, 1977.*)

Bibliography

CHAFEE, ZECHARIAH 1956 *Three Human Rights in the Constitution of 1787.* Lawrence: University of Kansas Press.

BILL OF CREDIT

A bill of credit is a promissory note issued by a government on its own credit and intended to circulate as money. Under Article I, section 10, of the Constitution the states are prohibited from emitting bills of credit. The prohibition was regarded as essential by the Framers of the Constitution, and it was included without significant debate or dissent by the CONSTITUTIONAL CONVENTION OF 1787.

Bills of credit are, in fact, unsecured paper currency. Both ALEXANDER HAMILTON and JAMES MADISON, referring to the prohibition in THE FEDERALIST (#44 and #80), wrote of a prohibition on "paper money." In the years immediately preceding the adoption of the Constitution, many states had issued unsecured currency in a deliberately inflationary policy intended to benefit borrowers. As long as local politicians had the power to stimulate inflation, there could be no stable economy. The "more perfect union" required that money have essentially the same purchasing power in every state and region.

The MARSHALL COURT, in CRAIG V. MISSOURI (1830), held that a state issue of certificates acceptable for tax payments violated the prohibition on bills of credit, since they were "paper intended to circulate through the community for its ordinary purposes, as money." But the TANEY COURT held that notes issued by a state-chartered bank—of which the state was the sole stockholder—did not violate the prohibition, since they were not issued "on the faith of the state." (See BRISCOE V. BANK OF KENTUCKY, 1837.)

DENNIS J. MAHONEY

BILL OF RIGHTS (ENGLISH)
(December 16, 1689)

During the controversy with Great Britain, from 1763 to 1776, American editors frequently reprinted the English Bill of Rights, and American leaders hailed it as "the second MAGNA CARTA." After the DECLARATION OF INDEPENDENCE, Americans framing their first state constitutions drew upon the Bill of Rights; certain clauses of the national Constitution and our own BILL OF RIGHTS, the first ten amendments, can also be traced to the English statute of 1689. Its formal title was, "An act for declaring the rights and liberties of the subject, and settling the succession of the crown." Like Magna Carta, the PETITION OF RIGHT, and other constitutional documents safeguarding "liberties of the subject," the Bill of Rights imposed limitations on the crown only. Indeed, the document capped the Glorious Revolution of 1688–1689 by which England hamstrung the royal prerogative and made the crown subservient to Parliament, which remained unrestrained by any constitutional document. In effect the Bill of Rights ratified parliamentary supremacy, which is the antithesis of the American concept of a bill of rights as a bill of restraints upon the government generally. Notwithstanding its inflated reputation as a precursor of the American Bill of Rights, the English bill was quite narrow in the range of its protections even against the crown. In fact it established no new principles, except, perhaps, for the provision against standing armies in time of peace without parliamentary approval. Sir William S. Holdsworth, the great historian of English law, declared, "We look in vain for any statement of constitutional principle in the Bill of Rights," a judgment that is too severe.

The Bill of Rights confirmed several old principles of major significance. NO TAXATION WITHOUT REPRESENTATION, which became the American formulation, here was limited to the assertion that levying money by royal prerogative "without grant of parliament" was illegal. The FREEDOM OF PETITION, protected by our FIRST AMENDMENT, and indirectly the FREEDOM OF ASSEMBLY go back to time immemorial, as the British say, but were here enshrined as part of the FUNDAMENTAL LAW. Article I, section 6, of the Constitution, protecting freedom of speech for members of Congress, derives from a clause in the Bill of Rights confirming a principle fought for by Parliament for a century and a half. Our Eighth Amendment follows closely the language of another provision of the Bill of Rights, which declares, "That excessive BAIL ought not to be required, no excessive fines imposed, nor CRUEL AND UNUSUAL PUNISHMENTS inflicted." The guarantee against excessive bail made the writ of HABEAS CORPUS effective by plugging the one loophole in the HABEAS CORPUS ACT OF 1679; the crown's judges had defeated that act's purpose by fixing steep bail that prisoners could not afford. The ACT OF TOLERATION OF 1689 preceded the Bill of Rights by a few months and is equally part of the constitutional inheritance of the Glorious Revolution.

The foremost significance of the English Bill of Rights, so called because it began as a declaration and ended as a bill enacted into law, probably lies in the symbolism of the name, conveying far more than the document itself actually protects. As an antecedent of the American Bill of Rights of 1791, the act of 1689 is a frail affair, though it achieved its purpose of cataloguing most of the rights that the Stuarts had breached. As a symbol of fundamental law and the RULE OF LAW it was a mighty precursor of the fuller catalogues of rights developed by the American states and in the Constitution.

LEONARD W. LEVY

Bibliography

SCHWOERER, LOIS G. 1981 *The Declaration of Rights, 1689.* Baltimore: Johns Hopkins University Press.

BILL OF RIGHTS (UNITED STATES)

On September 12, 1787, the only major task of the CONSTITUTIONAL CONVENTION OF 1787 was to adopt, engross, and sign the finished document reported by the Committee on Style. The weary delegates, after a hot summer's work in Philadelphia, were eager to return home. At that point GEORGE MASON remarked that he "wished the plan had been prefaced by a Bill of Rights," because it would quiet public fears. Mason made no stirring speech for CIVIL LIBERTIES; he did not even argue the need for a bill of rights or move the adoption of one, though he offered to second a motion if one were made. ELBRIDGE GERRY moved for a committee to prepare a bill, Mason seconded, and without debate the delegates, voting by states, defeated the motion 10–0. A motion to endorse FREEDOM OF THE PRESS was also defeated, after ROGER SHERMAN declared, "It is unnecessary. The power of Congress does not extend to the Press."

Not a delegate to the convention opposed a bill of rights in principle. The overwhelming majority believed "It is unnecessary." Although they were recommending a strong national government that could regulate individuals directly, Congress could exercise only ENUMERATED POWERS or powers necessary to carry out those enumerated. A bill of rights would restrain national powers, but, as Hamilton asked, "Why declare that things shall not be done which there is no power to do?" Congress had no power to regulate the press or religion.

Civil liberties, supporters of the Constitution believed, faced danger from the possibility of repressive state action, but that was a matter to be guarded against by state bills of rights. Some states had none, and no state had a comprehensive list of guarantees. That fact provided the supporters of ratification with another argument: if a bill were framed omitting some rights, the omissions might justify their infringement. The great VIRGINIA DECLARATION OF RIGHTS had omitted the FREEDOMS OF SPEECH, assembly, and petition; the right to the writ of HABEAS CORPUS; the right to GRAND JURY proceedings; the RIGHT TO COUNSEL; and freedom from DOUBLE JEOPARDY, BILLS OF ATTAINDER, and EX POST FACTO laws. Twelve states, including Vermont, had framed constitutions, and the only right secured by all was TRIAL BY JURY in criminal cases; although all protected religious liberty, too, five either permitted or provided for ESTABLISHMENTS OF RELIGION. Two passed over a free press guarantee. Four neglected to ban excessive fines, excessive BAIL, compulsory self-incrimination, and general SEARCH WARRANTS. Five ignored protections for the rights of assembly, petition, counsel, and trial by jury in civil cases. Seven omitted a prohibition on ex post facto laws. Nine failed to provide for grand jury proceedings, and nine failed to condemn bills of attainder. Ten said nothing about freedom of speech, while eleven were silent on double jeopardy. Omissions in a national bill of rights raised dangers that would be avoided if the Constitution simply left the rights of Americans uncatalogued. The Framers also tended to be skeptical about the value of "parchment barriers" against "overbearing majorities," as JAMES MADISON said. As realists they understood that the constitutional protection of rights would mean little during times of popular hysteria or war; any framer could cite examples of gross abridgments of civil liberties in states that had bills of rights.

The lack of a bill of rights proved to be the strongest argument of the opponents of ratification. The usually masterful politicians who dominated the Constitutional Convention had made a serious political error. Their arguments against including a bill of rights were neither politic nor convincing. A bill of rights could do no harm, and, as THOMAS JEFFERSON pointed out in letters persuading Madison to switch positions, might do some good. Moreover, the contention that listing some rights might jeopardize others not mentioned was inconsistent and easily answered. The inconsistency derived from the fact that the Constitution as proposed included some rights: no RELIGIOUS TEST for office; jury trials in criminal cases; the writ of habeas corpus; a tight definition of TREASON; and bans on ex post facto laws and bills of attainder. The argument that to include some rights would exclude others boomeranged; every right excluded seemed in jeopardy. Enumerated powers could be abused; the power to tax, opponents argued, might be used against the press or religion. Moreover, the argument that a bill of rights was unnecessary could not possibly apply to the rights of the criminally accused or to personal liberties of a procedural nature. The new national government would act directly on the people and be buttressed by an undefined executive power and a national judiciary to enforce laws made by Congress; and Congress had the authority to define crimes and prescribe penalties for violations of its laws. PATRICK HENRY contended that the proposed Constitution empowered the United States to torture citizens into confessing their violations of congressional enactments.

Mason's point that a bill of rights would quiet the fears of the people was unanswerable. Alienating him and his followers was bad politics and blunderingly handed them a stirring cause around which they could muster opposition to ratification. No rational argument—and the lack of a bill of rights created an extremely emotional issue not amenable to rational argument—could possibly allay the fears generated by demagogues like Henry and principled opponents like Mason.

In Pennsylvania, the second state to ratify, the minority demanded a comprehensive bill of rights. Massachusetts, the sixth state to ratify, was the first to do so with recommended amendments, although only two—jury trial in civil suits and grand jury INDICTMENT—belonged in a bill of rights. But Massachusetts led the way toward recommended amendments, and the last four states to ratify recommended comprehensive bills of rights. Every right that became part of the ten amendments known as the Bill of Rights was included in state recommendations, with the exception of JUST COMPENSATION for property taken.

Some Federalists—above all Madison, whose political position in Virginia deteriorated because of his opposition to a bill of rights—finally realized that statecraft and political expediency dictated a switch in position. In states where ratification was in doubt, especially New York, Virginia, and North Carolina, Federalists pledged themselves to subsequent amendments to protect civil liberties, as soon as the new government went into operation.

In the first Congress, Representative Madison sought to fulfill his pledge. His accomplishment in the face of opposition and apathy entitles him to be remembered as "father of the Bill of Rights" even more than as "father of the Constitution." Many Federalists thought that the house had more important tasks, like the passage of tonnage duties. The opposition party, which had capitalized on the lack of a bill of rights in the Constitution, hoped for either a second convention or amendments that would cripple the substantive powers of the government. They had used the bill of rights issue as a smokescreen for objections to the Constitution's provisions on DIRECT TAXES, the judicial power, and the commerce power; these objections could not be dramatically popularized, and now the Anti-Federalists sought to scuttle Madison's proposals. They began by stalling, then tried to annex amendments aggrandizing state powers, and finally depreciated the importance of the very protections of individual liberty that they had formerly demanded. Madison meant to prove that the new government was a friend of liberty, and he understood that his amendments, if adopted, would make extremely difficult the passage of genuinely Anti-Federalist proposals. He would not be put off; he was insistent, compelling, unyielding, and, finally, triumphant.

On June 8, 1789, he made his long masterful speech before an apathetic House, introducing amendments culled mainly from state constitutions and state ratification proposals. All power, he argued, is subject to abuse and should be guarded against by constitutional provisions securing "the great rights of mankind." The government had only limited powers, but it might, unless prohibited, use general warrants in the enforcement of its revenue laws. In Great Britain, bills of rights merely erected barriers against the powers of the crown, leaving the powers of Parliament "altogether indefinite," and in Great Britain, the constitution left unguarded the "choicest" rights of the press and of conscience. The great objective he had in mind, Madison declared, was to limit the powers of government, thus preventing legislative as well as executive abuse, and above all preventing abuses of power by "the body of the people, operating by the majority against the minority." Mere "paper barriers" might fail, but they raised a standard that might educate the majority against acts to which they might be inclined. To the argument that a bill or rights was not necessary because the states constitutionally protected freedom, Madison had two responses. One was that some states had no bills of rights, others "very defective ones." The states constituted a greater danger to liberty than the new national government. The other was that the Constitution should, therefore, include an amendment that "No State shall violate the equal rights of conscience, or the freedom of the press, or the trial by jury in criminal cases." This, Madison declared, was "the most valuable amendment in the whole list." To the contention that an enumeration of rights would disparage those not in the list, Madison replied that the danger could be guarded against by adopting a proposal of his composition that became the NINTH AMENDMENT. If his amendments were "incorporated" into the constitution, Madison said, using another argument borrowed from Jefferson, "independent tribunals of justice will consider themselves in a peculiar manner the guardians of those rights; they will be an impenetrable bulwark against every assumption of power in the legislative or executive; they will be naturally led to resist every encroachment upon rights expressly stipulated for in the constitution. . . ."

Supporters of Madison informed him that Anti-Federalists did not really want a bill of rights and that his proposals "confounded the Anties exceedingly. . . ." Madison's proposals went to a select committee, of which he was a member, though its chairman, John Vining of Delaware, thought the House had "more important business." The committee added freedom of speech to the recommended prohibitions on the states, made some stylistic changes, and urged the amendments, which the House adopted. Madison, however, had proposed to "incorporate" the amendments within the text of the Constitution at appropriate points. He did not, that is, recommend their adoption as a separate "bill of rights." Members objected that to incorporate the amendments would give the impression that the Framers of the Constitution had signed a document that included provisions not of their composition. Another argument for lumping the amendments together was that the matter of form was so "trifling" that the House should not squander its time debating the placement of the various amendments. Indeed, Aedanus Burke of South Carolina, an Anti-Federalist, thought the amendments were "not those solid and substantial amendments which the people expect; they are little better than whip-syllabub, frothy and full of wind . . . it will be better to drop the subject." Men of Burke's views in the Senate managed to kill the proposed restrictions on the states, and the Senate sought to cripple the clause against establishments of religion. A conference committee of the two houses, which included Madison, accepted the Senate's joining together several amendments but agreed to Madison's phrasing of the proposal that became the FIRST AMENDMENT. The House accepted the conference report on September 24, 1789, the Senate a day later. Virginia's senators, William Grayson and RICHARD HENRY LEE, both Anti-Federalists, opposed the amendments because they left "the great points of the Judiciary, direct taxation, &c to stand as they are. . . ." Lee informed Patrick Henry that they had erred in their strategy of accepting ratification on the promise of subsequent amendments. Grayson reported to Henry that the amendments adopted by the Senate "are good for nothing. . . ."

Within six months of the time the amendments, or Bill of Rights, were submitted to the states for approval, nine states ratified. Connecticut and Georgia refused to ratify on the ground that the Bill of Rights was unnecessary; they belatedly ratified on the sesquicentennial anniversary of the ratification of the Constitution in 1939. (Massachusetts ratified in 1939, too, although both houses of its legislature in 1790 had adopted most of the amendments, but they had failed to send official notice of ratification.) The admission of Vermont to the union in 1791 made necessary ratification by eleven states. Vermont's ratification of the amendments in November 1791 made Virginia's approval indispensable as the eleventh state. The battle there was stalled in the state senate, where the Anti-Federalists were in control. They first sought to sabotage the Bill of Rights and then, having failed in their chief objective to abolish the power of Congress to enact direct taxes, they irresolutely acquiesced two years later. Virginia finally ratified on December 15, 1791, making the Bill of Rights part of the Constitution.

The history of the framing and ratification of the Bill of Rights is sparse. We know almost nothing about what the state legislatures thought concerning the meanings of the various amendments, and the press was perfunctory in its reports, if not altogether silent. But for Madison's persistence the amendments would have died in Congress. Our precious Bill of Rights was in the main the result of the political necessity for certain reluctant Federalists to make their own a cause that had been originated, in vain, by the Anti-Federalists to vote down the Constitution. The party that had first opposed a Bill of Rights inadvertently wound up with the responsibility for its framing and ratification, while the party that had first professed to want it discovered too late that it was not only embarrassing but politically disastrous for ulterior party purposes.

LEONARD W. LEVY

Bibliography

BRANT, IRVING 1965 *The Bill of Rights: Its Origin and Meanings.* Indianapolis: Bobbs-Merrill.

DUMBAULD, EDWARD 1957 *The Bill of Rights and What It Means Today.* Norman: University of Oklahoma Press.

RUTLAND, ROBERT A. 1955 *The Birth of the Bill of Rights, 1776–1791.* Chapel Hill: University of North Carolina Press.

SCHWARTZ, BERNARD 1977 *The Great Rights of Mankind: A History of the American Bill of Rights.* New York: Oxford University Press.

BINGHAM, JOHN A. (1815–1900)

An Ohio attorney, John Armor Bingham was a congressman (1855–1863, 1865–1873), Army judge advocate (1864–1865), solicitor of the COURT OF CLAIMS (1864–1865), and ambassador to Japan (1873–1885). After President ABRAHAM LINCOLN's assassination, President ANDREW JOHNSON appointed Bingham as a special judge advocate (prosecutor) to the military commission trying the accused assassination conspirators. Bingham was particularly effective in answering defense objections during the trials and in justifying the constitutionality of trying the civilian defendants in military courts.

From 1865 to 1867 Bingham served on the JOINT COMMITTEE ON RECONSTRUCTION. As a Republican moderate Bingham supported congressional reconstruction but demanded strict adherence to the Constitution and favored early readmission of the ex-Confederate states. He offered numerous amendments to moderate the CIVIL RIGHTS ACT OF 1866, and although these passed he still voted against the bill, because he believed Congress lacked the authority to protect freedmen in this manner. Bingham wanted very much to protect them, and during the debates over the civil rights bill he argued that a new constitutional amendment was the answer. Bingham believed that the results of the war—including the death of both SLAVERY and state SOVEREIGNTY, as well as the protection of CIVIL LIBERTIES for blacks—could be secured only by an amendment that would nationalize the BILL OF RIGHTS. By working to apply the Fifth and FIRST AMENDMENTS to the states Bingham linked the antislavery arguments of the antebellum period to postbellum conditions.

In 1865 Bingham suggested an amendment that would empower Congress "to secure to all persons in every State of the Union equal protection in their rights, life, liberty, and property." Bingham believed the THIRTEENTH AMENDMENT had not only freed blacks but also made them citizens. As citizens of the United States they were among "the People of the United States" referred to in the PREAMBLE to the Constitution and protected by the Fifth Amendment. However, Bingham was unsure whether the enforcement provision of the Thirteenth Amendment allowed Congress to guarantee and protect CIVIL RIGHTS. Johnson's veto of the 1866 Civil Rights bill only increased Bingham's determination to place such protection beyond the reach of a presidential veto or repeal by a future Congress. Bingham therefore drafted what became Section 1 of the FOURTEENTH AMENDMENT, protecting the freedmen by explicitly making them citizens, prohibiting states from abridging their PRIVILEGES AND IMMUNITIES as United States citizens, and guaranteeing all persons DUE PROCESS and EQUAL PROTECTION of the law. In 1871 Bingham reaffirmed his belief that the amendment was designed to protect those privileges and immunities "chiefly defined in the first eight amendments to the Constitution of the United States." Thus, as Bingham saw it, the ABOLITIONIST CONSTITUTIONAL THEORY of the antebellum period became part of the Constitution.

By 1867 Bingham was at least temporarily a Radical Republican. He supported THADDEUS STEVENS's bill for military reconstruction after the ex-Confederate states refused to ratify the Fourteenth Amendment and after numerous outrages had been perpetrated against freedom. Initially opposed to IMPEACHMENT, he was elected to the impeachment committee and was made chairman after threatening to resign unless given that position. Bingham vigorously pursued the prosecution of Johnson, and after it failed he attempted to investigate the seven Republican senators who voted against impeachment.

Bingham had initially opposed linking black suffrage to readmission to the Union, and opposed efforts by Stevens to create such a linkage. He argued that Congress lacked the constitutional authority to do this. But by 1870 he supported the FIFTEENTH AMENDMENT and sought to extend the franchise even further, by prohibiting religious, property, or nationality limitations on the ballot. In 1871, with the three new amendments legitimizing congressional action, Bingham supported the three "force bills," which prohibited states and individuals from violating the newly acquired constitutional rights of the freedmen, gave the federal government supervisory powers over national elections, and made numerous acts federal crimes under the Ku Klux Klan Act. (See FORCE ACTS.) Bingham, the careful constitutionalist and moderate Republican leader, defended these acts because they were a response to the terror being inflicted against blacks, and because they were now constitutional.

PAUL FINKELMAN

Bibliography

HYMAN, HAROLD M. and WIECEK, WILLIAM M. 1982 *Equal Justice under Law: Constitutional Development, 1835–1875.* New York: Harper & Row.

SWIFT, DONALD C. 1968 John A. Bingham and Reconstruction: The Dilemma of a Moderate. *Ohio History* 77:76–94.

BINNEY, HORACE
(1780–1875)

A leading Philadelphia attorney, Horace Binney edited six volumes of the Pennsylvania Supreme Court's decisions, covering the years 1799–1814. In 1862 Binney published two pamphlets entitled *The Privilege of the Writ of Habeas Corpus under the Constitution,* in which he defended President ABRAHAM LINCOLN's suspension of the writ. Binney argued that the President, and not Congress, had the power to suspend HABEAS CORPUS, and that each branch of the government had the right to interpret the Constitution independently. In 1865 Binney answered the many critics of his earlier work with a third pamphlet of the same title.

PAUL FINKELMAN

Bibliography

BINNEY, CHARLES CHAUNCEY 1903 *The Life of Horace Binney, with Selections from His Letters.* Philadelphia: Lippincott.

BIRNEY, JAMES G.
(1792–1857)

A slaveholder, James Gillespie Birney studied law under ALEXANDER DALLAS, was a mildly antislavery politician in Kentucky and Alabama, and was a spokesman for the American Colonization Society. In 1834 he freed his remaining slaves, abandoned colonization, and formed the Kentucky Anti-Slavery Society. Finding Kentucky too dangerous for an abolitionist, Birney moved to Cincinnati, and in 1836 began publishing an antislavery newspaper, *The Philanthropist.* Unlike WILLIAM LLOYD GARRISON, whom he bitterly opposed, Birney believed that the United States Constitution could be a useful tool for abolitionists. He also argued for abolitionist political activity. In 1840 he was the Liberty party candidate for the presidency, but he drew only 7,069 votes. Four years later he won 62,300 votes, helping set the stage for more successful antislavery parties.

Birney was involved in three legal cases that helped develop his antislavery constitutionalism. In 1836 an anti-abolitionist mob in Cincinnati destroyed his press. Birney hired SALMON P. CHASE in a successful suit against the mob leaders for damages to the press. In 1837 Birney sheltered and hired a runaway slave named Matilda, and when she was captured, Chase and Birney defended her on the ground that having voluntarily been brought to Ohio, she therefore was not a fugitive slave; they also made the dubious argument that slaves who escaped from Kentucky into Ohio could not be recaptured, because the NORTHWEST ORDINANCE provided only for the return of slaves who escaped from the "original states." Matilda was returned south, but Chase and Birney were more successful in appealing Birney's conviction for harboring slaves, which the Ohio Supreme Court overturned. (See ABOLITIONIST CONSTITUTIONAL THEORY.)

PAUL FINKELMAN

Bibliography

FLADELAND, BETTY L. 1955 *James Gillespie Birney: Slaveholder to Abolitionist.* Ithaca, N.Y.: Cornell University Press.

BIRTH CONTROL

The American birth control movement began in the early twentieth century as a campaign to achieve a right of REPRODUCTIVE AUTONOMY in the face of hostile legislation in many states. By the time that campaign succeeded in getting the Supreme Court to espouse a constitutional RIGHT OF PRIVACY which allowed married couples to practice contraception, there was not a single state in which an anticontraception law was being enforced against private medical advice or against drugstore sales. GRISWOLD V. CONNECTICUT (1965) and its successor decisions thus did not create the effective right of choice; they recognized and legitimized the right, by subjecting restrictive legislation to strict judicial scrutiny and finding justifications wanting. (See FUNDAMENTAL INTERESTS.)

Contraception is only the most widely practiced method of birth control; others (apart from abstinence) are STERILIZATION and abortion. The Supreme Court, partly on the precedent of *Griswold,* recognized in ROE V. WADE (1973) a woman's constitutional right to have an abortion, qualified by the state's power to forbid abortion during the latter stages of pregnancy. The Court has had no occasion to recognize a person's right to choose to be sterilized, because the states have not sought to restrict that freedom. In any event the birth control movement has now won its most important constitutional battles; both married and single persons are free, both in fact and in constitutional theory, to choose not to beget or bear children.

"Birth control," however, has another potential meaning that is the antithesis of reproductive choice. The state may seek to coerce persons to refrain from procreating, either through compulsory sterilization or by other sanctions aimed at restricting family size. On present constitutional doctrine, the decision to procreate is "fundamental," requiring some COMPELLING STATE INTEREST to justify its limitation. (See SKINNER V. OKLAHOMA, 1942.) Although judicial recognition of such an interest is not inconceivable in some future condition of acute overpopulation, no such decision is presently foreseeable.

The constitutional right to choose whether to have a child or be a parent is properly rested today on SUBSTANTIVE DUE PROCESS grounds; "liberty" is precisely the point. Yet the interest in equality has also played a significant role in the development of these rights of choice. Justice BYRON R. WHITE, concurring in *Griswold,* pointed out how enforcement of an anticontraceptives law against birth control clinics worked to deny the disadvantaged from obtaining help in controlling family size. The well-to-do needed no clinics. And once *Griswold* recognized the right of married persons to practice contraception, the Supreme Court saw that EQUAL PROTECTION principles demanded extension of the right to be unmarried. (See EISENSTADT V. BAIRD, 1972; CAREY V. POPULATION SERVICES INTERNATIONAL, 1977.) Finally, judicial recognition of rights of reproductive choice has followed the progress of the women's movement. The breakdown of the traditional sexual "double standard" and the opening of new opportunities for women outside the "housewife marriage" have gone together, both socially and in constitutional development. No longer is the "erring woman" to be punished with unwanted pregnancy or parenthood. In 1920 Margaret Sanger wrote, "Birth control is woman's problem." Half a century later, the Supreme Court heard that message.

KENNETH L. KARST

Bibliography

CHARLES, ALAN F. 1980 Abortion and Family Planning: Law and the Moral Issue. Pages 331–356 in Ruth Roemer and George McKray (eds.), *Legal Aspects of Health Policy: Issues and Trends.* Westport, Conn.: Greenwood Press.

GREENAWALT, KENT 1971 Criminal Law and Population Control. *Vanderbilt Law Review* 24:465–494.

NOTE 1971 Legal Analysis and Population Control: The Problem of Coercion. *Harvard Law Review* 84:1856–1911.

BISHOP v. WOOD
426 U.S. 341 (1976)

Bishop worked a major change in the modern law of PROCEDURAL DUE PROCESS, enshrining in the law the view Justice WILLIAM H. REHNQUIST had unsuccessfully urged in ARNETT V. KENNEDY (1974): the due process right of a holder of a statutory "entitlement" is defined by positive law, not by the Constitution itself.

Here, a city ordinance that classified a police officer as a "permanent employee" was nonetheless interpreted by the lower federal courts to give an officer employment only "at the will and pleasure of the city." The Supreme Court held, 5–4, that this ordinance created no "property" interest in the officer's employment, and that, absent public disclosure of the reasons for his termination, he had suffered no stigma that impaired a "liberty" interest. The key to the majority's decision presumably lay in this sentence: "The federal court is not the appropriate forum in which to review the multitude of personnel decisions that are made daily by public agencies."

In dissent, Justice WILLIAM J. BRENNAN accurately commented that the Court had resurrected the "right/privilege" distinction, discredited in GOLDBERG V. KELLY (1970), and insisted that there was a federal constitutional dimension to the idea of "property" interests, not limited by state law and offering the protections of due process to legitimate expectations raised by government.

KENNETH L. KARST

BITUMINOUS COAL ACT
50 Stat. 72 (1937)

After CARTER V. CARTER COAL COMPANY (1936), Congress restored regulation of bituminous coal in INTERSTATE COMMERCE. The new act, designed to control the interstate sale and distribution of soft coal and to protect interstate commerce, levied a nineteen and one-half percent tax on all producers but remitted payment to those who accepted the new code. Price-fixing provisions constituted the crux of the act; Congress did not reenact any labor provisions, although it encouraged free COLLECTIVE BARGAINING.

The act established a National Bituminous Coal Commission to supervise an elaborate procedure for setting minimum prices. Unfair competition or sales below established prices violated the code. The act provided extensive PROCEDURAL DUE PROCESS and several means of enforcement, including CEASE-AND-DESIST ORDERS and private suits carrying treble damage awards for injured competitors.

An 8–1 Supreme Court sustained the act in *Sunshine Anthracite Coal Company v. Adkins* (1940). Conceding the tax was "a sanction to enforce the regulatory provisions of the Act," the majority held that Congress might nevertheless "impose penalties in aid of the exercise of any of its ENUMERATED POWERS." The Court thus upheld the act under the COMMERCE CLAUSE, declaring that the method of regulation was for legislative determination.

DAVID GORDON

BIVENS v. SIX UNKNOWN NAMED AGENTS OF THE FEDERAL BUREAU OF NARCOTICS
403 U.S. 388 (1971)

This is the leading case concerning IMPLIED RIGHTS OF ACTION under the Constitution. Federal agents conducted an unconstitutional search of Webster Bivens's apartment. Bivens brought an action in federal court seeking damages for a FOURTH AMENDMENT violation. Although no federal statute supplied Bivens with a cause of action, the Supreme Court, in an opinion by Justice WILLIAM J. BRENNAN, held that Bivens could maintain that action.

Two central factors led to the decision. First, violations of constitutional rights ought not go unremedied. The traditional remedy, enjoining unconstitutional behavior, plainly was inadequate for Bivens. And the

Court was unwilling to leave Bivens to the uncertainties of state tort law, his principal alternative source of action. Second, the implied constitutional cause of action makes federal officials as vulnerable as state officials for constitutional misbehavior. Prior to *Bivens,* state officials were subject to suits under SECTION 1983, TITLE 42, UNITED STATES CODE, for violating individuals' constitutional rights. An action against federal officials had to be inferred in *Bivens* only because section 1983 is inapplicable to federal officials.

Both factors emerged again in later cases. DAVIS V. PASSMAN (1979) recognized an implied constitutional cause of action for claims brought under the Fifth Amendment, and *Carlson v. Green* (1980) extended *Bivens* to other constitutional rights. BUTZ V. ECONOMOU (1978) extended to federal officials the good faith defense that state officials enjoy under section 1983.

Bivens raises important questions about the scope of federal JUDICIAL POWER. Chief Justice WARREN E. BURGER and Justices HUGO L. BLACK and HARRY BLACKMUN dissented on the ground that Congress alone may authorize damages against federal officials. The majority, and Justice JOHN MARSHALL HARLAN in a concurring opinion, required no congressional authorization. But they left open the possibility that Congress might have the last word in the area through express legislation.

THEODORE EISENBERG

BLACK, HUGO L.
(1886–1971)

When Hugo LaFayette Black was appointed to the Supreme Court in 1937, the basic tenets of his mature judicial philosophy had already been formed. Born in the Alabama hill country in 1886, Black received his law degree from the University of Alabama in 1906. He practiced law, largely handling personal injury cases, in Birmingham during the next twenty years and served brief terms as police court judge and county prosecutor. In 1926 he was elected to the United States Senate; after reelection in 1932 he became an outspoken advocate of the New Deal and a tenacious investigator. Throughout his career he read extensively in history, philosophy, and literary classics. From THOMAS JEFFERSON he took his view of the FIRST AMENDMENT. Aristotle, his "favorite author," and JOHN LOCKE offered appealing theoretical perspectives on the nature of government and society.

Coming to the bench in the aftermath of President FRANKLIN D. ROOSEVELT's Court-packing plan, which he vigorously espoused, Black searched for a jurisprudence of certainty, seeking clear, precise standards that would limit judicial discretion, protect individual rights, and give government room to operate. He saw the Constitution as a set of unambiguous commands designed to prevent the recurrence of historic evils. In its text and the intent of its Framers he found the authority for applying some provisions virtually open-ended, and others rather more strictly. All constitutional questions he considered open until he dealt with them; but when he came to a conclusion, he maintained it with single-minded devotion. His opinions never suggested that he entertained any doubts.

Black's Senate years left an indelible impression on his performance as Justice. Each of the popular branches must be left to carry out its duties according to the original constitutional understanding. Congress makes the laws, he noted in YOUNGSTOWN SHEET & TUBE COMPANY V. SAWYER (1952); the President's functions are limited to the recommending and vetoing of bills. Congress, Black believed, had the power to regulate whatever affected commerce. Likewise, unless states discriminated against INTERSTATE COMMERCE, they had the power to regulate in the absence of contrary congressional direction. Nor, under the DUE PROCESS clause of the FOURTEENTH AMENDMENT, might courts consider the appropriateness of legislation. In *Lincoln Federal Labor Union v. Northwestern Iron & Metal Company* (1949), he observed that the Court had rejected "the *Allgeyer-Lochner-Adair-Coppage* constitutional doctrine"; the states had power to legislate "so long as their laws do not run afoul of some specific federal constitutional provision, or of some valid federal law."

Black's adamant refusal to expand judicial power through the due process clause forced him to develop an alternative theory to protect the rights enumerated in the BILL OF RIGHTS. He had to overcome his initial "grave doubts" about the validity of JUDICIAL REVIEW. CHAMBERS V. FLORIDA (1940) was an early milestone. Courts, he stated in that case, "stand against any winds that blow as havens of refuge for those who might otherwise suffer because they are helpless, weak, outnumbered, or because they are non-conforming victims of prejudice and public excitement." Finally, in ADAMSON V. CALIFORNIA (1947), he laid down the formulation that guided him for the rest of his career:

> My study of the historical events that culminated in the Fourteenth Amendment . . . persuades me that one of the chief objects that the provisions of the Amendment's first section, separately, and as a whole, were intended to accom-

plish was to make the Bill of Rights applicable to the States. . . . I fear to see the consequences of the Court's practices of substituting its own concepts of decency and fundamental justice for the language of the Bill of Rights as its point of departure in interpreting and enforcing that Bill of Rights. . . . To hold that his Court can determine what, if any, provisions of the Bill of Rights will be enforced, and if so to what degree, is to frustrate the great design of a written Constitution.

Only by limiting judges' discretion, and demanding that they enforce the textual guarantees, could the protection of these rights be ensured. Black feared that the "shock the conscience" test, which Justice FELIX FRANKFURTER employed for the Court in *Rochin v. California* (1952), with its "accordion-like qualities" and "nebulous" and "evanescent standards," "must inevitably imperil all the individual liberty safeguards specifically enumerated in the Bill of Rights."

Black applied his INCORPORATION DOCTRINE in scores of cases. From his early days as a public official he hated coerced confessions, and he viewed POLICE INTERROGATIONS without counsel as secret inquisitions in flat violation of the FIFTH AMENDMENT's guarantee of the RIGHT AGAINST SELF-INCRIMINATION. "From the time government begins to move against a man," he said when the Court considered MIRANDA V. ARIZONA (1966), "when they take him into custody, his rights attach." He led the Court in expanding the RIGHT TO COUNSEL from his first term, when he held in JOHNSON V. ZERBST (1938) that in a federal prosecution counsel must be appointed to represent a defendant who cannot afford to hire an attorney. To his supreme satisfaction he wrote the opinion in GIDEON V. WAINWRIGHT (1963), overruling BETTS V. BRADY (1942) and making similar assistance mandatory in state FELONY trials. More of his dissents eventually became law than those of any other Justice.

Given his approach of allowing free play to the spirit of the Constitution while resting his justifications largely on its words, the generalities of the EQUAL PROTECTION clause presented problems of interpretation for Black. In his view, Article I conferred on qualified voters the rights to vote and to have their votes counted in congressional elections. Dissenting in COLEGROVE V. GREEN (1946), he argued that both Article I and the equal protection clause required that congressional district lines be drawn "to give approximately equal weight to each vote cast." Black formally buried *Colegrove* in WESBERRY V. SANDERS (1963). In every REAPPORTIONMENT case, as in every case involving an INDIGENT prosecuted for crime, he supported the equal protection claim. He shared in the widespread agreement that the Fourteenth Amendment had been designed primarily to end RACIAL DISCRIMINATION, and made the first explicit reference to race as a SUSPECT CLASSIFICATION which must be subjected to the "most rigid scrutiny." Ironically, this came in one of the JAPANESE AMERICAN CASES (1943), in which he upheld, over biting dissents, a conviction for violating a military order during World War II excluding all persons of Japanese ancestry from the West Coast. But as the Court moved beyond race in applying the equal protection clause, Black refused to follow. Classifications based on wealth or poverty were not "suspect"; and even though the claims in VOTING RIGHTS cases were essential for the democratic process to reach its full potential, he denied them.

During the first twenty-five years of his tenure, Black's opinions had remarkable constancy as he unflaggingly pursued his goal of human advancement within the bounds of constitutional interpretation. But new issues confronted the Court and the country in the 1960s. Black was fighting old age, and Court work, he admitted, was harder. Because of cataract operations he did not read nearly so much as he had. References in his opinions to books and articles became infrequent, and the cases he cited were often his old ones as he repeatedly accused his colleagues of going beyond their province. No longer was he reading the words of the Constitution expansively; his interpretations were restraining and cramped; and his categories of permissible legal action narrowed. Increasingly, he had trouble adjusting to a world that was changing. His opinions took on an essay-like quality, with a new structure and tone, and a note of anger crept into them.

From the beginning Black consistently interpreted the FOURTH AMENDMENT as restrictively as any Justice in the Court's modern history. Refusing to examine the term "unreasonable" in SEARCH AND SEIZURE cases, he generally accepted law enforcement actions. Almost invariably he validated WARRANTLESS SEARCHES including SEARCHES INCIDENT TO ARREST. His Fourth Amendment opinions emphasized the guilt of the accused, often starting with detailed descriptions of the crime; and, oddly, he ignored the amendment's rich history. After calling the EXCLUSIONARY RULE "an extraordinary sanction, judicially imposed," in *United States v. Wallace & Tiernan Company* (1949), he changed his mind: by linking the Fourth and Fifth Amendments in MAPP V. OHIO (1961), he found that "a constitutional basis emerges which not only justifies but actually requires" the rule. But his enthusiasm waned as the Court enlarged the

FOURTH AMENDMENT's scope. In his last search and seizure case, COOLIDGE V. NEW HAMPSHIRE (1971), he converted this limitation on government into a grant of power: "The Fourth Amendment provides a constitutional means by which the Government can act to obtain EVIDENCE to be used in criminal prosecutions. The people are obliged to yield to a proper exercise of authority under that Amendment."

By the time the RIGHT OF PRIVACY matured as an issue, Black had tied himself to the text as a mode of constitutional interpretation. Two heated dissents indicated his narrow conception of the Fourth Amendment. Seemingly oblivious to the dangers of WIRETAPPING, he wrote in BERGER V. NEW YORK (1967): "Had the framers of this amendment desired to prohibit the use in court of evidence secured by an unreasonable search and seizure, they would have used plain appropriate language to say that conversations can be searched and words seized. . . ." Finding no mention of privacy in the Constitution, he dismissed it as a "vague judge-made goal" and denigrated it: "the 'right of privacy' . . . , like a chameleon, has a different color for every turning," he wrote in *Berger.* He accurately viewed its elevation to separate constitutional status in GRISWOLD V. CONNECTICUT (1965) as the revival of SUBSTANTIVE DUE PROCESS. "Use of any such broad, unbounded judicial authority would make of this Court's members a day-to-day constitutional convention." Black rejected the idea of a living Constitution. His *Adamson* dissent not only had expanded horizons but had set limits.

Black was most famous for his views on the First Amendment. In *Milk Wagon Drivers Union v. Meadowmoor Diaries* (1941), his initial opinion on the subject, he said, "Freedom to speak and write about public questions . . . is the heart of our government. If that be weakened, the result is debilitation; if it be stilled, the result is death." He ceaselessly implored the Court to expand the amendment's protections, and embellished his opinions with moving libertarian rhetoric. But as in other areas during his last half-dozen years or so, Black narrowed his construction and retreated from many of his previous positions.

He subscribed fully to the "preferred position" doctrine of the First Amendment. He used, and reworked, the CLEAR AND PRESENT DANGER test in BRIDGES V. CALIFORNIA (1941), adding words that he repeated often: "the First Amendment does not speak equivocally. It prohibits any law 'abridging the freedom of speech, or of the press.' It must be taken as a command of the broadest scope that explicit language . . . will allow." But slowly "clear and present danger," with its inherent balancing of disparate interests, disillusioned Black. The First Amendment "forbids compromise" in matters of conscience, he argued in AMERICAN COMMUNICATIONS ASSOCIATION V. DOUDS (1950). The "basic constitutional precept" is that "penalties should be imposed only for a person's own conduct, not for his beliefs or for the conduct of those with whom he may associate"; those "who commit overt acts in violation of valid laws can and should be punished."

A new word began to appear as his opinions, invariably in dissent, grew more shrill and strident. "I think the First Amendment, with the Fourteenth, 'absolutely' forbids such laws without any 'ifs' or 'buts' or whereases,' " he wrote when the Court upheld a GROUP LIBEL statute in BEAUHARNAIS V. ILLINOIS (1952). The First Amendment "grants an absolute right to believe in any governmental system, discuss all governmental affairs, and argue for desired changes in the existing order," he proclaimed in *Carlson v. Landon* (1952)—"whether or not such discussion incites to action, legal or illegal," he added in YATES V. UNITED STATES (1957). He refined this speech-conduct distinction in BARENBLATT V. UNITED STATES (1959). Some laws "directly," while others "indirectly," affect speech; when in the latter cases the speech and action were intertwined, Black was willing to use a BALANCING TEST weighing "the effect on speech . . . in relation to the need for control of the conduct."

For many years Black voted to invalidate statutes as direct abridgments of First Amendment rights. He opposed such governmental actions as prescribing LOYALTY OATHS in WIEMAN V. UPDEGRAFF (1952); promulgating lists of "subversive" organizations in JOINT ANTI-FASCIST REFUGEE COMMITTEE V. MCGRATH (1952); demanding organizations' membership lists in GIBSON V. FLORIDA LEGISLATIVE INVESTIGATION COMMITTEE (1963); conducting LEGISLATIVE INVESTIGATIONS of suspected subversives in BARENBLATT V. UNITED STATES or prosecuting for subversive advocacy in DENNIS V. UNITED STATES (1951); and imposing penalties for Communist party membership in APTHEKER V. SECRETARY OF STATE (1965). Under his standard, OBSCENITY and LIBEL laws as well as the state's conditioning admission to the bar on an applicant's beliefs were unconstitutional. In cases of direct abridgment of speech, Black charged in UPHAUS V. WYMAN (1960), any balancing test substituted "elastic concepts" such as "arbitrary" and "unreasonable" for the Constitution's plain language, reducing the document's "absolute commands to mere admonitions." "Liberty, to be secure for any," he wrote in *Braden v. United States* (1961), "must be secure for all—even for the most miserable merchants of hated and unpopular ideas." The framers had ensured that liberty by doing all the balancing that was necessary.

Black was equally outspoken in RELIGIOUS LIBERTY cases, and played a key role in the development of the First Amendment's religious guarantees. He wrote the Court's opinion in EVERSON V. BOARD OF EDUCATION (1947), the first case declaring that the establishment clause applied to the states. After listing the clause's standards and stating that it was intended to erect, in Jefferson's words, "a wall of separation between Church and State," Black noted that government cannot "contribute tax-raised funds to the support of an institution which teaches the tenets and faith of any church." But for the state to pay the bus fares of all pupils, including those in parochial schools, served a secular purpose, and did not violate the establishment clause. In MCCOLLUM V. BOARD OF EDUCATION (1948), writing for the Court, he held unconstitutional a RELEASED TIME program in which religious instruction took place in a public school. In the school prayer case of ENGEL V. VITALE (1962), of all his opinions the one that produced the most vocal opposition, Black concluded that a state-sponsored "non-denominational" prayer was "wholly inconsistent" with the establishment clause. The clause prohibited any laws that "establish an official religion whether [they] operate directly to coerce non-observing individuals or not." Religion, he wrote, "is too personal, too sacred, too holy, to permit its 'unhallowed perversion' by a civil magistrate."

The direct action cases in the mid-1960s tested Black's First Amendment philosophy. He expounded the limitations that TRESPASS and BREACH OF THE PEACE statutes placed on FREEDOM OF SPEECH. Earlier, he had held, in GIBONEY V. EMPIRE STORAGE AND ICE COMPANY (1949), that legislatures could regulate PICKETING, but in *Barenblatt* he noted that they could not abridge "views peacefully expressed in a place where the speaker had a right to be." "Picketing," he now wrote in *Cox v. Louisiana* (1965), "though it may be utilized to communicate ideas, is not speech, and therefore is not of itself protected by the First Amendment." This was a very different Black from the one who in FEINER V. NEW YORK (1951) labeled the Court's decision sanctioning police action to silence a speaker as "a long step toward totalitarian authority."

New emphases emerged. The ownership of property became pivotal. A property owner, governmental or private, was under no obligation to provide a forum for speech; if owners could not control their property, Black feared, the result would be mob violence. The RULE OF LAW now took precedence over encouraging public discourse and protest. Focusing on maintaining "tranquility and order" in cases like *Gregory v. Chicago* (1969), Black deprecated protesters who "think they have been mistreated or . . . have actually been mistreated," and their supporters, who "do no service" to "their cause, or their country." Gone was much of his former admiration of dissenters, toleration of the unorthodox, and receptivity toward new ideas.

Nonetheless, Black remained uncompromising in protecting FREEDOM OF THE PRESS. In his view the people had the right to read any books or see any movies, regardless of content. In his final case, NEW YORK TIMES V. UNITED STATES (1971), he reexpressed his faith:

> Both the history and language of the First Amendment support the view that the press must be left to publish news, whatever the source, without censorship, INJUNCTIONS, or PRIOR RESTRAINTS.
>
> In the First Amendment the Founding Fathers gave the free press the protection it must have to fulfill its essential role in our democracy. The press was to serve the governed, not the governors. . . . The press was protected so that it could bare the secrets of government and inform the people. Only a free and unrestrained press can effectively expose deception in government. And paramount among the responsibilities of a free press is the duty to prevent any part of the government from deceiving the people and sending them off to distant lands to die of foreign fevers and foreign shot and shell.

Three months later he was dead.

Black is one of the handful of great judges in American history, second only to JOHN MARSHALL in his impact on the Constitution. Certain of his premises, and convinced that he and history were at one, he was a tireless, evangelical, constitutional populist. If the Court did not accept his most sweeping doctrines whole, it accepted them piece by piece. Incorporation stands as his monument, but equally enduring is his preeminence in sensitizing a whole generation to the value of the great freedoms contained in the Bill of Rights.

ROGER K. NEWMAN

Bibliography

FRANK, JOHN P. 1977 Hugo L. Black: Free Speech and the Declaration of Independence. *University of Illinois Law Forum* 2:577–620.

LANDYNSKI, JACOB W. 1976 In Search of Justice Black's

Fourth Amendment. *Fordham Law Review* 45:453–496.
REICH, CHARLES A. 1963 Mr. Justice Black and the Living Constitution. *Harvard Law Review* 76:673–754.
SNOWISS, SYLVIA 1973 The Legacy of Justice Black. *Supreme Court Review* 1973:187–252.
SYMPOSIUM 1967 Mr. Justice Black: Thirty Years in Retrospect. *UCLA Law Review* 14:397–552.

BLACK, JEREMIAH S. (1810–1883)

Jeremiah S. Black served on the Pennsylvania Supreme Court (1851–1857), as U.S. attorney general (1857–1860), U.S. secretary of state (1860–1861), and U.S. Supreme Court reporter (1861–1862). He advised ANDREW JOHNSON during the early phase of his IMPEACHMENT, and defended Samuel Tilden's claim to the presidency in the disputed election of 1876. A lifelong Democrat, Black was particularly antagonistic to abolitionists. During the winter of 1860–1861 Black opposed SECESSION and urged President JAMES BUCHANAN to reinforce federal military bases in the South. Buchanan appointed Black to the Supreme Court of the United States, but the Senate refused to confirm him.

PAUL FINKELMAN

Bibliography

BRIGANCE, WILLIAM N. 1934 *Jeremiah Sullivan Black, a Defender of the Constitution and the Ten Commandments.* Philadelphia: University of Pennsylvania Press.

BLACK CODES

In 1865–1866, the former slave states enacted statutes, collectively known as the "Black Codes," regulating the legal and constitutional status of black people. The Black Codes attempted to accomplish two objectives: (1) to enumerate the legal rights essential to the status of freedom of blacks; and (2) to provide a special criminal code for blacks. The latter objective reflected the two purposes of the antebellum law of slavery: race control and labor discipline.

In the view of white Southerners, emancipation did not of its own force create a civil status or capacity for freedmen. The southern state legislatures accordingly specified the incidents of this free status: the right to buy, sell, own, and bequeath property; the right to make contracts; the right to contract valid marriages, including so-called common-law marriages, and to enjoy a legally recognized parent–child relationship; the right to locomotion and personal liberty; the right to sue and be sued, and to testify in court, but only in cases involving black parties.

But the Codes also reenacted elements of the law of slavery. They provided detailed lists of civil disabilities by recreating the race-control features of the slave codes. They defined racial status; forbade blacks from pursuing certain occupations or professions; prohibited blacks from owning firearms or other weapons; controlled the movement of blacks by systems of passes; required proof of residence; prohibited the congregation of groups of blacks; restricted blacks from residing in certain areas; and specified an etiquette of deference to whites, such as by prohibiting blacks from directing insulting words at whites. The Codes forbade racial intermarriage and provided the death penalty for blacks raping white women, while omitting special provisions for whites raping black women. (See MISCEGENATION.) They excluded blacks from jury duty, public office, and voting. Some Black Codes required racial SEGREGATION in public transportation or created Jim Crow schools. Most Codes authorized whipping and the pillory as punishment for freedmen's offenses.

The Codes salvaged the labor-discipline elements of slave law in master-and-servant statutes, VAGRANCY and pauper provisions, apprenticeship regulations, and elaborate labor contract statutes, especially those pertaining to farm labor. Other provisions permitted magistrates to hire out offenders unable to pay fines. These statutes provided a basis for subsequent efforts, extending well into the twentieth century, to provide a legal and paralegal structure forcing blacks to work, restricting their occupational mobility, and providing harsh systems of forced black labor, sometimes verging on PEONAGE.

The Black Codes profoundly offended the northern ideal of equality before the law. Northerners lost whatever sympathies they might have entertained for the plight of southern whites trying to make the revolutionary transition from a slave society, based on a legal regime of status, to a free, capitalist society based on will and contract. Northerners determined to force the former slave states to create new structures of racial equality. Consequently, the Black Codes were repealed or left unenforced during the congressional phase of Reconstruction. Later Redeemer and Conservative state legislatures reenacted the Jim Crow provisions and labor contract statutes to provide the statutory component of the twilight zone of semifreedom that characterized the legal status of southern blacks through World War I.

WILLIAM M. WIECEK

Bibliography

WILSON, THEODORE B. 1965 *The Black Codes of the South.* University: University of Alabama Press.

BLACKMUN, HARRY A.
(1908–)

Nothing in Harry A. Blackmun's background presaged that within three years of his appointment he would write the most controversial Supreme Court opinion of his time—ROE V. WADE (1972)—providing significant constitutional protection to women and their doctors in the area of abortion.

After graduating from public school in St. Paul, Minnesota, where he and WARREN E. BURGER were elementary school classmates, young Blackmun attended Harvard College, having graduated in 1929 *summa cum laude,* and Harvard Law School, being graduated in 1932. He practiced law in St. Paul and then as resident counsel at the Mayo Clinic in Rochester, Minnesota. In 1959 President DWIGHT D. EISENHOWER appointed him to the Eighth Circuit, where he served for eleven unremarkable years until, in 1970, President RICHARD M. NIXON selected him to fill the vacancy on the Supreme Court created by the resignation of Justice ABE FORTAS.

Blackmun's early years on the Supreme Court did little to disturb his image as a judicial clone of his boyhood friend Warren Burger, at whose wedding he had served as best man. The two voted together so often that the press dubbed them the Minnesota Twins.

Blackmun's voting patterns shifted over the years until by the mid-1980s he was more likely to vote with Justices WILLIAM J. BRENNAN and THURGOOD MARSHALL in defense of a broad vision of constitutional rights than with Burger. When asked whether his views have changed, Blackmun asserts that he has remained constant while the Court has shifted, causing his recent opinions merely to appear more libertarian. If, however, one compares early and late Blackmun opinions, it is difficult to accept Blackmun's protestation that nothing has changed in his legal universe except the backdrop.

One widely held hypothesis seeking to explain Blackmun's apparent shift in views is linked to the stormy public reaction that greeted what is undoubtedly his most significant Supreme Court opinion—*Roe v. Wade.* In *Roe,* drawing on his years at the Mayo Clinic, Blackmun brought a medical perspective to the controversy over the constitutionality of state laws prohibiting abortion. In a now familiar construct, he divided pregnancy into trimesters, holding that the state had no compelling interest in preserving fetal life during the first two trimesters, but that the interest in viable fetal life became compelling in the final trimester. In the years following *Roe,* Blackmun vigorously defended the right of a pregnant woman, in consultation with her doctor, to decide freely whether to undergo an abortion, writing a series of opinions striking down state statutes designed to place obstacles in a woman's path and vigorously dissenting from the Court's willingness to uphold a ban on federal funds to poor women seeking abortions.

Public reaction to Blackmun's abortion decisions was intense. He was subjected to vigorous personal criticism by individuals who believe deeply in a moral imperative of preserving fetal life from the moment of conception. Critics called his opinion in *Roe* a classic example of judicial overreaching and even compared it to Chief Justice ROGER B. TANEY's infamous opinion in DRED SCOTT V. SANDFORD (1857).

Subjected to sustained personal and professional criticism after *Roe,* Blackmun was forced, according to one view, to confront fundamental questions about his role as a Supreme Court Justice. From the crucible of the personal and professional pressures generated by his abortion decisions, many believe that there emerged a Justice with a heightened commitment to the use of judicial power to protect individual freedom.

In fact, the linkage between Blackmun's defense of a woman's right to choose to undergo an abortion and his other major doctrinal innovation—the COMMERCIAL SPEECH doctrine—is a direct one. In *Bigelow v. Virginia* (1975) Blackmun wrote for the Court invalidating a ban on advertisements by abortion clinics and suggesting for the first time that a consumer's right to know might justify First Amendment protection for speech that merely proposed a commercial transaction. One year later, in VIRGINIA STATE BOARD OF PHARMACY V. VIRGINIA CITIZENS CONSUMER COUNCIL (1976) and BATES V. STATE BAR OF ARIZONA (1976), he struck down bans on advertising by pharmacists and lawyers, explicitly granting First Amendment protection for the first time to commercial speech. In his more recent commercial speech opinions, Blackmun's First Amendment analysis has become more trenchant, with his concurrence in CENTRAL HUDSON GAS & ELECTRIC CO. V. PUBLIC SERVICE COMMISSION (1980) ranking as a milestone in Supreme Court First Amendment theory.

Blackmun's third principal contribution to constitutional DOCTRINE—the defense of ALIENS—precedes his abortion decisions. In GRAHAM V. RICHARDSON, one of Blackmun's early majority opinions, he wrote the opinion that outlawed discrimination against resident aliens in granting WELFARE BENEFITS, holding that aliens, as a politically powerless group, were entitled to heightened judicial protection under the EQUAL PROTECTION clause. In later years, his majority opinions invalidated attempts to exclude aliens from all civil service jobs and from state-funded college scholarships; and, although he concurred in the Court's decision upholding the exclusion of aliens from the state police, he vigorously dissented from decisions upholding bans on alien public school teachers and deputy probation officers.

Blackmun's most significant FEDERALISM opinion dramatically illustrates his evolution on the Court. In 1976 he provided the crucial fifth vote for Justice WILLIAM H. REHNQUIST's opinion in NATIONAL LEAGUE OF CITIES V. USERY, invalidating congressional minimum wage protection for municipal employees as a violation of state SOVEREIGNTY. A decade later, however, Blackmun changed his mind and, abandoning the Rehnquist-Burger position, wrote the Court's opinion in GARCIA V. SAN ANTONIO METROPOLITAN TRANSPORTATION AUTHORITY (1985), rejecting their view of state sovereignty and overruling *Usery.*

The hypothesis that Blackmun's apparent drift toward the Brennan-Marshall wing of the Court is linked to the controversy over his abortion decisions is not wholly persuasive. It does not explain Justice Blackmun's pre-*Roe* decisions protecting aliens and it overlooks the fact that as a little known judge of the Eighth Circuit, Blackmun was among the first federal judges to declare prison conditions violative of the Eighth Amendment. Furthermore, it does not explain why, in the criminal law and CRIMINAL PROCEDURE area, Blackmun's post-*Roe* jurisprudence continues to construe Fourth, Fifth, and Sixth Amendment protections narrowly.

A more fruitful approach to Blackmun's voting patterns is to take seriously his protestation that a consistent judicial philosophy underlies his Supreme Court career. The task is difficult, for Blackmun's judicial philosophy defies easy categorization in terms of fashionable labels. He is "liberal" in cases involving racial minorities and aliens, but "conservative" in the criminal procedure area. His abortion decision in *Roe* has been called the most "activist" in the Court's history, but his *Garcia* federalism opinion counsels "judicial restraint." His commercial speech opinions are rigorously "libertarian," but his tax, antitrust law, and securities law opinions champion vigorous government intervention. Not surprisingly, therefore, attempts to evaluate Blackmun's work using currently fashionable yardsticks often lead to a critical judgment that he is doctrinally inconsistent. In fact, Blackmun's Supreme Court work appears linked by a unifying thread—a reluctance to permit preoccupation with doctrinal considerations to force him into the resolution of an actual case on terms that fail to do intuitive justice to the parties before the Court.

Blackmun's commitment to a jurisprudence of just deserts is reflected in three characteristic motifs that pervade his opinions. First, he is openly mistrustful of rigidly doctrinaire analyses that force him into unfair or unreasonable resolutions of cases. In rejecting the Court's two-tier equal protection analysis in favor of a more "flexible" doctrine, or expressing skepticism about prophylactic EXCLUSIONARY RULES in the criminal process, or searching for a federalism compromise based more on pragmatism than on theory, or rejecting automatic use of the OVERBREADTH DOCTRINE in FIRST AMENDMENT cases, Justice Blackmun refuses to allow doctrine to force him into dispute resolutions that seem intuitively unfair or that give an unjust windfall to one of the parties before the Court.

Second, his opinions are fact-oriented, canvassing both adjudicative and LEGISLATIVE FACTS in an attempt to place the dispute before the Court in a realistic context. In his more recent opinions, he frequently scolds the Court for slighting a case's factual context, often complaining that the Court's desire to announce law has taken it beyond the actual dispute before the Court.

Finally, he insists upon results that accord with his view of the "real" world. His decisions have tended to support efforts to undo the consequences of RACIAL DISCRIMINATION and have demonstrated an increasing empathy for the plight of the powerless, while demonstrating little sympathy for lawbreakers. Such a personal vision of "reality" must ultimately inject a dose of subjectivism into the decision-making process. Yet Justice Blackmun's qualities of mind and heart serve to remind the Court that a doctrinaire, intellectualized jurisprudence needs to be balanced by a jurisprudence grounded in intuitive fairness to the parties, human warmth, and pragmatic realism.

BURT NEUBORNE

Bibliography

FUQUA, DAVID 1980 Justice Harry A. Blackmun: The Abortion Decisions. *Arkansas Law Review* 34:276–296.

NOTE 1983 The Changing Social Vision of Justice Blackmun. *Harvard Law Review* 96:717–736.

SCHLESSINGER, STEVEN R. 1980 Justice Harry Blackmun and Empirical Jurisprudence. *American University Law Review* 29:405–437.

SYMPOSIUM 1985 Dedication to Justice Harry A. Blackmun—Biography; Tributes. *Hamline Law Review* 8:1–149.

BLACKSTONE, WILLIAM (1723–1780)

The influence of Sir William Blackstone's *Commentaries on the Laws of England,* first published at Oxford between 1765 and 1769, was pervasive in American jurisprudence for much of the nineteenth century, although the work affected constitutional thought more in the realm of philosophy rather than that of specific legal doctrine. The appeal of this four-volume summation of the COMMON LAW, in the beginning of the American federal system, may be explained in part by its highly readable style and its function as a ready reference for many lawyers and jurists whose professional preparation was often indifferent. The practical need for a comprehensive and coherent view of the parent stock more than offset a tentative effort to make the new nation entirely independent of English legal institutions; and after the first American annotations to Blackstone by ST. GEORGE TUCKER in 1804, the importing of successive English editions and the periodic publication of fresh American editions by jurists like THOMAS M. COOLEY of Michigan and scholars like William Draper Lewis of the University of Pennsylvania made the *Commentaries* a standard reference for more than a hundred years.

The almost instant appeal of Blackstone to the English New World colonies—soon to be arguing their entitlements to the "rights of Englishmen" which they finally concluded could be secured only through independence of England itself—lay not only in its comprehensiveness but also in its epitomizing of the creative mercantilist jurisprudence of Blackstone's friend and contemporary, WILLIAM MURRAY (Lord Mansfield), which demonstrated the adaptability of the common law to "modern" economic objectives. The colonial elite, who had devoted the last generation before independence to "Americanization" of the English law, had economic views substantially similar to the scions of the English ruling classes to whom Blackstone delivered his Oxford lectures as Vinerian professor of English law. It was not surprising, therefore, that the *Commentaries*—to be followed in the post-Revolutionary period by the published reports of Mansfield—should appeal to the ruling element in the new nation, which was eager to continue the rules of an ordered economy.

These American leaders, Edmund Burke reminded his listeners in his 1775 "Speech on Conciliation," had a sophisticated legal knowledge, and the proof was in the fact that at that date almost as many copies of the *Commentaries* had been sold in the colonies as in England. JOHN MARSHALL's father was a subscriber to the first Philadelphia printing of 1771–1772, and both the future Chief Justice and his great antagonist, THOMAS JEFFERSON, read assiduously in the volumes. Jefferson wrote that Blackstone's work was "the most elegant and best digested" of any English treatise, "rightfully taking [its] place by the side of the Justinian institutes." While he considered that its continuing popularity in the new nation encouraged a too-slavish reliance on English precedent, he applauded St. George Tucker's plan to bring out an edition with American annotations.

In constitutional thought, the obvious differences in the structure of British and American government stimulated Tucker and succeeding American editors to prepare elaborate essays distinguishing between the frames, although not necessarily the philosophies, of the two constitutional systems. Parliamentary supremacy, which Blackstone endorsed, was in one sense emulated in the organization of the legislative departments as provided in both state and national constitutions. The recent memory of arbitrary and preemptive authority exercised by royal governors led Tucker to make the "popular" branch dominant over the executive. Ironically, Chief Justice Marshall, however congenial he found Blackstone's definition of law in general, was to embody the general principles of the *Commentaries* into a judicial definition of American FEDERALISM which made the judicial an equal branch. Nevertheless, a succession of influential nineteenth-century jurists after Marshall converted the Blackstonian conservatism into the laissez-faire principles that dominated American constitutional law until the 1930s.

The Tucker interpretation of the *Commentaries* led, through his sons, NATHANIEL BEVERLEY TUCKER and HENRY ST. GEORGE TUCKER, to a strict constructionist or "STATES' RIGHTS" school of constitutional thought, which was brought to its zenith in the speeches and writings of Henry's son, John Randolph Tucker. His 1877 Saratoga Springs lecture on state–federal relations as affected by the post-Civil War amendments to the Federal Constitution culminated in his posthumously published *Commentaries on the Constitution* (1899). This view, merging with Cooley's edition of 1870, kept the conservative jurisprudence of Blackstone in a position of influence until the revolution in American constitutional doctrine in the New Deal crisis of the 1930s.

WILLIAM F. SWINDLER

Bibliography

BOORSTIN, DANIEL J. (1941)1973 *The Mysterious Science of the Law: An Essay on Blackstone's Commentaries.* Cambridge, Mass.: Harvard University Press; reprint, Gloucester, Mass.: Peter Smith.

KATZ, STANLEY M., ed. [William Blackstone] 1979 *Commentaries on the Laws of England: A Facsimile of the First Edition.* Chicago: University of Chicago Press.

KENNEDY, DUNCAN 1979 The Structure of Blackstone's Commentaries. *Buffalo Law Review* 28:205–382.

BLAINE AMENDMENT
(1875)

Representative James G. Blaine of Maine, with the support of President ULYSSES S. GRANT, introduced, in December 1875, a proposed constitutional amendment to prohibit state financial support of sectarian schools. The amendment was intended to prevent public support of the Roman Catholic schools which educated a large percentage of the children of European immigrants.

The first clause of the proposed amendment provided that "no State shall make any laws respecting an ESTABLISHMENT OF RELIGION or prohibiting the free exercise thereof." This is an indication that Congress did not believe that the FOURTEENTH AMENDMENT incorporated the religion clauses of the FIRST AMENDMENT. (See INCORPORATION DOCTRINE.)

The second clause would have prohibited the use or control by a religious sect or denomination of any tax money or land devoted to public education. Together with the first clause this prohibition suggests the connection between support of church-related schools and establishment of religion recognized in twentieth-century Supreme Court opinions beginning with EVERSON V. BOARD OF EDUCATION (1947).

The Blaine Amendment was approved by the House of Representatives, 180–7; but even a heavily amended version failed to carry two-thirds of the Senate, and so the proposal died.

DENNIS J. MAHONEY

(SEE ALSO: *Government Aid to Sectarian Institutions.*)

BLAIR, JOHN
(1732–1800)

John Blair was a member of the Virginia House of Burgesses when the American Revolution began. In 1776, as a delegate to the state CONSTITUTIONAL CONVENTION, he served on the committee that drafted the VIRGINIA DECLARATION OF RIGHTS and the VIRGINIA CONSTITUTION. In 1777 he was appointed a judge, and in 1780 he became chancellor of Virginia. As a justice of the Court of Appeals he joined in deciding COMMONWEALTH V. CATON (1782). He was a delegate to both the CONSTITUTIONAL CONVENTION OF 1787—at which he never made a speech—and the Virginia ratifying convention. In 1789 President GEORGE WASHINGTON appointed him one of the original Justices of the Supreme Court of the United States. He served on the Supreme Court until 1796, a period during which the Court handed down few important decisions. In the most noteworthy, CHISHOLM V. GEORGIA (1793), Blair joined in the decision to hear a case brought against a state by a citizen of another state, arguing that to refuse to do so would be to "renounce part of the authority conferred, and, consequently part of the duty imposed by the Constitution."

DENNIS J. MAHONEY

Bibliography

ROSSITER, CLINTON 1966 *1787: The Grand Convention.* New York: Macmillan.

BLASPHEMY

Defaming religion by any words expressing scorn, ridicule, or vilification of God, Jesus Christ, the Holy Ghost, the doctrine of the Trinity, the Old or New Testament, or Christianity, constitutes the offense of blasphemy. In the leading American case, *Commonwealth v. Kneeland* (1838), Chief Justice LEMUEL SHAW of Massachusetts repelled arguments based on FREEDOM OF THE PRESS and on RELIGIOUS LIBERTY when he sustained a state law against blasphemy and upheld the conviction of a pantheist who simply denied belief in God, Christ, and miracles. In all the American decisions, the courts maintained the fiction that the criminality of the words consisted of maliciousness or the intent to insult rather than mere difference of opinion.

The Supreme Court has never decided a blasphemy case. In BURSTYN, INC. V. WILSON (1951) the Court relied on FREEDOM OF SPEECH to void a New York statute authorizing the censorship of "sacrilegious" films. Justice FELIX FRANKFURTER, concurring, observed that blasphemy was a far vaguer term than sacrilege because it meant "criticism of whatever the ruling authority of the moment established as the orthodox religious doctrine." In 1968, when the last prosecution of blasphemy occurred in the United States, an appellate court of Maryland held that the prosecution violated the First Amendment's ban on ESTABLISHMENT OF RELIGION and its protection of freedom of religion. Should a blasphemy case ever reach the Supreme Court, that Court would surely reach a similar result.

LEONARD W. LEVY

Bibliography

LEVY, LEONARD W. 1981 *Treason Against God: A History of the Offense of Blasphemy.* New York: Schocken Books.

BLATCHFORD, SAMUEL (1820–1893)

Samuel Blatchford had been a federal judge for fifteen years when CHESTER A. ARTHUR appointed him to the Supreme Court in 1882. Like Horace Gray, Arthur's other appointee, Blatchford had initially made his mark on the profession as a reporter. Beginning in 1852, he published a volume of admiralty cases decided in the Southern District of New York, a volume of Civil War prize cases from the same JURISDICTION, and twenty-four volumes of Second Circuit decisions. He continued to report Second Circuit opinions following his appointment as district judge (1867), circuit judge (1872), and circuit justice. Blatchford's expertise in admiralty, PATENT, and construction of the national banking acts made him the Supreme Court's workhorse; he wrote 435 majority opinions during his eleven-year tenure, almost twenty percent more than his proportional share.

Two personal characteristics shaped Blatchford's modest contributions to American constitutional development. He was singularly uninterested in questions of statecraft, political economy, and philosophy; he was so committed to a collective conception of the judicial function that he dissented less frequently then any Justice since the era of JOHN MARSHALL. These attitudes, coupled with Chief Justice MORRISON R. WAITE's disinclination to assign him cases involving CONSTITUTIONAL INTERPRETATION, kept Blatchford out of the limelight during his first eight years on the Court. But his compromising tendency prompted MELVILLE W. FULLER, Waite's successor, to regard him as the logical spokesman for narrow, unstable majorities in two controversial FOURTEENTH AMENDMENT cases. Blatchford's lackluster performances in CHICAGO, MILWAUKEE & ST. PAUL RAILWAY V. MINNESOTA (1890) and *Budd v. New York* (1892) underscored his stolid approach to constitutional law.

At issue in the *Chicago, Milwaukee* case was the validity of an 1887 Minnesota statute establishing a railroad commission authorized to set maximum rate schedules that would be "final and conclusive." Because this scheme left no role for courts in reviewing railroad rates, the briefs focused on two previous statements by Chief Justice Waite. In *Munn v. Illinois* (1877) Waite had explained that "the controlling fact" in rate controversies was "the power to regulate at all." And he had added that "for protection against abuses by legislatures the people must resort to the polls, not the courts." In the *Railroad Commission Cases* (1886), however, Justice STANLEY MATTHEWS had persuaded Waite to acknowledge that "under the pretense of regulating fares and freights, the State cannot require a railroad corporation to carry persons or property without reward; neither can it do that which in law amounts to a taking of private property for PUBLIC USE without JUST COMPENSATION, or without DUE PROCESS OF LAW." Speaking for a 6–3 majority, Blatchford concluded that Waite's majority opinion in the Railroad Commission Cases presupposed at least some role for the courts; it followed that the Minnesota law could not be sustained. At one point Blatchford came very close to equating due process with judicial process, but he cautiously retreated and ultimately said nothing about either the scope of JUDICIAL REVIEW or its rationale, which went beyond Waite's enigmatic OBITER DICTUM. Only the dissent by JOSEPH P. BRADLEY forthrightly summarized what seemed to be the majority's premise. "In effect," he complained, the Court had now held "that the judiciary, and not the legislature, is the final arbiter in the regulation of fares and freights."

Budd brought both of the central issues in *Munn* back to the Court for reconsideration. Speaking again for a majority of six, Blatchford reiterated the Court's conclusion that bulk storage and handling of grain was a "business AFFECTED WITH A PUBLIC INTEREST." Consequently rates of charge for these services might be regulated by state governments. But what of *Chicago, Milwaukee,* which Bradley had described as "practically overrul[ing]" *Munn?* The two cases were "quite distinguishable," Blatchford insisted, "for in this instance the rate of charges is fixed directly by the legislature." Blatchford apparently regarded this formulation as an appropriate means of reconciling all previous decisions on the subject. But the distinction between legislative and commission regulation was so artificial that Justice JOHN MARSHALL HARLAN simply ignored it in his characteristically robust opinion for the Court in SMYTH V. AMES (1898). Seymour D. Thompson, editor of the *American Law Review*, was less gracious. "It was no great disparagement of him," Thompson remarked in a critical appraisal of Blatchford's constitutional law opinions, "to say that he was probably a better reporter than Judge."

CHARLES W. MCCURDY

Bibliography

PAUL, ARNOLD 1969 Samuel Blatchford. Pages 1401–1414 in Leon Friedman and Fred L. Israel, eds., *The Justices of the United States Supreme Court, 1789–1969: Their Lives and Major Opinions.* New York: Chelsea House.

BLOCK GRANTS

See: Federal Grants-in-Aid; Revenue Sharing

BLOOD SAMPLES

See: Testimonial Compulsion

BLOUNT, WILLIAM
(1749–1800)

William Blount was a delegate to the CONSTITUTIONAL CONVENTION OF 1787 from North Carolina and a signer of the Constitution. Blount did not speak at the Convention and, disliking the result, signed the Constitution only to attest to the fact that it was consented to by all of the states represented.

DENNIS J. MAHONEY

BLUE RIBBON JURY

Under the laws of some states, cases of unusual importance or complexity may be tried to special juries chosen from a venire with qualifications higher than those for the ordinary jury panel. Such juries are commonly called "blue ribbon juries." In *Fay v. New York* (1947) the Supreme Court affirmed (5–4) the constitutionality of using a blue ribbon jury in a criminal prosecution. Whether such juries would meet the contemporary standard of being drawn from a source fairly representative of the community is uncertain. (See JURY DISCRIMINATION; TAYLOR V. LOUISIANA, 1975.) In any event, blue ribbon juries have fallen into disuse.

DENNIS J. MAHONEY

BLUM v. YARETSKY
457 U.S. 991 (1982)
RENDELL-BAKER v. KOHN
457 U.S. 830 (1982)

Following the Supreme Court's decision in BURTON V. WILMINGTON PARKING AUTHORITY (1961), commentators and lower courts began to ask whether a significant state subsidy to a private institution might make that institution's conduct into STATE ACTION, subject to the limitations of the Fourteenth Amendment. *Blum* and *Rendell-Baker* ended two decades of speculation; by 7–2 votes, the Court answered "No."

In *Blum* patients in private nursing homes complained that they had been transferred to facilities offering lesser care without notice or hearing, in violation of their rights to PROCEDURAL DUE PROCESS. Through the Medicaid program, the state paid the medical expenses of ninety percent of the patients; the state also subsidized the costs of the homes and extensively regulated their operation through a licensing scheme. The Court rejected each of these connections, one by one, as an argument for finding state action. The Constitution governed private conduct only when the state was "responsible" for that conduct; normally, such responsibility was to be found in state coercion or significant encouragement; these features were missing here.

In *Rendell-Baker* employees of a private school complained that they had been discharged for exercising their rights of FREEDOM OF SPEECH, and fired without adequate procedural protections. The Court reached neither issue, because it concluded that the action of the school did not amount to state action. Although the school depended on public funding, no state policy—no coercion or encouragement—influenced the employees' discharge.

Dissents in the two cases were written by Justices WILLIAM J. BRENNAN and THURGOOD MARSHALL, respectively. They argued that a consideration of all the interconnections between the institutions and the states, including the heavy subsidies, amounted to the kind of "significant state involvement" found in *Burton.* But considering the totality of circumstances in order to find state action is precisely what a majority of the BURGER COURT has been unwilling to do.

KENNETH L. KARST

BOARD OF CURATORS v. HOROWITZ
435 U.S. 78 (1979)

A state university medical student was dismissed during her final year of study for failure to meet academic standards. The Supreme Court unanimously held that she had not been deprived of her PROCEDURAL DUE PROCESS rights, but divided 5–4 on the reasons for that conclusion. For a majority, Justice WILLIAM H. REHNQUIST commented that the student had not asserted any "property" interest, and strongly hinted that she had not been deprived of a "liberty" interest. Nevertheless, assuming the existence of an interest entitled to due process protections, Rehnquist said that a dismissal for academic rather than disciplinary reasons required no hearing or opportunity to respond. Four concurring Justices disagreed with the remarkable conclusion that due process required a fair procedure for the ten-day suspension of an elementary school pupil in GOSS V. LOPEZ (1975) but not for the academic dismissal of a medical student. Here, however, the four Justices agreed that the student had been given a sufficient hearing.

Horowitz illustrates the artificiality of the Court's recent narrowing of the "liberty" or "property" interests to which the guarantee of procedural due process attaches. A student's interest in avoiding academic termination fits awkwardly into those categories, in their recent restrictive definitions. Yet the student plainly deserves protection against termination procedures that are arbitrary. The specter of judges' having to read examination papers is no more than a specter. The concern of procedural due process is not the fairness of a particular student's termination, but the fairness of the procedural system for depriving a person of an important interest.

KENNETH L. KARST

BOARD OF EDUCATION v. ALLEN
392 U.S. 236 (1968)

New York authorized the loan of state-purchased textbooks to students in nonpublic schools. Justice BYRON R. WHITE, speaking for the Supreme Court, relied heavily on the "pupil benefit theory" which he purportedly derived from EVERSON V. BOARD OF EDUCATION (1947). If the beneficiaries of the governmental program were principally the children, and not the religious institutions, the program could be sustained.

Justice HUGO L. BLACK, the author of *Everson,* dissented. *Everson,* he recalled, held that transportation of students to church-related schools went "to the very verge" of what was permissible under the establishment clause. Justices WILLIAM O. DOUGLAS and ABE FORTAS also dissented.

Allen stimulated efforts to aid church-related schools in many state legislatures. Later opinions of the Court, invalidating many such aid programs, have limited *Allen's* precedential force to cases involving textbook loans.

RICHARD E. MORGAN

(SEE ALSO: *Government Aid to Religious Institutions.*)

BOARD OF EDUCATION v. PICO
457 U.S. 853 (1982)

Six students sued a school board in federal court, claiming that the board had violated their FIRST AMENDMENT rights by removing certain books from the high school and junior high school libraries. The board had responded to lists of "objectionable" and "inappropriate" books circulated at a conference of conservative parents. A fragmented Supreme Court, voting 5–4, remanded the case for trial.

Four Justices concluded that it would be unconstitutional for the school board to remove the books from the libraries for the purpose of suppressing ideas. Four others argued for wide discretion by local officials in selecting school materials, including library books. One Justice would await the outcome of a trial before addressing the constitutional issues. Thus, although the decision attracted national attention, it did little to solve the intractable constitutional puzzle of GOVERNMENT SPEECH.

KENNETH L. KARST

BOARD OF REGENTS v. ROTH
408 U.S. 564 (1972)

A nontenured state college teacher, hired for a one-year term, was told he would not be rehired for the following year. The Supreme Court held, 5–3, that he had not been deprived of PROCEDURAL DUE PRO-

CESS. Justice POTTER STEWART, for the majority, announced a restrictive view of the nature of the interests protected by the due process guarantee. Henceforth the Court would look for an impact on some "liberty" or "property" interest, rather than examine the importance of the deprivation imposed by the state. Here the teacher had no "property" interest beyond his one-year contract, and his nonrenewal required no hearing.

In a companion case, *Perry v. Sindermann* (1972), the Court found a "property" interest in an unwritten policy that was the equivalent of tenure for a state junior college teacher. Furthermore, the teacher had alleged that his contract had not been renewed because of his exercise of FIRST AMENDMENT freedoms—a "liberty" claim that did not depend on his tenured status.

KENNETH L. KARST

BOB JONES UNIVERSITY v. UNITED STATES

461 U.S. 574 (1983)

The Internal Revenue Service adopted a policy in 1969 of denying federal income tax exemption, available by statute to educational and religious institutions, to schools that practiced racial discrimination. Bob Jones University, an institution that had a multiracial student body but restricted interracial socializing, and Goldsboro Christian Schools, which practiced racial SEGREGATION on the basis of religious conviction, sought to have their tax-exempt status reinstated. In an opinion by Chief Justice WARREN E. BURGER, the Supreme Court held, 8–1, that the Internal Revenue Service had the power, even without explicit statutory authorization, to enforce by its regulations a "settled public policy" against racial discrimination in education. None of the Justices accepted the schools' claim that the regulations infringed on the First Amendment's guarantee of religious liberty, but Justice WILLIAM H. REHNQUIST, dissenting, warned of the danger of abrogating the SEPARATION OF POWERS.

DENNIS J. MAHONEY

BOB-LO EXCURSION COMPANY v. MICHIGAN

333 U.S. 28 (1948)

Although this decision unsettled interpretations of the COMMERCE CLAUSE, it nevertheless dealt SEGREGATION another blow. A Detroit steamship company violated a state CIVIL RIGHTS statute by refusing to transport a black girl to a local, though Canadian, destination. Justice WILEY RUTLEDGE's majority opinion distinguished MORGAN V. VIRGINIA (1946) and stressed the local nature of transportation in upholding the statute. Justices WILLIAM O. DOUGLAS and HUGO L. BLACK thought the law should be sustained because there could be no conflict with a congressional law; Chief Justice FRED M. VINSON and Justice ROBERT H. JACKSON dissented, arguing that *Morgan* and HALL V. DECUIR (1878) governed.

DAVID GORDON

BODDIE v. CONNECTICUT

401 U.S. 371 (1971)

An INDIGENT sought to file for divorce in a state court but was unable to pay the $60 filing fee. The Supreme Court held, 8–1, that the state had unconstitutionally limited the plaintiff's ACCESS TO THE COURTS. For a majority, Justice JOHN MARSHALL HARLAN rested decision on a PROCEDURAL DUE PROCESS theory. The marriage relationship was "basic" in our society, and the state had monopolized the means for legally dissolving the relationship. Justice WILLIAM O. DOUGLAS, concurring, would have rested decision on an EQUAL PROTECTION theory.

Two subsequent 5–4 decisions, *United States v. Kras* (1971) and *Ortwein v. Schwab* (1971), made clear that *Boddie* had not implied a general right of access in all civil cases. *Boddie*'s due process approach, rather than equal protection, has guided the Court's subsequent dealings with WEALTH DISCRIMINATION in the civil litigation process.

KENNETH L. KARST

BOLLING v. SHARPE

347 U.S. 497 (1954)

In the four cases now known as BROWN V. BOARD OF EDUCATION (1954), the Supreme Court held that racial SEGREGATION of children in state public schools violated the FOURTEENTH AMENDMENT's guarantee of the EQUAL PROTECTION OF THE LAWS. *Bolling*, a companion case to *Brown*, involved a challenge to school segregation in the DISTRICT OF COLUMBIA. The equal protection clause applies only to the states. However, in previous cases (including the JAPANESE AMERICAN CASES, 1943–1944) the Court had assumed, at least for argument, that the Fifth Amendment's guarantee of DUE PROCESS OF LAW prohibited arbitrary discrimination by the federal government.

The Court in *Bolling* also drew on OBITER DICTA in the Japanese American Cases stating that racial classifications were suspect, requiring exacting judicial scrutiny. Because school segregation was "not reasonably related to any proper governmental objective," the District's practice deprived the segregated black children of liberty without due process. Chief Justice EARL WARREN wrote for a unanimous Court.

The Court concluded its Fifth Amendment discussion by remarking that because *Brown* had prohibited school segregation by the states, "it would be unthinkable that the same Constitution would impose a lesser duty on the Federal Government." Critics have suggested that what was "unthinkable" was the political implication of a contrary decision. But the notions of liberty and equality have long been understood to overlap. The idea of national CITIZENSHIP implies a measure of equal treatment by the national government, and the "liberty" protected by the Fifth Amendment's due process clause implies a measure of equal liberties. Doctrinally as well as politically, a contrary decision in *Bolling* would have been unthinkable.

KENNETH L. KARST

BOLLMAN, EX PARTE, v. SWARTWOUT
4 Cranch 75 (1807)

The Supreme Court discharged the prisoners, confederates in AARON BURR's conspiracy, from an INDICTMENT for TREASON. The indictment specified their treason as levying war against the United States. Chief Justice JOHN MARSHALL, for the Court, distinguished treason from a conspiracy to commit it. He sought to prevent the crime of treason from being "extended by construction to doubtful cases." To complete the crime of treason or levying war, Marshall said, a body of men must be "actually assembled for the purpose of effecting by force a treasonable purpose," in which everyone involved, to any degree and however remote from the scene of action, is guilty of treason. But the levying of war does not exist short of the actual assemblage of armed men. Congress had the power to punish crimes short of treason, but the Constitution protected Americans from a charge of treason for a crime short of it.

Bollman is also an important precedent in the law of federal JURISDICTION. In OBITER DICTUM, Marshall stated that a federal court's power to issue a WRIT OF HABEAS CORPUS "must be given by written law," denying by inference that the courts have any inherent power to grant habeas corpus relief, apart from congressional authorization. (See EX PARTE MCCARDLE, 1869; JUDICIAL SYSTEM.)

LEONARD W. LEVY

BOND, HUGH LENNOX
(1828–1893)

President ULYSSES S. GRANT on July 13, 1870, commissioned Hugh Lennox Bond judge of the newly created Fourth Circuit Court, a position he filled until his death. The Maryland judge was immediately called upon to hold court in an eleven-county section of South Carolina that had been plagued by the Ku Klux Klan's reign of terror. The judge fearlessly restored the rights of freedmen in South Carolina, but he did so in the belief that the states retained responsibility for preserving most CIVIL RIGHTS. Congress, he insisted, could only impede the traditional power of the states over the franchise when there was evidence of direct STATE ACTION resulting in discrimination based on race, color, or previous condition of servitude. Bond rejected the view that the Civil War amendments incorporated rights deriving from natural law; the protection of such rights, he concluded, remained squarely within state discretion.

He refused to allow the concept of dual CITIZENSHIP to erect an absolute bar to FEDERAL PROTECTION. In *United States v. Petersburg Judges of Elections* (1874), election officials were charged with preventing voting by freedmen without any overt act of RACIAL DISCRIMINATION. Bond acknowledged that under the concept of dual citizenship the states could take away certain rights, such as the franchise. He held, however, that so long as states continued to grant those rights, the federal government could protect freedmen by inferring discriminatory intent from acts depriving them of the rights that had been granted.

Bond insisted on the supremacy of the national government in its proper sphere. In 1876 he ordered the release of the Board of Canvassers of South Carolina who had been imprisoned by the state supreme court for attempting to report election returns favorable to RUTHERFORD B. HAYES. Bond held that Article I, section 2, protected the Canvassers in their capacity as federal officials.

During Reconstruction Bond courageously extended federal judicial protection to freedmen. Yet even this most vigorous champion in the circuit courts of freedmen's civil rights eschewed the Radical Republicans' CONSTITUTIONAL INTERPRETATION of the Civil War amendments.

KERMIT L. HALL

Bibliography

HALL, KERMIT L. 1984 Political Power and Constitutional Legitimacy: The South Carolina Ku Klux Klan Trials, 1871–1872. *Emory Law Journal* 33:921–951.

BONHAM'S CASE
8 Coke 113b (1610)

Although the issue in *Bonham's Case* concerned the power of the Royal College of Physicians to discipline nonmembers, its importance principally derives from its subsequent use as a precedent for JUDICIAL REVIEW and the subordination of LEGISLATION to a higher, constitutional law. Thomas Bonham, holder of a doctorate from Cambridge University, continued to practice in London after being refused permission by the College. Acting under powers conferred by royal charter and parliamentary statutes, the college authorities accordingly fined Bonham and secured his incarceration, thus triggering his suit for false imprisonment before the Court of Common Pleas.

Chief Justice Sir EDWARD COKE ruled in Bonham's favor. Although most of his numerous grounds were technical, Coke also criticized the statutory power of the college to be the original judge in a case to which it had itself been a party and concluded that the COMMON LAW courts could "control" and render void those acts of Parliament that were "against Common Right, and Reason, or repugnant, or impossible to be performed."

Coke, nevertheless, invoked no judicial power to invalidate legislation or measure its constitutionality. He advised only that the statute be construed strictly, not nullified, thus prescribing a rule of statutory construction rather than a doctrine of constitutional superintendence. Coke assumed, moreover, that the defect in the law inhered not in UNCONSTITUTIONALITY but in want of reasonableness and in impossibility of performance. The common law court intervened here as the handmaiden, not the antagonistic overseer, of Parliament, a brother court, and only for the purpose of recapturing a reasonableness that permeated the immutable laws sought by bench and Parliament alike.

Coke's use of evidence was also defective. Coke misquoted, for example, a major precedent, *Tregor's Case* (1334), by infusing into it language that it actually lacked to secure the desired result.

Two antagonistic streams of interpretation devolve from *Bonham's Case.* The Glorious Revolution of 1688 signaled the dominance of Parliament over court as well as crown and, thus, the demise of the spacious judicial interpretation of legislation advocated by Coke. In 1765 WILLIAM BLACKSTONE definitively stated that no power could control unreasonable statutes, for such control subverted all government by setting the judiciary over the legislature. Although Coke's opinion in *Bonham* retained wide currency in the seventeenth century, its erosion began almost immediately and accelerated in the following century. In *The Duchess of Hamilton's Case* (1712), for example, Sir Thomas Powys insisted that judges must "strain hard" to avoid interpretations of statutes that would nullify them.

As the American Revolution approached, however, *Bonham's Case* evolved in the American colonies in the opposite direction as a fixed constitutional barrier against Parliament. Thus, in PAXTON'S CASE (1761) JAMES OTIS urged the Massachusetts Superior Court to impose a disabling interpretation on the British statute of 1662 that had codified WRITS OF ASSISTANCE. Although only private parties, not bench and Parliament, had directly clashed in *Bonham's Case,* Otis advanced it as a firm precedent for judicial evisceration of legislation. Coke questioned only the reasonableness of a statute; Otis and his followers challenged a law's constitutionality.

WILLIAM J. CUDDIHY

Bibliography

CORWIN, EDWARD S. 1929 *The "Higher Law" Background of American Constitutional Law.* Ithaca, N.Y.: Cornell University Press.

THORNE, SAMUEL 1938 The Constitution and the Courts: A Reexamination of the Famous Case of Dr. Bonham. Pages 15–24 in Conyers Read (ed.), *The Constitution Reconsidered.* New York: Columbia University Press.

BONUS BILL

See: Internal Improvements

BORDER SEARCH

A search at an international boundary of a person, a vehicle, or goods entering the United States may be carried out without a SEARCH WARRANT and in the absence of PROBABLE CAUSE or even suspicion. In *United States v. Ramsey* (1977) the Supreme Court said that this extraordinary power, which also allows the government to open international mail entering the United States, "is grounded in the recognized right of the sovereign to control . . . who and what may enter the country." The First Congress, in 1789, authorized WARRANTLESS SEARCHES of vessels suspected of carrying goods on which customs duty had been evaded, and similar provisions have been enacted subsequently. As the Court held in ALMEIDA-SANCHEZ V. UNITED STATES (1973), such a search may be conducted not only at the border itself but also at its "functional equivalent," such as "an established station near the border," or "a point marking the confluence of two or more roads that extend from the border," or an airplane arriving on a nonstop flight from abroad.

Under *United States v. Brignoni-Ponce* (1975) an automobile may not be stopped by a roving patrol car miles from the border (in an area that is not its legal equivalent) to determine whether the occupants are illegal aliens unless there is reasonable suspicion. Under *United States v. Martinez-Fuerte* (1976) automobiles may be stopped for this purpose at fixed checkpoints; in these circumstances the opportunity of officers to act arbitrarily is limited.

JACOB W. LANDYNSKI

Bibliography

LAFAVE, WAYNE R. 1978 *Search and Seizure: A Treatise on the Fourth Amendment.* Vol. 3:275–327. St. Paul, Minn.: West Publishing Co.

BORROWING POWER

Congress, under Article I, section 8, of the Constitution, may "borrow money on the credit of the United States." This power is ordinarily exercised through the sale of bonds or the issuance of BILLS OF CREDIT. The latter, sometimes called "treasury notes" or "greenbacks," are intended to circulate as currency and thus, in effect, to require the public to lend money to the government. In the GOLD CLAUSE CASES (1935) the Supreme Court held that the government, in borrowing, is bound by the terms of its contracts, but Congress, by invoking SOVEREIGN IMMUNITY, denied its creditors any legal remedy.

DENNIS J. MAHONEY

BOSTON BEER COMPANY v. MASSACHUSETTS
97 U.S. 25 (1878)

This case introduced the doctrine of INALIENABLE POLICE POWER, which weakened the CONTRACT CLAUSE's protections of property. The company's charter authorized it to manufacture beer subject to a reserved power of the legislature to alter, amend, or repeal the charter. The state subsequently enacted a prohibition statute. The RESERVED POLICE POWER should have been sufficient ground for the holding by the Court that the prohibition statute did not impair the company's chartered right to do business. However, Justice JOSEPH P. BRADLEY, in an opinion for a unanimous Court, found another and "equally decisive" reason for rejecting the argument that the company had a contract to manufacture and sell beer "forever." The company held its rights subject to the POLICE POWER of the state to promote the public safety and morals. "The Legislature," Bradley declared, "cannot, by any contract, devest itself of the power to provide for these objects." Accordingly the enactment of a statute prohibiting the manufacture and sale of intoxicating liquors did not violate the contract clause. Decisions such as this, by which the police power prevailed over chartered rights, produced a doctrinal response: the development of SUBSTANTIVE DUE PROCESS to protect property.

LEONARD W. LEVY

BOUDIN, LOUIS B.
(1874–1952)

Louis Boudianoff Boudin was a prominent New York attorney and the author of books and articles on constitutional law, jurisprudence, and government regulation of the economy. His most significant work was *Government by Judiciary* (2 vols., 1932), a massive, iconoclastic history of the doctrine of JUDICIAL REVIEW. Boudin argued that, beginning in 1803 with JOHN MARSHALL's opinion in MARBURY V. MADISON, the federal judiciary had gradually expanded its powers and authority at the expense of the legislative and executive branches, culminating in a "government by judiciary" hostile to the basic principles of the Constitution established by its Framers and to the tenets of democratic government. While Boudin's admirers praised his erudition and accepted his exposure of the weaknesses of the historical case for judicial review, his critics questioned his tendency to write as an advocate rather than as a historian and charged that his conclusions were not supported by an impartial examination of the historical evidence.

RICHARD B. BERNSTEIN

BOUNDS v. SMITH
430 U.S. 817 (1977)

Several state prisoners sued North Carolina prison authorities in federal court, claiming they had been denied legal research facilities in violation of their FOURTEENTH AMENDMENT rights. The Supreme Court, 6–3, upheld this claim in an opinion by Justice THURGOOD MARSHALL.

For the first time the Court explicitly recognized a "fundamental constitutional right of ACCESS TO THE COURTS." This right imposed on prison authorities the affirmative duty to provide either adequate law libraries or the assistance of law-trained persons, so that prisoners might prepare HABEAS CORPUS petitions and other legal papers. The three dissenters each wrote an opinion. Justice WILLIAM H. REHNQUIST complained that the majority had neither defined the content of "meaningful" access nor specified the source of the Fourteenth Amendment right; an EQUAL PROTECTION right, he pointed out, would conflict with ROSS V. MOFFITT (1974).

KENNETH L. KARST

BOWMAN v. CHICAGO & NORTHWESTERN RAILWAY COMPANY
125 U.S. 465 (1888)

The Supreme Court, by a vote of 6–3, held that a state statute prohibiting common carriers from importing intoxicating liquors into the state, except under conditions laid down by the state, violated the COMMERCE CLAUSE, because interstate transportation required a single regulatory system; the absence of congressional action made no difference.

LEONARD W. LEVY

(SEE ALSO: *State Regulation of Commerce.*)

BOYCOTT

A boycott is a group refusal to deal. Such concerted action is an effective way for society's less powerful members, such as unorganized workers or racial minorities, to seek fair treatment in employment, public accommodations, and public services. But as the Supreme Court recognized in *Eastern States Retail Lumber Dealers' Association v. United States* (1914): "An act harmless when done by one may become a public wrong when done by many acting in concert, for it then takes on the form of a conspiracy."

Boycotts by private entrepreneurs were illegal at common law as unreasonable restraints on commercial competition. The Sherman Act of 1890 made it a federal offense to form a "combination . . . in restraint of trade." The Supreme Court has interpreted that prohibition as covering almost every type of concerted refusal by business people to trade with others. The constitutionality of outlawing commercial boycotts has never seriously been questioned.

Employee boycotts may be either "primary" or "secondary." A primary boycott involves direct action against a principal party to a dispute. A union seeking to organize a company's work force may call for a strike, a concerted refusal to work, by the company's employees. A secondary boycott involves action against a so-called neutral or secondary party that is doing business with the primary party. The union seeking to organize a manufacturing company might appeal to the employees of a retailer to strike the retailer in order to force the retailer to stop handling the manufacturer's products.

Although early American law regarded most strikes as criminal conspiracies, modern statutes like the WAGNER NATIONAL LABOR RELATIONS ACT (NLRA) treat primary strikes in the private sector as "protected" activity, immune from employer reprisals. Even so, the Supreme Court has never held there is a constitutional right to strike. Furthermore, the Court sustained the constitutionality of statutory bans on secondary boycott strikes or related picketing in *Electrical Workers Local 501 v. NLRB* (1951). The use of group pressure to enmesh neutrals in the disputes of others was sufficient to enable government to declare such activity illegal.

Consumer boycotts present the hardest constitutional questions. Here group pressure may not operate directly, as in the case of a strike. Instead, the union or other protest group asks individual customers, typically acting on their own, not to patronize the subject firm. Yet if the appeal is to customers of a retailer not to shop there so long as the retailer stocks a certain manufacturer's goods, a neutral party is the target. The NLRA forbids union PICKETING to induce such a secondary consumer boycott. The Supreme Court held this limited prohibition constitutional in *NLRB v. Retail Clerks Local 1001* (1980), although there was no majority rationale. A plurality cited precedent concerning secondary employee boycotts, ignoring the differences between individual and group responses.

On the other hand, when a civil rights organization conducted a damaging boycott against white merchants to compel them to support demands upon elected officials for racial equality, the Supreme Court declared in *NAACP v. Claiborne Hardware Co.* (1982) that a state's right "to regulate economic activity could not justify a complete prohibition against a nonviolent, politically motivated boycott designed to force governmental and economic change and to effectuate rights guaranteed by the Constitution itself." The Court relied on the FIRST AMENDMENT rights of FREEDOM OF SPEECH, FREEDOM OF ASSEMBLY AND ASSOCIATION, and FREEDOM OF PETITION. The emphasis on the right to petition government raises the possibility of a different result if the merchants themselves, rather than the public officials, had been the primary target of the boycott. But that would appear incongruous. The Court needs to refine its constitutional analysis of consumer boycotts.

THEODORE J. ST. ANTOINE

Bibliography

HARPER, MICHAEL C. 1984 The Consumer's Emerging Right to Boycott: *NAACP v. Claiborne Hardware* and Its Implications for American Labor Law. *Yale Law Journal* 93:409–454.

KENNEDY, RONALD E. 1982 Political Boycotts, the Sherman Act, and the First Amendment: An Accommodation of Competing Interests. *Southern California Law Review* 55:983–1030.

BOYD v. UNITED STATES
116 U.S. 616 (1886)

Justice LOUIS D. BRANDEIS believed that *Boyd* will be remembered "as long as civil liberty lives in the United States." The noble sentiments expressed in JOSEPH P. BRADLEY's opinion for the Court merit that estimate, but like many another historic opinion, this one was not convincingly reasoned. To this day, however, members of the Court return to *Boyd* to grace their opinions with its authority or with an imperishable line from Bradley's.

Boyd was the first important SEARCH AND SEIZURE case as well as the first important case on the RIGHT AGAINST SELF-INCRIMINATION. It arose not from a criminal prosecution but from a civil action by the United States for the forfeiture of goods imported in violation of customs revenue laws. In such cases an 1874 act of Congress required the importer to produce in court all pertinent records tending to prove the charges against him or suffer the penalty of being taken "as confessed." The Court held the act unconstitutional as a violation of both the FOURTH and Fifth AMENDMENTS. The penalty made the production of the records compulsory. That compulsion, said Bradley, raised "a very grave question of constitutional law, involving the personal security and PRIVILEGES AND IMMUNITIES of the citizen. . . ." But did the case involve a search or a seizure, and if so was it "unreasonable," and did it force the importer to be a witness against himself in a criminal case?

Bradley conceded that there was no search and seizure as in the forcible entry into a man's house and examination of his papers. Indeed, there was no search here for evidence of crime. The compulsion was to produce records that the government required importers to keep; no private papers were at issue. Moreover, no property was confiscated as in the case of contraband like smuggled goods. The importer, who was not subject to a search, had merely to produce the needed records in court; he kept custody of them. But the Court treated those records as if they were private papers, which could be used as EVIDENCE against him, resulting in the forfeiture of his property, or to establish a criminal charge. Though the proceeding was a civil one, a different section of the same statute did provide criminal penalties for fraud.

Bradley made a remarkable linkage between the right against UNREASONABLE SEARCH and seizure and the right against self-incrimination. The "fourth and fifth amendments," he declared, "almost run into each other." That they were different amendments, protected different interests, had separate histories, and reflected different policies was of no consequence to Bradley. He was on sound ground when he found that the forcible production of private papers to convict a man of crime or to forfeit his property violated the Fifth Amendment and was "contrary to the principles of a free government." He was on slippery ground when he found that such a compulsory disclosure was "the equivalent of a search and seizure—and an unreasonable search and seizure—within the meaning of the fourth amendment." His reasoning was that though the case did not fall within the "literal terms" of either amendment, each should be broadly construed in terms of the other. Unreasonable searches and seizures "are almost always made for the purpose of compelling a man to give evidence against himself," and compulsion of such evidence "throws light on the question as to what is an 'unreasonable search and seizure.' . . ." In support of his reasoning Bradley quoted at length from Lord Camden's opinion (see WILLIAM PRATT) in ENTICK V. CARRINGTON (1765). Camden, however, spoke of a fishing expedition under GENERAL WARRANTS issued by an executive officer without authorization by Parliament. There was no warrant in this case, and there was authorization by Congress for a court to compel production of the specific records required by law to be kept for government inspection, concerning FOREIGN COMMERCE which Congress may regulate. In this case, however, Bradley thought meticulous analysis was out of place. He feared that unconstitutional practices got their footing in "slight deviations" from proper procedures, and the best remedy was the rule that constitutional protections "for the security of person and property should be liberally construed." Close construction, he declared, deprived these protections of their efficacy.

Justice SAMUEL F. MILLER, joined by Chief Justice MORRISON R. WAITE, concurred in the judgment that that offensive section of the act of Congress was unconstitutional. Miller found no search and seizure, let alone an unreasonable one. He agreed, however, that Congress had breached the right against self-incrimination, which he thought should be the sole ground of the opinion.

The modern Court no longer assumes that the Fifth Amendment is a source of the Fourth's EXCLUSIONARY RULE or that the Fourth prohibits searches for MERE EVIDENCE. Moreover, the production of private papers may be compelled in certain cases, as when the Internal Revenue Service subpoenas records in the hands of one's lawyer or accountant.

LEONARD W. LEVY

Bibliography

GERSTEIN, ROBERT S. 1979 The Demise of Boyd: Self-Incrimination and Private Papers in the Burger Court. *UCLA Law Review* 27:343–397.

LANDYNSKI, JACOB W. 1966 *Search and Seizure and the Supreme Court.* Pages 49–61. Baltimore: Johns Hopkins University Press.

BRADLEY, JOSEPH P. (1813–1892)

Joseph P. Bradley's appointment to the Supreme Court in 1870 by President ULYSSES S. GRANT was seen as part of Grant's supposed court-packing scheme. But whatever shadow that event cast on Bradley's reputation rapidly disappeared. For more than two decades on the bench, he commanded almost unrivaled respect from colleagues, lawyers, and legal commentators, and over time he consistently has been ranked as one of the most influential jurists in the Court's history.

When Bradley was appointed he already was a prominent railroad lawyer and Republican activist. Indeed, friends had been advocating his appointment to the Court nearly a year before his appointment. Shortly after Grant's inauguration in 1869, the Republicans increased the size of the court from eight to nine. While Grant and Congress haggled over the selection of a new Justice, the Court decided, 4–3, that the legal tender laws were unconstitutional. Justice ROBERT C. GRIER clearly was senile, and after he cast his vote against the laws his colleagues persuaded him to resign. That gave Grant two appointments and, on February 7, 1870, he nominated WILLIAM STRONG and Bradley—and the Court almost simultaneously announced its legal tender decision.

Within a year, Bradley and Strong led a new majority to sustain the constitutionality of greenbacks (unsecured paper currency). In his CONCURRING OPINION, Bradley saw the power to emit BILLS OF CREDIT as the essential issue in the case, and from that he contended that "the incidental power of giving such bills the quality of legal tender follows almost as matter of course." Bradley also emphasized the government's right to maintain its existence. He insisted it would be a "great wrong" to deny Congress the asserted power, "a power to be seldom exercised, certainly; but one, the possession of which is so essential, and as it seems to me, so undoubted." (See LEGAL TENDER CASES.)

Three months after his appointment, Bradley conducted circuit court hearings in New Orleans where he encountered the SLAUGHTERHOUSE CASES. He held unconstitutional the Louisiana statute authorizing a monopoly for slaughtering operations. Three years later, when the case reached the Supreme Court on appeal, Bradley dissented as the majority sustained the regulation. With Justice STEPHEN J. FIELD, Bradley believed that the creation of the monopoly and the impairment of existing businesses violated the PRIVILEGES AND IMMUNITIES clause of the FOURTEENTH AMENDMENT. Such privileges, Bradley had said earlier in his circuit court opinion, included a citizen's right to "lawful industrial pursuit—not injurious to the community—as he may see fit, without unreasonable regulation or molestation."

The antiregulatory views that Bradley advanced in *Slaughterhouse* did not persist as the major theme of his judicial career, as they did for Justice Field. JUDICIAL REVIEW and judicial superintendence of DUE PROCESS OF LAW could be maintained, he said, in *Davidson v. New Orleans* (1878), "without interfering with that large discretion which every legislative power has of making wide modifications in the forms of procedure." A year earlier, Bradley had vividly demonstrated his differences with Field when he provided Chief Justice MORRISON R. WAITE with the key historical sources and principles for the public interest doctrine laid down in *Munn v. Illinois* (1877). (See AFFECTATION WITH A PUBLIC INTEREST).

The Court largely gutted the *Munn* ruling when it held in WABASH, ST. LOUIS, AND PACIFIC RAILWAY V. ILLINOIS (1886) that states could not regulate interstate rates, even in the absence of congressional action. Bradley vigorously dissented, protesting that some form of regulation was necessary and that the Court had wrongly repudiated the public interest doctrine of the GRANGER CASES. Ironically, Bradley, the old railroad lawyer, found himself almost totally isolated when he dissented from the Court's finding that the judiciary, not legislatively authorized expert commisions, had the right to decide the reasonableness of railroad rates. That decision, in CHICAGO, MILWAUKEE AND ST. PAUL RAILWAY CO. V. MINNESOTA (1890), marked the triumph of Field's dissenting views in *Munn;* yet Bradley steadfastly insisted that rate regulation "is a legislative prerogative and not a judicial one."

Bradley insisted on responsibility and accountability from the railroads in numerous ways. In *New York Central R.R. v. Lockwood* (1873) he wrote that railroads could not, by contract, exempt themselves from liability for negligence. "The carrier and his customer do not stand on a footing of equality," he said. In *Railroad Company v. Maryland* (1875) he agreed that Maryland could compel a railroad to return one-fifth of its revenue in exchange for a right of way without compromising congressional control over commerce. But Bradley found clear lines of distinction between federally chartered and state chartered railroads. When the Court, in *Railroad Company v. Peniston* (1873), approved Nebraska's tax of a congressionally chartered railroad, Bradley disagreed, arguing that the carrier was a federal GOVERNMENT INSTRUMENTALITY; similarly, he joined Field in dissent in the SINKING FUND CASES (1879), arguing that Congress's requirement that the Union Pacific deposit some of its earnings to repay its debt to the federal government was tantamount to the "repudiation of government obligations."

Bradley generally advocated a broad nationalist view of the COMMERCE CLAUSE. He wrote, for example, the opinion of the Court in *Robbins v. Shelby Taxing District* (1887), one of the most famous of the "drummer" cases of the period, holding that discriminatory state taxation of out-of-state salesmen unduly burdened interstate commerce. He also maintained that states could not tax the gross receipts of steamship companies or telegraph messages sent across state lines. Yet he steadfastly resisted the attempts of business to avoid their fair share of tax burdens, and he ruled that neither goods destined for another state nor goods that arrived at a final destination after crossing state lines were exempt from state taxing. (See STATE TAXATION OF COMMERCE.)

Despite Bradley's broad reading of the Fourteenth Amendment in the *Slaughterhouse Cases,* he voted with the Court majority that failed in various cases to sustain national protection of the rights of blacks. He ruled against the constitutionality of the FORCE ACT of 1870 while on circuit, and the Court sustained his ruling in UNITED STATES V. CRUIKSHANK (1876). He acquiesced in UNITED STATES V. REESE (1876), crippling enforcement of the FIFTEENTH AMENDMENT, and in HALL V. DECUIR (1878) he agreed that a Louisiana law prohibiting racial segregation on railroads burdened interstate commerce. Unlike that of most of his colleagues, Bradley's interpretation of the commerce power was consistent, for he dissented with JOHN M. HARLAN when the Court in 1890 approved a state law requiring segregated railroad cars.

Bradley's most famous statement on racial matters came in the CIVIL RIGHTS CASES (1883). Speaking for all his colleagues save Harlan, Bradley held unconstitutional the CIVIL RIGHTS ACT OF 1875. He limited the scope of the Fourteenth Amendment when he wrote that it forbade only STATE ACTION and not private RACIAL DISCRIMINATION. Bradley eloquently—if unfortunately—captured the national mood when he declared: "When a man has emerged from slavery, and by the aid of beneficient legislation has shaken off the inseparable concomitants of that state, there must be some stage in the progress of his elevation when he takes the rank of a mere citizen and ceases to be the special favorite of the laws. . . ." Bradley concurred in BRADWELL V. ILLINOIS (1873), in which the Court held that Illinois had not violated the EQUAL PROTECTION clause of the Fourteenth Amendment when it refused to admit a woman to the bar. He stated that a woman's "natural and proper timidity" left her unprepared for many occupations, and he concluded that "the paramount destiny and mission of woman are to fulfill the noble and benign offices of wife and mother." Clearly, there were limits to the liberty that Bradley had so passionately advocated in the *Slaughterhouse Cases.*

The variety of significant opinions by Bradley demonstrates his enormous range and influence. In BOYD V. UNITED STATES (1886) he established the modern FOURTH AMENDMENT standard for SEARCH AND SEIZURE questions, advocating a narrow scope for governmental power: "It is the duty of courts to be watchful for the constitutional rights of the citizen, and against any stealthy encroachments thereon." In COLLECTOR V. DAY (1871) he dissented when the Court held that state officials were exempt from federal income taxes, and nearly sixty years later the Court adopted his position. He spoke for the Court in CHURCH OF JESUS CHRIST OF LATTER-DAY SAINTS V. UNITED STATES (1890), stipulating that forfeited Mormon property be applied to charitable uses, including the building of common schools in Utah. Finally, he helped resolve the Court's difficulties over the exercise of recently enacted JURISDICTION legislation and sustained the right of federal CORPORATIONS to remove their causes from state to federal courts. That opinion made possible a staggering number of new tort and corporate cases in the federal courts.

Bradley played a decisive role in the outcome of the disputed election of 1877 as he supported Rutherford B. Hayes's claims. He was the fifteenth member chosen on the Electoral Commission whose other members included seven Democrats and seven Republicans. Thus, Hayes and the Compromise of 1877 owed much to Bradley's vote.

Bradley, Field, Harlan, and SAMUEL F. MILLER are the dominant figures of late nineteenth-century judicial history. Field's reputation rests on his forceful advocacy of a conservative ideology that the Court embraced but eventually repudiated. Harlan's claims center on his CIVIL RIGHTS views. Miller's notions of judicial restraint continue to have vitality. But Bradley's range of expertise, his high technical competency, and the continuing relevance of his work arguably place him above those distinguished contemporaries. Indeed, a mere handful of Supreme Court Justices have had a comparable impact.

STANLEY I. KUTLER

Bibliography

FAIRMAN, CHARLES 1950 What Makes a Great Justice? *Boston University Law Review* 30:49–102.

MAGRATH, C. PETER 1963 *Morrison R. Waite: The Triumph of Character.* New York: Macmillan.

BRADWELL v. ILLINOIS
16 Wallace 130 (1873)

Bradwell is the earliest FOURTEENTH AMENDMENT case in which the Supreme Court endorsed sex discrimination. Mrs. Myra Bradwell, the editor of the *Chicago Legal News,* was certified by a board of legal examiners as qualified to be a member of the state bar. An Illinois statute permitted the state supreme court to make rules for admission to the bar. That court denied Mrs. Bradwell's application for admission solely on the ground of sex, although the fact that the applicant was married also counted against her: a married woman at that time was incapable of making binding contracts without her husband's consent, thus disabling her from performing all the duties of an attorney. She argued that the PRIVILEGES AND IMMUNITIES clause of the Fourteenth Amendment protected her CIVIL RIGHT as a citizen of the United States to be admitted to the bar, if she qualified.

Justice SAMUEL F. MILLER, speaking for the Court, declared that the right to be admitted to the practice of law in a state court was not a privilege of national CITIZENSHIP protected by the Fourteenth Amendment. Justice JOSEPH P. BRADLEY, joined by Justices NOAH SWAYNE and STEPHEN J. FIELD, concurred in the JUDGMENT affirming the state court, but offered additional reasons. History, nature, COMMON LAW, and the civil law supported the majority's reading of the privileges and immunities clause, according to Bradley. The "spheres and destinies" of the sexes were widely different, man being woman's protector; her "timidity and delicacy" unfit her for many occupations, including the law. Unlike Myra Bradwell, an unmarried woman might make contracts, but such a woman was an exception to the rule. "The paramount destiny and mission of woman are to fulfill the noble and benign offices of wife and mother. This is the law of the Creator." Society's rules, Bradley added, ought not be based on exceptions. Chief Justice SALMON P. CHASE dissented alone, without opinion, missing a chance to advocate the cause of SEX EQUALITY, at least in the legal profession.

LEONARD W. LEVY

BRANCH v. TEXAS

See: Capital Punishment Cases, 1972

BRANDEIS, LOUIS D.
(1856–1941)

The appointment of Louis D. Brandeis to the United States Supreme Court was not merely the crowning glory of an extraordinary career as a practicing lawyer and social activist. It was also the inauguration of an equally extraordinary career on the bench. In twenty-three years as a Justice, Brandeis acquired a stature and influence that few—before or since—could match. In part, this achievement reflected the fact that he was already a public figure when he ascended to the Court. But his skills as a jurist provided the principal explanation. He mastered details of procedure, remained diligent in researching the facts and law of the case, and, whatever the subject, devoted untold hours to make his opinions clear and logical. Perhaps the highest compliment came from colleagues who disagreed with his conclusions. "My, how I detest that man's ideas," Associate Justice GEORGE SUTHERLAND once observed. "But he is one of the greatest technical lawyers I have ever known."

Brandeis's opinions and votes on the Court were very much a product of his environment and experience. Born in Louisville, Kentucky, shortly before the Civil War, he grew up in a family that provided him with love and security. That background probably helped him in establishing skills as a tenacious lawyer in Boston, where he opened his office one year after graduating from Harvard Law School first in his class. Brandeis attained local and then national fame when he used his formidable talents to effect reform at the height of the Progressive movement in the early 1900s. He fought the establishment of a privately owned subway monopoly in Boston, was instrumental in developing a savings bank life insurance system to prevent exploitation of industrial workers by large insurance companies, developed the famed BRANDEIS BRIEF—a detailed compilation of facts and statistics—in defense of Oregon's maximum hour law for women, and even took on the legendary J. P. Morgan when the corporate magnate tried to monopolize New England's rail and steamship lines. Brandeis's renown as "the people's attorney" spread across the country when, in 1910, he led a team of lawyers in challenging Richard A. Ballinger's stewardship of the nation's natural resources as secretary of the interior in the administration of President WILLIAM HOWARD TAFT.

Because of Brandeis's well-known credentials as a lawyer who had single-handedly taken on the "trusts," WOODROW WILSON turned to him for advice in the presidential campaign of 1912. The relationship ripened, and after his election to the White House Wilson repeatedly called upon Brandeis for help in solving many difficult problems. Through these interactions Wilson came to appreciate Brandeis's keen intelligence and dedication to the public welfare. In January 1916 he nominated the Boston attorney to the Supreme Court. Brandeis was confirmed by the United States Senate almost six months later after a grueling and bitter fight.

For Brandeis, law was essentially a mechanism to shape man's social, economic, and political relations. In fulfilling that function, he believed, the law had to account for two basic principles: first, that the individual was the key force in society, and second, that individuals—no matter what their talents and aspirations—had only limited capabilities. As he explained to HAROLD LASKI, "Progress must proceed from the aggregate of the performances of individual men" and society should adjust its institutions "to the wee size of man and thus render possible his growth and development." At the same time, Brandeis did not want people coddled because of inherent limitations. Quite the contrary. People had to stretch themselves to fulfill their individual potentials.

In this context Brandeis abhorred what he often called "the curse of bigness." People, he felt, could not fully develop themselves if they did not have control of their lives. Individual control, however, was virtually impossible in a large institutional setting—whether it be a union, a CORPORATION, the government, or even a town. From this perspective, Brandeis remained convinced that democracy could be maintained only if citizens—and especially the most talented—returned to small communities in the hinterland and learned to manage their own affairs.

This commitment to individual development led Brandeis to assume a leadership position in the Zionist Movement in 1914 and retain it after he went on the Court. In Palestine, Brandeis believed, an individual could control his life in a way that would not be possible in the United States.

This theme—the need for individuals and local communities to control their own affairs—also threads the vast majority of Brandeis's major opinions on the Court. Some of the most controversial of Brandeis's early opinions concerned labor unions. Long before his appointment to the Court he had viewed unions as a necessary element in the nation's economy. Without them large CORPORATIONS would be able to exploit workers and prevent them from acquiring the financial independence needed for individual control. Brandeis made his views known on this matter in HITCHMAN COAL & COKE COMPANY V. MITCHELL

(1917). That case concerned the United Mine Workers' efforts to unionize the workers in West Virginia. As a condition of employment the mine owner forced his employees to sign a pledge not to join a union. A majority of the Court held that UMW officials had acted illegally in trying to induce the workers to violate that pledge.

Brandeis dissented. He could not accept the majority's conclusion that a union agreement would deprive the workers and mine owner of their DUE PROCESS rights under the FOURTEENTH AMENDMENT to FREEDOM OF CONTRACT. "Every agreement curtails the liberty of those who enter into it," Brandeis responded. "The test of legality is not whether an agreement curtails liberty, but whether the parties have agreed upon some thing which the law prohibits. . . ." Brandeis also saw no merit in the majority's concern with the UMW's pressure on workers to join the union. The plaintiff company's lawsuit was premised "upon agreements secured under similar pressure of economic necessity or disadvantage," he observed. "If it is coercion to threaten to strike unless plaintiff consents to a closed union shop, it is coercion also to threaten not to give one employment unless the applicant will consent to a closed non-union shop."

Brandeis adhered to these views in other labor cases that came before the Court. Eventually, the Court came around to Brandeis's belief that unions had a right to engage in peaceful efforts to push for a CLOSED SHOP. Brandeis himself added a finishing touch in an opinion he delivered in *Senn v. Tile Layers Union* (1937), where he upheld a state law restricting the use of INJUNCTIONS against PICKETING.

While concern for the plight of labor was vital to his vision of society, nothing concerned Brandeis more than the right of a state or community to shape its own environment. For this reason he voted to uphold almost every piece of social legislation that came before the Court. Indeed, he wanted to reduce federal JURISDICTION in part because, as he told FELIX FRANKFURTER, "in no case practically should the appellate federal courts have to pass on the construction of state statutes." Therefore, if the state wanted to regulate the practices of employment agencies, expand the disability protection to stevedores who worked the docks, or take other social actions, he would not stand in the way. As he explained for the Court in *O'Gorman & Young v. Hartford Insurance Company* (1931), "the presumption of constitutionality must prevail in the absence of some factual foundation of record for overthrowing the statute." This meant that the Court must abide by the legislature's judgment even if the Court found the law to be of doubtful utility.

Only a few months after *O'Gorman* Brandeis applied this principle in NEW STATE ICE COMPANY V. LIEBMANN (1932). The Oklahoma Legislature had passed a law that prohibited anyone from entering the ice business without first getting a certificate from a state corporation commission showing that there was a public need for the new business. A majority of the Court struck the law down because the ice business was not so AFFECTED WITH A PUBLIC INTEREST to justify a measure that would, in effect, restrict competition.

Brandeis was all for competition. He had long believed that large corporations were dangerous because they often eliminated competition and with it the right of individuals to control their lives, a proposition he examined in detail in *Liggett Company v. Lee* (1933). Whatever misgivings he had about the merits of the Oklahoma law, Brandeis had no trouble accepting the state's right to make its own decisions, especially at a time when the nation was grappling with the problems of the Depression. "It is one of the happy incidents of the federal system," he wrote in dissent, "that a single courageous State may, if its citizens choose, serve as a laboratory; and try novel social and economic experiments without risk to the rest of the country. This Court has the power to prevent an experiment. . . . But in the exercise of this high power, we must be ever on our guard, lest we erect our prejudices into legal principles."

It was, in a way, an ironic warning. For Brandeis himself sometimes allowed personal prejudice to govern his opinions. There was no better example than *Nashville, Chattanooga & St. Louis Railway v. Walters* (1935). A railroad challenged the application of a Tennessee law that required it to pay half the cost of an underpass—not to eliminate existing safety hazards but to help improve the national highway system and thereby facilitate its use by newer, high-speed automobiles. The challenge found a sympathetic listener in Brandeis. He hated cars. To him they represented the extravagance and overcapitalization that contributed to the Depression. Brandeis also opposed the construction of the national highway system because its maintenance would require too much public money. Primarily for these reasons the Justice was willing to uphold the railway's argument and ask the state court to reconsider. Nathaniel Nathanson, Brandeis's law CLERK at the time, protested (as Brandeis had in other cases) that the Court had no business second-guessing the state, and here there were many conceivable reasons why Tennessee felt justified in asking railroads to assume half the tab for grade crossings. It was all to no avail. "I apply the test of OLIVER WENDELL HOLMES," Brandeis told his clerk, "Does it make you puke?" This case flunked the test. "It may be shocking to mention them in the same breath," Nathanson wrote to Frankfurter afterward, "but I sometimes wonder whether the Justice or [Associate Justice JAMES C.] MCREYNOLDS votes more in accordance with his prejudices. . . ."

The Tennessee case was an exception to Brandeis's general inclination to protect the states' right to legislate. In fact, he was so devoted to states' rights that he once openly disregarded one of his most-oft stated juridical principles—never decide constitutional matters that can be avoided. Brandeis relied on this principle when he refused to join the Court's opinion in ASHWANDER V. TENNESSEE VALLEY AUTHORITY (1936) upholding the constitutionality of federal legislation establishing the TVA. In a CONCURRING OPINION he argued that they should have dismissed the case without deciding the constitutional issue because the plaintiffs had no STANDING to bring the lawsuit.

Brandeis was willing to ignore the teachings of his TVA opinion, however, when Chief Justice CHARLES EVANS HUGHES asked the aging Justice to write the Court's opinion in ERIE RAILROAD V. TOMPKINS (1938). The Court had voted to overrule SWIFT V. TYSON (1842), a decision that concerned cases arising under DIVERSITY JURISDICTION. Specifically, *Swift* allowed federal courts to ignore the laws of the states in which they were located and instead to apply FEDERAL COMMON LAW. *Swift* thus enabled litigants in certain cases to shop for the best forum in filing a lawsuit, for a federal court under *Swift* could and often did follow substantive law different from that applied by local courts.

Brandeis had long found *Swift* offensive. Not only did it mean that different courts in the same state could come to different conclusions on the same question; of greater importance, *Swift* undermined the ability of the state to control its own affairs. He was no doubt delighted when Hughes gave him the chance to bury *Swift;* and he wanted to make sure there could be no resurrection by a later Court or Congress. He therefore wrote an opinion holding that *Swift* violated the Constitution because it allowed federal courts to assume powers reserved to the states. The constitutional basis for the opinion was startling for two reasons: first, Brandeis could have just as easily overturned *Swift* through a revised construction of the JUDICIARY ACT OF 1789; and second, none of the parties had even raised the constitutional issue, let alone briefed it.

Brandeis would depart from his ready endorsement of state legislation if the law violated FUNDAMENTAL FREEDOMS and individual rights. It was not only a matter of constitutional construction. The BILL OF RIGHTS played a significant role in the individual's, and ultimately the community's, right to control the future. Brandeis knew, for example, that, without FIRST AMENDMENT protections, he never could have achieved much success as "the people's attorney" in battling vested interests. In those earlier times he had sloughed off personal attacks of the bitterest kind to pursue his goals. He knew that, in many instances, he would have been silenced if his right of speech had depended on majority approval. And he expressed great concern when citizens were punished—even during wartime—for saying or writing things someone found objectionable. "The constitutional right of free speech has been declared to be the same in peace and in war," he wrote in dissent in *Schaeffer v. United States* (1920). "In peace, too, men may differ widely as to what loyalty to our country demands; and an intolerant majority, swayed by passion or fear, may be prone in the future, as it has often been in the past, to stamp as disloyal opinions with which it disagrees." This point was later amplified in his concurring opinion in WHITNEY V. CALIFORNIA (1927). The Founding Fathers, Brandeis wrote, recognized "that fear breeds repression; that repression breeds hate; that hate menaces stable government; that the path of safety lies in the opportunity to discuss freely supposed grievances and proposed remedies; and that the fitting remedy for evil counsels is good ones."

Brandeis, then, often brought clear and deep-seated convictions to the conference table. He was not one, however, to twist arms and engage in the lobbying that other Justices found so successful. "I could have had my views prevail in cases of public importance if I had been willing to play politics," he once told Frankfurter. "But I made up my mind I wouldn't—I would have had to sin against my light, and I would have hated myself. And I decided that the price was too large for the doubtful gain to the country's welfare."

Brandeis therefore tried to use established procedures to persuade his colleagues. To that end he would often anticipate important cases and distribute his views as a "memorandum" even before the majority opinion was written. In OLMSTEAD V. UNITED STATES (1928), for example, he tried to convince the Court that the federal government should not be allowed to use EVIDENCE in a criminal case that its agents had obtained by WIRETAPPING. The eavesdropping had been done without a judicial warrant and in violation of a state statute. Brandeis circulated a memorandum reflecting views that had not been debated at conference. The government should not be able to profit by its own wrongdoing, he said—especially when, as here, it impinged on the individual's RIGHT TO PRIVACY (a right he had examined as a lawyer in a seminal article in the *Harvard Law Review*). The memorandum could not command a majority, and Brandeis later issued an eloquent dissent that focused on the contention that warrantless wiretaps violated the FOURTH AMENDMENT's protection against UNREASONABLE SEARCHES and seizures.

At other times Brandeis would use the Saturday conferences to urge a view upon his colleagues. On one occasion—involving *Southwestern Bell Telephone Company v. Public Service Commission* (1923)—an entire day was devoted to a seminar conducted by Brandeis to explain why a utility's rate of return should be based on prudent investment and not on the reproduction cost of its facilities. Few, if any, Justices shared Brandeis's grasp of rate-making principles. Hence, it took more than two decades of experience and debate before the Court—without Brandeis—accepted the validity of his position.

Brandeis took his losses philosophically. He knew that progress in a democracy comes slowly, and he was prepared to accept temporary setbacks along the way. But he rarely faded in his determination to correct the result. If his brethren remained impervious to his reasoning, he was willing to use other resources. He peppered Frankfurter and others with suggestions on articles for the *Harvard Law Review.* He also turned to the numerous congressmen and senators who frequently dined with him. Were they interested in introducing legislation to restrict federal jurisdiction or some other objective? If the answer was affirmative, Brandeis often volunteered the services of Frankfurter (whose expenses in public interest matters were generally assumed by Brandeis).

Few of these extrajudicial activities produced concrete results. Brandeis was apparently pleased, consequently, when Hughes became Chief Justice in 1930. Brandeis felt that the former secretary of state had a better command of the law than did Taft, the preceding Chief Justice, and would be able to use that knowledge to expedite the disposition of the Court's growing caseload. Of greater significance, Hughes and some other new members of the Court had views that closely coincided with Brandeis's. In fact, in 1937, BENJAMIN N. CARDOZO, HARLAN FISKE STONE, and Brandeis—the so-called liberal Justices—began to caucus in Brandeis's apartment on Friday nights to go over the cases for the Saturday conference.

With this kind of working relationship, plus the change in the times, Brandeis was able to join a majority in upholding New Deal legislation (he voted against only three New Deal measures). He also lived to see many of his earlier dissents become HOLDINGS of the Court, particularly in cases concerning labor and the right of states to adopt social legislation. After his death, many other dissents—including his First Amendment views and his contention that warrantless wiretaps were unconstitutional—would also become the law of the land. But Brandeis's overriding ambition—the desire to establish a legal framework in which individuals and communities could control their affairs—was frustrated by developments that would not yield to even the most incisive judicial opinion. Unions, like corporations and even government, continued to grow like Topsy. Almost everyone, it seemed, became dependent on a large organization. Brandeis, a shrewd realist, surely recognized the inexorable social, economic, and political forces that impeded the realization of his dreams for America. None of that, however, would have deterred him from pursuing his goals. As he once explained to his brother, the "future has many good things in store for those who can wait, . . . have patience and exercise good judgment."

LEWIS J. PAPER

Bibliography

BICKEL, ALEXANDER M. 1957 *The Unpublished Opinions of Mr. Justice Brandeis: The Supreme Court at Work.* Cambridge, Mass.: Harvard University Press.

FRANKFURTER, FELIX, ED. 1932 *Mr. Justice Brandeis.* New Haven, Conn.: Yale University Press.

FREUND, PAUL 1964 Mr. Justice Brandeis. In Allison Dunham and Philip B. Kurland, eds., *Mr. Justice.* Chicago: University of Chicago Press.

KONEFSKY, SAMUEL J. 1956 *The Legacy of Holmes and Brandeis: A Study in the Influence of Ideas.* New York: Macmillan.

MASON, ALPHEUS T. 1946 *Brandeis: A Free Man's Life.* New York: Viking Press.

PAPER, LEWIS J. 1983 *Brandeis.* Englewood Cliffs, N.J.: Prentice-Hall.

BRANDEIS BRIEF

The opinion of the Supreme Court in MULLER V. OREGON (1908) began with an unusual acknowledgment: the Court had found useful a brief by LOUIS D. BRAN-

DEIS, supporting Oregon's law regulating women's working hours. The brief had presented the views of doctors and social workers, the conclusions of various public committees that had investigated the conditions of women's labor, and an outline of similar legislation in the United States and overseas. The Court said that although these materials "may not be, technically speaking, authorities," they were "significant of a widespread belief that woman's physical structure, and the functions she performs in consequence thereof, justify special legislation." Its intimations of female dependency aside, this comment marked an important event: the Court's recognition of the utility of briefing and argument addressed to the factual basis for legislation.

Underlying the *Muller* opinion's comment lay a deeper change in the judiciary's conception of its proper role. Since around the time of the Civil War, lawyers and judges had commonly believed that the development of legal (including constitutional) doctrine was a pursuit of truth. In this view, there were answers to be found in authoritative documents such as laws and constitutions. The *Muller* opinion signaled a recognition that judges had a creative, legislative role, that they were properly concerned with the evaluation of the factual basis for legislation. This development, which sometimes bore the name of SOCIOLOGICAL JURISPRUDENCE and which culminated in the LEGAL REALISM of the 1920s and 1930s, represented a major shift in judicial attitudes. Judges came to see themselves as active participants in adapting the law to the needs of society. The technique of the Brandeis brief came to serve not only in cases involving ECONOMIC REGULATION but also in other constitutional contexts far removed. A famous modern example is BROWN V. BOARD OF EDUCATION (1954), in which an AMICUS CURIAE brief detailed the views of social scientists on the educational harm of racial SEGREGATION in schools.

It is possible to present such factual material as EVIDENCE in the trial of a constitutional case, and today it is not unusual for counsel to do so. However, the Brandeis brief has become a common technique in the Supreme Court and other appellate courts. In the *Muller* case, the Brandeis brief aimed at demonstrating that the Oregon legislature reasonably could have believed that certain evils existed and that a limit on women's working hours would mitigate them. Brandeis himself argued no more than that. The assumption was that the law was valid if there was a RATIONAL BASIS for the legislature's assumptions. Evidence on the other side of the factual questions would, in theory, be irrelevant. When the presumption of constitutionality is weaker—that is, when the state must justify its legislation by reference to a COMPELLING STATE INTEREST or some other heightened STANDARD OF REVIEW—the Brandeis brief technique may recommend itself to either side of the argument.

KENNETH L. KARST

(SEE ALSO: *Legislative Facts.*)

Bibliography

FREUND, PAUL A. 1951 *On Understanding the Supreme Court.* Chap. 3. Boston: Little, Brown.

BRANDENBURG v. OHIO
395 U.S. 444 (1969)

Libertarian critics of the CLEAR AND PRESENT DANGER test had always contended that it provided insufficient protection for speech because it depended ultimately on judicial guesses about the consequences of speech. Judges inimical to the content of a particular speech could always foresee the worst. Thus, to the extent that the test did protect speech, its crucial element was the imminence requirement, that speech was punishable only when it was so closely brigaded in time with unlawful action as to constitute an attempt to commit, or incitement of, unlawful action. When the Supreme Court converted clear and present danger to clear and probable danger in DENNIS V. UNITED STATES (1951) it actually converted the clear and present danger test into a BALANCING TEST that allowed judges who believed in judicial self-restraint to avoid enforcing the FIRST AMENDMENT by striking every balance in favor of the nonspeech interest that the government sought to protect by suppressing speech. The *Dennis* conversion, however, was even more damaging to the clear and present danger rule than a flat rejection and open replacement by the balancing standard would have been. A flat rejection would have left clear and present danger as a temporarily defeated libertarian rival to a temporarily triumphant antilibertarian balancing standard. The conversion to probable danger not only defeated the danger test but also discredited it among libertarians by removing the imminence requirement that had been its strongest protection for dissident speakers. Accordingly commentators, both libertarian and advocates of judicial self-restraint, were pleased to announce that *Dennis* had buried the clear and present danger test.

Some critics of the danger test had supported LEARNED HAND's approach in MASSES PUBLISHING

CO. V. PATTEN (1917), which had focused on the advocacy content of the speech itself, thus avoiding judicial predictions about what the speech plus the surrounding circumstances would bring. *Masses* left two problems, however: the "Marc Antony" speech which on the surface seems innocuous but in the circumstances really is an incitement, and the speech preaching violence in circumstances in which it is harmless. OLIVER WENDELL HOLMES himself had injected a specific intent standard alongside the danger rule, arguing that government might punish a speaker only if it could prove his specific intent to bring about an unlawful act.

Eighteen years after *Dennis,* carefully avoiding the words of the clear and present danger test itself, the Supreme Court brought together these various strands of thought in *Brandenburg v. Ohio,* a PER CURIAM holding that "the constitutional guarantees of free speech . . . do not permit a state to forbid or proscribe advocacy of the use of force or law violation except where such advocacy is directed to inciting or producing imminent lawless action and is likely to incite or produce such action." In a footnote the Court interpreted *Dennis* and YATES V. UNITED STATES (1957) as upholding this standard. The decision itself struck down the Ohio Criminal Syndicalism Act which proscribed advocacy of violence as a means of accomplishing social reform. The Court overruled WHITNEY V. CALIFORNIA (1927).

MARTIN SHAPIRO

BRANT, IRVING
(1885–1976)

Irving Newton Brant was a journalist, biographer, and constitutional historian. A strong supporter of President FRANKLIN D. ROOSEVELT, Brant published *Storm over the Constitution* in 1936; a vigorous defense of the constitutionality of the New Deal, it strongly influenced Roosevelt's later attempt to enlarge the membership of the Supreme Court. Brant's concentration in this book on the intent of the Framers of the Constitution led him to begin a biography of JAMES MADISON. Now regarded as definitive, his six-volume biography (1941–1961) had two aims: the rehabilitation of Madison's reputation as constitutional theorist and political leader, and the refutation of the STATES' RIGHTS interpretation of American history (which denied that the Revolutionary generation considered the newly created United States to be one nation). Brant's other works include *The Bill of Rights* (1965), a history championing the absolutist interpretation of the BILL OF RIGHTS espoused by Justices HUGO L. BLACK and WILLIAM O. DOUGLAS, and *Impeachment: Trials and Errors* (1972).

RICHARD B. BERNSTEIN

BRANTI v. FINKEL
445 U.S. 507 (1980)

Branti v. Finkel tightened the FIRST AMENDMENT restrictions on the use of patronage in public employment first established in *Elrod v. Burns* (1976). Justice JOHN PAUL STEVEN'S MAJORITY OPINION held that upon taking office a public defender could not constitutionally dismiss two assistants solely because they were affiliated with a different political party. The 6–3 majority held that these dismissals denied the employees' freedoms of belief and association. The employer had failed to show a sufficient connection between party loyalty and effective job performance.

Justice POTTER STEWART dissented, analogizing the public defender's office to private law practice. Justice LEWIS F. POWELL, joined by Justice WILLIAM H. REHNQUIST, also dissented, reiterating his dissenting view in *Elrod* that patronage plays an honorable, traditional role in American politics.

AVIAM SOIFER

BRANZBURG v. HAYES
408 U.S. 665 (1972)

Branzburg v. Hayes combined several cases in which reporters claimed a FIRST AMENDMENT privilege either not to appear or not to testify before grand juries, although they had witnessed criminal activity or had information relevant to the commission of crimes. The reporters' chief contention was that they should not be required to testify unless a GRAND JURY showed that a reporter possessed information relevant to criminal activity, that similar information could not be obtained from sources outside the press, and that the need for the information was sufficiently compelling to override the First Amendment interest in preserving confidential news sources.

Justice BYRON R. WHITE's opinion for the Court not only rejected these showings but also denied the very existence of a First Amendment testimonial privilege. Despite the asserted lack of any First Amendment privilege, the White opinion allowed that "news gathering" was not "without its First Amendment protections" and suggested that such protections would bar a grand jury from issuing SUBPOENAS to reporters "other than in good faith" or "to disrupt a reporter's relationship with his news sources." White rejected any requirement for a stronger showing of relevance, of alternative sources, or of balancing the need for the information against the First Amendment interest.

Nevertheless, Justice LEWIS F. POWELL, who signed White's 5–4 OPINION OF THE COURT, attached an ambiguous CONCURRING OPINION stating that a claim to privilege "should be judged on its facts by the striking of a proper balance between FREEDOM OF THE PRESS" and the government interest. Most lower courts have read the majority opinion through the eyes of Justice Powell. An opinion that emphatically denied a First Amendment privilege at various points seems to have created one after all.

STEVEN SHIFFRIN

(SEE ALSO: *Reporter's Privilege.*)

BRAUNFELD v. BROWN

See: Sunday Closing Laws

BREACH OF THE PEACE

Breach of the peace statutes are today popularly called disorderly conduct statutes. The wording of breach of the peace or disorderly conduct statutes varies significantly from one city or state to another. Generally, such statutes are violated if a person commits acts or makes statements likely to promote violence or disturb "good order" in a public place. Under modern statutes, as under the older COMMON LAW, it is possible to be guilty of committing a breach of the peace solely through the use of words likely to produce violence or disorder.

When a person is prosecuted for breach of the peace for his or her physical actions there is no significant FIRST AMENDMENT issue. Thus, if a person commits a breach of the peace by punching or shoving other persons in public no First Amendment issue arises. However, if a mixture of expression and physical activity forms the basis for the prosecution, the court must ask whether the person is being punished for the physical activity alone. Thus, a person might be convicted of a breach of the peace for using SOUNDTRUCKS OR AMPLIFIERS if the statute punished any use of a sound amplification device, regardless of the message communicated.

When a person is accused of committing a breach of the peace by speaking to others, a court must determine whether the guarantees of FREEDOM OF SPEECH and assembly have been violated. In addition, the court must determine whether the statute is tailored to avoid punishing constitutionally protected speech.

Although the Supreme Court has held that the First Amendment does not prohibit the punishment of FIGHTING WORDS, it has upheld few convictions for breach of the peace based solely upon verbal conduct. A considerable number of breach of the peace and disorderly conduct statutes have been held unconstitutional under the doctrine of VAGUENESS and OVERBREADTH.

A breach of the peace or disorderly conduct statute that can be constitutionally applied to persons who physically interfere with police officers engaged in police functions cannot constitutionally serve as the basis for punishing the use of insulting or annoying language to a police officer, short of actual interference with the officer's ability to perform police functions.

A person engaged in lawful speech in a public place may sometimes be confronted by a HOSTILE AUDIENCE. In such a situation the police must attempt to protect the individual speaker, or disperse the crowd, before ordering the speaker to cease his or her advocacy of the unpopular message. If it appears that the officers cannot otherwise prevent violence, they may order the speaker or speakers to cease their speech or assembly, and a refusal to comply can constitutionally be punished as disorderly conduct. Breach of the peace statutes may also be applied as consistent with the First Amendment to prohibit conduct that would interfere with the use of government property not traditionally open to speech. Thus, the state might prohibit activities near jails or school buildings if those activities interfere with the government's ability to operate the school or jail.

JOHN E. NOWAK

Bibliography

MONAGHAN, HENRY P. 1981 Overbreadth. *The Supreme Court Review* 1981:1–40.

NOWAK, JOHN E.; ROTUNDA, RONALD D.; and YOUNG, J. NELSON 1983 *Constitutional Law.* Pages 954–958, 973–987. St. Paul, Minn.: West Publishing Co.

BREARLY, DAVID
(1745–1790)

David Brearly represented New Jersey at the CONSTITUTIONAL CONVENTION OF 1787 and signed the Constitution. He was a spokesman for the small states, favoring equal representation of the states in Congress. He served on the Committee of Eleven on remaining matters, and delivered its reports to the Convention. He was later president of New Jersey's ratifying convention.

DENNIS J. MAHONEY

BRECKINRIDGE, JOHN
(1760–1806)

John Breckinridge studied law under Virginia's GEORGE WYTHE, then moved to Kentucky, serving as state attorney general (1795–1797), state representative (1798–1800), United States senator (1801–1805), and United States attorney general (1805–1806). During the ALIEN AND SEDITION ACT crisis Breckinridge traveled to Virginia, where he convinced THOMAS JEFFERSON, through an intermediary, that the vice-president's resolutions condemning the acts should be introduced in Kentucky, and not North Carolina, Jefferson's initial choice. Breckinridge revised Jefferson's draft by deleting the term NULLIFICATION, thus allowing Kentucky to condemn the acts and declare them unconstitutional without actually defying the federal government. Breckinridge then guided the resolutions through the Kentucky legislature while hiding Jefferson's authorship. In 1802 Breckinridge drafted and shepherded through the Senate an act to repeal the JUDICIARY ACT OF 1801—that eleventh-hour creation of the Federalists under JOHN ADAMS which allowed the outgoing President to appoint additional federal judges. Breckinridge argued that the repeal was constitutional, because if Congress had the power to create inferior courts, then Congress could also abolish them. He also contended against a judicial power to hold unconstitutional acts of Congress or of the President. Breckinridge initially doubted the constitutionality of the LOUISIANA PURCHASE, but in 1803 he introduced the Breckinridge Act which created territorial government for Louisiana. Like the Kentucky Resolutions, this act was secretly written by Jefferson.

PAUL FINKELMAN

(SEE ALSO: *Virginia and Kentucky Resolutions.*)

Bibliography

HARRISON, LOWELL H. 1969 *John Breckinridge: Jeffersonian Republican.* Louisville, Ky.: Filson Club.

BREEDLOVE v. SUTTLES
302 U.S. 277 (1937)

Georgia levied an annual POLL TAX of one dollar on every inhabitant between ages twenty-one and sixty except blind persons and women who did not register to vote. Voting registration was conditioned on payment of accrued poll taxes. A white male, denied registration for failure to pay poll taxes, challenged this scheme as a violation of the EQUAL PROTECTION and PRIVILEGES AND IMMUNITIES clauses of the FOURTEENTH AMENDMENT, and of the NINETEENTH AMENDMENT as well. In an opinion by Justice PIERCE BUTLER, a unanimous Supreme Court summarily rejected all these challenges and upheld the law. *Breedlove* was overruled in HARPER V. VIRGINIA BOARD OF ELECTIONS (1966).

KENNETH L. KARST

BREITHAUPT v. ABRAM
352 U.S. 432 (1957)

The taking of blood from an unconscious person to prove his intoxication and therefore his guilt for involuntary manslaughter was not conduct that "shocks the conscience" within the meaning of ROCHIN V. CALIFORNIA (1952), nor was it coercing a confession; accordingly the Supreme Court, in a 6–3 opinion by Justice TOM C. CLARK, found no violation of DUE PROCESS OF LAW.

LEONARD W. LEVY

BRENNAN, WILLIAM J.
(1906–)

William Joseph Brennan, Jr., was appointed an Associate Justice of the United States Supreme Court in October 1956. He quickly became, in both an intellectual and statistical sense, the center of gravity of what commentators have come to call the WARREN COURT, dissenting less than any other Justice, and fashioning many of that Court's most important opinions.

He came to the Court with more past judicial experience than any of his colleagues. For seven years he had been a New Jersey state judge, beginning his career at the trial level and rapidly advancing to the New Jersey Supreme Court. He had also been prominent in the movement to reform the antiquated New Jersey court system. He understood and cared about the practical workings of the justice system, and this concern was to prove important in the development of his constitutional perspective.

Brennan was a committed civil libertarian who believed in "providing freedom and equality of rights and opportunities, in a realistic and not merely formal sense, to all the people of this nation." He considered courts to be the particular guardians of constitutional rights. "[T]he soul of a government of laws," he once wrote, "is the judicial function, and that function can only exist if adjudication is understood by our people to be, as it is, the essentially disinterested, rational and deliberate element of our society." For Brennan, the judicial function demanded a continual effort to translate constitutional values into general doctrinal formulations. This emphasis on DOCTRINE distinguished Brennan from his colleague WILLIAM O. DOUGLAS, who was an equally committed civil libertarian.

Brennan viewed courts as the last resort of the politically disfranchised and the politically powerless. Constitutional litigation was for him "a form of political expression"; it was often, he wrote in NAACP v. BUTTON (1963), "the sole practicable avenue open to a minority to petition for redress of grievances." Litigation was thus an alternative, perhaps the only alternative, to social violence. For these reasons he seized every opportunity to enlarge litigants' access to federal courts. Exemplary is his opinion in BAKER v. CARR (1962), which held that the issue of unequal legislative representation was justiciable in federal court, and which Chief Justice EARL WARREN called "the most important case that we decided in my time." In opinion after opinion Brennan worked to open the doors of the federal courthouse, and to make available such federal judicial remedies for violations of the Constitution as HABEAS CORPUS, INJUNCTIONS, DECLARATORY JUDGMENTS, and DAMAGES. In later years Brennan dissented vigorously as many of these opinions were cut back by the BURGER COURT.

Because he believed that "the ultimate protection of individual freedom is found in judicial enforcement" of constitutional rights, Brennan did not flinch from the exercise of JUDICIAL POWER. When the time came, for example, to accelerate the ALL DELIBERATE SPEED with which BROWN v. BOARD OF EDUCATION (1955) had ordered the nation's public schools to be desegregated, Brennan, in GREEN v. NEW KENT COUNTY SCHOOL BOARD (1968), shattered the façade of southern "freedom-of-choice" plans and wrote that racial discrimination must end *"now"* and "be eliminated root and branch." In KEYES v. SCHOOL DISTRICT #1 OF DENVER (1973) Brennan took the lead in applying the requirement of *Brown* to northern school districts, and in cases like FRONTIERO v. RICHARDSON (1973) and CRAIG v. BOREN (1976) he played a major role in causing gender classifications to be subjected to substantial scrutiny under the EQUAL PROTECTION clause of the FOURTEENTH AMENDMENT.

Brennan was a nationalist. He believed in the power of Congress to define and protect CIVIL RIGHTS and to govern the national economy unrestrained by concerns of state SOVEREIGNTY. He disapproved of state regulations that interfered with interstate commerce. He favored the judicial imposition of national, constitutional values onto local decision-making processes. He believed, for example, that federal courts should fully incorporate almost all the guarantees of the BILL OF RIGHTS into the Fourteenth Amendment, and enforce them against the states. He dissented often and forcefully against the "federalist" leanings of the Burger Court. To Brennan the primary purpose of "the federal system's diffusion of governmental power" was to secure "individual freedom."

In his most enduring opinions, Brennan brought a unique and characteristic analysis to bear on the question of constitutional rights. Instead of inquiring into the power of government to regulate rights, he would instead focus on the manner in which the government's regulation actually functioned. The implications of this shift in focus were profound. They are perhaps most visible in the area of FIRST AMENDMENT adjudication.

To appreciate Brennan's contribution to First Amendment jurisprudence, it must be remembered that the Court to which Brennan was appointed was still reverberating from the effects of the constitutional crisis of the 1930s. It was, for example, groping for a means of reconciling judicial protection of First Amendment freedoms with the deep respect for majoritarian decision making that was the legacy of the Court's confrontation with President FRANKLIN D. ROOSEVELT's New Deal. At the time Brennan joined the Court, the Justices were embroiled in a vigorous but ultimately unproductive debate as to whether First Amendment freedoms were "absolutes" or whether they should be "weighed" against competing government interests in regulation. (See ABSOLUTISM and BALANCING TESTS.) Both sides of the debate viewed government interests and individual rights as locked in an indissoluble and paralyzing conflict.

Brennan's lasting contribution was to push the Court beyond this debate and to create a form of analysis in which this conflict receded from view. The essence of Brennan's approach was a precise and persistent focus on the processes and procedures through which government sought to regulate First Amendment freedoms.

Justice Brennan first used this approach in his second term on the Court in the modest but seminal case of SPEISER V. RANDALL (1958). The case involved a California law which denied certain tax exemptions to those who refused to execute an oath stating that they did "not advocate the overthrow of the United States or of the State of California by force of violence or other unlawful means." Significantly, Brennan did not approach the case in terms of an "absolute" right to engage in such advocacy. Nor did he inquire into California's "interests" in controlling such speech; he was willing to assume that California could deny tax exemptions to those who had engaged in proscribed speech.

Brennan focused his analysis instead on the procedures used to determine which taxpayers to penalize. He interpreted the California scheme as placing on taxpayers the burden of demonstrating that they had not engaged in unlawful speech. This procedure was unconstitutional, Brennan concluded, because it created too great a danger that lawful speech would be adversely affected. "The vice of the present procedure is that, where particular speech falls close to the line separating the lawful and the unlawful, the possibility of mistaken factfinding—inherent in all litigation—will create the danger that the legitimate utterance will be penalized. The man who knows that he must bring forth proof and persuade another of the lawfulness of his conduct necessarily must steer far wider of the unlawful zone than if the State must bear these burdens."

By focusing on the manner in which California had regulated speech, rather than on its power to do so, Brennan was led to inquire into the actual, practical effects of the regulatory scheme. He thus shifted the focus of judicial inquiry away from the particular speech of the litigant, and toward the impact of the legislation, as concretely embedded in its procedural setting, on concededly legitimate speech. This change in focus was central to Brennan's First Amendment jurisprudence, and it was the foundation of many of the Warren Court's innovations in this area. It had, for example, obvious relevance for the procedures used by government to regulate unprotected forms of speech like OBSCENITY. Brennan spelled out these implications in a series of influential obscenity decisions that demonstrated the substantive impact of such nominally procedural isses as BURDEN OF PROOF and the nature and timing of judicial HEARINGS.

Brennan's form of inquiry also led to a careful scrutiny of the VAGUENESS of government regulations of speech. Prior to *Speiser* the issue of "vagueness" was primarily conceived in terms of the rather weak NOTICE requirements of the DUE PROCESS clause. But Brennan's analysis offered a strict, new, and specifically First Amendment rationale for the doctrine. As Brennan explained in KEYISHIAN V. BOARD OF REGENTS (1967), a case involving a New York law prohibiting public school teachers from uttering "seditious" words, "[w]hen one must guess what conduct or utterance may lose him his position, one necessarily will 'steer far wider of the unlawful zone.' "

Brennan's focus on the practical impact of regulation also led him to the conclusion that the separation of legitimate from illegitimate speech had to be accomplished with "precision" and by legislation incapable of application to legitimate speech. As Brennan wrote in *Button,* First Amendment freedoms are "delicate and vulnerable," and "the threat of sanctions may deter their exercise almost as potently as the actual application of sanctions." In *Button* Brennan coined the term OVERBREADTH to capture this requirement that First Amendment regulations be narrowly tailored, and the term and the requirement have since become doctrinal instruments of major significance.

The framework of analysis developed by Brennan not only dominated the First Amendment jurisprudence of the Warren Court; it remained influential with the Burger Court that succeeded it. Its prominence was in large measure due to its apparent accommodation of government interests in regulation, if only the government could formulate its regulation more narrowly or more precisely. This accommodation, however, was in some respects illusory. The exact degree of constitutionally mandated precision or clarity was never specified, and the psychological assumptions that underlay the approach were not susceptible to empirical verification. As a result the requirements of clarity and precision could without explicit justification be loosened to uphold some government regulations, or tightened to strike down others. The indirection at the heart of this approach thus left it vulnerable to manipulation.

The approach was at its most compelling, therefore, when it was fused with an underlying substantive vision of the First Amendment. An illustration is the opinion which is Brennan's masterpiece, NEW YORK TIMES COMPANY V. SULLIVAN (1964). At issue in *Sullivan* was the Alabama law of LIBEL, which permitted a public official to recover damages for defamatory statements unless the speaker could prove that the statements were true. With reasoning similar to that in *Speiser* and *Button,* Brennan concluded that Alabama's allocation of the burden of proof was unconstitutional, because it "dampens the vigor and limits the variety of public debate" by inducing "self-censorship."

In *Sullivan,* however, Brennan took the unusual and penetrating step of lifting this analysis from its procedural setting and applying it to the substantive standards required by the First Amendment. Noting that the central purpose of the First Amendment was "the principle that debate on public issues should be uninhibited, robust, and wide-open," Brennan concluded that this purpose would be undermined if those who criticized public officials were subject to "any test of truth." He noted that an "erroneous statement is inevitable in free debate, and [it] must be protected if the freedoms of expression are to have the 'breathing space' that they 'need . . . to survive.' " The need for "breathing space" led Brennan to conclude that speech about public officials had to be constitutionally protected unless uttered with "actual malice"; that is, uttered "with knowledge that it was false or with reckless disregard of whether it was false or not." The actual malice standard thus incorporated into the substantive law of the First Amendment the insights Brennan had accumulated as a result of his prior focus on the process of regulation. The result, as ALEXANDER MEIKLEJOHN was moved to proclaim, was "an occasion for dancing in the streets."

Although Brennan's focus on process rather than power is most apparent in First Amendment opinions, it also pervades his entire approach to constitutional law. In *Speiser,* for example, California had argued that since a tax exemption was not a right but a privilege bestowed at the pleasure of the state, it could also be withdrawn by the state for any reason. The so-called RIGHT–PRIVILEGE DISTINCTION had a venerable judicial pedigree, and was supported by Supreme Court precedents as recent as *Barsky v. Board of Regents* (1954). Brennan, however, brought a fresh perspective to bear on this argument, for he was concerned not with California's power to withdraw the privilege but with the manner in which it did so. From this perspective the right–privilege distinction was beside the point.

Brennan repeatedly attacked the right–privilege distinction, and many of his most important opinions, contributing to or originating major lines of doctrinal development, were predicated upon its rejection. Examples include SHERBERT V. VERNER (1963), which resuscitated the doctrine of "unconstitutional conditions" as applied to the denial of unemployment compensation; SHAPIRO V. THOMPSON (1969), which created the FUNDAMENTAL RIGHTS strand of equal protection analysis and applied it to durational RESIDENCY REQUIREMENTS for welfare recipients; and GOLDBERG V. KELLY (1970), which for the first time applied the protections of PROCEDURAL DUE PROCESS to the recipients of government entitlements such as WELFARE BENEFITS.

Brennan's focus on process deeply influenced both the Warren and the Burger courts. As the welfare state increased in complexity, Brennan's approach provided the basis for flexible yet far-reaching judicial review of government action. We can recognize the consequences of this approach in the shape of modern constitutional inquiry, with its characteristic scrutiny into whether government has acted through appropriate procedures and in a manner not unduly burdening the exercise of constitutional rights.

It is noteworthy that the results of this scrutiny depend upon an apprehension of the actual impact of government action. In later years Brennan's views on this subject were informed by a compassion and empathy that were not always shared by his colleagues. With the advent of the Burger Court, Brennan increasingly became a dissenter. His dissents, like his majority opinions, tended to be careful and lawyerly, without the eloquence or sting that mark the most memorable examples of the genre. Often, however, both Brennan and the majority were writing within doctrinal frameworks that Brennan himself had helped to create. His success in redefining the major questions of constitutional law is the measure of his achievement.

ROBERT C. POST

Bibliography

BRENNAN, WILLIAM JOSEPH, JR. 1969 Convocation Address. *Notre Dame Lawyer* 44:1029–1033.

——— 1981 Justice Thurgood Marshall: Advocate for Human Need in American Jurisprudence. *Maryland Law Review* 40:390–397.

HECK, EDWARD V. 1980 Justice Brennan and the Heyday of Warren Court Liberalism. *Santa Clara Law Review* 20:841–887.

HUTCHINSON, DENNIS J. 1983 Hail to the Chief: Earl Warren and the Supreme Court. *Michigan Law Review* 81:922–930.

KALVEN, HARRY, JR. 1964 The New York Times Case: A Note on "The Central Meaning of the First Amendment." *Supreme Court Review* 1964:191–221.

LEVY, LEONARD W., ED. 1972 *The Supreme Court under Earl Warren.* New York: Quadrangle Books.

BREWER, DAVID J.
(1837–1910)

David Josiah Brewer forged conservative socioeconomic beliefs into constitutional DOCTRINE. From the time he assumed his seat on the Supreme Court in December 1889, Brewer unabashedly relied on judicial power to protect private property rights from the supposed incursions of state and federal legislatures. Through more than 200 DISSENTING OPINIONS, most of which came during his last ten years on the bench, Brewer emerged as the conservative counterpart of the liberal "Great Dissenter," JOHN MARSHALL HARLAN.

Like his uncle, Justice STEPHEN J. FIELD, Brewer moved from moderate liberalism as a state judge to strident conservatism on the federal bench. Increasing doubts about the power of the Kansas legislature to regulate the manufacture and sale of alcohol punctuated his twelve-year career on the state supreme court. Brewer refrained from directly challenging a constitutional amendment that destroyed the livelihood of distillers without compensation, although, in *State v. Mugler* (1883), he expressed serious reservations about it. After President CHESTER A. ARTHUR appointed him to the Eighth Circuit in 1884, Brewer adopted a more aggressive position. He held that Kansas distillers deserved JUST COMPENSATION for losses suffered because of PROHIBITION, a position that the Supreme Court subsequently rejected in MUGLER V. KANSAS (1887).

Brewer's CIRCUIT COURT opinions on railroad rate regulation proved more prophetic. He ignored the Supreme Court's HOLDING in *Munn v. Illinois* (1877) that state legislatures could best judge the reasonableness of rates. (See GRANGER CASES.) Instead, Brewer asserted that judges had to inquire broadly into the reasonableness of rates and to overturn LEGISLATION that failed to yield a FAIR RETURN ON FAIR VALUE of investment.

These views persuaded President BENJAMIN HARRISON to appoint Brewer the fifty-first Justice of the Supreme Court. The new Justice immediately lived up to expectations by contributing to the emerging doctrine of SUBSTANTIVE DUE PROCESS OF LAW. Brewer advocated use of the Fifth Amendment and the FOURTEENTH AMENDMENT to shelter corporate property rights from federal and state legislation. Three months after his appointment he joined the majority in the important case of CHICAGO, MILWAUKEE & ST. PAUL RAILWAY COMPANY V. MINNESOTA (1890) in striking down a state statute that did not provide for JUDICIAL REVIEW of rates established by an independent commission. More than other members of the Court, Brewer sought to expand the limits of substantive due process. Two years later, when the Court reaffirmed its *Munn* holding in *Budd v. New York* (1893), Brewer complained in dissent that the public interest doctrine granted too much discretion to the legislature. The Court ultimately accepted his position. In REAGAN V. FARMERS' LOAN AND TRUST COMPANY (1894) he spoke for a unanimous Court in holding that a state legislature could not force a railroad to carry persons or freight without a guarantee of sufficient profit. Brewer dramatically expanded the range of issues that the legislature had to consider when determining profitability, and, in so doing, he broadened the grounds for judicial intervention.

Brewer also applied judicial review to congressional acts. He joined the Court's majority in UNITED STATES V. E. C. KNIGHT COMPANY (1895) in narrowing Congress's power under the COMMERCE CLAUSE. He silently joined the same year with Chief Justice MELVILLE W. FULLER in POLLOCK V. FARMERS' LOAN AND TRUST COMPANY, a decision that obliterated more than one hundred years of PRECEDENT in favor of a federal income tax.

Brewer's important decision in IN RE DEBS (1895) coupled judicial power and property rights with a sweeping assertion of national power. The *Debs* case stemmed from the actions of the militant American Railway Union and its leader, Eugene V. Debs, in the Pullman strike of 1894. Debs had refused to obey an INJUNCTION granted by a lower federal court in Chicago that ordered the strikers to end their BOYCOTT of Pullman cars. President GROVER CLEVELAND dispatched troops to restore the passage of INTERSTATE COMMERCE and of the mails. The lower federal court then found Debs and other union members in contempt of court and imprisoned them. Debs petitioned the Supreme Court for a writ of HABEAS CORPUS on the ground that the lower court had exceeded its EQUITY power in issuing the injunction and that the subsequent EX PARTE contempt proceedings had resulted in conviction of a criminal offense without benefit of the procedural guarantees of the criminal law.

Brewer brushed aside Debs's claims with an opinion that blended morality, national supremacy, and the sanctity of private property. In JOHN MARSHALL-like strokes he concluded that the Constitution granted Congress ample power to oversee interstate commerce and the delivery of the mails. The President had acted properly in dispatching federal troops to quell the strikers, because the Constitution had pledged the power of the national government to preserve the social and economic order. The courts, Brewer concluded, had to protect property rights and this included the use of the CONTEMPT POWER to punish persons who refused to abide by injunctions. He disingenuously admonished Debs to seek social change through the ballot box.

Brewer in the post-*Debs* era retreated into STRICT CONSTRUCTION. This narrowing of his constitutional jurisprudence occurred at a time when most of the other Justices embraced the moderate middle class reformist ethos of the Progressive movement. Brewer, Chief Justice Fuller, and Justice RUFUS PECKHAM emerged as the conservative right wing of the Court.

Brewer disparaged Congress's resort to ENUMERATED POWERS to accomplish purposes not originally contemplated by the Framers. This contrasted sharply with his opinion in *Debs.* He dissented with Chief Justice Fuller in CHAMPION V. AMES (1903) on the ground that an act of Congress regulating interstate sale of lottery tickets threatened to destroy the TENTH AMENDMENT. More than issues of FEDERALISM troubled Brewer; his opinion reflected a socioeconomic agenda aimed at protecting property rights. In *South Carolina v. United States* (1905) he spoke for the Court in holding that the federal government could place an internal revenue tax on persons selling liquor, even though those persons acted merely as agents for the state. Brewer argued that state involvement, free from the federal TAXING POWER, in private business would lead inexorably to public ownership of important segments of the economy.

Brewer championed the concept of FREEDOM OF CONTRACT. He first articulated it for the Court in *Frisbie v. United States* (1895), and he joined with the majority two years later in ALLGEYER V. LOUISIANA when it struck down a Louisiana law affecting out-of-state insurance sales. Although the Court subsequently applied the concept unevenly, Brewer dogmatically clung to it. Between HOLDEN V. HARDY (1898) and McLean v. Arkansas (1909), Brewer routinely opposed state and federal laws designed to regulate labor. The single exception was MULLER V. OREGON (1908), and Brewer's opinion for a unanimous Court in that case ironically contributed to the new liberalism of the Progressive era.

LOUIS D. BRANDEIS in *Muller* submitted a massive brief based on extensive documentary evidence about the health and safety of women workers. It openly appealed to judicial discretion, and Brewer took the opportunity to infuse his long-held views of the dependent condition of women into constitutional doctrine. He denied an absolute right of liberty of contract; instead he concluded that under particular circumstances state legislatures might intervene in the workplace. The supposed physical disabilities of women provided the mitigating circumstances that made the Oregon ten-hour law constitutional. He emphatically argued that the Court had not retreated from substantive due process. Nevertheless, the *Muller* decision and the BRANDEIS BRIEF encouraged constitutional litigation that three decades later shattered Brewer's most cherished conservative values.

The son of a Congregationalist minister and missionary, Brewer never lost touch with his Puritan sense of character and obligation. His jurisprudence forcefully, although naively, proclaimed that material wealth and human progress went hand in hand.

KERMIT L. HALL

Bibliography

CRAMER, RALPH E. 1965 Justice Brewer and Substantive Due Process: A Conservative Court Revisited. *Vanderbilt Law Review* 18:61–96.

PAUL, ARNOLD M. 1969 David J. Brewer. Pages 1515–1549 in Leon Friedman and Fred L. Israel, eds., *The Justices of the Supreme Court, 1789–1969.* New York: Chelsea House.

BREWER v. WILLIAMS
430 U.S. 378 (1977)

This highly publicized case produced three concurring and three dissenting opinions and Justice POTTER STEWART's opinion for a 5–4 majority. Williams, who had kidnapped and murdered a child, was being transported by police who had read the MIRANDA RULES to him. But the police played on his religious beliefs. Although they had agreed not to interrogate him and he had declared that he wanted the assistance of counsel and would tell his story on seeing his counsel, a detective convinced him to show where he had buried the body so that the child could have a Christian burial. The Court reversed his conviction, ruling that the use of EVIDENCE relating to or resulting from his incriminating statements violated his RIGHT OF COUNSEL once adversary proceedings against him had begun, and he had not waived his right. (See NIX v. WILLIAMS.)

LEONARD W. LEVY

BREWSTER v. UNITED STATES
408 U.S. 501 (1972)

A 6–3 Supreme Court held that the SPEECH OR DEBATE CLAUSE does not protect a United States senator from prosecution for accepting a bribe in return for a vote on pending legislation. The clause, said Chief Justice WARREN E. BURGER, only forbids inquiry into legislative acts or the motives behind those acts. Justices WILLIAM J. BRENNAN and WILLIAM O. DOUGLAS attacked the majority's distinction between money-taking and voting and joined Justice BYRON R. WHITE who contended that the only issue was the proper forum for the trial.

DAVID GORDON

BRICKER AMENDMENT
(1952)

Senator John Bricker of Ohio in 1952 introduced a proposed constitutional amendment designed to limit the TREATY POWER and the President's power to make EXECUTIVE AGREEMENTS. The proposal was an outgrowth of widespread isolationist sentiment following the KOREAN WAR, and of fear of the possible consequences of the DOCTRINE of MISSOURI v. HOLLAND (1920) when combined with the United Nations Charter or the so-called Universal Declaration of Human Rights. The amendment, as introduced, would have declared that "a provision of a treaty or other international agreement which conflicts with this Constitution shall not be of any force or effect," and would have prohibited "self-executing" treaties by requiring separate, independently valid congressional action before a treaty could have force as "internal law."

President DWIGHT D. EISENHOWER opposed the Bricker Amendment, arguing that it would make effective conduct of FOREIGN AFFAIRS impossible and deprive the President "of his historic position as the spokesman for the nation." In February 1954, the Senate defeated the Bricker Amendment, and later it failed by one vote to give the required two-thirds approval to a weaker version written by Senator Walter F. George.

DENNIS J. MAHONEY

BRIDGES v. CALIFORNIA TIMES-MIRROR CO. v. CALIFORNIA
314 U.S. 252 (1941)

In these two companion cases, handed down by the Supreme Court on the same day, a bare majority of five Justices overturned exercises of the CONTEMPT POWER against Harry Bridges, a left-wing union leader, and the *Los Angeles Times,* then a bastion of the state's conservative business establishment, for their out-of-court remarks concerning pending cases. Bridges had been found in contempt for a telegram that predicted a longshoreman's strike in the event of a judicial decree hostile to his union; the *Times* had been punished for an editorial that threatened a judge with political reprisals if he showed leniency toward convicted labor racketeers.

Justice HUGO L. BLACK's majority opinion, joined by Justices WILLIAM O. DOUGLAS, FRANK MURPHY, STANLEY F. REED, and ROBERT H. JACKSON, held that both the telegram and the editorial had been protected by the FIRST AMENDMENT via the DUE PROCESS clause of the FOURTEENTH AMENDMENT against abridgment by the states; neither pronouncement constituted a CLEAR AND PRESENT DANGER to the administration of criminal justice in California courts. Justice FELIX FRANKFURTER, writing for himself and three others, dissented.

Frankfurter's dissent represented the original majority view when the cases were first argued in the spring of 1941. But the defection of Justice Murphy over the summer and the later addition of Justice Jackson produced a new majority for Black by October when the two cases were reargued.

MICHAEL E. PARRISH

BRIEF

Although the term may refer to a number of different kinds of legal documents, in American usage a "brief" ordinarily is a written summary of arguments presented by counsel to a court, and particularly to an appellate court. In the Supreme Court, counsel file briefs only after the Court has granted review of the case. Counsel's first opportunity to acquaint the Court with arguments in the case thus comes in the filing of a petition for a WRIT OF CERTIORARI (or, in the case of an APPEAL, a "jurisdictional statement"), and the papers opposing such a petition. By rule the Court prescribes the length and form of briefs, requires that they be printed (unless a party is permitted to proceed IN FORMA PAUPERIS, as one who cannot afford certain costs), and sets the number of copies to be filed. By the time of ORAL ARGUMENT, the Justices normally have had full opportunity to read and analyze the briefs (including reply briefs) of counsel for the parties and also for any AMICI CURIAE. At or after the argument, the Court may ask counsel to file supplemental briefs on certain issues.

KENNETH L. KARST

(SEE ALSO: *Brandeis Brief.*)

Bibliography

STERN, ROBERT L. and GRESSMAN, EUGENE 1978 *Supreme Court Practice,* 5th ed. Chaps. 6–7. Washington, D.C.: Bureau of National Affairs.

BRINEGAR v. UNITED STATES 338 U.S. 160 (1949)

In *Brinegar* the Supreme Court reaffirmed and broadened the rule in CARROLL V. UNITED STATES (1925) authorizing search of an automobile on the road where PROBABLE CAUSE exists to believe it contains contraband. The Court ignored the lack of congressional authorization for the WARRANTLESS SEARCH, a factor present, and emphasized, in *Carroll.*

JACOB W. LANDYNSKI

BRISCOE v. BANK OF COMMONWEALTH OF KENTUCKY 11 Peters 257 (1837)

This is one of the cases decided by the Supreme Court during the first term that ROGER B. TANEY was Chief Justice, and the decision panicked conservatives into the belief that the constitutional restraints which the MARSHALL COURT imposed on the states no longer counted. The case was decided during a depression year when an acute shortage of currency existed. Kentucky authorized a bank, which was state-owned and -operated, to issue notes that circulated as currency. Justice JOSEPH STORY made a powerful argument that the state notes violated the constitutional injunction against state BILLS OF CREDIT, but he spoke in lonely dissent. The Court, by a 6–1 vote, sustained the act authorizing the state bank notes. Justice JOHN MCLEAN, for the majority, assumed that the clause prohibiting bills of credit did not apply to notes not issued on the faith of a state by a CORPORATION chartered by the state. McLean's weak argument was dictated by the practical need for an expansion of the circulating medium. Economics rather than law governed the case.

LEONARD W. LEVY

BRITISH CONSTITUTION

Most eighteenth-century Englishmen believed that they were the freest people in the world. Foreign observers, such as MONTESQUIEU and Voltaire from France or Jean-Louis De Lolme from Geneva, concurred. Great Britain had somehow created and protected a unique heritage—a CONSTITUTION—that combined liberty with stability. This constitution was no single document nor even a collection of basic texts, although MAGNA CARTA, the BILL OF RIGHTS of 1689, and other prominent documents were fundamental to the tradition. It depended as much upon a series of informal understandings within the ruling class as upon the written word. And it worked. It "insures, not only the liberty, but the general satisfaction in all respects, of those who are subject to it," affirmed De Lolme. This "consideration alone affords sufficient ground to conclude without looking farther," he believed, "that it is also much more likely to be preserved from ruin." Not everyone agreed. English radicals insisted by the 1770s that only electoral reform and a reduction of royal patronage could preserve British liberty much longer. A vigorous press, the most open in Europe, subjected ministers to constant and often scathing criticism, which a literate and growing public thoroughly enjoyed. Yet until late in the prerevolutionary crisis of 1763–1775, North Americans shared the general awe for the British constitution and frequently insisted that their provincial governments displayed the same virtues.

Apologists explained Britain's constitutional achievement in both legal and humanistic terms. The role of "mixed government" in preserving liberty appealed to a broad audience. Even lawyers used this theme to organize a bewildering mass of otherwise disparate information drawn from the COMMON LAW, parliamentary statutes, and administrative practice. "And herein indeed consists the true excellence of the English government, that all parts of it form a mutual check upon each other," proclaimed Britain's foremost jurist, Sir WILLIAM BLACKSTONE, in 1765. "In the legislature, the people are a check upon the nobility, and the nobility a check upon the people; . . . while the king is a check upon both, which preserves the executive power from encroachment. And this very executive power is again checked, and kept within due bounds by the two houses. . . ."

To work properly, mixed government (or a "mixed and balanced constitution") had to embody the basic elements of the social order: the crown, consisting not just of the monarch but of the army and navy, the law courts, and all other officeholders with royal appointments; the titled aristocracy with its numerous retainers and clients; and landholding commoners. Each had deep social roots, a fixed place in government, and the power to protect itself from the others. United as king, lords, and commons (or as the one, the few, and the many of classical thought), they became a sovereign power beyond which there was no appeal except to revolution, as American colonists reluctantly admitted by 1775.

Although the king could do no wrong, his ministers could. Every royal act had to be implemented by a minister who could be held legally accountable for what he did. Into the early eighteenth century, this principle generated frequent IMPEACHMENTS, a cumbersome device for attempting to achieve responsible government. By mid-century, impeachment, like the royal veto, had fallen into disuse. Crown patronage had become so extensive that a parliamentary majority hostile to the government almost never occurred in the century after the Hanoverian Succession of 1714. When it did, or even when it merely seemed inevitable, as against Sir Robert Walpole in 1742 and Lord North in 1782, the minister usually resigned, eliminating the need for more drastic measures. When William Pitt the Younger refused to resign in the face of an implacably hostile commons majority in 1783–1784, his pertinacity alarmed many contemporaries. It seemed to portend a major crisis of the constitution until Pitt vindicated himself with a crushing victory in the general election of 1784.

British CONSTITUTIONALISM took for granted a thoroughly aristocratic society. Mixed government theory rested upon the recognition of distinct social orders, linked in countless ways through patron–client relationships. Its boast, that it provided a government of laws and not of men, had real merit, which an independent judiciary assiduously sustained. In like manner the House of Commons really did check the ambitions of the crown. The quest for responsible ministers still had not reached its nineteenth-century pattern of cabinet government, but it had moved a long way from the seventeenth-century reliance upon impeachment.

The Revolution converted American patriots from warm admirers to critics of British constitutionalism. Some, such as Carter Braxton of Virginia, hoped to change the British model as little as possible. Others, especially THOMAS PAINE, denounced the entire system of mixed government as decadent and corrupt, fit only for repudiation. Most Americans fell between these extremes. They agreed that they needed formal written constitutions. In drafting them, they discovered the necessity for other innovations. Lacking fixed social orders, they simply could not sustain a mixed government. Patron–client relations were also much weaker among the Americans, who had come to regard most crown patronage as inevitably corrupt, a sign of the decay of English liberty. Americans built governments with no organic roots in European social orders. In nearly every state, they separated the government into distinct branches—legislative, executive, and judicial—to keep each behaving legally and correctly. The SEPARATION OF POWERS thus became the American answer to the mixed and balanced constitution. This rejection of government by king, lords and commons led inexorably to a redefinition of SOVEREIGNTY as well. Americans removed sovereignty from government and lodged it with the people instead. To give this distinction substance, they invented the CONSTITUTIONAL CONVENTION and the process of popular ratification. This transformation made true FEDERALISM possible. So long as sovereignty remained an attribute of government, it had to belong to one level or the other—to Parliament or the colonial legislatures. But once it rested with the people, they became free to grant some powers to the states and others to a central government. In 1787–1788, they finally took that step.

JOHN M. MURRIN

Bibliography

BLACKSTONE, WILLIAM (1765–1769)1979 *Commentaries on the Laws of England,* ed. by Stanley N. Katz et al. Chicago: University of Chicago Press.

BREWER, JOHN 1976 *Party Ideology and Popular Politics at the Accession of George III.* Cambridge: At the University Press.

DE LOLME, J. L. 1775 *The Constitution of England, or An Account of the English Government; In which it is compared with the Republican Form of Government, and occasionally with the other Monarchies in Europe.* London: T. Spilsbury for G. Kearsley.

POCOCK, J. G. A. 1975 *The Machiavellian Moment: Florentine Political Thought and the Atlantic Republi-*

can Tradition. Princeton, N.J.: Princeton University Press.

ROBERTS, CLAYTON 1966 *The Growth of Responsible Government in Stuart England.* Cambridge: At the University Press.

BROADCASTING

Broadcasting is the electronic transmission of sounds or images from a single transmitter to all those who have the appropriate receiving equipment. It is thus a powerful medium for communicating ideas, information, opinions, and entertainment. In many countries broadcasting has become an arm of government. In the United States, however, Congress established the Federal Radio Commission in 1927 and then the Federal Communications Commission (FCC) in 1934 to award broadcasting licenses to private parties. Although a number of licenses were also designated for "public broadcasting," most were allocated to qualified applicants who promised to serve the public interest by acting as public trustees of the airwaves.

The asserted basis for government intervention in the United States was, initially, to eliminate the interference created when many different parties broadcast over the same frequency in the same area. Yet this chaos could have been eliminated with a mere registration requirement and the application of property rights concepts, allocating broadcast licenses by deed, as land is allocated. Instead, the potential interference was used to justify a complex and comprehensive regulatory scheme, embodied in the COMMUNICATIONS ACT of 1934.

In 1952, the FCC established a pattern of allocating television licenses to ensure that the maximum number of local communities would be served by their own local broadcast stations, a departure from the more centralized broadcasting systems of most other countries. Although this decision has added additional voices of local news in many communities, most local television stations affiliated with national networks to share the cost of producing programs of higher technical quality. Thus, while broadcast regulation always has been premised on the primacy of these local outlets, much of it has focused on the relationship between local stations and the powerful national broadcasting networks.

Government regulation of broadcasting obviously presents dangers to the FREEDOM OF SPEECH. Notwithstanding a statutory prohibition on censorship in the Communications Act, the existence of the licensing scheme has significantly influenced the content of programs. Holders of valuable licenses are careful not to offend the FCC, lest they jeopardize their chances of a license renewal. Raised eyebrows and stated concerns about aspects of content prevent station management from acting as freely as newspapers or magazines do. (See FAIRNESS DOCTRINE.) Indeed, only in the last quarter-century have broadcasters come to understand the dominant role that they can play in the distribution of news and information in the United States.

Until recently, the distinct constitutional status of broadcast regulation was premised on the assumption that only a limited number of broadcasting frequencies existed and on the right of the federal government to insure that this scarce commodity was used in the public interest. But recent technological developments have belied this basis for special intervention. Clearly, policy and not physics created the scarcity of frequencies, and now that economic conditions have made alternative media practical, the FCC has begun to open the broadcasting spectrum to new entrants, such as direct broadcast satellites, low-power television, and microwave frequencies.

Nevertheless, in FCC v. PACIFICA FOUNDATION (1978) the Supreme Court suggested that the extraordinary impact of broadcasting on society is itself a possible basis for special rules, at least during hours when children are likely to be listening and watching. This rationale appears to be the only remaining basis for giving broadcasting special constitutional treatment. Technology is rendering obsolete all other distinctions between broadcasting and printed material. For the receiver of ideas at a home console, all manner of data—words and hard copy and soft images—will come through the atmosphere, or over cables, or both. Distinctions based on the mode of delivery of information will have less and less validity. FCC efforts to repeal broadcast regulations, however, have often met with congressional disapproval.

MONROE E. PRICE

(SEE ALSO: *CBS, Inc. v. Federal Communications Commission, 1981.*)

Bibliography

COASE, R. H. 1959 The Federal Communications Commission. *Journal of Law & Economics* 2:1–40.

BROAD CONSTRUCTION

Broad construction, sometimes called "loose construction," is an approach to CONSTITUTIONAL INTERPRETATION emphasizing a permissive and flexible reading of the Constitution, and especially of the powers of the federal government. Like its opposite, STRICT CONSTRUCTION, the phrase has political, rather than technical or legal, significance.

ALEXANDER HAMILTON advocated broad construction in his 1791 controversy with THOMAS JEFFERSON over the constitutionality of the bill to establish the Bank of the United States. The essence of Hamilton's position, which was accepted by President GEORGE WASHINGTON and endorsed by the Supreme Court in MCCULLOCH V. MARYLAND (1819), was the doctrine of IMPLIED POWERS: that the delegated powers implied the power to enact legislation useful in carrying out those powers. The broad constructionists also argued that the NECESSARY AND PROPER CLAUSE empowered Congress to make any law convenient for the execution of any delegated power. Similarly, broad construction justified enactment of the ALIEN AND SEDITION ACTS and expenditures for INTERNAL IMPROVEMENTS.

In his Report on Manufactures (1792) Hamilton advocated a broad construction of the TAXING AND SPENDING POWER that would authorize Congress to spend federal tax money for any purpose connected with the GENERAL WELFARE, whether or not the subject of the appropriation was within Congress's ordinary LEGISLATIVE POWER. Broad construction of the COMMERCE CLAUSE and of the taxing and spending power now forms the constitutional basis for federal regulation of the lives and activities of citizens. Proponents of broad construction argue that the Constitution must be adapted to changing times and conditions. However, a thoroughgoing broad construction is clearly incompatible with the ideas of LIMITED GOVERNMENT and CONSTITUTIONALISM.

The Constitution both grants power to the government and imposes limitations on the exercise of governmental power. Consistent usage would describe the expansive reading of either, and not just of the former, as broad construction. Indeed, President RICHARD M. NIXON frequently criticized the WARREN COURT for its "broad construction" of constitutional provisions guaranteeing the procedural rights of criminal defendants. The more common usage, however, reserves the term for constitutional interpretation permitting a wider scope for governmental activity.

In the late 1970s and the 1980s, broad construction was largely displaced by a new theory of constitutional jurisprudence called "noninterpretivism." Unlike broad construction, which depends upon a relationship between government action and some particular clause of the Constitution, noninterpretivism justifies government action on the basis of values presumed to underlie the constitutional text and to be superior to the actual words in the document.

DENNIS J. MAHONEY

Bibliography

AGRESTO, JOHN 1984 *The Supreme Court and Constitutional Democracy.* Ithaca, N.Y.: Cornell University Press.

BROADRICK v. OKLAHOMA 413 U.S. 601 (1973)

The FIRST AMENDMENT doctrine of OVERBREADTH, developed by the WARREN COURT in the 1960s, came under increasing criticism from within the Supreme Court. In *Broadrick,* that criticism culminated in the invention of a "substantial overbreadth" DOCTRINE.

Oklahoma law restricted the political activities of state civil servants; such employees were forbidden to "take part in the management or affairs of any political party or in any political campaign," except to vote or express opinions privately. Three civil servants sued in a federal district court for a declaration that the law was unconstitutional for VAGUENESS and overbreadth. The district court upheld the law, and on direct review the Supreme Court affirmed, 5–4.

Justice BYRON R. WHITE, for the majority, concluded that the overbreadth doctrine should not be used to invalidate a statute regulating conduct (as opposed to the expression of particular messages or viewpoints) unless the law's overbreadth is "substantial, . . . judged in relation to the statute's plainly legitimate sweep." Although Oklahoma's law was theoretically capable of constitutionally impermissible application to some activities (the use of political buttons or bumper stickers were arguable examples), it was not substantially overbroad—not likely to be applied to a substantial number of cases of constitutionally protected expression. Thus the law's overbreadth did not threaten a significant CHILLING EFFECT on protected speech, and could be cured through "case-by-case analysis" rather than invalidation on its face. Appellants had conceded that their own conduct (campaigning for a superior state official) could be prohibited under a narrowly drawn statute.

Justice William J. Brennan, for three dissenters, called the decision "a wholly unjustified retreat" from established principles requiring facial invalidation of laws capable of applications to prohibit constitutionally protected speech. Justice WILLIAM O. DOUGLAS, dissenting, generally attacked the validity of laws restricting public employees' political activity.

On the same day the Court reaffirmed, 6–3, the validity of the HATCH ACT, which similarly restricts federal civil servants, in *Civil Service Commission v. National Association of Letter Carriers* (1973).

KENNETH L. KARST

BROCKETT v. SPOKANE ARCADES, INC.
472 U.S. (1985)

The *Brockett* opinion refined the DOCTRINE of OVERBREADTH in FIRST AMENDMENT cases. A Washington statute provided both civil and criminal sanctions against "moral nuisances"—businesses purveying "lewd" matter. Various purveyors of sexually oriented books and films sued in federal district court for a DECLARATORY JUDGMENT that the law was unconstitutional and an INJUNCTION against its enforcement. That court denied relief, but the court of appeals held the law INVALID ON ITS FACE. The defect, the court said, was the law's definition of "lewd" matter, which followed the Supreme Court's formula defining OBSCENITY, but defined the term "prurient" to include material that "incites lasciviousness or lust." That definition was substantially overbroad, the court said, because it included material that aroused only a normal, healthy interest in sex.

A 6–2 Supreme Court reversed, in an opinion by Justice BYRON R. WHITE. The Court agreed that, under MILLER V. CALIFORNIA (1973), a work could not be held obscene if its only appeal were to "normal sexual reactions" and accepted the lower court's interpretation that "lust" would embrace such a work. However, Justice White said, these plaintiffs were not entitled to a facial invalidation of the law. They had alleged that their own films and books were not obscene, but were constitutionally protected. In such a case, there is "no want of a proper party to challenge the statute, no concern that an attack on the statute will be unduly delayed or protected speech discouraged." The proper course would be to declare the statute's partial invalidity—here, to declare that the law would be invalid in application to material appealing to "normal . . . sexual appetites." In contrast, when the state seeks to enforce such a partially invalid statute against a person whose own speech or conduct is constitutionally *unprotected,* the proper course, assuming the law's substantial overbreadth, is to invalidate the law entirely. The result is ironic, but explainable. In the latter case, if the court did not hold the law invalid on its face, there would be a serious risk of a CHILLING EFFECT on the potential protected speech of others who were not in court.

The propriety of partial invalidation depended on the SEVERABILITY of the Washington statute, but that issue was easily resolved: the law contained a severability clause, and surely the legislature would not have abandoned the statute just because it could not be applied to material appealing to normal sexual interests.

Justice SANDRA DAY O'CONNOR joined the OPINION OF THE COURT but argued separately, joined by Chief Justice WARREN E. BURGER and Justice WILLIAM H. REHNQUIST, that the case was appropriate for federal court ABSTENTION, awaiting guidance from the state courts on the statutory meaning of "lust." Justice WILLIAM J. BRENNAN, joined by Justice THURGOOD MARSHALL, dissented, agreeing with the court of appeals.

KENNETH L. KARST

BRONSON v. KINZIE
1 Howard 311 (1843)

As a result of the depression of 1837 many states passed DEBTORS' RELIEF LEGISLATION to assist property holders who were losing their farms and homes by foreclosure. Illinois, for example, provided that foreclosed property could not be sold at auction unless it brought two-thirds of its appraised value, and that the property sold at foreclosure might be repurchased by the debtor within one year at the purchase price plus ten percent. Such legislation, which operated retroactively on existing contracts, did not directly affect their obligation, the duties of the contracting parties toward each other; it affected their remedies, the means by which the OBLIGATION OF CONTRACTS can be enforced.

By a vote of 7–1 the Supreme Court held the Illinois statutes unconstitutional on the ground that they violated the CONTRACT CLAUSE. The opinion of Chief Justice ROGER B. TANEY remained the leading one on the subject for ninety years, until distinguished away by HOME BUILDING LOAN ASSOCIATION V. BLAISDELL (1934). Taney conceded that the states have power to change the remedies available to creditors confronted by defaulting debtors, on condition that the changed remedy does not impair the obligation of existing contracts. "But if that effect is produced, it is immaterial whether it is done by acting on the remedy or directly on the contract itself." Taney reasoned that the rights of a contracting party could be "seriously impaired by binding the proceedings with new conditions and restrictions, so as to make the remedy hardly worth pursuing." In this case he found that if the state could allow the debtor to repurchase his lost property within a year, it might allow still more time, making difficult a determination of how much time the state might allow. Taney did not say why one year was too long, or why the Court could not fix a rule. He did say that the state requirement fixing two-thirds of the value as the minimum purchasing price "would frequently render any sale altogether impossible." He offered no test by which the state could know whether a change in the remedy adversely affected the obligation of a contract. Justice JOSEPH STORY privately wrote, "There are times when the Court is called upon to support every sound constitutional doctrine in support of the rights of property and of creditors."

LEONARD W. LEVY

BROOM, JACOB
(1752–1810)

Jacob Broom, a member of the CONSTITUTIONAL CONVENTION OF 1787 from Delaware, was a signer of the Constitution. He spoke briefly several times, exhibiting a desire to protect small-state interests and a distrust of a strong executive. When some delegates wanted to dissolve the Convention over the issue of REPRESENTATION, Broom argued against them.

DENNIS J. MAHONEY

BROWN, HENRY BILLINGS
(1836–1913)

Henry Billings Brown served on the Supreme Court from 1890 to 1906. During that period, he wrote more than 450 majority opinions and dissenting or CONCURRING OPINIONS in some fifty other cases, many of which had contemporary and historical significance. Justice Brown's jurisprudence revealed some hesitance, some ambivalence, even contradiction as he struggled to perform the judicial function.

The glorification of private property and free competition reflected one dimension of Brown's thought. He considered the right of private property "the first step in the emergence of the civilized man from the condition of the utter savage," and he joined the majority in LOCHNER V. NEW YORK (1905), striking down a state law that limited the hours of bakery workers to a maximum of sixty per week or ten per day. Yet Brown usually construed the STATE POLICE POWER broadly and sanctioned legislative modification of laissez faire principles. In HOLDEN V. HARDY (1898) Brown upheld Utah's maximum hours act for miners, rejecting arguments that the state had violated the CONTRACT CLAUSE and denied property without DUE PROCESS. He looked realistically at the disparity in bargaining position between employer and employee, recognizing that fear of losing their jobs prompted laborers to perform work detrimental to their health. Concern for public health and inequality of bargaining power justified the state regulation.

POLLOCK V. FARMERS' LOAN & TRUST CO. (1895) also revealed Brown's willingness to permit legislative regulation of private property. When the Court struck down a congressional tax on incomes, Brown eloquently dissented, protesting that the decision ignored a century of "consistent and undeviating" precedent and represented "a surrender of the TAXING POWER to the moneyed class." Although opponents of the tax had raised the specter of socialism to dissuade Congress from raising funds, Brown construed *Pollock* as "the first step toward the submergence of the liberties of the people in a sordid despotism of wealth."

Brown supported the gradual development of federal power as a necessary concomitant to a modern industrial economy. He also wrote many of the Court's ADMIRALTY opinions, broadly interpreting federal JURISDICTION and the scope of federal maritime law. Brown similarly endorsed an expansive federal power under the COMMERCE CLAUSE, joining, for example, Justice OLIVER WENDELL HOLMES's classic statement of the STREAM OF COMMERCE doctrine in SWIFT & CO. V. UNITED STATES (1905).

Brown's CRIMINAL PROCEDURE and CIVIL LIBERTIES opinions reflected the general attitude of late nineteenth-, early twentieth-century America toward criminals, blacks, and women. In BROWN V. WALKER (1896) he held that the Fifth Amendment RIGHT AGAINST SELF-INCRIMINATION was not violated if the state coerced testimony and afforded IMMUNITY from criminal prosecution. Social disgrace and ridicule might result from invoking the Fifth Amendment, but a "self-confessed criminal" did not deserve protection from his neighbors' negative judgment.

Brown's callousness to CIVIL RIGHTS is manifest in one of the most infamous decisions of the nineteenth century—PLESSY V. FERGUSON (1896). For the Court, Brown upheld a Louisiana statute requiring railroads to provide "equal but separate accommodations" for "white" and "colored" patrons. In a remarkably disingenuous opinion, he reasoned that the statute had "no tendency to destroy the legal equality of the two races" and did "not necessarily imply the inferiority of either race to the other." Brown rejected a Fourteenth Amendment EQUAL PROTECTION challenge, citing as precedent state cases decided prior to passage of the FOURTEENTH AMENDMENT. To Brown the Louisiana law was a reasonable legislative decision consistent with "the established usages, customs and traditions of the people." In other words, Brown conceived civil rights as adequately protected in the legislative process; he did not envision civil rights as enforceable by a minority against the majority. *Plessy* mirrored the late nineteenth-century's belief in physical and social differences between the races. Contemporary scientific and social science thought considered the Negro and Caucasian races as biologically separate and the Caucasian race as superior. In *Plessy,* Brown constitutionalized the prevailing prejudices of his era.

ROBERT JEROME GLENNON

Bibliography

GLENNON, ROBERT JEROME 1973 Justice Henry Billings Brown: Values in Tension. *University of Colorado Law Review* 44:553–604.

BROWN v. ALLEN
344 U.S. 443 (1953)

In *Brown v. Allen* the Supreme Court rejected the claim that North Carolina practiced unconstitutional JURY DISCRIMINATION. Speaking through Justice STANLEY F. REED, the Court held that the state did not deny EQUAL PROTECTION to blacks by randomly selecting jury panels from lists of property taxpayers, even though there was still a significantly smaller proportion of black jurors than black citizens. The Court declined to consider whether selecting for jury duty those with the most property constituted WEALTH DISCRIMINATION. Justices HUGO L. BLACK, FELIX FRANKFURTER, and WILLIAM O. DOUGLAS, dissenting, argued that the tax-list selection technique was not a "complete neutralization of RACIAL DISCRIMINATION."

DENNIS J. MAHONEY

BROWN v. BOARD OF EDUCATION
347 U.S. 483 (1954)
349 U.S. 294 (1955)

In the dual perspectives of politics and constitutional development, *Brown v. Board of Education* was the Supreme Court's most important decision of the twentieth century. In four cases consolidated for decision, the Court held that racial SEGREGATION of public school children, commanded or authorized by state law, violated the FOURTEENTH AMENDMENT's guarantee of the EQUAL PROTECTION OF THE LAWS. A companion decision, BOLLING V. SHARPE (1954), held that school segregation in the DISTRICT OF COLUMBIA violated the Fifth Amendment's guarantee of DUE PROCESS OF LAW.

Brown illustrates how pivotal historical events, viewed in retrospect, can take on the look of inevitability. To the actors involved, however, the decision was anything but a foregone conclusion. The principal judicial precedent, after all, was PLESSY V. FERGUSON (1896), which had upheld the racial segregation of railroad passengers, partly on the basis of an earlier Massachusetts decision upholding school segregation. More recent Supreme Court decisions had invalidated various forms of segregation in higher education without deciding whether *Plessy* should be overruled. Just a few months before the first *Brown* decision, Robert Leflar and Wylie Davis outlined eleven different courses open to the Supreme Court in the cases before it.

The four cases we now call *Brown* were the culmination of a twenty-year litigation strategy of the NAACP, aimed at the ultimate invalidation of segregation in education. (See SEPARATE BUT EQUAL DOCTRINE.) Part of that strategy had already succeeded; the Supreme Court had ordered the admission of black applicants to state university law schools, and had invalidated a state university's segregation of a black graduate student. The opinions in those cases had emphasized intangible elements of educational quality, particularly the opportunity to associate with persons of other races. (See SWEATT V. PAINTER, 1950). The doctrinal ground was thus prepared for the Court to strike down the segregation of elementary and secondary schools—if the Court was ready to occupy that ground.

The Justices were sensitive to the political repercussions their decision might have. The cases were argued in December 1952, and in the ordinary course would have been decided by the close of the Court's term in the following June or July. Instead of deciding, however, the Court set the five cases for reargument in the following term and proposed a series of questions to be argued, centering on the history of the adoption of the Fourteenth Amendment and on potential remedies if the Court should rule against segregation. The available evidence suggests that the Court was divided on the principal issue in the cases—the constitutionality of separate but equal public schools—and that Justice FELIX FRANKFURTER played a critical role in persuading his brethren to put the case over so that the incoming administration of President DWIGHT D. EISENHOWER might present its views as AMICUS CURIAE. It is clear that the discussion at the Court's CONFERENCE on the cases had dealt not only with the merits of the black children's claims but also with the possible reaction of the white South to a decision overturning school segregation. Proposing questions for the reargument, Justice Frankfurter touched on the same concern in a memorandum to his colleagues: ". . . for me the ultimate crucial factor in the problem presented by these cases is psychological—the adjustment of men's minds and actions to the unfamiliar and the unpleasant."

When Justice Frankfurter wrote of "the adjustment of men's minds," he had whites in mind. For blacks, Jim Crow was an unpleasant reality that was all too familiar. It is not surprising that the Justices centered their political concerns on the white South; lynchings of blacks would have been a vivid memory for any Justice who had come to maturity before 1930. In any event the Court handled the *Brown* cases from beginning to end with an eye on potential disorder and violence among southern whites.

Chief Justice FRED M. VINSON, who had written the opinions invalidating segregation in higher education, appeared to some of his brethren to oppose extending the reasoning of those opinions to segregation in the public schools. Late in the summer of 1953, five weeks before the scheduled reargument of *Brown*, Vinson died suddenly from a heart attack. With *Brown* in mind, Justice Frankfurter said, in a private remark that has since become glaringly public, "This is the first indication I have ever had that there is a God."

Vinson's replacement was the governor of California, EARL WARREN. At the *Brown* reargument, which was put off until December, he did not say much. In conference, however, Warren made clear his view that the separate but equal doctrine must be abandoned and the cases decided in favor of the black children's equal protection claim. At the same time, he though the Court should avoid "precipitous action that would inflame more than necessary." The conference disclosed an apparent majority for the Chief Justice's position, but in a case of such political magnitude, a unanimous decision was devoutly to be wished. The vote was thus postponed, while the Chief Justice and Justice Frankfurter sought for ways to unite the Court. Near-unanimity seems to have been achieved by agreement on a gradual enforcement of the Court's decision. A vote of 8–1 emerged late in the winter, with Justice ROBERT H. JACKSON preparing to file a separate concurrence. When Jackson suffered a heart attack, the likelihood of his pursuing an independent doctrinal course diminished. The Chief Justice circulated a draft opinion in early May, and at last Justice STANLEY F. REED was persuaded of the importance of avoiding division in the Court. On May 17, 1954, the Court announced its decision. Justice Jackson joined his brethren at the bench, to symbolize the Court's unanimity.

The opinion of the Court, by Chief Justice Warren, was calculatedly limited in scope, unilluminating as to doctrinal implications, and bland in tone. The South was not lectured, and no broad pronouncements were made concerning the fate of Jim Crow. *Plessy* was not even overruled—not then. Instead, the opinion highlighted two points of distinction: the change in the status of black persons in the years since *Plessy*, and the present-day importance of public education for the individual and for American society. Borrowing from the opinion of the lower court in the Kansas case (*Brown* itself), the Chief Justice concluded that school segregation produced feelings of inferiority in black children, and thus interfered with their motivation to learn; as in the graduate education cases, such intangibles were critical in evaluating the equality of the educational opportunity offered to blacks. In *Plessy*, the Court had brushed aside the argument that segregation stamped blacks with a mark of inferiority; the *Brown* opinion, on the contrary, stated that modern psychological knowledge verified the argument, and in a supporting footnote cited a number of social science authorities. (See LEGISLATIVE FACTS.) Segregated education was inherently unequal; the separate but equal doctrine thus had no place in education.

In the ordinary equal protection case, a finding of state-imposed inequality is only part of the inquiry; the Court goes on to examine into justifications offered by the state for treating people unequally. In these cases the southern states had argued that segregation promoted the quality of education, the health of pupils, and the tranquillity of schools. The *Brown* opinion omitted entirely any reference to these asserted justifications. By looking only to the question of inequality, the Court followed the pattern set in earlier cases applying the separate but equal doctrine. However, in its opinion in the companion case from the District of Columbia, the Court added this remark: "Segregation in public education is not reasonably related to any proper governmental objective. . . ." With those conclusory words, the Court announced that further inquiry into justifications for school segregation was foreclosed.

The *Brown* opinion thus presented a near-minimum political target, one that could have been reduced only by the elimination of its social science citations. Everyone understood the importance of educational opportunity. Nothing was intimated about segregation in PUBLIC ACCOMMODATIONS or state courthouses, hospitals, or prisons. Most important of all, the Court issued no orders to the defendant school boards, but set the cases for yet another argument at the next term on questions of remedy: should segregation be ended at once, or gradually? Should the Supreme Court itself frame the decrees, or leave that task to the lower courts or a SPECIAL MASTER?

A full year passed before the Court issued its remedial opinion. *Brown II,* as that opinion is sometimes called, not only declined to order an immediate end to segregation but also failed to set deadlines. Instead, the Court told the lower courts to require the school boards to "make a prompt and reasonable start" toward "compliance at the earliest practicable date," taking into account such factors as buildings, transportation systems, personnel, and redrawing of attendance district lines. The lower courts should issue decrees to the end of admitting the plaintiff children to the schools "on a racially nondiscriminatory basis with ALL DELIBERATE SPEED. . . ."

This language looked like—and was—a political compromise; something of the sort had been contemplated from the beginning by Chief Justice Warren. Despite the Court's statement that constitutional principles could not yield to disagreement, the white South was told, in effect, that it might go on denying blacks their constitutional rights for an indefinite time, while it got used to the idea of stopping. Unquestionably, whatever the Court determined in 1954 or 1955, it would take time to build the sense of interracial community in the South and elsewhere. But in *Brown II* the Court sacrificed an important part of its one legitimate claim to political and moral authority: the defense of principle. A southern intransigent might say: after all, if *Brown* really did stand for a national principle, surely the principle would not be parceled out for separate negotiation in thousands of school districts over an indefinite time. The chief responses of the white South to the Court's gradualism were defiance and evasion. (See DESEGREGATION.) In 1956 a "Southern Manifesto," signed by nineteen Senators and 82 members of the House of Representatives, denounced *Brown* as resting on "personal political and social ideas" rather than the Constitution. One Mississippi senator, seeking to capitalize on the country's recent anticommunist fervor, called racial integration "a radical, pro-Communist political movement." President Eisenhower gave the decision no political support, promising only to carry out the law of the land.

Criticism of another sort came from Herbert Wechsler, a Columbia law professor with impressive credentials as a CIVIL RIGHTS advocate. Wechsler argued that the Supreme Court had not offered a principled explanation of the *Brown* decision—had not supported its repeated assertion that segregation harmed black school children. Charles L. Black, Jr., a Texan and a Yale professor who had worked on the NAACP briefs in *Brown,* replied that all Southerners knew that Jim Crow was designed to maintain white supremacy. School segregation, as part of that system, must fall before a constitutional principle forbidding states deliberately to disadvantage a racial group. This defense of the *Brown* decision is irrefutable. But the *Brown* opinion had not tied school segregation to the system of Jim Crow, because Chief Justice Warren's strategy had been to avoid sweeping pronouncements in the interest of obtaining a unanimous Court and minimizing southern defiance and violence.

Within a few years, however, in a series of PER CURIAM orders consisting only of citations to *Brown,* the Court had invalidated state-supported segregation in all its forms. In one case *Plessy* was implicitly overruled. Jim Crow was thus buried without ceremony. Yet the intensity of the southern resistance to *Brown* shows that no one had been deceived into thinking that the decision was limited to education. Not only did the occasion deserve a clear statement of the unconstitutionality of the system of racial segregation; political practicalities also called for such a statement. The Supreme Court's ability to command respect for its decisions depends on its candid enunciation of the principles underlying those decisions.

Both *Brown* opinions, then, were evasions. Even so, *Brown* was a great decision, a personal triumph for a great Chief Justice. For if *Brown* was a culmination, it was also a beginning. The decision was the catalyst for a political movement that permanently altered race relations in America. (See SIT-IN; CIVIL RIGHTS ACT OF 1964; VOTING RIGHTS ACT OF 1965.) The success of the civil rights movement encouraged challenges to other systems of domination and dependency: systems affecting women, ALIENS, illegitimate children, the handicapped, homosexuals. Claims to racial equality forced a reexamination of a wide range of institutional arrangements throughout American society. In constitutional/doctrinal terms, *Brown* was the critical event in the modern development of the equal protection clause as an effective guarantee of equal CITIZENSHIP, a development that led in turn to the rebirth of SUBSTANTIVE DUE PROCESS as a guarantee of fundamental personal liberties. After *Brown,* the federal judiciary saw itself in a new light, and all Americans could see themselves as members of a national community.

KENNETH L. KARST

Bibliography

BELL, DERRICK 1980 Brown v. Board of Education and the Interest-Convergence Dilemma. *Harvard Law Review* 93:518–533.

BLACK, CHARLES L., JR. 1960 The Lawfulness of the Segregation Decisions. *Yale Law Journal* 69:421–430.

KLUGER, RICHARD 1975 *Simple Justice.* New York: Knopf.

LEFLAR, ROBERT A. and DAVIS, WYLIE H. 1954 Segregation in the Public Schools—1953. *Harvard Law Review* 67:377–435.

WECHSLER, HERBERT 1959 Toward Neutral Principles of Constitutional Law. *Harvard Law Review* 73:1–35.

WILKINSON, J. HARVIE, III 1979 *From Brown to Bakke.* New York: Oxford University Press.

BROWN v. MARYLAND
12 Wheat. 419 (1827)

The Court, over the sole dissent of Justice SMITH THOMPSON, held unconstitutional a state act imposing an annual license tax of $50 on all importers of foreign merchandise. Since the state charged only $8 for a retailer's license, the Court could have found that the license tax on wholesalers of imported goods discriminated against FOREIGN COMMERCE, but Chief Justice JOHN MARSHALL, for the Court, expressly declined to give an opinion on the discrimination issue. Marshall rested his opinion partly on a finding that the license tax constituted a state IMPOST or customs duty on imports, contrary to the IMPORT-EXPORT CLAUSE of Article I, section 16, clause 2, of the Constitution. The sale of an import, Marshall reasoned, is inseparably related to bringing it into the country under congressional tariff acts and paying the duty on it.

Marshall had still greater interests to protect. He turned this simple case of a prohibited state impost, or of a state discrimination against foreign commerce, into an opportunity to lay down a rule explaining when federal authority over foreign commerce ceased and the state power to tax its internal commerce began: as long as the importer retained the property in his possession in the "original package" in which he imported it, federal authority remained exclusive; but when the importer broke the package and mixed the merchandise with other property, it became subject to STATE TAXATION. Marshall therefore found that the state act was a violation of the COMMERCE CLAUSE interpreted as vesting an exclusive national power, as well as a violation of the import-export clause, and Marshall added, "we suppose the principles laid down in this case, to apply equally to importations from a sister State."

In the time of Chief Justice ROGER B. TANEY (who represented the state in *Brown*), the Court rejected that supposition and still later ruled that the ORIGINAL PACKAGE DOCTRINE applies only to foreign commerce. Although many imports, like crude oil and natural gas, no longer come in "packages," making the doctrine inapplicable, a state tax on foreign commerce still in transit remains an unconstitutional impost. But little remains today of the original package doctrine. In MICHELIN TIRE CORP. V. WAGES (1976) the Court abandoned the doctrine in cases involving nondiscriminatory *ad valorem* property taxes, ruling that such taxes, even on goods imported from abroad and remaining in their original packages, do not fall within the constitutional prohibition against state taxation of imports.

LEONARD W. LEVY

BROWN v. MISSISSIPPI
297 U.S. 278 (1936)

In this landmark decision, the Court for the first time held unconstitutional on DUE PROCESS grounds the use of a coerced confession in a state criminal proceeding. In a unanimous opinion reflecting outrage at the judicial system of Mississippi as well as at its law enforcement officers, Chief Justice CHARLES EVANS HUGHES found difficult to imagine methods "more revolting to the sense of justice" than those used by the state in this case. The record showed that prolonged "physical torture" of black suspects extorted their confessions; they were tried in a rush without adequate defense, were convicted solely on the basis of the confessions which they repudiated, and were quickly sentenced to death. The transcript read "like pages torn from some medieval account. . . ."

Yet the state supreme court, over dissenting opinions, had sustained the convictions on the basis of arguments later used by the state before the Supreme Court: under TWINING V. JERSEY (1908) the Constitution did not protect against compulsory self-incrimination in state courts, and counsel for the prisoners had not made a timely motion for exclusion of the confessions after proving coercion. To these arguments, Hughes replied, first, "Compulsion by torture to extort a confession is a different matter. . . . The rack and torture chamber may not be substituted for the witness stand" except by a denial of due process of law. The state could regulate its own CRIMINAL PROCEDURE only on condition that it observed the fundamental principles of liberty and justice. Second, Hughes regarded counsel's technical error as irrelevant compared to the fact that the wrong committed by the state was so fundamental that it made the whole proceeding a "mere pretense of a trial" and rendered the convictions void.

Brown did not revolutionalize state criminal procedure or abolish third-degree methods. But it proved to be the foundation for thirty years of decisions on POLICE INTERROGATION AND CONFESSIONS, finally resulting in an overruling of *Twining* and a constitutional law intended by the FOURTEENTH AMENDMENT.

LEONARD W. LEVY

BROWN v. SOCIALIST WORKERS '74 CAMPAIGN COMMITTEE
459 U.S. 87 (1982)

In BUCKLEY V. VALEO (1976) the Supreme Court refused to recognize a blanket FIRST AMENDMENT right of minor political parties to keep their contributors and their disbursements confidential. The Court said, however, that such a right would be recognized in particular cases when parties could show that political privacy was essential to their exercise of First Amendment rights. *Brown* was such a case. The party had shown a "reasonable probability of threats, harassment, or reprisals" in the event of disclosure. The Court thus held, unanimously, that Ohio could not compel the disclosure of contributions to the party, and held, 6–3, that the same logic protected against compulsory disclosure of the party's expenditures, such as wages or reimbursements paid to party members and supporters.

KENNETH L. KARST

BROWN v. UNITED STATES
381 U.S. 437 (1965)

This decision revitalized the Constitution's prohibitions on BILLS OF ATTAINDER. The TAFT-HARTLEY Act had made it a crime for a member of the Communist party to be a labor union officer. Brown, convicted under this law, argued that it violated the FIRST AMENDMENT, the Fifth Amendment's DUE PROCESS clause, and Article I, section 9, which forbids Congress to pass a bill of attainder. A 5–4 Supreme Court agreed with the latter argument. Citing CUMMINGS V. MISSOURI (1867), EX PARTE GARLAND (1867), and UNITED STATES V. LOVETT (1946), Chief Justice EARL WARREN said that the law amounted to legislative punishment of a specifically designated group. Congress might weed dangerous persons out of the labor movement, but it must use rules of general applicability, leaving adjudication to other tribunals. (See also IRREBUTTABLE PRESUMPTIONS.) Justice BYRON R. WHITE, for the dissenters, argued that Congress had shown no punitive purpose, but had intended to prevent future political strikes.

KENNETH L. KARST

BROWN v. WALKER
161 U.S. 591 (1896)

After COUNSELMAN V. HITCHCOCK (1892) Congress authorized transactional immunity to compel the testimony of anyone invoking the RIGHT AGAINST SELF INCRIMINATION in a federal proceeding. Appellant, despite a grant of immunity, refused to testify before a GRAND JURY investigating criminal violations of federal law. He argued that Congress could not supersede a constitutional provision by a mere statute and that the statute did not immunize him from all liabilities that might ensue from incriminating admissions. The Supreme Court, by a 5–4 majority, held that the act provided an immunity commensurate with the scope of the Fifth Amendment right and therefore constitutionally supplanted it.

Justice HENRY B. BROWN, for the Court, declared that if the compulsory disclosures could not possibly expose the witness to criminal jeopardy, the demand of the Fifth Amendment was satisfied. The statute did not have to protect him from every possible detriment that might result from his evidence, as long as it exempted the witness from prosecution for any crime to which he testified under compulsion. If his testimony "operates as a complete pardon for the offense to which it relates,—a statute absolutely securing to him such immunity from prosecution would satisfy the demands of the clause of question." But he could be compelled to be a witness against himself if a statute of limitations barred prosecution, if his evidence merely brought him into public disgrace, or if he had already received a pardon or absolute immunity and thus stood with respect to such offense "as if it had never been committed."

The dissenters argued that the act was unconstitutional because the amendment protected the witness from compulsory testimony that would expose him to INFAMY even in the absence of a prosecution. They added that the act also exposed the witness to a possible prosecution for perjury, which could not possibly be imputed if he did not have to testify. (See IMMUNITY GRANTS.)

LEONARD W. LEVY

BRYCE, JAMES
(1838–1922)

Educated at Oxford University and called to the bar at Lincoln's Inn, James Bryce was Regius Professor of Civil Law at Oxford from 1870 until 1893. A member of the Liberal party, he served in the House of Commons (1874–1906) and was a member of four cabinets. His writings on American government and politics were influential both in America and abroad and he was even elected president of the American Political Science Association.

Bryce's most noted work on America was *The American Commonwealth* (1888; last revised, 1910). Rejecting the model of ALEXIS DE TOCQUEVILLE's *Democracy in America,* Bryce set out to describe the American experience without deriving from it any general theories about democracy. A well-educated and widely traveled British politician, Bryce was most impressed by the very constitutional principles Americans frequently take for granted: FEDERALISM, SEPARATION OF POWERS, JUDICIAL REVIEW, and a fixed, written FUNDAMENTAL LAW beyond the amending power of the legislature. He thought the diffusion and limitation of governmental power in America were valuable safeguards against despotism, and that bicameralism and separation of powers provided the opportunity for full discussion of important measures; but he saw two great defects: the possibility that deadlock would prevent prompt action and the difficulty of fixing personal responsibility for policies and actions.

One of Bryce's important contributions as an empirical political scientist was his treatment of the POLITICAL PARTIES. The parties, he observed, constituted "a sort of second and unofficial government" directing the affairs of the legally constituted institutions. The party system counteracted the effects of federalism and separation of powers by linking the interests of legislative and executive officers and by making the results of local elections dependent upon national issues.

Bryce published thirteen other books, including *Studies in History and Jurisprudence* (1901) and *Modern Democracies* (1921), which present American government in comparative perspective, and numerous articles. He was the British ambassador to the United States from 1907 until 1913, and upon his retirement was elevated to the peerage as Viscount Bryce.

DENNIS J. MAHONEY

Bibliography

IONS, EDMUND S. 1970 *James Bryce and American Democracy, 1870–1920.* New York: Humanities Press.

BUCHANAN, JAMES
(1791–1868)

A Pennsylvania attorney, James Buchanan was a congressman (1821–1831), minister to Russia and Britain (1832–1834, 1853–1856), senator (1834–1845), secretary of state (1845–1849), and President (1856–1861). In 1831 Buchanan thwarted a repeal of the Supreme Court's APPELLATE JURISDICTION under section 25 of the JUDICIARY ACT OF 1789. The rest of his prepresidential career reflected his Democratic party regularity and support of STATES' RIGHTS. He attacked Chief Justice ROGER B. TANEY's nationalistic opinion in *Holmes v. Jennison* (1840), denounced the HOLDING in MCCULLOCH V. MARYLAND (1819), and urged a reduction in the number of Supreme Court Justices. In 1844 he declined an appointment to the Court. A close friend of many Southerners, Buchanan hated ABOLITIONISTS, always supported constitutional and congressional protection for slavery, and was the archetypal doughface—the northern man with southern principles. This outlook continued to his presidency and helped undermine it.

Before his inaugural address, Buchanan conversed with Chief Justice Taney while the audience looked on. In his address Buchanan observed that the question of SLAVERY IN THE TERRITORIES was of "little practical importance," in part because it was a "judicial question, which legitimately belongs to the Supreme Court of the United States, before whom it is now pending, and will, it is understood, be speedily and finally settled. To their decision, in common with all good citizens, I shall cheerfully submit. . . ." Two days later the decision was announced in DRED SCOTT V. SANDFORD (1857), and it appeared to many that Taney improperly had informed Buchanan of what the pending decision would hold. For over a month before the decision Buchanan had communicated with Justice JOHN CATRON of Tennessee and ROBERT C. GRIER of Pennsylvania about the case, successfully urging them to support Taney's position that the MISSOURI COMPROMISE was unconstitutional. Two years later, in his "House Divided Speech," ABRAHAM LINCOLN would accuse Buchanan of conspiring with Taney, President FRANKLIN PIERCE, and Senator STEPHEN A. DOUGLAS to force slavery into the territories. Although there was no conspiracy on this issue, Buchanan promoted slavery in the territories. In 1858 he unsuccessfully attempted to bring Kansas into the Union under the proslavery LECOMPTON CONSTITUTION. His support of slavery and southern Democrats helped split the party in 1860 over Douglas's nomination.

After Lincoln's election Buchanan presided over the disintegration of the Union, failing to act in any meaningful way. In December 1860 he blamed the crisis on the "long-continued and intemperate interference of the Northern people with the question of slavery in the Southern States. . . ." He asserted the Union "was intended to be perpetual," and that SECESSION "is revolution," but he also concluded that neither Congress nor the President had any constitutional authority "to coerce a State into submission which is attempting to withdraw" from the Union. The Union, he declared, rested "on public opinion." Buchanan spent his last few months in office vainly seeking a compromise which the South no longer wanted and whose terms the North found unacceptable. During these months Buchanan failed to protect military positions in the South, preserve national authority there, or prepare the nation for the impending war. Buchanan bequeathed to Lincoln a Union from which seven states had departed.

PAUL FINKELMAN

Bibliography

SMITH, ELBERT B. 1975 *The Presidency of James Buchanan.* Lawrence: University of Kansas Press.

BUCHANAN v. WARLEY 245 U.S. 60 (1917)

Buchanan was the most important race relations case between PLESSY V. FERGUSON (1896) and SHELLEY V. KRAEMER (1948). A number of southern border cities had adopted residential SEGREGATION ordinances. NAACP attorneys constructed a TEST CASE challenging the constitutionality of Louisville's ordinance, which forbade a "colored" person to move into a house on a block in which a majority of residences were occupied by whites, and vice versa. A black agreed to buy from a white a house on a majority-white block, provided that the buyer had the legal right to occupy the house. The seller sued to compel performance of the contract; the buyer defended on the basis of the ordinance. The Kentucky courts upheld the ordinance. In the Supreme Court, both sides focused the argument on the constitutionality of neighborhood segregation. An unusual number of AMICUS CURIAE briefs attested to the case's importance.

A unanimous Supreme Court reversed, holding the ordinance invalid. Justice WILLIAM R. DAY's opinion discussed at length the rights to racial equality and the "dignity of citizenship" established in the THIRTEENTH and FOURTEENTH AMENDMENTS, as well as the rights to purchase and hold property, established by the CIVIL RIGHTS ACT OF 1866. He lamely distinguished *Plessy* as a case in which no one had been denied the use of his property. Ultimately, however, he rested decision on a theory of SUBSTANTIVE DUE PROCESS: the ordinance unconstitutionally interfered with property rights.

Day's curious opinion may have aimed at persuading two of his brethren. Justice JAMES C. MCREYNOLDS generally attached greater weight to claims of constitutional property rights than to claims to racial equality. And Justice OLIVER WENDELL HOLMES had prepared a draft DISSENTING OPINION that was not delivered, arguing that the white seller lacked STANDING to assert the constitutional right of blacks.

Despite the ground for decision, *Buchanan* was seen by the press as a major CIVIL RIGHTS victory for blacks. And when the Supreme Court faced ZONING in a nonracial context, it upheld an ordinance in VILLAGE OF EUCLID V. AMBLER REALTY CO. (1926). *Buchanan* plainly was more than a property rights decision.

KENNETH L. KARST

Bibliography

SCHMIDT, BENNO C., JR. 1982 Principle and Prejudice: The Supreme Court and Race in the Progressive Era. Part 1: The Heyday of Jim Crow. *Columbia Law Review* 82:444, 498–523.

BUCK v. BELL 274 U.S. 200 (1927)

In *Buck* the Supreme Court upheld, 8–1, a Virginia law authorizing the STERILIZATION of institutionalized mental defectives without their consent. Justice OLIVER WENDELL HOLMES, for the Court, wrote an opinion notable for epigram and insensitivity. Virginia's courts had ordered the sterilization of a "feeble minded" woman, whose mother and child were similarly afflicted, finding that she was "the probable potential parent of socially inadequate offspring," and that sterilization would promote both her welfare and society's. Holmes, the Civil War veteran, remarked that public welfare might "call upon the best citizens for their lives"; these "lesser sacrifices" were justified to prevent future crime and starvation. There was no violation of SUBSTANTIVE DUE PROCESS. Citing JACOBSON V. MASSACHUSETTS (1905), he said, "The principle that sustains compulsory VACCINATION is broad enough to cover cutting the Fallopian tubes. . . . Three generations of imbeciles are enough."

Turning to EQUAL PROTECTION, which he called "the usual last resort of constitutional arguments," Holmes saw no violation in the law's reaching only institutionalized mental defectives and not others: "the law does all that is needed when it does all that it can." Justice PIERCE BUTLER noted his dissent.

Although *Buck* continues to be cited, its current authority as precedent is doubtful. (See SKINNER V. OKLAHOMA, 1942.)

KENNETH L. KARST

Bibliography

CYNKAR, ROBERT J. 1981 Buck v. Bell: "Felt Necessities" v. Fundamental Values? *Columbia Law Review* 81:1418–1461.

GOULD, STEPHEN JAY 1984 Carrie Buck's Daughter. *Natural History* July:14–18.

LOMBARDO, PAUL A. 1985 Three Generations, No Imbeciles: New Light on *Buck v. Bell. New York University Law Review* 60:30–62.

BUCKLEY v. VALEO
424 U.S. 1 (1976)

In *Buckley* the Supreme Court dealt with a number of constitutional challenges to the complex provisions of the FEDERAL ELECTIONS CAMPAIGN ACT. The act provided for a Federal Elections Commission, members of which were to be appointed variously by the President and certain congressional leaders. The Court held the congressional appointment unconstitutional; Article 2, section 2, prescribes a process for appointing all officers who carry out executive and quasi-judicial duties: appointment by the President, with confirmation by the Senate. Congress subsequently amended the statute to meet the Court's objections.

Rejecting both FIRST AMENDMENT and EQUAL PROTECTION challenges, the Court upheld, 7–2, the provision of public funds for presidential campaigns in amounts that favored major parties over minor parties.

The Court used a BALANCING TEST in considering First Amendment challenges to the provisions limiting expenditures by candidates and contributions to candidates in congressional elections. For both expenditures and contributions the Court defined the government's interest as preventing corruption and appearance of corruption.

The Court placed the interest of the candidate in FREEDOM OF SPEECH on the other side of the balance in striking down the expenditure provisions. Limiting expenditure limited the amount of speech a candidate might make. The Court rejected the argument that another legitimate purpose of the statute was to equalize the campaign opportunities of rich and poor candidates. The PER CURIAM opinion said that the government might not seek to equalize speech by leveling down the rights of rich speakers. High expenditures by rich candidates created no risk of corruption. Indeed, the opinion demonstrated that such a candidate was not dependent on others' money.

In upholding the contribution limits, the Court characterized the First Amendment interest of contributors not as freedom of speech but freedom of association. It reasoned that the initial contribution of $1,000 allowed by the statute completed the act of association and that further contributions did not significantly enhance the association. Further contributions did, however, increase the risk of corruption.

The statute's requirement that all contributions over $100 be a matter of public record were challenged as violating the right to anonymous political association previously recognized in NAACP v. Alabama (1958). The Court upheld the reporting provisions but said that individual applications to contributors to small unpopular parties might be unconstitutional.

MARTIN SHAPIRO

Bibliography

POLSBY, DANIEL D. 1976 Buckley v. Valeo: The Special Nature of Political Speech. *Supreme Court Review* 1976:1–44.

BUDGET

The federal budget is the comprehensive annual program of income and expenditure of the federal government. The budget is not a constitutional requirement, nor does it answer to either the "appopriations made by law" or the "regular statement of account" of Article I, section 9, of the Constitution. Rather the budget is a legislatively created device to regularize the exercise of the TAXING AND SPENDING POWER.

In the nineteenth century there was no overall annual spending program. Appropriations bills were formulated by various congressional committees, which thereby exercised considerable control over the executive departments. A national budget process was first recommended by the Commission on Economy and Efficiency, appointed by President WILLIAM HOWARD TAFT in 1908; and the BUDGET AND ACCOUNTING ACT, which governed the budget process for over half a century, was enacted in 1921.

Because expenditure is an executive function, the President, as chief executive, was given authority to prepare and submit the budget. This represented a major shift of power within the government in favor of the executive branch. President FRANKLIN D. ROOSEVELT further consolidated presidential authority in 1939 by transferring the Bureau of the Budget (created by the 1921 act) from the Treasury Department to the Executive Office of the President. In 1969, President RICHARD M. NIXON restyled the bureau OFFICE OF MANAGEMENT AND BUDGET and increased its control over the operations of executive departments and agencies.

Congress reasserted its role in fiscal policymaking by the CONGRESSIONAL BUDGET AND IMPOUNDMENT CONTROL ACT (1974). The act created a permanent budget committee in each house of Congress, established the Congressional Budget Office to provide independent evaluation of executive economic planning, and prescribed a timetable for each phase of the budget and appropriations process. Even after passage of this act, however, the budget process is necessarily dominated by the chief executive.

DENNIS J. MAHONEY

Bibliography

BORCHERDING, THOMAS E., ed. 1977 *Budgets and Bureaucrats: The Sources of Government Growth.* Durham, N.C.: Duke University Press.

MARINI, JOHN 1978 The Politics of Budget Control: An Analysis of the Impact of Centralized Administration on the Separation of Powers. Unpublished Ph.D. dissertation, Claremont Graduate School.

BUDGET AND ACCOUNTING ACT

42 Stat. 20 (1921)

Among the aims of the reform movement of the early twentieth century was the creation of neutral processes and agencies to perform public functions, substituting administration for politics in the delivery of government services. One key reform was the introduction of the federal BUDGET. Proposed by President WILLIAM HOWARD TAFT's Commission on Economy and Efficiency, enactment of a federal budget law was delayed by World War I. When Congress finally passed a bill in 1920, President WOODROW WILSON, although a longtime advocate of a budget system, vetoed it rather than submit to its limitation of his REMOVAL POWER. A virtually identical bill was passed the following year and signed into law by President Warren Harding, who called it "the greatest reformation in governmental practice since the beginning of the Republic."

Under the act, the President alone was responsible for submitting to Congress each year a statement of the condition of the treasury, the estimated revenues and expenditures of the government for the year, and proposals for meeting revenue needs. The act created the Bureau of the Budget, to receive, compile, and criticize the estimates and requests of the various departments, and the General Accounting Office, to audit the government's fiscal activities.

The Budget and Accounting Act caused a major change in the balance of power within the government, giving the President, rather than Congress, effective control over government spending. The act provided the machinery through which, during the middle third of the twentieth century, the national executive managed the whole economy.

DENNIS J. MAHONEY

Bibliography

MARINI, JOHN 1978 The Politics of Budget Control: An Analysis of the Impact of Centralized Administration on the Separation of Powers. Unpublished Ph.D. dissertation, Claremont Graduate School.

BUNTING v. OREGON

243 U.S. 426 (1917)

This decision upheld maximum hour legislation and approved state regulations of overtime wages as a proper exception to the prevailing constitutional standards of FREEDOM OF CONTRACT. A 1913 Oregon law prescribed a ten-hour day for men and women alike, thus expanding the law regulating women's hours which had been upheld in MULLER V. OREGON (1908). In addition, the measure required time and a half wages for overtime up to three hours per day. Justice JOSEPH MCKENNA's opinion for the 5–3 majority (there was no written dissent) assumed the validity of the working hours regulations, thus ignoring LOCHNER V. NEW YORK (1905) as well as Justice DAVID J. BREWER's careful distinction in *Muller* that the status of women required special legislative concern. Lawyers for Bunting had attacked the law for its wage-fixing provisions and had invoked *Lochner* and *Muller* to demonstrate that the Oregon statute had no reasonable relation to the preservation of public health. McKenna, focusing on the overtime provision, denied that it was a regulation of wages. The statute, he contended, was designed as an hours law, and the Court was reluctant to consider it as a "disguise" for illegal purposes. Somewhat ingenuously, McKenna argued that the overtime provision was permissive and that its purpose was to burden and deter employers from using workers for more than ten hours. He admitted that the requirement for overtime might not attain that end, "but its insufficiency cannot change its character from penalty to permission." The Oregon Supreme Court had construed the overtime provision as reflecting a legislative desire to make the ten-hour day standard; beyond that, McKenna and his colleagues were not willing to inquire into legislative motive.

Bunting provided frail support in behalf of wage legislation. A few weeks later, the Court split 4–4 on Oregon's minimum wage law (STETTLER V. O'HARA), but in 1923 the Court struck down such legislation in ADKINS V. CHILDREN'S HOSPITAL.

STANLEY I. KUTLER

Bibliography

MASON, ALPHEUS T. 1946 *Brandeis: A Free Man's Life.* New York: Viking Press.

BURBANK v. LOCKHEED AIR TERMINAL
411 U.S. 624 (1973)

The Supreme Court, in a 5–4 vote, struck down a city ordinance regulating air traffic as a violation of the SUPREMACY CLAUSE. The ordinance prohibited jets from taking off between 11 P.M. and 7 A.M. and also forbade the airport operator from allowing such flights. The Court, speaking through Justice WILLIAM O. DOUGLAS, applied the PREEMPTION DOCTRINE and found the ordinance in conflict with two federal statutes which provided for the regulation of navigable airspace. Justice WILLIAM H. REHNQUIST, for the dissenters, contended that these statutes did not supersede the STATE POLICE POWER.

DAVID GORDON

BURCH v. LOUISIANA
441 U.S. 130 (1979)

In *Burch v. Louisiana,* the Supreme Court held that conviction by a 5–1 vote of a six-person jury in a state prosecution for a nonpetty offense violates the accused's right to TRIAL BY JURY under the Sixth and FOURTEENTH AMENDMENTS. *Burch* involved a prosecution for exhibiting two obscene motion pictures.

In two earlier cases, APOCADA V. OREGON (1972) and JOHNSON V. LOUISIANA (1972), the Court had sustained 10–2 and 9–3 verdicts, and it had also previously ruled in BALLEW V. GEORGIA (1978) that juries of less than six persons were unconstitutional. In *Burch,* the Court concluded that "having already departed from the strictly historical requirements of jury trial, it is inevitable that lines must be drawn somewhere if the substance of the jury trial right is to be preserved." It relied mainly upon "the same reasons that led us in *Ballew* to decide that use of a five person jury threatened the fairness of the proceeding and the proper role of the jury." *Burch* did not resolve the constitutionality of different majority verdict systems for juries composed of seven through eleven members or majorities of 8–4 or 7–5 on a jury of twelve.

NORMAN ABRAMS

(SEE ALSO: *Jury Size; Jury Unanimity.*)

BURDEN OF PROOF

Although the Constitution does not mention burden of proof, certain principles are widely accepted as having constitutional status. The first and most significant of these is the rule that in a criminal case the government must prove its case "beyond a REASONABLE DOUBT." This is the universal COMMON LAW rule, and was said by the Supreme Court in IN RE WINSHIP (1970) to be an element of DUE PROCESS. This standard is commonly contrasted with proof "by a preponderance of the evidence" or "by clear and convincing evidence." The standard of proof is in practice not easily susceptible to further clarification or elaboration.

To what matters does the burden apply? The *Win-*

ship Court said it extended to "every fact necessary to constitute the crime with which [a defendant] is charged." The government must prove its case beyond a reasonable doubt. But suppose the defendant raises a defense of ALIBI, insanity, duress, or diplomatic immunity? With respect to such defenses the usual rule is that the defendant may be required to produce some evidence supporting his claim; if he does not, that defense will not be considered by the jury. By what standard should the jury be instructed to evaluate such a defense? Should they deny the defense unless they are persuaded by a preponderance of the evidence that the defendant has established it? Or does the "burden of persuasion" on the issue raised by the defendant remain on the government, so that the jury must acquit unless persuaded beyond a reasonable doubt that the defense falls? On this complicated question there is no settled view. The answer should probably vary with the kind of defense: alibi, for example, is not really an affirmative defense but a denial of facts charged. Such a defense as diplomatic immunity, however, might be regarded as one upon which the defendant should bear the burden of proof.

The foregoing structure is complicated by the existence of "presumptions," that is, legislative or judicial statements to the effect that if one fact is proved—say, possession of marijuana—another fact essential to conviction may be "presumed"—say, that the marijuana was illegally imported. The Supreme Court has held such a legislative presumption valid when the proved fact makes the ultimate fact more likely than not.

The burden of proof beyond a reasonable doubt is a critical element of due process. Like the requirements that laws be public and their prohibitions comprehensible and prospective, that trials be public and by jury, and that the defendant have counsel, the burden of proof limits the power of the government to impose arbitrary or oppressive punishments. It reinforces the rights of the defendant not to be a witness against himself nor to take the stand, for it imposes upon the government the task of proving its whole case on its own. A lower standard of proof would pressure defendants to involve themselves in the process of their own condemnation.

In civil cases, the rule is simply stated: the legislature may decide upon the burden of proof as it wishes, usually choosing the "preponderance of the evidence" test. In specialized proceedings, such as motions to suppress evidence for criminal trials, special rules have evolved. (See STANDARDS OF REVIEW.)

JAMES BOYD WHITE

Bibliography

MCCORMICK, CHARLES 1954 *Handbook of the Law of Evidence.* Chap. 6. St. Paul, Minn.: West Publishing Co.

BUREAUCRACY

The Constitution creates an executive branch that neatly fits into the SEPARATION OF POWERS and CHECKS AND BALANCES system that the Framers devised. But the Constitution does not explicitly provide for the kind of administrative branch, or bureaucracy, that evolved beginning in the late nineteenth century. Congress created both independent commissions, such as the Interstate Commerce Commission (established in 1887), and other executive agencies that regulated a wide range of economic activities, and delegated to those bodies the authority both to make law through rule-making and to adjudicate cases arising under their JURISDICTION.

The Framers of the Constitution understandably did not foresee the development of an executive branch that would be a dominant force in lawmaking and adjudication, functions that they expected to be carried out by Congress and the courts. They conceived of "administration" as the "mere execution" of "executive details," to use ALEXANDER HAMILTON's description in THE FEDERALIST #72. Article II makes the President chief executive by giving him the responsibility to "take care that the laws be faithfully executed." He has the authority to appoint public ministers and other executive branch officials designated by Congress, subject to the ADVICE AND CONSENT of the Senate. He may "require the opinion in writing, of the principal officer in each of the executive departments, upon any subject relating to the duties of their respective offices. . . ." Hamilton concluded in *The Federalist* #72: "The persons, therefore, to whose immediate management the different administrative matters are committed ought to be considered as assistants or deputies of the Chief Magistrate and, on this account, they ought to derive their offices from his appointment, at least from his nomination, and ought to be subject to his superintendence."

Hamilton thought, as did most of the Framers, that the President would be, to use Clinton Rossiter's characterization in *The American Presidency* (1956), chief administrator. From a Hamiltonian perspective—one that later turned up in the presidential supremacy school of thought in public administration, reflected in the Report of the President's Committee on Administrative Management in 1937—the President is constitutionally responsible for the administrative branch.

Whatever may have been the intent of the Framers, the Constitution they designed allows and even requires both congressional and judicial intrusion into executive branch affairs. Two factors help to explain the constitutional ambiguities surrounding executive branch accountability. First, the system of separation of powers and checks and balances purposely gives Congress both the motivation and the authority to share with the President control over the executive branch. Congress jealously guards its position and powers, and its constitutional incentive to check the President encourages legislators to design an executive branch that will, in many respects, be independent of the White House. Other political incentives support those of the Constitution in encouraging Congress to hold the reins of the bureaucracy. Political pluralism has fragmented congressional politics into policy arenas controlled by committees. They form political "iron triangles" with agencies and special interests for their mutual benefit. The resulting executive branch pluralism is a major barrier to presidential control.

Agency performance of quasi-legislative and quasi-judicial functions is the second factor complicating the Hamiltonian prescription for the President to be chief administrator. From the standpoint of constitutional theory, Congress and the courts are the primary legislative and judicial branches, respectively. Each has a responsibility to oversee administrative activities that fall within their spheres. Congressional, not presidential, intent should guide agency rule-making. Moreover, the constitutional system, as it was soon to be interpreted by the Supreme Court, gave to the judiciary sweeping authority to exercise JUDICIAL REVIEW over Congress and, by implication, over the President and the bureaucracy as well. Chief Justice JOHN MARSHALL stated in MARBURY V. MADISON (1803): "It is emphatically the province and duty of the Judicial Department to say what the law is. Those who apply the rule to particular cases must, of necessity, expound and interpret that rule." In concrete CASES AND CONTROVERSIES, where administrative action is appropriately challenged by injured parties, courts interpret and apply both statutory and constitutional law.

The hybrid character of the bureaucracy confuses the picture of its place in the governmental scheme. Constitutional prescriptions apply to the bureaucracy as they do to other branches. The bureaucracy must conform to the norms of separation of powers and checks and balances, PROCEDURAL DUE PROCESS, and democratic participation. The formal provisions of the Constitution and the broader politics of the system have shaped the administrative branch in various ways, limiting and controlling its powers.

Ironically, although the President alone is to be chief executive, Congress actually has more constitutional authority over the bureaucracy than does the White House as the result of its extensive enumerated powers under Article I. These do not mention the executive branch explicitly but by application of the doctrine of IMPLIED POWERS give the legislature the authority to create administrative departments and agencies and determine their course of action. Under the TAXING AND SPENDING POWER, the commerce power, and the WAR POWERS, Congress has authorized the creation of a vast array of agencies to carry out its responsibilities. The Legislative Reorganization Act of 1946 mandated Congress to establish oversight committees to supervise the bureaucracy and see to it that agencies were carrying out legislative intent. More important than legislative oversight, a responsibility most committee chairmen eschew because of its limited vote-getting value, is the appropriations and authorization process carried out by dozens of separate committees on Capitol Hill. Committee chairmen and their staffs indirectly sway administrative policymaking through committee hearings and informal contact with administrators who know that Congress strongly influences agency budgets.

The President's executive powers under Article II mean little unless Congress acquiesces in their exercise and buttresses the President's position in relation to the bureaucracy. It is congressional DELEGATION OF POWER to the President as much as, if not more than, the Constitution that determines to what extent he will be chief administrator. But the bureaucracy is always a pawn in the executive–legislative power struggle. Congressional willingness to strengthen presidential authority over the executive branch depends upon political forces that dictate the balance of power between Capitol Hill and the White House. Presidents have valiantly struggled but only intermittently succeeded in obtaining from Congress the powers they have requested to give them dominance over the bureaucracy.

From the New Deal of FRANKLIN D. ROOSEVELT through the Great Society of LYNDON B. JOHNSON, Congress often agreed to requests for increased powers over the bureaucracy. During Roosevelt's administration, Congress for the first time gave the President authority to reorganize the executive Branch, subject to LEGISLATIVE VETO by a majority vote of either the House or the Senate. Roosevelt issued a historic EXECUTIVE ORDER in 1939 creating the presidential bureaucracy—the Executive Office of the President—to help him carry out his executive responsibilities. Laws granting the President reorganization authority were periodically renewed and acted upon until 1973 when Congress, in reaction to the WATERGATE revelations and concern over the "imperial presidency," allowed the reorganization act to expire. Although Congress renewed the reorganization law during the subsequent administration of President GERALD FORD, presidential authority over the bureaucracy had been impaired by the CONGRESSIONAL BUDGET AND IMPOUNDMENT CONTROL ACT of 1974 and other laws. Under the Congressional Budget Act the President could no longer permanently impound funds appropriated by Congress, as President RICHARD M. NIXON had done on over forty separate occasions. The law prevented the President from interfering with administrative implementation of legislative programs.

The courts, too, have claimed administrative turf, by exercising judicial review. Most of the statutes of individual agencies as well as the Administrative Procedure Act of 1946 set forth broad standards of procedural due process that administrators must follow when their decisions directly affect private rights, interests, and obligations. The courts not only interpret these statutory requirements but also apply to the administrative realm constitutional criteria for procedural fairness. For example, the Supreme Court held, in *Wong Yang Sung v. McGrath* (1950), that the Fifth Amendment's DUE PROCESS clause requires the Immigration Service to hold a full hearing with an independent judge presiding, before ordering the DEPORTATION of an illegal ALIEN whose life and liberty might be threatened if he were forced to return to his native land.

Involvement of the three original branches of government in the operations of the bureaucracy does not by itself solve the problem administrative agencies pose to the constitutional theory and practice of the separation of powers. Agencies performing regulatory functions combine in the same hands executive, legislative, and judicial powers. The Administrative Procedure Act of 1946 required a certain degree of separation of functions within agencies by creating an independent class of ADMINISTRATIVE LAW judges who initially decide formal rule-making and adjudicatory cases, which are those that by statute require trial-type hearings. Administrative judges must make their decisions on the record; *ex parte* consultations outside of the agency are forbidden entirely and, within the agency, can be made only in rule-making proceedings. Attempts to impose a judicial model on the administrative process, however, have not solved the constitutional dilemma posed by the fusion of powers within the bureaucracy. Commissions, boards, and agency heads have virtually unlimited discretion to overturn, on the basis of policy considerations, the decisions made by administrative law judges. Courts have supported the imposition of a judicial model on lower-level administrative rule-making and adjudicatory decisions, but have recognized the need for the heads of agencies to have discretion in interpreting legislative intent and flexibility in implementing statutory policy.

Another problem that the bureaucracy poses to the constitutional system is that of democratic control and accountability. An unelected, semi-autonomous administrative branch with the authority to make law arguably threatens to undermine the principles of representative government by removing lawmaking powers from Congress. The solution, in this view, is to restore the delegation of powers doctrine expressed by the Supreme Court in SCHECHTER POULTRY CORPORATION V. UNITED STATES (1935), holding that the primary legislative authority resides in Congress and cannot be delegated to the administrative branch. The *Schechter* rule was never strictly followed, and executive branch lawmaking increased and was even supported by the courts after that decision. However, judges did require that legislative intent be fairly clearly expressed, and they encouraged Congress to tighten agency procedural requirements to guarantee both fairness and compilation of records sufficient to permit effective judicial review.

Administrative discretion in lawmaking and adjudication remains a reality regardless of the intricate network of presidential, congressional, and judicial controls over the bureaucracy. But administrative agencies are not conspiracies to undermine individual liberties and rights, nor to subvert democratic government, a view that conservatives and liberals alike have of the enormous power of the executive branch. Political demands have led to the creation of executive departments and agencies that continue to be responsive to the interests in their political constituencies, a democratic accountability that is narrow but, nevertheless, an important part of the system of administrative responsibility.

The bureaucracy performs vital governmental functions that the three original branches cannot easily carry out. Essential to any modern government is a relatively large and complex administrative branch capable of implementing the wide array of the programs democratic demands produce. American bureaucracy has added an important new dimension to the constitutional system. Because it is so profoundly shaped by the separation of powers, by the process of checks and balances, and by democratic political forces, it does fit, although imperfectly, into the system of constitutional democracy the Framers desired.

PETER WOLL

Bibliography

FRIENDLY, HENRY J. 1962 *The Federal Administrative Agencies.* Cambridge, Mass.: Harvard University Press.

LANDIS, JAMES M. 1938 *The Administrative Process.* New Haven, Conn.: Yale University Press.

WOLL, PETER 1977 *American Bureaucracy.* New York: Norton.

BURFORD v. SUN OIL COMPANY

See: Abstention Doctrines

BURGER, WARREN E. (1907–)

Warren Earl Burger was born in St. Paul, Minnesota. He attended the University of Minnesota and, in 1931, received a law degree from St. Paul College of Law (today known as the William Mitchell College of Law). After practicing law in St. Paul for several years, he became the assistant attorney general in charge of the Civil Division of the Department of Justice during the administration of DWIGHT D. EISENHOWER. In 1955, Burger was appointed a judge on the United States Court of Appeals for the District of Columbia Circuit. He served in that capacity until 1969, when he became the Chief Justice of the United States, having been nominated for that position by RICHARD M. NIXON.

In the years of his tenure as Chief Justice, the Supreme Court has been marked publicly as having a majority of Justices who hold a generally conservative orientation toward constitutional issues. Burger himself is widely viewed as a primary proponent of this conservative judicial posture and, at least during the early years of the BURGER COURT, he was expected to lead the other conservative Justices in a major, if one-sided, battle to undo as much as could be undone of the pathbreaking work of its predecessor, the quite distinctly liberal WARREN COURT.

To the surprise of many the record of the Burger Court has been extraordinarily complicated, or uneven, when viewed against both of its commonly assumed objectives of overturning Warren Court decisions and of achieving what is often called a "nonactivist" judicial posture toward new claims for constitutional rights. Although it is true that a few Warren Court innovations have been openly discarded (for example, the recognition of a FIRST AMENDMENT right to speak in the context of privately owned SHOPPING CENTERS was overturned) and several other doctrines significantly curtailed (for example, the well-known 1966 ruling in MIRANDA V. ARIZONA has been narrowed as new cases have arisen), it is also true that many Warren Court holdings have been vigorously applied and even extended (for example, the principle of SEPARATION OF CHURCH AND STATE has been forcefully, if still confusingly, applied). What is perhaps most surprising of all, whole new areas of constitutional jurisprudence have been opened up. The foremost example here, of course, is the Court's highly controversial decision in ROE V. WADE (1973), which recognized a woman's constitutional right to have an abortion—subject to a set of conditions that rivaled in their legislation-like refinement the Warren Court's greatly maligned rules for the *Miranda* warnings. Against this history of overrulings, modifications, extensions, and new creations in the tapestry of decisions of its predecessor Courts, it is difficult to characterize the constitutional course steered by the modern Supreme Court under the stewardship of Warren Burger.

The same difficulty arises if one focuses more specifically on the constitutional thought of Burger himself. Burger may properly be regarded as one of the Court's most conservative members. In the field of criminal justice, he has tended to support police and prosecutors. He has joined in a large number of decisions limiting would-be litigants' access to the federal courts. Although he played an important role in the Court's recognition of constitutional rights in areas such as SEX DISCRIMINATION, discrimination against ALIENS, and SCHOOL BUSING, in each of these areas he has resisted extension of the rights initially recognized. Nonetheless, he has been inclined to accept the validity of congressional CIVIL RIGHTS legislation, and to read those laws generously. And he has been a strong supporter of claims of RELIGIOUS LIBERTY. Generally, he has joined the majority as it has pursued this surprisingly labyrinthine constitutional course. The starting point, therefore, for thinking about the constitutional thought of Warren Burger (just as it is for the Court as a whole during his tenure) is the realization that his opinions do not reflect an especially coherent vision of the Constitution and its contemporary significance.

But to say that the decisions and opinions of Burger, taken together, do not add up to a coherent whole does not mean that there are no important themes working their way through them. It is in fact quite possible to locate several distinct threads of thought: for example, a desire to return greater political power to the states in the federal system and to give greater protection to property interests is frequently reflected in Burger's constitutional opinions. But perhaps the most important characteristic of Warren Burger's opinions while Chief Justice is to be found in the area of individual rights and freedoms. It is there that one feels the strongest tension between a commitment to constitutional standards that control and limit the legislative process and a desire to maintain legislative control over the moral and intellectual climate of the community. It is in the resolution of that tension that one is able to determine what is most distinctive about Burger's constitutional jurisprudence.

Burger has frequently displayed a willingness to protect individual freedom at the expense of the interests of the state. His opinion for the Court in *Reed v. Reed* (1971), for example, was the first to subject gender classifications to more rigorous EQUAL PROTECTION scrutiny than had theretofore been the case. But, that said, it is also critical to an understanding of Burger's approach to the BILL OF RIGHTS to see that the depth of his commitment to individual liberties has been limited by a seemingly equal reluctance to extend constitutional protection to individuals or groups whose challenged behavior has gone beyond what may be called the customary norms of good behavior.

Two areas of First Amendment decisions are revealing here. In WISCONSIN V. YODER (1972), for example, Burger wrote an opinion for the Court upholding the right of members of an Amish religious community to refuse, on religious grounds, to comply with the Wisconsin compulsory school-attendance law. In his opinion Burger repeatedly emphasized the fact that the Amish had adopted a traditional lifestyle, saying at one point how "the Amish communities singularly parallel and reflect many of the virtues of THOMAS JEFFERSON's ideal of the 'sturdy yeoman.'" On the other hand, in every case in which a speaker who used indecent language has sought the protection of the First Amendment, Burger has rejected the claim (though in these cases, usually in dissent) and, in doing so, has stressed the importance of maintaining community norms about proper and improper behavior.

In Burger's opinions, therefore, the protection of a specific liberty is often tied to his assessment of the respectability of the behavior. Sometimes this underlying attitude for a decision has been misinterpreted for other motivations. For example, in COLUMBIA BROADCASTING SYSTEM, INC. V. DEMOCRATIC NATIONAL COMMITTEE (1973), a major decision rejecting the claim that individuals and groups have a constitutional and statutory right to purchase airtime from broadcast stations in order to discuss public issues, Burger emphasized the importance of preserving the "journalistic autonomy" or "editorial discretion" of broadcasters, a theme reported in the press accounts of the case at the time. But this suggestion that the decision rested on a heightened respect for editorial freedom, and a preparedness to live with the consequent risks of bad editorial behavior, was considerably undermined by an additional thought Burger expressed. Freedom for broadcast journalists was to be preferred, he said, because broadcasters were regulated and therefore "accountable," while "[n]o such accountability attaches to the private individual, whose only qualifications for using the broadcast facility may be abundant funds and a point of view."

It is a noteworthy feature of Burger's constitutional work that in the area of FREEDOM OF THE PRESS he has written many of the Court's most prominent decisions upholding claims of the print media for protection against various forms of government regulation. Burger wrote for the Court in MIAMI HERALD PUBLISHING CO. V. TORNILLO (1974), holding that states could not require a newspaper to provide access to political candidates who had been criticized in the newspaper's columns; in NEBRASKA PRESS ASSOCIATION V. STUART (1976), holding that courts could not enjoin the media from publishing in advance of trial purported confessions and other evidence "implicative" of an accused individual; and in RICHMOND NEWSPAPERS, INC. V. VIRGINIA (1980), holding that courts could not follow a course of generally excluding the media from attending and observing criminal trials.

Yet, despite this strong record of extending constitutional protection to the press, the Burger Court, and especially Burger himself, has been strongly criticized by various segments of the press for retreating from earlier precedents and for being generally hostile to press claims. Burger, it is true, has sometimes voted along with a majority to reject press claims, as, for example, in BRANZBURG V. HAYES (1972), when the press urged the Court to recognize a limited constitutional privilege for journalists against being compelled to give testimony to grand juries, or in GERTZ V. ROBERT WELCH, INC. (1974), when the press sought to extend the "actual malice" standard in libel actions to all discussions of public issues, not just to those discussions concerning public officials and PUBLIC FIGURES. But an objective assessment of the holdings of the Burger Court does not seem to warrant the general accusation of its hostility to the press. It is too easy to lose sight of the basic truth that in virtually every case that involved significant issues of press freedom Burger has supported the press, and in many of them has written the majority opinions.

Is it possible to account for this discrepancy between criticism and performance? Here again the best explanation is to be found in Burger's disinclination to extend constitutional protection to activity judged as falling below conventional standards of good behavior. But in the area of freedom of the press this disinclination has manifested itself less in the actual results Burger has reached in particular cases and more in the craftsmanship and the tone of his judicial opinions.

The contrast between the opinions of the Warren Court and of Burger in the freedom of press area is remarkable. With Warren Court opinions the tone struck is almost uniformly that of praise for the role performed by the press in the American democratic political system. They extol the virtues of an open and free press. Although the same theme is to be found in Burger's judicial work, one often encounters rather sharp criticism of the press as well. Burger has actively used the forum of the Supreme Court judicial opinion to ventilate his feelings about the condition of the American press, and not everything he has had to say in that forum has been complimentary. One should consider in this regard one of the major cases in the free press area just mentioned, *Miami Herald Publishing Co. v. Tornillo.* In that case Burger's opinion for the Court begins with a lengthy and detailed description of the argument advanced by the state of Florida in support of its statute, which guaranteed limited access for political candidates to the columns of newspapers. The press has grown monopolized and excessively powerful, the state contended: "Chains of newspapers, national newspapers, national wire and news services, and one-newspaper towns, are the dominant features of a press that has become noncompetitive and enormously powerful and influential in its capacity to manipulate popular opinion and change the course of events. . . . Such national news organizations provide syndicated 'interpretive reporting' as well as syndicated features and commentary, all of which can serve as part of the new school of 'journalism.' " While ultimately rejecting the legal conclusion that the state sought to draw from this assumed social reality, Burger's opinion nevertheless strongly intimates sympathy with the general portrait of the press which the state's argument had painted. Thus, while the press may have had an ally in the constitutional result, it did not in the battle for public opinion generally.

Although Warren Burger retired from the Supreme Court at the end of the 1985–1986 term, what the lasting impact of his constitutional thought will be is of course impossible to tell. For the moment the most appropriate general assessment is that Burger's constitutional work displays a general disunity of character, while suggesting a responsiveness to generally conservative instincts, even when he is on the liberal side.

LEE C. BOLLINGER

Bibliography

BLASI, VINCENT, ED. 1983 *The Burger Court: The Counter-Revolution That Wasn't.* New Haven, Conn.: Yale University Press.

BOLLINGER, LEE C. 1986 *The Tolerant Society: Freedom of Speech and Extremist Speech in America.* New York: Oxford University Press.

CHOPER, JESSE 1980 *Judicial Review and the National Political Process.* Chicago: University of Chicago Press.

SYMPOSIUM 1980 The Burger Court: Reflections on the First Decade. *Law and Contemporary Problems* 43:1.

BURGER COURT (1969–1986)

The roots of the Burger Court lie in the JUDICIAL ACTIVISM of the WARREN COURT. The social vision of the Supreme Court under EARL WARREN was manifested on many fronts—dismantling racial barriers, requiring that legislative apportionment be based upon population, and vastly expanding the range of rights for criminal defendants, among others. At the height of its activity, during the 1960s, the Warren Court became a forum to which many of the great social issues of the time were taken.

Such activism provoked sharp attacks on the Court. Some of the criticism came from the ranks of the academy, other complaints from political quarters. In the 1968 presidential campaign, RICHARD M. NIXON objected in particular to the Court's CRIMINAL PROCEDURE decisions—rulings which, he said, favored the country's "criminal forces" against its "peace forces."

During his first term as President, Nixon put four Justices on the Supreme Court—WARREN E. BURGER, HARRY A. BLACKMUN, LEWIS F. POWELL, JR., and WILLIAM H. REHNQUIST. Rarely has a President been given the opportunity to fill so many vacancies on the Court in so short a time. Moreover, Nixon was explicit about the ideological basis for his appointments; he saw himself as redeeming his campaign pledge "to nominate to the Supreme Court individuals who share my judicial philosophy, which is basically a conservative philosophy."

Thus was born the Burger Court. For a time, pundits, at least those of liberal persuasion, took to calling it "the Nixon Court." Reviewing the 1971 TERM, *The New Republic* lamented that the "single-mindedness of the Nixon team threatens the image of the Court as an independent institution."

Inevitably, the work of the Burger Court was compared with that of its predecessor, the Warren Court. During the early Burger years, there was evidence that, with Nixon's four appointees on the bench, a new, and more conservative, majority was indeed in the making on the Court.

By the summer of 1976, a conservative Burger Court seemed to have come of age. For example, near the end of the 1975 term the Court closed the doors of federal courts to large numbers of state prisoners by holding that a prisoner who has had a full and fair opportunity to raise a FOURTH AMENDMENT question in the state courts cannot relitigate that question in a federal HABEAS CORPUS proceeding. In other criminal justice decisions, the Court whittled away at the rights of defendants, showing particular disfavor for claims seeking to curb police practices.

Decisions in areas other than criminal justice likewise showed a conservative flavor. For example, in the same term the Court used the TENTH AMENDMENT to place limits on Congress's commerce power, rejected the argument that claims of AGE DISCRIMINATION ought to trigger the higher level of JUDICIAL REVIEW associated with SUSPECT CLASSIFICATIONS (such as race), and refused to hold that CAPITAL PUNISHMENT is inherently unconstitutional.

By the mid-1970s, a student of the Court might have summarized the Burger Court, in contrast with the Warren Court, as being less egalitarian, more sensitive to FEDERALISM, more skeptical about the competence of judges to solve society's problems, more inclined to trust the governmental system, and, in general, more inclined to defer to legislative and political processes. By the end of the 1970s, however, such generalizations might have been thought premature—or, at least, have to be tempered. As the years passed, it became increasingly more difficult to draw clean distinctions between the years of Earl Warren and those of Warren Burger.

Cases involving claims of SEX DISCRIMINATION furnish an example. In 1973 four Justices (WILLIAM J. BRENNAN, WILLIAM O. DOUGLAS, BRYON R. WHITE, and THURGOOD MARSHALL) who had been on the Court in the Warren era sought to have the Court rule that classifications based on sex, like those based on race, should be viewed as "inherently suspect" and hence subject to STRICT SCRUTINY. The four Nixon appointees (together with Justice POTTER STEWART) joined in resisting such a standard. Yet, overall, the Burger Court's record in sex discrimination cases proved to be one of relative activism, even though the Court applied an intermediate STANDARD OF REVIEW in those cases, rather than one of strict scrutiny. In the 1978 term, for example, there were eight cases that in one way or another involved claims of sex discrimination; in six of the eight cases the Justices voted favorably to the claim, either on the merits or on procedural grounds.

In the early 1980s, with the Burger Court in its second decade, there was evidence that a working majority, conservative in bent, was taking hold. Two more Justices from the Warren era (William O. Douglas and Potter Stewart) had retired. Taking their place were appointees of Republican presidents—JOHN PAUL STEVENS (appointed by President GERALD R. FORD) and SANDRA DAY O'CONNOR (named by President RONALD REAGAN). While Stevens tended to vote with the more liberal Justices, O'Connor appeared to provide a dependable vote for the more conservative bloc on the Court.

In the 1983 term the conservatives appeared to have firm control. The Court recognized a "public safety" exception to the MIRANDA RULES and a "good faith" exception to the EXCLUSIONARY RULE in Fourth Amendment cases. The Justices upheld a New York law providing for the PREVENTIVE DETENTION of juveniles and sustained the Reagan administration's curb on travel to Cuba. As one commentator put it, "Whenever the rights of the individual confronted the authority of government this term, government nearly always won." The AMERICAN CIVIL LIBERTIES UNION's legal director called it "a genuinely appalling term," one in which the Court behaved as a "cheerleader for the government."

No sooner had such dire conclusions been drawn than the Burger Court once again confounded the Court-watchers. The very next term saw the Court return to the mainstream of its jurisprudence of the 1970s. The Court's religion cases are an example. Between 1980 and 1984 the Court appeared to be moving in the direction of allowing government to "accommodate" religion, thus relaxing the barriers the FIRST AMENDMENT erects between church and state. The Court rebuffed challenges to Nebraska's paying a legislative chaplain and Pawtucket, Rhode Island's displaying a Christmas crèche. Yet in the 1984 term the Court resumed a separationist stance, invalidating major programs (both federal and state) found to channel public aid to church schools, invalidating an Alabama statute providing for a "moment of silence or prayer" in public schools, and striking down a Connecticut law making it illegal for an employer to require an employee to work on the employee's chosen Sabbath. The Reagan administration had filed briefs in support of the challenged laws in all four cases, and in each of the four cases a majority of the Justices ruled against the program.

Even so brief a sketch of the Burger Court's evolution conveys something of the dialectical nature of those years on the Court. In reading Burger Court opinions, one is sometimes struck by their conservative thrust, sometimes by a liberal result. Here the Burger Court is activist, there it defers to other branches or bodies. There is continuity with the Warren years, but discontinuity as well. One is struck, above all, by the way in which the Court in the Burger era has become a battleground on which fundamental jurisprudential issues are fought out.

No simple portrait of the Burger Court is possible. Some measure of the Burger years may be had, however, by touching upon certain themes that characterize the Burger Court—the questions which observers of the Court have tended to ask and the issues around which decision making on the Court has tended to revolve.

At the outset of the Burger era, many observers thought that a more conservative tribunal would undo much of the work of the Warren Court. This prophecy has been unfulfilled. The landmarks of the Warren Court remain essentially intact. Among those landmarks are BROWN V. BOARD OF EDUCATION (1954) (school desegregation), REYNOLDS V. SIMS (1964) (legislative REAPPORTIONMENT), and the decisions applying nearly all of the procedural protection of the BILL OF RIGHTS in criminal trials to the states.

In all of these areas, there have been, to be sure, important adjustments to Warren Court doctrine. Sometimes, a majority of the Burger Court's Justices have shown a marked distaste for the ethos underlying those precedents. Thus, while leaving such precedents as MIRANDA V. ARIZONA (1956) and MAPP V. OHIO (1961) standing, the Burger Court has frequently confined those precedents or carved out exceptions. Yet, despite criticisms, on and off the bench, of the INCORPORATION DOCTRINE, there has been no wholesale attempt to turn the clock back to the pre-Warren era.

In school cases, while the Burger Court has rebuffed efforts to provide remedies for de facto SEGREGATION, where de jure segregation is proved the Court has been generous in permitting federal judges to fashion effective remedies (it was an opinion of Chief Justice Burger, in SWANN V. CHARLOTTE-MECKLENBURG BOARD OF EDUCATION (1971) that first explicitly upheld lower courts' use of busing as a remedy in school cases). In legislative apportionment cases, the Burger Court has permitted some deviation from strict conformity to a population basis in drawing state and local government legislative districts, but the essential requirement remains that REPRESENTATION must be based on population.

A common complaint against the Warren Court was that it was too "activist"—that it was too quick to substitute its judgment for decisions of legislative bodies or other elected officials. In opinions written during the Burger years, it is common to find the rhetoric of judicial restraint, of calls for deference to policy judgments of legislatures and the political process generally.

Some Burger Court decisions reflect a stated preference for leaving difficult social issues to other forums than the courts. In rejecting an attack of Texas's system of financing public schools through heavy reliance on local property taxes, Justice Powell argued against judges' being too ready to interfere with "informed judgments made at the state and local levels."

Overall, however, the record of the Burger Court is one of activism. One of the hallmarks of activism is the enunciation by the Court of new rights. By that standard, no judicial decision could be more activist than the Burger Court's decision in ROE V. WADE (1973). There Justice Blackmun drew upon the vague contours of the FOURTEENTH AMENDMENT's DUE PROCESS clause to decide that the RIGHT TO PRIVACY (itself a right not spelled out in the Constitution) implies a woman's right to have an ABORTION.

In the modern Supreme Court, the Fourteenth Amendment's due process and EQUAL PROTECTION clauses have been the most conspicuous vehicles for judicial activism. The Warren Court's favorite was the equal protection clause—the so-called new equal protection which, through strict scrutiny and other such tests, produced such decisions as *Reynolds v. Sims.* With the advent of the Burger Court came the renaissance of SUBSTANTIVE DUE PROCESS.

An example of the Burger Court's use of substantive due process is Justice Powell's plurality opinion in MOORE V. EAST CLEVELAND (1977). There the Court effectively extended strict scrutiny to a local ordinance impinging on the "extended family." Powell sought to confine the ambit of substantive due process by offering the "teachings of history" and the "basic values that underlie our society" as guides for judging. It is interesting to recall that, only a few years before *Roe* and *Moore,* even as activist a Justice as Douglas had been uncomfortable with using substantive due process (hence his peculiar "emanations from a penumbra" opinion in GRISWOLD V. CONNECTICUT, 1965). The Burger Court, in opinions such as *Roe* and *Moore,* openly reestablished substantive due process as a means to limit governmental power.

Another index of judicial activism in the Supreme Court is the Court's willingness to declare an act of Congress unconstitutional. Striking down a state or local action in order to enforce the Constitution or federal law is common, but invalidation of congressional actions is rarer. The Warren Court struck down, on average, barely over one federal statute per term; the Burger Court has invalidated provisions of federal law at about twice that rate. More revealing is the significance of the congressional policies overturned in Burger Court decisions. Among them have been CAMPAIGN FINANCE (BUCKLEY V. VALEO, 1976), the eighteen-year-old vote in state elections (OREGON V. MITCHELL, 1970), special bankruptcy courts (NORTHERN PIPELINE CONSTRUCTION CO. V. MARATHON PIPE LINE CO., 1982), and the LEGISLATIVE VETO (IMMIGRATION AND NATURALIZATION SERVICE V. CHADHA, 1983).

Yet another measure of judicial activism is the Court's oversight of the behavior of coordinate branches of the federal government, apart from the substantive results of legislative or executive actions. The Burger Court thrust itself directly into the WATERGATE crisis, during Nixon's presidency. Even as the IMPEACHMENT process was underway in Congress, the Supreme Court, bypassing the Court of Appeals, expedited its hearing of the question whether Nixon must turn over the Watergate tapes. Denying Nixon's claim of EXECUTIVE PRIVILEGE, the Court set in motion the dénouement of the crisis, resulting in Nixon's resignation. The Burger Court has similarly been willing to pass on the arnbit of Congress's proper sphere of conduct. For example, the Court's narrow view of what activity is protected by the Constitution's SPEECH OR DEBATE CLAUSE would have surprised WOODROW WILSON, who placed great emphasis on Congress's role in informing the nation.

Closely related to the question of judicial activism is the breadth and scope of the Court's business—the range of issues which the Court chooses to address. Justice FELIX FRANKFURTER used to warn against the Court's plunging into "political thickets" and was distressed when the Warren Court chose to treat legislative apportionment as appropriate for judicial resolution.

Reviewing the record of the Burger Court, one is struck by the new ground it has plowed. Areas that were rarely entered or went untouched altogether in the Warren years have since 1969 become a staple of the Court's docket. In the 1960s Justice ARTHUR J. GOLDBERG sought in vain to have the Justices debate the merits of capital punishment, but the Court would not even grant CERTIORARI. By contrast, not only did the Burger Court, in *Furman v. Georgia* (1972), rule that capital statutes as then administered were unconstitutional, but also death cases have appeared on the Court's calendar with regularity. (See CAPITAL PUNISHMENT CASES, 1972, 1976.)

Sex discrimination is another area that, because of Burger Court decisions, has become a staple on the Justices' table. In *Hoyt v. Florida* (1961) the Warren Court took a quite relaxed view of claims of sex discrimination in a decision upholding a Florida law making jury service for women, but not for men, completely voluntary. By the time Warren Burger became Chief Justice, in 1969, the women's movement had become a visible aspect of the American scene, and since that time the Burger Court has fashioned a considerable body of law on women's rights.

The Burger Court has carried forward—or has been carried along with—the "judicialization" or "constitutionalization" of American life. The victories won by blacks in court in the heyday of the CIVIL RIGHTS movement have inspired others to emulate their example. Prisoners, voters victimized by malapportionment, women, juveniles, inmates of mental institutions—virtually any group or individual failing to get results from the legislative or political process or from government bureaucracies has turned to the courts for relief. And federal judges have woven remedies for a variety of ills.

The Burger Court might have been expected to resist the process of constitutionalization. On some fronts, the Justices have slowed the process. SAN ANTONIO INDEPENDENT SCHOOL DISTRICT V. RODRIGUEZ (1973) represents a victory for a hands-off approach to SCHOOL FINANCE (although it is undercut somewhat by the Court's subsequent decision in *Plyler v. Doe,* 1982). But such decisions seem to be only pauses in the expansion of areas in which the judiciary is willing to inquire.

The Burger Court may sometimes reach a "liberal" result, sometimes a "conservative" one. In some cases the Justices may lay a restraining hand on the EQUITY powers of federal judges, and in some they may be more permissive. All the while, however, the scope of the Supreme Court's docket expands to include wider terrain. In constitutional litigation, there seems to be a kind of ratchet effect: once judges enter an area, they rarely depart. This pattern characterizes the Burger era as much as it does that of Warren.

Even in areas that seemed well developed in the Warren Court, the Burger Court has added new glosses. It was long thought that COMMERCIAL SPEECH fell outside the protection of the First Amendment; the Burger Court brought it inside. It was Burger Court opinions that enlarged press rights under the First Amendment to include, at least in some circumstances, a right of access to criminal trials. The jurisprudence by which government aid to sectarian schools is tested is almost entirely of Burger Court making. Most of the case law sketching out the contours of personal autonomy in such areas as abortion, BIRTH CONTROL, and other intimate sexual and family relations dates from the Burger era. If idle hands are the devil's workshop, the Burger Court is a temple of virtue.

The contour of rights consists not only of substantive doctrine; it also includes jurisdiction and procedure. Who shall have access to the federal forum, when, and for the resolution of what rights—these have been battlegrounds in the Burger Court. If a case may be made that the Burger Court has achieved a retrenchment in rights, it may be that the case is the strongest as regards the Court's shaping of procedural devices.

Warren Court decisions reflected a mistrust in state courts as forums for the vindication of federal rights. Burger Court decisions, by contrast, are more likely to speak of the COMITY owed to state courts. Thus, in a line of decisions beginning with YOUNGER V. HARRIS (1971), the Burger Court has put significant limitations on the power of federal judges to interfere with proceedings (especially criminal) in state courts. The Court also has sharply curtailed the opportunity for state prisoners to seek federal habeas corpus review of state court decisions.

Technical barriers such as STANDING have been used in a number of cases to prevent plaintiffs' access to federal courts. For example, in *Warth v. Selden* (1976) black residents of Rochester were denied standing to challenge exclusionary ZONING in the city's suburbs. Similarly, in SIMON V. EASTERN KENTUCKY WELFARE RIGHTS ORGANIZATION (1976) poor residents of Appalachia were held not to have standing to challenge federal tax advantages granted to private hospitals that refused to serve the INDIGENT.

By no means, however, are Burger Court decisions invariable in restricting access to federal courts or in limiting remedies for the violation of federal law. Some of the Court's interpretations of SECTION 1983, OF TITLE 42, UNITED STATES CODE (a civil rights statute dating back to 1871) have made that statute a veritable font of litigation. The Warren Court had ruled, in 1961, that Congress, in enacting section 1983, had not intended that municipalities be among the "persons" subject to suit under the statute; in 1978, the Burger Court undertook a "fresh analysis" of the statute and concluded that municipalities are subject to suit thereunder.

Going further, the Court ruled, in 1980, that municipalities sued under section 1983 may not plead as a defense that the governmental official who was involved in the alleged wrong had acted in "good faith"; the majority disregarded the four dissenters' complaint that "ruinous judgments under the statute could imperil local governments." And in another 1980 decision the Court held that plaintiffs could use section 1983 to redress claims based on federal law generally, thus overturning a long-standing assumption that section 1983's reference to federal "laws" was to equal rights legislation. The Burger Court's section 1983 rulings have been a major factor in the "litigation explosion" which in recent years has been the subject of so much legal and popular commentary.

The reach of federal courts' equity powers has been another hotly debated issue in the Burger Court. CLASS ACTIONS seeking to reform practices in schools, prisons, jails, and other public institutions have made INSTITUTIONAL LITIGATION a commonplace. Such suits go far beyond the judge's declaring that a right has been violated; they draw the judge into ongoing supervision of state or local institutions (recalling the quip that in the 1960s federal district judge Frank Johnson was the real governor of Alabama). Institutional litigation in federal courts raises serious questions about federalism and often blurs the line between adjudication, legislation, and administration.

Some Burger Court decisions have attempted to curb federal judges' equity power in institutional cases. For example, in RIZZO V. GOODE (1976) Justice Rehnquist, for the majority, reversed a lower court's order to the Philadelphia police department to institute reforms responding to allegations of police brutality; Rehnquist admonished the judge to refrain from interfering in the affairs of local government. Similarly, in prison cases, the Burger Court has emphasized the importance of federal judges' deference to state prison officials' judgment about questions of prison security and administration.

In important respects, however, the Burger Court has done little to place notable limits on federal courts' equity powers. Especially is this true in school DESEGREGATION cases. A wide range of remedies has been approved, including busing, redrawing of attendance zones, and other devices. Although the Court has maintained the distinction between DE FACTO AND DE JURE segregation (thus requiring evidence of purposeful segregation as part of a plaintiff's prima facie case), decisions such as those from Columbus and Dayton (both in 1979) show great deference to findings of lower courts used to support remedial orders against local school districts.

Painting a coherent portrait of the Burger Court is no easy task. An effort to describe the Court in terms of general themes, such as the Justices' attitude to judicial activism, founders on conflicting remarks in the Court's opinions. Likewise, an attempt to generalize about the Burger Court's behavior in any given area encounters difficulties.

Consider, for example, the expectation—understandable in light of President Nixon's explicit concern about the Warren Court's rulings in criminal justice cases—that the Burger Court would be a "law and order" tribunal. In the early years of the Burger Court (until about 1976), the Court, especially in its rulings on police practices, seemed bent on undermining the protections accorded in decisions of the Warren years. The majority showed their attitude to the exclusionary rule by referring to it as a "judicially created remedy," one whose benefits were to be balanced against its costs (such as to the functioning of a GRAND JURY). In the late 1970s, the Court seemed more sympathetic to *Miranda* and to other devices meant to limit police practices. But in the early 1980s, especially in SEARCH AND SEIZURE cases, the Court seemed once again markedly sympathetic to law enforcement.

Or consider the Court's attitudes to federalism. In some decisions, the Burger Court has seemed sympathetic to the interests of states and localities. In limiting state prisoners' access to federal writs of habeas corpus, the Court shows respect for state courts. In rebuffing attacks on inequalities in the financing of a state's public schools, the Court gives breathing room to local judgments about running those schools. In limiting federal court intervention in prison affairs, the Court gives scope for state judgments about how to run a prison.

Yet many Burger Court decisions are decidedly adverse to state and local governments' interests. The Court's section 1983 rulings have exposed municipalities to expensive damage awards. The Burger Court has been more active than the Warren Court in using the dormant COMMERCE CLAUSE to restrict state laws and regulations found to impinge upon national interests. And in the highly controversial decision of GARCIA V. SAN ANTONIO METROPOLITAN TRANSIT AUTHORITY (1985) the Court said that, if the states have Tenth Amendment concerns about acts of Congress, they should seek relief from Congress, not from the courts (in so ruling, the Court in *Garcia* overturned NATIONAL LEAGUE OF CITIES V. USERY, 1976, itself a Burger Court decision).

How does one account for such a mixed record, replete with conflicting signals about basic jurisprudential values? The temperament and habits of the Justices of the Burger Court play a part. Pundits often imagine the Justices coming to the Court's conference table with "shopping lists," looking for cases on which to hang doctrinal innovations. For most (although not necessarily all) of the Justices, this picture is not accurate. By and large, the Justices tend to take the cases as they come. This tendency is reinforced by the Court's workload pressures. Far more cases come to the Burger Court than came to the Warren Court. Complaints by the Chief Justice about the burden thus placed on the Court are frequent, and in 1975 it was reported that at least five Justices had gone on record as favoring the concept of a National Court of Appeals to ease the Supreme Court's workload.

The Burger years on the Court have lacked the larger-than-life figures of the Warren era, Justices like HUGO L. BLACK and Felix Frankfurter, around whom issues tended to polarize. Those were judges who framed grand designs, a jurisprudence of judging. Through their fully evolved doctrines, and their arm-twisting, they put pressure on their colleagues to think about cases in doctrinal terms. Since the departure of the great ideologues, the Justices have been under less pressure to fit individual cases into doctrinal tableaux. Ad hoc results become the order of the day.

The Burger Court has been a somewhat less ideological bench than was the Warren Court. Many of the Court's most important decisions have turned upon the vote of the centrists on the bench. It is not unusual to find, especially in 5–4 decisions, that Justice Powell has cast the deciding vote. Powell came to the bench inclined to think in the pragmatic way of the practicing lawyer; as a Justice he soon came to be identified with "balancing" competing interests to arrive at a decision. The Burger Court's pragmatism, its tendency to gravitate to the center, blurs ideological lines and makes its jurisprudence often seem to lack any unifying theme or principle.

A Burger Court decision—more often, a line of decisions—often has something for everyone. In *Roe v. Wade* the Court upheld the right of a woman to make and effectuate a decision to have an abortion. Yet, while invalidating state laws found to burden the abortion decision directly, the Court has permitted state and federal governments to deny funding for even therapeutic abortions while funding other medical procedures. In REGENTS OF THE UNIVERSITY OF CALIFORNIA V. BAKKE (1978) a majority of the Justices ruled against RACIAL QUOTAS in a state university's admissions process, but a university, consistent with *Bakke,* may use race as a factor among other factors in the admissions process.

Burger Court decisions show a distaste for categorical values. The Warren Court's fondness for prophylactic rules, such as *Miranda* or the Fourth Amendment exclusionary rule, is not echoed in the Burger Court. The Burger bench may not have jettisoned those rules outright, but most Justices of this era show a preference for fact-oriented adjudication rather than for sweeping formulae.

Burger Court opinions are less likely than those of the Warren Court to ring with moral imperatives. Even when resolving so fundamental a controversy as that over abortion, a Burger Court opinion is apt to resemble a legislative committee report more nearly than a tract in political theory. A comparison of such Warren Court opinions as *Brown v. Board of Education* and *Reynolds v. Sims* and a Burger Court opinion such as *Roe v. Wade* is instructive. Warren Court opinions often read as if their authors intended them to have tutorial value (Justice Goldberg once called the Supreme Court "the nation's schoolmaster"); Burger Court opinions are more likely to read like an exercise in problem solving.

For most of its existence, the Burger Court has been characterized by a lack of cohesive voting blocs. For much of its history, the Burger years have seen a 2–5–2 voting pattern—Burger and Rehnquist in one wing, Brennan and Marshall in the other wing, the remaining five Justices tending to take more central ground. Justice Stewart's replacement by Justice O'Connor (a more conservative Justice) tended to reinforce the Burger-Rehnquist wing, while Justice Stevens gravitated more and more to the Brennan-Marshall camp. Even so, the Burger Court was a long way from the sharp ideological alignments of the Warren years.

The Court's personalities and dynamics aside, the nature of the issues coming before the Burger Court help account for the mixed character of the Court's record. The Warren Court is well remembered for decisions laying down broad principles; *Brown, Mapp, Miranda,* and *Reynolds* are examples. The task of implementing much of what the Warren Court began fell to the Burger Court. Implementation, by its nature, draws courts into closer judgment calls. It is one thing to lay down the principle that public schools should not be segregated by race, but quite another to pick one's way through the thicket of de facto-de jure distinctions, interdistrict remedies, and shifting demographics. Had the Warren Court survived into the 1970s, it might have found implementation as difficult and splintering as has the Burger Court.

If the Warren Court embodied the heritage of progressivism and the optimistic expectations of post-World War II America, the Burger years parallel a period of doubt and uncertainty about solutions to social problems in the years after the Great Society, the VIETNAM WAR, and Watergate. In a time when the American people might have less confidence in government's capacity in other spheres, the Supreme Court might well intuitively be less bold in imposing its own solutions. At the same time, there appeared, in the Burger years, to be no turning back the clock on the expectations of lawyers and laity alike as to the place of an activist judiciary in public life. Debate over the proper role of the judiciary in a democracy is not insulated from debate over the role of government generally in a society aspiring to ORDERED LIBERTY. Judgments about the record of the Burger Court, therefore, tend to mirror contemporary American ideals and values.

A. E. DICK HOWARD

Bibliography

BLASI, VINCENT, ED. 1983 *The Burger Court: The Counter-Revolution That Wasn't.* New Haven, Conn.: Yale University Press.

FUNSTON, RICHARD Y. 1977 *Constitutional Counterrevolution?: The Warren Court and the Burger Court: Judicial Policy Making in Modern America.* Cambridge, Mass.: Schenkman.

LEVY, LEONARD W. 1974. *Against the Law: The Nixon Court and Criminal Justice.* New York: Harper & Row.

MASON, ALPHEUS T. 1979 *The Supreme Court from Taft to Burger,* 3rd ed. Baton Rouge: Louisiana State University Press.

WOODWARD, BOB and ARMSTRONG, SCOTT 1979 *The Brethren: Inside the Supreme Court.* New York: Simon & Schuster.

EMERSON, THOMAS I. 1980 First Amendment Doctrine and the Burger Court. *California Law Review* 68:422–481.

HOWARD, A. E. DICK 1972 Mr. Justice Powell and the Emerging Nixon Majority. *Michigan Law Review* 70:445–468.

REHNQUIST, WILLIAM H. 1980 The Notion of a Living Constitution. *Texas Law Review* 54:693–706.

SALTZBERG, STEPHEN A. 1980 Foreword: The Flow and Ebb of Constitutional Criminal Procedure in the Warren and Burger Courts. *Georgetown Law Journal* 69:151–209.

BURGESS, JOHN W.
(1842–1931)

John W. Burgess was professor of political science and constitutional law at Columbia University (1876–1912) where he founded America's first graduate department of political science. Trained in Germany, Burgess sought to develop an American political science based on historical determinism rather than the NATURAL RIGHTS assumptions of the DECLARATION OF INDEPENDENCE. He saw the Civil War as a necessary step in the process by which FEDERALISM gave way to nationalism. He understood the Constitution as creating the two spheres of government and liberty, and as granting rights to individuals rather than protecting preexisting rights. His most important book was *Political Science and Comparative Constitutional Law* (1890).

DENNIS J. MAHONEY

BURNS BAKING COMPANY v. BRYAN
264 U.S. 504 (1924)

The Supreme Court, speaking through Justice PIERCE BUTLER, declared unconstitutional a Nebraska statute that prohibited short-weighting as well as overweighting of bread as a violation of DUE PROCESS and an arbitrary interference with private business. Justice LOUIS D. BRANDEIS dissented, joined by OLIVER WENDELL HOLMES, decrying the decision as "an exercise of the powers of a super-legislature," and urging deference to the legislature's basis for state action.

DAVID GORDON

BURR, AARON
(1756–1836)

Aaron Burr of New York served as a Continental Army officer during the Revolutionary War and later practiced law in Albany and New York City. He was elected four times to the legislature and was for two years state attorney general before serving a term in the United States Senate (1791–1797). He organized the New York Republican party and was the first person to use the Tammany Society for political purposes.

In 1800 Burr was nominated for vice-president on the Republican ticket. Under the ELECTORAL COLLEGE system as it then existed, Burr received the same number of votes as his party's presidential nominee, THOMAS JEFFERSON. The House of Representatives took thirty-six ballots to break the tie and elect Jefferson President, and did so only after ALEXANDER HAMILTON interceded with Federalist congressmen.

After his term as vice-president ended in 1805, Burr became involved in a bizarre intrigue, generally supposed to have had as its object the creation of a separate nation southwest of the Appalachian Mountains. His expedition was thwarted, and Burr and several of his confederates were tried for TREASON. President Jefferson personally directed the prosecution and publicly proclaimed the conspirators guilty. In EX PARTE BOLLMAN AND SWARTOUT (1807) the Supreme Court released two of Burr's lieutenants on a writ of HABEAS CORPUS, refusing to extend the constitutional definition of treason to include conspiracy to commit the offense. A few months later Burr himself was tried before JOHN MARSHALL, sitting as circuit judge, and was acquitted on procedural grounds. The acquittal was the occasion of a renewed Jeffersonian assault against Marshall and the independence of the judiciary.

Burr spent the five years following his trial in European exile, and he never returned to public life.

DENNIS J. MAHONEY

Bibliography

LOMASK, MILTON 1979 *Aaron Burr: The Years from Princeton to Vice President, 1756–1805.* New York: Farrar, Straus & Giroux.

——— 1982 *Aaron Burr: The Conspiracy and Years of Exile, 1805–1836.* New York: Farrar, Straus & Giroux.

BURSTYN, INC. v. WILSON
343 U.S. 495 (1952)

The Supreme Court in this case unanimously overruled a 1915 decision that movies are a business "pure and simple," not entitled to constitutional protection as a medium for the communication of ideas. Justice TOM C. CLARK, for the *Burstyn* Court, ruled that expression by means of movies is included within the free speech and free press clauses of the FIRST AMENDMENT and protected against state abridgment by the FOURTEENTH. In this case New York authorized a state censor to refuse a license for the showing of any film deemed "sacrilegious," a standard that permitted unfettered and unprejudiced discretion.

(See VAGUENESS DOCTRINE.) The state, Clark declared, had no legitimate interest in protecting any religion from offensive views. Justice FELIX FRANKFURTER, concurring, emphasized the danger to the creative process and to RELIGIOUS LIBERTY from a standard so vague that it could be confused with BLASPHEMY.

LEONARD W. LEVY

BURTON, HAROLD
(1888–1964)

Probably no member of the United States Supreme Court enjoyed greater affection from his colleagues on the bench than Justice Harold Burton, whom FELIX FRANKFURTER once described as having "a kind of a boy scout temperament," and whom others praised for his kindness, reasonableness, and unfailing integrity. "There is no man on the bench now who has less pride of opinion," Frankfurter noted, ". . . or is more ready to change positions, if his mind can be convinced. And no vanity guards admission to his mind." Burton, a former mayor of Cleveland and United States senator from Ohio, enjoyed several other distinctions as well. Named to the Court in 1945, he was the only Republican appointed between 1933 and 1953; he also proved to be the most liberal of HARRY S. TRUMAN's four appointees, which, considering the nature of the competition, did not demand much liberalism.

Although dubbed by the press as one member of Truman's law firm, which also included FRED M. VINSON, TOM C. CLARK, and SHERMAN MINTON, Burton broke ranks with the President on the most crucial test of executive power during his tenure, when he joined Justice HUGO L. BLACK's opinion in YOUNGSTOWN SHEET & TUBE CO. V. SAWYER (1952), which declared Truman's seizure of the nation's steel mills illegal in the absence of congressional legislation.

With the notable exception of JOINT ANTI-FASCIST REFUGEE COMMITTEE V. MCGRATH (1951), however, Burton routinely upheld the Truman administration's efforts to destroy the American Communist party and to purge from the federal government suspected subversives during the high tide of the post-1945 Red Scare. He voted with the majority, for instance, in AMERICAN COMMUNICATIONS ASSOCIATION V. DOUDS (1950), in DENNIS V. UNITED STATES (1951), and in *Bailey v. Richardson* (1951), in which the VINSON COURT sustained the noncommunist oath provisions of the TAFT-HARTLEY ACT, the conviction of eleven top Communist party leaders under the Smith Act, and the federal government's LOYALTY AND SECURITY PROGRAM.

Apart from Minton and STANLEY F. REED, Burton became the most virulent antiradical on the bench during the 1950s. In SLOCHOWER V. BOARD OF EDUCATION (1956) he dissented against Clark's opinion voiding the dismissal of a professor who had invoked his right AGAINST SELF-INCRIMINATION during an investigation into his official conduct. He also dissented in SWEEZY V. NEW HAMPSHIRE (1957), when the Court reversed the conviction of another professor for refusing to answer questions about his classes posed by the state's attorney general. And he, Minton, and Reed were the only dissenters in PENNSYLVANIA V. NELSON (1956), when the Court invalidated the SEDITION law of that state and, by implication, similar statutes in other states.

Generally, Burton followed an equally conservative standard with respect to criminal justice issues. Here, too, he usually endorsed the claims of government rather than those of the individual. In *Bute v. Illinois* (1948) he wrote for a majority of five that reaffirmed the rule of BETTS V. BRADY (1942), which permitted the states to prosecute noncapital felonies without appointing counsel for indigent defendants. He also tolerated forms of police conduct that offended even Frankfurter's conception of DUE PROCESS. (See RIGHT TO COUNSEL.)

Moments of compassion and insight redeemed Burton's otherwise lackluster record in CIVIL LIBERTIES cases. In *Louisiana ex rel. Francis v. Resweber* (1947), perhaps his most famous opinion, he rebelled against Louisiana's efforts to execute a convicted murderer after the first grisly attempt failed because of low voltage in the electric chair. He also joined Black and Frankfurter in their futile efforts to secure a full hearing before the Supreme Court for Julius and Ethel Rosenberg, who were convicted of espionage at the depths of the cold war with the Soviet Union.

By the conclusion of his judicial career in 1956, moreover, he had emerged as one of the Court's most outspoken foes of racial SEGREGATION, despite an unpromising beginning in MORGAN V. VIRGINIA (1946), where he had been the lone dissenter against Black's opinion invalidating the application of that state's Jim Crow law to interstate buses. Four years before BROWN V. BOARD OF EDUCATION, Burton had been prepared to overrule the SEPARATE BUT EQUAL DOCTRINE in *Henderson v. United States* (1950). Reluctantly, he bowed to the preference of several colleagues for invoking the COMMERCE CLAUSE to topple segregation on southern railroads in that case, but he joined Chief Justice EARL WARREN's opinion eagerly in *Brown.* Suffering from a debilitating illness that later claimed his life, Burton retired from the Court in 1958.

MICHAEL E. PARRISH

Bibliography

BERRY, MARY F. 1978 *Stability, Security, and Continuity: Mr. Justice Burton and Decision-Making in the Supreme Court, 1945–1958.* Westport, Conn.: Greenwood Press.

BURTON v. WILMINGTON PARKING AUTHORITY

365 U.S. 715 (1961)

Burton exemplifies the interest-balancing approach to the STATE ACTION limitation of the FOURTEENTH AMENDMENT used by the Supreme Court during the Chief Justiceship of EARL WARREN. A private restaurant, leasing space in a publicly owned parking structure, refused to serve Burton because he was black. In a state court action, Burton sought declaratory and injunctive relief, claiming that the restaurant's refusal amounted to state action denying him the EQUAL PROTECTION OF THE LAWS. The state courts denied relief, but the Supreme Court reversed, 7–2, holding the Fourteenth Amendment applicable to the restaurant's conduct.

Public agencies owned the land and the building, had floated bonds, were collecting revenues to pay for the building's construction and maintenance, and received rent payments from the restaurant. The restaurant could expect to draw customers from persons parking in the structure; correspondingly, some might park there because of the restaurant's convenience. Profits earned from the restaurant's RACIAL DISCRIMINATION, the Court said, were indispensable elements in an integral financial plan. All these interrelated mutual benefits taken together amounted to significant involvement of the state in the private racial discrimination. Justice TOM C. CLARK, for the majority, disclaimed any pretensions of establishing a general rule about state aid to private discrimination, or even for the leasing of state property. Under "the peculiar facts or circumstances" here, the state action limitation was satisfied.

Justice POTTER STEWART, concurring, said simply that a state statute permitting a restaurant's proprietor to refuse service to persons offensive to a majority of patrons amounted to official authorization of private discrimination—a theme explored later in REITMAN v. MULKEY (1967). Justice JOHN MARSHALL HARLAN dissented, joined by Justice CHARLES E. WHITTAKER. Harlan complained that the majority had offered no guidance for determining when the state action limitation would be satisfied. Rather than pursue this inquiry, he urged a REMAND to the state courts for further illumination of the "authorization" question raised by Justice Stewart.

KENNETH L. KARST

BUSHELL'S CASE

6 State Trials 999 (1670)

A unanimous decision of the Court of Common Pleas, *Bushell's Case* stands for the proposition that a jury may not be punished for returning a verdict contrary to a court's direction. In medieval England, bribery and intimidation were commonly accepted methods of insuring "correct" verdicts, but the Privy Council and the Star Chamber had eliminated those practices by the sixteenth century. Nevertheless, the Star Chamber often handled as corrupt any acquittal that it felt contradicted the evidence. The popular view increasingly opposed punishment for jurors unless they returned a clearly corrupt verdict, and the House of Commons endorsed that position in 1667. The decision in *Bushell's Case* brought the law into line.

When jurors in a case against William Penn and other Quakers persisted in finding the defendants innocent—despite three days of starvation—Bushell and the other jurors were fined and imprisoned. Bushell obtained a writ of HABEAS CORPUS in the Court of Common Pleas and was subsequently discharged. Chief Justice John Vaughan delivered a powerful opinion distinguishing between the "ministerial" (administrative) and judicial functions of jurors. Violations of the former were finable but a verdict was judicial and therefore not subject to penalty. The Court only judged the law. The jury was obliged to deduce the facts from the evidence, and the court could not penalize them for disagreeing with its deductions and directions. Seventeenth-century jurors were expected and required to utilize their own knowledge of a case, private knowledge a judge likely did not have. Only by handpicking jurors could the Crown insure favorable verdicts.

DAVID GORDON

BUSING, SCHOOL

See: School Busing

BUTCHER'S UNION SLAUGHTERHOUSE v. CRESCENT CITY SLAUGHTERHOUSE
111 U.S. 746 (1884)

In this case the INALIENABLE POLICE POWER doctrine again defeated a VESTED RIGHTS claim based on the CONTRACT CLAUSE. Louisiana revoked a charter of monopoly privileges, which the Supreme Court had sustained in the first of the SLAUGHTERHOUSE CASES (1873). Although the contract was supposedly irrepealable for a period of twenty-five years, the Court, in an opinion by Justice SAMUEL F. MILLER, maintained that one legislature cannot bind its successors on a matter involving the GENERAL WELFARE, specifically the public health. No legislature can contract away the state's inalienable power to govern slaughterhouses, which affect the public health. Four Justices, concurring separately, argued that the original monopoly was unconstitutional and its charter revocable, because it violated the liberty and property of competing butchers; the four employed SUBSTANTIVE DUE PROCESS in construing the FOURTEENTH AMENDMENT.

LEONARD W. LEVY

BUTLER, BENJAMIN F.
(1818–1893)

A Massachusetts labor lawyer and Democratic politician, Benjamin Franklin Butler became a Union general in 1861. Butler declared that runaway slaves were "contrabands of war," and used them as noncombatants, refusing to return them to their masters. Later he supported the use of Negro soldiers and in 1864 forced the Confederacy to treat black Union prisoners of war according to the rules of war by retaliating against Confederate prisoners. In 1862 Butler directed the occupation of New Orleans, where his strict application of martial law kept a hostile population under control with virtually no violence. In 1865 Butler advocated that black veterans be given confiscated land and the franchise. After entering Congress in 1867, Butler was a manager of President ANDREW JOHNSON's IMPEACHMENT. Butler approached the trial as if he were prosecuting a horse thief. Butler's lack of dignity in presenting EVIDENCE probably contributed to Johnson's acquittal.

PAUL FINKELMAN

Bibliography

HOLZMAN, ROBERT S. 1978 *Stormy Ben Butler.* New York: Octagon Books.

BUTLER, PIERCE
(1744–1822)

Irish-born Pierce Butler represented South Carolina at the CONSTITUTIONAL CONVENTION OF 1787 and signed the Constitution. It was Butler who first proposed the Convention's secrecy rule. A frequent speaker, he favored a weak central government and championed the interests of slaveholders. He was later a United States senator.

DENNIS J. MAHONEY

BUTLER, PIERCE
(1866–1939)

President WARREN G. HARDING appointed Pierce Butler to the Supreme Court in 1922 in part because Harding wanted to name a conservative Democrat. He also preferred a Roman Catholic. As with other Harding judicial appointments, Chief Justice WILLIAM HOWARD TAFT had an influential role. Before his appointment, Butler had gained some fame as a railroad attorney, particularly for his defense of the carriers in the MINNESOTA RATE CASES (1913) and for his actions as a regent of the University of Minnesota, which led to the dismissal of faculty members who opposed World War I or who were socialists.

Progressive senators opposed Butler's confirmation, but marshaled only eight votes against him. The *New York Times* said that Butler's antagonists favored only judges who supported labor unions and opposed CORPORATIONS; the *St. Louis Post-Dispatch* countered that Butler's chief qualities were "bigotry, intolerance, narrowness, and partisanism." Taft predictably praised the appointment as "a most fortunate one." Until his death in 1939, Butler consistently followed the ideological direction friends and foes had anticipated.

Butler maintained his hostility to political dissenters while on the bench. He supported the majority in upholding a New York criminal anarchy law in GITLOW V. NEW YORK (1925). In UNITED STATES V. SCHWIMMER (1929) he sustained the government's denial of CITIZENSHIP to a sixty-year-old pacifist woman. In 1931 he broke with the majority in STROMBERG V. CALIFORNIA and in NEAR V. MINNESOTA to favor a state conviction of a woman who had displayed a red flag and a state court INJUNCTION against a newspaper editor who had harshly criticized public officials. In the *Near* case, Butler contended that FREEDOM OF THE PRESS should not protect an "insolent publisher who may have purpose and sufficient capacity to contrive and put into effect a scheme or program for oppression, blackmail, or extortion." Six years later Butler joined three others to protest the Court's revival of Justice OLIVER WENDELL HOLMES's CLEAR AND PRESENT DANGER doctrine in HERNDON V. LOWRY (1937). In one of his final statements, in *Kessler v. Strecker* (1939), he approved the DEPORTATION of an ALIEN who had once joined the Communist party but had never paid dues and long since had left the organization.

A Justice's views rarely are monolithic. In the area of CIVIL RIGHTS, for example, Butler stood alone in opposing state STERILIZATION of mental "defectives" in BUCK V. BELL (1927). Perhaps Butler's Catholicism motivated his vote; in any event, a half century later it was discovered that the sterilized woman had never been an imbecile, as Justice Holmes had callously characterized her. Butler also had strong views on the sanctity of the FOURTH AMENDMENT. In OLMSTEAD V. UNITED STATES (1928) he dissented from Taft's opinion upholding the use of WIRETAPPING for gaining evidence, and in another PROHIBITION case Butler insisted that the Fourth Amendment's prohibition of UNREASONABLE SEARCHES should be construed liberally. "Security against unlawful searches is more likely to be attained by resort to SEARCH WARRANTS than by reliance upon the caution and sagacity of petty officers," he wrote in *United States v. Lefkowitz* (1932).

His concern for the criminally accused, however, was not reflected in POWELL V. ALABAMA (1932), as he dissented with Justice JAMES C. MCREYNOLDS when the Court held that the "Scottsboro Boys" had been denied their RIGHT TO COUNSEL. He consistently opposed black claimants. For example, he dissented when the Court invalidated the Texas all-white primary election in NIXON V. CONDON (1932); he asserted in BREEDLOVE V. SUTTLES (1937) that payment of a POLL TAX as a condition to exercise VOTING RIGHTS did not violate the FOURTEENTH AMENDMENT; and he dissented when the Court first successfully attacked the SEPARATE BUT EQUAL DOCTRINE in MISSOURI EX REL. GAINES V. CANADA (1938). He also sustained state laws that prevented aliens from owning farm land in *Porterfield v. Webb* (1923).

Throughout the 1920s, Butler found the Court receptive to his conservative economic views. He was an aggressive spokesman for the claims of utilities, particularly in rate and valuation cases. He insisted on judicial prerogatives in such cases, relying on DUE PROCESS OF LAW to justify a court's determination of both law and facts. In general, Butler favored valuing utility property at reproduction costs in order to determine rate structures. He led the Court in striking down a state statute forbidding use of unsterilized material in the manufacture of mattresses in *Weaver v. Palmer Bros. Co.* (1924); and, in EUCLID V. AMBLER REALTY COMPANY (1926), he dissented when the Court, led by his fellow conservative, Justice GEORGE H. SUTHERLAND, sustained local zoning laws.

In the tumultuous New Deal years, Butler was one of the conservative "Four Horsemen," along with McReynolds, Sutherland, and WILLIS VAN DEVANTER. He opposed every New Deal measure that came before the Court. Butler rarely spoke in these cases, but before the Court reorganization battle he wrote the majority opinion narrowly invalidating a New York minimum wage law. Echoing LOCHNER V. NEW YORK (1905) and invoking ADKINS V. CHILDREN'S HOSPITAL (1923), Butler declared in MOREHEAD V. NEW YORK EX REL. TIPALDO (1936) that the state act violated the FOURTEENTH AMENDMENT's due process clause. Less than a year later, the *Tipaldo* decision was overturned. Thereafter, Butler and his fellow conservatives found themselves at odds with the new majority. To the end, however, they all resolutely kept the faith.

STANLEY I. KUTLER

Bibliography

BROWN, FRANCIS JOSEPH 1945 *The Social and Economic Philosophy of Pierce Butler.* Washington: Catholic University Press.

DANIELSKI, DAVID J. 1964 *A Supreme Court Justice Is Appointed.* New York: Random House.

BUTLER v. MICHIGAN
352 U.S. 380 (1957)

Michigan convicted Butler for selling to an adult an "obscene" book that might corrupt the morals of a minor. The Supreme Court unanimously reversed, in an opinion by Justice FELIX FRANKFURTER, who declared that the statute was not restricted to the evil with which it dealt; it reduced adults "to reading only what is fit for children," thereby curtailing their FIRST AMENDMENT rights as protected by the DUE PROCESS clause of the FOURTEENTH AMENDMENT.

LEONARD W. LEVY

BUTLER, UNITED STATES v.
297 U.S. 1 (1936)

In this historic and monumentally inept opinion, the Supreme Court ruled that the United States has no power to regulate the agrarian sector of the economy.

The AGRICULTURAL ADJUSTMENT ACT OF 1933 (AAA) sought to increase the purchasing power and living standards of farmers by subsidizing the curtailment of farm PRODUCTION and thus boosting farm prices. Congress raised the money for the subsidies by levying an EXCISE TAX on the primary processors of each crop, in this case a cotton mill, which passed on to the consumer the cost of the tax. AAA was the agricultural equivalent of a protective tariff. By a vote of 6–3 the Court held, in an opinion by Justice OWEN ROBERTS, that the statute unconstitutionally invaded the powers reserved to the states by the TENTH AMENDMENT. "It is a statutory plan," Roberts declared, "to regulate and control agricultural production, a matter beyond the powers delegated to the federal government. The tax, the appropriation of the funds raised, and the direction for their disbursement, are but parts of the plan. They are but means to an unconstitutional end." Roberts reached his DOCTRINE of DUAL FEDERALISM by simplistic MECHANICAL JURISPRUDENCE. He sought to match the statute with the Constitution and, finding that they did not square, seriously limited the TAXING AND SPENDING POWER.

Roberts did not question the power of Congress to levy an excise tax on the processing of agricultural products; he also conceded that "the power of Congress to authorize expenditures of public moneys for public purposes is not limited by the direct grants of legislative power found in the Constitution." He did not even deny that aiding the agrarian sector of the economy benefited the GENERAL WELFARE, in accord with the first clause of Article I, section 8; rather he reasoned that the Court did not need to decide whether an appropriation in aid of agriculture fell within the clause. He simply found that the Constitution did not vest in the government a power to regulate agricultural production. He ruled, too, that the tax was not really a tax, because Congress had not levied it for the benefit of the government; it expropriated money from processors to give to farmers. The tax power cannot, Roberts declared, be used as an instrument to enforce a regulation of matters belonging to the exclusive realm of the states, nor can the tax power be used to coerce a compliance which Congress has no power to command.

Despite Roberts's insistence on calling the crop curtailment program "coercive," it was in fact voluntary; a minority of farmers elected not to restrict production, foregoing subsidies. But Roberts added that even a voluntary plan would be unconstitutional as a "federal regulation of a subject reserved to the states." He added: "It does not help to declare that local conditions throughout the nation have created a situation of national concern; for that is but to say that whenever there is a widespread similarity of local conditions, Congress may ignore constitutional limitations upon its own powers and usurp those reserved to the states."

Justice HARLAN FISKE STONE, joined by Justices LOUIS D. BRANDEIS and BENJAMIN N. CARDOZO, wrote a scathing, imperishable dissent, one of the most famous in the Court's history. Strongly defending the constitutionality of the AAA on the basis of the power to tax and spend, Stone lambasted Roberts's opinion as hardly rising "to the dignity of an argument" and as a "tortured construction of the Constitution." Stone's opinion confirmed President FRANKLIN D. ROOSEVELT's belief that it was the Court, not the Constitution, that stood in the way of recovery. The AAA decision helped provoke the constitutional crisis of 1937.

LEONARD W. LEVY

Bibliography

HART, HENRY M. 1936 Processing Taxes and Protective Tariffs. *Harvard Law Review* 49:610–618.

MURPHY, PAUL L. 1955 The New Deal Agricultural Program and the Constitution. *Agricultural History* 29:160–169.

BUTZ v. ECONOMOU
438 U.S. 478 (1978)

In an action against the Department of Agriculture and individual department officials for alleged constitutional violations, the Court united two previously separate doctrinal strands governing official liability. *Butz* indicated that immunity from personal liability of federal executive officials in direct actions under the Constitution would be available only under circumstances in which state executive officials would be immune from analogous constitutional actions under SECTION 1983, TITLE 42, UNITED STATES CODE. *Butz* also extended absolute immunity to judicial and prosecutorial officials within an administrative agency.

THEODORE EISENBERG

(SEE ALSO: *Executive Immunity; Judicial Immunity.*)

BYRNES, JAMES F.
(1879–1972)

Few members of the United States Supreme Court in this century have led more varied political lives than James F. Byrnes of South Carolina, who served as congressman, United States senator, and governor of his state, czar of production during World War II, and secretary of state. In these other roles, Byrnes left a larger historical legacy than he did on the Court, where he remained for only the October 1941 term.

He wrote sixteen opinions for the Court, never dissented, and did not write a CONCURRING OPINION. As a Justice, he is remembered chiefly for his opinion in EDWARDS v. CALIFORNIA (1942), where he and four others invalidated as a burden on INTERSTATE COMMERCE a California "anti-Okie" law that made it a MISDEMEANOR to bring into the state indigent nonresidents. Initially, Byrnes had been inclined to strike down the law as a violation of the PRIVILEGES AND IMMUNITIES clause of the FOURTEENTH AMENDMENT (a position held by four other Justices), but he finally rejected this approach under pressure from Chief Justice HARLAN FISKE STONE and Justice FELIX FRANKFURTER. Although he also wrote for the Court in *Taylor v. Georgia* (1942), where the Justices voided that state's debt-peonage law, Byrnes did not usually exhibit great sensitivity to the claims of CIVIL LIBERTIES, or to the complaints of convicted felons and working-class people.

MICHAEL E. PARRISH

Bibliography

BYRNES, JAMES 1958 *All in One Lifetime.* New York: Harper & Row.

CABELL v. CHAVEZ-SALIDO

See: Aliens

CABINET

Whether or not the President should have a cabinet or council was a leading issue at the CONSTITUTIONAL CONVENTION. Such bodies were prevalent in the colonial governments and in the states that succeeded them. Another key element of the cabinet that also crystallized in the preconstitutional period was the concept of the department. Under the ARTICLES OF CONFEDERATION, Congress established four executive offices in 1781: a secretary of foreign affairs, a secretary of war, a superintendent of finance, and a secretary of marine.

At the Philadelphia Convention, GOUVERNEUR MORRIS proposed that there be a Council of State, consisting of the Chief Justice of the Supreme Court and the heads of departments or secretaries, of which there should be five, appointed by the President and holding office at his pleasure. The President should be empowered to submit any matter to the council for discussion and to require the written opinion of any one or more of its members. The President would be free to exercise his own judgment, regardless of the counsel he received. Morris's proposal was rejected in the late-hour efforts of the Committee of Eleven to complete the draft of the Constitution. Instead, the Committee made two principal provisions for advice for the President. Its draft specified that "The President, by and with the ADVICE AND CONSENT of the Senate, shall appoint ambassadors, and other public ministers, judges of the Supreme Court, and all other officers of the United States, whose appointments are not herein provided for." This provision is attributed to the New York state constitution in which the governor shared the appointment power with the Senate. The draft by the Committee of Eleven also provided that the President "may require the opinion, in writing, of the principal officer of each of the Executive Departments upon any subject relating to the duties of their respective offices."

GEORGE MASON resisted this plan, declaring that omission of a council for the President was an experiment that even the most despotic government would not undertake. Mason proposed an executive council composed of six members, two from the eastern, two from the middle, and two from the southern states. BENJAMIN FRANKLIN seconded the proposal, observing that a council would check a bad President and be a relief to a good one. Gouverneur Morris objected that the President might induce such a council to acquiesce in his wrong measures and thereby provide protection for them. Morris's view prevailed and Mason's plan was defeated. Doubtless a potent factor in the outcome was the expectation that the venerated GEORGE WASHINGTON would become the first President and that a council of some power might impede his functioning. CHARLES PINCKNEY, who once had advocated a council, now argued that it might "thwart" the President.

With the Constitution's prescriptions so sparse, it remained for Washington's presidency to amplify the concept of the cabinet. Congress in 1789 created three departments (State, War, and Treasury) and an attorney general who was not endowed with a department. Washington's appointees—THOMAS JEFFERSON as secretary of state, ALEXANDER HAMILTON as secretary of treasury, Major General Henry Knox as secretary of war, and EDMUND RANDOLPH as attorney general—reflected Mason's emphasis on geographic representation, for they were drawn from the three principal sections of the country. Washington frequently requested the written opinions of his secretaries on important issues and asked them for suggestions for the annual address to Congress.

In 1793, the diplomatic crisis arising from the war between Britain and France caused the cabinet to take firmer shape as an institution. Washington and his secretaries gathered in a series of meetings, including a notable one of April 19 at which the issuance of the PROCLAMATION OF NEUTRALITY was agreed upon. Jefferson recorded that the meetings occurred "almost every day." Because the crisis persisted throughout 1793, the collegial character of the cabinet became well established. Jefferson, Randolph, and Madison referred to the assembled secretaries as the "cabinet," but Washington did not employ the term. Although "cabinet" was long employed in congressional discussion, it did not appear in statutes until the General Appropriation Act of 1907.

The Constitution's meager provisions left Washington largely free to tailor the cabinet to his own preferences. He selected his secretaries on the basis of their individual talents, without regard to their political or policy predispositions. This procedure proved costly, leading to continuous dispute between Hamilton and Jefferson that required a remaking of the cabinet. Washington then resolved not to recruit appointees strongly opposed to his policies. Presidents have applied this principle in constituting their cabinets ever since.

Washington did not consider himself limited by the Constitution to seeking advice only from his department heads. Congressman JAMES MADISON was a frequent adviser on Anglo-American diplomatic issues, on executive appointments, and on the President's reply to the formal addresses of the two houses of Congress. Chief Justice JOHN JAY provided counsel on diplomatic questions, addresses to Congress, and on the political aspects of a presidential tour of the New England states.

Washington was less successful in seeking counsel from the Senate and the Supreme Court. He visited the Senate to discuss issues arising from an Indian treaty under negotiation, and was rebuffed when legislators made clear that his presence constrained their deliberations. The SUPREME COURT, equally self-protective, declined to render ADVISORY OPINIONS.

Washington set the pattern for future presidencies in reaffirming the constitutional arrangement of a strong, independent, single executive, and in rejecting any division of responsibility between the President and the cabinet. Ever since, the view has prevailed that the Constitution confers upon the President the ultimate executive authority and responsibility, which he does not share with the department heads individually or collectively.

Like the President, the cabinet is subject to such basic principles as SEPARATION OF POWERS and CHECKS AND BALANCES, on which the Constitution was constructed. Consequently, both the cabinet and the President are susceptible to the influence of the other two branches. The paucity of constitutional provision and the circumstances of the cabinet's beginning in Washington's administration, together with its continuous presence in all succeeding administrations, cause the cabinet's institutional status to rest upon custom. Since its founding in 1793, the cabinet, as Richard F. Fenno, Jr., has written, has continued to be "an extra-legal creation, functioning in the interstices of the law, surviving in accordance with tradition, and institutionalized by usage alone." Its influence and, to a large degree, its form rest on the will of the President of the moment.

Not surprisingly, given its acute dependence on the President, the cabinet has varied widely in its functions and its importance. Jefferson recruited a cabinet of supportive fellow partisans, but JOHN QUINCY ADAMS drew into his cabinet representatives of his party's great factions who had contested his rise to the Presidency. JAMES MONROE used his cabinet for the arduous crafting of the MONROE DOCTRINE, but ABRAHAM LINCOLN is one of many Presidents who used his cabinet sparingly. ANDREW JACKSON preferred the counsel of his "kitchen cabinet," an informal, unofficial body of friends who did not hold high position. JOHN TYLER rejected the request of his Whig cabinet that matters be decided by majority vote, with each secretary and the President having but one vote. ANDREW JOHNSON added fuel to the flames of his IMPEACHMENT when he removed Secretary of War EDWIN M. STANTON. Johnson's congressional foes contended that he violated the TENURE OF OFFICE ACT of 1867, which purported to deny the President the right to remove civil officials, including members of his cabinet, without senatorial consent.

The twentieth century, too, has seen wide variation

in the demeanors of Presidents toward their cabinets, from WARREN G. HARDING, who considered it his duty to build a cabinet comprised of the "best minds" in the nation, to WOODROW WILSON and JOHN F. KENNEDY, who used their cabinets little and chafed under extended group discussion. DWIGHT D. EISENHOWER endeavored to make the cabinet a central force in his administration through innovations to enhance its operating effectiveness. He created the post of secretary of the cabinet, empowered to arrange an agenda for cabinet meetings and to oversee the preparation of "cabinet papers" by the departments and agencies presenting proposals for cabinet deliberation and presidential decision. The results of cabinet discussions were recorded, responsibilities for implementation were allotted among the departments and agencies, and a system of follow-up was installed to check on accomplishment.

RICHARD M. NIXON designated four members of his cabinet counselors to the President and empowered them to supervise clusters of activity in several or more departments and agencies. With his popularity dropping and an election looming, JIMMY CARTER reshuffled his administration on an unprecedented scale in 1979 by ejecting discordant cabinet secretaries and replacing them with more supportive appointees. RONALD REAGAN instituted a structure of cabinet councils for broad policy areas with memberships of department secretaries and White House staff, supported by subcabinet working groups.

The cabinet's lack of specific delineation in the Constitution contributes to its weakness in coordinating the far-flung activities of the executive branch and in producing innovative policy on the scale and at the pace the President requires. These shortcomings have caused the cabinet to be overshadowed by more recent institutions of the modern presidency that assist in policy development and coordination. These are largely concentrated in the Executive Office of the President, which includes, among other units, the White House Office, the OFFICE OF MANAGEMENT AND BUDGET, the National Security Council, and the Council of Economic Advisers.

The cabinet's frail constitutional base has made the development of the departments susceptible to forces inimical to the cohesiveness that the concept of a "cabinet" implies. Often departments, such as Labor, Agriculture, and Commerce, were brought into being more by the pressures of their client groups than by the President's preference, and without a clear concept of what a department should be. Frequently alliances are formed between the client groups, the department's bureaus, and congressional committees with jurisdiction over the department. These alliances' combined strength has often exceeded the President's and frustrated his will. Even department heads have sometimes proved more responsive to their alliances than to the President.

Because the doctrines of separation of powers and checks and balances bring the cabinet and its departments within reach of the courts and Congress, those branches too have shaped those executive institutions. The Supreme Court, for example, in *Kendall v. United States* (1838), circumscribed the President's discretionary power over the department head when it upheld a lower court decision ordering the postmaster general to pay a complainant money owed by the United States. The payment was a MINISTERIAL ACT which gave the President "no other control over the officer than to see that he acts honestly, with proper motives." Despite the silence of the Constitution concerning the power of removal, Presidents have long removed department heads for any cause they see fit, and in MYERS V. UNITED STATES (1926) the Court upheld an order of the postmaster general to remove a first-class postmaster despite a statute requiring that the removal be by the advice and consent of the Senate.

The cabinet departments depend on Congress for money, personnel, and other resources necessary to function. In effect, department secretaries look to Congress for the means of survival, sometimes straining their ties with the President. Much of the substance of cabinet rank is provided by Congress: salary, title, membership in bodies such as the National Security Council, place in the line of presidential succession. Members of Congress often assert that department heads, notwithstanding their relation with the President, have responsibilities to the legislators. The powers and functions of the department head are conferred by acts of Congress. Although Congress respects the cabinet secretary's advisory role to the President, he is not solely the President's aide in his extracabinet functions, but performs in a shadow area of joint executive-legislative responsibility, and struggles with the resulting dilemmas. It is virtually indispensable that a department secretary attract the confidence of Congress as well as that of the President.

The cabinet's few moorings in the Constitution make its relationships with the POLITICAL PARTIES uncertain and fluctuating. Wilson once conceived of the cabinet as a potential link between the President and his party in Congress. He subsequently abandoned this view and like many other Presidents emphasized loyalty and competence in cabinet selection. JOHN QUINCY ADAMS, Warren G. Harding, HARRY

S. TRUMAN, and other Presidents used the cabinet to diminish intraparty factionalism, chiefly by appointing their rivals for the presidential nomination to cabinet posts. Eisenhower allotted several posts to persons with ties to his rival, ROBERT A. TAFT. Parties, however, have considerably less influence on the cabinet than the chief executive or Congress.

LOUIS W. KOENIG

Bibliography

FENNO, RICHARD F., JR. 1959 *The President's Cabinet.* Cambridge, Mass.: Harvard University Press.

HINSDALE, MARY 1911 *A History of the President's Cabinet.* Ann Arbor: University of Michigan Press.

HORN, STEPHEN 1960 *The Cabinet and Congress.* New York: Columbia University Press.

CAHN, EDMOND
(1906–1964)

Edmond Cahn's civil libertarianism emphasized the importance of a written Constitution and the role of the judiciary in upholding the guarantees of the BILL OF RIGHTS. JUDICIAL REVIEW is a historically "legitimate" device, he believed, for "converting promises on parchment into living liberties," and the Supreme Court is "the nation's exemplar and disseminator of democratic values." "The firstness of the FIRST AMENDMENT" ensures "the indefinitely continuing right to be exposed to an ideological variety." SEPARATION OF CHURCH AND STATE strengthens both entities and places sovereignty of choice in the populace. The First Amendment, by securing the basis for participation in the democratic process, provides an indispensable moral link between the governed and the governors.

Cahn's fact-skepticism, continually questioning factual assumptions, led him to indict CAPITAL PUNISHMENT, because a mistake-laden legal system should not impose an irreversible penalty. He insisted that the morally neutral social sciences occupy a subordinate place in judicial decisions and that "a judge untethered by a text is a dangerous instrument." He shared much in common with his friend, Justice HUGO L. BLACK, whose off-Court advocacy of First Amendment ABSOLUTISM he did not explicitly adopt. Cahn, a professor of law at New York University, had great confidence in the democratic citizen, freed from false certainties and protected by the mandates of the Bill of Rights, to prevent or repair injustice.

ROGER K. NEWMAN

CALANDRA, UNITED STATES v.
414 U.S. 338 (1974)

In *Calandra* the Court refused to apply the EXCLUSIONARY RULE to bar a GRAND JURY from questioning a witness on the basis of unlawfully seized EVIDENCE. The Court pointed out that although grand juries are subject to certain constitutional limitations, they are not bound by the restrictive procedures that govern trials. Since the exclusionary rule is not a constitutional right that redresses an invasion of privacy, but rather a deterrent against future police misconduct, its application should be restricted to situations where it will be most effective as a remedy. Exclusion at the grand jury level would deter only those searches in which evidence is intended solely for grand jury use; if the evidence should be presented at a subsequent trial, it would be excluded.

JACOB W. LANDYNSKI

CALDER v. BULL
3 Dallas 386 (1798)

Calder is the leading case on the meaning of the constitutional injunction against EX POST FACTO LAWS. Connecticut had passed an act setting aside a court decree refusing to probate a will, and the plaintiff argued that the act constituted an ex post facto law. In the Court's main opinion Justice SAMUEL CHASE ruled that although all ex post facto laws are necessarily "retrospective," retrospective laws adversely affecting the citizen in his private right of property or contracts are not ex post facto laws. The prohibition against the latter extended only to criminal, not civil, cases. An ex post facto law comprehends any retrospective penal legislation, such as making criminal an act that was not criminal when committed, or aggravating the act into a greater crime than at the time it was committed, or applying increased penalties for the act, or altering the rules of EVIDENCE to increase the chances of conviction.

The case is also significant in constitutional history because by closing the door on the ex post facto route in civil cases, it encouraged the opening of another door and thus influenced the course of the DOCTRINE OF VESTED RIGHTS. The CONTRACT CLAUSE probably would not have attained its importance in our constitutional history, nor perhaps the DUE PROCESS clause substantively construed, if the Court had extended the ex post facto clause to civil cases. In *Calder,* Chase endorsed the judicial doctrine of vested rights drawn from the HIGHER LAW, as announced by Justice WILLIAM PATERSON in VAN HORNE'S LESSEE v. DORRANCE (1795). Drawing on "the very nature of our free Republican governments" and "the great first principles of the social compact," Chase declared that the legislative power, even if not expressly restrained by a written CONSTITUTION, could not constitutionally violate the right of an antecedent and lawful private contract or the right of private property. To assert otherwise, he maintained, would "be a political heresy," inadmissible to the genius and spirit of our governmental system.

Justice JAMES IREDELL concurred in the judgment as well as the definition of ex post facto laws but maintained that judges should not hold an act void "merely because it is, in their judgment, contrary to the principles of natural justice," which he thought undefinable by fixed standards. (See FUNDAMENTAL LAW; SUBSTANTIVE DUE PROCESS.)

LEONARD W. LEVY

CALHOUN, JOHN C.
(1782–1850)

John C. Calhoun, foremost southern statesman of his time, was a product of the great Scots-Irish migration that took possession of the southern backcountry before the American Revolution. Born near Abbeville, South Carolina, young Calhoun received a smattering of education at a local academy and in his twentieth year went "straight from the backwoods" to Yale College. He excelled by force of intellect and zeal. In 1805, not long after graduating, he attended Litchfield Law School. This New England Federalist education left a permanent impression on Calhoun's mind, though all his political associations were Jeffersonian. Returning to South Carolina, he was admitted to the bar and hung out his shingle in Abbeville. But Calhoun did not take to the law. After making it the steppingstone to the political career he desperately wanted, he gave it up altogether. In 1807 he was elected to the legislature, taking the seat once held by his father. Sometime later he married Floride Bonneau Colhoun, who belonged to the wealthy lowcountry branch of the family, and brought her to the plantation he had acquired above the Savannah River. After two sessions at Columbia, Calhoun won election to the Twelfth Congress. He took his place with the "war hawks" and upon a brilliant maiden speech was hailed as "one of the master-spirits who stamp their name upon the age in which they live."

Calhoun's major biographer has conveniently divided his career into three phases: nationalist, nullifier, sectionalist. During the first, which ended in 1828, Calhoun was successively congressman, secretary of war, and vice-president. As a nationalist, he was the chief congressional architect of the Second Bank of the United States; he supported the tariff of 1816, including its most protective feature, the minimum duty on cheap cotton cloth; and he was a prominent advocate of INTERNAL IMPROVEMENTS. Many Republicans, headed by President JAMES MADISON, believed a constitutional amendment was necessary to sanction federally funded internal improvements. But Calhoun, speaking for his Bonus Bill to create a permanent fund for this purpose, declared that he "was no advocate for refined arguments on the Constitution. The instrument was not intended as a thesis for the logician to exercise his ingenuity on. It ought to be construed with plain, good sense. . . ." He held that the GENERAL WELFARE clause was a distinct power; to those who balked at that, he cited the ENUMERATED POWER to establish post roads. Deeply committed to a system of roads and canals and other improvements to strengthen the Union and secure its defenses, Calhoun, like Hamilton before him, viewed the Constitution as the starting-point for creative statesmanship. Later, when advocating internal improvements as secretary of war, he passed over the constitutional question in silence, thereby avoiding conflict with his chief, JAMES MONROE, who inherited Madison's scruples on the subject.

Calhoun made his first bid for the presidency in 1824 as an unabashed nationalist who professed "to be above all sectional or party feelings and to be devoted to the great interests of the country." He had to settle for the vice-presidency, however; and in that office he seized the first occasion to join the Jacksonian coalition against the National Republican administration of JOHN QUINCY ADAMS. Meanwhile, economic distress revolutionized the politics of South Carolina, driving Calhoun's friends off the nationalist platform and onto the platform of STATES' RIGHTS and STRICT CONSTRUCTION occupied for the past decade by his inveterate enemies. Calhoun was not a leader but a follower—a late one at that—in this movement. By 1827 he, too, had turned against the tariff as the great engine of "consolidation." It was unconstitutional, exploitative of the South, and, with other nationalist measures, it threatened "to make two of one nation." After the "tariff of abominations" the next year, Calhoun, at the request of a committee of the state legislature, secretly penned a lengthy argument against the tariff, showing its unconstitutionality, and expounded the theory of NULLIFICATION as the rightful remedy. (See EXPOSITION AND PROTEST.) The theory was speciously laid in the VIRGINIA AND KENTUCKY RESOLUTIONS. They, of course, were devised to secure the rule of the majority; Calhoun's theory, on the other hand, was intended to protect an aggrieved minority. Moreover, he was precise where those famous resolutions were ambiguous; and, unlike them, he invoked the constitution-making authority of three-fourths of the states. That authority might grant by way of amendment a federal power, such as the protection of manufactures, denied by any one of the states. Calhoun believed that the power of nullification in a single state would act as a healthy restraint on the law-making power of Congress; if not, and nullification occurred, the issue would be referred to a convention for decision. Each state being sovereign under this theory, SECESSION was always a last resort; but Calhoun argued that the Union would be strengthened, not weakened or dissolved, under the operation of nullification. Indeed, the Union could be preserved only on the condition of state sovereignty and strict construction—an exact reversal of his earlier nationalist position. The legislature published the *South Carolina Exposition* in December 1828. Although Calhoun's authorship was kept secret for several years, he had become the philosopher-statesman of a movement.

Calhoun hoped for reform from the new administration of ANDREW JACKSON, in which he was, again, the vice-president. But he was quickly disappointed. Personal differences, perhaps more than differences of principle or policy, caused his break with Jackson, completed early in 1831. Laying aside his presidential ambitions—he had hoped to be Jackson's successor—Calhoun issued his Fort Hill Address in July, publicly placing himself at the head of the nullification party in South Carolina. Named for the plantation near Pendleton that was ever after Calhoun's home, the address elaborated the theory set forth in the *Exposition.* When in the following year South Carolina nullified the tariff, it did so in strict conformity with the theory. Calhoun resigned the vice-presidency and was elected to the Senate to lead the state's cause in Washington. He denounced the President's FORCE BILL as a proposition to make war on a sovereign state. In a notable debate with DANIEL WEBSTER, he expounded the theory of the Union as a terminable compact of sovereign states and within that theory vindicated the constitutionality of nullification. (See UNION, THEORIES OF.) But Calhoun backed away from confrontation. He seized the olive branch of tariff reform HENRY CLAY dangled before him. The crisis was resolved peacefully. The nullifiers declared a victory, of course; and Calhoun vaunted himself on the basis of this illusion.

Henceforth, Calhoun abandoned nullification as a remedy and associated his constitutional theory with varying stratagems of sectional resistance to the alleged corruptions and majority tyranny of the general government. The idea of the "concurrent majority," in which the great geographical sections provided the balancing mechanism of estates or classes in classical republican theory, held a more and more important place in his thought. He came to believe that the government of South Carolina, with the balance of legislative power between lowcountry and upcountry established by "the compromise of 1808," embodied this theory. Slavery, of course, was at the bottom of the sectional interest for which Calhoun sought protection. In 1835 he proposed an ingenious solution to the problem of abolitionist agitation through the United States mail. Direct intervention, as Jackson proposed, was unconstitutional, Calhoun said; but the general government could cooperate in the enforcement of state laws that barred "incendiary publications." He thus invented the doctrine of "federal reenforcement" of state laws; and though his bill was defeated, his object was attained by administrative action. Calhoun led the fight in the Senate against the reception of petitions for the abolition of slavery in the DISTRICT OF COLUMBIA. He denied that there was an indefeasible right of petition. Regarding the attack on slavery in the District as an attack on "the outworks" of slavery in the states, he held that the mere reception of the petitions, even if they were immediately tabled, as would become the practice, amounted to an admission of constitutional authority over slavery everywhere. The fight was, therefore, the southern Thermopylae. In 1838, indulging his penchant for metaphysical solutions, Calhoun introduced in the Senate a series of six resolutions which, in principle, would throw a constitutional barricade around slavery wherever it existed—in the states, in the District, and in the territories (Florida then being the only territory). In an allusion to Texas, one resolution declared that refusal to annex territory lest it expand slavery violated the compact of equal sovereign states. This last resolution was dropped, others were modified, and as finally passed the resolutions advanced Calhoun's position by inches rather than yards.

Calhoun never naïvely believed that abolitionism constituted the chief danger to the South. The chief danger was from consolidation, from spoilsmen, from banks and other privileged interests fattening themselves at the public trough, and from the attendant corruption that undermined republican virtue and constitutional safeguards. The only remedy was to strip the government of its excessive revenues, powers, and patronage, and return to the Constitution as it came from the hand of the Framers. For a time, seeing Jackson as the immediate enemy, Calhoun worked with the Whigs; in 1840 he returned to the Democratic fold. He had become convinced that the Democratic party offered better prospects of security for the South. In addition, he hoped to realize his presidential ambition in succession to his old enemy, MARTIN VAN BUREN, in 1844. This was not to be.

The year 1844 found Calhoun secretary of state, engineering the ANNEXATION OF TEXAS, in the shattered administration of John Tyler. Returning to the Senate the following year, he lent his powerful voice to the Oregon settlement, opposed the Mexican War, then became the foremost champion of slavery in the new territories. He set forth his position in resolutions countering the WILMOT PROVISO in 1847: the territories are common property of the states; the general government, as the agent of the states, cannot discriminate against the citizens or institutions of any one in legislating for the territories; the restriction of slavery would be discriminatory; and finally, the people of the territories have the right to form state governments without condition as to slavery. Before long Calhoun repudiated the MISSOURI COMPROMISE and called for the positive protection of SLAVERY IN THE TERRITORIES. The leader of an increasingly militant South, he nevertheless acted, as in the past, to restrain disunionist forces. Secession was never an acceptable solution in his eyes.

The senator's last major speech—he was too ill to deliver it himself—occurred in March 1850 in response to Henry Clay's compromise plan. Calhoun did not so much oppose the measures of this plan as consider them inadequate. The balanced, confederate government of the Constitution had degenerated into a consolidated democracy before which the minority South was helpless. Only by restoring the sectional balance could the Union be saved, and he vaguely suggested a constitutional amendment for this purpose. Within the month he was dead. Two posthumous publications were his political testament. The *Disquisition on Government* contained his political theory, including the key idea of the concurrent majority. The *Discourse on the Constitution* specifically applied the theory to the American polity. After recommending various reforms, such as repeal of the 25th section of the JUDICIARY ACT OF 1789, the *Discourse* concluded with a proposal for radical constitutional change: a dual executive, elected by North and South, each chief vested with the VETO POWER. This was a metaphysical solution indeed! Yet it was one that epitomized Calhoun's paradoxical relationship to the Constitution. Although he made a fetish of the Constitution, he could never accept its workings and repeatedly advocated fundamental reforms. Although he proclaimed his love of the Union, his embrace was like the kiss of death. And while exalting liberty, he based his ideal republic on slavery and rejected majority rule as incompatible with constitutional government.

MERRILL D. PETERSON

Bibliography

CRALLE, RICHARD K., ED. 1853–1857 *The Works of John C. Calhoun.* 6 Vols. New York: D. Appleton & Co.

MERIWETHER, ROBERT L.; HEMPHILL, W. EDWIN; WILSON, CLYDE N.; and others, eds. 1959–1980 *The Papers of John C. Calhoun.* 8 Vols. to date. Columbia: University of South Carolina Press.

WILTSE, CHARLES M. 1944 *John C. Calhoun: Nationalist, 1782–1828.* Indianapolis: Bobbs-Merrill.

——— 1949 *John C. Calhoun: Nullifier, 1829–1839.* Indianapolis: Bobbs-Merrill.

——— 1951 *John C. Calhoun: Sectionalist, 1840–1850.* Indianapolis: Bobbs-Merrill.

CALIFANO v. GOLDFARB
430 U.S. 199 (1977)
CALIFANO v. WEBSTER
430 U.S. 313 (1977)

These decisions illustrated the delicacy of distinguishing between "benign" gender classifications and unconstitutional ones. *Goldfarb* invalidated, 5–4, a SOCIAL SECURITY ACT provision giving survivor's benefits to any widow but only to a widower who actually had received half his support from his wife. *Webster,* decided three weeks later, unanimously upheld the same law's grant of a higher level of old age benefits to women than to men.

In *Goldfarb* four Justices, led by Justice WILLIAM J. BRENNAN, saw the law as a discrimination against women workers, whose surviving families received less protection. The provision had not been adopted to compensate widows for economic disadvantage but to provide generally for survivors; Congress had simply assumed that wives are usually dependent. Saving the cost of individualized determinations of dependency was also insufficient to justify the discrimination. Four other Justices, led by Justice WILLIAM H.

REHNQUIST, saw the law as a discrimination against male survivors; because the discrimination was not invidious, implying male inferiority or burdening a disadvantaged minority, it should be upheld as "benign." Justice JOHN PAUL STEVENS agreed with Justice Rehnquist that the discrimination ran against men; however, it was only "the accidental byproduct of a traditional way of thinking about females." Lacking more substantial justifications, it was invalid. (See Justice Stevens's concurrence in CRAIG V. BOREN, 1976).

All the Justices in *Webster* agreed that the gender discrimination was not the product of "archaic and overbroad generalizations" about women's dependency but was designed to compensate for women's economic disadvantages. The *Goldfarb* dissenters, concurring separately in *Webster*, suggested that the fine distinction between the two results would produce uncertainty in the law.

KENNETH L. KARST

(SEE ALSO: *Sex Discrimination.*)

CALIFANO v. WEBSTER

See: *Califano v. Goldfarb*

CALIFANO v. WESTCOTT
443 U.S. 76 (1979)

The Supreme Court unanimously found unconstitutional SEX DISCRIMINATION in a federal law providing WELFARE BENEFITS to families whose children were dependent because fathers (but not mothers) were unemployed. The discrimination was based on sexual stereotyping that assumed fathers were breadwinners and mothers homemakers, and was not substantially related to the goal of providing for dependent children. Four Justices would have invalidated the benefits granted by the statute. A majority of five, speaking through Justice HARRY A. BLACKMUN, instead construed the statute to extend benefits to children of unemployed mothers as well as fathers.

KENNETH L. KARST

CALVIN'S CASE
(The Case of the *Post-Nati*)
2 Howell's State Trials 559 (1608)

The assumption of the English throne by King James VI of Scotland in 1603 raised the question of what rights accrued in England to Scotsmen born subsequently (the *post-nati*). The English House of Commons wrecked James's plan for a union of the two kingdoms by refusing to permit the NATURALIZATION of Scotsmen dwelling in England and thereby their right to acquire property as native-born Englishmen did. In *Calvin's Case,* however, Lord Chancellor Ellesmere, speaking for the Courts of Chancery and King's Bench, held that the COMMON LAW conferred such naturalization and, thereby, the rights to inherit, sue, and purchase property. In the final stage of the controversy with Parliament that led to the American Revolution, Americans relied on *Calvin's case* when claiming that they owed allegiance only to George III personally and were not subject to the authority of Parliament.

WILLIAM J. CUDDIHY

CAMARA v. MUNICIPAL COURT
387 U.S. 523 (1967)

In *Camara* the Supreme Court held that the householder may resist warrantless ADMINISTRATIVE SEARCHES of dwellings by inspectors implementing fire, health, housing, and similar municipal codes. However, because the inspection is not a criminal investigation, PROBABLE CAUSE for a warrant may be found without information about the individual dwelling, on the basis of such factors as the date of the last inspection and the condition of the area. Similar protection was accorded to commercial premises in *See v. Seattle* (1967).

JACOB W. LANDYNSKI

CAMDEN, LORD

See: Pratt, Charles

CAMINETTI v. UNITED STATES

See: *Hoke v. United States*

CAMPAIGN FINANCE

Enlargement of the electorate and development of modern communications have heightened the importance of campaign funds for communicating with voters, a purpose less patently wicked or easily regulated than vote-buying and bribery, which have long been illegal.

Modern attempts to regulate campaign financing, which raise sweeping constitutional issues, have been largely centered on the FEDERAL ELECTION CAMPAIGN ACT of 1971 and its various amendments. Federal law has developed along six identifiable lines: prohibitions of bribery and corrupt practices; disclosures of campaign contributions and expenditures; limits on the amount of contributions from individuals and groups; prohibitions against contributions from certain sources, such as corporate or union treasuries; limits on total expenditures; and public financing.

Although the regulation of bribery and corrupt practices does not generally raise significant constitutional issues, all of the other elements of the Federal Election Campaign Act and of comparable state laws do. In BUCKLEY V. VALEO (1976), the landmark case on the constitutionality of political finance regulations, the Supreme Court held that expenditures to advocate the election or defeat of candidates are constitutionally protected speech and may not be limited. Subsequent decisions have held that no limit may be imposed on expenditures in REFERENDUM OF INITIATIVE campaigns. And in *Common Cause v. Schmitt* (1982) an evenly divided Court sustained a lower court ruling that limits on expenditures by groups or individuals, acting independently, were impermissible, even when the candidate has agreed to limits as a condition for obtaining campaign public subsidies.

Campaign contributions embody a lesser element of constitutionally protected speech, but they are also an exercise of FREEDOM OF ASSEMBLY AND ASSOCIATION guaranteed in the FIRST AMENDMENT. Contributions may be limited to achieve COMPELLING STATE INTERESTS, such as avoidance of "the actuality and appearance of corruption." The Supreme Court has not yet identified any other compelling interest that justifies limits on campaign contributions. Hence, in *Buckley* the Court voided limits on a candidate's contributions to his own campaign and, in *Citizens Against Rent Control v. Berkeley* (1981), invalidated limits on contributions in referendum campaigns, because in neither case did the contributions pose a danger of corrupting candidates.

The rule against expenditures by and contributions from CORPORATIONS, labor unions, and other specified sources has not yet been tested in court, but its justification is largely undermined by FIRST NATIONAL BANK OF BOSTON V. BELLOTTI (1978), which struck down limits on referendum expenditures by corporations because First Amendment speech rights extend to corporations. Presumably the speech and association rights inherent in making contributions attach to corporations, unions, and other associations, and only limits necessary to avoid the actuality or appearance of corruption could be applied.

Public subsidies of campaigns and parties have been adopted by Congress and several states. In *Buckley* the Court held that such expenditures are within the ambit of the spending power of the general welfare clause. The Court also sustained a limit on expenditures for candidates who voluntarily accept public subsidies. No unconstitutional discrimination was found in limiting eligibility for subsidies to parties that had received a specified percentage of the vote in a prior election.

The Court has acknowledged that some persons may be deterred from making contributions and others may be subject to harassment if they exercise their constitutional right to make contributions, but substantial governmental interests warrant disclosure because it assists voters to evaluate candidates, deters corruption, and facilitates enforcement of contribution limits. Minor parties and independent candidates, however, because they have only a modest likelihood of coming to power and because they are often unpopular, need show only "a reasonable probability that compelled disclosure . . . of contributors will subject them to threats, harassment, or reprisals" in order to obtain relief from the disclosure requirements. Minor-party expenditures were also held exempt from disclosure, in BROWN V. SOCIALIST WORKERS '74 CAMPAIGN COMMITTEE (1982), to protect First Amendment political activity.

Equality and liberty, both values rooted in the Constitution, come into conflict in regulation of political finance. Limitations on contributions and expenditures have been justified as efforts to equalize the influence of citizens and groups in the political process. Money and the control of technology, especially communications media, pose special problems of scale; the magnitude of potential inequality between citizens far exceeds that which occurs in traditional or conventional political participation.

In balancing First Amendment liberties and the concern for political equality, the Supreme Court has, in the area of campaign finance, consistently given preference to speech and association rights, with little reference to the inequality this may produce between citizens. The Court has sustained limits on contributions only to avoid corruption, not to achieve equality. Similarly, the Court has permitted public subsidies, which equalize funds available to candidates, and expenditure limits attached to such subsidies, which create an equal ceiling on spending. But equality is not the controlling principle; the Court has made clear that candidate participation in public subsidy-and-limitation schemes must be voluntary and that such schemes do not impose ceilings on expenditures by persons acting independently of candidates.

Although equality in the political process has constitutional imprimatur in voting, contemporary constitutional doctrines relating to campaign finance neither acknowledge the validity of equality interests nor provide means for effecting them.

DAVID ADAMANY

Bibliography

NICHOLSON, MARLENE 1977 Buckley v. Valeo: The Constitutionality of the Federal Election Campaign Act Amendments of 1974. *Wisconsin Law Review* 1977:323–374.

CAMPBELL, JOHN A.
(1811–1889)

John Archibald Campbell was the TANEY COURT's most thoughtful advocate of STATES' RIGHTS and, with the exception of JOSEPH STORY, its most penetrating legal scholar. Although never a constitutional doctrinaire like PETER V. DANIEL, Campbell rooted his constitutional jurisprudence in a southern exceptionalism antagonistic to corporate and federal judicial power. Appointed by President Franklin Pierce in March 1853, Campbell served until April 1861 when he resigned to return to Alabama and eventual support for the Confederacy.

Campbell analyzed constitutional disputes as clashes between sovereign entities. He dissented from successful efforts by the majority to expand federal ADMIRALTY JURISDICTION to river waters above the ebb and flow of the tide. In *Jackson v. Steamboat Magnolia* (1858) he ridiculed these efforts as factually incorrect, historically superficial, and purposefully intended to diminish state SOVEREIGNTY. Campbell only once won acceptance for his narrow view of federal admiralty jurisdiction when he persuaded a bare majority in *Taylor v. Carry* (1858) that, where claims against a vessel rested on conflicting state and federal JURISDICTION, the claimants had to proceed under the former.

Justice Campbell's most important decisions involved CORPORATIONS. The Taney Court recognized corporations as citizens, a status that enabled them to seek relief from unfavorable state legislative and judicial action through federal DIVERSITY JURISDICTION. Campbell in 1853 dissented when the Court reaffirmed this position in *Marshall v. Baltimore and Ohio Railroad.* He charged that the majority perverted the meaning of CITIZENSHIP and crippled state economic regulation.

Campbell also dissented from the majority's view that corporate charters, even when narrowly construed, were contracts in perpetuity. In PIQUA BRANCH BANK V. KNOOP (1854) and DODGE V. WOOLSEY (1856) he insisted, respectively, that state legislatures and CONSTITUTIONAL CONVENTIONS could alter tax-exemption provisions of previously granted charters. The states, Campbell argued, had to retain sovereign power to tax corporations in order to promote the public interest. A political and economic agenda informed Campbell's thinking about corporate CITIZENSHIP and the CONTRACT CLAUSE: federal judicial protection of interstate corporations tilted the balance of national power in favor of northern manufacturing.

Campbell eased the dichotomy between state and federal sovereignty only on questions involving SLAVERY. In DRED SCOTT V. SANDFORD (1857) he concluded that the federal judiciary had a constitutional responsibility to protect slave property. He reiterated the primacy of federal judicial power in cases in the Fifth Circuit involving enforcement of the slave trade and neutrality laws. Like northern federal judges, who enforced the Fugitive Slave Acts, Campbell charged southern federal juries to adhere to a national RULE OF LAW.

During the post-Civil War era Campbell made his most lasting contribution to constitutional jurisprudence as an attorney for the corporations he once attacked. The Supreme Court in the SLAUGHTERHOUSE CASES (1873) narrowly rejected his arguments in behalf of the rights of corporate citizenship and SUBSTANTIVE DUE PROCESS under the FOURTEENTH AMENDMENT, but two decades later the Justices embraced them.

KERMIT L. HALL

Bibliography

SCHMIDHAUSER, JOHN R. 1958 Jeremy Bentham, the Contract Clause, and Justice John Archibald Campbell. *Vanderbilt Law Review* 11:801–820.

CANTWELL v. CONNECTICUT
310 U.S. 296 (1940)

Newton Cantwell and his sons, Jesse and Russell, were arrested in New Haven, Connecticut. As Jehovah's Witnesses and, by definition, ordained ministers, they were engaged in street solicitation. They distributed pamphlets, made statements critical of the Roman Catholic Church, and offered to play for passers-by a phonograph record including an attack on the Roman Catholic religion. The Cantwells were convicted of violating a Connecticut statute that prohibited persons soliciting money for any cause without a certificate issued by the state secretary of the Public Welfare Council. Jesse Cantwell was also convicted of the COMMON LAW offense of inciting a BREACH OF THE PEACE.

Justice OWEN J. ROBERTS delivered the opinion of a unanimous Court: although Connecticut had a legitimate interest in regulating the use of its streets for solicitation, the means the state had chosen infringed upon the RELIGIOUS FREEDOM of solicitors. The secretary appeared to have unlimited discretion to determine the legitimacy of a religious applicant and either issue or withhold the certificate. If issuance had been a "matter of course," the requirement could have been maintained, but so wide an official discretion to restrict activity protected by the free exercise clause was unacceptable. (See PRIOR RESTRAINT.)

The conviction of Jesse Cantwell for inciting breach of the peace was also constitutionally defective. Justice Roberts noted that the open-endedness of the common law concept of breach of the peace offered wide discretion to law enforcement officials. When such a criminal provision was applied to persons engaging in FIRST AMENDMENT-protected speech or exercise of religion there must be a showing of a CLEAR AND PRESENT DANGER of violence or disorder. Although Cantwell's speech was offensive to his listeners, it had not created such a danger.

As a religious freedom precedent, *Cantwell* is important in two ways: first, it made clear that the free exercise clause of the First Amendment applied to the states through the DUE PROCESS clause of the FOURTEENTH AMENDMENT; second, it suggested (in contrast to previous case law, for example, REYNOLDS V. UNITED STATES, 1879) that the free exercise clause protected not only beliefs but also some actions. The protection of belief was absolute, Roberts wrote, but the protection of action was not; it must give way in appropriate cases to legitimate government regulation. The implication was that at least some government regulations of religion-based conduct would be impermissible.

RICHARD E. MORGAN

CAPITAL PUNISHMENT

In 1971, the year before the Supreme Court began its long and tortured experiment in constitutional regulation of the death penalty, Justice JOHN MARSHALL HARLAN issued an ominous warning. In *McGautha v. California* he said that because of the irreducible moral complexity and subjectivity of capital punishment, any effort to impose formal legal rationality on the choice between life and death for a criminal defendant would prove futile: "To identify before the fact those characteristics of criminal homicides and their perpetrators which call for the death penalty, and to express these characteristics in language which can be fairly understood and applied by the sentencing authority, appear to be tasks which are beyond present human ability."

A constitutional interpreter who accepted Justice Harlan's pronouncement could draw one of at least two possible implications from it. She could conclude that in the face of this moral uncertainty, courts cannot interfere in legislative decisions about capital punishment, for judges have no objective principles to correct legislators. On the other hand, she could conclude that capital punishment must be constitutionally forbidden, because this moral uncertainty means that legislators cannot make the death penalty process conform to the minimal constitutional principles of the RULE OF LAW. But a constitutional interpreter might also conclude that Justice Harlan was unnecessarily cynical, and that an enlightened judicial effort might achieve an acceptable moral and instrumental rationality in the administration of the death penalty. The erratic constitutional history of capital punishment both before and after *McGautha* reflects the stubborn difficulty of these questions. That history reveals a complex, often confused experiment in lawmaking. It also illuminates the fundamental, recurring dilemma that Justice Harlan described, and lends sobering support to his pronouncement.

The Fifth Amendment says that no person "shall be deprived of life . . . without DUE PROCESS OF LAW." Thus, a strict textual reader would easily conclude that the Constitution does not forbid capital punishment per se. And indeed in early America, execution was the automatic penalty for anyone convicted of murder or any of several other felonies. Well into the nineteenth century, a jury that believed a defendant to be guilty of murder had no legal power to save him from death. As the states began to draw distinctions among degrees of murder, a prosecutor had to win a conviction on an aggravated or first-degree murder charge to ensure execution, but, after conviction, the death penalty still lay beyond the legal discretion of the jury.

One potential constitutional restraint on the death penalty lay in the Eighth Amendment prohibition of CRUEL AND UNUSUAL PUNISHMENT. But at least in the Supreme Court's contemporary historical interpretation, *Gregg v. Georgia* (1976), the authors of the cruel and unusual punishment clause did not intend to forbid conventional capital punishment for serious crimes. Rather, the Eighth Amendment, drawing on the English BILL OF RIGHTS of 1689, was intended merely to prohibit any punishments not officially authorized by statute or not lying within the sentencing court's jurisdiction, and any torture or brutal, gratuitously painful methods of execution.

For most of the nineteenth century, American courts placed virtually no constitutional restrictions on capital punishment. Nevertheless, the state legislatures gradually rejected the automatic death penalty scheme. Some legislators may have believed that the automatic death laws were too harsh, and that at least some murderers merited legal mercy. Others, paradoxically, may have felt that the automatic death penalty law actually proved too lenient. A jury that believed a defendant was guilty of first-degree murder, but did not believe he deserved execution, could engage in "jury nullification"—it could act subversively by acquitting the defendant of the murder charge.

In any event, by the early twentieth century most of the states had adopted an entirely new type of death penalty law that gave juries implicit, unreviewable legal discretion in the choice between life and death sentences. The jury was instructed that if it found the defendant guilty of the capital crime, it must then decide between life and death. The jury had no legal guidance in this decision. Moreover, the jury rarely received any general information about the defendant's background, character, or previous criminal record that might be relevant to sentence; it only had the evidence proffered on the guilt issue. Although a few states eliminated capital punishment entirely late in the nineteenth century or early in the twentieth century, the new unguided discretion statute was essentially the model American death penalty law until 1972.

Executions of murderers and rapists were fairly frequent in the United States until the 1960s, though the rate of execution peaked at about 200 per year during the Depression and then dropped during World War II. By the 1960s, however, the long-standing practice of death sentencing through unguided jury discretion began to face increasing moral and political opposition. Beyond any fundamental change in moral attitudes toward state killing itself, the opposition sounded essentially three themes. First, early empirical studies by social scientists cast grave doubt on the major instrumental justification for the death penalty—its general deterrent power over murderers. Second, even informal data on the patterns of execution under the unguided discretion laws suggested that the criminal justice system in general, and sentencing juries in particular, acted randomly and capriciously in selecting defendants for capital punishment. The process did not treat like cases alike, and no rational principle emerged to explain why some defendants were executed and others of similar crimes or character were not.

Third, to the extent that any pattern emerged at all, it was the unacceptable pattern of race. Critics of the death penalty offered empirical evidence that the race of the defendant was an important factor in a jury's choice between life and death, and that the race of the victim was potentially a still greater factor. Blacks were sentenced to death more often than whites, and people who committed crimes against whites were executed far more often than those who committed crimes against blacks. The racial pattern was absolutely overwhelming in the instance of rape, where virtually all executed rapists were black men convicted of raping white women, but the pattern was powerfully suggestive for murder as well.

As these themes emerged in academic commentary, legal argument, and even public opinion in the late 1960s, the courts faced increasing pressure to impose some legal restraint on the death penalty. In the most important and most enigmatic decision on capital punishment in American history, *Furman v. Georgia* (1972), a muddled consensus of the Supreme Court ignored Justice Harlan's warning and accepted the challenge, if not the ultimate conclusion, of the arguments against capital punishment. All nine Justices wrote separate opinions in *Furman,* and by a vote of 5–4 the Court reversed the death sentences before them. But the five opinions for reversal achieved at best a vague, thematic consensus about the problems with the death penalty, and no majority position on the solution.

Justices WILLIAM J. BRENNAN and THURGOOD MARSHALL alone were clearly persuaded that the death penalty was categorically unconstitutional in all cases. Responding to the powerful textualist argument that the authors of the Constitution and the Bill of Rights contemplated a legal death penalty, the Justices chose to read the Eighth Amendment's cruel and unusual punishments clause as a flexible instrument that could adjust constitutional law to American society's moral development. Thus, "evolving standards of decency," reflected in public opinion, jury behavior, and legislative attitudes, had come to condemn the death penalty. Moreover, the Eighth Amendment authorized judges to examine the moral and instrumental justification for capital punishment, and neither retribution nor general deterrence withstood scrutiny. Retribution was an unworthy moral principle, and general deterrence had no empirical support.

But the *Furman* majority hinged on the more cautious and cryptic views of Justices WILLIAM O. DOUGLAS, BYRON R. WHITE, and POTTER STEWART. They avoided the question of whether capital punishment had become an absolutely forbidden penalty, and instead seemed to conclude that, as administered under the unguided discretion laws, capital punishment had achieved impermissibly random or racially discriminatory effects. Thus, the official signal from *Furman* seemed to be that the states could try yet again to develop sound capital punishment laws that would resolve the dilemma between legal guidance and discretion, though the Court certainly suggested no particular formula for doing so. (See CAPITAL PUNISHMENT CASES OF 1972.)

The immediate effect of *Furman* was to suspend all executions for a few years while about three-fourths of the state legislatures prepared their responses. The responses took two statutory forms. Ironically, a few states "solved" the problem of unguided discretion by completely eliminating discretion. Essentially, they returned to the early nineteenth-century model of the automatic death penalty, at least for those convicted of the most serious aggravated murders. Most of the states that restored the death penalty, however, chose a subtler, compromise approach, which might be called the "guided discretion" statute. A rough common denominator of these guided discretion statutes is a separate hearing on the question of penalty after a defendant is convicted of first degree murder. This hearing is a novel cross between the traditional discretionary sentencing hearing conducted by a trial judge in noncapital cases, and a formal, if abbreviated, criminal trial. In most states, the jury decides the penalty, though in a few states the judge either decides the penalty alone or has power to override a jury recommendation on penalty.

The matters at issue in this hearing consist of aggravating and mitigating factors which the two sides may establish. These factors partly overlap with the issues that would be resolved at the guilt trial, but comprehend new information about the defendant's character or background, which would normally be legally irrelevant at the guilt trial. Thus, the prosecution may establish that the defendant committed the murder in an especially heinous or sadistic way; that the victim was a specially protected person such as a police officer; that the murder was for hire or for some other form of pecuniary gain; that the murder was committed in the course of a rape, robbery, or burglary; or that the defendant had a substantial record of earlier violent crimes. Conversely, the defense may introduce evidence that the defendant, though unable to prove legal insanity, was emotionally impaired or under the influence of drugs at the time of the crime; that he was young, or had no serious criminal record; that he had suffered serious abuse or neglect as a child; or that since arrest he had demonstrated remorse and model prison behavior.

The sentencing judge or jury hears these factors and orders execution only if, according to some statutory formula, the aggravating circumstances outweigh the mitigating. Most of the statutes expressly enumerated these factors, and in addition provided for automatic appellate review of the death sentence. Many also required the state appellate court to conduct periodic "proportionality reviews" of death and life sentences in comparable murder cases, to ensure that the new system avoided the problem of caprice denounced in *Furman*.

In 1976 the states returned to the Supreme Court to learn whether they had properly met the obscure challenge of *Furman*. In a cluster of five cases handed down the same day, the Court once again failed to produce a majority opinion. Justices Brennan and Marshall would have struck down both types of statutes. Chief Justice WARREN E. BURGER and Justices HARRY A. BLACKMUN, BYRON R. WHITE, and WILLIAM H. REHNQUIST would have upheld both types of statutes. The swing plurality of Justices Potter Stewart, LEWIS F. POWELL, and JOHN PAUL STEVENS thus decided the constitutional fate of capital punishment, and the outcome, at least, of the 1976 cases was clear: the automatic death penalty statutes fell and the new guided discretion statutes survived.

First, in *Woodson v. North Carolina*, the plurality rejected the new automatic death laws as misguided solutions to the problem of discretion. These statutes were too rigid to capture the quality of individualized mercy required in death sentencing, and only revived the problem of "jury nullification" that had plagued the old automatic sentencing more than a century earlier. Second, in the key opinion in *Gregg v. Georgia* (1976) the plurality upheld the new guided discretion statutes as the proper solution to the complex of problems discerned in *Furman*. To do so, of course, the plurality had to reject the categorical arguments against the death penalty made by Justices Marshall and Brennan in *Furman*, and so it squarely held that the death penalty does not inevitably violate the BILL OF RIGHTS. The plurality opinion accepted retribution as a justifiable basis for execution, in particular because state-enacted revenge on murderers might prevent the more socially disruptive risk of private revenge. The plurality also found the empirical evidence of the general deterrent power of capital punishment to be equivocal, and declared that in the face of equivocal evidence, judges had to defer to popular and legislative judgments. Thus, the simple fact that three-fourths of the state legislatures had chosen to reenact the death penalty after *Furman* became a primary ground for the general constitutional legitimacy of capital punishment. The plurality relied on the curious principle that the state legislatures, which are supposedly subject to the Eighth Amendment, had become a major source of the evolving moral consensus that could determine the meaning of the Eighth Amendment.

The plurality then examined the Georgia guided discretion statute, as well as the statutes of Florida and Texas, in *Proffitt v. Florida* and *Jurek v. Texas.* It concluded that the substantive and procedural elements of the new concept of the penalty hearing, combined with the promise of strict appellate review, indicated that these statutes, on their face, were constitutionally sufficient to prevent the random and racist effects of the old unguided discretion laws. (See CAPITAL PUNISHMENT CASES OF 1976).

A year later, with the execution of Gary Gilmore in Utah, capital punishment was effectively restored in America. But because of the uncertain meaning of *Gregg,* the rate of execution, compared to the rate of death sentencing, remained very low for several years thereafter. While *Gregg* probably foreclosed any argument that capital punishment was fundamentally unconstitutional, it confirmed that the operation of the death penalty laws remained subject to very strict due process-style constraints. Thus, the death penalty defense bar quickly found numerous legal arguments for challenging particular death sentences or particular elements of the new state statutes. Some of the new legal claims involved state law issues: The new aggravating circumstances that entered the law of homicide after *Furman* had made state substantive criminal law doctrine far more complex than before.

Most of the new claims, however, were constitutional. In one series of cases, the court extended "Eighth Amendment due process" by imposing a sort of revived WARREN COURT criminal procedure jurisprudence on the state death penalty hearing. It gave capital defendants a CONFRONTATION right to rebut aggravating evidence in *Gardner v. Florida* (1977), and a COMPULSORY PROCESS right to present hearsay mitigating evidence in *Green v. Georgia* (1979); it applied the due process "void-for-vagueness" principle to aggravating factors in *Godfrey v. Georgia* (1980) and the RIGHT AGAINST SELF-INCRIMINATION and RIGHT TO COUNSEL to penalty phase investigation in ESTELLE V. SMITH (1981); and it applied the principles of DOUBLE JEOPARDY to penalty phase determination in *Bullington v. Missouri* (1981). As the Court extended "Eighth Amendment due process," the defense bar pushed the lower courts still further to shape the penalty hearing into a formal criminal trial. It claimed, for example, that the Sixth and Eighth Amendments guaranteed the capital defendant a jury trial at the penalty phase, and that the jury had to apply the reasonable doubt standard to any choice of death over life.

At the same time, though it had foreclosed categorical arguments against the death penalty as a punishment for murder, the Court drew another line of decisions effectively limiting the death penalty to the crime of aggravated murder. In COKER V. GEORGIA (1977) the Court held that the death penalty was categorically disproportionate as a punishment for rape of adult women—and, by implication, for any nonhomicidal crime. In so holding, it noted that the great majority of states had repealed the death penalty for rape, and thus continued the method of legislation-counting as a form of constitutional jurisprudence. Yet the Court also engaged in its own moral balancing of the severity of the crime of rape and the severity of the sentence of death, claiming under the Eighth Amendment some independent power to determine when a punishment was so disproportionate as to be "cruel and unusual." The Court further applied this jurisprudence of legislative consensus finding and moral reasoning in ENMUND V. FLORIDA (1982). There, the Court forbade the death penalty as punishment for certain attenuated forms of unintentional felony murder.

After the Court had refined the new constitutional law of the death penalty, the process of appellate litigation in the state supreme courts—and even more so in federal district courts on HABEAS CORPUS petitions—became increasingly complex. It also became increasingly prolonged: the vast majority of defendants sentenced to death under the new laws were likely never to suffer execution, and for those that did, the time between original sentence and execution was often as long as ten years. Meanwhile, the Supreme Court encountered an ever increasing caseload of death penalty cases, in which it was continually asked to fine-tune still further the new constitutional regulation of capital punishment. But the Court's effort at formal legal regulation began to seem self-perpetuating, endlessly creating new grounds for reversible error. The appellate and habeas corpus courts were increasingly overwhelmed with death cases.

The Court recognized that it had exacerbated, not resolved, the inescapable tension between rational legal constraint and subjective jury discretion in the administration of capital punishment, and it began an effort to change course. The result, however, was that it was soon moving confusingly in both directions at once as it faced the fundamental—and perennial—legal issue: the feasibility of strict statutory rules, rather than open-ended discretionary standards, in choosing which defendants should die.

Ironically, perhaps the key decision in explaining the apparent unraveling of the Court's effort at constitutional regulation in the death penalty was a great defense victory—*Lockett v. Ohio* (1978). There, the Court held that the state must permit the sentencing judge or jury to give independent consideration to any mitigating factors about the defendant's character, crime, or record that the defense could reasonably proffer, even if those factors fell outside the state statute's carefully enumerated list of mitigating factors. The Court took the view that the moral principles of individualized sentencing demanded a degree of jury discretion that no formal statutory list could capture. The echo of Justice Harlan's 1971 warning was obvious. The Court faced the argument that *Lockett* had, ironically, revived all the problems of unguided jury discretion it had denounced in *Furman* and purported to resolve in *Gregg.*

The defense bar quickly lent support to this view, inundating the lower courts with *Lockett* claims that exploited the vast moral relativism of the concept of mitigation. Defendants sought to introduce evidence unrelated to technical criminal responsibility yet vaguely related to their moral deserts, such as evidence of upright, citizenlike conduct in prison while awaiting trial, or of late-found literary promise. The proffered mitigating evidence sometimes was not about the defendant's character at all: a defendant had a loving family that would suffer terribly if he died young; or, however culpable the defendant was, he had an equally culpable accomplice who had managed to gain a plea to a noncapital charge. Other defendants argued that a jury could not make a sound normative judgment about penalty unless it heard detailed evidence about the gruesome physical facts of execution. Still others read *Lockett* as mandating that a jury must receive an explicit instruction that it had full legal power to exercise mercy. It could spare a defendant after consulting its subjective assessment of his moral deserts, regardless of the technical outcome of its measurement of formal aggravating and mitigating factors.

A few years after *Lockett,* facing the complaint that it had revived, at least on the defendant's side, the very unguided discretion that *Furman* purported to prohibit, the Court arrived at a crudely symmetrical solution. In a bizarrely obscure pair of decisions, *Zant v. Stephens* and *Barclay v. Florida* (1983), the Court held that the state, in effect, had its own *Lockett* rights: so long as the sentencing judge or jury established at least one statutorily defined aggravating factor, it could also take account of aggravating factors about the defendant's crime or character that did not appear on the statute's enumerated list. Having taken an important, if ambivalent, step toward regulating capital punishment, the Court, perhaps reflecting simply its own weariness at the overload of death cases before it, had embarked on deregulation. Along with *Zant* and *Barclay,* the Court began, in *California v. Ramos* (1983) and *Pulley v. Harris* (1984), to remove most formal restrictions on such things as prosecution closing argument in the penalty phase and state appellate proportionality review. In *Spaziano v. Florida* (1984) the Court made clear that the apparent trial-like formality of the penalty phase did not create any defense right to jury sentencing. Once again, Justice Harlan echoed ominously.

In any event, partly because the Court has begun to narrow the grounds on which capital defendants can claim legal error, the execution rate has begun a slow but steady increase, with the number of post-*Furman* executions passing fifty in 1985. For the foreseeable future, a tired and conservative Court is not likely to entertain many dramatic procedural or substantive attacks on the death penalty, and so capital punishment has achieved political, if not intellectual stability.

A remarkable irony, though, lies in one remaining possibility for a very broad attack on the death penalty. In the years since *Furman,* social scientists have conducted more sophisticated empirical studies of patterns of death sentencing and have uncovered evidence of random and racially disparate effects similar to the evidence that helped bring down the old unguided discretion laws in *Furman.* Most important, studies using multiple regression analysis have found significant evidence that, holding all other legitimate factors constant, murderers of whites are far more likely to suffer the death sentence than murderers of blacks.

One of the obvious implications of this evidence is that though the new guided discretion statutes reviewed in *Gregg* at first looked like they would meet the demands of *Furman,* they now may have proved failures. If so, there is no reason not to declare capital punishment unconstitutional yet again. It would seem politically unrealistic to think that the court would now accept this implication. But it is nevertheless important to consider how one might reconcile this evidence with the modern constitutional doctrine of capital punishment.

One could finesse the issue by taking the view that no system can be perfect and that the statistical discrepancy is insignificant. Or one could acknowledge that the discrepancy is significant and disturbing, but still ascribe it to the inevitable, often unconscious prejudices of jurors, rather than to any deliberate racist conduct by legislators or prosecutors. If so, one might conclude that the Constitution requires the states to do only what is morally possible, not what is morally perfect. To put the matter in doctrinal terms, one could engage in some mildly revisionist history of *Furman* and *Gregg.* That is, one could say that *Furman* only required the state legislatures to make their best efforts to devise rational, neutral death penalty laws, that *Gregg* had upheld the new guided discretion statutes on their face as proof that the state legislatures had made that effort successfully, and that constitutional law has no more to say about capital punishment. Whatever the conclusion, capital punishment has given constitutional doctrine making one of its most vexing challenges.

ROBERT WEISBERG

(SEE ALSO: *Barefoot v. Estelle, 1983.*)

Bibliography

BEDAU, HUGO ADAM (1967)1982 *The Death Penalty in America.* Oxford: Oxford University Press.

BERNS, WALTER 1979 *For Capital Punishment.* New York: Basic Books.

BOWERS, WILLIAM J., with PIERCE, GLENN L. 1984 *Legal Homicide: Death as Punishment in America, 1864–1982.* Boston: Northeastern University Press.

DEATH PENALTY SYMPOSIUM 1985 *U.C. Davis Law Review* 18:865–1480.

GRANUCCI, ANTHONY F. 1969 Nor Cruel and Unusual Punishments Inflicted: The Original Meaning. *California Law Review* 57:839–865.

GROSS, SAMUEL R. and MAURO, ROBERT 1985 Patterns of Death: An Analysis of Racial Disparities in Capital Sentencing and Homicide Victimization. *Stanford Law Review* 37:27–153.

LEMPERT, RICHARD 1981 Desert and Deterrence: An Assessment of the Moral Bases of the Case for Capital Punishment. *Michigan Law Review* 79:1177–1231.

WEISBERG, ROBERT 1983 Deregulating Death. *Supreme Court Review* 1983:304–395.

CAPITAL PUNISHMENT CASES OF 1972

Furman v. Georgia
Jackson v. Georgia
Branch v. Texas
408 U.S. 238 (1972)

The Eighth Amendment clearly and expressly forbids the infliction of CRUEL AND UNUSUAL PUNISHMENTS (a prohibition that since 1947 has applied to the states as well as to the national government), and opponents of CAPITAL PUNISHMENT have long argued that to execute a convicted criminal, whatever his crime, is such a punishment. It was obviously not so regarded by the persons who wrote and ratified the BILL OF RIGHTS. They acknowledged the legitimacy of the death penalty when, in the Fifth Amendment, they provided that no person "shall be held to answer for a capital . . . crime, unless on a PRESENTMENT OR INDICTMENT of a GRAND JURY," and when in the same amendment they provided that no one shall, for the same offense, "be twice put in jeopardy of life or limb," and when they forbade not the taking of life as such but the taking of life "without DUE PROCESS OF LAW" (a formulation repeated in the FOURTEENTH AMENDMENT). The question of the original understanding of "cruel and unusual" is put beyond any doubt by the fact that the same First Congress that proposed the Eighth Amendment also provided for the death penalty in the first Crimes Act. In 1958, however, the Supreme Court, in the course of holding deprivation of CITIZENSHIP to be a cruel and unusual punishment, accepted the argument that the meaning of cruel and unusual is relative to time and place; the Eighth Amendment, the Court said in TROP V. DULLES (1958), "must draw its meaning from the evolving standards of decency that mark the progress of a maturing society." Implicit in this statement is the opinion that society, as it matures, becomes gentler, and as it becomes gentler, it is more disposed to regard the death penalty as cruel and unusual. According to one member of the five-man majority in the 1972 cases, that point had been reached: "capital punishment," wrote Justice THURGOOD MARSHALL, "is morally unacceptable to the people of the United States at this time in their history."

This assessment of the public's opinion could not reasonably provide the basis of the Court's judgment in these cases; contrary to Marshall, the polls showed a majority in favor of the death penalty and, more to the point, there were at that time some 600 persons on death row, which is to say, some 600 persons on whom the American people, acting through their federal and state courts, had imposed death sentences. Marshall's assessment was also belied by the reaction to the Court's decision: Congress and thirty-five states promptly enacted new death penalty statutes, and it is fair to assume that they did so with the consent of their respective popular majorities. The states remained authorized, or at least not forbidden, to do so, because the Court did not declare the death penalty as such to be a cruel and unusual punishment; only two members of the 1972 majority adopted that position. Justice WILLIAM J. BRENNAN said that the death penalty, for whatever crime imposed, "does not comport with human dignity." Marshall, in addition to finding it to be morally unacceptable, said its only possible justification was not that it was an effective deterrent (he accepted Thorsten Sellin's evidence that it was not) but as a form of retribution, a way to pay criminals back, and, he said, the Eighth Amendment forbade "retribution for its own sake." The other majority Justices found the death penalty to be cruel and unusual only insofar as the statutes permitted it to be imposed discriminatorily (WILLIAM O. DOUGLAS), or arbitrarily and capriciously (POTTER STEWART), or (because it is imposed infrequently) pointlessly or needlessly (BYRON R. WHITE).

That the death penalty has historically been imposed, if not capriciously, then at least in a racially and socially discriminatory fashion seems to be borne out by the statistics. Of the 3,859 persons executed in the United States during the years 1930–1967, when, for a time, executions ceased, 2,066, or fifty-four percent, were black. Georgia alone executed 366 persons, of whom 298 were black. Although American juries have shown increasing reluctance to impose the death penalty (despite the majority sentiment in favor of it in principle), they have been less reluctant to impose it on certain offenders, offenders characterized not by their criminality but by their race or class. "One searches our chronicles in vain for the execution of any members of the affluent strata in this society," said Douglas. "The Leopolds and Loebs are given prison terms, not sentenced to death." The three cases decided in 1972 illustrate his argument. The statutes (two from Georgia, one from Texas) empowered the juries to choose between death and imprisonment for the crimes committed (murder in the one case and rape in the other two), and in each case the jury chose death. As crimes go, however, those committed here were not especially heinous. In the *Furman* case, for example, the offender entered a private home at about 2 A.M. intending to burglarize it. He was carrying a gun. When heard by the head of the household, William Micke, a father of five children, Furman attempted to flee the house. He tripped and his gun discharged, hitting Micke through a closed door and killing him. Furman was quickly apprehended, and in due course tried and convicted. The salient facts would appear to be these: the offender was black and the victim was white, which was also true in the other two cases decided that day.

By holding that the death penalty, as it has been administered in this country, is a cruel and unusual punishment, the Supreme Court challenged the Congress and the state legislatures, if they insisted on punishing by executing, to devise statutes calculated to prevent the arbitrary or discriminatory imposition of the penalty.

WALTER BERNS

Bibliography

BERNS, WALTER 1979 *For Capital Punishment: Crime and the Morality of the Death Penalty.* New York: Basic Books.

BLACK, CHARLES L., JR. 1974 *Capital Punishment: The Inevitability of Caprice and Mistake.* New York: Norton.

LEVY, LEONARD 1974 *Against the Law: The Nixon Court and Criminal Justice.* Pages 383–420. New York: Harper & Row.

SELLIN, THORSTEN 1980 *The Penalty of Death.* Beverley Hills, Calif.: Sage Publications.

VAN DEN HAAG, ERNEST 1975 *Punishing Criminals: Concerning a Very Old and Painful Question.* Pages 225–228. New York: Basic Books.

CAPITAL PUNISHMENT CASES OF 1976

Gregg v. Georgia, 428 U.S. 153
Jurek v. Texas, 428 U.S. 262
Proffitt v. Florida, 428 U.S. 242
Woodson v. North Carolina, 428 U.S. 280
Roberts v. Louisiana, 428 U.S. 325
Green v. Oklahoma, 428 U.S. 907

Writing for the Supreme Court in *McGautha v. California* (1971), only a year before the CAPITAL PUNISHMENT CASES OF 1972, Justice JOHN MARSHALL

HARLAN said, "To identify before the fact those characteristics of criminal homicides and their perpetrators which call for the death penalty, and to express these characteristics in language which can fairly be understood and applied by the sentencing authority, appear to be tasks which are beyond present human ability." Yet, in *Furman v. Georgia* (1972), by declaring unconstitutional statutes that permitted arbitrary, capricious, or discriminatory imposition of the death penalty, the Court challenged the Congress and the various state legislatures to write new statutes that did express in advance the characteristics that would allow the sentencing authorities to distinguish between what is properly a capital and what is properly a noncapital case. The statutes involved in the 1976 cases were drafted in the attempt to meet these requirements.

Three states (North Carolina, Louisiana, Oklahoma) attempted to meet them by making death the mandatory sentence in all first-degree murder cases, thereby depriving juries of all discretion, at least in the sentencing process. By the narrowest of margins, the Court found these mandatory sentencing laws unconstitutional. Justices WILLIAM J. BRENNAN and THURGOOD MARSHALL held to their views expressed in the 1972 cases that the death penalty is unconstitutional per se. In the 1976 cases they were joined by Justices POTTER STEWART, LEWIS F. POWELL, and JOHN PAUL STEVENS (new on the Court since the 1972 decisions) who held, in part, that it was cruel and unusual to treat alike all persons convicted of a designated offense. Their view was that no discretion is as cruel as unguided discretion.

The three statutes upheld in 1976 (those from Georgia, Texas, and Florida) permitted jury sentencing discretion but attempted to reduce the likelihood of abuse to a tolerable minimum. All three statutes, and especially the one from Georgia, embodied procedures intended to impress on judge and jury the gravity of the judgment they are asked to make in capital cases. For example, all three required the sentencing decision to be separated from the decision as to guilt or innocence. In one way or another, all three implied that a sentence of death must be regarded as an extraordinary punishment not to be imposed in an ordinary case, even an ordinary case of first-degree murder. For example, the Georgia law required (except in a case of treason or aircraft hijacking) a finding beyond a REASONABLE DOUBT of the presence of at least one of the aggravating circumstances specified in the statute (for example, that the murder "was outrageously and wantonly vile, horrible and inhuman"), and required the sentencing authority to specify the circumstance found. In addition, the trial judge was required to instruct the jury to consider "any mitigating circumstances" (an element that was to play an important role in the 1978 capital punishment cases). Finally, Georgia required or permitted an expedited APPEAL to or review by the state supreme court, directing that court to determine whether, for example, "the sentence of death was imposed under the influence of passion, prejudice, or any other arbitrary factor," or was "excessive or disproportionate to the penalty imposed in similar cases, considering both the crime and the defendant."

These statutes went to great lengths to do what Harlan in *McGautha* had said could not be done but which, in effect, the Court in 1972 had said must be done: to characterize in advance the cases in which death is an appropriate punishment, or in which the sentencing authority (whether judge or jury) is entitled to decide that the death penalty is appropriate. With only Brennan and Marshall dissenting, the Court agreed that all three statutes met the constitutional requirements imposed four years earlier.

From the 1976 decisions emerged the following rules: the death penalty in and of itself is not a cruel and unusual punishment; a death sentence may not be carried out unless the sentencing authority is guided by reasonably clear statutory standards; in imposing the penalty, the sentencing authority must consider the characteristics of the offender and the circumstances of his offense; mandatory death sentences for murder (and presumably for all other offenses) are unconstitutional; the punishment must not be inflicted in a way that causes unnecessary pain; finally, the death penalty may not be imposed except for heinous crimes ("the punishment must not be grossly out of proportion to the severity of the crime").

The Court's decisions were a bitter disappointment not only to the hundreds of persons on death row who now seemingly faced the real prospect of being executed but also to the equally large number of persons who had devoted their time, talent, and in some cases their professional careers to the cause of abolishing the death penalty.

They had been making progress toward that end. In other Western countries, including Britain, Canada, and France, the death penalty had either been abolished by statute or been allowed to pass into desuetude; in the United States almost a decade had passed since the last legal execution. In this context it was easy for the opponents of capital punishment to see the Supreme Court's 1972 decision as a step along the path leading inevitably to complete and final abolition of the death penalty. This hope was dashed, at least temporarily, in 1976.

Not only did the Court for the first time squarely hold that "the punishment of death does not invariably violate the Constitution" but it also gave explicit support to the popular principle that punishment must fit the crime and that, in making this calculation, the community may pay back the worst of its criminals with death. Prior to 1976, the capital punishment debate had focused on the deterrence issue, and a major effort had been made by social scientists to demonstrate the absence of evidence showing the death penalty to be a more effective deterrent than, for example, life imprisonment. This opinion was challenged in 1975 by University of Chicago econometrician Isaac Ehrlich. Employing multiple regression analysis, Ehrlich concluded that each execution might have had the effect of deterring as many as eight murders. His findings were made available to the Court in an AMICUS CURIAE brief filed in a 1975 case by the solicitor general of the United States. In the 1976 opinion announcing the judgment of the Court, Stewart cited the Ehrlich study, acknowledged that it had provoked "a great deal of debate" in the scholarly journals, but nevertheless concluded that, at least for some potential murderers, "the death penalty undoubtedly is a significant deterrent." If this conclusion remains undisturbed, the focus of the capital punishment debate will shift to the issue of human dignity or the propriety of retribution. Thus, Stewart's statement on paying criminals back takes on added significance. With the concurrence of six Justices, he said, "the decision that capital punishment may be the appropriate sanction in extreme cases is an expression of the community's belief that certain crimes are themselves so grievous an affront to humanity that the only adequate response may be the penalty of death."

This sanctioning of the retributive principle especially disturbed Marshall, one of the two dissenters. Along with many opponents of the death penalty, he would be willing to allow executions if they could be shown to serve some useful purpose—for example, deterring others from committing capital crimes—but to execute a criminal simply because society demands its pound of flesh is, he said, to deny him his "dignity and worth." Why it would not deprive a person of dignity and worth to use him (by executing him) in order to influence the behavior of other persons, Marshall did not say; apparently he would be willing to accept society's calculations but not its moral judgments.

An unwillingness to accept society's moral judgments best characterizes the opposition to capital punishment, a fact reflected in the differences between popular and sophisticated opinion on the subject. Sophisticated opinion holds that the death penalty does not comport with human dignity because, as Brennan (the other dissenter) said, it treats "members of the human race as nonhumans, as objects to be toyed with and discarded." Popular opinion holds that to punish criminals, even to execute them, is to acknowledge their humanity, insofar as it regards them, as it does not regard other creatures, as responsible moral beings. Sophisticated opinion agrees with ABE FORTAS who, after he left the Supreme Court, argued that the "essential value" of our civilization is the "pervasive, unqualified respect for life"; this respect for life forbids the taking of even a murderer's life. Popular opinion holds that what matters is not *that* one lives but *how* one lives, and that society rightly praises its heroes, who sacrifice their lives for their fellow citizens, and rightly condemns the worst of its criminals who prey upon them.

In 1976, seven members of the Supreme Court agreed that society is justified in making this severe moral judgment, but this agreement on the principle may prove to be less significant than the Justices' inability to join in a common opinion of the Court. Embodied in that inability were differences in the extent to which the Justices were committed to the principle, and it could have been predicted that, in future cases, some of them would find reason not to apply it.

WALTER BERNS

Bibliography

BERNS, WALTER 1979 *For Capital Punishment: Crime and the Morality of the Death Penalty.* New York: Basic Books.

DAVIS, PEGGY C.; WOLFGANG, MARVIN E.; GIBBS, JACK P.; VAN DEN HAAG, ERNEST; and NAKELL, BARRY 1978 Capital Punishment in the United States: A Symposium. *Criminal Law Bulletin* 14:5–80.

EHRLICH, ISAAC 1975 The Deterrent Effect of Capital Punishment. *American Economic Review* 65:397–417.

ENGLAND, JANE C. 1977 Capital Punishment in the Light of Constitutional Evolution: An Analysis of Distinctions Between *Furman* and *Gregg. Notre Dame Lawyer* 52:596–610.

GILLERS, STEPHEN 1980 Deciding Who Dies. *University of Pennsylvania Law Review* 129:1–124.

LEMPERT, RICHARD O. 1981 Desert and Deterrence: An Assessment of the Moral Bases for Capital Punishment. *Michigan Law Review* 79:1177–1231.

CAPITATION TAXES

A capitation tax, or POLL TAX, is a tax levied on persons. A capitation tax takes a fixed amount for each person subject to it, without regard to income or property. Under Article I, section 9, any federal capitation tax must be apportioned among the states according to population, a restriction originally intended to prevent Congress from taxing states out of existence.

In the twentieth century some states made payment of capitation taxes a qualification for voting, usually in order to reduce the number of black voters. The TWENTY-FOURTH AMENDMENT and HARPER V. VIRGINIA BOARD OF ELECTIONS (1966) ended this practice.

DENNIS J. MAHONEY

(SEE ALSO: *Direct and Indirect Taxes; Excise Tax.*)

CAPTIVE AUDIENCE

The Supreme Court has encountered conflicts between FREEDOM OF SPEECH and PRIVACY. In some cases speech conflicts with a nonspeech interest, such as a claimed right to preserve one's peace and quiet. In other cases speech interests may be discerned on both sides; the listener objects to having to hear an uncongenial message. The notion of "captive audience" refers to both types of case. The right not to be compelled to listen to unwelcome messages may be viewed as a corollary to the right not to be compelled to profess what one does not believe, announced in WEST VIRGINIA BOARD OF EDUCATION V. BARNETTE (1943).

Justice WILLIAM O. DOUGLAS first argued the rights of captive auditors in a dissent in *Public Utilities Commission v. Pollak* (1952). His views reemerged in *Lehman v. Shaker Heights* (1974). There a city-owned transit system devoted transit advertising space solely to commercial and public service messages, refusing space to a political candidate. Four Justices held that placard space in city-owned buses and street cars did not constitute a PUBLIC FORUM because the space was incidental to a commercial transportation venture. Admitting, however, that city ownership implicated STATE ACTION, the four agreed that the transit system's advertising policies must not be "arbitrary, capricious, or invidious." The ban on political advertising was a reasonable means "to minimize chances of abuse, the appearance of favoritism and the risk of imposing upon a captive audience."

Justice Douglas concurred. His main point was that commuters, forced onto public transit as a economic necessity, should not be made a captive audience to placard advertising they cannot "turn off." They have a right to be protected from political messages that they are totally without freedom of choice to receive or reject.

The dissenters argued that, whether or not buses and streetcars were special-purpose publically owned property that could be denied public forum status, the city could not constitutionally discriminate among placard messages on the basis of their content.

A finding that a public forum did exist would likely be decisive for the captive audience issue. Surely there is only the most attenuated "right not to receive" when one enters a public forum whose very definition is that it is open to all senders; those who do not wish to receive a particular visual message are expected to turn away their eyes. *Lehman* and COHEN V. CALIFORNIA (1971) illustrate this tension between the public forum and captive audience concepts.

MARTIN SHAPIRO

Bibliography

BLACK, CHARLES 1953 He Cannot Choose but Hear: The Plight of the Captive Auditor. *Columbia Law Review* 53:960–974.

CAHILL, SHEILA M. 1975 The Public Forum: Minimum Access, Equal Access and the First Amendment. *Stanford Law Review* 28:117–148.

CARDOZO, BENJAMIN N. (1870–1938)

The towering professional and public reputation that OLIVER WENDELL HOLMES enjoyed when he retired from the Supreme Court in 1932 contributed to President HERBERT HOOVER'S selection of Benjamin Nathan Cardozo as his successor despite the fact that there were already two New Yorkers and one Jew on the Supreme Court. Cardozo was one of the very few lawyers in the country whose reputation resembled that of Holmes. A series of famous opinions, his extrajudicial writings, especially *The Nature of the Judicial Process,* his position as chief judge of an able New York Court of Appeals, and his almost saintlike demeanor propelled him into prominence and combined with the usual exigencies of fate and political calculation to put him onto the Supreme Court.

During his five and one-half terms on the Supreme Court from 1932 to 1938, one of Cardozo's major contributions was his demonstration of the utility of COMMON LAW techniques to elaboration of the FOURTEENTH AMENDMENT. Ever since the passage of that amendment, a substantial body of constitutional thought has sought to prevent, or at least to limit, the substantive interpretation of its open-ended provisions. The line stretches from the SLAUGHTERHOUSE CASES (1873) through LEARNED HAND to the current day. The arguments in the 1980s are considerably more complex and theoretical than they were in the nineteenth century and in the 1920s and 1930s. Yet the underlying theme remains essentially the same: the inappropriateness in a democratic society of a nonelected court giving substantive content to broad constitutional phrases such as DUE PROCESS OF LAW and EQUAL PROTECTION OF THE LAWS because of the lack of appropriate sources of judicial law for such an endeavor. The controversies in Cardozo's day revolved around the use of the due process clauses and the equal protection clause to test both the economic legislation that marked an increasingly regulatory society and the numerous infringements by government of individual rights. Although Cardozo's political and social outlook differed somewhat from those of his predecessors on the Court, Holmes, LOUIS D. BRANDEIS, and HARLAN FISKE STONE, he shared the general substantive constitutional outlook that they had espoused for many years: great deference to legislative judgments in economic matters but a more careful scrutiny to constitutional claims of governmental violation of CIVIL RIGHTS in noneconomic matters.

Thus Cardozo was consistently to be found joining those members of the Court, especially Brandeis and Stone, who voted to uphold ECONOMIC REGULATION against attack on COMMERCE CLAUSE, due process, and equal protection grounds. He wrote some of the more eloquent dissents, *Liggett v. Lee* (1933) (Florida chain store tax), PANAMA REFINING COMPANY V. RYAN (1935) (the "hot oil" provision of the NATIONAL INDUSTRIAL RECOVERY ACT), *Stewart Dry Goods Company v. Lewis* (1935) (graduated taxes on gross sales), and CARTER V. CARTER COAL COMPANY (1936) (The Guffey-Snyder Act), and two of the major Court opinions after the Court reversed itself and adopted the constitutional views of the former dissenters. In STEWARD MACHINE COMPANY V. DAVIS (1937) and HELVERING V. DAVIS (1937) Cardozo's opinions upholding the SOCIAL SECURITY ACT expounded Congress's power under the TAXING AND SPENDING clause of the Constitution and provided the theoretical basis for upholding major legislative policies in a way that complemented the parallel recognition of expansive congressional power under the commerce clause. He also viewed the commerce clause as imposing broad limits on the power of individual states to solve their economic problems at the expense of their neighbors (*Baldwin v. Seelig,* 1935), although he recognized at the same time that state financial needs required some tempering of those views (*Henneford v. Silas Mason Co.,* 1937).

Cardozo's special contribution lay in his discussion of the methodological approach to substantive results. Long before joining the Supreme Court, he had considered the appropriate factors that shape decision making for a judge, and although his primary experience was in the common law, he had considered the issue with respect to constitutional law as well. Many would sharply curtail the judiciary's role in constitutional, in contrast to common law, adjudication because of the legislature's inability to overturn most constitutional decisions, but Cardozo viewed the process of judicial decision making as unitary. In *The Nature of the Judicial Process* he had proposed a fourfold division of the forces that shape the growth of legal principles: logic or analogy (the method of philosophy); history (the historical or evolutionary method); custom (the method of tradition); and justice, morals, and social welfare (the method of sociology).

Those who have attacked the common law approach to Fourteenth Amendment adjudication have perceived the specter of subjectivism in employment of all these methods, but especially in the last. Cardozo saw "justice, morals, and social welfare," which he also labeled as "accepted standards of right conduct," as especially relevant in constitutional adjudication. He struggled to find an acceptable formula for deriving those standards, finally settling on "the principle and practice of the men and women of the community whom the social mind would rank as intelligent and virtuous."

Cardozo never directly met the charge of subjectivism, especially subjectivism in Fourteenth Amendment adjudication, for his message about judging was aimed at a different target: the regressive results produced by too slavish adherence to the so-called objective factors of precedent and logic. But he clearly did not believe that all was "subjective" or that complete reliance on "objective" factors was possible either. One did the best one could to avoid judging on the basis of purely personal values. "History or custom or social utility or some compelling sentiment of justice or sometimes perhaps a semi-intuitive apprehension of the pervading spirit of our law must come to the rescue of the anxious judge, and tell him where to go."

Cardozo brought these ideas with him to the Supreme Court and applied them to a number of notable issues. From its earliest days and notwithstanding bad experience with SUBSTANTIVE DUE PROCESS of law, epitomized by DRED SCOTT V. SANDFORD (1857) and LOCHNER V. NEW YORK (1905), the Court had become committed, in different guises and formulations, to the notion that various rights, liberties, privileges, or immunities existed that were not spelled out in the Constitution. Although there had been occasional discussion since the end of the nineteenth century of the question whether the Fourteenth Amendment "incorporated" specific provisions of the BILL OF RIGHTS (see INCORPORATION DOCTRINE), most major decisions in the twentieth century had used the due process clause on its own to assess whether a particular "liberty" had been denied. As the attack on the Court's use of the due process clause to strike down economic regulation increased throughout the 1930s, the Court began to refocus the issue of protection of noneconomic rights more in terms of incorporation of particular provisions of the Bill of Rights into the Fourteenth Amendment.

The classic reformulation was rendered by Cardozo in PALKO V. CONNECTICUT (1937). To be incorporated the claimed right must be "fundamental"; or one without which "neither liberty nor justice would exist"; or it must "be implicit in the concept of ORDERED LIBERTY." Without pursuing all the ramifications of the debate over "selective incorporation," as the *Palko* DOCTRINE came to be known, we should note that in the midst of the most severe attack on the Court's interpretation of the Fourteenth Amendment, Cardozo and the whole Court never questioned the notion that the amendment had a substantive content. The approach they chose, the selective incorporation doctrine, required the weighing of factors and building up of precedents in a common law fashion with only the general language of the Fourteenth Amendment as a starting point.

Two Fourteenth Amendment cases suffice to demonstrate specific attempts to apply a "common law" method of judging. In *Snyder v. Massachusetts* (1934) Cardozo wrote an opinion holding that due process was not violated when the defendant was not permitted to be present at a jury view of the scene of an alleged crime. After recognizing that the Fourteenth Amendment protected privileges "fundamental" to a FAIR TRIAL, he considered history, which showed that a view of the scene by a jury was not considered part of the "trial"; current practice in other states, which generally permitted the defendant to be present; and potential prejudice to defendant, which he found to be remote. The balance of these factors led him to conclude that there was nothing fundamental, on the facts of Snyder's case, about the right being asserted.

In GROSJEAN V. AMERICAN PRESS COMPANY (1936), Cardozo wrote an opinion, never published, concerning a Louisiana statute that placed a tax on newspapers that carried advertising and had a circulation over 20,000. The majority had originally agreed to hold the statute unconstitutional on equal protection grounds. After Cardozo wrote an opinion concurring on grounds of violation of FREEDOM OF THE PRESS, Justice GEORGE SUTHERLAND substituted a new opinion for a unanimous Court adopting the free press rationale, although in an ambiguous formulation that suggests unconstitutional motivation as at least one of its rationales. The opinion that Cardozo then withdrew is one of his best, and it discusses his methodology and substantive rationale quite clearly. What is a law "abridging the freedom of the press" may be somewhat more specific than the question whether a law denies liberty without due process of law (or denies a PRIVILEGE OR IMMUNITY of national CITIZENSHIP), but it was not much more of a specific starting point for the Court in the context of the Louisiana statute.

Cardozo's draft opinion considered exhaustively the English use first of licenses and then of taxation to control the press as part of the history that led to adoption of the FIRST AMENDMENT. That history led him to conclude that the tax involved was a modern counterpart of those repressive tactics. But he also recognized the financial needs of government. He thus concluded unambiguously—and innovatively—that while the press was not immune from taxation and while classifications were normally a matter of legislative discretion, freedom of the press could be safeguarded only if the press was not subjected to discriminatory taxation vis-à-vis other occupations and through use of internal classifications. The opinion is a splendid example of the use of history and reason combined with a sympathetic appreciation of the setting in which the press functions and of modern needs to assure its "freedom."

Another interesting substantive view was his analysis, before coming to the Supreme Court, of three due process cases that have become increasingly important to modern constitutional theory: MEYER V. NEBRASKA (1923) and *Bartel v. Iowa* (1923) (state laws forbidding teaching of foreign languages to young children held unconstitutional) and PIERCE V. SOCIETY OF SISTERS (1928) (state requirement that all children attend public school through eighth grade held unconstitutional). In *The Paradoxes of Legal Science* he characterized the unconstitutional legislation and the nature of the "liberty" that was upheld in the following prophetic language. "Restraints such as these are encroachments upon the free development of personality in a society that is organized on the basis of family." This emphasis on "free development of personality" and "family" is a stunning extrapolation of a second level of generalization from the constitutional principle of "liberty"; it places Cardozo a half century ahead of his time, for such a conception of the "liberty" protected by the Fourteenth Amendment did not resurface until GRISWOLD V. CONNECTICUT (1965) and ROE V. WADE (1973); and it is a graphic (and controversial) example of the operation of the "method of sociology" in CONSTITUTIONAL INTERPRETATION.

Cardozo was a judge for twenty-four years and he thought hard about what he did. If he was not wholly successful in making a useful statement that would clarify the basis for the creative leap of judgment that enabled him to value certain arguments more than others and thus to reach a conclusion, no one in the half century that followed has been more successful. More important, he provided assistance in his extrajudicial writings and in the reasoning of his opinions for the position, which continues to have considerable support among constitutional theorists and especially among judges, that asserts the validity of applying techniques of common law adjudication to the elaboration of Fourteenth Amendment doctrine. Finally and perhaps even more controversially, he demonstrated that an able, conscientious judge who believed that substantive Fourteenth Amendment adjudication was different from legislating might so comport himself on the bench as to offer hope to his successors a half century later that that position is desirable and capable of achievement.

ANDREW L. KAUFMAN

Bibliography

Collected essays on Cardozo in joint 1939 issues of *Columbia Law Review,* 39, #1; *Harvard Law Review,* 52, #3; *Yale Law Journal,* 48, #3; and *Cardozo Law Review,* 1, #1.

KAUFMAN, ANDREW L. 1969 Benjamin Cardozo. In Leon Friedman and Fred L. Israel, eds., *The Justices of the Supreme Court of the United States, 1789–1969,* 3:2287–2307. New York: Chelsea House.

——— 1979 Cardozo's Appointment to the Supreme Court. *Cardozo Law Review* 1:23–53.

CAREY *v.* POPULATION SERVICES INTERNATIONAL
431 U.S. 678 (1977)

By a 7–2 vote the Supreme Court in *Carey* invalidated three New York laws restricting the advertisement and sale of birth control devices. Justice WILLIAM J. BRENNAN wrote for a majority concerning two of the laws. First, he read GRISWOLD V. CONNECTICUT (1965) and ROE V. WADE (1973) to require STRICT SCRUTINY of laws touching the "fundamental" decision "whether to bear or beget a child." New York had limited the distribution of contraceptives to licensed pharmacists, and had not offered a sufficiently compelling justification. Second, he read the FIRST AMENDMENT to forbid a law prohibiting the advertising or display of contraceptives. (See COMMERCIAL SPEECH.)

The Court was fragmented in striking down the third law, which forbade distribution of contraceptives to minors under sixteen except under medical prescription. Justice Brennan, for himself and three other Justices, conceded that children's constitutional rights may not be the equivalent of adults' rights. Yet he found insufficient justification for the law in the state's policy of discouraging sexual activity among young people. He doubted that a limit on access to contraceptives would discourage such activity, and in any case the state could not delegate to doctors the right to decide which minors should be discouraged. Three concurring Justices expressed less enthusiasm for minors' constitutional rights to sexual freedom but found other paths to the conclusion that the New York law as written was invalid.

Chief Justice WARREN E. BURGER dissented without opinion, and Justice WILLIAM H. REHNQUIST filed a short dissent that was unusually caustic, even by his high standard for the genre.

Carey was not the last word on the troublesome problem of minors' rights concerning REPRODUCTIVE AUTONOMY; the Court has repeatedly returned to the issue in the ABORTION context. Yet *Carey*'s opinion invalidating the law limiting contraceptives sales to pharmacists was important for its recognition that *Griswold v. Connecticut* stood not merely for a right of marital PRIVACY but also for a broad FREEDOM OF INTIMATE ASSOCIATION.

KENNETH L. KARST

CAROLENE PRODUCTS COMPANY, UNITED STATES *v.*
Footnote Four
304 U.S. 144 (1938)

Footnote four to Justice HARLAN F. STONE's opinion in UNITED STATES V. CAROLENE PRODUCTS CO. (1938) undoubtedly is the best known, most controversial footnote in constitutional law. Stone used it to suggest categories in which a general presumption in favor of the constitutionality of legislation might be inappropriate. The issue of if and when particular constitutional claims warrant special judicial scrutiny has been a core concern in constitutional theory for nearly fifty years since Stone's three-paragraph footnote was appended to an otherwise obscure 1938 opinion.

The *Carolene Products* decision, handed down the same day as ERIE RAILROAD V. TOMPKINS (1938), itself reflected a new perception of the proper role for federal courts. It articulated a position of great judicial deference in reviewing most legislation. In his majority opinion, Stone sought to consolidate developing restraints on judicial intervention in economic matters, symbolized by WEST COAST HOTEL CO. V. PARRISH (1937). But in footnote four Stone also went on to suggest that legislation, if challenged with certain types of constitutional claims, might not merit the same deference most legislation should enjoy.

Stone's opinion upheld a 1923 federal ban on the interstate shipment of filled milk. The Court thus reversed a lower federal court and, indirectly, the Illinois Supreme Court, in holding that Congress had power to label as adulterated a form of skimmed milk in which butterfat was replaced by coconut milk. Today the decision seems unremarkable; at the time, however, not only was the result in *Carolene Products* controversial but the theory of variable judicial scrutiny suggested by its footnote four was new and perhaps daring.

Actually, only three other Justices joined that part of Stone's opinion which contained the famous footnote, though that illustrious trio consisted of Chief Justice CHARLES EVANS HUGHES, Justice LOUIS D. BRANDEIS, and Justice OWEN J. ROBERTS. Justice HUGO L. BLACK refused to agree to the part of Stone's opinion with the footnote because Black wished to go further than Stone in proclaiming deference to legislative judgments. Justice PIERCE BUTLER concurred only in the result; Justice JAMES C. MCREYNOLDS dissented; and Justices BENJAMIN N. CARDOZO and STANLEY F. REED did not take part.

In fact, the renowned footnote does no more than tentatively mention the possibility of active review in certain realms. The footnote is nonetheless considered a paradigm for special judicial scrutiny of laws discriminating against certain rights or groups. The first paragraph, added at the suggestion of Chief Justice Hughes, is the least controversial. The paragraph hints at special judicial concern when rights explicitly mentioned in the text of the Constitution are at issue. This rights-oriented, interpretivist position involves less of a judicial leap than the possibility, suggested in the rest of the footnote, of additional grounds for judicial refusal or reluctance to defer to judgments of other governmental branches.

The footnote's second paragraph speaks of possible special scrutiny of interference with "those political processes which can ordinarily be expected to bring about repeal of undesirable legislation." To illustrate the ways in which clogged political channels might be grounds for exacting judicial review, Stone cites decisions invalidating restrictions on the right to vote, the dissemination of information, freedom of political association, and peaceable assembly.

The footnote's third and final paragraph has been the most vigorously debated. It suggests that prejudice directed against DISCRETE AND INSULAR MINORITIES may also call for "more searching judicial inquiry." For this proposition Stone cites two commerce clause decisions, MCCULLOCH V. MARYLAND (1819) and *South Carolina State Highway Dept. v. Barnwell Bros.* (1938), as well as FIRST AMENDMENT and FOURTEENTH AMENDMENT decisions invalidating discriminatory laws based on religion, national origin, or race. Judicial and scholarly disagreement since 1938 has focused mainly on two questions. First, even if the category "discrete and insular minorities" seems clearly to include blacks, should any other groups be included? Second, does paragraph three essentially overlap with paragraph two, or does it go beyond protecting groups who suffer particular political disadvantage? The question whether discrimination against particular groups or burdens on certain rights should trigger special judicial sensitivity is a basic problem in constitutional law to this day.

Footnote four thus symbolizes the Court's struggle since the late 1930s to confine an earlier, free-wheeling tradition of judicial intervention premised on FREEDOM OF CONTRACT and SUBSTANTIVE DUE PROCESS, on the one hand, while trying, on the other, to create an acceptable basis for active intervention when judges perceive political disadvantages or racial or other invidious discrimination.

Dozens of Supreme Court decisions and thousands of pages of scholarly commentary since *Carolene Products* have explored this problem. In EQUAL PROTECTION analysis, for example, the approach introduced in footnote four helped produce a two-tiered model of judicial review. Within this model, legislation involving social and economic matters would be sustained if any RATIONAL BASIS for the law could be found, or sometimes even conceived of, by a judge. In sharp contrast, STRICT SCRUTINY applied to classifications based on race, national origin, and, sometimes, alienage. Similarly, judicial identification of a limited number of FUNDAMENTAL RIGHTS, such as VOTING RIGHTS, sometimes seemed to trigger a strict scrutiny described accurately by Gerald Gunther as " 'strict' in theory and fatal in fact."

Though this two-tiered approach prevailed in many decisions of the WARREN COURT, inevitably the system became more flexible. "Intermediate scrutiny" is now explicitly used in SEX DISCRIMINATION cases, for example. The Court continues to wrestle with the problem suggested in footnote four cases involving constitutional claims of discrimination against whites, discrimination against illegitimate children, and total exclusion of some from important benefits such as public education. Parallel with footnote four, the argument today centers on the question whether it is an appropriate constitutional response to relegate individuals who claim discrimination at the hands of the majority to their remedies within the political process. Yet, as new groups claim discriminatory treatment in new legal realms, the meaning of "discrete and insular minorities" grows more problematic. Undeniably, however, the categories suggested in footnote four still channel the debate. A good example is John Hart Ely's *Democracy and Distrust* (1980), an influential book that expands upon footnote four's theme of political participation.

Justice LEWIS H. POWELL recently stated that footnote four contains "perhaps the most far-sighted dictum in our modern judicial heritage." Yet Powell also stressed that, in his view, it is important to remember that footnote four was merely OBITER DICTUM and was intended to be no more. Even so, the tentative words of footnote four must be credited with helping to initiate and to define a new era of constitutional development. The questions raised by footnote four remain central to constitutional thought; controversy premised on this famous footnote shows no sign of abating.

AVIAM SOIFER

Bibliography

BALL, MILNER S. 1981 Don't Die Don Quixote: A Response and Alternative to Tushnet, Bobbitt, and the Revised Texas Version of Constitutional Law. *Texas Law Review* 59:787–813.

ELY, JOHN HART 1980 *Democracy and Distrust.* Cambridge, Mass.: Harvard University Press.

LUSKY, LOUIS 1982 Footnote Redux: A *Carolene Products* Reminiscence. *Columbia Law Review* 82:1093–1105.

POWELL, LEWIS F., JR. 1982 *Carolene Products* Revisited. *Columbia Law Review* 82:1087–1092.

CARPENTER, MATTHEW H.
(1824–1881)

A Wisconsin lawyer and senator (1869–1875, 1879–1881), Matthew Hale Carpenter was a vigorous Douglas Democrat who favored compromise to prevent SECESSION. Nevertheless, believing secession treasonous, Carpenter supported the war and became a Republican. During Reconstruction Carpenter successfully argued *Ex Parte Garland* (1867) which held the FEDERAL TEST ACT of 1865 unconstitutional. (See TEST OATH CASES.) Subsequently General ULYSSES S. GRANT hired Carpenter as counsel for the Army in EX PARTE MCCARDLE (1868). Carpenter's successful defense of the Army and of the right of Congress to limit Supreme Court JURISDICTION led to his election to the Senate in 1869. There he was generally a strong supporter of Grant's administration, but he only mildly supported CIVIL RIGHTS. In 1872 Carpenter vigorously opposed federal legislation mandating integrated schools and juries because, among other reasons, the statute would violate STATES' RIGHTS. Similarly, as defense counsel he successfully argued for a narrow reading of the FOURTEENTH AMENDMENT in the SLAUGHTERHOUSE CASES (1873). As a former railroad lawyer, however, Carpenter was a leader in protecting business interests. He led the debates supporting the JURISDICTION ACT of 1875, which greatly expanded the JURISDICTION OF FEDERAL COURTS to hear cases in which CORPORATIONS might claim constitutional rights. In 1876 he successfully defended Secretary of War William Belknap in his IMPEACHMENT trial. In 1877 Carpenter unsuccessfully represented Samuel Tilden before the presidential electoral commission. He was defeated for reelection in 1875 because of his connection with Grant administration scandals, but was reelected to the Senate in 1879, serving until his death.

PAUL FINKELMAN

Bibliography

THOMPSON, EDWING BRUCE 1954 *Matthew Hale Carpenter: Webster of the West.* Madison: State Historical Society of Wisconsin.

CARR, ROBERT K.
(1908–1979)

Robert Kenneth Carr was an educator and political scientist; he taught at Dartmouth College (1937–1959) and was president of Oberlin College (1960–1970).

In 1947 Carr served as Executive Secretary of the President's Committee on Civil Rights appointed by HARRY S. TRUMAN and played a leading role in framing its report, *To Secure These Rights* (1947); this report's detailed presentation of the legal and social disabilities imposed on America's black population sparked nationwide controversy. Carr's own book on the subject, *Federal Protection of Civil Rights: Quest for a Sword* (1947), set forth the history of federal civil rights laws and their enforcement and demonstrated their inadequacy in theory and practice. In *The House Committee on Un-American Activities, 1946–1950* (1952), Carr argued that the carelessness and irresponsibility displayed by members and staff of the HOUSE COMMITTEE ON UN-AMERICAN ACTIVITIES outweighed the benefits of alerting the public to the dangers posed by communism at home and abroad; he concluded that the committee's record argued strongly for its own abolition. Carr also wrote two books on the Supreme Court for general readers, *Democracy and the Supreme Court* (1936) and *The Supreme Court and Judicial Review* (1942), and several other books on education and American government.

RICHARD B. BERNSTEIN

CARROLL, DANIEL
(1730–1796)

Daniel Carroll, a wealthy, European-educated Roman Catholic from Maryland, was a signer of both the ARTICLES OF CONFEDERATION and the Constitution. Carroll, who favored a strong national government, spoke often and served on three committees. He was subsequently elected to the first House of Representatives.

DENNIS J. MAHONEY

CARROLL v. PRESIDENT AND COMMISSIONERS OF PRINCESS ANNE
393 U.S. 175 (1968)

After a meeting of a "white supremacist" group at which "aggressively and militantly racist" speeches were made to a racially mixed crowd, the group announced another rally for the next night. Local officials obtained an EX PARTE order enjoining the group from holding a rally for ten days. The Supreme Court, reviewing this order two years later, held that the case fell within an exception to the doctrine of MOOTNESS: rights should not be defeated by short-term orders "capable of repetition, yet evading review."

A unanimous Court held that the *ex parte* order violated the FIRST AMENDMENT. An INJUNCTION against expressive activity requires NOTICE to the persons restrained and a chance to be heard, absent a showing that it is impossible to give them notice and a hearing.

KENNETH L. KARST

CARROLL v. UNITED STATES
267 U.S. 132 (1925)

In *Carroll* the Supreme Court held that an officer can stop and search an automobile without a warrant if there is PROBABLE CAUSE to believe the vehicle contains contraband.

The Court noted that national legislation had routinely authorized WARRANTLESS SEARCHES of vessels suspected of carrying goods on which duty had been evaded. The analogy was shaky; Congress's complete control over international boundaries would justify searching any imports even without probable cause. The Court also approved this warrantless search on a dubious interpretation of the National Prohibition Act. But the Court had independent grounds beyond history and congressional intent for its decision: the search was justified as an implied exception to the FOURTH AMENDMENT's warrant requirement, because the vehicle might be driven away before a warrant could be obtained. Given these EXIGENT CIRCUMSTANCES, probable cause rather than a warrant satisfied the constitutional test of reasonableness. Indeed, legislative approval was not considered in the later AUTOMOBILE SEARCH cases.

JACOB W. LANDYNSKI

CARTER, JAMES COOLIDGE
(1827–1905)

One of the preeminent legal philosophers of his time, James Coolidge Carter frequently appeared before the Supreme Court. Stressing that the FREEDOM OF CONTRACT limited the commerce power, Carter lost two 5–4 decisions in antitrust cases: UNITED STATES V. TRANS-MISSOURI FREIGHT ASSOCIATION (1897) and *United States v. Joint Traffic* (1898). He also defended the constitutionality of the income tax in POLLOCK V. FARMERS' LOAN & TRUST COMPANY (1895).

The clearest exposition of his views appears in *Law: Its Origin, Growth and Function* (1905) where he contended that law must harmonize with customary beliefs.

DAVID GORDON

CARTER, JIMMY
(1924–)

As the first President elected after the WATERGATE scandal, Jimmy Carter was strongly oriented toward moral duties, Christian ethics, faith, trust, and personal rectitude. The "nobility of ideas" theme evoked in his inaugural address ranged broadly from human rights to the elimination of nuclear weapons. Missing from this pantheon of principles, however, was an understanding of the constitutional system and the mechanics of government needed to translate abstract visions into concrete accomplishments.

Carter considered himself an activist President and wanted to use the power of his office to correct social, economic, and political inequities. Some of his contributions to the legal system were long-lasting, such as the large number of women and persons from minority groups he placed on the federal courts. But comprehensive reforms for welfare, taxation, health, and energy became mired in Congress because of Carter's inability to articulate his beliefs and mobilize public opinion. He and his associates wrongly assumed that institutional resistance from Congress and the executive branch could be overcome simply by appealing to the people through the media.

Carter's congressional relations staff started off poorly and never recovered. By campaigning both against Congress and the bureaucracy, Carter had alienated the very centers of power he needed to govern effectively. He advocated "cabinet government" until the impression of departmental autonomy suggested weak presidential leadership. A major shake-up in July 1979 led to the firing or resignation of five cabinet secretaries, all with a history of friction with certain members of the White House staff. The abrupt nature of these departures cast doubt on Carter's judgment and stability, implying that in any contest between personal loyalty and professional competence, loyalty would prevail.

In foreign policy, the Camp David accord in 1978 marked a high point for Carter when he produced a "framework for peace" between Israeli Prime Minister Menachem Begin and Egyptian President Anwar Sadat. The ratification of the PANAMA CANAL TREATIES also marked a personal triumph, although Carter required last-minute assistance from several senators. His recognition of the People's Republic of China seriously damaged his relations with a number of members of Congress, who were offended by his lack of consultation and the breach of faith with Taiwan. When some of the congressional opponents challenged the termination of the defense treaty with Taiwan, however, the Supreme Court in GOLDWATER V. CARTER (1979) ordered the case dismissed for lack of JUSTICIABILITY. The Iranian revolution and the seizure of the American Embassy in Teheran produced a bitter fourteen months of "America held hostage." This development, including the abortive rescue attempt in 1980, exacerbated Carter's problems of weak leadership and perceived helplessness.

Carter and his associates from Georgia arrived in office with the reputation of amateurs, an image they would never dispel. Carter had campaigned as an outsider, treating that title as a virtue that would set him apart from politicians tainted by the "establishment." He came as a stranger and remained estranged. Having carefully dissociated himself he could not form associations. Throughout his four years he demonstrated little understanding of or interest in legislative strategy, the levers of power, or political leadership.

LOUIS FISHER

Bibliography

JOHNSON, HAYNES 1980 *In the Absence of Power: Governing America.* New York: Viking.

CARTER v. CARTER COAL CO.
298 U.S. 238 (1936)

This was the New Deal's strongest case yet to come before the Supreme Court, and it lost. At issue was the constitutionality of the BITUMINOUS COAL ACT, which regulated the trade practices, prices, and labor relations of the nation's single most important source of energy, the bituminous industry in twenty-seven states. No industry was the subject of greater federal concern or of as many federal investigations. After the Court killed the NATIONAL INDUSTRIAL RECOVERY ACT (NIRA) and with it the bituminous code, Congress enacted a "Little NIRA" for bituminous coal. Although the statute contained no provision limiting the amount of bituminous that could be mined, the Court held it unconstitutional as a regulation of PRODUCTION.

The statute had two basic provisions, wholly separable and administered separately by independent administrative agencies. One agency supervised the price and trade-practices section of the statute; the other the labor section, dealing with MAXIMUM HOURS AND MINIMUM WAGES, and COLLECTIVE BARGAINING. In NEBBIA V. NEW YORK (1934) the Court had sustained against a due process attack the principle of price-fixing in the broadest language. The labor sections seemed constitutional, because strikes had crippled INTERSTATE COMMERCE and the national economy on numerous occasions and four times required federal troops to quell disorders. The federal courts had often enjoined the activities of the United Mine Workers as restraining interstate commerce.

The Court voted 6–3 to invalidate the labor provisions and then voted 5–4 to invalidate the entire statute. Justice GEORGE SUTHERLAND for the majority did not decide on the merits of the price-fixing provisions. Had he attacked them, he might have lost Justice OWEN J. ROBERTS, who had written the *Nebbia* opinion. The strategy was to hold the price provisions inseparable from the labor provisions, which were unconstitutional, thereby bringing down the whole act, despite the fact that its two sections were separable.

Sutherland relied mainly on the stunted version of the COMMERCE CLAUSE that had dominated the Court's opinions in UNITED STATES V. E. C. KNIGHT CO. (1895) and more recently in the NIRA and AGRICULTURAL ADJUSTMENT ACT cases: production is local; labor is part of production; therefore the TENTH AMENDMENT reserves all labor matters to the states. That the major coal-producing states, disavowing STATES' RIGHTS, had supported the congressional enactment and emphasized the futility of STATE REGULATION OF COMMERCE meant nothing to the majority. Sutherland rejected the proposition that "the power of the federal government inherently extends to purposes affecting the nation as a whole with which the states severally cannot deal." In fact the government had relied on the commerce power, not INHERENT POWERS. But Sutherland stated that "the local character of mining, of manufacturing, and of crop growing is a fact, whatever may be done with the products." All labor matters—he enumerated them—were part of production. That labor disputes might catastrophically affect interstate commerce was undeniable but irrelevant, Sutherland reasoned, because their effect on interstate commerce must always be indirect and thus beyond congressional control. The effect was indirect because production intervened between a strike and interstate commerce. All the evils, he asserted, "are local evils over which the federal government has no legislative control." (See EFFECTS ON COMMERCE.)

Chief Justice CHARLES EVANS HUGHES dissented on the question whether the price-fixing provisions of the statute were separable. Justice BENJAMIN N. CARDOZO, supported by Justices LOUIS D. BRANDEIS and HARLAN F. STONE, dissented on the same ground, adding a full argument as to the constitutionality of the price-fixing section. He contended too that the issue on the labor section was not ripe for decision, because Carter asked for a decree to restrain the statute's operation before it went into operation. Cardozo's broad view of the commerce power confirmed the Roosevelt administration's belief that the majority's antilabor, anti-New Deal bias, rather than an unconstitutional taint on the statute, explained the decision.

LEONARD W. LEVY

Bibliography

STERN, ROBERT L. 1946 The Commerce Clause and the National Economy, 1933–1946. *Harvard Law Review* 49:664–674.

CARY, JOHN W.
(1817–1895)

As the general counsel of the Chicago, Milwaukee & St. Paul Railway, John W. Cary was involved in some of the most important court cases on ECONOMIC REGULATION in the late 1800s. In briefs submitted in the GRANGER CASES (1877), Cary went beyond the doctrine of VESTED RIGHTS and the guarantee of JUST COMPENSATION relied on by other railroad attorneys such as WILLIAM EVARTS. Cary contended that state fixing of prices (including railroad rates) deprived stockholders not only of their property but also of their *liberty,* that is their freedom to use and control their property. A legislative power to fix prices, he argued, would be "in conflict with the whole structure and theory of our government, hostile to liberty. . . ."

In CHICAGO, MILWAUKEE & ST. PAUL RAILWAY V. MINNESOTA (1890) Cary, along with WILLIAM C. GOUDY, successfully argued that the reasonableness of state-fixed rates was subject to JUDICIAL REVIEW.

DENNIS J. MAHONEY

CASES AND CONTROVERSIES

Article III of the Constitution vests the JUDICIAL POWER OF THE UNITED STATES in one constitutionally mandated Supreme Court and such subordinate federal courts as Congress may choose to establish. Federal judges are appointed for life with salaries that cannot be diminished, but they may exercise their independent and politically unaccountable power only to resolve "cases" and "controversies" of the kinds designated by Article III, the most important of which are cases arising under the Constitution and other federal law. The scope of the federal judicial power thus depends in large measure on the Supreme Court's interpretations of the "case" and "controversy" limitation applicable to the Court itself and to other Article III tribunals.

That limitation not only inhibits Article III courts from arrogating too much power unto themselves; it also prevents Congress from compelling or authorizing decisions by federal courts in nonjudicial proceedings and precludes Supreme Court review of state court decisions in proceedings that are not considered "cases" or "controversies" under Article III. The limitation thus simultaneously confines federal judges and reinforces their ability to resist nonjudicial tasks pressed on them by others.

The linkage between independence and circumscribed power is a continuously important theme in "case" or "controversy" jurisprudence, as is the connection between "case" or "controversy" jurisprudence and the power of JUDICIAL REVIEW of government acts for constitutionality—a power that MARBURY V. MADISON (1803) justified primarily by the need to apply the Constitution as relevant law to decide a "case." During the CONSTITUTIONAL CONVENTION OF 1787, EDMUND RANDOLPH proposed that the President and members of the federal judiciary be joined in a council of revision to veto legislative excesses. The presidential VETO POWER was adopted instead, partly to keep the judiciary out of the legislative process and partly to insure that the judges would decide cases independently, without bias in favor of legislation they had helped to formulate. Similar concerns led the convention to reject CHARLES PINCKNEY's proposal to have the Supreme Court provide ADVISORY OPINIONS at the request of Congress or the President. Finally, in response to JAMES MADISON's doubts about extending the federal judicial power to expound the Constitution too broadly, the Convention made explicit its understanding that the power extended only to "cases of a Judiciary nature." The Framers understood that the judicial power of constitutional governance would expand if the concept of "case" or "controversy" did.

What constitutes an Article III "case," of a "judiciary nature," is hardly self-evident. No definition was articulated when the language was adopted, but only an apparent intent to circumscribe the federal judicial function, and to insure that it be performed independently of the other branches. In this century, Justice FELIX FRANKFURTER suggested that Article III precluded federal courts from deciding legal questions except in the kinds of proceedings entertained by the English and colonial courts at the time of the Constitution's adoption. But the willingness of English courts to give advisory opinions then—a practice clearly inconsistent with convention history and the Court's steadfast policy since 1793—refutes the suggestion. Moreover, from the outset the SEPARATION OF POWERS aspect of the "case" or "controversy" limitation has differentiated CONSTITUTIONAL COURTS (courts constituted under Article III) from others. Most fundamentally, however, the indeterminate historical contours of "cases" or "controversies" inevitably had to accommodate changes in the forms of litigation authorized by Congress, in the legal and social environment that accompanied the nation's industrial growth and the rise of the regulatory and welfare state, and in the place of the federal judiciary in our national life.

After two centuries of elaboration, the essential characteristics of Article III controversies remain imprecise and subject to change. Yet underlying the various manifestations of "case" or "controversy" doctrine are three core requirements: affected parties standing in an adverse relationship to each other, actual or threatened events that provoke a live legal dispute, and the courts' ability to render final and meaningful judgments. These criteria—concerning, respectively, the litigants, the facts, and judicial efficacy—have both independent and interrelated significance.

As to litigants, only parties injured by a defendant's behavior have constitutional STANDING to sue. COLLUSIVE SUITS are barred because the parties' interests are not adverse.

As to extant factual circumstances, advisory opinions are banned. This limitation not only bars direct requests for legal rulings on hypothetical facts but also requires dismissal of unripe or moot cases, because, respectively, they are not yet live, or they once were but have ceased to be by virtue of subsequent events. The parties' future or past adversariness cannot substitute for actual, current adversariness. Disputes that have not yet begun or have already ended are treated as having no more present need for decision than purely hypothetical disputes. (See RIPENESS; MOOTNESS).

The desire to preserve federal judicial power as

an independent, effective, and binding force of legal obligation is reflected both in the finality rule, which bars decision if the judgment rendered would be subject to revision by another branch of government, and in the rule denying standing unless a judgment would likely redress the plaintiff's injury. These two rules are the clearest instances of judicial self-limitation to insure that when the federal courts do act, their judgments will be potent. To exercise judicial power ineffectively or as merely a preliminary gesture would risk undermining compliance with court decrees generally or lessening official and public acceptance of the binding nature of judicial decisions, especially unpopular constitutional judgments. Here the link between the limitations on judicial power and that power's independence and effectiveness is at its strongest.

Historically, congressional attempts to expand the use of Article III judicial power have caused the greatest difficulty, largely because the federal courts are charged simultaneously with enforcing valid federal law as an arm of the national government and with restraining unconstitutional behavior of the coequal branches of that government. The enforcement role induces judicial receptivity to extensive congressional use of the federal courts, especially in a time of expansion of both the federal government's functions and the use of litigation to resolve public disputes. The courts' checking function, however, cautions judicial resistance to congressional efforts to enlarge the scope of "cases" or "controversies" for fear of losing the strength, independence, or finality needed to resist unconstitutional action by the political branches.

The early emphasis of "case" or "controversy" jurisprudence was on consolidating the judiciary's independence and effective power. The Supreme Court's refusal in 1793 to give President GEORGE WASHINGTON legal advice on the interpretation of treaties with France—the founding precedent for the ban on advisory opinions—rested largely on the desire to preserve the federal judiciary as a check on Congress and the executive when actual disputes arose. Similarly, HAYBURN'S CASE (1792) established that federal courts would not determine which Revolutionary War veterans were entitled to disability pensions so long as the secretary of war had the final say on their entitlement: Congress could employ the federal judicial power only if the decisions of federal courts had binding effect. In the mid-nineteenth century the concern for maintaining judicial efficacy went beyond finality of substantive judgment to finality of remedy. The Supreme Court refused to accept appeals from the Court of Claims, which Congress had established to hear monetary claims against the United States, because the statutory scheme forbade payment until the Court certified its judgments to the treasury secretary for presentation to Congress, which would then have to appropriate funds. The Court concluded that Congress could not invoke Article III judicial power if the judges lacked independent authority to enforce their judgments as well as render them.

Preserving judicial authority remains an important desideratum in the twentieth century, but the growing pervasiveness of federal law as a means of government regulation—often accompanied by litigant and congressional pressure to increase access to the federal courts—inevitably has accentuated the law-declaring enforcement role of the federal judiciary and tended to expand the "case" or "controversy" realm. MUSKRAT V. UNITED STATES (1911) cited the courts' inability to execute a judgment as a reason to reject Congress's authorization of a TEST CASE to secure a ruling on the constitutionality of specific statutes it had passed. Similarly, the Court initially doubted the federal courts' power to give DECLARATORY JUDGMENTS. Yet, by the late 1930s, the Supreme Court had upheld both its own power to review state declaratory judgment actions and the federal DECLARATORY JUDGMENT ACT of 1934. The declaratory judgment remedy authorizes federal courts to decide controversies before legal rights are actually violated. The judge normally enters no coercive order, but confines the remedy to a binding declaration of rights. So long as the controversy is a live one, between adverse parties, and the decision to afford a binding remedy rests wholly with the judiciary, the advisory opinion and finality objections pose no obstacles. A controversy brought to court too early may fail Article III ripeness criteria, but the declaratory remedy itself does not preclude the existence of a "case" or "controversy."

Congress has succeeded in expanding the reach of federal judicial power not only by creating new remedies for the federal courts to administer but also by creating new substantive rights for them to enforce. The Supreme Court maintains as a fundamental "case" or "controversy" requirement that a suing party, to have standing, must have suffered some distinctive "injury in fact." The injury must be particularized, not diffuse; citizen or taxpayer frustration with alleged government illegality is insufficient by itself. In theory, Congress cannot dispense with this requirement and authorize suits by individuals who are not injured. Congress may, however, increase the potential for an injury that will satisfy Article III, simply by legislating protection of new rights, the violation of which amounts to a constitutional "injury in fact." For example, *Trafficante v. Metropolitan Life Insurance Company* (1972) held that a federal CIVIL RIGHTS ban on housing discrimination could be enforced not only by persons refused housing but also by current tenants claiming loss of desired interracial associations; the Court interpreted the statute to create a legally protected interest in integrated housing. To a point, then, Article III "cases" or "controversies" expand correspondingly with the need to enforce new federal legislation. Yet the scope of congressional power to transform diffuse harm into cognizable Article III injury remains uncertain and apparently stops short of providing everyone a judicially enforceable generalized right to be free of illegal governmental behavior, without regard to more individualized effects.

The historically approved image is that federal judges decide politically significant public law issues only to resolve controversies taking the form of private litigation. Over the years, however, this picture has had to accommodate not only congressional creation of enforceable rights and remedies but also the modern realities of public forms of litigation such as the CLASS ACTION, the participation of organized public interest lawyers, and lawsuits aimed at reforming government structures and practices. (See INSTITUTIONAL LITIGATION.) Public law adjudication, especially constitutional adjudication, is certainly the most important function of the federal courts. The inclination to stretch the boundaries of "cases" or "controversies" to provide desired legal guidance on important social problems, although it has varied among federal judges and courts of different eras, increases in response to congressional authorization and the perception of social need. Offsetting that impulse, however, are two countervailing considerations. First, the judges realize that the more public the issues raised, the more democratically appropriate is a political rather than a judicial resolution. Second, they understand the importance of a litigation context that does not threaten judicial credibility, finality, or independence; that presents a realistic need for decision; and that provides adequate information and legal standards for confident, well-advised decision making. These competing considerations will continue to shape the meaning of "cases" and "controversies," setting the limits of the federal judicial function in ways that preserve the courts' checking and enforcement roles in the face of changes in the forms and objectives of litigation, in the dimensions of federal law, and in the expectations of government officials and members of the public.

JONATHAN D. VARAT

Bibliography

BRILMAYER, LEA 1979 The Jurisprudence of Article III: Perspectives on the "Case or Controversy" Requirement. *Harvard Law Review* 93:297–321.

MONAGHAN, HENRY P. 1973 Constitutional Adjudication: The Who and When. *Yale Law Journal* 82:1363–1397.

RADCLIFFE, JAMES E. 1978 *The Case-or-Controversy Provision.* University Park: Pennsylvania State University Press.

TUSHNET, MARK V. 1980 The Sociology of Article III: A Response to Professor Brilmayer. *Harvard Law Review* 93:1698–1733.

CATEGORICAL GRANTS-IN-AID

See: Federal Grants-in-Aid

CATO'S LETTERS

Between 1720 and 1723 John Trenchard and Thomas Gordon, collaborating under the pseudonym of "Cato," published weekly essays in the London newspapers, popularizing the ideas of English libertarians, especially JOHN LOCKE. Gordon collected 138 essays in four volumes which went through six editions between 1733 and 1755 under the title, *Cato's Letters: Essays on Liberty, Civil and Religious.* CLINTON ROSSITER, who rediscovered "Cato," wrote, "no one can spend any time in the newspapers, library inventories, and pamphlets of colonial America without realizing that *Cato's Letters* rather than Locke's *Civil Government* was the most popular, quotable, esteemed source of political ideas in the colonial period." The essays bore titles such as "Of Freedom of Speech . . . inseparable from publick Liberty," "The Right and Capacity of the People to judge of Government," "Liberty proved to be the unalienable Right of all Mankind," "All Government proved to be instituted by Men," "How free Governments are to be framed to last," "Civil Liberty produces all Civil Blessings," and "Of the Restraints which ought to be laid upon publick Rulers." Almost every colonial newspaper from Boston to Savannah anthologized *Cato's Letters,* and the four volumes were imported from England in enormous quantities. The most famous of the letters were those on the FREEDOM OF SPEECH and FREEDOM OF THE PRESS. Cato conceded that freedom posed risks, because people might express themselves irreligiously or seditiously, but restraints on expression resulted in injustice, tyranny, and ignorance. "Cato" would not prosecute criminal libels because prosecution was more dangerous to liberty than the expression of hateful opinions. The sixth edition is available in an American reprint of 1971.

LEONARD W. LEVY

Bibliography

JACOBSON, DAVID L. 1965 Introduction to *The English Libertarian Heritage.* Indianapolis: Bobbs-Merrill.

CATRON, JOHN
(c.1786–1865)

President ANDREW JACKSON appointed John Catron, his fellow Tennessean and political disciple, to the Supreme Court in 1837. A man who reflected Jackson's own views, Catron had been chief justice of Tennessee. While on the state bench, Catron had undoubtedly endeared himself to Jackson by opposing the BANK OF THE UNITED STATES and challenging JOHN MARSHALL's *Worcester v. Georgia* (1832) opinion on Indian rights. Jackson's appointment of Catron filled one of two new positions created by the Judiciary Act of 1837. JOHN MCKINLEY of Alabama received the other appointment. The two decisively altered the geographic complexion of the Court, because five of the nine justices represented slaveholding circuits.

Catron's constitutional law decisions illustrated the judicial search for a balance between national and state power in the antebellum period. For example, in the LICENSE CASES (1847) Catron emphatically held that the commerce power could be exercised by Congress "at pleasure," but that absent such legislation, states might regulate INTERSTATE COMMERCE within their own boundaries. In the PASSENGER CASES (1849) he voted to strike down state taxes on immigrants because Congress had exercised its authority over foreign commerce.

Catron's opinions on the rights and powers of CORPORATIONS varied widely. He concurred in Chief Justice ROGER B. TANEY's opinion in BANK OF AUGUSTA V. EARLE (1839), holding that states could exclude foreign corporations, and he also agreed when the Court expanded federal court JURISDICTION over corporate activities in *Louisville Railroad Co. v. Letson* (1844). Except as a party to a diversity suit, however, a corporation, Catron insisted, was not a citizen within the sense of the Constitution. Catron resisted the TANEY COURT's accommodation with corporate interests in the Ohio bank cases of the 1850s. In PIQUA BRANCH BANK V. KNOOP (1854) he vigorously opposed the use of the CONTRACT CLAUSE to protect state legislative tax exemptions in corporate charters. In a companion case, Catron saw the burgeoning power of corporations as threatening to subvert the state governments that had created them. He believed that the community rights doctrine of CHARLES RIVER BRIDGE V. WARREN BRIDGE COMPANY (1837) had become "illusory and nearly useless, as almost any beneficial privilege, property, or exemption, claimed by corporations" might be construed into a contract to the corporation's advantage. He also protested when the Court, in DODGE V. WOOLSEY (1856), invalidated Ohio's constitutional amendment repealing corporate tax exemptions.

Catron's role in DRED SCOTT V. SANDFORD (1857) was more prominent for his extrajudicial activities than for his opinion. Before the decision, he wrote several letters to President-elect JAMES BUCHANAN, notifying him of the Court's resolution to "decide and settle a controversy which has so long and seriously agitated the country, and which *must* ultimately be decided by the Supreme Court." He also urged Buchanan to pressure his fellow Pennsylvanian, Justice ROBERT GRIER, to join in the effort to decide the constitutional question of congressional control over SLAVERY IN THE TERRITORIES. Catron's political maneuverings have overshadowed his opinion which deviated in some significant respects from Taney's. For example, he did not think that the Court could review the plea in abatement and he thought Taney's discussion of black CITIZENSHIP unnecessary. He also differed from the Chief Justice on the scope of congressional power over the TERRITORIES, acknowledging that it was plenary, save for a few exceptions, such as slavery.

Catron closed his long career with some measure of distinction. Unlike his colleague, Justice JOHN CAMPBELL, who resigned, or Taney, who bitterly opposed the Union's war efforts and President ABRAHAM LINCOLN's conduct of the war, Catron clung to a Jacksonian faith in the Union. He carried out his circuit duties in Tennessee, Kentucky, and Missouri, often at great personal risk. He lost much of his property in Nashville when he failed to respond to a local demand that he resign. Although he opposed Lincoln's blockade policy when he dissented in the PRIZE CASES (1863), on circuit he upheld the confiscation laws and the government's suspension of the writ of HABEAS CORPUS. "I have to punish Treason, & will,"

Catron wrote. With that expression, and through his judicial decisions, Catron faithfully reflected the spirit of his patron, Andrew Jackson.

STANLEY I. KUTLER

Bibliography

GATTELL, FRANK OTTO 1969 John Catron. In Leon Friedman and Fred L. Israel, eds., *The Justices of the Supreme Court,* Vol. 1:737–768. New York: Chelsea House.

SWISHER, CARL B. 1935 *Roger B. Taney.* New York: Macmillan.

CEASE AND DESIST ORDER

In ADMINISTRATIVE LAW, cease and desist orders require the cessation of specific violations of law or government regulations. The power to issue such orders may be granted to REGULATORY COMMISSIONS by Congress. Cease and desist orders are issued only after FAIR HEARING and are subject to review in the federal courts.

DENNIS J. MAHONEY

CENSORSHIP

See: Prior Restraint and Censorship

CENTRAL HUDSON GAS & ELECTRIC CORP. v. PUBLIC SERVICE COMMISSION 447 U.S. 557 (1980)

Central Hudson is the leading decision establishing ground rules for the Supreme Court's modern protection of COMMERCIAL SPEECH under the FIRST AMENDMENT. New York's Public Service Commission (PSC), in the interest of conserving energy, forbade electrical utilities to engage in promotional advertising. The Supreme Court held, 8–1, that this prohibition was unconstitutional.

Justice LEWIS F. POWELL, for the Court, used an analytical approach to commercial speech that combined a TWO-LEVEL THEORY with a BALANCING TEST. First, he wrote, it must be determined whether the speech in question is protected by the First Amendment. The answer to that question is affirmative unless the speech is "misleading" or it is "related to illegal activity" (for example, by proposing an unlawful transaction). Second, if the speech falls within the zone of First Amendment protection, the speech can be regulated only if government satisfies all the elements of a three-part interest-balancing formula: the asserted governmental interest must be "substantial"; the regulation must "directly advance" that interest; and the regulation must not be "more extensive than is necessary to serve that interest."

This intermediate STANDARD OF REVIEW seems loosely patterned after the standard used under the EQUAL PROTECTION clause in cases involving SEX DISCRIMINATION. In those cases, the Court typically accepts that the governmental interest is important; when a statute is invalidated, the Court typically regards gender discrimination as an inappropriate means for achieving the governmental interest. The *Central Hudson* opinion followed this pattern: the promotional advertising was protected speech, and the state's interest in conservation was substantial and directly advanced by the PSC's regulation. However, prohibiting all promotional advertising, including statements that would not increase net energy use, was not the LEAST RESTRICTIVE MEANS for achieving conservation.

Concurring opinions by Justices HARRY A. BLACKMUN and JOHN PAUL STEVENS, both joined by Justice WILLIAM J. BRENNAN, adopted more speech-protective doctrinal positions. Justice WILLIAM H. REHNQUIST, in lone dissent, argued that the PSC's regulation was only an ECONOMIC REGULATION of a state-regulated monopoly, raising no important First Amendment issue.

KENNETH L. KARST

CENTRAL PACIFIC RAILROAD CO. v. UNITED STATES

See: Sinking Fund Cases

CERTIFICATION

Certification may refer to a broad range of acts of government officials high and low: a clerk may certify the accuracy of a copy of a document; the Federal Power Commission may issue a certificate that a natural gas pipeline will serve "public convenience and necessity." In federal courts, however, certification has a narrower meaning. A court may certify questions of law to another court for authoritative decision.

The UNITED STATES COURTS OF APPEALS are authorized by Congress to certify "distinct and definite" questions of law for decision by the Supreme Court. The practice has been criticized for influencing the Supreme Court to decide issues in the abstract, without a complete factual record, and for weakening the Court's control over the questions it will decide. Partly for these reasons, this form of certification is rarely used.

More frequently, federal district courts certify doubtful questions of state law for decision by state courts. About half the states expressly authorize their courts to answer such certified questions, and the Supreme Court has applauded the technique. This form of certification is merely a variant form of abstention.

KENNETH L. KARST

Bibliography

BATOR, PAUL M., MISHKIN, PAUL J., SHAPIRO, DAVID L., and WECHSLER, HERBERT, eds. 1973 *Hart and Wechsler's The Federal Courts and the Federal System*, 2nd ed. Pages 1582–1586. Mineola, N.Y.: Foundation Press.

CERTIORARI, WRIT OF

A writ of certiorari is an order from a higher court directing a lower court to transmit the record of a case for review in the higher court. The writ was in use in England and America before the Revolution. Unlike the WRIT OF ERROR, which was used routinely to review final judgments of lower courts, certiorari was a discretionary form of review that might be granted even before the lower court had given judgment.

When Congress established the circuit courts of appeals in 1891, it expressly authorized the Supreme Court to review certain of these courts' decisions, otherwise declared to be "final," by issuing the writ of certiorari, which remained discretionary. In 1925, Congress expanded the Court's certiorari JURISDICTION and reduced the availability of the writ of error (renamed APPEAL). Certiorari is today the chief mode of the Supreme Court's exercise of APPELLATE JURISDICTION. Proposals to abolish the Court's theoretically obligatory jurisdiction over appeals would leave appellate review entirely to certiorari, and thus to the Court's discretion.

By statute the Court is authorized to grant certiorari in any case that is "in" a federal court of appeals. Thus in an appropriate case the Court can bypass the court of appeals and directly review the action of the district court, as it did in the celebrated case of UNITED STATES V. NIXON (1974).

The Supreme Court's rules have long stated some considerations governing the Court's discretionary grant or denial of certiorari. Three factors are emphasized: (1) conflicts among the highest courts of the states or the federal courts of appeals; (2) the resolution of important unsettled issues of federal law; and (3) the correction of error. These factors do not exhaust but only illustrate the considerations influencing the Court's certiorari policy.

KENNETH L. KARST

Bibliography

LINZER, PETER 1979 The Meaning of Certiorari Denials. *Columbia Law Review* 79:1227–1305.

CHAE CHAN PING v. UNITED STATES

(Chinese Exclusion Case)
130 U.S. 581 (1889)

The CHINESE EXCLUSION ACT of 1882 authorized the issuance of certificates to Chinese ALIENS, guaranteeing their right to reenter the United States after leaving. In 1888 Congress amended that act to prohibit reentry by voiding all outstanding certificates, destroying the right of Chinese to land. Justice STEPHEN J. FIELD, for a unanimous Supreme Court, admitted that this act "is in contravention of express stipulations of the Treaty of 1868 (and other agreements) . . . but it is not on that account invalid or to be restricted in its enforcement. The treaties were of no greater legal obligation than the Act of Congress." He asserted that the treaties were equivalent to federal statutes and they might thus be "repealed or modified at the pleasure of Congress." Because "no paramount authority is given to one over the other" the government could constitutionally exclude aliens from the United States as "an incident of SOVEREIGNTY."

DAVID GORDON

CHAFEE, ZECHARIAH, JR.

(1885–1957)

Modern scholarship in the area of free speech is indelibly stamped with the ideas of Zechariah Chafee, Jr., a distinguished professor of law and University Professor at Harvard, and a CIVIL LIBERTIES activist.

Chafee, scion of a comfortable business-oriented New England family, left the family's iron business to enter Harvard Law School, returning there in 1916 to teach. Inheriting ROSCOE POUND's third-year EQUITY course, in which Pound dealt with INJUNCTIONS against libel, Chafee, uncertain as to the meaning of FREEDOM OF SPEECH, read all pre-1916 cases on the subject. He concluded that the few existing decisions reached results unsatisfactory to one seeking precedents for free speech protection. This realization, coupled with stringent new wartime espionage and SEDITION laws, and their often arbitrary enforcement, persuaded him of the importance of developing a modern law of free speech. Starting with articles in the *New Republic* and the *Harvard Law Review*, and a 1920 book, *Freedom of Speech*, Chafee attempted workable delineations between liberty, which he felt must be safeguarded carefully, and the restraints that emergency situations might warrant. Unhappy with the insensitivity of OLIVER WENDELL HOLMES's initial CLEAR AND PRESENT DANGER construct in SCHENCK V. UNITED STATES (1919), Chafee, with the assistance of Judge LEARNED HAND, set out to persuade Holmes that the test for speech should consider not only the individual's interest in freedom but also the social desirability of injecting provocative thought into the marketplace. "Tolerance of adverse opinion is not a matter of generosity, but of political prudence," Chafee argued. Holmes embraced this position in his dissent in ABRAMS V. UNITED STATES (1919), having been newly convinced that the FIRST AMENDMENT established a national policy favoring a search for truth, while balancing social interests and individual interests. Contemporary traditionalists reacted negatively with a move to oust Chafee from Harvard Law School. Such action was thwarted when Harvard President A. Lawrence Lowell rallied to Chafee's defense.

Chafee, as one of the nation's leading civil libertarians in the 1920s became involved with a number of vital issues. He served on commissions to probe owner autocracy and brutality in the mining regions of the East, and he spoke out publicly against excessive use of the labor injunction to curtail legitimate union activities. In 1929 he headed a subcommittee of the Wickersham Commission which looked into police use of the "third degree" and improper trial procedures. He played a prominent role in the American Bar Association's Commission on the BILL OF RIGHTS in the late 1930s, and in the 1940s served on the Commission on Freedom of the Press, afterward performing similar duties for the United Nations.

Chafee maintained a deep commitment to legal education. He personally regarded as his principal professional accomplishment the Federal Interpleader Act of 1936, a statute creating federal court JURISDICTION when persons in different states make conflicting claims to the same shares of stock or the same bank accounts. His chief influence can be seen, however, in the work of generations of attorneys and judges, nurtured on his free speech and civil liberties view, who have rewritten First Amendment doctrine along Chafee's lines.

PAUL L. MURPHY

Bibliography

MURPHY, PAUL L. 1979 *World War I and the Origin of Civil Liberties in the United States.* New York: Norton.

CHAMBERS v. FLORIDA
309 U.S. 227 (1940)

Chambers was the first coerced confession case to come before the Court since the landmark decision in BROWN V. MISSISSIPPI (1936). In *Brown,* thc physical torture being uncontested, the state had relied mainly on the point that the RIGHT AGAINST SELF-INCRIMINATION did not apply to state proceedings. In *Chambers,* before the state supreme court finally affirmed the convictions it had twice reversed so that juries could determine whether the confessions had been freely and voluntarily made, and the record showed no physical coercion. Moreover, the state contested the JURISDICTION of the Supreme Court to review the judgments, arguing that there was no question of federal law to be denied. However, the Supreme Court, in an eloquent opinion by Justice HUGO L. BLACK, unanimously asserted jurisdiction and reversed the state court.

Black rejected the state's jurisdictional argument, declaring that the Supreme Court could determine for itself whether the confessions had been obtained by means that violated the constitutional guarantee of DUE PROCESS OF LAW. Reviewing the facts Black found that the black prisoners, having been arrested on suspicion without warrant, had been imprisoned in a mob-dominated environment, held incommunicado, and interrogated over five days and through a night until they abandoned their disclaimers of guilt and "confessed." POLICE INTERROGATION had continued until the prosecutor got what he wanted. On the basis of these facts Black wrote a stirring explanation of the relation between due process and free government, concluding that courts in our constitutional system stand "as havens of refuge for those who might otherwise suffer because they are helpless, weak, outnumbered, or because they are non-conforming victims of prejudice. . . ." Applying the exclusionary rule of *Brown,* the Court held that psychological as well as physical torture violated due process.

LEONARD W. LEVY

CHAMBERS v. MARONEY
399 U.S. 42 (1970)

In this important FOURTH AMENDMENT case involving the automobile exception to the SEARCH WARRANT clause, the police had seized a car without a warrant and had searched it later, without a warrant, after having driven it to the police station, where they impounded it. Justice BYRON R. WHITE for the Supreme Court acknowledged that the search could not be justified as having been conducted as a SEARCH INCIDENT TO ARREST; nor could he find EXIGENT CIRCUMSTANCES that justified the WARRANTLESS SEARCH.

White simply fudged the facts. He declared that there was "no difference between on the one hand seizing and holding a car before presenting the PROBABLE CAUSE issue to a magistrate and on the other hand carrying out an immediate search without a warrant." Either course was "reasonable under the Fourth Amendment," but the police had followed neither course in this case. Probable cause for the search had existed at the time of the search, and White declared without explanation that probable cause still existed later when the police made the search at the station, when the felons were in custody. However, the possibility that they might drive off in the car did not exist; that possibility had alone occasioned the automobile exception in the first place. Absent a risk that the culprits might use the vehicle to escape with the fruits of their crime, the constitutional distinction between houses and cars did not matter. White saw no difference in the practical consequences of choosing between an immediate search without a warrant, when probable cause existed, and "the car's immobilization until a warrant is obtained." That logic was irrefutable and irrelevant, because the failure of the police to obtain the warrant gave rise to the case. Only Justice JOHN MARSHALL HARLAN dissented from this line of reasoning.

Until this case mere probable cause for a search, as judged only by a police officer, did not by itself justify a warrantless search; the case is significant, too, because of its implied rule that exigent circumstances need not justify the warrantless search of a car. Following *Chambers,* the Court almost routinely assumed that if a search might have been made at the time of arrest, any warrantless search conducted later, when the vehicle was impounded, was a valid one.

LEONARD W. LEVY

CHAMPION v. AMES
188 U.S. 321 (1903)

As the twentieth century opened, the Supreme Court began to sustain use of the COMMERCE CLAUSE as an instrument to remedy various social and economic ills. (See NATIONAL POLICE POWER.) In 1895 Congress forbade interstate transportation of lottery tickets, seeking to safeguard public morals. Opponents challenged the act on three grounds: the tickets themselves were not SUBJECTS OF COMMERCE, Congress's power to regulate INTERSTATE COMMERCE did not extend to outright prohibition, and such a power would violate the TENTH AMENDMENT's reservation of certain powers to the states.

A 5–4 Court sustained the act, emphasizing Congress's plenary power over commerce. Because the tickets indicated a cash prize might be won, they were items liable to be bought or sold—thus, subjects of commerce and so subject to regulation. Citing the complete prohibition on FOREIGN COMMERCE in the EMBARGO ACT OF 1807, Justice JOHN MARSHALL HARLAN asserted that the power of regulation necessarily included the power of prohibition. Although he rejected the contention that "Congress may arbitrarily exclude from commerce among the states any article . . . it may choose," Harlan justified the ban on transporting lottery tickets on the ground that Congress alone had power to suppress "an evil of such appalling character," thus propounding the NOXIOUS PRODUCTS DOCTRINE. Harlan dismissed the Tenth Amendment objection: that provision was no bar to a power that had been "expressly delegated to Congress."

Chief Justice MELVILLE W. FULLER led Justices DAVID BREWER, RUFUS PECKHAM, and GEORGE SHIRAS in dissent. Fuller noted that the motive underlying the legislation was to suppress gambling, not to regulate commerce. He feared the disruption of distinct spheres of authority and the "creation of a centralized government." He also challenged Harlan's assertion that the commerce power included the right of prohibition. The Court, citing *Champion,* however, would soon uphold the PURE FOOD AND DRUG ACT (in HIPOLITE EGG COMPANY V. UNITED STATES, 1911), the MANN ACT (in HOKE V. UNITED STATES, 1913), and others, relying on its expansive view of the commerce clause.

DAVID GORDON

(SEE ALSO: *Hammer v. Dagenhart, 1918; United States v. Darby, 1941.*)

CHAMPION AND DICKASON v. CASEY

Cir. Ct., Rhode Island (1792)

Reported widely in newspapers in June 1792, this was the first case in which a federal court held a state act unconstitutional as a violation of the CONTRACT CLAUSE. Rhode Island had passed a stay law, postponing by three years the time for a debtor to pay his creditors.

The Circuit Court for the district, presided over by Chief Justice JOHN JAY, ruled that the stay law impaired the OBLIGATION OF CONTRACTS contrary to Article I, section 10.

LEONARD W. LEVY

CHANDLER v. FLORIDA

449 U.S. 560 (1981)

The Supreme Court here distinguished away ESTES V. TEXAS (1965), in which it had held that the televising of a criminal trial violated DUE PROCESS OF LAW because of the inherently prejudicial impact on criminal defendants. In *Chandler* an 8–0 Court ruled that the prejudicial effect must be actually shown by the facts of the particular case; Florida's statute, at issue here, imposed adequate safeguards on the use of electronic media in court, thereby insuring due process of law. Presumably the decision promoted FREEDOM OF THE PRESS and the principle of a PUBLIC TRIAL.

LEONARD W. LEVY

(SEE ALSO: *Free Press/Fair Trial.*)

CHAPLINSKY v. NEW HAMPSHIRE

315 U.S. 568 (1941)

In *Chaplinsky,* Justice FRANK MURPHY, writing for a unanimous Supreme Court, introduced into FIRST AMENDMENT jurisprudence the TWO-LEVEL THEORY that "There are certain well-defined and narrowly limited classes of speech, the prevention and punishment of which have never been thought to raise any constitutional problem. These include the lewd and obscene, the profane, the libelous, and the insulting or 'FIGHTING' WORDS—those which by their very utterance inflict injury or tend to incite an immediate breach of the peace." *Chaplinsky* itself arose under a "fighting words" statute, which the state court had interpreted to punish "words likely to cause an average addressee to fight." In this narrow context the decision can be seen as an application of the CLEAR AND PRESENT DANGER test. COHEN V. CALIFORNIA (1971), emphasizing this rationale, offered protection to an OBSCENITY that created no danger of violence.

In its broader conception of categories of speech excluded from First Amendment protection, the case served as an important doctrinal source for many later obscenity and libel decisions.

MARTIN SHAPIRO

CHAPMAN v. CALIFORNIA

See: Harmless Error

CHARLES RIVER BRIDGE v. WARREN BRIDGE COMPANY

11 Peters 420 (1837)

The Charles River Bridge case reflected the tension within ALEXIS DE TOCQUEVILLE's proposition that the American people desired a government that would allow them "to acquire the things they covet and which [would] . . . not debar them from the peaceful enjoyment of those possessions which they have already acquired." A metaphor for the legal strains that accompanied technological change, the case spoke more to the emerging questions of railroad development than to the immediate problem of competing bridges over the Charles River.

Following the Revolution, some investors petitioned the Massachusetts legislature for a charter to build a bridge over the Charles River, linking Boston and Charlestown. Commercial interests in both cities supported the proposal, and the state issued the grant in 1785. The charter authorized the proprietors to charge a variety of tolls for passage, pay an annual fee to Harvard College for the loss of its exclusive ferry service across the river, and then, after forty years, return the bridge to the state in "good repair."

Construction of the bridge began immediately, and in 1786, it was open to traffic, benefiting the proprietors, the communities, and the back country. The land route from Medford to Boston, for example, was cut from thirteen to five miles, and trade dramatically increased as the bridge linked the area-wide market. Success invited imitation, and other communities petitioned the legislature for bridge charters. When the state authorized the West Boston Bridge to Cambridge in 1792, the Charles River Bridge proprietors asked for compensation for the revenue losses they anticipated, and the state extended their charter from forty to seventy years. Ironically, that extension provided the basis for future political and legal assaults against the Charles River Bridge. Other bridges followed and no compensation was offered. The state specifically refuted any monopoly claims and the Charles River Bridge proprietors refrained from claiming any.

Increasing prosperity and population raised the collection of tolls to nearly $20,000 annually in 1805; the share values had increased over 300 percent in value. The toll rates having remained constant since 1786, profits multiplied. Swollen profits stimulated community criticism and animated a long-standing hostility toward monopolies. Opportunity was the watchword and special privilege its bane.

Beginning in 1823, Charlestown merchants launched a five-year effort to build a competing "free" bridge over the Charles. They argued that the existing facility was inadequate, overcrowded, and dangerous; but basically, they appealed for public support on the grounds that the tolls on the Charles River Bridge were "burdensome, vexatious, and odious." The proprietors, defending the bridge's utility, offered to expand and improve it. They consistently maintained that the legislature could not grant a new bridge franchise in the vicinity without compensating them for the loss of tolls. But the political climate persuaded legislators to support the new bridge, and in 1828, after rejecting various schemes for compensation, the legislature approved the Warren Bridge charter. The act established the bridge's termini at 915 feet from the existing bridge on the Boston side, and at 260 feet from it on the Charlestown side. The new bridge was given the same toll schedule as the Charles River Bridge, but the state provided that after the builders recovered their investment and five per cent interest, the bridge would revert to the commonwealth. In any event, the term for tolls could not exceed six years. Governor LEVI LINCOLN had previously vetoed similar legislation, but in 1828 he quietly acquiesced.

The new bridge, completed in six months, was an instant success—but at the expense of the Charles River Bridge. During the first six months of the Warren Bridge's operations, receipts for the old bridge rapidly declined. Net income for the Warren Bridge in the early 1830s consistently was twice that for the Charles River Bridge.

Counsel for the old bridge proprietors wasted little time in carrying their arguments to the courts. After DANIEL WEBSTER and LEMUEL SHAW failed to gain an INJUNCTION to prevent construction of the new bridge, they appeared in the state supreme court to argue the merits of the charter in 1829, nearly one year after the bridge's completion. Shaw and Webster contended that the Charles River Bridge proprietors were successors to the Harvard ferry's exclusive franchise. In addition, they argued that the tolls represented the substance of the 1785 charter. Although the charter for the new bridge did not take away the plaintiffs' franchise, the 1828 act effectively destroyed the tolls—the essence and only tangible property of the franchise. The lawyers thus contended that the new bridge charter violated the CONTRACT CLAUSE and the state constitutional prohibition against expropriation of private property without compensation. The Warren Bridge defendants denied the old bridge's monopoly claims and emphasized that the state had not deprived the Charles River Bridge proprietors' continued right to take tolls. They also maintained that the old bridge proprietors had waived exclusivity when they accepted an extension of their franchise in 1792 after the state had chartered the West Boston Bridge.

The state supreme court, dividing equally, dismissed the complaint to facilitate a WRIT OF ERROR to the United States Supreme Court. The Jacksonian Democrats on the state court supported the state and their Whig brethren opposed it. The former rejected monopoly claims and berated the Charles River Bridge proprietors for their failure to secure an explicit monopoly grant. Chief Justice Isaac Parker, acknowledging that the 1785 grant was not exclusive, agreed that the state could damage existing property interests for the community's benefit without compensation. But he insisted that "immutable principles of justice" demanded compensation when the forms of property were indistinguishable. He conceded that canals and railroads might legitimately destroy the value of a turnpike; but when the state chartered a similar franchise, then operators of the existing property could claim an indemnity.

The United States Supreme Court first heard arguments in the case in March 1831. Although absences and disagreements prevented any decision before JOHN MARSHALL's death in 1835, the Court's records offer good circumstantial evidence that he had supported the new bridge. Following several new appointments and ROGER B. TANEY's confirmation as Chief Justice, the Court heard reargument in January 1837. Webster again appeared for the plaintiffs; defendants engaged Simon Greenleaf of Harvard, a close associate of JOSEPH STORY and JAMES KENT. Both sides essentially continued the arguments advanced in the state court. Finally, in February 1837, after nearly nine years of litigation, the Court decisively ruled in behalf of the state's right to charter the new bridge.

Taney's opinion sought to balance property rights against community needs by strictly construing the old bridge charter. He rejected the proprietors' exclusivity claim, contending that nothing would pass by implication. "The charter . . . is a written instrument which must speak for itself," he wrote, "and be interpreted by its own terms." He confidently asserted that the "rule" of STRICT CONSTRUCTION was well settled and he particularly invoked Marshall's 1830 PROVIDENCE BANK V. BILLINGS opinion, rejecting a bank's claim to implied tax immunity. Like Marshall, Taney concluded that the implications of exclusivity constituted a derogation of community rights. He argued that the community's "interests" would be adversely affected if the state surrendered control of a line of travel for profit. Taney neatly combined old Federalist doctrines of governmental power with the leaven of Jacksonian rhetoric: "The continued existence of a government would be of no great value," he believed, "if by implications and presumptions, it was disarmed of the powers necessary to accomplish the ends of its creations; and the functions it was designed to perform, transferred to the hands of privileged CORPORATIONS."

But the touchstone of Taney's opinion was its practical response to the contemporary reality of public policy needs. Taking note of technological changes and improvements, such as the substitution of railroad traffic for that of turnpikes and canals, Taney argued that the law must be a spur, not an impediment, to change. If the Charles River Bridge proprietors could thwart such change, he feared that the courts would be inundated with suits seeking to protect established property forms. Turnpike companies, for example, "awakening from their sleep," would call upon courts to halt improvements which had taken their place. Railroad and canal properties would be jeopardized and venture capital would be discouraged. The Supreme Court, he concluded, would not "sanction principles" that would prevent states from enjoying the advances of science and technology. Taney thus cast the law with the new entrepreneurs and risk-takers as the preferred agents for material progress.

In his dissent Justice Story rejected Taney's reliance upon strict construction and advanced an imposing line of precedents demonstrating that private grants had been construed in favor of the grantees. "It would be a dishonour of the government," Story said, "that it should pocket a fair consideration, and then quibble as to the obscurities and implications of its own contract." But Story's dissent was not merely a defense of VESTED RIGHTS. Like Taney, he, too, was concerned with progress and public policy. But whereas Taney emphasized opportunity, Story maintained that security of title and the full enjoyment of existing property was a necessary inducement for private investment in public improvements. Story insisted that the proprietors were entitled to compensation. He thus discounted the potentially staggering social and economic costs implicit in a universal principle requiring JUST COMPENSATION when new improvement projects diminished the value of existing franchises.

Story's position reflected immediate reality. Several years earlier, the state's behavior in the bridge controversy had discouraged stock sales for the proposed Boston and Worcester Railroad. Lagging investment finally had forced the legislature to grant the railroad a thirty-year guarantee of exclusive privileges on the line of travel.

Given the materialism of the American people, Taney's arguments had the greater appeal and endurance. He allied the law with broadened entrepreneurial opportunities at the expense of past assets. Nothing threatened the economic aspirations of Americans more than the scarcity of capital; nothing, therefore, required greater legal encouragement than venture capital, subject only to the risks of the marketplace. These were the concerns that took a local dispute over a free bridge out of its provincial setting and thrust it into the larger debate about political economy. In a society that placed a premium on "progress" and on the release of creative human energy to propel that progress, the decision was inevitable. And throughout American economic development, the Charles River Bridge case has fostered the process that Joseph Schumpeter called "creative destruction," whereby new forms of property destroy old ones in the name of progress.

STANLEY I. KUTLER

Bibliography

KUTLER, STANLEY I. (1971)1977 *Privilege and Creative Destruction: The Charles River Bridge Case,* rev. ed. New York: Norton.

CHARTERS, COLONIAL

See: Colonial Charters; Particular Colonies

CHASE, SALMON P. (1808–1873)

Born in New Hampshire, Salmon Portland Chase enjoyed an elite education as a private pupil of his uncle, Episcopal Bishop Philander Chase of Ohio, as a Dartmouth student (graduating 1826), and as an apprentice lawyer (1827–1830) to United States Attorney General WILLIAM WIRT. Subsequently, Chase rose quickly as a Cincinnati attorney, beginning also his numerous, seemingly opportunistic, successive changes in political party affiliations. Abandoning Whig, then Democratic ties, Chase became in turn a member of the Liberty party and of the Republican organizations, winning elections to the United States Senate (1848–1855, 1860–1861), and to Ohio's governorship (1856–1860). He was an unsuccessful candidate for the Republican presidential nomination in 1860. ABRAHAM LINCOLN appointed Chase secretary of the treasury (1861–1864), and Chief Justice of the United States (1864–1873). Yet in 1864 Chase tried to thwart Lincoln's second term, in 1868 he maneuvered for the Democratic presidential nomination, and in 1872 he participated in the "Liberal Republican" schism against ULYSSES S. GRANT.

Such oscillations reflected more than Chase's large personal ambitions. Constitutional, legal, and moral concerns gave his public life coherence and purpose. These concerns derived from Chase's early conviction that men and society were easily corrupted, that SLAVERY was America's primary spoiling agent, and that political corruption was a close second. Although Chase, observing Wirt in the *Antelope* litigation (1825), found the doctrine in SOMERSET'S CASE (1772) an acceptable reconciliation of slavery and the Constitution as of that year, later events, especially those attending fugitive slave recaptures, unpunished assaults on abolitionists, and increases in slave areas due especially to the Mexican War and the treaties that closed it off, brought him to accept ABOLITIONIST CONSTITUTIONAL THEORY. Chase concluded that slavery's expansion beyond existing limits would demoralize white labor.

The first steps on this ultimately abolitionist road came from Chase's association with and brave defenses of Ohio antislavery activists, including JAMES BIRNEY, and of fugitive slaves; such defenses won Chase the nickname "attorney general for runaway negroes." A merely opportunistic Cincinnati lawyer would have had easier routes to success than this. Defending runaways and their abettors, Chase abjured HIGHER LAW pleadings popular among abolitionists; he focused instead on technical procedures and on a carefully developed restatement of state-centered FEDERALISM in which he insisted that nonslave jurisdictions also enjoyed STATES' RIGHTS. Slave states were able to export their recapture laws into free states via the federal FUGITIVE SLAVERY statutes. Chase argued that residents of free states also deserved to have the laws of their states concerning the status of citizens enjoy reciprocal effect and respect within slavery jurisdictions. Such a traffic of free state laws and customs across the federal system was impossible (and was to remain so until Appomattox). Chase insisted that residents of free states possessed at least the right to protect their co-residents of any race within those states from being reduced to servitude without DUE PROCESS.

Chase's evolving ideas culminated in a "freedom national" position, a general program for resolving the dilemma that slavery posed to a federal society based on assumptions of legal remedies, CIVIL RIGHTS, and CIVIL LIBERTIES. In his thinking, free labor was more than a marketplace phenomenon. It was a moral imperative, a complex of ethical relationships that the nation, under the Constitution, must nurture. Reformed, corruption-free two-party politics, with even blacks voting, was the way Chase discerned finally to nationalize freedom, a nationalization based upon acceptance of the DECLARATION OF INDEPENDENCE and the BILL OF RIGHTS as minimum definitions of the nation's interest in private rights adversely affected by state wrongs or private inequities.

The Civil War and the wartime and post-Appomattox Reconstruction of the southern states were the contexts in which Chase refined his thinking about individuals' rights and the nation's duty to protect them. Lincoln found a place in his cabinet for every one of the major competitors for the Republican presidential nomination in 1860, and Chase became secretary of the treasury. Once the war started, Chase had responsibility to provide an adequate circulating medium for the suddenly ballooning marketplace needs of the government, of the banking and commercial communities of the Union states, and of the millions of urban and rural entrepreneurs who rushed to expand production. Chase helped key congressmen to shape the historic wartime laws on national banking, income taxation, and legal tender (the legitimacy of the last of which Chase himself was to question as Chief Justice, in the LEGAL TENDER CASES).

The most outspoken abolitionist in Lincoln's cabinet, Chase also carved out a role for Treasury officials, who were responsible for administering rebels' confiscated property, in the Army's coastal experiments for abandoned, runaway, or otherwise freed blacks. He applauded the CONFISCATION ACTS, the EMANCIPATION PROCLAMATION, the major elements in Lincoln's MILITARY RECONSTRUCTION, the FREEDMEN'S BUREAU statute, and the THIRTEENTH AMENDMENT. Upon ROGER B. TANEY's death in late 1864, Lincoln, well aware of Chase's antipathy to the decision in DRED SCOTT V. SANDFORD (1857) and his commitment to irreversible emancipation, both of which the President shared, named the Ohioan to be Chief Justice.

After Appomattox, Chase, for his first years as Chief Justice, found that the work of the Court was almost exclusively with white men's rights rather than with the momentous, race-centered public questions that faced the Congress and the new President, ANDREW JOHNSON. On circuit, however, Chase's *In re Turner* opinion sustained broadly, in favor of a black female claimant, the provisions of the 1866 CIVIL RIGHTS ACT for enforcing the Thirteenth Amendment. In his opinion, Chase insisted that federal rights against servitude were defendable in national courts as against both state or private action or inaction, and he emphasized that a state's standard of right could serve as an adequate federal standard so long as the state did not discriminate racially.

Some contemporaries applauded *In re Turner* as an articulation of the new, nationalized federal system of rights that the Thirteenth Amendment appeared to have won. Chase's other circuit opinions did not, therefore, disturb race egalitarians, and generally won favor in professional legal and commercial media. These opinions dealt with numerous litigations concerning private relationships such as marriage licenses, trusts and inheritances, business contracts, and insurance policies made under rebel state dispensation. Chase recognized the validity of these legal arrangements. His decisions helped greatly to stabilize commerce and family relationships in the South.

The course of post-Appomattox Reconstruction as controlled both by President Johnson and by Congress, troubled Chase deeply. He knew, from his work in Lincoln's cabinet, how narrowly the Union had escaped defeat and tended, therefore, to sustain wartime measures. Yet he revered both the CHECKS AND BALANCES of the national government and the state-centered qualities of the federal system reflected in the Constitution. Therefore, in EX PARTE MILLIGAN (1866), Chase, still new on the Court, joined in the unanimous statement that Milligan, who had been tried by a military court, should preferably have been prosecuted in a civilian court for his offenses. But Chase, with three other Justices, dissented from the majority's sweeping condemnation of any federal military authority over civilians in a nonseceded state. The dissenters insisted instead that Congress possessed adequate WAR POWER to authorize military courts.

Chase again dissented from the 5–4 decision in the TEST OATH CASES (1867). Though privately detesting oath tests, Chase held to a public position that legislators, not judges, bore the responsibility to prescribe professional qualifications and licensing standards. By this time Congress had decided on Military Reconstruction. Mississippi officials, appointed earlier by Johnson, asked the Court for an INJUNCTION against the President's enforcing Congress's reconstruction law, and for a ruling that it was unconstitutional. For an unanimous Court, Chase refused to honor the petition (MISSISSIPPI V. JOHNSON, 1867), relying on the POLITICAL QUESTION doctrine. He agreed with his colleagues also in *Georgia v. Stanton* (1867) in refusing to allow the Court to intrude into political questions involving enforcement of the Reconstruction statutes. Mississippians again tried to enlist the Court against Congress. In early 1868 EX PARTE MCCARDLE raised *Milligan*-like issues of military trials of civilians, and of the Court's jurisdiction to hear such matters under the HABEAS CORPUS ACT OF 1867. Congress thereupon diminished the Court's APPELLATE JURISDICTION under that statute. Chase, for the Court, acquiesced in the diminution, though pointing out that all other habeas jurisdiction remained in the Court.

He supported Congress's Military Reconstruction as a statutory base for both state restorations and black suffrage, but he was offended by the Third Reconstruction Act (July 1867), providing that military decisions would control civil judgments in the South. The IMPEACHMENT of Andrew Johnson, with Chase presiding over the Senate trial, seemed to threaten the destruction of tripartite checks and balances. Chase drifted back toward his old Democratic states' rights position, a drift signaled by his advocacy of universal amnesty for ex-rebels and universal suffrage. He had tried, unsuccessfully, to have the FOURTEENTH

Amendment provide for both. His enhanced or renewed respect for states' rights was evident in *United States v. DeWitt* (1869), in which the Court declared a federal law forbidding the transit or sale of dangerous naphtha-adulterated kerosene, to be an excessive diminution of STATE POLICE POWERS.

This decision, the first in which the Court denied Congress a capacity to act for regulatory purposes under the COMMERCE CLAUSE, like the decisions on Reconstruction issues, suggests how far the CHASE COURT engaged in JUDICIAL ACTIVISM. Striking in this regard were the Legal Tender Cases. The first of these, *Hepburn v. Griswold* (1870), resulted in a 4–3 decision that the 1862 law authorizing greenbacks as legal tender was invalid as applied to contracts made before passage of the statute. Chase, for the thin majority, insisted that the statute violated the Fifth Amendment's due process clause, concluding that the spirit of the CONTRACT CLAUSE, though by its terms restraining only the states, applied also to the federal government. The trio of dissenters—all, like Chase, Republican appointees—saw the money and war powers as adequate authority for the statute.

Then, later in 1870, President ULYSSES S. GRANT named two new Justices to the Court: JOSEPH P. BRADLEY and WILLIAM STRONG. The new appointees created, in *Knox v. Lee* (1871), the second Legal Tender Case decision, a majority that overruled *Hepburn.* The new majority now upheld the nation's authority to make paper money legal tender for contracts entered into either before or after enactment of the statute, an authority not pinned necessarily to the war power.

Chase was in the minority in the SLAUGHTERHOUSE CASES (1873) in which the majority found no violation of the Thirteenth or Fourteenth Amendments in a state's assignment of a skilled-trade monopoly to private parties. The doctrine of *Slaughterhouse,* that the privileges of United States citizenship did not protect basic civil rights, signaled a sharp retreat from Chase's own *In Re Turner* position, and was a fateful step by the Court toward what was to become a general retreat from Reconstruction.

Slaughterhouse, along with Chase's anti-Grant position in 1872, closed off Chase's long and tumultuous career; he died in 1873. His career was consistent in its anticorruption positions and in its infusions of moral and ethical ideas into constitutional, legal, and political issues. Party-jumping was incidental to Chase's ends of a moral democracy, federally arranged in a perpetual union of perpetual states; he gave this concept effective expression in TEXAS V. WHITE (1869).

To be sure, neither Chase nor "his" Court created novel legal doctrines. But he, and it, helped greatly to reclaim for the Court a significant role in determining the limits of certain vital public policies, both national and state. In the tumults of Reconstruction, while avoiding unwinnable clashes with Congress, Chase bravely insisted that effective governmental power and individual rights could co-exist. He and his fellow Justices advanced novel constitutional doctrines drawn from the prohibitions against ex post facto laws and BILLS OF ATTAINDER, and from the commerce and money powers. In retrospect, such experiments with doctrine take on the quality of interim defenses of judicial authority between prewar reliance on the contract clause, as example, and the post-Chase development of the due process clause of the Fourteenth Amendment.

At the same time, Chase tried to focus the Court's attention on individuals' rights as redefined first by the Thirteenth and then by the Fourteenth Amendment, as against both private and public wrongs. As one who for years had observed at first hand the capacity of nation and states and private persons to wrong individuals, Chase, as Chief Justice, brought a particular sense of urgency to the goal of protecting individual rights. He failed to convert a majority of his brethren to this task. Instead, America deferred its constitutional commitments. (See CONSTITUTIONAL HISTORY, 1865–1877.)

HAROLD M. HYMAN

Bibliography

FAIRMAN, CHARLES 1971 *History of the Supreme Court of the United States: Reconstruction and Reunion, 1864–1888.* New York: Macmillan.

HUGHES, DAVID 1965 Salmon P. Chase: Chief Justice. *Vanderbilt Law Review* 18:569–614.

HYMAN, HAROLD M. and WIECEK, WILLIAM M. 1982 *Equal Justice under Law: Constitutional Development 1835–1875.* Chaps. 11–13. New York: Harper & Row.

WALKER, PETER F. 1978 *Moral Choices.* Chaps. 13–14. Baton Rouge: Louisiana State University Press.

CHASE, SAMUEL
(1741–1811)

Samuel Chase was one of the most significant and controversial members of America's revolutionary generation. Irascible and difficult, but also extremely capable, he played a central role in Maryland politics during the 1760s and 1770s, signed the DECLARATION OF INDEPENDENCE, and was a member of the Continental Congress from 1775 to 1778. In the latter year ALEXANDER HAMILTON denounced him for using confidential information to speculate in the flour market. During the 1780s Chase pursued various business interests, practiced law, rebuilt his political reputation, and became an important anti-Federalist leader. After the adoption of the Constitution, for reasons that remain unclear, he became an ardent Federalist.

In 1795 he was nominated for a position on the federal bench. President GEORGE WASHINGTON was at first wary of recommending him, but when he had trouble filling a vacancy on the United States Supreme Court, he offered the position to Chase, who accepted in 1796. As one of the better legal minds in the early republic, Chase delivered several of the Court's most important decisions in the pre-Marshall period. In WARE V. HYLTON (1796) he provided one of the strongest statements ever issued on the supremacy of national treaties over state laws. The decision invalidated a Virginia statute of 1777 that placed obstacles in the way of recovery of debts owed by Americans to British creditors, a law in clear violation of a specific provision of the treaty of peace with Great Britain (1783). In HYLTON V. UNITED STATES (1796) Chase and the Supreme Court for the first time passed upon the constitutionality of an act of Congress, upholding the carriage tax of 1794. Chase concluded that only CAPITATION TAXES were direct taxes subject to the constitutional requirement of apportionment among the states according to population. In CALDER V. BULL (1798), where the Supreme Court held that the prohibition against EX POST FACTO LAWS in the Constitution extended only to criminal, not civil, laws, Chase addressed the issue of constitutionality in natural law terms, presaging those late-nineteenth-century jurists who, in furthering the concept of SUBSTANTIVE DUE PROCESS, were to argue that the Supreme Court could properly hold laws invalid for reasons lying outside the explicit prohibitions of the constitutional text. Riding circuit, he ruled in *United States v. Worrall* (1798) that the federal courts had no jurisdiction over crimes defined by COMMON LAW. This position, which Chase abandoned, was adopted by the Supreme Court in *United States v. Hudson and Goodwin* (1812). (See FEDERAL COMMON LAW OF CRIMES.)

A fierce partisan, Chase refused to recognize the legitimacy of the Jeffersonian opposition in the party struggles of the late 1790s. He used his position on the bench to make speeches for the Federalists and he supported the passage of the ALIEN AND SEDITION ACTS in 1798. Riding circuit, he enforced the law with a vengeance when he presided over the trials of John Fries of Pennsylvania for TREASON and John Callendar of Virginia for SEDITION, sentencing the former to death (Fries was eventually pardoned by President JOHN ADAMS) and the latter to a stiff fine and a prison sentence. When THOMAS JEFFERSON and the Republicans came to power in 1801 and repealed the JUDICIARY ACT OF 1801, Chase vigorously campaigned behind the scenes for the Supreme Court to declare the repeal law unconstitutional, but the other Justices did not go along with him. Chase, however, remained adamant in his opposition to the Jeffersonians, refusing to alter his partisan behavior. "Things," he argued, "must take their natural course, from *bad* to *worse.*" In May 1803, in an intemperate charge to a GRAND JURY in Baltimore, he launched yet another attack on the Republican party and its principles.

Shortly thereafter, President Jefferson urged that Chase be removed from office. The House of Representatives voted for his IMPEACHMENT, and he came to trial before the United States Senate. The Constitution authorizes impeachment and conviction of federal government officers for "Treason, Bribery, or other high Crimes and Misdemeanors." Many of the more militant Republicans, unhappy with Federalist control of the judiciary, favored an expansive view of what should constitute an impeachable offense. As one put it: "Removal by impeachment was nothing more than a declaration by Congress to this effect: You held dangerous opinions and if you are suffered to carry them into effect, you will work the destruction of the Union. We want your offices for the purpose of giving them to men who will fill them better." Others, including a number of Republicans, favored a narrow definition: impeachment was permitted only for a clearly indictable offense.

Chase proved to be a formidable opponent. Aided by a prestigious group of Federalist trial lawyers, he put up a strong defense, denying that any of his actions were indictable offenses under either statute or common law. His attorneys raised various complicated and even moot legal questions such as the binding quality of local custom; the reciprocal rights and duties of the judge, jury, and defense counsel; the legality of bad manners in a court room; the rules of submitting EVIDENCE; and the problems involved in proving criminal intent. The prosecution was led by JOHN RANDOLPH, an extreme Republican and highly emotional man who badly botched the legal part of his argument. Chase was acquitted on all counts, even though most senators disliked him and believed his conduct on the bench had been improper. The final result was not so much a vote for Chase as it was against a broad definition of the impeachment clause—a definition that might be used to remove other judges, perhaps even to dismantle the federal judiciary altogether. Even Jefferson appears to have come around to this point of view; he made no attempt to enforce party unity when the Senate voted, and he was not unhappy with the outcome of the trial.

Although Chase served on the Supreme Court for the rest of his life, he no longer played an important role. JOHN MARSHALL had begun his ascendancy, and although Marshall was a staunch nationalist, he was less overtly partisan than Chase and less inclined to provoke confrontations with the Jeffersonians.

RICHARD E. ELLIS

Bibliography

ELLIS, RICHARD E. 1981 The Impeachment of Samuel Chase. Pages 57–78 in Michal Belknap, ed., *American Political Trials.* Westport, Conn.: Greenwood Press.

HAW, JAMES, et al. 1981 *Stormy Patriot: The Life of Samuel Chase.* Baltimore: Johns Hopkins University Press.

CHASE COURT
(1864–1873)

The decade of SALMON P. CHASE's tenure as Chief Justice of the United States was one of the more turbulent in the history of the Supreme Court. Laboring under the cloud of hostility engendered by DRED SCOTT V. SANDFORD (1857), hurt by partisan attacks from without and divisions within, staggering under loads of new business, the Chase Court nevertheless managed to absorb and consolidate sweeping new jurisdictional grants to the federal courts and to render some momentous decisions.

The Chase Court displayed an unusual continuity of personnel, which was offset by political and ideological heterogeneity. Of the nine men Chase joined on his accession (the Court in 1864 was composed of ten members), seven served throughout all or nearly all his brief tenure. But this largely continuous body was divided within itself by party and ideological differences. JOHN CATRON, who died in 1865, JAMES M. WAYNE, who died in 1867, and ROBERT C. GRIER, who suffered a deterioration in his faculties that caused his brethren to force him to resign in 1870, were Democrats. NATHAN CLIFFORD, an appointee of President JAMES BUCHANAN, and STEPHEN J. FIELD were also Democrats, the latter a War Democrat. SAMUEL F. MILLER, DAVID DAVIS, and JOSEPH P. BRADLEY were Republicans. Chase himself was an ex-Democrat who had helped form the Republican party in 1854, but he drifted back to the Democratic party after the war and coveted its presidential nomination. WILLIAM STRONG, Grier's replacement, and NOAH SWAYNE were also Democrats who turned Republican before the war. Like the Chief Justice, Davis never successfully shook off political ambitions; he accepted and then rejected the Labor Reform party's nomination for the presidency in 1872. From 1870, Republicans dominated the Court, which had long been controlled by Democrats.

The work of the Supreme Court changed greatly during Chase's tenure. In 1862 and 1866, Congress realigned the federal circuits, so as to reduce the influence of the southern states, which under the Judiciary Act of 1837 had five of the nine circuits. Under the Judiciary Act of 1866, the southern circuits were reduced to two. By the same statute, Congress reduced the size of the Court from ten to seven members, mainly to enhance the efficiency of its work, not to punish the Court or deprive President ANDREW JOHNSON of appointments to it. In 1869, Congress again raised the size of the Court to nine, where it has remained ever since. More significantly, the business of the Court expanded. By 1871, the number of cases docketed had doubled in comparison to the war years. This increase resulted in some measure from an extraordinary string of statutes enacted between 1863 and 1867 expanding the JURISDICTION OF THE FEDERAL COURTS in such matters as REMOVAL OF CASES from state to federal courts, HABEAS CORPUS, claims against the United States, and BANKRUPTCY.

The Chase Court was not a mere passive, inert repository of augmented jurisdiction: it expanded its powers of JUDICIAL REVIEW to an extent unknown to earlier Courts. During Chase's brief tenure, the Court held eight federal statutes unconstitutional (as compared with only two in its entire prior history), and struck down state statutes in thirty-six cases (as compared with thirty-eight in its prior history). The attitude that produced this JUDICIAL ACTIVISM was expressed in private correspondence by Justice Davis, when he noted with satisfaction that the Court in EX PARTE MILLIGAN (1866) had not "toadied to the prevalent idea, that the legislative department of the government can override everything." This judicial activism not only presaged the Court's involvement in policy during the coming heyday of SUBSTANTIVE DUE PROCESS; it also plunged the Chase Court into some of the most hotly contested matters of its own time, especially those connected with Reconstruction. The Court also attracted the public eye because of the activities of two of its members: Chase's and Davis's availability as presidential candidates, and Chase's firm, impartial service in presiding over the United

States Senate as a court of IMPEACHMENT in the trial of Andrew Johnson.

The Chase Court is memorable for its decisions in four areas: Reconstruction, federal power (in matters not directly related to Reconstruction), state regulatory and tax power, and the impact of the FOURTEENTH AMENDMENT.

Nearly all the cases in which the Supreme Court disposed of Reconstruction issues were decided during Chase's tenure. The first issue to come up was the role of military commissions. In EX PARTE VALLANDIGHAM, decided in February 1864 (ten months before Chase's nomination), the Court refused to review the proceedings of a military commission, because the commission is not a court. But that did not settle the issue of the constitutional authority of military commissions. The matter came up again, at an inopportune time, in *Ex parte Milligan,* decided in December 1866. Milligan had been arrested, tried, convicted, and sentenced to be hanged by a military commission in Indiana in 1864 for paramilitary activities on behalf of the Confederacy. The Court unanimously ruled that his conviction was illegal because Indiana was not in a theater of war, because the civil courts were functioning and competent to try Milligan for TREASON, and because he was held in violation of the provisions of the HABEAS CORPUS ACT OF 1863. But the Court split, 5–4, over an OBITER DICTUM in Justice Davis's MAJORITY OPINION stating that the Congress could never authorize military commissions in areas outside the theater of operations where the civil courts were functioning. The Chief Justice, writing for the minority, declared that Congress did have the power to authorize commissions, based on the several WAR POWERS clauses of Article I, section 8, but that it had not done so; hence Milligan's trial was unauthorized.

Milligan created a furor in Congress and deeply implicated the Court in the politics of Reconstruction. Assuming that military commissions were essential to the conduct of Reconstruction, Democrats taunted Republicans that *Milligan* implied that they were unconstitutional, and hence that proposed Republican measures providing for military trials in the CIVIL RIGHTS ACT OF 1866 and FREEDMEN'S BUREAU Act violated the Constitution. Taken together with subsequent decisions, *Milligan* caused Republicans some anxiety. But, as Justice Davis noted in private correspondence and as Illinois Republican LYMAN TRUMBULL stated on the floor of the Senate, the decision in reality had no application to the constitutional anomaly of Reconstruction in the South.

The Court next seemed to challenge congressional Reconstruction in the TEST OATH CASES, *Ex parte Garland* and *Cummings v. Missouri,* both 1867. The court, by 5–4 decisions, voided federal and state statutes requiring a candidate for public office or one of the professions to swear that he had never participated or assisted in the rebellion. The Court's holding, that they constituted BILLS OF ATTAINDER and EX POST FACTO LAWS, seemingly threatened programs of disfranchisement and oath qualification, another part of proposed Reconstruction measures. Then, in February 1868, the Court announced that it would hear arguments in EX PARTE MCCARDLE, another challenge to military commissions. William McCardle had been convicted by a military commission for publishing inflammatory articles. A federal circuit court denied his petition for a writ of habeas corpus under the HABEAS CORPUS ACT OF 1867, a measure that had broadened the scope of the writ, and he appealed the denial to the Supreme Court. Alarmed, congressional Republicans enacted a narrowly drawn statute known as the McCardle repealer, denying the Supreme Court appellate jurisdiction in habeas petitions brought under the 1867 act. In 1869, the Court accepted the constitutionality of the repealer, because Article III, section 2, made the Court's APPELLATE JURISDICTION subject to "such Exceptions . . . as the Congress shall make." But Chief Justice Chase pointedly reminded the bar that all the rest of the Court's habeas appellate authority was left intact. This broad hint bore fruit in *Ex parte Yerger* (1869), where the Court accepted jurisdiction of a habeas appeal under the JUDICIARY ACT OF 1789. Chief Justice Chase chastised Congress for the McCardle repealer and reaffirmed the scope of the Great Writ.

In the meantime, the Court had turned to other Reconstruction issues. As soon as Congress enacted the MILITARY RECONSTRUCTION ACTS of 1867, southern attorneys sought to enjoin federal officials, including the President and the secretary of war, from enforcing them. In MISSISSIPPI V. JOHNSON (1867), the Court unanimously rejected this petition. Chief Justice Chase drew on a distinction, originally suggested by his predecessor Chief Justice JOHN MARSHALL in MARBURY V. MADISON (1803), between ministerial and discretionary responsibilities of the President, stating that the latter were not subject to the Court's injunctive powers. In *Georgia v. Stanton* (1867), the Court similarly dismissed a petition directed at the secretary of war and General ULYSSES S. GRANT, holding that the petition presented POLITICAL QUESTIONS resolvable only by the political branches of the government. But the words of Justice Nelson's opinion seemed to suggest that if the petition had alleged a threat to private property (rather than the state's property), there might be a basis for providing relief. In May 1867, Mississippi's attorneys moved to amend their petition to specify such a threat. The Court, in a 4–4 order (Justice Grier being absent), rejected the motion. This minor, unnoticed proceeding was probably the truest index to the attitudes of individual Justices on the substantive policy questions of Reconstruction.

The Court's final involvement with Reconstruction came with TEXAS V. WHITE (1869) and *White v. Hart* (1872). In the former case, decided on the same day that the Supreme Court acknowledged the validity of the McCardle repealer, the postwar government of Texas sought to recover some bonds that the Confederate state government had sold to defray military costs. Because a state was a party, this was an action within the ORIGINAL JURISDICTION of the Supreme Court. But one of the defendants challenged the jurisdictional basis of the action, claiming that Texas was not a state in the constitutional sense at the time the action was brought (February 1867). This challenge directly raised important questions about the validity of SECESSION and Reconstruction. Chief Justice Chase, writing for the six-man majority (Grier, Swayne, Miller, dissenting) met the issue head on. He first held that secession had been a nullity. The Union was "indissoluble," "an indestructible Union, composed of indestructible States" in Chase's resonant, memorable phrasing. But, he went on, though the relations of individual Texans to the United States could not be severed, secession had deranged the status of the state within the Union. In language suggestive of the "forfeited-rights" theory of Reconstruction propounded by Ohio congressman Samuel Shellabarger which had provided a conceptual basis for Republican Reconstruction, Chase stated that the rights of the state had been "suspended" by secession and war. Congress was responsible for restoring the proper relationship, in wartime because of its authority under the military and MILITIA CLAUSES of Article I, section 8, and in peacetime under the guarantee of a REPUBLICAN FORM OF GOVERNMENT in Article IV, section 4. This was preponderantly a question to be resolved by Congress rather than the President, and hence the Lincoln and Johnson governments in power before enactment of the Military Reconstruction Acts were "provisional." Congress enjoyed wide latitude in working out details of Reconstruction policy. The sweeping language of Chase's opinion strongly implied the constitutionality of military Reconstruction. The majority opinion also offered a useful distinction between legitimate acts of the Confederate government of Texas, such as those designed to preserve the peace, and invalid ones in support of the rebellion.

In *White v. Hart* (1872) the Court reaffirmed its general position in *Texas v. White* and emphasized that the relationship of states in the union was a political question for the political branches to resolve. At the same time, the Court disposed of two lingering issues from the war in ways that reaffirmed the doctrine of *Texas v. White.* In *Virginia v. West Virginia* (1870) it accepted the creation of the daughter state, shutting its eyes to the obvious irregularities surrounding the Pierpont government's consent to the separation, and insisting that there had been a "valid agreement between the two States." And in *Miller v. United States* (1871), echoing THE PRIZE CASES (1863), a six-man majority upheld the constitutionality of the confiscation provisions of the Second Confiscation Act of 1862 on the basis of the Union's status as a belligerent.

The Chase Court decisions dealing with secession, war, and Reconstruction have stood well the test of time. *Milligan* and the *Test Oath Cases* remain valuable defenses of individual liberty against arbitrary government. The *McCardle* decision was a realistic and valid recognition of an explicit congressional power, while its sequel, *Yerger,* reaffirmed the libertarian implications of *Milligan.* The Court's position in the cases seeking to enjoin executive officials from enforcing Reconstruction was inevitable: it would have been hopeless for the Court to attempt to thwart congressional Reconstruction, or to accede to the Johnson/Democratic demand for immediate readmission of the seceded states. *Texas v. White* and *White v. Hart* drew on a sound prewar precedent, LUTHER V. BORDEN (1849), to validate actions by the dominant political branch in what was clearly a pure political question. Taken together, the Reconstruction cases evince a high order of judicial statesmanship.

The Chase Court made only tentative beginnings in issues of federal and state regulatory power, but those beginnings were significant. The first federal regulatory question to come up involved the currency. In VEAZIE BANK V. FENNO (1869) the Court sustained the constitutionality of sections of the Internal Revenue Acts of 1865 and 1866 that imposed a ten percent tax on state bank notes for the purpose of driving them out of circulation. Chase first held that the tax was not a DIRECT TAX (which would have had to be apportioned among the states) and then upheld Congress's power to issue paper money and create a uniform national currency by eliminating state paper.

The LEGAL TENDER CASES were more controversial. As secretary of the treasury, Chase had reluctantly acquiesced in the issuance of federal paper money. But when the issue came before the Court in the First Legal Tender Case (*Hepburn v. Griswold,* 1870), Chase, speaking for a 4–3 majority, held the Legal Tender Act of 1862 unconstitutional because it made greenbacks legal tender for preexisting debts. The division on the court was partisan: all the majority Justices were Democrats (Chase by this time had reverted to his Democratic antecedents), all the dissenters Republicans. Chase's reasoning was precipitate and unsatisfactory. He asserted that the act violated the OBLIGATION OF CONTRACTS, but the CONTRACT CLAUSE limited only the states. To this Chase responded that the act was contrary to the "spirit of the Constitution." He also broadly implied that the statute violated the Fifth Amendment's guarantee of DUE PROCESS.

An enlarged Court in 1871 reversed *Hepburn,* upholding the constitutionality of the 1862 statute in the Second Legal Tender Cases, with the two new appointees, Bradley and Strong, joining the three dissenters of the first case. Justice Strong for the majority averred that "every contract for the payment of money, simply, is necessarily subject to the constitutional power of the government over the currency." The Court's turnabout suggested to contemporaries that President Grant had packed the Court to obtain a reversal of the first decision. Grant was opposed to the decision, and he knew that Bradley and Strong were also opposed; but he did not secure from them any commitments on the subject, and he did not base his appointments solely on the single issue of legal tender.

Other Chase Court decisions involving federal power were not so controversial. In *United States v. Dewitt* (1870) Chase for the Court invalidated an exercise of what would come to be called the NATIONAL POLICE POWER, in this case a provision in a revenue statute prohibiting the mixing of illuminating oil with naphtha (a highly flammable mixture). Chase held that the COMMERCE CLAUSE conferred no federal power over the internal affairs of the states, and that the subject matter was remote from the topic of raising revenue. He simply assumed that there was no inherent national police power. In COLLECTOR V. DAY (1871) Justice Nelson for a divided Court held that federal revenue acts taxing income could not reach the salary of a state judge. Justice Bradley's dissent, maintaining the necessity of federal power to reach sources of income that included some functions of state government, was vindicated in GRAVES V. NEW YORK EX REL. O'KEEFE (1939), which overruled *Day.* In contrast to the foregoing cases, *The Daniel Ball* (1871) upheld the power of Congress to regulate commerce on navigable waterways, even where these were wholly intrastate.

The Chase Court decisions passing on the regulatory and taxing authority of the states caused less controversy. These cases are significant principally as evidence that the Court continued unabated its prewar responsibility of monitoring the functioning of the federal system, inhibiting incursions by the states on national authority and the national market, while at the same time preserving their scope of regulation and their sources of revenue intact. The first case of this sort, GELPCKE V. DUBUQUE (1864), involved a suit on bonds, issued by a city to encourage railroad building, which the city was trying to repudiate. The state courts had reversed their prior decisions and held that citizens could not be taxed to assist a private enterprise such as a railroad. The Supreme Court, in an opinion by Justice Swayne, reversed the result below, thus upholding the validity of the bonds. Swayne intemperately declared that "We shall never immolate truth, justice, and the law, because a state tribunal has erected the altar and decreed the sacrifice." The decision was welcomed in financial circles, particularly European ones, and presaged a Court attitude sympathetic to investors and hostile to repudiation, especially by a public agency.

The Court displayed less passion in other cases. In *Crandall v. Nevada* (1868), it struck down a state CAPITATION tax on passengers of public conveyances leaving the state as an unconstitutional interference with the right of persons to move about the country. The commerce clause aspects of the case were left to be decided later. Another case involving personal liberty, *Tarble's Case* (1872), vindicated the Court's earlier position in ABLEMAN V. BOOTH (1859) by holding that a state court in a habeas corpus proceeding could not release an individual held in federal custody (here, an allegedly deserting army volunteer).

But most cases testing the scope of state regulatory power dealt with commerce. In PAUL V. VIRGINIA (1869) the Court, through Chase, held that the negotiation of insurance contracts did not constitute commerce within the meaning of the commerce clause, and hence that a state was free to regulate the conduct of insurance companies as it pleased. This doctrine lasted until 1944. But one aspect of Justice Field's concurring opinion in *Paul* had momentous consequences. He asserted that, for purposes of the PRIVILEGES AND IMMUNITIES clause of Article IV, CORPORATIONS could not be considered "citizens," and were thus not entitled to the privileges and immunities of natural PERSONS. This caused attorneys to look to other sources, such as the due process clause (with its term "person") as a source of protection for corporations. During the same term, in WOODRUFF V. PARHAM (1868), the Chase Court upheld a municipal sales tax applied to goods brought into the state in INTERSTATE COMMERCE even though they were still in their original package, thus limiting Marshall's ORIGINAL-PACKAGE DOCTRINE announced in BROWN V. MARYLAND (1827) to imports from other nations.

Three 1873 cases demonstrated the Court carefully adjusting the federal balance. In the State Freight Tax Case the Court struck down a state tax on freight carried out of the state. But in the *Case of the State Tax on Railway Gross Receipts* the Court upheld a state tax on a corporation's gross receipts, even when the taxpayer was a carrier and the tax fell on interstate business. And in the *Case of the State Tax on Foreign-Held Bonds* the Court struck down a tax on interest on bonds as applied to the securities of out-of-state bondholders.

The last category of major Chase Court cases dealt with the scope of the Reconstruction Amendments, and the extent to which they would alter the prewar balances of the federal system. One of Chase's circuit court decisions, *In re Turner* (1867), suggested that this potential might be broad. Chase there held a Maryland BLACK CODE's apprenticeship provision unconstitutional on the ground that it imposed a condition of involuntary servitude in violation of the THIRTEENTH AMENDMENT. This decision might have been the prelude to extensive federal involvement in matters that before the war would have been considered exclusively within the STATE POLICE POWER. But this possibility was drastically narrowed in the SLAUGHTERHOUSE CASES (1873), the last major decision of the Chase Court and one of the enduring monuments of American constitutional law. Justice Miller for the majority held that "the one pervading purpose" of the Reconstruction Amendments was the liberation of black people, not an extension of the privileges and rights of whites. Miller construed the privileges and immunities, due process, and EQUAL PROTECTION clauses of the Fourteenth Amendment in light of this assumption, holding that none of them had deranged the traditional balance of the federal system. The states still remained the source of most substantive privileges and immunities, and the states remained primarily responsible for securing them to individuals. This ruling effectively relegated the definition and protection of freedmen's rights to precisely those governments—Redeemer-dominated southern states—least likely to provide that protection. Because "we do not see in those [Reconstruction] amendments any purpose to destroy the main features of the general system," Miller rejected a substantive interpretation of the new due process clause and restricted the equal protection clause to cases of "discrimination against the negroes as a class."

The future belonged to the *Slaughterhouse* dissenters, Justices Bradley and Field. Bradley articulated the doctrine of substantive due process, arguing that the right to pursue a lawful occupation is a property right which the state may not interfere with arbitrarily or selectively. Field, in a dissent in which Chase joined (Swayne dissented in a separate opinion) relied on the privileges and immunities clause of the Fourteenth Amendment, seeing in it a guarantee of "the fundamental rights" of free men, which cannot be destroyed by state legislation. His insistence on an "equality of right, with exemption from all disparaging and partial enactments, in the lawful pursuits of life" foreshadowed the doctrine of FREEDOM OF CONTRACT.

Yet Field's and Bradley's insistence on the right to follow a chosen occupation, free of arbitrary discrimination, did not avail Myra Bradwell in her effort to secure admission to the Illinois bar (BRADWELL V. ILLINOIS, 1873). Justice Miller for the majority (Chase being the lone dissenter) refused to overturn a decision of the Illinois Supreme Court denying her admission to the bar solely on the ground of her gender. "The paramount mission and destiny of woman are to fulfill the noble and benign offices of wife and mother. This is the law of the Creator," Bradley wrote in a concurrence. "And the rules of civil society . . . cannot be based upon exceptional cases." The emergent scope of the due process, equal protection, and privileges and immunities clauses were to have a differential application as a result of the *Slaughterhouse* dissents and *Bradwell* ruling, securing the rights of corporations and men in their economic roles, while proving ineffectual to protect others from discrimination based on race and gender. (See RACIAL DISCRIMINATION; SEX EQUALITY.)

During its brief span, the Chase Court made enduring contributions to American constitutional development. It handled the unprecedented issues of Reconstruction with balance and a due recognition of the anomalous nature of issues coming before it. Yet in those decisions, Chase and his colleagues managed to preserve protection for individual rights while at the same time permitting the victorious section, majority, and party to assure a constitutional resolution of the war consonant with its military results. In non-Reconstruction cases, the Chase court continued the traditional function of the Supreme Court in monitoring and adjusting the allocation of powers between nation and states. It was more activist than its predecessors in striking down federal legislation, while it displayed the same nicely balanced concern for state regulatory power and protection of the national market that was a characteristic of the TANEY COURT.

WILLIAM M. WIECEK

Bibliography

FAIRMAN, CHARLES 1939 *Mr. Justice Miller and the Supreme Court, 1862–1890.* Cambridge, Mass.: Harvard University Press.

——— 1971 *Reconstruction and Reunion, 1864–88, Part One* (vol. VI of the Oliver Wendell Holmes Devise *History of the Supreme Court of the United States*). New York: Macmillan.

HYMAN, HAROLD M. and WIECEK, WILLIAM M. 1982 *Equal Justice Under Law: Constitutional Development 1835–1875.* New York: Harper & Row.

KUTLER, STANLEY I. 1968 *Judicial Power and Reconstruction Politics.* Chicago: University of Chicago Press.

SILVER, DAVID M. 1957 *Lincoln's Supreme Court.* Urbana: University of Illinois Press.

SWISHER, CARL B. 1930 *Stephen J. Field: Craftsman of the Law.* Washington, D.C.: Brookings Institution.

WARREN, CHARLES 1937 *The Supreme Court in United States History,* rev. ed. Boston: Little, Brown.

CHATHAM, LORD

See: William Pitt

CHECKS AND BALANCES

In its precise meaning, "checks and balances" is not synonymous with SEPARATION OF POWERS; it refers instead to a system of rules and practices designed to maintain the separation of powers. The executive VETO POWER is considered part of this system, along with the power of JUDICIAL REVIEW, the IMPEACHMENT power, and other powers available to any of the branches of government for combating the encroachments of the others.

JAMES MADISON formulated the American theory of checks and balances in response to the Anti-Federalist charge that the proposed Constitution would contain an overlap of governmental functions, violating the principle of separated powers. Expressing a pessimistic view of human nature, he argued in THE FEDERALIST #10 that the way to avoid majority tyranny lay in creating a large national community of diverse and numerous economic interests, not in statesmanship or in religious and moral constraints. In *The Federalist* #47–49 Madison went on to argue that neither sharply drawn institutional boundaries nor appeals to the electorate could be relied upon to maintain the separation of powers. Both methods presupposed the virtues of official lawfulness and electoral nonpartisanship, virtues whose unreliability was attested by experience. Because such "external checks" were ineffective, said Madison in *The Federalist* #51, maintaining the separation of powers would require "internal checks" that linked the officeholders' personal ambitions to their duties. Officials would defend their constitutional prerogatives if they felt that doing so were a means to furthering their personal ambitions. "[A]mbition checking ambition"—not virtue—was the key to constitutional maintenance. And effective checks required each branch to have a hand in the others' functions. For example, the veto is the President's hand in the legislative function.

Madison knew, however, that this partial blending of power did not go far enough. Power might still be concentrated if all these branches were united in one interest or animated by the same spirit. Thinkers from Aristotle to MONTESQUIEU had taught that constitutions could be maintained at least partly through a balance of social groups such as estates or economic classes. But theorists with democratic pretensions could not institutionalize such social divisions. The problem for the Framers was to prevent a single interest from predominating in a society that had few official distinctions of status and class. Their answer was to rely on the different institutional psychologies of governmental branches whose personnel would represent the different constituencies and perspectives of a large and diverse society. Thus, Madison argued in *The Federalist* #62–63 that because of differences in age, period of CITIZENSHIP, tenure of office, constituency, and, to a lesser degree, legislative function, members of the House of Representatives and Senate would pursue different policies with different consequences for the long term and varying impact on local, national, and international opinion. ALEXANDER HAMILTON wrote in *The Federalist* #70–71 that presidential types would be likely to seek the acclaim that attends success in difficult tasks, especially tasks requiring leaders to stand against and change public opinion. Such differences in institutional psychology, compounded by the federal features of the electoral system and the pluralism of an essentially democratic, secular, and commercial society, were expected to impede the formation of political parties disciplined enough to overcome the moderating influence of separated institutions.

The American system of checks and balances envisions strong executive and judicial branches. Experience had taught the Framers that popular legislatures were a greater threat to the separation of powers than were executives or courts. Accordingly, *The Federalist* #51 rationalized the bicameralism of Congress and the independence of the executive and judicial branches as means of weakening the naturally strongest branch and strengthening the weaker ones. This positive feature of the system complements its negative function of preventing concentrations of power. The Framers thus sought to achieve separation of governmental institutions without sacrificing the capacity for coordinated leadership when times demanded.

The system of checks and balances has worked well in some respects, but not in all. It has discouraged concentrations of power through centralized and disciplined political parties. Although government is fragmented in normal times, the system does permit central leadership in times of crisis, as the presidencies of THOMAS JEFFERSON, ABRAHAM LINCOLN, and FRANKLIN D. ROOSEVELT attest. It has also helped to create a remarkable degree of judicial independence without producing a judiciary seriously at odds with public opinion on any given issue for too long. The system has not worked so well in the case of Congress, which has undermined its own position by a practice of broad DELEGATION OF POWER to the executive and independent agencies. Many such delegations are necessitated by the problems and complexities that have brought the triumph of the administrative state. But far too many delegations are little more than acts of political buckpassing explained by the perception that the way to reelection does not lie in clear positions on controversial questions, but in constituency services and publicity that is politically safe. After the Great Depression and before the Supreme Court's decision in IMMIGRATION AND NATURALIZATION SERVICE V. CHADHA (1983), Congress compounded avoidable offense to the separation of powers when it tried to straddle the question of legislative responsibility, limiting many of its buckpassing delegations of power with various versions of the LEGISLATIVE VETO.

Congress's experience shows that there is a limit to the ability of the system to maintain a constitutional arrangement through reliance on personal ambition. Personal ambition sometimes dictates surrendering institutional prerogatives. The same can be said when Presidents compromise firmness in anticipation of elections and when judges propose "judicial self-restraint" in response to threats like court-packing and withdrawals of JURISDICTION. Despite the Framers' theory of checks and balances, officials must at some point respect constitutional duty as something other than mere means to personal ambition.

SOTIRIOS A. BARBER

Bibliography

FISHER, LOUIS 1978 *The Constitution Between Friends: Congress, the President, and the Law.* New York: St. Martin's Press.

SHARP, MALCOLM 1938 The Classical American Doctrine of "the Separation of Powers." In Association of American Law Schools, *Selected Essays on Constitutional Law.* Vol. 4:168–194. Chicago: Foundation Press.

VILE, M. J. C. 1967 *Constitutionalism and the Separation of Powers.* Oxford: Clarendon Press.

CHEROKEE INDIAN CASES

Cherokee Nation v. *Georgia*
5 Peters 1 (1831)

Worcester v. *Georgia*
6 Peters 515 (1832)

The Cherokee Indian Cases prompted a constitutional crisis marked by successful state defiance of the Supreme Court, the Constitution, and federal treaties. The United States had made treaties with the Georgia Cherokee, as if they were a sovereign power, and pledged to secure their lands. Later, in 1802, the United States pledged to Georgia that in return for its relinquishment of the Yazoo lands (see FLETCHER V. PECK, 1810) the United States would extinguish the Cherokee land claims in Georgia. The Cherokee, however, refused to leave Georgia voluntarily in return for wild lands west of the Mississippi. In 1824 Georgia claimed LEGISLATIVE JURISDICTION over all the Indian lands within its boundaries. The Cherokee, who had a written language and a plantation economy, then adopted a CONSTITUTION and declared their sovereign independence. Georgia, which denied that the United States had authority to bind the state by an Indian treaty, retaliated against the Cherokee by a series of statutes that nullified all Indian laws and land claims and divided Cherokee lands into counties subject to state governance. President ANDREW JACKSON supported the state against the Indians, and Congress, too, recognizing that the Indians could not maintain a separate sovereignty within the state, urged them to settle on federally granted land in the west or, if remaining in Georgia, to submit to state laws.

The Cherokee turned next to the Supreme Court.

Claiming to be a foreign state within the meaning of Article III, section 2, of the Constitution, the Indians invoked the Court's ORIGINAL JURISDICTION in a case to which a state was a party and sought an INJUNCTION that would restrain Georgia from enforcing any of its laws within Cherokee territory recognized by federal treaties. By scheduling a hearing the Court exposed itself to Georgia's wrath. Without the support of the political branches of the national government, the Court faced the prospect of being unable to enforce its own decree or defend the supremacy of federal treaties against state violation.

The case of Corn Tassel, which suddenly intervened, exposed the Court's vulnerability. He was a Cherokee whom Georgia tried and convicted for the murder of a fellow tribesman, though he objected that a federal treaty recognized the exclusive right of his own nation to try him. On Tassel's application Chief Justice JOHN MARSHALL issued a WRIT OF ERROR to the state trial court and directed the governor of the state to send its counsel to appear before the Supreme Court. Georgia's governor and legislature contemptuously declared that they would resist execution of the Court's writ with all necessary force, denounced the Court's infringement of state SOVEREIGNTY, and hanged Corn Tassel. Justice JOSEPH STORY spoke of "practical NULLIFICATION." Newspapers and politicians throughout the nation took sides in the dispute between the Court and the state, and Congress in 1831 debated a bill to repeal section 25 of the JUDICIARY ACT OF 1789. Although the House defeated the repeal bill, Whigs despondently predicted that the President would not support the Court if it decided the *Cherokee Nation* case contrary to his view of the matter.

The Court wisely decided, 4–2, to deny jurisdiction on the ground that the Cherokee were not a foreign state in the sense of Article III's use of that term. Although Marshall for the Court declared that the Cherokee were a "distinct political society" capable of self-government and endorsed their right to their lands, he candidly acknowledged that the Court could not restrain the government of Georgia "and its physical force." That, Marshall observed, "savors too much of the exercise of political power" and that was what the bill for an injunction asked of the Court.

A year later, however, the Court switched its strategy. At issue in *Worcester* was the constitutionality of a Georgia statute that prohibited white people from residing in Cherokee territory without a state license. Many missionaries, including Samuel Worcester, defied the act in order to bring a TEST CASE before the Supreme Court, in the hope that the Court would endorse Cherokee sovereignty and void the state's Cherokee legislation. Worcester and another, having been sentenced to four years' hard labor, were the only missionaries to decline a pardon; they applied to the Court for a writ of error, which Marshall issued. Georgia sent the records of the case but again refused to appear before a Court that engaged in a "usurpation" of state sovereignty. The state legislature resolved that a reversal of the state court would be deemed "unconstitutional" and empowered the governor to employ all force to resist the "invasion" of the state's administration of its laws. The case was sensationally debated in the nation's press, and nearly sixty members of Congress left their seats to hear the argument before the Supreme Court.

In an opinion by Marshall, with Justice HENRY BALDWIN dissenting, the Court reaffirmed its jurisdiction under section 25, upheld the exclusive power of the United States in Indian matters, endorsed the authority of the Cherokee Nation within boundaries recognized by federal treaties, declared that the laws of Georgia had no force within these boundaries, and held that the "acts of Georgia are repugnant to the Constitution, laws, and treaties of the United States." The Court also reversed the judgment of the Georgia court and commanded the release of Worcester.

Why did the Court deliberately decide on the broadest possible grounds and challenge Georgia? In a private letter, Justice Story, noting that the state was enraged and violent, expected defiance of the Court's writ and no support from the President. "The Court," he wrote, "has done its duty. Let the nation do theirs. If we have a government let its commands be obeyed; if we have not it is as well to know it. . . ." Georgia did resist and Jackson did nothing. He might have made the famous remark, "John Marshall has made his decision; now let him enforce it." But Jackson knew Marshall's reputation for political craftiness, knew that a majority of Congress resisted all efforts to curb the Court, and knew that public opinion favored the Court and revered its Chief as the nation's preeminent Unionist. Jackson did nothing because he did not yet have to act. The state must first refuse execution of the Court's writ before the Court could order a federal marshal to free Worcester, and it could not issue an order to the marshal without a record of the state court's refusal to obey the writ. Not until the next term of the Court could it decide whether it had a course of action that would force the President either to execute the law of the land or disobey his oath of office. Marshall believed that public opinion would compel Jackson to execute the law. In the fall of 1832, however, Marshall pessimistically wrote that "our Constitution cannot last. . . . The Union has been prolonged thus far by miracles. I fear they cannot continue."

A miracle did occur, making the Court's cause the President's before the Court's next term; the SOUTH CAROLINA ORDINANCE OF NULLIFICATION intervened, forcing Jackson to censure state nullification of federal law. Georgia supported Jackson against South Carolina, and he convinced Georgia's governor that the way to dissociate Georgia from nullification was to free Worcester. The governor pardoned him. Worcester, having won the Supreme Court's invalidation of the Georgia Cherokee legislation, accepted the pardon. The lawyers for the Cherokee persuaded them to desist from further litigation in order to preserve a Unionist coalition against nullificationists. In 1838, long after the crisis had passed, the Cherokees were forcibly removed from their lands. The Court could not save them. It never could. It had, however, saved its integrity ("The Court has done its duty") by defending the supreme law of the land at considerable risk.

LEONARD W. LEVY

Bibliography

BURKE, JOSEPH C. 1969 The Cherokee Cases: A Study of Law, Politics, and Morality. *Stanford Law Review* 21:500–531.

WARREN, CHARLES 1923 *The Supreme Court in United States History,* 3 vols. Vol. 2:189–229. Boston: Little, Brown.

CHEROKEE NATION v. GEORGIA

See: Cherokee Indian Cases

CHICAGO, BURLINGTON & QUINCY RAILROAD v. CHICAGO
166 U.S. 226 (1897)

A 7–1 Supreme Court here sustained a $1 award as JUST COMPENSATION for a TAKING OF PROPERTY, holding that the SEVENTH AMENDMENT precluded it from reexamining facts, decided by a jury, which dictated that amount. Although due process required compensation, a nominal sum did not deprive the railroad of either due process or EQUAL PROTECTION. The Court required a "fair and full equivalent for the thing taken by the public" and stressed the necessity for understanding the spirit of due process. "In determining what is DUE PROCESS OF LAW, regard must be had to substance, not to form."

DAVID GORDON

CHICAGO, MILWAUKEE & ST. PAUL RAILWAY v. MINNESOTA
134 U.S. 418 (1890)

This decision, making the courts arbiters of the reasonableness of railroad rates, presaged the Supreme Court's final acceptance of SUBSTANTIVE DUE PROCESS ten years later. The Minnesota legislature had established a commission to inspect rail rates and alter those it deemed unreasonable. A 6–3 Court struck down the statute as a violation of both substantive and PROCEDURAL DUE PROCESS. Justice SAMUEL BLATCHFORD found that the statute neglected to provide procedural due process: railroads received no notice that the reasonableness of their rate was being considered, and the commission provided no hearing or other chance for the railroads to defend their rates. Moreover, Blatchford said that a rate's reasonableness "is eminently a question for judicial investigation, requiring due process of law for its determination." A company, denied the authority to charge reasonable rates and unable to turn to any judicial mechanism for review (procedural due process) would necessarily be deprived "of the lawful use of its property, and thus, in substance, and effect, of the property itself, without due process of law" (substantive due process). In dissent, Justice JOSEPH P. BRADLEY declared that the majority had effectively overruled MUNN V. ILLINOIS (1877). Bradley's opinion explicitly rejected the assertion that reasonableness was a question for judicial determination; it is, he said, "pre-eminently a legislative one, involving considerations of policy as well as of remuneration." If the legislature could fix rates (as precedent had shown), why could it make no such delegation of power to a commission? Indeed, the Court's next step, in REAGAN V. FARMERS' LOAN & TRUST COMPANY (1894), would be the claim of power to void statutes by which the legislature itself directly set rates, and, in SMYTH V. AMES (1898), the Court would reach the zenith, actually striking down a state act for that reason.

DAVID GORDON

CHIEF JUSTICE, ROLE OF THE

The title "Chief Justice" appears only once in the Constitution. That mention occurs not in Article III, the judicial article, but in connection with the Chief Justice's role as presiding officer of the Senate during an IMPEACHMENT trial of the President. With such a meager delineation of powers and duties in the Constitution, the importance of the office was hardly obvious during the early days of the Republic. Despite President GEORGE WASHINGTON's great expectations for the post, his first appointee, JOHN JAY, left disillusioned and convinced that neither the Supreme Court nor the chief justiceship would amount to anything. Yet, a little over a century later, President WILLIAM HOWARD TAFT stated that he would prefer the office to his own. During that intervening century, an office of considerable power and prestige had emerged from the constitutional vacuum. Since then, the Chief Justice's role has continued to evolve. Today, the office is the product of both the personalities and the priorities of its incumbents and of the institutional forces which have become stronger as the Supreme Court's role in our government has expanded and matured.

Like the other Justices of the Supreme Court, the Chief Justice of the United States is appointed by the President with the ADVICE AND CONSENT of the Senate. He enjoys, along with all other full members of the federal judiciary, life tenure "during his GOOD BEHAVIOR." With respect to the judicial work of the Court, he has traditionally been referred to as *primus inter pares*—first among equals. He has the same vote as each Associate Justice of the Court. His judicial duties differ only in that he presides over the sessions of the Court and over the Court's private CONFERENCE at which the cases are discussed and eventually decided. When in the majority, he assigns the writing of the OPINION OF THE COURT. Like an Associate Justice, the Chief Justice also performs the duties of a circuit Justice. A circuit Justice must pass upon various applications for temporary relief and BAIL from his circuit and participate, at least in a liaison or advisory capacity, in the judicial administration of that circuit. By tradition, the Chief Justice is circuit Justice for the Fourth and District of Columbia Circuits.

In addition to his judicial duties, the Chief Justice has, by statute, responsibility for the general administration of the Supreme Court. While the senior officers of the Court are appointed by the entire Court, they perform their daily duties under his general supervision. Other employees of the Court must be approved by the Chief Justice.

The Chief Justice also serves as presiding officer of the Judicial Conference of the United States. The Conference, composed of the chief judge and a district judge from each circuit, has the statutory responsibility for making comprehensive surveys of the business of the federal courts and for undertaking a continuous study of the rules of practice and procedure. The Chief Justice, as presiding officer, must appoint the various committees of the Conference which undertake the studies necessary for the achievement of those statutory objectives. He must also submit to the Congress an annual report of the proceedings of the Conference and a report as to its legislative recommendations. Other areas of court administration also occupy the Chief Justice's attention regularly. He has the authority to assign, temporarily, judges of the lower federal courts to courts other than their own and for service on the Panel on Multidistrict Litigation. He is also the permanent Chairman of the Board of the Federal Judicial Center which develops and recommends improvements in the area of judicial administration to the Judicial Conference.

From time to time, Congress has also assigned by statute other duties to the Chief Justice. Some are related to the judiciary; others are not. For instance, he must appoint some of the members of the Commission on Executive, Legislative, and Judicial Salaries; the Advisory Corrections Council; the Federal Records Council; and the National Study Commission on Records and Documents of Federal Officials. He also serves as Chancellor of the Smithsonian Institution and as a member of the Board of Trustees of both the National Gallery of Art and the Joseph H. Hirshhorn Museum and Sculpture Garden.

In addition to these formal duties, the Chief Justice is considered the titular head of the legal profession in the United States. He traditionally addresses the American Bar Association on the state of the judiciary and delivers the opening address at the annual meeting of the American Law Institute. He is regularly invited to other ceremonial and substantive meetings of the bar. Finally, as head of the judicial branch, he regularly participates in national observances and state ceremonies honoring foreign dignitaries.

The foregoing catalog of duties, while describing a burdensome role, does not fully indicate the impact of the Chief Justice on the Supreme Court's work. For instance, with respect to his judicial duties, the Chief Justice, while nominally only "first among equals," may exercise a significant influence on the Court's decision-making process and, consequently, on its final judicial work product. His most obvious opportunity to influence that process is while presiding at the Court's conference. He presents each case initially and is the first to give his views. Thus, he has the opportunity to take the initiative by directing the Court's inquiry to those aspects of the case he believes are crucial. Moreover, although the Justices discuss cases in descending order of seniority, they vote in the opposite order. Therefore, while speaking first, the "Chief," as he is referred to by his colleagues, votes last and commits himself, even preliminarily, only after all of the associates have explained their positions and cast their votes. If he votes with the majority, he may retain the opinion for himself or assign it to a colleague whose views are most compatible with his own. In cases where there is significant indecision among the Justices, it falls to the "Chief" to take the initiative with respect to the Court's further consideration of the case. He may, for instance, suggest that further discussion be deferred until argument of other related cases or he may request that several Justices set forth their views in writing in the hope that such a memorandum might form the basis of a later opinion.

There are also more indirect but highly significant ways by which the "Chief" can influence the decision-making process. As presiding officer during open session, he sets a "tone" which can make ORAL ARGUMENT either a formal, stilted affair or a disciplined but relaxed, productive dialogue between the Court and counsel. Even the Chief Justice's "administrative" duties within the Court can have a subtle influence on the Court's decision-making processes. The efficient administration of the Court's support services as well as the employment of adequate staff personnel can nurture an ambiance conducive to harmonious decision making.

While occupancy of the Court's center chair no doubt gives the incumbent an enhanced capacity to influence jurisprudential developments, there are clear limitations on the exercise of that power. The Court is a collegial institution; disagreement on important issues is a natural phenomenon. In such a context, as Justice WILLIAM H. REHNQUIST put it in a 1976 article: "The power to calm such naturally troubled waters is usually beyond the capacity of any mortal chief justice. He presides over a conference not of eight subordinates, whom he may direct or instruct, but of eight associates who, like him, have tenure during good behavior, and who are as independent as hogs on ice. He may at most persuade or cajole them." Political acumen is often as important as intellectual brilliance. Whatever the Chief's view of his power, he must remember that, in the eyes of the associates, "the Chief Justice is not entitled to a presumption that he knows more law than other members of the Court . . .," as Justice Rehnquist said in chambers in CLEMENTS v. LOGAN (1981). Other institutional concerns further constrain the Chief's ability to guide the Court's decisions. All Chief Justices have recognized, although to varying degrees, a responsibility to see not only that the Court gets its business done but also that it does so in a manner which maintains the country's confidence. Sometimes, those objectives require that the Chief refrain from taking a strong ideological stance and act as a mediator in the formation of a majority. Similarly, while the assignment power can be a powerful tool, it must be exercised to ensure a majority opinion that advances, not retards, growth in the law. Even the prerogative of presiding over the conference has a price. The Chief Justice must spend significant additional time reviewing all the petitions filed with the Court. As the performance of Chief Justice CHARLES EVANS HUGHES demonstrated, perceiving those areas of ambiguity and conflict that are most troublesome in the administration of justice is essential to leading effectively the discussion of the conference. For the same reason, the Chief must take the time to master the intricacies of the Court's procedure.

The extrajudicial responsibilities of the Chief Justice can also place him at a distinct disadvantage in influencing the Court's jurisprudential direction. The internal decision-making process of the Court is essentially competitive. There is nothing so humble as a draft opinion with four votes and nothing so arrogant as one with six. Such a process does not easily take into account that one participant must regularly divert his attention because of other official responsibilities. Moreover, there is a special intellectual and physical cost in shifting constantly between the abstract world of the appellate judge and the pragmatic one of the administrator. A Chief Justice who takes all his responsibilities seriously must experience the fatiguing tension that inevitably results from such bifurcation of responsibilities. Here, however, there may be compensating considerations. Whatever advantage the Chief may lose in the judicial bargaining because of administrative distractions may well be partially recovered by the prestige gained by his accomplishments beyond the Court. The Court has benefited from a strong Chief Justice's defense against specific political threats such as President FRANKLIN D. ROOSEVELT's Court-packing plan. It has also benefited when the Chief's efforts have resulted in legislation making its own workload more manageable. Chief Justice Taft's support of the JUDICIARY ACT OF 1925, for instance, gave the Court more control over its own docket and, consequently, increased capacity to address, selectively, the most pressing issues. In modern times, the tremors of the litigation explosion that has engulfed the lower courts have been felt on the Supreme Court. The accomplishments of a Chief Justice in alleviating these problems cannot be overlooked by his associates.

Certainly, with respect to nonjudicial matters, a Chief Justice's special responsibility for institutional concerns has commanded respect from the associates. Even such greats as Justice LOUIS D. BRANDEIS regularly consulted the Chief on matters that might have an impact on the reputation of the Court as an institution. This same identification of the Chief Justice with the Supreme Court as an institution has made some Chief Justices the acknowledged spokesperson for both the Supreme Court and the lower federal courts before the other branches of government and, indeed, before the public.

With no specific constitutional mandate to fulfill, early Chief Justices, most especially JOHN MARSHALL, molded the office in which they served just as they molded the courts over which they presided. In those formative periods, the dominance of personal factors was understandable. Today, however, significant institutional forces also shape the office. In addition to the extrajudicial duties imposed by Congress, the Court, now a mature institution of American government, exerts through its traditions a powerful influence over every new incumbent of its bench—including the person in the center chair.

KENNETH F. RIPPLE

Bibliography

FRANKFURTER, FELIX 1953 Chief Justices I Have Known. *Virginia Law Review* 39:883–905.

FREUND, PAUL A. 1967 Charles Evans Hughes as Chief Justice. *Harvard Law Review* 81:4–43.

REHNQUIST, WILLIAM H. 1976 Chief Justices I Never Knew. *Hastings Constitutional Law Quarterly* 3:637–655.

SWINDLER, WILLIAM F. 1971 The Chief Justice and Law Reform. *The Supreme Court Review* 1971:241–264.

CHILD BENEFIT THEORY

Protagonists of aid to religious schools have sought to justify the practice constitutionally through what has become known as the child benefit theory. The establishment clause, they urge, forbids aid to the schools but not to the children who attend them. Recognizing that the schools themselves benefit from the action, they argue that the benefit is secondary to that received by the pupils, and note that the courts have long upheld governmental assistance to children as an aspect of the POLICE POWER.

The recognition is at least implicit in Supreme Court decisions through BOARD OF EDUCATION V. ALLEN (1968). Thus, in *Bradfield v. Roberts* (1899), the Court upheld the validity under the establishment clause of a grant of federal funds to finance the erection of a hospital in the DISTRICT OF COLUMBIA, to be maintained and operated by an order of nuns. The Court reasoned that the hospital corporation was a legal entity separate from its incorporators, and concluded that the aid was for a secular purpose. Later court decisions ignored this fiction, consistently upholding grants to religious organizations, corporate or noncorporate, to finance hospitals that, though owned and operated by churches, nevertheless were nonsectarian in their admission policies, and generally benefited the patients.

In EVERSON V. BOARD OF EDUCATION (1947) the Court upheld use of tax-raised funds to finance transportation to religious schools, in part because the program had the secular purpose to enable children to avoid the risks of traffic or hitchhiking in going to school. In COCHRAN V. LOUISIANA STATE BOARD OF EDUCATION (1930) and *Board of Education v. Allen* (1968) the Court similarly sustained laws financing the purchase of secular textbooks for use in parochial schools. The beneficiaries of the laws, the Court asserted, were not the schools but the children who attended them.

More recent decisions, however, manifest a weakening of the theory. In *Board of Education v. Nyquist* (1973) the Court refused to uphold a law to finance costs of maintenance and repair in religious schools, notwithstanding a provision that the program's purpose was to insure the health, welfare, and safety of the school children.

Two years later, in *Meek v. Pittenger,* the Court refused to extend *Allen* to encompass the loan of instructional materials to church-related schools, even though the materials benefited nonpublic school children and were provided for public school children. Finally, in WOLMAN V. WALTER (1977) the Court, unwilling to overrule either *Everson* or *Allen,* nevertheless refused to extend them to encompass educational field trip transportation to governmental, industrial, cultural, and scientific centers.

In these later cases, the Court has rejected the argument that if public funds were not used for these support services, many parents economically unable to pay for them would have to transfer their children to the public schools in violation of their own and of their children's religious conscience.

LEO PFEFFER

(SEE ALSO: *Establishment of Religion; Separation of Church and State.*)

Bibliography

DRINAN, ROBERT F., S.J. 1963 *Religion, the Courts, and Public Policy.* Chap. 5. New York: McGraw-Hill.

PFEFFER, LEO 1967 *Church, State and Freedom,* rev. ed. Chap. 14. Boston: Beacon Press.

CHILD LABOR AMENDMENT

Two years after BAILEY V. DREXEL FURNITURE CO. (1922) when for the second time the Supreme Court invalidated a federal child labor law, Congress approved a constitutional amendment empowering it to regulate on the subject. But from 1924 until 1938, the amendment languished in state legislatures, with only twenty-eight of the requisite thirty-six having ratified it by 1938.

Led by the National Association of Manufacturers, critics contended that the proposed amendment endangered traditional state powers and local control of PRODUCTION. The Granges also lobbied in agricultural states in the South and Midwest, arguing that such congressional power would threaten the use of children on family farms. Religious groups maintained that the amendment would lead to federal control of education and increase the costs of educating children. Newspapers overwhelmingly opposed the amendment on the grounds that they would be deprived of delivery boys.

The Court's decision in the WAGNER ACT CASES (1937) renewed interest in congressional legislation. The FAIR LABOR STANDARDS ACT in 1938 outlawed child labor, and in UNITED STATES V. DARBY (1941), the Court sustained the legislation and overturned its own precedents. The new law and the *Darby* decision combined to make the amendment unnecessary.

The lengthy ratification process prompted Congress to impose time limits on many subsequent amendments. The child labor amendment also raised a knotty constitutional problem when one state reversed its position (in a disputed vote) and approved ratification. That action was challenged in COLEMAN V. MILLER (1939), but the Court sidestepped the issue as a POLITICAL QUESTION and left its resolution to Congress.

STANLEY I. KUTLER

Bibliography

WOOD, STEPHEN 1968 *Constitutional Politics in the Progressive Era: Child Labor and the Law.* Chicago: University of Chicago Press.

CHILD LABOR CASE

See: *Hammer v. Dagenhart*

CHILD LABOR TAX ACT
40 Stat. 1138 (1918)

In HAMMER V. DAGENHART (1918), a 5–4 Supreme Court voided the Child Labor Act of 1916, which had forbidden carriers from transporting the products of child labor in INTERSTATE COMMERCE, as a prohibition, not a regulation, of commerce. This distinction had been thought rejected as early as CHAMPION V. AMES (1903). Progressive reformers, intent on abolishing child labor, had shifted the basis of their efforts from the COMMERCE CLAUSE to the TAXING POWER, thus invoking a new set of powerful precedents, notably MCCRAY V. UNITED STATES (1904).

In late 1918 Congress passed a Revenue Act to which had been added an amendment known as the Child Labor Tax Act. A ten percent EXCISE TAX was imposed on the net profits from the sale of child labor-produced items. This tax extended to any factory, mine, or mill employing children under fourteen, or to the age of sixteen under certain circumstances. Congressmen from the major cotton textile manufacturing states, southern Democrats, cast nearly all the negative votes.

In BAILEY V. DREXEL FURNITURE CO. (1922) an 8–1 Court invalidated the act, *McCray* and UNITED STATES V. DOREMUS (1919) notwithstanding, as a violation of the powers reserved to the states by the TENTH AMENDMENT.

DAVID GORDON

Bibliography

WOOD, STEPHEN B. 1968 *Constitutional Politics in the Progressive Era: Child Labor and the Law.* Chicago: University of Chicago Press.

CHILD LABOR TAX CASE

See: *Bailey v. Drexel Furniture Company*

CHILDREN'S RIGHTS

The law of childhood is complex, but as a general legal proposition, a child is someone who has not yet reached the age of civil majority. Each state has the authority to determine the age of majority for its own residents, and in most states that age is now eighteen. Prior to 1971, the age of majority was typically twenty-one, but after the ratification of the TWENTY-SIXTH AMENDMENT, which gave eighteen-year-olds the right to vote in federal elections, most states lowered the age of majority, as well as the voting age for state elections.

In general, children have less liberty than adults and are less often held accountable for their actions. Parents have legal power to make a wide range of decisions for the child, although they are held responsible by the state for the child's care and support. Children have a special power to avoid contractual obligations but are not normally entitled to their own earnings and cannot manage their own property. Moreover, persons younger than certain statutory limits are not allowed to vote, hold public office, work in various occupations, drive a car, buy liquor, or be sold certain kinds of reading material, quite apart from what either they or their parents may wish.

Although a variety of civic and personal rights accrue at the age of majority, rights to engage in various "adult" activities may occur either before or after the age of eighteen. For example, many states restrict the legal access of nineteen- and twenty-year-olds to alcoholic beverages. On the other hand, most states permit sixteen- and seventeen-year-olds to secure licenses to drive automobiles. State child labor laws typically permit young people who are sixteen or seventeen to work, particularly outside of school hours, although federal law prohibits the employment of children under eighteen in hazardous occupations. A minor who is self-supporting and living away from home may, through emancipation, obtain a broad range of adult rights.

When advocates speak of children's rights, they may have in mind either of two quite contradictory notions. One notion focuses on children's basic needs, and the obligations to satisfy those needs. The other focuses on autonomy and choice.

At times, the word "right" is used to describe the duties of others—typically parents or state officials—to satisfy what are seen as a child's basic needs. Thus, claims are made that a child has or should have a legal right to education, adequate food and shelter, and even love, affection, discipline, and guidance. The federal Constitution has not been interpreted to give a child a substantive right to adequate education or care, although state law sometimes creates such duties. For example, every state provides for free public education, typically through high school, and many state constitutions require as much. Although the Supreme Court decided in SAN ANTONIO INDEPENDENT SCHOOL DISTRICT V. RODRIGUEZ (1973) that education is not a "fundamental" right, at least for purposes of requiring strict scrutiny under the EQUAL PROTECTION clause, the Court acknowledged in BROWN V. BOARD OF EDUCATION (1954) that education is "perhaps the most important function of state and local governments." There is no constitutional right to parental love, but opinions such as PIERCE V. SOCIETY OF SISTERS (1925) have suggested that children as well as parents have an interest of constitutional dimension in preserving the parent–child relationship. State child-neglect statutes do impose on parents an obligation to provide adequate custodial care. In all events, a child's "right" to such things as an education or minimally adequate care has little to do with the protection of choice on the part of a particular child. A judge usually does not ask a physically abused child whether she wants to remain with her parents when the responsible authorities believe they cannot protect her from further harm if she remains at home. Compulsory education laws and child labor laws do not give an unhappy eleven-year-old child the legal right to pursue an education by dropping out of school and taking a job.

A second, very different, notion of "children's rights" emphasizes autonomy, choice, and liberty. Claims asserting this sort of right have arisen in a variety of contexts: procedural claims in JUVENILE PROCEEDINGS and in schools (see GOSS V. LOPEZ, 1975); choices about abortion or BIRTH CONTROL; access to reading material (see GINSBERG V. NEW YORK, 1968); and involvement in political protests (see TINKER V. DES MOINES SCHOOL DISTRICT, 1969). Usually the challenge is to some form of state paternalism; but sometimes the minor's claim involves the assertion that he should have the "right" to act independently of his parents. Because the liberty of minors is much more restricted than that of adults, reformers have sometimes asserted that adolescents should have the right to adult status, at least in particular settings. A few have even suggested a children's liberation movement to end the double standard of morals and behavior for adults and children.

The definition of "children's rights" necessarily involves the allocation of power and responsibility among the child, the family, and the state. Taking contemporary constitutional doctrine at face value, three basic principles bear on this allocation. The first principle concerns the children themselves, and the notion that as individuals they have constitutional rights. The Supreme Court declared in IN RE GAULT (1967), the seminal children's rights case, "whatever may be their precise impact, neither the FOURTEENTH AMENDMENT nor the BILL OF RIGHTS is for adults alone."

The second principle concerns parents and the notion that parents have primary authority over the child. Children are part of families, and our traditions emphasize the primacy of the parental role in child-rearing. The rights of children cannot be defined without reference to their parents. The Court has suggested that parental authority also has a constitutional dimension: the state may not intrude too deeply into the parent–child relationship. Drawing on this principle, the Court held in WISCONSIN V. YODER (1972) that Wisconsin could not compel children to attend public schools when their old-order Amish parents believed that public schooling interfered with their raising of their children as their religion dictates. Nor may a state require all children to attend public school when there are private schools that meet legitimate regulatory standards.

The third principle concerns the state. It suggests that the state, in the exercise of its *parens patriae* power, has a special responsibility to protect children, even from their parents. The state's interest in protecting children has frequently been characterized as "compelling" and has been drawn on to justify a variety of child protective measures that constrain the liberty of parents and children alike. "Parents may be free," declared the Supreme Court in PRINCE V. MASSACHUSETTS (1944), "to become martyrs themselves. But it does not follow that they are free, under free and identical circumstances, to make martyrs of their children before they reach the age of full and legal discretion when they can make that choice for themselves."

Any one of these three principles, if taken very far, cuts deeply into the others. For example, to the extent that children, as individuals, are given autonomy rights, limits are necessarily imposed on parental rights to control their behavior or socialization. Recognition of child autonomy also limits the state's right to constrain a child's conduct in circumstances where adult conduct could not be similarly constrained. Some rights of child autonomy would disable the state from having special protective legislation for children. Broad interpretation of the state's *parens patriae* power to intervene to protect children necessarily will diminish both the parental role in child-rearing and the child's role in decision making. Similarly, an expansive interpretation of parents' rights to control and govern their children necessarily limits the state's ability to protect children, or to ensure child autonomy.

The Supreme Court's decisions concerning children's rights evidence these tensions. For example, the *Tinker* decision, emphasizing child autonomy, declared that children have First Amendment rights to engage in peaceful political protest within the schools. On the other hand, the *Ginsberg* decision, emphasizing state protection of children, determined that the state could criminally punish the sale to minors of sexually explicit materials that an adult would have a constitutional right to receive. (See OBSCENITY.) In its decisions concerning juvenile delinquency proceedings, the Court has extended a broad range of procedural rights to minors, and yet also determined that a juvenile court need not provide an accused young person with TRIAL BY JURY. In PARHAM V. J. R. (1979) the Court held that due process does not require a hearing before the commitment of a minor by a parent to a state mental hospital. Similarly, although the *Pierce* and *Yoder* opinions emphasized the primacy of the parental role in child-rearing, *Prince,* in enforcing a child labor law, emphasized the state's *parens patriae* obligation to protect children.

The Supreme Court's decisions involving the abortion rights of minors suggest that a state may not give parents an absolute "veto" over a pregnant minor's decision to have an abortion (PLANNED PARENTHOOD OF CENTRAL MISSOURI V. DANFORTH, 1976), but may require parental notification, at least for younger pregnant teenagers still living at home (*H. L. v. Matheson,* 1981). And in *Planned Parenthood v. Ashcroft* (1983) the Court upheld a state law requiring either parental or judicial consent to a minor's abortion; under the law the court must approve the abortion if the minor is sufficiently mature to make the abortion decision, or, alternatively, if the abortion is in the minor's best interests.

In sum, the Constitution has not been interpreted to prohibit the state from treating children differently from adults. Because children often lack adult capacity and maturity and need protection, and because of the special relationship of children to their families, giving children the same rights and obligations as adults would often do them a substantial disservice. To assume adult roles, children need to be socialized. The Constitution does not prohibit the use of state or parental coercion in this task of socialization. But, because ours is a society where adults are socialized for autonomous choice, there are necessarily some limits, even for children. In determining the contour of children's constitutional rights, then, the Supreme Court appears to be seeking to recognize the moral autonomy of children as individuals without abandoning children to their rights.

ROBERT H. MNOOKIN

Bibliography

HAFEN, BRUCE C. 1976 Children's Liberation and the New Egalitarianism: Some Reservations about Abandoning Youth to Their "Rights." *Brigham Young University Law Review* 1976:605–658.

MNOOKIN, ROBERT H. 1978 *Child, Family and State.* Boston: Little, Brown.

———, ed. 1985 *In the Interest of Children.* New York: W. H. Freeman & Co.

TEITELBAUM, LEE E. 1980 Foreword: The Meaning of Rights of Children. *New Mexico Law Review* 10:235–253.

WALD, MICHAEL S. 1979 Children's Rights: A Framework for Analysis. *University of California, Davis, Law Review* 12:255–282.

YOUTH LAW CENTER 1982 Legal Rights of Children in the United States of America. *Columbia Human Rights Law Review* 13:675–743.

CHILLING EFFECT

Law is carried forward on a stream of language. Metaphor not only reflects the growth of constitutional law but nourishes it as well. Since the 1960s, when the WARREN COURT widened the domain of the FIRST AMENDMENT, Justices have frequently remarked on laws' "chilling effects" on the FREEDOM OF SPEECH. A statute tainted by VAGUENESS or OVERBREADTH, for example, restricts the freedom of expression not only by directly subjecting people to the laws' sanctions but also by threatening others. Because the very existence of such a law may induce self-censorship when the reach of the law is uncertain, the law may be held INVALID ON ITS FACE. The assumed causal connection between vague legislation and self-censorship was made by the Supreme Court as early as HERNDON V. LOWRY (1937); half a century later, circulating the coinage of Justice FELIX FRANKFURTER, lawyers and judges express similar assumptions in the language of chilling effects.

The assumption plainly makes more sense in some cases than it does in others. For a law's uncertainty actually to chill speech, the would-be speaker must be conscious of the uncertainty. Yet few of us go about our day-to-day business with the statute book in hand. A statute forbidding insulting language may be vague, but its uncertainty is unlikely to have any actual chilling effect on speech in face-to-face street encounters. Yet a court striking that law down—even in application to one whose insults fit the Supreme Court's narrow definition of FIGHTING WORDS—is apt to speak of the law's chilling effects.

For chilling effects that are real rather than assumed, we must look to institutional speakers—publishers, broadcasters, advertisers, political parties, groups promoting causes—who regularly inquire into the letter of the law and its interpretation by the courts. Magazine editors, for example, routinely seek legal counsel about defamation. Here the uncertainty of the law's reach does not lie in any statutory language, for the law of libel and slander is largely the product of COMMON LAW judges. It was a concern for chilling effects, however, that led three concurring Justices in NEW YORK TIMES V. SULLIVAN (1964) to advocate an absolute rule protecting the press against damages for the libel of a public official. The majority's principle in the case, which would allow damages when a newspaper defames an official knowing that its statement is false, or in reckless disregard of its truth or falsity, may, indeed, chill the press. Even slight doubt about information may make an editor hesitate to publish it, for fear that it may turn out to be false—and that a jury years later will decide it was published recklessly. The concern is not to protect false information, but that doubtful editors will play it safe, suppressing information that is true.

Conversely, when the Justices are persuaded that the law's threat will not have the effect of chilling speech, they are disinclined to use the overbreadth doctrine. A prominent modern example is the treatment of COMMERCIAL SPEECH. Because advertising is profitable, and advertisers seem unlikely to be chilled by laws regulating advertising, such laws are not subject to challenge for overbreadth.

The worry, when a court discusses chilling effects, is that a law's uncertainty will cause potential speakers to censor themselves. Thus, an overly broad law is subject to constitutional challenge even by one whose own speech would be punishable under a law focused narrowly on speech lying outside First Amendment protection. The defendant in court stands as a surrogate for others whose speech would be constitutionally protected—but who have been afraid to speak, and thus have not been prosecuted, and cannot themselves challenge the law. Whether or not this technique amounts to a dilution of the jurisdictional requirements of STANDING or RIPENESS, it allows courts to defend against the chilling effects of unconstitutional statutes that would otherwise elude their scrutiny.

KENNETH L. KARST

Bibliography

AMSTERDAM, ANTHONY G. 1960 The Void-for-Vagueness Doctrine in the Supreme Court. *University of Pennsylvania Law Review* 109:67–116.

NOTE 1970 The First Amendment Overbreadth Doctrine. *Harvard Law Review* 83:844–927.

SCHAUER, FREDERICK 1978 Fear, Risk and the First Amendment: Unraveling the "Chilling Effect." *Boston University Law Review* 5:685–732.

CHIMEL v. CALIFORNIA
395 U.S. 752 (1969)

In *Chimel* the Supreme Court considerably narrowed the prevailing scope of SEARCH INCIDENT TO ARREST, by limiting the search to the person of the arrestee and his immediate environs. The Court thus ended a divisive, decades-long debate on the subject.

The principle that officers executing a valid arrest may simultaneously search the arrestee for concealed weapons or EVIDENCE has never been challenged; it is rooted in COMMON LAW, and was recognized by the Court in WEEKS V. UNITED STATES (1914) as an emergency exception to the FOURTH AMENDMENT's warrant requirement. That the search may extend beyond the person to the premises in which the arrest is made was recognized in AGNELLO V. UNITED STATES (1925). The extension, too, has never been challenged; it seems sensible to permit officers to eliminate the possibility of a suspect's seizing a gun or destroying evidence within his reach though not on his person. The permissible scope of a warrantless search of the premises has, however, embroiled the Court in controversy.

Some Justices would have allowed a search of the entire place, arguing that after an arrest, even an extensive search is only a minor additional invasion of privacy. The opposing camp, led by Justice FELIX FRANKFURTER, condemned such wholesale rummaging: to allow a search incident to arrest to extend beyond the need that justified it would swallow up the rule requiring a search warrant save in EXIGENT CIRCUMSTANCES. The latter view finally prevailed in *Chimel,* when the Court ruled that the search must be limited to the arrestee's person and "the area from which he might gain possession of a weapon or destructible evidence." It may not extend into any room other than the one in which the arrest is made, and even "desk drawers or other closed or concealed areas in that room itself" are off-limits to the officers if the suspect cannot gain access to them.

JACOB W. LANDYNSKI

CHINESE EXCLUSION ACT
22 Stat. 58 (1882)

Although Chinese IMMIGRATION to California probably raised both wages and living standards of white laborers, economic, political, and cultural arguments were adduced against the foreigners. Assimilation was said to be impossible: the Chinese were gamblers, opium smokers, and generally inferior. Anti-Chinese feeling became the hub for many political issues, and agitation for legislation increased. Senator John Miller of California contended that failure to enact exclusion would "empty the teeming, seething slave pens of China upon the soil of California." Although most of the nation was indifferent, opposition to exclusion was weak and disorganized; Congress thus passed its first exclusion law in 1882. The act prohibited Chinese laborers from entering the United States for ten years, although resident ALIENS might return after a temporary absence. Nonlaboring Chinese would be admitted only upon presentation of a certificate from the Chinese government attesting their right to come. Other sections provided for deportation of illegal immigrants and prohibited state or federal courts from admitting Chinese to CITIZENSHIP. Further exclusion acts or amendments passed Congress—eleven by 1902. The most important of these were the Scott Act of 1888 prohibiting the return of any departing Chinese and the Geary Act of 1892 which extended the 1882 law. (See CHAE CHAN PING V. UNITED STATES, 1889.)

DAVID GORDON

CHINESE EXCLUSION CASE

See: *Chae Chan Ping v. United States*

CHIPMAN, NATHANIEL
(1752–1843)

Federalist jurist and statesman Nathaniel Chipman was instrumental in securing Vermont's admission to the Union in 1791 as the first state with no history as a separate British colony. An ally and correspondent of ALEXANDER HAMILTON, Chipman was three times chief justice of Vermont and also the first federal judge in the Vermont district. He was professor of law at

Middlebury College (1816–1843) and author of *Principles of Government* (1793; revised edition 1833).

DENNIS J. MAHONEY

CHISHOLM v. GEORGIA
2 Dallas 419 (1793)

The first constitutional law case decided by the Supreme Court, *Chisholm* provoked opposition so severe that the ELEVENTH AMENDMENT was adopted to supersede its ruling that a state could be sued without its consent by a citizen of another state. Article III of the Constitution extended the JUDICIAL POWER OF THE UNITED STATES to all controversies "between a State and citizens of another State" and provided that the Supreme Court should have ORIGINAL JURISDICTION in all cases in which a state should be a party. During the ratification controversy, anti-Federalists, jealous of state prerogatives and suspicious about the consolidating effects of the proposed union, had warned that Article III would abolish state sovereignty. Ratificationists, including JOHN MARSHALL, JAMES MADISON, and ALEXANDER HAMILTON (*e.g.*, THE FEDERALIST #81) had argued that the clause intended to cover only suits in which a state had given its sovereign consent to being sued or had instituted the suit. Here, however, with Justice JAMES IREDELL alone dissenting, the Justices in SERIATIM OPINIONS held that the states by ratifying the Constitution had agreed to be amenable to the judicial power of the United States and in that respect had abandoned their SOVEREIGNTY.

The case arose when Chisholm, a South Carolinian executor of the estate of a Tory whose lands Georgia had confiscated during the Revolution, sued Georgia for restitution. The state remonstrated against the Court's taking jurisdiction of the case and refused to argue on the merits. The Justices, confronted by a question of sovereignty, discoursed on the nature of the Union, giving the case historical importance. Iredell, stressing the sovereignty of the states respecting reserved powers, believed that no sovereign state could be sued without its consent unless Congress so authorized. Chief Justice JOHN JAY and Justice JAMES WILSON, delivering the most elaborate opinions against Georgia, announced for the first time from the bench the ultra-nationalistic doctrine that the people of the United States, rather than the states or people thereof, had formed the Union and were the ultimate sovereigns. From this view, the suability of the states was compatible with their reserved sovereignty, and the clause in Article III neither excluded suits by outside citizens nor required state consent.

The decision, which seemed to open the treasuries of the states to suits by Tories and other creditors, stirred widespread indignation that crossed sectional and party lines. A special session of the Massachusetts legislature recommended an amendment that would prevent the states from being answerable in the federal courts to suits by individuals. Virginia, taking the same action, condemned the Court for a decision dangerous to the sovereignty of the states. The Georgia Assembly would have defied the decision by a bill providing that any United States officer attempting to enforce it should "suffer death, without benefit of clergy, by being hanged." Though the state senate did not pass the bill, Georgia remained defiant. Congress too opposed the decision and finally agreed on a remedy for it that took the form of the Eleventh Amendment.

LEONARD W. LEVY

Bibliography

MATHIS, DOYLE 1967 Chisholm v. Georgia: Background and Settlement. *Journal of American History* 54:19–29.

CHOATE, JOSEPH H.
(1832–1917)

A highly conservative lawyer and leader of the American bar, Joseph Hodges Choate often appeared before the Supreme Court in defense of property interests and removed from the concerns of a populace he inimitably referred to as the "Great Unwashed." In MUGLER V. KANSAS (1887), Choate sought in vain to convince the Court to embrace laissez-faire, but he succeeded in wresting, in OBITER DICTUM, future judicial examination of the reasonableness of exercises of STATE POLICE POWER. Choate unequivocally endorsed constitutional rights in private property, a position the Court would soon partly accept. Indeed, his most famous victory came in POLLOCK V. FARMERS' LOAN & TRUST COMPANY (1895), which he argued with WILLIAM GUTHRIE. Labeling the income tax "communistic" and heaping reactionary invective upon his opponent, JAMES COOLIDGE CARTER, Choate constructed a framework for the Court's decision; he attacked the tax as a DIRECT TAX on income from real property, history and judicial precedent to the contrary.

DAVID GORDON

Bibliography

HICKS, FREDERICK C. 1931 Joseph Hodges Choate. *Dictionary of American Biography*, Vol. 4. New York: Scribner's.

CHOICE OF LAW

In the system of American FEDERALISM, some transactions and phenomena are governed by supreme federal law and others by state law. In the latter situations, multistate transactions frequently raise the question which state's law is to be applied. "Choice of law" refers to the process of making this determination. Choice of law may usefully be viewed as an issue of distribution of legislative or lawmaking powers "horizontally" among the states in those areas not governed by overriding federal law.

A basic principle of choice of law theory under the Constitution is that determination of the allocation of lawmaking power among the states in such circumstances is, itself, an issue of state law. Each state has its own law on choice of law, which may differ from the choice of law doctrines of other states and which is applied in actions brought in that state both in state courts and in DIVERSITY JURISDICTION cases in federal courts. Thus the outcome of litigation involving a multistate transaction may in theory be determined by the choice of the forum in which the suit is brought. The basic principle might have been the contrary—that is, that conflicts of state laws within the federal system should be resolved by a comprehensive supreme federal law of choice of law, binding on the states. Such a body of national conflict of laws doctrine might have been derived from the FULL FAITH AND CREDIT clause, the COMMERCE CLAUSE, or the DUE PROCESS clause of the FOURTEENTH AMENDMENT. Alternatively, supreme federal choice of law doctrine might have been developed as FEDERAL COMMON LAW pertaining to the mutual relationships among the states in the federal union. Or Congress, under various ENUMERATED POWERS, might have enacted federal choice of law principles. None of these courses has been followed; the law of choice of law in the federal system has not developed, judicially or legislatively, as supreme federal law. The states remain the primary determiners of the legal aspects of their mutual relationships within the federal union.

A state's law of choice of law, like all state law, is subject to constitutional limitations. Two such provisions have occasionally been applied so as to limit state choice of law principles, but in general these are not significant limitations.

In an occasional early case the Supreme Court held that the application of the forum's own law to a multistate transaction violated due process, even though the forum state did have a legitimate interest in having its law prevail. Under more recent doctrine there would be no due process violation in such circumstances. The modern principle, enunciated in *Allstate Insurance Co. v. Hague* (1981), is that "for a State's substantive law to be selected in a constitutionally permissible manner, that State must have a significant contact or significant aggregation of contacts, creating state interests, such that choice of its law is neither arbitrary nor fundamentally unfair." The due process clause can also limit a state's choice of law doctrine where there would be unfair surprise to a litigant in the choice of law otherwise proposed to be made.

The Court also has occasionally held that the full faith and credit clause requires a state to apply the law of another state even though the forum state does have a legitimate interest in applying its own law. (Thus in a case of claims for benefits against a fraternal benefit association, the Court held that a national interest in having a single uniform law determine the mutual rights and obligations of members required all states to apply the law of the place where the association was incorporated.) In general, however, the full faith and credit clause does not require that a forum state apply the law of another state unless it would violate due process for the forum to apply its own law.

Other provisions of the Constitution are potentially applicable as limitations on state choice of law doctrine. The commerce clause might be the basis for channeling state choice of law principles regarding multistate commercial transactions. The EQUAL PROTECTION clause and the PRIVILEGES AND IMMUNITIES clause of Article IV might be held to limit distinctions made in state choice of law doctrine based upon the residence or domicile of parties to a transaction. These constitutional provisions have not been so developed.

HAROLD W. HOROWITZ

Bibliography

Symposium: Choice-of-Law Theory after *Allstate Insurance Co. v. Hague* 1981 *Hofstra Law Review* 10:1–211.

Symposium: Choice of Law 1981 *U. C. Davis Law Review* 14:837–917.

CHURCH OF JESUS CHRIST OF LATTER DAY SAINTS v. UNITED STATES
136 U.S. 1 (1890)

The Mormon Church was granted a charter of incorporation in February 1851 by the so-called State of Deseret; later an act of the territorial legislature of Utah confirmed the charter. In 1887 Congress, having plenary power over the TERRITORIES, repealed the charter and directed the seizure and disposal of church property.

Justice JOSEPH P. BRADLEY wrote for the Court. He held that the power of Congress over the territories was sufficient to repeal an act of incorporation. He also held that once the Mormon Church became a defunct CORPORATION, Congress had power to reassign its property to legitimate religious and charitable uses, as near as practicable to those intended by the original donors. The claim of RELIGIOUS FREEDOM could not immunize the Mormon Church against the congressional conclusion that, because of its sponsorship of polygamy, it was an undesirable legal entity.

Chief Justice MELVILLE WESTON FULLER dissented, joined by Justice STEPHEN J. FIELD and Justice L. Q. C. LAMAR. Fuller objected to according Congress such sweeping power over property.

RICHARD E. MORGAN

CIRCUIT COURTS

The JUDICIARY ACT OF 1789 fashioned a decentralized circuit court system. The boundaries of the three circuits coincided with the boundaries of the states they encompassed, a practice that opened them to state and sectional political influences and legal practices. The act assigned two Supreme Court Justices to each circuit to hold court along with a district judge in the state where the circuit court met. (After 1794, a single Justice and a district judge were a quorum.) The circuit-riding provision brought federal authority and national political views to the new and distant states, but also compelled the Justices to imbibe local political sentiments and legal practices.

For a century questions about the administrative efficiency, constitutional roles, and political responsibilities of these courts provoked heated debate. In the JUDICIARY ACT OF 1801, Federalists sought to replace the Justices with an independent six-person circuit court judiciary, but one year later the new Jeffersonian Republican majority in Congress eliminated the circuit judgeships and restored the Justices to circuit duties, although they left the number of circuits at six. (See JUDICIARY ACTS OF 1802.) Subsequent territorial expansion prompted the addition of new circuits and new Justices until both reached nine in the Judiciary Act of 1837. Slave state interests opposed further expansion because they feared the loss of their five-to-four majority on the high court. Congress in 1855 did create a special circuit court and judgeship for the Northern District of California to expedite land litigation.

Significant structural and jurisdictional changes accompanied the Civil War and Reconstruction. The Judiciary Act of 1869 established a separate circuit court judiciary and assigned one judge to each of the nine new circuits that stretched from coast to coast. Justices retained circuit-riding duties although the 1869 act and subsequent legislation required less frequent attendance.

Historically, these courts had exercised ORIGINAL and APPELLATE JURISDICTION in cases involving the criminal law of the United States, in other areas where particular statutes granted jurisdiction, and in cases resting on diversity of citizenship. The Judiciary Act of 1869 strengthened the appellate responsibilities of the circuit courts by denying litigants access to the Supreme Court unless the amount in controversy exceeded $5,000. The Jurisdiction and Removal Act of 1875 established a general FEDERAL QUESTION JURISDICTION and made it possible for, among others, interstate CORPORATIONS to seek the friendly forum of the federal as opposed to the state courts. The 1875 measure also transferred some of the original jurisdiction of the circuit courts to the district courts. However, because the circuit courts were given increased appellate responsibilities, along with only modest adjustments in staffing, their dockets became congested. The resulting delay in appeals, combined with similar congestion in the Supreme Court, persuaded Congress in 1891 to establish the Circuit Courts of Appeals which became the nation's principal intermediate federal appellate courts. (See CIRCUIT COURTS OF APPEALS ACT.) Although the old circuit courts became anachronisms, Congress delayed abolishing them until 1911.

Throughout the nineteenth century Supreme Court Justices held ambivalent attitudes toward circuit duty. The Justices complained about the rigors of circuit travel and the loss of time from responsibilities in the nation's capital, but most of them recognized that circuit judging offered a unique constitutional forum free from the immediate scrutiny of their brethren on the Court. "It is only as a Circuit Judge that the Chief Justice or any other Justice of the Supreme Court has, individually, any considerable power," Chief Justice SALMON P. CHASE observed in 1868.

Circuit court judges contributed to the nationalization of American law and the economy. Justice JOSEPH STORY, in the First Circuit, for example, broadly defined the federal ADMIRALTY AND MARITIME JURISDICTION. In perhaps the most important circuit court decision of the nineteenth century, Story held, in *De Lovio v. Boit* (1815), that this jurisdiction extended to all maritime contracts, including insurance policies, and to all torts and injuries committed on the high seas and in ports and harbors within the ebb and flow of the tide. This decision, coupled with Story's opinion eight years later in *Chamberlain v. Chandler* (1823), expanded federal control over admiralty and maritime-related economic activity and added certainty to contracts involving shipping and commerce.

The circuit courts extended national constitutional protection to property, contract, and corporate rights. Justice WILLIAM PATERSON's 1795 decision on circuit in VAN HORNE'S LESSEE V. DORRANCE was the first significant statement in the federal courts on behalf of VESTED RIGHTS. But in 1830 Justice HENRY BALDWIN anticipated by seven years the PUBLIC USE doctrine later embraced by the Supreme Court. In *Bonaparte v. Camden & A. R. Co.* he held that state legislatures could take private property only for public use, and that creation of a monopoly by a public charter voided its public nature. As new forms of corporate property emerged in the post-Civil War era, the circuit courts offered protection through the CONTRACT CLAUSE. In the early and frequently cited case of *Gray v. Davis* (1871) a circuit court held, and the Supreme Court subsequently affirmed, that a legislative act incorporating a railroad constituted a contract between the state and the company, and a state constitutional provision annulling that charter violated the contract clause.

The circuit courts' most dramatic nationalizing role involved commercial jurisprudence. Through their DIVERSITY JURISDICTION the circuit courts used SWIFT V. TYSON (1842) to build a FEDERAL COMMON LAW of commerce, thus encouraging business flexibility, facilitating investment security, and reducing costs to corporations. After the Civil War these courts eased limitations on the formation and operation of corporations in foreign states (*In Re Spain*, 1891), supported bondholders' rights, allowed forum shopping (*Osgood v. The Chicago, Danville, and Vincennes R. R. Co.*, 1875), and favored employers in fellow-servant liability cases.

Ambivalence, contradiction, and frustration typified circuit court decisions involving civil and political rights. In 1823 Justice BUSHROD WASHINGTON, in CORFIELD V. CORYELL, held that the PRIVILEGES AND IMMUNITIES clause guaranteed equal treatment of out-of-state citizens as to those privileges and immunities that belonged of right to citizens of all free governments, and which had at all times been enjoyed by citizens of the several states. After 1866 some circuit judges attempted to expand this narrow interpretation. Justice JOSEPH P. BRADLEY held, in *Live-Stock Dealers' & Butchers' Ass'n v. Crescent City Live-Stock Landing & Slaughter-House Co.* (1870), that the FOURTEENTH AMENDMENT protected the privileges and immunities of whites and blacks as national citizens against STATE ACTION. In 1871 the Circuit Court for the Southern District of Alabama, in *United States v. Hall,* decided that under the Fourteenth Amendment Congress had the power to protect by appropriate legislation all rights in the first eight amendments. And in *Ho Ah Kow v. Nunan* (1879) Justice STEPHEN J. FIELD struck down as CRUEL AND UNUSUAL PUNISHMENT, based on the Eighth Amendment and the EQUAL PROTECTION clause of the Fourteenth Amendment, a San Francisco ordinance that required Chinese prisoners to have their hair cut to a length of one inch from their scalps.

These attempts to nationalize civil rights had little immediate impact. The Supreme Court in 1873 rejected Bradley's reading of the Fourteenth Amendment, and in 1871 the Circuit Court for the District of South Carolina in *United States v. Crosby* concluded that the right of a person to be secure in his or her home was not a right, privilege, or immunity granted by the Constitution. Neither the Supreme Court nor any other circuit court adopted the theory of congressional power to enforce the Fourteenth Amendment set forth in *Hall.* Justice Field's *Nunan* opinion was most frequently cited in dissenting rather than majority opinions.

Political rights under the FIFTEENTH AMENDMENT fared only slightly better. In *United States v. Given* (1873) the Circuit Court for the District of Delaware held that the Fifteenth Amendment did not limit congressional action to cases where states had denied or abridged the right to vote by legislation. In the same year, however, Justice WARD HUNT, in *United States v. Anthony,* concluded that the right or privilege of voting arose under state constitutions and that the states might restrict it to males.

Despite a regional structure and diverse personnel, these circuit courts placed national over state interests, reinforced the supremacy of federal power, promoted national economic development, and enhanced the position of interstate corporations. However, in matters of civil and political rights they not only disagreed about the scope of federal powers but also confronted a Supreme Court wedded to a traditional state-centered foundation for these rights.

KERMIT L. HALL

Bibliography

FRANKFURTER, FELIX and LANDIS, JAMES M. 1927 *The Business of the Supreme Court: A Study in the Federal Judicial System.* Pages 3–86. New York: Macmillan.

HALL, KERMIT L. 1975 The Civil War Era as a Crucible for Nationalizing the Lower Federal Courts. *Prologue: The Journal of the National Archives* 7:177–186.

SWISHER, CARL B. 1974 *The Taney Period, 1836–1864.* Volume IV of *The Oliver Wendell Holmes Devise History of the Supreme Court of the United States.* Pages 248–292. New York: Macmillan.

CIRCUIT COURTS OF APPEALS ACT
26 Stat. 826 (1891)

The first substantial revision of the federal court system since its formation (except for the abortive JUDICIARY ACT OF 1801), this act established a badly needed level of courts just below the Supreme Court: the UNITED STATES COURTS OF APPEALS. Senator WILLIAM EVARTS led the reform movement to relieve pressure on the Supreme Court docket by providing intermediate appellate review for most district and circuit court decisions. By keeping the CIRCUIT COURTS but abolishing their APPELLATE JURISDICTION, Congress maintained two courts with substantially similar JURISDICTION, causing confusion until the circuit courts were abolished in the JUDICIAL CODE of 1911. The act established direct Supreme Court review, bypassing the courts of appeals, in cases of "infamous" crimes (an ill-considered description that actually increased the Court's business and had to be deleted in 1897), and introduced the principle of discretionary Supreme Court review by WRIT OF CERTIORARI.

The basic structure of today's system of appellate review of federal court decisions remains as it was established in the 1891 Act.

DAVID GORDON

Bibliography

FRANKFURTER, FELIX AND LANDIS, JAMES M. 1927 *The Business of the Supreme Court.* New York: Macmillan.

CITIES AND THE CONSTITUTION

Cities, unlike states, are not mentioned in the Constitution. Many other important collective institutions in our society, such as CORPORATIONS, are not mentioned in the Constitution either. In its effort to determine the constitutional status of cities, the Supreme Court has had to decide whether to treat cities like states or like corporations. In fact, the Court has been required to answer two separate questions concerning the constitutional status of cities. First, do cities, like private corporations, have rights that are protected from governmental power by the Constitution? Second, do cities, like states, exercise governmental power which is limited by the Constitution?

At the time the Constitution was written and adopted, there was no legal distinction between cities and other corporations. Neither WILLIAM BLACKSTONE's *Commentaries,* published the decade before the CONSTITUTIONAL CONVENTION OF 1787, nor the first treatise on corporations, published by Stuart Kyd in 1793, categorized corporations in a way that would distinguish the Corporation of the City of New York, for example, from manufacturing and commercial concerns or from universities. Each of these entities was considered a lay corporation, formed by its members and given legal status by a grant of power from the state. The ability of these corporations to pursue the purposes for which their charter was granted was a right that needed protection from governmental power. At the same time, however, all corporations wielded power delegated to them by the state and, therefore, posed a danger of abuse that required subjection to popular control.

The Supreme Court's first important attempt to settle the constitutional status of corporations created a distinction between cities and other corporations. In DARTMOUTH COLLEGE V. WOODWARD (1819) Justice JOSEPH STORY articulated a public/private distinction for American corporations, classifying cities with states and distinguishing them from private corporations. "Public corporations," he said, "are generally esteemed such as exist for public political purposes only, such as towns, cities, parishes, and counties; and in many respects they are so, although they involve some private interests; but strictly speaking, public corporations are such only as founded by the government for public purposes, where the whole interests belong also to the government."

When considering whether cities should have rights that protect them against state control, the Supreme Court has largely accepted Justice Story's proposition that the cities' whole interest belongs to the government; it has treated cities as if they were the state itself. At least insofar as they are considered "public" entities, cities, unlike private corporations, have virtually no constitutional protection against

STATE ACTION. The Supreme Court dramatically summarized the nature of state power over cities in *Hunter v. Pittsburg* (1907):

> Municipal corporations are political subdivisions of the State created as convenient agencies for exercising such of the governmental powers of the State as may be entrusted to them. . . . The State, therefore, at its pleasure may modify or withdraw all such powers, may take without compensation such property, hold it itself, or vest it in other agencies, expand or contract the territorial area, unite the whole or part with another municipality, repeal the charter and destroy the corporation. . . . In all these respects the State is supreme, and its legislative body, conforming its actions to the state constitution, may do as it will, unrestrained by any provision of the Constitution of the United States.

The Court in *Hunter* indicated, however, that there might be a limit to state power over cities, one it articulated in terms of a public/private distinction within the concept of a city. To some extent, cities act like private corporations, and this private aspect of city government, the Court said, could receive the same constitutional protection as other private interests. Even Justice Story had recognized in *Dartmouth College* that cities are not purely public entities but "involve some private interests" as well. But the proposition that cities are entitled to protection from state power under the Constitution in their "proprietary" (as contrasted to their "governmental") capacities has not yielded them much constitutional protection. The Supreme Court has never struck down a state statute on the grounds that it invaded such a private sphere. Indeed, in *Trenton v. New Jersey* (1923) Justice PIERCE BUTLER, noting that such a sphere could not readily be defined, expressed doubt whether there was a private sphere that limited the states' power over their own municipalities.

Whatever limited protection the Court has given cities under the Constitution has involved their public and not their private capacities. In GOMILLION V. LIGHTFOOT (1960) the Court held that the FIFTEENTH AMENDMENT restricted the state's ability to define the boundaries of its cities in a way that infringed on its citizens' VOTING RIGHTS; the Court narrowed the extravagant description of state power over cities in *Hunter* by construing the Court's language in that case to be applicable only to the particular constitutional provisions considered there. But the Court has not subsequently expanded on its distinction between the Fifteenth Amendment and other constitutional provisions, such as the FOURTEENTH AMENDMENT and the contract clause, as vehicles for limiting state power over cities. No subsequent case has given cities constitutional protection against state power.

From 1976 to 1985, during the short life of NATIONAL LEAGUE OF CITIES V. USERY (1976), the Supreme Court articulated the most expansive constitutional protection ever given cities, again a protection for their public and not their private activities. By treating them as if they were states the Court limited the power of the federal government to regulate cities; it held that cities, like states, were immunized from federal control under the TENTH AMENDMENT insofar as federal interference "directly impaired their ability to structure integral operations in areas of traditional governmental functions." In GARCIA V. SAN ANTONIO METROPOLITAN TRANSIT AUTHORITY (1985), however, *National League of Cities* was overruled. One reason for OVERRULING *National League of Cities,* the Court said, was that there was no practical way to make a public/private distinction between "traditional governmental functions" and other state and city functions. Hence, the Court reasoned, there was no principled basis for choosing some areas of state or city activity over others to be immune from federal control as a constitutional matter.

There is a second question concerning the constitutional status of cities: to what extent are cities like states, and, therefore, subject to those constitutional provisions that affect the power of states? The Supreme Court's answer to this question has been complex.

For some purposes, the Court has treated cities like states. City power is like state power, for example, in that it is equally limited by the DUE PROCESS and EQUAL PROTECTION clauses of the Fourteenth Amendment and by the dormant commerce clause. On the other hand, the Court has held that cities are not like states for purposes of the ELEVENTH AMENDMENT (dealing with states' immunity from suits in federal court). In a number of nonconstitutional cases the Supreme Court has also sought to distinguish cities from states. "We are a nation not of city-states but of States," the Court said in *Community Communications Co. v. City of Boulder* (1982), holding cities, like private corporations but unlike states, liable to federal antitrust laws.

Indeed, sometimes the Court has treated cities in a way that distinguishes them from both states and corporations. In MONELL V. DEPARTMENT OF SOCIAL SERVICES (1978) the Supreme Court interpreted SECTION 1983 OF TITLE 42 OF THE UNITED STATES CODE to allow damage suits against cities when they commit constitutional violations. City action is like state action in that cities are subject to constitutional limitations applicable to states. But states, unlike cities, have immunities under the Eleventh Amendment against suits in federal court to enforce these constitutional limitations. Thus, under *Monell,* cities are liable under section 1983 for constitutional violations in situations in which neither the states (because of the Eleventh Amendment) nor private corporations (because their power is not subject to constitutional limitations) would be liable.

Finally, at times cities are considered like states and private corporations simultaneously. Both cities and states can act in the marketplace just as private corporations do. Thus in *White v. Massachusetts Council of Construction Employers* (1983) the Supreme Court held that the commerce clause does not restrict a city's ability to require its contractors to hire city residents as long as it is acting as a market participant and not as a market regulator. The Court thus extended to cities the immunity from commerce clause restrictions that it had previously provided states when they act as market participants. The practical effect of the *White* case, however, is limited. In *United Building & Construction Trades Council v. Camden* (1984) the Court held that the privileges and immunities clause, unlike the commerce clause, limited a city's ability to require its contractors to hire city residents whether or not it acts as a market participant. In *Camden* the Court treated cities like states but distinguished them from corporations; the power of states and cities, unlike that of corporations, is restrained by the privileges and immunities clause of the Constitution.

The cities' historic link with corporations and their assimilation in the nineteenth century to the status of states have given them a divided status under the Constitution. Although the predominant linkage has been between cities and states, there remain occasions when the prior linkage with corporations is emphasized. The Court's ability to conceptualize cities as either states or corporations (indeed, to conceptualize them as both simultaneously or as distinguishable from both) opens up a multitude of possibilities for the Court as it defines the relationship between cities and the Constitution in the future.

GERALD E. FRUG

Bibliography

CLARK, GORDON 1985 *Judges and the Cities: Interpreting Local Autonomy.* Chicago: University of Chicago Press.

FRUG, GERALD 1980 The City as a Legal Concept. *Harvard Law Review* 93:1059–1154.

HARTOG, HENDRIK 1983 *Public Property and Private Power: The Corporation of the City of New York in American Law, 1730–1870.* Chapel Hill: University of North Carolina Press.

MICHELMAN, FRANK 1977–1978 Political Markets and Community Self-Determination: Competing Judicial Models of Local Government Legitimacy *Indiana Law Journal* 53:145–206.

CITIZENSHIP
(Historical Development)

The concept of citizenship articulated during the American Revolution and adjusted to the special circumstances of an ethnically diverse federal republic in the nineteenth century developed from English theories of allegiance and of the subject's status. Enunciated most authoritatively by Sir EDWARD COKE in CALVIN'S CASE (1608), English law held that natural subject status involved a perpetual, immutable relationship of allegiance and protection between subject and king analogous to the bond between parent and child. All persons born within the king's allegiance gained this status by birth. Conquest or NATURALIZATION by Parliament could extend the status to the foreign-born, but subjects adopted in such a manner were by legal fiction considered bound by the same perpetual allegiance as the native-born. The doctrine "once a subject, always a subject" reflected Coke's emphasis on the natural origins of the subject–king relationship and militated against the emergence of concepts of voluntary membership and EXPATRIATION.

The appearance of new SOCIAL COMPACT ideas modified but did not entirely supersede traditional concepts. By the mid-eighteenth century, Lockean theorists derived subject status from the individual's consent to leave the state of nature and join with others to form a society. To such theorists the individual subject was bound by the majority and owed allegiance to the government established by that majority. Barring the dissolution of society itself or the consent of the majority, expressed through Parliament, individual subjects were still held to a perpetual allegiance.

Colonial conditions eroded these ideas. Colonial naturalization policies especially contributed to a subtle transformation of inherited attitudes. Provincial governments welcomed foreign-born settlers in order to promote population growth vital to physical security and economic prosperity. Offering political and economic rights in exchange for the ALIEN'S contribution to the general welfare of the community, the colonists underscored the contractual, consent-based aspects of membership that had been subordinated in English law to older notions of perpetual allegiance.

Imperial administrators, concerned to protect England's monopoly of colonial trade, declared in 1700 that colonial naturalization could confer subject status only within the confines of the admitting colony; although a parliamentary statute of 1740 established administrative procedures whereby a colonial court could vest an alien with a subject status valid throughout the empire, such actions merely reinforced the conclusion that the origins, extent, and effects of subject status were determined not by nature but by political and legal compacts.

When Americans declared independence in 1776 they initially relied on the traditional linkage of allegiance and protection to define citizenship in the new republican states. Congress's resolution of June 24, 1776, declared that all persons then resident in the colonies and deriving protection from the laws were members of and owed allegiance to those colonies. Lockean theory was also useful, for if each colony were considered a separate society merely changing its form of government, then loyalist minorities could still be considered subject to the will of patriot majorities. Yet forced allegiance clashed with the idea that all legitimate government required the free consent of the governed. Wartime TREASON prosecutions contributed to a gradual reformulation of the theory of citizenship that stressed the volitional character of allegiance. Employing a doctrine stated most clearly in the Pennsylvania case of *Respublica v. Chapman* (1781), American courts came to hold that citizenship must originate in an act of individual consent.

Republican citizenship required the consent of the community as well as of the individual, and legislators concerned with establishing naturalization policies concentrated on defining the proper qualifications for membership. This preoccupation obscured the ill-defined nature of the status itself. The Revolution had created a sense of community that transcended state boundaries; the ARTICLES OF CONFEDERATION implied that state citizenship carried with it rights in other states as well (Article IV). Framers of the United States Constitution perpetuated this ambiguity: section 2 of Article IV provided that "The citizens of each State shall be entitled to all PRIVILEGES AND IMMUNITIES of citizens in the several States." Questions concerning the nature and relationship of state and national citizenship would not be resolved until the Civil War.

The Revolutionary idea that citizenship began with the individual's consent extended logically to the idea of expatriation. Although some states acknowledged this principle, it raised delicate questions of federal relations after 1789. The problem appeared as early as 1795 in *Talbot v. Janson,* when the United States Supreme Court wrestled with the question whether a Virginia expatriation procedure could release a citizen from national as well as state allegiance. Unwilling to resolve that issue, the Court looked to Congress to provide a general policy of expatriation. Although the propriety of such a measure was discussed a number of times during the antebellum period, congressional action foundered on the same issue of federal relations. As long as the question of the primacy of state or United States citizenship remained open, the idea that citizenship rested on individual choice would be more valid for aliens seeking naturalization than for persons whose citizenship derived from birth.

The problematic character of dual state and national citizenship appeared in its most intractable form in disputes over the status of free blacks. Many northern states acknowledged free blacks as birthright citizens, though often at the cost of conceding that important political rights were not necessarily attached to that status. From the 1820s on, slave states increasingly resisted the contention that such citizenship carried constitutional guarantees of "privileges and immunities" in their own jurisdictions. ROGER B. TANEY's opinion in DRED SCOTT V. SANDFORD (1857) that national citizenship was restricted to white state citizens of 1789, persons naturalized by Congress, and their descendants alone marked the final effort, short of SECESSION, to restrict the scope of citizenship.

The FOURTEENTH AMENDMENT finally defined national citizenship as the product of naturalization or birth within the JURISDICTION of the United States, leaving state citizenship dependent upon residency. On July 27, 1868, Congress declared that the right of expatriation was a fundamental principle of American government, thus allowing persons born to citizenship the same right as aliens to choose their ultimate allegiance.

JAMES H. KETTNER

Bibliography

KETTNER, JAMES H. 1978 *The Development of American Citizenship, 1608–1870.* Chapel Hill: University of North Carolina Press.

ROCHE, JOHN P. 1949 *The Early Development of United States Citizenship.* Ithaca, N.Y.: Cornell University Press.

CITIZENSHIP
(Theory)

Article I, section B, of the Constitution authorizes Congress "to establish a uniform Rule of NATURALIZATION." The power afforded Congress in this spare textual authorization has long been interpreted as plenary, effectively insulating from constitutional challenge congressional decisions about whom to admit to the national community. The theory of national community expressed through this constitutional interpretation was summarily sketched by the Supreme Court nearly a century ago in *Nishimura Eiku v. United States* (1891): "It is an accepted maxim of international law, that every sovereign nation has the power, inherent in SOVEREIGNTY, and essential to self-preservation, to forbid the entrance of foreigners within its domain, or to admit them only in such cases and upon such conditions as it may see fit to prescribe."

This still regnant theory of sovereignty has become, for most people, entirely natural and unimposed. Its inchoate justification, articulated in abstract terms, does have a natural and necessary air: one can understand nations asserting an absolute right to decide whom to admit or to exclude as advancing the universal right to form communities and the right to keep them distinctive and stable. While nations have grown significantly more interconnected and while the world's creatures are one for some important purposes, the notion of protecting the right to form and maintain special communities within larger communities resonates with our understanding of how America became a nation. Still, even for one who believes in protecting the national community, a moral question remains: what constitutes membership in the political community to be protected?

In a strictly positive sense, the answer is that citizenship in this country has been conferred by birth (either in the United States or abroad to American parents) or by naturalization. Although only "a natural born Citizen" can be President, naturalized citizens are otherwise the formal equals of citizens by birth. Moreover, the Constitution extends many of its protections to "persons" or "people" so that ALIENS are protected in much the same way as citizens even before they are naturalized.

But the United States has been a national community not readily inclined to ask what constitutes membership in the political community—or perhaps more accurately, not genuinely curious about the answer or willing to give it constitutional significance. Congress has long presumed that those who currently share citizenship (citizens and, during most but not all historical periods, documented residents) constitute the community to be protected and maintained.

The judiciary, in turn, has long deferred to whatever Congress decides. This deference, while varying across the range of immigration law disputes, radically diverges from the political relationship between judiciary and legislature that informs most constitutional jurisprudence. Consider a range of congressional "membership" decisions and the corresponding judicial response: Exclusion decisions and procedures are treated as extraconstitutional; congressional power to classify aliens is effectively unconstrained by EQUAL PROTECTION values; DEPORTATION is treated as a civil and not a criminal proceeding, thereby denying certain constitutional protections expressly limited or interpreted to apply only to criminal proceedings; the power to detain remains unlimited by any coherent set of values, and is available effectively to imprison individuals and groups for long periods and under disreputable conditions; immigration judges remain intertwined with government agencies responsible for administering and enforcing immigration law. In so deferring to Congress, the judiciary either denies the constitutional relevance of the always amending character of the national community or indulges absolutely Congress's habitual response to what constitutes membership in the political community.

If together Congress and the courts "freed" us from being genuinely curious about ourselves, they were not without help in constructing this reality. It has been commonplace for many to deny that citizenship does or should play a central role in our political community. No less a figure in recent constitutional jurisprudence than ALEXANDER M. BICKEL insisted that citizenship "was a simple idea for a simple government"; others entirely ignored the question, as if a view on membership in the process of self-determination were not itself constitutive of the national community's very nature. But, of course, citizenship in the United States never has been a simple idea. Naturalization laws, implementing the FOURTEENTH Amendment, were not extended to persons of African descent until 1870; citizens of Mexican descent were deported in 1930 raids; citizens of Japanese descent were interned during World War II because of their ancestry; women citizens were not allowed to vote until 1920; Puerto Ricans and people of other conquered territories were afforded only second-class citizenship status. Yet the relationship of these and other events to our conception of United States citizenship has been far more often ignored than attended to, as if the denial of contradictory acts would somehow save the regnant theory of national community.

These efforts notwithstanding, the experience of community is beginning to challenge the prevailing constitutionalized attitude toward membership in the political community. The presence of millions of undocumented workers—sharing neighborhoods, burdens, and laws—has prompted intense and frequently conflicting responses to the general question of citizenship and its role in the political community. In PLYLER v. DOE (1982) the Supreme Court compelled the state of Texas to provide the children of undocumented workers with a free public education. At the same time, attention to the relationship of citizenship to the political community has led the Court to intensify its scrutiny of laws that deny documented residents access to certain occupations. State laws barring aliens from permanent civil service positions and from the practice of law and civil engineering have been struck down. But where the position is intimately related to the process of democratic self-government (the so-called political function exception), the Court has upheld laws requiring police, public teachers, and probation officers to be citizens.

What this communitarian challenge foreshadows defies facile forecasting; a theory so long dominant as ours toward community membership and sovereignty resists predictable or simple change. Still, in its unwillingness to be silenced, in its refusal to accept uncritically the regnant theory, today's challenge focuses attention on our history, and on the relationship of work to full political life. At least in this sense, there is the hope that we will no longer blithely disregard the values formally expressed in our vision of citizenship. After all, whom we acknowledge as full members of the political community tells us much about who we are and why we remain together as a nation.

GERALD P. LÓPEZ

CITY COUNCIL OF LOS ANGELES v. TAXPAYERS FOR VINCENT 466 U.S. 789 (1984)

A Los Angeles ordinance prohibited the posting of signs on public property. Supporters of a candidate for city council sued to enjoin city officials from continuing to remove their signs from utility poles; they were joined as plaintiffs by the company that made and posted the signs for them. Of the 1,207 signs removed during one week of the campaign, 48 supported the candidate; most were commercial signs. The Supreme Court, 6–3, rejected constitutional attacks on the ordinance on its face and as applied.

The case seemed to call for analysis according to the principles governing rights of access to the PUBLIC FORUM—rights particularly valuable to people of limited means. Instead, Justice JOHN PAUL STEVENS, for the Court, applied the set of rules announced in UNITED STATES v. O'BRIEN (1968), suggesting the possibility that those rules might in the future be applied routinely to FIRST AMENDMENT cases involving regulations that are not aimed at message content. Here the government interest in aesthetic values was substantial; the city had no purpose to suppress a particular message; and the law curtailed no more speech than was necessary to its purpose. In a bow to public forum reasoning, Stevens noted that other means of communication remained open to the plaintiffs.

The dissenters, led by Justice WILLIAM J. BRENNAN, argued that the assertion of aesthetic purposes deserved careful scrutiny to assure even-handed regulation, narrowly tailored to aesthetic objectives that were both comprehensively carried out and precisely defined. The City had made no such showing here, they contended.

Critics of the decision have suggested that it is part of a larger inegalitarian trend in BURGER COURT decisions concerning the FREEDOM OF SPEECH and FREEDOM OF THE PRESS, a trend exemplified by BUCKLEY v. VALEO (1976) and HUDGENS v. N.L.R.B. (1976).

KENNETH L. KARST

CITY OF . . .

See: entry under name of city

CIVIL DISOBEDIENCE

Civil disobedience is a public, nonviolent, political act contrary to law usually done with the aim of bringing about a change in the law or policies of the government. The idea of civil disobedience is deeply rooted in our civilization, with examples evident in the life of Socrates, the early Christian society, the writings of Thomas Aquinas and Henry David Thoreau, and the Indian nationalist movement led by Gandhi.

The many occurrences of civil disobedience throughout American history have had a profound impact on the legal system and society as a whole. The Constitution does not provide immunity for those who practice civil disobedience, but because the United States is a representative democracy with deep respect for constitutional values, the system is uniquely responsive to acts of civil disobedience. Examples of civil disobedience in American history include the Quakers' refusal to pay taxes to support the colonial Massachusetts Church, the labor movement's use of the tactic in the early twentieth century, and citizens' withholding of taxes in protest of military and nuclear expenditures.

The fundamental justification for civil disobedience is that some persons feel bound by philosophy, religion, morality, or some other principle to disobey a law that they feel is unjust. As Martin Luther King, Jr., wrote in his *Letter from Birmingham Jail,* "I submit that an individual who breaks a law that his conscience tells him is unjust, and willingly accepts the penalty by staying in jail to arouse the conscience of the community over its injustice, is in reality expressing the very highest respect for law." Civil disobedience is most justifiable when prior lawful attempts to rectify the situation have failed; and when the acts of civil disobedience are done to force the society to recognize the problem; when performed openly and publicly; and when the actor will accept the punishment. Many proponents urge that civil disobedience be used only in the most extreme cases, arguing that the Constitution provides many opportunities to voice one's grievances without breaking the law.

Opponents of civil disobedience see it as a threat to democratic society and the forerunner of violence and anarchy. The premise of stable democracy, they contend, is that the minority will accept the will of the majority. Opponents argue that the lack of a coherent theory of civil disobedience can result in the abuse of the tactic.

Civil disobedience may be designed to change the Constitution itself. The responsiveness of the Constitution to the voice of dissent and civil disobedience is particularly evident in two movements in our history: the women's suffrage movement and the antislavery movement. These movements brought about great constitutional changes through a variety of political strategies, including civil disobedience.

The women's suffrage movement began in the first part of the nineteenth century. Increasing numbers of women were becoming active in political parties, humanitarian societies, educational societies, labor agitation groups, antislavery associations, and temperance associations. By 1848, the women had organized the National Women's Rights Convention at Seneca Falls where Elizabeth Cady Stanton and Lucretia Mott led the women in writing the Declaration of Sentiments. A main tenet of the declaration was that women should be granted the right to vote in order to preserve the government as one that has the consent of the governed. The women used a variety of tactics in their struggle to obtain the franchise, including conventional political tactics, lobbying at the national, state, and local levels, and petitions. An important tactic in the women's fight was the use of civil disobedience, which helped gain support and publicity for their cause. The methods of civil disobedience included voting in elections (which was illegal), refusing to pay taxes, and PICKETING the White House.

A visible act of civil disobedience used by the women's movement was to register and vote in elections. A prominent example occurred in 1872 when Susan B. Anthony and fourteen other women registered and voted in Rochester, New York. They were accused and charged with a crime "of voting without the lawful right to vote." The women argued that the FOURTEENTH AMENDMENT and FIFTEENTH AMENDMENT gave them the legal right to vote. This legal argument was dismissed by the Supreme Court in MINOR V. HAPPERSETT (1875), when the Court held that women were CITIZENS but were not entitled to vote. Once the Court refused to recognize the argument based on existing amendments, the suffragist organization concentrated their efforts on the fight for passage of a constitutional amendment that would ensure women the right to vote.

Another, more isolated instance of civil disobedience was performed by activist Abby Smith. Abby Smith refused to pay her property taxes until she was given the right to vote at the town meeting. This simple instance of a woman standing up for her rights served to publicize the women's cause to a certain extent.

A final tactic of the women's suffrage movement that amounted to both civil disobedience and lawful dissent was the practice of picketing the White House in order to gain presidential support for the proposed amendment. Although the women had a legal right to picket, the policemen at the time treated them with contempt, as if they were lawbreakers. The women were jailed for exercising constitutional rights, and it was not until later that they were vindicated by the courts.

During the antislavery movement in the mid-1850s, civil disobedience gained considerable acceptance in some parts of the country. Opposition to slavery reached new peaks after the passage of the FUGITIVE SLAVE Law of 1850. The act provided for a simplified procedure to return escaped slaves to their masters, with provisions excluding TRIAL BY JURY and writs of HABEAS CORPUS from fugitive slave cases, and providing a financial incentive for federal commissioners to decide cases in favor of southern claimants. Throughout the North, meetings were held where citizens denounced the new law and vowed their disobedience to the act. Many based their views on philosophical, legal, or religious grounds. Those publicly opposing the act included Lewis Hayden, William C. Nell, Theodore Parker, Daniel Foster, and Henry David Thoreau. Some commentators believe that a clear and direct line runs from the antislavery crusaders to the Fourteenth Amendment. The acts of civil disobedience to the Fugitive Slave Act represented the feelings of a substantial portion of the country at the time. This opinion was eventually transformed into the THIRTEENTH, Fourteenth, and Fifteenth Amendments, which abolished slavery, guaranteed the former slaves' citizenship, and protected their right to vote. Civil disobedience remains a potentially significant tool for effecting constitutional change.

The Constitution has been used to justify civil disobedience. Examples in our recent history include the CIVIL RIGHTS movement and military resistance. Some of the best-known uses of civil disobedience occurred during the civil rights movements of the 1950s and 1960s. Martin Luther King, Jr., and his followers felt compelled to disobey laws that continued the practice of SEGREGATION; they opposed the laws on moral, ethical, and constitutional grounds. In fact, some of the laws they allegedly disobeyed were unconstitutional. Although the movement initially attempted to change the system through conventional legal and political channels, it eventually turned to the tactics of civil disobedience in order to bring national attention to its cause. By appealing to the Constitution as justification for their acts of civil disobedience, the civil rights leaders made important contributions to the development of constitutional law in the areas of EQUAL PROTECTION, DUE PROCESS, and FREEDOM OF SPEECH.

The civil rights movement's tactics included SIT-INS, designed to protest the laws and the practice of segregated lunch counters and restaurants. Black students entered restaurants and requested to be served in the white part of the establishment. When they refused to leave upon the owner's request, they were arrested on grounds of criminal TRESPASS.

Quite a few of these cases were heard by the Supreme Court, where the blacks argued that the equal protection clause of the Fourteenth Amendment made these laws unconstitutional. In *Peterson v. City of Greenville* (1963) ten black students had been arrested after they refused to leave a segregated restaurant. The Supreme Court reversed their convictions, holding that the laws requiring segregation violated the equal protection clause of the Fourteenth Amendment. The court reasoned that there was sufficient STATE ACTION because of the existence of the statute, which indicated the state policy in favor of segregation. Many factually similar cases were reversed on the authority of the *Peterson* decision. In addition to using the equal protection clause, the courts sometimes held that the laws as applied to black citizens were VOID FOR VAGUENESS or for lack of NOTICE.

The sit-ins, freedom rides, and continued demonstrations eventually swayed public opinion and contributed to the passage of the CIVIL RIGHTS ACT OF 1964, which prohibited discrimination in many areas of life. Under the act, many acts that had previously amounted to civil disobedience became protected by law.

In addition to the successes achieved in RACIAL DISCRIMINATION law, the civil rights movement and its acts of civil disobedience have contributed to the FIRST AMENDMENT law regarding freedom of speech and FREEDOM OF ASSEMBLY AND ASSOCIATION. For example, in COX V. LOUISIANA (1964) peaceful civil rights demonstrators were convicted of disturbing the peace. The Court struck down the BREACH OF THE PEACE statute for vagueness and OVERBREADTH, thus expanding constitutional rights to free speech and assembly.

Although the civil rights movement involved acts of civil disobedience on a massive scale, resistance to the country's military policy has traditionally involved more solitary acts. Still, the resisters have based many of their arguments on constitutional provisions. These arguments have not always been successful, but the protesters succeeded in calling attention to causes such as opposition to war and military policy.

Those opposed to the country's military policy have used both indirect and direct methods of civil disobedience. Examples of indirect methods include DRAFT CARD BURNING, supplying false information on tax forms, and trespassing on government grounds. Although the protesters gained publicity from these tactics, the disobedient's claims of freedom of speech and RELIGIOUS LIBERTY under the First Amendment usually have not been accepted by the courts. A well-known example of the use of indirect civil disobedience is the Catonsville Nine case in which protesters entered the office of the local Selective Service Board and destroyed government records. Their defense, based on philosophical and moral grounds, was held insufficient by the courts.

Direct forms of civil disobedience to war have included resistance to the draft and refusal to pay taxes. The disobedience surrounding the draft has taken many forms, but many legal challenges have focused on the SELECTIVE SERVICE ACT. In several cases, the men who refused induction argued that the CONSCIENTIOUS OBJECTION provision was unconstitutional as it applied to the individual. They argued that to construe the provision as requiring a belief in a supreme being was a violation of the free exercise clause of the First Amendment. The Court has avoided the constitutional questions in these cases by giving a broad construction to statutory exemptions of the conscientious objectors. Another direct form of civil disobedience used to protest the country's involvement in war has been to withhold the payment of taxes, arguing that to support a war that one does not believe in is in violation of the free exercise clause. The Supreme Court has never decided the constitutional issues in these cases. Although both direct and indirect forms of civil disobedience in resistance to military policy have been equally unsuccessful in presenting legal challenges to laws, they have been successful in publicizing the disobedients' grievances.

The debate concerning the morality or justification for the use of civil disobedience as a method of effecting change in society will never be fully resolved. However, civil disobedience remains a significant and often successful tactic used in many movements in American society. The use of civil disobedience, when incorporated with other conventional political strategies, can lead to profound changes in the Constitution itself or in the interpretation of the document. American society's positive response to certain acts of civil disobedience can be seen in the civil rights movement, the women's suffrage movement, and the antislavery movement. Although not all acts of civil disobedience yield substantial changes, our democratic system provides the opportunity for civil disobedience to contribute to significant changes in society.

ROBERT F. DRINAN, S.J.

Bibliography

FORTAS, ABE 1968 *Concerning Dissent and Civil Disobedience.* New York: World Publishing Co.

GREENBERG, JACK 1968 "The Supreme Court, Civil Rights, and Civil Dissonance." *Yale Law Journal 77:1520–1544.*

KALVEN, HARRY, JR. 1965 *The Negro and the First Amendment.* Columbus: Ohio State University Press.

WEBER, DAVID R., ED. 1978 *Civil Disobedience in America.* Ithaca, N.Y.: Cornell University Press.

CIVIL LIBERTIES

WILLIAM BLACKSTONE described civil liberty as "the great end of all human society and government . . . that state in which each individual has the power to pursue his own happiness according to his own views of his interest, and the dictates of his conscience, unrestrained, except by equal, just, and impartial laws." As a matter of law, civil liberties are usually claims of right that a citizen may assert against the state. In the United States the term "civil liberties" is often used in a narrower sense to refer to FREEDOM OF SPEECH, FREEDOM OF THE PRESS, FREEDOM OF ASSEMBLY AND ASSOCIATION, RELIGIOUS LIBERTY, personal privacy, and the right to DUE PROCESS OF LAW, or to other limitations on the power of the state to restrict individual freedom of action. In this sense, civil liberties may be distinguished from rights to equality (sometimes called "civil rights"), although the latter have increasingly been recognized as important elements of individual freedom because they permit participation in society without regard to race, religion, sex, or other characteristics unrelated to individual capacity.

The concept of civil liberties is a logical corollary to the ideas of LIMITED GOVERNMENT and RULE OF LAW. When government acts arbitrarily, it infringes civil liberty; the rule of law combats and confines these excesses of power. The concept "government of laws, not of men" reflects this idea as does the vision of justice as fairness.

Although civil liberties are usually associated in practice with democratic forms of government, liberty and democracy are distinct concepts. An authoritarian government structure may recognize certain limits on the capacity of the state to interfere with the autonomy of the individual. Correspondingly, calling a state democratic does not tell us about the extent to which it recognizes civil liberty. Thus, "civil liberties" does not refer to a particular form of political structure but to the relationship between the individual and the state, however the state may be organized. But civil liberties do presuppose order. As Chief Justice CHARLES EVANS HUGHES said in COX V. NEW HAMPSHIRE (1941), "Civil liberties imply the existence of an organized society maintaining public order without which liberty itself would be lost in the excesses of unrestrained abuses."

In the final analysis, civil liberties are based on the integrity and dignity of the individual. This idea was expressed by George C. Marshall, who was chief of staff to the American army in World War II and later served as secretary of state: "We believe that human beings have . . . rights that may not be given or taken away. They include the right of every individual to develop his mind and his soul in the ways of his own choice, free of fear and coercion—provided only that he does not interfere with the rights of others."

There are two principal justifications for preferring individual liberties to the interests of the general community—justice and self-interest. At the very least, justice requires norms by which persons in authority treat those within their power fairly and evenly. Self-interest suggests that our own rights are secure only if the rights of others are protected.

Because these two justifications for civil liberties are abstractions to most people, they are often subordinated to more immediate concerns of the state or the majority. In America, even administrations relatively friendly to civil liberty have perpetrated some of the worst violations. The administration of FRANKLIN D. ROOSEVELT interned Japanese Americans during World War II. ABRAHAM LINCOLN suspended the right of HABEAS CORPUS. And as Leonard W. Levy has reminded us, THOMAS JEFFERSON was far more of a libertarian as a private citizen than when he was in power. Nevertheless, civil liberties have been more broadly defined and fully respected in the United States than in other nations.

The roots of American civil liberties can be traced to ancient times. The city-state of Athens made a lasting contribution to civil liberty. In the sixth century B.C., Solon, the magistrate of Athens, produced a constitution that, while flawed, gave the poor a voice in the election of magistrates and the right to call public officials to account. Solon is also credited with first expressing the idea of the rule of law. But Athens knew no limits on the right of the majority to adopt any law it chose, and there was no concept of individual rights against the state. Greek philosophers introduced the idea of "natural law" and the derivative concept of equality; all Athenians (except slaves) were equal citizens, for all possessed reason and owed a common duty to natural law.

The Romans also contributed to civil liberties, first through a rudimentary SEPARATION OF POWERS of government and later by the further development of natural law. Justinian's *Institutes* recites, "Justice is the fixed and constant purpose that gives every man his due." Nevertheless, the Roman emperors were autocratic in practice; there were no enforceable rights against the state, which practiced censorship, restricted travel, and coerced religion.

In the Middle Ages there was little manifestation of civil liberties. But the idea of a pure natural law was carried forward in Augustine's *City of God.* On the secular side, the contract between feudal lords and their vassals established reciprocal rights and responsibilities whose interpretation was, in some places, decided by a body of the vassal's peers.

Among English antecedents of civil liberties, the starting point is MAGNA CARTA (1215), the first written instrument that exacted from a monarch rules he was bound to obey. Although this document reflected the attempt of barons to secure feudal privileges, basic liberties developed from it—among them the security of private property, the security of the person, the right to judgment by one's peers, the right to seek redress of grievances from the sovereign, and the concept of due process of law. Above all, as Winston Churchill said, Magna Carta "justifies the respect in which men have held it" because it tells us "there is a law above the king."

Another great charter of English liberty was the 1628 PETITION OF RIGHT, a statute that asserted the freedom of the people from unconsented taxation and arbitrary imprisonment. The HABEAS CORPUS ACT OF 1679 was another major document of English liberty. The BILL OF RIGHTS of 1689, which also influenced American constitutional law, declared that parliamentary elections ought to be free and that Parliament's debates ought not to be questioned in any other place, and it condemned perversions of criminal justice by the last Stuart kings, including excessive BAIL and CRUEL AND UNUSUAL PUNISHMENTS.

The experience of the American colonies was important to the development of civil liberties in the United States. The COLONIAL CHARTERS set up local governments that built upon English institutions, and the colonists jealously opposed any infringements upon their rights. The VIRGINIA CHARTER OF 1606 reserved to the inhabitants "all liberties, Franchises and Immunities . . . as if they had been abiding and born, within this our Realm of England."

The MASSACHUSETTS BODY OF LIBERTIES of 1641 expressed in detail a range of fundamental rights later to be adopted in the American BILL OF RIGHTS. Rhode Island was the first colony to recognize religious liberty, largely through the efforts of its founder, ROGER WILLIAMS. The Puritans banished Williams from Massachusetts in 1635 for unorthodoxy, and he settled in Providence. There the plantation agreement of 1640 protected "liberty of Conscience," and this doctrine appeared in the Colony's charter in 1663. The Pennsylvania charter and those of other colonies were also influential in protecting individual rights. ZENGER'S CASE (1735), in which a jury acquitted a New York publisher on a charge of SEDITIOUS LIBEL, was a milestone in securing the freedom of the press.

By the time of the American Revolution, the colonists were familiar with the fundamental concepts of civil liberty that would be included in the Constitution and Bill of Rights. Unlike the contemporary French experience, where the promise of the Declaration of the Rights of Man went largely unfulfilled for want of institutional safeguards, the American Constitution of 1787 embodied a republican government elected by broad suffrage that was reinforced by judicial review and by CHECKS AND BALANCES among the three branches of government.

The original Constitution, a document devoted mainly to structure and the allocation of powers among the branches of the national government, contains some explicit safeguards for civil liberty. It provides that the "privilege" of habeas corpus, which requires a judge to release an imprisoned person unless he is being lawfully detained, may not be "suspended." The EX POST FACTO and BILL OF ATTAINDER clauses require the Congress to act prospectively and by general rule. Article III guarantees a jury trial in all federal criminal cases, defines TREASON narrowly, and imposes evidentiary requirements to assure that this most political of crimes will not be lightly charged.

Apart from the omission of a bill of rights, which was soon rectified, the Constitution's principal deficiency from a civil liberties standpoint was its countenance of slavery. Without mentioning the term, in several clauses it recognized the legality of that pernicious institution. DRED SCOTT V. SANDFORD (1857) cemented the legally inferior status of blacks and contributed to civil war by ruling that slaves or the descendants of slaves could not become citizens of the United States. The EMANCIPATION PROCLAMATION (1863) and the THIRTEENTH AMENDMENT (1865) freed the slaves, but the reaction that occurred after the end of Reconstruction in 1877 and decisions such as the CIVIL RIGHTS CASES (1883) and PLESSY V. FERGUSON (1896) undercut their purposes. The movement toward civil equality did not gain new momentum until the middle of the twentieth century.

The civil liberties of Americans are embodied primarily in the BILL OF RIGHTS (1791), the first ten amendments to the Constitution. JAMES MADISON proposed the amendments after the debates on RATIFICATION OF THE CONSTITUTION revealed wide public demand for additional protection of individual rights. The FIRST AMENDMENT guarantees the freedoms of speech, press, assembly, petition, and religious exercise, as well as the SEPARATION OF CHURCH AND STATE. The FOURTH AMENDMENT protects the privacy and security of home, person, and belongings and prohibits unreasonable SEARCHES AND SEIZURES. The Fifth, Sixth, and Eighth Amendments extend constitutional protection to the criminal process, including the right to due process of law, TRIAL BY JURY, CONFRONTATION of hostile witnesses, assistance of legal counsel, the RIGHT AGAINST SELF-INCRIMINATION, and protection against DOUBLE JEOPARDY and cruel and unusual punishment. The TENTH AMENDMENT reserves to the states and to the people powers not delegated to the federal government. Although the Bill of Rights was originally applicable only to the federal government, most of its provisions now have been applied to the states through the due process clause of the FOURTEENTH AMENDMENT. (See INCORPORATION DOCTRINE.) The amendment also provides a generalized guarantee of EQUAL PROTECTION OF THE LAWS as well as a virtually unenforced right to certain PRIVILEGES AND IMMUNITIES. Finally, the FIFTEENTH AMENDMENT and NINETEENTH AMENDMENT guarantee VOTING RIGHTS regardless of race or sex.

A practical understanding of civil liberties in the United States may be aided by illustrations of three main dimensions of the subject: freedom of speech, due process, and equal protection.

The First Amendment provides that "Congress shall make no law . . . abridging the freedom of speech, or of the press." The almost universal primacy given free speech as a "civil liberty" rests on several important values: the importance of freedom of speech for self-government in a democracy, its utility in probing for truth, its role in helping to check arbitrary government power, and its capacity to permit personal fulfillment of those who would express and receive ideas and feelings, especially unpopular ones, without fear of reprisal.

Consistent with the First Amendment, even revolutionary speech that is not "directed to inciting or producing imminent lawless action and is likely to incite or produce such action" is immunized from government control. (See INCITEMENT.) Similarly, highly offensive political speech and defamations of public officials and PUBLIC FIGURES that are not intentionally or recklessly false are protected. (See LIBEL AND THE FIRST AMENDMENT.) Because effective advocacy is enhanced by group membership, the First Amendment has also been interpreted to protect freedom of association from interference, absent a compelling state justification. The First Amendment provides particularly strong protection against PRIOR RESTRAINT—INJUNCTIONS or other means of preventing speech from ever being uttered or published.

Freedom of speech is not absolute. In addition to the limits just noted, OBSCENITY, child PORNOGRAPHY, and FIGHTING WORDS likely to provoke physical attacks are unprotected. All forms of speech, furthermore, are subject to reasonable time, place, and manner restrictions. The amendment has been interpreted to afford a lesser degree of protection to speech that is sexually explicit (although not obscene), to COMMERCIAL SPEECH, to SYMBOLIC SPEECH such as nonverbal displays intended to convey messages, and to

DEMONSTRATIONS (for example, PICKETING) that combine speech and action.

The concept of fair procedure, embodied in the due process clauses of the Fifth and Fourteenth Amendments, has been viewed as an element of civil liberties at least since Magna Carta, when the king was limited by "the LAW OF THE LAND." In principle, the guarantee of due process prevents government from imposing sanctions against individuals without sufficiently fair judicial or administrative procedures. Justice LOUIS D. BRANDEIS said: "In the development of our liberty insistence upon procedural regularity has been a large factor." Violations of this constitutional guarantee cover a wide range of official misconduct in the criminal process, from lynchings, to coerced confessions, to criminal convictions of uncounseled defendants, to interrogation of suspects without cautionary warnings. Beyond criminal cases, due process principles have been applied to protect juveniles accused of delinquency and individuals whose government jobs or benefits have been terminated. Whatever the context, civil liberty requires that individual interests of liberty and property not be sacrificed without a process that determines facts and liability at hearings that are fairly established and conducted. (See PROCEDURAL DUE PROCESS OF LAW, CRIMINAL; PROCEDURAL DUE PROCESS OF LAW, CIVIL).

The guarantee of equal protection is interpreted to forbid government, and in some cases private entities, to discriminate among persons on arbitrary grounds. The central purpose of the equal protection clause was to admit to civil equality the recently freed black slaves, and leading judicial decisions such as SHELLEY V. KRAEMER (1948) and BROWN V. BOARD OF EDUCATION (1954) and legislative enactments such as the CIVIL RIGHTS ACTS of 1866 and 1964 were particularly addressed to the condition of racial minorities. The constitutional guarantee of equality has been extended to women and to DISCRETE AND INSULAR MINORITIES—ethnic and religious groups, ALIENS, and children of unwed parents—whom the Supreme Court has deemed unable to protect their interests through the political process. In recent years, the Court has rejected attempts to broaden this category of specially protected groups. It has denied special protection to homosexuals, older persons, and the mentally retarded. The Court has also expressed the antidiscrimination ideal in holding that it is unconstitutional for a legislative districting system to accord votes in some districts significantly greater weight than votes in others.

A vexing equality issue is whether benign classifications of racial minorities or women are consistent with civil liberty on the theory that they prefer groups that historically were, and often still are, discriminated against. Against the background of slavery and legally enforced SEGREGATION, the Supreme Court has upheld AFFIRMATIVE ACTION programs for blacks that prefer them for employment and university admissions on the ground that a wholly "color blind" system would "render illusory the promise" of *Brown v. Board of Education.* It has also upheld some forms of preference for other minorities and for women. There is deep division over these programs. It is often charged that they are themselves an obnoxious use of racial or sexual classifications. Justice HARRY A. BLACKMUN responded to these contentions in REGENTS OF UNIVERSITY OF CALIFORNIA V. BAKKE (1978) by stating that "[i]n order to get beyond racism, we must first take account of race. . . . We cannot—we dare not—let the Equal Protection Clause perpetuate racial supremacy."

Some liberties in the United States are traceable to a natural law tradition that long antedated the Constitution and are only indirectly reflected in its text. In the American experience, for example, the VIRGINIA DECLARATION OF RIGHTS aserted that "all men are by nature equally free and independent, and have certain inherent rights . . . namely, the enjoyment of life and liberty, with the means of acquiring and possessing property." This sentiment was reflected in the DECLARATION OF INDEPENDENCE, which spoke of "inalienable rights," and in the Constitution itself, which embodied these principles. In CALDER V. BULL (1798) Justice SAMUEL CHASE expressed his view that NATURAL RIGHTS "form the very nature of our free Republican governments." Over the years the Supreme Court has recognized a number of rights not explicitly grounded in the constitutional text, including, for a season, FREEDOM OF CONTRACT, and, in recent years, the RIGHT TO TRAVEL, and the FREEDOM OF ASSOCIATION. The Court's most celebrated recent decisions of this kind have recognized a series of rights that reflect values of personal privacy and autonomy. These include the rights to marriage and to BIRTH CONTROL, to family relationships and to ABORTION. These liberties are fundamental conditions of the ability of a person to master his or her life. (See FREEDOM OF INTIMATE ASSOCIATION.)

The Supreme Court's decisions enunciating some of these rights have been challenged as unrooted in the original intention of the Framers and therefore subjective and illegitimate. But the Constitution was not frozen in time. Chief Justice JOHN MARSHALL said in MCCULLOCH V. MARYLAND (1819) for a unanimous

Court that it is an instrument "intended to endure for ages to come and, consequently, to be adapted to the various crises of human affairs." In the twentieth century, Justice BENJAMIN N. CARDOZO agreed: "The great generalities of the Constitution have a content and a significance that vary from age to age." Further, the NINTH AMENDMENT contemplated that the provisions of the Bill of Rights explicitly safeguarding liberty were not meant to be exhaustive: "The enumeration in the Constitution, of certain rights, shall not be construed to deny or disparage others retained by the people." Finally, the structure of the Constitution, and the premises of a free society, imply certain liberties, such as the freedom of association and the right to travel.

The uncertainty and even illogic of Supreme Court decisions protecting certain groups and rights—why illegitimate children and not homosexuals, why a right to travel and not a right to housing—should not be viewed as merely the product of politics or prejudice. There are inevitably disagreements and inconsistencies over the proper boundaries of civil liberties and the proper judicial role in their recognition. Filling in the "majestic generalities" of the Constitution has always been a long-range and uncertain task.

An example of the difficulty is CAPITAL PUNISHMENT—the question whether there is a constitutional right not to be executed even for a heinous crime. This liberty is widely accepted throughout the world, but the United States Supreme Court has not recognized it as a constitutional right, instead permitting states to impose sentences of death for murder, subject to due process limitations. Many consider capital punishment inherently a violation of civil liberties because of the randomness in its application, its finality in the face of inevitable trial errors, its disproportionate use against racial minorities, and its dehumanizing effect on both government and the people. The struggle over this and other claims of civil liberty continues in public opinion, legislatures, and the courts.

Another source of American civil liberties is the doctrine of separation of governmental powers, illuminated most notably in the eighteenth century by the *philosophe* MONTESQUIEU. Anticipating John Acton's dictum that absolute power corrupts absolutely, the Supreme Court recognized in LOAN ASSOCIATION v. TOPEKA (1875) that the "theory of our governments, State and National, is opposed to the deposit of unlimited power anywhere. The executive, the legislative, and the judicial branches of these governments are all of limited and defined powers." In the same vein, individual rights are enhanced by the existence of a diverse population. THE FEDERALIST #51 states: "In a free government the security for civil rights [consists] in the multiplicity of interests."

The Supreme Court has enforced the principle of separation of powers. In YOUNGSTOWN SHEET & TUBE CO. v. SAWYER (1952) it denied that the President had constitutional power, even in time of national emergency, to seize private companies without legislative authorization. Two Justices rested on the separation of powers doctrine in NEW YORK TIMES CO. v. UNITED STATES (1971) by holding that under all but extraordinary circumstances the President lacks inherent power to enjoin news organizations from publishing classified information. And in UNITED STATES v. NIXON (1974), while ruling that Presidents possess an EXECUTIVE PRIVILEGE to maintain the secrecy of certain communications, the Court rebuffed President RICHARD M. NIXON's attempt to withhold White House tapes from the Watergate special prosecutor. In form, these decisions dealt with questions of allocation of governmental powers; in fact they were civil liberties decisions effectuating a structure designed, in Justice Brandeis's words, "to preclude the exercise of arbitrary power."

Neither the original Constitution nor the Bill of Rights guaranteed the right to vote, a cornerstone of democratic government as well as a civil liberty; slaves, women, and those without property were disfranchised. During the early nineteenth century states gradually rescinded property qualifications; the Fifteenth Amendment (1868) barred voting discrimination by race or color, and the Nineteenth Amendment (1920) outlawed voting discrimination on the ground of sex. Nevertheless, various devices were employed to prevent nonwhites from voting. These were curtailed by the VOTING RIGHTS ACT of 1965, the TWENTY-FOURTH AMENDMENT's invalidation of POLL TAXES as a qualification for voting, and the Supreme Court's decision in HARPER v. VIRGINIA BOARD OF ELECTIONS (1966). The TWENTY-SIXTH AMENDMENT (1971) extended the franchise to all citizens eighteen years of age and older.

A controversial question is presented by the relationship between the right to property and civil liberties. As the Supreme Court stated in GRIFFIN v. ILLINOIS (1956), "Providing equal justice for poor and rich, weak and powerful alike is an age-old problem." Although some would reject any such link between economics and liberty, others disagree. ALEXANDER HAMILTON stated that "a power over a man's subsistence is a power over his will." More recently, Paul Freund, recognizing that economic independence provides a margin of safety in risk or protest, commented that the effective exercise of liberty may require "a degree of command over material resources."

To a limited extent the Supreme Court has concurred. It has prohibited discrimination against the poor in cases involving voting rights and ACCESS TO THE COURTS. It has also afforded procedural protection against loss of government entitlements, including a government employee's interest in his job and a recipient's interest in welfare benefits. On the other hand, the Court has refused to recognize a generalized constitutional right to economic security. The Court has permitted reduction of welfare benefits below a standard of minimum need, has permitted courtroom filing fees to keep indigents from obtaining judicial discharge of debts, and has refused to recognize a constitutional right to equalized resources for spending on public education. The Court said in DANDRIDGE V. WILLIAMS (1970): "In the area of economics and social welfare, a State does not violate [equal protection] merely because the classifications made by its laws are imperfect." The idea that civil liberties imply a degree of economic security is not yet a principle of constitutional law.

Invasions of liberty are usually committed by government. But individuals may also be victimized by private power. The authority of medieval lords over their vassals was not merely economic. Today large institutions such as corporations, labor unions, and universities may seek to limit the speech or privacy of individuals subject to their authority. For this reason federal and state legislation bars RACIAL DISCRIMINATION and other forms of arbitrary discrimination in the hiring, promotion, and firing of employees, in the sale and rental of private housing, and in admission to academic institutions. The courts likewise have recognized that private power may defeat civil liberties by barring the enforcement of private RESTRICTIVE COVENANTS not to sell real estate to racial minorities and by barring private censorship and interference with freedom of association when those restrictions are supported by STATE ACTION.

Civil liberties can never be entirely secure. Government and large private institutions often seek to achieve their goals without scrupulous concern for constitutional rights. In the eighteenth century Edmund Burke wrote: "Of this I am certain, that in a democracy the majority of citizens is capable of exercising the most cruel oppression upon the minority." More recently, Charles Reich observed that civil liberties are an "unnatural state for man or for society because in a short-range way they are essentially contrary to the self-interest of the majority. They require the majority to restrain itself." The legal rights of minorities and the weak need special protection, particularly under conditions of stress.

The first such condition is economic stringency. Mass unemployment and high inflation exacerbate ethnic rivalries and discrimination, and at times are offered to justify the repression of dissent. Minorities pay the heaviest price. The victims include the dependent poor, whose government benefits are often among the first casualties during economic recession.

War also strains the Bill of Rights, for a nation threatened from without is rarely the best guardian of civil liberties within. As noted, President Abraham Lincoln suspended habeas corpus during the Civil War and President Franklin D. Roosevelt approved the internment of Japanese Americans during World War II. In addition, President WOODROW WILSON presided over massive invasions of free speech during World War I; MCCARTHYISM, the virulent repression of dissent, was a product of the Cold War of the late 1940s and early 1950s; and President LYNDON B. JOHNSON authorized prosecution of protestors during the VIETNAM WAR. More recently, the deterioration of détente in the 1980s has led to interference with peaceful demonstrations, widespread surveillance of Americans, politically motivated travel bans and visa denials, and censorship of former government officials.

A third perennial source of trouble for civil liberties in America has been religious zeal. Anti-Catholic and Anti-Semitic nativism paralleled slavery during the nineteenth and twentieth centuries. The Scopes trial (STATE V. SCOPES, 1925), in which a public school teacher was convicted for teaching evolution, was the result of fundamentalist excesses. On the other hand, religious sentiments have often buttressed civil liberties by, for example, supporting the extension of civil rights to racial and other minorities and endorsing the claims of conscientious objectors to conscription in the armed services, even during wartime. But zealous groups threaten to infringe civil liberties when they seek government support to impose their own religious views on nonadherents. This has taken many forms, including attempts to introduce organized prayer in public schools, to outlaw birth control and abortion, and to use public tax revenues to finance religious schools.

If civil liberties exist simply as abstractions, they have no more value than the barren promises entombed in many totalitarian constitutions. To be real, rights must be exercised and respected. The political branches of government—legislators and executive officials—can be instrumental in protecting fundamental rights, and especially in preventing their sacrifice to the supposed needs of the nation as a whole. Yet majoritarian pressures on elected representatives are great during times of crisis, and the stress on liberty is most acute.

The vulnerability of politically accountable officials teaches that freedom is most secure when protected by life-tenured judges insulated from electoral retribution. The doctrine of JUDICIAL REVIEW, which gives the courts final authority to define constitutional rights and to invalidate offending legislation or executive action, is the most important original contribution of the American political system to civil liberty.

Since Chief Justice John Marshall wrote for a unanimous Supreme Court in MARBURY V. MADISON (1803) that the power of judicial review is grounded in the Constitution, tension has existed between this checking authority and the nation's commitment to majority rule. Challenges to the legitimacy of judicial review have been rejected with arguments based on the SUPREMACY CLAUSE in Article VI of the Constitution, on the pragmatic need for national uniformity, and on history. Thus, ROSCOE POUND, the long-time dean of Harvard Law School, concluded that the claim that judicial review is usurpation is refuted by the "clear understanding of American Lawyers before the Revolution, based on the seventeenth-century books in which they had been taught, the unanimous course of decision after independence and down to the adoption of the Constitution, not to speak of the writings of the two prime movers in the convention which drafted the instrument."

Judicial review reinforces the principle that even in a democracy the majority must be subject to limits that assure individual liberty. This principle is the essential premise of the Bill of Rights—the need to counteract the majoritarian pressures against liberty that existed in the eighteenth century and have persisted throughout American history. In the words of the Spanish writer José Ortega y Gassett, "[Freedom] is the right which the majority concedes to minorities and hence it is the noblest cry that has ever resounded in this planet." Further, the democratic political process requires civil liberties in order to function—the rights to vote, to speak, and to hear others. Elected legislatures and executive officials cannot be relied on to protect these rights fully and thus to assure the integrity of the democratic process; an insulated judiciary is essential to interpret the Constitution.

The role of the Supreme Court and other courts in exercising judicial review is valid even though their decisions may not reflect the view of the people at a given time. American democracy contemplates limitations on transient consensus and imposes long-term restrictions on the power of legislative majorities to act, subject to a constitutional amendment, because the democracy established by the Constitution is concerned not merely with effectuating the majority's will but with protecting minority rights. Further, as Burt Neuborne has pointed out, federal judges have a democratic imprimatur: "They are generally drawn from the political world; they are appointed by the President and must be confirmed by the Senate." It is for these reasons that James Madison viewed courts as the "natural guardian for the Bill of Rights."

The central role of independent courts in the enforcement of civil liberties has provoked efforts to weaken judicial review. The abolitionists, dissatisfied with federal judges who protected the rights of slaveholders, clamored for jury trials for alleged fugitive slaves; populists have long urged the popular election of judges; and Franklin D. Roosevelt sought to pack the Supreme Court to bend it to popular will. More recently, bills have been introduced in Congress to limit the JURISDICTION OF THE FEDERAL COURTS and to bar some legal remedies that are indispensable to the effectuation of certain constitutional rights. Whatever the perceived short-term advantages of such schemes to one group or another, the long-term effect would be erosion of judicial review and a consequent undermining of civil liberty.

The centrality of courts to the constitutional plan must not obscure the equally important role of legislatures. They can enhance or weaken civil liberty and, absent a declaration of unconstitutionality, their actions are final. During the period of the WARREN COURT, it was widely assumed that the judiciary alone would defend individual rights because legislatures were subject to immediate pressures from the electorate that prevented them from taking a long and sophisticated view of American liberties and protecting minorities and dissenters. But during the 1960s Congress prohibited discrimination in employment, housing, access to PUBLIC ACCOMMODATIONS, and voting; it passed the FREEDOM OF INFORMATION ACT; and it provided legal services for the poor. A few years later it enacted laws aimed at protecting the privacy of personal information. Congress can authorize expenditures, create and dismantle administrative agencies, and enact comprehensive legislation across broad subject areas—powers beyond the institutional capacity of courts.

Legislatures can also impair civil liberties in ways other than restricting judicial review. In recent years battles have raged in Congress over the Legal Services Corporation, the FREEDOM OF INFORMATION ACT, the VOTING RIGHTS ACT, school prayer, tuition tax credits to support private schools, the powers of the Central Intelligence Agency and the Federal Bureau of Investigation, and many other issues. This congressional agenda reflects an intense national debate over the meaning and scope of civil liberties in the 1980s.

Whatever the forum, the security of civil liberty requires trained professionals to press the rights of people. Throughout American history the services of paid counsel have been supplemented by lawyers who volunteer out of ideological commitment or professional obligation. Publicly supported legal services organizations and legislative provision for awarding attorneys' fees to prevailing plaintiffs in CIVIL RIGHTS cases have encouraged the growth of a sophisticated bar that litigates constitutional issues. Vital support for the defense of civil liberties is also provided by private organizations such as the AMERICAN CIVIL LIBERTIES UNION (ACLU) and more specialized groups such as the National Association for the Advancement of Colored People, the National Organization for Women, and public interest law firms ranging across the political spectrum. These bodies engage in litigation, legislative lobbying, and public education in order to advance the rights of their constituencies or constitutional rights generally.

History shows that civil liberties are never secure, but must be defended again and again, in each generation. Examples of frequently repetitive violations of civil liberties involve police misconduct, school book censorship, and interference with free speech and assembly. For instance, the ACLU found it necessary to assert the right of peaceful demonstration when that right was threatened by Mayor Frank Hague's ban of labor organizers in New Jersey in the 1930s, by Sheriff Bull Connor's violence to civil rights demonstrators in Alabama in the 1960s, by the government's efforts to stop antiwar demonstrators in Washington in the 1970s, and by the 1977–1978 effort of the city of Skokie, Illinois, to prevent a march by American Nazis.

The continuing defense of civil liberties is indispensable if often thankless. Strong and determined opponents of human rights have always used the rhetoric of patriotism and practicality to subvert liberty and to dominate the weak, the unorthodox, and the despised. Government efficiency, international influence, domestic order, and economic needs are all important in a complex world, but none is more important than the principles of civil liberties. As embodied in the Constitution and the Bill of Rights, these principles reflect a glorious tradition extending from the ancient world to modern times.

NORMAN DORSEN

Bibliography

BRANT, IRVING 1965 *The Bill of Rights.* Indianapolis: Bobbs-Merrill.

CHAFEE, ZECHARIAH, JR. 1956 *The Blessings of Liberty.* Philadelphia: Lippincott.

——— 1941 *Free Speech in the United States.* Cambridge, Mass.: Harvard University Press.

DEWEY, ROBERT E. AND GOULD, JAMES A., eds. 1970 *Freedom: Its History, Nature, and Varieties.* London: Macmillan.

DORSEN, NORMAN, ed. 1984 *Our Endangered Rights.* New York: Pantheon.

——— 1970 *The Rights of Americans: What They Are—What They Should Be.* New York: Pantheon.

EMERSON, THOMAS I. 1970 *The System of Freedom of Expression.* New York: Random House.

HAIMAN, FRANKLYN 1981 *Speech and Law in a Free Society.* Chicago: University of Chicago Press.

HAND, LEARNED 1960 *The Spirit of Liberty.* New York: Knopf.

MARSHALL, BURKE, ed. 1982 *The Supreme Court and Human Rights.* Washington, D.C.: Forum Series, Voice of America.

MULLER, HERBERT J. 1963 *Freedom in the Western World from the Dark Ages to the Rise of Democracy.* New York: Harper & Row.

SCHWARTZ, BERNARD 1971 *The Bill of Rights: A Documentary History.* New York: Chelsea House/McGraw-Hill.

TRIBE, LAURENCE H. 1978 *American Constitutional Law.* Mineola, N.Y.: Foundation Press.

CIVIL LIBERTIES AND THE ANTISLAVERY CONTROVERSY

Two civil liberties issues linked the freedom of communication enjoyed by whites with the cause of the slave: the mails controversy of 1835–1837 and the gag controversy of 1836–1844.

By 1835, southern political leaders, anxiety-ridden by threats to the security of slavery, were in no mood to tolerate a propaganda initiative of the American Anti-Slavery Society, which began weekly mailings of illustrated antislavery periodicals throughout the South. The first mailing was seized and burned by a Charleston, South Carolina, mob, an action condoned by Postmaster General Amos Kendall. President ANDREW JACKSON recommended legislation that would prohibit mailings of antislavery literature to the slave states. Senator JOHN C. CALHOUN denounced this as a threat to the SOVEREIGNTY of the states, while some northern political leaders objected to it on the grounds that it inhibited the FIRST AMENDMENT rights of FREEDOM OF SPEECH and FREEDOM OF THE PRESS of their constituents. In ensuing debates, the POSTAL POWER under Article I, section 8, and the First Amendment became the center of debates on Jackson's counterproposal, which would have mandated interstate cooperation in suppressing abolitionist mailings. Ironically, in 1836, Congress apparently inadvertently enacted legislation making it a misdemeanor to delay delivery of mail. But by 1837, abolitionists abandoned the campaign for more promising antislavery ventures.

The gag controversy proved to be longer-lived. Opponents of slavery had been petitioning Congress ever since 1790 on various subjects relating to slavery, such as the international and interstate slave trade. Such petitions were routinely either tabled or shunted to the oblivion of committees. Southerners in Congress were extremely inhospitable to such petitions, especially when the Anti-Slavery Society discontinued its mails campaign in favor of a stepped-up petition and memorial drive in 1836 focusing on the abolition of slavery in the DISTRICT OF COLUMBIA. To cope with the resulting flood of unwelcome petitions, Calhoun proposed that each house, acting under the rules of proceedings clause of Article I, section 5, refuse to receive petitions concerning slavery, rather than receiving and then tabling them. More moderate congressmen, however, adopted alternate resolutions providing for automatic tabling of such petitions. This only stimulated the antislavery societies to more successful petition drives. In response, each house annually adopted evermore stringent gag rules, the House of Representatives making its a standing rule in 1840.

Congressman JOHN QUINCY ADAMS, the former President who represented a Massachusetts district in the House, carried on an eight-year struggle to subvert the gags; he slyly introduced abolitionist petitions despite the standing rule. Enraged southern congressmen determined to stop his impertinence by offering a motion to censure him in 1842. The move backfired because it gave Adams a splendid forum to defend the First Amendment FREEDOM OF PETITION and to dramatize the threat to whites' CIVIL LIBERTIES posed by the attempted suppression of the antislavery movement. The Adams censure resolution failed. Proslavery congressmen then succeeded in censuring another antislavery Whig, Joshua Giddings of Ohio, for introducing antislavery resolutions in the House in 1842. He resigned his seat, immediately ran for reelection in what amounted to a referendum on his antislavery position, and was overwhelmingly reelected. Recognizing that the gags were not only tattered and ineffectual but now also counterproductive, stimulating the very debate they were meant to choke, Congress let them lapse in 1844.

WILLIAM M. WIECEK

Bibliography

WIECEK, WILLIAM M. 1977 *The Sources of Antislavery Constitutionalism in America, 1760–1848.* Ithaca, N.Y.: Cornell University Press.

CIVIL–MILITARY RELATIONS

The Constitution has a twofold impact on civil–military relations: first, through its specific provisions on this subject: and second, through the overall structure of government and division of powers it prescribes.

Several provisions of the Constitution deal directly with civil–military relations. The second clause of Article I, section 6, prohibits members of Congress from simultaneously holding other federal office. Article I, section 8, gives Congress the power to declare war, to grant LETTERS OF MARQUE AND REPRISAL, to make rules concerning captures, to raise and to support armies, to provide and to maintain a navy, to make rules for the regulation of the armed forces, to provide for calling the militia into federal service, and to provide for organizing, arming, and disciplining the militia. Article I, section 10, limits the military powers of the states. Article II, section 2, makes the President COMMANDER-IN-CHIEF of the armed forces and authorizes the appointment of officers. The SECOND AMENDMENT protects the right of the people to keep and bear arms, in order to constitute a "well-regulated militia." And the THIRD AMENDMENT severely restricts the quartering of troops in private homes.

These provisions constitute only a skeletal framework for the relations between civil government and military forces and between the military and society. Some of them (for example, those dealing with the quartering of troops, the two-year limit on appropriations for the army, the incompatibility of congressional and military office) have become obsolete, meaningless, or unobserved in practice. When written, however, these provisions reflected a broad consensus, expressed in the debates and actions of the CONSTITUTIONAL CONVENTION and the state ratifying conventions. Three key views underlay that consensus. The Framers believed that military power and military usurpation should be feared, that soldiering should be an aspect of citizenship, and that control of military power should be divided between state and national governments and between President and Congress.

The "supremacy of the civil over the military," said Justice FRANK MURPHY in DUNCAN V. KAHANAMOKU (1945), "is one of our great heritages." At the time of the framing of the Constitution, everyone agreed on the need to insure civil authority over the military. One of the indictments of George III in the DECLARATION OF INDEPENDENCE was that he had "affected to render the Military independent of and superior to the Civil Power." Several state constitutions, including the Virginia and Massachusetts Bills of Rights, contained declarations that the military should in all cases and at all times be subordinate to and governed by the civil power. CHARLES PINCKNEY vainly proposed inclusion of similar language in the federal Constitution, and the lack of such a provision was the target of much criticism in the state conventions. Objections were also raised because the Constitution had no provision guarding against the dangers of a peacetime standing army.

In practice civil supremacy prevailed for two reasons: the deeply ingrained antimilitary attitudes continuously prevalent in American political culture, and the equally deeply ingrained ideal of the apolitical, nonpartisan, impartial military professional that gained ascendancy in the officer corps after the Civil War. In the early nineteenth century, the line between professional officer and professional politician was unclear, and individual military officers were often involved in politics. After World War II many military officers were appointed to high civil positions in government. Yet at no time, in peace or war, did serious challenges to civilian authority issue from the central military institutions. When, as in the Civil War and the KOREAN WAR, individual military leaders challenged or seemed to challenge the authority of the President, they were removed from command. The Supreme Court, in EX PARTE MILLIGAN (1866), also limited military power by holding that martial law may operate only in situations where actual conflict forces civil courts to close. The Court has also narrowly defined the extent to which American civilians accompanying the armed forces overseas are subject to military justice, as in REID V. COVERT (1957).

In the 1780s there was general agreement that the militia should be the principal source of defense for a free society. Some members of the Constitutional Convention proposed prohibiting a standing army in peacetime or limiting the size of such an army. These proposals were rebutted both in the debates and in THE FEDERALIST by arguments that there was no way to prevent another nation with a standing army from threatening the United States, and that inability to maintain such a force would invite aggression. Everyone agreed, however, that in keeping with the tradition dating from the English BILL OF RIGHTS of 1689, the power to establish military forces rested with Congress. There was widespread belief that appropriations for the army should be limited to one year, and a two-year limit was approved only because it seemed likely that Congress might assemble only once every two years. The Constitution is silent on the means Congress may employ to recruit military manpower. CONSCRIPTION was, however, an accepted eighteenth-century practice, and the Supreme Court has held that the power to "raise and support" armies included, "beyond question," the power "to classify and conscript manpower for military service" in peace or in war.

The early consensus on the central role of the militia did not extend to the question of who should control it. Traditionally, the militias had been state forces, and it was widely accepted that they should remain under state control in time of peace. The national government, however, needed the power to call on the militia to deal with invasions or insurrections. Experience in the Revolution also had demonstrated the need to insure that the militia meet minimum national standards. JAMES MADISON remarked that control over the militia "did not seem in its nature to be divisible between two distinct authorities," but in the end that control was divided: the national government took responsibility for organizing, arming, and disciplining the militia, and the state governments were responsible for the appointment of officers and training. In the debates that led to this shared control, the most repeated and persuasive argument of the nationalists was the need to have a well-organized and disciplined militia under national control so as to reduce reliance on a standing army. Support in the state conventions for what subsequently became the SECOND AMENDMENT was based on similar reasoning.

In the Militia Act of 1792, Congress did not effectively exercise its powers to organize, arm, and discipline the militia. In effect, the states retained sole control over the militia in peacetime. When required, the militia was called into federal service for the limited constitutional purposes of executing the laws, suppressing insurrections, and repelling invasions. Even in wartime, however, the assertion of federal control was controversial because the states guarded their power to appoint officers. In addition, militia units could not be used outside the United States. Thus in the nineteenth century the militia was under state control in peace and under dual control in war. Laws passed between 1903 and 1933 in effect put the militia, now called the National Guard, under dual control in peace and national control in war. Federal support was greatly expanded, federal standards were more effectively imposed, and provision was made to order the National Guard into federal service in war under the army clause of the Constitution, thus precluding any assertion of state power.

In Great Britain the king was the COMMANDER-IN-CHIEF of the army and navy and in some states the governors played similar roles. The Federal Convention gave the President command of the national military forces and of the militia when in federal service. War Presidents, most notably ABRAHAM LINCOLN, FRANKLIN ROOSEVELT, and LYNDON B. JOHNSON, actively directed military operations. The commander-in-chief clause is unique in the Constitution in assigning power in terms of an office rather than a function. It is, consequently, unclear to what extent it gives the President powers extending beyond military command. In *The Federalist,* ALEXANDER HAMILTON wrote that the clause grants "nothing more than the supreme command and direction of the military and naval forces"; yet he also wrote that the clause makes the executive responsible for the "direction of war" and gives him "the power of directing and employing the common strength." The latter definition might justify a President's seizing a steel plant to insure the continuation of war production; the former clearly would not. Beginning with Lincoln, Presidents have, however, used the clause to justify the exercise of a wide range of war powers.

The ineligibility clause of the Constitution expressly prohibits appointment of congressmen to civil positions created while they are in Congress. The Framers specifically exempted military positions, because, in case of a war, citizens capable of conducting it might be members of Congress. The incompatibility clause, on the other hand, applies to both civil and military offices. Enforced in the nineteenth century, this prohibition against simultaneously holding legislative position and military office has been frequently and systematically violated in the twentieth century by congressmen holding reserve commissions in the military services.

The more fundamental provisions in the Constitution regarding the distribution of power have had an equal effect on shaping civil–military relations, complicating, and at times frustrating, the achievement of civilian control over the military. FEDERALISM required that authority over the militia be divided between state and national governments. This division has enhanced the power of the militia by giving them two masters that might be played off against each other. The division of control over the national forces between Congress and President has worked in comparable fashion. Military officers testifying before congressional committees have some freedom to determine how far they should go in defending the policies of their commander-in-chief and how far they should go in expressing their own views. Military officers working in implicit cooperation with influential members of Congress may be able to undermine policies of the President. In addition, the commander-in-chief clause has at times been interpreted to encourage a direct relationship between the President and the uniformed heads of the armed services, bypassing the civilian secretaries of those departments. The Framers clearly intended to establish firm civilian control over the military, and many specific provisions are designed to secure that goal. Yet, by limiting the power of each branch of the government, the constitutional system effectively limits the power those branches can exercise over the military.

SAMUEL P. HUNTINGTON

Bibliography

HUNTINGTON, SAMUEL P. 1957 *The Soldier and the State: The Theory and Politics of Civil–Military Relations.* Cambridge, Mass.: Harvard University Press.

RIKER, WILLIAM H. 1957 *Soldiers of the States: The Role of the National Guard in American Democracy.* Washington, D.C.: Public Affairs Press.

SMITH, LOUIS 1951 *American Democracy and Military Power.* Chicago: University of Chicago Press.

CIVIL RIGHTS

The core of the concept "civil rights" is freedom from RACIAL DISCRIMINATION. Although the term, not improperly, often refers to freedom from discrimination based on nationality, alienage, gender, age, sexual preference, or physical or mental handicap—or even RELIGIOUS LIBERTY, immunity from official brutality, FREEDOM OF ASSEMBLY AND ASSOCIATION, FREEDOM OF THE PRESS, FREEDOM OF SPEECH, the RIGHT OF PRIVACY, and additional rights found in the Constitution or elsewhere—other terms can characterize these rights. Sometimes they are referred to as CIVIL LIBERTIES or by particular names (for example, gender or handicap discrimination). Although the racial discrimination cases have influenced doctrinal development in many of these other areas, standards governing them often differ at the levels of both judicial scrutiny and appropriate remedies. Racial discrimination deserves separate treatment.

The constitutional law of civil rights begins in the THIRTEENTH, FOURTEENTH, and FIFTEENTH AMENDMENTS. These "Civil War Amendments" were adopted during Reconstruction to effect a radical revision of the status of blacks and a sharp change in relations between national and state governments. Until the end of the Civil War, the situation of black people had been dominated by SLAVERY in the South and a regime under which, in the words of the Supreme Court in DRED SCOTT V. SANDFORD (1857), they had no rights that a white man was bound to respect. Their legal rights or disabilities derived from state law, subject to no meaningful control by the national government. The Civil War amendments changed that. The Thirteenth Amendment abolished slavery; the Fourteenth, among other things, prohibited states from denying to any person DUE PROCESS OF LAW or EQUAL PROTECTION OF THE LAWS. (Other provisions of the Fourteenth Amendment had little practical effect). The Fifteenth Amendment protected VOTING RIGHTS against governmentally imposed racial discrimination.

Each amendment empowered Congress to adopt enforcing legislation. Such laws were enacted—most notably the CIVIL RIGHTS ACT OF 1866—but they were not implemented, were interpreted restrictively, or fell into disuse following the COMPROMISE OF 1877 which assured the Presidential election of RUTHERFORD B. HAYES in exchange for his pledge to withdraw Union troops from the South and end Reconstruction. During the same period southern states, effectively free from national control, implemented BLACK CODES, and later Jim Crow laws, which returned black people to a status that was only nominally free. No significant national civil rights law was adopted again until the mid-1960s.

Between Reconstruction and the mid-twentieth century, the judiciary sporadically found significant content in the Civil War Amendments; yet racial SEGREGATION and discrimination remained pervasive in the South and widespread elsewhere. During the same period, the Fourteenth Amendment was interpreted expansively to protect burgeoning business enterprise. Between BROWN V. BOARD OF EDUCATION (1954) and the CIVIL RIGHTS ACT OF 1964, the main period of the modern civil rights revolution, the doctrinal potential of the amendments to advance the cause of black people became largely realized. Implementation became the main task, taking the form of comprehensive civil rights statutes, lawsuits brought by the United States and private parties, and administrative enforcement. As a result of this process, some whites have charged that remedies for blacks violate *their* constitutional rights: for example, that AFFIRMATIVE ACTION constitutes "reverse discrimination," or that SCHOOL BUSING for integration injures them. Justice OLIVER WENDELL HOLMES's aphorism, "the life of the law has not been logic: it has been experience," is as least as true of civil rights law as of any other branch of law.

The concept of "equal protection of the laws" underwent its greatest evolution between 1896, when PLESSY V. FERGUSON upheld a state law requiring SEPARATE BUT EQUAL segregation of whites and blacks in intrastate rail travel, and 1954, when *Brown v. Board of Education* held that segregated public EDUCATION denied equal protection. Although *Plessy* dealt only with intrastate transportation and *Brown* only with education, each was quickly generalized to other aspects of life.

The very factors which the Supreme Court invoked to uphold segregation in 1896 were reassessed in *Brown* and used to justify a contrary result. The *Plessy* majority held that the framers of the Civil War Amendments did not intend to eliminate segregation in rail travel which the Court characterized as a social, not a political activity. It thereby distinguished STRAUDER V. WEST VIRGINIA (1880), in which the Supreme Court had held that excluding blacks from juries violated the Fourteenth Amendment because it stigmatized them. *Plessy* dismissed the argument that segregating blacks from whites could justify segregating Protestants from Catholics, because that would be unreasonable; racial segregation was reasonable, for state court decisions and statutes had authorized segregation in schools. Finally, the Court addressed what today is called social psychology, writing that although *Plessy* claimed segregation connoted black inferiority, whites would not consider themselves stigmatized if they were segregated by a legislature controlled by blacks. Any harmful psychological effects of segregation were self-inflicted.

Plessy became so deeply ingrained in jurisprudence that as late as 1927, in GONG LUM V. RICE, a Court in which Holmes, LOUIS D. BRANDEIS, and HARLAN F. STONE sat unanimously agreed that racial segregation in education "has been many times decided to be within the constitutional power of the state legislature to settle, without the intervention of the federal courts under the Federal Constitution."

Other Supreme Court decisions, however, offered hope that some day the Court might come to a contrary conclusion. In YICK WO V. HOPKINS (1886) the Court invalidated as a denial of equal protection a city ordinance which, under the guise of prohibiting laundries from operating in wooden buildings, where virtually all Chinese laundries were located, excluded Chinese from that business. In BUCHANAN V. WARLEY (1917) it invalidated racial zoning of urban land under the due process clause. Later it struck down state laws prohibiting blacks from participating in primary elections. By 1950, in SWEATT V. PAINTER and MCLAURIN V. OKLAHOMA STATE REGENTS, the Court invalidated segregation in law school and graduate education, without holding segregation unconstitutional per se and without abandoning the separate-but-equal formula. These and other decisions foreshadowed *Brown* and undermined precedents approving segregation.

Brown contradicted or distinguished *Plessy* on every score. It read the legislative history of the Civil War Amendments as inconclusive on the question of school segregation, pointing out that although after the Civil War public education had been undeveloped and almost nonexistent for blacks, it had become perhaps the most important function of state government. In effect the amendment was treated as embodying a general evolutionary principle of equality which developed as education became more important. The Court treated early precedents as not controlling school segregation and drew from the 1950 graduate school cases support for a contrary result.

In contrast to *Plessy*'s dismissal of the psychological effects of segregation, *Brown* held that "to segregate them [black children] from others of similar age and qualifications solely because of their race generates a feeling of inferiority as to their status in the community that may affect their hearts and minds in a way unlikely ever to be undone." The Court cited social science literature in support of this response to *Plessy*. This portion of the opinion provoked much adverse commentary, some condemning the decision as based on social science, not law. But of course, *Plessy* had come to its sociological conclusions without any evidence at all.

In BOLLING V. SHARPE, a companion case to *Brown*, the Court decided that the Fifth Amendment's due process clause prohibited school segregation in the District of Columbia. Any other result, the Court said, would be "unthinkable."

The contending arguments in *Plessy* and *Brown* not only exemplify the possibilities of legal advocacy but also raise the question how "equal protection" could be interpreted so differently at different times. After all, the arguments remained the same, but first one side prevailed, then the other. The reason for the change lies in the development of American history. Indeed, *Brown* suggests as much in describing how much public education had changed between Reconstruction and 1954, how essential education had become for personal development, and how much blacks had achieved. By 1954 black citizens had fought for their country in two major World Wars, the more recent of which was won against Nazi racism; had moved from concentration in the South to a more even distribution throughout the country; and had achieved much socially, politically, economically, and educationally, even though their status remained below that of whites.

The courtroom struggle leading to *Brown* showed that blacks were ready to participate effectively in securing their full liberation. It culminated a planned litigation campaign, building precedent upon precedent, directed by a group of mostly black lawyers headed by THURGOOD MARSHALL, then head of the NAACP LEGAL DEFENSE AND EDUCATIONAL FUND and later a Justice of the United States Supreme Court. This campaign had many ramifications, not the least of which was to become a model for development of public interest law, which grew rapidly in the 1970s.

The nation owed black people a debt which it acknowledged officially in several ways. In the late 1940s and in *Brown* itself the solicitor general of the United States joined counsel for black litigants in calling upon the Supreme Court to declare segregation unconstitutional. That the country was generally prepared to accept this argument was further evidenced in the 1947 Report of President HARRY S. TRUMAN's Committee on Civil Rights. The committee called for the end of racial segregation and discrimination in education, PUBLIC ACCOMMODATIONS, housing, employment, voting, and all other aspects of American life.

Despite the storm of controversy stirred by the 1954 decisions, they are firmly rooted in constitutional law and nowadays there is no longer significant criticism of their results. *Brown* was quickly followed by decisions applying its principles to all other forms of state imposed racial segregation. Courts soon ordered desegregation of parks, beaches, sporting events, hospitals, publically owned or managed accommodations, and other public facilities.

But *Brown* could not affect the rights of blacks against privately imposed discrimination, for the equal protection clause is a directive to the states. The admonition that "no state" shall deny equal protection was not addressed to private employers, property owners, or those who managed privately owned public accommodations. In the CIVIL RIGHTS CASES (1883) the Supreme Court made clear not only that the equal protection clause did not apply to private action but that Congress in enforcing the Fourteenth Amendment might not prohibit private persons from discriminating. As a consequence, national civil rights laws could not apply to private restaurants, hotels, transportation, employment, and housing—places where people spend most of their lives.

In 1960 the SIT-INS, freedom rides, and DEMONSTRATIONS burst upon the national scene, aimed first at racial exclusion from privately owned public accommodations and then at other forms of discrimination. This phase of the civil rights struggle sought to move antidiscrimination precepts beyond the limitation of state power to prohibitions against private discrimination. The cases arising out of these efforts necessarily examined the distinction between what is private and what is STATE ACTION, an issue long debated in political theory and constitutional law. On the one hand, it has been argued that privately asserted rights derive from power conferred and enforced by the state and that at bottom there is no such thing as a "private" right. According to this reasoning, applying the TRESPASS laws to enforce an owner's privately held preference against black patronage of his lunch counter would be prohibited by the Fourteenth Amendment: the owner's property interest is a function of state law; the law of trespass is a state creation; prosecution and its consequences are state conduct. Pursuing such reasoning, lawyers for sit-in demonstrators identified the governmental components of otherwise private action, arguing that the Fourteenth Amendment, therefore, protected blacks who were denied service on racial grounds and later prosecuted for refusing to leave the premises. They had some legal support for this argument. Even before 1954 the Supreme Court had held in MARSH V. ALABAMA (1946) that religious proselytizing on company town property was protected by the FIRST AMENDMENT against prosecution for trespass because the town was a governmental entity, notwithstanding private ownership. Similarly, the equal protection clause had been interpreted to forbid enforcement by state courts or racially RESTRICTIVE COVENANTS against purchase or occupancy of real estate by blacks or other minorities. These cases, and their rationales, followed to the end of their logic, would mean that governmental enforcement of private discrimination violates the equal protection clause.

But the courts were not prepared to follow the reasoning to its logical conclusion. In cases in which blacks were arrested and prosecuted for entering or remaining on privately owned public accommodations where they were not wanted because of race, the Supreme Court first avoided deciding whether there was state action by ruling for the defendants on various other grounds, for example, lack of evidence or VAGUENESS of the law. In other cases the Court found state action in special circumstances: a private owner segregated because required by law; an ordinance required segregated toilets, which tended to encourage exclusion of blacks; a private restaurant leased premises from a state agency; private security guards who enforced segregation were also deputy sheriffs. But the Court balked at finding state action in prosecution for trespass to enforce a proprietor's personal decision to discriminate. The resistance grew out of a fear that to extend the state action doctrine would make most private decisions subject to government control. Moreover, if one could not call upon the state to enforce private preferences, personal force might be employed.

Other legal theorists would have differentiated between conduct prohibited by the amendment and that which is not by factoring into the decision-making process the concept of privacy. They would find, for example, that impermissible state action existed in racial exclusion from a restaurant but not from a private home. The policy against racial discrimination would prevail in the restaurant case, where there was no countervailing interest of privacy, but in the private home case the privacy interest would outweigh strictures against racial discrimination.

In 1964 the Court held that the Civil Rights Act of that year invalidated convictions of sit-in demonstrators, even those convicted before its passage. The fundamental question of precisely what level of state involvement in private conduct constitutes state action was left undecided.

The uncertain scope of the state action doctrine was underscored by the constitutional basis advanced for congressional power to pass the 1964 Civil Rights Act. Congress relied on the COMMERCE CLAUSE in addition to the Fourteenth Amendment because the commerce clause does not require state action to justify congressional regulation. The initial Supreme Court decisions upholding the 1964 Civil Rights Act, HEART OF ATLANTA MOTEL V. UNITED STATES (1964) and KATZENBACH V. MCCLUNG (1964), relied on the commerce clause, and upheld applications of the law in cases of minimal effect upon commerce.

The impulse to define fully the meaning of state action was further damped by developments in Thirteenth Amendment law. The Thirteenth Amendment has no state action limitation and, therefore, covers private as well as state action. But early efforts to apply it to discrimination as a BADGE OF SERVITUDE were rejected by the Court, which held that the amendment forbade only slavery itself. The Civil Rights Act of 1866 had made illegal private racially discriminatory refusals to contract or engage in real estate transactions. But not until 1968 did the Supreme Court interpret these laws to forbid private discrimination. By the mid-1960s, through the civil rights acts of that period and the new judicial interpretation of Reconstruction legislation, it was no longer necessary to discover state action in ostensibly private conduct in order to prevent discrimination. With the passing of this need, concerted efforts to expand the courts' views of the state action concept came to a halt.

The contrast between the promise of the Constitution and its performance was nowhere better highlighted than in *Brown* itself. The Supreme Court treated constitutional right and remedy in two separate opinions, *Brown I* and *Brown II,* decided in 1955. *Brown I* decided only that racial segregation was unconstitutional, postponing decisions on the means and the pace of school desegregation. *Brown II* proclaimed that school segregation need not end immediately; it had to be accomplished with ALL DELIBERATE SPEED. The Court required a "prompt and reasonable" start, and permitted delay only for the time necessary for administrative changes. Opposition to desegregation, the Court said, would not justify delay. Nevertheless, southern schools actually integrated at an extremely slow pace. Not until 1969, when the Court announced that the time for "deliberate speed" had passed, did school integration proceed rapidly.

While the "deliberate speed" decision contributed to a sense that desegregation was not urgent and procrastination was tolerable, it is difficult to believe that a different formula would have materially affected the pace of integration. Armed physical opposition in Little Rock and elsewhere in the South was aimed at integration at any time, with or without deliberate speed. One hundred members of Congress signed the SOUTHERN MANIFESTO denouncing the Supreme Court, and Congress came within a single vote of severely restricting the Court's JURISDICTION. Congressional legislation implementing *Brown* would not be adopted until after the civil rights movement of the 1960s.

The refusal of school districts to desegregate was not susceptible to remedy because there was almost no one who would bring integration suits. No southern white lawyers would bring school suits until the 1970s; in many a southern state, there was only a handful of black lawyers with minimal resources; civil rights organizations were few, small, and overburdened; the United States Justice Department and the Department of Health, Education, and Welfare had no authority to bring suit. As a consequence, where school boards resisted or claimed to be in compliance with *Brown,* there was hardly any way to compel change. These conditions, not "deliberate speed," kept school segregation in place. Real opportunities for the judiciary to speed the pace of integration had to await political change. That change came in the 1960s, with the pro-civil rights policies of Presidents JOHN F. KENNEDY and LYNDON B. JOHNSON, culminating in the Civil Rights Act of 1964.

Supreme Court opinions stating in OBITER DICTUM that integration must be achieved rapidly began to be issued at the end of the 1960s. In the 1970s courts began to hand down detailed orders requiring the end of segregation "root and branch." Because black and white families were segregated residentially, the only way to integrate schools in many communities was to combine in single attendance zones areas separated by some distance, thus employing SCHOOL BUSING. Numerical standards also were employed to measure whether acceptable levels of integration had been reached. These techniques—particularly busing and RACIAL QUOTAS—have stimulated controversy and political opposition.

The integration of the 1970s in most instances was carried out as quickly as possible when courts ordered it. Although the deliberate speed doctrine had by then been overruled, such rapid desegregation met its literal requirements. In a typical case, the revision of boundaries and regulations and the reassignment of students and teachers took a few months. Conditions in the nation, not "deliberate speed," caused the long delay.

Brown, of course, concerned states where segregation had been required or permitted by statute. By the 1970s the Supreme Court faced the issue of northern segregation which was not caused by state statute. It differentiated between "de facto" segregation (resulting from racially segregated housing patterns) and "de jure" segregation (resulting from deliberate official decisions). Some commentators argued that there is no such thing as de facto segregation, for children always are assigned to schools by governmental action. But only where some intent to discriminate was demonstrated did the courts require desegregation. However, where an intent to discriminate has been shown in part of a district, a presumption has been held to arise that single-race schools elsewhere in the district have been the product of such intent. Under this doctrine many northern districts have been desegregated.

Often a city school district is nearly all black and

surrounded by white suburban districts. The Court held in MILLIKEN V. BRADLEY (1974) that integration across district lines may not be ordered without proof of an interdistrict violation. A number of lower courts have found such violations and have ordered integration across district lines.

All of these standards were implemented, particularly in the 1970s, by the Departments of Justice and Health, Education, and Welfare (later the Department of Education). The private bar brought a considerable number of cases facilitated by congressional legislation authorizing the award of counsel to prevailing parties in school segregation, to be paid by defendants. But the intimate relation between politics and implementation of constitutional civil rights became apparent once more in the 1980s when a new administration opposed to busing and numerical standards for gauging integration virtually ceased bringing school cases to court, undertook to modify or revoke INJUNCTIONS in already decided cases, and opposed private plaintiffs in others.

Following *Brown* and in response to the demonstrations of the 1960s, the Civil Rights Acts of 1964, 1965, and 1968 were enacted with the goal of implementing the ideals of the Civil War amendments. But results of these laws varied according to their political, social, and legal settings. Public accommodations, for example, integrated easily; housing has been intractable. Affirmative action policies have been devised to assure certain levels of minority participation, but they have stimulated opposition by whites who claim they are being disfavored and illegally so. Controversy has also developed over the question of whether antidiscrimination orders might be entered only upon a showing of official discriminatory intent, or whether such orders are also justified to remedy the racially discriminatory effects of official policies. Affirmative action and discriminatory intent, the twin central legal issues of civil rights in the 1980s, have in common a concern with distributive fairness. Both issues have been contested in political, statutory, and constitutional arenas.

In general, the courts have sustained the constitutionality of affirmative action as a congressional remedy for past discriminations and as an appropriate judicial remedy for past statutory or constitutional violations. In medical school admissions, for example, four Justices of the Supreme Court thought a fixed racial quota favoring minorities violated the Civil Rights Act of 1964, and a fifth Justice found an equal protection violation; a different majority, however, concluded that an admissions policy favoring racial and other diversity, which assured the admission of a substantial but not fixed number of minorities, would be valid as an aspect of a university's First Amendment exercise of academic freedom. The Court, with three dissents, has sustained a congressionally mandated quota assuring ten percent of certain government contracts to minority contractors. And in school integration numerical measures of integration have been commonplace. In employment and voting as well, affirmative action has been incorporated into efforts to undo discrimination and has been upheld by the courts. [See REGENTS OF UNIVERSITY OF CALIFORNIA V. BAKKE (1978), and FULLILOVE V. KLUTZNICK 1980).]

The courts usually have required a showing of discriminatory intent in order to establish an equal protection violation, but intent may be inferred from conduct. In any event, the intent requirement may be dispensed with where Congress has legislated to make discriminatory results adequate to trigger corrective action.

The public accommodations portions of the 1964 Act prohibited discrimination in specific types of establishments (typified by those providing food or amusement) that affect INTERSTATE COMMERCE. An exception for private clubs reflected uncertainty about the lack of power (perhaps arising out of countervailing constitutional rights of association) and the desirability of controlling discrimination in such places. But the meaning of "private" in this context has not been explicated. Clubs where a substantial amount of business is conducted may not be exempt and an amendment has been proposed to make this clear.

Immediately following passage of the law the Department of Justice and private plaintiffs brought successful suits against recalcitrant enterprises. Most public accommodations complied rapidly. Large national enterprises that segregated in the South integrated because they could not afford the obloquy of resistance, threat of boycott, and consequent loss of business in the North. Many small southern businesses opened to all without problems. Even proprietors who wished to continue discriminating soon bowed to the law's commands. Today one rarely hears of public accommodations discrimination.

Before adoption of the civil rights legislation of the 1960s, the only significant federal regulations of employment discrimination were the Fifth Amendment and Fourteenth Amendment, which prohibited federal and state employment discrimination, and executive order prohibition of discrimination by certain government contractors. The Railway Labor Act and the NATIONAL LABOR RELATIONS ACT were construed to forbid discrimination by covered unions. But all such limitations were difficult to enforce. The Civil Rights Act of 1964 and the 1968 Equal Employment Opportunity (EEO) Act were the first effective prohibitions against discrimination in employment. Private suits (with counsel fees payable to prevailing plaintiffs), suits by the Equal Employment Opportunity Commission against private defendants, and suits by the Justice Department against state and local government are the primary mechanisms of enforcement. As elsewhere in modern civil rights law, the two most important issues with constitutional overtones under this law have been whether a plaintiff must prove that discrimination was intentional and whether courts may award affirmative relief, including racial quotas. As to intent, the EEO statute has been interpreted to forbid hiring and promotion criteria that have an adverse impact on a protected group but bear no adequate relationship to ability to perform the job. Thus, an intelligence test for coal handlers, or a height requirement for prison guards, which screen out blacks or women and do not indicate ability to do the job, violate the statute even absent a showing of intent to discriminate. On the other hand, when the statute is not applicable, a plaintiff can secure relief under the Constitution only by showing intentional discrimination.

Affirmative action in the form of hiring and promotion goals and timetables have been prescribed by courts and all branches of the federal government with enforcement responsibility. Moreover, some private employers have adopted these techniques as a matter of social policy or to head off anticipated charges of discrimination. The legality of such programs has been upheld in the vast majority of cases. Affirmative action has substantially increased minority and female participation in jobs it covers but continues to be attacked by nonprotected groups as unconstitutional, illegal, or unwise. In 1984 the Supreme Court held that the EEO Act prohibits enjoining layoffs of black beneficiaries of a consent decree requiring certain levels of black employment where that would result in discharging whites with greater seniority.

Although the Fifteenth Amendment expressly protects the right to vote against racial discrimination and the Fourteenth Amendment's equal protection clause also has been interpreted to do so, voting discrimination was widespread and blatant well into the 1960s, and to some extent it still persists. Apart from physical violence and intimidation, which lasted until the mid-1960s, a long line of discriminatory devices has been held to be in violation of the Constitution and statutes, only to be succeeded by new ones. Very early, southern states adopted GRANDFATHER CLAUSES, requiring voters to pass literacy tests but exempting those who were entitled to vote in 1866, along with their lineal descendants—which meant whites only. When the courts struck down the grandfather clause, it was succeeded by laws permitting registration only during a very brief period of time without passing a literacy test. Thereafter even those who could pass the test were not permitted to register. Very few blacks could take advantage of this narrow window, but the stratagem was not outlawed until 1939. Most southern states through the 1920s had laws prohibiting blacks from voting in party PRIMARY ELECTIONS. In the South, the Democratic party excluded blacks, and the winner of the Democratic primary always was elected. These laws were held unconstitutional in the 1940s and 1950s on the grounds that the party primary was an integral part of the state's electoral system, despite its nominal autonomy. As the white primary fell, laws and practices were widely adopted requiring registrants to read and understand texts like the Alabama State Constitution or to answer registrars' questions such as "how many bubbles are there in a bar of soap." These tests were held unconstitutional. Racial GERRYMANDERING, a not uncommon practice where blacks in fact voted, also was enjoined as unconstitutional. Other impediments to voting were not motivated solely by racial considerations but affected blacks disproportionately, such as the POLL TAX, later prohibited by constitutional amendment. LITERACY TESTS also lent themselves to discriminatory administration.

The VOTING RIGHTS ACT OF 1965 invalidated any and all racially discriminatory tests and devices. But, more important, states in which there was a history of voting discrimination (identified by low registration or voter turnout) could not adopt new voting standards unless those standards were certified as nondiscriminatory by the Department of Justice. This prohibition ended the tactic of substituting one discriminatory device for another. Where they were needed, federal officials could be sent to monitor registration and voting or, indeed, to register voters.

Although the 1965 law significantly reduced racial discrimination in the electoral process, abuses persisted in the forms of inconvenient registration procedures, gerrymandering, occasional intimidation, and creation of MULTIMEMBER DISTRICTS. This last device has its roots in post-Reconstruction efforts to dilute black voting strength. The use of single-member districts to elect a city council would result in the election of blacks from those districts where blacks constitute a majority. By declaring the entire city a multimember district, entitled to elect a number of at-large candidates, the majority white population can, if votes are racially polarized, elect an all-white council—a result that has occurred frequently. The Supreme Court required a showing of discriminatory intent if such a voting system were to be held unconstitutional. But the interplay between Court and Congress produced an amendment of the Voting Rights Act in 1982, permitting proof of a violation of the act by a showing of discriminatory effect.

Affirmative action has been an issue in voting as in other areas. The Supreme Court has held that, upon a showing of past voting discrimination, the attorney general may condition approval of legislative redistricting upon a race-conscious drawing of district lines to facilitate election of minority candidates.

Until 1968, the most important federal prohibition of housing discrimination was the equal protection clause, which was held in SHELLEY V. KRAEMER (1948) to prohibit judicial enforcement of restrictive covenants among property owners forbidding occupancy of property by members of racial minorities. The Fifth and Fourteenth Amendments prohibit racial segregation in public housing, but the construction of public housing has virtually ceased.

The Fair Housing Act of 1968 marked the completion of the main statutory efforts to satisfy the prescriptions of President HARRY S. TRUMAN's 1947 Committee on Civil Rights. On the eve of the law's passage, the Supreme Court interpreted the Civil Rights Act of 1866 to forbid refusals to engage in real property transactions on racial grounds. Nonetheless, the 1866 and 1968 acts have been the least effective of the civil rights acts. Their failure owes to deep, persistent opposition to housing integration, to a lack of means of enforcement commensurate with the extent of the problem, and to a shortage in the housing market of houses in the price range which most minority buyers can afford. Because the housing market is atomized, a single court order cannot have widespread effect. (Housing is thus unlike education, where an entire district may be desegregated, or employment, where government agencies and other large employers can be required to take steps affecting thousands of employees.)

An effort to address the relationship between race and economics in housing foundered at the constitutional level when the Court held that large-lot zoning—which precluded construction of inexpensive housing, thereby excluding minorities—was not invalid under the Constitution absent a demonstration of racially discriminatory intent. The 1968 Fair Housing Act authorizes judicial relief when such laws produce discriminatory effects, without demonstration of intent. Nevertheless, economic factors and political opposition have prevented the statutory standard from having a significant practical impact. In several states where state law has invalidated such zoning, the actual change in racial housing patterns has been slight.

Some legislative efforts to desegregate housing have run into constitutional obstacles. A municipality's prohibition of "For Sale" signs to discourage panic selling by whites in integrated neighborhoods has been held to violate the First Amendment. A judge's award of damages for violation of the Fair Housing Act has been held to violate the Sixth Amendment right of TRIAL BY JURY (subsequently, contrary to civil rights lawyers' expectations, jury verdicts often have been favorable to plaintiffs). A large governmentally assisted housing development's racial quota, set up with the aim of preventing "tipping" (whites moving out when the percentage of blacks exceeds a certain point), was still being contested in the mid-1980s.

From constitutional adoption, through interpretation, and judicial and statutory implementation, the law of civil rights has interacted with the world that called it into being. No great departures from settled doctrine are to be anticipated in the near future. But similar assertions might have been made confidently at various points in the history of civil rights, only to be proved wrong in years to come.

JACK GREENBERG

Bibliography

BLACK, CHARLES L., JR. 1967 Foreword: State Action, Equal Protection, and California's Proposition 14. *Harvard Law Review* 81:69–109.

EASTLAND, TERRY and BENNETT, WILLIAM J. 1979 *Counting by Race.* New York: Basic Books.

GREENBERG, JACK 1968 The Supreme Court, Civil Rights and Civil Dissonance. *Yale Law Journal* 77:1520–1544.

JOINT CENTER FOR POLITICAL STUDIES 1984 *Minority Vote Dilution,* Chandler Davidson, ed. Washington, D.C.: Howard University Press.

KIRP, DAVID L. 1983 *Just Schools: The Idea of Racial Equality in American Education.* Berkeley: University of California Press.

KLUGER, RICHARD 1975 *Simple Justice: The History of Brown v. Board of Education and Black America's Struggle for Equality.* New York: Knopf.

KONVITZ, MILTON R. 1961 *Century of Civil Rights.* New York: Columbia University Press.

KUSHNER, JAMES A. 1983 *Fair Housing: Discrimination*

in Real Estate, Community Development, and Revitalization. New York: Shepard's/McGraw-Hill.

SCHLEI, BARBARA and GROSSMAN, PAUL 1983 *Employment Discrimination Law,* 2nd ed. Washington, D.C.: Bureau of National Affairs.

U.S. COMMISSION ON CIVIL RIGHTS 1981 *Affirmative Action in the 1980's: Dismantling the Process of Discrimination.* Washington, D.C.: U.S. Commission on Civil Rights.

CIVIL RIGHTS ACT OF 1866
(Framing)
14 Stat. 27

Responding to the Black Codes, Congress in 1866 passed its first CIVIL RIGHTS bill to enforce the THIRTEENTH AMENDMENT. The bill's definition of national CITIZENSHIP superseded the decision in DRED SCOTT V. SANDFORD (1857), which had excluded blacks. A citizen was any person not an Indian or of foreign allegiance born in any state or territory, regardless of color. All citizens were to enjoy full and EQUAL PROTECTION of all laws and procedures for the protection of persons and property, and be subject to like punishments without regard to former slave status. In all jurisdictions citizens were to have equal rights to sue, contract, witness, purchase, lease, sell, inherit, or otherwise convey personal or real property. Anyone who, "under color of any law . . . or custom," prevented any person from enjoying those rights, or who subjected any person to discriminatory criminal punishments because of race or previous involuntary servitude, was subject to MISDEMEANOR prosecutions in federal courts. Congress further authorized the REMOVAL OF CASES from state to federal courts of persons denied civil rights and of federal officer defendants, prosecuted by states, protecting civil rights; that provision connected the civil rights bill to the FREEDMEN'S BUREAU and the HABEAS CORPUS statutes. All federal officials could initiate proceedings under the bill. Federal judges were to appoint special commissioners to enforce judgments under the bill (a use of fugitive slave law processes for opposite purposes). Alternatively, judges could employ the army or state militias, under the President's command, as posses. Last, Congress expanded the Supreme Court's APPELLATE JURISDICTION to include questions of law arising from the statute.

President ANDREW JOHNSON's powerful veto of the Civil Rights Bill, though overridden by Congress, touched both honorable traditions of the states' monopoly of rights and ignoble concepts of race hierarchy. He insisted that the bill would create a centralized military despotism and invoked the recent EX PARTE MILLIGAN (1866) decision. Congress, he argued, was creating black citizens of the same states it was excluding from representation.

Though trenchant, the veto never touched on the question of the remedies available to injured citizens or the nation, when states failed to carry out their duty to treat their own citizens equally. If no statutory remedies existed, then both nation and states were returned to the conditions of 1860. Anxious to make clear the fact of the nation's advance from that pitiable condition, the Congress pushed ahead with a FOURTEENTH AMENDMENT proposal and, in 1867, resorted to military reconstruction as a desperate stop-gap.

But the Fourteenth Amendment, unlike the Thirteenth (which the Civil Rights Act enforced) constrained only STATE ACTION, at least according to Supreme Court judgments commencing with the *Slaughterhouse* case (1873). In May 1870, the Congress "re-enacted" the 1866 Civil Rights law, this time under the Fourteenth and FIFTEENTH AMENDMENTS (though section 16 of the 1870 law still punished discriminatory felonious private acts). In 1874, a revision of the federal statutes appeared, breaking up the text of the 1866 statute into scattered sections.

HAROLD M. HYMAN

(SEE ALSO: *Section 1983, Title 42, United States Code.*)

Bibliography

HOWE, M. A. DEWOLFE 1965 Federalism and Civil Rights. [Massachusetts Historical Society] *Proceedings* 77:15–27.

HYMAN, HAROLD M. and WIECEK, WILLIAM M. 1982 *Equal Justice under Law: Constitutional Development 1835–1875.* Chaps. 9–11. New York: Harper & Row.

KACZOROWSKI, ROBERT J. 1971 Nationalization of Civil Rights: Theory and Practice in a Racist Society, 1866–1883. Ph.D. diss., University of Minnesota.

CIVIL RIGHTS ACT OF 1866
(Judicial Interpretation)

Judicial interpretation has transformed the Civil Rights Act of 1866 from a simple effort to dismantle the BLACK CODES into one of the most important existing CIVIL RIGHTS laws. In assessing judicial treatment of the act, it is helpful to consider section one of the act separately from section three. Other sections have not led to noteworthy judicial development. Section one of the act, which granted all persons the same rights as white persons to make and enforce contracts, sue, be parties, give EVIDENCE, inherit, purchase, lease, sell, hold, and convey real and personal property, and to the full and equal benefit of all laws and proceedings for the security of person and property, was reenacted in modified form by the Civil Rights Act of 1870, was divided into two sections by the REVISED STATUTES OF 1874, and survives as sections 1981 and 1982 of Title 42, United States Code. Section three of the act, which set forth the procedures for vindicating rights protected by section one, was scattered throughout the United States Code. Portions of it survive as CIVIL RIGHTS REMOVAL statutes and as part of section 1988 of Title 42. Judicial interpretation of the 1866 act is not unrelated to these statutory reshufflings. Cut adrift from their moorings in the entire 1866 act, the act's remnants are amenable to many more interpretations than the original provision.

Cases decided in the years immediately following the 1866 act's passage are particularly important in ascertaining its original meaning. The REVISED STATUTES of 1874 would strip the act's descendants of any close resemblance to the original measure. And once the courts became accustomed to applying the FOURTEENTH AMENDMENT, much of the 1866 act would become superfluous. In addition, ratification of the Fourteenth Amendment eliminated most doubts about the act's constitutionality.

Prior to ratification of the Fourteenth Amendment, most courts were willing to sustain the act under Congress's THIRTEENTH AMENDMENT power to proscribe SLAVERY. But at least Kentucky's highest court in *Bowlin v. Commonwealth* (1867) declared the act unconstitutional. Other courts avoided such a declaration only by interpreting the act not to prohibit some forms of RACIAL DISCRIMINATION that the act's words arguably covered.

In the reported interpretations of the act, for example, courts divided over whether states could continue to outlaw marriages between whites and blacks. State courts in Tennessee (1871), Indiana (1871), and Alabama (1878) found marriage not to be a contract within the meaning of section 1, and therefore rejected attacks on antimiscegenation laws that relied on the 1866 act. State courts in Louisiana (1874) and Alabama (1872) relied at least in part on the 1866 act to find intermarriage legal, but the Alabama case was soon overruled. Not until LOVING V. VIRGINIA (1967) did the Supreme Court hold the Fourteenth Amendment to ban antimiscegenation laws.

State courts also divided over whether the 1866 act abrogated state laws prohibiting blacks from testifying against whites. The Kentucky court found Congress's effort to do so unconstitutional, but an 1869 Arkansas decision found the act to authorize such testimony. In 1869, the California Supreme Court relied on the 1866 act's evidentiary provision to dismiss an INDICTMENT against a mulatto, because Chinese witnesses had testified at his trial and state law prohibited them from testifying against white men. But a year later, despite the 1866 act, the California court sustained the state's evidentiary ban on testimony by Chinese against whites.

After the 1870s, section 1 diminished in importance. The state laws against which it most successfully operated, laws mandating racial discrimination in areas covered by section 1, could also be attacked directly under the Fourteenth Amendment. And with section 1 and the Fourteenth Amendment undermining the most egregious provisions of the Black Codes, there remained only one important area to which section 1 might be applied—private discrimination. When the CIVIL RIGHTS CASES (1883), UNITED STATES V. HARRIS (1883), and UNITED STATES V. CRUIKSHANK (1876) limited Congress's Thirteenth and Fourteenth Amendment power to legislate against private racial discrimination, there was doubt about whether section 1 constitutionally could be applied to private discrimination. One early lower federal court opinion, *United States v. Morris* (1903), suggested the 1866 act's applicability to private discrimination, but Supreme Court statements in *Virginia v. Rives* (1880) and CORRIGAN V. BUCKLEY (1926) suggested that the act did not apply to private conduct. (See STRAUDER V. WEST VIRGINIA, 1880.)

Hurd v. Hodge (1948), a companion case to SHELLEY V. KRAEMER (1948), gave section 1 some new life. The court applied section 1 to prohibit courts in the DISTRICT OF COLUMBIA from enforcing a racially RESTRICTIVE COVENANT. The breakthrough came in JONES V. ALFRED H. MAYER CO. (1968), where the Court held both that Congress meant the 1866 act to proscribe private discrimination and that Congress constitutionally could outlaw private discrimination under the Thirteenth Amendment. As the result of *Jones*, *Johnson v. Railway Express Co.* (1974), and RUNYON V. MCCRARY (1976), the remnants of the 1866 act were transformed from historical relics into federal laws broadly prohibiting private racial discrimination in the sale or lease of all housing, in schools, in employment and in virtually all other contracts. In many respects the 1866 act's newly discovered coverage exceeds that of comprehensive modern civil rights laws. *General Building Constructors Association, Inc. v. Pennsylvania* (1982) limited the 1866 act's reach by holding that liability may not be imposed under the act without proof of intentional discrimination.

Section 3 of the 1866 act traveled a less visible path through the courts. Its primary significance has been to determine when a violation of former section 1 authorizes an original or removal action in federal court. (See REMOVAL OF CASES.) In *Blyew v. United States* (1872), over the dissents of Justices JOSEPH P. BRADLEY and NOAH SWAYNE, the Court held that Kentucky's testimonial disqualification of black witnesses did not confer ORIGINAL JURISDICTION on a lower federal court to hear a state murder case at which the black witnesses were to testify. In a series of civil rights removal cases, the Court held that what had been section 3 authorized removal to federal court where state laws expressly mandated a racial distinction that prevented blacks from receiving equal justice, as when blacks were excluded from juries. But the Court found removal not to be authorized where the same result was achieved through other than formal state statutory command.

Under section 3's remnants, actions that arise under state law but are removed to federal court are tried in federal court by applying state law. In *Robertson v. Wegmann* (1978), however, the Court misconstrued the shred of the 1866 act commanding this result to require application of state law to cases arising under *federal* law. The same remnant, section 1988, also has been relied on in *Sullivan v. Little Hunting Park, Inc.* (1969) to authorize damages for violations of section 1 rights and in *Tomanio v. Board of Regents* (1980) to require the use of state statutes of limitations in federal civil rights cases.

THEODORE EISENBERG

Bibliography

BARDOLPH, RICHARD 1970 *The Civil Rights Record.* Pages 84–87, 94–96, 200–201, 532–533. New York: Thomas Y. Crowell.

CARR, ROBERT K. 1947 *Federal Protection of Civil Rights.* Ithaca, N.Y.: Cornell University Press.

EISENBERG, THEODORE 1981 *Civil Rights Legislation.* Charlottesville, Va.: Michie Co.

CIVIL RIGHTS ACT OF 1875
18 Stat. 335

On his deathbed Senator CHARLES SUMNER (Republican, Mass.) implored a congressional friend, "You must take care of the civil rights bill,—my bill, the civil rights bill, don't let it fail." Since 1870 Sumner had sought to persuade Congress to enact a law guaranteeing to all people, regardless of race or religion, the same accommodations and facilities in public schools, churches and cemeteries incorporated by public authority, places of public amusement, hotels licensed by law, and common carriers. Sumner had contended that racial SEGREGATION was discriminatory, that SEPARATE BUT EQUAL facilities were inherently unequal, and that compulsory equality would combat prejudice as much as compulsory segregation fostered it. Opponents claimed that the FOURTEENTH AMENDMENT protected the privileges of United States CITIZENSHIP only, not those of state citizenship to which the bulk of CIVIL RIGHTS attached. Opponents also claimed that Congress had no constitutional power to protect civil rights from violation by private persons or businesses.

School DESEGREGATION was unpopular among northern Republicans and hated by southern Democrats. After the election of 1874 resulted in a Democratic victory in the House, supporters of Sumner's bill settled for "half a loaf" by consenting to the deletion of the provisions on education, churches, and cemeteries. A black congressman from South Carolina agreed to the compromise because the school clause jeopardized the Republican party in the South and subordinated the educational needs of blacks to their right to be desegregated. Teaching the "three Rs" to the children of former slaves was more important than risking their educational opportunities by demanding their admission to "white" schools.

In February 1875 the lame-duck 43rd Congress, 2nd session, voting along party lines in both houses, passed the modified bill which President ULYSSES S. GRANT signed into law on March 1. The Civil Rights Act of 1875, the last Reconstruction measure and the last civil rights act until 1957, was the most important congressional enactment in the field of PUBLIC ACCOMMODATIONS until the CIVIL RIGHTS ACT OF 1964. The act of 1875 affirmed the equality of all persons in the enjoyment of transportation facilities, in hotels and inns, and in theaters and places of public amusement. Theoretically such businesses, though privately owned and operated, were like public utilities, exercising public functions for the benefit of the public and subject to public regulation. Anyone violating the statute was civilly liable for $500 damages and, on conviction in federal court, subject to a fine of not more than $1,000 or imprisonment for not more than one year. In 1883 the Supreme Court held the statute unconstitutional in the CIVIL RIGHTS CASES.

LEONARD W. LEVY

Bibliography

KONVITZ, MILTON R. 1961 *A Century of Civil Rights.* New York: Columbia University Press.

CIVIL RIGHTS ACT OF 1957
71 Stat. 634

Although this law marked the end of an eighty-two-year period of congressional inactivity in the field of CIVIL RIGHTS, it accomplished little. The act created the CIVIL RIGHTS COMMISSION but granted it only investigative and reporting powers. The act also created a separate CIVIL RIGHTS DIVISION within the Department of Justice to be headed by an additional assistant attorney general. More substantively, the act made it unlawful to harass those exercising their VOTING RIGHTS in federal elections and provided for federal initiation of proceedings against completed or potential violations. Offenders receiving more than slight penalties were entitled to TRIAL BY JURY, a watering-down provision inserted by Senate opponents.

The act is as significant for important deletions from the original bill as for what was ultimately enacted. Southern senators managed to eliminate a provision authorizing the ATTORNEY GENERAL to seek injunctive relief against all civil rights violators, a provision opponents feared would enhance the federal presence in school DESEGREGATION disputes and one they characterized as reimposing Reconstruction on the South. The emasculated act was viewed as a victory for southern segregationists. It was not even worth a filibuster.

THEODORE EISENBERG

Bibliography

BRAUER, CARL M. 1977 *John F. Kennedy and the Second Reconstruction.* New York: Columbia University Press.

CIVIL RIGHTS ACT OF 1960
74 Stat. 86

The insignificance and ineffectiveness of the CIVIL RIGHTS ACT OF 1957 generated pressure in the next Congress to enact a more effective CIVIL RIGHTS law. And the CIVIL RIGHTS COMMISSION established by the 1957 act added to the pressure by issuing a report documenting the abridgment of black VOTING RIGHTS in the South.

As enacted, the 1960 act required state election officers to retain for twenty-two months records relating to voter registration and qualifications in elections of federal officials. Where courts found patterns or practices of abridgment of the right to vote on account of race, they were authorized to declare individuals qualified to vote and to appoint federal voting referees to take EVIDENCE and report to the court on the treatment of black voters.

In a provision originally aimed at interference with school DESEGREGATION decrees, the act imposed criminal penalties for obstruction of all court orders. It also created a federal criminal offense of interstate flight to avoid prosecution for destroying buildings or other property.

Like the 1957 act, the 1960 act is noteworthy for its failure to include a proposed provision authorizing the United States to initiate actions on behalf of persons deprived of civil rights.

THEODORE EISENBERG

Bibliography

BRAUER, CARL M. 1977 *John F. Kennedy and the Second Reconstruction.* New York: Columbia University Press.

CIVIL RIGHTS ACT OF 1964
78 Stat. 241

The Civil Rights Act of 1964 signified many changes. For JOHN F. KENNEDY, prompted by southern resistance to DESEGREGATION orders and violent responses to peaceful CIVIL RIGHTS protests, proposing the measure symbolized an aggressive new attitude toward RACIAL DISCRIMINATION. For LYNDON JOHNSON, who supported the act after Kennedy's assassination, it marked a turn away from southern regionalism and toward national leadership on civil rights matters. For Congress, the act ended a century of nonexistent or ineffective civil rights laws and was the first civil rights measure with respect to which the Senate invoked CLOTURE. For blacks, the act was the first major legislative victory since Reconstruction and the most far-reaching civil rights measure in American history.

The act consists of eleven titles. Titles I and VIII reinforce voting rights provisions of the CIVIL RIGHTS ACTS OF 1957 and 1960 and limit the use of LITERACY TESTS to measure voter qualifications. (See also VOTING RIGHTS ACT OF 1970.) Titles III and IV, in provisions deleted from the bills that became the 1957 and 1960 acts, authorize court actions by the ATTORNEY GENERAL to challenge segregated public facilities and schools. Title V amends provisions governing the CIVIL RIGHTS COMMISSION. Title IX authorizes appeal from orders remanding to state courts civil rights cases that have been removed to federal court and authorizes the Attorney General to intervene in EQUAL PROTECTION cases. Title X establishes a Community

Relations Service to assist communities in resolving discrimination disputes. Title XI deals with miscellaneous matters. The most important parts of the law are Title II, forbidding discrimination in PUBLIC ACCOMMODATIONS; Title VI, forbidding discrimination in federally assisted programs; and Title VII, forbidding EMPLOYMENT DISCRIMINATION. In 1972, Congress extended Title VII's coverage to most government employees. It does not cover religious institutions.

Congress shaped the 1964 act with a keen awareness of previously declared constitutional limitations on ANTIDISCRIMINATION LEGISLATION. Title II's ban on discrimination in public accommodations and Title VII's ban on employment discrimination are limited to those entities whose operations affect INTERSTATE COMMERCE. By limiting these provisions to establishments and employers affecting commerce, Congress sought to avoid the CIVIL RIGHTS CASES' (1883) determination that Congress lacks power under the FOURTEENTH AMENDMENT to outlaw discrimination by private citizens, even in such a quasi-public area as that of public accommodations. Unlike its power to enforce the Fourteenth Amendment, Congress's COMMERCE CLAUSE power is not limited to STATE ACTION. In HEART OF ATLANTA MOTEL, INC. V. UNITED STATES (1964) and KATZENBACH V. MCCLUNG (1964) the Court upheld Title II as a valid exercise of the commerce power and the power to regulate interstate travel. Under the Court's subsequent decision in JONES V. ALFRED H. MAYER CO. (1968), much of Title II and Title VII would be valid as congressional enforcement of the THIRTEENTH AMENDMENT. Title VI's ban on discrimination in federally assisted programs was tied to another constitutional provision, Congress's TAXING AND SPENDING POWER.

Judicial interpretation seems to have avoided another potential constitutional problem attending Title VII. Under a 1972 amendment to Title VII, employers must accommodate an employee's religious practices if the employer is able to do so without undue hardship. In *Trans World Airlines, Inc. v. Hardison* (1977), the Supreme Court held that the statute does not require an employer to bear more than a DE MINIMIS cost to accommodate an employee's religious preferences. If Title VII were interpreted to mandate substantial concessions to religiously based employee work preferences, it might raise serious problems under the FIRST AMENDMENT'S ESTABLISHMENT OF RELIGION clause.

With the 1964 act's constitutional vulnerability minimized shortly after enactment, the way was clear for its development. Title II, banning racial discrimination in public accommodations, was the act's symbolic heart, providing immediate and highly visible evidence that blacks, as equal citizens, were entitled to equal treatment in the public life of the community. But Title II generated little litigation, for compliance was swift throughout the South once the principle of equal access was established. Equalizing employment opportunity was a goal that would take longer to accomplish. Thus in operation, Title VII has dwarfed all other titles combined, frequently generating a huge backlog of cases in the agency charged with Title VII's administration, the Equal Employment Opportunity Commission (EEOC), and leading to thousands of judicial decisions.

The proof necessary to establish a Title VII violation repeatedly occupies the Supreme Court. Two leading cases, *McDonnell Douglas Corp. v. Green* (1973) and GRIGGS V. DUKE POWER CO. (1971), approve alternative methods of proof in Title VII cases. Under *McDonnell Douglas,* a plaintiff alleging discrimination by an employer must, after exhausting the necessary remedies with the EEOC or a state antidiscrimination agency, show that the plaintiff applied and was rejected for a job for which the plaintiff was qualified, and that the employer continued to try to fill the position. An employer must then justify its actions. Under *Griggs,* in an extension of Title VII not necessarily contemplated by the 1964 Congress, proof that an employment selection criterion has a disproportionate adverse impact on minorities requires the employer to show that the selection standard is required by business necessity. After *Griggs,* statistically based Title VII cases, and threats to bring such cases, became a widespread method for pressuring employers to hire more minority and female workers. Few employers are both able to prove the business necessity of employment tests or other hiring criteria and willing to incur the expense of doing so.

The 1964 act, particularly Title VII, is not without its ironies. First, opponents of the act amended it to include sex discrimination in the hope that such an amendment would weaken the bill's chances for passage. But the bill passed with the additional ban that revolutionized at least the formal status of female workers. And in the case of sex discrimination, Title VII reaches beyond traditional refusals to hire or obvious pay disparities. When the Court held in *General Electric Co. v. Gilbert* (1976) that excluding pregnancy from a health plan does not constitute discrimination on the basis of sex, Congress amended Title VII to overturn the result. *Los Angeles Department of Water and Power v. Manhart* (1978) marks some sort of outer limit on Title VII's protection of female workers. The Court held Title VII to proscribe a requirement that females, who live longer than males and therefore can expect to receive greater total retirement benefits from a pension plan, contribute more to a pension than males contribute. In the case of sex, religion, or national origin discrimination, Title VII provides a defense if these factors constitute a bona fide occupational qualification, a defense sometimes difficult to separate from that of business necessity. The Supreme Court found in *Dothard v. Rawlinson* (1977) that a bona fide occupational qualification justifies requiring male prison guards for at least some classes of male prisoners.

Second, although the BURGER COURT generally has been viewed as conservative in the field of civil rights, Title VII owes much of its practical importance to Chief Justice WARREN E. BURGER's opinion for the Court in *Griggs v. Duke Power Co. Griggs* removed the requirement that discriminatory intent be an element of Title VII cases. This holding, in addition to its significance for Title VII, has been incorporated in other areas, including discrimination in housing under the CIVIL RIGHTS ACT OF 1968. *New York City Transit Authority v. Beazer* (1979), in which the Court refused to invalidate an employment selection standard (exclusion of drug users) with disparate impact on minorities, may signify some retrenchment from the full force of the *Griggs* principle. And in *International Brotherhood of Teamsters v. United States* (1977), the Court refused to extend *Griggs* to invalidate seniority systems that predate Title VII. But the Court never has directly questioned *Griggs.* In UNITED STEELWORKERS OF AMERICA V. WEBER (1979), the Burger Court concluded that Title VII permitted at least some private AFFIRMATIVE ACTION employment programs.

Although Title VII deservedly receives most of the attention paid to the 1964 act, Title VI is also an important antidiscrimination law. In REGENTS OF THE UNIVERSITY OF CALIFORNIA V. BAKKE (1978) it provided the setting for the Court's first important pronouncement on affirmative action programs. Many subsequent antidiscrimination laws, such as Title IX of the EDUCATION AMENDMENT OF 1972, the AGE DISCRIMINATION ACT OF 1975, and the REHABILITATION ACT of 1973 are modeled after Title VI. Title VI is the principal antidiscrimination measure for programs receiving federal funds that are not affected by other antidiscrimination measures. In the case of public institutions, however, there is much overlap between Title VI's prohibitions and those contained in the Fourteenth Amendment. The Supreme Court has been ambiguous in describing the relationship between the two. In *Bakke,* a majority of Justices suggested that Title VI and the Constitution are coterminous, but it did not purport to overturn the Court's earlier holding in LAU V. NICHOLS (1974), widely read as extending Title VI to cases of discrimination not banned by the Constitution.

The contributions of the 1964 act to racial equality defy precise measurement, but surely they have been weighty. Beyond the tangible changes the act brought to the public life of southern communities and to the entire American workplace lie enormous changes in attitudes and everyday personal relations. Those who believe that "you can't legislate morality" would do well to ponder the lessons of the Civil Rights Act of 1964.

THEODORE EISENBERG

(SEE ALSO: *Firefighters Local #1784 v. Stotts, 1984.*)

Bibliography

DORSEN, NORMAN; BENDER, PAUL; NEUBORNE, BURT; and LAW, SYLVIA 1979 *Emerson, Haber and Dorsen's Political and Civil Rights in the United States,* 4th ed. Vol. II:581–608, 902–1062, 1172–1220. Boston: Little, Brown.

LARSON, ARTHUR and LARSON, LEX K. 1981 *Employment Discrimination.* New York: Matthew Bender.

SCHLEI, BARBARA L. and GROSSMAN, PAUL 1976 *Employment Discrimination Law.* Washington, D.C.: Bureau of National Affairs.

SULLIVAN, CHARLES A.; ZIMMER, MICHAEL J.; and RICHARDS, RICHARD F. 1980 *Federal Statutory Law of Employment Discrimination.* Indianapolis: Bobbs-Merrill.

CIVIL RIGHTS ACT OF 1968
82 Stat. 696

This act capped the modern legislative program against RACIAL DISCRIMINATION that included the CIVIL RIGHTS ACT OF 1964 and the VOTING RIGHTS ACT of 1965. Title VIII of the act, which constitutes the nation's first comprehensive OPEN HOUSING LAW, prohibits discrimination in the sale, rental, financing, and advertising of housing, and in membership in real estate brokerage organizations. Ironically, soon after Title VIII's enactment, the Supreme Court, in JONES V. ALFRED H. MAYER CO. (1968), construed a remnant of the CIVIL RIGHTS ACT OF 1866 to outlaw private racial discrimination in housing. In dissent in *Jones,* Justice JOHN M. HARLAN, joined by Justice BYRON R. WHITE, relied in part on Title VIII's passage to challenge the need for the Court's decision. The 1968 act also contained criminal penalties to protect civil rights activity and comprehensive measures to protect rights of AMERICAN INDIANS. Different portions of the act, including antiriot provisions, represented a backlash against antiwar demonstrations, CIVIL RIGHTS protest, and other forms of domestic unrest.

Like the Civil Rights Act of 1964, the 1968 act survived a southern filibuster in the Senate. Efforts by House opponents to delay consideration of the bill backfired. The delay led to the bill's consideration in the aftermath of DR. MARTIN LUTHER KING, JR.'S assassination. Given that the bill passed the House by a small margin, the delay may have made all the difference.

THEODORE EISENBERG

Bibliography

HARVEY, JAMES C. 1973 *Black Civil Rights During the Johnson Administration.* Jackson, Miss.: University and College Press of Mississippi.

CIVIL RIGHTS CASES
109 U.S. 3 (1883)

In an opinion by Justice JOSEPH P. BRADLEY, with only Justice JOHN MARSHALL HARLAN dissenting, the Supreme Court ruled that Congress had no constitutional authority under either the THIRTEENTH or the FOURTEENTH AMENDMENT to pass the CIVIL RIGHTS ACT OF 1875. Holding that act unconstitutional proved to be one of the most fateful decisions in American history. It had the effect of reinforcing racist attitudes and practices, while emasculating a heroic effort by Congress and the President to prevent the growth of a Jim Crow society. The Court also emasculated the Fourteenth Amendment's enforcement clause, section five. The tragedy is that the Court made the Constitution legitimize public immorality on the basis of specious reasoning.

The *Civil Rights Cases* comprised five cases decided together, in which the act of 1875 had been enforced against innkeepers, theater owners, and a railroad company. In each of the five, a black citizen was denied the same accommodations, guaranteed by the statute, as white citizens enjoyed. The Court saw only an invasion of local law by the national government, contrary to the powers reserved to the states under the TENTH AMENDMENT. Bradley began his analysis with the Fourteenth Amendment, observing that its first section, after declaring who shall be a citizen, was prohibitory: it restrained only STATE ACTION. "Individual invasion of individual rights is not the subject-matter of the amendment." Its fifth section empowered Congress to enforce the amendment by appropriate legislation. "To enforce what? To enforce the prohibition," Bradley answered. He ignored the fact that the enforcement section applied to the entire amendment, including the CITIZENSHIP clause, which made all persons born or naturalized in the United States and subject to its jurisdiction citizens of the United States and of the states in which they reside. As Harlan pointed out, citizenship necessarily imports "equality of civil rights among citizens of every race in the same state." Congress could guard and enforce rights, including the rights of citizenship, deriving from the Constitution itself. Harlan reminded the Court of its opinion in STRAUDER V. WEST VIRGINIA (1880), where it had said that "a right or immunity created by the constitution or only guarantied by it, even without any express delegation of power, may be protected by congress."

But Bradley took the view that the legislative power conferred upon Congress by the Fourteenth Amendment does not authorize enactments on subjects "which are within the domain of state legislation. . . . It does not authorize congress to create a code of municipal law for regulation of private rights." Congress can merely provide relief against state action that violates the amendment's prohibitions on the states. Thus, only when the states acted adversely to the rights of citizenship could Congress pass remedial legislation. But its legislation could not cover the whole domain of CIVIL RIGHTS or regulate "all private rights between man and man in society." Otherwise, Congress would "supersede" the state legislatures. In effect the Court was saying that the Reconstruction amendments had not revolutionized the federal system. In effect the Court also warned the states not to discriminate racially, lest Congress intervene, as it had in the CIVIL RIGHTS ACT OF 1866, which the Court called "corrective" legislation against state action. In the cases under consideration, however, the discrimination derived from purely private acts unsupported by state authority. "The wrongful act of an individual, unsupported by any such authority, is simply a private wrong" that Congress cannot reach. Congress can, of course, reach and regulate private conduct in the normal course of legislation, penalizing individuals; but, Bradley explained, in every such case Congress possesses under the Constitution a power to act on the subject.

Under the Thirteenth Amendment, however, Congress can enact any legislation necessary and proper to eradicate SLAVERY and "all badges and incidents of slavery," and its legislation may operate directly on individuals, whether their acts have the sanction of state authority or not. The question, then, was whether the Thirteenth Amendment vested in Congress the authority to require that all persons shall have equal accommodations in inns, public conveyances, and places of public amusement. The Court conceded that the amendment established "universal civil and political freedom throughout the United States" by abolishing slavery, but it denied that distinctions based on race or color abridged that freedom. Where, Bradley asked, does slavery, servitude, or badges of either arise from race discrimination by private parties? "The thirteenth amendment," he declared, "has respect, not to distinctions of race, or class, or color, but to slavery." The act of the owner of an inn, or theater, or transportation facility in refusing accommodation might inflict an ordinary civil injury, recognizable by state law, but not slavery or an incident of it. "It would be running the slavery argument into the ground," Bradley insisted, "to make it apply to every act of discrimination which a person may see fit to make" as to his guests, or those he will take in his coach, or those he will admit to his concert. On the theory that mere discrimination on account of race or color did not impose badges of slavery, the Court held that the Thirteenth Amendment, like the Fourteenth, did not validate the Civil Rights Act of 1875.

The case involved questions of law, history, and public policy. Harlan, dissenting, had the weight of argument as to all three, but Bradley had the weight of numbers. It was an 8–1 decision, and the eight scarcely bothered to answer the dissenter. Ignoring him might have been more discreet than trying to rebut him. He met their contentions head-on, starting with a strenuous objection to their parsimonious interpretation of national powers under the Thirteenth and Fourteenth Amendments, both of which expressly made affirmative grants of power. By contrast, Harlan demonstrated, the Court had generously construed the Constitution to support congressional enactments on behalf of slaveholders. The fugitive slave acts, which operated on private individuals, were based on a clause in the Constitution, Article 4, section 2, paragraph 3, that did not empower Congress to legislate at all. The clause merely provided that a fugitive slave be delivered up upon the claim of his owner, yet the Court sustained the acts of 1793 (PRIGG v. PENNSYLVANIA, 1842) and of 1850 (ABLEMAN v. BOOTH, 1859), implying a national power to enforce a right constitutionally recognized. The Thirteenth Amendment, as the majority admitted, established a constitutional right: civil freedom for citizens throughout the nation. And, as the majority admitted, the abolition of slavery reached the BADGES OF SERVITUDE, so that the freedmen would have the same rights as white men. Similarly, the act of 1875 reached badges of servitude, because it, like the amendments to the Constitution, aimed at erasing the assumption that blacks were racially inferior. For Harlan, RACIAL DISCRIMINATION was a badge of servitude. Bradley had distinguished the act of 1866 from the act of 1875 on the ground that the earlier statute aimed at protecting rights that only the states might deny. Harlan replied that citizens regardless of race were entitled to the same civil rights.

Harlan also demonstrated that the rights allegedly violated by purely private parties were denied by individuals and CORPORATIONS that exercised public functions and wielded power and authority under the state. Relying on a broad concept of state action, he sought to prove that the parties whom the majority regarded as private were, in contemplation of law, public or quasi-public. A railroad corporation, an innkeeper, and a theater-manager had denied accommodations to black citizens. Railroads and streetcars were common carriers, that is, they were public highways, performing state functions; they were public conveyances which, though privately owned, had been established by state authority for a public use and were subject to control by the state for the public benefit. Free citizens of any race were entitled to use such facilities. Similarly, the COMMON LAW defined innkeepers as exercising a quasi-public employment that obligated them to take in all travelers, regardless of race. Theaters were places of public amusement, licensed by the public, of which the "colored race is a part," and theaters were clothed with a public interest, in accord with MUNN v. ILLINOIS (1877). Congress had not promiscuously sought to regulate the entire body of civil rights nor had it entered the domain of the states by generally controlling public conveyances, inns, or places of public amusement. Congress had simply declared that in a nation of universal freedom, private parties exercising public authority could not discriminate on ground of race; in effect the statute reached state instrumentalities whose action was tantamount to state action.

Under the Thirteenth Amendment, Congress could reach badges of servitude; under the Fourteenth, it could reach racial discrimination by state agencies. Contrary to the Court's assertion, Congress had not outlawed racial discrimination imposed by purely private action. It had aimed at such discrimination only in public places chartered or licensed by the state, in violation of the rights of citizenship which the Fourteenth Amendment affirmed. The amendment's fifth section empowered Congress to pass legislation enforcing its affirmative as well as its prohibitory clauses. Courts, in the normal exercise of JUDICIAL REVIEW, could hold unconstitutional state acts that violated the prohibitory clauses. Accordingly, section five was not restricted to merely corrective or remedial national legislation. Congress, not the Court, said Harlan, citing MCCULLOCH V. MARYLAND (1819), might choose the means best adopted to implementing the ends of the two amendments. Harlan insisted that Congress

> may, without transcending the limits of the constitution, do for human liberty and the fundamentals of American citizenship, what it did, with the sanction of this court, for the protection of slavery and the rights of the masters of fugitive slaves. If fugitive slave laws, providing modes and prescribing penalties whereby the master could seize and recover his fugitive slave, were legitimate exertions of an implied power to protect and enforce a right recognized by the constitution, why shall the hands of congress be tied, so that—under an express power, by appropriate legislation, to enforce a constitutional provision granting citizenship—it may not, by means of direct legislation, bring the whole power of this nation to bear upon states and their officers, and upon such individuals and corporations exercising public functions, assumed to abridge the supreme law of the land.

Some old abolitionists, deploring a ruling that returned the freedmen to a "reign of contempt, injury, and ignominy," denounced the "new DRED SCOTT decision," but most were resigned to defeat. Racial segregation was common throughout the country. Not surprisingly *The Nation* magazine, which approved of the decision, observed that the public's general unconcern about the decision indicated "how completely the extravagant expectations as well as the fierce passions of the war have died out." The Court served "a useful purpose in thus undoing the work of Congress," said the *New York Times*, and *Harper's Weekly* agreed. Public opinion supported the Court, but justice and judicial craftsmanship were on the side of Harlan, dissenting.

LEONARD W. LEVY

Bibliography

KONVITZ, MILTON R. 1961 *A Century of Civil Rights.* New York: Columbia University Press.

WESTIN, ALAN F. 1962 The Case of the Prejudiced Doorkeeper. Pages 128–144 in Garraty, John A., *Quarrels That Have Shaped the Constitution.* New York: Harper & Row.

CIVIL RIGHTS COMMISSION

THE CIVIL RIGHTS ACT OF 1957 created the Commission on Civil Rights to investigate alleged deprivations of VOTING RIGHTS, to study and collect information concerning denials of EQUAL PROTECTION, and to appraise federal laws and policies with respect to equal protection of the laws. Subsequent legislation restated and expanded the commission's concerns to include denials of rights on the basis of color, race, religion, national origin, sex, age, or handicap. Initially, the commission was to issue a series of reports and expire upon issuance of its final report, but Congress repeatedly has extended the commission's reporting duties and life. The commission lacks power to enforce any antidiscrimination or other CIVIL RIGHTS laws.

By the standards of later civil rights legislation, creation of the commission seems an innocuous event. But at the time even this mild gesture drew substantial southern opposition. The commission's "snoopers," one southern congressman argued, "would cause inestimable chaos, confusion, and unrest among [the South's] people and would greatly increase the tension and agitation between the races there."

Because of the commission's advisory nature, measuring its accomplishments is difficult. In the 1960s, the commission's early reports helped to inform Congress about the need for voting rights legislation. And it clearly has served the function, added to its mandate in 1964, of a national clearinghouse for information about denials of equal protection. But the commission also has played a somewhat larger political role. In most administrations the commission's views are more egalitarian than the President's. The commission thus serves as a gadfly that both makes official sounding pronouncements and commands media attention. Administrations hear the commission even if they do not always listen to it.

THEODORE EISENBERG

Bibliography

United States Commission on Civil Rights 1961 *Report.* Pages xv–xviii. Washington, D.C.: U.S. Government Printing Office.

CIVIL RIGHTS DIVISION

Created by Order of the Attorney General No. 3204, February 3, 1939, the Civil Rights Section (originally named the Civil Rights Unit) of the Justice Department became the federal government's principal CIVIL RIGHTS litigation unit. The order creating the Section called for a study of federal law to assess its utility in enforcing civil rights. The study, which stated the legal basis and goals of the Section's early civil rights enforcement efforts, suggested the need for TEST CASES to resolve uncertainties about the scope and constitutionality of the only statutory weapons then available to the Section, the surviving Reconstruction-era civil rights legislation. The Section's test cases include UNITED STATES v. CLASSIC (1941), an important precedent establishing authority to prosecute offenses relating to PRIMARY ELECTIONS, and SCREWS v. UNITED STATES (1945), which allowed the application of the criminal provisions of the CIVIL RIGHTS ACT OF 1866 to misconduct by state police officers.

The Civil Rights Section's growth reflects a general increase in national concern with civil rights matters. As of 1947, the Section is reported never to have had more than eight or ten lawyers and professional workers on its staff. In 1950, the section more than doubled in size. The CIVIL RIGHTS ACT OF 1957 upgraded the Section to the status of Division by providing for an additional assistant attorney general. By 1965, the Division had eighty-six attorneys and ninety-nine clerical workers. By 1978, there were 178 attorneys and 203 support personnel.

The Division's principal activity consists of litigation. It enforces the CIVIL RIGHTS ACTS OF 1957, 1960, 1964, and 1968, the VOTING RIGHTS ACT OF 1965, the Equal Credit Opportunity Act, the 1866 act's criminal provisions, laws prohibiting PEONAGE and involuntary servitude, and various other laws. It does so through direct actions or through AMICUS CURIAE appearances in private cases. An administration's civil rights priorities are reflected in the categories of cases emphasized by the Division. In the early 1960s the Division emphasized voting rights cases. From 1965 to 1967, DESEGREGATION of education was its priority issue. By 1967, employment litigation became a priority item. Creation of a Task Force on Sex Discrimination in 1977 reflected a growing concern with sex discrimination.

THEODORE EISENBERG

Bibliography

CARR, ROBERT K. 1947 *Federal Protection of Civil Rights: Quest for a Sword.* Ithaca, N.Y.: Cornell University Press.

CIVIL RIGHTS REMOVAL

Since the CIVIL RIGHTS ACT OF 1866, federal CIVIL RIGHTS laws have allowed REMOVAL OF CASES from state to federal courts. The 1866 and 1870 acts provided for removal to federal court of state criminal or civil cases affecting persons who were denied or could not enforce in state court rights guaranteed by the acts. In the REVISED STATUTES of 1874, Congress restated the removal power to encompass violations of "any law providing for . . . equal civil rights." Early removal cases, typified by STRAUDER v. WEST VIRGINIA (1880), allowed removal when state courts denied rights by enforcing state statutes but refused removal when state courts denied rights by following uncodified practices. With the vanishing of the BLACK CODES, removal became an insignificant remedy.

In the 1960s, civil rights protesters often were arrested under state TRESPASS, traffic, and other minor laws and were subjected to unfair state court proceedings. After a pause of eighty years, the Court again considered civil rights removal. In *Georgia v. Rachel* (1966) civil rights SIT-IN demonstrators being prosecuted for trespass in state court sought removal. The Court held removal authorized only for violations of "any law providing for specific civil rights stated in terms of racial equality." But, bending the *Strauder-Rives* line, the Court did not require that a state statute be the basis for the alleged deprivation of federal rights. The Court allowed removal on the grounds that the state prosecution violated the CIVIL RIGHTS ACT OF 1964, which outlaws even attempts to punish persons exercising rights of equal access to PUBLIC ACCOMMODATIONS.

On the same day, however, the Court decided in *City of Greenwood v. Peacock* (1966) that workers engaged in a voter registration drive could not rely on various voting statutes that prohibit RACIAL DISCRIMINATION to remove their state prosecutions for obstructing the public streets. The mere likelihood of prejudice was not enough to justify removal under the statute. The majority evidently shrank from the prospect of wholesale removal of criminal prosecutions of black defendants from southern state courts to federal courts. *Peacock* effectively precludes widespread modern use of civil rights removal.

THEODORE EISENBERG

Bibliography

AMSTERDAM, ANTHONY G. 1965 Criminal Prosecutions Affecting Federally Guaranteed Civil Rights: Federal Removal and Habeas Corpus Jurisdiction to Abort State Court Trial. *University of Pennsylvania Law Review* 113:793–912.

CIVIL RIGHTS REPEAL ACT
28 Stat. 36 (1894)

From the middle of the 1860s to 1875, Congress was favorably disposed toward ANTIDISCRIMINATION LEGISLATION and even enacted some such measures over presidential veto. But many of the provisions enacted encountered restrictive interpretations to outright invalidation in the Supreme Court. The Repeal Act of 1894 symbolizes formal reconvergence of congressional and judicial attitudes towards CIVIL RIGHTS statutes.

In 1892 the Democratic party, for the first time after the Civil War, gained control of both houses of Congress and the presidency. In the Repeal Act of 1894, which repealed portions of the Enforcement Act of 1870 and the FORCE ACT OF 1871, Congress eliminated most civil rights measures that had not already been undermined by the Court. The repealed provisions had provided for federal control of federal elections through the appointment of federal election officials, a control method revived in the CIVIL RIGHTS ACTS OF 1960 and 1964 and the VOTING RIGHTS ACT OF 1965.

THEODORE EISENBERG

Bibliography

EISENBERG, THEODORE 1981 *Civil Rights Legislation.* Page 741. Charlottesville, Va.: Michie Co.

CIVIL WAR AMENDMENTS

See: Fifteenth Amendment; Fourteenth Amendment; Thirteenth Amendment

CLAIMS COURT

The Claims Court hears actions for money damages against the United States, except for tort claims. The court thus hears claims for contract damages, tax refunds, and JUST COMPENSATION for property taken. With the consent of all parties to an action against the government under the FEDERAL TORT CLAIMS ACT, the court can substitute for a court of appeals and review the decision of a federal district court.

Under the doctrine of SOVEREIGN IMMUNITY, the United States cannot be sued without its consent. At first, persons with claims against the government had to ask Congress for relief under private acts. This practice became burdensome, and in 1855 Congress established the Court of Claims to hear nontort money claims against the United States, and report its recommendations to Congress. Much of the congressional burden remained; thus, in 1863, Congress empowered the court to give judgments against the government. In 1866 the process became fully "judicial" when Congress repealed a provision delaying payment of such a judgment until the Treasury estimated an appropriation.

The Court of Claims retained the nonjudicial function of giving ADVISORY OPINIONS on questions referred to it by the houses of Congress and heads of executive departments. However, its judges from the beginning had life tenure during GOOD BEHAVIOR. In 1933 the question arose whether the Court of Claims was a CONSTITUTIONAL COURT. Congress, responding to the economic depression, reduced the salaries of federal employees, except for judges protected by Article III against salary reductions. In *Williams v. United States* (1933), the Supreme Court, taking the preposterous position that claims against the government fell outside the JUDICIAL POWER OF THE UNITED STATES, held that the Court of Claims was a LEGISLATIVE COURT whose judges' salaries could constitutionally be reduced.

In 1953 Congress declared explicitly that the Court of Claims was established under Article III. In *Glidden v. Zdanok* (1962) the Supreme Court accepted this characterization on the basis of two separate (and incompatible) theories, pieced together to make a majority for the result. Two Justices relied on the 1953 Act; three others would have overruled *Williams* and held that the court had been a constitutional court since 1866 when Congress allowed its judgments to be paid without executive revision, and its business became almost completely "judicial." (The same decision confirmed that the COURT OF CUSTOMS AND PATENT APPEALS was a constitutional court.) The Court of Claims transferred new congressional reference cases to its chief commissioner, and Congress ratified this practice. The court's business became wholly "judicial."

In the FEDERAL COURTS IMPROVEMENT ACT (1982) Congress reorganized a number of specialized federal courts. The Court of Claims disappeared, and its functions were reallocated. The commissioners of that court became judges of a new legislative court, the United States Claims Court. They serve for fifteen-year terms. The Article III judges of the Court of Claims became judges of a new constitutional court, the UNITED STATES COURT OF APPEALS FOR THE FEDERAL CIRCUIT. That court hears appeals from a number of specialized courts, including the Claims Court.

The availability of a suit for damages in the Claims Court serves to underpin the constitutionality of some governmental action that might otherwise raise serious constitutional problems. Some regulations, for example, are arguable TAKINGS OF PROPERTY; if the regulated party can recover compensation in the

Claims Court, however, the constitutional issue dissolves (*Blanchette v. Connecticut General Insurance Corps.*, 1974).

KENNETH L. KARST

Bibliography

Symposium: The Federal Courts Improvement Act 1983 *Cleveland State Law Review* 32:1–116.

CLARK, CHARLES E.
(1889–1963)

Charles Edward Clark, the son of a Connecticut farmer and a graduate of Yale College, achieved distinction as a legal educator and a federal judge. In 1919 he began teaching at Yale Law School, where he had earned his law degree, and became its dean in 1929. Within the year he had modernized the curriculum, stressing interdisciplinary studies. Originally a Republican, Clark became a New Dealer and in 1937 was the only law school dean to testify in favor of President FRANKLIN D. ROOSEVELT's court reorganization plan. In 1939 Roosevelt appointed him to the UNITED STATES COURT OF APPEALS, Second Circuit. As a federal judge for twenty-five years he tended to be a liberal activist even though his opinions on the rights of the criminally accused strongly supported prosecutorial positions. But Clark's opinions favored trade unions, CIVIL RIGHTS, and government regulation of the economy. As a FIRST AMENDMENT absolutist, he eloquently and ardently championed views that Justices HUGO L. BLACK and WILLIAM O. DOUGLAS of the Supreme Court later endorsed.

LEONARD W. LEVY

Bibliography

SCHICK, MARVIN 1970 *Learned Hand's Court.* Baltimore: Johns Hopkins University Press.

CLARK, TOM C.
(1899–1977)

Tom Campbell Clark, Associate Justice of the Supreme Court and ATTORNEY GENERAL of the United States, was born September 23, 1899, in Dallas, Texas. He was educated at the University of Texas at Austin, receiving his B.A. in 1921 and his LL.B. in 1922. Admitted to the Texas Bar in 1922, he joined his family's firm in Dallas.

Clark began his twelve-year career with the Department of Justice in 1937 as a special assistant to the attorney general. He held a number of posts in the department, capped by his 1945 appointment as attorney general by President HARRY S. TRUMAN. With this promotion, Clark became the first person to become attorney general by working himself up from the lower ranks of the department.

Four years later, President Truman appointed Clark Associate Justice of the Supreme Court; he took his oath of office on August 24, 1949. His tenure on the bench spanned eighteen years, and he served on both the VINSON COURT and WARREN COURT. He retired from the Court on June 12, 1967, to avoid the appearance of a conflict of interests when his son, Ramsey Clark, was appointed attorney general by President LYNDON B. JOHNSON. Clark, however, continued to sit as a judge in the various courts of appeal, and to be a vigorous and vocal advocate of judicial reform until his death on June 13, 1977.

On the Supreme Court, Clark built a reputation as a pragmatic jurist. Early on, he voted regularly with Chief Justice FRED M. VINSON and the other Truman appointees. In time, however, he began to assert his independence. In YOUNGSTOWN SHEET AND TUBE COMPANY V. SAWYER (1952), the steel seizure case, Clark voted against Vinson and Truman, concurring in the Court's decision holding unconstitutional Truman's order for governmental seizure of the nation's steel mills.

While Clark was generally viewed as politically conservative, he was relatively nonideological, and his views changed throughout his tenure, especially during the years of the Warren Court (1953–1969). He was a nationalist, a liberal on racial matters, and, in general, a conservative on issues of CRIMINAL PROCEDURE and CIVIL LIBERTIES.

Clark's most significant opinions in the area of FEDERALISM are his landmark opinion on STATE REGULATION OF COMMERCE in DEAN MILK COMPANY V. MADISON (1951), and his dissent in *Williams v. Georgia* (1955), which provided the classic definition of "independent and ADEQUATE STATE GROUNDS" that insulate state court decisions from the Supreme Court. In the racial area, speaking for the Court in BURTON V. WILMINGTON PARKING AUTHORITY (1961), he rejected as unlawful STATE ACTION racial discrimination by private persons who had leased public property. In addition, he wrote for the Court in HEART OF ATLANTA MOTEL, INC., V. UNITED STATES (1964) where, in a case involving both national power and racial justice, a unanimous Court upheld the PUBLIC ACCOMMODATIONS provisions of the CIVIL RIGHTS ACT OF 1964.

In the areas of criminal procedure and civil liberties Clark was less consistent. Although he may be best known for his controversial opinion in MAPP V. OHIO (1961), declaring that illegally seized evidence must be excluded from a state criminal prosecution, this opinion was atypical. More often, especially in his later years on the bench, he disagreed with the liberalization of criminal procedure wrought by the Warren Court. For instance, he dissented strongly—indeed almost violently—in MIRANDA V. ARIZONA (1966).

Similarly, Clark's record on civil liberties, though generally conservative, was not completely consistent. Probably Clark was most consistent as to those issues arising out of anticommunist and LOYALTY-SECURITY PROGRAMS. As attorney general, he had been instrumental in setting up some of these programs, and as a Justice he continued to support government efforts to suppress what he regarded as the communist conspiracy. Thus, he dissented in WATKINS V. UNITED STATES (1957) and joined the majority in BARENBLATT V. UNITED STATES (1959). In addition, he was the sole dissenter in *Greene v. McElroy* (1959), a decision which badly damaged the loyalty-security program for employees of private companies.

On the other hand, Clark was generally less sympathetic to efforts by the states to cope with what he regarded as a national problem. Thus, he wrote for a unanimous Court in WIEMAN V. UPDEGRAFF (1952), which held unconstitutional an Oklahoma LOYALTY OATH statute requiring state employees to swear that they were not members of organizations designated by the attorney general as subversive or a "Communist front." Clark emphasized that under the Oklahoma law an individual could be guilty of perjury even though he did not know the character of the organization that he had innocently joined. And he joined the majority in PENNSYLVANIA V. NELSON (1956), which invalidated state SEDITION laws on the ground that Congress had preempted the field.

In other areas of civil liberties, Justice Clark tended more often to vote in favor of asserted constitution rights. Thus, in the area of church–state relations, he wrote the opinion in ABINGTON TOWNSHIP SCHOOL DISTRICT V. SCHEMPP (1963), which held unconstitutional a Pennsylvania statute that required that each school day start with the reading of at least ten verses from the Bible. Similarly, he voted with the majority in a series of cases that drastically narrowed court-martial jurisdiction over civilians, the most significant of which was *Kinsella v. Singleton* (1960).

JOHN KAPLAN

Bibliography

KIRKENDALL, RICHARD 1969 Tom C. Clark. In Leon Friedman and Fred L. Israel, eds., *The Justices of the United States Supreme Court, 1789–1969.* New York: Chelsea House.

CLARK DISTILLING CO. v. WESTERN MARYLAND RAILWAY CO.
242 U.S. 311 (1917)

With Justices OLIVER WENDELL HOLMES and WILLIS VAN DEVANTER dissenting without opinion, the Court upheld the WEBB-KENYON ACT. Chief Justice EDWARD D. WHITE, for the majority, rejected the assertion that the act constituted an unconstitutional legislative DELEGATION OF POWER to the states. No delegation occurred because Congress provided for uniform regulation throughout the states.

DAVID GORDON

CLARKE, JOHN H.
(1857–1945)

With the exception of OLIVER WENDELL HOLMES and LOUIS D. BRANDEIS, John H. Clarke was the most consistently progressive member of the Supreme Court during the final years of EDWARD D. WHITE's chief justiceship and the early tenure of WILLIAM HOWARD TAFT. A prosperous newspaper publisher and attorney who defended many midwestern railroads, Clarke belonged to the moderate wing of the Democratic Party in Ohio which defended the gold standard in 1896 and looked skeptically upon reform programs. WOODROW WILSON appointed Clarke to the federal district court in 1914 and two years later elevated him to the Supreme Court to fill the vacancy left by Wilson's presidential rival, CHARLES EVANS HUGHES.

Intellectually, Clarke could not fill Hughes's shoes, but he surprised many critics by his voting record in cases involving CORPORATIONS and labor. Despite his earlier representation of big business, Clarke became a strong judicial supporter of the antitrust laws. He dissented in the two leading cases of the period, *United States v. United Shoe Machinery Company* (1918) and *United States v. United States Steel Corporation* (1920), when the WHITE COURT spurned the government's efforts to convict these industrial giants for monopolistic behavior.

In 1920, however, Clarke won a majority to his side when the Justices ordered the dissolution of a major railroad monopoly in *United States v. Lehigh Valley Railroad,* and found the Reading Railroad guilty of restraint of trade in the anthracite coal industry. Over a powerful dissent by Holmes, Clarke also wrote for the Court that upheld indictments for open price agreements in the hardwood lumber industry.

Clarke rejected the dominant judicial ideology of FREEDOM OF CONTRACT, which had been used to stifle legislative reforms to benefit labor. He endorsed Oregon's ten-hour law for all industrial workers in BUNTING V. OREGON (1917), approved of the federal ADAMSON ACT which mandated an eight-hour day for railroad workers in WILSON V. NEW (1917), and refused to endorse the INJUNCTION at issue in the YELLOW DOG CONTRACT case of HITCHMAN COAL & COKE CO. V. MITCHELL (1917). He voted as well to sustain the constitutionality of the KEATING-OWEN CHILD LABOR ACT in HAMMER V. DAGENHART (1918), refused to sanction the prosecution of labor unions under the antitrust laws in UNITED MINE WORKERS V. CORONADO COAL CO. (1922), and upheld a union's right to conduct a SECONDARY BOYCOTT in the notorious case of DUPLEX PRINTING CO. V. DEERING (1921).

Despite his progressive record with respect to ECONOMIC REGULATION and the rights of labor, Clarke will probably always be remembered as the Justice who wrote for the majority in the case of ABRAMS V. UNITED STATES (1919), which sustained the conviction of pro-Bolshevik pamphleteers under the wartime ESPIONAGE ACT and SEDITION ACT. Clarke's opinion provoked Holmes's famous and biting dissent. Arguing that "men must be held to have intended and to be accountable for the effects which their acts were likely to produce," Clarke transformed Holmes's CLEAR AND PRESENT DANGER test into something approximating the BAD TENDENCY TEST that came to dominate the Court's FIRST AMENDMENT jurisprudence for several decades.

MICHAEL E. PARRISH

Bibliography

WARNER, HOYT L. 1959 *Life of Mr. Justice Clarke.* Cleveland, Ohio: Western Reserve University Press.

CLASS ACTION

The class action is a procedural device aggregating the claims or defenses of similarly situated individuals so that they may be tried in a single lawsuit. In recent decades the class action has frequently served as the vehicle by which various groups have asserted constitutional claims. For example, all the minority-race school children in various districts have sued (through their parents) to rectify alleged RACIAL DISCRIMINATION on the part of school authorities; or, to illustrate a nonconstitutional claim, the buyers of home freezers have sued as a group claiming that the dealer had made fraudlent misrepresentations. In both examples the members of the class could have sued separately. The class action pulled these potential individual actions into a single lawsuit making litigation feasible for the members of the class (by permitting a single lawyer to try all their claims together). For the party opposing the class the suit has the advantage of providing a single adjudication of all similar claims and the disadvantage, especially marked in suits for money damages, that the entire potential liability to a large group turns on a single suit.

The class action depends on representation, and that concept draws the Constitution into the picture. In the class action most class members are represented by an active litigant whose success or failure binds the class members. Opinions interpreting the DUE PROCESS clauses of the Constitution (in the Fifth and FOURTEENTH ADMENDMENTS) suggest that normally one may not be bound by the results of litigation to which one is not a party. Yet the class action purports to do just that—to bind the absentee class members to the results of a suit in which they played no active role.

The Supreme Court and the drafters of state and federal class action rules have supplied two solutions to this apparent tension. The Supreme Court's answer came in *Hansberry v. Lee* (1940), in which the justices indicated that class actions could bind absentee class members if the active litigants *adequately represented* the class. If not, the Court reasoned, binding the absentees would deprive them of due process of law.

Adequate representation has two aspects, competence and congruence of interests. All would agree that adequate representation implies some absolute level of competence and diligence on the part of the class representative and attorney. Though few cases have specifically discussed the question, it seems virtually a matter of definition that an adequate representative must pursue the cause with some minimum level of professional skill.

The second aspect of adequate representation presents a more difficult problem, forcing us to decide whether such representation requires the class members to have *agreed* that the action is in their interests, or whether it is possible to define such interests abstractly, without specific consent. Such an abstract definition relies on common intuitions about what would benefit persons in the class's circumstances. In *Hansberry* the Court did not need to decide between these definitions of interest because the attempted class representation failed on either count. Subsequent cases and procedural rules have not clearly resolved the question.

Contemporary procedural rules require that a judge presiding over a class action suit consider initially whether the action is in the class's interest, abstractly considered; that much seems constitutionally required. Beyond that, some rules also require that the absentee members receive individual notice permitting them to exclude themselves from the litigation.

Founded on the constitutional proposition that some form of representation will suffice to bind members of a class, the class suit has come to play an important role in twentieth-century American litigation.

STEPHEN C. YEAZELL

Bibliography

KALVEN, HARRY JR. and ROSENFIELD, MAURICE 1941 The Contemporary Function of the Class Suit. *University of Chicago Law Review* 8:684–721.

WRIGHT, CHARLES A. and MILLER, ARTHUR 1972 *Federal Practice and Procedure,* Vols. 7 & 7A. St. Paul, Minn.: West Publishing Co.

YEAZELL, STEPHEN C. 1980 From Group Litigation to Class Action; Part II: Interest, Class and Representation. *U.C.L.A. Law Review* 28:1067–1121.

CLASSIC, UNITED STATES v.
313 U.S. 299 (1941)

This became a TEST CASE used by the United States Attorney in Louisiana and the newly created CIVIL RIGHTS DIVISION of the Department of Justice to ascertain the federal government's power to protect VOTING RIGHTS in PRIMARY ELECTIONS. Louisiana election commissioners charged with willfully altering and falsely counting congressional primary election ballots were indicted under what are now sections 241 and 242 of Title 18, United States Code. To analyze the INDICTMENT under section 241, the Supreme Court had to determine whether the right to have one's ballot counted in a state primary election was a right or a privilege secured by the Constitution. Relying in part on Article I, section 2, of the Constitution, the Court held, 4–3, that the right to choose a congressman was "established and guaranteed" by the Constitution and hence secured by it. The Court then reaffirmed earlier holdings that Congress could protect federally secured voting rights against individual as well as STATE ACTION and squarely held that those rights included participation in state primary elections for members of Congress, thus overruling *Newberry v. United States* (1921).

In articulating those rights "secured by the Constitution" within the meaning of section 241, *Classic* forms a link between early interpretations of the phrase, as in EX PARTE YARBROUGH (1884), and later consideration of it, as in UNITED STATES V. GUEST (1966) and GRIFFIN V. BRECKENRIDGE (1971), the latter case decided under the civil counterpart to section 241, section 1985(3) of Title 42, United States Code. *Classic* also constitutes an important link in the chain of precedents specifically pertaining to federal power over elections. Later cases from the 1940s include SMITH V. ALLWRIGHT (1944) and *United States v. Saylor* (1944).

Because the *Classic* indictment also charged a violation of section 242, which requires action "under COLOR OF LAW," the case provides an early modern holding on the question whether action in violation of state law can be action under color of law. With virtually no discussion of the issue, the Court held such action to be under color of law, a holding later used to support similar holdings in *Screws v. United States* (1945) and MONROE V. PAPE (1961). Dissenters in *Screws* and *Monroe* would object to reliance on *Classic* because of its abbreviated consideration of the issue.

THEODORE EISENBERG

CLAY, HENRY
(1777–1852)

Henry Clay, distinguished politician and legislator, was a product of the Jeffersonian Republicanism that took possession of the Trans-Appalachian West, fought a second war against Great Britain, and was nationalized in the process. Born in Hanover County, Virginia, young Clay clerked for Chancellor GEORGE WYTHE and read law in Richmond before emigrating to Kentucky in his twentieth year. Settling in the rising metropolis of Lexington, Clay was promptly admitted to the bar, and by virtue of extraordinary natural talent, aided by the fortune of marriage into a prominent mercantile family, he soon became a leading member of the Bluegrass lawyer-aristocracy.

The chaos of land titles in Kentucky—a legacy of the state's Virginia origins—made it a paradise for lawyers. Clay mastered this abstruse branch of jurisprudence but earned his reputation as a trial lawyer in capital cases, in which he was said never to have lost a client. He rode the circuit of the county courts, acquiring a character for high spirits and camaraderie; he practiced before the court of appeals and also before the United States district court at Frankfort. When he first went to Congress in 1806, Clay was admitted to the bar of the Supreme Court. Occasionally in years to come he argued important constitutional cases before the court. He was chief counsel for the defendant in OSBORN V. BANK OF THE UNITED STATES (1824), for instance, in which the Court struck down a prohibitive state tax on branches of the bank. At about the same time he conducted Kentucky's defense of its Occupying Claimants Law, enacted years earlier in order to settle thousands of disputed land titles. Here Clay was unsuccessful, as the Court, in GREEN V. BIDDLE (1823), found the Kentucky law in violation of the CONTRACT CLAUSE. Justice JOSEPH STORY remarked after hearing Clay in this case that, if he chose, Clay might achieve "great eminence" at the bar. This interesting judgment would never be tested, however, for Clay sought eminence in politics rather than law.

Clay entered politics in 1798 as a Jeffersonian Republican protesting the ALIEN AND SEDITION ACTS and seeking liberal reform of the state constitution. Elected to the legislature in 1803, he became chief spokesman and protector of the Lexington-centered "court party." He was also very popular, rising rapidly to the speakership of the lower house. In 1806 he was sent to the United States Senate to complete three months of an unexpired term; this experience was repeated, upon the resignation of another incumbent, in 1810. Clay distinguished himself as a bold patriot and orator, as an advocate of federal INTERNAL IMPROVEMENTS and encouragement of domestic manufactures, both of great interest to Kentucky, and as the leading opponent of recharter of the national bank on strict Jeffersonian grounds. He then sought and won election to the Twelfth Congress. Upon its meeting in November 1811, he achieved recognition as chief of the "war hawks" who, though a small minority, took command of the House and elected Clay speaker. Whether or not the war hawks caused, in some significant degree, the War of 1812 is a matter in dispute among historians; but there is no doubt that they brought fresh westerly winds of nationalism into Congress and that Clay, as speaker, mobilized congressional action behind the JAMES MADISON administration's prosecution of the war. Clay transformed this constitutional office, the speakership, from that of an impartial moderator into one of political leadership. Five times he would be reelected speaker, always virtually without opposition; and when he finally retired from the House there was no one to fill his shoes.

After the Peace of Ghent, which he had helped negotiate as an American commissioner, Clay supported President Madison's national Republican platform with its broad constitutional principles. This support required an about-face on the constitutionality of a national bank. Clay candidly chalked up his error to experience, saying that the financial exigencies of the war had shown the necessity of a national bank; he now agreed with Madison on the need for a central institution to secure a stable and uniform currency. Henceforth, certainly, Clay's principal significance with respect to the Constitution lay in the affirmation of congressional powers.

The protective tariff was the core of the maturing national system of political economy that Clay named "the AMERICAN SYSTEM." The country ought not any longer, he argued, look abroad for wealth, but should turn inward to the development of its own resources. Manufactures would rise and flourish behind the tariff wall, consuming the growing surplus of American agriculture; and a balanced, sectionally based but mutually supportive, economy of agriculture, commerce, and manufactures would be the result. Because the system premised a positive role for the national government in economic development, it carried immense implications for the Constitution. When the protective tariff was first attacked on constitutional grounds in 1824, Clay rejected the narrow view that limited the TAXING POWER to raising revenue and continued the liberal interpretation of the COMMERCE CLAUSE that began with Jefferson's embargo. The infrastructure of the "home market" would be provided by a national system of INTERNAL IMPROVEMENTS. Madison, in his surprising veto of the Bonus Bill in 1817, interposed the constitutional objection that neither the funding nor the building of roads and canals was among the enumerated powers. When Madison's successor, JAMES MONROE, persisted in this view, Clay mounted a campaign to overturn it. He appealed to the Jeffersonian precedent of the National (Cumberland) Road; he appealed to the WAR POWERS (transportation as an element of national defense), to the power of Congress to establish post roads, and, above all, to the commerce power. To the old fears of a runaway Constitution Clay opposed his trust in democratic elections and the balance of interests to keep order. Monroe finally conceded the unlimited power of Congress to appropriate money for internal improvements, though not to build or operate them.

Clay protested that the concession was of greater scope than the principle he had advocated. But he took satisfaction in the result, most immediately in the General Survey Act of 1824.

Clay's coalition with JOHN QUINCY ADAMS in 1825, in which he secured the New Englander's election to the presidency and accepted appointment as his secretary of state, contributed to a growing sectional and partisan opposition to the American System and the constitutional doctrines that supported it. South Carolina's NULLIFICATION of the protective tariff in 1832 provoked a crisis that Clay, now in the Senate, helped to resolve with his Compromise Tariff Act. Under it protective duties would be gradually lifted until in 1842 they would be levied for revenue only. Without surrendering any constitutional principle, Clay nevertheless seemed to surrender the policy of protectionism. Some politicians said he courted southern votes in his quest for the presidency. As the National Republican candidate against President ANDREW JACKSON in the recent election, he had been badly defeated, winning nothing in the South, and he may have seen in this crisis an opportunity for a useful change of political direction. But Clay insisted he acted, first, to save the Union from the disaster of nullification, which was compounded by Jackson's threatened vengeance, and second, to save what he could of the American System. A high protective tariff could no longer be sustained in any event. The national debt was about to be paid off; the treasury faced an embarrassing surplus unless the revenue was drastically reduced. Clay sought to offset the impact of the surplus on the tariff by diverting the soaring revenue of public land sales to the states. Although Congress passed Clay's Distribution Bill in 1833, Jackson vetoed it.

This veto, with many others, above all JACKSON'S VETO OF THE BANK BILL, fueled Clay's assault on the alleged executive usurpations and monarchical designs of the President. The senator proposed to curtail the powers of the presidency. The abuse of the veto power should be corrected by a constitutional amendment allowing override by a majority of both houses. The despotic potential of the office, which Jackson was the first to disclose, should be curbed further by an amendment limiting the president to a single term, perhaps of six years. Clay also rejected the 1789 precedent on the REMOVAL POWER, arguing that the power of removal in the President effectively negated the Senate's agency in appointment. Removal, like appointment, should be a joint responsibility. The Whig Party, under Clay's leadership, consistently advocated these measures. None was ever enacted. Clay continued the campaign even after the Whigs came to power in 1841, assailing President John Tyler as he had earlier assailed Jackson.

Although Clay usually supported national authority in the debates of his time, he became increasingly cautious and protective of the Constitution under the threats posed, first, by reckless Jacksonian Democracy, and second, by the combination of abolitionism in the North and aggressive slavocracy in the South. He accepted the "federal consensus" on slavery: it was a matter entirely within the JURISDICTION of the states. Nevertheless, he raised no bar to the use of federal funds to advance gradual emancipation and colonization by the states, indeed advocated it in certain contexts. In the controversy over the right of petition for abolition of slavery in the DISTRICT OF COLUMBIA, he held that a gag was not only indefensible in principle but impolitic in practice, because it would make libertarian martyrs of the abolitionists. Clay opposed the ANNEXATION OF TEXAS, believing that the expansion of slavery it entailed must seriously disrupt the Union. When he seemed to equivocate on the issue in the election of 1844—his third run for the presidency—he lost enough northern votes to ensure his defeat. Returning to the Senate in 1849, he proposed a comprehensive plan for settlement of critical issues between North and South. It eventually became the COMPROMISE OF 1850. Here, as in all of his constructive legislative endeavors, Clay evaded spurious questions of constitutional law and sought resolution on the level of policy in that "spirit of compromise" which, he said, lay at the foundation of the American republic. From his earlier part in effecting the MISSOURI COMPROMISE (1820–1821) and the Compromise of 1833, he had earned the title of The Great Pacificator. The Compromise of 1850 added a third jewel to the crown.

Henry Clay was the most popular American statesman of his generation and one of the most respected. He helped to shape the course of constitutional development during forty years, not as a lawyer, judge, or theorist, but as a practical politician and legislator in national affairs.

MERRILL D. PETERSON

Bibliography

COLTON, CALVIN, ED. (1856)1904 *The Works of Henry Clay.* 10 Vols. New York: G. P. Putnam's.

HOPKINS, JAMES F. and HARGREAVES, MARY W. M., EDS. 1959–1981 *The Papers of Henry Clay.* Vols. 1–6. Lexington: University of Kentucky Press.

SEAGER, ROBERT II; WINSLOW, RICHARD E., III; and HAY, MELBA PORTER, EDS. 1982–1984 *Papers of Henry Clay.* Vols. 7–8. Lexington: University of Kentucky Press.

VAN DEUSEN, GLYNDON G. 1937 *The Life of Henry Clay.* Boston: Houghton, Mifflin.

CLAYTON ACT
38 Stat. 730 (1914)

Mistakenly hailed by Samuel Gompers as labor's MAGNA CARTA, the Clayton Act represented a new generation's attempt to deal with trusts. Acclaimed for its specificity, the new act in reality contained crucial ambiguities as vague as the SHERMAN ANTITRUST ACT it was intended to supplement. WOODROW WILSON'S ANTITRUST policy included both the FEDERAL TRADE COMMISSION ACT and the Clayton Act; in his view the latter would leave the Sherman Act intact while specifying conduct henceforth prohibited. Framed by Representative Henry Clayton, chairman of the House Judiciary Committee, the antitrust bill pleased no one: labor objected to the absence of an explicit guarantee of immunity for unions, many congressmen found the list of restraints of trade incomplete, and agrarian radicals believed that the bill betrayed Democratic pledges. In the face of this opposition, Wilson abandoned the Clayton bill in Congress. The House, unhappy over the vagueness of the Sherman Act and wishing to leave businessmen no loopholes, sought as specific a bill as possible. The Senate objected, but a compromise was reached naming only a few, particularly pernicious, practices which were declared unlawful "where the effect may be to substantially lessen competition or tend to create monopoly"—hardly a model of certainty. Four provisions of the Clayton Act contain this operative phrase. Section 7 prohibited the acquisition of stock by one corporation of another or mergers, but, by neglecting to forbid acquisitions of assets as well as stock, it provided a loophole not plugged until 1950. The act also placed strict limitations on interlocking directorates (section 8), and outlawed price discrimination (section 2) and exclusive dealing and tying contracts (section 3). The Federal Trade Commission would enforce these provisions by procedures paralleling those in the F.T.C. Act. In addition, the act rendered individual officers personally liable for corporate violations, permitted private individuals to secure INJUNCTIONS and to file treble damage suits, and allowed final judgments in government suits to be considered *prima facie* EVIDENCE in private cases.

Of two labor provisions, section 6, which declared that labor was "not a commodity or article of commerce" and that antitrust laws could not be used to forbid legitimate organizing activities, conceded nothing new. Section 20 prohibited the issuance of injunctions in labor cases unless "necessary to prevent irreparable injury to property." Together with a further clause which declared that peaceful strikes and boycotts were not in violation of federal antitrust laws, this section represented the only victory labor gained in this act.

DAVID GORDON

(SEE ALSO: *Labor and the Constitution.*)

Bibliography

NEALE, A. D. and GOYDER, D. G. 1980 *The Antitrust Laws of the United States of America,* 3rd ed. Cambridge: At the University Press.

CLEAN AIR ACT

See: Environmental Regulation

CLEAR AND PRESENT DANGER

The clear and present danger rule, announced in SCHENCK V. UNITED STATES (1919), was the earliest FREEDOM OF SPEECH doctrine of the Supreme Court. Affirming Schenck's conviction, Justice OLIVER WENDELL HOLMES concluded that a speaker might be punished only when "the words are used in such circumstances and are of such a nature as to create a clear and present danger that they will bring about the substantive evils that Congress has a right to prevent." Holmes was drawing on his own earlier Massachusetts Supreme Judicial Court opinion on the law of attempts. There he had insisted that the state might punish attempted arson only when the preparations had gone so far that no time was left for the prospective arsonist to change his mind, so that the crime would have been committed but for the intervention of the state. In the free speech context, Holmes and Justice LOUIS D. BRANDEIS assimilated this idea to the MARKETPLACE OF IDEAS rationale, arguing that the best corrective of dangerous speech was more speech rather than criminal punishment; government should intervene only when the speech would do an immediate harm before there was time for other speech to come into play.

In the context of *Schenck,* the danger rule made particular sense; the federal statute under which the defendant was prosecuted made the *act* of espionage a crime, not the speech itself. The danger rule in effect required that before speech might be punished under a statute that forbade action, a close nexus between the speech and the action be shown. The concentration of the rule on the intent of the speaker and the circumstances surrounding the speech also seem most relevant in those contexts in which speech is being punished as if it constituted an attempt at a criminal act. Opponents of the danger rule have often insisted that Holmes initially intended it not as a general FIRST AMENDMENT test but only for cases in which a statute proscribing action was applied to a speaker.

In *Schenck*, Holmes wrote for the Court. The most extended statement of the danger rule came some months later in ABRAMS V. UNITED STATES (1919), but by then it was to be found in a Holmes dissent, joined by Brandeis. In GITLOW V. NEW YORK (1925) the Court used the BAD TENDENCY TEST which openly rejected the imminence or immediacy element of the danger rule—again over dissents by Holmes and Brandeis. Brandeis kept the danger rule alive in a concurrence in WHITNEY V. CALIFORNIA (1927) in which he added to the immediacy requirement that the threatened evil be serious. The danger of minor property damage, for example, would not justify suppression of speech.

In the 1930s and 1940s the Court was confronted with a series of cases involving parades and street corner speakers in which the justification offered for suppressing speech was not concern for the ultimate security of the state but the desire to maintain peaceful, quiet, and orderly streets and parks free of disturbance. Behind the proffered justifications usually lurked a desire to muzzle unpopular speakers while leaving other speakers free. In this context the clear and present danger rule was well designed to protect unpopular speakers from discrimination. It required the community to prove that the particular speaker whom it had punished or denied a license did in fact constitute an immediate threat to peace and good order. In such cases as HERNDON V. LOWRY (1937) (subversion), THORNHILL V. ALABAMA (1941) (labor PICKETING), *Bridges v. California* (1941) (contempt of court), WEST VIRGINIA BOARD OF EDUCATION V. BARNETTE (1943) (compulsory flag salute), and *Taylor v. Mississippi* (1943) (state sedition law), the clear and present danger rule became the majority constitutional test governing a wide range of circumstances, not only for statutes punishing conduct but also those regulating speech itself.

Even while enjoying majority status the rule came under attack from two directions. The "absolutists" led by ALEXANDER MEIKLEJOHN criticized the rule for allowing too broad an exception to First Amendment protections. The rule made the protection of speech dependent on judicial findings whether clear and present danger existed; judges had notoriously broad discretion in making findings of fact, as FEINER V. NEW YORK (1951) and TERMINIELLO V. CHICAGO (1949) illustrated. When applied to radical or subversive speech, the danger test seemed to say that ineffectual speech would be tolerated but that speech might be stifled just when it showed promise of persuading substantial numbers of listeners. On the other hand, those favoring judicial self-restraint, led by Justice FELIX FRANKFURTER, argued that the rule was too rigid in its protection of speech and ought to be replaced by a BALANCING TEST that weighed the interests in speech against various state interests and did so without rendering the immediacy of the threat to state interests decisive.

Later commentators have also argued that the distinction between speech and conduct on which the danger rule ultimately rests is not viable, pointing to picketing and such SYMBOLIC SPEECH as FLAG DESECRATION which intermingle speech and action. The danger rule also engenders logically unresolvable HOSTILE AUDIENCE problems. If Holmes's formula had demanded a showing of the specific intent of the speaker to bring about violence or of specific INCITEMENT to crime in the content of the speech, it might have afforded greater protection to some speakers. The independent weight the danger formula gives to surrounding circumstances may permit the stifling of speakers because of the real or imagined act or threats of others. Yet focusing exclusively upon intent or upon the presence of the language of incitement may lead to the punishment of speakers whose fervently revolutionary utterances in reality have little or no chance of bringing about any violent action at all.

In DENNIS V. UNITED STATES (1951) the clear and *present* danger test was converted overtly into a clear and *probable* danger test and covertly into a balancing test. As its origin in the law of attempts reminds us, the cutting edge of Holmes's test had been the imminence or immediacy requirement. Speech might be punished only if so closely brigaded in time and space with criminal action that no intervening factor might abort the substantive evil. The probable danger test held that if the anticipated evil were serious enough the imminence requirement might be greatly relaxed. In practice this evisceration of the danger test left the Court free to balance the interests to be protected against the degree of infringement on speech, as the proponents of judicial self-restraint argued the Court had always done anyway under the danger standard.

Since *Dennis* the Court has consistently avoided the precise language of the clear and present danger test and with few exceptions commentators announced its demise. In BRANDENBURG V. OHIO (1969), however, the Court announced that "constitutional guarantees of free speech . . . do not permit a State to forbid . . . advocacy of the use of force or of law violation except where such advocacy is directed to inciting or producing imminent lawless action and is likely to incite or produce such action." The text and footnotes surrounding this pronouncement, its careful avoidance of the literal clear and present danger formula itself, plus the separate opinions of several of the Justices indicate that *Brandenburg* did not seek to revive Holmes's danger rule per se. Such earlier proponents of the rule as HUGO L. BLACK and WILLIAM O. DOUGLAS, feeling that it had been too corrupted by its *Dennis* conversion to retain any power to protect speech, had moved to the position of Meiklejohnian absolutism and its rejection of the danger standard. On the other hand, those Justices wishing to preserve low levels of protection for subversive speech and the high levels of judicial self-restraint toward legislative efforts to curb such speech that had been established in *Dennis* and YATES V. UNITED STATES (1957), shied away from the danger test because they knew that, in its Holmesian formulation, it was antithetical to the results that had been achieved in those cases. Apparently, then, Holmes's formula was avoided in *Brandenburg* because some of the participants in the PER CURIAM opinion thought the danger rule protected speech too little and others thought it protected speech too much.

Yet *Brandenburg* did revive the imminence requirement that was the cutting edge of the danger test, and it did so in the context of subversive speech and of OVERRULING *Whitney v. California,* in which the Brandeis and Holmes clear and present danger "concurrence" was in reality a dissent. Even when the danger test was exiled by the Supreme Court it continued to appear in state and lower federal court decisions and in popular discourse. Although the distinction between speech and action—like all distinctions the law seeks to impose—is neither entirely logical nor entirely uncontradicted by real life experience, clear and present danger reasoning survives because most decision makers do believe that the core of the First Amendment is that people may be punished for what they do, not for what they say. Yet even from this basic rule that speech alone must not be punished, we are compelled to make an exception when speech becomes part of the criminal act itself or a direct incitement to the act. Even the most absolute defenders of free speech would not shy from punishing the speaker who shouts at a mob, "I've got the rope and the dynamite. Let's go down to the jail, blow open the cell and lynch the bastard." However imperfectly, the Holmesian formula captures this insight about where the general rule of free speech ends and the exception of punishment begins. It is for this reason that the danger rule keeps reappearing in one form or another even after its reported demise.

The danger rule is most comforting when the speech at issue is an open, particular attack by an individual on some small segment of government or society, such as a street corner speech denouncing the mayor or urging an end to abortion clinics. In such instances the general government and legal system clearly retain the strength to intervene successfully should the danger of a substantive evil actually become clear and present. The emasculation of the danger test came in quite a different context, that of covert speech by an organized group constituting a general attack on the political and legal system as a whole. Unlike the situation in particularized attacks, where the reservoir of systemic power to contain the anticipated danger remains intact, should subversive speech actually create a clear and present danger of revolution the system as a whole might not have the capacity to contain the danger. It is one thing to wait until the arsonist has struck the match and quite another to wait until the revolution is ready to attack the police stations. For this reason the Court in *Dennis* reverted to the *Gitlow*-style reasoning that the government need not wait until the revolutionaries had perfected their campaign of conversion, recruitment, and organization. *Dennis* and *Yates* carve out a Communist party exception to the immediacy requirement of the clear and present danger rule. They say that where the speech is that of a subversive organization, the government need not prove a present danger of revolution but only that the organization intends to bring about the revolution as speedily as circumstances permit. Thus the government is permitted to intervene early enough so that its own strength is still intact and that of the revolutionaries still small. When in defense of the danger rule Holmes argued that time had overthrown many fighting faiths, he did so with a supreme confidence that it was the American, democratic, fighting faith that time favored and that subversive movements would eventually peter out in America's liberal climate. It was a failure of that faith in the face of the communist menace that led to the emasculation of the danger rule during the Cold War of the 1950s. With hindsight we can see that Holmes's confidence remained justified, and that communist subversion could not have created even a probable, let alone a present danger. Nonetheless American self-confidence has eroded sufficiently that the Supreme Court remains careful not to reestablish the full force of the danger rule lest it handicap the political and legal system in dealing with those who organize to destroy it.

MARTIN SHAPIRO

(SEE ALSO: *Judicial Activism and Judicial Restraint.*)

Bibliography

ANTIEAU, CHESTER JAMES 1950 "Clear and Present Danger"—Its Meaning and Significance. *Notre Dame Lawyer* 1950:3–45.

______ 1950 The Rule of Clear and Present Danger: Scope of Its Applicability. *Michigan Law Review* 48:811–840.

MENDELSON, WALLACE 1952 Clear and Present Danger—From Schenck to Dennis. *Columbia Law Review* 52:313–333.

______ 1953 The Degradation of the Clear and Present Danger Rule. *Journal of Politics* 15:349–355.

______ 1961 Clear and Present Danger—Another Decade. *Texas Law Review* 39:449–456.

STRONG, FRANK 1969 Fifty Years of "Clear and Present Danger": From Schenck to Brandenburg—And Beyond. *Supreme Court Review* 1969:427–480.

CLERKS

Each Justice of the Supreme Court employs two or more law clerks. (In recent years, typically each Justice, other than the CHIEF JUSTICE, has employed four clerks.) Most of the clerks are not long-term career employees, but honor law school graduates who have previously served for a year as clerk to a lower federal judge. Typically, the term of service for these noncareer clerks is one year.

The practice of employing recent law school graduates as short-term clerks began with Justice HORACE GRAY. Gray employed a highly ranked Harvard Law School graduate each year at his own expense while serving on the Massachusetts Supreme Judicial Court. He continued to do so when appointed to the United States Supreme Court in 1882. Congress assumed the cost of Justices' law clerks in 1886, but only Gray and his sucessor, OLIVER WENDELL HOLMES, continued the pattern of employing recent law school graduates. The widespread use of the Holmes-Gray practice began in 1919, when Congress authorized each Justice to employ both a "law clerk" and a "stenographic clerk." The use of young law school graduates as judges' law clerks for one- or two-year periods is now the prevailing pattern in most lower federal courts. A clerkship position with a Supreme Court Justice is prestigious, and former clerks have become prominent in the legal profession, government, the judiciary and academe. Three Justices had themselves served as law clerks to Supreme Court Justices (BYRON R. WHITE, WILLIAM H. REHNQUIST, and JOHN PAUL STEVENS).

The employment of noncareer clerks has been defended as exposing the Justices to fresh ideas and the new theories current in their clerks' law schools. Concern that clerks have too large a role in decisions has been expressed, but this is exaggerated, given the clerks' brief tenure and what is known of the Court's decision process. A distinct concern is that with employment of more clerks, they increasingly play an inappropriately large part in the drafting of opinions. That concern is not so easily rebutted, since each Justice has used clerks' services in a distinct fashion, and there is insufficient reliable public information of the roles played by the Court's current clerks. Court opinions, however, have become longer, more elaborate in their arguments, and studded with citations. The opinions of several Justices appear to be written in a uniform law review style, suggesting that staff plays a large part in their drafting.

WILLIAM COHEN

Bibliography

OAKLEY, JOHN B. and THOMPSON, ROBERT S. 1980 *Law Clerks and the Judicial Process.* Berkeley: University of California Press.

CLEVELAND, GROVER
(1837–1908)

The first Democratic President since JAMES BUCHANAN, Grover Cleveland supported civil service reform and tariff reduction. Cleveland devoted much of his two terms (1884–1888, 1892–1896) to eliminating corruption, inefficiency, and the exploitation of government for private benefit. Generally STATES' RIGHTS and probusiness in viewpoint, he insisted that the federal government function within constrained constitutional limits. As the first executive in decades willing to fight Congress, he frequently used the VETO POWER. A 6–3 Supreme Court sustained Cleveland's view of presidential removal power in *McAllister v. United States* (1891). (See APPOINTING AND REMOVAL POWER.)

Cleveland played almost no part in passage of the INTERSTATE COMMERCE ACT. He had no public reaction to the unpopular decision in POLLOCK V. FARMERS' LOAN & TRUST COMPANY (1895), voiding the income tax, for he believed criticism of the Court unseemly.

Cleveland was the second President with an opportunity to enforce the SHERMAN ANTITRUST ACT, but he expressed serious doubts about the act's effectiveness. Cleveland promised action "to the extent that [trusts] can be reached and restrained by Federal power," although he contended that state action provided the proper remedy. What antitrust successes his administration won (such as UNITED STATES V. TRANS-MISSOURI FREIGHT ASSOCIATION, 1897, and *United States v. Addyston Pipe & Steel Corp.*, 1899) belong to his second attorney general, Judson Harmon. Cleveland's last annual message even contains an exculpatory announcement about the "thus far . . . ineffective" act.

Cleveland and his first attorney general, RICHARD OLNEY, helped secure a federal INJUNCTION against the Pullman strike in 1894. Over the Illinois governor's objections, Cleveland sent 2,000 troops to Chicago to protect the mails and insure the free flow of INTERSTATE COMMERCE, purposes specifically approved by the Court in IN RE DEBS (1895). The troops broke the strike, killing twelve workers; this incident gave rise to the epithet "government by injunction."

Cleveland appointed four men to the Court—L. Q. C. LAMAR, MELVILLE FULLER, EDWARD WHITE, and RUFUS PECKHAM—but he was also the first President to suffer the embarrassment of having two successive appointments rejected by the Senate.

DAVID GORDON

Bibliography

MERRILL, HORACE 1957 *Bourbon Leader: Grover Cleveland.* Boston: Little, Brown.

CLEVELAND BOARD OF EDUCATION v. LAFLEUR
414 U.S. 632 (1974)

The Cleveland school board required a pregnant school teacher to take maternity leave, without pay, for five months before the expected birth of her child. A Virginia county school board imposed a similar four-month leave requirement. The Supreme Court, 7–2, held these rules unconstitutional. Justice POTTER STEWART, for the majority, invoked the IRREBUTTABLE PRESUMPTIONS doctrine. The school boards, by assuming the unfitness of pregnant teachers during the mandatory leave periods, had denied teachers individualized hearings on the question of their fitness, in violation of the guarantee of PROCEDURAL DUE PROCESS. Justice WILLIAM O. DOUGLAS concurred in the result, without opinion. Justice LEWIS F. POWELL rejected the irrebuttable presumptions ground as an EQUAL PROTECTION argument in disguise, but concluded that the boards' rules lacked rationality and denied equal protection. Justice WILLIAM H. REHNQUIST, for the dissenters, aptly characterized the irrebuttable presumptions doctrine as "in the last analysis nothing less than an attack upon the very notion of lawmaking itself."

KENNETH L. KARST

CLIFFORD, NATHAN
(1803–1881)

Nathan Clifford came to the Supreme Court in 1858 after an active political career. He served in the Maine legislature in the 1830s and in the House of Representatives in the early 1840s. He was JAMES K. POLK's attorney general, and during his term he represented (in a private capacity) the rebellious Dorr faction before the Supreme Court in LUTHER V. BORDEN (1849). Clifford's most significant political achievement came in 1848 when Polk dispatched him to persuade Mexico to accept the TREATY OF GUADALUPE HIDALGO as amended by Congress. A decade later, President JAMES BUCHANAN selected him to succeed Justice BENJAMIN R. CURTIS. At a time when the Court was perceived in many quarters as an instrument of southern and Democratic party interests, the choice of a Northerner with southern principles was viewed as blatant partisanship. After a lengthy confirmation battle, the Senate narrowly approved him.

Clifford, a "doughface" in politics, regarded himself as a Jeffersonian "strict constructionist" in constitutional matters. He resolutely opposed the centralization of governmental power during the 1860s and early 1870s. But in ABLEMAN V. BOOTH (1859) he voted to affirm federal judicial supremacy. During the war, Clifford generally supported the government. He wrote opinions upholding the seizure of slave-trading ships; he joined his colleagues in declining to decide any constitutional questions involving the legal tender laws; and he supported the Court's refusal to consider the martial law issues in EX PARTE VALLANDIGHAM (1864). In the PRIZE CASES (1863), however, Clifford joined the dissenters who questioned the legality of President ABRAHAM LINCOLN's blockade of southern ports.

Following the war, Clifford consistently opposed Republican Reconstruction policy. He joined the majority opinion in EX PARTE MILLIGAN (1866), which struck down trials by military commissions where the civil courts were functioning; he supported the majority in the TEST OATH CASES (1867); he agreed with the majority's narrow construction of the FOURTEENTH AMENDMENT in the SLAUGHTERHOUSE CASES (1873); and in separate opinions in several VOTING RIGHTS cases, including UNITED STATES V. REESE (1876) and UNITED STATES V. CRUIKSHANK (1876), he went beyond the majority opinions to condemn federal interference with state elections. Finally, he joined the Court's majority that overturned the legal tender laws in *Hepburn v. Griswold* (1870), but when that decision was reversed a year later in *Knox v. Lee* (1871), he dissented in a strict construction of Congress's power to regulate currency. (See LEGAL TENDER CASES.)

In HALL V. DECUIR (1878) Clifford wrote for the Court, nullifying a Louisiana law prohibiting segregation of steamboat passengers. "Governed by the laws of Congress," he wrote, "it is clear that a steamer carrying passengers may have separate cabins and dining saloons for white persons and persons of color, for the plain reason that the laws of Congress contain nothing to prohibit such an arrangement." In short, the absence of federal policy negated state policy—a strange position for an old STATES' RIGHTS Democrat.

Clifford generally supported state regulatory policies. His concurrence in *Slaughterhouse* signified his unwillingness to embrace a nationalizing interpretation of the Fourteenth Amendment; likewise, it reflected Clifford's traditionalist views of the STATE POLICE POWER. In *Munn v. Illinois* (1877), for example, he joined the majority to sustain Illinois's regulation of grain elevators. (See GRANGER CASES.) Clifford's most articulate statements on state powers came in his dissent in LOAN ASSOCIATION V. TOPEKA (1875). Rejecting the majority's invalidation of a state bonding authorization, Clifford struck at the Court's invocation of natural law doctrine and notions of judicial superintendence. Contending that state legislative power was "practically absolute," subject only to specific state and federal constitutional prohibitions, Clifford protested against JUDICIAL REVIEW that went beyond such limitations in tones reminiscent of older Jeffersonian doctrine: such power, he said, "would be to make the courts sovereign over both the constitution and the people, and convert the government into a judicial despotism."

Clifford dissented ninety-one times during his tenure, an extraordinarily high figure for the time. To some extent, it reflected his isolation and his archaic views. Throughout his judicial career, he consistently was perceived as a partisan Democrat. He served as president of the Electoral Commission to resolve the disputed election of 1876, and most accounts generally credit him with fairness in his conduct of the meetings. Nevertheless, the political purpose of his appointment in 1858 shadowed his work. He did not disappoint his benefactors; yet it was a career best characterized as dull and mediocre.

STANLEY I. KUTLER

Bibliography

CLIFFORD, PHILIP Q. 1922 *Nathan Clifford, Democrat.* New York: Putnam's.

FAIRMAN, CHARLES 1939 *Mr. Justice Miller and the Supreme Court, 1862–1890.* Cambridge, Mass.: Harvard University Press.

CLOSED SHOP

A workplace is a closed shop if, by virtue of a labor contract, only the members of a particular union may be hired. After passage of the TAFT-HARTLEY ACT (1947), the closed shop was replaced by the "union shop" wherein one must join the union after being hired.

DENNIS J. MAHONEY

CLOTURE

Cloture terminates debate in a legislative body. The rules of the Senate encourage extended debates and, by taking advantage of those rules, sectional or ideological cliques can prevent action on bills they oppose. Only after rules reforms in the early 1960s made cloture easier did Congress pass effective CIVIL RIGHTS ACTS.

DENNIS J. MAHONEY

CLYMER, GEORGE
(1739–1813)

George Clymer, who represented Pennsylvania at the CONSTITUTIONAL CONVENTION OF 1787, was a signer of both the DECLARATION OF INDEPENDENCE and the Constitution. Clymer did not speak often, but he was a member of the committees on state debts and the slave trade.

DENNIS J. MAHONEY

COCHRAN v. LOUISIANA
281 U.S. 370 (1930)

Louisiana provided books to all public and private school children. The private school support was challenged on FOURTEENTH AMENDMENT grounds as a use of public money for private purposes. Chief Justice CHARLES EVANS HUGHES held that the state's purpose was public.

Cochran is sometimes cited as an accommodationist precedent, but it was not decided under the establishment clause, which was not considered to apply to the states at that time.

RICHARD E. MORGAN

CODISPOTI v. PENNSYLVANIA
418 U.S. 506 (1974)

A 5–4 Court here extended its decision in DUNCAN V. LOUISIANA (1968) to persons receiving serious punishment for criminal contempt. Following their trial, two defendants were cited for contempt and given several consecutive sentences for contempt of court. *Bloom v. Illinois* (1968) served as the basis for Justice BYRON R. WHITE's opinion that the defendants were entitled to a TRIAL BY JURY. Even though no single sentence exceeded six months, the consecutive sentences could not be separated; they all stemmed from one trial conducted as a single proceeding by one judge.

DAVID GORDON

COEFFICIENT CLAUSE

See: Necessary and Proper Clause

COERCED CONFESSION

See: Police Interrogation and Confessions

COERCIVE ACTS

See: Constitutional History before 1776; First Continental Congress

COHEN, MORRIS R.
(1880–1947)

Morris Raphael Cohen came to the United States from Russia in 1892. After receiving his doctorate from Harvard in 1906, Cohen taught philosophy at the City College of New York from 1912 until 1938, when he retired to devote the rest of his life to writing.

A disciple of Justice OLIVER WENDELL HOLMES, Cohen rejected the conventional belief that judges decide cases by mechanical application of independently existing legal rules; he argued that the process of judicial lawmaking should be guided by the scientific method, a thorough understanding of the social consequences of judicial decisions, and a hierarchical set of social values. Believing natural law to be the measure of justice and advocating the philosophical analysis of legal systems, Cohen attacked such proponents of LEGAL REALISM as JEROME FRANK and THURMAN ARNOLD for their refusal to recognize any external standard by which positive law could be criticized. Cohen's legal writings are collected in *Law and the Social Order* (1933) and *Reason and Law* (1950).

RICHARD B. BERNSTEIN

Bibliography

HOLLINGER, DAVID A. 1975 *Morris R. Cohen and the Scientific Ideal.* Cambridge, Mass.: M.I.T. Press.

COHEN v. CALIFORNIA
403 U.S. (1971)

Cohen was convicted of disturbing the peace. He wore a jacket bearing the words "Fuck the draft" while walking down a courthouse corridor. In overturning the conviction, a 5–4 Supreme Court held that the FIGHTING WORDS exception to FIRST AMENDMENT protection did not apply where "no individual . . . likely to be present could reasonably have regarded the words . . . as a direct personal insult," and there was no showing that anyone who saw Cohen was in fact violently aroused or that . . . [he] . . . intended such a result." Both majority and dissenters suggested that the failure to show that violence was imminent as the result of the words was fatal to the state's case. The Court thus made clear that words, in the abstract, cannot be read out of the First Amendment; the "fighting words" doctrine depends on the context in which words are uttered.

The state's assertion of other justifications for punishing Cohen were similarly rejected: the jacket's message was not OBSCENITY, because it was not erotic; the privacy interests of offended passers-by were insubstantial in this public place, and anyone offended might look away; there was no CAPTIVE AUDIENCE.

Cohen's chief doctrinal importance lies in its rejection of the notion that speech can constitutionally be prohibited by the state because it is offensive. Because offensiveness is an "inherently boundless" category, any such prohibition would suffer from the vice of VAGUENESS. And the First Amendment protects not only the cool expression of ideas but also "otherwise inexpressible emotions."

MARTIN SHAPIRO

COHENS v. VIRGINIA
6 Wheat. 265 (1821)

In the rancorous aftermath of MCCULLOCH V. MARYLAND (1819), several states, led by Virginia and Ohio, denounced and defied the Supreme Court. State officers of Ohio entered the vaults of a branch of the Bank of the United States and forcibly collected over $100,000 in state taxes. (See OSBORN V. BANK OF THE UNITED STATES, 1824.) Virginia's legislature resolved that the Constitution be amended to create "a tribunal for the decision of all questions, in which the powers and authorities of the general government and those of the States, where they are in conflict, shall be decided." Widespread and vitriolic attacks on the Court, its doctrine of IMPLIED POWERS, and section 25 of the JUDICIARY ACT OF 1789 showed that MARTIN V. HUNTER'S LESSEE (1816) and *McCulloch* were not enough to settle the matters involved, especially as to the JURISDICTION of the Court over state acts and decisions in conflict with the supreme law of the land as construed by the Court. Accordingly a case appears to have been contrived to create for Chief Justice JOHN MARSHALL an opportunity to reply officially to his critics and to reassert both national supremacy and the supreme appellate powers of his Court.

Two brothers surnamed Cohen sold lottery tickets in Norfolk, Virginia, contrary to a state act prohibiting their sale for a lottery not authorized by Virginia. The Cohens sold tickets for a lottery authorized by an act of Congress to benefit the capital city. In Norfolk the borough court found the defendants guilty and fined them $100. By Virginia law, no appeal could be had to a higher state court. The Cohens, prosperous Baltimore merchants who could easily afford the paltry fine, claimed the protection of the act of Congress and removed the case on WRIT OF ERROR from the local court to the highest court of the land; moreover they employed the greatest lawyer in the nation, WILLIAM PINCKNEY, whose usual fee was $2,000 a case, and another distinguished advocate, David B. Ogden, who commanded a fee of $1,000. More was at stake than appeared. "The very title of the case," said the Richmond *Enquirer*, "is enough to stir one's blood"—a reference to the galling fact that the sovereign state of Virginia was being hauled before the Supreme Court of the United States by private individuals in seeming violation of the ELEVENTH AMENDMENT. The state governor was so alarmed that he notified the legislature, and its committee, referring to the states as "sovereign and independent nations," declared that the state judiciaries were as independent of the federal courts as the state legislatures were of Congress, the twenty-fifth section of the 1789 notwithstanding. The legislature, having adopted solemn resolutions of protest and repudiating federal JUDICIAL REVIEW, instructed counsel representing Virginia to argue one point alone: that the Supreme Court had no jurisdiction in the case. Counsel, relying on the Eleventh Amendment to argue that a state cannot be sued without its consent, also contended that not a word in the Constitution "goes to set up the federal judiciary above the state judiciary."

Marshall, for a unanimous Court dominated by Republicans, conceded that the main "subject was fully discussed and exhausted in the case of *Martin v. Hunter,*" but that did not stop him from writing a fifty-five-page treatise which concluded that under section 25 the Court had jurisdiction in the case. Marshall said little that was new, but he said it with a majestic eloquence and a forcefulness that surpassed JOSEPH STORY's, and the fact that the Chief Justice was the author of the Court's nationalist exposition, addressed to STATES RIGHTS' advocates throughout the country, added weight and provocation to his utterances. He was sublimely rhapsodic about the Constitution and the Union it created, sarcastic and disparaging in restating Virginia's position. Boldly he piled inference upon inference, overwhelming every particle of disagreement in the course of his triumphs of logic and excursions into the historical record of state infidelity. And he had a sense of the melodramatic that Story lacked, as when Marshall began his opinion by saying that the question of jurisdiction "may be truly said vitally to affect the Union." The defendant in error—Virginia—did not care whether the Constitution and laws of the United States had been violated by the judgment of guilt that the Cohens sought to have reviewed. Admitting such violation, Virginia contended that the United States had no corrective. Virginia, Marshall continued, maintained that the nation possessed no department capable of restraining, peaceably and by authority of law, attempts against the legitimate powers of the nation. "They maintain," he added, "that the constitution of the United States has provided no tribunal for the final construction of itself, or of the laws or treaties of the nation; but that this power may be exercised in the last resort by the courts of every state of the Union." Virginia even maintained that the supreme law of the land "may receive as many constructions as there are states. . . ." Marshall confronted and conquered every objection.

Quickly turning to Article III, Marshall observed that it authorizes Congress to confer federal jurisdiction in two classes of cases, the first depending on the character of the case and the second on the character of the parties. The first class includes "all" cases involving the Constitution and federal laws and treaties, "whoever may be the parties," and the second includes all cases to which states are parties. By ratifying the Constitution the states consented to judicial review in both classes of cases, thereby making possible the preservation of the Union. That Union is supreme in all cases where it is empowered to act, as Article VI, the SUPREMACY CLAUSE, insures by making the Constitution and federal law the supreme law of the land. The Court must decide every case coming within its constitutional jurisdiction to prevent the supreme law of the land from being prostrated "at the feet of every state in the Union" or being vetoed by any member of the Union. Collisions between the United States and the states will doubtless occur, but, said Marshall, "a constitution is framed for ages to come, and is designed to approach immortality as nearly as human institutions can approach it." To prevail, the government of the Union derived from the Constitution the means of self-preservation. The federal courts existed to secure the execution of the laws of the Union. History proved, Marshall declared, that the states and their tribunals could not be trusted with a power to defeat by law the legitimate measures of the Union. Thus the Supreme Court can take APPELLATE JURISDICTION even in a case between a state and one of its own citizens who relied on the Constitution or federal law. Otherwise Article III would be mere surplusage, as would Article VI. For the Court to decline the jurisdiction authorized by Article III and commanded by Congress would be "treason to the Constitution."

Although Marshall's rhetoric certainly addressed itself, grandiosely, to the question of jurisdiction, his critics regarded all that he had declared thus far as OBITER DICTA, for he had not yet faced the Eleventh Amendment, which Virginia thought concluded the case on its behalf. Upon finally reaching the Eleventh Amendment question, Marshall twisted a little history and chopped a little logic. The amendment, he said, was adopted not to preserve state dignity or sovereignty but to prevent creditors from initiating suits against states that would raid their treasuries. The amendment did not, therefore, apply to suits commenced by states and appealed by writ of error to the Supreme Court for the sole purpose of inquiring whether the judgment of a state tribunal violated the Constitution or federal law.

The argument that the state and federal judiciaries were entirely independent of each other considered the Supreme Court as "foreign" to state judiciaries. In a grand peroration, Marshall made his Court the apex of a single judicial system that comprehended the state judiciaries to the extent that they shared a concurrent jurisdiction over cases arising under the supreme law of the land. For most important purposes, Marshall declared, the United States was "a single nation," and for all those purposes, its government is supreme; state constitutions and laws to the contrary are "absolutely void." The states "are members of one great empire—for some purposes sovereign, for some purposes subordinate." The role of the federal judiciary, Marshall concluded, was to void state judgments that might contravene the supreme law; the alternative would be "a hydra in government."

Having sustained the jurisdiction of the Court, Marshall offered a sop to Virginia: whether the congressional lottery act intended to operate outside the DISTRICT OF COLUMBIA, he suggested, depended on the words of that act. The case was then reargued on its merits, and Marshall, again for a unanimous Court, quickly sustained the Cohens' conviction: Congress had not intended to permit the sale of lottery tickets in states where such a sale was illegal.

Virginia "won" its case, just as Madison had in *Marbury v. Madison* (1803), but no one was fooled this time either. The governor of Virginia in a special message to his legislature spoke of the state's "humiliation" in having failed to vindicate its sovereign rights. A legislative committee proposed amendments to the Constitution that would cripple not only the JUDICIAL POWER OF THE UNITED STATES but also (reacting to *McCulloch*) the powers of Congress in passing laws not "absolutely" necessary and proper for carrying out its ENUMERATED POWERS. In the United States Senate, enemies of the Court proposed constitutional amendments that would vest in the Senate appellate jurisdiction in cases where the laws of a state were impugned and in all cases involving the federal Constitution, laws, or treaties. Intermittently for several years senators introduced a variety of amendments to curb the Court or revoke section 25, but those who shared a common cause did not share a common remedy, though GREEN V. BIDDLE (1823) and OSBORN V. BANK OF THE UNITED STATES (1824) inflamed their cause.

In Virginia, where the newspapers published Marshall's long opinion to the accompaniment of scathing denunciations, SPENCER ROANE and JOHN TAYLOR returned to a long battle that had begun with the *Martin* case and expanded in the wake of *McCulloch.* Roane, as "Algernon Sydney," published five articles on the theme that *Cohens* "negatives the idea that the American states have a real existence, or are to be considered, in any sense, as sovereign and independent states." He excoriated federal judicial review, implied powers, and the subordination of the states, by judicial construction, to "one great consolidated government" that destroyed the equilibrium of the Constitution, leaving that compact of the states nonexistent except in name. Taylor's new book, *Tyranny Unmasked* (1822), continued the themes of his *Construction Construed* (1820), where he argued that the "federal is not a national government: it is a league of nations. By this league, a limited power only over persons and property was given to the representatives of the united nations." The "tyranny" unmasked by the second book turned out to be nationalist programs, such as the protective tariff, and nationalist powers, including the power of the Supreme Court over the states.

THOMAS JEFFERSON read Roane and Taylor, egged them on, and congratulated them for their orthodox repudiation of the Court's "heresies." To Justice WILLIAM JOHNSON, who had joined Marshall's opinion, Jefferson wrote that Roane's articles "appeared to me to pulverize every word which had been delivered by Judge Marshall, of the extra-judicial part of his opinion," and to Jefferson "all was extra-judicial"—and he was not wholly wrong—except the second *Cohens* opinion on the merits. Jefferson also wrote that the doctrine that courts are the final arbiters of all constitutional questions was "dangerous" and "would place us under the despotism of an oligarchy." Recommending the works of Roane and Taylor to a friend, Jefferson militantly declared that if Congress did not shield the states from the dangers originating with the Court, "the states must shield themselves, and meet the invader foot to foot." To Senator NATHANIEL MACON of Virginia, Jefferson wrote that the Supreme Court was "the germ of dissolution of our federal government" and "an irresponsible body," working, he said, "like gravity, by day and night, gaining a little today and a little tomorrow, and advancing its noiseless step, like a thief over the fields of jurisdiction, until all shall be usurped from the States, the government of all becoming a consolidated one."

JAMES MADISON deplored some of the Court's tactics, especially its mingling of judgments with "comments and reasoning of a scope beyond them," often at the expense of the states; but Madison told Roane flatly that the judicial power of the United States "over cases arising under the Constitution, must be admitted to be a vital part of the System." He thought Marshall wrong on the Eleventh Amendment and extreme on implied powers, but, he wrote to Roane, on the question "whether the federal or the State decisions ought to prevail, the sounder policy would yield to the claims of the former," or else "the Constitution of the U.S. might become different in every State."

The public reaction to *Cohens* depressed Marshall, because, as he wrote to Story, the opinion of the Court "has been assaulted with a degree of virulence transcending what has appeared on any former occasion." Roane's "Algernon Sydney" letters, Marshall feared, might be believed true by the public, and Roane would be hailed as "the champion of state rights, instead of being what he really is, the champion of dismemberment." Marshall saw "a deep design to convert our government into a mere league of States. . . . The attack upon the Judiciary is in fact an attack upon the Union." The whole attack originated, he believed, with Jefferson, "the grand Lama of the mountains." An effort would be made, predicted Marshall, accurately, "to repeal the 25th section of the Judiciary Act." Doubtless the personal attacks on him proved painful. A bit of anonymous doggerel, which circulated in Virginia after *Cohens,* illuminates public feeling.

Old Johnny Marshall what's got in ye
To side with Cohens against Virginny.
To call in Court his "Old Dominion."
To insult her with your foul opinion!
I'll tell you that it will not do
To call old Spencer in review.
He knows the law as well as you.
And once for all, it will not do.
Alas! Alas! that you should be
So much against State Sovereignty!
You've thrown the whole state in a terror,
By this infernal "Writ of Error."

The reaction to *Cohens* proves, in part, that the Court's prose was overbroad, but Marshall was reading the Constitution in the only way that would make the federal system operate effectively under one supreme law.

LEONARD W. LEVY

Bibliography

BEVERIDGE, ALBERT J. 1916–1919 *The Life of John Marshall,* 4 vols. Vol. IV: 340–375. Boston: Houghton-Mifflin.

HAINS, CHARLES GROVE 1944 *The Role of the Supreme Court in American Government and Politics, 1789–1835.* Pages 427–461. Berkeley: University of California Press.

KONEFSKY, SAMUEL J. 1964 *John Marshall and Alexander Hamilton.* Pages 93–111. New York: Macmillan.

COKE, EDWARD
(1552–1634)

Edward Coke (pronounced Cook) was an English lawyer, judge, and parliamentarian who influenced the development of English and American constitutional law by promoting the supremacy of the COMMON LAW in relation to parliamentary powers and the royal prerogative.

After studying at Trinity College, Cambridge, Coke entered the Inner Temple and was called to the Bar in 1578. His career was outstanding from the start. He was elected to Parliament in 1589 and in 1593 he became Speaker of the House of Commons. Appointed attorney-general in 1594, he prosecuted several notable TREASON cases, including that of Sir Walter Raleigh in 1603.

In 1600, Coke began publication of his *Reports.* Eleven volumes had been published by 1615; two additional volumes appeared after his death. These were not collections of appellate opinions; rather, they consisted of case notes made by Coke, legal history, and general criticism. Coke had mastered the precedents, and he brought symmetry to scattered authority. Thereafter, *The Reports,* as they were usually called, were the authoritative common law precedents in England and colonial America.

Coke was appointed Chief Justice of the Court of Common Pleas in 1606, serving until 1613, when he was appointed Chief Justice of the Court of King's Bench. His judicial career was terminated in 1616 when King James I removed him from office. During these years Coke began enunciating ideas concerning the supremacy of the common law, foreshadowing modern concepts of government under law.

Coke's judicial pronouncement most influential on the American doctrine of JUDICIAL REVIEW came in BONHAM'S CASE (1610). The College of Physicians had fined and imprisoned Dr. Bonham for practicing medicine without a license. The court held that because the College would share in the fine, the charter and parliamentary act conferring this authority were contrary to the common law principle that no man can be a judge in his own case. Coke stated: "And it appears in our books, that in many cases, the common law will control acts of parliament, and sometimes adjudge them to be utterly void: for when an act of parliament is against common right and reason, or repugnant, or impossible to be performed, the common law will control it, and adjudge such act to be void. . . ." Coke believed that the common law contained a body of fundamental, although not unchangeable, principles to be ascertained and enunciated by judges through the "artificial reason" of the law. In *Bonham's Case* he seemed to be reasoning that parliamentary acts must be interpreted consistently with those principles. Whatever Coke's precise meaning, however, the statement foreshadowed the American DOCTRINE of judicial review; it was influential in the developing concept of the supremacy of law as interpreted and applied by the judiciary.

Another incident of Coke's judicial career that contributed to the modern idea of government under law came in 1608 during a confrontation with James I. The king had claimed authority to withdraw cases from the courts and decide them himself. In a dramatic Sunday morning meeting convened by the king and attended by all the judges and bishops, Coke maintained that there was no such royal authority. He asserted, quoting Bracton, that the king was not under man "but under God and law," one of the earliest and most quoted expressions of this concept.

Coke returned to Parliament in 1620 and in the final phase of his career made two major contributions to constitutional government and English and American law.

Drawing on the provision in MAGNA CARTA that "no free man shall be taken [or] imprisoned . . . except by the . . . law of the land," he launched the concept of "due process of law." Coke asserted that this provision referred to the established processes of the common law. He expressed this view in the parliamentary debates leading to the PETITION OF RIGHT in 1628, raising Magna Carta to new heights with statements such as "Magna Carta is such a fellow that he will have no sovereign." Coke's arguments presaged the later American concept of a written constitution superior to other law. He also linked Magna Carta with HABEAS CORPUS, although there was little historical support for the connection. He believed that there must be a remedy for imprisonment contrary to common law process and the remedy was to be had through the writ of habeas corpus.

Coke's other major contribution in his last years was the writing of his *Institutes.* This four-part work, published in 1641, became a basic text in the education of lawyers in England and America. In America, where law books were few, the *Institutes* were the standard work before the publication of WILLIAM BLACKSTONE's *Commentaries* in 1767. As noted by the Supreme Court in one of its several twentieth-century references to Coke (KLOPFER V. NORTH CAROLINA, 1967): "Coke's Institutes were read in the American Colonies by virtually every student of the law. Indeed, THOMAS JEFFERSON wrote that at the time he studied law (1762–1767), *Coke Lyttleton* was the universal elementary book of law students. And to JOHN RUTLEDGE of South Carolina, the Institutes seemed to be almost the foundation of our law." Because few lawyers in England and America had either the inclination or the resources to go behind Coke's *Institutes* and his *Reports,* these works, despite historical inaccuracies revealed by later scholarship, became the authoritative legal source on both sides of the Atlantic.

Coke represents a transition from medieval to modern law. He lived in the dawn of the modern constitutional era, when the British colonization of North America was beginning. As the colonists later sought authority to support their arguments that royal power was limited by law, they found it in Coke. Since the American Revolution, Coke has been regarded as an early authority for the proposition that all government is under law and that it is ultimately for the courts to interpret the law.

DANIEL J. MEADOR

Bibliography

BOUDIN, LOUIS B. 1929 Lord Coke and the American Doctrine of Judicial Power. *New York University Law Review* 6:223–246.

BOWEN, CATHERINE D. 1957 *The Lion and the Throne: The Life and Times of Sir Edward Coke.* Boston: Little, Brown.

MULLETT, CHARLES F. 1932 Coke and the American Revolution. *Economica* 12:457–471.

COKER v. GEORGIA
433 U.S. 584 (1977)

Ehrlich Coker, an escaped felon, was convicted of rape with aggravating circumstances and sentenced to die. The Supreme Court, in a 7–2 decision, overturned the sentence. Justice BYRON R. WHITE, in a PLURALITY OPINION, argued that CAPITAL PUNISHMENT is "grossly disproportionate and excessive punishment for the crime of rape," and therefore unconstitutional under the Eighth Amendment, binding on the states through the FOURTEENTH AMENDMENT. Justice LEWIS F. POWELL's concurring opinion was applicable to the facts of this case only, while Justice WILLIAM J. BRENNAN and THURGOOD MARSHALL would have held the death penalty unconstitutional in any case whatsoever. Chief Justice WARREN E. BURGER and Justice WILLIAM H. REHNQUIST dissented, arguing that Coker's sentence was within the reserved power of the State.

DENNIS J. MAHONEY

COLEGROVE v. GREEN
328 U.S. 549 (1946)

Colegrove v. Green and BAKER V. CARR (which all but overruled *Colegrove* in 1962) bracket the passage of the ONE PERSON, ONE VOTE movement from failure to success. Migration had drastically enlarged urban electoral districts and reduced rural ones in most states, but legislators and voters were slow to reapportion, and reapportionists turned to courts for relief. But courts were wary of tampering with legislators' seats.

The Supreme Court dismissed Colegrove's suit to enjoin Illinois congressional elections in "malapportioned" districts. The Justices gave two reasons: the case wanted EQUITY to make an INJUNCTION appropriate, and it presented a POLITICAL QUESTION reserved for decision of the elected branches both by constitutional mandate and by lack of judicially appropriate standards of judgment. "Courts," said Justice FELIX FRANKFURTER, "ought not to enter this political thicket." Three Justices dissented, arguing that the case did not lack equity, that the question was not political, and that constitutional mandate and standards could be found in Article I, section 2, and the EQUAL PROTECTION clause of the FOURTEENTH AMENDMENT—a debatable assertion little argued in either *Colegrove* or *Baker.* Justice WILEY RUTLEDGE, the tiebreaker, thought the question nonpolitical but joined in the vote for dismissal for want of equity.

Though the Court dismissed all REAPPORTIONMENT cases for sixteen years, citing *Colegrove,* Rutledge's discretionary rationale left room for the debate between Justices WILLIAM J. BRENNAN and Frankfurter in *Baker,* and for the intervention that led to the reapportionment revolution. The applicability of the equal protection clause to reapportionment was not seriously debated until REYNOLDS V. SIMS (1964) and OREGON v. MITCHELL (1970). Justices HUGO L. BLACK and JOHN MARSHALL HARLAN debated the applicability of Article I, section 2, in WESBERRY v. SANDERS (1964), which finally overruled *Colegrove.*

WARD E. Y. ELLIOTT

Bibliography

AUERBACH, CARL A. 1964 The Reapportionment Cases: One Person, One Vote—One Vote, One Value." *Supreme Court Review* 1964:1–87.

COLEMAN v. MILLER
307 U.S. 433 (1939)

The lieutenant governor of Kansas had broken a tie vote in the Kansas senate to endorse a CHILD LABOR AMENDMENT, which Kansas had previously rejected. The losing senators, opponents of the amendment, challenged the vote because the lieutenant governor was not a part of the state "legislature" within the meaning of Article V and because the previous rejection of the amendment, plus the lapse of thirteen years, had cost the amendment its "vitality."

Over objections from dissenting Justices PIERCE BUTLER and JAMES C. MCREYNOLDS that the lapse of time issue had not been briefed or argued, Chief Justice CHARLES EVANS HUGHES declined to hear the challenge, citing the ratification of the FOURTEENTH AMENDMENT and arguing that efficacy of ratification—both as to lapse of time and as to the prior rejection—was a POLITICAL QUESTION, requiring "appraisal of a great variety of relevant conditions, political, social, and economic," not "within the appropriate range of EVIDENCE receivable in a court." Dominant considerations in political questions, he noted, are the "appropriateness of final action" by the elected branch and the "lack of satisfactory criteria for judicial determination."

Justice HUGO L. BLACK, writing for four concurring Justices, thought that Hughes had not sufficiently emphasized Congress's "exclusive power to control submission of constitutional amendments." An evenly divided Court expressed no opinion as to whether counting the lieutenant governor as part of the legislature was a political question.

WARD E. Y. ELLIOTT

Bibliography

SCHARPF, FRITZ W. 1966 Judicial Review and the Political Question: A Functional Analysis. *Yale Law Journal* 75:517–597.

COLGATE v. HARVEY
296 U.S. 404 (1935)

This case is a historical curiosity. Vermont taxed the income from money loaned out of state but exempted from taxation any income from money loaned in the state at not more than five percent interest. The Supreme Court, in an opinion by Justice GEORGE SUTHERLAND, held the act unconstitutional as a violation of the EQUAL PROTECTION and PRIVILEGES AND IMMUNITIES clauses of the FOURTEENTH AMENDMENT. Justices HARLAN F. STONE, LOUIS D. BRANDEIS, and BENJAMIN N. CARDOZO, in dissent, found difficulty in perceiving a privilege of national CITIZENSHIP which the state had violated, especially because the Court had decided forty-four cases since 1868 in which state acts had been attacked as violating the privileges and immunities clause and until this case had held none of them unconstitutional. MADDEN v. KENTUCKY (1940) overruled *Colgate.*

LEONARD W. LEVY

COLLATERAL ATTACK

As a general proposition a litigant gets one chance to present his case to a trial court; if he is dissatisfied with the result, he may APPEAL. What he cannot do, however, is to attack it "collaterally," starting the lawsuit all over again at the bottom, not so much asserting error in the first proceeding as ignoring it or trying to have the second trial court undo its results. This COMMON LAW doctrine forbidding collateral attack exists independently of the Constitution, which makes no direct mention of it. But the Constitution is frequently incomprehensible without some reference to its common law background. In this instance the document at three points implicates the doctrine of collateral attack. One section, the FULL FAITH AND CREDIT clause, seems to forbid collateral attack in civil cases (except where DUE PROCESS may require otherwise); the HABEAS CORPUS clause, by contrast, seems to require it in at least some criminal cases.

What constitutes collateral attack is itself often a difficult question; different JURISDICTIONS attach different significance to their judgments. As a general proposition, though, the full faith and credit clause requires that State A give the JUDGMENTS of State B the same effect State B would; to that extent the clause prohibits collateral attack in the interstate context. (A federal statute imposes the same requirements on federal courts.) The due process clause, however, limits the full faith and credit clause; if the courts of the state rendering the first judgment lacked jurisdiction over the defendant, the full faith and credit clause does not bar collateral attack. Due process requires that a defendant be able collaterally to attack a judgment rendered by a court that lacked authority over him. The due process clause, however, requires a court to permit collateral attack only when the party using it has not previously litigated the issue of jurisdiction; if he has, that question, like all others, is closed. Moreover, one who engages in litigation without raising the question of jurisdiction is generally treated as if he had done so and lost; the justification for such treatment is that the litigant had an opportunity to do so: due process does not require giving a second chance to one who has actually engaged in a lawsuit. The operation of this proposition leaves open to collateral attack only those judgments entered without any participation by the defendant—default judgments.

Collateral attack is thus available but is rather tightly circumscribed in civil cases; those held in detention on criminal charges have a somewhat wider scope of collateral attack available to them. The habeas clause requires federal courts (and arguably also those of the states) to entertain challenges to detention. Interpreting the federal statutes implementing the clause, federal courts have permitted those in custody to complain of various basic constitutional defects in the trials leading to their conviction; courts in some circumstances have permitted such collateral attack even though the asserted constitutional defect could have been raised in a direct appeal. To that extent present habeas practice, like the due process clause, requires courts to permit collateral attack. Unlike the due process clause, however, the habeas statute has been interpreted to permit litigants in some circumstances to raise again issues already litigated in the criminal trial.

At one level, then, the Constitution appears to issue contradictory commands: recognize judgments as conclusive—except when they are not. At another level the contradiction disappears, for both commands flow from the same impulse: under normal conditions only direct attack by appeal is permissible, but when the basic prerequisites of proper adjudication are absent (the basis of judicial authority or the incidents of a fair criminal trial), the normal rules must give way.

STEPHEN C. YEAZELL

Bibliography

AMERICAN LAW INSTITUTE 1971 *Restatement of the Law 2d, Conflicts of Laws.* St. Paul, Minn.: American Law Institute Publishers.

EISENBERG, THEODORE 1981 *Civil Rights Legislation.* Charlottesville, Va.: Michie Co.

NOTE 1957 The Value of the Distinction between Direct and Collateral Attacks on Judgments. *Yale Law Journal* 66:526–544.

COLLECTIVE BARGAINING

Collective bargaining is the process of negotiation between employers and labor unions to establish the wages, hours, and working conditions of employees. Collective bargaining has been regulated by the federal government since passage of the WAGNER (NATIONAL LABOR RELATIONS) ACT (1935) and the TAFT-HARTLEY ACT (1947).

DENNIS J. MAHONEY

(SEE ALSO: *Labor and the Constitution.*)

COLLECTOR v. DAY
11 Wallace 113 (1871)

In MCCULLOCH V. MARYLAND (1819) the Supreme Court had held unconstitutional a state tax on an instrumentality of the national government, and in *Dobbins v. Commissioners* (1842) the Court had forbidden a state to tax the salary of a federal officer. The Court had reasoned that a sovereign government must be immune from the taxes of another government to preserve its independence. Here the Court applied that doctrine reciprocally, holding that the United States had no constitutional power to tax the salary of a state judge. In GRAVES V. NEW YORK EX REL. O'KEEFE (1939) the Court overruled both *Dobbins* and *Collector,* vitiating the DOCTRINE of reciprocal tax immunities.

LEONARD W. LEVY

(SEE ALSO: *Intergovernmental Immunities.*)

COLLUSIVE SUIT

Article III of the Constitution limits the federal courts to the decision of CASES OR CONTROVERSIES. One component of that limitation bars adjudication of the merits of a claim absent a real dispute between parties who have conflicting interests. If nominally opposing parties manufacture a lawsuit to secure a judicial ruling, if one party controls or finances both sides of a case, or if both parties in fact desire the same ruling, the suit will be dismissed as collusive. The issues in a case need not be contested, so long as the parties' ultimate interests in the litigation are opposed. Hence, a default judgment can be entered, or a guilty plea accepted. Nor are all TEST CASES forbidden as collusive—only those where the contestants seek the same outcome. Of course, other JUSTICIABILITY barriers may prevent adjudication.

Like the ban on ADVISORY OPINIONS, the rule banning collusive suits saves judicial resources for disputes that need resolution, helps assure that federal courts act only on the basis of the information needed for sound decision making, and, in constitutional cases, prevents premature judicial intervention in the political process. The rule also may block efforts by supposed adversaries (but actual allies) to procure a ruling detrimental to opponents who are not represented in the collusive action.

JONATHAN D. VARAT

COLONIAL CHARTER

Perhaps no other American constitutional topic has been subject to such changing and contrary interpretations as has that of colonial charters. For example, GEORGE BANCROFT, who in 1834 had written that the Massachusetts charter of 1629 "established a CORPORATION, like other corporations within the realm," wrote in 1883 that the charter "constituted a body politic by the name of the Governor and Company of the Massachusetts Bay." Bancroft's apparent inconsistency is less contradiction than part of a constitutional controversy. Even during the colonial period constitutional experts disagreed about the legal nature of charters.

A few North American colonies (Plymouth, New Haven) had no charters. Most did, however, and the earliest charters were of two types. The first (Virginia, Massachusetts Bay), modeled on trading company charters granted to merchants, stressed commerce and settlement. The second (Maryland, Maine, Carolina) was based on the palatinate bishopric of Durham County, England. Later, a third type of charter was issued: "royal" charters for colonies in which the governor and other designated officers were appointed by the Crown. Containing more provisions directing government functions, royal charters generally defined a colony's relations with the mother country, not its internal constitution. No matter the type, charters were statements of privileges, not organic acts of government; they conferred immunities from prosecution and did not define structures of governance. Colonial charters, therefore, did not contribute significantly to constitutional law or history except when Americans claimed immunity from parliamentary authority.

American legal theory held that charters were contracts by which the king promised to protect and defend his American subjects in exchange for the subjects' allegiance. A better theory was that charters were evidence of a contract between the English crown and the first settlers of America. By either theory charters were not CONSTITUTIONS but one of the sources of constitutional rights along with the ancient English constitution, the current British constitution, the original contract, the second original contract, COMMON LAW, custom, and, to a minor degree, natural law. The first charter of Virginia stated a principle, repeated in later Virginia charters and in the charters of several other colonies, that the colonists "shall have and enjoy all Liberties, Franchises, and Immunities . . . to all Intents and Purposes as if they had been abiding and born within this our Realm of England. . . ." Americans of the Revolutionary period read such provisions as supporting their constitutional arguments against Britain. The legal theory subscribed to on the imperial side of the controversy held that charters created corporations not unlike municipal and commercial corporations in the mother country. As JOSEPH GALLOWAY declared, the colonies were only "corporations, or subordinate bodies politic, vested with *legislative* powers, to regulate their own internal police, under certain regulations and restrictions, and no more." A more extreme imperial theory held that charters were irrelevant; that the powers and limitations of colonial government came not from charters but from the instructions that British ministers issued to colonial governors. This theory, which American legislatures repudiated, contributed to the coming of the Revolution.

The American theory that charters were inviolable contracts confirming inalienable rights was premised on Old Whig constitutional definitions of LIMITED GOVERNMENT which still enjoyed some support in Britain during the second half of the eighteenth century and found expression in arguments that Parliament lacked constitutional authority to revoke or amend charters. This argument had little support in Britain, where all charters were viewed as revocable. In fact, a majority of colonies had their charters revoked and regranted at various times by the British government. Indeed, no single action so provoked the American Revolution as the Massachusetts Government Act asserting the authority of Parliament to amend colonial charters by unilateral decision.

When the Revolution commenced there were only two proprietary charters (Pennsylvania, Maryland) and two corporate charters (Connecticut, Rhode Island). Remaining colonies had royal charters, except Quebec and Georgia, which were governed by instructions. When Americans began to draft organic acts, they came more and more to think of charters as constitutions. To resist the Massachusetts Government Act, which revoked the charter of 1691, colonial leaders gave consideration to "resuming" the original charter of 1629 granted by Charles I. Connecticut and Rhode Island retained their charters as state constitutions, Connecticut until 1818 and Rhode Island until 1843.

JOHN PHILLIP REID

Bibliography

REID, JOHN PHILLIP 1976 In the First Line of Defense: The Colonial Charters, the Stamp Act Debate and the Coming of the American Revolution. *New York University Law Review* 51:177–215.

COLOR OF LAW

Some CIVIL RIGHTS statutes proscribe only behavior "under color of" state law, and this requirement has played an important role in the development of FEDERAL PROTECTION OF CIVIL RIGHTS. Ironically, civil rights statutes have been interpreted in a manner that strips the color of law requirement of most of its contemporary significance. Judicial interpretation usually equates the color of law requirement with STATE ACTION. Because in most contexts in which the color of law requirement appears state action also is required, there is no obvious independent role for the color of law requirement.

The phrase "under color of . . . law" appears in the nation's first civil rights act, the CIVIL RIGHTS ACT OF 1866. There it seemed to limit the act's coverage to actions taken pursuant to—under color of—the post-Civil War southern BLACK CODES. Subsequent revisions of the 1866 act and civil rights statutes modeled after it retained the concept as a way of limiting their coverage. It currently appears in section 242 of the federal criminal code, SECTION 1983, TITLE 42, UNITED STATES CODE, and section 1343(3) of the judicial code, the jurisdictional counterpart to section 1983.

In deciding what constitutes action under color of law, two extreme readings have been rejected. One view, advocated in dissenting opinions by Justices OWEN ROBERTS, FELIX FRANKFURTER, and ROBERT H. JACKSON in SCREWS V. UNITED STATES (1945) and by Justice Frankfurter in MONROE V. PAPE (1961), deems behavior to be under color of state law only when it is authorized by state law. In this view, any action by state officials in violation of state law cannot be under color of law. Where, as in *Screws,* a law officer murders his prisoner, in clear violation of state law, the officer's act would not be regarded as being under color of law and, therefore, would not be subject to civil or criminal penalties under federal statutes containing the requirement. This view of the color of law requirement would limit the significance of modern civil rights statutes, for much official behavior that civil rights litigants allege to violate the Constitution or federal law also violates state law. This view, however, would make the color of law requirement meaningful in the context of the times during which the requirement first appeared. During the post-Civil War era, much of the most disturbing official behavior, particularly behavior aimed at recently freed blacks, was authorized by state law.

The expansive extreme view of color of law arises not in interpreting the phrase itself but in interpreting it in conjunction with a series of nouns that accompany it. Section 1983, for example, refers to action "under color of any statute, ordinance, regulation, custom or usage." In *Adickes v. S. H. Kress & Co.* (1970), Justices WILLIAM J. BRENNAN and WILLIAM O. DOUGLAS interpreted "color of custom" to include virtually all segregative activity in the South, public or private, because the activity sprang from widespread custom. The majority in *Adickes* interpreted color of custom to include only action that constituted state action. Color of custom thus encompasses private behavior only to the extent that private persons act sufficiently in concert with public officials to render their action state action. This interpretation, combined with rejection in *Screws* and *Monroe* of the view limiting color of law to action authorized by law, leaves the color of law concept with little independent meaning. In general, action is under color of law if and only if the action satisfies the state action requirement.

There are, however, two areas in which it is useful to differentiate between state action and action under color of law. First, some constitutional rights, such as the THIRTEENTH AMENDMENT right not to be enslaved, are protected against both governmental and private infringement. A private person who caused the deprivation of such a right would be liable under statutes containing the "color of law" requirement even though his action was not state action. In these rare cases, action that is under color of law but that is not state action would lead to federal civil rights liability. Second, where a constitutional right, such as the right to DUE PROCESS, can be violated only by the government, private behavior authorized by statute may be action under color of law but, for want of state action, it may not subject the actor to civil rights liability. For example, when, pursuant to state statutes, creditors repossessed property without judicial proceedings, the Court in FLAGG BROS., INC. V. BROOKS (1978) held that the action taken was under color of law but that it was not state action.

In the pre-Civil War era, Congress employed the color of law requirement in a fashion related to its later use in civil rights statutes. States upset with expanding federal power and the behavior of federal officials would go so far as to initiate in state court criminal or civil proceedings against federal officers. Fearful of a biased forum, Congress, in a series of provisions commencing in 1815, provided federal officials with a right to remove these proceedings to federal court. (See REMOVAL OF CASES.) But Congress limited the power of removal to instances when the state proceedings were attributable to action by the officers under color of their office or of federal law. In this sense, as the Court noted in *Tennessee v. Davis* (1880), the color of law requirement clearly meant only action authorized by law, a point emphasized by the dissenters in *Screws.*

Nevertheless, it may be consistent with the purposes of both the removal and civil rights provisions to interpret color of law as limited to action authorized by law only in the case of the removal statute. If one views Congress in each case as desiring to protect only lawful behavior, it makes sense to interpret color of law in the removal statute to require action authorized by law and to interpret color of law in civil rights statutes to encompass official action, whether or not authorized by law. Use of the broad civil rights interpretation of color of law would immunize from state process action by federal officers not authorized by federal law. And in the context of civil rights statutes, adhering to the interpretation given the removal provision would immunize from federal remedies action by state officers not authorized by state law. The different interpretations serve a common function, subjecting a wrongdoer to liability.

THEODORE EISENBERG

Bibliography

EISENBERG, THEODORE 1982 Section 1983: Doctrinal Foundations and an Empirical Study. *Cornell Law Review* 67:507–510.

COLUMBIA BROADCASTING SYSTEM v. DEMOCRATIC NATIONAL COMMITTEE
412 U.S. 94 (1973)

The Supreme Court here considered a FIRST AMENDMENT challenge to a broadcaster's refusal to accept editorial advertisements except during political campaigns. Some Justices maintained that the broadcaster's action did not amount to governmental action, but the Court did not reach the question. Even assuming STATE ACTION, it held that the First Amendment permitted broadcasters to discriminate between commercial and political advertisements. Broadcasters, the Court observed, were obligated by the FAIRNESS DOCTRINE to cover political issues, and their choice to cover such issues outside of commercials protected CAPTIVE AUDIENCES and avoided a threat that the wealthy would dominate broadcast decisions about political issues.

STEVEN SHIFFRIN

COLUMBIA BROADCASTING SYSTEM, INC. v. FEDERAL COMMUNICATIONS COMMISSION
453 U.S. 367 (1981)

A 1971 amendment to the COMMUNICATIONS ACT OF 1934 permits the Federal Communications Commission (FCC) to revoke a broadcaster's license for failure to allow reasonable access to a candidate for federal office. The Supreme Court here interpreted this provision to create a right of access for an individual candidate. Further, reaffirming the much criticized precedent of RED LION BROADCASTING CO. V. FCC (1969), the Court sustained the law, as so interpreted, against a FIRST AMENDMENT challenge. The dissenters argued that the statute created no right of access.

KENNETH L. KARST

COLUMBUS BOARD OF EDUCATION v. PENICK
443 U.S. 449 (1979)
DAYTON BOARD OF EDUCATION v. BRINKMAN
433 U.S. 406 (1977); 443 U.S. 526 (1979)

These cases demonstrated the artificiality of the DE FACTO/DE JURE distinction in school DESEGREGATION litigation. Both cases arose in cities in Ohio, where racially segregated schools had not been prescribed by law since 1888. In both, however, blacks charged another form of de jure segregation: intentional acts by school boards aimed at promoting SEGREGATION.

When the *Dayton* case first reached the Supreme Court, a related doctrinal development was still a fresh memory. WASHINGTON V. DAVIS (1976) had held that RACIAL DISCRIMINATION was not to be inferred from the fact that governmental action had a racially disproportionate impact; rather the test was whether such an impact was intended by the legislative body or other officials whose conduct was challenged. (See LEGISLATION.) *Dayton I* in 1977 applied this reasoning to school segregation, emphasizing that a constitutional violation was to be found only in cases of established segregative intent. The Court remanded the case for more specific findings on the question of intent, and said that any remedy must be tailored to the scope of the segregation caused by any specific constitutional violations.

Many observers took *Dayton I* to portend the undermining of KEYES V. SCHOOL DISTRICT NO. 1 (1973). In *Keyes* the Court had held that, once a significant degree of de jure segregation was established, systemwide desegregation remedies (including SCHOOL BUSING) were appropriate unless the school board showed that any remaining racially separate schools were the product of something other than the board's segregative intent. When the case returned to the Supreme Court two years later, these predictions were confounded.

Dayton II came to the Court along with the *Columbus* case, and they were decided together. *Columbus,* decided by a 7–2 vote, provided the main opinions. Writing for a majority of five, Justice BYRON R. WHITE applied the *Keyes* presumptions approach so vigorously that the dissenters remarked that the de facto/de jure distinction had been drained of most of its meaning. None of the Justices disputed the finding that in 1954–1955, when BROWN V. BOARD OF EDUCATION was decided, the Columbus school board had deliberately drawn boundary lines and selected school sites to maintain racial segregation in a number of schools. What divided the Court was the question of inferences to be drawn from these undisputed facts.

Justice White reasoned that this de jure segregation placed the school board under an affirmative duty to dismantle its dual system. Its actions since 1954, however, had aggravated rather than reduced segregation; the foreseeability of those results helped prove the board's segregative intent. A districtwide busing remedy was thus appropriate under *Keyes.* Justice WILLIAM H. REHNQUIST, dissenting, pointed out the tension between this decision and *Dayton I.* Here there was no showing of a causal relationship between pre-1954 acts of intentional segregation and current racial imbalance in the schools. Thus present-day de facto segregation was enough to generate districtwide remedies, so long as some significant pre-1954 acts of deliberate segregation could be shown.

It will be a rare big-city school district in which such acts cannot be found—with a consequent presumption of current de jure segregation. A school board cannot overcome this presumption merely by relying on a neighborhood school policy and showing that the city's residences are racially separated. This analysis obviously blurs the de facto/de jure distinction.

Dayton II made clear that a school board's segregative purpose was secondary to its effectiveness in performing its affirmative duty to terminate a dual system—and that effectiveness was to be measured in the present-day facts of racial separation and integration. Justice White again wrote for the majority, but now there were four dissenters. Justice POTTER STEWART, the Court's one Ohioan, concurred in Columbus but dissented in *Dayton II,* deferring in each case to the district court's determination as to a continuing constitutional violation. In *Dayton II,* the district court had found pre-1954 acts of deliberate segregation, but had found no causal connection between those acts and present racial separation in the schools. That separation, the district judge concluded, resulted not from any segregative purpose on the part of the school board but from residential segregation. Justice Stewart would have accepted that judgment, but the majority, following the *Columbus* line of reasoning, held that the board had not fulfilled its affirmative duty to dismantle the dual system that had existed in 1954. Chief Justice WARREN E. BURGER joined Justice Stewart in both cases; Justice Rehnquist dissented in *Dayton II* chiefly on the basis of his *Columbus* dissent.

Justice LEWIS F. POWELL joined Justice Rehnquist's dissents, and also wrote an opinion dissenting in both cases. Justice Powell had argued in *Keyes* for abandoning the de facto/de jure distinction, and he did not defend that distinction here. Rather he repeated his skepticism that court orders could ever end racial imbalance in large urban school districts and his opposition to massive busing as a desegregation remedy. Justice Powell, a former school board president, argued that, twenty-five years after *Brown,* the federal courts should be limiting rather than expanding their control of public school operations.

KENNETH L. KARST

Bibliography

KITCH, EDMUND W. 1979 The Return of Color-Consciousness to the Constitution: Weber, Dayton, and Columbus. *Supreme Court Review* 1979:1–15.

COMITY, JUDICIAL

Comity is the deference paid by the institutions of one government to the acts of another government—not out of compulsion, but in the interest of cooperation, reciprocity, and the stability that grows out of the satisfaction of mutual expectations. When the courts of one nation give effect to foreign laws and the orders of foreign courts, that deference is called judicial comity. (See ACT OF STATE DOCTRINE.)

The states of the United States are, for many purposes, separate sovereignties. A state court, in deciding a case, starts from the assumption that it will apply its own state law. When it applies the law of another state, normally it does so as a matter of comity. (See CHOICE OF LAW, CONSTITUTIONAL LIMITS UPON.) Because comity is not so much a rule as an attitude of accommodation, state courts generally feel free to refuse to apply a law that violates their own state's public policy. In *Nevada v. Hall* (1979) California courts upheld a million-dollar verdict against the State of Nevada in an automobile injury case, rejecting Nevada's claim of SOVEREIGN IMMUNITY; the Supreme Court affirmed, saying that the Constitution left to California's courts the degree of comity they should afford to Nevada law.

A state court's enforcement of the valid judgment of a court of another state is not merely a matter of comity but is required by the FULL FAITH AND CREDIT CLAUSE. Similarly, the SUPREMACY CLAUSE binds state courts to enforce valid federal laws and regulations, along with the valid judgments of federal courts.

Notions of comity have recently taken on increased significance in the federal courts themselves. A federal court may, under some circumstances, stay its proceedings because another action between the same parties is pending in a state court. The Supreme Court in *Fair Assessment of Real Estate Association v. McNary* (1981) discovered in the Tax Injunction Act (1937) a general principle of comity forbidding federal courts not only to enjoin the collection of state taxes but also to award DAMAGES in state tax cases. And comity has been a major consideration in the development of the "equitable restraint" doctrine of YOUNGER V. HARRIS (1971), which generally forbids a federal court to grant an INJUNCTION against the continuation of a pending state criminal prosecution.

KENNETH L. KARST

(SEE ALSO: *Abstention Doctrine.*)

COMITY CLAUSE

See: Full Faith and Credit

COMMANDER-IN-CHIEF

In every state, the command of the armed forces is the ultimate component of executive power. Article II of the Constitution, adapting British practice, designates the President commander-in-chief both of the nation's armed forces and of the state militia when it is called into national service. Article IV, guaranteeing each state a REPUBLICAN FORM OF GOVERNMENT, somewhat qualifies that authority. It provides that the national force be used to suppress domestic violence only on application of the state legislature or of the governor when the state legislature cannot be convened.

With regard to domestic (and republican) tranquillity, it became apparent soon after 1789 that the deference of Article IV to STATES' RIGHTS did not permit the national government fully to protect the peace of the United States. Although state governments dealt with most episodes of domestic disorder—and still do—some of those episodes had a national dimension. As early as 1792, Congress declared that "it shall be lawful for the President" to use national troops or call forth the militia whenever he deems such action necessary to protect the functioning of the government or the enforcement of its laws. President GEORGE WASHINGTON leading more than 12,000 national guardsmen to suppress the WHISKEY REBELLION of 1793 is the classic symbol of an independent national power to enforce what the President, echoing Jean-Jacques Rousseau, called "the general will." This power has been invoked regularly, most notably during and after the Civil War, but also in major strikes affecting the national economy (IN RE DEBS, 1895) and in the enforcement of judicial decisions ordering racial DESEGREGATION during the 1950s and 1960s. President WILLIAM HOWARD TAFT used the national force to protect Asian ALIENS threatened by a local mob, relying on his duty as President to carry out the international responsibility of the United States for the safety of aliens.

The formula of the 1792 statute, like that used in

later statutes, straddles an unresolved controversy between the President and Congress. Congress insists that its power to pass laws NECESSARY AND PROPER to implement the President's authority as commander-in-chief includes the right to restrict the President's capacity to act. All Presidents, on the other hand, while recognizing the necessity for legislation in many situations, claim that statutes cannot subtract from their constitutional duty and power to preserve the Constitution and enforce the laws. Although the pattern of usage is by no means uniform, Presidents generally conform to statutes that purport to reinforce and structure the President's use of the armed forces in domestic disorders, at least as a matter of courtesy, unless "sudden and unexpected civil disturbances, disasters, or calamities," in the language of Army regulations, leave no alternative. Some Presidents have even paid lip service to the POSSE COMITATUS ACT (1878), a dubious relic of the end of Reconstruction. That act prohibits the use of the Army in suppressing domestic turbulence unless "expressly" authorized. Presidents have evaded this restriction by employing marines for the purpose.

Modern statutes usually retain the ancient requirement of a public proclamation before force is used to restore order, although Presidents sometimes ignore the tradition. The use of force by the President (or by a governor) in dealing with civil disorder does not alone justify suspending the writ of HABEAS CORPUS. According to the DOCTRINE of EX PARTE MILLIGAN (1867) and other cases, the writ cannot be suspended so long as the courts remain capable of carrying out their duties normally.

The use of force as an instrument of diplomacy, or of war and other extended hostilities, does not involve issues of dual SOVEREIGNTY but has presented significant constitutional conflicts both between Congress and the President, and between individuals and the state. (See WAR, FOREIGN AFFAIRS, AND THE CONSTITUTION.) The President's power as commander-in-chief under such circumstances goes far beyond the conduct of military operations. As the Supreme Court declared in *Little v. Barreme* (1804), it is also the President's prerogative to deploy troops and weapons at home and abroad in times of peace and war, and to use them when no valid law forbids him to do so. The purposes for which the President may use the armed forces in carrying on the intercourse of the United States with foreign nations are infinite and unpredictable. They include diplomatic ceremony and demonstrations of power; the employment of force in self-defense in order to deter, anticipate, or defeat armed attack against the interests of the United States, or any other act in violation of international law that would justify the use of force in time of peace; and the prosecution of hostilities after a congressional DECLARATION OF WAR. In actual hostilities, it is the President's sole responsibility to negotiate truces, armistices, and cease-fires; to direct the negotiation of peace treaties or other international arrangements terminating a condition of war; and to govern foreign territory occupied in the course of hostilities until peace is restored.

These powers are extensive. The use, threat, or hint of force is a frequent element of diplomacy. Military occupations lasted for years during and after the Civil War, the Philippine campaign, a number of Caribbean episodes, and both World Wars. The Cold War has required the apparently permanent deployment abroad of American armed forces on a large scale; novel legal arrangements have developed to organize these activities. Although the broad political and prudential discretion of both the President and Congress is taken fully into account by the courts in reviewing such exercises of the commander-in-chief's authority, constitutional limits have nonetheless emerged.

In recent years Congress has effectively employed its appropriation power to qualify the President's discretion as commander-in-chief in conducting military or intelligence operations that are not "public and notorious" general wars under international law. While such contests between the power of the purse and the power of the sword are largely political, they raise the principle of the SEPARATION OF POWERS applied in IMMIGRATION AND NATURALIZATION SERVICE V. CHADHA (1983). The judicial response to these contests can be expected further to clarify a particularly murky part of the boundary between the President and Congress.

EUGENE V. ROSTOW

Bibliography

BISHOP, JOSEPH W., JR. 1974 *Justice under Fire.* New York: Charter House.

CORWIN, EDWARD S. (1940)1957 *The President: Office and Powers 1787–1957.* New York: New York University Press.

WILCOX, FRANCIS 1971 *Congress, the Executive, and Foreign Policy.* New York: Harper & Row.

COMMENTATORS ON THE CONSTITUTION

The first important analysis of the Constitution appeared during the ratification contests of 1787 and 1788. ALEXANDER HAMILTON and JAMES MADISON, who had participated in the CONSTITUTIONAL CONVENTION, collaborated with JOHN JAY on THE FEDERALIST (1788), a series of essays defending the proposed new plan of government. Appealing to the rationalistic temper of the eighteenth century, they justified the creation of a strong central government on logical and philosophical grounds, and developed a model of CONSTITUTIONALISM that relied upon structural CHECKS AND BALANCES to promote harmony within the system. Ultimate SOVEREIGNTY, they argued, inhered in the American people; the Constitution, as an instrument of the popular will, defined and limited the powers of both the national government and the states. *The Federalist* provided valuable insights into the thinking of the Founding Fathers and established the guidelines for further constitutional commentary down to the Civil War.

Between 1789 and 1860 two major groups of commentators emerged in response to recurring political crises and sectional tensions. Legally trained publicists from New England and the middle states espoused a national will theory of government to justify the expansion of federal power, while southern lawyers and statesmen formed a state compact school of constitutional interpretation that championed decentralization and state sovereignty. Each group approached constitutional issues in a formal and mechanistic way, and relied upon close textual analysis to support its position.

The nationalists argued that the American people, acting in a collective national capacity, had divided sovereign power between the nation and the states and established the Constitution as the supreme LAW OF THE LAND. Under the resulting federal system, the states retained control of their internal affairs but were subordinate to the general government in all important national concerns, including taxation, INTERSTATE COMMERCE, and FOREIGN AFFAIRS. The Constitution, moreover, created a permanent union, whose basic features could be changed only by resort to a prescribed AMENDING PROCESS. Although several nationalists conceded that the Constitution had originated in a compact of the people of the several states, they insisted that such a compact, once executed, was inviolate, and could not be modified thereafter by the parties. Such was the message of NATHANIEL CHIPMAN's *Sketches of the Principles of Government* (1793) and William Alexander Duer's *Lectures on Constitutional Jurisprudence* (1843).

Other advocates of national supremacy rejected contractual assumptions altogether, and moved toward an organic theory of the Union. Nathan Dane, in *A General Abridgment and Digest of American Law* (1829), contended that the states had never been truly sovereign, because they owed their independence from British rule to the actions of the CONTINENTAL CONGRESS, a national body that represented the American people. The people, not the states, had ratified the Constitution through the exercise of majority will; therefore, any state efforts to nullify federal law or to withdraw from the Union amounted to illegal and revolutionary acts. JAMES KENT's *Commentaries on American Law* (1826–1830) and Timothy Walker's *Introduction to American Law* (1837) further noted that the Constitution provided for the peaceful resolution of federal–state disputes through the Supreme Court's power of JUDICIAL REVIEW.

In attacking the compact model of constitutionalism, these commentators stressed the noncontractual language of the PREAMBLE and the SUPREMACY CLAUSE. A similar preoccupation with formal textual analysis characterized JOSEPH STORY's *Commentaries on the Constitution of the United States* (1833), the most influential and authoritative statement of the nationalist position. Story, an associate Justice of the Supreme Court, interpreted the Constitution on a line-by-line basis, in light of the nationalistic jurisprudence of JOHN MARSHALL. Like Marshall, he insisted that the powers of the federal government had to be construed broadly, as the Framers had intended. On both theoretical and pragmatic grounds, Story defended the power of the Supreme Court to strike down unconstitutional state laws. Yet he also emphasized the limits of national authority, noting that the states retained control over matters of internal police that affected the daily lives of their citizens. Although Congress alone could regulate interstate commerce, for example, state legislatures might pass health and safety measures that indirectly affected such commerce. By focusing upon questions of terminology and classification, Story sought to demonstrate the stability of the federal system and to place the Constitution above partisan politics.

Nationalist historians described the formation of the Union in similarly legalistic and reverential terms. GEORGE TICKNOR CURTIS's *History of the Origin, Formation, and Adoption of the Constitution of the United States* (1854–1858), the first work to deal exclusively with a constitutional topic, quoted at length from the journals of the Continental Congress and other public records, but largely ignored surrounding political and economic circumstances. For Curtis and other romantic nationalists, the Founding Fathers were disinterested and divinely inspired patriots, who enjoyed the full confidence and support of the American people. Only RICHARD HILDRETH's *History of the United States of America* (1849–1852) presented a contrary view. Hildreth stressed the importance of conflicting economic groups in the new nation and pointed out that the Constitution had been ratified by conventions representing only a minority of American voters.

Although state compact theorists shared the prevailing belief in a fixed and beneficent Constitution, they deplored what they perceived as the aggrandizing tendencies of the national government. St. George Tucker's "View of the Constitution of the United States," appended to his edition of WILLIAM BLACKSTONE's *Commentaries* (1803), established the basic premises of the southern constitutional argument. The states and their respective citizens, Tucker contended, had entered into a compact—the Constitution—and had delegated some of their sovereign powers to the resulting federal government for specific and limited purposes. Because the Union remained subordinate to its creators, the states, and depended upon their cooperation for its continued existence, all positive grants of national power had to be construed strictly. If the federal government overstepped its constitutional powers, Tucker suggested that individuals might look to the state or federal courts for redress, while violations of STATES' RIGHTS would be answered by appropriate action from the state legislatures.

Later commentators refined Tucker's ideas and fashioned new remedies for the protection of state rights. The Philadelphia lawyer WILLIAM RAWLE introduced the possibility of peaceable SECESSION through the action of state CONSTITUTIONAL CONVENTIONS in *A View of the Constitution of the United States* (1825). Rawle's reasoning was hypothetical: because the people of each state had agreed to form a permanent union of representative republics, they could withdraw from their compact only by adopting a new state constitution based upon nonrepublican principles. A more realistic assessment of the nature and consequences of secession appeared in HENRY ST. GEORGE TUCKER's *Lectures on Constitutional Law* (1843). In Tucker's view, secession provided the only mode of resistance available to a state after a controversial federal law had been upheld by the judiciary. Secession was a revolutionary measure, however, because the Constitution had established the courts as the permanent umpires of federal–state relations.

Advocates of NULLIFICATION proposed a more extreme version of the state sovereignty argument, whose origins went back to JOHN TAYLOR of Caroline's *Construction Construed; and Constitutions Vindicated* (1820) and *New Views of the Constitution of the United States* (1823). Unlike the southern moderates, Taylor insisted that sovereignty was indivisible and inhered exclusively in the states. Each "state nation" thus retained the power to construe the terms of the federal compact for itself, and to interpose its authority at any time to protect its citizens against the consolidating tendencies of the federal government. Whenever a federal law violated the Constitution, asserted Abel Parker Upshur in *A Brief Inquiry into the Nature and Character of Our Federal Government* (1840), a state might summon its citizens to a special convention and declare the act null and void within its borders.

As the influence of the slaveholding South continued to decline in national politics, some commentators sought to preserve the Union by adding still more checks and balances to the constitutional structure. In *A Disquisition on Government* and *A Discourse on the Constitution and Government of the United States* (1851), JOHN C. CALHOUN called for amendments that would establish a dual executive and base REPRESENTATION upon broad interest groups, any one of which might block the enactment of undesirable congressional legislation. ALEXANDER H. STEPHENS's *A Constitutional View of the Late War Between the States* (1868–1870) and JEFFERSON DAVIS's *The Rise and Fall of the Confederate Government* (1881) confirmed the mechanistic cast of southern constitutional thought, as they summed up the case for secession in its final form. With the defeat of the Confederacy, the secessionist option ceased to exist, and later commentators treated the issue as a historical footnote. During the 1950s conservative Southerners tried unsuccessfully to circumvent federal CIVIL RIGHTS policy by reviving the idea of INTERPOSITION in such works as William Old's *The Segregation Issue: Suggestions Regarding the Maintenance of State Autonomy* (1955).

For Civil War Unionists the exercise of sweeping WAR POWERS by the President and Congress provoked vigorous constitutional debate. Conservative publicists, committed to a restrictive view of federal power, insisted that no departure from prewar constitutional norms was permissible, despite the wartime emergency. Former Supreme Court Justice BENJAMIN R. CURTIS charged in *Executive Power* (1862) that President ABRAHAM LINCOLN had acted illegally in authorizing the military to arrest and imprison suspected disloyal civilians in areas removed from a war zone. Joel Parker's *The War Powers of Congress, and of the President* (1863) denounced the EMANCIPATION PROCLAMATION and related CONFISCATION

ACTS for impairing property rights and revolutionizing federal–state relations.

A rival group of Lincolnian pragmatists defended the actions of federal authorities by appealing to an organic theory of constitutional development. Evolving national values and practices had shaped the Constitution far more than abstract legal rules, asserted FRANCIS LIEBER in *What Is Our Constitution—League, Pact, or Government?* (1861). The Founding Fathers had not anticipated the problem of secession; therefore, the Lincoln administration might, in conformity with natural law principles, take whatever measures it deemed necessary to preserve the nation. Sidney George Fisher's *The Trial of the Constitution* (1862) discovered new sources of federal power in the doctrine of popular sovereignty and other unwritten democratic dogmas. Charging that adherence to the checks and balances of the formal Constitution had immobilized the government in practice, Fisher urged Congress to create a new constitutional tradition by transforming itself into an American parliament immediately responsive to the popular will. William Whiting, solicitor of the War Department, contended that existent constitutional provisions authorized the federal government to pursue almost any wartime policy it chose. In *The War Powers of the President and the Legislative Powers of Congress in Relation to Rebellion, Treason, and Slavery* (1862), Whiting looked to the GENERAL WELFARE CLAUSE and other statements of broad national purpose to legitimize controversial Union measures.

The leading commentators of the late nineteenth century carried forward an organic view of the Constitution, but linked it to a laissez-faire ideology that sharply restrained the exercise of governmental power at all levels. Influenced by the conservative Darwinism of Herbert Spencer and William Graham Sumner, these economic libertarians feared legislative innovation and called upon the judiciary to preserve the fundamental economic rights of the individual against arbitrary state action. In *A Treatise on the Constitutional Limitations Which Rest upon the Legislative Power of the States of the American Union* (1868), THOMAS MCINTYRE COOLEY argued that a libertarian tradition stretching back to MAGNA CARTA protected private property from harmful regulation, even in the absence of specific constitutional guarantees. By appealing to these historic liberties, Cooley sought to broaden the scope of the DUE PROCESS clause, transforming it into a substantive restraint upon economic legislation. JOHN FORREST DILLON's *A Treatise on Municipal Corporations* (1872) discovered implied limits to the taxing power. Taxes could only be levied for a PUBLIC PURPOSE, Dillon maintained, and could not benefit one social class at the expense of another. CHRISTOPHER G. TIEDEMAN took an equally restrictive view of state and federal POLICE POWER in *A Treatise on the Limitations of Police Power in the United States* (1886), condemning usury laws and efforts to control wages and prices.

In the area of civil rights, commentators opposed "paternalistic" legislation and insisted that the Civil War had not destroyed the traditional division of power between the nation and the states. Amendments must conform to the general principles underlying the Constitution, asserted John Norton Pomeroy in *An Introduction to the Constitutional Law of the United States* (1868); and these principles included FEDERALISM, as defined by the Founding Fathers. Despite the broad language of the FOURTEENTH AMENDMENT, therefore, Congress lacked power to remedy most civil rights violations, which remained subject to state control. JOHN RANDOLPH TUCKER's *The Constitution of the United States* (1899) warned that federal attacks on customary racial practices in the South would undermine local institutions and create a dangerous centralization of power in the national government. The racist assumptions shared by most libertarians surfaced clearly in John Ordronaux's *Constitutional Legislation in the United States* (1891). Noting that national progress depended upon "race instincts," Ordronaux suggested that blacks, Orientals, and other non-Aryans were unfit for the full responsibilities of democratic CITIZENSHIP.

Constitutional historians of the late nineteenth century used a Darwinian model of struggle and survival to explain the rise of the American nation. HERMANN VON HOLST, the first scholar to make systematic use of the records of congressional debates, combined antislavery moralism with a laissez-faire attitude toward northern business in his ponderous *Constitutional and Political History of the United States* (1876–1892). Equally moralistic and libertarian was JAMES SCHOULER's *History of the United States under the Constitution* (1880–1913). In the growth of republican institutions and the triumph of Union arms Schouler discerned the unfolding of a divine plan. From a Social Darwinist perspective, William A. Dunning's *The Constitution of the United States in Civil War and Reconstruction, 1860–1867* (1885) and JOHN W. BURGESS's *Reconstruction and the Constitution, 1866–1876* (1902) criticized federal policymakers for enfranchising blacks at the expense of their Anglo-Saxon superiors.

In its mature form libertarian theory created a twilight zone on the borders of the federal system, within which neither the national government not the states could act. While the TENTH AMENDMENT prevented Congress from regulating local economic activities, state legislatures found their police powers circumscribed by the restrictive principles defined by Cooley and his associates. These extraconstitutional restraints also limited the federal government when it sought to exercise its express powers over taxation and commerce. Twentieth-century economic and racial conservatives have continued to defend the libertarian viewpoint and to protest the expansion of federal regulatory power. In *Neither Purse Nor Sword* (1936), James M. Beck and Merle Thorpe condemned early New Deal legislation for violating property rights and invading the reserved powers of the states. Charles J. Bloch's *States' Rights—The Law of the Land* (1958), written in the aftermath of the *Brown* decision, charged that the VINSON COURT and WARREN COURT had subverted the meaning of the Fourteenth Amendment in civil rights cases, and called upon Congress to revitalize the Tenth Amendment, "the cornerstone of the Republic."

As the excesses of a period of industrial growth threatened the welfare of workers and consumers, however, other commentators condemned the laissez-faire model of constitutionalism as archaic and unsuited to the needs of a modern democracy. Impressed by the empiricism of the emerging social sciences, these democratic instrumentalists approached constitutional questions from a pragmatic and reformist perspective. Although they did not deny the existence of fundamental principles, they argued that these principles needed to be adapted to changing environmental conditions. Through intelligent social planning, they maintained, federal and state lawmakers might control an expanding economy in accordance with the popular will.

Mechanistic eighteenth-century concepts, such as SEPARATION OF POWERS, impaired the efficiency of modern government, charged WOODROW WILSON in *Congressional Government* (1885) and *Constitutional Government in the United States* (1908). Constitutional grants of power to the national government established only "general lines of definition," he added, and should be broadly construed by the courts in response to developing societal needs. In a similar vein, WESTEL W. WILLOUGHBY's *The Constitutional Law of the United States* (1910) and FRANK J. GOODNOW's *Social Reform and the Constitution* (1911) criticized judges for obstructing progressive reforms through their continued adherence to laissez-faire idealism.

The advent of the welfare state in the 1930s magnified disagreements between libertarians and instrumentalists, and provoked a major confrontation between President FRANKLIN D. ROOSEVELT and the Supreme Court. EDWARD S. CORWIN, the most influential constitutional commentator of the time, applauded the programs of the early New Deal for establishing a new COOPERATIVE FEDERALISM. In *The Twilight of the Supreme Court* (1934), Corwin urged the Justices to uphold legislative policymaking in economic matters, and pointed to the nationalistic decisions of John Marshall as appropriate precedents. When judicial intransigence persisted, according to Attorney General ROBERT H. JACKSON in *The Struggle for Judicial Supremacy* (1941), the administration adopted a court-packing plan as the only apparent means of restoring the full constitutional powers of the national government. Although the plan failed, a majority of Justices began to redefine congressional power in more liberal terms. Corwin welcomed the Court's belated acceptance of sweeping federal regulation in *Constitutional Revolution, Ltd.* (1941), and correctly predicted that the Justices would thereafter focus their review power on protection of CIVIL LIBERTIES and the rights of minorities.

Instrumentalist historians tended to seek the causes of constitutional change in underlying social and economic developments. CHARLES A. BEARD's pathbreaking study, *An Economic Interpretation of the Constitution of the United States* (1913), encouraged Progressive reformers by demythologizing the work of the Philadelphia Convention. Using previously neglected Treasury and census records, Beard presented the Founding Fathers as a conspiratorial elite who had devised an undemocratic Constitution to protect their property from the attacks of popular legislative majorities. In *American Constitutional Development* (1943) CARL BRENT SWISHER drew upon other nontraditional sources to explain, and justify, the emergence of the positive state. With comparable erudition WILLIAM W. CROSSKEY's *Politics and the Constitution in the History of the United States* (1953) used linguistic analysis to demonstrate the legitimacy of New Deal regulatory measures. After an exhaustive inquiry into the eighteenth-century meaning of "commerce" and other key words, Crosskey concluded that the Framers had intended to create a unitary, centralized system in which "the American people could, through Congress, deal with any subject they wished, on a simple, straightforward, nation-wide basis."

Although the instrumentalists emphasized the need to adapt the Constitution to changing socioeconomic conditions, they remained committed to the RULE OF LAW and acknowledged the binding force of constitutional norms. This moderate position failed to satisfy a small group of radical empiricists, who argued that written codes were meaningless in themselves and merely served to rationalize the political decisions of legislators and judges. "The language of the Constitution is immaterial since it represents current myths and folklore rather than rules," asserted THURMAN W. ARNOLD in *The Folklore of Capitalism* (1937). "Out of it are spun the contradictory ideals of governmental morality." Howard L. McBain's *The Living Constitution: A Consideration of the Realities and Legends of Our Fundamental Law* (1927) similarly contended that law had no life of its own, but depended for its substance on the unpredictable actions of men. Because the American people believed the fiction of a government of law, they had grown politically apathetic, charged J. ALLEN SMITH in *The Growth and Decadence of Constitutional Government* (1930). Although constitutionalism had been designed to limit arbitrary power, he noted, it protected an irresponsible governing elite from popular scrutiny and control.

The empiricists were more successful in diagnosing ills than in prescribing remedies. Because they stressed the determining influence of ideology and personality upon decision making, they could find no satisfactory way to limit the discretionary power of public officials. The scope of administrative discretion must necessarily broaden as society grows more complex, contended William B. Munro in *The Invisible Government* (1928). He welcomed the trend, which promised to give government agencies greater flexibility in dealing with contemporary problems. Yet unrestrained power might also encourage irresponsible behavior, such as judges so often displayed in reviewing legislative measures. Both LOUIS B. BOUDIN's *Government by Judiciary* (1932) and Fred Rodell's *Nine Men: A Political History of the Supreme Court of the United States from 1790 to 1955* (1955) reduced jurisprudence to politics, and charged that judges wrote their conservative policy preferences into law under the guise of legal principles. The only remedy they could suggest, however, was the appointment to the bench of liberals who would promote the public welfare in a more enlightened, albeit equally subjective, fashion.

During the past quarter-century commentators, preeminently ALEXANDER M. BICKEL, have continued to debate the nature and scope of JUDICIAL REVIEW, in the context of the Supreme Court's enlarged role as guardian of individual and minority rights. The timely aspects of such recent studies attest to the constructive role that commentators have historically played in the shaping of American constitutional law. Responsive to changing trends in social and political thought, they have often helped to redefine and clarify the terms of constitutional discourse. As Corwin once quipped, "If judges make law, so do commentators."

MAXWELL BLOOMFIELD

Bibliography

BAUER, ELIZABETH K. 1952 *Commentaries on the Constitution, 1790–1860.* New York: Columbia University Press.

BELZ, HERMAN 1971 The Realist Critique of Constitutionalism in the Era of Reform. *American Journal of Legal History* 15:288–306.

HYMAN, HAROLD M. 1973 *A More Perfect Union: The Impact of the Civil War and Reconstruction on the Constitution.* New York: Knopf.

KONEFSKY, ALFRED S. 1981 Men of Great and Little Faith: Generations of Constitutional Scholars. *Buffalo Law Review* 30:365–384.

LARSEN, CHARLES E. 1959 Nationalism and States' Rights in Commentaries on the Constitution after the Civil War. *American Journal of Legal History* 3:360–369.

MURPHY, PAUL L. 1963 Time to Reclaim: The Current Challenge of American Constitutional History. *American Historical Review* 69:64–79.

NEWTON, ROBERT E. 1965 Edward S. Corwin and American Constitutional Law. *Journal of Public Law* 14:198–212.

COMMERCE CLAUSE

The commerce clause is the small part of the Constitution that provides that "The Congress shall have power . . . to regulate commerce with foreign nations, and among the several states, and with the Indian tribes."

The phrase relating to the Indians was derived from the provision in the 1781 ARTICLES OF CONFEDERATION which gave the federal congress "the sole and exclusive right and power of . . . regulating the trade and managing all affairs with the Indians." Despite the elimination of the sweeping second phrase, there never has been any question that the Indian part of the commerce clause (plus the TREATY and WAR POWERS) gave Congress power over all relations with the Indians, and no more need be said about it.

Nor has there been much question as to the scope of the federal power to regulate foreign commerce. Combined with the tax and WAR POWERS and the provisions prohibiting the states from entering treaties and agreements with foreign powers and from imposing duties on imports and exports, this power clearly gave the federal government complete authority over relations with foreign nations.

The short clause relating to "commerce among the several states," however, has become one of the most significant provisions in the Constitution. It has been in large part responsible for the development of the United States as a single integrated economic unit, with no impediments to the movement of goods or people at state lines.

The draftsmen of the commerce clause could not have envisaged the eventual magnitude of the national commercial structure or the breadth of the CONSTITUTIONAL INTERPRETATION which that structure would produce. Nevertheless the need for a national power over commerce led to the calling of the CONSTITUTIONAL CONVENTION OF 1787, and the seed for the growth of the power was planted in the early years.

In 1786 the Virginia General Assembly, and then a commission representing five states meeting at Annapolis, called for the appointment of commissioners to consider "the trade of the United States" and "how far a uniform system in their commercial regulation may be necessary to their common interest and their permanent harmony." The Congress created under the Articles of Confederation thereupon approved the calling of a convention to meet in Philadelphia in May 1787 for the purpose of revising the Articles and reporting its recommendations to the Congress and the States.

The Convention, after considerable debate, adopted a resolution generally describing the powers to be given the National Legislature, in the form proposed by the Virginia delegation led by GEORGE WASHINGTON, Governor EDMUND RANDOLPH, and JAMES MADISON. It was resolved that "the national legislature ought . . . to legislate in all cases for the general interests of the Union, and also in those to which the states are separately incompetent, or in which the harmony of the United States may be interrupted by the exercise of individual legislation." This and other resolutions were sent to a drafting committee, which reported out the commerce clause and other powers to be conferred on Congress in substantially the form finally adopted.

Although the needs of commerce had been principally responsible for the calling of the Convention, the clause was accepted with hardly any debate. The same was true in the state ratifying conventions. All reflected the view that in general the new Constitution gave the federal government power over matters of national but not of local concern.

The same view was expressed in the first commerce clause case in 1824 (GIBBONS V. OGDEN), written for a unanimous Supreme Court by Chief Justice JOHN MARSHALL, who had been a member of the Virginia ratifying convention. The Court declared that the commerce power did not extend to commerce that is completely internal, and "which does not extend to or affect other states." It "may very properly be restricted to that commerce which concerns more states than one. . . . The genius and character of the whole government seems to be, that its action is to be applied to all the concerns of the nation, and to these internal concerns which affect the States generally."

Of course, neither in 1787 nor in 1824 did those who wrote or ratified or interpreted the Constitution contemplate the tremendous and close-knit economic structure that exists today and the accompanying inability of the states, or of any agency but the nation, to meet the governmental problems that structure presents. Indeed, in the 1820s and into the 1850s many persons regarded even the construction of the principal highways within each state as purely internal matters not subject to federal power, as appeared from President JAMES MONROE's veto on constitutional grounds of an appropriation to construct what is now Interstate 70 from Maryland to the Western states. Although the MARSHALL COURT would not have agreed, some of the more STATES' RIGHTS-minded Supreme Court Justices of the 1840s and 1850s did.

In general, during the century from 1787 to 1887, the only national commercial problems concerned foreign trade and navigation and the removal of state-imposed barriers to interstate trade. Affirmative federal regulation applied almost entirely to matters of navigation on the oceans, lakes, and rivers. An early statute required vessels engaged in coastal traffic to obtain federal licenses. Reasonably enough, none of these were challenged as falling outside the commerce power.

All of the commerce clause cases during the first 100 years, and a great many of them thereafter, were concerned with the negative effect of the clause upon state legislation—even though the clause did not mention the states. The Constitution merely said that Congress should have the power to regulate commerce. Other clauses imposed specific prohibitions upon the states, but the commerce clause did not. On the other hand, it was well known during the early period that the principal evil at which the commerce clause was directed was state restrictions upon the free flow of commerce.

The issue first came before the Supreme Court in

GIBBONS V. OGDEN (1824). New York had granted Robert Fulton and ROBERT LIVINGSTON the exclusive right for thirty years to operate vessels propelled by steam in New York waters, thereby excluding steamboats coming from neighboring states. New Jersey, Connecticut, and Ohio had promptly passed retaliatory legislation forbidding the New York monopoly from operating in their waters. The case presented an example (though unforeseeable in 1787) of the type of interstate commercial rivalry which the commerce clause had been designed to prevent.

A unanimous Supreme Court held that Congress's commerce power extended to all commercial intercourse among the states, rejecting arguments that it did not apply to navigation and passenger traffic. The Court, speaking through Marshall, further concluded that Congress had exercised its power in the Coastal Licensing Act, that Gibbons's vessels were operating in compliance with that statute, and that New York's attempt to prohibit them from operating in New York waters was inconsistent with the federal statute and therefore unconstitutional under the SUPREMACY CLAUSE of the Constitution. The Court did not find it necessary to decide whether the power of Congress to regulate interstate commerce was exclusive or whether the states had CONCURRENT POWER in the absence of a conflicting federal law, although Marshall seemed to favor the former view. But Marshall recognized that, although the states had no power to regulate interstate or FOREIGN COMMERCE as such, they could exercise their preexisting powers to enact laws on such subjects as health, quarantine, turnpikes and ferries, and other internal commerce, even though that might overlap the subjects that Congress could reach under the commerce clause. Thus, as a practical matter, the Court recognized that the states had concurrent powers over many aspects of commerce, or of internal matters that might affect external commerce.

After ROGER B. TANEY became Chief Justice in 1835, a number of the Justices, including Taney, took the flat position that only state laws inconsistent with acts of Congress were preempted, and that the commerce clause itself had no preemptive effect. But in none of the cases could a majority of the Court agree on any theory.

This unhappy and unhealthy state of the law was formally resolved in 1852, when, speaking through newly appointed Justice BENJAMIN R. CURTIS, the Court sustained a Pennsylvania law governing the use of pilots in the port of Philadelphia in COOLEY V. BOARD OF WARDENS OF PHILADELPHIA (1852). Six Justices agreed that whatever subjects of this power are in their nature national, or admit only of one uniform system, or plan of regulation, may justly be said to be of such a nature as to require exclusive legislation by Congress. Where there was no need for regulation on a national scale, only state laws inconsistent with federal would fall.

The Court still cites the *Cooley* principle with approval, although the *Cooley* formula has been largely superseded by an interest-balancing approach to STATE REGULATION OF COMMERCE. (See SELECTIVE EXCLUSIVENESS; STATE POLICE POWER; STATE TAXATION OF COMMERCE.) But in a number of cases during the years following *Cooley,* the Court adopted a more simplistic approach. If the subject of the state regulation was interstate commerce, only Congress could regulate it; if it was not, only the states could. In these cases the Court held—or at least said—that the United States could not tax or regulate manufacturing or PRODUCTION because they were beyond the scope of the federal commerce power, a pronouncement that later caused substantial difficulty but was not explicitly disavowed until *Commonwealth Edison Co. v. Montana* (1981).

During the twenty years after the Civil War, the Court held that states could not directly tax or regulate interstate commerce, but that they could, for example, fix railroad rates between points in the same state. (See GRANGER CASES, 1877.) When, however, Illinois attempted to apply its prohibition against charging more for a shorter rail haul than a longer one to freight between Illinois cities and New York, the Court, applying the *Cooley* formula, held in WABASH, ST. LOUIS & PACIFIC RAILWAY V. ILLINOIS (1886) that the state had no such power. The opinion made it clear that interstate rates, even for the part of a journey within a state, were not subject to state regulation. Such transportation was "of that national character" that can be "only appropriately" regulated by Congress rather than by the individual states.

Because leaving shippers subject to unregulated rail rates was unthinkable at that time, Congress reacted in 1887 by adopting the INTERSTATE COMMERCE ACT, the first affirmative federal regulation of land transportation.

Three years later, in response to a similar public reaction against uncontrolled monopolies, Congress enacted the SHERMAN ANTITRUST ACT, which prohibited combinations that restrained or monopolized interstate and foreign trade or commerce. The Court easily upheld the applicability of the statute to interstate railroads, but, amazingly, by a vote of 8–1, held the act inapplicable to the Sugar Trust which combined all the sugar refiners in the United States.

UNITED STATES v. E. C. KNIGHT CO. (1895) held that such a combination concerned only manufacture and production, and not "commerce," as the act (and, presumably, the Constitution) used the word. This ruling left the country remediless against national monopolies of manufacturers. Since interstate manufacturers are of course engaged in interstate trade—selling, buying, and shipping—as well as manufacture, this was a strange decision. It was soon devitalized, though not expressly OVERRULED, in SWIFT & COMPANY v. UNITED STATES (1905), STANDARD OIL COMPANY v. UNITED STATES (1911), and UNITED STATES v. AMERICAN TOBACCO COMPANY (1911), which similarly involved combinations of manufacturers.

In a number of cases the Court upheld congressional regulation of interstate transportation for noncommercial reasons. Federal statutes forbidding the interstate sale of lottery tickets, the interstate transportation of women for immoral purposes, stolen motor vehicles, diseased cattle which might range across state lines, misbranded food and drugs, and firearms were all held valid, usually without much question. The effect was to establish that the commerce clause applied to things or persons moving across state lines, whether or not they had anything to do with trade or commerce in the usual sense. (See NATIONAL POLICE POWER.) This conclusion was consistent with Marshall's original definition of commerce as intercourse in GIBBONS v. OGDEN.

The Court's narrow approach to the commerce power in the early twentieth century was demonstrated by its invalidation in 1908 of a law creating a WORKER'S COMPENSATION system for all railroad employees, because it included those doing intrastate shop and clerical work, and a law prohibiting railroads from discharging employees because of membership in a labor organization. (See EMPLOYERS' LIABILITY CASES, 1908; ADAIR v. UNITED STATES, 1908.) In HAMMER v. DAGENHART (1918) the Court even held that Congress could not prohibit the interstate transportation of child-made goods because the prohibition's purpose was to prevent child labor in manufacturing plants within the states.

Decisions other than the monopoly cases during the same period recognized that the congressional commerce power could apply to intrastate transactions that had an effect upon or relation to interstate commerce. Although strikes blocking interstate shipments from manufacturing plants were found to affect interstate commerce only indirectly, the result was different when an intent to restrain interstate commerce was found, or when a SECONDARY BOYCOTT extended to other states. (See LOEWE v. LAWLOR, 1908.) Intrastate trains were held subject to federal safety regulations because of the danger to interstate trains on the same tracks. Intrastate freight rates were held subject to federal control when a competitive relationship to interstate rates or a general effect on all rail rates could be shown. (See SHREVEPORT DOCTRINE.) In 1930 the Court sustained the application of the Railway Labor Act to clerks performing intrastate work so as to protect the right to COLLECTIVE BARGAINING and thereby avert strikes disrupting interstate commerce, contrary to the *Adair* decision in 1908.

Perhaps of greatest significance were cases sustaining federal regulation of the stockyards and the Chicago Board of Trade which, even though located in a single city, were found to control interstate prices for agricultural products. (See STAFFORD v. WALLACE, 1922; CHICAGO BOARD OF TRADE v. OLSEN, 1923.) The Court was not disturbed by the fact that the sales of grain futures which had such an effect were often completely local, since most of them were not followed by any shipments of physical products.

Thus by 1930 there were lines of cases saying that the federal power did not extend to business activity occurring in a single state, and other cases holding the contrary where some kinds of relationship to interstate commerce were shown.

The Great Depression running from 1929 through the 1930s brought the nation its severest economic crisis. Inaction during HERBERT HOOVER'S administration proved ineffective and left thirteen million persons unemployed, prices and wages dropping in a self-perpetuating spiral, and banks, railroads, and many other businesses insolvent. The amount of revenue freight carried by railroad, a fair measure of the quantity of interstate commerce, had fallen by fifty-one percent. The public expected FRANKLIN D. ROOSEVELT, who took office in March 1933, to do something about the Depression. Although no one was sure what would work—and no one is yet quite sure what, if anything, did work—the President and Congress tried. Obviously the economy could not be restored by states acting separately. Only measures taken on a national scale could possibly be effective.

To stop the downward spiral in wages and prices, and to increase employment by limiting the number of hours a person could work, MAXIMUM HOURS AND MINIMUM WAGES were prescribed for industry generally, not merely for employees in interstate commerce. Collective bargaining was made mandatory, and protected against employer interference. The object was to increase national employment, national purchasing power, and the demand for and consumption of all products, which would benefit employers, employees, and the flow of commodities in interstate commerce. All this was originally sought to be accomplished by the NATIONAL INDUSTRIAL RECOVERY ACT (NIRA), which authorized every industry to prepare a code of competition designed to accomplish the above purposes; the code would become effective and enforceable when approved by the President.

The same statute and the AGRICULTURAL ADJUSTMENT ACT OF 1933 (AAA) attempted to cope with the overproduction of petroleum and agricultural products, which had forced prices down to absurd levels, such as five cents per barrel of crude oil and thirty-seven cents per bushel of wheat. The petroleum code under the NIRA and programs adopted under the AAA provided for the fixing of production quotas for oil producers and farmers.

The two lines of authorities summarized above supported opposing arguments as to the constitutionality of these measures under the commerce clause. For Congress to prescribe wages, hours, and production quotas for factories, farms, and oil wells undoubtedly would regulate intrastate activities, which prior opinions had frequently said were regulable only by the states.

On the other hand, the reasoning of opinions sustaining federal regulation of intrastate features of railroading and the intrastate marketing practices of stockyards and grain exchanges also supported the use of the commerce power to regulate intrastate acts that had an effect upon interstate commerce. The same was true of many of the antitrust cases referred to above. None of the relationships previously found insufficient to support federal regulation had involved general economic effects that halved the flow of interstate trade. But Congress had never sought to regulate the main body of manufacturing, mining, and agricultural production.

In the mid-1930s the Supreme Court included four Justices—WILLIS VAN DEVANTER, JAMES MCREYNOLDS, GEORGE SUTHERLAND, and PIERCE BUTLER—who looked askance at any enlargement of the scope of governmental power over business and who steadily voted against extension of the congressional commerce power, and also voted to invalidate both federal and state regulation under the due process clauses. Chief Justice CHARLES EVANS HUGHES and Justice OWEN J. ROBERTS sometimes voted with these four, while Justices LOUIS D. BRANDEIS, HARLAN FISKE STONE, and BENJAMIN N. CARDOZO usually voted to sustain the legislative judgments as to how to deal with economic problems.

In a series of cases in 1935 and 1936, passing upon the validity of the NIRA, the AAA, and the GUFFEY-SNYDER (BITUMINOUS COAL CONSERVATION) ACT regulating the bituminous coal industry, Hughes and Roberts joined the conservative four to hold these acts unconstitutional.

The government had hoped and planned to test the constitutionality of the NIRA in a case involving the nationally integrated petroleum industry, PANAMA REFINING CO. V. RYAN (January 1935). But the Court found it unnecessary to decide the commerce issue in the *Panama* case. Instead, that question came before the Court in SCHECHTER POULTRY CORP. V. UNITED STATES (May 1935), in which the defendant had violated the provisions of the Live Poultry Code with respect to wages and hours and marketing practices of seemingly little consequence. The poultry slaughtered and sold by the defendant had come to New York City from other states, but there was nothing in the record to show that this interstate movement was greatly affected by the practices in question.

The only persuasive argument supporting the constitutionality of the Poultry Code was that the depressed state of the entire economy and of interstate commerce in general could be remedied only by increasing national purchasing power, and that prescribing minimum wages and maximum hours for all employees, whether or not in interstate industries, was a reasonable method of accomplishing that purpose. None of the Justices was willing to go that far. Indeed, the opinion of Chief Justice Hughes for the Court and the concurring opinion of Justice Cardozo emphasized as a principal defect in the argument that it would extend federal power to all business, interstate or intrastate. The fact that little would be left to exclusive state control, rather than the magnitude of the effect on interstate commerce from a national perspective, was treated as decisive. On the same day, in RAILROAD RETIREMENT BOARD V. ALTON, an act establishing a retirement program for railroad employees was held, by a vote of 5–4, not to be within the federal commerce power.

In theory, the *Schechter* decision left open the power of Congress to regulate production in major interstate industries such as petroleum or coal. But that opening, if it existed, seemed to be closed by two decisions in 1936. Because of the foreseeable risks from reliance on the commerce power, Congress had utilized the taxing power to "persuade" farmers to limit the production of crops in order to halt the collapse of farm prices. In UNITED STATES V. BUTLER (1936), over Justice Stone's vigorous dissent, six Justices, speaking through Justice Roberts and including Chief Justice Hughes, thought it unnecessary to determine whether this legislative scheme came within the ENUMERATED POWERS of Congress. The majority avoided this inquiry by concluding that the law intruded upon the area of production reserved to the states by the TENTH AMENDMENT, which reserves to the states or the people "the powers not delegated to the United States." The Court invoked the same theory a few months later in CARTER V. CARTER COAL COMPANY (1936) to invalidate the Guffey Act's regulation of wages, hours, and collective bargaining in the coal industry. Although the evidence submitted in a long trial proved indisputably the obvious fact that coal strikes could and did halt substantially all interstate commerce moving by rail, as most commerce then did, five Justices, speaking through Justice Sutherland, found decisive not the magnitude of an effect on interstate commerce but whether the effect was immediate, without an intervening causal factor. Even Chief Justice Hughes concurred to this extent, although not in other parts of the majority opinion. Only Justices Brandeis, Stone, and Cardozo challenged the reasoning of the majority.

The *Butler* and *Carter* cases made it plain—or so it seemed—that the Constitution as construed by the Court completely barred the federal government from endeavoring to resolve the national economic problems which called for control of intrastate transactions at the production or manufacturing stage. As an economic matter, individual states were unable to set standards for their own industries that were in competition with producers in other states. The result was that in the United States no government could take action deemed necessary to deal with such matters no matter how crippling their effect upon the national economy might be.

In early 1937 the same type of collective bargaining regulation which the *Carter* case had stricken for the coal industry was on its way to the Supreme Court in the first cases under the WAGNER (NATIONAL LABOR RELATIONS) ACT of 1935. That statute by its terms applied to unfair labor practices that burdened or obstructed interstate commerce or tended to lead to a labor dispute that had such an effect. The courts of appeals, following the *Carter* case, had held that the act could not constitutionally reach a steel manufacturing company, a trailer manufacturer, and a small clothing manufacturer.

Three days before the arguments in these cases in the Supreme Court were to commence, President Roosevelt, who had recently been reelected by a tremendous majority, announced a plan to add up to six new Justices to the Supreme Court, one for each Justice over seventy years of age, purportedly for the purpose of providing younger judges who could enable the Court to keep up with its workload. The Court and many others vigorously opposed the plan. Two months later, in the WAGNER ACT CASES (1937), Chief Justice Hughes and Justice Roberts joined Justices Brandeis, Stone, and Cardozo to sustain the applicability of the National Labor Relations Act to the three manufacturers. The evidence as to the effect of their labor disputes upon interstate commerce was obviously much weaker than that presented in the *Carter* case as to the entire bituminous coal industry. Within the next few months, Justices Van Devanter and Sutherland retired, to be succeeded by Senator HUGO L. BLACK and Solicitor General STANLEY F. REED, and the court-packing plan gradually withered away, even though for a long time President Roosevelt refused to abandon it. No one can be certain whether the plan influenced the Chief Justice and Justice Roberts, but many persons thought the facts spoke for themselves.

Chief Justice Hughes's opinion for the Court in NATIONAL LABOR RELATIONS BOARD V. JONES & LAUGHLIN STEEL CORP. (1937) flatly declared that practices in productive industry could have a sufficient effect upon interstate commerce to justify federal regulation under the commerce clause. The test was to be "practical," based on "actual experience." The reasoning of the *Carter* and *Butler* cases was repudiated, although the majority opinion did not say so.

In 1938 a revised AGRICULTURAL ADJUSTMENT ACT and a new FAIR LABOR STANDARDS ACT were enacted. Under the former, the secretary of agriculture, after obtaining the necessary approval of two-thirds of the tobacco growers in a referendum, prescribed marketing quotas determining the maximum quantity of tobacco each grower could sell. Although the practical effect was to limit what would be produced, the object was to stabilize prices by keeping an excessive supply off the market. In MULFORD V. SMITH (1939), the Court, speaking through Justice Roberts, found that because interstate and intrastate sales of tobacco were commingled at the auction warehouses where tobacco was sold, Congress clearly had power to limit the amount marketed by each farmer. HAMMER V. DAGENHART, UNITED STATES V. BUTLER, and the Tenth Amendment were mentioned only in the dissenting opinion of Justice McReynolds and Butler.

The Fair Labor Standards Act of 1938 in substance reenacted the minimum wage and maximum hour provision of the NIRA for employees engaged in interstate commerce or the production of goods for such commerce, and also forbade the shipment in interstate commerce of goods produced under the proscribed labor conditions. The minimum wage then prescribed was twenty-five cents per hour. The prevailing wage in the lumber industry in the South ranged from ten cents to twenty-seven and a half cents per hour, which made it difficult for employers paying more than the lowest amount to compete. A case involving a Georgia sawmill (UNITED STATES V. DARBY LUMBER COMPANY) came to the Supreme Court late in 1940, and was decided in early 1941 after Justice Butler had died and Justice McReynolds had retired. By that time Justices FELIX FRANKFURTER and WILLIAM O. DOUGLAS had replaced Cardozo and Brandeis, and Justice FRANK MURPHY had succeeded Butler.

The Supreme Court, speaking unanimously through Justice Stone, upheld the statute. The Court held that Congress had the power to exclude from interstate commerce goods that were not produced in accordance with prescribed standards, and to prescribe minimum wages and maximum hours for employees producing goods which would move in interstate commerce. Overruling HAMMER V. DAGENHART, the Court declared that the power of Congress to determine what restrictions should be imposed upon interstate commerce did not exclude regulations whose object was to control aspects of industrial production. The Court invoked the interpretation of the NECESSARY AND PROPER CLAUSE in MCCULLOCH V. MARYLAND (1819): the commerce power extended not merely to the regulation of interstate commerce but also "to those activities intrastate which so affect interstate commerce or the exercise of the power of Congress over it as to make regulation of them appropriate means to the attainment of a legitimate end, the exercise of the granted power of Congress to regulate interstate commerce." The emphasis was not on direct or indirect effects, a judge-made concept not tied to constitutional language, or even to the substantiality of an effect. The Court found it sufficient that the establishment of federal minimum labor standards was a reasonable means of suppressing interstate competition based on substandard labor conditions. In KIRSCHBAUM V. WALLING (1942) the Court broadly construed the commerce clause to make the Fair Labor Standards Act apply to service and maintenance employees who were not directly engaged in the production of goods for commerce but in the performance of services ancillary to such production.

A year and a half after *Darby,* in WICKARD V. FILBURN (1942), a unanimous Court, speaking through Justice ROBERT H. JACKSON, upheld marketing quotas under the amended Agricultural Adjustment Act, even though they limited the amount of wheat allowed to be consumed on the farm as well as the amount sold. The object was to reduce the supply of wheat in order to increase the price—and the total supply of wheat, including the twenty percent of the crop consumed on the farm for feed or seed, not only was in at least potential competition with wheat in commerce but had a substantial influence on prices and market conditions for the wheat crop throughout the nation. Reviewing the prior law, and explicitly noting the cases that were being disapproved—*E. C. Knight, Employers' Liability, Hammer v. Dagenhart, Railroad Retirement Board, Schechter,* and *Carter*—Justice Jackson's opinion laid to rest the prior controlling effect attributed to nomenclature such as "production" and "indirect," as distinct from the actual economic effect of an activity upon interstate commerce. Even if an "activity be local" and not itself commerce, "it may still, whatever its nature, be reached by Congress if it exerts a substantial economic effect on interstate commerce." The proper point of reference was "what was necessary and proper to the exercise by Congress of the granted power." The Court further declared, as it had in *Darby,* that the magnitude of the contribution of each individual to the EFFECT ON COMMERCE was not the criterion but the total contribution of persons similarly situated, which meant that the insignificant effect of the amount consumed on any particular farm was not decisive.

In 1944 and 1946, in cases holding that Congress could regulate the insurance industry and public utility holding companies (UNITED STATES V. SOUTH-EASTERN UNDERWRITERS ASSOCIATION, 1944; *North American Co. v. Securities and Exchange Commission,* 1946), the Court broadly summarized the teachings of its prior cases beginning with the words of Chief Justice Marshall in *Gibbons v. Ogden:*

> Commerce is interstate . . . when it "concerns more States than one.". . . The power granted is the power to legislate concerning transactions which, reaching across State boundaries, affect the people of more states than one;—to govern affairs which the individual states, with their limited territorial jurisdictions, are not fully capable of governing. This federal power to determine the rules of intercourse across state lines was essential to weld a loose confederacy into a single, indivisible Nation; its continued existence is equally essential to the welfare of that Nation.

Since these decisions there has been no doubt that Congress possesses full power to regulate all aspects of the integrated national economy. The few commerce clause cases of importance since that time concerned the use of the commerce power for noncommercial purposes: to combat racial SEGREGATION, crime, and environmental problems.

In *Katzenbach v. McClung* (1964) the Court sustained the provisions of the CIVIL RIGHTS ACT OF 1964 prohibiting RACIAL DISCRIMINATION by restaurants serving interstate travelers or obtaining a substantial portion of their food from outside the state, both because discrimination had a highly restrictive effect upon interstate travel by Negroes and because it reduced the amount of food moving in interstate commerce (which seems quite doubtful). (See also HEART OF ATLANTA MOTEL V. UNITED STATES, 1964.)

PEREZ V. UNITED STATES (1971) upheld the application of the federal loanshark statute to purely intrastate extortion on the ground that Congress had rationally found that organized crime was interstate in character, obtaining a substantial part of its income from loansharking which to a substantial extent was carried on in interstate and foreign commerce or through instrumentalities of such commerce. Unmentioned rationales might have been the difficulty of proving that loansharking in a particular case had an interstate connection and the belief that it was necessary to prohibit all loansharking as an appropriate means of prohibiting those acts that did affect interstate commerce.

In *Hodel v. Virginia Surface Mining and Reclamation Association* (1981) the Court unanimously upheld federal regulation of surface or strip coal mining operations, rejecting the contention that this was merely a regulation of land use not committed to the federal government. There had been legislative findings that surface coal mining causes water pollution and flooding of navigable streams and that it harms productive farm land and hardwood forests in many parts of the country. The Court found, following *Darby,* that this was a means of preventing destructive interstate competition favoring the producers with the lowest mining and reclamation standards, that Congress can regulate the conditions under which goods shipped in interstate commerce are produced when that in itself affects interstate commerce, and that the commerce power permits federal regulation of activities causing air or water pollution, or other environmental hazards that may have effects in more than one state.

The more recent decisions, which in some respects went far beyond the classical statements as to the modern scope of the commerce power in *Darby* and *Wickard v. Filburn,* were expected and accepted with little comment or concern. The country now appears to recognize that the national government should have and does have power under the commerce clause to deal with problems that do not limit themselves to individual states—as Chief Justice Marshall had declared in 1824, though doubtless with no idea of how far that principle would eventually be carried.

The enlargement of the commerce power since 1789 is attributable not to the predilections of judges but to such inventions as steamboats, railroads, motor vehicles, airplanes, the telegraph, telephone, radio, and television. When the nation was young, composed mainly of farms and small towns, there was little interstate trade, except by water or near state lines. Now persons and goods can cross the continent in less time than a traveler in 1789 would have taken to reach a town thirty miles away. Business and the economy have adjusted to these changes. Somewhat more slowly than the people and Congress, the Supreme Court has recognized that an integrated national economy is predominantly interstate or related to interstate commerce, and must be subject to governmental control on a national basis.

The expansion of the concept of interstate commerce and of the subjects which Congress can regulate under the commerce power was not accompanied by a contraction of the powers of the states. Only those state laws that discriminate against or unduly burden interstate commerce are forbidden.

ROBERT L. STERN

Bibliography

CORWIN, EDWARD S. 1959 *The Commerce Power versus States Rights.* Princeton, N.J.: Princeton University Press.

FRANKFURTER, FELIX 1937 *The Commerce Clause under Marshall, Taney and Waite.* Chapel Hill: University of North Carolina Press.

GAVIT, BERNARD C. 1932 *Commerce Clause of the United States Constitution.* Bloomington, Ind.: Principia Press.

STERN, ROBERT L. 1934 That Commerce Which Concerns More States Than One. *Harvard Law Review* 47:1335–1366.

——— 1946 The Commerce Clause and the National Economy, 1933–1946. *Harvard Law Review* 59:645–693, 883–947.

——— 1951 The Problems of Yesteryear—Commerce and Due Process. *Vanderbilt Law Review* 4:446–468.

——— 1955 The 1955 Ross Prize Essay: The Scope of the Phrase "Interstate Commerce." *American Bar Association Journal* 41:823–826, 871–874.

——— 1973 The Commerce Clause Revisited—The Federalization of Interstate Crime. *Arizona Law Review* 15:271–285.

COMMERCE COURT

In 1910 Congress established the Commerce Court, with the JURISDICTION, formerly held by the district courts and courts of appeals, to review decisions of the Interstate Commerce Commission (ICC). Although the ICC acquiesced in the establishment of the new court, acceptance soon turned to opposition. The Commerce Court reversed the ICC's decisions in a number of important cases, and congressional Democrats saw the court as a threat to the program of railroad regulation. Two 1912 bills to abolish the court were vetoed by President WILLIAM HOWARD TAFT. In 1913, a third abolition bill received President WOODROW WILSON's blessing.

The creation of specialized federal courts is often proposed but not often enacted. The short, unhappy life of the Commerce Court is regularly offered as a cautionary tale.

KENNETH L. KARST

Bibliography

DIX, GEORGE E. 1964 The Death of the Commerce Court: A Study in Institutional Weakness. *American Journal of Legal History* 8:238–260.

COMMERCIAL SPEECH

Until 1976 "commercial speech"—a vague category encompassing advertisements, invitations to deal, credit or financial reports, prospectuses, and the like—was subject to broad regulatory authority, with little or no protection from the FIRST AMENDMENT. The early decisions, epitomized by *Valentine v. Chrestensen* (1942), followed the then characteristic judicial approach of defining certain subject-matter categories of expression as wholly outside the scope of First Amendment protection. Under this TWO-LEVEL THEORY, a "definitional" mode of First Amendment adjudication, commercial speech was considered to be, along with FIGHTING WORDS, OBSCENITY, and LIBEL, outside First Amendment protection.

When facing combinations of unprotected commercial speech and protected political speech in subsequent cases, the Court made First Amendment protection turn on the primary purpose of the advertisement. Thus, in MURDOCK V. PENNSYLVANIA (1943), the Court struck down an ordinance requiring solicitors of orders for goods to get a license and pay a fee as it applied to Jehovah's Witnesses who sold religious pamphlets while seeking religious converts. On the other hand, in *Bread v. Alexandria* (1951) the Court held that a door-to-door salesman of national magazine subscriptions was subject to a town ordinance barring such sales techniques, because his primary purpose was to sell magazines rather than to disseminate ideas.

The "primary purpose" test unraveled in NEW YORK TIMES V. SULLIVAN (1964), more prominently known for another rejection of the definitional approaches in its holding that defamation is not beyond First Amendment protection. In *Sullivan,* the *New York Times* had printed an allegedly defamatory advertisement soliciting funds for civil rights workers. Although the advertisement's primary purpose was, arguably, to raise money, the Court held that it was protected by the First Amendment because it "communicated information, expressed opinion, recited grievances, protested claimed abuses, and sought financial support on behalf of a movement whose existence and objectives are matters of the highest public interest and concern."

Recent decisions have gone well beyond *Sullivan* and moved advertising and other commercial speech—political or not—within the protection of the First Amendment. In the leading case, VIRGINIA PHARMACY BOARD V. VIRGINIA CITIZENS CONSUMER COUNCIL (1976), the Court struck down a state ban on prescription drug price advertising. The Court rejected the state's "highly paternalistic approach," preferring a system in which "people will perceive their own best interests if only they are well enough informed, and that the best means to that end is to open the channels of communication rather than to close them." The Court cautioned, however, that because untruthful speech has never been protected for its own sake government may take effective action against false and misleading advertisements. And it indicated a greater scope for regulating false or misleading commercial speech than is permitted in relation to false political statements, such as defamations of public officials, because advertising is more easily verifiable and is less likely to be "chilled" by regulation because it is a commercial necessity.

Virginia Pharmacy Board fixed the principle that advertising may be controlled when it is false, misleading, or takes undue advantage of its audience; but the case left open the issue whether whole categories of commercial speech deemed inherently misleading or difficult to police can be suppressed. This issue divided the Supreme Court with respect to lawyers' advertising, when a narrow majority extended First Amendment protection to price advertising of routine legal services, rejecting the dissenters' claim that the complex and variegated nature of legal services gave lawyers' advertising a high potential for deception and impeded effective regulation of particular deceptions. However, the Court held that "ambulance chasing"—in-person solicitation of accident victims for pecuniary gain—could be barred entirely because of its potential for deception and overbearing.

Where regulation of commercial expression is not directed at potential deception but intended to advance other interests such as aesthetics or conservation, the Supreme Court has followed a relatively permissive approach to state regulatory interests, while becoming hopelessly fragmented about the First Amendment principles that ought to govern. Thus, in METROMEDIA, INC. V. SAN DIEGO (1981) a shifting majority coalition of Justices made clear that commercial billboards could be entirely banned in a city for aesthetic or traffic safety reasons. Recent decisions, following CENTRAL HUDSON GAS & PUBLIC SERVICE COMMISSION (1980), have fashioned a four-part test to appraise the validity of restrictions on commercial speech. Protection will not be extended to commercial speech that is, on the whole, misleading or that encourages unlawful activity. Even protected commercial speech may be regulated if the state has a substantial interest, if the regulation directly advances that interest, and if the regulation is no broader than necessary to effectuate the state's interest. The elastic properties of this four-part test in actual application have generated considerable disarray within the Supreme Court.

The commercial speech decisions of the BURGER COURT have made clear that freedom of expression principles extend beyond political and religious expression, protecting not only the MARKETPLACE OF IDEAS but expression in the marketplace itself. Second, in affirming relatively broad regulatory power over commercial speech, even though it is deemed to be protected by the First Amendment, the Court has reinforced the notion that the First Amendment extends different levels of protection to different types of speech. The commercial speech decisions thus lend support to Justice ROBERT H. JACKSON's OBITER DICTUM in KOVACS V. COOPER (1949) that under the First Amendment each type and medium of expression "is a law unto itself."

BENNO C. SCHMIDT, JR.

Bibliography

JACKSON, THOMAS H. and JEFFRIES, J. C., JR. 1979 Commercial Speech: Economic Due Process and the First Amendment. *Virginia Law Review* 65:1–41.

WEINBERG, JONATHAN 1982 Constitutional Protection of Commercial Speech. *Columbia Law Review* 82:720–750.

COMMITTEE FOR PUBLIC EDUCATION AND RELIGIOUS LIBERTY v. NYQUIST
413 U.S. 752 (1973)
SLOAN v. LEMON
413 U.S. 825 (1973)

These cases, said Justice LEWIS F. POWELL in his opinion for a 6–3 SUPREME COURT, "involve an intertwining of societal and constitutional issues of the greatest importance." After LEMON V. KURTZMAN (1971), New York State sought to aid private sectarian schools and the parents of children in them by various financial plans purporting to maintain the SEPARATION OF CHURCH AND STATE. Avowing concern for the health and safety of the children, the state provided direct financial grants to "qualifying" schools for maintenance costs. But as Justice Powell observed, "virtually all" were Roman Catholic schools, and the grants had the inevitable effect of subsidizing religious education, thus abridging the FIRST AMENDMENT's prohibition against an ESTABLISHMENT OF RELIGION. New York, as well as Pennsylvania, also provided for the reimbursement of tuition paid by parents who sent their children to nonpublic sectarian schools; New York also had an optional tax relief plan. The Court found that the reimbursement plans constituted grants whose effect was the same as grants made directly to the institutions, thereby advancing religion. The tax benefit plan had the same unconstitutional result, because the deduction, like the grant, involved an expense to the state for the purpose of religious education. The Court distinguished outright tax exemptions of church property for reasons given in WALZ V. TAX COMMISSION (1970). By distinguishing *Nyquist* in MUELLER V. ALLEN (1983), the Court sustained the constitutionality of a tax benefit plan that aided the parents of children in nonpublic sectarian schools.

LEONARD W. LEVY

COMMITTEE FOR PUBLIC EDUCATION AND RELIGIOUS LIBERTY v. REGAN
444 U.S. 646 (1980)

A New York statute directed the reimbursement to nonpublic schools of costs incurred by them in complying with certain state-mandated requirements, including the administration of standardized tests. The participation of church-related schools in this program was challenged as an unconstitutional ESTABLISHMENT OF RELIGION, but the Supreme Court rejected the challenge.

Justice BYRON R. WHITE, writing for a narrowly divided Court, noted that a previous New York law authorizing reimbursement for test services performed by nonpublic schools had been found unconstitutional in *Levitt v. Committee* (1973). However, the new statute, unlike its predecessor, provided for state audit of school financial records to insure that public monies were used only for secular purposes.

Justice HARRY BLACKMUN, with whom Justices WILLIAM J. BRENNAN and THURGOOD MARSHALL joined, dissented. Blackmun stressed that New York's program involved direct payments by the state to a school engaged in a religious enterprise. Justice JOHN PAUL STEVENS also filed a brief dissent.

Committee v. Regan is another illustration of the blurred nature of the line the Court has attempted to draw between permissible and impermissible state support to church-related schools.

RICHARD E. MORGAN

COMMON LAW
(Anglo-American)

The common law is a system of principles and rules grounded in universal custom or natural law and developed, articulated, and applied by courts in a process designed for the resolution of individual controversies. In this general sense, the common law is the historic basis of all Anglo-American legal systems. It is also an important element in the origin and plan of the United States Constitution.

Though sometimes characterized as "unwritten" in reference to their ultimate source, the principles and rules of the Anglo-American common law are in fact found in thousands of volumes of written judicial opinions reporting the grounds of decision in countless individual cases adjudicated over the course of centuries. The process that produced this body of law has three important aspects. First, common law principles and rules derive their legitimacy from the adversary process of litigation. They are valid only if they are HOLDINGS, that is, propositions necessary to the resolution of actual controversies. Second, the common law is applied through a characteristic reasoning process that compares the facts of the present case to the facts of earlier cases. The holdings of those earlier cases are PRECEDENTS, which must be followed unless their facts can be distinguished or unless they can be overruled because their grounds are deemed unsound in light of changing social conditions or policy. In the latter situation, or if no existing precedent is applicable, a new rule may be fashioned from the logic of related rules or underlying principle. Third, the common law is a process in the procedural sense. Litigation is governed by rules designed to shape issues of fact and law so that a case may be fairly and efficiently presented to and decided by the jury, the traditional mode of trial.

The principles and rules of the common law grow and change within this threefold process at the initiative of parties to litigation as they bring forward issues falling outside, or challenging, existing precedents. The common law may also be changed by legislative enactment, but in Anglo-American countries legislation is relied on chiefly to supplement or revise or codify the common law in specific situations.

The Anglo-American common law evolved from decisions of the three great English courts of King's Bench, Common Pleas, and Exchequer, which were firmly established by the end of the thirteenth century. These courts, though created under the royal prerogative, became effectively independent by virtue of their ancient origins and the prestige and life tenure of their judges.

By the time of the American Revolution, two strands were apparent in the English common law. The private law, which developed in actions between subjects, included complex DOCTRINES of property, contract, and tort appropriate to a sophisticated landed and commercial society. The public law, product of actions in which the king was a litigant, consisted of rules defining and limiting his political and fiscal prerogatives, defining criminal conduct as a reflection of his role as peacekeeper, and establishing a series of procedural rights accorded to the criminally accused. In the largely unwritten English constitution, Parliament as supreme sovereign had power to alter or abolish even the most fundamental common law rules, but by convention basic governmental institutions and individual rights were ordinarily beyond legislative change.

The English common law had by 1776 been received in the American colonies. The full array of English law books was the source of common law principles and rules, and the courts followed the common law process. Though the colonists argued otherwise, the English view was that colonial reception of the common law was a matter of grace, not right. In legal theory, the colonies, as the king's dominions, were directly governed by the prerogative, free of common law constraints. Colonial governmental powers were expressly granted and defined by charter or statute. King and Parliament, when England's interests demanded, would set aside rights guaranteed by the common law. As the DECLARATION OF INDEPENDENCE shows, the Revolution was in part fought to rectify violations of charter grants of legislative and judicial power and invasions of individual rights such as TRIAL BY JURY and freedom from unreasonable SEARCH AND SEIZURE.

In reaction to the prerevolutionary experience, the people of the United States asserted SOVEREIGNTY through the federal and state constitutions, under which the executive, legislative, and judiciary were separate branches subject to the written FUNDAMENTAL LAW. The constitutions, however, were adopted against a common law backdrop. The states had expressly received the common law, assuming that their courts would develop it through application of the common law process. The federal Constitution contained no express reception provision, but it did authorize Congress to establish federal courts with JURISDICTION over cases arising under federal law and between citizens of diverse citizenship. Once the federal courts were established, important and difficult questions arose concerning their power to develop a FEDERAL COMMON LAW.

The result of two centuries of learned disputation is that today there is little federal common law. The Supreme Court in ERIE RAILROAD V. TOMPKINS (1938) settled the most enduring controversy by holding that in diversity-of-citizenship cases federal courts must apply the common law as though they were courts of the states where they sit, overruling Justice JOSEPH STORY's famous contrary decision in SWIFT V. TYSON (1842). Earlier the Court had concluded, as DUE PROCESS might have required, that there was no FEDERAL COMMON LAW OF CRIMES, even where federal interests were involved. In civil matters affecting federal interests the Court has held that there is no general federal common law, but the federal courts may articulate common law rules to supplement a comprehensive federal statutory scheme or implement an EXCLUSIVE JURISDICTION. These results are consistent with the basic premise of FEDERALISM that the national government is one of limited powers and other powers are reserved to the states, or to the people.

While the federal Constitution did not adopt the common law as a general rule of decision, many of its specific provisions were of common law origin. In its delineation of the SEPARATION OF POWERS, the Constitution incorporated common law limitations upon the prerogative and Parliament which had been honored in England and disregarded in the colonies. The BILL OF RIGHTS, adopted in part because of doubts about the existence and efficacy of a federal common law, codified specific common law procedural rights accorded the criminally accused. It also incorporated common law protections of more fundamental interests, including that basic guarantee of reason and fairness in governmental action, the right to due process of law.

Most important, the common law process has enabled the federal judiciary to attain its intended position in the constitutional plan. Chief Justice JOHN MARSHALL's opinion in MARBURY V. MADISON (1803), asserting judicial power to review legislation and declare it unconstitutional, was founded on the common law obligation of courts to apply all the relevant law, including the Constitution, in deciding cases. A declaration of unconstitutionality in one case is effective in other similar situations because of the force of precedent. In refining *Marbury*'s principle, the Supreme Court more recently has developed the doctrine of JUSTICIABILITY, designed to establish in constitutional cases the existence of a truly adversary CASE OR CONTROVERSY, to which decision of a constitutional issue is necessary. Together, these rules, by proclaiming that the federal courts are confined to the traditional common law judicial role, provide both legitimacy and effectiveness to court enforcement of the Constitution's limits upon the powers of the other branches and the states.

L. KINVIN WROTH

Bibliography

GOEBEL, JULIUS, JR. 1971 *Antecedents and Beginnings to 1801.* Volume 1 of *The Oliver Wendell Holmes Devise History of the Supreme Court of the United States.* New York: Macmillan.

LLEWELLYN, KARL N. 1960 *The Common Law Tradition: Deciding Appeals.* Boston: Little, Brown.

PLUCKNETT, THEODORE F. T. (1929)1956 *A Concise History of the Common Law.* Boston: Little, Brown.

TRIBE, LAURENCE H. 1978 *American Constitutional Law.* Mineola, N.Y.: Foundation Press.

COMMON LAW, CONSTITUTIONAL

See: Constitutional Common Law

COMMON LAW, FEDERAL CIVIL

See: Federal Common Law, Civil

COMMON LAW, FEDERAL CRIMINAL

See: Federal Common Law of Crimes

COMMONWEALTH v. ALGER

See: State Police Power

COMMONWEALTH v. AVES
18 Pickering (Mass.) 193 (1836)

This became the nation's leading case on sojourner slaves. It posed an unprecedented question: can a slave brought temporarily into a free state be restrained of liberty and be removed from the state on the master's return? Chief Justice LEMUEL SHAW rejected the contention that COMITY between the states compelled recognition of the laws of the master's domicile. SLAVERY, Shaw replied, was so odious that only positive local law recognized it. (See SOMERSET'S CASE, 1772.) In Massachusetts slavery was unconstitutional. Any nonfugitive slave entering Massachusetts became free because no local law warranted restraint and local laws could prevent involuntary removal.

LEONARD W. LEVY

COMMONWEALTH v. CATON
4 Call's (Va.) Reports (1782)

Decided by the highest court of Virginia in 1782, this case is a disputed precedent for the legitimacy of JUDICIAL REVIEW. The state constitution of 1776, which did not empower courts to void enactments in conflict with the constitution, authorized the governor to grant pardons except in impeachment cases. A statute on TREASON deprived the governor of his PARDONING POWER and vested it in the general assembly. Caton, having been sentenced to death for treason, claimed a pardon granted by the lower house, though the upper house refused to concur. The court had only to rule that the pardon was not valid.

Call's unreliable report of the case, a reconstruction made in 1827, indicates that the court considered the constitutionality of the statute on treason and that seven of the eight judges were of the opinion that the court had the power to declare an act of the legislature unconstitutional, though the court unanimously held the act constitutional. In fact, only one of the eight judges ruled the act unconstitutional, one held that it had no power to so rule, and another, GEORGE WYTHE, declared that the court had the power but need not exercise it in this case; he decided that the pardon had no force of law because it was not in conformity with the disputed act, which he found constitutional. A majority of the court, including Chief Justice EDMUND PENDLETON and Chancellor JOHN BLAIR, declined to decide the question whether they had the power to declare an act unconstitutional. Writing to JAMES MADISON a week later, Pendleton reported, "The great Constitutional question . . . was determined . . . by 6 Judges against two, that the Treason Act was not at variance with the Constitution but a proper exercise of the Power reserved to the Legislature by the latter. . . ." Both houses subsequently granted the pardon. The legitimacy of the case as a precedent for judicial review is doubtful.

LEONARD W. LEVY

COMMONWEALTH v. JENNISON
(Massachusetts, 1783, Unreported)

In 1781 Quock Walker, a Massachusetts slave, left his master, Nathaniel Jennison, to work as a hired laborer for Seth and John Caldwell. Jennison went to the Caldwell farm, seized Walker, beat him severely, and brought him home where he was locked up.

Three legal cases resulted from this event. In *Walker v. Jennison* (1781) Walker sued his former master for assault and battery. A jury ruled Walker was a free man and awarded him fifty pounds in damages. Jennison then successfully sued the Caldwells for twenty-five pounds for enticing away his "slave property." This decision was overturned by a jury in *Caldwell v. Jennison* (1781). Here attorney LEVI LINCOLN paraphrased arguments from SOMERSET V. STEWART (1772) in a stirring speech against slavery. In 1783 Jennison was convicted under a criminal INDICTMENT for assault and battery against Walker (*Commonwealth v. Jennison*). Chief Justice WILLIAM CUSHING charged the jury that the Massachusetts Constitution of 1780 abolished slavery by declaring "All men are born free and equal. . . ." Although some blacks were held as slaves after these cases, the litigation, known collectively as the "Quock Walker Cases," was instrumental in ending the peculiar institution in Massachusetts.

PAUL FINKELMAN

Bibliography

FINKELMAN, PAUL 1981 *An Imperfect Union: Slavery, Federalism, and Comity.* Chapel Hill: University of North Carolina Press.

COMMONWEALTH v. SACCO AND VANZETTI
(Massachusetts, 1921)

On August 23, 1927, the Commonwealth of Massachusetts electrocuted two Italian immigrants, Nicola Sacco and Bartolomeo Vanzetti, for the crimes of armed robbery and murder. The executions stirred angry protest in the United States and throughout the world by millions of people who believed that the two men had been denied a fair trial because of their ethnic background and political opinions.

Sacco and Vanzetti, ALIENS and anarchists who had fled to Mexico to avoid the draft during World War I, were arrested in 1920 and quickly brought to trial in Dedham, Massachusetts, for the murder of a paymaster and a guard during the robbery of a shoe factory. The trial took place at the end of the postwar Red Scare in a political atmosphere charged with hysteria against foreigners and radicals. Although the ballistics evidence was inconclusive and many witnesses, most of them Italian, placed the two men elsewhere at the time of the robbery, the jury returned guilty verdicts after listening to patriotic harangues from the chief prosecutor, Frederick Katzmann, and the trial judge, Webster Bradley Thayer.

During his cross-examination of the two defendants, Katzmann constantly emphasized their unorthodox political views and their flight to Mexico during the war. Thayer tolerated a broad range of political questions, mocked the two men's anarchism, and urged the members of the jury to act as "true soldiers . . . in the spirit of supreme American loyalty."

A diverse coalition of Bay State aristocrats, law professors such as FELIX FRANKFURTER, Italian radicals, and New York intellectuals attempted to secure a new trial for the condemned men during the next seven years. They marshaled an impressive amount of evidence pointing to Thayer's prejudice, the doubts of key prosecution witnesses, and the possibility that the crime had been committed by a gang of professional outlaws. The Massachusetts Supreme Judicial Court, however, relying on principles of trial court discretion that made it virtually impossible to challenge any of Thayer's rulings, spurned these appeals and refused to disturb either the verdict or the death sentences. A similar conclusion was reached by a special commission appointed by Governor Alvan T. Fuller and headed by Harvard University president A. Lawrence Lowell.

Last-minute efforts to secure a stay of execution from federal judges, including Supreme Court Justices OLIVER WENDELL HOLMES and LOUIS D. BRANDEIS, also proved unavailing. Attorneys for Sacco and Vanzetti argued that because of Thayer's hostility their clients had been denied a FAIR TRIAL guaranteed by the DUE PROCESS clause of the FOURTEENTH AMENDMENT. But with the exception of MOORE V. DEMPSEY (1923), where a state murder trial had been intimidated by a mob, the Supreme Court had shown great reluctance to intervene in local criminal proceedings. "I cannot think that prejudice on the part of a presiding judge however strong would deprive the Court of jurisdiction," wrote Holmes, "and in my opinion nothing short of a want of legal power to decide the case authorizes me to interfere. . . ." Whether Sacco and Vanzetti received a fair trial is questionable; however, Francis Russell has shown how illusory is the old contention that they were wholly innocent.

MICHAEL E. PARRISH

Bibliography

JOUGHN, G. LOUIS and MORGAN, EDMUND M. 1948 *The Legacy of Sacco and Vanzetti.* New York: Harcourt, Brace.

RUSSELL, FRANCIS 1962 *Tragedy in Dedham: The Story of the Sacco-Vanzetti Case.* New York: Harper & Row.

COMMONWEALTH STATUS

Commonwealths are TERRITORIES in free association with the United States, enjoying virtual autonomy in internal affairs but subject to the United States in foreign and defense matters. Citizens of commonwealths are citizens of the United States: they pay federal taxes and may move freely to, from, and within the United States. Public officials are elected by the people of the commonwealths and neither the officials nor their acts require approval by the President or Congress. Constitutional limitations on state legislation are applicable to commonwealth legislation; and APPEAL lies from the highest court of a commonwealth to the Supreme Court of the United States. When Congress established commonwealth status for the Philippines in 1934 it intended an interim state en route to independence, but commonwealth status has become a practically permanent condition for PUERTO RICO and the Northern Marianas.

The basis of the commonwealth relationship is a "covenant" between the American people and the people of the territory. Since Congress's authority to ratify the covenant derives from its plenary power over territories (Article IV, section 3, clause 2), most legal authorities maintain that Congress could repeal the covenant and impose direct rule. But any attempt to do so would constitute a grievous breach of faith and would excite overwhelming domestic and international political opposition.

DENNIS J. MAHONEY

COMMUNICATIONS ACT
48 Stat. 1064 (1934)

The Communications Act of 1934, enacted under Congress's COMMERCE POWER, provides the statutory basis for federal regulation of BROADCASTING and electronic communication. The act describes the electromagnetic spectrum as a national resource and permits private parties to use portions of it only as trustees in the public interest. To administer its provisions the act established the seven-member Federal Communications Commission (FCC), authorizing it to make regulations with the force of law and to issue licenses to broadcasters that may be granted, renewed, or revoked in accordance with "public interest, convenience, and necessity." Under the authority of the act the FCC has promulgated the FAIRNESS DOCTRINE, requiring broadcasters to provide equal time for replies to controversial messages, as well as regulations to prohibit the broadcasting of OBSCENITY.

The act was based on both technological and ideological considerations. The assumption that broadcasting channels are extremely limited has been disproved by improvements in technology; however, the ideological bias in favor of public ownership and regulation has not yet been overcome. Because of the Supreme Court's deference to Congress's findings of LEGISLATIVE FACT regarding the scarcity of broadcasting channels, as embodied in the Communications Act, in the face of the manifest reality that such channels are far more numerous than, for example, presses capable of producing a major metropolitan newspaper or an encyclopedia, the protection afforded broadcasters' FREEDOM OF SPEECH and FREEDOM OF THE PRESS is significantly reduced.

DENNIS J. MAHONEY

COMMUNIST CONTROL ACT
68 Stat. 775 (1954)

This measure marked the culmination of the United States government's program to prevent subversion from within during the loyalty-security years. Conservative senators, eager to facilitate removal of communists from positions of union leadership, and Senator HUBERT H. HUMPHREY, tired of hearing liberals smeared as "soft on communism," pushed the measure through Congress with large majorities in each chamber. Clearly tied to the 1954 elections, the act outlawed the Communist party as an instrumentality conspiring to overthrow the United States government. The bill as initially drafted made party membership a crime. Responding to criticism of the DWIGHT D. EISENHOWER administration that the membership clause would make the provisions of the 1950 INTERNAL SECURITY ACT unconstitutional, because compulsory registration would violate the RIGHT AGAINST SELF-INCRIMINATION, the bill's sponsors removed its membership clause. However, Congress deprived the Communist party of all "rights, privileges, and immunities attendant upon legal bodies created under the jurisdiction of the laws of the United States or any political subdivision thereof." The act added a new category of groups required to register—"communist-infiltrated" organizations. These, like communist and "front" organizations, although outlawed, were expected to register with the SUBVERSIVE ACTIVITIES CONTROL BOARD.

The measure, virtually inoperative from the beginning, raised grave constitutional questions under the FIRST AMENDMENT, the Fifth Amendment, and the ban against BILLS OF ATTAINDER. The Justice Department ignored it and pushed no general test of its provisions in the court. The act summarized well the official policy toward the Communist party at the time—to keep it legal enough for successful prosecution of its illegalities.

PAUL L. MURPHY

Bibliography

AUERBACH, CARL 1956 The Communist Control Act of 1954. *University of Chicago Law Review* 23:173–220.

COMMUNIST PARTY

See: Subversive Activities and the Constitution

COMMUNIST PARTY OF THE UNITED STATES v. SUBVERSIVE ACTIVITIES CONTROL BOARD
367 U.S. 1 (1961)

The Supreme Court upheld application to the Communist party of provisions of the Subversive Activities Control Act requiring "any organization . . . substantially controlled by the foreign government . . . controlling the world Communist movement" to register with the Board, providing lists of officers and members. The Court postponed considering self-incrimination objections, held that where an individual might escape regulation merely by ceasing to engage in the regulated activity no BILL OF ATTAINDER existed, and deferred to the congressional balance between national security and the FREEDOM OF ASSOCIATION arguing that any inhibition on communists' associational freedom caused by exposure was incidental to regulation of their activities on behalf of foreign governments.

MARTIN SHAPIRO

COMPACT THEORY

See: Social Compact Theory; Theories of the Union

COMPANION CASE

Cases decided by the Supreme Court on the same day are called companion cases when they involve the same issues or issues that are closely related. Sometimes a single opinion is used to explain two or more companion cases, and sometimes separate opinions are written. Occasionally a Justice writing for the Court will select the strongest of a group of companion cases for explanation in a full opinion, leaving the weaker cases to be discussed only briefly, with heavy reliance on the conclusions in the full opinion.

KENNETH L. KARST

COMPELLING STATE INTEREST

When the Supreme Court concludes that STRICT SCRUTINY is the appropriate STANDARD OF REVIEW, it often expresses its searching examination of the justification of legislation in a formula: the law is invalid unless it is necessary to achieve a "compelling state interest." The inquiry thus touches not only legislative means but also legislative purposes.

Even the permissive RATIONAL BASIS standard of review demands that legislative ends be legitimate. To say that a governmental purpose must be one of compelling importance is plainly to demand more. How much more, however, is something the Court has been unable to say. What we do know is that, once "strict scrutiny" is invoked, only rarely does a law escape invalidation.

Any judicial examination of the importance of a governmental objective implies that a court is weighing interests, engaging in a kind of cost-benefit analysis as a prelude to deciding on the constitutionality of legislation. Yet one would be mistaken to assume that the inquiry follows such a neat, linear, two-stage progression. Given the close correlation between employing the "strict scrutiny" standard and invalidating laws, the very word "scrutiny" may be misleading. A court that has embarked on a search for compelling state interests very likely knows how it intends to decide.

In many a case a court does find a legislative purpose of compelling importance. That is not the end of the "strict scrutiny" inquiry; there remains the question whether the law is necessary to achieve that end. If, for example, there is another way the legislature might have accomplished its purpose, without imposing so great a burden on the constitutionally protected interest in liberty or equality, the availability of that LEAST RESTRICTIVE MEANS negates the necessity for the legislature's choice. The meaning of "strict scrutiny" is that even a compelling state interest must be pursued by means that give constitutional values their maximum protection.

The phrase "compelling state interest" originated in Justice FELIX FRANKFURTER's concurring opinion in *Sweezy v. New Hampshire* (1957), a case involving the privacy of political association: "For a citizen to be made to forego even a part of so basic a liberty as his political autonomy, the subordinating interest of the State must be compelling." The Supreme Court uses some variation on this formula not only in FIRST AMENDMENT cases but also in cases calling for "strict scrutiny" under the EQUAL PROTECTION clause or under the revived forms of SUBSTANTIVE DUE PROCESS. The formula, in short, is much used and little explained. The Court is unable to define "compelling state interest" but knows when it does not see it.

KENNETH L. KARST

Bibliography

TRIBE, LAURENCE H. 1978 *American Constitutional Law.* Pages 1000–1002. Mineola, N.Y.: Foundation Press.

COMPETITIVE FEDERALISM

This is a term often used in analysis of constitutional DOCTRINE or working governmental practice. Competitive federalism is closely related to DUAL FEDERALISM, and in contrast with COOPERATIVE FEDERALISM stresses the conflict between the national government and the states.

HARRY N. SCHEIBER

COMPROMISE OF 1850

The Compromise of 1850 comprised a related series of statutes enacted by Congress in an attempt to settle sectional disputes related to SLAVERY that had flared since 1846, with the outbreak of the Mexican War and the introduction of the WILMOT PROVISO. After California's 1849 demand for admission as a free state and the concurrent appearance of southern disunionist sentiment, what had begun as a contest over the constitutional status of SLAVERY IN THE TERRITORIES absorbed other issues related to the security of slavery in the extant states and expanded into a crisis of the Union.

From proposals submitted by President Zachary Taylor and Senator HENRY CLAY, Senator STEPHEN A. DOUGLAS marshaled measures through Congress that admitted California as a free state; established the Texas-New Mexico boundary and compensated Texas and holders of Texas securities for territory claimed by Texas but awarded to New Mexico; abolished the slave trade in the DISTRICT OF COLUMBIA (but Congress rejected a proposal to abolish slavery itself there); amended the Fugitive Slave Act of 1793 by the drastic new measure known as the Fugitive Slave Act of 1850; and created Utah and New Mexico Territories. (See FUGITIVE SLAVERY.)

Both major parties hailed the Compromise as a final settlement of all problems relating to slavery. Southern disunion sentiment abated, while the Free Soil coalition, which had made a respectable beginning in the 1848 election, began to disintegrate. FRANKLIN PIERCE was elected President in 1852 on a platform extolling the finality of the Compromise and condemning any further agitation of the slavery issue.

But the territorial and fugitive-slave measures only extended and inflamed the slavery controversy. The New Mexico and Utah acts were couched in ambiguous language that left the status of slavery in those two immense territories unsettled, though Congress did decisively reject the Free Soil solution embodied in the Wilmot Proviso of 1846. The acts also contained sections providing for APPEAL of slavery controversies from the TERRITORIAL COURTS directly to the United States Supreme Court, an effort to resolve a politically insoluble problem by nonpolitical means.

The Fugitive Slave Act of 1850 was a harsh and provocative measure that virtually legitimated the kidnapping of free blacks. It thrust the federal presence into northern communities in obtrusive ways by potentially forcing any adult northern male to serve on slave-catching posses, by creating new pseudo-judicial officers encouraged by the fee structure to issue certificates of rendition, and by authorizing use of federal military force to enforce the act. It was therefore widely unpopular in the northern states. Subsequent recaptures, renditions, and rescues provided numerous real-life counterparts to the fictional drama of *Uncle Tom's Cabin.*

The finality supposedly achieved by the Compromise of 1850 was shattered by the controversy over the KANSAS-NEBRASKA ACT of 1854. But as ALEXANDER STEPHENS noted back in 1850, "the present adjustment may be made, but the great question of the permanence of slavery in the Southern states will be far from being settled thereby."

WILLIAM M. WIECEK

Bibliography

POTTER, DAVID M. 1976 *The Impending Crisis, 1848–1861.* New York: Harper & Row.

COMPROMISE OF 1877

Four of the sectional compromises in nineteenth-century America were efforts to settle quarrels by mutual concessions and forestall danger of violence. Three of the four efforts were temporarily successful, and only the fourth, that of 1861, broke down in failure. For the next sixteen years, during the Civil War and Reconstruction, differences were resolved by resort to force. The Compromise of 1877 differed from the earlier ones in several ways, one of them being that its main purpose was to foreclose rather than to forestall resort to armed force. Since the Republican party was committed to force when necessary to protect freedmen's rights under the constitutional amendments and CIVIL RIGHTS acts of the Reconstruction period, any repudiation of such commitments had to be negotiated discreetly.

Under President ANDREW JOHNSON and President ULYSSES S. GRANT, the government had been backing away from enforcement of freedmen's rights almost from the start. In part the result of white resistance in the South, this retreat from Reconstruction was also a consequence of the prevalence of white-supremacy sentiment in the North. In the elections of

1874, regarded by some as a referendum on Reconstruction, the Republican House majority of 110 was replaced by a Democratic majority of sixty. And in the ensuing presidential election of 1876 the Democratic candidate, Samuel J. Tilden, won a majority of the popular votes and was conceded 184 of the 185 electoral votes required for election. He also claimed all the nineteen contested votes of South Carolina, Florida, and Louisiana, the only southern states remaining under Republican control. But so did his Republican opponent, Rutherford B. Hayes, who also claimed the election. The impasse was solved by an agreement between the two political parties (not the sections) to create a bipartisan electoral commission of fifteen to count the votes. An unanticipated last minute change of one member of the commission gave the Republicans a majority of one, and by that majority they counted all contested votes for Hayes. That eliminated Tilden, but to seat Hayes required formal action of the House. The Democratic majority, enraged over what they regarded as a "conspiracy" to rob them of their victory, talked wildly of resistance and started a filibuster.

Foreseeing the victory of Hayes, southern Democrats sought to salvage whatever they could out of defeat. Their prime objective was "home rule," which meant not only withdrawal of troops that sustained Republican rule in South Carolina and Louisiana but also a firm Republican commitment to abandon use of force in the future for defending rights of freedmen, carpetbaggers, and scalawags. This amounted to the virtual nullification of the FOURTEENTH and FIFTEENTH AMENDMENTS and the CIVIL RIGHTS ACT. In return southern conservatives promised to help confirm Hayes's election, and many Democrats of the old Whig persuasion promised to cooperate with the new administration, but not to defect to the Republican party unless it abandoned "radicalism."

With control of the army and the submission of enough northern Democrats, Republicans could have seated Hayes anyway. But the southerners exploited Republican fears of resistance and skillfully played what they later admitted was "a bluff game." An old Whig himself, Hayes fell in with the idea of reconstituting his party in the South under conservative white leaders in place of carpetbaggers. He not only pledged "home rule" but promised to appoint a conservative southern Democrat to his cabinet and sweetened his appeal to that constituency by publicly pledging generous support to bills for subsidizing "INTERNAL IMPROVEMENTS of a national character" in the South. Hayes's election was confirmed only two days before he took office.

As in earlier sectional compromises, not all the terms of that of 1877 were fulfilled, but the main ones were. Hayes appointed a southern Democrat his postmaster general, chief dispenser of patronage, and placed many other white conservatives in southern offices. Bills for federal subsidies to internal improvements met with more success than ever before. The troops sustaining Republican rule in the two states were removed and Democrats immediately took over. In the CIVIL RIGHTS CASES (1883) the Supreme Court erected the STATE ACTION barrier, severely limiting the reach of the Fourteenth Amendment. The Court's opinion was written by Justice JOSEPH P. BRADLEY, who had been a member of the 1877 electoral commission. More important than all this was the pledge against resort to force to protect black rights. That commitment held firm for eighty years, until the military intervention at Little Rock, Arkansas, in 1957. This set a record for durability among sectional compromises.

C. VANN WOODWARD

Bibliography

GILLETTE, WILLIAM 1980 *Retreat from Reconstruction, 1869–1879.* Baton Rouge: Louisiana State University Press.

POLAKOFF, KEITH J. 1973 *The Politics of Inertia: The Election of 1876 and the End of Reconstruction.* Baton Rouge: Louisiana State University Press.

WOODWARD, C. VANN 1966 *Reunion and Reaction: The Compromise of 1877 and the End of Reconstruction.* Boston: Little, Brown.

COMPULSORY PROCESS, RIGHT TO

The first state to adopt a constitution following the Declaration of Independence (New Jersey, 1776) guaranteed all criminal defendants the same "privileges of witnesses" as their prosecutors. Fifteen years later, in enumerating the constitutional rights of accused persons, the framers of the federal BILL OF RIGHTS bifurcated what New Jersey called the "privileges of witnesses" into two distinct but related rights: the Sixth Amendment right of the accused "to be confronted with the witnesses against him," and his companion Sixth Amendment right to "compulsory process for obtaining witnesses in his favor." The distinction between witnesses "against" the accused and witnesses "in his favor" turns on which of the parties—the prosecution or the defense—offers the witness's statements in evidence as a formal part of its case. The CONFRONTATION clause establishes the government's obligations regarding the production and examination of witnesses whose statements the prosecution puts into evidence either in its case in chief or in rebuttal. The compulsory process clause establishes the government's obligations regarding the production and examination of witnesses whose statements the defendant seeks to put into evidence in his respective case.

The constitutional questions of compulsory process are twofold: What is "compulsory process?" Who are the "witnesses in his favor" for whom a defendant is entitled to compulsory process? The first is the easier of the two questions to answer. "Compulsory process" is a term of art used to denominate the state's coercive devices for locating, producing, and compelling evidence from witnesses. A common example is the SUBPOENA *ad testificandum,* a judicial order to a person to appear and testify as a witness, or suffer penalty of CONTEMPT for failing to do so. The right of compulsory process, in turn, is the right of a defendant to invoke such coercive devices at the state's disposal to obtain evidence in his defense. The right of compulsory process is therefore no guarantee that defendants will succeed in locating, producing, or compelling witnesses to testify in their favor; it does not entitle defendants to the testimony of witnesses who have died or otherwise become unavailable to testify through no fault of the state. Rather, it assures defendants that the state will make reasonable, good-faith efforts to produce such requested witnesses as are available to testify at trial. It gives a defendant access to the same range of official devices for producing available evidence on his behalf as the prosecution enjoys for producing available evidence on its behalf.

The more significant question for a defendant is: Who are the witnesses for whom a defendant is entitled to compulsory process? What law defines "witnesses in his favor"? Early commentators argued that a defendant might claim compulsory process only with respect to witnesses whose testimony had already been determined to be admissible, according to the governing rules of evidence in the respective jurisdiction. The Supreme Court in its seminal 1967 decision in *Washington v. Texas* rejected that narrow interpretation of "witnesses in his favor." The defendant had been tried in state court for a homicide that he asserted his accomplice alone had committed. The accomplice, who had already been convicted of committing the murder, had appeared at the defendant's trial and offered to testify that he, the accomplice, had acted alone in committing the homicide. The trial court, invoking a state rule of evidence disqualifying accomplices from testifying for one another in criminal cases, refused to allow the accomplice to testify in Washington's favor, and Washington was convicted. The Supreme Court held, first, that the compulsory process clause of the Sixth Amendment, like other clauses of the Sixth Amendment, had become applicable to the states through the DUE PROCESS clause of the FOURTEENTH AMENDMENT. Second, and more significantly, the Court held that the meaning of "witnesses in [a defendant's] favor" was to be determined not by state or federal evidentiary standards of admissibility but by independent constitutional standards of admissibility. The compulsory process clause, it said, directly defines the "witnesses" the defendant is entitled to call to the witness stand. The state in *Washington* violated the defendant's right of compulsory process by "arbitrarily" preventing him from eliciting evidence from a person "who was physically and mentally capable of testifying to events that he had personally observed, and whose testimony would have been relevant and material to the defense."

Having determined that the compulsory process clause operates to render exculpatory evidence independently admissible on a defendant's behalf, the Court found *Washington* to be an easy case; the accomplice's proffered testimony was highly probative of the defendant's innocence, and the state's reasons for excluding it were highly attenuated. The Court has since invoked the authority of *Washington* to prohibit a trial judge from silencing a defense witness by threatening him with prosecution for perjury; to prohibit a state from invoking state HEARSAY RULES to exclude highly probative hearsay evidence in a defendant's favor; and to prohibit a trial judge from instructing a jury that defense witnesses are less worthy of belief than prosecution witnesses. Lower courts have invoked the compulsory process clause to compel the government to disclose the identity of informers; to compel defense witnesses to testify over claims of EVIDENTIARY PRIVILEGES; and to compel the prosecution to grant use IMMUNITY to defense witnesses asserting the RIGHT AGAINST SELF-INCRIMINATION. Although the Supreme Court in *Washington* did not define the outer limits of the compulsory process clause, it subsequently emphasized in *Chambers v. Mississippi* (1973) that "few rights are more fundamental than the right of an accused to present witnesses in his defense."

The companion clause to compulsory process, the confrontation clause, is the more widely known and the more often litigated of the Sixth Amendment witness clauses. The issues of confrontation can be grouped into two questions: What does the right "to be confronted" with witnesses mean? Who are the "witnesses against him" whom a defendant is entitled to confront? The answer to the first question has become relatively clear in recent years. Some commentators, including JOHN HENRY WIGMORE, once argued that the right to be "confronted" with witnesses meant no more than the right of a defendant to be brought face to face with the state's witnesses and to cross-examine them in accord with the ordinary (nonconstitutional) rules of evidence. The Supreme Court in 1974 rejected that position in *Davis v. Alaska.* Davis was convicted in a state court on the basis of testimony for the prosecution by a juvenile delinquent. On cross-examination, the witness refused to answer impeaching questions relating to his current delinquency status, invoking a state-law privilege for the confidentiality of juvenile court records. The Supreme Court held that the right to be confronted with prosecution witnesses creates an independent right in defendants, overriding state rules of evidence to the contrary, to elicit probative evidence from the state's witnesses by cross-examining them for exculpatory evidence they may possess. The Court has yet to decide how far the right to examine prosecution witnesses extends in circumstances other than those presented in *Davis.* The parallel right of compulsory process suggests, however, that the confrontation clause entitles a defendant to elicit by cross-examination from prosecution witnesses the same range of probative evidence that the compulsory process clause entitles him to elicit by direct examination from defense witnesses. Both witness clauses serve the same purpose—to enable an accused to defend himself by examining witnesses for probative evidence in his defense.

The more difficult, and still uncertain, question of confrontation is the meaning of "witnesses against him." A defendant certainly has a right to face and cross-examine whichever witnesses the prosecution actually produces in court. The question is whether the confrontation clause also defines the "witnesses" whom the prosecution must call to the witness stand. Does the confrontation clause specify which witnesses the prosecution must produce in person? Or does it merely entitle a defendant to confront whichever witnesses the prosecution in its discretion chooses to produce? These questions arise most frequently in connection with hearsay, that is, evidence whose probative value rests on the perception, memory, narration, or sincerity of a "hearsay declarant," someone not present in court—and thus not subject to cross-examination. Most jurisdictions address the hearsay problem by treating hearsay as presumptively inadmissible, subject to numerous exceptions for particular kinds of hearsay that are admissible either because of their reliability or for other reasons. The Sixth Amendment potentially comes into play whenever the prosecution invokes such an exception to introduce hearsay evidence against the accused. The confrontation question is whether the hearsay declarant is a "witness against" the defendant, within the meaning of the Sixth Amendment, who must be produced for cross-examination under oath and in the presence of the jury.

The Supreme Court held in *Bruton v. United States* (1968) that a prosecutor must produce in person a declarant whose out-of-court statements are being offered against an accused, not to prove him guilty but to spare the state the administrative burden of conducting separate trials. The more difficult question is what other declarants are "witnesses" against an accused for constitutional purposes.

Some authorities have argued that hearsay declarants are always witnesses against the accused for Sixth Amendment purposes and, hence, must always be produced in person as a predicate for using their out-of-court statements against an accused, even if they are no longer available to appear or testify in person. Other authorities argue that hearsay declarants are never witnesses against the accused for Sixth Amendment purposes. The Supreme Court appears to have adopted a middle position. *Ohio v. Roberts* (1980) arguably held that although the state has a Sixth Amendment obligation to produce in person available hearsay declarants whom it can reasonably assume the defendant would wish to examine in person at the time their out-of-court statements are introduced into evidence, the state has no Sixth Amendment obligation to produce hearsay declarants who have become unavailable through no fault of the state. The state remains constitutionally free to use the hearsay statements of these declarants, provided that the statements possess sufficient "indicia of reliability" to afford the trier of fact "a satisfactory basis" for evaluating their truth—such as statements that fall within "firmly rooted hearsay exceptions." Significantly, the state's burden of production under the confrontation clause thus parallels its burdens under the compulsory process clause. Both clauses require the state to make reasonable, good-faith efforts to produce in person witnesses the defendant wishes to examine for evidence in his defense. Yet neither clause requires the state to produce witnesses whom a defendant is not reasonably expected to wish to examine for evidence in his defense, or witnesses who have died, disappeared, or otherwise become unavailable through no fault of the state.

Although the confrontation clause does not require the state to produce declarants who are unavailable to testify in person or whom a defendant is not reasonably expected to wish to examine in person, other constitutional provisions do regulate the state's use of their hearsay statements. *Manson v. Brathwaite* (1977) held that the due process clauses of the Fifth and Fourteenth Amendments require the state to ensure that every item of evidence it uses against an accused, presumably including hearsay evidence, possesses sufficient "features of reliability" to be rationally evaluated by the jury for its truth. The compulsory process clause, in turn, requires states to assist the defendant in producing every available witness, including available hearsay declarants, whose presence the defendant requests and who appears to possess probative evidence in his favor. It follows, therefore, that although the state has no obligation under the confrontation clause to produce hearsay declarants who are unavailable to testify in person, it has a residual due process obligation to ensure that their hearsay statements possess sufficient "indicia of reliability" to support a conviction of the accused. Although the state has no obligation under the confrontation clause to produce as prosecution witnesses available declarants whom it does not reasonably believe the defendant would wish to examine in person at the time their out-of-court statements are introduced into evidence, it has a residual obligation under the compulsory process clause to assist him in producing such declarants whenever the defendant indicates that he wishes to call and examine them as witnesses in his defense.

PETER WESTEN

Bibliography

WELLBORN III, OLIN GUY 1982 The Definition of Hearsay in the Federal Rules of Evidence. *Texas Law Review* 61:49–93.

WESTEN, PETER 1974 The Compulsory Process Clause. *Michigan Law Review* 73:73–184.

______ 1978 Confrontation and Compulsory Process: A Unified Theory of Evidence for Criminal Cases. *Harvard Law Review* 91:567–628.

______ 1979 The Future of Confrontation. *Michigan Law Review* 77:1185–1217.

CONCORD TOWN MEETING RESOLUTIONS (October 21, 1776)

The people of Concord, Massachusetts, at a town meeting in 1776, were the first to recommend a CONSTITUTIONAL CONVENTION as the only proper body to frame a CONSTITUTION. Earlier that year the provisional legislature of Massachusetts had requested permission from the people of the state to draw up a constitution. The legislature had recommended that the free males of voting age assemble in all the towns to determine that issue and also to decide whether the constitution should be made public for the towns to consider before the legislature ratified it. Nine towns objected to the recommended procedure on the grounds that a legislature was not competent for the purpose. Among the nine, Concord best described the procedure that should be followed.

Concord's resolutions declared that the legislature was not competent for three reasons: a constitution is intended to secure the people in their rights against the government; the body that forms a constitution has the power to alter it; a constitution alterable by the legislature is "no security at all" against the government's encroachment on the rights of the people. Accordingly, Concord resolved, a convention representing the towns should be chosen by all the free male voters. The sole task of the convention should be to frame the constitution. Having completed its task, the convention should publish the proposed constitution "for the Inspection and Remarks" of the people. One week later the town of Attleboro, endorsing the Concord principle of a convention, recommended that the constitution be ratified by the people of the towns rather than by the legislature.

The legislature, ignoring the dissident towns, framed a constitution but submitted it for ratification. The people overwhelmingly rejected it. In 1780 the people ratified a state constitution that was framed by a constitutional convention, the first in the history of the world to be so framed. Concord had designed an institution of government that conformed with the SOCIAL COMPACT theory of forming a FUNDAMENTAL LAW.

LEONARD W. LEVY

CONCURRENT JURISDICTION

The Constitution does not require Congress to create lower federal courts. The Framers assumed that state courts would be competent to hear the cases included in Article III's definition of the JUDICIAL POWER OF THE UNITED STATES. When Congress does choose to confer some of the federal judicial power on lower federal courts, state courts normally retain their JURISDICTION as well. This simultaneous or concurrent jurisdiction of state and federal courts normally exists unless Congress enacts a law stating that the federal power shall be exclusive. Only in unusual circumstances, as when state jurisdiction would gravely disrupt a federal program, has the Supreme Court required an explicit grant of congressional authority for concurrent state jurisdiction to exist. Indeed, in the limited instance of DIVERSITY JURISDICTION, the Framers intended concurrent jurisdiction to be mandatory, so that Congress could not divest state courts of judicial power they possessed before adoption of the Constitution.

Concurrent jurisdiction allows plaintiffs initial choice of a forum more sympathetic to their claims. In many circumstances, however, a defendant may supplant that choice by exercising a right under federal law to remove the case from state to federal court. (See REMOVAL OF CASES.)

State courts need not always agree to exercise their concurrent jurisdiction. If a state court declines to hear a federal claim for nondiscriminatory reasons tied to the sound management of the state judicial system, the Supreme Court will respect that decision.

When concurrent jurisdiction exists, state and federal courts may be asked to adjudicate the same rights or claims between parties at the same time. Ordinarily neither the federal nor the state court is required to stay its proceeding in such situations. However, the federal courts do possess a limited statutory power to enjoin pending state proceedings, and a state or federal court that is the first to obtain custody of property that is the subject of the dispute may enjoin the other.

CAROLE E. GOLDBERG-AMBROSE

Bibliography

CURRIE, DAVID 1981 *Federal Jurisdiction in a Nutshell,* 2nd ed. St. Paul, Minn.: West Publishing Co.

CONCURRENT POWERS

In THE FEDERALIST, JAMES MADISON wrote that in fashioning the federal relationship "the convention must have been compelled to sacrifice theoretical propriety to the force of extraneous circumstances." These sacrifices which produced a "compound republic, partaking both of the national and federal character" were "rendered indispensable" by what Madison termed "the peculiarity of our political situation." An important feature of the compound republic is the idea of concurrent powers.

Concurrent powers are those exercised independently in the same field of legislation by both federal and state governments, as in the case of the power to tax or to make BANKRUPTCY laws. As ALEXANDER HAMILTON explained in *The Federalist* #32, "the State governments would clearly retain all the rights of SOVEREIGNTY which they before had, and which were not, by that act, *exclusively* delegated to the United States." Hamilton goes on to explain that this "alienation" would exist in three cases only: where there is in express terms an exclusive delegation of authority to the federal government, as in the case of the seat of government; where authority is granted in one place to the federal government and prohibited to the states in another, as in the case of IMPOSTS; and where a power is granted to the federal government "to which a similar authority in the States would be absolutely and totally *contradictory* and *repugnant,* as in the case of prescribing naturalization rules." This last, Hamilton notes, would not comprehend the exercise of concurrent powers which "might be productive of occasional interferences in the *policy* of any branch of administration, but would not imply any direct contradiction or repugnancy in point of constitutional authority." The only explicit mention of concurrent power in the Constitution occurred in the ill-fated EIGHTEENTH AMENDMENT which provided that "the Congress and the several States shall have concurrent power to enforce this article."

The story of concurrent power in modern American constitutional history has largely been the story of federal PREEMPTION. The concurrent authority of the states is always subordinate to the superior authority of the federal government and generally can be exercised by the states only where the federal government has not occupied the field, or where Congress has given the states permission to exercise concurrent powers. Thus in MCCULLOCH V. MARYLAND (1819), Maryland's concurrent power of taxation had to give way when the state sought to tax a federal instrumentality, because such a tax was utterly repugnant to federal supremacy.

In the years since *McCulloch* the Supreme Court has devised an intricate system for determining when a federal exercise of power has implicitly or explicitly worked to diminish or extinguish the concurrent powers of the states. The federal government's steady expansion of power over the years has, of course, placed more restrictions on concurrent action by the states as, in more and more areas, the federal government has occupied the whole field of legislation.

The Court's decision in *Pacific and Electric Company v. Energy Resources Commission* (1983) provides a useful summary of the factors that determine whether federal preemption may be said to have taken place: whether Congress is acting within constitutional limits and explicitly states its intention to preempt state authority; whether the scheme of federal regulation is so pervasive as to make reasonable the inference that Congress intended for the state to be excluded from concurrent regulation; whether, even though the regulation of Congress is not pervasive, the operation of concurrent powers on the part of the state would actually conflict with federal law; and whether, in the absence of pervasive legislation, state law stands as an obstacle to the accomplishment of the full purposes and objectives of Congress. It is not difficult to see that most of the states' concurrent powers today exist at the forbearance of the federal legislature. This result was not entirely anticipated by the Framers of the Constitution; but it was the inevitable consequence of the centripetal forces embodied in the national features of the compound republic.

EDWARD J. ERLER

Bibliography

DODD, WALTER F. 1963 Concurrent Powers. In Edwin R. Seligman, ed., *Encyclopedia of the Social Sciences,* Vol. 4:173–174. New York: Macmillan.

STORY, JOSEPH 1833 *Commentaries on the Constitution of the United States,* Vol. 1:407–433. Boston: Hilliard, Gray & Co.

CONCURRENT RESOLUTION

Concurrent resolutions adopted by the Congress, unlike JOINT RESOLUTIONS, do not require the president's signature and do not ordinarily have the force of law. Concurrent resolutions may be used to express the "sense of Congress" or to regulate the internal affairs of Congress (such as expenditure of funds for congressional housekeeping).

Since 1939, concurrent resolutions have been the normal means of expressing the LEGISLATIVE VETO when by law that limit on PRESIDENTIAL ORDINANCE-MAKING POWER requires action by both houses. Recent examples of this requirement are found in the WAR POWERS ACT (1973) and the CONGRESSIONAL BUDGET AND IMPOUNDMENT CONTROL ACT (1974).

DENNIS J. MAHONEY

CONCURRING OPINION

When a member of a multi-judge court agrees with the DECISION reached by the majority but disagrees with the reasoning of the OPINION OF THE COURT or wishes to add his own remarks, he will customarily file a concurring opinion. The concurring opinion usually proposes an alternative way of reaching the same result. Once relatively rare, separate concurrences have become, in the late twentieth century, a normal part of the workings of the Supreme Court of the United States.

A concurring opinion may diverge from the majority opinion only slightly or only on technical points, or it may propose an entirely different line of argument. One example of the latter sort is found in ROCHIN V. CALIFORNIA (1952) in which the concurring opinions staked out a much bolder course of constitutional interpretation than the majority was willing to follow. In a constitutional system in which great issues of public policy are decided in controversies between private litigants, the principles of law enunciated in the opinions are usually of far greater importance than the decision with respect to the parties to the case. Sometimes dissenting Justices are closer to the majority on principles than are concurring Justices.

In the most important cases, several Justices may write separate opinions, even though there is substantial agreement on the grounds for deciding the case. DRED SCOTT V. SANDFORD (1857) and the CAPITAL PUNISHMENT CASES (1972) are examples of cases in which every Justice filed a separate concurring or DISSENTING OPINION.

Scholars generally agree that separate concurrences often diminish the authority of the court's decision and reduce the degree of certainty of the law. Some critics have suggested elimination of concurring opinions, especially when they are filed by Justices who also subscribe to the MAJORITY OPINION. But concurring opinions, no less than dissenting opinions, provide alternative courses for future constitutional development.

DENNIS J. MAHONEY

CONFEDERATE CONSTITUTION

The Constitution of the Confederate States of America, adopted in 1861, closely followed, and was in a sense a commentary upon, the Constitution of the United States. The most important points of divergence were: provision for the heads of executive departments to sit and speak in the Congress, a single six-year term for the President, a line-item VETO POWER over appropriations, explicit provision for presidential power to remove appointed officials, and the requirement of a two-thirds vote in each house to admit new states.

The Confederate Constitution prohibited laws impairing the right of property in slaves; but it also prohibited the foreign slave trade (except with the United States). Other innovations included a ban on federal expenditures for INTERNAL IMPROVEMENTS and provision for state duties on sea-going vessels, to be used for improvement of harbors and navigable waters. The AMENDING PROCESS provided for a convention of the states to be summoned by Congress upon the demand of state conventions; Congress did not have the power to propose amendments itself.

The provisions of the BILL OF RIGHTS of the United States Constitution were written into the body of the Confederate Constitution, as were those of the ELEVENTH and TWELFTH AMENDMENTS.

DENNIS J. MAHONEY

Bibliography

COULTER, E. MERTON 1950 *The Confederate States of America, 1861–1865.* Baton Rouge: Louisiana State University Press.

CONFERENCE

When the Justices of the Supreme Court refer to themselves in the aggregate as "the Conference"—as distinguished from "the Court"—they are alluding to their deliberative functions in reaching decisions. The Conference considers, discusses, even negotiates; the Court acts.

The name comes from the Justices' practice of meeting to discuss cases and vote on their disposition. Two kinds of questions are considered at these Conferences: whether the Court should review a case, and how to decide a case under review. Just before the beginning of each TERM, the Conference considers a great many applications for review. (See APPEAL; CERTIORARI, WRIT OF; APPELLATE JURISDICTION; ORIGINAL JURISDICTION.) During the term, in weeks when ORAL ARGUMENTS are scheduled, the Conference generally meets regularly to consider the cases argued within the preceding few days.

The Conference is limited to the nine Justices. Clerks and secretaries do not attend, and if messages are passed into the room, tradition calls for the junior Justice to be doorkeeper. By another tradition, each Justice shakes hands with all the other Justices before the Conference begins. The CHIEF JUSTICE presides.

The Chief Justice calls a case for discussion, and normally speaks first. The other Justices speak in turn, according to their seniority. (Interruptions are not unknown.) The custom has been for Justices to vote in inverse order of seniority, the Chief Justice voting last. Recent reports, however, suggest flexibility in this practice; when the Justices' positions are already obvious, a formal vote may be unnecessary. The vote at the Conference meeting is not final. Once draft opinions and memoranda "to the Conference" have begun to circulate, votes may change, and even the Court's decision may change.

KENNETH L. KARST

(SEE ALSO: *Opinion of the Court; Dissenting Opinion; Concurring Opinion.*)

Bibliography

HUGHES, CHARLES EVANS 1928 *The Supreme Court of the United States: Its Foundation, Methods and Achievements: An Interpretation.* New York: Columbia University Press.

WOODWARD, BOB and ARMSTRONG, SCOTT 1979 *The Brethren: Inside the Supreme Court.* New York: Simon & Schuster.

CONFESSIONS

See: Police Interrogation and Confessions

CONFIRMATIO CARTARUM 1297

Within two centuries after its adoption MAGNA CARTA was reconfirmed forty-four times. The reconfirmation of 1297 is significant because it was the first made after representatives of the commons were admitted to Parliament; because it embodied the inchoate principle that TAXATION WITHOUT REPRESENTATION is unlawful; and because it regarded Magna Carta as FUNDAMENTAL LAW. By one section the king agreed to exact certain taxes only "by the common assent of the realm. . . ." Another section declared that any act by the king's judges or ministers contrary to the great charter "shall be undone, and holden for nought." WILLIAM PENN ordered the charter and its reconfirmation of 1297 reprinted in the colonies for the first time in 1687. JOHN ADAMS, THOMAS JEFFERSON, and other lawyers of the era of the American Revolution were familiar with the principles of the statute of 1297, and in MARBURY V. MADISON (1803) the Supreme Court declared that any act contrary to the fundamental law of the written constitution is void.

LEONARD W. LEVY

Bibliography

PERRY, RICHARD L., ed. 1959 *Sources of Our Liberties.* Pages 23–31. New York: American Bar Foundation.

CONFISCATION ACTS
12 Stat. 319 (1861)
12 Stat. 589 (1862)

Congress enacted the Confiscation Acts "to insure the speedy termination of the present rebellion." Both statutes liberated the slaves of certain rebels and authorized the confiscation of other types of property by judicial procedures based on admiralty and revenue models. Both statutes were compromise measures, influenced by the progressive goal of emancipation of slaves and by a respect for the rights of private property.

The Supreme Court upheld the constitutionality of the acts in the 6–3 decision of *Miller v. United States* (1871), finding congressional authority in the WAR POWERS clauses of Article I. The majority shrugged off Fifth and Sixth Amendment objections on the grounds that the statutes were not ordinary punitive legislation but rather were extraordinary war measures.

The acts were indifferently and arbitrarily enforced, producing a total of less than $130,000 net to the Treasury. Property of Confederates was also virtually confiscated in proceedings for nonpayment of the wartime direct tax, under the Captured and Abandoned Property Act of 1863, and through President ABRAHAM LINCOLN's contraband emancipation policies.

WILLIAM M. WIECEK

Bibliography

RANDALL, JAMES G. 1951 *Constitutional Problems under Lincoln.* Urbana: University of Illinois Press.

CONFRONTATION, RIGHT OF

The confrontation clause of the Sixth Amendment, which guarantees an accused person the right "to be confronted with the witnesses against him," is one of the two clauses in the BILL OF RIGHTS that explicitly address the right of criminal defendants to elicit evidence in their defense from witnesses at trial. The other clause is its Sixth Amendment companion, the COMPULSORY PROCESS clause, which guarantees the accused the right to "compulsory process for obtaining witnesses in his favor." Together these two clauses provide constitutional foundations for the right of accused persons to defend themselves through the production and examination of witnesses at trial.

PETER WESTEN

(SEE ALSO: *Hearsay Rules.*)

CONGRESS AND THE SUPREME COURT

The delegates to the CONSTITUTIONAL CONVENTION OF 1787 confronted two fundamental problems in their quest to correct the political defects of the ARTICLES OF CONFEDERATION. First, they needed to bolster the powers of government at the national level so as to transform the "league of friendship" created by the Articles into a government with all the coercive powers requisite to government. Second, the Framers sought to create energetic but limited powers that would enable the new national government to govern, but in ways safe to the rights of the people. As JAMES MADISON put it in THE FEDERALIST #51, the task was to "enable the government to control the governed, but in the next place oblige it to control itself."

Their successful solution to this political problem was to separate the powers of government. Because the primary source of trouble in a popular form of government would be the legislative branch, the object was to bolster the coordinate executive and judicial branches, to offer "some more adequate defence . . . for the more feeble, against the more powerful members of the government." The arrangement of checked and balanced institutions would at once avoid "a tyrannical concentration of all the powers of government in the same hands" while rendering the administration of the national government more efficient.

When the Framers examined the existing federal system under the Articles to determine precisely what it was that rendered it "altogether unfit for the administration of the affairs of the Union," the want of an independent judiciary "crown[ed] the defects of the confederation." As ALEXANDER HAMILTON put it in *The Federalist* #22, "Laws are a dead letter without courts to expound and define their true meaning and operation." Thus the improved science of politics offered by the friends of the Constitution prominently included provision for "the institution of courts composed of judges, holding their offices during good behavior."

But to some Anti-Federalist critics of the Federalist-backed Constitution, the judiciary was too independent and too powerful. To the New York Anti-Federalist "Brutus," the proposed judiciary possessed such independence as to allow the courts to "mould the government into almost any shape they please." The "Federal Farmer" was equally critical: his fellow citizens were "more in danger of sowing the seeds of arbitrary government in this department than in any other." With such unanticipated criticism, the Federalists were forced to defend the judicial power more elaborately than had been done in the early pages of *The Federalist.*

So compelling were the Anti-Federalist arguments that Hamilton saw fit to explain and defend the proposed judicial power in no fewer than six separate essays (#78–83) in *The Federalist.* His task was to show how an independent judiciary was not only *not* a threat to safe popular government but was absolutely essential to it. In making his now famous argument in *The Federalist* #78 that the judiciary would be that branch of the new government "least dangerous to the political rights of the Constitution," Hamilton made the case that the courts were "designed to be an intermediate body between the people and the legislature, in order, among other things, to keep the latter within the limits assigned to their authority." By exercising neither force nor will but merely judgment, the courts would prove to be the "bulwarks of a limited constitution." Such an institution, Hamilton argued, politically independent yet constitutionally rooted, was essential to resist the overwhelming power of the majority of the community. Only with such a constitutional defense could the rights of individuals and of minor parties be protected against majority tyranny; only an independent judiciary could allow the powers of the national government to be sufficiently enhanced, while simultaneously checking the unhealthy impulses of majority rule that had characterized politics at the state level under the Articles.

To counter the Anti-Federalist complaint that the courts would be imperiously independent, Hamilton reminded them that the courts would not be simply freewheeling sources of arbitrary judgments and decrees. The Constitution, in giving Congress the power to regulate the APPELLATE JURISDICTION of the Supreme Court "with such exceptions, and under such regulations, as the Congress shall make," hedged against too expansive a conception of judicial power. "To avoid an arbitrary discretion in the courts," Hamilton noted, "it is indispensable that they should be bound down by strict rules and precedents, which serve to define and point out their duty in every particular case that comes before them." Thus the stage was set for a history of political confrontation between the Congress and the Court.

The tension between Congress and the Court has been a constant part of American politics at least since CHISHOLM V. GEORGIA (1793) led to the ELEVENTH AMENDMENT. Each generation has seen dramatic Supreme Court rulings that have prompted political cries to curb the courts. JOHN MARSHALL's now celebrated opinions in MARBURY V. MADISON (1803) and MCCULLOCH V. MARYLAND (1819), for example, caused him a good bit of political grief when he wrote them; the decision in DRED SCOTT V. SANDFORD (1857) soon came to be viewed as a judicially "self-inflicted wound" that weakened the Court and exacerbated the conflict that descended into civil war; and more recently, protests against the rulings in BROWN V. BOARD OF EDUCATION (1954) and ROE V. WADE (1973) have caused not only political demands for retaliation against the Court but social conflict and even violence as well. But through it all the Court has weathered the hostility with its independence intact.

Only once were the critics successful in persuading Congress to act against the Court, and the Court validated that move. In EX PARTE MCCARDLE (1869) the Court confirmed Congress's power to withdraw a portion of the Court's appellate jurisdiction. Fearing that the Court would use William McCardle's petition for a writ of HABEAS CORPUS under the HABEAS CORPUS ACT OF 1867 as a vehicle for invalidating the Reconstruction Acts *in toto,* the Congress repealed that portion of the act under which McCardle had brought his action—and after the Court had heard arguments in the case. The Court upheld the constitutionality of Congress's action in repealing this particular part of the Court's JURISDICTION. The extent of Congress's power to withdraw the Court's appellate jurisdiction remains a matter of constitutional controversy.

The constitutional relationship between Congress and the Court is one thing; their political relationship is another matter. Although there are often loud cries for reaction against the Court, the critics usually lack sufficient force to achieve political retribution. The reason is most often explained as a matter of political prudence. The courts by their decisions frequently irritate a portion of the community—but usually only a portion. For most decisions will satisfy certain public constituencies that are as vociferous as the critics. Even the most errant exercises of judicial decision making are rarely sufficient to undermine the public respect for the idea of an independent judiciary.

The reason for this is simple enough: an independent judiciary makes good political sense. To make the judiciary too much dependent upon "popularity" as that popularity may be reflected in Congress would be to lower the constitutional barriers to congressional power, barriers generally agreeable to most people most of the time. The arguments of Hamilton in *The Federalist* still carry considerable weight.

Thus in the constitutional design of separating the powers of government through the device of "partial agency"—mingling the powers enough to give each branch some control over the others—is to be found the inevitable gulf between legitimate power and prudent restraint. For Congress to be persuaded to restrict judicial power, the case must first be made that such restrictions are both necessary and proper.

Despite the dangers of legislative power, it was still considered by the Framers to be the cardinal principle of POPULAR SOVEREIGNTY. Basic to this principle is the belief that it is legitimate for the people through the instrumentality of law to adjust, check, or enhance certain institutions of the government. This belief embraces the power of the legislature to exert some control over the structure and administration of the executive and judicial branches.

The qualified power of the legislature to tamper with the judiciary is not so grave a danger to the balance of the Constitution as some see it. For even when a judicial decision runs counter to particular—and perhaps pervasive—political interests, the institutional arrangements of the Constitution are such as to slow down the popular outrage and give the people time for "more cool and sedate reflection." And given the distance between the people and LEGISLATION afforded by such devices as REPRESENTATION (with its multiplicity of interests), BICAMERALISM, and the executive VETO POWER, an immediate legislative backlash to judicial behavior is unlikely. Experience demonstrates that any backlash at all is likely to be "weak and ineffectual." But if the negative response is not merely transient and is widely and deeply felt, then the Constitution wisely provides well-defined mechanisms for a deliberate political reaction to what the people hold to be intolerable judicial excesses.

But ultimately the history of court-curbing efforts in America, from the failed IMPEACHMENT of Justice SAMUEL CHASE to the Court-packing plan of FRANKLIN D. ROOSEVELT, teaches one basic lesson: the American political system generally operates to the advantage of the judiciary. Presidential court-packing is ineffective as a means of exerting political influence, and impeachment is too difficult to use as an everyday check against unpopular decisions. Not since John Marshall saw fit pseudonymously to defend his opinion in *McCulloch v. Maryland* (1819) in the public press has any Justice or judge felt obliged to respond to public outrage over a decision.

Political responses to perceived excesses of judicial power tend to take one of two forms: either a policy response against a particular decision or an institutional response against the structure and powers of the courts. In either event, the response may be either partisan or principled. Usually a policy response will take the form of a proposed constitutional amendment or statute designed to overrule a decision. An institutional response will generally seek to make jurisdictional exceptions, to create special courts with specific jurisdiction, or to make adjustments regarding the personnel, administration, or procedures of the judicial branch. Whatever the response, court-curbing is difficult. Although a majority of one of the houses of Congress may object to particular cases of "judicial impertinence," as one congressman viewed Justice DAVID DAVIS's controversial opinion in EX PARTE MILLIGAN (1866), a variety of objections will issue in different views of what should be done.

On the whole, there has consistently been a consensus that tampering with judicial independence is a serious matter and that rash reprisals against the Court as an institution may upset the constitutional balance. Underlying the occasional outbursts of angry public sentiment against the court is that "moral force" of the community of which ALEXIS DE TOCQUEVILLE wrote. On the whole, the American people continue to view the judiciary as the "boast of the Constitution."

For any political attempt to adjust or limit the judicial power to be successful it is necessary that it be—and be perceived to be—a principled rather than a merely partisan response. Only then will the issue of JUDICIAL ACTIVISM be met on a ground high enough to transcend the more common—and generally fruitless—debates over judicial liberalism and conservatism. The deepest issue is not whether a particular decision or even a particular court is too liberal for some and too conservative for others; the point is whether the courts are exercising their powers capably and legitimately. Keeping the courts constitutionally legitimate and institutionally capable benefits both the liberal and the conservative elements in American politics.

The system the Framers devised is so structured that the branch the Framers thought "least dangerous" is not so malleable in the hands of Congress as to be powerless. Yet the threat of congressional restriction of the Court remains, a threat that probably helps to keep an otherwise largely unfettered institution within constitutional bounds.

GARY L. MCDOWELL

Bibliography

BERGER, RAOUL 1969 *Congress versus the Supreme Court.* Cambridge, Mass.: Harvard University Press.

BRECKENRIDGE, A. C. 1971 *Congress Against the Court.* Lincoln: University of Nebraska Press.

MORGAN, DONALD L. 1967 *Congress and the Constitution.* Cambridge, Mass.: Harvard University Press.

MURPHY, WALTER F. 1962 *Congress and the Courts.* Chicago: University of Chicago Press.

CONGRESSIONAL BUDGET AND IMPOUNDMENT CONTROL ACT
88 Stat. 297 (1974)

President RICHARD M. NIXON'S IMPOUNDMENT of billions of dollars appropriated by Congress for purposes which he did not approve amounted to the assertion of virtually uncontrollable power to block any federal program involving monetary expenditures. Nixon used impoundment as a weapon to alter legislative policy rather than to control the total level of government spending.

Congress, in the 1974 act, strengthened its own budgeting process, establishing new budget committees in each house and creating the Congressional Budget Office to give Congress assistance comparable to that given the President by the OFFICE OF MANAGEMENT AND BUDGET. The act required the President to recommend to Congress, in a special message, any proposal to impound funds. Thereafter, either house might veto the impoundment proposal by resolution, thereby forcing release of the funds. If the President refused to comply, the Comptroller General was authorized to seek a court order requiring the President to spend the money. The constitutionality of the LEGISLATIVE VETO was thrown into doubt by the IMMIGRATION AND NATURALIZATION SERVICE v. CHADHA (1983).

PAUL L. MURPHY

(SEE ALSO: *Constitutional History, 1961–1977.*)

CONGRESSIONAL INVESTIGATIONS

See: Legislative Investigations

CONGRESSIONAL MEMBERSHIP

Congress under the ARTICLES OF CONFEDERATION was a unicameral body representing thirteen states. But delegates to the CONSTITUTIONAL CONVENTION, influenced by the example of the British Parliament and almost all of the states, agreed rather early to the principle of a two-house legislature. Members of the House of Representatives were to be popularly elected, with each state's members proportionate to population. But membership in the Senate and selection of senators caused intense controversy.

The large states wanted the Senate also to represent population, but the smaller states were adamantly opposed. They forced a compromise under which every state would have two senators, elected by the state legislatures for six-year terms. This solution gave effect to the federal principle, the Senate representing the states and the House providing popular representation. However, legislative election of senators ultimately proved unacceptable. During the nineteenth century the elections were often marked by scandals and deadlocks, and a rising progressive temper in the country led to adoption of the SEVENTEENTH AMENDMENT in 1913 providing for direct popular election of senators.

The size of the House was initially set by Article I at sixty-five, to be revised thereafter on the basis of decennial censuses. As the population grew and more states were admitted to the Union, Congress increased the number of seats until it reached 435 after the 1910 census. Congress then concluded that further enlargement would make the House unwieldy, and by statute in 1929 fixed 435 as the permanent size of the House.

After each census the 435 House seats are apportioned among the states according to a statutory formula. It is then the responsibility of each state legislature to draw the lines for congressional districts. There was initially no legal obligation to assure equality of population among districts. Particularly in the early twentieth century rural-dominated state legislatures refused to revise district lines to provide equitable representation for growing urban areas. Judicial relief failed when the Supreme Court in COLEGROVE v. GREEN (1946) ruled that drawing the boundary lines of congressional districts was a POLITICAL QUESTION for decision by the state legislatures and Congress, not the courts. This HOLDING was implicitly overruled by the Court in BAKER v. CARR (1962), and in WESBERRY v. SANDERS (1964) the Court made equality of population in congressional districts a constitutional requirement.

The drawing of congressional district lines typically generates bitter legislative controversy as the majority party endeavors to protect its dominance by gerrymandering and incumbents of both parties seek to safeguard their own districts. In numerous states since 1964 legislative deadlocks have required the courts to intervene and draw the district lines.

Members of the House have two-year terms. Proposals for extending the term to four years have been made because of the increased costs of campaigning, longer sessions of Congress, and more complex legislative problems. In the Senate, the fact that only one-third of the seats fall vacant every two years gives it the status of a "continuing body," in contrast to the House which must reconstitute itself and elect its officers every two years.

The presiding officer of the House is its Speaker, chosen by the majority party from among its members. The Speaker has a vote and may on rare occasions participate in debate. The Senate's presiding officer is the vice-president; when serving in this capacity his title is President of the Senate. He has no vote except in case of a tie. The Constitution authorizes the Senate to choose a president *pro tempore* to preside in the absence of the vice-president. The president *pro tempore* is typically the senior member of the majority party.

Article I requires that a senator be thirty years of age, nine years a citizen of the United States, and an inhabitant of the state from which elected. A representative need be only twenty-five years of age and a citizen for seven years. By custom a representative should reside in the district from which elected. Members of Congress are disqualified for appointment to executive office, a provision that prevents the development of anything approaching a parliamentary system. To accept an executive post, a member of Congress must resign.

Each house is authorized to "be the judge of the elections, returns and qualifications of its own members" (Article I, section 5). The "qualifications," it has been established by POWELL v. MCCORMACK (1969), are only the age, residence, and CITIZENSHIP requirements stated in the Constitution. However, on several occasions both houses have in effect enforced additional qualifications by refusing to seat duly elected members who met the constitutional qualifications. In 1900 the House refused to seat a Utah polygamist; similar action was taken in 1919 against a Wisconsin socialist who had been convicted under the ESPIONAGE ACT for opposing American participation in World War I. The most prominent black member of Congress, Adam Clayton Powell, was denied his seat in 1967. There was a judgment of criminal contempt outstanding against him, and his conduct as a committee chairman had been irregular. The Supreme Court ruled, however, that he possessed the constitutional qualifications and so could not be denied his seat. Members of Congress cannot be impeached, but they are subject to vote of censure by their chamber, and to expulsion by two-thirds vote. The Court indicated that the House might have expelled Powell for his alleged conduct. Vacancies in the Senate can be filled by the state governor, but in the House only by special election.

Members of Congress have immunity from arrest during legislative sessions except for cases of "TREASON, FELONY and breach of the peace" (Article I, section 6). They are guaranteed FREEDOM OF SPEECH by the provision that "for any speech or debate in either house, they shall not be questioned in any other place." (See SPEECH OR DEBATE CLAUSE.) The purpose is to prevent intimidation of legislators by the executive or threat of prosecution for libel or slander. They can be held accountable for statements or actions in their legislative capacity only by their own colleagues. This immunity covers not only speeches in Congress but also written reports, resolutions offered, the act of voting, and all other things generally done in a legislative session. However, immunity does not extend to press releases, newsletters, or telephone calls to executive agencies, the Supreme Court held in HUTCHINSON v. PROXMIRE (1979). Also, taking a bribe to influence legislation is not a "legislative act," according to BREWSTER v. UNITED STATES (1972).

C. HERMAN PRITCHETT

Bibliography

DAVIDSON, ROGER H. and OLESZEK, WALTER J. 1985 *Congress and Its Members,* 2nd ed. Washington, D.C.: Congressional Quarterly.

CONGRESSIONAL PRIVILEGES AND IMMUNITIES

The Constitution specifically protects members of Congress against interference with their deliberative function. The special privileges and immunities attendant on CONGRESSIONAL MEMBERSHIP are contained in the first clause of Article I, section 6, of the Constitution. The Framers of the Constitution, familiar with the devices used by the British king against members of Parliament and by royal governors against members of the provincial legislatures, sought to insulate the members of the federal legislature against pressures that might preclude independence of judgment.

The PRIVILEGE FROM ARREST, other than for TREASON, FELONY, or BREACH OF THE PEACE, has been known in Anglo-American constitutional history since the advent of parliaments; WILLIAM BLACKSTONE cited an ancient Gothic law as evidence of the privilege's immemorial origins. The English Parliament claimed freedom of debate, that is, immunity from prosecution or civil lawsuit resulting from utterances in Parliament, at least from the thirteenth century; that immunity was finally established in the English BILL OF RIGHTS (1689). In America, privilege from arrest during legislative sessions was first granted in Virginia in 1623, and freedom of debate was first recognized in the FUNDAMENTAL ORDERS OF CONNECTICUT (1639).

The ARTICLES OF CONFEDERATION extended both the privilege from arrest and the freedom of debate to members of Congress, in words transcribed almost verbatim from the English Bill of Rights: "Freedom of speech and debate in Congress shall not be impeached or questioned in any court, or place out of Congress, and the members of Congress shall be protected in their persons from arrests and imprisonments, during the time of their going to and from, and attendance on Congress, except for treason, felony, or breach of the peace." At the CONSTITUTIONAL CONVENTION, these congressional privileges and immunities first appeared in the report of the Committee of Detail; they were agreed to without debate and without dissent. The Committee of Style gave final form to the wording of the clause.

The privilege from arrest, limited as it is to arrest for debt, no longer has any practical application. The immunity from having to answer in court, or in any other place out of Congress, for congressional SPEECH OR DEBATE is now primarily a shield against civil actions by private parties rather than against an executive jealous of his prerogative. That shield has been expanded to protect the whole legislative process, but not, as one senator learned to his chagrin in HUTCHINSON V. PROXMIRE (1979), to every public utterance of a member of Congress concerning a public issue.

DENNIS J. MAHONEY

Bibliography

WORMSER, MICHAEL D., ED. 1982 *Guide to Congress,* 3rd ed. Pages 850–855. Washington, D.C.: Congressional Quarterly.

CONGRESSIONAL VETO

See: Legislative Veto

CONKLING, ROSCOE (1829–1888)

A New York attorney, congressman (1859–1863, 1865–1867), and senator (1867–1881), Roscoe Conkling in 1861 initiated legislation creating the Joint Committee on the Conduct of the War. In 1865, as a member of the JOINT COMMITTEE ON RECONSTRUCTION, Conkling supported CIVIL RIGHTS for blacks. In 1867 he sponsored military reconstruction legislation. Conkling and other supporters of the bill argued that the South was still in the "grasp of war" and only a military occupation and Reconstruction would insure protection of the freedmen. After Reconstruction Conkling continued to support civil rights and helped Frederick Douglass become the first black Recorder of Deeds in Washington, D.C. Douglass placed Conkling alongside ULYSSES S. GRANT, CHARLES SUMNER, and BENJAMIN F. BUTLER as a protector of freedmen. In 1880 Conkling led a movement to renominate Grant because of disagreements with President RUTHERFORD B. HAYES over Reconstruction and patronage. In 1881 Conkling resigned his Senate seat to protest JAMES A. GARFIELD's appointments in New York State. As the undisputed leader of the New York Republican party, Conkling thought he, and not the President, should dispense patronage in the Empire State. Earlier he had opposed Hayes's attempts to remove federal officeholders in New York and had defended CHESTER A. ARTHUR from corruption charges. In 1873 Conkling declined Grant's offer of the Chief Justiceship of the United States; in 1882 the Senate confirmed him for an Associate Justiceship, but he declined to serve.

PAUL FINKELMAN

Bibliography

JORDON, DAVID M. 1971 *Roscoe Conkling of New York: Voice in the Senate.* Ithaca, N.Y.: Cornell University Press.

CONNALLY, THOMAS T. (TOM) (1877–1963)

A conservative Texas Democrat and internationalist, Tom Connally, as he officially called himself, served twelve years in the House of Representatives and twenty-four in the Senate. When he retired from politics in 1953, he said he was most proud of his leadership against FRANKLIN D. ROOSEVELT's Court-packing plan of 1937 and in favor of the creation of the United Nations. Connally's main achievements were in the field of FOREIGN AFFAIRS, from managing the Lend Lease Act to confirmation of the NORTH ATLANTIC TREATY. He was cool toward much of the New Deal, except when it benefited Texas cattle, oil, and cotton interests. The Supreme Court struck down the Connally "Hot Oil" Act in PANAMA REFINING CO.

v. RYAN (1935), but he secured a revised measure that constitutionally prohibited the shipment in INTERSTATE COMMERCE of oil produced in excess of government quotas. He opposed every CIVIL RIGHTS measure that came before the Senate and joined every southern filibuster, preventing the enactment of anti-lynching and anti-POLL TAX bills. Connally was one of the last of colorful, powerful, demagogic, and grandiloquent southern politicians who affected a drawl, string-tie, frock coat, and flowing hair.

LEONARD W. LEVY

Bibliography

CONNALLY, TOM and STEINBERG, ALFRED 1954 *My Name Is Tom Connally.* New York: Crowell.

CONNECTICUT COMPROMISE

See: Great Compromise

CONQUERED PROVINCES THEORY

"Conquered provinces" was one of a half dozen constitutional theories concerning the relationship of the seceded states and the Union. Representative THADDEUS STEVENS (Republican, Pennsylvania), the principal exponent of conquered provinces, argued that SECESSION had been de jure as well as de facto effective, and destroyed the normal constitutional status of the seceded states. Union victory required that they be governed under the principles of international law, which would have authorized essentially unlimited congressional latitude in setting Reconstruction policy. Congressional legislation for the ex-states had to be based on the premise that "the foundation of their institutions, both political, municipal, and social, must be broken up and relaid." This was to be accomplished through extensive confiscation of Confederates' properties and the abolition of slavery. The state constitutions would have to be rewritten and submitted to Congress, which would then readmit each "province" as a new state.

Other principal theories of Reconstruction were: territorialization, popular among some Republicans since 1861, which would have treated the seceded states as territories; STATE SUICIDE, expounded by CHARLES SUMNER since 1862; state indestructibility, the basis of varying southern and presidential views, and being the central assumption of ABRAHAM LINCOLN's programs; Richard Henry Dana's "Grasp of War" theory of 1865, which would have sanctioned congressional policy under the WAR POWERS; and forfeited rights, a theory propounded by Rep. Samuel Shellabarger (Republican, Ohio), which ultimately came as close as any to being the constitutional basis of congressional Republican Reconstruction.

Stevens's conquered provinces theory was logically consistent with Republican objectives, and Lincoln's policies concerning the wartime Reconstruction of Louisiana, Arkansas, and Tennessee resembled parts of Stevens's program. But because the idea of conquered provinces was widely considered unconstitutional and draconian, it was never adopted as the basis of Republican policy.

WILLIAM M. WIECEK

Bibliography

MCKITRICK, ERIC L. 1960 *Andrew Johnson and Reconstruction.* Chicago: University of Chicago Press.

CONSCIENTIOUS OBJECTION

A conscientious objector is a person who is opposed in conscience to engaging in socially required behavior. Since the genuine objector will not be easily forced into acts he abhors and since compelling people to violate their own moral scruples is usually undesirable in a liberal society, those who formulate legal rules face the question whether conscientious objectors should be excused from legal requirements imposed on others. The issue is most striking in relation to compulsory military service: should those whose consciences forbid killing be conscripted for combat? Historically, conscientious objection has been considered mainly in that context, and the clash has been understood as between secular obligation and the sense of religious duty felt by members of pacifist sects. The Constitution says nothing directly about conscientious objection, and for most of the country's existence Congress was thought to have a free hand in deciding whether to afford any exemption and how to define the class of persons who would benefit. By now, it is evident that the religion clauses of the FIRST AMENDMENT impose significant constraints on how Congress may draw lines between those who receive an exemption from military service and those who do not. The Supreme Court has never accepted the argument that Congress is constitutionally required to establish an exemption from military service, but it has indicated that the Constitution does entitle some individuals to exemption from certain other sorts of compulsory laws.

The principle that society should excuse conscientious objectors from military service was widely recognized in the colonies and states prior to adoption of the Constitution. JAMES MADISON's original proposal for the BILL OF RIGHTS included a clause that "no person religiously scrupulous of bearing arms shall be compelled to render military service in person," but that clause was dropped, partly because conscription was considered a state function. The 1864 Draft Act and the SELECTIVE SERVICE ACT of 1917 both contained exemptions limited to members of religious denominations whose creeds forbade participation in war. The 1917 act excused objectors only from combatant service, but the War Department permitted some of those also opposed to noncombatant military service to be released for civilian service.

The 1940 Selective Service Act set the basic terms of exemption from the system of compulsory military service that operated during World War II, the KOREAN WAR, and the Vietnam War, and during the intervening periods of uneasy peace. A person was eligible "who, by reason of religious training and belief, [was] conscientiously opposed to participation in war in any form." Someone opposed even to noncombatant service could perform alternate civilian service. In response to a court of appeals decision interpreting "religious training and belief" very broadly, Congress in 1948 said that religious belief meant belief "in relation to a Supreme Being involving duties superior to those arising from any human relation. . . ." What Congress had attempted to do was relatively clear. It wanted to excuse only persons opposed to participation in all wars, not those opposed to particular wars, and it wanted to excuse only those whose opposition derived from religious belief in a rather traditional sense. The important Supreme Court cases have dealt with these lines of distinction.

By dint of strained interpretation of the statute, the Court has avoided a clear decision whether Congress could limit the exemption to traditional religious believers. First, in UNITED STATES V. SEEGER (1965), a large majority said that an applicant who spoke of a "religious faith in a purely ethical creed" was entitled to the exemption because his belief occupied a place in his life parallel to that of a belief in God for the more orthodox. Then, in *Welsh v. United States* (1970), four Justices held that someone who laid no claim to being religious at all qualified because his ethical beliefs occupied a place in his life parallel to that of religious beliefs for others. Four other Justices acknowledged that Congress had explicitly meant to exclude such applicants. Justice JOHN MARSHALL HARLAN urged that an attempt to distinguish religious objectors from equally sincere nonreligious ones constituted a forbidden ESTABLISHMENT OF RELIGION; the three other Justices thought that Congress could favor religious objectors in order to promote the free exercise of religion. Because the plurality's view of the statute was so implausible, most observers have supposed that its members probably agreed with Justice Harlan about the ultimate constitutional issue, but this particular tension between "no establishment" and "free exercise" concepts has not yet been decisively resolved.

In *Gillette v. United States* (1971), a decision covering both religious and nonreligious objectors to the Vietnam War, the Court upheld Congress's determination not to exempt those opposed to participation in particular wars. Against the claim that the distinction between "general" and "selective" objectors was impermissible, the Court responded that the distinction was supported by the public interest in a fairly administered system, given the difficulty officials would have dealing consistently with the variety of objections to particular wars. The Court also rejected the claim that the selective objector's entitlement to free exercise of his religion created a constitutionally grounded right to avoid military service.

In other limited areas, the Court has taken the step of acknowledging a free exercise right to be exempt from a generally imposed obligation. Those religiously opposed to jury duty cannot be compelled to serve, and adherents of traditional religious groups that provide an alternative way of life for members cannot be required to send children to school beyond the eighth grade. (See WISCONSIN V. YODER, 1972.) Nor can a person be deprived of unemployment benefits when an unwillingness to work on Saturday is religiously based, though receptivity to jobs including Saturday work is a usual condition of eligibility. (See SHERBERT V. VERNER, 1963.) What these cases suggest is that if no powerful secular reason can be advanced for demanding uniform compliance, the Constitution may require that persons with substantial religious objections be excused. To this degree the Constitution itself requires special treatment for conscientious objectors. Beyond that, its recognition of religious liberty and of governmental impartiality toward religions provides a source of values for legislative choice and constrains the classifications legislatures may make.

KENT GREENAWALT

Bibliography

FINN, JAMES, ED. 1968 *A Conflict of Loyalties.* New York: Pegasus.

GREENAWALT, KENT 1972 All or Nothing At All: The Defeat of Selective Conscientious Objection. *Supreme Court Review* 1971: 31–94.

SIBLEY, MULFORD QUICKERT and JACOB, PHILIP E. 1952 *Conscription of Conscience: The American State and the Conscientious Objector, 1940–1947.* Ithaca, N.Y.: Cornell University Press.

CONSCRIPTION

The power of the federal government to conscript may derive either from its power to raise armies or, more debatably, from its broadly interpreted power to regulate commerce. It is restricted by the THIRTEENTH AMENDMENT's prohibition of involuntary servitude or, conceivably, by the Fifth Amendment's guarantee of liberty. The manner in which conscription is conducted must comport with a familiar range of constitutional protections, notably those that guarantee EQUAL PROTECTION and RELIGIOUS LIBERTY.

Though the nation has employed systems of military conscription during the Civil War, both World Wars, and for all but twelve months between 1945 and 1972, the interplay of these different constitutional considerations has been remarkably underdeveloped. Two hundred years after the Constitution was written, at least two fundamental questions about conscription remain unresolved. What is the power of Congress (or the states) to conscript for civilian purposes? How, if at all, is a conscription system obliged to take account of CONSCIENTIOUS OBJECTION?

The ambiguity surrounding these questions derives in part from the fact that although the constitutionality of military conscription is well settled, the issue has not been settled well. In SELECTIVE DRAFT LAW CASES (1917) the Supreme Court reviewed the World War I military conscription statute and declared that it was "unable to conceive" how the performance of the "supreme and noble duty" of military service in time of war "can be said to be the imposition of involuntary servitude." Therefore, in its view, this contention was "precluded by its mere statement."

This terse comment establishes no conceptual basis for the analysis of later questions. Unfortunately, also, history is not a particularly helpful guide. The intention of the Framers is not clear. At the time of the Constitution, it was accepted that state militias could conscript soldiers, but the central government could not do so. At the same time, the Constitution gave the Congress the power to "raise armies" and it was widely recognized that it could not tenably rely on volunteers. On the basis of this evidence some scholars have argued that to conclude that conscription (as opposed to enlistment) was a power given to Congress is logical, and others have called this conclusion absurd.

Legislative history and judicial PRECEDENT in this first century of the Republic are similarly uninformative. When the Supreme Court decided the *Selective Draft Law Cases* it had only two precedents for a military draft: first, Secretary of War JAMES MONROE's proposal for conscription during the War of 1812, a proposal still under compromise deliberation by Congress when peace arrived; and, second, the Civil War Enrollment Act, the constitutionality of which had been ruled on only by a sharply divided and perplexed Supreme Court of Pennsylvania.

The most significant judicial precedent, *Butler v. Perry* (1916), had been decided only a year before by the Supreme Court itself. Here the Court rejected a Thirteenth Amendment challenge to a Florida statute requiring adult men to work one week a year on public roads: "from colonial days to the present time, conscripted labor has been much relied on for the construction and maintenance of public roads," and the Thirteenth Amendment "certainly was not intended to interdict enforcement of those duties which individuals owe to the state."

No subsequent Supreme Court decision limits this sweeping view of the power to conscript. To the contrary, the Court held in *United States v. Macintosh* (1931) that the right of conscientious objection is only statutory and in ROSTKER V. GOLDBERG (1981) that the government can compel an all-male military registration in the face of equal protection contentions founded on a theory of SEX DISCRIMINATION.

Notwithstanding these decisions, it seems likely that a major constitutional issue would arise if the power to conscript were asserted more aggressively. Such an issue might arise if, for example, participation were coerced in a system of civilian national service or if the statutory right of conscientious objection were abolished. In that event, the question thus far begged—what "duties . . . individuals owe to the state"—would have to be, for the first time, seriously addressed.

RICHARD DANZIG
IRA NERKEN

Bibliography

ANDERSON, MARTIN and BLOOM, VALERIE 1976 *Conscription: A Select and Annotated Bibliography.* Stanford, Calif.: Hoover Institution Press.

FRIEDMAN, LEON 1969 Conscription and the Constitution: The Original Understanding. *Michigan Law Review* 67:1493–1552.

MALBIN, MICHAEL J. 1972 Conscription, the Constitution, and the Framers: An Historial Analysis. *Fordham Law Review* 40:805–826.

CONSENT DECREE

In a civil suit in EQUITY, such as a suit for an INJUNCTION or a DECLARATORY JUDGMENT, the court's order is called a decree. By negotiation, the plaintiff and the defendant may agree to ask the court to enter a decree that they have drafted. If the court approves, its order is called a consent decree. Federal courts frequently enter consent degrees in actions to enforce regulatory laws in fields such as antitrust, EMPLOYMENT DISCRIMINATION, and ENVIRONMENTAL REGULATION.

KENNETH L. KARST

(SEE ALSO: *Antitrust Law and the Constitution; Plea Bargaining.*)

CONSENT SEARCH

When an individual consents to a search, he effectively waives his rights under the FOURTH AMENDMENT and makes it unnecessary for the police to obtain a SEARCH WARRANT. In determining the validity of such a consent, the trial court must determine whether the consent was voluntary. The consent of a person illegally held is not considered voluntary. However, an explicit warning about one's constitutional rights, which MIRANDA V. ARIZONA (1966) made mandatory for custodial interrogation, is not a condition for effective consent to a search, under the decision in SCHNECKLOTH V. BUSTAMONTE (1973).

Consent must obviously be obtained from a person entitled to grant it. Not ownership of the premises but the right to occupy and use them to the exclusion of others is the decisive criterion. Thus, the consent of a landlord to search premises let to others is worthless. The consenting party controls the terms of the consent: it may be as broad or as narrow as he wishes to make it, allowing a search of an entire dwelling or merely of one small item.

For a consent by another person to be valid as against a defendant, it must be shown that the consenting party possessed common authority in the place or things searched. Anyone with joint access or control of the premises may consent to a search.

JACOB W. LANDYNSKI

Bibliography

LAFAVE, WAYNE R. 1978 *Search and Seizure: A Treatise on the Fourth Amendment.* Vol. 2:610–774. St. Paul, Minn.: West Publishing Co.

CONSPIRACY

See: Criminal Conspiracy

CONSTITUTION

At the time of the Stamp Act controversy, a British lord told BENJAMIN FRANKLIN that Americans had wrong ideas about the British constitution. British and American ideas did differ radically. The American Revolution repudiated the British understanding of the constitution; in a sense, the triumph in America of a novel concept of "constitution" *was* the "revolution." The British, who were vague about their unwritten constitution, meant by it their system of government, the COMMON LAW, royal proclamations, major legislation such as MAGNA CARTA and the BILL OF RIGHTS, and various usages and customs of government animating the aggregation of laws, institutions, rights, and practices that had evolved over centuries. Statute, however, was the supreme part of the British constitution. After the Glorious Revolution of 1688–1689, Parliament dominated the constitutional system and by ordinary legislation could and did alter it. Sir WILLIAM BLACKSTONE summed up parliamentary supremacy when he declared in his *Commentaries* (1766), "What Parliament doth, no power on earth can undo."

The principle that Parliament had unlimited power was at the crux of the controversy leading to the American Revolution. The American assertion that government is limited undergirded the American concept of a constitution as a FUNDAMENTAL LAW that imposes regularized restraints upon power and reserves rights to the people. The American concept emerged slowly through the course of the colonial period, yet its nub was present almost from the beginning, especially in New England where covenant theology, SOCIAL COMPACT THEORY, and HIGHER LAW theory blended together. THOMAS HOOKER in 1638 preached that the foundation of authority lay in the people who might choose their governors and "set bounds and limitations on their powers." A century later Jared Elliot of Massachusetts preached that a "legal government" exists when the sovereign power "puts itself under restraints and lays itself under limitations. This is what we call a legal, limited, and well constituted government." Some liberal theologians viewed God himself as a constitutional monarch, limited in power because he had limited himself to the terms of his covenant with mankind. Moreover God ruled a constitutional universe based on immutable natural laws that also bound him. Jonathan Mayhew preached in Boston that no one has a right to exercise a wanton SOVEREIGNTY over the property, lives, and consciences of the people—"such a sovereignty as some inconsiderately ascribe to the supreme governor of the world." Mayhew explained that "God himself does not govern in an absolute, arbitrary, and despotic manner. The power of this almighty king is limited by law; not indeed, by acts of Parliament, but by the eternal laws of truth, wisdom, and equity. . . ."

Political theory and law as well as religion taught that government was limited; so did history. But the Americans took their views on such matters from a highly selective and romanticized image of seventeenth-century England, which they perpetuated in America even as England changed. Seventeenth-century England was the England of the great struggle for constitutional liberty by the common law courts and Puritan parliaments against despotic Stuart kings. Seventeenth-century England was the England of EDWARD COKE, JOHN LILBURNE, and JOHN LOCKE. It was an England in which religion, law, and politics converged with theory and experience to produce limited monarchy and, ironically, parliamentary supremacy. To Americans, however, Parliament had bound itself by reaffirming Magna Carta and passing the HABEAS CORPUS ACT, the Bill of Rights, and the TOLERATION ACT, among others. Locke had taught the social contract theory; advocated that taxation without representation or consent is tyranny; written that "government is not free to do as it pleases," and referred to the "bounds" which "the law of God and Nature have set to the legislative power of every commonwealth, in all forms of government."

Such ideas withered but did not die in eighteenth-century England. CATO'S LETTERS popularized Locke on both sides of the Atlantic; Henry St. John (Viscount Bolingbroke) believed that Parliament could not annul the constitution; Charles Viner's *General Abridgment of Law and Equity* endorsed Coke's views in Dr. BONHAM'S CASE (1610); and even as Parliament debated the Declaratory Act (1766), which asserted parliamentary power to legislate for America "in all cases whatsoever," CHARLES PRATT (Lord Camden) declared such a power "absolutely illegal, contrary to the fundamental laws of . . . this constitution. . . ." Richard Price and Granville Sharpe were two of the many English radicals who shared the American view of the British constitution.

TAXATION WITHOUT REPRESENTATION provoked Americans to clarify their views. JAMES OTIS, arguing against the tax on sugar, relied on *Dr. Bonham's Case* and contended that legislative authority did not extend to the "fundamentals of the constitution," which he believed to be fixed. THOMAS HUTCHINSON, a leading supporter of Parliament, summed up the American constitutional reaction to the stamp tax duties by writing, "The prevailing reason at this time is, that the Act of Parliament is against Magna Charta and the NATURAL RIGHTS of Englishmen, and therefore according to Lord Coke, null and void." The TOWNSHEND ACT duties led to American declarations that the supreme legislature in any free state derives its power from the constitution, which limits government. JOHN DICKINSON, in an essay reprinted throughout the colonies, wrote that a free people are not those subject to a reasonable exercise of government power but those "who live under a government so constitutionally checked and controlled, that proper provision is made against its being otherwise exercised." J. J. Zubly of Georgia was another of many who argued that no government, not even Parliament, could make laws against the constitution any more than it could alter the constitution. An anonymous pamphleteer rhapsodized in 1775 about the "glorious constitution worthy to be engraved in capitals of gold, on pillars of marble; to be perpetuated through all time, a barrier, to circumscribe and bound the restless ambition of aspiring monarchs, and the palladium of civil liberty. . . ." TOM PAINE actually argued that Great Britain had no constitution, because Parliament claimed to exercise any power it pleased. To Paine a constitution could not be an act of the government but of "people constituting government. . . . A constitution is a thing antecedent to a government; a government is only the creature of the constitution."

Thus, by "constitution," Americans meant a supreme law creating the government, limiting it, unalterable by it, and above it. When they said that an act of government was unconstitutional, they meant that the government had acted lawlessly because it lacked the authority to perform that act. Accordingly the act was not law; it was null and void, and it could be disobeyed. By contrast when the British spoke of a statute being unconstitutional, they meant only that it was impolitic, unwise, unjust, or inexpedient, but not that it was beyond the power of the government to enact. They did not mean that Parliament was limited in its powers and had exceeded them.

The American view of "constitution" was imperfectly understood even by many leaders of the revolutionary movement as late as 1776. The proof is that when the states framed their first constitutions, the task was left to legislatures, although some received explicit authorization from the voters. THOMAS JEFFERSON worried because Virginia had not differentiated fundamental from ordinary law. Not until Massachusetts framed its constitution of 1780 by devising a CONSTITUTIONAL CONVENTION did the American theory match practice. When the CONSTITUTIONAL CONVENTION OF 1787 met in Philadelphia, the American meaning of a constitution was fixed and consistent.

LEONARD W. LEVY

Bibliography

ADAMS, RANDOLPH G. (1922)1958 3rd ed. *Political Ideas of the American Revolution.* New York: Barnes & Noble.

BAILYN, BERNARD 1967 *Ideological Origins of the American Revolution.* Cambridge, Mass.: Harvard University Press.

BALDWIN, ALICE M. (1928) 1958 *The New England Clergy and the American Revolution.* New York: Frederick Ungar.

MCLAUGHLIN, ANDREW C. 1932 *The Foundations of American Constitutionalism.* New York: New York University Press.

MULLETT, CHARLES F. 1933 *Fundamental Law and the American Revolution.* New York: Columbia University Press.

CONSTITUTIONAL COMMON LAW

"Constitutional common law" refers to a theory about the lawmaking competence of the federal courts. The theory postulates that much of what passes as constitutional adjudication is best understood as a judicially fashioned COMMON LAW authorized and inspired, but not compelled, by the constitutional text and structure. Unlike the "true" constitutional law exemplified by MARBURY V. MADISON (1803), constitutional common law is ultimately amenable to control and revision by Congress. The theory originated in an effort to explain how the Supreme Court could legitimately insist upon application of the EXCLUSIONARY RULE in state criminal proceedings, once the Court had recast the exclusionary rule as simply a judicially fashioned remedy designed to deter future unlawful police conduct rather than as part and parcel of a criminal defendant's underlying constitutional rights or a necessary remedy for the violation thereof. On this view of the exclusionary rule, why does the state court have a constitutional obligation to do more than provide an "adequate" remedy for the underlying constitutional violation, such as an action for DAMAGES? The source of the Supreme Court's authority to insist that the state courts follow any rule not required by the constitution or authorized by some federal statute is not evident. ERIE RAILROAD V. TOMPKINS (1938) makes plain that the federal courts have no power to create a general FEDERAL COMMON LAW. This limitation exists not simply because of Congress's express statutory command, applicable to civil cases in the federal district courts, but because of the perception that there is no general federal judicial power to displace state law. To the contrary, the courts must point to some authoritative source—a statute, a treaty, a constitutional provision—as explicitly or implicitly authorizing judicial creation of substantive federal law. That federal statutes can constitute such authority has long been clear, and the result has been in many areas judicial creation of a federal common law designed to implement federal statutory policies. There is no a priori reason to suppose that the Constitution itself should differ from statutes in providing a basis for the generation of an interstitial federal common law. Not surprisingly, therefore, a significant body of federal common law has been developed on the basis of constitutional provisions. For example, the Supreme Court has developed bodies of federal substantive law on the basis of the constitutional (and statutory) grants of jurisdiction to hear cases in ADMIRALTY, as well as cases involving disputes among the states or implicating FOREIGN AFFAIRS. Because the Court's decisions are ultimately reversible by Congress, its decisions holding statutes to be invalid burdens upon INTERSTATE COMMERCE are also best understood as federal common law created by the Court on the authority of the COMMERCE CLAUSE.

In the foregoing examples, constitutional common law has been created to govern situations where state interests are subordinated to interests of special concern to the national government, and thus come within the reach of the plenary national legislative power. They are FEDERALISM cases, in that the federal common law implements and fills out the authority that has been committed to the national government by the constitutional text and structure. Thus, the principle of these cases arguably is limited to the generation of federal constitutional common law in support of national legislative competence. These "federalism" cases do not by themselves establish that the Court may fashion a common law based solely upon constitutional provisions framed as *limitations* on governmental power in order to vindicate CIVIL LIBERTIES, such as those protected by the FIRST AMENDMENT and FOURTH AMENDMENT. Such a judicial rulemaking authority—which seeks to create federal rules in areas of primary *state* concern—intersects with federalism concerns in ways that sets these cases apart from the federalism cases. Moreover, at the national level judicial creation of common law implicates SEPARATION OF POWERS considerations. Nonetheless, the Court's constitutionally based common law decisions in areas of plenary national legislative authority at least invite inquiry whether the specific constitutional guarantees of individual liberty might also authorize the creation of a substructure of judicially fashioned rules to carry out the purposes and policies of those guarantees. Several COMMENTATORS have, directly or indirectly, argued for acceptance of judicial power to fashion such a subconstitutional law of civil liberties. They argue that recognition of such a power is the most satisfactory way to rationalize a large and steadily growing body of judicial decision, not only in the criminal procedure area but also with many of the Court's administrative DUE PROCESS cases, while at the same time recognizing a coordinate and controlling authority in Congress. There has, however, been no significant judicial consideration of this theory apart from the decision in *Turpin v. Mailet* (2d Cir., *en banc,* 1978–1979).

Whatever its perceived advantages, a theory that posits a competence in the courts to fashion a constitutionally inspired constitutional common law of civil liberties must deal adequately with a series of objections: that development of such a body of law is inconsistent with the original intent of the Framers; that the line between true constitutional interpretation and constitutional common law is too indeterminate to be useful; and that the existence of such judicial power is inconsistent with the autonomy of the executive department in enforcing law as well as the rightful independence of the states in the federal system. The theory of constitutional common law bears a family resemblance to the views of those commentators who hold that the Court may legitimately engage in "noninterpretive" review—that is, the Court may properly impose values on the political branches not fairly inferrable from the constitutional text or the structure it creates—but who insist that Congress may control those decisions by regulating the JURISDICTION of the Supreme Court. Other differences aside, the constitutional common law view would permit Congress to overrule the noninterpretive decisions directly, bypassing the awkward theoretical and political problems associated with congressional attempts to manipulate jurisdiction for substantive ends.

HENRY P. MONAGHAN

Bibliography

MONAGHAN, HENRY P. 1975 The Supreme Court, 1974 Term—Foreword: Constitutional Common Law. *Harvard Law Review* 89:1–45.

SCHROCK, THOMAS S. and WELSH, ROBERT C. 1978 Reconsidering the Constitutional Common Law. *Harvard Law Review* 91:1117–1176.

CONSTITUTIONAL CONVENTION

Constitutional conventions, like the written constitutions that they produce, are among the American contributions to government. A constitutional convention became the means that a free people used to put into practice the SOCIAL COMPACT THEORY by devising their FUNDAMENTAL LAW. Such a convention is a representative body acting for the sovereign people to whom it is responsible. Its sole commission is to frame a CONSTITUTION; it does not pass laws, perform acts of administration, or govern in any way. It submits its work for popular ratification and adjourns. Such a convention first came into being during the American Revolution. The institutionalizing of constitutional principles during wartime was the constructive achievement of the Revolution. The Revolution's enduring heroics are to be found in constitution-making. As JAMES MADISON exultantly declared, "Nothing has excited more admiration in the world than the manner in which free governments have been established in America; for it was the first instance, from the creation of the world . . . that free inhabitants have been seen deliberating on a form of government and selecting such of their citizens as possessed their confidence, to determine upon and give effect to it."

Within a century of 1776 nearly two hundred state constitutional conventions had been held in the United States. The institution is so familiar that we forget how novel it was even in 1787. At the CONSTITUTIONAL CONVENTION, which framed this nation's constitution, OLIVER ELLSWORTH declared that since the framing of the ARTICLES OF CONFEDERATION (1781), "a new sett [sic] of ideas seemed to have crept in. . . . Conventions of the people, or with power derived expressly from the people, were not then thought of. The Legislatures were considered as competent."

Credit for understanding that legislatures were not competent for that task belongs to JOHN LILBURNE, the English Leveller leader, who probably originated the idea of a constitutional convention. In his *Legall Fundamentall Liberties* (1649), he proposed that specially elected representatives should frame an Agreement of the People, or constitution, "which Agreement ought to be above Law; and therefore [set] bounds, limits, and extent of the people's Legislative Deputies in Parliament." Similarly, Sir Henry Vane, once governor of Massachusetts, proposed, in his *Healing Question* (1656), that a "convention" be chosen by the free consent of the people, "not properly to exercise the legislative power" but only to agree on "fundamentall constitutions" expressing the will of the people "in their highest state of soveraignty. . . ." The idea, which never made headway in England, was reexpressed in a pamphlet by Obadiah Hulme in 1771, recommending that a constitution should "be formed by a convention of delegates of the people, appointed for the express purpose," and that the constitution should never be "altered in any respect by any power besides the power which first framed [it]." Hulme's work was reprinted in Philadelphia in 1776 immediately before the framing of the PENNSYLVANIA CONSTITUTION by a specially elected convention. That convention, however, in accordance with prevailing ideas, simultaneously exercised the powers of government and after promulgating its constitution remained in session as the state legislature. Until 1780 American legislatures wrote constitutions.

The theory underlying a constitutional convention, but not the actual idea of having one, was first proposed in America by the town meeting of Pittsfield, Massachusetts, on May 29, 1776. Massachusetts then had a provisional revolutionary extralegal government. Pittsfield asked, "What Compact has been formed as the foundation of Government in this province?" The collapse of British power over the colonies had thrown the people, "the foundation of power," into "a state of Nature." The first step to restore civil government on a permanent basis was "the formation of a fundamental Constitution as the Basis & ground work of Legislation." The existing legislature, Pittsfield contended, although representative, could not make the constitution because, "They being but servants of the people cannot be greater than their Masters, & must be responsible to them." A constitution is "above the whole Legislature," so that the "legislature cannot certainly make it. . . ." Pittsfield understood the difference between fundamental and ordinary law, yet inconsistently concluded that the legislature should frame the constitution on condition that it be submitted to the people for ratification.

Pittsfield was merely inconsistent, but the Continental Congress was bewildered. The provisional government of Massachusetts, requesting advice from Congress on how to institute government, said that it would accept a constitution proposed by Congress. That was in May 1775. Many years later, when his memory was not to be trusted, JOHN ADAMS recalled in his autobiography that congressmen went around asking each other, "How can the people institute government?" As late as May 1776, Congress, still lacking an answer, merely recommended that colonies without adequate governments should choose representatives to suppress royal authority and exercise power under popular authority. By then the temporary legislatures of New Hampshire and South Carolina, without popular authorization, had already framed and promulgated constitutions as if enacting statutory law, and continued to operate as legislatures. Adams, however, credited himself with knowing how to "realize [make real] the theories of the wisest writers," who had urged that sovereignty resides in the people and that government is made by contract. "This could be done," he explained, "only by conventions of representatives chosen by the people in the several colonies. . . ." How, congressmen asked him, can we know whether the people will submit to the new constitutions, and he recalled having replied, if there is doubt, "the convention may send out their project of a constitution, to the people in their several towns, counties, or districts, and the people may make the acceptance of it their own act." Congress did not follow his advice, he wrote, because of his "new, strange, and terrible doctrines."

Adams had described a procedure followed only in Massachusetts, and only after the legislature had asked the people of the towns for permission to frame a constitution and submit it for popular ratification. Several towns, led by Concord (see CONCORD TOWN MEETING RESOLUTIONS) protested that the legislature was not a competent body for the task, because a constitution had been overwhelmingly rejected in 1778. Concord had demanded a constitutional convention. In 1779 the legislature asked the towns to vote on the question whether a state constitution should be framed by a specially elected convention. The towns, voting by universal manhood suffrage, overwhelmingly approved. In late 1779 the delegates to the first constitutional convention in world history met in Cambridge and framed the MASSACHUSETTS CONSTITUTION of 1780, which the voters ratified after an intense public debate. With pride Thomas Dawes declared in an oration, "The people of Massachusetts have reduced to practice the wonderful theory. A numerous people have convened in a state of nature, and, like our ideas of the patriarchs, have authorized a few fathers of the land to draw up for them a glorious covenant." New Hampshire copied the procedure when revising its constitution in 1784, and it rapidly became standard procedure. Within a few years American constitutional theory had progressed from the belief that legislatures were competent to compose and announce constitutions, to the belief that a convention acting for the sovereign people is the only proper instrument for the task and that the sovereign must have the final word. A constitution, then, in American theory, is the supreme fundamental law that creates the legislature, authorizes its powers, and limits the exercise of its powers. The legislature is subordinate to the Constitution and cannot alter it.

LEONARD W. LEVY

Bibliography

ADAMS, WILLI PAUL 1980 *The First American Constitutions: Republican Ideology and the Making of the State Constitutions in the Revolutionary Era.* Chapel Hill: University of North Carolina Press.

DODD, WALTER F. 1910 *The Revision and Amendment of State Constitutions.* Baltimore: Johns Hopkins University Press.

JAMESON, JOHN ALEXANDER 1887 *A Treatise on Constitutional Conventions: Their History, Powers, and Modes of Proceeding.* 4th ed. Chicago: Callahan & Co.

MCLAUGHLIN, ANDREW C. 1932 *The Foundations of American Constitutionalism.* New York: New York University Press.

WOOD, GORDON S. 1969 *The Creation of the American Republic, 1776–1787.* Chapel Hill: University of North Carolina Press.

CONSTITUTIONAL CONVENTION OF 1787

Over the last two centuries, the work of the Constitutional Convention and the motives of the Founding Fathers have been analyzed under a number of different ideological auspices. To one generation of historians, the hand of God was moving in the assembly; under a later dispensation, the dialectic replaced the Deity: "relationships of production" moved into the niche previously reserved for Love of Country. Thus, in counterpoint to the Zeitgeist, the Framers have undergone miraculous metamorphoses: at one time acclaimed as liberals and bold social engineers, today they appear in the guise of sound Burkean conservatives.

The "Fathers" have thus been admitted to our best circles; the revolutionary generation that confiscated all Tory property in reach and populated New Brunswick with outlaws has been converted into devotees of "consensus" and "prescriptive rights." Indeed, there is one fundamental truth about the Founding Fathers that every generation of Zeitgeisters has done its best to obscure: they were first and foremost superb democratic politicians. They were political men—not metaphysicians, disembodied conservatives, or agents of history—and, as recent research into the nature of American politics in the 1780s confirms, they were required to work within a democratic framework. The Philadelphia Convention was not a council of Platonic guardians working within a manipulative, predemocratic framework; it was a nationalist reform caucus which had to operate with great delicacy and skill in a political cosmos full of enemies to achieve the one definitive goal—popular approbation.

Perhaps the time has come, to borrow WALTON HAMILTON's fine phrase, to promote the Framers from immortality to mortality, to give them credit for their magnificent demonstration of the art of democratic politics: they made history and they did it within the limits of consensus. What they did was hammer out a pragmatic compromise that would both bolster the "national interest" and be acceptable to the people. What inspiration they got came from collective experience as politicians in a democratic society. As JOHN DICKINSON put it to his fellow delegates on August 13, "Experience must be our guide. Reason may mislead us."

When the Constitutionalists went forth to subvert the ARTICLES OF CONFEDERATION, they employed the mechanisms of political legitimacy. Although the roadblocks confronting them were formidable, they were also endowed with certain political talents. From 1786 to 1790 the Constitutionalists used those talents against bumbling, erratic behavior by the opponents of reform. Effectively, the Constitutionalists had to induce the states, by democratic techniques, to cripple themselves. To be specific, if New York should refuse to join the new Union, the project was doomed; yet before New York was safely in, the reluctant state legislature had to take the following steps: agree to send delegates to the Convention and maintain them there; set up the special ratifying convention; and accept that convention's decision that New York should ratify the Constitution. The same legal hurdles existed in every state.

The group that undertook this struggle was an interesting amalgam of a few dedicated nationalists and self-interested spokesmen of various parochial bailiwicks. Georgians, for example, wanted a strong central authority to provide military protection against the Creek Confederacy; Jerseymen and Connecticuters wanted to escape from economic bondage to New York; Virginians sought a system recognizing that great state's "rightful" place in the councils of the Republic. These states' dominant political figures therefore cooperated in the call for the Convention. In other states, the cause of national reform was taken up by the "outs" who added the "national interest" to their weapons systems; in Pennsylvania, for instance, JAMES WILSON's group fighting to revise the state Constitution of 1776 came out four-square behind the Constitutionalists.

To say this is not to suggest that the Constitution was founded on base motives but to recognize that in politics there are no immaculate conceptions. It is not surprising that a number of diversified private interests promoted the nationalist public interest. However motivated, these men did demonstrate a willingness to compromise in behalf of an ideal that took shape before their eyes and under their ministrations.

What distinguished the leaders of the Constitutionalist caucus from their enemies was a "continental" approach to political, economic, and military issues. Their institutional base of operations was the Continental Congress (thirty-nine of the fifty-five designated delegates to the Convention had served in Congress), hardly a locale that inspired respect for the state governments. One can surmise that membership in the Congress had helped establish a continental frame of reference, particularly with respect to external affairs. The average state legislator was probably about as concerned with foreign policy then as he is today, but congressmen were constantly forced to take the broad view of American prestige, and to listen to the reports of Secretary JOHN JAY and their envoys in Europe. A "continental" ideology thus developed, demanding invigoration of our domestic institutions to assure our rightful place in the international arena. Indeed, an argument with the force of GEORGE WASHINGTON as its incarnation urged that our very survival in the Hobbesian jungle of world politics depended upon a reordering and strengthening of our national SOVEREIGNTY.

MERRILL JENSEN seems quite sound in his view that to most Americans, engaged as they were in self-sustaining agriculture, the "Critical Period" was not particularly critical. The great achievement of the Constitutionalists was their ultimate success in convincing the elected representatives of a majority of the white male population that change was imperative. A small group of political leaders with a continental vision and essentially a consciousness of the United States' international impotence, was the core of the movement. To their standard rallied other leaders' parallel ambitions. Their great assets were active support from George Washington, whose prestige was enormous; the energy and talent of their leadership; a communications "network" far superior to the opposition's; the preemptive skill which made "their" issue The Issue and kept the locally oriented opposition on the defensive; and the new and compelling credo of American nationalism.

Despite great institutional handicaps, the Constitutionalists in the mid-1780s got the jump on the local oppositions with the demand for a Convention. Their opponents were caught in an old political trap: they were not being asked to approve any specific reform but only to endorse a meeting to discuss and recommend needed reforms. If they took a hard line, they were put in the position of denying the need for any changes. Moreover, because the states would have the final say on any proposals that might emerge from the Convention, the Constitutionalists could go to the people with a persuasive argument for "fair play."

Perhaps because of their poor intelligence system, perhaps because of overconfidence generated by the failure of all previous efforts to alter the Articles, the opposition awoke too late. Not only did the Constitutionalists manage to get every state but Rhode Island to appoint delegates to Philadelphia but they also dominated the delegations. The fact that the delegates to Philadelphia were appointed by state governments, not elected by the people, has been advanced as evidence of the "undemocratic" character of the gathering, but this argument is specious. The existing central government under the Articles was considered a creature of the states—not as a consequence of elitism or fear of the mob but as a logical extension of STATES' RIGHTS doctrine. The national government was not supposed to end-run the state legislatures and make direct contact with the people.

With delegations named, the focus shifted to Philadelphia. While waiting for a quorum to assemble, JAMES MADISON drafted the so-called VIRGINIA PLAN. This was a political masterstroke: once business got underway, this plan provided the framework of discussion. Instead of arguing interminably over the agenda, the delegates took the Virginia Plan as their point of departure, including its major premise: a new start on a Constitution rather than piecemeal amendment. This proposal was not necessarily revolutionary—a new Constitution might have been formulated as "amendments" to the Articles of Confederation—but the provision that amendments take effect after approval by nine states was thoroughly subversive. The Articles required unanimous state approval for any amendment.

Standard treatments of the Convention divide the delegates into "nationalists" and "states' righters" with various shadings, but these latter-day characterizations obfuscate more than they clarify. The Convention was remarkably homogeneous in ideology. ROBERT YATES and JOHN LANSING, Clinton's two chaperones for ALEXANDER HAMILTON, left in disgust on July 10. LUTHER MARTIN left in a huff on September 4; others went home for personal reasons. But the hard core of delegates accepted a grinding regimen throughout a Philadelphia summer precisely because they shared the Constitutionalist goal.

Basic differences of opinion emerged, of course, but these were not ideological; they were structural. If the so-called states' rights group had not accepted the fundamental purposes of the Convention, they could simply have pulled out and aborted the whole enterprise. Instead of bolting, they returned day after day to argue and to compromise. An index of this basic homogeneity was the initial agreement on secrecy: these professional politicians wanted to retain the freedom of maneuver that would be possible only if they were not forced to take public stands during preliminary negotiations. There was no legal means of binding the tongues of the delegates: at any stage a delegate with basic objections to the emerging project could have denounced the convention. Yet the delegates generally observed the injunction; Madison did not even inform THOMAS JEFFERSON in Paris of the course of the deliberations. Secrecy is uncharacteristic of any assembly marked by ideological polarization. During the Convention the *New York Daily Advertiser* called the secrecy "a happy omen, as it demonstrates that the spirit of party on any great and essential point cannot have arisen to any height."

Some key Framers must have been disappointed. Commentators on the Constitution who have read THE FEDERALIST but not Madison's record of the actual debates (secret until after his death in 1836), have credited the Fathers with a sublime invention called "Federalism." Yet the Constitution's final balance between the states and the nation must have dissatisfied Madison, whose Virginia Plan envisioned a unitary national government effectively freed from and dominant over the states. Hamilton's unitary views are too well known to need elucidation.

Under the Virginia Plan the general government was freed from state control in a truly radical fashion, and the scope of its authority was breathtaking. The national legislature was to be empowered to disallow the acts of state legislatures, and the central government would be vested, in addition to the powers of the nation under the Articles of Confederation, with plenary authority "wherever . . . the separate States are incompetent or in which the harmony of the United States may be interrupted by the exercise of individual legislation." Finally, the national Congress was to be given the power to use military force on recalcitrant states.

The Convention was not scandalized by this militant program for a strong autonomous central government. Some delegates were startled, some leery of so comprehensive a reform, but nobody set off any fireworks and nobody walked out. Moreover, within two weeks the general principles of the Virginia Plan had received substantial endorsement. The temper of the gathering can be deduced from its unanimous approval, on May 31, of a resolution giving Congress authority to disallow state legislation "contravening in its opinion the Articles of Union."

Perhaps the Virginia Plan was the delegates' ideological Utopia, but as discussions became more specific many of them had second thoughts. They were practical politicians in a democratic society, and they would have to take home an acceptable package and defend it—and their own political futures—against predictable attack. June 14 saw the breaking point between dream and reality. Apparently realizing that under the Virginia Plan, Massachusetts, Virginia, and Pennsylvania could virtually dominate the national government, the delegates from the small states demanded time for a consideration of alternatives. John Dickinson reproached Madison: "You see the consequences of pushing things too far. Some of the members from the small States wish for two branches in the General Legislature and are friends to a good National Government; but we would sooner submit to a foreign power than . . . be deprived of an equality of suffrage in both branches of the Legislature, and thereby be thrown under the domination of the large States."

Now the process of accommodation was put into action smoothly—and wisely, given the character and strength of the doubters. Madison had the votes, but mechanical majoritarianism could easily have destroyed the objectives of the majority: the Constitutionalists sought a qualitative as well as a quantitative consensus, a political imperative to attain ratification.

According to the standard script, the "states' rights" group now united behind the NEW JERSEY PLAN, which has been characteristically portrayed as no more than a minor modification of the Articles of Confederation. The New Jersey Plan did put the states back into the institutional picture, but to do so was a recognition of political reality rather than an affirmation of states' rights.

Paterson, the leading spokesman for the project, said as much: "I came here not to speak my own sentiments, but the sentiments of those who sent me. Our object is not such a Government as may be best in itself, but such a one as our Constituents have authorized us to prepare, and as they will approve." This is Madison's version; in Yates's transcription, a crucial sentence follows: "I believe that a little practical virtue is to be preferred to the finest theoretical principles, which cannot be carried into effect."

The advocates of the New Jersey Plan concentrated their fire on what they held to be the political liabilities of the Virginia Plan—which were matters of institutional structure—rather than on the proposed scope of national authority. Indeed, the SUPREMACY CLAUSE of the Constitution first saw the light of day in Paterson's Sixth Resolution; for Paterson, under either the Virginia or the New Jersey system the general government would "act on individuals and not on states." From the states' rights viewpoint, this was heresy.

Paterson thus reopened the agenda of the Convention, but within a distinctly nationalist framework. Paterson favored a strong central government but opposed putting the big states in the saddle. As evidence for this there is an intriguing proposal among Paterson's preliminary drafts of the New Jersey Plan:

> Whereas it is necessary in Order to form the People of the U.S. of America in to a Nation, that the States should be consolidated, . . . it is therefore resolved, that all the Lands contained within the Limits of each state individually, and of the U.S. generally be considered as constituting one Body or Mass, and be divided into thirteen or more integral parts.
>
> Resolved, That such Divisions or integral Parts shall be styled Districts.

He may have gotten the idea from his New Jersey colleague Judge DAVID BREARLEY, who on June 9 had commented that the only remedy to the dilemma over representation was "that a map of the U.S. be spread out, that all the existing boundaries be erased, and that a new partition of the whole be made into 13 equal parts." According to Yates, Brearley added at this point, "then a government on the present [Virginia Plan] system will be just."

Thus, the delegates from the small states announced that they were unprepared to be offered up as sacrificial victims to a "national interest" that reflected Virginia's parochial ambition. Caustic CHARLES PINCKNEY was not far off when he remarked sardonically that "the whole conflict comes to this: Give New Jersey an equal vote, and she will dismiss her scruples, and concur in the National system." What he rather unfairly did not add was that the Jersey delegates were not free agents who could adhere to their private convictions; they had to stake their reputations and political careers on the reforms approved by the Convention—in New Jersey, not Virginia.

Paterson spoke on Saturday, and the weekend must have seen a good deal of consultation, argument, and caucusing. One delegate prepared a full-length address: on Monday Alexander Hamilton, previously mute, rose and delivered a six-hour oration. It was a remarkably apolitical speech; the gist of his position was that both the Virginia and New Jersey Plans were inadequately centralist, and he detailed a reform program reminiscent of the Protectorate under the Cromwellian *Instrument of Government* of 1653. He wanted, to take a striking phrase from a letter to George Washington, a "strong well mounted government."

From all accounts this was a compelling speech, but it had little practical effect; the Convention adjourned, admired Hamilton's rhetoric, and returned to business. Hamilton, never a patient man, stayed another ten days and then left in disgust for New York. Although he returned to Philadelphia sporadically and attended the last two weeks of the Convention, Hamilton played no part in the laborious task of hammering out the Constitution. His day came later when he led the New York Constitutionalists into the savage imbroglio over ratification—an arena in which his unmatched talent for political infighting surely won the day.

On June 19 James Madison led off with a long, carefully reasoned speech analyzing the New Jersey Plan; although intellectually vigorous in his criticisms, Madison was quite conciliatory in mood: "The great difficulty lies in the affair of REPRESENTATION; and if this could be adjusted, all others would be surmountable." When he finished, a vote was taken on whether to continue with the Virginia Plan as the nucleus for a new constitution: seven states voted yes; New York, New Jersey, and Delaware voted No; and Maryland was divided.

Paterson, it seems, lost decisively; yet in a fundamental sense he and his allies had achieved their purpose: from that day onward, it could never be forgotten that the state governments loomed ominously in the background. Moreover, nobody bolted the convention. Paterson and his colleagues set to work to modify the Virginia Plan, particularly with respect to representation in the national legislature. They won an immediate rhetorical bonus; when OLIVER ELLSWORTH of Connecticut moved that the word "national" be expunged from the Third Virginia Resolution ("Resolved that a *national* Government ought to be established consisting of a *supreme* Legislative, Executive and Judiciary"), Randolph agreed and the motion passed unanimously. The process of compromise had begun.

For two weeks the delegates circled around the problem of legislative representation. The Connecticut delegation appears to have evolved a possible compromise early in the debates, but the Virginians, particularly Madison, fought obdurately against providing for equal representation of states in the second chamber. There was enough acrimony for BENJAMIN FRANKLIN to propose institution of a daily prayer, but on July 2, the ice began to break when the majority against equality of representation was converted into a dead tie. The Convention was ripe for a solution and the South Carolinians proposed a committee. Madison and James Wilson wanted none of it, but with only Pennsylvania dissenting, a working party was established to cope with the problem of representation.

The members of this committee, one from each state, were elected by the delegates. Although the Virginia Plan had held majority support up to that date, neither Madison nor Randolph was selected. This was not to be a "fighting" committee; the members could be described as "second-level political entrepreneurs."

There is a common rumor that the Framers divided their time between philosophical discussions of government and reading the classics in political theory. In fact, concerns were highly practical; they spent little time canvassing abstractions. A number of them had some acquaintance with the history of political theory, and it was a poor rhetorician indeed who could not cite JOHN LOCKE, MONTESQUIEU, or James Harrington in support of a desired goal. Yet up to this point no one had expounded a defense of states' rights or the SEPARATION OF POWERS on anything resembling a theoretical basis. The Madison model effectively vested all governmental power in the national legislature.

Because the critical fight was over representation of the states, once the GREAT COMPROMISE was adopted on July 17 the Convention was over the hump. Madison, James Wilson, and GOUVERNEUR MORRIS fought the compromise all the way in a last-ditch effort to get a unitary state with parliamentary supremacy. But their allies deserted them and after their defeat they demonstrated a willingness to swallow their objections and get on with the business. Moreover, once the compromise had carried (by five states to four, with one state divided), its advocates threw themselves into the job of strengthening the general government's substantive powers. Madison demonstrated his devotion to the art of politics when he later prepared essays for *The Federalist* in contradiction to the basic convictions he expressed in the Convention.

Two ticklish issues illustrate the later process of accommodation. The first was the institutional position of the executive. Madison argued for a chief magistrate chosen by the national legislature, and on May 29 this proposal had been adopted with a provision for a seven-year nonrenewable term. In late July this was reopened; groups now opposed election by the legislature. One felt that the states should have a hand in the process; another small but influential circle urged direct election by the people. There were a number of proposals: election by the people, by state governors, by electors chosen by state legislatures, by the national legislature. There was some resemblance to three-dimensional chess in the dispute because of the presence of two other variables: length of tenure and eligibility for reelection. Finally the thorny problem was consigned to a committee for resolution.

The Brearley Committee on Postponed Matters was a superb aggregation of talent and its compromise on the Executive was a masterpiece of creativity. Everybody present knew that under any system devised, George Washington would be the first President; thus they were dealing in the future tense. To a body of working politicians the merits of the Brearley proposal were obvious: everyone could argue to his constituents that he had really won the day. First, the state legislatures had the right to determine the mode of selection of the electors; second, the small states were guaranteed a minimum of three votes in the ELECTORAL COLLEGE while the big states got acceptance of the principle of proportional power; third, if the state legislatures agreed (as six did in the first presidential election), the people could be involved directly in the choice of electors; and finally, if no candidate received a majority in the College, the decision passed to the House of Representatives with each state having one vote.

This compromise was almost too good to be true, and the Framers snapped it up with little debate or controversy. Thus the Electoral College was neither an exercise in applied Platonism nor an experiment in indirect government based on elitist distrust of the masses. It was merely an improvisation which was subsequently, in *The Federalist* #68, endowed with high theoretical content.

The second issue on which some substantial bargaining took place was SLAVERY. The morality of slavery was, by design, not an issue; but in its other concrete aspects, slavery influenced the arguments over taxation, commerce, and representation. The THREE-FIFTHS RULE—that three-fifths of the slaves would be counted both for representation and for purposes of DIRECT TAXATION—had allayed some northern fears about southern overrepresentation, but doubts remained. Southerners, on the other hand, were afraid that congressional control over commerce would lead to the exclusion of slaves or to their prohibitive taxation as imports. Moreover, the Southerners were disturbed over "navigation acts" (tariffs), or special legislation providing, for example, that exports be carried only in American ships. They depended upon exports, and so urged inclusion of a proviso that navigation and commercial laws require a two-thirds vote in Congress.

These problems came to a head in late August and, as usual, were handed to a committee in the hope that, in Gouverneur Morris's words, "these things may form a bargain among the Northern and Southern states." The Committee reported its measures of reconciliation on August 25, and on August 29 the package was wrapped up and delivered. What occurred can best be described in George Mason's dour version. Mason anticipated JOHN C. CALHOUN in his conviction that permitting navigation acts to pass by majority vote would put the South in economic bondage to the North. Mainly on this ground, he refused to sign the Constitution. Mason said:

> The Constitution as agreed to till a fortnight before the Convention rose was such a one as he would have set his hand and heart to. . . . Until that time the 3 New England States were constantly with us in all questions . . . so that it was these three States with the 5 Southern ones against Pennsylvania, Jersey and Delaware. With respect to the importation of slaves, [decision making] was left to Congress. This disturbed the two Southernmost States who knew that Congress would immediately suppress the importation of slaves. Those two States therefore struck up a bargain with the three New England States. If they would join to admit slaves for some years, the two Southernmost States would join in changing the clause which required the ⅔ of the Legislature in any vote [on navigation acts]. It was done.

On the floor of the Convention there was a love-feast. When Charles Pinckney of South Carolina attempted to overturn the committee's decision, by insisting that the South needed protection from the imperialism of the northern states, General CHARLES COTEWORTH PINCKNEY arose to spread oil on the waters:

> It was in the true interest of the S[outhern] States to have no regulation of commerce; but considering the loss brought on the commerce of the Eastern States by the Revolution, their liberal conduct towards the views of South Carolina [on the regulation of the slave trade] and the interests the weak South. States had in being united with the strong Eastern states, he thought it proper that no fetters should be imposed on the power of making commercial regulations; and that his constituents, though prejudiced against Eastern States, would be reconciled to this liberality. He had himself prejudices against the Eastern States before he came here, but would acknowledge that he had found them as liberal and candid as any men whatever.

Drawing on their vast collective political experience, employing every weapon in the politician's arsenal, looking constantly over their shoulders at their constituents, the delegates put together a Constitution. It was a makeshift affair; some sticky issues they ducked entirely; others they mastered with that ancient instrument of political sagacity, studied ambiguity, and some they just overlooked. In this last category probably fell the matter of the power of the federal courts to determine the constitutionality of acts of Congress. When the judicial article was formulated, deliberations were still at the stage where the legislature was endowed with broad authority which by its own terms was scarcely amenable to JUDICIAL REVIEW. In essence, courts could hardly determine when "the separate States are incompetent or . . . the harmony of the United States may be interrupted"; the national legislature, as critics pointed out, was free to define its own jurisdiction. Later the definition of legislative authority was changed into the form we know, a series of stipulated powers, but the delegates never seriously reexamined the jurisdiction of the judiciary under this new limited formulation. All arguments on the intention of the Framers in this matter are thus deductive and *a posteriori.*

The Framers were busy and distinguished men, anxious to get back to their families, their positions, and their constituents, not members of the French Academy devoting a lifetime to a dictionary. They were trying to do an important job, and do it in such a fashion that their handiwork would be acceptable to diverse constituencies. No one was rhapsodic about the final document, but it was a beginning, a move in the right direction, and one they had reason to believe the people would endorse. In addition, because they had modified the impossible amendment provisions of the Articles of Confederation to one demanding approval by only three-quarters of the states, they seemed confident that gaps in the fabric which experience would reveal could be rewoven without undue difficulty.

So, with a neat phrase introduced by Benjamin Franklin that made their decision sound unanimous and an inspired benediction by the Old Doctor urging doubters to question their own infallibility, the delegates accepted the Constitution. Curiously, Edmund Randolph, who had played so vital a role throughout, refused to sign as did his fellow Virginian George Mason and ELBRIDGE GERRY of Massachusetts. Presumably, Randolph wanted to check the temper of the Virginia populace before he risked his reputation, and perhaps his job, in a fight with PATRICK HENRY. Events lend some justification to this speculation: after much temporizing and use of the conditional tense, Randolph endorsed ratification in Virginia and ended up getting the best of both worlds.

Madison, despite his reservations about the Constitution, was the campaign manager for ratification. His first task was to get the Congress in New York to light its own funeral pyre by approving the "amendments" to the Articles and sending them on to the state legislatures. Above all, momentum had to be maintained. The anti-Constitutionalists, now thoroughly alarmed and no novices in politics, realized that their best tactic was attrition rather than direct opposition. Thus they settled on a position expressing qualified approval but calling for a second Convention to remedy various defects (the one with the most demagogic appeal was the lack of a BILL OF RIGHTS). Madison knew that to accede to this demand would be equivalent to losing the battle, nor would he agree to conditional approval (despite wavering even by Hamilton). This was an all-or-nothing proposition: national salvation or national impotence, with no intermediate position possible. Unable to get congressional approval, he settled for second best: a unanimous resolution of Congress transmitting the Constitution to the states for whatever action they saw fit to take. The opponents then moved from New York and the Congress, where they had attempted to attach amendments and conditions, to the states for the final battle.

At first, the campaign for RATIFICATION went beautifully: within eight months after the delegates set their names to the document, eight states had ratified. Theoretically, a ratification by one more state convention would set the new government in motion, but in fact until Virginia and New York acceded to the new Union, the latter was a fiction. New Hampshire was the next to ratify; "Rogues' Island" was involved in its characteristic political convulsions; North Carolina's convention did not meet until July and then postponed a final decision. Finally in New York and Virginia, the Constitutionalists outmaneuvered their opponents, forced them into impossible political positions, and won both states narrowly.

Victory for the Constitution meant simultaneous victory for the Constitutionalists; the anti-Constitutionalists either capitulated or vanished into limbo—soon Patrick Henry would be offered a seat on the Supreme Court and Luther Martin would be known as the Federalist "bull-dog." And, irony of ironies, Alexander Hamilton and James Madison would shortly accumulate a reputation as the formulators of what is often alleged to be our political theory, the concept of "federalism." Arguments would soon appear over what the Framers "really meant"; although these disputes have assumed the proportions of a big scholarly business in the last century, they began almost before the ink on the Constitution was dry. One of the best early ones featured Hamilton versus Madison on the scope of presidential power.

The Constitution, then, was not an apotheosis of "constitutionalism," a triumph of architectonic genius; it was a patchwork sewn together under the pressure of time and events by a group of extremely talented democratic politicians. They refused to attempt the establishment of a strong, centralized sovereign on the principle of legislative supremacy for the excellent reason that the people would not accept it. They risked their political fortunes by opposing the established doctrines of state sovereignty because they were convinced that the existing system was leading to national impotence and, probably, to foreign domination. For two years, they worked to get a convention established. For over three months, in what must have seemed to the faithful participants an endless process of give-and-take, they reasoned, cajoled, threatened, and bargained amongst themselves. The results were a Constitution which the voters, by democratic processes, did accept, and a new and far better national government.

JOHN P. ROCHE

Bibliography

BROWN, ROBERT E. 1956 *Charles Beard and the Constitution.* Princeton, N.J.: Princeton University Press.

DINKIN, ROBERT J. 1977 *Voting in Provincial America.* Westport, Conn.: Greenwood Press.

ELKINS, STANLEY AND MCKITRICK, ERIC 1961 The Founding Fathers: Young Men of the Revolution. *Political Science Quarterly* 76:181–203.

FARRAND, MAX (ED.) 1937 *Records of the Federal Convention of 1787.* New Haven, Conn.: Yale University Press.

KENYON, CECELIA M. 1955 Men of Little Faith: The Anti-Federalists on the Nature of Representative Government. *William and Mary Quarterly,* 3rd series, 12: McDonald, Forrest T. 1958 *We the People.* Chicago: University of Chicago Press.

ROCHE, JOHN P. 1961 The Founding Fathers: A Reform Caucus in Action. *American Political Science Review* 55:799–816.

ROSSITER, CLINTON 1966 *1787: The Grand Convention.* New York: Macmillan.

WARREN, CHARLES (1928)1937 *The Making of the Constitution.* Boston: Little, Brown.

CONSTITUTIONAL COURT

Article III vests the federal judicial power in the Supreme Court and in any lower courts that Congress may create. The judiciary so constituted was intended by the Framers to be an independent branch of the government. The judges of courts established under Article III were thus guaranteed life tenure "during GOOD BEHAVIOR" and protected against the reduction of their salaries while they held office. The federal courts so constituted are called "constitutional courts." They are to be distinguished from LEGISLATIVE COURTS, whose judges do not have comparable constitutional guarantees of independence.

Constitutional courts, sometimes called "Article III courts," are limited in the business they can be assigned. They may be given JURISDICTION only over CASES AND CONTROVERSIES falling within the JUDICIAL POWER OF THE UNITED STATES. For example, Congress could not constitutionally confer jurisdiction on a constitutional court to give ADVISORY OPINIONS, or to decide a case that fell outside Article III's list of cases and controversies included within the judicial power. That list divides into two categories of cases: those in which jurisdiction depends on the issues at stake (for example, FEDERAL QUESTION JURISDICTION) and those in which jurisdiction depends on the parties to the case (for example, DIVERSITY JURISDICTION).

Congress can, of course, create bodies other than constitutional courts and assign them the function of deciding cases—even cases falling within the judicial power, within limits that remain unclear even after NORTHERN PIPELINE CONSTRUCTION CO. V. MARATHON PIPE LINE CO. (1982). Such a legislative court is not confined by Article III's specification of the limits of the federal judicial power, any more than an administrative agency would be so confined. However, a legislative court's decisions on matters outside the limits of Article III cannot constitutionally be reviewed by the Supreme Court or any other constitutional court.

KENNETH L. KARST

Bibliography

WRIGHT, CHARLES ALAN 1983 *The Law of Federal Courts,* 4th ed. Pages 39–52. St. Paul, Minn.: West Publishing Co.

CONSTITUTIONAL HISTORY BEFORE 1776

The opening words of the United States Constitution, "We the People," startled some of the old revolutionaries of 1776. PATRICK HENRY, after expressing the highest veneration for the men who wrote the words, demanded "What right had they to say, *We the People.* . . . Who authorized them to speak the language of *We, the People,* instead of *We, the States?*" It was a good question and, as Henry knew, not really answerable. No one had authorized the members of the CONSTITUTIONAL CONVENTION to speak for the people of the United States. They had been chosen by the legislatures of thirteen sovereign states and were authorized only to act for the governments of those states in redefining the relationships among them. Instead, they had dared not only to act for "the people of the United States" but also to proclaim what they did as "the supreme law of the land," supreme apparently over the actions of the existing state governments and supreme also over the government that the Constitution itself would create for the United States. Because those governments similarly professed to speak and act for the people, how could the Constitution claim supremacy over them and claim it successfully from that day to this, however contested in politics, litigation, and civil war? The answer lies less in logic than in the centuries of political experience before 1787 in which Englishmen and Americans worked out a political faith that gave to "the people" a presumptive capacity to constitute governments.

The idea that government originates in a donation by the people is at least as old as classical Greece. Government requires some sort of justification, and a donation of power by the governed or by those about to be governed was an obvious way of providing it. But such a donation has seldom if ever been recorded as historical fact, because it is virtually impossible for any substantial collection of people to act as a body, either in conveying powers of government or in prescribing the mode of their exercise. The donation has to be assumed, presumed, supposed, imagined—and yet be plausible enough to be acceptable to the supposed donors.

In the Anglo-American world two institutions have lent credibility to the presumption. The first to emerge was the presence in government of representatives chosen by a substantial portion of the people. With the powers of government thus shared, it became plausible to think of the representatives and the government as acting for the people and deriving powers from them. But as these popular representatives assumed a dominant position in the government, it was all too easy for them to escape from the control of those who chose them and to claim unlimited power in the name of the almighty people. A second device was necessary to differentiate the inherent sovereign powers of the people from the limited powers assigned to their deputed agents or representatives. The device was found in written CONSTITUTIONS embodying the people's supposed donation of power in specific provisions to limit and define the government.

Such written constitutions were a comparatively late development; the United States Constitution was one of the first. They came into existence not simply out of the need to specify the terms of the putative donation of power by the people but also out of earlier attempts by representatives or spokesmen of the people to set limits to governments claiming almighty authority from a different source. Although the idea of a popular donation was an ancient way of justifying government, it was not the only way. Indeed, since the fall of Rome God had been the favored source of authority: earthly rulers, whether in church or state, claimed His commission, though the act in which He granted it remained as shadowy as any donation by the people. Up to the seventeenth century, the persons who spoke for the people spoke as subjects, but they spoke as subjects of God as well as of God's lieutenants. While showing a proper reverence for divinely ordained authority, they expected those commissioned by God to rule in a godlike manner, that is, to abide by the natural laws (discernible in God's government of the world) that were supposed to guide human conduct and give force to the specific "positive" laws of nations derived from them. Even without claiming powers of government, those who spoke for the people might thus set limits to the powers of government through "fundamental" laws that were thought to express the will of God more reliably than rulers who claimed His commission. The link is obvious between such FUNDAMENTAL LAWS and written constitutions that expressed the people's will more reliably than their elected representatives could. The one grew out of the other.

Written constitutions were a deliberate invention, designed to overcome the deficiencies of representative government, but representative government itself was the unintended outcome of efforts by kings to secure and extend their own power. The story begins with the creation of the English House of Commons in the thirteenth century, when the English government centered in a hereditary king who claimed God-given authority but had slender means for asserting it. The king, always in need of funds, summoned two representatives from each county and from selected boroughs (incorporated towns) to come to his court for the purpose of consenting to taxes. He required the counties and boroughs in choosing representatives, by some unspecified electoral process, to give them full powers of attorney, so that no one could later object to what they agreed to. Although only a small part of the adult population shared in the choice of representatives, the House of Commons came to be regarded as having power of attorney for the whole body of the king's subjects; every man, woman, and child in the country was held to be legally present within its walls.

The assembly of representatives, thus created and identified with the whole people, gradually acquired an institutional existence, along with the House of Lords, as one branch of the king's Parliament. As representatives, the members remained subjects of the king, empowered by other subjects to act for them. But from the beginning they were somewhat more than subjects: in addition to granting the property of other subjects in taxes, they could petition the king for laws that would direct the actions of government. From petitioning for laws they moved to making them: by the sixteenth century English laws were enacted "by authority" of Parliament. Theoretically that authority still came from God through the king, and Parliament continued to be an instrument by which English monarchs consolidated and extended their government, never more so than in the sixteenth century. But in sharing their authority with Parliament the kings shared it, by implication, with the people. By the time the first American colonies were founded in the early seventeenth century, the king's instrument had become a potential rival to his authority, and the people had become a potential alternative to God as the immediate source of authority.

The potential became actual in the 1640s when Parliament, discontented with Charles I's ecclesiastical, military, and fiscal policies, made war on the king and itself assumed all powers of government. The Parliamentarians justified their actions as agents of the people; and at this point the presumption of a popular origin of government made its appearance in England in full force. The idea, which had been overshadowed for so long by royal claims to a divine commission, had been growing for a century. The Protestant Reformation had produced a contest between Roman Catholics and Protestants for control of the various national governments of Europe. In that contest each side had placed on the people of a country the responsibility for its government's compliance with the will of God. The people, it was now asserted, were entrusted by God with creating proper governments and with setting limits on them to insure protection of true religion. When the limits were breached, the people must revoke the powers of rulers who had betrayed their trust. For Roman Catholics, Protestant rulers fitted the definition, and vice versa.

When Englishmen, mostly Protestant, challenged their king, who leaned toward Catholicism, these ideas were ready at hand for their justification, and the House of Commons had long been recognized as the representative of the people. The House, the members now claimed, to all intents and purposes *was* the people, and the powers of the people were supreme. Both the king and the House of Lords, lacking these powers, were superfluous. In 1649 the Commons killed the king, abolished the House of Lords, and made England a republic.

By assuming such sweeping powers the members of the House of Commons invited anyone who felt aggrieved by their conduct of government not only to question their claim to represent the people but also to draw a distinction between the powers of the people themselves and of the persons they might choose, by whatever means, to represent them.

The first critics of the Commons to draw such a distinction were, not surprisingly, the adherents of the king, who challenged the Commons in the public press as well as on the field of battle. The House of Commons, the royalists pointed out, had been elected by only a small fraction of the people, and even that fraction had empowered it only to consent to positive laws and taxes, not to alter the government. Parliament, the royalists insisted, must not be confused with the people themselves. Even if it were granted that the people might create a government and set limits on it in fundamental laws, the House of Commons was only one part of the government thus created and could not itself change the government by eliminating the king or the Lords.

More radical critics, especially the misnamed Levellers, called not only for a reform of Parliament to make it more truly representative but also for a written "Agreement of the People" in which the people, acting apart from Parliament, would reorganize the government, reserving certain powers to themselves and setting limits to Parliament just as Parliament had formerly set limits to the king. Although the Levellers were unsuccessful, other political leaders also recognized the need to elevate supposed acts of the people, in creating a government and establishing its fundamental laws, above acts of the government itself. They also recognized that even a government derived from popular choice needed a SEPARATION OF POWERS among legislative, executive, and judicial branches, not merely for convenience of administration but in order to prevent government from escaping popular control.

Although the English in these years generated the ideas that have guided modern republican government, they were unable to bring their own government into full conformity with those ideas. By the 1650s they found that they had replaced a monarch, whose powers were limited, first with a House of Commons that claimed unlimited powers and refused to hold new elections, and then with a protector, Oliver Cromwell, whose powers knew only the limits of his ability to command a conquering army. In 1660 most Englishmen were happy to see the old balance restored with the return of a hereditary king and an old-style but potent Parliament to keep him in line. In 1688 that Parliament again removed a king who seemed to be getting out of control. This time, instead of trying to eliminate monarchy, they replaced one king with another who promised to be more tractable than his predecessor. William III at the outset of his reign accepted a parliamentary declaration of rights, spelling out the fundamental laws that limited his authority.

JOHN LOCKE, in the classic defense of this "Glorious Revolution," refined the distinction made earlier by the Levellers between the people and their representatives. Locke posited a SOCIAL COMPACT in which a collection of hitherto unconnected individuals in a "state of nature" came together to form a society. Only after doing so did they enter into a second compact in which they created a government and submitted to it. This second compact or constitution could be broken—the government could be altered or replaced—without destroying the first compact and throwing the people back into a state of nature. Society, in other words, came before government; and the people, once bound into a society by a social compact, could act without government and apart from government in order to constitute or change a government.

Locke could point to no historical occurrence that quite fitted his pattern. Even the Glorious Revolution was not, strictly speaking, an example of popular constituent action; rather, one branch of an existing government had replaced another branch. And the Declaration of Rights, although binding on the king, was no more than an act of Parliament that another Parliament might repeal. Moreover, the authority of the king remained substantial, and he was capable of extending his influence over Parliament by appointing members to lucrative government offices.

Locke's description of the origin of government nevertheless furnished a theoretical basis for viewing the entire British government as the creation of the people it governed. That view was expressed most vociferously in the eighteenth century by the so-called commonwealthmen, who repeated the call for reforms to make Parliament more representative of the whole people and to reduce the king's influence on its members. But it was not only commonwealthmen who accepted Locke's formulation. By the middle of the eighteenth century the doctrine of the divine right of kings was virtually dead in England, replaced by the sovereignty of the people, who were now accepted as the immediate source of all authority whether in king, lords, or commons.

In England's American colonies the idea that government originates in the people had been familiar from the outset, nourished not only by developments in England but also by the special conditions inherent in colonization. Those conditions were politically and constitutionally complex. The colonies were founded by private individuals or corporations under charters granted by the king, in which Parliament had no part. In the typical colony the king initially conveyed powers of government to the founders, who generally remained in England and directed the enterprise through agents. As time went on, the king took the powers of government in most colonies to himself, acting through appointed governors. But whether the immediate source of governmental authority in a colony rested in the king or in royally authorized corporations or individual proprietors, it proved impossible to govern colonists at 3,000 miles' distance without current information about changing local conditions. That kind of information could best be obtained through a representative assembly of the settlers, empowered to levy taxes and make laws. As a result, in each of England's colonies, within a short time of the founding, the actual settlers gained a share in the choice of their governors comparable to that which Englishmen at home enjoyed through their Parliament.

England's first permanent colony in America, Virginia, was the first to exhibit the phenomenon. The Virginia Company of London, which founded the colony in 1607 and was authorized to govern it in 1609, did so for ten years without participation of the actual settlers. The results were disastrous, and in 1618 the company instructed its agents to call a representative assembly. The assembly met in 1619, the first in the present area of the United States. When the king dissolved the Virginia Company and resumed governmental authority over the colony in 1624, he declined to continue the assembly, but the governors he appointed found it necessary to do so on their own initiative until 1639, when the king recognized the need and made the Virginia House of Burgesses an official part of the government.

In most other colonies representatives were authorized from the beginning or came into existence spontaneously when colonists found themselves beyond the reach of existing governments. The Pilgrims who landed at Plymouth in 1620 provided for their own government by the MAYFLOWER COMPACT, with a representative assembly at its center. The initial governments of Rhode Island and Connecticut began in much the same way. In these Puritan colonies religious principle worked together with pragmatic necessity to emphasize the popular basis of government. Puritans believed that government, though ordained by God, must originate in a compact (or covenant) between rulers and people, in which rulers promised to abide by and enforce God's laws, while the people in return promised obedience. Even in Massachusetts, where from the beginning the government rested officially on a charter from the king, Governor John Winthrop took pains to explain that he regarded emigration to Massachusetts as a tacit consent to such a covenant on the part of everyone who came. The emigrants themselves seem to have agreed; and because the king's charter did not spell out the laws of God that must limit a proper government, the representative assembly of the colony in 1641 adopted the MASSACHUSETTS BODY OF LIBERTIES, which did so.

The model for the colonial representative assemblies was the House of Commons of England; but from the beginning the colonial assemblies were more representative than the House of Commons, in that a much larger proportion of the people shared in choosing them. In England REPRESENTATION was apportioned in a bizarre fashion among the towns and boroughs, with nearly empty villages sending members while many populous towns sent none. In the colonies, although the extension of representation did not everywhere keep up with the spread of population westward, the imbalance never approached that in England, where virtually no adjustments to shifts of population were made after the sixteenth century and none at all between 1675 and the nineteenth century. And while in England a variety of property qualifications and local regulations excluded the great majority of adult males from voting, in the colonies, because of the abundance of land and its widespread ownership, similar restrictions excluded only a minority of adult males.

In addition to its broader popular base, representation in the colonies retained more of its original popular function than did the English counterpart. Representatives in both England and the colonies were initially identified more with a particular group of subjects than with their rulers. As representatives assumed a larger and larger role in government, they necessarily came to consider themselves as acting more in an authoritative capacity over the whole people and less as the designated defenders of their immediate constituents. This conception grew more rapidly in England, as the power of the king declined and that of Parliament increased, than it did in the colonies, where representatives continued to champion the interests of their constituents against unpopular directives from England. The divergence in the American conception of representation was to play a key role both in the colonies' quarrel with England and in the problems faced by the independent Americans in creating their own governments.

By 1763, when France surrendered its North American possessions, Great Britain stood at the head of the world's greatest empire. But the place of the American colonists in that empire remained constitutionally uncertain. Officially their governments still derived authority not from popular donation but directly or indirectly from the king. In two colonies, Rhode Island and Connecticut, the king had conveyed power to the free male inhabitants to choose their own governor, governor's council, and legislative assembly. In two more the king had conveyed governmental power to a single family, the Penns in Pennsylvania and the Calverts in Maryland, who exercised their authority by appointing the governor and his council. In the rest of the colonies the king appointed the governor and (except in Massachusetts) his council, which in all colonies except Pennsylvania doubled as the upper house of the legislature. Thus in every colony except Rhode Island, Connecticut, and Massachusetts, a representative assembly made laws and levied taxes, but neither the governor nor the members of the upper house of the legislature owed their positions even indirectly to popular choice.

It might have been argued that the king himself owed his authority to some sort of popular consent, however tacitly expressed, but it would have been hard to say whether the people who gave that consent included those living in the colonies. It would have been harder still to say what relationship the colonists had to the king's Parliament. In England the king's subordination to Parliament had become increasingly clear. It was Parliament that recognized the restoration of Charles II in 1660; it was Parliament that, in effect, deposed James II in 1688; it was Parliament that placed George I on the throne in 1714 and established the succession of the House of Hanover. Insofar as England's kings ruled Great Britain after 1714 they ruled through Parliament. But they continued to rule the colonies through royal governors and councils, and Parliament still had no hand officially in the choice of royal governors and councils or in the formulation of instructions to them.

Because each colony had its own little parliament, its representative assembly, the people of each colony could have considered themselves as a separate kingdom and a separate people, separate not only from the people who chose the representative assemblies of the other colonies but separate also from the people of Great Britain who chose the British Parliament. If any colonist thought that way—and probably few did before the 1760s or 1770s—he would have had to consider a complicating fact: the British Parliament did on occasion legislate for the colonies and the colonies submitted to that legislation, most notably to the Navigation Acts of 1660 and 1663, which limited the trade of the colonies for the benefit of English merchants. Did this submission mean that the people of the colonies, who elected no representatives to Parliament, were subordinate to, as well as separate from, the people of Great Britain?

In one sense the answer had to be yes: if the king was subordinate to Parliament and the colonists were subordinate to the king, that would seem to make the colonists subordinate to Parliament and thus to the people who elected Parliament. But since Parliament had so seldom legislated for the colonies, it could be argued that the colonists' subordination to it was restricted to those areas where it had in fact legislated for them, that is, in matters that concerned their trade. In other areas, they would be subordinate to Parliament only through the king, and the subordination of the colonial representative assemblies to the king was by no means unlimited. Through the taxing power the colonial assemblies had achieved, over the years, a leverage in the operation of their respective governments comparable to that which had raised Parliament above the king in Great Britain. To be sure, they had not arrived at so clear a position of superiority over their royal governors as Parliament enjoyed over the king. For example, while Queen Anne was the last monarch to veto an act of Parliament, royal governors regularly vetoed acts of colonial assemblies; and even an act accepted by the king's governor could still be vetoed by the king himself. The assemblies nevertheless enjoyed considerable power; by refusing to authorize taxation or to appropriate funds, they could thwart royal directives that they considered injurious to the interests or rights of their constituents. And in some ways they enjoyed a greater independence of royal influence than did Parliament. Because there were few sinecures or places of profit in colonial governments within the appointment of the king or his governors, it was difficult for a governor to build a following in an assembly through patronage.

Despite its constitutional and political ambiguities the British imperial system worked. It continued to work until the power of Parliament collided with the power of the colonial assemblies, thus requiring a resolution of the uncertainties in their relationship. The collision occurred when Parliament, facing a doubled national debt after the Seven Years War, passed the Revenue Act of 1764 (usually called the Sugar Act), levying duties on colonial imports, and the Stamp Act of 1765, levying direct taxes on legal documents and other items used in the colonies. In these acts, probably without intending to, Parliament threatened to destroy the bargaining power through which the colonial assemblies had balanced the authority of the king and his governors. If Parliament could tax the colonists directly, it might free the king's governors from dependence on the assemblies for funds and ultimately render the assemblies powerless.

In pamphlets and newspaper articles the colonists denounced the new measures. The assemblies, both separately and in a STAMP ACT CONGRESS, to which nine colonies sent delegates, spelled out in resolutions and petitions what they considered to be fundamental constitutional rights that Parliament had violated. In doing so the assemblies were obliged to define their constitutional relationship to Parliament with a precision never before required.

Parliament, it must be remembered, had been regarded for centuries as the bulwark of English liberties. It was the representative body of the English people, and through it the English had tamed their king as no other Europeans had. To question its supremacy might well seem to be a reactionary retreat toward absolute monarchy by divine right. The colonists were therefore hesitant to deny all subordination to Parliament. Yet, if they were to enjoy the same rights that other British subjects enjoyed in Great Britain, they must reserve to their own assemblies at the very least the power to tax. They acknowledged, therefore, the authority of Parliament to legislate for the whole empire as it had hitherto done in regulating colonial trade, but they drew a distinction between the power to legislate and the power to tax.

The colonists associated legislation with the sovereign power of a state, and they wanted to consider themselves as remaining in some still undefined way under the sovereign power of the British government. But taxation had from the time of England's first Parliaments been a function of representatives, authorized by those who sent them to give a part of their property to the king in taxes. Taxation, the colonial assemblies affirmed, was not a part of the governing or legislative power, but an action taken in behalf of the king's subjects. This distinction could be seen, they pointed out, in the form given to Parliamentary acts of taxation: such acts originated in the House of Commons and were phrased as the gift of the commons to the king.

Now the difference between American and British conceptions of representation began to appear. The colonists did not think of the English House of Commons as representing them, for no county or town or borough in the colonies sent members. The British government had never suggested that they might, and the colonists themselves rejected the possibility as impracticable. Given their conception of the representative's subservient relation to his constituents, it would have been impossible, they felt, to maintain adequate control over representatives at 3,000 miles' distance. Thus the colonists had not authorized and could not authorize any representative in Parliament to give their property in taxes. When Parliament taxed them, therefore, it deprived them of a fundamental right of Englishmen, sacred since before the colonies were founded. For a Parliament in which the colonists were not represented to tax them was equivalent to the king's taxing Englishmen in England without the consent of the House of Commons. The colonists called in vain on English courts to nullify this violation of fundamental law.

In answering the colonial objections, British spokesmen did not claim that the colonists could be taxed without the consent of their representatives. Thomas Whately, speaking for the ministry that sponsored the taxes, went even further than the colonists by denying that any legislation affecting British subjects anywhere could be passed without consent of their representatives. But he went on to affirm what to the colonists was an absurdity, that the colonists were represented in the House of Commons. Although they did not choose members, they were *virtually* represented by every member chosen in Britain, each of whom was entrusted with the interests not merely of the few persons who chose him but of all British subjects. The colonists were represented in the same way as Englishmen in towns that sent no members, in the same way also as English women and children.

However plausible this reasoning may have been to Englishmen, to the colonists it was sheer sophistry. They made plain in resolutions of their assemblies, as for example in Pennsylvania, "That the only legal Representatives of the Inhabitants of this Province are the Persons they annually elect to serve as Members of Assembly." Pamphlets and newspapers were even more scathing in rejecting the pretensions of Parliament to represent Americans. In Massachusetts JAMES OTIS asked, "Will any man's calling himself my agent, representative, or trustee make him so in fact?" On that basis the House of Commons could equally pretend "that they were the true and proper representatives of all the common people upon the globe." (See TAXATION WITHOUT REPRESENTATION.)

In reaction to the objections of the colonists and of the English merchants who traded with them, Parliament in 1766 repealed the Stamp Act and revised the Sugar Act. But at the same time it passed a Declaratory Act, affirming its right to legislate for the colonies "in all cases whatsoever." The framers of the act deliberately omitted specific mention of the power to tax, but in the following year Parliament again exercised that presumed power in the TOWNSHEND ACTS, levying more customs duties on colonial imports. The colonists again mounted protests, but they were still reluctant to deny all Parliamentary authority over them and clung to their distinction between legislation and taxation, which the great William Pitt himself had supported (unsuccessfully) in Parliamentary debate. Parliament, they said, could regulate their trade, even by imposing customs duties, but must not use the pretext of trade regulation for the purpose of raising revenue.

Once again the colonial protests, backed by boycotts, secured repeal of most of the offending taxes, but once again Parliament reaffirmed the principle of its unlimited power, not in a declaration, but by retaining a token tax on tea. The colonists, relieved of any serious burden, were left to ponder the implications of their position. In one sense Parliament was treating them as part of a single people, over all of whom, whether in England or elsewhere, Parliament reigned supreme. In rejecting the notion that they were, or even could be, represented in Parliament, the colonists implied that they were a separate people or peoples.

A reluctance to face this implication had prompted their continued recognition of some sort of authority in Parliament. If Parliament in the past had secured the rights of Englishmen, was it not dangerous (as Whately had indeed said it was) to rely instead on the powers of their own little assemblies? If they were a separate people, or peoples, not subject to Parliament, would they not be foregoing the rights of Englishmen, the very rights they were so vigorously claiming? Could they expect their own assemblies to be as effective defenders of those rights as the mighty British Parliament?

As the quarrel over taxation progressed, with the Boston Tea Party of 1773 and Parliament's punitive Coercive Act of 1774 against Massachusetts, more and more Americans overcame the doubts raised by such questions. The Coercive Acts regulated trade with a vengeance by interdicting Boston's trade, and the acts also altered the government of Massachusetts as defined by its royal charter (ending the provincial election of the governor's council), thereby showing once and for all that guarantees given by the king could not stand before the supremacy claimed by Parliament. In the treatment of Massachusetts the other colonies read what was in store for them, and the various colonial assemblies sent delegates to the FIRST CONTINENTAL CONGRESS in 1774 in order to concert their response.

As in the earlier Stamp Act Congress, the delegates had to determine what they considered to be the limits of Parliament's authority. This time, abandoning their distinction between legislation and taxation (which Parliament had never recognized), they denied that Parliament had or had ever had constitutional authority over them. As a last conciliatory gesture, they expressed a willingness voluntarily to submit to bona fide regulations of trade, but made clear that Parliament had no constitutional right to make such regulations. Following the lead given in tracts by JOHN ADAMS, JAMES WILSON, and THOMAS JEFFERSON, they elevated their separate representative assemblies to a constitutional position within their respective jurisdictions equal to that of Parliament in Great Britain. The only remaining link connecting them with the mother country was their allegiance to the same king, who must be seen as the king of Virginia, Massachusetts, and so on, as well as of England, Scotland, Wales, and Ireland. (Ireland, it was noted, also had its separate Parliament.) Over his peoples beyond the seas the king exercised his powers through separate but equal governments, each with its own governor, council, and representative assembly.

The king did not, of course, rule by divine right. In the colonies as in England he derived his authority from the people themselves, that is, from the separate consent or constituent act of each of the peoples of his empire. John Adams of Massachusetts, perceiving the need to identify such an act, pointed to the Glorious Revolution of 1688 as an event in which each of the king's peoples participated separately. "It ought to be remembered," he said, "that there was a revolution here, as well as in England, and that we as well as the people of England, made an original, express contract with King William." That contract, as Adams and other colonists now saw it, limited royal power in the same way it was limited in England and guaranteed in each colony the exclusive legislative and taxing authority of the representative assembly.

Although the First Continental Congress gave a terminal clarity to the colonists' views of their constitutional position in the empire, it looked forward uncertainly toward a new relationship among the colonies themselves. The membership of the Congress reflected the uncertainty. Some of the members had been chosen by regularly constituted assemblies; others had been sent by extralegal conventions or committees; and a few were self-appointed. What authority, if any, the members had was not clear. Given the view of representation that had guided colonial reaction to Parliamentary taxation, no one was ready to claim for Congress the powers denied to Parliament. Though delegates from every colony except Georgia were present, they had not been chosen by direct popular elections and therefore were not, by their own definition, representatives. At best, as one of them put it, they were "representatives of representatives."

Yet they had not come together simply for discussion. Boston was under military occupation and Massachusetts was under military government. Regular royal government throughout the colonies was fast approaching dissolution. It was time for action, and the Congress took action. Without pausing to determine by what authority, it adopted an ASSOCIATION forbidding not only exports to and imports from Great Britain but also the consumption of British goods. And it called for the creation of committees in every county, city, and town to enforce these restrictions.

In the misnamed Association (membership in which was scarcely voluntary) the Congress took the first steps toward creating a national government separate from that of the (not yet independent) states. If the members believed, as presumably they did, that the authority of government derives from the people, they implied, perhaps without quite realizing what they were doing, that there existed a single American people, distinct not only from the people of Great Britain but also from the peoples of the several colonies and capable of conveying a political authority distinct from that either of Great Britain or of the several colonies.

The implication would not become explicit until the Constitution of 1787, but the Second Continental Congress, which assembled in May 1775, looked even more like the government of a single people than had the First. Fighting had already broken out in April between British troops and Massachusetts militiamen, and Congress at once took charge of the war and began the enlistment of a Continental Army. It sent envoys to France to seek foreign assistance. It opened American commerce to foreign nations. It advised the peoples of the several colonies to suppress all royal authority within their borders. And finally, after more than a year of warfare, it declared the independence of the United States.

Despite the boldness of these actions, the DECLARATION OF INDEPENDENCE itself betrayed the ambiguities that Americans felt about their own identity. It unequivocally put an end to royal authority (parliamentary authority had already been rejected) and consequently to all remaining connection with the people of Great Britain. But it was not quite clear whether the independence thus affirmed was of one people, or of several, or of both one and several. While the preamble spoke of "one people" separating from another, the final affirmation was in the plural, declaring that "these United Colonies are, and of Right ought to be Free and Independent States." Yet in stating what constituted free and independent statehood, the Declaration specified only "power to levy war, conclude peace, contract alliances, establish commerce." These were all things, with the possible exception of the last, that had been done or would be done by the Congress.

But if the Congress sometimes acted like the government of a single free and independent state, the members still did not recognize the implication that they represented a single free and independent people. They did not consider their Declaration of Independence complete until it had been ratified by each of the separate states whose freedom and independence it declared. And when they tried to define their own authority, they found it difficult to reach agreement. ARTICLES OF CONFEDERATION, first drafted in 1776, were not ratified by the several states until 1781. The Articles entrusted Congress with the powers it was already exercising but declined to derive those powers from a single American people. The old local committees of the Association of 1774, tied directly to Congress, were now a thing of the past, and the enactments of Congress became mere recommendations, to be carried out by the various states as they saw fit.

Even before the Declaration of Independence, in response to the recommendation of the Congress, the states had begun to create governments resting solely on the purported will of the people within their existing borders. In every state a provisional government appeared, usually in the form of a provincial congress resembling the old colonial representative assembly. In most of the states, beginning with Virginia in June 1776, these provincial congresses drew up and adopted, without further reference to the people, constitutions defining the structure of their governments and stating limitations on governmental powers in bills of rights. In every case the constitution was thought or proclaimed to be in some way an act of the people who were to be governed under it, and therefore different from and superior to acts of representatives in a legislative assembly. But often the provincial congress that drafted a state constitution continued to act as the legislative body provided in it. Although a constitution might affirm its own superiority to ordinary legislation, the fact that it was created by legislative act rendered doubtful its immunity to alteration by the body that created it.

A similar doubt surrounded the principle, also enunciated in most of the constitutions, that (as in Virginia) "The legislative, executive, and judiciary departments shall be separate and distinct, so that neither exercise the powers properly belonging to the other." The several provincial congresses that drafted the constitutions inherited the aggressiveness of the colonial assemblies against executive and, to a lesser degree, judicial powers, which had hitherto rested in an overseas authority beyond their reach. In spite of the assertion of the separation of powers, and in spite of the fact that executives and judges would now derive authority solely from the people they governed, the state constitutions generally gave the lion's share of power in government to the representative assemblies.

The result was to bring out the shortcomings of the view of representation that had directed the colonists in their resistance to British taxation. For a decade the colonists had insisted that a representative must act only for the particular group of persons who chose him. They occasionally recognized but minimized his responsibility, as part of the governing body, to act for the whole people who were to be governed by the laws he helped to pass. Now the representative assemblies were suddenly presented with virtually the entire powers of government, which they shared only with a weak executive and judiciary and with a Continental Congress whose powers remained uncertain, despite Articles of Confederation that gave it large responsibilities without the means to perform them. Undeterred by any larger view of their functions, too many of the state assemblymen made a virtue of partiality to their particular constituents and ignored the long-range needs not only of their own state but of the United States.

The solution lay ahead in 1787. By 1776 the inherited ingredients of the settlement then adopted were in place. A rudimentary distinction between the constituent actions of a putative people and the actions of their government had been recognized, though not effectively implemented, in the state governments. All government officers were now selected directly or indirectly by popular choice, with their powers limited, at least nominally, by a reservation to the people of powers not specifically conveyed. And a national center of authority, not quite a government but nevertheless acting like a government, was in operation in the Continental Congress.

What was needed—and with every passing year after 1776 the need became more apparent—was a way to relieve popular government from the grip of short-sighted representative assemblies. Two political inventions filled the need. The first was the constitutional convention, an assembly without legislative powers, entrusted solely with the drafting of a constitution for submission to popular ratification, a constitution that could plausibly be seen as the embodiment of the popular will superior to the ordinary acts of representative assemblies. Massachusetts provided this invention in 1779, in the convention that drafted the state's first constitution. (See MASSACHUSETTS CONSTITUTION.)

The first invention made way for the second, which was supplied by JAMES MADISON and his colleagues at Philadelphia in 1787. They invented the American people. It was, to be sure, an invention waiting to be made. It had been prefigured in the assumptions behind the Continental Association and the Declaration of Independence. But it reached fulfillment only in the making of the Constitution. By means of a national constitutional convention the men at Philadelphia built a national government that presumed and thus helped to create an American people, distinct from and superior to the peoples of the states.

The idea of popular SOVEREIGNTY was, as we have seen, an old one, but only occasionally had it dictated the formation of popular governments, governments in which all the officers owed their positions directly or indirectly to popular election. Though the idea surfaced powerfully in the England of the 1640s and 1650s, it eventuated there in a restored monarchy, and it won only partial recognition in England's Revolution of 1688. In the American Revolution it had seemingly found full expression in thirteen separate state governments, but by 1787 the actions of those governments threatened once again to discredit the whole idea. The signal achievement of the constitutional convention was expressed in the opening words of the document it produced: "We the People of the United States." The United States Constitution rescued popular sovereignty by extending it. It inaugurated both a new government and a new people.

EDMUND S. MORGAN

Bibliography

ADAMS, WILLI PAUL 1980 *The First American Constitutions.* Chapel Hill: University of North Carolina Press.

BAILYN, BERNARD 1967 *The Ideological Origins of the American Revolution.* Cambridge, Mass.: Harvard University Press.

______ 1968 *The Origins of American Politics.* New York: Knopf.

FIGGIS, JOHN NEVILLE 1914 *The Divine Right of Kings.* Cambridge: At the University Press.

GREENE, JACK P. 1963 *The Quest for Power.* Chapel Hill: University of North Carolina Press.

KANTOROWICZ, ERNST H. 1957 *The King's Two Bodies.* Princeton: N.J.: Princeton University Press.

LABAREE, LEONARD W. 1930 *Royal Government in America.* New Haven, Conn.: Yale University Press.

MCILWAIN, CHARLES H. 1923 *The American Revolution.* New York: Macmillan.

MORGAN, EDMUND S. and MORGAN, HELEN M. 1953 *The Stamp Act Crisis.* Chapel Hill: University of North Carolina Press.

POCOCK, JOHN G. A. 1957 *The Ancient Constitution and the Feudal Law.* Cambridge: At the University Press.

RUSSELL, CONRAD 1979 *Parliaments and English Politics 1621–1629.* Oxford: Clarendon Press.

SCHUYLER, ROBERT L. 1929 *Parliament and the British Empire.* New York: Columbia University Press.

SKINNER, QUENTIN 1978 *The Foundations of Modern Political Thought.* Cambridge: At the University Press.

TUCKER, ROBERT W. and HENDRICKSON, DAVID C. 1982 *The Fall of the First British Empire.* Baltimore: Johns Hopkins University Press.

CONSTITUTIONAL HISTORY, 1776–1789

On July 4, 1776, King George III wrote in his diary, "Nothing of importance this day." When the news of the DECLARATION OF INDEPENDENCE reached him, he still could not know how wrong he had been. The political philosophy of SOCIAL COMPACT, NATURAL RIGHTS, and LIMITED GOVERNMENT that generated the Declaration of Independence also spurred the most important, creative, and dynamic constitutional achievements in history; the Declaration itself was merely the beginning. Within a mere thirteen years Americans invented or first institutionalized a bill of rights against all branches of government, the written CONSTITUTION, the CONSTITUTIONAL CONVENTION, FEDERALISM, JUDICIAL REVIEW, and a solution to the colonial problem (admitting TERRITORIES to the Union as states fully equal to the original thirteen). RELIGIOUS LIBERTY, the SEPARATION OF CHURCH AND STATE, political parties, SEPARATION OF POWERS, an acceptance of the principle of equality, and the conscious creation of a new nation were also among American institutional "firsts," although not all these initially appeared between 1776 and 1789. In that brief span of time, Americans created what are today the oldest major republic, political democracy, state constitution, and national constitution. These unparalleled American achievements derived not from originality in speculative theory but from the constructive application of old ideas, which Americans took so seriously that they constitutionally based their institutions of government on them.

From thirteen separate colonies the Second Continental Congress "brought forth a new nation," as ABRAHAM LINCOLN said. In May 1776, Congress urged all the colonies to suppress royal authority and adopt permanent governments. On that advice and in the midst of a war the colonies began to frame the world's first written constitutions. When Congress triggered the drafting of those constitutions, Virginia instructed its delegates to Congress to propose that Congress should declare "the United Colonies free and independent states." Neither Virginia nor Congress advocated state sovereignty. Congress's advice implied the erection of state governments with sovereign powers over domestic matters or "internal police."

On June 7, 1776, Congressman RICHARD HENRY LEE of Virginia introduced the resolution as instructed, and Congress appointed two committees, one to frame the document that became the Declaration of Independence and the other to frame a plan of confederation—a constitution for a continental government. When Lincoln declared, "The Union is older than the States, and in fact created them as States," he meant that the Union (Congress) antedated the states. The Declaration of Independence, which stated that the colonies had become states, asserted the authority of the "United States of America, in General Congress, Assembled."

The "spirit of '76" tended to be strongly nationalistic. The members of Congress represented the states, of course, and acted on their instructions, but they acted for the new nation, and the form of government they thought proper in 1776 was a centralized one. As a matter of fact BENJAMIN FRANKLIN had proposed such a government on July 21, 1775, when he presented to Congress "ARTICLES OF CONFEDERATION and perpetual Union." Franklin urged a congressional government with an executive committee that would manage "general continental Business and Interests," conduct diplomacy, and administer finances. His plan empowered Congress to determine war and peace, exchange ambassadors, make foreign alliances, settle all disputes between the colonies, plant new colonies, and, in a sweeping omnibus clause, make laws for "the General Welfare" concerning matters on which individual colonies "cannot be competent," such as "our general Commerce," "general Currency," the establishment of a post office, and governance of "our Common Forces." Costs were to be paid from a common treasury supplied by each colony in proportion to its male inhabitants, but each colony would raise its share by taxing its inhabitants. Franklin provided for an easy amendment process: Congress recommended amendments that would become part of the Articles when approved by a majority of colonial assemblies. Franklin's plan of union seemed much too radical in July 1775, when independence was a year away and reconciliation with Britain on American terms was the object of the war. Congress simply tabled the Franklin plan.

As the war continued into 1776, nationalist sentiment strengthened. THOMAS PAINE's *Common Sense* called for American independence and "a Continental form of Government." Nationalism and centralism were twin causes. JOHN LANGDON of New Hampshire favored independence and "an American Constitution" that provided for appeals from every colony to a national congress "in everything of moment relative to governmental matters." Proposals for a centralized union became common by the spring of 1776, and these proposals, as the following representative samples suggest, tended to show democratic impulses. Nationalism and mitigated democracy, not nationalism and conservatism, were related. A New York newspaper urged the popular election of a national congress with a "superintending power" over the individual colonies as to "all commercial and Continental affairs," leaving to each colony control over its "internal policy." A populistic plan in a Connecticut newspaper recommended that the congress be empowered to govern "all matters of general concernment" and "every other thing proper and necessary" for the benefit of the whole, allowing the individual colonies only that which fell "within the territorial jurisdiction of a particular assembly." The "Spartacus" essays, which newspapers in New York, Philadelphia, and Portsmouth printed, left the state "cantons" their own legislatures but united all in a national congress with powers similar to those enumerated by Franklin, including a paramount power to "interfere" with a colony's "provincial affairs" whenever required by "the good of the continent." "Essex" reminded his readers that "the strength and happiness of America must be Continental, not Provincial, and that whatever appears to be for the good of the whole, must be submitted to by every Part." He advocated dividing the colonies into many smaller equal parts that would have equal representation in a powerful national congress chosen directly by the people, including taxpaying widows. Carter Braxton, a conservative Virginian, favored aristocratic controls over a congress that could not "interfere with the internal police or domestic concerns of any Colony . . . ."

Given the prevalence of such views in the first half of 1776, a representative committee of the Continental Congress probably mirrored public opinion when it framed a nationalist plan for confederation. On July 12, one month after the appointment of a thirteen-member committee (one from each state) to write a draft, JOHN DICKINSON of Pennsylvania, the committee chairman, presented to Congress a plan that borrowed heavily from Franklin's. The Committee of the Whole of Congress debated the Dickinson draft and adopted it on August 20 with few changes. Only one was significant. Dickinson had proposed that Congress be empowered to fix the western boundaries of states claiming territory to the Pacific coast and to form new states in the west. The Committee of the Whole, bending to the wishes of eight states with extensive western claims, omitted that provision from its revision of the Dickinson draft. That omission became a stumbling block.

On August 20 the Committee of the Whole reported the revised plan of union to Congress. The plan was similar to Franklin's, except that Congress had no power over "general commerce." But Congress, acting for the United States, was clearly paramount to the individual states. They were not even referred to as "states." Collectively they were "the United States of America"; otherwise they were styled "colonies" or "colony," terms not compatible with sovereignty, to which no reference was made. Indeed, the draft merely reserved to each colony "sole and exclusive Regulation and Government of its internal police, in all matters that shall not interfere with the Articles of this Confederation." That crucial provision, Article III, making even "internal police" subordinate to congressional powers, highlighted the nationalist character of the proposed confederation.

The array of congressional powers included exclusive authority over war and peace, land and naval forces, treaties and alliances, prize cases, crimes on the high seas and navigable rivers, all disputes between states, coining money, borrowing on national credit, Indian affairs, post offices, weights and measures, and "the Defence and Welfare" of the United States. Congress also had power to appoint a Council of State and civil officers "necessary for managing the general Affairs of the United States." The Council of State, consisting of one member from each of the thirteen, was empowered to administer the United States government and execute its measures. Notwithstanding this embryonic executive branch, the government of the United States was congressional in character, consisting of a single house whose members were to be elected annually by the legislatures of the colonies. Each colony cast one vote, making each politically equal in Congress. On all important matters, the approval of nine colonies was required to pass legislation. Amendments to the Articles needed the unanimous approval of the legislatures of the various colonies, a provision that later proved to be crippling.

The Articles reported by the Committee of the Whole provoked dissension. States without western land claims opposed the omission of the provision in the Dickinson draft that gave Congress control over western lands. Large states opposed the principle of one vote for each state, preferring instead proportionate representation with each delegate voting. Sharp differences also emerged concerning the rule by which each state was to pay its quota to defray common expenses. Finally some congressmen feared the centralizing nature of the new government. Edward Rutledge of South Carolina did not like "the Idea of destroying all Provincial Distinctions and making every thing of the most minute kind bend to what they call the good of the whole. . . ." Rutledge resolved "to vest the Congress with no more Power than what is absolutely necessary." James Wilson of Pennsylvania could declare that Congress represented "all the individuals of the states" rather than the states, but Roger Sherman of Connecticut answered, "We are representatives of states, not individuals." That attitude would undo the nationalist "spirit of '76."

Because of disagreements and the urgency of prosecuting the war, Congress was unable to settle on a plan of union in 1776. By the spring of 1777 the nationalist momentum was spent. By then most of the states had adopted constitutions and had legitimate governments. Previously, provisional governments of local "congresses," "conventions," and committees had controlled the states and looked to the Continental Congress for leadership and approval. But the creation of legitimate state governments reinvigorated old provincial loyalties. Local politicians, whose careers were provincially oriented, feared a strong central government as a rival institution. Loyalists no longer participated in politics, local or national, depleting support for central control. By late April of 1777, when state sovereignty triumphed, only seventeen of the forty-eight congressmen who had been members of the Committee of the Whole that adopted the Dickinson draft remained in Congress. Most of the new congressmen opposed centralized government.

James Wilson, who was a congressman in 1776 and 1777, recalled what happened when he addressed the Constitutional Convention on June 8, 1787:

> Among the first sentiments expressed in the first Congs. one was that Virga. is no more. That Massts. is no more, that Pa. is no more &c. We are now one nation of brethren. We must bury all local interests and distinctions. This language continued for some time. The tables at length began to turn. No sooner were the State Govts. formed than their jealousy & ambition began to display themselves. Each endeavored to cut a slice from the common loaf, to add to

its own morsel, till at length the confederation became frittered down to the impotent condition in which it now stands. Review the progress of the articles of Confederation thro' Congress & compare the first and last draught of it [Farrand, ed., *Records,* I, 166–67].

The turning point occurred in late April 1777 when Thomas Burke of North Carolina turned his formidable localist opinions against the report of the Committee of the Whole. Its Article III, in his words, "expressed only a reservation [to the states] of the power of regulating the internal police, and consequently resigned every other power [to Congress]." Congress, he declared, sought even to interfere with the states' internal police and make its own powers "unlimited." Burke accordingly moved the following substitute for Article III, which became Article II of the Articles as finally adopted: "Each State retains its sovereignty, freedom and independence, and every power, jurisdiction and right, which is not by this confederation expressly delegated to the United States in Congress assembled." Burke's motion carried by the votes of eleven states, vitiating the powers of the national government recommended by the Committee of the Whole.

In the autumn of 1777 a Congress dominated by state-sovereignty advocates completed the plan of confederation. Those who favored proportionate representation in Congress with every member entitled to vote lost badly to those who favored voting by states with each state having one vote. Thereafter the populous wealthy states had no stake in supporting a strong national government that could be controlled by the votes of lesser states. The power of Congress to negotiate commercial treaties effectively died when Congress agreed that under the Articles no treaty should violate the power of the states to impose tariff duties or prohibit imports and exports. The power of Congress to settle all disputes between states became merely a power to make recommendations. The permanent executive branch became a temporary committee with no powers except as delegated by the votes of nine states, the number required to adopt any major measure. Congress also agreed that it should not have power to fix the western boundaries of states claiming lands to the Pacific.

After the nationalist spurt of 1776 proved insufficient to produce the Articles, the states made the Confederation feckless. Even as colonies the states had been particularistic, jealous, and uncooperative. Centrifugal forces originating in diversity—of economics, geography, religion, class structure, and race—produced sectional, provincial, and local loyalties that could not be overcome during a war against the centralized powers claimed by Parliament. The controversy with Britain had produced passions and principles that made the Franklin and Dickinson drafts unviable. Not even these nationalist drafts empowered Congress to tax, although the principle of no TAXATION WITHOUT REPRESENTATION had become irrelevant as to Congress. Similarly, Congress as late as 1774 had "cheerfully" acknowledged Parliament's legitimate "regulation of our external commerce," but in 1776 Congress denied that Parliament had any authority over America, and by 1777 Americans were unwilling to grant their own central legislature powers they preferred their provincial assemblies to wield. Above all, most states refused to repose their trust in any central authority that a few large states might dominate, absent a constitutionally based principle of state equality.

Unanimous consent for amendments to the Articles proved to be too high a price to pay for acknowledging the "sovereignty" of each state, although that acknowledgment made Maryland capable of winning for the United States the creation of a national domain held in common for the benefit of all. Maryland also won the promise that new states would be admitted to the union on a principle of state equality. That prevented the development of a colonial problem from Atlantic to Pacific, and the NORTHWEST ORDINANCE OF 1787 was the Confederation's finest and most enduring achievement.

The Constitution of 1787 was unthinkable in 1776, impossible in 1781 or at any time before it was framed. The Articles were an indispensable transitional stage in the development of the Constitution. Not even the Constitution would have been ratified if its Framers had submitted it for approval to the state legislatures that kept Congress paralyzed in the 1780s. Congress, representing the United States, authorized the creation of the states and ended up, as it had begun, as their creature. It possessed expressly delegated powers with no means of enforcing them. That Congress lacked commerce and tax powers was a serious deficiency, but not nearly so crippling as its lack of sanctions and the failure of the states to abide by the Articles. Congress simply could not make anyone, except soldiers, do anything. It acted on the states, not on people. Only a national government that could execute its laws independently of the states could have survived.

The states flouted their constitutional obligations. The Articles obliged the states to "abide by the determinations of the United States, in Congress assembled," but there was no way to force the states to comply. The states were not sovereign, except as to their internal police and tax powers; rather, they behaved unconstitutionally. No foreign nation recognized the states as sovereign, because Congress possessed the external attributes of sovereignty especially as to FOREIGN AFFAIRS and WAR POWERS.

One of the extraordinary achievements of the Articles was the creation of a rudimentary federal system. It failed because its central government did not operate directly on individuals within its sphere of authority. The Confederation had no independent executive and judicial branches, because the need for them scarcely existed when Congress addressed its acts mainly to the states. The framers of the Articles distributed the powers of government with remarkable acumen, committing to Congress about all that belonged to a central government except, of course, taxation and commercial regulation, the two powers that Americans of the Revolutionary War believed to be part of state sovereignty. Even ALEXANDER HAMILTON, who in 1780 advocated that Congress should have "complete sovereignty," excepted "raising money by internal taxes."

Congress could requisition money from the states, but they did not pay their quotas. In 1781 Congress requisitioned $8,000,000 for the next year, but the states paid less than half a million. While the Articles lasted, the cumulative amount paid by all the states hardly exceeded what was required to pay the interest on the public debt for just one year.

Nationalists vainly sought to make the Articles more effective by both interpretation and amendment. Madison devised a theory of IMPLIED POWERS by which he squeezed out of the Articles congressional authority to use force if necessary against states that failed to fulfill their obligations. Congress refused to attempt coercion just as it refused to recommend an amendment authorizing its use. Congress did, however, charter a bank to control currency, but the opposition to the exercise of a power not expressly delegated remained so intense that the bank had to be rechartered by a state. Congress vainly sought unanimous state consent for various amendments that would empower it to raise money from customs duties and to regulate commerce, foreign and domestic. In 1781 every state but Rhode Island approved an amendment empowering Congress to impose a five percent duty on all foreign imports; never again did an amendment to the Articles come so close to adoption. Only four states ratified an amendment authorizing a congressional embargo against the vessels of any nation with whom the United States had no treaty of commerce. Congress simply had no power to negotiate commercial treaties with nations such as Britain that discriminated against American shipping. Nor had Congress the power to prevent states from violating treaties with foreign nations. In 1786 JOHN JAY, Congress's secretary of foreign affairs, declared that not a day had passed since ratification of the 1783 treaty of peace without its violation by at least one state. Some states also discriminated against the trade of others. Madison likened New Jersey, caught between the ports of Philadelphia and New York, "to a cask tapped at both ends." More important, Congress failed even to recommend needed amendments. As early as 1784 Congress was so divided it defeated an amendment that would enable it to regulate commerce, foreign and domestic, and to levy duties on imports and exports. Often Congress could not function for lack of a quorum. The requisite number of states was present for only three days between October 1785 and April 1786. In 1786 Congress was unable to agree on any amendments for submission to the states.

The political condition of the United States during the 1780s stagnated partly because of the constitutional impotence of Congress and the unconstitutional conduct of the states. The controversy with Britain had taught that liberty and localism were congruent. The 1780s taught that excessive localism was incompatible with nationhood. The Confederation was a necessary point of midpassage. It bequeathed to the United States the fundamentals of a federal system, a national domain, and a solution to the colonial problem. Moreover the Articles contained several provisions that were antecedents of their counterparts in the Constitution of 1787: a free speech clause for congressmen and LEGISLATIVE IMMUNITY, a PRIVILEGES AND IMMUNITIES clause, a clause on the extradition of FUGITIVES FROM JUSTICE, a FULL FAITH AND CREDIT clause, and a clause validating United States debts. The Confederation also started an effective government bureaucracy when the Congress in 1781 created secretaries for foreign affairs, war, marine, and finance—precursors of an executive branch. When the new departments of that branch began to function in 1789, a corps of experienced administrators, trained under the Articles, staffed them. The courts established by Congress to decide prize and admiralty cases as well as boundary disputes foreshadowed a national judiciary. Except for enactment of the great Northwest Ordinance, however, the Congress of the Confederation was moribund by 1787. It had successfully prosecuted the war, made foreign alliances, established the national credit, framed the first constitution of the United States, negotiated a favorable treaty of peace, and created a national domain. Congress's accomplishments were monumental, especially during wartime, yet in the end it failed.

By contrast, state government flourished. Excepting Rhode Island and Connecticut, all the states adopted written constitutions during the war, eight in 1776. Madison exultantly wrote, "Nothing has excited more admiration in the world than the manner in which free governments have been established in America, for it was the first instance, from the creation of the world that free inhabitants have been seen deliberating on a form of government, and selection of such of their citizens as possessed their confidence to determine upon and give effect to it."

The VIRGINIA CONSTITUTION OF 1776, the first permanent state constitution, began with a Declaration of Rights adopted three weeks before the Declaration of Independence. No previous bill of rights had restrained all branches of government. Virginia's reflected the widespread belief that Americans had been thrown back into a state of nature from which they emerged by framing a social compact for their governance, reserving to themselves certain inherent or natural rights, including life, liberty, the enjoyment of property, and the pursuit of happiness. Virginia's declaration explicitly declared that as all power derived from the people, for whose benefit government existed, the people could reform or abolish government when it failed them. On the basis of this philosophy Virginia framed a constitution providing for a bicameral legislature, a governor, and a judicial system. The legislature elected a governor, who held office for one year, had no veto power, and was encumbered by an executive council. The legislature chose many important officials, including judges.

Some states followed the more democratic model of the PENNSYLVANIA CONSTITUTION OF 1776, others the ultraconservative one of Maryland, but all state constitutions prior to the MASSACHUSETTS CONSTITUTION OF 1780 were framed by legislatures, which in some states called themselves "conventions" or assemblies. Massachusetts deserves credit for having originated a new institution of government, a specially elected constitutional convention whose sole function was to frame the constitution and submit it for popular ratification. That procedure became the standard. Massachusetts's constitution, which is still operative, became the model American state constitution. The democratic procedure for making it fit the emerging theory that the sovereign people should be the source of the constitution and authorize its framing by a constitutional convention, rather than the legislature to which the constitution is paramount. Massachusetts was also the first state to give more than lip service to the principle of separation of powers. Everywhere else, excepting perhaps New York, unbalanced government and legislative supremacy prevailed. Massachusetts established the precedent for a strong, popularly elected executive with a veto power; elsewhere the governor tended to be a ceremonial head who depended for his existence on the legislature.

The first state constitutions and related legislation introduced significant reforms. Most states expanded VOTING RIGHTS by reducing property qualifications, and a few, including Vermont (an independent state from 1777 to 1791), experimented with universal manhood suffrage. Many state constitutions provided for fairer apportionment of REPRESENTATION in the legislature. Every southern state either abolished its ESTABLISHMENT OF RELIGION or took major steps to achieve separation of church and state. Northern states either abolished SLAVERY or provided for its gradual ending. Criminal codes were made more humane. The confiscation of Loyalist estates and of crown lands, and the opening of a national domain westward to the Mississippi, led to a democratization of landholding, as did the abolition of feudal relics such as the law of primogeniture and entail. The pace of democratic change varied from state to state, and in some states it was nearly imperceptible, but the Revolution without doubt occasioned constitutional and political developments that had long been dammed up under the colonial system.

The theory that a constitution is supreme law encouraged the development of judicial review. Written constitutions with bills of rights and the emerging principle of separation of powers contributed to the same end. Before the Revolution appellate judges tended to be dependents of the executive branch; the Revolution promoted judicial independence. Most state constitutions provided for judicial tenure during good behavior rather than for a fixed term or the pleasure of the appointing power. Inevitably when Americans believed that a legislature had exceeded its authority they argued that it had acted unconstitutionally, and they turned to courts to enforce the supreme law as law. The dominant view, however, was that a court holding a statute unconstitutional insulted the sovereignty of the legislature, as the reactions to HOLMES V. WALTON (1780) and TREVETT V. WEEDEN (1786) showed. COMMONWEALTH V. CATON (1782) was probably the first case in which a state judge declared that a court had power to hold a statute unconstitutional, though the court in that case sustained the act before it. In RUTGERS V. WADDINGTON (1784) Alexander Hamilton as counsel argued that a state act violating a treaty was unconstitutional, but the court declared that the judicial power advocated by counsel was "subversive of all government." Counsel in *Trevett* also contended that the court should void a state act. Arguments of counsel do not create precedents but can reveal the emergence of a new idea. Any American would have agreed that an act against a constitution was void; although few would have agreed that courts have the final power to decide matters of constitutionality, that idea was spreading. The TEN POUND ACT CASES (1786) were the first in which an American court held a state enactment void, and that New Hampshire precedent was succeeded by a similar decision in the North Carolina case of BAYARD v. SINGLETON (1787). The principle of MARBURY v. MADISON (1803) thus originated at a state level before the framing of the federal Constitution.

The Constitution originated in the drive for a strong national government that preceded the framing of the Articles of Confederation. The "critical period" of 1781–1787 intensified that drive, but it began well before the defects of the Articles expanded the ranks of the nationalists. The weaknesses of the United States in international affairs, its inability to enforce the peace treaty, its financial crisis, its helplessness during SHAYS' REBELLION, and its general incapacity to govern resulted in many proposals—in Congress, in the press, and even in some states—for national powers to negotiate commercial treaties, regulate the nation's commerce, and check state policies that adversely affected creditor interests and impeded economic growth. Five states met at the Annapolis Convention in 1786, ostensibly to discuss a "uniform system" of regulating commerce, but those who masterminded the meeting had a much larger agenda in mind—as Madison put it, a "plenipotentiary Convention for amending the Confederation."

Hamilton had called for a "convention of all the states" as early as 1780, before the Articles were ratified, to form a government worthy of the nation. Even men who defended state sovereignty conceded the necessity of a convention by 1787. William Grayson admitted that "the present Confederation is utterly inefficient and that if it remains much longer in its present State of imbecility we shall be one of the most contemptible Nations on the face of the earth. . . ." LUTHER MARTIN admitted that Congress was "weak, contemptibly weak," and Richard Henry Lee believed that no government "short of force, will answer." "Do you not think," he asked GEORGE MASON, "that it ought to be declared . . . that any State act of legislation that shall contravene, or oppose, the authorized acts of Congress, or interfere with the expressed rights of that body, shall be *ipso facto* void, and of no force whatsoever?" Many leaders, like THOMAS JEFFERSON, advocated executive and judicial branches for the national government with "an appeal from state judicatures to a federal court in all cases where the act of Confederation controlled the question. . . ." RUFUS KING, who also promoted a "vigorous Executive," thought that the needed power of Congress to regulate all commerce "can never be well exercised without a Federal Judicial." A consensus was developing.

The Annapolis Convention exploited and nurtured that consensus when it recommended to all the states and to Congress that a constitutional convention to "meet at Philadelphia on the second Monday in May next (1787), to take into consideration the situation of the United States, to devise such further provisions as shall appear to them necessary to render the constitution of the federal government adequate to the exigencies of the Union. . . ." Several states, including powerful Virginia and Pennsylvania, chose delegates for the Philadelphia convention, forcing Congress to save face on February 21, 1787, by adopting a motion in accord with the Annapolis recommendation, although Congress declared that the "sole and express purpose" of the convention was "revising the articles of confederation."

The CONSTITUTIONAL CONVENTION OF 1787, which formally organized itself on May 25, lasted almost four months, yet reached its most crucial decision almost at the outset. The first order of business was the nationalistic VIRGINIA PLAN (May 29), and the first vote of the Convention, acting as a Committee of the Whole, was the adoption of a resolution "that a *national* Government ought to be established consisting of a *supreme* legislative, Executive and Judiciary" (May 30). Thus the Convention immediately agreed on abandoning, rather than amending, the Articles; on writing a new Constitution; on creating a national government that would be supreme; and on having it consist of three branches.

The radical character of this early decision may be best understood by comparing it with the Articles. The Articles failed mainly because there was no way to force the states to fulfill their obligations or to obey the exercise of such powers as Congress did possess. "The great and radical vice in the construction of the existing Confederation," said Alexander Hamilton, "is the principle of legislation for states or governments, in their corporate capacities, and as contradistinguished from the individuals of which they consist." The Convention remedied that vital defect in the Articles, as George Mason pointed out (May 30), by agreeing on a government that "could directly operate on individuals." Thus the framers solved the critical problem of sanctions by establishing a national government that was independent of the states.

On the next day, May 31, the Committee of the Whole made other crucial decisions with little or no debate. One, reflecting the nationalist bias of the Convention, was the decision to establish a bicameral system whose larger house was to be elected directly by the people rather than by the state legislatures. Mason, no less, explained, "Under the existing confederacy, Congress represent the States not the people of the States; their acts operate on the States, not on the individuals. The case will be changed in the new plan of Government. The people will be represented; they ought therefore to choose the Representatives." Another decision of May 31 was to vest in the Congress the sweeping and undefined power, recommended by the Virginia Plan, "to legislate in all cases to which the separate States are incompetent; or in which the harmony of the U.S. may be interrupted by the exercise of individual [state] legislation; to negative all laws passed by the several States contravening in the opinion of the National Legislature the articles of Union, or any treaties subsisting under the authority of the Union." Not a state voted "nay" to this exceptionally nationalistic proposition. Nor did any state oppose the decision of the next day to create a national executive with similarly broad, undefined powers.

After deliberating for two weeks, the Committee of the Whole presented the Convention with its recommendations, essentially the adoption of the Virginia Plan. Not surprisingly, several of the delegates had second thoughts about the hasty decisions that had been made. ELBRIDGE GERRY reiterated "that it was necessary to consider what the people would approve." Scrapping the Articles contrary to instructions and failing to provide for state equality in the system of representation provoked a reconsideration along lines described by WILLIAM PATERSON of New Jersey as "federal" in contradistinction to "national." Yet injured state pride was a greater cause of dissension than were the powers proposed for the national government. Some delegates were alarmed, not because of an excessive centralization of powers in the national government but because of the excessive advantages given to the largest states at the expense of the others. Three states—Virginia, Massachusetts, and Pennsylvania—had forty-five percent of the white population in the country. Under the proposed scheme of proportionate representation, the small states feared that the large ones would dominate the others by controlling the national government.

On June 15, therefore, Paterson submitted for the Convention's consideration a substitute plan. It was a small states plan rather than a STATES' RIGHTS one, for it too had a strong nationalist orientation. Contemplating a revision, rather than a scrapping, of the Articles, it retained the unicameral Congress with its equality of state representation, thus appeasing the small states. But the plan vested in Congress one of the two critical powers previously lacking: "to pass Acts for the regulation of trade and commerce," foreign and interstate. The other, the power of taxation, appeared only in a stunted form; Congress was to be authorized to levy duties on imports and to pass stamp tax acts. Except for its failure to grant full tax powers, the PATERSON PLAN proposed the same powers for the national legislature as the finished Constitution. The Plan also contained the germ of the national SUPREMACY CLAUSE of the Constitution, Article Six, by providing that acts of Congress and United States treaties "shall be the supreme law of the respective States . . . and that the Judiciary of the several States shall be bound thereby in their decisions, any thing in the respective laws of the Individual States to the contrary notwithstanding." The clause also provided for a federal judiciary with extensive jurisdiction and for an executive who could muster the military of the states to compel state obedience to the supreme law. Compulsion of states was unrealistic and unnecessary. Paterson himself declared that the creation of a distinct executive and judiciary meant that the government of the Union could "be exerted on individuals."

Despite its nationalist features, the Paterson Plan retained a unicameral legislature, in which the states remained equal, and the requisition system of rising a revenue, which had failed. "You see the consequence of pushing things too far," said John Dickinson of Delaware to Madison. "Some of the members from the small States wish for two branches in the General Legislature and are friends to a good National Government; but we would sooner submit to a foreign power than submit to be deprived of an equality of suffrage in both branches of the Legislature, and thereby be thrown under the domination of the large states." Only a very few dissidents were irreconcilably opposed to "a good National Government." Most of the dissidents were men like Dickinson and Paterson, "friends to a good National Government" if it preserved a wider scope for small state authority and influence.

When Paterson submitted his plan on June 15, the Convention agreed that to give it "a fair deliberation" it should be referred to the Committee of the Whole and that "in order to place the two plans in due comparison, the other should be recommitted." After debating the two plans, the Committee of the Whole voted in favor of reaffirming the original recommendations based on the Virginia Plan "as preferable to those of Mr. Paterson." Only three weeks after their deliberations, had begun the Framers decisively agreed, for the second time, on a strong, independent national government that would operate directly on individuals without the involvement of states.

But the objections of the small states had not yet been satisfied. On the next day, Connecticut, which had voted against the Paterson Plan, proposed the famous GREAT COMPROMISE: proportionate representation in one house, "provided each State had an equal voice in the other." On that latter point the Convention nearly broke up, so intense was the conflict and deep the division. The irreconcilables in this instance were the leaders of the large-state nationalist faction, otherwise the most constructive and influential members of the Convention: Madison and James Wilson. After several weeks of debate and deadlock, the Convention on July 16 narrowly voted for the compromise. With ten states present, five supported the compromise, four opposed (including Virginia and Pennsylvania), and Massachusetts was divided. The compromise saved small-state prestige and saved the Convention from failure.

Thereafter consensus on fundamentals was restored, with Connecticut, New Jersey, and Delaware becoming fervent supporters of Madison and Wilson. A week later, for example, there was a motion that each state should be represented by two senators who would "vote per capita," that is, as individuals. Luther Martin of Maryland protested that per capita voting conflicted with the very idea of "the States being represented," yet the motion carried, with no further debate, 9–1.

On many matters of structure, mechanics, and detail there were angry disagreements, but agreement prevailed on the essentials. The office of the presidency is a good illustration. That there should be a powerful chief executive provoked no great debate, but the Convention almost broke up, for the second time, on the method of electing him. Some matters of detail occasioned practically no disagreement and revealed the nationalist consensus. Mason, of all people, made the motion that one qualification of congressmen should be "citizenship of the United States," and no one disagreed. Under the Articles of Confederation, there was only state citizenship; that there should be a concept of national citizenship seemed natural to men framing a constitution for a nation. Even more a revelation of the nationalist consensus was the fact that three of the most crucial provisions of the Constitution—the taxing power, the NECESSARY AND PROPER CLAUSE, and the supremacy clause—were casually and unanimously accepted without debate.

Until midway during its sessions, the Convention did not take the trouble to define with care the distribution of power between the national government and the states, although the very nature of the "federal" system depended on that distribution. Consensus on fundamentals once again provides the explanation. There would be no difficulty in making that distribution; and, the framers had taken out insurance, because at the very outset, they had endorsed the provision of the Virginia Plan vesting broad, undefined powers in a national legislature that would act on individuals. Some byplay of July 17 is illuminating. ROGER SHERMAN of Connecticut thought that the line drawn between the powers of Congress and those left to the states was so vague that national legislation might "interfere . . . in any matters of internal police which respect the Government of such States only, and wherein the general welfare of the United States is not concerned." His motion to protect the "internal police" of the states brought no debaters to his side and was summarily defeated; only Maryland supported Connecticut. Immediately after, another small-state delegate, GUNNING BEDFORD of Delaware, shocked even EDMUND RANDOLPH of Virginia, who had presented the Virginia Plan, by a motion to extend the powers of Congress by vesting authority "to legislate in all cases for the general interest of the Union." Randolph observed, "This is a formidable idea indeed. It involves the power of violating all the laws and constitution of the States, of intermeddling with their police." Yet the motion passed.

On July 26 the Convention adjourned until August 6 to allow a Committee on Detail to frame a "constitution conformable to the Resolutions passed by the Convention." Generously construing its charge, the committee acted as a miniature convention and introduced a number of significant changes. One was the explicit enumeration of the powers of Congress to replace the vague, omnibus provisions adopted previously by the Convention. Although enumerated, these powers were liberally expressed and formidable in their array. The committee made specific the spirit and intent of the Convention. Significantly the first enumerated power was that of taxation and the second that of regulating commerce among the states and with foreign nations: the two principal powers that had been withheld from Congress by the Articles.

When the Convention voted on the provision that Congress "shall have the power to lay and collect taxes, duties, imposts and excises," the states were unanimous and only one delegate, Elbridge Gerry, was opposed. When the Convention next turned to the commerce power, there was no discussion and even Gerry voted affirmatively.

Notwithstanding its enumeration of the legislative powers, all of which the Convention accepted, the Committee on Detail added an omnibus clause that has served as an ever expanding source of national authority: "And to make all laws that shall be necessary and proper for carrying into execution the foregoing powers." The Convention agreed to that clause without a single dissenting vote by any state or delegate. The history of the great supremacy clause, Article Six, shows a similar consensus. Without debate the Convention adopted the supremacy clause, and not a single state or delegate voted nay. Finally, Article One, Section 10, imposing restrictions on the economic powers of the states with respect to paper money, ex post facto laws, bills of credit, and contracts also reflected a consensus in the Convention. In sum, consensus, rather than compromise, was the most significant feature of the Convention, outweighing in importance the various compromises that occupied most of the time of the delegates.

But why was there such a consensus? The obvious answer (apart from the fact that opponents either stayed away or walked out) is the best: experience had proved that the nationalist constitutional position was right. If the United States was to survive and flourish, a strong national government had to be established. The Framers of the Constitution were accountable to public opinion; the Convention was a representative body. That its members were prosperous, well-educated political leaders made them no less representative than Congress. The state legislatures, which elected the members of the Convention, were the most unlikely instruments for thwarting the popular will. The Framers, far from being able to do as they pleased, were not free to promulgate the Constitution. Although they adroitly arranged for its ratification by nine state ratifying conventions rather than by all state legislatures, they could not present a plan that the people of the states would not tolerate. They could not control the membership of those state ratifying conventions. They could not even be sure that the existing Congress would submit the Constitution to the states for ratification, let alone for ratification by state conventions that had to be specially elected. If the Framers got too far astray from public opinion, their work would have been wasted. The consensus in the Convention coincided with an emerging consensus in the country that recaptured the nationalist spirit of '76. That the Union had to be strengthened was an almost universal American belief.

For its time the Constitution was a remarkably democratic document framed by democratic methods. Some historians have contended that the Convention's scrapping of the Articles and the ratification process were revolutionary acts which if performed by a Napoleon would be pronounced a coup d'état. But the procedure of the Articles for constitutional amendment was not democratic, because it allowed Rhode Island, with one-sixtieth of the nation's population, to exercise a veto power. The Convention sent its Constitution to the lawfully existing government, the Congress of the Confederation, for submission to the states, and Congress, which could have censured the Convention for exceeding its authority, freely complied—and thereby exceeded its own authority under the Articles! A coup d'état ordinarily lacks the deliberation and consent that marked the making of the Constitution and is characterized by a military element that was wholly lacking in 1787. A Convention elected by the state legislatures and consisting of many of the foremost leaders of their time deliberated for almost four months. Its members included many opponents of the finished scheme. The nation knew the Convention was considering changes in the government. The proposed Constitution was made public, and voters in every state were asked to choose delegates to vote for or against it after open debate. The use of state ratifying conventions fit the theory that a new fundamental law was being adopted and, therefore, conventions were proper for the task.

The Constitution guaranteed to each state a republican or representative form of government and fixed no property or religious qualifications on the right to vote or hold office, at a time when such qualifications were common in the states. By leaving voting qualifications to the states the Constitution implicitly accepted such qualifications but imposed none. The Convention, like the Albany Congress of 1754, the Stamp Act Congress, the Continental Congresses, and the Congresses of the Confederation, had been chosen by state (or colonial) legislatures, but the Constitution created a Congress whose lower house was popularly elected. When only three states directly elected their chief executive officer, the Constitution provided for the indirect election of the President by an ELECTORAL COLLEGE that originated in the people and is still operative. The Constitution's system of separation of powers and elaborate CHECKS AND BALANCES was not intended to refine out popular influence on government but to protect liberty; the Framers divided, distributed, and limited powers to prevent one branch, faction, interest, or section from becoming too powerful. Checks and balances were not undemocratic, and the Federalists were hard pressed not to apologize for checks and balances but to convince the Anti-Federalists, who wanted far more checks and balances, that the Constitution had enough. Although the Framers were not democrats in a modern sense, their opponents were even less democratic. Those opponents sought to capitalize on the lack of a BILL OF RIGHTS, and RATIFICATION OF THE CONSTITUTION became possible only because leading Federalists committed themselves to amendments as soon as the new government went into operation. At that time, however, Anti-Federalists opposed a Bill of Rights because it would allay popular fears of the new government, ending the chance for state sovereignty amendments.

Although the Framers self-consciously refrained from referring to slavery in the Constitution, it recognized slavery, the most undemocratic of all institutions. That recognition was a grudging but necessary price of Union. The THREE-FIFTHS CLAUSE of Article I provided for counting three-fifths of the total number of slaves as part of the population of a state in the apportionment of REPRESENTATION and DIRECT TAXATION. Article IV, section 2, provided for rendition of fugitive slaves to the slaveholder upon his claim. On the other hand, Article I, section 9, permitted Congress to abolish the slave trade in twenty years. Most delegates, including many from slaveholding states, would have preferred a Constitution untainted by slavery; but Southern votes for ratification required recognition of slavery. By choosing a Union with slavery, the Convention deferred the day of reckoning.

The Constitution is basically a political document. Modern scholarship has completely discredited the once popular view, associated with CHARLES BEARD, that the Constitution was undemocratically made to advance the economic interests of personalty groups, chiefly creditors. The largest public creditor at the Convention was Elbridge Gerry, who refused to sign the Constitution and opposed its ratification, and the largest private creditor was George Mason who did likewise. Indeed, seven men who either quit the Convention in disgust or refused to sign the Constitution held public securities that were worth over twice the holdings of the thirty-nine men who signed the Constitution. The most influential Framers, among them Madison, Wilson, Paterson, Dickinson, and Gouverneur Morris, owned no securities. Others, like Washington, who acted out of patriotism, not profit, held trifling amounts. Eighteen members of the Convention were either debtors or held property that depreciated after the new government became operative. On crucial issues at the Convention, as in the state ratifying conventions, the dividing line between groups for and against the Constitution was not economic, not between realty and personalty, or debtors and creditors, or town and frontier. The restrictions of Article I, section 10, on the economic powers of the states were calculated to protect creditor interests and promote business stability, but those restrictions were not undemocratic; if impairing the obligations of contracts or emitting bills of credit and paper money were democratic hallmarks, the Constitution left Congress free to be democratic. The interest groups for and against the Constitution were substantially similar. Economic interests did influence the voting on ratification, but no simple explanation that ignores differences between states and even within states will suffice, and many noneconomic influences were also at work. In the end the Constitution was framed and ratified because most voters came to share the vision held by Franklin in 1775 and Dickinson in 1776; those two, although antagonists in Pennsylvania politics, understood for quite different reasons that a strong central government was indispensable for nationhood.

LEONARD W. LEVY

Bibliography

ADAMS, WILLI PAUL 1980 *The First American Constitutions.* Chapel Hill: University of North Carolina Press.

BEARD, CHARLES 1935 *An Economic Interpretation of the Constitution of the United States.* New York: Macmillan.

BROWN, ROBERT E. 1956 *Charles Beard and the Constitution: A Critical Analysis of "An Economic Interpretation of the Constitution."* Princeton, N.J.: Princeton University Press.

BURNETT, EDMUND C. 1941 *The Continental Congress.* New York: Macmillan.

CROSSKEY, WILLIAM W. and JEFFREY, WILLIAM, JR. 1980 *Politics and the Constitution in the History of the United States.* Volume III: "The Political Background of the Federal Convention." Chicago: University of Chicago Press.

FARRAND, MAX, ed. 1937(1966) *The Records of the Federal Convention of 1787.* New Haven, Conn.: Yale University Press.

JENSEN, MERRILL 1940 *The Articles of Confederation.* Madison: University of Wisconsin Press.

KENYON, CECILIA, ed. 1966 *The Antifederalists.* Indianapolis: Bobbs-Merrill.

MCDONALD, FORREST 1958 *We the People: The Eco-*

nomic Origins of the Constitution. Chicago: University of Chicago Press.

McLaughlin, Andrew C. 1905 *The Confederation and the Constitution, 1783–1789.* New York: Harper & Brothers.

Murphy, William P. 1967 *The Triumph of Nationalism: State Sovereignty, the Founding Fathers, and the Triumph of the Constitution.* Chicago: Quadrangle Books.

Racove, Jack N. 1979 *The Beginnings of National Politics: An Interpretation of the Continental Congress.* New York: Knopf.

Warren, Charles 1928 *The Making of the Constitution.* Boston: Little, Brown.

CONSTITUTIONAL HISTORY, 1789–1801

George Washington was inaugurated the first President of the United States on April 30, 1789, in New York City. The First Congress, having been elected in February, was already at work. Most of the members were supporters of the Constitution. Fifty-four of them had sat either in the Constitutional Convention or in one of the state ratifying conventions; only seven were Anti-Federalists. A new government had been established. But in 1789 it was only a blueprint. The first business of the President and Congress was to breathe life into the Constitution. For a document of some 5,000 words, the Constitution was remarkably explicit and complete. Yet it left a great deal to the discretion and decision of the men entrusted with its care. They, too, were "founding fathers," for they transformed words engrossed on parchment into living institutions and defined the terms of debate on the Constitution.

James Madison was the Federalist leader in the House of Representatives, where most of the formative legislation of the new government originated. Among the first statutes were those establishing the three executive departments: state, treasury, and war. Madison wrote into his bill for the department of state a provision authorizing the President to remove the department head, thereby precipitating the first congressional debate over interpretation of the Constitution. The document was clear on the President's power to appoint, with the advice and consent of the Senate, but silent on his power to remove executive officers. Removal being the reverse of appointment, some congressmen argued that it should follow the same course. But Madison contended, successfully, that the President's responsibility to see that the laws were faithfully executed necessarily included the removal power. The action of the House set an enduring precedent. Thus it was that in the first year of the new government an unwritten constitution, unknown to the Framers, grew up alongside the written constitution. (See Appointing and Removal Power.)

Article II, it was sometimes said, had been framed with General Washington in mind; and so great was the confidence in him that Congress showed little jealousy of the chief executive. The act creating the treasury department, however, made its head responsible to Congress as well as to the President. This was recognition that "the power of the purse" was fundamentally a legislative power, and therefore the secretary of the treasury must answer to Congress in financial matters.

The Judiciary Act of 1789, which gave life to Article III, originated in the Senate. The act provided for an elaborate system of federal courts, created the office of attorney general, and in Section 25 authorized the Supreme Court to review on appeal decisions of state courts concerning questions of federal law involving the United States Constitution and the laws and treaties made under it. None of this had been settled in the Constitution itself, though Federalists said that Article III together with the supremacy clause of Article VI implicitly sanctioned Section 25.

The Federalists, with Madison in the lead, kept the promise made during the ratification campaign to add a bill of rights to the Constitution. Even before North Carolina and Rhode Island entered the new union, Congress approved twelve amendments and sent them to the states. Ten were ratified and on December 15, 1791, became part of the Constitution. In the founding of the nation the Bill of Rights was important less because it secured fundamental rights and liberties against the national government, which was without delegated power in this sphere, than because it strengthened public confidence in the government without impairing its powers as many Anti-Federalists had wished.

The principal executive offices were filled by Thomas Jefferson at state, Alexander Hamilton in the treasury, Henry Knox in the war department, and Edmund Randolph as the part-time attorney general. The unity of the executive was one of the claims made for it in The Federalist. Washington worked closely with his subordinates, and depended on them for initiative and advice, but there was never any doubt that the executive power belonged exclusively to him. The Constitution made no provision for a "cabinet," nor was one contemplated at first. The President seemed to think, on the basis of the advice and

CONSENT clause, that the Senate was meant to function as an advisory council. In August he appeared personally in the Senate to ask its advice on a proposed treaty with an Indian tribe. But the process proved awkward and cumbersome. It was not repeated. The President, instead, conducted his business with the Senate in writing, and met his need for collective consultation and advice, particularly in FOREIGN AFFAIRS, through the development of the cabinet. By 1793 it was an established institution. There were suggestions in the First Congress of a movement toward a generalized ministerial responsibility on the model of the treasury act; but this did not materialize. On the whole, the first presidency decisively enforced the theory of SEPARATION OF POWERS, associated with congressional government, rather than the ministerial responsibility characteristic of parliamentary government. In 1791 the President exercised the VETO POWER for the first time. The veto was potentially a means for controlling legislation, but Washington did not use it in that fashion (he vetoed only one other measure in eight years), and in the first forty years of the government Presidents used the veto sparingly.

The most important political and constitutional issues of Washington's first administration arose out of Hamilton's financial program. Exploiting his special relationship with Congress—conceiving of himself, indeed, as a kind of prime minister—Hamilton submitted a series of reports to Congress recommending measures to put the country's fiscal house in order, strengthen the government by appealing to the cupidity of the moneyed class, and stimulate the commercial and manufacturing sectors of the economy. His plan to fund the national debt at face value raised questions of equity between debtor and creditor interests but did not present a constitutional issue. The expectation of funding on the part of creditor groups had, of course, been a vital source of Federalist support for the Constitution. But Hamilton's plan also called for the assumption of the state debts. This proposal surprised many and aroused intense opposition in Congress, especially among Southerners sensitive to Anti-Federalist fears of undue concentration of power in the national government. Madison opposed Hamilton's plan, though on other grounds, and in doing so disclosed a division in the Federalist ranks on the direction of the new government. He was joined by his Virginia friend, Jefferson, who had just taken up his duties as secretary of state in the spring of 1790. Both were disposed to be conciliatory on this issue, however, and entered into a sectional bargain with Hamilton that would fix the permanent seat of government on the Potomac in exchange for the necessary southern votes to secure passage of the assumption bill. Still, the compromise failed to quiet Anti-Federalist fears. In December the Virginia legislature adopted a series of resolutions condemning the assumption of state debts as inimical to federal and republican institutions and pointedly questioning the constitutionality of the measure. Hamilton responded angrily. "This," he said, "is the first symptom of a spirit which must either be killed, or will kill the Constitution."

The constitutional question was brought to the fore a few months later on the bill to charter the BANK OF THE UNITED STATES. A national bank, as conceived and proposed by Hamilton, would function as the financial arm of the government and multiply the active capital of the country by mounting a large paper circulation. Because three-fourths of the initial bank capital would come in the form of public securities—securities issued to fund the debt—the institution was obviously an integral part of the funding system and would directly benefit the same creditor class. Madison vigorously opposed the bill in the House, less on grounds of policy than on grounds of unconstitutionality. The power to incorporate a bank was not among the powers delegated to Congress, nor could it be considered NECESSARY AND PROPER to execute those powers. But Congress adopted the bill and sent it to the President. Uncertain whether to sign or return it, Washington first sought the attorney general's opinion, which was adverse, and then requested Jefferson's. The secretary of state agreed with Madison and offered an even more emphatically STRICT CONSTRUCTION of the Constitution. The government was one of strictly delegated powers, as declared in the TENTH AMENDMENT still in the course of ratification. "To take a single step beyond the boundaries thus specifically drawn around the powers of Congress," Jefferson warned, "is to take possession of a boundless field of power, no longer susceptible to definition." To these objections Hamilton replied in a powerful opinion founded on the doctrine of IMPLIED POWERS. "Every power vested in a government is in its nature *sovereign,* and included, by *force* of the *term,* a right to employ all *means* requisite and fairly applicable to the attainment of the *ends* of such power, and which are not precluded by restrictions and exceptions specified in the Constitution . . ." (italics in original). The utility of a national bank in the execution of powers to tax, borrow money, and regulate commerce could not be denied. It was decisive in Hamilton's judgment. Washington concurred, and signed the Bank Bill into law.

In his Report on Manufactures, presented to the

Second Congress, Hamilton extended his nationalist program by way of the GENERAL WELFARE CLAUSE. Believing that extensive domestic manufactures were necessary to the wealth and welfare of the nation, Hamilton proposed a comprehensive system of aid and encouragement—tariffs, bounties, inspections, export controls, drawbacks—which he justified under the power to provide for the general welfare. No legislation resulted from the report, but it produced consternation in opposition ranks. "If not only the *means*, but the *objects* [of the government] are unlimited," Madison wrote, "The parchment had better be thrown into the fire at once" (italics in original). Virginia's two senators introduced constitutional amendments to limit the application of the clause to the ENUMERATED POWERS and deny the power of Congress to charter corporations.

Although the widening debate took its shape from the constitutional question, it involved much more. It involved the conflict of economic interests: debtors and creditors, landed property and fluid capital, the mass of people engaged in agriculture, and the enterprising class of merchants, bankers, and manufacturers. The fact that the former tended to be concentrated in the South, the latter in the Northeast, particularly in the coastal cities, gave the conflict a sectional character as well. The debate also involved competing strategies of economic development in the new nation, as well as contrasting ideas of the nature of freedom, the Union, and republican government. To an extent, certainly, the conflict was epitomized in the clash between the leading cabinet secretaries, Jefferson and Hamilton, who increasingly appeared as the protagonists of opposing doctrines and parties in the public eye. One despised, the other idolized governance. One located the strength of the republic in the diffuse energies of a free society, the other in the consolidation of the government's power. One believed that private interest corrupted public good, the other conscripted private interest for public benefit. One viewed the Constitution as a superintending rule of political action, the other, as a point of departure for heroic statesmanship. In the balance between authority and liberty, Hamilton was an apologist for the former, Jefferson for the latter. Hamilton feared most of the ignorance and turbulence of the people, while Jefferson preached "trust the people" and feared rulers independent of them.

The division on foreign policy deepened the division on domestic policy. Jefferson, Madison, and those who began to call themselves Republicans opposed British power and influence and openly championed the French Revolution. Hamilton and the Federalists, on the other hand, relied upon British trade, credit, and power to nurture American development; they feared the contagion of French ideas. The controversy over foreign policy assumed a constitutional dimension after Britain and France went to war in 1793. President Washington issued a proclamation pledging "a conduct friendly and impartial" toward the belligerents and warning citizens against hostile acts. Jefferson opposed this PROCLAMATION OF NEUTRALITY, as it came to be known, principally because it tended to defeat his foreign policy objectives to oppose Britain and support France. As an ally, France had a right to expect friendship from the United States; Britain, on the other hand, might have been made to pay a price for American neutrality, as in recognition of "free ships make free goods" and related guarantees of neutral rights. Viewing a declaration of neutrality as the negative side of a DECLARATION OF WAR, Jefferson also held that the proclamation invaded the authority of Congress. The popular reception of the new French minister to the United States, Edmond Genet, fueled criticism of the proclamation. Genet himself took advantage of this sentiment by arming privateers in American ports and issuing military commissions to American citizens. Hamilton, under the pseudonym "Pacificus," wrote a series of newspaper articles in defense of the presidential proclamation. Broadly construing Article II, Hamilton maintained that all executive power is vested in the President unless specifically qualified or withheld. The power to declare war belonged to Congress, of course, but did not preclude unilateral actions by the President bearing on the exercise of that power. To Republicans such a power looked suspiciously like the British royal prerogative in foreign affairs. Taking up his pen in reply, Madison, as "Helvidius," argued that all matters touching on the WAR POWER are necessarily legislative; the executive, therefore, cannot initiate a course of action that, in effect, confronts Congress with a *fait accompli.* Whatever the abstract merits of Madison's argument, it gave too little weight to realities in the conduct of foreign affairs, which inevitably favored the executive.

In the absence of statute, executive officers decided difficult questions of neutrality as they arose. Thus it was that the cabinet became a permanent institution. Jefferson and Hamilton were usually at odds, causing many split decisions. On July 18, 1793, the officers submitted to the Supreme Court a list of twenty-nine questions about international law. The Justices declined to rule, however, thereby setting a precedent against ADVISORY OPINIONS. The cabinet hammered out its own ADMINISTRATIVE LAW of neutrality, which prevailed until Congress convened and enacted the Neutrality Act of 1794.

Long before that the firebrand French minister had been recalled and Jefferson had retired from the government, ensuring Hamilton the same ascendancy in foreign affairs he had earlier enjoyed in domestic affairs. The upshot was JAY'S TREATY, negotiated in London in November 1794 and ratified by the Senate six months later. The treaty preserved peace with Britain but, in Republican opinion, at the cost of submission to British maritime power and risk of war with France. Like every great issue of Washington's presidency, the treaty caused significant constitutional debate. Because some provisions required appropriations to carry them into effect, the treaty came under the scrutiny of the House of Representatives. In this connection a Republican majority demanded that the President lay before the House a copy of the instructions given to JOHN JAY and other pertinent documents. The President emphatically rejected the call, holding that the House had no constitutional power with respect to treaties. The House, after reiterating its position and carefully differentiating the appropriation power from the TREATY POWER, which it disclaimed, proceeded to vote the money requested by the President.

The protracted battle over Jay's Treaty set the stage for the presidential election of 1796. Washington's decision to retire after two terms lifted the last restraint on partisanship, and two infant POLITICAL PARTIES, each with its own standard bearer, JOHN ADAMS for the Federalists, Jefferson for the Republicans, contested the election. The Constitution had been intended to work without parties. Parties, the Framers reasoned, fed the natural turbulence of the populace and served the ambitions of demagogues; they caused implacable rivalries in legislative councils, usurping the place of reason and moderation; they introduced whole networks of partisan allegiance at cross-purposes with the national welfare. Washington had attempted to govern independently of parties, but in an increasingly polarized political environment even he became a partisan. When the Republicans sought to channel popular enthusiasm for the French cause into "democratic societies," Washington publicly condemned the societies as illicit political engines, thereby betraying intolerance of political opposition from outside the constitutional channels of authority. WASHINGTON'S FAREWELL ADDRESS pointedly warned the people against the "baneful" effects of parties. The Republicans, however, were rapidly discovering in party organization outside the government the appropriate means for wresting power from the Federalists who, in their eyes, were the real bane of the country.

Adams was elected President by a slender ELECTORAL COLLEGE majority. Crisis with France, mounting since the British treaty, set the course of the administration. Angrily denouncing French decrees against American commerce, Adams sent a special commission to negotiate in Paris under threat of war. Intriguing agents of the French foreign ministry demanded money as the price of negotiations. The Americans indignantly refused. This affair—the XYZ Affair—then exploded in the United States, and the Federalists converted foreign crisis into domestic crisis. Under cover of whipped-up war hysteria, they assailed the patriotism of the Republicans, portraying them as Jacobin disorganizers in the country's bowels whose ultimate treachery only awaited the signal of an invading French army. Although the President refrained from asking for a declaration of war, he inflamed the war spirit. Congress abrogated the French treaties, expanded the army, established the Navy Department, and authorized an undeclared naval war against France. The Republicans fought this policy to no avail. Two years later the Supreme Court, in a prize case, *Bas v. Tingey* (1800), upheld the power of the government to make war without declaring it.

The war hysteria found domestic expression in the ALIEN AND SEDITION ACTS. The Republicans attacked the laws restrictive of ALIENS on grounds of policy and the Alien Act, in particular, for violating the Constitution by authorizing the President summarily to deport aliens deemed dangerous to the nation. The Sedition Act, the Republicans argued, was without congressional authority and directly violated the FIRST AMENDMENT. Despite the smokescreen of war, TREASON, and subversion, Republicans believed that the law aimed at suppressing their presses and crippling their party. Political freedom, as well as FREEDOM OF SPEECH and FREEDOM OF THE PRESS, was at stake. When the federal courts, manned by partisan Federalist judges, cooperated in enforcing the Sedition Act, closing off the judicial channel of redress, Jefferson and Madison turned to two Republican state legislatures to arouse opposition. The VIRGINIA AND KENTUCKY RESOLUTIONS interposed the authority of these states to declare the Alien and Sedition Acts unconstitutional and urged other states to join in forcing their repeal. The resolutions were especially significant as landmark statements of the THEORY OF THE UNION as a compact of sovereign states and of the right of a state, whether by INTERPOSITION or NULLIFICATION, to judge the constitutionality of acts of Congress. Northern state legislatures, in response, rejected the theory together with the appeal. Although the resolutions contributed to rising popular opposition against the administration, they did not force repeal of the hated laws. Whatever their later significance for the issue of STATES' RIGHTS and Union—the constitutional issue over which the Civil War would be fought—the resolutions originated in a struggle for political survival and addressed the fundamental issue of freedom and self-government descending from the American Revolution.

The foreign crisis passed in 1800. Adams seized the olive branch extended by France, broke with the Hamiltonian faction in his administration, and dispatched another commission to negotiate peace. The result was the Convention of 1800, which restored normal relations and formally terminated the Franco-American alliance of 1778. From the standpoint of the "war system," Adams's decision to make peace drove a sword into the Federalist party. In the ensuing presidential election, Hamilton and his friends conspired to defeat Adams.

The election of 1800 was bitterly contested by two organized political parties. The Republicans achieved unprecedented unity behind their ticket of Jefferson and AARON BURR. By party organization and electioneering tactics they turned the election of the President into a test of public opinion. This, of course, made a mockery of the Constitution, under which a body of electors separated from the people was to choose the President and vice-president. Electoral tickets became party tickets, and every presidential elector became an agent of the popular majority that elected him.

Jefferson won a decisive victory over Adams. Although the Federalists swept New England, took two of the small middle states (New Jersey and Delaware), and picked up scattered votes in three others, the Republicans won everything else, south, west, and north. The electoral vote, 73–65, failed to reflect the wide Republican margin at the polls. But the victory was jeopardized by political developments that played havoc with the electoral system. Under the Constitution each elector cast two votes for different candidates; the one with the most votes became President, while the runner-up became vice-president. The rise of political parties made the system an anachronism, for electors chosen on a party ticket would cast both votes for the party candidates, thereby producing a tie between them. So it happened in 1800: Jefferson and Burr received an equal number of electoral votes. The choice was thus thrown into the House of Representatives. There the lame-duck Federalist majority plotted to annul the popular verdict either by creating an interregnum or by dealing Burr into the presidency. Finally, on the thirty-sixth ballot, the stalemate was broken and Jefferson was elected.

The new Republican majority moved rapidly to amend the Constitution to prevent a similar occurrence in the future. The TWELFTH AMENDMENT (1804) provided for separate ballots for President and vice-president. The elaborate machinery devised by the Framers for the election of the President was thus radically revised in response to changing political realities. Not only was this an effective use of the AMENDING PROCESS, but it seemed to suggest frequent change by amendment in the future. However, the next amendment of the Constitution came only after the passage of sixty-one years and the convulsions of civil war.

MERRILL D. PETERSON

Bibliography

BUEL, RICHARD, JR. 1972 *Securing the Revolution: Ideology and American Politics, 1789–1815.* Ithaca, N.Y.: Cornell University Press.

MALONE, DUMAS 1962 *Jefferson and the Ordeal of Liberty.* Boston: Little, Brown.

MILLER, JOHN C. 1960 *The Federalist Era: 1789–1801.* New York: Harper & Row.

STOURZH, GERALD 1970 *Alexander Hamilton and the Idea of Republican Government.* Stanford, Calif.: Stanford University Press.

WHITE, LEONARD D. 1948 *The Federalist: A Study in Administrative History, 1789–1801.* New York: Free Press.

CONSTITUTIONAL HISTORY, 1801–1829

THOMAS JEFFERSON entered the presidency in 1801 with a rhetoric of return to constitutional first principles. Inaugurated in the new permanent capital on the Potomac, he offered a brilliant summation of these principles together with a lofty appeal for restoration of harmony and affection. "We are all republicans: we are all federalists," he declared. He hoped to achieve "a perfect consolidation" of political sentiments by emphasizing principles that ran deeper than party names or doctrines. He spoke of preserving "the whole constitutional vigor" of the general government yet called for "a wise and frugal government, which shall restrain men from injuring one another, which shall leave them otherwise free to regulate their own pursuits of industry and improvement, and shall not take from the mouth of labor the bread it has earned." Jefferson never doubted that "constitutional vigor" and individual liberty were perfectly compatible, indeed that the strength of republican government rested upon the freedom of the society. He named "absolute acquiescence in the decisions of the majority the vital principle of republics, from which there is no appeal but to force." This principle demanded freedom of opinion and debate, including the right of a minority to turn itself into a new majority, as the Republican party had done. "If there be any among us," Jefferson said, alluding to the delusions of 1798, "who would wish to dissolve this Union or to change its republican form, let them stand undisturbed as monuments of the safety with which error may be tolerated where reason is left free to combat it." He thus announced a commitment to ongoing change through the democratic process. Because of that commitment the Constitution became an instrument of democracy, change became possible without violence or destruction, and government went forward on the continuing consent of the governed.

The "revolution of 1800," as Jefferson later called it, introduced no fundamental changes in the structure or machinery of the general government but made that government a more effective instrument of popular leadership. Jefferson himself possessed great popular authority. Combining this with the constitutional authority of the office, he overcame Whiggish monarchical fears and gave the presidency a secure place in the republican system. Jefferson dominated his administration more surely and completely than even GEORGE WASHINGTON had done. The cabinet, which was composed of moderate Republicans, enjoyed unprecedented harmony, stability, and unity. It was the main agency of policy and decision making.

Jefferson also dominated Congress. For the first time, in 1801, the Republicans controlled both houses of Congress. The Federalists were a shrinking minority, though by no means powerless. In republican theory Congress should control the executive. Jefferson honored the theory in official discourse. Thus he declined to appear before Congress in person and sent his annual "State of the Union" message to be read by a clerk, setting a precedent that remained unbroken for 112 years. Practically, however, Jefferson recognized that the government demanded executive leadership if any majority, Federalist or Republican, was to carry out its program. How could he overcome the constraints of republican theory and the constitutional SEPARATION OF POWERS? The solution was found partly through the personal influence Jefferson commanded and partly through a network of party leadership outside constitutional channels. As the unchallenged head of the Republican party, Jefferson acted with an authority he did not possess, indeed utterly disclaimed, in his official capacity. Leaders of both houses of Congress were the President's political lieutenants. Despite the weak structural organization of the Republican party in Congress—the only formal machinery was the presidential nominating caucus which came into being every four years—the party was a pervasive functional reality. The President was chief legislator as well as chief magistrate. Nearly all the congressional legislation during eight years originated with the President and his cabinet. Lacking staff support, Congress depended on executive initiatives and usually followed them. Federalists complained of the "backstairs" influence of the President; eventually some Republicans, led by JOHN RANDOLPH, rebelled. But the system of presidential leadership worked with unerring precision during Jefferson's first term. It faltered during his second term when the Republicans, with virtually no opposition to contend with, began to quarrel among themselves; and it would not work at all under Jefferson's successor, JAMES MADISON, who lacked Jefferson's popular prestige and personal magnetism.

In matters of public policy, the Jefferson administration sought reform within the limits of moderation and conciliation. More doctrinaire Republicans, still infected with Anti-Federalism, were not satisfied with a mere change of leadership and demanded restrictive constitutional amendments to place the true principles of government beyond reversal or contradiction. While rejecting this course, Jefferson was never entirely happy with the consequences of his temporizing policies. Republican reform was bottomed on fiscal policy. The Hamiltonian system of public debt, internal taxes, and a national bank was considered an evil of the first magnitude. Secretary of the Treasury ALBERT GALLATIN developed a plan to extinguish the debt, which had increased under the Federalists, by large annual appropriations, yet, amazingly, reduce taxes at the same time. All internal taxes would be repealed and government would depend solely on revenue from the customs houses. The plan required deep retrenchment, especially in the army and navy departments. Of course, it was premised on peace. Congress embarked on it; and although the debt was dramatically reduced during the next seven years, the plan was initially upset by the exigencies of the Tripolitan War, then derailed by the Anglo-American crisis that led to the War of 1812. Jefferson agonized over

ALEXANDER HAMILTON's fiscal system. "When the government was first established," he wrote in 1802, "it was possible to have kept it going on true principles, but the contracted, English, half-lettered ideas of Hamilton destroyed that hope in a bud. We can pay off his debt in 15 years, but we can never get rid of his financial system. It mortifies me to be strengthening principles which I deem radically vicious, but the vice is entailed on us by the first error. . . . What is practicable must often control pure theory." A case in point was the Bank of the United States. Jefferson thought it an institution of "the most deadly hostility" to the Constitution and republican government. Yet he tolerated the Bank, in part because its charter ran to 1811 (when Republicans would refuse to renew it) and also because Gallatin found the bank highly useful to the government's operations.

Jefferson's "war on the judiciary" featured three main battles and several skirmishes, ending in no very clear outcome. The first battle was fought over the JUDICIARY ACT OF 1801. Republicans were enraged by this blatantly partisan measure passed in the waning hours of JOHN ADAMS's administration. It created a new tier of courts and judgeships, extended the power of the federal judiciary at the expense of state courts, and reduced the number of Supreme Court Justices beginning with the next vacancy, thereby denying the Republicans an early opportunity to reshape the Court. Jefferson promptly targeted the act for repeal. The Federalists had retreated to the judiciary as a stronghold, he said, from which "all the works of Republicanism are to be beaten down and erased." The Sedition Act had demonstrated the prostration of the judiciary to partisan purposes. After taking office Jefferson acted to pardon victims of the act, which he considered null and void, and to drop pending prosecutions. He often spoke of making judges more responsible to the people, perhaps by periodic review of their tenure; and although he recognized the power of JUDICIAL REVIEW, he did not think it binding on the executive or the legislature. According to his theory of "tripartite balance" each of the coordinate branches of government is supreme in its sphere and may decide questions of constitutionality for itself. The same theory was advanced by Republicans in Congress, as against the Federalist claim of exclusive power of the Supreme Court to declare legislation unconstitutional. Congress did not settle this issue; but after heated debate it repealed the offensive act and, with minor exceptions, returned the judiciary to its previous footing.

The second battle involved the case of MARBURY v. MADISON (1803). Although the Supreme Court's decision would later be seen as the cornerstone of judicial review, the case was understood at the time primarily as a political duel between the President and the Court, one in which Chief Justice JOHN MARSHALL took a gratuitous stab at the executive but then deliberately backed away from a confrontation he knew the Court could not win.

The third battle featured the IMPEACHMENT of federal judges. In 1803 Congress impeached, tried, and convicted Judge JOHN PICKERING of the district court in New Hampshire. The case was a hard one because Pickering's bizarre conduct on the bench stemmed from intoxication and possible insanity; but in the absence of any constitutional authorization for the removal of an incompetent judge, the Republicans took the course of impeachment and convicted him of "high crimes and misdemeanors." The subsequent impeachment of Supreme Court Justice SAMUEL J. CHASE was clearly a political act. A high-toned Federalist, Chase had earned Republican enmity as the convicting judge in several SEDITION trials and by harangues to grand juries assailing democracy and all its works. Nevertheless, his trial in the Senate ended in a verdict of acquittal in 1805. Jefferson and the Republican leaders turned away from impeachment in disgust. Although it may have produced salutary restraint in the federal judiciary, and enhanced the President's role as a popular leader, neither impeachment nor any other Jeffersonian action disturbed the foundations of judicial power.

During his second term, Jefferson used the TREASON trial of AARON BURR to renew the attack on the judiciary but without success. The former vice-president was charged with treason for leading a military expedition to separate the western states from the Union. Determined to convict him, Jefferson again faced an old enemy, John Marshall, who presided in the trial at Richmond. At Burr's request, Marshall subpoenaed Jefferson to appear in court with papers bearing on the case. Jefferson refused, citing his responsibility as chief executive. "The Constitution enjoins his constant agency in the concerns of six millions of people. Is the law paramount to this, which calls on him on behalf of a single one?" he asked. The court backed off. Nothing required Jefferson's presence. He offered to testify by deposition, but this was not requested. When the trial ended in Burr's acquittal, Jefferson denounced its whole conduct as political. He laid the proceedings before Congress and urged that body to furnish some remedy for judicial arrogance and error. Several Republican state legislatures instructed their delegations to seek amendment making judges removable on the address of both houses of Congress. Both President and Congress were preoccupied with FOREIGN AFFAIRS in the fall of 1807, however, and nothing came of this effort.

The first foreign crisis of the Jefferson administration culminated in the LOUISIANA PURCHASE. It was an ironic triumph for a President, an administration, and a party that made a boast of constitutional purity. For the Constitution made no provision either to acquire foreign territory or, as the purchase treaty mandated, to incorporate that territory and its inhabitants into the Union. Jefferson, therefore, proposed to sanction the acquisition retroactively by amendment of the Constitution. Actually, such an authorization was the lesser part of the amendment he drafted; the larger part undertook to control the future of the Trans-Mississippi West by prohibiting settlement above the thirty-third parallel. But neither part interested congressional Republicans, and Jefferson, though he said failure of the amendment made the Constitution "a blank paper by construction," acquiesced. A revolution in the Union perforce became a revolution in the Constitution as well. The expansion of the treaty-making power was only the beginning of the revolution. A series of acts for the government of the new territory vested extraordinary power in the President; and the President proposed, with the sanction of a constitutional amendment, a national system of INTERNAL IMPROVEMENTS to unite this far-flung "empire of liberty."

The foreign crisis of Jefferson's second administration continued under Madison and finally terminated in the War of 1812. With the formation of the Third Coalition against Napoleonic France in 1805, all Europe was engulfed in war. The United States became the last neutral nation of consequence—to the profit of its carrying trade. Unfortunately, each side, the British and the French, demanded the trade on its own terms, and submission to one side's demands entailed conflict with the other. Britain, the dominant sea power, was the greater problem. British ships attacked American carriers under interpretations of rules of blockade, contraband, and neutral commerce that were rejected by the United States. Britain claimed the right of impressment of seamen aboard American ships on the ground that they were actually British subjects who had deserted from His Majesty's Navy and shipped aboard American vessels with government connivance. There was some truth in this claim, but thousands of American citizens were, in fact, impressed by Britain. And every seizure was a stinging reminder of past colonial servitude. Diplomatic efforts to settle these issues proved abortive. Relations rapidly deteriorated after the *Chesapeake-Leopard* Affair in June 1807. The attack of HMS *Leopard* on an American naval vessel after its captain refused to permit boarding and search for deserters inflamed the entire country against Britain. Jefferson might have taken the country to war. Instead, in December, he proposed, and Congress swiftly passed, the EMBARGO ACT. Essentially a self-blockade of American commerce, the act was in some part a preparation for war and in some part an experiment to test the theory of "peaceable coercion." The idea that the United States might enforce reason and justice on European belligerents by withholding its commerce was a first principle of Jeffersonian statecraft. Under the trial now begun, that idea failed. While the policy had comparatively little effect abroad, it produced serious economic, political, and perhaps even constitutional damage at home.

The embargo raised a host of constitutional issues, all hotly debated by Federalists and Republicans, though the parties seemed to have changed places. First, and broadest, was the issue of the commerce power. Republicans said the power to regulate commerce included the power to prohibit it. Federalists, who were closely allied with eastern merchants and shipmasters, limited regulation to encouragement and protection. Yet it was a Federalist, John Davis, the United States District Judge for Massachusetts, who upheld the constitutionality of the embargo on a broad view of the commerce power backed up by the "inherent SOVEREIGNTY" of the United States. Second, wholesale violation of the embargo in the Lake Champlain region led the President to proclaim an insurrection and authorize military force to suppress it under the same law George Washington had earlier used to put down the WHISKEY REBELLION over Republican opposition. Third, enforcement of the embargo required ever tighter measures of control. The fourth in the series of five embargo acts empowered customs collectors to search without a SEARCH WARRANT and to detain vessels merely on suspicion of intent to violate the law. The FOURTH AMENDMENT, a part of the Bill of Rights, was thus jeopardized. Fourth, before Congress adjourned in April 1808 it authorized the President to suspend the embargo against either or both belligerents—an unprecedented DELEGATION OF POWER. Federalists, of course, denounced the embargo in terms that recalled the VIRGINIA AND KENTUCKY RESOLUTIONS.

A storm of protest in New England led Congress, at the end of Jefferson's presidency, to repeal the embargo. The Non-Intercourse Act, which replaced it, reopened trade with all the world except Britain and France. That course, too, failed; and for the next three years under the new president, Madison, the country drifted toward war. In the end, war was declared because both diplomacy and "peaceable coercion" had failed to resolve the conflict over neutral rights. But that conflict was a symbol of much more: the honor and independence of the nation, the freedom of its commerce, the integrity of American nationality, the survival of republican government. The war was thus morally justified as the second war for American independence. The nation was ill-prepared for war, however, and its conduct produced one disaster after another. One section of the Union, New England, vigorously opposed the war from the start.

This opposition gave rise to the principal constitutional controversy of the time. The governors of the New England states challenged congressional power to provide for organizing and calling forth the militia. The chief justice of Massachusetts's highest court advised the governor that the right to decide when the militia should be called belonged to him, not to Congress or the President; and later, in 1814, when the militia was activated it was in the state rather than the national service. Years later, in *Luther v. Mott* (1827), the Supreme Court fully sustained national authority over the militia. Interference with the prosecution of the war was accompanied by a steady stream of denunciation. Madison called this a "seditious opposition," but unlike his Federalist predecessors he made no move to restrain or suppress it. Ultra-Federalists had been hinting at disunion since the Louisiana Purchase threatened New England's power in the Union; some of them had plotted to establish a Northern Confederacy in 1804. Now, a decade later, Federalist delegates from all the New England states met secretly in the HARTFORD CONVENTION, not to plot disunion, for moderate forces were in control, but to organize resistance against "Mr. Madison's War." Resolutions adopted by the convention recommended a series of constitutional admendments, including elimination of the THREE-FIFTHS CLAUSE for the apportionment of representation and direct taxes, limitation of presidential tenure to one term, a two-thirds vote in Congress to admit new states and to declare war, and the disqualification of naturalized citizens from federal office.

The commissioners of the Hartford Convention arrived in Washington with their resolutions in the midst of jubilation over the Battle of New Orleans. They were ridiculed, of course; and from this nadir the Federalist party never recovered. News of the Peace of Ghent quickly followed. While it resolved none of the issues over which the war had begun, the treaty placed American independence on impregnable foundations and confirmed the strength of republican government. The American people erased the shame from a war so meager in victories, so marked by defeat, division, and disgrace, and put upon it the face of glory. In December 1815 Madison laid before Congress a nationalistic program that featured measures, such as a national bank, formerly associated with the defeated party. Yet the program was not a case of "out-Federalizing Federalism." The Republican nationalism that matured with the Peace of Ghent had nothing to do with Federalist nationalism, with its vitiating Anglophobia, its narrow class and sectional views, and its distrust of popular government. The American political experiment had vindicated itself, exorcising earlier fears for its survival and making possible the incorporation of principles of national improvement and consolidation into the Republican party.

A new era dawned in American politics in 1815. For a quarter-century the nation had directed its industry and commerce toward a Europe ravaged by war and revolution; now that era had ended, and with it the opportunity of rearing American prosperity on the misfortunes of the Old World. For almost as long, government had been carried on by party spirit; now one of the two parties, the Federalist, around which the rivalry of men, issues, and principles had turned, ceased to be a factor in national affairs, and it was by no means clear what political force would replace the force of party. A country that had hugged the Atlantic seaboard and sought its prosperity in foreign trade was about to explode in the Trans-Appalachian West. During the next six years five new western states would enter the Union. A wider Union and the rise of the West as a self-conscious section raised difficult problems of economic development, constitutional principle, and political power. Since its Revolutionary birth the nation had enjoyed astonishing continuity of leadership. Thomas Jefferson, author of the Declaration of Independence, was a gray eminence at Monticello; James Madison, Father of the Constitution, was the President who had finally, irrevocably, secured that independence in a second war against Great Britain. But a new generation of political leaders had burst on the scene during the war, and the fate of the nation now lay in their hands.

Nearly all Republicans united on the program of national improvement and consolidation that Madison laid before the Fourteenth Congress in December. This "Madisonian Platform" proceeded from an enlarged view of the general government's responsibility for the nation's welfare. A national bank had previously been recommended to Congress as an agency for financing the war. Now, facing the chaos of runaway state banking, Madison recommended it as a permanent institution to secure the constitutional object of a stable and uniform national currency. Madison, of course, had opposed the original Bank of the United States as unconstitutional, and Republicans in Congress had defeated its recharter in 1811. But conditions and needs had changed, and Madison, with most of these same Republicans, considered that experience had settled the question of constitutionality in favor of a national bank. The Madisonian platform called for continuing in peacetime high tariff duties on imports in order to protect the infant industries that had grown up behind the sheltering wall of war and embargo. The President called for a comprehensive system of internal improvements—roads and canals to bind the nation together, secure its defenses, and facilitate internal commerce. Any deficiency of constitutional power should be overcome by amendment. In a final appeal to the liberality of American patriotism, Madison proposed the establishment of a national university, in Washington, which would be "a central resort of youth and genius from every part of their country, diffusing on their return examples of those national feelings, those liberal sentiments, and those congenial manners which contribute cement to our union and strength to [its] great political fabric."

Congress responded with legislation to charter a national bank, establish a system of tariff protection, and create a permanent fund for financing a vast network of roads, canals, and other improvements. The last measure, dubbed the Bonus Bill because the fund was founded on the bonus to be paid for the bank charter, was vetoed by Madison on constitutional grounds in the last act of his presidency. In this surprising retreat to the doctrine of strict construction, Madison delivered the first shock to the postwar nationalism he had himself championed. His successor, JAMES MONROE, took the same position on internal improvements, holding that a constitutional amendment was necessary to authorize them. Republican leaders in Congress disagreed. They found sufficient constitutional warrant to build as well as to fund internal improvements in the commerce, post road, and general welfare clauses, and they declined to seek an amendment lest by the failure to obtain it the Constitution be weakened. In the end, however, Monroe conceded the unlimited power of Congress to appropriate money for internal improvements, while continuing to deny the power to construct and operate them. This concession provided a constitutional justification for the General Survey Act of 1824. Although the same argument supported important projects in the ensuing administration, no national system of internal improvements was ever realized. In the absence of constructive national action, the several states embarked upon ambitious projects of their own (New York's Erie Canal, for instance, begun in 1817); and soon the government even relinquished its one great enterprise, the National Road, to the states.

The period of Monroe's presidency was signalized as "The Era of Good Feelings." This reflected the dissolution of old party ties and feelings. The Republican party had become the grand party of the nation. In 1820 Monroe ran unopposed for reelection and only one erratic electoral vote was cast against him. But his success had little to do with party or popularity, nor did it translate into effective power and leadership. Power and leadership had shifted to Congress, particularly to the House of Representatives where HENRY CLAY had converted the office of speaker from that of an impartial moderator to one of policymaking leadership. To an extent, certainly, executive power receded because foreign affairs had taken a distant second place to domestic affairs on the nation's agenda. Interestingly, Monroe is best remembered not for any initiative or achievement in domestic affairs but for a masterly stroke of foreign policy, the Monroe Doctrine. But Clay even challenged the President in foreign policy; and congressional ascendancy owed much to the boldness and address of young leaders like Clay who sought to command the popular feeling and power of the country. Partly for this reason the postwar Republicans consensus was soon shattered and "good feelings" vanished on the winds of change. Great issues, such as the Missouri Compromise, split the nationalizing Republican party along its sectional seams. The Panic of 1819, which led to the first major depression in the country's history, released powerful currents that shriveled the bright hopes of 1815.

Although the Panic of 1819 broke banks, bankrupted merchants, idled workers, and emptied factories everywhere, it was centered in American agriculture, especially in the freshly burgeoning lands of the South and West. Many purchasers of these lands had availed themselves of the credit allowed by the Harrison Land Act of 1800. Also important to frontier farmers and planters, of course, was bank credit. State banks had generally met this need, but now they were aided and abetted by the new Bank of the United States, which established most of its branches in the South and West. Agricultural prices collapsed worldwide in 1818. A severe contraction of bank credit followed. The Bank of the United States barely survived, and did so only at the expense of bankrupting many thousands of farmers, merchants, and local bankers. Several western states enacted legislation in the interest of debtors. The controversy over the constitutionality of debtor relief laws rocked Kentucky for a decade. All along the frontier, in wheat lands and in cotton lands, people tended to blame their troubles on the Bank. There were calls for repeal of its charter, and state legislatures acted to restrain "The Monster." Ohio levied a prohibitive tax on resident branches; when it was not paid the state auditor seized $100,000 of the Bank's funds, thereby giving birth to the case of OSBORN V. THE BANK OF THE UNITED STATES (1824). Wherever the depression caused hostility to the Bank, it weakened the spring of support for economic nationalism generally. To nationalist leaders, on the other hand, the depression offered further confirmation of the colonial character of the American economy and pointed up the imperative need for higher protective tariffs and other government assistance to bring about a flourishing "home market" for the products of American industry. This AMERICAN SYSTEM, as Clay named it, had its fulfillment in the Tariff of 1824.

While the Panic was at its height, in March 1819, the Supreme Court handed down its unanimous decision in MCCULLOCH V. MARYLAND, upholding the constitutionality of the Bank and its freedom to operate without state interference. Chief Justice John Marshall drew upon the Hamiltonian doctrine of IMPLIED POWERS not only for the congressional authority to charter a bank but also for a sweeping vindication of national supremacy. In the same momentous term, which established the high-water mark of judicial nationalism, the court invoked the CONTRACT CLAUSE to strike down laws of two states. In DARTMOUTH COLLEGE V. WOODWARD it extended the protection of that clause to corporate charters; and in STURGES V. CROWNINSHIELD it struck down a New York law for the relief of debtors whose contracts antedated the law. Quite aside from their implications for national versus state authority, all these decisions placed the court unreservedly on the side of propertied interests against popular majorities in state legislatures.

The Bank case, in particular, provoked attack on the Supreme Court and more broadly on the growth of national power. In Virginia opposition to the Supreme Court, which Jefferson called a "subtle corps of sappers and miners constantly working under ground to undermine the foundations of our confederated fabric," sparked revival of the STATES' RIGHTS doctrines of the Virginia and Kentucky Resolutions and offered powerful reinforcement of the state's challenge to the court's appellate jurisdiction. The challenge had ridden on an old case involving the confiscation of Loyalist lands during the American Revolution. Taking the case on appeal from the Virginia Court of Appeals, the Supreme Court had overturned the state's confiscation law and found for the right of the English heir. To this Judge SPENCER ROANE, head of the Virginia court, responded by denying the Supreme Court's appellate jurisdiction, declaring section 25 of the Judiciary Act of 1789 unconstitutional, and refusing to execute the Supreme Court's decree. The court again took up the case, MARTIN V. HUNTER'S LESSEE (1816), and through Justice JOSEPH STORY reasserted the constitutionality of the appellate jurisdiction over state courts together with the judicial supremacy that went with it. But for the Bank case the controversy would have been quickly forgotten. As Marshall observed, however, that case "roused the Sleeping Giant of Virginia." Under the pseudonym "Hampden," in the columns of the Richmond *Enquirer,* Roane advanced a DUAL FEDERALISM philosophy of the Constitution. Under it there could be no ultimate appeal from the state courts to the Supreme Court. Marshall replied at length as "Friend of the Constitution" in the Alexandria *Gazette.* The veteran Old Republican JOHN TAYLOR of Caroline expounded the Virginia doctrines *ad nauseum* in *Construction Construed and Constitutions Vindicated* (1820). The doctrines still had a long course to run, but the controversy over appellate jurisdiction drew to a close in COHENS V. VIRGINIA (1821). In this arranged case Virginia became the defendant when the Cohens appealed their conviction in state court to the Supreme Court under Section 25. The Virginia assembly adopted resolutions backing the state cause. Surprisingly, perhaps because the case resulted in a nominal victory for the state, Marshall's broad assertion of national judicial supremacy provoked no official reaction in Virginia, and opposition collapsed in 1822.

The Missouri Compromise was enacted in the midst of these events and communicated its own passions to them. The proposal to restrict slavery in Missouri as a condition of statehood raised difficult questions about the constitutional authority of Congress, the nature of the Union, the future of the West, the morality of slavery, and the sectional balance of power. Congress had previously restricted SLAVERY IN THE TERRITORIES. That power was not seriously in dispute. But the Missouri constitution would provide for slavery, and it was by no means clear that Congress could overrule it, especially as slavery had always been considered an institution under local jurisdiction. The compromise resolved the issue by allowing Missouri to enter the Union as a slave state. A new problem arose, however, when the proffered Missouri constitution contained a provision for excluding "free negroes and mulattoes" from the state. Opponents of the compromise charged that this violated the PRIVILEGES AND IMMUNITIES clause of the United States Constitution, because Negroes who were citizens of northern states would be denied citizenship in Missouri. Laboriously, a new compromise had to be constructed to save the original one. Under it Missouri would be admitted to the Union only after the legislature agreed, despite the constitutional provision, never to pass a law that might abridge the privileges and immunities of citizens. Missouri acquiesced and gained admission to the Union in August 1821. Not for many years would the harmony of the Union again be disturbed by slavery. The Missouri Compromise, therefore, contributed mightily to peace and union. Yet to Thomas Jefferson, contemplating the exclusion of slavery above the 36' 30" parallel, the compromise was "like a fire-ball in the night," sounding "the knell of the Union." "It is hushed, indeed, for the moment. But this is a reprieve only, not the final sentence. A geographical line, once conceived and held up to the angry passions of men, will never be obliterated; and every new irritation will mark it deeper and deeper."

The Republican consensus vanished during Monroe's second term. The Missouri question had raised fears of sectional parties and politics that were not dispelled by the compromise. The growth of the West, with a maturing sectional consciousness of its own, and the scramble of economic interests for the bounty and favor of the general government put the National Republican system under heavy strain. While nationalists continued to believe that the Union would survive and prosper only through measures of consolidation, growing numbers of Republicans, inspired by the Virginia "Old Republicans," believed consolidation must tear the Union apart. They called for return to Jeffersonian austerity and states' rights.

In this unstable political environment, the contest for the presidential succession was especially disturbing. Monroe's chief cabinet officers, JOHN QUINCY ADAMS, William H. Crawford, and JOHN C. CALHOUN, were in the race from the start, and they were soon joined by Henry Clay and ANDREW JACKSON. In the absence of a single dominant leader or a clear line of succession, such as the Virginia dynasty had afforded, the Republican party split into personal followings and factions. The congressional caucus of the party, which had been the mechanism for nominating candidates for President and vice-president, could no longer be relied upon. The caucus itself had become an issue. In an increasingly democratic electorate it was assailed as a closed, elitist institution. Politicians grew wary of the caucus but saw no obvious substitute for it. "We are putting to the proof the most delicate part of our system, the election of the Executive," DANIEL WEBSTER remarked. What was most distressing about the present contest, among men nourished on traditional Whig fears of executive power, was that it made the presidency the center of gravity in the government. Great issues of public policy were submitted to the artifice and caprice of presidential politics; and senators and representatives, if elected on the basis of presidential preferences, must necessarily compromise their independence. This threatened subordination of the legislative to the executive power was an inversion of the proper constitutional order.

Given the multiplicity of candidates, each with his own following, and none able to command a majority of votes, the election of the President inevitably wound up in the House of Representatives. There Clay, the speaker, having been eliminated, threw his support to Adams, who was chosen over Jackson, the popular vote leader. Adams's subsequent appointment of Clay as secretary of state, the cabinet post which had furnished the President for the third successive time, brought cries of "corrupt bargain" from the Jacksonians, and from this canard the Adams administration never recovered. Boldly, in his first message to Congress, Adams proposed to rally the country behind a great program of national improvement, one which took conventional internal improvements—rivers and harbors, roads and canals—only as a starting point. "Liberty is power," Adams declared. A nation of liberty should be a nation of power, provided, of course, power is used beneficently. The Constitution presents no obstacle. Indeed, to refrain from exercising legitimate powers for good ends would be treachery to the people. "While foreign nations less blessed with that freedom which is power . . . are advancing with gigantic strides in the career of public improvement," Adams said, "were we to slumber in indolence or to fold up our arms and proclaim to the world that we are palsied by the will of our constituents, would it not be to cast away the bounties of Providence and doom ourselves to perpetual inferiority?"

In response to the message, all the old artillery of states' rights and STRICT CONSTRUCTION was hauled out and turned on the administration. Liberty is power? What dangerous nonsense. Liberty is the jealous restraint of power. Individuals, not governments, are the best judges of their own interests; and the national interest consists only in the aggregate of individual interests. These ideas had been employed in the attack on the American System. Now they entered deeply into the ideology of the emerging Jacksonian coalition. A new recruit to the coalition was Vice-President Calhoun, who began to shed the liberality and nationalism that had characterized his political career. In part, certainly, he was influenced by the rising states' rights frenzy in South Carolina. This movement was orchestrated by Calhoun's enemies in the Crawford faction. In 1825 they drove through the legislature resolutions declaring the protective tariff and federal internal improvements unconstitutional. This "Revolution of 1825," as it came to be known, showed how far out of step Calhoun was with the opinion of his state, and he hurried to catch up.

In Congress the anticonsolidation movement provided most of the rhetoric and some of the substance of opposition on every issue with the administration but was especially evident in debates on the judiciary and the tariff. Report of a bill in the House to reorganize the federal judiciary, mainly by the addition of three circuits—and three new judges—in the West, furnished a forum for advocates of reforming the judiciary. There was still no consensus on the role and authority of the Supreme Court. The Court had been a powerful ally of consolidation. Between 1816 and 1825 it had ruled in favor of national power seventeen times and of states' rights only six times, when they were at issue; and by 1825 it had invalidated in whole or in part the statutes of ten states. Various measures, most of them involving constitutional amendment, had been offered to curb judicial power: the withdrawal of opinions, or removal of Justices, on the address of both houses of Congress; the requirement of seriatim opinions; the use of the Senate as a tribunal of last resort on federal questions; and the repeal of section 25 of the Judiciary Act. All were aired in the 1826 debate. Nothing of substance emerged; the reorganization bill itself, after passing the House, failed in the Senate. Yet the debate, which was the "last hurrah" of reform, may have contributed to the increasing moderation of the Marshall Court after 1825.

The tariff had been a constitutional issue since the great debate on the American System in 1824. The power to tax, Virginia congressman PHILIP P. BARBOUR had then argued, was not a power to promote one industry over another, nor did any such power exist in the Constitution. Controversy was reignited three years later by demands for additional protection, particularly on behalf of the rising wool and woolens industry of the Northeast. Jacksonian politicians, who came into control of the new Congress, could not ignore the demand. Under the leadership of MARTIN VAN BUREN of New York they framed a tariff bill that was a political stratagem rather than a serious piece of economic legislation. Moreover, they persuaded their southern friends to go along with the bill on the spurious plea that it would finally fail because of provisions designed to trigger overwhelming New England opposition, thereby enabling the Jacksonians to claim credit in the North for protectionist efforts without inflicting further injury on the South. But in the Senate, where it was named the Tariff of Abominations, the bill was amended to become less objectionable to New England, and its great spokesman, Webster, heretofore a free-trader, dramatically declared his support. The TARIFF ACT OF 1828 became law. The South felt betrayed. In South Carolina, which had grasped the flagging torch of states' rights from Virginia, there were demands to "calculate the value of the Union." The legislature, in December, enacted a series of resolutions declaring the tariff oppressive and unconstitutional. It also published the South Carolina Exposition and Protest, which Calhoun had authored secretly at the invitation of a legislative committee. The Exposition repeated, with some elaboration, the litany of antitariff arguments South Carolina radicals had been urging for several years and it offered the first authoritative statement of "the Carolina doctrine" of nullification.

A motley coalition—western agrarians, southern planters, northern democrats—swept Andrew Jackson into the presidency in 1828. His inaugural address gave no clear sign of the direction his administration would take; but the dominant pressure of the men, ideas, and interests gathered around the President was toward dissolution of the National Republican platform and toward the rebirth of party government on specious Jeffersonian principles.

MERRILL D. PETERSON

Bibliography

ADAMS, HENRY 1891–1893 *History of the United States during the Administrations of Jefferson and Madison.* 9 Vols. New York: Scribner's.

BEVERIDGE, ALBERT J. 1919 *The Life of John Marshall,* vol. IV. Boston: Houghton Mifflin.

CUNNINGHAM, NOBLE E., JR. 1978 *The Process of Government under Jefferson.* Princeton, N.J.: Princeton University Press.

DANGERFIELD, GEORGE 1952 *The Era of Good Feeling.* New York: Harcourt, Brace.

GOODRICH, CARTER, ED. 1967 *The Government and the Economy: 1783–1861.* Indianapolis: Bobbs-Merrill.

JOHNSTONE, ROBERT M., JR. 1978 *Jefferson and the Presidency: Leadership in the Young Republic.* Ithaca, N.Y.: Cornell University Press.

KETCHAM, RALPH 1984 *Presidents above Party: The First American Presidency, 1789–1829.* Chapel Hill: University of North Carolina Press.

SOFAER, ABRAHAM D. 1976 *War, Foreign Affairs and Constitutional Power: The Origins.* Cambridge, Mass.: Ballinger.

TURNER, FREDERICK JACKSON 1906 *Rise of the New West, 1819–1829.* New York: Macmillan.

WHITE, LEONARD D. 1951 *The Jeffersonians: A Study in Administrative History, 1801–1829.* New York: Macmillan.

CONSTITUTIONAL HISTORY, 1829–1848

Constitutional change in the Jacksonian era began with the Virginia CONSTITUTIONAL CONVENTION of 1829–1830, and climaxed in the election controversies of 1848. Between these dates, the American people tried to renovate their constitutional order, especially with respect to the great issues of FEDERALISM, democratization, and slavery.

Virginia's venerable Constitution of 1776, like other early constitutions, had come to enshrine the related evils of malapportionment and disfranchisement. THOMAS JEFFERSON denounced these and other defects in the document from the founding of the commonwealth to his death. His criticism produced the convention of 1829, where the badly underrepresented Western delegates demanded reform, including white manhood suffrage and a REAPPORTIONMENT that would fairly represent the growing population of their region. The convention was a showcase of Virginia's political leadership, including as delegates JAMES MADISON (who had also been a delegate at the 1776 convention), JOHN MARSHALL, JAMES MONROE, JOHN RANDOLPH, as well as emergent conservative leaders like JOHN TYLER, Benjamin Watkins Leigh, and Abel Parker Upshur. The conservatives from the tidewater region, representing the interests of slaveholders, held the reformers at bay, conceding only a limited modification of the old freehold suffrage to include householders and leaseholders, far less than the taxpayer-militia qualification representing a compromise conceded by the western delegates. Reapportionment similarly fell short of western demands, as the convention adopted a complex system of regional representation. The conservative triumph on these two issues was assured partly because many delegates heeded Leigh's warning that reform would produce "the annihilation of all state rights." Implicit in this response were fears for the security of slavery. Those fears were bloodily confirmed by Nat Turner's 1831 slave insurrection in Southampton County, and reawakened the next year as the Virginia General Assembly debated and ultimately voted down a proposal for the gradual abolition of slavery.

Slavery, only hinted at in the 1828 Virginia debates, soon surfaced as a constitutional topic throughout the South. In *State v. Mann* (1829) Chief Judge Thomas Ruffin of the North Carolina Supreme Court held that the absolute subjection characteristic of slavery was "essential to the value of slaves as property, to the security of the master, and [to] the public tranquility." The South Carolina Court of Appeals later held that "a slave can invoke neither MAGNA CHARTA nor COMMON LAW. . . . In the very nature of things, he is subject to despotism." The political counterpart of this new proslavery jurisprudence was the "positive good" thesis, first advanced by South Carolina Governor George McDuffie in 1835 and amplified thereafter by JOHN C. CALHOUN in the United States Senate.

Southern judicial and political leaders found themselves compelled to erect defenses for the internal security of slavery after 1830 in part because a new cadre of abolitionists appeared in the northern states, led at first by William Lloyd Garrison. Repudiating both gradualism and projects for the colonization of free blacks in Liberia, this new generation of antislavery workers demanded the immediate and uncompensated abolition of slavery. They tried their hand at constitutional challenges to slavery. Although they conceded that the federal government had no power to interfere with slavery in the states, they found many areas for legitimate federal action, such as exclusion of slavery from the territories, abolition of slavery in the DISTRICT OF COLUMBIA, abolition of the interstate slave trade, and refusal to admit new slave states. At the state level, they sought, unsuccessfully, to have slavery declared unconstitutional in New Jersey, persuaded the Massachusetts and New York legislatures to enact PERSONAL LIBERTY LAWS, and provided invaluable support for fugitive slave rescues. In 1832, when they got their first taste of constitutional litigation in the Connecticut prosecution of Prudence Crandall, they attempted to define and secure the rights of free blacks under the PRIVILEGES AND IMMUNITIES CLAUSE of Article IV, section 2, of the Constitution.

By 1830 it was obvious that the South Carolinians were counting the costs of the Union, and weighing their alternatives. The fundamental concepts of state

SOVEREIGNTY and the right of SECESSION were commonplace at the time. Thus in the Webster-Hayne debates of 1830, South Carolina Senator Robert Y. Hayne was closer to orthodoxy than DANIEL WEBSTER when he supported a cluster of theories derived or extrapolated from the VIRGINIA AND KENTUCKY RESOLUTIONS of 1798–1799: he condemned the consolidationist tendencies of the federal government, asserted state sovereignty, insisted on a STRICT CONSTRUCTION of the Constitution, reiterated the compact theory of the Union (by which the Constitution and the national Union were the creation of a compact of sovereign states), and defended the legitimacy of INTERPOSITION and NULLIFICATION. Webster's famous rhetorical reply is better known but less analytical than other rebuttals by EDWARD LIVINGSTON, JOHN QUINCY ADAMS, and JOSEPH STORY between 1830 and 1833. These maintained that sovereignty had effectively been transferred to the national government by the Constitution, that the Union created thereby was perpetual, and that secession was extralegal. In his *Commentaries on the Constitution* (1833), Story flatly denied that the Constitution was a compact among sovereign states. James Madison joined his venerable voice to theirs, condemning all theories of nullification as perversions of the doctrines he and Thomas Jefferson had propounded in 1798 and 1799. All maintained that because the Union was perpetual, it was therefore indissoluble. But John Quincy Adams had the ominous last word when he wrote in 1831 that "it is the odious nature of [this] question that it can be settled only at the cannon's mouth." South Carolina's attempted nullification of the TARIFF ACT of 1828 and its 1832 revision forced a resolution of these conflicts that came close to the mode Adams had predicted.

Though ostensibly aimed at the tariff, and the larger but more nebulous problem of the "consolidation" of the federal government's powers, the nullification controversy at its heart concerned the security and perpetuity of slavery. The tariff controversy nonetheless provided a convenient vehicle for the Carolinians to reconfirm their traditional THEORIES OF THE UNION and state sovereignty. In November 1832 a specially elected convention adopted the SOUTH CAROLINA ORDINANCE OF NULLIFICATION, which prohibited collection of the tariff and appeals to the United States Supreme Court. President ANDREW JACKSON responded with his "Proclamation to the People of South Carolina," drafted by Secretary of State Livingston, which refuted nullification theories, asserted federal supremacy, insisted on obedience to federal laws, warned that "Disunion by armed force is treason," and, surprisingly in view of his Bank Veto Message five months earlier, maintained that the Supreme Court was the proper and final arbiter of disputes under the United States Constitution and laws. The FORCE ACT of 1833 gave teeth to the proclamation, while a compromise tariff assuaged Carolina's nominal grievance. The Carolinians suspended, then rescinded the ordinance of nullification, which had been universally condemned by other states. But the state convention consoled itself with the empty gesture of a second ordinance nullifying the Force Act. On this equivocal note, the nullification crisis dissolved. Both sides in reality suffered a long-term defeat. Nationalists led by Jackson had failed to quash ideas of state sovereignty and secession; Calhoun and the nullifiers had failed to forge a united front of slave states and had promoted the federal "consolidation" they feared and condemned.

The second party system, emergent at the time of the nullification crisis, produced its own constitutional controversies. HENRY CLAY had announced the basis of what he called the AMERICAN SYSTEM in 1824: a protective tariff, federal aid to INTERNAL IMPROVEMENTS, and support for the second Bank of the United States. In a decade this became the program of the Whig Party. Jacksonian Democrats denounced all three elements as being of dubious constitutionality. In 1830 President Andrew Jackson vetoed the MAYSVILLE ROAD BILL partly because he doubted that federal aid for internal improvements, at least those lying wholly within a state, was constitutional. Two years later, in his veto of the recharter bill for the second Bank of the United States, he similarly expressed reservations about the constitutional power of Congress to charter a bank. He brushed aside the binding force of Chief Justice John Marshall's decision on the subject in MCCULLOCH V. MARYLAND (1819) by asserting that "the authority of the Supreme Court must not, therefore, be permitted to control the Congress or the Executive when acting in their legislative capacities. . . ." In 1833 Jackson ordered his subordinates to remove all federal deposits from the bank, and to redistribute them in selected state-chartered banks.

The democratization of American politics was advanced by the Whigs' development of mass electioneering techniques in the 1840 presidential campaign. Whig success was short-lived, however, because of President William Henry Harrison's death in 1841. JOHN TYLER, a conservative Virginia Democrat, succeeded to the office, and in doing so established the important precedent that he was not merely the "acting President" but President in fact. One of the few positive accomplishments of the Whigs' brief accession to power was the enactment of the nation's second Bankruptcy Act in 1841. Its repeal in 1843 returned the matter of insolvency legislation to the states, where it was to remain until 1898. Direction of the nation's economy was to remain chiefly the responsibility of the states until the Civil War. (See BANKRUPTCY POWER.)

In the 1830s the states encouraged and subsidized economic development in numerous ways. Their role was almost entirely promotional; during the Jacksonian era, they essayed only the most diffident beginnings of ECONOMIC REGULATION. The state legislatures granted charters and franchises for banking, insurance, railroad, and manufacturing CORPORATIONS. Encouraged by the remarkable but unduplicated success of New York's Erie Canal in the 1820s, other states provided direct financial support for construction of turnpikes, canals, and railroads.

State jurists likewise supported economic development, sometimes by creating whole new domains of law (torts, nonmarine insurance), and sometimes by reworking traditional legal doctrines to provide instrumentalist approaches supportive of entrepreneurs. In 1831 Chancellor Reuben Walworth of New York upheld the power of the legislature to grant EMINENT DOMAIN powers to railroads, and Chief Justice LEMUEL SHAW of the Massachusetts Supreme Judicial Court afterward approved the extension of that power to manufacturing corporations as well. Chief Judge JOHN BANNISTER GIBSON of the Pennsylvania Supreme Court helped refashion the law of contracts in favor of the doctrine of *caveat emptor*, an impersonal and seller-oriented approach presumably suited to a national market. The new orientation of the law of contracts and sales emphasized the autonomy of the individual and private will, dismissing earlier insistence on equitable dealing and community standards of fairness.

But the public law of the states in the 1830s was not exclusively concerned with succoring nascent industrial capitalism. In fact, the common law itself, as well as its judicial exemplars, came under reformist attack. In the Jacksonian period, the movement toward an elective judiciary decisively gained ground, as Mississippi led the way in 1832 by making its entire bench elective. Other states followed suit, so that by the twentieth century only the federal judiciary remained wholly appointive and life-tenured. An even stronger assault on judge-made law emerged from the movement to codify all laws. Even legal conservatives like Joseph Story conceded that some restatement of law in certain areas (EVIDENCE, criminal law, and commercial law) might be both feasible and useful. More thoroughgoing codifiers, such as Edward Livingston and Robert Rantoul, condemned the common law as antidemocratic, mysterious, and prolix.

Meanwhile, the controversy over slavery intensified. From 1835 to 1840, mobs in all sections of the country harassed abolitionists and free blacks. The beleaguered abolitionists, for their part, mounted a propaganda campaign against slaveholding by weekly mailings of abolitionist literature throughout the South. Democrats and southern political leaders reacted violently, with Postmaster General Amos Kendall condoning destruction of mail in Charleston. President Jackson recommended congressional prohibition of abolitionist mailing in the southern states, but Senator John C. Calhoun objected, partly because such federal legislation would invade rights reserved to the states. The controversy dissipated when abolitionists redirected their energies to a petition campaign, garnering signatures throughout the north on petitions to Congress demanding various antislavery measures, such as abolition in the District of Columbia, interdiction of the interstate slave trade, and refusal to annex the slaveholding republic of Texas or to admit new slave states.

Abolitionists were active in legal-constitutional efforts against slavery at the state level, too. In Massachusetts, they scored a striking victory against the ingress of sojourners' slaves in COMMONWEALTH V. AVES (1836), when Chief Justice Shaw expounded an American version of the doctrine of SOMERSET'S CASE (King's Bench, 1772). Shaw held that a sojourning slave could not be held in slavery against her will in Massachusetts because no state law supported slavery and because the "all men are free and equal" provision of the 1780 Massachusetts Declaration of Rights was "precisely adapted to the abolition of negro slavery." Abolitionists enjoyed less success the next year in Ohio and Pennsylvania, however. Chief Judge Gibson held in 1837 that, under the Pennsylvania constitution, blacks were not "freemen" and hence could not vote. A state constitutional convention meeting that year took no action to reverse this holding. In Ohio, the abolitionist lawyers SALMON P. CHASE and JAMES G. BIRNEY developed an impressive range of legal and constitutional arguments in *Matilda's Case* (1837) to demonstrate that the 1793 federal Fugitive Slave Act was unconstitutional under the FOURTH AMENDMENT, the Fifth Amendment's DUE PROCESS clause, and the NORTHWEST ORDINANCE's guarantees of TRIAL BY JURY and HABEAS CORPUS. These arguments failed then, but they furnished an impressive stock of ideas to expanding ABOLITIONIST CONSTITUTIONAL THEORY.

At the national level, defenders of slavery launched a counterattack against this assault. The United States House of Representatives in 1836 adopted the first of the congressional "gag resolutions," declaring that all petitions coming into the House as a result of the antislavery petition campaign would be automatically tabled, without being referred or read. In subsequent years, the Senate adopted a similar rule, and the House made it a standing rule. But the gags proved insufficient bars to the determined evasions of a handful of antislavery congressmen, led by John Quincy Adams, who repeatedly introduced antislavery petitions. (See CIVIL LIBERTIES AND THE SLAVERY CONTROVERSY.)

Observing such assaults on slavery with alarm, Calhoun introduced into the Senate in 1837 a series of resolutions that in effect restated the nature of the Union and slavery's relation to it. These resolutions condemned antislavery agitation as "subversive"; declared that the federal government was the "common agent" of the states, bound to protect all their institutions, including slavery; that slavery was an "essential element" in the organization of the Union; that any congressional interference with slavery in the District of Columbia or the territories would be an "attack on the institutions" of the slave states; and that Congress could not discriminate against the interests of the slave states in the territories. Congress declined to adopt the last two, but its endorsement of the others threatened to give the slave states a constitutional predominance in the Union.

Abolitionists responded with innovative constitutional thinking of their own. In 1839 the hitherto unified movement began to split apart. The antislavery mainstream became involved in political action, forming the Liberty Party. They conceded exclusive state power over slavery in the states where it existed, but called for congressional action elsewhere, as, for example, by refusing to admit new slave states and by repealing the Fugitive Slave Act. Two splinter groups of the movement challenged this moderate position. Followers of William Lloyd Garrison, embracing the theological doctrine of perfectionism, by 1842 came to denounce the Constitution as a proslavery compact, and called for disunion. Radical abolitionists, led by the New York lawyer Alvan Stewart, discarded previous assumptions about slavery's legitimacy and contended that slavery was everywhere unconstitutional as a violation of various constitutional provisions, including the Fifth Amendment's due process clause (considered both in procedural and substantive senses), Article IV's guarantee of a REPUBLICAN FORM OF GOVERNMENT, and the same article's privileges and immunities clause.

Abolitionists harked back to the DECLARATION OF INDEPENDENCE and to the tenets of republican ideology of the Revolutionary era. So did contemporary suffrage reformers in Rhode Island, who faced the same problems of malapportionment and disenfranchisement as had Virginia two decades earlier. After concluding that the existing conservative regime would never concede reform, they called an extralegal constitutional convention to modernize the state's constitution, which until then had been the 1662 Charter. This "People's Constitution" was ratified by universal male suffrage. Its supporters then elected a new government for the state, with Thomas W. Dorr as governor. The existing regime refused to cede power, so for several months in 1842, Rhode Island had two governments, each claiming a different source of constitutional legitimacy: the Dorrites, a do-it-yourself, implicitly revolutionary popular sovereignty; and the extant regime, legality backed by force. With behind-the-scenes support of President Tyler, the regular government suppressed its opponents, then inaugurated the substance of what the reformers had demanded. The failure of the Dorr Rebellion demonstrated that the guarantees of self-government and equality in the Declaration of Independence would not be taken literally or programmatically in the Jacksonian era.

Constitutional change came to other states less turbulently in the 1840s. In neighboring Massachusetts, Chief Justice Shaw placed the Supreme Judicial Court in the forefront of legal and constitutional innovation in a series of decisions from 1842 to 1850 that created new doctrines and revolutionized old ones. In COMMONWEALTH V. HUNT (1842) Shaw legitimated labor union organization in the United States. The Philadelphia and New York *Cordwainers Cases* (1806, 1810), reaffirmed by New York decisions in the mid-1830s, had held labor organization and strikes to be CRIMINAL CONSPIRACIES at common law and illegal under state statutes prohibiting injury to commerce. But in *Hunt,* Shaw held that neither the objectives of the workers nor their means—unions and strikes—were inherently unlawful. Because it removed the taint of per se illegality from unions, the *Hunt* decision has been extravagantly called the "Magna Carta of organized labor."

Another Shaw decision of the same year, *Farwell v. Boston and Worcester Railroad,* proved as damaging to the cause of industrial workers as *Hunt* had been beneficial. In exempting an employer from liability for the injury to one of its employees caused by the negligence of another employee, Shaw enunciated the fellow-servant rule that stood as a bar to recovery in such situations.

Because Massachusetts was in the vanguard of industrialization, Shaw had an opportunity to influence the law of railroads and common carriers more than any other contemporary jurist, leading one scholar to conclude that he "practically established the railroad law for the country." In cases involving eminent domain and taxation, Shaw held railroads to be "a public work, established by public authority" whose property is held "in trust for the public." Shaw thereby hoped to secure legislative benefits granted railroads, while at the same time leaving open the possibility of some degree of public control through legislation. Yet he was solicitous to exempt railroads from forms of liability that would have drained investment capital.

The temperance movement proved to be as prolific a source of judicial lawmaking as innovations in transportation technology. Throughout the antebellum period, state appellate courts had kept alive the HIGHER LAW tradition enunciated by Justice SAMUEL CHASE in his opinion in CALDER V. BULL (1798). State judges, especially those of Federalist and Whig antecedents, readily struck down various state laws for the inconsistency with "the great principles of eternal justice" or "the character and genius of our government." In his *Commentaries on the Constitution* (3rd ed., 1858), Joseph Story summed up "the strong current of judicial opinion" that "the fundamental maxims of a free government seem to require, that the rights of personal liberty and private property should be held sacred." The Delaware Supreme Court used such nebulous concepts derived from the nature of republican government to void a local-option PROHIBITION statute in 1847. Higher law constitutional doctrine became all the more important after the United States Supreme Court's 5–4 decision in the LICENSE CASES (1847), upholding Massachusetts, Rhode Island, and New Hampshire statutes taxing and regulating liquor imported from outside the state. This trend culminated in the celebrated case of WYNEHAMER V. PEOPLE (1856), where the New York Court of Appeals struck down a state prohibition statute under the state constitution's LAW OF THE LAND and due process clauses.

Chief Justice Shaw was the author of a doctrine that provided a powerful offset to such higher law tendencies: the POLICE POWER. In COMMONWEALTH V. ALGER (1951) he stated that all property is held "under the implied liability that . . . use of it may be so regulated, that it shall not be injurious . . . to the rights of the community." He accorded the legislature sweeping power to subject property to "reasonable limitations." After the Civil War, the police power doctrine constituted the basis for an alternative to the dogmas of SUBSTANTIVE DUE PROCESS and FREEDOM OF CONTRACT.

Courts were by no means the sole font of constitutional innovation in the 1840s. State legislatures and constitutional conventions also modified the constitutional order. Reflecting the movement of the age from status to contract, as noted by Sir Henry Maine, the state legislatures in the 1840s extended some measure of control to married women over their own property through the married women's property acts. State courts sometimes reacted with hostility to these measures, seeing them either as a deprivation of the husband's property rights protected by higher law or as deranging gender and marital relationships.

Four New England states experimented with embryonic railroad regulatory commissions (Rhode Island, 1839; New Hampshire, 1844; Connecticut, 1850; Massachusetts, various ad hoc special commissions), but none of these proved successful or permanent. New York in the 1840s had to confront the legal consequences of the emergent nativist controversy. Roman Catholics sought public funding for parochial schools and objected to use of the King James Bible for devotional sessions in public schools. Nativists, for their part, demanded that the predominantly Catholic immigrants of the period be disfranchised.

The most significant state constitutional event of the decade was the drafting and ratification of the New York Constitution of 1846. This document was a compendium of constitutional trends of the era and profoundly influenced subsequent constitutions, especially those of Michigan and Wisconsin. It capped the decade's long movement toward general incorporation acts by restricting the granting of special corporate charters, and, for good measure, made all legislation respecting corporations, both general and special, subject to repeal or amendment at any time. It put to rest the controversies of the rent wars of the previous decade by abolishing all feudal real property tenures and perpetual leases, converting all long-term leaseholds into freeholds. It made the entire New York bench elective, and required appointment of a three-member commission to draw up a reformed procedural code.

Despite the sweep of innovation in the 1846 New York Constitution and its daughters in the west, the needs of certain groups in American society remained unmet. Chief among these were women. Feminists convened in Seneca Falls, New York, in 1848 and issued a manifesto on women's rights modeled on the Declaration of Independence, demanding VOTING RIGHTS, the recognition by law of full legal capacity, revision of male-biased divorce laws, access to the professions and to educational opportunity, and abolition of all discriminatory legislation.

Blacks in the northern states were no better off. After 1842, their situation, especially in areas near the slave states, became more precarious because of Justice Story's opinion in PRIGG V. PENNSYLVANIA (1842), upholding the constitutionality of the Fugitive Slave Act of 1793 and striking down inconsistent state legislation. After *Prigg,* most state personal liberty laws, such as those assuring jury trial to alleged fugitives or extending the writ of habeas corpus to them, were suspect. Abolitionists seized on a Story dictum in *Prigg,* stating that the states did not have to assist in fugitive recaptures under the federal act. They induced several state legislatures to enact statutes prohibiting state facilities from being used for temporary detention of alleged fugitives.

The slavery question briefly returned to Congress in 1842, in the form of the "*Creole* Resolutions" offered by Representative Joshua Giddings (Whig, Ohio). Slaves aboard the *Creole,* an American-flag vessel, mutinied on the high seas and made their way to the Bahamas, where most of them were freed by British authorities. Secretary of State Daniel Webster protested and demanded compensation for the liberated slaves. Giddings, despite the gag rule, introduced resolutions setting forth the *Somerset*-based position that the slaves had merely resumed their natural status, freedom, and could not be reenslaved. The federal government lacked authority to protect or reimpose their slave status, which was derived solely from Virginia law and hence confined to this JURISDICTION. The House defeated the resolutions and censured Giddings. But he was reelected by a landslide, in effect forcing and winning a REFERENDUM on his antislavery positions. This, together with the earlier and ignominious failure of an effort to censure Representative John Quincy Adams for flouting the gag, led to the demise of the gag rules in both houses in 1844.

Such inconclusive sparring between slavery and abolition might have gone on indefinitely had it not been for the Mexican War. But proslavery ambitions to expand into the southwestern empire fundamentally altered the character of the American Union, destabilizing extant constitutional settlements and requiring new constitutional arrangements to replace the now obsolete MISSOURI COMPROMISE.

ANNEXATION OF TEXAS had been controversial ever since Texan independence in 1836. When the issue reestablished itself on the national agenda in 1844, opponents of annexation, including Daniel Webster, Joseph Story, and John Quincy Adams, argued that annexation was not constitutionally permissible under the territories clause of Article IV, section 3, because previous annexations had been of dependent territories of sovereign nations, whereas Texas was itself an independent nation. Proponents dismissed this as an insignificant technicality, under the broad reading of the FOREIGN AFFAIRS power by Chief Justice Marshall in AMERICAN INSURANCE CO. V. CANTER (1828). Political opposition blocked ratification of an annexation treaty until President Tyler hit on the expedient of annexation by JOINT RESOLUTION of both houses, which required only a majority vote in each, rather than the two-thirds required for treaties in the Senate. Texas was thereby annexed in 1845.

Annexation hastened the deterioration of relations with Mexico, but Tyler was cautious and circumspect in his deployment of American forces in the areas disputed between Mexico and the United States. But the new President, JAMES K. POLK, ordered American ground forces into the area. After Mexican forces captured American soldiers, and the United States declared war, the question of the extent of the President's power to order American troops into combat areas reappeared regularly in congressional debates over military appropriations. In 1847, Whig Representative ABRAHAM LINCOLN offered the SPOT RESOLUTIONS, demanding to know the spot on American soil where, according to Polk, Mexican troops had attacked Americans. This led to House passage of a resolution early in 1848 declaring that the Mexican War had been "unconstitutionally begun by the President." Military victories and the TREATY OF GUADALUPE HIDALGO (1848) obviated this partisan measure, without providing any resolution to the question originally debated by James Madison and ALEXANDER HAMILTON in the Helvidius-Pacificus exchange of 1793 over whether there is an inherent executive prerogative that would embrace the power to commit troops to belligerent situations without explicit authorization by Congress. (See WAR, FOREIGN AFFAIRS, AND THE CONSTITUTION.)

In 1846, northern public opinion coalesced with remarkable unity behind the WILMOT PROVISO, which would have prohibited the extension of slavery into any territories to be acquired as a result of the Mexican War. Alarmed by the extent and fervor of grassroots support for such exclusion in the free states, administration Democrats and southern political leaders offered three alternatives to it, plus an expedient designed to depoliticize the whole question. The earliest proposal was to extend the old Missouri Compromise line of 36° 30′ all the way to the Pacific coast with slavery excluded north of the line and permitted south of it. After a short-lived flurry of interest in 1847, this suggestion withered. The northern Democratic alternative to the Wilmot Proviso was widely known as POPULAR SOVEREIGNTY or, pejoratively, "squatter sovereignty." First proposed by Vice-President George M. Dallas and then associated with Michigan Senator Lewis Cass, popular sovereignty called on Congress to refrain from taking any action concerning SLAVERY IN THE TERRITORIES, leaving it to the settlers of the territories to determine the future of slavery there. The idea's principal appeal derived from its superficial and simplistic democratic appearance. But its vitality was due to an ambiguity that could not be indefinitely postponed, namely, *when* were the settlers to make that determination? By the southern interpretation, that decision could not be made until the eve of statehood, by which time, presumably, slaveholders could avail themselves of the opportunity of settling there with their slaves and thus give the territory a proslavery impetus it would never lose. (All prior American territorial settlements had either guaranteed property rights in extant slaves, such as the LOUISIANA PURCHASE TREATY, or, like the Northwest Ordinance, had left existing pockets of slavery undisturbed as a practical matter despite their theoretical prohibition of slavery.) The northern assumption concerning popular sovereignty was that the territorial settlers could make their choice concerning slavery at any time in the territorial period, a position unacceptable to the South, which correctly believed that such an interpretation would exclude slavery.

The third alternative was embodied in resolutions offered by Calhoun in 1847. He proposed that the territories were the common property of all the states, and that Congress therefore could not prohibit citizens of any state from taking their property (including slaves) with them when they migrated into a territory. He also asserted that Congress could not refuse to admit a new state because it permitted slavery. After Calhoun's death in 1850, others advocated that Congress would have to protect the rights of slaveholders in all territories.

This selection of alternatives naturally influenced the presidential election of 1848. Democrats nominated Cass, thus providing some oblique endorsement of popular sovereignty, with its yet unresolved ambiguity. Whigs nominated the apolitical General ZACHARY TAYLOR and refused to endorse any party position at all on the various alternatives. Disgrunted elements of both parties in the northern states joined hands with the moderate, political-action abolitionists of the Liberty party to form the Free Soil party, which adopted the Wilmot Proviso as its basic plank, supplemented by the old Liberty party program of "divorce" of the federal government from support of slavery. Free Soil was an implicitly racist program, calling for the exclusion of all blacks from the territories to keep them open to white settlement, but that made it no less abominable to southern political leaders. The Whig victory in 1848 on its nonplatform merely postponed the resolution of what was rapidly becoming an urgent constitutional confrontation.

The American Union was in a far different condition in 1848 from what it had been at the onset of the Jacksonian era. The nation had increased in geographical extent by half. Such an immense increase necessitated a new or wholly revised constitutional order that could accommodate, if possible, the conflicting sectional expectations for the future of the western empire. All major constitutional events that had occurred at the national level since 1831 had made John Quincy Adams's prediction of that year all the more pertinent: the questions came ever closer to being settled at the cannon's mouth.

WILLIAM M. WIECEK

Bibliography

BLOOMFIELD, MAXWELL 1976 *American Lawyers in a Changing Society, 1776–1876.* Cambridge, Mass.: Harvard University Press.

DUMOND, DWIGHT L. 1961 *Antislavery: The Crusade for Freedom in America.* Ann Arbor: University of Michigan Press.

FRIEDMAN, LAWRENCE M. 1973 *A History of American Law.* New York: Simon & Schuster.

HAAR, CHARLES M., ED. 1965 *The Golden Age of American Law.* New York: Braziller.

HORWITZ, MORTON J. 1977 *The Transformation of American Law, 1780–1860.* Cambridge, Mass.: Harvard University Press.

HURST, JAMES WILLARD 1956 *Law and the Conditions of Freedom in the Nineteenth-Century United States.* Madison: University of Wisconsin Press.

HYMAN, HAROLD M. and WIECEK, WILLIAM M. 1982 *Equal Justice under Law: Constitutional Development, 1835–1875.* New York: Harper & Row.

LEVY, LEONARD W. 1957 *The Law of the Commonwealth and Chief Justice Shaw: The Evolution of American Law, 1830–1860.* Cambridge, Mass.: Harvard University Press.

WIECEK, WILLIAM M. 1977 *The Sources of Antislavery*

Constitutionalism in America, 1760–1848. Ithaca, N.Y.: Cornell University Press.

ZAINALDIN, JAMIL 1983 *Law in Antebellum Society: Legal Change and Economic Expansion.* New York: Knopf.

CONSTITUTIONAL HISTORY, 1848–1861

In American constitutional history, the years 1848 to 1861 ordinarily appear as a prelude to revolution, a time of intense controversy without significant change. Yet in at least two respects this impression is mistaken. First, constitutional change, though minimal in the national government, was widespread and vigorous among the states during the antebellum period. Second, if the structure of party politics is included (as it should be) in one's purview of the American constitutional system, then the 1850s, like the 1860s, were a decade of revolution.

Powerful social forces exerted pressure upon the constitutional order at mid-century. Mass immigration reached its first crest, with more than two million persons arriving in the years 1849–1854. This great influx caused much concern about the effects of ethnic diversity upon the quality of national life and upon the American experiment in self-government. At the same time, the progress of industrialization and business enterprise was rapidly changing the economic face of the agricultural nation for which the Constitution had been written. The railroads alone, as they tripled their mileage in the 1850s and thus accelerated their transformation of domestic commerce, confronted government with a host of new issues and problems, ranging from the regulation of capital formation to the determination of corporate liability in tort law. Still another major force at work was the continuing westward expansion of American SOVEREIGNTY and American people. The United States in 1848 was a transcontinental nation that had acquired forty percent of all its territory in the preceding three years. Occupation and assimilation of this new Western empire, extending from the mouth of the Rio Grande to the waters of Puget Sound, would absorb much national energy throughout the rest of the century. The process in itself placed no heavy strains upon the constitutional system. For the most part, it required only the further use of already tested forms and practices, such as territorial organization. But in the antebellum period, westward expansion became irredeemably entangled with still another formidable social force—the increasingly ominous sectional conflict over slavery.

The federal government, while extending its rule to the Pacific Ocean in the antebellum period, underwent little structural change. The Constitution had not been amended since 1803. Far fewer amendments than usual were proposed from 1848 to 1860, and none of them passed either house of Congress. (Prominent among those introduced were proposals for the popular election of senators and postmasters.) During the secession winter of 1860–1861, however, Congress received nearly two hundred proposed amendments. Most of them were aimed at dampening the crisis by offering concessions or guarantees to the South on such subjects as SLAVERY IN THE TERRITORIES and the DISTRICT OF COLUMBIA, the domestic slave trade, FUGITIVE SLAVES, and the right to travel with slaves in free states. Only one of these efforts proved successful to the point of passing both houses, but RATIFICATION in the states had scarcely begun before it was interrupted and canceled by the outbreak of hostilities. This abortive "Thirteenth Amendment" would have forbidden any amendment authorizing Congress to interfere with slavery as it existed in the states, thereby presumably fixing a double lock on the constitutional security of the institution. (See CORWIN AMENDMENT.)

Besides formal amendment, constitutional change may be produced by other means, such as legislative enactment and judicial decision. Congress altered the structure of the executive branch in 1849, for instance, by establishing a Department of the Interior. To it were transferred a number of agencies previously housed in other departments, notably those administering PATENTS, public lands, military pensions, and Indian affairs. Congress in 1849 also created the new office of "assistant secretary" for the Treasury Department, adding a similar position to the Department of State four years later. The federal bureaucracy as a whole grew appreciably in the antebellum period, but largely because of the necessary expansion of the postal system. Of the 26,000 civilian employees in 1851 and 37,000 in 1861, eighty percent were in the postal service. Only six percent performed their duties in the capital. On the eve of the Civil War, the whole Washington bureaucracy numbered about 2,200. The Department of State got along throughout the 1850s with a staff of thirty persons or fewer. The presidency remained a very simple affair with practically no official staff. Not until 1857 did Congress provide funds even for a private secretary and a messenger.

The federal government accepted few new responsibilities during the antebellum period. Enlargement of its role was inhibited by the economic principle of laissez-faire, by the constitutional principles of STRICT CONSTRUCTION and FEDERALISM, and by the inertial influence of custom. Most of the governmental activity affecting the lives of ordinary citizens was carried on by the states and their subdivisions. Any effort to extend national authority usually met resistance from Southerners worried about the danger of outside interference with slavery. Congressional reluctance to expand federal power is well illustrated in the history of the first successful telegraph line, run between Washington and Baltimore in the mid-1840s. Built with federal money and put in commercial operation as a branch of the postal system, it was very soon turned over to private ownership. When Congress did occasionally become venturesome, presidential disapproval might intervene. JAMES K. POLK and Franklin Pierce, citing constitutional reasons, vetoed several INTERNAL IMPROVEMENTS bills. JAMES BUCHANAN expressed similar scruples in vetoing homestead legislation and land grants for the support of colleges. Sometimes a new social problem or need did evoke federal intervention, such as laws providing for safety inspection of steamboats and for minimum health standards on ocean-going passenger ships. Perhaps most significant was the expanded use of federal subsidies, in the form of land grants or mail contracts, to support railroad construction, steamship lines, and overland stagecoach service to the Pacific.

Although the three branches of the federal government remained fairly stable in their relationships to one another during the antebellum period, there was some shift of power from the presidency to Congress. The change is commonly viewed as a decline in presidential leadership, but it must be attributed to other factors as well, including the intensity of the sectional conflict. Congress could quarrel violently over slavery, then arrange some kind of truce, and thus perform admirably its function as a deliberative assembly. The President, on the other hand, could take no vigorous action, make no substantial proposal in respect of slavery without infuriating one side or the other.

For various reasons, none of the Presidents between ANDREW JACKSON and ABRAHAM LINCOLN served more than a single term, and only one, MARTIN VAN BUREN, was even renominated. Polk's energetic foreign policy and successful prosecution of the war with Mexico strengthened the presidency for a time, but by 1848 sectional strains and party dissension had put his administration in disarray. Zachary Taylor and Millard Fillmore were committed as Whigs to the principle of limited executive power. They did not exercise the VETO POWER, for instance, and were the last Presidents in history to refrain from doing so. Taylor, to be sure, proved unexpectedly stubborn on the slavery issue and seemed headed for a collision with Congress until his sudden death in the summer of 1850 cleared the way for compromise. During the great sectional crisis of 1846–1850, the Senate reached its peak of oratorical splendor and national influence. JOHN C. CALHOUN, HENRY CLAY, and DANIEL WEBSTER were the most famous men in America, and the outstanding political figure of the decade that followed was not a President but a senator—STEPHEN A. DOUGLAS. Most of the leading cabinet members of the 1840s and 1850s (Webster, Calhoun, Buchanan, Robert J. Walker, John M. Clayton, JEFFERSON DAVIS, Lewis Cass) were recruited directly from the Senate. Lincoln, after his election in 1860, filled the three top cabinet positions with Republican senators. The appearance of presidential weakness in the 1850s was therefore partly a reflection of senatorial prestige.

If Pierce and Buchanan were among the most ineffectual of American Presidents, as they are commonly portrayed, it was not for lack of trying to be otherwise. Both men regarded themselves as Jacksonian executives. Together they exercised the veto as often as Jackson in his two terms (though Pierce's negatives were usually overridden). Both took stern attitudes toward groups whom they labeled rebellious—namely, the free-state forces in Kansas and the Mormons in Utah. Both conducted a vigorously expansionist foreign policy, having in mind especially the acquisition of Cuba. Both made energetic use of patronage to coerce votes from Congress on critical measures—the KANSAS-NEBRASKA ACT in 1854 and the admission of Kansas with a proslavery constitution in 1858. (See LECOMPTON CONSTITUTION.) Their fatal mistake was in misjudging the moral and political strength of the antislavery crusade. Seeking to discredit and dissipate the movement rather than accommodate it, they pursued policies that disastrously aggravated the sectional conflict and thereby brought the Presidency into disrepute. Then, in the final crisis of 1860–1861, Buchanan's constitutional scruples and his reluctance to use presidential power without specific congressional authorization lent substance to the *fainéant* image that history has fixed upon him. Again, as in 1850, the fate of the country seemed to rest primarily with the Senate, and when compromise failed in that body, little hope remained for peaceable preservation of the Union.

Meanwhile, the Supreme Court had tried its hand at resolving the slavery question and in the process had reasserted its power to review congressional legislation. The famous decision in DRED SCOTT V. SANDFORD (1857) invalidated a law that had been repealed three years earlier—the 36°30′ restriction of the MISSOURI COMPROMISE. Consequently, it did not put the Court into confrontation with Congress. Like the policies of Pierce and Buchanan, however, the decision outraged antislavery opinion and aggravated the sectional conflict. Thus the Court, like the presidency, entered the Civil War with lowered prestige.

At the level of state rather than national government, antebellum Americans acted very much in accord with the Jeffersonian credo that every generation should write its own fundamental law. The period 1830 to 1860 has been called "the high water mark for the making of constitutions among the states." During those three decades, ten new states framed their first constitutions, and eighteen of the other twenty-four revised their constitutions by means of conventions. In addition, many states added amendments from time to time through legislative action. The voters of Massachusetts, for instance, rejected a new constitution drafted by a convention in 1853, but they approved of six amendments in 1855, three in 1857, one in 1859, and two in 1860.

State constitutions became longer in the antebellum period, not only describing in greater detail the structure and functions of government but also incorporating many specific instructions and prohibitions intended to set public policy and control the substance of governmental action. The machinery for constitutional change remained heterogeneous, generally cumbersome, and, in some states, poorly defined. There was a clear trend, however, toward popular participation at every stage. Typically, voters decided whether a convention should be called, elected its members, and passed judgment on its handiwork. Legislative amendment, which bypassed the convention process and often had to be approved by two successive legislatures, was always submitted to the voters for ratification.

Democratization of the state constitutional systems, begun earlier in the century, proceeded unremittingly during the antebellum period. Two major categories of change were further extension of the franchise and further lengthening of the list of elective offices. With but a few exceptions, the old religious and property-holding qualifications for suffrage disappeared, although some states continued to require that voters be taxpayers. Under nativist influence, Connecticut in 1855 and Massachusetts in 1857 sought to curtail immigrant participation in politics by installing an English literacy test. But a stronger contrary tendency, exemplified in the constitutions of Wisconsin (1848), Michigan (1850), Indiana (1851), and Kansas (1859), was to expand the immigrant vote by enfranchising foreigners as soon as they had declared their intention to become citizens. Women were everywhere excluded from the polls, except in a few local elections, and blacks could vote only in a half-dozen northeastern states, but white male suffrage had become almost universal. The shift from appointive to elective offices was most dramatic in the case of the judiciary. Until 1846, only a few states had elective judgeships of any kind, and only in Mississippi were all judges elected. In that year both New York and Iowa followed the Mississippi example, and then the rush began. By 1861, twenty-four of the thirty-four states had written the election of judges into their constitutions, though in five of them the change did not extend to their supreme courts.

The antebellum state constitutions, like those written earlier, were primarily constructive. They established or redesigned systems of government and endowed them with appropriate powers. But in many there was also a conspicuous strain of negativism, reflecting disillusionment with state government and a determination to curb extravagance, corruption, and favoritism. Notably, the framers often placed new restrictions on legislative authority, particularly with reference to public finance, banks, and corporations. These subjects were political issues, of course, but then every CONSTITUTIONAL CONVENTION became to some extent a party battle. As a rule, Democrats were more hostile than their opponents to corporate enterprise and government promotion of it. Attitudes varied according to local circumstances, however, and much depended upon which party in the state had the upper hand at the time. The states of the Old Northwest, where prodigal internal improvement policies in the 1830s had proved disastrous, were especially emphatic in their restraint of legislative power. Their new constitutions approved in the years 1848–1851 forbade state investment in private enterprise and put strict limits on public indebtedness. They also restricted banking in various ways, such as ordering double liability for stockholders, prohibiting the suspension of specie payments, and requiring that any general banking act must be submitted to a popular REFERENDUM.

State constitutional change occurred in many ways and resulted from the work of many hands, including those of voters, convention delegates, legislators, governors, and judges. Appellate courts particularly often shaped or reshaped the fundamental law in the course of performing their routine duties, although JUDICIAL REVIEW of state legislation by state courts was a fairly rare occurrence until after the Civil War. Despite all the constitutional activity, innovation was by no means the dominant mode in the antebellum period. States borrowed much from one another, and old forms were sometimes retained well beyond the limits of their appropriateness. Vermont in 1860 still had its quaint Council of Revision, elected every seven years to examine the condition of the constitution and propose amendments. North Carolina had not yet given its governor a veto power, and in South Carolina, the legislature continued to choose the state's presidential electors. Yet the new problems of the age did encourage some experimentation. For example, certain states had begun to develop the quasi-judicial regulatory commission as an extra branch of government, and framers of the Kansas constitution in 1859 introduced the item veto, a device that most states would eventually adopt.

Although federal and state constitutional development proceeded in more or less separate grooves, the fundamental constitutional problem of the age was the relation between the nation and its constituent parts. The problem had been present and intermittently urgent since the birth of the republic, but after 1846 it became associated much more than ever before with the interrelated issues of slavery and expansion and with the dynamics of party politics.

In the federal system established by the Constitution, the national government and the state governments were each supreme within their respective spheres. This principle of DUAL FEDERALISM, even though it accorded rather well with the actual structure and distribution of governmental power in antebellum America, was by no means universally accepted as a true design of the Republic. Nationalists like Webster and Lincoln asserted the primacy of the nation, the sovereignty of its people, and the perpetuity of the Union. Sectionalists like Calhoun and Davis lodged sovereignty with the states, insisted upon strict construction of federal authority, and viewed the Union as a compact that could be abrogated. Logical consistency was not a characteristic of the intersectional debate, however. Both proslavery and antislavery forces invoked federal power and appealed to states' rights whenever either strategy suited their purposes. With regard to the recovery of fugitive slaves, for instance, Southerners demanded expansion and vigorous use of national authority, while the resistance to that authority of some northern state officials amounted to a revival of nullification. (See UNION, THEORIES OF THE.)

Most Americans agreed that slavery was a state institution, but from that premise they drew conflicting inferences. In the radical antislavery view of SALMON P. CHASE, the institution had no standing beyond the bounds of slave-state JURISDICTION, and the federal government had no constitutional power to establish it, protect it, or even acknowledge its legal existence. In short, slavery was local and freedom national. (See ABOLITIONIST CONSTITUTIONAL THEORY.) According to Calhoun, however, the federal government, as the mere agent of the states, was constitutionally obligated to give slavery as much protection as it gave any other kind of property recognized by state law. Only the sovereign power of a state could restrict or abolish the institution. In short, slavery was national and antislavery the local exception.

The practice of the United States government over the years ran closer to Calhoun's theory than to Chase's. All three branches recognized property rights in slaves and extended aid of some kind to their masters. Congress went beyond the requirements of the Constitution in making the recovery of fugitive slaves a federal business, and under congressional rule the national capital became a slave state in miniature, complete with a slave code, whipping posts, and a thriving slave trade. The image of the nation consistently presented in diplomatic relations was that of a slaveholding republic. With a persistence amounting to dedication, the Department of State sought compensation for owners of slaves escaping to foreign soil, and repeatedly it tried to secure Canadian cooperation in the return of fugitives. In the *Dred Scott* decision, Chief Justice ROGER B. TANEY laid down the one-sided rule that the federal government had no power over slavery except "the power coupled with the duty of guarding and protecting the owner in his rights."

To be sure, national authority was also used for antislavery purposes. In outlawing the foreign slave trade, Congress plainly acted within the letter and intent of the Constitution. In prohibiting slavery throughout much of the Western territory, however, the lawmakers probably drew as much sanction from the example of the NORTHWEST ORDINANCE as from the somewhat ambiguous passage in Article IV, section 3, that seemed to be relevant—namely, "The Congress shall have Power to dispose of and make all needful Rules and Regulations respecting the Territory or other Property belonging to the United States." By 1840, such prohibition had been enacted in six territorial organic acts, as well as in the Missouri Compromise. Furthermore, Chief Justice JOHN MARSHALL in AMERICAN INSURANCE COMPANY V. CANTER (1828) had given the territory clause a broad construction. In legislating for the TERRITORIES, he declared, "Congress exercises the combined powers of the general and of a State government." Since the authority of a state government to establish or abolish slavery was generally acknowledged, Marshall's words seemed to confirm Congress in possession of the same authority within the territories.

The constitutionality of legislation excluding slavery from federal territory did not become a major issue in American public life until after introduction of the WILMOT PROVISO in 1846. Although the question had arisen at times during the Missouri controversy of 1819–1820, the famous 36°30′ restriction had been approved without extensive discussion and with the support of a majority of southern congressmen. The subject had arisen again during the 1830s, but only as a secondary and academic consideration in the debate over abolitionist attacks upon slavery in the District of Columbia. As a practical matter, the Missouri Compromise had presumably disposed of the problem by reviving and extending a policy of having two different policies, one on each side of a dividing line. North of that line (first the Ohio River and then 36°30′), slavery was prohibited; south of the line, slavery was permitted if desired by the white inhabitants.

In the summer of 1846, with Texas annexed and admitted to statehood, with title to Oregon secured by treaty, and with the war against Mexico under way, the United States found itself engaged in territorial expansion on a grand scale. Texas entered the Union as a slaveholding state, and Oregon was generally understood to be free soil, but what about New Mexico and California, if they should be acquired by conquest? To many Americans, including President Polk, the obvious answer seemed to be extending the Missouri Compromise line to the Pacific Ocean. But the issue arose at a time when sectional antagonism had been inflamed by a decade of quarreling over abolitionist petitions, the GAG RULE, and the Texas question. Furthermore, whereas the 36°30′ line had meant partial abolition in a region previously open to slavery, extension of the line through New Mexico and California would have meant a partial rescinding of the abolition already achieved there by Mexican law. So David Wilmot's proposal to forbid slavery in any territory that might be acquired from Mexico won the overwhelming approval of northern congressmen when it was introduced in the House of Representatives on August 8, 1846. Southerners were even more united and emphatic in their opposition; for the Proviso would have completed the exclusion of slaveholders from all the newly acquired land in the Far West. Such injustice, they warned, could not fail to end in disunion.

The Proviso principle of "no more slave territory" quickly became the premier issue in American politics and remained so for almost fifteen years. Virtually the raison d'être of the Free Soil and Republican parties, the principle was rejected by Congress in 1850 and again in 1854, deprived of its legitimacy by the Supreme Court in 1857, and supported by less than forty percent of the electorate in the presidential contest of 1860. Yet forty percent proved sufficient to put a Republican in the White House and thereby precipitate SECESSION. During those years of intermittent sectional crisis from 1846 to 1861, the Southerners and northern conservatives who controlled government policy sought desperately and sometimes discordantly for a workable alternative to the Proviso. One thing that complicated their task was the growing tendency of all elements in the controversy to constitutionalize their arguments.

Southerners especially felt the need for constitutional sanction, partly because of their vulnerability as a minority section but also in order to offset the moral advantage of the antislavery forces. It was not enough to denounce the Proviso as unfair; they must also prove it to be unconstitutional despite the string of contrary precedents running back to the venerated Northwest Ordinance. One way of doing so was to invoke the Fifth Amendment, arguing that any congressional ban on slavery in the territories amounted to deprivation of property without DUE PROCESS OF LAW. But this argument, though used from time to time and incorporated rather vaguely in Taney's *Dred Scott* opinion, did not become a significant part of anti-Proviso strategy. For one thing, the Fifth Amendment had another cutting edge, antislavery in its effect. Free Soilers and Republicans could and did maintain that slavery was illegal in federal territory because it amounted to deprivation of *liberty* without due process of law.

More in keeping with the strict constructionism generally favored by Southerners was the principle of "nonintervention," that is, congressional nonaction with respect to slavery in the territories. Actually, nonintervention had been government policy in part of the West ever since 1790, always with the effect of establishing slavery. But in earlier years the policy had been given little theoretical underpinning. Then, after the introduction of the Wilmot Proviso, there were strenuous efforts to convert nonintervention into a constitutional imperative. The emerging argument ignored Marshall's opinion in *American Insurance Company v. Canter* and held that the territory clause of the Constitution referred only to disposal of public land. In providing government for a territory, Congress could do nothing more than what was absolutely necessary to prepare the territory for statehood. That did not include either the prohibition or the establishment of slavery. Thus nonintervention became a doctrine of federal incapacity. It left open, however, the question of what authority prevailed in the absence of congressional power. One answer, associated with Calhoun, was that property rights in slavery were silently legitimized in every territory by the direct force of the Constitution. Another answer, associated with Lewis Cass and Douglas, was that nonintervention meant leaving the question of slavery to be decided by the local territorial population. The latter theory, given the name POPULAR SOVEREIGNTY, had the advantage of seeming to be in tune with the spirit of Jacksonian democracy.

Thus, by 1848, when American acquisition of New Mexico and California was confirmed in the TREATY OF GUADALUPE HIDALGO, four distinct solutions to the problem of slavery in the territories had emerged. At one political extreme was the free soil doctrine requiring enactment of the Wilmot Proviso. At the other extreme was the Calhoun property rights doctrine legitimizing slavery in all federal territory by direct force of the Constitution. Between them were two formulas of compromise: extension of the 36°30′ line and the principle of popular sovereignty. Presumably the choice rested with Congress, but the constitutionalizing of the argument opened up another possibility—that of leaving the status of slavery in the territories to judicial determination. Legislation facilitating referral of the question to the Supreme Court was proposed in 1848 and incorporated in the historic set of compromise measures enacted two years later. The COMPROMISE OF 1850 admitted California as a free state, but for the rest of the Mexican Cession it adopted the principle of nonintervention. The effect was to reject the 36°30′ and Proviso solutions while leaving the field still open to popular sovereignty, the property rights doctrine, and judicial disposition.

Although neither of the major parties took a formal stand on the territorial question in the elections of 1848 and 1852, it was the Democrats who became closely associated with the principle of nonintervention. Cass, their presidential nominee in 1848, declared that Congress lacked the power to prohibit slavery in the territories and that the territorial inhabitants should be left free to regulate their internal concerns in their own way. This seemed to endorse popular sovereignty as the appropriate corollary to nonintervention, but for about a decade the Democratic party managed to invest both terms with enough ambiguity to accommodate both its northern and southern wings. More specifically, Southerners found that they could assimilate popular sovereignty to their own purposes by viewing it as the right of a territorial population to accept or reject slavery *at the time of admission to statehood.* That would presumably leave the Calhoun doctrine operative during the territorial period. At the same time, northern Democrats like Douglas went on believing that popular sovereignty meant the right of a territorial legislature to make all decisions regarding slavery, within the limits of the Constitution. The Whigs failed to achieve any such convenient doctrinal ambiguity, and that failure may have contributed to the disintegration of their party.

In 1854, a heavily Democratic Congress organized the territories of Kansas and Nebraska, repealing the antislavery restriction of the Missouri Compromise and substituting the principle of nonintervention. "The true intent and meaning of this act," the measure declared, "[is] not to legislate slavery into any Territory or State, nor to exclude it therefrom, but to leave the people thereof perfectly free to form and regulate their domestic institutions in their own way, subject only to the Constitution of the United States." This passage, since it could be interpreted to mean either the northern or the southern brand of popular sovereignty, preserved the ambiguity so necessary for Democratic unity. But of course the Kansas-Nebraska Act, by removing a famous barrier to slavery, provoked a storm of anger throughout the free states and set off a political revolution.

The crisis of the late 1850s was in one respect a confrontation between the emerging Republican party and the increasingly united South—that is, between the Wilmot Proviso and the principles of Calhoun. Yet it was also a struggle within the Democratic party over the meaning of nonintervention and popular sovereignty. The *Dred Scott* decision in March 1857 cleared the air and intensified the crisis. In ruling that Congress had no power to prohibit slavery in the territories, the Supreme Court officially constitutionalized the principle of nonintervention and virtually rendered illegal the main purpose of the Republican party. But Chief Justice Taney went further and disqualified the northern Democratic version of popular sovereignty. If Congress had no such power over slavery, he declared, then neither did a territorial legislature. Douglas responded with his FREEPORT DOCTRINE, insisting that a territorial government, by unfriendly legislation, could effectively exclude slavery, no matter what the Court might decide to the contrary. Southern Democrats, in turn, demanded federal protection of slavery in the territories, and on that issue the party split at its national convention in 1860.

By 1860 it had become apparent that slavery was

not taking root in Kansas or in any other western territory. Yet when secession began after Lincoln's election, the efforts at reconciliation concentrated on the familiar territorial problem. The centerpiece of the abortive Crittenden compromise was an amendment reviving and extending the 36°30′ line, so recently outlawed by the Supreme Court. This continued fascination with an essentially empty issue was not so foolish as it now may seem; for the territorial question had obviously taken on enormous symbolic meaning. Because of the almost universal agreement that slavery in the states was untouchable by the federal government, the territories had come to be the limited battleground of a fierce and fundamental struggle. Thus the sectional conflict of the 1850s, whatever its origins and whatever its substance, was decisively shaped by constitutional considerations.

DON E. FEHRENBACHER

Bibliography

BESTOR, ARTHUR 1961 State Sovereignty and Slavery: A Reinterpretation of Proslavery Constitutional Doctrine, 1846–1860. *Illinois State Historical Society Journal* 54:117–80.

DEALEY, JAMES QUAYLE 1915 *Growth of American State Constitutions.* Boston: Ginn & Co.

FEHRENBACHER, DON E. 1978 *The Dred Scott Case: Its Significance in American Law and Politics.* New York: Oxford University Press.

PARKINSON, GEORGE PHILLIP, JR. 1972 "Antebellum State Constitution-Making: Retention, Circumvention, Revision." Ph.D. dissertation, University of Wisconsin.

POTTER, DAVID M. 1976 *The Impending Crisis, 1848–1861.* Completed and edited by Don E. Fehrenbacher. New York: Harper & Row.

WHITE, LEONARD D. 1954 *The Jacksonians: A Study in Administrative History, 1829–1861.* New York: Macmillan.

CONSTITUTIONAL HISTORY, 1861–1865

If expediency and ideology ordinarily conflict with the constitutionalist desire for procedural regularity and limitations on government, in time of war they pose a fundamental challenge to CONSTITUTIONALISM and the RULE OF LAW. The first fact to be observed about the constitutional history of the Civil War, therefore, is that the federal Constitution, as in the prewar period, served as both a symbol and a source of governmental legitimacy and as a normative standard for the conduct of politics. Because the rule of the Constitution continued without interruption, it is easy to overlook the pressures that the war generated to institute a regime based exclusively on necessity and the public safety. To be sure, considerations of public safety entered into wartime constitutionalism, and there were those who believed passionately that the Union government in the years 1861 to 1865 did indeed cast aside the Constitution and resort to arbitrary rule. Yet, considered from either a comparative or a strictly American perspective, this judgment is untenable. The record abundantly demonstrates the persistence of constitutional controversy in Congress, in the executive branch, in the courts, and in the forum of public opinion—evidence that the nation's organic law was taken seriously in time of war, even if it was not applied in the same manner as in time of peace. Indeed, a constitutionalizing impulse may be said to have manifested itself in the business of warfare itself. General Order No. 100 for the government of Union armies in the field, promulgated by President ABRAHAM LINCOLN in 1863, was an attempt to limit the destructiveness of modern war that had resulted from developments in weaponry and from the emergence of other aspects of total war.

The most important constitutional question resolved by the events of the war concerned the nature of the Union. (See THEORIES OF THE UNION.) The Framers of the Constitution had created a mixed regime that in some respects resembled a confederation of autonomous states and in others a centralized unitary government. Its distinguishing feature—the chief characteristic of American FEDERALISM—was the division of SOVEREIGNTY between the federal government and the state governments. In constitutional law several decisions of the Supreme Court under Chief Justice JOHN MARSHALL had confirmed this dual-sovereignty system; yet periodically it was questioned by political groups who insisted that the Union was simply a league of sovereign states, and that the federal government possessed no sovereignty whatsoever except as the agent of the states. From 1846 to 1860 defenders of slavery asserted this state-sovereignty theory of the Union; although they never secured a congressional majority for the theory, they did force northern Democrats to adopt positions that virtually abandoned any claim to federal sovereignty in matters concerning slavery. The SECESSION policy of President JAMES BUCHANAN, which regarded secession as illegal but nonetheless tolerated the existence of the newly forming Confederate States of America, signified the constitutional and political bankruptcy of Democratic DUAL FEDERALISM and the practical repudiation of federal sovereignty.

The constitutional results of the Civil War must

be measured against the effective triumph of proslavery state sovereignty which permitted the disintegration of the Union in 1860–1861. Northern victory in the war established federal sovereignty in political fact and in public policy, and by the same token repudiated the state-sovereignty theory of the Union. From the standpoint of constitutional law, this result vindicated the divided-sovereignty concept of federalism asserted in the early national period. From the standpoint of federal–state relations in the field of public policy, the war produced a significant centralizing trend, evident principally in military recruitment and organization, internal security, the regulation of personal liberty and CIVIL RIGHTS, and the determination of national economic policy.

The changes in federalism produced by the war have usually been described—sometimes in almost apocalyptic terms—as the destruction of STATES' RIGHTS and the old federal Union and their replacement by a centralized sovereign nation. In fact, however, the changes in federal–state relations that occurred between 1861 and 1865 did not seriously erode or alter the decentralized constitutional system and political culture of the United States. The centralizing of policy was based on military need rather than the appeal of a new unitary constitutional model, and it was of limited scope and duration. In no comprehensive way did the federal government become supreme over the states, nor were states' rights obliterated either in law or in policy. The theoretical structure of American federalism, as explicated by John Marshall, persisted; the actual distribution of power between the states and the federal government, the result of policy struggles on questions raised by the war, was different.

Perhaps the best way to describe the change in federalism that occurred during the Civil War is to say that after a long period of disinclination to use the constitutional powers assigned to it, the federal government began to act like an authentic sovereign state. Foremost among its achievements was the raising of armies and the providing and maintaining of a navy for the defense of the nation.

At the start of the war the decision to resist secession was made by the federal government, but the task of raising a military force fell largely upon the states. The regular United States Army, at approximately 16,000 men, was inadequate for the government's military needs, and federal authorities were as yet unprepared to call for United States volunteers. To meet the emergency it was necessary to rely on the militia, a form of military organization that, while subject to national service, was chiefly a state institution. Accordingly President Lincoln on April 15, 1861, acting under the Militia Act of 1795, issued a call to the state governors to provide 75,000 militia for three months of national service. By August 1861, in pursuance of additional presidential requests, the War Department had enrolled almost 500,000 men for three years' duty. Yet, although carried out under federal authority, the actual recruiting of troops and to a considerable extent their preparation for combat were done by the state governors, acting as a kind of war ministry for the nation.

This arrangement did not last long. Within a year declining popular enthusiasm and the utility of centralized administrative management severely impeded state recruiting efforts and led to greater federal control. Eventually national CONSCRIPTION was adopted. Congress took a half-way step toward this policy in the Militia Act of July 1862, authorizing the President, in calling the militia into national service, to make all necessary rules and regulations for doing so where state laws were defective or inadequate. Under this statute a draft was planned by the War Department, to be enforced by provost marshals nominated by state governors and appointed by the department. Political resistance in the states prevented implementation of this plan. At length, in the Enrollment Act of March 1863, Congress instituted an exclusively national system of conscription. Directed at male citizens ages twenty to forty-five and foreigners who declared their intention to become citizens, the draft law omitted all reference to the state militia. Conscription was to be enforced by federal provost marshals under a Provost Marshal General, operating under an administrative structure organized according to congressional districts. The Civil War draft, which permitted substitutes and money commutation, aroused widespread and often violent opposition and was directly responsible for inducting only six percent of the total Union military force. Nevertheless, it proved to be a decisive constitutional precedent on which the federal government relied in meeting its manpower needs in the wars of the twentieth century. (See SELECTIVE SERVICE ACTS.)

Closely related to the raising of armies was the task of maintaining internal security on the home front against the treasonable and disloyal acts of persons interfering with the war effort. In this sphere too the Union government exercised previously unused powers, asserting an unwonted sovereignty in local affairs that challenged the states' exclusive power to regulate civil and political liberty.

The law against TREASON, the elements of which had been defined in the Constitution, was the most formidable instrument for protecting national security outside the theater of war. Yet in its various manifestations—the Treason Act of 1790 requiring the death penalty and the Seditious Conspiracies Act of 1861 and the treason provisions of the CONFISCATION ACT of 1862 imposing less severe penalties—it was inapplicable in the South as long as federal courts could not operate there. It was also unsuited to the task of containing the less than treasonable activities of Confederate sympathizers and opponents of the war in the North. Loyalty oaths were a second internal security measure. The third, and by far the most important, component of Union internal security policy was military detention of persons suspected of disloyal activities, suspension of the writ of HABEAS CORPUS, and the imposition of martial law.

In April 1861 and on several occasions thereafter, President Lincoln authorized military commanders in specific areas to arrest and deny the writ of habeas corpus to persons engaging in or suspected of disloyal practices, such as interfering with troop movements or discouraging enlistments. In September 1862 the President issued a general proclamation that such persons were liable to trial by military commission or court-martial. Initially the State Department supervised civilian arrests made by secret service agents, federal marshals, and military officers. In February 1862 the War Department assumed responsibility for this practice and created a commission to examine the causes of arrests and provide for the release of persons deemed to be political prisoners. Congress further shaped internal security policy in the HABEAS CORPUS ACT of March 1863, requiring the secretaries of war and state to provide lists of prisoners to federal courts for GRAND JURY consideration. If no indictment for violation of federal law should be forthcoming, a prisoner was to be released upon taking an oath of allegiance.

The Union government arrested approximately 18,000 civilians, almost all of whom were released after brief detention for precautionary rather than punitive purposes. The policy was extremely controversial, however, for what Unionists might consider a precaution to prevent interference with the war effort could easily be regarded by others as punishment for political dissent. Evaluation of internal security policy depended upon conflicting interpretations of CIVIL LIBERTIES guarantees under the Constitution, and differing perceptions of what critics and opponents of the government were in reality doing. As with conscription, however, there was no denying that internal security measures had a significant impact on federal–state relations.

In carrying out this policy the federal government for the first time intervened significantly in local regulation of civil and political liberty. Not only did the federal government make arbitrary or irregular arrests but it also temporarily suspended the publication of many newspapers. Not surprisingly, considering the traditional exclusivity of state power over civil liberty and the partisan context in which the internal security question was debated, the states resisted this extension of federal authority. In several states persons adversely affected by internal security measures, or by enforcement of federal laws and orders concerning conscription, trade restrictions, internal revenue, or emancipation, initiated litigation charging federal officers with violations of state law, such as false arrest, unlawful seizure, kidnaping, assault, and battery. Under prewar federalism no general recourse was available to national officials involved as defendants in state litigation of this sort. Congress remedied this defect, however, in the Habeas Corpus Act of 1863.

The 1863 act provided that orders issued by the President or under his authority should be a defense in all courts against any civil or criminal prosecution for any search, seizure, arrest, or imprisonment undertaken in pursuance of such an order. The law further authorized the removal of litigation against national officers from state to federal courts, and it imposed a two-year limit on the initiation of such litigation. On only two previous occasions, in 1815 and 1833 in response to state interference with customs collection, had Congress given protection for federal officers acting under authority of a specific statute by permitting removal of litigation from state to federal courts. The Habeas Corpus Act of 1863, by contrast, protected actions taken under any federal law or EXECUTIVE ORDER. Critics argued that the law gave immunity rather than indemnity, denied citizens judicial remedies for wrongs done by the government, and usurped state power. The logic of even a circumscribed national sovereignty demanded some means of protection against state JURISDICTION, however, and during reconstruction Congress extended the removal remedy and the federal judiciary upheld its constitutionality. The wartime action marked an important extension of federal jurisdiction that made the national government, at least in time of national security crisis, more able to compete with the states in the regulation of civil liberty.

The most novel and in the long run probably the most important exercise of federal sovereignty during the Civil War led directly to the abolition of slavery and the protection of personal liberty and civil rights by the national government. No constitutional rule was more firmly established than that which prohibited federal interference with slavery in the states that recognized it. The outbreak of hostilities did not abrogate this rule, but it did create the possibility that, under the war power, the federal government might emancipate slaves for military purposes. After prohibiting slavery where it could under its peacetime constitutional authority (in the DISTRICT OF COLUMBIA and in the TERRITORIES), Congress struck at slavery in the Confederacy itself. In the Confiscation Act of 1862, it declared "forever free" slaves belonging to persons in rebellion, those who were captured, or who came within Union army lines. Executive interference with slavery went considerably farther. After trying unsuccessfully in 1862 to persuade loyal slaveholding states to accept a federally sponsored plan for gradual, compensated emancipation to be carried out by the states themselves, Lincoln undertook military emancipation. In the EMANCIPATION PROCLAMATION of January 1, 1863, he declared the freedom of all slaves in states still in rebellion and pledged executive-branch protection of freedmen's personal liberty.

Federal power over personal liberty was further made manifest in the work of local police regulation undertaken by Union armies as they advanced into southern territory. All persons in occupied areas were affected by the rule of federal military commanders, and none more so than freed or escaped slaves. From the first incursions of national force in May 1861, War and Treasury Department officials protected blacks' personal liberty, provided for their most pressing welfare needs in refugee camps, and assisted their assimilation into free society by organizing their labor on abandoned plantations and by recruiting them into the army. In March 1865 Congress placed emancipation-related federal police regulation on a more secure footing by creating the Bureau of Refugees, Freedmen, and Abandoned Lands. Authorized to control all subjects relating to refugees and freedmen for a period of one year after the end of the war, the FREEDMEN'S BUREAU throughout 1865 established courts to protect freedmen's personal liberty and civil rights, in the process superseding the states in their most traditional and jealously guarded governmental function.

Federal emancipation measures, based on the war power, did not accomplish the permanent abolition of slavery as it was recognized in state laws and constitutions. To accomplish this momentous change, and the invasion of state power that it signified, amendment of the Constitution was necessary. Accordingly, Congress in January 1865 approved for submission to the states a constitutional amendment prohibiting slavery or involuntary servitude, except as a punishment for crime, in the United States or any place subject to its jurisdiction. Section 2 of the amendment gave Congress authority to enforce the prohibition by appropriate legislation.

Controversy surrounded this terse, seemingly straightforward, yet rather delphic pronouncement, which became part of the Constitution in December 1865. Though it appeared to be a legitimate exercise of the amending power under Article V, Democrats argued that the THIRTEENTH AMENDMENT was a wrongful use of that power because it invaded state jurisdiction over local affairs, undermining the sovereign power to fix the status of all persons within a state's borders and thus destroying the unspoken premise on which the Constitution and the government had been erected in 1787. The Republican framers of the amendment for their part were uncertain about the scope and effect of the guarantee of personal liberty that they would write into the nation's organic law. At the least, the amendment prohibited chattel slavery, or property in people; many of its supporters believed it also secured the full range of civil rights appurtenant to personal liberty that distinguished a free republican society. No determination of this question was required in order to send the amendment to the states, however, and when a year later the precise scope of the guarantees provided and congressional enforcement power became issues in reconstruction, more detailed and specific measures, such as the CIVIL RIGHTS ACT OF 1866 and the FOURTEENTH AMENDMENT, were deemed necessary. Constitutionally speaking, the Thirteenth Amendment played a minor role in reconstruction.

The federal government further exercised sovereignty characteristic of a nation-state in the sphere of economic policy. This development raised few questions of contitutional propriety; the instruments for accomplishing it lay ready to hand in the ALEXANDER HAMILTON-John Marshall doctrines of BROAD CONSTRUCTION and IMPLIED POWERS. These doctrines had fallen into desuetude in the Jacksonian era, when mercantilist-minded state governments effectively determined economic policy. The exodus of Southerners from the national government in 1861 altered the political balance, however, and Republicans in control of the wartime Congress seized the opportunity to adopt centralizing economic legislation. They raised the tariff for protective purposes, authorized construction of a transcontinental railway, facilitated settlement on the public domain (HOMESTEAD ACT), provided federal aid to higher education (MORRILL ACT), established a uniform currency, asserted federal control over the nation's banking institutions, and taxed the American people in innovative ways (income tax, DIRECT TAX). These measures laid the foundation for increasing federal ECONOMIC REGULATION in the late nineteenth and early twentieth centuries. Yet they did not make the determination of economic policy an exclusively national function. In this field, as in civil rights, the federal government's acquisition of a distinct and substantial share of sovereignty diminished, but by no means obliterated, state power.

As the federal government gained power relative to the states during the war, so within the SEPARATION OF POWERS structure of the national government the executive expanded its authority relative to the other branches. Lincoln was the instrument of this constitutional change. Unlike his predecessor Buchanan, Lincoln was willing to acknowledge the necessity of an inflexible defense of the Union during the secession crisis, and after the bombardment of Fort Sumter he acted swiftly and unhesitatingly to commit the nation to arms.

To raise a fighting force Lincoln called the state militia into national service, ordered—without authority from Congress—a 40,000-man increase in the regular army and navy, requested 42,000 volunteers, and proclaimed a blockade of ports in the seceded states. He also instituted the main elements of the internal security program previously described, closed the postal service to treasonable correspondence, directed that $2,000,000 be paid out of the federal treasury, and pledged the credit of the United States for $250,000,000. Lincoln did all this without congressional authority, but not without regard for Congress. Ordering the militia into national service, he called Congress into session to meet in mid-summer. Directing the enlargement of the army and navy, he said he would submit these actions to Congress. He did so, and Congress voted approval of the President's military orders, "as if they had been done under the previous express authority and direction of the Congress." Thereafter Lincoln was ever mindful of the lawmaking branch, and in some respects deferential to it. Yet in war-related matters he continued to take unilateral actions. Thus he proclaimed martial law, suspended habeas corpus, suppressed newspaper publication, issued orders for the conduct of armies in the field, ordered slave emancipation, and directed the political reorganization of occupied southern states.

How could these extraordinary actions be rationalized under the nation's organic law? The question aroused bitter controversy at the time, giving rise to charges of dictatorship which continued to find echo in scholarly debate. No more penetrating analysis of the problem has ever been offered than that presented by Lincoln himself.

In his message to Congress of July 4, 1861, Lincoln said his actions were required by "public necessity" and "popular demand." Referring to suspension of the writ of habeas corpus, he stated that if he violated "some single law," his doing so was justified on the ground that it would save the government." . . . are all the laws, *but one,* to go unexecuted, and the government itself go to pieces, lest that one be violated?" he asked. On another occasion Lincoln posed the question whether it was possible to lose the nation and yet preserve the Constitution. "By general law life and limb must be protected," he reasoned, "yet often a limb must be amputated to save a life; but a life is never wisely given to save a limb." This appears to mean that the Constitution might be set aside, as a limb is amputated, to save the life of the nation. The inference can be drawn that emergency action, while expedient, is unconstitutional.

What is required to understand the lawfulness of the emergency measures in question, however, is not legalistic analysis of the constitutional text but rather consideration of the fundamental relationship between the nation and the Constitution. Lincoln's principal argument was that the steps taken to defend the government were constitutional because the Constitution implicitly sanctioned its own preservation. The Constitution in this view was not a mere appendage of the living nation or a derivative expression or reflection of national life, as a legal code might be considered to be. Coeval and in an ultimate political sense coterminous with it, the Constitution *was* the nation. This conception is present in Lincoln's statement of April 1864 that "measures, otherwise unconstitutional, might become lawful, by becoming indispensable to the preservation of the constitution, through the preservation of the nation." "Is there," he asked in his message of July 1861, "in all republics, this inherent and fatal weakness? Must a government, of necessity, be too *strong* for the liberties of its own people, or too *weak* to maintain its own existence?" Not that Lincoln conceded to his critics at the level of positivistic, text-based constitutional argument. Concerning habeas corpus suspension, for example, he tenaciously insisted that as the Constitution did not specify who might exercise this power, he was justified in doing so when Congress was not in session. Congress, in fact, subsequently ratified Lincoln's suspension of habeas corpus. Although his argument conformed to the requirements of American constitutional politics, his principal justification of emergency actions was that they were necessary to preserve the substance of political liberty, which was the end both of the Constitution and the Union.

It is sometimes said that Lincoln established in American public law the principle of constitutional dictatorship. Yet at no time did Lincoln exercise unlimited power. The notion of constitutional dictatorship also obscures the fact that although Lincoln applied military power on a far wider scale than previous Presidents, in doing so he merely accelerated a tendency toward expansion of the executive's defensive war-making capability. In 1827 the Supreme Court, in MARTIN V. MOTT, had upheld the President's power under the Militia Act of 1795 to call out the militia (and by extension the army and navy) in the event of actual or imminent invasion. President JAMES K. POLK had used this defensive war-making power to commit the nation to war against Mexico, and Presidents Millard Fillmore and Franklin Pierce had employed military force in circumstances that could have led to wars with foreign states. In his exercise of executive power Lincoln merely widened a trail blazed by his predecessors.

Yet in minor matters unrelated to the war, emancipation, and reconstruction, Lincoln was a passive President. Although as party leader he made effective use of his patronage powers, he did little to influence congressional legislation aside from formal suggestions in annual messages. Moreover he exercised the veto sparingly, gave broad latitude to his department heads, and made little use of the cabinet for policymaking purposes. Lincoln's respect for legislative independence complemented and encouraged another important nineteenth-century constitutional trend—the strengthening of congressional power.

To an extent that is difficult to appreciate in the late twentieth century, nineteenth-century government was preeminently legislative in nature. Lawmakers shaped public policy, resolved constitutional controversies through debate and legislation, controlled the TAXING AND SPENDING process, and exercised significant influence over administration. The years between the presidencies of THOMAS JEFFERSON and ANDREW JACKSON had been a period of legislative assertiveness, and although the struggle over slavery had brought Congress to near-paralysis, still the political foundation existed for wartime exertions of power that anticipated the era of congressional government during and after reconstruction.

Although Congress approved Lincoln's emergency measures in 1861, its action by no means signified general deference to executive power. On the contrary, reciting constitutional provisions that gave Congress power to declare war and regulate the military establishment, members made vigorous claim to exercise the WAR POWER. Accordingly, they raised men and supplies for the war, attempted through the Joint Committee on the Conduct of the War to influence military strategy, modified internal security policy, and enacted laws authorizing confiscation, emancipation, and reconstruction. The need for party unity notwithstanding, the Republican majority in Congress insisted on civilian control over the military, monitored executive department administration, and, in an unusual maneuver in December 1862, even tried to force a change in the cabinet. Tighter internal organization and operational procedures made Congress more powerful as well as more efficient during the war. The speaker of the House, for example, assumed greater control over committee memberships and the flow of legislative business; the party caucus became a more frequent determinant of legislative behavior; and standing committees and their chairmen enjoyed enhanced prestige and influence, gradually superseding select committees as the key agencies for accomplishing legislative tasks. Exercising power conferred by statute in 1857 to punish recalcitrant or uncooperative witnesses, Congress used its investigative authority to extend its governmental grasp.

In the 1930s and 1940s, Civil War historiography regarded conflict between a radical-dominated Congress and the soberly conservative Lincoln administration as the central political struggle of the war. Recent research has shown, however, that disagreement between the Democratic and Republican parties was more significant in shaping the course of political and constitutional events than was the radical versus moderate tension within the Republican party. Conflict occurred between the executive and legislative branches, as much as a result of institutional rivalry inherent in the structure of separated powers as of programmatic differences. Congressional–presidential relations were not notably more strained than they have been in other American wars. Although Lincoln demonstrated the potentially vast power inherent in the presidency, his wartime actions did not measurably extend the executive office beyond the sphere of crisis government. He evinced no tendency toward the so-called stewardship conception of the presidency advanced by THEODORE ROOSEVELT in the early twentieth century. The power of Congress waxed, its wartime achievements in policymaking and internal organization providing a solid basis for a subsequent era of congressional government.

A significant portion of American constitutional history from 1861 to 1865 occurred south of the Potomac, where were manifested many of the same problems and tendencies that appeared in the wartime experience of the United States government. The CONFEDERATE CONSTITUTION, modeled closely on that of the United States, revealed the most bitterly contested issues that had led to the war. It recognized and protected the right of slave property; proclaimed state sovereignty as the basis of the Confederacy; omitted the GENERAL WELFARE clause and the TAXING AND SPENDING POWER contained in the United States Constitution; stated that all federal power was expressly delegated; and prohibited a protective tariff and INTERNAL IMPROVEMENTS appropriations. Yet the right of secession was not recognized, evidence that the Confederacy was intended to be a permanent government.

Confederate constitutional history was marked by war-induced centralization and conflicts between federal and state authority. The Confederate government conscripted soldiers; suspended the writ of habeas corpus and declared martial law; confiscated enemy property and seized for temporary use the property of its own citizens; taxed heavily and imposed tight controls on commerce and industry; and owned and operated munitions, mining, and clothing factories. These actions and policies aroused strong opposition as expressed in the rhetoric of states' rights and through the institutions of state government. Some governors refused to place their troops under the Confederacy's authority and challenged conscription and internal security measures. Many state judges granted writs of habeas corpus that interfered with military recruitment. Lack of effective leverage over the states seriously hampered the Confederate war effort.

The most significant difference between Union and Confederate constitutionalism centered on POLITICAL PARTIES. Driven by the desire to create national unity, Southerners eschewed political party organization as unnecessary and harmful. When political differences arose, they had to find resolution in the conflict-inducing methods of the system of states' rights. In the North, by contrast, political parties continued to compete, with beneficial results. Political disagreements between the government and its Democratic critics were kept within manageable bounds by the concept of a loyal opposition, while among members of the governing party differences were directed into policy alternatives. Moreover, party organization encouraged federal–state cooperation in the implementation of controversial measures like conscription, thus helping to minimize the centrifugal effects of federal organization. Indeed, the persistence of organized party competition, even in the critical year of 1864 when military success was uncertain and the Democratic party campaigned on a platform demanding a cessation of hostilities, was perhaps the most revealing fact in Civil War constitutional history. It showed that despite important changes in federal–state relations and reliance on techniques of emergency government, the American commitment to constitutionalism was firm, even amidst events that tested it most severely.

HERMAN BELZ

Bibliography

BELZ, HERMAN 1978 *Emancipation and Equal Rights: Politics and Constitutionalism in the Civil War Era.* New York: Norton.

CURRY, LEONARD P. 1968 *Blueprint for Modern America: Nonmilitary Legislation of the First Civil War Congress.* Nashville, Tenn.: Vanderbilt University Press.

FEHRENBACHER, DON E. 1979 Lincoln and the Constitution. In Cullom Davis, ed., *The Public and Private Lincoln: Contemporary Perspectives.* Carbondale: University of Southern Illinois Press.

HYMAN, HAROLD M. 1973 *A More Perfect Union: The Impact of the Civil War and Reconstruction on the Constitution.* New York: Knopf.

MCKITRICK, ERIC 1967 Party Politics and the Union and Confederate War Efforts. In Walter Dean Burnham and William N. Chambers, eds., *The American Party System: Stages of Political Development.* New York: Free Press.

MCLAUGHLIN, ANDREW C. 1936 Lincoln, the Constitution, and Democracy. *International Journal of Ethics* 47:1–24.

RANDALL, JAMES G. (1926)1951 *Constitutional Problems under Lincoln,* rev. ed. Urbana: University of Illinois Press.

WEIGLEY, RUSSELL F. 1967 *A History of the United States Army.* New York: Macmillan.

CONSTITUTIONAL HISTORY, 1865–1877

The great political and constitutional issue of the period 1865–1877 was the Reconstruction of the Union after the Civil War. Reconstruction presented several closely related issues. There were issues involving the nature of the federal system. One of these arose even before the war ended: what was the constitutional relationship to the Union of the states that had attempted to secede? Another arose after the southern states were restored to normal relations: what powers did the national government retain to protect the rights of its citizens? There was the problem of defining the constitutional status of black Americans—a problem that finally forced Americans to define American CITIZENSHIP and the rights incident to it. Also, because the President and Congress disagreed on these issues, Reconstruction brought about a crisis in legislative–executive relations that culminated in the only impeachment of an American President. Finally, the Reconstruction controversy had a powerful effect upon Americans' conception of the proper role of government, laying the groundwork for the development of laissez-faire constitutionalism.

These issues would be adjusted in the context of the established party system. During the war, the Republican party worked diligently and fairly successfully to broaden its support. Renaming their organization the Union party, Republican leaders accepted as colleagues men who had been influential Democrats until the outbreak of war. In 1864 the party nominated Tennessee's Democratic former governor and senator, ANDREW JOHNSON, to the vice-presidency. Despite this, the Union party, which would revive the name Republican after the war, was the heir to the governmental activism of the old Federalist and Whig parties. Likewise Republicans inherited nationalist theories of the federal system. (See UNION, THEORIES OF THE.) The war confirmed and extended their distrust of STATES' RIGHTS doctrines; yet many Republicans would resist going too far in the direction of "consolidation" of the Union at the expense of traditional areas of state jurisdiction. On the other hand, the majority of Democrats had remained loyal to their party and its heritage of states' rights and small government. Naturally, the Reconstruction issue, which involved both questions, found the two parties ranged against one another.

Northerners faced a paradox when they considered the status of the Confederate states at war's end. They had denied that a state could leave the Union, but few wanted the same governments that had attempted secession to return as if nothing had happened. Only so-called Peace Democrats argued that the Union should be restored through negotiations between the Confederate state governments and the national government. Somehow, Republicans and War Democrats insisted, the national government must have power to secure some changes in the South and in the federal system before final restoration. As the war progressed, and especially in 1865 and 1866, when they were forced to grapple with the problem, Republicans propounded a variety of constitutional justifications for such power. Unlike Democrats, who insisted that state government had existed before the Union and independent of it, Republicans insisted that states could exist only in the Union and by virtue of their connection with it. Thus, by trying to secede, the southern states had committed STATE SUICIDE, in the graphic language of Senator CHARLES SUMNER; or, as other Republicans put it, they had "forfeited their rights." Given this view, there were several ways to justify national power over Southerners. Many Republicans argued that if Southerners now lacked state governments, Congress must restore them under the clause of the Constitution requiring the national government to guarantee a REPUBLICAN FORM OF GOVERNMENT to each state. Moreover, in the 1849 case of LUTHER V. BORDEN the Supreme Court, citing this clause, had seemed to concede to the "political branches" of the government the power to recognize whether a state government was legitimate in case of doubt. The Court had held that the admission of state representatives to Congress was conclusive. With state governments defunct, Republicans argued, the Court's holding meant that the political branches of the national government would have final say about what government would be recognized as restored to the Union and when that recognition would take place. Implicit in this power was the authority to determine what sort of government would be acceptable.

But when some Republicans insisted that the GUARANTEE CLAUSE entitled the national government to require changes it believed necessary for states to be considered republican, most of their colleagues rebelled. Such an interpretation would give the national government power to modify "unrepublican" political and civil laws in states that had never left the Union.

Other Republicans found a safer source of power over states that had forfeited their rights: the national government had recovered control over the territory and citizens of the South through exercise of its WAR POWERS, which had overridded the peacetime provision of the Constitution that guaranteed citizens' and states' rights. The government could continue to hold Southerners in this "grasp of war" until they agreed to meet the government's conditions for the restoration of peace. On this theory, national power would be temporary, providing no precedent for intruding in states that had not been in rebellion.

Finally, other Republicans—those who wanted the most radical changes in southern society—argued that, having broken away from national authority de facto, the southern states were conquered provinces no different from any other newly acquired territory. Thus Southerners were subject to the direct control of the national government, which ought to provide ordinary territorial governments through which they could govern themselves under the revisory power of Congress. In this way the national government would retain authority to legislate directly for the South until new states were created there—establishing a public school system, for example, or confiscating the great landed estates and distributing them among the people as small farms. But this theory also seemed too radical for most Northerners, and most Republicans endorsed the more limited "grasp-of-war" doctrine.

Congress was adjourned in April and May 1865, as Lincoln was assassinated and the war ended. Lincoln's successor, the former Democrat Johnson, accepted the key elements of the WADE-DAVIS BILL developed during the war, but he followed Lincoln's policy of carrying it out under presidential authority, rather than calling Congress back into session to enact Reconstruction legislation. Johnson called for white, male voters in each southern state to elect a state constitutional convention as soon as fifty percent of them had taken a loyalty oath that would entitle them to AMNESTY. Thus blacks would have to depend on governments elected by whites for protection of life and property. The conventions were required to pronounce their states' SECESSION ordinances null and void, repudiate debts incurred by their Confederate state governments, and abolish slavery. Finally, the southern states would have to ratify the proposed THIRTEENTH AMENDMENT, which abolished slavery throughout the land. Then the conventions could organize elections to ratify the new constitutions, elect state officials, and elect congressmen. By December 1865, as Congress reconvened, this process had been completed in most of the southern states and would soon be completed in the remainder.

At first Johnson was vague about his constitutional theory of Reconstruction, but as congressional opposition developed his supporters articulated a position that left little power to Congress. Secession had merely "suspended" the operation of legal governments in the South, they insisted. As COMMANDER-IN-CHIEF of the armed forces, the President had the duty under the government's war powers to reanimate state governments. War powers were inherently presidential, Johnson insisted. He had exercised them in such a way as to preserve the traditional federal system. Congress could do no more than exercise its constitutional power to "judge of the elections, returns and qualifications of its own members" by deciding whether individual congressmen-elect were disqualified by their roles in the war; it could not deny REPRESENTATION to whole states. Gaining the support of northern Democrats for this states'-rights-oriented policy, Johnson set the stage for a bitter struggle over the relative powers of the branches of the national government.

A majority of congressmen might have acquiesced in the President's position had they been confident that loyalists would control the southern state governments or that the rights of the newly freed slaves would be respected there. However, it soon became apparent that the states were controlled by former rebels and that the rights of the freedmen would be severely circumscribed. Compounding the problem, the ex-Confederate-dominated South would increase its congressional representation now that slavery was abolished; the constitutional provision counting only three-fifths of the slave population would no longer apply. All this persuaded congressional Republicans to refuse immediate admission of southern state representatives to Congress and to seek a compromise with the President.

There were two thrusts to the congressional policy: protection of freedmen's rights and a new system of apportionment of representation in Congress. Most congressional leaders believed that the Thirteenth Amendment automatically conferred citizenship upon the freedmen when it abolished slavery. Moreover, the amendment's second section authorized Congress to pass legislation appropriate to enforce abolition. Republicans acted upon this understanding by passing a new FREEDMEN'S BUREAU bill, augmenting one passed during the war, and proposing the bill that became the CIVIL RIGHTS ACT OF 1866. The first, a temporary measure justified under the war powers, authorized an Army bureau to supervise the transition from slave to free labor, protecting the rights and interests of the freedmen in the process. The second was designed to secure permanent protection for the freedmen in their basic rights. Few Republicans thought that Americans would accept so drastic a change in the federal system as to give Congress instead of the states the job of protecting people in their ordinary rights. Therefore they adopted the idea of leaving that job to the states but requiring them to treat all groups equally. At the same time, Republicans intended to require equality only in the protection of *basic* rights of citizenship. This goal forced them to define just what those rights were. So the Civil Rights Act declared all persons born in the United States, except Indians who did not pay taxes, to be citizens of the United States; it granted all citizens, regardless of race, the same basic rights as white citizens. What were these basic rights of citizenship? "To make and enforce contracts; to sue, be parties, and give evidence; to inherit, purchase, lease, sell, hold, and convey real and personal property; and to full and equal benefit of all laws and proceedings for the security of persons and property" and to "be subject to like punishment, pains, and penalties." To secure these rights without centralizing power of ordinary legislation in Washington, the bill permitted citizens to remove legal cases from state to federal court jurisdiction in any state that did not end discrimination. (See CIVIL RIGHTS REMOVAL.) The idea was to force states to abolish RACIAL DISCRIMINATION in their own laws in order to preserve their jurisdictions. As its author explained, the act would "have no operation in any State where the laws are equal, where all persons have the same civil rights without regard to color or race."

At the same time Republicans prepared a fourteenth amendment to define citizenship and its rights; to change the way seats in Congress were apportioned, so as to reflect the number of voters rather than gross population; to disqualify leading Confederates from holding political office; and to guarantee payment of the United States debt while repudiating the Confederate debt. Congress was to have power to enforce this amendment, too, by "appropriate" legislation.

Republicans expected Johnson to endorse these measures, which after all did not attempt to replace the governments he had instituted in the South, and they expected Southerners to signify their acceptance of these "terms of peace" by ratifying the new amendment. However, Johnson insisted that the Republican program would revolutionize the federal system. He vetoed the legislation and urged Southerners to reject the proposed amendment. At the same time he attacked the Republicans bitterly. Republicans responded by passing the Civil Rights Act over Johnson's veto, enacting the new Freedman's Bureau Act, and sending the FOURTEENTH AMENDMENT to the states for RATIFICATION. To the voters, they stressed the moderation of their proposals, and Johnson's supporters were badly beaten in the congressional elections of 1866. Nonetheless, Southerners followed Johnson's advice and refused to ratify the amendment.

This refusal angered and frightened Republican congressmen. If the conflict drifted into stalemate, northern voters might tire of it and blame the Republicans for not completing restoration. Outraged at southern recalcitrance and Johnson's "betrayal," the Republicans passed new Reconstruction laws over his veto early in 1867. Designating Johnson's southern governments as temporary only, the Republicans instructed Southerners to begin the process anew. This time many leading Confederates would be disfranchised while the freedmen were permitted to vote. New state conventions would have to be elected to write new constitutions banning racial discrimination in civil and political rights. The voters would have to ratify these constitutions, and then newly elected state officials would have to ratify the Fourteenth Amendment. In 1869 the Republican Congress proposed to the states the FIFTEENTH AMENDMENT, banning racial discrimination in voting; southern states that had not yet finished the process of being readmitted would be required to ratify this amendment, too. In some ways the new program was a relief to Republicans. They expected that once southern blacks could vote, their state governments would have to provide them with the protection of the laws, thus rendering unnecessary the exercise of national power and preserving the old balance of the federal system.

Until the southern states complied with the new Reconstruction laws, they were to be under the control of the Army, subject to martial law and, if necessary, military courts. Southerners insisted that this whole program was unconstitutional, and they tried to persuade the Supreme Court to declare it so. In 1867 and 1868 representatives of Johnson's state governments asked the Supreme Court to enjoin Johnson and his secretary of war, respectively, from enforcing the MILITARY RECONSTRUCTION ACTS. They hoped for success, because the majority of the Justices were suspected of opposing the Republican program. In earlier cases, including EX PARTE MILLIGAN (1866), a narrow majority had held that military courts could not operate upon civilians where civil courts were functioning, and in the TEST OATH CASES the Court had ruled unconstitutional laws requiring persons to swear oaths of past loyalty in order to follow certain professions. However, even Johnson would not sustain an effort to secure Court intervention in so plainly a political issue, and the Court dismissed both suits. (See MISSISSIPPI V. JOHNSON, 1867.)

Southerners tried again in EX PARTE MCCARDLE (1869), where a Southerner convicted of murder in a military court asked for a write of HABEAS CORPUS, citing the Supreme Court's Milligan decision. At least some Reconstruction laws might be jeopardized if the Court endorsed this argument, and Republicans responded by repealing the law under which McCardle had brought his suit. The Court grudgingly acquiesced in the repeal but virtually invited a new application for the writ under another law.

These developments produced ambivalent feelings about the courts among Republicans. Before the war the judiciary had tended to sustain laws protecting slavery and discrimination against black Americans. During the war Chief Justice ROGER B. TANEY had seemed to obstruct the military effort, and the Court's course since the war had hardly been reassuring. Fearing judicial interference, several leading Republicans proposed narrowing the Court's jurisdiction and requiring a two-thirds majority of Justices to rule a congressional law unconstitutional, or denying that power altogether. On the other hand, the judiciary was the only national institution besides the military capable of enforcing the new laws protecting the rights of American citizens. Not only did Congress refrain from passing the court-limitation bills but it also expanded judicial authority by making the national judiciary the forum in which citizens and even businesses were to secure justice if their rights were denied in the states. Indeed, even as Republicans worried whether the Court would impair Reconstruction, in their roles as circuit court judges the Justices were upholding the power of the national government to protect rights under the Thirteenth and Fourteenth Amendments. Altogether, the Reconstruction era witnessed a great expansion of the jurisdiction and activity of the federal courts.

While the southern attack on the Reconstruction laws failed in the Supreme Court, Johnson was able to use against the laws the fact that they employed the military in their enforcement. As COMMANDER-IN-CHIEF of the armed forces, Johnson sought to limit the authority of military commanders and to give command of occupying forces to officers sympathetic to his position. When Secretary of War EDWIN M. STANTON resisted these efforts, Johnson suspended him from office and appointed the popular General ULYSSES S. GRANT in his place. By late 1867 Johnson's obstruction was so successful that Reconstruction was grinding to a halt, with white Southerners ready to prevent ratification of their new, egalitarian constitutions.

Many Republicans denied that the President had the constitutional right to obstruct legislation in this way, and they urged the House of Representatives to impeach him. However, most Republicans were frightened of taking so radical a step, and many insisted that IMPEACHMENT lay only for indictable crimes. Despite his obstructionism, Johnson had not clearly broken any law, and they would not support impeachment until he did. Therefore in December 1867 the first impeachment resolution failed.

However, in February 1868 Johnson did finally seem to break a law. As noted, Johnson had earlier suspended Secretary of War Stanton. He had done this while the Senate was adjourned, conforming to the TENURE OF OFFICE ACT, passed in 1867, which made all removals of government officers temporary until the Senate confirmed a successor, or, in certain circumstances, voted to accept the President's reasons for removal. In Stanton's case, the Senate in 1867 refused to concur in the removal, and Stanton returned to office. Now Johnson defied the Senate and the law, ordering Stanton's permanent removal. The House impeached him immediately, and from March through May the Senate established rules of procedure, heard arguments and testimony, and deliberated.

Although many questions were raised during Johnson's trial in the Senate, the decision finally turned for most senators on whether they believed Stanton was in reality covered by the Tenure of Office Act. Despite Johnson's initial compliance with the act, his lawyers persuaded just enough Republican senators that the act did not cover Stanton, and Johnson was acquitted. But the price for acquittal was Johnson's promise to end his obstruction of the Reconstruction laws. With that interference ended, most southern states adopted new state constitutions, and in nearly all those states Republicans took control of the governments.

The new southern constitutions and Republican governments were among the most progressive in the nation. Elected mainly by black voters, southern Republican leaders thought they could secure enough white support to guarantee continued victory by using government power to promote prosperity and provide services. Thus they emulated northern Republican policies, using state taxes and credit to subsidize railroads and canals, to develop natural resources, and to control flooding along the Mississippi River. They created the first centralized state public school systems and opened state hospitals and asylums. At the same time southern Republicans were committed to improving the conditions of former slaves, both on principle and to keep the support of their largest constituency. They passed laws to provide them with the same state services that whites received, put blacks in important positions, banned discrimination in many businesses, shaped labor laws to protect workers' interests, and appointed local judges who would be sympathetic to blacks in disputes with whites.

All these activities required the states to spend and borrow far more money than they had before the war. Because it was primarily whites who owned enough property to pay taxes, the Republican policies redistributed wealth, something not acceptable to nineteenth-century Americans. Bitterly, white Southerners charged that "ignorant," "brutal" voters were being duped by venal politicians with promises of "class legislation." Southern whites denied that such governments were really democratic. Unable to defeat Republicans at the polls in most states, they turned to violence and fraud. From 1868 through 1872, midnight riders, known by such names as the Ku Klux Klan, terrorized local Republican leaders. After 1872 the violence became more organized and more closely linked to anti-Republican political organizations.

A few southern Republican governors were at first able to suppress the violence. But by 1870 they were appealing to the national government for help, thus causing serious problems for national Republican leaders. Republicans had hoped that enfranchising the freedmen would protect them without a massive expansion of national power. Moreover, everyone believed that legislation must be based on the Fourteenth and Fifteenth Amendments, ignoring the earlier view that the Thirteenth Amendment gave power to protect citizens' basic rights. But the language of the two later amendments only protected rights against STATE ACTION, and Republicans had a difficult time justifying laws protecting blacks and white Republicans from attacks by private individuals. Nonetheless, in 1871 Republicans passed such laws and also authorized President Grant to take drastic action to crush violence, including suspension of the writ of habeas corpus. They insisted that the Fourteenth Amendment required states to protect their residents; failure to do so would amount to state denial of EQUAL PROTECTION.

At first this response seemed successful, and violence abated. However, it soon flared anew. In many southern states Republicans claimed that Democratic violence and intimidation should nullify apparent Democratic majorities in elections, and they refused to count Democratic votes from areas where violence was most intense. In return Democrats organized armed militia to press their claims. In state after state Republicans had to appeal for national troops to protect them against such opponents. Where it was difficult to afford protection, the Democratic militias—often called "White Leagues"—drove Republican officials from office.

It became ever more difficult for national Republicans to respond. More and more Northerners feared that continued national intervention in the South was undermining the federal system. At the same time the Supreme Court manifested its concern to preserve a balance between state and national authority. In *Texas v. White* (1869) the Justices emphasized the importance of states in the Union, and in *Collector v. Day* (1871) they seemed to endorse the doctrine of DUAL FEDERALISM, by denying the national government's power to tax the incomes of officers of the "sovereign" states. In the SLAUGHTERHOUSE CASES (1873) the Court, in an implicitly dual federalist opinion, ruled that national and state citizenships were distinct. The Fourteenth Amendment protected only a limited number of rights inherent in national citizenship; those rights usually identified as basic remained the sole province of the states. This decision severely curtailed national power to protect black Southerners and southern Republicans from violence. In UNITED STATES V. CRUIKSHANK (1876) the Court held invalid indictments against white conspirators who had massacred blacks, in part on the grounds that the Fourteenth Amendment was aimed only at state action and could not justify prosecution of private individuals.

At the same time a growing number of Northerners were coming to share Southerners' concern about "class legislation." To these Northerners, calls for a protective tariff, for artificial inflation of the currency, for repudiation of state-guaranteed railroad bonds, for regulation of railroad rates, and for government imposition of an eight-hour work day all indicated a growing clamor for "class legislation" in the North. City political organizations, which taxed urban property holders to provide services to the less wealthy, seemed to be engaging in the same kind of "plunder" that southern whites alleged against their Republican governments. Many Northerners began to argue that the state and national constitutions required judges to overturn class legislation. They had some initial successes. The Supreme Court ruled part of the Legal Tender Act unconstitutional, only to overrule itself a year later (see LEGAL TENDER CASES, 1870), and state courts ruled that business and railroad promotion laws exceeded legislative power. However, the courts generally declined the invitation to write the doctrine of "laissez faire" into the Constitution. The majority in the *Slaughterhouse Cases* rejected the argument, and the Court sustained broad state regulatory power over businesses AFFECTED WITH A PUBLIC INTEREST—railroads, grain warehouses, and others that were left undefined. (See GRANGER CASES, 1877.)

Nonetheless, the conviction was growing that the sort of wealth-redistributing policies followed by southern Republicans was fundamentally wrong and so was fear that such ideas might spread north. More and more Northerners agreed with southern whites that southern proponents of such policies were "carpetbaggers" and "scalawags." By 1875 President Grant was refusing to help his beleaguered political allies; all but three southern states had returned to Democratic control, often through force and intimidation; and white Southerners were planning similarly violent campaigns to "redeem" the last three in 1876. Their effort to do so led to one of the greatest political and constitutional crises in American history.

In the presidential election of 1876 the violence and fraud endemic in the South threatened to engulf the nation. In the three remaining Republican states in the South—South Carolina, Louisiana, and Florida—Democrats engaged in campaigns of violence and intimidation. Republican officials threw out votes from districts they claimed Democrats had carried by force. Democrats once again charged fraud and armed to confront Republicans; southern Republicans once again appealed to the national government for protection. However, this time the outcome of the presidential election itself turned upon who had carried these three states. Without them, Democrat Samuel J. Tilden was one electoral vote short of victory. Republican RUTHERFORD B. HAYES needed the electoral votes of all three to win.

As the time drew near to count the electoral vote and declare a winner, two sets of electoral votes were sent to Congress from each of the contested states—the Republican votes certified by appropriate state agencies, and Democratic competitors. The Constitution requires electoral votes to be counted by the president of the Senate (normally the vice-president of the United States) in the presence of both houses of Congress. Republicans insisted that, absent a specific congressional resolution governing the subject, the Republican president pro tempore of the Senate would have the power to decide which set of votes were the correct ones to count (the vice-president having died in office). Controlling the Senate, Republicans prepared to block any contrary resolution that might come from the Democratic House. Democrats, on the other hand, insisted that if the two houses of Congress could not agree upon which set of votes was legitimate, neither could be counted. Then no candidate would have a majority, and according to the Constitution the House would name the winner.

With no clear precedent, and with the Supreme Court not yet accepted as the usual arbiter of such constitutional disputes, it seemed that the conflict might be resolved by force. Republican President Grant controlled the Army; if he recognized a President counted in by the Republicans, a competitor named by the House would have a hard time pressing his claim. To counter this Republican program, Democrats threatened forcible resistance.

As Americans demanded a peaceful end to the crisis, the two sides were forced to compromise. Congress passed a resolution turning all disputed electoral votes over to an Electoral Commission of ten congressmen and five Supreme Court Justices for decision. The commission decision would stand in each case unless *both* houses voted to disagree to it—an early example of a LEGISLATIVE VETO.

To the Democrats' dismay, the three Republican Supreme Court Justices joined the five Republican congressmen on the commission to decide every disputed vote in favor of the Republican candidate. In each case the majority accepted the votes certified by the agency authorized by state law. Republicans insisted the commission had no power "to go behind" these returns.

Furious, Democrats charged that this was a partisan decision. Many of them urged Democratic congressmen to prevent the completion of the count by filibustering, saying that the House could name the President if the count were not completed by the constitutional deadline of March 3. But most Democrats felt that Americans would not support such a radical course after Democrats had agreed to the compromise. To strengthen these moderates, Hayes promised not to help southern Republicans against rival claimants for state offices. As a result Hayes was declared President just within the deadline. When he honored his commitment to the Democrats, the last southern Republican governments collapsed, even though the Republicans had claimed state victories based on the same election returns that elected Hayes. (See COMPROMISE OF 1877.)

The collapse of Reconstruction was related directly to the development of constitutional commitments that would dominate the last quarter of the nineteenth century. It marked a renewal of a state-centered federalism that would characterize succeeding years. Furthermore, it was a direct result of the growing fear of "class legislation" that would lead to the acceptance of "laissez-faire constitutionalism" in the 1890s.

MICHAEL LES BENEDICT

Bibliography

BENEDICT, MICHAEL LES 1975 *A Compromise of Principle: Congressional Republicans and Reconstruction, 1863–1869.* New York: W. W. Norton.

FAIRMAN, CHARLES 1971 *Reconstruction and Reunion, 1864–88—Part One,* Volume 6 of *The History of the Supreme Court of the United States.* New York: Macmillan.

GILLETTE, WILLIAM 1979 *Retreat from Reconstruction, 1869–1879.* Baton Rouge: Louisiana State University Press.

HYMAN, HAROLD M. 1973 *A More Perfect Union: The Impact of the Civil War and Reconstruction upon the Constitution.* New York: Knopf.

McKITRICK, ERIC L. 1960 *Andrew Johnson and Reconstruction.* Chicago: University of Chicago Press.
STAMPP, KENNETH M. 1965 *The Era of Reconstruction, 1865–1877.* New York: Knopf.

CONSTITUTIONAL HISTORY, 1877–1901

American public life during the Civil War-Reconstruction years was dominated by clashes over constitutional issues of the most basic sort: race and CITIZENSHIP; FEDERALISM, STATES' RIGHTS, and the Union; the power of the President, Congress, and the courts; and the bounds of military and civil authority. This was a time when the interpretation of the Constitution held center stage in American public life. The resolution of fundamental issues was sought in Congress and the courts, in party politics and elections, ultimately through force of arms. Merely to list the milestones of the period—the great debate over SLAVERY IN THE TERRITORIES; DRED SCOTT V. SANDFORD (1857); SECESSION and CIVIL WAR; the THIRTEENTH, FOURTEENTH, and FIFTEENTH AMENDMENTS; the CIVIL RIGHTS, Reconstruction, and Enforcement Acts; and the IMPEACHMENT OF ANDREW JOHNSON—is to make the point that during the years from 1850 to 1877 the Constitution provided the context in which Americans expressed, and fought over, their most fundamental social beliefs.

How different was the period that followed! The structure of government—the relationship of the states and territories to the Union; the powers of Congress, the courts, and the President; the role of the POLITICAL PARTIES—often was a matter of political but rarely of constitutional concern. Nor were the major economic and social issues of the time confronted primarily in constitutional terms. It is revealing that no amendment to the Constitution was adopted between 1870 and 1913.

This does not mean, though, that constitutional issues had no place in American public policy between 1877 and 1900. Rather, what happened was that a sea change was taking place in American life, and the issues generated by this change took time to assume a full-fledged constitutional guise. Just as the basic constitutional issues of states' rights and slavery did not fully emerge until the 1850s, so too the constitutional issues generated by the rise of an urban-industrial society did not come into their own until after 1900, in many respects not until the 1930s.

Where should we look, in the late nineteenth century, for the seeds of the great twentieth-century effort to adapt the Constitution to the realities of an urban-industrial society? The primary structural concern of the time was over the role of the judiciary, and here was a foreshadowing of the conflict between the administrative state and the representative state that would assume such great importance after 1900. Second, economic issues—in particular, those involving the regulation of large enterprises—were a fruitful area of contention in the late nineteenth century. And finally, questions of citizenship and race—partly a legacy of the Civil War-Reconstruction years but also a product of the social strains generated by an industrializing society—continued to engage the attention of the public and of policymakers.

Frank Goodnow in his *Comparative Administrative Law* (1893) observed that while constitutional issues set the terms of debate over the character of American government before the Civil War, administrative issues took center stage afterward. Certainly it seemed that, as much as anything could, the war had settled the question of the relationship of the states to the Union. Nor did the desuetude of the post-Reconstruction Presidency, the dominance of Congress, or the still-nascent administrative state generate much in the way of constitutional debate.

Late nineteenth-century Presidents were caught up in party politics and patronage and did relatively little to formulate and conduct public policy. But America's evolution into a powerful industrial nation began to leave its mark. RUTHERFORD B. HAYES and GROVER CLEVELAND used federal troops to restore order during the railroad strikes of 1877 and 1894. The federal bureaucracy, though small, was growing; and something like a professional civil service took form, in part under the aegis of the Civil Service Commission established by the PENDLETON ACT of 1883. Tariff and fiscal policy came to be more closely identified with presidential leadership. But in constitutional terms the chief executive at the end of the century was little changed from what he had been in 1877.

Congress, however, became a considerably more powerful and effective branch of government during this period. WOODROW WILSON in 1885 called "Congressional Government" the "predominant and controlling force, the centre and source of all motive and of all regulative power." This enhanced authority came from the fact that state and local party leaders served as senators and representatives; from congressional control over budgetary and fiscal policy; and from the increasing regularity and stability of congressional leadership and procedure.

Perhaps the most striking change in the balance of governmental powers during the late nineteenth century was the rise of JUDICIAL ACTIVISM. The Supreme Court found only two federal laws unconstitutional between 1790 and 1864, but it voided federal acts in seven cases between 1868 and 1877 and in eleven cases between 1878 and 1899. The Court voided state acts in thirty-eight cases before 1865, in thirty-five cases between 1865 and 1873, and in ninety-one cases between 1874 and 1899. A debate as old as the Constitution heated up once again in the 1890s: what were the proper limits of JUDICIAL REVIEW?

The belief was then widespread—and has been gospel since—that the late nineteenth-century courts declared open season on laws threatening corporate interests. The *American Law Review* observed in 1894 that "it has come to be the fashion . . . for courts to overturn acts of the State legislatures upon mere economical theories and upon mere casuistical grounds." Federal and state courts found in the DUE PROCESS and EQUAL PROTECTION clauses of the Fourteenth Amendment and in the doctrine of FREEDOM OF CONTRACT grounds for voiding laws that regulated working conditions or taxed CORPORATIONS. This judicial conservatism culminated in an unholy trinity of Supreme Court decisions in the mid-1890s: IN RE DEBS (1895), which sustained a federal INJUNCTION against striking railroad workers; UNITED STATES V. E. C. KNIGHT COMPANY (1895), which severely limited the scope of the SHERMAN ANTITRUST ACT; and POLLOCK V. FARMERS' LOAN AND TRUST (1895), which struck down the 1894 federal income tax law. Arnold Paul has called these decisions "related aspects of a massive judicial entry into the socioeconomic scene, . . . a conservative oriented revolution."

But the extent of the courts' antilabor and antiregulatory decision making has been exaggerated; and its purpose has been distorted. A review in 1897 of 1,639 state labor laws enacted during the previous twenty years found that 114 of them—only seven percent—were held unconstitutional. The STATE POLICE POWER to regulate working conditions was widely accepted legal doctrine: in ninety-three percent of 243 Fourteenth Amendment challenges before 1901 the Supreme Court upheld the state laws. By the late 1890s the influential New York and Massachusetts courts looked favorably on laws affecting the conditions of labor, as did the Supreme Court in HOLDEN V. HARDY (1898).

Nor did judicial policy rest only on a tender concern for the rights of property. The desire to foster a national economy was evident in many federal court decisions. And many Justices shared the widespread public sense that American society was being wrenched beyond recognition by industrialism and its consequences. Justice STEPHEN J. FIELD and jurist THOMAS M. COOLEY were as ill at ease with large corporate power as they were with legislative activism. The influential judge and treatise writer JOHN F. DILLON, who called all attempts "to pillage and destroy" private property "as baneful as they are illegal," insisted "with equal earnestness upon the proposition that such property is under many important duties toward the State and society, which the owners generally fail to appreciate."

By far the most important applications of the Constitution to issues of public policy during the late nineteenth century involved large corporate enterprise, that increasingly conspicuous and troubling presence on the American scene. Railroads led the way both in the scale of their corporate organization and in the consequent public, regulatory, and judicial response.

The roads were great beneficiaries of private and state loans before the Civil War. In the years after 1865, they received substantial federal and state land grants, and loans and subsidies from counties and townships. There were 35,000 miles of track in 1865; 93,000 in 1880. But by the mid-1870s railroads were staggering beneath the weight of their expansion. Fierce competition in the East and Midwest forced down rates and earnings. The overcapitalized lines, with high fixed costs, suffered also from the price deflation of the time. Bankruptcies and reorganizations, rate discrimination, and price-fixing pools were among the consequences. All had the effect of feeding popular anti-railroad sentiment.

That great Civil War venture in mixed enterprise, the Union Pacific Railroad, was a prolific breeder of controversy. Political and constitutional difficulties sprang up around the federal government's role in the capitalization and direction of the road. Congressmen bitterly assailed the Union Pacific's inability (or disinclination) to meet its financial obligations to the government. But not until the SINKING FUND CASES (1879) did the Supreme Court sustain the right of Congress to require this and other transcontinental lines to repay their debts. The Credit Mobilier scandal of 1872, in which stock in the construction company that built the Union Pacific was distributed to a number of influential politicians, epitomized the difficulty of fitting a semipublic enterprise into the American system of government. The Pacific Railroad Commission finally concluded: "The sovereign should not be mated with the subject."

Railroad land grants were no less a source of contention. The House unanimously resolved in 1870 that "the policy of granting subsidies in public lands to railroads and other corporations ought to be discontinued." Once again, the very principle of such aid came under attack: "These grants . . . have been made on the theory that government is an organized benevolence, and not merely a compact for the negative function of repelling a public enemy or repressing disorders."

The consequences of state and local railroad aid also were distressing, and were equally productive of doubts as to whether such aid was part of the proper role of government. The Supreme Court heard more than 350 bonding cases between 1870 and 1896. While the courts felt constrained to enforce most of those obligations, they made clear their displeasure with government subsidization. John F. Dillon condemned subsidies as "a coercive contribution in favor of private railway corporations" which violated "the general spirit of the Constitution as to the sacredness of private property." Thomas M. Cooley objected to railroad subsidies on similar grounds, arguing that "a large portion of the most urgent needs of society are relegated exclusively to the law of demand and supply." In LOAN ASSOCIATION v. TOPEKA (1875) the Supreme Court used this argument to block direct government subsidization of private enterprise.

During the years from 1880 to 1900, public, political, and (inevitably) judicial attention shifted from subsidization to regulation of the economy. The prevailing economic thought of the time, the weakness of government supervision, and the power of private interests worked against an effective system of ECONOMIC REGULATION. But inevitably the strains and conflicts attending the rise of an industrial economy produced demands on the state to intervene.

Journalist E. L. Godkin observed in 1873: "The locomotive is coming in contact with the framework of our institution. In this country of simple government, the most powerful centralizing force which civilization has yet produced must, within the next score years, assume its relation to that political machinery which is to control and regulate it." Nor surprisingly the railroads, the biggest of America's national enterprises, were the first to come under federal regulation.

During the 1870s, state railroad policy had moved from subsidy to containment. The 1870 Illinois constitution required the legislature to "pass laws establishing maximum rates of charges for the transportation of passengers and freight." That body in 1871 set maximum freight and grain elevator rates, forbade price discrimination, and created a railroad commission with supervisory and enforcement powers. Similar laws were adopted in Minnesota, Wisconsin, and Iowa. Because Grange members often were prominent advocates of rate regulation, these acts came to be known as the Granger laws.

The Supreme Court in *Munn v. Illinois* (1877), the first of the GRANGER CASES, upheld the regulatory power of the legislatures and opened up yet another path to regulation by resurrecting the old COMMON LAW doctrine that when private property was AFFECTED WITH A PUBLIC INTEREST it was subject to public accountability and control. But at the same time the Court conceded that "under some circumstances" legislation might be held to violate the Fourteenth Amendment: a portent of the conservative jurisprudence of later years.

Whatever constitutional authority might adhere to state regulation, its effectiveness was severely limited by compliant state railroad commissions, the political and legal influence of the roads, and above all the national character of the enterprise. From the mid-1880s on, federal courts increasingly struck down state railroad tax and rate laws that in their view interfered with the flow of INTERSTATE COMMERCE. The implicit policy decision was that ratemaking should be in the hands of the railroads—and be subject to the review of federal courts, not state courts and legislatures. One observer thought that "long tables of railway statistics, with the accompanying analyses, look strangely out of place in a volume of United States Reports": testimony to the fact that the courts of necessity were taking on a quasi-administrative role.

The scale and complexity of the interests affected by the railroads, the competitive problems of the lines themselves, the limited effectiveness of state regulation, and the growing intervention of the federal courts all fed a movement for national railroad regulation culminating in the INTERSTATE COMMERCE ACT of 1887. That act defined and laid down penalties for rate discrimination, and created an Interstate Commerce Commission (ICC) with the power to investigate and prosecute violators. Its primary purpose was negative: to block pooling and other cartel practices, not to secure a stable railroad rate structure. What the ICC gained thereby in constitutionality it lost in administrative effectiveness. Its early performance showed how difficult it was—given the power of private interests, popular distrust of government, and constitutional limits on the exercise of public power—to establish a bureaucratic mode of regulation. Instead, the ICC adopted what was in fact the only functioning American mode of economic supervision, that of the judiciary. Cooley, the judge and treatise writer who became the ICC's first chairman, announced: "The Commissioners realize that they are a new court,

. . . and that they are to lay the foundations of a new body of American law."

During the first ten years of its existence the ICC handed down rulings on more than 800 rate controversies. But the Commission's impact was limited by the size, complexity, and competitiveness of the railroad business and by its lack of supervisory power. Demands rose in the 1890s for government ownership and operation of the lines, or at least for more rigorous supervision by a national Department of Transportation. But, as Cooley observed, these proposals were beyond the range of the late nineteenth-century American polity: "The perpetuity of free institutions in this country requires that the political machine called the United States Government be kept from being overloaded beyond its strength. The more cumbrous it is the greater is the power of intrigue and corruption under it."

The regulation of large enterprise in general posed the same problems, and produced the same response, as did that of the railroads. Mid-nineteenth-century general incorporation acts, and the competition among states to attract corporation charters, guaranteed that the terms of incorporation would remain easy, the regulation of company affairs loose and permissive. In theory the internal affairs of corporations were the business of the states; in practice, the states exercised little control.

But as in the case of the railroads, the growth of business corporations into national enterprises created a demand for federal regulation. Once again, judicial interpretation fostered the growth of a national economy. State and federal courts strengthened the legal status of foreign (out-of-state) corporations, in effect reversing the severe constraints imposed on them by PAUL V. VIRGINIA (1869). In *Barron v. Burnside* (1887) the Supreme Court for the first time held that state regulation of foreign corporations could be of doubtful constitutionality. By the turn of the century the "liberal theory" of foreign corporations was the prevailing one.

Even more dramatic was the courts' use of the Fourteenth Amendment to protect corporate rights and privileges. During the 1870s, said Howard Jay Graham, "the rule that corporations were *not* to be regarded as constitutional 'PERSONS' theoretically was the LAW OF THE LAND." But this rule was more theory than fact, and during the late nineteenth century the judiciary explicitly brought corporations under the protection afforded to persons by the due process and equal protection clauses of the Amendment.

The rise of large enterprise in the late nineteenth century took forms that roused public concern and ultimately evoked a legislative and judicial response. The urge to override the limitations of state chartering led to the invention of the corporate trust and then the holding company. Although only about ten trusts were created during the 1880s, the word in the generic sense of a "huge, irrepressible, indeterminate" corporation came to be the object of great public concern. By 1890 several states had ANTITRUST laws, and six state supreme courts had held that trust agreements were against public policy or were illegal as monopolies or conspiracies in RESTRAINT OF TRADE. And public pressure grew for a federal antitrust law, as it had for railroad regulation.

The SHERMAN ANTITRUST ACT of 1890, passed overwhelmingly by Congress, relied on the legislature's power under the COMMERCE CLAUSE to outlaw "every contract, combination in the form of trust or otherwise, or conspiracy, in restraint of trade or commerce." The breadth of the law's formulation, and its dependence on the courts rather than on an administrative agency to define its provisions, testified to the still underdeveloped state of federal regulation. But in other ways the statute was sophisticated. By relying on the old common law concept of the illegality of conspiracies in restraint of trade, the drafters minimized the risk of having the law declared unconstitutional. And the Sherman Act was widely understood to be aimed at great combinations, not to fix an unrealistic standard of small-unit competition on the economy.

Even so, enforcement was full of difficulty. The Department of Justice in the 1890s lacked the manpower, the money, and the inclination to prosecute vigorously. The courts, too, severely limited the utility of the act. They held that a firm could come to dominate a sector of the economy without doing anything illegal, and they developed distinctions between reasonable and unreasonable restraint of trade, between legitimate business practices and "illegal commercial piracy." And in its Sugar Trust decision of 1895 (*United States v. E. C. Knight Company*) the Supreme Court dealt the law a heavy blow, holding that the Sherman Act applied only to "commerce" and not to manufacturing, and that the activities of the American Sugar Refining Company lay outside the act's coverage even though that firm controlled over ninety percent of the nation's sugar refining capacity.

The *American Law Review* called this decision "the most deplorable one that has been rendered in favor of incorporated power and greed . . . since the Dartmouth College case." In fact, the Court did take a narrow and mechanical view of interstate commerce. On that premise, its decision reflected a long-held distinction between state regulation of manufacturing and federal responsibility for interstate commerce. When private parties brought suit against trade and price cartels (particularly by those prime instances of enterprises in interstate commerce, the railroads), the Supreme Court was not reluctant to find that they violated the Sherman Act.

By the turn of the century it was apparent that the problem of corporate regulation was "rapidly assuming phases which seem beyond the scope of courts of justice." The rise of corporate capitalism, and the question of what to do about it, called as much for political-administrative will and wisdom as for legal-constitutional power and propriety.

The primary legal and, ultimately, constitutional justification for late nineteenth-century state regulation was the police power: the obligation of the states to protect the health, morals, safety, and welfare of their citizens. Many thought that the potential of that power was great indeed. The president of the American Bar Association estimated in 1897 that more than ninety percent of state legislation rested on the police power. CHRISTOPHER TIEDEMAN's *Limitations of the Police Power in the United States* (1886) was an elaborate attempt to find constitutional grounds for containing what he took to be a widely applied principle of government intervention. OLIVER WENDELL HOLMES caustically said of the police power: "We suppose the phrase was invented to cover certain acts of the legislature which are seen to be unconstitutional, but which are believed to be necessary."

The police power had its greatest appeal when public health and morals appeared to be at stake. A case in point was regulation of the liquor business. The Supreme Court upheld the right of the states to forbid the manufacture and sale of alcohol, and refused to accept the due process clause of the Fourteenth Amendment as a defense against state liquor legislation. (See INALIENABLE POLICE POWER.) Still more dramatic was judicial acceptance of extensive regulation—indeed, the near-crippling—of the oleomargarine industry. By 1886, twenty-two states either heavily taxed that product or required unattractive packaging or labeling. An 1886 federal law—"protection run mad," said an outraged critic—required that the product be called "oleo" (rather than "butterine" or other enticing names), and subjected it to a high license and manufacturing tax. The Supreme Court in *Powell v. Pennsylvania* (1888) upheld a similar Pennsylvania statute on the basis of the state's police power to protect public health.

The insufficiency of the state police power as a basis of state economic regulation became more and more apparent as the century neared its end. Corporate interests effectively espoused a laissez-faire, SUBSTANTIVE DUE PROCESS constitutionalism. More fundamentally, courts recognized the growing imbalance between state supervision and an economy that was becoming national in scope.

By 1899 the Supreme Court had held twenty-nine state laws unconstitutional because they conflicted with the commerce clause of the Constitution. In LEISY V. HARDIN (1890) the Court voided an Iowa law blocking the entry of liquor into the state, holding that the movement of an original package was protected by the national commerce power, so long as Congress had not authorized the state regulation. Responding to this invitation, Congress quickly passed the Wilson Act, which made liquor subject to state law regardless of where it was packaged. The Court validated the law on the grounds that "the common interest did not require entire freedom in the traffic in ardent spirits." But without similar congressional authorization, it continued to apply the original package doctrine against state laws restricting the entry of oleomargarine and cigarettes. And in CHAMPION V. AMES (1903) the Court upheld a statute forbidding the interstate transportation of lottery tickets, thus opening the prospect of NATIONAL POLICE POWER.

The constraints that limited the application of government authority to economic problems were at least as evident in the realm of social policy. During the period of the Civil War and Reconstruction, citizenship and race had been issues of prime importance not only in constitutional law but in politics and legislation as well. In the twentieth century these and other social concerns—education, crime, poverty, social mores, CIVIL LIBERTIES—would draw comparable attention from the public, Congress, and the courts. But such was not the case during the years between 1871 and 1900. With American society in transit from its small-unit agrarian past to its large-unit urban, industrial future, the political or constitutional standing of individual or social rights was largely ignored.

These years saw relatively little redefinition—in either constitutional law or legislative action—of the status of women, Orientals, blacks, or AMERICAN INDIANS. Legal barriers to female equality occasionally fell, but by legislation, not constitutional adjudication. Opposition to women's suffrage remained strong. Between 1870 and 1910 suffrage advocates conducted 480 campaigns in thirty-three states to get the issue on the ballot. Seventeen state REFERENDA (all but three west of the Mississippi) were held; only two were successful, in Colorado in 1893 and in Idaho in 1896.

The position of Orientals and blacks in society worsened. Organized labor agitated for the exclusion of Chinese immigrants, and anti-Chinese riots in the West testified to the intensity of public feeling. An 1882 federal law banned Chinese immigration for ten years. Supplementary acts in 1884 and 1888 tightened the exclusion law and imposed restrictions on Chinese already in the country. The Supreme Court in 1887 refused to apply the Civil Rights and Enforcement Acts of the Reconstruction period to Chinese, and in 1889 the Court upheld the restriction of Chinese immigration.

In 1892 Congress overwhelmingly renewed Chinese exclusion for another decade; it also required the registration of every resident Chinese laborer, with affidavits by one or more whites that the registrant had entered the country legally. The Supreme Court upheld this law in 1893. These policies had palpable consequences. About 100,000 lawful Chinese immigrants were in the United States in 1880; there were about 85,000 in 1900. In 1902 Chinese immigration was suspended indefinitely.

An even more pervasive white public opinion supported—or at least remained unconcerned about—discrimination against blacks. Late nineteenth-century northern courts generally upheld state laws that forbade discrimination in theaters, restaurants, and other public places, as a proper exercise of the police power. (The degree to which those laws were enforced is another matter.) But on similar grounds the courts accepted the growing number of SEGREGATION statutes. State laws separating the races in public transportation and accommodation, forbidding racial intermarriage, limiting access to the vote, and segregating schools met with no judicial obstacle.

In this sense the Supreme Court's acceptance of a Louisiana railroad segregation law in PLESSY V. FERGUSON (1896) represented the approval of an already widely established public policy, not the promulgation of new constitutional doctrine. When in 1903 the Court refused to agree that the Fifteenth Amendment might be used against Alabama officials who kept blacks from voting, Holmes suggested that relief "from a great political wrong" must come from "the legislative and political department of the government of the United States." At the same time the Court's invention of the STATE ACTION limitation on congressional power encouraged Congress to refrain from remedying private RACIAL DISCRIMINATION. (See CIVIL RIGHTS CASES, 1883.)

On the face of things, Indian public policy in the late nineteenth century had a different goal: it sought not to foster but to reduce separatism. Indian Commissioner Thomas J. Morgan declared in 1891: "The end at which we aim is that the American Indians shall become as speedily as possible Indian-Americans; that the savage shall become a citizen." But majority sentiment still regarded even nontribal Indians as inferior, and the Supreme Court went along. In *Elk v. Wilkins* (1884)—coterminous with the CIVIL RIGHTS CASES that invalidated the CIVIL RIGHTS ACT OF 1875—the Court held that Indians were not citizens within the understanding of the Fourteenth Amendment.

At the end of the century the acquisition of noncontiguous territory with substantial populations (Hawaii, the Philippines, Puerto Rico) raised old problems of statehood and citizenship in new forms. The Supreme Court in the INSULAR CASES (1901) limited the degree to which the Constitution applied to these peoples, much as the Court had been inclined to do with regard to Orientals, blacks, and Indians.

In most of the areas of social policy—education, crime, FIRST AMENDMENT freedoms—that in the twentieth century became important battlegrounds of public policy and constitutional law, there was little or no late nineteenth-century constitutional controversy. Only two such issues—prohibition and religion—raised substantial questions of constitutionality. New Hampshire Senator Henry W. Blair first proposed a national prohibition amendment to the Constitution in 1876, and a proposal to this effect was before Congress continuously until its adoption in 1918. State and local restrictions on the distribution and sale of liquor increased, and in general the courts sustained them against Fourteenth Amendment attacks, as proper applications of the police power.

The place of RELIGION IN THE PUBLIC SCHOOLS led to much political and legal conflict. State courts frequently dealt with the thorny issue of school Bible reading. Most states allowed this practice without exegesis, and the courts approved so long as attendance or participation was voluntary. The Iowa Supreme Court upheld a law that forbade the exclusion of Bible reading from the schools. But the Wisconsin court denied the constitutionality of such reading: "The connection of church and state corrupts religion, and makes the state despotic."

Protestant–Roman Catholic hostility underlay much of the conflict over school Bible reading, as it did the issue of state aid to parochial schools. Maine Republican James G. Blaine sought a constitutional amendment forbidding aid in the 1870s (see BLAINE AMENDMENT), and by 1900 twenty-three states had banned public grants to parochial schools. But the interrelationship of religion and education did not come before the Supreme Court until well into the twentieth century.

FELIX FRANKFURTER once told of a distinguished professor of property law who was called on to teach a course in constitutional law. Dutifully he did so. But he soon abandoned the effort, on the ground that the subject was "not law at all but politics." At no time in American history did this pronouncement seem more justified than in the period from 1877 to 1901. Except for the regulation of large enterprise, Americans debated the problems of a developing industrial society more in political than in constitutional terms. After 1900 the fit—or lack of fit—between those problems and the American constitutional system would be faced more directly.

MORTON KELLER

Bibliography

BETH, LOREN P. 1971 *The Development of the American Constitution 1877–1917.* New York: Harper & Row.

GRAHAM, HOWARD J. 1968 *Everyman's Constitution: Historical Essays on the Fourteenth Amendment, The 'Conspiracy Theory,' and American Constitutionalism.* Chaps. 10–13. Madison, Wisc.: State Historical Society.

KELLER, MORTON 1977 *Affairs of State: Public Life in Late Nineteenth Century America.* Cambridge, Mass.: Harvard University Press.

PAUL, ARNOLD M. 1960 *Conservative Crisis and the Rule of Law.* Ithaca, N.Y.: Cornell University Press.

SKOWRONEK, STEPHEN 1982 *Building a New American State: The Expansion of National Administrative Capacities 1877–1920.* Cambridge: At the University Press.

CONSTITUTIONAL HISTORY, 1901–1921

American public life profoundly changed during the early twentieth century. The policy agenda during the Progressive era stands in dramatic contrast, both quantitatively and qualitatively, to its nineteenth-century predecessors. A substantial body of state and national legislation sought to subject large corporations and public utilities to far greater regulation than had been the case before. A comparable surge of enactments dealt with social issues ranging from the hours and working conditions of women and children to housing, the quality of food and drugs, the conservation of land, and the control of drinking and prostitution.

More than at any time since the Civil War and Reconstruction, Americans paid substantial attention to the structure of their government. The pace of lawmaking that dealt with politics and government quickened, stimulated by the dual motives (not always complementary) of expanding popular democracy and of bringing greater honesty and efficiency to the workings of the American state. A burst of innovation led to the creation of direct PRIMARY ELECTIONS, the INITIATIVE and REFERENDUM, and new registration and voting laws, as well as to the direct election of senators and to women's suffrage. A flood of discussion and a lesser flow of administrative, judicial, and legislative action sought to increase the effectiveness of the executive branch and the BUREAUCRACY, to improve the workings of Congress and the functioning of the courts, and to modernize the relationship between federal and state authorities and the governance of the nation's cities.

American involvement in World War I was the capstone to the Progressive era. Federal involvement in the American economy and society reached new heights; and in both technique and spirit wartime governance drew heavily on the immediate prewar experience.

THEODORE ROOSEVELT, WILLIAM HOWARD TAFT, and WOODROW WILSON were far more activist than their predecessors both in leadership styles and in domestic and foreign policy. But perhaps the most dramatic result of the quickened pace of government and the new policy agenda was the adoption between 1913 and 1920 of four constitutional amendments, providing for a federal income tax, the direct election of senators, PROHIBITION, and women's suffrage. Only at the beginning of the Republic and during the Reconstruction era had constitutional revision occurred on so large a scale.

Insofar as there was a common denominator to the public policy of the Progressive era, it lay in the belief that the time had come to deal with some of the more chaotic and unjust aspects of a mature industrial society; to bring public policy (and the nation's political and governing institutions) into closer accord with new social and economic realities. This impulse cannot be simply explained away by the once fashionable label of "reform," or the now fashionable label of "social control." A quest for social justice coexisted in complex ways with a search for order. Some Progressives wanted society (and the polity) to be more efficient: more honest and economical, less wasteful and corrupt. Others sought policies that would make society safer: more secure from the threats of big business and corrupt political machines, or from the vagaries of competition and the business cycle, or from radicals, immigrants, or blacks. Still others wanted society to be fairer: more humane and less inequitable.

This was not solely an American development.

H. G. Wells observed in 1906 that "the essential question for America, as for Europe, is the rescue of her land, her public service, and the whole of her great economic process from the anarchic and irresponsible control of private owners . . . and the organization of her social life upon the broad, clear, humane conceptions of modern science."

Could it be said that a substantially changed constitutional order was one consequence of American Progressivism? Did the complex structure of ECONOMIC REGULATION embodied in the Interstate Commerce Commission, enforcement of the SHERMAN ACT, the Federal Trade Commission, railroad regulation, and a host of other economic measures fundamentally alter the relationship of the state to the economy? Did the interventionism embodied in the growing body of social legislation, accumulating restrictions on IMMIGRATION, the CIVIL LIBERTIES onslaught of the war years, and the passage of national prohibition fundamentally alter the relationship of government to American society and the individual rights of its citizens? Did the sequence of interventionist foreign policy actions, delimited at one end by the acquisition of overseas colonies after the Spanish-American War of 1898, and at the other by American intervention in World War I, fundamentally alter the place of FOREIGN AFFAIRS in the American political order?

In sum, did the early twentieth-century outburst of legislation, executive leadership, new agencies, and new government functions lead to what has been called "a qualitatively different kind of state"? Did a corporate-bureaucratic system of government supplant the nineteenth-century American "state of courts and parties"? JOHN W. BURGESS held in 1923 that the past generation had seen the transformation of American constitutional law from a stress on the protection of individual liberty to the imposition of "autocratic" governmental power over property, persons, and thought.

The distinctive American style of government that took form during the first century of the nation's history rested on the balance and SEPARATION OF POWERS among the executive, legislative, and judicial branches; on a FEDERALISM that rendered (through the POLICE POWER) to the states the things that were social; and on a conception of individual rights that, for all its abuses and distortions (the sacrifice of southern blacks to the not-so-tender mercies of southern whites; the use of the DUE PROCESS clause of the FOURTEENTH AMENDMENT to spare CORPORATIONS the indignity of state regulation and taxation), arguably gave nineteenth-century Americans more individual freedom from the interposition of the state than any other people in the world. To what degree was that constitutional order changed between 1901 and 1921?

Of course there can be no definitive answer: the glass of change inevitably will remain partially filled for some, partially empty for others. But an obscure chapter in the constitutional history of the United States may come into clearer focus if we abandon the traditional historiographical emphasis on Progressive "reform" in favor of an examination of the major instrumentalities of government: Congress, the presidency, the bureaucracy, and the mechanisms governing federal–state relations.

Congress was the branch of government that underwent the most overt and formal alteration during the early twentieth century. Two major changes, the popular election of senators through the passage of the SEVENTEENTH AMENDMENT, and the reduction of the powers of the speaker of the House of Representatives, came about in these years. These changes were products of the widespread view that Congress, like the parties, was under the control of corrupt, machine-bound politicos and sinister business interests.

Six times between 1893 and 1911 the House approved a direct election amendment. Finally, spurred by an arrangement whereby progressive Republicans agreed to drop the cause of black voting in the South in return for southern Democratic support, the Senate accepted the change. The Southerners assured that control of the time, place, and manner of holding senatorial elections would remain the province of each state.

A 1911 law sought also to assure that congressional districts would be compact, contiguous, and of roughly equal populations. But enforcement was so difficult, and the courts were so loath to intervene, that it had little effect. And although the direct election of senators gradually reversed the tendency (at least until recent times) for the Senate to become a "millionaires's club," it cannot be said that that body's role in the governmental process was substantially different in the 1920s from what it had been before 1900.

The controversy over the House speaker's authority was more intense. Joseph G. Cannon, the speaker from 1901 to 1911, appointed and was himself one of the five-member Committee on Rules, thus controlling assignments to the key committees of the House, which he populated with like-thinking conservatives. His power to expedite the work of an unwieldy legislature had been a late-nineteenth-century reform, designed to keep a boss-ridden legislature from working its will. Now it appeared to a majority of congressmen as an obstacle to the more programmatic demands of Progressive government. In 1910–1911 a coalition of Democrats and insurgent Republicans deprived Cannon of his power to serve on and appoint the Rules Committee, to choose standing committees, and to recognize members on the floor.

The seniority system came into general use as a more equitable means of choosing committee chairmen—a "reform" of the sort that Finley Peter Dunne's Mr. Dooley presumably had in mind when he commented on the Progressive predilection for structural change: "I wisht I was a German, and believed in machinery." But by the 1920s the House was as much under the control of the majority party leadership as it had ever been. During most of the decade, the Republican speaker, rules committee chairman, and floor leader ran the GOP Steering Committee and, hence, Congress. Surely Cannon would have nodded approval of floor leader John G. Tilson's estimate of his role in the 69th Congress (1929): "It will probably be said with truth that the most important work I have done during the session has been in the direction of preventing the passage of bad or unnecessary laws."

Much of the constitutional controversy of the early twentieth century focused on the character of the presidency—and of the Presidents. The Spanish-American War and the governance of territories afterward gave WILLIAM MCKINLEY's administration some of the attributes of the modern presidency, and led to concern over "The Growing Power of the President." But it was the chief executives of the Progressive years who gave a dramatically new shape to the office.

Theodore Roosevelt's executive vigor, his flamboyant efforts to turn the presidency into a "bully pulpit," his concern with issues such as the relations between capital and labor, the trusts, and conservation, and his assertiveness in foreign policy gave his presidency a cast of radicalism. Critics often spoke of him—more so than of any president since ABRAHAM LINCOLN—as having stretched the Constitution to its limits and beyond. Roosevelt himself thought that the power of the presidency enabled him "to do anything that the needs of the nation demanded. . . . Under this interpretation of executive power, I did and caused to be done many things not previously done. . . . I did not usurp power, but I did greatly broaden the use of executive power." But Roosevelt's innate conservatism, the traditionalist goals that informed most of his actions, and his political skill meant that few of his initiatives ran into constitutional difficulties. The most serious congressional objections on constitutional grounds came in the debate over the HEPBURN ACT expanding the power of the Interstate Commerce Commission (ICC); and Roosevelt adroitly compromised by leaving untouched the courts' power to review the ICC's decisions.

A contemporary said that the difference between Roosevelt and his successor, William Howard Taft, was that when a desirable course of action was proposed to Roosevelt he asked if the law forbade it; if not, then it should be done. Taft, on the other hand, tended to ask if the law allowed it; if not, then Congress must be asked. Taft brought a judicial temperament and experience (and almost no elective experience) to his office. He was thus a more self-conscious advocate of a limited presidency, and celebrator of the supremacy of law and of constitutional limitations, than any of his Republican predecessors.

Yet these views did not prevent his administration from adopting a more vigorous antitrust policy than that of Roosevelt. And Taft advocated innovations such as the establishment of a COMMERCE COURT to review ICC decisions and the institution of a federal BUDGET drawn up by the executive branch. The realities of early-twentieth-century American public life weighed more heavily than the niceties of constitutional theory.

Woodrow Wilson as a scholar of American government had long been critical of the traditional relationship between President and Congress. He often praised the British system of ministerial responsibility; his ideal President resembled the British Prime Minister. But as chief executive Wilson more closely followed Roosevelt's conception of the presidency as a bully pulpit (though perhaps with less bullying and more pulpit-pounding). And even more than Roosevelt he took the lead in formulating and seeing to the passage of legislation, a course symbolized by his breaking a tradition that dated from the time of THOMAS JEFFERSON by personally proposing legislation in a message to Congress.

The scope and coherence of Wilson's legislation was far greater than that of his predecessors. But it is worth noting that of the numerous major bills passed in his administration, including the FEDERAL RESERVE ACT, the FEDERAL TRADE COMMISSION ACT, the CLAYTON ANTITRUST ACT, the WEBB-KENYON ACT, the ESPIONAGE ACT, and the SEDITION ACT, only the KEATING-OWEN CHILD LABOR ACT was struck down by the Supreme Court.

With the entry of the United States into World War I, Wilson assumed presidential leadership of a sort that had not been seen since the time of Lincoln and the Civil War. The mobilization of American agriculture, industry, military manpower, and public opinion led to federal intervention into private activity on a massive scale. The creation of agencies such as the War Industries Board, the Food, Fuel, and Railroad Administrations, the War Finance Corporation, the National War Labor Board, and the Committee on Public Information, and statutes such as the SELECTIVE SERVICE ACT, the ESPIONAGE ACT, the Webb-Pomerene Act (which allowed exporters to organize cartels), and the Overman Act (which greatly expanded the President's power over federal bureaus and agencies) amounted to an unprecedented increase of federal power and its concentration under the President.

Did these circumstances in fact add up to a basic change in the constitutional character of the presidency? Certainly the administrations of WARREN G. HARDING and CALVIN COOLIDGE did not suggest so: they would have been comfortable with the most ardent (and least efficacious) practitioners of the limited presidency of the nineteenth century. Nor did HERBERT HOOVER, whose ambitions resembled those of his Progressive predecessors, exercise effective executive leadership on a bold new scale. And when FRANKLIN D. ROOSEVELT came into office in the trough of the Depression in 1933, he found it necessary to rest his call for a "temporary departure from [the] normal balance" of "executive and legislative authority" on the need for a "broad executive power to wage a war against the emergency as great as the power that would be given me if we were in fact invaded by a foreign foe."

For all the pressures of early-twentieth-century social, economic, and cultural change, the executive branch's constitutional position altered little if at all. After 1921, as before 1900, the powers of the presidency depended not upon alterations in Article II of the Constitution, or upon what the Supreme Court made of that article, but on the political skills of the incumbent and on the course of events: war and peace, prosperity and depression, the growth and alteration of government itself.

The argument that the character of American government underwent major change during the early twentieth century rests on the rise of an administrative state. Certainly one distinguishing characteristic of this period was the proliferation of administrative courts, boards, and commissions, with an attendant expansion of the powers, rules, and regulations of the public administration sector of the American state.

The ideal of expert administrators functioning through (or above) restraints such as party politics, federalism, or the balance of powers had a strong appeal to the Progressive generation. Abbot Lawrence Lowell warned: "If democracy is to be conducted with the efficiency needed in a complex modern society it must overcome its prejudice against permanent expert officials as undemocratic."

The courts had performed a number of essentially administrative and regulatory duties during the nineteenth century. Now, as economic and social problems became more complex and technical, so grew routinized and prescribed administrative processes, in which rule replaced discretion in public law. State laws and constitutions became ever more detailed and codelike; state regulatory agencies multiplied and gained substantially in independence. Federal laws increasingly left to administrative officers the "power to make supplementary law through rules and regulations."

The American involvement in World War I led to an exponential growth of administrative agencies and their power. The War Industries Board and its allied commissions had control over the American economy of a sort only dreamed of in Theodore Roosevelt's New Nationalism. Under the wartime ESPIONAGE ACT, the Post Office Department, the Department of Justice, and the Committee on Public Information wielded powers of suppression and persuasion over American thought and opinion that had no analogue in the nation's past.

Just where administrative law and its accompanying instrumentalities stood in the constitutional system was a matter of continuing concern. Woodrow Wilson observed in his pioneering 1887 essay "The Study of Administration" that "the field of administration is a field of business. It is removed from the hurry and strife of politics; it at most points stands apart even from the debatable ground of constitutional study." But administration was political in its relationship to law, to policy, and to interest group pressures; and it had an intimate relationship to—indeed, was very much a part of—the constitutional system of American government. In many ways the history of American public administration between 1900 and 1921 was a painful instruction in those home truths.

Administrative law of a sort had been part of the American constitutional system since the nineteenth century. Pensions, customs, internal revenue, land grants, and patents were administered by governmental agencies subject to little or no JUDICIAL REVIEW. There was continuing resistance to the idea that public administration had a distinct place in the constitutional order. Bruce Wyman, in one of the earliest systematic discussions of administrative law, set the subject in the context of Anglo-American COMMON LAW rather than constitutional law, holding that the central issue was whether public administration was subject to the same rules of law as governed the relations of citizens with one another.

Adolph Berle took another tack, arguing that administrative law was in fact the application of the will of the state by all three branches, for modern conditions made the traditional differentiation of functions impossible. Administrative law's constitutionality, he implied, rested on the proposition that all of the branches of government were essentially instruments for the expression of the popular will. Thus administrative law was "not a supplement to constitutional law. It is a redivision of the various bodies of law which previously had been grouped under the head of constitutional law."

The courts created evasive categories—"quasi-legislative," "quasi-judicial"—which enabled them to accept administrative powers without addressing the question of whether or not these threatened the separation of powers. By 1914 it appeared that "the exercise of certain discretionary power by administrative officers formally considered legislative is now held unobjectionable."

The growth of the federal bureaucracy, its increasing adherence to its own norms and standards, the fact that it was more and more under the civil service rather than political patronage—all of this has been taken to herald the arrival on the American scene of an autonomous administrative state. But the continuing subservience of government and public policy to the dictates of party politics, the competing governmental units of Congress and the courts, and underlying it all the persisting individualism, hostility to the state, and diversity of American life and thought, meant that the administrative expansion of the early twentieth century did not go on unchecked.

During the war, and immediately after, a number of intellectuals put forward schemes of postwar domestic economic and social reconstruction; they thought that the wartime infrastructure of governmental control and direction might be turned to more basic postwar problems. It soon became apparent, however, that both ideology and politics were working in another direction. Wilson himself told Congress in December 1918: "Our people . . . do not want to be coached and led. . . . [f]rom no quarter have I seen any general scheme of 'reconstruction' which . . . we could force our spirited businessmen and self conscious laborers to accept with due pliancy and obedience."

Similar forces worked to constrain the outward reach of postwar foreign policy embodied in the League of Nations. Both courts and legislatures after the mid-1920s began to turn from the radical-bashing of the Espionage Acts and the 1919–1920 Red Scare to begin the erection of the broad definition of FIRST AMENDMENT freedoms that would come to prevail in the modern American definition of civil liberties. A 1918 survey of American ADMINISTRATIVE LAW (probably by the young HAROLD LASKI, surely no enemy of the active state) warned that "with the great increase of state activity . . . there never was a time" when the value of the BILL OF RIGHTS "will have been so manifest."

As in so many other areas of American government, surface changes did not necessarily alter underlying continuities. Congressmen and party leaders may no longer have had the patronage power that once had been theirs. Yet Congress as an institution, and congressmen as party politicians, remained intensely sensitive to the political implications of administrative appointments, activities, and, perhaps most of all, budgets.

Attempts by the Presidents of the time to extend the control of the executive branch over the bureaucracy frequently ran afoul of congressional opposition. By 1921 it was an arguable point—as, indeed, it always had been—whether the bureaucracy was more subject to the direction of the President or to the will of Congress. One thing was certain: the autonomy of the bureaucracy—from Congress, from the parties, from politics—was not markedly greater than it had been a generation before.

True, administrative law as a field of theoretical concern and practical application would continue to develop. The New Deal did not spring fully armed from the brow of Franklin Roosevelt, but was built on a solid foundation of national and state precedents. From an international (and a later American) perspective, the New Deal's experiments did not seem especially bold and revolutionary. But the scale and passion of the charges of a broached constitutionalism raised by the New Deal's opponents in the 1930s suggests just how limited was the pre-1933 acceptance of an American administrative state.

One more aspect of the evolution (or non-evolution) of the American Constitution during the early twentieth century demands attention. That is the hoary principle of federalism: the distribution of functions between the state and federal governments.

In theory the Civil War and the postwar amendments had settled the nagging early-nineteenth-century question as to the degree to which the states were independent governmental entities. Relatively little attention was paid to the question of federalism during the late nineteenth century, in large part because the issues that most engaged the national government—tariff and currency policy, foreign relations, Indian affairs—were of marginal concern to the states. But as the full force of industrialism and urbanism began to change public policy in the early twentieth century, the relative roles of the federal and state governments once again became a matter of constitutional importance. The police power over health, safety, morals, and (from the late nineteenth century on) welfare, was the major legal basis for state social and economic legislation. For the most part the court accepted this; as ZECHARIAH CHAFEE, JR., observed in 1920, "The health, comfort, and general welfare of the citizens are in charge of the state governments, not of the United States."

But of the 194 Supreme Court decisions that invalidated state laws between 1899 and 1921, 102 were explained on the ground that the laws violated the distribution of powers embodied in the principle of federalism. By the 1920s and the early 1930s there was much talk of a judicial DUAL FEDERALISM that had created a "twilight zone" in which neither state nor federal power applied. And the attempt of the New Deal to create a new level of national intervention in the realms of economic regulation and social welfare led to one of the great constitutional controversies in American history. Once again, it would appear that the policy changes of the 1900–1921 period were not accompanied by a significant alteration of the constitutional order.

MORTON KELLER

Bibliography

BERLE, A. A., JR. 1916–1917 The Expansion of American Administrative Law. *Harvard Law Review* 30:430–448.

BETH, LOREN 1971 *The Development of the American Constitution 1877–1917.* New York: Harper & Row.

BLUM, JOHN M. 1954 *The Republican Roosevelt.* Cambridge, Mass.: Harvard University Press.

BURGESS, JOHN W. 1923 *Recent Changes in American Constitutional Theory.* New York: Columbia University Press.

HASBROUCH, PAUL D. 1927 *Party Government in the House of Representatives.* New York.

LOWELL, A. LAWRENCE 1913 Expert Administrators in Popular Government. *American Political Science Review* 7:45–62.

NOTE 1915 Delegation of Legislative Power to Administrative Officials. *Harvard Law Review* 28:95–97.

NOTE 1918 The Growth of Administrative Law in America. *Harvard Law Review* 31:644–646.

SKOWRONEK, STEPHEN 1982 *Building a New American State: The Expansion of National Administrative Capacities, 1877–1920.* Cambridge: At the University Press.

WYMAN, BRUCE 1903 *The Principles of Administrative Law Governing the Relations of Public Officers.* St. Paul, Minn.: Keefe-Davidson Co.

CONSTITUTIONAL HISTORY, 1921–1933

If reverence for the federal Constitution had diminished in the Progressive era, it was revitalized in the 1920s, as the Constitution again became a symbol of national unity and patriotism. Organizations such as the American Bar Association and the National Security League launched national campaigns of patriotism, circulating leaflets and pamphlets by the hundreds of thousands, encouraging Constitution worship, promoting an annual Constitution Day, and working for state laws to require Constitution instruction in the public schools. Forty-three states passed laws mandating the study of the the Constitution; often such laws required loyalty oaths for teachers. Such laws were intended to affirm one hundred percent Americanism from every public school instructor.

The Constitution which was so apotheosized, however, was one geared primarily to the service of property interests. This meant, on the one hand, the protection of business from government regulation and from assault by radical and liberal critics; and, on the other, active intervention of courts and the executive branch to see that constitutional ways were found to insure that the free use of one's property be protected by positive government policies, both formal and informal. Thus, while constitutional changes did occur during the decade and new emphases were developed, these modulations were contained within the dominant ideological construct of free enterprise and individual property rights—rights, it was argued, that had been secured for all time by the sacred document and its amendments.

The most influential constitutionalist of the 1920s was Chief Justice WILLIAM HOWARD TAFT. Taft set the tone for national political leadership. He was fully committed to the protection of a social order explained and justified by the tenets of JOHN LOCKE, Adam Smith, the Manchester Economists, WILLIAM BLACKSTONE, THOMAS COOLEY, and Herbert Spencer. Espousing a social ethic that stressed self-reliance, individual initiative and responsibility, and the survival of the fittest, Taft emphasized the virtually uninhibited privilege of private property and rationalized the growth of corporate collectivism in terms of individual liberty and private enterprise. For Taft it was time to move away from Progressive expansivism and restore the country to its traditional constitutional bases through a legal system that rested primarily upon judicial defense of a static Constitution and an immutable natural law.

In specific constitutional terms, these goals required restrictive, although selectively restrictive, interpretations of the federal government's taxing and commerce power; an emphasis upon the TENTH AMENDMENT as an instrument for precluding federal intrusion into the reserved powers of the states; and a limitation on the states themselves, through an interpretation of the FOURTEENTH AMENDMENT that emphasized SUBSTANTIVE DUE PROCESS and FREEDOM OF CONTRACT. These constitutional constructs would protect property against restrictive state laws but leave the states free through their police power to legislate against private activities that might threaten that property.

Operating from these assumptions, the Supreme Court majority in this period was activist in its hostility to legislative enactments that threatened or constrained the rights or privileges of the "haves" of society. Thus, between 1921 and 1933, that body ruled unconstitutional fourteen acts of Congress, 148 state laws placing governmental restraints on one or another form of business activity, and twelve city ordinances. Conversely, its majority had no trouble sustaining federal measures that aided business and sanctioning numerous state laws and city ordinances that abridged the CIVIL LIBERTIES of labor, radicals, too outspoken pacifists, and other critics of the capitalist system. In 1925, Taft took the further step of lobbying through Congress a new JUDICIARY ACT, granting the Supreme Court almost unlimited discretion to decide for itself what cases it would hear. (See CERTIORARI, WRIT OF.) Henceforth the Court could choose to take no more cases than it could handle expediently and could restrict adjudication to matters of more general interest. The result was an upgrading of the importance of the cases that the body did agree to hear and a commensurate enhancement of the Court's own prestige and power. Such a looming judicial presence dampened the enthusiasm of activist legislators, state and national, for pushing social reform legislation and made progressive members of REGULATORY COMMISSIONS cautious about exercising their frequently limited authority. Hence bodies such as the Interstate Commerce Commission and the Federal Trade Commission remained largely passive during the period, except when their business-oriented majorities sought to act solicitiously toward those being regulated.

The three presidential administrations of the period, while sharing a common constitutional philosophy, differed in concrete legislative and policy accomplishments. WARREN G. HARDING had begun his presidency with an ambitious legislative docket. His proposals included a National BUDGET AND ACCOUNTING ACT (previously vetoed by WOODROW WILSON), a new farm credit law, the creation of a system of national highways, the enactment of a Maternity Bill, the immediate development and effective regulation of aviation and radio, the passing of an antilynching law, and the creation of a Department of Public Welfare. A surprised Congress was confused over priorities and wound up passing little legislation. The PACKERS AND STOCKYARDS ACT of 1921 made it unlawful for packers to manipulate prices, create monopolies, and award favors to any person or locality. The regulation of stockyards provided for nondiscriminatory services, reasonable rates, open schedules, and fair charges. The measure, which was constitutionally based on a broad interpretation of the COMMERCE CLAUSE, gave the secretary of agriculture authority to entertain complaints, hold hearings, and issue CEASE AND DESIST ORDERS. The bill was a significant part of the agrarian legislation of the early 1920s, and its validation by the Supreme Court in STAFFORD V. WALLACE (1922) provided a constitutional basis for later New Deal legislation. The 1921 Congress also passed the FESS-KENYON ACT, appropriating money for disabled veteran rehabilitation, and the SHEPPARD-TOWNER MATERNITY ACT, subsidizing state infant and maternity welfare activities. Aside from the bill setting up a Budget Bureau in the Treasury Department with a director appointed by the President, little else was forthcoming. By the end of 1921 the *New York Times* observed: "It is evident, and it is clearly admitted in Washington, that the public is not counting any longer upon sound and constructive legislation from Congress." Indeed, Congress supported only occasional further legislation through the decade. One effect of such congressional inaction, along with the increasingly desultory Harding leadership and the even more quiescent CALVIN COOLIDGE presidency, was to direct the attention of reformers to the AMENDING PROCESS.

The immediate post-World War I years had seen the ratification of the EIGHTEENTH AMENDMENT (prohibition) and the NINETEENTH AMENDMENT (woman suffrage). In the 1920s certain fallout from both occurred. Prohibition was unpopular from the start. In fact, noncompliance became such a problem that by the late 1920s President HERBERT HOOVER appointed a special commission, headed by former Attorney General GEORGE WICKERSHAM to "investigate problems of the enforcement of prohibition under the 18th Amendment." As the report of the commission stated, "the public was irritated at a constitutional 'don't' in a matter where the people saw no moral question." More specifically, the commission pointed to enforcement problems, emphasizing the lack of an American tradition of concerned action between independent government instrumentalities. This, it felt, was now being painfully demonstrated by the Eighteenth Amendment's policy of state enforcement of federal laws, with responsibility too often falling between the two stools and enforcement occurring not at all. Not surprisingly, during the twelve years that the Eighteenth Amendment was in force, more than 130 amendments affecting the Eighteenth in some manner were introduced. Most of these amendments provided for outright repeal; others weakened the amendment in varying degrees. When FRANKLIN D. ROOSEVELT opposed prohibition in 1932, he attracted wide support. The TWENTY-FIRST AMENDMENT repealing the Eighteenth was ratified in December 1933, although prohibition's legal residue took some years to settle. (This measure came only nine months after passage of the relatively uncontroversial TWENTIETH AMENDMENT, eliminating the "lame duck" session of Congress and changing the time for the inauguration of presidents from March to January).

The momentum that carried woman suffrage to a successful amendment continued to some degree into the early 1920s. Some feminist leaders continued to push for improved working conditions for women, for minimum wage laws, and for laws bettering the legal status of women in marriage and DIVORCE. In 1922, Congress passed the Cable Act, providing that a married woman would thereafter retain and determine her own citizenship and make her own application for naturalization after lawful admission for permanent residence, which the Act reduced to three years. Supporters of the political emancipation of women, especially the National Women's Party, got the EQUAL RIGHTS AMENDMENT (ERA) introduced in Congress in 1923 and worked for its adoption by lobbying and exerting political pressure in the early years of the decade. At that time the ERA was opposed by most of the large women's organizations, by trade unions, and by the Women's Bureau primarily because it was seen as a threat to labor-protective legislation. Opponents contended that the ERA would deprive most working women and the poor of hard-won economic gains and would mainly benefit middle and upper class women. Thus the measure floundered at the time, not to be revived until toward the end of World War II. The same period saw all native-born American Indians granted full citizenship through the Curtis Act of 1924. The measure, however, did not automatically entitle them to vote, and some states still disfranchised Indians as "persons under guardianship." In 1925 Congress passed the Federal Corrupt Practices Act, extending federal regulation of political corruption to the choice of presidential electors.

A CHILD LABOR AMENDMENT fared only slightly better. With the Supreme Court striking down federal child labor laws as unconstitutional under both the commerce and the taxing powers, advocates of children's rights turned to the amending process and Congress adopted a proposed Child Labor Amendment in June 1924. Opposed by manufacturers' associations and certain religious groups, the measure, by 1930, had secured ratification in only five states. More than three-fourths had rejected it, with the greatest hostility coming from the south and from agricultural regions, where child labor was seen as essential to family economic stability. The measure was eventually superseded by the FAIR LABOR STANDARDS ACT of 1938. By that time the evils of child exploitation were no longer felt to be beyond the constitutional reach of federal legislative power.

Other amendments were proposed: providing minimum wages for women; establishing uniform national marriage and divorce laws; giving the president an item veto in appropriation bills; abolishing congressional immunity for speeches and debates in either house; providing representation for the DISTRICT OF COLUMBIA; changing the amending process itself; providing for the election of judges; providing for the independence of the Philippine Islands; prohibiting sectarian legislation; defining the right of states to regulate employment of ALIENS; requiring teachers to take an oath of allegiance; preventing governmental competition with private enterprise; conferring upon the House of Representatives coordinate power for the ratification of treaties; limiting the wealth of individual citizens; providing for legislation by INITIATIVE; extending the civil service merit system; regulating industry; and prohibiting loans to any except allies. Varying support for all reflected, to a greater or lesser degree, public discontent with aspects of the political-constitutional system of the time. A segment of this discontent crystallized in the La Follette Progressive Party's 1924 platform, which even proposed the RECALL of judges, much to the alarm and ire of Chief Justice Taft. Such straws in the wind did not, however, portend a successful assault upon property-oriented constitutional interpretation. That assault would await the depths of the Depression.

The middle to later years of the decade saw continued congressional hostility to government interference in economic and personal activities, but no reluctance to use power when the result supported President Coolidge's aphorism that "the business of America is business." Antilynching legislation failed during the decade; northern conservatives joined white southerners in deploring it as an assault upon STATES' RIGHTS and individual freedom. In 1927, Congress enacted the McNary-Haugen Farm Bill, an elaborate measure calling for federal support for agricultural prices. The measure countered the prevailing temper of constitutional conservatism, for it extended national regulatory authority over agricultural PRODUCTION and thus not only invaded a sphere of authority traditionally reserved to the states but also interfered extensively with private property rights. President Coolidge vetoed the measure, denouncing it as "economically and constitutionally unsound." When Congress persisted, he vetoed a second McNary-Haugen Bill the following year on the same grounds.

Somewhat similar antistatist sentiments emerged when, in 1925, newly appointed Attorney General HARLAN FISKE STONE took the Bureau of Investigation out of politics and terminated its pursuit of radicals. "There is always the possibility," Stone stated in taking the action, "that a secret police may become a menace to free government and free institutions because it carries with it the possibility of abuses of power which are not always quickly apprehended or understood. The Bureau . . . is not concerned with political or other opinions of individuals. It is concerned with their conduct, and then only with such conduct as is forbidden by the laws of the United States." Store's action was popular with all but some patriotic and right-wing groups for whom radical, or even unorthodox, ideas were a threat which the government did have a responsibility actively to check.

On the other hand, Congress met little opposition when it enacted a broad, restrictive IMMIGRATION Act in 1924 imposing stringent quotas on entry to the United States, heavily biased against southern and eastern European and Asiatic peoples. Such action was consonant with the strong tendency of the courts in the period to define the rights of aliens narrowly, with an eye to keeping such people in their proper place, particularly as easily exploitable members of the work force.

To the extent that an alternative constitutional tradition existed or was developed in the 1920s, its impact was not fully felt until Depression days. There were undertones of protest, however, coming from disparate sources. Justice LOUIS D. BRANDEIS, in his dissent in *Gilbert v. Minnesota* (1920), a decision sustaining a sedition conviction for criticism of the government's wartime policies, had stated: "I cannot believe that liberty guaranteed by the Fourteenth Amendment includes only liberty to acquire and to enjoy property." Others quickly picked up on the contradiction in this double standard, particularly when the same "liberty" was not then deemed applicable to FREEDOM OF SPEECH, FREEDOM OF THE PRESS, and FREEDOM OF ASSEMBLY. The AMERICAN CIVIL LIBERTIES UNION (ACLU), a product of the war, itself an opponent of strong government intervention in people's personal lives, worked through the decade to strengthen the power of labor and working people. The ACLU operated on the assumption that BILL OF RIGHTS freedoms flowed from economic power and that artificial impediments to the achievement of that power had to be removed. The National Association for the Advancement of Colored People was active in the decade in behalf of the constitutional rights of minorities, although its successes in producing constitutional change were decidedly limited. Similarly, organized labor saw itself as a beleaguered "minority" throughout the decade, attributing its position partly to conservation constitutionalism. Samuel Gompers stated shortly before his death: "The Courts have abolished the Constitution as far as the rights and interest of the working people are concerned."

The impact of such criticism ultimately was not so great as that from popularly elected constitutional liberals and an influential segment of the legal community. Senators William E. Borah and GEORGE NORRIS openly opposed the appointment of CHARLES EVANS HUGHES to the Chief Justiceship, arguing that there was a need for judges who would stop treating the Fourteenth Amendment only as a protection of property and recognize it as a guarantee of individual liberty. Although this opposition failed, partly because of Hughes's constitutional record and the public image of him as more progressive than reactionary, the Senate did block the subsequent nomination of John J. Parker, a prominent North Carolina Republican, to the Supreme Court in 1930; opponents particularly emphasized his racist and antilabor record. Both actions constituted unignorable Depression calls for constitutional liberalization, echoed increasingly by liberal lawyers, particularly in the law schools, many of which has been influenced by the LEGAL REALISM movement of the times. Such criticism combined with growing disillusionment with the business establishment and cynicism about a Supreme Court that could be aggressively activist in the protection of property rights and a paragon of self-restraint when it came to protecting human rights. Pressure for altered uses of government power mounted fairly early in Depression days.

Herbert Hoover was undoubtedly the most competent of the 1920s Presidents. A successful mining engineer and government bureaucrat, he had served effectively as war-time food administrator under Woodrow Wilson and as secretary of commerce in the Harding and Coolidge administrations. Hoover was eager to overhaul the executive branch of the government and reorganize it in ways that would achieve greater efficiency and greater economies in government. Saddled quickly with the worst depression in American history, Hoover was pressed to launch a large-scale national attack on the depression through federal governmental action. Such action had to fit his constitutional views, which were decidedly Taftian. For Hoover, "unless the enterprise system operated free from popular controls, constitutional freedoms would die." "Under the Constitution it was impossible to attempt the solution of certain modern social problems by legislation." "Constitutional change must be brought about only by the straightforward methods provided by the Constitution itself." Such a commitment to laissez faire economics and constitutional conservatism precluded sweeping federal actions and permitted only such remedial legislation as the AGRICULTURAL MARKETING ACT of 1929, designed to assist in the more effective marketing of agricultural commodities. Congress created the Reconstruction Finance Corporation in 1932 to rescue commercial, industrial, and financial institutions through direct government loans. Both measures so limited the scope of permissible federal activity that neither proved adequate to the challenge of providing successful depression relief.

A more specific example of Hoover's constitutionalism involved congressional enactment of the Muscle Shoals Bill of 1931. In 1918 President Wilson had authorized, as a war-time measure, the construction of government plants at Muscle Shoals on the Tennessee River for the manufacture of nitrates and of dams to generate electric power. After the war the disposition of these plants and dams produced bitter national controversy. Conservatives insisted that they be turned over to private enterprise. Congress twice enacted measures providing for government ownership and operation for the production and distribution of power and the manufacture of fertilizers. In vetoing the second of these bills (Coolidge had vetoed the first in 1928), Hoover reiterated his belief that government ownership and operation was an approach to socialism designed to break down the initiative and enterprise of the American people. He argued that such a measure was an unconstitutional federal entrance into the field of powers reserved to the states and as such deprived the people of local communities of their liberty.

A growing number of congressmen and senators, however, were convinced that such constitutional negativism was no longer useful. In 1932, Congress passed and sent to a reluctant President the NORRIS-LAGUARDIA ACT, probably the most important measure of the period. Ever since the 1890s, labor had protested against business's turn to the courts for INJUNCTIONS to prohibit its legitimate activities. Congress's only response was a Railway Labor Act, in 1926, giving railway labor the right to bargain collectively through its own representatives. By the late 1920s, a national campaign against the labor INJUNCTION was launched with liberal congressional leaders joined by groups as disparate as the ACLU, the Federal Council of Churches, and the American Federation of Labor, all protesting the unfairness and unconstitutionality of enjoining labor's legitimate use of speech, press, and assembly. The Great Depression intensified this discontent. The Norris-LaGuardia Act made YELLOW DOG CONTRACTS unenforceable in federal courts; forbade the issuance of injunctions against a number of hitherto outlawed union practices; and guaranteed jury trials in criminal prosecutions based on violations of injunctions. The act thus removed the machinery for a variety of informal antilabor devices.

Hoover's response was to seek assurance from his attorney general, William Mitchell, that the more rigorous terms of the measure could be successfully bypassed. Having gained such assurance, he signed the bill, leaving Senator Norris to remark, bitterly, that the President dared not veto but did everything he could to weaken its effect. Yet the measure was generally popular, as was its symbolism, which presaged a more active role for the federal government in the achievement of social justice.

Such response was not lost on Franklin D. Roosevelt. During the presidential campaign of 1932, he called for a new, more liberal view of the Constitution and a BROAD CONSTRUCTION of congressional legislative power as a way of solving the nation's difficult problems. His overwhelming election victory seemed to assure that the minority liberal constitutional arguments of the 1920s would become majority ones when the New Deal program was enacted.

PAUL L. MURPHY

Bibliography

HICKS, JOHN D. 1960 *Republican Ascendancy, 1921–1933.* New York: Harper & Row.

LEUCHTENBURG, WILLIAM E. 1958 *The Perils of Prosperity, 1914–1932.* Chicago: University of Chicago Press.

MURPHY, PAUL L. 1972 *The Constitution in Crisis Times, 1918–1969.* New York: Harper & Row.

——— 1972 *The Meaning of Freedom of Speech: First Amendment Freedoms from Wilson to F.D.R.* Westport, Conn.: Greenwood Press.

CONSTITUTIONAL HISTORY, 1933–1945

With the exception of the Civil War-Reconstruction era and the turbulent decade of the 1960s, no period in our history generated more profound changes in the constitutional system than the years of the Great Depression and World War II. Although the tenure of a Chief Justice of the United States often marks the boundary of a particular constitutional epoch, in this period it was a single President, FRANKLIN D. ROOSEVELT, whose personality and policies dominated the nation's political landscape, first as the leader of a domestic "war" against economic chaos, and, finally, as the architect of victory over the Axis powers. "Most of us in the Army have a hard time remembering any President but Franklin D. Roosevelt," remarked one soldier at the time of Roosevelt's death in April 1945. "He was the COMMANDER-IN-CHIEF, not only of the armed forces, but of our generation."

Roosevelt, described by Justice OLIVER WENDELL HOLMES as having a "second-rate intellect, but a first-rate temperament," was a charming, politically astute country squire from Hyde Park, New York. Crippled by polio at thirty-nine, elected President a decade later, he presided over five momentous revolutions in American life. The first, arising from his confrontation with the Supreme Court, has been aptly termed the "constitutional revolution" of 1937. The Court abandoned its long campaign, dating from the 1880s, to shape the content of the nation's economic policy by means of the judicial veto. The second revolution elevated the presidency, already revitalized by THEODORE ROOSEVELT and WOODROW WILSON in the Progressive era, to the pinnacle of leadership within the American political system. FDR did not invent the "imperial presidency," but his mastery of the radio, his legislative skills, and his twelve-year tenure went far toward institutionalizing it, despite several notable setbacks at the hands of Congress and the Court.

The third revolution, symbolized by the expansion of FEDERAL GRANT-IN-AID programs, the SOCIAL SECURITY ACT of 1935, and the efforts by the Department of Justice to protect CIVIL RIGHTS under the old Reconstruction-era statutes, significantly transformed American FEDERALISM by making the national government the chief custodian of economic security and social justice for all citizens. The fourth, marked by the revitalization of old independent REGULATORY COMMISSIONS such as the Interstate Commerce Commission, saw the final denouement of laissez-faire capitalism and the birth of state capitalism, managed by a bureaucratic elite drawn from the legal profession, the academic world, and private business. And the fifth revolution, characterized by the unionization of mass-production industries, the growing influence of urban-labor representatives in the Congress, and Roosevelt's successful effort to attract support from ethnic minorities, brought a major realignment in voting blocs and party strength that lasted three decades.

The triumph of Roosevelt and the Democratic party in the 1932 elections represented both the outcome of short-term political forces and the culmination of voting realignments that began much earlier. The inability of the HERBERT HOOVER administration to stop the slide into economic depression after the stock market crash of 1929 represented the most obvious and immediate source of Roosevelt's appeal. More significantly, his victory ended an era of Republican domination in national politics that began with WILLIAM MCKINLEY in 1896, and it ushered in a Democratic reign that lasted well into the 1980s. From McKinley to Hoover, the Republicans controlled the White House, except for Wilson's two terms (1913–1921), a Democratic interlude that rested mostly upon divisions in Republican ranks.

The Republicans also controlled both houses of Congress for twenty-eight of the thirty-six years between McKinley and Franklin Roosevelt, elected a majority of the nation's governors and state legislators outside the South, and even enjoyed great popularity in big cities among trade unionists, middle class professionals, and many ethnic-religious minorities. On a platform of high tariffs, sound money, low taxes, and rising prosperity, the GOP built a formidable national coalition.

The Republican coalition developed signs of collapse during the WARREN G. HARDING–CALVIN COOLIDGE–Herbert Hoover years as economic distress increased among farmers and industrial workers despite the vaunted prosperity of the Republican New Era. In 1924, running as an independent on the Progressive party ticket, the aging Senator Robert LaFollette garnered a healthy share of votes from both urban workers and staple-crop farmers, who protested with their ballots against the economic conservatism of Coolidge and his Democratic rival, John W. Davis, a prosperous Wall Street lawyer. Hoover easily defeated New York governor Alfred E. Smith in 1928, but Smith—Irish, Roman Catholic, opposed to prohibition, and urban to the core—detached millions of ethnic, working class voters from the Republican party. Three years of economic distress which also alienated farmers, businessmen, and the once-affluent middle classes, completed the realignment process and assured Roosevelt victory in 1932.

From 1932 until his death, Roosevelt forged his own national coalition. Anchored in the lily-white South and the big cities where the Democratic party had been powerful since the days of ANDREW JACKSON and MARTIN VAN BUREN, Roosevelt welded together a collection of social, ethnic, regional, and religious minorities into a new political majority. In peace and war, the New Deal gave power, status, and recognition to those who had been outsiders in American society before the Great Depression—Irishmen, Jews, Slavs, white Southerners, and blacks.

Within this broad, diverse "Roosevelt coalition," the power and influence of organized labor and the urban wing of the Democratic party grew impressively, especially after the elections of 1934 and 1936 and the passage of the WAGNER (NATIONAL LABOR RELATIONS) ACT in 1935. Roosevelt's nomination in 1932 had been made possible by the support of key southern leaders. The success of the New Deal after 1934 and Roosevelt's electoral victories in 1940 and 1944, however, rested upon the political acumen and money provided by big labor through the political action committees of the Congress of Industrial Organizations. Roosevelt built well. His coalition ran both houses of Congress in every year but eight during the next half century. It elected HARRY S. TRUMAN in 1948, JOHN F. KENNEDY in 1960, LYNDON B. JOHNSON in 1964, and JIMMY CARTER in 1976.

Neither of the two amendments to the Constitution ratified during this period owed their inspiration directly to Roosevelt or the New Deal, although the TWENTIETH AMENDMENT, eliminating the lame-duck session of Congress, had been pushed by leading progressives for over a decade, and the TWENTY-FIRST AMENDMENT, repealing national PROHIBITION of liquor, had been endorsed by the Democratic party in its 1932 platform. Both amendments were proposed in 1932, the first time since 1789 that a single Congress had sent to the states for RATIFICATION more than one amendment. Congress also specified an unusual ratification procedure for the Twenty-First Amendment, requiring the states to convene special ratifying conventions instead of submitting the measure to their legislatures. Proponents of prohibition repeal feared that the legislatures, most of them malapportioned in favor of rural constituencies, would not be sympathetic to ratification.

Supporters of the Twentieth Amendment, led by the venerable progressive senator from Nebraska, GEORGE NORRIS, argued that the existing short session of Congress which met from December until March was a barrier to effective majoritarian democracy. By an accident of history, Congresses elected in November of even-numbered years did not meet in regular session until December of the odd-numbered year. Norris's amendment, first passed by the Senate in 1923, proposed to correct this situation by moving forward to January 3 from December the date on which sessions of Congress began and shifting back to January 3 and 20 from March 4 the date on which the terms of office began for members of Congress, and the President and Vice-President, respectively. A newly elected Congress, reflecting the fresh mandate of the people, would meet two months after an election rather than thirteen months later.

The Senate passed the Norris plan five times after 1923, but it failed to advance in the Republican-dominated House of Representatives, where the Speaker, Nicholas Longworth, opposed it. Longworth wished to keep the lame-duck session as a check upon the turbulent masses and he also objected to a provision in the Norris amendment that allowed Congress to determine the date of its own adjournment each year. Such flexibility, he believed, would only encourage more lawmaking by Congress, a prospect that he and other conservatives viewed with great distaste. The 1930 elections returned Democratic majorities to both houses of Congress, who quickly passed the Twentieth Amendment and sent it on to the states where it was ratified three years later.

American temperance organizations struggled for more than a century to achieve their goal with the adoption of the EIGHTEENTH AMENDMENT in 1919. It took the "wet" forces little more than a decade to bring the brewery, the distillery, and the saloon back to American life through ratification of the Twenty-First Amendment nine months after Roosevelt took office. Like the resurgence of the Democratic party, the repeal of national prohibition reflected a fundamental shift in political forces. The Congress that passed the Eighteenth Amendment during World War I was overwhelmingly rural, with House seats apportioned on the basis of the 1910 census, the last to record a majority for the countryside rather than the cities. The 72nd Congress, on the other hand, reflected the reapportionment of the House in 1929, where twenty-one states (mostly from the rural South and West) lost representation and eleven states (mostly in Eastern metropolitan areas) increased their share of seats.

In addition to providing urban-ethnic voters with a measure of symbolic revenge for the inconvenience of a "dry" decade, the repeal of prohibition had wide appeal in a nation reeling from economic depression and plagued by criminal violence. Sponsors argued that repeal would boost employment, raise tax revenues, and permit law enforcement personnel to concentrate upon the apprehension of major criminals such as John Dillinger. With equal vehemence, defenders of the "dry" faith claimed that repeal had been hatched by millionaires and rich corporations, eager to shift their tax burdens onto poor consumers of alcohol, and that Satan would conquer America. Thirty-six states, more concerned for the nation's fiscal problems than for the wiles of Satan, ratified the repeal amendment by December 1933.

The legislative program of the New Deal had a more direct impact upon the fate of the old CHILD LABOR AMENDMENT, which had passed Congress in 1924 but had failed to secure ratification by three-fourths of the states. As late as 1937, only twenty-eight state legislatures had ratified the proposal which would have authorized Congress to regulate or prohibit the labor of persons under eighteen years of age. Fifteen states, mostly in the South and border regions, had rejected it; five had failed to act. The amendment became moot, however, when Congress in 1938 passed the FAIR LABOR STANDARDS ACT, which contained a similar restriction, and when the Supreme Court upheld its constitutionality in UNITED STATES V. DARBY LUMBER COMPANY (1941).

As usual, formal constitutional revision on the state level during these years was more extensive and diverse than for the federal government, although only three states (New York, Missouri, and Georgia) entirely rewrote their constitutions. At one extreme were states such as Tennessee and Illinois, where constitutional innovation remained minimal. The fundamental law of Tennessee had not been amended since 1870, while the Illinois Constitution of 1890 had been revised only twice since that date. On the other hand, voters in Louisiana were asked to adopt twenty-eight constitutional amendments in 1938, nineteen in 1940, ten in 1942, and nineteen in 1944, creating an organic law that filled nearly 300 pages with 200,000 words. California ran a distant second. By the end of World War II, its constitution of 1879 had been amended 250 times and totaled close to 50,000 words.

Unlike the United States Constitution with its broad, sweeping language, most state charters in this period included detailed declarations of public policies; the amendment process often served as a surrogate for statutory changes. In 1944, for instance, 100 proposed amendments were put before the voters in thirty different states. In California, Arizona, Oregon, and Washington the electorates defeated amendments to enact old-age pension schemes. Arkansas and Florida adopted right-to-work amendments that banned union shops, while California spurned a similar amendment. In the same year voters in other states were asked to pass upon amendments dealing with the location of airports, POLL TAXES, dog racing, and preferential civil service hiring for veterans.

Because of the era's economic crisis, which combined high unemployment, business failures, and falling tax revenues, all of the states confronted similar constitutional crises, because their organic laws usually limited state indebtedness. Escalating relief burdens placed a severe strain upon the states' fiscal resources, especially before the New Deal picked up a larger share of these costs after 1935. Legislatures and governors often found paths around these obstacles through constitutional experimentation: amendment, REFERENDUM, and judicial interpretation.

The age of Roosevelt, marked by class conflict and intense political controversy over both the economy and FOREIGN AFFAIRS, spawned many durable myths about the presidency, the growth of federal authority, and the relationship between government and the private sector. Roosevelt's critics, who hated the New Deal and distrusted his diplomacy, accused him of erecting a Presidential dictatorship. The New Deal and the mobilization of the war economy, it has been argued, also transformed the federal union as well as business–government relationships by subjecting local government and business corporations to the despotism of Washington bureaucrats. There is some truth in these generalizations but also considerable exaggeration.

Few political leaders in our history could match

Roosevelt's oratorical gifts, his skill at dispensing patronage, and his deft manipulation of subordinates, the press, Congress, and opponents. But Roosevelt also experienced a number of profound setbacks between 1933 and 1939 that limited presidential power even during the unparalleled economic crisis of the Great Depression. It was World War II that shifted the balance decisively in his favor, but even during those turbulent years he usually functioned within boundaries set by Congress and public opinion.

Under the New Deal, the years of presidential preeminence in the shaping of domestic policy were remarkably fertile but brief. During the so-called Hundred Days, from Roosevelt's inauguration to early June 1933, Congress rubber-stamped dozens of White House proposals, including new banking laws, the first federal securities statute, a complete overhaul of the nation's monetary system, legislation creating the Tennessee Valley Authority, as well as laws setting up the controversial National Recovery Administration and the New Deal's basic farm program. Acting under the dubious authority of the World War I Trading with the Enemy Act, Roosevelt banned gold exports and all foreign exchange transactions until Congress approved of the administration's monetary plans that nullified gold clauses in private and public contracts and devalued the dollar by almost twenty-five percent. Equating the Depression with war, Roosevelt asked for and received from Congress the resources appropriate for a military commander battling a foreign invader.

The 1934 elections gave the President even larger majorities in Congress. This mandate encouraged a second burst of New Deal reforms in 1935. Again responding to presidential initiatives, Congress adopted a series of path-breaking laws, including the Social Security Act, the Wagner National Labor Relations Act, a $4.8 billion relief and public works measure, and a significant revision of the federal tax code that closed many loopholes and levied new surcharges on the very rich. Despite the judicial mutilation of key administration measures in 1935–1936, executive power probably stood at its peacetime zenith after Roosevelt's crushing reelection victory in 1936.

Even during these years of strong presidential leadership, Roosevelt's claims to authority did not go unchallenged. The federal courts remained a bastion of conservative Republicanism. Federal judges had issued hundreds of INJUNCTIONS against New Deal programs by early 1935, when the Supreme Court began to invalidate many of the laws of the Hundred Days, including the NATIONAL INDUSTRIAL RECOVERY ACT (NIRA) and the AGRICULTURAL ADJUSTMENT ACT. The most serious rebuff to the President came in the *Schechter* case, where the Justices invalidated the NIRA on the ground of improper DELEGATION OF POWER to the executive, and HUMPHREY'S EXECUTOR V. UNITED STATES (1935), where they curbed the President's power to remove members of independent regulatory commissions.

These judicial affronts to presidential authority became a war during FDR's second term, beginning with his ill-devised scheme to "pack" the Supreme Court with additional Justices. His proposed "Judicial Reform Act of 1937" inspired criticism both from conservatives and from many of the President's liberal friends in the Congress as well. This bitter legislative struggle divided the New Deal coalition, squandered much of the political capital that Roosevelt had accumulated during the previous four years, and gave rise to cries of "dictatorship," "tyranny," and "fascism." When the dust settled, the Court-packing plan had been defeated by Chief Justice CHARLES EVANS HUGHES and opponents in the Congress, but the Supreme Court never again seriously challenged the New Deal.

The economic recession of 1937–1938 and Roosevelt's attempt to restructure the executive branch dealt new blows to presidential leadership and prestige. Having taken credit for the economic upturn in 1935–1936, the President had to absorb the blame for the "Roosevelt recession," which had been triggered in part by his own desire to cut federal expenditures and balance the budget. Congress also scuttled his plans to reorganize the executive branch which rested upon the recommendations of a blue-ribbon committee on administrative management. The original bill called for an enlargement of the White House staff, creation of the Executive Office of the President to include the Bureau of the Budget, and a consolidation of existing bureaus, agencies, and commissions into twelve superdepartments under the President's control. The independent regulatory commissions such as the Federal Trade Commission, the Interstate Commerce Commission, and the Securities Exchange Commission would have been regrouped under the authority of these executive departments.

Congressional opponents denounced the plan as another presidential power grab. Working in tandem with rebellious bureaucrats who hoped to protect their own fiefdoms from the White House, they easily defeated the most controversial features of the plan. Roosevelt got his Bureau of the Budget and a larger staff, but little more. His political fortunes hit rock bottom in the 1938 elections, when several conservative Democratic senators won reelection despite Roosevelt's effort to purge them during bitter primary campaigns. Confronted by an emerging conservative congressional coalition of southern Democrats and midwestern Republicans, Roosevelt had lost the initiative on domestic policy by the time German troops marched into Austria and Czechoslovakia.

The growth of presidential power, checked at the end of the 1930s, received new impetus after 1938 from the coming of World War II. Although the Supreme Court had reaffirmed in the broadest possible terms the President's constitutional authority over foreign policy in UNITED STATES v. CURTISS-WRIGHT EXPORT CORPORATION (1936), the actual limits of that authority remained to be tested. Sometimes alone and sometimes with congressional support, between 1939 and 1945 Roosevelt enlarged presidential power to an extent unknown even during World War I and the early New Deal.

Facing substantial isolationist sentiment both in Congress and among the public, Roosevelt initially attempted to counter Germany and Japan by means of EXECUTIVE AGREEMENTS and EXECUTIVE ORDERS that rested exclusively upon his claims to inherent presidential authority to conduct foreign relations and command the armed forces. He applied economic sanctions against Japan, terminating a 1911 commercial treaty, banning sales of scrap iron and steel, and freezing all Japanese financial assets in the United States. He ordered naval patrols of the western Atlantic—virtually assuring hostilities with German U-boats—and he ordered the military occupation of Iceland, with attendant naval convoys to protect ships supplying the occupation troops. In brief, Roosevelt waged an economic war in Asia and shooting war in the Atlantic without the consent of Congress.

The most extraordinary assertion of presidential power before Pearl Harbor was the destroyer-bases executive agreement in September 1940, by which Roosevelt transferred fifty over-age American destroyers to the British government in return for leases on seven naval bases in the Caribbean. This transaction, through which the President gave away a substantial portion of the United States Navy, rested upon a generous interpretation of an old nineteenth-century statute which permitted the President to dispose of worn-out ships. Most observers have believed that this action subverted the intention of Congress and violated a 1917 law specifically prohibiting the President in any foreign war "to send out of the jurisdiction of the United States any vessel built, armed, or equipped as a vessel of war." Attorney General ROBERT H. JACKSON, who advised Roosevelt on the legality of the transfer, dismissed this statute on the grounds that it applied only to ships built with the specific intention of giving them to a nation at war.

After the Japanese attack on Pearl Harbor Congress rapidly augmented presidential control over both military policy and the domestic economy. By means of the renewal of Lend-Lease, the Second WAR POWERS ACT, the EMERGENCY PRICE CONTROL ACT, the War Labor Dispute Act, and other laws, Congress gave the President the discretion, among other things, to allocate $50 billion of war supplies to America's allies, to reorganize all executive departments and agencies at will, to fix rents and prices throughout the land, and to seize industrial plants closed by strikes. In 1935, invalidating the NIRA, the Supreme Court had scolded Congress for vesting unbridled authority in the President to regulate the economy. Ten years later, as World War II drew to a close, executive discretion over the nation's economic structure far transcended that of the NIRA years.

A substantial enlargement of presidential discretion was essential for effective prosecution of World War II, but the growth of executive power carried with it threats to CIVIL LIBERTIES and unfathomable dangers to the survival of the human race. The Congress that permitted the President to restructure the executive branch also approved of the administration's plans to remove Japanese Americans from the West Coast. (See JAPANESE AMERICAN CASES.) The Congress that permitted the President to ration sugar and gasoline also gave the Commander-in-Chief a blank check for research, development, and potential use of nuclear weapons. This was truly, in Justice BENJAMIN N. CARDOZO's memorable phrase, "delegation run riot."

The expansion of federal responsibility for economic management and social services paralleled the growth of presidential power between 1933 and 1945. In a series of cases beginning with the WAGNER ACT CASES (1937) and ending with WICKARD v. FILBURN (1942), the Supreme Court laid to rest the antiquated notions of DUAL FEDERALISM, which had postulated the existence of rigid constitutional boundaries separating appropriate federal activities from those reserved exclusively to the states. In the wake of these decisions and those upholding the Social Security Act, there seemed to be no constitutional limitation upon the authority of Congress to regulate INTERSTATE COMMERCE and to tax and spend on behalf of the GENERAL WELFARE, even where these federal efforts intruded deeply into areas of social and economic life traditionally left to local government. Practice often preceded formal doctrinal legitimation. In 1934, for instance, the Bureau of Biological Survey in the Department of Commerce eradicated over seven million disease-carrying rodents in three states with a $8.7 million grant from the Civil Works Administration. Although this project produced no constitutional objection, a more sweeping federal intrusion into the domain of local health authorities is hard to imagine.

The most far-reaching instrument of expanding federal policymaking became the myriad programs of FEDERAL GRANTS-IN-AID which provided federal money for specific activities to be administered by state officials under federal guidelines. As early as 1862, the MORRILL ACT had conveyed federal lands to the states on condition that they be used for the construction and support of colleges and universities. In the Weeks Act of 1911, Congress had extended this principle to include cash grants to the states for fighting forest fires in the watersheds of navigable streams. Similar grant-in-aid programs flourished during the Wilson administration for vocational education, highways, and agricultural extension work, but budget-conscious Republican administrations had put a cap on new programs during the 1920s.

In their efforts to fight the depression, both the Hoover and Roosevelt administrations increasingly used the grant-in-aid technique. The Emergency Relief and Construction Act of 1932, approved reluctantly by Hoover, offered over $600 million in federal loans to the states for work-relief projects. The Roosevelt administration substituted grants for loans in the relief programs of the New Deal. By 1940, in addition to these vast relief activities and the continuation of old programs from the Progressive era, the New Deal had undertaken grant-in-aid programs for employment services and unemployment compensation, old age assistance, child welfare services, and maternity care. Social Security, the largest New Deal grant-in-aid program, assisted the blind, the disabled, and the unemployed through combined federal–state efforts.

The growth of federal grant-in-aid programs during the New Deal years rested upon the realization that many social and economic problems required national attention and that only the federal government commanded the fiscal resources to deal with them. Between 1932 and the end of World War II, the federal government's share of total taxes collected rose from twenty-four percent to nearly seventy-four percent. At the same time, grant-in-aid programs avoided the growth of an even larger federal bureaucracy and left many important administrative decisions in the hands of state and local officials.

In addition to grant-in-aid programs, state and local elites played a major role in the implementation of other New Deal efforts as well, a pattern of political decision making that refuted simplistic ideas about rampant centralization of power in federal bureaucrats. The heart of the New Deal's farm program, the domestic allotment system, vested important decisions in county committees composed of farmers and extension-service personnel chosen by local authorities. Under the Taylor Grazing Act, local livestock ranchers determined the extent of grazing rights on the vast public lands in the western states. And the most coercive federal program in this period, the SELECTIVE SERVICE ACT of 1940, left life-and-death decisions about the drafting of millions of American citizens in the hands of local draft boards appointed by state governors. Without the active participation of state and local officials, the wartime rationing programs for gasoline, sugar, coffee, and butter would have broken down for lack of enforcement.

When New Deal reformers ignored the interests and sensibilities of local elites, they provoked instant political protest and retaliation. Roosevelt quickly dismantled the innovative Civil Works Administration in 1934 because it drew intense criticism from governors, county supervisors, and mayors who objected to the complete nationalization of its extensive work-relief efforts. The subsequent Works Projects Administration program gave a larger share of decision making to local officials, who systematically used the machinery to punish political enemies and to discriminate against racial minorities, especially in the South. When idealistic young lawyers in the Agricultural Adjustment Administration attempted to protect sharecroppers and tenants from wholesale eviction under the farm program, they stirred up a revolt by commercial farmers, who forced their removal from the agency. Much of the opposition from southern Democrats to the New Deal after 1935 grew out of their anger at the Department of Justice for attempting to protect blacks from local violence under the old Reconstruction-era civil rights laws. The New Deal nourished a new brand of COOPERATIVE FEDERALISM in many areas of American life, but it was not a federalism without conflict and tensions, especially when national reformers challenged entrenched local customs and power relationships.

While encouraging the growth of big labor and ministering to the needs of the elderly and the poor, the New Deal also provided substantial benefits to American capitalists. Business opposition to Roosevelt was intense, but it was narrowly based in labor-intensive corporations in textiles, automobiles, and steel which had the most to lose from collective bargaining. The New Deal found many business allies among firms in the growing service industries of banking, insurance, and stock brokerage where government regulations promised to reduce cutthroat competition and to weed out marginal operators. Because of its aggressive policies to expand American exports and investment opportunities abroad, the New Deal also drew support from high-technology firms and from the large oil companies who were eager to penetrate the British monopoly in the Middle East.

Sophisticated businessmen discovered that they could live comfortably in a world of government regulation. The "socialistic" Tennessee Valley Authority lowered the profits of a few utility companies, but cheap electric power for the rural South translated into larger consumer markets for the manufacturers of generators, refrigerators, and other appliances. In addition to restoring public confidence in the stock exchanges and the securities industry, the Securities and Exchange Commission promoted self-regulation among over-the-counter dealers. Motor trucking firms received a helping hand from the Interstate Commerce Commission in reducing rate wars, and the major airlines looked to the Civil Aeronautics Board to protect them from the competitive rigors of the marketplace. When "Dr. Win-the-War" replaced "Dr. New Deal" after 1942, businessmen began to play key roles as well in the wartime agencies that regulated production, manpower, and the allocation of raw materials. The New Deal thus laid the foundations of both the welfare state and the permanent warfare state.

MICHAEL E. PARRISH

Bibliography

CAREY, JANE PERRY 1865 *The Rise of a New Federalism: Federal–State Cooperation in the United States.* New York: Russell & Russell.

HAWLEY, ELLIS P. 1965 *The New Deal and the Problem of Monopoly.* Princeton, N.J.: Princeton University Press.

LEUCHTENBURG, WILLIAM E. 1963 *Franklin D. Roosevelt and the New Deal.* New York: Harper & Row.

PATTERSON, JAMES T. 1969 *The New Deal and the States: Federalism in Transition.* Princeton, N.J.: Princeton University Press.

POLENBERG, RICHARD 1972 *War and Society: The United States 1941–1945.* Philadelphia: Lippincott.

SCHLESINGER, ARTHUR M., JR. 1957, 1959, 1960 *The Age of Roosevelt,* 3 vols. Boston: Houghton Mifflin.

CONSTITUTIONAL HISTORY, 1945–1961

Reconversion to a peacetime society required reestablishing balance among the branches of the government and a careful reassessment of the role of each. The same process occasioned a reexamination of the relations between government and private power. These immediate problems of reconstruction were joined by the emergence of a "cold war" with the Communist bloc of nations. Americans defined that struggle as one against totalitarian rule—the antithesis of constitutional democracy.

The wartime period had seen massive government regulation of the economy and the personal lives of citizens. Congress had authorized governmental reorganization in 1941, reenacting a World War I measure giving the President almost unlimited power to reorganize federal agencies directing the nation's resources in wartime. (See WAR POWERS ACT.) At the end of World War II, Congress created a bipartisan Commission on Organization of the Executive Branch of the government headed by ex-President HERBERT HOOVER. It recommended reforms designed to reduce administrative disorder and bureaucracy. Congress in 1947 proposed the TWENTY-SECOND AMENDMENT (ratified in 1951) limiting presidential service to two terms.

Although many congressional conservatives hoped to roll back various New Deal programs, few were prepared to return the nation's economy to the unregulated control of private business leaders. Depression lessons had been painful. The FULL EMPLOYMENT ACT of 1946 declared that it was the government's task to take all steps necessary to maximize employment, production, and purchasing power. And while certain conservative congressmen were disturbed by the economic management this measure obviously necessitated, few opposed its goal of securing national economic stability. The Housing and Rent Act of 1947, continuing the wartime Price Control Act, raised an important question: does the WAR POWER continue after the shooting has ceased? The Supreme Court, in WOODS V. MILLER (1948), answered affirmatively as to legislation responding to wartime dislocations.

The issue of restraints on organized labor dissolved presidential–congressional harmony. President HARRY S. TRUMAN in 1946 vetoed the TAFT-HARTLEY ACT, an amendment to the 1935 WAGNER ACT, the nation's principal labor law. Taft-Hartley sought to eliminate an alleged prolabor bias by arming management with new rights and imposing limitations on long-established trade union practices. Truman called the act "completely contrary to the national policy of economic freedom," and "a threat to the successful working of our democratic society." But Congress passed it over his veto, and thirty states also enacted antilabor statutes, including RIGHT-TO-WORK LAWS and antipicketing measures. The LANDRUM-GRIFFIN ACT of 1959 sought to combat growing charges of union scandal, extortion, and deprivation of members' rights by imposing more direct federal authority over internal union procedures.

Executive-legislative cooperation resulted in passage of the Cellar-Kefauver Act of 1950, authorizing more rigid enforcement of the antitrust laws against corporate mergers. Two years later, following a Supreme Court ruling striking at "fair trade" laws, Congress passed the McGuire Act exempting state-approved fair trading from the federal antitrust laws. Seen as a consumer protection law, the measure was politically acceptable at the time.

In the FOREIGN AFFAIRS area, Congress and the President clashed. Truman had inherited a presidency whose prerogatives in foreign policy had been greatly expanded. Committed to the realization of Roosevelt's postwar programs, Truman backed American participation in the new United Nations. Such action entailed expanding presidential prerogatives at the expense of congressional power. American participation meant applying military sanctions against an aggressor state at the discretion of the United States delegate to the Security Council, who was under the control of the President. By the United Nations Participation Act of 1945 Congress recognized that the President could not commit the United States to participation in United Nations military sanctions without congressional consent, but it acknowledged implicitly that Congress's warmaking power was conditioned by the necessity of international security action. Similarly, when the United States joined the NORTH ATLANTIC TREATY Organization in 1950, it pledged automatic intervention if any member suffered armed attack. The question was raised whether such a commitment upset the traditional balance between the executive and legislative branches in questions of war and peace.

With the invasion of South Korea by Communist forces, presidential discretion rather than congressional action provided a dramatic answer. Truman, on June 25, 1950, without asking for a formal DECLARATION OF WAR or consulting Congress, ordered United States POLICE ACTION in the area. This order brought charges from Senator ROBERT A. TAFT that Truman had "usurped power and violated the Constitution and the laws of the United States." In the "great debate" that followed, Truman's actions and presidential war power generally were condoned, but not without a strong attempt, led by Senator John Bricker, to curb the treaty-making power of the President by constitutional amendment. One form of the unsuccessful BRICKER AMENDMENT would have declared: "A provision of a treaty or other international agreement which conflicts with this Constitution shall not be of any force or effect."

The Supreme Court ultimately eased the minds of Bricker's supporters. The circumstances were constitutionally significant. As new treaties of alliance grew in the late 1940s and early 1950s, American military and civilian personnel spanned the globe. Questions grew regarding the legal status of American citizens living abroad. Did the Constitution follow the flag? In REID v. COVERT (1957) the Court held that an EXECUTIVE AGREEMENT was subject to the limits of the Constitution, and thus could not confer on Congress power to authorize trial by COURT-MARTIAL of a civilian dependent of a serviceman stationed overseas. "We must not," wrote Justice HUGO L. BLACK, "break faith with this nation's tradition of keeping military power subservient to civilian authority."

Earlier, Congress had enacted a NATIONAL SECURITY ACT, creating the National Security Council and reorganizing the means by which war powers were exercised. The measure constricted the President's foreign policy prerogatives by requiring him to consult Congress before taking certain actions. In practice, however, it did not constrain willful Presidents. The ATOMIC ENERGY ACT of 1946 sought to insure civilian control over atomic energy production and precluded dissemination of technical information to other nations. By the 1950s, however, President Eisenhower sought and obtained an amendment, as the basis for an international cooperation program, to develop peaceful applications of nuclear energy. Nuclear power was apparently to become an important bargaining chip in the international arena.

One incident growing out of the KOREAN WAR revealed public feelings regarding the swelling authority of the executive and the proper nature of constitutional government. During the war, the President felt that constitutional history was on his side, given earlier validated presidential interventions in national emergency crises. He authorized his secretary of commerce to seize and operate struck steel mills, thereby insuring production of vital defense materials. His executive order was not based on statutory authority, but only on the ground that a threatened strike of the nation's steelworkers created a national emergency. When the steel companies sought an INJUNCTION against the government, federal spokesmen argued that the seizure was based upon Article II of the Constitution, and "whatever inherent, implied, or residual powers may flow therefrom." The President's actions drew sharp criticism, especially his refusal to use the Taft-Hartley Act provisions hated by his labor constituency. Before the Supreme Court, government counsel stressed expanded presidential prerogative during national emergencies, but the Supreme Court drew a line between public regulation and governmental operation of private business. In one of its most celebrated postwar constitutional decisions, the Court, speaking through Justice Black, rejected claims for presidential EMERGENCY POWERS and INHERENT POWERS in domestic affairs. Truman promptly announced compliance with the ruling, and the public reacted favorably to JUDICIAL ACTIVISM in curtailing excessive federal power. (See STEEL SEIZURE CONTROVERSY; YOUNGSTOWN SHEET & TUBE V. SAWYER.)

Constitutional development in the Truman years had been heavily influenced by considerations of national security at home and abroad, some serious, some specious, and all heavily political. Republican and conservative southern Democratic opponents of the New Deal had begun in 1938 to "red-bait" the Roosevelt administration by associating its personnel with un-Americanism or by representing the government's extension of powers as socialistic or communistic. Wartime investigations of federal employees and postwar revelations of inadequate security procedures intensified conservative demands for a housecleaning of the executive branch. Capitalizing on this issue during the 1946 congressional elections, the Republicans secured control of both houses of Congress, insuring that the subsequent Congress would investigate the loyalty of federal employees. During this period, the HOUSE COMMITTEE ON UN-AMERICAN ACTIVITIES (HCUA) was given permanent committee status, and between 1947 and 1948 Congress instituted thirty-five committee investigations of federal personnel and policies.

Lacking Roosevelt's political capital, and alarmed by leaks of classified information, Truman moved quickly to take control of the loyalty issue. In November 1946 he appointed a special presidential commission to investigate the problem, and in 1947 he formally instituted, by EXECUTIVE ORDER 9835, a permanent federal employee LOYALTY-SECURITY PROGRAM. To disarm congressional opposition further, Truman appointed conservatives to the loyalty program's major administrative positions. Under this program, negative information from any source was the potential basis for a security dismissal or the denial of government service. An ATTORNEY GENERAL'S LIST of subversive organizations was drawn up, with membership a basis for dismissal. The only guideline the order provided was that a designated organization must be "totalitarian, Fascist, Communist, or subversive," or one adopting a policy "approving the commission of acts of force or violence to deny to others their constitutional rights."

Civil libertarians attacked the program on constitutional grounds, charging that it presumed employees to be subversive and subject to dismissal unless they could prove themselves innocent. Critics of the program also charged that it lacked procedural protections, a charge raised chronically against HCUA. However, the administration moved with regard for justice and fair play during its loyalty probes, and by early 1951 the Civil Service Commission had cleared more than three million federal employees; the Federal Bureau of Investigation had made 14,000 investigations of doubtful cases; over 2,000 employees had resigned, although in very few cases because of the investigation; and 212 persons had been dismissed because of reasonable doubts of their loyalty. In 1948 the executive branch also sought to demonstrate concern for national security by obtaining indictments of the eleven national leaders of the Communist party under the Smith Act. A long and bombastic trial followed, ending in convictions for conspiracy to advocate overthrow of the government by force and violence. (See DENNIS V. UNITED STATES.)

Conservative critics claimed that the Truman administration's loyalty efforts were window dressing to divert attention from more serious problems. The sensational Alger Hiss-Whittaker Chambers hearings and the resultant conviction of Hiss, a former New Deal official, for perjury in connection with disclosures of secret security information, catalyzed Congress into launching its own loyalty program. The MUNDT-NIXON BILL, seeking to force communists out into the open by requiring them to register with the Justice Department, was caught in 1948 election year politics and failed passage; but by 1950, following the reelection of Truman, the INTERNAL SECURITY ACT, a similar measure, was passed resoundingly over the President's veto. The act went beyond the Truman loyalty program for government employees. It attempted to extend loyalty probes into nongovernmental areas of American life and generally assumed a need to shift the authority for security matters to congressional leadership. Civil libertarians challenged the measure as violative particularly of FIRST AMENDMENT guarantees. But in the Korean War period, with burgeoning security apprehensions fed aggressively by Senator JOSEPH R. MCCARTHY of Wisconsin, the possibility of launching a successful test case of even the act's most extreme provisions promised little success. Instead, Senator Patrick A. McCarran of Nevada, one of the measure's principal champions, persuaded Congress in 1952 to pass, over another Truman veto, a revised immigration law. The act contained provisions to prevent the admission of possible subversives, and it authorized DEPORTATION of immigrants with communist affiliations even after they had become citizens.

The expanded activities of congressional committees in LEGISLATIVE INVESTIGATIONS of loyalty and security raised important constitutional questions about committee prerogatives and behavior. While practice varied, some of the more flamboyant committees, such as HCUA, Senator McCarthy's Committee on Governmental Operations, or McCarran's Senate Internal Security Committee with large, aggressive, and ruthless staffs, pried into federal activities and even investigated subversion in the movie and entertainment industries, various private organizations, the academic community, and the churches. Committee actions alarmed civil libertarians, because of growing disregard for the type of procedural guarantees and safeguards of individual liberty normally afforded any citizen in a court of law. The committees browbeat witnesses, denied a RIGHT TO COUNSEL, and afforded no opportunity to examine charges, which were often irresponsible and from dubious sources. Opportunity to cross-examine witnesses was denied. Individuals' past affiliations and activities were used as evidence of guilt, and they were expected to prove themselves innocent to an obviously biased congressional "jury." As a result many witnesses invoked the Fifth Amendment, refusing to testify on the grounds that any statement made might tend to incriminate them. This led to charges that such citizens were "Fifth Amendment Communists." Congress in 1954 passed a FEDERAL IMMUNITY ACT to force testimony in return for promises of immunity from prosecution. (See IMMUNITY GRANT.) Generally the courts, including the Supreme Court, were cautious about thwarting government measures, deciding cases on the narrowest of grounds and proscribing only the most overt abuses.

Postwar demands for greater constitutional protections for minorities within American society expanded CIVIL RIGHTS. Many Americans believed that the United States should extend first class CITIZENSHIP to all. The struggle with the Communist world for the minds of Third World people added urgency. Early in 1946, President Truman established a Committee on Civil Rights affirming that "the preservation of civil rights, guaranteed by the Constitution, is essential to domestic tranquillity, national security, the general welfare, and the continued existence of our free institutions." In 1947 the committee proposed extension of an approach initiated by Attorney General FRANK MURPHY in the late 1930s, stressing that the federal government should be a shield in protecting citizens against those who would endanger their rights, and a sword to cut away state laws violating those rights. The report called for strengthening the CIVIL RIGHTS DIVISION of the Justice Department, using the Federal Bureau of Investigation in cases involving violations of civil rights, enacting antilynching and anti-POLL TAX laws, and establishing a permanent Fair Employment Practices Commission. However, with Southerners dominating many key congressional committees, prospects were dim for any program extending full civil rights to black Americans.

Truman determined to make the effort. In early 1948 he sent Congress a message calling for prompt implementation of the commission's report. A southern revolt in the Congress culminated in the secession of members from the Democratic Party. These "Dixiecrats" ran their own presidential candidate, J. Strom Thurmond, on a STATES' RIGHTS platform calling for "segregation of the races" and denouncing national action in behalf of civil rights as a "totalitarian concept, which threatens the integrity of the states and the basic rights of their citizens." Although Truman won the election, in the civil rights area he had available only executive remedies. These he utilized, strengthening the Civil Rights Division and encouraging the Justice Department to assist private parties in civil rights cases. He also ordered that segregation be ended in federal employment and that the armed services be fully integrated. (See EXECUTIVE ORDERS 9980 AND 9981.) These developments encouraged civil rights activists to look to the courts for constitutional action in behalf of minority rights. Truman's Supreme Court appointees, however, were consistently conservative and espoused a narrow view of the judicial power. Only a few cautious rulings proscribed some forms of RACIAL DISCRIMINATION. (See SHELLEY V. KRAEMER, 1948; SWEATT V. PAINTER, 1950.)

Although DWIGHT D. EISENHOWER shared many of Truman's views regarding the President's vital and dominant leadership role in foreign policy, he conceived the domestic presidency in a different light. No social crusader, Eisenhower also had no desire to undo major programs of the New and Fair Deals. Rather he saw the presidency as a mediating agency, harmonizing the functioning of the team, and ratifying decisions and policies carefully prepared by responsible subordinates or by congressional leadership. Thus during Eisenhower's eight years in office Congress reasserted considerable domestic initiative, and when the President acted he usually complemented congressional desires.

During the 1952 campaign, Republicans made much of the "Communists in government" issue. Eisenhower realized that loyalty-security actions had to be taken to satisfy a nervous public. In 1953, he established a new executive loyalty program that expanded the criteria of the earlier Truman program. Discharge from federal service was now based on a simple finding that the individual's employment "may not be clearly consistent with the interests of national security." Several thousand "security risks" were dismissed. HCUA, cheering from the sidelines, then attempted to subpoena former President Truman to explain his security inadequacies. Truman responded with a polite letter giving the committee a lecture on SEPARATION OF POWERS and the independence of the executive.

Critics of the program focused on the absence of PROCEDURAL DUE PROCESS, the prevalence of GUILT BY ASSOCIATION, and the use of "faceless informers" as sources of damaging accusations. As long as Senator McCarthy was riding high such allegations remained just that. Tired of being smeared as "soft on Communists," frustrated liberal Democrats pushed through Congress a COMMUNIST CONTROL ACT in 1954, outlawing the party and initially seeking to make party membership a crime. The act proved virtually unenforceable. With the Senate censure and eventual demise of Senator McCarthy and the growing lack of enthusiasm of the Eisenhower administration for fueling the loyalty hysteria, security issues drifted into the background. By the late 1950s respectable bodies such as the New York City Bar Association and the League of Women Voters called for more precise standards for the federal government's loyalty-security program. With the Supreme Court also questioning aspects of that program's constitutional insensitivity, the President in early 1960 established a new industrial security program with vastly improved procedural safeguards. It included FAIR HEARINGS, the right of CONFRONTATION, and the right to examine all charges under ordinary circumstances. The same spirit came to prevail in the operation of other security programs.

The Eisenhower administration showed concern for state prerogatives and the need for balancing them against the rights of the individual. The federal government's growth in size and power since the late 1930s had been paralleled in state governments. During this period the states collected more money, spent more, employed more people, and engaged in more activities than ever before. When the expenditure and employment were assisted by FEDERAL GRANTS-IN-AID, lack of state compliance with federal standards meant potential loss of federal revenues. But states acted enthusiastically on their own in areas ranging from education and social services to a struggle with the federal government over control of natural resources. In 1947 the Supreme Court ruled that the United States had dominion over the soil under the marginal sea adjoining California. That state had maintained it was entitled, by virture of the "equal footing" clause in the act admitting it to the Union, to the rights enjoyed by the original states and that those states owned such offshore areas. The Court concluded that such ownership had not been established at the time of the Constitution, and the interests of SOVEREIGNTY favored national dominion. But following the victorious Eisenhower campaign of 1952, in which the Republicans had courted the West and the South with promises of offshore riches, Congress passed the Submerged Lands Act of 1953, vesting in the states the ownership of lands beneath the marginal sea adjacent to the respective states. The Supreme Court subsequently denied leave to file complaints challenging the statute's constitutionality.

At another level, states and municipalities became so concerned in the 1950s with employees' loyalty that they enacted restrictive security measures. These included prohibiting the employment of Communist party members, LOYALTY OATHS as a condition of employment for teachers, service personnel, and candidates for public office, and measures authorizing state prosecution for SEDITION against the United States. State bar associations in turn moved to exclude from admission candidates who were allegedly former Communist party members or who refused to answer questions regarding former suspect affiliations. When the Supreme Court struck at such state sedition laws (PENNSYLVANIA V. NELSON, 1956) and bar restraints (SCHWARE V. NEW MEXICO BOARD OF BAR EXAMINERS, 1958; KONIGSBERG V. CALIFORNIA STATE BAR, 1957) its actions were denounced by the Conference of Chief Justices of the States as "the high-water mark . . . in denying to a state the power to keep order in its own house." Bills were introduced in Congress to deny the Court APPELLATE JURISDICTION in cases of this kind.

In this atmosphere, national leaders were hesitant to push for early implementation of the Supreme Court's DESEGREGATION mandate, and preferred to interpret the command "with ALL DELIBERATE SPEED" by emphasizing deliberation. A pattern of "massive resistance" emerged in the southern states, constituting a crazy quilt of INTERPOSITION proclamations, pupil-assignment or placement laws, freedom-of-choice laws, TUITION GRANT plans, and state statutes prescribing discipline of teachers for violation of state policies on the school segregation question. Meanwhile, federal authorities sat on their hands until after the 1956 election. Then they took cautious steps to bring the federal government more directly into the civil rights area. Eisenhower's attorney general proposed a federal statute to authorize an investigation of rights violations, particularly VOTING RIGHTS. The CIVIL RIGHT ACT OF 1957 passed after Southerners had so amended it as to make it virtually toothless. When Eisenhower signed the act into law early in September, he could have used a much stronger bill. One week earlier Governor Orville Faubus of Arkansas, an acknowledged segregationist, had ordered state troops into Little Rock to prevent implementation of a federal court order approving the admission of a handful of black students into that city's Central High School. Confronted with military defiance of federal authority, Eisenhower had no choice but to respond. He reluctantly dispatched several companies of the United States Army to Little Rock, under a provision of the United States Code, which authorized the suppression of insurrection and unlawful combinations that hindered the execution of either state or federal law. (See POSSE COMITATUS ACT.) He also nationalized and thus neutralized the Arkansas National Guard. Black children attended school for a year under military protection and Arkansas's massive resistance was held at bay by bayonets.

After the Little Rock case was decided by the Supreme Court in COOPER V. AARON (1958), which sustained the school desegregation order, Congress also acted. The CIVIL RIGHTS ACT OF 1960 made it a federal crime for a person to obstruct or interfere with a federal court order, or to attempt to do so by threats of force. Other provisions expanded federal remedies for enforcing voting rights. The measure, for which the Republicans claimed credit in their 1960 platform, put Congress and the executive branch on record as committed to push ahead with rights enforcement.

For minority groups without the political constituency of blacks, little positive action was forthcoming. Women's rights in this period was a subliminal theme at best. Women's work in World War II had gone a long way toward shattering the stereotype of the helpless, weaker sex in need of protective legislation. Some leaders in Congress moved toward proposal of the EQUAL RIGHTS AMENDMENT as a vote of thanks to women for their magnificent wartime performance. Both parties endorsed the measure at war's end, and Harry Truman spoke publicly in its support. But Eleanor Roosevelt, with the support of organized labor, insisted that protective legislation was more valuable for working women than the establishment of an abstract principle of legal rights. Despite two attempts in the Senate to pass a bill proposing the amendment in the late 1940s, and a third in 1953 with a rider specifying that no protective legislation was to be affected, the measure was not seriously revived in this period.

The rights of American Indians suffered even more. In 1953, the Eisenhower administration set out on a policy of "termination," supporting a program designed to reduce the federal government's involvement in Indian affairs and to "free" Indians from federal supervision. Specifically, termination sought to end the existing supportive federal–tribal relationship and transfer almost all responsibilities and powers from the federal government to the states. The effects on "terminated" tribes was disastrous; many tribal members were soon on public assistance rolls. Indians detested the law embodying this policy, seeing it as an instrument for tribal extinction. They expended their energies to defeat it, and finally achieved victory in 1968. The Indian Civil Rights Act of that year encouraged Indian self-determination with continuing government assistance and services.

The judicial branch in the period from 1945 to 1961 changed from a cautious and accommodating agency, under Chief Justice FRED M. VINSON, to an active, aggressive, and controversial storm-center under Chief Justice EARL WARREN. Just as WILLIAM HOWARD TAFT had made the Supreme Court the principal instrument for the determination of constitutionality in the 1920s, Earl Warren, who assumed the chief justiceship 1953, came to play a similar role in the late 1950s. Often backlash resulted, but in Warren's case, from conservatives and not liberals. Statistically, the WARREN COURT'S record was not so activist as that of the 1920s. Four acts of Congress, eighty-five state acts, and sixteen ordinances were ruled unconstitutional from 1945 through 1960, with the Justices overruling twenty-two prior decisions. But the activist image was strong because the Court entered explosive areas of sensitive public policy.

The Court's unanimous decision in BROWN V. BOARD OF EDUCATION (1954) had shocked southern states-righters into defensive and retaliatory actions. The Court's consistent pushing ahead in the civil rights area sustained and intensified this antipathy. But Warren, supported by a liberal majority, was not prepared to stop. In the loyalty-security area, the Court limited the more sweeping provisions of the Smith Act, the Internal Security Act of 1950, and state loyalty measures. The rights of individuals and their protection from the abuses of government seemed to come first to the Justices' minds. The Court struck at departures from fair procedure by congressional committees. In *Jencks v. United States* (1957) it ruled that a defendant in a criminal case should have access to prior recorded statements of witnesses against him. Congress promptly sought to limit that ruling by the passage of the JENCKS ACT. By the late 1950s, the Justices began the process of critically examining state anti-OBSCENITY and censorship laws. In Congress there was talk of the need to curtail the Court's authority through legislation limiting its appellate jurisdiction. National action by right-wing groups quickly emerged to bolster such a movement, contributing to a broad public dialogue on the Court's proper function.

Defenders and critics of the Warren Court's liberal activism debated the proper role of the Constitution in the American polity. Champions of liberal judicial activism defended the legitimacy of judicial activity to shape constitutional law in accordance with democratic values. Supporters of judicial restraint advocated deference to popularly elected legislatures with courts confined to a narrowly circumscribed role. To conservative constitutionalists, the rule of law meant more than the imposition by a liberal Court of its own ethical imperatives, with little concern for orthodox doctrinal consistency.

There were no winners in this debate. But it proved apropos to the developments of the 1950s and to the institutional interrelationships of those years.

PAUL L. MURPHY

Bibliography

MURPHY, PAUL L. 1969 *The Constitution in Crisis Times, 1918–1969.* New York: Harper & Row.

MURPHY, WALTER F. 1962 *Congress and the Court.* Chicago: University of Chicago Press.

PRITCHETT, C. HERMAN 1954 *Civil Liberties and the Vinson Court.* Chicago: University of Chicago Press.

CONSTITUTIONAL HISTORY, 1961–1977

An examination of nonjudicial constitutional development from the administration of President JOHN F. KENNEDY to that of President GERALD R. FORD reveals at the outset an unusual amount of constitutional change through the process of constitutional amendment. Indeed, counting the adoption of the BILL OF RIGHTS in 1791 as only one episode of constitutional change via the AMENDMENT PROCESS, the period from 1961 to 1977 was characterized by an exceptionally high level of constitutional amending activity, with four amendments adopted during the period. In contrast, again counting the adoption of the Bill of Rights as one amendment episode, there were thirteen constitutional amendments adopted between 1789 and 1961.

Three of the constitutional amendments adopted during the 1961–1977 period were clear reflections of the expansion of egalitarianism that found expression in other fields in the policies of DESEGREGATION, REAPPORTIONMENT, and the enlargement of the protection of CIVIL RIGHTS. The TWENTY-THIRD AMENDMENT, adopted on March 19, 1961, extended the right to vote in presidential elections to the residents of the DISTRICT OF COLUMBIA although restricting the District to the number of electoral votes allotted to the least populous state. The TWENTY-FOURTH AMENDMENT, ratified on January 23, 1964, outlawed the imposition of POLL TAXES in presidential and congressional elections and therefore removed a form of WEALTH DISCRIMINATION in federal elections. The addition of this amendment to the Constitution was subsequently rendered superfluous by the Supreme Court's holding in HARPER V. VIRGINIA BOARD OF ELECTIONS (1966) that poll taxes were a form of INVIDIOUS DISCRIMINATION prohibited by the Constitution. Further extension of VOTING RIGHTS occurred with the adoption of the TWENTY-SIXTH AMENDMENT on June 30, 1971, which extended the right to vote in both federal and state elections to eighteen-year-old citizens. The Twenty-Sixth Amendment was necessitated by the Supreme Court's holding in OREGON V. MITCHELL (1974) that Congress lacked the constitutional power to legislate the eighteen-year-old vote in state and local elections.

In contrast with the Twenty-Third, Twenty-Fourth, and Twenty-Sixth Amendments, the Twenty-Fifth Amendment, relating to PRESIDENTIAL SUCCESSION and disability and adopted in 1967, was the result of years of debate with regard to the problems that might arise if an incumbent president were temporarily or permanently disabled. Serious consideration of such an amendment to the Constitution was prompted by the illnesses afflicting President DWIGHT D. EISENHOWER during his term of office, and additional impetus for constitutional change in this area was created by the assassination of President Kennedy in 1963.

Under the provisions of the Twenty-Fifth Amendment, the President may declare his own disability to perform the duties of the office by informing the president pro tempore of the Senate and the speaker of the House of Representatives in writing of his own disability. Alternatively, the President's disability may be declared in writing to the same congressional officers by the vice-president and a majority of the Cabinet. In either instance, the vice-president assumes the duties of the presidency as acting President. A period of presidential disability may be ended either by the President's informing the congressional officers in writing of the termination of his disability, or if there is disagreement between the President and the vice-president and a majority of the Cabinet on the issue of the President's disability, the Congress may resolve the dispute. A two-thirds majority of both houses of Congress, however, is required to declare the President disabled; otherwise, the President resumes the duties of his office.

Although the disability provisions of the Twenty-Fifth Amendment have not been applied, Section 2 of the amendment had an important impact on the succession to the presidency during the administration of President RICHARD M. NIXON. Section 2 provides that whenever a vacancy in the office of vice-president occurs, the President shall appoint a new vice-president with the approval of a majority of both houses of Congress. These provisions of the Twenty-Fifth Amendment came into play when Vice-President Spiro T. Agnew resigned his office in 1973 under the threat of prosecution for income tax evasion. Pursuant to Section 2, President Nixon appointed Congressman Gerald R. Ford of Michigan as Agnew's successor, and the Congress confirmed Ford as vice-president. Subsequently, President Nixon resigned his office on August 9, 1974, when his IMPEACHMENT for his involvement in the WATERGATE affair and other abuses of office seemed imminent, and Vice-President Ford succeeded Nixon in the office of President. Under the provisions of the Twenty-Fifth Amendment, Ford thus became the first appointed vice-president as well as the first unelected vice-president to assume the office of the presidency.

The Watergate affair that led to President Nixon's resignation involved not only charges of bugging the Democratic National Committee headquarters, and the obstruction by the executive of the subsequent investigation of that incident, but also more generalized abuses of power by the executive. In addition to the issue of the scope of EXECUTIVE PRIVILEGE, which was ultimately resolved by the Supreme Court adversely to the President's claims in UNITED STATES v. NIXON (1974), the Watergate affair raised major constitutional issues concerning the nature of the impeachment process, as the impeachment of a President was seriously considered by the Congress for the first time since the impeachment of President ANDREW JOHNSON in 1868. Because the Constitution provides that governmental officers including the President may be removed from office on impeachment for TREASON, bribery, or other high crimes and MISDEMEANORS, the consideration of the impeachment of President Nixon by the Congress involved the determination of what constituted an impeachable offense, an issue that had also been at the heart of the debate over the Johnson impeachment.

In the deliberations of the Judiciary Committee of the House of Representatives regarding ARTICLES OF IMPEACHMENT against President Nixon, the President's supporters argued that the President could be impeached only within the meaning of the Constitution for an indictable criminal offense. The President's opponents, on the other hand, contended that articles of impeachment could embrace political offenses, such as the abuse of power by the President, which were not indictable under the criminal law. The latter position ultimately prevailed among a majority of the Judiciary Committee when the committee adopted three articles of impeachment against President Nixon that contained charges that were essentially political, abuse of power offenses which were not indictable.

Article one of the articles of impeachment charged the President with obstruction of justice and with violating his oath of office requiring him to see to it that the laws were faithfully executed, but the second and third articles charged him with violating the constitutional rights of citizens, impairing the administration of justice, misusing executive agencies, and ignoring the SUBPOENAS of the Judiciary Committee through which it had sought EVIDENCE related to its impeachment inquiry. Although these charges included some indictable offenses, in adopting the articles the majority of the committee obviously construed the words "high crimes and misdemeanors" to include offenses that did not involve indictable crimes. In reaching this conclusion, the committee majority took a position that conformed with the view of the nature of the impeachment process that the House of Representatives had adopted in the Johnson impeachment proceedings in 1868.

Whether this broad view of the nature of impeachable offenses would have been sustained by a majority of the House of Representatives or the required two-thirds majority in the Senate remained an unanswered question because of President Nixon's resignation in August 1974. The Supreme Court rejected the President's claim of executive privilege and ordered the disclosure of the White House tape recordings relevant to the trial of those indicted in the Watergate affair. On the tapes thus released there appeared conversations clearly indicating President Nixon's participation in a conspiracy to obstruct justice, an indictable offense. In light of almost certain impeachment by the House of Representatives and likely conviction in the Senate, President Nixon resigned. With the impeachment process thus aborted, the answer to what properly could be considered an impeachable offense was left unresolved, as it had been in the proceedings against President Johnson over a hundred years earlier.

The Watergate affair and the abuses of presidential power associated with it, along with the involvement of the United States in the Vietnam War, had a profound impact upon the principal nonjudicial constitutional issue during the 1961–1977 period—the issue of the proper relation between the powers of the executive branch of the government and the powers of the Congress. Beginning at least as early as the administrations of FRANKLIN D. ROOSEVELT in the 1930s and 1940s, the presidency had increasingly become the dominant political institution at the national level, and Roosevelt's successors refined and added to the assertions of PRESIDENTIAL POWER that had characterized his administrations. By the late 1960s and early 1970s, therefore, the "Imperial Presidency" had become the focus of considerable attention and constitutional controversy, and a reassertion of congressional power against the aggrandizement of presidential power had clearly begun.

This reassertion of congressional power was to a great extent a reaction to the expansion of the powers of the presidency to new extremes during the administration of President Nixon. Although previous presidents had asserted the power to impound and to refuse to expend funds appropriated by Congress in limited areas, President Nixon asserted a much broadened IMPOUNDMENT power as a presidential prerogative. Instead of the relatively isolated instances of presidential refusals to spend congressionally appropriated monies that had occurred previously, during the 1970s the Nixon administration impounded billions of dollars in congressional appropriations and effectively asserted a presidential power to enforce only those congressionally authorized programs that received the president's approval.

The involvement of the United States in the war in Vietnam and Southeast Asia contributed to further controversy regarding the scope of presidential power to commit the armed forces to foreign military conflicts in the absence of a DECLARATION OF WAR by the Congress. The involvement of the United States in Vietnam had begun under President Kennedy with the dispatch of military advisers to the South Vietnamese armed forces, but under Presidents LYNDON B. JOHNSON and Nixon the American military presence in Southeast Asia grew to hundreds of thousands of troops. The failure of the American military efforts in Southeast Asia and the high cost of those efforts in lives and resources bolstered the arguments of critics that the power of the President to commit the United States to foreign military conflicts must be reined in.

Because of the impoundment policy of the Nixon administration and the presidential war in Southeast Asia, a reassertion of congressional power occurred in the field of domestic as well as FOREIGN AFFAIRS. The congressional response to the impoundment controversy was the enactment of the CONGRESSIONAL BUDGET AND IMPOUNDMENT CONTROL ACT OF 1974. This legislation provided that if the President resolved to eliminate the expenditure of funds appropriated by Congress, he was required to inform both houses of Congress of: the amounts involved; the agencies and programs affected; and the fiscal, budgetary, and economic effects of, and the reasons for, the proposed impoundment of funds. Both houses of Congress, the act provided, must approve the impoundment within forty-five days. If the President proposed instead to defer the spending of congressionally authorized appropriations, the act provided that he must similarly inform Congress of his intention to defer expenditures, and within forty-five days either house of Congress could require the expenditure of the funds by passing a resolution disapproving the President's proposed action. If the President refused to abide by congressional disapproval of impoundments, the act further authorized the Comptroller General to initiate legal action in the federal courts to force compliance with the will of the Congress.

In addition to addressing the problem of presidential impoundments, the Congressional Budget and Impoundment Control Act was directed at strengthening the powers of Congress over the budgetary process. To replace the practice of enacting appropriations without regard to the total amount that should be appropriated in a given fiscal year, the act provided that the Congress should agree upon a BUDGET resolution at the outset of the appropriations process, setting the total amount of money to be appropriated during the fiscal year. The amount so specified would then govern the actions of Congress in considering individual appropriations bills.

Finally, the act created a new agency, the Congressional Budget Office, and authorized that agency to advise Congress regarding revenue estimates, the likely amount of deficits or revenue surpluses and other economic data important to the budgetary process. Congress thus created a congressional agency, beyond the control of the executive, which would be an independent source of economic and budgetary information in competition with the executive branch's Treasury Department and Office of Management and Budget.

This reassertion of congressional power over domestic policy was matched in the field of foreign policy by the WAR POWERS RESOLUTION of November 7, 1973, passed over the veto of President Nixon. In the War Powers Resolution, Congress sought to deal with the problem of presidential wars such as the military involvement of the United States in Southeast Asia. Congress therefore not only imposed restrictions upon the power of the President to commit the country's armed forces in foreign conflicts but also sought to define the war-making powers of both the President and the Congress.

With regard to the war-making power of the President, the War Powers Resolution declared that the President could introduce United States armed forces into hostilities, or into a situation in which imminent involvement in hostilities was clearly indicated by the circumstances, only pursuant to a declaration of war, or under specific statutory authorization, or in response to a national emergency created by an attack upon the United States, its territories or possessions, or its armed forces. The language of the resolution thus clearly repudiated the argument, frequently asserted in the past, that the President was constitutionally authorized to take whatever action deemed necessary to protect the national interest. The impact of the resolution as an authoritative congressional interpretation of the President's constitutional war-making power was diluted, however, by the decision of Congress to include the interpretation of the President's war-making power in the "Purpose and Policy" section of the act, with the result that it did not purport to have legally binding effect.

The parts of the War Powers Resolution that did purport to be legally binding required the President to consult with Congress in every possible instance before committing the armed forces in hostilities or hostile situations. If the armed forces are introduced by the President into hostilities or hostile situations in the absence of a declared war, the resolution provided, the President must report the situation in writing to the presiding officers of the Congress within forty-eight hours and continue to report every six months thereafter. The resolution further required that in the absence of a declared war, the introduction of the armed forces must be terminated within sixty days, or ninety days if the military situation makes their safe withdrawal impossible within sixty days. Finally, in the absence of a declared war or congressional authorization, the President must withdraw the armed forces from hostilities occurring outside the territory of the United States if Congress directs him to do so by CONCURRENT RESOLUTION, which is not subject to the President's veto power.

Although the War Powers Resolution was plainly an attempt by Congress to reassert its authority over presidential war-making and over the conduct of foreign affairs generally, its impact upon presidential power did not appear to have been so great as its supporters hoped or it critics feared at the time of its passage. During the administration of President Ford, American armed forces were introduced into hostile situations during the evacuation of Vietnam as well as during the recapture of the American merchantman *Mayaguez* and its crew from Cambodia. President Ford nevertheless did not feel bound in these actions by the terms of the War Powers Resolution but rather made plain his conviction that he was acting under his constitutional powers as COMMANDER-IN-CHIEF and as chief executive. The War Powers Resolution was thus subjected to early challenge as an authoritative construction of the President's war-making power. Given the ability of Presidents to marshal public support for their actions in foreign affairs, particularly in times of crisis, it was clear that the act could not be considered the last word regarding the relative power of Congress and the President in the field of foreign policy and war-making.

Just as the War Powers Resolution and the Congressional Budget and Impoundment Control Act symbolized the reassertion of congressional power in relation to the executive, both also embodied the device which Congress increasingly used in reasserting power over executive policymaking—the LEGISLATIVE VETO. The legislative veto first emerged as a congressional device for controlling the executive during the 1930s when Congress reserved the right to veto presidential proposals to reorganize the executive branch, but by the 1970s the legislative veto in various forms had proliferated and had been embodied in almost two hundred statutes enacted by Congress. The increased use of the legislative veto reflected Congress's dissatisfaction with its relationship with the executive and a desire to reassert policymaking power that had been eroded during the previous decades of heightened executive power.

Congress employed the legislative veto to disapprove proposed presidential actions, to disapprove rules and regulations proposed by the executive branch or administrative agencies, and to order the termination of presidential actions. The device took several forms, with some statutes requiring a resolution of approval or disapproval by only one house of Congress, others requiring both houses to act through a concurrent resolution, and still others conferring upon congressional committees the power to exercise the legislative veto.

Despite its increased use by Congress, the legislative veto was frequently opposed by the executive branch since its introduction in the 1930s on the grounds that the practice violates the Constitution. The executive and other critics of the legislative veto argued that the practice violated the principle of SEPARATION OF POWERS, ignored the principle of bicameralism in the exercise of legislative power, and allowed Congress to avoid the President's veto power which is normally applicable to legislation passed by Congress.

The constitutional principle of separation of powers, critics of the legislative veto noted, permits Congress to shape national policy by passing statutes, but, properly construed, does not permit Congress to interfere in the enforcement or administration of policy—a power properly belonging to the executive branch. The legislative veto, it was argued, thus violated a fundamental constitutional principle, especially insofar as it was used to allow Congress to veto rules and regulations proposed by executive or administrative agencies under DELEGATIONS OF POWER from the Congress.

Opponents also argued that the Constitution contemplates that Congress's policy-making role ordinarily requires the passage of statutes by both houses of Congress with the presentation of the statutes to the President for his approval or disapproval. By allowing the approval or disapproval of national policy through single house resolutions, JOINT RESOLUTIONS, or decisions of congressional committees, it was argued, the legislative veto ignored the bicameral legislative process contemplated by the Constitution and in addition permitted congressional policymaking through mechanisms not subject to the President's veto power, as the Constitution also contemplated.

Congress, on the other hand, clearly viewed the legislative veto as a useful weapon in exercising oversight over the executive and the bureaucracy, both of which were recipients of massive delegations of legislative power since the 1930s. Striking at another source of the imperial presidency, Congress thus embodied the legislative veto in the National Emergencies Act of 1976, which terminated national emergencies declared by the President in 1933, 1950, 1970, and 1971, and required the President to inform the Congress of the existence of national emergencies and the powers the executive intends to use in managing the emergency. Such emergencies, the act provided, could be terminated at any time by Congress via a concurrent resolution. (See EMERGENCY POWERS.)

Despite the long-standing controversy regarding the constitutional legitimacy of the legislative veto, the Supreme Court did not pass upon the validity of the device until 1983. In IMMIGRATION AND NATURALIZATION SERVICE V. CHADHA (1983), however, the Court declared the legislative veto invalid on the ground that it violated the constitutional principles requiring legislative enactments to be passed by both houses of Congress and to be subject to the veto powers of the President.

Just as the period from the administration of President Kennedy to that of President Ford witnessed significant readjustments of presidential–congressional relations, dramatic changes also occurred during the period in the nature of the political party system and the electoral process. Perhaps the most significant development was the decline in the power and influence of the major political parties. The decline in the percentage of the public who identified with the Republican and Democratic parties that began in the 1950s continued during the 1960s and 1970s. In 1952 twenty-two percent of the voters indicated a strong identification with the Democratic party, while thirteen percent indicated such an identification with the Republican party. By 1976, these percentages had declined to fifteen and nine percent, respectively, while the number of voters identifying themselves as independents had risen significantly.

This decline in voter identification with the two major political parties was accompanied by a decline in the importance of the national conventions of the two parties in the selection of presidential candidates. In 1960, only sixteen states selected their delegations to the national party conventions through presidential primaries, but by 1976 thirty states used the primary system for the selection of national party convention delegates, with the result that almost three-quarters of the Democratic national convention delegates and well over sixty percent of the Republican delegates were selected through the presidential primary process. Nominations of presidential candidates were consequently no longer the products of negotiations among party leaders at the national conventions;

rather the national conventions merely ratified the selection of a presidential candidate as determined in the presidential primaries. And this decline in the significance of the national conventions was furthered, in the Democratic party, by the adoption of rules during the 1970s diminishing the power of party leaders and requiring proportional representation of women, minority groups, and other constituent groups within the party.

The decline of power of the political parties was furthered by the adoption of federal CAMPAIGN FINANCING laws in 1971, 1974, and 1976 which limited the amounts that could be contributed to election campaigns by individuals and groups and provided for federal financing of presidential elections. The result was a further diminution of the importance of traditional party organizations to presidential candidates, who increasingly relied upon personal campaign organizations both to win nomination and to conduct their national election campaigns. In a governmental system based upon the separation of powers, the decline of the party system, which traditionally had served to bridge the gap between the executive and legislative branches, could only have profound effects upon the capacity of Presidents to lead as well as upon the formation of national policy.

The period between 1961 and 1977 witnessed an acceleration of a long-term trend toward the centralization of power in the national government, although by the end of the period a significant reaction to this trend had become apparent. Two primary factors contributed to this centralizing trend: increased subsidization by the national government of programs at the state and local levels, and the assumption of responsibility by the national government over vast areas that had traditionally been left to state and local governments.

When John F. Kennedy was elected in 1960, for example, FEDERAL GRANTS-IN-AID to state and local governments stood at just over seven billion dollars and accounted for approximately fifteen percent of the total expenditures of state and local governments. By 1976, these federal grants-in-aid had mushroomed to almost sixty billion dollars and constituted almost twenty-five percent of total state and local expenditures.

Not only did state and local governments become increasingly dependent financially upon federal largess during this period but the character of federal grant-in-aid programs was also significantly altered. Before the 1960s, federal aid was primarily directed at subsidizing programs identified by state and local governments, but during the 1960s the identification of program needs increasingly shifted to the national government, with federal funds allocated according to national priorities. In addition, many federal grants, especially during President Johnson's War on Poverty program, were distributed at the local community level, by-passing state governors and officials who had traditionally had a voice in the administration of federal grants. As a result of the ensuing outcry from state and local officials, during the late 1960s and 1970s the federal government resorted to the device of block grants to state and local governments, grants involving fewer nationally imposed restrictions on their use and thus allowing the exercise of greater discretionary power by state and local officials. In 1972, Congress also adopted the State and Local Fiscal Assistance Act, which embraced the principle of federal revenue sharing with state and local governments. Despite the greater flexibility allowed state and local decision makers under REVENUE SHARING and block grants, the financial dependence of state and local governments on the national government in 1976 was eight times what it had been in 1960.

During the same period, the federal government's power was significantly expanded through congressional passage of a host of new statutes that expanded the regulatory role of the federal government in numerous new fields. Civil rights, the environment, occupational safety, consumer protection, and many other fields for the first time were subjected to extensive federal regulation. Since almost all of the new regulatory statutes involved extensive delegation of legislative power by Congress to the bureaucracy, the new expansion of federal regulatory authority involved a massive increase in administrative rules and regulations, as the bureaucracy exercised the legislative powers that had been delegated to it.

This increased intrusion of the federal government into the lives and affairs of the public ultimately produced a backlash of hostility toward the federal bureaucracy. John F. Kennedy had campaigned for the presidency in 1960 with the promise to get the country moving again, a promise suggesting an activist role for the national government. Because of the backlash against the expansion of the regulatory role of the federal government, however, presidential candidates in 1976 found that attacks on the federal bureaucracy and the national government as a whole hit a responsive chord with the public and proved to be popular campaign rhetoric.

This unpopularity of the bureaucracy, however, was only one symptom of the American public's shaken confidence in its major political institutions that had become manifest by the mid-1970s. Between 1961 and 1976, one President had been assassinated, one had resigned in disgrace, the long and costly war in Vietnam had concluded in disaster, and the Watergate affair had revealed the betrayal of the public trust at the highest levels of the government as well as abuses of power with sinister implications for the liberties of the American people. Such traumatic events not only undermined public confidence in political institutions but also profoundly affected the course of constitutional development. The office of the presidency, which since the 1930s had evolved into the dominant political institution at the national level, was consequently diminished considerably by 1976 in both power and prestige. Although a resurgence of congressional power had occurred in the 1970s, there was little evidence that Congress was institutionally capable of assuming the role of national leadership previously performed by the presidency, and effective national leadership had been made even more difficult by the decline of the political party system.

The most basic problem confronting the American polity by 1976 was nevertheless the problem of the loss of public confidence in governmental institutions. And the restoration of that confidence was the most profoundly difficult and fundamentally important task American public leadership faced as this period of constitutional development came to a close.

RICHARD C. CORTNER

Bibliography

ALEXANDER, HERBERT 1976 *Financing Politics: Money, Elections and Political Reform.* Washington, D.C.: Congressional Quarterly.

DRY, MURRAY 1981 The Congressional Veto and the Constitutional Separation of Powers. In Bessette, Joseph M. and Tulis, Jeffry, *The Presidency in the Constitutional Order.* Baton Rouge: Louisiana State University Press.

JACOB, HERBERT AND VINES, KENNETH N., eds. 1976 *Politics in the American States: A Comparative Analysis,* 3rd ed. Boston: Little, Brown.

KEECH, WILLIAM R. AND MATTHEWS, DONALD R. 1977 *The Party's Choice.* Washington, D.C.: Brookings Institution.

KURLAND, PHILIP B. 1977 *Watergate and the Constitution.* Chicago: University of Chicago Press.

SCHLESINGER, ARTHUR M., JR. 1973 *The Imperial Presidency.* Boston: Houghton Mifflin.

SCIGLIANO, ROBERT 1981 The War Powers Resolution and the War Powers. In Bessette, Joseph M. and Tulis, Jeffry, *The Presidency in the Constitutional Order.* Baton Rouge: Louisiana State University Press.

SUNDQUIST, LEONARD D. 1981 *The Decline and Resurgence of Congress.* Washington, D.C.: Brookings Institution.

CONSTITUTIONAL HISTORY, 1977–1985

As America moved from commemorating the bicentennial of the DECLARATION OF INDEPENDENCE to commemorating the bicentennial of the Constitution, the political order was in apparent disarray. Constitutional history is, primarily, an account of changes in the distribution of power and authority within a regime. At least since 1933, political power in the American regime had shifted toward the federal government, and, within the federal government, toward the executive branch. Commentators referred to an "imperial presidency"; and yet no one since DWIGHT D. EISENHOWER had held the presidential office for two full terms. JOHN F. KENNEDY had been assassinated; LYNDON B. JOHNSON had abandoned the quest for reelection; RICHARD M. NIXON had been forced to resign; GERALD R. FORD, the appointed vice-president who succeeded Nixon, lost his bid for election in his own right. JIMMY CARTER, who defeated Ford, was to prove unable to carry the burden of the presidency, and so to be crushed in his bid for reelection by the landslide that elected RONALD REAGAN.

The national consensus about what the government should be and should do, at bottom a consensus about the meaning of the Constitution, was breaking down. No longer did national majorities automatically form behind the notions of positive government, of redistribution of wealth and incomes, or of solving anything identified as a "national problem" by creating a new administrative agency within the federal BUREAUCRACY. There were indications that a new consensus was forming, but it was not yet fully formed. Less clearly than in the past—say, in 1800, 1832, 1860, or 1932—was the new consensus readily identified with the program of a particular POLITICAL PARTY, although the revitalization of the Republican party gave it the better claim to such identification.

Constitutional history can be understood either broadly or narrowly. In the broad sense, the constitution is the arrangement of offices and the distribution of powers in a country, it is how the country governs itself. In a narrow sense, the Constitution is a document in which the framework for self-government is spelled out. The process of constitutional change in the United States most often involves redistribution of power without constitutional amendment.

Formal amendment of the Constitution is a rare

event. Only thirty-two amendments have ever been proposed by Congress, and two of those were pending as 1977 began; by 1985 both had died for want of RATIFICATION. The EQUAL RIGHTS AMENDMENT (ERA), ostensibly a guarantee that women and men would be treated equally under the law, but potentially a blank check for expansion of federal and judicial power, had been proposed in 1972. The DISTRICT OF COLUMBIA REPRESENTATION AMENDMENT, which would have made the national capital the equivalent of a STATE for most purposes, had been proposed in 1978. Even as those proposals failed to obtain the necessary votes in state legislatures, there was popular demand for more amendments: to mandate a balanced federal BUDGET; to proscribe SCHOOL BUSING as a remedy for de facto school segregation; to permit prayer in public schools; and to overturn the Supreme Court's proclamation of a constitutional right to abortion.

Amendments to accomplish each of these objectives were introduced in Congress, and the ERA was reintroduced, but none was proposed to the states. Indeed, only one amendment received a two-thirds vote in either house of Congress: the balanced budget amendment passed the Senate, but died when the House of Representatives failed to act on it. In the case of the balanced budget amendment, there were petitions from thirty-three states (one less than constitutionally required) calling for a convention to frame the proposal. Although there was much speculation among politicians, academicians, and pundits about how such a convention might work and whether it could be restricted in its scope, the failure of a thirty-fourth state to act made the speculation at least temporarily moot.

For three decades, constitutional innovation had been centered on the judicial branch. Between 1977 and 1985, however, constitutional development centered on the contest between Congress and the executive branch for predominance. The most important constitutional decision of the Supreme Court during the period, IMMIGRATION AND NATURALIZATION SERVICE v. CHADHA (1983), passed on a phase of that contest.

The only uniquely American constitutional doctrine is that of the SEPARATION OF POWERS attended by CHECKS AND BALANCES. The embodiment of that doctrine in the Constitution set up a constant rivalry for preeminence between the political branches and an intense jealousy of powers and prerogatives. Beginning in the FRANKLIN D. ROOSEVELT era, the President—or the institutionalized presidency—seemed to acquire ever more power within the political system, and appeared to have acquired a permanent position of dominance. But the VIETNAM WAR and the WATERGATE crisis led to a resurgence of Congress, represented especially in the War Powers Resolution of 1973 and the CONGRESSIONAL BUDGET AND IMPOUNDMENT CONTROL ACT of 1974.

The seizure of the American embassy in Iran by Islamic revolutionary guards in 1979 set the stage for reassessment of the constitutional status of the WAR POWERS. President Carter in April 1980 ordered the armed forces to attempt a rescue of the American citizens held hostage in Tehran. The secrecy necessarily surrounding such an attempt precluded the "consultations" mandated by the War Powers Resolution. When, through the coincidence of bad planning and bad weather, the operation proved a costly failure, congressional critics were quick to denounce Carter for his defiance of the law—some going so far as to call for his IMPEACHMENT. The hostages subsequently were released as the result of an EXECUTIVE AGREEMENT by which Carter canceled the claims of some Americans against the revolutionary government of Iran and caused other claims to be submitted to an international tribunal rather than to American courts. This settlement of the hostage crisis appeared to some observers to exceed the scope of presidential power, but it was upheld by the Supreme Court in DAMES & MOORE v. REGAN (1981).

The War Powers Resolution continued to bedevil presidential conduct of FOREIGN AFFAIRS during the Reagan administration; but the real character of that controversial resolution was revealed by the contrast between two incidents involving American military forces. In 1981 President Reagan, at the request of all of the governments of the region, and in conjunction with two foreign allies, detailed a battalion of marines to Beirut, Lebanon, as part of an international peacekeeping force. The operation was not of the sort explicitly covered by the War Powers Resolution, and Reagan, although he communicated with members of Congress, did not take steps to comply with the consultation or reporting requirements of the resolution. Congress, however, unilaterally acted to approve the President's course of action rather than precipitate a confrontation over either the applicability of the resolution or its constitutionality. Several months after a suicide bomber killed more than 200 marines, the President withdrew the rest of the marines from Lebanon, conceding a major foreign policy failure; but Congress, because it had acted affirmatively to approve the operation, was in no position to condemn the President for that failure.

Subsequently, in 1984, the President authorized

a military operation to rescue American citizens trapped in the small Carribean nation of Grenada and to liberate that country from a Cuban-sponsored communist dictatorship. Such an operation was precisely within the terms of the War Powers Resolution, but it was planned and executed in secrecy and, again, the President complied with neither the consultation nor the reporting requirements of the resolution. However, because the operation was perceived as a success, most members of Congress refrained from complaining about the breach of the War Powers Resolution.

As the War Powers Resolution represented the resurgence of Congress in the foreign policy arena, the Congressional Budget Act was designed to reassert congressional control over government spending priorities. The federal budgetary process had been introduced in the 1920s to replace the chaotic amalgam of uncoordinated appropriations by which Congress had theretofore allocated federal revenues. But the executive budget, while coordinating expenditures and subjecting them to a common annual plan, remained detached from the appropriations process; hence disputes arose between the branches, especially when the aggregate of appropriations exceeded the executive's estimate of revenues. The deferral and cancellation of appropriated expenditures—called IMPOUNDMENT—became especially controversial when President Nixon was accused of using them for political, rather than economic, reasons.

The 1974 act purported to solve the problem by making budget planning a congressional function and by linking budgeting and appropriations in a single process. But, because the internal structure of Congress is not conducive to unified decision making and because the executive branch has not conceded that the detailed planning of expenditures is properly a legislative activity, the revised budget process has not been successful. The national government commonly operates for most of the year on the basis of resolutions authorizing continued spending at some percentage increase over the previous year's spending plus numerous special appropriations.

Between 1977 and 1985, as, to a lesser degree, between World War II and 1977, one of the great tests of constitutional government in America was the fiscal crisis resulting from persistent excesses of governmental expenditures over governmental revenues. Under constant political pressure to maintain or increase expenditure levels, but facing the unpopularity of increases in taxation (combined with the economic difficulty that increased tax rates may, by diminishing the tax base, actually result in lower revenues), Congress has resorted to borrowing to finance chronic deficits. At the end of 1985, Congress enacted, and President Reagan signed, a law providing for automatic reductions of appropriations when projected deficits reached specified levels. However, the ink was hardly dry before that measure (the GRAMM-RUDMAN-HOLLINGS ACT) was challenged as unconstitutional, even by some members of Congress and some representatives of the administration.

State legislatures, commonly required by their state constitutions to balance their own annual budgets, have petitioned Congress for a convention to propose a balanced budget amendment to the federal constitution. How even a constitutional mandate could be enforced to make Congress do what it seems unable to do, that is, to make difficult choices about public affairs, remains unclear. Meanwhile, the Congressional Budget Act exists to frustrate any attempt of the executive branch to supply the decision making.

Yet another device by which Congress attempted to reassert itself in the contest for dominance under a constitution that separates powers was the LEGISLATIVE VETO. Long before 1977, the DELEGATION OF POWER to the executive branch and to various INDEPENDENT REGULATORY AGENCIES was so great that the published volumes of federal regulations exceeded in number by many times the volumes of federal statutes. In statutes delegating legislative power to administrative bodies, Congress began to include provisions allowing Congress, or one house of Congress, to deprive agency actions of effect by simple resolution. In June 1983 the Supreme Court, in IMMIGRATION AND NATURALIZATION SERVICE V. CHADHA, held that the legislative veto, in some or all of its forms, was unconstitutional. The effect of the *Chadha* decision on legislative veto provisions that differed significantly from that in the Immigration and Nationality Act remained unclear for some time after the decision, and Congress continued to enact new legislative veto provisions after the decision. The real winner in that struggle for power, however, was not the President, but the bureaucracy.

Congress also asserted itself in more traditional ways, especially by exploiting the constitutional requirement that certain presidential actions have the Senate's ADVICE AND CONSENT. One category of such action is treaty making. President Carter suffered embarrassment over the PANAMA CANAL TREATIES and defeat on the second Strategic Arms Limitation Treaty. The Panama Canal debate was the first extended debate on a major treaty since that on the

Treaty of Versailles in 1919. The treaty was signed in September 1977 but the Senate did not consent to its ratification until the spring of 1978. The vote was 68–32 (only one affirmative vote more than required) and the Senate attached a "reservation" to the treaty, asserting that the United States could intervene militarily if the canal should ever be closed; the reservation nearly caused Panama to rescind its ratification of the treaty. President Carter signed the strategic arms treaty in July 1979 at a summit meeting with President Leonid Brezhnev of the Soviet Union. Although trumpeted as a major foreign policy achievement, the treaty was delayed in Senate hearings and finally shelved in 1980 after the Soviet Union invaded Afghanistan.

President Carter vigorously asserted the presidential treaty power when, after recognizing the People's Republic of China in Beijing as the lawful government of all of China he unilaterally abrogated the longstanding mutual defense treaty between the United States and the Republic of China on Taiwan. An affronted Congress immediately provided for a United States Institute to represent American interests in the Republic of China while delaying for over a year Carter's request that trade preferences be granted to the mainland regime. Congress was unable to salvage the mutual defense treaty, however; and the Supreme Court held in GOLDWATER V. CARTER (1979) that members of Congress lacked STANDING to challenge the President's action in court.

The other category of action requiring Senate approval is appointments. The Senate, although nominally controlled by the President's own party, frequently used confirmation hearings and votes to express disapproval of certain Reagan administration policies, especially the administration's reluctance to impose and enforce AFFIRMATIVE ACTION requirements. The Senate delayed for over a year appointment of Edwin Meese to be ATTORNEY GENERAL, and rejected outright the promotion of William Bradford Reynolds to be associate attorney general. Although Reagan's nomination of SANDRA DAY O'CONNOR to the Supreme Court (the only nomination to the Court between 1977 and 1985) was approved rapidly and without serious controversy, several other judicial appointments were delayed or rejected.

Another signal characteristic of American constitutionalism is FEDERALISM. From the mid-1930s on, the balance of power between the national government and the states has been shifting steadily in favor of the national government. President Reagan came to office pledging a reversal of that trend. However, his proposal for a "new federalism," in which governmental functions assumed by the national government would be relinquished to the states, was coolly received not only by Congress but also by state politicians, who feared that their responsibilities would increase even as their revenues continued to decrease. Somewhat more successful was Reagan's proposal to replace the myriad of categorical FEDERAL GRANTS-IN-AID, by which the national government partially funded certain mandated programs and set the standards by which the programs were to be run, with block grants.

Congress, however, has increasingly imposed conditions and restrictions on the use of block grant funds; so even the limited victory may prove hollow. Although conservatives like President Reagan frequently express a principled aversion to the use of conditional grants of money as a means to coerce the states into acceding to federal goals and programs, they have not been so averse in practice. Examples of new uses of the TAXING AND SPENDING POWER to accomplish legislative goals not strictly within Congress's ENUMERATED POWERS include: a requirement that hospitals receiving federal funds perform certain lifesaving measures on behalf of handicapped newborn children; a requirement that states, as a condition of receiving highway building funds, enact certain provisions to counter drunken driving; and a requirement that schools, as a condition of receiving federal aid, permit religious groups to meet in their facilities on the same basis as do other extracurricular organizations.

Whether the election of 1980 wrought an enduring change in the constitution of American government remains an open question. Although President Reagan decisively defeated former Vice-President Walter F. Mondale in 1984, the House of Representatives remained under the control of Carter's and Mondale's party. And the Senate, even with a Republican majority, did not prove to be so committed as the President to reduction of the role of the federal government in American society. Nevertheless, Reagan had considerable success in achieving the deregulation of some kinds of businesses and in returning to private enterprise some activities that had come under the ownership and management of the federal government. On the other hand, the heralded "new federalism" did not cause a resurgence in the relative importance of the state governments, and federal control continued to be maintained through the use of conditions attached to grants-in-aid. At the bicentennial of the Constitution, it is still too early to say whether

Reagan effected, as he said he would, "another American revolution."

DENNIS J. MAHONEY

Bibliography

CARTER, JIMMY 1984 *Keeping the Faith.* New York: Bantam.

FISHER, LOUIS 1984 *Congressional Conflicts between Congress and the President.* Princeton, N.J.: Princeton University Press.

GINSBERG, BENJAMIN 1987 *Reconstituting American Politics: Cleavages and Coalitions in the Age of Ronald Reagan.* New York: Oxford University Press.

HOWITT, ARNOLD M. 1984 *Managing Federalism: Studies in Intergovernmental Relations.* Washington: Congressional Quarterly.

SCHRAMM, PETER W. and MAHONEY, DENNIS J., EDS. 1986 *The 1984 Election and the Future of American Politics.* Durham, N.C.: Carolina Academic Press.

CONSTITUTIONAL INTERPRETATION

"Constitutional interpretation" comprehends the methods or strategies available to people attempting to resolve disputes about the meaning or application of the Constitution. The possible sources for interpretation include the text of the Constitution, its "original history," including the general social and political context in which it was adopted as well as the events immediately surrounding its adoption, the governmental structures created and recognized by the Constitution, the "ongoing history" of interpretations of the Constitution, and the social, political, and moral values of the interpreter's society or some subgroup of the society. The term "originalist" refers to interpretation concerned with the first three of these sources.

The extraordinary current interest in constitutional interpretation is partly the result of controversy over the SUPREME COURT's expansive readings of the FOURTEENTH AMENDMENT; it also parallels developments in literary theory and more generally the humanities. Received notions about the intrinsic meaning of words or texts, access to an author's intentions, and the very notion of "validity" in interpretation have been forcefully attacked and vehemently defended by philosophers, literary theorists, social scientists, and historians of knowledge. Legal writers have imported scholarship from these disciplines into their own, and some humanists have become interested in legal interpretation.

Issues of interpretive methodology have always been politically charged—certainly so in constitutional law. JOHN MARSHALL's foundational decisions asserting the power of the central government were met by claims that he had willfully misconstrued the document. In our own time, modernist interpretive theories tend to be invoked by proponents of JUDICIAL ACTIVISM, and more conventional views by its opponents. The controversy within the humanities and the social sciences is itself deeply political, for the modernist assertion that truth or validity is socially constructed and hence contingent is often perceived as destabilizing or delegitimating.

The Constitution is a political document; it serves political ends; its interpretations are political acts. Any theory of constitutional interpretation therefore presupposes a normative theory of the Constitution itself—a theory, for example, about the constraints that the words and intentions of the adopters should impose on those who apply or interpret the Constitution. As Ronald Dworkin observed, "Some parts of any constitutional theory must be independent of the intentions or beliefs or indeed the acts of the people the theory designates as Framers. Some part must stand on its own political or moral theory; otherwise the theory would be wholly circular."

The eclectic practices of interpreters and the continuing debate over the appropriate methods or strategies of constitutional interpretation suggest that we have no unitary, received theory of the Constitution. The American tradition of constitutional interpretation accords considerable authority to the language of the Constitution, its adopters' purposes, and the implications of the structures created and recognized by the Constitution. But our tradition also accords authority to precedents and the judicial exegesis of social values and practices, even when these diverge from plausible readings of the text and original understandings.

Any theory of constitutional interpretation must start from the fact that we have a written Constitution. Why is the written Constitution treated as binding? Because, as Chief Justice Marshall asserted in MARBURY V. MADISON (1803), it is law—the supreme law of the land—and because since 1789 public institutions and the citizenry have treated it as an authoritative legal document. It is no exaggeration to say that the written Constitution lies at the core of the American "civil religion."

Doubtless, the most frequently invoked canon of textual interpretation is the "plain meaning rule." Marshall wrote in STURGES V. CROWNINSHIELD (1819):

[A]lthough the spirit of an instrument, especially of a constitution, is to be respected not less than its letter, yet the spirit is to be collected chiefly from its words. . . . [I]f, in any case, the plain meaning of a provision, not contradicted by any other provision in the same instrument, is to be disregarded, because we believe the framers of that instrument could not intend what they say, it must be one in which the absurdity and injustice of applying the provision to the case, would be so monstrous that all mankind would, without hesitation, unite in rejecting the application.

Marshall did not equate "plain" meaning with "literal" meaning, but rather (as Justice OLIVER WENDELL HOLMES later put it) the meaning that it would have for "a normal speaker of English" under the circumstances in which it was used. The distinction is nicely illustrated by Chief Justice Marshall's opinion in MCCULLOCH V. MARYLAND (1819), decided the same year as *Sturges.* Maryland had argued that the NECESSARY AND PROPER clause of Article I authorized Congress only to enact legislation "indispensable" to executing the ENUMERATED POWERS. Marshall responded with the observation that the word "necessary," as used "in the common affairs of the world, or in approved authors, . . . frequently imports no more than that one thing is convenient, or useful, or essential to another." He continued:

Such is the character of human language, that no word conveys to the mind, in all situations, one single definite idea; and nothing is more common than to use words in a figurative sense. Almost all compositions contain words, which, taken in their rigorous sense, would convey a meaning different from that which is obviously intended. It is essential to just construction that many words which import something excessive, should be understood in a more mitigated sense—in that sense which common usage justifies. . . . This word, then, like others, is used in various senses; and in its construction, the subject, the context, the intention of the person using them, are all to be taken into view.

To read a provision without regard to its context and likely purposes will yield either unresolvable indeterminacies or plain nonsense. An interpreter could not, for example, decide whether the FIRST AMENDMENT's "FREEDOM OF SPEECH" encompassed singing, flag-waving, and criminal solicitation; or whether the "writings" protected by the COPYRIGHT clause included photographs, sculptures, performances, television broadcasts, and computer programs. She would not know whether the provision in Article II that "No person except a natural born Citizen . . . shall be eligible to the Office of President" disqualified persons born abroad or those born by Caesarian section. We can identify interpretations as compelling, plausible, or beyond the pale only because we think we understand the concerns that underlie the provisions.

One's understanding of a provision, including the concerns that underlie it, depends partly on the ideological or political presuppositions one brings to the interpretive enterprise. Marshall could so readily label Maryland's construction of the word "necessary" as excessive because of his antecedent conception of a "constitution" as essentially different from a legal code—as a document "intended to endure for ages to come"—and because of his beliefs about the structure of FEDERALISM implicit in the United States Constitution. A judge starting from different premises might have found Maryland's construction more plausible.

A meaning thus is "plain" when it follows from the interpreter's presuppositions and when these presuppositions are shared within the society or at least within the relevant "community of interpretation"—for example, the legal profession. Kenneth Abraham has remarked, "The plain is plain because it is constantly recurring in similar contexts and there is general agreement about the meaning of language that may be applied to it. In short, meaning is a function of agreement. . . ."

When a provision is interpreted roughly contemporaneously with its adoption, an interpreter unconsciously places it in the social and linguistic context of her society. Over the course of several centuries, however, even a relatively stable nation will undergo changes—in social and economic relations, in technology, and ultimately in values—to an extent that a later interpreter cannot readily assume that she has direct access to the contexts in which a constitutional provision was adopted. This poses both a normative and a methodological question for the modern interpreter: should she attempt to read provisions in their original social and linguistic contexts, or in a modern context, or in some way that mediates between the two? And, to the extent that the original contexts are relevant, how can she ascertain them?

Original history includes "legislative history"—the debates and proceedings in the conventions and legislatures that proposed and adopted constitutional provisions—and the broader social, economic, and political contexts surrounding their adoption. Although it is widely acknowledged that original history should play a role in constitutional interpretation, there is little agreement over the aims and methods of historical inquiry. The controversy centers on the level of generality on which an interpreter should try to apprehend the adopters' intentions. On the highest or broadest level, an interpreter poses the questions: "What was the general problem to which this provision was responsive and how did the provision respond to it?" On the most specific level, she inquires: "How would the adopters have resolved the particular issue that we are now considering?"

The first or "general" question elicits answers such as: "The purpose of the COMMERCE CLAUSE was to permit Congress to regulate commerce that affects more than one state, or to regulate where the states are separately incompetent to regulate." Or: "The purpose of the EQUAL PROTECTION clause was to prohibit invidious discrimination." These characterizations do not purport to describe the scope of a provision precisely. On the contrary, they are avowedly vague or open-ended: the claim is not that the equal protection clause forbids every conceivable invidious discrimination (it may or may not) but that it is generally concerned with preventing invidious discriminations.

The general question is an indispensable component of any textual interpretation. The interpreter seeks a "purpose" that she can plausibly attribute to everyone who voted for the provision, and which, indeed, must have been understood as their purpose even by those who opposed its adoption. The question is often couched in objective-sounding terms: it seeks the "purpose of the provision" rather than the "intent of the framers." And its answer is typically sought in the text read in the social and linguistic context in which it was adopted. As Marshall wrote in *McCulloch,* "the spirit of an instrument . . . is to be collected chiefly from its words." If the status of the written Constitution as "law" demands textual interpretation, it also entails this general inquiry, without which textual interpretation cannot proceed.

The second inquiry, which can be called "intentionalist," seeks very specific answers, such as: "Did the adopters of the Fourteenth Amendment intend to prohibit school SEGREGATION?" or "Did they intend to prohibit 'reverse' discrimination?" One rationale for this focus was asserted by Justice GEORGE H. SUTHERLAND, dissenting in HOME BUILDING & LOAN ASSOCIATION V. BLAISDELL (1934): "[T]he whole aim of construction, as applied to a provision of the Constitution, is . . . to ascertain and give effect to the intent of its framers and the people who adopted it." Another rationale is that recourse to the adopters' intentions constrains the interpreter's discretion and hence the imposition of her own values. Some methodological problems are presented by any interpretive strategy that seeks to specify the adopters' intentions.

The procedures by which the *text* of a proposed constitutional provision is adopted are usually straightforward and clear: a text becomes a law if it is adopted by the constitutionally prescribed procedures and receives the requisite number of votes. For example, an amendment proposed in Congress becomes a part of the Constitution when it is approved by two-thirds of the members of each House and ratified by the legislatures in three-fourths of the states, or by conventions in three-fourths of the states, as Congress may prescribe.

How does an *intention* acquire the status of law? Some interpreters assume, without discussion, that by ratifying the framers' language, the thousands of people whose votes are necessary to adopt a constitutional provision either manifest their intent to adopt, or are somehow bound by, the intentions of certain of the drafters or framers—even if those intentions are not evident from the text itself. This view is not supported by anything in the Constitution, however, or by eighteenth- or nineteenth-century legal theory or practice.

If one analogizes the adoption of "an intention" concerning the text of the Constitution to the adoption of a text, an intention would become binding only when it was held by the number and combination of adopters prescribed by Article V. This poses no particular difficulty for an interpreter who wishes to understand the general aims or purposes of a provision. Statements by framers, proponents, and opponents, together with the social and political background against which the provision was adopted, often indicate a shared understanding. But these sources cannot usually answer specific questions about the adopters' intentions. The intentionalist interpreter thus often engages in a degree of speculation that undermines the very rationale for the enterprise.

The adopters of a provision may intend that it prohibit or permit some activity, or that it *not* prohibit or permit the activity; or they may have no intentions at all regarding the matter. An intentionalist interpreter must often infer the adopters' intentions from opaque sources, and must try to describe their intentions with respect to situations that they probably never thought about.

The effort to determine the adopters' intentions is further complicated by the problem of identifying the intended specificity of a provision. This problem is nicely illustrated by an example of Ronald Dworkin's. Consider the possible intentions of those who adopted the CRUEL AND UNUSUAL PUNISHMENT clause of the Eighth Amendment. They might have intended the language to serve only as a shorthand for the Stuart tortures which were their exemplary applications of the clause. Somewhat more broadly, they might have intended the clause to be understood to incorporate the principle of *ejusdem generis*—to include their exemplary applications and other punishments that they found, or would have found, equally repugnant.

More broadly yet, they might have intended to delegate to future decision makers the authority to apply the clause in light of the general principles underlying it. To use Dworkin's terms, they might have intended future interpreters to develop their own "conceptions" of cruel and unusual punishment within the framework of the adopters' general "concept" of the clause. If so, then the fact that they viewed a certain punishment as tolerable does not imply that they intended the clause "not to prohibit" such punishments. Like parents who instill values in their children both by articulating and applying a moral principle, the adopters may have accepted the eventuality that the principle would be applied in ways that diverged from their own particular views.

Whether or not such a motivation seems likely with respect to applications of the clause in the adopters' contemporary society, it may be more plausible with respect to applications by future interpreters, whose understandings of the clause would be affected by changing knowledge, values, and forms of society. On the other hand, the adopters may have thought of themselves as more virtuous or less corruptible than unknown future generations, and for that reason may have intended this and other clauses to be construed narrowly.

How can an interpreter determine the breadth of construction intended by the adopters of any particular provision? Primarily, if not exclusively, from the language of the provision itself. Justice FELIX FRANKFURTER wrote in *National Mutual Insurance Company v. Tidewater Transfer Company* (1949):

> The precision which characterizes [the jurisdictional provisions] . . . of Article III is in striking contrast to the imprecision of so many other provisions of the Constitution dealing with other very vital aspects of government. This was not due to chance or ineptitude on the part of the Framers. The differences in subject-matter account for the drastic difference in treatment. Great concepts like "Commerce among the several states," "due process of law," "liberty," "property," were purposely left to gather meaning from experience. For they relate to the whole domain of social and economic fact, and the statesmen who founded this nation knew too well that only a stagnant society remains unchanged. But when the Constitution in turn gives strict definition of power or specific limitations upon it we cannot extend the definition or remove the translation. Precisely because "it is a *constitution* we are expounding," M'Culloch v. Maryland, we ought not to take liberties with it.

Charles Curtis put the point more generally: "Words in legal documents are simply delegations to others of authority to give them meaning by applying them to particular things or occasions. . . . And the more imprecise the words are, the greater is the delegation, simply because then they can be applied or not to more particulars. This is the only important feature of words in legal draftsmanship or interpretation."

This observation seems correct. Yet it is worth noting that the relative precision of a word or clause itself depends both on context and on interpretive conventions, and is often uncertain and contestable. For example, in UNITED STATES V. LOVETT (1946) Justice Frankfurter characterized the BILL OF ATTAINDER clause as among the Constitution's very "specific provisions." Yet he construed that clause to apply to punishments besides death, ignoring the technical eighteenth-century distinction between a bill of attainder, which imposed the death penalty, and a bill of "pains and penalties," which imposed lesser penalties.

The effort to characterize clauses as relatively open or closed confronts a different sort of historical problem as well. The history of interpretation of written constitutions was not extensive in 1787. Marshall's assertion that it is the nature of a constitution "that only its great outlines should be marked" (*McCulloch*) drew more on theory than on practice. But Marshall and his successors practiced this theory. Whatever assumptions the adopters of the original Constitution might have made about the scope of their delegations of authority, the Reconstruction amendments were adopted in the context of decades of "latitudinarian" constitutional interpretation. What bearing should this context have on the interpretation of provisions adopted since the original Constitution?

The intentionalist interpreter's initial task is to situate the provision and documents bearing on it in their original linguistic and social contexts. She can draw on the accumulated knowledge of American social, political, and intellectual history. Ultimately, however, constitutional interpretation is subject to the same limitations that attend all historical inquiry. Quentin Skinner has described the most pervasive of these:

> [I]t will never in fact be possible simply to study what any given classic writer has *said* . . . without bringing to bear some of one's own expectations about what he must have been saying. . . . [T]hese models and preconceptions in terms of which we unavoidably organize and adjust our

perceptions and thoughts will themselves tend to act as determinants of what we think or perceive. We must classify in order to understand, and we can only classify the unfamiliar in terms of the familiar. The perpetual danger, in our attempts to enlarge our historical understanding, is thus that our expectations about what someone must be saying or doing will themselves determine that we understand the agent to be doing something which he would not—or even could not—himself have accepted as an account of what he *was* doing.

Trying to understand how the adopters intended a provision to apply in their own time and place is, in essence, doing history. But the intentionalist interpreter must take the further step of translating the adopters' intentions into the present. She must decide how the commerce power applies to modes of transportation, communication, and economic relations not imagined—perhaps not imaginable—by the adopters; how the cruel and unusual punishment clause applies to the death penalty in a society that likely apprehends death differently from a society in which death was both more commonplace and more firmly integrated into a religious cosmology. The Court invoked difficulties of this sort when it concluded that the history surrounding the adoption of the Fourteenth Amendment was "inconclusive" with respect to the constitutionality of school DESEGREGATION almost a century later. Noting the vastly different roles of public education in the mid-nineteenth and mid-twentieth centuries, Chief Justice EARL WARREN wrote in BROWN V. BOARD OF EDUCATION (1954): "[W]e cannot turn back the clock to 1868 when the Amendment was adopted. . . . We must consider public education in the light of its full development and its present place in American life throughout the Nation. Only in this way can it be determined if segregation in public schools deprives these plaintiffs of the equal protection of the laws." In sum, even the historian who attempts to meet and understand the adopters on their own ground is engaging in a creative enterprise. To project the adopters into a world they could not have envisioned borders on fantasy.

In an important lecture given in 1968, entitled "Structure and Relationship in Constitutional Law," Professor Charles L. Black, Jr., described a mode of constitutional interpretation based on "inference from the structure and relationships created by the constitution in all its parts or in some principal part." Professor Black observed that in *McCulloch v. Maryland*, "Marshall does not place principal reliance on the [necessary and proper] clause as a ground of decision. . . . [Before] he reaches it he has already decided, on the basis of far more general implications, that Congress possesses the power, not expressly named, of establishing a bank and chartering corporations: . . . [h]e addresses himself to the necessary and proper clause only in response to counsel's arguing its *restrictive* force." Indeed, the second part of *McCulloch*, which held that the Constitution prohibited Maryland from levying a tax on the national bank, rested exclusively on inferences from the structure of the federal system and not at all on the text of the Constitution. Similarly, *Crandall v. Nevada* (1868) was not premised on the PRIVILEGES AND IMMUNITIES clause of either Article IV or the Fourteenth Amendment. Rather, the Court inferred a right of personal mobility among the states from the structure of the federal system: "[The citizen] has the right to come to the seat of government to assert any claim he may have upon that government, or to transact any business he may have with it . . . and this right is in its nature independent of the will of any State over whose soil he must pass to exercise it."

Citing examples like these, Professor Black argued that interpreters too often have engaged in "Humpty-Dumpty textual manipulation" rather than relying "on the sort of political inference which not only underlies the textual manipulation but is, in a well constructed opinion, usually invoked to support the interpretation of the cryptic text."

Institutional relationships are abstractions from the text and the purposes of provisions—themselves read on a high level of abstraction. The implications of the structures of government are usually vague, often even ambiguous. Thus, while structural inference is an important method of interpretation, it shares the limitations intrinsic to other interpretive strategies. It seldom yields unequivocal answers to the specific questions that arise in the course of constitutional debates.

For the most part, the Supreme Court—the institution that most systematically and authoritatively interprets and articulates the meaning of the Constitution—has construed the language, original history, and structure of the Constitution on a high level of abstraction. It has treated most provisions in the spirit suggested by Chief Justice Marshall in *McCulloch v. Maryland*. This view of the Constitution is partly a political choice, based on the desire to accommodate a venerated and difficult-to-amend historical monument with changing circumstances, attitudes, and needs. But it is no less a consequence of the nature of language and history, which necessarily leave much of the meaning of the Constitution to be determined by its subsequent applications.

Constitutional disputes typically arise against the

background of earlier decisions on similar subjects. A complete theory of constitutional interpretation therefore must deal with the role of precedent. Interpreting a judicial precedent is different from interpreting the constitutional provision itself. A precedent consists of a JUDGMENT based on a particular set of facts together with the court's various explanations for the judgment. The precedent must be read, not only in terms of its own social context, but against the background of the precedents it invokes or ignores. Lon Fuller wrote:

> In the common law it is not too much to say that the judges are always ready to look behind the words of a precedent to what the previous court was trying to say, or to what it would have said if it could have foreseen the nature of the cases that were later to arise, or if its perception of the relevant factors in the case before it had been more acute. There is, then, a real sense in which the written words of the reported decisions are merely the gateway to something lying behind them that may be called, without any excess of poetic license, "unwritten law."

The American doctrine of STARE DECISIS accords presumptive but not indefeasible authority to precedent. Courts sometimes have overruled earlier decisions to return to what is said to be the original understanding of a provision. They have also overruled precedents that seem inconsistent with contemporary norms. For example, in HARPER V. VIRGINIA STATE BOARD OF ELECTIONS (1966), the Supreme Court overruled a twenty-year-old precedent to invalidate, under the equal protection clause, a state law conditioning the right to vote in state election on payment of an annual POLL TAX of $1.50. After surveying intervening decisions protecting political participation and other interests, Justice WILLIAM O. DOUGLAS concluded: "In determining what lines are unconstitutionally discriminatory, we have never been confined to historic notions of equality, any more than we have restricted due process to a fixed catalogue of what was at a given time deemed to be the limits of fundamental rights. . . . Notions of what constitutes equal treatment for purposes of the Equal Protection clause *do* change."

The process of constitutional adjudication thus has a dynamic of its own. It creates an independent force which, as a DOCTRINE evolves, may compete with the text and original history as well as with older precedents. Whether or not, as Justice JOHN MARSHALL HARLAN argued in dissent, *Harper* was inconsistent with the original understanding of the Fourteenth Amendment, the decision would have been inconceivable without the intervening expansion of doctrine beyond applications contemplated by the adopters of the Fourteenth Amendment.

Disagreements about the propriety of this evolutionary process are rooted in differing theories of constitutional law. To a strict intentionalist like Raoul Berger, the process appears to be simply the accretion of errors, which should be corrected to the extent possible. Others hold that the process properly accommodates the Constitution to changing needs and values. As Justice Holmes wrote in MISSOURI V. HOLLAND (1920):

> [W]hen we are dealing with words that are also a constituent act, like the Constitution of the United States, we must realize that they have called into life a being the development of which could not have been foreseen completely by the most gifted of its begetters. It was enough for them to realize or to hope that they had created an organism; it has taken a century and cost their successors much sweat and blood to prove that they created a nation. The case before us must be considered in the light of our entire experience and not merely in that of what was said a hundred years ago. . . . We must consider what this country has become in deciding what the Amendment has reserved.

Chief Justice CHARLES EVANS HUGHES's opinion in *Home Building & Loan* stands as the Court's most explicit assertion of the independent force of precedents and of the changing values they reflect. The Court upheld a law, enacted during the Depression, which postponed a mortgagor's right to foreclose against a defaulting mortgagee. In dissent, Justice Sutherland argued that the CONTRACT CLAUSE, which had been adopted in response to state debtor-relief legislation enacted during the depression following the Revolutionary War, was intended to prohibit precisely this sort of law. Given his intentionalist premise this disposed of the case. Hughes did not dispute Sutherland's account of the original history. Rather, he reviewed the precedents interpreting the contract clause to conclude:

> It is manifest . . . that there has been a growing appreciation of public needs and of the necessity of finding ground for a rational compromise between individual rights and public welfare. The settlement and consequent contraction of the public domain, the pressure of a constantly increasing density of population, the interrelation of the activities of our people, and the complexity of our economic interests, have inevitably led to an increased use of the organization of society in order to protect the very bases of individual opportunity. . . . [T]he question is no longer merely that of one party to a contract as against another, but of the use of reasonable means to safeguard the economic structure upon which the good of all depends.

The views articulated by Holmes, Hughes, and Douglas reflect the Court's actual practice in adjudication under the BILL OF RIGHTS, the Fourteenth Amendment, and other provisions deemed relatively open-textured. The process bears more resemblance to COMMON LAW adjudication than to textual exegesis.

In an influential essay, Thomas Grey observed that the American constitutional tradition included practices of nonoriginalist adjudication purportedly based on principles of natural rights or FUNDAMENTAL LAW, or on widely shared and deeply held values not readily inferred from the text of the written Constitution. Several of the Supreme Court's contemporary decisions involving procreation and the family have invoked this tradition, and have given rise to a heated controversy over the legitimacy of adjudication based on "fundamental values."

Originalist and nonoriginalist adjudication are not nearly so distinct as many of the disputants assume. Constitutional provisions differ enormously in their closed- or open-texturedness. Indeed, a provision's texture is not merely a feature of its language or its original history, but of the particular situation in which it is applied. One's approach to a text is determined by tradition and by social outlooks that can change over time. Depending on one's political philosophy, one may bemoan this inevitability, or embrace it. For better or for worse, however, Terrance Sandalow described an important feature of our constitutional tradition when he remarked that "[t]he Constitution has . . . not only been read in light of contemporary circumstances and values; it has been read *so that* the circumstances and values of the present generation might be given expression in constitutional law."

Most disputes about constitutional interpretation and fundamental values concern interpretation in particular institutional contexts. Today's disputes center on the judicial power to review and strike down the acts of legislatures and agencies and are motivated by what ALEXANDER M. BICKEL dubbed the "counter-majoritarian difficulty" of JUDICIAL REVIEW. Urgings of "judicial restraint" or of a more expansive approach to constitutional adjudication tend to reflect differing opinions of the role of the judiciary in a democratic polity and, more crudely, differing views about the substantive outcomes that these strategies yield. The question, say, whether Congress, the Supreme Court, or the states themselves should take primary responsibility for elaborating the equal protection clause is essentially political and cannot be resolved by abstract principles of interpretation. But this observation also cautions against taking interpretive positions based on particular institutional concerns and generalizing them beyond the situations that motivated them.

Constitutional interpretation is as much a process of creation as one of discovery. If this view is commonplace among postrealist academics, it is not often articulated by judges and it probably conflicts with the view of many citizens that constitutional interpretation should reflect the will of the adopters of the Constitution rather than its interpreters.

So-called STRICT CONSTRUCTION is an unsatisfactory response to these concerns. First, the most frequently litigated provisions do not lend themselves to "strict" or unambiguous or literal interpretation. (What are the strict meanings of the privileges or immunities, due process, and equal protection clauses?) Second, attempts to confine provisions to their very narrowest meanings typically produce results so ludicrous that even self-styled strict constructionists unconsciously abandon them in favor of less literal readings of texts and broader conceptualizations of the adopters' intentions. (No interpreter would hold that the First Amendment does not protect posters or songs because they are not "speech," or that the commerce clause does not apply to telecommunications because the adopters could not have foreseen this mode of commerce.) An interpreter must inevitably choose among different levels of abstraction in reading a provision—a choice that cannot itself be guided by any rules. Third, the two modes of strict interpretation—literalism and strict intentionalism—far from being synergistic strategies of interpretation, are often antagonistic. (Although the adopters of the First Amendment surely did not intend to protect obscene speech, the language they adopted does not exclude it.) A strict originalist theory of interpretation must opt either for literalism or for intentionalism, or must have some extraconstitutional principle for mediating between the two.

To reject these strategies is not to shed constraints. The text and history surrounding the adoption of a provision originate a line of doctrine, set its course, and continue to impose limitations. Some interpretations are more plausible than others; some are beyond the pale. And the criteria of plausibility are not merely subjective. Rather, they are intersubjective, constituted by others who are engaged in the same enterprise. Beyond the problem of subjectivity, however, the demographic characteristics of the legal interpretive community gives rise to an equally serious concern: the judiciary and the bar more generally have tended to be white, male, Anglo-Saxon, and well-to-do, and one might well wonder whether their interpretations do not embody parochial views or class interests. The concerns cannot be met by the choice of interpretive strategies, however, but only by addressing the composition and structure of the institutions whose interpretations have the force of law.

PAUL BREST

Bibliography

ABRAHAM, KENNETH 1981 Three Fallacies of Interpretation: A Comment on Precedent and Judicial Decision. *Arizona Law Review* 23:771–783.

BERGER, RAOUL 1977 *Government by Judiciary: The Transformation of the Fourteenth Amendment.* Cambridge, Mass.: Harvard University Press.

BLACK, CHARLES L., JR. 1969 *Structure and Relationship in Constitutional Law.* Baton Rouge: Louisiana State University Press.

CURTIS, CHARLES 1950 A Better Theory of Legal Interpretation. *Vanderbilt Law Review* 3:407–437.

DWORKIN, RONALD 1981 The Forum of Principle. *New York Law Review* 56:469–518.

ELY, JOHN HART 1980 *Democracy and Distrust.* Cambridge, Mass.: Harvard University Press.

FULLER, LON 1968 *Anatomy of Law.* New York: Praeger.

GREY, THOMAS 1975 Do We Have an Unwritten Constitution? *Stanford Law Review* 27:703–718.

HOLMES, OLIVER W. 1899 The Theory of Interpretation. *Harvard Law Review* 12:417.

MONAGHAN, HENRY 1981 Our Perfect Constitution. *New York University Law Review* 56:353–376.

SANDALOW, TERRANCE 1981 Constitutional Interpretation. *Michigan Law Review* 79:1033–1072.

SKINNER, QUENTIN 1969 Meaning and Understanding in the History of Ideas. *History & Theory* 8:3–53.

SYMPOSIUM 1985 Constitutional Interpretation. *University of Southern California Law Review* 58:551–725.

SYMPOSIUM ON LAW AND LITERATURE. 1982 *Texas Law Review* 60:373–586.

TEN BROEK, JACOBUS 1938–1939 Admissibility and Use by the Supreme Court of Extrinsic Aids in Constitutional Construction. *California Law Review* 26:287–308, 437–454, 664–681; 27:157–181, 399–421.

Encyclopedia of the American Constitution

Editorial Board

Encyclopedia of the American Constitution

LEONARD W. LEVY, Editor-in-Chief
Claremont Graduate School, Claremont, California

KENNETH L. KARST, Associate Editor
University of California, Los Angeles

DENNIS J. MAHONEY, Assistant Editor
Claremont Graduate School, Claremont, California

MACMILLAN PUBLISHING COMPANY
A Division of Macmillan, Inc.
NEW YORK

Collier Macmillan Publishers
LONDON

Macmillan Publishing Company
A Division of Macmillan, Inc.
866 Third Avenue, New York, NY 10022

Collier Macmillan Canada, Inc.

Printed in the United States of America

printing number
1 2 3 4 5 6 7 8 9 10

Library of Congress Catalog in Publication Data

Encyclopedia of the American Constitution.

Includes index.
1. United States—Constitutional Law—Dictionaries.
I. Levy, Leonard Williams, 1923– II. Karst, Kenneth L. III. Mahoney, Dennis J.
KF4548.E53 1986 342.73′023′03 86–3038
ISBN 0–02–918610–2 347.3022303
ISBN (this edition) 0-02-918695-1

STAFF:

Charles E. Smith, *Publisher*
Elly Dickason, *Project Editor*
Morton I. Rosenberg, *Production Manager*
Joan Greenfield, *Designer*

Complete and unabridged edition 1990

(*Continued*)

CONSTITUTIONALISM

Constitutionalism is a term not altogether congenial to American lawyers. It seems to share the characteristics of other "isms": it is neither clearly prescriptive nor clearly descriptive; its contours are difficult to discern; its historical roots are diverse and uncertain. Legal realist WALTON H. HAMILTON, who wrote on the subject for the *Encyclopedia of the Social Sciences,* began his article in an ironic vein: "Constitutionalism is the name given to the trust which men repose in the power of words engrossed on parchment to keep a government in order."

Historians, on the other hand, employ the concept with some confidence in its meaning. American historians tend to use it as a shorthand reference to the constitutional thought of the founding period. European historians have a somewhat harder time. Given a largely UNWRITTEN CONSTITUTION and the SOVEREIGNTY of Parliament, what does it mean to refer to British constitutionalism? What is the significance of Dicey's distinction between the "conventions of the constitution" and the "law of the constitution"? How meaningful is the distinction? As Dicey noted: "Whatever may be the advantages of a so-called unwritten constitution, its existence imposes special difficulties on teachers bound to expound its provisions." French authors view constitutionalism as an important element of the French Revolution, but run into difficulties as they contemplate the fact that, since the constitution of 1791, France has had fifteen of them—and by no means all democratic. German historians tend to restrict the use of the term *Konstitutionalismus* to the Central European constitutional monarchies of the nineteenth century, though German-language equivalents for constitutionalism (*Verfassungsstaat, Verfassungsbegriff*) are frequently encountered in the literature. The German constitutionalist trauma is, of course, the ease with which the Weimar constitution, in its time viewed as one of the most progressive in the world, could be brought to collapse at the hands of determined enemies who then managed to organize arbitrariness in the form of law.

Constitutionalism has both descriptive and prescriptive connotations. Used descriptively, it refers chiefly to the historical struggle for constitutional recognition of the people's right to "consent" and certain other rights, freedoms, and privileges. This struggle extends roughly from the seventeenth century to the present day. Its beginnings coincide with the "enlightenment" of the seventeenth and eighteenth centuries. Used prescriptively, especially in the United States, its meaning incorporates those features of government seen as the essential elements of the American Constitution. Thus F. A. Hayek called constitutionalism the American contribution to the RULE OF LAW.

Constitutionalism obviously presupposes the concept of a CONSTITUTION. A Swiss authority of some influence in the American revolution, EMERICH DE VATTEL, in his famous 1758 treatise, *The Law of Nations or the Principles of Natural Law,* provided a definition: "The FUNDAMENTAL LAW which determines the manner in which the public authority is to be exercised is what forms the *constitution of the State.* In it can be seen the organization by means of which the Nation acts as a political body; how and by whom the people are to be governed; and what are the rights and duties of those who govern. This constitution is nothing else at bottom than the establishment of the system, according to which a Nation proposed to work in common to obtain the advantages for which a political society is formed."

This rather neutral definition has to be read against the background of Vattel's theory of natural law. Vattel recognized the right of the majority to reform its government and, most important, excluded fundamental laws from the reach of legislators, "unless they are expressly empowered by the nation to change them." Moreover, Vattel believed that the ends of civil society were "to procure for its citizens the necessities, the comforts, and the pleasures of life, and in general their happiness; to secure to each the peaceful enjoyment of his property and a sure means of obtaining justice; and finally to defend the whole body against all external violence."

Later in the eighteenth century strong prescriptive elements became part of the very definition of a constitution. Two examples are equally famous. On October 21, 1776, the town of Concord, Massachusetts, resolved "that a Constitution in its Proper Idea intends a System of Principles Established to Secure the Subject in the Possession and enjoyment of their Rights and Privileges, against any Encroachment of the Governing Part." (See CONCORD RESOLUTION.) Article 16 of the French Declaration of the Rights of Man of 1789 put it even more bluntly: "A society in which the guarantee of rights is not assured nor the SEPARATION OF POWERS provided for, has no constitution."

Although it would be impractical to make such substantive features a necessary part of one's definition of a written or unwritten constitution, a proper understanding of constitutionalism as a historical phenomenon depends on them. Constitutionalism does not refer simply to having a constitution but to having a particular kind of constitution, however difficult it may be to specify its content. This assertion holds true even in the case of the interplay of old forces (monarchies and estates) with new forces (the middle class in particular) which characterized the emergence of constitutional monarchies in Central Europe during the nineteenth century. Seen from a constitutionalist perspective, many of the German constitutional monarchies were influenced by concepts that had much in common with constitutionalist thought. The most important of these concepts was the *Rechtsstaat:* a state based on "reason" and a strict regulation of government by law.

The concepts of a constitution and of fundamental laws have not had a constant meaning over time. Since the eighteenth century (though not before), it has become customary to translate Aristotle's word *politeia* as "constitution": "A constitution is the arrangement of the offices in a *polis,* but especially of the highest office." This definition precedes Aristotle's differentiation among six forms of government—those for the common good (monarchy, aristocracy, and "polity") and their perversions, which serve individual interests (tyranny, oligarchy, and democracy). Aristotle thus introduced substantive, not merely formal, criteria into his teachings about constitutional arrangements.

Cicero is usually credited with first giving the Latin term *constitutio* something like its modern meaning. About a mixed form of government, he said in *De Re Publica:* "This constitution has a great measure of equability without which men can hardly remain free for any length of time." Indeed, Roman law was characterized by constitutional notions. The constitution of the Roman republic, putting other substantive arrangements aside, was marked by the power of the plebs to pass on laws which bound the entire Roman people. While this republican prerogative of the plebs was later replaced by Senate lawmaking and eventually by the emperor's legislative monopoly, its status is perhaps best illustrated by Augustus's repeated refusal, on "constitutional" grounds, to accept extraordinary powers to renew law and morals. Though this Augustan reticence may have been a triumph of form over substance, "triumphs" of this kind have frequently illustrated how constitutional notions have become deeply entrenched.

In subsequent Roman usage the term *constitutio* came to identify imperial legislation that preempted all other law. The understanding of *constitutio* as signifying important legislation was retained during the Middle Ages in the Holy Roman Empire, in the church, and throughout Europe. A well-known English example is the Constitution of Clarendon issued by Henry II in 1164.

In England, the modern use of constitution as referring to the nature, government, and fundamental laws of a state dates from the early seventeenth century. In the House of Commons, in 1610, James Whitelock argued that the imposition of taxes by James I was "against the natural frame and constitution of the policy of this kingdom, which is ius publicum regni, and so subverteth the fundamental law of the realm and induceth a new form of State and government."

In Europe, perception that some laws were more fundamental than others were well established before the eighteenth century. MAGNA CARTA (1215), the PETITION OF RIGHT (1628), and the HABEAS CORPUS

Act (1679) are the best known English illustrations of this point. In addition, by their coronation oaths English kings obliged themselves "to hold and keep the laws and righteous customs which the community of [the] realm shall have chosen." Even if the law could not reach the king, the king was viewed as under the law (and, of course, under God). The bounds of the king's discretion were defined by the ancient laws and customs of England or, put differently, the COMMON LAW. By the seventeenth century, EDWARD COKE was even prepared to claim that acts of Parliament were subject to review under the common law (and natural law).

Though the status of French kings was considerably more mysterious and legal constraints on them were far fewer than in England, they too were viewed as subject to fundamental laws. The French Protestant political theorists of the sixteenth century expressed far-reaching views on the matter. François Hotman subtitled the XXVth chapter of the third edition of his *Francogallia* (1586): "The king of France does not have unlimited domain in his kingdom but is circumscribed by settled and specific law."

Beginning in the seventeenth century, the struggle over the limits of power, the ends of government, and the limits of obedience was frequently expressed in terms of social contract theory. Johannes Althusius, Hugo Grotius, JOHN LOCKE, and Jean-Jacques Rousseau all influenced the civil struggles of their age. Although the differences among these writers are profound, all of them stipulate a SOCIAL COMPACT as the foundation for the constitutional arrangements of the state. While such a contract is not necessarily based on an assumption of popular sovereignty, a social contract without the assumed or actual consent of "the people" or their representatives is unthinkable. Once this notion spread widely, it was difficult to maintain the divine right of kings, and it became almost irresistible to relocate sovereignty in the people—Thomas Hobbes notwithstanding.

One must not confuse the concept of a social contract with that of a constitution. For the "contractarians," constitutions follow from the social contract; they are not identical with it. Although the social contract is mostly a logical stipulation, at times the contract seems real enough, embodying or justifying specific constitutional arrangements. The Glorious Revolution in England, the American Revolution, the French Revolution—all appealed to the social contract.

The Glorious Revolution, like the English Civil War before it, was seen in contractarian terms. The Convention Parliament of 1689 resolved that James II "having endeavored to subvert the constitution of the kingdom by breaking the original contract between king and people . . . has abdicated the government and the throne is hereby vacant." The Declaration of Rights of 1689 was part of Parliament's contract with William and Mary and, later that year, was incorporated into the act of Parliament known as the BILL OF RIGHTS. After reciting Parliament's grievances against the absolutist tendencies of James II, the Bill of Rights prohibited the suspension of the laws by regal authority; provided for the election and privileges of Parliament (including a prohibition of prerogative taxation); and dealt with the right to petition, excessive bail, and the jury system.

Although this catalogue of constitutional concerns is modest by contemporary standards, the Bill of Rights, in conjunction with other British traditions and the "mixed government" confirmed by the Glorious Revolution, led MONTESQUIEU to celebrate England as the one nation in the world "that has for the direct end of its constitution political liberty." Montesquieu concluded his chapter on "The Constitution of England" in *The Spirit of the Laws* with the wry comment that it was not his task to examine whether the English actually enjoyed this liberty. "Sufficient it is for my purpose to observe, that it is established by their laws; and I inquire no further." When Montesquieu's book was published in 1748, some questions about constitutional liberty in England might indeed have been examined. For instance, the right to vote was extremely restricted and even that small electorate was not consulted when, by the Septennial Act of 1716, Parliament extended its own duration by another four years. For the American colonists who fought more against the British Parliament than against their monarch, this example of the "sovereignty of Parliament" marked the limit of British constitutionalism. As JAMES MADISON wrote in THE FEDERALIST #53, citing the Septennial Act: "Where no constitution paramount to the government, either existed or could be obtained, no constitutional security similar to that established in the United States, was to be attempted."

American constitutionalism during the colonial and revolutionary periods included the notions of a constitution as superior to legislation and the notion of a written constitution. As concerns the "writing" of constitutions, Gerald Stourzh has remarked, for the period after 1776, that Americans clearly differentiated "between the functions of constitution-*making* (with an additional differentiation between drafting and ratifying functions), of *amending* constitutions, and of *legislating* within the framework of the constitution."

One formal element in the American colonies was bound to have a profound impact on American constitutionalism, especially its choice of written constitutions as the means for anchoring the organization of their governments and the protection of their rights and privileges. COLONIAL CHARTERS, fundamental orders, and other written documents were used in the establishment of the colonies. These contracts between rulers and ruled provided for the government of the colonies, secured property rights, and even extended the guaranteed liberties and privileges of the English constitution. The 1629 CHARTER OF MASSACHUSETTS BAY is an important early example.

Pennsylvania, however, provides the most vivid illustration of the essential features and conundrums of American constitutionalism. In England, in 1682, a "frame of government of the province of Pensilvania" was agreed to by the Governor, WILLIAM PENN, and "divers freemen" of the province. It was a revision of an earlier plan drawn up by Penn which he had called "Fundamental Constitutions of Pennsylvania." The frame of government was replaced by a new frame as early as 1683. Its place was taken in 1701 by the Pennsylvania Charter of Privileges, granted by Penn during his second visit to the province and formally approved by the General Assembly. (See PENNSYLVANIA COLONIAL CHARTERS.) Though the focus here is on the Charter of Privileges, William Penn's preface to the Frame of Government deserves quotation: "*Any government is free to the people under it* (whatever be the frame) *where the laws rule, and the people are a party to those laws,* and more than this is tyranny, oligarchy, or confusion." Having invoked the notions of government of laws and popular consent, Penn went on, however, to warn against excessive optimism about the RULE OF LAW: "Governments, like clocks, go from the motion men give them; and as governments are made and moved by men, so by them they are ruined too." It is difficult to imagine a better reflection on the challenges faced by the American constitution makers of the eighteenth century.

The Pennsylvania Charter of Privileges of 1701 was a remarkable constitutional document. First of all, the charter itself was adopted in a constitutional manner, according to the provisions for amending the Frame of Government. Second, it began, not with the organization of government, but with an issue of fundamental rights: it guaranteed the freedom of conscience and made all Christians eligible for public office. Third, the charter provided for a unicameral representative assembly to be elected annually by the freemen with the right to initiate LEGISLATION and with all parliamentary powers and privileges "according to the Rights of the free-born Subjects of *England,* and as is usual in any of the King's Plantations in *America.*" Fourth, far ahead of its time, it gave to all "criminals" "the same Privileges of Witness and Council as their Prosecutors." Fifth, it guaranteed the "ordinary Course of Justice" in all disputes concerning property. Sixth, the proprietor committed himself and his heirs not to breach the liberties of the charter; anything done to the contrary should "be held of no Force or Effect." Seventh, the liberties, privileges, and benefits granted by the charter were to be enjoyed, "any Law made and passed by this General Assembly, to the Contrary hereof, notwithstanding." Eighth, the charter could be amended only by a vote of "*Six* Parts of *Seven*" of the Assembly and the consent of the governor. Ninth, the guarantee of liberty of conscience was placed even beyond the power of constitutional amendment "because the Happiness of Mankind depends so much upon the Enjoying of Liberty of their Consciences."

This colonial charter, granted by a feudal landowner, embodies the most significant elements of American constitutionalism as it emerged in the course of the century—the concept of consent and the concept of a written constitution sharply differentiated from ordinary legislation and with provisions for its amendment and a bill of rights, however rudimentary. Indeed, by placing the liberty of conscience beyond the amending power it posed the ultimate conundrum of constitutionalism—the possibility of unconstitutional constitutional amendments.

The concept of consent had direct consequences for questioning the powers of Parliament over America and for the American understanding of REPRESENTATION. In terms of constitutionalism, the most important part of the long list of grievances against George III with which the DECLARATION OF INDEPENDENCE began (following the model of the Declaration of Rights of 1689) was the passage which stated that the king had "combined with others to subject us to a JURISDICTION foreign to our constitutions, and unacknowledged by our laws; giving his assent to their acts of pretended legislation." The nation began with an assertion of the right to consent.

In the decades of constitution-making following independence the main organizational task of American constitutionalism was to spell out in detail the implications of popular sovereignty for the structure of government. What, for instance, should follow from the famous formulation in the VIRGINIA DECLARATION OF RIGHTS, of June 12, 1776, "that all power is vested in, and consequently derived from, the people; the magistrates are their trustees and servants, and at all times amenable to them"? Four subjects were of overriding importance: the franchise; the separation of powers; the amending process; and the protection of individual rights.

Political status in the colonies had mostly depended on property ownership, and the Revolution had not done away with these requirements. The federal CONSTITUTIONAL CONVENTION of 1787 could not agree on who should have the right to vote. Sovereignty of the people did not mean all the people. But who should have the right to vote was discussed frequently and with great seriousness. The voters of the Massachusetts town of Northampton, for instance, concluded in 1780 that restricting the franchise for the Massachusetts house to freeholders and other men of property was inconsistent with the concepts and principles of native equality and freedom, the social compact, personal equality, and no TAXATION WITHOUT REPRESENTATION. Their objections pertained only to elections to the house; indeed, they were based on the notion that in a bicameral legislature one chamber should represent property, the other persons. A few more decades had to elapse before property and taxpaying qualifications disappeared. The franchise was expanded in all Western societies in the course of the nineteenth century. The earliest and most inclusive expansion, however, came in the United States—although even here the vote was withheld from women, AMERICAN INDIANS, slaves, and, as a rule, free blacks.

The colonists widely believed that their governments were "mixed" in accord with the British model. A London compendium from 1755 said of the colonial governments: "By the governor, representing the King, the colonies are monarchical; by a Council they are aristocratical; by a house of representatives, or delegates from the people, they are democratical." While this was more an "ideal type" than an accurate description of the constitutional facts, the post-Revolution problem for those who had grown up within the tradition of mixed or balanced government was how to institute it under radically changed conditions. The question was not really whether to have balanced government, though some advocates of "simple" government existed.

The separation of powers doctrine, as put forward most influentially by Montesquieu, sought to limit power by separating factions and, to some extent, associating them with the executive and legislative functions of government. To Montesquieu the separation of powers was a necessary if not a sufficient condition of liberty. By 1776 the American constitutional problem had become not the separation of "powers" but the distribution of power flowing from a single source—the people.

Though the Americans continued to view the separation of powers as necessary to liberty and therefore indispensable to constitutionalism, they faced a formidable challenge in attempting to implement the concept. The towns of Essex County, Massachusetts, wrote "the Essex Result," a veritable dissertation on the subject in voicing their objections to the proposed Massachusetts constitution of 1778, which they considered insufficiently mindful of the separation of powers. They propounded the principle "that the legislative, judicial, and executive powers are to be lodged in different hands, that each branch is to be independent, and further, to be so balanced, and be able to exert such checks upon the others, as will preserve it from dependence on, or an union with them."

Practical problems were inevitable. The different powers of government do not imply clearly differentiated functions; they will necessarily be closely intertwined—especially if one adds the notion, urged in the Essex Result, of CHECKS AND BALANCES. In the major state constitutions enacted in 1776 and immediately after, the legislative branch usually dominated, but the constitutions distinguished conceptually between legislative, executive, and judicial functions. They made members of one branch ineligible to serve in the others, and they gave some measure of autonomy to the judiciary. However, with respect to such crucial features as the structure and election of the executive and the power of appointments, they differed radically one from the other.

As successful revolutionaries, the Americans faced a difficult political task. They needed to justify the power of the people to change their government and at the same time to assure the stability of the new order based on popular sovereignty. If, as a practical matter, consent meant consent by a majority, was that majority not also at liberty to change the states' new constitutions? If not, why not? Vattel had struggled valiantly to develop a satisfactory framework for thinking about constitutional change, though without much success. His argument in *The Law of Nations* that the legislative power could not amend the constitution is hardly a model of tight reasoning. Concluding his essay, Vattel observed: "However, in discussing changes in a constitution, we are here speaking only of the right; the expediency of such changes belongs to the field of politics. We content ourselves with the general remark that it is a delicate operation and one full of danger to make great changes in the State; and since frequent changes are hurtful in themselves, a Nation ought to be very circumspect in this matter and never be inclined to make innovations, except for the most urgent reasons or from necessity."

In America, THOMAS JEFFERSON was the foremost theorist of constitutional change. He believed that each generation has "a right to choose for itself the form of government it believes most promotive of its happiness. . . ." The same man who provided us with this theory of constitutional change wanted to be remembered in his epitaph for the VIRGINIA STATUTE OF RELIGIOUS LIBERTY (1786), which ended with a proviso that sought to secure the statute forever: we "do declare, that the rights hereby asserted are of the NATURAL RIGHTS of mankind, and that if any act shall be hereafter passed to repeal the present or to narrow its operation, such act will be an infringement of natural right."

In a way, the matter was simple. Jefferson and many of his fellow citizens were for change, stability, and inalienable rights all at the same time. These disparate aims were somewhat reconciled in practice by having the constitutions provide for their own amendment and for bills of rights. This course had important practical implications: it legitimized the concept of constitutional change and thus dramatically reduced the need for revolutions; and it advised the majority that it had no power to regulate at will the structure of government or basic rights of individuals. Enlightened America was anything but unanimous on the status of specific rights. Not every state constitution had a bill of rights; those that did almost always included the liberty of conscience, FREEDOM OF PRESS, trial by jury, and protection of property. Some of the rights, as Penn and Jefferson suggested, were considered so fundamental that their amendment would conflict with the very nature of constitutional government.

The CONSTITUTIONAL CONVENTION OF 1787 and the main features of the federal constitution, after a decade of state constitutions, further defined American constitutionalism. The Constitution precariously provided for a mode of RATIFICATION hardly in accord with the ARTICLES OF CONFEDERATION. Among the ironies of history is the fact that the Constitutional Convention's preference for the convention method of ratification (rather than ratification by all state legislatures as required by the Articles) resulted in attaching to the Constitution, in 1791, a BILL OF RIGHTS, which the Framers of Philadelphia had considered unnecessary.

The most important aspect of the Constitution was its implementation of the goal "to form a more perfect Union." Carl J. Friedrich characterized the claim that FEDERALISM is an American invention a defensible overstatement. The Constitution's effort to delineate clearly the powers of the federal government as against those of the states is remarkable indeed. Its main accomplishment was not to get bogged down by the metaphysics of sovereignty and to enable the federal government to legislate and tax in a manner binding the people directly, without using the states as intermediaries. This structure of "dual sovereignty" assured the viability of the federal government and, at least well into the twentieth century, the viability of the states. It underwent one substantial modification. When the "perpetual" nature of the Union was challenged over the issue of SLAVERY, constitutional amendments were enacted at the end of the Civil War for the primary purpose of securing equal rights to recently emancipated black citizens. These amendments eventually legitimized a great expansion of federal influence on the law of the states in the interest of greater equality for blacks and other minorities.

The constitutional organization of the federal government is delineated by the organization of the constitutional text. The PREAMBLE speaks of the people of the United States as ordaining and establishing the Constitution. The first (and presumably most important) article deals with the election and LEGISLATIVE POWERS OF CONGRESS. Article II vests the executive power in a President. Article III concerns the JUDICIAL POWER and its jurisdiction. Although this organization seems to provide us with a rather pure example of the separation of powers, the Constitution combines elements of separate and independent powers (such as an independent judiciary or a President not dependent on Congress for his term of office) with a thorough mixing of powers, best summarized by the concept of checks and balances.

Superficially, the legislative and executive branches seem to be assigned separate functions: lawmaking and law executing. The judicial branch, through dispute-settling, performs one part of the executive function under special conditions and special procedures. In reality, however, both the executive and the judiciary engage in lawmaking through interpretation and rule-making. The executive intrudes into the legislative function by exercising the VETO POWER. Congress, on the other hand, performs executive functions through legislative oversight, appropriations decisions, and confirming appointments. One might better forgo the Framers' own characterization of the system as one of separation of powers. American constitutionalism indulged itself in heaping checks upon checks so that the love of power of officials occupying the various branches of government could be harnessed.

On one of the most important of these checks and the most distinctly American contribution to constitutionalist doctrine, the Constitution of 1787 was silent. Nowhere does the constitutional text grant the power of JUDICIAL REVIEW of legislation. On the basis of the debates in the Constitutional Convention one can make a strong case that some of the most influential Framers thought that judicial review was implied, but this is not the same as saying that the Constitution implies it. How then did the American judiciary end up as the guardian of the Constitution?

There had been instances of courts exercising the power of judicial review as well as public debate of the issue in the new states. The case for judicial review was based on a peculiarly American amalgam of various strands of constitutionalism. First, there was the notion of a constitution as fundamental law. If Lord Coke could claim the common law as a basis for reviewing acts of Parliament, how much more plausible the claim that judges were bound to obey a fundamental charter viewed as supreme law. Second, if the constitutions derived their authority from the sovereignty of the people, and if legislators and other government officials were simply the people's trustees and servants, it was no great leap to reason that judges had to obey the will of the whole people as expressed in the constitution. Third, the special procedures for constitutional amendment typically denied the legislatures the power to amend by ordinary legislation, which suggested that attempts of that kind should go unenforced. Fourth, those constitutions containing bills of rights reenforced the notion of a constitution as superior law with the aim of protecting the rights of individuals against tyrannical majorities. Fifth, in the case of the federal constitution there was the added need to assure its status as supreme law throughout the Union. The arguments for and practice of judicial review of state legislation served to consolidate the understanding of the American Constitution as the supreme law of the land to which all government actors were subject.

Chief Justice JOHN MARSHALL in MARBURY V. MADISON (1803) to the contrary notwithstanding, the issue of judicial review was an intricate one. No simple constitutionalist syllogism could be constructed that invariably led one to conclude that judges had the power of judicial review. The amalgam, however, proved powerful under the conditions prevailing in the United States. When the Supreme Court went ahead and in effect appointed itself and the other judges guardians of the Constitution (in the case of the Supreme Court, eventually to become the preeminent guardian), the people, by and large, acquiesced.

The American institution of judicial review has influenced developments abroad. Various forms of constitutional review exist in Austria, Germany, India, Italy, Japan, and, now, even France—to name the most important. While their historical roots are many and their institutional characteristics diverse, the American model was highly visible when they came into being. One of the most instructive contemporary instances is that of the Court of Justice of the European Community. Starting with the need of assuring the uniformity of Community law throughout the member nations, the Court of Justice has transformed the treaties underlying the European Community (especially the Treaty of Rome) into the constitution of the community. These are radical developments. The constitutionalization of the Treaty of Rome has led to the introduction of judicial review, or what one might more appropriately call Community review, even into countries that have not previously recognized the power of their courts to pass on the constitutionality of legislation.

As constitutionalism does not refer to having a constitution but to structural and substantive limitations on government, it would be a gargantuan task to determine its incidence in a world full of written constitutions, of which many do not mean what they say, while others do not accomplish what they mean. The need to distinguish between form and substance would necessitate impossibly vast empirical assessments. The distinction between form and substance would also make desirable a detailed examination of the legal situation in countries, such as Great Britain, that meet most substantive requirements of constitutionalism without a written constitution, an entrenched bill of rights, or the power of judicial review.

Constitutionalism matured in the context of the liberal democracies with their emphasis on civil and political rights and their attempts clearly to define the public and the private sphere. The rights guaranteed, with the exception of certain rights to participate in the exercise of governmental power, were rights of the citizen against infringement by government of his own sphere, or "defensive" rights (German constitutional law has coined the term *Abwehrrechte* for this category). The eighteenth- and nineteenth-century constitutions do not contain social rights aimed at guaranteeing citizens a fair measure of well-being. A notable aspect of the Weimar constitution was its effort to formulate rights that would guarantee everyone a worthwhile existence. As the concept of CITIZENSHIP expanded from the formal equality of sharing legal capacities to the substantive equality of sharing goods, the contemporary welfare state became clearly committed to some undefined (and probably undefinable) minimum of such substantive equality. The predominant means for accomplishing such goals has been legislation rather than constitutionalization. Certain legislation of this kind has been viewed by some as in actual conflict with the constitutionalist scheme. This alleged conflict has, in turn, led to substantial efforts in the United States and other countries to reinterpret the liberal constitutions as not only permitting but demanding government intervention on behalf of the underprivileged.

In conjunction with these difficulties, but by no means restricted to them, American constitutional scholarship engages in periodic debates about methods of CONSTITUTIONAL INTERPRETATION. Much of the discussion reinvents the interpretive wheels of earlier generations. Its main focus is the degree of fidelity which may be owed the words of the Constitution and the intentions of its Framers. Some contemporary writing argues that the Constitution can incorporate contemporary value preferences of a highly subjective kind. The tension is between the need to expound an essentially unaltered eighteenth-century Constitution in a manner consistent with "the progress of the human mind," on the one hand, and the danger of dissolving the Constitution in the process. The dispute is further complicated by endless varieties of highly refined theories concerning the proper scope of judicial review.

Over its two hundred years the American Constitution has been assigned the role of a national ideology. It has performed this role for a people that has grown from a few million to almost 250 million citizens of very diverse background. While the historical disinclination to amend the Constitution by means other than judicial review may help account for its durability, it has also subjected the Constitution to considerable strain. As the secular equivalent of the Bible, as Walton Hamilton observed, "it became the great storehouse of verbal conflict, and rival truths were derived by the same inexorable logic from the same infallible source." More often than not, Americans invoke constitutional principles in order to understand and resolve conflicts. This fact attests to the extraordinary vitality of American constitutionalism. It may also endanger its viability. Too frequent crossings of the line between "constitution as ideology" and "ideology as constitution" will blur the line. The American concept of the legitimacy of government is closely tied to the Constitution. Its limitless manipulation may endanger the very legitimacy that has been the great accomplishment of American constitutionalism.

GERHARD CASPER

Bibliography

ADAMS, WILLI PAUL 1980 *The First American Constitutions.* Chapel Hill: University of North Carolina Press.

BAILYN, BERNARD 1967 *The Ideological Origins of the American Revolution.* Cambridge, Mass.: Belknap Press.

COOKE, JACOB E., ed. 1961 *The Federalist.* Middletown, Conn.: Wesleyan University Press.

DICEY, A. V. (1885)1959 *Introduction to the Study of the Law of the Constitution.* London: Macmillan.

FRANKLIN, JULIAN H., ed. 1969 *Constitutionalism and Resistance in the Sixteenth Century.* Indianapolis: Bobbs-Merrill.

FRIEDRICH, CARL J. 1941 *Constitutional Government and Democracy.* Boston: Little, Brown.

FRIEDRICH, CARL J. 1967 *The Impact of American Constitutionalism Abroad.* Boston: Boston University Press.

HAMILTON, WALTON H. 1931 Constitutionalism. Pages 255–258 in Edwin R. A. Seligman et al. (eds.), *Encyclopedia of the Social Sciences.* New York: Macmillan.

MAITLAND, F. W. 1926 *The Constitutional History of England.* Cambridge: At the University Press.

MCILWAIN, CHARLES HOWARD (1940)1947 *Constitutionalism: Ancient and Modern.* Ithaca, N.Y.: Cornell University Press.

PENNOCK, J. RONALD and CHAPMAN, JOHN W., eds. 1979 *Constitutionalism.* New York: New York University Press.

PERRY, RICHARD L., ed. 1972 *Sources of Our Liberties.* New York: New York University Press.

STOURZH, GERALD 1977 The American Revolution, Modern Constitutionalism, and the Protection of Human Rights. Pages 162–176 in Kenneth Thompson et al. (eds.), *Truth and Tragedy: A Tribute to Hans J. Morgenthau.* Washington, D.C.: New Republic Book Co.

WOOD, GORDON S. 1969 *The Creation of the American Republic 1776–1787.* New York: Norton.

WORMUTH, FRANCIS D. 1949 *The Origins of Modern Constitutionalism.* New York: Harper.

CONSTITUTIONALISM AND THE AMERICAN FOUNDING

Between 1776 and 1789 the American people constituted themselves a nation by creating republican governments in the thirteen former English colonies and then, in the CONSTITUTIONAL CONVENTION OF 1787, by transforming the Union of confederated states into a genuine law-giving government. The novelty of this achievement was epitomized in the seal of the new nation, which, by incorporating the phrase "Novus Ordo Seclorum," announced "a new order of the ages." Yet in founding political societies Americans pursued a goal that had occupied Western man since antiquity: the establishment of government power capable of maintaining the stability and order necessary to realize the purposes of community, yet so defined and structured as to prevent tyranny. This age-old quest for the forms, procedures, and institutional arrangements most suitable for limiting power and implementing a community's conception of political right and justice, we know as CONSTITUTIONALISM.

Constitutionalism takes as its purpose resolution of the conflict that characterizes political life and makes government necessary, through procedures and institutions that seek to limit government and create spheres of individual and community freedom. Based on the paradoxical idea that the power to make law and to rule can be at once sovereign and effective, yet also defined, reasonable, and responsible, constitutionalism contains an inherent tension that sets it against utopianism and anarchism, which deny the reality of power, and against absolutism and totalitarianism, which tolerate no limitations on power. Nevertheless, although constitutionalists can in retrospect be seen as sharing common assumptions, differences among them have sometimes led to irreconcilable conflict. One such division occurred in the eighteenth century when the American people separated from the English and adopted a new type of constitutional theory and practice for the conduct of their political life.

Perhaps the most obvious feature of American constitutionalism was its apparent dependence upon legally binding written instruments prescribing the organization of government and fixing primary principles and rules to guide its operation. Texts had of course long been used in law, government, and politics, and the English constitution comprised written elements. Americans' resort to documentary, positive law techniques of government was so much more systematic and complete than any previous undertaking, however, as to amount to constitutional innovation. Following the American example, peoples everywhere in the modern world have adopted the practice of forming governments by writing constitutions. But Americans in the founding era did more than invent a new approach to the old problem of limited government. Their constitution-making was informed with a new purpose—the liberal purpose of protecting the NATURAL RIGHTS of individuals. American charters of FUNDAMENTAL LAW were not simply ordinances of government; they were also constitutions of liberty. The meaning of liberty, especially the relation between the individual and the community that was central to any practical definition of it, was a deeply controversial issue that divided Americans in state and national constitution-making. The adoption of the federal Constitution in 1787, however, marked a decisive shift toward protection of individuals in the pursuit of their interests, and away from enforcement of community consensus aimed at making citizens virtuous and moral as the central purpose of constitutional government in America.

American constitutionalism is thus concerned with organizational and procedural matters, on the one hand, and with substantive questions of political purpose, on the other. Most constitutional politics in the United States deals with the former concern, as groups and individuals assert or deny the existence of proper governmental power or challenge methods used to employ it. Nevertheless, constitutionalism is ultimately normative and purposive. Every state may be said to have a constitution, in the sense of an institutional structure and established procedures for conducting political affairs. But not every state is a constitutional state. In the Western political tradition constitutional government exists where certain forms and procedures limit the exercise of power. American constitutionalism goes farther by pursuing not only the negative goal of preventing tyranny but also the positive end of promoting individual liberty, both in the passive sense of protection against government power and in the active sense of participation in the decisions of the political community. Viewed in this light, American constitutionalism raises basic questions of political purpose that connect it with the mainstream of Western political philosophy.

In the history of constitutionalism the great problem has not been to create power but to define and limit it. The Western constitutional tradition has employed two methods toward this end. The first is the theory and practice of arranging the internal structure of government so that power is distributed and balanced. A second method of constitutionalism has been to subject government to legal limitations, or the RULE OF LAW.

English constitutionalism in the period of American colonization comprised both strands of the constitutional tradition. The common law courts in the early seventeenth century insisted on the superiority of law to the royal prerogative. Sir EDWARD COKE gave famous expression to the idea of a higher law controlling government in asserting that " 'sovereign power' is no parliamentary word. . . . MAGNA CARTA is such a fellow, that he will have no sovereign." Coke also said that "when an act of Parliament is against common right and reason, or repugnant, or impossible to be performed, the common law will control it and adjudge such act to be void." Parliament itself, however, subsequently claimed supremacy in lawmaking, and vindication of its authority in the Glorious Revolution of 1688 effectively precluded development of the rule of law into a politically relevant form of HIGHER LAW constitutionalism. An internally balanced institutional structure, expressed in the revised and revitalized theory of mixed government in the eighteenth century, became the principal model of constitutional government in England.

Essentially descriptive in its connotation, the English constitution was the structure of institutions, laws, conventions, and practices through which political issues were brought to resolution and carried out in acts of government. Yet the constitution was also prescriptive or normative, or at least it was supposed to be. More specifically, as MONTESQUIEU, WILLIAM BLACKSTONE, and other eighteenth-century writers affirmed, the end of the English constitution was civil and political liberty. From the standpoint of modern constitutionalism the legislative supremacy that contemporaries regarded as the foundation of English liberty was incompatible with effective restraints on governments. Nevertheless, Parliament was believed to be under a moral obligation to protect the rights and liberties of Englishmen, and the sanctions of natural law were still seen as effective restraints. Moreover, political accountability to public opinion through elections operated as a limitation on government. Englishmen thus continued to see their constitution as fixed and fundamental, notwithstanding legislative SOVEREIGNTY.

American constitutionalism began in the seventeenth century when English settlers founded political societies and institutions of government in North America. Two things stand out in this early constitutional experience. First, the formation of government was to a considerable extent based on written instruments. In corporate and proprietary colonies the founding documents were COLONIAL CHARTERS granted by the crown conferring enumerated powers on a particular person or group within a designated geographical area for specific purposes. Under these charters the colonists adopted further agreements, organic acts, ordinances, combinations, and frames of government giving more precise form to political institutions. In religiously motivated colonies government was more clearly the result of mutual pledging and association under civil-religious covenants. American colonists thus used constitutionlike instruments to create political community, define fundamental values and interests, specify basic rights, and organize governmental institutions.

The second outstanding fact in early American constitutional history was substantial community control over local affairs. To be sure, the colonies employed the forms and practices of English government and generally emulated the metropolitan political culture. Their institutions at the provincial and local level were patterned after English models, and the theory of mixed government and the balanced constitution was accepted as valid. Yet discordant tendencies pointed to a distinctive course of constitutional development. The fact that in most colonies the power of the governor depended on royal authority while the power of the assembly rested on a popular base, as well as frequent conflict of interest between them, made separation and division of power a political reality discrepant with the theory of mixed government. Furthermore, popularly elected assemblies responsive to growing constituencies and enjoying de facto local sovereignty under written charters introduced a republican element into American politics.

As English subjects, Americans believed they lived under a free and fixed English constitution. Long before the Revolution they expressed this view in the course of conflicts with imperial officials. Numerous writers asserted that the constitution was a SOCIAL COMPACT between the people and their rulers; that the legislature could not alter the fundamental laws from which government derived its form, powers, and very existence; that government must exercise power within limits prescribed by a compact with the people. Moreover, the compact chosen to organize and direct government, as a colonial sermon of 1768 put it, must coincide with "the moral fitness of things, by which alone the natural rights of mankind can be secured." Disputing the descriptive English constitution that included parliamentary sovereignty, Americans were coming to think of a constitution as normative rules limiting the exercise of power for the purpose of protecting the people's liberty, property, and happiness.

In declaring their independence from England, Americans in a sense reenacted the founding experience of the seventeenth century. They took what their history and political circumstances determined to be the logical step of writing constitutions to organize their political communities. Before issuing the DECLARATION OF INDEPENDENCE, Congress recommended that the colonies adopt governments that "in the opinion of representatives of the people, best conduce to the happiness and safety of their constituents in particular, and America in general." Although some argued that the people acting in convention should form the government, political exigencies and Whig political theory conferred legitimacy on legislatures which, in all but two instances, were responsible for writing or adopting the first state constitutions.

The most distinctive feature of the state constitutions, their documentary character, followed the decision to form new governments as a matter of course. Given the long tradition of founding documents in America, it seemed obvious that the purposes of political community and limitations on government could be better achieved by writing a constitution than by relying on an unstipulated, imprecise constitution like England's, which did not limit government and was not really a constitution after all. Although consisting in part of written documents, the English constitution was too subjective, ultimately existing in men's minds and premised on the idea that "thinking makes it so." Americans insisted that the principles and rules essential to organizing power and preserving liberty be separated from the government and objectively fixed in positive form. Old in the tendency it reflected, though new in its comprehensive application, American constitutionalism rested on the idea that "saying it makes it so," or at least the hope that putting something in writing so it can be authoritatively consulted makes it easier to achieve specified ends.

The state constitutions stood in a direct line of descent from colonial documents that created political communities and established institutions of government. One type of founding document (compact or covenant) signified mutual promise and consent by which individuals formed a political community and identified basic values, rights, and interests. A second type of document (ordinance or frame) specified governmental institutions. Half the state constitutions written between 1776 and 1789 were described as compacts and contained bills of rights that defined basic community values. In the other constitutions the design of government received principal attention. All the constitutions reflected tendencies of previous political development; none created institutions on a completely clean slate. This fact appeared more clearly in documents that were mainly concerned with establishing a framework of government. In these more modern documents, which anticipated the course of American constitutional development, community consensus yielded in importance to protection of individual rights as the main purpose of constitution-making.

Republicanism was the political philosophy of the American Revolution. Although lacking in precise meaning, the concept is most accurately defined as government resting on the consent of the people and directed by the public will expressed through representative institutions. In the perspective of Western political thought republican philosophy was formulated in the seventeenth century to defend liberty against absolutism. The state constitutions were republican insofar as they limited government by prescribing public decision-making procedures that prevented government officials from aggrandizing power for private benefit rather than for the public good. The constitutions were liberal also in confirming and extending the right of political participation that according to republican philosophy constituted true liberty for individuals. In many respects, however, state constitutionalism in the revolutionary era was a doctrine of community power and control that restricted individual rights in a way that would now be seen as illiberal.

Under the state constitutions the most important power in modern government—the power to make law and to compel obedience—was lodged in the legislature. Unimpeded by internal governmental checks under the extreme version of the SEPARATION OF POWERS that prevailed in the first phase of state making, and sustained by presumptive identity with POPULAR SOVEREIGNTY as the source of political authority after the rejection of monarchy, legislatures acted forcefully to promote public virtue and the common good. Requirements of public virtue frequently took the form of restrictions on individual liberty through sumptuary laws and statutes regulating the transfer and use of property. Bills of rights that were part of state constitutions had little effect on curbing legislative power because they were treated as hortatory rather than legally binding. In the name of popular sovereignty and patriotism, state legislatures fashioned a constitutionalism of unity and power in government.

The concentrated power of republican virtue acting through institutions of community control was a useful and perhaps necessary expedient in the wartime emergency. In the doctrines of state sovereignty and the POLICE POWER revolutionary republicanism entered into the American constitutional tradition, and has offered a compelling model of constitutional government throughout our history to reformers and radicals on both the left and the right. However, the actions of the state legislatures too plainly contradicted the constitutional meaning of the Revolution to become accepted as the principal or exclusive expression of American constitutionalism. That meaning was nowhere better stated than by the MASSACHUSETTS CIRCULAR LETTER of 1768, which declared: ". . . in all free States the Constitution is fixed; & as the supreme Legislative derives its Power & Authority from the Constitution, it cannot overleap the Bounds of it, without destroying its own foundation." Yet this was precisely what was happening in the American republics.

The state constitutions may have been fundamental law in the sense of ordaining a framework of government, but they were not fundamental in the sense of controlling legislative power. In all but two states the constitution was written by the legislature and could be altered or abolished by that body. More than language of urging and admonition, contained in many of the constitutions, was needed to transform them into effective restraints on the actual exercise of power. Nor was the technique of internal institutional balance effectively employed to limit the state legislatures.

Attempts to restrict state legislative power in the 1780s broadened and reformed American constitutionalism. Writing and amending of constitutions by popularly elected conventions clarified the distinction between legislative law and fundamental law. Massachusetts in 1780 and New Hampshire in 1784 wrote their constitutions in conventions and required them to be ratified by the people in special elections. In theory this was the most effective way to make the constitution an antecedent higher law secure against legislative alteration. Further restriction of legislative power resulted from changes in the internal structure of government. Executive officers were given greater powers as CHECKS AND BALANCES—that is, a partial and limited sharing or mixing of functional powers among the departments—were introduced in some states as modification of the separation of powers. BICAMERALISM, a carry-over from colonial government, was recognized as a means of making legislative action more deliberate. And courts began to play a more prominent political role by treating constitutions as higher law in relation to legislative enactments.

So strong was the tradition of community self-government under legislative sovereignty, however, that it could not easily be dislodged as the main reliance of constitutionalism. Certainly little could be done to alter it by isolated efforts in the several states. Effective reform, if that was what was needed, could only come from an interstate collaboration working through the state system created by the colonies when they declared their independence. Heretofore peripheral to republican political development, the Union of the states in the Confederation became the focus of constitutional change.

The CONTINENTAL CONGRESS had been formed by the colonies in 1774 as a coordinating and advisory body to protect American interests and eventually to pursue the cause of national independence. Exigencies of war and common concerns among the states had given Congress political power, which it had exercised through informal rules and practices that were codified in the ARTICLES OF CONFEDERATION. Considered from a constitutional perspective as a limiting grant of power, the Articles were inadequate because, although they gave Congress ostensible power to do many things, they did not confer the lawmaking authority that is essential to government. Congress could at best make resolutions and recommendations, which in practice amounted to requests that the states could ignore. The Articles were unconstitutionlike in consequence of having been written by Congress and ratified by the states, rather than based in any direct way on popular authority. They were also unconstitutionlike with respect to institutional structure. Whether considered analogous to a legislative or executive body, Congress was the sole governmentlike organ, and only an evolving departmental system saved it from complete incompetence.

As an alliance or league of friendship, the Articles were a successful founding instrument. Yet in the form given it in the Articles, the confederation was incapable of addressing in a constructive manner the defects in American government revealed in the actions of the states. The confederation provided a field of political action, however, on which the reform of republican constitutionalism could take place. The practical impossibility of amending the Articles so as to strengthen Congress having been demonstrated, and the insecurity of liberty and property in the states apparently increasing, proponents of constitutional reform made a desperate move—the calling of a convention of the states at Philadelphia in May 1787—into an enduring achievement of statesmanship and constitutional invention.

Perhaps most significant, the Framers gave institutional expression to the idea that a constitution, in order to function as a limiting grant of power, must be higher as well as fundamental law. In addition to originating or organizing power, it must be maintained separate from and paramount to government. In a formal sense the Constitution as a founding document was superficially similar to the state constitutions. A preamble explained the reasons for the document, proclaimed the existence of a people and political community, defined specific purposes, and ordained a framework of government. In reality, however, the Framers departed from the model of the state constitutions. It was unnecessary to return to the fundamentals of the social compact and the purposes of republican government, as state constitution writers to varying degrees were inclined to do. The authors of the Constitution observed that they were not addressing the natural rights of man not yet gathered in society but natural rights modified by society and interwoven with the rights of the states. They knew that the nation whose existence they were recognizing was loosely related in its constituent parts and united by few principles and interests. It was far from the kind of cohesive, integrated community that the states by contrast seemed to be, and most unlike the nation-states of Europe. Hence the Framers briefly addressed in the PREAMBLE those few basic unifying purposes and values—liberty, justice, domestic peace, military defense, the general welfare—and gave virtually the entire document to stipulating the institutions and procedures of government. As fundamental law the Constitution thus was less a social compact for a coherent, like-minded community and more a contractlike specification of the powers, duties, rights, and responsibilities among the diverse polities and peoples that constituted the American Union.

Far more effectively than writers of earlier founding instruments, the Framers made the Constitution a paramount, controlling law. In a practical sense this was merely a question of law enforcement. Creating a real government to operate directly on individuals throughout a vast jurisdiction raised a new and potentially difficult compliance issue, but this received little attention at the Convention. It was the old compliance problem of the states that stood in the way of making the Constitution binding and effective. At first the delegates considered a congressional veto on state legislation to deal with this issue, but this was rejected as impracticable and was replaced by the SUPREMACY CLAUSE. This clause expressed the paramountcy of the federal Constitution over the states, and by inference, over national legislative law as well. Not explicitly stated, but implied in the judicial article, was the idea that the superior force of the Constitution depended on its application and interpretation by the courts.

The higher law character of the Constitution was further affirmed and institutionalized in the method of its drafting and in provisions for its ratification and amendment. Although delegates to the Philadelphia Convention were appointed by the state legislatures rather than elected by the people, the Constitution was a more genuine expression of the will of the people than were the Articles of Confederation, which were written by Congress. The Framers' apprehension about unlimited popular rule does not gainsay their commitment to the republican idea that government derives its just powers from the consent of the governed. Consistent with this commitment, institutions of direct popular consent that were still exceptional at the state level were incorporated into the national constitution. Ratification would be decided by conventions in the states, presumably popularly elected. Amendment of the Constitution could occur through popular approval, in state legislatures or special conventions, of proposals recommended by Congress or by a convention to be called by Congress on the application of two-thirds of the state legislatures. The superiority of the Constitution to legislative law was enhanced by this provision for amendment, as an utterly fixed and inflexible political law would become irrelevant to the task of governing an expanding society. If the Constitution required change, however, the people would have to amend it. Thus were popular sovereignty and the higher law tradition incorporated into American constitutionalism.

To make the Constitution paramount law in operational fact, however, it was not enough to assert its supremacy and assume that the people's innate law-abidingness would give it effect. This was to rely on "paper barriers," concerning the efficacy of which there was much skepticism among the Framers. It was necessary also to structure the organs of government so that power would be internally checked and limited. Although the Framers' objective was to create coercive authority where none existed, they rejected concentrated sovereign power as a constitutional principle. Delegated, divided, reciprocally limiting power formed the motif of their institutional design.

Unlike the state constitutions, which organized the inherent plenary power of the community, the Constitution delegated specific powers to the general government. The contrast was most significant in the plan of the legislative department, to which the state constitutions assigned the LEGISLATIVE POWER and which the federal constitutions defined by the ENUMERATED POWERS. Stable and energetic government seeming to require a strong executive and independent judiciary, the Constitution made grants of power of a more general nature to these branches, which under the separation of powers were counterweights to the lawmaking department. The separation principle by itself, however, as the state experience showed, was not a sufficient limitation on legislative power. Accordingly, checks and balances, by which each branch was given a partial and limited agency in the others' power (for example, executive participation in legislation through the VETO POWER or legislative judging in the IMPEACHMENT process) built further restraints into the Constitution.

The structure of the Union, of course, presented the most urgent question of institutional arrangements affecting the constitutional reality of a supreme political law. A division of power was already evident in the plan of the Articles of Confederation; what was needed was to transform the Union's political authority into a genuine power to impose lawful requirements on its constituent parts. This was achieved by reconstituting the Confederation as a compound republic, based on both the people and the states. Once this was accomplished, the pertinent fact for the paramountcy of the Constitution was the division of sovereignty. By giving the central government power over objects of general concern and allowing the states to retain almost all of their authority over local matters, the Framers divided sovereignty, thereby effectively eliminating it from the constitutional order. Arguments were certain to arise about the nature and extent of the powers of the several governments in the American state system, but the effect of such controversy would be to focus attention on the Constitution as the authoritative source of answers to questions about the rights of constituent members.

The Constitution was both fundamental and higher law because it expressed the will of the people, the ultimate source of authority in America. But it would truly limit power only if it was superior to the people themselves as a political entity, as well as to the legislative law. At the time some theorists of popular sovereignty argued that the people could alter their government at will, exercising the right of peaceful revolution and disregarding legalities of form and procedure, even as the Framers did in drafting and securing RATIFICATION OF THE CONSTITUTION against the express requirements of the Articles of Confederation. However we view their action, the authors of the Constitution rejected the notion of unlimited popular sovereignty. They provided restraints on the people in the form of a limited number of offices, long terms of office, indirect elections, large electoral districts, and separated and balanced departments of government. Although these provisions have often been viewed as antidemocratic and in conflict with republican theory, they are more accurately seen as modifying the popular form of government adopted during the Revolution. The Framers' intent, as JAMES MADISON wrote in THE FEDERALIST #10, was to supply "a republican remedy for the diseases most incident to republican government." And it should not be forgotten that despite careful distribution and balancing of authority, Congress remained potentially the most powerful branch of the government, most responsive to the people and possessed of the lawmaking power.

Making the Constitution effective as a permanent higher law involved matters of form, procedure, and institutional structure. Yet as procedural issues carry substantive implications, and means sometimes become ends in themselves, it is also necessary to ask what a constitution is for. To prevent tyranny, the constitutionalist goal, is to create a space in which differences among people become manifest, in which politics can appear and questions of purpose arise. If running a constitution always reflects political concerns, making a constitution is all the more a form of political action that derives from or partakes of political philosophy.

Americans were emphatic in declaring liberty to be the purpose of their constitutions. Moreover, if the purpose of politics is to protect men's natural rights, then American constitutions were liberal in purpose. Yet the concept of liberty, universally embraced as a political good, can be defined in different ways. And while recognition of natural rights gave modern politics a new purpose, it is equally true that virtue and moral excellence did not disappear from political discourse. These considerations give rise to two conceptions of political freedom in the constitutionalism of the founding period. The first is the liberty of self-governing political communities that were thought to have an obligation to make men virtuous and on which individuals depended for their happiness and well-being. The second rests on the primacy of natural rights and generally asserts individual liberty over community consensus as the purpose of government.

Although these conceptions of liberty stand in theoretical opposition to each other, they coexisted in the revolutionary era. After protesting imperial policies in the language of English constitutional rights, Americans justified national independence by appealing to universal natural rights. Wartime exigencies required decisive political action, however, which was based on the right of local communities to control individuals for the sake of the common good. States interfered with the liberty and property of individuals by controlling markets, restricting personal consumption, awarding monopoly privileges, and limiting imports and exports. They also regulated the speech and press freedoms of persons suspected of disloyalty to the patriot cause. In many ways revolutionary republicanism subordinated the rights of individual citizens to those of the community, defining true liberty as the pursuit of public happiness through political action.

Reacting against state encroachments on liberty and property, the constitution makers of 1787 emphasized protection of individual rights rather than promotion of virtue and community consensus as the purpose of government. Rather than an unattainable ideal of public virtue in ordinary citizens, they appealed to enlightened self-interest as the social reality on which the Constitution would rest. The Framers recognized factional conflict as a limiting condition for creating a constitution, yet also as an opportunity for broadening and redefining republican government. Alongside the communitarian ideal, which remained strong in many states, they created a new constitutional model in the complex and powerful government of the extended republic, based partly on the people yet so structured and limited that individual liberty, property, and pursuit of personal interests would be substantially protected against local legislative interference. This is not to say that mere private enrichment at the expense of the community good or general welfare was the end of the Constitution. The concepts of virtue and the public interest remained integral to political thought and discourse. But virtue assumed a new meaning as the prudent and rational pursuit of private commercial activity. Instead of telling people how to live in accordance with a particular conception of political right or religious truth, the Framers would promote ends believed beneficial to all of society—peace, economic growth, and intellectual advancement—by accommodating social competition and upholding citizens' natural rights against invasion by the organized power of the community, whether local, state, or national.

The Founding Fathers often appear antidemocratic because they created a strong central government, removed from direct popular and local community control, which they expected to be managed by an aristocratic elite. Notwithstanding its foundation in popular sovereignty and protection of individual liberty and rights, the Constitution contradicted rule by local communities guided by republican civic virtue as the real meaning of the Revolution. Although the Revolution stood for government by consent, there is no sound reason for regarding revolutionary state making as the single true expression of the republican principle. Essential parts of that principle were that government should operate through laws to which all were subordinate, both citizens and government officials, and that legislative law should be controlled by the higher law of the constitution. This was the meaning of the rule of law in the United States, and its more complete realization in the Constitution of 1787 signified climax and fulfillment of the Revolution.

The Framers' purpose must also be considered in relation to the threat of national disintegration, either from internal discord or foreign encroachment. The weakness of Congress in discharging its responsibilities was surely an impediment to protecting American interests, and an embarrassment to patriotic men. Yet the problem in 1787 was not the threat of total rupture of the Union attended by actual warfare among the states; the problem was the character of American politics and government, or the nature and tendency of republican government. Republicanism was the defining idea of the nation, and without it America would no longer have existed. The country was growing in the 1780s as population expanded, economic development occurred, and westward settlement continued. Yet the state system of 1776 was incapable of adequately accommodating and guiding this development. The states were too strong for the good of republican principles, the Union not strong enough. By restructuring the state system, by reconstituting the Union on the basis of a republican constitution that crystallized tendencies in congressional–state relations in the 1780s, the Framers sought to reform American government to the end of securing the republican ideals of the Revolution.

A constitution must recognize and conform to a people's principal characteristics and nature. Considered from this point of view the achievement of the Founding Fathers is undeniable. They created a complex government of delegated and dispersed, yet articulated and balanced, powers based on the principle of consent. Confirmation of that principle was in turn required by the Constitution in the cooperation and concurrence among the branches of government that were necessary for the conduct of public business. Made for an open, acquisitive, individualistic, competitive, and pluralistic society, the Constitution ordered the diverse constituent elements of American politics. More than merely a neutral procedural instrument for registering the play of social forces, it was a statement of ends and means for maintaining the principles that defined Americans as a national people. The Framers made a liberal constitution for a liberal society.

The Constitution was not only formally ratified but also quickly accorded full political legitimacy. The state constitutions, although not merely pretextual or façade documents, were not invoked and applied in the actual conduct of government as the United States Constitution was. And the new federal instrument was more than accepted: it rapidly became an object of veneration. The Constitution took a deep and abiding hold on the American political mind because it reflected a sober regard for the propensities of ordinary human nature and the realities of republican society; created powerful institutions capable of attracting men of talent, ambition, and enlarged civic outlook; and introduced changes in the conduct of public affairs that most people saw as improvements and that caused them to form an interest in the government it created.

The Constitution stipulated institutions, rules, and procedures embodying and symbolizing the principles of republican liberty, national unity, and balance and limitation of power. It was a fixed, objective document that could be consulted and applied, not a formless assemblage of principles, statutes, and decisions carried about in men's minds and dependent on social internalization for its effect. Yet the Constitution's principles and provisions were general and ambiguous enough to allow varying interpretations. Liberty, union, and reciprocally limiting power meant different things to different people, as did the rules and institutional arrangements expressing and embodying them. At a superficial level this circumstance produced conflict, but at a deeper level the effect was unifying. For groups and individuals were encouraged to pursue political goals within the framework of rules and requirements established by the Constitution. Thus the document became permanent and binding. Only the most extreme groups (radical abolitionists and slaveholders in the nineteenth century, totalitarian parties in the twentieth) have repudiated the Constitution as a framework for political action.

The Constitution possessed force and effect because it was useful and relevant to political life. Responsive to the social environment, it had instrumental value. At the same time, repeated reference to the document as the source and symbol of legitimate authority confirmed its intrinsic value, apart from the practical results of specific controversies. People believed, in other words, that it was important to follow the Constitution for its own sake or for the common good, rather than for a particular political reason. The intrinsic value of the Constitution lay not only in the wisdom and reasonableness of its principles in relation to the nature of American society but also in the form those principles were given in a written instrument. The effect of the Constitution as binding political law has much to do with its textual character.

The Framers addressed this issue in discussing "parchment barriers." The state constitutions were evidence that written stipulations were no guarantee of performance, especially when it came to limiting legislative power. Madison in particular said that it was not enough to erect parchment barriers in the form of constitutional provisions stating that the legislative department must confine itself to lawmaking. It was further necessary to arrange the interior structure of government so the constituent parts would limit each other. Personal motives of ambition and interest, Madison reasoned, when linked with constitutional offices would lead men to resist encroachments from other departments. These were the "auxiliary precautions" (supplementing accountability to the people) that would oblige government to control itself. Madison was saying that pluralistic differences in opinion and interest are necessary to make the prescriptions of the text function effectively.

Nevertheless, American constitutionalism insists that the text of the fundamental law be given its due. Madison's auxiliary precautions are in fact rules written into the document. Although the written text may not be sufficient, it is necessary to achieve the purposes of constitutionalism, or so it has seemed most of the time to most Americans. In the Constitutional Convention RUFUS KING said that he was aware that an express guarantee of STATES' RIGHTS, which he favored, would be regarded as "a mere paper security." But "if fundamental articles of compact are not sufficient defence against physical power," King declared, "neither will there be any safety against it if there be no compact."

Reference to the constitutional text has been a fixed feature of American politics. Its significance and effect have been variously estimated. A long tradition of criticism holds that the document has failed to limit government, especially the federal government in relation to the states. Others argue that constant invoking of the Constitution has trivialized politics by translating policy debate into legalistic squabbles that discourage dealing with issues on their merits. Reformers seeking a more programmatic politics have lamented that the Constitution by fragmenting power prevents responsible party government. And still others contend that the Constitution has worked precisely as intended: to eliminate genuine political action and make citizens passive subjects interested in private economic pursuits rather than public happiness and civic virtue.

These criticisms misunderstand the nature of constitutional politics and hence the binding and configurative effect of the Constitution. If politics is concerned with the end or purpose of political community, the proper role of government, the relationship between the individual and society, then it is difficult to see how the Constitution can be said to have brought an end to politics or prevented political action. As an expression of modern liberalism, however, the Constitution did signify a change in the nature of politics. To elevate natural rights into constitutionally protected CIVIL RIGHTS, as the Framers did, was to discourage an older politics based on the pursuit of glory, honor, conquest, and political or religious truth, as well as a newer ideological politics born of modern revolution. The Framers' constitutionalism was a way of organizing political life that paradoxically placed certain principles, rules, and procedures beyond politics, according them the status of fundamental and paramount law. Premised on the idea that citizens could pursue private interests while preserving community, it was intended to limit the scope and intensity of politics, preventing a total absorption of society that would impose tyranny in the name of ruler, party, people, or community.

Starting in the 1790s and continuing with remarkable continuity to the present day, public policy advocates have charted courses of action with reference to the Constitution. Using constitutional language firmly embedded in political rhetoric, such as DUE PROCESS OF LAW, EQUAL PROTECTION OF THE LAW, separation of powers, and so forth, they invoke its principles and values to justify their goals, argue over the meaning of its requirements, and align themselves with its manifest tenor as explicated in constitutional law and legislation. Political leaders do this not because they are unwaveringly committed to a specific constitutional principle; in different circumstances they might advocate a different principle. The decisive fact is the high public status accorded the Constitution: policymakers and political actors know that the people take the Constitution seriously, regard it as supreme law, believe that it is powerful because it embodies sound principles of government and society's basic values, and, indeed, venerate it. Aware of this popular prejudice in favor of the Constitution, and seeking the approval of public opinion, political groups and individuals are constrained to act in conformity with its provisions. Thus the Constitution as binding political law shapes the form and content of policies and events.

The constraining effect of the Constitution might nevertheless be questioned, for it will appear obvious that while some requirements are unequivocally clear (for example, the minimum age of the President), many provisions are ambiguous and imprecise in meaning. Confronted with this fact, many scholars have concluded that there is no single, true meaning of the Constitution, but rather that there are several possible readings of it, none of which possesses exclusive legitimacy. Some contend there is no real Constitution against which arguments about it can be evaluated, only different assertions as to what the Constitution is at any given time, or as to what we want it to be. Expressed in the oft-cited statement that the Constitution is what the Supreme Court says it is, this view, carried to its logical conclusion, would mean that the American Constitution is a developing, evolving, growing thing that is changed by the actions of judges, lawmakers, and executive officers. In that case the Constitution ceases to be a fixed, prescriptive, paramount law.

Politically and historically realistic as this analysis appears, it has never been accepted as legitimate in constitutional theory or in the conduct of constitutional politics. From the standpoint of the people and their representatives, the Constitution, in both its procedural requirements and its essential principles, has a true, fixed, ascertainable meaning. This popular understanding has existed from the beginning of constitutional politics in the debate over ratification, and it will probably continue until the popular belief, that the Constitution as a document says what it means and means what it says, is eroded or superseded by a more sophisticated view of the character of texts and political language. There is still a strong tendency in public opinion to think that written constitutions, in THOMAS JEFFERSON's words, "furnish a text to which those who are watchful may again rally and recall the people: they fix too for the people principles for their political creed."

The importance of the constitutional text in American government has been raised anew in recent years in the controversy over original intent jurisprudence. Many legal scholars have expressed doubt about the wisdom and legitimacy of consulting the original intent of the Constitution or of its authors in settling constitutional disputes. The words of the text, it is argued, apart from anything that its authors may have written or said about its meaning, must be considered as expressing the original intent. And the text must be read and understood according to the accepted meaning of words in the interpreter's own time, place, and historical situation. Some dispose of original intent more directly by asserting that constitutional interpretation need not be bound by the constitutional text, but may be based on fundamental social values and conceptions of justice and moral progress that judges are specially qualified to understand and apply. Either way, the Constitution is assured of its status as a "living document" adaptable to changing social conditions.

Although there may be sound reasons for disconnecting constitutional politics from original intent, from a historical standpoint it seems clear that neither the Framers nor the people over 200 years have taken so narrow a view of the meaning and relevance of original intent. The purpose of making a fixed, objective constitution was to decide the most important basic questions about politics and government once and for all—or until the people changed their mind and amended the document. The idea was to bind future generations in fundamental ways. This purpose would be defeated if those who later ran the Constitution were free to substitute their own definitions of its key terms. Yet the fact remains that constitutional principles and rules have been reinterpreted and redefined, in apparent contradiction of the Framers' intent, in decisions and statutes that have been accepted as politically legitimate. The Supreme Court has, in a sense, acted as a continuing constitutional convention.

Although the Founding Fathers intended the Constitution to be permanent and binding, the language of the document cannot realistically or reasonably, in a categorical sense, be frozen in its eighteenth-century meaning. It is the Constitution's essential purposes and its fundamental principles and procedures that were not intended to change. The question to be asked is whether fundamental principles and values—the values of individual liberty, national union, distributed and balanced power, the consent of the people—can be defined in an authoritative text and thereby realized in public law and policy to the satisfaction of the political community. American political history generally provides an affirmative answer to this question. But it is important to remember that an overriding imperative in American politics, law, and government has been to reconcile public policy with constitutional principles and rules as embodied in the text, and in accordance with the Framers' intentions. Moreover, original intent has not been viewed in a narrowly positivistic manner. The text was thought to have a definite and lasting meaning; and speeches, writings, and letters of the authors of the Constitution have always been thought pertinent to the task of elucidating its meaning. Whatever the practical effect of dismissal of the text and repudiation of original intent would be, such a step would alter the historic character of American constitutionalism.

Diverse in ethnic, religious, cultural, and social characteristics, Americans were united in 1776 by the political principles set forth in the Declaration of Independence. Inchoate though it was, the new nation was defined by these principles—liberty, equality, government by consent, the pursuit of happiness as an individual right—which in various ways were written into the state constitutions. By establishing a republican government for the nation, the Framers of the Constitution confirmed these principles, completing the Revolution and making it permanent. Since then American politics has derived from and been shaped by the Constitution, and has periodically been renewed by popular movements resulting in electoral realignments that have included a return to the first principles of the Founding as an essential element.

Understanding this attachment to the constitutional text has often been difficult for scholars and intellectuals, who tend to disparage it as "constitution worship." Perhaps reverence for the Constitution expresses not so much a naive literalism, however, as an awareness of the act of foundation as a source of authority. Considered in this perspective the constitutional text stands for the Founding, and the principles written into the document symbolically represent values evident in the actions of the Framers. The Founding required rational discussion, deliberation, compromise, and choice; consent, concurrence, and mutual pledging. These procedural values are embodied in constitutional provisions that require government under a fixed institutional structure and by deliberative processes that depend on compromise and concurrence, in accordance with substantive principles of natural rights, consent, and limited and balanced power.

HERMAN BELZ

Bibliography

CORWIN, EDWARD S. 1955 *The "Higher Law" Background of American Constitutional Law.* Ithaca, N.Y.: Cornell University Press.

FRIEDRICH, CARL J. 1968 *Constitutional Government and Democracy.* Cambridge, Mass.: Harvard University Press.

GOUGH, J. W. 1955 *Fundamental Law in English Constitutional History.* Oxford: Oxford University Press.

LIENESCH, MICHAEL 1980 The Constitutional Tradition: History, Political Action, and Progress in American Political Thought. *Journal of Politics* 42:2–30.

LUTZ, DONALD 1980 From Covenant to Constitution in American Political History. *Publius* 10:101–133.

MCILWAIN, CHARLES H. (1940)1947 *Constitutionalism: Ancient and Modern.* Ithaca, N.Y.: Cornell University Press.

VILE, M. J. C. 1967 *Constitutionalism and the Separation of Powers.* New York: Oxford University Press.

WRIGHT, BENJAMIN F. 1958 *Consensus and Continuity: 1776–1787.* New York: Norton.

CONSTITUTIONAL REASON OF STATE

Reason of state is one of the illimitable silences of the Constitution. Derived directly from Niccolò Machiavelli and JOHN LOCKE (who called it the "prerogative"), it is "the doctrine that whatever is required to insure the survival of the state must be done by the individuals responsible for it, no matter how repugnant such an act may be to them in their private capacity as decent and moral men." Not labeled "reason of state" by the Supreme Court, the doctrine often travels under the banner of NATIONAL SECURITY or the "interests of society."

National survival is the ultimate value protected by the doctrine. But more is covered; it is used whenever an important interest of the state is jeopardized, as perceived by those who wield effective control over the state's apparatus (government). Wartime use is the most obvious, stated classically by ABRAHAM LINCOLN in 1861: "Is there in all republics this inherent and fatal weakness? Must a government of necessity be too *strong* for the liberties of its people, or too *weak* to maintain its own existence?" Other instances in which reason of state has been the validating principle include the treatment of American Indians, wars of conquest (such as the Mexican War), economic depressions, and the control of dissident groups. Justification for both the Korean and Vietnam "wars" rests on the doctrine. (See KOREAN WAR.)

The basic constitutional problem is to distinguish between the circumstances fit for republican (that is, democratic) rule and those suited for personal rule. With rare exceptions—the principal ones are the *Steel Seizure Case* (YOUNGSTOWN SHEET AND TUBE V. SAWYER, 1952) and UNITED STATES V. UNITED STATES DISTRICT COURT (1972)—the Supreme Court has deferred to the political branches of government. The President normally is the moving force, with Congress usually acquiescing in executive actions designed to meet perceived emergencies. The PRIZE CASES (1863) were the leading early judicial statement approving the doctrine. (See also JAPANESE AMERICAN CASES.)

To the extent that the doctrine of reason of state finds acceptance, the theory of LIMITED GOVERNMENT recedes. Government in the United States has always been relative to circumstances, precisely as strong as conditions necessitated. The Constitution, accordingly, has been updated by successive generations of Americans, often at least tacitly employing reason of state principles.

No criteria exist by which to determine whether reason of state has been validly invoked. The Supreme Court has thus far failed to define such synonymous terms as "national security" and "society." By employing a BALANCING TEST, the Justices rule for society—for the state—whenever the vital interests of the state are considered to be in danger. In so doing, the Court never divulges how it determines what the interests of society are or the weights to be given to them. Reason of state, therefore, often amounts to government by fiat, but with the legitimizing imprimatur of the Supreme Court.

The BILL OF RIGHTS was an effort to limit the application of reason of state. However, Supreme Court interpretations have converted many of those seemingly absolute commands into mere hortatory admonitions to act reasonably in the circumstances. For example, the FIRST AMENDMENT's presciption that "no law" should abridge freedom of speech or press has been interpreted into relative standards. Reason of state thus has been resurrected by the Supreme Court after the constitutional Framers tried to hem it in.

Every nation employs a variation of reason of state, whether or not it has a written constitution. France, for example, expressly provides for EMERGENCY POWERS in Article 16 of the constitution of the Fifth Republic. The United States has accomplished the same result without an express constitutional provision or even a stated constitutional principle.

If, as many assert, the United States has entered a period of great danger, one in which its constitutional institutions will be sorely tested, reason of state will doubtless often be invoked—probably tacitly—as emergencies and crises arise. The doctrine can and will be employed to justify presidential use of violence without congressional authorization, as Presidents have almost routinely done in the past. It is the ultimate basis for expansion of presidential powers in many directions.

The Constitution was written at a propitious time in history, a time when a coalescence of factors—geography, natural resources, freedom from external pressures, a small population, capital and cheap labor from Europe—provided a favorable milieu for the FUNDAMENTAL LAW and its structure of government to flourish. Today, Americans face polar opposites—a shrinking planet, dwindling resources, total immersion in FOREIGN AFFAIRS, a burgeoning population, a slowing of productivity and of economic growth. Crisis government, accordingly, is becoming the norm. More and more, government will call upon emergency powers—upon reason of state—in efforts to cope. The large meaning is that a new fundamental law is emerging, one that can be called the "Constitution of Control." It exists as another layer on the palimpsest that is the Constitution of 1787.

ARTHUR S. MILLER

Bibliography

FRIEDRICH, CARL J. 1957 *Constitutional Reason of State.* Providence, R.I.: Brown University.

MILLER, ARTHUR SELWYN 1981 *Democratic Dictatorship: The Emergent Constitution of Control.* Westport, Conn.: Greenwood Press.

ROSSITER, CLINTON 1948 *Constitutional Dictatorship: Crisis Government in the Modern Democracies.* Princeton, N.J.: Princeton University Press.

CONTEMPT POWER (Judicial)

The Constitution nowhere mentions contempt of court. The courts' powers in this area flow instead from a COMMON LAW tradition of debated antiquity and legitimacy. Contempt power has, however, become entangled with the Constitution in two respects: first, courts have had to explain how they came to exercise a power that in some respects seems antithetical to constitutional values; second, the Constitution has been held to limit some aspects of the courts' exercise of contempt power.

Contempt is the disobedience of a court's order or interference with its processes. Most judicial decrees are not orders to do or refrain from doing some act. Contempt would not arise, for example, from the simple failure to pay a money judgment. Some judgments, however, directly order a party to perform or refrain from performing some act. A court might order a party to transfer land, to integrate a school system, to cease polluting a stream, to answer questions put by the other side, or to refrain from obstructive behavior in the courtroom.

Having disobeyed such an order, one might be charged with a crime (since many jurisdictions make such acts criminal) or with contempt. Either charge might result in a fine or jail sentence, but the accompanying process might differ. For some categories of contempt the contemnor may suffer punishment without many of the rights normally attaching to criminal trials: to be represented by counsel, to prepare for trial, to present testimony, to cross-examine witnesses, or to have a TRIAL BY JURY. The list is extreme and would not apply to all of the often confusing categories of contempt developed by the courts, but it illustrates the potentially drastic nature of the power.

Courts employ such "criminal" contempt sanctions to redress judicial dignity, but individual litigants may also use contempt sanctions to gain the benefit of court orders. A party seeking to compel obedience to an INJUNCTION entered at his request may ask a court for a "civil" contempt sanction. Such a sanction typically orders the contemnor to jail or to the payment of a progressively mounting fine until he "purges" himself of the contempt by obeying the injunction in question. Though an accused civil contemnor enjoys the rights of counsel, testimony, and cross-examination, his hearing has none of the protections accorded criminal defendants, for the courts have held that this is a "civil" rather than a "criminal" proceeding in spite of the risk of imprisonment. Nor is the duration of the imprisonment or the size of the fine subject to any limitation save the discretion of the judge and the contemnor's continuing ability to perform the act required of him.

Justifying the use of apparently criminal penalties without protections constitutionally accorded criminal defendants, the courts have relied on claims of history, necessity, and categorization. The claim of history has rested on the propositions that at the time the Constitution was framed courts had long exercised contempt powers and that the Framers did not intend to alter them. Those claims have been challenged but are still made. The claim of necessity still urges the need for orderly adjudicatory proceedings and enforceable orders. The argument rests on the hypothesis that, were the usual restrictions of the BILL OF RIGHTS to apply to contempt proceedings, the courts would be unable to function. The argument from categorization involves simply the assertion that because neither civil nor criminal contempts involve "crimes," the portions of the Bill of Rights applicable to crimes do not apply. In the case of imprisonment for civil contempt this argument is bolstered by the circumstance that the contemnor has the power at any time to obtain his release by complying with the order—a power not enjoyed by a convicted criminal.

Though the courts' exercise of contempt power has thus been remarkable for the absence of constitutional constraints, some limits do exist. First, state and federal legislatures have statutorily required greater protections that the Constitution mandates. Second, the Supreme Court has imposed some constitutional limits: in criminal contempts the judge must find the defendant guilty beyond a reasonable doubt; in "indirect" contempts (those not committed before a judge or involving judicial officers) the contemnor is, in addition, accorded the rights of counsel, testimony, and cross-examination. Even in cases of direct contempt the contemnor may have a trial by jury if the judge proposes to inflict a serious penalty. Yet even in enunciating these protections, the Court has steadfastly insisted that the judge has a wide power to impose sentence on the spot for contemptuous behavior in the courtroom.

Judicial use of contempt power involves a collision between two *desiderata:* that of having tribunals able to conduct their proceedings and enforce their orders; and that of having persons whose freedom stands in jeopardy enjoy the protections of the Bill of Rights. Thus far the courts have concluded that in many situations the first goal necessitates subordinating the second.

STEPHEN C. YEAZELL

Bibliography

GOLDFARB, RONALD L. 1963 *The Contempt Power.* New York: Columbia University Press.

CONTEMPT POWER, LEGISLATIVE

See: Legislative Contempt Power

CONTINENTAL CONGRESS

On September 5, 1774, delegates from the colonies convened in Philadelphia in a "Continental" Congress, so called to differentiate it from local or provincial congresses. The FIRST CONTINENTAL CONGRESS adopted a Declaration and Resolves to protest British measures and promote American rights; it also adopted the ASSOCIATION. The Congress dissolved on October 24, 1774, having decided that the colonies should meet again if necessary on May 10, 1775. By that time, the colonies and Great Britain were at war. The Second Continental Congress adopted a Declaration of the Causes and Necessity of Taking Up Arms on July 6, 1775, and the DECLARATION OF INDEPENDENCE a year later. The Congress appointed GEORGE WASHINGTON as commander-in-chief of its armies, directed the war, managed FOREIGN AFFAIRS, and adopted a plan of union designated as the ARTICLES OF CONFEDERATION. After the thirteenth state ratified the Articles in 1781, the official governing body of the United States became known as "the Congress of the Confederation," but it was a continuation of the Continental Congress and was not reconstituted until 1789, when a Congress elected under the Constitution of the United States took office.

LEONARD W. LEVY

Bibliography

BURNETT, EDMUND C. 1941 *The Continental Congress.* New York: Macmillan.

CONTRACEPTION

See: Birth Control; *Griswold v. Connecticut;* Reproductive Autonomy

CONTRACT CLAUSE

In a flashing aperçu Sir Henry Maine observed that "the movement of progressive societies has hitherto been a movement from Status to Contract." In feudal systems a person acquired a fixed, social status by birth, one's legal rights and duties being determined thereby for life. The decline of feudalism was a fading away of the status system in favor of personal rights and duties based largely on contractual relationships. Obligations imposed by ancestry gave way to obligations voluntarily undertaken. Generally thereafter a person's place in society depended upon success or failure in covenants with respect, for example, to wages, raw materials, farm and industrial goods, or artistic talent. In such a setting it is crucial that agreements be dependable—not merely to promote the individual's security and mobility but for the good of a society that relies for its sustenance upon a vast network of voluntary, contractual relationships. Thus Article I, section 10, of the Constitution, reflecting in part unfortunate experience under the ARTICLES OF CONFEDERATION, forbids *inter alia* state laws "impairing the OBLIGATION OF CONTRACTS." In THE FEDERALIST #44, JAMES MADISON observed that such laws "are contrary to the first principles of the SOCIAL COMPACT and to every principle of sound legislation." In his view "the sober people of America" were "weary of fluctuating" legislative policy, and wanted reform that would "inspire a general prudence and industry, and give a regular course to the business of society."

Indeed the sanctity of contracts was deemed so vital to personal security that in fifty-five years following the Supreme Court's first contract clause decision (FLETCHER V. PECK, 1810), twenty-two states put such provisions in their own constitutions. With one exception each of them was included in the state's bill of rights. Prior to 1810 four states had already done this. All of them protected contracts generally (per *Fletcher*), not merely private contracts as in the NORTHWEST ORDIANCE. Plainly in JOHN MARSHALL'S day and long thereafter his Court's broad view of the contract clause was widely accepted—along with FREEDOM OF PRESS, FREEDOM OF RELIGION, and FAIR TRIALS—as one of those restrictions on government "which serve to protect the most valuable rights of the citizen."

Obviously those who thus equated property rights and civil liberty were—like the Founding Fathers and the MARSHALL COURT—disciples of JOHN LOCKE. He had taught that property and liberty go hand in hand; that neither thrives without the other; that to protect them both as indispensable to life itself is the reason for government. Generations later, in a radically changed economic setting, some Americans came to believe that property hampers liberty. Inevitably then (having forgotten Locke) they would misunderstand both the founders and our early judges—Lockians all. Thus the Progressive movement convinced itself and its heirs that the Marshall Court had erred in holding the contract clause applicable to state, that is, public, covenants and that in so holding the judges had revealed a pro-property bias. Both of these views—derived largely from *Fletcher* and *Dartmouth College v. Woodward* (1819)—seem erroneous. The first rests on the strange idea that unambiguous language of the Constitution means not what it plainly says, but rather something else, because of the supposed intent of its authors. (Of course authors' intent may be a proper key to the meaning of ambiguous terminology, but that is a very different matter.)

Had the CONSTITUTIONAL CONVENTION OF 1787 wanted the clause to cover only private agreements, that is, those between individuals, it need only have said so. The Continental Congress had done just that in the Northwest Ordinance: ". . . no law ought ever to be made, or to have force in the said territory, that shall in any manner whatever, interfere with or affect private contracts. . . ." Six weeks later, RUFUS KING moved to include its private contract approach in the Constitution. Following a brief discussion of possible ramifications of such a provision, it was dropped. A few days later, at the suggestion of the Committee of Style, the Constitutional Convention adopted the contract clause, which refers comprehensively to "contracts" without qualification. Nothing in our record of the proceedings explains the change of mind or the change of terminology. But this is certain: not a word there or in *The Federalist* even hints that the founders were concerned only with private covenants—that they thought a state should be free to violate its own agreements. ALEXANDER HAMILTON would later observe: "It is . . . impossible to reconcile the idea of a [state] promise which obliges, with a power to make a law which can vary the effect of it." Hamilton, of course, had been a member of the Constitutional Convention.

Long before John Marshall became a judge, Justice JAMES WILSON, in CHISHOLM V. GEORGIA (1793), had asked rhetorically: "What good purpose could this constitutional provision secure if a state might pass a law impairing the obligation of its own contracts, and be amendable, for such a violation of right, to no controlling judiciary power?" This from one who had been perhaps the second most important leader of the Constitutional Convention. Justice WILLIAM PATERSON, too, had been influential at the Convention. Years before *Fletcher* in a similar case, VAN HORNE'S LESSEE V. DORRANCE (1795), he had held that a state could not impair its own contractual obligations. So did the highest court of Massachusetts in *Derby v. Blake* (1799) and in *Wales v. Stetson* (1806). *Fletcher* was not without significant judicial precedent.

The argument that the contract clause does not mean what it says rests essentially on the proposition that the crucial contract problem in late eighteenth-century America was erosion of private contract obligations by DEBTORS' RELIEF LEGISLATION. No doubt this was a vexing and well-known difficulty. Yet surely it is no *ipso facto* basis for excluding related problems plainly covered by explicit constitutional language. State negligence with respect to state obligations was after all a matter of experience. Even if it were known that the Framers intended the written words to embrace only private contracts, judges could not properly adopt that view. For those who ratified can hardly be said to have ratified something other than the words of the document. To hold otherwise is to undermine the basic premise of a written constitution. As the Marshall Court put it in orthodox manner in *Dartmouth:* "This case being within the words of the Contract Clause, must be within its operation likewise, unless there be something in the literal construction so obviously absurd or mischievous, or repugnant to the general spirit of the instrument, as to justify those who expound the constitution in making it an exception. . . ." No such basis for an exception having been discovered, the Supreme Court ever since has found the contract clause applicable as written to contracts generally, whether public or private.

A related problem in *Fletcher* concerned the scope of the term "contract." The Georgia legislature had sold and granted to speculators millions of acres of public land. A subsequent legislature had repealed the grant on the ground that it had been obtained by bribery. Meanwhile part of the land had been conveyed to innocent third-party purchasers. The issue in *Fletcher* was whether the initial grant entailed obligations protected against impairment by the contract clause. The Court responded affirmatively. Of course, in modern usage a grant is not a contract, but that does not solve the problem. For it is quite clear that in the late eighteenth century the term "contract" had far broader connotations than it does today. As Dean ROSCOE POUND has explained:

> Contract was then used, and was used as late as Parsons on Contracts in 1853 to mean [what] might be called "legal transaction." . . . Not merely contract as we now understand it, but trust, will, conveyance, and grant of a franchise are included. . . . The writers on natural law considered that there was a natural legal duty not to derogate from one's grant. . . . This is the explanation of *Fletcher*, . . . and no doubt is what the [contract clause] meant to those who wrote it into the Constitution. ["The Charles River Bridge Case," *Massachusetts Law Quarterly* 27:19–20.]

In sum, in the context of the times a grant included an executory, contractual obligation of the grantor not to violate the terms of his grant.

On this and the public contract aspect of Marshall's opinions one finds no criticism or disagreement in a random selection of twelve legal treatises published before 1870, including THOMAS M. COOLEY's famous *Constitutional Limitations* (1868). Twelve years later, however, Cooley's *General Principles of Constitutional Law* (1880) took a somewhat critical stand. The change apparently reflected attacks upon the Marshall Court by C. M. Hill, R. Hutchinson, and J. M. Shirley writing separately in the *American Law Review* and the *Southern Law Review* from 1874 to 1879. In due course the Progressives would pick up these charges that the Marshall Court had erred, and they would add that "the great Chief Justice" was in fact "a stalwart . . . reactionary," a servant of property interests. It seems no coincidence that the Hill-Hutchinson-Shirley attacks germinated in an era (1865–1873) when nearly sixty percent of laws challenged under the contract clause were held invalid—an all-time high. Many such cases of course "favored" business interests and thus tended to offend Progressives. The result was that John Marshall became for them a villain.

Fletcher, of course, upheld the property claims of innocent, third-party purchasers. The alternative would have been to sustain the property claims of the innocent people of Georgia. Either way the judges would be deciding in favor of some, and against other, property interests. Either way innocent people would suffer. One fails to see how *Fletcher* can be said to reveal a property bias. Was there, however, bias of another sort in deciding for the ultimate buyers rather than for the initial owners? Far from exceptional, the choice was informed by a long settled (and still prevailing) rule of Anglo-American EQUITY jurisprudence. Although a fraudulent purchaser takes a good title *at law*, it is subject to cancellation by a chancery decree. Thus in a clash between a cheating buyer and his innocent victim the latter prevails. But *Fletcher* involved a clash between the innocent victim and an equally innocent, subsequent purchaser for value. With the equities thus in balance and the social interest in security of transactions on the side of the purchaser in possession, the chancellor does not intervene (the victim's recourse being an action for damages against the fraudulent party). In short, Marshall and his Court read the contract clause in the light of a long familiar rule of equity.

In the *Dartmouth* case, a group of philanthropists had received a public charter to create a college in New Hampshire. Later the state tried to take over and govern the school contrary to the charter provisions. Marshall's Court, following *Fletcher*, held that the charter was a contract which the state was not free to violate. Viewed narrowly the case was won by the college trustees, but they had no beneficial interest in the college property. They won on behalf of the donor-philanthropists (presumably deceased) and generations of future students.

The Progressive response is that the *Dartmouth* decision was a crafty gambit purposefully designed for an ulterior purpose: protection of corporation charters from legislative interference. That it was highly successful is demonstrated, we are told, by the enormous growth of corporate enterprise thereafter. This is make-believe. Justice JOSEPH STORY in *Dartmouth* pointed out that no state need grant irrevocable or nonamendable charters—that the power to amend or revoke may be reserved. Damage resulting from failure to do so can hardly be held a fault of the judges. In fact reservation of power to alter corporate charters became widespread after *Dartmouth* and was not unknown before. (See RESERVED POLICE POWER.)

Fletcher and *Dartmouth* are not pro-property, but rather pro-transaction, cases. They mean that when judges find no clearly overriding public interest such as they found in GIBBONS V. OGDEN (1824) they will not disturb the contractual arrangements, that is, the *transactions*, by which women and men conduct their affairs—be they philanthropists (*Dartmouth*) or land speculators and farmers (*Fletcher*). As Marshall put it, "the intercourse between man and man would be very seriously obstructed, if this principle be overturned." Incidentally, by killing New York's restrictive steamboat law *Gibbons* too promoted transactional freedom.

An inclination toward unfettered private activity was deep in the temper of the times. Americans were on the make. They had escaped the old-world fetters: king, feudal aristocracy, and established church. They were the "new men." A vast geographical frontier invited initiative and ingenuity. The standard of living was low, but natural resources were plentiful. These conditions put a high premium on private, developmental effort. Such was the setting in which contract clauses found their way into bills of rights along with other basic protections then deemed indispensable to personal freedom and social well-being.

If the Marshall Court found that the Constitution forbade reneging on state obligations, it also recognized that public agreements raised special problems justifying a special rule of strict construction. In PROVIDENCE BANK V. BILLINGS (1830) Rhode Island had chartered the Providence Bank "in the usual form" with no reference of stipulation concerning taxation. Later, when the state enacted a bank tax, Providence Bank argued that a power (taxation) which might be used to destroy its charter was foreclosed by implication. The Court demurred: "as the whole community is interested in retaining [the power to tax] undiminished, that community has a right to insist that its abandonment ought not to be presumed, in a case in which the deliberate purpose to abandon it does not appear." Obviously the mere grant of a corporate charter for an ordinary banking operation could not rationally be held to imply an immunity from routine, nondiscriminatory taxation.

Marshall's Jacksonian successors under Chief Justice ROGER B. TANEY followed the established path with two modifications: a temporary enlargement of the rule of strict construction, and a decision that a state may not by covenant fetter its power of EMINENT DOMAIN. The former occurred in CHARLES RIVER BRIDGE CO. V. WARREN BRIDGE CO. (1837). Massachusetts had authorized private investors to build, operate, and maintain a public drawbridge in exchange for toll rights for a period of forty (later extended to seventy) years. Before that period expired the state authorized a competing, in effect toll-free, bridge only yards away from the original facility. Was the state free thus to jeopardize the revenue of the first bridge, or did the forty-year provision implicitly preclude such interference? It must have been clear at the outset to all concerned that investors would not provide, maintain, and operate for forty years a public facility, if the state were free at any time to disrupt their only source of compensation. Surely in these circumstances the Marshall rule of strict construction was satisfied; the state's "deliberate purpose" to permit unimpeded toll collection for the period in question seems obvious.

The Taney Court did not repudiate—indeed it purported to follow—the *Providence Bank* rule of strict construction. In fact, it simply ignored the "deliberate purpose" aspect of that rule, and substituted an incompatible principle derived from English precedents: "nothing passes by implication in public grants." (Thus did Harvard College lose part of its endowment.) Justices Story and SMITH THOMPSON dissented on implied agreement grounds. Justice JOHN MCLEAN agreed with them on the merits, but thought the Court lacked JURISDICTION. In substance *Charles River* was a 4–3 decision—although five of the Justices had been appointed by President ANDREW JACKSON, the other two by his Jeffersonian predecessors.

The majority position—exalting form over substance—would have permitted construction of an adjacent, toll-free bridge immediately after construction of the first one. Yet surely no court would so decide. If this be true, the Taney rule against implied agreements must be untenable. The Court seems rarely to have used it, having returned long ago to the Marshall approach. See, for example, NORTHWESTERN FERTILIZING CO. V. HYDE PARK (1878): "Nothing is to be taken as conceded but what is given in unmistakable terms, *or by an implication equally clear*" (emphasis added). The major upshot of the Taney Court's stricter rule of construction was that those who covenanted with a state took care to secure elaborately explicit commitments.

Charles River Bridge exudes liberalism, stressing as it does the social interest in progress. Property rights, the Court proclaimed, must not impede developing technology. Old turnpike charters, for example, should be construed "strictly" lest they block new railroads. But no such clash of old and new was at issue before the Court. The real problem was that after some forty years the Massachusetts legislature had come to believe the tolls were no longer justified—the bridge having long since paid for itself. A severely split Court decided not the real, but a hypothetical, case—demonstrating once again that the framing of the issue largely determines the outcome of a controversy.

The other innovation of the Taney era came in *West River Bridge Co. v. Dix* (1848). Vermont had granted exclusive bridge rights. This did not prevent it from confiscating the grantees' bridge during the life of the grant—subject of course to JUST COMPENSATION. The Court's rationale was that all contracts are subject to HIGHER LAW conditions. "Such a condition is the right of eminent domain." The indispensable power of taxation, however, is not such a "condition" and thus may be limited by state covenants, as the Court held in PIQUA BRANCH OF THE STATE BANK v. KNOOP (1854). Surely the distinction rests not on "higher law"—whatever that meant to the Court in the *Piqua* opinion—but upon the just compensation requirement in the one situation but not in the other, and the fact that there are many taxpayers and many ways to secure public revenue, but only one recourse when a specific piece of private property stands in the way of the public welfare.

The WAITE COURT followed a similar approach in generously defining the so-called STATE POLICE POWER. Thus a charter to operate a lottery does not bar enforcement of a later antilottery law. "All agree that the legislature can not bargain away the police power," the Court declared in STONE v. MISSISSIPPI (1880). Of course neither the state in question, nor any other, has ever undertaken to "bargain away" its POLICE POWER. The DOCTRINE as enunciated in *Stone* is at best a truism providing no standard for judgment. Had it been used in *Dartmouth,* the school would have lost its case and its independence. In fact, as Gerald Gunther has remarked, the *Stone* police power rule has been used mainly in cases "involving prohibitions of matters widely regarded as 'evil' ": for example, lotteries and intoxicating beverages, in an era when "Court invalidations of state laws impairing corporate charter privileges reached its highest frequency." (See INALIENABLE POLICE POWER.)

The epidemic of railroad fever that began in the Midwest in the 1850s was a prolific source of contract clause litigation. Many towns, cities, counties, and states issued railroad-aid bonds at an overall face value exceeding half a billion dollars. The purpose was to induce railroad companies to build lines convenient to the various bond issuers. Some of the desired construction never materialized. Many, perhaps all, of the railroad companies were overcapitalized. Stock watering was common. Some public and company officials were less than honest. These developments produced widespread resentment which some communities may have used for selfish purposes. In any case, what Henry Adams called the "mortgaged generation" (1865–1895) tried in one form or another to evade or repudiate much of its bond obligation. These circumstances are reflected in the path-breaking case of GELPCKE v. DUBUQUE (1864). After several decisions upholding the authority of cities to issue railroad-aid bonds, the Iowa Supreme Court, reinterpreting state law, reversed itself. On review the nation's highest Court upheld the claims of the adversely affected bondholders. In doing so it intimated that the state court's shift of position, retroactively altering the position of investors, was incompatible with contract clause principles. Popularly elected state judges apparently were more responsive to public sentiment than were appointed members of the federal Supreme Court. Ten years later *Pine Grove Township v. Talcott* (1874) brought the most extreme application of *Gelpcke* doctrine: to situations in which the state judiciary held bond issues invalid without overruling any prior decisions. The Supreme Court's rationale was that similar bond issues had been upheld in many other states before issuance of the bonds in question.

The contract clause intimations in *Gelpcke* and *Pine Grove* became an explicit basis of decision in *Douglass v. Pike* (1880). Much later the Court said that state court decisions did not produce contract obligations, and that neither *Gelpcke* nor its numerous offspring had in fact held otherwise. (*Tidal Oil Co. v. Flanagan,* 1924.)

Along with these bond cases another numerically important group involved the old problem of tax exemption. Without foregetting Marshall's *Providence Bank* rule of strict construction, the Court blocked a series of state efforts to annul pledges of corporate tax immunity.

After 1890 the contract clause as applied to state covenants gradually declined in favor or a more comprehensive, new device called SUBSTANTIVE (economic) DUE PROCESS—a gross perversion of the FOURTEENTH AMENDMENT. Years later, after the demise of that perversion, two cases suggested a possible renaissance of the contract clause. In UNITED STATES TRUST CO. v. NEW JERSEY (1977), the Court expounded a new principle of "particular" (more careful) scrutiny for cases involving public covenants "because the State's self-interest is at stake." New Jersey had issued transportation-system bonds pledging it would not substantially divert to other transportation needs the reserves and revenues securing them. Later it repealed this pledge. State courts upheld the repeal as a police power measure designed to promote additional transportation facilities. The Supreme Court reversed. No longer willing to defer to state determination of such issues, it ruled that judges must decide whether the contract impairment is "reasonable and necessary to serve an important public purpose." In this case it found that the state's needs could be served by less drastic means. In a bitter dissent Justices WILLIAM J. BRENNAN, BYRON R. WHITE, and THURGOOD MARSHALL insisted that for a century the "central principle" had been this: "unusual deference to [state and local] law-making authority." They could not accept a departure "from the virtually unbroken line of our cases" holding that "lawful" exercises of the police power are "paramount to private rights held under contract." The question remains, however, whether a particular exercise of power is lawful.

We turn now from public to private contract problems. No doubt the contract clause was inspired largely by debtor's relief laws, for example, measures authorizing postponed repayment of debts, installment payments, or payment in goods (often at a discount). In the Supreme Court's first encounter with this private contract problem it struck down a New York law discharging debts upon surrender of the debtor's property however inadequate to meet his obligations. Chief Justice Marshall's opinion for a unanimous Court in STURGES V. CROWNINSHIELD (1819) is noteworthy for two points: the "mere existence" of the national BANKRUPTCY POWER does not preclude state insolvency legislation; and, while a state may not impair contract obligations, it may alter the legal sanctions (remedies, such as imprisonment for debt) for enforcement of such obligations. Eight years later OGDEN V. SAUNDERS (1827) construed *Sturges* to prohibit only retrospective application of insolvency measures. Prospective application was deemed a different matter. The Court's rationale was that a debtor relief act in existence at the time of a contract became part of the contract; later enforcement thus would not constitute an impairment. On this basis, however, a retroactive insolvency law could also be upheld. After all, a state's power to adopt future insolvency measures may equally be deemed part of every contract. In his only recorded constitutional dissent "the great Chief Justice" along with Justices GABRIEL DUVALL and Story objected: the 4–3 majority had reduced a safeguard for contract rights to no more than a prohibition on "retrospectivity." Later, we shall see, even this restriction faded away.

Marshall's dissenting view in *Ogden* finds support in two separate votes in the Constitutional Convention. The contract clause of the Northwest Ordinance applied only to "private contracts . . . previously formed." In "copying" it, the Founders (as we have seen) dropped the limiting word "private." *They also dropped the limiting term "previously formed."* Later, on September 15, the Convention reaffirmed this position by rejecting George Mason's motion to insert the word "previous" after the words "obligation of" in the contract clause. Thus on two occasions the convention *rejected* the limitation that *Ogden v. Saunders* read into the Constitution.

The *Sturges* distinction between impairment of obligations and alteration of remedies threatened in later years to undermine the contract clause. Thus BRONSON V. KINZIE (1843), a leading Taney Court decision, taught that the allowable scope of remedial changes depends on their "reasonableness," provided "no substantial right" is impaired. As Justice BENJAMIN N. CARDOZO wrote with characteristic restraint in *Worthen Co. v. Kavanaugh* (1935), the dividing line "is at times obscure." The leading modern case, HOME BUILDING AND LOAN ASSOCIATION V. BLAISDELL (1934), upheld a Minnesota "mortgage moratorium" law that extended the time of payment of mortgage loans, thus saving many homeowners, farmers, and businesses from foreclosure. The Court used the remedy and police power gambits to escape the *Sturges-Ogden* rule against retroactivity. The significance of the case is this: it is the culmination early in the Great Depression of a long, step-by-step process that replaced the absolute approach of the Constitution with a judicial balancing or "reasonableness" approach in private contract cases. Yet all agree these are the cases that above all else produced the unqualified language of the contract clause. Such absolutism does not mean that the founders were hard-hearted, preferring creditors to debtors. It means merely that, giving debtor-relief authority to Congress via the bankruptcy power, they opted for uniform, national treatment of the ubiquitous debtor/creditor tension.

Notwithstanding *Blaisdell* the "old Court" thereafter struck down several insolvency measures. One of them was LOUISVILLE JOINT STOCK LAND BANK V. RADFORD (1935). In effect it read the contract clause into the Fifth Amendment to invalidate a federal mortgage moratorium law (a matter of reverse INCORPORATION). Then with the advent of the Roosevelt Court in 1937 (until *United States Trust* in 1977) the contract clause all but vanished as a safeguard for contractual obligations—public or private. The only exceptions are *Indiana ex rel. Anderson v. Brand* (1938), protecting teacher tenure claims, and *Wood v. Lovett* (1941), protecting a tax-sale purchaser against repeal of a law that cured possible defects in his title. *Wood* is particularly interesting because it rests on the *Fletcher* principle that a state land grant entails an implied contractual obligation not to repudiate the grant in question. Then came ALLIED STRUCTURAL STEEL CO. V. SPANNAUS (1978). There an employer had adopted an employee pension agreement. The state tried to alter it by enlarging the employer's obligations retroactively. Finding the alternation too "severe" to be upheld, the Court observed: "If the Contract Clause is to retain any meaning at all . . . it must be understood to impose *some* limits upon the power of a State to abridge existing contractual relationships, even in the exercise of its otherwise legitimate police power." As in *United States Trust,* Justices Brennan, White, and Marshall dissented bitterly. Stressing again their view of minimal (or no) protection of economic interests vis-à-vis the police power, they added this: the contract clause at most prevents diminution, not enlargement, of contractual obligations.

All of these cases from *Fletcher* to *Spannaus* entail a common theme: the precept of reasonable expectations. To what extent, if any, is government free to disturb those formal pledges on which men and women acting in good faith have planned their lives? A healthy legal system accommodates changing social needs. When ours was a rich and vigorous, yet underdeveloped, nation with a low overall standard of living, our law encouraged capital formation, transactional freedom, and respect for contract obligations. The "design"—not always and everywhere fully perceived—was to encourage production in the interest of a more comfortable life for everyone. Given the propensity of successful institutions to press beyond the limits of their logic, such encouragement may take grotesque forms, for example, the judicial abuses called DUAL FEDERALISM and substantive due process. If eventually a "backward" nation becomes highly developed, emphasis seemingly shifts from economic rights to "personal rights," from production to welfare, as in the United States beginning in the 1930s. If such a shift results in overreaction, threatening the source of the "golden eggs," emphasis may focus again on production along with protection for property and contractual rights, as in *New Jersey Trust* and *Spannaus.*

WALLACE MENDELSON

Bibliography

HALE, ROBERT L. 1944 The Supreme Court and the Contract Clause. *Harvard Law Review* 57:512–557, 621–674, 852–892.

HURST, WILLARD 1956 *Law and the Conditions of Freedom.* Madison: University of Wisconsin Press.

SCHWARTZ, BERNARD 1980 Old Wine in Old Bottles? The Renaissance of the Contract Clause. *Supreme Court Review* 1979:95–121.

WRIGHT, BENJAMIN F. 1938 *The Contract Clause of the Constitution.* Cambridge, Mass.: Harvard University Press.

CONTRACT THEORY

See: Social Compact Theory

COOLEY, THOMAS M.
(1824–1898)

Thomas McIntyre Cooley was a distinguished law teacher, state judge, first chairman of the Interstate Commerce Commission, and author of the influential 1868 *Treatise on the Constitutional Limitations Which Rest upon the Legislative Power of the States of the American Union.* Born in western New York to a family with a Jeffersonian "bias," Cooley absorbed an anticorporate equal-rights ideology, fearful of "class legislation" that aided the few at the expense of many.

In 1843 Cooley went west to Michigan and combined activities in law, journalism, politics, and poetry. He helped organize the Free Soil Party in the state and in 1856 became a Republican. Narrowing his concerns to the law, he rapidly attained professional recognition. Appointed Compiler of the state's laws in 1857 and Reporter to the Supreme Court in 1858, he was selected in 1859 as a professor at the newly opened University of Michigan Law Department. In 1864 he was elected to the Michigan Supreme Court.

Cooley tempered his preoccupation with the law with historical and political values and naturally turned to constitutional questions. To Francis Thorpe's 1889 query on books for a constitutional law library he replied that "constitutional law is so inseparably connected with constitutional history and that is so vital a part of general history that I should not know where to draw the line."

Historical, COMMON LAW, and Jacksonian sensibilities were the presuppositions of Cooley's 1868 treatise, although his aim was merely to write "a convenient guidebook of elementary constitutional principles." The book was that; it had gone through six editions by 1890 and had a broader circulation, a greater sale, and more frequent citations than any other law book published in the second half of the nineteenth century.

The treatise was useful because no one prior to Cooley had systematically analyzed the cases and principles dealing with constitutional limitations on state legislative power. Chapters on constitutional protection to personal liberty, to liberty of speech, and to RELIGIOUS LIBERTY were supplemented with chapters on municipal government, EMINENT DOMAIN, taxation, and the POLICE POWER. Chapter Eleven, "Of the Protection to Property by the Law of the Land" attracted the most attention, for here Cooley discussed DUE PROCESS OF LAW and gave it a significant substantive definition. Cooley said that legislative restraints on property should be tested by "those principles of civil liberty and constitutional defense which have become established in our system of law, and not by any rules that pertain to forms of procedure only." His test of due process was historical: the "established principles" and "settled usuages" of the common law protected property rights.

Cooley's definition of due process was used in the briefs of corporation lawyers who also distorted his comprehensive definition of the liberty protected by the FOURTEENTH AMENDMENT as embracing "all our liberties—personal, civil, and political" to a FREEDOM OF CONTRACT doctrine. Twentieth-century commentators have often accepted these briefs, misinterpreting Cooley as a zealous advocate of the judicial protection of property rights. To Cooley, however, due process did not necessarily mean judicial process nor did individual property rights mean corporate property rights. His views on judicial self-restraint were summarized in his treatise comment that judges "cannot run a race of opinions upon points of right, reason, or expediency with the law-making power." And Cooley repeated Justice LEMUEL SHAW'S views on a strong police power.

When Cooley was writing his treatise he was lecturing students on "the struggle between corporations and the rights of the people," condemning the decision in DARTMOUTH COLLEGE V. WOODWARD (1819), issuing opinions criticizing special privileges for corporations, and using the principle of equal rights and the maxims of "no taxation except for a PUBLIC PURPOSE" and of "due process of law" to declare tax aid to railroad corporations unconstitutional.

Cooley anxiously observed the growth of corporate capitalism in post-Civil War America. Deploring the national sentiment "to become immediately rich and great," he worried over the conflict of labor and capital and felt "that *class legislation* has been making the rich richer and the poor poorer," adding that "property is never so much in danger of becoming master as when capital unjustly manipulates the legislation of the country." These remarks in an 1879 lecture at Johns Hopkins University have been overlooked, as has a similar warning in an 1884 article on "Labor and Capital Before the Law" that when constitutional protection to property especially benefits those who have possessions, "the Constitution itself may come to be regarded by considerable classes as an instrument whose office it is to protect the rich in the advantages they have secured over the poor, and one that should be hated for that reason."

In court decisions Cooley evidenced older Jeffersonian values, upholding free public education, the FREEDOM OF THE PRESS, the rights of local self-government, and the necessity for judicial self-restraint. But the changing America of the late nineteenth century diminished earlier Jeffersonian hopes. In a melancholic mood in 1883 he admitted that "the political philosophy of Burke never grows stale and is for all times and all people."

By the 1880s Cooley had a national reputation, earned by judicial duties and constant lecturing, editing, and writing, including editions of SIR WILLIAM BLACKSTONE and JOSEPH STORY and treatises on torts and taxation. Aspirations for a United States Supreme Court appointment were dashed in 1881 when railroad interests, Cooley thought, successfully lobbied for STANLEY MATTHEWS. But Cooley had given up on Republicans, and in 1886 wondered whether the Party "possesses any good reason for existence." He admired GROVER CLEVELAND and accepted his offer of the chairmanship of the Interstate Commerce Commission. Regulating the American railway system was a task beyond Cooley's declining powers, and the effort led to a breakdown that left him a semi-invalid after 1890.

An 1889 comment to the South Dakota Constitutional Convention reveals that Cooley had modified older beliefs in constitutional limitations to legislative power: "Even in the millennium people will be studying ways whereby—by means of corporate power—they can circumvent their neighbors. Don't do that to any such extent as to prevent the legislative power hereafter from meeting all the evils that may be within the reach of proper legislation."

ALAN R. JONES

Bibliography

JONES, ALAN R. 1986 *The Constitutional Conservatism of Thomas McIntyre Cooley: A Study in the History of Ideas.* New York: Garland Publishing.

TWISS, BENJAMIN 1942 *Lawyers and the Constitution: How Laissez-Faire Came to the Constitution.* Princeton, N.J.: Princeton University Press.

COOLEY v. BOARD OF WARDENS OF PORT OF PHILADELPHIA
12 Howard 299 (1851)

The chaos in judicial interpretation that characterized the TANEY COURT'S COMMERCE CLAUSE cases was ended in *Cooley*, the most important decision on the subject between GIBBONS V. OGDEN (1824) and

UNITED STATES v. E. C. KNIGHT CO. (1895). The Taney Court finally found a doctrinal formula that allowed a majority to coalesce around a single line of reasoning for the first time since the days of the MARSHALL COURT. That formula was the DOCTRINE of SELECTIVE EXCLUSIVENESS, announced for the majority by Justice BENJAMIN R. CURTIS. The doctrine was a compromise, combining aspects of the doctrines of CONCURRENT POWERS over commerce and EXCLUSIVE POWERS, but three Justices of the eight who participated rejected the compromise. Justices JOHN MCLEAN and JAMES M. WAYNE, whom Curtis privately called "high-toned Federalists," persisted in their nationalist view, expressed in dissent, that congressional powers over INTERSTATE and FOREIGN COMMERCE were always exclusive, while PETER V. DANIEL, an intransigent states-rightist, concurred in the majority's result on the ground that congressional power over commerce was never exclusive.

At issue in *Cooley* was the constitutionality of a Pennsylvania statute requiring ships of a certain size entering or leaving the port of Philadelphia to employ local pilots in local waters. Cooley, claiming that the state act unconstitutionally regulated foreign commerce, refused to pay the pilotage fee. The fact that the first Congress had provided that the states could enact pilotage laws did not alter Cooley's claim. Curtis for the Court acknowledged that if the grant of commerce powers to Congress had divested the states of a power to legislate, the act of Congress could not confer that power on the states. The problem was whether the power of Congress in this case was exclusive.

Commerce, Curtis declared, embraces a vast field of many different subjects. Some subjects imperatively demand a single uniform rule for the whole nation, while others, like pilotage, demand diverse local rules to cope with varying local situations. The power of Congress was therefore selectively exclusive. If the subject required a single uniform rule, the states could not regulate that subject even in the absence of congressional legislation. In such a case congressional powers would be exclusive. Such was the nationalist half of the doctrine. The other half, by which the Court sustained the state act, maintained that the states did possess concurrent powers over commerce if the subject required diversity of regulation. Thus Congress's power was exclusive or concurrent depending on the nature of the subject to be regulated. "It is the opinion of a majority of the court," Curtis declared, "that the mere grant to Congress of the power to regulate commerce, did not deprive the States of power to regulate pilots, and that although Congress has legislated on this subject, its legislation manifests an intention . . . to leave its regulation to the several States."

The Court's doctrine of selective exclusiveness gave it a point of departure for analyzing commerce clause issues. The doctrine, however, had to be interpreted. It did not even suggest how the Court could determine which subjects required national legislation, thus excluding state action, and which required diverse local regulations. The doctrine could be manipulated by Justices who employed nationalist doctrine to invalidate state enactments.

LEONARD W. LEVY

Bibliography

SWISHER, CARL BRENT 1974 *History of the Supreme Court.* Vol. 5:404–407. New York: Macmillan.

COOLEY RULE

See: *Cooley v. Board of Wardens;* Selective Exclusiveness

COOLIDGE, CALVIN
(1872–1933)

John Calvin Coolidge, the thirtieth President of the United States, succeeded WARREN G. HARDING upon Harding's death in August 1923 and served until 1929. The heart of his legislative program was a series of tax reductions for individual taxpayers in all brackets, economy in government, and a balanced BUDGET.

The chief legislative controversy of the 1920s concerned the McNary-Haugen bills, which Coolidge vetoed in 1927 and 1928. These bills, proposed in response to a prolonged agricultural recession, would have authorized the federal government to buy and sell farm products in an effort to raise their prices. Coolidge opposed the bills as unworkable and as an unconstitutional expansion of the commerce power. The Congress, he argued, was limited to those powers granted to it or implied as incidental to the express powers. In language anticipating the opposition to the New Deal, Coolidge cautioned against the dangers of bureaucracy. He also observed that the people of the United States could reallocate the constitutional powers of the federal government and the states by means of the AMENDING PROCESS. Coolidge supported national legislation to regulate child labor, but he believed that a constitutional amendment would be required first to grant such power to the federal government.

Coolidge's only appointment to the Supreme Court was of his Amherst College classmate, Attorney General HARLAN FISKE STONE.

THOMAS B. SILVER

Bibliography

SILVER, THOMAS B. 1983 *Coolidge and the Historians.* Durham, N.C.: Carolina Academic Press.

COOLIDGE, UNITED STATES v.

See: Federal Common Law

COOLIDGE v. NEW HAMPSHIRE
403 U.S. 443 (1971)

In *Coolidge v. New Hampshire,* police officers, acting pursuant to a SEARCH WARRANT issued by the state attorney general, seized and later searched an automobile parked in the driveway of a murder suspect's home. The Supreme Court ruled the warrant invalid because a prosecutor could not be regarded as a neutral and detached magistrate. The automobile seizure was too far removed in time and space from the suspect's arrest to be considered incident to that arrest, was not grounded in any EXIGENT CIRCUMSTANCES to qualify for an AUTOMOBILE SEARCH or PLAIN VIEW exception nor was the discovery of the automobile inadvertent. Later decisions have confined *Coolidge* to its facts, emphasizing the automobile's location on a private driveway and the fact that the automobile was not contraband, stolen, or itself dangerous.

STEVEN SHIFFRIN

COOPER, THOMAS
(1759–1839)

Dr. Thomas Cooper, an English radical who settled in the United States in 1794, was an intellectual jack-of-all-trades, master of most, and the author of treatises on philosophy, law, religion, government, political economy, and various sciences. When he was a Jeffersonian editor, he was convicted of violating the SEDITION ACT OF 1798. His *Political Essays* and the report of his trial advocated a radically broad theory of FREEDOM OF THE PRESS. Later a Pennsylvania judge, he was removed from office and soured on liberalism, although his friend THOMAS JEFFERSON called him the "greatest man in America, in the powers of mind and in acquired information." When Cooper was president of what later became the University of South Carolina, he revised the state statutes and wrote *On the Constitution* (1826), which spoke for SLAVERY, state SOVEREIGNTY, and NULLIFICATION.

LEONARD W. LEVY

COOPER v. AARON
358 U.S. 1 (1958)

For several years after its decision in BROWN V. BOARD OF EDUCATION (1954–1955), the Supreme Court gave little guidance or support to the lower courts charged with supervising the DESEGREGATION of the public schools. In this case, however, the Court was confronted with direct defiance of *Brown* by a state's highest officials, and it met that challenge head-on.

Even before the *Brown* remedial opinion in 1955, the school board of Little Rock, Arkansas, had approved a plan for gradual desegregation of the local schools, and the federal district court had upheld the plan. Just before the opening of the fall 1957 term, the state governor, Orval Faubus, ordered the state's National Guard to keep black children out of Little Rock's Central High School. The attorney general of the United States obtained an injunction against the governor's action, and the children entered the school. A hostile crowd gathered, and the children were removed by the police. President DWIGHT D. EISENHOWER was thus prodded into his first significant act supporting desegregation; he sent Army troops to Central High to protect the children, and eight black students attended the school for the full academic year.

In February 1958, the school board asked the district court, in *Cooper v. Aaron,* for a delay of two and one-half years in the implementation of its plan, and in June the court agreed, commenting on the "chaos, bedlam and turmoil" at Central High. In August the federal court of appeals reversed, calling for implementation of the plan on schedule. The Supreme Court, in an unusual move, accelerated the hearing to September 11, and the next day it issued a brief order affirming the decision of the court of appeals. Later the Court published its full opinion, signed by all nine Justices to emphasize their continued unamimous support of *Brown.*

The opinion dealt quickly with the uncomplicated merits of the case, saying that law and order were not to be achieved at the expense of the constitutional rights of black children. The Court then added a response to the assertion by the Arkansas governor and legislature that the state was not required to abide by *Brown,* because *Brown* itself was an unconstitutional assumption of judicial power.

The response scored two easy points first: the Constitution, under the SUPREMACY CLAUSE, is "the supreme Law of the Land," and MARBURY V. MADISON (1803) had held that it was the province of the judiciary to "say what the law is." The Court's next step, however, was not self-evident: *Marbury* meant that the federal courts are supreme in expounding the Constitution; thus *Brown* was the supreme law of the land, binding state officers. This view, which carried the assertion of judicial power further than *Marbury* had taken it, has been repeated by the Court several times since the *Cooper* decision.

Cooper's importance, however, was not so much doctrinal as political. It reaffirmed principle at a crucial time. The televised pictures of black children being escorted into school through a crowd of hostile whites galvanized northern opinion. The 1960 election brought to office a president committed to a strong civil rights program—although it took his death to enact that program into law.

KENNETH L. KARST

(SEE ALSO: *John F. Kennedy; Civil Rights Act of 1964.*)

COOPERATIVE FEDERALISM

The theory of cooperative federalism postulates that the relationship between the national government and the states is one in which: governmental functions typically are undertaken jointly by federal and state (including local) agencies, rather than exclusively by one or the other; a sharing of power characterizes an integrated system instead of an exclusive SOVEREIGNTY at either level of government; and power tends not to concentrate at either level, or in any one agency, because the fragmented and shared nature of responsibilities gives citizens and interest groups "access" to many centers of influence.

Cooperative federalism is a modern phenomenon. Its main features—sharing of policy responsibilities and financial resources, interdependence of administration, overlapping of functions—are associated mainly with the FEDERAL GRANT-IN-AID programs. Collaboration, grants-in-aid from the national government to the states, bypassing of the states through establishment of grant programs aiding local or special-district governments directly, and development of auditing procedures and conditional grant requirements all have characterized cooperative federalism in the period after 1933.

Numerous analysts who celebrate these developments as signifying that old-style FEDERALISM is "dead," displaced by "intergovernmental relations," argue that the tension, pretensions at autonomy, and the notion of separateness of responsibilities that characterized governance in the pre-New Deal periods of constitutional development no longer form part of the reality of the federal system. Some scholars argue that relative power distribution is no longer a relevant issue. Forgotten is the elementary notion that "sharing" does not necessarily mean equality. Characteristically, in the modern grant-in-aid programs, the national government has not only raised and distributed the revenues, it has also designed the programs and established the goals, quite apart from overseeing administration.

Fascination with the alleged "non-centralization of power," which is seen to result from cooperative federalism, also can obscure the evidence of the vast additions of discretionary power in the national executive branch since 1933. Presidents from both parties have contributed to the growth of the "Imperial Presidency," and the process of centralization of power that has gone forward in this century has been profoundly influenced by this development.

The decision in MASSACHUSETTS V. MELLON (1923) established the juridical foundation of modern grant-in-aid constitutional theory. The Court there dismissed the complaint of Massachusetts that state prerogatives were improperly invaded by conditional grant programs (in that instance, the maternity-aid program of national grants). The interpretation of the TENTH AMENDMENT as "but a truism," in UNITED STATES V. DARBY (1941), further advanced the constitutional basis for cooperative federalism in action. Subsequently the Court upheld the principle of making grants conditional, even in *Oklahoma v. United States Civil Service Commission* (1947), when the federal legislation required adherence to HATCH ACT restraints on political activity by state officials. A contrary note was sounded by the Court in NATIONAL LEAGUE OF CITIES V. USERY (1976), in which the

Court asserted that "Congress may not exercise power in a fashion that impairs the states' integrity of their ability to function effectively in a federal system." Yet this assertion was made as the Court invalidated only a regulatory measure affecting hours and wages of local government employees, not a grant-in-aid or collaborative program. In GARCIA V. SAN ANTONIO TRANSIT AUTHORITY (1985) the Court overruled *Usery,* the majority declaring that case-by-case development since 1976 had failed to produce any principled basis for identifying " 'fundamental' elements of state sovereignty." The Court specifically cited the history of federal grants-in-aid as evidence that cooperative federalism and the political process gave adequate protection to the interests of the states.

HARRY N. SCHEIBER

Bibliography

CORWIN, EDWARD 1941 *Constitutional Revolution, Ltd.* Claremont, Calif.: Claremont Colleges.

COPPAGE v. KANSAS
236 U.S. 1 (1915)

In ADAIR V. UNITED STATES (1908), the Supreme Court had held that the section of the ERDMAN ACT that outlawed YELLOW DOG CONTRACTS was outside Congress's power to regulate INTERSTATE COMMERCE. Now, facing a question "not distinguishable in principle," a 6–3 Court struck down a Kansas statute banning yellow dog contracts. Justice MAHLON PITNEY for the majority, finding no reason to depart from *Adair,* reaffirmed the doctrine of FREEDOM OF CONTRACT. That "fundamental and vital" freedom fused rights of liberty and property so that any "arbitrary interference with that freedom of contract would impair those rights." Only a "legitimate" exercise of STATE POLICE POWER could limit it, and the majority could see no relation between the avowed purpose of the statute and the state's responsibility to protect the safety, morals, and health of its citizens. Indeed, "an interference with the normal exercise of personal liberty and property rights is the primary object of the statute." Concluding that it deprived employers and employees of the right to contract freely on their own terms, the majority voided the statute as a violation of SUBSTANTIVE DUE PROCESS guaranteed by the FOURTEENTH AMENDMENT.

In a brief dissent, Justice OLIVER WENDELL HOLMES reiterated the position he had stated in LOCHNER V. NEW YORK (1905). He saw nothing in the Constitution forbidding the Kansas statute, and he declined to substitute the courts' judgment for the legislature's on this policy question. In a lengthier dissent joined by Justice CHARLES EVANS HUGHES, Justice WILLIAM R. DAY, who had voted with the majority in *Adair,* asserted that Kansas had enacted the statute to promote the general welfare, thereby validly limiting the freedom of contract.

DAVID GORDON

COPYRIGHT

The Framers of the Constitution delegated to the national government authority to enact copyright laws. The copyright power, together with the PATENT power, is found in Article I, section 8, clause 8, which empowers Congress "to promote the progress of science and useful arts, by securing for limited times to authors and inventors the exclusive right to their respective writings and discoveries." Because there is no record of any debate on this clause at the CONSTITUTIONAL CONVENTION OF 1787, and mention of it in THE FEDERALIST is perfunctory, the meaning of the clause must be found in case law.

The phrase "to promote the progress of science" states what the Supreme Court, in *Mazer v. Stein* (1954), described as "the economic philosophy behind the clause," which is "the conviction that encouragement of individual effort by personal gain is the best way to advance public welfare through the talents of authors. . . ." Most courts, however, would deny that the introductory phrase permits the denial of copyright to any particular work on the ground that it does not contribute to such "progress." In fact, a United States Court of Appeals held in 1979 that obscene content does not invalidate copyright.

The words "by securing" came into contention in *Wheaton v. Peters* (1834), the first important copyright case decided by the Supreme Court, and a case involving two of the Court's own reporters. The plaintiff there argued that the federal copyright statute merely added additional remedies to a right that already existed at COMMON LAW. To bolster this position, he argued that the word "secure" meant to protect, insure, save, and ascertain, not to create. The Court rejected this contention, holding that the federal statute had created a new right, but that the author had not complied with the act's conditions.

Because the clause contains the words, "for limited times," a federal copyright statute that purported to grant copyright protection in perpetuity would clearly be unconstitutional. So too would a term that is nominally "limited" but is in fact the equivalent of perpetual protection (for example, a one thousand year term). The term currently provided for newly created works, the life of the author plus fifty years, conforms with the "limited times" requirement.

Only "authors" may be granted copyright in the first instance, although, once granted, copyright is transferable by an author to others. The term "authors" in the Constitution gives rise to the "originality" requirement in the law of copyright, which excludes from copyright protection material copied from others. An author is no less an author because others have anticipated his work, as long as he did not copy from such others. This Judge Frank contrasted with an "inventor" under the patent power, who must by definition produce something "novel," that is, not anticipated in the prior art. By reason of the phrase "exclusive right," it is clear that Congress has the power to grant to authors the "exclusive right" to exploit their works. But Congress is under no compulsion to exercise its full powers under the Constitution. If it may withhold copyright protection altogether from a given category of works, it may also grant something less than exclusive rights. The phrase "to their respective writings" means that only "writings" may be the subject of copyright. But the concept of a "writing" for copyright purposes has been liberally construed. The Court has held that photographic portraits and sound recordings constitute a "writing." Indeed, in *Goldstein v. California* (1973), the Court defined "writings" as "any physical rendering of the fruits of creative intellectual or aesthetic labor." A work that has not been physically fixed is ineligible for copyright protection.

In *Goldstein* the Court held that the copyright power is not exclusive, so that, subject to the SUPREMACY CLAUSE, the states retain concurrent power to enact copyright laws. Until adoption of the current Copyright Act in 1978 this reserved state power was significant, because most unpublished works were protected by so-called common law (or state law) copyright. However, under the current Copyright Act this area of state law has been largely preempted, so that most works, published or unpublished, are protected, if at all, under the federal act.

In recent years the courts have begun to question whether, and to what extent, the copyright laws are subject to the FREEDOM OF SPEECH and FREEDOM OF THE PRESS guarantees of the FIRST AMENDMENT. If the First Amendment were literally applied it would invalidate the Copyright Act, since the act clearly abridges the freedom of speech and press of those who would engage in copyright infringement by copying from others. Nothing in the First Amendment limits the freedom protected thereunder to speech that is original with the speaker. Nor does the fact that the Constitution also grants to Congress the power to enact copyright laws render the First Amendment inapplicable. The First Amendment and the remainder of the BILL OF RIGHTS limit only those powers that have otherwise been confided to the federal government. If it did not modify such powers, it would have no meaning at all. The conflict between these two socially useful, yet antithetical, interests is, of course, capable of resolution. The Ninth Circuit held in *Krofft v. McDonald's Corp.* (1977), and the Supreme Court implicitly agreed in *Zacchini v. Scripps-Howard Broadcasting Co.* (1977), that "ideas" lie in the domain of the First Amendment, so that copyright may not be claimed therein, but that the form of "expression" of ideas may be the subject of copyright, notwithstanding the First Amendment.

MELVILLE B. NIMMER

Bibliography

NIMMER, MELVILLE B. 1978 *Copyright.* 4 Vols. Albany, N.Y.: Matthew Bender & Co.

CORFIELD v. CORYELL

4 Wash. C.C. 371 (1823), 6 Fed. Case 546 (No. 3,230)

The importance of Justice BUSHROD WASHINGTON's circuit opinion derives from the fact that it contains the only exposition of Article IV, section 2, prior to the adoption of the FOURTEENTH AMENDMENT, that also uses the phrase PRIVILEGES AND IMMUNITIES. The clause in Article IV declares: "The Citizens of each state shall be entitled to all Privileges and Immunities of Citizens in the several states." *Corfield* arose because the plaintiff's vessel had been condemned under a state law forbidding nonresidents to take shell fish from state waters; in his TRESPASS action, the plaintiff relied upon the privileges and immunities clause. Washington declared, however, that the clause protected only the "fundamental" rights of CITIZENSHIP, such as the protection of government, the enjoyment of life, liberty, and property, the right to move about freely, the right to claim the benefit of the writ of HABEAS CORPUS, the right to sue, and the right to vote if qualified. This category did not include the right to exploit the state's oyster beds.

LEONARD W. LEVY

(SEE ALSO: *Slaughterhouse Cases, 1873.*)

CORNELIUS v. NAACP LEGAL DEFENSE AND EDUCATIONAL FUND, INC.
473 U.S. (1985)

This decision demonstrated how cumbersome the Supreme Court's analysis of PUBLIC FORUM issues has become since its decision in PERRY EDUCATION ASSOCIATION v. PERRY LOCAL EDUCATORS' ASSOCIATION (1983).

A 1983 EXECUTIVE ORDER limited the Combined Federal Campaign (CFC), a charity drive among federal employees, to charities that provide direct health and welfare services, and expressly excluded legal defense and advocacy groups. Seven such groups sued in federal district court, challenging their exclusion as a violation of the FIRST AMENDMENT. That court agreed, and issued an INJUNCTION forbidding exclusion of the groups from CFC. The court of appeals affirmed, but the Supreme Court reversed, 4–3, in an opinion by Justice SANDRA DAY O'CONNOR.

The Court held that the government had not designated either the federal workplace or CFC in particular as a public forum, in the sense of the *Perry* opinion. Rather, each of these was a "nonpublic forum"—a government operation in which communications could be limited to those promoting the operation's mission. CFC's purpose was to provide a means for government employees to lessen the government's burden in meeting human health and welfare needs, by making their own contributions to those ends. It was not necessary, in excluding the plaintiffs from CFC, to show that their solicitations would be incompatible with the goals of CFC; the relevant standard was the reasonableness of the exclusion. The President could reasonably conclude that money raised for direct provision of food or shelter was more beneficial than money raised for litigation or advocacy on behalf of the needy. Furthermore, the government could properly avoid the appearance of political favoritism by excluding all such groups. Those organizations had alternative means for raising funds from government employees, including direct mail advertising and in-person solicitation outside the workplace.

The Court, recognizing that other groups not in the business of direct provision of health and welfare services had been allowed to participate in CFC, remanded the case for determination whether the government had excluded the plaintiff groups for the purpose of suppressing their particular viewpoints.

Justice HARRY A. BLACKMUN, joined by Justice WILLIAM J. BRENNAN, dissented, arguing that any governmental exclusion of a class of speakers from any forum must be justified by a showing that the would-be speakers' intended use of the forum was incompatible with the relevant governmental operation. Here no such incompatibility had been shown, he said. Justice JOHN PAUL STEVENS, also dissenting, expressed skepticism about the value of a DOCTRINE founded on a series of categories of forum. In this case, he said, the government's own arguments supported "the inference of bias" against the excluded groups.

KENNETH L. KARST

CORONADO COAL COMPANY v. UNITED MINE WORKERS

See: *United Mine Workers v. Coronado Coal Company*

CORPORATIONS AND THE CONSTITUTION

The United States is the organizational or the corporate society par excellence. Seen sociologically, numerous societal entities of a corporate nature exist. From the perspective of constitutional law, only the business corporation has the status of being a PERSON. Those enterprises are social organizations midway between the state and the individual, owing their existence to the latter's need for organization and the former's reluctance to supply it. They are part of the greatest silence of the Constitution—the nature and operation of the economy. Except for a few nebulous provisions in Article I, plus the OBLIGATION OF CONTRACTS clause and the property provisions of the Fifth Amendment, all is left to inference. Neither business corporations nor unions nor any other private organization (for example, universities, farmers' legions, veterans' leagues, and the like) are mentioned.

As a consequence, corporate organizations fit uneasily into constitutional theory. As collectivities, they are the principal units of today's political pluralism. The giant corporations dominate the economy, both domestically and internationally. It was not always so. As late as 1800, only about 300 business corporations existed. Industrialization, coupled with massive governmental aid (pursuant to ALEXANDER HAMILTON'S principles), so burgeoned corporate growth that during the 1850s more were formed than ever before.

After the Civil War, the "trusts"—the forerunners of today's corporate giants—flowered.

The large corporations do not fit into democratic theory. Centers of economic and thus of political power, some are so mighty as to challenge the SOVEREIGNTY of the state. Constitutional decisions of the Supreme Court have formed a major part of the legal basis for that dominating position. DARTMOUTH COLLEGE V. WOODWARD (1819) set the tone. Chief Justice JOHN MARSHALL read the CONTRACT CLAUSE to nullify New Hampshire's attempt to alter Dartmouth's charter, originally granted by the English crown. In well-known language, Marshall called the corporation "an artificial being, invisible, intangible, and existing only in contemplation of law." He thus made it clear that corporations, although collectivities, were private entities, and by labeling them "artificial beings" he paved the way for the Court in 1886 to declare that corporations are PERSONS protected by the FOURTEENTH AMENDMENT. (Also in 1819, Marshall ruled that Congress had IMPLIED POWER to form corporations when "NECESSARY AND PROPER" to carry out its expressly granted powers. The decision, MCCULLOCH V. MARYLAND, is also noteworthy for its theory of BROAD CONSTRUCTION of the Constitution.)

As constitutional persons, corporations were able to invoke the DUE PROCESS clauses to fend off adverse regulations. By inventing the concept of SUBSTANTIVE (or economic) DUE PROCESS, the Supreme Court helped to defang the Granger, Populist, and nascent labor movements. FREEDOM OF CONTRACT was read into the Constitution; laissez-faire economics became constitutional DOCTRINE. By that one development the Court catapulted JUDICIAL REVIEW into a powerful instrument of governance.

LOCHNER V. NEW YORK (1905) is the best known economic due process decision. Over a famous dissent by Justice OLIVER WENDELL HOLMES, the Court invalidated a statute regulating the hours of workers in bakeries, because both the company's and the workers' freedoms to contract were improperly invaded. So many similar decisions were rendered that by 1924 John R. Commons called the Court "the first authoritative faculty of political economy in the world's history."

That practice was altered by the Great Depression: in 1937 the Court grudgingly conceded that economic policy was a province of federal legislation. The turning point came in WEST COAST HOTEL CORP. V. PARRISH (1937) and the WAGNER ACT CASES (*National Labor Relations Board v. Jones & Laughlin Steel Corp.*, 1937). The latter decision in practical effect "constitutionalized" political pluralism. FERGUSON V. SKRUPA (1963) illustrates the modern, and doubtless permanent, attitude of the Court toward ECONOMIC REGULATION.

Noneconomic regulation is a different matter. In FIRST NATIONAL BANK OF BOSTON V. BELLOTTI (1978) the Court invalidated a Massachusetts statute prohibiting corporations from spending money to influence elections. Corporate managers now have an unabridgeable right not only to spend their personal funds to further their political views but to use the money of others (in legal theory, corporations are owned by the stockholders). Although fictional persons, corporations by judicial legislation are attaining many of the rights of natural persons.

Neither political theorists nor economists have produced a satisfactory theory of conscious economic cooperation and its effect on the constitutional order. The Supreme Court refuses to recognize the corporation for what it is—a private government that, save in label, differs little from public government. Americans are governed as much—perhaps more—by corporations as they are by the official organs of government. Corporations, moreover, have such an influence upon the governmental structure that a version of corporatism is in process of creation.

Corporations were originally considered to be arms of the state—divisions of society established to get some of the public's business done. Today, paradoxically, they are both associations of individuals and constitutional persons. As such, they challenge orthodox constitutional theory. Their governmental character could be acknowledged by the Supreme Court; but the Justices have usually refused to do so. However, SMITH V. ALLWRIGHT (1944) did apply constitutional norms to a corporate body (albeit not a chartered corporation)—the Democratic party; and in MARSH V. ALABAMA (1946) a business corporation operating a "company town" was subjected to the limits of the FIRST AMENDMENT.

The giant corporations have assets that overshadow those of most of the states (and, indeed, most nation-states). They have created a national economic system that makes a decentralized political order impractical. Traditional concepts of FEDERALISM have consequently had to give way to notions of nationalism. In recent decades, many corporations have become transnational and they are creating an international economic order. They thus challenge the political order of the nation-state much as their predecessors altered the original federal system.

Corporate bodies, whether business or otherwise,

have become so socially significant that in one perspective they have replaced the individual (the natural person) as the basic unit of society. The modern corporation has created societies with structural foundations different from those of the past. Constitutional theory must therefore adapt itself to the corporation on three levels: federalism (in many respects corporations are in effect the most important units of local government); nationalism (where the transnational corporation challenges the sovereignty of the nation-state); and individualism (the natural person must become adapted to living in a hierarchic, bureaucratic society). To date, little scholarly activity has addressed any of these levels.

ARTHUR S. MILLER

Bibliography

COLEMAN, JAMES S. 1974 *Power and the Structure of Society.* New York: W. W. Norton.

COMMONS, JOHN R. 1924 *Legal Foundations of Capitalism.* Madison: University of Wisconsin Press.

MILLER, ARTHUR SELWYN 1976 *The Modern Corporate State: Private Governments and the Constitution.* Westport, Conn.: Greenwood Press.

CORRIGAN v. BUCKLEY
271 U.S. 323 (1926)

Reviewing a RESTRICTIVE COVENANT case from the DISTRICT OF COLUMBIA, the Supreme Court unanimously held that it presented no substantial constitutional question. The Court dismissed Fifth and FOURTEENTH AMENDMENT claims because they referred to government and state, not individual, actions. (Surprisingly, the Court failed to mention that the Fourteenth did not apply in the District.) Although these amendments provide for equal rights, they did not in any manner prohibit or invalidate contracts entered into by private individuals in respect to the control and disposition of their own property. The Court therefore dismissed the case for want of JURISDICTION.

DAVID GORDON

(SEE ALSO: *State Action; Shelley v. Kraemer, 1948.*)

CORWIN, EDWARD S.
(1878–1963)

Edward S. Corwin, McCormick Professor of Jurisprudence at Princeton University, succeeded the nineteenth-century titans JAMES KENT, JOSEPH STORY, and THOMAS M. COOLEY. Corwin's understanding of constitutional and political thought distinguished him from these lawyers and judges, who exemplified Edmund Burke's maxim that the study of law sharpens the mind by narrowing it. Matchless learning in government and history made him an eminent COMMENTATOR ON THE CONSTITUTION.

Corwin's *Liberty against Government* (1948) was a major defense of liberty as the fundamental American principle. *The Twilight of the Supreme Court* (1934) upheld the New Deal with an idea of national power that left presidential and congressional power without statable limits. Corwin later more persuasively and moderately pondered the New Deal's extension of governmental power in relationship to the Founders' intention. In UNITED STATES V. DARBY (1941) Chief Justice HARLAN FISKE STONE had cited Chief Justice JOHN MARSHALL'S definition of congressional power over INTERSTATE COMMERCE in GIBBONS V. OGDEN (1824) and Marshall's interpretation of NECESSARY AND PROPER in MCCULLOCH V. MARYLAND (1819). Corwin persuasively denied that Marshall would have consented to be "thus conscripted in the service of the New Deal": "Liberty, the spacious liberty of an expanding nation, not social equality, was the lodestar of his political philosophy." Corwin's bow to the "great Chief Justice" Marshall showed that Corwin, too, championed liberty.

Public law, said Corwin, is the "law that governs government itself"; political theory is the branch that explains the moral source of the law's authority. Corwin identified his topics and accomplishments in public law as the origins and development of the idea of liberty against government, "the most important theme of American constitutional legal history"; JUDICIAL REVIEW in historical perspective; DUAL FEDERALISM; and the Presidency.

The Constitution and What It Means Today (1920, 1958), his best known work, combined scholarship and simplicity. Popular education for Corwin kept the Constitution from becoming a "craft mystery," whether one of bench and bar or of behaviorism. Corwin's most important work was *The President: Office and Powers* (1957), which concluded that the autonomous and self-directing idea of the Presidency had triumphed. Decades before the WATERGATE crimes he prophetically challenged the excesses of presidential power with the idea of liberty against government. The most important condition of the people's moderation in liberty was religious instruction. Corwin's *Constitution of Powers in a Secular State* (1951) opposed Supreme Court decisions against religious instruction in the public schools, arguing that the American people understand democracy as a system of ethical principles "grounded in religion." Hence, religion in effect should habituate Americans to virtue; virtue should guide the use of liberty.

Corwin's preeminence arose in part from his emphasis on fundamentals, restoration of natural law, explanations of doctrine, grasp of the perennial themes of American politics and history, and understanding of the enduring principles that prop the Constitution. In teaching future scholars, Corwin had, according to Alpheus T. Mason, the gift "of reaching within each person, of discovering something firm and worthwhile, of encouraging him to stand on it." As Corwin himself put it, "a noble emulation is the true source of excellence."

RICHARD LOSS

Bibliography

LOSS, RICHARD 1977 Edward S. Corwin: The Constitution of the Dominant Presidency. *Presidential Studies Quarterly* 7:53–65.

______, ed. 1981 *Corwin on the Constitution,* Volume I, *The Foundations of American Constitutional and Political Thought, the Powers of Congress, and the President's Power of Removal.* Ithaca, N.Y.: Cornell University Press.

STEVENS, RICHARD G. 1980 The Constitution and What It Meant to Corwin. *Political Science Reviewer* 10:1–53.

CORWIN AMENDMENT
(1861)

On 2 March 1861, in a futile attempt to prevent the secession of the slaveholding states, Congress proposed, and sent to the states for ratification, a constitutional amendment designed to protect SLAVERY in the states where it existed. The amendment, written by Representative Thomas Corwin of Ohio, would have prohibited any future constitutional amendment authorizing Congress to abolish or interfere with the "domestic institutions" of any state. Although the amendment went on specifically to include the institution of "persons held to service or labor," it is not clear what other domestic institutions, if any, might have been protected.

The Corwin Amendment was proposed after President-elect ABRAHAM LINCOLN rejected the CRITTENDEN compromise proposals, which would have permitted slavery in some federal territories. Its intended effect was that, although slavery would survive in the existing slave states, there would never be any new slave states admitted to the union, and slaveholders would be an ever diminishing minority. In any case, the Corwin Amendment was largely a symbolic gesture of conciliation, as six southern states had already seceded by the time it was proposed. The legislatures of only two states (Ohio and Maryland) voted to ratify the Corwin Amendment.

DENNIS J. MAHONEY

Bibliography

HYMAN, HAROLD M. 1967 The Narrow Escape from the Compromise of 1860: Secession and the Constitution. Pages 149–166 in Harold M. Hyman and Leonard W. Levy, eds., *Freedom and Reform.* New York: Harper & Row.

COUNSEL, RIGHT TO BE REPRESENTED BY

See: Right to Counsel

COUNSELMAN v. HITCHCOCK
142 U.S. 547 (1892)

The first Supreme Court decision on immunity statutes, *Counselman* remained the leading case until it was distinguished away in KASTIGAR V. UNITED STATES (1972). Appellant refused to testify before a federal GRAND JURY on the ground that he might incriminate himself, though he had been granted USE IMMUNITY under an 1887 act of Congress guaranteeing that his evidence would not be used against him criminally, except in a prosecution for perjury. *Counselman* thus raised the question whether a grant of use immunity could supplant the Fifth Amendment right of a person not to be a witness against himself in a criminal case. The government contended that an investigation before a grand jury was not a criminal case, which could arise only after an INDICTMENT should be returned, but that in any instance, Counselman had received immunity in return for his testimony.

Justice SAMUEL BLATCHFORD for a unanimous Court declared that it is "impossible" that the clause of the Fifth Amendment could mean only what it says, for it is not limited to situations in which one is compelled to be a witness against himself in a "criminal case." The object of the clause is to insure that no person should be compelled as a witness "in any investigation" to testify to anything that might tend to show he had committed a crime. "The privilege is limited to criminal matters, but it is as broad as the mischief against which it seeks to guard," and therefore it applied to grand jury proceedings that might result in a prosecution. Clearly, said Blatchford, a statute cannot abridge a constitutional privilege nor replace one, "unless it is so broad as to have the same extent in scope and effect." The statute did not even do what it purported to do; it did not bar use of the compelled testimony, for its fruits could be used against the witness by searching out any leads, originating with his testimony, to other evidence that could convict him. No statute leaving the witness subject to prosecution after answering incriminating questions can have the effect of supplanting the constitutional provision. The 1887 act of Congress was unconstitutional because it was not a "full substitute" for that provision.

Thus the Court introduced the extraordinary doctrine that a statute could be a substitute for a provision of the Constitution, after having said that a statute could not "replace" such a provision. But the statute, to be constitutional, must serve "co-extensively" with the right it replaces. The Court laid down the standard for TRANSACTIONAL IMMUNITY: to be valid the statute "must afford absolute immunity against future prosecution for the offense to which the question relates."

LEONARD W. LEVY

(SEE ALSO: *Right Against Self-Incrimination*).

COURT MARTIAL

See: Military Justice and the Constitution

COURT OF CLAIMS

See: Claims Court of the United States

COURT OF CUSTOMS AND PATENT APPEALS

The Court of Customs Appeals was established by Congress in 1909 to hear appeals from the Board of General Appraisers, a body that itself heard appeals from decisions by customs collectors. (In 1926 the Board became the United States Customs Court, and in 1980 that court was converted into the United States COURT OF INTERNATIONAL TRADE.) In 1929 Congress renamed the court and expanded its jurisdiction. The new Court of Customs and Patent Appeals (CCPA) heard, in addition, appeals from the Patent Office in both patent and trademark cases.

In 1958 Congress declared the CCPA to be a CONSTITUTIONAL COURT, created under Article III. In *Glidden Co. v. Zdanok* (1962) the Supreme Court held, 5–2, that the CCPA was, indeed, an Article III court, despite its statutory authorization to do some nonjudicial business. There was no opinion of the Court, and the theories supporting the decision were in conflict. Justice JOHN MARSHALL HARLAN, for three Justices, concluded that the CCPA had been an Article III court since 1930, when Congress had granted its members life tenure during good behavior. Justice TOM C. CLARK, for the other two majority Justices, said that the 1958 declaration of Congress had converted the CCPA into a constitutional court. Justice WILLIAM O. DOUGLAS, joined by Justice HUGO L. BLACK, dissented, arguing that the court remained a LEGISLATIVE COURT despite the congressional declaration. Thus, while a majority rejected each theory argued in support of the decision, the result was acceptance of the CCPA's Article III status.

In the FEDERAL COURTS IMPROVEMENT ACT (1982) Congress abolished the CCPA, transferring its JURISDICTION to a newly established UNITED STATES COURT OF APPEALS FOR THE FEDERAL CIRCUIT.

KENNETH L. KARST

COURT OF INTERNATIONAL TRADE

In 1926 Congress converted the Board of General Appraisers, which had been hearing APPEALS from decisions of customs collectors, into the United States Customs Court. In 1956, Congress declared that the court was established under Article III. Because the court's business is strictly "judicial" and its members are appointed for life during good behavior, it is probably a CONSTITUTIONAL COURT on the same reasoning that was applied to the COURT OF CUSTOMS AND PATENT APPEALS (CCPA).

In 1980 Congress changed the Customs Court's name to the United States Court of International Trade and extended its JURISDICTION to include additional noncustoms matters relating to international trade. Its decisions, formerly reviewed by the CCPA, today are reviewed by the UNITED STATES COURT OF APPEALS FOR THE FEDERAL CIRCUIT.

KENNETH L. KARST

COURT OF MILITARY APPEALS

In the Uniform Code of Military Justice, enacted in the aftermath of World War II, Congress established the Court of Military Appeals (COMA). A civilian body, whose three judges serve for fifteen-year terms, COMA reviews questions of law arising in certain serious court-martial cases. COMA, which heard its first case in 1951, has never been part of the federal judiciary. The whole military justice system, COMA included, is part of the governance of the armed forces. Since 1983, however, many of COMA's decisions have been reviewable by the Supreme Court on petition for CERTIORARI. Whether or not such a review has taken place, a person in custody as a result of a court-martial decision can apply for HABEAS CORPUS in a federal district court. (See MILITARY JUSTICE AND THE CONSTITUTION.)

Like many another judicial or military institution, COMA has sought to expand its jurisdiction. It has developed a notion of its own "inherent powers," which it has used to nudge the military justice system toward increasing resemblance to the civilian system of criminal justice, notably by tightening the requirements of procedural fairness. Although some military officers have strongly criticized COMA's "constitutionalizing" innovations, most proposals for statutory restoration of the old order have died in congressional committees.

KENNETH L. KARST

Bibliography

WILLIS JOHN T. 1972 The Constitution, the United States Court of Military Appeals and the Future. *Military Law Review* 57:27–97.

——— 1972 The United States Court of Military Appeals: Its Origin, Operation and Future. *Military Law Review* 55:39–93.

COURT REORGANIZATION

See: Judicial System

COURTS, RELATIONSHIP OF STATE AND FEDERAL

See: Judicial System

COURTS OF APPEAL

See: United States Courts of Appeal

COX v. LOUISIANA
379 U.S. 536 (1965)
379 U.S. 559 (1965)

Some black students were jailed in a courthouse for PICKETING segregated lunch counters. About 2,000 other black students marched there and, in accordance with police instructions, lined a sidewalk 101 feet away. Whites gathered. Cox made a speech that elicited some grumbling from whites; the police ordered the demonstration broken up; the students were dispersed.

Justice ARTHUR GOLDBERG writing for the Supreme Court reversed Cox's BREACH OF THE PEACE conviction, finding that Cox's actions threatened no violence and that the police could have handled any threat from the whites. The Court also held the breach of peace statute unconstitutionally vague and overbroad as construed by the state supreme court to define breach as "to arouse from a state of repose . . . to disquiet."

In striking down Cox's conviction for obstruction of public passages because the statute's actual administration had vested discretion in city officials to forbid some parades and allow others, the Court emphasized that violation of nondiscriminatory traffic laws would not be protected by the FIRST AMENDMENT. The court reversed Cox's conviction for picketing near a courthouse because the police, by directing the demonstrators to a particular sidewalk, had led them to believe that it was not near the courthouse within the terms of the statute so that a subsequent conviction created a "sort of entrapment," in violation of DUE PROCESS. Nevertheless, in dictum it invoked the old doctrine that picketing was subject to reasonable regulation as "speech plus" and supported the authority of a state legislature to forbid picketing near a courthouse because of its danger to the administration of justice.

Although *Cox* is often cited as a case establishing the concept of a PUBLIC FORUM, the Court went out of its way to say "We have no occasion . . . to consider the constitutionality of the . . . non-discriminatory application of a statute forbidding all access to streets and other public facilities for parades and meetings."

MARTIN SHAPIRO

COX v. NEW HAMPSHIRE
312 U.S. 569 (1941)

In this seminal decision, Chief Justice CHARLES EVANS HUGHES, writing for a unanimous Supreme Court, synthesized a series of cases involving speeches, parades, and meetings in parks and on streets. He held that there was a "right of assembly . . . and . . . discussion of public questions immemorially associated with resort to public places," but that such a right was limited by the authority of local government to make reasonable regulations governing "the time, place and manner" of such speech, if the regulations did not involve "unfair discrimination" among speakers. The Court upheld a state law requiring parade licenses issued by local governments on the grounds that, as construed by the state supreme court, it authorized only such reasonable and nondiscriminatory regulations. *Cox* is one of the building blocks in the creation of the doctrine of the PUBLIC FORUM.

This case took on renewed importance in the context of the CIVIL RIGHTS demonstrations of the 1960s. The crucial problem under the *Cox* test is often whether a law purporting to be a neutral regulation of traffic and noise control is actually a façade behind which local authorities seek to deny a public forum to speakers whose speech they dislike.

MARTIN SHAPIRO

COX BROADCASTING CORP. v. COHN
420 U.S. 469 (1975)

In *Cox Broadcasting Corp. v. Cohn* the Supreme Court held that broadcasting the name of a rape victim, derived from public court documents open to public inspection, could not constitutionally be made the basis for civil liability. The Court left open the questions whether liability could be imposed for a similar broadcast if the name had been obtained in an improper fashion, or if the name had not been directly derived from the public record, or if the name had not appeared in a public record open to public inspection, or if the public record were inaccurate.

STEVEN SHIFFRIN

COYLE v. SMITH
221 U.S. 559 (1911)

This decision construed the guarantee of a REPUBLICAN FORM OF GOVERNMENT in a case involving a state's admission to the Union. The enabling act admitting Oklahoma specified the location of the state capital, a condition which the Oklahoma legislature soon violated. The Supreme Court struck down the limitation as outside the limits of Congress's power over admission.

DAVID GORDON

CRAIG v. BOREN
429 U.S. 190 (1976)

It is ironic that the leading modern decision setting the STANDARD OF REVIEW for claims of SEX DISCRIMINATION involved discrimination against men, concerning an interest of supreme triviality. Oklahoma allowed women to buy 3.2 percent beer upon reaching the age of eighteen; men, however, had to be twenty-one. A young male would-be buyer and a female beer seller challenged the law's validity. The young man became twenty-one before the Supreme Court's decision; his challenge was thus rejected for MOOTNESS. The Court held that the seller had STANDING to raise the young man's constitutional claims, and further held, 8–1, that the law denied EQUAL PROTECTION OF THE LAWS. Justice WILLIAM H. REHNQUIST dissented.

Speaking through Justice WILLIAM J. BRENNAN, the Court held that classifications based on gender were invalid unless they served "important governmental objectives" and were "substantially related to achievement of those objectives." This intermediate standard was a compromise between the two views of the majority in FRONTIERO V. RICHARDSON (1973) as to the level of judicial scrutiny of both legislative objectives and legislative means. Under the RATIONAL BASIS standard of review, the objective need be only legitimate, and the means (in equal protection language, the classification) only rationally related to its achievement. At the opposite end of the continuum of standards of review, STRICT SCRUTINY demands a legislative objective that is a COMPELLING STATE INTEREST, and means that are necessary to achieving that objective. The *Craig* standard appears to have been deliberately designed to fall between these two levels of judicial scrutiny of legislation.

In the years since *Craig*, the Supreme Court has often invalidated classifications based on sex but typically has not challenged the importance of legislative objectives. Instead, the Court generally holds that a sex classification is not "substantially related" to a legislative goal. In *Craig* itself, the Court admitted that traffic safety, the state's objective, was important, but said maleness was an inappropriate "proxy for drinking and driving."

Justice JOHN PAUL STEVENS, concurring, doubted the utility of multitiered levels of judicial scrutiny in equal protection cases, and commented that men, as a class, have not suffered "pervasive discrimination." The classification was objectionable, however, because it was "based on the accident of birth," and perpetuated "a stereotyped attitude" of young men and women. Because the state's traffic safety justification failed, the law was invalid.

KENNETH L. KARST

CRAIG v. MISSOURI
4 Peters 410 (1830)

Craig defined BILLS OF CREDIT, which no state may issue without violating Article I, section 10, of the Constitution. By a 4–3 vote the Supreme Court ruled that bills of credit mean any paper medium intended to circulate as money on the authority of a state, even if not designated as legal tender in payment of debts. Missouri, lacking currency, authorized state loan offices to issue loan certificates, on collateral, to private citizens, in amounts ranging from fifty cents to ten dollars; the certificates could be used for payment of taxes and official salaries. Chief Justice JOHN MARSHALL's opinion invalidating the state act, though constitutionally correct, ignored economic realities: many states desperately needed a circulating medium. Senator THOMAS H. BENTON, for Missouri, defending its certificate law before the Court, thunderingly defended state sovereignty. The disastrous consequences of *Craig* provoked denunciations of the court and yet another movement in Congress to repeal section 25 of the JUDICIARY ACT OF 1789, the grant of APPELLATE JURISDICTION under which the Court had reversed state court judgments and held state acts unconstitutional. The repeal movement failed, but a solid South ominously opposed the Court.

LEONARD W. LEVY

(SEE ALSO: *Briscoe v. Bank of Kentucky, 1837.*)

CRAMER v. UNITED STATES
325 U.S. 1 (1945)

On the night of June 12, 1942, several specially trained saboteurs were put ashore from a German submarine near Amagansett, New York, with orders to disperse throughout the United States and to sabotage the American war effort. Anthony Cramer, a naturalized American citizen of German background, befriended two of the saboteurs, met with them, and was suspected of assisting them in their mission. However, the only overt acts to which two witnesses could testify were two meetings between Cramer and one of the saboteurs, who was an old friend of Cramer's. The prosecution was unable to produce the testimony of two witnesses concerning what took place at the meetings or to establish that Cramer gave information, encouragement, shelter, or supplies to the saboteurs. Cramer was tried for and convicted of TREASON, and he appealed his conviction to the Supreme Court.

The *Cramer* case marked the first time that the Supreme Court passed on the meaning of the treason clause of Article III, section 2, of the Constitution. Justice ROBERT H. JACKSON, for a 5–4 Court, held that the overt acts testified to by two witnesses must be sufficient, in their setting, to sustain a finding that actual aid and comfort was given to an enemy of the United States. Although there was other EVIDENCE of Cramer's Nazi sympathies and of his assistance to the saboteur, the overt acts—the meetings—were not in themselves treasonable, and the conviction could not stand.

DENNIS J. MAHONEY

(SEE ALSO: *Haupt v. United States; Ex Parte Quirin.*)

Bibliography

BELKNAP, MICHAL R. 1980 The Supreme Court Goes to War: The Meaning and Implications of the Nazi Saboteur Case. *Military Law Review* 89:59–95.

CRANCH, WILLIAM
(1779–1855)

President JOHN ADAMS in March 1801 commissioned his nephew, William Cranch, assistant judge of the newly created Circuit Court for the DISTRICT OF COLUMBIA. President THOMAS JEFFERSON in 1806 surprised Cranch, a loyal Federalist, by elevating him to chief judge, a post he filled until his death, half a century later.

Cranch simultaneously undertook the unofficial position of reporter of the decisions of the Supreme Court of the United States. His nine volumes of reports, for which he derived compensation at public sale, covered the period from the August Term, 1801, to the February Term, 1815. The role of the law reporter in Cranch's time commanded professional respect and even glamour. These reports, which added luster to the judge's reputation, received favorable comment, even from Jeffersonian opponents.

Cranch's first major constitutional opinion, *United States v. Bollman et al.* (1807), stressed the independence and power of the federal judiciary, themes that pervaded his other major opinions. President Jefferson in early 1807 had sought a bench warrant for the arrest of Erik Bollman and Samuel Swartwout on charges of TREASON in the Burr Conspiracy. Cranch dissented from the decision by the court's other two judges to issue the warrant. He took exception to the English doctrine of constructive treason. He also rejected the proposition that an executive communication from the President, without either an oath or affirmation, established sufficient probability of treasonous activity.

Three decades later Cranch spoke for a unanimous court in upholding the power of the judiciary to intervene in executive affairs. *United States ex rel. Stokes v. Kendall* (1837) stemmed from an alleged debt due Stokes and others for services they claimed to have rendered to the Post Office. When Postmaster General Amos Kendall refused to pay, despite congressional direction to do so, Stokes sought a WRIT OF MANDAMUS. Although no circuit court had ever issued such a writ against the executive branch, Cranch held that his court could do so. He found that the judicial power could properly issue a writ to command performance of a purely ministerial function by the head of an executive department.

Cranch remained a thoroughgoing Federalist long after that party ceased to exist. His opinions powerfully affirmed the role of the federal judiciary. His most important legacy was the establishment of the Circuit Court and its successors in the District of Columbia as the major forums in which to adjudicate causes involving executive departments and agencies.

KERMIT L. HALL

Bibliography

CARNE, WILLIAM F. 1901 Life and Times of William Cranch, Judge of the District Circuit Court, 1801–1855. *Records of the Columbia Historical Society* 5:294–310.

CRAWFORD v. BOARD OF EDUCATION
458 U.S. 527 (1982)
WASHINGTON v. SEATTLE SCHOOL DISTRICT NO. 1
458 U.S. 457 (1982)

By statewide votes, both Washington and California sought to limit the use of SCHOOL BUSING for purposes of DESEGREGATION. A 1978 Washington INITIATIVE effectively prohibited school boards from assigning children to public schools outside their residential neighborhoods for purposes of racial integration. A 1979 amendment to the California Constitution prohibited state courts from ordering school busing unless busing would be available in a federal court as a remedy for a violation of the FOURTEENTH AMENDMENT. The Supreme Court sustained the California measure, 8–1, but held the Washington measure invalid, 5–4.

In the *Seattle* case, Justice HARRY A. BLACKMUN wrote for the majority. Following the precedent of HUNTER V. ERICKSON (1969), he concluded that the Washington law placed a special burden on racial minorities, using an issue's racial nature to define the local decision-making structure. For the dissenters, Justice LEWIS F. POWELL argued that the Washington law had not altered the political process at all, but had merely adopted a neighborhood school policy—something a local school board itself remained free to do, within the limits of the Fourteenth Amendment.

Justice Powell wrote for the Court in the *Crawford* case. The California courts had previously read the state constitution to forbid DE FACTO as well as DE JURE school SEGREGATION. There was, however, no "ratchet" principle in the Fourteenth Amendment; the state could constitutionally adopt federal EQUAL PROTECTION standards. The amendment, Powell said, was not adopted with a racially discriminatory purpose; it chiefly reflected a choice for the neighborhood school policy. Justice THURGOOD MARSHALL, dissenting, considered the two cases indistinguishable. Indeed, the opinions of Justice Powell in the two cases bear marked similarities; yet, if *Hunter* be taken as the critical precedent, the distinction is supportable. A line is none the worse for being thin.

KENNETH L. KARST

CRIMINAL CONSPIRACY

The modern crime of conspiracy punishes the act of agreement with another to do something unlawful, and the vagueness and breadth of its scope are the legacies of seventeenth-century English judges who invented its COMMON LAW progenitor. Constitutional DOCTRINE has not shaped the boundaries of this crime; it is, indeed, the other way around. Most paradoxically, the crime has served both as a tool for the suppression of FIRST AMENDMENT freedoms and as a weapon for the defense of rights to racial equality. Like all political issues, the definition of "unlawful" conspiracies fluctuates with the moral hemlines of history.

In the eighteenth century, the English crime came to encompass the agreement to do any "immoral" acts, even noncriminal ones. This became an element of American conspiracy law as well, and one of its early critics was Chief Justice LEMUEL SHAW of the Massachusetts Supreme Judicial Court. In COMMONWEALTH V. HUNT (1842) Shaw put an end to conspiracy prosecutions of laborers who organized to seek such noncriminal goals as higher wages or a CLOSED SHOP. Criminal goals, of course, remained punishable, and trade union conspiracy prosecutions died out in the 1890s only because they were replaced by judicial resort to the labor INJUNCTION. Statutes prohibiting noncriminal conspiracies remained on the books, but their demise was hastened by state court decisions holding them void for VAGUENESS or violative of the EX POST FACTO clause.

Federal conspiracy prosecutions commenced in 1867 with the enactment of a Federal Criminal Code provision prohibiting conspiracies to defraud the United States. The rise of organized crime during Prohibition provided the impetus for the expansion of federal conspiracy offenses; the Racketeer Influenced and Corrupt Organizations Act of 1970 is an exemplar of their sweeping scope. In 1925, Judge LEARNED HAND labeled conspiracy "the darling in the prosecutor's nursery," because of the progovernment features that mark conspiracy trials. HEARSAY statements of co-conspirators are admissible in evidence, and conspiratorial membership may be inferred solely from conduct showing a desire to further the conspiracy's goals. In *Pinkerton v. United States* (1946) the Court held conspirators liable for every crime committed by co-conspirators, including those of participants whose existence was unknown but foreseeable. The DOUBLE JEOPARDY clause does not bar separate, consecutive sentences for these offenses and the conspiracy itself. VENUE will lie anywhere an act is committed in furtherance of the conspiracy, often effectively nullifying the SIXTH AMENDMENT right to be tried where a crime is committed. Conspirators may be tried en masse, and fringe participants thus become tainted with the culpability of the ringleaders.

It is small wonder that in *Krulewitch v. United States* (1949) Justice ROBERT H. JACKSON declared that the "elastic, sprawling and pervasive" nature of the crime of conspiracy poses a "serious threat to fairness" in the administration of justice. Yet while many commentators call for limitations on the crime, DUE PROCESS arguments meet with recurrent failure in the courts. This amoeboid offense remains entrenched in state and federal law and in legislative proposals for criminal code reform.

Conspiracy was a potent weapon for the prosecution of political dissidents during World War I, and these cases brought the Supreme Court to its first important encounter with the First Amendment's guarantees of FREEDOM OF SPEECH and FREEDOM OF THE PRESS. The ESPIONAGE ACT of 1917 prohibited conspiracies to obstruct the draft or cause insubordination in the armed services, and in SCHENCK V. UNITED STATES (1919) and FROHWERK V. UNITED STATES (1919) a unanimous Court affirmed the conspiracy convictions of dissidents who had circulated antidraft publications. In *Schenck*, Justice OLIVER WENDELL HOLMES declared that only a CLEAR AND PRESENT DANGER of a conspiracy's success would justify conviction, but this formula was not an important limitation in these cases, where the danger was assumed. Justices Holmes and LOUIS D. BRANDEIS later argued for greater speech protections, but their pleas went unheeded for a generation. Conspiracy convictions of eleven national Communist party leaders were affirmed in DENNIS V. UNITED STATES (1951), even though the danger posed by their conspiracy to advocate the overthrow of the government was evidenced only by the party's structure and tenets. The doctrinal thaw came in 1957, with Justice JOHN MARSHALL HARLAN's opinion in YATES V. UNITED STATES portending the formula of BRANDENBURG V. OHIO (1969). *Brandenburg* allows prosecution for speech crimes—including conspiracy to advocate—only when advocacy of imminent, illegal action is likely to incite such action.

Brandenburg's weakness as a limit on conspiracy prosecutions is that it only guarantees defendants the benefit of appellate court scrutiny of jury verdicts. It provides no more than an indirect caution for legislative reliance on conspiracy statutes or prosecutorial decisions to seek indictments. Protection of speech interests rests ultimately in the court of public opinion, and the VIETNAM WAR era dissidents found an uncertain haven there. The "Chicago Seven" protesters at the 1968 Democratic National Convention were acquitted of conspiring to travel interstate with intent to incite a riot, but they were convicted of other INCITEMENT offenses. Benjamin Spock and William Sloane Coffin were convicted of conspiring to counsel draft evasion, based on their support of a DRAFT CARD BURNING rally in Boston. After appellate court reversals in *United States v. Dellinger* (1972) and *United States v. Spock* (1969), reprosecution was halted only because the government decided to give up trying. The CHILLING EFFECT of such prosecutions is irremediable, and judicial vindication of speech rights often becomes a matter of better late than never.

The concept of conspiracy can serve CIVIL LIBERTIES as aptly as it defeats them. After the Civil War,

Congress prohibited conspiracies "to injure, oppress, threaten or intimidate" any citizen's free exercise of constitutional rights, and also provided a civil action for DAMAGES against conspirators. Narrow judicial construction of these rights defeated their enforcement in the era of UNITED STATES V. HARRIS (1883) and the CIVIL RIGHTS CASES (1883). But Justice WILLIAM O. DOUGLAS's opinion in SCREWS V. UNITED STATES (1945) revived prosecutions of state officials, while UNITED STATES V. GUEST (1966) brought similar vindication against private individuals, and GRIFFIN V. BRECKENRIDGE (1971) opened the damage remedy door. Debate continues over the scope of rights protected by these remedies. But conspiracy's contribution toward curbing civil rights violators remains as notable as its role in rounding up racketeers.

CATHERINE HANCOCK

Bibliography

FILVAROFF, DAVID B. 1972 Conspiracy and the First Amendment. *University of Pennsylvania Law Review* 121:189–253.

JOHNSON, PHILLIP E. 1973 The Unnecessary Crime of Conspiracy. *California Law Review* 61:1137–1188.

CRIMINAL JUSTICE ACT
78 Stat. 552 (1964)

By the Criminal Justice Act Congress provided that counsel must be furnished at public expense for INDIGENT defendants in federal criminal cases. The act requires each district court to formulate a plan for furnishing counsel, subject to supervision by the circuit judicial council and the Judicial Conference of the United States. The act provides that counsel shall be furnished from the defendant's first appearance before a court or magistrate through the APPEAL process, and authorizes reimbursement for such expenses as investigations and expert testimony.

DENNIS J. MAHONEY

(SEE ALSO: *Right to Counsel.*)

CRIMINAL PROCEDURE

"It was a great day for the human race," Charles E. Merriam wrote in *Systematic Politics* (1945), "when the idea dawned that every man is a human being, an end in himself, with a claim for the development of his own personality, and that human beings had a dignity and a worth, respect for which is the firm basis of human association." This idea is the predicate for that branch of American constitutional law which is concerned with criminal procedure, for this body of law is deliberately weighted in favor of persons accused of crime. This pronounced tilt of the law is based on the assumption that it is vitally necessary to protect the dignity inherent in all human beings, regardless of their station in society.

The commitment of the Constitution to protect in some emphatic way the rights of criminal defendants is reflected in the fact that such protection is a principal theme of the federal BILL OF RIGHTS. Similar protections appear in the bills of rights that form parts of all state CONSTITUTIONS. Even before the ratification of the Bill of Rights in 1791, however, the Constitution in its original form did not ignore the subject altogether. Thus, the privilege of the writ of HABEAS CORPUS was guaranteed, and both BILLS OF ATTAINDER (legislative convictions for crime) and EX POST FACTO laws (laws making criminal acts that were innocent when done) were forbidden (Article I, sections 9 and 10). TRIAL BY JURY "for all crimes" was also guaranteed (Article III, section 2), and the offense of TREASON was defined with meticulous care to prevent abuse of a charge often made on flimsy grounds in moments of great political excitement (Article III, section 3).

The Bill of Rights filled in many more details by spelling out a long list of guarantees designed to protect criminal defendants: freedom from "unreasonable SEARCHES AND SEIZURES" (FOURTH AMENDMENT), INDICTMENT by GRAND JURY, freedom from DOUBLE JEOPARDY, the RIGHT AGAINST SELF-INCRIMINATION, the right to DUE PROCESS OF LAW (Fifth Amendment), the right to a speedy and PUBLIC TRIAL by an impartial local jury, the right to notice of charges, the right to confront adverse witnesses (*i.e.*, cross-examination), the right to have the assistance of counsel (SIXTH AMENDMENT), and freedom from excessive BAIL and from the infliction of CRUEL AND UNUSUAL PUNISHMENT (Eighth Amendment). In addition, section 1 of the FOURTEENTH AMENDMENT, with its provision that no state shall "deprive any person of life, liberty, or property, without due process of law," eventually opened the door to considerable supervision of criminal justice in the states by the federal courts.

This commitment to the safeguarding of the rights of defendants in criminal cases was deeply rooted in the COMMON LAW system which the earliest settlers brought with them from England. In ancient Anglo-Saxon and Norman times, questions of guilt or innocence were determined by such ritualistic devices as trial by battle or ordeal, or by compurgation (oath-taking), which were largely appeals to God to work a miracle establishing the defendant's innocence. Actually, private vengeance, taking the form of private war or blood feuds, was the principal check on criminal conduct. But by the time the first colonies were established in America, the basic procedures characteristic of modern jurisprudence had taken form. The essence of modern adjudication is the discovery of innocence or guilt through the presentation of proofs and reasoned argument.

Furthermore, it is important that under common law a person accused of crime carries with him the presumption of innocence, which means that the defendant is not obliged to prove his innocence, but rather that the BURDEN OF PROOF is on the prosecution to prove guilt. In addition, jurors must be instructed by the presiding judge that they may convict only if they find that guilt has been established "beyond a REASONABLE DOUBT," which is the greatest quantum of proof known to the law. In most civil litigation a preponderance of evidence suffices to support a verdict. Thus, in a landmark English case, *Woolmington v. D.P.P.* (1935), the House of Lords ruled clearly wrong an instruction of the trial judge to the effect that since the accused had shot his wife, the law presumed him to be guilty of murder unless he could satisfy the jury that death was due to an accident. "No matter what the charge or where the trial," Lord Sankey declared, "the principle that the prosecution must prove the guilt of the prisoner is part of the common law of England and no attempt to whittle it down can be entertained."

The common law rules relating to the presumption of innocence and the burden of proof are part of the law prevailing in every American state. For example, following the completion of a modern, revised criminal code in Wisconsin, the legislature adopted a statute that declared: "No provision of the criminal code shall be construed as changing the existing law with respect to presumption of innocence or burden of proof." These principles are also firmly rooted in federal jurisprudence. As Justice FELIX FRANKFURTER, dissenting in *Leland v. Oregon* (1952), wrote, "From the time that the law which we have inherited has emerged from dark and barbaric times, the conception of justice which has dominated our criminal law has refused to put an accused at the hazard of punishment if he fails to remove every reasonable doubt of his innocence in the minds of jurors. It is the duty of the Government to establish his guilt beyond a reasonable doubt." Similarly, the Supreme Court has ruled that the standard of proof beyond a reasonable doubt in criminal cases is a due process requirement binding upon the state courts. It is, Justice WILLIAM J. BRENNAN asserted in IN RE WINSHIP (1970), "a prime instrument for reducing the risk of convictions resting on factual error. The standard provides concrete substance for the presumption of innocence. . . ." According to the Supreme Court, the states are required to prove beyond a reasonable doubt all elements of the crime with which the defendant was charged, and the jury must be so instructed. An instruction is improper if it has the effect of reducing substantially the prosecution's burden of proof or of requiring the defendant to establish his innocence beyond a reasonable doubt.

The solicitude of American constitutional law for the rights of the accused is so great that the American system has been described as a defendant's law, in contrast with inquisitorial systems of other countries which give the prosecution many advantages not available in the United States. American public law on this important subject rests upon the recognition of several important considerations that are not the product of abstract theorizing or mere sentimentalism but rather the result of historical experience over centuries of time. For one thing, it is an unquestionably legitimate, indeed essential, function of government to apprehend, try, and punish convicted criminals. But it is also the duty of those public officials who operate the criminal justice system to avoid violating the law themselves in their zeal to combat crime. Of course, our society has a serious crime problem which government cannot and should not ignore, but it has long been recognized that at some point the price of law enforcement may be exorbitant. As Justice Frankfurter observed in *Feldman v. United States Oil Refining Co.* (1944), "The effective enforcement of a well designed penal code is of course indispensable for social security," but he went on to say: "The Bill of Rights was added to the original constitution in the conviction that too high a price may be paid even for the unhampered enforcement of the criminal law and that, in its attainment, other social objects of a free society should not be sacrificed."

Surely, one of the indispensable objectives of a free society is to avoid the disorganizing consequences of lawlessness by public officials. Thus Justice OLIVER WENDELL HOLMES observed in his celebrated dissenting opinion in the Supreme Court's first WIRETAPPING case, OLMSTEAD V. UNITED STATES (1928), that "we must consider two objects of desire, both of which we cannot have, and make up our minds which to choose. It is desirable that criminals should be detected and to that end that all available evidence should be used. It is also desirable that the government should not itself foster and pay for other crimes, when they are the means by which the evidence is to be obtained. . . . We have to choose, and for my part I think is a less evil that some criminals should escape than that the Government should play an ignoble part." In a separate dissenting opinion in the same case, Justice LOUIS D. BRANDEIS warned that government forcefully teaches by example, that crime is contagious, and that "if the Government becomes a lawbreaker, it breeds contempt for law; it invites every man to become a law unto himself; it invites anarchy." To permit the government to commit crimes, he asserted, in order to convict criminals, "would bring terrible retribution."

Without question, if unrestrained by law, the police could apprehend and prosecutors could secure the conviction of far more lawbreakers than they now manage to catch and convict. For example, if the police had a free hand to break into any dwelling or other building and to rummage around as they please, looking for stolen goods or other contraband, such as controlled substances, unquestionably they would solve more crimes and put more thieves, burglars, drug peddlers, and other criminal characters in jail. But the price would be prohibitively high, since it would entail the destruction of a cherished aspect of privacy. Similarly, if the police were completely free to torture suspects, more confessions would be secured, and the conviction rate would rise significantly, but again, other values must be weighed in the balance. These values include avoiding the risk of convicting innocent people who cannot endure the pain and avoiding the danger of encouraging unprofessional, brutal police conduct which employs uncivilized methods shocking to the conscience. Obviously, choices must be made between the desire to catch and punish lawbreakers and our concern for maintaining the legal amenities of a civilized society. The search for a tolerable balance between these competing objectives is what much of our constitutional law is all about. As Justice WILLIAM O. DOUGLAS remarked, in *An Almanac of Liberty* (1954), "a degree of inefficiency is a price we necessarily pay for a civilized, decent society. The free state offers what a police state denies—the privacy of the home, the dignity and peace of mind of the individual." Aside from the fact that one hundred percent law enforcement would make the building of additional jails the highest priority of the country, it simply cannot be achieved without devoting resources far beyond what we can afford, considering all the other important functions for which government is responsible, and without resorting to methods that are almost universally deplored in civilized countries.

The various rights secured for the accused by our constitutional law are not technicalities; due process of law is at the center of our concept of justice. The overall purpose of our legal system is not so much to secure convictions as to render justice. Our rules of constitutional law are not only designed to protect people who are in trouble with the law but also to assure us that those who are engaged in the often exciting business of law enforcement will observe those time-tested rules which in large measure constitute the essence of fair procedure. "Let it not be overlooked," Justice ROBERT H. JACKSON, dissenting in SHAUGHNESSY V. UNITED STATES (1953), wrote, "that due process of law is not for the sole benefit of the accused. It is the best insurance for the Government itself against those blunders which leave lasting stains on a system of justice. . . ."

There are additional compelling reasons that explain and support our legal system's concern for protecting the rights of persons accused of crime. For one thing, a criminal case is essentially a contest between an individual and a government, that is to say, between parties of vastly unequal strength. This disparity in the strength of the parties is especially visible in the modern age of powerful governments. The teaching of experience the world over is that inequality tends to beget injustice, and where the parties are so unequal, a determined effort must be made to redress the imbalance of power. Thus, the accused is entitled to seek a reversal of a conviction in an appellate court, but the prosecution may not get an acquittal reversed, for the double jeopardy principle forbids it. In this respect, the scales of justice are tipped in favor of the weaker party.

In addition, our concern for the defendant's rights rests upon an understanding that for most people it is a very serious matter indeed to be accused by the government of having committed a crime. The possible consequences range from loss of employment to disruption of family life, injury to reputation, and, ultimately, loss of personal liberty. It follows that one accused of crime is likely to be in such deep trouble that he or she must have every opportunity to combat the charges, as fully, as quickly, and as decisively, as possible. Many rights—bail, a public and SPEEDY TRIAL, CONFRONTATION of accusers, and assistance of counsel—facilitate an early and effective defense, or at the very least, make one possible.

Furthermore, one of the major purposes of assuring a full measure of due process of law is to promote the sense of community by giving all of us the feeling that even guilty persons have been treated fairly. As Justice Douglas observed in BRADY V. MARYLAND (1963), "Society wins not only when the guilty are convicted but when criminal trials are fair; our system of the administration of criminal justice suffers when any accused is treated unfairly." As Justice Brennan said in FURMAN V. GEORGIA (1972), "Even the vilest criminal remains a human being possessed of common human dignity."

In a larger sense, our body of procedural law in the criminal field seeks to combat abuse of the POLICE POWER of the state. Police brutality is the hallmark of totalitarian and dictatorial systems of government. The twentieth century has been well schooled in the fearful menace of the midnight knock on the door, the ransacking of private dwellings by the police without legal warrant, the use of torture to break the will, and the ultimate indignity of incarceration in brutal concentration camps. For these compelling reasons our constitutional law was deliberately formulated to prevent the unrestrained exercise of police power.

Indeed, if one looks closely at the elements of the constitutional right to a FAIR TRIAL it becomes clear that for every rule there is a persuasive reason. The basic rights of the accused are responses to our concrete historical experience. Why, for example, does American constitutional law assure defendants representation by counsel? The answer was explained with convincing clarity by Justice GEORGE SUTHERLAND in POWELL V. ALABAMA (1932):

> The right to be heard would be, in many cases, of little avail if it did not comprehend the right to be heard by counsel. Even the intelligent and educated layman has small and sometimes no skill in the science of law. If charged with crime, he is incapable, generally, of determining for himself whether the indictment is good or bad. He is unfamiliar with the rules of evidence. Left without the aid of counsel he may be put on trial without a proper charge, and convicted upon incompetent evidence, or evidence irrelevant to the issue or otherwise inadmissible. He lacks both the skill and knowledge adequately to prepare his defense, even though he has a perfect one. He requires the guiding hand of counsel at every step in the proceedings against him.

In GIDEON V. WAINWRIGHT (1963), the case that extended the RIGHT TO COUNSEL in state courts to all persons charged with felonies, Justice HUGO L. BLACK argued that it was an obvious truth that a person too poor to hire a lawyer cannot be assured a fair trial. He pointed out that government spends vast sums of money to engage the services of lawyers to prosecute, and that few defendants who can afford them fail to hire the best lawyers they can find to present their defenses, from which it follows that "lawyers in criminal courts are necessities, not luxuries."

To cite another example, in all American jurisdictions, state and federal, double jeopardy—which means essentially putting a person on trial twice for the same offense—is forbidden. Once a defendant has been tried and acquitted, he may not be put on trial a second time, even though the prosecution has found fresh relevant evidence not previously available to it or has discovered that serious legal errors were made at the trial. As explained by Justice Black in GREEN V. UNITED STATES (1957): "The underlying idea, one that is deeply ingrained in at least the Anglo-American system of jurisprudence, is that the State with all its resources and power should not be allowed to make repeated attempts to convict an individual for an alleged offense, thereby subjecting him to embarrassment, expense, and ordeal and compelling him to live in a continuing state of anxiety and insecurity, as well as enhancing the possibility that even though innocent he may be found guilty."

There are equally persuasive reasons for the guarantee of trial by jury. Justice BYRON R. WHITE noted, in the landmark case of DUNCAN V. LOUISIANA (1968), that the right of trial by jury is "an inestimable safeguard against the corrupt or overzealous prosecutor and against the compliant, biased, or eccentric judge." The jury, one of the distinctive features of Anglo-American jurisprudence, is the result of several centuries of concrete experience; it has changed in the past, in many different ways, and it is still a dynamic institution. The authors of the Constitution were thoroughly familiar with the jury system and made careful provision for it in the original document, before the Bill of Rights filled in additional details. Thus, our criminal law procedure has always reflected a reluctance to entrust prosecutors and judges with unchecked powers over life and liberty.

Similarly, there are compelling reasons why American constitutional law protects the individual against UNREASONABLE SEARCHES AND SEIZURES, the main reason being the desire to protect the RIGHT OF PRIVACY. This "right to be left alone," as Justice Brandeis asserted in his notable dissenting opinion in *Olmstead*, is "the most comprehensive of rights and the right most valued by civilized man." Fresh from his Nuremberg experience, Justice Robert Jackson wrote, in a spirited dissent in BRINEGAR V. UNITED STATES (1949), that the Fourth Amendment rights "are not mere second-class rights but belong in the catalog of indispensable freedoms. Among deprivation of rights, none is so effective in cowing a population, crushing the spirit of the individual and putting terror in every heart. Uncontrolled search and seizure is one of the first and most effective weapons in the arsenal of every arbitrary government." Justice Jackson also pointed out that because police officers are themselves the chief invaders of this right, the responsibility for protection against unreasonable searches and seizures has fallen on the courts.

An ancient teaching of English and American law is that to compel a person to convict himself or herself of a crime by being coerced into giving unwilling testimony is inadmissible. Our criminal jurisprudence makes the assumption that everyone is innocent until proved guilty beyond a reasonable doubt on the basis of competent evidence; the prosecution has the duty to prove guilt. Because the accused is not required to establish his innocence, it follows that he cannot be required to supply testimony that would lead to a conviction. The Fifth Amendment's guarantee against compulsory self-incrimination is thus neither an alien nor a novel doctrine but rather, as Justice Douglas wrote in *An Almanac of Liberty,* "one of the great landmarks in man's struggle to be free of tyranny, to be decent and civilized. It is our way of escape from the use of torture. It is part of our respect for the dignity of man."

The rights of the accused in American criminal procedure are not static but respond to changing social values and moral concepts. This dynamism is reflected in the judicial interpretation of the Eighth Amendment's prohibition of cruel and unusual punishment. Thus Chief Justice EARL WARREN wrote in TROP V. DULLES (1958): "The Amendment must draw its meaning from the evolving standards of decency that mark the progress of a maturing society." Similarly, in FURMAN V. GEORGIA, the Supreme Court for the first time held that the death penalty is unconstitutional under certain circumstances, Justice THURGOOD MARSHALL observing that "a penalty that was permissible at one time in our Nation's history is not necessarily permissible today." The court similarly made new law when it ruled in ESTELLE V. GAMBLE (1976) that deliberate indifference of a jailer to the medical needs of prisoners constituted an "unnecessary and wanton infliction of pain" proscribed by the Eighth Amendment. Similarly, the right to be free from unreasonable searches or seizures had to be given a progressively broadened scope as we moved into the age of electronic gadgetry. Given the dynamic character of American life, flexibility of interpretation was inevitable if a living Constitution was to retain its vitality, and the broad and generous character of constitutional language contributed to that flexibility.

Many policy questions relating to criminal procedure must be understood in the context of the federal character of the American system of government. Certain important powers are delegated by the Constitution to the national government, and except as the states are limited by that Constitution—which is the supreme law of the land—the TENTH AMENDMENT confirms that the states retain power over all other matters. One of the most important residual powers of the states is the power to define and punish crimes. Although Congress was not expressly empowered to enact a general code of criminal statutes, it was assumed from the beginning that the national government could enforce its laws by imposing criminal sanctions. The doctrine of IMPLIED POWERS provided the necessary doctrinal underpinning. For example, the delegated power to tax includes by implication the power to punish persons who commit tax frauds. The federal criminal code has expanded steadily since 1789 and is today a lengthy document. Even so, most criminal laws are state laws, and a very large majority of persons in jail are incarcerated in state institutions. That the criminal law in all its facets is mainly state law is a well-understood fact of American life. In a special message to Congress in 1968, President LYNDON B. JOHNSON pointed out that crime "is essentially a local matter. Police operations—if they are to be effective and responsible—must likewise remain basically local. This is the fundamental premise of our constitutional structure and of our heritage of liberty." It follows, said the President, that "the Federal Government must never assume the role of the Nation's policeman."

Decisions of state courts are not reviewable by the Supreme Court if they involve only issues of state law, as to which the highest state court speaks the last word. For example, a 1967 case involved an appeal from the Texas courts regarding the state's habitual-criminal statute. Under this statute, the trial jury is fully informed of previous criminal convictions and the state is not obliged to have a two-stage trial, one devoted to the pending charge and a second to a consideration of the previous convictions. On appeal, the Supreme Court ruled in SPENCER V. TEXAS that as a matter of national constitutional law the state is not required to provide a two-stage trial. Declining to interfere, the Court held that this matter is controlled by state procedural law; the Court is not "a rule-making organ for the promulgation of state rules of procedure."

There are, in fact, two avenues available to seek federal judicial review of the decisions of state courts in criminal cases. First of all, if a convicted defendant has taken whatever appeals are available to him under state law in the state courts and if he has sought review of a substantial federal (as distinguished from state law) question, then the Supreme Court has JURISDICTION to review the judgment on direct review if it chooses to do so. Second, one who is in custody following conviction in a state court and has exhausted his available postconviction state remedies may, in a proper case, assert his federal legal claim by applying to a federal district court for a writ of habeas corpus. Accordingly, whether through direct review by the Supreme Court or through habeas corpus proceedings, federal courts often correct state courts where federal rights have been denied. But federal courts do not sit merely to correct errors alleged to have occurred in state courts. As the Supreme Court said in *Herb v. Pitcairn* (1945), "Our only power over state judgments is to correct them to the extent that they incorrectly adjudge federal rights."

The key question, then, is: what is a federal right? A short answer is: any right arising under the Constitution of the United States, statutes of Congress, or treaties. But the provisions of the Constitution relating to basic rights are stated in vague and general language that does not in terms apply to the states. Indeed the Court held in a landmark case, BARRON V. BALTIMORE (1833), that the Bill of Rights did not apply to the states. This holding was based on the proposition that the Bill of Rights was intended only to supply additional protection from violations by the new, untested national government, and that wherever the states were limited by the constitution, the language to this effect was always explicit. Prior to the Civil War, federal court review of state criminal convictions under the Bill of Rights was not possible.

A major change in our whole system of government began in 1868 with the adoption of the Fourteenth Amendment, which provides that no state shall "deprive any person of life, liberty, or property, without due process of law." Not until 1923, however, did the Supreme Court undertake to employ this clause as a limit on state criminal procedure. In the leading case of MOORE V. DEMPSEY, the Court held that a conviction in a trial dominated by a mob was a violation of due process and could be remedied by a federal court through issuance of a writ of habeas corpus. In such a proceeding the federal court must make an independent evaluation of the facts, even though the state's highest appellate court has upheld the correctness of the conviction. The Supreme Court, too, on direct review, began to reverse state convictions as violations of due process. In 1932 the Court ruled that the Sixth Amendment right to representation by counsel, at least in capital cases, is an indispensable element of a fair trial which is guaranteed by the Fourteenth Amendment's due process clause. Later decisions extended the constitutional right to counsel in state courts to include any offense punishable by imprisonment for any period of time. Other decisions, most of which were made after World War II by the WARREN COURT, applied to the states, as due process requirements, most of the other provisions of the Bill of Rights which are designed to protect persons accused of crime. For example, in MAPP V. OHIO (1961) the Court extended to the states the EXCLUSIONARY RULE, long applicable in federal prosecutions by reason of the Fourth Amendment. Henceforth state courts, too, would be required to exclude from criminal trials all evidence secured as a result of unreasonable searches and seizures. Similarly, a state violates due process if it subjects a person to compulsory self-incrimination (MALLOY V. HOGAN, 1964), if it denies trial by jury at least where nonpetty offenses are involved (DUNCAN V. LOUISIANA, 1968), or if it subjects a defendant to the hazards of double jeopardy (BENTON V. MARYLAND, 1969). In fact, by 1970 all of the criminal procedure provisions of the Bill of Rights were made applicable to the states by way of Fourteenth Amendment due process, except the Fifth Amendment guarantee of indictment by grand jury and the Eighth Amendment prohibition of excessive bail. The bail guarantee very likely will be incorporated into the Fourteenth Amendment when the issue comes to the Supreme Court in the proper form. All the other rights of the accused guaranteed by the Bill of Rights are now regarded as elements of Fourteenth Amendment due process, enforceable against the states through federal judicial process. In the words of the Court, they are "fundamental principles of liberty and justice," or are "basic in our system of jurisprudence," or are "FUNDAMENTAL RIGHTS essential to a fair trial," or are "the very essence of a scheme of ordered liberty." (See INCORPORATION DOCTRINE.)

Not only does Fourteenth Amendment due process now incorporate most of the Bill of Rights, it also has an independent force wholly outside of the Bill of Rights. For example, in the famous case of *Mooney v. Holohan* (1935), the Court ruled that a state has denied the accused due process of law if the prosecution has deceived the court and jury by presenting testimony known to be perjured. Similarly, in *Jackson v. Virginia* (1979), the Court ruled that a state court conviction can pass the test of Fourteenth Amendment due process only if a rational trier of fact could find that each essential element of the crime had been established "beyond a reasonable doubt."

The expansion of the list of federally enforceable constitutional rights available to defendants in state courts has come a long way in enlarging both the review powers of the Supreme Court and the habeas corpus jurisdiction of the federal district courts. The federal courts are establishing more and more standards in the area of criminal justice which the states are obliged to observe.

In operating the criminal justice system, government must make some hard choices, since basic objectives undergirding that system often conflict. On the one hand, there is the due process model, preferred by the courts, which stresses our concern for maintaining the legal amenities of a civilized community. This process, adversarial and judicial in character, seeks to protect the dignity and autonomy of the individual. On the other hand, there is the crime control model, preferred by most law enforcement officials, which emphasizes the need to apprehend, try, and punish lawbreakers. The principal procedural objective is the quick, efficient, and reliable handling of persons accused of crime. The method is essentially administrative and managerial in character, operating, especially in respect to MISDEMEANORS, on assembly-line principles. Accordingly, many law enforcement officials are critical of what they see as the Supreme Court's tenderness on the subject of defendants' rights, arguing that change has been too rapid and too far-reaching. Impatience has even been expressed by a few Justices of the Court itself. An experienced California trial judge, Macklin Fleming, has gone so far as to accuse the Court of pursuing the unattainable objective of "perfect justice." It is difficult, perhaps impossible, to locate the exactly right balance between the due process model and the crime control model. But in seeking to achieve a tolerable balance the Supreme Court has moved with considerable caution, deciding one case at a time, and always within the mainstream of American culture and its dominant legal traditions.

DAVID FELLMAN

Bibliography

CASPER, JONATHAN D. 1972 *American Criminal Justice: The Defendant's Perspective.* Englewood Cliffs, N.J.: Prentice-Hall.

CORTNER, RICHARD C. 1980 *The Supreme Court and the Second Bill of Rights.* Madison: University of Wisconsin Press.

FELLMAN, DAVID 1976 *The Defendant's Rights Today.* Madison: University of Wisconsin Press.

FLEMING, MACKLIN 1974 *The Price of Perfect Justice.* New York: Basic Books.

FRIENDLY, HENRY J. 1967 The Bill of Rights as a Code of Criminal Procedure, in *Benchmarks.* Chicago: University of Chicago Press.

GOLDSTEIN, ABRAHAM S. 1960 The State and the Accused: Balance of Advantage in Criminal Procedure. *Yale Law Journal* 69:1149–1199.

PACKER, HERBERT L. 1964 Two Models of the Criminal Process. *University of Pennsylvania Law Review* 113:1–68.

CRIMINAL SYNDICALISM LAWS

Criminal syndicalism statutes were but one of several kinds of statutes punishing manifestations of unpopular thought and expression for their probable bad tendency enacted during and just after World War I by many midwestern and western states. The laws were a response to the economic unrest of the postwar period, specifically to the doctrines and activities of the Industrial Workers of the World (IWW), and to the antiradical hysteria prompted by the Russian Revolution of 1917. Twenty-two states and territories enacted—and eight other states considered but rejected—criminal syndicalism statutes between 1917 and 1920. Attempts to enact a federal criminal syndicalism law in 1919 and 1920 came to nothing, but the Smith Act of 1940 was patterned after the earlier model.

The Idaho statute, the first of its kind and a model for those adopted by other states, defined criminal syndicalism as "the doctrine which advocates crime, sabotage, violence or other unlawful methods of terrorism as a means of accomplishing industrial or political reform." Offenses punished as FELONIES under such statutes included oral or written advocacy of criminal syndicalism; justifying commission of or attempts to commit criminal syndicalism; printing or displaying written or printed matter advocating or advising criminal syndicalism; organizing or being or becoming a member of any organization organized or assembled to teach or advocate criminal syndicalism, or even presence at such an assembly. Though most citizens and state legislators believed that these statutes were directed solely against the use or advocacy of force and violence, in practice they jeopardized FREEDOM OF SPEECH, because they were used to punish those who expressed or even held opinions offensive to the majority of the community.

Criminal syndicalism statutes almost uniformly survived constitutional challenges in the state courts. In WHITNEY V. CALIFORNIA (1927) the United States Supreme Court upheld the California Criminal Syndicalism Act; Justice LOUIS D. BRANDEIS's eloquent opinion, concurring only in the result, set forth the most sophisticated formulation of the theoretical foundations and practical applications of the CLEAR AND PRESENT DANGER test previously formulated in other FIRST AMENDMENT cases. In *Fiske v. Kansas* (1927), the first decision overturning a conviction under a criminal syndicalism statute, the Supreme Court merely invalidated the statute's application, holding that the state had not shown that the defendant had advocated any but lawful methods to achieve the goals of the IWW. In DE JONGE V. OREGON (1937) a unanimous Court struck down the application of the Oregon Criminal Syndicalism Act to defendants who had merely attended a peaceful meeting of the Communist party; the Oregon legislature later repealed the statute. The labor troubles of the 1930s prompted efforts to strengthen existing criminal syndicalism laws, but these came to nothing, and several states followed Oregon's example in repealing their criminal syndicalism statutes. State criminal syndicalism statutes fell into disuse after the 1930s; in BRANDENBERG V. OHIO (1969) the Supreme Court declared the Ohio Criminal Syndicalism Act unconstitutional on its face, overruling *Whitney*, adopting the principles of Justice Brandeis's concurring opinion, and making successful prosecutions under criminal syndicalism statutes virtually impossible.

RICHARD B. BERNSTEIN

Bibliography

CHAFEE, ZECHARIAH, JR. 1941 *Free Speech in the United States.* Cambridge, Mass.: Harvard University Press.

DOWELL, ELDRIDGE FOSTER 1939 *A History of Criminal Syndicalism Legislation in the United States.* Baltimore: Johns Hopkins University Studies in Historical and Political Science, Series 57, No. 1.

CRITTENDEN, JOHN J.
(1787–1863)

A Kentucky lawyer, John Jordan Crittenden was a United States attorney general (1841, 1850–1853) and senator (1817–1819, 1835–1841, 1842–1848, 1855–1861). In late 1828 President JOHN QUINCY ADAMS nominated him to the Supreme Court, but the Senate's Democratic majority killed the appointment. A border state Whig, Crittenden always supported compromise on slavery. Thus, as President Millard Fillmore's attorney general, Crittenden vigorously enforced the 1850 fugitive slave law. But he also opposed ANNEXATION OF TEXAS, the Mexican War, the KANSAS-NEBRASKA ACT, and Kansas statehood, because these issues raised the politically disruptive question of SLAVERY IN THE TERRITORIES. In December 1860 Crittenden proposed four resolutions and six constitutional amendments to settle the SECESSION crisis. The resolutions condemned the northern PERSONAL LIBERTY LAWS and reasserted the constitutionality of the fugitive slave laws. The amendments—one of which declared the others "unrepealable"—would have compensated masters for unrecovered fugitive slaves and given permanent protection to slavery where it already existed and in all existing territories or those "hereafter acquired" which were south of the MISSOURI COMPROMISE line. Crittenden's only concession to northern sentiments was to propose the permanent prohibition of slavery north of the Missouri Compromise line; however, many Northerners read "hereafter acquired" as an invitation for proslavery filibustering in Latin America. Furthermore, Republicans opposed any western extension of slavery. Southern extremists, on the other hand, wanted secession, and not compromise. Thus, only the amendment permanently protecting slavery in the existing states was approved by Congress. From 1861 to 1863 Crittenden worked to prevent Kentucky's secession and limit the war to preserving the Union. Thus, he opposed the EMANCIPATION PROCLAMATION, the CONFISCATION ACTS, the use of black troops, West Virginia statehood, and other administration policies.

PAUL FINKELMAN

Bibliography

KIRWAN, ALBERT D. 1962 *John J. Crittenden: The Struggle for the Union.* Lexington: University of Kentucky Press.

CROLY, HERBERT
(1869–1930)

New York journalist and social critic Herbert David Croly was the leading intellectual of the Progressive movement. Croly's *The Promise of American Life* (1909) became the programmatic handbook of the reformers: in it he advocated strengthening the federal government as the special protector of working people and the creation of a "welfare state." His inspiration was the nationalism of ALEXANDER HAMILTON rather than the individualism of THOMAS JEFFERSON. Croly believed that the process of government should be separated from politics and placed in the hands of experts. Croly advised President WOODROW WILSON, but his greatest influence on public affairs was as editor of *The New Republic.*

DENNIS J. MAHONEY

CROSS-EXAMINATION, RIGHT OF

See: Confrontation, Right of

CROSSKEY, WILLIAM W. (1894–1968)

William Winslow Crosskey's reputation as a constitutional historian rests upon his *Politics and the Constitution in the History of the United States* (1953, 1960), a learned, controversial reinterpretation of the framing of the Constitution. Crosskey, a professor of law at the University of Chicago, argued that the Framers of the Constitution sought to create a unitary system of government with virtually unlimited legislative powers, that Congress would have supreme authority within the constitutional system, and that the power of JUDICIAL REVIEW was intended merely as a means for the judiciary to defend itself against encroachments by the other branches of government. Crosskey began with two premises: first, that the words of the Constitution should be understood according to the meanings they had in common usage in 1787; and, second, that the source relied upon by most historians to determine the intent of the Framers, JAMES MADISON's *Notes of the Debates in the Federal Convention of 1787,* had been deliberately distorted by Madison to support the "limited-powers" interpretation of the Constitution favored by Jeffersonian Republicans. Crosskey's third volume, completed posthumously by William W. Jeffrey, Jr., and published in 1980, asserted that nationalist sentiments and ideas pervaded the political climate in the United States from the Revolution to the opening of the CONSTITUTIONAL CONVENTION OF 1787.

RICHARD B. BERNSTEIN

CRUEL AND UNUSUAL PUNISHMENT

The Eighth Amendment provides that "excessive BAIL shall not be required . . . nor cruel and unusual punishment inflicted." Similar provisions now exist in virtually all state constitutions. Even if they did not, the federal constitutional prohibition has been held in *Robinson v. California* (1962) to be binding on the states through the FOURTEENTH AMENDMENT'S DUE PROCESS CLAUSE.

A legal prohibition against cruel and unusual punishment appears to have originated in the English BILL OF RIGHTS in 1688. Its purpose then was to curtail the shockingly barbarous punishments that were so common during that period.

How the prohibition was to be applied to American society, with its different values and legal system, remained unclear a century after the enactment of the American BILL OF RIGHTS. In the late nineteenth and early twentieth centuries, the Supreme Court did occasionally interpret the cruel and unusual punishment language, mostly as it related to the means for executing CAPITAL PUNISHMENT. However, not until the 1970s did the Supreme Court begin to give extensive consideration to the scope and meaning of the prohibition apart from capital punishment. The Court did not decide until 1977, for example, whether the cruel and unusual punishment clause applied to persons who had not been convicted of crime. INGRAHAM V. WRIGHT (1977) raised the question whether the corporal punishment of school children constituted cruel and unusual punishment. The Court held that it did not, stating that the Eighth Amendment provision is applicable only to persons convicted and incarcerated for crimes. In the Court's view, the prohibition was not necessary to protect children in public institutions, as other protections were available. Since *Ingraham,* the Supreme Court has also held that the Eighth Amendment is inapplicable to persons detained for treatment or detention and not punishment, such as persons committed to mental institutions (*Youngblood v. Romero,* 1982) or detained awaiting trial (*Bell v. Wolfish,* 1979). Any protection against improper punishments in such situations derives from due process of law and not the Eighth Amendment prohibition against cruel and unusual punishment.

Since the late 1970s, in a number of cases involving noncapital sentences and the treatment of prison inmates, the Court has generally given a narrow interpretation of the cruel and unusual punishment clause.

Prior to Supreme Court review of the issue, several federal and state courts had held that a sentence could be invalid on cruel and unusual punishment grounds if its length was disproportionate to the offense. Courts used several measures to determine whether a particular sentence violated the Eight Amendment: the nature of the crime, and particularly whether violence was involved; comparison of the individual sentence or statutory sentencing scheme with sentences or schemes for similar crimes in other jurisdictions; and comparison of the individual sentence or statutory sentencing scheme for the particular crime with those for other similar or more serious crimes in the same jurisdiction. Thus a federal court of appeals struck down a life sentence imposed on an offender under a Texas statute authorizing a life sentence for a person convicted of felonies on three separate occasions. In this case, the three felonies included: fraudulently using a credit card to obtain $80.00 worth of services; passing a forged check for $28.36; and obtaining $120.75 by false pretenses. The three convictions occurred over a nine-year period. In RUMMEL V. ESTELLE the Supreme Court reversed; the 5–4 majority refused to apply the comparative measures used by lower courts. Instead, it gave great weight to legislative judgments on criminal sentences and to the deterrence of habitual offenders. The fact that Rummel was eligible for early release on parole apparently eased the majority's decision. After *Rummel,* it was uncertain what circumstances might justify judicial intervention on cruel and unusual punishment grounds in cases not involving habitual offender statutes. In *Hutto v. Davis* (1982), in a PER CURIAM opinion, the Court, over three dissents, held that a forty-year sentence for possession of nine ounces of marijuana did not constitute cruel and unusual punishment. The Court reiterated the *Rummel* majority's view that federal courts should be "reluctan[t] to review legislatively mandated terms of imprisonment" and that "successful challenges to the proportionality of particular sentences" should be "exceedingly rare."

In 1983, in SOLEM V. HELM, however, the Supreme Court invalidated a life sentence without possibility of parole for a person convicted under a recidivist statute. The immediate charge involved passing a check for one hundred dollars written on a nonexistent account; all his prior felony convictions were for nonviolent crimes against property. The Court, in a 5–4 decision, applied a proportionality test in applying the cruel and unusual punishment clause. Even after this decision, it appears that the burden of attacking a sentence of a term of years on disproportionality grounds, at least in the federal courts, will be difficult to carry. Some state supreme courts have been more willing to use state constitutional counterparts to the Eighth Amendment to strike down terms that seem excessive relative to the crime committed.

In earlier cases, the Supreme Court did reverse some sentences involving issues other than their length. In TROP V. DULLES (1958), for example, the Court concluded that depriving a person of nationality for conviction by court-martial of wartime desertion constituted cruel and unusual punishment. Also, in WEEMS V. UNITED STATES (1909), the Court held that the crime of being an accessory to the falsification of a public document could not justify a twelve-to-twenty-year sentence at hard labor with chains and a permanent deprivation of civil rights.

The Supreme Court has also applied the Eighth Amendment to reverse the punishment of a person simply because of his status or condition. In *Robinson v. California* (1962) the Court held that punishing a person for being a drug addict constitutes cruel and unusual punishment. The Court refused, however, to apply this same reasoning six years later when it was asked to invalidate an alcoholic's conviction of public drunkenness in *Powell v. Texas* (1968).

In summary, the Supreme Court has rarely relied on the federal prohibition against cruel and unusual punishment to overturn a criminal sentence. The Court has also applied the prohibition sparingly to challenges by prisoners to prison conditions, even though courts have frequently found these conditions to be shocking.

Without question, most prisons throughout the country are archaic, overcrowded, filthy, and understaffed, and provide few worthwhile vocational or recreational activities for prisoners. Because the prison population is growing dramatically at a time when resources to maintain it are shrinking proportionately, prison conditions are deteriorating. In several cases in the late 1970s and early 1980s, the Supreme Court attempted to articulate standards for applying the prohibition against cruel and unusual punishment to challenges against prison conditions. In *Rhodes v. Chapman* (1981) the Court summarized these standards as follows: "Today the Eighth Amendment prohibits punishments which, although not physically barbarous, involve the unnecessary and wanton infliction of pain, or are grossly disproportionate to the severity of the crime. Among unnecessary and wanton infliction of pain are those that are totally without penological justification." The Court has not yet applied these standards to the intentional physical abuse of prisoners. It has, however, cited with approval a court of appeals decision, *Jackson v. Bishop* (1968), which proscribed the whipping of prisoners.

Holt v. Finney (1978) confronted the Supreme Court with its first Eighth Amendment challenge to prison conditions. The lower courts had declared that the general conditions of the Arkansas state prison system constituted cruel and unusual punishment. Among the conditions challenged were: administration of much of the prisons' activities by inmate trustees; dangerous barracks; overcrowded and filthy conditions in isolation or punishment cells and the poor diet of prisoners in these cells; and lack of any rehabilitation programs. The lower courts entered sweeping orders requiring major improvements in the prisons. Among these improvements were restrictions on the numbers of prisoners placed in isolation cells, a requirement that bunks be placed in these cells, a discontinuation of the "grue" diet, and a limit of thirty days in an isolation cell. The state appealed the thirty-day limitation. In a cautious opinion, the Supreme Court upheld the lower court's conclusion. Although it held that confinement in punitive isolation is not a per se violation of the Eighth Amendment, the Court stated that such confinement may become a violation depending on the conditions of isolation. If violations do occur, the Court said, remedies may include a limit on the time to be spent in isolation; the thirty-day restriction of the lower court seemed supportable in this case.

The Supreme Court reached a different result in a constitutional challenge to overcrowding in an Ohio prison. In *Rhodes v. Chapman* (1981) the issue was "double-bunking" prisoners in cells originally designed for single inmates. The courts below had found this practice to violate the Eighth Amendment because prisoners were serving long sentences; the prison was thirty-eight percent over capacity; decency required more living space; prisoners spent much of their time in their cells; and double-bunking was a regular practice, not a temporary condition.

The Supreme Court reversed, holding that there was no evidence that double-bunking in this case "inflicted unnecessary or wanton pain or [was] grossly disproportionate to the severity of crimes warranting punishment." The Court found that double-bunking did not lead to "deprivation of essential food, medical care, or sanitation" or to increased violence among inmates. In the Court's view, the Constitution "does not mandate comfortable prisons," and judges should be reluctant to intervene in prison condition cases unless the conditions were "deplorable" or "sordid": "In discharging [their] oversight responsibility, however, [federal] courts cannot assume that State legislatures and prison officials are insensitive to the requirements of the Constitution or to the perplexing sociological problems of how best to achieve the penal function in the criminal justice system."

In another opinion, *Estelle v. Gamble* (1976), the Supreme Court established some minimum requirements for the provision of health care in prisons. Stating that the government must provide medical care to those whom it punishes by incarceration, the Court held that "deliberate indifference to the serious medical needs of prisoners constitutes unnecessary and wanton infliction of pain proscribed by the Eighth Amendment." The Court placed several limits on successful claims, however. For example, an inadvertent failure to provide adequate medical care would not constitute "unnecessary and wanton infliction of pain." Nor would an accident, simple negligence, or a disagreement as to treatment options.

Thus, although the Supreme Court had indicated that the Eighth Amendment does protect prisoners from deplorable conditions, for the most part the Court has not shared the view of many lower courts or of prison experts as to what conditions are deplorable.

The Supreme Court has yet to consider a number of other important questions, such as the factors that must be weighed in assessing challenges to the conditions of a prison as a whole; the constitutional limits on behavior modification programs, including drug usage programs; and the minimum requirements for providing a secure environment for prisoners. Precedent suggests that the Supreme Court will be as cautious in addressing these and other related prison condition issues as it has been in confronting other asserted impositions of cruel and unusual punishment.

SHELDON KRANTZ

(SEE ALSO: *Institutional Litigation.*)

Bibliography

GRANNUCCI, ANTHONY F. 1969 Nor Cruel and Unusual Punishment Inflicted: The Original Meaning. *California Law Review* 57:839–865.

JOINT COMMITTEE ON THE LEGAL STATUS OF PRISONERS 1977 American Bar Association Standards Relating to the Legal Status of Prisoners. *American Criminal Law Review* 14:377–629.

KRANTZ, SHELDON 1983 *Corrections and Prisoners' Rights in a Nutshell*, 2nd ed. St. Paul, Minn.: West Publishing Co.

SHERMAN, MICHAEL and HAWKINS, GORDON 1981 *Imprisonment in America: Choosing the Future.* Chicago: University of Chicago Press.

UNIFORM LAW COMMISSION 1978 *Model Sentencing and Convictions Act.* New York: National Conference of Commissioners on Uniform State Laws.

UNITED NATIONS ECONOMIC AND SOCIAL COUNCIL 1957 *Minimum Rules for the Treatment of Prisoners.* New York: United Nations Publications.

CRUIKSHANK, UNITED STATES v. 92 U.S. 542 (1876)

Cruikshank paralyzed the federal government's attempt to protect black citizens by punishing violators of their CIVIL RIGHTS and, in effect, shaped the Constitution to the advantage of the Ku Klux Klan. The case arose out of a federal prosecution of nightriders responsible for the Colfax Massacre of 1873 in Grant Parish, Louisiana. Several hundred armed whites besieged a courthouse where hundreds of blacks were holding a public assembly; the attackers burned down the building and murdered about 100 people. The United States tried Cruikshank and others involved in the massacre and convicted three for violating section six of the FORCE ACT OF 1870. That act, which survives as section 241 of Title 18 of the United States Code, is a general conspiracy statute making it a federal crime, then punishable by a $5,000 fine and up to ten years in prison, for two or more persons to conspire to injure or intimidate any citizen with the intent of hindering his free exercise of any right or privilege guaranteed him by the Constitution or laws of the United States.

In a unanimous opinion by Chief Justice MORRISON R. WAITE, the Court ignored the statute and focused on the INDICTMENT to ascertain whether the rights Cruikshank and others interfered with were granted or secured by the United States. Reasserting the theory of dual CITIZENSHIP advanced in the SLAUGHTERHOUSE CASES (1873), Waite concluded that the United States cannot grant or secure rights not under its JURISDICTION. Examining in turn each right named in the indictment as having been deprived, Waite found that they were all "left under the protection of the States." None was a federal right. The right to peaceably assemble predated the Constitution and remained "subject to state jurisdiction." The United States could neither infringe it nor protect it, for it was not an attribute of United States citizenship. So too the right to bear arms. The right to be secure in one's person, life, and liberty was protected by the FOURTEENTH AMENDMENT against state deprivation, but for protection of that right, sovereignty "rests alone with the States." The amendment, said Waite, "adds nothing to the rights of one citizen as against another." Thus the violence here conducted by private persons could not be reached by Congress, which was limited to assuring that the states do not violate the amendment's prohibitions. As for the right to vote, the FIFTEENTH AMENDMENT merely protected against discrimination based on race. The Constitution did not confer the right to vote on anyone; that right was not, Waite said, an attribute of national citizenship.

By such reasoning the Court held that the indictment did not show that the conspirators had hindered or prevented the enjoyment of any right granted or secured by the Constitution. Accordingly, no conviction based on the indictment could be sustained, and the Court ordered the defendants discharged. The conspiracy statute remained impotent until revived in recent times by the Department of Justice, but the Court did not sustain a conviction under the statute until 1966 (UNITED STATES V. PRICE; UNITED STATES V. GUEST), when the Court vitiated *Cruikshank*.

LEONARD W. LEVY

Bibliography

MAGRATH, C. PETER 1963 *Morrison R. Waite.* Pages 120–134. New York: Macmillan.

CRUZ v. BETO

See: Religious Liberty

CULTS (RELIGIOUS) AND THE CONSTITUTION

The term "cult," currently used to designate a particular unpopular and feared new religious group often claiming a personal relationship between its leader and the Divinity, is not found explicitly in the original Constitution, the FIRST AMENDMENT's free exercise or establishment clause, or the FOURTEENTH AMENDMENT's EQUAL PROTECTION clause. Among the most prominent of these groups in recent times have been the Unification Church, the Worldwide Church of God, Inc., the Church of Scientology, and the International Society for Krishna Consciousness.

Cults, which have experienced varying degrees of discrimination and persecution by law enforcement officials, have consistently claimed that the Constitution does not sanction legal distinctions between them on the one hand and long-established and respected faiths on the other. They note, too, that historically most of the now well-established and fully respected faiths, including Baptists, Roman Catholics, Jews, Mormons, Christian Scientists, and Jehovah's Witnesses, have been subjected to governmental discrimination before achieving acceptability and equal treatment.

The claim to equal treatment was upheld in LARSON v. VALENTE (1982) where the Supreme Court held unconstitutional a Minnesota statute, enforced against the Unification Church, that imposed special registration and reporting requirements upon religious groups that received more than half of their income from nonmembers, a provision the Court found to have been aimed at unpopular cults. This provision, the Court said, constituted precisely the sort of official denominational preference and discrimination forbidden by the establishment clause in the absence of a compelling interest not otherwise amenable to protection. Moreover, the statute also violated the clause by authorizing excessive governmental entanglement with and politicizing of religion.

Compelling registration is only one comparatively mild sanction imposed by government upon religious cults. Although that term had not yet become popular in 1944, when *United States v. Ballard* was decided by the Supreme Court, that decision ruled unconstitutional a mail fraud conviction of "I Am" members who obtained donations by representing that their leader was divinely appointed with supernatural powers to heal the incurably ill. To allow a jury to determine the truth or falsity of religious doctrines, the Court said, would render vulnerable representations concerning the miracles of the New Testament, the divinity of Christ, life after death, and the power of prayer. The First Amendment permits only a determination whether the defendants themselves actually believed that what they recounted was true, not whether it was actually true.

Other devices applied against cults include denial of tax exemption, dissolution of the corporate structure and seizure of assets (as in CHURCH OF JESUS CHRIST OF LATTER DAY SAINTS v. UNITED STATES, 1890), and prosecution for disturbance of the peace (as in CANTWELL v. CONNECTICUT, 1940, involving Jehovah's Witnesses).

Whatever may have been the Court's response in earlier times, today it accords cults the same constitutional protection accorded to long-standing and commonly accepted faiths.

LEO PFEFFER

Bibliography

New York University Review of Law and Social Change 1979–1980 Volume 9, #1: *Proceedings of Conference on Alternative Religions, Government Control and the First Amendment.*

CUMBERLAND ROAD BILL

See: Internal Improvements

CUMMINGS, HOMER S. (1870–1956)

A prominent Connecticut Democrat, Homer S. Cummings served as attorney general under President FRANKLIN D. ROOSEVELT from 1933 to 1939, defending much of the New Deal legislation in the Supreme Court. He broke with recent practice when he personally argued the GOLD CLAUSE CASES (1935), and the Court reiterated much of his argument in its opinions. Cummings strongly supported Roosevelt's court packing plan as "clearly constitutional" and privately suggested a constitutional amendment requiring justices to retire at seventy. With Carl McFarland, he wrote *Federal Justice* (1937), a history of the Department of Justice based on previously neglected manuscript materials. Cummings instituted reform of federal criminal and administrative procedures, helping secure adoption of the FEDERAL RULES OF CIVIL PROCEDURE in 1938.

DAVID GORDON

CUMMINGS v. MISSOURI

See: Test Oath Cases

CURTIS, BENJAMIN R. (1809–1874)

Benjamin Robbins Curtis of Massachusetts generally rates high marks for his six-year tenure on the Supreme Court. His bold dissent in DRED SCOTT v. SANDFORD (1857), followed by his dramatic resignation, largely accounts for his reputation. Yet Curtis's contributions to the development of constitutional law transcend that one case.

Curtis's prominence in the *Dred Scott* case is ironic, considering the fact that he received his appointment in 1851 because he was a northern Whig, acceptable to southern slave interests. By that time, he already was a leading figure in Boston legal circles. He had been selected in 1846 to succeed Justice JOSEPH STORY as an overseer (trustee) of Harvard College, and he was highly regarded for his promotion of procedure and litigation reforms. In 1851 he represented the Boston school board against the desegregationists in ROBERTS V. CITY OF BOSTON. But most important, Curtis had also endorsed Senator DANIEL WEBSTER's efforts in the COMPROMISE OF 1850, had advocated strict enforcement of the new Fugitive Slave Act, and had fought abolitionists and free-soilers, even opposing CHARLES SUMNER's successful Senate campaign in 1851. Shortly afterward, President MILLARD FILLMORE, following Webster's recommendation, nominated Curtis to succeed Justice LEVI WOODBURY. The only criticism came from the abolitionist press. Southern politicians, however, were satisfied and the Democratic Senate quickly confirmed the appointment.

Curtis's first major opinion, in COOLEY V. BOARD OF WARDENS (1851), reflected both his legal skills and his willingness to follow the middle ground of his patron, Daniel Webster. The case involved the limiting effects of the COMMERCE CLAUSE on state regulation, a subject that had divided the TANEY COURT since 1837. Southerners feared congressional regulation of interstate traffic in slaves, and consequently sought to interpret the commerce power narrowly. In *Cooley* Curtis acknowledged broad congressional authority over foreign and INTERSTATE COMMERCE, but the case challenged the validity not of congressional action but of local pilotage regulations for the port of Philadelphia. Curtis devised a compromise between the EXCLUSIVE POWER and CONCURRENT POWER views. His doctrine of SELECTIVE EXCLUSIVENESS recognized exclusive congressional power over subjects demanding uniform national regulation, but invited state regulation, in cases where Congress had not acted, of subjects admitting of diverse local regulation.

Curtis again demonstrated a shrewd practicality coupled with an ability to make law responsive to new conditions when he upheld federal regulations of steamboat operations. In *Steamboat New World v. King* (1854) Curtis applied the emerging law of negligence to the rapidly expanding technology of steamboating. In addition, he confirmed that federal admiralty jurisdiction applied to all inland, navigable waters. A year before the *Dred Scott* controversy over the content of the Fifth Amendment's DUE PROCESS clause, Curtis had discussed the subject in MURRAY'S LESSEE V. HOBOKEN LAND AND IMPROVEMENT COMPANY (1856) and had followed a traditional procedural interpretation of the clause.

The understanding of Curtis's role in *Dred Scott* has shifted with historiographical tides. When it was fashionable to view the Civil War as a "reconcilable conflict," Curtis was seen as a *provocateur;* but when the *Dred Scott* decision is seen as Chief Justice ROGER TANEY's attempt to make the nation safe for slavery, Curtis's opinion emerges as a calm, reasoned historical and legal brief properly explicating national authority to regulate SLAVERY IN THE TERRITORIES. Curtis's opinion differed from Taney's conclusions in nearly every respect. He demonstrated historically that blacks could be American citizens, and hence could sue in the federal courts. Equally important, he offered constitutional language and long-standing historical precedent to justify congressional regulation of slavery in the territories. Curtis's comments on the need for judicial restraint were pointed: "To engraft on any instrument a substantive exception not found in it must be admitted to be a matter attended with great difficulty. . . . To allow this to be done with the Constitution, upon reasons purely political, renders its judicial interpretation impossible because judicial tribunals . . . cannot decide upon political considerations."

Curtis resigned a few months after the *Dred Scott* decision. He was dissatisfied with his circuit duties and his inadequate salary, and the *Dred Scott* imbroglio convinced him that he and his colleagues could no longer work together effectively and harmoniously.

During the Civil War, Curtis emerged as an outspoken critic of Lincoln's unprecedented exercise of PRESIDENTIAL POWERS. In good Whig fashion, he leveled constitutional attacks on Lincoln for suspending the writ of HABEAS CORPUS and for issuing the EMANCIPATION PROCLAMATION. Yet, following the war, he endorsed the sentiments of the National Union Convention in 1866 and advocated exclusive presidential control of reconstruction. Two years later, he joined WILLIAM M. EVARTS and others to represent President ANDREW JOHNSON in his IMPEACHMENT trial. Curtis's defense of the President argued that Johnson was not an "acting President," as some claimed, and that the TENURE OF OFFICE ACT unduly interfered with the President's constitutional prerogative to remove executive officers—an argument the Supreme Court came to accept half a century later. Finally, he offered a ringing affirmation of the FIRST AMENDMENT to defend Johnson against the charge that he had "improperly" spoken of Congress.

In his last years, Curtis had a lucrative law practice and argued more than fifty cases before the Supreme Court. Most noteworthy were his briefs in behalf of federal regulation of the insurance industry in PAUL V. VIRGINIA (1869) and his defense of the legal tender laws in HEPBURN V. GRISWOLD (1870).

Curtis's all too brief career on the Supreme Court must exclude him from a short list of truly great jurists. But he displayed uncommon skills, especially a talent for closely reasoned and logical arguments. His defense and understanding of the Constitution, on and off the bench, mark contributions that have been affirmed by the passage of time.

STANLEY I. KUTLER

Bibliography

CURTIS, GEORGE TICKNOR and CURTIS, BENJAMIN R., EDS. 1879 *Life and Writings of Benjamin Robbins Curtis.* Boston: Little, Brown.

FEHRENBACHER, DON E. 1978 *The Dred Scott Case: Its Significance in American Law and Politics.* New York: Oxford University Press.

LEACH, RICHARD H. 1952 Benjamin Robbins Curtis: Judicial Misfit. *New England Quarterly* 25:507–523.

CURTIS, GEORGE T. (1812–1894)

A leading Boston attorney, George Ticknor Curtis ordered the rendition to slavery of Thomas Sims in 1852 while serving as a Fugitive Slave Law Commissioner. (See SIMS' CASE.) In 1856 he represented Dred Scott before the United States Supreme Court in DRED SCOTT V. SANDFORD. Curtis wrote numerous legal treatises, three political biographies, and a two-volume *History of the Origin, Formation, and Adoption of the Constitution* (1854–1858)—revised as *Constitutional History of the United States* (1889–1896). This work presents a classic Federalist-Whig interpretation of American political and constitutional history. It was begun at the suggestion of DANIEL WEBSTER and reflects the senator's approach to the Constitution and the Union.

PAUL FINKELMAN

Bibliography

FISH, CARL RUSSELL 1930 George T. Curtis. *Dictionary of American Biography,* Vol. 4:613–614.

CURTISS-WRIGHT EXPORT CORPORATION, UNITED STATES v. 299 U.S. 304 (1936)

Nearly two years after Paraguay and Bolivia went to war in 1932, Congress authorized President FRANKLIN D. ROOSEVELT to embargo American arms shipments to the belligerents if he found that the action might contribute to reestablishing peace. Indicted in January 1936 for conspiring to violate the embargo resolution and Roosevelt's implementing proclamation, Curtiss-Wright Export Corporation demurred on grounds of unconstitutional DELEGATION OF POWER. Recent rulings against New Deal legislation in PANAMA REFINING CO. V. RYAN (1935) and SCHECHTER POULTRY CORP. V. UNITED STATES (1935) lent weight to the company's position, and the district court sustained the demurrer. On appeal, however, the Supreme Court approved the embargo resolution and proclamation with a ringing endorsement of independent presidential authority in the area of FOREIGN AFFAIRS.

For a 7–1 majority, Justice GEORGE SUTHERLAND defended the embargo measures by distinguishing between powers of internal and external SOVEREIGNTY, a distinction the government had not employed in arguing *Curtiss-Wright.* For him, the federal government's domestic authority derived from states having delegated power via the Constitution. External sovereignty had passed, however, from the British Crown to the United Colonies and then to the United States in their collective capacities, with the states severally never possessing it nor delegating it. "Rulers come and go; governments end and forms of government change; but sovereignty survives." In the realm of foreign relations, the authority of the federal government therefore equaled that of any sovereign nation, and the usual constitutional divisions between the President and Congress were largely irrelevant, as was the normal prohibition on delegation of legislative power. Keenly aware of the need for energy and dispatch in the delicate business of conducting foreign relations, the Framers had endorsed this arrangement, Sutherland claimed, and early statesmen put it into practice. Although dissenting, Justice JAMES C. MCREYNOLDS filed no opinion.

Later characterized as dictum-laden, Sutherland's argument made sense within the constitutional climate of the 1930s and in view of his own commitments. The government, for example, had claimed that the 1934 embargo resolution and proclamation met the straited *Panama-Schechter* requirement that delegatory legislation specify the findings of fact the President must make before taking the anticipated action. Such an approach ignored the plausible objection that findings involving diplomatic and military imponderables were no firmer than those already disallowed as "opinion" in *Schechter.* An alternative was simply to rely on judicial precedent and legislative practice regarding delegation in areas cognate to foreign relations. Sutherland did examine earlier embargo, tariff, and kindred measures in which Congress had given latitude to the President, but he did so primarily as a means of showing that his view of external sovereignty had been accepted from the beginning. Neither judicial nor legislative iterations carried the same weight as the original intent and first principles he valued so highly. Perhaps most important, Sutherland himself had broached the external–internal distinction the previous May, in CARTER V. CARTER COAL COMPANY (1936), and had earlier explicated his full theory of sovereignty in his book *Constitutional Power and World Affairs* (1919).

The real weakness of Sutherland's opinion was its faulty history. Scant evidence exists that the Framers held the extraconstitutional understanding of the foreign relations power he attributed to them. Sutherland also misconstrued many of the earlier episodes and commentaries that, he argued, were informed by his theories of sovereignty and plenary executive authority. *Curtiss-Wright* nevertheless had timing on its side. It soon provided a base for upholding EXECUTIVE AGREEMENTS as domestic law in UNITED STATES V. BELMONT (1937) and UNITED STATES V. PINK (1942). More broadly, Sutherland's opinion appealed to proponents of an expanded presidential role as the United States acquired global responsibilities, engaged in nuclear diplomacy, fought undeclared wars, and debated the requirements of internal security.

CHARLES A. LOFGREN

Bibliography

LEVITAN, DAVID M. 1946 The Foreign Relations Power: An Analysis of Mr. Justice Sutherland's Theory. *Yale Law Journal* 55:467–497.

LOFGREN, CHARLES A. 1973 *United States v. Curtiss-Wright Export Corporation:* An Historical Reassessment. *Yale Law Journal* 83:1–32.

CUSHING, WILLIAM
(1732–1810)

William Cushing served on the United States Supreme Court, in an undistinguished manner, for nearly twenty-one years. Born into a politically well-connected, upper middle class Massachusetts family, he graduated from Harvard College, and then studied law; he was admitted to the bar in 1755. He practiced law in Maine, where he represented the interests of large landholders against squatters and debtors. In 1771 he succeeded his father as a judge of the Massachusetts Superior Court. Because many of his family had loyalist leanings and he owed his position to a royal appointment, Cushing expressed his political views cautiously during the 1770s, when colonial resistance to British policies turned into revolution. Although he chose the patriot side in 1776, some ardent radicals doubted his enthusiasm for independence. Nonetheless he was appointed to the newly created superior court and became chief justice for the state in 1777 when JOHN ADAMS resigned the post. He also served as a member of the convention that wrote the MASSACHUSETTS CONSTITUTION of 1780.

While chief justice, Cushing played an important role in bringing about the end of slavery in Massachusetts, beginning with COMMONWEALTH V. JENNISON (1783). In his charge to the jury, Cushing interpreted the clause of the state constitution that declared that "all men are born free and equal" as abolishing slavery in the state. Unsympathetic to the debtors in western Massachusetts who prevented the collection of taxes and closed the courts during SHAYS' REBELLION, Cushing opposed their activities while riding circuit and presided over the TREASON trial of the leaders; some of his sentences included the death penalty. He advocated RATIFICATION OF THE CONSTITUTION in 1788 and served as vice-president of the state ratifying convention.

GEORGE WASHINGTON appointed Cushing the first associate Justice of the United States Supreme Court in 1789. Despite his extensive judicial experience he did not play a very active role on the Court. Although he participated in many of the most important cases of the 1790s—CHISHOLM V. GEORGIA (1793), WARE V. HYLTON (1796), HYLTON V. UNITED STATES (1796), and CALDER V. BULL (1798)—his opinions tended to be brief, and dealt with narrow legal and procedural questions. Ceremonious in his deportment, Cushing was the last member of the Court to wear a wig. His affability and courtesy enabled him to enforce the Sedition Act with minimal rancor. After 1800, illness, age, and the difficulties of riding circuit caused him considerable hardship. He could no longer adequately perform his duties, and he probably would have retired early if a federal pension had been available. He died, while still a member of the Supreme Court, in 1810.

RICHARD E. ELLIS

Bibliography

JOHNSON, HERBERT ALAN 1969 William Cushing. Pages 57–70 in Leon Friedman and Fred L. Israel, eds., *Justices of the Supreme Court, 1789–1969,* Vol. I. New York: Chelsea House.

CUSHMAN, ROBERT E.
(1889–1969)

Robert Eugene Cushman taught constitutional law for many years at Cornell University. His landmark anthology, *Leading Constitutional Decisions* (1925; 16th ed. by Robert F. Cushman, 1982), quickly established itself as a standard casebook for constitutional law and history courses. Cushman founded and edited the Cornell Studies on Civil Liberty; the contributors to this series of monographs included Robert K. Carr, Milton R. Convitz, Walter Gellhorn, James Morton Smith, and Cushman himself. Cushman described his monograph, *Civil Liberties in the United States* (1956), as "a guide to current problems and experience." A synoptic description of the state of the law and an attempt to chart its future development, it was well-received, although some critics questioned its formalistic approach and its skeletal coverage of various issues. Cushman's major scholarly work, *The Independent Regulatory Commissions* (1941), a byproduct of his service with the President's Committee on Administrative Management (1937); prophetically proposed the separation in independent regulatory commissions of the prosecutorial and adjudicative functions. For many years he wrote the *American Political Science Review*'s annual survey of the work of the Supreme Court. From 1958 until his death, Cushman was editor-in-chief of the *Documentary History of the Ratification of the Constitution;* he was succeeded by MERRILL JENSEN.

RICHARD B. BERNSTEIN

CUSTODIAL INTERROGATION

See: Police Interrogation and Confessions

DAIRY QUEEN, INC. v. WOOD
369 U.S. 469 (1962)

The owners of the "Dairy Queen" trademark sued a licensee alleging breach of contract and trademark infringement and asking for injunctive relief and an "accounting." Since this was a case in EQUITY, U. S. District Judge Wood denied the defendant's motion for a jury trial.

A unanimous Supreme Court, speaking through Justice HUGO L. BLACK, held that Wood's decision deprived Dairy Queen of its SEVENTH AMENDMENT rights: although the complaint asked for an "accounting," it was really a suit for damages or debt. As Black wrote, "the constitutional right of TRIAL BY JURY cannot be made dependent upon the choice of words used in the pleadings."

DENNIS J. MAHONEY

DALLAS, ALEXANDER J.
(1759–1817)

Admitted to the bar in 1785, Alexander James Dallas practiced law in Philadelphia. He supplemented his income by reporting the opinions of the courts that sat in that city, including the Supreme Court of the United States (1790–1800). From 1801 to 1814 he was United States attorney for eastern Pennsylvania.

As secretary of the treasury under President JAMES MADISON (1814–1816), Dallas secured enactment of the highest federal taxes to that date, restored confidence in the currency, and dictated terms of the second BANK OF THE UNITED STATES ACT (1816). In 1815 he was also acting secretary of war.

DENNIS J. MAHONEY

DAMAGES

From the earliest days of COMMON LAW, courts have ordered the payment of money ("damages") to compensate for legal wrongs. Two related but separable lines of cases shape the availability of damages for violations of constitutional rights. One line of cases involves interpretation of SECTION 1983, TITLE 42, UNITED STATES CODE, and its express provision for "an action at law" to redress deprivations of constitutional rights by state officials. Since the revival of section 1983 in MONROE V. PAPE (1961), it has been understood that damages are available to compensate for constitutional violations by state officials. CAREY V. PIPHUS (1978) reaffirmed this understanding, but held that substantial damages could not be recovered for PROCEDURAL DUE PROCESS violations without proof of injury. *Smith v. Wade* (1983) clarified the standards governing awards of punitive damages under section 1983.

In actions against federal officials, which are not governed by section 1983, the Court, in BIVENS V. SIX UNKNOWN NAMED AGENTS OF THE FEDERAL BUREAU OF NARCOTICS (1971), inferred a damages action based on the FOURTH AMENDMENT. Later cases, such as DAVIS V. PASSMAN (1979), extended the implied constitutional damages action to other constitutional provisions. The *Bivens* line of cases may be viewed as an extension of EX PARTE YOUNG (1908) and other decisions that allowed actions for injunctive relief to be based directly on the Constitution.

THEODORE EISENBERG

Bibliography

NEWMAN, JON O. 1978 Suing the Lawbreakers: Proposals to Strengthen the Section 1983 Damages Remedy for Law Enforcers' Misconduct. *Yale Law Journal* 87:447–467.

DAMES & MOORE v. REGAN
453 U.S. 654 (1981)

The United States hostage crisis was settled by the 1981 Algerian Agreement under which, *inter alia*, the United States undertook to terminate certain litigation by American claimants against Iran and its agencies. Under the agreement, the claims involved were required to be submitted to binding international arbitration. By EXECUTIVE ORDER, President JIMMY CARTER suspended various claims pending in American courts. Certain American claimants challenged this action as exceeding presidential authority. The Supreme Court upheld the President's authority to conclude and implement this part of the agreement on the basis of his constitutional FOREIGN AFFAIRS powers. It relied on congressional acceptance of broad presidential power during crises in foreign affairs, and on Congress's historic acquiescence in the practice of settling American claims by EXECUTIVE AGREEMENT. The Court also held that if the agreement caused a TAKING OF PROPERTY within the scope of the Fifth Amendment, American nationals had a remedy for compensation in the CLAIMS COURT OF THE UNITED STATES.

The decision effectively permitted the President to remove a category of cases from federal court JURISDICTION (although the Court characterized its action as only approving a change in the "applicable substantive law"). And it opened the way to subsequent "takings" litigation over a broad area of foreign economic policy. In both respects the Court went beyond previous decisions involving presidential executive agreement authority, and treated the presidential executive agreement as fully equivalent to a Senate-approved treaty. Accordingly, it seems to be the most sweeping judicial recognition to date of presidential foreign relations power.

PHILLIP R. TRIMBLE

Bibliography

MARKS, LEE R. and GRABOW, JOHN C. 1982 The President's Foreign Economic Powers after Dames & Moore v. Regan: Legislation by Acquiescence. *Cornell Law Review* 68:68–103.

TRIMBLE, PHILLIP R. 1984 Foreign Policy Frustrated—Dames & Moore, Claims Court Jurisdiction and a New Raid on the Treasury. *Columbia Law Review* 84:317–385.

DANDRIDGE v. WILLIAMS
397 U.S. 471 (1970)

Dandridge stifled the infant DOCTRINE, born in cases such as GRIFFIN V. ILLINOIS (1956) and DOUGLAS V. CALIFORNIA (1963), that governmental WEALTH DISCRIMINATION, like RACIAL DISCRIMINATION, demanded strict judicial scrutiny of its justifications. Maryland provided welfare aid to dependent children on the basis of need, partly determined by the number of children in a family. However, payment to any one family was limited to $250 per month, irrespective of the family's size. A 6–3 Supreme Court, speaking through Justice POTTER STEWART, characterized the case as one involving "social and economic" regulation, and applied the RATIONAL BASIS standard of review. Here there were legitimate state interests in encouraging employment and avoiding distinctions between welfare recipients and the working poor. Although some welfare beneficiaries were unemployable, the maximum-grant rule was generally reasonable.

Justice THURGOOD MARSHALL, dissenting, rejected the idea of two separate STANDARDS OF REVIEW, rational basis and STRICT SCRUTINY. He argued for a "sliding scale" of judicial supervision that would demand progressively more state justification as the classification in question bore more heavily on the powerless and in proportion to the importance of the interest at stake. Here, where indigent children were being deprived of basic subsistence as defined by the state's own standards of need, the permissive rational basis standard was inappropriate. Marshall also argued that the maximum-grant rule was invalid even under that permissive standard, given the state's aim of aiding children and the unemployability of a large proportion of welfare recipients.

After *Dandridge*, it became futile to argue to the Supreme Court either that welfare subsistence was a FUNDAMENTAL INTEREST or that wealth discrimination implied a SUSPECT CLASSIFICATION. Since 1970 the Court has regularly shied away from decisions that would place the judiciary in the position of allocating state resources.

KENNETH L. KARST

DANE, NATHAN
(1752–1835)

A loyal graduate of Harvard College, Nathan Dane of Beverly, Massachusetts, became a lawyer, politician, and scholar. In 1787, while representing his state in Congress, he single-handedly composed the NORTHWEST ORDINANCE. Its provision outlawing slavery derived from THOMAS JEFFERSON'S LAND ORDINANCE OF 1785, but Dane deserves credit for writing the various other provisions that amounted to the first national BILL OF RIGHTS. It included, too, a precursor of the CONTRACT CLAUSE.

After serving in various state offices, Dane was forced by deafness to retire to his law practice and to legal scholarship as the century ended. Although he attended the HARTFORD CONVENTION, he spent most of his energies on a compendium of American law, published in eight volumes between 1820 and 1829 and known as "Dane's Abridgment." The work earned him the name of "the American Blackstone" and the money that he gave to develop Harvard Law School. Dane Hall was the first building and Dane himself chose the first Dane Professor, Justice JOSEPH STORY.

LEONARD W. LEVY

Bibliography

JOHNSON, ANDREW W. 1986 *The Life and Constitutional Thought of Nathan Dane.* New York: Garland Publishing.

DANIEL, PETER V.
(1784–1860)

Peter Vivian Daniel, a Virginian born in 1784, served as an Associate Justice of the Supreme Court of the United States from 1841 until his death in 1860. His opinions were notable for the extremist positions he adopted on constitutional issues, including the powers of the federal and state governments, the status of corporations, and slavery.

Daniel, a Republican and later a Jacksonian Democrat, served in the Virginia General Assembly, as privy councillor, and as lieutenant governor. President ANDREW Jackson appointed him to the U. S. District Court in 1836 and President MARTIN VAN BUREN to the Supreme Court in 1841. There the bulk of his work involved cases concerning land titles, procedure, and EQUITY. However, he did participate in most of the major constitutional decisions of the TANEY COURT. But in all instances save one, he spoke either in a concurring or in a dissenting opinion.

Viewing the federal Constitution as a compact among sovereign states, Daniel opposed the extension of federal regulatory authority in COMMERCE CLAUSE cases and extolled the states' POLICE POWER (LICENSE CASES, 1847; PASSENGER CASES, 1849). He concurred in COOLEY V. BOARD OF WARDENS (1851) because he denied that the subject matter of that case (pilotage regulation) was within the federal commerce power at all. In the first *Pennsylvania v. Wheeling Bridge* case (1851), Daniel condemned the use of the commerce power to restrict commerce on navigable rivers. Daniel's hostility to federal ADMIRALTY JURISDICTION sprang from the same source and was buttressed by his insistence on preservation of JURY TRIAL. He dissented in PROPELLER GENESEE CHIEF V. FITZHUGH (1851), one of the few times in which he disagreed with Chief Justice ROGER B. TANEY, opposing the extension of federal admiralty jurisdiction to nontidal waters. In his *Searight v. Stokes* dissent (1845), Daniel insisted that the federal government lacked any power at all to finance INTERNAL IMPROVEMENTS, going far beyond the constitutional doctrine of Jackson's MAYSVILLE ROAD BILL veto (1830).

Daniel was an inveterate foe of banks and corporations, seeking unsuccessfully to deny them access to federal courts as the "Citizens" requisite to Article III jurisdiction (*Rundle v. Delaware and Raritan Canal Co.*, 1852, dissent). In his dissent in *Planters Bank v. Sharp* (1848), he sought to limit the CONTRACT CLAUSE'S scope as a restraint on state regulatory power over corporations. In the only significant constitutional case where he spoke for the Court, WEST RIVER BRIDGE V. DIX (1848), Daniel upheld the state's use of EMINENT DOMAIN and police power to condemn corporate property.

In his later years, Daniel came to despise the institutions and values of the free states. His concurrence in DRED SCOTT V. SANDFORD (1857) was remarkable for its intemperate condemnation of the MISSOURI COMPROMISE and for his insistence that no free blacks could be citizens.

Daniel himself best evaluated his contribution to the work of the Court in his *Genesee Chief* dissent: "My opinions may be deemed to be contracted and antiquated, unsuited to the day in which we live, but they are founded upon deliberate convictions as to the nature and objects of LIMITED GOVERNMENT."

WILLIAM M. WIECEK

Bibliography

FRANK, JOHN P. 1964 *Justice Daniel Dissenting: Peter V. Daniel.* Cambridge, Mass.: Harvard University Press.

DARBY LUMBER COMPANY, UNITED STATES v.
312 U.S. 100 (1941)

This decision held the FAIR LABOR STANDARDS ACT of 1938 to be a valid exercise of federal power under the COMMERCE CLAUSE. That was no surprise after the 1937 decisions upholding the WAGNER (NATIONAL LABOR RELATIONS) ACT and after the retirement of the four Justices who had voted consistently for a narrow interpretation of the commerce clause. The opinion of Justice HARLAN FISKE STONE was nevertheless of great significance. For instead of speaking in terms of such nonconstitutional concepts as "direct" and "indirect," it returned to basic constitutional principles as to the scope of the power of Congress.

The commerce clause itself precluded states with high labor standards from protecting their wage levels by forbidding the entry of goods produced elsewhere at lower wages. This meant that in the absence of federal legislative action, states with the lowest labor standards could drive the standards down throughout the country. In 1916 Congress first sought to meet this problem by barring the interstate transportation of goods produced by children. Although that statute was clearly a regulation of INTERSTATE COMMERCE the Supreme Court held it unconstitutional by a vote of 5–4 in HAMMER V. DAGENHART (1918) because the purpose of the act was to control what occurred during the course of intrastate PRODUCTION. Five years later, in ADKINS V. CHILDREN'S HOSPITAL (1923), the Court ruled, 6–3, that the DUE PROCESS clause forbade the fixing of minimum wages by either federal or state governments.

The downward spiral of prices and wages during the Great Depression of the 1930s forced employers seeking to survive to reduce wages to incredibly low levels. Congress sought to deal with this problem by requiring the codes of fair competition under the NATIONAL INDUSTRIAL RECOVERY ACT to prescribe MAXIMUM HOURS AND MINIMUM WAGES. SCHECHTER POULTRY CORP. V. UNITED STATES (1935), holding the NRA unconstitutional, brought this program to a halt, and CARTER V. CARTER COAL COMPANY (1936), holding that Congress lacked power to regulate labor conditions and relations in the coal industry, seemed to create an insurmountable impediment. Unpredictably, this lasted for only a year, when *Carter* was in substance overruled in the WAGNER ACT CASES (1937) and *Adkins* was overruled in WEST COAST HOTEL CO. V. PARRISH (1937). The result was passage of the Fair Labor Standards Act in June 1938.

That statute prescribed a minimum wage of twenty-five cents per hour for employees engaged in interstate commerce or in producing goods for such commerce. Payment of fifty percent more for overtime was required for all hours over forty-four per week (to be reduced to forty after two years). The act penalized violation of those standards or interstate shipment of goods produced in violation of them.

The lumber industry was typically afflicted with depressed wage rates; wages ranged from ten to twenty-seven and one-half cents per hour. The annual average wage for all lumber industry employees in Georgia in 1937 was $389. Fred Darby was paying his employees twelve and one-half to seventeen cents per hour; he devised a scheme to continue doing so after the Fair Labor Standards Act became effective, and he was indicted.

Although the other federal lower courts had seen the light after the Labor Board cases and sustained the new statute, the Georgia district judge deemed himself bound to follow HAMMER V. DAGENHART and CARTER until the Supreme Court explicitly overruled them. Accordingly, he dismissed the INDICTMENT as an invalid regulation of manufacture, not interstate commerce, and the government appealed directly to the Supreme Court.

In upholding the statute Justice Stone spoke for a unanimous Court—undoubtedly because Justice JAMES C. MCREYNOLDS had retired three days before. The Court first held that the prohibition against the interstate shipment of goods produced under substandard labor conditions was "indubitably a regulation of [interstate] commerce." And this was none the less so because the motive or purpose may have been to control the "wages and hours of persons engaged in manufacture." The commerce power of Congress, as defined in GIBBONS V. OGDEN (1824), "may be exercised to its utmost extent, and acknowledges no limitations other than are prescribed in the Constitution." "The motive and purpose of a regulation of interstate commerce are matters for the legislative judgment upon which the courts are given no control." The contrary decision in HAMMER V. DAGENHART "by a bare majority of the Court over the powerful and now classic dissent of Mr. Justice [OLIVER WENDELL] HOLMES" was accordingly overruled.

In determining the validity of the regulation of wages and hours for manufacturers, the Court adopted the approach approved in MCCULLOCH V. MARYLAND (1819), the initial pronouncement on the scope of the ENUMERATED POWERS. The test was whether a regulation of intrastate activities was an "appropriate means to the attainment of a legitimate end, the exercise of the granted power of Congress to regulate interstate commerce." The directness or indirectness of the effect on such commerce was not mentioned, although the substantiality of the effect was. (See EFFECTS ON COMMERCE). The Court noted that legislation under other powers had often been sustained "when the means chosen, although not themselves within the granted power, were nevertheless deemed appropriate aids to the accomplishment of some purpose within an admitted power. . . ." The policy of excluding from interstate commerce goods produced under substandard labor conditions could reasonably be effectuated by prohibiting such conditions for manufacturers producing for interstate distribution. That would suppress a method of interstate competition Congress deemed unfair.

The opinion flatly rejected the contention that the TENTH AMENDMENT restricted the enumerated powers. That amendment, which provides that "the powers not delegated to the United States by the Constitution nor prohibited by it to the states are reserved to the states respectively or to the people," did not deprive the federal government of "authority to resort to all means for the exercise of a granted power which are appropriate and plainly adapted to the permitted end." "The amendment states but a truism that all is retained which has not been surrendered."

Darby was followed a year later by WICKARD V. FILBURN in which the Court alluded to the NECESSARY AND PROPER clause, which MCCULLOCH V. MARYLAND had emphasized, as the source of the power of Congress to regulate intrastate transactions. It also identified the cases which *Darby* had disapproved by implication, among others *Hammer*, *Schechter*, and *Carter*. *Darby* and *Wickard* together have provided the foundation for commerce clause interpretation thereafter. They firmly establish that the national economic system is subject to the control of the only entity that can possibly control it, the federal government.

ROBERT L. STERN

Bibliography

DODD, E. MERRICK 1946 The Supreme Court and Fair Labor Standards, 1941–1945. *Harvard Law Review* 59:321–375.

STERN, ROBERT L. 1946 The Commerce Clause and the National Economy, 1933–1946. *Harvard Law Review* 59:645–693, 883–947.

DARNEL'S CASE (FIVE KNIGHTS CASE)

See: Petition of Right

DARTMOUTH COLLEGE v. WOODWARD
4 Wheaton 518 (1819)

The most famous and influential CONTRACT CLAUSE case in our history, *Dartmouth College* was a boon to higher education and to corporate capitalism. The case established the DOCTRINE, never overruled, that a CORPORATION charter or the grant by a state of corporate rights to private interests comes within the protection of the contract clause. Although the case involved a small college in New Hampshire rather than a manufacturing concern, a bank, or a transportation company, the Court seized an opportunity to broaden the contract clause by making all private corporations its beneficiaries. DANIEL WEBSTER, counsel for the college, said that the judgment was a "defense of VESTED RIGHTS against Courts and Sovereignties," and his co-counsel, Joseph Hopkinson, asserted that it would "secure corporations . . . from legislative despotism. . . ." Corporations were still a recent innovation; JAMES KENT, in his *Commentaries on American Law* (1826), remarked that their rapid multiplication and the avidity with which they were sought by charter from the states arose as a result of the power that large, consolidated capital gave them over business of every sort. The Court's decision in the *Dartmouth College* case, Kent said, more than any other act proceeding from the authority of the United States, threw "an impregnable barrier around all rights and franchises derived from the grant of government; and [gave] solidity and inviolability to the literary, charitable, religious, and commercial institutions of our country." Actually, FLETCHER V. PECK (1810) had made the crucial and original extension of the contract clause, construing it to cover public and executed contracts as well as private executory ones. The *Dartmouth College* doctrine was a logical implication.

The college case was a strange vehicle for the doctrine that emerged from it. Dartmouth, having been chartered in 1769 in the name of the crown to christianize and educate Indians, had become a Christian college for whites and a stronghold of the Congregationalist Church, which had benefited most from the laws establishing the Protestant religion in New Hampshire. The college had become embroiled in state politics on the side of the Federalists, who supported the establishment. When in 1815 the trustees removed the president of the college, they loosed a controversy that drew to the ousted president a coalition of Jeffersonians and religious denominations demanding separation of church and state. The reformers having swept the state elections in 1816, the legislature sought to democratize the college by a series of statutes that converted it into a state university under public control, rather than a private college as provided by the original charter. The state supreme court sustained the state acts, reasoning that the institution had been established with public aid for public purposes of an educational and religious nature. The state court held that the contract clause did not limit the state's power over its own public corporations.

On APPEAL, the Supreme Court held that Dartmouth was a private eleemosynary corporation whose VESTED RIGHTS could not be divested without infringing a continuing obligation to respect inviolably the trustees' control of property given to the corporation for the advancement of its objectives. The Court held unconstitutional the state acts subjecting Dartmouth to state control and ordered Woodward, the treasurer of the institution who had sided with the state, to return to the trustees the records, corporate seal, and other corporate property which he held.

At every step of his opinion Chief Justice JOHN MARSHALL misstated the facts about the history of the original charter in order to prove that it established a purely private corporation. That, perhaps, was a matter primarily of interest to the college, which, contrary to Marshall, had received its charter not from George III but from the governor of the colony; moreover, the private donations, which Marshall said had been given to Dartmouth on condition of receiving the charter, had been given unconditionally to an entirely different institution, Moor's Charity School for Indians, and had been transferred to Dartmouth over the donors' objections. Also, the funds of the college, contrary to Marshall, did not consist "entirely of private donations," because the endowment of the college at the time of the issuance of the chapter derived mainly from grants of public lands. Even if the grant of the charter were a contract, as Marshall said it "plainly" was, Parliament could have repealed it at will. The Chief Justice conceded the fact but added that a repeal would have been morally perfidious. If, however, the charter were subject to revocation at the will of the sovereign authority, or the grantor, the "contract" did not bind that party and created no obligation that could be impaired.

Marshall conceded that at the time of Independence, the state suceeded to the power of Parliament and might have repealed or altered the charter at any time before the adoption of the Constitution. The provision in Article I, section 10, preventing states from impairing the obligation of a contract, altered the situation. That clause, Marshall conceded, was not specifically intended to protect charters of incorporation: "It is," he said boldly, "more than possible that the preservation of rights of this description was not particularly in the view of the framers of the constitution," but the clause admitted no exceptions as far as private rights were concerned. "It is not enough to say that this particular case was not in the mind of the convention when the article was framed, nor of the American people when it was adopted." In the absence of proof that the language of the Constitution would have been altered had charters of incorporation been considered, the case came within its injunction against state acts impairing the OBLIGATION OF CONTRACTS.

Although Marshall can be doubted when he said, "It can require no argument to prove that the circumstances of this case constitute a contract," his general doctrine, that any state charter for a private corporation is a constitutionally protected contract, was not far-fetched. The Court must construe the text, not the minds of its framers, and, as he said, "There is no exception in the constitution, no sentiment delivered by its contemporaneous expounders, which would justify us in making it." If a state granted a charter of incorporation to private interests, the charter has "every ingredient of a complete and legitimate contract," should it be made on a valuable consideration for the security and disposition of the property conveyed to the corporation for management by its trustees in perpetuity. Unless, as Justice JOSEPH STORY stressed in his concurring opinion, the government should reserve, in the grant of the charter, a power to alter, modify, or repeal, the rights vested cannot be divested, except by the consent of the incorporators, assuming they have not defaulted. Whether, however, a modification of the charter, as in this case, impairs an obligation, if the charter be executed and by its terms should not specify a term of years for the corporation's existence, is another question. In *Fletcher v. Peck,* however, the Court had brought executed as well as public contracts within the meaning of the contract clause. Marshall construed contract rights sweepingly, state powers narrowly.

Max Lerner's comment on the case, referring to Webster's peroration, is provocative. "Every schoolboy," he wrote, "knows Webster's eloquent plea and how Marshall, whom the Yazoo land scandals had left cold, found his own eyes suffused with tears, as Webster, overcome by the emotion of his words, wept. But few schoolboys know that the case had ultimately less to do with colleges than with business corporations; that sanctity of contract was invoked to give them immunity against legislative control, and that business enterprise in America never had more useful mercenaries than the tears Daniel Webster and John Marshall are reputed to have shed so devotedly that March day in Washington. . . ." In fact, the reserved power to alter or repeal, of which Story spoke, limited corporate immunity from legislative control. Moreover, the protection given by the Court to corporate charters came into play after the legislatures, not the Court, issued these charters, often recklessly and corruptly, without consideration of the public good; Marshall's opinion should have put the legislatures and the public on guard. Finally, the case had a great deal to do with higher education as well as business. *Dartmouth College* is the MAGNA CARTA of private colleges and universities, and, by putting them beyond state control, provided a powerful stimulus, not only to business corporations but also to the chartering of state institutions of higher learning. Unable to make private institutions public ones, the states established state universities.

LEONARD W. LEVY

Bibliography

BEVERIDGE, ALBERT J. 1916–1919 *The Life of John Marshall,* 4 vols. Vol. IV:220–281. Boston: Little, Brown.

HAINES, CHARLES GROVE 1944 *The Role of the Supreme Court in American Government and Politics, 1789–1835.* Pages 378–419. Berkeley: University of California Press.

SHIRLEY, JOHN M. (1879)1971 *The Dartmouth College Causes and the Supreme Court.* New York: Da Capo Press.

STITES, FRANCIS N. 1972 *Private Interest and Public Gain: The Dartmouth College Case, 1819.* Amherst: University of Massachusetts Press.

DAVIS, DAVID
(1815–1883)

David Davis's Supreme Court appointment in 1862 stemmed from his longtime legal and political association with ABRAHAM LINCOLN. Throughout the Civil War, Davis loyally supported the administration in the PRIZE CASES (1863) and EX PARTE VALLANDIGHAM (1864), but he opposed the president regarding emancipation and military trials of civilians. At one point, Davis urged Lincoln to withdraw the EMANCIPATION PROCLAMATION, believing that it would only increase southern resistance and border-state hostility toward the Union. The military trial issue, however, aroused Davis's unrelenting enmity and criticism. Appropriately, Davis delivered the Court's unanimous opinion in EX PARTE MILLIGAN in 1866, holding that civilian trials by presidentially created military commissions were unconstitutional. Davis, joined by the four Democrats on the bench, added that Congress could not authorize such commissions, provoking sharp dissent from Chief Justice SALMON P. CHASE and the other three Republicans.

Democrats and Southerners claimed that the subsequent Republican military reconstruction program was unconstitutional on the basis of *Milligan.* But Davis's opinion really offered little comfort on this point. While he found that the "laws and usages of war" could not apply where civil courts were open, he qualified this conclusion by specifying those "states which have upheld the authority of the government." In his private correspondence, Davis showed that he was disturbed by contemporary interpretations. He noted that there was "not a word said in the opinion about reconstruction, & the power is conceded in insurrectionary states."

Disenchanted with the Republicans, and equally wary of the Democrats, Davis castigated the partisan wrangling that characterized the Reconstruction period. He opposed suffrage for blacks, stating that "the thrusting on them [of] political rights is to their injury." He advocated the preservation of traditional state powers, and he expressed alarm "at the tendency to consolidated Govt manifested by the Republican party." Yet he believed that the military reconstruction program would have been avoided if the Democrats and the South had accepted the FOURTEENTH AMENDMENT. Davis displayed little inclination to have the judiciary thwart the Republican program, however. He was with the majority in TEXAS V. WHITE (1869). He also resisted the attempts of some colleagues to force a decision in EX PARTE MCCARDLE

(1868) before Congress repealed the appropriate JURISDICTION legislation, thinking "it was unjudicial to run a race with Congress." Finally, he opposed a motion to challenge the Reconstruction Act on property rights grounds in *Mississippi v. Stanton* (1868).

Davis's sense of restraint characterized his votes in most of the other issues involving the Civil War and Reconstruction. Despite the libertarian concerns he had expressed in *Milligan,* he joined the dissenters who favored upholding both federal and state TEST OATHS. He also joined the dissenters who favored sustaining LEGAL TENDERS in *Hepburn v. Griswold* (1870) and then joined the new majority a year later when the decision was reversed. His political conservatism, combined with his notions of JUDICIAL RESTRAINT, best explains his adherence to the majority view in the SLAUGHTERHOUSE CASES (1873).

Davis's literal reading of the compact clause (Article I, section 10), however, led him to dissent in *Virginia v. West Virginia* (1871) when he denied the legality of West Virginia's annexation of two western Virginia counties during the Civil War. And in *Miller v. United States* (1871), a key case testing the CONFISCATION ACT of 1862, he supported the act's constitutionality but found reversible error. In a number of circuit rulings involving confiscation, his insistence on procedural fairness largely masked his distaste for the law.

In the Court's consideration of emerging economic questions in the 1870s, Davis again adopted rather traditional views on federalism and state prerogatives. He dissented, for example, in PHILADELPHIA & READING RAILROAD V. PENNSYLVANIA (the *State Freight Tax Case,* 1873), arguing that a state tax imposed on freight tonnage was simply a business tax and not an interference with INTERSTATE COMMERCE. In a long series of municipal bond cases in the 1860s and 1870s, Davis usually supported Justice SAMUEL F. MILLER's vigorous battle against the Court's attempts to provide bondholders protection from state taxation or repudiation. In his most notable statement on the issue, Davis dissented when the Court held that the interest of nonresident bondholders could not be taxed. In *State Tax on Foreign-Held Bonds* (1873), Davis relied on traditional state statutes requiring taxation of "all mortgages [and] money owned by solvent debtors." Such taxation, he said, did not impair any contractual obligations between creditors and those who issued bonds. A quarter-century later, Davis's views were adopted by a new majority.

Despite his prominence and reputation, Davis produced few noteworthy constitutional opinions beyond his contribution in *Milligan.* In truth, he was misplaced as a Supreme Court Justice. He preferred the involvement of political life or trial court work. Davis eagerly sought the presidency and he courted anti-Grant elements within the Republican party in 1872. He finally resigned in 1877 when the Illinois legislature elected him to the Senate. He eventually was elected President *pro tem,* prompting Chief Justice MORRISON R. WAITE, who deplored Davis's political ambitions, to remark that the position was "as near to the Presidency as he can get."

Davis himself offered the most candid and fitting estimate of his judicial career. "[A]s I never did like hard study, the work is not always agreeable," he wrote to his brother-in-law in 1870. "I believe I write the shortest opinions of any one on the bench, & if I had to elaborate opinions & write legal essays as some Judges do, I would quit the concern. I like to hold trial court, but this work on an appellate bench is too much like hard labor."

STANLEY I. KUTLER

(SEE ALSO: *Constitutional History,* 1861–1865 and 1865–1877.)

DAVIS, JEFFERSON
(1808–1889)

A Mississippi planter, Jefferson Davis graduated from West Point, served with distinction in the Mexican War, and was a congressman (1845–1846), senator (1847–1851, 1857–1861) and secretary of war (1853–1857). In 1861 he reluctantly resigned from the Senate when Mississippi left the Union. Davis served as Confederate President (1861–1865) and at the end of the Civil War was indicted for TREASON and jailed but never tried because prosecutors were unsure they could legally convict him. Stripped of his CITIZENSHIP, Davis never returned to politics, but he did write a tedious and defensive two-volume history of SECESSION and his presidency, *The Rise and Fall of the Confederate Government* (1881).

Davis came to national political prominence with his opposition to the COMPROMISE OF 1850. He was one of ten senators who voted against California statehood. Davis supported only the 1850 Fugitive Slave Act, which he thought should be passed and enforced "as a right not to be estimated . . . by the value of the property, but for the principles involved." Unlike JOHN C. CALHOUN, with whom he usually agreed, Davis opposed a constitutional amendment to secure southern rights in all the TERRITORIES. Davis supported extending the MISSOURI COMPROMISE line to California.

After Calhoun's death Davis was the Senate's foremost supporter of southern rights and STATES' RIGHTS. He asserted that secession was constitutional because: the Constitution did not prohibit it nor provide power to coerce a state to remain in the Union; the national government was created by "the states," not "the people," and therefore the states could exist separately from the national government; and the Union "was in the nature of a partnership between individuals without limitation of time" and could be dissolved by the unilateral action of any of the parties.

Davis was ambivalent, however, on whether the theoretical right of secession should be implemented. He opposed secession at the NASHVILLE CONVENTION (1850), arguing that southern rights could be protected within the Union. In 1851 he unsuccessfully sought the Mississippi governorship on a "states' rights" ticket, but later in the decade he opposed states' rights parties because he thought southern interests could best be protected by alliances with sympathetic northern Democrats. In 1860 he attempted to mediate a compromise that would have taken John Bell, JOHN C. BRECKINRIDGE, and STEPHEN A. DOUGLAS out of the presidential contest, in favor of a single Democratic candidate. In 1858 he said publicly that if a Republican were elected "I should deem it your duty to provide for your safety outside the Union." In 1859 he said that the John Brown raid meant that loyalty to the Constitution required secession. Even so, after ABRAHAM LINCOLN's election Davis urged compromise, and served on the Committee of Thirty-Three. Only when this committee failed did he support secession.

Davis was ambivalent in other ways. He believed that blacks were inferior to whites, that congressional prohibition of the African slave trade was unconstitutional, and that the federal government should not interfere with slavery. Yet his plantation was a model, surpassed only by his brother's for treating blacks with compassion and for giving them a great deal of self-government. He opposed reopening the slave trade on moral grounds and in 1865 advocated emancipation to save the Confederacy. He saw secession as a conservative measure to protect the Constitution from tyranny by Lincoln and the national government. But as Confederate president, Davis implemented CONSCRIPTION, suspension of HABEAS CORPUS, and impressment of supplies. A lifelong states' rights man, Davis was vilified by politicians and governors as he sought, unsuccessfully, to create a Confederate national policy.

PAUL FINKELMAN

Bibliography

DODD, WILLIAM E. 1907 *Jefferson Davis.* Philadelphia: George Jacobs.

MCCARDELL, JOHN 1979 *The Idea of a Southern Nation.* New York: Norton.

DAVIS, JOHN W. (1873–1955)

One of the nation's most celebrated lawyers, John William Davis served as SOLICITOR GENERAL under WOODROW WILSON, winning WILSON V. NEW (1917) and the SELECTIVE DRAFT LAW CASES (1918). In 1924 he was the Democratic candidate for President. He remained prominent at the Supreme Court bar, successfully challenging New Deal legislation, and in 1952 Davis attacked HARRY S. TRUMAN's seizure of the steel mills as a "usurpation" of power "without parallel in American history." (See YOUNGSTOWN SHEET AND TUBE COMPANY V. SAWYER, 1952.) He won that case but would lose his last one: *Briggs v. Elliott* (1954). Arguing this companion case to BROWN V. BOARD OF EDUCATION (1954), Davis dismissed arguments about SEGREGATION's psychological harm and urged the continued validity of the SEPARATE BUT EQUAL rule.

DAVID GORDON

DAVIS v. ALASKA

See: Compulsory Process

DAVIS v. BEASON 130 U.S. 333 (1890)

Davis involved an Idaho territorial statute directed at POLYGAMY. The law required voters to foreswear membership in any organization that "teaches, advocates, counsels or encourages" its members to undertake polygamous relationships. Davis was convicted of swearing falsely.

Justice STEPHEN J. FIELD, speaking for the Supreme Court, saw the case as identical to REYNOLDS V. UNITED STATES (1879). The free exercise clause of the FIRST AMENDMENT protected religious beliefs not acts that prejudiced the health, safety, or good order of society as defined by the legislature operating under its POLICE POWER. Field concluded that if something is a crime, then to teach, advise, or counsel it cannot be protected by evoking religious tenets.

The decision became one of the principal underpinnings of what later came to be called the "secular regulation" approach to the free exercise clause whereby no religious exemptions are required from otherwise valid secular regulations.

RICHARD E. MORGAN

DAVIS v. PASSMAN
442 U.S. 228 (1979)

Congressman Otto Passman fired Davis, a female member of his staff, because "it was essential that the [job] be [held by] a man." Such sex discrimination normally violates Title VII of the CIVIL RIGHTS ACT OF 1964 but Congress had exempted itself from that act's coverage. Davis therefore brought suit directly under the Constitution, alleging that sex discrimination by members of Congress violates the EQUAL PROTECTION guarantees contained in the Fifth Amendment. The Supreme Court, in an opinion by Justice WILLIAM J. BRENNAN and over four dissents, found that Davis had stated a cause of action. The Court extended its holding in BIVENS V. SIX UNKNOWN NAMED AGENTS OF THE FEDERAL BUREAU OF NARCOTICS (1971) to allow direct private damage actions under the Fifth Amendment. The majority did not discuss the SPEECH OR DEBATE CLAUSE's effect, if any, on the action.

THEODORE EISENBERG

DAVIS v. SCHNELL

See: Literacy Test

DAY, WILLIAM R.
(1849–1923)

William Rufus Day was named to the Supreme Court by THEODORE ROOSEVELT in 1903, after WILLIAM HOWARD TAFT had declined the nomination to remain at his post in the Philippines. Coincidentally, Day had replaced Taft on the Sixth Circuit Court of Appeals in 1899 when President WILLIAM MCKINLEY dispatched Taft to the Pacific outpost.

Day's tenure spanned the Progressive era. He generally favored the movement's interventionist thrust, particularly state regulatory actions. Day's decisions relating to federal power, however, were more ambivalent, as reflected by his famous opinion in HAMMER V. DAGENHART (1918), which invalidated a congressional attempt to regulate child labor premised on the COMMERCE CLAUSE. Unlike many STATES' RIGHTS advocates, he consistently supported state police regulations.

Justice Day faithfully followed the precedent of UNITED STATES V. E. C. KNIGHT COMPANY (1895), holding that Congress's INTERSTATE COMMERCE power did not extend to PRODUCTION. For example, in *Delaware, Lackawanna and Western Railroad Company v. Yurkonis* (1915) he declined to extend coverage of the federal EMPLOYERS LIABILITY ACT to coal miners even though the coal they produced eventually was used in interstate commerce. Three years later, in the child labor case, Day elaborated his conception of FEDERALISM with an expansive discussion of the TENTH AMENDMENT and its limitations on national power. He found that a congressional law prohibiting the interstate transportation of goods made by child labor unconstitutionally regulated production.

Generally, however, Day supported federal regulation of business. In *Atchison, Topeka and Santa Fe Railway Company v. Robinson* (1914), he wrote an opinion sustaining amendments to the HEPBURN ACT that greatly expanded federal JURISDICTION in railroad regulation, and in *Harriman v. Interstate Commerce Commission* (1908) he vigorously dissented from an opinion by Justice OLIVER WENDELL HOLMES that weakened the commission's SUBPOENA powers. Day also consistently sided with the government in antitrust suits. Soon after his appointment, he provided the decisive vote for the government in NORTHERN SECURITIES COMPANY V. UNITED STATES (1904). Although he acquiesced in the Court's RULE OF REASON doctrine in STANDARD OIL COMPANY V. UNITED STATES and UNITED STATES V. AMERICAN TOBACCO COMPANY (1911), Day expressed reservations toward the doctrine in a number of opinions that strongly supported the SHERMAN ACT. Finally, in UNITED STATES V. UNITED STATES STEEL CORPORATION (1920), he led the dissenters who hotly disputed the Court's approval of the corporation's control of most of the steel industry. Consistently acting as a principled foe of monopoly, Day advocated governmental intervention to destroy concentrated power and insure competition.

Despite Day's views in the child labor case, he supported the concept of a NATIONAL POLICE POWER based on the commerce clause. In *Pittsburgh Melting Company v. Totten* (1918) he sustained the Meat Inspection Act of 1906, and in HOKE V. UNITED STATES

(1913) he offered a classic defense of the police power to uphold the MANN ACT. Congress's control over commerce, he said, was "complete in itself," and Congress might adopt "not only means necessary but convenient to its exercise, and the means may have the quality of police considerations."

Similarly, Day upheld widespread uses of state police powers. He joined Justice JOHN MARSHALL HARLAN's dissent in LOCHNER V. NEW YORK (1905), and he supported the Court's approval of compulsory VACCINATION in JACOBSON V. MASSACHUSETTS (1905). Day consistently rejected the rigid FREEDOM OF CONTRACT dogma of *Lochner.* In *McLean v. Arkansas* (1909) he wrote to sustain state mining safety regulations and deferred to legislative prerogative: "The [state] legislature being familiar with local conditions is, primarily, the judge of the necessity of such enactments." Although the judiciary might have different views of social policy, Day insisted judges had no warrant to interfere. When the Court invalidated a state law prohibiting YELLOW DOG CONTRACTS in COPPAGE V. KANSAS (1915), Day protested against a literalist view of liberty of contract and, ignoring the *Lochner* precedent, he argued that "liberty of contract may be circumscribed in the interest of the State and the welfare of its people."

Day served on the Court until 1922. His opinions, though not memorable, were relatively free from rigid dogma. He contributed significantly to the Court's general approval of the expanded scope of governmental authority, federal and state. In the latter part of his career, that support extended to the prosecution of dissenters and radicals as he consistently sided with the government in the "Red Scare" cases. His 1918 child labor opinion unfortunately has served to obscure his more enduring contributions to constitutional law, such as his support for national regulatory power and an expanded state police power authority.

STANLEY I. KUTLER

Bibliography

MCLEAN, JOSEPH E. 1946 *William Rufus Day: Supreme Court Justice from Ohio.* Baltimore: Johns Hopkins University Press.

DAYTON, JONATHAN
(1760–1824)

Jonathan Dayton, the youngest signer of the Constitution, represented New Jersey at the CONSTITUTIONAL CONVENTION OF 1787. He spoke several times at the Convention in support of small-state positions. He was afterward speaker of the House of Representatives and a senator. In 1807 he was arrested for conspiring with AARON BURR but was not tried.

DENNIS J. MAHONEY

DAYTON BOARD OF EDUCATION v. BRINKMAN

See: *Columbus Board of Education v. Penick*

DAYTON-GOOSE CREEK RAILWAY COMPANY v. UNITED STATES
263 U.S. 456 (1924)

A unanimous Supreme Court here sustained the constitutionality of the recapture provision of the ESCH-CUMMINGS TRANSPORTATION ACT of 1920. The Dayton-Goose Creek Railway earned a return exceeding six percent of its property value, prompting the Interstate Commerce Commission to ask what arrangements it had made to contribute to the fund for which the act had provided. The railroad then sought an INJUNCTION against enforcement of the act, alleging the provision's unconstitutionality. Sixteen railroads, including some of the most powerful of the day, filed AMICUS CURIAE briefs.

Chief Justice WILLIAM HOWARD TAFT asserted that Congress's power over INTERSTATE COMMERCE was not limited to prescribing reasonable rates and voiding unjust ones. Its regulatory power was "intended . . . to foster, protect, and control the commerce with appropriate regard to the welfare of those who are immediately concerned, as well as the public at large, and to promote its growth and insure its safety." Because private railroads offered a public service, Congress might regulate them in order to assure performance of that function. After considering the necessity and justification for the recapture provisions, Taft concluded that the railroad's obligation to serve the public limits it to only "fair or reasonable profit." Reducing a carrier's income to what the Court deemed a FAIR RETURN did not constitute a TAKING OF PROPERTY without compensation because the act made the carrier only a trustee of any "excess." The government was entitled to appropriate that amount for "public uses because the appropriation takes away nothing which equitably belongs either to the shipper or to the carrier."

DAVID GORDON

DEAN MILK COMPANY v. CITY OF MADISON
340 U.S. 349 (1951)

A Madison, Wisconsin, city ordinance that prohibited the sale of milk pasteurized at a plant more than five miles outside city limits provided the basis for clarification of the limits on STATE REGULATION OF COMMERCE. A 6–3 Supreme Court invalidated the law as an "undue burden on INTERSTATE COMMERCE" because it effectively barred the sale of milk from firms in neighboring Illinois. Justice TOM C. CLARK also found a discrimination against outside producers which could not be sustained as an exercise of the state's POLICE POWER when "reasonable nondiscriminatory alternatives" were available, as here.

DAVID GORDON

DEATH PENALTY

See: Capital Punishment

DEBS, IN RE
158 U.S. 564 (1895)

Eugene V. Debs, head of the American Railway Union, petitioned for a writ of HABEAS CORPUS on the ground that he had been imprisoned illegally, for contempt of court, because of his defiance of an INJUNCTION issued by a United States CIRCUIT COURT. That draconian injunction, which became a model for subsequent injunctions in American labor disputes, sought to end the strike by Debs's union against railroads hauling Pullman sleeping cars. The Pullman Company and the managers association of twenty-four railroad CORPORATIONS, according to a later federal investigation, sought to crush the strike and the union rather than accept any peaceable solution. The managers jubilantly described the injunction as a "gatling gun on paper." It prohibited the strikers from attempting to obstruct the movement of mail or INTERSTATE COMMERCE by the struck railroads. It also forbade the use of "persuasion" aimed at preventing workers from doing their jobs.

Justice DAVID J. BREWER, speaking for a unanimous Supreme Court, delivered a breathtakingly broad opinion based not on any statutory authority for the injunction, but on general principles of national supremacy. "The strong arm of the national government," he declared, "may be put forth to brush away all obstructions to the freedom of INTERSTATE COMMERCE or the transportation of the mails. If the emergency arises, the army of the Nation, and all its militia, are at the service of the Nation to compel obedience to its laws." Similarly, Brewer added, the United States might invoke the power of its courts to remove obstructions by injunctions. Brewer's opinion transcended the particular injunction in this case; he failed to examine its terms, though it outlawed persuasion as well as force and assumed that the refusal to work for a railroad is an obstruction of commerce and the mails.

National supremacy, which the Court rendered nearly impotent to cope with obstructions to commerce caused by giant corporations, triumphed against the militant union. The union never recuperated from its defeat in this case and soon disintegrated. *Debs* taught that injunctions could be effective union-smashing devices. They became common afterward. The case also foreshadowed the use of the SHERMAN ANTITRUST ACT against unions. The circuit court had issued the injunction mainly on the ground that the strike was a combination in restraint of interstate commerce. The Supreme Court said that it did not dissent from that conclusion but preferred to rest its judgment on "broader ground."

LEONARD W. LEVY

Bibliography

LINDSEY, ALMONT 1942 *The Pullman Strike.* Chicago: University of Chicago Press.

DEBS v. UNITED STATES
249 U.S. 211 (1919)

During his long and controversial career as a labor leader and radical, Eugene V. Debs twice ran afoul of the federal government, which looked upon his activities as a threat to the nation's economic and political orthodoxy. In 1894 he was sentenced to six months' imprisonment for contempt of court as part of the GROVER CLEVELAND administration's efforts to crush the Pullman boycott in Chicago. In IN RE DEBS (1895) the United States Supreme Court affirmed this conviction and upheld the sweeping labor INJUNCTION which Debs and other leaders of the American Railway Union were alleged to have violated. Two decades later, as the leader of the American Socialist Party and one of the most visible critics of the WOODROW WILSON administration's decision to enter World War I, Debs again found himself in federal court, this time charged with violating the ESPIONAGE ACT of 1917.

Debs was tried and convicted on the basis of a speech he delivered at a socialist, antiwar rally in Canton, Ohio, for inciting insubordination, disloyalty, and mutiny in the armed forces and for obstructing military recruitment. In his oration, Debs praised other imprisoned leaders of the party who had been convicted for aiding and abetting resistance to the draft. In the course of his speech Debs also accused the government of using false testimony to convict another antiwar activist and he labeled the war as a plot by "the predatory capitalist in the United States" against the working class, "who furnish the corpses, having never yet had a voice in declaring war and . . . never yet had a voice in declaring peace." He told the audience that "you need to know that you are fit for something better than slavery and cannon fodder," and he ended by noting: "Don't worry about the charge of TREASON to your masters; but be concerned about the treason that involves yourselves." Debs was sentenced to ten years in prison.

When the *Debs* case reached the Supreme Court, a postwar "red scare" had descended on the nation. CRIMINAL CONSPIRACY trials of leaders of the Industrial Workers of the World were still underway. The Department of Justice had embarked on a large-scale program that would culminate in the PALMER RAIDS and the deportation of hundreds of ALIEN radicals.

Without even a reference to the CLEAR AND PRESENT DANGER test enunciated a week earlier, a unanimous Supreme Court affirmed Debs's conviction in an opinion written by Justice OLIVER WENDELL HOLMES. Although Holmes conceded that "the main theme" of Debs's speech had concerned socialism, its growth, and its eventual triumph, he argued that "if a part of the manifest intent of the more general utterance was to encourage those present to obstruct recruiting . . . the immunity of the general theme may not be enough to protect the speech." As Harry Kalven has remarked, "It is somewhat as though George McGovern had been sent to prison for his criticism of the [Vietnam] war." Holmes saw the case as a routine criminal appeal; in a letter to Sir Frederick Pollock, Holmes referred to the *Debs* case, saying, "there was a lot of jaw about free speech."

Debs remained in federal prison long after the armistice. Although a convicted felon, he received the Socialist Party nomination for President in 1920 and nearly a million votes. President Wilson, in failing health and embittered by the war and its critics, refused to pardon Debs before leaving the White House in 1921. His successor, the Republican conservative WARREN G. HARDING, displayed greater compassion by granting the socialist leader a pardon.

MICHAEL E. PARRISH

Bibliography

FREUND, ERNST 1919 The Debs Case and Freedom of Speech. *The New Republic,* May 3, 1919, p. 13. Reprinted in *University of Chicago Law Review* 40:239–42 (1973).

DECISION

A decision is the final determination by a competent tribunal of matters of law and fact submitted to it in a CASE OR CONTROVERSY. The decision is ordinarily in writing and comprises the JUDGMENT or decree in the case. The decision is not itself law, but only evidence of the law; and the value of a case as precedent derives less from the decision than from the reasoning behind the decision. The term "decision" is one of popular usage and not a technical legal term.

The Supreme Court reaches its decisions in CONFERENCE following the ORAL ARGUMENT of a case. A vote is taken after each Justice has had a chance to state his or her views. The decision is announced by means of a memorandum order or as part of a formal opinion.

In casual usage, the decision is often confounded with the OPINION OF THE COURT, a usage sanctioned by certain law dictionaries and a number of court opinions. In precise usage, however, the decision is the conclusion reached by the court, while the opinion is a statement of the reasoning by which the decision was reached. In the simplest terms, the decision answers the question: who won the case.

DENNIS J. MAHONEY

DECLARATION AND RESOLVES OF FIRST CONTINENTAL CONGRESS

See: First Continental Congress

DECLARATION OF INDEPENDENCE

1 Stat. 1 (July 4, 1776)

America's most fundamental constitutional document was adopted by the United States in Congress on July 4, 1776. The Declaration of Independence may carry little weight in the courts; it may, for all its being placed at the head of the *Statutes at Large* and described in the United States Code as part of the "organic law," have no legally binding force. Yet it is the Declaration that constitutes the American nation. JOHN HANCOCK, president of the Continental Congress, transmitting the Declaration to the several states, described it as "the Ground & Foundation of a future Government." JAMES MADISON, the Father of the Constitution, called it "the fundamental Act of Union of these States."

The Declaration of Independence is the definitive statement for the American policy of the ends of government, of the necessary conditions for the legitimate exercise of political power, and of the SOVEREIGNTY of the people who establish the government and, when circumstances warrant, may alter or abolish it. No mere tract in support of a bygone event, the Declaration was and remains the basic statement of the meaning of the United States as a political entity.

The historical event, the Revolution, provided the occasion for making that statement. RICHARD HENRY LEE, on instructions from the Virginia convention, introduced three resolutions on June 7, 1776: to declare the colonies independent, to establish a confederation, and to seek foreign alliances. Each of the resolutions was referred to a select committee, one of which was charged with preparing "a declaration to the effect of the first resolution." Lee's motion was adopted on July 2, the Declaration two days later.

Although the Congress had appointed for the task a distinguished committee, including JOHN ADAMS of Massachusetts, BENJAMIN FRANKLIN of Pennsylvania, ROGER SHERMAN of Connecticut, and ROBERT LIVINGSTON of New York, THOMAS JEFFERSON of Virginia actually penned the Declaration. So well did Jefferson express the sentiments of the Congress that his committee colleagues made only a few changes in his draft.

Jefferson, by his own account, turned to neither book nor pamphlet for ideas. Nor did he seek to expound a novel political theory. His aim was to set forth the common sense of the American people on the subject of political legitimacy. To be sure, there are ideas, and even phrases, that recall JOHN LOCKE: the Declaration follows Locke in stressing the NATURAL RIGHTS of man as the foundation of the political order. But the concept of man's natural autonomy, modifiable only by his consent to the rule of others in a SOCIAL COMPACT, was long acknowledged in the American colonies; it inhered in congregational church polity, and it was transmitted through such theoretical and legal writers as EMERICH DE VATTEL, Jean-Jacques Burlamaqui, and Samuel Pufendorf, as well as by the authors of CATO'S LETTERS and other popular works.

The Declaration of Independence has a structure that emphasizes its content. It begins with a preamble, by which the document is addressed not to the king of Great Britain or to the English public, but to the world at large, to the "opinion of mankind." Moreover, the purpose of the document is said explicitly to be to "declare the causes" that impelled the Americans to declare their independence from Britain.

There had been other revolutions in British history, but this one was different. From the barons at Runnymede to the Whigs who drove James II from the throne, British insurgents had appealed to the historic rights of Englishmen. The declarations they extracted—from MAGNA CARTA to the BILL OF RIGHTS—were the assurances of their kings that the ancient laws obtaining in their island would be respected. The preamble of the Declaration of Independence makes clear that this is not the case with the American Revolution. The case of Britain's rule in America was to be held up to a universal standard and exposed as tyrannical before a "candid world." Against the selfsame standard all government everywhere could be measured. Everyone who reads the Declaration with his eyes open must be struck by this fact: the Declaration justifies the independence of the American nation by appeal not to an English or an Anglo-American standard, but to the universal standard of human rights.

There follows next a statement of the ends of government and of the conditions under which obedience to government is proper. "All men are created equal . . . endowed by their Creator with certain unalienable rights . . . among [which] are life, liberty, and the pursuit of happiness." Equality is the condition of men prior to government—logically prior, not chronologically. But that equality is not equality of condition, or even equality of opportunity; certainly it is not equality of intelligence, strength, or skill. The equality that men possess by nature is equality of *right.* There is, among human beings, none with a right to rule the others; God may claim to rule human beings by right, human beings may rule the brutes by right, but no human being has a claim to rule another by right.

The rights with which men are endowed are said to be "unalienable." That is, human rights may be neither usurped nor surrendered, neither taken away nor given up. The Declaration rejects the false doctrine of Thomas Hobbes (more gently echoed by WILLIAM BLACKSTONE) that men on entering society and submitting to government yield their natural rights and retain only "civil" rights, dispensed and revoked at the pleasure of the sovereign.

"To secure these rights, governments are instituted among men." The purpose of government is to protect the natural rights which men possess, but which, in the absence of government, they are not secure enough to enjoy. Government in society is not optional, it is a necessary condition for the enjoyment of natural rights. But the institution of government does not create an independent motive or will in society. All just powers of government derive "from the consent of the governed."

The Declaration asserts that the people retain the right of revolution, the right to substitute new constitutions for old. But it also asserts that the exercise of that right is properly governed by prudence—a prudence that the Americans had shown in the face of great provocation.

The next section of the Declaration is a bill of indictment against George III on the charge of attempted tyranny. The specifications are divided almost evenly between procedural and substantive offenses. The fact that the king—by his representatives in America—assembled the provincial legislatures at places far from their capitals or required persons accused of certain crimes to be transported to England for trial, evinced a tyrannical design by disregard of procedural safeguards. But even when the established procedures were followed, as in giving or withholding assent to legislation, the result could be tyrannical; for example, the suppression of trade, the discouragement of population growth, and the keeping of standing armies in peacetime were acts according to the forms of due process that unjustly deprived the Americans of their liberty. Still other acts, such as making the royal assent conditional on surrender of the right of representation and withholding assent from bills to create provincial courts, were tyrannical in both form and substance.

The most critical charge, the thirteenth, was that the king had conspired with others—the British Parliament—to subject the Americans to a JURISDICTION foreign to their constitution. The Americans had come to see that a compact existed between the British king and each of his American provinces by which the king exercised executive power in each even as he did in the home island, and that the common executive was the sole governmental connection between America and Britain. The imperial constitution, as the Americans had come to understand it, no more permitted the British legislature to regulate the internal affairs of Massachusetts or Virginia than it did the provincial legislatures to regulate the internal affairs of England or Scotland. But the British legislature could not breach the compact between the king and the provinces because Parliament was not a party to that compact. The king, however, by conniving at that usurpation, did breach the compact.

The final five accusations deal with the fact that Britain and America were at war. One charge that Jefferson included, but Congress struck out, accused the king of waging "cruel war against human nature itself" by tolerating the introduction of SLAVERY into the colonies and sanctioning the slave trade. Only two states, Georgia and South Carolina, objected to the passage, but the others acquiesced to preserve unanimity. In any case, the condemnation of slavery was implicit in the opening paragraphs of the Declaration.

The conclusion of the document asserts that the Americans had tried peaceably to resolve their differences with the mother country while remaining within the empire, and in a final paragraph contains the actual declaration that the erstwhile colonies were now independent states.

Whether the colonies became independent collectively or individually was a matter of debate for at least a hundred years. At the CONSTITUTIONAL CONVENTION OF 1787, JAMES WILSON and ALEXANDER HAMILTON advanced the former position, while LUTHER MARTIN maintained the latter position. At least until the Civil War, different THEORIES OF THE UNION arose based on differing interpretations of the act of declaring independence.

Considered as a tract for the times, as a manifesto for the Revolutionary cause, the Declaration marks an important step in American constitutional development. The resistance to British misrule in America had, at least since the French and Indian Wars, been based on an appeal to the British constitution. The Americans had charged that the imposition of taxes by a body in which they were not represented and the extension to them of domestic LEGISLATION by a Parliament to whose authority they had not consented violated the ancient traditions of British government. The constitution, that is, the arrangement of offices and powers within the government and the privileges of the subjects, had been overridden or altered by the British Parliament. Although the differences between the American provinces and the mother country were great, they were differences about, and capable of resolution within, the British constitutional framework. The liberties that the colonists had claimed were based on prescription.

When independence was declared, the British constitution became irrelevant. The liberties claimed in the Declaration are grounded in natural law; they are justified by reason, not by historical use. The American Revolution was, therefore, the first and most revolutionary of modern revolutions. Not the quantity of carnage but the quality of ideas distinguishes the true revolution. In the Declaration was recognized a HIGHER LAW to which every human law—constitution or statute—is answerable. The British constitution, as it then existed, was tried by the standards of that higher law and found guilty of tyranny. As the British constitution, so every constitution, including the American Constitution, may be tried; and on conviction the sentence is that the bonds of allegiance are dissolved.

Much of American constitutional history has revolved around the attempt to reconcile the nation's political practice with the teachings of the Declaration. The gravest problem in our constitutional history was SLAVERY. Although the Congress struck out Jefferson's condemnation of slavery as "cruel war against human nature," the founders clearly understood that slavery was incompatible with the principles of liberty and equality that they espoused.

Chief Justice ROGER B. TANEY, in DRED SCOTT V. SANDFORD (1857), tried to read the black man out of the Declaration. But this was a distortion of the history and the plain meaning of the document. Even JOHN C. CALHOUN had not stooped to this, choosing rather to denounce the Declaration than to pervert its meaning. The antithesis between the Declaration and the existence of chattel slavery was recognized by the slave power in Congress when, during the gag rule controversy, any petition referring to the Declaration of Independence was automatically treated as a petition against slavery and laid on the table.

The intimate connection between the Declaration of Independence (and therefore of antislavery) and the Constitution became the theme of the political career of ABRAHAM LINCOLN. When the slavery question divided the nation, Lincoln, with the voice of an Old Testament prophet, called for rededication to the principles of the Declaration. During Lincoln's presidency, the Civil War, begun as a challenge to the Union, was won as a struggle to vindicate the Declaration of Independence. It was fought to prove that a nation "dedicated to the proposition that all men are created equal" could endure.

The putative antagonism between America's two basic documents, invented by the slave power in the nineteenth century, was revived as a political theme during the Progressive movement. Authors like J. ALLEN SMITH and CHARLES A. BEARD contended that the Constitution's system of FEDERALISM, SEPARATION OF POWERS, CHECKS AND BALANCES, and BICAMERALISM frustrated the unfettered will of the people allegedly set free by the Declaration. Smith and Beard posited a virtually bloodless coup d'état by wealthy conservatives—a "Thermidorian reaction" to the success of the democratic revolution. Thus constitutional forms were attacked as illegitimate, notwithstanding that they were intended to preserve the Declaration's regime of LIMITED GOVERNMENT.

The Beard-Smith thesis remained popular as long as the Constitution seemed to be a barrier to social reform and redistribution of wealth and income by the government. The later twentieth century, however, witnessed another change in the attitude of intellectuals toward the two documents. President FRANKLIN D. ROOSEVELT appointed a sufficient number of Supreme Court Justices to insure that the Court would ratify his policies as constitutional. Later, the WARREN COURT devised a host of new "constitutional" rights and remedies for criminal defendants, ethnic minorities, and political dissenters. The Constitution was transformed into a "living" document, that is, one almost infinitely malleable in the hands of enlightened judges. History, understood as progress, rather than nature thereafter dictated the ends of government. The Declaration of Independence, with its references to "the laws of nature and of nature's God," although revered as a symbol of American nationality, ceased to be regarded as the source of authoritative guidance for American politics.

The Constitution of the United States is sometimes pronounced, by scholars or politicians, to be neutral with respect to political principles. But the Constitution was not framed in a vacuum. It was devised as the Constitution of the nation founded by the Declaration of Independence. The Declaration prescribes the ends and limits of government, and proclaims the illegitimacy of any government that fails to serve those ends or observe those limits. The Constitution is thus ruled by the Declaration. The Constitution provides for the government of the regime created by the Declaration: the regime of equality and liberty.

DENNIS J. MAHONEY

Bibliography

BECKER, CARL L. 1922 *The Declaration of Independence.* Cambridge, Mass.: Harvard University Press.

DIAMOND, MARTIN 1975 The Declaration and the Constitution: Liberty, Democracy and the Founders. *The Public Interest* 42:39–55.

HAWKE, DAVID 1964 *A Transaction of Free Men: The Birth and Course of the Declaration of Independence.* New York: Scribner's.

JAFFA, HARRY V. 1959 The Universal Meaning of the Declaration of Independence. Chap. 14 of *The Crisis of the House Divided.* New York: Doubleday.

WHITE, MORTON 1978 *The Philosophy of the American Revolution.* New York: Oxford University Press.

DECLARATION OF WAR

The Constitution gives Congress the power "to declare War . . ." (Article I, section 8, clause 11). There is no explicit provision for any other exercise by the United States of its sovereign power to make war, although the President is made "COMMANDER IN CHIEF of the Army and Navy of the United States . . ." (Article II, section 2). But the draftsmen were certainly familiar with the concept of undeclared war, usually with limited purposes and theaters of operation, such as the French and Indian War of 1754–1756 and the opening campaign of the Seven Years War between England and France, in which GEORGE WASHINGTON had fought as a lieutenant colonel. Indeed, ALEXANDER HAMILTON observed that "the ceremony of a formal denunciation [*i.e.*, declaration] of war has of late fallen into disuse" (THE FEDERALIST #25). Whether the Framers intended to give Congress the paramount power to wage war against other sovereigns is a question that has ever since been debated but not formally resolved. The problem had not, of course, arisen under the ARTICLES OF CONFEDERATION, when all federal (or confederate) power was vested in the Continental Congress. The records of the CONSTITUTIONAL CONVENTION furnish no clear answer. The draft submitted by the Committee on Detail on August 6, 1787, gave Congress the power "to make war." When it was considered eleven days later, on motion by ELBRIDGE GERRY and JAMES MADISON, "make" was changed to "declare." The brief debate gives no indication of any effect the change was intended to have on the allocation of war-making power between President and Congress. For what it is worth, some years later Hamilton expressed the view that making war was essentially an executive function, while Madison thought the power belonged primarily to Congress.

Whatever the Framers may have intended, the practice has clearly been in accord with the Hamiltonian view. The United States has fought only five declared wars (the War of 1812, the Mexican War, the Spanish War, and World Wars I and II), but the President has committed the armed forces to combat on more than 150 other occasions, from JOHN ADAMS's undeclared naval war with France in 1798–1799 to the KOREAN WAR and the VIETNAM WAR. (See also POLICE ACTION; STATE OF WAR.) The Civil War was, of course, undeclared, since a declaration would have constituted a recognition of Confederate SOVEREIGNTY, but it was treated as war for the purposes of international law. (See PRIZE CASES, 1863.) As a practical matter, whether a formal declaration of war adds much to the power of the President is doubtful, so long as Congress furnishes the necessary men and money. Thus, during the Vietnam War the lower federal courts held that Congress, by supplying troops and arms, made the President's actions constitutional; and the Supreme Court let their decisions stand. (See MASSACHUSETTS V. LAIRD, 1971.)

Congress has occasionally attempted to assert its primacy in war, but without much success. In 1896, when a group of congressmen proposed to declare war on Spain, GROVER CLEVELAND scotched the project by informing them that as Commander in Chief he had no intention of using the Army and Navy for any such purpose. The WAR POWERS RESOLUTION of 1973, enacted over President RICHARD M. NIXON's veto, provides in substance that before the President can commit the armed forces to actual or potential combat he must first "consult" with Congress and must withdraw the forces within ninety days unless Congress declares war or provides "specific authorization" for their continued employment.

Scholars disagree on the constitutionality of the War Powers Resolution. In any case, it seems unlikely to have much practical effect, as President GERALD R. FORD demonstrated in 1975 when he immediately, and with a minimum of "consultation," used the armed forces to rescue an American vessel, the *Mayaguez,* and its crew, who had been seized by the communist regime in Cambodia. History suggests that it will be politically very difficult for Congress to deny support when the troops are actually fighting. If there is any historical difference between wars declared by Congress and other wars, it seems to be that the former have usually been larger in scale and have had as their goal not some more or less limited objective, such as rescuing American citizens or defending an ally from attack, but the total defeat of the enemy.

JOSEPH W. BISHOP, JR.

Bibliography

CRUDEN, JOHN C. 1975 The War-Making Process. *Military Law Review* 69:35–143.

LOFGREN, CHARLES A. 1972 War-Making Power under the Constitution: The Original Understanding. *Yale Law Journal* 81:672–702.

ROSTOW, EUGENE V. 1972 Great Cases Make Bad Laws: The War Powers Act. *Texas Law Review* 50:833–900.

DECLARATORY JUDGMENT

Until the beginning of the twentieth century, most American courts would entertain lawsuits only when plaintiffs sought redress for harm already suffered or imminently threatened. Except in certain real property actions, the plaintiff was not deemed harmed simply because uncertainty about his or her legal rights made potentially beneficial conduct too risky to undertake. For example, if a manufacturer were uncertain about whether a new product would infringe another's patent, or a would-be demonstrator were uncertain whether the planned demonstration was protected under the FIRST AMENDMENT, the only choices were to refrain from acting or to proceed and wait to be sued or prosecuted.

The declaratory judgment is a judicial remedy that allows the uncertain individual instead to file suit, asking a court to determine the legal rights in question. It reflects the view, long accepted in land title law, that paralysis due to uncertainty is real harm that courts should alleviate.

Over the first decades of the twentieth century, the states and the federal government adopted this remedy by statute. Declaratory judgments came into use not only to eliminate uncertainty but also to provide a similar but less coercive remedy to individuals eligible for injunctive relief.

Under Article III, the life-tenured federal judiciary may not give ADVISORY OPINIONS but may hear only real disputes between adverse, concretely interested parties. Because declaratory judgments are typically sought in advance of liability-causing conduct, there were early doubts that declaratory judgment actions would satisfy this requirement, known as RIPENESS. To allay this concern, the drafters of the federal declaratory judgment statute limited the remedy to "case[s] of actual controversy within [the courts'] JURISDICTION."

The Supreme Court held in *Perez v. Ledesma* (1971) that, for reasons of comity, a person being prosecuted in a state court for violation of a state criminal law may not seek a declaratory judgment in a federal court that the law is unconstitutional. Prior to a state prosecution, however, an individual may obtain a federal declaration of constitutional rights. That individual may have to flirt so dangerously with actual prosecution in order to satisfy the ripeness requirement, however, that the declaratory judgment may not be able to perform its salutary function of encouraging constitutionally protected conduct.

The plaintiff in a declaratory judgment action is frequently the person who would be a defendant in a more traditional lawsuit, and the elements of a complaint for declaratory relief often differ from those of a more traditional complaint. In applying legal doctrines that antedated the declaratory remedy to this new form of litigation, courts sometimes require that the suit be transposed to what it would have been had the declaratory remedy not existed. Thus, in determining whether the right to TRIAL BY JURY exists in a suit for a declaratory judgment, the courts must ascertain whether the claim could have been filed as an action at COMMON LAW had the declaratory judgment not been invented. Similarly, in determining whether a suit arises under federal law within the meaning of the FEDERAL QUESTION statute, the courts must ascertain whether the federal element would have appeared in the plaintiff's *prima facie* case had the suit been brought for a conventional remedy. Unfortunately, there is not always only one conventional alternative to a given declaratory judgment action, and this cumbersome transposition process has been difficult to administer.

CAROLE E. GOLDBERG-AMBROSE

Bibliography

NOTE 1949 Developments in the Law: Declaratory Judgments, 1941–1949. *Harvard Law Review* 62:787–885.

DE FACTO/DE JURE

De facto and de jure are old COMMON LAW terms meaning, respectively, "in fact" and "in law." In older usage, de facto carried at least a hint of reference to illegitimacy or illegality. Thus, a usurper might be called a de facto king, or a corporation whose formation was irregular might be called a de facto corporation. As these examples suggest, the connotation often was that for some legal purposes the person or institution would be treated *as if* there were no irregularity. De jure, on the other hand, carried a suggestion of lawfulness or rightfulness.

In modern constitutional law, these terms have come to be used almost exclusively in the context of racial SEGREGATION, and particularly segregation in the public schools. In this context the connotations concerning lawfulness are reversed. De jure segregation refers to the separation of pupils by race resulting from deliberate action by state officials, such as the legislature or the school board. De facto segregation refers to the racial separation of pupils by other causes, and particularly through the adoption of the "neighborhood school" policy in a community characterized by residential separation of the races. The Supreme Court has held that only de jure segregation violates the Constitution. (See COLUMBUS BOARD OF EDUCATION V. PENICK, 1979; DAYTON BOARD OF EDUCATION V. BRINKMAN, 1977–1979.)

There is some artificiality in this distinction. When a school board's members are aware of racial patterns in residential neighborhoods, and they draw school attendance district lines in ways that do not minimize the racial separation of pupils, it would not do violence to the language to call the results of their action de jure segregation. Yet the courts tend not to "find" the "fact" of de jure segregation in this circumstance.

On the other hand, deliberately segregative actions of the school board in the rather distant past may be held to constitute de jure segregation, so that the school board remains under a continuing obligation to dismantle a "dual" (segregated) system by taking affirmative remedial action, such as the busing of children. The *Columbus* and *Dayton* cases, cited above, exemplify this line of reasoning.

KENNETH L. KARST

(SEE ALSO: *Swann v. Charlotte-Mecklenburg Board of Education,* 1971; *Keyes v. School District No. 1,* 1973; *School Busing.*)

Bibliography

SEDLER, ROBERT ALAN 1979–1980 The Constitution and School Desegregation: An Inquiry into the Nature of the Substantive Right. *Kentucky Law Journal* 68:879–969.

DEFAMATION

See: Libel and the First Amendment

DEFUNIS v. ODEGAARD
416 U.S. 312 (1974)

DeFunis challenged the constitutionality of the University of Washington law school's use of racial preferences in admitting students. The case was expected to be a decisive test for AFFIRMATIVE ACTION programs in higher education. Instead, by a 5–4 vote, the Supreme Court held that the case was moot, because the law school would graduate DeFunis at the end of the current term, however the case might be decided. Cynics, remembering how the Court had recently dealt with the argument of MOOTNESS in ROE V. WADE (1973), suggested that the majority had been readier to reach the merits of the ABORTION issue in *Roe* than it was to face the problem presented by *DeFunis.*

Justice WILLIAM O. DOUGLAS, who thought the case was not moot, wrote an opinion on the merits. He concluded that the law school had denied DeFunis, a nonminority applicant, the EQUAL PROTECTION OF THE LAWS by awarding a preference solely on the basis of race. Justice Douglas commented that minority applicants should be evaluated specially to avoid cultural bias in admissions, but he did not explain how a school could evaluate minority applicants separately without devising a scale to measure them against other applicants. Such a scale would necessarily involve setting goals for minority representation. *DeFunis* was Justice Douglas's last chance to speak to these issues, which returned to the Court in REGENTS OF UNIVERSITY OF CALIFORNIA V. BAKKE (1978), after his retirement.

KENNETH L. KARST

DE JONGE v. OREGON
299 U.S. 353 (1937)

The Oregon Criminal Syndicalism Law was declared unconstitutional as applied to a person who conducted a meeting of the Communist party at which "neither CRIMINAL SYNDICALISM nor any unlawful conduct was taught or advocated." The Supreme Court held that peaceful speech at a peaceful, open meeting could not be punished constitutionally simply because of party sponsorship even if it were assumed that the party advocated violent overthrow of government. "Peaceable assembly for lawful discussion," declared Chief Justice CHARLES EVANS HUGHES for an 8–0 Court, "cannot be made a crime."

This is one of the early cases "incorporating" the FREEDOM OF SPEECH and FREEDOM OF ASSEMBLY provisions of the FIRST AMENDMENT into the DUE PROCESS clause of the Fourteenth Amendment, thus making them binding on the states. Unlike many other speech cases of the 1920s and 1930s, *De Jonge* rests firmly on freedom of speech rather than on collateral due process grounds such as VAGUENESS. It also foreshadows later, not altogether successful, attempts by the Court to distinguish between those Communist party members and activities devoted to constitutionally protected advocacy and those implicated in incitement to revolutionary violence.

MARTIN SHAPIRO

DELEGATION OF POWER

Early in American constitutional history the Supreme Court announced a rule that Congress could not delegate its power to the President or others. Yet the practical demands of an increasingly complex governmental environment have forced Congress to delegate, often quite broadly. The Court has rationalized all but a few delegations without abandoning the rule of nondelegation. This has been accomplished through successively more permissive formulations of the rule. Though the rule is in a state of desuetude, some revival is possible in the aftermath of the Court's invalidation of a LEGISLATIVE VETO in IMMIGRATION AND NATURALIZATION SERVICE V. CHADHA (1983).

A few commentators call the rule against delegations a judge-made doctrine lacking genuine constitutional status. This suggests the untenable proposition that genuine rules of constitutional law must be explicit in the constitutional document. Building on a COMMON LAW maxim against redelegation of delegated authority and on JOHN LOCKE's observation that only the sovereign people can determine the legitimate location of legislative authority, most commentators have found nondelegation implicit in the SEPARATION OF POWERS and in concepts of representative government and DUE PROCESS OF LAW. The status of the rule thus secured, debate has concentrated on exactly what it prohibits.

As if the rule prohibited all delegations, nineteenth-century judges tried to reconcile it with the practical needs of government by denying that delegations in fact were delegations in law. In *The Brig Aurora* (1813) the Supreme Court held that Congress had not breached the rule by empowering the President to make factual finding on which the application of a previously declared congressional policy—an embargo—was contingent. In *Wayman v. Southard* (1825) the Court permitted a delegation to federal judges for "filling up the details" of part of the Federal Process Act of 1792. Though the rules announced in these cases were modest when stated in the abstract, the delegations themselves were the objects of acrimonious political conflict. By the early 1900s, power to declare facts and fill up details had become the foundation for the delegation of such discretionary authority to the President and administrative agencies as power to decide which grades of tea to exclude from import, to make rules regulating grazing on lands in national forests, and even to vary tariffs on imported goods.

In J. W. HAMPTON & COMPANY V. UNITED STATES (1928) the Court formulated a more realistic delegation doctrine when it acknowledged that transfers of discretionary authority were essential to the effectiveness of Congress's will in modern conditions. The new rule was that congressional delegation is permissible if governed by adequate "legislative standards," a term that now includes statutory specifications of facts to be declared, preambulatory statements of legislative purpose, and even judicial imputations of legislative purpose inferred from legislative and administrative history.

The Court has rarely taken the standards requirement seriously. Illustrative of a pattern that prevails to the present, *Federal Radio Commission v. Nelson Brothers* (1933) found adequate guidance for issuing radio station licenses in what Congress called the "public convenience, interest, and necessity." This pattern was interrupted when the Court unexpectedly used the delegation doctrine against the NATIONAL INDUSTRIAL RECOVERY ACT (1933) in PANAMA REFINING COMPANY V. RYAN (1935) and SCHECHTER POULTRY CORPORATION V. UNITED STATES (1935). But the spirit of these decisions was not to survive, and by the middle of World War II the Court had returned to using the delegation doctrine more for rationalizing than for limiting transfers of congressional power.

As if delegations were not broad enough, the Court in *United States v. Mazurie* (1975) suggested an even more permissive approach. UNITED STATES V. CURTISS-WRIGHT EXPORT CORPORATION (1936) had seemed to hold that because the President had independent powers in the field of FOREIGN AFFAIRS, the standards requirement for congressional delegations to the President could be relaxed in that area. At a time when *Panama* and *Schechter* had recently limited the scope of delegated power, *Curtiss-Wright* was a reasonable move toward flexibility in foreign affairs. But *Curtiss-Wright* featured an unorthodox theory of extraconstitutional or inherent governmental power, and the need for a special approach to foreign affairs delegations disappeared as the Court returned to its old permissiveness toward delegations generally. During the VIETNAM WAR, however, the nondelegation doctrine was raised in opposition to American policy, and, although the Court successfully avoided the issue, government lawyers invoked *Curtiss-*

Wright before congressional committees. One of these lawyers was WILLIAM H. REHNQUIST, who later led the Court to its first reaffirmation of *Curtiss-Wright*'s delegation doctrine in *Mazurie,* a relatively noncontroversial case involving a delegation to the tribal council of an American Indian tribe over liquor sales on a reservation. The tribe's council, said Justice Rehnquist, had "independent authority over tribal life," just as the President had over foreign affairs, and *Curtiss-Wright* was cited for a new rule that the standards requirement is "less stringent in cases where the entity exercising the delegated authority itself possesses independent authority over the subject matter." In light of what "less stringent" can mean today, *Mazurie* has a potential for rationalizing virtual abdications of congressional responsibility, not only to the President but to the states, whose legal claims to "independent authority" are stronger than that of Indian tribal councils.

Since the 1930s and with accelerated frequency after the Vietnam War, Congress used the legislative veto to recapture power lost through broad delegations. To the extent—perhaps modest—that regulatory and political conditions permit, Congress may choose to delegate more narrowly now that the legislative veto is unavailable. And if the Court really has renewed its commitment to the separation of powers, it may honor the standards requirement with something more than mere lip service.

SOTIRIOS A. BARBER

Bibliography

BARBER, SOTIRIOS A. 1975 *The Constitution and the Delegation of Congressional Power.* Chicago: University of Chicago Press.

DAVIS, KENNETH C. 1958 *Administrative Law Treatise.* St. Paul, Minn.: West Publishing Co.

DELIBERATE SPEED

See: All Deliberate Speed

DELIMA v. BIDWELL

See: Insular Cases

DEMEANOR EVIDENCE

See: Confrontation, Right of

DE MINIMIS NON CURAT LEX

(Latin: "The law does not concern itself with trifles.") It is a maxim of the COMMON LAW that the courts will not intervene in disputes where the substance of the controversy is insignificant. For example, a court will not hear a case that turns on an amount less than a dollar or a time period shorter than a day.

DAVID GORDON

(SEE ALSO: *Cases and Controversies.*)

DEMONSTRATION

The FIRST AMENDMENT guarantees the right of persons to congregate peaceably in large numbers in appropriate public spaces in order to communicate ideas or grievances. In *Edwards v. South Carolina* (1963) the Court described an assemblage of 187 protesters on the grounds of a state capitol as "an exercise of . . . basic constitutional rights in their most pristine and classic form." Mass demonstrations cannot be prohibited simply on account of their size or their need to occupy public land.

Constitutional litigation over demonstrations tends to focus on three issues. First is the question of what public spaces must be made available to demonstrators. By virtue of the number of persons involved, mass demonstrations can be disruptive of other activities even when the demonstrators remain peaceable and orderly. When must those other activities give way to the First Amendment claims of persons who wish to engage in a mass demonstration?

The Supreme Court has never given a definitive and comprehensive answer to that question, and probably never could. The Court has indicated, however, that demonstrations in PUBLIC FORUMS such as streets, sidewalks, and parks cannot be subjected to a blanket prohibition. On the other hand, the Court has upheld regulations that entirely prohibited demonstrations in a jailyard and in areas of a military base otherwise open to the public.

Second, the issue has arisen whether a demonstration can be prohibited or postponed on the ground that audience hostility to the demonstrators threatens to produce a BREACH OF THE PEACE. The Court has inveighed against any such "heckler's veto" in OBITER DICTUM, and has reversed disorderly conduct convictions of speakers who continued their orderly protests in the face of potentially threatening crowds. In language quoted many times in the United States Reports, the Court stated in TERMINIELLO V. CHICAGO (1949):

> [A] function of free speech under our system of government is to invite dispute. It may indeed best serve its high purpose when it induces a condition of unrest, creates dissatisfaction with conditions as they are, or even stirs people to anger. Speech is often provocative and challenging. It may strike at prejudices and preconceptions and have profound unsettling effects as it presses for acceptance of an idea. That is why freedom of speech . . . is . . . protected against censorship or punishment, unless shown likely to produce a clear and present danger of a serious substantive evil that rises far above public inconvenience, annoyance, or unrest.

Despite strong dicta and case outcomes favorable to speakers, it cannot be said with assurance that a hostile audience can in no circumstances provide a basis for disallowing a demonstration. The Court has yet to decide a case in which the regulatory authority was confined by a narrowly drawn statute and the police could not contain the HOSTILE AUDIENCE by the exercise of due diligence. There is also the unresolved question of whether demonstrators who wish to proceed in the face of a hostile audience have a First Amendment right to do so on repeated occasions, or whether at some point the mounting costs of police protection for the demonstrators might justify a prohibition on the continuation of their expressive activity.

A third set of issues that arise frequently in disputes over demonstrations concerns the doctrine of prior restraint. Demonstrators who wish to assemble in large numbers can be required to obtain permits in advance, despite the general presumption in First Amendment law against licensing. Officials who administer permit systems for marches and rallies are required to rule upon permit requests expeditiously, and to validate denials in court on a strict timetable. Thus, administrative delay is not permitted to serve as an indirect means of prohibiting mass demonstrations. If a permit request is under administrative or judicial consideration by the time a demonstration is scheduled to take place, the demonstrators may be permitted to proceed without a permit and defend against a prosecution on the ground that they exhausted all channels of prior approval and were entitled under the First Amendment to have their permit request granted. However, demonstrators who do not both apply for a permit and pursue all channels of appeal may be prosecuted for holding a march or rally without a permit, despite the fact that had they applied for a permit they would have been entitled under the Constitution to have it issued.

A fourth issue concerning demonstrations that has not generated a great deal of litigation to date but could do so in the future is whether persons who engage in mass demonstrations can be made to pay the costs of municipal services that attend the event. The Court has indicated in dictum that reasonable costs for such services as clean-up, police protection, and the provision of toilets can be assessed against the demonstrators. However, such assessments can be quite large for major events and can be used as a means of discouraging demonstrations. This issue of cost assessment was important in the litigations during the 1970s over the proposed march of American Nazis in the predominantly Jewish community of Skokie, Illinois, and could emerge as a focus of controversy in other cases.

VINCENT BLASI

Bibliography

BAKER, C. EDWIN 1983 Unreasoned Reasonableness: Mandatory Parade Permits and Time, Place, and Manner Regulations. *Northwestern University Law Review* 78:937–1024.

BOLLINGER, LEE C. 1982 The Skokie Legacy: Reflections on an "Easy Case" and Free Speech Theory. *Michigan Law Review* 80:617–633.

DENATURALIZATION

American CITIZENSHIP can be lost in two ways: denaturalization and EXPATRIATION. Denaturalization is the official cancellation, for cause, of a certificate of naturalization. It can be employed only against a person who has secured his citizenship by NATURALIZATION. Once denaturalized, a person is again an ALIEN in the eyes of the law; unlike the expatriate, he is considered never to have been a citizen. As an alien, the denaturalized former citizen is vulnerable to DEPORTATION and, in the case of a denaturalized criminal, to extradition.

Denaturalization, like naturalization, is governed by statute—currently, the Immigration and Nationality Act of 1952. Congress derives the implied power to denaturalize from its express power set forth in Article I, section 8, to "establish a uniform Rule of Naturalization." Congress has provided for denaturalization when a person's citizenship has been "illegally procured" or "procured by concealment of a material fact or by willful misrepresentation."

Denaturalization has been employed against naturalized citizens because of their membership in communist, Nazi, or other organizations espousing doctrines deemed antithetical to American allegiance. In such cases, the ground for denaturalization is that citizenship has been illegally procured because the applicant failed to comply with the statutory condition that he be attached to the principles of the American Constitution for the five years immediately preceding his naturalization. Also under the act, membership in such an organization within five years of naturalization is "prima facie evidence" of a lack of attachment prior to naturalization.

Denaturalization has also been employed against criminals and racketeers (thereby rendering them subject to deportation), on the ground that they obtained their American citizenship by lying about their criminal past. In such a case, even though the courts have held that denaturalization proceedings are suits in EQUITY and are governed by the FEDERAL RULES OF CIVIL PROCEDURE, the government must prove that the naturalized citizen lied about his criminal past, and thus, in effect, must prove the crime. The Supreme Court has stated, however, that the government need not meet the usual standard of proof for criminal guilt, as the defendant is subject not to penal sanctions but only to denaturalization.

Recently denaturalization suits have also been brought against Nazi war criminals. The central issue in these cases has been falsification or concealment of objective facts about the person's past. Although the courts have been unanimous that the alleged misrepresentations must be material, they have disagreed over whether a misrepresentation is sufficiently material if the truth, which by itself would not have been sufficient to bar the granting of citizenship, would nevertheless have provided leads for uncovering facts of the person's past that would have precluded his naturalization.

Litigants sometimes challenge the constitutionality of denaturalization, arguing either that it reduces naturalized citizens to second class status (in that they can be stripped of citizenship on grounds and by procedures that cannot be applied to native-born citizens), or that Congress's power to naturalize does not carry with it the implied power to denaturalize. To date such arguments have proven unsuccessful.

RALPH A. ROSSUM

Bibliography

GORDON, CHARLES and ROSENFIELD, HARRY N. 1984 *Immigration Law and Procedure,* Vol. 3, chap. 20. New York: Matthew Bender.

ROCHE, JOHN P. 1952 Statutory Denaturalization. *University of Pittsburgh Law Review* 13:276–327.

DENNIS v. UNITED STATES
341 U.S. 494 (1951)

Eugene Dennis and other high officials of the Communist party had been convicted of violating the ALIEN REGISTRATION ACT of 1940 (the Smith Act) by conspiring to advocate overthrow of the government by force and violence. LEARNED HAND, writing the Court of Appeals opinion upholding the constitutionality of the act and of the conviction, was caught in a dilemma. He was bound by the Supreme Court's CLEAR AND PRESENT DANGER rule, and the government had presented no evidence that Dennis's activities had created a present danger of communist revolution in the United States. Hand, however, believed that courts had limited authority to enforce the FIRST AMENDMENT. His solution was to restate the danger test as: "whether the gravity of the evil, discounted by its improbability, justifies such invasion of free speech as is necessary to avoid the danger." Because Dennis's conspiracy to advocate was linked to a grave evil, communist revolution, he could be punished despite the remote danger of communist revolution. Hand's restatement allowed a court to pay lip service to the danger rule while upholding nearly any government infringement on speech. If the ultimate threat posed by the speech is great enough, the speaker may be punished even though there is little or no immediate threat.

The Supreme Court upheld Dennis's conviction with only Justices HUGO L. BLACK and WILLIAM O. DOUGLAS dissenting. Chief Justice FRED M. VINSON's plurality opinion adopted Hand's restatement of the danger rule. At least where an organized subversive group was involved, speakers might be punished so long as they intended to bring about overthrow "as speedily as circumstances would permit."

Justice FELIX FRANKFURTER's concurrence openly substituted a BALANCING TEST for the danger rule, arguing that the constitutionality of speech limitations ultimately depended on whether the government had a weighty enough interest. Congress, he said, surely was entitled to conclude that the interest in national security outweighed the speech interests of those advocating violent overthrow.

Decided at the height of the Cold War campaign against communists, *Dennis* allied the Court with anticommunist sentiment. No statute would seem more flatly violative on its face of the First Amendment than one that made "advocacy" a crime. Indeed, in YATES V. UNITED STATES (1957) the Court later sought to distinguish between active urging or incitement to revolution, which was constitutionally punishable "advocacy," and abstract teaching of Marxist doctrine, which was constitutionally protected speech.

Defenders of the clear and present danger rule criticize *Dennis* for abandoning that rule's essential feature, the immediacy requirement. Such commentators see the Court as correcting its *Dennis* error in BRANDENBURG V. OHIO (1969) in which the Court returned to something like "clear and present danger" and placed heavy emphasis on the immediacy requirement. Justices Black and Douglas subsequently treated *Dennis* as a case applying the clear and present danger rule and thus as an illustration of the failure of the rule to provide sufficient protection for speech and of the need to replace it with the more "absolute" free speech protections urged by ALEXANDER MEIKLEJOHN. Proponents of balancing applaud Hand's "discounting" formula as one of the roots of the balancing doctrine, although only the most ardent proponents of judicial self-restraint support Frankfurter's conclusion that Congress, not the Court, should do the final balancing.

It is possible to read *Dennis, Yates,* and *Brandenburg* together as supporting the following theory. The clear and present danger rule, including a strong immediacy requirement, applies to street-corner speakers; so long as their speech does not trigger immediate serious harms, others will have the opportunity to respond to it in the marketplace of ideas, and the government will be able to prepare protective measures against violence that may follow. However, where organized, subversive groups engage in covert speech aimed at secret preparations that will suddenly burst forth in revolution, the "as speedily as circumstances will permit" test is substituted for the immediacy requirement. Covert speech cannot easily be rebutted in the marketplace of ideas; by the time underground groups pose a threat of immediate revolution, they may be so strong that a democratic government cannot stop them or can do so only at the cost of many lives.

Whether or not the Communist party of Eugene Dennis constituted such a covert, underground group impervious to the speech of others and posing a real threat of eventual revolution, a theory such as this is probably the reason the Smith Act was never declared unconstitutional and *Dennis* was never overruled although both have been drastically narrowed by subsequent judicial interpretation.

MARTIN SHAPIRO

Bibliography

CORWIN, EDWARD S. 1951 Bowing Out Clear and Present Danger. *Notre Dame Lawyer* 27:325–359.

MENDELSON, WALLACE 1952 Clear and Present Danger—From Schenk to Dennis. *Columbia Law Review* 52:313–333.

DEPARTMENT OF AGRICULTURE v. MORENO

See: *Department of Agriculture v. Murry*

DEPARTMENT OF AGRICULTURE v. MURRY
413 U.S. 508 (1973)
DEPARTMENT OF AGRICULTURE v. MORENO
413 U.S. 528 (1973)

Piqued by the activities of protesting students and members of "hippie communes" during the Vietnam years of agony, Congress in 1971 amended the Food Stamp Act to deny eligibility for food subsidies to two classes of applicants: "unrelated" persons living together and persons claimed by others in the previous year as tax dependents. On the same day the Supreme Court struck down both these amendments. *Moreno,* 7–2, invalidated the "unrelated" limitation on "Fifth Amendment EQUAL PROTECTION" grounds; the amendment was irrelevant to the act's goals of nourishing the needy and aiding agriculture, and harming "hippies" for their unpopularity was not a legitimate legislative purpose. The law thus lacked a RATIONAL BASIS. *Murry,* 5–4, held the "tax dependency" limitation an unconstitutional IRREBUTTABLE PRESUMPTION. A claimant might be needy during the current year although dependent on another during a previous year; yet the law denied any opportunity to qualify for aid by demonstrating need.

KENNETH L. KARST

DEPORTATION

Deportation is the removal of an ALIEN out of the country. Congress has plenary power to deport aliens, even of long residence; its power rests upon the same grounds and is as unqualified as its power to exclude aliens from entering the country. Aliens permitted to enter and reside in the United States remain subject to the power of Congress to order them deported. Congress may direct that all aliens leave the country, or that some leave and others stay, distinguishing between the two by such tests as it thinks appropriate. While aliens cannot be deported without DUE PROCESS OF LAW, guaranteed to them by the Fifth Amendment, they are entitled only to PROCEDURAL DUE PROCESS: NOTICE and a HEARING at which they may seek to show that they do not come within the classification of aliens whose deportation Congress has directed. (A resident of the United States who claims to be a citizen cannot be deported without a judicial trial.)

Initially, deportation was conceived of only as a method for expelling aliens who had entered the country illegally. Soon, however, Congress employed it to remove aliens who had entered legally but had violated conditions attached to continued residence. Thus, for example, the Immigration Act of 1917 provided for the deportation of aliens convicted of crimes involving moral turpitude. Other statutory grounds for deportation, now codified in the Immigration and Nationality Act of 1952, include violation of alien registration requirements, drug trafficking, addiction to narcotics, becoming a public charge within five years after entry, or membership in the Communist party or other subversive organizations.

By its express terms, the Immigration and Nationality Act applies retroactively to any alien belonging to any class enumerated in the statute, notwithstanding that the alien entered the United States prior to the date of the statute or that the facts alleged to justify deportation occurred prior to that date. Because deportation is not considered a punishment, the prohibition of the EX POST FACTO clause of the Constitution does not apply, and retroactive application of provisions specifying grounds for deportation was upheld in *Lehmann v. Carson* (1957).

In *Harisiades v. Shaughnessy* (1952) Justice WILLIAM O. DOUGLAS declared in his dissent that "an alien, who is assimilated in our society, is treated as a citizen so far as his property and his liberty are concerned. . . . If those rights, great as they are, have constitutional protection, I think the more important one—the right to remain here—has a like dignity." To date, this view has not been able to overcome the two basic propositions announced in the Court's seminal deportation case, *Fong Yue Ting v. United States* (1893), that Congress has the INHERENT POWER to order deportation and that deportation is not a criminal punishment.

RALPH A. ROSSUM

Bibliography

GORDON, CHARLES and ROSENFIELD, HARRY N. 1984 *Immigration Law and Procedure,* Vol. 1, chaps. 4–5; Vol. 2, chaps. 6–8. New York: Matthew Bender.

NOTE 1962 Deportation and Exclusion. *Yale Law Journal* 71:760–792.

DESEGREGATION

Freed finally of slavery's shackles, blacks in America began the long quest for racial equality. Desegregation, a generic term used to describe elimination of the SEGREGATION and RACIAL DISCRIMINATION that nonwhites confronted at life's every turn, has been the equivalent of their Holy Grail.

While blacks have attacked barriers based on color across a spectrum that includes VOTING, employment, housing, the administration of justice, access to public facilities, and even sex and marriage, the elimination of discrimination in the public schools has been and remains the most important goal for black Americans in their continuing struggle against racism in this country.

At an early time in the nation's history, blacks hoped an already hostile society might at least share their fear, as a black minister phrased it, "for our rising offspring to see them in ignorance in a land of gospel light." That petition presented in 1787 to the Massachusetts legislature sought a separate school for Boston's black children whose parents had withdrawn them from the harassment and ridicule heaped on them by white teachers and students in some of the new nation's first public schools.

The legislature denied the petition, which reflected fears shared by succeeding generations of black parents who all during the nineteenth century filed dozens of law suits with state courts seeking relief from the racial discrimination they found in the public schools. Depending on the times and the character of the discrimination they faced, black parents have sought equal educational opportunity for their children through the advocacy of either racially separate or integrated schools.

With few exceptions, the courts were no more sympathetic to these petitions than were the school boards whose policies sometimes excluded black children from the public schools entirely and always subjected them to conditions that left little doubt as to which students were deemed members of the superior race. In ROBERTS V. CITY OF BOSTON (1850) a state court rejected a school desegregation petition almost two decades before the adoption of the FOURTEENTH AMENDMENT; three decades after its ratification, the United States Supreme Court concluded in PLESSY V. FERGUSON (1896) that the Fourteenth Amendment did not prohibit state-sanctioned segregation, citing the *Roberts* decision as support for the reasonableness of what it called SEPARATE BUT EQUAL facilities. *Plessy* provided the Constitution's blessing for laws throughout the South that required racial segregation not only in public schools, but in every possible public facility, including cemeteries and houses of prostitution.

The law and much of society enforced the "separate" phase of the *Plessy* standard to the letter, but the promise of "equal" facilities received only the grudging attention of a public whose racial attitudes ranged from apathy to outright hostility. Deep-South states spent far less for the schooling of black children than for whites. Despite a major effort to equalize segregated schools as a means of forestalling the steadily increasing number of CIVIL RIGHTS challenges in the 1950s, the South as a whole expended an average of $165 for every white child, and only $115 for each black in 1954, the year in which segregated schools were ruled unconstitutional.

More than a half century after its *Plessy* decision, the Supreme Court in BROWN V. BOARD OF EDUCATION (1954) reviewed the "separate but equal" DOCTRINE in the light of education's importance for children in a modern society, and concluded that the Fourteenth Amendment's EQUAL PROTECTION clause was violated by segregated schools "even though the physical facilities and other 'tangible" factors may be equal. . . ."

Chief Justice EARL WARREN's ringing rhetoric in the *Brown* opinion condemned racially segregated schooling as "inherently unequal." He found that the separation by the state of children in grade and high schools solely on the basis of race "generates a feeling of inferiority as to their status in the community that may affect their hearts and minds in a way unlikely ever to be undone."

This decision was the result of long years of planning and litigation by the NAACP, and the committed work of lawyers including THURGOOD MARSHALL and Robert L. Carter, social scientists like Kenneth Clark, and hundreds of courageous black parents and their children. The decision, most blacks were convinced, required the elimination of segregated school facilities. Black parents knew that state-mandated black schools were a racial insult, and most hoped that if their children attended schools with whites, they would more likely gain access to the same educational resources as white children.

But the determination of civil rights groups representing an ever-increasing number of black parents seeking to join in school desegregation suits was met by the equally determined and, at least initially, far more powerful resistance of southern whites who strongly opposed sending their children to school with blacks and greatly resented the federal coercion involved in school desegregation orders which they equated with the occupation of the region by Union forces following the Civil War.

Arguably, opposition by southern working class whites could be predicated on the basis that, by invalidating segregation laws, *Brown* betrayed post-Reconstruction promises of white superior status made to them by policymakers in return for political support given during periods when populist movements sought to challenge the monopoly of economic power held by the upper class.

Although the Supreme Court refused to turn the clock back to 1868 to determine whether the framers of the Fourteenth Amendment had intended to condone segregated schools, an examination of post-Reconstruction history shows that policies of segregation reflected a series of political compromises through which working class whites settled their demands for social reform and greater political power. C. Vann Woodward and other historians have shown that segregated schools and facilities were established by legislatures at the insistence of the white working classes who saw color barriers as official confirmation that the society's policymakers would maintain even the poorest whites in a permanent status superior to that designated for blacks.

While not willing to acknowledge that its school desegregation decision would deprive whites of long-held rights of superior status based on race, the Court in *Brown v. Board of Education II* (1955), signaled that it was aware of the major social upheaval its ruling would require. Rejecting the black petitioners' requests for immediate relief, the Court chose a procedure that would permit the individual resolution of administrative and academic problems. It mandated only a "prompt and reasonable start toward full compliance," and returned the cases to the district courts with the admonition that orders and decrees be entered to admit plaintiffs to public schools on a racially nondiscriminatory basis "with ALL DELIBERATE SPEED. . . ."

But the Court's conciliatory efforts did not avoid

and may have encouraged a period of massive resistance by southern elected officials, a rise in the Ku Klux Klan and other white supremacist groups, and a general upswing in economic intimidation and threats of physical violence against blacks deemed responsible for or participants in the civil rights movement. The Court met open resistance in Little Rock, Arkansas, and elsewhere with firm resolve, as in COOPER V. AARON (1958), but for several years condoned pupil placement laws and other procedural devices clearly designed to frustrate any meaningful compliance with the *Brown* mandate.

Federal courts were far less cautious in applying the *Brown* decision as the controlling precedent in cases challenging racial segregation in other public facilities. Thus, in the first half-dozen years following *Brown,* civil rights groups succeeded in desegregating state-operated places of recreation, government buildings, and transportation facilities.

Finally, in 1964, during the height of the SIT-IN protest movement that was bringing an end to "Jim Crow" policies in many hitherto segregated privately owned facilities not covered by the Fourteenth Amendment, the Court indicated that the time for mere deliberate speed had run out, in GRIFFIN V. SCHOOL BOARD OF PRINCE EDWARD COUNTY (1964). But the success of a decade of white resistance to school desegregation was reflected in the statistics. In the eleven states of the old Confederacy, a mere 1.17 percent of black students were attending school with white students by the 1963–1964 school year. The dirgelike progress of school desegregation finally gained momentum through a series of far-reaching lower court orders combined with the federal government's enforcement of Title VI of the CIVIL RIGHTS ACT OF 1964. This provision required the cut-off of federal financial assistance to entities that followed racially discriminatory policies. The federal government's enforcement of Title VI was seldom vigorous, but even the threat of losing the federal monies made available under a host of new antipoverty and educational assistance programs in the late 1960s persuaded hundreds of southern school districts that some form of compliance was in their best interests.

In 1968, the Supreme Court in GREEN V. NEW KENT COUNTY SCHOOL BOARD virtually eliminated the offer by a school board of "freedom of choice" to all children as a sufficient compliance with desegregation requirements. The decision was hailed by civil rights lawyers who believed that the *Brown* mandate could not be implemented unless public schools were rendered nonidentifiable by race. This goal, articulated in the *Green* case by Justice WILLIAM J. BRENNAN as requiring school boards to formulate plans that promise "realistically to convert promptly to a system without a 'white' school and a 'Negro' school, but just schools," was furthered when the Court applied the *Green* standard to a large, urban school district in North Carolina in SWANN V. CHARLOTTE-MECKLENBURG BOARD OF EDUCATION (1971). A few years later, the Court held a large northern school district subject to a similar standard in KEYES V. SCHOOL DISTRICT NO. 1 OF DENVER, COLORADO (1973). (See SCHOOL BUSING.)

But while the percentage of children attending desegregated schools increased impressively, opposition to school desegregation remained. Resistance focused on plans like those approved in both *Swann* and *Keyes* requiring the transportation of children in order to achieve a measure of desegregation in each school roughly equivalent to the percentages of white and nonwhite children in the district as a whole. Opponents had gained national political strength, and their support likely played an important role in the election of RICHARD M. NIXON as President in 1968. The Nixon administration adopted policies that had the effect of slowing the federal government's participation in the school desegregation campaign, but the Supreme Court rejected Administration-sponsored delay requests in ALEXANDER V. HOLMES COUNTY BOARD OF EDUCATION (1969) and *Carter v. West Feliciana Parish School Board* (1970), although not without cracks in the solid front of unanimous opinions the Court had handed down in school desegregation cases since *Brown I.*

By 1974, in MILLIKEN V. BRADLEY, an APPEAL from lower court orders requiring the consolidation with the seventy percent black Detroit school system of fifty-three predominantly white suburban school districts, those cracks had grown into a chasm between divergent viewpoints on the appropriateness of school desegregation remedies. The insistence of civil rights lawyers that courts had unlimited discretion to impose racial-balance oriented plans to remedy proven segregation resulted in a significant change in the standards for proving school district liability for violating the Constitution.

In a 5–4 decision, the Court in *Milliken* held that federal courts could not impose multidistrict remedies to cure a single district's segregation absent findings that the other included school districts had failed to operate unitary school systems within their districts, or were responsible for the segregation in the other districts. Proof of this character could be found in few districts without histories of official, state-mandated segregation, and thus plans to desegregate large, urban school districts through metropolitan-wide plans were rendered inoperable.

By the late 1970s, roughly half of all nonwhite children in the nation resided in the country's twenty to thirty largest school districts. Minority children averaged sixty percent of the school population in these districts and close to seventy percent in the ten largest districts. Politically if not physically, desegregation in these districts on the *Green-Swann* model became increasingly difficult.

Lower courts, impressed by detailed prescriptions of racial wrongdoing by urban school boards, continued at the urging of civil rights lawyers to grant relief requiring reassignments and busing to change the racial makeup of schools. But the Supreme Court, now quite divided, set increasingly difficult liability standards in cases from Dayton and Columbus, Ohio; Omaha, Nebraska; Austin, Texas; Milwaukee, Wisconsin; and Indianapolis, Indiana. Plans requiring wholesale reassignment of children in these districts were finally approved, mainly because the proof of past discrimination was so clear. There was little judicial enthusiasm for continued reliance on a remedial process about which there was so much controversy as to its effectiveness even among civil rights proponents.

By this time, a great many black communities were questioning the continued validity of the "neither black schools nor white schools" desegregation approach that had stood as an article of faith since the early post-*Brown* years. Disenchantment was prompted by the hundreds of black schools closed and the scores of black teachers and principals dismissed in the course of the school desegregation process. In addition, black parents were discovering that the sacrifice involved in busing children across town to mainly white schools did not always eliminate racial discrimination. More litigation had to be prosecuted to challenge resegregation tactics as varied as the use of standardized tests to track black students into virtually all-black classrooms, to the exclusion of blacks from extracurricular programs. In most desegregated school systems, black students were far more likely to be suspended and expelled for disciplinary violations than white students. Black parents able to enroll their children in desegregated schools all too often found themselves protesting policies of in-school discrimination quite similar to those that had led their late eighteenth-century predecessors to petition for separate schools.

The NAACP and the few other groups who sponsored most school desegregation litigation remained firm in their belief that identifiably black schools would always be inferior and must be eliminated. But local black groups in several cities including Atlanta, St. Louis, Detroit, Dallas, Boston, and Portland, Oregon, decided that mainly black schools in black neighborhoods might provide effective schooling for their children if black parents could be involved more closely in faculty hiring, curriculum selection, and other policymaking aspects of these schools.

In 1975, a court of appeals approved in CALHOUN V. COOK, over the vigorous objection of the national NAACP office, a settlement of a twenty-year-old Atlanta school case providing full faculty and employee desegregation but only limited pupil desegregation in exchange for a school board promise to hire a number of blacks in top administrative positions, including a black superintendent of schools.

A few years later, in *Milliken v. Bradley II* (1977), the Supreme Court approved without dissent a Detroit desegregation plan that gave priority to a range of "educational components" while limiting pupil desegregation in the district that was by now more than eighty percent black to a provision that no school be less than thirty percent black. The Court though was unable to decide and left standing a lower court ruling that an almost all-black subdistrict created by the Dallas school desegregation plan met school desegregation standards. The record showed both that housing patterns and geographical conditions would have made desegregation difficult and that much of the black community in the subdistrict supported its retention.

Public resistance to school desegregation continued into the 1980s even though the likelihood of new court orders was lessened by the Supreme Court's application of higher standards of proof even in litigation where metropolitan relief was not sought. For example, California voters approved an amendment to their state constitution barring state courts from ordering racial balance remedies in cases where, absent a finding that the school board was guilty of a specific intent to discriminate, the Fourteenth Amendment would not require racial balance relief. The Supreme Court upheld this provision in *Crawford v. Los Angeles Unified School District* (1982).

Civil rights organizations mobilized to meet such challenges, but local black groups increasingly opted for programs that promised to provide equal educational opportunity in neighborhood schools. At the same time, many black parents either moved to suburban areas or sent their children out of their neighborhoods to enable them to attend predominantly white schools.

The quest for effective schooling in the 1980s mirrors those made by black parents in the 1780s and during all the periods between. They and their children have recognized that neither separate schools nor integrated schools will automatically eliminate racist policies intended to provide priority to white children for scarce educational resources. School desegregation programs mandated by the *Brown* decision, and earnestly sought in hundreds of court cases, have served to slow but have not otherwise much discouraged those policies.

Beyond the real gains made by blacks during the *Brown* years, there remain millions of black and other minority children whose schooling remains both segregated and inferior. For them, there is ample basis for parental fears as they watch their rising offspring grow "in ignorance in a land of gospel light."

DERRICK A. BELL

Bibliography

BELL, DERRICK A. (1973)1980 *Race, Racism and American Law.* Boston: Little, Brown.

KALODNER, HOWARD I. and FISHMAN, JAMES J., EDS. 1978 *Limits of Justice: The Courts' Role in School Desegregation.* Cambridge, Mass.: Ballinger.

KLUGER, RICHARD 1976 *Simple Justice: The History of Brown v. Board of Education and Black America's Struggle for Equality.* New York: Knopf.

WOODWARD, C. VANN (1955)1974 *The Strange Career of Jim Crow.* New York: Oxford University Press.

DEVELOPMENTALLY DISABLED ASSISTANCE AND BILL OF RIGHTS ACT
89 Stat. 486 (1975)

This statute established a grant program under which participating states receive federal financial assistance to aid them in creating programs for the developmentally disabled, a term that refers mainly to the mentally retarded. To qualify for federal funds states must take AFFIRMATIVE ACTION to hire qualified handicapped individuals, submit a plan to evaluate the services provided under the act, have a habitation plan for each person receiving services under a program funded under the act, and have in effect a system to protect and advocate the rights of persons with developmental disabilities. The act's "bill of rights" for the developmentally disabled includes the rights to appropriate treatment in a setting least restrictive of the patient's liberty, to a well-balanced diet, to sufficient medical and dental services, to be free of restraint as punishment, to be free of excessive use of chemical restraints, to be visited by relatives, and to a safe environment. In PENNHURST STATE SCHOOL AND HOSPITAL V. HALDERMAN (1981) the Supreme Court, in an opinion by Justice WILLIAM H. REHNQUIST and over three dissents, held that the "bill of rights" portion of the act does not confer on the developmentally disabled any substantive rights to appropriate treatment in the least restrictive setting. The act "does no more than express a congressional preference for certain kinds of treatment."

THEODORE EISENBERG

Bibliography

EISENBERG, THEODORE 1981 *Civil Rights Legislation.* Pages 886–887. Charlottesville, Va.: Michie Co.

DIAMOND v. CHAKRABARTY

See: Patents

DICEY, ARTHUR V.

See: Rule of Law

DICKINSON, JOHN
(1732–1808)

The conservative patriot leader John Dickinson, scion of a wealthy Quaker family, was called to the bar at the Middle Temple in London in 1757 and soon after returning to America became one of the most prosperous lawyers in Philadelphia. He served in the colonial legislatures of both Delaware and Pennsylvania, and in 1765 he rose to continental prominence with his pamphlets opposing the Sugar Act and the Stamp Act.

A delegate to the STAMP ACT CONGRESS (1765), Dickinson was the author of that body's Declaration of Rights and Grievances, ostensibly a loyal, even humble, petition to the king. Dickinson's resolutions condemned as unconstitutional the levying of internal taxes upon the colonists by the British Parliament and denounced as subversive of liberty the trial of offenses against tax laws by admiralty courts without juries. Dickinson himself later referred to the Declaration of Rights and Grievances as the first American BILL OF RIGHTS.

After the passage of the TOWNSHEND ACTS in 1767 Dickinson established himself as the preeminent American interpreter of the constitutional relationship between the colonies and Britain. His "Letters from a Farmer in Pennsylvania" (1767–1768), published in all but four American newspapers, advanced an understanding of the British constitution that made Parliament supreme in imperial matters but proscribed all TAXATION WITHOUT REPRESENTATION. Moreover, he abandoned the distinction between external and internal taxes in favor of a distinction based on purpose: if a duty was laid for the purpose of raising revenue, rather than regulating commerce, then it was taxation and fell under the constitutional proscription. The Farmer's Letters counseled petition for repeal of, rather than resistance to, unconstitutional legislation.

By the time he wrote his long essay on "The Constitutional Power of Great Britain" in 1774, Dickinson had come to think of the British Empire as federal—comparable to the Swiss Confederation or the United Netherlands. The British king was king of the American colonies, but "a parliamentary power of internal legislation over these colonies appears . . . equally contradictory to humanity and to the Constitution, and illegal."

In 1774 Dickinson represented Pennsylvania in the First Continental Congress. The petition to the king and the address to the inhabitants of Canada, adopted pursuant to the DECLARATION AND RESOLVES, were products of Dickinson's pen. In 1775, at the Second Continental Congress, he worked with THOMAS JEFFERSON drafting the Declaration of the Causes and Necessity of Taking Up Arms. But Dickinson was still committed to the idea of a resolution of the crisis within the constitutional system of the British Empire. He opposed immediate separation from Britain and refused to sign the DECLARATION OF INDEPENDENCE.

On June 12, 1776, the Congress, anticipating independence, appointed a committee to draft a plan of union. Dickinson was the dominant member of that committee and the principal author of the draft ARTICLES OF CONFEDERATION reported to Congress on July 12. Dickinson's draft called for no mere alliance or league of sovereign states but for a permanent union with a national government. The "United States assembled" was to be heir to those powers of regulation and general legislation legitimately exercised before independence by the British Parliament, while each "colony" retained "sole and exclusive Regulation and Government of its internal police, in all matters that shall not interfere with the Articles of this Confederation." True to the "Farmer's" principles, Dickinson inserted a provision that "the United States assembled shall never impose or levy any Taxes or Duties, except in managing the Post-Office." Dickinson's draft Articles were regarded by many in Congress, especially Southerners, as too centralizing, and even some who favored Dickinson's position despaired of securing ratification. Only after considerably weakening the government to be established by the Articles did Congress finally propose them to the states.

When his stand on independence cost Dickinson his seat in Congress and his colonelcy in the militia, he enlisted in the army as a private soldier. But in November 1776 he was elected to Congress by Delaware, and he was later made a brigadier general in the Delaware militia. In 1779 he signed the Articles of Confederation to signify Delaware's ratification.

Dickinson served as president of Delaware in 1781–1782 and as president of Pennsylvania in 1782–1785. In both states he was recognized as a leader of the conservative party. Although a slaveholder, he favored abolition of SLAVERY, and he opposed its extension into the Northwest Territory.

In 1785 he retired to his estate in Delaware, but he was recalled to public service in 1786 and elected a delegate from Delaware to the ANNAPOLIS CONVENTION. Dickinson was chosen president of the convention, which discussed commercial problems under the Confederation and which issued the first call for a federal constitutional convention.

Notwithstanding his poor health, Dickinson accepted appointment to represent Delaware at the CONSTITUTIONAL CONVENTION OF 1787. Although he was an active and conscientious delegate, his contribution to the work of the convention was not among the most important. A nationalist of long standing, he represented a small state and often had to balance competing interests. He was the first to propose a bicameral congress with equal REPRESENTATION of the states in one house and representation apportioned by population or financial contribution in the other—a proposal that later became the basis of the GREAT COMPROMISE. He favored abolition of the slave trade but acquiesced in the compromise that imposed a twenty-year moratorium on congressional power to accomplish it. He wanted Congress to be the dominant branch of government, with full authority to remove Presidents and judges; and he wanted to limit executive power and to create a council to share the President's appointing power. Forced by illness to leave the convention early, Dickinson authorized a colleague to sign his name to the finished Constitution.

Dickinson wrote a series of nine newspaper essays (signed "Fabius") in support of RATIFICATION OF THE CONSTITUTION; they were influential, especially in

Pennsylvania. He declined appointment as a United States senator from Delaware and never held public office under the new Constitution.

DENNIS J. MAHONEY

Bibliography

FORD, PAUL LEICESTER, ed. 1970 *Political Writings of John Dickinson.* New York: Da Capo.

JACOBSON, D. L. 1965 *John Dickinson and the Revolution in Pennsylvania.* Berkeley: University of California Press.

STILLE, CHARLES J. 1891 *Life and Times of John Dickinson.* Philadelphia: Historical Society of Philadelphia.

DICTA

See: Obiter Dictum

DIES, MARTIN
(1900–1972)

Martin Dies, an anti-New Deal Democrat from Texas, served in the House of Representatives from 1931 to 1945 and from 1953 to 1961. In 1938 he became chairman of the special Committee to Investigate Un-American Activities, forerunner of the HOUSE COMMITTEE ON UN-AMERICAN ACTIVITIES. Dies and his committee attained national prominence through sensational exposés of supposed Fascist, Nazi, and communist activity in government, labor unions, and industry. His published lists of government employees who were "Communists or Communist dupes," the publicity he gave to unsubstantiated accusations, and his disregard of normal CIVIL LIBERTIES foreshadowed the activities of Senator JOSEPH MCCARTHY.

DENNIS J. MAHONEY

DIFRANCESCO, UNITED STATES v.
449 U.S. 117 (1980)

In this case on the DOUBLE JEOPARDY clause of the Fifth Amendment a 5–4 Supreme Court sustained the constitutionality of the ORGANIZED CRIME CONTROL ACT of 1970, which in special instances granted to the United States the right to APPEAL a criminal sentence. Justice HARRY L. BLACKMUN for the majority, rejecting the dissenters' contention that review of a sentence is comparable to the review of a verdict of acquittal, held that a government appeal that succeeded in increasing a sentence did not constitute double jeopardy.

LEONARD W. LEVY

DILLON, JOHN F.
(1831–1914)

Elected a member of the Iowa Supreme Court at thirty-one, John Forrest Dillon was a leading advocate of the PUBLIC PURPOSE doctrine. In 1869 President ULYSSES S. GRANT appointed Dillon to the Eighth Circuit Court, but after ten years' service Dillon resigned to accept a professorship at Columbia University Law School. Within three years he left that post to enter private practice, and he soon represented major business interests including Jay Gould and the Union Pacific Railroad.

Although Dillon was not an original thinker, his writings and speeches helped establish his tremendous reputation. He served as president of the American Bar Association in 1892 and delivered the prestigious Storrs Lectures at Yale University shortly thereafter. These were published in 1895 as *The Laws and Jurisprudence in England and America,* and in them Dillon claimed that the DUE PROCESS CLAUSE of the FOURTEENTH AMENDMENT "in the most impressive and solemn form places life, liberty, contracts, and property . . . among the fundamental and indestructible rights of all the people of the United States." He endorsed SUBSTANTIVE DUE PROCESS and rhapsodized on the distinction of America's written CONSTITUTIONS: their limitations on government. Restraints such as SEPARATION OF POWERS and CHECKS AND BALANCES were just two of the many means available to prevent "despotism of the many,—of the majority." Dillon also wrote an influential treatise on *Municipal Corporations* (1872).

As a judge, Dillon narrowly construed the public purpose DOCTRINE. He believed that a municipal corporation had the authority to tax to support a public purpose, but incidental public benefits did not justify such taxation. Moreover, he believed that the judiciary could inquire into the legislative purpose and that private enterprises (with the sole exception of railroads) did not qualify under the doctrine. He thus wrote laissez-faire ideas into the law as limitations on legislative power (*Loan Association v. Topeka, Commercial National Bank of Cleveland v. Iola,* both 1873). Dillon appeared frequently before the Supreme Court where, in UNITED STATES V. TRANS-MISSOURI FREIGHT ASSOCIATION (1897) he urged the

Court to adopt the RULE OF REASON whereby the SHERMAN ANTITRUST ACT would be read to prohibit only unreasonable restraints of trade, a position finally adopted in STANDARD OIL COMPANY V. UNITED STATES (1911).

DAVID GORDON

Bibliography

JACOBS, CLYDE E. (1954)1973 *Law Writers and the Courts.* New York: Da Capo Press.

DIONISIO, UNITED STATES v. 410 U.S. 1 (1973)

A gambling suspect refused a federal court's order to provide a voice sample to a GRAND JURY, and was adjudged in civil contempt and committed to custody. The Supreme Court affirmed. The Court rejected, 7–2, a claim that the order violated the suspect's RIGHT AGAINST SELF-INCRIMINATION, saying that the voice sample was to be used only for identification, not for the content of the statements. A 6–3 majority also rejected a claim that the order violated the FOURTH AMENDMENT. Because there was no "seizure" here, there was no need to demonstrate the reasonableness of the grand jury's request.

DAVID GORDON

DIRECT AND INDIRECT TAXES

The Constitution imposes two major limitations on the federal power to tax. Direct taxes can be levied only if allocated among the states according to population. All other taxes (indirect taxes) must be uniform among the United States.

The requirement of apportioning direct taxes apparently was included because the southern states feared that they would bear excessive burdens on land and slaves—a fear demonstrated by the fact that (until the FOURTEENTH AMENDMENT) only three-fifths of slaves were counted in the population. Nobody in the Convention appeared to be very clear, however, on just what was a direct tax that had to be allocated.

The issue first came to the Supreme Court in HYLTON V. UNITED STATES (1796). A duty laid on carriages was challenged as being a direct tax. The Court pointed out the difficulties with direct taxes, particularly the fact that while the total amount allocated to each state related to the population of that state, the individual taxpayers (in this case the owners of carriages) would pay quite different amounts depending not only on population but also on the relative numbers of the taxable subjects within the state. The Court expressed doubt that any taxes other than a capitation tax or a tax on the value of land could be called direct taxes. Over the next century the issue seldom arose, for Congress levied very few taxes beyond customs duties until the Civil War. However, the Court did hold that a tax of ten percent on state-issued currency (VEAZIE BANK V. FENNO, 1869), a tax on the succession to a decedent's property (*Scholey v. Rew,* 1875), and income taxes (*Springer v. United States,* (1881) were all indirect, not direct taxes.

The income tax involved in *Springer* had remained in effect only until 1872. By the 1890s, however, many groups called for a reduction in federal dependence on tariffs for revenue and for an income tax on wealthier persons. In 1894 a statute was passed imposing a tax on all incomes over $4,000. Facing a challenge to this tax, the Supreme Court reversed its earlier stand and in POLLOCK V. FARMERS' LOAN & TRUST CO. (1895) held the tax a direct tax and so invalid because not apportioned. The Court's new position was that taxes on the rents or income of real estate and taxes on personal property or the income from personal property were direct taxes and must be apportioned, though taxes on income from other sources would not be direct taxes.

A few years later there was another attempt to enact an income tax law. More conservative members of Congress countered by presenting a proposal to amend the Constitution to provide that income taxes need not be apportioned. Perhaps to their surprise, the SIXTEENTH AMENDMENT was proposed by Congress in 1909 and secured ratification by three-fourths of the states in 1913. The result, of course, was to open the door to the major federal revenue producer.

During the twentieth century there have been occasional attempts to litigate various taxes as being direct—but never with success. Congress does not impose capitation taxes nor property taxes—and all other kinds of taxes apparently are indirect.

The requirement that indirect taxes be uniform has given little difficulty. In upholding a federal tax on legacies in *Knowlton v. Moore* (1900), the Court said that what is required is geographical uniformity. A tax is uniform when it operates with the same force and effect in every place where the subject of it is found. It does not matter that the subject may exist in some states and not in others so long as the tax is the same. Thus, the Court in *Fernandez v. Wiener* (1945) upheld a federal statute imposing death taxes on community property—even though such property existed in only the few states that had adopted the community property system. In *United States v. Ptasynski* (1983) the Court cast some doubt on the geographical limitation by upholding a provision exempting Alaskan oil from a crude oil windfall profit tax. (See TAXING AND SPENDING POWER.)

EDWARD L. BARRETT, JR.

Bibliography

PAUL, RANDOLPH E. 1954 *Taxation in the United States.* Pages 46–58. Boston: Little, Brown.

DIRECT ELECTIONS

Whenever there has been dissatisfaction with the performance of appointing officials, whether party, legislative, or electoral college, there has been a demand for direct elections. The Progressive Era (1890–1920) marked a heyday for such demands, producing direct election of senators (SEVENTEENTH AMENDMENT), direct nomination of state party candidates (through PRIMARY ELECTIONS), and, in many cities and states, direct legislation through INITIATIVE and REFERENDUM, and direct RECALL of candidates. After most close presidential elections, there has also been talk of direct election of the President in place of the ELECTORAL COLLEGE.

Direct election of the President and direct party primaries have been criticized on policy (but not constitutional) grounds for weakening the two-party system. Initiative and referendum, besides being criticized as "plebiscitary," have been challenged as violative of the GUARANTEE CLAUSE, but such challenges have uniformly been found nonjusticiable. The leading case is *Pacific States Telephone Company v. Oregon* (1912).

WARD E. Y. ELLIOTT

Bibliography

BONFIELD, ARTHUR E. 1962 The Guarantee Clause of Article IV, Section 4: A Study in Constitutional Desuetude. *Minnesota Law Review* 46:513–572.

DIRKSEN, EVERETT M.
(1896–1969)

Everett McKinley Dirksen represented Illinois as a United States congressman (1933–1949) and senator (1951–1969). Despite a previous record as an isolationist in FOREIGN AFFAIRS and a reactionary in domestic affairs, he contributed to the legislative successes of the Democratic Presidents when he was the Republican leader of the Senate in the 1960s. Dirksen was an eccentric—flamboyant in style, florid in oratory, and organ-voiced; he was also a superb parliamentary tactician and a politician who was exceptionally inconsistent in his policies. On matters of constitutional interest, he supported MCCARTHYISM and opposed the censure of Senator Joseph R. McCarthy, and savagely criticized the Supreme Court for opinions he disliked, especially on REAPPORTIONMENT, SEPARATION OF CHURCH AND STATE, and the rights of the criminally accused. Dirksen favored bills to curb the Court's APPELLATE JURISDICTION, proposed a constitutional amendment to allow prayers in public schools, and led a movement that failed by the vote of one state to convene a constitutional convention. Yet the CIVIL RIGHTS ACT OF 1964 and the VOTING RIGHTS ACTS of 1965 would not have been passed without his support.

LEONARD W. LEVY

Bibliography

SCHAPSMEIER, EDWARD L. 1985 *Dirksen of Illinois: Senatorial Statesman.* Urbana: University of Illinois Press.

DISANTO v. PENNSYLVANIA
273 U.S. 34 (1927)

Protection of the public health and welfare temporarily lost ground to the COMMERCE CLAUSE in this case. A Pennsylvania statute required the licensing of persons selling steamship tickets to or from foreign countries. The Court declared the law a "direct" interference with FOREIGN COMMERCE, over the dissents of Justices HARLAN FISKE STONE, OLIVER WENDELL HOLMES, and LOUIS D. BRANDEIS. Stone found the direct/indirect test of EFFECTS ON COMMERCE "too mechanical, too uncertain . . . and too remote . . . to be of value." He proposed a more pragmatic test: "the actual effect on the flow of commerce," a view which prevailed in 1941 when this decision was overruled by CALIFORNIA V. THOMPSON.

DAVID GORDON

(SEE ALSO: *Parker v. Brown, 1943.*)

DISCOVERY

Discovery is a procedure by which one party obtains information from the adverse party in his case. This disclosure of information in criminal proceedings includes statements, documents, test results, reports, and other similar items. Although there is a very broad power to discover items in the exclusive possession of an adverse party in civil proceedings, the Supreme Court stated in *Weatherford v. Bursey* (1977) that "there is no general constitutional right to discovery in a criminal case."

In civil cases, the predominant means for discovery are depositions and interrogatories. In criminal cases, no jurisdiction expressly permits the defense to discover prosecutorial information through interrogatories. Most jurisdictions allow depositions in criminal cases only for the purpose of preserving testimony. Most jurisdictions also have statutes or court rules similar to FEDERAL RULE OF CRIMINAL PROCEDURE 16 governing defense discovery which require the prosecution to disclose items such as: (1) written or recorded statements (including GRAND JURY testimony) of the defendant and, in some states, of any co-defendant; (2) the substance of any oral statement of the defendant (and, in some states, of a co-defendant) that the prosecution intends to use at trial; (3) the defendant's prior criminal record; (4) relevant documents and other tangible objects; and (5) results and reports of physical or mental examinations and of scientific tests or experiments.

The prosecutorial duty to disclose exculpatory information is based on the view that the primary task of the prosecutor is to see justice done and DUE PROCESS upheld through the fair treatment of accused persons. If this duty is breached, the defendant is entitled to a new trial.

The leading modern case on this duty is *Brady v. Maryland* (1963). In separate trials, the petitioner and a companion were convicted of murder and sentenced to death. At his trial, the petitioner admitted participating in the crime but claimed that his companion had done the actual killing. Prior to trial the petitioner's attorney requested the prosecution to allow him to examine all the companion's statements to the police. One such statement, in which the companion admitted the actual killing, was withheld by the prosecution and did not come to the petitioner's attention until after his conviction was affirmed on APPEAL. The Supreme Court held that "the suppression by the prosecution of EVIDENCE favorable to an accused upon request violates due process where the evidence is material either to guilt or to punishment, irrespective of the good faith or bad faith of the prosecution."

In order to determine whether particular information should have been disclosed, courts consider whether the defendant made a specific request for the information at issue or a more general request for exculpatory information. They also consider to what extent the information was material to the outcome of the trial. When a specific request is made, withholding information is seldom excusable. Even when a general request is made or the defense fails to request exculpatory information, withholding clearly material information, such as the fact that particular testimony is perjured, is not permissible. In determining materiality, the test is whether the withheld information creates a reasonable doubt in the mind of the trial judge as to the defendant's guilt.

There is no clear rule as to when exculpatory information must be disclosed, but it would seem that some circumstances would require pretrial disclosure in order to permit the defense adequate time to prepare its case.

Generally, the prosecutor decides what evidence should be disclosed, although the trial court may occasionally decide *in camera* whether a particular piece of evidence is favorable to the defendant and should therefore be disclosed to him.

Finally the Supreme Court indicated in *United States v. Agurs* (1976) and *Smith v. Phillips* (1982) that the focus should be whether the prosecutor's failure to disclose rendered the trial fundamentally unfair, not the extent of prosecutorial culpability.

CHARLES H. WHITEBREAD

Bibliography

SALTZBURG, STEPHEN 1980 *American Criminal Procedure.* St. Paul, Minn.: West Publishing Co.

WHITEBREAD, CHARLES H. 1980 *Criminal Procedure.* Mineola, N.Y.: Foundation Press.

DISCRETE AND INSULAR MINORITIES

The idea of the "discrete and insular minority" originated in the now famous footnote four of the opinion in UNITED STATES V. CAROLENE PRODUCTS COMPANY (1938). Justice HARLAN F. STONE, writing for only a plurality of the Court, queried—without answering the question—"whether prejudice against discrete and insular minorities may be a special condition, which tends seriously to curtail those political processes ordinarily to be relied upon to protect minorities, and which may call for a correspondingly more searching judicial inquiry." In the wake of the Court's about-face in 1937, Justice Stone was serving notice that the Court might not accord the same deference to statutes directed at "discrete and insular minorities" that it would to statutes directed at ECONOMIC REGULATION.

The Court made little use of the concept until the early 1970s, when it began to delineate the class characteristics of such groups. Included were groups that had been "saddled with such disabilities, or subjected to such a history of purposeful unequal treatment, or relegated to such a position of political powerlessness as to command extraordinary protection from the majoritarian political process." Although race, nationality, and alienage seem to have been firmly established as class characteristics of the "discrete and insular minority," the Court has refused to extend such class status to illegitimates, the poor, or conscientious objectors.

REGENTS OF THE UNIVERSITY OF CALIFORNIA V. BAKKE (1978) presented the question of the "discrete and insular minority" in a new light. The question in *Bakke* was whether the same "solicitude" should be applied to test a governmental action designed to benefit rather than injure a "discrete and insular" minority. The university, citing *Carolene Products*, argued that STRICT SCRUTINY was reserved exclusively for "discrete and insular minorities." Four Justices agreed that a white male needed no special protection from the political process that authorized the actions of the university. Justice LEWIS F. POWELL rejected this argument: "the 'rights created by the . . . FOURTEENTH AMENDMENT are, by its terms, guaranteed to the individual. The rights established are personal rights. . . .' The guarantee of EQUAL PROTECTION cannot mean one thing when applied to one individual and something else when applied to a person of another color."

In FULLILOVE V. KLUTZNICK (1980) the Court, for the first time since the JAPANESE AMERICAN CASES (1943–1944), upheld a racial classification that was expressed on the face of a law. *Fullilove* involved a challenge to an act of Congress authorizing federal funds for local public works projects and setting aside ten percent of those funds for employment of businesses owned by Negroes, Hispanics, Orientals, AMERICAN INDIANS, and Aleuts. Chief Justice WARREN E. BURGER, writing for a plurality, called for judicial deference to Congress's power under section 5 of the Fourteenth Amendment, as equivalent to "the broad powers expressed in the NECESSARY AND PROPER CLAUSE. . . ." The irony was that the idea of the "discrete and insular minority" in its inception was designed to curtail such deference when racial classifications were involved.

BENIGN RACIAL CLASSIFICATIONS, it is sometimes said, are justified because they do not involve the stigma of INVIDIOUS DISCRIMINATION. The recipients of the benefits that accrue from the "benign" classification are not branded as members of an "inferior race" as they would be if the classification were an invidious one. This theory erects "stigma" as the standard for equal protection rights. Absent any such stigma the implication is that the Constitution is not offended, even if individuals must bear burdens created by a classification that otherwise would be disallowed by the equal protection clause. As Burger stated in *Fullilove*, " 'a sharing of the burden' by innocent parties is not impermissible." To use the idea of stigma as a racial class concept is, in effect, to translate equal protection rights into class rights.

But the intrusion of class into the Constitution is a dangerous proposition, one that is at odds with the principles of the constitutional regime—principles ultimately derived from the proposition that "all men are created equal." Class considerations explicitly deny this equality because they necessarily abstract from the individual and ascribe to him class characteristics that are different—and necessarily unequal—from those of individuals outside the class. A liberal jurisprudence must disallow all class considerations. When there is a conflict between two different "discrete and insular minorities," which should be accorded preference? No principle can answer this question. And the question is not merely theoretical. The Court has already faced this dilemma in cases such as UNITED JEWISH ORGANIZATIONS V. CAREY (1977) and *Castenada v. Partida* (1977), and in a pluralistic society it is inevitable that many more such cases will arise. Equal protection can be the foundation of a genuine liberal jurisprudence only if it applies to individuals. As Justice JOHN MARSHALL HARLAN remarked in his powerful dissent in PLESSY V. FERGUSON (1896), the case that established the SEPARATE-BUT-EQUAL DOCTRINE, "[o]ur Constitution is color-blind, and neither knows nor tolerates classes among citizens. In respect of CIVIL RIGHTS, all citizens are equal before the law." This is undoubtedly still the essential principle of liberal government.

JAMES MADISON argued, in THE FEDERALIST #10, that in a large, diverse republic with a multiplicity of interests it was unlikely that there would ever be permanent majorities and permanent minorities; thus there would be little probability that "a majority of the whole will have a common motive to invade the rights of other citizens." On this assumption, the majorities that do form will be composed of coalitions of minorities that come together for limited self-interested purposes. The majority will thus never have a sense of its own interest as a majority.

By and large, the solution of the Founders has worked remarkably well. There have been no permanent majorities, and certainly none based exclusively on race. Understanding American politics in terms of monolithic majorities and "discrete and insular minorities"—as the Supreme Court appears to do—precludes the creation of a common interest that transcends racial class considerations. By transforming the Fourteenth Amendment into an instrument of class politics, the Court risks either making a majority faction more likely by heightening the majority's awareness of its class status as a majority, or transforming the liberal constitutional regime into one no longer based on majority rule.

EDWARD J. ERLER

Bibliography

ELY, JOHN H. 1980 *Democracy and Distrust: A Theory of Judicial Review.* Pages 75–77 and 135–179. Cambrige, Mass.: Harvard University Press.

ERLER, EDWARD J. 1982 Equal Protection and Personal Rights: The Regime of the "Discrete and Insular Minority." *Georgia Law Review* 16:407–444.

KARST, KENNETH L. and HOROWITZ, HAROLD W. 1974 Affirmative Action and Equal Protection. *Virginia Law Review* 60:955–974.

DISMISSED TIME

See: Released Time

DISORDERLY CONDUCT

See: Breach of the Peace

DISSENTING OPINION

In cases in which the judges of a multijudge court are divided as to the decision, it is customary for those in the minority to file a dissenting opinion. This practice is followed in the Supreme Court of the United States. In recent years, dissenting opinions have been filed in as many as seventy percent of all cases decided by the Court. In a typical TERM over 150 separate dissenting opinions are filed by Justices who find themselves on the losing side.

The author of a dissenting opinion tries to explain why the Court should have decided the case differently. Often a dissenting Justice will attempt to provide the public with an interpretation of the MAJORITY OPINION in order to narrow its scope or to restrict its impact. A strong dissenting opinion may go far to weaken the decision and may point the way for future litigation.

The OPINION OF THE COURT is written by a Justice on the prevailing side designated by the Chief Justice (or the senior Justice in the majority), and must reflect a consensus of the majority. Dissenters have a freer hand: they can make their point more sharply because they do not need to accommodate colleagues who might balk at aspects of their argument. Before the decision of a case is announced, the draft opinions circulate among the Justices. A well-argued dissent can induce the author of the majority opinion to modify its content, either to retain majority support, as in EVERSON V. BOARD OF EDUCATION (1947), or to respond in kind to a particularly harsh attack, as in DRED SCOTT V. SANDFORD (1857). In an extraordinary case, the dissent may attract enough support actually to become the majority opinion.

Dissents are most common during change in the ideological composition of the Court. For a time the dissents portend an imminent revolution in the tendency of judicial thought and point to the future course of decisions. Once the revolution is perfected there follows a time when the dissents resist the new orientation and recall the old orthodoxy. Two of the Court's great dissenters were Justices JOHN MARSHALL HARLAN (1833–1911) and OLIVER WENDELL HOLMES, each of whom stood against the majority of his day and took positions that much later were adopted by the Court.

CHARLES EVANS HUGHES once wrote that "a dissent in the court of last resort is an appeal to the brooding spirit of the law, to the intelligence of a future day. . . ." Contemporaneously, HARLAN F. STONE wrote that "dissents seldom aid in the right development of the law. They often do harm."

DENNIS J. MAHONEY

DISTRICT OF COLUMBIA

"If any of their officers, or creatures, should attempt to oppress the people, or should actually perpetrate the blackest deed, he has nothing to do but get into the ten miles square. Why was this dangerous power given?" The "dangerous power" to which GEORGE MASON objected so vehemently at the Virginia ratifying convention was that vested in Congress by the seventeenth clause of Article I, section 8, "to exercise exclusive legislation in all cases whatsoever, over such district (not exceeding ten miles square) as may . . . become the seat of the government of the United States." That the power to legislate for the capital district should be controversial was a surprise to JAMES MADISON, who had proposed it in the CONSTITUTIONAL CONVENTION OF 1787. He defended the provision as the means by which the federal government might "be guarded from the influence of particular states, or from insults."

The district was established on the banks of the Potomac River between Maryland and Virginia, at a site chosen by GEORGE WASHINGTON, and Congress assumed JURISDICTION over it on February 27, 1801. The location of the capital was agreed to by northern Federalists in exchange for southern acquiescence in federal assumption of state revolutionary war debts. But that location, south of Mason's and Dixon's line, resulted in the greatest national disgrace before the Civil War, namely, that the federal capital was a bastion of slavery and the home of a flourishing slave market. Not until the COMPROMISE OF 1850 was even abomination of slave trading extinguished.

Originally, the District of Columbia comprised one hundred square miles of land ceded by Virginia and Maryland, and three municipal corporations, Washington, Georgetown, and Alexandria. Alexandria was retroceded to Virginia in 1846, at the request of its inhabitants, and the district has since comprised less than seventy square miles. Since 1871, there has been a single municipal corporation coextensive with the district. The 1980 population of over 600,000 was larger than the populations of each of four states.

During most of its history the district's lawmaking was done directly by Congress. There was a brief period of home rule, under a government like those of the TERRITORIES, from 1871 to 1874, during which the district plunged deeply into debt. From 1878 until 1974 the district was governed by three commissioners appointed by the President. Home rule was restored by passage of the DISTRICT OF COLUMBIA GOVERNMENT REORGANIZATION AND SELF-GOVERNING ACT in 1973 and adoption of a city charter in 1974. Since that time the district has been governed by an elected mayor and council, although Congress must approve the budget and retains a veto over other legislation.

The legal status of residents of the District of Columbia is anomalous. The Framers of the Constitution apparently did not foresee a large permanent population in the district distinct from the population of the surrounding states. Even the CITIZENSHIP of district residents, who were not citizens of any state, was uncertain until adoption of the FOURTEENTH AMENDMENT (1868). At least from *Hepburn v. Ellzey* (1805) until the Supreme Court sustained an amendment to the JUDICIAL CODE in *National Mutual Insurance Company v. Tidewater Transfer Company* (1949), citizens of the district could not sue or be sued in federal court under DIVERSITY JURISDICTION. Moreover, district residents were unable to vote for presidential electors until passage of the TWENTY-THIRD AMENDMENT (1961), and they remain unrepresented in Congress to this day (except, since 1970, by a nonvoting delegate). In 1978, Congress proposed the DISTRICT OF COLUMBIA REPRESENTATION AMENDMENT, which would have given the district a status equivalent to statehood, but the amendment failed of RATIFICATION by the state legislatures.

The district has often been the site of experiments in "model legislation," such as the DISTRICT OF COLUMBIA MINIMUM WAGE ACT (1918) and the District of Columbia Crime Control Act (1970). The district is also the focus of demonstrations, small and great, against government policies, ranging from Coxey's army (1894) and the bonus marchers (1932) to Resurrection City (1968) and the marches against the VIETNAM WAR. The right to carry demands for redress of grievances directly to the seat of government is a unique expression of FREEDOM OF PETITION.

Creation of a capital district outside the jurisdiction of any of the constituent states has been copied by other federal unions, including Australia, Brazil, India, and Mexico. The idea that no one member of the federation should control the conditions under which the central government works has thus become a part of the modern theory of FEDERALISM. The all-too-real practical difficulty is that the conditions come to be controlled instead by those who make up the permanent infrastructure of the government and whose perceived interest is in the perpetual growth of that government. In the United States itself, the District of Columbia remains an anomaly, a city dependent almost entirely upon the public payroll serving as the capital of a republic dedicated to the principle of free private enterprise.

DENNIS J. MAHONEY

DISTRICT OF COLUMBIA MINIMUM WAGE LAW
40 Stat. 960 (1918)

Congress, in its capacity as legislature for the DISTRICT OF COLUMBIA, enacted this minimum wage law for women and minors "to maintain them in good health and to protect their morals." Seeking to ground the act on the POLICE POWER, Congress established a Minimum Wage Board with power to compel testimony and other EVIDENCE. The act authorized the board to investigate wage conditions of women and minors in the District of Columbia and to fix their minimum wages on the basis of adequacy "to supply the necessary cost of living." The act required the board to provide PROCEDURAL DUE PROCESS; it also provided for APPEALS to courts of the District and made violations punishable as MISDEMEANORS. The Supreme Court declared the act unconstitutional in ADKINS V. CHILDREN'S HOSPITAL (1923) as a violation of SUBSTANTIVE DUE PROCESS OF LAW, but when the Court overruled *Adkins* in WEST COAST HOTEL CO. V. PARRISH (1937), Attorney General HOMER CUMMINGS declared that the law was in effect without any need for congressional reenactment.

DAVID GORDON

(SEE ALSO: *Unconstitutionality.*)

DISTRICT OF COLUMBIA REPRESENTATION AMENDMENT

92 Stat. 3795 (1978)

Twenty-three times since 1800, congressional representation for the DISTRICT OF COLUMBIA had been sought, mainly on the grounds that taxation of District residents without REPRESENTATION in Congress was undemocratic. The modern District's predominantly black population is larger than that of each of ten states. In 1978 Congress proposed a constitutional amendment that would treat the district as a state is treated for purposes of congressional and ELECTORAL COLLEGE representation and for participation in presidential elections and RATIFICATION OF CONSTITUTIONAL AMENDMENTS. It would have repealed the TWENTY-THIRD AMENDMENT, which had allowed district residents to vote for President and vice-president, while limiting district representation in the electoral college to that of the least populous state. As with other recent amendments, Congress fixed a seven-year time limit for ratification and provided that it would implement the amendment by legislation at a later date.

Although both houses of Congress passed the proposed amendment enthusiastically, it had slight chance of ratification because it would have added two senators and one representative to Congress, all almost certain to be both black and Democrats. In 1985, the period for ratification expired.

PAUL L. MURPHY

Bibliography

BEST, JUDITH 1983 *National Representation of the District of Columbia.* Frederick, Md.: University Publications of America.

DISTRICT OF COLUMBIA SELF-GOVERNING AND GOVERNMENT REORGANIZATION ACT

87 Stat. 774 (1973)

Limited home rule in the DISTRICT OF COLUMBIA had been a long-time desire of its inhabitants. Since 1874, the President had chosen the city's administrators and Congress had acted as the city's governing council. Washingtonians elected only their school board and a nonvoting delegate to the House of Representatives.

This 1973 act granted the District a council, a mayor, and increased self-government. It provided a charter for local government, subject to approval by a majority of the registered voters. Although Congress sought to avoid day-to-day responsibility for District affairs, it retained ultimate legislative authority as provided in Article I, section 8, including the power to legislate generally for the District and to veto local laws. The city government exercised the functions of several quasi-federal agencies: the Redevelopment Land Agency, the National Capital Housing Authority, and the District of Columbia Manpower Administration. The Act reorganized the National Capital Planning Commission, giving the mayor responsibility for District planning, excepting federal and international projects. Further, it required the President, in appointing judges to the District of Columbia Court of Appeals and the Superior Court, to choose from candidates submitted to him by a newly created District of Columbia Judicial Nomination Commission.

The act, while still denying the District congressional REPRESENTATION, satisfied a number of city residents' demands for local control over city affairs.

PAUL L. MURPHY

DIVERSITY JURISDICTION

Under Article III of the Constitution, the JUDICIAL POWER OF THE UNITED STATES extends to "Controversies between Citizens of different States . . . and between . . . the Citizens [of a State] . . . and foreign . . . Citizens or Subjects." This power is called diversity jurisdiction because its basis is the difference in CITIZENSHIP of the parties.

The accepted justification for diversity jurisdiction has been the need to protect out-of-state citizens against discrimination in state courts. However, the extent of such discrimination as of the time the Constitution was written is uncertain, and there is evidence that financial and commercial interests supported diversity jurisdiction in the hope of finding shelter from state laws and judicial systems favorable to debtors.

In fact, the diversity jurisdiction authorized in Article III is not confined to situations in which out-of-state citizens require protection. For example, a plaintiff may file a diversity action in her home state's federal court if she can obtain personal JURISDICTION over the defendant there. Also, it is constitutionally permissible for Congress to confer diversity jurisdiction even when citizens of the same state are on both sides of the litigation, so long as some out-of-state citizens are also parties. Congress has conferred jurisdiction in just such cases in the federal interpleader statute.

Congress has the power to determine how much of the constitutionally authorized diversity jurisdiction the lower federal courts may exercise. It has enacted a general statute that allows the federal courts to hear some but not all types of diversity cases either originally or on REMOVAL. Examples of excluded cases are those in which less than a required amount is in controversy, those in which there is incomplete diversity (that is, at least one plaintiff is from the same state as at least one defendant), and those which the defendant seeks to remove from his or her home state's court.

In 1946 Congress first provided expressly for diversity jurisdiction over suits involving citizens of the DISTRICT OF COLUMBIA and TERRITORIES. In *National Mutual Insurance Co. v. Tidewater Co.* (1949), the Supreme Court upheld the law because two Justices were willing to declare that the District of Columbia was a "state" within the meaning of the diversity clause of Article III, and three Justices concluded that Congress could confer the jurisdiction even if it were not within the Article III judicial power.

The citizenship of parties for purposes of applying the general diversity statute is not always obvious. Some problems have been solved by statute. For example, problems arising from the Court's 1844 decision that a CORPORATION is a citizen of its state of incorporation were resolved by a congressional declaration that a corporation is a citizen of both the state of its incorporation and of the state where its principal place of business is located. Others have been handled by judicial interpretation, which has held, for example, that an individual is a citizen of the state in which he or she is domiciled at the time suit is filed. Difficult interpretive problems remain, however.

Under the Rules of Decision Act, as interpreted in ERIE RAILROAD V. TOMPKINS (1938), a federal court hearing a diversity case must apply the substantive law of the state in which it is located. It must also employ that state's CHOICE OF LAW rules and any of the state's procedural rules that have a predictable effect on the outcome of the case and do not conflict with the FEDERAL RULES OF CIVIL PROCEDURE or some overriding federal policy. In cases in which state law is unclear or has not yet been decided, the federal court must strive to resolve the case as the state's highest court would, drawing direction from trends and policies manifest in state judicial opinions at all levels. The state courts are not bound by the federal court's decisions interpreting state law.

It is doubtful that Congress could constitutionally enact a law giving to the federal courts or assuming for itself the power to develop substantive law for diversity cases. Although the *Erie* opinion avoided this constitutional issue, fundamental notions of state sovereignty and the limited role of the federal government dictated the decision's interpretation of the Rules of Decision Act. Notwithstanding these limitations, Congress may enact and has enacted rules of procedure regulating diversity cases, even though the rules also affect substantive rights. And because of the federal interest in the orderly and fair treatment of individuals engaged in multistate transactions, Congress likely could also constitutionally enact a body of federal choice of law rules applicable to diversity actions.

Declining concern over the need to protect out-of-state citizens against discrimination in state courts, coupled with rising distress over the heavy caseload of the federal courts, has spawned proposals to eliminate the federal courts' general diversity jurisdiction. While some continue to praise diversity jurisdiction for the continued acquaintance it offers federal judges with the common law process and the access it offers litigants (albeit selectively) to the often superior federal procedural system, those who support congressional repeal of diversity jurisdiction seem to be approaching success. Eventually it may come to be used only in complex, multistate cases, such as CLASS ACTIONS and interpleaders, in which the federal courts' power to issue process nationwide offers substantial advantages over state jurisdiction.

CAROLE E. GOLDBERG-AMBROSE

Bibliography

ELY, JOHN HART 1974 The Irrepressible Myth of *Erie*. *Harvard Law Review* 87:693–740.

SHAPIRO, DAVID 1977 Federal Diversity Jurisdiction: A Survey and a Proposal. *Harvard Law Review* 91:317–355.

DIVORCE AND THE CONSTITUTION

The constitutional power of the states to prescribe conditions for marriage and divorce went largely unchallenged until the mid-twentieth century. Once Americans became highly mobile, however, new constitutional questions emerged. Divorce might be difficult under some states' laws, and well-nigh impossible under others', but in some places the courthouse doors were open. Could two North Carolinians go to Nevada, stay there for six weeks of "residence," obtain EX PARTE divorces from their respective North Carolina spouses, marry each other, and return to live in North Carolina without being guilty of bigamous cohabitation? In two cases entitled *Williams v. North Carolina* (1942, 1945), the Supreme Court answered that question conditionally. The Nevada divorces were valid, and must be given FULL FAITH AND CREDIT by North Carolina, if the travelers really were domiciled in Nevada when they received their divorces. However, domicile was a jurisdictional requirement for the Nevada courts; North Carolina might constitutionally retry the issue of the previous Nevada domicile, and, if its courts found that domicile lacking, might punish its straying residents.

The *Williams* "solution" soon crumbled. The Court held in 1948 that if both husband and wife entered appearances in the Nevada proceeding, then neither of them could later challenge the Nevada divorce by way of COLLATERAL ATTACK. Nor could a third party attack such a JUDGMENT. Perhaps the "true" domiciliary state might prosecute for bigamy in a case just like *Williams*, but few states had North Carolina's zeal for such prosecutions.

Since mid-century American law in this area has undergone two distinct but related revolutions. First, almost all the states now permit the dissolution of marriage on at least one "no fault" ground. Second, in a variety of contexts the Supreme Court has recognized not only a constitutional right to marry but a broad FREEDOM OF INTIMATE ASSOCIATION. It is doubtful that a state's interest in preserving a marriage against the will of one spouse would be given the same weight today that the Court gave it in the 1940s. In SOSNA V. IOWA (1975) the majority did remark that domicile was still a jurisdictional requirement for divorce, but the Court might take a different view if a latter-day prosecutor were to bring bigamy charges in circumstances closely resembling the *Williams* facts. (See MARRIAGE AND THE CONSTITUTION.)

Sosna itself upheld Iowa's one-year durational RESIDENCE REQUIREMENT as a condition on access to the state's divorce court, rejecting the argument that this limitation denied the constitutional RIGHT TO TRAVEL with the comment that the state had not denied divorce but only delayed it. Lawyers, including Justices, are experts in rationalizing; each day's delay in getting a divorce is surely a denial of one day's single status and of the right to remarry. The *Sosna* rationalization was aimed at distinguishing the Court's earlier decision in BODDIE V. CONNECTICUT (1971). *Boddie* held, on PROCEDURAL DUE PROCESS grounds, that INDIGENTS could not constitutionally be denied ACCESS TO THE COURTS in divorce cases for inability to pay filing fees. The Court there remarked on the "basic importance" of marriage, and took note that the state had a monopoly over its dissolution—and thus the availability of lawful remarriage.

The Court has not recognized a "right to divorce" analogous to the "right to marry" confirmed in LOVING V. VIRGINIA (1967) and ZABLOCKI V. REDHAIL (1978). However, we are not far from the recognition that the Constitution demands important justification for any significant interference with a spouse's freedom to terminate a marriage. Although the virtual disappearance of highly restrictive divorce laws makes less urgent the recognition of this constitutional liberty, that same change in state law surely alters the climate in which the Justices would evaluate the state's interests urged in opposition to the claim of associational freedom.

The collateral issue of child custody can also raise constitutional issues. Of necessity, a domestic relations court must have wide discretion in awarding custody. Yet because the parent–child relation is itself an intimate association of "fundamental" importance, it is vital that the custody decision not be made arbitrarily. The presumption of custody for the mother over a child of "tender years," for example, raises grave issues concerning SEX DISCRIMINATION. Racial and religious grounds for custody obviously raise constitutional danger signals, as PALMORE V. SIDOTI (1984) shows. And for a court to deny custody to a parent simply because he or she is living with another adult outside marriage, or is involved in a homosexual relationship, would also raise serious problems of associational freedom. Of course, at some level of maturity well below the age of adulthood, the child's preference—his or her own associational freedom—takes on constitutional weight that may dominate the custody decision. The Supreme Court has only begun its exploration of these painful subjects. Surely an early priority for the Court will be the reexamination of its old assumptions about the interests that justify a state's imposing its own preferred family patterns on the individuals who must live in them.

KENNETH L. KARST

Bibliography

GARFIELD, HELEN 1980 The Transitory Divorce Action: Jurisdiction in the No-Fault Era. *Texas Law Review* 58:501–547.

KARST, KENNETH L. 1980 The Freedom of Intimate Association. *Yale Law Journal* 89:624–692.

NOTE 1980 Developments in the Law: The Constitution and the Family. *Harvard Law Review* 93:1156, 1308–1350.

DOCTRINE

In constitutional law as in other pursuits of revelation, initiates commonly refer to "doctrines": bodies of rules or principles either authoritatively declared or systematically advocated. Some such doctrines have been simple; the ORIGINAL PACKAGE DOCTRINE is an example. Others, such as the INCORPORATION DOCTRINE, may become shorthand references to larger and more complex creations of the legal mind. More inclusively, one may speak of a doctrine as the body of principles ruling any branch of law, including constitutional law: the doctrine governing PRIOR RESTRAINTS on speech, for example, or the doctrine governing discrimination based on ILLEGITIMACY. In any such use, "doctrine" refers to a body of judicial interpretations of a particular branch of law.

Even more generally, one may speak of constitutional "doctrine" in the abstract, referring to the whole body of rules and principles resulting from the judicial process of CONSTITUTIONAL INTERPRETATION. Our constitutional law, apart from a few rules explicitly stated in the text of the Constitution (such as the requirement that a senator be thirty years old), consists almost entirely of doctrine made by judges in the tradition of the Anglo-American COMMON LAW. Doctrine thus develops as precedents are made by decisions in particular cases. One branch of constitutional doctrine, in fact, is designed in part to assure that the federal courts' lawmaking is informed by the need to apply doctrine to concrete facts. (See CASES AND CONTROVERSIES.) There is therefore a human quality in nearly every constitutional case; a court's opinion normally begins with a recitation of actual facts touching the lives of named individuals. One danger in an era of CLASS ACTIONS and INSTITUTIONAL LITIGATION is that those techniques carry some risk of squeezing the human flavor out of a case, with attendant costs to the process of keeping doctrine attuned to life. Yet implied in the idea of doctrine is the elaboration of principles transcending the concerns of particular individuals, to provide guidance—or comfort—to people in the aggregate.

Doctrinal formulas may outlive their usefulness, as the "original package doctrine" has. When they do, they fall into disuse or are explicitly abandoned. One of the paradoxes of law is that it strives to provide the security of enduring rules and principles yet is compelled to adjust to the demands of an evolving human society. Constitutional doctrine is rarely tidy and nearly always susceptible to manipulation; it is full of ambiguity and vagueness; "absolute" rules either give way to interest-balancing or serve as interest-balancing's disguises. Doctrine was ever history's handmaiden.

Yet constitutional doctrine has had generating force of its own. It is hard to imagine what this country would have been like but for the nation-building doctrinal contributions of the MARSHALL COURT. And the doctrinal development begun by BROWN V. BOARD OF EDUCATION (1954) has been a major influence in our twentieth-century social and political life. If constitutional doctrine sometimes seems no more than a chapter in a given era's political story, it is sometimes a chapter that advances the plot.

KENNETH L. KARST

Bibliography

BICKEL, ALEXANDER M. 1962 *The Least Dangerous Branch: The Supreme Court at the Bar of Politics.* Indianapolis: Bobbs-Merrill.

DODGE v. WOOLSEY
18 Howard 331 (1856)

The PIQUA BRANCH BANK V. KNOOP (1854) decision striking down the tax on banks enraged the people of Ohio. They exercised SOVEREIGNTY by amending their state CONSTITUTION to empower and require their legislature to tax all banks, regardless of any tax-immunity or tax-preference clauses in their charters. Woolsey, a stockholder of a bank, sued the bank, as well as the tax collector, in a state court to enjoin the collection of a tax authorized by the state legislature under the new amendment to the state constitution. The Supreme Court, by a vote of 6–3, for the first time sustained its JURISDICTION in a STOCKHOLDER'S SUIT and ruled that the state could no more impair the OBLIGATION OF A CONTRACT, contrary to the CONTRACT CLAUSE, by its constitution than by a statute. Justice JOHN A. CAMPBELL, one of the dissenters, angrily asserted that his brethren had established the DOCTRINE that the final power over public revenues was to be found not in the people "but in the numerical majority of the judges of this court. . . ." Besides his heat, he raised a profound question: "Should it be that a state of this Union had become the victim of vicious legislation, its property alienated, its powers of taxation renounced in favor of chartered associations, and the resources of the body politic cut off, what remedy has the people against the misgovernment?" Chief Justice ROGER B. TANEY answered for the majority by saying that the people govern themselves, wisely or not, and are bound to their contracts by the Constitution. By 1862 the Court handed down five more decisions involving the taxation of Ohio banks. The state finally capitulated, and the Court irrevocably committed itself to the doctrine that a grant of tax privileges could not be repealed for the life of the contract.

LEONARD W. LEVY

DOE, CHARLES
(1830–1896)

Charles Cogswell Doe, associate justice of the New Hampshire Supreme Court from 1859 to 1874, and chief justice from 1876 to 1896, is remembered as one of the country's greatest COMMON LAW judges. He is less renowned for his contributions to constitutional law. One reason may have been his bold originality. During his years on the bench, constitutional law was less tolerant of the unorthodox and less receptive to eccentric genius than was the common law. And Doe was original if not eccentric. The perspective from which he viewed the state constitution is an example. The drafters of the document had adopted words indicating they were writing a SOCIAL COMPACT and Doe insisted it had to be interpreted as a social compact. Under the other types of constitutions—those that were organic laws, not compacts—the government, Doe maintained, possesses INHERENT POWERS limited by certain enumerated provisions (for example, the federal *Bill of Rights*). When the liberty of a citizen is pitted against the authority of the state, the citizen must find specific wording to restrain government. A constitution that is a compact, by contrast, has no place for inherent power. As a result, Doe held in WOOSTER V. PLYMOUTH (1882), CIVIL RIGHTS are not immunities but "privileges which society has engaged to provide in lieu of the natural liberties so given up by individuals" under the "contract." The proposition that the compact made government an agent, and individual rights absolute except when specifically surrendered, permitted Doe to relieve the citizen of the burden of establishing constitutional limits on state authority. The state had to demonstrate that the power it claimed had, by compact, been delegated to it.

The chief constitutional DOCTRINE resulting from the social compact doctrine was equality. "The bill of rights," Doe ruled in STATE V. U.S. & CANADA EXPRESS CO. (1880), "is a bill of their equal, private rights, reserved by the grantors of public power." Equality, he added, is "practically the source and sum of all rights, and the substance of the constitution." Doe sought to make equality the most fundamental civil right protecting nineteenth-century Americans.

The national development in constitutional law most troublesome to Judge Doe was the United States Supreme Court's decision in the SINKING FUND CASES (1879). Fearing that the ruling endangered private property rights, he wrote several opinions hoping to diminish those cases' influence. In *Corbin's Case* (1891) Doe even invented the concept of "constitutional estoppel" to bar the state government from taking an action that in a corporate charter it had expressly reserved the right to take. Doe's particular genius even led him to criticize FLETCHER V. PECK (1810) and DARTMOUTH COLLEGE V. WOODWARD (1819), two decisions most contemporaries thought protected property rights. Doe believed they weakened property rights and increased arbitrary legislative power. Better had they been decided on the SEPARATION OF POWERS principle than on the CONTRACT CLAUSE.

In Doe's hands, the separation of powers principle became a means of enlarging his court's JURISDICTION. His distrust of legislative power resulted in support of laissez-faire principles, but his belief that courts should impose common law tests of reasonableness on business supported a measure of regulation. The supremacy of constitutional limitations was his foremost principle.

JOHN PHILLIP REID

Bibliography

REID, JOHN PHILLIP 1967 *Chief Justice: The Judicial World of Charles Doe.* Cambridge, Mass.: Harvard University Press.

DOE v. BOLTON

See: *Roe v. Wade*

DOMBROWSKI v. PFISTER
380 U.S. 479 (1965)

Dombrowski marks the high point of the Supreme Court's willingness to authorize federal district court interference with pending state criminal proceedings. When decided, *Dombrowski* seemed to suggest that such interference was warranted when the state statutes forming the basis of the prosecution were alleged to violate the FIRST AMENDMENT OVERBREADTH DOCTRINE. The CHILLING EFFECT—a term first used in *Dombrowski*—on First Amendment rights of prosecutions under such statutes derived from the fact of the prosecution, thereby rendering successful defense of the prosecution an inadequate remedy for the chilling effect. *Dombrowski* was "reinterpreted" in YOUNGER V. HARRIS (1971) and has since been of little precedential or practical importance.

THEODORE EISENBERG

DOMESTIC COMMERCE

See: Intrastate Commerce

DOREMUS, UNITED STATES v.
249 U.S. 86 (1919)

Congress moved to suppress illegal drug trafficking in the HARRISON ACT of 1919 by compelling persons dealing in narcotics to register with the federal government. The act further imposed a $1 annual license tax, an exercise of the NATIONAL POLICE POWER. Justice WILLIAM R. DAY, for a 5–4 Supreme Court, sustained the entire act even though the provision at issue was the one requiring the use of federal forms for recording transactions. "The act may not be declared unconstitutional," Day said, "because its effect may be to accomplish another purpose as well as the raising of revenue." He found the tax section closely related to the rest of the act. By ignoring LEGISLATIVE INTENT—and his own recent opinion in HAMMER V. DAGENHART (1918) where such intent had been dispositive—he chose to follow the line of precedents beginning with CHAMPION V. AMES (1903). A single-sentence dissent found that the act overstepped Congress's delegated powers and invaded the states' RESERVED POLICE POWER.

DAVID GORDON

(SEE ALSO: *Drug Regulation; Taxing and Spending Power.*)

DOREMUS v. BOARD OF EDUCATION
342 U.S. (1952)

A New Jersey statute provided for the reading, without comment, of five verses of the Old Testament at the opening of each public school day. This was challenged as an ESTABLISHMENT OF RELIGION by a taxpayer of the town of Hawthorne who had had a child in its school system.

Justice ROBERT H. JACKSON, writing for the Supreme Court, rejected the STANDING of the plaintiff to raise the constitutional question. His child had been graduated from school, so that his claim as a parent suffered from MOOTNESS. Furthermore, because there was no showing that public money was spent on the practice, the plaintiff's taxpayer status gave him no stake in the litigation.

Justice WILLIAM O. DOUGLAS, with whom Justices STANLEY F. REED and HAROLD BURTON agreed, dissented. A taxpayer, Douglas argued, had a general interest in how the schools of the community were managed. The effect of this disposition was to defer for a decade decision on the constitutional merits of religious exercises in public schools.

RICHARD E. MORGAN

DORMANT POWERS

A constitutional power is called dormant if it is granted by the constitution but is not currently being exercised. For a variety of reasons Congress may not see fit to exercise power which it has been granted by the Constitution. These dormant powers may be "awakened" whenever Congress chooses to exercise them.

The federal system of the United States presumes that the states possess the governmental powers not taken away from them by the Constitution. In vesting powers in the federal government, the Constitution grants the national government EXCLUSIVE POWER over some matters of national scope, but CONCURRENT POWERS with the states over other matters. When a power granted to the federal government lies dormant, its effect depends on whether it is an exclusive or concurrent power. When the Supreme Court concludes that the subject matter requires uniform national regulation, then the states are not free to exercise the power even though Congress has not legislated in the area. By its silence Congress is presumed to have decreed that the subject shall remain free of regulation. If, on the other hand, the subject of the power admits of locally diverse regulation, as in COOLEY V. BOARD OF WARDENS (1851), states may legislate until Congress intervenes.

When Congress awakens a dormant power by legislating, its act will preempt inconsistent state laws by force of the SUPREMACY CLAUSE of Article VI. However, the courts do not always hold that Congress has preempted state law simply because it has granted power to a federal administrative agency to regulate an area. If the agency has not exercised the power given to it, then the states may yet be free to regulate the subject just as if the power were still dormant.

GLEN E. THUROW

Bibliography

PRITCHETT, C. HERMAN 1977 *The American Constitution*, 3d ed. Pages 150–216. New York: McGraw-Hill.

DORR v. UNITED STATES

See: Insular Cases

DOUBLE JEOPARDY

Double jeopardy is the most ancient procedural guarantee provided by the American BILL OF RIGHTS. Rooted in Greek, Roman, and canon law, the right not to be put twice in jeopardy may be regarded as essential to a right to TRIAL BY JURY, and is well established in the law of other nations.

The Fifth Amendment of the Constitution includes the simple phrase: "nor shall any person be subject for the same offense to be twice put in jeopardy of life or limb." Yet this phrase, which has been copied in most American state constitutions, conceals a number of complex policy issues, many of which are still unsettled in American law in spite of numerous judicial interpretations since its birth in 1791.

In the course of time American courts abandoned any insistence that the jeopardy required involve a risk of life or limb, even though that had been an important consideration under the harsh criminal law of eighteenth-century England. Thus, the policy underlying the double jeopardy protection does not depend upon the hazard of severe physical punishment or death.

The English COMMON LAW recognizes the pleas of *autrefois acquit* (former acquittal) and *autrefois convict* (former conviction) to preclude retrial of an accused person, but American law has taken a more expansive view of the right. In America a prior accusation without a verdict could result in a successful plea of double jeopardy. The American version of the right is more generous to accused persons in many other respects, making double jeopardy an important potential source of protection.

In *Green v. United States* (1957) Justice HUGO L. BLACK provided a persuasive explanation of the American concept of double jeopardy. He suggested that the guarantee against double jeopardy is aimed primarily at three potential abuses of governmental power: "The underlying idea, one that is deeply ingrained in at least the Anglo-American system of jurisprudence, is that the state with all its resources and power should not be allowed to make repeated attempts to convict an individual for an alleged offense, thereby (1) subjecting him to embarrassment, expense and ordeal and (2) compelling him to live in a continuing state of anxiety and insecurity, as well as (3) enhancing the possibility that even though innocent he may be found guilty."

Double jeopardy policy embodies a conflict between a defendant's interest in "being able once and for all, to conclude his confrontation with society," as the Court said in *United States v. Jorn* (1970), and the public interest in a full and accurate prosecution. To preclude retrial of an accused person on some technical defect in the presentation of the prosecution's case is not in the public interest. Conversely, individuals must be protected against repeated risks of criminal punishment so that they may conclude their confrontation with society in a just manner and resume their normal lives as free citizens.

Surprisingly, it was not until 1969 that the Supreme Court extended the Fifth Amendment's double jeopardy prohibition to state criminal prosecutions. In BENTON V. MARYLAND (1969) the Court finally held "that the double jeopardy prohibition of the Fifth Amendment represents a fundamental ideal in our constitutional heritage." Since then the Court has been deeply involved in reviewing double jeopardy questions, refining and reconsidering many of its earlier interpretations of the clause. Now the Supreme Court is the chief source of policymaking in double jeopardy matters, although some state legislatures have begun to reexamine the DOCTRINE in the process of revising state criminal codes to eliminate overlapping criminal offenses.

Double jeopardy law involves at least four distinct policy questions. The first concerns the time when jeopardy begins or "attaches." Clearly, pretrial proceedings are not covered by double jeopardy, but at some point after a trial opens jeopardy is said to "attach." The second double jeopardy question is the legal significance to be accorded political boundaries such as state/federal, state/municipal, national/international. Third is the problem arising from the numerous definitions of crime which sometimes carve up criminal deeds into small parcels of criminalized behavior. These multiple offense categories could give rise to multiple prosecutions unless bounded by the double jeopardy protection. Finally, there is the issue raised by a criminal appeal (by the defendant or the state) with its potential of a new trial reviving the same risks to the liberty of the defendant.

All these issues are embraced within the American doctrine of double jeopardy and none has been definitively resolved. American double jeopardy law has become one of the most complex areas of JUDICIAL POLICYMAKING. English law on the subject lacks the complexity of American law because it is confined largely to the issue of the effect of a prior final judgment. American law is distinctive in its subtle interplay among the interests of the accused person, the prosecution, and the society at large. However, American double jeopardy law is confused by the judicial failure to separate the strands of double jeopardy and to pursue the essential purposes served by double jeopardy. Indeed, close reading of Supreme Court decisions reveals some conflict among the Justices concerning the goals of double jeopardy policy.

In *Crist v. Betz* (1978) the issue of attachment of double jeopardy was called "the lynchpin for all double jeopardy jurisprudence," but it still is not clearly settled. The federal rule is that jeopardy attaches at the time when the jury is sworn, and this federal rule now extends to state proceedings as well. The rule takes effect when the first witness is sworn in a case tried before a judge. After this point, in the absence of exceptional circumstances, the defendant's jeopardy begins, and it cannot be begun again merely because the prosecution wishes to retry a stronger case at a later time.

However, it is possible for the prosecution to retry a case that has been aborted short of FINAL JUDGMENT if it can bear the heavy burden of showing "manifest necessity" for repetitious proceedings. Courts have wrestled vainly in an effort to define the nature of the "manifest necessity" that justifies reprosecution. Recently the Supreme Court has developed a balancing test to weigh the interests of the prosecution and the defendant. Now, if a mistrial is based upon an error by the state that could be manipulated to strengthen the prosecution's case, a defendant is entitled to immunity from reprosecution if he chooses to oppose the mistrial, but not if he requests it. But the Supreme Court has wavered in its mistrial decisions, even overruling itself at times.

Attachment doctrines apply to JUVENILE PROCEEDINGS as well as to adult criminal trials, so that jeopardy attaches to an adjudicatory finding in juvenile court, preventing a subsequent trial in the criminal court for the same conduct. However, a closed master's hearing for a juvenile has been treated as a pretrial event, not an attachment of jeopardy.

The clearest interpretation of double jeopardy policy appears in the area of separate prosecutions for the same offense by federal and state governments. According to BARTKUS V. ILLINOIS (1959), double jeopardy is inapplicable when a defendant is charged with having violated the laws of two or more different "sovereigns." Yet, after a barrage of criticism of the Supreme Court ruling, the attorney general adopted a policy of avoiding federal reprosecution of a matter already tried by a state where the state prosecution rested upon the same act or acts. This discretionary policy remains an administrative restraint upon federal prosecution. In 1970 the Supreme Court held in *Waller v. Florida* that a state and its municipalities were not "separate sovereigns" in this sense; successive prosecutions thus were barred by the double jeopardy clause.

The most complex and least settled area of double jeopardy involves the meaning of "same offense" in the Fifth Amendment clause. The basic federal rule does not prohibit imposition of two or more punishments for the same activity. Instead, the Supreme Court has largely left it to the Congress and the state legislatures to carve up a single act or series of acts into an appropriate set of criminal offenses. The possibility of fragmentation of a single act into a number of criminal offenses with separate trials for each generally is not an occasion for judges to invoke the double jeopardy protection, although the Supreme Court has made some limited attempts to do so.

The double jeopardy clause is not a barrier to an APPEAL by the prosecution in a criminal case. The government may appeal decisions in a criminal case only if authorized by statute. Since the ORGANIZED CRIME CONTROL ACT of 1970, which grants the right to appeal a sentence imposed upon a "dangerous special offender," reviews of sentences are available to the federal government. The Supreme Court has held in *United States v. DiFrancesco* (1980) that the increase of a sentence on review under this statute does not constitute multiple punishment in violation of the double jeopardy clause. Whenever a defendant appeals from his own conviction he is usually said to have "waived" his right to plead double jeopardy.

Taken together, double jeopardy doctrines appear still to be somewhat unsettled in the United States. The general contours of double jeopardy have been described since 1969 in increasing detail. Yet inconsistencies and uncertainties continue. This most ancient of American rights is subject to judicial balancing. Increasingly, the balance has been more favorable to the prosecution, contracting the generous scope of double jeopardy evident in earlier years. Since the Supreme Court has been deeply divided on double jeopardy issues we may expect continued developments of policy with changes in judicial personnel. States may have more stringent views of double jeopardy policy under their own double jeopardy provisions. Therefore some states may set higher standards than the Supreme Court for the protection of defendants.

JAY A. SIGLER

Bibliography

FRIEDLAND, MARTIN 1969 *Double Jeopardy.* Oxford: Clarendon Press.

SIGLER, JAY A. 1969 *Double Jeopardy: The Development of a Legal and Social Policy.* Ithaca, N.Y.: Cornell University Press.

WESTIN, PETER and DRUBEL, RICHARD 1979 Toward a General Theory of Double Jeopardy. *Supreme Court Review* 1978:81–169.

DOUGLAS, STEPHEN A. (1813–1861)

An Illinois lawyer and judge, Stephen Arnold Douglas served in the House of Representatives (1843–1847) and the Senate (1847–1861), where he chaired the powerful committee on the TERRITORIES from 1847 until 1859. Throughout his career Douglas was a strong Democratic partisan who advocated western expansion, railroad development, and compromise on slavery. A major political figure throughout the 1850s, Douglas closed his career with his losing presidential campaign in 1860. When the Civil War began Douglas rallied to the cause of the Union despite his hostility toward Lincoln and his familial and residual political ties to the South.

Throughout his career Douglas attempted to finesse the issue of SLAVERY IN THE TERRITORIES while supporting territorial acquisition and western settlement. Douglas hoped such a policy would lead to a presidential nomination from a united Democratic party. Practical politics dovetailed with Douglas's personal beliefs that blacks were inferior to whites, that slavery was a legitimate institution deserving of constitutional and political protection, and that ABOLITIONISTS were troublemakers or worse.

The key to Douglas's program was POPULAR SOVEREIGNTY, which would allow settlers to decide the slavery issue for themselves, and thus not require Congress, and the national Democratic party, to take a position on slavery in any particular territory. Ultimately, Douglas's position proved costly. Proslavery Democrats eventually demanded federal protection for slavery in the territories and opposed any Democrat who would not support them. On the other hand, Northerners, in Illinois and elsewhere, came to oppose the spread of slavery into the western territories. By 1858 Douglas discovered he could not satisfy the voters at home and remain a viable presidential candidate in the South.

As early as 1844–1845 Douglas had advocated that settlers in the West be allowed to decide for themselves the status of slavery. In Congress he urged the organization of the Oregon Territory without slavery because settlers there did not want slavery. In the House and Senate Douglas enthusiastically supported all American claims in Oregon and the Mexican War, and he opposed the WILMOT PROVISO. As chairman of the Committee on the Territories, Douglas secured the organization of the Oregon and Minnesota territories without slavery. In August 1850, Douglas resurrected the compromise measures of HENRY CLAY's "Omnibus Bill" and adroitly guided them through the Senate, one bill at a time, as the COMPROMISE OF 1850. The Compromise included the infamous Fugitive Slave Law of 1850, the admission of California without slavery, and organization of the rest of the Mexican Cession with slavery. The compromise satisfied few, but it halted a SECESSION movement then building in the South and probably delayed the Civil War by ten years.

In 1854 Douglas supported the KANSAS-NEBRASKA ACT in the expectation that it would stimulate western expansion and set the stage for a transcontinental railroad, which he hoped would begin in Chicago. The act repealed the MISSOURI COMPROMISE, refused "to legislate slavery into any Territory of State, nor to exclude it therefrom," and left the settlers "perfectly free to form and regulate their domestic institutions in their own way." Northern resentment of this sellout to slavery resulted in Democratic electoral defeats and formation of the Republican party, while popular sovereignty in the territories quickly degenerated into "bleeding Kansas." Douglas lost political support throughout the North, but he explained to hostile constituents that popular sovereignty would lead to a free

Kansas. In 1858, however, Kansas petitioned for statehood under the proslavery LECOMPTON CONSTITUTION. Douglas opposed the Lecompton Constitution because it was ratified by fraud, did not represent the majority in Kansas, and thus was not a fair expression of popular sovereignty. For this opposition Douglas was virtually read out of his party. Later that year, in debate with ABRAHAM LINCOLN during the Senate race, Douglas defended the Supreme Court's decision in DRED SCOTT V. SANDFORD (1857) and the Kansas-Nebraska Act by asserting in the FREEPORT DOCTRINE that territorial governments could prevent slavery by denying it police protection or supportive legislation. Despite opposition from the Buchanan wing of his own party, as well as Lincoln, Douglas was reelected to the Senate. In 1859 his party, dominated by Southerners, stripped him of his Territorial Committee chairmanship because of his apostasy on the Lecompton Constitution and his Freeport Doctrine. Openly a presidential candidate since 1852, Douglas led a divided party in 1860. He ran second in popular votes and a distant fourth in electoral votes. Douglas opposed SECESSION and before his death in 1861 urged Lincoln to call out enough troops to defend the Union.

PAUL FINKELMAN

Bibliography

JAFFA, HARRY V. 1959 *Crisis of the House Divided: An Interpretation of the Lincoln-Douglas Debates.* Garden City, N.Y.: Doubleday.

JOHANNSEN, ROBERT W. 1973 *Stephen A. Douglas.* New York: Oxford University Press.

DOUGLAS, WILLIAM O. (1898–1980)

William Orville Douglas was appointed to the Supreme Court by President FRANKLIN D. ROOSEVELT on April 15, 1939, the youngest appointee since JOSEPH STORY, 128 years earlier. Illness forced his retirement on November 12, 1975, but he had surpassed by nearly two years the record for longevity of service previously held by STEPHEN J. FIELD.

As a child, Douglas contracted polio and overcame the residual weakness in his legs through long solitary hikes. When his father died before Douglas's sixth birthday, his mother was left nearly penniless with three children. Douglas knew grinding poverty and from his childhood, through all of his education, he worked to support himself and his family. Three views that colored his outlook on life emerged from this period and strongly influenced his legal views. Above all an individualist, he believed that, if given enough room by society, one could achieve full potential through self-reliance and hard work. At the same time, he formed a deep sympathetic bond with the outcasts and disadvantaged of society, particularly the poor, racial minorities, and political radicals. Finally, he harbored a lingering resentment of "the establishment," a view that later matured into a distrust of concentrations of power, whether of the private sector, the police, or government generally. A number of Douglas's legal positions trace their origin to these three linked premises, from his populist view of the antitrust laws to his repeated insistence that the function of the BILL OF RIGHTS was to take government off the backs of the people.

Douglas's career prior to his appointment to the Court also explains the hallmarks of his judicial style. (Over the years, even admirers of the Justice's substantive conclusions criticized his opinions for insufficiently explaining the origins of novel legal DOCTRINES, for carelessness in setting out the limits and definitions of the principles announced, and for unnecessary inconsistency in arguments made from one case to another.) Douglas was always a superior student, with an intellect in the genius range, yet from high school through law school, as he explained in his autobiography, "I had been trotting while I learned." His work obligations and his other activities left little time for reflection. Douglas was a quick study.

Douglas described both his initial appointment as a law teacher and his appointment to the Supreme Court as furnishing new leisure for intellectual contemplation. Intellectual habits, however, are not so easily set aside. Douglas was never contemplative. His habit was to analyze swiftly mountains of data, get to the heart of a controversy, and decide. He was impatient with extended discussion as an aid to decision, with long indecision prior to decision, and with excessive concern for peripheral issues. He remained a loner who spent little time trying to proselytize other members of the Court to his own views. In the Court's conferences and in his separate opinions, he was content to state his positions without adapting them to gain greater acceptance from either his brethren or the scholarly community.

Douglas's impatience with traditional legal style in opinions is also easily explained. As a law professor at Columbia and Yale, Douglas was at the center of the realist movement in jurisprudence. (See LEGAL REALISM.) The realists shared the view that traditional judicial opinions obscured rather than explained the reasons for decision. Douglas's own approach to his fields of business organization, securities regulation, and bankruptcy was to study the political, economic, and social institutions with which the law dealt and to shape the law to cope with contemporary problems presented by those institutions. And so it was with his approach to constitutional law. Douglas viewed much of the elaborate argument in standard Court opinions as so much "Harvard fly paper." Indeed, he delighted in sharp criticism of his opinion-writing style, which he viewed as the carping of the conservative legal establishment. He remained a pragmatist who did not try to develop a general theory of constitutional adjudication. Often he was content to let Justices with whom he agreed develop the overarching theories. He was indifferent to scholarly debates about the abstract limits of JUDICIAL ACTIVISM, and he did not have a consistent theory explaining his own pattern of judicial restraint and active judicial intervention.

The substance of Douglas's constitutional jurisprudence can best be explained by contrast with the views of the two other major figures among Roosevelt's appointees to the Court—FELIX FRANKFURTER and HUGO L. BLACK. Between 1937 and 1939, when these three joined the Court, the chief constitutional controversies were still perceived as those of the previous decade—the Court's "economic due process" theory had restrained state ECONOMIC REGULATION, and its "dual federalism" theory had limited federal power to regulate the national economy. The mainstream of constitutional law thought was still preoccupied by the mistakes of the "old Court" in writing its own notions of laissez-faire economics into constitutional limits on state and federal power. All of Roosevelt's appointees shared the opinion that these decisions of the old Court had been erroneous. The major battles surrounding economic due process, and the legitimate scope of federal economic regulatory authority, however, were over before Roosevelt appointed a single Justice to the Court. (See WAGNER ACT CASES; WEST COAST HOTEL V. PARRISH, 1937.)

The early 1940s brought new problems, with personal liberty claims asserted under the FIRST AMENDMENT, and attacks on criminal convictions for procedural irregularities of constitutional dimension. For Frankfurter, the lessons of the Court's previous excesses in second-guessing state and federal economic regulation applied here. It was inappropriate for judges to block decisions of political majorities simply because judges held deep personal views that those decisions were wrong. Issues of personal liberty involved a balance between legitimate interests of government and claims of constitutionally protected liberty. Judges must defer to reasonable governmental accommodations of these competing interests. Moreover, in the case of challenged state laws, interests of FEDERALISM imposed additional constraints.

For a brief initial period, Black and Douglas accepted the Frankfurter position. In *Minersville School District v. Gobitis* (1940), the first of the FLAG SALUTE CASES, Justice Frankfurter wrote for the Court, sustaining a law compelling salute to the flag against a challenge by children of Jehovah's Witnesses, whose religious beliefs forbade their participation. (Only Justice HARLAN FISKE STONE dissented.)

The break with Frankfurter came soon. Black and Douglas shared similar concerns about the rights of minorities and about fair procedures in state and federal criminal trials. In 1942, dissenting in *Jones v. Opelika,* a case sustaining a state license tax applied to the sale of religious literature, they announced that they had recanted their position in *Gobitis. Jones* was overruled a year later in MURDOCK V. PENNSYLVANIA (1943), with Douglas writing for the Court. The same year, West Virginia State Board of Education v. Barnette overruled *Gobitis,* with Black and Douglas joining Justice ROBERT H. JACKSON's opinion.

Even though Black and Douglas often wrote jointly in constitutional cases involving claims of constitutionally protected liberty, it was Black who was the theoretician. Black gradually evolved the views that protection of liberty required the Court to give liberal—and even literal—construction to the Bill of Rights, and that the Bill of Rights restricted not only the national government but also state governments, because, historically, it had been "incorporated" into section one of the FOURTEENTH AMENDMENT. (See INCORPORATION DOCTRINE.) Douglas and Black often clashed with Frankfurter on both issues throughout the 1940s and 1950s.

In ADAMSON V. CALIFORNIA (1947) the Court decided, 5–4, that the RIGHT AGAINST SELF-INCRIMINATION of the Fifth Amendment was inapplicable to the states. Justice Frankfurter, concurring, defended the Court's position that the historic and practical meaning of due process was not contained in the specific provisions of the Bill of Rights, but he also insisted that working out the limits of DUE PROCESS OF LAW required more than personal judgments according to a judge's idiosyncratic sense of justice. Black, joined by Douglas, wrote a lengthy dissent arguing that the Fourteenth Amendment incorporated the "specific" standards of the Bill of Rights.

As time passed, Black, again joined by Douglas, further insisted that the guarantees of the Bill of Rights were specific indeed. Characteristic was their position concerning the First Amendment—that it literally forbade all government restrictions upon the content of "speech," leaving to the government power only to regulate "conduct" (for example, YATES V. UNITED STATES, 1957, separate opinion). Justice Frankfurter predictably insisted that free speech claims involved a balance between competing interests and required deference to legislative choices (BEAUHARNAIS V. ILLINOIS, 1952). During the 1950s, the Frankfurter position usually prevailed. Black and Douglas were often in lonely dissent as the Court sustained a series of state and federal antisubversion measures. With the appointment of Chief Justice EARL WARREN and Justice WILLIAM J. BRENNAN in the mid-1950s, the dissenting group grew to four.

After Frankfurter's retirement in 1962, the substance, if not the rhetoric, of many of the Black and Douglas dissenting opinions prevailed. Although the Court rejected total "incorporation" of the Bill of Rights, a process of "selective incorporation" of "fundamental" provisions applied nearly all of its provisions to state governments (for example, GRIFFIN V. CALIFORNIA, 1965, overruling *Adamson v. California*). The provisions of the Bill of Rights governing procedure in criminal trials were expansively construed in cases such as MIRANDA V. ARIZONA (1966). And while no other Justice accepted the Black-Douglas theory that the First Amendment literally protected all speech, the Court's cases of the 1960s rejected the Frankfurter position that the First Amendment tolerated all reasonable governmental restriction on speech. (See NEW YORK TIMES V. SULLIVAN, 1964; BRANDENBURG V. OHIO, 1969.)

The 1960s, however, brought new constitutional problems and a noticeable split between Justices Black and Douglas. There was a negative side to Black's theory pinning activist protection of liberty to the literal meaning of the Bill of Rights. For Black, the Bill of Rights defined not only the minimum guarantees of constitutionally protected liberty but also the maximum. As with Frankfurter's approach, the restrictive branch of Black's theory could be traced to the judicial excesses of the past. The "old Court" had used a natural law approach to write into the Constitution laissez-faire economic policies not fairly reflected in the document's history or text. For Black it was equally wrong for judges to import subjective notions of personal liberty into the Constitution. If judges balanced competing interests in interpreting the Constitution, there was danger beyond the certainty that judges would "balance away" constitutional restrictions with which they were unsympathetic. Judges might also use an open-ended balancing process to create rights according to their subjective predilections.

In *Adamson v. California,* two other dissenting Justices—FRANK MURPHY and WILEY B. RUTLEDGE—had agreed with Black and Douglas that the Fourteenth Amendment incorporated the Bill of Rights as restrictions on state government. They had disagreed, however, with the contention that the Bill of Rights was the outer limit of constitutionally protected liberty. In their view, the Fourteenth Amendment's conception of due process required "fundamental standards of procedure . . . despite the absence of a specific provision of the Bill of Rights." Black and Douglas, on the other hand, had condemned the "natural law-due process formula" which allowed courts "to roam at large in the broad expanse of policy and morals and to trespass, all too freely, on the legislative domain. . . ."

In the late 1940s and the 1950s Douglas continued to support Black's literalist position. Occasional votes can be identified during this period, however, to suggest that his agreement with Black was only skin deep. In *Francis v. Resweber* (1947), decided only months before *Adamson,* the Court permitted a state to electrocute a man after a first attempt at his execution had failed. The vote was again 5–4. This time Black concurred in the result, without opinion. Douglas, along with Murphy and Rutledge, joined Justice HAROLD BURTON's dissent. The same year, another 5–4 vote, in *Kotch v. Board of River Pilot Commissioners* (1947), sustained a Louisiana law that limited the occupation of river pilots to friends and relatives of incumbents. Black wrote for the Court, but Douglas and Murphy joined Rutledge's dissent.

In the late 1960s, more cases arose testing the negative side of Black's constitutional literalism and the break with Black had become apparent. (Interestingly, Douglas never openly conceded that he had recanted his agreement with Black in the *Adamson* case. Only in the posthumously published second volume of his autobiography does he admit that the Murphy and Rutledge position was one with which he "in the years to come, was inclined to agree.") The pattern of voting disagreements with Black in the 1960s was no longer episodic but dramatic. Their differences can be seen on a wide range of issues, all centering on Black's consistent rejection of what he called the "natural law" approach to constitutional adjudication and Douglas's growing willingness to go beyond the literal text of the document.

Douglas wrote the Court's opinion in HARPER V. VIRGINIA STATE BOARD OF ELECTIONS (1966), striking down poll taxes in state elections under the EQUAL PROTECTION clause. Black dissented. Douglas also wrote for the Court in LEVY v. LOUISIANA (1968), striking down a state law discriminating against children born out of wedlock. Again, he relied on an expansive interpretation of the equal protection clause. Justice Black was in dissent and, three years later (*Labine v. Vincent,* 1971), wrote an opinion for the Court that seemed at the time to overrule *Levy.* Here, Black emphasized the absence of any "specific constitutional guarantee." Douglas, of course, was in dissent. Douglas endorsed open-ended theories extending the Fourteenth Amendment's restrictions on STATE ACTION to actions by private business. Black disagreed, insisting that in the absence of federal legislation, the Fourteenth Amendment was inapplicable to private conduct. (See BELL v. MARYLAND, 1973.) With reference to limitations on the time, place, or manner of speech activities on public property, Douglas was prepared to balance the need for available avenues of dissent against competing state interests, if the balance favored freedom of expression. Black disagreed. In ADDERLEY v. FLORIDA (1966), a 5–4 decision sustaining a sheriff's order that protesters leave a jail driveway, Black wrote for the Court and Douglas for the dissent. Finally, Douglas was prepared to interpret the Constitution to require government to follow fair criminal, civil, and administrative procedures even where those requirements could not be tied to specific guarantees of the Bill of Rights. Black, of course, disagreed. (See IN RE WINSHIP, 1970; GOLDBERG v. KELLY, 1970.)

The most dramatic clash between the two former judicial allies occurred in GRISWOLD v. CONNECTICUT (1965). Douglas wrote for the Court, striking down a state law forbidding the use of contraceptive devices. In that case, Black's dissent was predictable, since no provision of the Bill of Rights dealt with the issue. Douglas made a valiant attempt in his opinion to maintain the façade of his agreement with Black eighteen years earlier in *Adamson.* The opinion explained that the right of marital privacy was within "penumbras, formed by emanations" of specific guarantees of the Bill of Rights. (See PENUMBRA THEORY.) The façade was thin, particularly as Douglas relied on the NINTH AMENDMENT for the proposition that constitutionally protected liberty was not limited to the specific guarantees of the Bill of Rights. Just how far removed from even the "penumbras" of the Bill of Rights was Douglas's own conception of the constitutional guarantee of privacy became apparent years later in his concurrence in the abortion cases (*Doe v. Bolton* and ROE v. WADE, 1973; see also RIGHT OF PRIVACY.) Here, he explained that the term "liberty" in the Fourteenth Amendment, as he read it, was broader than the Court's conception of a right to freedom of choice in the areas of marriage, divorce, procreation, contraception, and the education and upbringing of children. It included "the freedom to care for one's health and person, freedom from bodily restraint or compulsion, freedom to walk, stroll or loaf." These, too, were rights that he insisted could not be abridged by government absent a COMPELLING STATE INTEREST.

Douglas had come to believe that the excesses of the old Court in the economic due process cases had not been that the judges read personal values into the fabric of the Constitution. The problem was, rather, that the Court's laissez-faire economic values were the wrong values. For Douglas, the "right" values had been clear all along. They required protecting the individual's right to self-fulfillment, protecting the politically powerless from unsympathetic legislative majorities, insulating the individual from excess concentrations of governmental and private power, and insisting that government procedures be fundamentally fair.

These values best explain Douglas's decisions, up until the end. In his own written instructions for his funeral service, conducted in Washington, D.C., in January 1980, Douglas requested that Woody Guthrie's song "This Land is Your Land" be sung. He patiently explained that some had falsely assumed the song to be a hymn to socialism. Quite to the contrary, he said, the song was in praise of the freedom to wander from place to place which had received constitutional protection in his opinion for the Court in *Papachristou v. City of Jacksonville* (1972).

The *Papachristou* decision was a fitting epitaph. Douglas had written for a unanimous Court striking down a local VAGRANCY ordinance under the due process clause of the Fourteenth Amendment. The technical basis for the decision was that the ordinance was unconstitutionally vague. Insofar as activities that were "normally innocent" were made crimes, an unfettered discretion was placed in the hands of the police. But, quoting Walt Whitman, Henry David Thoreau, and Vachel Lindsay, he went on to argue that wandering and strolling were more than merely "innocent" activities. They were "historically part of the amenities of life as we have known them. They are not mentioned in the Constitution or in the Bill of Rights. These unwritten amenities have been in part responsible for giving our people the feeling of independence and self-confidence, the feeling of creativity. These amenities have dignified the right of dissent and have honored the right to be nonconformists and the right to defy submissiveness. They have encouraged lives of high spirits rather than hushed, suffocating silence." The *Papachristou* opinion, in its results, its style, and the values it enshrined, was vintage Douglas.

WILLIAM COHEN

Bibliography

COUNTRYMAN, VERN 1977 *The Douglas Opinions.* New York: Random House.

DOUGLAS, WILLIAM O. 1974 *Go East, Young Man: The Early Years.* New York: Random House.

——— 1980 *The Court Years: 1939–1975.* New York: Random House.

KARST, KENNETH L. 1969 Invidious Discrimination: Justice Douglas and the Return of the "Natural-Law-Due-Process Formula." *UCLA Law Review* 16:716–750.

POWE, L. A., JR. 1974 Evolution to Absolutism: Justice Douglas and the First Amendment. *Columbia Law Review* 74:371–411.

SIMON, JAMES F. 1980 *Independent Journey: The Life of William O. Douglas.* New York: Harper & Row.

DOUGLAS v. CALIFORNIA
372 U.S. 353 (1963)

Douglas, decided the same day as GIDEON V. WAINWRIGHT (1963), established an EQUAL PROTECTION right for INDIGENTS to be supplied counsel by the state, free of charge, to represent them in direct APPEALS from their criminal convictions. Justice WILLIAM O. DOUGLAS, for a 6–3 majority, followed the lead of GRIFFIN V. ILLINOIS (1956): DUE PROCESS might not require the state to offer appellate review of convictions, but once appeals were granted as of right, they must be made *effectively* available for all. The state's procedure, which provided appellate counsel only when the appeals court found such an appointment appropriate, denied "that equality demanded by the FOURTEENTH AMENDMENT."

Justice JOHN MARSHALL HARLAN, dissenting, elaborated on his *Griffin* dissent. The Fourteenth Amendment had enacted no "philosophy of leveling"; the state had no affirmative duty to relieve the poor from the handicaps of poverty. Due process was satisfied by the reasonableness of the state's procedure for appointing counsel.

Douglas appeared to be a major precedent pointing toward strict judicial scrutiny of WEALTH DISCRIMINATION. However, the BURGER COURT ended such speculations, even in the field of criminal justice. (See ROSS V. MOFFITT, 1974; STRICT SCRUTINY.)

KENNETH L. KARST

DOWDELL v. UNITED STATES

See: Insular Cases

DOWLING, NOEL T.
(1885–1969)

Constitutional problems of FEDERALISM were the chief interest of Noel Thomas Dowling, Columbia University's principal teacher of constitutional law for three decades (1926–1956). Joining the Columbia faculty in 1922, Dowling, a gentle Alabamian, moved into constitutional law when the more corrosive THOMAS REED POWELL departed for Harvard. The main sources of Dowling's influence were his casebook, his articles, and his consulting activities.

Dowling's widely used book, *Cases on Constitutional Law,* was first published in 1937, at the height of the New Deal crisis. Its major theme reflected his lifelong concern: "the regulatory power of government, national and state." His teaching stressed the lawyer's role in constitutional litigation. His emphasis on statutes and LEGISLATIVE FACTS reflected his long participation in the work of Columbia's Legislative Drafting Research Fund.

Dowling advised on the drafting of a number of federal and state statutes. PRUDENTIAL INSURANCE CO. V. BENJAMIN (1946), upholding the MCCARRAN ACT of 1945 granting congressional permission for continued state regulation of insurance, was a special vindication for Dowling's emphasis on the broad scope of the congressional "consent" power. Similarly, Chief Justice HARLAN F. STONE's "balancing" opinion in SOUTHERN PACIFIC CO. V. ARIZONA (1945) vindicated Dowling's advocacy of a significant judicial role in curbing state intrusions on free trade in the absence of congressional action.

GERALD GUNTHER

Bibliography

SYMPOSIUM 1958 A Tribute to Noel Thomas Dowling. *Columbia Law Review* 58:589–613.

DOWNES v. BIDWELL

See: Insular Cases

DRAFT CARD BURNING

The burning of Selective Service registration certificates—or "draft cards"—was a brief and dramatic episode that punctuated the early opposition to the VIET-

NAM WAR. Many draft registrants, often before television cameras, publicly burned their cards to demonstrate their refusal to participate in the draft. These events attracted wide attention and often served as a rallying point for war protesters.

Congress responded in 1965 by amending the Universal Military Training and Service Act to make it a FELONY when any person "knowingly destroys [or] knowingly mutilates" his registration certificate. This law was challenged by David O'Brien with the aid of the AMERICAN CIVIL LIBERTIES UNION. O'Brien had burned his registration certificate before a sizable Boston crowd, including several FBI agents. He was indicted, tried, convicted, and sentenced to prison in the Massachusetts District Court, but the United States Court of Appeals held that the 1965 law unconstitutionally abridged FREEDOM OF SPEECH because it interfered with O'Brien's "symbolic" protest against the war.

In *United States v. O'Brien* (1968), the Supreme Court in an opinion by Chief Justice EARL WARREN reversed the Court of Appeals and upheld the challenged law and O'Brien's conviction. The Court first ruled that the Government has a "substantial interest in assuring the continued availability" of draft cards—for example, so that the individual can prove he has registered and so communication between registrants and local boards can be facilitated, particularly in an emergency. Second, in a more far-reaching holding, the Court rejected O'Brien's claim that the 1965 amendment was unconstitutional because Congress sought to suppress freedom of speech. The Court did not determine whether that in fact was Congress's purpose. Instead it ruled that such a purpose would not invalidate the law in light of the principle that courts may not "restrain the exercise of lawful [congressional] power on the assumption that a wrongful purpose or motive has caused the power to be exercised." (See MCCRAY V. UNITED STATES, 1903.)

Only Justice WILLIAM O. DOUGLAS dissented from the Court's decision, in an opinion that dwelt less on draft card burning than on the power of Congress to initiate a peacetime draft. The *O'Brien* case led to a sharp curtailment of draft card burning and opponents of the Vietnam War turned to other forms of protest.

NORMAN DORSEN

Bibliography

ALFANGE, DEAN, JR. 1968 Free Speech and Symbolic Conduct: The Draft Card Burning Case. *Supreme Court Review* 1968:1–52.

DRAPER v. UNITED STATES
358 U.S. 307 (1959)

In *Draper* the Supreme Court held that information provided by a previously reliable informer, even though hearsay and not within the personal knowledge of the police, is sufficient to establish PROBABLE CAUSE for an arrest, at least when there is substantial corroboration for the information.

JACOB W. LANDYNSKI

DR. BONHAM'S CASE

See: Bonham's Case

DRED SCOTT v. SANDFORD
19 Howard 393 (1857)

Closely associated with the coming of the Civil War, DRED SCOTT V. SANDFORD remains one of the most famous decisions of the United States Supreme Court. It is certainly the prime historical example of judicial power exercised in the interest of racial subordination, and, as such, it stands in sharp contrast with BROWN V. BOARD OF EDUCATION (1954), handed down almost a century later.

Scott was a Missouri slave owned by an army medical officer named John Emerson, who took him to live at military posts in Illinois and in federal territory north of 36°30′ where SLAVERY had been prohibited by the MISSOURI COMPROMISE. In 1846, Scott brought suit against Emerson's widow in St. Louis, claiming that he had been emancipated by his residence on free soil. Missouri precedent was on his side, and after two trials he won his freedom. In 1852, however, the state supreme court reversed that judgment. By a 2–1 vote and in bitterly sectional language, it declared that the state would no longer enforce the antislavery law of other jurisdictions against Missouri's own citizens. Scott's residence elsewhere, it held, did not change his status as a slave in Missouri.

Normally, the next step should have been an APPEAL to the United States Supreme Court, but a recent decision in the somewhat similar case of STRADER V. GRAHAM (1851) may have persuaded Scott's legal advisers that the Court would refuse to accept JURISDICTION. They decided instead to initiate a brand new suit for freedom in the federal CIRCUIT COURT for Missouri against Mrs. Emerson's brother, John F. A.

Sanford of New York, who had been acting as her agent in the Scott litigation and may even have become the slave's owner. Sanford's New York CITIZENSHIP provided the foundation for DIVERSITY JURISDICTION. So began the case of *Dred Scott v. Sandford* (with Sanford's name misspelled in the official record).

Up to this point, the principal issue in Scott's suit had been how residence on free soil affected the legal status of a slave. It was a familiar issue that dated back to the noted British case of *Somerset v. Stewart* (1772) and had been dealt with in a number of state court decisions. (See SOMERSET'S CASE.) During the early decades of American independence, a tacit sectional accommodation had prevailed. Southerners accompanied by slaves were generally able to travel and sojourn in free states without interference. At the same time, southern courts joined in upholding the rule that a slave domiciled in a free state became forever free. Beginning in the 1830s, however, this arrangement broke down under antislavery pressure. State after state in the North withdrew the privilege of maintaining slaves while sojourning, and there was growing judicial acceptance of the view that any slave other than a fugitive became free the moment he set foot on free soil. (See COMMONWEALTH V. AVES, 1836.) To Southerners the change meant not only inconvenience but also insult, and by the 1850s they were retaliating in various ways.

Dred Scott v. Sandford raised an additional issue. In order to maintain a suit in federal court, Scott had to aver that he was a citizen of Missouri. Sanford's counsel challenged this assertion with a plea in abatement arguing that Negroes were not citizens and that the Court therefore lacked jurisdiction. The trial judge ruled that any person residing in a state and legally capable of owning property was qualified to bring suit under the diverse-citizenship clauses of the Constitution and the JUDICIARY ACT. On the merits of the case, however, he instructed the jury in favor of the defendant. Like the Missouri Supreme Court in *Scott v. Emerson,* he declared that Scott's status, after returning to Missouri, depended entirely upon the law of that state, without regard to his residence in Illinois and free federal territory. The jury accordingly brought in a verdict for Sanford.

The case then proceeded on WRIT OF ERROR to the United States Supreme Court, whose membership at the time consisted of five southern Democrats, two northern Democrats, one northern Whig, and one Republican. Argument before the Court in February 1856 introduced another new issue. For the first time, Sanford's lawyers maintained that Scott had not become free in federal territory because the law forbidding slavery there was unconstitutional. This, of course, was the issue that had inflamed national politics for the past decade and would continue to do so in the final years of the sectional crisis. With a presidential contest about to begin, the Justices prudently ordered the case to be reargued at the next session. On March 6, 1857, two days after the inauguration of James Buchanan, Chief Justice ROGER B. TANEY finally read the decision of the Court.

Although Taney spoke officially for the Court, every other member had something to say, and only one concurred with him in every particular. The effect of the decision was therefore unclear, except that Dred Scott had certainly lost. Seven Justices concluded that at law he remained a slave. Taney, in reasoning his way to that judgment, also ruled that free blacks were not citizens and that Congress had no power to prohibit SLAVERY IN THE TERRITORIES. But were these declarations authoritative parts of the decision?

According to some contemporary critics and later historians, Taney did not speak for a majority of the Court in excluding Negroes from citizenship. Their conclusion rests upon the assumption that only those Justices expressly agreeing with him can be counted on his side. Yet, since Taney's opinion was the authorized opinion of the Court, it seems more reasonable to regard only those Justices expressly disagreeing with him as constituting the opposition. By this measure, the opinion never encountered dissent from more than two Justices at any major point. Furthermore, five Justices in their opinions spoke of the citizenship question as having been decided by the Court. In other words, the authoritativeness of that part of Taney's opinion was attested to by a majority of the Court itself.

More familiar is the charge that Taney indulged in OBITER DICTUM when he ruled against the constitutionality of the Missouri Compromise restriction after having decided that Scott was not a citizen and so had no right to bring suit in a federal court. "Obiter dictum" was the principal battle cry of the Republicans in their attacks on the decision. By dismissing Taney's ruling against territorial power as illegitimate, they were able to salvage the main plank of their party platform without assuming the role of open rebels against judicial authority. What the argument ignored was Taney's not unreasonable contention that throughout his opinion he was canvassing the question of jurisdiction. Having concluded that Scott could not be a citizen because he was a *Negro,* the Chief Justice elected to fortify the conclusion by demonstrating also that Scott could not be a citizen because he was a *slave.* Such reinforcement was especially appropriate because some of the Justices were convinced that the Court could not properly review the citizenship question.

It therefore appears that none of Taney's major rulings can be pushed aside as unauthoritative. In any case, the long-standing argument over what the Court "really decided" has been largely beside the point; for Taney's opinion was accepted as the opinion of the Court by its critics as well as its defenders. As a matter of historical reality, the *Dred Scott* decision is what he declared it to be.

Taney devoted about forty-four percent of his opinion to the question of Negro citizenship, thirty-eight percent to the territorial question, sixteen percent to various technical issues, and only two percent to the original question of whether residence on free soil had the legal effect of emancipating a slave. Throughout the entire document, he made not a single concession to antislavery feeling but instead committed the JUDICIAL POWER OF THE UNITED STATES totally to the defense of slavery. Behind his mask of judicial propriety, the Chief Justice had become privately a fierce southern sectionalist, seething with anger at "Northern insult and Northern aggression." His flat legal prose does not entirely conceal the intensity of emotion that animated his *Dred Scott* opinion.

The citizenship issue concerned the status of free Negroes only; for everyone agreed that slaves were not citizens. Yet Taney persistently lumped free Negroes and slaves together as one degraded class of beings who "had been subjugated by the dominant race, and, whether emancipated or not, yet remained subject to their authority." Thus all blacks, in his view, stood on the same ground. Emancipation made no difference. Negroes could not have been regarded as citizens by the Framers of the Constitution, he declared, because at the time they "had no rights which the white man was bound to respect." These notorious words were not mere historical commentary as defenders of the Chief Justice have often insisted. Taney also held that the constitutional status of Negroes had not changed at all since 1787, which meant that in 1857 they still had no federal rights that white men were bound to respect. His reasoning excluded blacks not only from citizenship but also from every protection given to *persons* by the Constitution.

Much more forceful in its political impact was Taney's ruling against the constitutionality of the antislavery provision in the Missouri Compromise. He began by dismissing as irrelevant the one clause of the Constitution in which the word "territory" appears, preferring instead to derive the territorial power of Congress by implication from the power to admit new states. No less remarkable is the fact that he never said precisely why the antislavery provision was unconstitutional. Historians have inferred from one brief passage that he based his holding on the DUE PROCESS clause of the Fifth Amendment. Yet there is no explicit statement to that effect, and in the end he did not declare that congressional prohibition of slavery in the territories *violated* any part of the Constitution; he said only that it was "not warranted" by the Constitution, a phrasing that suggests reliance on the principle of strict construction.

Not satisfied with ruling in effect that the Republican party was organized for an illegal purpose, the Chief Justice also struck a hard blow at northern Democrats and the doctrine of POPULAR SOVEREIGNTY. If Congress could not prohibit slavery in a territory, he said, neither could it authorize a territorial legislature to do so. This statement, being on a subject that did not arise in the case, was *dictum.* It exemplified Taney's determination to cover all ground in providing judicial protection for slavery. The dissenting Justices, JOHN MCLEAN and BENJAMIN R. CURTIS, rejected Taney's blanket exclusion of Negroes from citizenship. Having thus affirmed Scott's capacity to bring suit in a federal court, they proceeded to the merits of the case while denying the right of the Court majority to do so. Both men upheld the constitutionality of the Missouri Compromise restriction by interpreting the territory clause, in Republican style, as an express and plenary delegation of power to Congress. They went on to maintain that antislavery law, state or federal, dissolved the legal relationship between any master and slave coming within its purview, thereby working irrevocable emancipation.

Antislavery critics made good use of the dissenting opinions in launching an angry, abusive attack upon the Court majority and its judgment. The influence of the decision on the sectional conflict is difficult to assess. No doubt it contributed significantly to the general accumulation of sectional animosity that made some kind of national crisis increasingly unavoidable. It also aggravated the split in the Democratic party by eliciting STEPHEN A. DOUGLAS's FREEPORT DOCTRINE and inspiring southern demands for a territorial slave code. At the same time, there is reason to doubt that the decision enhanced Republican recruiting or had a critical effect on the election of ABRAHAM LINCOLN.

For the two principals in the case, the verdict of the Court made little difference. John Sanford died in an insane asylum two months after the reading of the decision. Dred Scott was soon manumitted, but he lived only sixteen months as a free man before succumbing to tuberculosis. The constitutional effect of the decision likewise proved to be slight, especially after the outbreak of the Civil War. The wartime Union government treated *Dred Scott v. Sandford* as though it had never been rendered. In June 1862, Congress abolished slavery in all the federal territories. Later the same year, Lincoln's ATTORNEY GENERAL issued an official opinion holding that free men of color born in the United States were citizens of the United States. The THIRTEENTH AMENDMENT (1865) and the FOURTEENTH AMENDMENT (1868) completed the work of overthrowing Taney's decision.

The *Dred Scott* case damaged Taney's reputation but did not seriously weaken the Supreme Court as an institution. Aside from its immediate political effects, the case is significant as the first instance in which a major federal law was ruled unconstitutional. It is accordingly a landmark in the growth of JUDICIAL REVIEW and an early asserton of the policymaking authority that the Court would come to exercise more and more.

DON E. FEHRENBACHER

Bibliography

EHRLICH, WALTER 1979 *They Have No Rights: Dred Scott's Struggle for Freedom.* Westport, Conn.: Greenwood Press.

FEHRENBACHER, DON E. 1978 *The Dred Scott Case: Its Significance in American Law and Politics.* New York: Oxford University Press.

SWISHER, CARL B. 1974 *The Taney Period, 1836–1864,* Volume V of the Oliver Wendell Holmes Devise *History of the Supreme Court of the United States.* New York: Macmillan.

DRUG REGULATION

Congress's power to regulate the manufacture, distribution, and use of narcotic drugs, formerly limited by a considerable body of constitutional DOCTRINE based on the TENTH AMENDMENT, today is regarded as plenary, limited only by the guarantees of the BILL OF RIGHTS.

The Constitution nowhere expressly grants to Congress power to regulate narcotics. Congress's efforts to regulate the area have thus relied on its powers to tax and regulate foreign and interstate commerce, and on its implied power to make laws enforcing treaty obligations. In the early part of this century, though, the Supreme Court viewed these powers as being constrained by the Tenth Amendment, which, the Court repeatedly held, reserved the POLICE POWER exclusively to the states; federal laws attempting to usurp the police power were void.

Thus, for example, tax statutes were void unless they indicated on their face a revenue purpose rather than an intent to exercise reserved police power. As the Court stated in *United States v. Jin Fuey Moy* (1916), a tax statute would be upheld where it was clearly designed to raise revenue, even though it had "a moral end as well as revenue in view," provided that moral ends were reached "within the limits of a revenue measure." In practice, purported taxes would seldom be voided, but ambiguities in statutory language would be resolved by reference to the purported revenue purpose.

The requirement of a revenue purpose has become less important over time. Congress quickly became adept at structuring tax measures to pass the facial scrutiny of the courts. At the same time, the Court's review of purpose became more cursory. Indeed, at least one lower court expressed the view that a tax purpose is no longer required. In any case, the expansion of the COMMERCE CLAUSE power has made the use of the TAXING POWER unnecessary, and the Comprehensive Drug Abuse Prevention and Control Act of 1970 repealed most prior federal statutes based on the taxing power.

The development of the commerce power largely paralleled that of the taxing power. The Court for many years distinguished sharply between the commerce power granted to the federal government and the police power reserved to the states. The Court's decision in CHAMPION V. AMES (1903), though, established that Congress had the power to ban goods dangerous in themselves from interstate and FOREIGN COMMERCE. Under this power, Congress was free to ban trade in narcotics with foreign countries and between states, but had no power to regulate the intrastate manufacture or sale of narcotics. Thus, prosecution of narcotics violators under federal law required a case-by-case showing that the drugs in question were involved in foreign or interstate commerce, although Congress could create a statutory presumption that drugs of a type normally imported from foreign countries had been so imported.

Now that the courts have sweepingly interpreted the commerce clause, Congress may impose sanctions without showing in each prosecution that the narcotics transaction affected interstate commerce. Challenges to recent federal narcotics regulations have been routinely brushed aside by the courts.

Congress has also occasionally regulated drugs through the TREATY POWER. Thus, a law requiring narcotics addicts to register with customs upon leaving the United States was valid as a measure to carry out the nation's obligations under the Hague Convention of 1912, a treaty ratified by the Senate. With the rise of the commerce power, however, Congress has had little need for the treaty power in regulating narcotics.

Congress's power to regulate narcotics is, of course, limited by the Bill of Rights. In general, these limits are the same in narcotics cases as in other criminal cases; for example, Congress may not authorize unreasonable SEARCHES AND SEIZURES or CRUEL AND UNUSUAL PUNISHMENT of narcotics violators. Nonetheless, the BURGER COURT's contraction of the reach of the Fourth Amendment has led some commentators to speak ironically of a "narcotics exception" to that guarantee.

One issue unique to the narcotics laws, however, has arisen from the FIRST AMENDMENT's guarantee of RELIGIOUS LIBERTY. Several religious groups in the United States use drugs in their observance. The question thus arises whether the federal and state governments may constitutionally forbid the possession and use of drugs for religious purposes. The Supreme Court has held that only a COMPELLING STATE INTEREST can justify substantial infringement of the right to free exercise of religion. This compelling interest must, under the holding in SHERBERT V. VERNER (1963), be "some substantial threat to public safety, peace or order."

Two state courts have found that this standard bars legislative prohibition of the use of peyote by members of the Native American Church in their religious ceremonies. California, indeed, has found that the same ban applies to any person who uses peyote in connection with a bona fide religious practice, even if the person is not a member of any recognized religious group. In a 1964 case involving a "self-styled peyote preacher" the California Supreme Court granted a new trial to determine whether the defendant's professed religious belief was bona fide. Most courts, however, have rejected this view. As of 1983, courts in at least five states have held that the interest of defendants in free exercise of religion is outweighed by the compelling governmental interest in controlling the distribution and use of dangerous drugs.

Whether or not Congress is constitutionally compelled to do so, it has occasionally granted exemptions for the sacramental use of otherwise controlled substances. Just as sacramental wine was exempted from the provisions of the National Prohibition Act (1919), the Controlled Substances Act of 1970 exempted from its prohibitions the sacramental use of peyote. Although the Drug Enforcement Agency has consistently interpreted this exemption as being available only to members of the Native American Church, at least one lower court has held that Congress intended to exempt all bona fide religious groups using peyote for sacramental purposes and regarding the drug as a deity.

Other than this single exemption for peyote, however, the federal narcotics laws have not authorized sacramental use of otherwise forbidden drugs. Nor have the courts yet recognized any religious claims other than those made for peyote. The Supreme Court has not yet spoken on the matter, and constitutional claims for religious exemptions to the narcotics laws cannot be regarded as wholly frivolous. Still, neither the Supreme Court nor the lower courts seem currently to view these claims with favor.

JOHN KAPLAN

Bibliography

BONNIE, RICHARD J. 1980 *Marijuana Use and Criminal Sanctions.* Charlottesville, Va. Michie Co.

KAPLAN, JOHN 1970 *Marijuana: The New Prohibition.* New York: World Publishing Co.

——— 1983 *The Hardest Drug: Heroin and Public Policy.* Chicago: University of Chicago Press.

MOORE, MARK H. and GERSTEIN, DEAN R., EDS. 1981 *Alcohol and Public Policy: Beyond the Shadow of Prohibition.* Washington, D.C.: National Academy Press.

NATIONAL COMMISSION ON MARIHUANA AND DRUG ABUSE 1973 *Drug Use in America: Problem in Perspective.* Washington, D.C.: Government Printing Office.

DUAL FEDERALISM

EDWARD S. CORWIN devised the term "dual federalism" to describe a constitutional theory enunciated by the Supreme Court and by many COMMENTATORS ON THE CONSTITUTION at various times (and to various purposes) in the nation's history—a theory concerning the proper relationships between the national government and the states. This theory, Corwin wrote, embodied four postulates of constitutional interpretation: "1. The national government is one of ENUMERATED POWERS only; 2. Also, the purposes which it may constitutionally promote are few; 3. Within their respective spheres the two centers of government are 'sovereign' and hence 'equal'; 4. The relation of the two centers with each other is one of tension rather than collaboration."

This theory gives enormous importance to the TENTH AMENDMENT, with its declaration that powers not delegated to the national government and not prohibited to the states by the Constitution "are reserved to the States respectively, or the people." (The ARTICLES OF CONFEDERATION had reserved to the states powers that were not "expressly delegated" to Congress.) Confronted with the competing concept of national authority in the Constitution's SUPREMACY CLAUSE, proponents of dual federalism have insisted that the Tenth Amendment holds a superior position. The TANEY COURT, especially in the LICENSE CASES, often portrayed the states' reserved powers as a constitutional limitation on the legitimate authority of Congress. In the post-Civil War period, the Court built another constitutional monument to dual federalism theory in its doctrine of INTERGOVERNMENTAL IMMUNITIES. In the hands of a conservative, property-minded judiciary in the late nineteenth century, dual federalism became a potent instrument for invalidation of federal regulatory measures. In HAMMER V. DAGENHART (1918) the Court's majority took an extreme view of the Tenth Amendment, declaring that it forbade even a federal regulation of interstate commerce when the regulation's purpose was to invade the province of the states' reserved powers.

A series of decisions in the late 1930s, however, put to rest the formal constitutional theory of dual federalism. The Court's revised interpretations of the COMMERCE POWER, the CONTRACT CLAUSE, and the TAXING AND SPENDING POWER all rejected Tenth Amendment limitations on national authority. Meanwhile, the Court also validated the administrative innovations of COOPERATIVE FEDERALISM, in the form of extensive programs of FEDERAL GRANTS-IN-AID to the states.

The only serious reappearance of dual federalism theory in post-New Deal constitutional law has been in NATIONAL LEAGUE OF CITIES V. USERY (1976), in which a concept of inviolable powers and functions of the "states as states" became a limitation on congressional regulatory power, in this instance the power to establish wages and hours for municipal workers.

HARRY N. SCHEIBER

Bibliography

CORWIN, EDWARD S. 1950 The Passing of Dual Federalism. *Virginia Law Review* 36:1–24.

MASON, ALPHEUS THOMAS 1968 Federalism: Historic Questions and Contemporary Meanings. The Role of the Court. In Valerie, Earl, ed., *Federalism: Infinite Variety in Theory and Practice.* Itasca, Ill.: F. E. Peacock Publishers.

SCHEIBER, HARRY N. 1978 American Federalism and the Diffusion of Power. *University of Toledo Law Review* 9:619–680.

DUANE, JAMES
(1733–1797)

James Duane, a wealthy New York lawyer and conservative political leader of the Revolutionary period, served in the Continental Congress (1774–1784) and helped write and secure ratification of the ARTICLES OF CONFEDERATION. As mayor of New York City (1784–1789) he presided over the Mayor's Court case of RUTGERS V. WADDINGTON (1784), a disputed precedent for JUDICIAL REVIEW. Not named, because of his nationalist views, as a delegate to the CONSTITUTIONAL CONVENTION OF 1787, he attended the New York convention and worked for RATIFICATION OF THE CONSTITUTION. He was later the first UNITED STATES DISTRICT COURT judge in New York (1789–1794).

DENNIS J. MAHONEY

DUE PROCESS OF LAW

A 1354 act of Parliament reconfirming MAGNA CARTA paraphrased its chapter 29 as follows: "That no man . . . shall be put out of Land or Tenement, nor taken, nor imprisoned, nor disinherited, nor put to death, without being brought in Answer by due Process of Law." This was the first reference to due process in English legal history. Chapter 29 of the 1225 issue of Magna Carta originally concluded with the phrase "by the LAW OF THE LAND." Very probably the 1354 reconfirmation did not equate "the law of the land" with "due process of law"; the two were not synonymous. Due process in the 1354 enactment, and until the seventeenth century, meant an appropriate COMMON LAW writ.

In the Five Knights Case (see PETITION OF RIGHT), JOHN SELDEN, the great parliamentarian, said in defense of the accused that "No freeman shall be imprisoned without due process of law," meaning that the "law of the land" was an equivalent for "either INDICTMENT OR PRESENTMENT." Sir EDWARD COKE, in his commentary on Magna Carta, also equated due process with the law of the land, meaning regularized courses of proceeding in common law prosecutions for crime. Coke's primary claim was that the law of the land was the common law, one of several rival systems of law then prevalent in England. When abolishing the courts of High Commission and Star Chamber, Parliament in 1641 quoted the due process phraseology of the act of 1354 and added that trials by "ordinary Courts of Justice and by the ordinary course of law" protected property right against arbitrary proceedings. JOHN LILBURNE and his Levellers agreed, but they also asserted that due process signified a cluster of procedural protections of the criminally accused, including TRIAL BY JURY, the RIGHT TO COUNSEL, and the RIGHT AGAINST SELF-INCRIMINATION. By the mid-seventeenth century due process and the law of the land referred to PROCEDURAL DUE PROCESS in both civil and criminal cases. The "law of the land" usage, however, was the dominant one, and "due process" continued to be used in the very limited sense of a writ appropriate to a legal proceeding. A century later WILLIAM BLACKSTONE discussed various processes—original, mesne, and final—without discoursing on due process of law per se. After referring to indictment in capital cases and the principle that "no man can be put to death without being brought to answer by due process of law," Blackstone referred to the different writs that summoned an accused to trial in MISDEMEANOR and FELONY cases.

In the American colonies the usage was similar. In deference to Magna Carta, the "law of the land" formulation was by far the most common, although a variety of paraphrases existed. The MASSACHUSETTS BODY OF LIBERTIES (1641) guaranteed that one's life, liberty, and property could not be deprived except by "some expresse law of the Country warranting the same, established by a generall Court and sufficiently published"—that is, by known, standing law. West New Jersey protected the same substantive rights by a clause guaranteeing "due trial and judgment passed by twelve good and lawful men." New York in 1683 sought a charter that incorporated the famous chapter of Magna Carta with a clause requiring "by due course of law." Probably the first American reference to "due process of law" was in a Massachusetts act of 1692 endorsing chapter 29 of Magna Carta.

During the controversy with Great Britain leading to the American Revolution, Americans frequently spoke of trial by jury, FUNDAMENTAL LAW, the law of the land, no TAXATION WITHOUT REPRESENTATION, and a gamut of CIVIL LIBERTIES, but rarely referred to due process of law. Their references to the "law of the land" had no fixed or single meaning. They meant by it a variety of safeguards against injustice and abuses of CRIMINAL PROCEDURE; they equated it with NOTICE, hearing, indictment, trial by jury, and, more generally, with regular forms of common law procedure and even the fundamental law itself or constitutional limitations on government. The "law of the land" was an omnibus phrase whose content ranged from specific writs to the concept of CONSTITUTIONALISM, and the phrase connoted protection of substantive rights—life, liberty, and property—as well as various precedural rights. Later, due process inherited all the content and connotations of law of the land.

All the first state constitutions used the "law of the land" phraseology, as did the NORTHWEST ORDINANCE of 1787. No state constitution included a due process clause until New York's of 1821, although Mississippi's constitution of 1817 referred to "due course of law." Before the Civil War, only five state constitutions referred to "due process of law." All others had the older "law of the land" equivalent.

The first American constitution to include a due process clause was the Constitution of the United States in its Fifth Amendment, ratified in 1791. The clause reflected JAMES MADISON's preference. For reasons unknown, he recommended that no person should be "deprived of life, liberty, or property without due process of law." The four states which had ratified the Constitution with recommendations for a comprehensive BILL OF RIGHTS urged versions of chapter 29 of Magna Carta, although only one, New York, referred to "due process of law" rather than "law of the land." The due process clause of the Fifth Amendment was ratified without any discussions that illumine its meaning. Although every clause of the Constitution is supposed to have its own independent meaning, rendering no clause tautological, the due process clause was an exception. It pacified public apprehensions, bowed toward Magna Carta, and reinforced specific rights such as trial by jury.

When the Supreme Court construed the due process clause of the Fifth Amendment for the first time in MURRAY V. HOBOKEN LAND COMPANY (1856), it declared that although due process limited all branches of the government, it had only the procedural connotations that derived from the settled usages and modes of proceeding which characterized old English law suited to American conditions. Chief Justice ROGER B. TANEY's opinion in DRED SCOTT V. SANDFORD (1857) passingly employed SUBSTANTIVE DUE PROCESS OF LAW, which had cropped up in some state decisions and in ABOLITIONIST CONSTITUTIONAL THEORY as well as proslavery theory. The

FOURTEENTH AMENDMENT's due process clause, taken verbatim from the Fifth's, proved to be the turning point in the national acceptance of "due process of law" as the common usage rather than the "law of the land" usage. In the last third of the nineteenth century, state constitutions finally substituted "due process" for "law of the land," and judicial decisions, state and federal, as well as legal treatises, expounded "due process of law," making it the most important and influential term in American constitutional law.

LEONARD W. LEVY

Bibliography

HOWARD, A. E. DICK 1968 *The Road from Runnymede: Magna Carta and Constitutionalism in America.* Charlottesville: University Press of Virginia.

JUROW, KEITH 1975 Untimely Thoughts: A Reconsideration of the Origins of Due Process of Law. *American Journal of Legal History* 19:265–279.

MOTT, RODNEY 1926 *Due Process of Law.* Indianapolis: Bobbs-Merrill.

DUE PROCESS OF LAW, PROCEDURAL

See: Procedural Due Process of Law

DUE PROCESS OF LAW, SUBSTANTIVE

See: Substantive Due Process of Law

DULANY, DANIEL
(1722–1797)

Daniel Dulany was a member of the Delaware governor's council (1757–1774) and one of the most prominent lawyers in America. In 1765 he published a pamphlet opposing the Stamp Act and arguing that "there is a clear distinction between an Act imposing a Tax for the single Purpose of raising a Revenue, and those Acts which have been made for Regulation of Trade." He denounced the doctrine of virtual representation as a "cobweb, spread to catch the unwary, and intangle the weak."

Dulany was a delegate to the STAMP ACT CONGRESS but later opposed the American Revolution.

DENNIS J. MAHONEY

DUN & BRADSTREET, INC. v. GREENMOSS BUILDERS, INC.
472 U.S. (1985)

The PLURALITY OPINION in this case may portend significant changes in the constitutional DOCTRINE governing LIBEL AND THE FIRST AMENDMENT. Dun & Bradstreet, a credit reporting business, falsely and negligently reported to five subscribers that Greenmoss had filed a petition in bankruptcy, and also negligently misrepresented Greenmoss's assets and liabilities. In an action for defamation, Greenmoss recovered substantial compensatory and punitive damages. Vermont's highest court held that the principle of GERTZ V. ROBERT WELCH, INC. (1974) did not apply in actions against defendants who were not part of the press or broadcast media. A fragmented Supreme Court avoided this question but affirmed, 5–4.

Justice LEWIS F. POWELL, for a three-Justice plurality, concluded that *Gertz*—which had held, among other things, that punitive damages could not be awarded against a magazine without proof of knowing or reckless disregard of the falsity of the statement—was applicable only to "expression on a matter of public concern." Justice Powell spoke only generally about the content of the "matter of public concern" standard, but hinted that "media" speech might qualify automatically for protection under *Gertz.* Dun & Bradstreet's report, however, involved "matters of purely private concern." Although such speech is "not wholly unprotected" by the FIRST AMENDMENT, he concluded, it can be the basis of a punitive damages award even absent a showing of reckless disregard of the truth. Chief Justice WARREN E. BURGER and Justice BYRON R. WHITE, in separate CONCURRING OPINIONS, expressed willingness to abandon *Gertz* altogether, but meanwhile agreed with this radical surgery on *Gertz.*

In a footnote pregnant with meaning, Justice Powell remarked that some kinds of constitutionally protected speech are entitled only to "reduced protection"—COMMERCIAL SPEECH, for example. But he did not place Dun & Bradstreet's report in the latter category, and thus raised speculation that the majority may be prepared to adopt a "sliding scale" for the FREEDOM OF SPEECH, with varying (and, as yet, unspecified) degrees of constitutional protection for each kind of speech, depending on the Justices' determinations about the value of the speech and the context in which it is uttered.

Justice WILLIAM J. BRENNAN, for the four dissenters, agreed that credit reports were not central to

First Amendment values, but argued nonetheless that the *Gertz* requirements should apply to this case: credit and bankruptcy information was "of public concern." Justice Brennan noted with satisfaction that six Justices (the dissenters and authors of the concurring opinions) had rejected a distinction between the First Amendment rights of "media defendants" and of others sued for defamation.

KENNETH L. KARST

DUNCAN v. KAHANAMOKU
327 U.S. 304 (1946)

Interpreting the scope of MARTIAL LAW established in Hawaii after the bombing of Pearl Harbor, Justice HUGO L. BLACK, for the Supreme Court, concluded that the Hawaiian Organic Act of 1900 extended constitutional guarantees to that TERRITORY. The creation of military courts empowered to try civilians violated the SIXTH AMENDMENT right to a FAIR TRIAL, thus contravening the intent of Congress. Chief Justice HARLAN FISKE STONE and Justice FRANK MURPHY wrote separate CONCURRING OPINIONS. Stone would have given greater scope to martial law but found the claim of EMERGENCY POWER unjustified here. Murphy joined the Court's opinion but preferred to rest on constitutional grounds, citing EX PARTE MILLIGAN (1866). Justices HAROLD BURTON and FELIX FRANKFURTER, in dissent, argued that the military situation and the conduct of the war, as an executive function, justified the emergency steps taken here.

DAVID GORDON

DUNCAN v. LOUISIANA
391 U.S. 145 (1968)

A 7–2 Supreme Court here overruled several earlier decisions and held that the FOURTEENTH AMENDMENT incorporated the Sixth Amendment right to TRIAL BY JURY. Louisiana tried Duncan for battery, a MISDEMEANOR charge punishable by up to two years' imprisonment. The court denied his request for a jury trial and sentenced him, upon conviction, to sixty days and a $150 fine. On appeal to the Supreme Court, the Justices abandoned the approach used in PALKO V. CONNECTICUT (1937) and ADAMSON V. CALIFORNIA (1947), where the Court had examined the circumstances to determine whether they preserved the implicit DUE PROCESS requirement of "fundamental fairness." In his opinion in *Duncan,* Justice BYRON R. WHITE asked instead whether trial by jury was "fundamental to the American scheme of justice" and concluded that history supported an affirmative response. Conceding a court's duty to distinguish between petty and serious offenses to determine which cases warranted this protection, White declined to do so as a general rule. He declared that an offense punishable by more than two years' imprisonment was sufficiently serious to apply the Sixth Amendment guarantee. Penalties involving less than six months' time were not accorded that right. As usual, Justices HUGO L. BLACK and WILLIAM O. DOUGLAS, concurring separately, advocated the total INCORPORATION DOCTRINE. Justices JOHN MARSHALL HARLAN and POTTER STEWART, dissenting, asserted that "the Court's approach and its reading of history are altogether topsy-turvy." Later decisions in WILLIAMS V. FLORIDA (1970) and *Apodaca v. Oregon* (1972) have limited the extent of the right incorporated.

DAVID GORDON

DUNN v. BLUMSTEIN
405 U.S. 330 (1972)

Tennessee restricted voting to persons with one year of residence in the state and three months in the county. The Supreme Court, 6–1, speaking through Justice THURGOOD MARSHALL, held this limitation a denial of the EQUAL PROTECTION OF THE LAWS. The durational RESIDENCE REQUIREMENTS had to pass the test of STRICT SCRUTINY, both because they penalized exercise of the RIGHT TO TRAVEL interstate and because they restricted the FUNDAMENTAL INTEREST in voting. The state's asserted justifications for the requirements were not necessary for achieving COMPELLING STATE INTERESTS. Fraud could be prevented by the LESS RESTRICTIVE MEANS of requiring registration thirty days before an election. The objective of an informed electorate bore only a tenuous relation to length of residence. Chief Justice WARREN E. BURGER dissented. The recently appointed Justices LEWIS F. POWELL and WILLIAM H. REHNQUIST did not participate.

The following year, the Court approved fifty-day residency requirements in *Marston v. Lewis* (1973) and *Burns v. Fortson* (1973).

KENNETH L. KARST

DUPLEX PRINTING PRESS COMPANY v. DEERING
254 U.S. 443 (1921)

In a case that brought the apparently prolabor provisions of the CLAYTON ACT before the Supreme Court, a 6–3 majority held that the act had placed no substantial bar to issuing INJUNCTIONS against labor unions. Section 6 of the act allowed unions to "lawfully [carry] out . . . legitimate objects," and section 20 denied the issuance of injunctions in a labor dispute unless essential to protect property. Duplex sought an injunction against a SECONDARY BOYCOTT which had been brought to force unionization of their open shop, claiming injury to and destruction of INTERSTATE COMMERCE. The Court declared that the boycott, even though peaceful, was not a "lawful method" of achieving the union's ends and thus violated the antitrust laws. According to the Court, section 6 only approved methods not expressly forbidden. Moreover, the majority redefined section 20: "labor dispute" was not meant generically but applied only "to parties standing in proximate relation to a controversy," an unwarranted gloss. They thus confined the section to a mere reflection of precedent, undoing congressional action.

Justice LOUIS D. BRANDEIS, joined by Justices OLIVER WENDELL HOLMES and JOHN H. CLARKE, dissented. Brandeis argued that the defendants shared a "common interest" with the employees, and the majority's denial of the existence of a dispute, within the act's meaning, simply ignored reality. Section 20, said the dissenters, attempted to render both sides equal. Although the Court refused to acknowledge that the Clayton Act had legalized any new methods for labor's use, a similar decision in BEDFORD CUT STONE V. JOURNEYMEN STONECUTTERS (1927) prompted enactment of the NORRIS-LAGUARDIA ACT in 1932, reversing the doctrinal direction.

DAVID GORDON

(SEE ALSO: *Labor and Antitrust Laws.*)

DU PONCEAU, PETER S.
(1760–1844)

Peter S. Du Ponceau arrived in America from France as Baron von Steuben's interpreter. Following service in the Revolution, he became a citizen of Pennsylvania where he was admitted to the bar in 1785. He defended the radical state CONSTITUTION of 1776 and was an Anti-Federalist, but as time passed he became a Jeffersonian Republican. He declined THOMAS JEFFERSON's offer of the chief justiceship of Louisiana. Du Ponceau was a founder and provost of the Law Academy of Pennsylvania. Among his books were *A Dissertation on the Nature and Extent of the Jurisdiction of the Courts of the United States* (1824), in which he advocated a FEDERAL COMMON LAW, and *A Brief View of the Constitution of the United States* (1834), in which he sought a middle course between a consolidated government and STATES' RIGHTS. In general he taught moderate nationalism and the supremacy of the union.

LEONARD W. LEVY

Bibliography

BAUER, ELIZABETH K. 1952 *Commentaries on the Constitution.* Pages 65–78. New York: Columbia University Press.

DUVALL, GABRIEL
(1752–1844)

Although he served as a Justice of the United States Supreme Court for nearly a quarter of a century, Gabriel Duvall had a relatively small impact on the development of American constitutional law. Born into a prominent Maryland Huguenot family, he studied law and was admitted to the bar in 1788. He supported the movement for independence during the 1770s, and held a number of minor posts under the revolutionary government. Following the adoption of the Maryland Constitution of 1777 he served as clerk of the State House of Delegates. In 1782 he was elected to the Maryland State Council and in 1787 to the House of Delegates as a representative from Annapolis. He was selected to be a delegate to the CONSTITUTIONAL CONVENTION, but, for reasons that are unclear, he declined to serve. He supported THOMAS JEFFERSON during the political battles of the 1790s, and was elected as a Democratic-Republican to Congress in 1794. He resigned the position less than two years later to become a judge of the Maryland Supreme Court. He helped to organize Maryland successfully for the Republicans in 1800 and often advised Jefferson and JAMES MADISON on appointments there. In December 1802 Jefferson appointed him to be the first comptroller of the United States Treasury.

In 1811 President Madison appointed Duvall to the United States Supreme Court. On the most important and controversial cases of the period—MARTIN V. HUNTER'S LESSEE (1816), GIBBONS V. OGDEN (1824), and BROWN V. MARYLAND (1827)—Duvall followed the lead of JOSEPH STORY and JOHN MARSHALL, and he even supported the Chief Justice when he dissented in OGDEN V. SAUNDERS (1827). DARTMOUTH COLLEGE V. WOODWARD was the only major case in which he failed to support Marshall, but since he dissented without opinion, it is not possible to determine his reasons. It is clear that Duvall knew and understood the law, and he did write straightforward and creditable opinions for the Court in several minor commercial law and maritime cases: *Archibald Freeland v. Heron, Lenox and Company* (1812); *United States v. January and Patterson* (1813), *Prince v. Bartlett* (1814); and *The Frances and Eliza v. Coates* (1823).

Although no abolitionist, Duvall had definite antislavery leanings. Dissenting from a Supreme Court ruling in *Mina Queen and Child v. Hepburn* (1812), in which HEARSAY evidence had been excluded "from a trial in which two black persons attempted to establish their freedom," he argued, with some force, "It appears to me that the reason for admitting hearsay evidence upon a question of freedom is much stronger than in cases of pedigree or in controversies relative to the boundaries of land. It will be universally admitted that the right to freedom is more important than the right of property." In another case, *LeGrand v. Darnall* (1829), speaking on behalf of the Court, Duvall ruled that a slaveholder's deeding of property to his ten-year-old son by a slave woman implied an intention to free the boy, despite a Maryland law that denied manumission to any slave under forty-five years of age.

As he grew older, Duvall's increasing infirmities and deafness caused numerous problems and considerable embarrassment for the Court. For almost a decade his resignation was expected, but he did not step down until January 1835, when he received assurances that ANDREW JACKSON planned to appoint fellow Marylander ROGER B. TANEY to the bench. Duvall died nine years later at the age of ninety-two.

RICHARD E. ELLIS

Bibliography

DILLARD, IRVING 1969 Gabriel Duvall. Pages 419–429 in Leon Friedman and Fred L. Israel, eds., *Justices of the Supreme Court 1789–1969.* New York: Chelsea House.

EAKIN v. RAUB
12 Sargeant & Rawle 330 (Pa. 1825)

In this otherwise insignificant Pennsylvania case, JOHN BANNISTER GIBSON offered the classic rationale for JUDICIAL RESTRAINT. His opinion is an explicit refutation of JOHN MARSHALL's arguments for JUDICIAL REVIEW in MARBURY V. MADISON (1803), a position which Gibson confessed he had once accepted, but more as "a matter of faith than of reason."

Gibson's major premise was that the judiciary had no right or power to void legislation without express constitutional warrant. Like Marshall, Gibson agreed that under a written CONSTITUTION, no branch of government could claim more than its granted powers. But as the legislature was supreme within the limits of its grant, Gibson argued, the judiciary could not annul those powers without "direct authority" from the constitution, "either in terms or by irresistible implication." While the judiciary might interpret legislation, it had no power to "scan the authority of the lawgiver." The legislature was superior, Gibson concluded, because "the power to will and to command is essentially superior to the power to act and obey."

Legislative indiscretions and abuses severely tested Gibson's fidelity to his principles. In *Norris v. Clymer* (1845) Gibson acknowledged that he had altered his views on judicial review because the Pennsylvania constitutional convention of 1837, by its silence, apparently sanctioned the power, and also "from experience of the necessity of the case." While Gibson undoubtedly moderated his views for some circumstances, he remained generally faithful to the notion of legislative superiority and the wisdom of judicial restraint. The "experience of the necessity of the case" involved legislative private acts that granted equity. The legislature had given substantially complete EQUITY jurisdiction to the courts in 1836, yet continued to act on its own, inevitably provoking clashes with the judiciary. In *Greenough v. Greenough* (1849) Gibson strongly defended an exclusive sphere for judicial power: "[T]he judicial power . . . is . . . so distributed . . . that the legislature cannot exercise any part of it." The next year, in *De Chastellux v. Fairchild,* he struck down an act ordering a new trial in an action of TRESPASS. "The power to order new trials is judicial," he said; "but the power of the legislature is not judicial."

In the *Eakin* opinion Gibson emphasized judicial independence, and he acknowledged legislative sovereignty, but only "within the limit of its powers." Further, he anticipated cases such as *De Chastellux* when he said that a legislative act directing a reversal of a court judgment would be "a usurpation of judicial power." Finally, he declared that when the judiciary was the prescribed organ to execute the constitution, such as in the conduct of trials, the judges were bound to follow the constitution, a legislative act notwithstanding.

Throughout the remainder of his long career, Gibson adhered to the spirit of *Eakin.* He insisted that the legislature's apprehension of public sentiment, not the fear of judicial interposition, offered the most effective barrier to unconstitutional action. With language similar to later opinions by MORRISON R. WAITE and OLIVER WENDELL HOLMES, Gibson declared that the responsibility for overcoming abusive acts rested not with the courts, but with the people, who were "wise, virtuous, and competent to manage their own affairs."

STANLEY I. KUTLER

E.C. KNIGHT CO., UNITED STATES v.

See: *Knight Co., E.C., United States v.*

ECONOMIC ANALYSIS AND THE CONSTITUTION

To what extent do "economic" ideas and concepts better enable us to understand the American Constitution?

One persisting characterization of the Constitution is that it succeeded both in arresting a decline in the American economy occurring under (and because of) the ARTICLES OF CONFEDERATION and in initiating an epoch of great prosperity. In reality, the shape of the economy during the 1780s was not particularly unsatisfactory. Indeed, in 1786 BENJAMIN FRANKLIN was willing to declare that "America was never in higher prosperity." But deflation injured creditors such as farmers, thereby provoking SHAYS' REBELLION in Massachusetts as well as inducing the enactment by the states of DEBTORS' RELIEF LEGISLATION.

The 1789 Constitution authorized the federal government to tax and to regulate commerce and centralized in the national government the power to print money. The long-range economic implications of these particular grants of power have been profound; their short-range consequences, however, may well have been modest. The federal power to tax was lightly exercised for many decades, and the federal power to print money was of limited importance in an era when "monetary policy" had not yet been recognized as a major instrument of national economic policy. The burst of prosperity in the decades following adoption of the Constitution owed largely to a surge in foreign trade, promoted by America's neutrality during the Napoleonic Wars—a neutrality that had been facilitated, to be sure, by the Constitution's recognition of centralized authority over foreign policy.

The first comprehensive "Economic Interpretation of the Constitution" to attract great attention was that of CHARLES A. BEARD in his celebrated 1913 study. Rejecting the popular view of the Constitution as the noble product of patriotic impulses, Beard assessed the Constitution as an "economic document" designed to advance certain economic interests to the detriment of others. In particular, he believed that "personalty" interests—"money, public security, manufacturers, and trade and shipping"—prevailed at the expense of "landed" interests of farmers and others, as well as at the expense of the unpropertied general public. Beard further asserted that the entire constitutional process had been initiated by a small group of men "immediately interested through their personal possessions in the outcome of their labors." In the preface to his 1935 edition, however, Beard denied that he had meant to suggest that the Framers were merely seeking to enrich themselves personally; rather, Beard explained, the Framers' own economic holdings merely made them receptive to the claims of more general economic groups.

The empirical ambitions that Beard displayed in his research remain commendable. But his particular empirical conclusions have been disputed by more recent scholarship. For example, those attending the CONSTITUTIONAL CONVENTION owned more in realty than they owned in securities; and it is not clearly true that creditors as a class supported the Constitution's RATIFICATION. Those portions of the Constitution that Beard singled out as establishing its economic preferences were the Constitution's general system of CHECKS AND BALANCES, which supposedly served to inhibit the unpropertied majorities; Congress's powers over taxation, war, commerce, and public lands; and the prohibitions on state coinage of money and on state impairment of contractual obligations. The DUE PROCESS clause of the FIFTH AMENDMENT Beard barely mentioned—even though the due process clause of the FOURTEENTH AMENDMENT had served as the basis for the Supreme Court's notorious decision in LOCHNER V. NEW YORK (1905) just eight years previously. Much of Beard's analysis of the Constitution now seems badly forced. In particular, his treatment of checks and balances is extraordinarily reductionistic in its failure to acknowledge that they were designed to serve any purpose other than the protection of certain property interests. In all, Beard's economic interpretation—though a major event in constitutional historiography—no longer commands adherents.

Economists have long been concerned with the objective of economic efficiency, and modern economists have developed an elaborate analysis in support of this objective. Might it be that the goal of efficiency has constitutional status? Insofar as original intent is relevant, information is needed on the economic views of the Framers. One philosophy common in eighteenth-century America was classical republicanism, which, in commending community, equality, and public virtue, was capable of disparaging commercial activity. The Framers, however, were also exposed to the newer tradition of Lockean liberalism, which strongly endorsed individualism and commercial activity. Propitiously, Adam Smith's *The Wealth of Nations* was published in 1776, the year of the DECLARATION OF INDEPENDENCE. Consistent with Smith's free market approach, ALEXANDER HAMILTON in THE FEDERALIST #11 espoused the idea of an open national economy: "The veins of commerce in every part will be replenished and will acquire additional motion and vigor from a free circulation of the commodities of every part." Hamilton began that paper with the observation that "the prosperity of commerce" is "a primary object of [enlightened statesmen's] political cares"—an observation that evidently contemplated mercantilist, rather than laissez-faire, policies. In *The Federalist* #10, JAMES MADISON made clear that he was hardly an economic egalitarian. "The first object of government" is to protect "the diversity of faculties of man, from which the rights of property originate." Elsewhere, however, *The Federalist* set forth theories that were imbued with republicanism; and in a 1792 essay Madison recommended policies that would "raise extreme indigence towards a state of comfort." In all, the free market interests of the Framers should neither be ignored nor exaggerated.

From the early nineteenth century on, free-market norms have exerted their most continuing influence upon constitutional doctrine through the negative underside of the COMMERCE CLAUSE. According to Justice ROBERT JACKSON in *H. P. Hood & Sons v. DuMond* (1949), "Our system . . . is that every farmer and every craftsman shall be encouraged to produce by the certainty that he will have free access to every market in the nation, that no home embargoes will withhold his exports, and that no foreign state will by custom duties or regulation exclude them. Likewise, every consumer may look to the free competition from every producing area in the Nation to protect him from exploitation by any." The Supreme Court has frequently endeavored to protect out-of-state sellers, out-of-state buyers, and multistate transportation concerns from discriminatory or excessive burdens imposed by self-interested state governments. In SOUTHERN PACIFIC COMPANY V. ARIZONA (1945), for example, the Court invalidated an Arizona statute limiting the lengths of trains operating in Arizona: the Court found that the statute's burdens on INTERSTATE COMMERCE were substantial, its safety benefits probably trivial. At times, however, the Court has been reluctant to intervene even when the prospect of Justice Jackson's "exploitation" has seemed keen. If a state enjoys a monopoly on an important natural resource, then the state, by imposing a substantial tax on the extraction of that resource, can "export" its tax burden, enriching its local treasury at the expense of consumers throughout the nation. Yet in *Commonwealth Edison Company v. Montana* (1981) a divided Supreme Court declined to hold that Montana's thirty percent severance tax on coal violated the commerce clause. The Court majority did not clearly disagree with the proposition that an "exported" state tax violates commerce clause ideals if it is not "fairly related to the services provided by the state." But the majority seemed to regard it as beyond the judicial function to assess the incidence of such a tax and to compute the value of those state-provided "services." (See STATE REGULATION OF COMMERCE; STATE TAXATION OF COMMERCE.)

Though the commerce clause imposes some limits on the states, its primary and explicit purpose is to confer powers on the federal Congress. In GIBBONS V. OGDEN (1824) the Court, in expansively interpreting what counts as interstate commerce, upheld a congressional enactment that implicitly abrogated a New York rule creating a steamboat monopoly between certain New York and New Jersey ports. Because this monopoly plainly offended free-market norms, the federal statute in *Gibbons* vindicated what Justice Jackson in *Hood* regarded as the "vision of the Founders." But what would the result have been in *Gibbons* had it been Congress, rather than the state, that had insisted on a monopoly? In exercising its commerce clause powers in the twentieth century, Congress has frequently chosen to restrict rather than enhance the competitive process. What is noteworthy is that the Supreme Court has found this in no way problematic. Justice Jackson's opinion in WICKARD V. FILBURN (1942) was shrewd in its perception of how intra-farm (and hence intrastate) events could have an aggregate impact on interstate economic arrangements. But the opinion was strikingly uninterested in the extent to which the federal statute it was approving brought about the cartelization of the otherwise highly competitive agricultural economy, thereby curtailing production and elevating consumer prices. Perhaps the point is that the "vision of the Founders," as understood by the Court, is not a competitive economy as such, but merely an economy free of anti-competitive restrictions imposed by the states. Besides accounting for the assumed irrelevance of free-market norms to congressional action under the commerce clause, this attribution of purpose can also explain the fact that the negative underside of the commerce clause has never been thought directly applicable to private monopolies that might severely restrict competition. Consider, however, Paul Freund's view that the spirit—though not the letter—of the commerce clause anticipates a "free national market," and that the commerce clause therefore needs to be supplemented by a strong federal antitrust program.

In the first third of the Twentieth Century, the Court did engage in a rather broad-ranging implementation of free-market values. The Court proceeded primarily in the name of the due process clauses of the Fourteenth and Fifth Amendments, clauses which enabled it to review all state and federal legislation, without regard to interstate impacts. During these years, the quite sophisticated approach of an Adam Smith was frequently replaced by the insensitive dogmatism of the Social Darwinist movement, thereby provoking Justice OLIVER WENDELL HOLMES's *Lochner* quip that "the Fourteenth Amendment does not enact Mr. Herbert Spencer's Social Statics." Since 1937, by contrast, the Court has consistently declined to invalidate "economic" legislation on substantive due process grounds and has stubbornly refused to subject that legislation to even minimal review. In WILLIAMSON v. LEE OPTICAL CO. (1955), for example, the Court unanimously and unhesitatingly upheld an Oklahoma statute requiring consumers to employ a licensed doctor merely in order to fit old eyeglass lenses into new frames.

Judicial tolerance of inefficient economic enactments is probably for the best. Economic analysis is an acquired taste; courts should not insist that legislators be educated in basic economic concepts, let alone that they keep abreast of the current literature on externalities and public goods. Moreover, most economists would acknowledge that a legislature might properly choose to sacrifice economic efficiency in order to achieve some desired distribution of wealth among societal groups. Also, even if certain private conduct is economically acceptable, a legislature could properly conclude that the conduct is interpersonally unfair in the particular way it enables A to cause harm to B.

Nevertheless, the argument favoring somewhat greater judicial scrutiny of inefficient legislation is not altogether without merit. In *Lynch v. Household Finance Corp.* (1972), a PROCEDURAL DUE PROCESS case, the Court—drawing on JOHN LOCKE, JOHN ADAMS, and WILLIAM BLACKSTONE—recognized an important connection between property and liberty. In addition, recent "commercial speech" cases such as VIRGINIA STATE BOARD OF PHARMACY v. VIRGINIA CITIZENS CONSUMER COUNCIL, INC. (1976) have attached considerable constitutional significance to marketplace norms. Moreover, aggressive JUDICIAL REVIEW is often defended on the ground of its ability to correct predictable breakdowns in the legislative process. *Southern Pacific* itself relied, for commerce clause purposes, on the Court's idea that out-of-state railroads are likely to be unrepresented in the state's legislative processes. For due process purposes, "consumers" as such are anything but a DISCRETE AND INSULAR MINORITY. But—as an economic analysis of the legislative process lucidly suggests—the very diffusion of consumers throughout society signifies that consumers may fare poorly in the legislature when challenged by producer groups, which are far better able to mobilize themselves in seeking protective legislation.

In any event, given the Supreme Court's position that neither the commerce clause (as a grant of power) nor the due process clause (as a restriction of power) includes any significant free-market content, it appears likely that Congress, if it chooses, could enact socialism (the ultimate rejection of market values) as this country's form of economic organization. It seems hard to deny that Congress could offer a RATIONAL BASIS on behalf of a socialist program that would satisfy the trivial demands of the commerce and due process clauses. To be sure, the takings clause would require that the nationalization of industry achieve a PUBLIC USE. But recent interpretations of the public use doctrine make it doubtful that the doctrine places any limits on Congress's choice of economic philosophy.

It is true that the takings clause would require Congress to afford JUST COMPENSATION to the shareholders of any companies nationalized. As a general matter, the just compensation requirement serves to rule out at least certain legislative efforts to redistribute wealth, whether by socialism or by more modest measures. It should not be forgotten that the progressive federal income tax—a central feature of federal policy during the last forty years—required for its legality a constitutional amendment. Still, the Supreme Court's invalidation of a pre-amendment federal income tax in POLLOCK v. FARMERS LOAN & TRUST COMPANY (1895) rested on a dubious interpretation of the DIRECT TAXES clause. Consider, moreover, a general tax on wealth or property, the proceeds of which are dedicated to financing welfare programs: it seems entirely clear that such a tax would not constitute a prohibited "taking." It appears, then, that wealth redistribution is constitutionally quite acceptable so long as it is both candid and evenhanded.

When a "taking" does occur, the "just compensation" that the takings clause requires has long been defined in terms of "fair market value." This "fair market value" gloss introduces, almost by hypothesis, certain capitalist values into constitutional doctrine. Yet that gloss can also be critiqued precisely from a free-market perspective. Assume a neighborhood of homes which, if individually available for sale, would each yield a price of $100,000. At any one time, however, only a limited number of houses are in fact offered for sale. To state that a homeowner is not interested in selling for $100,000 is to acknowledge that he presently values his ownership of the house at some figure in excess of $100,000. That excess is what economists call "consumer surplus." "Fair market value" provides less than full compensation in that it deprives the homeowner of this consumer surplus. From an ethical perspective, compensation that is less than full is arguably less than "just." Moreover, economic analysis can make clear that a "fair market value" standard for compensation has the practical effects of subsidizing government in its land acquisitions (by negating consumer surplus) and distorting government EMINENT DOMAIN choices (by encouraging government to ignore variations in consumer surplus among property owners).

Yet an economic analysis also verifies that the problem of measuring full compensation resists easy solution. Rendering consumer surplus compensable would not be satisfactory: consumer surplus would be notably difficult to quantify on an individual basis, and compensability would invite owners to dissemble in representing their surpluses' magnitude. Reminded of the difficulties involved in establishing the proper price for an eminent-domain forced sale, an economist might question the very practice of forced sales: he might suggest that the government be deprived of the eminent domain power altogether, thereby remitting the government to the opportunities afforded by the ordinary real estate market for purposes of acquiring land. Yet it is precisely the economist who can explain why this solution, too, would not always be satisfactory. Without the government's power of eminent domain, the owner of the final parcel within a tract of land that the government has otherwise succeeded in acquiring would be in a position—knowing of the government's situation—to extract an excessive monopoly price from the government-buyer. Because governments engage in tract acquisition more frequently than private parties do (only governments build superhighways, for example), it may make sense to limit the eminent domain power to governmental bodies. Obversely, the fact that the eminent domain power *is* generally limited to governments helps explain why private parties often are not in a good position to initiate large-tract projects.

As suggested above, an economic analysis is at least able to deepen understanding of the implications of constitutional doctrine. Correspondingly, such an analysis can correct what would otherwise be misunderstandings. In SHAPIRO V. THOMPSON (1969), for example, the Supreme Court considered the states' argument that WELFARE BENEFITS can be properly be denied to indigents who move into a state in order to collect higher benefits. Such an argument, the Court suggested, rested on the implicit premise that such welfare applicants are not "deserving"—a premise that the Court then rejected as unsound. But from the economist's useful perspective, the problem is not the grantee's desert but rather the grantor's incentives. States, anticipating an influx of indigents if welfare benefits are increased, may be dissuaded from raising those benefits, a dissuasion that might ill serve whatever the public's preference may be for compassionate welfare programs. Given an economic point of view, *Shapiro* unwittingly reduces the feasibility of state-administered welfare programs, thereby strengthening the argument in favor of the nationalization of welfare.

At the minimum, economic analysis can assist in identifying the costs or inefficiences of any proposed constitutional ruling. It is, of course, for the courts then to determine what weight to accord these costs in interpreting constitutional doctrine. The economist would be disturbed, however, by any disparagement of these costs that seems naive or inadequately considered. In *Shapiro*, for example, there is language stating that administrative inefficiencies, no matter what their magnitude, are automatically "uncompelling" for purposes of STRICT SCRUTINY review. But it is far from clear that the Court really adheres to such a position. In recent procedural due process opinions such as MATHEWS V. ELDRIDGE (1976), the Court has taken the efficiency criterion significantly into account.

In a number of important ways, then, an economic analysis can be clearly beneficial in the process of constitutional analysis. Nevertheless, economics will probably never achieve, in constitutional studies, the influence that it has secured in certain other fields of law. There are too many constitutional doctrines that endorse ideas or values that are largely beyond the economist's jurisdiction. To employ an extreme example, the economist's recognition of people's "taste for discrimination" is of little help in understanding the Constitution's moral assessment that racial discriminations are inherently invidious.

GARY T. SCHWARTZ

Bibliography

BEARD, CHARLES A. (1913)1935 *An Economic Interpretation of the Constitution.* New York: Macmillan.

BROWNLEE, W. ELLIOT (1941)1979 *Dynamics of Ascent.* New York: Knopf.

EPSTEIN, DAVID F. 1984 *The Political Theory of the Federalist.* Chicago: University of Chicago Press.

EPSTEIN, RICHARD A. 1985 *Takings.* Cambridge, Mass.: Harvard University Press.

FREUND, PAUL A. 1961 *The Supreme Court of the United States.* Cleveland, Ohio: World Publishing Co.

GOLDWIN, ROBERT A. and SCHAMBRA, WILLIAM A., EDS. 1982 *How Capitalist Is the American Constitution?* Washington, D.C.: American Enterprise Institute.

LEE, SUSAN P. and PASSELL, PETER 1979 *A New Economic View of American History.* New York: Norton.

MCDONALD, FORREST 1979 *We the People: The Economic Origins of the Constitution.* New York: Samuel Insull.

POSNER, RICHARD A. 1977 *Economic Analysis of Law.* Boston: Little, Brown.

WOOD, GORDON S. 1969 *The Creation of the American Republic, 1776–1787.* Chapel Hill: University of North Carolina Press.

WRIGHT, ESMOND 1978 *Fabric of Freedom 1763–1800.* New York: Hill & Wang.

ECONOMIC LIBERTIES AND THE CONSTITUTION

Contrary to its existing practice, the United States Supreme Court was once a strong guarantor of economic liberties. This was the period (1897–1937) of "economic due process." The Fifth Amendment and FOURTEENTH AMENDMENT provide that neither the federal nor state governments shall deprive any person "of life, liberty, or property, without DUE PROCESS OF LAW." The Court interpreted these prohibitions to mean that government could not, except in specified or extraordinary circumstances, prevent individuals or corporations from freely engaging in the production and distribution of goods and services.

However, since 1936 the Supreme Court has abandoned this interpretation; economic regulations now are subject to a very low level of review pursuant to which they are upheld whenever rationally related to the achievement of legitimate state purposes. Supporters of the more recent policy conclude that as a result, the Court has wisely steered a neutral role in the nation's economic affairs. Another interpretation of this policy, however, is that it has denied many people a fundamental liberty in a society dedicated to liberty—the opportunity to engage in economic activity. Our Constitution, it is argued, was not intended to be neutral in the conflict between liberty and authority, especially in the economic area.

There is little question that the Framers of the Constitution sought to limit greatly the commercial powers of the states. The tariffs and other economic barriers erected by the states against each other were a major source of discontent with the existing confederation. The regulatory abuses of the state legislatures are not so well detailed, but probably were no less responsible for such sentiments. According to ALEXANDER HAMILTON, writing in 1801, "creditors had been ruined or in a very extensive degree, much injured, confidence in pecuniary transactions had been destroyed, and the springs of industry have been proportionately relaxed" because of the failure of the states to safeguard commercial freedoms.

The deterioration of the economy that followed the revolutionary period led the states to what CHARLES EVANS HUGHES once described as "an ignoble array of legislative schemes for the defeat of creditors and invasion of contractual relations." Among other things, the states passed stay laws extending the due dates of notes and installment laws allowing debtors to pay their obligations in installments after they had fallen due. (See DEBTOR RELIEF LEGISLATION.)

JOHN MARSHALL, later Chief Justice, said in Virginia's ratification convention that economy and industry were essential to happiness, but the ARTICLES OF CONFEDERATION took away "the incitement to industry by rendering property insecure and unprotected." The Constitution, on the contrary, would "promote and encourage industry." JAMES MADISON stated that the passage of laws infringing contractual obligations "contributed more to that uneasiness which produced the convention . . . than those which accrued . . . from the inadequacy of the Confederation to its immediate objectives." During the CONSTITUTIONAL CONVENTION OF 1787 Madison said that an important object of the Union was "the necessity of providing more effectively for the security of private rights, and the steady dispensation of justice. . . . Was it to be supposed that Republican liberty could long exist under the abuses of it, practiced in [some of the] states?" ALBERT J. BEVERIDGE, Marshall's biographer, understandably concluded that the "determination of commercial and financial interests to get some plan adopted under which business could be transacted, was the most effective force that brought about [the Philadelphia convention]."

Several provisions of the Constitution appear to have been intended to curtail the economic regulatory authority of government. These are the prohibitions on the passage of EX POST FACTO laws which affect both the state and federal governments, and the ban on state laws impairing the OBLIGATION OF CONTRACTS. At the time the Constitution was framed and ratified, the term "ex post facto law" was applied to both penal and civil retroactive laws. In the criminal law, it was accepted that an ex post facto law was one that rendered an act punishable that was not punishable when it was committed. The term also described civil laws that operated retroactively to the detriment of a private owner of an iterest acquired or existing under prior law. Justice JOSEPH STORY of the MARSHALL COURT asserted that "every statute, which takes away or impairs VESTED RIGHTS acquired under existing laws, or creates a new obligation, imposes a new duty, or attaches a new disability, in respect to the transactions or considerations already passed, must be deemed retrospective."

Newspapers and judges of that period considered that stay and installment laws operated ex post facto. Members of Congress used the term in the broad sense. Some leading constitutional scholars held similar views on the meaning of the clauses. Although accounts of the CONSTITUTIONAL CONVENTION do not disclose precisely how the Framers defined the term, they are consistent with the view that ex post facto included retroactive civil laws. Nevertheless, a 1798 Supreme Court decision, CALDER V. BULL, interpreted the ex post facto clauses as applying solely to penal laws, thereby removing them as an important restraint on the regulatory powers of the federal and state legislatures.

In Chief Justice Marshall's opinion, the CONTRACT CLAUSE was intended to safeguard FREEDOM OF CONTRACT—which made it, under this view, a severe curb on state economic regulation. According to the Chief Justice, if a law limited the written understanding of the parties, it impaired their contractual obligation whether it was enacted before or after execution of the agreement.

However, the Supreme Court, in a 4–3 decision in OGDEN V. SAUNDERS (1827), ruled that the clause did not cover contracts executed subsequent to the adoption of a law: that is, it applied only to retroactive and not to prospective laws. The case involved a New York bankruptcy law, adopted prior to the execution of the promissory obligation in issue. In his only dissent on a constitutional issue in his thirty-four years as Chief Justice, Marshall vigorously contended that the New York law, although passed before the execution of the note, changed the understanding of the parties, and therefore impaired the obligation of their contract. The majority decision in the case followed a quarter of a century of failure to obtain a national bankruptcy law. Marshall's interpretation would have greatly limited the operation of state bankruptcy laws, and the majority rejected this outcome.

The BILL OF RIGHTS also evidences constitutional concern for material rights. The TAKINGS clause of the Fifth Amendment states that private property shall not be taken for PUBLIC USE without JUST COMPENSATION. The Fifth Amendment also states that no person shall be deprived of life, liberty, or property without due process of law. The SECOND AMENDMENT prohibits the confiscation of arms. The THIRD AMENDMENT restricts the quartering of troops. The FOURTH AMENDMENT prohibits unreasonable SEARCHES AND SEIZURES, and the Eighth Amendment prohibits excessive BAIL and fines.

Those who doubt that the Constitution protects the material rights from infringement by the states should consider section 1 of the Fourteenth Amendment, the second sentence of which reads: "No state shall make or enforce any law which shall abridge the privileges or immunities of citizens of the United States: nor shall any State deprive any person of life, liberty, or property, without due process of law; nor deny to any person within its jurisdiction the equal protection of the law." The framers of this amendment, the Congress of 1866, were concerned about protecting property and economic liberties as well as other personal rights.

While opinion is divergent as to the full meaning of the quoted language, commentators generally agree that it was primarily intended to make constitutional the CIVIL RIGHTS ACT OF 1866, placing it beyond the power of any subsequent Congress to repeal. The chief purpose of this act was to provide federal protection for the freed blacks in the exercise of certain described liberties.

The 1866 law was not confined to the protection of blacks. It was also intended to secure equality of rights for most other citizens. Thus Senator Lyman Trumbull, who wrote the original bill, viewed it as affecting state legislation generally, quoting in his introductory statement from a note to WILLIAM BLACKSTONE's commentaries: "In this definition of civil liberty it ought to be understood, or rather expressed, that the restraints introduced by the law should be equal to all, or as much as the nature of things will admit." The statute emphasized material, and not political or intellectual, considerations. It protected against discriminatory treatment the rights of most native-born citizens "to make and enforce contracts . . . and to inherit, purchase, lease, sell, hold and convey real and personal property."

The debates on section 1 of the Fourteenth Amendment further spell out Congress's commitment to preserving the material rights. Frequently quoted in the debates was Justice BUSHROD WASHINGTON's definition in CORFIELD V. CORYELL (1823), stating that privileges and immunities included "the right to acquire and possess property of every kind." For the thirty-ninth Congress, Sir William Blackstone and Chancellor JAMES KENT were highly authoritative on the powers and purposes of government. Both strongly emphasized the importance of economic and property rights in a free society.

There should be little doubt that the values of foremost importance to the Framers of many provisions of the Constitution encompassed the protection of economic and property rights.

BERNARD H. SIEGAN

Bibliography

CORWIN, EDWARD S. 1948 *Liberty Against Government.* Baton Rouge: Louisiana State University Press.

MCCLOSKEY, ROBERT G. 1962 Economic Due Process and the Supreme Court. *Supreme Court Review* 1962:34–62.

SIEGAN, BERNARD H. 1981 *Economic Liberties and the Constitution.* Chicago: University of Chicago Press.

______ 1984 The Economic Constitution in Historical Perspective. In Richard M. McKenzie, ed., *Constitutional Economics.* Pages 39–53. Lexington, Mass.: D.C. Heath.

ECONOMIC OPPORTUNITY ACT
78 Stat. 580 (1964)

Moving rapidly to consolidate his control over the administration he inherited from JOHN F. KENNEDY, President LYNDON B. JOHNSON in January 1964 declared "war on poverty" and announced his aim of building a "Great Society." The Economic Opportunity Act of 1964 was the centerpiece of the Johnson program.

Building on a BROAD CONSTRUCTION of the TAXING AND SPENDING POWER, the architects of the act erected a new conception of the role of the federal government. The government was to eliminate the "culture of poverty" that kept some people in economic distress. The act established several new agencies, the most important of which was the Office of Economic Opportunity (later the Community Services Administration) within the Executive Office of the President. It also created a plethora of new programs: Job Corps, Neighborhood Youth Corps, Head Start, etcetera.

From the beginning the war on poverty faced problems, and no poor person ever benefited from it as much as the bureaucrats who ran it. Funds were targeted on the basis less of economic need than of political patronage. And simultaneous expenditure for the war on poverty and the war in Vietnam depleted the treasury and fueled runaway inflation.

DENNIS J. MAHONEY

ECONOMIC REGULATION

In the field of economic policy, the composite constitutional powers of American governments—federal, state, and local—are extremely broad. Granted that governments may not implement economic policies that would violate the guarantees of the BILL OF RIGHTS or a few other constitutional limitations, within these spacious constraints there is little that governments may not do. But what they must or should do is more complex. As to macroeconomic policy, whose main instruments are monetary and fiscal, powers amount virtually to duties, for government could not function without taxing and borrowing, nor could the economy run at all smoothly if government declined to issue any money or take any steps to control its value. (See BORROWING POWER; MONETARY POWER; TAXING AND SPENDING POWER.) Just how these essential functions should be carried out is a matter of art and of debate, but few contend that the functions need not be carried out at all. However, as to microeconomic policies—those identified by usage as the substance of "economic regulation"—constitutional powers have not been regarded as inescapable duties. Although governments may intervene directly to regulate prices, wages, quality of products, and various other aspects of markets, they need not do so. Wages, for instance, have been regulated at some times but not others, in some occupations but not all, and so as to set minima but not maxima. In short, economic regulation is constitutionally optional.

Nonetheless, American governments have always practiced economic regulation, albeit in varying forms and degrees. Moreover, they have always been considered to possess broad authority to regulate, even if during a relatively short interval at the beginning of this century the federal courts invalidated a few particular forms of economic regulation without, however, casting doubt on the legitimacy of most other forms. This historically continuous practice of economic regulation shows that American governments were never dogmatically addicted to laissez-faire, notwithstanding a broad though sometimes faltering preference for private enterprise, and that the Constitution, as intended, written, and interpreted, is not a manifesto in favor of laissez-faire.

Before the Civil War, the constitutional authority of the states to carry on any and every form of economic regulation was seldom questioned. And this acceptance was not for want of regulations to question. On the contrary, state and local governments set the prices to be charged by wagoners, wood sawyers, chimneysweeps, pawnbrokers, hackney carriages, ferries, wharfs, bridges, and bakers; required licensing of auctioneers, retailers, restaurants, taverns, vendors of lottery tickets, and slaughterhouses; and inspected the quality of timber, shingles, onions, butter, nails, tobacco, salted meat and fish, and bread. This very incomplete list attests to an intention to exercise detailed control over the operation of markets, especially (though not only) those that have since been characterized as providing "public services" and those thought to be morally dubious because of association with usury, betting, intoxication, or excessive jubilation.

In the few instances before the Civil War when such regulations came before its eyes, the Supreme Court roundly affirmed their constitutional propriety, always provided (for so the issues arose) that the state's legislation did not collide with the federal commerce power. So in GIBBONS V. OGDEN (1824) JOHN MARSHALL referred to "the acknowledged power of a state to regulate . . . its domestic trade" and to adopt "inspection laws, quarantine laws, health laws . . . , and those which respect turnpike roads, ferries, etc." In the LICENSE CASES (1847) ROGER B. TANEY defined the STATE POLICE POWER as "nothing more or less than the powers of . . . every sovereignty . . . to govern men and things," including commerce within its domain, powers absolute except as restrained by the Constitution. Again, in COOLEY V. BOARD OF WARDENS (1851) the Court upheld the constitutionality of a state law requiring ships in the port of Philadelphia to employ local pilots, and further regulating the qualifications of pilots and their fees. Only one notable judgment of the time, by the highest court of New York, seems on casual reading to cast doubt on a state's regulatory power. In WYNEHAMER V. PEOPLE (1856) that court invalidated a law prohibiting the sale, and even the possession, of hard liquor on the ground that the statute acted retroactively and thus fell afoul of the DUE PROCESS clause in the state's constitution. The Justices agreed that a PROHIBITION law framed to operate prospectively would lie entirely within the legislature's power, and the only Justice who expressed reservations about outright prohibition went on to say: "It is . . . certain that the legislature can regulate trade in property of all kinds." Long and widespread practice throughout the country confirmed that state legislatures can indeed regulate the terms and conditions not only of trade but also of PRODUCTION, as well as entry into various occupations—though courts repeatedly insisted that the states' police powers, broad though they were, must be limited by profound constitutional antipathy to arbitrary action, such as that instanced by Justice SAMUEL CHASE in CALDER V. BULL (1798): "a law that takes property from A. and gives it to B."

Nor was this broad scope of the police power curtailed by decisions following shortly after the ratification of the FOURTEENTH AMENDMENT in 1868. In the SLAUGHTERHOUSE CASES (1873) the majority of the Supreme Court upheld a Louisiana law that closed down all slaughtering inside New Orleans, confined it to a designated area outside the city, and gave a single private company the right to operate a slaughterhouse there, despite the complaint by butchers that the statute, by depriving them of part of their usual trade, violated the PRIVILEGES AND IMMUNITIES and due process clauses of the Fourteenth Amendment. The Court concluded that the police power undoubtedly authorized regulation of slaughtering, and that the prohibitions imposed on the states by the amendment should not be interpreted as a limitation on reasonable exercises of the police power.

A broadly similar view prevailed in *Munn v. Illinois* (1877), which concerned the validity of a statute fixing the maximum charge to be levied by grain elevators in Chicago. Against the defendants' plea that the ceiling thus set on their earnings effectively deprived them of property without due process, Chief Justice MORRISON R. WAITE marshaled the long history of adjudication prior to 1868: "It was not supposed that statutes regulating the use, or even the price of the use, of private property necessarily deprived an owner of his property without due process of law." The word "necessarily" signaled a departure from the majority's blunt assertion in *Slaughterhouse* that due process should not box in the police power. Instead, the Court adopted in *Munn* the pared-down principle that states could, without offending against due process, regulate the prices of some kinds of business, "those AFFECTED WITH A PUBLIC INTEREST" or, as later usage had it, public service businesses. The tempting inference, that ordinary, "private" businesses are immune to economic regulation, though lent plausibility by some hints in the text, is not confirmed by any forthright judicial statement. (See GRANGER CASES.)

The "affectation with a public interest" DOCTRINE, though frequently invoked by courts in support of state regulation of railroads and public utilities, did not always carry the day. The first notable deviation, not only from *Munn* but from the longer previous tradition, took place in ALLGEYER V. LOUISIANA (1897). In question was Allgeyer's right to buy marine insurance from a New York company despite a Louisiana statute prohibiting out of state insurance companies from doing business there without a license. While conceding the state's power to regulate or even to exclude insurance companies domiciled in other states, the Court concentrated on every American citizen's privilege to pursue an "ordinary calling or trade" and, in the course of it, to make such contracts as might be useful and proper. By interfering with a person's exercise of that privilege, the Court unanimously held, Louisiana had abridged the Fourteenth Amendment's guarantee of liberty and property. To believe, however, as the decision's admirers and detractors alike have believed, that the Court thus read a sweeping FREEDOM OF CONTRACT into the Fourteenth Amendment, so as to equate all economic regulation with denial of due process, is to ignore a vital passage in the opinion, where RUFUS PECKHAM declared that the police power of a state "cannot extend to prohibiting a citizen from making contracts . . . outside the limits and JURISDICTION of the State, and which are also to be performed outside of such jurisdiction." Cavalier disregard of that essential qualification has made the *Allgeyer* opinion seem what it was not. If further evidence were needed, it was supplied by the Court's decision one year later in HOLDEN V. HARDY (1898), where the majority of seven upheld an act of Utah regulating the hours of labor in mines and smelters, without any suggestion that mines and smelters are businesses affected with a public interest, and notwithstanding considerable interference with freedom of contract.

Supposedly initiated by *Allgeyer,* the triumph of "economic due process" or SUBSTANTIVE DUE PROCESS—a triumph never fully consummated—was supposedly completed by LOCHNER V. NEW YORK (1905). Inasmuch as the Supreme Court there struck down a statute that limited the work of bakers to sixty hours a week, the decision could be so represented. But a close reading of the opinions, including the dissents, leads to the sounder conclusion that the statute was invalidated because, while purporting to be a measure for the public health, it adopted means that (in the majority's view) had no reasonable relation to that end, or alternatively because it was really an effort to interfere in the bargaining between master and employee, an effort lying outside the proper scope of the police power as constrained by the due process clause.

That the *Lochner* decision did not undermine economic regulation was demonstrated three years later in MULLER V. OREGON (1908), when the Supreme Court (with only one new member) upheld a restriction on hours of work of women as a reasonable means of achieving the proper end of public health, and was demonstrated again in BUNTING V. OREGON (1917), where the statute applied to men as well as women and to overtime wage rates as well as to hours. In ADKINS V. CHILDREN'S HOSPITAL (1923), however, the Court once again sailed closer to the *Lochner* tack, when it disallowed a minimum wage law. Nevertheless, despite the *Lochner-Adkins* line and reliance on decisions before, during, and after the brief era of laissez-faire activism, many states continued to pass and enforce laws regulating the conditions of labor as well as other economic relations, especially after the onset of the Great Depression.

The older line of interpretation, temporarily obscured but not reversed, was restored to predominance by the Supreme Court's decision in NEBBIA V. NEW YORK (1934). Here, while apparently relying on *Munn v. Illinois* (1877), the Court effectively reversed it by holding "that the private character of a business does not necessarily remove it from the realm of regulation of charges or prices." Indeed, the Court went on to say that it had upheld an extensive variety of economic regulations, a statement the accuracy of which it vindicated by citing some hundred PRECEDENTS that it had laid down during the three or four decades earlier. A further step toward closing the *Lochner* episode was taken in WEST COAST HOTEL V. PARRISH (1937); and the final (at least until the present) bit of punctuation was supplied in UNITED STATES V. CAROLENE PRODUCTS COMPANY (1938) when the Court committed itself not to invalidate regulatory legislation unless the law's irrationality offended against due process or it otherwise contravened specific constitutional guarantees such as those in the Bill of Rights.

Meanwhile, economic regulation by the federal government had been undergoing a roughly parallel development. Substantively it was less extensive, because until about the Civil War economic activity within the several states far outweighed that which crossed the boundaries of any state, because the federal government spent less and did less than state and local governments, and not at all because the federal government was more attached than were state and local governments to laissez-faire. Ample evidence to the contrary is afforded by the protective tariffs so vigorously advocated by ALEXANDER HAMILTON and HENRY CLAY and so widely supported, by the subsidies granted to transportation facilities in the name of INTERNAL IMPROVEMENTS, and by close regulation of ships and sailors involved in interstate and foreign navigation. If nevertheless the federal government did little to implement the COMMERCE CLAUSE during its first century, Congress's latent constitutional power was recognized and approved. When Marshall wrote in GIBBONS V. OGDEN (1824) that the commerce power "is complete in itself, may be exercised to its utmost extent, and acknowledges no limitations, other than are prescribed in the constitution," he prefigured later judicial pronouncements that the commerce power is effectively the NATIONAL POLICE POWER.

As might have been expected, the coexistence of two tiers of police power occasioned increasing collisions when, after the Civil War, the federal government expanded the exercise of its own power. Such collisions might have been resolved by simple-minded recourse to the SUPREMACY CLAUSE, but that solution would not have appealed strongly to judges who remembered that the professed objective of the Civil War had been, on the one side, to protect the autonomy of the states and, on the other side, to preserve a Union (rather than replace it by a unitary state). Recollections of the crisis reinforced the traditional effort to delineate clear boundaries between the domains of the states and that of the federal government.

A striking specimen of this issue arose from the increasing efforts of state governments after the Civil War to regulate railroad rates, and in particular to prohibit what many shippers regarded as iniquitous discrimination. In this instance a railroad had charged a shipper a certain amount for sending goods from one place in Illinois to New York City while charging another shipper less for sending the same sort of goods from another place in Illinois to New York City, though the latter distance was greater than the former. This habitual practice, known as LONG-HAUL–SHORT-HAUL DISCRIMINATION, violated an Illinois statute. In WABASH, ST. LOUIS, PACIFIC RAILWAY V. ILLINOIS (1886) the Supreme Court decided that, although the Illinois courts had confined application of the statute to transportation within the state, the statute was nevertheless invalid as applied to contracts for continous transportation through several states, so "interfering with and seriously embarrassing" interstate commerce. The counterargument, that state statutes of this sort might be permitted to stand until the federal government might occupy the field, became moot when in the following year Congress passed the INTERSTATE COMMERCE ACT, which among other things established the first federal REGULATORY AGENCY, the Interstate Commerce Commission. For twenty-seven years thereafter, until announcement of the SHREVEPORT DOCTRINE, a relatively comfortable equilibrium recognized the exclusive power of states to regulate purely intrastate transportation and of the federal government to regulate purely interstate transportation, though controversy occasionally erupted as to whether some particular regulation by one tier of government materially spilled over into the other's domain.

Concerning enterprises other than transportation, it was harder to draw a neat line between what is a fixture within a state and what though within a state is visiting it as a bird of passage or, according to a habitual metaphor, "flowing" through it. This difficulty was manifested in UNITED STATES V. E. C. KNIGHT CO. (1894), the Supreme Court's first ruling on the SHERMAN ANTITRUST ACT. It arose from a suit asking that the courts invalidate contracts by which the "Sugar Trust" had purchased four independent refineries, so achieving an almost complete monopoly of refining. Considering that the government had attacked the contracts rather than the trust itself, that the contracts concerned factories necessarily installed within a state, and that no proof had been offered to connect the contracts with a scheme to restrain interstate commerce, the Court held that the contracts were not reached by the Sherman Act; as so construed, the act was valid. In dissent, Justice JOHN MARSHALL HARLAN objected that the nub of the case was not the sugar trust's acquisition of the four refineries but its monopolization of interstate commerce. One may suppose that, contrary to Chief Justice MELVILLE W. FULLER'S pronouncement that "commerce succeeds to manufacture," Harlan would have preferred to say that manufacture, when ancillary to interstate commerce, falls within federal legislative power.

Similar partitioning of state and federal domains persisted in most such decisions down to 1936, accompanied by judicial reminders that if the reach of the commerce power were excessively widened, the states would be rendered economically otiose. So in HAMMER V. DAGENHART (1918) the Supreme Court, while agreeing that the working hours of children in mines and factories should be regulated (and in fact was regulated by every state), invalidated a federal child labor law on the ground that it would disturb the desirably "harmonious" balance between the police power and the commerce power. Similarly, when ruling in SCHECHTER POULTRY CORPORATION V. UNITED STATES (1935) that poultry slaughterers in New York City could not be reached by federal regulation, Chief Justice CHARLES EVANS HUGHES wrote: "If the commerce clause were construed to reach all enterprises and transactions which could be said to have an indirect effect upon interstate commerce, the Federal authority would embrace practically all the activities of the people and all the authority of the State over its domestic concerns would exist only by sufferance of the Federal Government."

That traditional view was substantially revised by *National Labor Relations Board v. Jones & Laughlin Steel Corporation* (1937), decided while President Franklin D. Roosevelt's Court reorganization plan was being vigorously debated. Technically the turn hinged on the Court's finding that the defendant company, besides owning steel mills and mines, owned and operated interstate railroads and water carriers and sales offices throughout the country; as the company was "a completely integrated enterprise," one in which manufacture and commerce might be said to have been completely unified, its relations with labor unions in its steelworks and mines as well as in its railroads and water carriers were properly subject to federal regulation. On a narrow view, the Court continued to adhere to the principle that state and federal regulation must coexist—as the Court took trouble to emphasize in UNITED STATES V. DARBY LUMBER COMPANY (1941)—and merely found federal power applicable to "national" firms; on a broader view the Court had considerably shifted the dividing line. The virtual obliteration of the line was confirmed by WICKARD V. FILBURN (1942), where the Court upheld federal regulation of wheat farming, by reinterpreting production as well as consumption on the farm, previously understood to be inherently local, as ingredients of an "economic market" which, being national and indeed international, was properly subject to federal regulation.

Rash though it may be to suppose that one can identify historical patterns, it might nevertheless be ventured that economic regulation by the states was never impeded by laissez-faire nor, except briefly and partially, by the doctrine of substantive due process, and that economic regulation by the federal government has expanded, generally though unsteadily, as a proportion of the whole. This summary, assuming it to be accurate, does not of course endorse the logical rigor of CONSTITUTIONAL INTERPRETATION that underlay those tendencies, nor does it prejudge their political desirability. Those who see private enterprise as self-serving and chaotic conclude that extensive economic regulation is a condition of social welfare; whereas minimalists maintain that economic regulation is desirable only in the event of market failure, that is, only in relation to enterprises that give rise to oppressive externalities or to industries that are natural monopolies. The Constitution provides ample scope for the former view but imposes no restrictions corresponding to the latter view. Despite some indications of "deregulation" in legislation and adjudication since 1960, it would be foolhardy to predict whether economic regulation will diminish or increase during the future.

WILLIAM LETWIN

Bibliography

HALE, ROBERT L. 1952 *Freedom Through Law: Public Control of Private Governing Power.* New York: Columbia University Press.

HAMMOND, BRAY 1957 *Banks and Politics in America from the Revolution to the Civil War.* Princeton, N.J.: Princeton University Press.

HANDLIN, OSCAR 1947 *Commonwealth: A Study of the Role of Government in the American Economy.* New York: Oxford University Press.

KOONTZ, HAROLD and GABLE, RICHARD W. 1956 *Public Control of Economic Enterprise.* New York: McGraw-Hill.

LETWIN, WILLIAM 1965 *Law and Economic Policy in America: The Evolution of the Sherman Antitrust Act.* Chicago: University of Chicago Press.

LIEBHOFSKY, H. H. 1971 *American Government and Business.* New York: Wiley.

MORRIS, RICHARD B. 1946 *Government and Labor in Early America.* New York: Columbia University Press.

WILSON, JAMES Q., ED. 1980 *The Politics of Regulation.* New York: Basic Books.

ECONOMIC STABILIZATION ACT
84 Stat. 799 (1970)

This measure authorized the most comprehensive peacetime ECONOMIC REGULATION in American history. The act extended a temporary sweeping DELEGATION OF POWER which authorized the President "to issue such orders and regulations as he may deem appropriate to stabilize prices, rents, wages, and salaries at levels not less than those prevailing on May 25, 1970." It authorized federal courts to issue INJUNCTIONS to enforce the presidential orders and mandated a $5,000 penalty for violation. A Democratic Congress passed the act at a time of persistent inflation; Republicans charged it was an election-year ploy attacking President RICHARD M. NIXON for failure to curtail rising unemployment, high interest rates, and a balance of payments deficit.

Nixon signed the measure but indicated he would have preferred to veto it and had no intention of using its authority. He opposed committing vast regulatory power to presidential discretion; if Congress favored controls, he said, it should "face up to its responsibilities and make such controls mandatory." One year later, amid growing disapproval of his economic policies, Nixon used the act to impose a ninety-day freeze on wages, prices, and rents. The President twice requested and received congressional extension as "in the public interest." The act was allowed to expire in 1974.

PAUL L. MURPHY

Bibliography

SILK, LEONARD 1973 *Nixonomics.* New York: Praeger.

EDELMAN v. JORDAN
415 U.S. 651 (1974)

This decision defines states' ELEVENTH AMENDMENT immunity from suit in federal court. Plaintiffs, alleging that Illinois welfare officials were unconstitutionally administering a welfare program financed by state and federal funds, sought the payments wrongfully withheld. The Supreme Court, in an opinion by Justice WILLIAM H. REHNQUIST, held the Eleventh Amendment to bar the request for retroactive relief but suggested that, as in EX PARTE YOUNG (1908), the Eleventh Amendment would not bar relief requiring the state to pay the costs of future constitutional compliance. In MILLIKEN V. BRADLEY (1977), the Court reconfirmed *Edelman* by requiring a state to pay the costs of future constitutional compliance.

Edelman also developed the principles regulating Congress's power to modify the states' Eleventh Amendment immunity. First, limiting earlier holdings such as *Parden v. Terminal Railway* (1964), *Edelman* held that mere participation by a state in a federal welfare program does not constitute a waiver of the state's Eleventh Amendment protection. It thus confirmed the narrow approach to waiver signaled by *Employees v. Department of Public Health and Welfare* (1973). Second, despite Congress's power to abrogate states' Eleventh Amendment immunity, *Edelman* stated that actions brought under SECTION 1983, TITLE 42, UNITED STATES CODE, are limited by the Eleventh Amendment. At the time, the state's protection from section 1983 actions seemed to stem from the Court's holding in MONROE V. PAPE (1961) that Congress had not meant to render cities liable under section 1983. With the overruling of that portion of *Monroe* in MONELL V. DEPARTMENT OF SOCIAL SERVICES (1978), the question whether section 1983 abrogated the states' Eleventh Amendment immunities reemerged. In QUERN V. JORDAN (1979), a sequel to *Edelman,* the Court held that section 1983 was not meant to abrogate the states' Eleventh Amendment protection.

THEODORE EISENBERG

EDUCATION AMENDMENTS OF 1972 (TITLE IX)
86 Stat. 373

Title VI of the CIVIL RIGHTS ACT OF 1964 prohibits discrimination on the ground of race, color, or national origin in programs receiving federal financial assistance. Title IX of the Education Amendments of 1972 extends Title VI's ban to discrimination on the basis of sex in federally assisted education programs. Title IX excludes from its coverage fraternities, sororities, Girl Scouts, Boy Scouts, and similar organizations, and scholarships awarded to beauty contest winners; the act does not require sexually integrated living facilities. Title IX instructs federal departments to implement its provisions through rules or regulations and authorizes termination of funding in cases of noncompliance.

Title IX has played a major role in increasing female athletic opportunities at educational institutions, and *North Haven Board of Education v. Bell* (1982) held that Title IX could reach sexually discriminatory employment practices. In *Cannon v. University of Chicago* (1979) the Supreme Court held that Title IX may be enforced through private civil actions. (See SEX DISCRIMINATION.)

THEODORE EISENBERG

Bibliography

DORSEN, NORMAN; BENDER, PAUL; NEUBORNE, BURT; and LAW, SYLVIA 1979 *Emerson, Haber and Dorsen's Political and Civil Rights in the United States,* 4th ed. Vol. II: 771–774, 883–893. Boston: Little, Brown.

EDUCATION AND THE CONSTITUTION

Basic to any discussion of the role of courts in educational decision making is the primacy of education in American ideology. Americans believe that education is central to the realization of a truly democratic and egalitarian society. It is through education that the skills necessary to exercise the responsibilities of citizenship and to benefit from the opportunities of a free economy will be imparted, no matter how recently arrived or previously disadvantaged the individual. Thus courts are concerned with protecting access to education. Moreover, since decision making by those charged with the administration of public education is seen as one of the most significant areas of law in terms of its effects on the lives of individuals and groups in our society, courts are inevitably drawn into reviewing the legitimacy of those decisions.

Education is primarily a state function in large part delegated to local school districts; the federal government has no direct constitutional responsibility for education. Nevertheless, Congress has enacted laws providing FEDERAL GRANTS-IN-AID to state and local educational agencies, as well as laws protecting the CIVIL RIGHTS of various categories of students. The constitutional authority for these statutes and their implementing regulations comes from Article I, section 8, clause 1, of the Constitution—the TAXING AND SPENDING POWER—which has been interpreted to permit Congress to attach conditions to the receipt of federal funds. Constitutional authority for congressional civil rights mandates governing educational institutions may also lie in section 5 of the FOURTEENTH AMENDMENT.

In the absence of federal legislation, are there constitutional constraints on the extent to which school authorities can control education and regulate the lives of students and teachers? Conversely, do students and teachers have the same constitutional rights as all citizens in our society, or are these rights limited within the school environment? The courts have acknowledged the importance of education to our democratic society and the importance of schools in preserving and transmitting the values—social, moral, or political—on which our society rests. The challenge is to inculcate those values without stifling the exercise of the freedom of expression, the freedom of religion, and other constitutional rights.

Until the middle of the twentieth century, education was almost the sole prerogative of school administrators and local boards of education. There were few legal constraints on school authorities and even fewer legal entitlements for teachers and students. Today various competing groups and individuals seek to control educational decision making—school boards, school administrators, teachers, parents, students, community leaders, minority groups, and federal and state agencies. Their struggles for control have often ended up in the courts. Since BROWN V. BOARD OF EDUCATION (1954), the Supreme Court has decided cases involving nearly every major area of educational policy.

Whether states may constitutionally compel all children to be educated in state-run schools was resolved by the Supreme Court in PIERCE V. SOCIETY OF SISTERS (1925), which held that while the state may compel all children to obtain schooling, parents have a constitutional right to choose between public and private schools. Nearly fifty years after *Pierce,* however, the Court held that there are certain constitutional interests of parents and children that may outweigh the state's interest in compelling children to attend school. The Court, in WISCONSIN V. YODER (1972), emphasized that parental direction of the religious upbringing of their children is an important interest to be protected. Although education is important to our democratic society, the interest of the state in compelling two more years of education beyond the eighth grade was outweighed by the burden on the RELIGIOUS LIBERTY of Amish parents. Only the dissent discussed the possibility that the child's interest might differ from that of the parent. In this perspective, *Yoder* seems not so much a case about the rights of children as a contest between parents and state over the power to inculcate values.

The state has a much greater role to play in selecting the curriculum and regulating what is taught in its own schools than it does in private schools. Education necessarily involves the process of selection; it also requires some degree of order to carry out the educational mission. However, as the Supreme Court noted in TINKER V. DES MOINES INDEPENDENT SCHOOL DISTRICT (1969), students (and teachers) do not "shed their constitutional rights . . . at the schoolhouse gate." Nevertheless, these rights may be circumscribed because of the "special characteristics of the school environment." The constitutional claims made on the courts with regard to schooling have been directed principally toward the protection of individual freedom and the attainment of equality. In the first instance, the countervailing factors are the stability and order of the educational enterprise; in the second instance, they center on differing conceptions of equality and the extent to which the educational enterprise is constitutionally obligated to respond to the equity-based claims of various groups absent a showing of intentional discrimination.

There has been much litigation regarding constitutional limitations on the inculcation of religious, political, and moral values in the public schools. The principal cases resolving the question of the proper place of RELIGION IN THE PUBLIC SCHOOLS were decided in the early 1960s. In ENGEL V. VITALE (1962) the Supreme Court held that a nondenominational prayer written by the New York Board of Regents for use in the public schools violated the FIRST AMENDMENT's prohibition of an ESTABLISHMENT OF RELIGION. A year later, in ABINGTON SCHOOL DISTRICT V. SCHEMPP (1963), the Court struck down the practice of reading verses from the Bible and the recitation of the Lord's Prayer in public schools, holding that the state's obligation to be neutral with regard to religion forbids it to conduct a religious service even with the consent of the majority of those affected. Justice TOM C. CLARK was careful, however, to distinguish between the study of religion or of the Bible "when presented objectively as part of a secular program of education" and religious exercises. In *Stone v. Graham* (1980), the Court held unconstitutional a Kentucky law that required that the Ten Commandments be posted on the walls of public school classrooms. The Court indicated, however, that the case would be different if the Ten Commandments were integrated into the school's curriculum, where the Bible could be studied as history, ethics, or comparative religion.

Although the extent to which religious socialization can be undertaken by school authorities has been sharply limited by the courts, the constitutional limits on political and moral socialization are less clear. *West Virginia State Board of Education v. Barnette* acknowledged the right of school authorities to attempt to foster patriotism in the schools, but held that the Constitution protects the right of nonparticipation in a patriotic ritual that, in effect, coerces an expression of belief. So too, the First Amendment appears to prevent the editing out of particular ideas with a view to prescribing orthodoxy in politics, religion, or other matters of opinion, but the removal of books and curricular materials from the school library may be permitted when it is done for educational reasons. In so holding, the plurality opinion in BOARD OF EDUCATION V. PICO (1982) recognized a limited right of students to receive information, at least in the context of removal of books from a school library, that was protected by the First Amendment.

The reverse side of the coin involves the extent to which parents have a constitutional right to exempt their children from being socialized by public schools to values to which they object. Absent a clear establishment clause claim, it is unlikely that parents can demand, on moral or philosophical grounds, that certain books or courses be excluded from the public school curriculum approved by school authorities. And absent a clear free exercise claim, it is also unlikely that parents can exempt their children from courses to which they may object, particularly as *Pierce* protects the option of sending their children to private schools if they disagree with the values being taught in the public school.

To what extent does the Constitution protect the right of free expression of students and teachers in the school environment? Complete freedom of expression is inconsistent with the schooling enterprise, which requires order and control. In *Tinker v. Des Moines Independent Community School District* (1969) the Court said that although an "undifferentiated fear or apprehension of disturbance is not enough to overcome the right to freedom of expression," school officials could limit expression if they showed that "the forbidden conduct would 'materially and substantially interfere with the requirements of appropriate discipline in the operation of the school.' "

With regard to First Amendment protection for student organizations, the Supreme Court, in *Healy v. James* (1972), held that "associational activities need not be tolerated where they infringe reasonable campus rules, interrupt classes, or substantially interfere with the opportunity of other students to obtain an education." Nevertheless, because the denial of recognition of a student organization is a form of prior restraint, school authorities have a heavy burden of proving the likelihood of disruption. Although the college in the *Healy* case had denied Students for a Democratic Society access to campus facilities, various other student organizations were permitted such access. Thus, *Healy* might be read as concerned with equal treatment—that is, if a college generally permits student organizations access to its facilities, although it could exclude all such organizations, it may not exclude an organization based on the political or social views it espouses. (See also WIDMAR V. VINCENT, 1981.)

May a teacher's right of expression be restricted in light of the special demands of the school environment? This question arises in a variety of contexts. Is the right of the teacher as citizen to free expression circumscribed by being an employee of the school system? Does the teacher as a professional have the right to determine course content, the selection of books, and the ideas and values to be presented in the classroom? Another question, not yet clearly resolved, is whether there is an independent right of ACADEMIC FREEDOM protected by the Constitution or whether that freedom is merely a corollary of the students' RIGHT TO KNOW.

The Supreme Court has never decided a case that squarely dealt with academic freedom in the classroom. Although KEYISHIAN V. BOARD OF REGENTS (1967) noted that academic freedom is "a special concern of the First Amendment" and that "the classroom is peculiarly the 'MARKETPLACE OF IDEAS'," the case involved neither the classroom nor the teacher's right to choose the curriculum or to teach in any particular way. Justice HUGO L. BLACK, in his concurring opinion in EPPERSON V. ARKANSAS (1968), expressed a narrow view of the "academic freedom" protected by the First Amendment: "I am . . . not ready to hold that a person hired to teach school children takes with him into the classroom a constitutional right to teach sociological, economic, political, or religious subjects that the school's managers do not want discussed. . . . I question whether . . . 'academic freedom' permits a teacher to breach his contractual agreement to teach only the subjects designated by the school authorities that hired him."

Although lower court decisions vary significantly as to whether "academic freedom" in the classroom is constitutionally protected, OBITER DICTUM in the plurality opinion in *Pico* suggested that school authorities have unfettered discretion to inculcate community values through the curriculum. If this view prevails, the teacher would appear to have no unilateral right to dictate the lessons (especially value lessons) to which the student will be exposed. If the classroom is the vehicle for imparting values, it cannot also be an open "marketplace of ideas."

Other issues of "academic freedom" actually involve the extent to which the freedom of expression of teachers as citizens, outside the classroom, must be balanced against the interest of the state as employer. For example, the Supreme Court held in *Pickering v. Board of Education* (1968) that, "absent proof of false statements knowingly or recklessly made by him, a teacher's exercise of his right to speak on issues of public importance may not furnish the basis for his dismissal from public employment." However, if the teacher's statements had been shown to have impeded his or her performance in the classroom or otherwise interfered with the regular operation of the schools, the speech might not be protected. And it is not clear whether protection would extend to teachers who voice their criticisms in the classroom.

The extent to which the Constitution constrains school authorities in the manner in which institutional rules and regulations are applied to students and teachers has been extensively litigated. Must certain procedures be followed before a student can be searched for EVIDENCE of the commission of a crime or a violation of a school rule, or before disciplinary action can be taken for failure to comply with institutional rules and norms?

A search made of private property is ordinarily held to be "unreasonable" under the FOURTH AMENDMENT if made without a valid SEARCH WARRANT. Even when the circumstances are such that courts have permitted warrantless searches, however (such as when necessary to prevent concealment or destruction of evidence), such searches usually require a showing of a PROBABLE CAUSE. However, the Supreme Court, in balancing school authorities' "substantial" interest in maintaining discipline against students' legitimate expectations of privacy, has fashioned a less protective standard. In NEW JERSEY V. T.L.O. (1985) the Court held that a search by school authorities is constitutional when there are reasonable grounds for suspecting that the search will turn up evidence, and when "the measures adopted are reasonably related to the objectives of the search and not excessively intrusive in light of the age and sex of the student and the nature of the infraction." Moreover, there is no warrant requirement for school searches.

Important constitutional values are incorporated in our notions of procedural fairness. GOSS V. LOPEZ (1975) held that state-created entitlements to a public education are protected by the due process clause of the Fourteenth Amendment; thus, the right to attend school may not be withdrawn on the ground of misconduct, absent fair procedures for determining whether the misconduct has occurred. However, having decided that some process is due, the procedural requirements in the school environment are minimal. In the case of a ten-day suspension of a student for disciplinary reasons, *Goss* required only that the student be given notice of the charges and an opportunity to explain his or her version of the story. Immediate removal from school may be justified in some cases even before the hearing. The hearing itself may simply be a brief meeting between the student and the administrator minutes after the alleged transgression. More stringent safeguards, however, may be required for deprivations of education significantly longer than the ten-day period involved in *Goss*. Just two years after *Goss*, the Court held, in INGRAHAM V. WRIGHT (1977), that although the administration of corporal punishment for violating school rules implicated a constitutionally protected liberty interest, "the traditional COMMON LAW remedies were fully adequate to afford due process." Thus, no advance procedural safeguards were constitutionally required. Because, according to the Supreme Court in BOARD OF CURATORS V. HOROWITZ (1978), academic grades and evaluations typically involve more subjective and evaluative judgments than do disciplinary decisions, the determination of "what process is due" turns on whether the disputed action is deemed to be academic or disciplinary in nature.

Yet another constitutional constraint on the public schools is embodied in the Fourteenth Amendment's EQUAL PROTECTION clause. The assertion of an entitlement to a minimum educational opportunity, to equal access to the schooling process, or to a specified educational outcome seeks to impose an affirmative obligation upon public schools. The most fully matured and litigated definition of equal educational opportunity is the right of minority students to be free of RACIAL DISCRIMINATION. The principal issues have concerned the requirements for finding that the Constitution has been violated, and the scope of the remedy once a constitutional violation has been established. The courts have held that intentional actions of school authorities constitute de jure SEGREGATION and, in some cases, that intent to segregate can be inferred from actions that have the foreseeable effect of fostering segregation. The courts have also held that the lapse of time between past acts and present segregation does not alone eliminate the presumption of causation and intent. Courts have also coped with the question whether RACIAL QUOTAS or AFFIRMATIVE ACTION to assist minorities who have been handicapped by past discrimination are unconstitutional, what are permissible remedial techniques (such as zoning, pairing of schools, or SCHOOL BUSING), when a systemwide remedy is permissible and what proof is required before a systemwide remedy can be ordered, and whether a court may require that school district boundaries be reorganized in order to devise an effective remedy.

Some students seeking equal educational opportunity are asserting a right to be free of discrimination on the basis of gender. However, most of the case law has developed under Title IX of the EDUCATION AMENDMENTS OF 1972 and its implementing regulations, and few of these cases have been decided on constitutional grounds.

In CRAIG V. BOREN (1976) the Supreme Court indicated that gender would not be treated as a SUSPECT CLASSIFICATION as is race, but as a category requiring an intermediate level of judicial scrutiny. Thus, a gender classification must serve important governmental objectives and must be substantially related to the achievement of those objectives before it can be upheld. MISSISSIPPI UNIVERSITY FOR WOMEN V. HOGAN (1982), involving the exclusion of males from MUW's School of Nursing, held that the state had failed to meet this standard. The state had argued that its single-sex admissions policy was designed to compensate for discrimination against women, but was unable to show that women had suffered discrimination in the field of nursing. For the majority, not only was the policy excluding males from the School of Nursing not compensatory, it tended "to perpetuate the stereotyped view of nursing as an exclusively women's job." The state also failed to show that the gender-based classification was substantially related to its purported compensatory objective. SEPARATE but equal educational offerings, if truly equal, and policies that are truly compensatory may still be constitutionally permitted in the case of gender.

Equal educational opportunity has sometimes been defined in terms of financial resources. The school finance reform movement of the early 1970s concerned inequalities in educational resources among school districts within a state. The issue in those cases was whether such inequalities were constitutionally impermissible. In SAN ANTONIO INDEPENDENT SCHOOL DISTRICT V. RODRIGUEZ (1973) the Supreme Court held that because Texas's school finance system neither employed a SUSPECT CLASSIFICATION nor touched on a fundamental interest, the financing scheme must be assessed in terms of the RATIONAL BASIS standard of review. The Supreme Court's opinion distinguished differences among school districts from a state "financing system that occasioned an absolute denial of educational opportunities to any of its children." Those statements raise two related questions: First, under what circumstances, if any, is exclusion of a class of children from public schools constitutionally justifiable? Second, if absolute deprivation of an education is unconstitutional, can this principle be extended to certain children who, although attending public schools, are "functionally excluded?" PLYLER V. DOE (1982) raised the first question and LAU V. NICHOLS (1974) the second.

In *Plyler v. Doe* the Court held invalid a state statute that permitted school districts to bar illegal alien children from public schooling. *Lau v. Nichols* involved non-English-speaking children who, even though they had the same access as other children to teachers and books, were "functionally excluded" because they could not understand what went on in the classroom where only English was spoken. The Court struck down this "functional exclusion" of students on statutory grounds.

Although students with limited English proficiency and handicapped students, like minorities or women generally, have sought equal treatment with respect to educational offerings, in some circumstances they have sought to impose affirmative duties on government to remove barriers to their opportunity to obtain an equal education—barriers that were not of the government's making. If they do not receive special treatment, the argument goes, they do not have an opportunity equal to that of others to take advantage of the education the government offers to all. The Supreme Court has not yet held that this latter approach to equal educational opportunity, focusing on an affirmative duty to provide special, additional services for certain groups, is constitutionally dictated; the only cases to come before the Court have been decided on statutory grounds.

Cleburne v. Cleburne Living Center, Inc. (1985) suggested in OBITER DICTUM that the handicapped are entitled only to application of the rational relationship standard to their equal protection claims. However, now that *Plyler v. Doe* has recognized the importance of education, perhaps the handicapped will receive some special solicitude for their claims to education. On the other hand, *Plyler v. Doe* involved the total exclusion of undocumented alien children from public schooling. Even in *Rodriguez,* the Court suggested that the total deprivation of education might be constitutionally impermissible. Thus, arguably, the total exclusion—or perhaps even the functional exclusion—of handicapped children from education would be unconstitutional, but there would be no constitutional violation in a state's failure to provide the special treatment and additional educational resources needed to bring them to the same starting line as other children.

Since Americans view education as of utmost importance to the maintenance of both their political and their economic systems, as well as to the well-being of the individual and his or her family, schooling is compulsory. The school is, on the one hand, the agency of government closest to the day-to-day lives of people and, on the other hand, the most inherently coercive. Thus courts have been concerned with the appropriate balance between individual liberties and societal interests as well as equal access to an education.

BETSY LEVIN

Bibliography

GOLDSTEIN, STEPHEN R. 1976 The Asserted Constitutional Right of Public School Teachers to Determine What They Teach. *University of Pennsylvania Law Review* 124:1293–1357.

HIRSCHOFF, JON 1977 Parents and the Public School Curriculum: Is There a Right to Have One's Child Excused from Objectionable Instruction? *Southern California Law Review* 50:871–959.

LEVIN, BETSY 1977 Current Trends in School Finance Reform Litigation: A Commentary. *Duke Law Journal* 1977:1099–1137.

VAN ALSTYNE, WILLIAM W. 1970 The Constitutional Rights of Teachers and Professors. *Duke Law Journal* 1970:841–879.

YUDOF, MARK G.; KIRP, DAVID L.; VAN GEEL, TYLL; and LEVIN, BETSY 1982 *Educational Policy and the Law.* Berkeley, Calif.: McCutchan.

EDUCATION OF HANDICAPPED CHILDREN ACTS

84 Stat. 175, 88 Stat. 579, 89 Stat. 773, 91 Stat. 230

Title VI of the Elementary and Secondary Education Amendments of 1970, the Education for All Handicapped Children Act of 1975 (EAHCA), and the Education of the Handicapped Amendments of 1974 and 1977 provide funds and a variety of federal programs to assist states in educating and training handicapped individuals. In states receiving federal educational assistance for handicapped children, the acts require a state policy assuring all handicapped children the right to a free appropriate public education, assuring private school education at no cost to parents if children are placed in private schools as the means of fulfilling state responsibilities under the acts, offering an individual educational plan for every handicapped child, and providing education with nonhandicapped children to the "maximum extent appropriate." The acts require substantial procedural safeguards to assure receipt of a free appropriate public education. EAHCA provides a private right of action, after exhaustion of administrative remedies, to compel compliance.

Board of Education v. Rowley (1982), the Supreme Court's first interpretation of EAHCA, held that the statutorily mandated "free appropriate public education" need not provide each child an opportunity to achieve her full potential. The statute mandates only an "adequate" education, one reasonably calculated to enable the child to achieve passing marks and advance from grade to grade.

THEODORE EISENBERG

Bibliography

BURGDORF, ROBERT L., JR. 1980 *The Legal Rights of Handicapped Persons.* Pages 213–245. Baltimore: Paul H. Brookes.

EDWARDS v. ARIZONA
451 U.S. 477 (1981)
OREGON v. BRADSHAW
462 U.S. 1039 (1983)

In *Edwards,* involving application of the MIRANDA RULES, the Court held that when an accused has invoked his right to have counsel present during interrogation, he has not waived that right simply by responding to further POLICE INTERROGATION unless he himself initiated additional communication. In *Bradshaw* the defendant, who had been advised of his rights and had asked for an attorney, later initiated a conversation with an officer who reminded him that he had no obligation to speak to the police. The prisoner said he understood, continued talking, and confessed. A plurality of the Court decided that the conviction in *Bradshaw* involved no breach of the rule of *Edwards,* which was meant to prevent badgering by the police.

LEONARD W. LEVY

EDWARDS v. CALIFORNIA
314 U.S. 160 (1941)

The years of the Great Depression were especially harsh for residents of the Dust Bowl. Many migrated to the West, and particularly California, in conditions of poverty graphically detailed in John Steinbeck's novel, *The Grapes of Wrath* (1939). California's hospitality to this "huge influx of migrants" was reflected in its "Okie law," making it a MISDEMEANOR knowingly to assist an indigent person in entering the state. Edwards, a Californian, went to Texas and drove his indigent brother-in-law back to California. For his troubles, he was given a six-month suspended jail sentence for violating the Okie law.

The Supreme Court unanimously reversed the conviction. Justice JAMES F. BYRNES, for the Court, concluded that the law violated the COMMERCE CLAUSE. The state's concerns with health and the integrity of its welfare funds were insufficient to justify so severe a burden on INTERSTATE COMMERCE. Justice WILLIAM O. DOUGLAS, concurring, would have rested decision on the PRIVILEGES AND IMMUNITIES clause of the FOURTEENTH AMENDMENT. Interstate travel was a privilege of national CITIZENSHIP, and to deny that privilege to indigents would create an inferior class of citizens. Justices HUGO L. BLACK and FRANK MURPHY joined this opinion.

Justice ROBERT H. JACKSON, concurring, agreed with Justice Douglas but also remarked that indigence was "a neutral fact—constitutionally an irrelevance, like race, creed, or color."

KENNETH L. KARST

(SEE ALSO: *Wealth Discrimination; Equal Protection of the Laws.*)

EFFECTS ON COMMERCE

"At the beginning Chief Justice [JOHN] MARSHALL described the federal commerce power with a breadth never yet exceeded." So said Justice ROBERT H. JACKSON for a unanimous Supreme Court in WICKARD V. FILBURN (1946), in the course of an opinion recognizing the broad sweep of Congress's modern power to regulate the national economy under the COMMERCE CLAUSE. Marshall's opinion in GIBBONS V. OGDEN (1824) read that clause's reference to commerce "among the several States" to mean "that commerce which concerns more States than one."

For the Constitution's first century, however, Congress did little to regulate INTERSTATE COMMERCE. The first major national regulatory laws were the INTERSTATE COMMERCE ACT of 1887, regulating railroads, and the SHERMAN ANTITRUST ACT of 1890. It fell to another Supreme Court to define the scope of congressional power, and at first the Court's definition was narrow. In UNITED STATES V. E. C. KNIGHT CO. (1895) the Court interpreted the Sherman Act, which prohibited monopolizing "any part of the trade or commerce among the several States," to exclude from its coverage a monopoly of sugar refining. Manufacturing was not commerce, said the Court; that "commerce might be indirectly affected" by a manufacturing combination producing ninety-eight percent of the nation's refined sugar was insufficient to bring the combination under the act's terms.

"Direct" effects on commerce, however, were found in a series of Sherman Act cases culminating in SWIFT & CO. V. UNITED STATES (1905). (See also STAFFORD V. WALLACE, 1922). Yet the Court persisted in its assertion that manufacturing was not commerce, even to the extent of holding in HAMMER V. DAGENHART (1918) that a congressional regulation of the interstate transportation of goods made by child labor was invalid because its purpose was to regulate manufacturing.

Meanwhile, the Court was developing quite another view of congressional power to regulate railroads. In HOUSTON, EAST AND WEST TEXAS RAILWAY CO. V. UNITED STATES, the "Shreveport case" (1914), the Court upheld an Interstate Commerce Commission order requiring a railroad to equalize certain interstate and intrastate rates. Such railroads were "common instrumentalities" of interstate and local commerce; the ICC was regulating only the relation between local and interstate rates. Taken seriously, the SHREVEPORT DOCTRINE implies congressional power to regulate intrastate activity because of its effect on interstate commerce.

After two decades of resisting the implications of the Shreveport case, the Court returned to its logic in NATIONAL LABOR RELATIONS BOARD V. JONES & LAUGHLIN STEEL CORPORATION (1937), the most important judicial victory for FRANKLIN ROOSEVELT's New Deal. There the Court upheld the WAGNER ACT's regulation of collective bargaining in application to a large steel manufacturer that obtained its raw materials in interstate commerce, manufactured steel in Pennsylvania, and shipped finished products to many other states. The opinion was written by Chief Justice CHARLES EVANS HUGHES, who had written the Shreveport case's opinion. A strike by manufacturing employees, said Hughes, would "directly" obstruct interstate commerce. "It is the effect upon commerce, not the source of the injury, which is the criterion."

In every succeeding case, the Supreme Court has applied this "effects on commerce" rationale to sustain congressional power. WICKARD V. FILBURN was the culminating case of ECONOMIC REGULATION, upholding congressional control of a small farmer's on-the-farm consumption of wheat, on the theory that Congress had a RATIONAL BASIS for believing that the aggregate of all such farmers' consumption would have "a substantial economic effect" on commerce. More recently the Court has employed similar reasoning to sustain congressional regulations aimed at distinctly noneconomic purposes. (See PEREZ V. UNITED STATES, 1971, extortion through "loan sharking"; HEART OF ATLANTA MOTEL V. UNITED STATES, 1964, racial segregation). Today, the "effects on commerce" rationale effectively allows Congress to be the judge of its own commerce clause powers.

KENNETH L. KARST

Bibliography

STERN, ROBERT L. 1946 The Commerce Clause and the National Economy, 1933–1946. *Harvard Law Review* 59:645–693, 883–947.

EIGHTEENTH AMENDMENT

The Eighteenth Amendment was framed and adopted to give a peacetime constitutional basis to the national PROHIBITION of alcoholic beverages, originally imposed as a war measure. Congress proposed the amendment in December 1917, and ratification was completed thirteen months later. Congress adopted the National Prohibition Act (VOLSTEAD ACT) to provide a mechanism for enforcement and penalties for violation of the prohibition.

The prohibition amendment provided the occasion for several controversies about the character and extent of the amending power. In Ohio, for example, the voters, by REFERENDUM, attempted to rescind their legislature's ratification of the amendment; but the Supreme Court held that procedure unconstitutional in *Hawke v. Smith* (1920). The Court, in the *National Prohibition Cases* (1920), rejected a number of arguments that the amendment was itself unconstitutional because of purported inherent limitations on the AMENDING POWER, including the contention that ordinary legislation cannot be made part of the Constitution and the assertion that the Constitution cannot be amended so as to diminish the residual SOVEREIGNTY of the states. In the same case the Court held that the requirement of a two-thirds vote in each house to propose amendments was met by the vote of two-thirds of the members present and voting and that amendments automatically become part of the Constitution when ratified by three-fourths of the states, whether or not promulgated by Congress or the secretary of state. In UNITED STATES V. SPRAGUE (1931) the Court rejected the argument that the amendment should have been ratified by state conventions rather than by state legislatures, holding that the mode of RATIFICATION OF CONSTITUTIONAL AMENDMENTS was a matter of congressional discretion.

Prohibition, a product of the reforming impulse that characterized PROGRESSIVE CONSTITUTIONAL THOUGHT, proved very difficult to enforce; and the widespread disregard of federal law scarcely tended toward that moral improvement that the authors intended. In 1933, the Eighteenth Amendment became the only constitutional amendment ever to be wholly rescinded when it was repealed by passage of the TWENTY-FIRST AMENDMENT.

DENNIS J. MAHONEY

EIGHTH AMENDMENT

See: Bail; Capital Punishment; Cruel and Unusual Punishment

EISENHOWER, DWIGHT D. (1890–1969)

The nation has often rewarded its military heroes by electing them to the presidency. General of the Army Dwight David Eisenhower, who had commanded the Allied forces in Europe during World War II, was President from 1953 to 1961. A 1915 graduate of West Point, Eisenhower held no public office—except his military command—before being elected President.

Eisenhower was a "moderate" Republican: conservative on economic matters but often liberal on social issues. Although he privately expressed to Chief Justice EARL WARREN his disapproval of BROWN V. BOARD OF EDUCATION (1954), he proposed, and successfully pressed for passage of, the CIVIL RIGHTS ACTS OF 1957 and 1960, the first such acts since Reconstruction. They expanded VOTING RIGHTS and created the CIVIL RIGHTS COMMISSION. In 1957, when the governor of Arkansas resisted a federal court's SCHOOL DESEGREGATION order (see COOPER V. AARON), the Eisenhower administration obtained an INJUNCTION forbidding the use of the National Guard to prevent INTEGRATION. When anti-integration rioting broke out in Little Rock, and the local authorities proved unable or unwilling to suppress it, Eisenhower ordered regular federal troops to the city.

Perhaps because of his military background Eisenhower was more cautious than some Presidents in exercising his power as COMMANDER-IN-CHIEF. He brought the KOREAN WAR to an end and, thereafter, no American troops were actively engaged in combat during his administration. When Chinese communists bombarded the Nationalist-held islands of Quemoy and Matsu, Eisenhower sought, and obtained, a JOINT RESOLUTION of Congress authorizing American military action, if necessary. In 1958, again authorized by congressional resolution, he ordered Marines to Lebanon to maintain order, but they did no actual fighting.

In foreign affairs, Eisenhower's was an activist administration. During the Eisenhower presidency the mutual defense treaty with Nationalist China and the Southeast Asia (SEATO) Treaty were signed, each committing the United States to the defense of distant—and not necessarily democratic—countries. Under the SEATO pact Eisenhower in 1954 began the American policy of assistance to South Vietnam that continued through the Vietnam War (1965–1973). Eisenhower supported the United Nations campaign of "anticolonialism," opposing America's European allies in Suez and Africa.

Domestically, Eisenhower was criticized for not speaking out forcefully against Senator Joseph R. McCarthy of Wisconsin, whose inquiries into communist influence in government threatened CIVIL LIBERTIES and often involved GUILT BY ASSOCIATION. Eisenhower promulgated EXECUTIVE ORDER 10450, which revamped the existing LOYALTY-SECURITY PROGRAM for federal employees.

During his two terms in the White House Eisenhower suffered three serious illnesses and was, for a time, virtually incapacitated. During those periods, Vice-President RICHARD M. NIXON presided over the cabinet and the National Security Council while routine matters were handled by a powerful White House staff. Eisenhower's illnesses raised questions about PRESIDENTIAL SUCCESSION in case of disability that were not resolved until passage of the TWENTY-FIFTH AMENDMENT.

Eisenhower made four APPOINTMENTS OF SUPREME COURT JUSTICES: Chief Justice EARL WARREN (1953) and Associate Justices JOHN MARSHALL HARLAN (1955), WILLIAM J. BRENNAN (1956), and CHARLES E. WHITTAKER (1957). Ironically, the moderate conservative Eisenhower made his most lasting mark on American constitutional history by appointing Justices who turned the Court toward liberal activism.

DENNIS J. MAHONEY

Bibliography

GREENSTEIN, FRED I. 1982 *The Hidden Hand Presidency: Eisenhower as Leader.* New York: Basic Books.

EISENSTADT v. BAIRD 405 U.S. 438 (1972)

At a BIRTH CONTROL lecture, Baird gave contraceptive foam to a woman presumed to be unmarried. Convicted in a Massachusetts court for distributing a contraceptive device, Baird sought federal HABEAS CORPUS. On appeal the Supreme Court, 6–1, held the conviction unconstitutional. Four Justices, concluding that GRISWOLD V. CONNECTICUT (1965) would bar prosecution for distribution of contraceptives to married persons, held that the EQUAL PROTECTION clause forbade the state to outlaw their distribution to the unmarried. Two Justices relied on *Griswold* alone, saying the record had not shown the recipient to be unmarried. Chief Justice WARREN BURGER dissented.

KENNETH L. KARST

(SEE ALSO: *Right of Privacy; Freedom of Intimate Association.*)

EISNER v. MACOMBER
252 U.S. 189 (1920)

A 5–4 Supreme Court declared that stock dividends did not constitute income subject to taxation under the SIXTEENTH AMENDMENT. Justice MAHLON PITNEY agreed that dividends were a "mere readjustment of the evidence of a capital interest already owned." Justices OLIVER WENDELL HOLMES, WILLIAM R. DAY, and JOHN H. CLARKE joined the DISSENTING OPINION of LOUIS D. BRANDEIS, who argued that the dividends represented profit (and thus income) and that the power conferred by the amendment ought to be measured by "the substance of the transaction, not its form." The Court subsequently narrowed the DOCTRINE of *Eisner* through a series of exquisite distinctions.

DAVID GORDON

ELASTIC CLAUSE

See: Necessary and Proper Clause

ELECTIONS, REGULATION OF

Defining "democracy," Henry B. Mayo has argued that the "one institutional embodiment . . . universally regarded as indispensable in modern democracies is that of choosing the policy-makers [representatives] at elections held at more or less regular intervals." In addition to their central democratic function of providing a mechanism for popular choice of officials, parties, and policies, elections have also been credited with two other important democratic functions: offering a forum for public participation and education in politics; and legitimizing the state's coercive authority and peacefully resolving social conflicts, because the public will generally accept officials and policies selected through fair, participative processes.

The Constitution, by its terms, mandates elections only for members of the House of Representatives and of the Senate. Article I, section 2, provides that members of the House shall be elected by the people of the respective states, and the SEVENTEENTH AMENDMENT provides similarly for senators. Persons meeting the qualifications necessary to vote for members of the larger house of the legislature in each state are constitutionally eligible to vote for representatives and senators. The Supreme Court, in WESBERRY V. SANDERS (1964), held also that "as nearly as practicable one man's vote in a congressional election is to be worth as much as another's." Subsequently, the Court has reaffirmed, in *Kirkpatrick v. Preisler* (1969), that in drawing congressional district boundaries states must "make a good-faith effort to achieve precise mathematical equality."

Characterizing its previous decisions, the Supreme Court, in *Rivera-Rodriguez v. Popular Democratic Party* (1982), said that it has "rejected claims that the Constitution compels a fixed method of choosing state or local officers or representatives." The guarantee clause of Article IV, section 4, has been construed to raise only POLITICAL QUESTIONS within the exclusive jurisdiction of Congress and does not, therefore, make state methods for selecting officials subject to constitutional adjudication in the federal courts. Nonetheless, every state employs popular elections to select presidential electors and its governor and legislature. Other state executive, administrative, and judicial officials, and all manner of local officials are also elected. In all, about 540,000 federal, state, and local offices are filled by election. In addition, the prevailing method of selecting political party nominees and of choosing final contenders in nonpartisan elections is the primary election.

Thirty-seven states provide for popular review of policymaking by the use of referenda, and twenty-one states allow popular instigation of policy through initiative elections. Referendum elections are also widely used in local governments throughout the nation, especially to review tax levies and charter revisions; and initiative elections are available in some local jurisdictions.

Although the Constitution prescribes elections only for Congress, virtually all elections have gradually been constitutionalized and therefore in some degree nationalized. The FIFTEENTH AMENDMENT prohibits the states from impairing the franchise on the basis of race, color, or previous condition of servitude. The NINETEENTH AMENDMENT forbids discrimination in electoral qualification based on sex; and the TWENTY-FOURTH AMENDMENT prevents the states from imposing "any poll tax or other tax" as a condition of voting for a candidate for federal office. The TWENTY-SIXTH AMENDMENT effectively grants the right to vote to all eligible citizens at eighteen years of age.

In the modern era, the right to vote has been declared a "fundamental right" under the FOURTEENTH AMENDMENT, in REYNOLDS v. SIMS (1964), because it is "preservative of other basic civil and political rights." The Supreme Court has therefore declared, in KRAMER v. UNION FREE SCHOOL DISTRICT (1969) and HARPER v. VIRGINIA BOARD OF ELECTIONS (1966), that every classification defining the right to vote in elections must be subject to strict judicial scrutiny and can be sustained only by independent judicial examination which finds "important," "compelling," or "overriding" state interests justifying restrictions on voting rights.

Mayo has argued that elections effectively promote democracy only if two conditions obtain. First, there must be "political equality in which [each] person should have one vote . . . and each vote should count equally." Second, citizens must have the "freedom to oppose," consisting of "formal rules . . . of effective choice—secret ballot, freedom to run for office, and freedom to speak, assemble, and organize for political purposes." It is these conditions for effective elections that the Supreme Court has generally promoted by declaring the vote a fundamental right and by rejecting poll taxes, residence requirements of extended duration, race and sex qualifications, limits on campaign spending, wide deviations from the ONE PERSON, ONE VOTE principle, and impediments to candidacy that significantly narrow voters' choices.

DAVID ADAMANY

(SEE ALSO: *Brown v. Socialist Workers '74 Campaign Committee, 1982.*)

Bibliography

MAYO, HENRY B. 1960 *An Introduction to Democratic Theory.* New York: Oxford University Press.

NOTE 1975 Developments in the Law—Elections. *Harvard Law Review* 88:1111–1339.

ELECTORAL COLLEGE

The Electoral College was hurriedly improvised by the Framers to placate all factions, provide a mechanism for electing GEORGE WASHINGTON, and leave hard questions for the states to resolve after Washington's retirement. Yet it turned out, unexpectedly, to be the forming and sustaining mold of the American party system.

At conception, the College was partly democratic and responsive to the large states, partly aristocratic and answerable to small states. It was apportioned mostly by population, with a delegate for each congressman and senator, and a state could select its delegates in any way it pleased. The Framers seem to have expected that, after Washington, the delegates—acting deliberatively or as agents of state legislatures—would normally fail to muster a majority for one candidate, and that most elections would be settled in the House of Representatives, with one vote per state.

This happened only in 1824, when the House chose JOHN QUINCY ADAMS over ANDREW JACKSON, the frontrunner in popular and electoral votes. In 1800 the House also elected THOMAS JEFFERSON, who tied with his running mate AARON BURR in the Electoral College. This deadlock led to the adoption of the TWELFTH AMENDMENT, which separated the votes for President and vice-president and gave the College its essential modern written constitutional constraints.

In the same decades, the College acquired two powerful unwritten constraints: party control and unit vote. Party control originated in congressional nominating caucuses in 1796 and shifted to state and national nominating conventions during the 1830s. It ended the notion of unbound, deliberative delegates seeking "continental" leadership. POLITICAL PARTIES, not delegates, did the deliberation.

The unit vote, chosen by all but one state by 1836, delivered each state's delegation as a unit to the winner of its popular vote. Unit voting already prevailed in the House and in most state elections, but the Electoral College gave it its widest leverage. It is kind to winners, hard on second parties, and almost prohibitive of third parties. It forces competition for shiftable votes, and it rewards inclusive, center-seeking, accommodational parties (and groups) while discouraging narrow, ideological, exclusive ones. Many scholars believe that the American two-party system has its roots in the unit vote and its taproot in the Electoral College.

The College has prompted two complaints, both largely, but not wholly, theoretical. It might elect as President an "unrepresentative" candidate who had won a minority of the popular vote or had been chosen deliberatively by "unfaithful" delegates, or who was chosen by a House manipulated by splinter groups. Or it might favor some voters against others: urban against rural, liberal against conservative, North against South, or large state against small. Yet we have had only two clear minority Presidents (RUTHERFORD B. HAYES and BENJAMIN HARRISON), one House-chosen President (John Quincy Adams), no Presidents chosen by the rare, unfaithful delegate, and no constitutional crisis over any of these contretemps.

The College was once thought to favor "pivotal" large-state over small-state voters, and hence urban, liberal over rural, conservative interests, but political change and closer analysis have qualified this impression. Liberals who defended the College in the 1950s fought unsuccessfully to abolish it, in favor of direct election, in the 1960s and 1970s.

Any of the major reform proposals—direct election, proportional representation by state, and election by congressional district—arguably would change outcomes of close elections. JOHN F. KENNEDY would have lost the 1960 election, with the same votes cast, under the proportional or district systems. But surely the same vote would not have been cast, for any alternative system would have changed voting and campaign strategies. The district system might have given more weight to rural voters, the direct or proportional systems to third parties. Changes in the party system in either case could have been profound.

These complexities may explain why Congress, which considers proposing an amendment to abolish the Electoral College after most close elections, has never actually done so. The Supreme Court has been likewise acquiescent, upholding state delegate allocations against all challenges and refusing, in *Delaware v. New York* (1966), to hear Delaware's complaint that New York voters had 2.3 times better odds of affecting the outcome of a presidential election.

WARD E. Y. ELLIOTT

Bibliography

CEASER, JAMES W. 1979 *Presidential Selection: Theory and Development.* Princeton, N.J.: Princeton University Press.

ELLIOTT, WARD E. Y. 1975 *The Rise of Guardian Democracy: The Supreme Court's Role in Voting Rights Disputes, 1845–1969.* Cambridge, Mass.: Harvard University Press.

PIERCE, NEAL R. 1968 *The People's President: The Electoral College in American History and the Direct-Vote Alternative.* New York: Simon & Schuster.

ELECTRONIC EAVESDROPPING

A Constitution written in the eighteenth century does not easily accommodate events and developments two centuries later. This has been especially true of the FOURTH AMENDMENT guarantee against unreasonable SEARCHES AND SEIZURES. Originally designed to deal with British soldiers breaking into buildings to search for smuggled goods under overly broad GENERAL WARRANTS, in this century it has had to deal with electronic eavesdropping. In 1928 Justice LOUIS D. BRANDEIS, dissenting in OLMSTEAD V. UNITED STATES, observed that "WRITS OF ASSISTANCE and GENERAL WARRANTS are but puny instruments of tyranny and oppression when compared with wiretapping." Today, there are surveillance devices far more penetrating and efficient than wiretapping, such as tiny microphones that catch the softest utterance hundreds of feet away; pen registers that record telephone numbers; "beepers" that trace movements over miles and for days; and electronic intensifiers that permit photography in almost complete darkness. Continuing advances in miniaturization and surveillance technology will produce even more intrusive and undetectable devices.

At first, the Supreme Court refused to apply any of the BILL OF RIGHTS to these technologies. The FIRST AMENDMENT ramifications were emphasized by Justice Brandeis in his *Olmstead* dissent when he pointed out the link between freedom of expression and invasions of personal security, a link established as early as the WILKES CASES (1763–1770), the first great English cases establishing the right of personal security against governmental intrusion. The *Olmstead* majority did not even mention the First Amendment, however, and that silence continues—the First Amendment has played an insignificant role in constitutional analyses of electronic surveillance, although in UNITED STATES V. UNITED STATES DISTRICT COURT (1972) the Supreme Court did address First Amendment considerations relevant to domestic NATIONAL SECURITY intelligence surveillance. In *Olmstead* the Fifth Amendment was explicitly ruled inapplicable, and electronic surveillance was held not to be a form of compelled self-incrimination. That ruling has been reaffirmed in cases such as HOFFA V. UNITED STATES (1966).

It is the Fourth Amendment that has become the primary constitutional instrument for control of electronic surveillance, and even that development was delayed some forty years. In 1928, the Supreme Court ruled in *Olmstead,* over dissents by Justices Brandeis and OLIVER WENDELL HOLMES, that the Fourth Amendment was limited to physical intrusions on property (TRESPASSES) that "seized" material objects, not intangible conversations. *Olmstead* was gradually eroded in the 1950s and 1960s, particularly with respect to conversations. The trespass aspect of *Olm-*

stead remained applicable, however, until 1967, when KATZ V. UNITED STATES extended Fourth Amendment protection to conversations and other things that people reasonably expect to keep private.

During the forty years between *Olmstead* and *Katz,* electronic surveillance was not left completely uncontrolled, however. Although the trespass requirement produced the ruling in GOLDMAN V. UNITED STATES (1942) that a room microphone placed against the outside of a wall did not violate the Fourth Amendment, telephone wiretapping itself was held to be prohibited by section 605 of the COMMUNICATIONS ACT of 1934, and this prohibition was applied to both federal and state law enforcement officers in NARDONE V. UNITED STATES (1937) and *Benanti v. United States* (1955). New York State also established statutory procedures for regulating electronic surveillance.

Empirical studies of wiretapping prior to 1968 showed that the controls established by these laws were ineffective. The Justice Department construed section 605 so narrowly that it was rarely invoked; judicial supervision of state wiretapping was virtually nonexistent. In addition, two forms of wiretapping and bugging remained completely uncontrolled: national security wiretapping, done pursuant to presidential directives; and surveillance with the consent of one of the parties to the conversation.

As to national security surveillances, the Federal Bureau of Investigation installed over 7,000 wiretaps and room microphones during 1940–1960, and one treasury agent additionally admitted to having installed over 10,000 wiretaps and microphones between 1934 and 1948; other federal agencies also did electronic eavesdropping. Although all of these intrusions were purportedly for national security purposes, many were revealed to be for crime control or political purposes, the most notorious of which was the massive electronic surveillance of MARTIN LUTHER KING, JR., between 1963 and 1968 ordered by FBI Director J. EDGAR HOOVER.

Consent surveillance, either on a telephone extension or with informers equipped with secret radio transmitters or recorders, is probably the most widely practiced type of electronic surveillance, although so much of electronic surveillance remains secret that one cannot be certain. The Supreme Court had consistently held, before and after the *Katz* decision, that under both the Constitution and the Communications Act, consent surveillance is free from virtually all constitutional or statutory controls. Leading cases on this point include ON LEE V. UNITED STATES (1952) and UNITED STATES V. WHITE (1971). The only federal restriction prior to 1968 was a very limited rule of the Federal Communications Commission barring secret recordings.

Ever since the 1937 *Nardone* decision, the Justice Department had sought authority for electronic surveillance. This effort gained impetus from Attorney General ROBERT F. KENNEDY's campaign against organized crime in 1961–1963 and the revelation that FBI Director Hoover had illegally installed hundreds of taps and bugs on alleged organized crime figures under the "national security" authority, many of which stayed in place for many years; the disclosure of these surveillances placed scores of convictions in jeopardy. With the Court's decisions in BERGER V. NEW YORK (1967) and *Katz,* the stage was set for congressional action. In these two decisions the Court discarded the "trespass" requirement imposed by *Olmstead,* ruled that electronic surveillance was subject to Fourth Amendment requirements, and set out relatively detailed requirements for a valid statute, including: (1) a specification and detailed description of the place to be searched, the conversations to be overheard, and the crime under investigation; (2) a limit on the period of intrusion; and (3) adequate NOTICE of the eavesdropping to the people overheard.

Six months after *Katz,* Congress passed the OMNIBUS CRIME CONTROL AND SAFE STREETS ACT (1968), Title III of which legitimated electronic surveillance for law enforcement purposes. The statute provides that electronic surveillance of conversations is prohibited, upon pain of a substantial jail sentence and fine, except for: (1) law enforcement surveillance under a court order; (2) certain telephone company monitoring to ensure adequate service or to protect company property; (3) surveillance of a conversation where one participant consents to the surveillance; and (4) national security surveillance insofar as it is within the President's inherent constitutional powers, whatever those may be. Law enforcement surveillance must meet certain procedural requirements, which include: (1) an application by a high ranking prosecutor; (2) surveillance for one of the crimes specified in Title III; (3) PROBABLE CAUSE to believe that a crime has occurred, that the target of the surveillance is involved, and that EVIDENCE of that crime will be obtained by the surveillance; (4) a statement indicating that other investigative procedures are ineffective; and (5) an effort to minimize the interception.

A judge must pass on the application and may issue the order and any extensions if the application meets the statutory requirements. Shortly after the surveillance ends, notice must be given of the surveillance to some or all of the persons affected, as the judge decides, unless he agrees to postpone the notice. Illegally obtained evidence may not be used in any official proceedings, and a suit for damages may be brought for illegal surveillance, though a very strong good faith defense is allowed. In addition, the manufacture, distribution, possession, and advertising of devices for electronic surveillance for private use are prohibited.

The legislation is written in terms of federal officials but it also authorizes state surveillance if a state passes a law modeled on the federal statute, though the state may (as have some states, like Connecticut) impose more stringent requirements. More than half the states plus the DISTRICT OF COLUMBIA have passed such statutes, though many rarely use the authority. State surveillance is concentrated in New York, New Jersey, and Florida, mostly for narcotics and gambling offenses.

Title III raised many constitutional issues but almost all have been resolved in its favor. For example, a common contention is that electronic eavesdropping is inherently uncontrollable and necessarily intrudes on vast numbers of innocent people who use phones or rooms under surveillance, thus violating the particularization requirements of the Fourth Amendment. In order to meet this objection, and to avoid turning the surveillance authorization into a general warrant, Title III requires that interceptions be minimized. The Supreme Court, however, made this requirement very easy to meet by its decision in *Scott v. United States* (1978). The lower courts do not impose sanctions for the failure to minimize interception, partly because minimization is often very difficult to achieve or supervise. One federal judge in a major drug case excused the interception of seventy-three calls between a suspect's babysitter and her friends and classmates with the comment that although these conversations were indeed "teenage trivia . . . the eavesdropper, unless possessed of the prescience of a clairvoyant, could hardly predict when they might become relevant, or when they might be interrupted by an adult with more pressing problems." There are also many cases where police do not minimize interceptions even though they could. For example, some police listen to every conversation, including privileged conversations between lawyers and their clients, but record only those they think appropriate. In one case, it was accidentally revealed that police had recorded all conversations but had prepared a minimized set for use in court. Where room microphones are used, minimizing the interceptions is virtually impossible, especially if the microphones are placed in areas to which the public has access.

The *Berger* case also seemed to require that the interception be limited to specific and quite short time periods. Title III, however, permits thirty-day authorizations on a twenty-four-hour per day basis, with an unlimited number of extensions, and many interceptions remain in continuous operation for many months. The Report on Applications for Orders Authorizing or Approving the Interception of Wire or Oral Communications for 1981, issued by the Administrative Office of the United States Court, indicates that almost half the 106 federal interceptions reported for 1981 lasted thirty or more days.

One of the most significant ways of enforcing Fourth Amendment requirements is by imposing sanctions for their violation. Imposing these sanctions, of course, requires an awareness by the victim that a search has taken place, and of how it was conducted. With a conventional search, such conditions are easy to meet, but electronic surveillance is surreptitious and may never be discovered. The Supreme Court has therefore insisted that notice of the interception be given to the persons named in the application as targets of the surveillance. The statute, however, permits indefinite postponement of this notice, and this provision, too, has been upheld.

Critics have charged that judicial supervision has been minimal and ineffective, particularly on the state level. At hearings before the National Commission for the Review of Federal and State Laws Relating to Electronic Surveillance, many witnesses lamented the inability or unwillingness of state judges to supervise the process closely.

Passage of the statute, while effectively ending the constitutional debate, has not ended the dispute over the value of electronic eavesdropping. Critics have charged that the device is used almost exclusively for minor crimes involving gambling and drugs; is quite useless for major crimes and especially those involving organized crime, the avowed target of the statute; is very expensive; is largely unsupervised by the judiciary; and has invaded the privacy of millions. For support, they rely on the staff studies of the National Commission. Proponents reply that the technique has produced some very useful results, that many of the problems are those attending any new technique, and that more sophisticated use will produce better results. The opposing views were set out in detail in the Report of the National Commission; over a vigorous minority dissent the majority of the commission supported the use of electronic surveillance under the statute, with some modification.

Two types of surveillance remain uncontrolled by Title III: consent intrusions and national security surveillance. Title III totally exempts interceptions by government officials if an official is a party to the conversation of if there is consent by one of the parties; a private interception that is consented to is also exempt, unless the interception is for the purpose of committing a tortious, criminal, or "other injurious act," the meaning of which is not clear. Several states, however, have imposed more stringent requirements on consent surveillance than the federal statute, such as a warrant, either by statute (California, Georgia) or under their own state constitutions (Alaska, Montana). The Supreme Court, however, continues to rule in cases like *United States v. White* (1971) that consent surveillance does not implicate the Fourth Amendment.

National security surveillance continues to pose difficult constitutional questions. Presidents since FRANKLIN D. ROOSEVELT have claimed inherent executive power to use electronic surveillance to obtain intelligence for national security purposes, and have authorized such intrusions on their own, without prior judicial approval. Most courts have upheld such a power, where national security surveillance involving foreign powers and agents is concerned. But where American citizens or groups are targeted for domestic security purposes, the Supreme Court, in *United States v. United States District Court,* ruled unanimously that the President has no INHERENT POWER to use warrantless electronic surveillance. The Court did suggest that Congress could authorize procedures for domestic intelligence gathering that are less stringent than those of Title III for law enforcement, but so far Congress has not done so.

Intelligence gathering for foreign security purposes is now governed by statute. The 1976 Report of the Senate Select Committee to Study Governmental Operations with Respect to the Intelligence Agencies disclosed massive abuses of executive power to tap telephones and bug rooms for national security purposes, often with the approval of the incumbent President. These abuses included taps on the telephones of National Security Agency advisers authorized by President RICHARD M. NIXON in 1969; on the Los Angeles Chamber of Commerce in 1941; on congressmen in the early 1960s in connection with the "sugar lobby"; and FBI taps and bugs on Martin Luther King, Jr., to find "communist" influence. From 1940 to 1975, the FBI alone installed some 10,000 taps and bugs; the National Security Agency, the Central Intelligence Agency, local police, and many other governmental agencies have also engaged in national security surveillance.

These disclosures resulted in the passage in 1978 of the Foreign Intelligence Surveillance Act, which requires approval from a court for national security surveillances of foreign powers or agents. The President is denied extrastatutory inherent or other power to use electronic surveillance for foreign intelligence within the United States—though not outside—and no Americans may be eavesdropped upon unless their activities have some element of criminality about them. The court operates secretly, and there have been very few published rulings and very little public information about it. The constitutionality of this act and its procedures—which are much less demanding than those under Title III for law enforcement purposes—has been sustained.

The courts have also tried to grapple with other forms of electronic surveillance. In *Smith v. Maryland* (1979) pen registers, which record the telephone numbers called, were held outside Title III and not in conflict with the Fourth Amendment; the Supreme Court concluded that the user has no reasonable expectation of privacy in the numbers called. Electronic signaling devices ("beepers") attached to cars to enable their movements to be traced have also been held to be without Fourth Amendment protection because cars are generally traced while on public streets and highways (*United States v. Knotts, 1983*); if the device is attached to a container or other item that is taken into a private area, however, a warrant and probable cause are required (*United States v. Karo,* 1984).

In 1928, after describing the dangers that the emerging modern technology presented to individual liberty, Justice Brandeis asked, "Can it be that the Constitution affords no protection against such invasions of individual security?" Almost a half century later, it is clear that such protection is available—if the nation wants it.

HERMAN SCHWARTZ

Bibliography

ADMINISTRATIVE OFFICE OF THE UNITED STATES COURTS 1968–1982 *Reports on Applications for Orders Authorizing or Approving the Interception of Wire or Oral Communications.* Washington, D.C.: Administrative Office.

AMERICAN BAR ASSOCIATION PROJECT ON STANDARDS FOR CRIMINAL JUSTICE 1974 *Standards Relating to the Administration of Criminal Justice; Electronic Surveillance.* Pages 33–52. New York: Institute of Judicial Administration.

CARR, JAMES G. 1977 (with 1983 supp.) *The Law of Electronic Surveillance.* New York: Clark Boardman.

NATIONAL COMMISSION FOR THE REVIEW OF FEDERAL AND STATE LAW RELATING TO ELECTRONIC SURVEILLANCE 1976 *Report* and *Staff Studies.* Washington, D.C.: Government Printing Office.

SCHWARTZ, HERMAN 1977 *Taps, Bugs, and Fooling the People.* New York: Field Foundation.

——— 1968 The Legitimation of Electronic Eavesdropping: The Politics of "Law and Order." *Michigan Law Review* 67:455–510.

UNITED STATES CONGRESS, SENATE SELECT COMMITTEE TO STUDY GOVERNMENTAL OPERATIONS WITH RESPECT TO INTELLIGENCE ACTIVITIES 1976 *III Final Report.* 94th Congress, 2d session.

ELEMENTARY AND SECONDARY EDUCATION ACT

79 Stat. 27 (1965)

This first general school aid bill in American history broke an impasse that had long stymied legislation to provide federal moneys to elementary and secondary schools. Previous efforts toward such action had foundered on the question whether education was a state, not federal, function; whether segregated school systems should receive federal aid; and whether aid to private as well as public schools would violate the FIRST AMENDMENT's establishment clause. The segregation issue had been settled by the CIVIL RIGHTS ACT OF 1964. The 1964 elections had filled Congress with federal aid advocates untroubled by STATES' RIGHTS issues. The church–state controversy over federal assistance to parochial schools continued but was generally resolved here for the first time.

As passed, the measure, which appealed to the CHILD BENEFIT THEORY, authorized specialized aid to districts with children from low-income families. Private schools would share in aid to some specialized services such as shared-time projects and educational television. The act gave school districts wide discretion in using the federal funds; it required, however, that the funds be used to meet the special needs of educationally deprived children and that private schools be included in any benefit sharing. The act also authorized for five years grants to states for purchase of textbooks and library material, and for funding supplementary community educational services that schools could not provide. It expanded the 1954 Cooperative Research Act, authorizing a five-year program of grants for new research and training in teacher methods, and it provided for grants to strengthen state departments of education.

Despite overwhelming congressional support for the act, critics continued to express constitutional doubts. The use of public funds for books in parochial schools and special educational centers could not be justified, it was argued, because funds would be channeled directly to religious schools. The AMERICAN CIVIL LIBERTIES UNION contended that providing instructional materials and supplementary services to church schools was an unconstitutional subversion of the principle of SEPARATION OF CHURCH AND STATE. In FLAST V. COHEN (1968) the measure was challenged on First Amendment grounds, but the Court did not rule on the constitutional issues in the case.

PAUL L. MURPHY

ELEVENTH AMENDMENT

The Eleventh Amendment of the Constitution provides that "the JUDICIAL POWER OF THE UNITED STATES shall not be construed to extend to any suit in law or EQUITY, commenced or prosecuted against one of the United States by citizens of another State, or by citizens or subjects of a foreign State." Congress submitted this amendment, on votes of twenty-three to two in the Senate and eighty-one to nine in the House of Representatives, for ratification in March 1794. By February 1795, the legislatures of three-fourths of the states had ratified, but, because of delays in certification of this action, adoption of the amendment was not proclaimed until 1798.

According to traditional theory the purpose of the amendment was to correct an erroneous interpretation of the Constitution by the Supreme Court. Impetus for the amendment undoubtedly was the unpopular decision in CHISHOLM V. GEORGIA (1793)—one of seven early suits instituted against a state by citizens of other states or by ALIENS. In *Chisholm* the Court, voting 4–1, held that the judicial power of the United States and the JURISDICTION of the Court reached such suits under the provision in Article III extending the federal judicial power to "Controversies between a State and Citizens of another State . . . and between a State . . . and foreign States, Citizens or Subjects."

Although the language of Article III is broad enough to support the *Chisholm* holding, proponents of the theory that the amendment was adopted to correct an error in constitutional interpretation have argued that (1) the doctrine of SOVEREIGN IMMUNITY, exempting the sovereign from unconsented suits, was part of the COMMON LAW heritage at the time the Constitution was adopted, and hence implicitly qualified some delegations of judicial power in Article III; and (2) an understanding to that effect emerged during the ratification debates.

Existence of an implicit common law qualification upon the various delegations of federal judicial power is doubtful, however. While the supposition that the immunity doctrine was already incorporated into American law appears sound, at least some state immunity surely was surrendered under the Constitution. The purpose behind the various delegations of judicial power to the United States was to create a judiciary competent to decide all cases "involving the National peace and harmony." Surrender—rather than retention—of state immunity is consonant with that objective. Nor is the argument that the ratification debates evidenced an understanding that the states would be immune from suit persuasive. While ALEXANDER HAMILTON, JAMES MADISON, and JOHN MARSHALL offered assurances to that effect in reply to Anti-Federalist objections, these objections were not quieted; and other leading Federalists, including EDMUND RANDOLPH and JAMES WILSON—members of the Committee of Detail where most provisions of Article III were drafted—took the contrary view.

While some proponents of the Eleventh Amendment probably understood it to be corrective, the broad support enlisted for its adoption can be better explained in terms of diverse perceptions and objectives. These ranged from the desire of STATES' RIGHTS advocates to repudiate the extravagant nationalism manifested by Federalist justices in their *Chisholm* opinions, to Federalist perceptions that the amendment effected only a relatively insignificant restriction upon part of the DIVERSITY JURISDICTION of the federal judiciary. Experience was accumulating that suit against a state in the Supreme Court was cumbersome and unnecessary for the maintenance of federal supremacy. Moreover, assumption of a major portion of state indebtedness and rapid liquidation of the remainder had allayed a Federalist concern that partially accounted for the original grant of federal judicial power.

Judicial construction of the amendment has been shaped by the view that as a corrective measure, it restored common law sovereign immunity as an implicit qualification upon some grants of judicial power in Article III. As interpreted, the amendment bars any suit against a state, including those raising federal questions, instituted by private plaintiffs, regardless of CITIZENSHIP (*Hans v. Louisiana,* 1890), as well as by foreign states (*Monaco v. Mississippi,* 1934) in federal court. In general, only where another state or the United States is plaintiff, is a state subject to unconsented suit in federal court (*Virginia v. West Virginia,* 1907; (*United States v. Mississippi,* 1965). The amendment does not affect Article III rights of a state to institute suits in federal courts, nor does it preclude appeals by private plaintiffs in actions commenced by a state. (See COHENS V. VIRGINIA, 1821.)

Although the amendment literally limits the federal judicial power—which, by general rule, may not be modified by consent of the parties—as shorthand for the doctrine of sovereign immunity, it has always been interpreted to permit exercises of Article III powers upon a state's waiver of immunity from suit in federal court. Such waivers ordinarily must be explicit (EDELMAN V. JORDAN, 1974); however, implied and imputed waivers, although exceptional, are not unknown (*Parden v. Terminal Railway,* 1964).

The amendment imposes an absolute bar against unconsented suits commenced in federal court by private plaintiffs against state governments and their agencies. To this generalization, there is a single but increasingly important exception. Congress, pursuant to its enforcement powers under the FOURTEENTH AMENDMENT, may create federal causes of action against the states and thereby deprive them of immunity (FITZPATRICK V. BITZER, 1976). Whether such authority can be inferred from other powers delegated to the national government has not been settled.

The exemption from suit enjoyed by the states under the amendment does not extend to their political subdivisions nor, in general, to governmental corporations (*Lincoln County v. Luning,* 1890). Of paramount importance in restricting the impact of the amendment is the availability of relief in suits instituted against state officers for acts performed or threatened under color of unconstitutional state legislation. The issues whether and to what extent the amendment bars suits against state officers for official acts have occasioned more litigation under the amendment than any others, and the course traversed by the Court from OSBORN V. BANK OF THE UNITED STATES (1824) through *In re Ayers* (1887) to EX PARTE YOUNG (1908) was tortuous. In some early cases the amendment was held applicable only to suits in which a state was a defendant of record, but this rule was never firmly established. Later cases turned on whether a suit against a state officer was substantially a suit against the state itself. In *Ayers* the Court held that a suit against a state officer is a suit against the state unless the officer's act, if stripped of its official character, constitutes a private wrong; but this rigorous test was abandoned in *Ex parte Young,* a landmark case which, despite its unpopularity at the time, fixed the law for the future. While adhering to the general rule that a suit against a state officer is barred by the amendment if it is substantially against the state itself, the Court adopted the fiction that mere institution of state judicial proceedings by a state officer pursuant to an allegedly unconstitutional statute is a wrong for which federal equitable relief is available. The theoretical difficulties posed by this formulation are grave and many, but in facilitating direct access to the federal courts to test the validity of state legislation, *Young* is of transcendent importance in maintaining federal supremacy and the RULE OF LAW. Adopted as the instrument of judicial protection of the rights of property and enterprise, the *Young* principle today does the same essential service in the protection of personal rights and liberties. Even so, not every act of a state may be reached through suit against its officers. Where such suits are adjudged to be against the state itself—actions affecting the public treasury for past wrongs and those seeking to dispossess the state of property—the Eleventh Amendment remains a bar (*Edelman v. Jordan,* 1974).

CLYDE E. JACOBS

(SEE ALSO: *Atascadero State Hospital v. Scanlon, 1985; Pennhurst State School v. Halderman, 1981, 1984.*)

Bibliography

JACOBS, CLYDE E. 1972 *The Eleventh Amendment and Sovereign Immunity.* Westport, Conn.: Greenwood Press.

NOWAK, JOHN E. 1975 The Scope of Congressional Power to Create Causes of Action Against State Governments and the History of the Eleventh and Fourteenth Amendments. *Columbia Law Review* 75:1413–1469.

ELFBRANDT v. RUSSELL
384 U.S. 11 (1966)

By a 5–4 vote, the WARREN COURT struck down a section of Arizona's Communist Control Act of 1961, which subjected state employees to perjury prosecutions if they subscribed to a state LOYALTY OATH while members of the Communist party, later joined the party, or joined "any other organization" having for "one of its purposes" the overthrow of the government. For the majority, Justice WILLIAM O. DOUGLAS argued that even knowing membership in the Communist party could not expose one to criminal punishment without proof of specific intent to further the organization's illegal goals of violent revolution. Such a law "infringes unnecessarily on protected freedoms. It rests on the doctrine of 'GUILT BY ASSOCIATION' which has no place here. . . ."

The dissenters were led by Justice BYRON R. WHITE. "If a government may remove from office . . . and . . . criminally punish . . . its employees who engage in certain political activities," White wrote, "it is unsound to hold that it may not, on pain of criminal penalties, prevent its employees from affiliating with the Communist Party or other organizations prepared to employ violent means to overthrow constitutional government."

MICHAEL E. PARRISH

ELKINS v. UNITED STATES
364 U.S. 206 (1960)

In Elkins the Supreme Court overthrew the SILVER PLATTER DOCTRINE, an exception to the EXCLUSIONARY RULE allowing use in federal prosecutions of evidence seized by state officers in illegal searches. Two changes had undermined the authority of the doctrine since it was formulated in WEEKS V. UNITED STATES (1914). First, the extension of the constitutional prohibition of unreasonable searches to the states in WOLF V. COLORADO (1949) meant that the doctrine now permitted federal courts to admit evidence unconstitutionally seized. Second, the doctrine vitiated the policies of about half the states, which had in the meantime independently adopted an exclusionary rule.

The *Elkins* opinion, in addition, contains the most thorough and convincing analysis in favor of the exclusionary rule to be found in any opinion of the Court; it thus laid the groundwork for imposition of the rule on the states the following year in MAPP V. OHIO (1961).

JACOB W. LANDYNSKI

ELKINS ACT
32 Stat. 847 (1903)

The decisions in INTERSTATE COMMERCE COMMISSION V. CINCINNATI, NEW ORLEANS & TEXAS PACIFIC RAILWAY (1897) and its companion case, *ICC v. Alabama Midland Railway Company,* had stripped the Interstate Commerce Commission of much of its regulatory power. As a result, many of the evils the INTERSTATE COMMERCE ACT had been designed to remedy had revived. One of the most pernicious abuses was the practice of rebating. Federal legislation forbidding the practice would not only save the railroads money but also protect them against demands imposed by the trusts. Sponsored by the railroads, the Elkins Act made any deviation from the published rate schedule (whether a rebate or a general rate reduction) a criminal offense. Although Congress repealed the imprisonment penalty, it quadrupled the fine and directly subjected the corporations to the penalty; no longer could the principal escape punishment for its agents' acts. Anyone who sought or received a rebate (or other rate concession) was equally liable to criminal penalties. Despite the act's significance, further legislation would prove necessary. Charges were now enforced, but the ICC was still powerless to replace discriminatory rates. Congress would expand ICC powers and extend regulatory control over the rails in the HEPBURN and MANN-ELKINS ACTS.

DAVID GORDON

Bibliography

SHARFMAN, ISAIAH L. 1931–1937 *The Interstate Commerce Commission.* Vol. 1. New York: Commonwealth Fund.

ELLSWORTH, OLIVER
(1745–1807)

Oliver Ellsworth played a key role in the creation of the United States Constitution in 1787 and the establishment of a national judiciary during the Constitution's first decade.

Born into a well-established Connecticut family, he entered Yale in 1762, but left after two years to attend the College of New Jersey (Princeton) where he was graduated with a B.A. in 1766. Ellsworth returned to Connecticut and studied theology for about a year, but abandoned it for the law and was admitted to the bar in 1771. One of the ablest lawyers of his day, he built up an extremely lucrative practice. He also entered politics and was elected to the state's General Assembly in 1773. A warm supporter of the patriot cause against Great Britain, he helped supervise the state's military expenditures during the war for independence, was appointed state attorney for Hartford in 1777, a member of the Governor's Council in 1780, and a judge of the Connecticut Supreme Court in 1785. He also served as one of the state's representatives to the Continental Congress for six terms (1777–1783). While in Congress he became a member of the Committee of Appeals which heard appeals from state admiralty courts, and in this capacity he ruled on the important case of Gideon Olmstead and the British sloop *Active* which eventually culminated in UNITED STATES v. PETERS (1809).

In 1787 Connecticut selected him to be one of its three delegates to the federal CONSTITUTIONAL CONVENTION in Philadelphia. He played an active role at the convention and won respect for his orderly mind and his effectiveness as a debater. Ellsworth favored the movement to establish a strong and active federal government with the power to act directly on individuals and to levy taxes, as a substitute for the weak central government created by the ARTICLES OF CONFEDERATION. But he also thought that the VIRGINIA PLAN went too far in a nationalist direction. "The only chance of supporting a general government lies in grafting it on those of the original states," he argued. In particular, he opposed the idea of apportioning representation in both houses of Congress according to population, to the clear advantage of larger states. To resolve the differences between the large and the small states he helped forge the successful GREAT COMPROMISE which apportioned representation in the lower house according to population and in the Senate by a rule of equality, with each state having two senators. Ellsworth also played an active role on the Committee on Detail which produced the basic draft of the United States Constitution.

Following adoption of the Constitution, Connecticut elected Ellsworth to the United States Senate. He recognized that the Constitution as written and ratified was only a basic outline; an actual government had to be created and its powers implemented. He supported ALEXANDER HAMILTON's financial program and was opposed to attempts to ally the United States too closely with France, but his most important contribution was the drafting of the JUDICIARY ACT OF 1789. This law was in many ways an extension of the Constitution itself, for it fleshed out the terse third article of that document which dealt with the nature and powers of the federal judiciary. The Judiciary Act of 1789 specified that the Supreme Court should consist of six Justices, that each state should have a district court, and that there should be three circuit courts consisting of two Supreme Court Justices sitting with a district judge. Under this law the fedral courts were given exclusive JURISDICTION in a number of important areas and CONCURRENT JURISDICTION with the state courts in other matters. The act also provided that decisions of the state courts involving the Constitution or laws or treaties of the United States could be appealed to the Supreme Court.

In 1796 President GEORGE WASHINGTON appointed Ellsworth Chief Justice of the United States. He held the post for three years but had little impact. The cases he heard were not very significant, illness limited his participation in the duties of the Court, and a diplomatic mission took him out of the country. Perhaps his most important decision came in *Wiscart v. Dauchy* (1796) in which he examined the relationship of the Supreme Court to the district and circuit courts, established a series of important rules dealing with WRITS OF ERROR, and extended COMMON LAW procedures in APPEALS to EQUITY and ADMIRALTY jurisdiction as well. His opinions tended to be brief, to the point, and nationalist in orientation. In *United States v. La Vengeance* (1796) he expanded the admiralty jurisdiction of the federal courts to inland navigable rivers, the Great Lakes, and other water routes away from the high seas; and while riding circuit in *United States v. Isaac Williams* (1799) he upheld the English common law DOCTRINE that citizens of a country did not have a right to expatriate themselves without their native country's consent.

As Chief Justice, Ellsworth encouraged the practice of the Supreme Court's handing down PER CURIAM opinions, with a single decision representing the will of the entire court, as opposed to having separate SERIATIM opinions by the individual Justices. JOHN MARSHALL, who succeeded Ellsworth as Chief Justice, considered the continuation and further development of this practice all-important in maintaining respect for the authority of the Court when it handed down controversial decisions.

In 1799 Ellsworth, over the protest of some of his closest associates, agreed to a request from President JOHN ADAMS to be part of a special diplomatic mission to resolve the undeclared naval war with France. The mission was a success, but Ellsworth became ill while abroad, resigned the chief justiceship in October 1800, and stayed in England to recuperate. By the time he returned to America the Jeffersonians had triumphed and he retired from public life.

RICHARD E. ELLIS

Bibliography

BROWN, WILLIAM GARROTT 1905 *The Life of Oliver Ellsworth.* New York: Macmillan.

GOEBEL, JULIUS, JR. 1971 *History of the Supreme Court of the United States, Vol. 1: Antecedents and Beginnings to 1801.* New York: Macmillan.

ELLSWORTH COURT

See: Supreme Court, 1789–1801

EMANCIPATION PROCLAMATION
12 Stat. 68 (1863)

ABRAHAM LINCOLN, employing the Constitution's WAR POWERS, announced the Emancipation Proclamation on September 22, 1862. It had its roots in ABOLITIONIST CONSTITUTIONAL THEORY. Although Lincoln's swift rise in the Republican party was due in part to his outspoken opposition to the extension of slavery, on the outset of the war he was bound by the Constitution (Article IV, section 2) and federal laws on fugitive slaves that required federal officials to return runaways, even to disloyal owners. Politically ambitious Union general George B. McClellan, a conservative would-be Democratic presidential candidate, sternly enforced the 1850 law; generals BENJAMIN F. BUTLER and John Charles Frémont, by contrast, refused to return runaways in their commands and armed some against rebel guerrillas. Lincoln countermanded the latter's orders to dim the issue of arming Negroes and to keep policy in civilians' hands.

Negroes continued to flee to Union lines no matter what orders civilians or generals issued. Awareness grew in the Union army and among bluecoats' families and other correspondents that almost the only trustworthy southerners were blacks. Gradually, sentiment increased that to return runaways was indecent and illogical, for slaves were the South's labor force. In Congress, with few exceptions, Democrats remained uneducable on the runaway issue and damned as unconstitutional any mass emancipation whether by EXECUTIVE ORDER or statute and whether or not involving colonization of freedmen abroad or compensation to loyal owners. Republicans, from Lincoln down, altered their opinions on race matters. Some northern states softened racist BLACK CODE clauses in constitutions and civil and criminal laws; some made laws color-blind. Congress, in addition to the CONFISCATION ACTS and with Lincoln's assent, enacted laws in March, April, and June 1862, respectively, that prohibited military returns of disloyal owners' runaways without requiring a judicial verdict of disloyalty, ended slavery in the DISTRICT OF COLUMBIA with compensation to owners, and forbade slavery in the federal TERRITORIES, thus challenging part of DRED SCOTT V. SANDFORD (1857). In effect, Republicans, retaining their basic view of the Constitution as an adaptable instrument, were adopting aspirations that abolitionist constitutionalists had long advanced.

Fearing conservative gains in the 1862 congressional and state elections, congressional Republicans then marked time. Lincoln did not have this option. He determined to reverse two centuries of race history *if* continued Confederate intransigence forced further changes and *if* the Union won the war.

Therefore, following the Antietam "victory," Lincoln proclaimed that unless slaveowners in still-unoccupied states of the Confederacy (he excluded unseceded slaveholding states) publicly renounced the rebellion by January 1, 1863, their slaves "shall be then, thenceforward, and forever free." All Union military personnel must positively assist, not merely not impede, runaways from slavery. With respect to unseceded slaveholding states, Lincoln encouraged "immediate or gradual" emancipation by state initiative, with compensation to loyal owners and colonization of freedmen abroad.

The Proclamation was not an immediate success. It diminished opinion abroad favoring recognition of the Confederacy. Few southern whites abjured the rebellion before the deadline. Lincoln, on New Year's Day 1863, announced the Proclamation to be in effect. But he had enlarged his horizons, adding an announcement that he would recruit blacks for the Union's armies. Relatively few blacks lived in northern states. Lincoln's new policy, if successful—which meant if Union voters persevered, if enough slaves kept coming into Union lines, and if Union forces occupied enough Confederate areas—could drain the South of its basic labor force and augment the Union's military power.

The policy eventually succeeded. Almost 200,000 black bluecoats, overwhelmingly southern in origin, helped to crush the rebellion. *Dred Scott* was made irrelevant. Though black Union soldiers and sailors suffered inequities in rank, pay, and dignity compared to whites, their military record made it impossible for the nation to consider them again as submen in law, though racists advocated the retrograde view. Compared to their prewar status even in the free states, blacks' legal and constitutional conditions improved as a result of the Proclamation. It initiated also an irreversible revolution in race relationships leading to the WADE-DAVIS BILL, the THIRTEENTH AMENDMENT, and the CIVIL RIGHTS ACT OF 1866. But the eventual consequence of the Emancipation Proclamation was Appomattox; thereby, alternatives forbidden by *Dred Scott,* by the 1861 Crittenden Compromise, and by the aborted Thirteenth Amendment of 1861, became options. This society could be slaveless, biracial, and more decently equal in the constitutions, laws, and customs of the nation and the states.

HAROLD M. HYMAN

Bibliography

BELZ, HERMAN 1978 *Emancipation and Equal Rights: Politics and Constitutionalism in the Civil War Era.* New York: Norton.

HYMAN, HAROLD M. and WIECEK, WILLIAM M. 1982 *Equal Justice under Law: Constitutional Development 1835–1875.* Pages 252–255. New York: Harper & Row.

OATES, STEPHEN B. 1977 *With Malice Toward None: The Life of Abraham Lincoln.* New York: Harper & Row.

VOEGELI, V. JACQUES 1967 *Free But Not Equal: The Midwest and the Negro During the Civil War.* Chicago: University of Chicago Press.

EMBARGO ACTS
(1807–1809)

For fifteen months the United States under President THOMAS JEFFERSON pursued a policy of economic coercion against foreign powers as an alternative to war. In retaliation for attacks on American commerce during the Napoleonic wars, a compliant Congress gave Jefferson everything he requested, including five embargo acts which sought to compel England and France to respect American maritime rights in return for a restoration of American trade. The first three acts, which interdicted that trade, could be constitutionally defended by a doctrine of IMPLIED POWERS that Jefferson once thought inimical to American liberty. In *United States v. The William* (1808) a federal district court invoked a BROAD CONSTRUCTION of the COMMERCE CLAUSE, reinforced by the NECESSARY AND PROPER CLAUSE, to justify a ruling that the power to regulate commerce included the power to prohibit it. Justice WILLIAM JOHNSON of the Supreme Court, a Jefferson appointee, rebuked the President in a circuit case, *Gilchrist v. Collector* (1808), for having exceeded his statutory authority in enforcing the embargo acts, and another Jefferson appointee, Justice BROCKHOLST LIVINGSTON, in *United States v. Hoxie* (1808), scathed the President for insinuating the doctrine of constructive treason into a prosecution for violation of the acts. The draconian fourth embargo act carried the administration to the precipice of unlimited enforcement powers and mocked Republican principles by its concentration of authority in the President, its employment of the navy for enforcement, and its disregard of the FOURTH AMENDMENT's protection against UNREASONABLE SEARCHES and seizures. Unconstitutional military enforcement characterized the fifth embargo act, which rivaled any legislation in American history for its suppressiveness. The embargo acts, having failed their purpose, lapsed when Jefferson left office.

LEONARD W. LEVY

EMERGENCY BANK ACT
48 Stat. 1 (1933)

When FRANKLIN D. ROOSEVELT took office on March 4, 1933, banks had closed in thirty-eight states. The next day Roosevelt declared a national bank holiday, suspended all gold transactions, and called a special session of Congress for March 9. On that day Congress rushed through, and that same evening Roosevelt signed, a bill submitted by the White House aimed at ending the panic that had begun earlier that year. The bill ratified Roosevelt's actions, which he had based on the questionable authority of the 1917 Trading With the Enemy Act. The act gained constitutional significance by thus expanding executive authority. Congress also gave the President discretionary authority over national and Federal Reserve banks. The act provided for calling in all gold and gold certificates in circulation and assessed criminal penalties for hoarding. The government could appoint conservators for the assets of insolvent banks, and the Treasury could license the reopening of sound ones and reorganize the remainder. The act further authorized the emergency issuance of paper notes up to a limit of one hundred percent of the value of government bonds in its member banks.

DAVID GORDON

EMERGENCY COURT OF APPEALS

In the Emergency Price Control Act of 1942, Congress established a comprehensive system of administrative control over prices, as a means of checking the inflation that accompanied this country's entry into World War II. The Act created a temporary Emergency Court of Appeals, staffed by federal judges from the district courts and courts of appeals, with exclusive JURISDICTION to determine the validity of price control regulations. Regulated persons thus could not challenge the administrative regulations' constitutionality or statutory authorization in the ordinary state or federal courts—either in injunctive proceedings or by way of defense to criminal prosecutions for their violation. The only course open was to obey the regulations and challenge their validity in the newly created court.

In a series of decisions, the most important of which was YAKUS V. UNITED STATES (1944), the Supreme Court upheld the validity of this scheme (LOCKERTY V. PHILLIPS, 1943; BOWLES V. WILLINGHAM, 1944; see also JUDICIAL SYSTEM).

A Temporary Emergency Court of Appeals, established in 1971, is similarly staffed by judges from other federal courts. It hears appeals from the district courts in cases arising under various congressional statutes regulating allocation and pricing of certain commodities.

KENNETH L. KARST

Bibliography

BATOR, PAUL M., MISHKIN, PAUL J., SHAPIRO, DAVID L., and WECHSLER, HERBERT, eds. 1973 *Hart and Wechsler's The Federal Courts and the Federal System*, 2nd ed. Pages 317–322. Mineola, N.Y.: Foundation Press.

EMERGENCY POWERS

As justifications for taking emergency action without first receiving legislative authority, chief executives from different countries have relied on "reason of state" (*raison d'état*) and "prerogative." JOHN LOCKE, in the *Second Treatise on Civil Government* (1690), defined prerogative as the power to act "according to discretion for the common good, without the prescription of the law and sometimes even against it. . . ." More concise is the maxim *salus populi suprema lex:* the safety of the people is the supreme law.

The United States Constitution contains few provisions for emergency power. Congress has the power to meet emergencies by passing LEGISLATION. Under Article I, Section 8, Congress may declare war and call forth the militia to suppress insurrections and to repel invasions. Article II authorizes the President to convene Congress "on extraordinary Occasions" for the purpose of enacting emergency legislation.

An exception to this statutory process is implied in the debates at the CONSTITUTIONAL CONVENTION. The Framers recognized that the President might have to begin military operations for defensive purposes before Congress could act. When one of the delegates proposed that Congress be empowered to "make war," it was objected that legislative proceedings might at times be too slow for the safety of the country. "Declare" was substituted for "make," giving Congress the power to declare war but allowing the President discretionary authority "to repel sudden attacks."

For twentieth-century America, the concept of "defensive war" has expanded to include military actions far beyond the nation's borders. The long drawn-out war in Southeast Asia led to the WAR POWERS RESOLUTION of 1973, an effort to reconcile the war-making power of the President with the war-declaring power of Congress. The statute attempts to insure the "collective judgment" of both branches by requiring the President to consult with Congress "in every possible instance," to report to Congress within forty-eight hours after introducing forces into hostilities, and to withdraw those forces unless he receives congressional support within sixty or ninety days. Congress may at any time during this period pass a CON-

CURRENT RESOLUTION (which is not subject to veto) directing the President to remove forces engaged in hostilities. The consultation and reporting provisions have had mixed results. The LEGISLATIVE VETO mechanism in the War Powers Resolution was declared invalid in IMMIGRATION AND NATURALIZATION SERVICE V. CHADHA (1983).

Article I, section 9, permits the suspension of the writ of HABEAS CORPUS "in Cases of Rebellion or Invasion [when] the public Safety may require it." It has never been determined conclusively whether this power resides solely in Congress or is shared with the President. History supports the latter interpretation. In April 1861, while Congress was in recess, President ABRAHAM LINCOLN issued proclamations ordering a number of emergency actions, including the suspension of the writ of habeas corpus. Congress supported his initiatives, as did a sharply divided Supreme Court in the PRIZE CASES (1863).

Although Chief Justice ROGER B. TANEY had earlier placed the power of suspension exclusively with Congress, in *Ex parte Merryman* (1861), Lincoln ignored the court order and continued to exercise emergency powers. His attorney general, EDWARD BATES, argued that the President shared with Congress the power to suspend the writ of habeas corpus. In such cases as EX PARTE MILLIGAN (1866) and DUNCAN V. KAHANAMOKU (1946), the Supreme Court has held illegal the establishment of military tribunals to try civilians in areas where the civil courts are open. In these decisions, however, the Court took care to assert judicial control at the close of, rather than during, hostilities.

The President's emergency power has also grown because of authority delegated to him by Congress. These authorities would sometimes come to life whenever the President issued a proclamation declaring the nation to be in a state of emergency. A report issued by a Senate special committee in 1973 disclosed that four proclamations (issued by FRANKLIN D. ROOSEVELT in 1933, HARRY S. TRUMAN in 1950, and RICHARD M. NIXON in 1970 and 1971) brought to life 470 provisions of federal law. Each statute conferred upon the President some facet of control over the lives and property of American citizens.

The NATIONAL EMERGENCIES ACT of 1976 restricted the use of presidential emergency powers. The statute terminated emergency authorities two years from the date of the bill's enactment (September 14, 1976). For future national emergencies the President must publish a declaration in the *Federal Register*. Congress could terminate the national emergency by passing a concurrent resolution. After the *Chadha* decision, Congress substituted a joint resolution for the concurrent resolution. To prevent "emergencies" from lingering for decades without congressional attention or action, the 1976 statute contained an action-forcing mechanism. No later than six months after the President declares a national emergency, and at least every six months thereafter while the emergency continues, each House of Congress must meet to consider a vote to terminate the emergency.

The 1976 statute exempted certain provisions of law, including section 5(b) of the Trading With the Enemy Act, first enacted in 1917. This section had become a source of presidential authority in peacetime as well as wartime. President Roosevelt, for example, used section 5(b) in 1933 to declare a national emergency. Legislation in 1977 attempted to strengthen congressional control, allowing Congress to terminate an emergency by passing a concurrent resolution (a joint resolution would now be required). It was under the 1977 legislation that President Jimmy Carter seized Iranian assets in 1979, an action upheld by the Supreme Court two years later in DAMES & MOORE V. REGAN (1981).

LOUIS FISHER

Bibliography

ROSSITER, CLINTON 1963 *Constitutional Dictatorship: Crisis Government in the Modern Democracies.* New York: Harcourt, Brace & World.

U.S. CONGRESS 1976 *The National Emergencies Act (Public Law 94–412). Source Book: Legislative History, Texts, and Other Documents.* Senate Committee on Government Operations and Senate Special Committee on National Emergencies and Delegated Emergency Powers. 94th Congress, 2d session.

EMERGENCY PRICE CONTROL ACT

56 Stat. 23 (1942)

The most important independent administrative agency set up during World War II was the Office of Price Administration (OPA). The agency began studying plans for rationing and price fixing in April 1941 without benefit of statutory authority. The Emergency Price Control Act of 1942 gave the OPA official status, with broad powers for price regulation and a price administrator to make the act effective. The administrator was given broad discretion to supervise and fix prices and rent ceilings, combat profiteering and speculation, expedite defense purchases without excessive waste, and place limits on wages and other income from PRODUCTION. From 1942 to

1945, the OPA approached complete regulation of prices and rents. To prevent sellers and landlords from seeking INJUNCTIONS in state or federal courts against enforcement of particular price orders, the statute directed all determinations of the legality of price orders, including their constitutionality, to an EMERGENCY COURT OF APPEALS, established in Washington, D.C.

Unlike most wartime agencies, the OPA was challenged in the courts. The Supreme Court was supportive, upholding in YAKUS V. UNITED STATES (1944) those portions of the EPCA delegating to the OPA power to fix prices; in *Bowles v. Willingham* (1944) the Court upheld an OPA rent-fixing directive. *Yakus* also upheld the channeling of issues of legality to the Emergency Court of Appeals, which had the effect of requiring other courts to enforce price orders irrespective of the question of their lawfulness. In *Steuart and Bros. v. Bowles* (1944), the system of "indirect sanctions," whereby the OPA imposed its controls on the economy without formal resort to the judicial process, was sustained; the Court refused to interfere with the principal coercive device whereby various executive agencies gave practical force to their directives.

PAUL L. MURPHY

Bibliography

United States Office of Temporary Controls 1947 *The Beginnings of OPA.* Washington, D.C.: Office of Temporary Controls.

EMINENT DOMAIN

In his argument as counsel in WEST RIVER BRIDGE COMPANY V. DIX (1848), the first case in which the Supreme Court ruled directly on the constitutionality of the states' power of eminent domain, DANIEL WEBSTER thundered against the whole concept of state discretion in "takings." Only in the past few years, he contended, had this power of eminent domain been recognized in American law. Claims for its legitimacy, moreover, were "adopted from writers on other and arbitrary [civil law] governments," he declared; and eminent domain could easily become an instrument for establishment by the states of "unlimited despotisms over the private citizens." Webster tried, in effect, to get the court to impose Fifth Amendment standards on the states.

Webster was engaged in a failing cause. Besides, his history was inaccurate and his predictions of disaster were simplistic. He was certainly right, however, in seeing the eminent domain power as a formidable threat to VESTED RIGHTS, corporate or individual. He understood that eminent domain condemnations might become a proxy for regulation under the POLICE POWER, undermining the CONTRACT CLAUSE as a bulwark of property rights. He was right in raising the alarm when he did; when *West River Bridge* was argued there had been a vast increase in activity by government and private CORPORATIONS in exercise of eminent domain. The transportation revolution in America was in an expansionary phase; extensive new railroad construction reinforced the effects on property law already felt from canal, turnpike, and bridge enterprises. All these ventures required use of the "taking" power in order to accomplish their purposes.

Contrary to Webster's version of legal history, government's power to expropriate privately owned property for a variety of public purposes had long been an element of Anglo-American law. The power of eminent domain was the power to compel transfers to government or government's assignees. In its constitutional version, even in the 1840s, it was understood as a power that could be exercised legitimately only for a PUBLIC USE or PUBLIC PURPOSE, and that required the payment of JUST COMPENSATION. In English decisions and statutes going back several centuries, in American colonial law, and in the state law of the early republic, this power of taking by governmental authority had been exercised for such purposes as road-building, fortifications, drainage (including the great Fens projects of England in the seventeenth century), navigational improvement on rivers, and construction of bridges and canals. In colonial Massachusetts, statute had extended a variant of the power into the manufacturing sector by authorizing builders of mills to dam up streams, flooding neighboring lands; these "milldam laws" provided for assessment of damages and payment of compensation in cash.

The Fifth Amendment—which the Supreme Court would rule in BARRON V. BALTIMORE (1833) was not applicable to the states—expressed the views and used language already embodied in several of the state constitutions adopted during the Revolutionary era. Thus the amendment's requirement that property could be taken "for public use" and on payment of "just compensation" had been foreshadowed by such documents as the 1780 Massachusetts Declaration of Rights, which declared that "whenever the public exigencies require that the property of any individual should be appropriated to public uses, he shall receive reasonable compensation therefor."

Although several early state constitutions lacked such language, uniformly the state courts, in reviewing takings cases, ruled that general principles of justice, the writings of the natural-law jurists, or the constitutional values reflected in the Fifth Amendment justified imposition by judges of both a "public use" and a "just compensation" limitation upon their legislatures' uses of the eminent domain power. It was a singular feature of legal development in the states, however, that despite the widespread formal adoption of such limitations, in fact only slight constraints were placed on the legislatures. In practice, compensation paid to persons suffering from takings was far below market value (and, because of offsetting benefits commonly calculated against damages, often they were paid nothing in cash); hence, eminent domain became an instrument for the subsidization, through cost reduction, of both governmental enterprises and favored private undertakings. "Public convenience" became, in most states, a legitimate reading of the "public use" requirement; and in practice, the legislatures enjoyed wide discretion in deciding what types of enterprise might be vested with the power to expropriate private property. Ironically, the very bridge and railroad corporations that Webster represented so often were among the greatest beneficiaries of eminent domain devolution in that era.

The Court in *West River Bridge* wholly rejected Webster's contentions, ruling that state eminent domain powers were "paramount to all private rights vested under the government." It left the state courts to decide for themselves whether compensation payments were just in particular cases, or whether DUE PROCESS requirements of state constitutions had been met.

So stood constitutional doctrine until the adoption of the FOURTEENTH AMENDMENT. Under its due process clause, the door was opened to challenges in federal courts of state eminent domain actions. Increasingly, too, in the late nineteenth century, the Supreme Court was called upon to rule upon the constitutionality of regulatory measures that activist state legislatures were enacting. The issue tended to take the form of defining a "taking," with the constitutional requirement it connoted, as opposed to bona fide use of the police power, which did not require compensation. The Court ruled in a succession of cases that the Fourteenth Amendment embodied the requirements of "public use" and "just compensation." It took a broad view, however, of what types of enterprise the states might aid with devolutions of the eminent domain power; in a series of cases on irrigation districts, drainage companies, individual enterprises and corporation activities in other areas such as logging and mining, and the more traditional areas of state activity, the Court upheld legislative discretion under a permissive "public use" standard.

In MUGLER V. KANSAS (1887), the Court attempted to distinguish between a taking, which required compensation, and uses of the police power, which it defined as laws abating nuisances or limiting uses of property that were harmful to "health, morals, or safety of the community," not compensable. But drawing the police power/eminent domain line proved difficult; indeed, it perplexes the Court to the present day. In *Pennsylvania Coal Company v. Mahon* (1922), Justice OLIVER WENDELL HOLMES argued that the police power and eminent domain power are on a single continuum; differences are a matter of degree, not qualitative. The Court has continued to struggle with the issue, and in modern land-use ZONING cases from EUCLID V. AMBLER REALTY (1926) to *Agins v. Tiburon* (1980) it has sought a firmer ground to replace the distinction Holmes found so appropriate.

The Court has upheld congressional discretion in deciding what purposes of federal eminent domain met the Fifth Amendment's "public use" requirement. In *United States v. Gettysburg Electric Railway Company* (1896), the Court declared acceptable any use "which is legitimate and lies within the scope of the Constitution." In *United States ex rel. Tennessee Valley Authority v. Welch* (1946) the Court carried the doctrine to an extreme, concluding that a congressional decision to authorize expropriation of property "is entitled to deference until it is shown to involve an impossibility." A few years later, *Berman v. Parker* (1954) upheld federal eminent domain takings to conduct an urban redevelopment project in the District of Columbia. Here the end was the public welfare, a "broad and inclusive" concept, the Court declared, that certainly embraced slum clearance and an urban development designed to be "beautiful as well as sanitary." Given the validity of this purpose, it was legitimate to invoke eminent domain, which was only a means. Congress must decide as to the need for the project and its design.

In its quest to develop standards to distinguish takings from legitimate exercise of the police power, the Court has probed to the heart of property concepts. What rights are "vested," how "reasonable expectations" should be defined, what obligations inhere in the ownership of private property—all are questions that come to the surface repeatedly in continuing litigation. Nearly 150 years ago, Chief Justice LEMUEL SHAW of Massachusetts admonished, in *Boston Water Power Company v. Railroad* (1839), that the eminent domain power "must be large and liberal, so as to meet the public exigencies, and it must be so limited and constrained, as to secure effectually the rights of the citizen; and it must depend, in some instances, upon the nature of the exigencies as they arise, and the circumstances of individual cases." Shaw's view may have lacked prescriptive potential, but it has proved remarkably accurate in predicting the direction that the law would take—and the perplexities that would beset the best efforts of lawmakers and judges to produce definitive formulae.

HARRY N. SCHEIBER

(SEE ALSO: *Hawaii Housing Authority v. Midkiff, 1984.*)

Bibliography

DUNHAM, ALLISON 1962 *Griggs v. Allegheny County* in Perspective: Thirty Years of Supreme Court Expropriation Law. *Supreme Court Review* 1962:63–106.

GRANT, J. A. C. 1931 The "Higher Law" Background of the Law of Eminent Domain. *Wisconsin Law Review* 6:67–85.

HURST, JAMES WILLARD 1964 *Law and Economic Growth: The Legal History of the Lumber Industry in Wisconsin, 1836–1915.* Cambridge, Mass.: Harvard University Press.

SCHEIBER, HARRY N. 1971 The Road to *Munn:* Eminent Domain and the Concept of Public Purpose in the State Courts. *Perspectives in American History* 5:327–402.

STOEBUCK, WILLIAM B. 1972 A General Theory of Eminent Domain. *Washington Law Review* 47:553–608.

——— 1980 Police Power, Takings, and Due Process. *Washington and Lee Law Review* 37:1057–1099.

EMPLOYERS' LIABILITY ACTS
34 Stat. 232 (1906)
35 Stat. 65 (1908)

In the first Employers' Liability Act of June 1906, Congress extended nationwide protection to railroad workers against the arsenal of COMMON LAW defenses which employers had so effectively used to defeat personal injury suits. This act rendered every common carrier engaged in INTERSTATE COMMERCE liable to its employees for all damages resulting from negligence. Congress thus discarded the "fellow-servant" rule which had exculpated employers in accidents caused by another workman's negligence. Moreover, contributory negligence would not bar recovery and the law directed juries, not judges, to determine questions of negligence and assess damages proportionally. The act also prohibited the use of insurance or other benefits as a defense against damage suits. When a 5–4 Supreme Court declared this act unconstitutional because it extended to railroad employees not engaged in interstate commerce, Congress passed a second version of the act in April 1908. Although substantially the same, the new act covered only employees actually working in interstate commerce. Congress also added several sections further protecting employees and extended the period of limitation on actions from one to two years. As it had implied in its first decision, the Court unanimously sustained the act in the second set of EMPLOYERS' LIABILITY CASES (1912).

DAVID GORDON

EMPLOYERS' LIABILITY CASES
207 U.S. 463 (1908)
223 U.S. 1 (1912)

The first EMPLOYERS' LIABILITY ACT, passed in 1906, made a common carrier liable for the on-the-job injury or death of any employee and eliminated the "fellow-servant" rule by which an employer had been relieved of liability for an injury to one worker caused by another's negligence. In the first *Employers' Liability Cases,* a 5–4 Supreme Court held that Congress had exceeded its INTERSTATE COMMERCE power.

Justice EDWARD D. WHITE's opinion for the Court (only Justice WILLIAM R. DAY concurred completely in his opinion) addressed two objections to the act: that Congress had no power to regulate the subject, and that the act regulated things outside the scope of the commerce power. He dismissed the first objection. The COMMERCE CLAUSE set no limits on subjects regulated. Indeed, the Court decided only the extent of Congress's power, not the wisdom of its action. "We fail to perceive any just reason for holding that Congress is without power to regulate the relation of master and servant . . . [as a subject of] interstate commerce." The argument that the act had unconstitutionally regulated INTERSTATE COMMERCE proved more troublesome. Because the act imposed liability on employers "without qualification or restriction as to the business in which the carriers or their employees may be engaged at the time of injury, of necessity [it] includes subjects wholly outside the power of Congress to regulate commerce." White refused to accept the contention that the Court ought to interpret the act as applying solely to interstate commerce even though it did not explicitly say so.

Chief Justice MELVILLE W. FULLER and Justice DAVID J. BREWER concurred in Justice RUFUS PECKHAM's opinion endorsing White's result but retreating from White's statement about Congress's power over master–servant relations. In a lengthy dissent, Justice WILLIAM MOODY argued that the Court was obliged to read the statute so as to preserve its constitutionality. "We think that the act, reasonably and properly interpreted, applies . . . only to cases of interstate commerce . . . and not to domestic commerce."

After Congress enacted another version of the law accommodating the majority's objections, a unanimous Court upheld its constitutionality. Justice WILLIS VAN DEVANTER's opinion broadly asserted the reach of Congress's power over the subject. He disposed of the objection that the act, by discarding COMMON LAW doctrines, had exceeded Congress's power: "A person has no property, no vested interest, in any rule of common law." The act also promoted safety and advanced commerce, and Van Devanter dismissed the contention that it violated the DUE PROCESS CLAUSE's guarantee of FREEDOM OF CONTRACT.

DAVID GORDON

EMPLOYMENT DISCRIMINATION

Employment discrimination on grounds of race, sex, nationality, or religion may be challenged under two acts of Congress. One of the statutes, now codified as Title 42 of the United States Code, Section 1981, is a survivor of the CIVIL RIGHTS ACT OF 1866, enacted for the protection of former slaves. As originally enacted, the statute was not seen as an employment discrimination statute. It conferred upon blacks the right to make and enforce contracts, to sue and to enjoy on a par with whites the protection of laws. The act was passed pursuant to Congress's authority under Section 2 of the THIRTEENTH AMENDMENT, and Congress proposed the FOURTEENTH AMENDMENT in order to assure the act's validity. After the Reconstruction era, however, it and other Reconstruction-era civil rights legislation fell into disuse until the 1960s. Not until *Johnson v. Railway Express Agency, Inc.* (1975) did the United States Supreme Court confirm the application of Section 1981 to RACIAL DISCRIMINATION in private-sector employment. This statute's use in employment discrimination cases has become secondary to reliance on Title VII of the CIVIL RIGHTS ACT OF 1964, which was enacted by Congress as part of a comprehensive statute prohibiting discrimination on grounds of race, sex, religion, or national origin in employment, PUBLIC ACCOMMODATIONS, and federally funded programs.

Enactment of the 1964 Act followed a long period of civil rights DEMONSTRATIONS against the kinds of discrimination the act prohibited. For twenty years preceding the enactment of Title VII, more than 200 fair employment practice bills had been proposed in the Congress, but none had passed. Allegations of a Title VII violation often are accompanied by additional allegations of a Section 1981 violation.

Another survivor of Reconstruction-era legislation now codified as 42 United States Code 1985(c), was originally designed to protect blacks from Ku Klux Klan violence. The Supreme Court, in *Great American Federal Savings and Loan Association v. Novotny* (1979), rejected the view that Section 1985(c) provides an independent remedy for the adjudication of rights protected by Title VII.

The constitutionality of Title VII of the 1964 act was never seriously questioned. The power of Congress to enact Title VII, either under the COMMERCE CLAUSE or to enforce the FOURTEENTH AMENDMENT, seems to have been assumed. In 1972 Congress extended the coverage of Title VII to include employment discrimination by state and local governments. Subsequently, it was argued that back-pay awards and attorneys' fees levied by a federal court against a state under the amended Title VII violated the jurisdictional limitations of the ELEVENTH AMENDMENT. However, in FITZPATRICK V. BITZER (1976) the Supreme Court rejected that argument, holding that the 1972 amendment was a valid exercise of Congress's enforcement power under Section 5 of the FOURTEENTH AMENDMENT.

REGINALD ALLEYNE

Bibliography

COMMENT 1980 Developments in the Law—Section 1981. *Harvard Civil Rights–Civil Liberties Law Review* 15:29–277.

DEAN, JOHN P. 1978 Title VII and Public Employers: Did Congress Exceed Its Powers? *Columbia Law Review* 78:372–408.

HILL, HERBERT 1977 The Equal Employment Opportunity Acts of 1964 and 1972: A Critical Analysis of the Legislative History and Administration of the Law. *Industrial Relations Law Journal* 2:1–96.

EN BANC

(French: "As a bench.") The term often applies to appellate courts, and in particular to the UNITED STATES COURTS OF APPEALS. Commonly only a three-member panel of a federal court of appeals hears a case. When the full membership is sitting—whether by its own choice or at a litigant's request—the case is heard before them *en banc.* In the federal courts of appeals, the decision of a panel is reconsidered *en banc* if a majority of the full court's members agree on such a hearing.

DAVID GORDON

ENDO, EX PARTE

See: Japanese American Cases

ENFORCEMENT ACTS

See: Force Acts

ENGEL v. VITALE
370 U.S. 421 (1962)

The Board of Regents of the State of New York authorized a short prayer for recitation in schools. The Regents were seeking to defuse the emotional issue of religious exercises in the classroom. The matter was taken out of the hands of school boards and teachers, and the blandest sort of invocation of the Deity was provided: "Almighty God, we acknowledge our dependence upon Thee, and beg Thy blessings upon us, our teachers, and our country." School districts in New York did not have to use the prayer, and if they did, no child was required to repeat it. But if there were any prayer in a New York classroom it would have to be this one. The Board of Education of New Hyde Park, New York, chose to use the Regents' Prayer and directed its principals to cause it to be said aloud at the beginning of each school day in every classroom.

Use of the prayer was challenged as an ESTABLISHMENT OF RELIGION. Justice HUGO L. BLACK, writing for the Court, concluded that neither the nondenominational nature of the prayer nor the fact that it was voluntary could save it from unconstitutionality under the establishment clause. By providing the prayer, New York officially approved theistic religion. With his usual generous quotations from JAMES MADISON and THOMAS JEFFERSON, Black found such state support impermissible.

Justice WILLIAM O. DOUGLAS concurred separately. He had more trouble than Black concluding that the prayer established religion "in the strictly historic meaning of these words." What Douglas feared was the divisiveness engendered in a community when government sponsored a religious exercise.

Only Justice POTTER STEWART dissented, concluding that "the Court has misapplied a great constitutional principle." Stewart could not see how a purely voluntary prayer could be held to constitute state adoption of an official religion. For Stewart, an official religion was the only meaning of "establishment of religion." He noted that invocations of the Deity in public ceremonies of all sorts had been a feature of our national life from its outset. Without quite saying so, Stewart asked his brethren how the Regents' Prayer could be anathematized on establishment clause grounds without scraping "In God We Trust" off the pennies.

Engel v. Vitale was the first of a series of cases in which the Court used the establishment clause to extirpate from the public schools the least-common-denominator religious invocations which had been a traditional part of public ceremonies—especially school ceremonies—in America.

The decision proved extremely controversial. It has been widely circumvented and there have been repeated attempts to amend the Constitution to undo the effect of *Engel.*

RICHARD E. MORGAN

Bibliography

BERNS, WALTER 1976 *The First Amendment and the Future of American Democracy.* Pages 33–76. New York: Basic Books.

MUIR, WILLIAM K., JR. 1967 *Prayer in the Public Schools.* Chicago: University of Chicago Press.

ENGLISH BILL OF RIGHTS

See: Bill of Rights (English)

ENGLISH CONSTITUTION

See: British Constitution

ENMUND v. FLORIDA
458 U.S. 782 (1982)

Before this decision, nine states permitted infliction of the death penalty on one who participated in a FELONY resulting in a murder, even if committed by confederates. Earl Enmund drove the getaway car in a robbery at which co-defendants killed the victims when he was not present and had not premeditated murder. A 5–4 Court held that the CRUEL AND UNUSUAL PUNISHMENT clause of the EIGHTH AMENDMENT, which the FOURTEENTH AMENDMENT extended to the states, prevented imposition of the death penalty. Capital punishment was disproportionate to the crime when Enmund had not himself killed, attempted to kill, intended to kill, or even intended the use of lethal force.

LEONARD W. LEVY

ENTANGLEMENT TEST

See: Government Aid to Sectarian Institutions

ENTRAPMENT DEFENSE

The entrapment defense is not constitutionally safeguarded and raises no constitutional issue unless a guilty defendant claims that law enforcement conduct violates the fundamental fairness mandated by DUE PROCESS OF LAW; if such a constitutional defense were to be recognized by the Supreme Court the effect would, like an EXCLUSIONARY RULE, be aimed at deterring unlawful police conduct.

Entrapment is a means of securing evidence to convict by luring a person into the commission of a crime of which he is suspected. Ordinarily the duty of an officer of the law is to deter crime and apprehend those who commit it, not to incite or instigate it. Certain offenses of a clandestine or consensual character, however, are difficult to expose and punish except by some degree of covert government participation. Official deceit is not necessarily illegal or unconstitutional. Undercover police work is particularly effective in uncovering crimes that involve gambling, drugs, prostitution, and official corruption. Nevertheless the government should not fight crime with crime.

When an undercover officer has gained the confidence of a radical organization and encouraged its members to engage in terrorist activities and provided them with the weapons and explosives to do so, he has become an *agent provocateur* who has conceived and procured the commission of a crime that would not have occurred but for him. If an officer posing as an imposter approaches a law-abiding person with no criminal record and induces him to smuggle contraband, the officer has passed the law's tolerance and the smuggler's guilty conduct may be legally excusable. When entrapment goes too far, it creates a legal defense which, like insanity or killing to save one's own life, merits a verdict of not guilty. The question in any case is whether the evidence shows that entrapment is a sufficient defense by a person who has in fact committed the crime charged against him. The mere fact that a government agent provides a favorable opportunity to one willing and ready to break the law is not entrapment for the purpose of making good a defense; if, however, the defendant had no previous intent to commit the offense and did so only because the police induced him, the verdict should be an acquittal.

Entrapment comes before the Supreme Court as a nonconstitutional defense in cases involving federal crimes. The Justices have always divided into two wings: one focuses on the criminal intent or predisposition of the defendant to commit the crime; the other focuses on the conduct of law enforcement officers. The view that has always prevailed, from the first case, *Sorrells v. United States* (1932), to *Hampton v. United States* (1976), is that it is no entrapment for the police merely to instigate the crime; they must also instigate its commission by luring an innocent person with no previous disposition to commit it. The criminal design, as Chief Justice CHARLES EVANS HUGHES said in 1932, must originate with the authorities who implant the predisposition in the mind of an otherwise innocent person and incite him to commit it so that they may prosecute. Thus, in *United States v. Russell* (1973), the Court sustained the conviction of the manufacturer of an illegal drug, who claimed that the government had violated due process when an undercover agent supplied him with an essential chemical ingredient. But the ingredient was harmless, its possession was not illegal, and, above all, the defendant was already engaged in the criminal enterprise. In *Hampton,* however, a government informant supplied an illegal drug and arranged its sale by the defendant to undercover agents. Although the government deliberately set him up, the Court stressed that his previous propensity to commit the crime negated his entrapment defense. He was, in a phrase of Chief Justice EARL WARREN, "an unwary criminal" rather than an "unwary innocent."

Justice WILLIAM H. REHNQUIST wrote the entrapment opinions of the BURGER COURT, from which Justices POTTER STEWART, WILLIAM J. BRENNAN, and THURGOOD MARSHALL dissented. The dissenters insisted that the majority's focus on the criminal's predisposition is "subjective," and they preferred an "objective" test: whether, despite predisposition, police conduct instigated the offense. The objectivity of that view, however, can be deceptive, and it ignores criminal intent. Doubtless, though, the trend of decision has made the entrapment defense nearly useless if a jury does not accept it. If the "outrageousness" of police conduct should pass the threshold of judicial tolerance in some future case, the Court may find a due process basis for the entrapment defense.

LEONARD W. LEVY

Bibliography

DUNHAM, DAN S. 1977 Hampton v. United States: Last Rites for the "Objective" Theory of Entrapment? *Columbia Human Rights Law Review* 9:223–262.

O'CONNER, PETER J. 1978 Entrapment versus Due Process: A Solution to the Problem of the Criminal Conviction Obtained by Law Enforcement Misconduct. *Fordham Urban Law Journal* 7:32–53.

ROSSUM, RALPH A. 1978 The Entrapment Defense and the Teaching of Political Responsibility. *American Journal of Criminal Law* 6:287–306.

ENUMERATED POWERS

Instead of establishing a national government with a general power to do whatever it might deem in the public interest, the Constitution lists the authorized powers of Congress. The chief source of these "enumerated powers" is Article I, section 8, which authorizes Congress to regulate commerce among the several states, tax and spend, raise and support military forces, and so on. This enumeration has been supplemented by other grants, including authority to enforce the Civil War Amendments.

The enumeration of powers has both a negative and a positive implication. Enumerating or specifying powers implies that some of government's ordinary concerns are beyond the constitutional competence of the national government. This implication is made explicit by the TENTH AMENDMENT. Nevertheless, the founding generation wanted to solve such specific problems as commercial hostility among the states and an unpaid war debt. When THE FEDERALIST defended the proposed national powers it cited the desiderata that might be achieved through their successful exercise. The enumeration of powers thus implies affirmative responsibilities as well as limited concerns. These competing implications are associated with competing approaches to constitutional interpretation and different conceptions of the normative character of the Constitution as a whole. As a reminder of a line between national and state powers, the enumeration of powers suggests THOMAS JEFFERSON's view of the Constitution as a contract between sovereign states to be construed with an eye to preserving state prerogatives. As a reminder of affirmative responsibilities the enumeration suggests JOHN MARSHALL's view of the Constitution as a charter of government to be construed in ways that permit achievement of the social objectives it envisions. History has not favored the Jeffersonian view.

ALEXANDER HAMILTON, in *The Federalist* #84, cited the enumeration of powers as one reason for opposing a BILL OF RIGHTS. Not only were bills of rights unnecessary in countries whose governments possessed only those powers that their people had expressly granted, specifying rights could undermine the enumeration of powers by suggesting "to men disposed to usurp" that the Constitution authorized all that the bill of rights did not prohibit. The result Hamilton ostensibly feared was achieved through constitutional doctrines that accompanied the nation's progress toward the economically integrated industrial society Hamilton favored. These doctrines included Hamilton's own theories of the SUPREMACY CLAUSE and the NECESSARY AND PROPER CLAUSE, theories that influenced John Marshall's doctrine of IMPLIED POWERS in MCCULLOCH V. MARYLAND (1819).

Marshall's original theory of implied powers was consistent with the idea of enumerated powers because it removed STATES' RIGHTS burdens on national power while insisting that national concerns were limited. In the twentieth century, however, the Supreme Court changed the meaning of implied powers and gave nationalist readings to the general welfare clause and other powers. The aggregate and practical effect of these interpretations was to empower the national government to deal with anything that Congress may perceive as a national problem. This development has all but eliminated the restrictive implication of the enumeration of powers, leaving the Bill of Rights and the Constitution's institutional norms as the principal limitations on national power.

SOTIRIOS A. BARBER

(SEE ALSO: *General Welfare Clause; Tenth Amendment.*)

Bibliography

ALFANGE, DEAN, JR. 1969 Congressional Power and Constitutional Limitations. *Journal of Public Law* 18:103–134.

BARBER, SOTIRIOS A. 1984 *On What the Constitution Means.* Chap. 4. Baltimore: Johns Hopkins University Press.

ENVIRONMENTAL QUALITY IMPROVEMENT ACT

See: Environmental Regulation

ENVIRONMENTAL REGULATION AND THE CONSTITUTION

Indirectly, at least, the Constitution provides the federal government with power to regulate on behalf of environmental quality, but it also sets limits on the power. It sets limits, likewise, on the regulatory power of the states. What it does not do, at present, is grant the "constitutional right to a clean environment" so avidly sought in the heyday of environmental concern, the decade of the 1970s. Thus, the one unique aspect of the general topic considered here has no doctrinal standing; the remaining aspects are matters of doctrine, but they are not unique to environmental regulation. It is quite sufficient, then, merely to illustrate the wide range of constitutional issues that arise in the context of environmental regulation, and to suggest the nature of the debate on the question of a constitutional right to an environment of good quality.

Environmental lawmaking at the national level of government—whether by Congress, the executive, or indeed the federal courts—became important only in the 1970s, but the beginnings reach back well into the nineteenth century, if not farther. This history, especially the strong federal presence of recent years, makes apparent the significant constitutional authority of the central government in regard to the environment. Granting that it is a government of LIMITED POWERS, and mindful of occasional suggestions "that these powers fall short of encompassing the breadth of concerns potentially subject to environmental regulation," one can still conclude, with Philip Soper, "that no conceivable measure reasonably intended to protect the environment is beyond the reach" of federal authority.

The most important source of federal power to regulate in the environmental field is found in the COMMERCE CLAUSE. The clause, especially as it pertains to congressional authority to regulate activities *affecting* commerce, has been so expansively applied by the federal courts as to justify federal control of virtually any problem of environmental pollution. Some pollution sources, such as automobiles and ships, move in INTERSTATE COMMERCE; other sources manufacture products that do so; pollution affects such mainstays of interstate commerce as agricultural commodities, livestock, and many raw materials; pollutants themselves can be seen as products, or at least byproducts, moving "in commerce" across state lines. An imaginative federal district court relied upon this last theory to sustain the Clean Air Act in *United States v. Bishop Processing Company* (D.Md. 1968).

These views lend support not only to the federal air pollution control program but also to programs concerning noise, pesticides, solid waste, toxic substances, and water pollution. Regarding the last especially, Congress can draw on its unquestioned authority over navigable waters, and on the willingness of the federal courts to regard as navigable any waters of a depth sufficient, as someone once said, to float a Supreme Court opinion.

The federal government can draw on other sources of power, at least on a selective basis, to support programs of environmental regulation. The property clause of Article IV, section 3, for example, gives Congress the power to "make all needful Rules and Regulations respecting" the property of the United States. In *Kleppe v. New Mexico* (1976) the clause was relied upon to sustain the Wild Free-Roaming Horses and Burros Act of 1971 as a "needful regulation" "respecting" public lands, against New Mexico's claim that the federal government lacked authority to control the animals unless they were moving in interstate commerce or damaging public lands. It seems clear that under the property clause Congress may regulate the use of its own lands, and perhaps adjacent lands as well, to protect environmental conditions and promote ecological balance on government property.

Other powers relevant to environmental regulation include the TAXING POWER, which presumably would authorize effluent and emission fees to control pollution; perhaps the ADMIRALTY power, as a basis for controlling pollution from ships; and the power to approve INTERSTATE COMPACTS, as an indirect means by which to impose federal environmental standards on compacting states, as the Court suggested in *West Virginia ex rel. Dyer v. Sims* (1951), involving a compact among eight states to control pollution in the Ohio River system. And the Supreme Court may draw on its ORIGINAL JURISDICTION to shape a FEDERAL COMMON LAW of pollution in suits between states or between a state and the citizens of another state.

The TREATY POWER provides yet another basis for federal environmental quality and conservation measures. The leading case here is MISSOURI V. HOLLAND

(1920), sustaining the Migratory Bird Act of 1918. Congress enacted the legislation in question in order to give effect to a treaty between the United States and Great Britain. Missouri, claiming "title" to birds within its borders, sought to prevent a federal game warden from enforcing the Act. The Court, through Justice OLIVER WENDELL HOLMES, rejected the state's contention. Treaties, under the SUPREMACY CLAUSE, are the "supreme Law of the Land"; so too are acts of Congress "NECESSARY AND PROPER for carrying into Execution" the treaty power vested in the president and the Senate. *Missouri v. Holland* is of particular interest because the Court upheld the Migratory Bird Act notwithstanding the fact that a similar act, not based on a treaty, had earlier been invalidated as beyond the scope of congressional power. As Soper remarks, the case "accordingly seems to stand for the proposition that Congress may do by statute and treaty what it has no power to do by statute alone."

The specific basis for the state's claim in *Missouri v. Holland* was the TENTH AMENDMENT, which reserves to the states powers not delegated to the United States by the Constitution. The provision introduces the subject of constitutional limitations (as opposed to powers) that may apply to programs of environmental regulation, and illustrates a limitation applicable only to the federal government, and not to the states.

The Tenth Amendment figured prominently in a series of cases involving the federal Clean Air Act and decided by several courts of appeals in the 1970s. A central question in the cases was whether the amendment foreclosed the federal Environmental Protection Agency from promulgating regulations compelling various implementation and enforcement measures by the states, under threat of fines and imprisonment for recalcitrant state and local officials. The courts of appeals divided on the question, at least one of them intimating a constitutional violation, one explicitly finding no violation, and one interpreting the Clean Air Act in such a way as to sidestep the issue. The Supreme Court granted certiorari and heard argument in several of the cases, but it ultimately declined to reach the merits because counsel for the United States conceded that the regulations in question would have to be rewritten to eliminate requirements that states adopt implementation and enforcement measures. The Court's later decisions in HODEL V. VIRGINIA SURFACE MINING AND RECLAMATION ASSOCIATION (1981) and *Federal Energy Regulatory Commission v. Mississippi* (1982) show that Congress can constitutionally place great pressures on the states to regulate, so long as it uses indirect means for doing so.

Another constitutional limitation operating upon state but not federal environmental protection programs arises from the supremacy clause. The limitation may come into play in two common respects. One of these involves PREEMPTION and is illustrated by BURBANK V. LOCKHEED AIR TERMINAL, INC. (1973), where the Court concluded that federal legislation, including the Noise Control Act of 1972, reflected a congressional intention to "occupy the field" of aircraft noise regulation; hence, Burbank's noise ordinance was held invalid under the supremacy clause. The second application of the clause is illustrated in *Hancock v. Train* (1976) and *Environmental Protection Agency v. State Water Resources Control Board* (1976), in which the Court held that the supremacy clause sheltered federal facilities from permit requirements imposed by state governments pursuant to the Clean Air Act and the Federal Water Pollution Control Act, respectively, absent a clear congressional indication to the contrary.

The remaining constitutional limitations on environmental regulation apply more or less equally to state and federal government alike. We can put aside the general question of state *authority* to regulate on behalf of the environment. States, unlike the federal government, are not creatures of limited powers. It has long been acknowledged that the STATE POLICE POWER justifies the widest range of health and safety measures insofar as the federal Constitution is concerned, absent some conflict with supreme federal law. This generalization stood fairly firm even during the most active period of SUBSTANTIVE DUE PROCESS review by the federal judiciary. And it bears mention, regarding health and safety measures, as the Court said in *Northwestern Laundry v. Des Moines* (1916), that "the harshness of such legislation, or its effect upon business interests, short of a merely arbitrary enactment, are not valid constitutional objections. Nor is there any valid Federal constitutional objection in the fact that the regulation may require the discontinuance of the use of property or subject the occupant to large expense in complying with the terms of the law or ordinance."

The BILL OF RIGHTS may bear on state and federal environmental regulation just as it may bear on regulation generally. Recent cases illustrate the point. Thus the FIRST AMENDMENT came into play in *Metromedia, Inc. v. San Diego* (1981), where a local ordinance controlling billboards and the like for the sake of safety and aesthetics was invalidated insofar as it pertained to noncommercial advertising. In *Air*

Pollution Variance Board of Colorado v. Western Alfalfa Corporation (1974), the issue was whether the FOURTH AMENDMENT prohibition of unreasonable searches and seizures was violated when a health inspector entered the grounds of a pollution source to make an opacity check of smoke coming from a chimney. The Court held the entry lawful under a line of cases sustaining "open field" searches. In *United States v. Ward* (1980), the Court held that civil penalties imposed for violating certain provisions of the Federal Water Pollution Control Act pertaining to oil spills were not "quasi-criminal" so as to implicate the Fifth Amendment RIGHT AGAINST SELF-INCRIMINATION (or, presumably, the Sixth Amendment's procedural restrictions applicable to criminal prosecutions). Similarly, *Atlas Roofing Co. v. Occupational Safety and Health Review Commission* (1976) held that administrative civil penalty provisions of the Occupational Safety and Health Act did not contravene the SEVENTH AMENDMENT right to TRIAL BY JURY.

In principle, the takings clause of the Fifth Amendment might be thought to contain the most significant restriction on state and federal environmental regulation. The clause, which applies to the states through the FOURTEENTH AMENDMENT, provides: "nor shall private property be taken for PUBLIC USE, without JUST COMPENSATION." It is clearly recognized that a government regulation can work a taking, but it is seldom held that it actually does. Most environmental regulations challenged on taking grounds are alleged to reach too far, to reduce value too much, and thus to transgress the bounds drawn by Justice Holmes in one of his most famous—and least informative—generalizations, uttered in *Pennsylvania Coal Co. v. Mahon* (1922): "that while property may be regulated to a certain extent, if regulation goes too far it will be recognized as a taking." The statement suggests that if a regulation reduces property value by a great deal, a taking will be found. In practice, however, the courts tend to look not at value lost but value left. If the regulation leaves significant value intact, then usually it will be upheld. The central case in point is PENN CENTRAL TRANSPORTATION COMPANY v. NEW YORK CITY (1978), upholding New York's historic landmark preservation law as applied to Grand Central Terminal, notwithstanding very large losses to the terminal's owners. In any event, the takings clause has little bite in the context of conventional environmental regulation because control of nuisance-like activities has long escaped takings challenges even if the value of the regulated property is reduced to zero. Because virtually any environmental regulation can be characterized as a nuisance control measure, virtually none is likely to be regarded as a taking.

The state and federal governments, then, may regulate rather freely on behalf of environmental quality, but are they constitutionally obliged to do so? Nothing in the federal Constitution says as much. There are arguments that diligent and imaginative searching would find the right between the lines of text, chiefly in the "penumbra" of the Bill of Rights, or as a fundamental personal right protected by the NINTH Amendment, or as a right "implicit in the concept of ORDERED LIBERTY" and guaranteed by the DUE PROCESS clause. The Supreme Court and all but a few federal district courts have been unmoved by these arguments. Courts generally have displayed an unwillingness to make the difficult business of environmental policy a matter of constitutional principle, a point reflected in state court decisions holding that state constitutional amendments setting out environmental rights are not self-executing but require, rather, legislative implementation. The courts, quite obviously, feel ill-equipped to play a role thought better suited to legislatures. It is not that the environment is somehow less important than other recognized constitutional values, but rather that it is less amenable to adjudication.

Richard B. Stewart summarizes the arguments in this regard: a constitutional right to environmental quality would give courts ultimate responsibilities for making resource allocation decisions beyond their analytic capabilities; for trading off allocative efficiency and distributional equity without any principled means by which to do so; and for engineering and implementing dynamic policies through the clumsy and apolitical means of litigation. Stewart adds:

> A familiar justification for constitutional protection of given interests is that they are held by a "discrete and insular" minority or are otherwise chronically undervalued because of basic structural defects in the political process. This rationale has been utilized by advocates of a constitutional right to environmental quality, buttressing it by claims that environmental degradation violates "fundamental" interests in health and human survival and implicates the fate of future generations that are unrepresented in the political process. But the spate of environmental legislation enacted by federal and state governments over the past ten years flatly contradicts the general claim that the political process suffers from structural defects that necessitate a constitutional right to environmental quality [*Development,* 1977: 714–715].

Whether future generations will agree is an open question.

JAMES E. KRIER

Bibliography

SOPER, PHILIP 1974 The Constitutional Framework of Environmental Law. Pages 20–125 in E. Dolgin and T. Guilbert, eds., *Federal Environmental Law.* St. Paul, Minn.: West Publishing Co.

STEWART, RICHARD B. 1977 The Development of Administrative and Quasi-Constitutional Law in Judicial Review of Environmental Decisionmaking: Lessons from the Clean Air Act. *Iowa Law Review* 62:713–769.

——— 1977 Pyramids of Sacrifice? Problems of Federalism in Mandating State Implementation of National Environmental Policy. *Yale Law Journal* 86:1196–1272.

EPPERSON v. ARKANSAS
393 U.S. 97 (1968)

Arkansas prohibited the teaching in its public schools "that mankind ascended or descended from a lower order of animals." In dealing with a challenge to the law based on establishment clause and FREEDOM OF SPEECH grounds, Justice ABE FORTAS, speaking for the Supreme Court, concluded that the Arkansas law violated the establishment clause. "There can be no doubt," he said, "that Arkansas sought to prevent its teachers from discussing the theory of evolution because it is contrary to the beliefs of some that the book of Genesis must be the exclusive source of the doctrine of the origin of man."

Justice HUGO L. BLACK and Justice POTTER STEWART concurred in brief opinions resting on VAGUENESS grounds. The Black opinion raised important GOVERNMENT SPEECH issues that are still unresolved.

RICHARD E. MORGAN

EQUAL EMPLOYMENT OPPORTUNITY COMMISSION (EEOC) v. WYOMING
460 U.S. 226 (1983)

The EEOC sought to enforce the AGE DISCRIMINATION IN EMPLOYMENT ACT (ADEA) against the state of Wyoming in a case involving the involuntary retirement of a fifty-five-year-old game warden. The Supreme Court, 5–4, upheld the ADEA as so applied. Justice WILLIAM J. BRENNAN, for the Court, found congressional power in the COMMERCE CLAUSE, and rejected the state's claim, based on NATIONAL LEAGUE OF CITIES V. USERY (1976), that it was immune to this form of congressional regulation. The majority was composed of the four dissenters in *Usery* plus Justice HARRY A. BLACKMUN.

Wyoming, Brennan said, failed the third part of the formula of *Hodel v. Virginia Surface Mining and Reclamation Association* (1981): the ADEA did not "directly impair" Wyoming's ability to "structure integral operations in areas of traditional governmental functions." Wyoming could use other means to test the fitness of game wardens—or, as the ADEA allowed, justify the necessity of the age limit. The ADEA would affect state finances and state policies only marginally. Chief Justice WARREN E. BURGER, for the four dissenters, employed the same *Hodel* formula and concluded that the ADEA was unconstitutional as applied to a state.

This decision helped set the stage for *Usery's* overruling in GARCIA V. SAN ANTONIO METROPOLITAN TRANSIT AUTHORITY (1984).

KENNETH L. KARST

(SEE ALSO: *Intergovernmental Immunities.*)

EQUAL PROTECTION OF THE LAWS

The ancient political ideal of equality did not find explicit recognition in the text of the Constitution until the FOURTEENTH AMENDMENT was ratified in 1868. Yet equality was an American ideal from the earliest colonial times. There was irony in the expression of the ideal in the DECLARATION OF INDEPENDENCE; the newly independent states generally limited voting to white male property owners, and THOMAS JEFFERSON, the Declaration's author, was the troubled owner of slaves. Even so, one feature of white American society that set it apart from Europe was an egalitarian climate for social relations. The Constitution's ban on TITLES OF NOBILITY symbolized the nation's determination to leave behind the old world's privileges of monarchy and aristocracy.

Jefferson, who believed in an aristocracy of "virtue and talents," understood that equality of opportunity was consistent with wide disparities among individuals' wealth and power. The equality he envisioned was, above all, equality before the law. The principle of universal laws, equally applicable to all citizens, itself provided a foundation for a market economy whose competitive struggles would lead to further inequalities. An equality that was formal, or legal, thus would undermine the "equality of condition" that attracted some of Jefferson's contemporaries. Yet formal equality was something that mattered greatly in the nation's first decades, and it matters greatly today. When Europeans remark, as they still do, on America's relatively high degree of equality, they are referring not to equality of wealth or political power but to equality of social status. With pardonable literary exaggeration, Simone de Beauvoir said it this way: "the rich American has no grandeur; the poor man no servility; human relations in daily life are on a footing of equality. . . ."

The Fourteenth Amendment's wording emphasizes legal equality. A state is forbidden to "deny to any person within its jurisdiction the equal protection of the laws." On its face this language seems to demand no more than even-handed enforcement of laws as they are written. Such a reading, however, would drain all life from the guarantee of equal protection. On this view even a law barring blue-eyed persons from state employment would pass constitutional muster if the state applied it equally, without discrimination, to all applicants, refusing jobs only to those who were blue-eyed. No one has ever seriously argued for so restricted a scope for the equal protection clause. The Supreme Court casually dismissed the idea with a passing comment in YICK WO V. HOPKINS (1886): "the equal protection of the laws is a pledge of the protection of equal laws."

At the other extreme of silliness, the *Yick Wo* statement might be taken literally, interpreting the equal protection clause to forbid the enforcement of any law that imposed any inequality. As Joseph Tussman and JACOBUS TEN BROEK showed nearly forty years ago, so sweeping a reading would convert the clause into a constitutional prohibition on legislation itself. All laws draw lines of classification, applying their rules only to some people (or some transactions or phenomena) and not to others. Furthermore, the very existence of law—that is, of governmental regulation of human behavior—implies inequality, for some individuals must evaluate the behavior of others and enforce the state's norms by imposing sanctions on the recalcitrant. In Ralf Dahrendorf's biting formulation, "all men are equal *before* the law but they are no longer equal *after* it." Given the diverse characteristics of humans, the achievement of equality as to one aspect of life necessarily implies inequalities as to other aspects. And if it were possible to construct a society characterized by total, uncompromising equality, no one would want to live in that society.

Then what kinds of inequality are prohibited by the equal protection clause? The abstraction, equality, cannot resolve cases; the question always remains, equality as to what? To give meaning to the equal protection clause requires identification of the substantive values that are its central concern. The inquiry begins in the history leading to the adoption of the Fourteenth Amendment, but it does not end there. To understand the substantive content of the equal protection clause, we must consider not only what it meant to its framers, but also what it has come to mean to succeeding generations of judges and other citizens.

Just what role the framers had in mind for the equal protection clause remains unclear; the amendment's sketchy "legislative history" has been given widely divergent interpretations. All the interpreters agree, however, that the framers' immediate objective was to provide an unshakable constitutional foundation for the CIVIL RIGHTS ACT OF 1866. That act had been passed over the veto of President ANDREW JOHNSON, who had asserted that it exceeded the powers of Congress.

The 1866 act had declared the CITIZENSHIP of all persons born in the United States and subject to its JURISDICTION. This declaration, later echoed in the text of the Fourteenth Amendment, had been designed to "overrule" the assertion by Chief Justice ROGER B. TANEY in his opinion for the Supreme Court in DRED SCOTT V. SANDFORD (1857) that black persons were incapable of being citizens. Taney had said that blacks—not just slaves but any blacks—were incapable of citizenship, because blacks had not been members of "the People of the United States" identified in the Constitution's PREAMBLE as the body who adopted that document. Blacks has been excluded from membership in the national community, according to Taney, because they were "considered as a subordinate and inferior class of beings, who had been subjugated by the dominant race, and, whether emancipated or not, yet remained subject to their authority. . . ." Discriminatory state legislation in force when the Constitution was adopted, Taney said, negated the conclusion that the states "regarded at that time, as fellow-citizens and members of the sovereignty, a class of beings whom they had thus stigmatized; . . . and upon whom they had impressed such deep and enduring marks of inferiority and degradation. . . ."

This dubious reading of history is beside the point; *Dred Scott*'s relevance to our inquiry is that Taney's assumptions about racial inferiority and restricted citizenship were just what the drafters of the 1866 act sought to destroy. There was to be no "dominant race" and no "subordinate and inferior class of beings," but only citizens. Indeed the act's conferral of various CIVIL RIGHTS was aimed at abolishing a new system of serfdom designed to replace SLAVERY in the southern states. That system rested on the BLACK CODES, laws methodically imposing legal disabilities on blacks for the purpose of maintaining them in a state of dependency and inferiority.

The 1866 act, after its declaration of citizenship,

provided that "such citizens, of every race and color [including former slaves], shall have the same right [to contract and sue in court and deal with property, etc.] as is enjoyed by white citizens. . . ." The "civil rights" thus guaranteed were seen as the equal rights of citizens. When President Johnson vetoed the bill, he similarly linked the ideas of citizenship and equality, and argued that the THIRTEENTH AMENDMENT was an insufficient basis for congressional power. Congress overrode Johnson's veto, but from the time of the veto forward, a major purpose of the promoters of the Fourteenth Amendment, then under consideration in Congress, was to secure the constitutional foundations of the 1866 act.

The amendment, like the act, begins with a declaration of citizenship. In the same first section, the amendment goes on to forbid a state to "abridge the PRIVILEGES OR IMMUNITIES of citizens of the United States," to "deprive any person of life, liberty, or property, without DUE PROCESS OF LAW," or to deny a person "the equal protection of the laws." No serious effort was made during the debates on the amendment to identify separate functions for the three clauses that followed the declaration of citizenship. The section as a whole was taken to guarantee the equal enjoyment of the rights of citizens.

Beyond those specific goals, nothing in the consensus of the Fourteenth Amendment's framers would have caused anyone to anticipate what the Supreme Court made of the amendment in the latter half of the twentieth century. Yet the Fourteenth Amendment was not written in the language of specific rights, such as the right to contract or buy or sell property, but was deliberately cast in the most general terms. The broad language of the amendment strongly suggests that its framers were proposing to write into the Constitution not a "laundry list" of specific civil rights but a principle of equal citizenship.

To be a citizen is to enjoy the dignity of membership in the society, to be respected as a person who "belongs." The principle of equal citizenship presumptively forbids the organized society to treat an individual either as a member of an inferior or dependent caste or as a nonparticipant. As Taney recognized in his *Dred Scott* opinion, the stigma of caste is inconsistent with equal citizenship, which demands respect for each individual's humanity. Further, a citizen is a participant in society, a member of a moral community who must be taken into account when community decisions are made. Citizenship also implies obligations to one's fellow citizens. The values of participation and responsibility contribute to the primary citizenship value of respect, but they are also independently significant as aspects of citizenship.

For the first eight decades of the Fourteenth Amendment's existence, its interpretation by the Supreme Court was largely a betrayal of the constitutional ideal of equal citizenship. First by inventing the STATE ACTION limitation on the Fourteenth Amendment in the CIVIL RIGHTS CASES (1883), and then by giving racial SEGREGATION the stamp of constitutional validity in the SEPARATE BUT EQUAL decision of PLESSY V. FERGUSON (1896), the Supreme Court delivered virtually the entire subject of race relations back into the hands of the white South. The equal citizenship principle was left to be articulated in dissenting opinions. Notable among those dissents were the opinions of Justice JOSEPH P. BRADLEY in the SLAUGHTERHOUSE CASES (1873) and of Justice JOHN MARSHALL HARLAN in the *Civil Rights Cases* and *Plessy v. Ferguson.* The latter dissent included a passage that is now famous: "In view of the Constitution, in the eye of the law, there is in this country no superior, dominant, ruling class of citizens. There is no caste here. Our Constitution is color-blind, and neither knows nor tolerates classes among citizens." For half a century, those words expressed not a reality but a hope.

Outside the field of RACIAL DISCRIMINATION, the equal protection clause had little force even during the period when the due process clause of the Fourteenth Amendment was in active use as a defense against various forms of ECONOMIC REGULATION. By the 1920s, Justice OLIVER WENDELL HOLMES could say in BUCK V. BELL (1927), with accuracy if not with compassion, that the equal protection clause was the "usual last resort of constitutional arguments."

Even during the years when Holmes's "last resort" epithet summarized equal protection jurisprudence, the NAACP was pinning its hopes for racial justice on the federal judiciary, and was winning some victories. The Supreme Court had struck down LITERACY TESTS for voting that contained GRANDFATHER CLAUSES exempting most white voters, in GUINN V. UNITED STATES (1915) and *Lane v. Wilson* (1939); the Court had begun the process of holding "white primaries" unconstitutional; and it had invalidated racial zoning in BUCHANAN V. WARLEY (1917). And after the nation had emerged from the Great Depression and World War II, the judicial climate was distinctly more hospitable to equal protection claims.

The Depression had brought to dominance a new political majority, committed to active governmental intervention in economic affairs for the purpose of achieving full employment and major improvements in wages and the conditions of labor. The judiciary's main contribution to those egalitarian goals was to free the legislative process from the close judicial supervision of economic regulation that had attended the flowering of SUBSTANTIVE DUE PROCESS doctrines in the recent past. The war not only ended the Depression; it was a watershed in race relations. The migration of blacks from the rural South to northern and western cities, which had slowed during the Depression, dramatically accelerated, as wartime industry offered jobs that black workers had previously filled only rarely. Urban blacks were soon seen as a potent national political force. By the end of the war, the Army had begun the process of racial integration. Wartime ideology, with its scorn for Nazi racism, had lasting effects on the public mind. Even as the Supreme Court was upholding severe—and racist—wartime restrictions in the JAPANESE AMERICAN CASES (1943–1944), it reflected a new national state of mind in its celebrated OBITER DICTUM in KOREMATSU V. UNITED STATES (1944): "All legal restrictions which curtail the civil rights of a single racial group are immediately suspect. . . . [C]ourts must subject them to the most rigid scrutiny."

In the immediate postwar years the Supreme Court held unconstitutional the judicial enforcement of RESTRICTIVE COVENANTS in SHELLEY V. KRAEMER (1948), and it even ruled that the equal protection clause forbade some forms of segregation in state universities. (See SWEATT V. PAINTER, 1950.) The expected return to economic depression did not materialize. Instead, the country entered a period of unprecedented economic expansion. Good times are the most propitious for egalitarian public policies; it is relatively easy for "haves" to share with "have-nots" when they see their own conditions as steadily improving. The time was ripe, in the 1950s, for important successes in the movement for racial equality.

On the national scene, however, the political branches of government remained disinclined to act. One-party politics in the South had given disproportionate influence in the Congress to Southerners whose seniority gave them chairs of major committees. With President DWIGHT D. EISENHOWER reluctant to intervene, the prospects for effective civil rights legislation seemed dim. Thus was the stage furnished when Eisenhower appointed EARL WARREN to the Chief Justiceship in 1953.

In Warren's first term the Court decided BROWN V. BOARD OF EDUCATION (1954)—still the leading authoritative affirmation that the Constitution forbids a system of caste—and in so doing began what Philip Kurland has called an "egalitarian revolution" in constitutional law. *Brown* was a major event in modern American history. Race relations in America would never again be what they were on the eve of the decision. The political movement for racial equality took on new vitality, and other egalitarian movements drew encouragement from that example. The constitutional law of equal protection gained powerful momentum, and the doctrinal effects went well beyond the subject of racial equality. If *Brown* itself represented JUDICIAL ACTIVISM, it was no more than a shadow of what was to come. The equal protection clause became the cutting edge of the WARREN COURT's active intervention into realms that previously had been left to legislative choice.

Two doctrinal techniques served these egalitarian ends. First, the Court heightened the STANDARD OF REVIEW used to test the constitutionality of certain laws, insisting on STRICT SCRUTINY by the courts of legislation that employed a SUSPECT CLASSIFICATION or discriminated against the exercise of a FUNDAMENTAL INTEREST. Second, the Court relaxed the "state action" limitation on the Fourteenth Amendment, bringing new forms of private conduct under the amendment's reach. Although the BURGER COURT later revitalized the "state action" limitation and slowed the advance of equal protection into new doctrinal territory, it made its own contributions to the development of the principle of equal citizenship.

Once the Court had firmly fastened the "suspect classification" label to racial discrimination, other forms of discrimination were attacked in the same terms. Some Justices have refused to find any legislative classification other than race to be constitutionally disfavored, but most of them have been receptive to arguments that at least some nonracial discriminations deserve heightened scrutiny. Thus, while only discrimination against ALIENS has been assimilated to the "suspect classifications" category—and even that assimilation is a sometime thing—the Court has announced clearly that judicial scrutiny should be heightened in some significant degree for SEX DISCRIMINATION or legislative classifications based on ILLEGITIMACY. Not only in these opinions but also in opinions refusing to apply similar reasoning to other forms of discrimination, the Court has developed a consensus on two sets of factors that are relevant in determining a classification's degree of "suspectness" or disfavor, and thus the level of justification which courts should demand for it.

The first set of factors emphasizes the equal citizenship value of respect; these factors reflect the judiciary's solicitude for the victims of stigma. A classification on the basis of a trait that is immutable and highly visible—such as race or sex—promotes stereotyping, the automatic assignment of an individual to a general category, often implying inferiority. The second set of factors, emphasizing the equal citizenship value of participation, focuses on the historic disadvantages (especially political disadvantages) of DISCRETE AND INSULAR MINORITIES. Both the phrase and the idea antedate Warren Court activism; they come from Justice HARLAN FISKE STONE's opinion for the Court in UNITED STATES V. CAROLENE PRODUCTS CO. (1938). Legislation that burdens a group likely to be neglected by the legislature is a natural candidate for special judicial scrutiny.

The equal citizenship themes of respect, participation, and responsibility also informed the Warren Court's decisions demanding close examination of the justifications for legislative discrimination against the exercise of "fundamental interests." Those decisions, in theory, might have been rested on grounds of substantive due process rather than equal protection. In fact, the Burger Court, which refused to recognize any new "fundamental" interests in equal protection doctrine, employed similar reasoning under the heading of due process, with corresponding attention to the values of equal citizenship. (See ABORTION AND THE CONSTITUTION; FAMILY AND THE CONSTITUTION; RIGHT OF PRIVACY.) The equal protection cases, however, identify only three clusters of interests as "fundamental": VOTING RIGHTS and related interests in equal access to the electoral process; certain rights of ACCESS TO THE COURTS (which have come to be explained more recently on due process grounds); and rights concerning marriage, procreation, and family relations. (See FREEDOM OF INTIMATE ASSOCIATION.)

Voting, of course, is one of the core responsibilities of citizenship. Perhaps more important, it is the citizen's preeminent symbol of participation as a valued member of the community. Access to the courts, like voting, is instrumentally valuable as a way to protect other interests. But—also like voting—the chance to be heard is an important citizenship symbol. To be listened to, to be treated as a person and not an object of administration, is to be afforded the dignity owed to a citizen. Finally, the marriage and family cases similarly implicate the citizenship values of respect, responsibility, and participation. Marriage and parenthood do not merely define one's legal obligations; they define one's status and social role and self-concept. For the state to deny a person the right and responsibility of choice about such matters is to take away the presumptive right to be treated as a person, one of equal worth among citizens. None of these "fundamental" interests is entirely immune from state interference; what the principle of equal citizenship requires is that government offer weighty justification before denying their equal enjoyment.

In retrospect the whole apparatus of differential standards of review can be seen as judicial interest-balancing, thinly disguised: the more important the interest in equality, the more justification was required for its invasion by the government. Perhaps the Warren Court's majority chose to clothe its decisions in a "judicial"-sounding system of categories because the Justices were sensitive to the charge that they were writing their own policy preferences into the equal protection clause, and not just "interpreting" it. As a consequence, the Court extended the reach of equal protection without ever explicitly articulating the substantive content of the equal protection clause.

The Warren Court, in its final years, was well on the way to effective abandonment of the "state action" limitation on the Fourteenth Amendment, finding "significant state involvement" in all manner of private racial discriminations that denied their victims full participation in the public life of the community. Once Congress passed the CIVIL RIGHTS ACT OF 1964, however, it became unnecessary for the Court to complete its dismantling job; now there was a federal statutory right of access to PUBLIC ACCOMMODATIONS such as hotels, restaurants, and theaters. When the Court in JONES V. ALFRED H. MAYER CO. (1968) discovered the Thirteenth Amendment as a source of congressional power to forbid most other private racial discrimination, the chief practical motivation for doing away with the "state action" doctrine was removed. In later years, a different majority of Justices has gone far to restore the "state action" limitation to its former status but at the same time it has both reaffirmed the power of Congress to stamp out private racial discrimination and promoted that purpose with an expansive interpretation of existing civil rights acts.

The right to participate in the community's public life—even those portions of public life that are owned and managed by private persons—is an essential ingredient of effective citizenship, part of what it means to be a respected member of society. The "state action" limitation, when the Supreme Court invented it, insulated the "private" choices of the owners of public accommodations and other commercial businesses not only from the direct reach of the Fourteenth Amendment's guarantee of equal protection but also from congressional vindication of the rights of equal citizenship. Although "state action" remains an impediment to the application of the equal protection clause to some private conduct, Congress can protect, and has protected, the most important claims to participation by all citizens in society's public life.

To say that the principle of equal citizenship is the substantive core of the equal protection clause, and that the Supreme Court's recent equal protection jurisprudence has centered on the values of equal citizenship, is not to decide particular cases. Equal citizenship is not a decisional machine but a principle that informs judgment by reference to certain substantive values. Like other constitutional principles, it is inescapably open-ended. The Warren Court's expansion of the content of equal protection doctrine was regularly greeted with the criticism that the Court had not specified exactly how far its egalitarian principles would reach. The critics did no more than echo what Jeremy Bentham had said more than a century earlier: the abstraction, equality, is insatiable; where would it all end?

This "stopping-place" problem is implicit in any constitutional guarantee of equality. Most obviously, it lies at the center of the question of affirmative governmental obligations to reduce inequality. In a few decisions over the past three decades the Supreme Court has imposed on government the duty to compensate for the inability of INDIGENTS to pay various costs or fees required for effective access to the courts. The Burger Court's consciousness of the stopping-place problem produced two types of response. Some claims of access, although accepted, were explained as resting on rights to procedural fairness, and thus on due process rather than equal protection grounds. (See BODDIE V. CONNECTICUT, 1971.) Other access claims were rejected, halting further extension of the demands of equal protection. (See ROSS V. MOFFITT, 1974.) Yet the Court has not been willing to put an end to the notion that some inequalities, although not caused directly by the state, are constitutionally intolerable, requiring governmental action to relieve their victims from some of their consequences.

Similarly, consciousness of the stopping-place problem has influenced the Court's definition of what constitutes a legislative discrimination based on race, or gender, or, presumably, any other disfavored classification. After flirting in some school segregation cases with a view that would equate de facto with de jure segregation, the Court declared in the employment discrimination case of WASHINGTON V. DAVIS (1976) that it was not enough, in making a claim of racial discrimination, to show that legislation had a racially discriminatory impact. To succeed, such a claim must be based on a showing of official discriminatory purpose. (See LEGISLATION.) The "impact" principle, said the Court, "would be far reaching and would raise serious questions about, and perhaps invalidate, a whole range of tax, welfare, public service, regulatory, and licensing statutes that may be more burdensome to the poor and to the average black than to the more affluent white." In other words, where would it all end?

What is needed, in dealing with the stopping-place problem as with any other aspect of equal protection interest-balancing, is the guidance that can be found in the Fourteenth Amendment's substantive values. Some inequalities will invade the core values of equal citizenship, and others will touch them hardly at all. The level of justification required for governmental action—or failure to act—will vary according to the magnitude of that invasion. Some economic inequalities may be so severe as to impose a stigma of caste, but most do not. Part of our tradition of responsible citizenship, after all, is to provide for oneself and one's family. The principle of equal citizenship is not a charter for economic leveling but a presumptive guarantee against those inequalities that dehumanize or seriously impair one's ability to participate as a member of society. To say that such determinations turn on questions of degree is merely to acknowledge that no constitutional principle is a substitute for judicial judgment.

Since the late 1960s a number of governmental and private bodies have voluntarily taken steps to compensate for inequalities that are the legacy of past societal discrimination, and generally to integrate various institutions by race and by gender. These AFFIRMATIVE ACTION programs, sometimes in the form of racial or gender-based quotas for employment or housing or admission to higher education, do not merely equalize. Every equality begets another inequality. Even absent a quota, when a person's race becomes a relevant qualification for a job, all other relevant factors are diminished in weight. To put the matter more concretely, an individual can lose the competition for the job on the basis of his or her race. If affirmative action is constitutionally justified—and the Supreme Court has largely validated it—the reasons lie not in any lack of sympathy for such arguments, but in the weight of countervailing considerations supporting the programs. The Justices' various opinions upholding affirmative action have mainly sounded the theme of remedying past discrimination, but other arguments emphasize the urgency of integrating American institutions in the present generation.

The debate over affirmative action has touched a more general issue: the appropriate role of groups in equal protection analysis. In one view, group membership is simply irrelevant. The text of the equal protection clause provides its guarantees to "any person," and much of our constitutional tradition is individualistic. Yet, inescapably, a claim to equality is a claim made on behalf of a group. If every law draws some line of classification, then it is also true that every individual is potentially classifiable according to an enormous variety of characteristics. Legislative classification implies a selection of certain attributes as the relevant ones—the "merits" that justify conferring a benefit (or "demerits" that justify a burden). Once such a classification is written into law, any individual is classified either with the group of persons who possess the "merits" (or "demerits") or with the group of those who do not. To complain against a classification scheme is not merely to say "I am wronged," but to say "We—the whole group of individuals disadvantaged—are wronged." Indeed, any claim based on a rule of law is intelligible only as a demand to be treated the same as other members of a group, that is, all others who share the relevant "individual" attributes specified by the rule.

The origins of the Fourteenth Amendment strongly suggest that a group, defined by race just as the *Dred Scott* opinion had defined it, was intended to be the amendment's chief beneficiary. If today the equal protection clause prohibits other forms of inequality, there is nothing incongruous about viewing that development in one perspective as the recognition of the claims of groups of people: women, aliens, illegitimate children, homosexuals, the handicapped. When equal citizenship is denied, the denial typically takes a form that affects not merely isolated individuals but classes of people.

The equal protection clause limits only the states; nothing in the constitutional text expressly imposes an analogous limit on the federal government. Yet since BOLLING V. SHARPE (1954) the Supreme Court has consistently interpreted the Fifth Amendment's due process clause to guarantee equal protection against federal denial. This interpretation has roots in the original Constitution's assumption that the new national government would have a direct relationship with individuals. The idea of national citizenship was current long before the Civil Rights Act of 1866. And that citizenship, as Justice Bradley argued in his dissent in the *Slaughterhouse Cases,* implies some measure of equality before the law. *Bolling,* a companion case to *Brown v. Board of Education,* presented a challenge to school segregation in the District of Columbia. *Brown* held the segregation of state schools unconstitutional, and Chief Justice Warren said it would be "unthinkable" if a similar principle were not applied to the national government. After the Fourteenth Amendment's reaffirmation of national citizenship, such a result would, indeed, have been unthinkable.

The Warren Court's expansion of constitutional guarantees of equality necessarily implied an expansion of the powers of the national government. The Civil War amendments were reinterpreted to give Congress sweeping powers to reach virtually all racial discriminations, public and private. The Fourteenth Amendment's equal protection clause became the basis for intensified intervention by the federal courts into areas previously governed by local law and custom, as a new body of uniform national law replaced local autonomy. As the "state action" limitation was relaxed, the Constitution brought the commands of law to areas previously regulated by private institutional decision. In ALEXANDER BICKEL's phrase, the Warren Court's main themes were "egalitarian, legalitarian, and centralizing."

The desegregation of places of public accommodations in the South is an instructive example. The Supreme Court first held unconstitutional all forms of state-sponsored segregation, including segregation of public beaches, parks, golf courses, and restaurants. Then, cautiously, it began to apply the same reasoning to some privately owned public accommodations, finding "state action" in the most tenuous connections between public policy and the private decision to segregate. Finally, in HEART OF ATLANTA MOTEL CO. V. UNITED STATES (1964) the Court moved swiftly to validate the Civil Rights Act of 1964, which forbade segregation in most public accommodations that mattered. In all these actions the Court promoted the extension of a body of uniform national law to replace the local laws and customs that had long governed southern communities, with an earlier Supreme Court's blessing.

These changes in the law governing racial discrimination in public accommodations were, in one perspective, a repetition of a course of events that had been common in the Western world since the seventeenth century. An older system, basing a person's legal rights on his or her status in a hierarchical structure, came to be replaced by a newer law that applied impersonally to everyone. The abolition of slavery, the 1866 Civil Rights Act, the Civil War amendments—all had been earlier episodes in this same historical line. And the law that liberated individuals from domination based on race, like the law that previously had broken feudal hierarchies and the power of the guilds, was the law of the centralized state. If one were asked to compress three centuries of Western political history into three words, the words might be: "egalitarian, legalitarian, and centralizing."

Justice ROBERT H. JACKSON, concurring in EDWARDS V. CALIFORNIA (1941), remarked that the Fourteenth Amendment's privileges and immunities clause was aimed at making United States citizenship "the dominant and paramount allegiance among us." Whatever the historical warrant for that assertion, it reflects today's social fact. We think of ourselves primarily as citizens of the nation, and only secondarily as citizens of the several states. The Constitution itself has become our pre-eminent symbol of national community, and the judiciary's modern contributions to our sense of community have centered on the principle of equal citizenship.

It is hard to overstate the importance of the ideal of equality as a legitimizing force in American history. For the SOCIAL COMPACT theorists of the eighteenth century whose thinking was well-known to the Framers of the original Constitution, some measure of equality before the law was implicit in the idea of citizenship. DANIEL WEBSTER, speaking of "the LAW OF THE LAND," agreed: "The meaning is, that every citizen shall hold his life, liberty, property, and immunities, under the protection of the general rules which govern society." By Webster's time, support for the principle of equality of opportunity could be found even among the most comfortable Americans, who saw in that principle a way to justify their advantages. More generally, the egalitarian spirit that has promoted a national consciousness has also lent legitimacy to government. There has been just enough truth in the belief that "anyone can grow up to be President" to provide a critical measure of the diffuse loyalty that is an essential ingredient of nationhood.

Never in our history has it been true that *anyone* might aspire to the presidency. Slavery and racial discrimination are only the most obvious and uglier counterexamples; not until our own time have women's aspirations to such high position become realistic. Yet the guarantee of equal protection of the laws, even during the long decades when lawyers deemed it a constitutional trifle, stood as a statement of an important American ideal. Much of the growth in our constitutional law has resulted when the downtrodden have called the rest of us to account, asking whether we intend to live up to the principles we profess. Vindication of the constitutional promise of equal citizenship did not take its rightful place on our judicial agenda for an unconscionably long time, and it remains far from complete. What is most remarkable, however, is the nourishment that the promise—the promise alone—has provided for a national community.

KENNETH L. KARST

Bibliography

BELL, DERRICK A., JR. 1980 *Race, Racism, and American Law*, 2nd ed. Boston: Little, Brown.

BICKEL, ALEXANDER M. 1970 *The Supreme Court and the Idea of Progress.* New York: Harper & Row.

BLACK, CHARLES L., JR. 1969 *Structure and Relationship in Constitutional Law.* Pages 51–66. Baton Rouge: Louisiana State University Press.

ELY, JOHN HART 1980 *Democracy and Distrust: A Theory of Judicial Review.* Cambridge, Mass.: Harvard University Press.

FISS, OWEN M. 1976 Groups and the Equal Protection Clause. *Philosophy and Public Affairs* 5:107–177.

KARST, KENNETH L. 1977 The Supreme Court, 1976 Term—Foreword: Equal Citizenship under the Fourteenth Amendment. *Harvard Law Review* 91:1–68.

KINOY, ARTHUR 1967 The Constitutional Right of Negro Freedom. *Rutgers Law Review* 21:387–441.

MICHELMAN, FRANK I. 1969 The Supreme Court, 1968 Term—Foreword: On Protecting the Poor Through the Fourteenth Amendment. *Harvard Law Review* 83:7–59.

POLE, J. R. 1978 *The Pursuit of Equality in American History.* Berkeley: University of California Press.

RAE, DOUGLAS 1981 *Equalities.* Cambridge, Mass.: Harvard University Press.

TOCQUEVILLE, ALEXIS DE 1945 *Democracy in America,* P. Bradley, ed., 2 vols. New York: Vintage Books.

TUSSMAN, JOSEPH and TEN BROEK, JACOBUS 1949 The Equal Protection of the Laws. *California Law Review* 37:341–381.

WESTEN, PETER 1982 The Empty Idea of Equality. *Harvard Law Review* 95:537–596.

EQUAL RIGHTS AMENDMENT

In March 1972, Congress proposed an Equal Rights Amendment (ERA) to the United States Constitution. The amendment provided:

Section 1. Equality of rights under the law shall not be denied or abridged by the United States or by any State on account of sex.
Section 2. The Congress shall have the power to enforce, by appropriate legislation, the provisions of this article.
Section 3. The Amendment shall take effect two years after the date of ratification.

In May 1982, the extended deadline for ratification expired without the necessary approval from three-fourths of the states; fifteen had never ratified and five had voted to rescind their ratification. Challenges to the legality of those rescissions and to Congress's extension of the ratification deadline became moot.

Proponents subsequently reintroduced the amendment in Congress, thus continuing a campaign that began a half-century earlier. Some version of an equal rights amendment had surfaced in every congressional term between 1923 and 1972. In the view of most proponents, the text adopted in 1972 was designed to prohibit gender classifications except those concerning personal privacy, physical characteristics, or past discrimination. The rationale was that a constitutional prohibition would avoid piecemeal remedies for various forms of discrimination. Such a mandate would also subject sex-based classifications to a more rigorous standard of review than that prevailing under FOURTEENTH AMENDMENT doctrine, which allows discrimination substantially related to an important state purpose.

Although conceived as a measure to unite women, the amendment has often divided them. Throughout its history, the ERA campaign has triggered fundamental controversies about the meaning of equality and the means to attain it in a society marked by significant disparities in sexual roles. Much debate has centered not on legal entitlements but on cultural aspirations. Dispute has focused on the amendment's effect concerning laws purportedly advantaging women, such as protective labor legislation, marital support requirements, and military service exemptions. Particularly during the earlier part of the century, opponents contended that equality in formal mandates could never secure equality in fact. So long as female wage earners and homemakers were more economically vulnerable than men, a demand for equal rights appeared out of touch with social realities. By contrast, ERA proponents contended that protective legislation had often "protected" women from opportunities for higher paid vocations, and had legitimated stereotypes on which invidious discrimination rested. Supporters also noted that by the time Congress proposed the amendment in 1972, much sex-based regulation had been either invalidated or extended to men, and that which remained could be cast in sex-neutral terms.

So too, much of the discrimination that the amendment was originally designed to redress was, by the 1970s, illegal under various judicial, executive, and legislative mandates. Accordingly, the ERA ratification campaign frequently focused on symbolic rather than legal implications. To proponents, a constitutional mandate would serve as an important affirmation of women's equal status and as a catalyst for change in social practices beyond the scope of legal regulation. For opponents, however, the amendment's symbolic subtext represented an assault less on gender discrimination than on gender differences, and an invitation for further encroachments on states' rights.

In the ratification struggle of the 1970s, ERA supporters lacked the leverage to make their interests felt. But if the equal rights campaign helps inspire and empower women to expand their political influence, then the struggle itself may prove more important than its constitutional consequences.

DEBORAH L. RHODE

Bibliography

BOLES, JANET 1979 *The Politics of the Equal Rights Amendment: Conflict and the Decision Process.* New York: Longmans.

BROWN, BARBARA A.; EMERSON, THOMAS I.; FALK, GAIL; and FREEDMAN, ANN E. 1971 The Equal Rights Amendment: A Constitutional Basis for Equal Rights for Women. *Yale Law Journal* 80:872–985.

RHODE, DEBORAH L. 1983 Equal Rights in Retrospect. *Journal of Law and Inequality* 1:1–72.

EQUITABLE RESTRAINT

See: Abstention Doctrines

EQUITY

First named (in Article III) among the subjects to which the judicial power "shall extend" are "all Cases, in Law and Equity, arising under this Constitution, the Laws of the United States, and Treaties made, or which shall be made, under their authority." The word "equity" has here a technical meaning well comprehended by American lawyers of the eighteenth century, and today still generally familiar to lawyers in all legal systems derived from that of England. The explanation is necessarily historical.

In a development more than well begun in the Middle Ages, and pretty much completed by Stuart times, England developed a unique double system of courts at the national level—the courts of "law," or COMMON LAW courts, and the "court of equity"—or, as it was often called, the "court of chancery."

The common law courts administered a system of law that was radically deficient, first as to remedies available, and, second, as to the breadth of considerations that could be taken into account in the formation of decisions. These courts could in most cases award only damages in money, in many cases a step inadequate to the doing of full justice. The common law courts were also excessively formalistic. If, for example, an error occurred in the transcription of a written contract, the common law courts had no conceptual apparatus for dealing with the mistake. Similarly, they had little capacity for taking into account the problems created by fraud. And the "trust," an institution of great importance, was utterly unknown to the "common law."

During the Middle Ages, suitors who could not get full justice out of the common law courts began to appeal to the Lord Chancellor, a high royal official, for supplementary or corrective help. By Tudor times, this practice had become firmly institutionalized, so that the Lord Chancellor became in some sense a judicial officer, hearing and dealing with such pleas. Little by little, the "chancery" came to be a court. This court had at its disposal a remedy enormously more versatile and efficient than the award of damages—the remedy of the order, or command, that the defendant do or refrain from doing something. The chancery court, in contrast to the courts of common law, knew nothing of the jury; the Chancellor decided all issues of fact and law.

This "court of chancery" opened its eyes, moreover, to many things the common law courts were institutionally disabled from seeing. While a suitor in the common law courts might, for example, get a JUDGMENT in his favor on a written contract procured by fraud on his part, the chancery court might order him to give up the fraudulently procured instrument, or to refrain from suing on it, or even to refrain from collecting on a "law" judgment he had already procured by using it.

Because this chancery court so often intervened in the name of a higher justice or of "conscience," it came to be thought of as (and called) a "court of equity." By the time of the drafting of the Constitution, the doctrines and practices of this kind of "equity" had become well systematized. And most of the new states had borrowed from English practice the two-part system of "law" courts and "chancery" courts, with the doctrines and remedial apparatus of equity available in the latter. It is against this background that the constitutional phrase, "cases in law and equity," is to be understood. "Cases in law" were such cases as would be heard by the common law courts; "cases in equity" were such as would be heard by the Court of Chancery, in England or in a state mirroring the English division.

At the very beginning, the new national government rejected (in the JUDICIARY ACT OF 1789) the idea of totally separate courts of "law" and of "equity." The lower federal courts combined "legal" and "equitable" JURISDICTION in the same judges. But the ancient division was in some sense continued. Down to 1938, the federal district court had the two separate sides of "law" and "equity," respectively—in addition to such special jurisdictions as admiralty and bankruptcy. Even today, after the formal merger of "law" and "equity" cases under the single name of "civil action," lawyers still refer, for example, to the INJUNCTION (an order to do or not to do something) as "equitable relief."

"Equity" cases, in the language of Article III, are of great importance. The injunction is enormously more flexible and powerful than the remedies—mostly the award of damages—available to the court in a "case at law." Dramatic examples abound. It would have been impossible even to begin thinking about the lower federal courts' desegregating the schools if those courts had not had jurisdiction over "cases in equity" seeking orders to state officials. On this jurisdictional grant, indeed, rests the whole elaborate development of efficacious relief against official action thought to be unconstitutional—ranging from injunctions against the enforcement of unconstitutional laws (as in PIERCE V. SOCIETY OF SISTERS, 1925, enjoining state enforcement of a law requiring all pupils to go to public schools) to the running of state prisons by an Alabama district judge. (See INSTITUTIONAL LITIGATION.) The modern history of practical constitutional safeguards is a history of the use of the "equitable" remedy of injunction, together with the remedy of the DECLARATORY JUDGMENT—a remedy that would probably have been judged outside the "judicial power" were it not for its close analogy to "cases in equity."

Another characteristic of "cases in equity," overpoweringly important in the use of the national judicial power to protect constitutional rights against action of the states, is that the "court of equity" does not use the jury. This, as far as we can tell, is a gift of history; there appears to be no intrinsic reason why a local jury should not find "the facts" in, say, school desegregation cases. Experience shows that local juries will not often convict, for example, in prosecutions for CIVIL RIGHTS crimes, where the jury is constitutionally required. The whole course of development of national protection of human rights against local oppression might have been quite different if it were not for the fact that the "court of equity," the Lord Chancellor's court, sat without a jury—so that the federal judge, wielding the vital weapons in the "equity" remedial armory, does the same.

CHARLES L. BLACK, JR.

Bibliography

FISS, OWEN M. 1972 *Injunctions.* Mineola, N.Y.: Foundation Press.

MCCLINTOCK, HENRY LACY 1948 *Handbook of the Principles of Equity.* St. Paul, Minn.: West Publishing Co.

ERDMAN ACT
30 Stat. 424 (1898)

The report of a commission appointed by President GROVER CLEVELAND to investigate the Pullman strike of 1894 (see IN RE DEBS) prompted this act, one of the earliest federal acts providing for the arbitration of railway labor disputes. The act applied to all railroads and their employees engaged in INTERSTATE COMMERCE and provided mediation of any labor dispute "seriously interrupting or threatening to interrupt" interstate commerce. If mediation failed to resolve the dispute, the parties could turn to an arbitration board whose award would be binding and enforceable through EQUITY proceedings. Neither strikes nor lockouts were permitted during arbitration or ninety days after an award. Section 10 made it a MISDEMEANOR for any employer to require, as a condition of employment, any discriminatory agreements, particularly with regard to union membership. Clearly aimed at outlawing YELLOW DOG CONTRACTS, section 10 fell in ADAIR V. UNITED STATES (1906) as a violation of FREEDOM OF CONTRACT. The act otherwise operated quite successfully, and Congress fortified its mediation provisions in 1913. A bitter nationwide strike in which both sides refused to invoke mediation, however, forced replacement of the act three years later with the ADAMSON EIGHT-HOUR ACT.

DAVID GORDON

Bibliography

TAYLOR, BENJAMIN J. and WITNEY, FRED 1971 *Labor Relations Law,* 2nd ed. Englewood Cliffs, N.J.: Prentice-Hall.

ERIE RAILROAD CO. v. TOMPKINS
304 U.S. 64 (1938)

The Supreme Court in *Erie* posed the question whether the "oft-challenged doctrine of SWIFT V. TYSON (1842) shall now be disapproved," and answered that it should. The Court rejected its earlier construction of the Rules of Decision Act, originally section 34 of the JUDICIARY ACT OF 1789, and held that the "laws of the several states"—which, except as otherwise required by federal law, are to be "regarded as rules of decision" in civil actions in the federal courts "in cases where they apply"—included all of the decisional or COMMON LAW of the states.

Erie, like *Swift,* involved an exercise of the DIVERSITY JURISDICTION of the federal courts. In *Erie,* plaintiff Tompkins brought a federal court suit against the railroad for personal injuries, and the court of appeals upheld a substantial jury verdict in the face of the railroad's claim that it had not violated the limited duty owned to plaintiff under the decisional law of the state where the injury occurred. That court concluded that, in the absence of a state statute, the question of the scope of the railroad's duty was one not of "local" but of "general" law, and under the general law the railroad had a duty of care that the jury could properly find to have been broken.

The Supreme Court, in an opinion by Justice LOUIS D. BRANDEIS, reversed and remanded for application of state law with respect to the scope of the railroad's duty. The Court concluded that (1) the refusal in *Swift* to read the mandate of the Rules of Decision Act as embracing all of the decisional law of the states was based on an incorrect construction of the purpose of that act; (2) the construction in *Swift* had prevented uniformity in the administration of state law and had permitted "grave discrimination by noncitizens [of a state] against citizens"; and (3) the doctrine of *Swift* represented "an unconstitutional assumption of powers by the Courts of the United States." Justices PIERCE BUTLER and JAMES C. MCREYNOLDS dissented; Justice STANLEY F. REED concurred in part, believing it unnecessary to reach the constitutional issue addressed by the Court.

Although the parties in *Erie* had not briefed the question whether *Swift* should be overruled, there had been intimations of the Court's intentions in earlier majority and dissenting opinions. And while the *Erie* result itself still finds general acceptance, the years since the decision have seen much debate about its rationale, scope, and application.

DAVID L. SHAPIRO

(SEE ALSO: *Federal Common Law, Civil.*)

ERNST, MORRIS
(1888–1976)

With his colleague ARTHUR GARFIELD HAYS, Morris Ernst served as general counsel to the AMERICAN CIVIL LIBERTIES UNION from 1929 to 1954. Together with Hays and ROGER BALDWIN, Ernst fought to protect individual rights against government action. Although he excoriated both the Ku Klux Klan and the Communist party, he defended members of both organizations. He was a staunch opponent of government censorship and defended James Joyce's novel against OBSCENITY charges in the ULYSSES trial (1934). Ernst participated in a number of well-known cases, including COMMONWEALTH OF MASSACHUSETTS V. SACCO AND VANZETTI (1921), HAGUE V. C.I.O. (1939), and the *Associated Press v. N.L.R.B.* (1937), one of the WAGNER ACT CASES. He wrote several popular books championing civil liberties.

DAVID GORDON

ERROR, WRIT OF

A writ of error is an order of an appellate court, directing a lower court to transmit the record of a case that it has decided, for review by the appellate court. The JUDICIARY ACT OF 1789 established the writ of error as the means of invoking the APPELLATE JURISDICTION of both the CIRCUIT COURTS and the Supreme Court. For a century, the writ of error was, in practice, virtually the exclusive method of invoking review by the Supreme Court. In the cases specified by law for issuance of the writ, review by the Supreme Court was obligatory. In 1891 Congress reorganized the federal judiciary, establishing the circuit courts of appeals. (See CIRCUIT COURTS OF APPEALS ACT.) In some cases, these courts' decisions were final, unless the courts certified questions for review by the Supreme Court, or the Supreme Court in its discretion granted WRITS OF CERTIORARI to review their decisions. In 1925, in the course of reducing the Supreme Court's obligatory JURISDICTION and expanding the Court's discretionary control of its docket, Congress changed the name of the writ of error; since that time the Supreme Court's theoretically obligatory appellate jurisdiction has been invoked by APPEAL.

KENNETH L. KARST

Bibliography

ROBERTSON, REYNOLDS and KIRKHAM, FRANCIS R. 1951 *Jurisdiction of the Supreme Court of the United States,* ed. Richard F. Wolfson and Philip B. Kurland. Pages 191–196, 756, 806–807. Albany, N.Y.: Matthew Bender.

ERVIN, SAMUEL J.
(1896–1985)

A conservative Democrat who graduated from Harvard Law School in 1922, Samuel J. Ervin described himself as an "ol' country lawyer" from North Carolina, his native state. In 1954 he left that state's supreme court to enter the United States Senate. During his two decades as a senator, he supported business against labor and opposed CIVIL RIGHTS legislation, equal rights for women, voting by eighteen-year-olds, and federal encroachments on STATES' RIGHTS. He also became a strict separationist on church–state issues, and he opposed intrusive searches, computer invasions of privacy, preventive detention, and any other measures he deemed subversive of the Constitution. By 1973 he was respected as the Senate's expert on the Constitution. Central casting destined him to be chairman that year of the Senate's Select Committee on Presidential Campaign Activities—the WATERGATE Committee. As chairman, he was a relentless but fair interrogator who expressed outrage when witnesses equivocated or lied. The televised hearings made him a national celebrity as the watchdog of the Constitution who preached the constitutional responsibilities of those entrusted with public office. Ervin projected a grandfatherly image of a judicious moralist, the very model of integrity when models were in short supply. The public adored "Senator Sam," and he adored the Constitution.

LEONARD W. LEVY

Bibliography

ERVIN, SAMUEL J., JR. 1980 *The Whole Truth: The Watergate Conspiracy.* New York: Random House.

ERZNOZNIK v. CITY OF JACKSONVILLE
422 U.S. 205 (1975)

An ordinance prohibited drive-in movie theaters from showing films containing nudity on screens visible from public streets or places. Conceding that the films were constitutionally protected speech, the city asserted an authority to protect its citizens, particularly minors, against unwilling exposure to offensive materials. The Supreme Court declared the ordinance unconstitutional, holding that people on public streets, unlike people in their homes or people on buses who are a captive audience, have only a limited interest in privacy which does not justify the city's discrimination among movies based solely on content.

KIM MCLANE WARDLAW

(SEE ALSO: *Obscenity.*)

ESCH-CUMMINGS TRANSPORTATION ACT
41 Stat. 456 (1920)

Congress favored the return of the railroads to private ownership and operation after government control during World War I. This act accomplished that objective and altered Congress's regulatory approach. It did not seek to prevent abuses so much as to strengthen the industry and foster the public interest. The act granted the Interstate Commerce Commission extensive new powers including the authority to set minimum rates, oversee fiscal operation of the roads, regulate acquisitions and consolidations, and supervise services. One provision prescribed a rate-making rule to assure "a FAIR RETURN upon the aggregate value of the railroad property," allowing the ICC to determine what constituted such a return. A recapture clause, inserted to protect weaker lines, required that roads earning a return over six percent divide that profit between a reserve fund for their own stability and a general fund (administered by the ICC) to compensate those railroads earning under four and one-half percent. The Supreme Court sustained this clause in DAYTON-GOOSE CREEK RAILWAY V. UNITED STATES (1924). The act also established labor boards with JURISDICTION over a variety of disputes.

DAVID GORDON

Bibliography

SHARFMAN, ISAIAH L. 1931–1937 *The Interstate Commerce Commission.* Vol. 1. New York: Commonwealth Fund.

ESCOBEDO v. ILLINOIS
378 U.S. 478 (1964)

Daniel Escobedo was arrested and taken to the police station for questioning. Over the course of several hours, his repeated requests to see his lawyer were refused and his lawyer sought unsuccessfully to consult with him. The Supreme Court held that Escobedo's subsequent confession was obtained in violation of his Sixth Amendment RIGHT TO COUNSEL. For the first time, the Court spoke of "an absolute constitutional right to remain silent," which the presence of a lawyer would facilitate. *Escobedo* is important also because it presaged MIRANDA V. ARIZONA (1966) in discussing the possibility that warnings about the right to counsel might serve to cure the infirmity of in-custody interrogation.

Although *Escobedo* retains historical significance, the arguments in POLICE INTERROGATION AND CONFESSION cases have largely shifted from the Sixth to the Fifth Amendment with an emphasis on whether warnings were given, and given correctly, and whether the right to remain silent was waived.

The case has lost authority as precedent in another respect. It seemed to establish a practical flexible standard for the time when Sixth Amendment rights would come into play: when "the investigation is no longer a general inquiry into an unresolved crime but has begun to focus on a particular suspect." This approach was specifically abandoned in *Kirby v. Illinois* (1972), when the court limited *Escobedo* to its facts and ruled that the right to counsel does not attach until adversary judicial proceedings have been initiated.

BARBARA ALLEN BABCOCK

ESPIONAGE ACT
40 Stat. 451 (1917)

When on April 2, 1917, President WOODROW WILSON asked Congress to recognize a STATE OF WAR, he included in his indictment of Germany the activities of German agents in the United States. Such activity, he said, should be treated with "a firm hand of stern repression." Nine weeks later, a much discussed and much amended Espionage Act was signed into law.

The initial measure, an amalgamation of seventeen bills prepared in the attorney general's office, was intended to "outlaw spies and subversive activities by foreign agents." Critics, particularly in the American press, quickly complained that the measure was far too restrictive and imposed a type of PRIOR RESTRAINT AND CENSORSHIP potentially destructive to basic American liberties. Thus, despite Wilson's contention that the administration must have authority to censor the press since this was "absolutely necessary to the public safety," the most overt censorship provisions were removed. The belief of a majority of national lawmakers that now the bill could not be used to suppress critical opinion overlooked the fact that two of the twelve titles of the act as passed still bore directly on freedom of expression. One provided punishment for (1) making or conveying false reports for the benefit of the enemy; (2) seeking to cause disobedience in the armed forces; and (3) willfully obstructing the recruiting or enlistment service. Another section closed the mails to any item violating any of the act's provisions.

The constitutional basis of these two provisions rested on a broad interpretation of the federal WAR POWERS and upon the argument that a denial of use of the mails did not constitute censorship, since the federal courts had ruled that the mails constituted an optional federal service. Thus, it was argued, refusal to extend the facility did not deprive anyone of a constitutional right. Further, the measure's supporters argued that FREEDOM OF SPEECH was not absolute and could not protect a person who deliberately sought to obstruct the national war effort.

The difficulty of applying the law, however, was clear from the outset, since the statute sought to punish questionable intent, a difficult factor to measure. With punishment set at a $10,000 fine, imprisonment for up to twenty years, or both, and with its interpretation largely in the hands of patriotic enforcers, many suffered under the measure and its subsequent amendments. The Justice Department prosecuted more than 2,000 cases. At least 1,050 citizens were convicted under its terms, including Industrial Workers of the World leaders, Socialists (especially Eugene V. Debs), and a number of suspect hyphenates, particularly German-Americans, whose verbal criticism of aspects of the war were often brutally repressed. The Supreme Court upheld the constitutionality of the act's prohibitions on causing disobedience in the armed forces and obstructing enlistment in a series of postwar decisions: SCHENCK V. UNITED STATES (1919), FROHWERK V. UNITED STATES (1919); DEBS V. UNITED STATES (1919).

Under the mails provisions, the postmaster general exercised virtually dictatorial authority over the effective circulation of the American press, a power which he used capriciously and subjectively for punitive reasons. In an effort to preserve FIRST AMENDMENT values through the process of statutory construction, Judge LEARNED HAND construed the mails provision narrowly to exclude its application to ordinary criticism of government policies, including war policy. Hand's decision, however, was reversed by the court of appeals. (See MASSES PUBLISHING CO. V. PATTEN, 1917.)

The measure remained on the books through the 1920s and 1930s and was reenacted in March 1940, Congress increasing its penalties for peacetime violation. The Supreme Court narrowed its application in *Hartzel v. United States* (1944) by interpreting its provisions through a literal application of Holmes's clear and present danger test. The government again turned to it in 1971, seeking unsuccessfully to prevent the publication by the *New York Times* of the "Pentagon papers," which the government called harmful to the security of the United States. (See NEW YORK TIMES CO. V. UNITED STATES, 1971.)

PAUL L. MURPHY

Bibliography

CHAFEE, ZECHARIAH 1941 *Free Speech in the United States.* Cambridge, Mass.: Harvard University Press.

MURPHY, PAUL 1979 *World War I and the Origin of Civil Liberties in the United States.* New York: Norton.

ESTABLISHMENT CLAUSE

See: Establishment of Religion; First Amendment; Religious Liberty; Separation of Church and State

ESTABLISHMENT OF RELIGION

The FIRST AMENDMENT begins with the clause, "Congress shall make no law respecting an establishment of religion. . . ." There are two basic interpretations of what the framers meant by this clause. In EVERSON V. BOARD OF EDUCATION (1947), the first decision on the clause, the Supreme Court unanimously adopted the broad interpretation, although the Justices then and thereafter disagreed on its application. (See SEPARATION OF CHURCH AND STATE.) Justice HUGO L. BLACK declared that the clause means not only that government cannot set up a church but also that government cannot aid all religions impartially or levy a tax for the support of any religious activities, institutions, or practices. "In the words of [THOMAS] JEFFERSON," Black said, "the clause against establishment of religion by laws was intended to erect 'a wall of separation between Church and State.' "

EDWARD S. CORWIN, a distinguished constitutional scholar who espoused the narrow view of the clause, asserted that the Court's interpretation was "untrue historically." What the clause does, he wrote, "and all that it does, is to forbid Congress to give any religious faith, sect, or denomination preferred status.

. . . The historical record shows beyond peradventure that the core idea of 'an establishment of religion' comprises the idea of preference; and that any act of public authority favorable to religion in general cannot, without manifest falsification of history, be brought under the ban of that phase" (Corwin, "Supreme Court as National School Board," pp. 10, 20). Justice POTTER STEWART, dissenting in ENGEL V. VITALE (1962), endorsed the narrow view when he noted that a nondenominational school prayer did not confront the Court with "the establishment of a state church" or an "official religion."

The debate in the First Congress, which proposed the First Amendment, provides support for neither the broad nor the narrow interpretation. The history of the drafting of the clause, however, is revealing. Congress carefully considered and rejected various phrasings that embraced the narrow interpretation. At bottom the amendment was an expression of the intention of the Framers of the Constitution to prevent Congress from acting in the field of religion. The "great object" of the BILL OF RIGHTS, JAMES MADISON had said, when introducing his draft of amendments to the House, was to "limit and qualify the powers of Government" for the purpose of making certain that none of the powers granted could be exercised in forbidden fields, including religion. The history of the drafting of the establishment clause does not provide a clear understanding of what was meant by the phrase "an establishment of religion." But the narrow interpretation, which permits government aid to religion in general or on a nonpreferential basis, leads to the impossible conclusion that the First Amendment *added* to Congress's powers. The amendment meant to restrict Congress to the powers that it possessed, and since it had no power to legislate on matters concerning religion, and therefore could not support religion on any basis, Congress would have had no such power even in the absence of the First Amendment. To suppose that an express prohibition on power vests or creates power is capriciously unreasonable. The Bill of Rights, as Madison said, was not framed "to imply powers not meant to be included in the enumeration."

Congress did not define "an establishment of religion" because its members knew from common experience what they meant. At the time of the framing of the amendment, six states maintained or authorized establishments of religion. That amendment denied to Congress the power to do what those states were doing, and since *Everson* the states come under the same ban. An establishment meant to the framers of the amendment what it meant in those states. Thus, reference to the American experience with establishments at the time of the framing of the Bill of Rights is essential to any understanding of what the clause in question meant.

The narrow interpretation is based on European precedents but the European form of an establishment was not the American form, except in the Southern colonies before the American Revolution, and the European meaning of establishment was not the American meaning. The revolution triggered a pent-up movement for separation of church and state in the nine states that had establishments. Of these nine, North Carolina (1776), New York (1777), and Virginia (1786) separated church and state. Each of the remaining six states made concessions to anti-establishment sentiment by broadening their old establishments. After the Revolution, none maintained a single or exclusive establishment. In all six an establishment of religion was not restricted to a state church or a system of public support of one denomination; in all an establishment meant public support of all denominations and sects on a nonpreferential basis.

Three of these six states were in New England. The MASSACHUSETTS CONSTITUTION (1780) authorized its towns and parishes to levy taxes for the support of Protestant churches, provided that each taxpayer's money go to the support "of his own religious sect or denomination" and added that "no subordination of any one sect or denomination to the other shall ever be established by law." An establishment in Massachusetts meant government support of religion. Congregationalists, for a few decades, benefited the most, because they were the most numerous and resorted to various tricks to fleece non-Congregationalists out of their share of religious taxes. But the fact remains that Massachusetts had a multiple, not a single, establishment under which Baptist, Episcopalian, Methodist, and Unitarian churches were publicly supported until the establishment ended in 1833. In 1784 Connecticut and New Hampshire modeled their multiple establishments after that of Massachusetts, ending them in 1818 and 1819, respectively.

In the South, where the Episcopal Church was the sole established church before the revolution, three states either maintained or permitted establishments of religion, and in each the multiple form was the only legal one. Maryland (1776) permitted its legislature to tax for the support of "the Christian religion," with the proviso that every person had the right to designate the church of his choice, making every Christian church an established church on a nonpreferential basis. The legislature sought to pass an enabling act in 1785, but the nonpreferential system was denounced as an establishment and defeated. The situation in Georgia was the same as in Maryland, and a revised constitution (1789), which was in effect when the First Amendment was adopted, continued the multiple establishment system, allowing each person to support only his own church. South Carolina restricted its multiple nonpreferential establishment to Protestant churches. The last Southern establishment died in 1810. Virginia sought to emulate the Maryland system, but a general assessment bill benefiting all Christian churches failed, thanks to the opposition of most non-Episcopal denominations and to MADISON'S MEMORIAL AND REMONSTRANCE; the VIRGINIA STATUTE OF RELIGIOUS FREEDOM (1786) then separated church and state.

In none of the six states maintaining or allowing establishments at the time of the framing of the First Amendment was any church but a Christian one established. The multiple establishments of that time comprehended the churches of every denomination and sect with a sufficient number of adherents to form a church. Where Protestantism was established it was synonymous with religion; there were either no Jews or no Roman Catholics or too few of them to make a difference. Where Christianity was established, as in Maryland, which had a significant Roman Catholic minority, Jews were scarcely known. To contend that exclusive establishments of one religion existed in each of the six states ignores the novel American experiment with multiple establishments on an impartial basis. Europe knew only single-church establishments. An establishment of religion in the United States at the time of the First Amendment included nonpreferential government recognition, aid, or sponsorship of religion. The framers of the amendment looked to their own experience, not Europe's.

LEONARD W. LEVY

(SEE ALSO: *Grand Rapids School District v. Ball, 1985; Larkin v. Grendel's Den, 1983; Lynch v. Donnelly, 1984; Marsh v. Chambers, 1983; Mueller v. Allen, 1983; Thornton v. Caldor, Inc., 1985; Valley Forge Christian Schools v. Americans United, 1982; Wallace v. Jaffree, 1985; Widmar v. Vincent, 1984.*)

Bibliography

ANTIEAU, CHESTER JAMES, ET AL. 1964 *Freedom from Federal Establishment: Formation and Early History of the First Amendment Religion Clauses.* Milwaukee, Wisc.: Bruce Publishing Co.

COBB, SANFORD H. 1902 *The Rise of Religious Liberty in America.* New York: Macmillan.

CORWIN, EDWARD S. 1949 The Supreme Court as National School Board. *Law and Contemporary Problems* 14:3–22.

LEVY, LEONARD W. 1986 *The Establishment Clause: Religion and the First Amendment.* New York: Macmillan.

ESTELLE v. SMITH
451 U.S. 454 (1981)

A unanimous Supreme Court held that the protection of the MIRANDA RULES applied to every phase of an in-custody prosecution, and that a psychiatrist's testimony introduced at the penalty phase of a capital trial violated the RIGHT AGAINST SELF-INCRIMINATION. At the pretrial interview on which the testimony was based, the defendant had not received the appropriate warnings about his right to silence.

LEONARD W. LEVY

ESTES v. TEXAS
381 U.S. 532 (1965)

The trial of Billy Sol Estes for swindling involved a FREE PRESS/FAIR TRIAL confrontation in which the Supreme Court held that televising trials was inherently prejudicial to a FAIR TRIAL. Circuslike live television and radio broadcasts of Estes's pretrial hearings involved such extensive disruption of the courtroom that many changes were ordered for coverage of the trial. Although live broadcasts of the actual trial were forbidden, excerpts from the proceedings were broadcast regularly.

The Court split 5–4 on the constitutionality of televising the proceedings. Justices HUGO L. BLACK, WILLIAM J. BRENNAN, POTTER STEWART, and BYRON R. WHITE called the practice unwise and dangerous, but not constitutionally objectionable. Chief Justice EARL WARREN and Justices ARTHUR J. GOLDBERG and WILLIAM O. DOUGLAS joined an opinion by Justice TOM C. CLARK seeking to ban television completely from the courts—subject to future developments (see CHANDLER V. FLORIDA, 1981)—as a violation of the right to a fair trial. Both the jury and the witnesses, Clark declared, would be under great pressure and be more self-conscious, aware of a large public audience; prospective witnesses might be influenced by the proceedings. The judge would have additional responsibilities (and temptations), and the defendant would be subject to "a form of mental—if not physical—harassment." Clark said, "A defendant on trial for a specific crime is entitled to his day in court, not in a stadium, or a city or nationwide arena." Justice JOHN MARSHALL HARLAN approved the ban here, but indicated he would do so only in cases of "great notoriety."

DAVID GORDON

EUCLID v. AMBLER REALTY COMPANY
272 U.S. 365 (1926)

This case established the constitutionality of ZONING laws to regulate land use. In *Euclid* a Cleveland suburb sought to preserve an area of single-family dwellings by excluding even two-family dwellings and apartment houses, as well as commercial properties and public buildings. Against claims drawn from supposed deprivations of liberty and property without DUE PROCESS OF LAW and a supposed denial of the EQUAL PROTECTION OF THE LAWS, a 6–3 Supreme Court, speaking through Justice GEORGE SUTHERLAND, sustained the comprehensive zoning ordinance. It was, the Court ruled, a legitimate STATE POLICE POWER measure intended to maintain the residential area and thus protect the community's health, peace, and safety. As a result of this leading decision on comprehensive zoning laws, no argument drawn from the FOURTEENTH AMENDMENT or from the takings clause is likely to survive judicial scrutiny in the absence of an ordinance that is demonstrably unrelated to the improvement of a community.

LEONARD W. LEVY

EUTHANASIA

Euthanasia, or mercy killing, has long engaged the attention of philosophers and others concerned with the morality of offering the incurably ill the dignity of a choice whether to end their lives. Only recently, however, has euthanasia become a subject of constitutional debate. Active assistance to suicide remains a crime throughout the country, and the sort of euthanasia actively practiced on the defective newborn and on some very old persons who are ill beyond hope is also murder. Neither of these forms of euthanasia raises any serious constitutional issue. It is "passive euthanasia"—the withholding of aids to the preservation of life—that has been discussed in constitutional terms. Unfortunately, "the right to die," perhaps because it is so effective a slogan, has beclouded discussion of genuine issues of personal choice.

The Supreme Court has not yet confronted these matters. Undoubtedly, however, there is some constitutional right to refuse medical treatment. Compulsory VACCINATION has been upheld against the claim that it deprived its reluctant beneficiary of liberty without DUE PROCESS OF LAW. A strong governmental interest in protecting public health justified that invasion of an unwilling person's body, however, and no such interest is present in the ordinary case of a person who refuses medical treatment. Even absent any claim to RELIGIOUS LIBERTY, the idea of a right to refuse treatment follows easily from the Supreme Court's modern recognition of constitutional rights to personal autonomy, offered in the name of "privacy." The Court's decisions affirming the right of a woman to have an abortion are cases in point.

In the context of euthanasia, however, the constitutional right to refuse treatment fits awkwardly into the typical dilemma a patient's doctors and relatives face. Even if a person has previously directed her doctors not to use artificial means to prolong life, she will ordinarily be unconscious for a time before dying and thus incapable of forming any present intention to refuse aid. Usually, of course, the problem of passive euthanasia arises in connection with patients in a persistent vegetative state who have given no directions whatever to their doctors. To invoke the concept of a constitutional right to die in such a case, as New Jersey's supreme court did in *Matter of Quinlan* (1976), is to beg the critical question whether someone in such a state can have any rights at all. The decision of the *Quinlan* court authorizing the termination of artificial life supports seems justified, but surely its justification appropriately responds to interests of the patient's relatives, not the patient's constitutional RIGHT OF PRIVACY.

KENNETH L. KARST

Bibliography

SYMPOSIUM 1977 In Re Quinlan. *Rutgers Law Review* 30:243–328.

EVANS v. ABNEY
396 U.S. 435 (1970)

The 1911 will of U.S. Senator Augustus O. Bacon gave land to the city of Macon, Georgia, in trust for use as a park for white persons only. The city's operation of the park on these terms could not survive the Supreme Court's decisions invalidating state-sponsored SEGREGATION, and the city was replaced by private trustees. When the Supreme Court held, in *Evans v. Newton* (1966), that the park must still be open to all races, Bacon's residuary heirs claimed the land, arguing that the trust had failed. The Georgia courts agreed, and the Supreme Court held, 5–2, that this judicial enforcement of Bacon's racially discriminatory disposition of property did not constitute STATE ACTION in violation of the FOURTEENTH AMENDMENT. Justice HUGO L. BLACK, for the majority, distinguished SHELLEY V. KRAEMER (1948), saying that *Abney* involved no RACIAL DISCRIMINATION: the terminated park was unavailable for blacks and whites alike. Justices WILLIAM O. DOUGLAS and WILLIAM J. BRENNAN dissented.

Abney's importance lay in showing that *Shelley* did not stand for a broad principle forbidding judicial enforcement of any and all private racial discrimination. It also began the BURGER COURT's revitalization of the state action limitation as a barrier to enforcement of the Fourteenth Amendment.

KENNETH L. KARST

EVARTS, WILLIAM MAXWELL (1818–1901)

William Maxwell Evarts, called "the Prince of the American Bar," was probably the most famous, successful, and influential lawyer of his time. He defended ANDREW JOHNSON in the President's IMPEACHMENT trial, and he served as attorney general, secretary of state, and United States senator (Republican, New York). Twice Evarts almost became CHIEF JUSTICE of the United States. His lasting impact on American constitutional law derived from his pathbreaking arguments as counsel and his authorship of the CIRCUIT COURTS OF APPEALS ACT (1891). In the GRANGER CASES (1877) he argued that rate regulation interfered with the management and beneficial use of private property, reducing profits and thereby taking private property without JUST COMPENSATION or DUE PROCESS OF LAW. He lost that case, but his argument was destined for eventual acceptance. IN RE JACOBS (1885) was his greatest constitutional triumph. His argument, which the New York Court of Appeals adopted, advanced SUBSTANTIVE DUE PROCESS OF LAW and the doctrine of FREEDOM OF CONTRACT. Evarts was a stalwart champion of VESTED RIGHTS and an opponent of government regulation. The Circuit Courts of Appeals Act (Evarts Act) created the modern three-tier structure of the federal courts and the discretionary WRIT OF CERTIORARI by which the Supreme Court manages its APPELLATE JURISDICTION.

LEONARD W. LEVY

Bibliography

TWISS, BENJAMIN 1942 *Lawyers and the Constitution.* Pages 93–109. Princeton, N.J.: Princeton University Press.

EVARTS ACT

See: Circuit Courts of Appeals Act (1891)

EVERSON v. BOARD OF EDUCATION 330 U.S. 1 (1947)

A New Jersey statute authorized local school boards to reimburse parents for the cost of public transportation of students to both public and private schools. Such reimbursement for the cost of transportation to church-related schools was challenged as an unconstitutional ESTABLISHMENT OF RELIGION.

Justice HUGO L. BLACK delivered the opinion of a 5–4 Supreme Court. He began with a consideration of the background of the establishment clause, which relied heavily on the writings of JAMES MADISON and THOMAS JEFFERSON, but he had little to say about the actual legislative history of the FIRST AMENDMENT's language in the First Congress. Black concluded that the establishment clause "means at least this":

> Neither a state nor the federal government can set up a church. Neither can pass laws which aid one religion, aid all religions or prefer one religion over another. . . . No tax in any amount, large or small, can be levied to support any religious activities or institutions, whatever they may be called, or whatever form they may adopt to teach and practice religion. . . . In the words of Jefferson, the clause against the establishment of religion by law was intended to erect "a wall of separation between church and State."

But after this sweeping separationist pronouncement, Justice Black pirouetted neatly and upheld the New Jersey program on the grounds that the state aid in that case was a public safety measure designed to protect students and could in no way be construed as aid to church-related schools.

Four dissenters were convinced that Justice Black had missed the point. Justice ROBERT H. JACKSON likened Black's MAJORITY OPINION to Byron's Julia who, "whispering I will ne'er consent, consented." What could be more helpful to a school, Jackson asked, than depositing the students at its door? Justice WILEY B. RUTLEDGE, with whom Justices Jackson, FELIX

FRANKFURTER, and HAROLD BURTON joined, also filed a lengthy dissent. Justice Rutledge also made lavish use of the writings of Madison and Jefferson, and argued that the New Jersey program could not be justified as a public safety expenditure.

Everson stands at the entrance to the maze of law and litigation concerning participation by church-related schools in public programs. It was the first major utterance by the Supreme Court on the meaning of the establishment clause. Those favoring strict separation between religious institutions and government were pleased by Black's rhetoric and dismayed by his conclusion; those favoring a policy of flexibility or accommodation in church–state relations reacted the opposite way. That *Everson* satisfied no one and enraged many was portentous.

RICHARD E. MORGAN

Bibliography

JOHNSON, RICHARD M. 1967 *The Dynamics of Compliance.* Evanston, Ill.: Northwestern University Press.

MORGAN, RICHARD E. 1972 *The Supreme Court and Religion.* Pages 76–122. New York: Free Press.

EVIDENCE

Excepting cases that may be decided by applying legal rules to undisputed facts, the determination of disputed factual propositions must be central to adjudicating the rights and liabilities of litigants. As an initial matter, a society might adopt an "inquisitorial" system, under which a public official investigates and decides the facts. In the Anglo-American legal tradition, however, we structure the litigation process so that every dispute has at least two parties, each charged with the primary responsibility for proving its factual propositions and therefore discovering and presenting the evidence to support its version of the facts before an impartial arbiter.

In criminal cases, this adversary system is reinforced by rules that place the BURDEN OF PROOF on the prosecution, presuming that the defendant is innocent, and that grant the defendant a RIGHT AGAINST SELF-INCRIMINATION—thus shielding him from being forced to be a witness against himself, and depriving the prosecution of an obvious source of evidence. The structuring of criminal litigation as a contest between the state as prosecutor and the defendant—with the judge as arbiter—has two major consequences. First, this procedure gives greater weight to the autonomy of the individual litigant. Second, placing responsibility on each party to advance its own cause will, in general, result in the production of more evidence for the finder of fact than would be produced by disinterested—and perhaps bored and overworked—public officials. Though our prototypical case is the criminal case, we use similar procedures and rules in civil cases.

In both civil and criminal cases, TRIAL BY JURY means that a group of laymen decides issues of disputed fact. A great many of the intricacies of our laws of evidence result from two specific worries about the jury. The first is that the jury may systematically overvalue or undervalue some kinds of evidence, such as HEARSAY. The second is that the ad hoc nature of the jury, which is empaneled to decide a particular case, will produce a verdict at odds with the values of a legal system handling many cases over a long period of time. Often a rule of evidence will keep out testimony not so much because a jury might overweigh it but simply because other policies of the law are entitled to equal weight along with the proper resolution of factual issues. In this category fall the exclusion of reliable evidence because it has been unconstitutionally seized; because it has been obtained in violation of the MIRANDA RULES; because it is a coerced confession (which, though typically unreliable, may in a particular case be thoroughly corroborated); or because its exclusion is necessary to enforce a privilege, such as that protecting confidential communications between the attorney and the client.

Nor is the exclusion of evidence confined to cases where we choose this means of vindicating the rights of the individual. Though it is by no means clear that the rule is of constitutional dimension, every Anglo-American JURISDICTION in civil and (until the passage of California's "Victims' Bill of Rights" initiative) in criminal cases kept from the jury certain evidence of the prior character of the accused—not so much because the jury might overvalue it as out of fear that the jury might succumb to the temptation to be lawless and decide that the defendant was either so bad a person that he should be punished regardless of his fault in the particular case at issue. That kind of jury behavior might appeal to common sense, but it would be at odds with our principles requiring a particular act as a precondition of guilt and requiring fair NOTICE of the charge made against a defendant.

Despite the huge body of statutory and COMMON LAW evidence law, the Constitution nowhere states flatly a rule as to admissibility of evidence and refers to evidence in only one place—the requirement of two witnesses to the same overt act before a conviction of TREASON may be returned. Moreover, apart from the rules as to SEARCH AND SEIZURE and self-incrimination, the rules of evidence have largely escaped the Supreme Court's constitutional supervision. In criminal cases, however, two lines of cases have partially constitutionalized the law of evidence. The first involves the defendant's right to exclude inculpatory hearsay evidence that otherwise would be admitted under one or another of the exceptions to the general rule excluding hearsay; the second involves the defendant's rights to introduce exculpatory evidence notwithstanding common or statutory law purporting to exclude such evidence. Both these lines grow out of the Sixth Amendment. The first grows out of the CONFRONTATION clause, which guarantees that "[i]n all criminal prosecutions, the accused shall enjoy the right . . . to be confronted with the witnesses against him." The second line also stems in part from the Sixth Amendment right of the accused to "COMPULSORY PROCESS for obtaining witnesses in his favor," and in part from the DUE PROCESS clause.

Historically, courts read the confrontation clause as guaranteeing only the right of the accused to be present at his trial and to cross-examine any witnesses testifying there. In the 1960s, however, the Supreme Court began to view the clause as forbidding use in a criminal trial of certain inculpatory hearsay declarations. Thus, the Court held in POINTER V. TEXAS (1965) that the clause rendered inadmissible at a criminal trial a transcript of inculpatory testimony elicited during a preliminary hearing at which the defendant was not represented by counsel from a prosecution witness who was no longer available to testify. Likewise, a codefendant's out-of-court confession that also implicated the accused was held inadmissible in *Bruton v. United States* (1968) when the codefendant invoked his right against self-incrimination and refused to take the stand at the trial. Similarly, in *Barber v. Page* (1968) the Court held that preliminary hearing testimony of an absent witness was inadmissible when the prosecutor had failed to make a good-faith effort to obtain the presence of the witness at the trial. These rulings by the Court threw the validity of inculpatory hearsay evidence into doubt. The Court seemed to be drifting toward a rule that would in effect preclude the use of all such hearsay.

California v. Green (1970) arrested this drift. In *Green,* a prosecution witness testified adversely to the defendant during a preliminary hearing at which the defendant's attorney subjected him to a rigorous cross-examination. At the later trial, however, the witness claimed to have suffered a memory lapse and refused to repeat his testimony. The prosecutor then read into evidence portions of the preliminary hearing testimony. The Court held that, under these circumstances, admission of the hearsay did not violate the confrontation clause. The Court stated that its previous confrontation clause decisions had all rested on the inability of the defendant effectively to cross-examine witnesses, and that where, as here, defendant had once had a full and fair opportunity to cross-examine, there was no constitutional impediment to the hearsay.

Green made it clear that when the declarant was unavailable at the trial, his declaration would be admissible if he had been subject to meaningful cross-examination by defendant's counsel at the time he made the declaration. The meaning of "unavailability" and the nature of "meaningful cross-examination" were left open to interpretation, but clearly where these criteria were met, the evidence was admissible. By the same token, *Green* left little doubt that when the declarant was available at the trial for meaningful cross-examination, evidence of his out-of-court declaration would be admissible even if he had not been subject to cross-examination at the time he made the statement.

Since *Green,* the Court's decisions have withdrawn even further from the constitutionalization of hearsay law. The Court made apparent in *Ohio v. Roberts* (1980) that hearsay evidence of a declarant's out-of-court statements will be admissible, even when the defendant has never had an opportunity to cross-examine the declarant, provided that the declarant is truly unavailable and that the statements bear adequate "indicia of reliability." "Reliability can be inferred without more in a case where the evidence fails within a firmly footed hearsay exception," that is, an exception "rest[ing] upon such solid foundations" that "virtually any evidence within them" will in fact be reliable. Thus, dying declarations are admissible, as are properly administered business and public records. Hearsay evidence is admissible even under less "firmly rooted" exceptions when there is a particularized showing of its trustworthiness under the circumstances. Thus, under some circumstances, at least, declarations against penal interest and party admissions by coconspirators (such as a spontaneous admission by a coconspirator to his prison cellmate) are admissible.

The Court's decisions since *Green* thus have confined the pre-*Green* decisions narrowly to their facts. Apparently, the Court is unlikely to find that evidence admitted under an established hearsay exception offends the confrontation clause, unless, as in *Barber v. Page,* a prosecutor falsely alleges for purposes of the exception that a declarant is unavailable, or, as in *Bruton v. United States,* the hearsay consists of a codefendant's confession which ostensibly is read into evidence against him alone but in fact contains statements inculpating other defendants in the same trial, and the codefendant refuses to take the stand. Moreover, even when a defendant alleges a *Barber* or *Bruton* violation, the Court is unlikely to find that the facts of the case at hand justify reversal. Twice since *Green* the Court has refused to sustain arguments that a prosecutor had failed to make a good-faith effort to find absent declarants, and repeatedly the Court has found even clear and admitted violations of the *Bruton* rule to result in merely HARMLESS ERROR not justifying reversal.

It would seem, then, that the Court has substantially withdrawn from the field of writing hearsay law. While it has not explicitly reverted to the traditional view of the confrontation clause in this area, the manner in which it has analyzed hearsay exceptions in recent cases leaves little doubt of its reluctance significantly to reduce the prosecutor's ability to introduce evidence falling within ancient, recognized exceptions.

The rules of evidence traditionally have been held to bind defendants as well as the state. The first significant developments in the line of cases recognizing defendants' rights to introduce exculpatory evidence despite rules of evidence excluding it grew out of the compulsory process clause. In *Washington v. Texas* (1967) the Court overturned a Texas statute that rendered accomplices incompetent to testify for each other. The Court held that the compulsory process clause forbade the state "arbitrarily [to] den[y defendants] the right to put on the stand a witness who was physically and mentally capable of testifying to events that he had personally observed and whose testimony would have been relevant and material to the defense."

In *Chambers v. Mississippi* (1973) the Court faced a case in which it might have used compulsory process reasoning but used the due process clause instead. In *Chambers* the defendant was charged with murder for shooting a police officer during a crowd incident. Another man, McDonald, who had been in the crowd, had confessed to the shooting, and substantial evidence pointed to the truth of this confession, but McDonald had repudiated the confession and had not been charged in the case. The trial judge allowed Chambers to present two witnesses who claimed actually to have seen McDonald fire the shots, but the judge barred the testimony of witnesses who had not seen the incident but to whom McDonald had made damaging admissions, ruling that this testimony did not fall within any applicable state hearsay exception. In addition, the judge permitted Chambers to call McDonald to the stand and to read his prior confession into evidence, but when McDonald repudiated the confession on the stand and offered an alibi, the judge refused to allow Chambers to examine McDonald as an "adverse witness," ruling that because McDonald had not actually alleged the defendant's guilt, his testimony was not "adverse" within the meaning of Mississippi's exception to the rule that a party may not impeach his own witness.

The Supreme Court reversed, holding that the trial judge's exclusion of this exculpatory evidence had violated the due process clause of the FOURTEENTH AMENDMENT. The trial judge's refusal to allow Chambers to examine McDonald, who was a "witness against him" even if not an "adverse" witness under Mississippi law, constituted prejudicial error. In addition, the Court held that the trial judge's refusal to allow the exculpatory hearsay testimony of the three witnesses to whom McDonald had confessed violated Chambers's right "to present witnesses in his own defense." Although the language used by the Court in discussing these issues is reminiscent of the confrontation and compulsory process clauses of the Sixth Amendment, the Court did not explicitly rest its decision on these clauses. Rather, the Court announced only that "[t]he right of an accused in a criminal trial to due process is, in essence, the right to a fair opportunity to defend against the State's accusations," and that "under the facts and circumstances of this case the rulings of the trial court deprived Chambers of a fair trial."

The Court has applied *Chambers* in only one other case. In *Green v. Georgia* (1979) the defendant was convicted of rape and murder, and a second trial was then held to decide whether CAPITAL PUNISHMENT would be imposed. At this trial, the defendant sought to introduce a witness who had previously testified for the prosecution at the trial of Moore, the defendant's coconspirator. The witness intended to testify, as he had testified at Moore's trial, that Moore had admitted to him that Moore alone had fired the shots that killed the victim, and that the defendant had not been present when the shots were fired. The trial judge, however, ruled this testimony inadmissible as hearsay. At Moore's trial the witness's repetition of Moore's declaration had fallen within the admission exception to the hearsay rule, but its repetition at Green's trial did not fall within the exception. In a brief opinion, the Supreme Court reversed. It noted that the excluded evidence was highly relevant to a critical issue in the trial and that substantial reasons existed to assume its reliability: it was a statement against Moore's penal interest made spontaneously by him to a close friend and for which there was ample corroborating evidence. Most important, the prosecution had considered the evidence reliable enough to use against Moore at his trial. Under these circumstances, the Court ruled, "the hearsay rule may not be applied mechanistically to defeat the ends of justice."

The future of this line of cases is not easy to foresee. The cases may stand for no more than the proposition that the Court will reverse a conviction when it is convinced that a gross injustice has been done. But they seem to stand for more. They seem to suggest that the Court has begun to read into the Constitution the ethical rule that the state's proper goal is not merely to get a conviction but to get a conviction only if justice demands it. Thus, the cases suggest, the prosecutor may not object to evidence that the defense seeks to introduce on any ground other than that it is wasteful of time, or likely to distract the jury's attention from the real issues of the case. This consideration, always important ethically, rises to constitutional significance when failure to abide by it leads to the exclusion of strongly credible exculpatory evidence that is highly relevant to critical issues in the trial.

JOHN KAPLAN

Bibliography

MAGUIRE, JOHN M. 1947 *Evidence, Common Sense, and Common Law.* Mineola, N.Y.: Foundation Press.

MCCORMICK, CHARLES T. 1954 *Handbook of the Law of Evidence.* St. Paul, Minn.: West Publishing Co.

MORGAN, EDMUND M. 1961 *Basic Problems of Evidence.* Philadelphia: American Bar Association.

THAYER, JAMES BRADLEY 1898 *Preliminary Treatise on Evidence at Common Law.* Boston: Little, Brown.

WIGMORE, JOHN HENRY 1961 *Evidence in Trials at Common Law,* rev. by John T. Naughton. Boston: Little, Brown.

EVIDENTIARY PRIVILEGE

To say that a person possesses an evidentiary privilege means that he or she cannot be compelled, as a witness, to disclose certain ("privileged") information. The possessor of the privilege (the privilege "holder") may also be entitled to prevent others who share the privileged information from disclosing it. The holder may waive the privilege by failing to assert it in timely fashion, by explicitly consenting to the disclosure of privileged information, or by engaging in conduct interpreted as consent (for example, voluntarily testifying to a portion of the privileged matter). In state courts, the contours of evidentiary privileges are determined by state law. In federal courts, they are determined by federal law, though at times the federal approach has been to defer to state rules of privilege, as specified, for example, in Federal Rule of Evidence 501.

Unlike most of the evidentiary rules of exclusion (such as those excluding HEARSAY or irrelevant evidence), the testimonial privileges do not exclude EVIDENCE because it is unreliable, prejudicial, or lacking in fact-finding utility. Rather, they exclude it *despite* its potential value; the privileges promote goals other than rational fact-finding. To be aware of these goals is to understand why traditional evidentiary privileges can readily take on constitutional dimensions. The interests served by the privileges are commonly phrased in terms that are uncompromisingly utilitarian. For example, privileges concerned with the protection of confidential communications—such as those between husband and wife, attorney and client, doctor and patient, priest and penitant, parent and child (a developing privilege)—are commonly justified on such reasoning: first, that the free flow of communication is indispensable to these important relationships; second, that confidentiality is essential to their free flow. An alternative perspective would support the claims of confidentiality not for such narrowly instrumental reasons but because confidentiality serves the participants' interest in privacy, whether or not the possibility of compulsory disclosure would hinder free communication.

Similar justifications, both instrumental and noninstrumental, could be generated in support of another kind of privilege, protecting interests other than confidentiality. An example is the phase of the husband–wife privilege permitting one spouse to refuse to testify against another, whether or not the testimony may concern intraspousal communications.

Although these privileges were not in their original conception constitutionally based, today they are often seen as implicating constitutional values. The justifications for many of the privileges could be reformulated in terms of constitutional principles. The attorney–client privilege, invoked by a criminal defendant, could draw support from the RIGHT TO COUNSEL, the RIGHT AGAINST SELF-INCRIMINATION, and the DUE PROCESS clauses of the Constitution. Indeed, if the attorney–client privilege were not a common law privilege, some version of it probably would have to be invented to satisfy constitutional requirements. FIRST AMENDMENT arguments could likewise be mustered in support of the priest–penitent privilege and the REPORTER'S PRIVILEGE (which in some states protects against compelled disclosure of a newsperson's sources of information). And, efforts to pierce the confidentiality of certain communications—such as those between husband and wife, priest and penitent, or psychiatrist and patient—could be challenged as infringements of a constitutionally protected RIGHT OF PRIVACY.

On the other hand, just as evidentiary privileges sometimes draw support from constitutional principles, sometimes their enforcement may prove incompatible with other constitutional requirements. Thus to deny a criminal defendant the use of testimony important to his or her defense, out of respect for a privilege invoked by a witness, might run afoul of the defendant's right of CONFRONTATION, to COMPULSORY PROCESS, or to due process of law; the conflicting constitutional claims of the defendant and the witness would then have to be resolved.

LEON LETWIN

Bibliography

CLEARY, E. 1984 *McCormick on Evidence,* 3rd ed. Pages 170–187. St. Paul, Minn.: West Publishing Co.

NOTE 1985 Developments in the Law—Privileged Communications. *Harvard Law Review* 98:1450–1666.

EVITTS v. LUCEY
469 U.S. (1985)

Interpreting DOUGLAS V. CALIFORNIA (1963), the Supreme Court held, 7–2, in an opinion by Justice WILLIAM J. BRENNAN, that the DUE PROCESS clause of the FOURTEENTH AMENDMENT requires the effective assistance of counsel during a defendant's first appeal, as of right, from a criminal conviction. (The Court had previously held that the RIGHT TO COUNSEL at the trial level comprehended effective assistance.) The procedural posture of this case made it unnecessary to spell out standards for judging the effectiveness of counsel on appeal; the Court thus left those standards for another day. Justice WILLIAM H. REHNQUIST and Chief Justice WARREN E. BURGER dissented, arguing that the trial and appellate levels presented different degrees of need for counsel's assistance, and predicting that the decision would allow convicted defendants to "tie up the courts" with petitions for HABEAS CORPUS based on claims of ineffectiveness of appellate counsel.

KENNETH L. KARST

EXCISE TAX

In its original meaning an excise was a tax on goods manufactured or produced within the taxing country, as opposed to a duty or IMPOST on imports. Undoubtedly, this was the sense in which it was used in the constitutional grant of power to Congress to collect "taxes, duties, imposts and excises." In modern times an excise tax is any tax imposed on the manufacture or sale of a commodity, engaging in an occupation, or enjoying any other privilege. It is distinguished from a direct tax, such as a POLL TAX or an *ad valorem* property tax.

EDWARD L. BARRETT, JR.

(SEE ALSO: *Direct and Indirect Taxes; State Taxation of Commerce.*)

EXCLUSIONARY RULE

When the police obtain evidence by violating the BILL OF RIGHTS, the victim of their misconduct may lack any effective legal remedy. Yet some enforcement mechanism is necessary if several important constitutional guarantees are to be a reality and not merely expressions of hope. The Supreme Court responded to this concern by developing a series of rules that have come to be known in the aggregate as the exclusionary rule. In typical application, the rule is that evidence obtained in violation of a person's constitutional rights cannot be used against that person in his or her trial for a criminal offense. The rule is most frequently applied to exclude evidence produced by SEARCHES OR SEIZURES made in violation of the FOURTH AMENDMENT. However, a coerced confession obtained in violation of the defendant's Fifth Amendment RIGHT AGAINST SELF-INCRIMINATION, or a statement taken from the defendant in violation of his Sixth Amendment's guarantee of the RIGHT TO COUNSEL, would also be inadmissible at his trial.

The term "exclusionary rule" is of modern origin, but even at COMMON LAW a coerced confession was excluded or inadmissible as evidence, because its involuntariness cast serious doubt on its reliability. No one today seriously argues that this long-standing rule of evidence should be abandoned. Other aspects of the exclusionary rule, however, have been the source of major controversy among members of the judiciary, professional commentators, law enforcement officials, and the public.

The controversy did not become intense until the era of the WARREN COURT. But as far back as WEEKS

v. UNITED STATES (1914) the Supreme Court had unanimously held that evidence seized in violation of the Fourth Amendment was inadmissible in a *federal* criminal prosecution. However, even after the Court had held in WOLF v. COLORADO (1949) that the Fourth Amendment's guarantee against unreasonable searches and seizures was applicable to the states, the Court had continued until 1961 to resist the argument that the exclusionary rule should also be extended to *state* prosecutions. In that year, in MAPP v. OHIO, the Warren Court held that the Fourteenth Amendment did, indeed, impose on the states the exclusionary rule derived from the Fourth Amendment. Subsequent decisions broadened the Sixth Amendment guarantee of the right to counsel to govern the procedures for police interrogation and for the use of LINEUPS; each of these developments was accompanied by an extension of the exclusionary rule to state-court proceedings. Since the "FRUIT OF THE POISONOUS TREE" DOCTRINE requires the exclusion not only of evidence immediately obtained by these various forms of constitutional violation but also of other evidence derived from the initial violations, the exclusionary rule in its modern form results in the suppression of many items of evidence of unquestioned reliability and the acquittal of many persons who are guilty.

The primary purpose of the exclusionary rule, as the Supreme Court said in *Elkins v. United States* (1960), "is to deter—to compel respect for the constitutional guaranty in the only effectively available way—by removing the incentive to disregard it." Yet this deterrent function is only part of the exclusionary rule's justification. A court that allows the government to profit from unconstitutional police action sullies the judicial process itself, by becoming an accomplice in an unlawful course of conduct. When the Court first applied the rule in *Mapp* to state-court prosecutions, it said:

> There are those who say, as did Justice (then Judge) [BENJAMIN N.] CARDOZO, that under our constitutional exclusionary doctrine "the criminal is to go free because the constable has blundered." . . . In some cases this will undoubtedly be the result. But, . . . "there is another consideration—the imperative of judicial integrity." . . . The criminal goes free, if he must, but it is the law that sets him free. Nothing can destroy a government more quickly than its failure to observe its own laws, or worse, its disregard of the charter of its own existence. As Mr. Justice LOUIS D. BRANDEIS, dissenting, said: . . . "Our government is the potent, the omnipresent teacher. For good or for ill, it teaches the whole people by its example. . . . If the government becomes a lawbreaker, it breeds contempt for law."

The evidence seized in an illegal search—a knife, a packet of heroin, counterfeit plates—is as trustworthy and material as if the search had been lawful. The rule's critics argue that to protect the privacy of the search victim by letting a guilty person escape responsibility for his crime is illogical. It would make more sense, they say, to use the evidence (as do the courts in Great Britain, for example) and provide civil or criminal remedies against the errant police officers. If the rule's purpose is to deter police lawlessness, the critics argue, the rule misses the point: prosecutors, not police officers, feel the immediate effects of the rule. If the rule is designed to maintain respect for the courts, they ask how the public can be expected to respect a system that frees criminals by suppressing trustworthy evidence of their guilt.

How many criminals do go free when the constable blunders? Inadequate studies provide no clear-cut answer, except that opponents of the exclusionary rule grossly exaggerate the number of felons it sets loose, and they tend to dramatize the worst cases. In California, whose supreme court has created the most stringent exclusionary rule in the nation, a study by the National Institute of Justice showed that .78 percent of all accused felons are not prosecuted because of search and seizure problems, and of those released, nearly three-fourths were involved in drug-related cases. The effect of the exclusionary rule is slight in cases involving violent crimes. When the charge is murder, rape, assault, or robbery, prosecutors decide not to proceed in one out of every 2,500 cases. Studies of felony court records in other states reach similar conclusions. Only 0.4 percent of all cases that federal prosecutors decide not to prosecute are rejected because of search problems. At the trial level, motions to suppress illegally seized evidence are rarely granted in cases of violent crime. If the exclusionary rule were abolished, the conviction rate in all felony cases would increase by less than half of one percent. Translated into absolute figures, however, thousands of accused felons are released nationally as a result of the exclusionary rule, most of them in drug and weapons possession cases. Street crime does not flourish, though, because of the exclusionary rule, even though it does protect criminals, as do all constitutional rights. They also protect society and help keep us free.

The rule's effectiveness in deterring illegal searches is hotly debated. The critics point out that some ninety percent of criminal prosecutions do not go to trial but are disposed of by pleas of "guilty." (The figure varies from state to state, and according to the nature of the crime.) Without a trial, there is no evidence for the rule to exclude. In the huge number of cases in which the police make arrests but the persons arrested are not prosecuted, the exclusionary rule has, of course, no immediate application. The rule's proponents reply that the decision whether to prosecute or accept a defendant's "guilty" pleas on a lesser offense may itself be influenced by the prosecutor's estimate of the potential operation of the exclusionary rule if the case should go to trial. (In jurisdictions where separate procedures are established to rule on motions to suppress evidence, the rule normally will have operated in advance of the trial.)

Undeniably, however, the exclusionary rule has no application at all to the cases that cry out most for a remedy: cases of police misconduct against innocent persons, who are never even brought to the prosecutors' attention, and cases of illegal searches and seizures made for purposes other than collecting evidence to support prosecutions. In TERRY V. OHIO (1968) Chief Justice EARL WARREN admitted: "Regardless how effective the rule may be where obtaining conviction is an important objective of the police, it is powerless to deter invasions of constitutionally guaranteed rights where the police either have no interest in prosecuting or are willing to forego successful prosecution in the interest of serving some other goal." The police may deliberately engage in illegal searches and seizures for a number of reasons: to control crimes such as gambling or prostitution; to confiscate weapons or contraband or stolen property; or to maintain high visibility either to deter crime or to satisfy a public clamoring for aggressive police action. In none of these cases will the exclusionary rule inhibit police violations of the Bill of Rights.

The rule does not in fact significantly impede the police, despite contentions from the rule's opponents that it handcuffs the police. A 1984 report prepared for the National Center for State Courts concluded that a properly administered search warrant process can protect constitutional rights without hampering effective law enforcement. Nevertheless, police try when possible to conduct search and seizure under some exception to the warrant requirement. The overwhelming number of searches and seizures are warrantless. In 1980, for example, only about 1,000 warrants were issued in Los Angeles in about 300,000 cases. Police usually try to make CONSENT SEARCHES or searches under what they claim to be EXIGENT CIRCUMSTANCES, or they conduct a search to confiscate contraband or harass criminals, without attempting a prosecution. In the few cases in which they seek warrants, they get them almost as if magistrates rubber-stamp their applications, and almost all warrants survive in court despite motions to suppress. Motions to suppress are made in about five percent of all cases but are successful in only less than one percent of all cases. Still more important is the fact that only slightly over half of one percent of all cases result in acquittals because of the exclusion of evidence.

Even when the rule does operate to exclude evidence in a criminal trial, it has no direct, personal effect on the police officer whose misconduct caused the rule to be invoked. The rule does not require discipline to be imposed by the officer's superiors, nor does either civil or criminal responsibility follow as a matter of course. Police officers are prosecuted only extremely rarely for their official misdeeds. Suits for damages by victims are inhibited not only by the defense of "good faith" and PROBABLE CAUSE but also by the realization that most officers are neither wealthy nor insured against liability for their official acts. Unsurprisingly, most victims conclude that a lawsuit is not worth its trouble and expense. In the typical case of an illegal search, neither the judge who excludes the fruits of the search from evidence nor the prosecutor whose case is thereby undermined will explain to the officer the error of his ways. The intended educational effect of judicial decisions is also diminished by the time-lag between the police action and its final evaluation by the courts. Even if an officer should hear that a court has excluded the evidence he found in an illegal search some months ago, he will probably have forgotten the details of the event. Incentives and sanctions that might influence the officer's future behavior are not within the exclusionary rule's contemplation. On the other hand, advocates of the rule emphasize that it is meant to have an institutional or systemic effect on law enforcement agencies generally, not necessarily on particular officers.

The officer is apt to respond not to judicial decisions (which he may regard as unrealistic if they impede his work) but to departmental policies and the approval of his colleagues and superiors. One whose main job is the apprehension of criminals and the deterrence of crime will have a low tolerance for what he sees as procedural niceties. He may even shade the truth in making out a report on a search or when testifying in court. It is not unheard of for the police to arrange to make a valid arrest at a place where they can conduct a warrantless SEARCH INCIDENT TO THE ARREST, and thus evade the requirement of a SEARCH WARRANT based on probable cause to believe that evidence of crime is in that place. To the extent that the courts have used the exclusionary rule to educate the police, then, the main things learned seem to have been the techniques for evading the rule.

Summarizing the criticisms of the exclusionary rule, Dallin H. Oaks has said:

> The harshest criticism of the rule is that it is ineffective. It is the sole means of enforcing the essential guarantees of freedom from unreasonable arrests and searches and seizures by law enforcement officers, and it is a failure in that vital task.
>
> The use of the exclusionary rule imposes excessive costs on the criminal justice system. It provides no recompense for the innocent and it frees the guilty. It creates the occasion and incentive for large-scale lying by law enforcement officers. It diverts the focus on the criminal prosecution from the guilt or innocence of the defendant to a trial of the police. Only a system with limitless patience with irrationality could tolerate the fact that where there has been one wrong, the defendant's, he will be punished, but where there have been two wrongs, the defendant's and the officer's, both will go free. This would not be an excessive cost for an effective remedy against police misconduct, but it is a prohibitive price to pay for an illusory one.

Despite the severity of criticisms, the exclusionary rule's chief critics have not proposed its total abolition. However, the Supreme Court has limited the rule's application in significant ways. Thus, for the most part, only the victim of an illegal search has standing to claim the benefits of the exclusionary rule; if A's house is searched in violation of the Fourth Amendment, and evidence is found incriminating B, the evidence can be used in B's trial. (State courts are free to extend the exclusionary rule to such cases; some state courts have done so, concluding that the point of the rule is not to protect people against being convicted but to deter the police.) Similarly, in UNITED STATES v. CALANDRA (1974) the Court held that illegally obtained evidence is admissible in grand jury proceedings, and it ruled in HARRIS v. NEW YORK (1971) that it can be used for the purpose of impeaching the testimony of the accused at his trial. Some uses of illegally obtained evidence have been tolerated as HARMLESS ERROR. More important, the GOOD FAITH EXCEPTION to the exclusionary rule allows the use of evidence obtained with a search warrant if the police reasonably believed the warrant to be valid, even though it later proves to be illegal. The rule has also been held inapplicable to collateral proceedings for postconviction relief such as HABEAS CORPUS. The Court's opinions in these cases have repeated the familiar criticisms of the exclusionary rule; their logic would seem to suggest abandonment of the rule altogether.

Yet the exclusionary rule remains, largely because no one has yet suggested an effective alternative means for enforcing the Bill of Rights against police misconduct. A federal statute dating from Reconstruction authorizes the award of damages against state or local officials (including police officers) who violate individuals' constitutional rights. In 1971, the Supreme Court found that the Fourth Amendment itself implicitly authorized similar damages awards against federal officers who violated the Amendment. The future effectiveness of such remedies will depend in part on the Supreme Court itself, as it spells out the victim's BURDEN OF PROOF in these cases and the measure of damages. Partly, however, the civil-damages alternative depends for its effectiveness on legislation to provide for real compensation to victims when the police officers are judgment-proof, and for real punishment of officers for constitutional violations when the payment of damages is unrealistic.

Meanwhile, the Supreme Court has only the exclusionary rule, which everyone agrees is an imperfect deterrent to police misbehavior. The rule survives, then, for want of better alternatives. But it also stands as a symbol that government itself is not above the law.

LEONARD W. LEVY

(SEE ALSO: *Electronic Eavesdropping; New York v. Quarles, 1984; Police Interrogation; Wiretapping; Warrantless Searches.*)

Bibliography

LAFAVE, WAYNE R. 1978 *Search and Seizure: A Treatise on the Fourth Amendment,* 3 vols. St. Paul: West Publishing Co.

OAKS, DALLIN H. 1970 Studying the Exclusionary Rule. *University of Chicago Law Review* 37:665–757.

SCHROEDER, WILLIAM 1981 Deterring Fourth Amendment Violations: Alternatives to the Exclusionary Rule. *Georgetown Law Review* 68:1361–1426.

STEWART, POTTER 1983 The Road to *Mapp v. Ohio* and Beyond: The Origins, Development and Future of the Exclusionary Rule in Search-and-Seizure Cases. *Columbia Law Review* 83:1365–1404.

EXCLUSIVE POWERS

The Constitution divides governmental power in two ways: between the states and the federal government, and among the three branches of the federal government. Some powers are vested exclusively in one authority, and may not be exercised by any other authority.

The exclusive powers of the federal government include not only all power over foreign affairs but also certain domestic powers that affect the whole country. Not all of the powers granted to the federal government by the Constitution are exclusive in character; some may be exercised concurrently and independently by both state and federal governments, or may be exercised by the states until Congress acts.

The Constitution makes clear the exclusive character of some powers by explicitly prohibiting the states from exercising them (such as the treaty power). In some other cases, the courts have held the grant to be exclusive when the subject of the power is national in character or requires one uniform system or plan. In some cases the states, with the express permission of Congress, may exercise an exclusive power of the national government.

The states also possess exclusive powers. Because the Constitution establishes a government of limited powers, any domestic governmental power not granted to the federal government by the Constitution and not prohibited by it to the states remains an exclusive power of the state government.

Within the federal government a power may be possessed exclusively by one of the three branches of government. The separation of powers implies that each branch of government has its exclusive sphere of power, which it can independently exercise and from which the other branches are excluded. In theory the legislative power, executive power, and judicial power each belong exclusively to one branch of government. This exclusive power is compatible with the influence of other branches over some part of its exercise. Only Congress may legislate, but legislation may be affected by the President's veto power and the power of the courts to declare statutes unconstitutional. Powers not explicitly granted to one branch have been found by the courts to belong exclusively to Congress, the President, or the courts when they are in their nature exclusively legislative, executive, or judicial.

Although the complexities of modern government require much sharing of power among governmental authorities, the constitutional principles of federalism and the separation of powers require also the maintenance of the proper exclusive spheres of power.

GLEN E. THUROW

Bibliography

PRITCHETT, C. HERMAN 1977 *The American Constitution,* 3d ed. Pages 150–216. New York: McGraw-Hill.

EXECUTIVE AGREEMENT

Executive agreements—that is, international agreements concluded between heads of state or their representatives, commonly without the necessity of parliamentary approval—are nowhere explicitly authorized in the Constitution. The Constitution is silent about international agreement-making except as it vests in the President, in cooperation with the Senate, the power to make and enter into treaties. Nevertheless the principle has long been established that the capacity of the United States to negotiate and enter into international agreements is not exhausted by the TREATY POWER. This principle has been repeatedly recognized in the actual conduct of United States FOREIGN AFFAIRS since the early days of the Republic. Since the mid-nineteenth century, but especially since World War II, the use of executive agreements in United States practice has exceeded the use of treaties by an increasingly wide margin.

The expression "executive agreement," which is not widely used outside the United States but which has its equivalents abroad, is understood by the Department of State to refer, in general, to any international agreement brought into force relative to the United States without the ADVICE AND CONSENT of the Senate that is constitutionally required for treaties. In particular, it is understood to refer to three kinds of agreements: those made pursuant to, or in accordance with, an existing treaty; those made subject to congressional approval or implementation ("congressional-executive agreements"); and those made under, and in accordance with, the President's constitutional powers ("sole executive agreements"). None of these executive agreements is subject to the formal treaty-making process specified in Article II, section 2, clause 2, of the Constitution.

A treaty-based executive agreement, provided that it is within the intent, scope, and subject matter of the parent treaty, has the same validity and effect as the treaty itself and is subject to the same constitutional limitations. Deriving from one of the elements of "the supreme law of the land," it takes precedence over all inconsistent state laws and follows the customary rule favoring the instrument later in time in case of inconsistency with a federal statute. A conspicuous example of a treaty-based executive agreement is the traditional *compromis* defining the terms of submission to adjudication or arbitration under a basic convention. Another is found in the hundreds of STATUS OF FORCES AGREEMENTS and other agreements required to carry out the NORTH ATLANTIC TREATY, the linchpin of United States policy in Europe since World War II.

A congressional-executive agreement is based on either a prior or a subsequent act of Congress authorizing the making of the agreement or providing general authority for the executive action needed internationally to implement the legislation in question. The scope or subject matter of the agreement is the same whether the congressional act comes before or after the negotiation of the agreement; the act of Congress often takes the form of an authorization to enter into or effectuate an agreement already negotiated. In principle, however, the agreement must reside within the joint powers of Congress and the President in order to have constitutional validity. An agreement outside the legal competence of Congress or the President, authorities generally agree, would be unconstitutional. On the other hand, as the American Law Institute has commented, "the source of authority to make a congressional-executive agreement may be broader even than the sum of the respective powers of Congress and the President," and "in international matters the President and Congress together have all the powers of the United States inherent in its SOVEREIGNTY and nationhood and can therefore make any international agreement on any subject." In any event, partly out of a concern to CHECK AND BALANCE the President in the conduct of foreign affairs, the vast majority of executive agreements entered into by the United States—for example, the Lend-Lease Agreements of World War II and the Trade Expansion Acts of 1934 and 1962—are of this type. Like its treaty-based counterpart, deriving from one of the elements of "the supreme law of the land," the congressional-executive agreement supersedes all inconsistent state law and follows the customary rule favoring the instrument later in time in case of inconsistency with a federal statute.

Sole executive agreements are international agreements entered into by the President without reference to treaty or statutory authority, that is, exclusively on the basis of the President's constitutional powers as chief executive and COMMANDER-IN-CHIEF, responsible for United States foreign relations and military affairs. Department of State records indicate that only a small percentage of executive agreements are of this type and that the great majority have dealt with essentially routine diplomatic and military matters. Accordingly, with relatively minor exception (such as agreements settling pecuniary and personal injury claims of citizens against foreign governments), they have had little direct impact on private interests and therefore have given rise to little domestic litigation. However, in part out of fear that the President might undertake by international agreement what would be unconstitutional by statute, as in fact occurred in MISSOURI V. HOLLAND (1920), such agreements have not been free of controversy. Two issues in particular continue to stand out.

First there is the question, not yet conclusively settled, of whether Congress may legislate to prohibit or otherwise limit sole executive agreements. Although comprehensive limitations on such agreements, including the proposed BRICKER AMENDMENT of 1953–1954, have so far failed to be adopted, Congress has nonetheless occasionally restricted presidential authority in ways that appear to preclude some executive agreements. For example, the War Powers Resolution of 1973, requiring congressional authorization to introduce combat troops into hostile situations, arguably restrains the President from making agreements that would commit United States armed forces to undeclared foreign wars. Similarly, the Arms Control and Disarmament Act of 1961 forbids the limitation or reduction of armaments "except pursuant to the treaty making power . . . or unless authorized by further legislation of the Congress of the United States." The validity of such restrictions upon presidential authority has been challenged by Presidents and has yet to be determined by the Supreme Court.

Second, while it is widely accepted that the President, under the "executive power" clause, has the authority to conclude sole executive agreements that are not inconsistent with legislation in areas where Congress has primary responsibility, there is a question as to whether the President alone may make an agreement inconsistent with an act of Congress or, alternatively, whether a sole executive agreement may supersede earlier inconsistent congressional legislation. The prevailing view, rooted in the belief that it would be unconscionable for an act of a single person—the President—to repeal an act of Congress, is that sole executive agreements are inoperative as law in the United States to the extent that they conflict with a prior act of Congress in an area of congressional competence. This is the position taken by a federal appeals court in *United States v. Guy W. Capps, Inc.* (4th Circuit, 1953) and by the American Law Institute. The Supreme Court has not yet rendered a definitive decision in these respects, however.

The foregoing two issues aside, there is broad agreement about the scope and effect of sole executive agreements as a matter of constitutional law. Like the other two kinds of executive agreements, they are subject to the same limitations applicable to treaties, they are not limited by the TENTH AMENDMENT, and they supersede all inconsistent state law.

In sum, all three categories of executive agreements bespeak a historic trend toward strong executive leadership in foreign affairs. Only three final points need be added. First, the judgment to resort to these agreements in lieu of the treaty alternative is essentially a political one, affected more by surrounding circumstances than by abstract theories of law. Second, once in force, executive agreements are presumptively binding upon the United States and the other parties to them under international law, to the same extent and in the same way as treaties. Third, the international obligations assumed under such agreements survive all subsequent limitations or restrictions in domestic law.

BURNS H. WESTON

Bibliography

AMERICAN LAW INSTITUTE 1965 *Restatement of the Law, Second: Foreign Relations Law of the United States.* Pages 361–448. St. Paul, Minn.: American Law Institute.

——— 1980 *Restatement of the Law: Foreign Relations Law of the United States (Revised), Tentative Draft No. 1.* Pages 71–144. Philadelphia: American Law Institute.

BERGER, RAOUL 1972 The Presidential Monopoly of Foreign Relations. *Michigan Law Review* 71:1–58.

BORCHARD, EDWIN 1944 Shall the Executive Agreement Replace the Treaty? *Yale Law Journal* 53:664–683.

HENKIN, LOUIS 1972 *Foreign Affairs and the Constitution.* Pages 173–188. Mineola, N.Y.: Foundation Press.

MCDOUGAL, MYRES and LANS, ASHER 1945 Treaties and Congressional-Executive Agreements: Interchangeable Instruments of National Policy. *Yale Law Journal* 54:181–351, 534–615.

EXECUTIVE IMMUNITY

In tracing the development of executive immunity in the United States, one should separate immunity for constitutional violations from immunity for nonconstitutional violations and immunity of federal officials from immunity of state officials. State officials' immunity for nonconstitutional violations is a matter left to each state's laws. At least since enactment in 1871 of SECTION 1983, TITLE 42, UNITED STATES CODE, state officials have been liable for some federal constitutional violations. Until well into the twentieth century, however, their immunity in constitutional cases had not been fully explored because there were relatively few federal constitutional restrictions on state officials' behavior. By the middle of the twentieth century, federal officials, who are not covered by section 1983, seemed immune from actions for both constitutional and nonconstitutional misbehavior. Within a few decades, however, with the exception of the President, no executive official, state or federal, was fully immune from damage actions for constitutional violations.

In the Massachusetts case of *Miller v. Horton* (1891) Justice OLIVER WENDELL HOLMES, writing for the majority, narrowly restricted state officials' state-law immunity from suit. Even reasonable, good-faith behavior might trigger liability if found to violate the Constitution or some other legal limit. But in *Spaulding v. Vilas* (1896) and other cases, the Supreme Court was more protective of federal executives. And in subsequent years, many states provided their executives with more generous protection from suits in state courts, particularly when their acts were viewed as discretionary rather than ministerial.

Gregoire v. Biddle (1949) highlighted the movement away from *Miller v. Horton.* In an influential opinion by Judge LEARNED HAND for the United States Court of Appeals, *Gregoire* suggested that a federal executive officer's malice would not render him liable for an otherwise lawful act. *Gregoire* was read as conferring broad immunity upon federal officials. *Barr v. Matteo* (1959) accentuated this trend when, in a case generating no majority opinion, the Supreme Court seemed to hold federal officials absolutely immune from defamation suits.

After *Barr,* the Supreme Court paused in its treatment of federal executive immunity to explore the liability, under section 1983, of state officers charged with constitutional violations. In a series of cases, including PIERSON V. RAY (1967), SCHEUER V. RHODES (1974), and WOOD V. STRICKLAND (1975), the Court held that unconstitutional acts by state executive officials would not trigger liability under section 1983 if the officials acted under a reasonable, good-faith belief that their behavior was constitutional. But they enjoyed no absolute immunity. *Scheuer v. Rhodes,* in which a governor was found not to have absolute immunity, dispelled illusions some had entertained about special status for high officials.

This experience with state officials undoubtedly influenced the Court's subsequent treatment of federal officials. In BUTZ V. ECONOMOU (1978), over four dissents, the Supreme Court held that the good-faith defense, and not the rule of *Barr,* applied to damage actions against federal officials for constitutional violations. Prior statements about absolute immunity, and the importance of the ministerial/discretionary dichotomy, in effect were limited to cases involving common law torts. *Harlow v. Fitzgerald* (1982) reaffirmed and modified the limited immunity of high federal executive officials and NIXON V. FITZGERALD (1982) found the federal chief executive, the President, to enjoy the absolute immunity that *Scheuer* had denied to state chief executives.

THEODORE EISENBERG

Bibliography

JAFFE, LOUIS L. 1963 Suits against Governments and Officers: Damage Actions. *Harvard Law Review* 77:209–239.

SCHUCK, PETER H. 1981 Suing Our Servants: The Court, Congress, and the Liability of Public Officials for Damages. *Supreme Court Review* 1980:281–368.

EXECUTIVE ORDER

Executive orders, a class of presidential documents, primarily regulate actions of government officials and agencies. Although most executive orders are issued under specific statutory authorization, some, including President HARRY S. TRUMAN's STEEL SEIZURE order and executive orders affecting CIVIL RIGHTS, are issued on the President's own authority under Article II. Executive orders were not numbered until 1907 and were not required to be published until 1935.

Executive orders have taken on particular importance in times of war and in the field of civil rights. President FRANKLIN D. ROOSEVELT's executive orders played a key role in the World War II Japanese relocation program, sustained in the JAPANESE AMERICAN CASES (1943–1944). Most executive orders concerning civil rights relate to employment by government contractors. Executive Order 8802 (1941), generated by a wartime need for labor, established a Committee on Fair Employment Practices to carry out a policy of nondiscrimination in defense industries. EXECUTIVE ORDERS 9980 AND 9981 (1948) declared a national policy of nondiscrimination in federal employment and sought to foster equality of treatment in the armed services. Executive Order 11603 (1962) attempted to promote nondiscrimination in federally assisted housing. On the more mundane level, executive orders also have been a vehicle through which Presidents promulgate the never-ending plans for reorganizing the executive branch of government.

With the enactment of ANTIDISCRIMINATION LEGISLATION in the 1960s and the expansion of constitutional prohibitions on government discrimination, executive orders prohibiting discrimination became less important. They continue, however, to provide internal authority regulating the federal government's employment and contracting policies. And in requiring employers to take AFFIRMATIVE ACTION to hire minorities and women, EXECUTIVE ORDER 11246 (1965) goes further than fair employment statutes. It has been a significant factor in pressuring government contractors to hire minority and female workers.

THEODORE EISENBERG

(SEE ALSO: *Presidential Ordinance-Making Power.*)

Bibliography

MORGAN, RUTH P. 1970 *The President and Civil Rights: Policy-Making by Executive Order.* New York: St. Martin's Press.

EXECUTIVE ORDER 9066 AND PUBLIC LAW 503 (1942): JAPANESE AMERICAN RELOCATION

On February 19, 1942, citing the necessity for "every possible protection against espionage and against sabotage," President FRANKLIN D. ROOSEVELT issued an EXECUTIVE ORDER authorizing various military commanders to designate any area in the United States from which "any or all persons may be excluded" at their discretion. Although based on a 1918 WAR POWERS act, the order resulted from vigorous anti-Japanese sentiment on the West Coast. Despite its broad wording, the order was enforced almost exclusively against persons of Japanese ancestry. The order conveyed a remarkably broad DELEGATION OF POWER but failed to distinguish between American citizens and ALIENS or even between loyal and disloyal citizens. To provide for enforcement, the War Department drafted a bill making it a federal crime for a civilian to disobey a military relocation order. The bill passed Congress without dissent and Roosevelt signed it into law on March 21. Few spoke out against the use of these two measures to deprive some 110,000 people (an entire community was relocated in ten "camps") of their CIVIL RIGHTS. The Supreme Court sustained the evacuation and relocation in three JAPANESE AMERICAN CASES (1943–1944), despite a vigorous dissent by Justice FRANK MURPHY objecting to the "legalization of racism."

DAVID GORDON

EXECUTIVE ORDER 10340 (1952)

On April 8, 1952, on the eve of a nationwide strike of steelworkers, President HARRY S. TRUMAN issued Executive Order 10340, directing the secretary of commerce to take possession of and operate the plants and facilities of eighty-seven major steel companies. The order anticipated that the plants would continue to be run by company managers, preserving the rights and obligations of the companies until corporation officials and union leaders settled their dispute. As justification for averting a work stoppage, the order referred to Truman's proclamation of December 16, 1950, declaring the existence of a national emergency and the dispatch of American fighting men to Korea. The order called steel "indispensable" for producing weapons and war materials, for carrying out the programs of the Atomic Energy Commission, and for maintaining the health and vitality of the American economy.

Although Truman based the order on authority under "the Constitution and laws of the United States, and as President of the United States and COMMANDER-IN-CHIEF of the armed forces of the United States," the Justice Department later argued in court that Truman had acted solely on inherent executive power without any statutory support. On June 2, 1952, the Supreme Court declared the Executive Order invalid.

LOUIS FISHER

(SEE ALSO: *Youngstown Sheet and Tube Co. v. Sawyer,* 1952; *Steel Seizure Controversy.*)

Bibliography

MARCUS, MAEVA 1977 *Truman and the Steel Seizure Case: The Limits of Presidential Power.* New York: Columbia University Press.

EXECUTIVE ORDER 11246 (1965)

Executive Order 11246 required government contractors to take AFFIRMATIVE ACTION to ensure nondiscriminatory employment practices. Employers complying with the order may encounter employees or potential employees who claim that affirmative action violates Title VII of the CIVIL RIGHTS ACT OF 1964 or the Constitution. UNITED STEELWORKERS OF AMERICA V. WEBER (1979), which sustained some affirmative action by private employers, does not foreclose all such claims. Efforts to undermine the order by amending the 1964 act have failed. Part I of the order, which banned discrimination and required affirmative action by the federal government, was superseded by Executive Order 11478 (1969) and by the 1972 extension of the 1964 act to government employees.

THEODORE EISENBERG

EXECUTIVE ORDERS 9835 AND 10450 (1947, 1953)

As a result of domestic political and security pressures after 1945, Presidents HARRY S. TRUMAN and DWIGHT D. EISENHOWER instituted sweeping loyalty investigations of federal workers. Truman's Executive Order 9835, affecting over two million employees, established loyalty review boards in executive departments to evaluate information provided by Federal Bureau of Investigation or Civil Service Commission investigations and informants. The basic standards for dismissal required "reasonable grounds for belief in disloyalty," which included evidence of affiliation with groups on the ATTORNEY GENERAL'S LIST of subversive organizations. Critics who alleged widespread subversion nevertheless demanded more stringent measures, and Truman's Executive Order 10241 (April 28, 1951) altered the criterion to one of "reasonable doubt" of loyalty. The change effectively shifted the burden of proof to the accused or suspected employee. Eisenhower, however, later complained that the Truman program reflected "a complacency . . . toward security risks," such as homosexuals and alcoholics, and in April 1953, he issued Executive Order 10450 that made security, not loyalty, the primary concern.

The loyalty probes produced new bureaucracies, with agendas of their own and standards and practices that varied widely in different departments. Between 1947 and 1956, approximately 2,700 employees were dismissed and another 12,000 resigned because of the inquiries. After 1953, the security program provided for immediate suspension without pay, and many employees undoubtedly resigned to avoid the stigma of combating the charges, however flimsy. Then, too, the program's shroud of secrecy, including the use of unknown informants, made challenges difficult.

The Supreme Court responded cautiously to the program. In *Bailey v. Richardson* (1951) an evenly divided bench sustained Bailey's dismissal even though she had been denied an opportunity to confront her accusers. The same day, in JOINT ANTI-FASCIST REFUGEE COMMITTEE V. MCGRATH, the Court questioned the procedures for compiling the attorney general's list of subversive organizations, yet did not prevent its continued use. Some individuals successfully challenged their dismissals, but courts carefully avoided broader constitutional issues. In *Peters v. Hobby* (1955) the Supreme Court overturned a medical professor's dismissal because his position was nonsensitive, yet the Justices ignored Peters's challenge against secret informers. Similar reasoning was employed in *Cole v. Young* (1956) to reverse the discharge of an employee who had challenged the use of the attorney general's list as a violation of rights of association. The real turning point came in *Service v. Dulles* (1957) when the Court reversed the dismissal of one of the "China Hands" who had been purged from the State Department. Finally, in *Greene v. McElroy* (1959), Chief Justice EARL WARREN condemned the use of "faceless informers," unknown to the accused. Without determining constitutional issues, the Court held that the government's evidence must be disclosed to the individual to give him an opportunity to refute it.

Although the Court's decisions undoubtedly demonstrated that abusive, illegal governmental actions could be brought to account, such challenges required extraordinary individual persistence and courage as well as financial and emotional cost. For all the government's efforts, the results were dubious. Judith Coplon, convicted of passing Justice Department documents to a Soviet agent, had escaped the program's net. And in 1954, the Civil Service Commission acknowledged that no communist or fellow traveler had been uncovered in its probes.

STANLEY I. KUTLER

Bibliography

HARPER, ALAN D. 1969 *The Politics of Loyalty.* Greenwich, Conn.: Greenwood Press.

EXECUTIVE ORDERS 9980 AND 9981: INTEGRATION OF THE FEDERAL GOVERNMENT (1948)

When issued by President HARRY S. TRUMAN, Executive Orders 9980 and 9981 were among the most far-reaching federal antidiscrimination measures adopted since Reconstruction. Executive Order 9980 authorized the establishment of review boards within federal executive departments and agencies to which employees claiming racially discriminatory treatment could appeal. It also established a Fair Employment Board to coordinate and supervise executive antidiscrimination policy and to hear appeals from agency and department review boards.

Executive Order 9981 declared it "to be the policy of the President that there shall be equality of treatment and opportunity for all persons in the armed services without regard to race, color, religion or national origin." To this end, the order established the President's Committee on Equality of Treatment and Opportunity in the Armed Services to study and resolve the problem of SEGREGATION in the armed forces. Issued under pressure from black leaders, and in the midst of a reelection campaign, the order and the committee's recommendations were crucial first steps to desegregating the armed services.

THEODORE EISENBERG

Bibliography

BERMAN, WILLIAM C. 1970 *The Politics of Civil Rights in the Truman Administration.* Pages 116–120. Columbus: Ohio State University Press.

EXECUTIVE PRIVILEGE

Executive privilege refers to a right of the chief executive to refuse to produce documents within his control in response to a demand from either the legislative or judicial departments of the national government. There would seem to be no question that the chief magistrate need not respond to such demands from departments of state governments. Raoul Berger has asserted that "executive privilege is a myth," a creature of the Presidents who have asserted this claim to immunity without foundation in the Constitution. Although the Constitution does provide for legislative privilege, there are no words in the Constitution on which to base any such executive privilege. Nevertheless, the Supreme Court, in UNITED STATES V. NIXON (1974), wrote executive privilege into the Constitution on the grounds that it inheres in the notion of SEPARATION OF POWERS that is immanent in our basic document:

> The expectation of a President to the confidentiality of his conversations and correspondence, like the claim of confidentiality of judicial deliberations, for example, has all the values to which we accord deference for the privacy of all citizens and, added to these values, is the necessity for protection of the public interest in candid, objective, and even blunt or harsh opinions in presidential decision-making. A President and those who assist him must be free to explore alternatives in the process of shaping policies and making decisions and to do so in a way many would be unwilling to express except privately. These are the considerations justifying a presumptive privilege for Presidential communications. The privilege is fundamental to the operation of Government and inextricably rooted in the separation of powers under the Constitution.

The privilege as created by the Court in *Nixon* is not, however, an absolute one. Interests of the other branches of government may override the presidential interest in the privilege. And in *Nixon* the executive privilege was held subordinate to the claim of a GRAND JURY for EVIDENCE "that is demonstrably relevant in a criminal trial." Thus, the weight of the privilege to withhold information differs according to its function. It is at its lowest force when it "is based only on the generalized interest in confidentiality." It is at its strongest when the claim is based on the ground of "military or diplomatic secrets."

The Supreme Court's constitutional DOCTRINE of executive privilege is still in its nascency. The Court, in *Nixon*, particularly eschewed passing on "the balance between the President's generalized interest in confidentiality and the need for relevant evidence in civil litigation, [or] with that between the confidentiality interest and congressional demands for information, [or] with the President's interest in preserving state secrets." In the absence of constitutional language, the constitutional meaning of executive privilege depends totally on judicial creation, for "it is the province and duty of this Court 'to say what the law is.' "

Prior to the *Nixon* decision, the question of executive privilege, especially as it related to demands of Congress on the executive branch, was resolved in the political rather than the judicial arena. It was a contest of wills, with each side exerting its own powers and its own claims on public opinion, which was frequently dispositive of the issue. The strongest power of the Congress lies in its control over the purse and its threat to cut off funding from programs as to which Congress makes inquiry and as to which the executive branch declines to produce the documents sought. The greatest force on the side of the executive branch lies in its capacity to delay acquiescence, since most executive privilege questions become moot or stale through the passage of time.

The problem has a long history in this country, going back to the time that President GEORGE WASHINGTON declined to deliver to the House of Representatives documents relating to JAY'S TREATY, on the grounds that it was none of the business of the House to participate in the treaty process and that all relevant information had, indeed, been delivered to the Senate, whose job it was to advise and consent on the content of treaties. When in the *Burr* case JOHN MARSHALL subpoenaed communications in the hands of President THOMAS JEFFERSON, Jefferson decided which he would and which he would not provide. In *Burr* the judiciary proved helpless against the adamancy of the President to withhold documents, although the Court might have tried to invoke the CONTEMPT POWER.

Since the investigatory or oversight power of Congress is itself an implied rather than a granted power, its claim to access to presidential papers generally rests on as weak a reed as does the President's claim to immunity from producing the information. Both are implicit rather than express constitutional rights. But the case differs where Congress, particularly the House, is investigating the question of misbehavior of executive branch officials. The Congress is particularly charged by the IMPEACHMENT provisions of the Constitution with the duty of "throwing the rascals out." And surely they must have access to relevant information to determine whether an executive official, be it the President himself, has committed "high crimes and misdemeanors" for which he might be impeached and convicted. But the problem of executive privilege has not arisen in the impeachment context. Rather the impeachment power is used to justify a general congressional power of investigation.

It is with regard to Congress's legislative duty to secure knowledge on which to base its laws or to assure itself that the President is, indeed, engaged in the faithful execution of the laws which Congress has enacted that "executive privilege" problems tend to arise. History provides us with no doctrinal answer to the correct meaning of executive privilege here. Most are agreed that the privilege can be claimed only by the President himself or by a government official at the command of the President. It is not to be invoked even by the vice-president or the secretary of state except through the President. There is little other consensus. Impeachable offenses aside, the privilege is strong where, as the Court noted, it is concerned with military or state secrets. Beyond this, history shows only that the balance between the two constitutional claims, Congress's to be able to perform its duties and the President's to perform his own, has been resolved on an ad hoc basis, with the President having the greater ability to manipulate public opinion, and Congress being able to invoke only the time-consuming processes of contempt and fiscal restraints.

Now that the Supreme Court seems to have made the question of executive privilege a judicial rather than a political one, some further elucidation may be forthcoming. But, except in times of crisis such as the Watergate affair, the mills of the courts, like the mills of the gods, grind so very slowly that they may prove inadequate to provide greater definition to the amorphous concept of executive privilege. This is especially the case since the Court recognized the privilege as a conditional one and not an absolute one, requiring balancing by a judicial arbiter without any special competence to perform the task. It may be predicted, however, that where the conflict is between the judicial and executive branches, as it was in the *Nixon* case, the judicial branch is more likely to prevail, at least in a criminal case or one in which the government itself is seeking the information. But, as between Congress and the President, the Court is likely to be found where it is usually found, aligned with the executive branch.

Executive privilege could cover immunities other than the right to reject a demand for information from another branch. In the Nixon period, the question arose, speculatively, whether a President of the United States could be arrested, indicted, and tried for crime while still in office. That a successful impeachment would leave the person charged with no immunity to arrest, INDICTMENT, and trial is made clear by the words of the Constitution itself. On the other hand, it says nothing about executive immunity while in office. Without judicial precedent or judgment, there appeared to be agreement that the President of the United States and only the President must be immune from interruption of his duties while he holds office, subject only to the necessity for responding to impeachment charges. There is no moment when the President is not on duty, even while on vacation. This immunity, whether termed executive privilege or not, derives from the implications of the Constitution much more readily than his right to refuse to produce documents, which need not interrupt his presidential obligations.

One must assume, too, that the President, like everyone in the nation, can claim the RIGHT AGAINST SELF-INCRIMINATION both in Congress and in the courts. The practical effects on the electorate of such a claim make it highly unlikely that it will ever be invoked. And again, the privilege not to incriminate himself is not the executive privilege as that term is generally used.

The contours of executive privilege remain hard to define, and certainty is not likely to come soon, if ever.

PHILIP B. KURLAND

Bibliography

BERGER, RAOUL 1974 *Executive Privilege: A Constitutional Myth.* Cambridge, Mass.: Harvard University Press.

KURLAND, PHILIP B. 1978 *Watergate and the Constitution.* Chicago: University of Chicago Press.

UNITED STATES SENATE, JUDICIARY COMMITTEE, SUBCOMMITTEE ON SEPARATION OF POWERS 1971 *Executive Privilege: The Withholding of Information by the Executive.* 92nd Congress, 1st session. Washington, D.C.: Government Printing Office.

———, SUBCOMMITTEE ON ADMINISTRATIVE PRACTICE AND PROCEDURE AND SEPARATION OF POWERS, AND COMMITTEE ON GOVERNMENT OPERATIONS, SUBCOMMITTEE ON INTERGOVERNMENTAL RELATIONS 1973 *Freedom of Information: Executive Privilege; Secrecy in Government.* 3 Vols. 93rd Congress, 1st session. Washington, D.C.: Government Printing Office.

EXHAUSTION OF REMEDIES

Exhaustion-of-remedies questions arise in at least two areas of constitutional adjudication. Since *Ex parte Royall* (1886), state prisoners have been required to exhaust available, effective state court remedies before seeking federal HABEAS CORPUS relief from allegedly unconstitutional state convictions. Congress codified this result more than half a century later. The exhaustion requirement, which is not constitutionally mandated, is said to reflect the Court's sensitivity to relations between federal and state courts; a federal court is prevented from reviewing a state conviction until state courts have had a chance to correct constitutional errors.

In another class of cases seeking to vindicate constitutional rights, the Supreme Court does not require exhaustion of state judicial remedies. In MONROE V. PAPE (1961) and a series of later cases, the Court has stated that there is no requirement of exhaustion of state judicial remedies before bringing an action against state officials under SECTION 1983, TITLE 42, UNITED STATES CODE. *Patsy v. Board of Regents* (1982) held that litigants bringing section 1983 cases also need not exhaust state administrative remedies and thereby resolved a long-standing conflict among the courts of appeal. In the Civil Rights of Institutionalized Persons Act (1980), Congress imposed an exhaustion-of-administrative-remedies requirement upon certain prisoners bringing actions under section 1983.

The exhaustion requirement in habeas corpus cases, and its absence in section 1983 cases, generates difficulty in deciding whether to require exhaustion in constitutional actions brought by prisoners, many of which may be brought either as habeas actions or as section 1983 cases. In *Preiser v. Rodriguez* (1973) the Court held that exhaustion was required in a case close to "the core of habeas corpus," that is, one attacking the validity of a prisoner's conviction or otherwise challenging the fact or duration of confinement. When the prisoner challenges the conditions of confinement, the Court said, the nonexhaustion rule applicable to section 1983 cases governs. Perhaps inspired in part by the long-standing exhaustion requirement in habeas corpus cases, much modern CIVIL RIGHTS legislation reflects sensitivity to state prerogatives by requiring complainants initially to present claims to state authorities. Title VII of the CIVIL RIGHTS ACT OF 1964 requires resort to state antidiscrimination agencies before the Equal Employment Opportunity Commission may act on a complaint. Title VIII of the CIVIL RIGHTS ACT OF 1968 requires federal administrators to allow state and local housing agencies the first chance at a housing discrimination complaint. But post-Civil War ANTIDISCRIMINATION LEGISLATION, such as the CIVIL RIGHTS ACTS OF 1866 and 1870, reflected no such sensitivity. And the practice is not uniform in modern statutes. The VOTING RIGHTS ACT OF 1965 expressly rejects any requirement of exhaustion of administrative or other remedies before initiation of actions in federal court. Other civil rights statutes simply do not address the issue.

THEODORE EISENBERG

Bibliography

COMMENT 1974 Exhaustion of State Administrative Remedies in Section 1983 Cases. *University of Chicago Law Review* 41:537–556.

NAHMOD, SHELDON H. 1979 *Civil Rights & Civil Liberties Litigation.* Pages 143–148. Colorado Springs, Colo.: Shepard's.

EXIGENT CIRCUMSTANCES SEARCH

Although the Supreme Court has denounced WARRANTLESS SEARCHES as *"per se* unreasonable under the FOURTH AMENDMENT," it has recognized "a few specifically established and well-delineated exceptions" to this rule based on exigent circumstances. A SEARCH WARRANT, which in ordinary circumstances provides constitutional reasonableness for a search, may be dispensed with if the delay involved in obtaining the warrant might defeat the purpose of the search. In fact, far more searches are made without warrants than with them. The warrantless search is "exceptional" only in the sense that exceptional (that is, exigent) circumstances are needed to justify it.

Five types of warrantless searches have thus far received the Court's sanction. In WEEKS V. UNITED STATES (1914) the Court upheld SEARCH INCIDENT TO ARREST of a person—and, in later cases, of the area under the arrestee's control— in order to disarm him and prevent the destruction of EVIDENCE. The search of an automobile on the road is constitutional when there is PROBABLE CAUSE to believe the automobile is transporting contraband. As the Court said in CARROLL V. UNITED STATES (1925), to delay the AUTOMOBILE SEARCH is to risk the escape of driver and vehicle. "Hot pursuit" of a suspected felon into a building was held reasonable in WARDEN V. HAYDEN (1967). Delaying to obtain a warrant might endanger the lives of the pursuing officers and others. Such a search may continue until the suspect is apprehended and his weapons are seized. In SCHMERBER V. CALIFORNIA (1966) the Court permitted the compulsory taking of blood from an individual to determine whether he was intoxicated while driving when there was probable cause to believe that he was. The exigency in such cases is furnished by the fact that the level of alcohol in the blood diminishes after its intake ceases. In TERRY V. OHIO (1968) the Court upheld the practice of stopping a suspect and frisking his outer clothing to discover concealed weapons, even when probable cause for an arrest is lacking, provided that circumstances entitle an officer to believe that a criminal venture is about to be launched and that his safety or that of others is endangered.

The concept of exigent circumstances is an open one. Indeed, in *Mincey v. Arizona* (1978) the Court indicated that officers may enter and search without a warrant upon reasonable belief that there is a "need to protect or preserve life or avoid serious injury. . . ."

JACOB W. LANDYNSKI

Bibliography

LANDYNSKI, JACOB W. 1971 The Supreme Court's Search for Fourth Amendment Standards: The Warrantless Search. *Connecticut Bar Journal* 45:2–39.

EX PARTE

(Latin: "From the part [of]. . . .") A legal proceeding is said to be *ex parte* if it occurs on the application or for the benefit of one party without NOTICE to or contest by an adverse party. In the reports such a case is entitled *"Ex parte . . ."* followed by the name of the party at whose instance the case is heard. A proceeding of which an adverse party has notice, but at which he declines to appear, is not considered *ex parte.* Writs, INJUNCTIONS, etcetera, are said to be *ex parte* when they are issued without prior notice to an affected party.

DENNIS J. MAHONEY

EX PARTE . . .

See under name of party

EXPATRIATION

Expatriation was defined by the Supreme Court in *Perkins v. Elg* (1939) as "the voluntary renunciation or abandonment of nationality and allegiance." It refers to the loss of CITIZENSHIP as a result of voluntary action taken by a citizen, either native-born or naturalized. By expatriation, a citizen becomes an ALIEN; he divests himself of the obligations of citizenship and loses the rights connected with those obligations. In general, he can regain citizenship only by the process of NATURALIZATION.

At COMMON LAW, a person owed perpetual allegiance to the country of his birth and could not expatriate himself without the consent of that country. Initially, there was an inclination in the United States to follow this rule. In 1868, however, Congress explicitly broke with that tradition and declared by statute that "the right of expatriation is a natural and inherent right of all people, indispensable to the enjoyment of the rights of life, liberty, and the pursuit of happiness." Congress did so in order to establish that persons naturalized in the United States did not continue to owe allegiance to foreign governments. Congress seemed to rely on the simple mechanism of formal renunciation to determine whether a citizen actually wished to expatriate himself. Because the statute made expatriation dependent upon the voluntary action of the individual, it raised no constitutional questions about Congress's power over expatriation.

Determination of volition, however, has never been limited to formal renunciation, and through a series of nationality statutes, culminating in the Immigration and Nationality Act of 1952, Congress has identified various actions that indicate a citizen's desire voluntarily to expatriate himself. These actions include obtaining naturalization in a foreign state, taking an oath of allegiance to a foreign state, serving in a foreign army, voting in a foreign election, desertion from the armed forces, TREASON against the United States, assuming public office under the government of a foreign state for which only nationals of that state are eligible, formal renunciation of citizenship either in the United States or abroad, and leaving or remaining outside the United States during either a war or a national emergency for the purpose of evading military service.

Congress's power to declare that such actions constitute voluntary renunciation, even when the individual who so acts claims not to have intended to renounce his citizenship, was rarely challenged by the courts until the 1960s. Nationality laws were shielded from judicial scrutiny because the courts believed it was beyond their competence to examine matters so intimately related to foreign affairs. However, in the landmark decision of AFROYIM V. RUSK (1967), the Supreme Court restored citizenship to a naturalized citizen who was considered by the government to have expatriated himself by voting in an Israeli parliamentary election. The Court held that although Congress can provide a mechanism by which an individual can voluntarily expatriate himself, volition is a judicially ascertainable quality and the government bears the BURDEN OF PROOF that the citizen's renunciation was truly voluntary. Put simply, *Afroyim* made the statutory presumption of volition rebuttable rather than conclusive.

While the BURGER COURT seemed to retreat from these principles in *Rogers v. Bellei* (1971), in *Vance v. Terrazas* (1980) it reaffirmed *Afroyim* and held that the government must prove specific intent to surrender citizenship and not simply the voluntary commission of an expatriating act. At the same time, the Court upheld the rebuttable presumption that an act of expatriation is performed with the specific intention of relinquishing citizenship and held that Congress is free to prescribe as the evidentiary standard for proving this intention the "preponderance-of-the-evidence" standard of proof.

RALPH A. ROSSUM

Bibliography

GORDON, CHARLES and ROSENFIELD, HARRY N. 1984 *Immigration Law and Procedure,* Vol. 3, chap. 20. New York: Matthew Bender.

SCHWARTZ, DAVID F. 1975 American Citizenship after *Afroyim* and *Bellei:* Continuing Controversy. *Hastings Constitutional Law Quarterly* 2:1003–1028.

EXPOSITION AND PROTEST (1828–1829)

JOHN C. CALHOUN drafted the *Exposition* in 1828. The next year, the legislature of South Carolina published the *Exposition* in amended form along with its own resolution of protest against the TARIFF ACT OF 1828. Like most of the great controversial documents in American politics it took the form of a discourse on the meaning of the Constitution. It argued the case for STRICT CONSTRUCTION of the powers of the federal government and spelled out the doctrine of NULLIFICATION.

Rejecting the argument that a protective tariff was justified by custom and precedent, the *Exposition* declared: "Ours is not a government of precedent. . . . The only safe rule is the Constitution itself." But even the Constitution was not a safe rule if its interpretation were left to Congress and the Supreme Court, which were its creatures. The only authoritative interpreter was the constituent body itself, the people of the states in convention.

According to the *Exposition,* if a convention in any state declared a federal law unconstitutional, the law was null and void in that state until the Constitution was amended to authorize the disputed act. Should an amendment pass the state would have no recourse but SECESSION.

DENNIS J. MAHONEY

Bibliography

FREEHLING, WILLIAM W. 1965 *Prelude to Civil War: The Nullification Controversy in South Carolina, 1816–1865.* New York: Harper & Row.

EX POST FACTO

In THE FEDERALIST #84 ALEXANDER HAMILTON argued that "the creation of crimes after the commission of the fact, or, in other words, the subjecting of men to punishment for things which, when they were done, were breaches of no law" has been "in all ages" one of "the favorite and most formidable instruments of tyranny." Indeed, ex post facto legislation has generally been regarded as a violation of the fundamental DUE PROCESS requirement that there must be fair warning of the conduct which gives rise to criminal penalties. The Framers of the Constitution believed so strongly that ex post facto laws were contrary to the principles of republican government that they proscribed their use in two different provisions of the Constitution: Article I, section 9, as a specific exception to the powers of the United States Congress, and Article I, section 10, as a specific prohibition on the powers of state legislatures.

Justice SAMUEL CHASE in CALDER V. BULL (1798) provided what has since come to be regarded as the authoritative delineation of the kinds of LEGISLATION that fall within the Constitution's prohibition against ex post facto enactments:

> 1st. Every law that makes an action done before the passing of the law, and which was *innocent* when done, criminal; and punishes such action. 2d. Every law that *aggravates a crime,* or makes it *greater* than it was, when committed. 3d. Every law that *changes the punishment,* and inflicts a *greater punishment,* than the law annexed to the crime, when committed. 4th. Every law that alters the *legal* rules of *evidence,* and received less, or different, testimony, than the law required at the time of the commission of the offence, *in order to convict the offender.*

Although there is some question about the Framers' intent, the Supreme Court has consistently followed Chase's lead in restricting the ex post facto rule to criminal laws. Thus the Court has held that the deportation of ALIENS, the loss of a passport, and the denial of certain benefits do not fall within the ex post facto exception because they are not punishments in a criminal sense even though they may be "burdensome and severe." In the TEST OATH CASES (1867), however, the Court held that oaths that disqualified people from holding certain offices or practicing certain professions constituted ex post facto laws.

The essential ingredient of an ex post facto law is its retrospective character; but not all retrospective laws are ex post facto in the technical meaning of the term. An ex post facto law not only is retrospective but also injures those to whom it is directed by imposing or increasing criminal penalties. For example, *Weaver v. Graham* (1981) invalidated retroactive application to a prisoner of a law reducing "good time" credits against a sentence. Retrospective laws that ameliorate penalties, however, are not ex post facto.

The rights affected by retrospective legislation must be substantial. As the Court held in *Beazell v. Ohio* (1925), statutory changes in trial procedures or rules of EVIDENCE "which do not deprive the accused of a defense and which operate only in a limited and unsubstantial manner to his disadvantage, are not prohibited." Thus, the ex post facto prohibition secures "substantial personal rights against arbitrary and oppressive legislation without limiting legislative control of remedies and procedures that do not affect matters of substance." Of its own weight, the ex post facto prohibition applies only to legislative acts, and not to changes in the law effected by judicial decisions. But where an unforeseeable statutory construction by a court is applied retrospectively in a manner that is tantamount to ex post facto legislation, that construction is barred by the due process clause. Although the particular application of the ex post facto clause has generated much controversy and debate, and involves, on occasion, the most intricate and detailed considerations, there seems to be almost universal agreement that the Constitution's prohibition against ex post facto legislation remains one of the mainstays of constitutional government.

EDWARD J. ERLER

Bibliography

FIELD, OLIVER P. 1922 Ex Post Facto in the Constitution. *Michigan Law Review* 20:315–331.

NOTE 1975 Ex Post Facto Limitations on Legislative Power. *Michigan Law Review* 73:1491–1516.

EXTRADITION

See: Fugitive from Justice

EXTRATERRITORIALITY

Around the turn of the century, the Supreme Court placed strict territorial limits on the application of United States constitutional and statutory law. In the case of *In re Ross* (1891) the Court held that a citizen could be tried by an American consular court, without INDICTMENT by GRAND JURY and without TRIAL BY JURY, for crimes aboard an American ship in Japan. The Court flatly declared that "[t]he Constitution can have no operation in another country." And in *American Banana Co. v. United Fruit Co.* (1909) Justice OLIVER WENDELL HOLMES asserted that "[a]ll legislation is prima facie territorial." Although he acknowledged that exceptions could be found in the case of laws applying on the high seas or in "uncivilized" countries, Holmes said "the general and almost universal rule is that the character of an act as lawful or unlawful must be determined wholly by the law of the country where the act is done." No doubt these sweeping statements, even then, were not literally followed. In any event, today DOCTRINES limiting the extraterritorial application of both the Constitution and statutory law have been abandoned.

In REID V. COVERT (1956) the Court effectively overruled *Ross* and held that Congress could not deprive a citizen of the right to a jury trial in a court-martial abroad where CAPITAL PUNISHMENT was potentially involved. Justice HUGO L. BLACK said: "When the Government reaches out to punish a citizen who is abroad, the shield which the BILL OF RIGHTS and other parts of the Constitution provide to protect his life and liberty should not be stripped away just because he happens to be in another land." This decision signaled the end of territorial limitations on the Constitution.

In *United States v. Toscanino* (2d Cir. 1974) a lower court applied the FOURTH and Fifth AMENDMENTS where American officials instigated enforcement activity by foreign officials that included torture and violated United States treaty obligations. Although other courts have declined to apply CONSTITUTIONAL REMEDIES in the circumstances of particular cases before them, they agree that the Bill of Rights may apply where the United States government instigates conduct that "shocks the conscience." The JUST COMPENSATION clause of the Fifth Amendment has also been held applicable to TAKINGS OF PROPERTY abroad in several lower court cases. As a general rule, therefore, the Constitution now unquestionably applies to acts of government abroad.

At the same time the special circumstances that are invariably present in these cases influence the scope of constitutional protection afforded. Although the court only occasionally confronts these questions, it seems clear that protection against government action abroad is more difficult to obtain than in similar cases without a foreign element. This is especially true when foreign policy or national security interests are at issue, as was the case in UNITED STATES V. CURTISS-WRIGHT EXPORT CORP. (1936). Indeed, in HAIG V. AGEE (1981) the Supreme Court questioned whether the FIRST AMENDMENT would apply at all to government suppression of speech abroad, where the speech threatened American intelligence activity.

Perhaps the most accurate description of the modern approach to extraterritorial application of constitutional law was made by Justice JOHN MARSHALL HARLAN in *Reid v. Covert.* He took exception to the broad suggestion that "every provision of the Constitution must be deemed automatically applicable to American citizens in every part of the world." He believed that "the question is *which* guarantees of the Constitution *should* apply in view of the particular circumstances, the practical necessities, and the possible alternatives which Congress had before it." The Harlan view seems more likely to prevail in a world of increased American involvement and interdependence than the absolutist approach of Justice Black.

A related issue of historical interest was whether the Constitution applied to TERRITORIES acquired by the United States. Constitutional guarantees limiting legislative and executive power were applicable only when Congress, expressly or by clear implication, "incorporated" the acquired territory into the United States. In unincorporated territories only undefined "fundamental" liberties were guaranteed.

Finally, the courts have repeatedly applied federal statutes to conduct abroad, assuming other jurisdictional prerequisites were met. Occasionally limitations on the application of a particular statute have been imposed, but those limitations have normally been based on the presumed intent of Congress or on international comity, not the Constitution.

PHILLIP R. TRIMBLE

Bibliography

COUDERT, FREDERIC R. 1926 The Evolution of the Doctrine of Territorial Incorporation. *Columbia Law Review* 26:823–850; *Iowa State Bar Association Report* 1926:180–228.

HENKIN, LOUIS 1972 *Foreign Affairs and the Constitution.* Pages 266–269. Mineola, N.Y.: Foundation Press.

KAPLAN, STEVEN M. 1977 The Applicability of the Exclusionary Rule in Federal Court to Evidence Seized and Confessions Obtained in Foreign Countries. *Columbia Journal of Transnational Law* 16:495–520.

NOTE 1985 Predictability and Comity: Toward Common Principles of Extraterritorial Jurisdiction. *Harvard Law Review* 98:1310–1330.

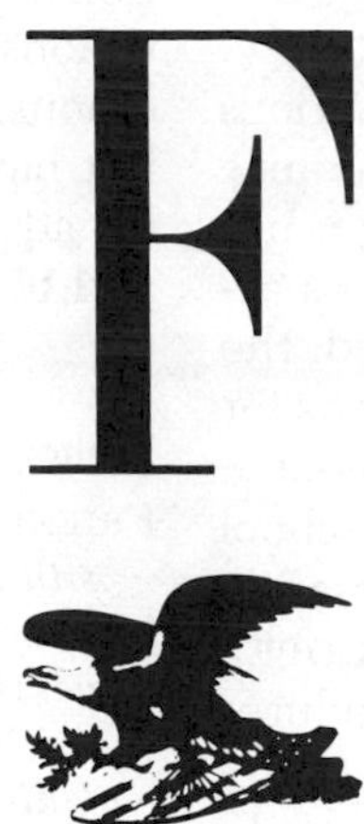

FAIR COMMENT

See: Libel and the First Amendment

FAIR HEARING

In numerous contexts the Constitution requires the state to afford its citizens DUE PROCESS, which frequently includes an adversarial voicing of opposed contentions. "Fair hearing" in this broadest sense could thus include both the specific constitutional guarantees that attach to criminal trials and the more general requirement that civil litigation meet minimal standards of fairness. Among lawyers, however, the term more narrowly refers to the procedure that must be afforded to persons involved not in judicial trials but in some less formal dispute with the state. Speaking to that issue, the Supreme Court has asked when the Constitution requires any process and what that process should be. For some time the Court focused on the first question, assuming that if any process was due, it would resemble a formal trial; later decisions emphasized the flexibility of appropriate process.

For due process requirements to attach to any proceedings, they must, by involving governmental action that threatens life, liberty, or property, fall within the requirements of the Fifth and FOURTEENTH AMENDMENTS. Following in the wake of the welfare state, the Court has expanded its definition of property to include entitlements to various government benefits (for example, welfare and disability payments, tenured positions in state employment). Many threatened deprivations of such benefits consequently require due process, and the question becomes what that process must be. The Court has never answered that question in categorical terms, insisting that each situation calls for a rather individualized judgment. It has, however, suggested some minimal criteria and a set of factors to be considered in striking the balance from case to case. In deciding what process is due, one must consider "first, the private interest . . . affected by the official action; second, the risk of an erroneous deprivation of such interest through the procedures used, and the probable value, if any, of additional or substitute procedural safeguards; and finally, the government's interest, including the function involved and the fiscal and administrative burdens that the additional or substitute procedural requirements would entail" (MATHEWS V. ELDRIDGE, 1976). These factors represent an attempt to arrive at conclusions about two aspects of process: timing and elaborateness.

At a minimum, due process requires notice that tells the person threatened with deprivation the reason for the action and how he can challenge its factual and legal bases. Usually notice and such an opportunity must precede the deprivation, but even this proposition is not invariable; thus in a case of a threat to public health or other emergency situation, a seizure could occur first and notice and hearing afterward.

More difficult than the question of the timing of the required process is its nature. Because the Court has been unable to articulate guidelines applicable to all situations, it defines appropriate processes on a case-by-case basis. Consequently one can fully understand the requirements of due process only by sampling a large number of cases. It is, however, possible to suggest some rough guidelines and some distinctions. The first might be the line between situations requiring formal adjudicatory hearings, as for the termination of WELFARE BENEFITS in GOLDBERG V. KELLY (1970), and those that do not: the more serious the deprivation, the more likely the Court is to require a trial-type hearing. Even when such a hearing is not required, one can further differentiate situations according to the formality of the process required: the state must provide a written statement of reasons for ending disability benefits and give the recipient a chance to respond (*Mathews v. Eldridge*), but a school official need engage only in a brief oral conversation before suspending a student, as in GOSS V. LOPEZ (1975). Indeed, the Court has approved procedures that are not even adversarial in the normal sense, for example, an expulsion proceeding in which a medical student has an opportunity to demonstrate her medical skills to several local doctors over several days. (See BOARD OF CURATORS V. HOROWITZ, 1978.)

The consequence of such flexibility is that a constitutionally "fair hearing" need not entail a hearing at all, and even if it does that hearing may occupy various points along a continuum of adjudicatory formality. Such flexibility results from the Court's attempts, once it has concluded that due process attaches, to tailor the process to the situation at hand, taking some account of the stakes for the adversaries and of the goals of process. Some commentators have criticized the Court for the narrowness of its focus, arguing that the goals of process include the dignity of the participants as well as the accuracy of the result; the Court has seemed unpersuaded of this point.

The constitutional focus on fair hearings in administrative law has drawn attention to a number of areas presenting similar profiles—to which, however, due process does not apply, either because the institutions involved are private or because life, liberty, or property is not threatened. Nevertheless, under the influence of the constitutional cases many institutions (such as private schools or trade associations) have adopted processes that resemble those that might be required if due process did apply. Some of these procedures have resulted from legislation or regulation and an occasional judicial decision using COMMON LAW; others have come voluntarily. In either case the consequence has been a softening of the lines between the practices of public and private institutions; there is thus a sense in which one can speak of a fair hearing as a practice (though not a constitutional requirement) of many areas of institutional life.

If fairness does not always require a hearing, it is nevertheless true that the constitutional ideal described by the term has permeated many areas of life where neither fairness nor a hearing is constitutionally required. The result, in a society of large institutions and sometimes uncertain responsibility for decisions, has been a requirement taking many forms but having at its basis the idea that persons about to be adversely affected have the right to know why and to respond.

STEPHEN C. YEAZELL

Bibliography

FRIENDLY, HENRY 1975 Some Kind of Hearing. *University of Pennsylvania Law Review* 123:1267–1317.

MASHAW, JERRY L. 1976 The Supreme Court's Due Process Calculus for Administrative Adjudication in *Mathews v. Eldridge:* Three Factors in Search of a Theory of Value. *University of Chicago Law Review* 44:28–59.

VERKUIL, PAUL 1975 The Ombudsman and the Limits of the Adversary System. *Columbia Law Review* 75:845–861.

FAIR HOUSING LAWS

See: Open Housing Laws

FAIR LABOR STANDARDS ACT
52 Stat. 1060 (1938)

The Fair Labor Standards Act (FLSA), usually called the federal wage and hour law, was adopted in 1938. For all covered employees the act required the payment of a minimum wage (initially 25 cents an hour) and time and one-half for all hours worked over forty a week. Child labor was forbidden under certain circumstances. The act prohibited the shipment in INTERSTATE COMMERCE of goods produced under substandard conditions. There were numerous and complicated exemptions.

The constitutionality of the act under the COMMERCE CLAUSE was sustained by the Supreme Court in UNITED STATES V. DARBY LUMBER CO. (1940). Since then the act has been amended many times, principally to increase periodically the minimum wage, which reached $3.35 an hour in 1981, to expand coverage, and to provide more effective enforcement.

The act originally covered employees engaged in commerce or in the PRODUCTION of goods for commerce. Production was defined to include activities necessary to the actual production.

Coverage based on engagement in commerce includes employees engaged in the actual movement of commerce, such as transportation, shipping, and communications. It also includes employees whose work involves the distribution or receipt of goods across state lines. The Supreme Court upheld application of the act to employees who did construction or repair work on interstate instrumentalities and even to employees who prepared plans and specifications for the construction or repair of interstate instrumentalities.

Under the extended production definition, many fringe activities were found necessary to production. Thus, the Court upheld application to employees of an office building occupied by a corporation which at other locations produced goods for commerce and to employees of an independent contractor washing windows in industrial plants that produced goods for commerce.

These decisions, although they involved statutory construction, demonstrated the enormous scope of the commerce power even under coverage formulas less extensive than that used to describe the constitutional maximum, "affecting" commerce. The breadth of the Court's holdings led Congress in 1949 to amend the statute to confine the extended production definition to activities "closely related" and "directly essential" to production.

The reduced coverage effectuated by this change was largely nullified, however, by a 1961 amendment providing for "enterprise" coverage. Before 1961 coverage was determined for each employee; thus, some employees of an employer could be covered while others were not. "Enterprise" coverage extended to all an employer's employees, if at least two employees were covered individually and the enterprise did a requisite annual dollar volume of business. The constitutionality of "enterprise" coverage was upheld by the Court in *Maryland v. Wirtz* (1967).

Other aspects of the act have also received expansive interpretation. Thus, the term "employee" has been defined in accordance with "economic reality" rather than COMMON LAW rules, and applied to persons who in other contexts would be independent contractors. These cases illustrate the peculiar American phenomenon of defining "employee" differently under various statutes, so that an employee may be covered under one statute and not under another.

What constitutes compensable work time has presented a special problem under the FLSA. In *Armour & Co. v. Wantoch* (1944), involving firefighters, the Court held that inactive waiting time was compensable work time. Time spent in travel between the mine entrance and the underground cutting face was held compensable in *Tennessee Coal, Inc. & Railroad v. Muscoda Local* (1944). Finally, in *Anderson v. Mt. Clemens Pottery Co.* (1946), the Court required payment for time spent by employees walking between the factory gate and their work place. Many lawsuits were promptly filed claiming billions of dollars in back wages. Congress responsed by enacting the Portal-to-Portal Act of 1947, which distinguished between an employee's compensable principal activity and noncompensable preliminary and after-working activities. Employers were thus absolved in most cases from liability under the *Mt. Clemens Pottery* decision. The Court held, however, that time spent changing clothes, when necessitated by the nature of the work, is a principal activity and thus compensable.

The FLSA applies on a work week basis. Overtime is required for hours in excess of forty a week. The required time and one-half premium is applied to the employee's "regular rate of pay" which is determined by dividing the total weekly compensation (including straight wages plus all fringe benefits) by the number of hours worked. Because employee pay plans are of great variety, determination of the regular rate of pay frequently is a difficult problem.

Among the principal exemptions from the FLSA are executive, administrative, and professional employees (which terms have special definitions), employees of small retail or service establishments, and some employees engaged in agriculture. Special provision is made for learners, apprentices, students, and the handicapped.

The act is enforced by individual employee suits for back wages, or suits by the secretary of labor seeking an INJUNCTION as well as back wages. Individual suits are preempted by suits by the secretary. Liquidated DAMAGES are authorized. TRIAL BY JURY is available in employee suits, but generally is denied in combined injunction–back-wage suits by the secretary. The FLSA is unique in labor legislation in providing criminal prosecution for willful violators. Such actions are handled by the Justice Department, but have not been a major aspect of the statute's enforcement.

Originally the FLSA applied only to private employment. In 1966 it was extended to employees of state hospitals and schools; this extension was sustained in *Maryland v. Wirtz* (1967). In 1974 Congress extended the FLSA to almost all state and local government employees. In NATIONAL LEAGUE OF CITIES V. USERY (1976) the Court held that the TENTH AMENDMENT protected state sovereign functions against commerce power regulation and overruled *Maryland v. Wirtz. Usery* in turn was overruled by GARCIA V. SAN ANTONIO METROPOLITAN TRANSIT

AUTHORITY (1985). Congress responded the same year with legislation authorizing states and cities to reimburse employees for overtime with compensatory time off in lieu of cash payment.

In 1938 the principal purpose of the FLSA was to combat the Depression by increasing the purchasing power in the hands of the lowest-paid workers. Thus, it has been called the original antipoverty law. Fifty years later, the wisdom of the act and its effect on the economy are still debated, but the FLSA survives as a permanent and major piece of American labor legislation.

WILLIAM P. MURPHY

Bibliography

PLAYER, MACK 1975 Enterprise Coverage under the Fair Labor Standards Act: An Assessment of the First Generation. *Vanderbilt Law Review* 28:283–347.

WILLIS, ROBERT N. 1972 The Evolution of the Fair Labor Standards Act. *University of Miami Law Review* 26:607–634.

FAIRNESS DOCTRINE

Born out of a progression of decisions by the Federal Communications Commission (FCC) and then codified by Congress in 1959, the fairness doctrine requires a BROADCASTING license holder "to operate in the public interest and to afford reasonable opportunity for the discussion of conflicting views on issues of public importance." Although the doctrine was upheld against a FIRST AMENDMENT challenge in RED LION BROADCASTING COMPANY V. FCC (1969), it has been perceived increasingly as an intrusive exception to the First Amendment, with diminishing justification.

The doctrine, applicable to radio and television licensees and to some cable operators, requires a licensee that presents a controversial issue to provide a reasonable amount of time for contrasting viewpoints. A less frequently litigated aspect of the doctrine requires affirmative coverage of issues important to the public. Finally, the doctrine assures persons who are disparaged on the airwaves a limited right to respond.

The doctrine reflects a distinction in the way Congress and the courts have conceived of newspapers, on the one hand, and broadcasters on the other. Thus, in MIAMI HERALD V. TORNILLO (1974) the Supreme Court held unconstitutional on First Amendment grounds a Florida statute that required a newspaper to grant a right of reply to persons attacked in its columns. The Court did not distinguish *Red Lion* but ignored it.

Recently a campaign to narrow, if not eliminate, the fairness doctrine has gained momentum. When the fairness doctrine was in full sway, its justification was a supposed scarcity of the channels available for transmission of broadcast signals. Those who wished to communicate by the printed word were not curtailed by government action or the rationing of resources. On the other hand, the number of channels for radio and television transmission was demonstrably limited. Cable television and other new technologies have undermined the "scarcity" justification for regulation by providing abundant new channels.

Some have argued that the spectrum of broadcasting channels is a public resource, and thus that the federal government can insist that a private user of that resource give voice to many speakers. In another perspective, emphasis on the right of the licensee to be an unencumbered editor is misplaced. Expressing this view, in *Red Lion,* the Court said that "it is the right of the viewers and listeners, not the right of broadcasters, which is paramount." (See LISTENERS' RIGHTS.)

Recent commentary has proposed quite a different solution to the "fairness" issue: setting aside segments of broadcast time, or even whole channels, for public access. Owners of broadcasting stations would have no editorial control over these "soapboxes of the air." Broadcasters generally consider the fairness doctrine a badge of second-class citizenship in the ranks of the press. The FCC, in the early 1980s, confined the fairness doctrine's scope and considered its repeal. As an interim measure the FCC announced that asserted violations would not be adjudicated individually, but would be considered when a broadcaster sought renewal of a license. Still, despite these limits, the doctrine continues to influence the culture of television. Producers of national and local television news programs take great care to present at least two sides of important controversial issues.

MONROE E. PRICE

Bibliography

BOLLINGER, LEE 1976 Freedom of the Press and Public Access: Toward a Theory of Partial Regulation of the Mass Media. *University of Michigan Law Review* 75:1–42.

FAIR RETURN ON FAIR VALUE

The DOCTRINE of a fair return on a fair value, which the Supreme Court propounded in SMYTH V. AMES (1898), provided that any government regulation of rate schedules charged by railroads or utilities must allow a reasonable profit or fair rate of return based on a fair valuation of the property. The principal considerations were the original cost of the property, and the cost of reproducing it at the time of the rate regulation. Having entered the business of supervising the details of ratemaking, the Court remained in that business until 1944.

The Court first provided the basis for the doctrine by equating rate regulation with EMINENT DOMAIN: just compensation must accompany a TAKING OF PROPERTY, and to the Court a rate regulation was comparable to a taking. In CHICAGO, MILWAUKEE, AND ST. PAUL RAILWAY COMPANY V. MINNESOTA (1890) the Court declared that the failure to allow a company to charge reasonable rates for the use of its property constituted an unconstitutional taking of property or a violation of SUBSTANTIVE DUE PROCESS OF LAW comparable to a taking. In REAGAN V. FARMERS' LOAN AND TRUST COMPANY (1894) the Court voided rates because they were fixed so low that they virtually took property without compensation. (See GRANGER CASES.) In *Smyth v. Ames* the Court, in a unanimous opinion by Justice JOHN M. HARLAN, proclaimed that a company was entitled to receive a reasonable profit based on the rates it could charge and that a reasonable rate must be determined by the fair value of the property. To ascertain that value, Harlan declared that among the matters to be considered "and given such weight as may be just and right in each case" are the following: "the original cost of construction, the amount expended in permanent improvements, the amount and market value of its bonds and stock, the present as compared with the original cost of construction, the probable earning capacity of the property under particular rates prescribed by statute, and the sum required to meet operating expenses. . . ."

Prior to World War I, the Court usually relied on original costs in determining whether a particular rate schedule yielded a fair return. The Court switched to reproduction costs after the war, when prices and costs rose, thereby challenging more rates. *Smyth*'s vague and flexible standards allowed the Court to act as it wished, without restraints. In UNITED RAILWAYS & ELECTRIC COMPANY V. WEST (1930), for example, the Court voided rates allowing a profit of 6.26 percent on the ground that anything less than 7.5 percent was "confiscatory."

Fair value governed fair return standards against the opposition of Justices LOUIS D. BRANDEIS and OLIVER WENDELL HOLMES, who attacked the doctrine as legally and economically unsound. In 1939, Justices FELIX FRANKFURTER and HUGO L. BLACK called for the rejection of the doctrine, and in 1942 the Court indicated that the determination of property value, although useful, was not indispensable. Finally, in FEDERAL POWER COMMISSION V. HOPE NATURAL GAS (1944), the Court rejected the fair value doctrine. Thereafter the Court permitted government ratemaking bodies to fix rates without judicial interference, on condition that the ratemaking process respected PROCEDURAL DUE PROCESS.

LEONARD W. LEVY

Bibliography

HALE, ROBERT L. 1952 *Freedom through Law.* New York: Columbia University Press.

FAIR TRIAL

The requirement of a fair trial in criminal proceedings has its constitutional source in the due process clause of the Fifth and FOURTEENTH AMENDMENTs, which declares that no person shall be deprived of "life, liberty, or property, without DUE PROCESS OF LAW." Other provisions of the BILL OF RIGHTS deal explicitly with particular aspects of a criminal trial. Historically, the coverage of those provisions has tended to expand, narrowing the application of the more general provision. The "incorporation" of provisions of the Fifth and SIXTH AMENDMENTs into the due process clause of the Fourteenth Amendment is especially noteworthy in this respect, having had the effect of eliminating the need for fair-trial analysis of issues in state cases covered by those provisions. While important elements of a fair trial are thus treated individually, the requirements can be summarized generally as a hearing before a competent, impartial tribunal, at which the prosecutor does not present the government's case inaccurately or unfairly and the defendant has an opportunity to present his case fully and effectively.

Ordinarily, any judge of a court having JURISDICTION is presumed to be competent to hear a criminal case. However, a judge is presumed not to be impartial if he has a substantial personal interest in a verdict against the defendant. The requirement of a fair trial prohibits a judge from sitting in that circumstance. In *Tumey v. Ohio* (1927) the Supreme Court held invalid a local practice assigning the mayor of a village as judge in criminal cases, because the compensation for his judicial services and other income for the village accrued only if the defendant were convicted and a fine imposed. In *In re Murchison* (1955) the Court overturned convictions for criminal contempt following a trial before the same judge who was the defendants' accuser and the principal witness against them.

The Sixth Amendment gives a criminal defendant the right to be tried by an "impartial jury." That provision, which applies to federal and state trials, entitles the defendant to a jury selected from a representative cross-section of the community, without inclusions or exclusions because of sex, nationality, race, or other impermissible classifications. (See JURY DISCRIMINATION.) The jury finally chosen need not have any particular composition or be representative of the community as a whole.

The defendant must have a reasonable opportunity to uncover bias or prejudice of an individual juror. This is afforded by VOIR DIRE, the examination of prospective jurors. The trial judge or the prosecutor and defense counsel question the members of the jury panel to reveal any basis for disqualification in the particular case. The trial judge has broad discretion to direct the conduct and scope of the examination, provided it is adequate to ensure the jurors' impartiality. Counsel for either side may challenge a juror "for cause" if there is a basis for disqualification and then exercise a limited number of "peremptory" challenges without explanation. In an effort to secure an impartial jury, the prosecutor may, under the DOCTRINE of SWAIN V. ALABAMA (1965), exercise peremptory challenges on the basis of group factors such as race or nationality.

However fair the formal means for ensuring an impartial tribunal, a trial conducted in an atmosphere of mob violence or insistent public pressure for conviction does not meet the constitutional standard. (See MOORE V. DEMPSEY, 1923.)

The Sixth Amendment gives a criminal defendant the RIGHT TO BE INFORMED OF THE ACCUSATION. This right, which is essential to a fair trial, requires that the statement of the offense charged identify the criminal conduct and the circumstances of the alleged crime precisely enough for the defendant to prepare his defense.

Although the constitutional guarantee of a fair trial does not ordinarily entitle the defendant to PRETRIAL DISCLOSURE of the EVIDENCE against him, all jurisdictions allow limited pretrial DISCOVERY of evidence and some allow rather full discovery subject only to special exceptions. Whenever evidence against the accused is disclosed, the defendant is entitled to enough time to prepare to meet it; if evidence is not disclosed before trial, the defendant may be entitled to a continuance. Furthermore, as the Court held in *Wardius v. Oregon* (1973), the defendant cannot be obliged to disclose evidence before trial unless the prosecution has a reciprocal obligation; fundamental fairness requires that discovery be "a two-way street."

Most of the evidentiary requirements of a fair trial are now subsumed under the CONFRONTATION and COMPULSORY PROCESS clauses of the Sixth Amendment, which, as incorporated into the Fourteenth, are applied to state criminal trials. A defendant has the rights "to be confronted with the witnesses against him" and "to have compulsory process for obtaining witnesses in his favor." As part of his right to hear and challenge the evidence against him, the defendant has a right to be present at the trial. (He may lose this right by absenting himself voluntarily or interfering with the orderly conduct of the trial.) Like other constitutional rights, the right to be present cannot be unnecessarily burdened; accordingly, since *Estelle v. Williams* (1976) a defendant cannot be required to appear at trial in prison clothing. Where jurors have obtained information from a person who did not appear as a witness, some courts have treated the event as a violation of the right to confront witnesses.

The confrontation clause also limits the use of out-of-court statements of persons who are not present in court. With few exceptions, an available witness must testify in person, so that he can be cross-examined by the defense. If a witness is not available, his out-of-court statement can be used as evidence only if there are indications of reliability sufficient to satisfy the purpose of confrontation at trial. (See HEARSAY RULES.)

The right to compulsory process assures the defendant that he will be able to present evidence favorable to his case. On occasion, the Supreme Court has held that the application of a state procedural requirement or the trial judge's conduct of the trial denied the defendant an opportunity to present critical evidence and has reversed the conviction, relying on the compulsory process clause or directly on the due process clause.

The Sixth Amendment gives a defendant the right "to have the assistance of counsel for his defense," which requires that counsel be appointed for an INDIGENT defendant in any case in which a sentence of imprisonment is imposed. Before this provision was made applicable to the states by incorporation into the Fourteenth Amendment, an indigent state defendant had a right to appointed counsel only if counsel were necessary to a fair trial. The appointment of counsel was required for defendants who were unable to defend themselves effectively because of their ignorance, or illiteracy, or youth, or because the circumstances of the case made professional skills essential; capital cases were invariably deemed to require the appointment of counsel. Since the decisions in GIDEON V. WAINWRIGHT (1963) and ARGERSINGER V. HAMLIN (1972), the RIGHT TO COUNSEL applies alike in federal and state cases. It is possible although unlikely that in a minor case in which the Sixth Amendment's provision was inapplicable, the defense would be so difficult and complex that counsel would be required for a fair trial.

The requirements of a fair trial embodied in the due process clause continue to govern the conduct of the prosecution, which is not the subject of another, particular provision of the Bill of Rights. Although the prosecution is responsible for the presentation of the case against the defendant, its concern must be, as the Court said in BERGER V. NEW YORK (1967), "not that it shall win a case, but that justice shall be done. . . . It is as much [the prosecutor's] duty to refrain from improper methods calculated to produce a wrongful conviction as it is to use every legitimate means to bring about a just one."

The prosecutor's obligation of fairness requires him to avoid conduct calculated or likely to mislead the jury. The knowing use of false evidence, including testimony of a witness, is ground for reversal of a conviction. If the prosecutor knows that a witness has testified falsely about a material fact, he must take steps to correct the falsehood. The obligation not to use false evidence extends to the government as a whole; even if the prosecutor at trial is unaware that evidence is false, a blameworthy failure of the police or others in the prosecutor's office or elsewhere in the government to avoid or remedy the falsehood is a denial of a fair trial.

The prosecutor has a parallel obligation to disclose evidence favorable to the defendant if, as the Court said in *United States v. Agurs* (1976), the "evidence is obviously of such substantial value that elementary fairness requires it." The constitutional obligation of fairness does not require the prosecution to disclose all evidence that might possibly be helpful to the defense. The test following a conviction is whether the undisclosed evidence "creates a REASONABLE DOUBT that did not otherwise exist." The duty to disclose evidence in response to a specific request by the defense is greater; if the evidence is material at all the prosecutor must either honor the request or inform the court of his refusal.

Aside from his obligation to present the evidence fully, the prosecutor must avoid arguments or conduct before the jury that might mislead it or prejudice it against the defendant. In his opening and closing arguments as well as his questioning of witnesses, the prosecutor is expected not to depart from the evidence or to lead the jury away from a dispassionate judgment based on the evidence. Isolated improper remarks of a prosecutor usually are not deemed to have denied a fair trial, especially if they do not appear to have been a deliberate violation and the trial judge has taken corrective action such as instructing the jury to disregard the remarks. In order to determine whether the standard of fair trial has been met, the prosecutor's conduct is examined in the context of the whole trial.

In a number of situations, the demands of a fair trial are opposed by conflicting demands based on the FIRST AMENDMENT's protection of FREEDOM OF THE PRESS. Pretrial publicity of a case may make it more difficult or impossible to impanel an impartial jury. A fair trial does not require that jurors have been entirely ignorant of the facts of a case but only that, having in mind the news coverage and atmosphere of the community, they be able to decide according to the evidence. The Supreme Court has occasionally reversed a conviction because members of the jury were presumed to have, or acknowledged that they had, strong preconceptions of the defendant's guilt because of extensive coverage of the case in local news media.

A similar problem has sometimes arisen during trial. In *Sheppard v. Maxwell* (1966) the Supreme Court concluded that prejudicial pretrial publicity in the news media as well as the "carnival atmosphere" created by the media in and around the courtroom during trial had denied the defendant a fair trial. In ESTES V. TEXAS (1965) the Court concluded that television coverage of portions of a sensational trial that had also been the subject of massive pretrial publicity was impermissible. There is, however, no absolute constitutional prohibition against radio, television, or photographic coverage of a trial, which may, as the Court held in CHANDLER V. FLORIDA (1981), be allowed if it is conducted in a manner consistent with a fair trial.

The Supreme Court held, in RICHMOND NEWSPAPERS, INC. V. VIRGINIA (1980), that the First Amendment protects the right of the public to attend criminal trials. (In contrast, the right to a PUBLIC TRIAL in the Sixth Amendment is a right of the defendant alone.) Therefore, all other measures for ensuring a fair trial, such as sequestration of witnesses or jurors, must be considered before the public can be excluded, whether or not the defendant asks for exclusion. The Court has indicated strongly that a trial court should exercise its authority in whatever manner will afford a fair trial without closing it to the public.

Unlike some of the more particular provisions of the Bill of Rights that have to do with criminal process, the requirement of a fair trial retains the flexibility of a general standard and is not susceptible to precise definition by a set of rules. While important aspects of a fair trial are covered by other constitutional provisions, some remain within the ambit of the general standard. Jurisprudentially, the principal difference is that, unlike some particular constitutional rules, the general standard does not invalidate a conviction for a single instance of prejudicial error or unfairness. Rather it is set in the context of the whole trial, and a conviction will be reversed only if the trial as a whole was unfair. The standard of a fair trial also serves as a reminder of the government's relationship with an individual even when it seeks to convict him of a crime and as the repository of changing or enlarged conceptions of what fairness in the criminal process requires.

LLOYD L. WEINREB

Bibliography

AMERICAN BAR ASSOCIATION 1968 *Standards Relating to Fair Trial and Free Press.* New York: Institute of Judicial Administration.

FELLMAN, DAVID 1976 *The Defendant's Rights Today.* Madison: University of Wisconsin Press.

KAMISAR, YALE; LAFAVE, WAYNE R.; and ISRAEL, JEROLD H. (1965)1986 *Modern Criminal Procedure.* St. Paul, Minn.: West Publishing Co.

LEVY, LEONARD W. 1974 *Against the Law.* New York: Harper & Row.

WEINREB, LLOYD L. (1969)1987 *Criminal Process.* Mineola, N.Y.: Foundation Press.

FAMILY AND THE CONSTITUTION

Family relations have an uncertain, even ambivalent constitutional status in Supreme Court decisions. If the Constitution protects the family against external interference, it also permits the establishment of public moral standards to regulate social relations among adults and to protect children from apparently harmful parental conduct.

This ambivalence appeared early. In MEYER V. NEBRASKA (1923) the Supreme Court opined that FOURTEENTH AMENDMENT "liberty" included the right "to marry, establish a home and bring up children." The Court did not explain, however, why this right stopped short at monogamy. In REYNOLDS V. UNITED STATES (1878) it had upheld Congress's power to forbid POLYGAMY in the TERRITORIES notwithstanding the religiously grounded objections of Mormon settlers. Nor did the Court subsequently explain how the right "to bring up children" was consistent with the compulsory STERILIZATION of a woman considered retarded by state authorities upheld in BUCK V. BELL (1927). One discernible principle did unify these early cases: the Constitution protects only family relations that judges consider "normal" and "wholesome." This principle might occasionally lead judges to substitute their views of normality for legislative impositions (as in *Meyer* where the state had forbidden schoolroom teaching of children in any language but English); it hardly serves, however, as a MAGNA CARTA for the protection from state interference of family sanctity and autonomy.

The prospect that constitutional doctrine might be elevated to serve this broader protective purpose emerged in the 1960s, as cases involving family relations began to appear in unprecedented numbers on the Supreme Court's docket. But in fact the decided cases exemplify the same conflicting strains as before. The first of the modern cases was GRISWOLD V. CONNECTICUT (1965), striking down a state law that prohibited anyone including married couples from using contraceptives. The Court spoke of marriage as "intimate to the degree of being sacred" and found a constitutionally protected "RIGHT OF PRIVACY surrounding the marriage relationship." In subsequent cases, however, the Court has been reluctant to extend this familial privacy right beyond the conventionally conceived marriage bond. Although EISENSTADT V. BAIRD (1972) recognized the right of unmarried persons to practice contraception, in *Doe v. Commonwealth's Attorney* (1976) the Court summarily affirmed a lower court's rejection of a constitutional attack on a state law criminally proscribing homosexual relations even among consenting adults in private. Similarly in *Belle Terre v. Boraas* (1974) the Court upheld a municipal ZONING restriction excluding communal families unless they were "related by blood, adoption or marriage"; and yet in MOORE V. CITY OF EAST CLEVELAND (1977) the Court struck down zoning restrictions that limited residence to nuclear families and excluded multigenerational families with blood ties. The theme that runs through these two zoning cases and through *Griswold* and *Doe* is that the Constitution protects "families" when they reflect conventional social definitions of decency and morality.

The Court does not unquestioningly defer to legislative conceptions of appropriately conventional family relations. The Court has struck down familial regulations reflecting RACIAL DISCRIMINATION as in LOVING V. VIRGINIA (1967), or SEX DISCRIMINATION regarding alimony entitlements as in *Orr v. Orr* (1979), or required consent for adoptive placement as in *Caban v. Mahammed* (1979). But even in these cases the Justices appear guided more by their own conceptions of appropriate social conventions for family relations than by any principle of protection of individuals against state interference with their autonomous choices in family matters.

The constitutional status of parent–child relations is the result of similar conflicting impulses. In the adult relations cases, the underlying conflict is essentially between principles of individual autonomy and of community, between the individual's FREEDOM OF INTIMATE ASSOCIATION and the right of a group to define and enforce common standards of conduct on every group member. For state regulation of parent–child relations, these same conflicting principles are at stake, but the conflict extends even into these principles' very definition.

Thus the state can plausibly claim that it must restrict parental conduct to protect and enhance the child's developing capacity for individual autonomy. The claim is implicit in compulsory education laws, in laws permitting state intervention to override parental directives in disputes between parent and child (particularly adolescent children), and in laws proscribing child abuse or neglect. Parents, however, can plausibly claim that a child's capacity to develop as an autonomous individual is impaired by state impositions on parental conduct beyond the most minimal standards to protect the child's physical integrity. Thus even if constitutional DOCTRINE should give priority to individual autonomy over communitarian claims in adult relations, this priority does not resolve disputes regarding state regulation of parental conduct when both the state and the parents can plausibly claim to speak for the child's developing capacity for individual autonomy.

These disputes have occurred in three different contexts: claims by state authorities that parents' conduct was harmful to children; claims by parents that their children were harmed by state conduct, particularly in public schools; and claims by children, particularly older children, that state authorities should take their sides in disputes with their parents. In none of these contexts do the decided cases yield consistent constitutional principles.

The unresolved tension between competing principles was particularly evident in two Supreme Court decisions in successive terms that considered the application of constitutional norms to state abuse and neglect statutes. In SANTOSKY V. KRAMER (1982) the Court held that states must meet a higher burden of proof than the ordinary civil standard before the parent–child relationship could be terminated on grounds of harmful parental conduct; but in *Lassiter v. Department of Social Services* (1981) the Court had held that the parental relationship was not of sufficient constitutional weight to require the appointment of counsel to give indigent parents effective assistance against state actions for termination.

A similar if less blatant inconsistency is evident in the Court's rulings regarding the rights of parents to constrain state impositions on their children in public schools. Thus in INGRAHAM V. WRIGHT (1977) the Court ruled that school officials were free to inflict corporal punishment on students notwithstanding parental objections that the punishment was physically and psychologically harmful to their children; but in WISCONSIN V. YODER (1972) the Court had ruled that school officials could not require Amish children to attend secondary schools in the face of their parents' objections that this imposition was harmful to the children and inconsistent with the parents' views on proper child-rearing practices.

In the Amish case, the Court emphasized the religious basis for the parents' claims, a factor that might serve to distinguish the parents' claim in the corporal punishment case. But parental claims to preclude state interference in their decisions regarding children were not similarly honored, notwithstanding the religious grounding of such claims, in PLANNED PARENTHOOD V. DANFORTH (1976) where the parents objected to their unmarried pregnant daughters' wish to obtain an abortion. The minors' abortion and the Amish case might be distinguished on the ground that the pregnant minors openly disagreed with their parents while the Amish students apparently concurred with theirs. But this view of the abortion case—that the Constitution not only permits but requires state intervention to protect the autonomous wishes of older children from being overridden by their parents—cannot readily be squared with the Court's subsequent ruling in PARHAM V. J. R. (1979) essentially upholding parents' authority to confine their adolescent children in psychiatric institutions, notwithstanding the children's objections and claims for independent judicial protection.

These decisions raise at least the suspicion that the same guiding principle is at work in these parent–child–state cases as appeared in the cases regarding state regulation of adult familial relations—the principle that the Justices are not prepared to find constitutional protection for family status as such but only for those families whose conduct meets the Justices' particular approval. This principle could explain the Court's deference to Amish parents who generally succeed in imposing rigid behavioral controls on their children, as the Court repeatedly stressed in *Yoder*, or its deference to parents' wishes to confine their socially disruptive children in psychiatric institutions. A judicial preference for such behavior controls might also explain the Court's refusal to defer to parents' objections to school corporal punishment or to parents' resistance to abortions when they had failed effectively to constrain their unmarried daughters' indulgence in sexual relations.

The Court has not been unanimous in these cases, and no Justice has explicitly defended this particular child-rearing principle as a constitutional norm. Yet the logical plausibility of this harmonizing principle does suggest that current constitutional doctrine gives no special status to family relations as such, either between parents and child or among adults. The occasional rhetorical flourishes in Supreme Court opinions about the "constitutional sanctity" of the family does not yet reflect any consistent constitutional principle.

ROBERT A. BURT

Bibliography

BURT, ROBERT A. 1979 The Constitution of the Family. *The Supreme Court Review* 1979:329–395.

GOLDSTEIN, J.; FREUD, A.; and SOLNIT, A. 1973 *Beyond the Best Interests of the Child.* New York: Free Press.

______ 1979 *Before the Best Interests of the Child.* New York: Free Press.

KARST, KENNETH L. 1980 The Freedom of Intimate Association. *Yale Law Journal* 89:624–692.

FARETTA v. CALIFORNIA
422 U.S. 806 (1975)

In *Faretta* the Supreme Court reversed the conviction of a defendant forced to accept the services of a public defender in a FELONY case, holding that the Sixth Amendment guarantees the right to self-representation when a defendant "knowingly and intelligently" requests it.

This is a major decision about the WAIVER OF CONSTITUTIONAL RIGHTS because the argument of the state and the dissent was that society has an interest in a FAIR TRIAL, independent of the defendant's desires. Recognition of such an interest would necessarily mean that the trial judge must have discretion to reject even a knowing and intelligent waiver of the RIGHT TO COUNSEL.

Standby counsel may be appointed over the defendant's objection to aid him should he request help at the trial, or to intervene if the termination of self-representation becomes necessary.

BARBARA ALLEN BABCOCK

FARRAND, MAX
(1869–1945)

Anyone who cares seriously to study the work of the CONSTITUTIONAL CONVENTION OF 1787 owes a debt to Max Farrand. Farrand, professor of history at Stanford (1901–1908) and Yale (1908–1925) Universities and later director of research at the Huntington Library, compiled and edited all the known *Records of the Federal Convention* (1911, revised 1937). That work was more influential than his narrative history books, which were intended for undergraduate or popular audiences.

DENNIS J. MAHONEY

FAY v. NOIA
372 U.S. 391 (1963)

The Great Writ of HABEAS CORPUS allows state prisoners to seek federal court review of constitutional errors made at their trials, but the JUDICIAL CODE requires EXHAUSTION OF REMEDIES in state court, in order to preserve comity between state and federal courts. Charles Noia's 1942 murder conviction was based solely on a coerced confession procured in violation of his FOURTEENTH AMENDMENT rights to DUE PROCESS. He chose not to file a state APPEAL, however, because he feared that a new trial might end in a death sentence. Years later, he sought review of his due process claim in state courts, but they held that his original failure to appeal was a procedural default that barred further review. In *Fay*, a 6–3 Supreme Court held that his failure was not a "deliberate bypass" of state procedures and thus no bar to habeas corpus relief.

Justice WILLIAM J. BRENNAN, speaking for the majority, posited a "manifest federal policy" that liberty rights should not be denied without the fullest opportunity for federal JUDICIAL REVIEW. The concept of comity could not justify denying habeas corpus relief for failure to exhaust a remedy no longer available.

As for the state's interests in insuring finality of criminal judgments, or exacting compliance with its procedures through default rules, these could not outweigh the "ideal of fair procedure" and the historic habeas corpus policy favoring the free exercise of federal judicial power to enforce this ideal. Finally, the state's rejection of Noia's claim could not be treated as an ADEQUATE STATE GROUND, for this jurisdictional deference would unduly burden the vindication of federal rights. Only when a defendant deliberately evaded state adjudication would FEDERALISM concerns justify the denial of habeas corpus review.

As dissenting Justice JOHN MARSHALL HARLAN noted, *Fay* marked a dramatic expansion of federal power to supervise state criminal justice. The concepts of exhaustion and adequate state grounds were modified to make room for a generous view that excused defendants from uncalculated WAIVER OF CONSTITUTIONAL RIGHTS in state proceedings. The "deliberately bypassing" defendant was a rare one, and *Fay*'s scope freed most defendants from forfeiting their rights through procedural defaults of every kind. Simultaneously, the WARREN COURT's application of the Fourth, Fifth, and Sixth Amendments to the states codified a BILL OF RIGHTS for criminal defendants. *Fay* insured a broad federal path of enforcement for these new guarantees, in an era when the state path of review was not always open or receptive to constitutional claims.

The BURGER COURT era brought a less hospitable federal climate for criminal defendants and, not surprisingly, also brought a corresponding change in the habeas corpus barometer, emerging clearly in WAINRIGHT v. SYKES (1977). *Fay*'s deliberate bypass rule did not endure as an exclusive measure of federalism interests, because a new "manifest" federal policy came to elevate the state's interest in finality above the ideal of fair procedure. With this new federalism, the whole point of habeas corpus review was transformed from the protection of constitutional rights to the protection of those with a claim to innocence.

CATHERINE HANCOCK

Bibliography

COVER, ROBERT M. and ALEINIKOFF, T. ALEXANDER 1977 Dialectical Federalism: Habeas Corpus and the Court. *Yale Law Journal* 86:1035–1102.

FEDERAL . . . ACT

See also under word following "Federal"

FEDERAL COMMON LAW, CIVIL

In the English legal tradition to which this country is heir, judge-made COMMON LAW—law developed by courts in the absence of applicable LEGISLATION—has played a critical role in the determination of rights, duties, and remedies. But because our federal government is one of limited, delegated powers, the questions whether and under what circumstances the federal courts are empowered to formulate federal common law have been the subject of much debate. Although it is now settled that the federal courts do have such authority in civil matters, the debate continues over the sources of that authority and the proper scope of its exercise.

The Supreme Court's decision in ERIE RAILROAD CO. v. TOMPKINS (1938) marks a watershed in the evolution of this problem. Prior to that decision, the federal courts did not strive to develop a federal, or national, common law binding on the states and indeed on occasion denied that it existed (*Wheaton v. Peters,* 1834; *Smith v. Alabama,* 1888). Yet the Supreme Court, in SWIFT v. TYSON (1842), upheld the authority of the federal courts, in cases within the DIVERSITY JURISDICTION, to determine certain controversies on the basis of "general principles and doctrines" of jurisprudence and without regard to the common law decisions of the state courts. Thus, during the reign of *Swift v. Tyson,* the federal courts exercised considerable common law authority over a variety of disputes, ultimately extending well beyond the interstate commercial controversy involved in *Swift* itself and involving matters apparently not subject to federal legislative power. The decisions rendered in these cases, however, did not purport to bind the state courts, and the result was often the parallel existence of two different rules of law applicable to the same controversy, with the governing rule dependent on the forum in which the controversy was adjudicated.

Historians disagree on the justification—statutory and constitutional—of the *Swift* decision. In one view, the decision was not rooted in contemporary understanding of the nature of the common law but instead represented the use of judicial power to aid in the redistribution of wealth to promote commercial and industrial growth. A contrasting position is that the decision was fully consistent with the perception of the time that the common law of commercial transactions was not the command of the sovereign but rather was both the embodiment of prevailing customs and a process of applying them to the case at hand.

There is general agreement, however, that the

Court expanded *Swift* well beyond its originally intended scope and that its OVERRULING, in *Erie*, reflected a very different perception of the proper role of the federal courts. The Court in *Erie*, speaking through Justice LOUIS D. BRANDEIS, concluded that there was no "general" federal common law—that the Rules of Decision Act, originally section 34 of the JUDICIARY ACT OF 1789, required adherence to state decisional or common law in controversies such as *Erie* itself, a case that fell within federal JURISDICTION solely on the basis of the parties' diversity of citizenship.

But the *Erie* decision helped bring to the surface the existence of what has been called a "specialized" federal common law, operating in those areas where the application of federal law seems warranted even though no federal constitutional or legislative provision points the way to a governing rule. Indeed, on the very day that *Erie* was decided, the Court in *Hinderlider v. La Plata River & Cherry Creek Ditch Co.* (1938), again speaking through Justice Brandeis, said that "whether the water of an interstate stream must be apportioned between the two States is a question of 'federal common law' upon which neither the statutes nor the decisions of either State can be conclusive."

What is the source of the authority to formulate federal common law—law that, unlike decisions rendered pursuant to *Swift*, binds state and federal courts alike? To some extent, the source may be traced to specific constitutional provisions, such as the grant of ADMIRALTY AND MARITIME JURISDICTION in Article III, or the prohibition of unreasonable SEARCHES AND SEIZURES in the FOURTH AMENDMENT. (See BIVENS V. SIX UNKNOWN NAMED AGENTS (1971), declaring the existence of a damage remedy for a Fourth Amendment violation.) But the line between CONSTITUTIONAL INTERPRETATION, on the one hand, and the exercise of common law authority, on the other, is indistinct, and there is often disagreement among both judges and commentators about the function the courts are performing. The significance of this disagreement is more than semantic, for the ability of the legislative branch to modify or reject a Supreme Court ruling is plainly more circumscribed if the ruling is seen to be required by the Constitution than if the ruling is a common law one authorized but not compelled by the FUNDAMENTAL LAW.

In other instances, the source of judicial authority may be found in a particular federal statute. Infrequently, the congressional command is explicit, as in the mandate in Rule 501 of the Federal Rules of Evidence that in certain cases questions of evidentiary privilege "shall be governed by the principles of the common law as they may be interpreted by the courts of the United States in the light of reason and experience." More often, the legislative direction is, at best, implicit and the judicial role may be viewed as that of implementing federal legislative policy by filling the gaps left by the legislation itself. Once again, the line between statutory construction and the exercise of common law authority is not easily drawn.

In a significant number of cases, the exercise of authority to formulate federal common law is difficult to trace to a specific provision in the Constitution or in a statute. In such cases, the authority may be attributed more broadly to the nature of the judicial process, to the structure of our federal constitutional system, and to the relationships created by it. The authority, in other words, may be rooted in necessity. As Justice ROBERT H. JACKSON put it, concurring in *D'Oench Duhme & Co. v. F.D.I.C.* (1942): "Were we bereft of the common law, our federal system would be impotent. This follows from the recognized futility of attempting all-complete statutory codes and is apparent from the terms of the Constitution itself."

Some examples of the exercise of this authority may help to clarify its scope. Perhaps most important is the category of those interstate or international disputes that, in the words of the Supreme Court, "implicate conflicting rights of States or our foreign relations" (*Texas Industries, Inc. v. Radcliff Materials, Inc.*, 1981). Such disputes do not always fall within the specific jurisdictional grants of Article III applicable to certain interstate or international controversies. In any event, the existence of a conflict between the interests of two states may make it inappropriate for the law of either to govern of its own force. And controversies affecting our relations as sovereign with foreign nations may require a single federal response rather than a cacophony of responses rooted in varying state laws. (See ACT OF STATE DOCTRINE.)

Another leading instance of the exercise of common law authority embraces controversies involving the rights, obligations, or proprietary interests of the United States. In such controversies, especially those arising in the administration of nationwide programs, formulation of federal common law may be warranted by the need for uniform treatment of the activities of the federal government or, more modestly, for some degree of federal supervision of the application of state law to those activities.

The amorphous origins and uncertain scope of the federal common law power underscore the need to recognize certain limitations that are anchored in the concerns of FEDERALISM and of SEPARATION OF POW-

ERS. The first of these concerns focuses on the interests of the states in preserving a measure of autonomy on matters properly within their sphere—interests reflected in the TENTH AMENDMENT. Because federal law is often interstitial in character—written against a background of state laws governing basic human affairs—the concern for federalism supports a presumption that state law ought not to be displaced in the absence of a clear legislative direction, a sharp conflict between the state law and federal program, or the existence of a uniquely federal interest requiring protection. To some extent, this presumption is supported by and reflected in the provision of the Rules of Decision Act that state laws shall constitute the rules of decision except where otherwise required by the Constitution or by federal treaty or statute. But the last phrase of that act—limiting its command to "cases where they (the rules of decision) apply"—gives the provision a circularity that affords little guidance to the resolution of particular problems of potential conflict between federal and state authority.

Even when the exercise of federal authority is warranted, a careful balancing of state and federal interests may lead to the adoption of state laws rather than to the imposition of a uniform federal rule, so long as the state laws in question are compatible with federal interests. Such results were reached, for example, in *De Sylva v. Ballentine* (1955), involving a definition of "children" under the Federal Copyright Act, and *United States v. Kimbell Foods, Inc.* (1979), dealing with the priority of federal government liens arising from federal lending programs.

The second concern—that of separation of powers—springs from the belief that the primary responsibility for lawmaking should rest with the democratically elected representatives in the legislative branch. At a time when the common law function was seen in terms primarily of the application of established customs and usages, the concern for the proper separation and allocation of federal powers had less force than it does today, when there is more emphasis on the creative potential of the common law. Moreover, the separation of powers question is not unrelated to the regard for state interests, since the bicameral federal legislature is structured in such a way as to protect the states against action that might be taken by a legislature apportioned solely on the basis of population.

Concern that the courts not usurp a function that is properly legislative has led to an emphasis on LEGISLATIVE INTENT in many instances in which the federal courts have been asked to articulate new rights or develop new remedies not specifically provided for by statute. Moreover, the Supreme Court has stressed the ability of Congress to displace federal common law with statutory regulations, even in some instances in which the source of authority is the Constitution itself.

The problems inherent in the exercise of common law power have been highlighted in the Supreme Court's struggle with the question of implied remedies for federal constitutional or statutory violations. Since BIVENS V. SIX UNKNOWN NAMED AGENTS (1971), the Court has generally been willing to allow a person harmed by unconstitutional action to sue for damages, despite the lack of any constitutional or statutory provision for suit. But persons harmed by violations of federal statutes have frequently been held unable to obtain relief in the absence of an express statutory remedy or strong evidence of legislative intent to permit such a remedy.

In both types of cases the Supreme Court has perhaps too readily yielded its authority to exercise a principled discretion in determining whether traditional common law remedies should be available to implement federal policy. The tendency toward formalistic insistence on a remedy for every wrong in cases involving constitutional violations, and toward ritualistic invocation of legislative intent in order to deny a remedy in cases of statutory infractions, suggests a relinquishment of the judicial responsibility that lies at the heart of our common law heritage.

DAVID L. SHAPIRO

Bibliography

BATOR, PAUL; MISHKIN, PAUL J.; SHAPIRO, DAVID L.; and WECHSLER, HERBERT (1953) 1973 and 1981 Supp. *Hart and Wechsler's The Federal Courts and the Federal System.* Pages 691–832. Mineola, N.Y.: Foundation Press.

BRIDWELL, RANDALL and WHITTEN, RALPH U. 1977 *The Constitution and the Common Law.* Lexington, Mass.: Lexington Books.

FIELD, MARTHA A. 1986 Sources of Law: The Scope of Federal Common Law. *Harvard Law Review* 99:883–984.

FRIENDLY, HENRY J. 1964 In Praise of Erie—And of the New Federal Common Law. *New York University Law Review* 39:383–422.

FREYER, TONY ALLAN 1979 *Forums of Order: The Federal Courts and Business in American History.* Greenwich, Conn.: JAI Press, Inc.

HILL, ALFRED 1967 The Law-Making Power of the Federal Courts: Constitutional Preemption. *Columbia Law Review* 67:1024–1081.

HORWITZ, MORTON J. 1977 *The Transformation of American Law, 1780–1860.* Pages 211–252. Cambridge, Mass.: Harvard University Press.

REDISH, MARTIN H. 1980 *Federal Jurisdiction: Tensions*

in the Allocation of Judicial Power. Pages 79–107. Indianapolis: Bobbs-Merrill.

FEDERAL COMMON LAW OF CRIMES

One of the leading Jeffersonian jurists, ST. GEORGE TUCKER, noted with alarm that Chief Justice OLIVER ELLSWORTH and Justice BUSHROD WASHINGTON had laid down the general rule that the COMMON LAW was the unwritten law of the United States government. The question whether the Constitution adopted the common law, Tucker wrote,

> is of very great importance, not only as it regards the limits of the JURISDICTION of the *federal courts;* but also, as it relates to the extent of the powers vested in the *federal government.* For, if it be true that the common law of England has been adopted by the United States in their national, or federal capacity, the jurisdiction of the *federal courts* must be co-extensive with it; or, in other words, *unlimited:* so also, must be the jurisdiction, and authority of the *other branches* of the federal government [Tucker, *Blackstone's Commentaries,* 1803, I, 380].

Tucker's answer to the question was that the JUDICIAL POWER OF THE UNITED STATES under Article III was limited to the subjects of congressional legislative power and that common law did not give jurisdiction in any case where jurisdiction was not expressly given by the Constitution. Tucker's view eventually prevailed, but it was probably not the view of the Constitution's Framers.

Article III extends the judicial power of the United States to all cases in law and EQUITY arising under the Constitution, treaties, and "Laws of the United States." The latter phrase could include common law crimes. At the CONSTITUTIONAL CONVENTION OF 1787, the Committee of Detail reported a draft declaring that the Supreme Court's jurisdiction extended to "all Cases arising under the Laws passed by the Legislature of the United States." The Convention without dissenting vote adopted a motion striking out the words "passed by the Legislature." That deletion suggests that "the Laws of the United States" comprehended the common law of crimes, as well as other nonstatutory law.

The legislative history of the JUDICIARY ACT OF 1789 suggests a similar conclusion. A draft of that statute relating to the jurisdiction of both the federal district and federal circuit courts (sections nine and eleven as enacted) gave these courts "cognizance of all crimes and offenses that shall be cognizable under the authority of the United States and *defined by the laws of the same.*" The italicized phrase, deleted from the act's final text, might have restricted criminal jurisdiction to statutory crimes. Whether a federal court was to apply a federal common law of crimes or apply the common law of the state in which a crime was committed is not clear.

What is clear is that the first generation of federal judges assumed jurisdiction in cases of nonstatutory crimes. Justice JAMES WILSON, an influential Framer of the Constitution, at his state's ratifying convention had endorsed federal prosecutions at common law for criminal libels against the United States. In 1793 he instructed a federal GRAND JURY on the virtues of the common law, which included, he said, the law of nations. The grand jury indicted Gideon Henfield for breaching American neutrality by assisting a French privateer in the capture of a British ship; the INDICTMENT referred to "violation of the laws of nations, against the laws and constitution of the United States and against the peace and dignity of the United States." ALEXANDER HAMILTON prepared the indictment, which Attorney General EDMUND RANDOLPH (another Framer) helped prosecute. Justice Wilson, joined by Justice JAMES IREDELL and Judge RICHARD PETERS, constituted the federal CIRCUIT COURT that tried Henfield's nonstatutory offense. Henfield, having been at sea when President GEORGE WASHINGTON proclaimed American neutrality, pleaded ignorance. Secretary of State THOMAS JEFFERSON, who had urged Henfield's prosecution and endorsed Wilson's opinion as to the indictability of the offense, explained that the jury acquitted because the crime was not knowingly committed. JOHN MARSHALL, in his *Life of Washington,* described the prosecution as having been based on an offense "indictable at common law, for disturbing the peace of the United States."

Subsequent common law prosecutions were not so fuzzy. In 1793 a federal grand jury indicted Joseph Ravara, a consul from Genoa, for attempting to extort money from a British diplomat. Justice Wilson, joined by Peters, ruled that the circuit court had jurisdiction, although Congress had passed no law against extortion. Justice Iredell argued that the defendant's diplomatic status brought him within the exclusive ORIGINAL JURISDICTION of the Supreme Court. Ravara was tried in 1794 by a circuit court consisting of Jay and Peters, who instructed the jury that the offense was indictable at common law, part of the LAW OF THE LAND. The jury convicted. In 1795 a federal court in New York, at the instigation of Attorney General Randolph, indicted Greenleaf, the editor of the *New-York Journal,* for criminal libel, a common law crime. The case was dropped, but in 1797 the editor was again indicted for the same crime and convicted by a court presided over by Chief Justice Oliver Ellsworth, an influential Framer and chief author of the Judiciary Act of 1789. In Massachusetts in 1797 Ellsworth ruled that the federal circuit court possessed jurisdiction over crimes against the common law, which the laws of the United States included, and therefore might try persons indicted for counterfeiting notes of the Bank of the United States (not then a statutory offense).

In the same year a federal grand jury followed Justice Iredell's charge and indicted a congressman, Samuel J. Cabell, for the common law crime of SEDITIOUS LIBEL, but the prosecution was aborted for political reasons. In 1798, before Congress passed the Sedition Act, prosecutions for seditious libel were begun against Benjamin Bache, who soon died, and John Burke, who fled the country before Justice WILLIAM PATERSON could try him. In 1799 Ellsworth and Iredell, in separate cases, told federal grand juries that the federal courts had common law jurisdiction over seditious libel and, in Ellsworth's words, over "acts manifestly subversive of the national government." He added that an indictable offense need be defined only by common law, not statute.

The sole dissenting voice in this line of decision was that of Justice SAMUEL CHASE in *Worrall's Case* (1798), where the common law indictment was for attempted bribery of a federal official. Judge Peters disagreed with Chase's argument that no federal common law of crimes existed, and the jury convicted. Chase, however, changed his opinion in *United States v. Sylvester* (1799), when he presided over a common law prosecution for counterfeiting. Thus, Chief Justices Jay and Ellsworth and Justices Wilson, Paterson, Iredell, and Chase endorsed federal court jurisdiction over common law crimes. The Jeffersonians, by then, vehemently opposed such views, arguing that only the state courts could try common law crimes. When Jefferson was President, however, Judge Pierpont Edwards, whom he had appointed to the federal district court in Connecticut, sought and received common law indictments against several persons for seditious libel against the President and the government. Jefferson knew of the common law prosecutions by the federal court and did not criticize them or take any actions to halt them, until he learned that one of the defendants could prove the truth of his accusation that the President had once engaged in a sexual indiscretion. The prosecutions were dropped except for those against Hudson and Goodwin, editors of Hartford's *Connecticut Courant*, who challenged the jurisdiction of the federal court.

By this time the administration had a stake in a ruling against federal jurisdiction over common law crimes. After much government stalling until a majority of Jeffersonian appointees controlled the Supreme Court, UNITED STATES V. HUDSON AND GOODWIN was finally decided in 1812. Without hearing ORAL ARGUMENTS and against all the precedents, a bare majority of the Court, in a brief opinion by Justice WILLIAM JOHNSON, ruled that the question whether the federal courts "can exercise a common law jurisdiction in criminal cases" has been "settled in public opinion," which opposed such jurisdiction. Moreover, the Constitution had not expressly delegated to the federal courts authority over common law crimes. "The legislative authority of the Union must first make an act a crime, affix a punishment to it, and declare the Court that shall have jurisdiction of the offense."

Justice JOSEPH STORY, who had not made known his dissent at the time, did so in a circuit opinion in 1813 and forced a reconsideration of the rule of *Hudson and Goodwin.* In UNITED STATES V. COOLIDGE (1816), decided without argument, Johnson, noting that the Court was still divided (Marshall and Washington probably supported Story), refused to review the 1812 decision in the absence of "solemn argument." Thus the great question was resolved without reasoned consideration, to the enormous detriment of the power of the United States courts to define criminal acts.

Although "judge-made" or nonstatutory federal crimes disappeared after the *Coolidge* decision, federal courts continued to exercise common law powers to enforce law and order within their own precincts (see CONTEMPT POWER) and continued to employ a variety of common law techniques, forms, and writs in the enforcement of congressionally defined crimes. The FEDERAL RULES OF CRIMINAL PROCEDURE reflect that fact, as does *Marshall v. United States* (1959). By its "supervisory powers" over lower federal courts and, through them, over federal law enforcement officers, the Supreme Court can still be said, loosely, to exercise an interstitial common law authority with respect to federal crimes.

LEONARD W. LEVY

Bibliography

CROSSKEY, WILLIAM W. 1953 *Politics and the Constitution in the History of the United States,* 2 vols. Chaps. 20–24. Chicago: University of Chicago Press.

GOEBEL, JULIUS, JR. 1971—*Antecedents and Beginnings to 1801.* Volume 1 of Freund, Paul, ed., *The Oliver Wendell Holmes Devise History of the Supreme Court.* New York: Macmillan.

PRESSER, STEPHEN B. 1978 "A Tale of Two Judges: Richard Peters, Samuel Chase, and the Broken Promise of Federalist Jurisprudence." *Northwestern Law Review* 73:26–111.

TUCKER, ST. GEORGE 1803 *Blackstone's Commentaries, with Notes of Reference to the Constitution and Laws of the Federal Government of the United States and of the Commonwealth of Virginia,* 5 vols. Philadelphia: Young & Small.

WARREN, CHARLES 1923 "New Light on the History of the Federal Judiciary Act of 1789." *Harvard Law Review* 37:49–132.

WHARTON, FRANCIS, ed. 1849(1970) *State Trials of the United States During the Administrations of Washington and Adams.* New York: Burt Franklin.

FEDERAL COMMUNICATIONS COMMISSION

See: Broadcasting; Communications Act; Regulatory Commissions

FEDERAL COMMUNICATIONS COMMISSION v. LEAGUE OF WOMEN VOTERS

See: Government Speech

FEDERAL COMMUNICATIONS COMMISSION v. PACIFICA FOUNDATION

438 U.S. 726 (1978)

In *FCC v. Pacifica Foundation* the Court held that limited civil sanctions could constitutionally be invoked against a radio broadcast containing many vulgar words. The Court stressed that its holding was limited to the particular context, that is, to civil sanctions applied to indecent speech in an afternoon radio broadcast when, the Court assumed, children were in the audience. The opinion did not address criminal sanctions for televised or closed circuit broadcasts or late evening presentations, nor did it illuminate the concept of indecent speech except to suggest that occasional expletives and Elizabethan comedies may be decent enough even in the early afternoon.

STEVEN SHIFFRIN

FEDERAL COURTS IMPROVEMENT ACT

96 Stat. 25 (1982)

This act reorganized several specialized federal courts. It merged the former COURT OF CLAIMS and COURT OF CUSTOMS AND PATENT APPEALS into a new UNITED STATES COURT OF APPEALS FOR THE FEDERAL CIRCUIT, transferring to the new court the former courts' JURISDICTION, and staffing it with the judges of the superseded courts. The Federal Circuit is a CONSTITUTIONAL COURT, staffed by twelve judges with life terms.

The act also created a new CLAIMS COURT to handle the trial functions formerly performed by commissioners (later called trial judges) of the old Court of Claims. The Claims Court is a LEGISLATIVE COURT; its sixteen judges serve for fifteen-year terms. Appeals go to the Federal Circuit.

KENNETH L. KARST

Bibliography

SYMPOSIUM 1983/1984 The Federal Courts Improvement Act. *Cleveland State Law Review* 32:1–116.

FEDERAL ELECTION CAMPAIGN ACTS

Presidential Election Campaign Fund Act
85 Stat. 497 (1971)

Federal Election Campaign Act
86 Stat. 3 (1971)

Federal Election Campaign Act
88 Stat. 1263 (1974)

The success of constitutional democracy depends upon the integrity and autonomy of the electoral process. But whether that integrity is threatened more seriously by wealthy individuals and organizations than by regulations that prevent individuals and organizations from using their resources to promote candidates and policies is a matter for debate. During the 1970s several attempts at campaign finance "reform" were enacted, resulting in an almost complete switch from private to public financing at least of the presidential general election campaigns.

Two reform statutes were enacted in 1971: the Federal Election Campaign Act (FECA) and the Presidential Election Campaign Fund Act. The former required any committee receiving or spending more than $1,000 in a campaign for federal office to register with the federal government and publish reports of contributions and expenditures. It also prohibited contributions under names other than that of the actual donor and limited total expenditures on campaign advertising. The second statute created a fund of public money to replace private contributions in financing presidential election campaigns. By means of a "check-off" device, taxpayers would nominally designate one dollar of their annual federal income tax payment for the election campaign fund. Acceptance of these public funds precluded a party or campaign committee from accepting any private contributions.

The FECA of 1974 was an extremely comprehensive effort to regulate the "time, place, and manner" of electing federal officials. Among the provisions of the 1974 act were: maximum spending limits for presidential nominating and general election campaigns; federal matching funds for qualifying candidates in major party nominating campaigns; complete federal funding of major party candidates in the general election campaign; limits on contributions of individuals, organizations, and political action committees to campaigns for Congress and for the presidential nominations; limits on campaign spending per state in presidential nomination campaigns; and rigorous accounting and reporting requirements for campaign finance committees. In addition, the 1974 act created a six-member Federal Elections Commission to enforce the other provisions of the act; the commission was to comprise members appointed by the President, the speaker of the House of Representatives, and the president pro tempore of the Senate.

The Supreme Court heard major constitutional challenges to the 1974 act even as the first campaign was being conducted under it. In BUCKLEY V. VALEO (1976) the Court held unconstitutional the method of appointment of the commission (because the Constitution grants to the President alone the power to appoint federal officers) and all the spending limitations imposed other than as a condition for receiving federal matching funds. The rationale for the latter holding was that the commitment of funds in support of a candidate or cause was a form of expression protected under the FIRST AMENDMENT.

The tendency toward public financing of electoral campaigns, with accompanying regulation, works to the advantage of incumbents and to the disadvantage of challengers, who usually need to spend more than their opponents to overcome the advantages of incumbency. The scheme for financing and regulating the presidential election campaigns serves to insulate the two major parties from challenges by third parties or independent candidates. While claiming to protect the people from the "fat cats," federal politicians have taken steps to protect themselves from the people.

DENNIS J. MAHONEY

Bibliography

ALEXANDER, HERBERT E. 1980 *Financing Politics: Money, Elections and Political Reform.* Washington, D.C.: Congressional Quarterly.

FEDERAL ENERGY AGENCY v. ALGONQUIN SNG, INC. 426 U.S. 548 (1976)

A unanimous Supreme Court, through Justice WILLIAM J. BRENNAN, upheld the constitutionality of oil import licensing fees imposed under the Trade Expansion Act (1962) and the Trade Act (1974). Under those statutes the President was authorized to "adjust" imports of commodities if the importation was in such quantities or under such conditions as to threaten national security. This was not an improper DELEGATION OF POWER, as the laws established preconditions for and limits upon its exercise. Furthermore, the court ruled, license fees were as acceptable a means of adjusting levels of importation as quotas.

DENNIS J. MAHONEY

FEDERAL GRANTS-IN-AID

Federal grants-in-aid are subventions to state or local governments, private institutions, or individuals in support of a wide variety of undertakings. Early in the nineteenth century, governmental transfers of land were used to support road construction and agricultural education. Cash grants to states for diverse functions, such as vocational EDUCATION, forest fire prevention, and maternal health, came of age in the decades preceding the New Deal. The public welfare programs established in 1935 greatly expanded the federal role in state finances. But it is the proliferation of categorical grants since 1960 that has rendered them the principal instrument of federal influence over social services and urban affairs. This recent extraordinary growth reflects an unplanned series of fragmented national responses to state fiscal inadequacy in the face of increased demand for collective goods.

Most of the current 500 or so national grant programs are intergovernmental, and federal monies under them constitute about one-quarter of the annual expenditures of both state and local governments. Notwithstanding federalism-inspired movements toward less directive federal grants, known as REVENUE SHARING and block grants, most aid programs remain categorical, with narrowly defined undertakings and detailed conditions imposed on the receiving agencies.

Grants are made pursuant to Congress's broad discretion to spend for the GENERAL WELFARE and common defense. Like other national powers, grant-making authority rests on permissive and expansive constitutional principles established during the post-New Deal era of judicial reaction and retreat, typified by such cases as STEWARD MACHINE CO. v. DAVIS (1937) and *Oklahoma v. Civil Service Commission* (1947). The recurrent use of grant conditions to impose national solutions on traditionally local issues suggests that the political safeguard of FEDERALISM constraining Congress in the use of national regulatory power is less operative in the exercise of grant-making authority. (See TAXING AND SPENDING POWER.)

For many years intergovernmental relationships in grant programs were understood to be administrative, cooperative, professional, and donative. Consequently, federal judges declined to intervene in grievances founded on grant programs. This aloofness markedly changed with the advent of antipoverty litigation in the late 1960s, when courts acknowledged that private beneficiaries of public WELFARE BENEFITS were entitled to relief against state and local laws and practices inconsistent with federal grant conditions. Litigation over grants soon became a staple of federal court dockets, with suits by federal grantor agencies and local government grantees as well as by private parties. The judicial decisions, while providing a novel and potent injunctive remedy, broadly construed and uniformly validated federal goals and conditions. Federal courts thus placed their stamp of approval on Congress's expansive use of federal grants.

Grants differ from regulation in that they entail expenditures, not direct commands and sanctions, as the inducement for conforming activity. Because of this difference, courts maintain that state and local governmental participation in grant-in-aid programs is voluntary, not coerced. They consequently reject attacks on grant conditions, on the ground that onerous or intrusive requirements can be avoided by the "simple expedient" of not yielding and of refusing the grant. This choice of the state or city is largely fictional in light of citizen-industry mobility and the competition among states for resources. But courts cannot intelligibly resolve the question of whether federal grants have overborne the "free will" of government units.

On several recent occasions Congress has further reduced the difference between grants and regulation through the creation of new grant-in-aid directives without additional federal funding. Instead of monetary inducements, Congress has chosen to condition continuation of eligibility under well-established, and usually large, aid programs on conformity with its new requirements. This tying arrangement has the look of regulation, but its validity seems beyond question so long as there is a plausible relationship between the new program or condition and the national purposes of the older one.

For example, states may be required to supplement or to provide welfare payments in order to remain eligible for large Medicaid health care grants; the justification is that income maintenance and health-care support once were within a single grant program, and, more fundamentally, that subsistence payments significantly affect the health of the impoverished. Similarly Congress has tied the availability of federally insured mortgages to state participation in a flood control program; has tied the entire portmanteau of federal health dollars to state adoption of an elaborate apparatus for health systems planning and cost control; and has tied highway grants to state regulation of billboards, state enforcement of a federal speed limit, and state adoption of a national minimum age for drinking. There may be constitutional limits on tying new conditions to older grant programs, but the limits remain unenforced and unexplored.

The basic constitutional constraint on grant conditions is that they must be relevant to the purpose of a grant program. Here, as elsewhere, Congress has an exceedingly large discretion to determine relationships between means and goals. Fair treatment of private beneficiaries and efficiency are the two primary categories of relatedness, and they obviously can carry a good deal of baggage. In addition, Congress of late has established a web of elaborate "cross-cutting" conditions applicable to all or most grant-in-aid programs concerning, for example, the handicapped, environmental impacts, labor and procurement standards, citizen participation, merit hiring, and CIVIL RIGHTS. Administrative enforcement of grant conditions played a major role in the DESEGREGATION of southern schools. To be sure, many of these restrictions would fall within congressional powers under the COMMERCE CLAUSE and the FOURTEENTH AMENDMENT, but there is significance in Congress's casting them as grant-in-aid conditions. The judicial assumption that states have the option not to accept the grants apparently makes it easier for Congress to impose new and controversial obligations on the states.

The TENTH AMENDMENT limit established in NATIONAL LEAGUE OF CITIES v. USERY (1976) has not been applied to grants founded on the spending power, no doubt because such a ruling would eviscerate the current system of federal grants. Numerous federal grant conditions directly affect the structure and operation of state and local governments. Grant programs not only pervasively alter the spending priorities of governmental units, but, through the imposition of conditions, also allocate power between state and local governments (and occasionally between governors and legislatures), dictate hiring practices and employment benefits, and, by barring partisan political activity, limit the occasions on which officials administering departments having grants may be elected.

There is, finally, the Supreme Court's assimilation of grant programs to regulatory ones in its holding that state laws inconsistent with the terms of federal grants are invalid under the SUPREMACY CLAUSE. Although not fully explicated, this theory has been used repeatedly to warrant injunctive relief against grantee noncomplicance with national conditions. Traditionally, federal administrative enforcement of grant conditions had been exceptionally lax, perhaps designedly so. Third-party suits for injunctive relief have altered this convention, while enlarging the role of federal courts in monitoring and enforcing grant programs. As a consequence, there is now more law and less discretion defining and governing the relationships under national grants.

LEE A. ALBERT

Bibliography

LAPIERRE, D. BRUCE 1983 The Political Safeguards of Federalism Redux. *Washington University Law Quarterly* 60:779–1056.

MAXWELL, J. and ARONSON, J. R. (1965)1977 *Financing State and Local Government.* Washington, D.C.: Brookings Institution.

FEDERAL IMMUNITY ACT
68 Stat. 745 (1954)

The growing tendency in the early 1950s of witnesses before congressional committees to refuse to testify by relying on the Fifth Amendment's RIGHT AGAINST SELF-INCRIMINATION led Congress in 1954 to amend previous statutes and provide revised immunity arrangements. The purpose of the measure was to bypass the Fifth Amendment by giving Congress the power to grant a reluctant witness immunity from prosecution and compel the individual to testify. Either house of Congress by majority vote or a congressional committee by a two-thirds vote could grant immunity from prosecution to a witness in a national security investigation, provided an order was first obtained from a United States District Court judge. The statute required the attorney general to be given advance notification and an opportunity to offer objections. The law also permitted UNITED STATES DISTRICT COURTS to grant immunity to witnesses before courts or GRAND JURIES. Witnesses thus immunized faced the choice of testifying or going to jail. The Fifth Amendment could not be raised as a barrier to compulsory testimony.

In ULLMAN V. UNITED STATES (1956) the Supreme Court sustained its constitutionality.

PAUL L. MURPHY

(SEE ALSO: *Immunity Grant.*)

FEDERALISM
(History)

Reflecting on the achievements of the CONSTITUTIONAL CONVENTION, JAMES MADISON wrote in 1831 that the Framers had lacked even "technical terms or phrases" to describe accurately the governmental system they designed. Prior to 1787, the term "federal" had been used to signify confederation, a system in which SOVEREIGNTY remained with the constituent states that ceded certain elements of authority to a central government—and in which the central authority's legislature merely could propose measures to the states for approval. By contrast, in what was known as "consolidated" government, typical of the modern European nation-state, the central authority was the repository of sovereignty and the power of the locally based units of government depended entirely upon it. The Founders departed from all the historical precedents in both these modes, Madison declared, to produce a system that was "a novelty and a compound." It is this system that we know as American federalism, with its combination of features associated with both the consolidated (or unitary) nation-state and the old-style confederational form of government.

Nearly two centuries of colonial history in North America had afforded only rare examples of cooperation and coordination that presaged even in a remote way the system devised in 1787. In 1643, Plymouth, Massachusetts, Connecticut, and New Haven formed a league called the United Colonies of New-England. Commissioners appointed by the four governments dealt with boundary questions, missions to the Indians, and even coordination of military operations in the Indian war of 1675–1676; but the organization soon faded into obscurity. The only serious effort at united action after that time and involving surrender of any colonial powers was the abortive Albany Plan of Union of 1754. Designed by BENJAMIN FRANKLIN and

THOMAS HUTCHINSON, the plan would have created a council of the colonies and an executive appointed by the Crown. In addition to being empowered to declare war, conclude treaties with the Indian nations, and regulate territories outside the existing colonial boundaries, the council would have been given authority to impose taxes. But the plan foundered, with not a single colonial assembly giving assent to the proposal.

Certain qualities of the British colonial system itself had foreshadowed American federalism. Although formal authority remained squarely in the hands of the British government, still the colonies were given significant latitude in governing their own affairs. The sudden centralization of power after 1763, when the British decided to tighten the reins and impose new taxes and administrative reforms, precipitated the Revolutionary crisis. Even the exigencies of newly declared independence and armed conflict with Britain had not induced the American states, however, to surrender claims to sovereignty in the interest of national unity. Indeed, the ARTICLES OF CONFEDERATION specifically provided that each state would retain "its sovereignty, freedom, and independence, and every power, JURISDICTION and right, which is not by this confederation expressly delegated to the United States, in Congress assembled." Article III, moreover, described the government only as "a firm league of friendship." The notorious weaknesses of government under the Articles, leading to demands for basic reform by 1786–1787, derived from precisely this perpetuation of the states' prerogatives.

What the Convention sought to create in 1787 was a system in which some measure of sovereignty would be retained for the states; but the national government would be given powers ample enough to govern effectively, operate directly upon the citizens, and establish the nation as a credible presence in international affairs. The continued existence of the states as separate legal entities was an essential component of the original understanding embodied in the Constitution. Structural features that assured the states of great influence included the system of REPRESENTATION in Congress (including equal representation for each state in the Senate), the AMENDING PROCESS, and the voting by state in the House of Representatives in presidential elections not resolved in the ELECTORAL COLLEGE.

Equally important was the concept of enumerated powers. The jurisdiction of the proposed national government, wrote Madison in THE FEDERALIST #39, extended "to certain enumerated objects only, and [left] to the several states a residuary and inviolable sovereignty over all other objects." The "general principle" underlying enumeration of the central government's powers, as JAMES WILSON later wrote, was "that whatever object was confined in its nature and operation to a particular State ought to be subject to the separate government of the States; but whatever in its nature and operation extended beyond a particular State, ought to be comprehended within the federal jurisdiction." On this principle was designed Article I, section 8, with its enumeration of the specific powers of Congress, including control over foreign and INTERSTATE COMMERCE, coinage, and the military and naval forces; the power to establish roads and post offices, inferior federal courts, and an organized militia; and authority as well to declare war and conclude treaties, to create a federal district as the seat of government, and to govern TERRITORIES and regulate property of the United States. Specific limitations were also embraced in the original document of 1787: the prohibition against import and export taxes, grants of TITLES OF NOBILITY, BILLS OF ATTAINDER, suspension of HABEAS CORPUS except during rebellions or invasions, or congressional interference with the slave trade for a period of twenty years. Demarcating the boundaries of the states' authority were provisions in Article I, section 10, that prohibited the states from enactment of EX POST FACTO LAWS, bills of attainder, or laws impairing the OBLIGATION OF CONTRACT. The Constitution also forbade the states from entering into treaties or imposing duties or tonnage fees without permission of Congress.

The seeds of controversy over the proper reach of the bounds of national power were to be found, however, in the GENERAL WELFARE CLAUSE and in the NECESSARY AND PROPER CLAUSE. Article VI, moreover, included the SUPREMACY CLAUSE, holding that all laws and treaties made under the Constitution "shall be the supreme Law of the Land." Opponents of the Constitution cited all these provisions as evidence that the Constitution could easily justify a dangerous centralization of power, overwhelming the states and rendering their alleged residual sovereignty a nugatory matter. A new tyranny, according to this view, could easily be the result of consolidated, unitary government.

Anticipating exactly such objections, the Framers built into the federal design a guarantee of a REPUBLICAN FORM OF GOVERNMENT to each state. The FULL FAITH AND CREDIT, FUGITIVE SLAVE, PRIVILEGES AND IMMUNITIES, and extradition provisions further buttressed state authority. The most important consequence of concern about the centralization of power and potential tyranny, however, was the movement for a BILL OF RIGHTS. The first nine amendments, together with the original provisions of the Constitution prohibiting the states from enacting bills of attainder or abrogating contracts, represented an effort to establish national ideals of justice—defining boundaries beyond which government must respect the rights of individual citizens. The Bill of Rights served to reinforce federalism itself as a bulwark of defense for liberty against concentrated governmental power.

What values were intended to be served by this new system of federalism, a system described by a New York judge in 1819 as a "complex and peculiar structure" that permitted the states and the national government to move "in different spheres but occupying the same territorial space, operating upon and for the benefit of the same people"? The first value, designed to protect liberty and to give republican principles full play, was maintenance of government "close to the people." The champions of the Constitution contended that by giving a continuing—and vital—role to the states, popular oversight of governmental operations would be effective and there would be a high degree of participation in public affairs. These same contentions have been heard ever since in the arguments for a federal division of powers in American government.

A second value given a high place in the rationale for federalism was diversity itself. Regional differences in cultural values and local preferences on matters of law and policy would be permitted and find expression when important powers of government remained with the states. Providing in this manner for diversity meant, as Justice LOUIS D. BRANDEIS argued in NEW STATE ICE COMPANY V. LIEBMANN (1932), that "a single courageous state may, if its citizens choose, serve as a laboratory, and try novel social and economic experiments without risk to the rest of the country."

Efficiency was another value intended to be promoted by federalism. Loading all the functions of government upon authority at the center is not only potentially dangerous to liberty; it is also potentially the cause of congestion, complexity, and ineffectiveness. Even unitary, consolidated governments find it necessary to devolve certain functions on subnational or local authority. As Madison wrote in *The Federalist* #14, even if the states were to be abolished, "the general government would be compelled, by the principle of self-preservation, to reinstate them in their proper jurisdiction." What distinguishes a system founded on the principles of federalism from a consolidated system, however, is that federalism recognizes the legitimacy of exclusive state claims to some meaningful autonomy in important areas of law and policy. Power to control at least some of the things that really matter, in the regulation of society's affairs, must be left to the states.

A notable distinguishing feature of American federalism, consistent with the effective pursuit of these values, is the provision for constitutional amendment. What seemed a rational division of authority in the largely agrarian-commercial nation of 1787 will not be rational (or even minimally workable) two hundred years later in an integrated industrial nation with over fifty times the population of 1787. Most of the major changes in the American federal system, both in formal doctrine and in actual governmental practice, have occurred in response to that problem. By a remarkable insight of the Framers, expressed through the amendment process explicitly and the judicial processes by implication, they provided mechanisms for successful adaptation to changing circumstances and national values.

The principles of a federal system require that major changes in the boundaries of authority between the states and the national government should be accomplished by the prescribed amendment process. Such fundamental change should not occur through a process of ordinary legislation or mere administrative innovations in policy. The actual operation of the American system has sometimes conformed to this ideal: fundamental change in the structure of powers within the system were initiated, for example, by the Civil War and Reconstruction amendments. Yet at other times basic changes in federal–state relationships were effected without resort to the amendment process. Even the THIRTEENTH, FOURTEENTH, and FIFTEENTH AMENDMENTS, for example, ratified decisions already made on the bloody battlefields of the Civil War. The doctrine of IMPLIED POWERS was a judicial invention in MCCULLOCH V. MARYLAND (1819). The dramatic swing in antebellum interpretation of the COMMERCE CLAUSE—first the MARSHALL COURT's nationalistic interpretation; then, the TANEY COURT's assertion of DUAL FEDERALISM and concurrent powers—came about by judicial innovations in doctrine. Vast changes in law and policy, not least the abandonment of economic due process and the emergence of new presidential EMERGENCY and WAR POWERS, have occurred since 1933 without benefit of constitutional amendments.

Provisions for accommodating new states in the course of national expansion is another important feature of the federal scheme. The thirteen original states took the chance, in effect, that they would be confronted by new sectional alignments and powerful interests hostile in some measure to their own. It was a certainty that each new state taken into the Union would significantly dilute the power of the original states in the Senate, and, as population grew in newer areas, would dilute even more their power in the House of Representatives and in the Electoral College. This provision for the admission of new states underlined the values fundamental to the original understanding: government close to the people, diversity, and efficiency.

A legacy of the Founders not easily separated from their creation of a federal system is the "federal creed" that has been as influential in shaping political behavior as constitutional provisions have been in shaping the dynamics of government. By "federal creed" is meant habitual skepticism with regard to centralized power. It was expressed vividly in Walt Whitman's *Leaves of Grass:*

> To the States or any of them or any city of the States,
> *Resist much, obey little.*
> Once unquestioning obedient, once fully enslaved, no nation state, city of this earth, ever afterward resumes its liberty.

These lines express a political reality of the nineteenth century, namely, that whenever a policy was considered, debate typically centered not only on the wisdom of the policy itself but also on the cognate question: what level of government—the states or Washington—ought legitimately to have responsibility? It was the enduring popular commitment to the values of federalism, some historians contend, that kept the nation from accepting full-scale reorganization as a consolidated, unitary government in the Civil War years. Instead, despite such centralizing measures as the wartime banking laws and the postwar adoption of the Fourteenth Amendment, there remained a strong faith in the desirability of a meaningful "state sovereignty." The culture of federalism was expressed in the enigmatic pronouncement of the Supreme Court in TEXAS V. WHITE (1869) that "the Constitution in all its provisions looks to an indestructible Union composed of indestructible states." Similar convictions about the states' continuing importance found voice in COLLECTOR V. DAY, two years later, when the Court asserted that surviving aspects of state sovereignty made the states "as independent of the general government as [it] is independent of the states."

Opponents of centralized power appealed to such convictions in the late nineteenth century and early twentieth century, when they argued for narrow construction of the commerce clause and found in the due process clause of the Fifth Amendment authority for declaring unconstitutional congressional regulatory measures. The same federal creed led many reformers in the Progressive era to prefer uniform state codes to outright imposition of uniformity in law by congressional action. In the New Deal years and down to the present day, moreover, opponents of the welfare and regulatory features of modern policy have expressed their views in terms that extolled state sovereignty and deplored the centralizing of power in Washington as contrary to the Framers' intent.

The variety and ingenuity of such arguments have led many commentators to conclude that the federal creed is a convenient, all-purpose shield behind which to advocate special-interest positions. The most egregious example in the nation's history has been the invocation of STATES' RIGHTS as a justification for policies of RACIAL DISCRIMINATION. Conservative jurists also created a constitutional void within which neither the national government nor the states could legislate to regulate economic interests; federalism became the handmaiden of laissez-faire. Inconsistency in the application of federal principles in the 1920s led THOMAS REED POWELL to remark that "the sacred slogan of states' rights is easily forgotten when employers wish their laborers sober but unctuously invoked when they wish them young" (a reference to southern opposition to child-labor laws and support of national prohibition). In the post-World War II era, moreover, some of the most outspoken champions of "small government" and states' rights, and opponents of the nationalization of economic and social policy, have also been most consistently in favor of massive increases in the size of the national armed forces and even of federal surveillance of political activists and other infringements on CIVIL LIBERTIES.

Even if one concedes that federalism can be a smokescreen behind which special interests can pursue selfish aims or hide inconsistencies, the prominence of the traditional values of federalism in political rhetoric indicates that such arguments are regarded as effective. They are, in effect, appeals to the values of a "federal" political culture: American political consciousness retains inherited and much-reiterated notions that certain important values are best served by decentralization of power.

Some prominent contemporary students of American federalism claim that the abstract concept of separate governments (state and national), with separate responsibilities and constituencies, is—and indeed always has been—a fiction. According to this view, despite the "fiction" of ENUMERATED POWERS there has always been an overlap of responsibilities and a significant measure of federal–state sharing of power. "Dual federalism"—the concept of state and national governments occupying distinct, separate spheres of authority—is in this version of our history only a myth. Contrary to this view is another that contends that until 1861 the federal system in actuality functioned much as the model of "dual federalism" prescribed, and after the Civil War, there began a progressive centralization of power which continued until the 1980s.

The evaluation of such contending views depends upon analysis not only of doctrinal development but also of the system's practical operation. How has government actually behaved, and to what extent has power been centralized or decentralized in important areas of policy, at different stages of the nation's history? In fact, the story of American federalism is one of progressive centralization. Except for the overarching continuity infusing the whole record—the progressive centralization of power, step by step—distinct stages in the history of federalism indicate fundamental discontinuities.

The first stage was the period from the founding, in 1787–1789, to the Civil War. In this period, a remarkable array of governmental functions were exclusively, or nearly so, in the hands of the states. Power was diffused, and what "sharing" was found tended to be confined to the most superficial types of cooperation between state and national governments. Criminal law, definition of the requirements of due process, prison management, and criminal punishment were all state functions. So was the definition of property rights, confined only by the contract clause decisions of the Supreme Court. The power of EMINENT DOMAIN was exercised by the states virtually without a check by federal authority. Public education and labor relations, even slavery, were state matters. The states controlled the content of commercial law, family law, and such COMMON LAW matters as the rules of torts, nuisance, and liability. Also decentralized were CORPORATION law, most of taxation policy, and the design and control of the nation's transport system. At no other time after 1861 were the theoretical maxims of dual federalism so closely approximated by government in action.

The decentralization of real power before 1861 persisted even though the Marshall Court was handing down a series of landmark "nationalizing" decisions that lay the doctrinal groundwork for centralization. Even the Marshall Court left the door open for robust state regulatory activity. By the late 1830s, moreover, the Taney Court had begun to develop the doctrine of "concurrent powers," and it had shored up the STATE POLICE POWER with its decision in CHARLES RIVER BRIDGE V. WARREN BRIDGE (1837). Congress simply abstained from acting in many areas of policy that had been left open to it by the Marshall Court's doctrines. The state governments, therefore, held the reins in many vital areas of policy; the structure and dynamics of power were decentralized. One consequence of this decentralization was significant state-to-state variation in the substantive content of law in property, labor, family, and criminal law. The differences between law in slave states and free states were only the most dramatic illustration of such diversity.

The period from 1861 to 1890 was the second stage in the development of American federalism. Formal constitutional change came with the Civil War and had transforming doctrinal and practical consequences, deriving from the Thirteenth, Fourteenth, and Fifteenth Amendments. Meanwhile, Congress in the 1860s was enacting CIVIL RIGHTS laws, instituting an income tax (terminated after the war), inaugurating a national banking system, subsidizing transcontinental railroad projects, and expanding the size and reach of the federal bureaucracy generally. Thus power was centralized at an entirely unprecedented level, both in control of the economy and in protection of individual rights. Laws expanding the jurisdiction of the federal courts further concentrated power in the national government. In 1887, the INTERSTATE COMMERCE ACT inaugurated federal ADMINISTRATIVE LAW and centralized the regulation of the railroads. In 1890, the SHERMAN ACT marked the beginning of federal business law. Although such measures continued the centralizing trend in the distribution of real power, nonetheless elements of dual federalism persisted: property law, criminal justice, family relations, labor law, and most of an infant system of business regulation all remained nearly exclusively with the states.

The third stage of American federalism occupied the years 1890–1933. It was an era of accelerating centralization of policy responsibilities—although diversity persisted and the states did continue to exercise a wide-ranging discretionary authority, without substantial federal interference or direction, in many areas of law. Large-scale aid for irrigation in the West commenced with the Carey Act of 1894; and the Newlands Act of 1902 established an even larger national policy presence in that area. The PURE FOOD AND DRUG ACT (1906) signaled a trend toward exercise of the NATIONAL POLICE POWER, augmenting controls imposed through use of the TAXING AND SPENDING POWER, POSTAL POWER, and commerce power. Both the Federal Reserve Act of 1913 and the CLAYTON

ANTITRUST ACT of 1914 greatly extended federal administrative law, displacing state regulatory powers. Over the next seventy years, one of the most influential changes was the SIXTEENTH AMENDMENT, which set the stage for the national government's use of income taxes as a major source of revenues. Midway in this period, moreover, came the dramatic temporary expansion of centralized power occasioned by World War I. Although the conservative dominance of Congress in the Republican 1920s slowed the centralizing trend, even in that decade new responsibilities were assumed or expanded by the national government. They included the institution of FEDERAL GRANTS-IN-AID to the states for infant and maternity care, and expansion of the federal roads program, established earlier. The 1920 Transportation Act and the Federal Power Act of the same year also enlarged the regulatory powers of the federal government.

Ironically, these expansions of centralized power occurred in counterpoint with recurrent expressions of dual federalism and LIMITED GOVERNMENT doctrines by the Supreme Court. The most important initiatives of Congress struck down by the Court were the income tax instituted in 1893 and the 1916 KEATING-OWENS CHILD LABOR ACT. Matters such as labor relations were "entrusted to local authority" by the Constitution, the Court asserted in HAMMER v. DAGENHART (1918); child labor was "a purely local matter in which federal authority does not extend," and to permit Congress to regulate child labor risked permitting "our system of government [to] be practically destroyed"! Yet the same judges who subscribed to such doctrines of federalism also adhered to the doctrine of economic due process. Hence, when the Court reviewed regulatory and welfare legislation enacted by the states, it frequently struck down such laws under the Fourteenth Amendment. The Court thus immunized many business interests against regulation by either the state or the national government. The federal judiciary's activism in the cause of laissez-faire and dual federalism, ironically, was evidence of a negative type of centralization: the Supreme Court stood as censor of the states in vital social and economic matters.

Against this background of mixed constitutional doctrine and new centralizing initiatives, intergovernmental relations in the modern "sharing" mode emerged. Its most important feature was grants of cash aid to the states. Congress often tied strings to such aid, requiring planning of state programs and some degree of auditing by federal officers. By 1920, eleven programs were paying $30 million annually to the states—about 2.5 per cent of state revenues, or about a tenth the proportion paid by such grants-in-aid in the early 1980s—with most of the payments representing highway construction funds.

In the field of civil rights, the Court made only a small dent in the solid shield of states' rights behind which Jim Crow legislation, disfranchisement of blacks, and control of racial violence remained the exclusive responsibility of state governments. In the South, white supremacy reigned. In the area of FREEDOM OF SPEECH and FREEDOM OF THE PRESS, however, there was some movement by the Court toward applying Fourteenth Amendment constraints on state action.

The fourth stage of American federalism's development embraced the New Deal and World War II years, from 1933 to 1945. This period witnessed the wholesale centralization of policy responsibilities, a movement spurred by the worst economic depression in the nation's history and by four years of total mobilization for war. In the wake of centralizing initiatives by Congress came a dramatic shift in constitutional doctrine by the Supreme Court. To be sure, the Court initially erected doctrinal barriers to the innovations of FRANKLIN D. ROOSEVELT's New Deal administration; but by 1937–1938 a modern "constitutional revolution" had occurred without benefit of formal constitutional amendment. The Court discarded the doctrine of economic due process, and it adopted an interpretation of the commerce clause that validated unprecedented expansion of federal interventions in the economy and of social welfare and relief programs.

One policy area after another that previously had been in the states' hands came into the domain of federal action. Congress made agriculture a managed sector beginning in 1933; and the NATIONAL INDUSTRIAL RECOVERY ACT had much the same effect in the manufacturing sector from 1933 to 1935. The TENNESSEE VALLEY AUTHORITY ACT inaugurated regional development under federal auspices, and national programs proliferated in the conservation and reclamation fields. The WAGNER ACT of 1935 established a comprehensive federal policy of collective bargaining in labor relations, instituting national administrative law in the labor field; and by 1938 wages and hours legislation had augmented the basic labor law by setting uniform national standards. Congress authorized massive federal relief and subsidized work programs; and the SOCIAL SECURITY ACT and unemployment-compensation legislation of 1935 marked a new era of nationally sponsored and directed welfare policy. The net of federal regulatory power was thrown over many areas of industry formerly controlled, if at all, by the states: BROADCASTING, trucking, waterways, the securities exchanges, and previously unregulated segments of the banking industry. Meanwhile grants-in-aid—and the model of COOPERATIVE FEDERALISM of which they were an essential component—began to dominate federal–state relationships. True "sharing," in which the bulk of funding came from Congress, thus became a prominent feature of the working federal system; yet decisions tended to be made at the center, both as to policy and as to funding, with the states exercising administrative functions and serving as conduits for federal money.

Still, except for the three and a half years of war, when emergency powers extended to the national control of virtually every feature of the nation's life, the states remained a source of diversity in the American system of government. Yet the number and the significance of policy areas under their control had been so reduced that a new-modeled federal system had clearly become dominant.

The final stage in the history of federalism dates from 1945 to the present day. Its main feature, at least until the administration of RONALD REAGAN beginning in 1981, was a continued trend toward centralization. Four characteristics of this centralization movement are particularly important. First is the permanent status of large-scale standing military forces, their support taking as much as half of the federal government's operating expenses—something without precedent in peacetime prior to 1940. Second is the tendency toward stronger federal guarantees of civil rights. All three branches of government contributed to the civil rights expansion. The executive branch enforced racial integration of the armed forces and required AFFIRMATIVE ACTION programs of firms taking government contracts. Congress defined new guarantees of rights in areas such as VOTING, PUBLIC ACCOMMODATIONS, and employment; it also enacted legislation under which executive departments instituted affirmative action and equal opportunity policies in labor relations, education, and other areas. The judiciary played a leading role, with the line of DESEGREGATION cases elaborating the principles of BROWN V. BOARD OF EDUCATION (1954). The Court also carved out new areas of federal constitutional rights, such as the RIGHT OF PRIVACY and rights against SEX DISCRIMINATION.

The third major characteristic of centralization since 1945 is the rapid growth in the 1960s and 1970s, and the continued importance since then, of federal grants-in-aid to the states. The design and initiation of new grant programs, especially those associated with the "Great Society" measures of the LYNDON B. JOHNSON administration, led some analysts to speak of a "near monopolization of innovation by the central government" as a novel form of primary centralization. A fourth characteristic of post-1945 centralization is the continued enlargement of the scope of congressional regulatory concerns. Congress instituted far-reaching controls over air and water pollution, occupational health and safety, food and drug quality, and energy resources. Despite a strong movement in the Jimmy Carter and especially the Reagan years toward "deregulation," the federal regulatory presence in the mid-1980s remained far greater than that of the 1950s.

The Supreme Court seldom has stood in the way of such trends. Indeed, its role has been that of leader in the REAPPORTIONMENT and civil rights areas. In reviewing regulatory measures, only once since 1937 has the Court invoked states' rights or the commerce clause in such a way as to limit congressional power; that one exception was NATIONAL LEAGUE OF CITIES V. USERY (1976), a decision of limited application although notable for its assertion of the rights of the states "as states." Some state activities, the Court held, were beyond the reach of national wage and hour standards. Yet the Court has validated all other federal regulatory measures.

The scores of modern grant-in-aid programs have included many that bypassed the state governments: federal funds were awarded directly to cities and local special-purpose districts. Another hallmark of recent intergovernmental relations is what may be termed "managerialism," taking the form of program realignments, reliance on new budgeting concepts, oversight of programs by regional-level federal offices, and increased attention by Congress to the quality of governmental services at all levels. In 1958, Congress created the Advisory Commission on Intergovernmental Relations, which became a major proponent of reforms in aid programs and also an exemplar of the new-style managerialism in action.

Successive Presidents have championed the realignment of powers and policy responsibilities, as between the nation and the states. Thus Lyndon Johnson called for a "creative federalism" that would involve private-sector institutions as well as all levels of government in jointly administered programs. Some of Johnson's Great Society program complicated intergovernmental relations by permitting community organizations to challenge the existing governmental and political establishments. A reaction to the Johnson-era programs and politics was embodied in RICHARD M. NIXON's call for a "new federalism." His proposals took the form of combining increased executive power with increasing reliance on REVENUE SHARING and "block grants" instead of categorical or conditional grants-in-aid. Although during Jimmy Carter's administration general revenue sharing was continued, the President sought to reemphasize the problems of major urban centers and depressed minority populations; he also sought to impose tighter control on grants-in-aid, to assure the realization of congressional objectives.

Ronald Reagan announced his own brand of "new federalism" on taking office in 1981. Both in his rhetoric and by administrative actions, he sought to turn the clock back dramatically on many features of modern federalism. National political dialogue was infused, for the first time in many years, with an orthodox small-government, anticentralist ideology little heeded since New Deal days. Previous Republican Presidents—DWIGHT EISENHOWER, Nixon, and GERALD R. FORD—had all accepted in varying degrees, and even expanded in some respects, the permanent legacy of the New Deal. But in the 1980s, Reagan led a much more deeply rooted challenge to some of the welfare state and regulatory state foundations of the modern federal system. At the same time, he endorsed legislation designed to curb the authority of the federal courts, especially in the civil rights and CRIMINAL PROCEDURE areas; and he gave his support to constitutional amendments designed to permit school prayer in public schools, to require balanced BUDGETS, and to permit the states to prohibit abortions. Reagan's programs underlined his admiration for the constitutional doctrines and policies of federalism dominant in Republican circles in the 1920s.

Once again, therefore, in the Reagan years, federalism was at the center of political debate in America; and once again, the values of federalism were being invoked for purposes that transcended the mere reordering of federal–state relationships. The classic concerns of federalism in theory—diffusion of power, diversity, liberty, efficiency—remained in the forefront of public attention. How to square the ideals expressed in the original understanding with the social and economic realities of the late twentieth century remained a profoundly important issue.

HARRY N. SCHEIBER

Bibliography

BEER, SAMUEL 1973 The Modernization of American Federalism. *Publius* 3:49–95.

DAVIS, RUFUS 1978 *The Federal Principle: A Journey through Time in Quest of Meaning.* Berkeley: University of California Press.

GRODZINS, MORTON 1966 *The American System: A New View of Government in the United States,* ed. Daniel Elazar. Chicago: Rand, McNally.

MACMAHON, ARTHUR W., ED. 1955 *Federalism: Mature and Emergent.* New York: Columbia University Press.

PATTERSON, JAMES 1969 *The New Deal and the States: Federalism in Transition.* Princeton, N.J.: Princeton University Press.

SCHEIBER, HARRY N. 1975 Federalism and the American Economic Order, 1789–1910. *Law & Society Review* 10:57–118.

_____ 1978 American Federalism and the Diffusion of Power. *University of Toledo Law Review* 9:619–680.

WALKER, DAVID 1981 *Toward a Functioning Federalism.* Cambridge, Mass.: Winthrop.

WRIGHT, DEIL 1978 *Understanding Intergovernmental Relations.* North Scituate, Mass.: Duxbury Press.

FEDERALISM
(Theory)

The American federal system came into existence when the United States declared its independence in 1776. Indeed, the very process of declaring independence involved a series of reciprocal initiatives and actions on the part of the colonies; the CONTINENTAL CONGRESS declared independence for all thirteen colonies in one act, federal to the extent that the declaration itself was a culmination of this interplay and was undertaken by delegates from the states, each state speaking with one voice.

The foundation of the United States was a federal act par excellence, involving a consistent and protracted interplay between the colonies (later states) and the Congress, which they created as a single, national body to speak in their collective name. In the year that the representatives of the people of the colonies collectively declared the independence of the United States, other representatives of the same people were reconstituting the colonies themselves as states. Four colonies—New Hampshire, South Carolina, Virginia, and New Jersey—adopted state CONSTITUTIONS in 1776 before the adoption of the DECLARATION OF INDEPENDENCE, and four more—Pennsylvania, Maryland, Delaware, and North Carolina—did likewise before the year was out. Within sixteen months, all the former colonies except Massachusetts had adopted constitutions.

At one time this fact was used to argue that considerable disagreement existed over whether the states preceded the Union. Today it is generally agreed that both came into existence simultaneously—in the original federal act of the United States as such. In sum, all of the ambiguities of diversity in unity endemic to federalism were present at the creation. Even local governments (in this case the towns and counties) participated in the constitutional drafting and ratifying processes.

As Americans moved westward, they created new states "from scratch," in virtually every case establishing local and territorial institutions under the aegis of the federal government, but generally as a result of local initiatives. Ultimately, these new polities, with their new populations, would be admitted to the federation as states, fully equal to their sisters under the Constitution. Thus the American federation expanded from the Atlantic to the Pacific by settling what were, to white Americans, empty lands and organizing them politically.

The last of the forty-eight contiguous states was admitted in 1912; and Alaska and Hawaii, the two noncontiguous states, were added in 1959 and 1960, respectively, after relatively long periods of territorial status. In the same decade, the United States embarked upon a new experiment in federalism by creating a category of commonwealth or "free associated state," whose people, as American citizens, voted to associate their polity with the United States under a special charter. This new arrangement was devised for Puerto Rico, which became the first "free associated state" in 1952. In 1976 a similar arrangement was made with the Northern Mariana Islands. In both cases small, populated TERRITORIES sought that status to increase their autonomy, not to diminish it. (See COMMONWEALTH STATUS.)

Historically, then, the United States model is that of a political entity that was federal from its founding. The American states did not have to find a common cultural denominator because they had one from the first. All of their regimes were of the same character and their level of economic development was roughly equal. No plan for intercolonial union was ever put forth that was not federal in character. The American colonial period, indeed, had been a period of incubation for a uniquely American approach to governance, which properly can be termed "federal democracy."

Federal democracy is the authentic American contribution to democratic thought and republican government. Its conception represents a synthesis of the Puritan idea of the covenant relationship as the foundation of all proper human society and the constitutional ideas of the English natural rights school of the seventeenth and early eighteenth centuries. Contractual noncentralization—the structured dispersion of power among many centers whose legitimate authority is constitutionally guaranteed—is the key to the widespread and entrenched diffusion of power that remains the principal characteristic of and argument for federal democracy.

Federal democracy is a composite notion that includes a strong religious component. The religious expression of federalism was brought to the United States through the theology of the Puritans, who viewed the world as organized through the covenants that God had made with mankind, binding God and man into a lasting union and partnership to work for the redemption of the world, but in such a way that both parties were free, as partners must be, to preserve their respective integrities. Implicit in the Puritan view is the understanding that God relinquished some of His own omnipotence to enable men to be free to compact with Him.

According to federal theology, all social and political relationships are derived from that original covenant. This theological perspective found its counterpart in congregationalism as the basis of church polity and the town meeting as the basis of the civil polity. Thus, communities of believers were required to organize themselves by covenant into congregations just as communities of citizens were required to organize themselves by covenant into towns. The entire structure of religious and political organization in New England reflected this application of a theological principle to social and political life.

Even after the eighteenth-century secularization of the covenant idea, the behavioral pattern resurfaced on every frontier, whether in the miners' camps of southwestern Missouri, central Colorado, and the mother lode country of California, in the agricultural settlements of the upper Midwest, or in the wagon trains that crossed the plains, whose members compacted together to provide for their internal governance during the long trek westward.

It should not be surprising that Americans early became socialized into a kind of federalistic individualism that recognized the subtle bonds of partnership linking individuals even as they preserved their individual integrities. William James was later to write about the federal character of these subtle bonds in his prescription for a pluralistic universe as a "republic of republics."

In strictly governmental terms, federalism is a form of political organization that unites separate polities within an overarching political system, enabling all to maintain their fundamental political integrity and distributing power among general and constituent governments so that they all share in the system's decision-making and executing processes. In a larger sense, federalism represents the linking of free people and their communities through lasting but limited political arrangements to protect certain rights or liberties and to achieve specific common ends while preserving their respective integrities. To reverse the order, federalism has to do, first and foremost, with a relationship among entities, and then with the structure that embodies that relationship and provides the means for sustaining it. Originally federalism was most widely recognized as a relationship to which structural questions were incidental; but since the creation of the American federal system, in which a new structure was invented to accommodate that relationship, federalism has become increasingly identified in structural terms. This usage in turn has contributed to a certain emphasis on legal and administrative relations between the units and to a neglect of the larger question of the relationships federalism is designed to foster throughout the polity.

Although, in a strictly constitutional sense, American federalism is a means by which the national government shares authority and power with the states, the influence of federal principles actually extends far beyond the institutional relationships that link the federal, state, and local governments. The idea of the federal commonwealth as a partnership is a key principle of federalism and the basis of its integrative powers. Like all partnerships, the commonwealth is bound by a compact—the Constitution—that sets the basic terms of the partnership to insure, among other things, the preservation and continued political viability of its basic political units.

The principle of partnership has been extended far beyond its simple sense of a relationship between the federal and state governments. It has come to serve as the guiding principle in most of the political relationships that tie institutions, groups, interests, and individuals together in the American system. The term "partnership" describes a relationship that allows the participants freedom of action while acknowledging the ties that require them to function in partnership.

Partnership implies the distribution of power among several centers that must negotiate cooperative arrangements with one another in order to achieve common goals. Although the basic forms of the partnership are set forth in the United States Constitution, the actual character of the federal system is delineated, maintained, and made functional only partly by constitutional devices. The role of the Constitution (and of its primary interpreters, the courts) should not be minimized; yet equally important is the way in which the institutions and purposes of federalism are maintained through the political process. The political process, as it affects the federal–state–local relationship most directly, is made manifest through four basic political devices: territorial democracy, the dual system of laws and courts, the POLITICAL PARTY system, and the system of public–private "complexes."

The basic pattern of political organization in the United States is territorial. That is to say, American politics is formally organized around units of territory rather than economic or ethnic groups, social classes, or the like. The nation is divided into states, and the states are divided into counties, and the counties are divided into townships or cities or special districts, and the whole country is divided into election districts of varying sizes. This organization means that people and their interests gain political identity and formal representation through their location in particular places and their ability to capture political control of territorial political units.

A second basic device is the multiple system of laws and courts tied to the federal division of powers. In the nation as a whole, state law is the basic law. Federal law is essentially designed to fill in the gaps left by the existence of fifty different legal systems. Thus both state and federal courts are bound by state-made law unless it is superseded by the Constitution or by federal statutory law. The complexity of this system is compounded by the nature of the dual court structure, with each state and the federal government having its own complete court system. The federal courts have asserted extensive superiority in interpreting the manner in which the United States Constitution protects the rights of American citizens (who, of course, are also citizens of their states). Led by the United States Supreme Court, which is constitutionally placed at the apex of both court systems, the federal courts interpret federal law, review the work of the state courts, and enforce the laws of the states in which they are located in cases that come under federal JURISDICTION.

The third basic political channel is the party system. The Democratic and Republican parties represent two broad confederations of otherwise largely independent state party organizations that unite on the national plane primarily to gain public office. Despite the greater public attention given to the national parties, the real centers of party organization, finance, and power are on the state and local planes. This noncentralization of the parties helps to maintain generally noncentralized governments and to perpetuate a high degree of local control even in the face of "big government." Thus the party system is of great importance in maintaining the basic structure of

American politics and basic American political values, including those of federalism.

The fourth political device, the system of public–private "complexes," is partly reflected in the character of interest group activity. The partnership system extends outward to include private elements as well as governments—both public nongovernmental bodies, such as civic, philanthropic, educational, health, and welfare associations, and private profit-making bodies. These private associations and bodies often work so closely with their governmental allies that it is difficult to distinguish where the public interest ends and the private interest begins.

As a federation, the United States differs from a confederation of essentially separate political systems where the overarching authority is deliberately weak. At the same time, in the noncentralized American system, there is no central government with absolute authority over the states, but there is a strong national or general government coupled with strong state and local governments that share authority and power, constitutionally and practically.

The first important feature of a federation, following the American pattern, is the fundamental role and importance of the federal constitution as an organic law. The American Constitution reflects a federal approach to political SOVEREIGNTY, rejecting the idea that states or governments are sovereign as such, and holding that the people are the ultimate repositories of sovereignty and that governments have only "powers," delegated to them by the people. That approach precludes any notion of INHERENT POWERS. Under the Constitution, all powers possessed by the federal government are delegated to it by the people. The federal government has no inherent powers, although, as a result of those delegated, it gains some inherent extensions of its power. So, for example, because the people have delegated to the federal government the power to conduct some aspects of FOREIGN AFFAIRS, the President is understood to have acquired certain IMPLIED POWERS to negotiate with foreign governments. Once the people delegated the principal power, the implied power flowed automatically, but the second is theoretically dependent upon the first. From time to time, Presidents have claimed that they have inherent powers in the fields of foreign affairs and defense that are not subject to constitutional limitations but, rather, flow from the status of the United States as a sovereign state. Although the United States Supreme Court has recognized the existence of inherent powers, it has clearly limited them. This approach has been possible in the United States because of the dual character of the American founding, which enabled Americans to avoid confronting the issue of sovereignty head on.

Accordingly, as ANDREW C. MCLAUGHLIN suggested, the American federal system was designed to provide for the government of a large civil society without reliance upon hierarchical principles. In its original form, the American political system was designed as a matrix of polities, an indefinite number of structured political arenas linked to one another within the framework provided by the national and state constitutions. These arenas were to be distinguished from one another not on the basis of being "higher" or "lower" in importance but on the basis of the relative size of the constituencies they served. It was further assumed that the arenas were essentially equal, because size, of itself, was no measure of importance. Tasks were designed to be assumed or shared within the matrix on the assumption that sometimes a smaller arena is more appropriate than a larger one and that sometimes the reverse is true. The federal government was constitutionally mandated to serve the largest arena and to maintain the entire structure by assuring the continuity of the matrix itself. The role of the state governments in serving the basic divisions in the matrix was affirmed in the constitutional arrangement, and the states established local governments to serve the smallest arenas. Today the matrix consists of thousands of local arenas within the national framework, divided into fifty basic units—the states of the federal Union.

The American system has increasingly emphasized COOPERATIVE FEDERALISM rather than DUAL FEDERALISM as the basis of its operations. The American pattern of federalism has been cooperative since its beginnings, because since its inception most powers and competences have been treated as concurrent, shared by the various planes of government. In Morton Grodzins's terms, it is not a layer cake but a marble cake. Therefore, in the American polity, it is especially difficult to define what is exclusively in the federal sphere of competence, or in the state sphere, or in the local sphere.

The American federal system is at once extraordinarily simple and unusually complex. The simplicity of the federal system lies in a formal structure of federal, state, and local governments and in the outline of formal relationships between them. The complexity of the system lies in the myriad relationships that have developed between the governments and those who make them work. People often tend to take it for granted that national problems are handled in Washington; state problems in the state capital; and local problems at city hall or in the county courthouse. But, although it is easy to say that this is how things should be, it is well-nigh impossible to take a specific issue or function and to determine that it is exclusively national, state, or local.

The constitutional place of the states in the federal system is determined by four elements: the provisions in the federal and state constitutions that either limit or guarantee the powers of the states vis-à-vis the federal government; the provisions in the federal Constitution that give the states a role in the composition of the national government; the subsequent interpretations of both sets of provisions by the courts (particularly the United States Supreme Court); and the unwritten constitutional traditions that have evolved informally and have only later been formally recognized through the first three, directly or indirectly. The federal constitutional provisions outlining the general position of the states must always be taken into consideration even if some of them can be transcended through politics in specific situations. The specific limitations and guarantees of state powers fall into four basic categories: general concern for the integrity of the states as well as their subordination to the Union; some brief provisions ensuring the states a role in the common defense; a delineation of the role of the states in the two central areas of positive governmental activity at home, management of commerce and raising of revenues; and a description of state responsibilities in the administration of justice.

The procedure by which the basic status of the Union may be revised is found in Article V of the United States Constitution.

Similar procedures are found in most federal constitutions in the world. They underline one of the paramount characteristics of a federation: the revision of the basic status of the union is not totally dependent on the member states. Individual states have no right to veto changes adopted through the accepted procedure. When they oppose an amendment to the constitution—or demand an amendment—they are not sure to win.

One of the most important features of American federalism lies in the impossibility of the member states to abandon the federation. As the Civil War dramatically affirmed, there is no right of SECESSION. The United States Supreme Court, responding to that war, set down the accepted definition of the American federation in TEXAS v. WHITE (1869): "The Constitution in all its provisions, looks to an indestructible Union, composed of indestructible States."

Another characteristic of federalism in the United States is the existence of federal norms, whether legal, administrative, or judicial, that bear directly upon the federation citizens, without any need of intervention of the member states. The architects of the American system recognized that a successful federal system, something more than a loose confederation of states, required that both the national and the state governments be given substantial autonomy. They also recognized that each had to have some way to influence the other from within as well as through direct negotiation. The federal government has the power to deal directly with the public, that is to say, with the citizenry of the states. The states, in turn, have a major role in determining the composition of the federal government and the selection of those who make it work.

DANIEL J. ELAZAR

Bibliography

ELAZAR, DANIEL J. 1962 *The American Partnership: Intergovernmental Cooperation in the Nineteenth Century United States.* Chicago: University of Chicago Press.

——— 1984 *American Federalism: A View from the States.* New York: Harper & Row.

GRODZINS, MORTON 1966 *The American System: A New View of Government in the United States.* Chicago: Rand McNally.

HART, HENRY and WECHSLER, HERBERT 1953 *The Federal Courts and the Federal System.* Mineola, N.Y.: Foundation Press.

MCLAUGHLIN, ANDREW C. (1932)1972 *The Foundations of American Constitutionalism.* Gloucester, Mass.: Peter Smith.

OSTROM, VINCENT 1971 *The Political Theory of the Compound Republic.* Blacksburg: Virginia Polytechnic Institute, Center for the Study of Public Choice.

VILE, M. J. C. 1961 *The Structure of American Federalism.* Oxford: Oxford University Press.

WRIGHT, DEIL S. 1978 *Understanding Intergovernmental Relations.* North Scituate, Mass.: Duxbury Press.

FEDERALIST, THE

In the eight months following the adjournment of the CONSTITUTIONAL CONVENTION OF 1787, ALEXANDER HAMILTON, JAMES MADISON, and JOHN JAY wrote a series of eighty-five essays in support of the proposed Constitution. These essays were published in newspapers and as a two-volume book under the title *The Federalist.* This work was intended to influence voters electing delegates to the ratifying conventions and the delegates themselves; and the length, detail, and subtlety of its argument suggest an additional intention of enlightening later generations. While some contemporaries thought other, simpler and briefer, writings better calculated to influence the decision of 1787–1788, *The Federalist* was regarded as a work of enduring value by THOMAS JEFFERSON ("the best commentary on the principles of government which ever was written"), GEORGE WASHINGTON, and others. It has remained the most comprehensive and profound defense ever written of the American form of government; and it has been, as Chief Justice JOHN MARSHALL wrote in MCCULLOCH V. MARYLAND (1819), "justly supposed to be entitled to great respect" by courts engaged in "expounding the constitution."

The first section of *The Federalist* (#2 through #14) explains the advantages of a union as compared to independent American states. A large country is better suited than small countries to avoid or win wars, to pursue profitable commercial arrangements, and to raise revenue. Moreover, a large country's relative freedom from fear of war makes it more likely to preserve a free government. (Small countries facing frequent wars eventually accept the risk of being less free in order to be more safe.) Most novel was *The Federalist*'s claim that a popular form of government would be more likely in a large country than in a small country to secure private rights and the public good. MONTESQUIEU and the Anti-Federalist writers who quoted him acknowledged that large countries ruled by monarchs enjoyed certain advantages in FOREIGN AFFAIRS, but insisted that only small republics could enjoy the internal advantages of a patriotic citizenry ruling itself for its own good. In the famous *Federalist* #10 Madison argued that even in the smallest republic the citizenry is not an "it" but a collection of diverse individuals. Those individuals' rights deserve protection, but their passions and interests can unite them in groups that oppose the rights of others or the public good. Madison offered a twofold defense of a large republic. First, the diversity of a large country makes it less likely that any single group will constitute a majority of the voters and therefore be able to oppress other groups by virtue of the republican principle of majority rule. Second, in a large republic elections will be more likely to choose "fit characters" who will pursue the public good. The conclusion that republican government was possible, indeed better, in a large country served to reconcile the unpleasant necessities that seem to require largeness with the deep-rooted desire to have a popular government.

Essays #15 through #36 explain the necessity of "energetic" government. Although the national government has limited purposes, it must be able to tax and raise armies. Under the ARTICLES OF CONFEDERATION, Congress could demand the necessary money and men but had to address its demands to the state governments, whose disobedience could not be punished and whose compliance therefore could not be counted on. The decisive innovation of the new Constitution was the government's ability to address its commands to individual citizens, each of whose inability to contemplate forcible resistance made him respectful of "the arm of the ordinary magistrate." By defending this innovation in the name of FEDERALISM, *The Federalist* transformed the meaning of that term. Whereas others regarded true federalism as requiring what Montesquieu called a "society of societies"—that is, a union composed of and ruling over political communities rather than individuals—*The Federalist* regarded that as a prescription for disunion, thus deserving the name "antifederal" for its inevitable tendency.

The prospect that the new government would be able to exercise its nominal powers and coerce citizens raised the question of how such an energetic government could be confined to its proper purposes and restrained from oppression. *The Federalist* did not look to a careful enumeration of granted or excluded powers to control the government, because mere "parchment" would do little by itself and because certain formidable powers (for example, taxation) could not be excluded or even limited in their extent. The government could only be controlled by being "well modeled," by having a "general genius" and "internal structure" that made it trustworthy. This meant first of all that the government was "wholly popular"; its whole power was entrusted to the representatives of the people, and could therefore be controlled by the people in elections. *The Federalist* #37 through #84 explains the "conformity of the proposed Constitution to the true principles of republican government."

The fact that popular elections permit the people to "oblige the government to control itself" exhausts neither *The Federalist*'s prescription for a well-modeled government nor its argument for popular government. For one thing, the people are vulnerable to rulers who deceive them, misuse their powers between elections, or cancel elections. "A dependence on the people is no doubt the primary control on the government; but experience has taught mankind the necessity of auxiliary precautions." The auxiliary precautions are of various sorts, but all are designed to make ambition counteract ambition, so that no ruler's love of power is given free rein. A SEPARATION OF POWERS, legislative, executive, and judicial, insures that the people will be ruled in accordance with known laws that are enforced even against those who adopt them. The executive's VETO POWER both preserves this functional separation and, together with the legislature's BICAMERALISM, inhibits hasty lawmaking. The judiciary enjoys a tenure of GOOD BEHAVIOR to fortify judges in their task of preventing illegal executive acts and unconstitutional legislative acts. This last activity, now known as JUDICIAL REVIEW, was given its first sustained intellectual defense by Hamilton in *The Federalist* #78. Hamilton insisted on the court's duty to enforce the Constitution as law and indeed, because it was solemnly and authoritatively adopted by the people, as superior to the laws passed by the legislature, even if the legislature's laws were supported or instigated by the people themselves. The legislature's power of IMPEACHMENT provided a remedy against abuse of this judicial authority, or of the President's formidable powers. And the existence of state and national governments with independent powers to serve their own distinct objects gives each a platform and a motive to expose the other's encroachments.

The Federalist defended such auxiliary precautions (that is, precautions in addition to the people's electoral power) as reducing the chance that the government would betray and oppress the people as a whole. A more difficult problem, already explained in *The Federalist* #10, was that the people are not a whole, and that rulers elected by the majority might oppress the rights of minorities. The longer terms of senators, Presidents, and judges enabled them to oppose sudden and transient unjust impulses of the majority. A grateful people might reward such service once the heat of passion had cooled, or an excellent ruler might do his duty without reward; but the Constitution's institutions could not defend against an enduring majority's unjust passion or interest—hence the importance of a large country's diversity in making such majorities less likely.

The Federalist defends the "particular structure" of the Constitution not only as discouraging oppression but as encouraging good government. The task of a good national government is to secure the nation against foreign and domestic violence and to regulate its commerce so as to promote the general welfare. These activities in turn serve the most fundamental object of government, which is justice, meaning the protection of each individual's right to exercise his own faculties in the acquisition of property and in other activities. Thus an important accomplishment for any government is that it not itself be a source of injustice, that it achieve "the negative merit of not doing harm."

Further, positive merit of doing some good is encouraged by the Constitution's creation of offices in relatively small numbers and with relatively long terms, so as to encourage more capable candidates to seek office and to be elected and (more important) to put those elected in a situation in which they feel a personal motive to do some good. The experience officials could gain in office would help them devise means to promote the public good; and the distance of the people from direct rule would enable them to judge dispassionately and retrospectively the merit of their officials' policies according to their experience of the apparent effects of those policies. In the best case, officials moved by "the love of fame, the ruling passion of the noblest minds" would have an opportunity to "undertake extensive and arduous enterprises for the public benefit." Even in more ordinary cases, a durable senate would tend to foster stability in the laws and a single executive would be able to enforce them energetically.

The Federalist's defense of these institutions does not, however, deduce them entirely from the requirements of safe and good government. By those standards, *The Federalist* would not have found indefensible the "mixed" government of England, whose popularly elected House of Commons permits the people to restrain the government from oppression, whose king is an energetic executive, and whose House of Lords provides a source of stability and of protection for the rights of a minority. *The Federalist* emphatically defends the "strictly republican," "wholly popular" character of the American Constitution, which is made necessary by "that honorable determination, which animates every votary of freedom, to rest all our political experiments on the capacity of mankind for self-government." Not a knowledge of human fitness for self-government but an assertion of that fitness, or a knowledge of the human impulse to assert that fitness, justifies popular government. To protect the faculties of men requires protecting their faculty of passionately defending their own opinions, respecting their "pretension" to rule. *The Federalist* defended the American Constitution not only for its likely service of the interests of Americans but also for its tendency to "vindicate the honor of the human race."

The Federalist remains America's most important political book because it offers an explanation and defense of our form of government written by men who could not take the goodness or permanence of that regime for granted. Americans who study *The Federalist* today may find not only new reasons to appreciate the Constitution they inherit but also an account of government somewhat different from that assumed in contemporary opinion. For example, to *The Feder-*

alist justice means impartial protection of the right to exercise one's faculties, not equal provision for the satisfaction of one's needs or desires. CONSTITUTIONALISM means that the people's solemn choice of their own form of government can be overridden only by a new, deliberate popular choice, not silently and gradually improved by judges trying to make the Constitution a living document. And REPRESENTATION is an arrangement that allows an opinionated people to select capable rulers and periodically pass formal judgment on their service of the public good, not an imperfect simulation of ancient direct democracy or a primitive version of modern opinion polling. *The Federalist* is thus both a source of understanding and appreciation of the American Constitution and a guide to reflection on its subsequent development.

DAVID F. EPSTEIN

Bibliography

ADAIR, DOUGLASS 1974 *Fame and the Founding Fathers.* New York: Norton.

DIAMOND, MARTIN (1963)1972 The Federalist. Pages 631–651 in Leo Strauss and Joseph Cropsey, eds., *History of Political Philosophy.* Chicago: Rand McNally.

EPSTEIN, DAVID F. 1984 *The Political Theory of The Federalist.* Chicago: University of Chicago Press.

FEDERAL POWER COMMISSION

See: Regulatory Agencies

FEDERAL POWER COMMISSION v. HOPE NATURAL GAS COMPANY
320 U.S. 591 (1944)

In SMYTH V. AMES (1898) the Supreme Court saddled state REGULATORY COMMISSIONS with a specious DUE PROCESS rule for setting public utility rates. Forty-six years later the Justices repudiated the rule of a FAIR RETURN ON FAIR VALUE. Prior to *Hope,* the Court relied primarily on original construction costs and reproduction costs as a means of determining property value.

Justice WILLIAM O. DOUGLAS, speaking for a 5–3 Court, based rate regulation on the POLICE POWER. Douglas declared: "In so far as the power to regulate involves the power to reduce net earnings, it must involve the power to destroy." He adhered to the recent trend of decisions which removed the Court from such determinations. Without mentioning *Smyth,* Douglas accorded regulatory commissions broad power to choose methods of evaluating property: "The Constitution does not bind rate-making bodies to the service of any single formula or combination of formulas." Henceforth, the determination of the reasonableness of a rate would be made by looking to the "end result" or "total effect." This pragmatic approach returned the burden of decision to the commissions because a rate order was "the product of expert judgment," carrying a presumption of validity. Even the dissenters did not feel bound to adhere to *Smyth;* they disagreed over the applicable statutory standard. In *Hope,* the Court eliminated judicial obstruction to effective administrative rate regulation.

DAVID GORDON

FEDERAL PROTECTION OF CIVIL RIGHTS

Although the story of federal protection of CIVIL RIGHTS is most conveniently told chronologically, two themes warrant separate mention. First, federal protection of civil rights has a paradoxical relationship with STATES' RIGHTS. All civil rights legislation has been opposed or limited in response to the argument that the federal government ought not involve itself in areas of state responsibility. The Supreme Court repeatedly has voiced this concern and, in the past, invalidated civil rights legislation partly on this ground. Deference to state law enforcement prerogatives always has been a centerpiece of Justice Department civil rights enforcement policy. And for many years Congress repeatedly rebuffed so basic a measure as antilynching legislation in the name of states' rights. Yet the original federal civil rights statutes, and their underlying constitutional amendments, were responses to outrages by states or to private outrages that states failed to ameliorate. Given the origins of the need for federal protection of civil rights, states' interests may have received undue weight in shaping federal civil rights policy.

Second, there is a seedy underside to the topic of federal protection of civil rights. For many years the federal government was more involved with denying blacks' rights than with protecting them. Well into the twentieth century federal employment policy included racial SEGREGATION and exclusion. DE JURE segregation in Washington, D.C., and the armed forces, government participation in segregated and racially isolated housing projects, racially prejudiced federal judges, and other circumstances demonstrate the depth of federal involvement in discrimination.

Since the 1940s, however, there has been a trend toward increased federal protection of civil rights.

The Bureau of Refugees, Freedmen, and Abandoned Lands (the FREEDMEN'S BUREAU), created near the end of the Civil War, may be viewed as the federal government's initial civil rights enforcement effort. The Bureau's statutory charge, "the control of all subjects relating to refugees and freedmen from rebel states," enabled it to perform a variety of social welfare functions. But this first effort to assist blacks was tainted by, among other factors, the Bureau's role in establishing the oppressive system of southern labor contracts. Although Bureau agents invalidated particularly harsh terms, such as those providing for corporal punishment, much depended on the local agent's views. The Bureau and the Union Army, no less than southern legislatures, felt most comfortable when blacks were on plantations under contract and not seeking their fortune in urban areas.

With few exceptions, federal protection of blacks via the Freedmen's Bureau terminated in 1868. Congress's other Reconstruction legislation employed a variety of techniques to protect civil rights. The CIVIL RIGHTS ACT OF 1866 and the FORCE ACT of 1870 imposed penalties on those who enforced discriminatory features of the southern BLACK CODES, and the 1870 act made it a crime to conspire to hinder a citizen's exercise of federal rights. The 1870 act also provided special protection for black VOTING RIGHTS and the Force Act of 1871 went further by providing for the appointment of federal supervisors to scrutinize voter registration and election practices. The Civil Rights Act of 1871 authorized civil actions and additional criminal penalties against those who violated constitutional rights and authorized the president to use federal forces to suppress insurrections or conspiracies to deprive "any portion or class of . . . people" of federal rights. The CIVIL RIGHTS ACT OF 1875, the culmination of the Reconstruction period civil rights program, imposed civil and criminal sanctions for discrimination in PUBLIC ACCOMMODATIONS, public conveyances, and places of amusement.

Armed with the criminal provisions of the civil rights program, federal prosecutors brought thousands of cases in southern federal courts and established criminal actions as the primary vehicle through which the federal government protected civil rights. This burst of protective activity, along with the rest of Reconstruction, disintegrated with the COMPROMISE OF 1877 and the attendant withdrawal of federal troops from the South. In 1878, only twenty-five federal criminal civil rights prosecutions were brought in southern federal courts.

There are many reasons why federal criminal prosecutions were and are ineffective to protect civil rights. First, shortly after enactment of the post-Civil War ANTIDISCRIMINATION LEGISLATION, the Supreme Court limited Congress's power to protect civil rights. UNITED STATES V. REESE (1876) and JAMES V. BOWMAN (1903) invalidated portions of the 1870 act. UNITED STATES V. HARRIS (1883) and *Baldwin v. Franks* (1887) struck down the CRIMINAL CONSPIRACY section of the 1871 act and the CIVIL RIGHTS CASES (1883) found the 1875 act to be unconstitutional. These and other cases, including the SLAUGHTERHOUSE CASES (1873) and UNITED STATES V. CRUIKSHANK (1876), also narrowly construed constitutional provisions and statutory provisions that were not struck down. The entire federal statutory civil rights program therefore depended upon those provisions that, almost by happenstance, survived judicial scrutiny. And some of these were eliminated by the CIVIL RIGHTS REPEAL ACT of 1894 and a reorganization of federal law in 1909.

The principal criminal provisions that survived, now sections 241 and 242 of Title 18, United States Code, are not well suited to protecting civil rights. They always have been plagued by doubts about the particular rights they protect and the conduct they reach, and more generally by doubt about the federal government's role in law enforcement. Similar difficulties characterized federal civil remedies to protect civil rights. Finally, southern juries, until recently all white, have rarely convicted whites for violating the rights of blacks.

From the Compromise of 1877 until about 1940, reference to federal "protection" of civil rights would be misleading. Racism in America peaked in the early twentieth century, a fact reflected in the federal government's attitude toward blacks. THEODORE ROOSEVELT'S lunch with Booker T. Washington summarized his administration's concern with civil rights. Roosevelt's successor, WILLIAM HOWARD TAFT, did not even lunch with Washington, and under Taft and WOODROW WILSON segregation in federal employment was adopted. Neither Warren Harding nor Calvin Coolidge showed any inclination to rise above the worst racial attitudes of their times. As secretary of commerce, HERBERT HOOVER did desegregate the Census Bureau.

Attorney General FRANK MURPHY'S decision in 1939 to establish a CIVIL RIGHTS DIVISION within the Department of Justice represented a noticeable shift in federal enforcement activity. The new section studied the dormant post-Civil War statutes and adopted an enforcement program that led to such important decisions as UNITED STATES V. CLASSIC (1941) and SCREWS V. UNITED STATES (1945). Federal criminal civil rights prosecutions, however, did not grow beyond several dozen cases a year. But two decades later, in MONROE V. PAPE (1961), these cases served as precedents in establishing private enforcement of civil rights through SECTION 1983, TITLE 42, UNITED STATES CODE.

Creation of the Civil Rights Division combined with other events to generate pressure for progress in the civil rights field. In June 1941, President FRANKLIN D. ROOSEVELT issued an EXECUTIVE ORDER creating a Fair Employment Practices Committee (FEPC). A response to defense needs and black political pressure, the executive order prohibited discriminatory employment practices on account of race, color, creed, or national origin in government service, in defense industries, and by trade unions. The order, administered by the FEPC, helped many northern blacks to obtain defense jobs and encouraged many southern blacks to move north.

But the nation was not ready for an aggressive federal civil rights program. Roosevelt himself was reluctant to propose or endorse civil rights legislation. In the 1930s, he even refused to endorse an antilynching bill pending in Congress. And where Roosevelt did act, Congress balked. Until 1944, the President's Emergency Fund financed the FEPC. Congress then required congressional approval for all executive expenditures. In 1946, the FEPC expired for lack of funds and subsequent efforts to establish a statutory FEPC failed.

The end of World War II seemed to trigger or coincide with renewed violence against blacks. Following a Democratic party defeat in the 1946 congressional elections, President HARRY S. TRUMAN, in Executive Order 9008, created a presidential civil rights committee to conduct inquiries and to recommend civil rights programs. In its report, *To Secure These Rights,* the committee made far-reaching recommendations in the areas of voting, employment, and federally assisted programs, many of which would be enacted in the 1960s. Although President Truman recommended legislation based on the commission's report, his administration's civil rights accomplishments were to be on other fronts.

Truman, like other presidents, fostered civil rights most effectively in areas not requiring legislative action. Southern political power in Congress precluded significant civil rights legislation. In 1947, under black and liberal pressure, Truman authorized the Justice Department to submit an amicus curiae brief opposing judicial enforcement of racially RESTRICTIVE COVENANTS. Some believe this brief to have been influential in the Supreme Court's decision in SHELLEY V. KRAEMER (1948), which rendered racially restrictive housing covenants judicially unenforceable. From 1948 through 1951, Truman issued a series of executive orders which prohibited discrimination by defense contractors, established a committee to study compliance with government contract provisions prohibiting discrimination, provided processes for handling EMPLOYMENT DISCRIMINATION complaints in federal departments and agencies, and called for equality of treatment and opportunity in the armed services.

Civil rights enforcement received little attention early in the administration of DWIGHT D. EISENHOWER, but there were important exceptions to this pattern. Executive Order 10479 (1953) extended the antidiscrimination provisions previously required in defense contracts to all government procurement contracts. And after BROWN V. BOARD OF EDUCATION (1954), Eisenhower could not avoid civil rights issues. Southern recalcitrance in the face of *Brown* led to a federal–state confrontation in Little Rock, Arkansas, which was settled through the presence of federal troops. (See COOPER V. AARON, 1958.) But Little Rock marked no general turning point in the administration's enforcement efforts. Even when armed with increased authority to investigate denials of voting rights by the CIVIL RIGHTS ACT OF 1957, the Justice Department brought few cases.

JOHN F. KENNEDY'S administration also began with little impetus toward substantial civil rights achievement. But the rising tide of civil rights activity, increased public awareness, and continued southern resistance to DESEGREGATION made new federal–state confrontations inevitable. In May 1961, federal marshals were employed to protect freedom-riders. In September 1962, in connection with efforts to integrate the University of Mississippi, heavily outnumbered federal marshals and federalized National Guard troops withstood an assault by segregationists. Only the arrival of thousands of federal troops restored order. In the Birmingham crisis of 1963, which gained notoriety for the brutal treatment of demonstrators by state and local law enforcement officers, the federal government tried to act as a mediator. The administration's inability under federal law to deal forcefully with situations like that in Birmingham led Kennedy to propose further federal civil rights legislation.

Within the executive branch, the Interstate Commerce Commission, at the administration's request, promulgated stringent rules against discrimination in terminals. Armed with the CIVIL RIGHTS ACTS OF 1957 and 1960, the Civil Rights Division established by the 1957 Act conducted massive voter registration suits but secured only token improvements in black registration. Sometimes the judges blocking progress were Kennedy appointees. In November 1962 President Kennedy issued an executive order prohibiting discrimination in public housing projects and in projects covered by direct, guaranteed federal loans. And in executive orders in 1961 and 1963 Kennedy both required AFFIRMATIVE ACTION by government contractors and extended the executive branch's antidiscrimination program in federal procurement contracts to all federally assisted construction projects.

Soon after LYNDON B. JOHNSON succeeded to the presidency, he publicly endorsed Kennedy's civil rights legislation. Due in part to his direct support, Congress enacted the CIVIL RIGHTS ACT OF 1964, the most comprehensive civil rights measure in American history. The act outlaws discrimination in public accommodations, in federally assisted programs, or by large private employers, and it extends federal power to deal with voting discrimination. Title VII of the act created a substantial new federal bureaucracy to enforce antidiscrimination provisions pertaining to employment. The 1964 act also marked the first time that the Senate voted cloture against an anti-civil rights filibuster.

Despite the efforts of the Kennedy and Johnson Justice Departments, the Civil Rights Acts of 1957, 1960, and 1964 proved inadequate to protect black VOTING RIGHTS. Marches and protests to secure voting rights led to violence, including an infamous, widely reported confrontation in Selma, Alabama, in which marchers were beaten. In March 1965, President Johnson requested new voting rights legislation. He included in his speech to the nation and a joint session of Congress the words of the song of the civil rights movement, "We shall overcome," thus emphasizing the depth of the new federal involvement in civil rights. By August, the VOTING RIGHTS ACT OF 1965 was in place. Within ten years of its passage many more than a million new black voters were registered without great fanfare, with corresponding gains in the number of black elected officials. In 1968, after the assassination of Martin Luther King, Jr., Congress enacted a fair housing law as part of the CIVIL RIGHTS ACT OF 1968.

Unlike the Reconstruction civil rights program, Congress's 1960s civil rights legislation survived judicial scrutiny. In a series of cases from 1964 to 1976, the Supreme Court both sustained the new civil rights program and revived the Reconstruction-era laws. In *Katzenbach v. McClung* (1964) and HEART OF ATLANTA MOTEL V. UNITED STATES (1964) the Court rejected constitutional attacks on the public accommodations provisions of the 1964 act. In SOUTH CAROLINA V. KATZENBACH (1966) and KATZENBACH V. MORGAN (1966) the Court rebuffed state challenges to the Voting Rights Act of 1965. And in JONES V. ALFRED H. MAYER CO. (1968) and RUNYON V. MCCRARY (1976) the Court interpreted the Civil Rights Act of 1866 to fill important gaps in the coverage of the 1964 and 1968 acts.

With the passage and sustaining of the 1964, 1965, and 1968 acts and the revival of the 1866 act, the legal battle against RACIAL DISCRIMINATION at least formally was won. The federal civil rights program encompassed nearly all public and private purposeful racial discrimination in public accommodations, housing, employment, education, and voting. Future civil rights progress would have to come through vigorous enforcement, through programs aimed at relieving poverty, through affirmative action, and through laws benefiting groups other than blacks.

Just as the civil rights movement was running out of traditional civil rights laws to support, two other issues brought federal civil rights protection near its outer limits. The comprehensive coverage of federal civil rights laws did not eliminate the inferior status of blacks in American society. Pressure mounted for assistance in the form of affirmative action programs. But these programs divided even the liberal community traditionally supportive of civil rights enforcement. Affirmative action, unlike antidiscrimination standards, meant black progress at the expense of what many believed to be legitimate opportunities of innocent individuals. In its most important aspects affirmative action survived the initial series of statutory and constitutional attacks.

In the 1970s, civil rights enforcement became engulfed in another controversy: whether to bus school children for purposes of desegregation. (See SCHOOL BUSING.) President RICHARD M. NIXON's 1968 "Southern strategy" included campaigning against busing. Within six months of Nixon's inaugural, the Justice Department for the first time opposed the NAACP LEGAL DEFENSE AND EDUCATION FUND in a desegregation case. But under the pressure of Supreme Court decisions, and given the momentum of the prior administration's civil rights efforts, the Nixon administration did help promote new levels of southern integration. The administration, however, continued to lash out at "forced busing."

School desegregation also triggered a legislative backlash. In the 1970s the Internal Revenue Service, under the pressure of court decisions, sought to foster integration by denying tax benefits to private segregated academies and their benefactors. Congress, however, intervened to limit the Service's use of funds for such purposes. Similarly, Congress restrained executive authority to seek busing as a remedy for school segregation.

In the 1960s and 1970s, federal protection of civil rights reached beyond race. In the Age Discrimination in Employment Act, the AGE DISCRIMINATION ACT OF 1975, the REHABILITATION ACT OF 1973, and other measures, Congress acted to protect the aged and the handicapped. And the Equal Pay Act of 1963, the Civil Rights Act of 1964, and the EDUCATION AMENDMENTS OF 1972 increased federal protection against sex discrimination. In each of these areas, attachment of antidiscrimination conditions to federal disbursements became a significant vehicle for civil rights enforcement.

THEODORE EISENBERG

Bibliography

BERMAN, WILLIAM C. 1970 *The Politics of Civil Rights in the Truman Administration.* Columbus: Ohio State University Press.

BRAUER, CARL M. 1977 *John F. Kennedy and the Second Reconstruction.* New York: Columbia University Press.

CARR, ROBERT K. 1947 *Federal Protection of Civil Rights: Quest for a Sword.* Ithaca, N.Y.: Cornell University Press.

GRESSMAN, EUGENE 1952 The Unhappy History of Civil Rights Legislation. *Michigan Law Review* 50:1323–1358.

HARVEY, JAMES C. 1973 *Black Civil Rights During the Johnson Administration.* Jackson: University and College Press of Missouri.

KONVITZ, MILTON R. 1961 *A Century of Civil Rights.* New York: Columbia University Press.

LITWACK, LEON F. 1979 *Been in the Storm So Long: The Aftermath of Slavery.* New York: Knopf.

FEDERAL QUESTION JURISDICTION

Article III of the Constitution provides that the JUDICIAL POWER OF THE UNITED STATES shall extend to all "Cases . . . arising under this Constitution, the laws of the United States, and Treaties. . . ." This power is called federal question jurisdiction, because typically it entails the construction, application, or enforcement of federal law, including federal COMMON LAW. Performance of this function includes interpretation of the Constitution itself; thus federal question jurisdiction provides the jurisdictional basis for the federal courts' important power of JUDICIAL REVIEW. It is also the means by which Congress can secure a sympathetic and uniform interpretation of federal laws.

Although Congress has the power to make exceptions to the Supreme Court's APPELLATE JURISDICTION over federal questions, it currently makes few of them. A few federal trial court decisions, such as those remanding cases to state court following removal, are unreviewable. The Supreme Court reviews state court decisions only when they are FINAL JUDGMENTS that have been rendered by the highest state court in which judgment is available. Such a judgment will not be reviewed if it rests on an independent and ADEQUATE STATE GROUND or if it lacks a substantial federal question (for example, raises only a federal issue already resolved in an earlier case).

Apart from these restrictions, the appellate federal question jurisdiction extends to every federal issue, factual or legal, part of the plaintiff's case or part of a defense, in either a civil or a criminal case. Even if federal law appears in a case solely because a state statute refers to and incorporates it, the Supreme Court may exercise its federal question jurisdiction if it finds an independent federal interest in assuring proper interpretation of the incorporated federal matter.

In contrast, when Congress first created the lower federal courts in 1789, it authorized them to hear only a few federal question cases of special importance, such as PATENT suits and suits involving treaty rights. After the Civil War, Congress realized that state courts would be reluctant to enforce newly created federal CIVIL RIGHTS, and authorized the federal courts to hear the enforcement actions. Then, in 1875, Congress used almost the exact language of Article III to empower federal courts to hear "all suits of a civil nature . . . arising under the Constitution or laws of the United States, or treaties made. . . ." The 1875 act, known as the general federal question statute, required that at least $500 be in controversy in the suit, a requirement that was increased gradually over time.

Notwithstanding the breadth of the general federal question statute, Congress has continued to enact more limited laws authorizing federal jurisdiction over particular kinds of federal questions. These laws, designed to aid in enforcing the vast array of federal rights created in recent decades, have not required any amount in controversy. The range of these specialized federal question statutes is so great that by 1970 few federal question cases drew only upon the general statute. In 1976 Congress eliminated the amount in controversy requirement for the only remaining significant group of such cases, suits alleging unconstitutional conduct by federal officers; and in 1980, it repealed the requirement altogether.

Because Congress's legislative powers are enumerated and limited, a complaint filed in federal court frequently invokes a combination of state and federal law. The issue then arises whether the federal element warrants labeling the case one that "arises under" federal law. For a federal court to have federal question jurisdiction, this inquiry must be determined affirmatively, both under Article III and under the general federal question statute.

Although some Supreme Court decisions, notably Justice BENJAMIM N. CARDOZO'S opinion in *Gully v. First National Bank* (1936), have announced an equally demanding construction for both the Constitution and the statute, the currently accepted view is that the statute should be construed more narrowly than Article III despite the near identity of their language. In other words, Congress has a broad power but is assumed not to have exercised all of it. Interpretations of Article III have required that the plaintiff invoke some federal law to support a part of the claim for relief, whether or not the federal right is actually disputed by the defendant. (See OSBORN V. BANK OF UNITED STATES, 1824.) In a theory known as "protective jurisdiction," some judges and scholars have advanced the view that Congress should have the power to confer federal question jurisdiction even over a case arising under state law, when the claim implicates a strong, legistimate federal interest. The Supreme Court has not yet been required to decide whether Article III extends this far, although in some fields, such as BANKRUPTCY, the Court has approved federal question jurisdiction over suits involving only minor elements of federal law.

The Supreme Court has struggled to develop a narrower interpretive principle for the general federal question statute, seeking to allow adequate implementation of federal policy while avoiding an unnecessary deluge of cases into federal courts. For example, the statute is read to require the plaintiff's reliance on federal law to be revealed in the complaint according to traditional rules of pleading. It also appears that if plaintiff's reliance on federal law is not at the forefront of the claim, as when there is a dispute over present property rights that at some remote time had their source in federal law, jurisdiction will be denied under the general statute even though Congress could constitutionally confer it more specifically. Also, if the plaintiff relies on, refers to, and incorporates state law, the Court may refuse to allow the claim into federal court under the general statute because federal law will not be sufficiently at issue.

No single principle explains all the cases interpreting the general federal question statute. Despite this confusion, most types of cases have been classified either within or outside the federal question jurisdiction. To determine whether a new type of case combining federal and state elements falls within the statute's scope, the courts pragmatically assess the degree of federal interest in the subject matter of the litigation, the relative prominence of state and federal issues, and the likely burden on the federal judicial system of accepting jurisdiction in cases of that type.

The federal question jurisdiction authorized in Article III encompasses cases removed from state to federal court upon the defendant's assertion of a federal defense. Congress has not, however, conferred such broad federal question removal jurisdiction upon the federal courts. With a few exceptions, it has limited removal to cases that fall within original federal question jurisdiction under the general statute.

CAROLE E. GOLDBERG-AMBROSE

Bibliography

COHEN, WILLIAM 1967 The Broken Compass: The Requirement That a Case Arise "Directly" under Federal Law. *University of Pennsylvania Law Review* 115:890–916.

MISHKIN, PAUL J. 1953 The Federal "Question" in the District Courts. *Columbia Law Review* 53:157–196.

FEDERAL RULES OF CIVIL PROCEDURE

Article I of the Constitution empowers Congress to "constitute" lower federal courts and thus, by conventional assumption, to regulate practice and procedure in the cases heard in those courts. When the lower federal courts were first created in 1789, Congress enacted a law, known as the Conformity Act, that required each federal trial court to follow, in civil actions at law, the procedural rules of the state in which it was situated. By contrast, Congress directed the Supreme Court to promulgate federal procedures for federal admiralty and EQUITY cases respectively.

Under the Conformity Act, hypertechnical and arbitrary state procedures hampered the federal courts.

Also, uniform procedures were not available for administration of federal law nationwide under the general FEDERAL QUESTION JURISDICTION first conferred on the federal courts in 1875. Finally, in 1934, Congress adopted the Rules Enabling Act, which authorized the Supreme Court to promulgate federal procedural rules, subject to a congressional veto. Both Congress's power to delegate this authority and the Supreme Court's power to exercise it, consistent with the CASE OR CONTROVERSY requirement of Article III, have been upheld.

In accordance with the Act, the Supreme Court issued the Federal Rules of Civil Procedure in 1938. Congress declined to veto them. The new rules combined law and equity into a single form of action while preserving the SEVENTH AMENDMENT right to TRIAL BY JURY on any issue that would have been so tried before the merger. While they incorporated state law with respect to some matters, such as provisional remedies, the rules also made important innovations, such as simplified pleading, liberal joinder of claims and parties, and greater emphasis on pretrial discovery of facts. Many state procedures have come to resemble the Federal Rules. And the new joinder rules have resulted in enlargement of the definition of a "case" for purposes of determining ANCILLARY and PENDENT JURISDICTION in the federal courts. In 1966, admiralty actions were made subject to the Federal Rules of Civil Procedure, as amended to retain a few specialized rules for suits designated as admiralty actions in the pleadings.

Special constitutional problems have arisen when the Federal Rules have been employed in diversity actions. Congress and the federal courts do not have general substantive lawmaking power over cases simply because they are within the DIVERSITY JURISDICTION. Thus, when a Federal Rule of Civil Procedure differs from the procedural rule that would be applied in state court, and the difference in rules could affect the outcome of the case, the question arises whether the Federal Rule exceeds federal lawmaking authority and impermissibly intrudes on reserved state power. In *Hanna v. Plumer* (1963) the Supreme Court held that so long as a rule is "rationally capable of classification" as procedural, it is an appropriate subject of legislation under Congress's Article I power to create and regulate the lower federal courts, even though the rule may also affect substantive rights. It is unlikely that the Supreme Court, which promulgates the rules of civil procedure, would decide that those rules are not rationally classifiable as "procedural."

CAROLE E. GOLDBERG-AMBROSE

Bibliography

WRIGHT, C. 1976 *Federal Courts,* 3rd ed. St. Paul, Minn.: West Publishing Co.

FEDERAL RULES OF CRIMINAL PROCEDURE

After the FEDERAL RULES OF CIVIL PROCEDURE (1938) established a uniform set of procedures for the trial of civil cases in federal courts, Congress authorized the SUPREME COURT to make rules for the trial of federal criminal cases as well. With two Justices dissenting, the Supreme Court adopted the rules in 1944 and submitted them to Congress, which, by silence, approved them.

Before adoption of the rules, the trial of federal criminal cases was regulated by a varying and uncertain mixture of state and federal rules. The first achievement of the Federal Rules was simplification and clarification. The second was uniformity: the same rules would govern the major aspects of federal criminal trials all over the country. The federal appellate courts would now need to know only one body of procedural law, and all federal defendants would now enjoy similar rights and bear similar burdens.

Certain of the changes worked by the rules—for example, the substitution of a simplified complaint for the old, highly technical forms of INDICTMENT, and the consolidation of defense motions under a single heading—were clear gains by any measure. But probably the most significant achievement of the rules was to focus national attention on the regulation of the criminal process, which has consumed an enormous amount of professional and public attention ever since. Surely it was no accident that *McNabb v. United States* (1943), holding inadmissible a statement obtained from a suspect whom federal officers illegally detained, was decided while the rules were being considered; nor that *McNabb* was later reaffirmed in *Mallory v. United States* (1957) on the basis of Rule 5. (See MCNABB-MALLORY RULE.)

The rules have played a significant part in the expansion and clarification of defendants' rights: as an independent source of law, as a model for constitutional judgments, and as a means by which constitutional judgments could be elaborated. Two examples are illustrative. Rule 11, governing guilty pleas, was used as a guide in constitutional decision making and was itself amended to reflect and to elaborate case law. Rule 41, governing SEARCH WARRANTS, has likewise been modified to elaborate Supreme Court holdings, with respect, for example, to the permissible objects of search, and has also been used as a guide by the Court.

The administration, amendment, and interpretation of the Federal Rules have been heavily charged with constitutional significance, especially in a time of fundamental rethinking of the relation between government and the accused. For the most part this process has been carried on in a public and open-minded way, largely immune from politically motivated oversimplifications.

JAMES BOYD WHITE

Bibliography

MOORE, JAMES WILLIAM and WAXNER, MARVIN 1985 *Rules of Criminal Procedure.* Volume 8 of *Moore's Federal Practice,* 2nd ed. New York: Matthew Bender.

FEDERAL TEST ACTS

12 Stat. 430 (1862)
12 Stat. 502 (1862)
13 Stat. 424 (1865)
23 Stat. 21 (1868)

Early in the Civil War northern state and federal officials on an ad hoc basis administered oaths of allegiance to civilians suspected of disloyalty. In June 1862 Congress enacted the "jurors' test oath" which required persons sitting on federal GRAND and PETIT JURIES to swear to future loyalty and that they had not, in the past, voluntarily supported or given "aid or comfort" to the rebellion. The "Ironclad Test Oath" statute, enacted by Congress in July 1862, required all federal officeholders, except the President and vice-president, to swear they had "never voluntarily borne arms against the United States," aided the rebellion, nor "sought nor accepted nor attempted to exercise" any office under the Confederacy. In 1864 the United States Senate required that its members take this oath. In 1865 the "ironclad oath" was extended to attorneys practicing in federal courts, but in *Ex parte Garland* (1867) (one of the TEST OATH CASES) this extension was declared unconstitutional. From 1864 until 1868 the "ironclad oath" kept former Confederates from holding federal offices or being seated in Congress. After 1868 the Republican-dominated Congress allowed exceptions for members of their party (and later Democrats) who had served the Confederacy. The "jurors' oath" was used to prevent former Confederates from serving on juries until the repeal of all test oaths in 1884.

PAUL FINKELMAN

Bibliography

HYMAN, HAROLD M. 1954 *Era of The Oath: Northern Loyalty Tests During the Civil War and Reconstruction.* Philadelphia: University of Pennsylvania Press.

FEDERAL TORT CLAIMS ACT

60 Stat. 842 (1946)

The Federal Tort Claims Act, enacted in 1946, relinquished an important part of the SOVEREIGN IMMUNITY of the United States and was part of a larger twentieth-century trend toward relaxing absolute barriers to suits against governments and officials. By this act, the United States consented to be sued for its agents' torts when private persons would be liable for such torts under the law of the place where the tort occurred. But the act fell short of imposing liability for all torts of United States agents. Generally, the tort must be compensable under state law. In addition, the act excluded liability for a vague category of behavior known as "discretionary functions." As originally enacted, the act also excluded liability for many torts that might arise in the context of law enforcement, including assault, battery, false imprisonment, and false arrest. In 1974, however, the Intentional Tort Amendment Act expanded government liability to include these and other torts. The act continues to exclude liability for defamation, misrepresentation, deceit, and interference with contract rights.

THEODORE EISENBERG

Bibliography

SCHUCK, PETER H. 1983 *Suing Government: Citizen Remedies for Official Wrongs.* New Haven, Conn.: Yale University Press.

FEDERAL TRADE COMMISSION

See: Regulatory Agencies

FEDERAL TRADE COMMISSION v. GRATZ

253 U.S. 421 (1920)

Section 5 of the FEDERAL TRADE COMMISSION (FTC) ACT outlawed, but did not define, "unfair methods of competition." Justice JAMES MCREYNOLDS, for a 7–2 Supreme Court, upheld a contract exclusively binding customers to one supplier. Confining FTC orders against unfair methods to those previously found illegal (a HOLDING reversed in 1934), the courts, not the commission, were henceforth to determine what section 5 meant. Justice LOUIS D. BRANDEIS, joined by Justice JOHN H. CLARKE, dissented. They would have voided this practice, contending that "the Act left the determination to the Commission." They agreed that courts might determine whether—based on FTC findings—a practice was unfair, but they cautioned against overturning commission decisions without substantial reason.

DAVID GORDON

(SEE ALSO: *Regulatory Commissions; Economic Regulation and the Constitution.*)

FEDERAL TRADE COMMISSION ACT

38 Stat. 717 (1914)

When the decisions in STANDARD OIL COMPANY V. UNITED STATES (1911) and *United States v. American Tobacco* (1911) demonstrated that trusts could be dissolved, public calls for a policy regulating combinations and monopolies increased. Responding to President WOODROW WILSON's appeal, Congress created the Federal Trade Commission (FTC) on September 26, 1914. The act created no criminal offenses; the commission would advise business on how to conform to a policy of competition. Congress vested the commission with broad powers of investigation and recommendation regarding enforcement of the ANTITRUST laws, but the act did not cover banks or common carriers. (See INTERSTATE COMMERCE ACT.) Consisting of five commissioners, the FTC is a quasi-judicial tribunal whose findings of fact, if supported by testimony, are binding on the courts and whose decisions are reviewable there.

In furtherance of its goal of fostering competition, section 5 stated that "unfair methods of competition in commerce and unfair or deceptive acts or practices in commerce are hereby declared illegal." Intentionally vague, this provision relied on judicial decisions and experience to give it meaning. By outlawing methods, it improved upon earlier statutes which prohibited only specific acts. Other sections (6 and 9) granted the commission power to require compliance: it could require written responses to inquiries, secure access to corporate books and records, and subpoena witnesses.

DAVID GORDON

(SEE ALSO: *Federal Trade Commission v. Gratz, 1920.*)

FEINER v. NEW YORK

340 U.S. 315 (1951)

Feiner was convicted of BREACH OF THE PEACE for derogatory remarks concerning President HARRY S. TRUMAN which provoked hostility and some threats from a "restless" crowd. Two police officers, fearing violence, ordered Feiner to stop. When he refused, they arrested him. Feiner marked the post-1920s Court's first use of the CLEAR AND PRESENT DANGER rule to uphold the conviction of a speaker. Chief Justice FRED M. VINSON spoke for the majority. JUSTICE FELIX FRANKFURTER'S concurrence urged a balancing approach to replace the danger rule. This case, like TERMINIELLO V. CHICAGO (1949), raised the HOSTILE AUDIENCE problem.

MARTIN SHAPIRO

FELONY

The most common classification of crimes is between MISDEMEANORS and felonies. The Constitution does not control the definitions of felony and misdemeanor; the distinction usually is made by a state statute, or, in a few instances, by state constitution. Federal statutes define the scope of federal felonies and misdemeanors.

A state statute commonly will define a felony as a crime for which a person may be imprisoned in a state penitentiary (rather than a local jail) or as an offense for which a person may be imprisoned for a minimum length of time (such as six months or one year). The distinction between a felony and a misdemeanor may determine whether a police officer had statutory authority to arrest a person without a warrant, which state court has jurisdiction over a criminal charge, or whether the defendant will be subject to punishment under a habitual criminal statute which provides for increased punishment after conviction for several felonies.

Although the distinction between felonies and misdemeanors is an important one under state law, it is not significant for constitutional law purposes. There are three constitutional provisions, applicable to the prosecution of criminal cases, whose meaning or impact is dependent in part upon the seriousness of the crime charged, not upon the felony–misdemeanor distinction. These provisions are the Fifth Amendment GRAND JURY clause, the Sixth Amendment RIGHT TO COUNSEL, and the Sixth Amendment right to TRIAL BY JURY.

The Supreme Court has held that the FOURTEENTH AMENDMENT does not incorporate the Fifth Amendment's grand jury clause; that clause, therefore, is not applicable to state or local criminal prosecutions. In *Ex parte Wilson* (1885) the Supreme Court defined the federal crimes to which the grand jury clause applied as those "punishable by imprisonment at hard labor" in a federal penitentiary. Federal statutes and the FEDERAL RULES OF CRIMINAL PROCEDURE define a federal felony as any federal offense punishable by imprisonment for a term exceeding one year. A federal felony prosecution must be initiated by a grand jury indictment. Someone charged with a federal misdemeanor may be prosecuted based on either an INFORMATION filed by the federal prosecutor or a grand jury indictment.

The Sixth Amendment guarantee of a right to counsel in all criminal prosecutions applies to the states through the Fourteenth Amendment. The Supreme Court has held that the Sixth Amendment also gives an INDIGENT defendant the right to have the government provide him with an attorney in some, but not all, criminal cases. A defendant convicted of a crime cannot be sentenced to imprisonment for even one day unless he has had the opportunity to be represented by counsel at his trial. The government, however, need not appoint attorneys for indigent persons who are convicted of crimes that in fact are not punished by imprisonment. The determination whether the state is required to appoint counsel to represent an indigent defendant is not based on a felony–misdemeanor distinction. A state is not required to provide counsel to an indigent defendant charged with a serious crime so long as the conviction in fact does not result in imprisonment. Any right to an attorney in a case in which incarceration is not imposed would be based upon a case-by-case DUE PROCESS analysis.

The Sixth Amendment also provides that an accused person has a right to "an impartial jury." The jury trial provision of the Sixth Amendment has been incorporated into the Fourteenth Amendment; it governs both state and federal prosecutions. Although the Sixth Amendment refers to the right to a jury trial in "all criminal prosecutions," the Supreme Court has ruled that the accused has a right to a jury trial, rather than a trial before a judge, only when he is charged with an offense that is not "petty." The Court has held that any offense punishable by incarceration for more than six months cannot be deemed "petty." Thus, regardless of the sentence a defendant actually receives, if the defendant is accused of an offense for which there is a possible sentence of more than six months of incarceration, he has a Sixth Amendment right to a trial by jury. The Supreme Court has not explained how courts are to distinguish between "petty" and "nonpetty" offenses where the crime is punishable by no more than six months' imprisonment.

JOHN E. NOWAK

Bibliography

LAFAVE, WAYNE, and ISRAEL, JEROLD 1984 *Criminal Procedure.* St. Paul, Minn.: West Publishing Co.

FERGUSON v. SKRUPA
372 U.S. 726 (1963)

This decision is often cited as a leading modern example of the Supreme Court's permissive attitude toward ECONOMIC REGULATION challenged as a violation of SUBSTANTIVE DUE PROCESS.

Kansas prohibited "the business of debt adjusting" except as an incident of the practice of law. The Court unanimously upheld this statute against a challenge to its constitutionality. Justice HUGO L. BLACK wrote for the Court. Any argument that the business of debt adjusting had social utility should be addressed to the legislature, not the courts. "We refuse to sit as a 'super legislature to weigh the wisdom of legislation.' " The Court had given up the practice, common during the years before WEST COAST HOTEL CO. V. PARRISH (1937), of using "the 'vague contours' of the Due Process Clause to nullify laws which a majority of the Court believed to be economically unwise." Justice Black, unlike many of his brethren, carried this same view of the judicial function into other areas of CONSTITUTIONAL INTERPRETATION; see his dissents in GRISWOLD V. CONNECTICUT (1965) and HARPER V. VIRGINIA BOARD OF ELECTIONS (1966).

In *Ferguson* Justice JOHN MARSHALL HARLAN concurred separately on the ground that the law bore "a rational relation to a constitutionally permissible objective." Apparently Justice Harlan wanted to maintain some level of judicial scrutiny of economic regulations, even if it were only the relaxed RATIONAL BASIS standard, and thought the Black opinion suggested a complete abdication of the judicial role in such cases.

KENNETH L. KARST

FESSENDEN, WILLIAM PITT
(1806–1869)

A Maine lawyer, congressman (1841–1843; 1853–1854), senator (1854–1864; 1865–1869), and secretary of the treasury (1864–1865), William Pitt Fessenden chaired the Senate Finance Committee during the Civil War and later the Joint Committee on Reconstruction. Although sympathetic to many radical goals, Fessenden always demanded strict adherence to constitutional principles. Thus, he opposed aspects of the EMANCIPATION PROCLAMATION, the legal tender acts, the CONFISCATION ACTS, and the TENURE OF OFFICE ACT. Although Senate majority leader, he voted to acquit ANDREW JOHNSON in his 1867 IMPEACHMENT trial, because he did not believe the President had committed an impeachable offense within the meaning of the Constitution.

PAUL FINKELMAN

Bibliography

JELLISON, CHARLES ALBERT 1962 *Fessenden of Maine, Civil War Senator.* Syracuse, N.Y.: Syracuse University Press.

FEW, WILLIAM
(1748–1828)

William Few represented Georgia at the CONSTITUTIONAL CONVENTION OF 1787 and signed the Constitution. He attended the Convention irregularly (leaving to attend Congress), spoke infrequently, and served on only one committee. He afterward served as a senator and federal judge.

DENNIS J. MAHONEY

FIELD, DAVID D.
(1805–1894)

David Dudley Field, older brother of Justice STEPHEN J. FIELD, won a number of important cases before the Supreme Court in his career as a highly successful lawyer, EX PARTE MILLIGAN (1866), *Cummings v. Missouri* (1867), and UNITED STATES V. CRUIKSHANK (1876) among them. His appearance on behalf of Jay Gould and Jim Fisk in the celebrated Erie Railroad scandal brought him popular criticism and charges of misconduct from his peers. He would later represent the Tweed Ring when his free services were rejected by the prosecution. As one biographer remarked, Field "was essentially a protestant, an originator, a breaker of precedents."

Field devoted his last decades to codification of municipal and international law. He also played a fundamental role in reforming the substantive and procedural codes of New York State; those codes would serve as models for many other states. He served as president of the American Bar Association, 1888–1889.

DAVID GORDON

FIELD, STEPHEN J.
(1816–1899)

Stephen Johnson Field is a massive figure in the history of the United States SUPREME COURT. Appointed by ABRAHAM LINCOLN in 1863 following six years of distinguished service on the California Supreme Court, Field remained on the bench until 1897 and established a record for length of tenure since surpassed only by WILLIAM O. DOUGLAS. For two generations he preached a radically new gospel of constitutional interpretation that fused natural law concepts, a theory of adjudication based on formally bounded categories of public power and private right, and a designing foresight about the Court's unique capacity to shape American public life. Field's contributions to American constitutional development are conventionally summed up in the phrase laissez-faire CONSTITUTIONALISM. But his profound impact on the institutional character of the Court outlasted his doctrinal formulations. Field was arguably the Court's first self-conscious "activist," and he was certainly the first Justice to describe judicial protection of substantive rights as a democratic endeavor. "As I look back over the more than a third of a century that I have sat on this bench," Field wrote in his valedictory letter, "I am more and more impressed with the immeasurable importance of this court. Now and then we hear it spoken of as an aristocratic feature of a Republican government. But it is the most Democratic of all. Senators represent their states, and Representatives their constituents, but this court stands for the whole country, and as such it is truly 'of the people, by the people, and for the people. " It was this fundamentally new conception of the Court's position in the American system of government and the manifold ways Field acted upon it during his long career that prompted EDWARD S. CORWIN to describe him as "the pioneer and prophet of our modern constitutional law."

Field's jurisprudence was essentially a constitutional version of the equal rights creed expounded by ANDREW JACKSON in his veto of the bill rechartering the Second Bank of the United States. Field understood democracy in terms of "the natural equal rights of the citizen," particularly equality in the marketplace; he was quick to distinguish the common good of the whole people from the focused demands of interest seekers that sometimes generated legislation favoring some and discriminating against others. Since the Court, like the President, represented "the whole country" rather than a narrow constituency, Field claimed that JUDICIAL REVIEW of legislation was at once the moral equivalent of the executive veto and a consummately democratic power. His two most famous opinions resonated with the substantive concerns of antebellum Jacksonians. The first was designed to protect the rights of the many against legal privileges granted to a few. Dissenting in the SLAUGHTERHOUSE CASES (1873) Field denounced the "odious monopoly" produced by legislative skulduggery in Louisiana and claimed that the newly adopted FOURTEENTH AMENDMENT would become "a vain and idle enactment, which accomplished nothing" if the Court continued to permit state legislatures "to farm out the ordinary avocations of life" to favored corporations. In the second, POLLOCK V. FARMERS LOAN & TRUST CO. (1895), Field resisted a statute that, in his view, was designed to enable the many to steal from the few under color of law. There he attacked the mildly progressive federal tax on incomes as an "assault on capital . . . the stepping stone to others, larger and more sweeping, till our political contests . . . become a war of the poor against the rich; a war constantly growing in intensity and bitterness." If Field had been successful in persuading his colleagues to conceptualize the case as he did, the income tax would have been invalidated not because it was a DIRECT TAX but on the ground that its graduated rates violated the Constitution's requirement that "all duties, imposts and excises shall be uniform throughout the United States." For Field, uniformity mandated equal treatment; the chief defect of the statute was that it created a different rule for rich and poor, thereby violating the first principle of republicanism articulated by his Jacksonian mentors.

Field's penchant for pouring his ideological predispositions into open-ended textual phrases such as "uniform" and "due process" was apparent to colleagues throughout his career. Many were alarmed by his expansive conception of the judicial function; some regarded him as a dangerous man. DAVID DAVIS called him a "damned rascal" in 1866 and HORACE GRAY likened him to a "wild bull" three decades later. HENRY B. BROWN said he was "a man of great determination and indomitable courage, though lacking in judicial temperament." Yet it was impossible to ignore him. What made Field so formidable was his skill in translating the featureless generalities of the Constitution into a coherent system of principled standards. He had an uncanny ability to diagnose recurrent problems almost immediately and to frame rules derived from the COMMON LAW or the structure of the federal system that accommodated his value-laden premises. He anticipated future controversies and supplied mutually consistent solutions to all of them. For Field, these solutions were neither contingent nor variable; they were "true."

Few of the twenty-eight men with whom Field sat on the bench perceived the whole truth in precisely the way he did. But every Justice shared at least some of his premises, and most were willing to articulate one or more of his pet doctrinal formulations in an opinion for the Court. With each new handhold Field secured, however, his colleagues found it increasingly difficult to resist the entire array of rules he had proposed at the outset. The analogies linking each component of his system to the others were very compelling. As late as 1890, Field remained confident that the whole truth, as he understood it, would eventually be embraced by the Court. "[A]ny grave departure from the purposes of the Constitution . . . will not fit harmoniously with other rulings," he explained at the Centennial Celebration of the Organization of the Federal Judiciary. "[I]t will collide with them, and thus compel explanations and qualifications until the error is eliminated. . . . [T]ruth alone is immortal, and in the end will assert its rightful supremacy."

The system of rules Field proposed for integrating the Fourteenth Amendment into the existing corpus of constitutional law was breathtaking in scope. It also had a deceptively simple and, in its day, alluring structure. First, he called for a clear and immutable boundary between the public and private spheres in order to forestall legislation that emptied one pocket only to fill another. Here the operable phrase in the amendment was not due process so much as "take property." Beginning in the *Slaughterhouse Cases,* Field claimed that some businesses were purely private while others were public in "use." Firms that necessarily "held franchises of a public character appertaining to government," such as those that exercised the EMINENT DOMAIN power or occupied the public rivers or public streets, were public in "use." Consequently government might confer monopoly privileges on such firms, subsidize their operations with tax funds, and regulate their rates of charge. But manufacturers, food processors, warehouse operators, and other businesses that did not need to exercise public franchises were purely private. Those businesses had to be open to all entrants as a matter of common right and their operations could be subject neither to price regulations nor to public subsidy. In the GRANGER CASES

(1877) Field added one corollary to this scheme. When government regulated the rates of firms public in "use," he asserted, the prices fixed must be subject to judicial review in order to ensure that service to the public was not "required without reward, or upon conditions amounting to the TAKING OF PROPERTY for PUBLIC USE without compensation." The Court's duty, he said, was "to draw the line between regulation and confiscation."

Field repeatedly claimed that judicial application of these doctrines required no great departure in constitutional interpretation. All the Court had to do was constitutionalize under the Fourteenth Amendment and apply in a systematic fashion the principles of "general constitutional law" articulated by SAMUEL F. MILLER in *Pumpelly v. Green Bay Co.* (1872) and LOAN ASSOCIATION V. TOPEKA (1874). There the Court proscribed exercises of the eminent domain and tax powers that amounted to "robbery," in the one case by designating irreparable injury to property as a taking and in the other by barring public spending "for purposes of private interest instead of public use." When the Court refused to apply the same principles to the POLICE POWER under the Fourteenth Amendment in the *Granger Cases,* Field dissented. "Of what avail is the constitutional provision that no State shall deprive any person of property except by DUE PROCESS OF LAW," he asked, "if the State can, by fixing the compensation which he may receive for its use, take from him all that is valuable in the property?" Beginning in STONE V. FARMER'S LOAN AND TRUST CO. (1886), however, the majority made one concession after another to Field's position. By 1898 only the doctrine of business AFFECTED WITH A PUBLIC INTEREST, which Field considered dangerously protean, remained to be pulled down before "the truth . . . asserted its rightful supremacy."

The second component of Field's Fourteenth Amendment system dealt with intergovernmental relations. His general theory was based on the Jacksonian principle of DUAL FEDERALISM: "a national government for national purposes, local governments for local purposes," and each "sovereign" within its assigned sphere such that neither was dependent upon or subordinate to the other nor, indeed, capable of clashing with it as long as the powers of each were properly defined. Thus Field eagerly joined majorities that imposed implied limitations on Congress's MONETARY POWER in *Lane County v. Oregon* (1869), its taxing power in COLLECTOR V. DAY (1871), and its commerce power in UNITED STATES V. E. C. KNIGHT CO. (1895). Beginning in *Tarble's Case* (1871) he also developed implied limitations on the states' authority to impair the national government's independent energy in the exercise of its "acknowledged powers." Yet Miller, speaking for the majority in the *Slaughterhouse Cases,* claimed that the Fourteenth Amendment threatened to unravel these "main features of the federal system." What frightened Miller most was the assumption that if the Court had JURISDICTION to protect FUNDAMENTAL RIGHTS under the amendment's first section, Congress must have jurisdiction to enact statutes affecting the same rights under the fifth section vesting it with power "to enforce, by appropriate legislation" the amendment's substantive provisions. One reason the majority gutted the PRIVILEGES OR IMMUNITIES clause, then, was to avoid articulating doctrine that might ultimately "fetter and degrade the State governments by subjecting them to the control of Congress."

In Field's view, the *Slaughterhouse* majority was afraid of a phantom, for a STATE ACTION doctrine could stay the hand of Congress without disturbing the Court's jurisdiction. Here the operable phrase in the text was: "No State shall make or enforce any law." The Fourteenth Amendment, he asserted in dissent, only "ordains that [fundamental rights] shall not be abridged by State legislation." "The exercise of these rights . . . and the degree of enjoyment received from such exercise," he added in anticipation of UNITED STATES V. CRUIKSHANK (1876), "are always more or less affected by the condition and the local institutions of the State, or city, or town where he resides." These rights had never been a concern of the United States and the amendment did not make them one. The enabling clause in the fifth section, whatever its meaning, could not constitutionally enlarge the modest accretion to national authority envisioned by the first section. Because the amendment was not a grant of power but a series of limitations on state legislation, moreover, the Court could readily distinguish between national remedies for prohibited state action (laws that were not "true" exercises of the eminent domain, taxing, and police powers reserved to the states) and inappropriate acts of Congress invading the sphere of state authority. In practical application, the amendment would affect the federal system in a way comparable to the clauses of the Constitution forbidding the states from passing BILLS OF ATTAINDER, EX POST FACTO laws, and laws impairing the obligation of contracts.

The WAITE COURT tentatively endorsed the state action doctrine in *Cruikshank,* and invoked it with a vengeance in UNITED STATES V. HARRIS (1883) and the CIVIL RIGHTS CASES (1883). These decisions not only assuaged previous doubts about Congress's authority to use the Fourteenth Amendment as a grant of power but also prompted the Court to reconsider Field's blueprint for judicial intervention in government–business relations. Meanwhile, Field elaborated the third component of his Fourteenth Amendment theory. It addressed what he called INVIDIOUS DISCRIMINATION. Here Field was a singularly important pioneer, for he decided the federal case of first impression on circuit. At issue in *Ho Ah Kow v. Nunan* (1879) was the San Francisco "queue ordinance" requiring county prisoners to have their hair cropped. As it was "universally understood" that the regulation had been designed "to be enforced only against [the Chinese] race," Field explained, the ordinance violated the equal protection clause. This decision, along with Field's 1882 opinion striking down an anti-Chinese laundry ordinance, supplied the conceptual foundations for the Court's ringing proclamation of the antidiscrimination principle in YICK WO V. HOPKINS (1886).

Yet Field's understanding of "invidious discrimination" did not compel state governments to be colorblind. Dissenting in STRAUDER V. WEST VIRGINIA (1880), where the Court invalidated a statute that limited jury service to whites, Field claimed that the equal protection clause dealt only with the CIVIL RIGHTS described in *Ho Ah Kow.* It "leaves political rights . . . and social rights . . . as they stood previous to its adoption." "Civil rights," he explained, "are absolute and personal and [a]ll persons within the jurisdiction of the State, whether permanent residents or temporary sojourners, whether young or old, male or female, are to be equally protected." But nobody in the *Strauder* majority was prepared to hold that the Fourteenth Amendment forbade the states from excluding Chinese aliens, women, or children from the jury box. The conclusion was inescapable that jury service could not be regarded as a "civil right," for which the amendment mandated "universality of the [equal] protection secured," but only as a "political right . . . conditioned and dependent upon the discretion of the elective or appointing power, whether that be the People acting through the ballot, or one of the departments of their government." The "social rights" to which Field only alluded in the *Strauder* stood on a similar footing. The capacity of individuals to marry or to have access to public goods such as libraries and schools had always been regulated by law on the basis of age, sex, race, and citizenship. "Such legislation is not obnoxious to the [equal protection] clause of the 14th Amendment," he said, "if all persons subject to it are treated alike under similar circumstances and conditions."

The *Strauder* majority flatly rejected the classification of rights that Field proposed. "The Fourteenth Amendment makes no attempt to enumerate the rights it is designed to protect," WILLIAM STRONG declared for the Court. "It speaks in general terms, and those are as comprehensive as possible." But once again a Field dissent proved to be prophetic. Three years later, speaking for a unanimous Court in PACE V. ALABAMA (1883), Field held that antimiscegenation laws were not forbidden by the Fourteenth Amendment as long as both parties received the same punishment for their crimes. Equal protection mandated equal treatment, not freedom of choice; antimiscegenation laws restricted the liberty of blacks and whites alike. Underlying this ruling was an unarticulated premise of enormous importance: the legal classification "Negro" was not suspect per se. The doctrine of SEPARATE BUT EQUAL enunciated in PLESSY V. FERGUSON (1896) followed almost as a matter of course, especially after the Court had distinguished "civil rights" from "social rights" under the THIRTEENTH AMENDMENT in the *Civil Rights Cases.* Even Field's distinction between "civil rights" and "political rights" eventually got incorporated into the Court's Fourteenth Amendment jurisprudence, albeit in a form substantially different from what he proposed in *Strauder.* The Waite Court conceded from the outset that jury selection officials might constitutionally employ facially neutral yet impossibly vague tests of good character, sound judgment, and the like. In the absence of state laws expressly restricting participation to whites, JOHN MARSHALL HARLAN explained in *Bush v. Kentucky* (1883), the Court had no choice but to presume that jury commissioners had acted properly. When the "civil right" of equal opportunity to pursue an "ordinary trade" was at issue in *Yick Wo,* however, the Court unanimously invalidated the law not only because it had been administered with "an evil eye and an unequal hand" but also because it lacked adequate standards for controlling the discretion of public officials authorized to license the regulated trade.

Simply to sketch the basic contours of Field's jurisprudence is to suggest the degree to which his views, forged into a coherent system at an astonishingly early date and reiterated with great force throughout his record-shattering tenure on the Court, shaped the course of American constitutional law. His associates resisted the whole "truth," as Field understood it, to the very end, and Harlan predicted that he would spend even the final days with "his face towards the setting sun, wondering . . . whether the Munn case or the eternal principles of right and justice will ultimately prevail." Yet appellate judging in America is inherently a collective enterprise. The remarkable thing about Field's career is not that he failed to win every battle but that he eventually celebrated so many victories when the stakes were so very high. What endured was his claim that the Court was "the most [d]emocratic of all" governmental institutions. By acting on that belief Field not only transformed the character of judicial power in America but also influenced debate on the Court's legitimate role long after the structure of doctrine he helped to forge had been annihilated.

CHARLES W. MCCURDY

Bibliography

CORWIN, EDWARD S. 1909 The Supreme Court and the Fourteenth Amendment. *Michigan Law Review* 7:643–672.

GRAHAM, HOWARD J. 1968 *Everyman's Constitution: Historical Essays in the Fourteenth Amendment, the "Conspiracy Theory," and American Constitutionalism.* Madison: State Historical Society of Wisconsin.

MCCURDY, CHARLES W. 1975 Justice Field and the Jurisprudence of Government–Business Relations. *Journal of American History* 61:970–1005.

SWISHER, CARL B. 1930 *Stephen J. Field: Craftsman of the Law.* Washington, D.C.: Brookings Institution.

FIELD v. CLARK
143 U.S. 649 (1892)

This is a leading case on the subject of DELEGATION OF POWER. The Tariff Act of 1890 authorized the President to suspend its free-trade provisions indefinitely as to countries discriminating against American products. The Supreme Court held, 7–2, that though the act invested the President with discretion, it did not invest him with "legislative power"; Congress had fixed adequate standards for his guidance.

Field is also often cited as a POLITICAL QUESTION precedent. Appellants argued that the enrolled act contained one section that the House of Representatives had not passed. The Court refused to examine this question; the act's transmission by the congressional leadership and its enrollment by the secretary of state conclusively established its content.

LEONARD W. LEVY

FIFTEENTH AMENDMENT
(Framing and Ratification)

In January 1869 adult black males could vote in only twenty states. Blacks had received the franchise in ten states of the South under the Reconstruction Act of March 1867 as part of the price of readmission to the Union set by the Republicans in Congress. Because Republicans also controlled the state government of Tennessee, blacks were enfranchised there. But many lived in the ex-slave border states that had been loyal to the Union, and they were not enfranchised. In the North, most blacks did not have the right to vote; however, there were minor exceptions in those states where the black population was small. The New England states except Connecticut allowed black suffrage, as did four midwestern states, Wisconsin, Nebraska, Minnesota, and Iowa. But especially in the lower North, where most northern blacks lived, white voters in REFERENDUM after referendum had rejected their unrestricted enfranchisement. Indeed in 1868 the issue of black suffrage was thought to be so dangerous and debilitating to the Republican party that at the party's national convention the framers of the platform devised a double standard by endorsing black voting in the South while trying not to antagonize white voters in the North: thus each northern state could decide black suffrage without federal interference, but southern states must accept black voting as a matter of national policy.

In the presidential election of 1868 Republican candidate ULYSSES S. GRANT captured most of the electoral vote and the Republicans retained control of Congress. But beneath the surface the situation was not reassuring. Grant's electoral victory was much greater than his popular vote (only 52 percent). Without the southern black voter Grant would have lost the popular, though not the electoral, vote. In state after state Grant squeaked by with narrow margins. Indeed, a switch of a mere 29,862 votes out of the 5,717,246 cast for the two major party candidates (.52 percent) would have made the Democratic candidate president. Moreover, the Democrats gained seats in the House of Representatives in Washington. And Republican majorities in state after state were slim indeed. Finally, Republican politicians throughout the South reported that little reliance could be placed on the southern black voter in the long run because of strong white influence and intimidation and because of black poverty, illiteracy, and inexperience. Danger signals in the South, defeats in state referenda in the North, and a narrow escape from defeat in the presidential election of 1868 taught the Republicans that their platform pledge to the North had to be ignored. Something must be done by the final session of the Fortieth Congress before the Democrats arrived in force.

The Republicans decided it was necessary to augment their strength by enfranchising more blacks, who could be expected to vote Republican en masse. Although egalitarians had begun the advocacy of black enfranchisement, politicians had made its achievement possible. Two years before, Congress had enfranchised blacks in the South because the Republicans then needed southern black votes to counter southern white votes. Now the Republicans also needed the support of northern and border blacks, especially in closely balanced states, and were willing to run limited risks and promote political reform in order to maintain power.

Therefore, during early 1869 the Republicans in the lame-duck Congress pressed for a constitutional amendment to secure impartial manhood suffrage in every state, thereby avoiding further popular rejection in state referenda. They opted for the usual but more indirect method of having Republican state legislatures that were still in session ratify the amendment. Thus they avoided the risk of possible rejection by special conventions.

The amendment finally passed Congress in late February 1869 after a number of compromises. To secure enough moderate votes, the sponsors had to omit a clause that would have outlawed property qualifications and LITERACY TESTS. Such a clause was dispensable because the tests would affect more Negroes in the South than in the North, and because the proponents of the amendment were intent primarily upon securing the northern Negro voter for the Republican party. For the same reasons, they omitted any provision banning RACIAL DISCRIMINATION in qualifications for officeholding. A provision for federal authority over voter qualifications was defeated, and so the potential for evasion in the southern and border states was left wide open.

The legislative history of the Fifteenth Amendment indicated no triumph of radical idealism but rather served to demonstrate its failure—a fact underscored by the fury and frustration of that band of radicals who had favored idealistic and uncompromising reforms. A moderate measure, the amendment had the support of those who understood the limits of party power and who had practical goals in mind; they took into account the possible difficulties of ratification. Time was short, the pressures were great, and the options were limited.

The primary objective—the enfranchisement of blacks in the northern and border states—was clearly understood, stated, and believed by the politicians, the press, and the people during the time when the amendment was framed and then considered by the state legislatures. As the abolitionist organ, the *National Anti-Slavery Standard,* declared, "evenly as parties are now divided in the North, it needs but the final ratification of the pending Fifteenth Amendment, to assure . . . the balance of power in national affairs." A black newspaper, the Washington *New National Era,* predicted the same for the border states. Indeed, most newspapers both in the North and in the South during 1869 and 1870 unequivocally, incontrovertibly, and repeatedly spoke of the Republican objective of ensuring party hegemony by means of the Fifteenth Amendment. Moreover, congressmen and state legislators, in arguing for passage and ratification, referred again and again to the partisan need for those votes. The southern black, already a voter, was not irrelevant; an important secondary purpose of the amendment was to assure the continuance of black suffrage in the South by forbidding racial discrimination as to the franchise in a virtually unrepealable amendment to the federal Constitution. Still, the anticipated importance of the black electorate in the North and in the borderland was clearly the overriding concern.

To be sure, the political motives of many Republican politicians were not incompatible with a sincere moral concern. The idealistic motive reinforced the pragmatic one: there was no conflict at the outset between the ideal and the practical or between the interests of the black electorate and those of the Republican party. A radical Republican congressman declared, "party expediency and exact justice coincide for once." A black clergyman from Pittsburgh observed that "the Republican Party had done the negro good but they were doing themselves good at the same time." Indeed, the amendment as framed was both bold and prudent: bold in enfranchising blacks despite concerted opposition and in ordering change by establishing constitutional guidelines; prudent in adapting methods to circumstances so that the amendment would not only pass Congress but also be ratified by the states.

Although the struggle over ratification lasted only thirteen months, it was hard going and the outcome was uncertain until the very end. To be sure, ratification was easy in safe Republican territory (New England and most of the Middle West) and in the South where Republican legislators did their duty. But the fight was especially close in the Middle Atlantic states and in Indiana and Ohio, where the parties were competitive and a black electorate had the potential for deciding victory or defeat. In the Democratic border states and on the Pacific Coast, where racial feeling ran high, Republicans feared that pushing the amendment would lose them votes; so they refrained from pressing for ratification in these regions. Nevertheless, in clear-cut conflicts of interest between state and national Republican party organizations, the national party was everywhere victorious. Mutinies in Rhode Island and Georgia were suppressed. The amendment had the backing of the Grant administration, with its rich patronage. By endorsing the amendment in his inaugural address, Grant placed the indispensable prestige of the presidency behind it; he then went beyond pronouncements by swinging Nebraska to ratify it. Those Republican politicians who held or aspired to hold national office added the weight of their influence. As one Ohioan advised, "By hook or by crook you must get the 15th amendment through or we are gone up."

The Fifteenth Amendment became law on March 30, 1870. Republican euphoria followed the hard battle for ratification. Grant, in his message to Congress, wrote that the amendment "completes the greatest civil change and constitutes the most important event that has occurred since the nation came to life." Blacks everywhere celebrated; they regarded the Fifteenth Amendment as political salvation, as a solemn written guarantee that would never be abridged. They now felt secure, protected by both the vote and the "long strong arm of the Government." Whites believed that since the Negro was now a citizen and a voter, he could take care of himself. Antislavery societies throughout the country disbanded, now confident that equality before the law was sufficient and that in any event, "no power ever permanently wronged a voting class without its own consent." But subsequent events made a mockery of such predictions in the South where Democrats denied blacks the franchise for almost a century.

WILLIAM GILLETTE

Bibliography

GILLETTE, WILLIAM (1979)1981 *Retreat from Reconstruction, 1869–1879.* Baton Rouge: Louisiana State University Press.

——— (1965)1969 *The Right to Vote: Politics and the Passage of the Fifteenth Amendment.* Baltimore: Johns Hopkins University Press.

MITTRICK, ROBERT 1985 *A History of Negro Voting in Pennsylvania during the Nineteenth Century.* Unpublished Ph.D. dissertation, Rutgers University, chap. 5.

FIFTEENTH AMENDMENT
(Judicial Interpretation)

The judicial interpretation of the Fifteenth Amendment has been closely intertwined with that of the FOURTEENTH AMENDMENT, largely in a Southern context. Within a year of ratification (1870) Congress passed three FORCE ACTS forbidding both public and private interference with voting on the basis of race or color. Federal officials tried hard at first to enforce these laws, but they were daunted by hostility in the South and growing indifference in Congress and the Supreme Court. Prosecutions dropped sharply in 1874; Reconstruction ended in 1877; the Jim Crow era of systematic SEGREGATION began around 1890; and the conspiracy provisions of the Force Acts were dropped in 1894.

From Reconstruction to World War I the Supreme Court showed more ingenuity in voiding VOTING RIGHTS actions than in upholding them. Although it was willing, under Article I, section 4, to uphold convictions and damage awards for ballot box fraud in federal elections, as in EX PARTE YARBROUGH (1884), it would not allow INDICTMENTS for conspiracy to bribe, even in federal elections as in JAMES V. BOWMAN (1903). It steadfastly refused to uphold convictions for private interference with voting rights in state or local elections in UNITED STATES V. REESE (1875) and UNITED STATES V. CRUIKSHANK (1876), or to uphold civil actions for a state official's refusal to register blacks, in *Giles v. Teasley* (1904).

The Court did shrug off arguments in *Myers v. Anderson* (1915) that the Fifteenth Amendment was itself void for diluting the votes of enfranchised whites and thereby depriving their states of equal suffrage in the Senate without their consent. But it did almost nothing to thwart the new franchise restrictions of the Jim Crow era—literacy, property, POLL TAX, residence, character, and understanding tests—designed to cull black and upcountry white voters. (See WILLIAMS V. MISSISSIPPI, 1898.) Only in GUINN V. UNITED STATES (1915) did it strike down a GRANDFATHER CLAUSE exempting descendants of 1867 voters from Oklahoma's LITERACY TEST—without, however, striking down the test itself. *Guinn* had no practical impact on voting registration, but it was important for serving notice that the Fifteenth Amendment bars subtle as well as blatant discrimination.

The Court moved against white PRIMARY ELECTIONS with more deliberation than speed. Party primary elections emerged in response to the regional party monopolies, Republican in the North, Democratic in the South, which followed the "realigning" election of 1896. By World War I, primaries were universal. The dominant party's nomination became the choice that counted, and general elections merely rubber-stamped the dominant party's nominee. This trend was earliest and most pronounced in the South. It weakened party discipline, lowered turnout drastically in general elections, strengthened the dominance of plantation whites, and froze out blacks almost completely.

Blacks challenged this exclusion in a famous series of Texas cases. In NIXON v. HERNDON (1927) and NIXON v. CONDON (1932) NAACP attorneys successfully attacked statutes barring blacks, and letting the parties bar blacks, from voting in primary elections. Counsel for both sides in *Herndon* argued the Fifteenth Amendment, but Justice OLIVER WENDELL HOLMES, speaking for a unanimous Court, found the statute instead a "direct and obvious infringement of the Fourteenth." The Court followed this precedent in *Condon.*

In attacking the discriminatory law under the Fourteenth, rather than the denial of a voting right under the Fifteenth, the Court ignored its earlier view that the pertinent section of the Fourteenth was not intended to protect voting rights. (See MINOR v. HAPPERSETT, 1875.) It also left Texas free to repeal the *Condon* statute, while permitting the Democrats to exclude blacks legally through their own "private" action. (See GROVEY v. TOWNSEND, 1935.)

The Court returned to the Fifteenth Amendment to overrule *Grovey* in SMITH v. ALLWRIGHT (1944), finding STATE ACTION in laws governing the timing and conduct of primary elections and by the "fusing [in UNITED STATES v. CLASSIC (1941)] of primary and general elections into a single instrumentality for the choice of officers." Later, in TERRY v. ADAMS (1953), the Court extended this concept of "fusion into a single instrumentality" to invalidate a whites-only "preprimary" election used by the Jaybird party since 1889 to capture Democratic nominations in a Texas county.

Without the white primary, segregationist whites had only franchise restrictions to block black votes. These restrictions had reduced black registrations by a third in the nineteenth century, but they had only limited and temporary effect by the 1950s. Black literacy was up, and only three of the eleven Southern states—Alabama, Mississippi, and Louisiana—retained blatantly discriminatory literacy tests. These the Court struck down, along with nondiscriminatory tests where blacks had been segregated in inferior schools.

Congress greatly aided in expanding the black vote with judicial protection in the CIVIL RIGHTS ACTS OF 1957, 1960, and 1964, and especially with the VOTING RIGHTS ACT OF 1965, which authorized suspension of state literacy and character tests and provision of federal examiners to register blacks where discrimination was found. In 1970, Congress wholly forbade literacy tests as a condition on voting in state elections.

Though the Court took almost seventy-five years to give the Fifteenth Amendment much practical effect, its interventions since World War II have greatly changed both the constitutional and political landscapes. *Smith v. Allwright,* with its broad reading of the Fifteenth Amendment looking through form to substance foreshadowed such great Fourteenth Amendment cases as SHELLEY v. KRAEMER (1948) and BROWN v. BOARD OF EDUCATION (1954). GOMILLION v. LIGHTFOOT (1960), which struck down a racial GERRYMANDER under the Fifteenth Amendment, was a bridge to BAKER v. CARR (1962).

Opening the primaries and the franchise to blacks brought them out of political exile. Black registration in the South, only five percent in 1940, grew to twenty-eight percent in 1960 and sixty-three percent in 1976, narrowing the gap between black and white registrations from forty-four percent to five percent. Black elected officials in the South increased from fewer than 100 to more than 1,000. White politicians stopped waving ax handles, standing in the doorways of segregated schools, and using terms like "burrhead" in public debate. The Court's enforcement of the Fifteenth Amendment may properly be described as late, but not little.

WARD E. Y. ELLIOTT

Bibliography

ELLIOTT, WARD E. Y. 1975 *The Rise of Guardian Democracy: The Supreme Court's Role in Voting Rights Disputes, 1845–1969.* Cambridge, Mass.: Harvard University Press.

KEY, V. O., JR. 1949 *Southern Politics.* New York: Knopf.

KOUSSER, J. MORGAN 1974 *The Shaping of Southern Politics: Suffrage Restriction and the Establishment of the One-Party South, 1880–1910.* New Haven, Conn.: Yale University Press.

LAWSON, STEVEN F. 1976 *Black Ballots: Voting Rights in the South, 1944–1969.* New York: Columbia University Press.

FIFTH AMENDMENT

See: Double Jeopardy; Due Process of Law; Eminent Domain; Right Against Self-Incrimination; Taking of Property

FIGHTING WORDS

In CHAPLINSKY v. NEW HAMPSHIRE (1942) the Supreme Court upheld the conviction of a Jehovah's Witness who called a policeman "a God damned racketeer" and "a damned Fascist," holding that "fighting words"—face-to-face words plainly likely to provoke the average addressee to fight—were not protected by constitutional free speech guarantees. Viewed narrowly, the fighting words doctrine can be seen as a per se rule effectuating the CLEAR AND PRESENT DANGER principle, relieving the government of proving an actual INCITEMENT by taking the words themselves as decisive. Taken broadly, *Chaplinsky* strips "four-letter words" of free speech protection. "It has been well observed," Justice FRANK MURPHY said, "that such utterances are no essential part of any exposition of ideas, and are of such slight social value as a step to the truth that any benefit that may be derived from them is clearly outweighed by the social interest in order and morality."

The modern tendency of the Court has been to extend partial FIRST AMENDMENT protection to even the "excluded" areas of speech. To the extent that *Chaplinsky* refuses protection to four-letter words because they offend against taste or morality, it has been limited by recent decisions such as COHEN V. CALIFORNIA (1971), *Gooding v. Wilson* (1972), and *Rosenfeld v. New Jersey* (1972). The Justices appear to have been engaging in ad hoc analysis of what persons in what situations are entitled to a measure of protection from the shock to their sensibilities generated by words that, in the language of *Chaplinsky*, "by their very utterances inflict injury."

The shock aspect of four-letter words is obviously related to the shock element in OBSCENITY. In FCC V. PACIFICA FOUNDATION (1978) the Court upheld FCC regulation of "indecent" broadcasting that involved "patently offensive" four-letter words but was not obscene. While admitting that the words in question would warrant constitutional protection under certain circumstances, the Court held that in view of their capacity to offend, their slight social value in the conveying of ideas, and the intrusive character of speech broadcast into the home, their repeated use might constitutionally be banned at least in time slots and programming contexts when children might be listening.

The recent decisions suggest that outside the direct incitement to violence context the Court is prepared to balance PRIVACY against speech interests where four-letter words are at issue. Where statutes go beyond prohibiting incitement to violence, and also bar cursing or reviling, or using opprobrious, indecent, lascivious, or offensive language, they are likely to be held unconstitutionally vague or overbroad. (See *Lewis v. New Orleans*, 1974.)

MARTIN SHAPIRO

(SEE ALSO: *Freedom of Speech; Balancing Test.*)

Bibliography

KONVITZ, MILTON 1978 *Fundamental Liberties of a Free People.* Chap. 17. Westport, Conn.: Greenwood Press.

SHEA, THOMAS 1975 Fighting Words and the First Amendment. *Kentucky Law Journal* 63:1–22.

FILLMORE, MILLARD
(1800–1874)

A Buffalo, New York, lawyer and Whig politician, Millard Fillmore was elected vice-president in 1848 and became President when ZACHARY TAYLOR died in 1850. Unlike Taylor, Fillmore enthusiastically supported passage of the COMPROMISE OF 1850 which he believed necessary to preserve the Union. His administration was particularly vigorous in enforcing the Fugitive Slave Law through the Christiana Treason Trials, and prosecutions of those involved in the Shadrach Rescue, the Jerry Rescue, and the abortive Sims Rescue. Fillmore was not renominated by the Whigs in 1852 and ran unsuccessfully as a Know-Nothing in 1856.

PAUL FINKELMAN

Bibliography

RAYBACK, ROBERT J. 1959 *Millard Fillmore: Biography of a President.* Buffalo, N.Y.: Buffalo Historical Society.

FINAL JUDGMENT RULE

By congressional statute the federal courts of appeals are permitted, in the usual case, to exercise their APPELLATE JURISDICTION only over final judgments of the district courts. An additional provision authorizes review of district court orders granting, denying, or otherwise dealing with INJUNCTIONS, and of certain other INTERLOCUTORY orders less frequently given. Furthermore, a district judge may certify an interlocutory order for review by the court of appeals, and that court can, in its discretion, review such a nonfinal order. The Supreme Court's appellate jurisdiction over cases coming from the state courts also is limited to final judgments of those courts. (The Supreme Court is not limited by this final judgment rule in hearing cases coming to it from a federal court of appeals; it can grant CERTIORARI in any case "in" the court of appeals.)

The final judgment rule, which aims at avoiding piecemeal appellate review, has so many judge-made exceptions that it has aptly been called "a permeable screen." Thus, a "collateral" order, unrelated to the merits of the case, may be reviewed if it presents an issue that might never be decided if the final judgment rule were strictly applied. Similarly, if rigorous application of the rule would do irreparable injury to some important federal policy, the Supreme Court has held that a nonfinal order can be reviewed. And in UNITED STATES v. NIXON (1974) the Court permitted review of a nonfinal order of a district court ordering the President of the United States to turn over the "Watergate tapes," in order to avoid putting the President to the "unseemly" choice between obeying the order and refusing and being cited for contempt. It is hard to avoid the conclusion that the final judgment "rule" has been made into a technique for allowing review of those interlocutory orders the Supreme Court thinks should be reviewed even though they are not final.

KENNETH L. KARST

Bibliography

WRIGHT, CHARLES ALAN 1983 *The Law of Federal Courts,* 4th ed. Pages 697–717, 739–743. St. Paul, Minn.: West Publishing Co.

FIREFIGHTERS LOCAL UNION NO. 1784 v. STOTTS
467 U.S. 561 (1984)

The City of Memphis, Tennessee, laid off white firefighters with more seniority to protect the positions of less senior blacks who had been employed under a "race conscious" AFFIRMATIVE ACTION plan. The white firefighters sued, alleging that their seniority rights were explicitly protected by the CIVIL RIGHTS ACT OF 1964.

Justice BYRON R. WHITE, writing for the Supreme Court's majority, agreed, noting that "mere membership in the disadvantaged class is insufficient to warrant a seniority award; each individual must prove that the discriminatory practice had an impact on him." White thus affirmed the proposition, which is explicit from the plain language of Title VII, that rights vest in the individual and not in the racial class, and that this fact demands a close fit between injuries and remedies. White's opinion raises some doubt about the power of courts to fashion classwide remedies where, as in race-conscious affirmative action plans, benefited individuals are not required to demonstrate individual injury. This case signals an important move toward the restoration of the principle that rests at the core of liberal jurisprudence—that rights adhere to the individual, and not to the racial class that one happens to inhabit.

EDWARD J. ERLER

FIRST AMENDMENT

The First Amendment today protects the overlapping realms of the spirit—of belief, emotion, and reason—and of political activity against intrusion by government. The amendment directly forbids federal violation of the individual's RELIGIOUS LIBERTY, freedom of expression, FREEDOM OF ASSEMBLY, and associated political liberties. The amendment indirectly forbids state violation because it is held to be incorporated into the FOURTEENTH AMENDMENT's restrictions upon the powers of the states. The body of law presently defining First Amendment liberties has been shaped not so much by the words or intent of the original sponsors as by the actors and events of much later history. The story is one of the continual expansion of individual freedom of expression, of the FREEDOM OF THE PRESS, and, until 1980, of widening SEPARATION OF CHURCH AND STATE.

The CONSTITUTIONAL CONVENTION OF 1787 saw no need to include guarantees of religious liberty, FREEDOM OF SPEECH, or other human rights. Most of the Framers believed in some such rights but supposed that the powers proposed for the new federal government were so severely limited by specific enumeration as to leave scant opportunity for either Congress or President to threaten individual liberty. The threats would come from state law and state governments. For protection against these, the Framers looked to the constitutions of the individual states. In the struggle for RATIFICATION OF THE CONSTITUTION, however, those who feared abuse of federal power exacted an undertaking that if the proposed Constitution were ratified by the states, the first Congress would be asked to propose amendments constituting a BILL OF RIGHTS. The First Amendment is thus the first and most far-reaching of the ten articles of amendment submitted by JAMES MADISON, proposed by Congress, and ratified by three-quarters of the states in 1791 solely as restrictions upon the new federal government, the powers of which were already severely limited.

The assumption that the amendment would have only a narrow function made it possible to ignore fundamental differences that would produce deep divisions more than a century later, after the amendment had been extended to the several states. The colonists held a variety of religious beliefs, though nearly all were Christian and a majority were Protestant. Whatever the limits of their tolerance back home in their respective states where one church was often dominant, they had reason to understand that the coherence of the federal union could be fixed only if the new federal government were required to respect the free exercise of religion. The men of South Carolina with their state-established religion and of Massachusetts with religion appurtenant to their state government could therefore support a prohibition against any *federal* ESTABLISHMENT OF RELIGION shoulder to shoulder with the deist THOMAS JEFFERSON and other eighteenth-century rationalists who opposed any link between church and state. Similarly, in applying ROGER WILLIAMS's vision of "the hedge or wall of separation between the garden of the church and the wilderness of the world," there was originally no need to choose between his concept of protection for the church against the encroachments of worldly society and Jefferson's concept of protection for the state against the encroachments of religion.

The conditions and political assumptions of 1791 also made it easy to guarantee "the freedom of speech or of the press" without accepting or rejecting the Blackstonian view that these guarantees bar only licensing and other previous restraints upon publication, leaving the government free to punish SEDITIOUS LIBELS and like unlawful utterances. Because the original amendment left the states unhampered in making and applying the general body of civil and criminal law, except as the people of each state might put restrictions into its own constitution, there was no need to consider how the First Amendment would affect the law of LIBEL and slander, the power of the judges to punish CONTEMPT of court, or the operation of laws punishing words and demonstrations carrying a threat to the public peace, order, or morality. Such questions could and would arise only after the First Amendment was extended to the states.

The fulcrum for extending the First Amendment to the states was set in place in 1868 by the adoption of the Fourteenth Amendment, which provides in part: ". . . nor shall any State deprive any person of life, liberty or property without DUE PROCESS OF LAW."

The effects of the new amendment upon religious and political liberty and upon freedom of expression were slow to develop. As late as 1922 the Court declared in *Prudential Insurance Co. v. Cheek* that "neither the Fourteenth Amendment nor any other provision of the Constitution of the United States imposes upon the States any restrictions about 'freedom of speech.' " Within another decade, however, the First Amendment's guarantee of freedom of expression had been incorporated into the Fourteenth by judicial interpretation. INCORPORATION of the other clauses, including the prohibition against laws "respecting an establishment of religion," followed somewhat later. Today the First Amendment restricts both state and federal governments to the same extent and in the same fashion.

Yet the historic sequence is important. Many questions of First Amendment law cannot be resolved truly in terms of the original intention because the questions could not arise while the original assumption held. Resolution of the issues was thus postponed until the middle decades of the twentieth century, an era in which liberalism, secularism, and individualism dominated American jurisprudence.

Disparate strains of thought were merged even in the writing of the First Amendment. Subsequent events, including current controversies, have poured new meaning into the words, yet the juxtaposition of the key phrases still tells a good deal about the chief strains in the philosophy underpinning and binding together guarantees of several particular rights.

The Framers put first the prohibition against any law "respecting an establishment of religion or prohibiting the free exercise thereof." The sequence attests the primacy ascribed to religion. The colonists belonged to diverse churches. Many had fled to the New World to escape religious oppression. Rigid though some might be in their own orthodoxy, probably a majority rejected the imposition of belief or the use of government to stamp out heresy. Certainly, they rejected use of federal power.

It was natural for the authors of the amendment to link "the freedom of speech, or of the press" with freedom of religious belief and worship. The one church was breaking up in late sixteenth- and seventeenth-century Britain. New faiths were emerging based upon individual study of the Holy Word. The man or woman who has discovered the road to salvation has a need, even feels a duty, to bring the gospel to others. Liberty of expression benefits more than the speaker. Suppression would deny the opportunity to hear and read the word of God, and thus to discover the road to salvation. Modern legal analysis recognizes the importance of the hearers' and readers' access to information and ideas in cases in which the author's interest lacks constitutional standing or would, if alone involved, be subject to regulation. (See LISTENERS' RIGHTS.)

Concern for a broader spiritual liberty expanded from the religious core. The thinking man or woman, the man or woman of feeling, the novelist, the poet or dramatist, and the artist, like the evangelist, can experience no greater affront to his or her humanity than denial of freedom of expression. The hearer and reader suffer violation of their spiritual liberty if they are denied access to the ideas of others. The denial thwarts the development of the human potential, the power and responsibility of choice. Although concerned chiefly with religion, John Milton stated the broader concern in *Areopagitica* (1644), the single most influential plea, known to the Framers, for unlicensed access to the printing press.

The Enlightenment gave the argument a broader, more rationalistic flavor. Thomas Jefferson and other children of the Enlightenment believed above all else in the power of reason, in the search for truth, in progress, and in the ultimate perfectibility of man. Freedom of inquiry and liberty of expression were deemed essential to the discovery and spread of truth, for only by the endless testing of debate could error be exposed, truth emerge, and men enjoy the opportunities for human progress.

After John Stuart Mill one should perhaps speak only of the ability to progress *toward truth,* and of the value of the process of searching. The compleat liberal posits that he has not reached, and probably can never reach, the ultimate truth. He hopes by constant search—by constant open debate, by trial and error—to do a little better. Meanwhile he supposes that the process of searching has inestimable value because the lessons of the search—the readiness to learn, the striving to understand the minds and hearts and needs of other men, the effort to weigh their interests with his own—exemplify the only foundation upon which men can live and grow together.

It was not chance that America's most eloquent spokesman for freedom of speech, OLIVER WENDELL HOLMES, was also a profound skeptic. Dissenting in ABRAMS V. UNITED STATES (1919), he wrote:

> When men have realized that time has upset many fighting faiths, they may come to believe even more than they believe the very foundations of their own conduct that the ultimate good desired is better reached by free trade in ideas—that the best test of truth is the power of the thought to get itself accepted in the competition of the market, and that truth is the only ground upon which their wishes safely can be carried out. That at any rate is the theory of our Constitution.

On the far side of the First Amendment's guarantee of freedom of speech and of the press one finds the political rights "peaceably to assemble, and to petition the Government for a redress of grievances." (See FREEDOM OF PETITION; FREEDOM OF ASSEMBLY AND ASSOCIATION.) The juxtaposition recalls that freedom of speech and of the press have a political as well as a spiritual foundation; and that the First Amendment protects political activity as part of and in addition to the world of the spirit. American thought, especially in Supreme Court opinions, puts the greater emphasis on the political function of free expression. In GARRISON V. LOUISIANA (1964), for example, the Court explained that "speech is more than self-expression; it is the essence of self-government." ALEXANDER MEIKLEJOHN, perhaps the foremost American philosopher of freedom of expression, argued that whereas other constitutional guarantees are restrictions protecting the citizens against abuse of the powers delegated to government, the guarantees of freedom of speech and of the press hold an absolute, preferred position because they are measures adopted by the people as the ultimate rulers in order to retain control over the government, the people's legislative and executive agents. James Madison, the author of the First Amendment, expressed a similar thought in a speech in 1794. "If we advert to the nature of Republican Government, we shall find that the censorial power is in the people over the Government, and not in the Government over the people."

Despite the eloquence of Justice Holmes, most of us reject the notion that the ability of an idea to get itself accepted in free competition is the best test of its truth. Some propositions seem true or false beyond rational debate. Some false and harmful, political and religious doctrines gain wide public acceptance. Adolf Hitler's brutal theory of a "master race" is sufficient example. We tolerate such foolish and sometimes dangerous appeals not because they may prove true but because freedom of speech is indivisible. The liberty cannot be denied to some persons and extended to others. It cannot be denied to some ideas and saved for others. The reason is plain enough: no man, no committee, and surely no government, has the infinite wisdom and disinterestedness accurately and unselfishly to separate what is true from what is debatable, and both from what is false. To license one to impose his truth upon dissenters is to give the same license to all others who have, but fear to lose, power. The judgment that the risks of suppression are greater than the harm done by bad ideas rests upon faith in the ultimate good sense and decency of free people.

Constitutional law has been remarkably faithful to this philosophy in dealing with both religious and political ideas. In the prosecution of the leader of a strange religious cult for obtaining money by false pretenses, as in UNITED STATES V. BALLARD (1963), the truth or falsity of the leader's claims of miraculous religious experiences is legally irrelevant; conviction depends upon proof that the defendant did not believe his own pretenses. Similarly, although distaste for political ideology may have influenced some of the decisions in the 1920s affirming the convictions of anarchists and communists for advocacy of the overthrow of the government by force and violence, the social, political, or religious activists seeking changes that frighten or annoy all "right-minded" people receive wide protection in their resort to the SIT-INS, PICKETING, marches, mass demonstrations, coarse expletives, affronts to personal and public sensibilities, and other unorthodox vehicles that are so often their most effective means of expression. Such methods of expression may prejudice opposing public and private interests because of the time, place, or manner of communication, regardless of the content of the message; therefore, the amendment allows regulation of particular forms of expression, or of expression at a particular time or place, regardless of content, provided that the restriction protects important interests that cannot be secured by less restrictive means. The courts have typically scrutinized such restrictions, however, with an eye zealous to condemn as unconstitutional any statute or ordinance ostensibly designed to protect the public peace and order but phrased in such loose words as either to deter constitutionally protected expression or to invite discrimination by police, public prosecutors, or judges against radical "troublemakers" and other unpopular minorities. Thus, the American Nazis were secured the right to parade in uniform with swastikas in an overwhelmingly Jewish community many of whose residents had fled the Holocaust.

Distrust of official evaluation of the worth of ideas may also lie behind the decisions barring regulation of political debate in the interest of "fairness" or equality of opportunity. In BUCKLEY V. VALEO (1976), holding that the freedom of speech clause bars laws restricting the dollars that may be spent in a political campaign, the Court observed: "The concept that government may restrict the speech of some elements of our society in order to enhance the relative voice of others is wholly foreign to the First Amendment." Similarly, in MIAMI HERALD V. TORNILLO (1974) the Court held a state law granting a political candidate a right of space in which to reply to a newspaper's attacks upon his or her record to be unconstitutional interference with the editorial freedom of the newspaper. Only in the area of BROADCASTING has the Court thus far recognized that realization of the ideal of free competition of ideas may be irreconcilable with total freedom from regulation in an era in which the public's chief sources of ideas and information are expensive media of mass communication, which are often under monopolistic control. Federal statutes and regulations subject radio and television broadcasters to loosely defined duties to present public issues fairly and to give a degree of access to political candidates and parties.

Although only deliberately false religious or political representations fall wholly outside the First Amendment, the law is more willing to try to separate the worthless from the valuable in the field of literature and the arts. The amendment gives no protection to "obscene" publications. For many years the definition of OBSCENITY was broad enough to cover works containing individual words or short passages that would tend to excite lustful thoughts in a particularly susceptible person. This standard condemned *Lady Chatterley's Lover, An American Tragedy,* and *Black Boy.* From 1930 to 1973 the legal definition of obscenity was gradually narrowed so tightly that many jurists concluded that the First Amendment would protect the most prurient of matter unless it was "utterly without redeeming social value." After 1973 changes in the composition of the Court led to a somewhat less permissive formulation. A work is obscene if a person applying contemporary community standards would find that it appeals to the prurient interest; if it represents or describes ultimate sexual acts, excretory functions, or the genitals in a patently lewd or offensive manner; and if it lacks serious literary, artistic, political, or scientific value. YOUNG V. AMERICAN MINI THEATRES (1976) suggests that explicity sexual books and motion pictures, even when not obscene, may be regulated as to the places and perhaps the time and manner of their distribution in ways that are forbidden for other materials.

These exceptions from the principle that bars any branch of government, including the judiciary, from judging the value of ideas and sensations seem attributable partly to the emphasis that American law puts upon the political values of the First Amendment, partly to the diminishing but still traditional concern of government for public morals, and partly to the actual or supposed links between producers and distributors of commercial pornography and the criminal underworld.

So long as one is dealing with beliefs and expressions separable from conduct harmful to other individuals or the community, the essential unity of the philosophical core of the First Amendment makes it unnecessary to distinguish for legal purposes among religious beliefs, political ideologies, and other equally sincere convictions. In upholding the First Amendment privilege of Jehovah's Witnesses to refuse to join other school children in a daily salute to the United States flag, the Court pointedly refrained from specifying whether the privilege arose under the free exercise clause or the guarantee of freedom of speech: ". . . compelling the flag salute and pledge . . . invades the sphere of intellect and spirit which it is the purpose of the First Amendment to reserve from all official control." (See FLAG SALUTE CASES, 1940, 1943.) Test oaths, like particular beliefs, cannot be required for holding public office or receiving public grants. In upholding the conviction of a Mormon for POLYGAMY in REYNOLDS V. UNITED STATES (1879), despite his plea that the free exercise clause protected him in obeying his religious duty, the Supreme Court sought to erect this distinction between the realm of ideas and the world of material action into a constitutional principle: "Congress was deprived of all legislative power over mere opinion, but was left free to reach actions which were in violation of social duties or subversive of good order."

As the guarantees of the freedoms of speech and press and of free exercise of religion seek to bar hostile governmental intrusion from the realm of the spirit, so do modern interpretations of the establishment clause bar state sponsorship of, or material assistance to, religion. In the beginning religion and established churches were dominant forces in American life. Nearly all men and women were Christians; Protestants were predominant. In South Carolina the Constitution of 1778 declared the "Protestant religion to be the established religion of this State." Church and state were intertwined in Massachusetts. Where there was no official connection, both the laws and practices of government bore evidence of benevolent cooperation with the prevailing creeds. SUNDAY CLOSING LAWS were universal. Oaths were often required of state officials. Legislative sessions began with prayer. The crier in the United States Supreme Court still begins each session by invoking divine blessing. The coinage states, "In God We Trust." Church property was and remains exempt from taxation. As public education spread, prayers and Bible-reading became the first order of each school day.

These traditional links between church and state were challenged after incorporation of the First Amendment into the Fourteenth Amendment, not only by anticlerical secularists but also by religious minorities whose members were set apart by official involvement in religious practices and who were fearful that their isolation would hamper full assimilation into all aspects of American life and might stimulate INVIDIOUS DISCRIMINATION. The Supreme Court was then forced to choose among the competing strains of religious and political philosophy whose adherents had agreed only that the federal government, but not the States, should be barred from "an establishment of religion." The majority's inclination during the years 1945–1980 toward Jefferson's strongly secular, anticlerical view of the wall of separation between church and state led to two important lines of decision.

One line bars both state and federal governments from giving direct financial aid to sectarian primary and secondary schools even though the same or greater aid is given to the public schools maintained by government. The decisions leave somewhat greater latitude not only for aid to parents but also to include religious institutions in making grants for higher education. (See GOVERNMENT AID TO SECTARIAN INSTITUTIONS.)

The second important line of decisions required discontinuance of the widespread and traditional practice of starting each day in the public schools with some form of religious exercise, such as saying an ecumenical prayer or reading from the Bible. The latter decisions provoked such emotional controversy that in the 1980s, more than two decades after the decisions were rendered, fundamentalist groups were actively pressing for legislation abolishing the Supreme Court's JURISDICTION to enforce the establishment clause in cases involving school prayer, thus leaving interpretation of the clause to the vagaries of judges in individual states. (See RELIGION IN PUBLIC SCHOOLS.)

Even though the line between the realm of the spirit and the world of material conduct subject to government regulation is fundamental to the jurisprudence of the First Amendment, the simple line between belief and conduct drawn in the polygamy cases was too inflexible to survive as a complete constitutional formula. Religious duties too often conflict with the commands of civil authority. Conversely, the public has compelling interests in the world of conduct that sometimes cannot be secured without interference with the expression of ideas.

Two cases suggest the line limiting constitutional protection for religious disobedience to the commands of the state. In WISCONSIN V. YODER (1972) the Supreme Court held that the free exercise clause secured Amish parents the privilege of holding fourteen- and fifteen-year-old children out of high school contrary to a state compulsory attendance law but pursuant to their religious conviction that salvation requires simple life in a church community apart from the world and worldly influence. The Court's constitutional, judicial duty—the Court said—required balancing the importance of the interests served by the state law against the importance to believers of adherence to the religious practice in question. Striking such a balance, the Court held in NEGRE V. LARSEN (1971) that a faithful Roman Catholic's belief that the "unjust" nature of the war in Vietnam required him to refuse to participate did not excuse his refusal to be inducted into the armed forces.

When belief is invoked to justify otherwise unlawful conduct, it may become significant that the First Amendment speaks of the free exercise of "religion," but not of other kinds of belief held with equal sincerity. In UNITED STATES V. SEEGER (1965) the Court skirted establishment clause questions by refusing to make any distinction between the teachings of religion and other moral convictions for the purposes of the Selective Service Act. That act exempted from military service CONSCIENTIOUS OBJECTORS opposed to war in any form by reason of their "religious training and belief" and defined such belief as one "in relation to a Supreme Being involving duties superior to those arising from any human relation." A majority held that, despite the references to religion and a belief in a Supreme Being, the exemption extended "to any belief that occupies a place in the life of its possessor parallel to that filled by the orthodox belief in God of one who clearly qualifies for the exemption." In the *Yoder* case, on the other hand, the opinion of the Court by Chief Justice WARREN E. BURGER, calling upon the example of Henry D. Thoreau, stated that a "philosophical and personal" belief "does not rise to the demands of the Religion Clauses." Perhaps this declaration of orthodoxy puts an end to the question, but in an age of subjectivism it is likely to press for fuller debate and deliberation.

Where religious objectors seek exemption from laws of general application, both federal and state governments must walk a narrow line. On the one hand, the free execise clause may require exception. On the other hand, excepting religious groups from laws of general application may be an unconstitutional "establishment of religion." Here again the decisions call for ad hoc balancing of the individual and public interests affected by the particular legislative act.

The requirement of self-preservation exerts the strongest pressures upon government to violate the realm of the spirit by suppressing the publication of ideas and information. Here, as in other areas, judicial elaboration of the First Amendment has been increasingly favorable to freedom of expression.

The expansion of the freedom by interpretation began within a decade from ratification. WILLIAM BLACKSTONE had taught that the freedoms of speech and press were freedoms from PRIOR RESTRAINTS, such as licensing, and did not bar subsequent liability or punishment for unlawful words, including seditious libels. Dispute arose when Congress enacted a Sedition Act and the Federalist party then in office prosecuted the editors of journals supporting their political opponents, the Jeffersonian Republicans, for publishing false, scandalous, and malicious writings exciting the hatred of the people. (See ALIEN AND SEDITION ACTS.) Thomas Jefferson and James Madison led the attack upon the constitutionality of the Sedition Act by drafting the VIRGINIA AND KENTUCKY RESOLUTIONS declaring that the act violated the First Amendment. The lower federal courts followed the orthodox teaching of Blackstone, upheld the act, and convicted the Republican editors. Jefferson pardoned them after his election to the presidency. Still later, Congress appropriated funds to repay their fines. Events thus gave the speech and press clauses an interpretation extending the guarantees beyond mere prohibition of previous restraints. The Supreme Court subsequently ratified the teaching of history.

The modern law defining freedom of expression began to develop shortly after World War I when pacifists and socialists who made speeches and published pamphlets urging refusal to submit to conscription for the armed forces were prosecuted for such offenses as willfully obstructing the recruiting or enlistment service of the United States. In affirming the conviction in SCHENCK V. UNITED STATES (1919), Justice Holmes coined the famous CLEAR AND PRESENT DANGER test: "The question in every case is whether the words used are of such a nature as to create a clear and present danger that they will bring about the substantive evils that Congress has a right to prevent." When Justice Holmes wrote these words, they gave little protection to propaganda held subversive by dominant opinion. Speaking or circulating a paper, the Justice held, is not protected by the First Amendment if the "tendency" of the words and the intent with which they are uttered are to produce an unlawful act. Later, after Justice Holmes's sensitivity to the dangers of prosecution for words alone had been increased by the prosecution of tiny groups of anarchists and communists for holding meetings and distributing political pamphlets in time of peace, criticizing the government, and preaching its overthrow by force and violence, he and Justice LOUIS D. BRANDEIS in a series of dissenting opinions tightened their definition of "clear and present danger" and laid the emotional and philosophical foundation for the next generation's expansion of the First Amendment guarantees. Justice Brandeis's eloquent opinion in WHITNEY V. CALIFORNIA (1927) is illustrative:

> Those who won our independence by revolution were not cowards. They did not fear political liberty. To courageous, self-reliant men, with confidence in the power of free and fearless reasoning applied through the processes of popular government, no danger flowing from speech can be deemed clear and present, unless the incidence of the evil apprehended is so imminent that it may befall before there is opportunity for full discussion. If there be time to expose through discussion the falsehood and fallacies, to avert the evil by the processes of education, the remedy to be applied is more speech, not enforced silence. Only an emergency can justify repression. Such must be the rule if authority is to be reconciled with freedom. Such, in my opinion, is the command of the Constitution. It is, therefore, always open to Americans to challenge a law abridging free speech and assembly by showing that there was no emergency justifying it.
>
> Moreover, even imminent danger cannot justify resort to prohibition of these functions essential to effective democracy, unless the evil apprehended is relatively serious. . . . There must be the probability of serious injury to the state. Among freemen, the deterrents ordinarily to be applied to prevent crime are education and punishment for violations of the law, not abridgement of the rights of free speech and assembly.

In the 1920s a majority of the Justices consistently rejected the views expressed by Justices Holmes and Brandeis. GITLOW V. NEW YORK (1925) held that (1) a state, despite the First Amendment, may punish utterances inimical to the public welfare; (2) a legislative finding that a class of utterances is inimical to the public welfare will be accepted by the Court unless the finding is arbitrary or capricious; (3) the Court could not set aside as arbitrary or capricious a legislative finding that teaching the overthrow of the government by force or violence involves danger to the peace and security of the State because the spark of the utterance "may kindle a fire that, smoldering for a time, may burst into a sweeping and destructive conflagration"; and (4) the Court would not consider the kind or degree of evil threatened by a particular utterance if it fell within a class of utterances found by the legislature to be dangerous to the state.

Ironically, in the very years in which the Court was deferential to legislative restrictions upon radical political expression, the Court was going behind legislative judgment to invalidate minimum wage laws, the regulation of prices and other restrictions upon FREEDOM OF CONTRACT. Beginning in 1937, however, a philosophy of judicial self-restraint became dominant among the Justices. "We have returned to the original proposition that courts do not substitute their social and economic beliefs for the judgment of legislative bodies, who are elected to pass laws," the Court declared in FERGUSON V. SKRUPA (1963). (See JUDICIAL ACTIVISM AND JUDICIAL RESTRAINT.)

Such sweeping denigration of JUDICIAL REVIEW put civil libertarians in a dilemma. On the one hand, the need for consistency of institutional theory cautioned against activist judicial ventures even under the First Amendment. On the other hand, self-restraint would leave much CIVIL LIBERTY at the mercy of executive or legislative oppression. The only logical escape was to elevate civil liberties to a "preferred position" justifying standards of judicial review stricter than those used in judging economic regulations. The dissenting opinions by Justices Holmes and Brandeis seemed to point the way. Three rationales were offered:

(i) In a famous footnote in UNITED STATES V. CAROLENE PRODUCTS COMPANY (1938), Justice HARLAN FISKE STONE suggested that legislation restricting the dissemination of information or interfering with political activity "may be subject to more exacting judicial scrutiny . . . than most other types of legislation" where the legislation "restricts those political processes which can ordinarily be expected to bring about the repeal of undesirable legislation." The rationale fails to justify STRICT SCRUTINY in cases involving religious liberty, freedom of expression in literature, entertainment, and the arts, and other nonpolitical, personal liberties.

(ii) "Personal liberties" deserve more stringent protection than "property rights." The rationale does not explain why holding property is not a preferred "personal" liberty.

(iii) Stricter review is appropriate in applying the First Amendment, and the First when incorporated into the Fourteenth, because the guarantees of the First Amendment are more specific than the general constitutional prohibitions against deprivation of life, liberty, or property without due process of law. The difference in specificity is considerable, but its relevance is less obvious. Justice HUGO L. BLACK stood almost alone in the supposition that the language of the First Amendment could be read literally. (See ABSOLUTISM.) Perhaps the most that can be said is that the Bill of Rights marks particular spheres of human activity for which the Framers deemed it essential to provide judicially enforced protection against legislative and executive oppression. During the debate in Congress, James Madison observed: "If they [the Amendments] are incorporated into the Constitution, independent tribunals of justice will consider themselves in a peculiar manner the guardian of those rights; they will be an impenetrable bulwark against every assumption of power in the Legislative or Executive. . . ."

At bottom all the rationales assert that the ultimate protection for minorities, for spiritual liberty, and for freedom of expression, political activity, and other personal liberties comes rightfully from the judiciary. In this realm the political process, filled with arbitrary compromises and responsive, as in some degree it must be, to short-run pressures, is deemed inadequate to enforce the long-range enduring values that often bespeak a people's aspirations instead of merely reflecting their practices.

Propelled by this judicial philosophy, the Court greatly expanded the First Amendment guarantees of freedom of expression. The Court avowedly adopted the strict Holmes-Brandeis "clear and present danger" test for judging whether prosecution for a subversive utterance is justified by its proximity to activities the government has a right to prevent. The amendment bars restrictions upon the publication of information or ideas relating to public affairs because of harm which the government asserts will result from the impact of the message unless the government shows pressing necessity to avoid an immediate public disaster. The case of the Pentagon Papers (1971) illustrates the principle. (See NEW YORK TIMES V. UNITED STATES.) A consultant to the Department of Defense, cleared for access to classified information, gave copies of highly secret papers describing military operations and decision making to newspapers for publication. The Department of Justice upon instructions from the President asked the courts to enjoin publication, making strong representations that the risks of injury to national interests included "the death of the soldiers, the destruction of alliances, the greatly increased difficulty of negotiation with our enemies, the inability of our diplomats to negotiate . . . and the prolongation of the war." All the weight of these executive representations was insufficient to induce the Court to bar disclosure.

After 1940 the PREFERRED FREEDOMS theory coupled with the incorporation of the First Amendment into the Fourteenth led to Supreme Court review and invalidation or modification of many familiar state statutes and well-established COMMON LAW doctrines restricting or penalizing sundry forms of expression: libel and slander, contempt of court, obscenity, BREACH OF THE PEACE, and laws limiting access to the streets, parks, or other public places for the purposes of expression. A short reference to the law of contempt will illustrate the trend.

The interest in the impartial disposition of judicial business solely upon the evidence and arguments presented in court often conflicts with the interest in free discussion of public affairs. Newspaper editorials and like public pressures upon a judge may improperly influence or seem to influence the disposition of a pending judicial proceeding. In English and early American law such publications were enjoinable and punishable as contempt of court. Today the First Amendment is held to protect such expression. Similarly, the English law and some American decisions treated the pretrial publication of EVIDENCE as contempt of court where, as in a notorious criminal case, the publicity might reach actual or prospective jurors and serve to make it difficult to assure the accused a FAIR TRIAL and a jury verdict based solely upon the evidence presented in the court room. The Supreme Court has now set its face firmly against GAG ORDERS forbidding newspapers to print or broadcast or publicize confessions or other damaging evidence before their admissibility has been determined and they have been received in court.

The heavy emphasis that constitutional law puts upon the role of the First Amendment in the operation of representative government has led some commentators to ascribe special significance to the amendment's particular mention of "the freedom of the press" in addition to the more general guarantee of "the freedom of speech." In a crowded society, newspapers, radio, and television not only are the most effective vehicles for disseminating ideas and information but also have by far the best, if not the only, adequate resources for gathering information concerning the conduct of public affairs by the vast and omnipresent agencies of government. Starting from this premise, proponents of a "structural view" of the First Amendment argue that the special functions of the "fourth estate" entitle its members to special protection. Some of the claims to exemption from laws of general applicability have been patently excessive, such as the claims to exemption from antitrust laws, labor relations laws, and wage and hour regulation. With much greater force but scarcely greater success, the media have claimed that the First Amendment protects reporters in refusal to disclose their sources or give unpublished information to a court or GRAND JURY in compliance with the general testimonial obligation of all citizens. (See REPORTER'S PRIVILEGE.) On the other hand, the near-immunity from liability for libels upon public figures which the Court has granted to the press under the First Amendment has not yet been extended by that Court to other writers and publishers.

The words of the First Amendment move from religion to speech and press and then to the purely political rights of free assembly and petition for redress of grievances. Denials of the rights of assembly and petition have been infrequent. The express mention of a "right of the people peaceably to assemble" is also taken, however, to symbolize the much broader freedom of association that the amendment is held to secure.

The freedom of association thus far held to be protected by the First Amendment, while broad, is narrower than the freedom of individuals to associate themselves for all purposes in which they may be interested, the right debated by Thomas Hobbes and Jean-Jacques Rousseau, on one side, and, on the other side, by JOHN LOCKE. The enactment of labor relations acts securing employees the right to form, join, and assist labor unions made it unnecessary for workers to appeal to a constitutional right of freedom of association. Only the antitrust laws barring unreasonable restraints on competition impose substantial restrictions upon business combinations. In consequence, the decisional law treats association as a necessary and therefore protected incident of other First Amendment liberties: speech, political action, and religious purposes. Associations formed to provide legal services in litigation have been treated as "political" not only in the plausible instances of suits to establish civil liberties and CIVIL RIGHTS but also in the incongruous instances of actions for damages for personal injuries.

Legislative efforts to outlaw associations formed for religious or political purposes have been infrequent, except in the case of the Communist party. A decision in 1961 sustained the power of Congress to require the party to register and disclose its membership as a foreign-dominated organization dedicated to subversion of the government, but the sanctions directed at members, for example, denial of passports and employment in defense facilities, were held unconstitutional. Associations and their members have had more occasion to complain of coerced disclosure under disclosure laws and in LEGISLATIVE INVESTIGATIONS. Prima facie the First Amendment protects privacy of association. Governmentally compelled disclosure must be justified by a showing of important public purpose. Where the unpopularity of the association makes it likely that disclosure will result in reprisals, an even stronger justification may be required. Similarly, a state must justify by a strong public purpose any interference with the conduct of a religious organization's or political party's internal affairs.

Any pressure for substantial new growth in First Amendment interpretation will probably come in three areas. First, the amendment was intended and has nearly always been construed as a prohibition against active government interference. Today government has a near-monopoly upon much information essential to informed self-government. Although FREEDOM OF INFORMATION ACTS may at least partially satisfy the need, there is likely to be pressure to read into the First Amendment's explicit verbal barrier to abridgment affirmative governmental duties to provide access to official proceedings and even to supply otherwise inaccessible information in the government's possession.

Second, in the crowded modern world broadcasters, newspapers, and other media of mass communication dominate the dissemination of information and formation of public opinion. New technologies make prediction hazardous, but the concentration of control over the most influential media appears to be increasing. In this context the old assumption, that the widest dissemination of information and freest competition of ideas can be secured by forcing government to keep hands off, is open to doubt. Such questions as whether the First Amendment permits government regulation to secure fair access to the mass media and whether the amendment itself secures a right of access to media licensed by government may well multiply and intensify.

Third, the electoral influence of political advertising through the mass media, coupled with its high cost, gives great political power to the individuals and organizations that can raise and spend the largest sums of money in political campaigns. Even though decisions already rendered tend to accord political expenditures the same protection as speech, important future litigation over legislative power to limit the use and power of money in elections seems assured. (See CAMPAIGN FINANCING.)

The First Amendment secures the people of the United States greater freedom against governmental interference in the realms of the spirit, intellect, and political activity than exists in any other country. The future may bring shifts of boundary lines and emphasis. A threat to national survival could revive earlier restrictions. Generally speaking, however, the modern First Amendment appears to meet the nation's needs.

ARCHIBALD COX

Bibliography

ABERNATHY, GLENN 1961 *The Right of Assembly and Association.* Columbia: University of South Carolina Press.

CHAFEE, ZECHARIAH, JR. 1948 *Free Speech in the United States.* Cambridge, Mass.: Harvard University Press.

COX, ARCHIBALD 1981 *Freedom of Speech in the Burger Court.* Cambridge, Mass.: Harvard University Press.
EMERSON, THOMAS I. 1970 *The System of Freedom of Expression.* New York: Random House.
HOWE, MARK DEWOLFE 1965 *The Garden and the Wilderness.* Chicago: University of Chicago Press.
KONVITZ, MILTON 1957 *Fundamental Liberties of a Free People: Religion, Speech, Press, Assembly.* Ithaca, N.Y.: Cornell University Press.
LEVY, LEONARD W. 1963 *Freedom of Speech and Press in Early American History: Legacy of Suppression.* New York: Harper & Row.
______ 1972 "No Establishment of Religion: The Original Understanding." Pages 169–224 in *Judgments: Essays in American Constitutional History.* Chicago: Quadrangle.
MEIKLEJOHN, ALEXANDER 1960 *Political Freedom: The Constitutional Powers of the People.* New York: Harper & Bros.
PFEFFER, LEO 1967 *Church, State, and Freedom.* Rev. ed. Boston: Beacon Press.
STOKES, ANSON PHELPS 1950 *Church and State in the United States.* 3 Vols. New York: Harper & Bros.
______ 1964 *Church and State in the United States.* Rev. ed., with Leo Pfeffer. New York: Harper & Row.

FIRST CONTINENTAL CONGRESS, DECLARATIONS AND RESOLVES OF
(October 1, 1774)

The Coercive or Intolerable Acts, passed by Parliament in 1774, threatened colonial self-government. The Boston Port Act sought to starve Boston into paying a tax on tea and making reparations for the "Boston Tea Party." The Massachusetts Government Act altered the charter of the colony: it stripped the lower house of power to choose the upper house, which became the creature of the royal governor; it took from the town meetings the power to choose jurors and vested that power in sheriffs appointed by the governor; and it banned all town meetings not approved by the governor. The Administration of Justice Act allowed the governor to transfer to England trials involving the enforcement of revenue acts. The Quartering Act and the Quebec Act also contained provisions deemed reprehensible by many colonists.

To decide on measures for the recovery of American liberties, delegates from all colonies but Georgia assembled in Philadelphia. After defeating the plan of union proposed by JOSEPH GALLOWAY, the congress adopted a statement that defined the American constitutional position on the controversies with Parliament. Congress grasped a rudimentary principle of FEDERALISM, asserted various American rights, and condemned as "unconstitutional" the Coercive Acts and all the acts by which Parliament sought to raise a revenue in America. Rejecting Parliament's claim of unlimited power to legislate for America, the congress repudiated TAXATION WITHOUT REPRESENTATION and any parliamentary governance over "internal polity" but recognized Parliament's power to regulate "external commerce." Congress also grounded American rights, for the first time, in "the immutable laws of nature" as well as the British CONSTITUTION and COLONIAL CHARTERS. Among the rights claimed were free government by one's own representatives, TRIAL BY A JURY of the VICINAGE according to the COMMON LAW, FREEDOM OF ASSEMBLY and petition (holding town meetings), freedom from standing armies in time of peace, and, generally, the rights to life, liberty, property, and all the liberties of English subjects. The document was a forerunner of the first state bills of rights. (See PENNSYLVANIA CONSTITUTION and VIRGINIA CONSTITUTION.)

LEONARD W. LEVY

Bibliography

BURNETT, EDMUND CODY 1941 *The First Continental Congress.* Pages 33–59. New York: Macmillan.

FIRST NATIONAL BANK OF BOSTON v. BELLOTTI
435 U.S. 765 (1978)

Although the Supreme Court had extended FIRST AMENDMENT protections to newspapers that were organized as CORPORATIONS, this was the first case to hold explicitly that the FREEDOM OF SPEECH was not a "purely personal" right such as the RIGHT AGAINST SELF-INCRIMINATION and so might be claimed by corporations. In this case and in VIRGINIA STATE BOARD OF PHARMACY V. VIRGINIA CITY CONSUMER COUNCIL (1976), the Justices adopted the position that where there is a willing speaker, he may be protected by the First Amendment not so much because of his own speech interest but because of the societal interest in maximizing the stock of information upon which the public may draw. Thus a banking corporation was held to have speech rights because limiting its speech would limit the electorate's access to vital information.

After defeat of a REFERENDUM authorizing a personal income tax, which was attributed by some to corporation-funded advertising, Massachusetts adopted a statute forbidding a corporation to spend money for the purpose of influencing the vote on referenda not directly affecting the corporation, including referenda on individual income taxation. In the face of this obvious attempt of protax legislators to muzzle their opponents, Justice LEWIS F. POWELL for the Court had little trouble concluding under a BALANCING TEST that the asserted state interests in preserving the integrity of the electoral process were not compelling and that the statute was not narrowly drawn to protect the interests of stockholders.

The dissent by Justices BYRON R. WHITE, WILLIAM J. BRENNAN, and THURGOOD MARSHALL sounds the theme of a legitimate state interest in limiting the influence of money on elections raised in BUCKLEY V. VALEO (1976). Justice WILLIAM H. REHNQUIST dissented alone on STATES' RIGHTS grounds.

With the recognition of corporate speech rights and the recognition of some First Amendment protection for COMMERCIAL SPEECH, the Court set the stage for a whole new area of freedom-of-speech jurisprudence, particularly in the light of the high levels of corporate institutional and issue advertising engendered by environmental, energy, and deregulation policies. Among the difficult problems are the rights of stockholders who oppose advertised corporate stances and the extent to which laws against false and misleading advertising constitutionally can be applied to advertisements that do more than offer a product for sale.

MARTIN SHAPIRO

FISHER, SYDNEY GEORGE

See: Commentators on the Constitution

FISKE, JOHN
(1842–1901)

A conservative Yankee educated at Harvard, where he later taught, John Fiske was a man of letters who published about a book a year, as many on science, philosophy, and religion as on history. He was essentially a great popularizer. His books were captivatingly written, bold in interpretation, and widely read. His most influential work as a historian was *The Critical Period in American History, 1783–1789* (1888), which vividly depicted the weaknesses and deficiencies of the United States under the ARTICLES OF CONFEDERATION. For Fiske the Constitution was "a Fifth Symphony of statesmanship" that saved the nation from Balkanizing into petty states.

LEONARD W. LEVY

FITZPATRICK v. BITZER
427 U.S. 445 (1976)

This case concerned Congress's power to modify states' ELEVENTH AMENDMENT immunity from suit in federal court. In the 1972 amendments to Title VII of the CIVIL RIGHTS ACT OF 1964, Congress extended Title VII to forbid employment discrimination by state employers. In *Fitzpatrick,* in an opinion by Justice WILLIAM H. REHNQUIST, the Court held that Congress, in exercising its FOURTEENTH AMENDMENT powers, and despite the Eleventh Amendment, could subject states to suit in federal courts for discriminatory behavior. *Fitzpatrick* was an important counterpoint to *Employees v. Department of Public Health and Welfare* (1973) and EDELMAN V. JORDAN (1974), cases that had held that other federal statutes were not meant to abrogate the states' Eleventh Amendment immunity.

THEODORE EISENBERG

FITZSIMONS, THOMAS
(1741–1811)

An Irish-born Roman Catholic and a successful merchant, Thomas FitzSimons signed the Constitution as a Pennsylvania delegate to the CONSTITUTIONAL CONVENTION OF 1787. He spoke infrequently and always in favor of a strong national government to foster and regulate commerce. He served in the first three Congresses under the Constitution, where he supported ALEXANDER HAMILTON's policies.

DENNIS J. MAHONEY

FIVE KNIGHTS' CASE (DARNEL'S CASE)

See: Petition of Right

FLAG DESECRATION

The American flag, as a unique symbol embodying national pride and patriotism, evidences the unity and diversity which the country represents, and the varying ideals and hopes of its people. By the same token, the flag has frequently been used by those who wish to communicate opposition to—or even ridicule of—government policies.

Congress has enacted statutes that prescribe how

the flag may be displayed and disposed of, and how and for what purposes it may be used. Many state laws prohibit flag "desecration" (casting "contempt" on a flag by "mutilating, defacing, defiling, burning or trampling upon" it) and "improper use" of flags (placing on a flag "any word, figure, mark, picture, design, drawing or advertisement").

In *Halter v. Nebraska* (1907) the Supreme Court upheld a state statute prohibiting flag desecration and use of the flag for advertising purposes. But that decision was rendered twenty years before the Court applied the FIRST AMENDMENT to the States, and it was not dispositive when protesters later challenged the constitutionality of flag desecration statutes.

In *Smith v. Gorguen* (1973), the Court reversed a conviction for wearing an American flag on the seat of the pants, ruling that the Massachusetts flag desecration statute was void for VAGUENESS. In *Spence v. Washington* (1974) the Court invalidated a Washington statute prohibiting the affixing of a symbol to the flag, holding that the display of a flag with a peace symbol superimposed on it was protected free expression. The *Spence* decision was consistent with other cases in which the Supreme Court recognized SYMBOLIC SPEECH as a form of activity protected by the First Amendment. On the other hand, the Court has upheld statutes forbidding flag burning, concluding as in *Sutherland v. Illinois* (1976) that they rested on a "valid governmental interest unrelated to expression—that is, the prevention of breaches of the peace and the preservation of public order."

NORMAN DORSEN

FLAGG BROS., INC. v. BROOKS
436 U.S. 149 (1978)

Brooks is one of a series of BURGER COURT decisions reestablishing the STATE ACTION limitation as a barrier to judicial enforcement of FOURTEENTH AMENDMENT rights against private persons acting under state authority. The Uniform Commercial Code, as adopted in New York, authorizes a warehouse operator to sell goods stored in order to pay overdue warehousing charges. This notion of a "warehouseman's lien" is an ancient COMMON LAW remedy. When Brooks and her family were evicted from their apartment, a city marshal had her goods stored with Flagg Bros. Ten weeks later, Flagg Bros. wrote to Brooks, demanding payment of storage charges and threatening to sell her goods to satisfy the charges accrued. Brooks brought a CLASS ACTION against Flagg Bros. for damages and injunctive relief under federal CIVIL RIGHTS laws claiming DUE PROCESS and EQUAL PROTECTION violations. (See INJUNCTION.) The Supreme Court held, 5–3, that the proposed sale did not amount to state action; thus there had been no constitutional violation.

Justice WILLIAM H. REHNQUIST wrote for the majority, as he had done in other recent cases strengthening the state action limitation. The proposed sale did not fit the "public function" DOCTRINE of state action (here renamed the "sovereign function" doctrine), because the function of dispute resolution historically had not been the exclusive province of the states. Nor had the state authorized or encouraged the use of this creditor's remedy in such a way as to take responsibility for its exercise. The Uniform Commercial Code "permits but does not compel" a warehouse operator's threat to sell goods stored and merely announces the circumstances in which the state will not intervene with that private sale.

Justice WILLIAM J. BRENNAN did not participate in the decision. Justice JOHN PAUL STEVENS dissented, joined by Justices BYRON R. WHITE and THURGOOD MARSHALL. The distinction between state permission and state compulsion was untenable, Stevens argued; on the Court's theory, for example, the state could "announce" its intention not to intervene when a finance company entered a private home to repossess property, with no finding of state action. He also argued persuasively that the "exclusive sovereign function" notion had no basis in the Court's prior decisions. What the state had done here was to "order binding, nonconsensual resolution of a conflict between debtor and creditor"—which is "exactly the sort of power with which the Due Process Clause is concerned."

KENNETH L. KARST

FLAG SALUTE CASES
MINERSVILLE SCHOOL DISTRICT v. GOBITIS
310 U.S. 586 (1940)
WEST VIRGINIA BOARD OF EDUCATION v. BARNETT
319 U.S. 624 (1943)

The Supreme Court's encounter in the early 1940s with the issue of compulsory flag salute exercises in the public schools was one of the turning points in American constitutional history. It presaged the civil libertarian activism that culminated in the WARREN COURT of the 1960s.

The flag salute ceremony developed in the latter half of the nineteenth century. In the original ceremony the participants faced the flag and pledged "allegiance to my flag and the republic for which it stands, one nation indivisible, with liberty and justice for all." While repeating the words "to my flag" the right hand was extended palm up toward the flag. Over the years the ceremony evolved slightly, with minor changes of wording and with the extended arm salute dropped in 1942 because of its similarity to the Nazi salute. At this point in its evolution, however, the salute had official standing; Congress had prescribed the form of words and substituted the right hand over the heart for the extended arm.

Beginning in 1898 with New York, some states began requiring the ceremony as part of the opening exercise of the school day. The early state flag salute laws did not make the ceremony compulsory for individual pupils, but many local school boards insisted on participation. Many patriotic and fraternal organizations backed the flag salute; opposition came from civil libertarians and some small religious groups. The principal opponents of the compulsory school flag salute were the Jehovah's Witnesses, a tightly knit evangelical sect whose religious beliefs commanded them not to salute the flag as a "graven image."

The Witnesses were blessed with legal talent. "Judge" Joseph Franklin Rutherford, who had become head of the sect, brought in Hayden Covington, who, as chief counsel for the Witnesses in the *Gobitis* litigation and in many other cases influenced the development of First Amendment doctrine.

The first flag salute case to reach the Supreme Court came out of Minersville, a small community in northwest Pennsylvania. Because of Rutherford's bitter opposition to required flag salute exercises, Lillian and William Gobitis stopped participating in the ceremony in their school and were expelled.

The argument for the Gobitis children was that requiring them to salute the flag, an act repugnant to them on religious grounds, denied that free exercise of religion protected against state action by the DUE PROCESS clause of the FOURTEENTH AMENDMENT. Arguments for the Minersville School Board relied on REYNOLDS V. UNITED STATES (1878), JACOBSON V. MASSACHUSETTS (1905), and the doctrine that a religious objection did not relieve an individual from the responsibility of complying with an otherwise valid secular regulation. The Gobitis children won in the lower federal courts, but the Supreme Court granted CERTIORARI.

The Court in the spring of 1940 had a very different cast from that which had survived FRANKLIN D. ROOSEVELT's effort to "pack" it three years before. Of the hard-core, pre-1937 conservatives only Justice JAMES C. MCREYNOLDS remained. Chief Justice CHARLES EVANS HUGHES and Justices HARLAN F. STONE and OWEN J. ROBERTS also remained. With them, however, were five Roosevelt appointees: FELIX FRANKFURTER, HUGO L. BLACK, WILLIAM O. DOUGLAS, STANLEY F. REED, and FRANK MURPHY. On three previous occasions the Court had sustained compulsory flag salutes against religious objection in PER CURIUM opinions. Whether because of the extraordinary persistence of the Jehovah's Witnesses or because of the nonconformance of the lower federal courts in this case, the Justices now gave the matter full dress consideration.

Speaking for the majority Justice Frankfurter concluded that "conscientious scruples have not, in the course of the long struggle for religious toleration, relieved the individual from obedience to a general law not aimed at the persecution or a restriction of religious beliefs."

To Justice Stone, dissenting, the crucial issue was that the Gobitis children were forced to bear false witness to their religion. The flag salute compelled the expression of a belief, and "where that expression violate[d] religious convictions," the free exercise clause provided protection.

The reaction to the decision in the law reviews was negative. In the popular press the reaction was mixed but criticism predominated. Most important, the decision seems to have produced a wave of persecution of Jehovah's Witnesses which swept through the country. *Gobitis* emboldened some school authorities. The State Board of Education of West Virginia in January 1942 made the salute to the flag mandatory in the classrooms of that state.

Meanwhile, new decisions of the Supreme Court, notably the 5–4 division of the Justices in *Jones v. Opelika,* raised the hopes of opponents of the mandatory flag salute. Hayden Covington sought an INJUNCTION barring enforcement of West Virginia's new rule against Walter Barnett and other Jehovah's Witness plaintiffs. After a three-judge District Court issued an injunction, the State Board of Education appealed to the Supreme Court.

The case was argued on March 11, 1943, and the decision came down on June 14. Justice ROBERT H. JACKSON, who had joined the Court after *Gobitis,* wrote for a 6–3 majority, overruling the prior decision. Chief Justice Stone was with Jackson, as were Justices Douglas, Black, and Murphy, who had changed their minds. Justice Frankfurter, the author of *Gobitis,* wrote a long and impassioned dissent.

For Justice Jackson and the majority the crucial point was that West Virginia's action, while not intended either to impose or to anathematize a particular religious belief, did involve a required affirmation of belief: "If there is any fixed star in our constitutional constellation, it is that no official, high or petty, can prescribe what shall be orthodox in politics, nationalism, religion, or other matters of opinion or force citizens to confess by word or act their faith therein." West Virginia was pursuing the legitimate end of enhancing patriotism, but had not borne the heavy burden of justifying its use of coercive power.

Justice Frankfurter began his dissent by noting that were the matter one of personal choice he would oppose compulsory flag salutes. But it was not for the Court to decide what was and was not an effective means of inculcating patriotism. West Virginia had neither prohibited nor imposed any religious belief. For Frankfurter this fact was controlling, and he reminded his brethren that a liberal spirit cannot be "enforced by judicial invalidation of illiberal legislation."

Barnett was a landmark decision in the strict sense of that overworked word. By 1943 the Roosevelt Court had largely completed its task of dismantling the edifice of SUBSTANTIVE DUE PROCESS erected by its predecessors to protect economic liberty. Now the Court set out on the path to a new form of JUDICIAL ACTIVISM in the service of individual rights. *Barnett* was the first long step on that path.

Barnett had doctrinal significance both for FREEDOM OF SPEECH and for RELIGIOUS LIBERTY. Jackson's opinion suggested that there were significant limitations on the kinds of patriotic affirmations that government might require, and the decision also moved away from the "secular regulation" rule that had dominated free exercise doctrine.

Barnett also had a significant effect on the Supreme Court. Justice Frankfurter was deeply offended by the majority's treatment of his *Gobitis* opinion and even more alarmed at what he regarded as a misuse of judicial power. The split between the activist disposition of Justices Black and Douglas and the judicial self-restraint championed by Frankfurter date from *Barnett.*

RICHARD E. MORGAN

Bibliography

MANWARING, DAVID R. 1962 *Render unto Caesar: The Flag Salute Controversy.* Chicago: University of Chicago Press.

FLAST v. COHEN
392 U.S. 83 (1968)

A WARREN COURT landmark regarding the JUDICIAL POWER OF THE UNITED STATES, *Flast* upheld taxpayer STANDING to complain that disbursements of federal funds to religious schools violate the FIRST AMENDMENT prohibition of an ESTABLISHMENT OF RELIGION. The decision carved an exception from, but did not overturn, the rule of FROTHINGHAM V. MELLON (1923) that federal taxpayers lack a sufficiently individual or direct interest in spending programs to be allowed to attack them in federal court. To Justice JOHN MARSHALL HARLAN's dissenting chagrin, the Court so ruled knowing that Congress, cognizant of *Frothingham,* had decided against granting taxpayers a right to JUDICIAL REVIEW of federal support for religious education.

The Court was unanimous on one fundamental point: the taxpayers in *Flast* presented an Article III "case." (See CASES AND CONTROVERSIES.) For the majority, Chief Justice EARL WARREN reaffirmed the traditional Article III requirement of a "personal stake in the outcome of the controversy," but deemed that requirement satisfied whenever a taxpayer claims that Congress exercised its TAXING AND SPENDING POWER in derogation of specific constitutional limits on that power. The Court found the establishment clause a specific limit, because, historically, the clause was designed to block taxation to support religion.

Dissenting, Justice Harlan could not agree that taxpayers challenging spending, rather than their tax liability, had a personal stake. They had no financial stake, because victory would only change how the government's general revenues are spent—not their tax bill. Nor was the Court's exception tailored to the requirement of a personal stake. A taxpayer's interests did not vary with the power Congress exercised in appropriating funds or with the constitutional provision ("specific" or not) invoked to oppose the expenditures. For Harlan, the taxpayer's interest in government spending was not personal but public—a citizen's concern that official behavior be constitutional. Nonetheless, he thought the "public action" would satisfy Article III, apparently because the parties were sufficiently adversary. But because "public actions" would press judicial authority vis-à-vis the representative branches to the limit, he concluded the Court should not entertain them without congressional authorization.

The bearing of SEPARATION OF POWERS on taxpayer standing was the pivotal dividing point in *Flast.*

Justice WILLIAM O. DOUGLAS, too, thought *Flast* a public action, the attempt to distinguish *Frothingham* a failure, and the requirements of Article III met. But he found *Frothingham* deficient, not *Flast,* for he perceived the judicial role as enforcement of basic rights against majoritarian control without awaiting congressional authorization—even in "public actions." Chief Justice Warren's view fell between the Harlan and Douglas poles by disavowing the connection between standing and the separation of powers. JUSTICIABILITY requires that a suit be appropriate in form for judicial resolution and implicates separation of powers, said Warren, but standing, with its focus on the party suing, not the issues raised, looks only to form.

Under the BURGER COURT, separation of powers considerations have resurfaced in TAXPAYER SUITS, stunting the potential growth of *Flast* into the mature "public action." Typical of the Burger Court approach was VALLEY FORGE CHRISTIAN COLLEGE V. AMERICANS UNITED FOR SEPARATION OF CHURCH AND STATE (1982). The *Flast* landmark has become a historical marker.

JONATHAN D. VARAT

FLETCHER v. PECK
6 Cranch 87 (1810)

Fletcher was the Court's point of departure for converting the CONTRACT CLAUSE into the chief link between the Constitution and capitalism. The case arose from the Yazoo land scandal, the greatest corrupt real estate deal in American history. Georgia claimed the territory within her latitude lines westward to the Mississippi, and in 1795 the state legislature passed a bill selling about two-thirds of that so-called Yazoo territory, some 35,000,000 acres of remote wilderness comprising a good part of the present states of Alabama and Mississippi. Four land companies, having bribed every voting member of the state legislature but one, bought the Yazoo territory at a penny and a half an acre. Speculation in land values was a leading form of capitalist enterprise at that time, provoking an English visitor to characterize the United States as "the land of speculation." Respectable citizens engaged in the practice; the piratical companies that bought the Yazoo included two United States senators, some governors and congressmen, and Justice JAMES WILSON. In a year, one of the four companies sold its Yazoo holdings at a 650 percent profit, and the buyers, in the frenzy of speculation that followed, resold at a profit. But in 1796 the voters of Georgia elected a "clean" legislature which voided the bill of sale and publicly burned all records of it but did not return the $500,000 purchase price. In 1802 Georgia sold its western territories to the United States for $1,250,000. In 1814 a Yazooist lobby finally succeeded in persuading Congress to pass a $5,000,000 compensation bill, indemnifying holders of Yazoo land titles.

Fletcher v. Peck was part of a twenty-year process of legal and political shenanigans related to the Yazoo land scandal. Georgia's nullification of the original sale imperiled the entire chain of Yazoo land speculations, but the ELEVENTH AMENDMENT made Georgia immune to a suit. A feigned case was arranged. Peck of Massachusetts sold 15,000 acres of Yazoo land to Fletcher of New Hampshire. Fletcher promptly sued Peck for recovery of his $3,000, claiming that Georgia's nullification of the sale had destroyed Peck's title: the acreage was not his to sell. Actually, both parties shared the same interest in seeking a judicial decision against Georgia's nullification of the land titles—the repeal act of 1796. Thus, by a collusive suit based on DIVERSITY OF CITIZENSHIP, a case involving the repeal act got into the federal courts and ultimately reached the Supreme Court. The Court's opinion, by Chief Justice JOHN MARSHALL, followed the contours of Justice WILLIAM PATERSON's charge in VAN HORNE'S LESSEE V. DORRANCE (1795).

Although the fraud that infected the original land grants was the greatest scandal of the time, the Court refused to make an exception to the principle that the judiciary could not properly investigate the motives of a legislative body. (See LEGISLATION.) The Court also justifiably held that "innocent" third parties should not suffer an annihilation of their property rights as a result of the original fraud. The importance of the case derives from the Court's resolution of the constitutionality of the repeal act.

Alternating in his reasoning between extraconstitutional or HIGHER LAW principles and constitutional or textual ones, Marshall said that the repealer was invalid. Before reaching the question whether a contract existed that the Constitution protected, he announced this doctrine: "When, then, a law is in its nature a contract, when absolute rights have been vested under that contract, a repeal of the law cannot devest those rights. . . ." In the next sentence he asserted that "the nature of society and of government" limits legislative power. This higher law doctrine of judicially inferred limitations protecting vested rights was the sole basis of Justice WILLIAM JOHNSON's concurring opinion. A state has no power to revoke its grants, he declared, resting his case "on a general principle, on the reason and nature of things: a principle which will impose laws even on the Deity." Explicitly Johnson stated that his opinion was not founded on the Constitution's provision against state impairment of the OBLIGATION OF CONTRACTS. The difficulty, he thought, arose from the word "obligation," which ceased once a grant of lands had been executed.

The difficulty with Marshall's contract clause theory was greater than even Johnson made out. The clause was intended to prevent state impairment of executory contracts between private individuals; it had been modeled on the provision of the NORTHWEST ORDINANCE, which had referred to "private contracts, or engagements *bona fide,* and without fraud previously formed." What was the contract in this case? If there was one, did its obligation still exist at the time of the repeal bill? Was it a contract protected by the contract clause, given that it was a land grant to which the state was a party? If the land grant was a contract, it was a public executed one, not a private executory one. The duties that the parties had assumed toward each other had been fulfilled, the deal consummated. That is why Johnson could find no continuing obligation. Moreover, the obligation of a contract is a creature of state law, and the state in this instance, sustained by its courts, had recognized no obligation.

Marshall overcame all difficulties by employing slippery reasoning. A contract, he observed, is either executory or executed; if executed, its object has been performed. The contract between the state and the Yazoo land buyers had been executed by the grant. But, he added, an executed contract, as well as an executory one, "contains obligations binding on the parties." The grant had extinguished the right of the grantor in the title to the lands and "implies a contract not to reassert that right." Moreover, the Constitution uses only the term "contract, without distinguishing between those which are executory and those which are executed." Having inferred from the higher law that a grant carried a continuing obligation not to repossess, he declined to make a distinction that, he said, the Constitution had not made. Similarly he concluded that the language of the contract clause, referring generally to "contracts," protected public as well as private contracts. Marshall apparently realized that the disembodied or abstract higher law doctrine on which Johnson relied would provide an insecure bastion for property holders and a nebulous precedent for courts to follow. So he found a home for the VESTED RIGHTS doctrine in the text of the Constitution.

Marshall seemed, however, to be unsure of the text, because he flirted with the bans on BILLS OF ATTAINDER and EX POST FACTO laws, giving the impression that Georgia's repeal act somehow ran afoul of those bans, too, although the suit was a civil one. Marshall's uncertainty emerged in his conclusion. He had no doubt that the repeal act was invalid, but his ambiguous summation referred to both extraconstitutional principles and the text: Georgia "was restrained, either by general principles which are common to our free institutions, or by the particular provisions of the Constitution. . . ." He did not, in the end, specify the particular provisions.

In the first contract clause decision by the Court, that clause became a repository of the higher law DOCTRINE of vested rights and operated to cover even public, executed contracts. The Court had found a constitutional shield for vested rights. And, by expanding the protection offered by the contract clause, the Court invited more cases to be brought before the judiciary, expanding opportunities for judicial review against state legislation.

LEONARD W. LEVY

Bibliography

MAGRATH, C. PETER 1966 *Yazoo: Law and Politics in the New Republic, The Case of Fletcher v. Peck.* Providence, R.I.: Brown University Press.

FOLEY v. CONNELIE
435 U.S. 291 (1978)

New York excluded ALIENS from employment as state troopers. In an opinion by Chief Justice WARREN E. BURGER, the Supreme Court held, 6–3, that this discrimination did not violate the EQUAL PROTECTION clause of the FOURTEENTH AMENDMENT. The Court took its cue from OBITER DICTA in SUGARMAN V. DOUGALL (1973) concerning "political community." Although the admission of aliens for permanent residence showed congressional intent to grant them full participation in earning a livelihood and receiving such state benefits as welfare and education, the "right to govern" could be limited to citizens. Police officers, like high executive officials, exercise discretionary governmental power, whose abuse can have "serious impact on individuals." (The Chief Justice may have had a vision of an alien trooper inviting a citizen to spreadeagle over the hood of a car.)

Justices THURGOOD MARSHALL, WILLIAM J. BRENNAN, and JOHN PAUL STEVENS dissented: the "execution of broad public policy" mentioned in *Sugarman* had not included the day-to-day execution of the law but the formulation of broad policy. The disloyalty of aliens could not be conclusively presumed.

KENNETH L. KARST

FOOD, DRUG, AND COSMETIC ACT

52 Stat. 1040 (1938)

Grounded on the COMMERCE CLAUSE, this act was a sweeping revision of the PURE FOOD AND DRUG ACT of 1906. It passed Congress after a five-year struggle and then only because of an uproar caused by nearly one hundred deaths from a new drug. Despite extensive compromise, this act substantially strengthened earlier legislation, affording greater consumer protection. Different chapters of the law dealt at length with food, drugs, and cosmetics, expanding coverage and increasing penalties. The act prohibited shipment in INTERSTATE COMMERCE of adulterated or misbranded products and broadened the definition of these terms. Indicative of the act's thrust, one section authorized the secretary of agriculture to establish standards of quality for foods to "promote honesty and fair dealing in the interest of consumers." Misbranding received special attention: imitations were to be clearly marked, flavoring or coloring additives noted, and the use of habit-forming ingredients was to be indicated on the label. Drugs had to meet federal formulations or disclose the differences. New drugs would have to pass rigorous tests. Congress partly remedied one of the act's weaknesses, a less stringent control over false advertising, in the Wheeler-Lea Act of the same year. The Supreme Court sustained the act in UNITED STATES v. SULLIVAN (1947).

DAVID GORDON

FORCE ACT

4 Stat. 632 (1833)

Restive over the threat to slavery that they saw implicit in the growth of federal power, South Carolinians devised doctrines of NULLIFICATION and SECESSION in response to the Tariff Act of 1828. When the Tariff of 1832 failed to satisfy their demands for reduction, a special convention adopted an Ordinance of Nullification (1832), nullifying the tariff. President ANDREW JACKSON responded with his PROCLAMATION TO THE PEOPLE OF SOUTH CAROLINA (1832), denouncing the theory of secession, and with a request to Congress to enact legislation that would simultaneously avoid a military clash with the state over the collection of duties and permit a more prompt resort to federal force if confrontation could not be evaded.

Congress responded with the Force Act (Act of 2 March 1833), reaffirming the power of the President to use federal military and naval force to suppress resistance to the enforcement of federal laws, even if the source of resistance was the state itself. The act empowered him to call up states' militias after issuing a proclamation calling on those obstructing to disperse. It also permitted him to revise the procedure for collecting customs duties. Though South Carolina subsequently nullified the Force Act, federal authority had been vindicated.

WILLIAM M. WIECEK

Bibliography

FREEHLING, WILLIAM W. 1966 *Prelude to Civil War: The Nullification Controversy in South Carolina, 1816–1836.* New York: Harper & Row.

FORCE ACTS

16 Stat. 140 (1870)
16 Stat. 433 (1871)
17 Stat. 13 (1871)

Congress enacted three statutes in 1870 and 1871 to protect the right of blacks to vote in the southern states and to suppress anti-Reconstruction terrorism. They are sometimes called the Enforcement Acts. The Act of May 31, 1870, prohibited all forms of infringement of the RIGHT TO VOTE, not merely the exclusion prohibited by the FIFTEENTH AMENDMENT, and made nightriding a federal FELONY. The Act of February 28, 1871, provided for federal supervision of voter registration and congressional elections to prohibit ballot-box frauds and intimidation of black voters. The Act of April 20, 1871, commonly called the Ku Klux Klan Act, provided civil remedies to persons deprived of rights and privileges secured by the federal Constitution; prohibited violent resistance to federal authority, in order to protect civilian and military officials enforcing Reconstruction measures; authorized the President to use militia and federal military force to suppress insurrections and domestic violence when a state was unable to do so; defined "rebellion" against the federal government; and provided that when the president proclaimed that a rebellion exists, he could suspend the writ of HABEAS CORPUS in the rebellious district. Under authority of the Klan Act, President ULYSSES S. GRANT proclaimed nine counties in South Carolina to be in rebellion during October 1871, suspended the writ of habeas corpus, and used federal troops to suppress violence there and elsewhere in the South. The Klan Act was instrumental in breaking the power of the Klans and other terrorist organizations for the time being.

In UNITED STATES v. REESE (1876), the Supreme Court held sections of the 1870 Act unconstitutional on the grounds that "the Fifteenth Amendment does not confer the right of suffrage upon any one." The Court anticipated its later STATE ACTION doctrine in UNITED STATES v. CRUIKSHANK (1876), voiding INDICTMENTS under the Klan Act on the grounds that the FOURTEENTH AMENDMENT "adds nothing to the rights of one citizen as against another. It simply furnishes a federal guaranty against any encroachment by the States." The Court held parts of the Klan Act unconstitutional in UNITED STATES v. HARRIS (1883) because they were directed at the actions of private persons, not at the states or their officers. (These decisions have lost most of their force today. See UNITED STATES v. GUEST, 1966.) Later Congresses in 1894 and 1909, hostile to the goals of Reconstruction, repealed most of the 1870 Act and the Klan Act, but the prohibitions of conspiracies and nightriding survive today in the United States Code, and the civil remedies provided by the Klan Act are today the foundation for an overwhelming majority of federal court lawsuits challenging the constitutionality of actions of state officers. (See SECTION 1983, TITLE 42, UNITED STATES CODE.)

WILLIAM M. WIECEK

Bibliography

HYMAN, HAROLD M. 1973 *A More Perfect Union: The Impact of the Civil War and Reconstruction on the Constitution.* New York: Knopf.

FORD, GERALD R. (1913–)

Gerald Rudolph Ford, Jr., a graduate of the University of Michigan and Yale University Law School, served in the House of Representatives from 1949 to 1973. A moderately conservative Republican who opposed most social welfare legislation but supported all of the CIVIL RIGHTS ACTS, Ford was his party's floor leader in the House from 1965 to 1973. Among his more controversial undertakings in that capacity was his attempt to secure the IMPEACHMENT of Supreme Court Justice WILLIAM O. DOUGLAS in 1970.

President RICHARD M. NIXON appointed Ford vice-president of the United States when the office fell vacant in 1973; this was the first application of procedures set forth in the Twenty-Fifth Amendment. When Nixon resigned the presidency in August 1974, Ford succeeded him, thereby becoming the first President to serve without winning a national election. In September 1974 Ford granted Nixon a full pardon for any offense against the United States that he might have committed while in office. (See WATERGATE AND THE CONSTITUTION.)

As President, Ford used the VETO POWER extensively, disapproving some forty-eight bills. In 1974, after Congress failed to act, Ford granted conditional AMNESTY to VIETNAM WAR deserters and draft evaders, exercising the presidential PARDONING POWER. His dispatch of Marines to free the freighter *Mayaguez* from Cambodia in May 1975 demonstrated that the "consultation" provisions of the WAR POWERS RESOLUTION OF 1973 did not prevent the COMMANDER-IN-CHIEF from taking decisive action in an emergency. Ford sought election in his own right in 1976 but was narrowly defeated by JIMMY CARTER.

DENNIS J. MAHONEY

FOREIGN AFFAIRS

The words "foreign affairs" are not to be found in the United States Constitution. There are scattered references to "commerce with foreign nations," to TREATIES and ambassadors, to the law of nations, but there is nothing to suggest that the relations of the United States with other nations form a significantly discrete constitutional category. Yet every major theme of constitutional jurisprudence is played differently in respect of foreign affairs. Foreign affairs provide a unique exception to the dogma that the federal government has only the powers expressly enumerated in the Constitution. For the relations of the United States with other countries, FEDERALISM is virtually irrelevant and the United States is essentially a unitary state. The separation and allocation of authority among the branches of the federal government for conducting foreign affairs are different from what they are in respect to domestic matters. Individual rights, strongly safeguarded by the Constitution in the internal life of the country, bow quite readily before the foreign interests of the United States. In this and in other respects foreign affairs discourage JUDICIAL REVIEW and intervention, the hallmark of United States constitutionalism.

The Constitution vests some foreign affairs powers in the federal government in the same manner in which it vests domestic powers, by bestowing them on one or another of the three branches of that government. Thus, Congress in Article I, section 8, is given the power to regulate commerce with foreign nations, to define offenses against the law of nations, and to declare war. The President has the power under Article II, section 2, to appoint ambassadors and make treaties (with the ADVICE AND CONSENT of the Senate). The JUDICIAL POWER OF THE UNITED STATES extends, according to Article III, section 2, to cases arising under treaties, and to certain controversies involving foreign states, their public ministers, or their citizens. Many powers of government relating to foreign affairs, however, are not mentioned: for example, the power to control IMMIGRATION, to regulate ALIENS in the United States or United States nationals abroad, to assert the rights of the United States and to respond to claims by other governments, to participate in the international process of developing customary law, to make international agreements other than treaties, to recognize states and governments, or generally to determine national policy and attitudes on friendship and intercourse with other nations. While some missing powers can plausibly be inferred from ENUMERATED POWERS, others cannot, and, under general principles, powers not enumerated and not fairly to be inferred from expressed powers were not granted to the federal government: the legislative powers of Congress are limited to those "herein granted" (Article I, section 1), and the powers not delegated to the United States are reserved to the states or to the people by the TENTH AMENDMENT. Yet the federal government has exercised all these foreign affairs powers and others from the beginning, and no one has doubted that the federal government had that authority, and that the states did not.

In foreign affairs, then, the principle that the federal government has only the enumerated powers does not apply. All foreign affairs are delegated to the federal government as though that were expressly provided. A hundred years ago the Supreme Court, in CHAE CHAN PING V. UNITED STATES (1889), held, for example, that Congress has the power to regulate immigration because the power to exclude or admit aliens is inherent in the nationhood and SOVEREIGNTY of the United States. In UNITED STATES V. CURTISS-WRIGHT EXPORT CORP. (1936) the Supreme Court expounded a special constitutional principle:

> The broad statement that the federal government can exercise no powers except those specifically enumerated in the Constitution, and such implied powers as are NECESSARY AND PROPER to carry into effect the enumerated powers, is categorically true only in respect of our internal affairs. In that field, the primary purpose of the Constitution was to carve from the general mass of legislative powers *then possessed by the states* such portions as it was thought desirable to vest in the federal government, leaving those not included in the enumeration still in the states. . . . And since the states severally never possessed international powers, such powers could not have been carved from the mass of state powers but obviously were transmitted to the United States from some other source. . . .
>
> As a result of the separation from Great Britain by the Colonies acting as a unit, the powers of external sovereignty passed from the Crown not to the colonies severally, but to the colonies in their collective and corporate capacity as the United States of America. . . .
>
> The Union existed before the Constitution, which was ordained and established among other things to form "a more perfect Union." Prior to that event, it is clear that the Union, declared by the ARTICLES OF CONFEDERATION to be 'perpetual,' was the sole possessor of external sovereignty and in the Union it remained without change save in so far as the Constitution in express terms qualified its exercise. The Framers' Convention was called and exerted its powers upon the irrefutable postulate that though the states were several their people in respect of foreign affairs were one. . . .
>
> It results that the investment of the federal government with the powers of external sovereignty did not depend upon the affirmative grants of the Constitution. The powers to declare and wage war, to conclude peace, to make treaties, to maintain diplomatic relations with other sovereignties, if they had never been mentioned in the Constitution, would have vested in the federal government as necessary concomitants of nationality. . . . As a member of the family of nations, the right and power of the United States in that field are equal to the right and power of the other members of the international family. Otherwise, the United States is not completely sovereign. The power to acquire territory by discovery and occupation . . . the power to expel undesirable aliens . . . the power to make such international agreements as do not constitute treaties in the constitutional sense . . . , none of which is expressly affirmed by the Constitution, nevertheless exist as inherently inseparable from the conception of nationality. This the court recognized, and . . . found the warrant for its conclusions not in the provisions of the Constitution, but in the law of nations.

Although the theory underlying *Curtiss-Wright* has been criticized, it has never been questioned by the Supreme Court. In any event, the DOCTRINE resulting from the theory—plenary power of the federal government in matters relating to foreign affairs, beyond those explicitly granted in the Constitution—is firmly established. The Supreme Court has not often found it necessary to resort to "sovereignty" or "nationhood" as a source of power for the federal government. In large part, the foreign activities of the federal government that have come to court are amply supported by enumerated powers of Congress or the President, by powers reasonably implied in enumerated powers, or by construction of the Constitution as a whole. But sovereignty, nationhood, and their implications in international law and in the practice of other nations are ever available as a source of authority to supply any lack of enumerated power for the federal government in matters relating to foreign affairs. The network of regulation of immigration and of aliens in the United States, for a principal example, rests ultimately on United States sovereignty, and other exercises of authority not easily rooted in enumerated powers have been supported as exercises of "the foreign affairs powers" of Congress, with citations to *Curtiss-Wright.*

The powers expressly conferred upon branches of the federal government, and those additional powers implied in sovereignty, give the federal government full authority to act in the United States and for the United States in respect to its foreign affairs. Since plenary power has been delegated, state authority, STATES' RIGHTS, even state immunity (except in remote, hypothetical respects) do not limit federal authority in foreign affairs. When the federal government acts, its action is supreme, superseding any inconsistent state law. Federal action may also preempt, "occupy a field," excluding state action even if it is not inconsistent.

Some state actions in foreign affairs are excluded by Article I, section 10, even when the federal government has not acted. A state may not make a treaty. It may enter into an "Agreement or Compact" with a foreign nation only with the consent of Congress. Although here, as for other purposes, the difference between a treaty and another international agreement is uncertain, presumably if Congress should consent to an agreement by a state with a foreign government the agreement would not be successfully challenged as being a treaty to which Congress could not consent. An agreement requiring the consent of Congress may be formal or informal, even tacit. But, by analogy to doctrine that has developed in cases such as *Virginia v. Tennessee* (1893), with respect to compacts between states of the United States, probably a state may make a compact with a foreign government without congressional consent if the agreement does not tend to "the increase of political power in the states, which may encroach upon or interfere with the just supremacy of the United States."

The states are limited also by implication of the grant to Congress of power "to regulate commerce with foreign Nations and among the several States." Although that doctrine of implied limitations developed principally in respect of INTERSTATE COMMERCE it applies in essentially the same way to FOREIGN COMMERCE. The COMMERCE CLAUSE bars regulation by the states that excludes or discriminates against foreign commerce, or burdens such commerce unduly, as determined by weighing the local against the national interest. The courts continue to monitor such state regulations.

A single case, *Zschernig v. Miller* (1968), has held, more broadly, that even if the federal government has not acted, and even if there is no undue burden on foreign commerce, a state may not intrude on the federal monopoly in foreign affairs. In that case Oregon law required state courts to deny an inheritance to an alien unless the court were satisfied that the government of the alien's state of nationality would allow a United States national to inherit in reciprocal circumstances, and that the alien would be allowed to enjoy his inheritance without confiscation. That state law, the Supreme Court ruled, was impermissible under the Constitution because it involved the state courts in sitting in judgment on the policies of foreign governments. No other case has been decided on that principle.

"In respect of foreign relations generally, State lines disappear. As to such purpose the State . . . does not exist," the Supreme Court said in UNITED STATES V. BELMONT (1937). But while federal authority in foreign affairs is plenary, it is not exclusive. Federal law generally is superimposed on a network of state law; state law of property and contract, state tort and criminal law, state corporate law, tax law, and estate law govern activities and interests that implicate or impinge on foreign trade and other foreign relations of the United States. If in principle all of that state law could be superseded or excluded by federal statute or treaty, it has not been and could not effectively be done in fact, and foreign relations continue to be greatly affected by state law. State influence is reflected also in the system of selection of the national government—the President, the Senate, and the House of Representatives—and particular state interests weigh heavily in the determination of national interest by every branch of the federal government. Increasingly, states have also entered, independently if informally, on the international scene by commercial missions to promote local produce and industry abroad, and by participation in international cultural activities.

The principal field of constitutional uncertainty and the focus of constitutional controversy in foreign affairs have been the respective powers and authority of President and Congress.

The Framers of the Constitution, reflecting the painful lessons of the early years of independence, created the office of President and vested it with "executive power." They gave the President authority to appoint ambassadors and to make treaties but required that he obtain the advice and consent of the Senate. They designated the President the COMMANDER-IN-CHIEF of the army and navy. At the same time the Framers gave Congress the power to impose tariffs and otherwise regulate commerce with foreign nations; to define and punish piracy and other offenses against the law of nations; and to declare war. Other general powers given to Congress reach to foreign as well as domestic matters: the powers to tax and spend, to borrow and regulate the value of money, to establish post offices, to authorize and appropriate funds, to create and regulate a federal bureaucracy, and to make other laws necessary and proper to carry out the power of Congress and other federal powers.

Both Congress and the presidency have developed and changed, the President in particular now exercising his constitutional authority through a huge bureaucracy. The enumerated powers of each branch have grown as the United States has grown and achieved its large place in a transformed world. But the division of authority between President and Congress remains today essentially as it was expressly prescribed by the Framers. Although the President may propose, and his proposals weigh heavily, Congress exercises its expressed powers as they have developed. Congress decides whether the United States shall be at war or at peace, and passes the laws necessary to prepare for war, and to wage war successfully, and to deal with the consequences of war. Congress regulates "commerce with foreign nations"—trade, transportation, communication, and other intercourse—in its innumerable forms. Congress enacts laws to effectuate the powers of the federal government deriving from the sovereignty and nationhood of the United States. It passes laws constituting national policy toward other nations, for example, laws fixing the rights of their nationals in the United States or in our coastal waters. It also passes laws regulating our relations with other nations, for example, the 1976 statute determining the immunity of foreign governments in American courts. Congress enacts the laws—including any federal criminal law—necessary and proper for carrying out its own foreign affairs powers, the country's treaty obligations, and the foreign affairs powers of the President, including laws protecting the processes for making foreign policy or conducting foreign relations, *e.g.*, statutes protecting classified documents, or forbidding the harassment of foreign diplomats or the picketing of foreign embassies. Congress also uses its general lawmaking powers for foreign as for domestic affairs. Congress decides how much to spend for defense, and how much for foreign aid and to which countries. Its power to borrow money and to regulate the value of money (of the United States and that of other countries) has major transnational applications and implications. By its authority to establish post offices Congress has approved American participation in an international postal system; it has used its authority over PATENTS and COPYRIGHTS to authorize dealing with them by international arrangements. Congress appropriates money for the BUDGET of the State Department, or to pay our obligations to the United Nations. Congress creates and regulates the Foreign Service. It investigates so that it can legislate (or not legislate).

For his part, the President (not Congress) makes treaties and appoints ambassadors (with the consent of the Senate) and receives ambassadors. Only the President acts as commander-in-chief of the armed forces; only he can take care that the laws are faithfully executed. A few powers have been inferred from those listed: for example, only the President speaks for the United States to other nations and only the President negotiates with other nations. The President recognizes governments, enters into diplomatic relations with them or terminates these relations, and gives his ambassadors their instructions and receives their reports.

There is more to foreign affairs, however, than is accounted for in the express allocations of the Constitution, and issues have arisen as to matters not clearly implied in those allocations or where argument can support allocation to one of the political branches as plausibly as to the other. The President makes treaties, but who can terminate them on behalf of the United States? Congress declares war, but who can decide to terminate a war? Who can make international agreements other than treaties, or otherwise commit the power and resources of the United States? Who can deploy forces for purposes short of war? Who can determine those general principles, guidelines, and attitudes that go to make up "foreign policy?"

There is no ready principle of allocation of authority between Congress and President, or of CONSTITUTIONAL INTERPRETATION generally, to determine to whom these unmentioned yet clearly federal powers are assigned. In domestic affairs the principle of allocation of authority between Congress and the President is reasonably clear: Congress makes the law; the President executes the law. In foreign affairs that principle of allocation did not obtain even in the original conception, and surely it does not as the two branches have developed. Clearly, the President has substantial authority to "legislate," to determine national policy, as well as to execute it. The President makes foreign policy when he makes treaties and other international agreements; he also makes law, since international agreements create international law, and some treaties and agreements have domestic effect and are the LAW OF THE LAND under the SUPREMACY CLAUSE. The President makes foreign policy also in representing the United States in the international arena—by recognizing states or governments and deciding on the character of relations with them; by making or responding to international claims; by declaring the attitudes of the United States, many of which he can implement or reflect in actions on his own authority. Inevitably, the President makes foreign policy also by the manner in which he conducts foreign relations.

The President and Congress have asserted opposing principles of constitutional jurisprudence to determine allocation of the unallocated federal powers in foreign affairs. The President has claimed a source of plenary authority in that he is the "sole organ of the United States in its international relations." He has argued that Article II, section 2, of the Constitution vests in him not only the power to execute laws but the whole "executive power" of the United States. It is urged that the Framers understood the executive power to include the whole of foreign relations, except insofar as the Constitution expressly limits the President's authority (as by requiring that he obtain the consent of the Senate to appoint ambassadors or to make treaties), or has expressly given some foreign affairs power to Congress, such as the power to regulate foreign commerce or to declare war. Congress, on the other hand, has claimed that its constitutional authority over foreign "commerce" includes all aspects of intercourse with foreign nations; by that authority, and by its control of war and peace, it has been claimed, Congress is the principal political organ of the nation and has all the authority of the United States in international relations except that expressly given to the President.

The competing constitutional doctrines have rarely come to court and the issue remains largely unresolved in principle. Constitutional history, however, has supplied some of the answers that constitutional law has left unanswered. From the beginning, many powers not expressly delegated by the Constitution have flowed to the President and have made his the predominant part in the foreign policy process. Presidential authority grew early and steadily by a kind of "accretion." Even when United States diplomatic missions abroad were few and United States international relations simple and minimal, the conduct of foreign affairs was a continuing process, and it raised issues every day. These came to the President, through his ambassadors and his secretary of state; Congress did not hear of them unless the President saw necessary or fit to tell Congress. The early issues—whether to declare our neutrality in European wars, or send a misbehaving French minister home—were not matters which the Constitution expressly left to Congress or expressly denied to the President. They did not call for general policy best reflected in formal legislation or resolution, but for ad hoc judgment and particular measures tailored to the case. Sometimes decision was urgent, and the President was always "in session" while Congress was not, and could readily or easily be informed and convened, especially in the conditions of communications and transportation of the early days. The President could act quickly and informally, often discreetly or secretly, while action by Congress would have been public and formal, slow and sometimes unduly dramatic. Often, unless the President acted, the United States could not act at all.

And so President GEORGE WASHINGTON declared neutrality, President JAMES MONROE his famous doctrine; later Presidents opened Japan, traded in China, intervened in Latin America. Presidents appointed "agents" (without Senate consent), concluded EXECUTIVE AGREEMENTS (without consent of Congress or the Senate), sent troops abroad, expanded intelligence and "covert activities," acted in the world arena for the United States, making its policies, committing its honor and credit. What early Presidents did became precedents for their successors to do likewise or to exceed. What successive Presidents did became the basis for assertions of authority to do them, supported in constitutional terms in the President's "foreign affairs power" often implemented by his power as commander-in-chief.

Congress contributed to the steady growth of presidential power. Congress early recognized and confirmed the President's control of daily foreign intercourse, and the resulting monopoly of information and experience promoted the President's claim of expertise and Congress's sense of inadequacy. A growing practice of informal consultations between the President and congressional leaders disarmed them as well as members of Congress generally, and helped confirm presidential authority to act without formal congressional participation. Often Congress later ratified or confirmed what the President had done, as in the KOREAN WAR. And repeatedly it delegated its own huge powers to the President in broad terms, so that he could later claim to act under the authority of Congress as well as his own, as in the VIETNAM WAR.

Congress has never formally conceded all these unspecified powers to the President. At most Congress has silently acquiesced in his power to act. Frequently, Congress asserted authority for itself to act in areas where the President also claimed authority. For example, although in 1945, President HARRY S. TRUMAN, without congressional participation, claimed for the United States the resources of its continental shelf, Congress in 1976 acted to declare an exclusive 200-mile fishing zone for the United States, and did so against the wishes of the executive branch. At times, Congress has also insisted on its authority to preclude, supersede, or control presidential action. In foreign affairs, as elsewhere, it has insisted that the President must execute the laws that Congress enacts and must spend (not impound) money that Congress appropriates. In foreign as in domestic affairs Congress has repudiated EXECUTIVE PRIVILEGE when its committees have sought information or documents. In foreign affairs, too, Congress has provided for LEGISLATIVE VETO to recoup delegation of authority and to oversee executive execution of the law. Whether the general invalidation of the legislative veto (IMMIGRATION AND NATURALIZATION SERVICE V. CHADHA, 1983) will totally bar its use in foreign affairs legislation as well is yet to be determined.

A principal unresolved issue between President and Congress has been the claimed authority of the President to deploy the armed forces of the United States. The issue has not been about the WAR POWERS, expressed in the Constitution. The power to decide for war or peace is indisputably with Congress: Congress can declare war or authorize it by other resolution; it can decide for limited war, and though Presidents have claimed plenary authority as commanders-in-chief, theoretically Congress can probably regulate the conduct of war in general though perhaps not in detail. Wars apart, Presidents have claimed authority to deploy the armed forces for political ends and have done so on numerous occasions, sometimes engaging them in hostilities short of war. In Korea in 1950–1952 troops were engaged in war, President Truman claiming authority to act under a treaty—the UNITED NATIONS CHARTER—and Congress soon acquiesced in and ratified his action. In Vietnam, Congress gave two Presidents blanket authority to engage in hostilities. Members of Congress have often challenged the President's authority, although Congress has rarely done so formally. After Vietnam, however, in the WAR POWERS RESOLUTION adopted over President RICHARD M. NIXON's veto, Congress purported to regulate the power of the President to deploy armed forces in circumstances where they are or might be engaged in hostilities. Although Presidents have questioned the resolution's constitutionality, they have acquiesced in principle, but in several instances they may not have respected the resolution in fact.

The power that Presidents have claimed to enter into international agreements or otherwise commit the United States has also been an unresolved subject of controversy. Again, it is not the treaty power, expressed in the Constitution, that has raised serious issues. The President can make a treaty if the Senate consents, and the Senate can ask for changes and impose other relevant conditions upon its consent. The power to terminate treaties has been exercised by the President, often on his own authority. A challenge to the President's authority to terminate the treaty with the Republic of China (Taiwan) in 1979 did not prevail, although the Supreme Court did not decide the merits of the controversy in GOLDWATER V. CARTER (1980).

Since the beginnings of the nation, Presidents have made many international agreements other than by treaty. An agreement authorized or approved by resolution of Congress, by majority vote in both Houses (rather than by consent of two-thirds of the Senate to a treaty), is the equivalent of a treaty for virtually all purposes. But Presidents have also made agreements on their own authority. Some authority to do so is conceded. It is not disputed that the President can make agreements as commander-in-chief during war (for example, an armistice). He can make agreements also to implement his established foreign affairs power, for example, agreements incidental to recognizing a foreign government, as in the Litvinov agreements with the Union of Soviet Socialist Republics in 1933. (See *United States v. Belmont,* 1937; UNITED STATES V. PINK, 1942). At least some other international agreements have been held to be within his authority, for example, the Iranian Hostages Agreement, since, the Supreme Court said, in DAMES & MOORE V. REGAN (1981), the President's exercise of authority to resolve international claims had been acquiesced in by Congress. On the other hand, some agreements clearly require Senate consent (to a treaty) or congressional approval. There has been no authoritative determination, nor any accepted guidelines, as to which agreements the President can make on his own authority and which he cannot. The suggestion that "important" agreements cannot be made by the President alone is not self-defining, and Presidents have in fact made "important" agreements alone, especially when they desired to keep them confidential. The Senate has expressed its sense that the President cannot commit the forces or resources of the United States except by treaty or pursuant to act of Congress. Congress has considered numerous bills to regulate international agreements by the President on his own authority. But it has legislated only a limited measure, requiring the executive branch to transmit any executive agreement to Congress, if only to a congressional committee in confidence.

In general, Presidents and Congress have worked together even when Congress is not controlled by the President's POLITICAL PARTY. That party politics "stop at the water's edge" and do not trouble American foreign relations is not wholly true, and in the view of many would not be desirable. But throughout most of our national history the dominant voices in the two major parties have not differed sharply in foreign policy, and Congress has more or less willingly followed the President's lead, while Presidents have tried to lead chiefly where Congress would not be too reluctant to follow.

The respective authority of the political branches apart, there have been other constitutional issues relating to treaties and other international agreements. Some early issues have been resolved. Treaties and other international agreements, like other acts of the United States government, are subject to the BILL OF RIGHTS and other constitutional limitations. There are no limitations on the subject matter of such agreements other than those implied in the fact that there must be a bona fide agreement between the United States and one or more other nations in a matter related to foreign policy interests of the United States. A treaty or other agreement may deal with matters that might otherwise be regulated by the states or by congressional statute.

Treaties and international agreements have their own place in constitutional law. Some treaties or agreements are "self-executing": they are intended to be enforced by the executive or applied by the courts without waiting for implementation by Congress. Whether a treaty is self-executing is a matter of interpretation of the agreement, usually determined by the intent of the United States government in the matter. If a treaty or other agreement is self-executing it will be treated like a federal law, supreme over state law and superseding any earlier, inconsistent federal law. But the treaty is not superior to later federal law, and although the courts will interpret a statute, where fairly possible, consistently with international obligations of the United States, when Congress passes a law clearly inconsistent with a pre-existing treaty, the courts will apply the later statute, in effect putting the United States in default on its international obligation.

The role of the courts in foreign affairs is not essentially different from their role in domestic affairs. The JURISDICTION OF THE FEDERAL COURTS under Article III of the Constitution extends to cases arising under treaties of the United States as well as those arising under other international agreements of the United States or under customary international law. Foreign affairs may be implicated also in cases arising under the Constitution and various laws of the United States. The federal courts have jurisdiction also over "cases affecting Ambassadors, other public ministers and consuls," and over controversies between a foreign state or foreign citizen and a state or citizen of the United States, but such controversies have not loomed large in the history of the Constitution or of our foreign relations.

Thanks to both political and institutional limitations, the judicial prerogative of invalidating acts of the political branches has not troubled United States foreign affairs. Most constitutional issues in foreign affairs, including some big issues of competition between President and Congress, rarely come to court because in general there is not the required CASE OR CONTROVERSY and there is no one with the necessary STANDING to raise the issue. Challenge to an exercise of national authority in foreign affairs on grounds of "states' rights" is generally futile in view of the established monopoly of the federal government. Foreign affairs have also been a principal source of the POLITICAL QUESTION DOCTRINE, under which the courts have declared some foreign affairs issues "political" and therefore not justiciable. Federalism does provide the court a role relevant to foreign affairs when they scrutinize state activities that, a private party claims, unduly burden foreign commerce or that may be inconsistent with or preempted by congressional policy.

The courts exercise their usual lawmaking function in foreign affairs also. In addition to interpreting the Constitution and laws, the courts have determined and developed the maritime law which remains largely judge-made. They have also developed rules, if only for their own guidance, such as the "ACT OF STATE" DOCTRINE, that courts will not sit in judgment on the acts of a foreign state in its own territory, as in *Banco Nacional de Cuba v. Sabbatino* (1964). Courts also make foreign relations law when they determine and apply customary international law. "International law is part of our law, and must be ascertained and administered by the courts of justice of appropriate jurisdiction, as often as questions of right depending on it are duly presented for their determination," the Court said in *The Paquete Habana* (1900).

Nothing in the Constitution suggests that the rights of individuals in respect of foreign affairs are different from what they are in relation to other exercises of governmental power. But although arguments that individual rights and protections are fewer and narrower in foreign affairs than elsewhere have not prevailed in principle, constitutional guarantees sometimes look different and afford less protection.

In principle, constitutional safeguards apply in foreign as in domestic affairs and apply to governmental activities abroad as at home. The Bill of Rights limits the Congress and the President, foreign affairs legislation as well as treaties and other international agreements. Even temporary or unauthorized aliens in the United States are entitled to the protections of the Bill of Rights, for example, the safeguards for those accused of crime. But where an individual right is not absolute but might be outweighed by an important public interest, national interests in war and peace, and even lesser concerns of foreign relations, would have important weight in the balance. So, for example, courts have upheld prohibitions on picketing near embassies (*Frend v. United States,* 1938), or the cancellation of a passport of someone engaged in systematically identifying U.S. intelligence agents abroad (AGEE V. HAIG, 1981).

In regard to foreign relations as to other matters, DUE PROCESS OF LAW requires fair procedures, and that requirement applies to aliens as to citizens, in the United States or abroad. Trial under the authority of the United States, at least in time of peace, must provide a jury, RIGHT TO COUNSEL, and other constitutional safeguards for those accused of crime. An alien in the United States, subject to DEPORTATION on grounds prescribed by law, is entitled to a FAIR HEARING, and the government must prove by clear, unequivocal, and convincing evidence that the alien is deportable on the grounds provided by Congress. But an alien seeking admission to the United States is due no process beyond consideration and decision by the designated administrative officer.

Due process also limits the substance of what government can do, requiring that it not be "unreasonable, arbitrary or capricious, and [that] the means selected have real and substantial relation to the object sought to be attained," as the Court said in NEBBIA v. New York (1934). Courts have long refrained, however, from invalidating economic and social regulations, and they are even less likely to do so in matters affecting foreign relations. But SUBSTANTIVE DUE PROCESS protects also a person's liberty, and here the constitutional limitation has been greater, and judicial deference to the political branches far less. The Supreme Court declared in KENT V. DULLES (1955) that the RIGHT TO TRAVEL abroad is "a part of the liberty of which the citizen cannot be deprived without due process of law." In AFROYIM V. RUSK (1967) the Court invalidated a statutory provision making it a crime for members of certain communist organizations to obtain or use a passport, because the law "too broadly and indiscriminately restricts the right to travel and thereby abridges the liberty guaranteed by the Fifth Amendment." However, in *Agee v. Haig* the Court upheld withdrawal of a passport from one who systematically exposed the identity of United States intelligence agents. And to date the courts have held that even an alien lawfully admitted and long resident in the United States can be deported for whatever reasons commend themselves to Congress.

The EQUAL PROTECTION OF THE LAWS is required in foreign affairs matters as elsewhere. States cannot discriminate against aliens to deny them WELFARE BENEFITS, EDUCATION, access to the general civil service, or the right to practice their profession. States may not deny educational opportunities even to "undocumented" alien children, not lawfully admitted to the United States (*Plyer v. Doe,* 1982). But a state may reserve for citizens jobs as teachers, policemen, other "peace officers" (including deputy probation officers), and others involved in "the political function of governing." (See FOLEY V. CONNELIE, 1978; AMBACH V. NORWICK, 1979.) Some state discriminations against aliens are invalid because inconsistent with, or preempted by, the immigration laws or other acts of Congress (HINES V. DAVIDOWITZ, 1941; TAKAHASHI V. FISH & GAME COMMISSION, 1948). Unlike the states, however, Congress can limit the federal Civil Service to citizens, and may discriminate against aliens in other respects that do not infringe their basic rights. An act of Congress or treaty may give some rights to aliens on the basis of reciprocity, *i.e.,* that the country of which the alien is a national give such benefits to United States citizens.

Aliens may be denied the right to acquire some kinds of property or invest in some kinds of enterprises in the United States. But an alien (other than an enemy alien in time of war) may not be deprived of his property without due process of law, and it cannot be taken for public use without JUST COMPENSATION.

The constitutional provision that property not be taken for public use without just compensation may have special application in foreign affairs. The United States has frequently in its history entered into an agreement with another government to settle claims of United States citizens against that government. Although the settlements sometimes did not have authorization or approval by the individual claimants, and often gave them only partial recovery, the courts have upheld such agreements as within the authority of the President to make, and have rejected claims that the agreements deprived the claimants of property without just compensation. But where private claims are sacrificed by the United States in settlement of other national interests, as was apparently the case in the early French spoliation cases, and as was claimed in the Iranian Hostages Agreement, the courts may yet find that there has been a taking of the claims requiring compensation.

There is much uncertainty in the constitutional law of foreign relations but it should not be exaggerated. The abiding uncertainties lie principally—almost wholly—in the separation, distribution, and fragmentation of powers between the President and Congress (or between President and Senate), a division different from those prevailing in domestic affairs. Some of the uncertainties and conflicts arise out of different constitutional interpretations, which might in theory be resolved but are not likely to be resolved soon, for courts are reluctant to step into intense confrontation between President and Congress or inhibit either when the other does not object. If the courts do speak to such "separation" issues occasionally, they are likely to reach for the narrowest ground, resolving as little as possible.

Much of the controversy in the conduct of foreign affairs, moreover, does not stem from constitutional uncertainty, but rather reflects what the Framers intended, or were willing to accept, when they separated powers and subdivided functions. If Congress refuses to authorize an anti-ballistic missile program requested by the President, if the President vetoes a tariff adopted by Congress, if the Senate refuses consent to a human rights treaty negotiated by the President, the controversy does not involve competition for constitutional power but the kind of conflict "prescribed" by the Constitution. There is no constitutional issue when the complaint is not that the Constitution has been violated but that it is not working to taste. For a contemporary example, the real complaint in the national crisis over Vietnam was not that the President usurped constitutional power, but that, acting within his powers, he virtually compelled Congress to go along. That is a complaint against the Constitution.

That under a less-than-certain and less-than-happy constitutional arrangement, the conduct of foreign relations continues to function with reasonable effectiveness owes in substantial part to extraconstitutional arrangements, including varieties of congressional committees and staff that have become integral to the foreign policy process. But the Framers thought they had good reasons for prescribing limits to cooperation, even some conflict. If effective government, in foreign relations as elsewhere, requires cooperation, democratic government, in foreign relations as elsewhere, abhors congressional abdication, and even enjoins it to provide legal opposition. The President provides initiative and efficiency, but Congress is the more representative branch and brings to bear the influence of public opinion, diversity, concern for local and individual rights. At its best, there is a counterpoint of presidential expertise and some inexpert congressional wisdom producing foreign policy and foreign relations not always efficient but supporting larger, deeper national interests.

LOUIS HENKIN

Bibliography

CORWIN, EDWARD S. 1957 *The President: Office and Powers.* 4th rev. ed. New York: New York University Press.

HENKIN, LOUIS 1972 *Foreign Affairs and the Constitution.* Mineola, N.Y.: Foundation Press.

LOFGREN, CHARLES A. 1972 War-Making Power Under the Constitution: The Original Understanding. *Yale Law Journal* 81:672–797.

MCDOUGAL, MYRES S. and LANS, ASHER 1954 Treaties and Congressional-Executive or Presidential Agreements: Interchangeable Instruments of National Policy. *Yale Law Journal* 54:181–351, 534–615.

Report of the Commission on the Organization of the Government for the Conduct of Foreign Policy, and Appendices. 1975.

SOFAER, ABRAHAM D. 1976 *War, Foreign Affairs and Constitutional Power.* Cambridge, Mass.: Ballinger Publishing Co.

WRIGHT, QUINCY 1922 *The Control of American Foreign Relations.* New York: Macmillan.

FOREIGN COMMERCE

The Constitution grants to Congress the power "To regulate Commerce with foreign Nations, and among the several States. . . ." A few cases in the 1800s indicated that the power to regulate foreign commerce was the same as the power to regulate INTERSTATE COMMERCE. Later, in *Brolan v. United States* (1915), the Supreme Court indicated that the power given Congress to regulate foreign commerce was so complete that it was limited only by other portions of the Constitution. So the Court upheld Congress in its regulating, prohibiting, and taxing commerce with other nations while sometimes restricting its power to regulate interstate commerce.

Today the issue is of no significance. The power of Congress to regulate interstate commerce is so great as to make any distinctions meaningless. Congress need only concern itself with the specific constitutional restrictions on the foreign commercial power: those preventing the taxation of exports and giving any preference to the ports of one state over those of another state.

In *Japan Line, Ltd. v. Los Angeles* (1979), however, the Court held that the foreign COMMERCE CLAUSE may serve to limit state taxation in cases in which the interstate commerce clause would not. The Court held invalid a nondiscriminatory, apportioned, state property tax on the value of shipping containers belonging to a Japanese shipping company. The Court said that the tax would have been valid if it had been applied to interstate shipments, but was not here because the containers were taxed on full value in Japan and the Court had no authority to require apportioned taxation in foreign lands. The Court said that state taxes on foreign commerce had to meet all the tests for interstate commerce; in addition, the Court must inquire whether even with apportionment a substantial risk of international multiple taxation persists, and whether the tax prevents the federal government from speaking with one voice when regulating commerce with foreign governments.

EDWARD L. BARRETT, JR.

(SEE ALSO: *State Regulation of Commerce; State Taxation of Commerce.*)

Bibliography

HENKIN, LOUIS 1972 *Foreign Affairs and the Constitution.* Pages 69–71. Mineola, N.Y.: Foundation Press.

NOWAK, JOHN E.; ROTUNDA, RONALD D.; and YOUNG, NELSON J. 1980 *Handbook on Constitutional Law.* Pages 129–131. St. Paul, Minn.: West Publishing Co.

FORTAS, ABE
(1910–1982)

Abe Fortas of Tennessee, a graduate of Yale Law School, became a New Deal lawyer. As undersecretary of state, he opposed the removal and internment of Japanese Americans. In 1946 Fortas cofounded a Washington law firm whose corporate clients made him rich and influential, but he contributed his time to defending the rights of underdogs and alleged security risks. One client, LYNDON B. JOHNSON, became a close friend. Fortas continued as his adviser after Johnson became President, and Johnson later appointed Fortas to the Supreme Court.

Justice Fortas served for less than four years, from October 4, 1965, to May 14, 1969. In 1968, President Johnson nominated him to serve as Chief Justice of the United States, succeeding EARL WARREN, but a Senate delay in confirming him, initiated primarily by Republicans eager to save the appointment in case a Republican was victorious in November, caused Fortas to withdraw from consideration before the 1968 Supreme Court Term opened. Before that term was over, Justice Fortas had resigned his seat because of revelations of alleged improprieties in his financial activities.

Four years away from practice is a very brief period in which to develop an overall judicial philosophy. Nevertheless, Fortas developed a distinctive style, notable for flowery prose, the artful phrase, and emphasis on the underlying facts of the particular case. He also developed distinctive positions on particular issues.

Fortas's FIRST AMENDMENT analysis was the most well-developed aspect of his constitutional theory. He disparaged the speech-conduct distinction adhered to by Justice HUGO L. BLACK and others; Fortas thought both speech and conduct could warrant First Amendment protection. But while he gave full protection in cases like TINKER V. DES MOINES INDEPENDENT COMMUNITY SCHOOL DISTRICT (1969) to nonviolent, nondisruptive speech and conduct, he believed, as he said in BARKER V. HARDWAY (1969), that speech or conduct that is "violent and destructive interference with the rights of others" falls outside the scope of First Amendment protections. In drawing this line in individual cases, Fortas focused tightly on the specific facts of the case. For instance, in BROWN V. LOUISIANA (1966), the arrest of demonstrators for conducting a SIT-IN in a segregated public library was unconstitutional because the particular sit-in was "neither loud, boisterous, obstreperous, indecorous, nor impolite."

Those who disagreed with Fortas's approach asked, as in ADDERLEY V. FLORIDA (1966), whether the *type* of demonstration at issue could be disruptive and so was legitimately subject to state prohibition. Fortas reached opposite conclusions by weighing the potential for violence only of the *particular* demonstration involved. He thus gave greater protection to expression in cases the Supreme Court reviewed. But his opinions gave little guidance, simply reporting his own reactions to the facts of the case. Moreover, Fortas occasionally strayed from this approach. Dissenting in STREET V. NEW YORK (1969), he was willing to affirm a conviction under a state FLAG DESECRATION statute, not because the particular flag-burning threatened disorder but because a government seeking to avoid fire hazards could have prohibited all public burning. There, Fortas stated "action, even if clearly for serious protest purposes, is not entitled to the pervasive protection that is given to speech alone." Seemingly, it again was reaction to the particular factual situation that stirred Fortas, but he was unable to articulate persuasively the reasons for the particular sanctity he attached to the American flag.

When appointed, Fortas already was well-known as the victorious attorney in GIDEON V. WAINWRIGHT (1963), establishing indigents' RIGHT TO COUNSEL in criminal cases. As a Justice, he continued to stress procedural regularity and the need for law enforcement officers to obey the law. He was not afraid to extend protections further than the WARREN COURT majority, as he urged in ALDERMAN V. UNITED STATES (1969) and DESIST V. UNITED STATES (1969). One example is the Fifth Amendment RIGHT AGAINST SELF-INCRIMINATION which the majority limited to evidence of a testimonial or communicative nature in SCHMERBER V. CALIFORNIA (1966) and UNITED STATES V. WADE (1967). Fortas disagreed, saying it violated the privilege to subject a defendant to blood tests, or to make him repeat words uttered by the perpetrator of the crime, or to give a handwriting sample. His principle was that the privilege forbade compelling any evidence the gathering of which requires "affirmative, volitional action" on the part of the defendant. He applied that test in a somewhat conclusory fashion, however, maintaining that the accused could be made to stand in a LINEUP, "an incident of the state's power to ARREST, and a reasonable and justifiable aspect of the state's custody resulting from the arrest."

In EPPERSON V. ARKANSAS (1968) Fortas, for the Court, struck down an Arkansas statute that prohibited teaching evolution. *Epperson* suggests that the fact that a prohibition owes its existence to a particular religious dogma or religious campaign may be sufficient to invalidate it under the ESTABLISHMENT OF RELIGION clause—a position that Fortas might have preferred as an explanation for the invalidity of anti-abortion legislation, had he remained on the Court to decide that issue. That case and those in which Fortas championed the rights of children, such as *Tinker* and his landmark opinion IN RE GAULT (1967), or suggested the desirability of parents making some important decisions with their children rather than having a state-prescribed rule, such as GINSBURG V. NEW YORK (1968) (dissent), foreshadowed themes that have since proved important in other contexts (health services, EDUCATION, contraception, and abortion, for example). They suggest that Fortas would have had much to contribute to the Court had his service not been so limited in duration.

MARTHA A. FIELD

Bibliography

GRAHAM, FRED 1969 Abe Fortas. Pages 3015–3027 in Leon Friedman and Fred L. Israel, eds., *The Justices of the United States Supreme Court, 1789–1969.* New York: Chelsea House.

MASSARO, JOHN 1982–1983 LBJ and the Fortas Nomination for Chief Justice. *Political Science Quarterly* 97:603–621.

SHOGAN, ROBERT 1972 *A Question of Judgment: The Fortas Case and the Struggle for the Supreme Court.* Indianapolis: Bobbs-Merrill.

FOURTEENTH AMENDMENT
(Framing)

The Fourteenth Amendment to the United States Constitution consists of a variety of provisions addressed to several problems that arose when the Civil War and the abolition of slavery transformed the American political order. One sentence—"No State shall make or enforce any law which shall abridge the PRIVILEGES OR IMMUNITIES of citizens of the United States; nor shall any State deprive any person of life, liberty, or property without DUE PROCESS OF LAW; nor deny to any person within its jurisdiction the EQUAL PROTECTION OF THE LAWS"—has become the text upon which most twentieth-century constitutional law is a gloss. But this sentence may not have been the most important part of the amendment as it was conceived by its framers, adopted by Congress, and ratified by the states between 1865 and 1868.

The sentence was addressed most pointedly to one of the lesser problems that Congress faced in the winter of 1865–1866. During that winter congressional legislation protecting the CIVIL RIGHTS of former slaves had been vetoed by President ANDREW JOHNSON in part, he contended, because the Constitution entrusted the protection of civil rights to the states.

The Republican proponents of the CIVIL RIGHTS ACT OF 1866 mustered the necessary two-thirds vote to override the veto, but doubt remained about the power of the federal government to protect civil rights. The quoted sentence in section 1 of the Fourteenth Amendment was written, at least in part, to resolve that doubt.

Another concern of some Northerners in the winter of 1865–1866 was that some future Congress might repudiate the debt that the federal government had amassed during the Civil War or might undertake to pay the Confederate debt or compensate former slaveholders for the loss of their slaves. Section 4 of the amendment guaranteed the national debt, prohibited the payment of the Confederate debt, and barred compensation to slaveholders.

However, the most urgent task that the Thirty-ninth Congress confronted when it began its first session in December 1865 was to establish governments in the South that would be loyal to the Union and send loyal representatives to Congress. The problem was compounded by the ratification of the THIRTEENTH AMENDMENT, which not only abolished slavery but also put an end to the original Constitution's THREE-FIFTHS CLAUSE. With the abolition of slavery, the former slaves would be fully counted as part of the population of the former Confederate states; as a result those states would have more power in Congress and the ELECTORAL COLLEGE than they had had before the Civil War. Something had to be done to insure that the war did not increase the political power of the disloyal groups that had brought the war about.

Three solutions were advanced to prevent those who had lost the Civil War from enhancing their power as a result of it. One was to confer the franchise on Southern blacks, whose votes were expected to bring about the election of loyal candidates. A second solution was to deny political rights—both the right to vote and the right to hold office—to some or all who had participated in the rebellion against national authority. This scheme would increase the number of districts in which Union loyalists had a majority or at least some power to tip the electoral balance in favor of loyal candidates.

A third solution was to alter the basis of representation: to base a state's number of representatives in the House and hence its votes in the Electoral College not on total population but on the number of people eligible to vote. Thus, if a state excluded blacks from the right to vote, they would not be counted in determining its representation in Congress and its vote in the Electoral College. Thus the abolition of slavery and the end of the three-fifths compromise would reduce Southern political power in Congress unless Southern states gave blacks the right to vote and hence a share in that power.

The JOINT COMMITTEE ON RECONSTRUCTION, established by CONCURRENT RESOLUTIONS of the House and Senate in the opening days of the Congress, sought to put the possible solutions into some sort of order. Four members of this fifteen-man committee were most prominent in its activities: JOHN A. BINGHAM and THADDEUS STEVENS from the House and WILLIAM PITT FESSENDEN and JACOB M. HOWARD from the Senate.

At the third meeting of the Joint Committee on January 12, 1866, Bingham proposed a constitutional amendment that would give Congress "power to make all laws necessary and proper to secure to all persons in every State within this Union equal protection in their rights of life, liberty and property." The proposal was referred to a subcommittee which eight days later returned it to the Joint Committee in the following form: "Congress shall have power to make all laws necessary and proper to secure to all citizens of the United States, in every State, the same political rights and privileges; and to all persons in every State equal protection in the enjoyment of life, liberty, and property." In this form the proposal addressed two of the problems then pending, because it gave Congress power to protect civil rights and to legislate VOTING RIGHTS for blacks. This proposal, however, was never presented to Congress. The committee spent two weeks debating its language, finally agreeing on February 3 to the following: "The Congress shall have power to make all laws which shall be necessary and proper to secure to citizens of each State all privileges and immunities of citizens in the several States [Art. IV, Sec. 2]; and to all persons in the several States equal protection in the rights of life, liberty and property [5th Amendment]." A key issue that subsequent judges and scholars have long debated is whether this change in language was meant to deprive Congress of power to legislate black suffrage or merely to put that power into more acceptable language.

On the same day that the subcommittee submitted the early version of the amendment to the Joint Committee, it also submitted a proposal basing representation on population, but further providing "[t]hat whenever the elective franchise shall be denied or abridged in any State on account of race or color, all persons of such race or color shall be excluded from the basis of representation." Thus, the total package as of January 20 not only gave Congress power to legislate civil rights and black suffrage—power which Congress might or might not exercise—but also deprived a state of representation based on its black population if blacks were not given suffrage either by Congress or by the state. The package, as altered by the language change of February 3, was submitted to the full House as two separate constitutional amendments.

On February 28, the House postponed consideration of the Bingham amendment conferring legislative power on Congress, and never again considered that amendment as a separate entity. Earlier it had passed and sent to the Senate the amendment depriving states of representation if blacks were denied the right to vote. The Senate, however, never acted on the proposal. Thus, by the end of February 1866, the two forerunners of the Fourteenth Amendment had come to nought.

Both reappeared in slightly different language, however, in the omnibus measure which the Joint Committee presented to both houses of Congress on April 30, 1866. Section 1 of the measure was the sentence containing today's privilege and immunities, due process, and equal clauses, while section 2 reduced the representation of states who denied the right to vote to males over the age of twenty-one. Section 3 deprived all persons who had voluntarily supported the Confederate cause of the right to vote in federal elections prior to 1870, while section 4 dealt with the war debt. Section 5 gave Congress power to enforce the other four sections.

The omnibus amendment passed the House as proposed, but it faced difficulties in the Senate. When it emerged from the Senate on June 8, it had been changed in two significant respects. One of the changes added to section 1 a definition of CITIZENSHIP. The Senate also weakened section 3; instead of disfranchising those who had supported the Confederacy, it merely barred from federal office those Confederate supporters who prior to the Civil War had taken an oath to support the Constitution.

After the House had concurred on June 13 in the Senate's changes, the amendment was sent to the states. Twelve days later, on June 25, Connecticut became the first state to ratify. Five additional states ratified the amendment in 1866, and eleven added their RATIFICATIONS in January 1867. By June of 1867, one year after the amendment had been sent to the states, a total of twenty-two had ratified it.

Ratification by six more states was needed, however, and that did not occur until July 1868. By that time two of the states that had previously ratified the amendment, New Jersey and Ohio, had voted to withdraw their assent. Nonetheless Congress ruled that their ratifications survived the subsequent efforts at withdrawal and remained valid. On July 28, 1868, Secretary of State WILLIAM SEWARD accordingly proclaimed the Fourteenth Amendment part of the Constitution of the United States.

In recent decades, historians and judges have extensively debated three questions about the meaning which the Thirty-Ninth Congress and the ratifying states attached to the Fourteenth Amendment, especially to section 1. First, does section 1 give Congress power to protect voting rights? Second, does section 1 overrule BARRON V. BALTIMORE (1833) and require the states to abide by the provisions of the BILL OF RIGHTS? Third, does section 1 prohibit compulsory racial SEGREGATION?

Did section 1 of the Fourteenth Amendment give Congress power to protect voting rights? The Justices of the Supreme Court have been divided in their answer to this question, although the weight of historical scholarship leans toward the view that section 1 was not concerned with voting rights. As the above summary of the progress of the amendment in Congress suggests, resolution of the issue depends on whether the privileges and immunities language in section 1 was meant to alter the substance or only the form of an earlier version of the section, which explicitly gave Congress power to secure to all citizens in every state "equal political rights and privileges." The question can never be answered definitively, for the substitution was made in committee and the committee left no record of its reasoning. The record of congressional debates is equally ambiguous. When the present language of section 1 was on the floor, some congressmen suggested that the section gave Congress power to protect voting rights, but others disagreed. Similarly, some congressmen claimed after the amendment had been adopted that it gave them power to legislate protection of voting rights—and again others disagreed.

Was section 1 meant to overrule *Barron v. Baltimore* and compel the states to abide by the provisions of the Bill of Rights? Justice HUGO L. BLACK, relying on explicit statements during congressional debates that the section would accomplish that end, declared in a dissenting opinion in ADAMSON V. CALIFORNIA (1947) that the Fourteenth Amendment did incorporate the Bill of Rights and apply it to the states. Some scholars have supported Black's position. However, two years after *Adamson* Charles Fairman wrote an article challenging Black. Fairman noted that many states in the 1860s did not follow procedures mandated by the Bill of Rights, but that no one during state ratification proceedings seemed concerned that adoption of the Fourteenth Amendment would require changes in state practice. He thought it probable that, if the states were concerned that the amendment, through INCORPORATION of the Bill of Rights, would require changes in their practices, they would at least have discussed the issue. He concluded from the lack of discussion that the amendment had no such purpose. The view of several recent scholars has been that, in light of the conflicting and insubstantial evidence, the question raised by Justice Black can never be conclusively answered.

Finally, there is the question whether section 1 was intended to prohibit racial segregation. After asking the litigants in BROWN V. BOARD OF EDUCATION (1954) to address this question, the Court concluded that the historical evidence was too ambiguous to permit an answer. Some scholars, however, have been more confident. Raoul Berger concluded that the framers of the amendment did not intend to prohibit racial segregation. On the other hand, ALEXANDER BICKEL had argued some years earlier that the framers had consciously framed section 1 in broad, open-ended language that would permit people in the future to interpret it as prohibiting the practice of segregation. The historical record itself is sparse. During the debates in Congress on the amendment, little was said about segregation. Earlier, however, Congress had engaged in lengthy debates about the legality of segregation on DISTRICT OF COLUMBIA streetcars. Moreover, school segregation was opposed by some members of Congress, notably CHARLES SUMNER who had been counsel in ROBERTS V. CITY OF BOSTON, an 1849 school desegregation case. In the 1860s, however, Congress was permitting racially segregated schools to exist in the District of Columbia.

Questions about whether the Thirty-Ninth Congress and the states that ratified the Fourteenth Amendment intended it to protect voting rights, make the Bill of Rights binding on the states, or outlaw segregation can never be answered confidently. All that the person who inquires into the historical record in search of an answer can do is make a guess—a guess more likely to reflect his political beliefs than to reflect the state of the historical record. The questions that judges and historians have asked about the original meaning of the Fourteenth Amendment are simply the wrong ones, because they do not address the issues that Congress and the ratifying states in fact debated and decided during the era of Reconstruction.

On one point of political philosophy, nearly all Americans of the 1860s agreed. President Andrew Johnson stated the point in his 1865 State of the Union address: "Monopolies, perpetuities, and class legislation are contrary to the genius of free government, and ought not to be allowed. Here there is no room for favored classes or monopolies; the principle of our Government is that of equal laws. . . . We shall but fulfill our duties as legislators by according 'equal and exact justice to all men,' special privileges to none." Innumerable Republicans argued that the purpose of section 1 of the Fourteenth Amendment was to enact this political principle into law. John A. Bingham, the draftsman of section 1, said what others repeated: that he proposed "by amending the Constitution, to provide for the efficient enforcement, by law, of these 'equal rights of every man' "—of "the absolute equality of all men before the law." Even Democrats from former slave states accepted the principle that the law should treat all persons equally. There was neither division nor sustained debate in the Thirty-Ninth Congress over the contrary principle that people who are in fact the same should receive equal treatment before the law and that people who are different may be treated differently. The issue on which Republicans and Democrats divided was whether black people, in essence, were equal to white people or inherently inferior.

Garrett Davis, a Democratic senator from Kentucky, used typical racist rhetoric. During an 1866 debate on the question whether blacks should be permitted to vote in the District of Columbia, Davis said:

> [T]he proposition that a nation of a superior race should allow an inferior race resident in large numbers among them to take part in their Government, in shaping, and controlling their destinies, is refuted by its mere statement. And the further proposition that a nation composed of the Caucasian race, the highest type of man, having resident in it more than four million negroes, the lowest type, of which race no nation or tribe, from the first dawning of history to the present day, has ever established a polity that could be denominated a Government, or has elaborated for itself any science or literature or arts or even an alphabet, or characters to represent numbers, or been capable of preserving those achievements of intellect when it has received them from the superior race; such a proposition is, on examination, revolting to reason, and in its practical operation would be productive of incalculable mischief.

Republicans responded to this "prejudice," which "belong[ed] to an age of darkness and violence, and is a poisonous, dangerous exotic when suffered to grow in the midst of republican institutions." Jacob M. Howard, a key member of the Joint Committee, told the Senate:

> For weal or for woe, the destiny of the colored race in this country is wrapped up with our own; they are to remain

in our midst, and here spend their years and here bury their fathers and finally repose themselves. We may regret it. It may not be entirely compatible with our taste that they should live in our midst. We cannot help it. Our forefathers introduced them, and their destiny is to continue among us; and the practical question which now presents itself to us is as to the best mode of getting along with them.

Justin Morrill of Vermont added: "We have put aside the creed of the despot, the monarchist, the aristocrat, and have affirmed the right and capacity of the people to govern themselves, and have staked the national life on the issue to make it good in practice. . . . To deny any portion of the American people civil or political rights common to the citizen upon pretense of race or color, is to ignore the fundamental principles of republicanism." The only proper policy for the Government, according to Lyman Trumbull, chairman of the Senate Judiciary Committee, was "to legislate in the interest of freedom. Now, our laws are to be enacted with a view to educate, improve, enlighten, and Christianize the negro; to make him an independent man; to teach him to think and to reason; to improve that principle which the great Author of all has implanted in every human breast, which is susceptible of the highest cultivation, and destined to go on enlarging and expanding through the endless ages of eternity."

Trumbull and his fellow Republicans understood that God had created blacks as the equals of whites and that, if the law gave blacks an opportunity, they would demonstrate their equality. The Republicans made this equalitarian faith the basis of the Fourteenth Amendment. Although the faith was forgotten within a decade of the Fourteenth Amendment's ratification, it still offers a perspective from which to begin analysis of the issues of Fourteenth Amendment jurisprudence that confront us today.

WILLIAM E. NELSON

(SEE ALSO: *Abolitionist Constitutional Theory.*)

Bibliography

BERGER, RAOUL 1977 *Government by Judiciary: The Transformation of the Fourteenth Amendment.* Cambridge, Mass.: Harvard University Press.

BICKEL, ALEXANDER M. 1955 The Original Understanding and the Segregation Decision. *Harvard Law Review* 69:1–65.

FAIRMAN, CHARLES 1949 Does the Fourteenth Amendment Incorporate the Bill of Rights? The Original Understanding. *Stanford Law Review* 2:5–173.

HYMAN, HAROLD M. and WIECEK, WILLIAM M. 1982 *Equal Justice under Law: Constitutional Development 1835–1875.* New York: Harper & Row.

JAMES, JOSEPH B. 1956 *The Framing of the Fourteenth Amendment.* Urbana: University of Illinois Press.

TEN BROEK, JACOBUS 1951 *The Antislavery Origins of the Fourteenth Amendment.* Berkeley: University of California Press.

FOURTH AMENDMENT
(Historical Origins)

Appended to the United States Constitution as part of the BILL OF RIGHTS in 1789, the Fourth Amendment declares that "The right of the people to be secure in their persons, houses, papers and effects against UNREASONABLE SEARCHES and seizures shall not be violated, and no warrants shall issue but upon PROBABLE CAUSE, supported by oath or affirmation, and particularly describing the place to be searched and the persons or things to be seized." In identifying the "specific" warrant as its orthodox method of search, the amendment constitutionally repudiated its antithesis, the GENERAL WARRANT.

The general warrant did not confine its reach to a particular person, place, or object but allowed its bearer to arrest, search, and seize as his suspicions directed. In 1763, a typical warrant by the British secretaries of state commanded "diligent search" for the unidentified author, printer, and publisher of a satirical journal, *The North Briton, No. 45,* and the seizure of their papers. At least five houses were consequently searched, forty-nine (mostly innocent) persons arrested, and thousands of books and papers confiscated. Resentment against such invasions ultimately generated an antidote in the Fourth Amendment and is crucial to its understanding.

General warrants and general searches without warrant had a lengthy pedigree. In 1662, a statute codified WRITS OF ASSISTANCE that allowed searching all suspected places for goods concealed in violation of the customs laws. Such writs had been used since at least 1621 and themselves absorbed the language of royal commissions that had for centuries authorized general searches without warrant. Similarly promiscuous searches had existed for numerous applications: the pursuit of felons, suppression of political and religious deviance, regulation of printing, medieval craft guilds, naval and military impressment, counterfeiting, bankruptcy, excise and land taxes, vagrancy, game poaching, sumptuary behavior, and even the recovery of stolen personal items.

Colonial America copied Britain's machinery of search but varied its applications. Most jurisdictions instituted general searches to collect taxes, discourage poaching, capture felons, or find stolen merchandise. In the southernmost colonies, general searches without warrant blossomed into a comprehensive system of social regulation of the civilian population by quasi-military "slave patrols."

Although general warrants were the basic method of search, numerous restraints qualified their operation. Writs of assistance were invalid at night; certain areas of legislation touching the guilds and excises confined the general searches involved to the persons vocationally concerned. Yet such measures were not a comprehensive guarantee, systematically applied. Moreover, social philosophy outweighed civil libertarianism as a motive for the most conspicuous restraints, for while general "privy searches" plagued the poor, the elite enjoyed immunity from whole classes of similar searches. Covered by a thin veneer of restraints different from the specific warrant, the centrality of the general search remained starkly visible. Conversely, although specific warrants existed in legal manuals, they were rare before 1750, thereby indicating that they were not the intended constitutional successor to the general warrant.

English legal thinkers, however, expressed far greater hostility to the general warrant than did the law itself. As early as 1589 Robert Beale charged that the general search warrants used by the "High Commission" against Puritans violated MAGNA CARTA (1215). In the next two centuries, such titans of English law as Sir EDWARD COKE, Sir Matthew Hale, and Sir WILLIAM BLACKSTONE embellished similar themes with citations from the COMMON LAW.

Such evidence, however, was more embroidery than substance. Magna Carta was a profoundly feudal document that said nothing on the intersection of searches, houses, and warrants. The master case usually cited against the general warrant, *Semayne's Case* (1602, 1604), actually drew a rigid line exempting the Crown from the protections elsewhere extended against invasion of the dwelling by private citizens. Unlike later scholars, the court had there emphasized that a man's house was *not* his castle against the government.

Like legal theorists, ordinary critics of the general search did not identify the specific warrant as its solution. Those whose houses were searched were more likely to execrate being searched than the generality of the authorizing warrant. Indignation that the victim of a general search was a member of the nobility deflected hostility from the search process and implied that it could properly be inflicted on the overwhelming majority who were not nobles. Ubiquitous laments that pregnant wives had miscarried during violent searches simply substituted appeals to the reader's sympathy for criticism of the absence of the concrete laws against such actions. Yet these very mythologies provided legitimacy and impulse for a right against unreasonable SEARCH AND SEIZURE. Although the Magna Carta of the thirteenth century said nothing against general searches, that of the eighteenth century had swollen into a formidable ideological weapon against them.

The movement against general warrants accelerated from 1761 to 1787. The *North Briton* controversy culminated in dozens of trials and in resolutions by the House of Commons against the use of those warrants. In *Wilkes v. Wood* (1763) and *Huckle v. Money* (1763–1765), CHARLES PRATT (Lord Camden) and WILLIAM MURRAY (Lord Mansfield), the chief justices of the Courts of Common Pleas and King's Bench, respectively, condemned the general warrants of search and arrest used by the secretaries of state as incompatible with statute, natural justice, the common law, and Magna Carta. A dozen derivative cases surrounding *Entick v. Carrington* ended in decisions against the seizure of personal papers. (See WILKES CASES.)

Writs of assistance came under attack in the American colonial courts. JAMES OTIS, a fiery young Massachusetts attorney, made a brilliant "higher law" assault on the writs in PAXTON'S CASE (1761). Although Otis lost, most colonial courts refused to issue such writs when requuired to do so by the Townshend Act of 1767, and a series of pamphlets beginning with JOHN DICKINSON'S *Farmer's Letters* joined in the assault. Eight states inserted some guarantee against general warrants in their constitutions of 1776–1784. Finally, four state conventions urged a corresponding restraint on searches by the new national government in ratifying the federal Constitution of 1787. JAMES MADISON of Virginia duly responded by including what became the Fourth Amendment among the Bill of Rights which he proposed to Congress on June 8, 1789.

Neither Britain nor the separate American states, however, immediately abolished general searches. Rhetorical implications notwithstanding, the British abandoned only the isolated form of general warrants issued by state secretaries. Writs of assistance and other kinds of statutory general SEARCH WARRANTS survived, for no comprehensive statute to the contrary ever emerged from the House of Commons. Despite their constitutions, the American states retained general search warrants not only as devices for [prosecuting the American Revolution] but also for a wide range of other purposes into the 1780s.

Although the right against unreasonable search and seizure has lengthy British roots, its cornerstone, the confinement of all searches, seizures, and arrests by warrant to the particular place, persons, and objects enumerated, derives from Massachusetts. A cluster of Massachusetts statutes and court decisions from 1756 to 1766, the third stage in a century-long process, uniformly restrained searches and arrests to the person or location designated in the warrant. Legislation in the 1780s extended this specificity to the objects of seizure. The Fourth Amendment is thus the marriage of an ancient British right and a new, colonial interpretation that vastly extended its meaning.

WILLIAM J. CUDDIHY

Bibliography

CUDDIHY, WILLIAM and HARDY, B. CARMON 1980 A Man's House Was Not His Castle: Origins of the Fourth Amendment to the United States Constitution. *William and Mary Quarterly* 3:371–400.

LASSON, NELSON 1937 *The History . . . of the Fourth Amendment.* Baltimore: Johns Hopkins University Press.

FRAENKEL, OSMOND K. (1888–1981)

Trained at Columbia University Law School, Osmond Kessler Fraenkel made his mark on American constitutional law as a CIVIL LIBERTIES advocate. He was counsel for the New York Civil Liberties Union from 1934 to 1955 and for the AMERICAN CIVIL LIBERTIES UNION from 1955 to 1977. During most of that time he was also an official of the National Lawyers Guild. In addition to being involved in much of the important civil liberties litigation of his time, Fraenkel wrote four books, including *Our Civil Liberties* (1945) and *The Supreme Court and Civil Liberties* (1960), as well as many law review articles.

DENNIS J. MAHONEY

FRANK, JEROME N. (1889–1957)

Jerome Frank held important positions in FRANKLIN D. ROOSEVELT's New Deal, pioneered American legal realism, taught at Yale Law School, and served on the United States Court of Appeals for the Second Circuit from 1941 until his death in 1957. During this period the Second Circuit was one of the most illustrious courts in the nation's history. On the court Frank developed a highly refined concept of his role as intermediate appellate judge. His decisions greatly influenced the United States Supreme Court by crystallizing and focusing legal issues and by articulating major considerations of precedent and policy. His opinions, even if written as concurrences or dissents, frequently became the law of the land when the Supreme Court followed Jerome Frank's lead. When the VINSON COURT and WARREN COURT protected CIVIL LIBERTIES, they often relied on the spadework of lower federal judges, prominently including Jerome Frank.

In his opinions Frank frequently addressed the Supreme Court as an advocate—urging, persuading, coaxing, and cajoling the Court to move in desired directions. At the same time, he recognized the limits imposed by his subordinate position, and he gracefully accepted those bounds. Frank faithfully followed Supreme Court precedent, but, if a rule seemed misguided, he would criticize the DOCTRINE and urge the Supreme Court to reexamine it. *United States v. Roth* (1956) illustrates Frank's technique. Although he considered a federal OBSCENITY statute unconstitutional, several Supreme Court decisions had assumed the statute's validity without squarely facing the issue. In a new challenge to the law, Frank did not dodge these earlier rulings by describing them as OBITER DICTA. Rather, he followed them and voted to uphold the convictions. At the same time, in a concurrence, he analyzed the serious constitutional issues with a coherence and lucidity that has not yet been surpassed. Frank's seminal effort anticipated many later Supreme Court cases which, over the next two decades, relied on Frank's opinion and reasoning. (See *Roth v. United States*, 1957.)

Protection for civil liberties was a persistent theme in Frank's judicial opinions. He believed that republican government maximized free choice and affirmed the dignity of the individual. On the Second Circuit he struggled to protect this vision. He regularly challenged the Supreme Court to expand the definition of, and protection for, civil liberties. For instance, he tried valiantly to humanize IMMIGRATION and DEPORTATION laws which perennially had treated ALIENS cavalierly. Frank wrote his most passionate opinions in the area of criminal law and procedure. He considered ELECTRONIC EAVESDROPPING a dangerous invasion of privacy which should be limited by the FOURTH AMENDMENT's prohibition on UNREASONABLE SEARCHES and seizures. His skepticism about the accuracy of the law's fact-finding processes led him to believe that courts wrongly convicted many innocent persons. He thought that police investigation practices frequently degenerated into brutal "third degree" tactics which coerced confessions in violation of the Fifth and Sixth Amendments. Following in Frank's path, the Supreme Court moved to curb prolonged POLICE INTERROGATIONS and to control offensive police practices. The progressive constitutionalization of American criminal process secured by the Vinson and Warren Courts reflected not merely the judgment of a majority of the Supreme Court but rather a broader legal movement led prominently by Jerome Frank.

ROBERT JEROME GLENNON

Bibliography

GLENNON, ROBERT JEROME 1985 *The Iconoclast as Reformer: Jerome Frank's Impact on American Law.* Ithaca, N.Y.: Cornell University Press.

FRANK v. MANGUM
237 U.S. 309 (1915)

Vicious anti-Semitism and bitter resentment against encroaching industrialization joined in Atlanta, Georgia, in the spring of 1913. Leo Frank, a young Jewish businessman from the North, was arrested and convicted of murdering a thirteen-year-old girl in a factory he superintended. Prejudice, disorder, and blatant public hostility characterized the trial and its coverage. The Georgia Supreme Court denied Frank a new trial, 4–2, dismissing claims of procedural errors, irregularities, and the trial judge's stated doubts about Frank's guilt.

Justices JOSEPH R. LAMAR and OLIVER WENDELL HOLMES each turned down requests for WRITS OF ERROR on procedural grounds (though Holmes was not convinced that Frank had received DUE PROCESS), as did the entire Supreme Court, without opinion. Frank then petitioned for a writ of HABEAS CORPUS because mob domination had effectively denied him PROCEDURAL DUE PROCESS. The Court likewise denied this relief, 7–2. Justice MAHLON PITNEY declared that habeas corpus could not be substituted for a writ of error to review procedural irregularities. Further, when Frank neglected to object during the trial, he effectively waived the right to claim a denial of due process later. Justices Holmes and CHARLES EVANS HUGHES dissented, pointing to the lack of a FAIR TRIAL: "Mob law does not become due process of law by securing the assent of a terrorized jury." Less than two months after the Georgia governor commuted his death sentence to life imprisonment, Frank was kidnapped from prison and lynched. That he was innocent of the crime for which he was convicted is no longer doubted.

The Supreme Court subsequently embarked on a series of decisions insuring the observance of the constitutional safeguards of procedural due process. In MOORE V. DEMPSEY (1923), the turning point, Holmes wrote for the Court, permitting the use of habeas corpus as a means of preserving criminal defendants' rights. *Frank*'s rule of forfeiture through failure to object, however, returned with only slight modification in WAINWRIGHT V. SYKES (1977).

In 1982 a witness came forward and stated that shortly after the murder he had seen another man carrying the victim's body. In 1986 the governor of Georgia posthumously pardoned Leo Frank.

DAVID GORDON

Bibliography

DINNERSTEIN, LEONARD 1968 *The Leo Frank Case.* New York: Columbia University Press.

FRANKFURTER, FELIX
(1882–1965)

The immigrant son of Austrian Jews, Felix Frankfurter acquired a legendary reputation as a lawyer, law professor, intellectual gadfly, and presidential adviser even before President FRANKLIN D. ROOSEVELT named him to the Supreme Court in 1939. Unable to speak or write a word of English when he entered the public schools of New York City in the 1890s, he was graduated with honors from City College of New York and compiled a distinguished record at the Harvard Law School, where he fell under the influence of Dean James Barr Ames's historical methods, absorbed the constitutional theories of JAMES BRADLEY THAYER, and generally adopted the social and cultural trappings of the New England Brahmins, without their intellectual boorishness or political conservatism.

As a law professor at Harvard, Frankfurter introduced several generations of students to constitutional and ADMINISTRATIVE LAW, and invented a new field of study: the JURISDICTION of the federal courts. His students and protégés, including Dean Acheson, JAMES LANDIS, David Lilienthal, and Tom Corcoran, populated the federal bureaucracy from the days of WOODROW WILSON to those of JOHN F. KENNEDY. His 1917 report on the deportation of striking miners from Arizona by local vigilantes and his severe criticism of the procedural unfairness of the COMMONWEALTH V. SACCO & VANZETTI (1921) showed his deep concern for CIVIL LIBERTIES and political reform. That he should come to be known, at the end of his judicial career, as a conservative on many of these issues reflected not a weakening of personal convictions, but a strongly held view about the proper limits of the judicial function.

Frankfurter served on the Court between the two great periods of JUDICIAL ACTIVISM in this century. He arrived on the bench two years after the HUGHES COURT, retreating from its activism of 1935–1936, laid to rest the DUE PROCESS clause and the COMMERCE CLAUSE as instruments of judicial control over legislative ECONOMIC REGULATION. His retirement and replacement in 1962 by ARTHUR J. GOLDBERG permitted the Warren Court to enter its most activist phase through the expansion of due process and EQUAL PROTECTION to provide Americans with extensive new CONSTITUTIONAL REMEDIES against governmental encroachments upon personal liberties.

Frankfurter deplored both the conservative activism of the Hughes years and the liberal activism of the Warren era. From 1939 until 1962, he attempted to discover some middle ground for the Court to occupy that would be intellectually respectable, politically defensible, and morally satisfying. Although his ultimate posture of institutional self-restraint won him few plaudits from liberals and captured the fancy of only a minority among the legal intelligentsia, it had the virtue of predictability.

He rejected the PREFERRED FREEDOMS doctrine articulated by Justice HARLAN FISKE STONE in UNITED STATES v. CAROLENE PRODUCTS CO. (1938), where the latter urged the Court to adopt a two-tiered system of JUDICIAL REVIEW that would take the justices out of the business of shaping economic policy at large but expand their role as the arbiters of civil liberties, race relations, and criminal justice. When passing upon all constitutional questions, Frankfurter responded, the Justices should always act with restraint, avoid ultimate issues of power, and insist only upon a RATIONAL BASIS test for legislation, whether the challenged law concerned filled milk, labor relations, FREEDOM OF SPEECH, or CRIMINAL PROCEDURE. This judicial posture led Frankfurter to uphold a broad range of social and economic measures adopted by the states and the federal government after 1940, but it also earned him the enmity of constitutional liberals when he applied the same tolerant standards to less enlightened manifestations of the political process, including the SMITH ACT, the McCarran Act (see INTERNAL SECURITY ACT), a GROUP LIBEL statute, and the investigative techniques of the HOUSE COMMITTEE ON UN-AMERICAN ACTIVITIES.

Frankfurter also spurned Justice HUGO L. BLACK's arguments for incorporating the BILL OF RIGHTS into the FOURTEENTH AMENDMENT's due process clause. Like Frankfurter, the Alabama-born justice wished to chain the arbitrary power of judges in the wake of the Great Depression's constitutional crisis, and he urged the Court to replace "the vague contours of due process" with the specific prohibitions and guarantees of the first nine amendments. But beneath Black's façade of positivistic neutrality, Frankfurter suspected, there beat the heart of a judicial fundamentalist, moved by the plight of the poor and the oppressed but no less unbending than PIERCE BUTLER's or GEORGE SUTHERLAND's. Frankfurter eschewed mechanical formulas such as Black's, and he believed that the INCORPORATION DOCTRINE lacked any historical basis in the Fourteenth Amendment. Incorporation, he feared, would encourage the Supreme Court to impose a single code of criminal procedure upon the states and would establish a more rigid judicial tyranny than even the conservative "Four Horsemen" had espoused during the 1930s.

From BETTS v. BRADY (1942) to MAPP v. OHIO in 1961, he insisted that the framers of the Fourteenth Amendment had not intended to subject state criminal proceedings to the precise requirements of the federal Bill of Rights. That amendment, he argued in ADAMSON v. CALIFORNIA (1947), was "not the basis of a uniform code of criminal procedure federally imposed. . . . In a federal system it would be a function debilitating to the responsibility of state and local agencies."

But this did not mean for Frankfurter that the Supreme Court of the United States had no obligation to review state criminal convictions under the due process clause. That clause, he believed, represented no explicit commands, but a requirement of fairness and reasonableness, above all, a prohibition against official conduct that "shocked the conscience" or offended contemporary standards of civilized behavior. Within this broad, subjective framework, the states had flexibility to manage their own affairs in the realm of criminal justice. Police officers could not, in the absence of friends or counsel, interrogate a suspect for days and claim that his confession had been voluntary; they could not recover physical evidence with the aid of a stomach pump (as in ROCHIN v. CALIFORNIA, 1952); or place a listening device in a suspect's bedroom (as in IRVINE v. CALIFORNIA, 1953, dissenting opinion). But due process did not require, in Frankfurter's judgment, that the state provide legal counsel in all felony cases; exclude evidence seized illegally by the police; or refrain from executing a person after a first attempt had failed, although he had strong personal objections to all of these practices

(*Louisiana ex rel. Francis v. Resweber,* 1947, concurring opinion; *Mapp v. Ohio,* 1961, dissenting).

An early high point of Frankfurter's doctrinal influence came in the summer of 1940, when, over Stone's lone dissent, the Justices rejected a FIRST AMENDMENT–due process attack on the mandatory flag salute in the public schools of West Virginia. Within a year of that decision, however, Frankfurter's majority disintegrated. (See FLAG SALUTE CASES, 1940–1943.) Led by Black and WILLIAM O. DOUGLAS, a coalition of from five to six Justices carved out a generous area of constitutional protection for both religious and political minorities under the First Amendment and the due process clause. This same majority also began to impose sharp limitations upon the conduct of state criminal trials and local police methods and to afford state prisoners greater ACCESS to federal courts by means of HABEAS CORPUS proceedings.

Throughout his judicial career, Frankfurter remained skeptical of absolutes. He preached a gospel of relativism and "balancing" that usually encouraged judicial modesty and retrenchment, yet, he too could be a fundamentalist on many constitutional questions. Few Justices took more literally the First Amendment's prohibition against an ESTABLISHMENT OF RELIGION, and his views in EVERSON V. BOARD OF EDUCATION (1947) and MCCOLLUM V. BOARD OF EDUCATION (1948) remained as uncompromising as Black's on freedom of speech. He abhorred CAPITAL PUNISHMENT and used every weapon in his considerable legal arsenal to set aside convictions that carried the death penalty.

Moreover, he consistently championed the FOURTH AMENDMENT by refusing to bend its language to accommodate SEARCHES AND SEIZURES made without a valid warrant or PROBABLE CAUSE as demonstrated by his dissenting opinion in UNITED STATES V. RABINOWITZ (1950). Finally, although he resisted the extension of the EXCLUSIONARY RULE to the states via the due process clause, he expected federal judges, prosecutors, and law enforcement officials to follow a strict code of fairness and decency when confronting persons accused or suspected of crimes (*McNabb v. United States,* 1943, see MCNABB-MALLORY RULE; *Nye v. United States,* 1941; *Rosenberg v. United States,* 1953, dissenting opinion).

In addition to institutional self-restraint, Frankfurter found in FEDERALISM—perhaps the oldest of our constitutional values—a major, articulate premise of his jurisprudence. His concern for maintaining the vitality of local governmental units distinguished him sharply from most other post-1937 Justices. "The states," he wrote, nine years before joining the Court, "need the amplest scope for energy and individuality in dealing with the myriad problems created by our complex industrial civilization. . . . For government means experimentation. To be sure, constitutional limitations confine the area of experiment. But these limitations are not self-defining and were intended to permit government. Opportunity must be allowed for vindicating reasonable belief by experience. The very notion of our federalism calls for the free play of local diversity in dealing with local problems." From 1939 until 1962, he attempted to apply these convictions.

A great many of Frankfurter's conflicts with other Justices, often viewed as disputes over civil liberties or judicial self-restraint, actually focused for him upon questions of federalism. A good example is the famous 1941 case of BRIDGES V. CALIFORNIA, which, many scholars agree, marked a turning point in his relationship with Justice Black and remains a landmark in the Court's post-1937 concern for civil liberties. In *Bridges,* speaking through Black, the Court reversed contempt sentences imposed by California judges upon a militant union leader and the Los Angeles *Times* for out-of-court publications that the local courts believed had disrupted pending cases. Unless such statements represented a CLEAR AND PRESENT DANGER to the orderly administration of justice, Black wrote, the due process clause (incorporating the First Amendment's protection of speech and press) prohibited judicial punishment of this kind.

Frankfurter took issue with Black on several points, but the heart of his dissenting opinion reflected powerful federalist concerns for the independence and autonomy of local courts. "We are, after all," he noted, "sitting over three thousand miles away from a great state, without intimate knowledge of its habits and its needs, in matters which do not cut across the affirmative powers of the national government. . . . How are we to know whether an easy-going or stiffer view of what affects the actual administration of justice is appropriate to local circumstances?" Nine months earlier, in a similar contempt case that did not raise the problem of a direct conflict with state courts, Frankfurter had no difficulty in joining an opinion by Justice Douglas in *Nye v. United States* (1941) that sharply curtailed the power of federal judges to punish disruptive litigants. For Frankfurter, what distinguished *Nye* from *Bridges* was not the First Amendment, "the clear and present danger" test, or the degree of judicial misconduct involved, but the simple matter of the constitution's limited reach into the processes of state courts.

A passionate New Dealer, Frankfurter consistently

upheld the power of Congress, acting under the commerce clause, to regulate the nation's economic affairs, even when these regulations touched activities within the traditional domain of the states. He sustained, for example, the judgment of the National Labor Relations Board that local newspaper boys, employed by the Hearst chain, were "employees" within the coverage of the WAGNER (NATIONAL LABOR RELATIONS) ACT, and he agreed that the administrator of the FAIR LABOR STANDARDS ACT could entirely prohibit homework in the embroidery industry as a reasonable means to enforce minimum wage decrees.

At the same time, he tended to read congressional regulation of commerce as permitting complementary state legislation, except where the national legislature acted with clarity to preempt local regulations. He insisted that Congress speak with precision on this matter, and he abhorred judicial expansion of congressional intentions, especially where the results limited local authority. In *Cornell Steamboat Co. v. United States* (1944), for instance, he rejected Black's interpretation of the 1940 Transportation Act that gave the Interstate Commerce Commission authority to fix the rates of tugboats operating on the Hudson River, where ninety-five percent of their business took place between New York ports, but where they passed briefly over the territorial waters of New Jersey. He rejected the idea that Congress had intended in the Wagner Act to exempt union officials from state regulation that did not touch directly upon the employee–employer relationship. In close cases, he often supported a solution that expanded federal authority the least.

In commerce clause cases, despite his concern for maintaining local authority, he refused to endorse the extreme views of Justice Black and others, who mechanically endorsed state economic regulations in the absence of specific federal legislation preempting certain fields. He voted to overturn, for example, Arizona's Train Limit Law and he likewise objected to a local milk ordinance that discriminated against competing products pasteurized beyond five miles of the city. On the other hand, he often allowed the states considerable latitude when they attempted to tax or regulate other aspects of interstate commerce, and he did not support wholeheartedly the economic nationalism of Justice ROBERT H. JACKSON, with whom he disagreed in cases such as *Duckworth v. Arkansas* (1941); *Northwest Airlines v. Minnesota* (1944); and *H. P. Hood & Sons v. DuMond* (1949; dissenting).

Frankfurter believed that federalism required the national judiciary, above all the Supreme Court, to respect the autonomy, sagacity, and integrity of state courts. He was a strong supporter of Justice LOUIS D. BRANDEIS's views (which had become law in ERIE V. TOMPKINS, 1938) that required federal judges to apply state law in cases involving diversity of state citizenship, and he often voted to restrict the role of federal courts in this area. (See DIVERSITY JURISDICTION.) State courts, he believed, could efficiently and honestly protect the interests of nonresidents. The Supreme Court should not construe federal statutes in such a manner as to preempt local judicial procedures unless that construction seemed inescapable. For instance, he rejected the idea that Congress intended in the federal bankruptcy laws to strip local courts of their control over their own procedures. "The state courts belong to the States," he wrote. "They are not subject to the control of Congress though of course state law may in words or by implication make the federal rule for conducting litigation the rule that should govern suits to enforce federal rights in the state courts."

America's continuing racial ordeal probably tested the limits of his deference to state authority more severely than did any other constitutional issue. An early member of the NAACP and the first Justice to hire a black clerk, he detested racial discrimination in all of its forms. Yet he refused to interpret the Reconstruction-era CIVIL RIGHTS ACTS to impose criminal and civil penalties on local officials who abused their authority and acted in a hostile manner against minorities. In SCREWS V. UNITED STATES (1945), Frankfurter, dissenting, argued that Congress had intended in the Reconstruction statute to attack only discrimination sanctioned by positive state laws, not the abuse of authority by local officials. "We should leave to the States," he said, "the enforcement of their criminal law, and not relieve States of the responsibility for vindicating wrongdoing that is essentially local or weaken the habits of local law enforcement by tempting reliance on federal authority for an occasional unpleasant task of local enforcement."

Two decades later, Frankfurter still reaffirmed these views in MONROE V. PAPE (1961), when the Court sustained a civil action against several Chicago police officers who invaded a black family's home and illegally arrested a member of the household without a SEARCH WARRANT. The conduct of the police infuriated him, but in Frankfurter's judgment they had not acted with the approval of state law and therefore they could not be sued under the federal statute for damages. "To be sure," he wrote, "this leaves certain cases unprotected. . . . But the cost of ignoring the distinction in order to cover those cases—the cost, that is, of providing a federal judicial remedy for every constitutional violation—involves preemption by the National Government . . . of matters of intimate concern to state and local government."

History treated neither Justice Frankfurter nor his federalism kindly. By means of the commerce clause and its TAXING AND SPENDING POWERS, the federal government continued to absorb more and more authority at the expense of the states, usually with the Supreme Court's approval. Horrified by local police brutality and by the failure of local political elites to eradicate racial SEGREGATION, the federal judiciary became a powerful instrument of social reform in the decade after Frankfurter left the bench. Even during his tenure, American society was not usually prepared to pay the price of his attachment to federalism. As the *Screws* and *Monroe* cases demonstrated, the price could be very high: the inability of the national government to correct glaring denials of constitutional rights that the states themselves refused to correct, and the failure of the states to correct local ills of a kind already eliminated in the conduct of the national government.

From the perspective of many of his colleagues, Frankfurter too often sacrificed efficiency, uniformity, and morality on behalf of an archaic devotion to localism. They hoped to create a new world of prodigious economic growth and humanitarian social policy, where the enlightened judiciary helped to sweep away the provincial forces of commercial and political reaction. For Justice Frankfurter, however, federalism remained both a constitutional command as well as a viable method for ordering American life through the slower process of self-education and social experimentation.

Frankfurter enlivened American politics and immeasurably enriched the nation's legal literature for a half-century. "There is some talk here of replacing him on the Supreme Court," James Reston wrote when he retired in 1962, "but this is as silly as the doctor's bulletins. They may eventually put somebody in his place, but they won't replace him."

MICHAEL E. PARRISH

Bibliography

FREEDMAN, MAX, ED. 1967 *Roosevelt and Frankfurter: Their Correspondence, 1928–1945.* Boston: Little, Brown.

HIRSCH, HARRY N. 1981 *The Enigma of Felix Frankfurter.* New York: Basic Books.

LASH, JOSEPH P. 1975 *From the Diaries of Felix Frankfurter.* New York: Norton.

PARRISH, MICHAEL E. 1982 *Felix Frankfurter and His Times.* Volume One. New York: Macmillan.

PHILLIPS, HARLAN B., ED. 1960 *Felix Frankfurter Reminisces.* New York: Reynal & Co.

FRANKLIN, BENJAMIN
(1706–1790)

Benjamin Franklin, president of Pennsylvania, was the oldest delegate to the CONSTITUTIONAL CONVENTION OF 1787. A beloved elder statesman of the young Republic, Franklin lent prestige to the Convention by his presence. His signature on the new Constitution was a symbol of the continuity of revolutionary principles and a warranty of the democratic character of the document.

Franklin's public career began in 1736, when he was appointed clerk of the Pennsylvania Assembly, and lasted for more than half a century. He served as a member of the assembly and as postmaster of British North America even while pursuing a private career as a printer and inventor.

In 1754, as a delegate to the Albany Congress, Franklin proposed the "Albany Plan" of colonial union. Under his plan, the British Crown would have appointed a president-general and the colonial legislatures would have chosen delegates to a Grand Council with power to raise an army and navy, to make war and peace with the Indian tribes, to control commerce with the Indians, and to levy taxes and customs duties to pay the expenses of the union. The plan, one of the earliest moves toward American FEDERALISM, was too consolidated to find support in the colonies and too democratic to be acceptable in England.

From 1757 to 1762, and again from 1766 to 1775, Franklin was the agent in England of Pennsylvania and several other colonies. In that capacity he explained to Parliament American opposition to the Stamp Act, that is, to TAXATION WITHOUT REPRESENTATION, and persuaded WILLIAM PITT to propose a plan of colonial union within the British Empire.

Returning to Pennsylvania in 1775, Franklin was named a delegate to the Second Continental Congress, where, in July, he proposed ARTICLES OF CONFEDERATION establishing a "league of friendship" among the colonies with a Congress that would exercise considerable legislative power. The following year he served on the committee that drafted the DECLARATION OF INDEPENDENCE.

From 1776 to 1785, Franklin served as minister of the United States to France (and was accredited to several other European governments as well). He negotiated the French military and financial assistance that was crucial to the success of the Revolution, and he carried out a propaganda campaign to win European support for the American cause. In

1781 he was named a commissioner to the peace negotiations that resulted in the Treaty of Paris and formal British recognition of American independence.

At the Constitutional Convention, Franklin was a conciliator and mediator. Although, at eighty-one, he was in failing health and had to have his speeches read by fellow delegate JAMES WILSON, Franklin attended almost all sessions. Such proposals as he put forward (for example, unicameral legislature, plural executive, elected judges, unpaid officials) were too radical to attract much support; but Franklin, with his humorous anecdotes and his commitment to the Union, served the Convention well by cooling tempers and encouraging compromise.

According to a legend, which serves as a warning still, Franklin, emerging from the Convention, was asked, "What have you given us?" "A republic," he replied, "if you can keep it."

DENNIS J. MAHONEY

Bibliography

VAN DOREN, CARL 1938 *Benjamin Franklin.* New York: Viking.

FRAZIER-LEMKE ACTS

Federal Farm Bankruptcy Act 48 Stat. 1289 (1934)

Farm Mortgage Moratorium Act 49 Stat. 942 (1935)

Congress passed the Federal Farm Bankruptcy Act in June 1934 in an effort to stem the flow of foreclosures caused by the Depression. Enacted as an amendment to a general bankruptcy act of 1898, the first Frazier-Lemke Act allowed bankrupt farmers two choices. Under the first, court-appointed appraisers would assess the "fair and reasonable value, not necessarily the market value" of the property, which the debtor could then repurchase within six years according to a graduated scale of interest. Alternatively, a court could halt all proceedings for five years, during which time the debtor would retain possession "provided he pays a reasonable rent annually," preserving the right to buy it after five years.

Within a year a unanimous Supreme Court struck down the act as a TAKING OF PROPERTY belonging to the creditor without JUST COMPENSATION in LOUISVILLE JOINT STOCK LAND BANK v. RADFORD (1935). Congress passed a second Frazier-Lemke (Farm Mortgage Moratorium) Act in August 1935, effectively similar legislation to which they added a declaration of emergency and a discretionary provision allowing courts to shorten the stay of proceedings during which time the creditor retained a lien on the property. This act received the Court's approval in WRIGHT v. VINTON BRANCH OF MOUNTAIN TRUST BANK OF ROANOKE (1937).

DAVID GORDON

FREEDMAN v. MARYLAND

380 U.S. 51 (1965)

Although the Supreme Court often remarks that the FIRST AMENDMENT imposes a heavy presumption against the validity of any system of PRIOR RESTRAINT on expression, the Court has tolerated state censorship of motion pictures through advance licensing. Typically, such a law authorizes a censorship board to deny a license to a film on the ground of OBSCENITY. Other substantive standards ("immoral," "tending to corrupt morals") have been held invalid for VAGUENESS. In addition, the Court insists that the licensing system's procedures follow strict guidelines designed to avoid the chief evils of censorship. *Freedman* is the leading decision establishing these guidelines.

In a test case, a Baltimore theater owner showed a concededly innocuous film without submitting it to the state censorship board, and he was convicted of a violation of state law. The Supreme Court unanimously reversed the conviction. The *Freedman* opinion, by Justice WILLIAM J. BRENNAN, set three procedural requirements for film censorship. First, the censor must have the burden of proving that the film is "unprotected expression" (for example, obscenity). Second, while the state may insist that all films be submitted for advance screening, the censor's determination cannot be given the effect of finality; a judicial determination is required. Thus the censor must, "within a specified brief period, either issue a license or go to court to restrain showing of the film." Advance restraint, before the issue gets to court, must be of the minimum duration consistent with orderly employment of the judicial machinery. Third, the court's decision itself must be prompt. Maryland's statute failed all three parts of this test and accordingly was an unconstitutional prior restraint. Justices WILLIAM O. DOUGLAS and HUGO L. BLACK, concurring, would have held any advance censorship impermissible.

KENNETH L. KARST

FREEDMEN'S BUREAU

Congress created the Bureau of Refugees, Freedmen, and Abandoned Lands in March 1865, assigning it the disposition of rebels' lands and distribution of emergency relief to freed blacks and refugees of both races uprooted by the war. Though the Freedmen's Bureau was the first federal human-services organization, its establishment reflected Congress's resistance to constitutional innovation, combined with the pervasive nineteenth-century belief that relief and welfare were beyond the constitutional authority of the federal government. Hence the Bureau was a public–private hybrid, drawing its personnel from the army, assisted by volunteers from the various private relief and welfare organizations working with blacks and soldiers in the South.

The 1865 Act provided that the agency would expire a year after cessation of hostilities. In February 1866, Congress enacted a bill to extend the Bureau's life indefinitely. The bill permitted the President "to extend military protection and jurisdiction over all cases" in which blacks were denied CIVIL RIGHTS enjoyed by whites or were punished in ways whites were not. This provision reflected Republicans' resentment at the de jure and de facto discrimination against blacks in the South, especially that authorized by the BLACK CODES. Democrats and other conservatives denounced trials before military commissions or "courts" composed of Freedmen's Bureau agents, citing the absence of guarantees of INDICTMENT or PRESENTMENT as violative of the prohibition against military trials of civilians implied in the Fifth Amendment. Republicans countered that the bill was authorized by the enforcement clause (section 2) of the recently ratified THIRTEENTH AMENDMENT. The bill thus provided the first opportunity to explore the meaning and extent of this new provision. President ANDREW JOHNSON vetoed the bill, charging its Republican sponsors with racial favoritism and a disregard of FEDERALISM. Congress narrowly sustained the veto, but a similar bill became law four months later over his veto.

In existence until 1874, the Bureau helped blacks to adjust to freedom in the turbulent conditions of the postwar South.

WILLIAM M. WIECEK

Bibliography

NIEMAN, DONALD G. 1979 *To Set the Law in Motion: The Freedmen's Bureau and the Legal Rights of Blacks, 1865–1868.* Milwood, N.Y.: KTO Press.

FREEDOM OF . . .

See also under Right . . .

FREEDOM OF ASSEMBLY AND ASSOCIATION

The FIRST AMENDMENT's "right of the people peaceably to assemble" and the FOURTEENTH AMENDMENT have supplied a basis for federal protection of undefined FUNDAMENTAL RIGHTS from violation by the states. In the landmark case of UNITED STATES V. CRUIKSHANK (1876), the Supreme Court, in the course of allowing some lynchers to escape federal prosecution, said by way of OBITER DICTUM that the right peaceably to assemble was an attribute of CITIZENSHIP under a free government that antedated the Constitution, and that it was a privilege of national citizenship provided that the assembly in question concerned matters relating to the national government. (See PRIVILEGES AND IMMUNITIES.)

With respect to STATE ACTION, the right of peaceable assembly is now regarded as a Fourteenth Amendment DUE PROCESS right. Thus, in DEJONGE V. OREGON (1937), the Supreme Court reversed a conviction for CRIMINAL SYNDICALISM under an Oregon statute of a man who had participated in a peaceful meeting called by the Communist party for a lawful purpose, on the grounds that the due process clause of the Fourteenth Amendment had been violated. Chief Justice CHARLES EVANS HUGHES wrote for a unanimous Court: "The right of peaceable assembly is a right cognate to those of free speech and free press and is equally fundamental," and "peaceable assembly for lawful discussion cannot be made a crime," no matter under whose auspices the meeting is held.

In addition, the rights of assembly and petition are mentioned in rather standardized language in all but two of the fifty state CONSTITUTIONS. The first such statement appeared in the North Carolina constitution of 1776, and the New Hampshire constitution of 1784 began the practice of adding the word "peaceable" to the right of assembly guarantee. Furthermore, the constitutions of Missouri, New Jersey, and New York specifically guarantee a particular form of association, the right of employees to bargain collectively through representatives of their own choosing; the North Carolina constitution forbids "secret political societies" as being "dangerous to the liberties of a free people"; and there is a declaration in the Georgia constitution, of dubious validity, that "freedom from compulsory association at all levels of public education shall be preserved inviolate."

The right of assembly, like nearly all other rights, is not and cannot be regarded as without limit. As Justice LOUIS D. BRANDEIS wrote in 1927, concurring in WHITNEY V. CALIFORNIA, "although the rights of free speech and assembly are fundamental, they are not in their nature absolute. Their exercise is subject to restriction, if the particular restriction proposed is required in order to protect the State from destruction or from serious injury, political, economic or moral." The right of assembly does not protect an unlawful assembly, usually defined in American law as a gathering of three or more people for the purpose of committing acts that will give firm and courageous people in the neighborhood grounds to apprehend a BREACH OF THE PEACE. It must be shown that those who assembled intended to do an unlawful act or a lawful act in a violent, boisterous, or tumultuous manner. Thus the right to engage in peaceful PICKETING is protected by the Constitution, but picketing in a context of violence or having the purpose of achieving unlawful objectives, may be forbidden.

In American law the right of assembly extends to meetings held in such PUBLIC FORUMS as the streets and parks. This point was first spelled out in HAGUE V. C.I.O. (1939), extending constitutional protection to street meetings since, in the words of Justice OWEN J. ROBERTS, streets "have immemorially been held in trust for the use of the public and, time out of mind, have been used for purposes of assembly, communicating thoughts between citizens, and discussing public questions." Public authorities may be given the power to license parades or processions on the public streets as to time, place, and manner, provided that the licensing law does not confer an arbitrary or unbridled administrative discretion upon them. (See PRIOR RESTRAINT.) In addition, Justice Roberts wrote in CANTWELL V. CONNECTICUT (1940) that "When a CLEAR AND PRESENT DANGER of riot, disorder, interference with traffic upon the public streets, or other immediate threat to public safety, peace, or order, appears, the power of the State to prevent or punish is obvious." Thus, a leading decision has upheld the right to assemble on the grounds of a state house, but the Court has drawn the line at the picketing of a courthouse or holding a demonstration on jail grounds. The Court extended the concept of the right of assembly in RICHMOND NEWSPAPERS, INC. V. VIRGINIA (1980) by ruling invalid a state judge's order barring all members of the public and the press from the courtroom where a murder case was being tried, on the grounds that the First Amendment rights of speech, press, and assembly were violated.

Although the right of association is not mentioned specifically either in the United States Constitution or in the state constitutions, it is now recognized through judicial interpretation of various constitutional clauses, particularly those dealing with the rights of assembly and petition, the right of free press, and the privileges and immunities of citizens. The first forthright recognition by a majority of the Supreme Court that due process embraces the right to freedom of association, as distinguished from the more limited concept of assembly, came in NAACP V. ALABAMA (1958), although the idea had been advanced in several earlier minority opinions. In the *Alabama* case, the Court unanimously held unconstitutional a statute that required the NAACP to give to the state's attorney general the names and addresses of all its members, reasoning that such compelled disclosure of affiliation could constitute an effective restraint on freedom of association. Justice JOHN MARSHALL HARLAN wrote: "Effective advocacy of both public and private points of view, particularly controversial ones, is undeniably enhanced by group association, as this Court has more than once recognized by remarking upon the close nexus between the freedoms of speech and assembly. . . . Of course, it is immaterial whether the beliefs sought to be advanced by association pertain to political, economic, religious or cultural matters, and state action which may have the effect of curtailing the freedom to associate is subject to the closest scrutiny." In later years the Supreme Court, in a series of decisions, protected the NAACP's associational rights from various forms of harassment, subtle as well as heavy-handed, by local authorities.

A leading case involving education was SHELTON V. TUCKER (1960), where the Supreme Court, by a 5–4 vote, declared unconstitutional an Arkansas statute requiring every teacher in the public schools to file annually an affidavit listing all organizations to which the teacher belonged or contributed money during the preceding five years, because disclosure of every associational tie undoubtedly impaired the teacher's right of free association. Furthermore, in HEALY V. JAMES (1972), the Court upheld the right of a student association to receive university recognition, including access to various campus facilities, even though the president of the college regarded the group's philosophy as abhorrent; the Court added that the university might lawfully require the group to agree to obey reasonable rules relating to student conduct.

The Court took an even more generous view of

the right of association in GRISWOLD V. CONNECTICUT (1965), in which a state anticontraceptive statute was held unconstitutional. Justice WILLIAM O. DOUGLAS reasoned that the statute operated directly on the intimate relationship of husband and wife, thus invading the right of association broadly construed. In his opinion there was a first suggestion that although the right of association grows out of the PENUMBRA of the First Amendment, its scope is larger and extends to the marriage relationship. (See FREEDOM OF INTIMATE ASSOCIATION.)

The right of association, however vital it may be in a society committed to maximum freedom of speech and action, is not absolute but is subject to reasonable limitations required by substantial public interests. For example, the right of workers to organize and bargain collectively through representatives of their own choosing is firmly established in statute and judge-made law. But trade unions are not free to organize or participate in SECONDARY BOYCOTTS, since Congress did not intend "to immunize labor unions who aid and abet manufacturers and traders in violating the SHERMAN ACT. . . ." (See ALLEN BRADLEY CO. V. LOCAL UNION #3, 1945.) On the other hand, the Court has ruled that a labor leader cannot be required to secure a license to give a speech soliciting new members.

The right to form or engage in the activities of POLITICAL PARTIES is protected by the constitutional right of association. "The First Amendment," the Supreme Court said in BUCKLEY V. VALEO (1976), "protects political association as well as political expression." In that case the Court upheld a federal statute imposing limitations on contributions to political parties, on the theory that the limitations were designed to prevent corruption and the appearance of corruption, and to open up the political system to candidates who lacked access to large amounts of money. In addition, the right of political association extends to members of minor parties as well as to the two major parties. Many cases hold that government may protect the right to vote in party primaries, and ensure that voters cast ballots of approximately equal weight, but the two large parties are not obliged to apportion national convention delegates among the states according to the ONE-PERSON, ONE-VOTE concept, because party strength varies from state to state, and the parties must have the freedom to operate effectively. Similarly, the Supreme Court has ruled that a national party convention is not bound by state law and state judicial power in deciding which of two slates of delegates from a state should be seated. A state does have the power to decide upon the strength a party must demonstrate in order to get a place on the election ballot, but such a statute may not impose a rigid and arbitrary formula that applies equally to sparsely settled and populous counties, and unreasonably large signature requirements will not be permitted. Furthermore, the Supreme Court has conceded that, in order to protect the integrity of the electoral process, states may require some sort of party registration during a reasonable period before a primary election is held. Similarly, a state may require that candidates for party nominations pay filing fees, but the fees must not be so excessive as to be patently exclusionary.

Finally, in the unusual case of ELROD V. BURNS (1976), a bare majority of the Court read something new into party membership by holding that in discharging persons in non-civil service positions because they were Republicans, the newly elected Democratic sheriff of Cook County was placing an unconstitutional restraint on freedom of belief and association. This ruling does not apply, however, to persons holding policymaking positions involving broad functions and goals.

Membership in the Communist party or subversive organizations has for some years posed complex issues of constitutional law. (See SUBVERSIVE ACTIVITIES AND THE CONSTITUTION.) In AMERICAN COMMUNICATIONS ASSOCIATION V. DOUDS (1950), the Court upheld a section of the TAFT-HARTLEY ACT of 1947 which denied access to the facilities of the National Labor Relations Board to any union whose officers were members of the Communist party. The Court reasoned that the act validly protected INTERSTATE COMMERCE from the obstruction caused by political strikes and applied only to those who believed in the violent overthrow of the government as a concrete objective and not merely as a prophecy. Similarly, in SCALES V. UNITED STATES (1961), the Court upheld the clause in the SMITH ACT of 1940 making membership in any organization advocating the overthrow of government by force or violence (in that instance, membership in the Communist party) a criminal offense. But the Court stressed that it was reading the statute to mean that the Smith Act did not proscribe mere membership in the Communist party as such but only membership of an individual who knew of the party's unlawful purposes and specifically intended to further those purposes; the proscribed membership must be active and not nominal, passive, or merely theoretical. This construction of the Smith Act was fully consistent with the position the Court had taken in YATES V. UNITED STATES (1957). The distinction between INCITEMENT and abstract teaching was underscored by the Court in the important case of BRANDENBURG V. OHIO (1969), which held the Ohio Criminal Syndicalism Act unconstitutional. Thus, mere membership in the Communist party, without more, cannot be made a predicate for the denial of a passport, or a job in a defense facility, or of public employment. The Court has recognized that membership may be innocent, and that groups may change their positions from time to time.

Whether unions or other associations may engage the services of such regulated professionals as doctors and lawyers has been the subject of much recent litigation. Because the practice of medicine is subject to comprehensive and detailed regulation by the state under its POLICE POWER for compelling reasons, a state statute prohibiting laymen from forming CORPORATIONS for the delivery of medical care has been upheld on the theory that limiting the formation of such corporations to licensed physicians tends to preserve important doctor–patient relationships and prevents possible abuses which may result from lay control.

The constitutionality of regulation of lawyers presents more complex issues. The Supreme Court has ruled that a state may lawfully compel all lawyers in the state to belong to an integrated bar, and a state bar association may be authorized to discipline a lawyer for personally soliciting clients for pecuniary gain, although the Court ruled in BATES V. STATE BAR OF ARIZONA (1977) that a state, through its bar association, may not forbid lawyers to engage in truthful advertising of routine legal services. Furthermore, the Court held in KONIGSBERG V. STATE BAR OF CALIFORNIA (1961) that a state may refuse to admit to the practice of law a candidate who refuses to reply to questions regarding membership in the Communist party, although the Court has also ruled that there must be a showing of knowing, active membership before an applicant can be excluded on this ground.

The Supreme Court has decided that such associations as trade unions, the NAACP, and the AMERICAN CIVIL LIBERTIES UNION may employ lawyers to provide legal services for their members. In BROTHERHOOD OF RAILROAD TRAINMEN V. VIRGINIA EX REL. VIRGINIA STATE BAR (1964), the Court held that a union has an associational right to advise injured members to use the services of specific approved lawyers. Moreover, a labor union is constitutionally entitled to employ a licensed attorney on a salary basis to represent any of its members who desire his services in prosecuting workers' compensation claims. In NAACP V. BUTTON (1963), the Court upheld the right of this association to finance certain types of litigation through its own staff of lawyers. The Court noted that NAACP litigation is not a mere technique for resolving private differences but a means of achieving the lawful objective of legal equality. Similarly, the Court has affirmed the right of the American Civil Liberties Union to employ attorneys in the pursuit of its objectives.

The right of association has been explored in a wide variety of other situations. Many years ago, in WAUGH V. BOARD OF TRUSTEES OF THE UNIVERSITY OF MISSISSIPPI (1915), the Supreme Court held constitutional a Mississippi statute prohibiting Greek-letter fraternities and other secret societies in all public educational institutions of the state, on the theory that this was a reasonable moral and disciplinary regulation which the legislature might believe would save the students from harmful distraction. Several state appellate courts have sustained the validity of such regulations as applied to high schools. In NEW YORK EX REL. BRYANT V. ZIMMERMAN (1928), the Supreme Court upheld a state statute, aimed at the Ku Klux Klan, which required all secret oath-bound organizations having over twenty members to supply to a designated public official a roster of its members and a list of its officers. In NAACP V. ALABAMA (1958), holding unconstitutional a similar disclosure requirement of the NAACP, the Court noted that the *Zimmerman* decision "was based on the particular character of the Klan's activities, involving acts of unlawful intimidation and violence, which the Court assumed was before the state legislature when it enacted the statute, and of which the Court itself took judicial notice." (See COMMUNIST PARTY V. SUBVERSIVE ACTIVITIES CONTROL BOARD, 1961.) On the other hand, in LANZETTA V. NEW JERSEY (1939), the Court ruled unconstitutional a state statute that purported to make it illegal to associate with gangsters, on the ground that the key words in the statute were so vague, indefinite, and uncertain that it lacked the specificity required of penal enactments.

Although the right of association as such is not mentioned in the Constitution, it holds a firm, indeed expanding, place in American constitutional law. This right is partly an emanation from the First Amendment's cognate guarantees of freedom of speech and assembly, partly a privilege or immunity of citizenship, and partly a by-product of democratic voting and representative government. However the right of association is tied to the text of the Constitution, it is regarded by the judges as such a fundamental right that doubts are resolved in favor of protecting the right of association from governmental restraints.

DAVID FELLMAN

Bibliography

ABERNATHY, GLEN 1961 *The Right of Assembly and Association.* Columbia: University of South Carolina Press.

FELLMAN, DAVID 1963 *The Constitutional Right of Association.* Chicago: University of Chicago Press.

HORN, ROBERT A. 1956 *Groups and the Constitution.* Stanford, Calif.: Stanford University Press.

KALVEN, HARRY, JR. 1965 The Concept of the Public Forum. *Supreme Court Review* 1965:1–32.

RAGGI, REENA 1977 An Independent Right to Freedom of Association. *Harvard Civil Rights-Civil Liberties Law Review* 12:1–30.

FREEDOM OF CONTRACT

Freedom of contract in the United States means that the law accepts and protects broad scope for private individuals and business firms to decide the uses of economic resources in seeking profits. Through the country's history, sharp controversies have centered on exercise of freedom of contract as it has affected concerns for the worth of individuals, the vitality of private markets, the natural and social environment, and the structure of practical as well as formal legal power in the society. Few other concepts touch as many dimensions of the history of American public policy and constitutional law.

The law's attention to freedom of contract has centered on fostering and sustaining the private market as a major institution of social control (ranking in importance with the law itself). Even the assessment of the interactions of freedom of contract and other values, not defined in market, has typically resulted from community reactions to the effects of market operations. Thus, to examine the place of freedom of contract in constitutional law entails examining the roles and working character of the market.

Law and public policy have historically responded to four salient characteristics of private contract activity in market, carrying both constructive and damaging aspects. These responses have provided the institutional setting within which the substantive legal/constitutional meaning of freedom of contract has emerged.

(1) Under the protection of the law of contract, private contract activity seeking profit in market energizes private will in producing and distributing goods and services. This activity promises efficiency in allocating limited resources, partly because the actors are motivated to obtain the most output for the least input, and partly because market bargaining allows flexibility in coordinating a great volume and diversity of private decisions. In the country's constitutional tradition, social and political values also favor freedom of contract. Proponents argue that individuals gain self-respect from the initiatives of will they exercise in markets, as well as courage to participate in and criticize government because their means of livelihood are not dependent on official favor. The law reflects this appraisal of positive values by presuming the legality of private contracts until a challenger demonstrates their unlawfulness, and by casting some constitutional protections around private contract activity and the property interests it produces. (See CONTRACT CLAUSE; SUBSTANTIVE DUE PROCESS; TAKING OF PROPERTY; ECONOMIC REGULATION AND THE CONSTITUTION.) But the driving dynamic of private contract activity is the focused self-interest of the bargainers. We value this dynamic because it counters the inertia prevalent in social relationships, but it largely ignores the impact of bargains on people other than the bargainers. A factory producing to meet its contractual obligations may deposit in a handy stream industrial wastes harmful to the public's interest in pure drinking water or recreational opportunities. The law responds to this narrow focus of the market with ENVIRONMENTAL REGULATIONS, the constitutionality of which may or may not be challenged.

(2) Large-scale markets cannot operate by barter but require use of money (including money-measured credit). Law responds to this need by regulating the money supply. But the money calculus required by extended contract activity carries dangers of a bias in identifying and weighing matters of public interest. Public opinion, public policymakers (including judges), and market-oriented pressure groups seeking to influence legislators and other public officers tend to identify interests deserving law's promotion or protection only with interests readily calculable in dollar terms. Thus, nineteenth-century COMMON LAW readily gave JUDGMENT for money damages if a factory failed to deliver promised goods to a buyer but was grudging in recognizing a community right to redress for more diffuse detriments—hard to measure in dollars—caused by the factory's deposit of industrial waste in a nearby stream. Today's public policy, with the blessings of today's constitutional law, increasingly seeks to offset the bias injected by a monetized calculus of interests by legislating to protect diffuse values and establishing administrative agencies to implement them.

(3) Whether tailored to particular transactions or standardized as in such commercial instruments as promissory notes or warehouse receipts, private contracts can be multiplied to any number of dealings

and varied to shifting conditions of supply and demand. Contracts and the market thus permit flexible adaptation to changes in the conditions of the economy and the parties. Public policy recognizes the value of this adaptability in the law's readiness to enforce such terms of dealing as the parties choose and in legal/constitutional doctrine protecting the play of market competition. However, when change proceeds in this manner, its increments are so small that even the parties, let alone the environing society, may not be aware that the accumulation of relatively limited incremental shifts is producing basic alterations in the social context which no one has predicted, assessed, or chosen to bring about.

(4) Private contracting parties and the markets in which they operate typically work within the distribution of wealth and income in society as they find it. Contract and property law reinforce this distribution; only in rare hard cases will courts set aside a bargain as unconscionable, and normally they will not examine the adequacy of the consideration a party accepted in return for what he promised to perform. But underlying the social utility of freedom of contract and the resource-allocations role of markets lies an assumption: that private bargainers enjoy a considerable range of practical and legal options in dealing with each other. Great inequalities of wealth may grossly distort some bargaining relations, so that freedom of contract becomes illusory and markets sharply accentuate inequalities of bargaining power. While constitutional law only rarely addresses such inequalities (see INDIGENTS; WEALTH DISTRIBUTION), it consistently validates legislation to this end. (See SUBSTANTIVE DUE PROCESS; ECONOMIC REGULATION; COMMERCE CLAUSE.) Sometimes lawmakers seek to encourage private organization of countervailing power, as in the law regarding COLLECTIVE BARGAINING between management and LABOR. Sometimes they interpose between focused centers of private market power and diffused bodies of customers a public bargaining agency, as in the law of public utilities. Such legal interventions and their constitutional underpinnings depart from an abstract model of freedom of contract in order to promote more real freedom of bargaining.

The span from the 1880s through the 1920s witnessed increased resort to state and national law to correct imperfections of private contract activity in market. In this period opponents of government intervention made "freedom of contract" a code phrase for imposing constitutional and other limits on legal regulation. This emphasis has been so prominent in past policy debate that there is danger of equating the idea of freedom of contract with limitations on the use of law. In fact, law operates at least as much to promote market activity as to regulate it. A realistic assessment of the relation of constitutional law to freedom of contract must recognize the range of such promotional roles of legal processes.

By the late eighteenth century, in this country of abundant land, the law of land titles made land fully transferable and thus readily marketable—thus promoting private contract activity. By the mid-nineteenth century, common law had established a strong presumption in favor of the legality of private agreements for market dealing. By the second half of the nineteenth century, state legislatures were actively removing the common law disability of married women to make binding contracts. The married women's property acts may have responded more to the wish of the husband's creditors to acquire effective pledge of the wife's assets to secure her husband's debts than to any concern for sex equality. Still, these statutes enlarged the potential scope for contract activity in market.

Legal development, often supported by constitutional law, has consistently fostered entrepreneurial energy. Contract law legitimized and standardized a growing range of trade documents and instruments for capital investment. In three respects law especially promoted increased reach and pervasive effect of private contract activity. Though often inefficiently, law provided a money supply to facilitate increased volumes of trade. Particularly under the commerce clause of the national Constitution, Congress and the Supreme Court protected markets of sectional or national scope against intrusion of state parochial interest. (See STATE REGULATION OF COMMERCE; STATE TAXATION OF COMMERCE.) With increasing liberality lawmakers made the device of incorporation available for the general run of business, providing means for mustering and directing otherwise scattered assets. (See CORPORATIONS AND THE CONSTITUTION.)

Many individuals had only their labor to offer in market, and only their wages to spend. For them law gave other positive promotion to freedom of contract. In the nineteenth century, statutes created mechanics' liens, exempted workers' tools from creditors' execution, and abolished imprisonment for debt. In the twentieth century, legislation created administrative agencies to implement laws designed to help consumers get money's worth for their purchases. The most dramatic expansion of freedom of contract for labor was the abolition of SLAVERY. Fulfillment of the substance of that policy through the THIRTEENTH AMENDMENT and the supplementary provisions of the FOURTEENTH AMENDMENT and the CIVIL RIGHTS

ACT OF 1866 had a long and tortured history, but the general line of policy was clear. In the 1960s, CIVIL RIGHTS legislation gave that policy additional impetus, placing the affirmative support of law behind opening markets for labor, goods, and services free of barriers raised on grounds of race, sex, or religion. (See FEDERAL PROTECTION OF CIVIL RIGHTS; EMPLOYMENT DISCRIMINATION.)

Granted that law plays positive, promotional roles in fostering markets, freedom of contract also insists that law protect a substantial area of autonomy for private contract and market activity, to allow operative room for the efficiency criteria which legitimize private contract and market functions. Threats of invasion of this zone come from both private and official power. Accordingly the autonomy that public policy provides for private contract and private markets has two dimensions, relating to private and to official action.

The law protects market autonomy against private interference not only by enforcing contractual obligations through damages or other relief against breach of contract but also by providing sanctions against interference by outsiders with the performance of those obligations. Furthermore, an elaborate body of statutory, judge-made, and ADMINISTRATIVE LAW offers criminal and civil sanctions against efforts to defeat market bargaining by achieving monopoly, or by fixing prices or other terms of trade, or by engaging in such predatory forms of competition as geographical price discriminations so as to limit or destroy competition. (See ANTITRUST AND THE CONSTITUTION.)

More controversy has surrounded the creation of legal/constitutional protections of limited autonomy for private contract activity in market as against interventions by government. Experience shows two quite different sources of concern. Some battles over legal regulation are fought on claims that one set of private interests seeks to handicap another by persuading a legislature to create barriers to free competition as when producers of dairy products obtained laws regulating the sale of oleomargarine. Other battles are fought on claims that in pursuing nonmarket objectives, such as protecting public health, lawmakers impose unreasonable costs on market-measured profit-seeking—as when environmental regulations are opposed on the ground that they hamper "productivity" (meaning that they limit money-measured gains of regulated firms). Common to both types of concern is the objection that law is used in ways that interfere with economic efficiency defined according to the profit and loss calculus of the immediate bargainers in a competitive private market. "Efficiency" in this sense and freedom of contract are the same thing.

Common law imposes some limits on freedom of bargainers to set terms for which they may invoke the law's support and sets the standards for determining what constitutes an enforceable contract. Generally, however, the courts presume that private bargains are valid. The principal legal battlegrounds for defending freedom of contract against official invasion lie in constitutional law. Both national and state constitutions limit legislative restrictions on the freedom of private contract.

The national and state constitutions forbid government to take private property for PUBLIC USE without JUST COMPENSATION. These guarantees primarily protect property titles rather than contracts not yet performed. However, they help safeguard private contract activity; contracts that call for performance over time are likely to require commitments of assets which bargainers will not make if they do not consider the commitments secure against government appropriation. Some uncertainty attends the definition of what public action amounts to a "taking." However, these guarantees do not require government to pay all costs incurred by those subjected to laws regulating economic affairs. Particularly, when government intervenes in a situation where some detriment will in fact occur to either of two competing private interests whether government acts or not, there is no "taking" requiring compensation when the law determines which interest must bear the burden. (See TAKING OF PROPERTY.)

The national Constitution forbids any state to make a law that impairs the OBLIGATION OF CONTRACTS. This clause limits only retroactive state legislation; it does not affect state laws that operate only on future events. No comparable clause limits the Congress, and the Supreme Court applies a presumption of constitutionality to federal statutes of retroactive impact. (See RETROACTIVITY OF LEGISLATION.) The CONTRACT CLAUSE has not figured in so much litigation as the constitutional guarantees of DUE PROCESS and EQUAL PROTECTION OF THE LAWS. Where litigants invoke the clause, however, judges generally give it firm application in the types of situation that most directly challenge respect for outstanding private agreements in market—that is, where a retroactive state statute undertakes to readjust the terms of a contract or its legal context in order to give one party what the legislature in hindsight sees as a socially more acceptable exchange. The usual case of this kind has arisen when a legislature intervenes to relieve distressed debtors of the full measure of claims or remedies afforded their creditors. Moreover, the Supreme Court requires a state to enforce a contract between the state itself and a private party when the retroactive change has given the state an economic advantage not conferred by the original terms. On the other hand, the Supreme Court treats the contract clause more flexibly when the prime object of the challenged legislation appears to be not to alter terms of dealing between the bargaining parties but to protect public interests in a healthy social context without which private contracts have no meaning. Care for social context may include care for preserving the market itself. Thus the Supreme Court upheld a state statute that imposed a limited moratorium on foreclosing mortgages contracted before the statute was passed, where the Court was persuaded that the legislature reasonably believed the moratorium necessary not mainly to benefit mortgagors but to save the general economy from destruction by averting distress sales of land that would undermine the financial integrity of the banking and insurance systems of the state. (See HOME BUILDING AND LOAN ASSOCIATION V. BLAISDELL, 1934.) The Court has taken a like approach where the challenged legislation seeks to safeguard other than market interests; thus it has sustained against contract clause challenges retroactive legislation that, in the interest of public morals, abrogated an earlier statutory charter for a lottery and that, to protect public health, abrogated an earlier statutory charter for a slaughterhouse.

Another relatively specific constitutional limit on state legislation affecting freedom of contract developed under the COMMERCE CLAUSE of the national Constitution. The core purpose of granting Congress authority to regulate INTERSTATE COMMERCE was to use national law to protect from parochial state legislation contract activity that ranged over state lines into markets of interstate scope. Congress has used this authority notably to provide uniform national regulation of the terms on which private business provides interstate transportation and communication services. Most often, however, the commerce clause has operated to limit state interference with interstate contract activity through the United States Supreme Court. In the Court's construction, the commerce clause of its own force authorizes judges to rule invalid state legislation that discriminates against or unduly burdens interstate transactions. The Court most strictly limits state laws that in their terms or by their practical effect lay legal or economic burdens on dealings in an interstate market that they do not impose on intrastate transactions. Here the Court puts on the supporter of a challenged state statute a heavy burden of persuading the Court that some overriding local public interest warrants legislation that thus singles out interstate dealing for special regulation. But if a nondiscriminatory state statute affects interstate transactions for a nonmarket purpose, such as protecting public safety on the highways, it enjoys the benefit of a presumption of constitutionality, so that the challenger must persuade the Court that local interests are insufficient to warrant the regulation.

Constitutional guarantees of due process and equal protection are the protections most often invoked on behalf of substantial autonomy of private contract activity in market, as against government intervention. At the threshold of any examination of this body of constitutional law stands an issue of institutional legitimacy. Anglo-American political tradition includes high regard for public policy that favors initiatives of private will in the economy. JOHN LOCKE gave this tradition classic expression in seventeenth-century England, asserting that the individual normally needs no official license before he may make productive use of natural resources. Locke recognized that legislation might properly care for "commonwealth" interests, and particularly that the elected legislature might exercise the power to tax for public purposes. But the legislative authority, he said, was held in "trust," permitting the legislature to act only for the public interest (foreshadowing the Supreme Court's later standard of SUBSTANTIVE DUE PROCESS) and by equal laws. Of course, this English inheritance did not provide authority for judges to hold invalid legislation that infringed standards of public interest and equal protection. When judges in the United States asserted that authority—with some limited warrant in the history of adoption of the national Constitution—it was another, long step for them to conclude that the guarantee of due process of law included judicial protection of some extent of private contract autonomy. In its origins, "due process of law" meant assurance of fair procedures for applying law, not authority of courts to set limits on the substantive content of the policy legislatures might adopt. And the core historic meaning of the equal protection standard referred to application of law rather than to its substantive classifications. However, by the mid-twentieth century, some seventy-five years of Supreme Court practice had outweighed historic doubts; the live issue in the twentieth century is, rather, how the Court will use the authority it has staked out for itself. The fact that judges were able to extend their power of review beyond historic foundations attests to the strength of values which conservative opinion in the past has put on freedom of contract in market. On the other hand, the doubt which history has cast on the political legitimacy of the expanded judicial role correspondingly helps account for the limits set by the Court since the 1930s on its exercise of JUDICIAL REVIEW of economic regulations challenged as violations of due process and equal protection.

Early in the development of the doctrine of substantive due process, in *Powell v. Pennsylvania* (1888), the Court set sharp limits on the scope of judicial review. There a state had banned the sale of oleomargarine, for the declared goals of protecting public health and preventing fraud on consumers. The Court ruled that it would uphold the statute unless the challenger showed beyond a reasonable doubt that the legislature could not reasonably find that the act was an appropriate means to serve some public interest. Nonetheless, in some cases judges, especially state courts interpreting state constitutions, will enforce respect for some degree of autonomy of private contract activity in market. In some cases parties have successfully rebutted the strong presumption of constitutionality by showing that one set of business interests has won the law's favor simply in order to obtain a legal advantage against other socially useful competitors. Such resort to law violates the social justification of legally protected freedom of contract: the promotion of efficient allocation of limited resources through market competition. Thus, in a later case, where the challenger demonstrated that an anti-oleomargarine statute had no reasonable basis in protecting health or preventing fraud, the Wisconsin court held, in *John F. Jelke Co. v. Emery* (1927), that the act violated constitutional standards of due process and equal protection.

In counterpoint with the pattern of judicial self-restraint indicated by *Powell v. Pennsylvania*, over the span from about 1890 into the mid-1930s the Supreme Court developed three other interrelated doctrinal lines which promoted aggressive judicial protection of private contract autonomy.

First, the Court identified freedom of private contract as a key component of the "liberty" protected by the due process and equal protection clauses. The founding decision was ALLGEYER V. LOUISIANA (1897). There the Court held unconstitutional a Louisiana statute forbidding performance of a contract to insure property in the state with a company not licensed to do business there. The Court ruled that in denying the parties the liberty to make the contract the statute violated limits that the due process clause put on the substantive policies which the legislature might enact into law.

Second, in the standard of substantive due process the Court found warrant for a judicial veto over legislative goals. Judicial scrutiny of these goals had two aspects. One concerned the relationship between private contract and the social context in which the contracting went on. Even in decisions most restrictive of legislative power, the Supreme Court did not deny that legislation might properly pay some regard to the impact of private contract activity on the lives and concerns of individuals or groups other than the contracting parties. However, the Court often spoke of legislative authority as the sum of a limited, closed number of categories of goals traditionally recognized as serving public interest, notably protection of health, safety, or morals. (See STATE POLICE POWER; NATIONAL POLICE POWER). The indication was that a statute would violate substantive due process if its objective did not fit handily under one of these familiar designations. Conspicuous in this approach were ADAIR V. UNITED STATES (1908), COPPAGE V. KANSAS (1915), and WOLFF PACKING COMPANY V. COURT OF INDUSTRIAL RELATIONS (1923). These rulings refused to recognize promotion of peace in management–labor relations as a sufficient public-interest goal to sustain statutes that outlawed employment contracts binding employees not to join a union or providing for compulsory arbitration of labor disputes.

The third aspect of heightened judicial scrutiny of statutory goals was more specific. Substantive due process demanded that legislation serve what the Court regarded as the general welfare. A statute might appear to serve one of the judicially approved public-interest goals, such as protection of health. But also, it might have the purpose or likely effect of bringing about a different distribution of gains and costs among private bargainers than might result if bargainers operated simply within the frame of common law contract and property law. Between about 1890 and the mid-1930s many decisions treated the presence of a purpose or effect to alter the distribution of gains and costs among private bargainers as enough to show that a challenged statute did not meet the due process standard of serving the public interest; the redistributive character of such a statute made it "class legislation" or an effort, forbidden by constitutional law, to "take property from A and give it to B." Judges would accept statutes that protected groups commonly recognized as subject to exceptional hazards or weaknesses in bargaining power. Thus, in HOLDEN V. HARDY (1898), the Supreme Court upheld a statutory limit on working hours of men mining coal underground, emphasizing the well-known special hazards of the occupation and the accepted fact that in practice the employers fixed the terms of the employment contracts. So, too, in MULLER V. OREGON (1908), the Court sustained a working hours limit for women, to protect a class which the judges saw as peculiarly dependent. But where a statute apparently sought to offset the weak bargaining power of workers in situations not conventionally regarded as deserving law's special care, the fact that the statute would confer particular benefit on labor was taken as enough to show a lack of justifying public interest. Such was the Court's approach in LOCHNER V. NEW YORK (1905), which held invalid a statutory limit on working hours of bakers. Of similar character was Court doctrine that confined statutory regulation of prices and services of private contractors to what judges regarded as businesses AFFECTED WITH A PUBLIC INTEREST—those conventionally deemed public utilities. On this basis, in TYSON V. BANTON (1927) and in RIBNIK V. MCBRIDE (1928), the Court held invalid statutes regulating resale prices of theater tickets and fees of employment agencies.

There was unreconciled tension between many of these decisions and the approach taken in *Powell v. Pennsylvania.* In *Powell,* the fact that the statutory ban on selling oleomargarine might serve both the private, competitive interest of sellers of butter and the public interest in health was held insufficient to invalidate the regulation. In *Powell,* the favored private interest was that of one set of businessmen, the sellers of butter. In *Lochner* and in *Ribnik,* the interest the statutes immediately protected was that of labor. So, also, in *Adair, Coppage,* and *Wolff Packing,* the interest of labor suffered when the challenged legislation was upset. The pattern suggested a definite bias of policy.

Between 1890 and the mid-1930s the Supreme Court also usually required a positive showing of a "real and substantial" relation between the legislature's goal and the means it provided to reach the goal. That the Court could conceive of other, less burdensome means of achieving the desired result was likely, as in *Lochner v. New York,* to be treated as a distinct and sufficient basis for invalidating the statute. The climax of both lines of doctrine—regarding challenges to the end or to the means adopted by the legislature—came in ADKINS V. CHILDREN'S HOSPITAL (1923), when the Supreme Court held unconstitutional legislation setting minimum wages for women workers. There a Court majority in effect repudiated the presumption of constitutionality by declaring that "Freedom of contract is . . . the general rule and restraint the exception; and the exercise of legislative authority to abridge it can be justified only by the existence of exceptional circumstances." As late as MOREHEAD V. NEW YORK EX REL. TIPALDO (1936), a Court majority in effect reaffirmed the *Adkins* approach, but a new alignment of Justices repudiated that approach in WEST COAST HOTEL V. PARRISH (1937).

The Court's readiness through some forty years after 1890 to upset legislation limiting freedom of contract had serious implications for the role of legislatures and the interests legislatures sought to advance or protect. But we should not exaggerate the impact of judicial review. One inventory counts 197 cases between 1899 and 1937 in which the Supreme Court invalidated state or federal regulations under the standard of substantive due process, but another estimate notes that between 1889 and 1918 the Court upheld some 369 challenged statutes enacted under the state police power. Other tallies emphasize the more vigorous use of the judicial veto in the later years of the forty-year span; one count finds fifty-three state police power acts held invalid between 1889 and 1918, while another shows almost 140 laws held unconstitutional between 1920 and 1930. All such inventories must be seen in a wider perspective; a great bulk of economic regulatory legislation never came under constitutional challenge in lawsuits.

However, in a sharp turnabout beginning in the mid-1930s, the Court disavowed these enlargements of judicial protection for autonomy of private contract in market. In NEBBIA V. NEW YORK (1934) it ruled that a legislature might regulate pricing practices outside the field of traditional public utilities if legislators could reasonably find that regulation would serve a public interest. In UNITED STATES V. CAROLENE PRODUCTS COMPANY (1938), it ruled that no particular sanctity attached to the "liberty" or "property" interests involved in private contract activity; all regulatory legislation affecting ordinary commercial transactions enjoyed the presumption of constitutionality. *Nebbia* also made clear that there is no closed category of public interests to which legislatures may extend protection; even if a statute intervenes in private contract activity for a purpose not within familiar concerns with public health, safety, or morals, it is valid unless the judges determine that no reasonable legislators could find justification for it. Finally, in WEST COAST HOTEL COMPANY V. PARRISH (1937), the Court expressly overruled the formula declared in *Adkins;* that a statute limits freedom of contract does not cast on its supporter a burden of justifying it; rather, the general presumption of constitutionality applies.

The Court's permissive modern doctrine leaves the autonomy of private contract activity mostly in the hands of the legislature. Given the realities of the legislative process, in two respects this outcome implies a lessening of the preferred status of the private market. Statute law tends to speak more and more for interests of the general social context, as in regulation of burdens—such as air or water pollution—which private contract activity otherwise may place on parties outside the bargaining circle. Less appealing is the practical operation of the presumption of constitutionality to allow special interest lobbies to obtain legal favors, protected by plausible arguments of action taken for a presumed public interest. But this increased scope for lobby influence seems an inescapable cost of a proper division of functions between legislatures and courts in the area of economic regulation. In a more favorable light, the presumption of constitutionality as the Supreme Court defines it means that a statute is not invalid merely because in serving some public interest it may operate concurrently to provide special gain to some private interest. This result seems appropriate. Concurrence of public and private gain from legislation is so common in this society of diverse, interweaving interests that judges would substantially abrogate the legislative function if they held that such parallel effects alone made a statute unconstitutional.

Finally, we should recall that constitutional law is by no means the whole of what determines the realities of freedom of contract. In the second half of the twentieth century several factors other than direct legal regulation work to reduce, or at least realign, the operation of the freedom of contract. One element is the growth in relative economic importance of large-scale business corporations. In a big corporate organization many decisions that once would have been made by private bargains over supply of goods and services now occur through relations of hierarchy, as boards of directors instruct managers and managers plan and instruct subordinates. Thus, much resource allocation is done through internal discipline of firms, rather than by transactions in market. This internalizing of decisions has generated new concerns about the balance of power among affected interests. Such concerns have prompted new government regulation, as in the WAGNER (NATIONAL LABOR RELATIONS) ACT, in legislation governing corporate finance and administered by the Securities and Exchange Commission, and in the regulation of workplace safety under state and federal laws.

Statutes and administrative regulations now standardize many areas of contract dealing, sometimes providing optional standard forms, sometimes requiring adherence to forms fixed by law. Thus, large areas which are still governed by contract, in the sense that parties enter into relationships only by exchange of consents, are nonetheless areas in which individuals and firms no longer bargain out the details of their transactions. Such is the case with most contracts of insurance, contract relations between corporate stockholders and their corporations, collective bargaining contracts for the supply of labor, and lending contracts.

From the 1930s on, national monetary and fiscal policy has greatly affected the practical scope of freedom of private contract. Government's roles in providing and regulating the money supply are not neutral ones; the qualities of public monetary policy affecting rates of deflation or inflation profoundly affect the extent to which people can control their affairs by private bargains. Similarly, as government enlarges the reach of its TAXING AND SPENDING POWERS, it enlarges or restricts practical freedom of private contract. Government-induced transfer payments—payment of interest on public debt, or payments of Social Security allowances or of unemployment compensation—shift purchasing power among groups. Government spending on goods or services for its own needs removes some proportion of material or labor from the field of private contract in market. In the late twentieth century the cumulative effects of public monetary and fiscal programs spell substantial complication of the patterns of private contract activity and public resource allocation, in comparison with the patterns that existed from the late eighteenth century to the end of the nineteenth century. Freedom of contract in the United States continues to stand for important propositions concerning the structure and working procedures of society, but the content of the idea has undergone significant change from the vision of society held by John Locke or by the Justices of the Supreme Court who spoke for strict judicial review of economic regulations between the 1890s and the middle 1930s.

JAMES WILLARD HURST

Bibliography

CHANDLER, ALFRED D., JR. 1977 *The Visible Hand.* Cambridge, Mass.: Belknap Press of Harvard University Press.

FRIEDMAN, LAWRENCE M. 1973 *A History of American Law.* New York: Simon & Schuster.

HORWITZ, MORTON J. 1977 *The Transformation of American Law, 1760–1860.* Cambridge, Mass.: Harvard University Press.

HURST, JAMES WILLARD 1982 *Law and Markets in United States History.* Madison: University of Wisconsin Press.

JACOBS, CLYDE 1954 *Law Writers and the Courts.* Berkeley: University of California Press.

MACAULAY, STEWART 1963 Non-Contractual Relations in Business: A Preliminary Study. *American Sociological Review* 28:55–67.

PAUL, ARNOLD M. 1960 *Conservative Crisis and the Rule of Law: Attitudes of Bar and Bench, 1887–1895.* Ithaca, N.Y.: Cornell University Press.

POUND, ROSCOE 1909 Liberty of Contract. *Yale Law Journal* 18:454–487.

TRIBE, LAURENCE H. 1978 *American Constitutional Law.* Chap. 8. Mineola, N.Y.: Foundation Press.

TWISS, BENJAMIN R. 1942 *Lawyers and the Constitution: How Laissez Faire Came to the Supreme Court.* Princeton, N.J.: Princeton University Press.

FREEDOM OF INFORMATION ACT

80 Stat. 378 (1966)

The Freedom of Information Act of 1966 establishes a public disclosure policy for information in the custody of the executive branch of the federal government. It authorizes public access to government records and provides administrative and judicial APPEAL of decisions to withhold them. The law mandates that unreleased executive branch records be made available on request; however, it permits the withholding of information in nine categories upon government justification. Among them are classified national security information, information protected by other statutes, internal advisory memoranda, invasions of privacy, certain law enforcement records, and certain confidential business information.

The idea of a freedom of information law was first championed by journalists concerned with the effects of government censorship and discretionary bureaucratic secrecy on FREEDOM OF THE PRESS and the accountability of public officials. After eleven years of congressional hearings, the Freedom of Information Act was passed in 1966, amending the Administrative Procedures Act which had allowed the withholding of almost all government records. Initial compliance with the new law fell short of congressional expectations, and effectuating amendments were passed over a presidential veto in 1974.

As the keystone of "open government" legislation, the act was the first of several statutes that subject certain records and activities of the federal government to public scrutiny. These include the Federal Advisory Committee Act of 1972, the PRIVACY ACT of 1974, the Government in the Sunshine Act of 1976, and the Presidential Records Act of 1978.

The freedom of information policy established by the law does not flow from an express, constitutional RIGHT TO KNOW. Some controversy surrounds the question of whether a public right to know is merely political rhetoric or is an unenumerated constitutional right protected by the NINTH AMENDMENT. A majority of the Justices of the Supreme Court concluded, in RICHMOND NEWSPAPERS, INC. V. VIRGINIA (1980), that the FIRST AMENDMENT gave the public a right of access to criminal trials, which rests on the traditional importance of citizen scrutiny of the judicial trial process. In a separate opinion, Justice WILLIAM J. BRENNAN argued that the theory of citizen participation in self-government also supports the right, and that this logic is not confined to access to courtrooms. In another CONCURRING OPINION, Justice JOHN PAUL STEVENS pointed out that in this case the Court recognized for the first time a protected right of access to important government information.

EXECUTIVE PRIVILEGE is embodied in several exemptions to the 1966 Act. Although the scope of the privilege remains in dispute, the Supreme Court in OBITER DICTUM in UNITED STATES V. NIXON (1974) recognized the authority to withhold military and diplomatic national security information, as well as internal memoranda that are advisory and not factual in nature. Later that year, in his veto message returning the 1974 amendments to Congress, President Ford declared that the provision for judicial review of executive branch determinations as to national security classification violates constitutional principles. However, the government has never pressed that argument in litigation.

Individuals have found the act useful for obtaining business information and as an alternative to judicial discovery. Open government policies have affected administrative behavior. Federal law enforcement practices were somewhat restrained after dubious covert investigative activities were disclosed. A government study following the 1974 amendments found that attitudes in the bureaucracy had become more positive toward the release of information and that the quality of some government work had improved because of public scrutiny.

EVERETT E. MANN, JR.

Bibliography

MANN, EVERETT E. 1984 The Public Right to Know Government Information: Its Affirmation and Abridgment. Ph.D. dissertation, Claremont Graduate School.

FREEDOM OF INTIMATE ASSOCIATION

Since the 1960s the Supreme Court has decided scores of cases dealing with marriage and divorce, family relationships, the choice whether to procreate, and various forms of intimate association outside the traditional family structure. Although the factual settings of these cases and their opinions' doctrinal explanations have been diverse, in the aggregate they represent the emergence of a constitutional freedom of intimate association.

The Court had asserted as early as MEYER V. NEBRASKA (1923) and PIERCE V. SOCIETY OF SISTERS (1925) that the Constitution protected the freedom to marry and raise one's children, and SKINNER V. OKLAHOMA (1942) had subjected a compulsory STERILIZATION law to STRICT SCRUTINY. But the modern beginning for the freedom of intimate association was Justice WILLIAM O. DOUGLAS's opinion for the Court in GRISWOLD V. CONNECTICUT (1965). Although that case involved a prosecution of the operators of a BIRTH CONTROL clinic for dispensing advice on contraception and the means to achieve it, the focus of the opinion was a married couple's right to use contraceptive devices. Justice Douglas located that right in a "zone of privacy," created by "penumbras" of various specific guarantees in the BILL OF RIGHTS. He did not specify the scope of the new RIGHT OF PRIVACY, and one product of *Griswold* has been a distinguished body of literature rich with suggested approaches to that issue. In *Griswold* itself, however, the chief object of constitutional protection was the marital relationship.

Griswold has become a major precedent for several lines of doctrinal development. The right to marry has been recognized as a SUBSTANTIVE DUE PROCESS right in LOVING V. VIRGINIA (1967) and ZABLOCKI V. REDHAIL (1978). The right to use contraceptives has been extended to unmarried persons in EISENSTADT V. BAIRD (1972) on an EQUAL PROTECTION theory, and even the right to advertise and sell them has been defended in CAREY V. POPULATION SERVICES INTERNATIONAL (1977) on the basis of the FIRST AMENDMENT and the privacy right of potential buyers, married or not. These protections of intimate relationships outside marriage have been complemented by heightened scrutiny of legislative classifications visiting disadvantage on the status of ILLEGITIMACY. *Griswold*'s most famous doctrinal outgrowth was ROE V. WADE (1973), which squarely placed the new constitutional right of privacy within the liberty protected by substantive due process, and held that the right included a woman's freedom to choose to have an ABORTION.

Here as elsewhere, constitutional doctrine has followed in the wake of social change. After World War II the movement for racial equality accelerated, bringing new awareness and new acceptance of a cultural diversity extending well beyond differences based on race. By the 1970s the feminist movement had succeeded in engaging the nation's attention and changing attitudes of both men and women toward questions of "woman's role," and in particular toward marriage and the family. The white, middle-class "housewife marriage," with the father working and the mother and children at home in a one-family suburban house, may still be the image most often called to mind by general references to "the family." The image, however, represents less than half of America's population. The "wife economy" is now obsolete; increased longevity will place further strains on lifetime marriage; women now know they can choose marriage without motherhood, or motherhood without marriage; racial and ethnic minorities will not again accept the idea that the diversity of their forms of intimate association is merely pathological. Indeed, large numbers of middle-class white couples are openly living together without marrying. What has changed is not so much the fact of diversity as the range of the acceptable in intimate association.

A strong egalitarian theme runs through our society's collective recognition of these changes; it is natural that both due process and equal protection have provided doctrinal underpinnings for the freedom of intimate association. As abstractions, "liberty" and "equality" may sometimes be in tension, but here they have nourished each other. As the civil rights movement sought to advance equality under the banner of "freedom," so the abortion rights movement has sought a new status for women under the banner of "choice."

Taking account of doctrinal development in this area, the Supreme Court, in its opinion in *Roberts v. United States Jaycees* (1984), referred for the first time to a "freedom of intimate association." "[C]ertain kinds of highly personal relationships," said the Court, had been afforded substantial constitutional protection: "marriage; childbirth; the raising and education of children; and cohabitation with one's relatives." The Court noted that these relationships tended to involve relatively small numbers of persons; a high degree of selectivity in beginning and maintaining the affiliations; and "seclusion from others in critical aspects of the relationship." Their constitutional protection reflected "the realization that individuals draw much of their emotional enrichment from close ties with others. Protecting these relationships from unwarranted state interference therefore safeguards the ability independently to define one's identity that is central to any concept of liberty."

For half a century the Court has performed much of its judicial interest-balancing by adjusting the STANDARDS OF REVIEW of the constitutionality of legislation. As the *Jaycees* opinion noted, heightened judicial scrutiny results when the Court perceives the importance of the values or interests impaired when government restricts freedom or imposes inequality. The Court has spoken of procreation as a "basic" right, and has labeled "fundamental" both the right to marry and the freedom of choice "whether to bear or beget a child." To understand what these characterizations may imply for the constitutional status of other forms of intimate association, it is necessary to ask why REPRODUCTIVE AUTONOMY and the freedom to marry are so important. To answer that question requires analysis of the substantive values that may be at stake in intimate associations.

The term "intimate association" is used here to mean a close and familiar personal relationship with another that is in some significant way comparable to a marriage or family relationship. Its connecting links may take the form of living together in the same quarters, or sexual intimacy, or blood ties, or a formal relationship, or some mixtures of these, but in principle the idea of intimate association also includes close friendship, with or without any such links. The values of intimate association are undeniably elusive; they are not readily reducible to items on a list. Yet such an exercise is implicit in any attempt to illuminate the principle underlying the decisions on marriage and reproductive choice. The potential values in intimate associations can be grouped in four clusters: society, caring and commitment, intimacy, and self-identification.

Intimate association implies some expectation of access of one person to another's physical presence, some opportunity for face-to-face encounter. A couple's claim of the right to live together, with or without a sexual relationship, directly implicates this interest in another's society; so does a divorced parent's claim of a right of access to a child in a former spouse's custody, or a prison rule wholly denying visitation rights. Other impairments of the interest in an intimate's society are indirect, as when welfare aid to a mother's family is terminated because she is living with a man. The latter case offers opportunity for manipulation; it might be characterized as a denial of no more than a money payment, or as a denial of the society of an intimate. To allow a claim of constitutional right to turn on such question-begging seems intolerable; yet that is just what the Supreme Court typically does in cases of indirect interference with the values of intimate association. Concededly, not every impairment of the freedom to enjoy an intimate's society requires the same degree of justification, but there is little to be said for distracting attention from substantive interest-balancing by engaging in definitional legerdemain.

For most people, mutual caring and commitment are the chief values of intimate association. Caring implies commitment, for it requires an effort to know another, trust another, hope for another, and help another develop. The commitment in question is not a legal commitment enforceable by law, but a personal commitment, the sense that one is pledged to care for another and intends to keep the pledge. It is possible to be committed to an association one has not chosen; a young child exercises no choice in forming an association with her family and yet may feel wholly committed to them. Still, the value of commitment is usually heightened for the partners to an intimate association when they know there is real and continuing choice to maintain the association. The caring partner continually reaffirms her autonomy and responsibility by choosing the commitment, and the cared-for partner gains in self-respect by seeing himself through his partner's eyes as one who is worth being cared for. Furthermore, although commitment means an expectation of constancy over time, it is not paradoxical to say that effective legal shelter for this value must offer protection to casual intimate associations as well as lasting ones. Such a casual association may ripen into a durable one, and the value of commitment is fully realizable only in an atmosphere of freedom to choose whether a particular association will be fleeting or enduring. Finally, to limit the law's protection to lasting intimate associations would require intolerable inquiries into private behavior and private intentions.

Intimacy, in the context of intimate associations, is more than privacy in its ordinary sense of nondisclosure. When we speak of intimate friends, or of persons who share an intimate relationship, we refer to the intimacy of a close and enduring association, that is, intimacy in the context of caring and commitment. This sort of intimacy is something that a person can share with only a limited number of others, for it requires time and effort to know another and deal with her as a whole person.

Intimate associations are powerful influences over

the development of most people's personalities. Not only do these associations give an individual his best chance to be seen (and thus to see himself) as a whole person rather than an aggregate of social roles; they also serve as statements to others. As the legal consequences of cohabitation come to approximate those of marriage, and as divorce becomes more readily available, marriage itself takes on a special significance for its expressive content as a statement that the couple wish to identify with each other. The decision whether to have a child is also a major occasion for self-identification. To become a parent is to assume a new status in the eyes of oneself and others. Plainly the freedom to choose one's intimate associations is at the heart of this notion of association-as-statement. And, just as the freedom of political nonassociation is properly recognized as a FIRST AMENDMENT right, the freedom not to form an intimate association is similarly linked to the freedom of expression.

These four sets of intimate associational values—society, caring and commitment, intimacy, and self-identification—coalesce in an area of the human psyche that is awkward to discuss in lawyers' language. Yet even before the *Jaycees* opinion the Supreme Court had occasionally suggested its awareness of the reasons why such values are important. In *Eisenstadt*, for example, Justice WILLIAM J. BRENNAN spoke of "unwarranted governmental intrusion into matters so fundamentally affecting a PERSON as the decision whether to bear or beget a child." Although the word "person" usually is no more than a prosaic reference to an individual, its use in this passage resonates in the registers of matters personal and the human personality. If freedoms relating to marriage and family and reproductive choice are "fundamental," the reason is that these concerns lie close to the center of one's sense of self.

Not all governmental restrictions on associational freedom are intrusive in the same degree on the values of intimate association. The constitutional freedom of intimate association is not a rule for decision but an organizing principle, demanding justification for governmental intrusions on close personal relationships in proportion to the magnitude of invasion of intimate associational values. One complicating feature of this interest-balancing is that the law's interference with the freedom of intimate association usually is not direct. Instead, government typically conditions some material benefit (employment, inheritance, welfare payments, Social Security) on the candidate's associations in fact or formal associational status.

In DANDRIDGE V. WILLIAMS (1970), for example, a state proportioned welfare benefits to family size but set an absolute limit on aid to any one family. The Supreme Court, treating the law as a restriction on money payments and ignoring its potential effects on family size, subjected it only to RATIONAL BASIS scrutiny. In CLEVELAND BOARD OF EDUCATION V. LAFLEUR (1974), however, pregnant school teachers were required to take a long maternity leave. The Court, emphasizing the right to procreate, rigorously scrutinized the law under the IRREBUTTABLE PRESUMPTIONS doctrine. This sort of question-begging without explanation, far from being aberrational, has been the norm for the Court's treatment of indirect restrictions on intimate association. It is not unusual for the Court to conceal its interest-balancing behind definitional assumptions.

When a state conditions a benefit on a formal associational status such as marriage or legitimacy of parentage, a further analytical complication arises. The state controls entry into the status as well as its legal consequences. Judicial evaluation of such a restriction on benefits must take into account the ease of entry. Alternatively, a law restricting entry into a formal associational status must be evaluated partly on the basis of the consequences of the status, including eligibility for benefits. The opportunities for circular reasoning are evident; only close attention to the associational values at stake will permit noncircular resolutions. The formal status of marriage, for example, must be seen not merely as a bureaucratic hurdle on the road to material benefits but also as a statement of the partners' commitment and self-identification.

In protecting the freedom of intimate association the Supreme Court has followed several different doctrinal paths. The *Griswold* opinion drew on the First Amendment's freedom of political association partly by way of analogy and partly in support of the Court's "zone of privacy" theory. Later decisions have both extended *Griswold*'s results in the name of equal protection and recharacterized its right of privacy as a substantive due process right. For a brief time in the 1970s the Court even used the rhetoric of PROCEDURAL DUE PROCESS and irrebuttable presumptions to defend the freedom of intimate association—a development which some Justices called a disguised form of equal protection or substantive due process. Today the freedom's most secure doctrinal base is substantive due process; yet both the First Amendment and the equal protection clause counsel judicial sensitivity to the need to protect intimate associations that are unconventional or that may offend majoritarian morality. In a society that expresses its cultural diversity in a rich variety of family forms and other personal relationships, these constitutional claims of freedom and equality will overlap.

Whatever its doctrinal context, a claim to freedom of intimate association depends on the nature and magnitude of the intrusion into the substantive values of intimate association, weighed against the governmental interests asserted to justify the intrusion. To give life to this abstraction it is necessary to examine the freedom of intimate association in operation as an organizing principle in particular subject areas. The Supreme Court's decisions can be grouped in seven overlapping categories: marriage and husband–wife relations; divorce; nonmarital relationships; procreation; illegitimacy; family autonomy; and homosexual relationships.

The Supreme Court's clear recognition of a constitutional right to marry by no means forecloses a state from regulating entry into marriage. Some restrictions, in fact, promote the principle of associational choice: minimum age requirements, for example, or requirements demanding minimum competency to understand the nature of marriage. Other restrictions aimed at promoting public health, such as mandatory blood tests, also seem likely to pass the test of strict judicial scrutiny. It is less clear that the balance of state interests against the freedom of associational choice should uphold a prohibition against POLYGAMY, or a refusal to allow homosexuals a status comparable to marriage, or a prohibition on marriage between first cousins. Yet it is safe to predict that homosexual marriage will not gain judicial blessing in the immediate future, and that the constitutionality of incest and polygamy laws will not be questioned seriously in any future now foreseeable. The Supreme Court, after all, is an instrument of government in a human society. Still, in theory, any direct state prohibition of marriage must pass the test of strict scrutiny, and indirect restriction on the right to marry requires justification proportioned to the restriction's likely practical effects as a prohibition.

The freedom of intimate association speaks not only to state interference with the right to marry but also to state intrusion into the relations between husband and wife. A marriage is more than a list of contractual duties; the partners deal with each other on many levels, both practical and emotional, and their relations are necessarily diffuse rather than particularized, exploratory rather than fixed. Spouses who are committed to stay together in an intimacy characterized by caring need to heal their relationship for the future, not settle old scores. Long before *Griswold* recognized a married couple's constitutional right to autonomy over the intimacies of their relationship, our nonconstitutional law largely maintained a "hands-off" attitude toward interspousal disputes. This tradition once supported a system of patriarchy now discredited; today the values of intimate association counsel the state to leave the partners to an ongoing marriage alone and let them work out their own differences—or, if they cannot, to terminate the marriage with a minimum of state interference.

Although the Supreme Court has not formally recognized a constitutional "right to divorce" comparable to the right to marry, both in principle and in practical effect such a right can be derived from the Court's decisions. The freedom of intimate association demands significant justification for state restrictions on exit from a marriage. The relevance to divorce of the associational value of self-identification is evident. Even the value of commitment bears on such a case, and not merely because divorce is the legal key to remarriage. For those who choose to stay married, their commitment is heightened by the knowledge that it is freely chosen. The Constitution apart, state laws setting conditions for divorce have virtually eliminated the requirement of a showing of one partner's fault. The restrictions that remain concern ACCESS TO THE COURTS, and involve limitations such as filing fees, as in BODDIE V. CONNECTICUT (1971), or RESIDENCE REQUIREMENTS, as in SOSNA V. IOWA (1975).

When a marriage terminates, nothing in the principle of associational choice militates against judicial enforcement of interspousal contracts governing the division of property. Once the union is dissolved, application of the usual rules of contract law to postdissolution obligations threatens none of the values of intimate association and demands no special justification. (Issues of child custody, which do require careful balancing of associational values, are discussed along with other parent–child questions.)

When a couple live together in a sexual relationship without marrying, the associational values of society, caring, and intimacy are all present in important degrees. Although the couple's association may not be so definitive a statement of self-identification as marriage would be, such a statement it surely is. Even the commitment implicit in such a union, although it may be tentative, usually is not trivial. If the couple see the union as a trial marriage, it takes on the instrumental quality that the *Griswold* court saw in sexual privacy. The Supreme Court's decisions on contraception and abortion have extended that right of privacy to unmarried persons. In 1968 the Court construed federal welfare legislation to prevent a state from terminating a mother's benefits merely because she had a man, not her husband, living in the house; Justice Douglas, concurring, would have held the state's attempted regulation of the mother's morals a denial of equal protection, by analogy to the Court's then recent decisions on illegitimacy. Some classifications based on marital status plainly are unconstitutional.

It seems no more than a matter of time before the Court, recognizing the expansion of the boundaries of the acceptable in intimate association, follows the logic of the contraception cases and holds invalid state laws forbidding fornication and unmarried cohabitation. Many lower courts have reached similar results, typically without addressing constitutional issues. Most of the cases have involved the claims of unmarried women denied employment, or child custody, or admission to the bar because they were living with men. The freedom of intimate association is, in important part, a product of the movement for equality between the sexes.

So are the Supreme Court's decisions on reproductive choice. "Birth control is woman's problem," said Margaret Sanger in 1920; it still is. The right to procreate, which another generation's Court called "one of the basic civil rights to man," is now matched with the constitutional right of man and woman alike to practice contraception and with a woman's right to have an abortion, even over her husband's objection. Although the right to choose "whether to bear or beget a child" is not reducible to an aspect of the freedom of intimate association, it is in part an associational choice. Given today's facility of contraception and abortion, generally one can choose whether to be a parent. The *Skinner* opinion properly connected marriage and procreation. An unmarried couple living together recognize this linkage when they decide to marry because they "want to have a family." Children are valued not only for themselves and the associations they bring but also as living expressions of their parents' caring for—and commitment to—each other. The decision whether to have a child is, in part, a choice of social identification and self-concept; it ranks in importance with any other a person may make in a lifetime.

Not only the right to be a parent, protected in *Skinner,* but also the right to choose to defer parenthood or to avoid it altogether implicates the core values of intimate association. *Griswold* and its successor decisions, defending these values in the context of nonassociation, protect men and women—but particularly women—against the enforced intimate society of unwanted children, against an unchosen commitment and a caring stained by reluctance, against a compelled identification with the social role of parent. Coerced intimate association in the shape of forced child-bearing or parenthood is no less serious an invasion of the sense of self than is forced marriage.

Griswold and its successors also protect the autonomy of a couple's association, whether it be a marriage or an association of unmarried intimates. The point was explicitly made in the *Griswold* opinion concerning marital autonomy, and *Eisenstadt v. Baird* (1972) effectively gave unmarried couples the same power to govern the intimacies of their association. What emerges from these decisions, along with *Skinner* and *LaFleur,* is not an absolute rule but a requirement of appropriate justification when the state burdens the decision whether to procreate.

The Supreme Court has focused on equal protection in dealing with the constitutionality of laws defining the incidents of illegitimacy. There is obvious unfairness in visiting unequal treatment on an illegitimate child in order to express the state's disapproval of her parents. Yet the freedom of intimate association suggests an additional perspective: the unfairness of state-imposed inequality between persons in traditional marriage/family relationships and those in other comparable forms of intimate association. In particular, the illegitimacy laws discriminate against unmarried women and their children—as, indeed, such laws have done from their medieval beginnings. The principle of legitimacy of parentage assumes not only that a child needs a male link to the rest of the community but also that the claim of the child's mother to social position depends on her being granted the status of formal marriage. In historical origin and in modern application, the chief function of the law of illegitimacy is to assure male control over the transmission of wealth and status. Deviance from the principle of legitimacy is most likely in subgroups whose fathers lack wealth and status; it is no accident that the incidence of illegitimacy in our society is highest among the nonwhite poor.

As increased numbers of middle-class couples live together without marrying, surely there will be changes in the legal status of unmarried mothers and their children. In the perspective of the freedom of intimate association, the constitutional basis for the whole system of illegitimacy appears shaky. If the informal union of an unmarried couple is constitutionally protected, the relationship between that union's children and their parents is also protected. Significant impairment of the substantive values of such an intimate association must find justification, in proportion to the impairment, in state interests that cannot be achieved by other less intrusive means.

Ever since *Meyer v. Nebraska* (1923) and *Pierce*

v. Society of Sisters (1925) judges and commentators have assumed that the Constitution protects the autonomy of the traditional family against excessive state interference. Those two decisions rested on substantive due process grounds, and they have been cited often by the Supreme Court during the modern revival of substantive due process as a guarantee of personal liberty. When a family is united concerning such matters as the children's education, only a COMPELLING STATE INTEREST will justify state interference with the family's choice.

When a family is not united, however, the constitutional principle of family autonomy is an imperfect guide. Generally, the law assumes that children prosper under their parents' control. For very young children, this assumption is little more than a corollary of the family autonomy principle. As children mature, however, it becomes sensible to speak of the continuing family relationship as a matter of choice. Within the family that stays together, parent–child relations are, from some point in a child's teenage years forward, a matter of intrafamily agreement. Even when parental discipline is the rule, it rests on the child's consent, once the child is capable of making an independent life. Not surprisingly, the Supreme Court held invalid a state law giving an unmarried minor female's parents the right to veto her decision to have an abortion. (See PLANNED PARENTHOOD OF MISSOURI V. DANFORTH, 1976.)

The freedom of intimate association thus counsels severe restrictions on the state's power to intervene either to enforce parental authority or to oppose it—just as considerations of intramarital associational choice and harmony dictate that state intervention into the husband–wife relationship be limited to cases of urgent necessity, such as wife abuse. Conceding that most children want and need parental discipline, it remains true that invoking the state's police officers and juvenile halls to enforce that discipline is destructive of the values of intimate association. For mature children, those values depend on their willingness to identify with their parents and to be committed to maintaining a caring intimacy with them. In cases of a parent's incapacity or serious neglect, state intervention into the zone of family autonomy may be constitutionally justified. Yet removals of children from parental custody and terminations of parental rights are extreme measures, intruding deeply into the values of intimate association—not only for parents but also for children. The most compelling justification is therefore required for so drastic a state intervention, justification found in the child's needs, not any interest the state may have in punishing parental misbehavior. The Supreme Court's refusal in LASSITER V. DEPARTMENT OF SOCIAL SERVICES (1981) to extend the full reach of the RIGHT TO COUNSEL to indigent parents in termination proceedings seems an unstable precedent.

While a marriage lasts, the law is no more likely to interfere in interspousal disputes over child-rearing than it is in other controversies between husband and wife. When a marriage ends, an agreement between the separating parents over child custody usually will prevail, absent some overriding factor such as the associational choice of a mature child. A custody contest upon divorce, involving competing claims of rights of association, demands discretionary, whole-person evaluations rather than application of specific rules of law. The Constitution comes to bear on such decisions only marginally, as appellate courts seek to assure that trial judges do, in fact, consider the whole persons before them and do not disqualify parents from custody by informally substituting unconstitutional "rules" for the discretion that is appropriate. Such a "rule," for example, might disqualify on the basis of a parent's race—or, as in PALMORE V. SIDOTI (1984), the race of the parent's spouse—or religion, or unmarried cohabitation, or sexual preference. *Stanley v. Illinois* (1972) is an instructive analogy; there the Supreme Court held that a law disqualifying a natural father from custody of his illegitimate child upon the mother's death was an unconstitutional irrebuttable presumption of unfitness.

It is now established beyond question that the "liberty" protected by the two due process clauses protects "freedom of personal choice in matters of marriage and family life"—Justice POTTER STEWART's words, concurring in *Zablocki v. Redhail* (1978). If the logic of that freedom extends beyond formal marriage and beyond the nuclear family, the reason is that the human family is a social artifact, not an entity defined in nature. In MOORE V. CITY OF EAST CLEVELAND (1977) a plurality of four Justices admitted the traditional "extended family" into the circle of due process protection, and that opinion is now regularly cited as if it were an OPINION OF THE COURT. The freedom Justice Stewart described is comprehensible only in the light of intimate associational values that are also found in families that depart significantly from traditional models. One result of the movement for women's liberation has been the increased adoption of alternative living arrangements: couples living together outside marriage; single mothers with children, sometimes combining with other similar families. Other groupings such as communes for the young and the old are responses to what their members see as the failings of traditional arrangements. These people do not risk prosecution under cohabitation laws or other "morals" statutes; they may, however, risk the loss of material benefits.

Any governmental intrusion on personal choice of living arrangements requires substantial justification, in proportion to its likely influence in coercing people out of one form of intimate association and into another. In DEPARTMENT OF AGRICULTURE V. MORENO (1973) the Supreme Court demanded such justification for a law denying food stamps to households composed of "unrelated" persons, and found it lacking. Yet in *Village of Belle Terre v. Boraas* (1974) the Court made no search for justification beyond minimum rationality, and upheld a ZONING ordinance designed to screen out nontraditional families and applied to exclude occupancy of a home by six unrelated students. In design, the *Belle Terre* ordinance was a direct assault on the freedom of intimate association, an attempt to stamp out forms of personal association departing from a vision of family life that no longer fit a large proportion of the population. *Belle Terre*'s standing as a precedent surely will weaken as the Court comes to take seriously its own rhetoric about "family" values in nontraditional families. One occasion for such rhetoric was the opinion in *Smith v. Organization of Foster Families* (1977), recognizing the values of intimate association in a foster family.

Laws prohibiting homosexual conduct are only rarely enforced against private consensual behavior. The middle-class homosexual couple thus have each other's society, including whatever sort of intimacy they want; they care for each other and are committed to each other in the degree they choose. What government chiefly denies them is the dignity of self-identification as equal citizens, along with certain forms of employment and other material benefits that may be reserved for partners to a formal marriage.

Whatever may have been the original purpose of laws forbidding homosexual sex, today one of their chief supports is a wish to regulate the content of messages about sexual preference. One fear is that the state, by repealing its restrictions, will be seen as approving homosexual conduct. The selective enforcement of these laws is itself evidence that one of the main policies being pursued is the suppression of expression; the laws are enforced mainly against those who openly advertise their sexual preferences. The immediate practical effect of this enforcement pattern is to penalize public self-identification and expression, some of which is political expression in support of "gay liberation." Even thoroughgoing enforcement would severely impair expression, along with the values of caring and intimacy. For a homosexual, a violation of these laws is the principal form that a sexual expression of love can take.

The denial of the status of marriage, or some comparable status, does not merely limit homosexuals' opportunities for expressive self-identification; material benefits also are frequently conditioned on marriage. Some commentators argue that a state's refusal to recognize homosexual marriage raises a problem of sex discrimination, and others contend that homosexuality should be regarded as a SUSPECT CLASSIFICATION for equal protection purposes. In any case, the heart of the constitutional problem lies in the freedom of intimate association. Although the denial of formal recognition of a homosexual couple's union may not demand the same compelling justification that would be required by a total prohibition of homosexual relations, it nonetheless seems unlikely that government could meet any requirement of justification that was not wholly permissive.

The burden of justification is of critical importance in the area of regulation of homosexual conduct, precisely because most such regulations are the product of folklore and fantasy rather than evidence of real risk of harm. If, for example, the state had to prove that a lesbian mother, by virtue of that status alone, was unfit to have custody of her child, the effort surely would demonstrate that the operative factor in the disqualification was not risk of harm, but stigma. The results of serious constitutional inquiry into harms and justifications in such cases are easy to predict. First, however, that serious inquiry must be made, and the Supreme Court showed in *Doe v. Commonwealth's District Attorney* (1976) that it was not eager to embark on that course.

The freedom of intimate association serves as an organizing principle mainly by focusing attention on substantive associational values. In a given case, the impairment of those values is matched against the asserted justifications for governmental regulation. Those justifications are hard to discuss systematically, for they can be asserted on the basis of a range of interests as broad as the public welfare. One cluster of justifications, however, deserves attention: the promotion of a political majority's view of morality. The state may claim a role in socializing its citizens, and especially the young, to traditional values. When a legislature prohibits unmarried cohabitation or homosexual relations or other disapproved forms of intimate association, it does so primarily to promote a moral view and to protect the sensibilities of those who share that view. The freedom of intimate association does not wholly disable government from seeking these ends; however, as *Griswold* and its successor decisions show, neither can the state defeat every claim to the freedom of intimate association simply by invoking conventional morality.

The judicial interest-balancing appropriate to the evolution of many claims of freedom of intimate association thus must consider not only degrees of impairment of associational values but also questions of the kind raised by GOVERNMENT SPEECH cases involving official promotion of particular points of view. There is a difference, for example, between a "baby bonus" designed to assist parents with child-rearing and a state's offer of cash to any woman entering an abortion clinic, conditioned on her agreement to forgo an abortion. To say that the difference is one of degree is to remind ourselves that the judicial function in constitutional cases is one of judgment. The freedom of intimate association is not a machine that, once set in motion, must run to all conceivable logical conclusions. It is instead a constitutional principle, requiring significant justification when the state seeks to lay hands on life-defining intimate associational choices.

KENNETH L. KARST

Bibliography

BURT, ROBERT A. 1979 The Constitution of the Family. *Supreme Court Review* 1979:329–395.

Developments in the Law—The Constitution and the Family 1980 *Harvard Law Review* 93:1156–1383.

GERETY, TOM 1977 Redefining Privacy. *Harvard Civil Rights-Civil Liberties Law Review* 12:233–296.

GLENDON, MARY ANN 1977 *State, Law and Family.* New York: North-Holland Publishing Company.

KARST, KENNETH L. 1980 The Freedom of Intimate Association. *Yale Law Journal* 89:624–692.

SYMPOSIUM 1975 Children and the Law. *Law and Contemporary Problems* 39, no. 3:1–293.

SYMPOSIUM 1979 Children and the Law. *University of California, Davis Law Review* 12:207–898.

SYMPOSIUM 1985 The Legal System and Homosexuality—Approbation, Accommodation, or Reprobation? *University of Dayton Law Review* 10:445–813.

TRIBE, LAURENCE H. 1978 *American Constitutional Law.* Chap. 15. Mineola, N.Y.: Foundation Press.

WILKINSON, J. HARVIE, III and WHITE, G. EDWARD 1977 Constitutional Protection for Personal Lifestyles. *Cornell Law Review* 62:563–625.

FREEDOM OF PETITION

The freedom to petition the government for redress of grievances was recognized in MAGNA CARTA in 1215 and was well established in English law before the American Revolution. The king would summon Parliament to supply funds for the running of government and Parliament developed the habit of petitioning for a redress of grievances as the condition of supplying the money. The growing recognition of the right of subjects as well as of Parliament to petition the Crown culminated in the explicit affirmation in the English BILL OF RIGHTS of 1689 "That it is the right of the subjects to petition the King and all commitments and prosecutions for such petitioning are illegal."

In the United States Constitution, the FIRST AMENDMENT protects "the right of the people peaceably to assemble, and to petition the Government for a redress of grievances." Historically, the FREEDOM OF ASSEMBLY was regarded as ancillary to the right of petition, as if the amendment guaranteed the right to assemble *in order to* petition the government. This view was expressed by the Supreme Court in UNITED STATES V. CRUIKSHANK (1876). Today, however, the right of assembly has independent significance equal to that of the FREEDOMS OF SPEECH, PRESS, and religion. (See DEJONGE V. OREGON, 1937.) The right to petition has received less judicial attention than the other First Amendment rights. Nevertheless, it is one of the freedoms protected by the DUE PROCESS clause of the FOURTEENTH AMENDMENT against infringement by the states. (See HAGUE V. C.I.O., 1939.) Comparable protections of the right of petition are found, expressly or by clear implication, in the constitutions of all the states. And the right to petition Congress for redress of grievances has been recognized as one of the privileges of national CITIZENSHIP protected against state infringement by the PRIVILEGES OR IMMUNITIES clause of the Fourteenth Amendment. (See TWINING V. NEW JERSEY, 1908.)

The right of petition includes the right not only to approach public officials directly with requests for redress of grievances but also to circulate petitions for signature so as to generate mass pressure on the Congress and other public bodies. It is in this context that the right of petition may have its greatest contemporary significance. For the exercise of the right of petition involves the exercise of other First Amendment rights, including not only the right of expression but the right of other people to be exposed to the ideas expressed in the petition. The act of preparing and circulating a petition is itself an exercise of the freedom to associate with others for the expression of political and other opinions. Justice WILLIAM J. BRENNAN, dissenting in BOSTON V. GLINES (1980), remarked: "The petition is especially suited for the exercise of all these rights: It serves as a vehicle of communication; as a classic means of individual affiliation with ideas or opinions; and as a peaceful yet effective method of amplifying the views of the individual signers." As with other First Amendment rights, the freedom of petition cannot be infringed in the absence of a compelling governmental interest justifying the infringement; the right of petition is an essential component of the political liberties protected by the First Amendment.

CHARLES E. RICE

FREEDOM OF RELIGION

See: Religious Liberty

FREEDOM OF SPEECH

Freedom of speech is guaranteed in the American Constitution by the FIRST AMENDMENT. Adopted in 1791 as the first provision of the BILL OF RIGHTS, the First Amendment reads (excluding the clauses on religion): "Congress shall make no law . . . abridging the freedom of speech, or of the press, or the right of the people peaceably to assemble, and to petition the Government for a redress of grievances." Although the provision names four specific rights—freedom of speech, FREEDOM OF THE PRESS, FREEDOM OF ASSEMBLY, and FREEDOM OF PETITION—the several guarantees have never been clearly differentiated; rather the First Amendment has been construed as guaranteeing a composite right to freedom of expression. The term "freedom of speech," therefore, in popular usuage as well as in legal doctrine, has been considered roughly coextensive with the whole of the First Amendment.

The precise intentions of the framers of the First Amendment have never been entirely clear. The debates in Congress when the amendment was proposed do not throw much light upon the subject. The right to freedom of speech derives from English law and tradition. And it is agreed that the English law of the time, following the lapse of the censorship laws at the end of the seventeenth century, did not authorize advance censorship of publication. The English law of SEDITIOUS LIBEL, however, did provide punishment, after publication, for speech that criticized the government, its policies or its officials, or tended to bring them into contempt or disrepute. These features of English law were under severe attack, both in England and in the American colonies, but whether the First Amendment was meant to abolish or change them has been a matter of dispute. Similarly, the application of the First Amendment to other aspects of free speech, such as civil libel, BLASPHEMY, OBSCENITY, and the like, remained obscure.

Passage of the ALIEN AND SEDITION ACTS in 1798, which incorporated much of the English law of seditious libel, stimulated public discussion of the meaning of the First Amendment. The constitutional issues, however, never reached the Supreme Court. Nor, despite widespread suppression of speech at certain times in our history, such as took place during the abolitionist movement, the Civil War, and the beginnings of the labor movement, did the Supreme Court have or take the occasion to address in any major way the development of First Amendment doctrine. The reason for this failure of the constitutional guarantee to be translated into legal action seems to lie partly in the fact that the Bill of Rights had been construed by the Court to apply only to action of the federal government, not to state or local governments; partly in the fact that, insofar as suppression emanated from federal sources, it was the executive not the legislature that was involved; and partly in the fact that the role of the courts in protecting CIVIL LIBERTIES had not matured to the point it has reached today.

In any event this state of affairs ended at the time of World War I. Legislation enacted by Congress in 1917 and 1918, designed to prohibit interference with the war effort, raised clear-cut issues under the First Amendment. Beginning in 1919, a series of cases challenging the wartime legislation came before the Supreme Court. These were followed by cases arising out of the Red scare of the early 1920s. In 1925, in GITLOW V. UNITED STATES, the Court accepted the argument that the First Amendment was applicable to the state and local governments as a "liberty" that could not be denied without DUE PROCESS OF LAW under the FOURTEENTH AMENDMENT. It also became clear that, while the First Amendment literally refers only to "Congress," its provisions extend not only to the legislature but to the executive and judicial branches of government as well. As the First Amendment has come to be applied to more and newer problems growing out of the operation of a modern technological society, there has developed an extensive network of principles, legal rules, implementing decisions, and institutional practices which expand and refine the constitutional guarantee.

The fundamental values underlying the concept of freedom of speech, and the functions that principle serves in a democratic society, are widely accepted. They have been summarized in the following form:

First, freedom of speech is essential to the development of the individual personality. The right to express oneself and to communicate with others is central to the realization of one's character and potentiality as a human being. Conversely, suppression of thought or opinion is an affront to a person's dignity and integrity. In this respect freedom of speech is an end in itself, not simply an instrument to attain other ends. As such it is not necessarily subordinate to other goals of the society.

Second, freedom of speech is vital to the attainment and advancement of knowledge. As John Stuart Mill pointed out, an enlightened judgment is possible only if one is willing to consider all facts and ideas, from whatever source, and to test one's conclusion against opposing views. Even speech that conveys false information or maligns ideas has value, for it compels us to retest and rethink accepted positions and thereby promotes greater understanding. From this function of free speech it follows that the right to express oneself does not depend upon whether society judges the communication to be true or false, good or bad, socially useful or harmful. All points of view, even a minority of one, are entitled to be heard. The MARKETPLACE OF IDEAS should be open to all sellers and all buyers.

Third, freedom of speech is a necessary part of our system of self-government. ALEXANDER MEIKLEJOHN, the leading exponent of this view of the First Amendment, stressed that under our Constitution, sovereignty resides in the people; in other words, the people are the masters and the government is their servant. If the people are to perform their role as sovereign and instruct their government, they must have access to all information, ideas, and points of view. This right of free speech is crucial not only in determining policy but in checking the government in its implementation of policy. The implication of this position is that the government has no authority to determine what may be said or heard by the citizens of the community. The servant cannot tell the master how to make up its mind.

Fourth, freedom of speech is vital to the process of peaceful social change. It allows ideas to be tested in advance before action is taken, it legitimizes the decision reached, and it permits adaptation to new conditions without the use of force. It does not eliminate conflict in a society, but it does direct conflict into more rational, less violent, channels. From this it follows, in the words of Justice WILLIAM J. BRENNAN in NEW YORK TIMES V. SULLIVAN (1964), that speech will often be "uninhibited, robust, and wide-open."

There is also general agreement that speech is entitled to special protection against abridgment by the state. Freedom of thought and communication are central to any system of individual rights. Most other rights of the person against the collective flow from and are dependent upon that source. Moreover, speech is considered to have less harmful effects upon the community—to be less coercive—than other forms of conduct. And, as a general proposition, the state possesses sufficient power to achieve social goals without suppressing beliefs, opinions, or communication of ideas. Hence, in constitutional terms, freedom of speech occupies a "preferred position."

One further background factor should be noted. Toleration of the speech of others does not come easily to many people, especially those in positions of power. As Justice OLIVER WENDELL HOLMES remarked in ABRAMS V. UNITED STATES (1919), "If you have no doubt of your premises or your powers and want a certain result with all your heart you naturally express your wishes in law and sweep away all opposition." Hence the pressures leading to suppression of speech are widespread and powerful in our society. The mechanisms for protecting freedom of speech, therefore, must rely heavily upon an independent judiciary, standing somewhat outside the fray, and upon the creation of legal DOCTRINES that are precise and realistic.

The principal controversies that have engaged our system of freedom of speech have concerned the formulation of these implementing rules. In general the issues have centered on two basic questions. The first is what kind of conduct is to be considered "speech" entitled to special protection under the First Amendment. The second concerns what degree of protection, or encouragement, must be given that speech under the constitutional mandate.

As to the first question—the issue of coverage—it has been argued from time to time that certain categories of speech are totally outside the purview of the First Amendment. Thus it has been contended that totalitarian and racist groups should not be permitted to advance antidemocratic ideas. The argument has been that political groups that would destroy democratic institutions if they came to power should not be entitled to take advantage of these institutions in order to promote their cause; only those who adhere to the rules of the game should be allowed to participate. Similarly it has been urged that racist speech violates the dignity and integrity of fellow persons in the community, performs no social function, and should not be tolerated in a civilized society dedicated to human rights.

While this position has been strongly urged it has not prevailed in the United States. For both theoretical and practical reasons the concept of freedom of speech has been interpreted to mean that all persons should be allowed to express their beliefs and opinions regardless of how obnoxious or "fraught with death" those ideas may be. As a matter of principle, all ideas must be open to challenge; even totalitarian and racist speech serves a useful purpose in forcing a society to defend and thereby better comprehend its own basic values. Moreover, groups that promote totalitarian or racist ideas do not operate in a political vacuum. Their speech reflects fears, grievances, or other conditions which society should be aware of and in some cases take action to deal with. Suppression of such speech simply increases hostility, diverts attention from underlying problems, and ultimately weakens the society.

In practical terms, experience has shown that it is difficult or impossible to suppress any set of ideas without endangering the whole fabric of free speech. The dividing line between totalitarian and racist speech, on the one hand, and "acceptable" speech, on the other, cannot be clearly drawn and thus is open to manipulation. The apparatus necessary to suppress a political movement—involving government investigation into beliefs and opinions, the compiling of dossiers, the employment of agents and informers—inevitably creates an atmosphere damaging freedom of all speech. Frequently actions ostensibly directed against the outlawed group are merely a pretext for harassment of unwanted political opposition. Most important, once the dike has been broken all unorthodox or minority opinion is in danger. The only safe course is to afford protection to all who wish to speak.

The Supreme Court, accepting the prevailing view, has consistently taken the position that antidemocratic forms of speech are within the coverage of the First Amendment. Thus, while upholding the conviction of the Communist party leaders under the Smith Act for advocating overthrow of the government by force and violence in DENNIS V. UNITED STATES (1951), the Court never suggested that the defendants were not entitled to the protection of the First Amendment. Likewise in BRANDENBURG V. OHIO (1969) racist speech by members of the Ku Klux Klan was given full First Amendment protection. The viewpoint taken by the Court was perhaps most dramatically formulated by Justice Holmes when he said in *Gitlow v. New York:* "If in the long run the beliefs expressed in proletarian dictatorship are destined to be accepted by the dominant forces of the country, the only meaning of free speech is that they should be given their chance and have their way."

It has also been contended that the coverage of the First Amendment should be limited to speech that relates to "political issues." Meiklejohn, who emphasized the role of the First Amendment in the process of self-government, advocated this interpretation, although he ultimately reached a broad definition of "political speech." Other commentators, arguing for a similar limitation, have adopted a far more restrictive concept of "political speech." The position has not, however, been accepted. For one thing, the proposed restriction has no inner logic; virtually all speech has political overtones or ramifications. In any event, there is no convincing reason for restricting the coverage of the First Amendment in this way. Speech concerned with literature, music, art, science, entertainment, ethics, and a host of other matters serves the functions sought by the First Amendment and should be equally entitled to its protection. The Supreme Court has consistently so held.

Other, narrower, categories of speech have also been said to be excluded from First Amendment coverage. In CHAPLINSKY V. NEW HAMPSHIRE (1942) the Supreme Court observed that restrictions on speech that was obscene, profane, libelous, or involved FIGHTING WORDS had "never been thought to raise any Constitutional problem." But this OBITER DICTUM has been eroded in the course of time. Obscenity is still, in theory, excluded from First Amendment protection; but in formulating the definition of "obscenity" the Court has brought constitutional considerations back into the decision. The exception for profanity has been disregarded. The dictum concerning libel has been expressly overruled. And the "fighting words" exemption, which has been narrowly construed to apply only to face-to-face encounters, turns more on the proposition that "fighting words" are not really speech at all than upon a concept of exclusion from First Amendment protection. Thus virtually all conduct that can be considered "speech" falls within the coverage of the First Amendment.

There are certain areas of speech where, although the First Amendment is applicable, the governing rules afford somewhat less protection than in the case of speech generally. These areas include speech in military institutions, which are not structured according to democratic principles, and speech by or addressed to children, who are "not possessed of that full capacity for individual choice which is the presupposition of First Amendment guarantees." COMMERCIAL SPEECH, that is, speech concerned solely with buying or selling goods or services for a profit, was at one time excluded from First Amendment protection. It is now covered by the First Amendment but is entitled to less stringent safeguards than noncommercial speech.

The most controversial aspect of the coverage question concerns not whether conduct that is recognized as speech is exempted from First Amendment protection but what conduct is to be considered speech and what is to be held non-speech, or "action," and hence not protected by the First Amendment. The resolution of this problem poses obvious difficulties. Clearly some verbal conduct, such as words exchanged in planning a CRIMINAL CONSPIRACY, does not constitute "speech" within the intention of the First Amendment. Likewise some nonverbal conduct, such as operating a printing press, is an integral part of the speech which it is the purpose of the First Amendment to protect. Some conduct, such as PICKETING, combines elements of speech and action.

Two approaches to this dilemma are possible. One is to attempt to define "speech" or "action" in light of the values and functions served by the First Amendment. The other is to abandon any effort at a sharp definition of "speech" and to hold that any conduct containing an "expressive element" is within the coverage of the First Amendment. The advantage of the first approach is that it allows the development of more clear-cut rules for protecting conduct found to be "speech," that is, all "speech" or most "speech" could be fully protected without the need for devising elaborate qualifications difficult to apply. The advantage of the second approach is that it avoids the necessity of making refined, and in some cases unpersuasive, distinctions between "speech" and "action." The Supreme Court has, on the whole, tended to follow the second path of analysis. However, in the overwhelming majority of cases where First Amendment protection is invoked, there is no serious question but that the conduct involved is properly classified as "speech."

The second major problem in interpreting and applying the First Amendment is the determination of what degree of protection from government interference, or encouragement by government, is to be afforded "speech." Most of the controversy over the meaning of the First Amendment has involved this issue. The Supreme Court has varied its approach from time to time and no consistent or comprehensive theory has emerged. The question arises in a great variety of situations, and only a brief summary of some of the principal results is possible.

The starting point is that, as a general proposition, the government cannot prohibit or interfere with speech because it objects to the content of the communication. Legitimate government interests must be achieved by methods other than the control of speech. Thus speech that is critical of the government or its officials, that interferes with government efficiency, that makes the attainment of consensus in the society more difficult, that urges radical change, or that affects similar societal interests cannot be abridged.

Somewhat less stringent rules have been applied where the speech is of such a character as to lead to concern that it will provoke violence or other violation of a valid law. Many of the Supreme Court decisions have involved issues of this nature, and a series of legal doctrines emerged. In the earlier cases, mostly growing out of legislation designed to prevent interference with the conduct of World War I or to suppress emerging radical political parties, the Court adopted a BAD TENDENCY TEST under which any speech that had a tendency to cause a violation of law could be punished. Such a test, of course, gives very little protection to nonconforming speech. Subsequently, on the initiative of Justices Holmes and LOUIS D. BRANDEIS, the Court accepted the CLEAR AND PRESENT DANGER TEST. Under this doctrine speech could be penalized only when it created a clear and present danger of some significant evil that the government had a right to prevent. In some cases the Court has used an ad hoc BALANCING TEST, by which the interest in freedom of speech is balanced against the social interest in maintaining order. Ultimately the Court appears to have settled upon the so-called *Brandenburg* test. "[T]he constitutional guarantees of free speech and free press," the Court said in *Brandenburg v. Ohio,* "do not permit a State to forbid or proscribe advocacy of the use of force or of law violation except where such advocacy is directed to inciting or producing imminent lawless action and is likely to incite or produce such action." An approach which attempts to separate "speech" from "action" and gives full protection to speech has never appealed to a majority of the Justices. But the Court has progressively tightened the originally loose restrictions on the government's power to punish militant political rhetoric.

In recent years the question has been posed in various forms whether or not speech can be curtailed where it may cause injury to NATIONAL SECURITY. The term "national security" has never been precisely defined and could of course include virtually every aspect of national life. Generally speaking it is clear that the usual First Amendment principles apply in national security cases; the society must seek to achieve national security by methods that do not abridge freedom of speech. Nevertheless, qualifications of the general rule have been urged with increasing vigor. The chief issues have involved publication of information alleged to jeopardize national security and the conduct of intelligence agencies seeking to acquire information relating to national security matters.

The Supreme Court in NEW YORK TIMES V. UNITED STATES (1971) (the Pentagon Papers case), a landmark decision in this area, rejected attempts by the government to enjoin the *New York Times* and the *Washington Post* from publishing a secret classified history of the VIETNAM WAR obtained illicitly by a former government employee, despite government claims that publication would cause "grave and irreparable injury" to the national security. The decision rested on the ground that the government had not met the "heavy burden of showing justification for the imposition of [a PRIOR] RESTRAINT." The majority were unable to agree, however, upon a single theory of the case. Three Justices thought that an INJUNCTION against publication of information should never, or virtually never, be allowed, but others, including the dissenters, would have accepted less rigorous standards. In UNITED STATES V. UNITED STATES DISTRICT COURT (1972), another critical decision in the national security area, the Court ruled that government intelligence agencies were bound to adhere to constitutional limitations (in that case the FOURTH AMENDMENT) in gathering information pertaining to national security, but it expressed no opinion as to "the issues which may be involved with respect to activities of foreign powers or their agents." The degree to which the Supreme Court will accept claims to national security as ground for qualifying First Amendment rights thus remains uncertain.

Cases where the exercise of free-speech rights runs into conflict with other social or individual interests frequently come before the Supreme Court. Interests invoked as ground for limiting speech have included the right of an accused person to obtain a FAIR TRIAL free from prejudice caused by adverse newspaper publicity; the interest of society in assuring fair elections through regulation of contributions and expenditures in political campaigns; the patriotic interest of the community in protecting the American flag against desecration by political dissenters; the aesthetic interests of the public in maintaining certain areas free from unsightly billboards; and many others. Where the countervailing interest is an appealing one the Court has tended to apply a balancing test: individual and social interests in freedom of speech are balanced against the opposing interests at stake. Likewise, where a government regulation is ostensibly directed at some other objective but has the effect of restricting speech, as in the case of government LOYALTY-SECURITY PROGRAMS or LEGISLATIVE INVESTIGATIONS, the balancing test is usually employed.

The balancing test has come to assume various forms. When most protective of free speech it requires that the government (1) has the burden of justifying any restriction on speech (2) by demonstrating "compelling" reasons and (3) showing that less intrusive means for advancing the government interest are not available. On the other hand, in some cases the balancing test is applied without giving any special weight to First Amendment considerations. The consequence of using a balancing test is that the outcome in any particular case is difficult to predict. Thus in BUCKLEY V. VALEO (1976) the Supreme Court held, in substance, that limitations on the amount of funds that can be contributed to a candidate in a political campaign are permissible but limitations on expenditures are not. Moreover, the balancing test is such a loose standard that, in times of stress, it might afford very little protection to freedom of speech. Thus far, however, the balances struck by the Court have given a substantial degree of support to free-speech rights.

Special rules for measuring the protection accorded speech have evolved in several areas. With respect to laws punishing obscene publications the Supreme Court, as noted above, still adheres to the theoretical position that obscenity is not covered by the First Amendment but it does take constitutional factors into account in determining whether or not a particular publication is obscene. As set forth in MILLER V. CALIFORNIA (1972), the current definition of obscenity is "(a) whether the average person, applying contemporary community standards, would find that the work, taken as a whole, appeals to the prurient interest; (b) whether the work depicts or describes, in a patently offensive way, sexual conduct specifically defined by the applicable state law; and (c) whether the work, taken as a whole, lacks serious literary, artistic, political, or scientific value." In practical application, as nearly as it can be articulated, the *Miller* test allows regulation only of "hard-core pornography."

The Supreme Court has also imposed substantive limitations upon actions for libel. Criminal libel laws have been narrowly construed and, although a GROUP LIBEL law was upheld in BEAUHARNAIS V. ILLINOIS (1952), subsequent developments have cast doubt upon the present validity of that decision. In the field of civil libel the Supreme Court held, in *New York Times v. Sullivan,* that public officials could maintain a suit for libel only when they can establish that a damaging statement about them was not only false but was made with "actual malice," that is, "with knowledge that it was false or with reckless disregard of whether it was false or not." Later the "actual malice" rule was extended to "public figures." As to others, namely "private individuals," the Court has held that the state or federal government could adopt any rule respecting libel so long as it required at least a showing of negligence on the part of the defendant. Although the Court in recent years has tended to take a narrow view of who is a "public figure," and the costs of defending libel actions frequently operate as a restraint upon speech, the curtailment of public discussion through libel laws has been somewhat held in check.

Constitutional doctrine for reconciling the right to freedom of speech with the RIGHT OF PRIVACY remains unformed. In most respects the two constitutional rights do not clash but rather supplement each other. Conflict may arise, however, at several points, such as where a communication contains information that is true, and hence is not covered by the libel laws, but relates to the intimate details of an individual's personal life that are not relevant to any issue of public concern. The scope of the constitutional right of privacy has never been clearly delineated. Nor has the Supreme Court ever held that the right of privacy prevails over the right to freedom of speech. Nevertheless the issue is a recurring one and sooner or later an accommodation between the two constitutional rights will have to be formulated.

The degree of protection afforded speech under the First Amendment may also hinge on various other factors. Where the physical facilities for communication are limited, and the government is therefore forced to allocate available facilities among those seeking to use them, the government has the power, indeed the obligation, to lay down certain conditions in order to assure that the scarce facilities will be used in the public interest. This is the situation with respect to radio and television BROADCASTING where, at least at the present time, the number of broadcast channels is limited. On this theory, government regulations such as the FAIRNESS DOCTRINE, requiring that broadcasting stations give adequate coverage to public issues and that such coverage be fair in accurately reflecting opposing views, have been upheld by the Supreme Court. Such regulatory powers, however, extend only to what might be termed a "macro level" of intervention. The government may require that a broadcasting station devote a certain proportion of its time to public interest programs, but it may not censor or determine the content of particular programs, that is, it may not exercise control at the "micro level."

Likewise special considerations enter when a person seeking to exercise rights to freedom of speech is an employee of the government or is confined in a government institution such as a mental hospital or a prison. Here the relationship of the individual to the government is somewhat different from the relationship of the ordinary citizen to the general community; the goals and interests of the particular institution involved are entitled to more immediate recognition. The Supreme Court has dealt with these issues by applying a balancing test, but the weights have been cast largely on the government side of the scales.

One further aspect of government attempts to regulate the content of speech should be noted. The letter and spirit of the EQUAL PROTECTION clause have had an important bearing upon the right to freedom of speech. The equal protection element guarantees the universality of the rules protecting the right to speak. It means that the government cannot differentiate, at least without a compelling reason, between speakers on the basis of the content of their communications. Hence if the government allows a patriotic organization to march down the main street of town it must grant equal opportunity to unpopular or radical organizations. If it grants the use of a public building for a meeting to a group of one political persuasion it must grant the same use to all political groups. This combination of the First Amendment and the equal protection clause thus helps to assure that unorthodox speech will receive the same treatment as conventional speech.

Apart from attempts to control the content of speech, government regulation has also dealt with various issues in the administration of the free speech system. Thus the requirement of a permit to hold a meeting in a public building, or to conduct a demonstration that may interfere with traffic, clearly constitutes a justifiable regulation. Likewise, a municipal ordinance may legitimately keep soundtrucks from operating in a residential area during certain hours of the night. It is frequently said that "time, place, and manner" restrictions on speech are permissible so long as they are "reasonable." Such generalizations, however, are overbroad. In many situations, "time, place, and manner" restrictions can be used to curtail freedom of speech to the same degree as content regulations. And to accord them all validity would be inconsistent with the basic premise that the right of free speech is entitled to a preferential position among competing interests. A more precise statement of the applicable legal doctrine would be to say that administrative regulations dealing with physical incompatibilities between the exercise of free speech rights and other interests are permissible. Thus government could validly allocate use of the streets between those seeking to hold a demonstration and those using the streets for passage. And the physical intrusion of noises from soundtrucks would also be subject to control. The principle for resolving such physical conflicts is not mere "reasonableness" but a fair accommodation between the competing interests.

Other legal doctrines play an important role in maintaining the system of freedom of speech. Thus the courts have held that the rules against undue VAGUENESS or OVERBREADTH in legislation or administrative regulation will be applied with special rigor where First Amendment rights are affected. And the prohibition in the Fourth Amendment against UNREASONABLE SEARCHES and seizures is given added force when invoked to protect freedom of speech. Perhaps the most significant supportive doctrine of this nature is the rule against prior restraint. Attempts by the government to prevent publication in advance, through a system of censorship, an injunction, or similar measures, are presumptively invalid and rarely allowed. Thus the silencing of speech before it is uttered—a particularly effective form of suppression—is normally not available as a method of control.

The constitutional doctrines thus far discussed have been of a negative character in that they have been directed against government interference with freedom of speech. In recent years, however, increasing attention has been given to questions relating to the affirmative side of the constitutional guarantee: to what extent does the First Amendment allow or require the government to encourage or promote a more effective system of free speech? These issues are important because of growing distortions within the system. More and more, as the mass media have become concentrated in fewer hands and have tended to express a single economic, social, and political point of view, the concept of a marketplace of diverse ideas has failed to conform to original expectations. The problems are difficult to solve because they involve using the government to expand freedom of speech while at the same time continuing to prohibit the government from controlling or inhibiting speech.

Not only does government itself engage in speech, for example, through schools and libraries and the statements of officials (see GOVERNMENT SPEECH), but government also promotes the freedom of speech in many ways. One of the most significant involves assuring access to the means of communication. The courts have gone some distance in recognizing the obligation of government to make facilities for communication available. Thus the courts have held that the streets, parks, and other public places must be open for meetings, parades, demonstrations, canvassing, and similar activities. Other public facilities have likewise been considered PUBLIC FORUMS and available, to the extent compatible with other uses, for free speech purposes. At one time the Supreme Court ruled that SHOPPING CENTERS and malls, privately owned but open to the public, could not exclude persons seeking to engage in speech activities. However, the Court later withdrew from this position. A very limited right of access to radio and television, justified by the scarcity principle, has been upheld. On the other hand, the Court has refused to allow a right of access to the columns of privately owned newspapers, on the grounds that intervention of this nature would destroy the independence of the publisher. Expansion of a right of access, without jeopardizing the rights of those already using the facilities of communication, remains a critical problem, the solution to which appears to depend more upon legislative than judicial action.

Affirmative governmental promotion of speech also takes the form of subsidies. Government contributions to educational, cultural, research, and other speech activities are widespread. Most of these subsidies have gone unchallenged in the courts. In *Buckley v. Valeo*, however, the Supreme Court did consider the constitutionality of legislation providing for the public financing of presidential election campaigns, upholding that measure upon the grounds that the use of "public money to facilitate and enlarge public discussion . . . furthers, not abridges, pertinent First Amendment values." The decision apparently accepts the basic validity of all government funding that can be found to promote public discussion. Nevertheless certain limitations on the power of government to finance nongovernment speech would seem to be clear. Thus government subsidy of religious speech would certainly be prohibited under the religion clauses of the First Amendment. And although the government would be free to choose at the "macro" level of intervention, that is, to determine the nature of the speech activity to be subsidized, it would have no power to intervene at the "micro" level, that is, to control the content of a particular communication. Likewise some rules against INVIDIOUS DISCRIMINATION, though giving government more leeway than when it is undertaking to regulate speech, would certainly apply. Development of these and other limiting principles, however, remains for the future.

Further support for affirmative promotion of speech rests on the constitutional doctrine of the RIGHT TO KNOW. The concept of a right to know includes not only the right of listeners and viewers to receive communications but also the right of those wishing to communicate to obtain information from the government. In earlier decisions the Supreme Court rejected right-to-know arguments that news reporters had a constitutional right to be admitted to prisons in order to observe conditions and interview inmates. But in RICHMOND NEWSPAPERS V. VIRGINIA (1980) the Court, changing directions, ruled that the public and the press could not be excluded from criminal trials, thereby holding for the first time that some right to obtain information from the government existed. How much further the Court will go in compelling the government to disclose information remains to be seen. Most likely the right of would-be speakers to obtain information from the government will continue to rest primarily upon FREEDOM OF INFORMATION and sunshine laws.

Efforts to expand and improve the system of free speech by affirmative governmental action, although they incur serious risks, remain essential to the continued vitality of the system. Major progress in this area will probably depend, however, more on legislative than judicial action.

The right to freedom of speech embodied in the First Amendment has expanded into an elaborate constitutional structure. This theoretical framework has some weaknesses. At some points it does not extend sufficient protection to speech, and at other places loosely formulated doctrine may not stand up in a crisis. On the whole, however, the legal structure provides the foundation for a workable system. The extent to which freedom of speech is actually realized in practice depends, of course, upon additional factors. The underlying political, economic, and social conditions must be favorable. Above all, freedom of speech, a sophisticated concept, must rest on public interest and understanding.

THOMAS I. EMERSON

Bibliography

CHAFEE, ZECHARIAH, JR. (1920)1941 *Free Speech in the United States.* Cambridge, Mass.: Harvard University Press.

DORSEN, NORMAN; BENDER, PAUL; and NEUBORNE, BURT 1976 Emerson, Haber and Dorsen's *Political and Civil Rights in the United States,* 4th ed. Vol. 1. Boston: Little, Brown.

EMERSON, THOMAS I. 1970 *The System of Freedom of Expression.* New York: Random House.

HAIMAN, FRANKLYN S. 1981 *Speech and Law in a Free Society.* Chicago: University of Chicago Press.

HUDON, EDWARD G. 1963 *Freedom of Speech and Press in America.* Washington, D.C.: Public Affairs Press.

LEVY, LEONARD W. 1960 *Legacy of Suppression.* Cambridge, Mass.: Harvard University Press.

MEIKLEJOHN, ALEXANDER (1948)1960 *Political Freedom.* New York: Harper.

MILL, JOHN STUART 1859 *On Liberty,* R. B. McCallum, ed., London: Oxford University Press.

NIMMER, MELVILLE B. 1984 *Nimmer on Freedom of Speech.* New York: Mathew Bender.

REDISH, MARTIN H. 1984 *Freedom of Expression: A Critical Analysis.* Charlottesville, Va.: Michie Co.

FREEDOM OF SPEECH, LEGISLATOR'S

See: Legislative Immunity; Speech or Debate Clause

FREEDOM OF THE PRESS

The constitutional basis for freedom of the press in the United States is the FIRST AMENDMENT, which provides: "Congress shall make no law . . . abridging the FREEDOM OF SPEECH, or of the press, or the right of the people peaceably to assemble, and to petition the Government for a redress of grievances." In a constitutional interpretation the separate rights enumerated in the First Amendment are merged into a composite right to freedom of expression. Within this general system freedom of the press focuses on the right to publish. Originally concerned with the product of printing presses—newspapers, periodicals, books, pamphlets, and broadsides—the term "press" now includes the electronic media. In general the constitutional issues involving freedom of the press are similar to those pertaining to other aspects of freedom of expression. However, certain areas are of special interest to the press, particularly to the mass media.

Freedom of the press has its roots in English history. When printing presses were introduced into England at the end of the fifteenth century they were quickly brought under total official control. Through a series of royal proclamations, Parliamentary enactments, and Star Chamber decrees a rigid system of censorship was established. No material could be printed unless it was first approved by a state or ecclesiastical official.

Further, no book could be imported or sold without a license; all printing presses were required to be registered; the number of master printers was limited; and sweeping powers to search for contraband printed matter were exercised. (See PRIOR RESTRAINT AND CENSORSHIP.)

In 1695, when the then current licensing law expired, it was not renewed and the system of advance censorship was abandoned. The laws against SEDITIOUS LIBEL remained in effect, however. Under the libel law any criticism of the government or its officials, or circulation of information that reflected adversely upon the government, regardless of truth or falsity, was punishable by severe criminal penalties. Sir WILLIAM BLACKSTONE, summarizing the English law as it existed when he published his *Commentaries* in 1769, put it in these terms: "The liberty of the press is indeed essential to the nature of a free state; but this consists in laying no *previous* restraints upon public actions, and not in freedom from censure for criminal matter when published. Every free man has an undoubted right to lay what sentiments he pleases before the public; to forbid this, is to destroy the freedom of the press; but if he publishes what is improper, mischievous or illegal, he must take the consequences of his own temerity."

Developments in the American colonies followed those in England. Censorship laws existed in some of the colonies well into the eighteenth century. Likewise, prosecutions for seditious libel were not uncommon. in both England and America, however, there was strong opposition to the seditious libel laws. Thus in the famous ZENGER'S CASE, where the publisher of a newspaper was prosecuted for printing satirical ballads reflecting upon the governor of New York and his council, the defense argued vigorously (but unsuccessfully) that truth should be a defense, and urged the jury (successfully) to give a general verdict of not guilty.

The law was in this state of flux when the First Amendment, with its guarantee of freedom of the press, was added to the Constitution in 1791. The specific intention of the Framers was never made explicit. It is generally agreed that the First Amendment was designed to make unconstitutional any system of advance censorship of the press, or "prior restraint," but its impact upon the law of seditious libel has been the subject of controversy. The latter issue was brought into sharp focus when the ALIEN AND SEDITION ACTS, which did include a modified seditious libel law, were enacted by Congress in 1798. Prosecutions under the Sedition Act were directed largely at editors of the press. The constitutionality was upheld by a number of trial judges, including some members of the Supreme Court sitting on circuit, but the issues never reached the Supreme Court. The lapse of the Alien and Sedition Acts after two years ended public attention to the problem for the time being.

For well over a century, although freedom of the press was at times not realized in practice, the constitutional issues did not come before the Supreme Court in any major decision. This situation changed abruptly after World War I as the Court confronted a series of First Amendment problems. Two of these early cases were of paramount importance for freedom of the press. In NEAR V. MINNESOTA (1931) the Court considered the validity of the so-called Minnesota Gag Law. This statute provided that any person "engaged in the business" of regularly publishing or circulating an "obscene, lewd and lascivious" or a "malicious, scandalous and defamatory" newspaper or periodical was "guilty of a nuisance," and could be enjoined from further committing or maintaining such a nuisance. The Court held that the statutory scheme constituted a "prior restraint" and hence was invalid under the First Amendment. The Court thus established as a constitutional principle the doctrine that, with some narrow exceptions, the government could not censor or otherwise prohibit a publication in advance, even though the communication might be punishable after publication in a criminal or other proceeding. In a second decision, GROSJEAN V. AMERICAN PRESS CO. (1936), the Court struck down a Louisiana statute, passed to advance the political interest of Senator Huey Long, that imposed a two percent tax on the gross receipts of newspapers and periodicals with circulations in excess of 20,000 a week. The *Grosjean* decision assured the press that it could not be subjected to any burden, in the guise of ECONOMIC REGULATION, that was not imposed generally upon other enterprises.

In the years since *Near* and *Grosjean* an elaborate body of legal doctrine, interpreting and applying the First Amendment right to freedom of the press in a variety of situations, has emerged. Before we turn to a survey of this constitutional structure, two preliminary matters need to be considered.

First, the functions that freedom of the press performs in a democratic society are, in general, the same as those served by the system of freedom of expression as a whole. Freedom of the press enhances the opportunity to achieve individual fulfillment, advances knowledge and the search for understanding, is vital to the process of self-government, and facilitates social change by the peaceful interchange of ideas. More particularly the press has been conceived as playing a special role in informing the public and in monitoring the performance of government. Often referred to as the "fourth estate," or the fourth branch of government, an independent press is one of the principal institutions in our society that possesses the resources and the capacity to confront the government and other centers of established authority. This concept of a free press was forcefully set forth by Justice HUGO L. BLACK in his opinion in NEW YORK TIMES CO. v. UNITED STATES (1971) (the Pentagon Papers case): "In the First Amendment the Founding Fathers gave the free press the protection it must have to fulfill its essential role in our democracy. The press was to serve the governed, not the governors. The Government's power to censor the press was abolished so that the press would remain forever free to censure the Government. The press was protected so that it could bare the secrets of government and inform the people. Only a free and unrestrained press can effectively expose deception in government."

A second preliminary issue is whether the fact that the First Amendment specifically refers to freedom "of the press," in addition to "freedom of speech," means that the press is entitled to a special status, or special protection, different from that accorded other speakers. It has been suggested that the First Amendment should be so construed. Thus Justice POTTER STEWART has argued that the Framers of the Constitution intended to recognize "the organized press," that is, "the daily newspapers and other established news media," as "a fourth institution outside the Government," serving as "an additional check on the three official branches." As such an institution, he suggested, the press was entitled to enjoy not only "freedom of speech," available to all, but an additional right to "freedom of the press." Some commentators have echoed Justice Stewart's argument.

There are obvious drawbacks to according a special status to the "organized press." It is difficult to draw a line between "the press" and others seeking to communicate through the written or spoken word, such as scholars, pamphleteers, or publishers of "underground" newspapers. Nor are there persuasive reasons for affording the one greater advantages than the other. Any attempt to differentiate would merely tend to reduce the protection given the "nonorganized" publisher. In any event the Supreme Court has never accepted the distinction.

However, there are some situations where the capacities and functions of the "organized press" are taken into account. Thus where there are physical limitations on access to the sources of information, as where a courtroom has only a limited number of seats, or only a limited number of reporters can ride on the President's airplane, representatives of the "organized press" may legitimately be chosen to convey the news to the general public. Beyond this point, however, the rights of the "organized press" to freedom of expression are the same as those of any writer or speaker.

The constitutional issues that have been of most concern to the press fall into two major categories. One involves the constraints that may be placed upon the publication of material by the press. The other relates to the rights of the press in gathering information.

On the whole the press has won its battle against the law of seditious libel. The Sedition Act of 1798 has never been revived. In NEW YORK TIMES CO. v. SULLIVAN (1964) the Supreme Court, declaring that the Sedition Act violated the central meaning of the First Amendment, said: "Although the Sedition Act was never tested in this Court, the attack upon its validity has carried the day in the court of history." Many states still retain criminal libel laws upon the books, but they have been so limited by the Supreme Court as to be largely inoperative. Even vigorous attacks upon the courts for their conduct in pending cases, traditionally a sensitive matter, are not punishable unless they present a CLEAR AND PRESENT DANGER to the administration of justice. (See CONTEMPT POWER.) Only the civil libel laws impose restrictions. The result is that the press is free to criticize the government, its policies, and its officials, no matter how harsh, vituperative, or unfair such criticism may be. Likewise it is free to publish information about governmental matters, even though incorrect, subject only to civil liability for false statements knowingly or recklessly made.

The extent to which the press can be prevented from publishing material claimed to be injurious to NATIONAL SECURITY has become a matter of controversy in recent years. The issues are crucial to the operation of a democratic system. Clearly there are some areas, particularly those relating to tactical military operations, where government secrecy is justified. On the other hand, the process of self-government cannot go on unless the public is fully informed about matters pending decision. Moreover, the very concept of "national security," or "national defense," is virtually open-ended, capable of covering a vast area of crucial information. Hence any constitutional doctrine allowing the government to restrict the flow of information alleged to harm national security would be virtually without limits. In addition, claims of danger to national security can be, and have been, employed to hide incompetence, mistaken judgments, and even corruption on the part of government officials in power.

For these reasons no general statutory ban on the publication of material deemed to have an adverse effect upon national security has ever been enacted by Congress. Laws directed at traditional espionage do, of course, exist. And Congress has passed legislation, thus far untested, instituting controls in certain very narrow areas. Thus the Intelligence Identities Protection Act (1982) forbids disclosure of any information that identifies an individual as the covert agent of an agency engaged in foreign intelligence. Beyond this, however, statutory controls on freedom of the press in the national security area have never been attempted. Even during wartime, censorship of press reporting on information pertaining to military operations has taken place only on a voluntary basis.

The constitutional authority of the government to restrict the publication of national security information was considered by the Supreme Court in the Pentagon Papers case. There the government sought an INJUNCTION against the *New York Times* and the *Washington Post* to prevent the publication of a government-prepared history of United States involvement in the Vietnam War. The documents had been classified as secret but were furnished to the newspapers by a former government employee who had copied them. The government contended that publication of the Pentagon Papers would result in "grave and irreparable injury" to the United States.

The Supreme Court ruled, 6–3, that the attempt at prior restraint could not stand, concluding that the government had not met "the heavy burden of showing justification for the imposition of such a restraint." Several theories of the right of the government to prohibit the publication of national security information emerged, none of which commanded a majority of the Court. At one end of the spectrum Justices Black and WILLIAM O. DOUGLAS thought that the government possessed no power to "make laws enjoining publication of current news and abridging freedom of the press in the name of 'national security.'" Justice WILLIAM J. BRENNAN held the same view, except that he would have allowed the government to stop publication of information that "must inevitably, directly and immediately cause the occurrence of an event kindred to imperiling the safety of a transport already at sea." Justices Stewart and BYRON WHITE believed that a prior restraint was permissible if the government could demonstrate "direct, immediate, and irreparable damage to our Nation or its people," a showing they concluded had not been made in the case before them. Justice THURGOOD MARSHALL, not passing on the First Amendment issues, took the position that, in the absence of express statutory authority, the government had no power to invoke the JURISDICTION OF THE FEDERAL COURTS to prevent the publication of national security information. At the other end of the spectrum Chief Justice WARREN E. BURGER and Justices JOHN M. HARLAN and HARRY L. BLACKMUN, the dissenters, urged that the function of the judiciary in reviewing the actions of the executive branch in the area of FOREIGN AFFAIRS should be narrowly restricted and that in such situations the Court should not attempt "to redetermine for itself the probable impact of disclosure on national security."

The result in the Pentagon Papers case was a significant victory for the press. Had the decision gone the other way the road would have been open for the government to prevent publication of any material when it could plausibly assert that national security was significantly injured. Yet the failure of the Court to agree upon a constitutional doctrine to govern in national security cases left the press vulnerable in future situations. Moreover, the issues were limited to an effort by the government to impose a prior restraint. The Justices did not address the question whether, if appropriate legislation were enacted, a criminal penalty or other subsequent punishment for publication of national security information would be valid.

In two subsequent cases the Supreme Court revealed some reluctance to restrict the executive branch in its efforts to control the publication of information relating to foreign intelligence. In SNEPP V. UNITED STATES (1980) the Court upheld an injunction to enforce an agreement, which the Central Intelligence Agency required each of its employees to sign, that the employee would not publish any information or material relating to the agency, either during or after employment, without the advance approval of the agency. The Court treated the issue primarily as one of private contract law; it dealt with First Amendment questions only in a footnote, saying that the government has "a compelling interest in protecting both the secrecy of information important to our national security and the appearance of confidentiality so essential to effective operation of our foreign intelligence service." Likewise in HAIG V. AGEE (1981) the Court upheld the action of the secretary of state in revoking the passport of a former CIA employee traveling abroad, on the grounds that he was causing "serious damage to the national security [and] foreign policy of the United States" by exposing the names of undercover CIA officers and agents. The constitutional RIGHT TO TRAVEL abroad, said the majority opinion, is "subordinate to national security and foreign policy considerations," adding that [m]atters intimately related to foreign policy and national security are rarely proper subjects for judicial intervention." Unless these later decisions are limited to their somewhat unusual facts, the right of the press to publish national security information that the government wishes to keep secret could be sharply curtailed.

Civil libel laws have also been a matter of paramount concern to the press. For many years it was assumed that the First Amendment was not intended to restrict the right of any person, under COMMON LAW or statute, to bring a suit for damages to reputation arising out of false and defamatory statements. In its well-known OBITER DICTUM in CHAPLINSKY V. NEW HAMPSHIRE (1942) the Supreme Court had declared that there were "certain well-defined and narrowly limited classes of speech," including the "libelous," which had never been thought to raise any constitutional problem.

In time it became clear, however, that libel laws could be used to impair freedom of the press and other First Amendment rights. In 1964 the issue came before the Supreme Court in *New York Times Co. v. Sullivan.* In that case the commissioner of public affairs in Montgomery, Alabama, sued the *New York Times* for publication of an advertisement, paid for by a New York group called the Committee to Defend Martin Luther King, which criticized certain actions of the police in dealing with CIVIL RIGHTS activity in Montgomery. Some of the statements in the advertisement were not factually correct. The Alabama state courts, after a jury trial, awarded the police commissioner $500,000 in damages. The majority opinion of the Court, stating that "libel can claim no talismanic immunity from constitutional limitations," went on to say: "Thus we consider this case against the background of a profound national commitment to the principle that debate on public issues should be uninhibited, robust, and wide-open, and that it may well include vehement, caustic, and sometimes unpleasantly sharp attacks on government and public officials." The Court ruled that public officials could recover damages in a libel action only if they could prove that a false and defamatory statement was made with "actual malice," that is, "with knowledge that it was false or with reckless disregard of whether it was false or not." Three Justices would have gone further and given the press full protection against libel suits regardless of proof of actual malice.

The "actual malice" rule for reconciling First Amendment rights with the libel laws was extended in 1967 to suits brought by "public figures," and in 1971 to all suits involving matters "of public or general interest." At this point it appeared that, although a majority of the Supreme Court had not gone the full distance, the press did have substantial protection against harassing libel suits. Weaknesses in the press position, however, soon developed. In 1974 the Court, changing directions, held that, apart from cases involving "public officials" and "public figures," libel laws would be deemed to conform to First Amendment standards so long as they did not impose liability in the absence of negligence. Moreover, the Court greatly narrowed the definition of "public figure," holding in one case that a person convicted of contempt of court for refusing to appear before a GRAND JURY investigating espionage was not a "public figure." In addition, juries in some cases began to award large sums in damages, legal expenses skyrocketed, and the costs in time and money of defending libel suits, even where the defense was successful, often became a heavy burden. By the same token, persons or organizations without substantial resources found it difficult to finance libel actions.

Efforts to dispose of unjustified libel suits at an early stage by motions to dismiss received a setback from the Supreme Court in HERBERT V. LANDO (1979). Lieutenant Colonel Anthony Herbert brought a libel suit against Columbia Broadcasting System because of a program on "60 Minutes" which suggested that Herbert had falsely accused his superior officers of covering up war crimes. Conceding he was a "public figure" and had to show "actual malice," Herbert sought in DISCOVERY proceedings to inquire into the mental states and editorial processes of the CBS officials who were responsible for the program. The Court held that, despite the CHILLING EFFECT of such probing and the resulting protraction of libel proceedings, the right to make such inquiries was inherent in the "actual malice" rule. The result of the *Herbert* case has been to diminish substantially the value to the press of the "actual malice" doctrine.

Because of these considerations, sections of the press as well as some commentators have urged that libel laws are incompatible with the First Amendment and should be abolished, at least where matters of public interest are under discussion. The courts, however, have shown no disposition to follow this course. The solution most in accord with First Amendment principles would be to provide for a right of reply by the person aggrieved. Yet this poses other difficulties. The press argues, with considerable justification, that it would be impossible for the government to supervise and enforce an effective right of reply system without sacrificing the independence of the media in the process. Federal Communication Commission regulations now grant a limited right of reply where "personal attacks" are made over radio or television and, because of the pervasive governmental controls already in place, such regulation probably does not appreciably reduce existing freedoms of the electronic media. But any broad extension to the printed press or to other forms of communication would almost certainly be seriously inhibiting. Indeed in MIAMI HERALD PUBLISHING CO. V. TORNILLO (1974) the Supreme Court unanimously invalidated a state statute requiring a newspaper to grant equal space for a political candidate attacked in its columns to reply. Moreover, practical difficulties, such as finding a suitable forum, would greatly limit the effectiveness of any attempt to substitute a right of reply for an action for damages. Thus the tension between the libel laws and freedom of the press is likely to continue.

A similar tension exists between freedom of the press and the RIGHT OF PRIVACY. Common law and statutory actions for invasion of privacy are permitted in most states. Moreover, the Supreme Court has recognized a constitutional right of privacy, running against the government, which would seem to impose restrictions upon disclosure to the press of certain information in the government's possession. The Supreme Court has held that the publication of material already in the public domain, such as the name of a rape victim which is available from public records, cannot be prohibited. However, it has never ruled upon the broad issue whether publication of information that is true but is alleged to invade the privacy of an individual can under some circumstances be restricted. The press has expressed concern over the possibility that the right of privacy might be used to curtail its freedom to publish. If the right of privacy is not narrowly limited—and there is presently no agreement upon the scope of the right—the chilling effect upon the press could be substantial. Nevertheless, in view of the current power of the press and the relative weakness of persons seeking to preserve privacy, any danger to the independence of the press from recognition of the right of privacy would seem to be remote.

Another conflict between freedom of the press and rights of the individual arises over the publication of news relating to criminal proceedings. The administration of justice is, of course, a matter of great public concern, and the role of the press in informing the public about such matters is crucial to the maintenance of a fair and effective system of justice. In most cases no conflict arises. On the other hand press reporting of occasional sensational crimes can be of such a nature as to prejudice the right of an accused to a FAIR TRIAL guaranteed by the DUE PROCESS clause and the Sixth Amendment. (See FREE PRESS/FAIR TRIAL.)

A number of remedies are available to the courts by which fairness in criminal proceedings can be assured without imposing restrictions upon the conduct of the press. These include change of VENUE, postponement of the trial, careful selection of jurors to weed out those likely to be prejudiced by the publicity, warning instructions to the jury, sequestration of witnesses and jurors, and, as a last resort, reversing a conviction and ordering a new trial. By and large the courts have found the use of these devices adequate. In some cases, however, trial courts have issued "gag" orders prohibiting the press from printing news about crimes or excluding the press from courtrooms.

In NEBRASKA PRESS ASSOCIATION V. STUART (1976) the Supreme Court dealt at some length with the "gag order" device. The majority opinion pointed out that the trial judge's order constituted a prior restraint, "the most serious and least tolerable infringement on First Amendment rights," but declined to hold that the press was entitled to absolute protection against all restrictive orders. The issue, the Court ruled, was whether in each case the newspaper publicity created a serious and likely danger to the fairness of the trial. And that issue in turn depended upon what was shown with respect to "(a) the nature and extent of pretrial news coverage; (b) whether other measures would be likely to mitigate the effects of unrestrained pretrial publicity; and (c) how effectively a restraining order would operate to prevent the threatened danger." The Court's ruling thus left the issue open to separate decision in each instance. The conditions laid down by the Court for issuance of a restrictive order, however, afford little room for use of that device except under rare circumstances. Three Justices urged that a prior restraint upon publication in this situation should never be allowed.

The exclusion of the press from courtrooms in criminal cases has also received the attention of the Supreme Court. Initially the Court rejected the contention that the Sixth Amendment's guarantee of a PUBLIC TRIAL entitled the press and the public to attend criminal trials, holding that the right involved was meant for the benefit of the defendant alone. Subsequently, however, in RICHMOND NEWSPAPERS, INC. V. VIRGINIA (1980) the Court recognized that the First Amendment extended some protection against exclusion from criminal trials. The Court again refused to hold that the First Amendment right was absolute, but it did not spell out the nature of any exceptions. Because it is always possible in a criminal trial for the judge to sequester the jury, few occasions for closing trials are likely to arise. On the other hand, the right of the press to attend pretrial hearings, where opportunity for sequestration does not exist, was left uncertain.

For many years the press has urged the courts to permit the use of radio, television, and photographic equipment in courtrooms. The courts have been reluctant to allow such forms of reporting. And in 1964 the Supreme Court overturned the conviction of Billie Sol Estes, accused of a notorious swindle, on the grounds that the broadcasting of parts of the trial by radio and television had been conducted in such a manner as to deprive him of a fair trial. Recently the courts have been more willing to open the courtroom to the electronic media and many of them have done so. The movement received the sanction of the Supreme Court in CHANDLER v. FLORIDA (1981) when an experimental program in Florida, which allowed broadcast and photographic coverage of trials subject to certain guidelines and under the control of the trial judge, was upheld by a unanimous vote.

The right of the press to gather news, as distinct from its right to publish the news, raises somewhat different issues. Freedom of the press implies in some degree a right to obtain information free of governmental interference. Indeed the Supreme Court in BRANZBURG v. HAYES (1972) expressly recognized that news-gathering did "qualify for First Amendment protection," saying that "without some protection for seeking out the news, freedom of the press could be eviscerated." But the limits of the constitutional right are difficult to define and remain undeveloped. The issue has arisen in three principal areas: REPORTER'S PRIVILEGE, the application of the FOURTH AMENDMENT to the press, and the right of the press to obtain information from the government.

The press has consistently asserted a right to refuse to disclose the sources of information obtained under a pledge of confidentiality—a claim known as "reporters' privilege." From the point of view of the press the right to honor a commitment to secrecy is essential to much reporting, particularly investigative reporting into organized crime, government corruption, and similar sensitive areas. On the other hand, under certain circumstances the need to obtain evidence in the possession of a reporter is also pressing, particularly where the information is necessary for defense in a criminal prosecution or to prove malice in a libel suit. Over the years the courts have generally refused to recognize the reporters' privilege, but they have attempted to avoid open conflict with the press. Reporters nevertheless continued to urge their claim, often to the point of going to jail for CONTEMPT OF COURT. A number of states have passed legislation recognizing the privilege in whole or in part, but the courts have tended to construe such statutes in a grudging manner, sometimes invoking constitutional objections.

The question whether reporters could invoke the privilege as a constitutional right under the First Amendment came before the Supreme Court in the *Branzburg* case. The reporters, who had refused to appear before grand juries, did not assert an absolute privilege but claimed they should not be compelled to give testimony unless the government demonstrated substantial grounds for believing they possessed essential information not available from other sources. The Court, in a 5–4 decision, rejected their claims. The majority opinion said that reporters had no greater claims to refuse testimony than other citizens. However, Justice LEWIS F. POWELL, whose vote was necessary to make the majority, expressed a more qualified position in a CONCURRING OPINION: "if the newsman . . . has reason to believe that his testimony implicates confidential source relationships without a legitimate need of law enforcement," the court should strike the "balance of these vital constitutional and societal interests on a case-by-case basis." In practice the courts appear to have accepted the Powell formula. Thus, although reporters cannot count on substantial constitutional protection the courts still prefer to avoid direct confrontation with the press tradition that reporters will not reveal confidential sources.

The First Amendment right to freedom of the press and the Fourth Amendment right to be secure from unreasonable SEARCHES AND SEIZURES have historically been closely linked. It was the GENERAL WARRANTS, used in America to obtain evidence of customs violations (and in England to find seditious publications), that in large part prompted the framing of the Fourth Amendment. At times the Supreme Court has recognized that Fourth Amendment protection extends with particular rigor to governmental intrusions affecting First Amendment rights. In the much discussed case of ZURCHER v. STANFORD DAILY (1978), however, the Court displayed less sympathy for the traditional position. The issue was whether the police could search the offices of a student newspaper for evidence of criminal offenses growing out of a student demonstration, or whether they should be confined to the issuance of a SUBPOENA requiring the newspaper to produce what evidence it had. Despite the vulnerability of the press to police searches tht could result in the ransacking of their news rooms, the Court by a 5–3 vote approved the warrant procedure. The press greeted the decision with strong criticism, mixed with alarm.

The third major issue with respect to operations of the press relates to the right of the press to obtain information from the government. The constitutional basis for such a claim grows out of the broader doctrine of the RIGHT TO KNOW. For many years the Supreme Court has recognized that the First Amendment embraces not only a right to communicate but also a right to receive communications. (See LISTENERS' RIGHTS.) The press has insisted that this feature of the First Amendment includes a right to have access to information in the possession of the government. Because a major purpose of the First Amendment is to facilitate the process of self-government, a strong constitutional argument can be advanced that, apart from a limited area of necessary secrecy, all material relating to operations of the government should be made available to the public. The press urged this position in a series of cases where it sought access to prisons in order to interview inmates and report on conditions inside. The Supreme Court, however, was not receptive. In rejecting the press proposals four of the Justices expressly declared in *Houchins v. KQED* (1978) that "the First and Fourteenth Amendments do not guarantee the public a right of access to information generated or controlled by government."

In 1980, in the Richmond Newspapers case, the Supreme Court shifted its position. In ruling that the press had a First Amendment right to attend criminal trials the majority relied heavily upon the right-to-know doctrine. Moreover, the concurring Justices were plainly willing to carry the right-to-know concept beyond the confines of the particular case before them. As Justice JOHN PAUL STEVENS correctly observed, the decision constituted "a watershed case": "never before has [the Court] squarely held that the acquisition of newsworthy material is entitled to any constitutional protection whatsoever." The full scope of the right to obtain information from the government remains to be seen. The development, however, is potentially one of great significance for the press.

Taken as a whole, freedom of the press in the United States rests upon a relatively firm constitutional footing. The press has not been granted any special status in the First Amendment's structure, but its general right to publish material, regardless of potential impacts on government operations or other features of the national life, has been accepted. There are some weaknesses in the position of the press. The law with respect to publication of national security information is obscure and, in its present form, poses some threat to press freedoms. The press is also vulnerable to libel suits, as the protections thought to have been afforded by the "actual malice" rule have not been altogether realized. Likewise the courts have been reluctant to assist the press in its news-gathering activities. From an overall view, however, constitutional developments have left the press in a position where it is largely free to carry out the functions and promote the values sought by the Framers of the First Amendment.

THOMAS I. EMERSON

Bibliography

ANDERSON, DAVID A. 1983 The Origins of the Press Clause. *University of California at Los Angeles Law Review* 30:455–537.

BARRON, JEROME A. 1973 *Freedom of the Press for Whom?* Bloomington: Indiana University Press.

LEVY, LEONARD W., ED. 1966 *Freedom of the Press from Zenger to Jefferson.* Indianapolis: Bobbs-Merrill.

LOFTON, JOHN 1980 *The Press as Guardian of the First Amendment.* Columbia: University of South Carolina Press.

NELSON, HAROLD L., ED. 1967 *Freedom of the Press from Hamilton to the Warren Court.* Indianapolis: Bobbs-Merrill.

SCHMIDT, BENNO C., JR. 1976 *Freedom of the Press vs. Public Access.* New York: Praeger.

SIEBERT, FREDRICK SEATON 1952 *Freedom of the Press in England 1476–1776.* Urbana: University of Illinois Press.

SYMPOSIUM 1975 First Amendment and the Media. *Hastings Law Journal* 26:631–821.

FREE EXERCISE OF RELIGION

See: Religious Liberty

FREEMAN v. HEWITT
329 U.S. 249 (1946)

Justice FELIX FRANKFURTER, for a 6–3 Supreme Court, here voided an Indiana tax levied on proceeds realized from the sale of securities in another state. Frankfurter struck down the tax as a greater burden than police regulations on INTERSTATE COMMERCE.

Justice WILLIAM O. DOUGLAS, dissenting, denied the existence of any interstate commerce.

DAVID GORDON

FREEPORT DOCTRINE

During the LINCOLN-DOUGLAS DEBATES of 1858, Senator STEPHEN A. DOUGLAS attacked ABRAHAM LINCOLN and the Republicans for their unwillingness to accept the Supreme Court's decision in DRED SCOTT V. SANDFORD (1857), which held that Congress could not proscribe SLAVERY in federal territories. But at the same time, Douglas and the Northern Democrats contended that the issue of slavery was to be decided by the people who lived in each territory, a position for which Douglas appropriated the name POPULAR SOVEREIGNTY. At Freeport, Lincoln asked Douglas: "Can the people of a United States territory, in any lawful way, . . . exclude slavery from its limits prior to the formation of a state constitution?"

Douglas's reply is known as the "Freeport Doctrine." It was that "slavery cannot exist a day or an hour anywhere, unless it is supported by local police regulation." In other words, a territorial legislature could exclude slavery by "unfriendly legislation" or simply by failing to pass the laws necessary to enforce slaveholding. The Freeport Doctrine appeared intended to neutralize the *Dred Scott* decision, and it effectively cut Douglas off from the slaveholding interests and divided the Democratic party.

DENNIS J. MAHONEY

Bibliography

JAFFA, HARRY V. 1959 *Crisis of the House Divided: An Interpretation of the Issues in the Lincoln–Douglas Debates.* Garden City, N.Y.: Doubleday.

FREE PRESS/FAIR TRIAL

Although press coverage has challenged the fairness and dignity of criminal proceedings throughout American history, intensive consideration of free press/fair trial issues by the Supreme Court has mainly been a product of recent decades. The first free press/fair trial issue to receive significant attention was the extent of press freedom from judges' attempts to hold editors and authors in contempt for criticizing or pressuring judicial conduct in criminal proceedings. The next category of decisions to receive attention, reversals of convictions to protect defendants from pretrial publicity, began rather gingerly in 1959, but in the years following the 1964 Warren Commission Report the Supreme Court reversed convictions more readily and dealt in considerable detail with the appropriate treatment of the interests of both the press and defendants when those interests were potentially in conflict. More recently, the Court has considered whether the press can be enjoined from publishing prejudicial material, and whether the press can be excluded from judicial proceedings.

In view of the large number of free press/fair trial decisions handed down over the years by the Supreme Court, this particular corner of the law of FREEDOM OF THE PRESS is probably the best developed of any, and offers a particularly instructive model of how the Supreme Court seeks to accommodate colliding interests of constitutional dimension. Overall, the Court has sought a balance that respects Justice HUGO L. BLACK's OBITER DICTUM in the seminal case of BRIDGES V. CALIFORNIA (1941) that "free speech and fair trial are two of the most cherished policies of our civilization, and it would be a trying task to choose between them."

In one of our history's pivotal FIRST AMENDMENT cases, the Supreme Court in 1941 sharply restricted the power of state judges to hold persons in contempt for publishing material that attacked or attempted to influence judicial decisions. By a 5–4 vote in *Bridges* the Supreme Court struck down two contempt citations, one against a newspaper based on an editorial that stated that a judge would "make a serious mistake" if he granted probation to two labor "goons," the second against a union leader who had sent a public telegram to the secretary of labor criticizing a judge's decision against his union and threatening to strike if the decision was enforced. Black's majority opinion held that the First Amendment protected these expressions unless they created a CLEAR AND PRESENT DANGER of interfering with judicial impartiality. From the start, this test as applied to contempt by publication has been virtually impossible to satisfy. Black insisted that "the substantive evil must be extremely serious and the degree of imminence extremely high before utterances can be punished," and, in order to remove predictions about the likelihood of interference from the ken of lower courts, the Court reinforced the strictness of this standard by using an apparently IRREBUTTABLE PRESUMPTION that judges would not be swayed by adverse commentary. "[T]he law of contempt," wrote Justice WILLIAM O. DOUGLAS in *Craig v. Harney* (1947), echoing a position taken in *Bridges,* "is not made for the protection of judges who may be sensitive to the winds of public opinion. Judges are supposed to be men of fortitude, able to thrive in a hardy climate." Under these decisions, it seems doubtful that anything short of a direct and credible physical threat against a judge would justify punishment for contempt.

For general First Amendment theory and more specifically for the rights of the press in free press/fair trial contexts, the chief significance of the contempt cases is the emergence of a positive conception of protected expression under the First Amendment. As Black put it in *Bridges*, "it is a prized American privilege to speak one's mind, although not always with perfect good taste, on all public questions." Drawing upon the decisions in NEAR V. MINNESOTA (1931) and DE JONGE V. OREGON (1937), which stressed the Madisonian conception of free expression as essential to political democracy, opinions in the contempt cases shifted the clear and present danger rule toward a promise of constitutional immunity for criticism of government. The contempt cases are thus the primary doctrinal bridge between the Court's unsympathetic approach to political dissent during and after World War I and the grand conception of NEW YORK TIMES CO. V. SULLIVAN (1964) that the central meaning of the First Amendment is "the right of free discussion of the stewardship of public officials." Beyond this, the contempt cases make it clear that protecting expressions about judges and courts is itself a core function of the First Amendment. Douglas put it this way in *Craig*, in words that have echoed in later free press/fair trial cases: "A trial is a public event. What transpires in the court room is public property. . . . There is no special perquisite of the judiciary which enables it, as distinguished from other institutions of democratic government, to suppress, edit, or censor events which transpire in proceedings before it."

Although the contempt cases focused on the rights of the press and others who sought to publicize information about trials, the next set of free press/fair trial cases, without dealing with the right to publish, looked with a sympathetic eye toward defendants who might have been convicted because of prejudice caused by such publications. Although individual Justices had objected bitterly to the prejudicial effects of media coverage on jurors, not until 1959 did the Supreme Court reverse a federal conviction because of prejudicial publicity. The first reversal of a state court conviction followed two years later in IRVIN V. DOWD (1961), where 268 of 430 prospective jurors said during their VOIR DIRE examination that they had a fixed belief in the defendant's guilt, and 370 entertained some opinion of guilt. News media had made the trial a "cause célèbre of this small community," the Court noted, as the press had reported the defendant's prior criminal record, offers to plead guilty, confessions, and a flood of other prejudicial items.

In 1963, the special problems of television were introduced into the pretrial publicity fray by *Rideau v. Louisiana*, producing another reversal by the Supreme Court of a state conviction. A jailed murder suspect was filmed in the act of answering various questions and of confessing to the local sheriff, and the film was televised repeatedly in the community that tried and convicted him. The Supreme Court held that "[a]ny subsequent court proceedings in a community so pervasively exposed to such a spectacle could be but a hollow formality." Two years later, in ESTES V. TEXAS (1965), a narrowly divided Court held that, at least in a notorious case, the presence of television in the courtroom could generate pressures that added up to a denial of due process.

In the mid-1960s the Court took a more categorical and more aggressive stance against prejudicial publicity. The shift was consistent with the WARREN COURT's growing impatience toward ad hoc evaluations of fairness in its review of state criminal cases. This period of heightened concern for the defendant was triggered by the disgraceful media circus that surrounded the murder trial of Dr. Sam Sheppard. Before Sheppard's trial, most of the print and broadcast media in the Cleveland area joined in an intense publicity barrage proclaiming Sheppard's guilt. During the trial, journalists swarmed over the courtroom in a manner that impressed upon everyone the spectacular notoriety of the case. "The fact is," wrote Justice TOM C. CLARK in his most memorable opinion for the Court, "that bedlam reigned at the courthouse during the trial and newsmen took over practically the entire courtroom, hounding most of the participants in the trial, especially Sheppard." The deluge of publicity outside the courtroom, and the disruptive behavior of journalists inside, combined to make the trial a " 'Roman holiday' for the news media" that "inflamed and prejudiced the public."

In *Sheppard v. Maxwell* (1966) Clark adumbrated the techniques by which trial judges may control prejudicial publicity and disruptions of the judicial process by the press. The opinion is a virtual manual for trial judges, suggesting proper procedures initially by listing the particular errors in the case: that Sheppard was not granted a continuance or a change of VENUE, that the jury was not sequestered, that the judge merely requested jurors not to follow media commentary on the case rather than directing them not to, that the judge failed "to insulate" the jurors from reporters and photographers, and that reporters invaded the space within the bar of the courtroom reserved for counsel, created distractions and commotion, and hounded people throughout the courthouse.

But the *Sheppard* opinion went beyond these essentially traditional judicial methods for coping with publicity and the press. The Court identified the trial judge's "fundamental error" as his view that he "lacked power to control the publicity about the trial" and insisted that "the cure lies in those remedial measures that will prevent the prejudice at its inception." Specifically, Clark admonished trial judges to insulate witnesses from press interviews, to "impos[e] control over the statements made to the news media by counsel, witnesses, and especially the Coroner and police officers," and to "proscrib[e] extrajudicial statements by any lawyer, party, witness, or court official which divulged prejudicial matters. . . ."

Sheppard left open the central question whether the courts could impose direct restrictions on the press by INJUNCTIONS that would bar publications that might prejudice an accused. In NEBRASKA PRESS ASSOCIATION V. STUART (1976) the Supreme Court, unanimous as to result though divided in rationale, answered this question with a seemingly definitive No. The Nebraska state courts had ordered the press and broadcasters not to publish confessions or other information prejudicial to an accused in a pending murder prosecution. Some of the information covered by the injunction had been revealed in an open, public preliminary hearing, and the Supreme Court made clear that a state could in no event bar the publication of matters disclosed in open judicial proceedings. As to other information barred from publication by the state courts, Chief Justice WARREN E. BURGER's majority opinion went by a curious and circuitous route to the conclusion that the impact of prejudicial publicity on prospective jurors was "of necessity speculative, dealing . . . with factors unknown and unknowable." Thus, the adverse effect on the fairness of the subsequent criminal proceeding "was not demonstrated with the degree of certainty our cases on PRIOR RESTRAINT require." Burger's opinion made much of the fact that the state court had not determined explicitly that the protections against prejudicial publicity set out in *Sheppard* would not suffice to guarantee fairness, as if trial court findings to this effect might make a difference in judging the validity of a prior restraint against publication. And Burger said again and again that he was dealing with a particular case and not laying down a general rule. But because Burger termed the evils of prejudicial publicity "of necessity speculative," and viewed the prior restraint precedents as requiring a degree of certainty about the evils of expression before a prior restraint should be tolerated, his opinion for the Court seems to be, in the guise of a narrow and particularistic holding, a categorical rejection of prior restraints on pretrial publicity. Lower courts have read the decision as an absolute bar to judicial injunctions against the press forbidding the publication of possibly prejudicial matters about pending criminal proceedings.

Beyond its rejection of prior restraints against the press to control pretrial publicity, the *Nebraska Press Association* decision emphatically affirmed all the methods of control set out in *Sheppard,* including the validity of judicial orders of silence directed to parties, lawyers, witnesses, court officers, and the like not to reveal information about pending cases to the press. Such orders, indeed, have flourished in the lower courts since the *Nebraska Press Association* decision.

The free press/fair trial conundrum has also presented the Supreme Court with the only occasion it has accepted to shed light on the very murky question whether the First Amendment protects the right to gather information, as against the right to publish or refuse to publish. No doubt in response to the Supreme Court's rejection of direct controls on press publication, either by injunctions or by the CONTEMPT POWER, several lower courts excluded news reporters and the public from preliminary hearings and even from trials themselves to prevent the press from gathering information whose publication might be prejudicial to current or later judicial proceedings. Initially, in GANNETT CO. V. DE PASQUALE (1979), reviewing a closing of a preliminary hearing dealing with the suppression of EVIDENCE, the Supreme Court found no guarantee in the Sixth Amendment of public and press presence. The decision produced an outcry against secret judicial proceedings, and only a year later, in one of the most precipitous and awkward reversals in its history, the Court held in RICHMOND NEWSPAPERS V. VIRGINIA (1980) that the First Amendment barred excluding the public and the press from criminal trials except where special considerations calling for secrecy, such as privacy or national security, obtained. The decision marks the first and only occasion to date in which the Court has recognized a First Amendment right of access for purposes of news gathering, and the Court was careful to limit its holding by resting on the long tradition of open judicial proceedings in English and American law. One year later, in *Chandler v. Florida* (1981), the

Court held that televising a criminal trial was not invariably a denial of due process, thus removing *Estes* as an absolute bar to television in the courtroom.

The pattern of constitutional law formed by the free press/fair trial decisions has several striking aspects. While direct judicial controls on the right of publication have been firmly rejected, the courts have proclaimed extensive power to gag sources of information. (See GAG ORDERS.) Participants in the process can be restrained from talking, but the press cannot be restrained from publishing. However, the broad power to impose secrecy on sources does not go so far as to justify closing judicial proceedings, absent unusual circumstances. The interests of freedom of expression and control over information to enhance the fairness of criminal trials are accommodated not by creating balanced principles of general application but rather by letting each interest reign supreme in competing aspects of the problem. Moreover, the principles fashioned in the cases tend to be sweeping, as if the Supreme Court were acting with special confidence in fashioning First Amendment standards to govern the familiar ground of the judicial process. And in dealing with its own bailiwick, the judicial process, the Supreme Court has acted not defensively but with a powerful commitment to freedom of expression.

BENNO C. SCHMIDT, JR.

Bibliography

FRIENDLY, ALFRED and GOLDFARB, RONALD 1967 *Crime and Publicity.* New York: Twentieth Century Fund.

JAFFE, LOUIS 1965 Trial by Newspaper. *New York University Law Review* 40:504–524.

LEWIS, ANTHONY 1980 A Public Right to Know about Public Institutions: The First Amendment as Sword. *Supreme Court Law Review* 1980:1–25.

SCHMIDT, BENNO C., JR. 1977 Nebraska Press Association: An Expansion of Freedom and Contraction of Theory. *Stanford Law Review* 29:431–476.

TAYLOR, TELFORD 1969 *Two Studies in Constitutional Interpretation.* Evanston, Ill.: Northwestern University Press.

FREUND, ERNST
(1864–1932)

Ernst Freund, professor of law at the University of Chicago, is best remembered today for his huge and immensely influential *Police Power: Public Policy and Constitutional Rights* (1904), the first systematic exposition of its subject. POLICE POWER, said Freund, was the "power of promoting the public welfare by restraining and regulating the use of liberty and property." Because Freund saw the power "not as a fixed quantity, but as the expression of social, economic, and political conditions," he praised that elasticity which helped adapt the law to changing circumstances. This endorsement, along with only minimal approval of laissez-faire doctrines such as FREEDOM OF CONTRACT, helped provide support for the Progressive movement. His views strongly contrasted with those of CHRISTOPHER TIEDEMAN, a vigorous and authoritative exponent of laissez-faire who decried the use of the police power. In *Standards of American Legislation* (1917), Freund attempted to formulate positive principles to guide legislators and to give DUE PROCESS OF LAW a more definite meaning.

DAVID GORDON

FRIES' REBELLION

In 1798 Congress levied a tax on houses, land, and slaves, to finance a possible war with France. There was considerable resistance to the tax and, in February 1799, an armed band led by John Fries rescued tax resisters from the United States marshal at Bethlehem, Pennsylvania. President JOHN ADAMS ordered the army and militia to suppress the uprising.

Fries and his followers were arrested and some seventy-two insurrectionists were tried for various offenses relating to the incident. Fries and two companions were tried before Justice SAMUEL CHASE and Judge RICHARD PETERS and were convicted of TREASON, the prosecution arguing that armed resistance to the enforcement of federal law amounted to levying war against the United States. President Adams, against the advice of his cabinet, subsequently granted a general pardon to all participants in the "rebellion."

DENNIS J. MAHONEY

FROHWERK v. UNITED STATES
249 U.S. 204 (1919)

In the second major test of the wartime ESPIONAGE ACT to reach the Supreme Court, the Justices unanimously affirmed the conviction of the publisher of a pro-German publication for conspiring to obstruct military recruitment through publication of antidraft articles. Justice OLIVER WENDELL HOLMES invoked the CLEAR AND PRESENT DANGER test. "We do not lose our right to condemn either measures or men because the Country is at war," he wrote, "But . . . it is impossible to say that it might not have been found that the circulation of the paper was in quarters where a little breath would be enough to kindle a flame. . . ." Holmes and his brethren declined to inquire themselves into the degree or probability of the danger represented by the publication.

MICHAEL E. PARRISH

FRONTIERO v. RICHARDSON
411 U.S. 677 (1973)

In *Reed v. Reed* (1971) a unanimous Supreme Court had invalidated a state law preferring the appointment of men, rather than women, as administrators of decedents' estates. The Court had used the rhetoric of the RATIONAL BASIS standard of review but had in fact employed a more rigorous standard of JUDICIAL REVIEW. Conceding the rationality of eliminating one type of contest between would-be administrators, the Court had concluded that the preference for men was an "arbitrary legislative choice" that denied women the EQUAL PROTECTION OF THE LAW.

In *Frontiero,* two years later, the Court came within one vote of radically restructuring the constitutional doctrine governing SEX DISCRIMINATION. Under federal law, a woman member of the armed forces could claim her husband as a "dependent" entitled to certain benefits only if he was, in fact, dependent on her for more than half his support; a serviceman could claim "dependent" status for his wife irrespective of actual dependency. Eight Justices agreed that this discrimination violated the Fifth Amendment's equal protection guarantee, but they divided 4–4 as to their reasoning.

Justice WILLIAM J. BRENNAN, for four Justices, concluded that sex, like race, was a SUSPECT CLASSIFICATION demanding STRICT SCRUTINY of its justifications. Four other Justices merely rested on the precedent of *Reed.* Justice LEWIS F. POWELL, writing for three of them, added that it would be inappropriate for the Court to hold that gender was a suspect classification while debate over ratification of the EQUAL RIGHTS AMENDMENT was still pending. Justice WILLIAM H. REHNQUIST dissented.

The confusion in the wake of *Frontiero* ended three years later, in CRAIG V. BOREN (1976), when the Justices compromised on an intermediate STANDARD OF REVIEW.

KENNETH L. KARST

FROTHINGHAM v. MELLON MASSACHUSETTS v. MELLON
262 U.S. 447 (1923)

In the SHEPPARD-TOWNER MATERNITY ACT of 1921, a predecessor of modern FEDERAL GRANTS-IN-AID, Congress authorized federal funding of state programs "to reduce maternal and infant mortality." These companion cases involved suits to halt federal expenditures under the act, challenging it as a deprivation of property without DUE PROCESS OF LAW and a violation of the TENTH AMENDMENT. Justice GEORGE SUTHERLAND, for a unanimous Supreme Court, dismissed the *Massachusetts* case for failing to present a justiciable controversy. The state's suit in its own behalf presented a POLITICAL QUESTION calling on the Court to adjudicate "abstract questions of political power," not rights of property or even "quasi-sovereign rights actually invaded or threatened." The state was under no obligation to accept federal monies. The state also lacked STANDING to represent its citizens, who were also citizens of the United States.

Frothingham's due process argument relied on the premise that spending under the act would increase her tax liability. Sutherland concluded that she, too, lacked standing to sue. Any personal interest in federal tax monies "is comparatively minute and indeterminable; and the effect upon future taxation, of any payment out of the funds, so remote, fluctuating and uncertain, that no basis is afforded for an appeal." Because Frothingham could not demonstrate direct injury, her suit must fail. An OBITER DICTUM implying the constitutionality of grants-in-aid was the Court's only pronouncement on such programs until approved in STEWARD MACHINE COMPANY V. DAVIS (1937).

DAVID GORDON

FRUIT OF THE POISONOUS TREE

No doctrine in constitutional CRIMINAL PROCEDURE has created more confusion than the disarmingly simple proposition that when the state has violated FUNDAMENTAL RIGHTS, it may receive no benefit from the violation. The "poisonous tree" is the violation, an illegal search for instance, in which the key to a safe deposit is found. Clearly under the EXCLUSIONARY RULE the government may not use as EVIDENCE the discovery of the key; but neither may it use whatever incriminating items are in the safe deposit box. These are the "fruits."

The existence of a "poisonous tree," however, does not mean that all that is discovered after the tree sprouts is automatically a "fruit." The issue in its classic though grammatically inelegant formulation is: "whether, granting establishment of the primary illegality, [the evidence] has been come at by exploitation of that illegality or instead by means sufficiently distinguishable to be purged of the primary taint" (WONG SUN V. UNITED STATES, 1963). Many exceptions to the fruits doctrine have evolved from these words and have been variously named by courts and commentators, although the basic question is always how far from the tree the fruit has fallen.

The exception used most often is "attenuation": too much has intervened between the primary illegality and the gathering of the fruit. In *Wong Sun* itself, a confession made after an illegal ARREST was found not to be a fruit because of the passage of time between the arrest and confession, during which the accused was free on BAIL. Another exception is labeled "independent source"; the idea is that although the evidence could have been a fruit, it was actually uncovered by means distinguishable from the primary illegality. Closely allied to the independent source exception is that of "inevitable discovery," which the Supreme Court endorsed in NIX V. WILLIAMS (1984). Although the body of the deceased was discovered through a blatant violation of the defendant's Sixth Amendment RIGHT TO COUNSEL, the Court held that it would have been found through other proper investigative techniques that the police were employing at the time that the primary illegality was committed. The burden is on the government to show that the discovery would have been "inevitable." Finally, while refusing to establish an across-the-board rule that eyewitness testimony could never be a fruit, the Supreme Court has indicated that the free will of a witness expressed in the desire to testify would, in virtually every case, attenuate the taint, even when the witness would never have been found without the primary illegality.

As can be seen from the number and nature of the exceptions, the fruit of the poisonous tree doctrine is subject to much interpretation. For instance, in *Harrison v. United States* (1968) the Court held that the defendant's testimony at trial was a fruit of illegally obtained confessions introduced into evidence. Two years later, in *McMann v. Richardson* (1970), the Court found that a guilty plea entered after an arguably illegal confession was not induced by the prospect of the admission of the confessions. These cases can be reconciled by applying the attenuation exception—the defendant's decision to plead guilty was an intervening event that dissipated the poison. But this is hardly a satisfying distinction.

The case that most strikingly reveals the difficulties with the fruits doctrine and is also the key to future interpretation is *United States v. Crews* (1980). In connection with his illegal arrest, the police obtained Crews's photograph which would not otherwise have been available. They showed it in an array of pictures to the victims who made an immediate identification. Next, Crews was placed in a fair LINEUP where the victims also identified him. The first question was whether testimony about the pretrial identifications was fruit; this was easily resolved because the prosecution conceded that it was. The harder issue was whether the victim's identification at trial of Crews must be suppressed. In the metaphoric language that seizes courts when dealing with this doctrine, the Court concluded that: "At trial, [the victim] retrieved the [mental image of her assailant], compared it to the figure of the defendant, and positively identified him as the robber. No part of this process was affected by respondent's illegal arrest. . . . [T]he toxin in this case was injected only after the evidentiary bud had blossomed; the fruit served at trial was not poisoned."

The Court in *Crews* went on to say that there could be cases where the victim's in-court identification was a result of the primary illegality—in other words, that the photograph and lineup identifications had led to the ability to point to the defendant at trial. In finding that this was not such a case the Court implicitly emphasized that the analysis of whether evidence is the fruit of the poisonous tree will continue in a case-by-case, highly pragmatic, and utterly unpredictable vein.

BARBARA ALLEN BABCOCK

Bibliography

LAFAVE, WAYNE R. 1978 *Search and Seizure: A Treatise on the Fourth Amendment.* Vol. 3:621–681. St. Paul, Minn.: West Publishing Co.

FUGITIVE FROM JUSTICE

The second clause of Article IV, section 2, of the Constitution provides that a person charged with a crime in one state, who has fled to another to escape justice, "shall, on demand of the executive authority of the state from which he fled, be delivered up. . . ." The clause makes rendition (or extradition) of fugitives from justice a duty of state officials.

Although extradition of escaped felons from one political JURISDICTION to another was long recognized as an obligation of comity in international law, the process is not automatic. Between sovereign nations, extradition normally occurs only when there is a treaty providing for it. Permanent extradition arrangements were not common before the nineteenth century.

Among the earliest standing arrangements for extradition of accused criminals was the one embodied in the articles of the New England Confederation (1643), which provided for the surrender of a fugitive to the colony from which he had fled when demand was made by two magistrates of that colony. Interstate extradition has been from the first, therefore, a feature of American FEDERALISM. The ARTICLES OF CONFEDERATION contained a provision identical to that in the Constitution. The Constitution's fugitive from justice clause was proposed in the CONSTITUTIONAL CONVENTION as part of the New Jersey Plan and was given its present form by the committee of detail.

EDMUND RANDOLPH, the first attorney general, issued an opinion that the fugitive from justice clause was not self-executing, that is, the Constitution did not specify what official was to render fugitives or establish enforcible procedures. Congress therefore, in 1793, passed a law imposing the duty of rendition on state governors.

The first test of the clause in the Supreme Court was in *Kentucky v. Dennison* (1861). The governor of Ohio had refused to honor Kentucky's demand that he render a fugitive wanted in Kentucky for aiding the escape of a slave. Chief Justice ROGER B. TANEY, for the Court, rejected Ohio's contention that the crime in question was not one contemplated by the Framers of the Constitution as within the scope of the clause; the clause extends to any act defined as a crime in the place where it was committed. The Court held that rendition of a fugitive was a MINISTERIAL ACT, one which a state governor has a duty to perform and not one over which he has any discretion. However, the Court also held that there was no power in the federal courts to compel compliance with the duty. Subsequently, governors have occasionally refused, for various reasons, to deliver fugitives to the states in which they were wanted.

Fugitives' careers are complicated by other factors. In 1934, Congress made it a federal crime to travel in INTERSTATE COMMERCE with the intent to avoid prosecution or confinement. The federal crime must be tried in the state from which the fugitive fled, and one practical effect of the statute is to return fugitives to the states in which they are wanted, facilitating arrest on state charges. Interstate rendition has also been facilitated by INTERSTATE COMPACTS and by adoption in most states of the Uniform Criminal Extradition Act.

DENNIS J. MAHONEY

FUGITIVE SLAVERY

The problem of runaways plagued American slave societies since the seventeenth century and was not solved until the abolition of slavery itself during the Civil War. Statutes of the colonial period dealing with indentured servants and slaves contained extensive provisions providing for punishment of runaways. Those relating to black slaves became increasingly severe over time, culminating in various eighteenth-century provisions permitting death, whipping, branding, outlawry, castration, dismemberment, and ear-slitting for runaways and compensation by the colony to masters of "outlying" slaves who were killed.

Provisions for interjurisdictional rendition of fugitives began with the fugitive-servant provisions of the New England Confederation (1643), but until 1787 rendition was a matter of comity between the colonies/states. The NORTHWEST ORDINANCE (1787) contained a fugitive slave/servant clause. The Constitution contained a clause providing that a "Person held to Service or Labour" shall not be freed when he absconds into another state, "but shall be delivered up." The use of the passive voice and the location of the clause in Article IV blurred responsibility for its enforcement, which caused protracted constitutional controversies in the 1840s and 1850s.

In 1793, Congress enacted the first Fugitive Slave Act, which provided that any slave holder or his "agent or attorney" could seize an alleged runaway, take him before a federal judge or local magistrate, prove title to the slave by affidavit or oral testimony, and get a certificate of rendition entitling him to take the slave back to the master's domicile. The constitutionality of the statute was repeatedly upheld by eminent authority: implicitly in JOSEPH STORY's *Commentaries on the Constitution of the United States* (1833); explicitly by Chief Justice William Tilghman of the Pennsylvania Supreme Court in *Wright v. Deacon* (1819) and Chief Justice Isaac Parker of the Massachusetts Supreme Judicial Court in *Commonwealth v. Griffin* (1823). Early abolitionist societies worked to prevent free blacks from being kidnapped through the instrumentality of the 1793 act and provided counsel to alleged fugitives. Abolitionists challenged the statute on the grounds that Congress exceeded its powers in forcing state officials to participate in federal rendition proceedings, in permitting rendition from TERRITORIES as well as states, and in interfering with the rights of the states to protect their free citizens.

Before 1843, a few states enacted PERSONAL LIBERTY LAWS that provided various procedural safeguards, such as HABEAS CORPUS or TRIAL BY JURY, to alleged fugitives. The slave states resented these and challenged their constitutionality in PRIGG v. PENNSYLVANIA (1842). Speaking for a majority of the Court, Justice Joseph Story held that: the fugitive slave clause of the Constitution was an essential compromise necessary to ratification of the Constitution by the southern states; the 1793 act was constitutional; the master had a right of recapture of a runaway slave, derived either from the COMMON LAW or from the fugitive slave clause; and the Pennsylvania personal liberty law was unconstitutional because it infringed on masters' rights protected by the federal statute. In an OBITER DICTUM, Story stated that the federal government could not constitutionally oblige state officials to participate in enforcement of the act.

Insubstantial as this suggestion was, northern states after 1842 enacted new personal liberty laws prohibiting state officials from participating in enforcement of the federal statute and prohibiting the use of state facilities such as jails for detaining runaways. Abolitionists then mounted a more sophisticated, wide-ranging attack on the constitutionality of the 1793 statute, alleging that it violated the Fifth Amendment's DUE PROCESS clause and the FOURTH AMENDMENT'S SEARCHES AND SEIZURES clause.

Congress, as part of the COMPROMISE OF 1850, enacted a new Fugitive Slave Act, which was an extension of the 1793 Act, not a replacement for it. It contained these novel features: owners and agents were authorized to seize alleged fugitives with or without legal process; certificates of rendition could be granted by federal commissioners as well as federal judges; any adult male could be drafted into a posse to assist in capture and rendition; obstruction of the act was punishable by a fine of $1,000; the commissioner's fee was $5 if he determined that the black was not a runaway, but $10 if he awarded the certificate of rendition, prompting an abolitionist's remark that the statute set the price of a Carolina Negro at $1,000 and a Yankee soul at $5.

Residents of the free states objected vehemently to the new statute. Throughout the 1850s, dramatic rescues and recaptures of runaways provided real-life drama to accompany the sensational success of the serialized, book, and stage versions of *Uncle Tom's Cabin,* with its melodramatic runaway scene. Federal authorities and northern conservatives responded to abolitionist challenges and to rescues of fugitives by affirming the constitutionality of the 1850 Act (Chief Justice LEMUEL SHAW of the Massachusetts Supreme Judicial Court in IN RE SIMS, 1851) and by demanding that resistance to enforcement of the measure be prosecuted as treason. Two efforts at doing so, however (resulting from the Jerry rescue, Syracuse, New York, 1851, and the Oberlin-Wellington rescue, northern Ohio, 1858), ended in inglorious failure for the prosecution. In general, however, the northern states attempted to comply with the statute, and most blacks seized as fugitives under the act were sent into slavery.

In a dictum in ABLEMAN v. BOOTH (1859) Chief Justice ROGER B. TANEY declared the 1850 statute constitutional, but the question was soon to be mooted. After the outbreak of the Civil War, the policies of some Union commanders discouraged the return of runaways who fled behind Union lines. Congress partially repealed the Fugitive Slave Acts in 1862 and then fully in 1864. The whole issue, and the fugitive slave clause of the Constitution, became dead letters with the abolition of slavery in 1864–1865.

WILLIAM M. WIECEK

Bibliography

CAMPBELL, STANLEY W. 1968 *The Slave Catchers: Enforcement of the Fugitive Slave Law, 1850–1860.* Chapel Hill: University of North Carolina Press.

DUMOND, DWIGHT L. 1961 *Antislavery: The Crusade for Freedom in America.* Ann Arbor: University of Michigan Press.

HYMAN, HAROLD M. and WIECEK, WILLIAM M. 1982 *Equal Justice under Law: Constitutional Development, 1835–1875.* New York: Harper & Row.

FULL EMPLOYMENT ACT
60 Stat. 23 (1946)

Despite the post-World War II desire to shake off wartime economic controls, Congress passed a Full Employment Act in February 1946, establishing a new concept of the relation of the government to the national economy. The measure declared officially that it was the responsibility of the national government to insure effective operation of the country's economic system and maintain maximum employment, production, and purchasing power. Through a newly created three-person Presidential Council of Economic Advisors, the nation's economic patterns were studied and analyzed with the government responsible for evolving new controls essential to the nation's economic security. These included: tax rates designed to produce a predetermined deficit or surplus based on whether the administration sought to stimulate or cool off the economy; controlling the ease or tightness of credit; raising or lowering public spending levels; and maintaining wage and price guidelines. Such use of deficit financing, public works, and economic controls might alleviate the negative effects of the business cycle and avoid another major economic depression.

The measure was a constitutional landmark. It formally rejected the concept that the government's main role in the economic sphere was negative: to maintain a free enterprise system by preserving, through laws and court decisions, a hands-off policy toward American economic activities.

PAUL L. MURPHY

Bibliography

BAILEY, STEPHEN K. 1950 *Congress Makes a Law: The Story Behind the Employment Act of 1946.* New York: Columbia University Press.

FULLER, MELVILLE W. (1833–1910)

Melville Weston Fuller, eighth Chief Justice of the United States, was appointed by GROVER CLEVELAND in 1888 and presided over the Court until his death on July 4, 1910. Fuller's twenty-two-year tenure as Chief Justice, the longest during the Court's second century, spanned one of the most significant periods of constitutional development in American history. Fuller and his associates circumscribed the rights of state criminal defendants under the FOURTEENTH AMENDMENT, established an inferior legal status for residents of the new overseas colonies, articulated the infamous SEPARATE BUT EQUAL DOCTRINE, and devised a spate of other juristic strategies for avoiding interventions on behalf of black petitioners in the fields of education and VOTING RIGHTS. At the same time the FULLER COURT made so many new departures in decisions affecting the economic order that one scholar has described its work as "the new judicialism." Fuller and his colleagues invalidated the federal income tax, emasculated the Interstate Commerce Commission, put the Court's imprimatur on the labor INJUNCTION, construed the commerce clause so that the SHERMAN ANTITRUST ACT frustrated the activities of labor unions yet failed to impede the fusion of manufacturing corporations, and elaborated the concept of SUBSTANTIVE DUE PROCESS as a guarantor of VESTED RIGHTS and LIBERTY OF CONTRACT.

The vast bulk of the Fuller Court's work in constitutional law reflected the Chief Justice's constitutional understanding, the contours of which had been firmly fixed before Fuller came to the bench. Beginning in 1856, when he left his native Maine and settled in Chicago, Fuller was an active stump speaker and essayist for the Illinois Democratic party; he styled himself a disciple of Thomas Hart Benton and STEPHEN A. DOUGLAS long after both were dead. Fuller spoke often in favor of free trade, hard money, and equal opportunity in the market. "Paternalism, with its constant intermeddling with individual freedom," he wrote in 1880, "has no place in a system which rests for its strength upon the self-reliant energies of the people." But Fuller's version of the equal rights creed had no place for blacks. An exponent of a conservative naturalism that stressed the importance of homogeneous communities and local autonomy in American public life, Fuller believed that union and republican liberty were possible only if the federal government acquiesced in local racial arrangements on the same ground that it acquiesced in state laws regulating the status of women. He objected to the EMANCIPATION PROCLAMATION on the ground that it was "predicated upon the idea that the President may annul the constitutions and laws of sovereign states." He claimed that the THIRTEENTH AMENDMENT and Fourteenth Amendment protected only the "common rights" of individuals against discriminatory classification. And he never ceased to insist that Congress's powers to regulate persons or property were limited, derivable only from specific grants and not from any assumption of an underlying national SOVEREIGNTY. Fuller's longest, most plaintive dissents came in the INSULAR CASES (1901), where he denied Congress's power to levy tariffs on the products of colonial possessions, and in CHAMPION V. AMES (1903), where he contended that Congress could not exercise police powers on the pretense of regulating commerce.

Fuller did not grapple with the Court's role in the American system of government following his appointment as Chief Justice. For Fuller, as for Benton, Douglas, and Cleveland, the Constitution was more than a text that allocated specific powers and secured particular rights against government. The Constitution was significant above all as the repository of values so integral to the existence of republicanism that any public official who failed to protect and defend them was guilty of a breach of trust. Consequently, Fuller conceptualized the judicial function in terms of duty rather than in terms of role; his approach to judging was instinctive rather than ratiocinative. Since he had long associated the Constitution with the Democratic party's mid-nineteenth-century dogmas, Fuller impulsively enforced those dogmas as the law of the land. It was no accident that JAMES BRADLEY THAYER published his path-breaking assessment of "The Origins and Scope of the American Doctrine of Constitutional Law" five years after Fuller's appointment or that a school of jurisprudence dedicated to "judicial self-restraint" grew increasingly large and vocal during his tenure. Other critics accused his Court of aiding the rich and powerful at the expense of the poor and helpless in the name of judicial neutrality. But Fuller neither replied to them nor sought to persuade others to do so. He simply hoped it would always be said of him, as he said of Cleveland in a 1909 eulogy, that "he trod unswervingly the path of duty, undeterred by doubts, single-minded and straight-forward."

The Chief Justice's constitutional understanding may have been "single-minded and straight-forward," but the Fuller era abounds with anomalies all the same. First there is the matter of Fuller's reputation. Until EARL WARREN's day, no Court was subjected to more strident criticism for a more sustained period of time than Fuller's. Yet when Fuller died the press concurred that none of his predecessors had been so successful in earning the respect and confidence of the country. Even THEODORE ROOSEVELT's *Outlook* conceded that Fuller was "perhaps the most popular" though "not the strongest or most famous Chief Justice." Perceptions of Fuller's capacity for judicial leadership were equally anomalous. The Chief Justice voted with the majority in virtually every leading case decided during his tenure. If STEPHEN J. FIELD is to be believed, moreover, Fuller was effective in setting the tenor of conference discussion. "Field told me on the bench this morning," Fuller informed his wife in 1891, "that in the conference I was almost invariably right. He said I was remarkably quick in seizing the best point." Yet contemporary observers invariably described him as a weak Chief Justice who neither led his Court nor exerted a substantial influence on its outlook.

The greatest anomaly of the Fuller era was the doctrinal structure of "the new judicialism." When Fuller contemplated the future of the republic in a centennial address on GEORGE WASHINGTON, two fears loomed especially large. One was that "the drift toward the exertion of the national will" might ultimately result in "consolidation," which in turn would impair the "vital importance" of the states and undermine self-government by extending the sphere of legislative authority to such a degree that the people no longer controlled it. The other was "the drift . . . towards increased interference by the State in the attempt to alleviate inequality of conditions." Fuller admitted that "[s]o long as that interference is . . . protective only," it was not only legitimate but necessary. "But," he added, "the rights to life, to use one's faculties in all lawful ways, and to acquire and enjoy property, are morally fundamental rights antecedent to constitutions, which do not create, but secure and protect them." It was imperative, he said, that Americans never grow "unmindful of the fact that it is the duty of the people to support the government and not of the government to support the people." Each of these concerns soon reappeared as major premises in the Court's construction of Congress's COMMERCE POWER and in its articulation of the liberty of contract protected by the Fifth and Fourteenth Amendments. But the Chief Justice directed a cacophonous band, not an orchestra. Decisions which, in Fuller's view, were consistent with one another looked antithetical to other observers because different Justices expressed the Court's opinions in different language.

Fuller regarded the liberty of contract doctrine as a juristic device for distinguishing between "paternalism," which he thought was unconstitutional, and legislation that "is protective only." Thus the maximum hours law for miners at issue in HOLDEN V. HARDY (1898) was valid because it protected the health and safety of workers employed in an inherently dangerous occupation. But the maximum hours law for bakery workers invalidated in LOCHNER V. NEW YORK (1905) and the ERDMAN ACT of Congress prohibiting discrimination against union members were unconstitutional because neither statute was "protective only." In Fuller's view, government had no authority to redress inequalities in the bargaining relation. "The employer and the employee have equality of right," JOHN MARSHALL HARLAN explained for the Court in ADAIR V. UNITED STATES (1908), "and any legislation that disturbs that equality is an arbitrary interference with liberty of contract, which no government can legally justify in a free land." Yet in *Holden* HENRY BROWN spoke at length about the inequality of bargaining power between employees and employers; he also implied that the worker's inability to contract for fair terms provided a legitimate rationale for government intervention. Although Brown apparently retreated from that position when he joined the *Lochner* majority seven years later, the language he used in *Holden* was never expressly disapproved.

The disparity between Fuller's constitutional understanding and the language used by colleagues in opinions he assigned was even more pronounced in the commerce field. Speaking for the Court in UNITED STATES v. E. C. KNIGHT CO. (1895), Fuller held that the Sherman Act could not be constitutionally construed to require the dissolution of manufacturing corporations when the transactions deemed unlawful in the government's complaint involved neither interstate transportation nor interstate sales. "Commerce succeeds to manufacturing," he explained, "and is not part of it." Underlying this distinction were three assumptions which Fuller elaborated with varying degrees of clarity. Congress could not regulate manufacturing combinations under the commerce clause, he said, for if that were permitted there was nothing to prevent Congress from regulating "every branch of human activity." Fuller also contended that that line between manufacturing and commerce was readily ascertainable. In a spate of recent dormant commerce clause decisions the Court had invalidated state tax laws and police regulations that burdened interstate transactions yet had sustained such legislation when it burdened the production process. With the exception of state laws that burdened commerce "indirectly" and might therefore be sustained under the rule of COOLEY v. BOARD OF WARDENS (1851), then, Congress could regulate only what the states could not and vice versa. Finally, Fuller made it clear that when manufacturing firms made "contracts to buy, sell, or exchange goods to be transported among the several states," the federal government had a duty to intervene under the Sherman Act if those contracts, or agreements pursuant to them, were in restraint of trade. In *Robbins v. Shelby County Taxing District* (1887), a leading dormant commerce clause case, the Court had held that "the negotiation of sales of goods which are in another state . . . is INTERSTATE COMMERCE."

Fuller believed that his construction of Congress's powers under the Sherman Act had two important virtues. It forestalled "consolidation" and it was easy to apply. Congress could certainly reach the agreement at issue in *Addyston Pipe & Steel Co. v. United States* (1899), for there a pool had been devised to allocate the interstate distribution of goods among the cooperating firms. And in LOEWE v. LAWLOR (1908) the hatter's union had not only gone on strike, thus disrupting the production process, but had engaged in a secondary boycott to prevent the sale of hats in interstate commerce. SWIFT & CO. v. UNITED STATES (1905) posed equally simple issues for Fuller. Some thirty firms had agreed to refrain from bidding against one another when livestock was auctioned prior to its delivery for slaughter at the Chicago packinghouses. Clearly, as the Court explained, "the subject-matter [was] sales and the very point of the combination . . . to restrain and monopolize commerce among the states in respect to such sales." But Fuller had designated OLIVER WENDELL HOLMES to speak for the Court in *Swift,* and Holmes had a great deal more to say. Holmes remarked that "commerce among the States is not a technical legal conception, but a practical one, drawn from the course of business." He spoke metaphorically about a current of commerce, suggesting that local production and interstate marketing were not distinct processes so much as parts of a single, undifferentiated process. (See STREAM OF COMMERCE DOCTRINE.) And he cast a pall of doubt on the idea, implicit in Fuller's *Knight* opinion, "that the rule which marks the point at which State taxation or regulation becomes permissible necessarily is beyond the scope of interference by Congress in cases where such interference is deemed necessary for the protection of commerce among the States."

Each of the anomalies of the Fuller years is attributable to the personality of the Chief Justice and his conception of the office. Fuller was a self-effacing, amiable man who was gracious and courteous, even deferential, to his colleagues. He made every effort to secure harmonious relations among the Justices. Fuller inaugurated the custom, still followed today, that each Justice greet and shake hands with every other Justice each morning. And he used his authority to assign opinions when in the majority not to enhance his own reputation or to elaborate favorite doctrines but to cultivate the good will of his associates. The opinion in a leading case ordinarily went to the colleague who, in Fuller's judgment, was most likely to want to speak for the Court. Cases involving questions of JURISDICTION and practice or mundane matters of private law Fuller kept to himself. Thus he let Field deliver the Court's opinions in *Georgia Banking & Railroad Co. v. Smith* (1889), a rate regulation case, and *Chae Chan Ping v. United States* (1889), the Chinese Exclusion Case. Both controversies raised issues of enormous importance to Field; for that very reason Fuller's predecessor had been disinclined to permit Field to address them for the Court.

Fuller also assumed that Brown would consider *Holden* a plum, for he had recently addressed the American Bar Association on the labor question. RUFUS PECKHAM had earned the right to speak for the majority in *Lochner* by dissenting without opinion in every previous case involving legislative regulation of the labor contract. The *Adair* decision provided Fuller with an opportunity to elaborate his own liberty of contract views in a systematic fashion, but he gave the opinion to Harlan instead. Harlan had dissented in *Lochner* on the grounds that the Court had no authority to reject the legislature's reasonable claim that long hours affected the health and safety of bakery workers. In *Adair* the government advanced no such claim and Harlan's opinion barely noticed the Court's prior liberty of contract rulings. Holmes was the logical choice for *Swift,* for the opinion would show Roosevelt that the administration had drawn spurious conclusions about Holmes's antitrust views from NORTHERN SECURITIES CO. V. UNITED STATES (1904).

The Chief Justice's obsession with courtesy also accounts for the striking differences between his own views and the Court's language in opinions which he assigned. He stubbornly defended his convictions in conference and, if necessary, in dissent. But once he had voted with the majority and had authorized an associate to speak for the Court, Fuller never criticized the work produced by a colleague. Good will among the Justices might be lost forever because of a single quarrel; incongruities of DOCTRINE could always be repaired later. Fuller let it be known that forthright yet polite concurring opinions were preferable to postconference haggling over doctrine, and silent acquiescence in the opinion of the Court was more preferable still. Fuller's own behavior set high standards for his associates; he wrote only seven concurring opinions in twenty-two years.

Underlying Fuller's management of the Court was a belief that the Chief Justice's primary duty was to convey to the public the impression that in the Court, more than in any other institution of government, reason triumphed over partisanship and statesmanship prevailed over pettiness. Fuller's success in achieving that goal while rarely speaking for the Court in landmark cases accounts for misperceptions of his capacity for intellectual leadership and for his great popularity despite persistent criticism of his Court's work. But Fuller's winning personality and the apparent anomalies it produced should not overshadow the relationship between his convictions and the new principles of law his Court articulated. Not since JOHN MARSHALL's day had the constitutional understanding of the Chief Justice been more at odds with that of voters and party leaders for such a prolonged period of time. Nevertheless, Fuller presided over a Court that made fundamentally new departures in constitutional interpretation which, in the main, incorporated the values he had imbibed during the party battles of a bygone era in American public life. Although Fuller hoped that eulogists would compare him with Cleveland, it might be more appropriate to analogize his career with that of another charming nineteenth-century Democrat. Like MARTIN VAN BUREN, he rowed to his objectives with muffled oars.

CHARLES W. MCCURDY

Bibliography

FULLER, MELVILLE 1890 *Address in Commemoration of the Inauguration of George Washington as First President of the United States, Delivered Before the Two Houses of Congress, December 11, 1889.* New York: Banks & Brothers.

KING, WILLARD L. 1950 *Melville Weston Fuller: Chief Justice of the United States, 1888–1910.* Chicago: University of Chicago Press.

PAUL, ARNOLD M. 1959 *Conservative Crisis and the Rule of Law: Attitudes of Bar and Bench, 1887–1895.* Ithaca, N.Y.: Cornell University Press.

FULLER COURT
(1888–1910)

MELVILLE W. FULLER was Chief Justice of the United States from 1888 to 1910. Lawyers and historians know the period, and its significance for constitutional law, but do not generally identify it with Fuller's name—and for good reason. He was no leader. Fuller discharged his administrative duties effectively, and in "good humor," to borrow a phrase from OLIVER WENDELL HOLMES, one of his admirers, but he was not an important source of the ideas and vision that shaped the work of the Court.

The year of Fuller's appointment, 1888, was nonetheless an important date in the life of the Court because it marked the beginning of a period of rapid turnover. From 1888 to 1895 there were a considerable number of vacancies, and the two Presidents then in office, GROVER CLEVELAND, a Democrat, and BENJAMIN HARRISON, a Republican—whose politics were conservative and largely indistinguishable—appointed six of the Justices. One was Fuller himself. At the time of his appointment he was a respected Chicago lawyer and, perhaps more significantly, a friend of Cleveland's. The others were DAVID J. BREWER, a federal circuit judge in Kansas; HENRY BILLINGS BROWN, a federal district judge in Detroit; RUFUS PECKHAM, a judge on the New York Court of Appeals; GEORGE SHIRAS, a lawyer from Pittsburgh; and EDWARD D. WHITE, a senator from Louisiana. (LUCIUS Q. C. LAMAR and HOWELL JACKSON were also appointed during this period, but served for relatively short periods.) The intellectual leaders of this group of six were Brewer and Peckham. They appeared in their written opinions as the most powerful and most eloquent, and the Chief Justice usually turned to one or the other to write for the Court in the major cases.

In constructing their majorities, Brewer and Peckham could usually count on the support of STEPHEN J. FIELD (Brewer's uncle), who earlier had achieved his fame by protesting various forms of government regulation in the SLAUGHTERHOUSE CASES and the GRANGER CASES. In the late 1890s Field was replaced by JOSEPH MCKENNA, who was chosen by WILLIAM MCKINLEY, a President who continued in the conservative tradition of Cleveland and Harrison. Another ally of this Cleveland-Harrison group, though perhaps not so steadfast as Field or McKenna, was HORACE GRAY. Gray was appointed in 1881 by President CHESTER A. ARTHUR and served until 1902.

As a result of these appointments, the Court over which Fuller presided was perhaps one of the most homogeneous in the history of the Supreme Court. Even more striking, its composition did not significantly change for most of Fuller's tenure. Fuller died in July 1910, just months after Brewer and Peckham. It was almost as though he could not go on without them. Brown resigned in 1906 and Shiras in 1903, but their replacements—WILLIAM H. MOODY and WILLIAM R. DAY—did not radically alter the balance of power. The only important break with the past came when THEODORE ROOSEVELT appointed Oliver Wendell Holmes, Jr., to replace Gray.

At the time of his appointment, Holmes was the Chief Justice of the Supreme Judicial Court of Massachusetts and had already written a number of the classics of American jurisprudence. Brown described Holmes's appointment as a "topping off." On the Court, however, Holmes played a different role, for he had no taste for either the method of analysis or general philosophical outlook of the Cleveland-Harrison appointees. His stance was fully captured by his quip in LOCHNER V. NEW YORK (1905) that "The FOURTEENTH AMENDMENT does not enact Mr. Herbert Spencer's Social Statics." In this remark Holmes was finally vindicated in 1937 with the constitutional triumph of the New Deal, but in the early 1900s he spoke mostly for himself, at least on the bench, and had no appreciable impact on the course of decisions. No other Justice joined his *Lochner* dissent.

The other significant presence on the Court at the turn of the century was JOHN MARSHALL HARLAN. He was originally appointed by President RUTHERFORD B. HAYES in 1877 and served until 1911. He is greatly admired today for his views on the rights of the newly freed slaves and on the power of the national government. But, like Holmes, Harlan suffered the fate of a prophet: He was a loner. He had his own agenda, and though he sometimes spoke for the Cleveland-Harrison group, Harlan seemed most comfortable playing the role of "the great dissenter."

At the turn of the century, as in many other periods of our history, the Court was principally concerned with the excesses of democracy and the danger of tyranny of the majority. In one instance, the people in Chicago took to the streets and, through a mass strike, tied up the rail system of the nation and threatened the public order. President Cleveland responded by sending the army, and the judiciary helped by issuing an INJUNCTION. In IN RE DEBS (1895) Brewer, writing for a unanimous Court, upheld the contempt conviction of the leader of the union, and legitimated the use of the federal injunctive power to prevent forcible obstructions of INTERSTATE COMMERCE. For the most part, however, the people fought their battles in the legislative halls, and presented the Court with a number of statutes regulating economic relationships. The question posed time and time again was whether these exercises of state power were consistent with the limitations the Constitution imposed upon popular majorities. Sometimes the question was answered in the affirmative, but the Court over which Fuller presided is largely remembered for its negative responses. It stands as a monument to the idea of limited government.

The most important such response consists of POLLOCK V. FARMERS' LOAN & TRUST CO. when, in the spring of 1895, the Court invalidated the first federal income tax enacted in peacetime. The statute imposed a 2 percent tax on all annual incomes above $4,000, and it was estimated that, due to the exemption, the tax actually fell on less than 2 percent of the population, the wealthy few who resided in a few northeastern states. The tax was denounced by JOSEPH CHOATE, in arguments before the Supreme Court, as an incident in the "communistic march," but the Court chose not to base its decision on a rule that would protect the wealthy few from redistribution. The Court instead largely relied upon that provision of the Constitution linking REPRESENTATION and taxation and requiring the apportionment among the states according to population of all DIRECT TAXES.

The Constitution identified a POLL TAX as an example of a direct tax. It was also assumed by all that a real estate tax would be another example of a direct tax, and the Court first decided that a tax upon the income from real estate is a direct tax. This ruling resulted in the invalidation of the statute as applied to rents (since the tax was not apportioned according to population), but on all other issues the Court was evenly divided, 4–4. The ninth justice, Howell Jackson, was sick at the time. A second argument was held and then the Court continued along the path it had started. Just as a tax on income from real property was deemed a direct tax, so was the tax on income from personal property (such as dividends). This still left unresolved the question whether a tax on wages was a direct tax, but the majority held that the portions of the statute taxing rents and dividends were not severable and that as a result the whole statute would fall. As Fuller reasoned, writing for the majority, if the provision on wages were severable, and it alone sustained, the statute would be transformed, for "what was intended as a tax on capital would remain in substance a tax on occupations and labors."

A decision of the Court invalidating the work of a coordinate branch of government is always problematic. *Pollock* seemed especially so, however, because the Court was sharply divided (5–4), and even more so because one of the Justices (whose identity is still unknown) seems to have switched sides after the reargument. The Justice who did not participate the first time (Jackson) voted to uphold the statute, yet the side he joined lost. It was no surprise, therefore, that *Pollock*, like *Debs*, became an issue in the presidential campaign of 1896, when William Jennings Bryan—a sponsor of the income tax in Congress—wrested control of the Democratic Party from the traditional, conservative elements and fused it with the emerging populist movement. Bryan lost the election, but remained the leader of the party for the next decade or so, during which the political elements critical of the Court grew in number and persuasiveness. By 1913 a constitutional amendment—the first since Reconstruction—was adopted. The SIXTEENTH AMENDMENT did not directly confront the egalitarian issue, any more than did the Court, but simply declared that an income tax did not have to be apportioned.

The Court's first encounter with the SHERMAN ACT of 1890 was negative and thus bore some resemblance to *Pollock*. In UNITED STATES v. E. C. KNIGHT COMPANY, also announced in 1895, just months before *Debs* and *Pollock*, the Court refused to read the Sherman Act to bar the acquisition of a sugar refinery even though it resulted in a firm that controlled 98 percent of the market and aptly was described (by Harlan in dissent) as a "stupendous combination." The Court reasoned that manufacturing was not within the reach of Congress's power over "commerce." The difference with *Pollock*, however, lay in the fact that this decision (written by Fuller) was in accord with long-standing interpretations of the COMMERCE CLAUSE, which equated "commerce" with the transportation of goods and services across state lines. And this decision was not denounced by the populists; they had no desire whatsoever to have the federal government assume jurisdiction over productive activities such as agriculture. In any event, by the end of Fuller's Chief Justiceship, *E. C. Knight* was in effect eradicated by the Court itself. The Court fully indicated that it was prepared to apply the act to manufacturing enterprises, provided the challenged conduct impeded or affected the flow of goods across state lines.

In the late 1890s, almost immediately after *E. C. Knight*, the Court, speaking through Peckham, applied the Sherman Act to prohibit open price-fixing arrangements by a number of railroads. There was little issue in these cases about the reach of the commerce power, because they involved transportation, but the Court was sharply divided over an issue that was presented by these early antitrust cases, namely, whether such an interference with what was then perceived as ordinary or accepted business practices (supposedly aimed at preventing "ruinous competition") was an abridgment of FREEDOM OF CONTRACT. At first the argument about freedom of contract was presented as a constitutional defense of the application of the Sherman Act, wholly based on the DUE PROCESS clause, but starting with Brewer's separate concurrence in UNITED STATES v. NORTHERN SECURITIES COMPANY (1903) and then again in White's opinions for a near-unanimous Court in the STANDARD OIL COMPANY v. UNITED STATES (1911) and UNITED STATES v. AMERICAN TOBACCO COMPANY (1911), the liberty issue dissolved into a question of statutory interpretation. The Sherman Act was read to prohibit not all but only "unreasonable" restraints of trade, and if a business practice was "unreasonable," then it was, almost by definition, the proper subject of government regulation.

In the late 1890s and early 1900s, antitrust sentiments were the principal cause of the growing Progressive movement. While populists extolled cooperative activity, progressives tried to use the legislative power to preserve the market and the liberties that it implied. They condemned activities (such as mergers or price fixing) that stemmed from the ruthless pursuit of self-interest but that, if carried to their logical extreme, would destroy the social mechanism that both legitimates and is supposed to control such self-interested activity. Progressives were also concerned, however, with stopping certain practices that did not threaten the existence of the market, but rather offended some standard of "fairness" or "decency" that had a wholly independent source. And they used the legislative power for this end.

The Justices were not unmoved by the moralistic concerns that fueled the progressives, but they were also determined—as they had been in *Pollock*—to make certain that the majorities were not using the legislative power to redistribute wealth or power in their favor. In some instances the Court allowed redistributive measures that benefited some group that was especially disadvantaged and thus could be deemed a ward of the state. On that theory, the Court, in a unanimous opinion by Brewer, upheld in MULLER V. OREGON (1908) a statute creating a sixty-hour maximum work week for women employed in factories or laundries. More generally, however, the Court voiced the same fears that had animated *Pollock* and insisted that there be a "direct" connection between the legislative rule and an acceptable (that is, nonredistributive) end such as health. The statute at issue in *Lochner v. New York,* for example, was defended on the ground that a work week for bakers in excess of sixty hours would endanger their health. Justice Peckham's opinion for the majority acknowledged that there might be some connection between a maximum work week and health, but suspected redistributive purposes and argued that if, in the case of bakers, this connection with health were deemed sufficient—that is, direct—the same could be said for virtually every occupation or profession: "No trade, no occupation, no mode of earning one's living, could escape this all-pervading power."

Just as it was fearful of state intervention to control the terms of employment, the Court was also wary of legislation regulating consumer prices—a practice initiated by the Granger movement of the 1870s but continued by the populists and progressives in the 1890s and the early 1900s. In this instance the Court feared that the customers would enrich themselves at the expense of the investors. The danger was, as Brewer formulated it, one of legalized theft. In contrast to cases like *Lochner,* however, the Court took up this issue with a viable and highly visible precedent on the books, namely, *Munn v. Illinois* (1877). Some consideration was given to OVERRULING the decision (there was no limit to the daring of some of the Justices), but the Court finally settled upon a more modest strategy—of cabining *Munn.*

For one thing, the *Munn* formula for determining which industries would be regulated—a formula that allowed the state to reach "any industry AFFECTED WITH A PUBLIC INTEREST"—was narrowed. In *Budd v. New York* (1892) the Court upheld the power of the legislature to regulate the rates of grain operators, but placed no reliance on the *Munn* public interest formula. Instead, it stressed the presence of monopoly power and the place of the grain operation in the transportation system. Second, the Court began to surround the rate-settling power with procedural guarantees. Legislatures were now delegating the power of setting prices to administrative bodies, such as railroad commissions, and the Court, in CHICAGO, MILWAUKEE & ST. PAUL RAILWAY CO. V. MINNESOTA (1890), required agencies of that type to afford investors a full, quasi-judicial hearing prior to setting rates. Finally, the Court ended the tradition of judicial deference initiated by *Munn* by authorizing judicial review of the rate actually set. The purpose was to insure against confiscation and to this end Brewer articulated in REAGAN V. FARMERS' LOAN & TRUST (1894) a right of FAIR RETURN ON FAIR VALUE. In that case the rate was set so low as to deny the investors any return at all. In the next case, SMYTH V. AMES (1898), there was some return to the investors, but the Court simply concluded that the rate was "too low."

Reagan v. Farmers' Loan & Trust and *Smyth v. Ames* were both unanimous and thrust the federal judiciary into the business of policing state rate regulations. A particularly momentous and divisive exercise of this supervisory jurisdiction occurred when a federal judge in Minnesota enjoined the attorney general of that state from enforcing a state statute that set maximum railroad rates. The attorney general disobeyed the injunction and was held in criminal contempt. Peckham wrote the opinion for the Court in EX PARTE YOUNG (1908) affirming the contempt conviction, and in doing so, constructed a theory that, notwithstanding the ELEVENTH AMENDMENT, provided access to the federal EQUITY courts to test the constitutionality of state statutes—an avenue of recourse that was to become critical for the CIVIL RIGHTS movement of the 1960s. Ironically, Harlan, who, by dissenting in the CIVIL RIGHTS CASES (1883) and in PLESSY V. FERGUSON (1896), had already earned for himself an honored place in the history of civil rights, bitterly dissented in *Ex parte Young,* because, he argued, the Court was opening the doors of federal courts to test the validity of all state statutes.

The confrontations between the Court and political branches in economic matters such as antitrust, maximum hours, and rate regulation were considerable—*Northern Securities, Lochner,* and *Ex Parte Young* were important public events of their day. Some of these decisions were denounced by political forces, particularly by the Progressive movement, which had begun to dominate national politics. Roosevelt made his disappointment with Holmes's performance in *Northern Securities* well known ("I could carve out of a banana a judge with more backbone than that"—a comment that seems only to have either amused or pleased Holmes) and finished his presidency in 1908 with a speech to Congress sharply critical of the Court. By 1912 the Supreme Court and its work were once again the subject of debate in a presidential election, as it had been in the election of 1896. It was as though the body politic was scoring the Court over which Fuller had presided for the past twenty years. Now the critical voices were more respected and covered a wider political spectrum than in 1896, but the results were mixed.

In the 1912 election the Democratic candidate, Woodrow Wilson, beat the incumbent WILLIAM HOWARD TAFT, who was generally seen as the defender, indeed the embodiment, of the judicial power. On the other hand, Wilson was less critical of the Court than Roosevelt, who ran as a Progressive. The legislation of this period also was two-sided. The CLAYTON ACT of 1914, for example, exempted labor from antitrust legislation (thus reversing the *Danbury Hatters* decision of 1908), and also imposed procedural limits on the use of the labor injunction (thus revising *Debs*), but it did not in fact have as critical an edge as the Sixteenth Amendment of 1913. The Clayton Act did not repudiate the idea of the labor injunction altogether nor did it repudiate the rule of reason in antitrust cases. Similarly, although Congress reacted in 1910 to *Ex Parte Young*, it did so only in a trivial, near-cosmetic way, by requiring three judges (as opposed to one) to issue an injunction against the enforcement of state statutes.

In attempting to construct limits on the power of the political branches, and to guard against the tyranny of the majority as it did in *Pollock*, *Ex Parte Young*, and *Lochner*, the Court assumed an activist posture. The Justices were prepared to use their power to frustrate what appeared popular sentiments. The activist posture was, however, mostly confined to economic reforms—redistributing income, regulating prices, controlling the terms of employment—as though the constitutional conception of liberty were structured by an overriding commitment to capitalism and the market. This characterization of their work, voiced in a critical spirit in their day and in ours, is strengthened when a view is taken of the Justices' overall receptiveness to the antitrust program of the progressives, and even more when account is taken of the pattern of decisions outside the economic domain, respecting human rights as opposed to property rights. The Justices were passive about human rights—by and large willing to let majorities have their way.

A particularly striking instance of this passivity consists of their reaction to the treatment of Chinese residents. Ever since the Civil War the Chinese were by statute denied the right to become naturalized citizens, but in the late 1880s and the early 1900s their situation worsened. The doors of the nation were closed to any further IMMIGRATION, and Congress (in the Geary Act of 1892) created an oppressive regime for those who had previously been admitted. Chinese residents were required to carry passes, and failure to have the passes subjected them to DEPORTATION proceedings that were to be conducted by commissioners (rather than judges or juries) and that put them to the task of producing "at least one credible white witness." YICK WO V. HOPKINS (1886), which invalidated, on EQUAL PROTECTION grounds, a San Francisco laundry ordinance that had disadvantaged the Chinese, was already on the books. But neither it nor the passionate dissent of Brewer ("In view of this enactment of the highest legislative body of the foremost Christian nation, may not the thoughtful Chinese disciple of Confucius fairly ask, why do they send missionaries here?") was of much avail. The Court sustained the Geary Act in *Fong Yue Ting v. United States* (1893) in virtually all its particulars.

A few years later the Court held in UNITED STATES V. WONG KIM ARK (1898) that Chinese children born here were, by virtue of the FOURTEENTH AMENDMENT, citizens of the United States. But this decision sharply divided the Court, despite the straightforward language of the amendment ("All persons born . . . in the United States and subject to the jurisdiction thereof are citizens of the United States"), and did not materially improve the quality of the process the Chinese received. There was, by virtue of *Wong Kim Ark*, a chance that a Chinese person whom the government was trying to deport was a natural born citizen, yet the Court did not even require that this claim of CITIZENSHIP be tried by a judge. Holmes wrote the opinion in these cases, *United States v. Sing Tuck* (1904) and *United States v. Ju Toy* (1905), and once again Brewer, now joined by Peckham, dissented with an intensity equal to that he had exhibited in *Fong Yue Ting*.

The same spirit of acquiescence was manifest in the cases involving the civil rights of blacks, though here it was Harlan who kept the nation's conscience. In *Plessy v. Ferguson* (1896) the Court upheld a Louisiana statute requiring racial SEGREGATION of rail cars; Harlan dissented and, borrowing a line from Plessy's lawyer, Albion Tourgee, insisted that "our Constitution is colorblind." In HODGES V. UNITED STATES (1906) the Court dismissed a federal INDICTMENT against a group of white citizens in Arkansas who forced a mill owner to discharge the blacks who had been hired. Brewer, for the majority, said that the power of the federal government under the Civil War-Reconstruction amendments (and thus under the criminal statute in question) extended only to acts by state officials. He reaffirmed the principle of the CIVIL RIGHTS CASES of 1883 by which the Court effectively ceded to the states exclusive jurisdiction to govern the treatment of one citizen by another. In *Hodges,* Harlan, the Union general from Kentucky, replayed his dissent in the *Civil Rights* cases, and denounced this principle as a fundamental distortion of the Thirteenth and Fourteenth Amendments. And in BEREA COLLEGE V. KENTUCKY (1908) the Court, over Harlan's dissent, upheld a state law that prohibited a private educational corporation from conducting its educational programs on an integrated basis.

Berea College was also written by Brewer. He was mindful of the contrast with a case such as *Lochner,* where the judicial power had been used to the utmost to protect the contractual freedom of worker and employer. Accordingly, Brewer stressed the fact that this law was applicable only to CORPORATIONS, which, to pick up a theme he had previously articulated in his concurring opinion in *Northern Securities,* were merely artificial entities created by government, not entitled to the same degree of protection as natural persons. He specifically left open the question of the validity of a similar statute if it regulated the conduct of natural persons. Harlan, in an equally equivocal dissent, said that a different result might follow if the statute regulated public rather than private education. In fact, the distorting impact of public subsidies upon the articulation of civil rights had been implicitly acknowledged some years earlier in *Cumming v. Board of Education* (1899). In that case Harlan dismissed a challenge by black parents to a decision of a local county, which ran its schools on a segregated basis, to close the only black high school and to send the black students out of the county for their education.

In the 1890s and early 1900s blacks, through one scheme or another, were disenfranchised on a grand scale. The FIFTEENTH AMENDMENT was reduced to a nullity, as Jim Crow was becoming more firmly entrenched. On several occasions, the Court was presented with challenges to these electoral practices, yet it was unable to respond with the energy that it had summoned in *Pollock* or *Lochner* or *Reagan* or, even more to the point, *Debs.* Holmes, the spokesman in these early VOTING RIGHTS cases, saw judicial relief as nothing but an "empty form": "[R]elief from a great political wrong, if done, as alleged, by the people of a State and the State itself, must be given by them or by the legislative and political department of the government of the United States." Harlan dissented, as might be expected, but so did Brewer. They realized that, because the disenfranchisement was the work of state officials, something more was at issue than the allocation of power between states and nation approved in the *Civil Rights Cases.* What was at issue, according to Brewer and Harlan, was nothing less than the integrity of the judicial power and the duty of the judiciary, to borrow a line from *Debs,* to do whatever it could to fulfill the promise of the Constitution.

The principal issue before the Court at the turn of the century was democracy and, more specifically, the determination of what limits should be placed on popular majorities. As was evident in the civil rights cases, however, the Court was also asked to allocate power between the states and the national government. The FEDERALISM issue arose in many contexts, including antitrust, labor, and rate regulation, but the one in which it proved most troublesome was PROHIBITION. By the late 1880s the prohibition movement was an active force in the states, and Fuller began his Chief Justiceship with a set of constitutional decisions that were unstable. In MUGLER V. KANSAS (1887) the Court had held that prohibition was within the STATE POLICE POWER, yet, just weeks before Chief Justice MORRISON R. WAITE's death, the Court in *Bowman v. Iowa* (1888) had also held that the states were without power to prohibit the importation of liquor from other states. The Court seemed to take away in one decision what it gave in the other. Fuller confronted this problem early on in LEISY V. HARDIN (1890), and in probably his most lasting contribution to constitutional law, fashioned an odd response. First, he announced that the commerce clause barred the states from prohibiting the sale of imported liquor (as well as its actual importation). Second, he invited Congress to intervene, and to authorize states to pass laws that would prohibit out-of-state liquor. Congress quickly responded to this invitation, and in the Wilson Act of 1890 authorized states to enact measures aimed at erecting walls to out-of-state liquor.

The state laws in question in *Leisy v. Hardin* were invalidated on the theory that they sought to regulate a matter that required nationwide uniformity. When it came to judging the congressional response, Fuller found the requisite uniformity since it was Congress that had spoken (even though it did no more than allow the states to choose) and on that theory, in *In re Rahrer* (1891), upheld the Wilson Act. In 1898, however, after some change in the composition of the Court and after the responsibility of speaking on this issue had shifted to one of the new appointees, Edward White, a sharply divided Court cut back on the Wilson Act. *Rhodes v. Iowa* (1890) held that the Wilson Act authorized a ban on sales of imported liquor within the state but not a ban on the importation itself. White insisted that any other construction would raise grave constitutional doubts as to the validity of the Wilson Act. Fuller joined White's opinion.

Over the next decade, mail order business in out-of-state liquor grew. The conflict between the Court and the prohibition movement escalated. Then in 1913 Congress, as part of the same era that saw the Sixteenth Amendment and the Clayton Act, passed the WEBB-KENYON ACT to remove any ambiguity over what it sought to accomplish in the Wilson Act. Congress allowed states to bar both the sale and the importation of out-of-state liquor. After considerable struggle and deliberation, the Webb-Kenyon Act was upheld in an opinion by White (then Chief Justice) on the theory (if that is what it can be called) that "liquor is different." For all other goods, the common market was deemed a constitutional necessity.

The federalism issue has recurred throughout the entire history of the Supreme Court. The Court over which Fuller presided did, however, confront one issue pertaining to structure of government that was unique to the times: colonialism. The issue arose from the "splendid little war," as Secretary of State John Hay called the Spanish-American War of 1898, which left the United States with two former Spanish colonies, PUERTO RICO and the Philippines. (Much earlier the United States had purchased Alaska, and in the late 1890s it had also taken possession of Hawaii.) The assumption was that the United States would hold these territories as territories, for an indefinite period, and perhaps ultimately build a colonial empire along the European model. The question posed for the Supreme Court—not just by the litigants but by the nation at large—was whether colonialism was a constitutionally permissible strategy for the United States. Technically, the case involved a challenge to a statute imposing a tariff on goods (sugar) imported from Puerto Rico into the states. The Constitution bars Congress from imposing duties on the importation of goods from one state to another, and so the issue was whether a territory was to be treated the same as a state, or, as phrased in the language of the day, whether the Constitution followed the flag.

Three positions emerged in a series of decisions beginning in 1901 known as the INSULAR CASES. The first, most in keeping with the position of the Court in *Pollock* and the other economic cases, proclaimed the idea of limited government. The government of the United States was formed and established by the Constitution, and thus it was impossible to conceive of a separation of Constitution and government. This was the position taken by Brewer, Peckham, Fuller, and Harlan. At the opposite end of the spectrum was the so-called annexation position. It proclaimed the separation of Constitution and flag, and generally left the government unrestricted in its activities in the territories; whatever restrictions there were flowed from natural law or from a small group of provisions of the Constitution deemed essential (the tariff provision was not one). This position was most congenial to the government and yet at odds with the general jurisprudence of the Court. Only Justice Brown subscribed to it.

The remaining four Justices, in an opinion written by White, put forth what was called the incorporation theory. It tried to chart a middle course, as appeared to be White's trade. It made the Constitution fully applicable to a territory, but only after that territory was incorporated into the United States. (Prior to incorporation the government would be subject only to the restraints of natural law.) Justice White's opinion also made it clear that the decision to incorporate a territory resided in Congress. In the case before it the Court decided that the territory was not incorporated, but White also acknowledged that incorporation could be done by implication and, even more to the point, he reserved for the judiciary the power to determine whether that act of incorporation had taken place.

Ultimately incorporation was adopted as the position of the Court. But this did not occur until 1905, after an insurrection in the Phillipines and other developments in the world (such as the Boer War) had made the idea of a colonial empire seem less attractive, and the danger of further imperial acquisitions seemed to have waned. In fact, incorporation became majority doctrine in *Rassmussen v. United States* (1905) in which the Court held that Alaska had been *implicitly* incorporated and that the United States was bound by the BILL OF RIGHTS in its governance of that territory. The outcome in this case affirmed the idea of limited government and JUDICIAL SUPREMACY, the hallmarks of this Court, and made it possible for Fuller, and perhaps even more significantly, for Brewer and Peckham, to abandon their absolutist position and to support the middle-of-the-road theory of White—perhaps a sign of what was to come in 1910, when Fuller died and Taft, who had once served as the commissioner in the Philippines, replaced him with White.

OWEN M. FISS

Bibliography

DUKER, WILLIAM 1980 Mr. Justice Rufus W. Peckham: The Police Power and the Individual in a Changing World. *Brigham Young University Law Review* 1980:47–67.

——— 1980 Mr. Justice Rufus W. Peckham and the Case of *Ex Parte Young:* Lochnerizing *Munn v. Illinois. Brigham Young University Law Review* 1980:539–558.

GOODWYN, LAWRENCE 1976 *Democratic Promise: The Populist Movement in America.* New York: Oxford University Press.

KING, WILLARD 1967 *Melville Weston Fuller, Chief Justice of the United States, 1888–1910.* Chicago: University of Chicago Press.

KOLKO, GABRIEL 1963 *The Triumph of Conservatism: A Reinterpretation of American History 1900–1916.* New York: Free Press.

PAUL, ARNOLD 1960 *Conservative Crisis and the Rule of Law: Attitudes of Bar and Bench 1887–1895.* Ithaca, N.Y.: Cornell University Press.

PIERCE, CARL 1972 A Vacancy on the Supreme Court: The Politics of Judicial Appointment, 1893–1894. *Tennessee Law Review* 39:555–612.

ROCHE, JOHN 1974 *Sentenced to Life.* New York: Macmillan.

ROGAT, YOSAL 1963 The Judge as Spectator. *University of Chicago Law Review* 31:231–278.

THORELLI, HANS 1954 *The Federal Antitrust Policy: Origination of an American Tradition.* Baltimore: Johns Hopkins University Press.

TWISS, BENJAMIN 1942 *Lawyers and the Constitution: How Laissez Faire Came to the Supreme Court.* Princeton, N.J.: Princeton University Press.

WESTIN, ALAN 1953 The Supreme Court, the Populist Movement and the Campaign of 1896. *Journal of Politics* 15:3–41.

——— 1958 Stephen J. Field and the Headnote to *O'Neil v. Vermont:* A Snapshot of the Fuller Court at Work. *Yale Law Journal* 67:363–383.

WOODWARD, C. VANN 1966 *The Strange Career of Jim Crow,* rev. ed. New York: Oxford University Press.

FULL FAITH AND CREDIT

The full faith and credit clause of the Constitution (Article IV, section 1) provides that: "Full Faith and Credit shall be given in each State to the public Acts, Records and judicial Proceedings of every other State. And the Congress may by general Laws prescribe the Manner in which such Acts, Records and Proceedings shall be proved, and the Effect thereof."

The first sentence of the clause closely tracked language contained in Article IV of the ARTICLES OF CONFEDERATION, the precursor of our present Constitution. The second sentence, which authorizes Congress to enact implementing legislation, was new. "Faith and credit" was a familiar term in English law where it had been used on occasion for some centuries to describe the respect owed to judgments and other public records. Its precise meaning, however, was obscure; it was not clear whether it was concerned only with the admission of public records, including judgments, into evidence or whether it was intended to deal likewise with the effect as RES JUDICATA to which a judgment was entitled. There is similar uncertainty with respect to the meaning which the term was intended to bear in the Articles of Confederation.

The subject of full faith and credit evoked little discussion in the CONSTITUTIONAL CONVENTION, and it seems unlikely that there was any general understanding among the delegates of what the clause was designed to accomplish. In any event, Congress was quick to exercise its power to pass implementing legislation. The initial statute was enacted in 1790 by the First Congress. It provided for the manner of authenticating the acts of the legislatures and of the records and judicial proceedings of the several states and concluded that "the said records and judicial proceedings shall have such faith and credit given to them in every court of the United States, as they have by law or usage in the courts of the State from whence the said records are or shall be taken." The second congressional act, that of 1804, extended the scope of full faith and credit by requiring that the same measure of respect should be given to the records and judicial proceedings of the TERRITORIES of the United States and of the countries subject to its JURISDICTION.

Judicial decisions have now made clear many things that the full faith and credit clause and its implementing statutes left uncertain. The Supreme Court has decided that, provided the requirements of jurisdiction, NOTICE, and opportunity to be heard have been satisfied, a judgment rendered in one state, territory, or possession of the United States shall in general be given the same res judicata effect that it has in the state of its rendition. Exceptions to this rule, if any there be, are few indeed. A state cannot, for example, deny effect to a judgment on the ground that the underlying claim was contrary to its public policy. Initially, some might have wondered whether Congress was empowered to extend the protection of full faith and credit to the records and judicial proceedings of territories and possessions of the United States. The full faith and credit clause itself gives no such authority, but the Supreme Court has held that this is to be found in those provisions of the Constitution that afford the United States with JUDICIAL POWER (Article III), authorize LEGISLATION that is NECESSARY AND PROPER to execute the powers entrusted to the federal government (Article II, section 8), and provide that the Constitution and the laws and treaties of the United States shall be the supreme law of the land (Article VI). Neither the clause nor the implementing statute refer to judgments of the federal courts. The Supreme Court has filled this gap by holding that these judgments are entitled to the same respect that is owed to state judgments.

A sharp distinction must be drawn between the recognition and the enforcement of judgments. With respect to recognition, the Supreme Court has held, as has already been said, that a judgment must be given the same res judicata effect that it enjoys under the law of the state of its rendition. On the other hand, the method of enforcing a judgment is determined by the law of the state where enforcement is sought. It is therefore for this latter law to determine whether a new action in the nature of debt must be brought on the judgment or whether it can be enforced by means of a registration procedure.

Full faith and credit is not owed to the judgments of foreign countries. Each state of the United States determines for itself the measure of respect that such judgments are to receive in its courts. Perhaps because of their experience in giving full faith and credit to federal and sister state judgments, American courts are extremely liberal, perhaps the most liberal in the world, in giving respect to the judgments of other countries.

The intentions of the original Framers may have been obscure. But the Supreme Court has said that the full faith and credit clause should become "a nationally unifying force" by establishing "throughout the federal system the salutory principle of the COMMON LAW that a litigation once pursued to judgment shall be as conclusive of the rights of the parties in every other court as in that where the judgment was rendered."

It will have been noted that whereas the full faith and credit clause speaks of "public Acts, Records and judicial Proceedings," the implementing statutes of 1790 and 1804 required only that full faith and credit be given to records and judicial proceedings. No definite information is available on why public acts were omitted, but it can be surmised that this omission was deliberate and stemmed from the realization that the circumstances, if any, in which one state should be required to apply another's law presented considerations infinitely more complex than those involving the recognition and enforcement of judgments. (See CHOICE OF LAW.) After some years, the Supreme Court held that the clause was self-executing and that there were limited circumstances in which a state was required to apply another's laws. By and large, the Supreme Court has now withdrawn from its earlier opinions and today the command of full faith and credit with respect to public acts is slight indeed. The Supreme Court has, however, held that full faith and credit imposes limitations upon the power of a state to refuse on public policy grounds to entertain suit on a claim arising under the law of a sister state. It can be expected that in due course restrictions will likewise be placed upon a state's power to dismiss a suit on the ground that the claim involved is one for a penalty.

The implementing statute remained substantially unchanged from 1804 to 1948. In the latter year, it was amended as part of a general revision of Title 28 of the United States Code. This revision was not intended to make controversial substantive changes in the law. Nevertheless, the implementing statute was amended to require that full faith and credit be given not only to records and judicial proceedings, as had been the case heretofore, but to acts as well. It seems improbable that this change in wording will lead to any substantial change in the law. No such change was presumably intended by the revisers, and, to date, the amendment has not influenced the decisions of the courts. But, taken literally, the statute, as now worded, requires the same measure of respect for statutes that it does for judgments. There is always the possibility that at some time in the future the courts will seize upon this new language to make substantial changes in what is owed under full faith and credit to the statutes of sister states and of United States territories and possessions.

WILLIS L. M. REESE

Bibliography

AMERICAN LAW INSTITUTE 1971 *Restatement of the Law: Conflict of Laws, Second.* Chap. 5, pages 271–348. St. Paul, Minn.: American Law Institute Publishers.

NADELMANN, KURT 1957 Full Faith and Credit to Judgments and Public Acts. *Michigan Law Review* 56:33–88.

WHITTEN, RALPH U. 1981 The Constitutional Limitations on State-Court Jurisdiction: An Historical-Interpretative Reexamination of the Full Faith and Credit and Due Process Clauses. *Creighton Law Review* 14:499–606.

FULLILOVE v. KLUTZNICK 448 U.S. 448 (1980)

The Supreme Court's fragmentation in REGENTS OF UNIVERSITY OF CALIFORNIA V. BAKKE (1978) left open the question of the constitutionality of government-imposed RACIAL QUOTAS or preferences. The following year, in UNITED STEELWORKERS V. WEBER, the Court held that a voluntary AFFIRMATIVE ACTION plan, calling for a racial quota in hiring by a private employer and approved by a union, did not violate Title VII of the CIVIL RIGHTS OF 1964. *Fullilove* reopened *Bakke*'s question: Can government impose a racial quota to remedy the effects of past discrimination?

Congress, in a public works statute aimed at reducing unemployment, provided that ten percent of the funds distributed to each state should be set aside for contracts with "minority business enterprises" (MBE). An MBE was defined as a business at least half owned by persons who are "Negroes, Spanish-speaking, Orientals, Indians, Eskimos and Aleuts." Nonminority contractors challenged this limitation as a denial of the Fifth Amendment's guarantee of EQUAL PROTECTION, as recognized in BOLLING V. SHARPE (1954) and later cases.

The Supreme Court held, 6–3, that the MBE limitation was valid. Three Justices, speaking through Chief Justice WARREN E. BURGER, paid great deference to Congress's judgment that the racial quota was a "limited and properly tailored remedy to cure the effects of past RACIAL DISCRIMINATION." Emphasizing the flexibility provided for the law's administration, they said that the funds could be limited to MBEs that were in fact disadvantaged because of race. The other three majority Justices, speaking through Justice THURGOOD MARSHALL, took the position they had taken in *Bakke*, concluding that the racial quota was "substantially related to . . . the important and congressionally articulated goal of remedying the present effects of past racial discrimination."

Justice POTTER STEWART, joined by Justice WILLIAM H. REHNQUIST, dissented; they would forbid any statutory racial classification, allowing race-conscious remedies only in cases of proven illegal discrimination. Justice JOHN PAUL STEVENS was not prepared to take so absolute a position but dissented here because Congress had not sufficiently articulated the reasons for its racial quota and tailored its program to those reasons.

KENNETH L. KARST

FUNDAMENTAL INTERESTS

The idea that some interests are fundamental, and thus deserving of a greater measure of constitutional protection than is given to other interests, is an old one. Justice BUSHROD WASHINGTON, sitting on circuit in CORFIELD V. CORYELL (1823), held that the PRIVILEGES AND IMMUNITIES clause of Article IV of the Constitution protected out-of-staters against discriminatory state legislation touching only those privileges that were "in their very nature, fundamental; which belong, of right, to the citizens of all free governments." Washington's list of such interests was limited but significant: free passage through a state; HABEAS CORPUS; the right to sue in state courts; the right to hold and dispose of property; freedom from discriminatory taxation.

Although the *Corfield* doctrine suggested an active role for the federal judiciary in protecting NATURAL RIGHTS against state interference—at least on behalf of citizens of other states—the doctrine was not embraced by the full Supreme Court during Washington's lifetime. If some hoped that the FOURTEENTH AMENDMENT's privileges and immunities clause would breathe new life into the fundamental rights theory, those hopes were disappointed in the SLAUGHTERHOUSE CASES (1873). Rejecting the theory as propounded in two eloquent dissenting opinions, the Court again refused to find any special federal constitutional protection against state invasions of preferred rights.

Within a generation, however, the Court had identified a cluster of preferred rights of property and the FREEDOM OF CONTRACT, to be defended against various forms of ECONOMIC REGULATION. The Court did not use the language of fundamental interests; for doctrinal support it avoided both privileges and immunities clauses, relying instead on a theory of SUBSTANTIVE DUE PROCESS. When this doctrinal development played out in the late 1930s, the Court abandoned its STRICT SCRUTINY of business regulation in favor of a STANDARD OF REVIEW demanding no more than a RATIONAL BASIS for legislative judgments.

Even as the Court adopted its new permissive attitude toward economic regulation, it was laying the groundwork for another round of protections of preferred rights. (See UNITED STATES v. CAROLENE PRODUCTS CO., 1938; SKINNER v. OKLAHOMA, 1942.) When the WARREN COURT set about its expansion of the reach of EQUAL PROTECTION doctrine, it not only followed these precedents but also revived the rhetoric of fundamental interests. A state law discriminating against the exercise of such an interest, the Court held, must be justified as necessary for achieving a COMPELLING STATE INTEREST.

The Warren Court hinted strongly that it would expand the list of fundamental interests demanding strict judicial scrutiny to include all manner of claims to equality. In fact, the Court's holdings placed only a limited number of interests in the "fundamental" category: VOTING RIGHTS and related interests in the electoral process; some limited rights of ACCESS TO THE COURTS; and rights relating to marriage, the family, and other intimate relationships. Even so modest a doctrinal development evoked the strong dissent of Justice JOHN MARSHALL HARLAN: "I know of nothing which entitles this Court to pick out particular human activities, characterize them as 'fundamental,' and give them added protection under an unusually stringent equal protection test."

The BURGER COURT, making Harlan's lament its theme song, called a halt to the expansion of fundamental interests occasioning strict judicial scrutiny under the equal protection clause. However, in cases touching marriage and other close personal relationships, the Court continued to promote the notion of fundamental liberties deserving of special protection—now on a substantive due process theory. (See ABORTION AND THE CONSTITUTION; ILLEGITIMACY; FREEDOM OF INTIMATE ASSOCIATION.) The notion of natural rights as part of our constitutional law is deeply ingrained. Our modern doctrines about fundamental rights are novel only in the particular interests they have termed fundamental.

KENNETH L. KARST

Bibliography

TRIBE, LAURENCE H. 1978 *American Constitutional Law.* Chaps. 8, 11, 15, and 16. Mineola, N.Y.: Foundation Press. 000 002

FUNDAMENTAL LAW
(History)

The institution of a written CONSTITUTION as fundamental law superior to and limiting ordinary statutory law and government, which we now take for granted, was distinctively American. The concept of fundamental law embodied in a written constitution was one of the most influential and radical ideas to emerge from the American Revolution. It involved a break with the recent English past.

The notion of fundamental law has had a continuing history in Western political thought. Mid-seventeenth century Englishmen anticipated the use of a written constitution as the foundation of government, but the half-hearted experiment did not last. Fundamental law remained an ill-defined and vague term then, standing for the customary constitution as distinguished from revolutionary change. Parliamentarians accused Charles I and James II of attempting by arbitrary acts to subvert the fundamental laws of the realm, especially the traditional rights of liberty and property. Although interest in fundamental law declined in the eighteenth century, the concept never lost its attractiveness for the English. However, the growing acceptance of the omnipotence of Parliament made the idea of a single written instrument creating and limiting the government decidedly obsolete, because no restraints existed on parliamentary power, and for that reason Americans would finally repudiate the unwritten English constitution as less than the embodiment of truly fundamental law.

Reformist ideas about law, current in early seventeenth-century England, influenced the settlers of early America in the creation of their legal systems. The colonists developed a conception of the sources and nature of law that was much more expansive than the traditionally narrow conception of the English COMMON LAW. This broad approach reflected the fundamentally altered state of many aspects of law in the New World. Leaders of the American colonies also assimilated new currents in political thought which led to the conclusion that fundamental or natural law lay behind the civil law of every nation. Fundamental law became equated in their minds with natural law or the law of nature. Many residents of the New World regarded their charters from the crown as a fundamental source for their basic rights as Englishmen.

The revolutionary ferment of the 1760s and 1770s in the American colonies produced the idea of a written constitution embodying fundamental law. Americans regarded as unconstitutional several of Parliament's statutes governing America. In 1761 JAMES OTIS argued that WRITS OF ASSISTANCE were "against the fundamental Principles of Law." Like the English a century earlier, Americans gravitated toward an understanding of a constitution as something antecedent and paramount to all branches of government, including even their legislative representatives. Fundamental law controlled statutory law. A 1760 *Letter to the People of Pennsylvania* noted the relevance to forming a plan of government of "the fundamental laws and rules of the constitution, which ought never to be infringed. . . ." Writing against the authority of Parliament over the colonies in 1774, JOHN ADAMS regarded New Englanders as deriving their laws "not from parliament, not from common law, but from the law of nature and the compact made with the king in our charter. . . . English liberties are but certain rights of nature, reserved to the citizen by the English constitution, which rights cleaved to our ancestors when they crossed the Atlantic. . . ."

The process of state constitution-making that began in 1776 led to eleven written constitutions by 1780, but the basic and largely unchanging nature of such documents was not fully recognized in practice in the first decade, mainly because the first constitutions granted predominant power to the legislatures. Criticisms of excessive legislative activity in the 1780s led to general acceptance of the idea that constitutions should serve as fundamental laws to control legislatures. THOMAS JEFFERSON eagerly sought a Virginia constitution that the legislature could not easily change.

The American states gradually came to regard their written constitutions as fundamental or HIGHER LAWS superior to ordinary legislative acts—which meant restrictions on legislative power, because ordinary courts of law eventually implemented the written constitutions through a process of JUDICIAL REVIEW. The argument in favor of the innovative practice of judicial review was that fundamental laws were predominant. Thus the CONSTITUTIONAL CONVENTION that met in Philadelphia in 1787 accepted the notion that a legislature could not change a constitution without the calling of a special constitutional convention. The recognition of the new federal Constitution as a fundamental law required the calling of special ratifying conventions to avoid disputes about its legitimacy. This process of creating fundamental law through constitution-making was the source of the basic appeal of the American Revolution to continental Europeans.

DAVID H. FLAHERTY

Bibliography

GOUGH, J. W. (1955)1971 *Fundamental Law in English Constitutional History.* Oxford: Clarendon Press.

MULLETT, CHARLES F. (1933)1966 *Fundamental Law and the American Revolution 1760–1776.* New York: Octagon.

WOOD, GORDON S. 1969 *The Creation of the American Republic, 1776–1787.* Chapel Hill: University of North Carolina Press.

FUNDAMENTAL LAW AND THE SUPREME COURT

The DECLARATION OF INDEPENDENCE explicitly invoked the concept of natural justice—a HIGHER LAW, timeless and universal—as a defense against tyranny. By the late eighteenth century there had evolved a conviction that the essence of this fundamental law could at one stroke be captured in a document that would endure for ages to come. Of the original state constitutions several were declared in force without constituent ratification and some made no provision for amendment. By the time of the federal CONSTITUTIONAL CONVENTION OF 1787, these extreme forms of immutability had given way. Article V provided a formalized process of constitutional amendment, while Article VII conditioned adoption on ratification by state conventions. But the concept of written constitutions as the embodiment of fundamental law was central to the federal Constitution and to later state constitutions.

The issue whether fundamental law had other appropriate functions in the American constitutional scheme arose early among Justices of the Supreme Court of the United States, and remains critical at the Constitution's bicentenary. Debate opened in CALDER V. BULL (1798). The Connecticut legislature had set aside a court decree refusing to probate a will, granting a new hearing at which the will was admitted. Denied relief in the state courts, the disappointed heir appealed to the Supreme Court. Outraged at the destruction of the heir's expectancy, Justice SAMUEL CHASE declared "it is against all reason and justice, for a people to intrust a legislature with such powers, and therefore, it cannot be presumed that they have done it." In Chase's view, the fundamental law could not tolerate "a law that takes property from A and gives it to B," even in the absence of constitutional prohibition. Justice JAMES IREDELL challenged this claim of extraconstitutional power to nullify legislation, insisting that if legislation is within constitutional limits "the Court cannot pronounce it to be void, merely because it is, in their judgment, contrary to the principles of natural justice."

Iredell's logic prevailed in *Calder* but in the long run could not hold the line. Chief Justice JOHN MARSHALL hedged on the question in FLETCHER V. PECK (1810), declaring that Georgia's attempt to revoke fraudulent land grants was void "either by general principles which are common to our free institutions, or by the particular provisions of the constitution of the United States. . . ." Similarly, Justice JOSEPH STORY rested the Court's opinion in TERRETT V. TAYLOR (1815) upon several grounds, among them "the principles of natural justice" and "the spirit and letter of the [federal] constitution. . . ." LOAN ASSOCIATION V. TOPEKA (1874), although decided following ratification of the FOURTEENTH AMENDMENT, was grounded by Justice SAMUEL F. MILLER on extraconstitutional principles founded in fundamental law. The taking from A (by taxation) in aid of B (bridge manufacturer not a public utility) was stricken as an "unauthorized invasion of private right." In contrast, DRED SCOTT V. SANDFORD (1857) and HEPBURN V. GRISWOLD (1869) invalidated congressional "takings" under the Fifth Amendment's due process clause.

At the turn of the century the issue of extraconstitutional adjudication intensified with an OBITER DICTUM in ALLGEYER V. LOUISIANA (1897). With LOCHNER V. NEW YORK (1905) and ADAIR V. UNITED STATES (1908), the majority of the court opened a period in which much economic and social legislation was held unconstitutional, ostensibly under the due process clauses. However, the basis given was violation of FREEDOM OF CONTRACT, for which there was no constitutional warrant. Justice OLIVER WENDELL HOLMES, in his celebrated *Lochner* dissent, insisted that the Fourteenth Amendment, properly construed, should accord with "fundamental principles as they have been understood by the traditions of our people and our law." Yet to him that amendment correctly embraced condemnation of governmental expropriation of property from A for B's benefit, as he made clear in PENNSYLVANIA COAL CO. V. MAHON (1922). Justice LOUIS D. BRANDEIS there dissented, but he later invoked the identical principle under both due process clauses: the Fifth Amendment clause in *Wright v. Vinton Branch of Mountain Trust Bank* (1937) upholding a revised moratorium law, and the Fourteenth Amendment clause in *Thompson v. Consolidated Gas Utilities Corp.* (1937). In the latter he declared, "Our law reports present no more glaring instance of the taking of one man's property and giving it to another."

The *Lochner-Adair* venture into noninterpretive constitutionalism was rejected by a split vote in NEBBIA V. NEW YORK (1934), followed by unanimity in LINCOLN FEDERAL LABOR UNION V. NORTHWESTERN IRON & METAL CO. (1949). Yet only two years after categorical repudiation in FERGUSON V. SCRUPA (1963), the seductive appeal of the philosophy of *Lochner* and its progeny was back, this time in the service of noneconomic interests. In GRISWOLD V. CONNECTICUT (1965) the due process clause was used to invalidate an anticontraception law; in HARPER V. VIRGINIA BOARD OF ELECTIONS (1966) the EQUAL PROTECTION clause provided the basis for invalidating the POLL TAX as a condition for exercise of VOTING RIGHTS. In both cases the majority sought to ground decision in constitutional provisions, but Justice HUGO L. BLACK, unpersuaded, accused the Court of invoking "the old 'natural-law–due-process formula,'" which, he declared, "is no less dangerous when used to enforce this Court's views about personal rights than those about economic rights." ROE V. WADE (1973), insulating from governmental intervention a woman's decision to have an abortion during the first trimester of pregnancy, rested upon a doctrine of "personhood" demonstrably beyond the ambit of constitutional text, context, or structure. Reaffirmed in AKRON V. AKRON CENTER FOR REPRODUCTIVE HEALTH, INC. (1983) out of respect for STARE DECISIS, *Roe* highlights the Supreme Court's continuing temptation to give constitutional force to extraconstitutional values it finds lying in the recesses of unwritten fundamental law.

FRANK R. STRONG

Bibliography

GREY, THOMAS 1978 Origins of the Unwritten Constitution: Fundamental Law in American Revolutionary Thought. *Stanford Law Review* 30:843–893.

HAND, LEARNED 1960 *The Spirit of Liberty,* 3rd ed. New York: Knopf.

PERRY, MICHAEL 1982 *The Constitution, the Courts, and Human Rights,* chap. 4. Columbus: Ohio State University Press.

FUNDAMENTAL LAWS OF WEST NEW JERSEY

See: New Jersey, Colonial Charters of

FUNDAMENTAL ORDERS OF CONNECTICUT
(January 14, 1639)

Historians almost invariably refer to this document as a CONSTITUTION, indeed as the first written constitution of the modern world. It was very probably a statute enacted by a provisional legislative body representing the freemen of three towns meeting in Hartford. It was not, however, an ordinary statute, because it described a frame of government, though the statute lacked any explicit provision for amendment. The assembly or "general court" which enacted it, derived its powers from it but could and did alter it.

THOMAS HOOKER, the founder of Hartford and the leading divine of the colony, was probably the principal author of the document. In a 1638 sermon he had declared that the foundation of authority in both state and church was the free consent of the people expressed in a covenant or SOCIAL COMPACT; the people, according to Hooker, had power to appoint officers for their governance and "to set the bounds and limitations of the power and place unto which they call them." But the Fundamental Orders did not impose such limitations or reserve any rights that the government could not abridge.

The preamble stated that the inhabitants of the towns joined together to become "one Public State or Commonwealth" to preserve their churches and be governed according to laws made and administered by the officers described in the document. The people, "all that are admitted inhabitants," chose an assembly or "general court" which in turn annually elected a governor and magistrates, who together exercised the judicial power. The document empowered the general court to make laws, impose taxes, dispose of lands, and admit freemen and deputies from other towns. The general court, "the supreme power of the Commonwealth," consisted of the governor, magistrates, and deputies, who were guaranteed "liberty of speech," probably the progenitor of the SPEECH OR DEBATE CLAUSE in Article I, section 6, of the Constitution.

LEONARD W. LEVY

Bibliography

ANDREWS, CHARLES MCLEAN 1936 *The Colonial Period of American History.* Vol. 2, pages 94–113. New Haven, Conn.: Yale University Press.

FUNDAMENTAL RIGHTS

Inherent in the Anglo-Saxon heritage of DUE PROCESS OF LAW, the concept of fundamental rights defies facile analysis. Yet it constitutes one of those basic features of democracy that are the test of its presence. As defined by Justice FELIX FRANKFURTER, dissenting in *Solesbee v. Balkcom* (1950), it embraces "a system of rights based on moral principles so deeply embedded in the traditions and feelings of our people as to be deemed fundamental to a civilized society. . . ." The Justice whom Frankfurter succeeded on the high bench, BENJAMIN N. CARDOZO, had spoken in *Snyder v. Massachusetts* (1934) of "principles of justice so rooted in the traditions and conscience of our people as to be deemed fundamental." Three years later, in PALKO V. CONNECTICUT, Cardozo articulated fundamental rights as "implicit in the concept of ORDERED LIBERTY." Because these rights are "fundamental," they have been accorded special protection by the judiciary, which has thus viewed them as PREFERRED FREEDOMS that command particularly STRICT SCRUTINY of their infringement by legislative or executive action. In other words, to pass judicial muster, laws or ordinances affecting fundamental rights must demonstrate a more or less "compelling need," whereas those affecting lesser rights need only be clothed with a RATIONAL BASIS justifying the legislative or executive action at issue.

But which among our rights fall on the "fundamental" and which on the "nonfundamental" side of constitutional protection? The Supreme Court commenced to endeavor to draw a dichotomous line in the turn-of-the-century INSULAR CASES: on the "fundamental" side now fell such rights as those present in the FIRST AMENDMENT (religion, FREEDOMS OF SPEECH, PRESS, ASSEMBLY, and PETITION); on the other side, styled "formal rights," fell such "procedural" rights or guarantees as those embedded in the FOURTH, Fifth, SIXTH, SEVENTH, and Eighth AMENDMENTS, including, for example, TRIAL BY JURY. Justice Cardozo reconfirmed the dichotomy with his *Palko* division, adding to the roster of "fundamental" rights those of assigned counsel to INDIGENT defendants in major criminal trials and the general right to a FAIR TRIAL. He relegated other procedural rights to the nonfundamental sphere, noting that "justice would not perish" in the absence of such "formal rights" at the state level.

Cardozo's dichotomy did not apply to the federal BILL OF RIGHTS, which was wholly enforceable against federal abridgment or denial by the terms of its specific provisions. He used it instead to explain which provisions of the Bill of Rights were, and which were not, made applicable to the states by the FOURTEENTH AMENDMENT. While the "formal" rights, as he explained, do have "value and importance . . . they are not of the essence of a scheme of ordered liberty. To abolish them is not to violate a principle of justice so rooted in the traditions and conscience of our people as to be deemed fundamental. . . . Few would be so narrow as to maintain that a fair and enlightened system of justice would be impossible without them." This dichotomy stood until the 1960s when, through acceleration of the process known as INCORPORATION or "absorption," most of the enumerated safeguards in the Bill of Rights were made applicable to the states by judicial decisions. The Supreme Court's rationale for these decisions was its expanding view of the nature and reach of "fundamental" rights. In practical affect, the incorporation doctrine no longer draws an appreciable distinction between "formal" and "fundamental" rights.

Yet concurrently the WARREN COURT gave new life to the notion that certain fundamental rights should be protected by heightened judicial scrutiny of laws limiting them. This development built on Justice HARLAN FISKE STONE's famed formulation in UNITED STATES V. CAROLENE PRODUCTS CO. (1938). Voting rights and rights concerning marriage, procreation, and family relationships were identified as "fundamental" and clothed with special judicial protection. The Warren Court's other chief category of occasions for strict scrutiny of legislation—that of SUSPECT CLASSIFICATIONS—can also be seen in a similar light. If race is a suspect classification, surely the reason is that no interest in civil society is more fundamental than being treated as a full-fledged member of the community.

In effect, although all but a few of the enumerated rights in the Constitution and its amendments are now regarded as *fundamental,* and thus fully entitled to thorough judicial protection and scrutiny, the Court has embraced a hierarchical or "tiered" formulation. Some fundamental rights thus remain preferred. To what extent that arrangement will stand the test of time and experience will depend chiefly upon the judiciary's perception.

HENRY J. ABRAHAM

Bibliography

ABRAHAM, HENRY J. 1987 *Freedom and the Court: Civil Rights and Liberties in the United States,* 5th ed. New York: Oxford University Press.

CORTNER, RICHARD C. 1981 *The Supreme Court and the Second Bill of Rights.* Madison: University of Wisconsin Press.

GUNTHER, GERALD 1972 The Supreme Court: 1971 Term; In Search of Evolving Doctrines on a Changing Court: A Model for a Newer Equal Protection. *Harvard Law Review* 86:1–48.

FURMAN v. GEORGIA

See: Capital Punishment Cases, 1972

FURNEAUX, PHILIP
(1726–1783)

Philip Furneaux, an English dissenter minister, in 1770 published a volume criticizing WILLIAM BLACKSTONE's exposition of the laws of toleration. Furneaux opposed all restraints on the expression of religious or irreligious opinions. He flatly rejected the BAD TENDENCY TEST, proposing in its place punishment of overt acts only. His book of 1770 was republished in Philadelphia in 1773 under the title *The Palladium of Conscience.* Furneaux influenced THOMAS JEFFERSON and the writing of the VIRGINIA STATUTE OF RELIGIOUS FREEDOM.

LEONARD W. LEVY

GAG ORDER

"Gag order" is the press's pejorative term for a judicial order forbidding public comment, usually about a pending criminal case. Judges issue the order in an effort to prevent publicity that might make it impossible for a criminal defendant to receive a fair trial by an impartial jury. The orders came into use as a result of criticism by the American Bar Association (ABA) and others of press coverage of notorious cases such as the 1932 kidnap-murder of Charles Lindbergh's baby, the murder trial of Dr. Sam Sheppard in 1954, and the assassination of President JOHN F. KENNEDY in 1963. Each of those cases generated a torrent of publicity, much of it prejudicial to the accused's right to a fair trial.

The Supreme Court first discussed gag orders in *Sheppard v. Maxwell* (1966), when it reversed Sheppard's conviction on the ground that he had been denied DUE PROCESS OF LAW. Although the decision turned on the trial judge's failure to control "the carnival atmosphere at trial" rather than prejudicial pretrial publicity, the Court went out of its way to suggest that the judge "should have made some effort to control the release of leads, information, and gossip to the press by police officers, witnesses, and the counsel for both sides."

This *obiter dictum* finally made pretrial publicity a constitutional, rather than merely ethical, issue. In 1968 an ABA committee promulgated new "Standards on Fair Trial and Free Press," endorsing prohibitions against release of information by lawyers and law enforcement officers. Gag orders then came into widespread use, usually over the vehement opposition of the press.

The ABA report distinguished between gag orders directed at lawyers and other trial participants and those directed at the press itself. It did not endorse the latter, fearing that restrictions on the press would violate the FIRST AMENDMENT. This distinction is still widely observed, even though gag orders against lawyers operate as prior restraints on speech just as surely as those against the press.

The constitutionality of gag orders reached the Supreme Court in NEBRASKA PRESS ASSOCIATION V. STUART (1976). In a multiple murder case a state trial judge had forbidden the local press to publish confessions or "other information strongly implicative of the accused as the perpetrator of the slayings." The Supreme Court treated the order as a prior restraint on publication, and held it unconstitutional because there was no showing that less drastic alternatives, such as postponement or sequestration of jurors, would have been insufficient to protect the defendant's right to a fair trial. The Court also doubted the efficacy of the order, because of difficulties in controlling publicity by media beyond the trial judge's jurisdiction and by word of mouth within the community.

The *Stuart* opinion stopped short of saying that all gag orders against the press are unconstitutional, but three members of the Court would have said so, and two others doubted that such orders could ever be justified. Since *Stuart,* gag orders against the press have been rare. The Court reserved judgment on orders against trial participants, however, and these continue to be issued with some frequency. The lower courts generally have upheld narrowly drawn restrictions against lawyers and defendants when judges have determined that they are necessary to prevent a "reasonable likelihood" or "a serious and imminent threat" of interference with a fair trial.

DAVID A. ANDERSON

(SEE ALSO: *Free Press/Fair Trial.*)

Bibliography

BARRON, JEROME A. and DIENES, C. THOMAS 1979 *Handbook of Free Speech and Free Press.* Boston: Little, Brown.

HALLAM, OSCAR 1940 Some Object Lessons on Publicity in Criminal Trials. *Minnesota Law Review* 24:454–508.

PORTMAN, SHELDON 1977 The Defense of Fair Trial from *Sheppard* to *Nebraska Press Association:* Benign Neglect to Affirmative Action and Beyond. *Stanford Law Review* 29:393–410.

GAG RULE

See: Civil Liberties and the Slavery Controversy; Freedom of Petition; Slavery and the Constitution

GALLAGHER v. CROWN KOSHER SUPER MARKET

See: Sunday Closing Laws

GALLATIN, ALBERT (1761–1849)

Born in Geneva, Switzerland, Albert Gallatin came to America in 1780 and settled in western Pennsylvania. He opposed RATIFICATION OF THE CONSTITUTION because he thought the union too consolidated and the presidency too monarchial. In 1788–1789, as a delegate to the Pennsylvania state CONSTITUTIONAL CONVENTION, Gallatin spoke out for virtually universal suffrage and for popular election of United States senators.

Gallatin served three terms in the Pennsylvania Assembly (1790–1792), where he was leader of the Republican minority. He there advocated public education and INTERNAL IMPROVEMENTS. In 1792 he was secretary of a convention called to denounce ALEXANDER HAMILTON's federal whiskey excise, and he drafted a petition to Congress against the excise; but two years later he publicly opposed the violence of the WHISKEY REBELLION.

Elected to the United States Senate in 1793, Gallatin was denied his seat on the grounds that he had not been a citizen for the requisite nine years. From 1795 until 1801 he served in the House of Representatives, the last four years as Republican floor leader; he rigorously opposed the ALIEN AND SEDITION ACTS.

As secretary of the treasury under Presidents THOMAS JEFFERSON and JAMES MADISON (1801–1814) Gallatin attempted to reorganize public finance on a Republican basis by abolishing both the national debt and all internal taxes and supporting the government by revenue from the tariff and sale of public lands. That design was ultimately frustrated by the War of 1812. During his tenure at the Treasury, Gallatin introduced more efficient statistical accountability and began the practice of issuing annual reports to Congress of revenues and expenditures.

In 1814 Gallatin helped negotiate peace with Great Britain. He continued his diplomatic career as minister to France (1816–1823) and to Britain (1826–1827). He later became a bank president and devoted his leisure to the study of American Indian languages.

DENNIS J. MAHONEY

GALLOWAY, JOSEPH (1731–1803)

A conservative political leader, Joseph Galloway long sought compromise with England. At the First Continental Congress (1774) he proposed establishment of an "inferior and distinct" branch of Parliament in America. A president-general, chosen by the king, would preside over a "grand council," execute its acts (to which he must assent), and direct all matters concerning more than one colony. Approval by both this council and Parliament would be required for all "general acts," but each colony would retain its own government. Galloway's plan lost by one vote. Although he opposed a parliamentary tax and defended the colonies' right to govern themselves, he accepted parliamentary supremacy and understood English attempts to have the colonies share in the cost of their defense. Galloway's loyalism doomed him to exile after Philadelphia's capture by American forces in 1778.

DAVID GORDON

Bibliography

WERNER, RAYMOND C. 1931 Joseph Galloway. In *Dictionary of American Biography.* New York: Scribner's.

GANNETT CO., INC. v. DEPASQUALE
443 U.S. 368 (1978)

In *Gannett* the trial judge excluded the public, including the press, from a pretrial hearing involving evidence of an involuntary confession in a highly publicized murder case. The Supreme Court rejected arguments that the Sixth Amendment provided a constitutional public right to attend criminal trials. Reasoning that the constitutional guarantee of a public trial is designed to benefit the defendant, not the public, the Court concluded that where the litigants agree to close a pretrial proceeding to protect the defendant's right to a FAIR TRIAL, the Constitution does not require that it remain open to the public. The Court declined to address the corollary issue whether the FIRST AMENDMENT created a right of access to the press to attend criminal trials—a question later answered affirmatively in RICHMOND NEWSPAPERS, INC. V. VIRGINIA (1980).

Justice LEWIS F. POWELL, concurring, conceded that the press had an interest, protected by the First Amendment, in being present at the pretrial hearing, but said that this interest should be balanced against the defendant's right to a fair trial. The order excluding the press from attending the pretrial hearing in *Gannett* was distinguished from the GAG ORDER in NEBRASKA PRESS ASSOCIATION V. STUART (1976) because the press was merely excluded from one source of information; it was not told what it might or might not publish.

Justice HARRY A. BLACKMUN, joined by Justices WILLIAM J. BRENNAN, BYRON R. WHITE, and THURGOOD MARSHALL, also framed the issue as one of access to the judicial proceeding, not one of prior restraint on the press. Blackmun, upon a lengthy historical examination, concluded that the criminally accused did not have a right to compel a private pretrial proceeding or trial. Only in certain circumstances, with appropriate procedural safeguards, might a court give effect to the accused's attempts to waive the right to a public trial.

KIM MCLANE WARDLAW

(SEE ALSO: *Free Press/Fair Trial.*)

GARCIA v. SAN ANTONIO METROPOLITAN TRANSIT AUTHORITY
469 U.S. (1985)

In NATIONAL LEAGUE OF CITIES V. USERY (1976) a 5–4 majority of the Supreme Court sought to establish a new doctrinal foundation for the concept of STATES' RIGHTS. Overruling its eight-year-old PRECEDENT in *Maryland v. Wirtz* (1968), the Court held unconstitutional the application of the wage and hour provisions of the federal FAIR LABOR STANDARDS ACT to state and local government employees in areas of "traditional governmental functions" such as police and fire protection. After eight more years, *Garcia* followed *Wirtz* and overruled *Usery*—again by 5–4 vote. Justice HARRY A. BLACKMUN, whose change of vote produced this second about-face, wrote the OPINION OF THE COURT.

Lower court decisions following *Usery,* said Justice Blackmun, had failed to establish any principle for determining which governmental functions were "traditional" and essential to state sovereignty, and thus immune from impairment by congressional regulations. Justice Blackmun did not mention his own contribution to the confusion, first in his *Usery* concurrence, which suggested that the reach of Congress's power depended on the importance of the national interests at stake, and later in his votes to uphold congressional power in cases only doubtfully distinguishable from *Usery,* such as *Federal Regulatory Commission v. Mississippi* (1982) and EQUAL EMPLOYMENT OPPORTUNITY COMMISSION V. WYOMING (1983). The reasoning in those opinions—heatedly disputed by the four *Garcia* dissenters—had sapped *Usery*'s strength as a precedent by making the states pass through a doctrinal labyrinth before *Usery* could be applied.

The aspect of the *Garcia* opinion that drew the most fire, from within the Court and from the outside, was its announcement of the Court's virtual abdication from JUDICIAL REVIEW of acts of Congress challenged as invasions of state SOVEREIGNTY. The principal remedy for such potential abuses of congressional power, said Justice Blackmun, is not judicial but political. The constitutional structure assures the states a significant role in the selection of the national government; the influence of the states was demonstrated in the federal government's financial aid to the states and in the numerous exemptions for state activities provided in congressional regulations. The Court's abdication was not complete; Justice Blackmun acknowledged that some "affirmative limits . . . on federal action affecting the States" may remain. Yet he explicitly left to another day the specification of what those limits might be.

Justice LEWIS F. POWELL wrote the main opinion for the four dissenters. He began with a lament for the demise of STARE DECISIS—which he had not mourned when *Usery* overruled *Wirtz.* The *Usery* principle had been "reiterated consistently over the past eight years," he said—not mentioning that those same opinions uniformly had sustained congressional regulations against challenges founded on *Usery.* Justice Powell argued that the majority had abandoned the FEDERALISM envisioned by the Framers, leaving the states' role to "the grace of elected federal officials." In any event, he contended, the "political safeguards of federalism" are not what they used to be. Congressional regulatory techniques have changed, increasingly displacing or commandeering the states' sovereign functions. Furthermore, although the people of the states are represented in the federal government, the state governments as institutions are apt to have little influence on national decision making, in comparison with nationwide interest groups.

Some of the dissenters left no doubt that they expect the *Usery* principle to return when members of the *Garcia* majority are replaced by new Justices more attuned to the symbolism of states' rights. But symbolism may be all that is left of that once vital principle, whatever the future may hold for the *Garcia* precedent. First, Congress can dragoon the state into its regulatory schemes as it did in HODEL V. VIRGINIA SURFACE MINING AND RECLAMATION ASSOCIATION (1981): regulating private conduct directly, but allowing a state to opt out of the federal regulation by adopting its own law under federal guidelines. Furthermore, if Congress wants to buy state sovereignty, it will find willing sellers. By placing conditions on FEDERAL GRANTS-IN-AID—which now amount to about one-fifth of state budgets—Congress can achieve through the spending power virtually anything it might achieve by direct regulation. Even if *Garcia* should be overruled and *Usery* reinstated, Congress can offer subsidies that are vital to local transit authorities or police departments, conditioned on promises to pay transit and police employees the federal minimum wage. The passion of the Justices on both sides may indicate that in these cases the symbolism is what counts.

KENNETH L. KARST

Bibliography

FIELD, MARTHA A. 1985 Garcia v. San Antonio Metropolitan Transit Authority: The Demise of a Misguided Doctrine. *Harvard Law Review* 99:84–118.

VAN ALSTYNE, WILLIAM W. 1985 The Second Death of Federalism. *Michigan Law Review* 83:1709–1733.

GARFIELD, JAMES A. (1831–1881)

A Civil War general, James Abram Garfield served in Congress from 1863 until 1881, when he became President of the United States. In Congress Garfield was a skilled parliamentarian and self-taught expert on finance. After 1868 he was one of the most powerful Republicans in Congress, and served as minority leader from 1876 until 1880. In a period of pervasive corruption Garfield remained relatively untainted. In 1876 he helped frame the legislation that led to the COMPROMISE OF 1877 that settled the disputed presidential election. He served on the electoral commission, supporting President Rutherford B. Hayes on every issue. In 1880 the Ohio legislature chose him for the United States Senate, for a term beginning in 1881. However, that summer he became a compromise candidate for the presidency, after the Republican convention deadlocked. As President, Garfield attempted to root out corruption in the Post Office Department and the notorious New York customs house. Garfield's insistence that he, as President, should make all appointments, regardless of longstanding notions of senatorial privilege, led ROSCOE CONKLING of New York to resign from the Senate. In July 1881 Garfield was shot and killed by a disappointed office seeker who shouted that he was a party "stalwart" and that now CHESTER A. ARTHUR would be President. In the wake of this tragedy Arthur continued Garfield's investigation of the Post Office and secured the passage of the first civil service reform law, the PENDLETON ACT.

PAUL FINKELMAN

Bibliography

PESKIN, ALAN 1978 *Garfield.* Kent, Ohio: Kent State University Press.

GARLAND, AUGUSTUS H. (1832–1899)

Augustus Hill Garland, a Whig lawyer, opposed SECESSION in 1861 but represented Arkansas in the Confederate Congress throughout the Civil War. He won readmission to the federal bar in *Ex parte Garland* (1867), one of the TEST OATH CASES; but the same year the United States Senate, to which he had been elected, denied him his seat. He served as governor of Arkansas (1874–1876) and United States senator (1877–1885) before becoming President GROVER CLEVELAND's attorney general (1885–1889). He was later a prominent lawyer practicing in Washington, D.C. He was co-author of a treatise on federal court JURISDICTION.

DENNIS J. MAHONEY

GARLAND, EX PARTE

See: Test Oath Cases

GARRISON, WILLIAM LLOYD (1805–1879)

William Lloyd Garrison edited America's leading abolitionist newspaper, *The Liberator* (1831–1865), and helped found the New England Anti-Slavery Society (1831) and the American Anti-Slavery Society (1833; president, 1843–1865). Garrison believed pacifism, nonresistance, and moral suasion could end slavery. He argued that the Constitution supported slavery and was "a covenant with death and an agreement with Hell." Thus, he refused to vote or voluntarily support civil government, and after 1843 Garrison and his followers advocated a peaceful dissolution of the Union under the slogan "No Union with Slaveholders." More moderate abolitionists rejected Garrison's analysis of the Constitution, his opposition to antislavery political candidates and parties, and his extreme tactics, such as publicly burning the Constitution and declaring "So perish all compromises with tyranny." Despite his disunionist beliefs, he ultimately gave tacit support to ABRAHAM LINCOLN and the Union during the Civil War.

PAUL FINKELMAN

Bibliography

THOMAS, JOHN L. 1963 *The Liberator.* Boston: Little, Brown.

GARRITY v. NEW JERSEY 385 U.S. 493 (1967)

Justice WILLIAM O. DOUGLAS, for a 6–3 majority, ruled that coercion had tainted confessions exacted from police officers suspected of fixing traffic tickets, when they were made to choose between exercising their RIGHT AGAINST SELF-INCRIMINATION and retaining their jobs. The dissenters argued that the state could require police officers to assist in detecting unlawful activities, that the officers' confessions were not involuntary, and that their constitutional right was not burdened.

LEONARD W. LEVY

GAULT, IN RE 387 U.S. 1 (1967)

In re Gault is the Supreme Court's most important landmark concerning juveniles, both because of its specific requirements for delinquency proceedings and because of its unequivocal declaration of the broad principle that young persons, as individuals, have constitutional rights of their own. Rejecting the informality that had long characterized state juvenile courts, the Supreme Court held that DUE PROCESS OF LAW required four procedural safeguards in the adjudicatory (or guilt-determining) phase of delinquency proceedings: adequate written NOTICE to the juvenile and his parents of the specific charges; notification of the RIGHT TO COUNSEL, with appointed counsel for those who lack the means to retain a lawyer; the right of CONFRONTATION and cross-examination of witnesses; and the notification of the RIGHT AGAINST SELF-INCRIMINATION. For the first time the Supreme Court declared boldly, in a seminal opinion by Justice ABE FORTAS, that "whatever may be their precise impact, neither the FOURTEENTH AMENDMENT nor the BILL OF RIGHTS is for adults alone."

The facts of the case dramatically suggested the risks of procedural informality and "unbridled discretion," which the Court saw as a poor substitute for "principle and procedure." Fifteen-year-old Gerald Gault was found to be a delinquent and was committed for up to six years to the Arizona Industrial School for an offense that would have subjected an adult to a small fine and no more than two months' imprisonment. Neither Gerald nor his parents were ever served with a petition that disclosed the factual basis of the juvenile court proceedings. It was claimed that Gerald and a friend had made an obscene telephone call to a neighbor who never appeared in the proceedings. Although the judge subsequently reported that Gerald had made some sort of admission to him, no transcript was made of what was said at either of Gerald's two appearances before the judge, nor was Gerald offered counsel.

Although a few states had anticipated the Court's rulings in *Gault* by adopting new juvenile justice acts that provided greater safeguards, procedural informality had characterized most juvenile courts since their creation around 1900. This was typically justified on two interrelated grounds. First, the goal of JUVENILE PROCEEDINGS was said to be treatment and rehabilitation, not punishment or deterrence. Second, investigation, diagnosis, and treatment required individualized determinations of what was best for each particular child. Legalistic formalities were seen as inconsistent and counterproductive in a benevolent and paternalistic institution committed to the rehabilitative ideal. State courts had refused to impose safeguards that "restrict the state when it seeks to deprive a person of his liberty," typically with conclusory statements that minors had no interest in liberty (because they would be subject in all events to parental control) or that delinquency proceedings were civil, rather than criminal, because their purpose was not punitive.

Gault rejected these traditional justifications. Pointing to various empirical studies, the *Gault* majority challenged the rehabilitative effectiveness of the juvenile justice system by suggesting that juvenile crime had increased since the establishment of the juvenile courts; questioned the value of procedural informality as a means to shape desirable attitudes about justice in the young people caught up by the system; and disparaged the significance, in terms of loss of liberty, of the difference between detention in a "home" or "school" after a finding of delinquency and incarceration after conviction of a crime. The strength of much of the social science evidence cited by the Court has been subsequently challenged, but the Court's willingness to attach substantial weight to the interest of a young person in avoiding the serious practical consequences of an erroneous determination of delinquency is certainly justified.

The Court did not suggest in *Gault* or in its subsequent decisions that the Constitution requires the state to treat a juvenile accused of delinquency in all respects like an adult accused of a similar act. The Court has extended other procedural safeguards to juveniles in delinquency proceedings—in IN RE WINSHIP (1970) it required proof beyond a REASONABLE DOUBT, for example, and in *Breed v. Jones* (1975) it held that the prohibition against DOUBLE JEOPARDY applied—but it has refused, as in MCKEIVER V. PENNSYLVANIA (1971), to require TRIAL BY JURY in delinquency proceedings. Although the traditional goals of the juvenile courts do not justify the absence of certain safeguards, *Gault* and its progeny suggest that the Constitution does not require abolition of the separate juvenile court system with some distinctive procedural features. Nor does *Gault* require the states to impose identical sanctions on minors and adults after a determination that a criminal statute has been violated. Indeed, by emphasizing that the procedural requirements extended only to the adjudicatory phase, and not to the dispositional phase, of delinquency proceedings, the Court in *Gault* argued that its decision did not threaten the emphasis juvenile courts have traditionally claimed to place on individualized treatment and rehabilitation.

ROBERT H. MNOOKIN

(SEE ALSO: *Children's Rights.*)

Bibliography

STAPLETON, W. VAUGHAN and TEITELBAUM, LEE E. 1972 *In Defense of Youth: A Study of the Role of Counsel in American Juvenile Courts.* New York: Russell Sage Foundation.

GELBARD v. UNITED STATES
408 U.S. 41 (1972)

The Supreme Court held that a witness who refuses to answer a GRAND JURY question derived from illegal electronic surveillance may not be held in CONTEMPT. Title III of the OMNIBUS CRIME CONTROL AND SAFE STREETS ACT excludes from grand jury proceedings any EVIDENCE obtained from illegal surveillance and a witness need not answer a question based on such information.

HERMAN SCHWARTZ

GELPCKE v. DUBUQUE
1 Wallace 175 (1864)

In his introduction to the 1864 reports of the Supreme Court, John Wallace, the Supreme Court reporter, remarked that in *Gelpcke* the Court imposed "high moral duties . . . upon a whole community seeking apparently to violate them." The community was Dubuque, Iowa, which attempted to enhance its property values by issuing municipal bonds, backed by local taxes, to promote railroad development that would put Dubuque on the map. Dubuque acted on authority granted by the Iowa legislature, although the state constitution prevented the legislature from investing in private railroads, as Dubuque did, and from increasing the state's indebtedness as much as the legislature authorized the city to increase its indebtedness. Responding to railroad shenanigans and the objections of taxpayers, Dubuque repudiated its debt, and the Iowa Supreme Court held that the legislature had violated the state constitution when authorizing Dubuque to issue the bonds.

Bondholders, seeking federal relief against default, persuaded the Supreme Court to rule that a contract once valid under state law cannot have its validity or obligation impaired by the subsequent action of a state court. Justice NOAH H. SWAYNE, speaking for all but Justice SAMUEL F. MILLER, who dissented, refused to accept the state supreme court's ruling on a matter of state constitutional law. Swayne took the high ground by declaring, "We shall never immolate truth, justice, and the law, because a state tribunal has erected the altar and decreed the sacrifice." However, the ground of decision was not clear, and the Supreme Court construed a state judicial decision as a "law," contrary to conventional usage.

Justice OLIVER WENDELL HOLMES later remarked that the decision in *Gelpcke* took the Court a good while to explain. In fact, the explanation subsequently provided by the Court was that the state judicial decision had violated the CONTRACT CLAUSE. However construed, *Gelpcke* was a means of the Supreme Court's expansion of its JURISDICTION, either under the doctrine of SWIFT v. TYSON (1842) or under the contract clause, which had previously applied only to statutes, not judicial decisions. And the Court established a basis for curbing municipal repudiation of debts and protecting municipal bondholders.

LEONARD W. LEVY

GENDER DISCRIMINATION

See: Sex Discrimination

GENERAL LAWS AND LIBERTIES OF MASSACHUSETTS

See: Massachusetts General Laws and Liberties

GENERAL WARRANT

General warrants command either apprehension for unstated causes or the arrest, search, or seizure of unspecified persons, places, or objects. Since the *Five Knights Case* (1628) English courts have consistently disallowed the first category of warrant, although its use survived a century later. The general warrant of the second sort, which allowed its bearer to search wherever or seize whomever or whatever he wished, was more common. It existed by the early fourteenth century and found ever growing applications. The Star Chamber and "High Commission" of the Tudor-Stuart period used such warrants vigorously to suffocate political and religious dissent. By the middle of the eighteenth century, general warrants were or had also been used to combat vagrancy, regulate publications, impress persons into the army and navy, pursue felons, collect taxes, and find stolen merchandise. A close relative, the WRIT OF ASSISTANCE, allowed customs officers to search all houses in which they suspected concealed contraband.

Beginning with the WILKES CASES (1763–1770), British courts undermined the use of general SEARCH WARRANTS by secretaries of state. Although they were widely used in colonial and revolutionary America, eight state constitutions of 1776–1784 forbade them, as does the FOURTH AMENDMENT to the federal Constitution.

WILLIAM CUDDIHY

Bibliography

CUDDIHY, WILLIAM and HARDY, B. CARMON 1980 A Man's House Was Not His Castle: Origins of the Fourth Amendment to the United States Constitution. *William and Mary Quarterly* 37:371–400.

GENERAL WELFARE CLAUSE

With no enforceable power to tax under the ARTICLES OF CONFEDERATION, Congress "requisitioned" funds from the states each of which then decided how and whether to raise its share of the confederation's needs. Uneven responses brought resentment among the states and frequent frustration of congressional policies. Dissatisfaction with this system was a leading cause of the failure of the Articles. As a remedy, the CONSTITUTIONAL CONVENTION proposed to empower the new Congress to "lay and collect Taxes, Duties, IMPOSTS, and EXCISES, to pay the Debt and provide for the common Defense and general welfare of the United States." Some Anti-Federalists said this language defeated the principle of ENUMERATED POWERS because it could be read to authorize action for the common defense and general welfare by any legislative means whatever. JAMES MADISON disclaimed this interpretation in THE FEDERALIST #41, saying that the general welfare clause conferred power to tax and spend only for purposes indicated by the enumerated powers that followed in Article

I, section 8. Congress could tax and spend for armies and navies, for example, but not for purposes reserved to the states.

Later, during conflicts with the Jeffersonians over national economic policy, ALEXANDER HAMILTON argued that the enumerated powers did not exhaust the concept of "the general welfare" and that Congress could tax and spend for purposes beyond the enumerated powers, so long as it acted in the general interest. Constitutional history has thus produced three theories of the general welfare clause: as the Anti-Federalists charged, that Congress could claim unrestricted power to act in the general interest; that Congress could tax and spend only for purposes indicated by the enumerated powers, as Madison claimed; and that Congress could tax and spend for purposes beyond the enumerated powers, as Hamilton claimed. In OBITER DICTUM, the Supreme Court adopted the Hamiltonian theory in UNITED STATES V. BUTLER (1936).

In *Butler,* the court voided a federal tax as part of an unconstitutional scheme to use the spending power to invade powers reserved to the states. After first declaring that Congress could tax and spend for purposes beyond the enumerated powers, the Court then ignored the Hamiltonian theory by holding the act unconstitutional as an attempt to invade an area (agricultural production) beyond Congress's enumerated powers. Later decisions that were friendlier to the New Deal effectively reversed this holding and rescued the Hamiltonian theory. The Court enlarged the scope of the COMMERCE CLAUSE by affirming Congress's authority directly to regulate any social or economic activity with an "effect" upon INTERSTATE COMMERCE, regardless of Congress's motives relative to the reserved powers of the states. (See UNITED STATES V. DARBY LUMBER COMPANY, 1941; IMPLIED POWERS.) In SONZINSKY V. UNITED STATES (1937) the Court refused to scrutinize Congress's motives for taxing socially harmful activities so long as the tax produced some revenue. And in STEWARD MACHINE COMPANY V. DAVIS (1937) the Court upheld the taxing scheme that was the foundation of the Social Security system, irrespective of any other enumerated power of Congress.

Such decisions eliminated doubts about the Court's acceptance of the Hamiltonian theory, and the era following World War II saw a great increase in federal regulatory taxes and subsidies conditioned on conformity with policies (such as racial integration) which some state and local governments otherwise would more actively have opposed. The Hamiltonian theory has also supported federal regulatory taxes on narcotics, gambling, and other morally injurious practices. (See UNITED STATES V. KAHRIGER, 1953.) No development has had a more corrosive effect on the old idea that some concerns lay beyond the reach of Congress. Given the broad regulatory uses of the TAXING AND SPENDING POWERS, the triumph of Hamilton's theory vindicated the Anti-Federalists' predictions of what the general welfare clause eventually would become.

SOTIRIOS A. BARBER

(SEE ALSO: *National Police Power.*)

Bibliography

BARBER, SOTIRIOS A. 1984 *On What the Constitution Means.* Baltimore: Johns Hopkins University Press.

GEORGIA v. STANTON

See: *Mississippi v. Johnson*

GERENDE v. BOARD OF SUPERVISORS OF ELECTIONS 341 U.S. 56 (1951)

A Maryland statute barred from public employment or office anyone who belonged to a "subversive" organization. In this unanimous PER CURIAM OPINION, the VINSON COURT sustained the law upon an understanding that the term "subversive" was limited to those somehow engaged in the attempt to overthrow the government by force or violence. The Court assumed that an affidavit negating such activity would satisfy the state's LOYALTY OATH required of those running for office.

MICHAEL E. PARRISH

GERRY, ELBRIDGE (1744–1814)

A Massachusetts merchant, Elbridge Gerry was particularly active in Revolutionary politics and served as a delegate to the Second Continental Congress. He signed the DECLARATION OF INDEPENDENCE as an early and vigorous supporter of separation from a government and people that he believed had become "corrupt and totally destitute of Virtue."

Gerry devoted most of his life to public service. He represented Massachusetts in Congress from 1779 to 1785, signing the ARTICLES OF CONFEDERATION. As a Massachusetts delegate to the CONSTITUTIONAL

CONVENTION OF 1787, Gerry was, at the outset, a moderate nationalist who favored a strong central government although emphasizing the need for certain "federal features." Gerry opposed democracy—"the evils we experience flow from the excess of democracy"—and he often supported his own business interests. Indeed, he early recognized the need for congressional power "competent to the protection of" FOREIGN COMMERCE in order for Congress to "command reciprocal advantages in trade." A firm believer in republicanism, Gerry insisted on the need for a SEPARATION OF POWERS and the inclusion of additional checks on the national government. He chaired the committee that formulated the GREAT COMPROMISE and helped secure its adoption. The absence of a BILL OF RIGHTS, however, and the concentration of power in the federal government led Gerry to oppose RATIFICATION OF THE CONSTITUTION.

Elected to Congress in 1789, he served for four years as a strong supporter of ALEXANDER HAMILTON's financial program. Gerry retired from Congress in 1793 and was elected Republican governor of Massachusetts in 1810 and 1811. He so opposed the idea of legitimate opposition that his second term saw the passage of a bill radically redistricting the state to assure the Republicans greater representation in the state legislature than their actual strength justified. This political technique was satirized in a cartoon showing one oddly shaped district in the form of a salamander, hence the name GERRYMANDER. JAMES MADISON selected Gerry as his vice-presidential running mate in 1812, and until his death in 1814 Gerry championed Madison's administration.

DAVID GORDON

Bibliography

BILLIAS, GEORGE A. 1976 *Elbridge Gerry, Founding Father and Republican Statesman.* New York: McGraw-Hill.

GERRYMANDER

A gerrymander is a political district drawn to advantage some and disadvantage others: candidates, parties, or interest groups. The name comes from a particularly spectacular partisan apportionment engineered by ELBRIDGE GERRY in 1812. Technically, any winner-take-all district can be called a gerrymander, for district lines inevitably favor some against others. But common usage limits the term to districts deemed unnatural in form or unfair in intent or effect. The Supreme Court boldly and unanimously attacked a blatant racial gerrymander in GOMILLION V. LIGHTFOOT (1960), but it has been almost uniformly acquiescent since then.

Gomillion voided an "uncouth, 28-sided figure" surgically excluding almost all of the blacks in Tuskegee, Alabama, from voting in the city while retaining every white. It cleared the way for BAKER V. CARR (1962) and the REAPPORTIONMENT revolution. But, apart from a few cases of municipal expansion challenged under the VOTING RIGHTS ACT OF 1965, the Court has never since been able or willing to find "cognizable discrimination" in gerrymandering cases.

The leading cases, *Wright v. Rockefeller* (1964) and UNITED JEWISH ORGANIZATIONS V. CAREY (1977), both involved packing of New York black and Puerto Rican voters into what dissenting Justice WILLIAM O. DOUGLAS (in *Wright*) called a "racial borough." Its packed nonwhite majority, if unpacked and spread to adjacent districts, might have formed two or three nonwhite majorities.

But it is difficult to tell clearly what packing does to a group's power, because "wasted" surplus votes in good years can be badly needed in bad years. In *Wright* the black plaintiffs wanted more "effective" black votes through dispersion, while the black incumbent, siding with the defendants, argued for strength through concentration: better one safe seat than two marginal ones. The baffled Court claimed it could find "no evidence of racial discrimination" in the obvious gerrymander, but the Court's real lack was simple rules for making sense of the evidence it had.

It is also impossible to equalize everyone's effective REPRESENTATION, short of ordering proportional representation, which could be a cure worse than the disease. In *UJO v. Carey* the United States attorney general had found the ethnically packed district discriminatory under the Voting Rights Act and ordered the state to create two more districts with nonwhite majority quotas. To do so, the state had to dismember a Hasidic Jewish community, which objected to the explicit RACIAL QUOTAS as a violation of the FOURTEENTH and FIFTEENTH AMENDMENTS. But the Court, ignoring the constitutional attack, argued that the racial quotas served the purposes of the Voting Rights Act by enhancing the black vote and did not involve "cognizable discrimination" against the Jews, who, as "whites in Kings County," might be submerged in their own districts but would have vicarious "fair representation" by white representatives of other districts.

Only in a few cases under the Voting Rights Act, with its heavy statutory burden on the state to prove nondiscrimination, has the Court intervened against racial gerrymandering since *Gomillion.* In constitutional terms, partisan and incumbent-favoring gerrymanders are deemed tolerable, perhaps because political districting is indeed a "mathematical quagmire" ill-suited for resolution with simple rules. The Court all but announced its retreat in *Gaffney v. Cummings* (1973).

Gerrymandering, largely unregulated, has flourished in reapportionment years. Theoretically, it could give the dominant party a manifold advantage over a numerically equal rival. In practice, it gives a thirty to forty percent advantage to the dominant party in seats per vote, often rewarding a minority of votes with a majority of seats.

Once it was hoped that objective standards—of compactness, contiguity, or competitiveness—or impartial judges or commissioners would curb gerrymandering. But standards have been largely ineffectual and judges and commissioners overwhelmingly partisan. A few states have limited partisan gerrymanders with bipartisan commissions, and roughly half the states have found protection through the happenstance of divided, two-party control of the elected branches. Ironically, despite *Gomillion* and the reapportionment revolution, the chief protection against gerrymandering has not come from courts but from the "weak" CHECKS AND BALANCES—FEDERALISM, SEPARATION OF POWERS, and multiplication of competing factions—that court intervention was supposed to supplant.

WARD E. Y. ELLIOTT

Bibliography

DIXON, ROBERT G. 1968 *Democratic Representation: Reapportionment in Law and Politics.* New York: Oxford University Press.

ELLIOTT, WARD E. Y. 1975 *The Rise of Guardian Democracy: The Supreme Court's Role in Voting Rights Disputes, 1845–1969.* Cambridge, Mass.: Harvard University Press.

SICKELS, ROBERT J. 1966 "Dragons, Bacon Strips, and Dumbbells—Who's Afraid of Reapportionment?" *Yale Law Journal* 75:1300–1308.

GERTZ *v.* ROBERT WELCH, INC.
418 U.S. 323 (1974)

In this major case on LIBEL AND THE FIRST AMENDMENT, the Supreme Court in an opinion by Justice LEWIS F. POWELL held, 5–4, that the rule of NEW YORK TIMES V. SULLIVAN (1964) did not apply when the party seeking damages for libel is not a public official or a public figure. *New York Times* had applied the rule of "actual malice": the First Amendment bars a public official from recovering damages for a defamatory falsehood relating to his conduct in office unless he proves that the publisher or broadcaster made the statement knowing it to be false or "with reckless disregard of whether it was false or not." The Court had extended that rule in 1967 to PUBLIC FIGURES. In *Rosenbloom v. Metromedia, Inc.* (1971) a plurality ruled that if the defamation concerned a public issue the actual malice rule extended also to private individuals, who were not public figures. In *Gertz* the Court, abandoning that rule, held that a private plaintiff had to prove actual malice only if seeking punitive damages; the FIRST AMENDMENT did not require him to produce such proof merely to recover actual damages for injury to reputation.

Powell reasoned that public officers and public figures had a far greater opportunity to counteract false statements than private persons. Moreover, an official or a candidate for public office knowingly exposes himself to close public scrutiny and criticism, just as public figures knowingly invite attention and comment. The communications media cannot, however, assume that private persons similarly expose themselves to defamation. Powell declared that they "are not only more vulnerable to injury than public officials and public figures; they are also more deserving of recovery." Their only effective redress is resort to a state's libel laws. So long as a state does not permit the press or a broadcaster to be held liable without fault and applies the actual malice rule to requests for punitive damages, the Court held that the First Amendment requires a "less demanding showing than that required by *New York Times*" and that the states may decide for themselves the appropriate standard of liability for media defendants who defame private persons.

Each of the dissenting Justices wrote a separate opinion. The dissents covered a wide spectrum from greater concern for the defamed party to alarm about the majority's supposedly constrictive interpretation of the First Amendment. Chief Justice WARREN E. BURGER worried that the party libeled in this case was a lawyer who ought not to be invidiously identified with his client. Justice WILLIAM O. DOUGLAS thought all libel laws to be unconstitutional. Justice WILLIAM J. BRENNAN preferred the actual malice test to be applied to private individuals in matters of public concern. Justice BYRON R. WHITE, opposing the Court's restriction of the COMMON LAW of libels, condemned the nationalization of so large a part of libel law.

LEONARD W. LEVY

GIBBONS v. OGDEN
9 Wheaton 1 (1824)

Chief Justice JOHN MARSHALL's great disquisition on the COMMERCE CLAUSE in this case is the most influential in our history. *Gibbons* liberated the steamship business and much of American INTERSTATE COMMERCE from the grip of state-created monopolies. More important, Marshall laid the doctrinal basis for the national regulation of the economy that occurred generations later, though at the time his opinion buttressed laissez-faire. He composed that opinion as if statecraft in the interpretation of a constitutional clause could decide whether the United States remained just a federal union or became a nation. The New York act, which the Court voided in *Gibbons*, had closed the ports of the state to steamships not owned or licensed by a monopoly chartered by the state. Other states retaliated in kind. The attorney general of the United States told the *Gibbons* Court that the country faced a commercial "civil war."

The decision produced immediate and dramatic results. Within two weeks, a newspaper jubilantly reported: "Yesterday the Steamboat *United States*, Capt. Bunker, from New Haven, entered New York in triumph, with streamers flying, and a large company of passengers exulting in the decision of the United States Supreme Court against the New York monopoly. She fired a salute which was loudly returned by huzzas from the wharves." Senator MARTIN VAN BUREN (Democrat, New York), who had recently advocated curbing the Court, declared that even those states whose laws had been nullified, including his own, "have submitted to their fate," and the Court now justly attracted "idolatry," its Chief respected as "the ablest Judge now sitting upon any judicial bench in the world." For a Court that had been under vitriolic congressional and state attack, *Gibbons* wedded a novel popularity to its nationalism.

One of the ablest judges who ever sat on an American court, JAMES KENT of New York, whose opinion Marshall repudiated, grumbled in the pages of his *Commentaries on American Law* (1826) that Marshall's "language was too general and comprehensive for the case." Kent was right. The Court held the state act unconstitutional for conflicting with an act of Congress, making Marshall's enduring treatise on the commerce clause unnecessary for the disposition of the case. The conflict between the two statutes, Marshall said, "decides the cause." Kent was also right in stating that "it never occurred to anyone," least of all to the Congress that had passed the Coastal Licensing Act of 1793, which Marshall used to decide the case, that the act could justify national supremacy over state regulations respecting "internal waters or commerce." The act of 1793 had been intended to discriminate against foreign vessels in the American coastal trade by offering preferential tonnage duties to vessels of American registry. Marshall's construction of the statute conformed to his usual tactic of finding narrow grounds for decision after making a grand exposition. He announced "propositions which may have been thought axioms." He "assume[d] nothing," he said, because of the magnitude of the question, the distinction of the judge (Kent) whose opinion he scrapped, and the able arguments, which he rejected, by Thomas Emmett and Thomas Oakely, covering over 125 pages in the report of the case.

Except for the arguments of counsel, the Court had little for guidance. It had never before decided a commerce clause case, and the clause itself is general: "Congress shall have power to regulate commerce with foreign nations and among the several states. . . ." The power to regulate what would later be called "interstate commerce" appears in the same clause touching FOREIGN COMMERCE, the regulation of which is necessarily exclusive, beyond state control. But the clause does not negate state regulatory authority over interstate commerce, and the framers of the Constitution had rejected proposals for a sole or EXCLUSIVE POWER in Congress. Interstate commerce could be, as counsel for the monopoly contended, a subject of CONCURRENT POWER. Marshall had previously acknowledged that although the Constitution vested in Congress bankruptcy and tax powers, the states retained similar powers. THE FEDERALIST #32 recognized the principle of concurrent powers but offered no assistance on the commerce clause. Congress had scarcely used the commerce power except for the EMBARGO ACTS, which had not come before the Supreme Court. Those acts had interpreted the power to "regulate" as a power to prohibit, but they concerned commerce with foreign nations and were an instrument of foreign policy.

Prior to *Gibbons* the prevailing view on the interstate commerce power was narrow and crossed party lines. Kent, a Federalist, differed little from the Jeffersonians. JAMES MADISON, for example, when vetoing a congressional appropriation for INTERNAL IMPROVEMENTS, had declared in 1817 that "the power to regulate commerce among the several states cannot include a power to construct roads and canals, and to improve the navigation of water courses." In 1821, when JAMES MONROE had vetoed the CUMBERLAND ROAD BILL, whose objective was to extend national authority to turnpikes within the states, he had virtually reduced the commerce power to the enactment of duties and imports, adding that goods and vessels are the only SUBJECTS OF COMMERCE that Congress can regulate. "Commerce," in common usage at the time of *Gibbons,* meant trade in the buying and selling of commodities, not navigation or the transportation of passengers for hire. That was the business of Mr. Gibbons, who operated a steamship in defiance of the monopoly, between Elizabethtown, New Jersey, and New York City, in direct competition with Ogden, a licensee of the monopoly. Had Gibbons operated under sail, he would not have violated New York law; as it was, the state condemned his vessel to fines and forfeiture.

In *Gibbons,* then, the Court confronted a stunted concept of commerce, a STRICT CONSTRUCTION of the commerce power, and an opinion bearing Kent's authority that New York had regulated only "internal" commerce. Kent had also held that the commerce power was a concurrent one and that the test for the constitutionality of a state act should be practical: could the state and national laws coexist without conflicting in their operation? Marshall "assumed nothing" and in his step-by-step "axioms" repudiated any argument based on such premises.

He began with a definition of "commerce." It comprehended navigation as well as buying and selling, because "it is intercourse." This sweeping definition prompted a disgruntled states-rightist to remark, "I shall soon expect to learn that our fornication laws are unconstitutional." That same definition later constitutionally supported an undreamed of expansion of congressional power over the life of the nation's economy. Having defined commerce as every species of commercial intercourse, Marshall, still all-embracing, defined "commerce among the several states" to mean commerce intermingled with or concerning two or more states. Such commerce "cannot stop at the external boundary line of each State, but may be introduced into the interior"—and wherever it went, the power of the United States followed. Marshall did not dispute Kent's view that the "completely internal commerce" of a state (what we call INTRASTATE COMMERCE) is reserved for state governance. But that governance extended only to such commerce as was completely within one state, did not "affect" other states, "and with which it is not necessary to interfere, for the purpose of executing some of the general powers of the [United States] government." Marshall's breath-taking exposition of the national commerce power foreshadowed the STREAM OF COMMERCE DOCTRINE and the SHREVEPORT DOCTRINE of the next century. "If Congress has the power to regulate it," he added, "that power must be exercised whenever the subject exists. If it exists within the States . . . then the power of Congress may be exercised within a State."

Having so defined the reach of the commerce power, Marshall, parsing the clause, defined the power to "regulate" as the power "to prescribe the rule by which commerce is to be governed." It is a power that "may be exercised to its utmost extent, and acknowledges no limitations. . . ." In COHENS v. VIRGINIA (1821) he had said that the United States form, for most purposes, one nation: "In war, we are one people. In making peace, we are one people. In all commercial regulations, we are one and the same people," and the government managing that people's interests was the government of the Union. In *Gibbons* he added that because the "sovereignty of Congress" is plenary as to its objects, "the power over commerce with foreign nations, and among the several states, is vested in Congress as absolutely as it would be in a single government. . . ." Were that true, the commerce power would be as exclusive as the TREATY POWER or WAR POWERS and could not be shared concurrently with the states.

Marshall expressly denied that the states possessed a concurrent commerce power; yet he did not expressly declare that Congress possessed an exclusive commerce power, which would prevent the states from exercising a commerce power even in the absence of congressional legislation. That was DANIEL WEBSTER's argument in *Gibbons,* against the monopoly, and Marshall found "great force" in it. Notwithstanding the ambiguity in Marshall's opinion, he implicitly adopted Webster's argument by repeatedly rejecting the theory of concurrent commerce powers. He conceded, however, that the states can reach and regulate some of the same subjects of commerce as Congress, but only by the exercise of powers distinct from an interstate commerce power. Referring to the mass of state regulatory legislation that encompassed inspection laws, health laws, turnpike laws, ferry laws, "etc.," Marshall labeled them the state's "system of police," later called the POLICE POWER. But his jurisprudence-by-label did not distinguish interstate from intrastate commerce powers. Having declared that Congress might regulate a state's "internal" commerce to effectuate a national policy, he allowed the state police power to operate on subjects of interstate commerce, in subordination, of course, to the principle of national supremacy. (See WILLSON v. BLACK-BIRD CREEK MARSH CO., 1829.)

Following his treatise on the commerce clause, Marshall turned to the dispositive question whether the New York monopoly act conflicted with an act of Congress. The pertinent act of 1793 referred to American vessels employed in the "coasting trade." It made no exception for steamships or for vessels that merely transported passengers. The New York act was therefore "in direct collision" with the act of Congress by prohibiting Gibbons's steamship from carrying passengers in and out of the state's ports without a license from the monopoly.

Justice WILLIAM JOHNSON, although an appointee of THOMAS JEFFERSON, was even more nationalistic than Marshall. Webster later boasted that Marshall had taken to his argument as a baby to its mother's milk, but the remark better suited Johnson. Concurring separately, he declared that the commerce clause vested a power in Congress that "must be exclusive." He would have voided the state monopoly act even in the absence of the Federal Coastal Licensing Act: "I cannot overcome the conviction, that if the licensing act was repealed tomorrow, the rights of the appellant to a reversal of the decision complained of, would be as strong as it is under this license." Johnson distinguished the police power laws that operated on subjects of interstate commerce; their "different purposes," he claimed, made all the difference. In fact, the purpose underlying the monopoly act was the legitimate state purpose of encouraging new inventions.

In a case of first impression, neither Marshall nor Johnson could lay down DOCTRINES that settled all conflicts between state and national powers relating to commerce. Not until 1851 did the Court, after much groping, seize upon the doctrine of SELECTIVE EXCLUSIVENESS, which seemed at the time like a litmus paper test. (See COOLEY v. BOARD OF PORT WARDENS OF PHILADELPHIA, 1852.) Yet *Gibbons* anticipated doctrines concerning the breadth of congressional power that emerged in the next century and still govern. Marshall was as prescient as human ability allows. The Court today cannot construe the commerce clause except in certain state regulation cases without being influenced by Marshall's treatise on it. "At the beginning," Justice ROBERT JACKSON declared in WICKARD v. FILBURN (1941), "Chief Justice Marshall described the federal commerce power with a breadth never exceeded."

LEONARD W. LEVY

Bibliography

BAXTER, MAURICE G. 1972 *The Steamboat Monopoly: Gibbons v. Ogden, 1824.* New York: Knopf.

BEVERIDGE, ALBERT J. 1916–1919 *The Life of John Marshall.* 4 vols. Vol. IV:397–460. Boston: Houghton Mifflin.

FRANKFURTER, FELIX 1937 *The Commerce Clause under Marshall, Taney and Waite.* Pages 1–45. Chapel Hill: University of North Carolina Press.

GIBONEY v. EMPIRE STORAGE & ICE CO.
336 U.S. 490 (1949)

Speaking through Justice HUGO L. BLACK, the Supreme Court unanimously sustained an INJUNCTION issued by a Missouri court against labor pickets who attempted to pressure a supplier of ice not to deal with nonunion peddlers. The pickets claimed that the injunction violated their right to FREEDOM OF SPEECH and also conflicted with THORNHILL v. ALABAMA (1940), where the Justices had protected peaceful PICKETING. The Court rejected these arguments, by pointing out that the dominant purpose of the picketing here was to induce a violation of state law forbidding agreements in RESTRAINT OF TRADE. The FIRST AMENDMENT, Black noted, does not protect speech used as part of conduct that violates a valid state criminal statute.

MICHAEL E. PARRISH

GIBSON, JOHN BANNISTER
(1780–1853)

John Bannister Gibson was a Pennsylvania judge for forty years, thirty-seven of which were spent on the state supreme court. Born in 1780, he studied at Dickinson College and was admitted to the bar in 1803. After a brief legislative experience, the governor appointed him to the Court of Common Pleas in 1813 and three years later elevated him to the state's highest court. In 1827, Gibson became chief justice, a position he retained until 1851 when a constitutional change inaugurated a rotation system. He spent the remaining two years of his life as an associate justice.

Gibson's views on judicial power form the bedrock of his reputation. In particular, his dissent in EAKIN V. RAUB (1825) presented the most important response to JOHN MARSHALL's opinion in MARBURY V. MADISON (1803). Gibson insisted that without specific constitutional authorization, the judiciary had no power to nullify legislative acts. His permissive view of legislative power complemented the "commonwealth idea." For example, he held that state-created monopolies were not constitutionally prohibited and, furthermore, that they were "useful institutions" (*Case of "The Philadelphia and Trenton Railroad Company,"* 1840).

Legislative interference with the judicial process resulted in the only exception to Gibson's temporizing course. The Pennsylvania legislature traditionally had exercised EQUITY powers through private acts. But after the courts were granted substantially complete equity jurisdiction in 1836, Gibson and his colleagues struck down attempts by the legislature to maintain their own practice. When the legislature ordered a new trial in a simple trespass action, Gibson ruled that "the power to order new trials is judicial; but the power of the legislature is not judicial" (*De Chastellux v. Fairchild,* 1850).

Gibson's views of judicial power were eclipsed by the judicial activism of the post-Civil War era. But subsequent demands for judicial restraint in the twentieth century resulted in renewed interest in Gibson and respect for his ideas. ROSCOE POUND ranked him among the ten leading American jurists, and MORRIS R. COHEN praised him as one of the "great creative minds" in American law.

STANLEY I. KUTLER

Bibliography

KUTLER, STANLEY I. 1965 John Bannister Gibson: Judicial Restraint and the "Positive State." *Journal of Public Law* 14:181–197.

GIBSON v. FLORIDA LEGISLATIVE INVESTIGATION COMMITTEE
372 U.S. 539 (1963)

The committee ordered the president of the Miami branch of the NAACP to produce his membership records and refer to them when the committee asked whether specific individuals, suspected of being communists, were NAACP members. Earlier committee attempts to expose the NAACP's entire membership list showed that the communist issue was a screen behind which the state sought to use publicity to weaken a group engaged in activities aimed at racial equality and DESEGREGATION.

The Supreme Court, 5–4, held that Gibson's conviction for contempt for refusal to produce the records infringed the FREEDOM OF ASSOCIATION, which protected associational privacy. The Court, in an opinion by Justice ARTHUR GOLDBERG, was prepared to balance the state interest in legislative investigation against this FIRST AMENDMENT interest, but it held that such an infringement could be constitutional only if "the state convincingly show[s] a substantial relation between the information sought and a subject of overriding and COMPELLING STATE INTEREST," and that Florida had not done so in this instance. Accordingly Gibson's conviction was invalidated.

Gibson and its predecessor, *Bates v. Little Rock* (1960), must be read in conjunction with the BALANCING TEST applied to a congressional investigation into communist activity in BARENBLATT V. UNITED STATES (1959). The later cases may be read narrowly to distinguish *Barenblatt* and provide greater constitutional protection from investigative exposure only for "groups which themselves are neither engaged in subversive or other illegal . . . activities nor demonstrated to have any substantial connections with such activities." Alternatively, *Bates* and *Gibson* can be seen to modify the balancing test of *Barenblatt* to a "preferred position" balancing in which the government must show a compelling interest before it can invade associational privacy.

MARTIN SHAPIRO

GIDEON v. WAINWRIGHT
372 U.S. 335 (1963)

From time to time in constitutional history an obscure individual becomes the symbol of a great movement in legal doctrine. Character and circumstance illuminate a new understanding of the Constitution. So it was in the case of Clarence Earl Gideon.

Gideon was a drifter and petty thief who had served four prison terms when, in 1961, he was charged with breaking and entering the Bay Harbor Poolroom in Panama City, Florida, and stealing a pint of wine and some coins from a cigarette machine. At the age of fifty he had the look of defeat: a gaunt wrinkled face, white hair, a trembling voice. But inside there was still passion—a concern for justice that approached obsession. Through it, in a manner of speaking, Gideon changed the Constitution.

When he went to trial in the Circuit Court of Bay County, Florida, on August 4, 1961, he asked the judge to appoint a lawyer for him because he was too poor to hire one himself. The judge said he was sorry but he could not do that, because the laws of Florida called for appointment of counsel only when a defendant was charged with a capital offense. Gideon said: "The United States Supreme Court says I am entitled to be represented by counsel." When the Florida courts rejected that claim, he went on to the Supreme Court. From prison he submitted a petition, handwritten in pencil, arguing that Florida had ignored a rule laid down by the Supreme Court: "that all citizens tried for a felony crime should have aid of counsel."

Gideon was wrong. The rule applied by the Supreme Court at that time was in fact exactly the opposite. The Constitution, it had held, did *not* guarantee free counsel to all felony defendants unable to retain their own. That was the outcome—the bitterly debated outcome—of a line of cases on the right to counsel.

The Supreme Court first dealt with the issue in 1932, in the Scottsboro Case, POWELL V. ALABAMA. DUE PROCESS OF LAW required at least a "hearing," Justice GEORGE H. SUTHERLAND said, and the presence of counsel was "fundamental" to a meaningful hearing.

But Sutherland said that the Court was not deciding whether poor defendants had a right to free counsel in all circumstances, beyond the aggravated ones of this case: a capital charge, tried in haste and under public pressure.

In JOHNSON V. ZERBST (1938) the Court read the Sixth Amendment to require the appointment of counsel for all indigent *federal* criminal defendants. But in BETTS V. BRADY (1942), when considering the right of poor *state* defendants to free counsel in noncapital cases, the Court came out the other way. Justice OWEN J. ROBERTS said that "the states should not be straitjacketed" by a uniform constitutional rule. Only when particular circumstances showed that want of counsel denied FUNDAMENTAL FAIRNESS, he said, were such convictions invalid.

For twenty years the rule of *Betts v. Brady* applied. Counsel was said to be required only when a defendant suffered from "special circumstances" of disability: illiteracy, youth, mental illness, the complexity of the charges. But during that period criticism of the case mounted. No one could tell, it was said, when the Constitution required counsel. More and more often, too, the Supreme Court found "special circumstances" to require counsel.

That was the situation when Clarence Earl Gideon's petition reached the Court. The Justices seized on the occasion to think again about the Constitution and the right to counsel. Granting review, the Court ordered counsel to discuss: "Should this Court's holding in *Betts v. Brady* be reconsidered?" And then it appointed to represent Gideon, who had had no lawyer at his trial, one of the ablest lawyers in Washington, ABE FORTAS—later to sit on the Supreme Court himself.

On March 18, 1963, the Court overruled *Betts v. Brady*. Justice HUGO L. BLACK, who had dissented in *Betts*, wrote the opinion of the Court: a rare vindication of past dissent. He quoted Justice Sutherland's words on every man's need for the guiding hand of counsel at every step of the proceeding against him. "The right of one charged with crime to counsel may not be deemed fundamental and essential to fair trials in some countries," Justice Black said, "but it is in ours."

The decision in *Gideon v. Wainwright* was an important victory for one side in a general philosophical debate on the Court about whether constitutional protections should apply with the same vigor to state as to federal action: a victory for Justice Black over Jusitce Felix Frankfurter's more deferential view of state power. But on this particular issue changing ideas of due process would have led Justice Frankfurter in 1963 to impose a universal rule; retired and ill, he told a friend that he would have voted to overrule *Betts*. The case thus showed how time may bring a new consensus on the meaning of the Constitution.

And, not least, the *Gideon* case showed that the courts still respond to individuals in a society where most institutions of government seem remote and unresponsive. The least influential of men, riding a wave of legal history, persuaded the Supreme Court to reexamine a premise of justice. The case in fact represented more than an abstract principle. It was a victory for Clarence Earl Gideon. After the Supreme Court decision he was tried again in Bay County, Florida, this time with a lawyer—and the jury acquitted him. Gideon stayed out of prison until he died, on January 18, 1972.

ANTHONY LEWIS

Bibliography

LEWIS, ANTHONY 1964 *Gideon's Trumpet.* New York: Random House.

GILES, WILLIAM B.
(1762–1830)

Virginia Anti-Federalist William Branch Giles served in six of the first seven Congresses and opposed the policies of ALEXANDER HAMILTON, especially the

BANK OF THE UNITED STATES (1791). He opposed the ALIEN AND SEDITION ACTS, endorsed the VIRGINIA AND KENTUCKY RESOLUTIONS, and advocated repeal of the JUDICIARY ACT OF 1801. As a Jeffersonian leader in the Senate (1804–1815) he voted to convict Justice SAMUEL CHASE, arguing that "if the judges of the Supreme Court should . . . declare an act of Congress unconstitutional, . . . it was the undoubted right of the House of Representatives to impeach them, and of the Senate to remove them." After the acquittal of AARON BURR (1807), Giles, at President THOMAS JEFFERSON's behest, introduced a bill to expand the definition of TREASON. In his declining years Giles was an outspoken champion of STATES' RIGHTS.

DENNIS J. MAHONEY

GILMAN, NICHOLAS
(1755–1814)

Nicholas Gilman represented New Hampshire at the CONSTITUTIONAL CONVENTION OF 1787 and signed the Constitution. Gilman was not an active participant in the deliberations or committee work of the Convention. He later served in Congress, first as a Federalist, later as a Republican.

DENNIS J. MAHONEY

GINSBERG v. NEW YORK
390 U.S. 629 (1968)

In *Ginsberg* the Supreme Court upheld the validity under the FIRST AMENDMENT and FOURTEENTH AMENDMENT of a New York criminal statute that prohibited the sale to persons under seventeen years of age of sexually explicit printed materials that would not be obscene for adults. Drawing upon the criteria suggested in ROTH V. UNITED STATES (1957) and MEMOIRS V. MASSACHUSETTS (1966), the New York statute broadly defined sexually explicit descriptions or representations as "harmful to minors" when the material: "(i) predominantly appeals to the prurient, shameful or morbid interest of minors, and (ii) is patently offensive to prevailing standards in the adult community as a whole with respect to what is suitable material for minors, and (iii) is utterly without redeeming social importance for minors." Convicted for selling two "girlie" magazines to a sixteen-year-old, Ginsberg claimed that the statute was unconstitutional because the state was without the power to deny persons younger than seventeen access to materials that were not obscene for adults. Justice WILLIAM J. BRENNAN, for the 6–3 majority, rejected this challenge by introducing the concept of "variable obscenity." According to the majority, the New York statute had "simply adjust[ed] the definition of OBSCENITY to social realities by permitting the appeal of this type of material to be assessed in terms of the sexual interests . . . of such minors."

Although the decision rests on the legitimacy of protecting children from harm, the Court found it unnecessary to decide whether persons under seventeen were caused harm by exposure to materials proscribed by the statute. After suggesting that scientific studies neither proved nor disproved a causal connection, the majority held that it was "not irrational" for the New York legislature to find that "exposure to material condemned by the statute is harmful to minors."

To what extent does a minor's own First Amendment rights constrain the state's power to limit a minor's access to written or pictorial materials? Because of the nature of Ginsberg's challenge to the statute, the Court did not concern itself with the question whether a minor might have the constitutional right to buy "girlie" magazines. In ERZNOZNIK V. JACKSONVILLE (1975) the Court later indicated that while the First Amendment rights of minors are not coextensive with those of adults, "minors are entitled to a significant measure of First Amendment protection" and that under the *Ginsberg* variable obscenity standard "all nudity" in films "cannot be deemed as obscene even as to minors."

ROBERT H. MNOOKIN

(SEE ALSO: *Children's Rights.*)

GINZBURG v. UNITED STATES

See: *Memoirs v. Massachusetts*

GIROUARD v. UNITED STATES
328 U.S. 61 (1946)

An applicant for United States CITIZENSHIP declared that he could take the oath of allegiance ("support and defend the Constitution and laws of the United States against all enemies . . .") only with the reservation that he would not serve in the military in a combatant role.

The Court, speaking through Justice WILLIAM O. DOUGLAS, held that despite UNITED STATES V.

SCHWIMMER (1929), *United States v. MacIntosh* (1931), and *United States v. Bland* (1931), Girouard met the requirements for NATURALIZATION. Justice Douglas argued that Congress had not specifically insisted upon willingness to perform combatant service. Chief Justice HARLAN F. STONE dissented, joined by Justices STANLEY F. REED and FELIX FRANKFURTER.

This case established the eligibility of CONSCIENTIOUS OBJECTORS to be naturalized as citizens of the United States.

RICHARD E. MORGAN

GITLOW v. NEW YORK
268 U.S. 652 (1925)

Gitlow was convicted under a state statute proscribing advocacy of the overthrow of government by force. In a paper called *The Revolutionary Age,* he had published "The Left Wing Manifesto," denouncing moderate socialism and prescribing "Communist revolution." There was no evidence of any effect resulting from the publication. Rejecting the CLEAR AND PRESENT DANGER test which OLIVER WENDELL HOLMES and LOUIS D. BRANDEIS reasserted in their dissent, Justice EDWARD SANFORD for the Court upheld the statute. Enunciating what subsequently came to be called the remote BAD TENDENCY TEST, Sanford declared that the state might "suppress the threatened danger in its incipiency." "It cannot reasonably be required to defer the adoption of measures for its own . . . safety until the revolutionary utterances lead to actual disturbances of the public peace or imminent and immediate danger of its own destruction."

Unwilling to reverse its decision in SCHENCK v. UNITED STATES (1919), the Court limited the clear and present danger test enunciated there to the situation in which a speaker is prosecuted under a statute prohibiting acts and making no reference to language. Under such a statute the legislature has made no judgment of its own as to the danger of any speech, and the unlawfulness of the speech must necessarily depend on whether "its natural tendency and probable effect was to bring about the substantive evil" that the legislature had proscribed. In short, Sanford sought to confine the danger test to its origin in the law of attempts and to strip it of its imminence aspect. He argued that where a legislature itself had determined that a certain category of speech constituted a danger of substantive evil, "every presumption [was] to be indulged in favor of the validity" of such an exercise of the police power.

The PREFERRED FREEDOMS doctrine that became central to the speech cases of the next two decades was largely directed toward undermining the *Gitlow* position that state statutes regulating speech ought to be subject to no more demanding constitutional standards than the reasonableness test applied to state economic regulation.

The *Gitlow* formula was rejected in the 1930s, but the Court returned to some of its reasoning in the 1950s, particularly to the notion that where revolutionary speech is involved, government need not wait until "the spark . . . has enkindled the flame or blazed into the conflagration." Such reasoning, bolstered by the *Gitlow* distinction between advocacy and abstract, academic teaching informed the DENNIS v. UNITED STATES (1951) and YATES v. UNITED STATES (1951) decisions that upheld the Smith Act, a federal statute in part modeled on the New York criminal anarchy statute sustained in *Gitlow.*

The Court's language in *Gitlow* was equivocal, and it provided no rationale. Indeed, *Gitlow* is most often cited today for its dictum, "incorporating" FIRST AMENDMENT free speech guarantees into the DUE PROCESS clause of the FOURTEENTH AMENDMENT, thus rendering the Amendment applicable to the states as well as to Congress. (See INCORPORATION DOCTRINE.)

Holmes's *Gitlow* dissent did not address the question so troublesome to believers in judicial self-restraint: why should courts not defer to the legislature's judgment that a particular kind of speech is too dangerous to tolerate when, in applying the due process clause, they do defer to other legislative judgments? He did attack the majority's distinction between lawful abstract teaching and unlawful INCITEMENT in language that has become famous:

> Every idea is an incitement. It offers itself for belief and if believed it is acted on unless some other belief outweighs it. . . . The only difference between the expression of an opinion and an incitement in the narrower sense is the speaker's enthusiasm for the result. . . . If in the long run the beliefs expressed in proletarian dictatorship are destined to be accepted by the dominant forces of the community, the only meaning of free speech is that they should be given their chance and have their way.

MARTIN SHAPIRO

Bibliography

CHAFEE, ZECHARIAH 1941 *Free Speech in the United States.* Cambridge, Mass.: Harvard University Press.

GLIDDEN v. ZDANOK

See: Claims Court; Legislative Court

GLOBE NEWSPAPER COMPANY v. SUPERIOR COURT
457 U.S. 596 (1982)

Writing for a 7–2 Court, Justice WILLIAM J. BRENNAN sweepingly broadened the right of the public and press to attend criminal trials. On FIRST AMENDMENT grounds the Court held unconstitutional a state act intended to protect the juvenile victims of sex crimes by closing the trial proceedings. The exclusion of the press and public rested chiefly on the state's interest in safeguarding those victims from additional trauma and humiliation by not requiring them to testify in open court. The Supreme Court did not find that interest adequately compelling to warrant a mandatory closure rule. The decision created an anomalous condition of law: states can close trials to protect juvenile rapists but not to protect their victims. Chief Justice WARREN E. BURGER and Justice WILLIAM H. REHNQUIST dissented.

LEONARD W. LEVY

GLONA v. AMERICAN GUARANTEE AND LIABILITY INS. CO.

See: *Levy v. Louisiana*

GODCHARLES v. WIGEMAN

See: *Millett v. People*

GODFREY v. GEORGIA
100 S. Ct. 1759 (1980)

This is another case in which the Supreme Court reversed a death sentence because it was imposed under the state's standardless discretion: death for murder "outrageously or wantonly vile, or inhuman." Justice POTTER STEWART for a PLURALITY ruled that those words lacked objectivity and provided no principled basis for distinguishing the few cases in which death is imposed from the many in which it is not. Georgia's standard therefore placed no restraint on arbitrary and capricious infliction of the ultimate penalty. Two Justices argued that the death penalty is always CRUEL AND UNUSUAL. Three found Georgia's standard unobjectionable.

LEONARD W. LEVY

GOESAERT v. CLEARY
335 U.S. 464 (1948)

Goesaert typified the Court's SEX DISCRIMINATION decisions in the century between BRADWELL V. ILLINOIS (1873) and the 1970s. Michigan denied a woman a bartender's license unless she were "the wife or daughter of the male owner" of a licensed establishment. The Supreme Court, 6–3, rejected an EQUAL PROTECTION attack on this limitation. For the majority, Justice FELIX FRANKFURTER applied a RATIONAL BASIS standard of review: the legislature might rationally have believed that the presence of a barmaid's husband or father would help avoid "moral or social problems." Thus the Court could not "give ear to the suggestion that the real impulse behind this legislation was the unchivalrous desire of male bartenders to try to monopolize the calling."

Justice WILEY B. RUTLEDGE, for the dissenters, argued that the law failed to serve these protective ends, because unrelated, nonowner males might be present in some cases, and related male owners might be absent.

KENNETH L. KARST

GOLDBERG, ARTHUR J.
(1908–)

Arthur Joseph Goldberg's tenure on the Supreme Court was a brief chapter in a long and distinguished career. He served fewer than three years, from October 1, 1962, until he resigned on July 25, 1965, to become the United States ambassador to the United Nations. Goldberg consistently voted with the WARREN COURT majority on CIVIL LIBERTIES and CRIMINAL PROCEDURE issues, although three terms as the Court's junior Justice scarcely gave him enough time to develop a distinctive voice on the major constitutional questions of that active period.

When Goldberg came to the Court, the unanimity of the earlier Warren years had begun to erode. The Court was struggling to give specific content to the broad principles established in the landmark rulings of the 1950s and early 1960s. Goldberg's appointment to replace FELIX FRANKFURTER allowed the flowering of the liberal JUDICIAL ACTIVISM for which the Warren Court is best remembered. Frequently his vote helped to create a bare majority for a FIRST AMENDMENT claim or for the rights of a criminal defendant.

ESCOBEDO V. ILLINOIS (1964), Justice Goldberg's best known opinion for the Court, was such a case. A year before, in GIDEON V. WAINWRIGHT, the Court had ruled unanimously that the state was required to provide counsel for an indigent defendant accused of a serious crime. The question in *Escobedo* was at what stage in the process from arrest through INDICTMENT the Sixth Amendment RIGHT TO COUNSEL attached. Voting 5–4, the Court overturned the murder conviction of a man whose request to consult a lawyer during interrogation by the police had been denied. In his opinion, Goldberg wrote: "The fact that many confessions are obtained during this period points up its critical nature as a 'stage when legal aid and advice' are surely needed. The right to counsel would indeed be hollow if it began at a period when few confessions were obtained." Escobedo thus pried open the door for MIRANDA V. ARIZONA (1966).

Goldberg's opinions for the Court also contributed to the growth of the First Amendment's protection of the freedoms of expression and association. COX V. LOUISIANA (1965) promoted the development of the concept of the "public forum." GIBSON V. FLORIDA LEGISLATIVE INVESTIGATION COMMITTEE (1963) remains a major precedent for protecting the privacy of political association. And APTHEKER V. SECRETARY OF STATE (1964) struck down a section of the Subversive Activities Control Act of 1950, which denied passports to members of various communist organizations. The law, Goldberg wrote for the Court, "sweeps too widely and too indiscriminately across the liberty guaranteed in the Fifth Amendment." *Aptheker* was an important stop in the elaboration of the First Amendment doctrine of OVERBREADTH. Goldberg also wrote the opinion for the Court in KENNEDY V. MENDOZA-MARTINEZ (1963), striking down a federal law that automatically revoked the CITIZENSHIP of anyone who left the country during a time of war or national emergency in order to evade the draft.

Goldberg's area of professional expertise was labor law, and he was widely regarded as the nation's most eminent labor lawyer. But because he joined the Court directly from eighteen months as secretary of labor in the cabinet of President JOHN F. KENNEDY, he excused himself from participation in many of the labor cases that reached the Court during his tenure.

Goldberg was born in Chicago on August 8, 1908, and received his law degree from Northwestern University in 1929. He built a labor law practice in Chicago before moving to Washington, D.C., in 1948 to serve as general counsel to both the Congress of Industrial Organizations (CIO) and the United Steelworkers. He was instrumental in the 1957 merger of organized labor's two factions, the CIO and the American Federation of Labor (AFL), and continued to play a key role in AFL-CIO affairs until he joined the Kennedy cabinet in 1961. His appointment to the Supreme Court followed the next year.

In 1965, President LYNDON B. JOHNSON persuaded him to leave the Court to fill the United Nations post made vacant by the death of Ambassador Adlai Stevenson. He resigned his ambassadorship in 1968 and practiced law briefly in New York, where he ran unsuccessfully for governor on the Democratic ticket in 1970. He then returned to Washington, where he continued to practice law and to speak out on civil liberties issues.

LINDA GREENHOUSE

Bibliography

CARMEN, IRA H. 1966 One Civil Libertarian among Many: The Case of Mr. Justice Goldberg. *Michigan Law Review* 65:301–336.

FRIEDMAN, STEPHEN J. 1969 Arthur J. Goldberg. In Leon Friedman and Fred L. Israel, eds., *The Justices of the United States Supreme Court 1789–1969.* New York: Chelsea House.

GOLDBERG v. KELLY
397 U.S. 254 (1970)

Residents of New York receiving WELFARE BENEFITS brought suit challenging the state's procedures authorizing termination of a beneficiary's benefits without a prior hearing on his or her eligibility. The Supreme Court, 6–3, held that these procedures denied PROCEDURAL DUE PROCESS.

For the majority, Justice WILLIAM J. BRENNAN rejected the state's argument that because welfare benefits were a "privilege" and not a "right," their termination could not deprive a beneficiary of "property" within the meaning of the due process clause. Those benefits, said Brennan, were "a matter of statutory entitlement for persons qualified to receive them" and thus qualified as "property" interests whose termination must satisfy the requirements of due process.

These requirements included an evidentiary hearing prior to the termination of welfare benefits, including timely notice of the reasons for the proposed termination, the right to retain counsel, opportunity to confront any adverse witnesses, and opportunity to present the beneficiary's own evidence. The procedural safeguards thus required approximated those available in judicial proceedings; the Court underscored the point by insisting on an impartial decision maker who would "state the reasons for his determination and indicate the evidence he relied on."

Goldberg was the leading decision extending the guarantees of procedural due process in civil proceedings beyond the protection of traditional COMMON LAW property interests to "entitlements" defined by statute, administrative regulation, or contract. It was aptly called the beginning of a "procedural due process revolution." By the mid-1970s, however, the counterrevolution had begun. (See BISHOP V. WOOD, 1976; PAUL V. DAVIS, 1976; MATHEWS V. ELDRIDGE, 1976.)

KENNETH L. KARST

GOLD CLAUSE CASES

Norman v. Baltimore & Ohio Railroad Co.
294 U.S. 240 (1935)
Nortz v. United States
294 U.S. 317 (1935)
Perry v. United States
294 U.S. 330 (1935)

The decisions in these cases were virtually the only Supreme Court opinions upholding congressional New Deal legislation before the judicial "revolution" of 1937. The Depression had caused an emergency in which contracts calling for payment in gold, rather than paper, "obstruct[ed] the power of Congress." So declaring, Congress passed the JOINT RESOLUTION of June 5, 1933, which asserted its regulatory power over gold as an item that "affect[ed] the public interest." Such gold clauses were "against public policy," and henceforth debtors could legally discharge their obligations in any other legal tender. Creditors resisted this action because, in conjunction with earlier legislation that had reduced the gold value of the dollar, it effectively devalued debts by allowing paper to be substituted for gold. Even though these suits involved relatively small amounts, they represented one hundred billion dollars in outstanding gold obligations (three-fourths of which were private debts) at a time when the Treasury had only some four billion dollars in gold reserves.

In *Norman v. Baltimore & Ohio Railroad Company*, the plaintiffs sought to enforce payment of $38.10 in currency, the equivalent of the value of the gold ($22.50) specified in the contract, a sixty-nine percent markup. Chief Justice CHARLES EVANS HUGHES, for a 5–4 Court, reviewed the MONETARY POWER and, resting on *Knox v. Lee* (1871), insisted on the government's power to void any private OBLIGATION OF CONTRACTS that interfered with the exercise of Congress's power to regulate currency. The majority said that requiring debtors to pay sixty-nine percent more in currency to match the gold value of their debts would cause "dislocation of the domestic economy." The majority opinion, while reaching perhaps the only possible satisfactory result for the stability of the economy, was, in the conventional constitutional wisdom of the time, tenuous. In a spiteful dissent, Justice JAMES MCREYNOLDS attacked Hughes's purely pragmatic approach as a monstrous miscarriage of justice. Delivering his opinion orally, he exclaimed, "This is Nero at his worst. The Constitution is gone!"

In cases involving public obligations, the majority rested on sturdier constitutional ground. In accordance with the EMERGENCY BANK ACT, E. C. Nortz had surrendered his gold certificates after the government refused his demand for payment in gold. He sued for the difference between the currency he received and the value of the gold, over $64,000. Hughes, writing in *Nortz v. United States*, declared that gold certificates were only one form of currency and were thus replaceable by any other valid currency. Because Nortz suffered only "nominal" damages, his suit failed. In so deciding, the Court avoided the question whether gold certificates amounted to a contract with the government. In *Perry v. United States*, however, an 8–1 Court admitted that a government Liberty bond was a contractual obligation. Insofar as the joint resolution abrogated gold clauses in public contracts, it must be unconstitutional. A 5–4 majority quickly moved to destroy the force of this concession, however. Because the rise in gold prices which formed the basis of Perry's suit resulted from government manipulation of monetary values, payment in excess of a simple dollar-for-dollar exchange would constitute "unjust enrichment." Perry, like Nortz, had sustained only minimal damages and his suit likewise failed.

As McReynolds's dissent aptly noted, the majority was more concerned with economic and political consequences than constitutional precedent. ROBERT H. JACKSON, later on the Court himself, wrote that "in the guise of private law suits involving a few dollars, the whole American economy was haled before the Supreme Court." In these cases, by theoretically destroying thousands of obligations, the Court sustained Congress's exercise of the monetary power—

a course it found itself unable to follow when later confronted by other major New Deal legislation.

DAVID GORDON

Bibliography

DAWSON, JOHN P. 1935 Gold Clause Decisions. *Michigan Law Review* 33:647–684.

GOLDFARB v. VIRGINIA STATE BAR
421 U.S. 773 (1975)

By extending antitrust liability to the legal profession, this decision afforded consumers further protection against illegal business practices. The minimum fee schedule of the Fairfax County Bar Association, enforced by the Virginia State Bar, fixed the lowest charge for title searches at one percent of the value of the property involved. A unanimous eight-member Supreme Court, led by Chief Justice WARREN E. BURGER, sustaining a CLASS ACTION against the state and county bars, found violations of the price-fixing provisions of the SHERMAN ANTITRUST ACT as well as restraint of INTERSTATE COMMERCE.

DAVID GORDON

GOLD RESERVE ACT
48 Stat. 337 (1934)

Following the Gold Content Rider of mid-1933, the government sought to stabilize the gold value of the dollar in an effort to raise prices. Congress, fulfilling a request from President FRANKLIN D. ROOSEVELT, passed the Gold Reserve Act on January 30, 1934, under its MONETARY POWER and extended broad authority to establish a sound currency system. The act called in all gold and gold certificates in circulation, with specified exceptions, and granted the Treasury title to all monetary gold. The act also established an Exchange Stabilization Fund with which the secretary of the treasury was empowered to deal in gold in international markets to preserve a favorable balance of exchange and support the dollar. Congress also granted the President authority to regulate the gold content of the dollar. Further sections dealt with silver coinage and retroactively approved actions taken under authority of the EMERGENCY BANK ACT.

On January 31, Roosevelt reduced the gold content of the dollar to just under sixty percent of its former value. By mid-year the absence of circulating gold necessitated a congressional joint resolution abrogating clauses in private contracts and government bonds that called for payment in gold; the Supreme Court sustained this action in the GOLD CLAUSE CASES (1935).

DAVID GORDON

GOLDWATER v. CARTER
444 U.S. 285 (1979)

Members of Congress sued the President for declaratory and injunctive relief, claiming he had exceeded his powers in terminating a treaty with the Republic of China (Taiwan) without any congressional participation. Without briefing or ORAL ARGUMENT, a fragmented Supreme Court held, 6–3, that the case was not justiciable. Justice WILLIAM H. REHNQUIST, for four Justices, concluded that the case presented a POLITICAL QUESTION. Justice LEWIS F. POWELL rejected this argument but concluded that the case lacked RIPENESS because the President and Congress had not reached an impasse. Justice THURGOOD MARSHALL concurred in the result. Justice WILLIAM J. BRENNAN would have affirmed the court of appeals's decision upholding the President's action, and the other dissenting Justices would have set the case for full argument.

KENNETH L. KARST

GOMILLION v. LIGHTFOOT
364 U.S. 339 (1960)

Alabama redrew the boundaries of the city of Tuskegee in "an uncouth twenty-eight-sided figure" that excluded from the city all but a handful of black voters while excluding no whites. The lower federal courts refused to grant any relief from this racial GERRYMANDER, concluding on the basis of COLEGROVE V. GREEN (1946) that municipal boundaries, like legislative districting, presented only POLITICAL QUESTIONS that lacked JUSTICIABILITY.

The Supreme Court unanimously held the case justiciable, and eight Justices, speaking through Justice FELIX FRANKFURTER, concluded that the gerrymander violated the FIFTEENTH AMENDMENT. The effect of the law was so clear as to demonstrate a purpose to deprive blacks of their vote for city officials. Justice CHARLES E. WHITTAKER concurred, on the basis of the EQUAL PROTECTION clause of the FOURTEENTH AMENDMENT.

The door which *Gomillion* pried open was flung wide in BAKER V. CARR (1962), when the Court held that the malapportionment of state legislative districts presented a justiciable controversy under the equal protection clause.

KENNETH L. KARST

GOMPERS v. BUCK'S STOVE & RANGE COMPANY
221 U.S. 418 (1911)

In a decision that presaged the CLAYTON ACT, a unanimous Supreme Court held that an advertisement encouraging a SECONDARY BOYCOTT was unlawful and not protected by the FREEDOM OF SPEECH or of the PRESS. To support a local affiliate, the American Federation of Labor had run a notice in its magazine, the *American Federationist,* which transformed a local dispute into a national boycott by including the firm in a "We Don't Patronize" list. Prompted by a local strike, the company obtained an INJUNCTION prohibiting the AFL, its officers, and the local from obstructing sales or furthering any boycott, including use of the firm's name on the "We Don't Patronize" list. When Samuel Gompers and other union leaders ignored the injunction, they were jailed for contempt. Their APPEAL to the Court maintained that they could lawfully ignore the injunction because it abridged their rights of free speech and press.

Speaking for the Court, Justice JOSEPH R. LAMAR dismissed the free speech claim. Publication might provide a means of continuing an illegal boycott because the printing of words in an unlawful conspiracy might foster actions, thereby "exceeding any possible right of speech which a single individual might have." The resultant "verbal acts" would necessarily be subject to injunction. In this case, the publicity destroyed business and illegally restrained commerce. Here Lamar introduced the analogy of a SHERMAN ANTITRUST ACT violation, an analogy that has misled many authorities to believe that the case found such a violation—which it did not, for the company had not sought such relief. Declaring that the decision in LOEWE V. LAWLOR (1908) extended to any unlawful method of restraint, Lamar asserted that a failure to "hold that the restraint of trade under the Sherman anti-trust act, or on general principles of law, could be enjoined . . . would be to render the law impotent." This was no more than an analogy. Because the boycott constituted an illegal conspiracy, the Court had the power and the duty to sustain the injunction.

With the effectiveness of the boycott reduced by this decision, labor turned to politics to influence elections and legislation. In a well-intentioned, if ambiguous, attempt to eliminate the confusion over labor's rights and obligations under the Sherman Act, Congress passed the Clayton Act in 1914. Section 20 of this act, ostensibly addressed to the *Gompers* issue, prohibited the issuance of injunctions restraining unions from maintaining secondary boycotts or "from recommending, advising, or persuading others by peaceful and lawful means so to do." Although the Court would virtually divest this section of meaning in DUPLEX PRINTING PRESS COMPANY V. DEERING (1921), Congress had the last word, passing the NORRIS-LAGUARDIA ACT in 1932.

DAVID GORDON

Bibliography

BERMAN, EDWARD (1930)1969 *Labor and the Sherman Act.* New York: Russell & Russell.

GONG LUM v. RICE
275 U.S. 78 (1927)

Classifying a youngster of Chinese ancestry as "colored," thereby compelling her to attend a black school, did not deny her EQUAL PROTECTION under the FOURTEENTH AMENDMENT. By so ruling, a unanimous Supreme Court upheld a Mississippi decision. The Court declined to consider the issue at length; citing ROBERTS V. BOSTON (Massachusetts, 1850) and PLESSY V. FERGUSON (1896), the Court concluded that PRECEDENT had clearly established a state's right to settle such issues of racial SEGREGATION without "intervention of the federal courts."

DAVID GORDON

GOOD BEHAVIOR

Until the late seventeenth century, royal judges held their offices "during the king's good pleasure." After the Glorious Revolution (1688–1689), judges in England (but not in the colonies) were appointed "during good behavior." This was a crucial step toward insuring the independence of the judiciary. The phrase was used in several revolutionary state constitutions, and the CONSTITUTIONAL CONVENTION OF 1787 unanimously adopted it to define the tenure of federal judges. ALEXANDER HAMILTON, in THE FEDERALIST, defended such tenure on the grounds that judicial independence is as necessary in a republic as in a monarchy.

It is by no means certain that a judge deviates from "good behavior" only when he commits "high crimes and misdemeanors"; however, the Constitution provides for no means of removal except IMPEACHMENT.

DENNIS J. MAHONEY

GOOD FAITH EXCEPTION

The good faith exception to the EXCLUSIONARY RULE created to enforce the FOURTH AMENDMENT allows prosecutorial use of illegally seized EVIDENCE if the police made the seizure in good faith reliance on the validity of a SEARCH WARRANT, even though an appellate court later finds that the warrant was unconstitutionally issued. As Justice BYRON R. WHITE for the Supreme Court stated the doctrine in UNITED STATES V. LEON (1984), the Court "modified" the exclusionary rule "so as not to bar the use in the prosecution's case-in-chief of evidence seized on a search warrant issued by a detached and neutral magistrate but ultimately found to be unsupported by PROBABLE CAUSE."

Those who support the good faith exception claim that it does not prevent either the Fourth Amendment or the exclusionary rule from achieving its intended functions. They see the exclusionary rule as a judicially created remedy designed to deter violations of the amendment; and they stress that the substantial costs exacted by the rule often outweigh its benefits. By excluding genuine evidence from the truth-finding process, the rule allows guilty persons to escape punishment and offends basic concepts of criminal justice. These costs can be justified only if the rule deters police misconduct. Advocates of the good faith exception assert, too, that the rule does not lower the probable cause standard and that it loses its deterrent capability when the officer has acted on a good faith belief that he was executing a warrant properly issued by a neutral magistrate and based on probable cause.

Opponents of the exception defend the exclusionary rule as inherent in the Fourth Amendment, preventing law enforcement officials from making any use of evidence obtained through their misconduct or misjudgment. Opponents claim that the amendment itself, not just the rule, makes convictions difficult. They stress that empirical studies show that the social cost of the exclusionary rule in lost prosecutions and acquittals has been exaggerated, and they argue that the rule improves police work by giving real effect to requirements to which law enforcement officials must conform. The good faith exception, on the other hand, places a premium on police ignorance of the law. Although they concede that no individual officer is likely to be deterred from unconstitutional conduct by exclusion of evidence seized in reliance on a defective warrant, the opponents argue that a good faith exception weakens the rule's influence toward a systemic or institutional compliance with the Fourth Amendment. They point out, too, that an objectively reasonable reliance on an UNREASONABLE SEARCH or on a warrant lacking probable cause is *impossible*, because no search and seizure can simultaneously be reasonable and unreasonable. The warrant requirement lies at the heart of the amendment, they contend; and the good faith exception erodes the requirement of probable cause. The Framers of the amendment sought to condition search and seizure on probable cause. They were primarily concerned with illegal warrants—GENERAL WARRANTS and WRITS OF ASSISTANCE. The exception admits illegally seized evidence and in so doing implicates the integrity of the judicial process. The exclusionary rule exists to deter violations of the amendment by all law enforcement agencies, the courts included.

Proponents of the good faith exception regard the courts, including the magistrates who issue warrants, as independent of, not part of, law enforcement agencies. Proponents and opponents of the exception, and of the exclusionary rule, argue from different premises and rarely confront each other's arguments.

LEONARD W. LEVY

Bibliography

KAMISAR, YALE 1984 Gates, "Probable Cause," "Good Faith," and Beyond. *Iowa Law Review* 69:551–615.

GOODNOW, FRANK J.
(1859–1939)

Frank Johnson Goodnow, founding president of the American Political Science Association (1903–1905), professor at Columbia University (1891–1912) and subsequently president of Johns Hopkins University (1914–1929), was one of the leading proponents of PROGRESSIVE CONSTITUTIONAL THOUGHT. Rejecting the traditional doctrine of SEPARATION OF POWERS, he urged a new separation of political decision making from public administration. In *Social Reform and the*

Constitution (1911) he condemned the STRICT CONSTRUCTION of the Constitution that blocked implementation of progressive reforms. He advocated a flexible CONSTITUTIONALISM that would reflect the pace of social change.

DENNIS J. MAHONEY

Bibliography

MAHONEY, DENNIS J. 1984 A New Political Science for a World Made Wholly New: The Doctrine of Progress and the Emergence of American Political Science. Ph.D. dissertation, Claremont Graduate School.

GORDON, THOMAS

See: Cato's Letters

GORHAM, NATHANIEL
(1738–1796)

Nathaniel Gorham, a prominent businessman and political leader, signed the Constitution as a representative of Massachusetts. One of the handful of most active delegates to the CONSTITUTIONAL CONVENTION OF 1787, Gorham presided over the Committee of the Whole, served on several committees, including the Committee on Detail, and spoke frequently. He was a supporter of strong national government.

DENNIS J. MAHONEY

GOSS v. LOPEZ
419 U.S. 565 (1975)

Ohio law authorized a public school principal to suspend a misbehaving student for up to ten days, without a hearing. A 5–4 Supreme Court held that this law violated a student's right to PROCEDURAL DUE PROCESS. For the majority, Justice BYRON R. WHITE found a "property" interest in the state's statute setting out a student's "entitlement" to attend school, and a "liberty" interest in the loss of reputation attending suspension for misconduct. While trivial school discipline might not require any hearing, a ten-day suspension demanded notice of the charges against the student, and, if the charges were denied, an explanation of the EVIDENCE and an opportunity to present his or her story. Justice LEWIS F. POWELL, a former school board president, led the dissenters. The statute authorizing suspension gave only a conditional entitlement to attend school—as Justice WILLIAM H. REHNQUIST had argued in ARNETT V. KENNEDY (1974)—and the injury to reputation was not serious enough to invade a "liberty" interest. Thus, Powell argued, the school discipline here did "not assume constitutional dimensions."

KENNETH L. KARST

GOUDY, WILLIAM CHARLES
(1824–1893)

The leader of the Chicago bar, William Goudy was a creative constitutional lawyer and railroad counsel who argued many cases before the Supreme Court. He familiarized the Court with the relationship of laissez-faire tenets and constitutional limitations on STATE POLICE POWER. In *Munn v. Illinois* (see GRANGER CASES, (1877), WABASH, ST. LOUIS, AND PACIFIC RAILROAD V. ILLINOIS (1886), and CHICAGO, MILWAUKEE, AND ST. PAUL RAILROAD V. MINNESOTA (1890), he advanced SUBSTANTIVE DUE PROCESS of law in the context of arguments, stressing that the right to property included its unfettered use as well as its title and possession. State regulation of rates, by reducing profits, constituted a TAKING OF PROPERTY without JUST COMPENSATION and a denial of due process, according to Goudy.

LEONARD W. LEVY

Bibliography

TWISS, BENJAMIN 1942 *Lawyers and the Constitution.* Pages 76–84. Princeton, N.J.: Princeton University Press.

GOVERNMENT AID TO RELIGIOUS INSTITUTIONS

Constitutionality of governmental aid to religious institutions, generally, though not exclusively, in the form of financial subsidies, is most often challenged under the FIRST AMENDMENT's ban on laws respecting an ESTABLISHMENT OF RELIGION. When the purpose of the subsidy is to finance obviously religious activities, such as the erection or repairing of a church building, UNCONSTITUTIONALITY is generally recognized. In large measure the purpose of the establishment clause was to forbid such grants, as is indicated by the Court's opinion and Justice WILEY RUTLEDGE's dissenting opinion in EVERSON V. BOARD OF EDUCATION (1947). On the other hand, where the funds are used for what would generally be considered secular activities, such as maintaining hospitals or providing meals for pupils in church-related (often called parochial) schools, constitutional validity is fairly unanimously assumed.

Constitutional controversy revolves largely around governmental financing of church-related schools that combine the inculcation of religious doctrines and beliefs with what is generally considered the teaching of secular subjects, substantially, though not necessarily entirely, as they are taught in public schools.

In *Everson,* the Court upheld as a valid exercise of the POLICE POWER a state statute financing bus transportation to parochial schools, on the ground that the legislative purpose was not to aid religion by financing the operations of the schools but to help insure the safety of children going to or returning from them. A law having the former purpose would violate the establishment clause, which forbids government to set up a church, aid one or more religions, or prefer one religion over others. "No tax in any amount, large or small," the Court said, "can be levied to support any religious activities or institutions, whatever they may be called, or whatever form they may adopt to teach or practice religion."

The *Everson,* or "no-aid," interpretation of the establishment clause as applied to governmental financing of religious schools next reached the Supreme Court in the case of BOARD OF EDUCATION V. ALLEN (1968). There the Court upheld a New York statute providing for the loan to pupils attending nonpublic schools of secular textbooks authorized for use in public schools. The Court concluded that the statute did not impermissibly aid religious schools within the meaning of *Everson,* nor did it violate the establishment clause ban on laws lacking a secular legislative purpose or having a primary effect that either advances or inhibits religion, as that clause had been interpreted in ABINGTON SCHOOL DISTRICT V. SCHEMPP (1963). In upholding the New York law, the Court recognized that the police power rationale of *Everson* was not readily applicable to textbook laws, but it adjudged that the processes of secular and religious training are not so intertwined that secular textbooks furnished to students by the public are in fact instrumental in the teaching of religion.

It is fairly obvious that the *Allen* rationale could be used to justify state aid to religious schools considerably more extensive than mere financing of transportation or provision of secular textbooks. It could, for example, justify state financing of supplies other than textbooks, costs of maintenance and repair of parochial school premises, and, most important, salaries of instructors who teach the nonreligious subjects, which constitute the major part of the parochial school curriculum.

That this extension was intended by Justice BYRON R. WHITE, the author of the *Allen* opinion, is indicated by the fact that he thereafter dissented in all the decisions barring aid to church-related schools. The first of these decisions came in the companion cases of LEMON V. KURTZMAN and *Earley v. DiCenso* (1973). In *Lemon,* Pennsylvania purchased the services of religious schools in providing secular education to their pupils. In *DiCenso,* Rhode Island paid fifteen percent of the salaries of religious school teachers who taught only secular subjects.

A year earlier, in WALZ V. TAX COMMISSION (1970), the Court had expanded the purpose–effect test by adding a third dimension: a statute violated the establishment clause if it fostered excessive governmental entanglement with religion. The statutes involved in *Lemon* and *DiCenso* violated the clause, the Court held, because in order to insure that the teachers did not inject religion into their secular classes or allow religious values to affect the content of secular instruction, it was necessary to subject the teachers to comprehensive, discriminating, and continuing state surveillance, which would constitute forbidden entanglement of church and state.

In other cases the Court held unconstitutional laws enacted to reimburse religious schools for the cost of preparing, conducting, and grading teacher-prepared tests, of maintaining and repairing school buildings, of transporting students on field trips to museums and concerts as part of secular courses, and of purchasing instructional materials and equipment susceptible of diversion to religious use. The Court also held unconstitutional state tuition assistance to the parents of parochial school pupils, whether by direct grant or through state income tax benefits.

On the other hand, the Court has upheld the constitutionality of reimbursement for noninstructional health and welfare services supplied to parochial school pupils, such as meals, medical and dental care, and diagnostic services relating to speech, hearing, and psychological problems. In COMMITTEE FOR PUBLIC EDUCATION AND RELIGIOUS LIBERTY V. REGAN (1980) the Court allowed reimbursement for the expense of administering state-prepared and mandated objective examinations.

The Court has manifested a considerably more tolerant approach in cases challenging governmental aid to church-related institutions of higher education. While the purpose–effect–entanglement test is in principle equally applicable, the Court held that where a grant is used to finance facilities in colleges and universities used only for secular instruction, the primary effect of the law is not to advance religion. As for entanglement, religion does not necessarily so permeate the secular education provided by church-related colleges nor so seep into the use of their facilities as to require a ruling that in all cases excessive surveillance would be necessary to assure that the facilities were not used for religious purposes. The Court also gave consideration to the skepticism of college students, the nature of college and postgraduate courses, the high degree of academic freedom characterizing many church-related colleges, and their nonlocal constituencies. For all these reasons, in TILTON V. RICHARDSON (1973) the Court sanctioned substantial governmental financing of church-related institutions of higher education.

In *Walz v. Tax Commission* the Court upheld the constitutionality of tax exemption accorded to property used exclusively for worship or other religious purposes. Exemption, it held, does not entail sponsorship of religion and involves even less entanglement than nonexemption, since it does not require the government to examine the affairs of the church and audit its books or records. The longevity of exemption, dating as it does from the time the Republic was founded, constitutes strong evidence of its constitutionality.

The Court, in *Walz,* did not hold that the free exercise clause would be violated if exemption were disallowed (although it was urged to do so in the AMICUS CURIAE brief submitted by the National Council of Churches). Nor, on the other hand, did it decide to the contrary. As of the present, therefore, it seems that governments, federal or state, have the constitutional option of granting or denying exemption.

LEO PFEFFER

(SEE ALSO: *Separation of Church and State.*)

Bibliography

MORGAN, RICHARD E. 1972 *The Supreme Court and Religion.* New York: Free Press.

PFEFFER, LEO 1967 *Church, State and Freedom.* Rev. ed. Boston: Beacon Press.

——— 1975 *God, Caesar and the Constitution.* Boston: Beacon Press.

TRIBE, LAURENCE 1978 *American Constitutional Law.* Chap. 14. Mineola, N.Y.: Foundation Press.

GOVERNMENT INSTRUMENTALITY

Government instrumentalities are agencies, including government-owned corporations, created by Congress or the state legislatures to carry out public functions or purposes. Since MCCULLOCH V. MARYLAND (1819) the doctrine of INTERGOVERNMENTAL IMMUNITY has precluded the state and federal governments from directly taxing one another's governmental instrumentalities.

DENNIS J. MAHONEY

GOVERNMENT REGULATION OF THE ECONOMY

See: Economic Regulation

GOVERNMENT SPEECH

FIRST AMENDMENT commentary has emphasized the danger of government as censor; thus lavish attention has been given to whether government can prevent Nazis from marching in Skokie, Illinois, Communists from advocating revolution, pornographers from selling their wares, or eccentrics from yelling fire in crowded theaters. Much less attention has been paid to the role of government as speaker; yet, one need only notice the ready access of government officials to the mass media, the constant stream of legislative and executive reports and publications, and the massive system of direct grants and indirect subsidies to the communications process (including federal financing of elections) to recognize that speech financed or controlled by government plays an enormous role in the marketplace of ideas. Sometimes the government speaks as government; sometimes it subsidizes speech without purporting to claim that the resulting message is its own. The term "government speech," therefore, includes all forms of state-supported communications: official government messages; statements of public officials at publicly subsidized press conferences; artistic, scientific, or political subsidies; even the classroom communications of public school teachers.

Basic assumptions of First Amendment law are sharply modified when governments speak. A basic canon of First Amendment law is that content distinctions are suspect. Indeed, in POLICE DEPARTMENT

OF CHICAGO V. MOSLEY (1972) the Court insisted that government could not deviate " 'from the neutrality of time, place and circumstances into a concern about content.' This is never permitted." When governments speak, however, content distinctions are the norm. Government does not speak at random; it makes editorial judgments; it decides that some content is appropriate for the occasion and other content is not. The public museum curator makes content distinctions in selecting exhibits; the librarian, in selecting books; the public official, in composing press releases. If government could not make content distinctions, it could not speak effectively.

The government speech problem is to determine the constitutional limits, if any, on the editorial decisions of government. BUCKLEY V. VALEO (1976) squarely presented the issue. Certain minor party candidates argued that their exclusion from the system of public financing of presidential elections violated the First Amendment and the DUE PROCESS CLAUSE of the Fifth Amendment. The Court briskly dismissed the relevance of the First Amendment challenge on the ground that a subsidy "furthers, not abridges, pertinent First Amendment values." This cryptic response has prompted criticism on the ground that it ignores the equality values in the First Amendment. One wonders, for example, how the Court would have reacted if the Congress had funded Democrats but not Republicans. Nonetheless, the Court did consider an equality claim grounded in Fifth Amendment due process, and concluded that the financing scheme was in "furtherance of sufficiently important government interests and has not unfairly or unnecessarily burdened the political opportunity of any party or candidate."

Buckley is important for two reasons. First, it affirms that government subsidies for speech enhance First Amendment values, recognizing that our "statute books are replete with laws providing financial assistance to the exercise of free speech, such as aid to public broadcasting and other forms of educational media . . . and preferential postal rates and antitrust exceptions for newspapers." Second, it seems to recognize that political subsidies are subject to constitutional limits under the equality principle, if not under the principle of free speech.

The First Amendment issues given short shrift in *Buckley* were fully aired in BOARD OF EDUCATION V. PICO (1982). Students alleged that the school board had removed nine books from school libraries because "particular passages in the books offended their social, political and moral tastes and not because the books, taken as a whole, were lacking educational value." The case produced seven different opinions and no clear resolution of the First Amendment issues. Over the dissent of four Justices, the Court ruled that the students' complaint could survive a summary judgment motion. Four of the Justices in the majority stated that if the allegations of the complaint were vindicated, the First Amendment barred the board's action. The fifth Justice, BYRON R. WHITE, thought that because of unresolved questions of fact the case should proceed to trial; he maintained, however, that discussion of the First Amendment issues was premature.

Most of the eight Justices who did discuss the issues expressed three important notes of agreement. First, they agreed that a major and appropriate purpose of government speech in the public schools is to transmit community values "promoting respect for authority and traditional values be they social, moral, or political." There was substantial disagreement, however, about the relevance of this purpose to book selections for a school library. Second, the Justices agreed that local authorities had wide latitude in making content decisions about library materials. Finally, most agreed that discretion could not be employed in a "narrowly partisan or political manner," such as removing all books written by Republicans. Beyond these agreements, however, the Justices struggled over differences between libraries and classrooms, between lower and higher levels of education, between acquiring books and removing books. *Pico* stands for little more than the proposition that government's broad discretion in subsidizing speech is not entirely unfettered by the First Amendment.

Perhaps the most serious challenges of government speech have surrounded government spending to influence the outcome of election campaigns. In many lower court cases, taxpayers have challenged the constitutionality of spending by cities or administrative agencies to influence the outcome of initiative campaigns. Lower courts have frequently avoided constitutional issues, concluding that state law does not authorize the city or administrative agency to spend the money. At least one question is implicitly resolved by these decisions, however, namely, that cities and administrative agencies do not have First Amendment rights against the state, at least none comparable to the rights of individuals or business corporations. The decisions have left open the question of the extent to which the Constitution permits governments to use their treasuries to help one side in an election campaign.

The establishment clause unquestionably prohibits some forms of religious government speech, and the

EQUAL PROTECTION clause presumably prohibits some forms of racially discriminatory government speech. It remains to be seen what other limits the First Amendment or the equal protection clause may place on government's massive role in subsidizing speech.

STEVEN SHIFFRIN

Bibliography

SHIFFRIN, STEVEN 1983 Government Speech. *UCLA Law Review* 27:565–655.

YUDOF, MARK 1983 *When Government Speaks: Politics, Law, and Government Expression in America.* Berkeley and Los Angeles: University of California Press.

GRACE v. UNITED STATES
461 U.S. 171 (1983)

A federal statute forbids display of any flag or device designed to "bring into public notice any party, organization, or movement" in the United States Supreme Court building or on its grounds. The Supreme Court held this statute invalid, on FIRST AMENDMENT grounds, as applied to lone individuals engaging in expressive activity on the sidewalk adjoining the Court's building. The Court did not address the law's validity as applied to the building or the grounds inside the sidewalk, or to parades or demonstrations on the sidewalk.

KENNETH L. KARST

GRAHAM v. RICHARDSON
403 U.S. 365 (1971)

Arizona denied certain WELFARE BENEFITS to ALIENS who had not lived in the country fifteen years. Pennsylvania denied similar benefits to all aliens. The Supreme Court unanimously held these restrictions unconstitutional. Justice HARRY A. BLACKMUN, for the Court, said that alienage, like race, was a SUSPECT CLASSIFICATION, demanding STRICT SCRUTINY by the Court of its justification. The state argued that its "special public interest" in aiding its own citizens justified discriminating against aliens, but the Court, citing TAKAHASHI V. FISH AND GAME COMMISSION (1948), rejected the argument. The discrimination thus denied aliens the EQUAL PROTECTION OF THE LAWS.

Again citing *Takahashi,* the Court concluded that the two state laws invaded the province of Congress to regulate aliens, encroaching on an area of "exclusive federal power." Justice JOHN MARSHALL HARLAN concurred only as to this FEDERALISM ground, refusing to join in the equal protection ground.

KENNETH L. KARST

GRAMM-RUDMAN-HOLLINGS ACT
99 Stat. 1037 (1985)

The Balanced Budget and Emergency Deficit Control Act of 1985 is better known by the names of its three principal Senate sponsors, Phil Gramm (Republican, Texas), Warren B. Rudman (Republican, New Hampshire), and Ernest Hollings (Democrat, South Carolina). Attached as a rider to the bill that raised the national debt ceiling to $2 trillion, the act amended the CONGRESSIONAL BUDGET AND IMPOUNDMENT CONTROL ACT of 1974. Under the Gramm-Rudman-Hollings Act the maximum budget deficit for fiscal year 1986 was set at $180 billion, and maximum deficits were set for the next four fiscal years, with deficits to be completely eliminated beginning in fiscal year 1991. To enforce the deficit limitation, the act established an automatic mechanism according to which the OFFICE OF MANAGEMENT AND BUDGET (an executive agency) and the Congressional Budget Office (a congressional agency) were required annually to report their estimates of the deficit to the comptroller general (the head of the General Accounting Office, another congressional agency), who was to average the two estimates and report the result to the President. The President would be required to issue an executive order "sequestering" appropriated funds to the extent that the estimated deficit exceeded the deficit authorized by the act. Other provisions of the act divided the sequestration equally between defense appropriations and nondefense domestic programs and exempted from sequestration funds appropriated for Social Security, interest payments on the national debt (the total of previous deficits), and certain other programs.

The constitutionality of some aspects of the act was questioned even before the act was passed by Congress; and President RONALD REAGAN alluded to outstanding constitutional questions even as he signed the act into law. Indeed, the act contained provisions facilitating JUDICIAL REVIEW. It authorized members of Congress to file suit challenging the constitutionality of the act, it provided for challenges to be heard by a special three-judge federal court with direct appeal to the Supreme Court, and it set up an expedited process at each level of the judiciary.

Within hours of President Reagan's signing the act, Representative Michael Synar (Democrat, Oklahoma) filed suit charging that Congress, in the act, unconstitutionally delegated its power to control federal spending and that, even if the DELEGATION OF POWER were constitutional, delegation to the comptroller general, who serves at the pleasure of Congress, was unconstitutional. The latter argument was based on the modern understanding of SEPARATION OF POWERS, exemplified by the Supreme Court's decision in IMMIGRATION AND NATURALIZATION SERVICE V. CHADHA (1983). Should Synar's suit prevail, the deficit limits would be left intact, but the automatic enforcement provisions would be eliminated and imposition of spending controls to meet the limits would depend on the ability of members of Congress to agree to a JOINT RESOLUTION reducing spending. In early 1986, a three-judge federal court in the District of Columbia heard Synar's suit and held that the automatic provisions of the act, insofar as they delegated authority other than to executive branch officials, were unconstitutional.

DENNIS J. MAHONEY

GRANDFATHER CLAUSE

This expression, born of legislative skulduggery, has survived to serve more acceptable purposes. A number of southern states, seeking to circumvent the FIFTEENTH AMENDMENT's prohibition against RACIAL DISCRIMINATION in the field of VOTING RIGHTS, adopted LITERACY TESTS for voter eligibility. These provisions standing alone would have disqualified not only most black registrants but also a large number of whites. Under a typical exception, however, an illiterate might be registered if he had been eligible to vote before some date in 1865 or 1866, or if he were the descendant of a person eligible at that time. The Supreme Court, in GUINN V. UNITED STATES (1915) and *Lane v. Wilson* (1939), held such grandfather clauses invalid.

More recently, the same term has described any legislative exception relieving from regulation a person who has been engaging in a certain practice for a period of time. A new ZONING law, for example, might limit LAND USE in one zone to single-family residences, but contain a grandfather clause allowing the continuation of businesses or apartment houses already operating there. In part, such an exception is designed to avoid constitutional problems that arguably might arise in its absence. (See TAKING OF PROPERTY; VESTED RIGHTS; SUBSTANTIVE DUE PROCESS.) But the exception itself may be challenged as unconstitutional. In NEW ORLEANS V. DUKES (1976), the city had prohibited the sale of food from pushcarts in the French Quarter, but had exempted pushcart vendors who had been operating there more than eight years. The Supreme Court unanimously upheld this grandfather clause against an EQUAL PROTECTION attack. Quite properly, the Court omitted mention of *Lane v. Wilson;* it did say, however, that in cases of ECONOMIC REGULATION, "only the INVIDIOUS DISCRIMINATION" was invalid.

KENNETH L. KARST

Bibliography

SCHMIDT, BENNO C., JR. 1982 Principle and Prejudice: The Supreme Court and Race in the Progressive Era. Part 3: Black Disfranchisement from the KKK to the Grandfather Clause. *Columbia Law Review* 82:835–905.

GRAND JURY

Historians date the grand jury to King Henry II's Assize of Clarendon in 1166. That ancient ancestor was markedly different from its American descendants. The Grand Assize, as it was known, was comprised of local gentry, relying on personal knowledge and local rumor to report alleged cases of misconduct. Today's grand jury—surviving in America, but since 1933 abolished in England—normally considers events and people unknown to the grand jurors, who receive fairly formal testimony and other EVIDENCE, presented by prosecutors to decide whether or not alleged wrongdoers ought to be indicted.

Between 1166 and 1791, when the American BILL OF RIGHTS was adopted, the grand jury had come to be viewed as a safeguard for the people rather than an investigative arm of the executive. This is reflected in the portion of the Fifth Amendment that says: "No person shall be held to answer for a capital, or otherwise infamous crime, unless on a PRESENTMENT OR INDICTMENT of a Grand Jury, except in cases arising in the land or naval forces, or in the Militia, when in actual service in time of War or public danger."

This means that nobody outside the armed forces may be put to trial for a serious federal crime unless a grand jury has heard enough evidence to satisfy it that there is PROBABLE CAUSE (enough evidence on the prosecution side, largely or wholly ignoring what the defendant may show, to make it reasonable) to issue an indictment. The good sense of the safeguard is the realization that "merely" being brought to trial can be an agonizing, expensive, destructive experience. In this light, the grand jury stands as a shield against arbitrary or wicked or careless prosecutors bringing people to trial on insufficient or improper grounds.

In modern times, this role as bulwark retains an exceedingly limited reality. As a practical matter, grand juries, especially in the busy urban settings where they do the bulk of their work, function largely as the investigative and indicting arms of prosecutorial officials. There could be no other feasible or acceptable way for them to operate. The detection of crime, the decision to investigate, the judgment as to where prosecution resources should be invested are no longer, if they ever were, subjects suitable for amateur, part-time management. Inevitably, then, grand jurors work almost entirely under the guidance and effective control of prosecutors. They consider cases brought to them by the government's lawyers. They tend almost always to indict when they are advised to indict, and not otherwise.

Although this quality of "rubber stamp" is markedly unlike the constitutional ideal, there is no agreeable alternative if we are to keep the grand jury as a body of lay citizens. The grand jury is a potent instrument for invading PRIVACY, threatening reputations, and cutting a swath of terror and anxiety if it proceeds without a prudent awareness of its impact and a deep sense of its duty to be fair and discreet. In the hands of untrained people, it would be an engine of destruction. Such considerations might point in the end to abolishing the grand jury altogether. But while and wherever it survives, the leadership role of professionals is probably desirable as well as inevitable.

The passive character of the grand jury should not, however, be overstated. In strict law, the grand jury is an agency of the court rather than of the prosecution. A judge of the court is required to instruct the jurors concerning their powers and responsibilities. A judge should be available to answer questions and give guidance as the group proceeds with its work. Properly performed, these judicial directions can promote some measure of the independent judgment and common-sense wisdom that grand jurors are in principle expected to supply. Grand jurors do in fact decline now and again to return indictments sought by the prosecution. In far fewer cases "runaway" grand juries may contrive to investigate and indict people whom the prosecutors, for reasons that may be good or bad, do not deem suitable targets. These occurrences are, however, rare indeed, and usually happen in circumstances of local disarray and political upset.

In its normal functioning, the grand jury operates as a peculiar variant of the familiar Anglo-American judicial process—in some measure aping courtroom procedures but differing in fundamental respects. The similarity consists mainly in the types of evidence and, partially, in the mode of presentation. Grand juries hear witnesses under oath, proceeding by question and answer in something close to the style of the courtroom, with a prosecuting attorney doing most or all of the interrogation. Similarly, the grand jurors are given documents or other things as "exhibits" to assist in the attempted reconstruction, or partial reconstruction, of the events under inquiry. A critical difference from the courtroom is the one-sidedness of the presentation. In a system that prides itself on being "adversarial"—as distinguished from the so-called inquisitorial system of the European continent and many other countries—the grand jury is more purely inquisitorial and nonadversarial than almost any other criminal law agency anywhere. Subject to some variations among the states, the norm is that only one side, the prosecution, is heard. There is no opposing lawyer to object to questions or answers on grounds of relevance, fairness, privilege, or anything else. Nobody impartial presides; there are no disputes to umpire. In some places a potential defendant may be allowed on request to appear and present evidence that may persuade the grand jurors not to indict. More commonly, the prospective target will be heard only upon being summoned (and duly warned about the RIGHT AGAINST SELF-INCRIMINATION) by the prosecution.

The EX PARTE character of the proceeding means, in most states and in the federal courts, that the trial rules of evidence are not applicable. These rules require for effective operation the presence of an opposing lawyer to object and a judicial officer to rule on objections as the evidentiary record is being made. Free (or deprived) of all that, the grand jury may receive, and base indictments upon, hearsay or other evidence that would be excluded on objection in a trial.

Still more thoroughly ex parte, the grand jury's proceedings, until an indictment is published, are almost totally secret. This aspect accounts for a good part of what is perceived (and not infrequently functions) as fearsome and threatening in the grand jury. The concealed tribunal is by its nature more likely than the open courtroom to be a place where corners are cut and abuses are perpetrated, ranging from the tricking and bullying of witnesses to the misleading of the grand jurors themselves. Still, the received doctrine thought to justify the secrecy retains considerable vitality. As they were summarized in 1958 by the Supreme Court, the reasons are:

> (1) To prevent the escape of those whose indictment may be contemplated; (2) to insure the utmost freedom to the grand jury in its deliberations, and to prevent persons subject to indictment or their friends from importuning the grand jurors; (3) to prevent subornation of perjury or tampering with the witnesses who may testify before [the] grand jury and later appear at the trial of those indicted by it; (4) to encourage free and untrammeled disclosures by persons who have information with respect to the commission of crimes; (5) to protect [the] innocent accused who is exonerated from disclosure of the fact that he has been under investigation, and from the expense of standing trial where there was no probability of guilt. [*United States v. Procter & Gamble Company,* 356 U.S. 677, 681 n. 6 (1958).]

Granting these salutary concerns, the concealed proceedings of grand juries are pregnant with grave possibilities of abuse, too often realized in the work of insensitive or malevolent prosecutors. As mentioned, witnesses in the grand jury room face dangers of abuse, oppression, harassment, and entrapment. Judge LEARNED HAND, never tender in enforcing the criminal law, noted this familiar problem in *United States v. Remington* (2d Cir. 1953) where he thought decent bounds had been overstepped: "Save for torture, it would be hard to find a more effective tool of tyranny than the power of unlimited and unchecked ex parte examination."

A grand jury has the power to compel witnesses to testify. (See IMMUNITY GRANTS; BRANZBURG V. HAYES, 1972.) The plight of a grand jury witness is aggravated by the standard rule, in federal and most state courts, barring lawyers from accompanying witnesses to the grand jury room. Abstruse questions of privilege, the ever present dangers of later perjury prosecutions, and problems of relevance or other evidentiary objections must be discerned by the lay witness and somehow handled on the spot or made the subject of hurried consultation with counsel outside the grand jury room, an ungainly procedure that often has witnesses trotting back and forth between lawyer and grand jurors during hours or days of interrogation.

Among other grievances evoked by grand juries is the superficially paradoxical complaint against failures of secrecy. The grand jury "leak" is a familiar and pernicious phenomenon, scarring reputations and threatening the right to a FAIR TRIAL. The problems of preventing and sanctioning leaks remain among the unresolved doubts concerning the grand jury's net worth as an institution. Probably all these criticisms have helped persuade the Supreme Court not to extend the INCORPORATION DOCTRINE, applying the "right" to indictment by grand jury to state felony prosecutions. (See HURTADO V. CALIFORNIA, 1884.)

These unresolved doubts are subjects of ongoing debate. Many distinguished jurists and scholars argue that the grand jury has outlived its usefulness and should be abolished. That is a tall order at the federal level, where it would require amendment of the Fifth Amendment (which would be the first change in any portion of the Bill of Rights since its adoption). On the other hand, over half the states have dispensed with the requirement of grand jury indictment, permitting felonies to be prosecuted by INFORMATION (a written accusation by the prosecutor), and that trend seems likely to continue.

Still, at the federal level and in at least a number of states, total abolition seems highly improbable through at least the remainder of the twentieth century. In this setting, grand jury reform is a recurrently lively topic. Among the proposals (and changes already effected in some states) are provisions that would allow counsel to accompany witnesses before the grand jury; require closer control and supervision by judges; prescribe more detailed accounting by prosecutors and records of grand jury proceedings; better advise and protect prospective defendants; and confine the abuses of leaks and prejudicial publicity by prosecutorial staffs. The prospects for sound reform are greatest when citizens outside the legal profession take an informed interest in the problems.

MARVIN E. FRANKEL

Bibliography

DASH, SAMUEL 1972 The Indicting Grand Jury: A Critical Stage. *American Criminal Law Review* 10:807–828.

FRANKEL, MARVIN E.and NAFTALIS, GARY P. 1975 *The Grand Jury.* New York: Hill & Wang.

NOTE 1961 The Grand Jury as an Investigatory Body. *Harvard Law Review* 74:590–605.

YOUNGER, RICHARD D. 1963 *The People's Panel: The Grand Jury in the United States.* Providence, R.I.: Brown University Press.

GRAND RAPIDS SCHOOL DISTRICT v. BALL

See: *Aguilar v. Felton*

GRANGER CASES
(1877)
Munn v. Illinois, 94 U.S. 113
Chicago, Burlington & Quincy Railroad v. Iowa, 94 U.S. 155
Peik v. Chicago & Northwestern Railway Co., 94 U.S. 164
Chicago, Milwaukee & St. Paul Railroad Co. v. Ackley, 94 U.S. 179
Winona and St. Peter Railroad Co. v. Blake, 94 U.S. 180
Stone v. Wisconsin, 94 U.S. 181

The *Granger Cases,* decided on March 1, 1877, included *Munn v. Illinois,* in which state regulation of grain warehouse and elevator rates and practices was challenged, and five railroad cases in which the companies attacked the validity of state legislatures' imposition of fixed maximum rates. In these decisions, the Supreme Court upheld the state regulations. Conservative, pro-business voices—and Justice STEPHEN J. FIELD, in vigorous dissent in *Munn*—regarded the decisions as a catastrophic surrender of DUE PROCESS values in law and a mortal blow to entrepreneurial liberty. They left legislatures, Field contended, with an unfettered power over private property rights of business firms. To the Court's majority, speaking through Chief Justice MORRISON R. WAITE, however, the issue of state regulation's legitimacy must turn on the difference in nature between business that was purely private and business that was AFFECTED WITH A PUBLIC INTEREST, hence peculiarly subject to regulation.

Laws for the regulation of railroads and grain warehouses, enacted in Illinois, Wisconsin, Iowa, and Minnesota during the period 1871–1874, were at issue in the 1877 decisions. Until recent years, historians and students of constitutional law have tended to accept the view that the Grange and other farm organizations provided the political muscle in the midwestern reform movements that produced those laws. Indeed, it was customary to regard the legislation as radical, antibusiness, and anti-private property in intent and content. Recent research (particularly the work of historian George L. Miller) has shown, however, that there was no general antagonism between agrarian and business interests in the debates over the regulatory laws. Instead, reform was sought by coalitions, in a pattern of intrastate sectionalism; farmers lined up with commercial interests in some sections that favored regulation, and similar interests joined against regulation in other sections. The division of views depended much more upon calculations of local advantage and disadvantage from regulation than upon political ideology, "agrarian" or otherwise, or even upon political party alignments.

Contrary to another view long held by scholars, the Granger laws did not lack legislative precedent. The charters of early railway companies typically had carried maximum rate provisions and other features that bespoke the state's interest in the efficient provision of transport services. And in the 1850s several states (notably New York and Ohio) had prohibited local discrimination in railroad rate-making and had levied special taxes on railroad companies to offset the effects of rail competition on state-owned canals. The Granger laws may be seen as an extension of a regulatory tradition well established in American railway law.

Still another common error of interpretation concerns the doctrinal basis of the "affectation" doctrine as employed in Waite's majority opinion in *Munn.* The concept of "business affected with a public interest," according to a long-standard view, was a surprising resort to a forgotten antiquity of English COMMON LAW—a concept reintroduced into American law after a lapse of nearly two centuries. In fact, the concept of affectation was well known in American riparian and ADMIRALTY law; and equally familiar was the jurist from whose writings Waite drew the affectation concept for use in *Munn,* for Lord Chief Justice Matthew Hale's tracts on common law had been cited in scores of important American cases in riparian and EMINENT DOMAIN law.

The Court's majority in the *Granger Cases* rejected the contention of railroad counsel that if state legislatures were permitted to mandate fixed, maximum rates, the result would be to deprive business of fair profits, and thus to produce effective "confiscation" of private property. The majority also rejected the view that the EQUAL PROTECTION and due process clauses of the Fourteenth Amendment warranted judicial review of the fairness of rates. Such regulatory power was subject to abuse, Waite conceded, but this was "no argument against its existence. For protection against abuses by legislatures the people must resort to the polls, not to the courts."

Thus the *Granger Cases* decisions held back, at least for a time, the conservative efforts to make the Fourteenth Amendment a fortress for VESTED RIGHTS against the STATE POLICE POWER. The decisions were also of enduring importance in constitutional development for their elaborate formulation of the "affectation with a public interest" doctrine. Relying upon the advice of his colleague Justice JOSEPH P. BRADLEY, who was learned in the English law of common carriers and in admiralty law, Waite explored in his opinion the legitimate reach of the police power in regulation of business. He concluded that modern railroad companies and warehouses played a role in commerce that was analogous to the role played by ferry operators and others who in the seventeenth century had exercised a "virtual monopoly" of vital commercial services, hence were held subject to regulations not ordinarily imposed on other businesses. Thus the Court indicated, by implication at least, that businesses not so affected with a special public interest could not be regulated.

Not long after publication of the decisions, Waite wrote privately: "The great difficulty in the future will be to establish the boundary between that which is private, and that in which the public has an interest. The Elevators furnished an extreme case, and there was no difficulty in determining on which side of the line they properly belonged." This proved an accurate forecast of the Court's future travails, until in *Nebbia v. New York* (1934) the Court finally abandoned the "affectation" doctrine, holding that *all* businesses were subject to state regulation under the police power.

Within fifteen years after the *Granger Cases,* moreover, the Court had begun to invoke both the COMMERCE CLAUSE and the Fourteenth Amendment to strike down state regulations of interstate railroad operations and to review both procedural and substantive aspects of state regulation of business. The drive to establish a new constitutional foundation for vested rights, in sum, for many years relegated the *Granger Cases'* support of a broad legislative discretion to the status of a doctrinal relic.

HARRY N. SCHEIBER

Bibliography

FAIRMAN, CHARLES 1953 "The So-Called Granger Cases, Lord Hale, and Justice Bradley." *Stanford Law Review* 5:587–679.

MAGRATH, C. PETER 1963 *Morrison R. Waite: The Triumph of Character.* New York: Macmillan.

MILLER, GEORGE L. 1971 *Railroads and the Granger Laws.* Madison: University of Wisconsin Press.

SCHEIBER, HARRY N. 1971 The Road to *Munn:* Eminent Domain and the Concept of Public Purpose in the State Courts. *Perspectives in American History* 5:327–402.

GRANT, ULYSSES SIMPSON (1822–1885)

Next to President ABRAHAM LINCOLN, Ulysses S. Grant was the most important individual in the struggle to maintain the Union and the reconstruction of the nation in the Civil War period. A West Point graduate, Grant left the military in 1854 but returned as a colonel in the Illinois Volunteers in 1861. By 1864 Grant had risen to become America's first lieutenant general since Washington, and commander of all Union forces. Throughout the war Grant understood that victory was synonymous with preserving the Union and the Constitution. He developed strategies that devastated the South, because he believed that only a decisive defeat of the Confederacy, with a military abolition of slavery and an unconditional surrender of southern troops, would remove SECESSION from the American constitutional vocabulary.

In 1866 Grant became America's first full general, and he gradually challenged ANDREW JOHNSON's leadership. Grant accepted an interim appointment as secretary of war, in defiance of the TENURE OF OFFICE ACT, but he relinquished the post to EDWIN M. STANTON, paving the way for Johnson's IMPEACHMENT. As President (1869–1877) Grant supported the FIFTEENTH AMENDMENT (1870), the Ku Klux Klan Act (1871), the CIVIL RIGHTS ACT of 1875, and the creation of a Department of Justice and SOLICITOR GENERAL's office to help enforce these new measures. However, after 1872 Grant gave little support to the freedmen and their white allies. He dismissed his aggressively integrationist attorney general, Amos Akerman, and in 1875–1876 he refused to send federal troops to protect black voters.

Three of Grant's Supreme Court nominees were never confirmed while a fourth, Edwin Stanton, died before he could take office. Apart from JOSEPH BRADLEY, Grant's successful Court appointments to the Court, WILLIAM STRONG, WARD HUNT, and MORRISON WAITE, were lackluster. Grant's administration was scandal-ridden. His secretary of war was impeached and avoided conviction only through resignation.

PAUL FINKELMAN

Bibliography

MCFEELY, WILLIAM S. 1981 *Grant: A Biography.* New York: Norton.

GRANTS-IN-AID

See: Federal Grants-in-Aid

GRAVEL v. UNITED STATES
408 U.S. 606 (1972)

In the midst of efforts by the United States government to enjoin publication of the classified Pentagon Papers (see NEW YORK TIMES CO. V. UNITED STATES, 1971), Senator Mike Gravel (Democrat, Alaska) held a "meeting" of his subcommittee, read extensively from the papers, and placed their entire text in the record. In this case a federal GRAND JURY sought to question Gravel's aide concerning the senator's action and the subsequent private publication of the papers. The Supreme Court, in an opinion by Justice BYRON R. WHITE and over four dissents, confirmed that reading the papers in subcommittee was protected by the SPEECH OR DEBATE CLAUSE. The clause also extended its protection to congressional aides acting as alter egos to members of Congress. But *Gravel* held that dissemination of the papers to a private publisher was not a legislative act, and thus was not protected by the speech or debate clause. Therefore, Gravel's aide could be questioned about the private publication of the papers.

THEODORE EISENBERG

GRAVES v. NEW YORK ex rel. O'KEEFE
306 U.S. 466 (1939)

For practical purposes the decision in *Graves* by a 7–2 Supreme Court toppled an elaborate structure of INTERGOVERNMENTAL TAX IMMUNITIES, which the Justices had erected from assumptions about the federal system. The right of self-preservation immunized the United States and the states from taxation by competing governments within the system. Obviously the United States cannot tax the Commonwealth of Massachusetts or the state capitol in Sacramento, California, any more than the states can tax a congressional investigation. From a sensible assumption first advanced in MCCULLOCH V. MARYLAND (1819) protecting a national instrumentality from state taxation, the Court made progressively sillier decisions that hampered the TAXING POWER of the state and national governments and allowed many commercial activities to escape taxation. COLLECTOR V. DAY (1871) made the salaries of state judges exempt from federal income taxes. In time the Court held unconstitutional a federal tax on the income of a private corporation leasing state land, and a federal sales tax on a motorcycle sold by a private corporation to city police.

By 1939 the Court had already begun to retrench its doctrines of reciprocal tax immunities enjoyed by "government" instrumentalities. In *Graves,* Justice HARLAN FISKE STONE faced the question whether a state tax on the salary of an employee of a federal instrumentality created by Congress violated the principles of national supremacy. Stone observed that the tax was imposed on an employee's salary, not on the instrumentality itself. Because the Constitution did not mandate tax immunity and such immunity should attach only to a government instrumentality, the Court not only sustained the tax but also overruled *Day* and several related cases. A state may tax the income of officers or employees of the national government, and vice versa. In *New York v. United States* (1946), the Court upheld a national tax on soft drinks bottled by the state. To the extent that government functions cannot be be taxed by another government the core doctrine from *McCulloch* endures.

LEONARD W. LEVY

GRAY, HORACE
(1828–1902)

Horace Gray, Jr., reporter of the Supreme Judicial Court of Massachusetts (1854–1861) and Associate Justice (1864–1873) and Chief Justice (1873–1881) of the same court, was appointed to the United States Supreme Court in 1882 and served until his death twenty years later. Anglo-American legal history was his forte; he was the nation's leading judicial exponent of Harvard-style "legal science" during the second half of the nineteenth century. Like Dean Christopher Columbus Langdell, his Harvard classmate and lifelong friend, Gray viewed the law neither as the changing product of specific historical struggles nor as an imperfect reflection of "the spirit of the age" but rather as an array of immanent principles firmly rooted in a vibrant COMMON LAW tradition. Consequently he insisted on a radical separation of law from politics, linking the former with reason and the latter with will and power. According to John Chipman Gray, his commitment to these central concepts of "legal science" was complete yet unreflexive. "My brother's historical knowledge was confined to a knowledge of legal precedents," he wrote in 1902. "In this sphere he was not only learned, but his treatment of historical matter was strong and broad: but, outside of that, he made and had no pretensions. He was neither a philosophical historian nor a political economist."

Gray's understanding of Anglo-American legal history produced an idiosyncratic style of judging with significant implications for CONSTITUTIONAL INTERPRETATION. His treatise-like opinions were bereft of appeals to public policy or social advantage; because he assumed that the validity of legal rules was unrelated to particular historical contexts, Gray was virtually immune to both historicist and functionalist arguments against the constitutionality of legislation. In WABASH, ST. LOUIS & PACIFIC RAILWAY V. ILLINOIS (1886), *Robbins v. Shelby County Taxing District* (1887), and LEISY V. HARDIN (1890), for example, he dissented when the majority invoked national market imperatives to invalidate state police regulations and tax laws of a sort that had never before run afoul of the COMMERCE CLAUSE. Gray also resisted the majority's contraction of what he regarded as venerable SOVEREIGN IMMUNITY doctrines in *United States v. Lee* (1882) and the *Virginia Coupon Cases* (1885).

Gray's metahistorical approach to judging was especially apparent in Fourteenth Amendment cases. In *Head v. Amoskeag Manufacturing Company* (1884) and *Wurts v. Hoagland* (1885) he conceded that mill acts and drainage laws invariably disturbed valuable rights of property. In each case, however, Gray provided a lengthy digest of statutes to demonstrate that the several states had authorized compulsory flooding or drainage of property for one hundred years or more. It was simply too late, then, for the Court to suggest that such legislation took property either for private use or without JUST COMPENSATION in violation of the DUE PROCESS clause. Similar considerations prompted Gray's dissent in the landmark SUBSTANTIVE DUE PROCESS case of CHICAGO, MILWAUKEE & ST. PAUL RAILWAY V. MINNESOTA (1890). And in *Budd v. New York* (1892), where the Court upheld a New York statute fixing rates of charge for grain storage, he supplied the majority's spokesman with a long memorandum "showing that the prices of necessary articles were controlled by the legislature, in England and America, at the time of the adoption of the State and National Constitutions." His authorities included Hening's statutes of colonial Virginia and a 1709 act of Parliament regulating coal prices.

Gray voted with the majority in every case involving the rights of racial minorities decided during his tenure on the Court. Yet his route to the results often differed substantially from that of his colleagues. If Gray had been assigned PLESSY V. FERGUSON (1896), for example, he would no doubt have supplied a thorough digest of state legislation, as well as acts of Congress pertaining to the DISTRICT OF COLUMBIA, in an attempt to show that racial classifications in "social" contexts had been just as common in American law after ratification of the FOURTEENTH AMENDMENT as before. Legal history, not the conservative sociology that figured so prominently in HENRY B. BROWN's opinion or the natural justice to which JOHN MARSHALL HARLAN appealed in dissent, shaped Gray's construction of minority rights. Thus his associates were not surprised by his opinion in UNITED STATES V. WONG KIM ARK (1898), confirming the CITIZENSHIP claim of a Chinese child born in the United States, even though he had also spoken for the Court in *Elk v. Wilkins* (1884), denying the same claim when filed by an American Indian who had left a government reservation and renounced all privileges of tribal membership. In Gray's view, the anomalous status of Indians as wards of the nation had already been fixed by nine decades of administrative usage. But the status of persons born of unnaturalizable ALIENS was a new question in American law. Consequently he assumed that *Wong Kim Ark* could be decided only after an examination of all the juridical authorities on birthright citizenship running back to CALVIN'S CASE (1608).

It is ironic that Gray is best known as the probable "vacillating Justice" in POLLOCK V. FARMER'S LOAN & TRUST CO. (1895). We shall never know for certain whether he changed his vote on the validity of the income tax following the second hearing; but, as EDWARD S. CORWIN observed, "the surprising thing would be not that Gray was the last Justice to line up against the act, but that he should have done so at all." Gray's extraordinarily BROAD CONSTRUCTION of Congress's IMPLIED POWERS in *United States v. Jones* (1883), *Juilliard v. Greenman* (1884), and *Fong Yue Ting v. United States* (1893) underscored his constitutional nationalism. Yet he set a face of flint to HOWELL E. JACKSON's claim, in dissent, that *Pollock* was "the most disastrous blow ever struck at the constitutional power of Congress." It is equally astonishing that a self-conscious practitioner of historical method concurred in an opinion that, as Corwin put it, "played ducks and drakes with the precedents." The unkind verdict of modern scholarship is that even Gray, a jurist for whom the separation of law and politics ordinarily served as the very touchstone for judging, succumbed in *Pollock* to the reactionary impulse that gripped the legal profession at large during the turbulent 1890s.

CHARLES W. MCCURDY

Bibliography

CORWIN, EDWARD S. 1938 *Court over Constitution.* Princeton, N.J.: Princeton University Press.

FILLER, LOUIS 1969 Horace Gray. Pages 1379–1389 in Leon Friedman and Fred L. Israel, eds., *The Justices of the United States Supreme Court, 1789–1969: Their Lives and Major Opinions.* New York: Chelsea House.

GRAY v. SANDERS
372 U.S. 368 (1963)

Gray, along with WESBERRY V. SANDERS (1964), was a way-station between BAKER V. CARR (1962) (legislative districting presents a justiciable controversy) and REYNOLDS V. SIMS (1964) (the ONE PERSON–ONE VOTE principle governs the issue). In *Gray,* the Supreme Court, 8–1, invalidated Georgia's "county unit system," which weighed rural votes more heavily than urban votes in PRIMARY ELECTIONS for statewide offices. The state, said Justice WILLIAM O. DOUGLAS, was the electoral unit; within that unit, EQUAL PROTECTION demanded the principle of one person, one vote. Justice JOHN MARSHALL HARLAN dissented, drawing an analogy to the ELECTORAL COLLEGE.

KENNETH L. KARST

GREAT ATLANTIC & PACIFIC TEA CO. v. COTTRELL
424 U.S. 366 (1976)

Mississippi allowed the resale of milk from another state only if that state reciprocally accepted Mississippi milk. A. & P. stores were refused a permit to sell Louisiana milk in Mississippi, even though Louisiana milk satisfied all Mississippi quality standards, because Louisiana had not entered a reciprocity agreement with Mississippi. Citing DEAN MILK CO. V. MADISON (1951), the Supreme Court, 8–0, held that the Mississippi law was an unconstitutional STATE REGULATION OF COMMERCE. The law severely burdened INTERSTATE COMMERCE without significantly promoting public health objectives; sales of Louisiana milk would have been allowed in the state if Louisiana had signed a reciprocity agreement. Mississippi could not "use the threat of economic isolation" to force other states into such agreements.

KENNETH L. KARST

GREAT COMPROMISE

The defeat of the NEW JERSEY PLAN provoked the fiercest battle at the CONSTITUTIONAL CONVENTION OF 1787. Small-state nationalists believed that they could not obtain ratification of any constitution that put their states at the political mercy of the large ones. The struggle focused on representation in the bicameral Congress. Small-state delegates, seeking compromise, would accept representation in the lower house based on population, but as to the upper house they would not retreat from the principle of state equality. ROGER SHERMAN of Connecticut declared that he would agree to two houses with "proportional representation in one of them, provided each State have an equal voice in the other." WILLIAM S. JOHNSON of Connecticut explained that in one house "the people ought to be represented, in the other, the States." State representation was essential to a Union "partly national, partly federal," declared OLIVER ELLSWORTH of Connecticut. But the stubbornness of the large state faction resulted in a 5–5 tie vote on what would later be called the "Connecticut Compromise." Its initial defeat brought the convention, in Sherman's words, "to a full stop," and the convention stood at the brink of failure. Concessions were politically necessary. A special committee shrewdly recommended the compromise urged by Connecticut. That recommendation carried by the slimmest majority, averting a breakup of the convention. The principle of state equality having been won, small-state nationalists then supported a motion allowing members of the Senate to vote as individuals, although LUTHER MARTIN objected that individual voting violated "the idea of the *States* being represented."

LEONARD W. LEVY

Bibliography

BRANT, IRVING 1950 *James Madison: Father of the Constitution, 1787–1800.* Pages 79–100. Indianapolis: Bobbs-Merrill.

GREEN v. BIDDLE
8 Wheaton 1 (1823)

This case extended the CONTRACT CLAUSE to INTERSTATE COMPACTS, the obligation of which a state may not impair. The Supreme Court, in an opinion by Justice JOSEPH STORY, voided Kentucky acts that failed to protect property rights guaranteed by that state's compact with Virginia, entered into when Kentucky became an independent state. On reargument, Senator HENRY CLAY defended the state. His Kentucky colleague, Senator Richard Johnson, inveighing against judicial "despotism" and "oligarchy," demanded repeal of section 25 of the JUDICIARY ACT OF 1789, proposed packing the Court, and sought a restriction of JUDICIAL REVIEW. Justice BUSHROD WASHINGTON, grounding the Court's second opinion in the contract clause, declared that "we hold ourselves answerable to God, our consciences and our country . . . be the consequences of the decision what they may." Kentucky passed state-sovereignty resolves, but congressional measures to limit judicial review and to repeal section 25 failed, because the Court's enemies were unable to unite behind one bill. Nevertheless hostility to the Court, further aggravated by OSBORN V. BANK OF THE UNITED STATES (1824), remained intense.

LEONARD W. LEVY

GREEN v. COUNTY SCHOOL BOARD OF NEW KENT COUNTY
391 U.S. 430 (1968)

In states where racial segregation of school children had been commanded or authorized by law, the process of DESEGREGATION following BROWN V. BOARD OF EDUCATION (1954–1955) was impeded by officials' tactics of delay and evasion. One such tactic was the "freedom of choice" plan, which allowed pupils to select their schools. This "freedom" was often restricted by the fear of black parents that sending their children to formerly white schools would be followed by the loss of a job, or by violence and harassment directed at them or their children. In *Green,* the Supreme Court held that a rural Virginia county's "freedom of choice" plan was an insufficient remedy for segregation.

The Court took note of the practical restrictions on the freedom of black parents but did not rest decision on that ground. Instead the Court adopted a doctrinal position that reshaped the course of school desegregation. Justice WILLIAM J. BRENNAN, writing for a unanimous Court, reinterpreted *Brown II* (1955) to require "the dismantling of well-entrenched dual [segregated] systems." A school board had an affirmative duty "to come forward with a plan that . . . promises realistically to work *now.*" A "freedom of choice" plan might possibly suffice, but where other alternatives were "more promising" the board must use them. The Court left no doubt that it had in mind the actual integration of black and white children as the index of success in dismantling a dual system.

In a small rural county with no residential segregation, integration would be easily achieved through geographical attendance zones and neighborhood schools. The question remained whether the Court would similarly insist on integrative results in large cities where housing was segregated. That question was answered affirmatively, three years after *Green.* (See SWANN V. CHARLOTTE-MECKLENBURG BOARD OF EDUCATION, 1971; SCHOOL BUSING.)

KENNETH L. KARST

GREEN v. OKLAHOMA

See: Capital Punishment Cases, 1976

GREGG v. GEORGIA

See: Capital Punishment Cases, 1976

GRIER, ROBERT C.
(1794–1870)

The Senate on August 4, 1846, unanimously confirmed Robert Cooper Grier as the thirty-third Justice of the Supreme Court. President JAMES K. POLK nominated Grier because of his STATES' RIGHTS Democratic principles, his position on the FUGITIVE SLAVERY issue, and his familiarity through thirteen years of previous judicial experience with Pennsylvania's unique law of real property. The bar of Pennsylvania thought the last of these particularly important since Grier's duties included presiding over the Third Circuit which included Pennsylvania.

Grier embraced the concept of dual SOVEREIGNTY. He believed that the inherent state police powers included the power to curb the flow of liquor for purposes of public health and morality. (See LICENSE CASES, 1847.) Yet Grier also believed that the states could not interfere in areas of responsibility granted by the COMMERCE CLAUSE to the Congress. Thus, he sided with the narrow majority in the PASSENGER CASES (1849) in striking down taxes levied by two states on ship masters bringing immigrants to the United States.

Grier contributed significantly to the constitutional law of CORPORATIONS and PATENTS. He formulated an important legal fiction in *Marshall v. Baltimore and Ohio Railroad* (1853) by holding that for purposes of establishing federal JURISDICTION federal judges could assume that corporate officers resided in the state of incorporation. The decision aided litigants seeking access to federal courts and prevented a corporation from electing officers in the state of a complaining party in order to avoid a suit in federal court.

Because of his experience with patent litigation in the Third Circuit, Grier spoke for the Court in several important patent cases. He wrote the opinions in *Seymour v. McCormick* (1854) and *McCormick v. Talbot* (1858), which involved the exclusivity of Cyrus McCormick's patent on the reaper. In the 1864 case of *Burr v. Duryee,* the most important patent decision to that time, Grier, writing for the Court, held that the patent clause protected inventors of machinery but did not extend to scientific principles. The decision guaranteed accessibility to technical information in a rapidly expanding economy while protecting manufacturers in recovering the costs of developing new machinery.

Grier staunchly enforced the fugitive slave acts. He regularly charged circuit court juries to find for the rights of masters, even when it meant a hostile public reaction. Contrary to the position of Justice JOSEPH STORY in PRIGG V. PENNSYLVANIA (1842), Grier employed the dual sovereignty theory (in *Moore v. Illinois,* 1852) to assert that state and national governments shared a CONCURRENT POWER of rendition over fugitive slaves so long as the states did not interfere with the performance of federal officers.

Grier compromised his dual sovereignty principles in DRED SCOTT V. SANDFORD (1857). He initially opposed any decision that addressed the issues, and he urged his colleagues to adopt the rule of STRADER V. GRAHAM (1851) that the laws of the state in which a slave resided should prevail. President JAMES BUCHANAN, at the urging of Justice JOHN CATRON, wrote Grier urging him to add bisectional unity to a forceful resolution by the Court of the SLAVERY controversy. Grier succumbed, although he did so equivocally. His one-paragraph opinion concurred in Chief Justice ROGER B. TANEY's holding that the MISSOURI COMPROMISE was unconstitutional and in Justice SAMUEL NELSON's position that the laws of Missouri established Dred Scott's legal status.

Grier's participation in the *Scott* case faded before his loyal unionism. His most notable constitutional contribution while a member of the Court came during the PRIZE CASES (1863). The owners of vessels and cargoes seized as prizes at the beginning of the Civil War argued that President ABRAHAM LINCOLN had imposed an unconstitutional blockade of southern ports, because Congress had not declared war. Grier spoke for a 5–4 majority in holding that Lincoln had acted constitutionally when confronted with hostilities of sizable proportions. The Justice circumvented the constitutional issues of presidential ursurpation and the definition of the conflict by stressing the President's inherent obligation to preserve the Union.

Grier tarnished his reputation by lingering on the Court after senility had taken its toll. The crisis came when the Justices considered the constitutionality of the Legal Tender Acts. In conference Grier voted in favor of the acts in *Hepburn v. Griswold* (1870), but when the Justices moved to consider the next case involving the same issue Grier's mind wandered. He switched his vote. (See LEGAL TENDER CASES, 1870–1884.) With the prodding of Justice STEPHEN J. FIELD, Grier submitted his resignation in December 1869 and left the Court the following February. Six months later he died at his home in Philadelphia.

KERMIT L. HALL

Bibliography

GATELL, FRANK O. 1969 Robert C. Grier. Pages 873–892 in Leon Friedman and Fred L. Israel, eds., *The Justices of the United States Supreme Court 1789–1969: Their Lives and Major Opinions.* New York: Chelsea House.

GRIFFIN v. BRECKENRIDGE
403 U.S. 88 (1971)

This decision provided a generous construction of section 1985(3) of Title 42 of the United States Code and of Congress's power to reach private deprivations of CIVIL RIGHTS. Casting aside some constitutional considerations that had led to a more constricted reading of section 1985(3) in *Collins v. Hardyman* (1951), and effectively overruling UNITED STATES V. HARRIS (1883), the Court, in an opinion by Justice POTTER STEWART, concluded that section 1985(3) provides a cause of action against private conspiracies to violate constitutional rights. To avoid the "constitutional shoals that would lie in the path of interpreting §1985(3) as a general federal tort law," the Court required that the conspiracy be the product of some racial or other class-based animus.

THEODORE EISENBERG

GRIFFIN v. CALIFORNIA
380 U.S. 609 (1965)

Overruling ADAMSON V. CALIFORNIA (1947) without saying so, the Court, speaking through Justice WILLIAM O. DOUGLAS, held that state laws allowing adverse comment on the failure of a criminal defendant to take the stand and deny or explain evidence of which he had knowledge violated his RIGHT AGAINST SELF-INCRIMINATION. A jury acting on its own might infer what it wished, said Douglas, but what it infers "when the court solemnizes the silence of the accused into evidence against him is quite another thing" and imposes a penalty on the exercise of a constitutional right. Two dissenters argued that adverse comment on the right to silence did not compel the accused to be a witness against himself.

LEONARD W. LEVY

GRIFFIN v. COUNTY SCHOOL BOARD OF PRINCE EDWARD COUNTY

377 U.S. 218 (1964)

Griffin, one of the school segregation cases decided with BROWN V. BOARD OF EDUCATION (1954–1955), arose in Prince Edward County, Virginia. In 1956 Virginia adopted legislation aimed at closing mixed-race schools and providing state aid to private schools. The state courts held much of this "massive resistance" legislation unconstitutional in 1959. The legislature responded by making compulsory school attendance a matter of local option and by authorizing TUITION GRANTS and property tax credits to help support private schools.

Meanwhile, the federal district court in *Griffin* had ordered the commencement of DESEGREGATION in the 1959–1960 year. The county school commissioners refused to levy school taxes for the year, and in the fall of 1959 the public schools of Prince Edward County remained closed. Private schools for white children were established, taking advantage of the state's financial aid. The *Griffin* plaintiffs challenged the constitutionality of this new response to *Brown,* and the case returned to the Supreme Court.

In an opinion by Justice HUGO L. BLACK, the Court held that closing the schools denied EQUAL PROTECTION to black pupils in the county. The Court acknowledged that no general equal protection principle required a state to treat all counties alike. However, the only reason for different treatment of this county's children was to ensure the continuation of racial segregation—an unconstitutional objective. (See LEGISLATION.)

Only the question of remedy divided the Court. All the Justices agreed that the TUITION GRANTS and tax credits should be enjoined while the public schools remained closed. (A federal court of appeals later enjoined them, irrespective of the closure of the public schools.) But the majority went further, authorizing the district court to order county officials to open the schools and, if necessary, to levy taxes to support them: "the time for mere 'deliberate speed' has run out." Justices TOM C. CLARK and JOHN MARSHALL HARLAN briefly noted their disagreement with the holding that the federal courts had power to order the opening of the county's schools.

Griffin's doctrinal importance is twofold. It is an early suggestion of the state's affirmative obligation to equalize educational opportunity, and it is an early example of federal court intervention deep in the processes of local government. (See INSTITUTIONAL LITIGATION.) In practical terms, the episode also provides a sad example of "white flight." (See DESEGREGATION.) The county's public schools opened, but they were populated almost entirely by black pupils. A whites-only private school flourished, even without the aid of the state's money. Today, while it is true that such "segregation academies" cannot lawfully exclude applicants on account of race (see RUNYON V. MCCRARY, 1976), it is also true that their tuition fees are beyond the reach of most black families. When middle-class white children withdraw from desegregated schools—in Chicago and Los Angeles as well as Prince Edward County—the result is segregation by economic status and the likely continuation of continued racial segregation.

KENNETH L. KARST

GRIFFIN v. ILLINOIS

351 U.S. 12 (1956)

Griffin was the first decision giving constitutional status to an INDIGENT person's claim to invalidate an economic barrier to his or her ACCESS TO THE COURTS.

Illinois normally required persons appealing from their criminal convictions to provide trial transcripts to the appellate courts. The state supplied free transcripts to INDIGENTS appealing in capital cases, but not in other cases. The Supreme Court held, 5–4, that the state must furnish a free transcript to an appellant in a noncapital case.

The opinion of Justice HUGO L. BLACK, for four Justices, rested on both due process and EQUAL PROTECTION grounds, asserting the state's constitutional obligation to provide "equal justice for poor and rich." Justice FELIX FRANKFURTER, concurring, emphasized the irrationality of the capital/noncapital distinction. The dissenters found this distinction reasonable and argued that the state had no affirmative duty to alleviate the consequences of economic inequality.

Griffin, along with DOUGLAS V. CALIFORNIA (1963), raised expectations that the equal protection clause would be interpreted as a broad guarantee against WEALTH DISCRIMINATION, but these decisions are seen today as standing for a more modest proposition: that the right to state criminal appeals must not be foreclosed to the poor because of their poverty. (See ROSS V. MOFFITT, 1974.)

KENNETH L. KARST

GRIFFITHS, IN RE

See: *Sugarman v. Dougall*

GRIGGS v. DUKE POWER CO. 401 U.S. 924 (1971)

Although subject to narrower interpretations, *Griggs* is viewed as establishing that employment selection criteria that disqualify blacks at higher rates than whites may violate Title VII of the CIVIL RIGHTS ACT OF 1964 even if the selection criteria are not chosen for discriminatory purposes. *Griggs* opened the door to vast numbers of Title VII actions seeking to establish violations through statistical analysis of the relative effect of employment criteria on minorities. *Griggs*'s emphasis on effects also influenced non-Title VII cases. Until WASHINGTON V. DAVIS (1976) was decided, many courts and analysts relied in part on *Griggs* to interpret the EQUAL PROTECTION clause to prohibit unequal effects. Even after *Davis, Griggs*'s effects test continued to influence litigation under Title VI of the Civil Rights Act of 1964, Title VIII of the CIVIL RIGHTS ACT OF 1968, and other provisions.

THEODORE EISENBERG

(SEE ALSO: *Legislation.*)

GRIMAUD, UNITED STATES v. 220 U.S. 506 (1911)

In 1905, Congress authorized the secretary of agriculture to administer public lands set aside as forest reservations. Varying local conditions had made congressional regulation impractical, so the act designated him to make regulations respecting the use of these lands, violation of which would constitute a criminal offense. A federal district court judge held the act unconstitutional on the grounds that it constituted a delegation of legislative power to the executive and that it empowered the secretary to define federal crimes.

Justice JOSEPH R. LAMAR, speaking for a unanimous Supreme Court, sustained the act. The Court validated the delegation of broad discretion because "the authority to make administrative rules is not a delegation of legislative power." Even the imposition of criminal penalties did not render the regulations legislative. When a statute prescribes the penalty for a violation of administrative regulations, Congress—not the administrative officer—fixes the penalty. The notion, nurtured by this and other cases, that legislative DELEGATION OF POWER had become unimportant received a shock when the Court revived it in 1935 to strike down portions of the NATIONAL INDUSTRIAL RECOVERY ACT. (See PANAMA REFINING COMPANY V. RYAN.)

DAVID GORDON

GRISWOLD v. CONNECTICUT 381 U.S. 479 (1965)

Seen in the perspective of the development of constitutional doctrine, *Griswold* stands among the most influential Supreme Court decisions of the latter part of the twentieth century. A full understanding of its effect on the constitutional future requires a look at *Griswold's* antecedents. Even seen narrowly, *Griswold* was something of a culmination. The birth control movement had made two previous unsuccessful attempts to get the Court to invalidate Connecticut's law forbidding use of contraceptive devices. In *Tileston v. Ullman* (1943) a doctor was held to lack STANDING to assert his patients' constitutional claims, and in *Poe v. Ullman* (1961), when a doctor and his patients sued in their own rights, the Court again dismissed—this time on jurisdictional grounds that could charitably be called ingenuous. *Griswold* proved to be the charm; operators of a birth control clinic had been prosecuted for aiding married couples to violate the law, furnishing them advice and contraceptive devices. The Supreme Court held the law invalid, 7–2.

Griswold fanned into flames a doctrinal issue that

had smoldered in the Supreme Court for nearly two centuries: the question whether the Constitution protects NATURAL RIGHTS or FUNDAMENTAL INTERESTS beyond those specifically mentioned in its text. (See CALDER V. BULL, 1798; FUNDAMENTAL LAW AND THE SUPREME COURT; HIGHER LAW.) In the modern era, that question of CONSTITUTIONAL INTERPRETATION had focused on Justice HUGO L. BLACK's argument that the FOURTEENTH AMENDMENT fully incorporated the specific guarantees of the BILL OF RIGHTS and made them applicable to the states. Black's dissent in ADAMSON V. CALIFORNIA (1947) had scorned the competing view, limiting the content of the Fourteenth Amendment DUE PROCESS to the fundamentals of ORDERED LIBERTY. This "natural-law–due-process formula," said Black, not only allowed judges to fail to protect rights specifically covered by the Constitution but also permitted them "to roam at large in the broad expanses of policy and morals," trespassing on the legislative domain. In *Adamson* Justice FRANK MURPHY had also dissented; accepting the INCORPORATION DOCTRINE, Murphy argued that other "fundamental" rights, beyond the specific guarantees of the Bill of Rights, were also protected by due process. *Griswold* offered a test of the Black and Murphy views.

Justice WILLIAM O. DOUGLAS, who had agreed with Black in *Adamson,* recognized that the Connecticut birth control law violated no specific guarantee of the Bill of Rights. A number of other guarantees, however, protected various aspects of PRIVACY, and all of them had "penumbras, formed by emanations from those guarantees that [helped] give them life and substance." The *Griswold* case concerned "a relationship lying within the zone of privacy created by several fundamental constitutional guarantees." The NINTH AMENDMENT recognized the existence of other rights outside those specifically mentioned in the Bill of Rights, and the right of marital privacy itself was "older than the Bill of Rights." Enforcement of Connecticut's law would involve intolerable state intrusion into the marital bedroom. The law was invalid in application to married couples, and the birth control clinic operators could not be punished for aiding its violation.

In form, this "penumbras" theory was tied to the specifics of the Bill of Rights; in fact, it embraced the Murphy contention. Justices JOHN MARSHALL HARLAN and BYRON R. WHITE, concurring, candidly rested on SUBSTANTIVE DUE PROCESS grounds. Justice Black, dissenting, expressed distaste for the Connecticut law but could find nothing specific in the Constitution to prevent the state from forbidding the furnishing or the use of contraceptives. He chided the majority for using natural law to "keep the Constitution in tune with the times"—a function that lay beyond the Court's power or duty.

Griswold served as an important precedent eight years later when the Court held, in ROE V. WADE (1973), that the new constitutional right of privacy included a woman's right to have an abortion. (See REPRODUCTIVE AUTONOMY.) The *Roe* opinion, abandoning the shadows of *Griswold's* penumbras, located the right of privacy in the "liberty" protected by Fourteenth Amendment due process. *Griswold* thus provided a bridge from the Murphy view in *Adamson* to the Court's modern revival of substantive due process. Underscoring this transition, later decisions such as EISENSTADT V. BAIRD (1972) and CAREY V. POPULATION SERVICES INTERNATIONAL (1977) have made plain that *Griswold* protected not only marital privacy but also the marital relationship—and, indeed, a FREEDOM OF INTIMATE ASSOCIATION extending to unmarried persons. If substantive due process is a vital part of today's constitutional protections of personal liberty, much of the credit goes to the *Griswold* decision and to Justice Douglas.

KENNETH L. KARST

Bibliography

KAUPER, PAUL G. 1965 Penumbras, Peripheries, Emanations, Things Fundamental and Things Forgotten: The Griswold Case. *Michigan Law Review* 64:235–258.

GROSJEAN v. AMERICAN PRESS CO., INC.
297 U.S. 233 (1936)

In this unique case the Court unanimously held unconstitutional, as abridgments of the FREEDOM OF THE PRESS, any "taxes on knowledge"—a phrase, from British history, used to designate any punitive or discriminatory tax imposed on publications for the purpose of limiting their circulation. Louisiana, under the influence of Governor Huey Long, exacted a license tax (two percent of gross receipts) on newspapers with a circulation exceeding 20,000 copies weekly. By no coincidence the tax fell on thirteen publications, twelve of which were critics of Long's regime, and missed the many smaller papers that supported him. The large publishers sued to enjoin enforcement of the license tax and won a permanent INJUNCTION.

Justice GEORGE SUTHERLAND, writing for the

Court, reviewed the history of taxes on knowledge, concluding that mere exemption from PRIOR RESTRAINT was too narrow a view of the freedom of the press protected by the FIRST and FOURTEENTH AMENDMENTS. In addition to immunity from censorship, that freedom barred any government action that might prevent the discussion of public matters. Sutherland declared that publishers were subject to the ordinary forms of taxation, but the tax here was an extraordinary one with a long British history, known to the framers of the First Amendment, of trammeling the press as a vital source of public information. Similarly, Louisiana's use of the tax showed it to be a deliberate device to fetter a selected group of newspapers. To allow a free press to be fettered, Sutherland said, "is to fetter ourselves." Deciding that the tax abridged the freedom of the press made unnecessary a determination whether it also denied the EQUAL PROTECTION OF THE LAWS. In subsequent cases the Court sustained nondiscriminatory taxes on publishers but extended the principle of *Grosjean* to strike down taxes inhibiting RELIGIOUS LIBERTY.

LEONARD W. LEVY

GROSSCUP, PETER S. (1852–1921)

Peter Stenger Grosscup served nineteen years in the lower federal courts, the last twelve (1899–1911) on the Seventh Circuit Court of Appeals. Controversy dogged his judicial career. He preached the inevitability of industrial consolidation and the need for reasonable regulation of capital and labor. The judge's numerous critics within the Progressive movement charged that his conception of reasonableness merely disguised a probusiness bias.

Grosscup in 1894 gained national attention during the violent confrontation between Eugene V. Debs's American Railway Union and the Pullman Palace Car Company. The judge's sympathies were clear. Grosscup issued an INJUNCTION ordering the strikers to cease disruption of INTERSTATE COMMERCE and the mails. Grosscup, describing the strikers to a federal GRAND JURY, observed that "neither the torch of the incendiary, or the weapon of the insurrectionist, nor the inflamed tongue of him who incites to fire and sword is the instrument to bring about reform."

Grosscup's pronouncements in favor of reasonable regulation clashed with his advocacy of the abolition of the SHERMAN ANTITRUST ACT and his evanescent enforcement record. In *United States v. Swift & Co.* (1903) he did hold that since the commerce power included intercourse brought about by sale or exchange, application of the Sherman Act to outlaw price fixing by the Beef Trust was constitutional. However, in *Standard Oil Co. of Indiana v. United States* (1908), he spoke for a unanimous circuit court in reversing a district court fine of $29,240,000 against an oil company valued at $1,000,000. Grosscup testily wrote that the holding company—which could have afforded to pay—had not been on trial. The judge responded with mocking indifference to President THEODORE ROOSEVELT's sharp denunciation of the opinion.

Grosscup was publicly perceived as a tool of the corporations. His involvement as a shareholder and director of several businesses further undermined his judicial credibility. After resigning under pressure, Grosscup successfully defied his critics to prove misconduct.

KERMIT L. HALL

Bibliography

VANCE, JOHN T. 1964 Peter Stenger Grosscup. *Dictionary of American Biography,* Vol. 4:21–22. New York: Scribner's.

GROSSMAN, EX PARTE 267 U.S. 87 (1925)

This opinion, elucidating the scope of the PARDONING POWER, declared executive discretion absolute in the matter. The President had commuted Grossman's sentence, but a court ordered him reimprisoned to serve a sentence for contempt. The Supreme Court, recurring to history, rejected arguments that extension of the pardoning power to criminal contempts would violate judicial independence or the SEPARATION OF POWERS: "Whoever is to make [the pardoning power] useful must have full discretion to exercise it."

DAVID GORDON

GROUNDS OF OPINION

The grounds of opinion are the stated reasons given by a court or a judge for the DECISION (or dissent) in a case. The grounds are the principles, precedents, and logical steps relied upon to support the conclusion. In the OPINION OF THE COURT, the grounds are the RATIO DECIDENDI, as opposed to the OBITER

DICTA. In CONCURRING and DISSENTING OPINIONS, the grounds are, correspondingly, the points necessary to establish the desired result.

DENNIS J. MAHONEY

GROUP LIBEL

Group libel statutes pose uniquely difficult issues, for they produce a clash between two constitutional commitments: to equality and to FREEDOM OF SPEECH. Such laws impose punishments on the defamation of racial, ethnic, or religious groups. Group libel statutes were first enacted following World War II. It was widely believed that the Nazis had come to power in Germany by means of systematic calumny of their opponents and of Jews and other groups that might serve as scapegoats. Group libel statutes were enacted to afford remedies for defamation, to prevent breaches of the peace, and ultimately to protect democracy against totalitarianism. On the other hand, as the Supreme Court stated in NEW YORK TIMES CO. V. SULLIVAN (1964), the FIRST AMENDMENT manifests "a profound national commitment to the principle that debate on public issues should be uninhibited, robust and wide-open." Group libel statutes test that commitment.

The Court purported to settle the question in BEAUHARNAIS V. ILLINOIS (1952). A deeply divided Court upheld an Illinois group libel statute by resort to constitutional premises that have been substantially eroded by subsequent decisions. Although the continuing force of *Beauharnais* as a precedent is subject to serious doubt, it has not been overruled and was cited by the Court with seeming approval in *New York v. Ferber* (1982).

Beauharnais had been convicted for circulating a leaflet calling on officials in Chicago "to halt the further encroachment, harassment and invasion of white people, their property, neighborhoods, and persons, by the Negro." Calling upon white people to unite, Beauharnais's leaflet counseled that "if persuasion and the need to prevent the white race from becoming mongrelized by the Negro will not unite us, then the . . . rapes, robberies, knives, guns and marijuana of the Negro surely will."

One of the dissenting Justices, WILLIAM O. DOUGLAS, found it an easy case. In his view, if the "plain command of the First Amendment was to be overridden, the state was required to show that "the peril of speech" was "clear and present."

Justice FELIX FRANKFURTER, writing for the Court's majority, found it unnecessary to consider any CLEAR AND PRESENT DANGER test; libel, he said, is beneath First Amendment protection. Given the history of racial violence in Illinois, he argued, the legislature was not "without reason" in concluding that expressions like Beauharnais's had contributed to the violence and should be curbed.

In dissent, Justice HUGO L. BLACK challenged the Court's equation of group libel and ordinary libel. He suggested that the limited scope of libel assured that it applied to "nothing more than purely private feuds." The move from libel to group libel, he declared, was a move "to punish discussion of matters of public concern" and "a corresponding invasion of the area dedicated to free expression by the First Amendment."

Although Justice Black's characterization of the law of libel exaggerated its limits, constitutional developments since *Beauharnais* strongly support his general perspective. In *New York Times Co. v. Sullivan* the Court ruled that despite prior history, fresh assessment of the First Amendment yielded the conclusion that some libel was indeed within the scope of First Amendment protection. In a trail of decisions from *Sullivan* to GERTZ V. ROBERT WELCH, INC. (1974), the Court concluded that the First Amendment afforded some protection for a broad range of defamatory material. The driving force behind this constitutionalization of the tort of defamation was *Sullivan's* recognition of the First Amendment's commitment to uninhibited debate; moreover, the profound First Amendment importance of expression on public issues has been echoed in many subsequent opinions.

Sullivan and its successor decisions undermine the premises of *Beauharnais.* No Justice today could write an opinion saying that because libel is beneath First Amendment protection, so is group libel. First, most libel is clearly entitled to some measure of First Amendment protection. Second, putting group libel aside, if some libel remains entirely outside the First Amendment's scope, it would be speech of a private or commercial character. Justice Black's point that the move from libel to group libel is a move from the private sphere to the public sphere describes today's doctrine more accurately than it described the doctrine of 1952.

Another reason to doubt *Beauharnais's* continuing vitality is the Court's statement in *Gertz v. Robert Welch, Inc.* that "under our Constitution, there is no such thing as a false idea." That expression has generally been interpreted to mean that opinions are immune from any imposition of liability based on their asserted falsity. Although the line between fact and opinion is hard to draw, and although some group libel contains false assertions of fact, the sting of most group libel comes from unverifiable opinions. For example, what evidence could have proved the "truth" of Beauharnais's pejorative comments about black Americans? A separate issue is whether it is desirable for American trials to be conducted about the truth or falsity of various pejorative statements about ethnic groups. In the case of religious groups, the legal resolution of such questions could pose serious issues under the religion clauses of the First Amendment.

If group libel statutes are to find constitutional refuge, the necessary constitutional principles will have to be found beyond the defamation decisions. A growing body of opinions resonate with the theme of *Paris Adult Theatre v. Slaton* (1973) pronouncing the right to maintain "a decent society." From *Young v. American-Mini Theatres, Inc.* (1976) to FEDERAL COMMUNICATIONS COMMISSION v. PACIFICA FOUNDATION (1978) and a series of dissents in decisions involving FIGHTING WORDS, there is support for arguments based on concepts of civility, decency, and dignity. Whether or not these arguments succeed in validating group libel statutes, the conflict between public morality and freedom of speech will persist as an abiding theme of constitutional law.

STEVEN SHIFFRIN

Bibliography

ARKES, HADLEY 1974 Civility and the Restriction of Speech: Rediscovering the Defamation of Groups. *Supreme Court Review* 1974:281–335.

KALVEN, HARRY, JR. 1965 *The Negro and the First Amendment.* Columbus: Ohio State University Press.

GROVES v. SLAUGHTER
15 Peters 449 (1841)

Groves was the only case to come before the United States Supreme Court involving the relative powers of the state and federal governments over the interstate slave trade. Mississippi's Constitution forbade the importation of slaves for sale. In suit on a defaulted note given for an imported slave, the Court majority, speaking through Justice SMITH THOMPSON, held that the state constitutional provision was not self-executing and was unenforceable without legislation implementing it. Concurring opinions revealed a wide divergence of opinion among the justices on slavery-related questions. Justice JOHN MCLEAN asserted that slaves were essentially persons, not property. Chief Justice ROGER B. TANEY insisted that state power over blacks, slave or free, was exclusive and superseded any exercise of federal power under the slave-trade or COMMERCE CLAUSE. Justice HENRY BALDWIN denied that states could exclude the slave trade.

WILLIAM M. WIECEK

GROVEY v. TOWNSEND
295 U.S. 45 (1935)

Following the decision in NIXON v. CONDON (1932), the Texas state convention of the Democratic party adopted a rule limiting voting in PRIMARY ELECTIONS to whites. Grovey, a black, was refused a primary ballot and sued for damages. The Supreme Court unanimously held that the party's rule did not amount to STATE ACTION under the FOURTEENTH or FIFTEENTH AMENDMENT and thus violated no constitutional rights. Grovey was merely denied membership in a private organization. The Court distinguished *Nixon v. Condon* as a case in which the party's executive committee had acted under state authorization. Only nine years later, in SMITH v. ALLWRIGHT (1944), the Court overruled *Grovey.*

KENNETH L. KARST

GUARANTEE CLAUSE

Article IV, section 4, of the Constitution provides that "The United States shall guarantee to every State in this Union a REPUBLICAN FORM OF GOVERNMENT. . . ." Anticipated between 1781 and 1787 in various state and federal legislative requirements that territorial governments be republican, the clause as drafted at the CONSTITUTIONAL CONVENTION embodied the aspirations of republican ideology in the Confederation era. At a minimum, it prohibited regression to monarchical and aristocratic government, but it also incorporated the principles of POPULAR SOVEREIGNTY, representative government, majority rule, SEPARATION OF POWERS, and federal supremacy.

The guarantee clause was first invoked under circumstances JAMES MADISON anticipated in THE FEDERALIST #43: to suppress an insurrectionary challenge to the authority of one of the states (Dorr's Rebellion, Rhode Island, 1842). Then, and in the earlier WHISKEY REBELLION (western Pennsylvania, 1794), it took on a repressive character as a bulwark of extant institutions, affirming GEORGE WASHING-

TON's insistence in his Farewell Address (1796) that "the constitution which at any time exists till changed by . . . the whole people is sacredly obligatory upon all."

In the first significant judicial interpretation of the clause, LUTHER V. BORDEN (1849), Chief Justice ROGER B. TANEY declined to overturn the Rhode Island government established in the aftermath of the Dorr Rebellion. Taney held that the determination of whether a state government was republican rested exclusively with Congress, whose action was binding on the courts. In this case, Taney invoked the POLITICAL QUESTION doctrine, asserting that the issue presented "belonged to the political power and not to the judicial."

The guarantee clause figured prominently in debates on reconstruction of the Union during and after the Civil War. Democrats opposed to effective Reconstruction measures relied on a conservative interpretation of the clause as securing extant, nonmonarchical governments; they extolled self-government but limited it to whites. Republicans rejected the static, backward-looking, and racist implications of the Democratic view. Echoing earlier abolitionist contentions that slavery was incompatible with republican government, Republicans fashioned Reconstruction policies (including military Reconstruction, federal guarantees of blacks' CIVIL RIGHTS, and enfranchisement) that were conceptually derived from Taney's assertion of the exclusive power of Congress to assure republican government in the states. Chief Justice SALMON P. CHASE validated the Republican uses of the clause in TEXAS V. WHITE (1869).

The clause has played a less prominent role in public affairs during the twentieth century. The Supreme Court rejected a conservative interpretation of the clause that would have invalidated the initiative and referendum (*Pacific States Telephone and Telegraph Co. v. Oregon*, 1912). Together with the political question doctrine, the clause became linked with the concept of JUSTICIABILITY (a characteristic of cases requisite to their resolution by judicial tribunals). But the majority opinion of Justice WILLIAM J. BRENNAN in BAKER V. CARR (1962) restricted the scope of the political question doctrine, thus creating the possibility of future judicial, as well as congressional, reliance on the clause to evaluate the republican character of state institutions.

WILLIAM M. WIECEK

Bibliography

WIECEK, WILLIAM M. 1972 *The Guarantee Clause of the U. S. Constitution.* Ithaca, N.Y.: Cornell University Press.

GUEST, UNITED STATES v.
383 U.S. 745 (1966)

This case raised important questions about Congress's power to enforce the FOURTEENTH AMENDMENT and about the scope of section 241 of Title 18 of the United States Code, a federal criminal CIVIL RIGHTS statute deriving from section 6 of the FORCE ACT of 1870. Section 241 outlaws conspiracies to interfere with rights or privileges secured by the Constitution or laws of the United States. A group of whites allegedly murdered Lemuel A. Penn, a black Army officer, while he was driving through Georgia on his way to Washington, D.C. Two of the whites were charged with murder and acquitted by a state court jury. They and others then were indicted under section 241 for conspiracy to deprive blacks of specified constitutional rights by shooting, beating, and otherwise harassing them and by making false criminal accusations causing the blacks to be arrested. The rights allegedly deprived included the right to use state facilities free of RACIAL DISCRIMINATION and the RIGHT TO TRAVEL freely throughout the United States. The Supreme Court held that the alleged conduct constituted a crime under section 241, punishable by Congress under the Fourteenth Amendment.

Guest's principal significance stems from two separate opinions, joined by a total of six Justices, that addressed the question whether the Fourteenth Amendment empowers Congress to outlaw private racially discriminatory behavior. In an opinion concurring in part and dissenting in part, Justice WILLIAM J. BRENNAN, joined by Chief Justice EARL WARREN and Justice WILLIAM O. DOUGLAS, stated that section 5 of the Fourteenth Amendment grants Congress authority to punish individuals, public or private, who interfere with the right to equal use of state facilities. Justice TOM C. CLARK, in a concurring opinion joined by Justices HUGO L. BLACK and ABE FORTAS, in effect agreed with the portion of Justice Brennan's opinion relating to Congress's power. Justice Clark's opinion stated that there could be no doubt about Congress's power to punish all public and private conspiracies that interfere with Fourteenth Amendment rights, "with or without STATE ACTION."

Guest also raised the question whether, in light of the state action doctrine, the defendants, all private persons, were legally capable of depriving others of Fourteenth Amendment rights within the meaning of section 241. Justice POTTER STEWART's opinion for the Court, which, as to this point, Justice Clark's opinion expressly endorsed, avoided the issue by construing the INDICTMENT's allegation that the conspiracy was accomplished in part by "causing the arrest of Negroes by means of false reports that such Negroes had committed criminal acts" to be an allegation of state involvement. Justice Brennan read Justice Stewart's opinion to mean that a conspiracy by private persons to interfere with Fourteenth Amendment rights was not a conspiracy to interfere with a right secured by the Constitution within the meaning of section 241. Justice Brennan rejected this interpretation, arguing that private persons could deprive blacks of rights "secured" by the Constitution "even though only governmental interferences with the exercise of that right are prohibited by the Constitution itself."

Other aspects of *Guest* generated less disagreement among the Justices. The case revived a question addressed in SCREWS V. UNITED STATES (1945) when the Court interpreted section 242 (a remnant of the CIVIL RIGHTS ACT OF 1866). Sections 241 and 242 define proscribed behavior as conduct violating constitutional rights. Since constitutional standards change, defendants argued that the sections were unconstitutionally vague. As in *Screws,* the Court construed the statute to require a specific intent to violate constitutional rights and, therefore, found section 241 not unconstitutionally vague. And the Court found the right to travel throughout the United States to be a basic constitutional right that, like freedom from INVOLUNTARY SERVITUDE, is protected even as against private interference. Only Justice JOHN MARSHALL HARLAN dissented from the HOLDING that the right to travel is protected against private interference.

Both the suggestion by six Justices (through the Brennan and Clark opinions) concerning Congress's power under section 5 of the Fourteenth Amendment and Justice Brennan's views about the scope of section 241 are difficult to reconcile with important nineteenth-century decisions. In UNITED STATES V. CRUIKSHANK (1876), one of the first cases construing Reconstruction-era civil rights legislation, indictments charging violations of section 6 of the FORCE ACT of 1870 were ordered dismissed in part on the ground that Fourteenth Amendment rights could not be violated by private citizens. In UNITED STATES V. HARRIS (1883) the Court held unconstitutional a civil rights statute that punished private conspiracies to interfere with rights of equality. The provision struck down in *Harris,* which stemmed from section 2 of the Civil Rights Act of 1871, was so similar to section 241 that, until *Guest,* it seemed unlikely that section 241 could be applied to private conspiracies to interfere with rights of equality. And *Guest*'s expansive view of Congress's Fourteenth Amendment powers is difficult to reconcile with the Court's decision in the CIVIL RIGHTS CASES (1883).

Guest thus represents a shift in attitude toward Congress's Fourteenth Amendment power to reach private discrimination. But *Guest* also is part of a larger shift in attitude toward the Civil War amendments. In KATZENBACH V. MORGAN (1966) and SOUTH CAROLINA V. KATZENBACH (1966), cases decided during the same term as *Guest,* the Court for the first time found Congress to have broad powers to interpret and define the content of the Fourteenth and FIFTEENTH AMENDMENTS.

Guest's generous attitude toward Congress's power has had less influence than might have been expected. Prior to *Guest,* HEART OF ATLANTA MOTEL, INC. V. UNITED STATES (1964) and KATZENBACH V. MCCLUNG (1964) already had found Congress to have broad power under the COMMERCE CLAUSE to reach discrimination in facilities affecting INTERSTATE COMMERCE. In JONES V. ALFRED H. MAYER CO. (1968), the Court found Congress to have broad THIRTEENTH AMENDMENT powers to reach private discrimination in all areas. *Jones* and the Commerce Clause cases rendered moot much of the question about Congress's Fourteenth Amendment powers. GRIFFIN V. BRECKENRIDGE (1971), where the Court again faced the question of Congress's power to reach private discriminatory conspiracies, underscores *Guest*'s modest influence. *Griffin* involved a civil statute, section 1985(3), that is similar to section 241. By the time of *Griffin,* however, the Court could rely on Congress's Thirteenth Amendment powers to sustain legislation proscribing private racial conspiracies. *Guest*'s possible implications will be realized only in cases, if any, to which Congress's Thirteenth Amendment and commerce clause powers are inapplicable.

THEODORE EISENBERG

Bibliography

COX, ARCHIBALD 1966 Foreword: Constitutional Adjudication and the Promotion of Human Rights. *Harvard Law Review* 80:91–122.

NOTE 1974 Federal Power to Regulate Private Discrimination: The Revival of the Enforcement Clauses of the Reconstruction Era Amendments. *Columbia Law Review* 74:449–527.

NOTE 1967 Fourteenth Amendment Congressional Power to Legislate Against Private Discrimination: The *Guest* Case. *Cornell Law Quarterly* 52:586–599.

TRIBE, LAURENCE H. 1978 *American Constitutional Law.* Pages 273–275. Mineola, N.Y.: Foundation Press.

GUFFEY-SNYDER (BITUMINOUS COAL CONSERVATION) ACT

See: *Carter v. Carter Coal Company*

GUILT BY ASSOCIATION

The United States Supreme Court frequently proclaims that guilt by association has no place in our constitutional system (for example, *Schneiderman v. United States,* 1943; WIEMAN V. UPDEGRAFF, 1952). Sanctions imposed for membership in a group are said to be characteristic of primitive cultures, or elements of the early COMMON LAW long since eliminated with prohibitions against such punishments as attaint and forfeiture.

In 1920, CHARLES EVANS HUGHES made what is probably still the most famous statement attacking guilt by association as inconsistent with our individualistic legal norms. In protesting the action of the New York Assembly, which had suspended five elected members because they were members of the Socialist Party, Hughes argued: "It is the essence of the institutions of liberty that it be recognized that guilt is personal and cannot be attributed to the holding of opinion or of mere intent in the absence of overt acts."

Other Justices frequently quoted or paraphrased this argument by Hughes, made between the two periods Hughes served on the Court, in decisions invalidating deportations, employment dismissals, and denials of licenses, as well as in criminal prosecutions. It is obvious, however, that frequently ascription of guilt by association is permitted. For example, members of a CRIMINAL CONSPIRACY may be found guilty for actions by their co-conspirators based entirely on their association in the conspiracy. The Supreme Court recognized the potential for abuse in criminal conspiracy in *Krulewitch v. United States* (1949), but convictions of coconspirators still may be upheld without proof of their direct knowledge or participation in the range of crimes committed by other members of the conspiracy.

There are also striking examples of the Court's condoning of government action based on the presumption of guilt by association in constitutional law. These include the JAPANESE AMERICAN CASES (1943–1944), which upheld the internment of West Coast residents of Japanese ancestry during World War II, and numerous decisions during the 1950s, such as AMERICAN COMMUNICATIONS ASSOCIATION V. DOUDS (1950) and BARENBLATT V. UNITED STATES (1959), which allowed sanctions for membership in communist organizations.

Despite reiteration of the unacceptability of punishment premised upon guilt by association, judgments about individuals based upon their membership in groups frequently—perhaps even necessarily—are made in a bureaucratized world in which personal knowledge of others seems increasingly elusive. Nevertheless, the assignment of individual guilt premised on one's associations remains anathema. It is still thought to be an important premise of constitutional law that the government may not use a gross shorthand such as guilt by association to stigmatize or to punish citizens.

Constitutional safeguards derived primarily from the FIRST AMENDMENT and the DUE PROCESS clauses are said to surround FREEDOM OF ASSOCIATION. When the government employs the technique of guilt by association, it endangers this freedom, which the Court proclaimed in DEJONGE V. OREGON (1937) to be among the most fundamental of constitutional protections. Guilt by association also is inconsistent with basic premises of individual responsibility, which lie close to the core of much of America's legal culture.

AVIAM SOIFER

Bibliography

EMERSON, THOMAS I. 1970 *The System of Freedom of Expression.* Pages 105–110, 126–129, 161–204, 235–241. New York: Random House.

O'BRIAN, JOHN L. 1948 Loyalty Tests and Guilt by Association. *Harvard Law Review* 61:592–611.

GUINN v. UNITED STATES 238 U.S. 347 (1915)

In an 8–0 decision, the Supreme Court sustained the conviction of two Oklahoma election officials of conspiracy to deprive blacks of their VOTING RIGHTS. In an opinion by Chief Justice EDWARD D. WHITE, the court held that a state constitutional amendment enacting a GRANDFATHER CLAUSE, which exempted from the literacy test the descendants of persons who had been entitled to vote before 1866, violated the FIFTEENTH AMENDMENT, and that officials could be prosecuted for attempting to enforce it. In a companion case (MYERS V. ANDERSON) the Court held that Maryland officials were liable for civil damages for enforcing that state's grandfather clause.

DENNIS J. MAHONEY

GULF OF TONKIN RESOLUTION
73 Stat. 384 (1964)
84 Stat. 2053 (1971) (repeal)

One criticism of American participation in the VIETNAM WAR was based on the Constitution: half a million troops had been committed to combat without a DECLARATION OF WAR by Congress. In 1964 President LYNDON B. JOHNSON reported that North Vietnamese boats had attacked United States naval vessels in the Gulf of Tonkin. Accepting the truth of these reports, Congress adopted a resolution supporting the President in "taking all necessary measures to repel any armed attack against the forces of the United States and to prevent further aggression." The resolution further approved the use of armed force to defend other nations that had signed the Southeast Asia treaty. Massive escalation of the American involvement in South Vietnam soon followed; the President cited this resolution and successive appropriations measures as evidence of congressional ratification of his actions.

In 1971 Congress repealed the Gulf of Tonkin Resolution. President RICHARD M. NIXON did not oppose the repeal; he asserted that his power as COMMANDER-IN-CHIEF of the armed forces authorized continuation of American participation. After the American troops were withdrawn in 1973, Congress reasserted its authority, adopting the WAR POWERS RESOLUTION over Nixon's veto.

KENNETH L. KARST

GUN CONTROL

See: Second Amendment

GUTHRIE, WILLIAM D.
(1859–1935)

A corporation lawyer and professor of law at Columbia (1913–1922), William D. Guthrie was one of several prominent attorneys who successfully challenged the federal income tax in POLLOCK V. FARMERS' LOAN & TRUST COMPANY (1895). His most famous appearance before the Supreme Court, however, came in a losing cause: CHAMPION V. AMES (1903). In that case, he advocated a doctrine EDWARD S. CORWIN would later call DUAL FEDERALISM (and which the Supreme Court itself would adopt in HAMMER V. DAGENHART, 1918). Drawing on his *Lectures on the Fourteenth Article of Amendment to the Constitution* (1898), Guthrie argued that the suppression of lotteries did not fall under the national commerce power because no commerce was involved. Such regulation belonged solely to the STATE POLICE POWER, to which Guthrie accorded great deference. He also favored the RULE OF REASON in ANTITRUST cases (though he was unable to convince the Court to accept it in UNITED STATES V. TRANS-MISSOURI FREIGHT ASSOCIATION, 1897) and he vigorously opposed the SIXTEENTH AMENDMENT on dual federalism grounds.

DAVID GORDON

HABEAS CORPUS

(Latin: "You shall have the body.") Habeas corpus is the most celebrated of Anglo-American judicial procedures. It has been called the "Great Writ of Liberty" and hailed as a crucial bulwark of a free society. Compared to many encomia, Justice FELIX FRANKFURTER's praise in BROWN V. ALLEN (1953) is measured:

> The uniqueness of habeas corpus in the procedural armory of our law cannot be too often emphasized. It differs from all other remedies in that it is available to bring into question the legality of a person's restraint and to require justification for such detention. Of course this does not mean that prison doors may readily be opened. It does mean that explanation may be exacted why they should remain closed. It is not the boasting of empty rhetoric that has treated the writ of *habeas corpus* as the basic safeguard of freedom in the Anglo-American world. "The great writ of habeas corpus has been for centuries esteemed the best and only sufficient defence of personal freedom." Mr. Chief Justice [SALMON P.] CHASE, writing for the Court, in *Ex parte Yerger,* 8 Wall. 85, 95. Its history and function in our legal system and the unavailability of the writ in totalitarian societies are naturally enough regarded as one of the decisively differentiating factors between our democracy and totalitarian governments.

Though even this rhetoric may be a bit overdone, it nonetheless reflects the importance that has come to be attached to habeas corpus. It is a symbol of freedom, as well as an instrument. What is significant in the rhetoric is not the degree of exaggeration but rather the extent of truth.

Habeas corpus is accorded a special place in the Constitution. Article I, section 9, of the basic document, included even before the BILL OF RIGHTS was appended, contains the following provision: "The privilege of the Writ of Habeas Corpus shall not be suspended, unless when in Cases of Rebellion or Invasion the public Safety may require it."

This text of course presumes an understanding of what habeas corpus is. Technically, it is simply a writ, or court order, commanding a person who holds another in custody to demonstrate to the court legal justification for that restraint of personal liberty. The name "habeas corpus" derives from the opening words of the ancient COMMON LAW writ that commanded the recipient to "have the body" of the prisoner present at the court, there to be subject to such disposition as the court should order. A writ of habeas corpus, even one directed to an official custodian, can be obtained routinely by the prisoner or by someone on his behalf. As at common law, the writ that starts proceedings also defines the nature of those proceedings (and lends its name to them and, sometimes, to the final order granting relief). Thus, habeas corpus not only requires the custodian promptly to produce the prisoner in court but also precipitates an inquiry into the justification for the restraint and may result in an order commanding release.

The writ itself is no more than a procedural device that sets in motion a judicial inquiry. Yet the importance attached to habeas corpus necessarily posits that a court will not accept a simple showing of official authority as sufficient justification for imprisonment. Otherwise, the constitutional provision would indeed be much ado about nothing. "The privilege of the

Writ" would hardly be worth guaranteeing if it did not invoke substantial criteria for what are sufficient legal grounds for depriving a person of liberty.

The principle that even an order of the king was not itself sufficient basis had been established in England before the time of our Constitution. In *Darnel's Case* (1627), during the struggle for parliamentary supremacy, a custodian's return to a writ of habeas corpus asserted that the prisoner was held by "special command" of the king, and the court accepted this as sufficient justification. This case precipitated three House of Commons resolutions and a PETITION OF RIGHT, assented to by the king, declaring habeas corpus available to examine the underlying cause of a detention and, if no legitimate cause be shown, to order the prisoner released. But even these actions did not resolve the matter. Finally, two HABEAS CORPUS ACTS, of 1641 and 1679, together established habeas corpus as an effective remedy looking beyond formal authority to examine the sufficiency of the actual cause for holding a prisoner.

Although the Habeas Corpus Acts did not extend to the American colonies, the principle that the sovereign had to show just cause for imprisoning an individual was carried over to the colonies. After the Revolution, the underlying principle was implicitly incorporated in the constitutional provision guaranteeing the regular availability of habeas corpus against suspension by the new central national government.

The broad assumptions underlying the Great Writ have been well articulated by HENRY HART. Speaking in the particular context of PROCEDURAL DUE PROCESS for ALIENS, but with general implications, he wrote of:

> the great and generating principle . . . that the Constitution always applies when a court is sitting with JURISDICTION in habeas corpus. For then the Court has always to inquire, not only whether the statutes have observed, but whether the petitioner before it has been "deprived of life, liberty, or property, without due process of law," or injured in any other way in violation of the FUNDAMENTAL LAW. . . .
>
> That principle forbids a CONSTITUTIONAL COURT with JURISDICTION in habeas corpus from ever accepting as an adequate return to the writ the mere statement that what has been done is authorized by act of Congress. The inquiry remains, if MARBURY V. MADISON still stands, whether the act of Congress is consistent with the fundamental law. Only upon such a principle could the Court reject, as it surely would, a return to the writ which informed it that the applicant for admission [to the United States] lay stretched upon a rack with pins driven in behind his fingernails pursuant to authority duly conferred by statute in order to secure the information necessary to determine his admissibility. The same principle which would justify rejection of this return imposes responsibility to inquire into the adequacy of other returns [Hart, 1953: 1393–1394].

It hardly requires demonstration that an executive directive can provide no more justification than an act of Congress. In fact the Supreme Court very early held in EX PARTE BOLLMAN AND SWARTWOUT (1807) that a President's order was not itself a sufficient basis for a return to a writ of habeas corpus.

The purpose of the habeas corpus clause of Article I, section 9, is to assure availability of the writ, but the provision clearly allows its suspension when necessary in the event of rebellion or invasion. The power to suspend the writ has been rarely invoked. Suspensions were proclaimed during the Civil War; in 1871, to combat the Ku Klux Klan in North Carolina; in 1905, in the Philippines; and in Hawaii during World War II. Furthermore, two of these suspensions were limited by the Supreme Court. In the first case, EX PARTE MILLIGAN (1866), the Supreme Court held that the writ was not suspended in states (*e.g.*, Indiana) where the public safety was not threatened by the Civil War. In the last case, DUNCAN V. KAHANAMOKU (1946), the Supreme Court held that the writ was not suspended in Hawaii eight months after the attack on Pearl Harbor because the public safety was no longer threatened by invasion.

The point is not the rarity with which the power to suspend the writ of habeas corpus has been invoked in this country's history. That can be seen as a function of the relative stability and insulation that the nation has enjoyed. Rather, the significant point is the basic acceptance of the proposition that the courts remain open in habeas corpus proceedings to consider the validity of an attempted suspension of the writ and, if they find it invalid, to examine the validity of the detention. This position has not always been respected by the immediately affected executive or military authorities, and such holdings by the Supreme Court have been handed down after immediate hostilities have ended. Nevertheless, the ultimate verdict of history has upheld the courts' position. The existence of those Supreme Court precedents, and their acceptance and perceived vindication by history, help bolster the likelihood of similar judicial action in response to future emergencies.

The habeas corpus writ described by Article I is not necessarily one issued by a federal court. The Constitution posits the existence of state courts as the basic courts of the nation; it does not require the creation of lower federal courts at all. Thus, the suspension clause was designed to protect habeas corpus in state courts from impairment by the new national government.

The clause may nonetheless have reflected a wider sense of moral duty. The first Congress, in establishing a system of lower federal courts, gave federal judges the power to issue the writ on behalf of prisoners held "under or by colour of the authority of the United States." The federal courts have always retained that habeas corpus jurisdiction, and it has since been much expanded.

Perhaps the most dramatic example of the use of habeas corpus occurred in *Ex parte Milligan.* Milligan, a civilian living in Indiana, was sentenced to death by a court-martial during the Civil War though the local GRAND JURY had refused to indict him. The Supreme Court held that courts-martial do not have jurisdiction to try civilians so long as the civilian courts are open. The Court further held that the writ of habeas corpus was not suspended, despite the general language of a statute purporting to suspend the writ during the Civil War, because the public safety was not threatened in Indiana.

Habeas corpus also provided an effective remedy for challenging an extraordinary extension of military power during World War II. The government relocated Japanese Americans away from their homes on the West Coast to detention camps inland. Although the Supreme Court in *Korematsu v. United States* (1944) held the relocation to be constitutional, the Court on the same day held in a habeas corpus case, *Ex parte Endo* (1944), that the government was not authorized to confine Japanese Americans in the camps against their will. (See JAPANESE AMERICAN CASES, 1943–1944.)

Nor is the availability of habeas corpus to challenge extraordinary military actions limited to American citizens or residents. Even German saboteurs, landed in this country by submarine, were permitted during wartime to challenge the power of a special military commission over them. Though the Court rejected that challenge in EX PARTE QUIRIN (1942), the exercise of military power was drawn into question and examined; the Court denied relief on the merits, holding that the asserted jurisdiction was constitutional.

Habeas corpus is not restricted to testing major or extraordinary extensions of power. Particularly in the last few decades, the writ has provided a means by which federal courts have regularly controlled the reach and exercise of fairly commonplace court-martial jurisdiction. For example, in UNITED STATES EX REL. TOTH V. QUARLES (1955), military police arrested an ex-serviceman in Pennsylvania and flew him to Korea to stand trial in a court-martial on charges related to his time in service. (See MILITARY JUSTICE AND THE CONSTITUTION.) A writ of habeas corpus issued, Toth was returned to the United States, and the civilian court that had issued the writ ordered him released on the ground that he was a civilian not subject to military jurisdiction. More generally and more routinely, habeas proceedings have provided the means to define and enforce constitutional boundaries determining which persons and events may be tried without civilian courts and their procedures. Habeas corpus is a residual font of authority to ensure that the Constitution is not violated whenever individuals are imprisoned.

Indeed, habeas corpus proceedings are not limited to the enforcement of constitutional rights; they also open for scrutiny other issues of basic legal authority. For example, the writ has been used as a means to invoke JUDICIAL REVIEW of individual administrative orders for military CONSCRIPTION or alien DEPORTATION. The issues raised have included questions of statutory authority and the existence of a basis in fact for the official order. Most significant, the federal courts were unwilling to take general language precluding judicial review as barring habeas corpus; habeas corpus proceedings were held to be available even though the applicable statutes expressly provided that the administrative action should be final. Here again that position, insisting on the primacy of habeas corpus, was subsequently vindicated, and indeed, ratified by Congress in statutory revisions. Whether the Constitution entitles an individual to judicial review of military draft or IMMIGRATION orders still has not been authoritatively resolved. One of the strengths of habeas corpus, however, is that it permitted that issue to be finessed. The availability of *habeas corpus* facilitated avoidance of an ultimate confrontation—which might well have resulted in a rejection of the constitutional claim—while securing reaffirmation of the principle that government is subject to the RULE OF LAW as applied in the ordinary courts.

Our focus to this point has been on the writ from a federal court directed to a federal officer or custodian. The matter becomes more complex when the issues involve the relationships between federal and state governments. Seizure of one government's agents by the other, and their release from resulting custody, can be crucial factors in a struggle for political power. It is no accident, then, that the writ has been involved—and had evolved—in jurisdictional battles within or among governments. This involvement was evident, as mentioned earlier, in the battle for parliamentary supremacy over the crown in Britain. The writ has also played an important role in the changing relationships of federal and state governments in this country, and has in turn been shaped by these evolving relationships.

When the first Congress gave the lower federal courts power to issue the writ, it limited the power to federal prisoners and, even as to them, did not provide for exclusive jurisdiction. The state courts, then, had CONCURRENT JURISDICTION to issue habeas corpus for federal prisoners and exclusive *habeas* jurisdiction for state prisoners. The succeeding centuries have witnessed a huge expansion of federal power, including a shift of much power from the states to the central government. As the power of the federal government grew, the federal courts gradually gained the power to issue writs of habeas corpus for state prisoners. At the same time, the power of state courts to issue habeas corpus for federal prisoners has narrowed and today is practically extinguished.

As with many American legal institutions the conflict over slavery figured prominently in the development. The Fugitive Slave Act of 1850, which was enacted as part of the COMPROMISE OF 1850, increased federal power at the expense of the states. Enforcement of the act, which required return of escaped slaves to their owners, met strong resistance in Northern states. State courts would order the arrest of federal officers who attempted to enforce the act and would issue writs of habeas corpus to release individuals charged with violating the act. The federal officers were not helpless, however. Although the federal courts did not have general power to issue writs of habeas corpus for state prisoners, they had been empowered to release state prisoners imprisoned for actions taken pursuant to federal law. Congress had granted this power in 1833 in response to South Carolina's threat to arrest anyone who attempted to collect the federal tariff. The federal courts exercised the power in the 1850s and 1860s to release federal agents arrested for enforcing the Fugitive Slave Act. (See FUGITIVE SLAVERY.)

A more intractable problem was posed by state court writs of habeas corpus releasing individuals convicted in federal court of violating the Fugitive Slave Act. The Supreme Court resolved this problem in ABLEMAN V. BOOTH (1859), holding that state courts did not have the power to release prisoners held pursuant to proceedings in federal court. Otherwise, the laws of the United States could be rendered unenforceable in states whose courts were in opposition. After the Civil War, the Supreme Court went further and held in *Tarble's Case* (1872) that state courts could not issue habeas corpus to release someone held under authority, or color of authority, of the federal government. A state court may only require the federal officer to inform it of the authority for a prisoner's detention; all further questions as to actions under color of federal authority are to be resolved in the federal courts. Habeas corpus cannot be entirely barred, but so long as the writ is available from the federal courts, state courts are effectively precluded from issuing habeas corpus on behalf of persons held in custody by the federal government.

The power of federal courts to issue habeas corpus for state prisoners followed the opposite course. The JUDICIARY ACT OF 1789 did not give the federal courts any such power and, until after the Civil War, these courts were granted it only in a limited number of circumstances. An example was the release of those seized for enforcing federal law, mentioned earlier. The HABEAS CORPUS ACT OF 1867, however, was general, giving federal courts power to issue the writ "in all cases where any person may be restrained of his or her liberty in violation of the constitution, or of any treaty or law of the United States. . . ." Jurisdiction in essentially these terms continues to the present day.

The precise objectives of the 1867 act were never defined. The act aimed generally at extending the effectiveness of federal authority, particularly against resistance in the former slave states. Its terms extended to prisoners in state custody as to all other persons. Until well into the twentieth century, its thrust was principally against restraints without (or before) trial. Among other reasons, the federal Constitution had not yet been construed to impose any significant requirements for state criminal proceedings. In more recent times, federal habeas corpus has become a forum for challenging state criminal convictions on constitutional grounds. In terms of volume, this is the federal writ's principal use today.

This pattern evolved only sporadically, and only after a number of limiting concepts had been loosened. The first of these was a principle of long standing that habeas corpus was available to persons imprisoned under authority of a court, particularly following criminal trial and conviction, only on the grounds that the court had no jurisdiction to try him. If that court had jurisdiction, all challenges, including constitutional ones, were to be raised there. Trial court decisions were to be reviewable, if at all, by higher courts, not by COLLATERAL ATTACK in other courts of the same level. It was often stated that habeas corpus was not to serve as a substitute for appeal.

The formal doctrine that the habeas corpus court

would not look beyond whether the holding or convicting court had jurisdiction prevailed until near the middle of the twentieth century. Nevertheless, the scope of federal habeas corpus grew substantially even before that time. The concept of "lack of jurisdiction" is not inelastic, and the Supreme Court gradually expanded the meaning of that term to include constitutional violations that might be said to preclude a fair trial.

The first step in this expansion of the meaning of the issue of jurisdiction was to allow habeas corpus relief for a prisoner convicted of violating an unconstitutional law. Unconstitutional laws were null and void, it could be rationalized; thus the state court was without jurisdiction because *no* law authorized the conviction. The next step was to issue habeas corpus to remedy constitutional violations so gross as effectively to deprive the prisoner of a real trial. Such violations were held to be so fundamental that a court, proceeding in those circumstances, lost jurisdiction. Examples included mob-dominated trials and denial to defendants of opportunity to be heard. Reliance on the concept of lack of jurisdiction became more and more attenuated until, in *Waley v. Johnston* (1942), the Supreme Court explicitly abandoned that formal concept as linch-pin. From that time forward, the Court focused on more realistic considerations: whether the constitutional claims being asserted could not have been presented effectively in the original court that tried the case or on direct review of the conviction.

The concerns over the proper "deference" to be accorded by the habeas corpus court to the court that originally tried and convicted a prisoner arose even where both courts were federal. When federal habeas corpus was being sought by a state-convicted prisoner, these concerns were reinforced by further considerations of mutual respect and comity between state and federal systems. In response to these considerations, there developed early two substantial limits on the availability of federal habeas corpus for state prisoners: if the state courts had fully and fairly litigated the prisoner's claim, or if the prisoner failed to exhaust all state remedies, federal habeas corpus would not lie.

The requirement that state remedies be exhausted was established in *Ex parte Royall* (1886). To meet it, the prisoner must first press his claims to be free based on federal law, through the state courts. Thus, the prisoner must appeal his conviction or must seek state habeas corpus or other available postconviction remedy. (See EXHAUSTION OF REMEDIES.) Under the Constitution's SUPREMACY CLAUSE, state courts are required to follow and apply federal constitutional law. Principles of comity—essentially respect for the state courts' responsibility and ability to reach a correct decision—were seen to require that state courts be allowed an opportunity to correct their own errors before federal habeas corpus could be issued. The general exhaustion requirement is now codified in the statute governing habeas corpus.

In view of the exhaustion requirement, it may seem ironic that for many years presentation of the federal claim in state proceedings might mean that it could not thereafter be considered in federal habeas corpus. Federal collateral attack was barred if the state courts had sufficiently considered and passed upon the prisoner's constitutional claim. This is not so perverse as might first appear. Habeas corpus, as a collateral remedy, was to deal with serious constitutional problems involving circumstances outside the record or cognizance of the state courts. It would also serve where appellate consideration was unavailable or ineffective. If the state courts had adjudicated the federal constitutional contention adversely to the prisoner, on full and fair consideration and with effective appellate review, the remedy for error was to seek review in the United States Supreme Court. This was another aspect of the principle that habeas corpus was not to do service as an appeal.

The soundness of this reasoning depends, of course, upon Supreme Court reviews being available and effective. But whatever may once have been true, by the middle of the twentieth century that premise had clearly become unreliable. The Court's docket had grown to the point that it could pass on the merits of no more than a sixth of the cases in which its review was sought. The percentage has become even smaller in recent years. Moreover, even when available, appellate review in particular cases may be innately limited in significant respects because it must be conducted on the basis of a "cold" written record. Tones, attitudes, inflections of voice, and other subtle factors may exert powerful influences on outcomes and yet not be evident on the record. Beyond that, in many criminal proceedings an adequate written record may not even be produced. The significance of these factors in limiting the utility of Supreme Court review is greatly heightened when the applicable federal law is developing rapidly, and particularly if state judges are hostile to or less than entirely sympathetic with the direction of that development. Both of these conditions existed in the 1930s and 1940s and both intensified in the period following World War II, when the Supreme Court greatly expanded the procedural requirements imposed by federal constitutional law in state criminal prosecutions. Many requirements that previously governed only federal CRIMINAL PROCEDURE were "incorporated" into the FOURTEENTH AMENDMENT and made applicable in state trials. (See INCORPORATION DOCTRINE.) Moreover, and surely of no less import, the Supreme Court was also expansively construing the EQUAL PROTECTION CLAUSE of the Fourteenth Amendment to heighten prohibitions against RACIAL DISCRIMINATION. That attitude enhanced federal scrutiny of jury selection and other elements of state criminal proceedings. Particularly in the early stages of the development of these growing constitutional demands, there was reason to believe that many state judges might be less than fully sympathetic, if not directly hostile, to these new federal principles and DOCTRINES.

Under these conditions, direct appellate review by the Supreme Court could not alone provide reliable and effective enforcement of federal constitutional guarantees in the state courts. Indeed, any tendency toward heel-dragging or resistance might well be encouraged by the knowledge that the statistical probability of federal appellate review was very low. Moreover, by diverting Supreme Court energy to enforcement of earlier holdings, resistance might effectively retard further development of the new doctrines.

Habeas corpus from federal courts probing the validity of state convictions could offer an alternative mode for securing effective enforcement of the new constitutional rights. Federal judges generally could be relied upon to be more in tune with Supreme Court developments than their state counterparts. Because the entire federal judiciary would be involved, caseload capacity would be much more equal to the task. Moreover, because trial-type hearings were possible, habeas corpus had the further advantage that the federal courts need not be dependent upon the state court record. These gains could, of course, be achieved only by abandoning the rule that barred consideration on federal habeas corpus of contentions that had been adjudicated previously in the state courts. The Supreme Court took that step in 1953 in *Brown v. Allen.*

Brown v. Allen represented a major extension of the functions of habeas corpus. Its holding, allowing federal reconsideration of issues previously considered fully by state courts, also effectively opened wide the range of constitutional contentions that could serve as sufficient grounds for seeking federal habeas corpus. From that point forward, it was clear that at the very least any constitutional claim that could be said to raise any significant issue of trial fairness would be open to consideration. That expansion of the scope of habeas corpus serves important ends, but it has significant costs.

One of these costs is the adverse reaction of many state judges. The result of *Brown v. Allen* is that federal courts on habeas corpus may reexamine a state prisoner's constitutional challenges to his conviction after a state court has considered and rejected those same challenges. Because the prisoner must exhaust his state remedies before federal habeas corpus, normally the federal constitutional claims have been pressed not only at the state trial but throughout the state court system, including the state supreme court. The upshot of the new role of federal habeas corpus, then, is that a single federal district judge routinely may review the determination of the highest court of a state and, if he disagrees with it, overturn the conviction that the collegial, multimember court had upheld.

People and state officials in general, and state supreme court justices in particular, long since have become accustomed to review by the Supreme Court of the United States. Whatever may have been thought in their time of the challenges raised and rejected in MARTIN V. HUNTER'S LESSEE (1816) and COHENS V. VIRGINIA (1821), the higher authority of the Supreme Court in matters of federal law has been fully accepted. There has not been a corresponding acceptance of the habeas corpus authority of lower federal court judges. That federal judges may be more in accord with developing Supreme Court doctrines, though offered as justification, does not palliate the felt insult. On the contrary, if state judges are hostile to those developments, that fact exacerbates it. If the state court justices see themselves as entirely in accord with the Supreme Court's developing doctrines, the routine reexamination by a single district judge may still be offensive, to some perhaps even more so. On occasion, state courts have even openly refused to pass upon a constitutional claim on the grounds that a federal judge would pass on it anyway. On balance, the expansion of federal habeas corpus jurisdiction has almost certainly enhanced even state court enforcement of federal constitutional rights, but the felt slight to status and the consequent resentment are real.

At least as important as the resentment of state judges is the concern that the wide availability of federal habeas corpus may dilute the deterrent effect of the criminal law. Part of this concern grows out of the belief that deterrence is enhanced by certainty of punishment and that the expansion of federal habeas corpus increases the possibility that a conviction may be overturned. Certainly, the availability of federal habeas corpus, after the full range of state court remedies, does mean that the finality of a conviction is greatly delayed, even when the conviction is ultimately upheld. Moreover, the knowledge that the ultimate decision can always be greatly delayed itself diminishes any general sense in the community that punishment may be swift or certain.

When the conviction is overturned years after the trial and even longer after the alleged crime, these effects are exacerbated. Although the usual habeas corpus remedy is to order release only if the prisoner is not retried and convicted within a reasonable time, retrial after considerable delay may be practically impossible: witnesses may have died or disappeared; memories inevitably fade; other evidence may be lost. In those instances a reversal on procedural grounds amounts to a full release.

In fact, the proportion of habeas corpus proceedings that result in any victory for the prisoner is exceedingly small. But the effect of those few cases may be far greater than their number, particularly if a case was notorious in the community. Each such incident attracts attention and presumably lessens the deterrent effect of the criminal law. It may also be important that each raises questions for the citizenry at large who are already fearful about the capacity of the system to cope with crime.

Finally, the rehabilitative functions of the penal system may be affected. It has been suggested that demonstration of society's deep concern for fair procedure is useful, and even that channeling prisoners' efforts into litigation may be helpful. But it is more likely that the indefinite stringing-out of a conclusion is counterproductive. As Justice LEWIS F. POWELL, concurring in SCHNECKLOTH V. BUSTAMONTE (1973), wrote: "No effective judicial system can afford to concede the continuing theoretical possibility that there is error in every trial and that every incarceration is unfounded. At some point the law must convey to those in custody that a wrong has been committed, that consequent punishment has been imposed, that one should no longer look back with the view to resurrecting every imaginable basis for further litigation but rather should look forward to rehabilitation and to becoming a constructive citizen."

The concerns expressed are real and significant, but they can be accommodated only by restricting the scope of federal habeas corpus. That in turn involves a judgment as to the necessity of having federal judges routinely available to consider particular claims of constitutional violations. Every constitutional claim is important. But the issue here is not whether a constitutional right shall be declared, or whether rights so declared shall be binding on state courts and subject to review and enforcement by the federal Supreme Court. The issue is whether there should be an additional, collateral channel for routine reexamination of every state court rejection of every constitutional claim asserted in a criminal proceeding.

While perhaps in theory all constitutional rights are equal, there are differences among them. For one thing, there may be substantial differences in the justifications for, and consequences of, seeking thoroughgoing enforcement of particular rights in every case where they may be colorably claimed. The Supreme Court has recognized as much in holding that some newly established constitutional rights should be given full retroactive effect (applying to all habeas corpus cases regardless of when the original conviction was obtained) and others should not. In at least one sense it is fair to characterize these decisions as holding some constitutional rights to be more fundamental than others.

Furthermore, constitutional rights serve different sets of purposes. Most procedural requirements in criminal prosecutions are designed to minimize the likelihood of an erroneous conviction, for example, the RIGHT TO COUNSEL or the right to confront prosecution witnesses. (See CONFRONTATION.) Others are designed to protect personal privacy or dignity at trial or in the society; among these are the rules against UNREASONABLE SEARCHES or seizures, and the RIGHT AGAINST SELF-INCRIMINATION. Finally, there may be relevant distinctions between rights and remedies. Thus, the rule excluding evidence obtained by prohibited police actions may be viewed as a means to deter official misconduct rather than an independent right.

These distinctions may be highly relevant in determining the appropriate scope of federal habeas corpus in reexamining state court convictions. Consider, for example, the EXCLUSIONARY RULE that evidence obtained by an unconstitutional search may not be used in a criminal prosecution. State convictions obtained after such evidence has been introduced are invalid and subject to reversal on direct Supreme Court review. (See MAPP V. OHIO, 1961). But if in a particular case the state courts should decide that the search was legal, how important is it that the decision be reviewable on federal habeas corpus—even assuming that the state decision might be wrong and yet not important enough to warrant Supreme Court attention? Illegally seized evidence does not mean actually unreliable evidence; in fact, such evidence is generally highly probative (for example, the drugs themselves in a prosecution for possession or sale of narcotics). The ban on unreasonable searches and the exclusionary rule do not protect against convicting the wrong person; they aim to protect individual privacy and control police conduct. Thus the sole purpose of extending habeas corpus to encompass the exclusionary rule would be to enhance the rule's deterrent effect. But that enhancement would be only marginal, *i.e.*, only to the extent of whatever additional disincentive might be generated by the extra possibility of a conviction, upheld by the state courts, being overturned years later on federal habeas corpus. At the same time, any such gain could be only obtained at the cost of the side effects of habeas corpus already described, including particularly the problems involved in releasing individuals who have been proven to have violated the law.

The Supreme Court has vacillated on precisely this issue. After many years in which federal habeas corpus was held to encompass claims under the exclusionary rule, the Court in STONE V. POWELL (1976) decided that it would not be available to review decisions of SEARCH AND SEIZURE issues reached after full consideration.

That decision stirred much debate. Perhaps as a result of the prominent role of lawyers and judicial review in interpreting the Constitution, there is a tendency to focus attention on the borderlines of case law development. That perspective can be misleading. What is more important than the decision to exclude search and seizure issues is the scope of federal habeas corpus for state prisoners that remains available. Constitutional claims need not be related to ultimate accuracy of conviction in order to be included. Moreover, despite strong suggestions from respected sources that the prisoner's factual innocence ought to be a major element in the availability of habeas corpus relief, the Court has not adopted that position. By any measure, the range of constitutional claims that may be raised and relitigated in federal habeas corpus is far greater than those few precluded—and then only after full and fair state consideration.

Similarly, much of the legal writing concerning habeas corpus today deals with its use to challenge criminal convictions. It is sometimes even suggested that Congress could not constitutionally restrict the scope of that kind of habeas corpus. Related to this, but more generally, it is argued that the provision of Article I, section 9, against the suspension of the privilege of habeas corpus should now be interpreted as prohibiting Congress from suspending or limiting federal habeas corpus—including habeas corpus for state convicted prisoners. The argument generally acknowledges that this was not the original intention of the suspension clause. It contends, rather, that in view of subsequent developments and present conditions, the original purpose now calls for extending it to cover habeas corpus from federal courts.

While these arguments, and the general issue of federal habeas corpus for persons held under state court convictions, are important, too exclusive a focus on them risks distorted perspective. Far more significant than the existence of these arguments, or their validity, is their currently academic nature. Despite strenuous objections to the jurisdiction, Congress has not significantly restricted the scope of federal habeas corpus for state prisoners. Moreover, it does not derogate from the importance of this use of habeas corpus to point out that at base the availability of the Great Writ to challenge executive or military actions or other imprisonments without semblance of judicial process is far more vital to the maintenance of liberty. Even the most ardent advocates of collateral attack on judicial convictions are not likely to disagree.

It is surely a measure of the state of liberty in the United States that so much can be taken for granted. Habeas corpus for extraordinary assertions of executive, military, or other nonjudicial authority comes to the fore only rarely—and that is a measure of freedom's health in the nation. Yet it is that general freedom from that kind of arbitrary authority that is most crucial. Habeas corpus has helped to secure that freedom in the past, and its continuing availability helps secure it continually. It is true that liberty is most prevalent when habeas corpus is needed least. It is also true that the effectiveness of the remedy of habeas corpus is dependent upon the substantive criteria that come into play. Yet the existence of the Great Writ, indeed precisely in its taken-for-granted quality, plays a major role in supporting and reinforcing the conditions of freedom.

PAUL J. MISHKIN

Bibliography

BATOR, PAUL M.; MISHKIN, PAUL J.; SHAPIRO, DAVID L.; and WECHSLER, HERBERT 1973 Supplement 1981 Chaps. I, IV, and X in *Hart & Wechsler's The Federal Courts and the Federal System,* 2nd ed. Mineola, N.Y.: Foundation Press.

CHAFEE, ZECHARIAH, JR. 1952 *How Human Rights Got into the Constitution.* Pages 51–74. Boston: Boston University Press.

COVER, ROBERT M. and ALEINIKOFF, T. ALEXANDER 1977 Dialectical Federalism: Habeas Corpus and the Court. *Yale Law Journal* 86:1035–1102.

DUKER, WILLIAM F. 1980 *A Constitutional History of Habeas Corpus.* Westport, Conn.: Greenwood Press.

FRIENDLY, HENRY J. 1970 Is Innocence Irrelevant? Collateral Attack on Criminal Judgments. *University of Chicago Law Review* 38:142–172.

HART, HENRY M. 1953 The Power of Congress to Limit the Jurisdiction of the Federal Courts: An Exercise in Dialectic. *Harvard Law Review* 66:1362–1402.

NOTE 1970 Developments in the Law—Federal Habeas Corpus. *Harvard Law Review* 83:1038–1280.

OAKS, DALLIN H. 1966 Legal History in the High Court—Habeas Corpus. *Michigan Law Review* 64:451–472.

HABEAS CORPUS ACT OF 1679
31 Charles II c.2 (1679)

The right to the writ of HABEAS CORPUS, as ZECHARIAH CHAFEE, JR., said, is "the most important human rights provision in the Constitution" (Article I, section 9) because it safeguards personal liberty, without which other liberties cannot be exercised. This act of Parliament created no new right; the writ was already about a century old as a mechanism by which a prisoner could test in court the legality of his imprisonment. But crown officers knew a variety of stratagems that hamstrung the writ. This statute, which runs on and on in dull detail without a word about the liberty of the subject or any high-sounding principle, sought to seal off every means of circumventing the writ. It is a technical instruction manual—how and what to do in any situation—to make the writ enforceable as a practical remedy for illegal imprisonment. It imposed steep penalties on every officer of government, from the local jailor to the lord high chancellor for breach, evasion, or delay. The only loophole in the statute, a failure to prohibit excessive BAIL, was plugged in 1689 by the BILL OF RIGHTS. Although the statute did not extend to the colonies, it provided a model, and Americans regarded the great writ as a fundamental right protected by COMMON LAW and gave it constitutional status.

LEONARD W. LEVY

Bibliography

PERRY, RICHARD L., ed. 1959 *Sources of Our Liberties.* Pages 189–203. New York: American Bar Foundation.

HABEAS CORPUS ACT OF 1863
12 Stat. 755 (1863)

Justice, before the Civil War and Reconstruction, was overwhelmingly state justice. Under the Constitution's Article III, implemented in the JUDICIARY ACT of 1789, few litigants qualified for federal JURISDICTION. The 1863 Habeas Corpus law lessened this imbalance at least for federal officials who, enforcing EXECUTIVE ORDERS or statutes, were defendants in state courts. After legitimizing Lincoln's HABEAS CORPUS suspensions since 1861 and authorizing future suspensions, Congress, in the Habeas Corpus Act, indemnified federal officials who had been found guilty in state courts of wrongs against civilians. Further, the law authorized a federal officer facing a state court proceeding to remove the case to a federal court. United States attorneys would act for the defendant if the state proceeding were prejudiced against him and if the defendant had been carrying out orders in a proper manner. Though federal proceedings were to flow from state rules, blacks could testify even adversely to whites, and all court officers and jurors were sworn to the TEST OATH. In extending these protections to its officials, the nation bridged, for them at least, ancient interstices in the dual system of courts. Congress exacted a price from the executive, however, by requiring relevant Cabinet department heads to report to federal judges on civilians arrested by soldiers for allegedly violating draft, internal security, emancipation, or trade-control policies. In the HABEAS CORPUS ACT of 1867, Congress further expanded the classes of protected persons who could resort to federal justice.

HAROLD M. HYMAN

Bibliography

DUKER, WILLIAM F. 1980 *A Constitutional History of Habeas Corpus.* Pages 126–224. Westport, Conn.: Greenwood Press.

HABEAS CORPUS ACT OF 1867
14 Stat. 385 (1867)

This act, whose intent one expert has called "unusually murky," fundamentally amended the HABEAS CORPUS provisions of the JUDICIARY ACT OF 1789. Where that act limited availability of the writ to those persons jailed under federal authority, the new act applied "in all cases where any person may be restrained of his or her liberty in violation of the constitution, or of any treaty or law of the United States." Section 1 vested power to issue the writ in all United States courts and judges, established procedures, and authorized APPEALS from inferior courts to CIRCUIT COURTS and to the Supreme Court. A writ could issue at any point in state court proceedings, halting them until the federal habeas corpus action ended. The second section made available WRITS OF ERROR from the Supreme Court in specified instances.

The act gave the Supreme Court JURISDICTION over the appeal of a Mississippi editor who challenged the constitutionality of military reconstruction, but in 1868 Congress withdrew the provisions establishing the Supreme Court's APPELLATE JURISDICTION, and in EX PARTE MCCARDLE (1869) the Court declined to hear the editor's case. The Court nevertheless asserted authority on another statutory basis in *Ex parte Yerger* (1869), and Congress restored the Court's power to hear habeas corpus appeals in 1885.

The federal courts' statutory authority to grant writs of habeas corpus to state prisoners unconstitutionally held in custody continues to this day.

DAVID GORDON

HAGUE v. CONGRESS OF INDUSTRIAL ORGANIZATIONS
307 U.S. 496 (1939)

In separate opinions yielding no majority, over two dissents, and with only seven Justices participating, the Court enjoined enforcement of a local ordinance used to harass labor organizers. Justices OWEN ROBERTS and HUGO L. BLACK and Chief Justice CHARLES EVANS HUGHES deemed the right to organize under and discuss the WAGNER (NATIONAL LABOR RELATIONS) ACT a privilege or immunity of national CITIZENSHIP. Justices HARLAN FISKE STONE and STANLEY F. REED held it a right protected by the FIRST AMENDMENT. Justice Stone's separate opinion, which suggested that SECTION 1983's jurisdictional counterpart authorized federal courts to hear actions involving personal liberty but not to hear actions involving property rights, influenced subsequent CIVIL RIGHTS cases. Some courts accepted the distinction and applied the dichotomy to section 1983 itself. *Lynch v. Household Finance Corp.* (1972) discredited the distinction.

THEODORE EISENBERG

HAIG v. AGEE
453 U.S. 280 (1981)

Philip Agee, a former employee of the Central Intelligence Agency (CIA) who was familiar with its covert intelligence gathering, revealed the identities of its agents and sources, disrupting the intelligence operations of the United States, and exposing CIA operatives to assassination. The secretary of state revoked Agee's passport because his activities abroad damaged national security. Agee objected that revocation of his passport violated his constitutional RIGHT TO TRAVEL, FREEDOM OF SPEECH, and PROCEDURAL DUE PROCESS. An 8–2 SUPREME COURT found his claims meritless, because his freedom to travel abroad was subordinate to national security considerations, his disclosures obstructed intelligence operations and therefore were unprotected by the FIRST AMENDMENT, and his right to due process was satisfied by the opportunity for a prompt hearing after revocation. The dissenters did not rely on constitutional grounds.

LEONARD W. LEVY

HAINES, CHARLES G.
(1879–1948)

Charles Grove Haines was an eminent scholar of American constitutional history who taught political science at the University of California, Los Angeles. In 1939 he was president of the American Political Science Association. His major books continue to be among the best on their subjects. His *Revival of Natural Law Concepts* (1930) is a comparative study of theories of FUNDAMENTAL LAW. *The American Doctrine of Judicial Supremacy* (revised edition, 1932) is the finest book on the history of JUDICIAL REVIEW from the standpoint of a critic of the institution. His *Role of the Supreme Court in American Government and Politics* (volume I, 1944; volume II, posthumous and coauthored by Forest Sherwood, 1957), covering the period 1789 to 1864, is a trenchant history from the viewpoint of a Jeffersonian democrat.

LEONARD W. LEVY

HALL v. DECUIR
95 U.S. 485 (1877)

In 1870 the operator of a steamboat regularly traveling between New Orleans, Louisiana, and Vicksburg, Mississippi, refused a black woman accommodation in the cabin reserved for whites. He thereby violated a Louisiana statute, adopted during the period of MILITARY RECONSTRUCTION, which prohibited RACIAL DISCRIMINATION by common carriers operating within the state. Speaking for the Court, Chief Justice MORRISON R. WAITE sought to avoid the "great inconvenience and unnecessary hardship" which might arise if all states bordering the Mississippi River were to enact divergent and conflicting laws. Waite stressed the importance of uniform regulations and struck down the state act as a "direct burden upon INTERSTATE COMMERCE" in violation of Article I, section 8. Nearly seventy years later, in MORGAN V. VIRGINIA (1946), the Supreme Court struck down a law requiring racial SEGREGATION on buses, on a similar commerce ground. Neither opinion discussed the EQUAL PROTECTION clause.

DAVID GORDON

HAMILTON, ALEXANDER
(1755–1804)

Alexander Hamilton, American statesman, member of the Constitutional Convention (1787), coauthor of THE FEDERALIST, first secretary of the Treasury (1789–1795), and leading member of the Federalist party in New York, was born on the island of Nevis in the British West Indies. He came to New York in 1773 and enrolled in King's College; he served with distinction in the Revolutionary War, from 1777 to 1781 as GEORGE WASHINGTON'S aide-de-camp. Hamilton was a leading member of the New York bar before and after he served in President Washington's cabinet.

During the prelude to independence, Hamilton participated in the pamphlet controversies between American Whigs and supporters of Britain. His most important pamphlet, "The Farmer Refuted" (1775), expressed a conventional natural rights philosophy. He asserted that "nature has distributed an equality of rights to every man." He also upheld the right to resort to first principles above and beyond the "common forms of municipal law." He subscribed to the theory of government as a social compact between ruler and ruled (a model used by WILLIAM BLACKSTONE rather than JOHN LOCKE) and, like JOHN ADAMS and THOMAS JEFFERSON, argued that the British king was "King of America, by virtue of a compact between us and the King of Great Britain."

Hamilton, who by origin was not rooted in any one of the thirteen states, became an early and perhaps the most outspoken advocate of a stronger and more centralized government for the United States. In 1780 he developed a far-reaching program of constitutional reform. First, he pleaded for a vast increase in the power of Congress and asked for a convention for the purpose of framing a confederation, to give Congress complete sovereignty in all matters relating to war, peace, trade, finance, and the management of FOREIGN AFFAIRS. Second, he called for a more efficient organization of the executive tasks of Congress. Individuals were better suited than boards of administration (with the possible exception of trade matters), because responsibility was then less diffused; "men of the first pretentions" would be more attracted to these tasks if offered individual responsibility. Hamilton developed his plea for strengthening Congress in "The Continentalist" (1781–1782) in which he revealed his future political program by pointing to the need "to create in the interior of each state a mass of influence in favour of the Foederal Government." As a delegate from New York to Congress (1782–1783), Hamilton criticized the ARTICLES OF CONFEDERATION. Only in September 1786 did he succeed having the Annapolis Convention endorse his resolution for calling a convention to meet in Philadelphia in May 1787 "to devise such further provisions as shall appear to them necessary to render the constitution of the Foederal Government adequate to the exigencies of the Union."

Hamilton took a strong stand during that period against New York state legislation discriminating against Loyalists. His "Letters of Phocion" (1784) defended individual rights and the rule of law against "arbitrary acts of legislature," as well as the supremacy of the state constitution over acts of the legislature. As counsel for the defense in the New York case of RUTGERS V. WADDINGTON (1784) Hamilton argued that the New York Trespass Act (1783), which enabled people who had fled New York when British forces occupied the city to recover damages from persons who had held their premises during the occupation, was incompatible with higher law—that of the law of nations, of the peace treaty, and of commands of Congress. The Court did not accept the argument for JUDICIAL REVIEW, but followed another of Hamilton's arguments: that the legislature could not have meant to violate the law of nations.

At the CONSTITUTIONAL CONVENTION OF 1787, Hamilton was somewhat an outsider for two reasons. First, the other two members of the New York delegation, JOHN LANSING and ROBERT YATES, opposed a stronger central government. Second, Hamilton's views, presented to the Convention in a five-hour speech on June 18, were extreme on two counts: he advocated the abolition of states as states, favoring a system that would leave them only subordinate jurisdiction; and he advocated tenure during GOOD BEHAVIOR both for members of the Senate and for the chief executive. He admitted that in his private opinion the British government was "the best in the world." Hamilton's constitutional proposals reflected the idea of "mixed government": the lower house of Congress should be elected on the basis of democratic manhood suffrage, yet the Senate and the President ought to be elected by electors with high property qualifications. A chief reason for Hamilton's "high-toned" constitutional ideas was that "he was much discouraged by the amazing extent of Country"; he feared disruptive tendencies, originating particularly from the larger and more powerful states.

Could his constitutional proposals influenced by the British model still be termed republican? Hamilton held that the standards of republican government were respected as long as "power, mediately, or immediately, is derived from the consent of the people," or as long as all magistrates were appointed by "the people, or a process of election originating with the people." Against later charges of "monarchism," Hamilton replied that his plan submitted at Philadelphia was conformable "with the strict theory of a Government purely republican; the essential criteria of which are that the principal organs of the Executive and Legislative departments be elected by the people and hold their offices by a responsible and temporary or defeasible tenure."

Though Hamilton absented himself during much of the Convention's work, he signed the Constitution on September 17, 1787, as the only member from New York, indicating that he saw only an alternative between anarchy, on the one hand, and "the chance of good to be expected from the plan," on the other.

During the struggle for ratification of the Constitution (1787–1788), Hamilton's two major achievements were the publication of *The Federalist* essays and his part in the New York ratifying convention at Poughkeepsie. He organized and coordinated publication of *The Federalist,* which appeared over the signature of "Publius" from late October 1787, to late May 1788. Of the eighty-five essays, Hamilton wrote fifty-one. In them he developed several major themes, some of which also recurred in his speeches in the New York Ratifying Convention.

Hamilton proved the utility of the union to America's political prosperity chiefly by painting a somber picture of international rivalry, ever ready to exploit dissensions among the states; he raised the specter of a disrupted Confederation, of war between the states, and of the rise of partial confederations, the most likely and most dangerous contingency being the formation of a northern and a southern confederacy. Hamilton then demonstrated the insufficiency of the Confederation to preserve the union by pointing to the necessity that the federal government, to be effective, "carry its agency to the persons of the citizens." He envisaged a broad scope for the powers granted to the federal government. The powers needed to provide for the common defense of the members of the Union "ought to exist without limitation." A vast scope for the federal power to regulate commerce and to provide for the financial needs of the Union, and the maxim that "every POWER ought to be in proportion to its OBJECT," foreshadowed Hamilton's later constructions of the Constitution while he directed the Treasury. The Constitution ought to allow a capacity "to provide for future contingencies," which were illimitable.

Hamilton's most important contribution to the analysis of institutions and procedures is his discussion of the executive branch in *The Federalist* #67–77. Believing that efficient administration was the very core of good government, he supported an individual executive who would be less likely than a plural executive "to conceal faults, and destroy responsibility." The office of chief magistrate, if not shackled by brief duration or restrictions on reeligibility, might attract men imbued with "the love of fame, the ruling passion of the noblest minds" (#72).

Hamilton's analysis of the federal judiciary is best known for the justification of judicial review in *The Federalist* #78. There Hamilton tried to refute the argument presented by the Anti-Federalist "Brutus" that judicial review implied JUDICIAL SUPREMACY. Hamilton invoked the superiority of the will of the people as declared in the Constitution and the duty of the judges to be governed by that will. A constitution "is in fact, and must be regarded by the judges as fundamental law." His statement in *The Federalist* #81 "that the Constitution ought to be the standard of construction for the laws, and that wherever there is an evident opposition, the laws ought to give place to the Constitution" is similarly significant.

Hamilton argued against a federal bill of rights in *The Federalist* #84. His main point that bills of rights were not needed in constitutions founded upon the power of the people is rhetorical; it is contradicted by his own admission that the Constitution as drafted did in fact contain a rudimentary bill of rights, including provisions on habeas corpus, the prohibition of BILLS OF ATTAINDER and EX POST FACTO laws and the guarantee of TRIAL BY JURY in criminal cases.

The office of secretary of the Treasury, coveted by Hamilton more than any other, afforded him the opportunity to initiate policies for strengthening the public support, and particularly the support of the moneyed community, for the federal government. He considered leadership not only as compatible with, but incumbent on, executive office, and once spoke of the "executive impulse." He seems to have considered his office as that of a prime minister on the British model. Hamilton's major effort and achievement was the establishment of public credit for the new federal government. His measures included funding the foreign and domestic debt at par, assumption of the revolutionary state debts, creation of the Bank of the United States, and levying of federal excise taxes; his most important policy papers were his Report on Public Credit (January 1790) and his Report on the National Bank (December 1790). As a program for the future, Hamilton, in the Report on Manufactures (1791), envisaged protective tariffs, aid for agriculture, and INTERNAL IMPROVEMENTS. Increasingly, his policies encountered and provoked opposition from Thomas Jefferson, JAMES MADISON, and the Republican party forming around them.

There were two great constitutional issues on which Hamilton spoke out during his membership in Washington's cabinet: the constitutionality of the proposed Bank of the United States (1791), and the constitutionality of the President's PROCLAMATION OF NEUTRALITY (1793). In the dispute on the bank, both Attorney General EDMUND RANDOLPH and Secretary of State Jefferson denied that the United States had the power to incorporate a bank, this power not being enumerated in the catalogue of powers granted to Congress by the Constitution. Hamilton, in his "Opinion on the Constitutionality of an Act to Establish a Bank," developed the theory of IMPLIED POWERS granted by the Constitution, arguing that implied powers as well as express powers were in fact delegated by the Constitution; he also asserted the existence of such resulting powers as those resulting from the conquest of neighboring territory. Grants of power included means to attain a specified end, the criterion of constitutionality being met if the end was specified in the Constitution. To attain the objective of the "effectual administration of the finances of the United States," there was no "parsimony of power." Also, Hamilton argued that the NECESSARY AND PROPER CLAUSE ought to be construed "to give a liberal latitude to the exercise of specified powers" rather than construing the word "necessary" restrictively, as had Jefferson. These arguments were later adopted by the Supreme Court in MCCULLOCH V. MARYLAND (1819), and still guide the interpretation of Congress's legislative powers.

Hamilton's second major constitutional pronouncement concerned the power of the executive to issue a declaration of neutrality. In the first of his "Pacificus" articles justifying the President's action against Jeffersonian criticism, he presented an extremely broad construction of Article II. The grant of "executive power" (singular) as opposed to the "powers" (plural) granted to Congress meant a general grant of power; the enumeration of specific powers of the executive was merely demonstrative, "intended by way of greater caution." Hamilton also argued that the executive conducted the nation's foreign policy and that his duty obligated him to execute the laws including the law of nations.

During the years after his retirement from the Treasury, Hamilton, as leading Federalist politician, yet without federal office except for a brief spell as Inspector of the Army (1798–1800), on several occasions commented on constitutional matters.

Controversy over JAY'S TREATY (1794) involved constitutional issues between the executive and the House of Representatives. Was the President bound to submit papers pertaining to the treaty negotiations to the legislature? Did the treaty power, jointly exercised by President and Senate, oblige the legislature to appropriate the needed funds without any liberty of exercising legislative discretion? Hamilton denied any obligation on the part of the President to transmit papers, arguing that such a transmittal would "tend to destroy" the confidence of foreign governments in the "prudence and delicacy" of the government. He further argued that a treaty could obligate the legislature to appropriate funds.

Representing the federal government in HYLTON V. UNITED STATES (1796), his only appearance as counsel before the Supreme Court, Hamilton argued that a federal tax on carriages (levied by Congress in 1794 on Hamilton's recommendation) was an excise rather than a direct tax, and so did not have to be apportioned among the states according to the census. Hamilton argued that as an excise the tax was constitutional, and the Court upheld his view.

In 1796 Hamilton was approached for a legal opinion on the Yazoo land grant affair in Georgia. An act of the Georgia legislature had repealed an earlier act providing for the sale of vast tracts of land, the repeal having been prompted by charges of fraud in the original transaction and a political changeover in the legislature. Hamilton argued that Article I, section 10, of the Constitution, prohibiting the states from passing any law "impairing the obligation of contracts," applied not merely to contracts between individuals but to contracts between states and individuals as well, and that a land grant was a contract covered by the contract clause. Hamilton's views became the basis of the Supreme Court's decision in FLETCHER V. PECK (1810).

When New York State election results in the spring

of 1800 made it virtually certain that the state legislature would elect presidential electors favoring Jefferson as President, Hamilton suggested that Governor JOHN JAY call the outgoing legislature into special session to elect anti-Jefferson electors. Hamilton believed that it "is easy to sacrifice the substantial interests of society by a strict adherence to ordinary rules." Jay rejected this proposal, which shows Hamilton's readiness to neglect, in cases he considered extraordinary crises or emergencies, "ordinary rules." Hamilton approved, incidentally, the LOUISIANA PURCHASE.

Although not technically concerning the Constitution, Hamilton's defense of freedom of the press in PEOPLE V. CROSWELL (1804) deserves notice. Hamilton was counsel for the appellant before the high court of New York, the appellant having been convicted of LIBEL for publishing an anti-Jefferson piece. Hamilton's two main points, based on the successful plea of Andrew Hamilton in ZENGER'S CASE (1735), were that truth of an alleged libel should be admitted as evidence and that juries, in libel cases, ought to decide both on fact and on law. The Court divided and thus the conviction was allowed to stand, though no sentence was passed. State legislation to give effect to Hamilton's points was enacted soon afterward.

Hamilton's understanding of the federal Constitution was informed by his vision of the United States as one nation rather than thirteen states, and also by his conviction that the United States constituted one nation among many nations in a state of permanent rivalry. In his interpretation of the Constitution, three points stand out: the broad construction of federal powers as opposed to state powers; the broad construction of executive powers; and the doctrine of judicial review.

GERALD STOURZH

Bibliography

COOKE, JACOB ERNEST 1982 *Alexander Hamilton.* New York: Scribner's.

GOEBEL, JULIUS, JR., et al., eds. 1964–1980 *The Law Practice of Alexander Hamilton: Documents and Commentaries.* 4 Vols. New York: Columbia University Press.

MITCHELL, BROADUS 1957–1962 *Alexander Hamilton.* 2 Vols. New York: Macmillan.

ROSSITER, CLINTON 1964 *Alexander Hamilton and the Constitution.* New York: Harcourt, Brace.

STOURZH, GERALD 1970 *Alexander Hamilton and the Idea of Republican Government.* Stanford, Calif.: Stanford University Press.

SYRETT, HAROLD E. et al., eds. 1961–1978 *The Papers of Alexander Hamilton.* 26 Vols. New York: Columbia University Press.

HAMILTON, ANDREW

See: Zenger's Case

HAMILTON, WALTON HALE
(1881–1958)

Although Walton Hale Hamilton never formally studied law, he became an influential member of the faculty of Yale Law School and one of the nation's leading experts on government regulation of the economy. Hamilton's many books discussing the relationship between the government and the economic order include *Prices and Price Policies* (1938), *The Patterns of Competition* (1940), *Patents and Free Trade* (1941), and *The Politics of Industry* (1957). In these and other works, Hamilton criticized as unrealistic the traditional view of the American economy as a self-regulating free market; he pointed out that the government is deeply enmeshed in the economy, often at the urgent request of the private sector. Hamilton's most substantial contribution to constitutional scholarship, *The Power to Govern,* written with Douglass Adair (1937), followed naturally from his other interests. Exploring the intellectual background of the framing of the Constitution, Hamilton and Adair focused on the meaning of the word "commerce"; they concluded that the Framers intended to grant the national government broad powers through the Constitution's COMMERCE CLAUSE to regulate all forms of economic activity resulting in transactions across state lines, thus implicitly supporting the constitutionality of New Deal federal regulation.

RICHARD B. BERNSTEIN

HAMILTON v. BOARD OF REGENTS OF THE UNIVERSITY OF CALIFORNIA
292 U.S. 245 (1934)

This case raised the problem of CONSCIENTIOUS OBJECTION to military service in a state context. California required that male freshman and sophomore state university students enroll in a course of military science. Hamilton, a religious objector, argued that this requirement violated the liberty guaranteed him by the FOURTEENTH AMENDMENT. Justice PIERCE BUTLER spoke for a unanimous Supreme Court, and concluded that nothing in the Constitution relieved a conscientious objector from the obligation to bear arms.

RICHARD E. MORGAN

HAMMER v. DAGENHART
247 U.S. 251 (1918)

From 1903 to 1918, the Supreme Court consistently had approved NATIONAL POLICE POWER regulations enacted under the COMMERCE CLAUSE. But in *Hammer v. Dagenhart,* the Court deviated from this tradition and invalidated the KEATING-OWEN CHILD LABOR ACT, which prohibited the interstate shipment of goods produced by child labor. The Court's restrictive DOCTRINE nevertheless proved vulnerable and the decision itself eventually was overruled.

In CHAMPION V. AMES (1903) the Justices had sustained a congressional prohibition against the interstate shipment of lottery tickets. The ruling actually was quite narrow, holding that such tickets were proper SUBJECTS OF COMMERCE and that Congress could prevent the "pollution" of INTERSTATE COMMERCE. A more general, expansive doctrine seemed to emerge as the Court soon approved similar regulations of the interstate flow of adulterated foods and impure drugs, prostitutes, prize fight films, and liquor. The Court abruptly deviated from this course in the child labor case, perhaps signaling a reaction against some of the Progressive era's social reforms and the Court's prior tendency toward liberal nationalism.

Justice WILLIAM R. DAY, speaking for a 5–4 majority, maintained at the outset that in each of the other cases the Court had acknowledged that the "use of interstate transportation was necessary to the accomplishment of harmful results." But the child labor regulations, Day held, were different because the goods shipped were of themselves harmless in contrast with lottery tickets, impure foods, prize fight films, and liquor. It was an unsound distinction, but one perhaps anticipated by Justice JOHN MARSHALL HARLAN's remarks in the *Lottery Case* that the Court would not allow Congress arbitrarily to exclude every article from interstate commerce.

The Court refuted any suggestions that congressional authority extended to prevent unfair competition among the states, thus enabling it to ignore any discussion of the evils or deleterious effects of child labor. This argument was grounded in the majority's revival of rigid notions of DUAL FEDERALISM. PRODUCTION, Day said, as he resurrected an older, dubious, and arbitrary distinction, was not commerce; the regulation of production was reserved by the TENTH AMENDMENT to the states. "If it were otherwise," Day noted, "all manufacture intended for interstate shipment would be brought under federal control to the practical exclusion of the authority of the States, a result certainly not contemplated by the . . . Constitution." The regulation of child labor, he maintained, not only exceeded congressional authority but also invaded the proper sphere of local power. To allow such a measure, Day concluded, would end "all freedom of commerce," eliminate state control over local matters, and thereby destroy the federal system.

In dissent, Justice OLIVER WENDELL HOLMES uttered his oft-quoted remark that "if there is any matter upon which civilized countries have agreed—far more unanimously than they have with regard to intoxicants and some other matters over which this country is now emotionally aroused—it is the evil of premature and excessive child labor." But Holmes offered more than his customary philosophical discourse on judicial restraint. Congress plainly had the power to regulate interstate shipments, and its motives of doing so were no less legitimate here than they had been in the regulations.

Whether "evil precedes or follows the transportation" was irrelevant, Holmes said; once states transported their goods across their boundaries, they were "no longer within their rights."

The *Hammer* decision did not significantly diminish the Court's willingness or ability to sustain congressional police regulations under the commerce clause. The ruling revealed that the Court seemed less concerned with the evils of child labor than Congress and was more interested in maintaining the purity of the federal system. In BAILEY V. DREXEL FURNITURE (1922), the Justices invalidated a congressional attempt to regulate child labor by using the TAXING POWER, again despite ample precedents justifying national power. But three years later, Chief Justice WILLIAM HOWARD TAFT, who had written the child labor tax opinion, reverted to the Court's earlier POLICE POWER decisions and broadly approved the National Motor Vehicle Act (1919) which made the transportation of stolen automobiles across state lines a federal crime. In *Brooks v. United States* (1925), Taft agreed that Congress could forbid the use of interstate commerce "as an agency to promote immorality, dishonesty or the spread of any evil or harm of other States from the State of origin." *Hammer v. Dagenhart* marred an otherwise consistent pattern in the precedents, but Taft quickly disposed of it by reiterating the distinction that the products of child labor were not harmful. Yet his 1925 opinion refuted such doctrine as he demonstrated that a perceived evil required national action and the question of harmfulness was secondary.

Throughout the 1920s, the Supreme Court, following Taft's strong views, generally approved an ever expanding scope to the commerce clause. There was some retreat during the bitter constitutional struggle over the New Deal, but it proved temporary. After 1937, a number of decisions reaffirmed a broad nationalistic view of the commerce power. Finally, in 1941, the Court specifically overruled *Hammer.* Justice HARLAN FISKE STONE, in UNITED STATES V. DARBY, rebuked the earlier decision as "novel," "unsupported," "a departure," and "exhausted" as a precedent.

The most poignant historical commentary on *Hammer* came from the supposed victor, Reuben Dagenhart, whose father had sued in order to sustain his "freedom" to allow his fourteen-year-old boy to work in a textile mill. Six years later, Reuben, a 105-pound man, recalled that his victory had earned him a soft drink, some automobile rides from his employer, and a salary of one dollar a day; he had also lost his education and his health.

STANLEY I. KUTLER

Bibliography

WOOD, STEPHEN 1968 *Constitutional Politics in the Progressive Era: Child Labor and the Law.* Chicago: University of Chicago Press.

HAMPTON v. MOW SUN WONG
426 U.S. 88 (1976)

In this case the Supreme Court declined to extend to federal government action the constitutional limits it had imposed on the states' discrimination against ALIENS. The Court recognized that "overriding national interests" might justify a limitation of employment in the federal civil service to citizens—as required by the Civil Service Commission (CSC) here—despite the invalidity of a parallel state law. (See SUGARMAN V. DOUGALL, 1973.) But the interests identified by CSC were insufficient: some of them could be asserted only by the President or Congress; others, within CSC's purview, were after-the-fact rationalizations that had not been considered before the regulation was adopted. The regulation thus violated the Fifth Amendment's guarantee of DUE PROCESS OF LAW; that amendment's EQUAL PROTECTION component need not be reached. The vote was 5–4.

Shortly after the Court's decision in *Hampton,* President GERALD R. FORD issued an order embracing the policy of the invalidated CSC rule.

KENNETH L. KARST

HAMPTON & CO. v. UNITED STATES
276 U.S. 394 (1928)

In *J. W. Hampton, Jr., & Co. v. United States,* a unanimous Supreme Court, speaking through Chief Justice WILLIAM HOWARD TAFT, upheld Congress's DELEGATION OF POWER to the President to adjust tariffs in order to protect American business. The delegation was not improper because the law provided an intelligible standard to which tariffs had to conform. The Court also sustained the protective tariff itself, holding that, because its effect was to raise revenue, Congress's motive in enacting it was irrelevant.

DENNIS J. MAHONEY

HAND, AUGUSTUS N.
(1868–1954)

Born in upstate New York to a prominent legal family, Augustus Noble ("Gus") Hand, after graduating from Harvard College and Harvard Law School, practiced law in New York City from 1897 to 1914. President WOODROW WILSON appointed him in 1914 to the UNITED STATES DISTRICT COURT for the Southern District of New York. A defendant in a trial over which Hand presided described him as a judge of such integrity and impartiality that he could have sustained the dignity of the law in a hurricane. In 1927 President CALVIN COOLIDGE, deferring to the acclaim of the bench and bar, promoted Hand, a Democrat, to the UNITED STATES COURT OF APPEALS, Second Circuit, where he joined his famous cousin, LEARNED HAND.

No appellate judge was more austere than Gus Hand, who commanded the respect and influenced the votes of his brethren for a quarter of a century. He preferred judicial self-restraint to JUDICIAL ACTIVISM. A moderate, he once declared that the ignorance of conservatives hardly exceeded the intolerance of liberals obsessed with change. The ardent crusaders who administered New Deal agencies, he declared, should be left to "fry in their own fat" until Congress reformed them.

Hand dissented rarely and cultivated a passionless style, though he could be eloquent. His opinions tended to favor prosecutors in cases involving the rights of the criminally accused and the government in cases involving subversive activities. For example, he sustained the summary contempt conviction of the lawyers who defended the Communist party leaders tried under the SMITH ACT, even though the trial judge who convicted the lawyers gave them no hearing and waited until the trial's end, months after their contemptuous acts. Hand upheld the SEPARATE BUT EQUAL DOCTRINE and ruled that the Army's racially based quota system during World War II did not violate the SELECTIVE SERVICE ACT. But he championed RELIGIOUS LIBERTY and extended the benefits of conscientious objection to persons who founded their claims on philosophical and political considerations as well as purely religious ones. "A mighty oak has fallen," said one of his colleagues on his death.

LEONARD W. LEVY

Bibliography

SCHICK, MARVIN 1970 *Learned Hand's Court.* Baltimore: Johns Hopkins University Press.

HAND, LEARNED
(1872–1961)

Learned Hand is widely viewed, with OLIVER WENDELL HOLMES, LOUIS D. BRANDEIS, and BENJAMIN N. CARDOZO, as among the leading American judges of the twentieth century. His influence on constitutional law stems more from his extrajudicial advocacy of judicial restraint and his modest, yet creative, performance on lower federal courts in fifty-two years of judging than from the relatively few constitutional rulings among his nearly 3,000 decisions.

Christened Billings Learned Hand, the son and grandson of upstate New York lawyers and judges, Hand dropped the Billings after graduating from Harvard Law School in 1896. Hand surrendered to family pressures in turning to law rather than pursuing his interest in philosophy engendered by his Harvard College teachers, including William James, Josiah Royce, and George Santayana. In six years of practice in Albany and seven in New York City, he performed competently but considered himself inadequate. But the young lawyer's associations with New York City intellectuals and reformers prompted President WILLIAM HOWARD TAFT to name the thirty-seven-year-old Hand to the federal trial bench in 1909. President CALVIN COOLIDGE elevated him to the Court of Appeals for the Second Circuit in 1924, where Hand served for the rest of his life.

Hand's persistent belief in judicial restraint antedated his appointment to the bench. He had been strongly influenced by JAMES BRADLEY THAYER at Harvard Law School. His major publication before the judgeship was an article attacking LOCHNER V. NEW YORK (1905). His deepseated skepticism and allergy to absolutes, as well as his devotion to democratic policymaking and his unwillingness to be ruled by a bevy of Platonic Guardians, made him disdainful of judges ready to pour subjective philosophies into vague constitutional phrases. He was unwilling to suppress his hostility to JUDICIAL ACTIVISM, developed in the era of the Nine Old Men and its use of SUBSTANTIVE DUE PROCESS to strike down ECONOMIC REGULATION, in the post-1937 years, when the philosophy of HARLAN FISKE STONE's footnote to UNITED STATES V. CAROLENE PRODUCTS COMPANY (1937), with its preference for personal rather than economic rights, gained ascendancy.

In his early years as a federal judge, Hand participated widely in extrajudicial activities. He was a member of the group that founded *The New Republic* magazine, and he helped draft THEODORE ROOSEVELT's Bull Moose platform in 1912. Indeed, he was so devoted to the Progressive cause that he permitted his name to be entered as that party's candidate for the New York Court of Appeals in 1913.

After World War I, Hand decided that his position precluded extrajudicial involvements in controversial issues. But he had frequent occasion to continue airing his views of the judicial role in papers and addresses, many of which are collected in *The Spirit of Liberty* (1952). Hand's Holmes Lectures, delivered at Harvard three years before his death and published under the title *The Bill of Rights,* were an extreme restatement of Hand's hostility to the *Lochner* interventionist philosophy. The lectures even questioned the judicial enforceability of vague BILL OF RIGHTS provisions.

Hand's judicial reputation rests mainly on his craftsmanlike performance in operating creatively within the confines set by the political branches. His strength is best revealed in the way he handled many small cases in private law and statutory interpretation. He probed deeply to discover underlying questions, rejecting glib formulations and striving for orderly sense amidst the chaos of received legal wisdoms. Although constitutional issues seldom came before his court, he touched upon a wide range of them, from favoring strong enforcement of FOURTH AMENDMENT guarantees in *United States v. Rabinowitz* (1949) to offering innovative views on defining OBSCENITY in *United States v. Kennerley* (1913).

Hand's most important judicial contributions dealt with political speech under the FIRST AMENDMENT. His most enduring impact stems from his controversial decision in MASSES PUBLISHING CO. V. PATTEN

(1917). The ruling, overturned on appeal, protected the mailing of antiwar materials in the midst of national hostility to dissent. Hand's approach shielded all speech falling short of direct INCITEMENT TO UNLAWFUL CONDUCT. Two years later, the Supreme Court, in its first confrontation with the problem, refused to go so far as Hand had. Instead, SCHENCK V. UNITED STATES (1919) launched the CLEAR AND PRESENT DANGER test, under which the protection of speech turned on guesses about its probable impact. In a rare disagreement with his one judicial idol, Oliver Wendell Holmes, Hand criticized Holmes's approach, in ABRAMS V. UNITED STATES (1919) as well as *Schenck,* as an inadequate bulwark against majoritarian passions. With the Supreme Court adhering to Holmes's standard for decades, Hand assumed that his *Masses* approach had failed. But in 1969, Hand's incitement test, combined with the best elements of Holmes's approach, became the modern standard for First Amendment protection, in BRANDENBURG V. OHIO (1969).

Hand is equally well known for recasting and, many believe, diluting the clear and present danger test by affirming convictions of the Communist leaders in UNITED STATES V. DENNIS (1950). This ruling reflected not only Hand's mounting skepticism about judicial protection of fundamental rights but also his consistent obedience to Supreme Court pronouncements. In affirming the *Dennis* convictions, Chief Justice FRED M. VINSON's plurality opinion adopted Hand's reformulation as the proper criterion. Hand, however, remained convinced even in the 1950s that his *Masses* approach offered better protection to dissenters.

The distinctive traits of Hand's model of judging—open-mindedness, impartiality, skepticism, restless probing—came naturally to him. Those traits were ingredients of his personality by the time Hand became a judge. Philosopher and humanist as well as judge, Hand remained intellectually engaged, ever ready to reexamine his own assumptions.

Hand's unmatched capacity to behave according to the model of the modest judge was not wholly a conscious deduction from the theory of judicial restraint instilled by Thayer and confirmed by Hand's early experiences. It was at least as much a product of Hand's temper and personality. The doubting, open-minded human being could not help but act that way as a judge. Hand's major legacy, to constitutional law as well as to all other areas of the law, lies in his demonstration that detached and open-minded judging is within human reach.

GERALD GUNTHER

Bibliography

HAND, LEARNED (1952)1960 *The Spirit of Liberty: Papers and Addresses,* ed. Irving Dilliard. New York: Knopf.

——— 1958 *The Bill of Rights.* Cambridge, Mass.: Harvard University Press.

SHANKS, HERSHEL, ED. 1968 *The Art and Craft of Judging: The Decisions of Judge Learned Hand.* New York: Macmillan.

HARDING, WARREN G.
(1865–1923)

Warren Gamaliel Harding, twenty-ninth President of the United States, served one of the shortest presidential terms, from his inauguration on March 4, 1921, until his death on August 2, 1923. An Ohio newspaperman and politician, and a United States senator (1915–1921), Harding was nominated as a compromise candidate at the deadlocked 1920 Republican party convention and won a landslide victory over his Democratic opponent, James Cox.

Harding's policies flowed from an understanding of the American Constitution very different from that of his predecessor, WOODROW WILSON. His economic policy consisted of tax reduction, economy in government, a higher tariff, and various measures to aid agriculture in its recovery from the postwar depression. His foreign policy consisted of opposition to American participation in the League of Nations (but support for membership in the World Court), reduction of armaments, and refusal to forgive war debts owed to the United States or its citizens.

Harding's presidency was marred by scandals, which were exposed fully only after his death and in which he was not personally implicated. Despite his brief tenure as President, Harding appointed four Supreme Court Justices: WILLIAM HOWARD TAFT, PIERCE BUTLER, GEORGE H. SUTHERLAND, and EDWARD T. SANFORD.

THOMAS B. SILVER

Bibliography

MURRAY, ROBERT K. 1969 *The Harding Era: Warren G. Harding and His Administration.* Minneapolis: University of Minnesota Press.

HARLAN, JOHN MARSHALL
(1833–1911)

Among the Justices of the Supreme Court, few have provoked more diverse reactions from colleagues, contemporaries, and later generations than the first

Justice John Marshall Harlan. Despite a distinguished tenure of over thirty-three years (1877–1911), during which he participated in many cases of constitutional significance and established himself as one of the most productive, independent, and voluble members of the Court, both jurists and historians were inclined to hold Harlan in low esteem from his death in 1911 to the middle of the twentieth century. But two signal events in 1954—the Court's implicit adoption of Harlan's famous solitary dissent in PLESSY V. FERGUSON (1896) in its decision of the public school SEGREGATION cases, BROWN V. BOARD OF EDUCATION and BOLLING V. SHARPE, and President DWIGHT D. EISENHOWER's appointment of his distinguished grandson and namesake to the highest bench—prompted historians to reevaluate the first Justice Harlan. No longer belittled and neglected, Harlan now began to be recast as a great dissenter who had foretold many of the most fundamental developments in later constitutional interpretation: the virtually complete INCORPORATION of the BILL OF RIGHTS into the FOURTEENTH AMENDMENT; the inherent inequality of racial segregation; and the plenary power of Congress under the COMMERCE CLAUSE. How can one account for the wide disparity between the traditional and revisionist interpretations of Mr. Justice Harlan?

Harlan was born in 1833 in Kentucky, the son of a two-term Whig member of the United States House of Representatives. A stern Presbyterian, young Harlan grew up during the worsening estrangement of the South and the Union. Kentucky, as a border state, was sharply divided. Harlan was graduated from Centre College, and, at twenty, completed his law courses at Transylvania University and was admitted to the Kentucky bar.

Harlan participated actively as a moderate in the political struggles that racked the country on the eve of the Civil War. In 1859 he ran for Congress, but was narrowly defeated. A traditional southern gentleman and conservative, he refused to join the Republican party or to support ABRAHAM LINCOLN's 1860 campaign. He supported the Constitutional Union party which sought the peaceful preservation of the status quo.

After the attack on Fort Sumter, Kentucky declined to furnish troops. Harlan volunteered to fight on the northern side and, in the fall of 1861, organized the Tenth Kentucky Volunteer Infantry. Harlan rose rapidly to the rank of colonel and served as acting commander of a brigade until he resigned his military commission in 1863 upon the death of his father.

Shortly after returning to civilian life, Harlan campaigned for the Constitutional Union party and was elected attorney general of Kentucky, a post he held until 1867. Harlan stumped for General George McClellan in the presidential election of 1864, bitterly criticizing the Lincoln administration. He opposed the THIRTEENTH AMENDMENT and continued to hold slaves until forced to free them.

In 1867, however, Harlan changed his party affiliation, becoming the unsuccessful Republican gubernatorial candidate. As a southern slaveholder and Whig he had long sought to support both slavery and a strong national government—a position that grew increasingly difficult in the political environment of *antebellum* Kentucky, where supporters of slavery based their political programs on opposition to the federal government. In the end Harlan resolved his dilemma in favor of the national government. Contending that he would rather be right than consistent, Harlan publicly repudiated his views favoring slavery and defended the civil war amendments as necessary to the reconstruction of the Union. A second try for the Kentucky governorship in 1871 also ended in failure.

At the national level, Harlan supported ULYSSES S. GRANT in the presidential election of 1868 and had attained sufficient prominence by 1872 to have been proposed as a vice-presidential candidate. Four years later Harlan led the Kentucky delegation to the Republican convention. When it became apparent that his friend, Benjamin Bristow, could not win, Harlan threw the Kentucky delegation's support to RUTHERFORD B. HAYES, enabling Hayes narrowly to defeat James G. Blaine and obtain the nomination.

On October 16, 1877, President Hayes nominated Harlan to the Supreme Court, an appointment that was widely regarded as a payment for political services rendered. Until five days before his death on October 15, 1911, for almost thirty-four years, Harlan served on the Court. With the exception of JOHN MARSHALL and JOSEPH STORY, none of its members up to that time had taken part in so many decisions that ultimately so crucially affected the future of American constitutionalism.

Harlan served on the Supreme Court during a period of rapid social and economic change. Although the era of Reconstruction had passed, the effect of the postwar amendments on the federal system remained a topic of bitter constitutional dispute. The Court was also increasingly obliged to rule on constitutional challenges to the validity of state and federal statutes purporting to regulate the economy in the public interest.

Harlan brought to the Court two fundamental convictions drawn from his upbringing and early experiences in Kentucky politics. He believed in a strong national government, especially in the spheres of commerce and economic development. Hence Harlan would view federal laws regulating the economy much more favorably than similar state initiatives. Second, he would ardently support the rights of blacks, although he had developed that posture only late in his political career. While Harlan never wavered in his judicial support for black rights and a strong national economy, the political implications of his Whig principles varied widely during his judicial tenure. When he came to the Court in 1877 Harlan quickly established himself as its foremost defender of private contracts against state regulation since Marshall. Indeed, throughout his long career Harlan closely scrutinized any state law that impinged on private property rights. He often voted to invalidate such statutes under the contract, JUST COMPENSATION, or EQUAL PROTECTION clauses.

After the passage of the INTERSTATE COMMERCE ACT of 1877 and the SHERMAN ANTITRUST ACT of 1890, however, Harlan came to look quite favorably upon national, as opposed to state, regulation of the economy. Harlan's Whig philosophy explains much of his apparent inconsistency in decisions concerning private property rights. Harlan generally upheld national ECONOMIC REGULATION, but often voted to strike down state economic regulations that discriminated against interstate commerce without furthering significantly an important state interest under the POLICE POWER.

During his thirty-four years on the Court, Harlan articulated a broad body of constitutional principles respecting both governmental powers and individual rights. A convinced believer in legislative authority and judgment, he abhorred and denounced what he viewed as "judicial legislation" and advocated a straightforward application of the law as set forth in the Constitution and legislative enactments. But when it came to determining the provisions of a given law, his view was unique: "It is not the words of the law but the internal sense of it that makes the law: the letter is the body; the sense and reason of the law is the soul" (CIVIL RIGHTS CASES, 1883).

Justice Harlan lifted the practice of employing LEGISLATIVE INTENT as a guide to the sound construction of the law to the level of a philosophical principle. In addition, he, above all others, had an all but religious reverence for the Constitution as the fundamental instrument of the ideals of American democracy. A fervent Marshall disciple, he viewed the Court as the ultimate guardian of the Constitution. Harlan also adhered to Marshall's views on the proper distribution of powers within the federal system.

With respect to congressional power under the INTERSTATE COMMERCE clause, Harlan was a liberal national constitutionalist, with an almost slavish devotion to Chief Justice Marshall's opinions in general, and GIBBONS V. OGDEN (1824) in particular. Harlan displayed his broad interpretation of the commerce power most forcefully in opinions construing the Interstate Commerce Act of 1887 and the Sherman Antitrust Act of 1890. He dissented in *Texas & Pacific Railroad Co. v. Interstate Commerce Commission* (1896) and INTERSTATE COMMERCE COMMISSION V. ALABAMA MIDLAND RAILWAY CO. (1897) when the Court interpreted the Interstate Commerce Act as not granting the commission the power either to void discriminatory railroad rates or to set nondiscriminatory rates itself. Harlan believed that these decisions went far "to make that commission a useless body for all practical purposes, and to defeat many of the important objectives designed to be accomplished by the various enactments of Congress relating to interstate commerce. . . ." Congress eventually agreed, amending the Interstate Commerce Act to give the commission the powers for which Harlan had contended in his dissents.

When the Court emasculated the Sherman Antitrust Act, Justice Harlan, again in dissent, registered his strong advocacy of congressional power and the spirit of the law. In UNITED STATES V. E. C. KNIGHT CO. (1895) the Court narrowly interpreted the Sherman Act as applying to monopolies in interstate commerce but not to intrastate monopolies in manufacture of goods; it also stated that Congress lacked power under the commerce clause to regulate manufacturing. In the majority's view, "Commerce succeeds to manufacture, and is not a part of it." Yet Harlan insisted that the statute applied because the goods, although manufactured in one state, entered into interstate commerce. Four decades later, in the WAGNER ACT CASES (1937), Harlan's expansive view of congressional power under the commerce clause would become the generally accepted view.

Although Harlan held to a broad interpretation of national power under the commerce clause, he nonetheless supported some positive uses of STATE POLICE POWER that affected interstate commerce. He believed that, although a state might not—under the guise of inspection laws—discriminate against meat imported from out of state (MINNESOTA V. BARBER, 1890), it might require certain passenger stops of interstate railroad trains unless Congress had superseded local laws. Indeed, Harlan thought that state power should prevail if the statute in question affected interstate commerce "only incidentally" and furthered an important state interest under the police power—as was the case with state laws prohibiting the importation or sale of intoxicating liquor (BOWMAN V. CHICAGO & NORTHWESTERN RAILWAY, 1888). Whether agreeing or dissenting, however, Harlan consistently stood for the freedom of commerce and the rights of citizens of other states. While he upheld state enactments genuinely aiming to protect the public morals, safety, health, or convenience, he strongly expressed his disapproval of those that appeared to have been enacted for the ulterior purpose of discriminating against commerce from other states.

Although fervently opposed to Justice STEPHEN J. FIELD'S NATURAL RIGHTS philosophy, Harlan strongly defended the Bill of Rights and, in spite of his border state origin, became a vigorous and eloquent advocate of a nationalistic interpretation of the Thirteenth, Fourteenth, and FIFTEENTH AMENDMENTS. Harlan's most celebrated CIVIL RIGHTS dissent, *Plessy v. Ferguson* (1896), became law in the unanimous Warren Court holding in *Brown v. Board of Education* (1954). It was in *Plessy,* dissenting alone from the Court's decision upholding a Louisiana "Jim Crow" train-segregation statute under the SEPARATE BUT EQUAL doctrine, that Harlan had warned: "The thin disguise of 'equal' accommodations . . . will not mislead anyone, nor atone for the wrong this day done. . . ."

However, it was his dissent in the CIVIL RIGHTS CASES (1883) that Harlan considered as his most notable. There the majority ruled that Congress lacked power under the Fourteenth Amendment to protect blacks against private discrimination; Harlan, in contrast, argued that Congress could prohibit discrimination "by individuals or CORPORATIONS exercising public functions or authority, against any citizen because of his race or previous condition of servitude."

In these and other cases involving racial discrimination, Harlan demonstrated his belief that the Thirteenth Amendment meant more than the mere prohibition of one person's owning another as property. He urged that the framers of the Thirteenth, Fourteenth, and Fifteenth Amendments could not have expected the very states that had held blacks in bondage willingly to protect their new civil rights. Harlan thus championed congressional authority to define and regulate the entire body of civil rights of citizens.

Although Justice Harlan's dissents in racial segregation cases have received widespread attention, some of the most critical questions presented to the Court during his tenure centered on what later came to be termed the INCORPORATION DOCTRINE. Harlan joined the Court after a pattern of decisions had been set. Alone, except for Field, among Justices of his time, Harlan viewed the due process clause of the Fourteenth Amendment as encompassing at least the first eight amendments of the Bill of Rights (for example, HURTADO V. CALIFORNIA, 1884), a stand for which he was still severely castigated more than sixty years later by Justice FELIX FRANKFURTER, in ADAMSON V. CALIFORNIA (1947). The process of "selective incorporation" of Bill of Rights guarantees, which was nearly complete by the end of the Warren Court, vindicated Justice Harlan's position in practice, if not in theory.

Interestingly, the emphasis accorded Harlan's famous dissents in civil rights cases concerning life and liberty interests resulted in a widespread neglect of his staunch defense of property rights. In CONTRACT CLAUSE cases involving states' attempts either to void or alter their obligations to bondholders, or to amend corporate charters without express reservation of the right to do so, Harlan strongly asserted the contractual rights of the individual. Under the equal protection clause Harlan voted to strike down state laws that imposed special contractual duties on corporations without imposing similar obligations on individuals.

More significant, Harlan wrote the opinion in CHICAGO, BURLINGTON & QUINCY RAILROAD CO. V. CHICAGO (1898), frequently cited as the first "incorporation" of a Bill of Rights provision, the Fifth Amendment's just compensation clause, into the Fourteenth Amendment's due process clause. The famous rate case of SMYTH V. AMES (1898) provided an indication of how far Harlan would go in striking down, under SUBSTANTIVE DUE PROCESS principles, an exercise of state police power. Speaking for the Court, he voided a Nebraska statute that pegged intrastate freight rates, on the grounds that the rates were so low as to deprive railroads of property without due process of law. A public utility, asserted Harlan, has a judicially enforceable constitutional right to a "reasonable return" upon the "fair value" of its operating assets. (See FAIR RETURN ON FAIR VALUE.)

Harlan's constitutional doctrines evoked diverse reactions from contemporaries and later generations: patronization, neglect, disdain, and praise. His colleague and friend, Justice DAVID J. BREWER, described Harlan as a simple man who "retired at eight, with one hand on the Constitution and the other on the Bible, safe and happy in perfect faith in justice and righteousness." Justice OLIVER WENDELL

HOLMES patronized him in private as "old Harlan . . . the last of the tobacco-spitting judges." Contemporaneous observers of the Court viewed Harlan as a militant dissenter who was inflexible on civil rights.

How could Harlan's contemporaries and historians in the first half of the twentieth century have held him in such low esteem when the prophetic nature of his many dissents appears so obvious today? Part of the answer is that traditional and revisionist interpreters of Justice Harlan have employed widely different analytical perspectives. Viewed narrowly in comparison with his contemporaries, Harlan was simply an "eccentric exception" on the Court. Many of his most famous dissents were solos. His constitutional doctrines were often "out of tune with the times."

Harlan's eccentricity, however, was principled. In a letter of 1870 Harlan described his conception of the proper role of a Justice as that of "an independent man, with an opportunity to make a *record* that will be remembered long after he is gone." Throughout his tenure on the Court Harlan was constantly concerned with broad questions of the public interest; consequently his opinions often contained extraneous matter, referring to circumstances with no direct bearing on the case at hand.

When the Court in POLLOCK V. FARMERS' LOAN & TRUST COMPANY (1895) decided that a tax on the income from land and personal property constituted DIRECT TAXATION and thereby held unconstitutional the recently enacted Federal Income Tax Act, Harlan vehemently dissented. He correctly warned that the Court's decision would make a constitutional amendment necessary for the imposition of the income tax. Harlan's contemporaries, however, saw his denunciation of judicial legislation and his appeals to practical considerations as ignorance of the principles of legal argumentation.

Recent admirers have perhaps too strongly emphasized Harlan's opinion on civil rights and CIVIL LIBERTIES, recasting him as a Jeffersonian Democrat. Although he strongly defended the Bill of Rights against STATE ACTION and private action clothed in public functions, Harlan viewed himself as a staunch adherent to the views of John Marshall and rejected THOMAS JEFFERSON's states' rights views. Moreover, Harlan was one of the most vigorous defenders of individual property rights ever to sit on the Court, as his opinion in ADAIR V. UNITED STATES (1908) illustrated. His STRICT CONSTRUCTION of the contract and just compensation clauses and his adherence to substantive property protections under the due process clause have been soundly rejected by subsequent Courts.

The composite figure emerging from history is that of a Southern gentlemen of the nineteenth century—absolute confidence in the correctness of his own views; a firm belief that human beings could clearly discern between right and wrong; and an inability to understand, once he had made this distinction, how any reasonable man could disagree with him. An ardent disciple of Chief Justice Marshall's views of the proper judicial role and the nature of the federal system, Harlan was an egalitarian when confronted with questions of civil rights.

But today's distinction between property and liberty interests, with enhanced judicial solicitude for the latter, found no place in Harlan's constitutional philosophy. This antebellum slaveholder applied substantive due process equally to liberty and property interests.

Although Harlan's legacy thus contains elements out of tune with contemporary constitutional fashion, many of his dissents presaged what our nation would become in the second half of the twentieth century. Succeeding generations owe a great debt to this solitary dissenter. Because his philosophy contained a touch of immortality, he will be numbered among the great Justices of the Supreme Court (and he was so voted as one of but twelve "greats" in a 1970 study).

HENRY J. ABRAHAM

Bibliography

ABRAHAM, HENRY J. 1955 John Marshall Harlan: A Justice Neglected. *Virginia Law Review* 41:871–891.

CLARK, FLOYD B. 1915 *The Constitutional Doctrines of John Marshall Harlan.* Baltimore: Johns Hopkins University Press.

FRIEDMAN, LEON and ISRAEL, FRED L. 1969 Pages 1281–1295 in *The Justices of the United States Supreme Court, 1789–1969.* New York: Chelsea House.

WATT, RICHARD F. and ORLIKOFF, RICHARD M. 1953 The Coming Vindication of Mr. Justice Harlan. *Illinois Law Journal* 44:13–40.

WESTIN, ALAN F. 1958 The First Justice Harlan: A Self-Portrait from his Private Papers. *Kentucky Law Journal* 46:321–357.

WHITE, G. EDWARD 1975 John Marshall Harlan I: The Precursor. *American Journal of Legal History* 19:1–21.

HARLAN, JOHN MARSHALL (1899–1971)

John Marshall Harlan, grandson of the Justice of the same name, served as Associate Justice of the United States Supreme Court from 1955 to 1971. Educated principally at Princeton and Oxford, he enjoyed a highly successful career as a New York trial lawyer, with intervals for military service and in various public positions. Immediately prior to his appointment to the Supreme Court he served briefly on the United States Court of Appeals for the Second Circuit. His work on the Supreme Court was marked by rigorous intellectual honesty, unflagging industry, and an uncommon dedication to judicial craftsmanship. No Justice sought more earnestly to evaluate fairly every relevant fact and authority, and none labored more carefully to decide, not policies or causes, but actual and concrete cases. In the "measured" assessment of Judge Henry Friendly, no other Justice has "so consistently maintained a high quality of performance" or has enjoyed "so nearly uniform respect."

Influenced in his first years on the Court by FELIX FRANKFURTER, Harlan ultimately developed a constitutional philosophy distinctly his own. He combined dignity with an attractive modesty, personal qualities that were reflected in his conception of the judicial function. In REYNOLDS V. SIMS (1964) he emphasized that the Constitution required a "diffusion of governmental authority" within which the Court was assigned a "high" but "limited" function. Rigidly nonpolitical after his appointment to the bench, he believed that the Court could effectively perform its "limited" constitutional role only by studiously respecting the powers variously entrusted to the states, Congress, or the federal executive. He denied that courts are entitled to promote or compel reform whenever others fail to act, and warned that judges should not seek solutions to every social ill in the Constitution.

More than any Justice in recent years, Harlan regarded FEDERALISM as an important limitation upon the Court's authority. He believed, with Justice LOUIS D. BRANDEIS, that the states could serve as laboratories for the solution of social and political issues, and he willingly afforded them freedom to seek such solutions. In FAY V. NOIA (1963), MIRANDA V. ARIZONA (1966), and other cases he resisted the Court's imposition of federal standards upon the conduct of state criminal proceedings, arguing in *Fay* that the federal system would "exist in substance as well as form" only if the states were permitted, within the limits of FUNDAMENTAL FAIRNESS, to devise their own procedures. In HARPER V. VIRGINIA BOARD OF ELECTIONS (1966) he dissented from the Court's invalidation of a state's use of a POLL TAX as a condition on voting, despite his obvious doubts as to the law's wisdom, in part because the issue should be left for decision by the state itself. In ROTH V. UNITED STATES (1957) he urged that the states be permitted greater leeway than the federal government to control "borderline" PORNOGRAPHY because the risks of nationwide censorship were "far greater." Because the Court could not devise clear rules for regulating OBSCENITY, he saw "no overwhelming danger" if the states were given room to seek their own answers.

Harlan's federalism did not, however, prevent him in appropriate cases from denying the constitutionality of state legislation. In *Poe v. Ullman* (1961) he wrote one of the most important of his opinions, dissenting from the Court's refusal to decide a challenge to a Connecticut statute prohibiting the use of contraceptive devices. Observing that the statute intruded upon "the most intimate details of the marital relation" in order to enforce "a moral judgment," Harlan declared marital privacy to be a "most fundamental" right, any invasion of which requires STRICT SCRUTINY. He defined DUE PROCESS in terms of evolving national traditions and the balance between "liberty and the demands of organized society," and concluded on that basis that the statute was unconstitutional. Four years later, in GRISWOLD V. CONNECTICUT (1965), a majority of the Court reached the same result.

One of the issues most revealing of Harlan's constitutional outlook was the INCORPORATION DOCTRINE, by which large portions of the BILL OF RIGHTS have been held applicable to the states through "incorporation" in the FOURTEENTH AMENDMENT. Harlan vigorously resisted both the "total" incorporation theory advanced by Justice HUGO L. BLACK and the "selective" version adopted by other Justices. In POINTER V. TEXAS (1965), DUNCAN V. LOUISIANA (1968), and other cases he argued that the doctrine lacks historical basis and creates a "constitutional straitjacket" that risks preventing the states from responding to the nation's "increasing experience and evolving conscience." He preferred to test state LEGISLATION and procedures by a standard of fundamental fairness derived from the due process clause of the Fourteenth Amendment, whose generality affords room for future constitutional development. Indeed, in *Griswold* he expressed the fear that the incorporation doctrine might "restrict" the reach of the due process clause, limiting the Court's review of future state actions.

Due process formed the heart of Harlan's constitutional outlook, and two cases illustrate both the breadth of his conception and the restraint with which he employed it. In BODDIE V. CONNECTICUT (1971) Harlan held for the Court that filing and service fees imposed by the state upon persons seeking divorce were denials of due process when applied to INDIGENTS. Carefully avoiding reliance upon the EQUAL PROTECTION clause, whose scope and implications he evidently distrusted, he held that as a matter of fundamental fairness a state could not preempt the right to dissolve marriages unless all its citizens were afforded access to the mechanism prescribed for that purpose. The opinion provoked Justice Black in dissent to reiterate that Harlan's conception of due process permitted judges to determine constitutionality merely by their "sense of fairness." Quoting *Williams v. North Carolina* (1945), Black added that due process afforded judges "a blank sheet of paper" on which to order constitutional change.

The deaths of the two close friends prevented Harlan and Black from continuing their debate after *Boddie,* but part of Harlan's response may be inferred from IN RE GAULT (1967), in which the Court first addressed the constitutional issues presented by state systems of juvenile justice. Such systems often imposed penalties similar to those in criminal cases without the accompanying procedural protections. Harlan's concurring opinion emphasized the novelty of the questions, and urged caution in imposing detailed constitutional requirements. He feared that the hasty adoption of rigid standards might "hamper enlightened development," and found room in the spacious contours of due process to impose only selected procedural requirements. Harlan's caution illustrated his conviction, previously expressed in *Poe v. Ullman,* that the discretion afforded judges by the due process clause must be exercised with "judgment and restraint."

Harlan also made significant contributions to the development of FIRST AMENDMENT principles. In COHEN V. CALIFORNIA (1971) he wrote the opinion for a divided Court overturning the conviction of a man wearing a jacket bearing an antidraft expletive in the halls of a Los Angeles courthouse. Although the protest's form was "distasteful," Harlan explained that "fundamental societal values" are implicated even in "crude" exercises of First Amendment rights. In GINZBURG V. UNITED STATES (1966), he dissented from the affirmance of a federal obscenity conviction in which the Court held that evidence of "commercial exploitation" could tip the balance toward a determination that a publication was obscene. Harlan responded that the Court, by "judicial improvisation," had created a new and impermissibly vague statutory standard, under which "pandering" could justify the censorship of otherwise protected materials. In contrast to his less rigid attitude toward state obscenity prosecutions, he argued that the federal government should be permitted to ban from the mails only hardcore pornography.

The concern for privacy interests expressed in *Poe v. Ullman* was also reflected in Harlan's First Amendment opinions. In NAACP V. ALABAMA (1958) he wrote the Court's opinion overturning an order holding the NAACP in civil contempt for failing to reveal the names of its members and agents in Alabama. He found that such disclosures had previously resulted in threats and reprisals, and explained the "vital relationship" between organizational privacy and freedom of association. Because the contempt order would adversely affect the NAACP's ability to foster beliefs it was constitutionally entitled to advocate, the association's privacy interests overrode the state's regulatory goals. In *Time, Inc. v. Hill* (1967) he argued that where private individuals had by misadventure become involuntary subjects of publicity, the state could constitutionally require the press to conduct a reasonable investigation and to limit itself to fair comment upon the facts. The denial of such state authority, he contended, would create a "severe risk of irremediable harm" to those who had not sought public exposure and were "powerless to protect themselves against it."

Harlan's contributions to constitutional law are not fully measured by the opinions he wrote or conclusions he reached. Time and again, his prodding compelled the Court to revise or reconsider its first assessment of a fact or an issue, drawing from others a higher quality of performance than they might otherwise have achieved. No Justice labored more earnestly to act with care and fairness, and none adhered to a more rigorous standard of judicial integrity. His reassuring example of craftsmanship and rectitude meant much in a period of rapid constitutional change, when the Court and its members were frequently the subject of hostility or question.

CHARLES LISTER

Bibliography

DORSEN, NORMAN 1969 John Marshall Harlan. Pages 2803–2820 in Leon Friedman and Fred L. Israel, eds., *The Justices of the United States Supreme Court 1789–1969.* New York: Chelsea House.

FRIENDLY, HENRY J. 1971 Mr. Justice Harlan, as Seen by a Friend and Judge of an Inferior Court. *Harvard Law Review* 85:382–389.

SHAPIRO, DAVID L. 1969 *The Evolution of a Judicial Philosophy: Selected Opinions and Papers of Justice John M. Harlan.* Cambridge, Mass.: Harvard University Press.

HARLOW v. FITZGERALD

See: *Nixon v. Fitzgerald*

HARMLESS ERROR

Not all denials of a defendant's federal constitutional rights compel reversal of a conviction. The Supreme Court announced in *Chapman v. California* (1967) as a matter of federal constitutional law that, in criminal proceedings, if the beneficiary of the error can prove beyond a REASONABLE DOUBT that the error in no way contributed to the result, the case need not be reversed. This standard applies to state as well as federal proceedings and state rules requiring only a lesser showing of the harmlessness of error are not controlling when federal constitutional error has been shown.

Although the Supreme Court's standard is stricter than that of many state courts (which may adhere to a lesser standard than reasonable doubt or even in some cases shift the BURDEN OF PROOF to the victim of the error), it nevertheless falls short of a per se rule requiring automatic reversal for all violations of federal constitutional rights. Thus, for example, where EVIDENCE obtained through an UNREASONABLE SEARCH in violation of the FOURTH AMENDMENT is improperly admitted into a trial, reversal of a guilty verdict is not always required. The Supreme Court has stated that certain kinds of violations do, indeed, require automatic reversal—such as coerced confessions or unconstitutionally obtained guilty pleas—but these kinds of violation are few in number.

Chapman itself concerned a prosecutor's comments to the jury upon the defendants' failure to testify, in violation of defendants' Fifth Amendment RIGHT AGAINST SELF-INCRIMINATION, and cases involving harmless error doctrine may arise from any part of the Constitution. The bulk of the decided cases, though, have involved application of the EXCLUSIONARY RULE to evidence unconstitutionally seized.

Where illegally obtained evidence is the sole or primary basis for a conviction, of course, the conviction must be reversed. On the other hand, where independent, admissible evidence of defendant's guilt is overwhelming, or illegally obtained evidence is noninflammatory and merely cumulative, reversal is not required. But such a finding will often involve difficult determinations. First, which evidence is actually admissible, and which is a fruit of the federal constitutional error? Second, since the prosecutor in introducing the tainted evidence has represented that it tended to prove guilt, the Supreme Court may look carefully at later claims that the evidence was in fact harmless.

The Court has not yet definitively settled the issue of whether a federal constitutional error can be cured through the trial judge's instructions to the jury. *Chapman* suggests that such instructions may render the error harmless, if they are shown beyond a reasonable doubt to have prevented the error from affecting the jury's verdict. But none of the cases decided by the Court since *Chapman* has found this standard to have been met.

JOHN KAPLAN

Bibliography

SALZBURG, STEPHEN A. 1984 *American Criminal Procedure,* 2nd ed. St. Paul, Minn.: West Publishing Co.

HARPER v. VIRGINIA BOARD OF ELECTIONS
383 U.S. 663 (1966)

Harper epitomizes the WARREN COURT'S expansion of the reach of the EQUAL PROTECTION clause of the FOURTEENTH AMENDMENT. Virginia levied an annual $1.50 POLL TAX on residents over twenty-one, and conditioned voter registration on payment of accrued poll taxes. The Supreme Court, 6–3, overruled BREEDLOVE V. SUTTLES (1937), holding that the condition on registration denied the equal protection of the laws.

The *Harper* opinion, by Justice WILLIAM O. DOUGLAS, played an important part in crystallizing equal protection DOCTRINE by justifying heightened levels of judicial scrutiny. The Court did not quite hold that wealth or indigency was a SUSPECT CLASSIFICATION, saying only that "lines drawn on the basis of wealth of property, like those of race, are traditionally disfavored." It did say, following REYNOLDS V. SIMS (1964), that voting was a FUNDAMENTAL INTEREST, requiring STRICT SCRUTINY of its restriction. The poll tax by itself might be constitutionally unobjectionable; wealth as a condition on voting, however, not only failed the test of strict scrutiny; it was a "capricious or irrelevant factor."

For Justice HUGO L. BLACK, dissenting, *Harper* represented a relapse into judicial subjectivism through a variation on the "natural-law–due-process" formula he had decried in ADAMSON V. CALIFORNIA (1947). The Virginia scheme was not arbitrary; it might increase revenues or ensure an interested electorate. The Court should not substitute its judgment for the Virginia legislature's. Justice JOHN MARSHALL HARLAN also dissented, joined by Justice POTTER STEWART. Harlan, who shared Black's views, added that it was arguable that "people with some property have a deeper stake in community affairs, and are consequently more responsible, more educated, more knowledgeable, more worthy of confidence, than those without means." That this belief was not his own did not matter; it was arguable, and that was all the RATIONAL BASIS standard demanded.

Commentators saw in *Harper* and other contemporary decisions a major shift away from the tradition of minimal judicial scrutiny of laws challenged under the equal protection clause. Invasions of interests of great importance, or discrimination against disadvantaged groups, appeared to call for judicial scrutiny more demanding than that required by the relaxed rational basis standard. Soon the Court found a formula for two levels of review: rational basis for most "social and economic" legislation, and strict scrutiny for laws invading fundamental interests or employing suspect classifications.

The Court has not pursued *Harper's* suggestion that WEALTH DISCRIMINATION is suspect. VOTING RIGHTS, however, are firmly established as interests whose invasion demands strict scrutiny. Implicitly, as in cases involving ALIENS or ILLEGITIMACY, and explicitly, as in cases on SEX DISCRIMINATION, the Court has transformed its two levels of judicial scrutiny into a sliding-scale approach that is interest balancing by another name: the more important the interest invaded, or the more "suspect" the classification, the more the state must justify its legislation. In broad outline this development was portended in *Harper,* which exemplified not only Warren Court egalitarianism but also Justice Douglas's doctrinal leadership.

KENNETH L. KARST

Bibliography

KARST, KENNETH L. 1969 Invidious Discrimination: Justice Douglas and the Return of the "Natural-Law–Due-Process Formula." *UCLA Law Review* 16:716–750.

HARRIS, UNITED STATES v.
106 U.S. 629 (1883)

Harris, like UNITED STATES V. CRUIKSHANK (1876), involved a federal prosecution under a general conspiracy statute, and like *Cruikshank* it was a victory for the Ku Klux Klan. The Supreme Court had gutted the *Cruikshank* statute but allowed it to survive; the *Harris* statute, though similar, did not survive. Section two of the FORCE ACT of 1871 made it a federal crime, punishable by fine and up to six years in prison, for two or more persons to conspire for the purpose of depriving anyone of the EQUAL PROTECTION OF THE LAWS or hindering lawful authorities from securing equal protection for others. The United States prosecuted Harris who, at the head of an armed lynch mob, had broken into a Tennessee jail and captured four black prisoners, despite the efforts of the sheriff to protect them. The mob had beaten the four, killing one. Could the United States try them under the act of 1871? With Justice JOHN MARSHALL HARLAN dissenting silently, the Court held, in an opinion by Justice WILLIAM WOODS, that the act of Congress was unconstitutional. Woods declared that the FOURTEENTH AMENDMENT merely authorized Congress to take remedial measures against STATE ACTION that violated the amendment; it applied only to acts of the states, not to acts of private individuals. The THIRTEENTH AMENDMENT did not apply to the acts of private individuals, but this statute could apply to conspiracies by whites against whites, a subject having nothing to do with slavery. The statute, therefore, had no constitutional basis.

LEONARD W. LEVY

HARRIS v. MCRAE
448 U.S. 297 (1980)

A 5–4 Supreme Court here sustained a series of restrictions on congressional appropriations for the Medicaid program. The restrictions went beyond the law sustained in MAHER V. ROE (1977) by refusing funding even for medically necessary abortions.

Justice POTTER STEWART'S opinion for the Court relied heavily on *Maher* in rejecting claims based on the SUBSTANTIVE DUE PROCESS right of PRIVACY and on the EQUAL PROTECTION clause. A woman's right to be free from governmental interference with her decision to have an abortion did not imply a right to have government subsidize that decision. Equal protection demanded only a RATIONAL BASIS for the law's discrimination between therapeutic abortions and other medical necessities, and such a basis was found in the protection of potential life. Justice Stewart also rejected a claim that the law amounted to an ESTABLISHMENT OF RELIGION. Opposition to abortion might be a tenet of some religions, but the establishment clause did not forbid governmental action merely because it coincided with religious views.

The *Maher* dissenters were joined in *McRae* by Justice JOHN PAUL STEVENS, who had joined the *Maher* majority. The cases were different, he argued; here an indigent woman was denied a medically necessary abortion for lack of funds, at the same time that the government was funding other medically necessary services. ROE V. WADE (1973), allowing a state to forbid abortions in the later stages of pregnancy, had excepted abortions necessary to preserve pregnant women's lives or health. The government could not create exclusions from an aid program, Justice Stevens argued, solely to promote a governmental interest (preservation of potential life) that was "constitutionally subordinate to the individual interest that the entire program was designed to protect."

KENNETH L. KARST

(SEE ALSO: *Abortion and the Constitution; Reproductive Autonomy.*)

HARRIS v. NEW YORK 401 U.S. 222 (1971)

This case is significant as a limitation on MIRANDA V. ARIZONA (1966). Harris sold narcotics to undercover police officers. The police failed to inform him, after his arrest, that he had a RIGHT TO COUNSEL during a custodial POLICE INTERROGATION and they ignored his request for an attorney. Harris eventually admitted that he had acted as an intermediary, buying heroin for the undercover agent, but he denied selling it to the agent. During the trial Harris contradicted the statement that he had made during interrogation; the judge overruled defense objections that the custodial statement was inadmissible under the MIRANDA RULES because it was made involuntarily and in violation of his rights. The judge instructed the jury that although the statement was unavailable as EVIDENCE OF GUILT, they might consider it in assessing Harris's credibility as a witness.

The Supreme Court, 5–4, upheld Harris's conviction. *Miranda* dissenters JOHN MARSHALL HARLAN, BYRON R. WHITE, and POTTER J. STEWART along with Justice HARRY A. BLACKMUN joined in Chief Justice WARREN E. BURGER's opinion holding that testimony secured without the necessary warnings could nevertheless be used to impeach contradictory testimony at trial. Burger flatly asserted that Harris made "no claim that the unwarned statements were coerced or involuntary"—a statement clearly controverted by the record. Burger also dismissed, as OBITER DICTUM, the assertion in *Miranda* that all such statements were inadmissible for any purpose. The majority relied heavily on *Walder v. United States* (1954), in which evidence secured in an UNREASONABLE SEARCH was admitted to impeach testimony although the EXCLUSIONARY RULE would have prohibited its use as evidence of guilt.

Justice WILLIAM J. BRENNAN, dissenting, said that *Miranda* prohibited the use of any statements obtained in violation of its guarantees and denied the contention that that was obiter dictum. Brennan also distinguished *Walder:* the statement there had no connection to the crime with which the defendant had been charged; in *Harris* the defendant's statements related directly to the crime. Moreover, the evidence there could have been used to assess credibility; here the jury could have misused it as evidence of guilt because the statement provided information about the crime charged.

DAVID GORDON

Bibliography

LEVY, LEONARD W. 1974 *Against the Law: The Nixon Court and Criminal Justice.* New York: Harper & Row.

HARRIS v. UNITED STATES

See: Search Incident to Arrest

HARRISON, BENJAMIN (1833–1901)

One of a series of "caretaker" Presidents in the last quarter of the nineteenth century, Benjamin Harrison exercised only minimal influence on constitutional issues during his administration from 1889 to 1893. Though Harrison favored civil service reform and a reduction in the labor workday, and opposed southern disenfranchisement of blacks, his philosophy of the executive function limited his actions. Harrison believed his duty lay solely in enforcing the public will, as expressed by Congress.

Although he had called for federal antitrust action in his first message to Congress, claiming that trusts "are dangerous conspiracies against the public good, and should be made the subject of prohibitory and even penal legislation," Harrison's only contribution to the SHERMAN ANTITRUST ACT, passed during his term, was his signature. His administration, moreover, was rather indifferent to the act; of seven cases instituted by the government, only two resulted in a government victory and none was pressed to the Supreme Court. Harrison appointed four Justices to the Court: DAVID J. BREWER, HENRY B. BROWN, GEORGE SHIRAS, and HOWELL E. JACKSON, all conservatives. These appointments indicated Harrison's desire to secure property interests and vested rights against the assaults of reformers.

DAVID GORDON

Bibliography

VOLWILER, ALBERT T. 1932 Harrison, Benjamin. In *Dictionary of American Biography*, Vol. 8, pp. 331–335. New York: Scribner's.

HARRISON ACT
38 Stat. 785 (1914)

Congress passed this act at the behest of the Treasury Department to implement the 1912 Hague Convention banning narcotics trafficking. As with other legislation of the period, the act reflected a belief in the necessity of federal regulation to curb social evils. Although most such acts relied on the COMMERCE CLAUSE, Congress here used the TAXING POWER to establish a complex network of national drug control.

The act required all manufacturers and dealers in certain narcotics to register with the government and to pay a $1 annual license tax. The act also mandated the use of federal forms to complete transactions and ordered these forms kept for two years, accessible to federal inspection. Sale or shipment of specified drugs in INTERSTATE COMMERCE—even their possession by an unregistered person—was illegal. The act exempted physicians and other professionals from filing the federal forms but required them to maintain separate records. A 5–4 Supreme Court sustained the act in UNITED STATES V. DOREMUS (1919). Justice WILLIAM R. DAY asserted Congress's complete discretion to levy taxes, subject merely to the constitutional requirement of geographical uniformity.

DAVID GORDON

HART, HENRY M., JR.
(1904–1969)

At Harvard Law School, Henry Hart was a disciple of FELIX FRANKFURTER. After a clerkship with Justice LOUIS D. BRANDEIS, Hart returned to Harvard as a member of the law faculty, where he remained—with an interruption during World War II—all his life.

Hart was one of a handful of the most authoritative academic lawyers of his time. He was, above all, a teacher; his most important scholarship is embodied in two books designed for law school courses. In *The Federal Courts and the Federal System* (1953), co-authored with Herbert Wechsler, Hart introduced students to a conception of the functions of the federal judiciary that still dominates the thinking of courts and commentators. In *The Legal Process* (1958), co-authored with Albert Sacks, Hart expounded a view of the role of courts in lawmaking focused on "reasoned elaboration" of principle. For a generation that view was so influential that today's critics speak of a "legal process school" as the focus for their attack.

For Hart, reason was "the life of the law." His intellectual integrity was legendary. Nor was the integrity merely intellectual. He was a decent man, as generous and humane in personal dealings as he was formidable in print. During his last illness, he continued to meet his classes until he was physically unable to get to the classroom. To the end, he taught everyone around him.

KENNETH L. KARST

Bibliography

HART, HENRY M., JR. FESTSCHRIFT 1971 *Southern California Law Review* 44:i-x, 305–498.

HARTFORD CONVENTION
(December 15, 1814–January 5, 1815)

The Hartford Convention, called by the Federalists of the Massachusetts legislature, consisted of delegates chosen by the legislatures of Massachusetts, Connecticut, and Rhode Island. The delegates sought to promote the interests and policies of the New England Federalists, who vehemently opposed the War of 1812. Although secessionist sentiment flourished among extremists, moderates—those who opposed a separate New England confederacy and civil war—controlled the convention. The fact that it was held showed a respect for the Constitution, however perverse. Despite the convention's endorsement of theories of state NULLIFICATION and INTERPOSITION similar to those of the VIRGINIA AND KENTUCKY RESOLUTIONS of 1798–1799, the delegates unanimously advocated amendments to the Constitution as a means of curtailing federal powers. After a manifesto assailing the war, American foreign policy, national control of state militias, and the admission of western states, the convention proposed that congressional REPRESENTATION and federal taxation be based on the number of free persons only; embargoes be restricted to sixty days; Congress be prevented from declaring war, restricting foreign trade, or admitting new states except by a two-thirds majority; federal offices be restricted to native-born citizens; and the President be restricted to one term.

The convention had the misfortune of meeting while events were making it irrelevant. As three delegates left for Washington to present its proposals for constitutional amendments, the news arrived of ANDREW JACKSON's victory at New Orleans, and when the delegates arrived in Washington, the town celebrated peace reports from Ghent. President JAMES MADISON excoriated the convention as a "rebel Parliament" that had engaged in a treasonable conspiracy, and the public ridiculed it. It accomplished nothing, left a bitter heritage, and enhanced the respectability of the doctrine of interposition.

LEONARD W. LEVY

Bibliography

BANNER, JAMES M., JR. 1970 *To the Hartford Convention.* New York: Knopf.

HASTIE, WILLIAM HENRY (1904–1976)

William Henry Hastie was the first black federal judge. He studied law at Harvard Law School, where he was elected to the *Harvard Law Review.* After graduation in 1930 he pursued a career that included service to the national government, the Howard Law School, and the NAACP.

Hastie in 1939 took the chair of that CIVIL RIGHTS organization's National Legal Committee, a post he used to influence the course of civil rights litigation. He argued successfully with THURGOOD MARSHALL in SMITH V. ALLWRIGHT (1941) that a Texas all-white PRIMARY ELECTION law violated the Fifteenth Amendment. He also joined with Marshall five years later in arguing MORGAN V. VIRGINIA. They persuaded the Court that a Virginia law imposing SEGREGATION on interstate buses unconstitutionally burdened the uniform flow of commerce. *Smith* and *Morgan* were critical victories in the NAACP's attack on the South's dual system of race relations: the former leveled a barrier to black voting; the latter marked the first victory in a transportation case.

Following appointment as judge of the Third Circuit in 1949, Hastie had few judicial opportunities to advance the cause of civil rights. Scarcely two dozen of his 486 opinions dealt with civil rights, and these reveal a commitment to constitutional law rooted in principle and judicial restraint. In *Lynch v. Torquato* (1965) Hastie declined to expand the STATE ACTION theories he had advanced in *Smith.* He held that the EQUAL PROTECTION clause of the FOURTEENTH AMENDMENT did not embrace the management of the internal affairs of the Democratic party. In an article he spurned AFFIRMATIVE ACTION programs that used "race alone as a determinant of eligibility or qualification."

William Hastie stood in the front rank of civil rights leaders. Notably, a strong sense of Madisonian constitutionalism balanced his commitment to legal activism.

KERMIT L. HALL

Bibliography

RUSCH, JONATHAN J. 1978 William H. Hastie and the Vindication of Civil Rights. *Howard Law Journal* 21:749–820.

HATCH ACT 53 Stat. 1147 (1939) 54 Stat. 767 (1940)

The Hatch Act prohibits most federal employees from engaging in any of a broad range of partisan political activities. It was adopted in 1939, but its antecedents go back well into the nineteenth century. The act has twice been challenged on FIRST AMENDMENT, VAGUENESS, and OVERBREADTH grounds, and has twice been upheld: CIVIL SERVICE COMMISSION V. NATIONAL ASSOCIATION OF LETTER CARRIERS (1973) and UNITED PUBLIC WORKERS V. MITCHELL (1947). Similar state legislation was upheld in BROADRICK V. OKLAHOMA (1973).

Although public employee organizations are among the most formidable lobbies in Congress and state legislatures, laws like the Hatch Act severely restrict the individual employee's political activities. These restrictions have been justified as assuring impartiality in public service, preventing the incumbent party from constructing a political machine, and preventing coercion of public employees.

The Hatch Act cases contrast sharply with later BURGER COURT decisions such as BUCKLEY V. VALEO (1976), protecting unlimited campaign spending, and FIRST NATIONAL BANK OF BOSTON V. BELLOTTI (1978), protecting corporate spending in ballot measure campaigns.

These decisions, in combination with the Hatch Act cases, suggest that, in the Burger Court's view, no liberty may be sacrificed to prevent unfair grasping of power by the use of concentrated wealth, but a great deal of liberty may be sacrificed to prevent unfair grasping of power by a mass-based device such as political patronage.

DANIEL H. LOWENSTEIN

Bibliography

COMMISSION ON POLITICAL ACTIVITY OF GOVERNMENT PERSONNEL 1968 *A Commission Report.*

ROSE, HENRY 1962 A Critical Look at the Hatch Act. *Harvard Law Review* 75:510–526.

HAUPT v. UNITED STATES
330 U.S. 1 (1947)

Herbert Haupt, a German-American, infiltrated into the United States during World War II from a German submarine as part of a Nazi plot to sabotage American war industry. His father, Hans Max Haupt, allowed him to stay at the latter's home, bought a car for him, and helped him to get a job in a factory where Norden bomb sights were manufactured. There were at least two witnesses to each of these three acts, and on the basis of that testimony Hans Haupt was convicted of TREASON.

The Supreme Court sustained Haupt's conviction in an 8–1 decision. In an opinion by Justice ROBERT H. JACKSON, the Court held that the overt acts testified to met the test laid down in CRAMER V. UNITED STATES (1945): each constituted the actual giving of aid and comfort to an enemy spy. Unlike Anthony Cramer's public meetings with the saboteurs, Hans Haupt's "harboring and sheltering" of his son were of direct support to the enemy mission.

DENNIS J. MAHONEY

(SEE ALSO: *Ex Parte Quirin, 1942.*)

HAWAII v. MANKICHI

See: Insular Cases

HAWAII HOUSING AUTHORITY v. MIDKIFF
467 U.S. 229 (1984)

The system of feudal land tenure developed under the Hawaiian monarchy had modern consequences. Seventy-two landowners owned forty-seven percent of the land in the state, and the federal and state governments owned forty-nine percent; only four percent of the land was left for other owners. The Hawaii legislature, finding that this system distorted the land market, in 1967 adopted a land reform act. The law authorized use of the state's EMINENT DOMAIN power to condemn residential plots and to transfer ownership to existing tenants. Landowners challenged the law as authorizing TAKINGS OF PROPERTY for private benefit rather than PUBLIC USE. The Supreme Court unanimously rejected this argument, upholding the law's validity. The legislature's purpose to relieve perceived evils of land concentration was legitimately public, and the courts' inquiry need extend no further. Apart from issues of JUST COMPENSATION, the taking of property has virtually ceased to present a judicial question.

KENNETH L. KARST

HAYBURN'S CASE
2 Dallas 409 (1792)

Hayburn's Case was regarded in its time and has been regarded by many historians since as the first case in which a federal court held an act of Congress unconstitutional. Congress in 1791 directed the CIRCUIT COURTS to rule on the validity of pension claims made by disabled Revolutionary War veterans; the findings of the courts were to be reviewable by the secretary of war and by Congress. The circuit court in New York, presided over by Chief Justice JOHN JAY, and the circuit court in North Carolina, presided over by Justice JAMES IREDELL, addressed letters to President GEORGE WASHINGTON explaining why they could not execute the act in their judicial capacities but that out of respect for Congress they would serve voluntarily as pension commissioners.

In the Pennsylvania circuit, Justices JAMES WILSON and JOHN BLAIR, confronted by a petition from one Hayburn, decided not to rule on his petition, and they also explained themselves in a letter to the President. They would have violated the Constitution to have ruled on the petition, they said, because the business directed by the act was not of a judicial nature and did not come within the JUDICIAL POWER OF THE UNITED STATES established by Article III. They objected to the statute because it empowered officers of the legislative and executive branches to review court actions, contrary to the principle of SEPARATION OF POWERS and judicial independence.

Hayburn's Case thus presented no suit, no controversy between parties, and, technically, no "case," and none of the courts rendered judicial decisions; they reported to the President their refusal to decide judicially. (See CASES AND CONTROVERSIES.) Some congressmen thought that *Hayburn's Case* was "the first instance in which a Court of Justice had declared a law of Congress to be unconstitutional," and the same opinion was delightedly trumpeted in anti-administration newspapers, which praised a precedent that they hoped would lead to judicial voiding of Hamiltonian legislation. The "case" reported in 2 Dallas 409 involved a motion for a WRIT OF MANDAMUS to compel the circuit court to grant a pension to Hayburn, but the court held the case over, and Congress revised the statute, providing a different procedure for the relief of pension-seeking veterans.

LEONARD W. LEVY

HAYES, RUTHERFORD B. (1822–1893)

An Ohio lawyer and Civil War general, Rutherford Birchard Hayes briefly served in Congress and was thrice elected Governor. A compromise Republican presidential candidate in 1876, Hayes received a minority of the popular vote and probably should not have been elected. However, the electoral vote was uncertain because of disputed results in South Carolina, Florida, Louisiana, and Oregon. Claims of vote fraud and threats of civil war led to a crisis which was resolved by the COMPROMISE OF 1876 which gave the election to Hayes on the condition that federal troops would be removed from the South. During his Presidency the rights of the freedmen were severely undermined as Reconstruction came to an end.

PAUL FINKELMAN

Bibliography

KENNETH E. DAVISON 1972 *The Presidency of Rutherford B. Hayes.* Westport, Conn.: Greenwood Press.

HAYNE, ROBERT YOUNG (1791–1839)

As a United States senator from South Carolina, Robert Young Hayne debated DANIEL WEBSTER of Massachusetts in the famous Webster-Hayne Debate of 1830. The debate began over a bill to slow down the sale of western lands but developed into a heated discussion over slavery, the nature of the Union, and the relationship between the states and the federal government. Hayne argued for the right of states to nullify federal laws. After the debate—which most contemporaries and historians agree was won by Webster—Hayne was a key participant in the South Carolina NULLIFICATION Convention of 1833. The Convention asserted that the federal tariffs of 1828 and 1832 were unconstitutional and null and void in South Carolina. Hayne was then elected governor of the state. In his inaugural address he asserted "we will STAND OR FALL WITH CAROLINA." As governor he organized troops to defend South Carolina's SOVEREIGNTY from the federal government, but he ultimately accepted a compromise that peacefully ended the "Nullification Crisis."

PAUL FINKELMAN

Bibliography

JERVEY, THEODORE D. (1909)1970 *Robert Y. Hayne and His Times.* New York: Da Capo Press.

HAYNES, UNITED STATES v.

See: *Marchetti, United States v.*

HAYNES v. WASHINGTON 373 U.S. 503 (1963)

This was the last of many confessions cases, prior to ESCOBEDO V. ILLINOIS (1964), in which the Supreme Court decided the voluntariness of a confession by a DUE PROCESS standard. In 1944 the Court had held that due process was violated if the police obtained a confession by continuous interogation while the prisoner was held incommunicado in an inherently coercive situation. Thereafter, however, the Court frequently had deferred to a determination of voluntariness by state courts. *Haynes* was the first case since 1944 in which the Court revived the standard of inherent coerciveness where the facts showed incommunicado detention and the prisoner was not allowed to call his lawyer. The case foreshadowed *Escobedo* and MIRANDA V. ARIZONA (1966).

LEONARD W. LEVY

HAYS, ARTHUR GARFIELD (1881–1954)

A leading defense counsel for and later director of the AMERICAN CIVIL LIBERTIES UNION, Arthur Garfield Hays devoted his career to protecting CIVIL LIBERTIES and FREEDOM OF SPEECH. Two of his books, *Let Freedom Ring* (1928) and *Trial by Prejudice* (1933), recount his participation in the Scottsboro cases (see NORRIS V. ALABAMA, 1935), the Scopes antievolution trial in Tennessee with Clarence Darrow (see STATE V. SCOPES, 1925), and on behalf of Sacco and Vanzetti (see COMMONWEALTH V. SACCO AND VANZETTI, 1921). Hays maintained a laissez-faire attitude toward government regulation of business and vigorously championed democracy, positions he elucidated in *Democracy Works* (1939).

DAVID GORDON

HEALTH INSURANCE FOR THE AGED ACT (MEDICARE)

79 Stat. 286 (1965)

The 1965 amendment of the SOCIAL SECURITY ACT establishing a system of health insurance operated by the Social Security Administration culminated thirty years of controversy over the proper role of the federal government in relation to medical care. Medicare provided hospital insurance and a variety of medical benefits for citizens sixty-five years or older. The act was designed to meet the serious problem of providing care for those who faced old age fearful of the financial ravages of illness.

Medicare's two insurance programs operated differently. The Hospital Benefit program automatically covered anyone over sixty-five with no "needs" test. It paid for hospitalization, nursing home care, home visits, and diagnostic services. It was financed by compulsory contributions from the protected persons and their employers and provided benefits as a matter of entitlement. The Supplementary Medical Insurance section created a voluntary individual program subsidized and administered by the government, using private insurance companies to assist in its administration.

Medicare influenced the entire pattern of medical care in the United States. With government financing a growing share of total health care expenditures, its power and role within the American health care system expanded proportionately. Not only administrators but also doctors and nurses adjusted their conduct to comply with newly mandated rules and procedures.

PAUL L. MURPHY

Bibliography

FEDER, JUDITH 1977 *Medicare: The Politics of Federal Hospital Insurance.* Lexington, Mass.: Lexington Books.

HEARING

See: Fair Hearing

HEARSAY RULE

The hearsay rule is a nonconstitutional rule of EVIDENCE which obtains in one form or another in every JURISDICTION in the country. The rule provides that in the absence of explicit exceptions to the contrary, hearsay evidence of a matter in dispute is inadmissible as proof of the matter. Although jurisdictions define "hearsay" in different ways, the various definitions reflect a common principle: evidence that derives its relevance in a case from the belief of a person who is not present in court—and thus not under oath and not subject to cross-examination regarding his credibility—is of questionable probative value.

The Constitution does not explicitly refer to the hearsay rule or implicitly constitutionalize the hearsay rule in civil or criminal cases generally; but it does contain two provisions that share common purposes with the hearsay rule. The TREASON clause of Article III, section 3, prohibits a conviction for treason "unless on the testimony of two witnesses to the same overt act, or on a confession in open court." In CRAMER V. UNITED STATES (1945) the Supreme Court construed this clause to require the federal government to produce witnesses who possessed direct evidence—as opposed to circumstantial evidence—of the same overt act. Although *Cramer* itself did not involve hearsay evidence, its reasoning applies as well to hearsay evidence of overt acts, because hearsay evidence is itself a kind of circumstantial evidence.

The other provision of the Constitution that bears on the hearsay rule is the Sixth Amendment's CONFRONTATION clause, which entitles the accused in a criminal case "to be confronted with the witnesses against him." In contrast to the hearsay rule, the confrontation clause does not treat hearsay evidence as presumptively inadmissible against the accused, and it does not treat traditional exceptions to the hearsay rule as automatically admissible. Nevertheless, the confrontation clause addresses the questionable nature of hearsay evidence by requiring the state to produce at trial the hearsay declarants whose statements it uses against the accused, when it appears that the declarants are available to testify in person and that the defendant could reasonably be expected to wish to examine them in person at the time their hearsay statements are introduced into evidence.

PETER WESTEN

(SEE ALSO: *Compulsory Process.*)

Bibliography

MCCORMICK, CHARLES 1972 *Evidence,* 2nd ed. Pages 579–756. St. Paul, Minn.: West Publishing Co.

HEART OF ATLANTA MOTEL v. UNITED STATES
379 U.S. 241 (1964)
KATZENBACH v. MCCLUNG
379 U.S. 294 (1964)

In these cases the Supreme Court unanimously upheld the portion of the CIVIL RIGHTS ACT OF 1964 forbidding RACIAL DISCRIMINATION by hotels, restaurants, theaters, and other PUBLIC ACCOMMODATIONS.

Congressional debates had discussed the appropriate source of congressional power to prohibit private racial discrimination. The COMMERCE CLAUSE was proposed as a safe foundation for the bill; since 1937 the Supreme Court had upheld every congressional regulation of commerce that came before it. Because Congress obviously was seeking to promote racial equality, some thought the commerce clause approach "artificial" and thus "demeaning." They argued for reliance on the power of Congress to enforce the FOURTEENTH AMENDMENT. That amendment's STATE ACTION limitation, however, seemed to obstruct reaching private discrimination. As enacted, the 1964 act's public accommodations provisions were limited to establishments whose operations "affect commerce" or whose racial discrimination is "supported by state action."

The Supreme Court moved swiftly, accelerating decision in these two cases. The majority relied on the commerce power, validating the act in application not only to a large whites-only motel that mainly served out-of-state guests but also to a restaurant with no similar connection to interstate travel. The latter case, *McClung*, illustrates how far the commerce power has been stretched in recent years to allow Congress to legislate on matters of national concern. The restaurant mainly served a local clientele; it served blacks, but only at a take-out counter. Almost half the food used by the restaurant had come from other states, but even the Court recognized that this fact was trivial. More persuasive was the fact, fully documented in congressional hearings, that discrimination in public accommodations severely hindered interstate travel by blacks. Justices WILLIAM O. DOUGLAS and ARTHUR J. GOLDBERG, concurring, argued that both the commerce clause and the Fourteenth Amendment empowered Congress to impose these regulations.

In retrospect the pre-enactment debate over which power Congress should assert seems unimportant, in either institutional or doctrinal terms. Congress need not, after all, specify which of its powers it is using. And the Supreme Court has not needed to explore the full reach of Congress's Fourteenth Amendment power, because in JONES V. ALFRED H. MAYER CO. (1968) it held that the THIRTEENTH AMENDMENT empowered Congress to prohibit private racial discrimination. (See BADGES OF SERVITUDE.)

KENNETH L. KARST

HEFFRON v. INTERNATIONAL SOCIETY FOR KRISHNA CONSCIOUSNESS , INC.
452 U.S. 640 (1981)

One rule governing the Minnesota State Fair allows the sale or distribution of literature, or the solicitation of funds, only at fixed booths. The International Society for Krishna Consciousness (ISKCON) sued in a state court challenging this rule's validity on its face and as applied. ISKCON contended that the rule violated its FIRST AMENDMENT rights of FREEDOM OF SPEECH and RELIGIOUS LIBERTY. The Minnesota Supreme Court held the law invalid as applied to ISKCON, saying that the state authorities had not shown that exempting ISKCON from the rule would significantly interfere with crowd control at the fair.

The Supreme Court reversed, upholding the rule on its face and as applied to distribution (5–4) and to sales and solicitation (9–0). Justice BYRON R. WHITE wrote for the Court. He concluded that the rule, which made no distinctions based on speech content and allowed no discretion to the licensing authorities, was valid as a regulation of the time, place, and manner of speech. The fair was a PUBLIC FORUM, but differed significantly from a public street. Considerations of safety and crowd control amounted to substantial state interests, justifying the rule restricting sales, distribution, and solicitation to booths. Exempting ISKCON would require exempting all applicants. Other less restrictive means for achieving those interests, such as penalizing disorder or limiting the number of solicitors, were unlikely to deal with the problems posed by large numbers of solicitors roaming the fairgrounds.

Justice WILLIAM J. BRENNAN'S partial dissent, joined by two other Justices, argued that the rule was invalid in application to ISKCON's proposed distribution of literature. Such distribution, he argued, was no more disruptive than the making of speeches, or face-to-face proselytizing, both of which were permitted. Justice HARRY A. BLACKMUN also dissented as to the distribution of literature.

KENNETH L. KARST

HELVERING v. DAVIS
301 U.S. 619 (1937)

Plaintiff, a stockholder of an affected CORPORATION, challenged Titles II and VIII of the 1935 SOCIAL SECURITY ACT. Title II creates the old age benefits program, popularly known as "social security," and Title VIII contains the funding mechanism for that program. Under Title VIII, an employer must take a payroll deduction from each employee's wages and pay it, together with an equal amount directly from the employer, to the treasury.

Plaintiff's primary argument was that Congress lacked constitutional power to levy a tax for the purpose of providing old age benefits. Justice BENJAMIN N. CARDOZO, writing an opinion in which six other Justices joined, resoundingly rejected the argument that Congress had transgressed the TENTH AMENDMENT reservation to the states of powers not delegated to the federal government. Only Justices JAMES C. MCREYNOLDS and PIERCE BUTLER dissented. The majority classified the old age benefits program as a legitimate exercise of Congress's power "to lay and collect taxes . . . to . . . provide . . . for the GENERAL WELFARE of the United States." The Court adopted a fluid definition of the general welfare. "Nor is the concept of the general welfare static. Needs that were narrow or parochial a century ago may be interwoven in our day with the well-being of a nation." The Court then examined the effects on older workers of the "purge of nation-wide calamity that began in 1929" and concluded that the problem was national in scope, acute in severity, and intractable without concerted federal effort. State governments were deficient in economic resources and reluctant to finance social programs that would place them at comparative economic disadvantage with competitor states: industry would flee the new taxes and INDIGENTS would flock to any state that provided the new social benefits. (Justice Cardozo's analysis proved prescient. In the 1960s and 1970s a number of socially progressive northeastern and western states experienced these twin problems when they far exceeded national benefit norms in the federal-state cooperative programs of Aid to Families with Dependent Children and Medicaid.) Having determined that the purpose of Title II was well within the scope of the "general welfare" clause, the Court sustained the Title VIII funding provisions.

In its broad, though imprecise, reading of the term "general welfare," *Helvering v. Davis,* even more than its companion case, STEWARD MACHINE CO. V. DAVIS (1937), rejects the view that Congress, in exercising its power to tax for the general welfare, is required by the Tenth Amendment to eschew regulation of matters historically controlled by the states. In so doing, it repudiates that vein of case law, exemplified by UNITED STATES V. BUTLER (1936), that treats the Tenth Amendment as a limitation on the federal TAXING AND SPENDING POWER. Though *Butler* is factually distinguishable, the analysis used by Justice Cardozo in *Steward Machine Co.* and *Helvering v. Davis* would surely have sustained the agricultural price support provisions struck down in *Butler* a year earlier.

GRACE GANZ BLUMBERG

HENRY, PATRICK
(1736–1799)

Unsuccessful as a merchant, Patrick Henry turned to the law. He was admitted to the Virginia bar in 1760 and rose rapidly to prominence and prosperity. In 1765 Henry was elected to the House of Burgesses and, in his first term, won fame and popularity with a series of resolutions opposing the STAMP ACT as an unconstitutional imposition of TAXATION WITHOUT REPRESENTATION. A flamboyant and persuasive orator, Henry became the leader of the radical patriot faction in Virginia. As a delegate to the FIRST CONTINENTAL CONGRESS Henry favored both issuance of a declaration of grievances and formation of the ASSOCIATION. At home, he successfully urged the arming of the militia and served briefly as commander-in-chief of Virginia's forces. He was a member of the convention that, in 1776, adopted the VIRGINIA DECLARATION OF RIGHTS AND CONSTITUTION and instructed the state's congressional delegation to call for a DECLARATION OF INDEPENDENCE. Henry was himself a delegate to Congress but resigned in June 1776 when he was elected first governor of Virginia. In 1776 Governor Henry supported a BILL OF ATTAINDER (written by THOMAS JEFFERSON) against a notorious Tory brigand. When Jefferson and JAMES MADISON proposed to end the ESTABLISHMENT OF RELIGION in Virginia, Henry countered with a plan for general assessment to support all Christian churches and teachers.

Although Henry was a longtime self-proclaimed nationalist and had often called for enlargement of the powers of Congress under the ARTICLES OF CONFED-

ERATION, he declined appointment as a delegate to the CONSTITUTIONAL CONVENTION OF 1787. In the Virginia state convention of 1788 he was the leader of the anti-Federalists and spoke and voted against RATIFICATION OF THE CONSTITUTION. He argued that the document lacked a BILL OF RIGHTS and infringed on state SOVEREIGNTY, and he warned that the new federal Congress might someday abolish SLAVERY.

Henry later converted to the Federalist cause; in 1795 President GEORGE WASHINGTON offered to make Henry secretary of state, but Henry declined. In the 1796 case of WARE V. HYLTON Henry appeared with JOHN MARSHALL as counsel for Virginians who claimed that, the Treaty of Paris notwithstanding, state law precluded their obligation to repay debts due to British subjects. That same year Henry turned down Washington's offer of appointment as Chief Justice of the United States. Like SAMUEL ADAMS of Massachusetts, Henry proved better suited to making a revolution than to erecting a stable constitutional order.

DENNIS J. MAHONEY

HEPBURN ACT
34 Stat. 584 (1906)

A string of adverse decisions by the Supreme Court left the Interstate Commerce Commission (ICC) with few effective powers. Abuses abounded despite the ELKINS ACT of 1903, and in December 1905 THEODORE ROOSEVELT reiterated his earlier calls for corrective legislation. The resulting bill, which met significant opposition only in the Senate, expressly vested the ICC with the power to prescribe "reasonable" maximum rail rates only after current rates and practices had been condemned in a hearing. The bill, which became law on June 29, 1906, nonetheless failed to establish any standards for those rates, thus leaving the Court to apply the FAIR RETURN rule of SMYTH V. AMES (1898). Rates initiated by the ICC were subject to narrow JUDICIAL REVIEW; new rates became effective upon issuance unless challenged in the CIRCUIT COURTS and successfully enjoined, in which case they took effect only when sustained by the courts. The "commodities clause," which forbade carriers from transporting goods produced by railroads or in which they had an interest, was primarily addressed to rail lines serving mining interests. Additional provisions, effective immediately, shifted the burden of APPEALS to the carriers, not the commission. Congress followed this with the MANN-ELKINS ACT in 1910, further supporting the commission.

DAVID GORDON

(SEE ALSO: *Interstate Commerce Commission v. Illinois Central Railroad,* 1910.)

Bibliography

SHARFMAN, ISAIAH L. 1931–1937 *The Interstate Commerce Commission,* 4 vols. New York: Commonwealth Fund.

HERBERT v. LANDO
441 U.S. 153 (1979)

In *Herbert v. Lando* a majority of the Supreme Court soundly rejected the argument that the constitutional protections afforded journalists should be expanded to bar inquiry into the editorial processes of the press in libel actions. Anthony Herbert, a Vietnam veteran, received widespread media attention when he accused his superior officers of covering up atrocities and other war crimes. Herbert sued for libel when CBS broadcast a report and *The Atlantic Monthly* published an article, both by Barry Lando, about Herbert and his accusations. Herbert conceded that he was a PUBLIC FIGURE required by NEW YORK TIMES V. SULLIVAN (1964) to prove that the media defendants acted with "actual malice." During pretrial discovery, Lando refused to answer questions on the ground that the FIRST AMENDMENT precluded inquiry into the state of mind of those who edit, produce, or publish, and into the editorial process.

The Court recognized that the FIRST AMENDMENT affords substantial protection to media defendants in libel actions, citing specifically the *Sullivan* requirement that public figures and officials must prove knowing or reckless untruth. The Court noted, however, that the Framers did not abolish civil or criminal liability for defamation when adopting the First Amendment. It reasoned that upholding a constitutional privilege that barred inquiry into facts relating directly to the central issue of the defendant's state of mind would effectively deprive plaintiffs of the very evidence necessary to prove their case. That result would substantially eliminate recovery by plaintiffs who were public figures or public officials.

Justice LEWIS F. POWELL separately elaborated upon the majority's admonition that in supervising discovery in libel actions, trial judges should exercise appropriate controls to prevent abuse, noting the courts' duty to consider First Amendment interests along with plaintiffs' private interest. Justice WILLIAM J. BRENNAN, dissenting in part, asserted that the First Amendment provided a qualified editorial privilege which would yield once the plaintiff demonstrated a *prima facie* defamatory falsehood. Separately dissenting, Justice POTTER J. STEWART argued that inquiry into the editorial process is irrelevant, and Justice THURGOOD MARSHALL rejected the majority's balance of the competing First Amendment and private interests.

KIM MCLANE WARDLAW

(SEE ALSO: *Balancing Test; Evidence; Freedom of the Press.*)

HERNDON v. LOWRY
301 U.S. 242 (1937)

Herndon was a black organizer convicted of attempting to incite insurrection in violation of a state law. Herndon had sought to induce others to join the Communist party. At the time the party was seeking to organize southern blacks and calling for separate black states in the South. While only indirectly adopting the CLEAR AND PRESENT DANGER test, the Court refused to apply the BAD TENDENCY TEST of GITLOW v. NEW YORK (1925) and stressed the absence of any immediate threat of insurrection. In an opinion by Justice OWEN ROBERTS, a 5–4 Court held (1) that the evidence presented failed "to establish an attempt to incite others to insurrection" even at some indefinite future time; and (2) that the statute was unconstitutionally vague as applied and contrued because "every person who attacks existing conditions, who agitates for a change in the form of government, must take the risk that if a jury should be of opinion he ought to have foreseen that his utterances might contribute in any measure to some future forcible resistance to the existing government he may be convicted of the offense of inciting insurrection." The VAGUENESS DOCTRINE invoked was not specifically articulated as a FIRST AMENDMENT standard; instead, the general criminal standard of "a sufficiently ascertainable standard of guilt" was applied.

The state supreme court believed that a conviction would be justified if the defendant intended that insurrection "should happen at any time within which he might reasonably expect his influence to continue to be directly operative in causing such action by those whom he sought to induce. . . ." This formula, which the Supreme Court found constitutionally infirm, must be compared with its own of the 1950s upholding convictions for conspiracy to advocate overthrow of the government where the intention was that of an organized group to bring about overthrow "as speedily as circumstances would permit."

MARTIN SHAPIRO

HICKLIN v. ORBECK
437 U.S. 518 (1978)

A unanimous court, speaking through Justice WILLIAM J. BRENNAN, held unconstitutional an Alaska law requiring private firms working on oil and gas leases or pipelines to give preference in hiring to Alaska residents. By discriminating against nonresidents, the "Alaska Hire" law violated the PRIVILEGES AND IMMUNITIES clause of Article IV of the Constitution.

DENNIS J. MAHONEY

HIGHER LAW

Americans have never been hesitant to argue that if a law is bad it must be unconstitutional. When no written constitutional provision suggests an interpretation that undermines the law under attack, American lawyers have often looked to the ancient tradition of unwritten higher law for support.

It is worth distinguishing two kinds of unwritten higher law. The first is natural law, conceived by the ancient Stoics as, in Cicero's words, "right reason, harmonious, diffused among all, constant, eternal." The Stoic conception was integrated with Christian theology by the medieval scholastics, and later was reformulated in a secular and individualistic direction by the NATURAL RIGHTS theorists of the Enlightenment. In this latter form, the natural law tradition provided the intellectual background for the American colonists' assertion of "certain inalienable rights" in the DECLARATION OF INDEPENDENCE.

The second kind of unwritten higher law, which we may call FUNDAMENTAL LAW, derives from those conventional and largely unquestioned values and practices that need be neither constant, eternal, nor dictated by reason. The members of a society may see their fundamentals as contingent, peculiar to themselves, and mutable—though, because fundamental, not easily or quickly mutable. On the other hand, those who see their own society's basic conventions as the only possible ones do not accept, perhaps cannot even understand, the distinction between "natural" and "fundamental" law.

In the practice of legal argument either natural or fundamental law can have priority, with the other regarded as ancillary. Thus one can argue that a principle is legally binding because it comports with right reason, as is incidentally confirmed by its acceptance in society; or one can reverse the priorities, leaving reason to confirm what convention and tradition primarily establish. Until about the mid-nineteenth century, American lawyers alternated between these rhetorical strategies, but since the Civil War the fundamental law strand has predominated.

The American idea of fundamental law derived originally from the seventeenth-century English habit of conducting political disputes in terms of an "ancient constitution," unwritten and believed (like the COMMON LAW itself) to be of "immemorial antiquity." Sir EDWARD COKE exemplified this habit when he merged natural with traditional law and both with English common law, and then asserted judicial authority to override legislation in the name of this powerful conglomerate. His declaration in BONHAM'S CASE (1608) that "when an Act of Parliament is against common right and reason . . . the common law will control it, and adjudge such act to be void" supplied a significant argument in the American colonists' struggle with Parliament between 1761 and 1776.

During the prerevolutionary period, the Americans argued for limitations on Parliament's authority over them on the basis of this same conglomerate of reason, common law, and constitutional tradition. Only when they broke with the English crown altogether in 1776—an avowedly revolutionary step—was their justification purely in terms of natural right.

With independence, the new states enacted popularly ratified written constitutions, a process later repeated in the adoption of the federal Constitution. The question then arose whether the new constitutions subsumed the older idea of unwritten constitutional law based on reason or tradition. The classic debate on this question was the exchange of OBITER DICTA between Justices JAMES IREDELL and SAMUEL CHASE of the Supreme Court in CALDER V. BULL (1798). Iredell argued that a law consistent with the applicable written constitutions was immune from further JUDICIAL REVIEW; because the "ablest and the purest minds differ" concerning the requirements of natural justice, judges should assume no special authority to enforce so indeterminate a standard. Chase insisted that "certain vital principles in our free Republican governments" would invalidate inconsistent legislation whether the principle were enacted or not; thus a law that took the property of A and gave it to B could not stand, even if the applicable written constitution did not explicitly protect private property.

Chase's dictum followed the tenor of the NINTH AMENDMENT to the federal Constitution (1791): "The enumeration in the Constitution, of certain rights, shall not be construed to deny or disparage others retained by the people." But the Ninth Amendment does not settle the Chase–Iredell dispute, as it might if it said explicitly whether the unenumerated and retained rights have enforceable constitutional status.

During the first years of the republic, a number of state courts, as in *Ham v. McClaws* (South Carolina, 1789), anticipated Chase by invoking unenacted constitutional law to invalidate legislation. On the other hand, the most influential discussions of judicial review during the early federal period—ALEXANDER HAMILTON'S THE FEDERALIST #78 (1787) and JOHN MARSHALL'S opinion in MARBURY V. MADISON (1803)—echoed Iredell's view in basing power solely on the judicial authority to construe the written constitution, itself conceived as the expressed will of a fully sovereign people.

On the whole, judicial practice before 1830, particularly in the state courts but in a few federal cases as well, adopted Chase's view while also invoking his natural-law language with its appeal to "general principles of republican government." Marshall himself, in FLETCHER V. PECK (1810), ambiguously justified invalidation of a Georgia statute "either by general principles which are common to our free institutions, or by the particular provisions of the constitution of the United States." The particular provision in question was the CONTRACT CLAUSE, which Marshall heroically stretched to fit the case, perhaps out of reluctance to rest decision solely on "general principles." In a few later cases, such as TERRETT V. TAYLOR (1815), the Supreme Court did invalidate state legislation without reference to constitutional text.

Even during their heyday before 1830, the "general principles" of the unwritten constitution were never regarded as federal constitutional law, binding on the states under the SUPREMACY CLAUSE. Because they did not count as "the Constitution or laws of the United States," unwritten general principles would not support appeal to the Supreme Court from the decision of a state court; federal courts invoked these principles against state legislatures only when acting as substitute state courts under DIVERSITY OF CITIZENSHIP JURISDICTION.

In their content, the unwritten "general principles" applied during this period were largely confined to the protection of traditional vested property rights against retroactive infringement. As such, they were equally well supported by common law tradition and by contemporary ideas of natural justice.

From about 1830 on, judicial assertion of pure unwritten constitutional law became less common, perhaps because of its conflict with Jacksonian ideas of popular sovereignty. The process of stretching the language of vague constitutional provisions to encompass notions of natural or traditional justice continued, however, and there began a historic shift in the favored vague provision from the federal contract clause to the clauses of state constitutions guaranteeing the LAW OF THE LAND and DUE PROCESS OF LAW—phrases that began to be construed to mean more than their originally understood sense as guarantees of customary common law procedures. Thus was born the concept bearing the oxymoronic name of SUBSTANTIVE DUE PROCESS, which ever since has been the main vehicle for the implementation of higher law notions in American constitutional law.

A leading case in this development was *Taylor v. Porter* (New York, 1843), which incorporated in "due process" the prohibition, earlier invoked by Chase as an unwritten general principle, against the state's taking the property of the worthy A only to give it to the undeserving B. In these early substantive due process decisions the language of immutable natural law mixed indiscriminately with talk of historically based common law and tradition; there was no felt conflict between the two rhetorical strands.

By contrast, the discourses of natural justice and of customary practice did conflict in the great constitutional debates over SLAVERY that occurred, largely outside the courts, during the period 1830–1860. Proslavery forces occasionally argued that the natural right of property protected the owners of human as of other chattels. Indeed, in the most notorious of constitutional slavery cases, DRED SCOTT V. SANDFORD (1857), Chief Justice ROGER B. TANEY held that congressional prohibition of SLAVERY IN THE TERRITORIES violated slaveholders' property rights guaranteed by the Fifth Amendment's due process clause. But the legal defenders of slavery did not generally have to rely on unwritten higher law; they could point to the positive guarantees the slave states had insisted on inserting in the federal Constitution.

On the other hand, antislavery lawyers had almost no basis for legal argument except the increasingly widespread conviction that slavery was intolerably unjust. With positive law and custom against them, they tried to translate natural law directly into constitutional doctrine. To this end, they invoked the PRIVILEGES AND IMMUNITIES clause of Article IV; the "liberty" protected by substantive due process; and the proclamation of human equality in the Declaration of Independence, for which they claimed constitutional status. More radical abolitionists opposed these efforts to accommodate the Constitution, the "covenant with Hell," to the antislavery cause; on the other hand, the pre-Civil War courts found the antislavery constitutional arguments unacceptable because too radical. But abolitionist constitutional theory triumphed in larger arenas; it became part of the political program of the Republican party, and thus part of the world view of the politicians who led the war against slavery and afterward framed the Reconstruction amendments.

The language of section 1 of the FOURTEENTH AMENDMENT (1868) directly echoes the old triad of antislavery constitutional arguments in its guarantees of due process, EQUAL PROTECTION OF THE LAW, and the privileges and immunities of national citizenship. These general clauses have ever since provided the main textual basis for the continuation of the higher law tradition in constitutional law.

In the SLAUGHTERHOUSE CASE (1874) the Supreme Court at first by a 5–4 vote rejected the argument that the new amendment constitutionally bound the states to the whole array of unenumerated rights. But by the end of the century, the courts had accepted the arguments of commentators, chief among whom was THOMAS M. COOLEY (*Constitutional Limitations*, 1868), that due process prohibited all legislative intrusions upon basic liberties and property rights that did not reasonably promote the limited ends of public health, safety, or morals. Of the protected liberties, the dearest to the courts of this period was FREEDOM OF CONTRACT, and in a series of decisions epitomized by LOCHNER V. NEW YORK (1905) the courts invalidated economic regulatory laws on the grounds that they unreasonably constrained the terms on which adults could contract with each other.

In developing this doctrine, courts and commentators sometimes echoed the old language of natural law, but the more characteristic note of this aggressive laissez-faire constitutionalism was struck by Justice RUFUS PECKHAM, who condemned a price regulation law as a throwback to the past that ignored "the more correct ideas which an increase of civilization and a fuller knowledge of the fundamental laws of political economy . . . have given us today" (*Budd v. State*, New York, 1889). The notion of evolution had taken hold, and it not only supported the doctrines of Social Darwinism but also promoted the idea that fundamental legal principles evolved—a progress that the courts should accommodate by developing the law of the due process clause through a "gradual process of judicial inclusion and exclusion" (*Davidson v. New Orleans,* 1878). Tradition continued to play a role as well; thus the courts invalidated much new legislation regulating the price charged for goods while accepting old usury laws that regulated the price charged for the use of money, and generally tolerating public regulation of those businesses that had traditionally been treated as AFFECTED WITH A PUBLIC INTEREST.

The legal supporters of Progressive politics fiercely attacked "liberty of contract" and its associated doctrines in the name of popular sovereignty, which they argued required repudiation of the very idea of unwritten constitutional law. When laissez-faire constitutionalism was finally put to rest in the mid-1930s under the combined influence of FRANKLIN D. ROOSEVELT's court-packing plan and more long-run historical forces, it appeared that the higher law tradition might finally have come to the end of its long influence on American constitutionalism.

Only if higher law is given its narrower sense derived from classic natural law has this come to pass. The New Deal and post-New Deal courts found a new active role in the program of correcting for legislative failures sketched by the famous footnote four of the opinion in UNITED STATES V. CAROLENE PRODUCTS (1938). They promoted racial equality and electoral reform while protecting political dissidents, religious deviants, and criminal defendants, a role that reached its peak during the years of the WARREN COURT (1953–1969). The doctrinal vehicles for these projects have been the gradual incorporation within due process of the specific guarantees of the BILL OF RIGHTS and above all the evolutionary interpretation of the equal protection clause as a vehicle of fundamental law.

One of the most effective promoters of these developments, Justice HUGO L. BLACK (1937–1971), did wholly repudiate any invocation of higher law in their support; his characteristic stance was a rigorously exclusive appeal to constitutional text as a source of doctrine. While Justice Black's colleagues did not share his strict constructionist views, they too generally avoided invoking notions of natural or universal human rights, often resting decision on imaginative readings of original intent. Frequently, however, the Justices have openly construed vague constitutional language in light of an evolving fundamental law specific to American history and culture. During these years the Court has said that "notions of what constitutes equal treatment . . . do change" (HARPER V. VIRGINIA BOARD OF ELECTIONS, 1966); that due process requires states to institute criminal procedures that are "fundamental" in the sense of "necessary to an Anglo-American regime of ordered liberty" (DUNCAN V. LOUISIANA, 1968); and that the prohibition of CRUEL AND UNUSUAL PUNISHMENT is to be construed in the light of "those evolving standards of decency that mark the progress of a maturing society" (*Furman v. Georgia,* 1972).

Its association with laissez-faire constitutionalism had discredited substantive due process as a doctrinal tool during the generation following the New Deal, but beginning with GRISWOLD V. CONNECTICUT (1965) the Court moved toward reviving the use of this old rubric for the protection of substantive liberties. The role once held by "liberty of contract" was now taken by the RIGHT OF PRIVACY, a misleading name for what was at its core a constitutional protection for freedom of REPRODUCTIVE CHOICE, surrounded by a periphery of other doctrines limiting governmental power to regulate the FAMILY. The privacy decisions openly used as precedents substantive due process cases decided before the New Deal. Like those earlier decisions, the privacy cases avoided reference to universal right or natural law in support of their doctrines, with a plurality of Justices stating in MOORE V. EAST CLEVELAND (1977) that "the Constitution protects the sanctity of the family precisely because the institution of the family is deeply rooted in this Nation's history and tradition."

The natural law strand of argument, though much muted in this century, has never entirely disappeared from American constitutional rhetoric. Justice WILLIAM O. DOUGLAS was at times inclined to argue in this vein; before the *Griswold* decision he supported constitutional protection for marriage and procreation on the grounds that they were, as he said in SKINNER V. OKLAHOMA (1945), "basic CIVIL RIGHTS of man." Since the 1970s a number of constitutional commentators have argued for the use of "the methods of moral philosophy" in constitutional decision, referring to philosophical theories that claim universality for their results, and in this sense directly descend from classic natural law approaches. Whether there will be a revival of natural law discourse in constitutional doctrine remains an open question. On the other hand, the broader tradition of an unwritten higher law of the Constitution, encompassing both fundamental and natural law, seems by now too firmly entrenched to be dislodged.

THOMAS C. GREY

Bibliography

CORWIN, EDWARD S. (1928–1929) 1955 *The "Higher Law" Background of American Constitutional Law.* Ithaca, N.Y.: Cornell University Press.

——— 1948 *Liberty Against Government.* Baton Rouge: Louisiana State University Press.

GRAHAM, HOWARD JAY 1968 *Everyman's Constitution.* Madison: State Historical Society of Wisconsin.

HAINES, CHARLES GROVE 1930 *The Revival of Natural Law Concepts.* Cambridge, Mass.: Harvard University Press.

TEN BROEK, JACOBUS (1951)1965 *Equal under Law.* New York: Collier Books.

WRIGHT, BENJAMIN F., JR. 1931 *American Interpretations of Natural Law.* Cambridge, Mass.: Harvard University Press.

HILDRETH, RICHARD
(1807–1865)

A prolific pamphleteer, Richard Hildreth passionately opposed SLAVERY and took a Federalist or Whig stance on most issues. He was also a nationalist and an economic determinist who insisted on free competition. His *History of the United States* (1849–1852), ending in 1821, is meticulous in detail, scrupulously presenting each argument on major issues. His bias is nevertheless apparent in his championing of Federalist legislation; he minimized the effects of the ALIEN AND SEDITION ACTS, stressed the "virulence" of the VIRGINIA AND KENTUCKY RESOLUTIONS, and decried the repeal of the JUDICIARY ACT OF 1801. This six-volume study is still extraordinary for its realism and rejection of nineteenth-century romantic and heroic traditions.

DAVID GORDON

HILLS v. GAUTREAUX
425 U.S. 284 (1976)

Two years after MILLIKEN V. BRADLEY (1974) rejected metropolitan relief for school DESEGREGATION absent a showing of a constitutional violation by both city and suburban districts or by state officials, the Supreme Court encountered a parallel issue in the field of housing discrimination. The United States Department of Housing and Urban Development (HUD) had aided a Chicago city agency in locating low-income housing sites for the purpose of maintaining residential SEGREGATION. HUD, citing *Milliken,* argued that relief should be limited to the city. However, the Court approved the district court's order, which had regulated HUD's conduct beyond Chicago's boundaries. No restructuring or displacement of local government would result here, the Court said.

KENNETH L. KARST

HINES v. DAVIDOWITZ
312 U.S. 52 (1941)

Hines held that under the PREEMPTION doctrine, enforcement of a state alien registration law was barred by the federal ALIEN REGISTRATION ACT. Justice HUGO L. BLACK, for the Court, emphasized the broad power of Congress over ALIENS. Justice HARLAN FISKE STONE, for three dissenters, noted the absence of any conflict between state and federal laws or any express congressional prohibition of state regulation.

KENNETH L. KARST

HIPOLITE EGG COMPANY v. UNITED STATES
220 U.S. 45 (1911)

A unanimous Supreme Court relied on the decision in CHAMPION V. AMES (1903) to sustain the PURE FOOD AND DRUG ACT's prohibition on the interstate transportation of adulterated food. Justice JOSEPH MCKENNA's opinion acknowledged few limits on congressional power over INTERSTATE COMMERCE, declaring that there was no trade "carried on between the states to which it does not extend," and that it was "subject to no limitations except those found in the Constitution." McKenna did not consider the purpose or intent of the act as the Court had previously done in *Champion* and would do so again in HOKE V. UNITED STATES (1913) and HAMMER V. DAGENHART (1918).

DAVID GORDON

HIRABAYASHI v. UNITED STATES

See: Japanese American Cases

HITCHMAN COAL & COKE CO. v. MITCHELL
245 U.S. 229 (1917)

In this case a 6–3 Supreme Court approved use of an INJUNCTION to enforce YELLOW DOG CONTRACTS. The injunction prohibited the union from inducing breach of contract by communicating with employees or potential employees of the company. The majority emphasized that Hitchman had as much right to condition employment contracts on promises not to join a union as the workers had to decline job offers. Indeed, "this is a part of the constitutional right of personal liberty and private property" protected by SUBSTANTIVE DUE PROCESS of law. The Court thus held that these workers were not free because they had signed the yellow dog contracts.

Justice LOUIS D. BRANDEIS dissented, joined by Justices OLIVER WENDELL HOLMES and JOHN H. CLARKE. The union, they said, had merely sought promises to join, and the yellow dog contracts were not genuine contracts because they were not freely entered into by the workers. The Court's hostility to LABOR would not change until 1937. (See HUGHES COURT.)

DAVID GORDON

H. L. v. MATHESON

See: Reproductive Autonomy

HODEL v. VIRGINIA SURFACE MINING AND RECLAMATION ASSOCIATION
452 U.S. 264 (1981)

The *Hodel* opinion provided a formula for interpreting the demands of NATIONAL LEAGUE OF CITIES v. USERY (1976). The Supreme Court unanimously upheld an act of Congress stringently regulating private stripmining operations, but providing for relaxation of the federal regulations when a state undertook to regulate the same activities according to standards set out in the act. Justice THURGOOD MARSHALL, for the Court, wrote that an act of Congress would not be held invalid under the *Usery* principle unless it satisfied three conditions: that the law regulated "the States as States"; that it addressed "matters that are indisputably 'attributes of state SOVEREIGNTY' "; and that it directly impaired the states' ability "to structure integral operations in areas of traditional governmental functions." In *Hodel* itself, the law failed the first part of the test, for it regulated only private parties. All three requirements were taken from the *Usery* opinion; in combination, they proved an insuperable hurdle to states seeking to rely on *Usery* to invalidate federal regulation of state activities, and ultimately led to the overruling of *Usery* in GARCIA v. SAN ANTONIO METROPOLITAN TRANSIT AUTHORITY (1985). Justice WILLIAM H. REHNQUIST, who concurred only in the judgment, wrote separately to decry the majority's assumptions concerning the breadth of Congress's commerce power.

KENNETH L. KARST

HODGES v. UNITED STATES
203 U.S. 1 (1906)

Black laborers had agreed to work for a lumber firm. Hodges and the other white defendants, all private citizens, ordered the blacks to stop working, assaulted them, and violently drove them from their workplace. The defendants were indicted for violating federal CIVIL RIGHTS laws. In a decision reconfirming much of the CIVIL RIGHTS CASES (1883) opinion, the Supreme Court indicated that the federal prosecution could not be supported under the FOURTEENTH or FIFTEENTH AMENDMENTS because those amendments restrict only STATE ACTION. The THIRTEENTH AMENDMENT did not support a federal prosecution because group violence against blacks was not the equivalent of reducing them to SLAVERY. In JONES v. ALFRED H. MAYER CO. (1968) and GRIFFIN v. BRECKENRIDGE (1971) the Court adopted a more generous attitude towards Congress's Thirteenth Amendment power to prohibit private discrimination.

THEODORE EISENBERG

HODGSON AND THOMPSON v. BOWERBANK
5 Cranch 303 (1809)

Hodgson is a constitutional trivium, of little doctrinal importance. Its interest today is captured in a question: Was *Hodgson* the one occasion between MARBURY v. MADISON (1803) and DRED SCOTT v. SANDFORD (1857) when the Supreme Court held an act of Congress unconstitutional? Various scholars have answered that question differently.

Article III of the Constitution does not explicitly authorize Congress to confer JURISDICTION on federal courts to decide a case in which one ALIEN sues another. The JUDICIARY ACT OF 1789, however, conferred such jurisdiction on the circuit court when "an alien is a party." In *Hodgson,* plaintiffs were British subjects; defendants' CITIZENSHIP was unknown. Chief Justice JOHN MARSHALL, responding to counsel's claim of jurisdiction, was quoted by the reporter, Cranch, as saying only this: "Turn to the article of the constitution of the United States, for the statute cannot extend the jurisdiction beyond the limits of the constitution."

Hodgson plainly holds that Congress cannot constitutionally confer federal court jurisdiction in the alien-versus-alien case. But was Marshall merely limiting the 1789 act's construction to avoid constitutional problems, or was he holding a part of the act's reach unconstitutional? Eighteen decades after the event, the debate goes on.

KENNETH L. KARST

(SEE ALSO: *Unconstitutionality.*)

Bibliography

MAHONEY, DENNIS J. 1982 A Historical Note on *Hodgson v. Bowerbank*. *University of Chicago Law Review* 49:725–740.

HOFFA v. UNITED STATES
385 U.S. 293 (1966)

Information received from a secret government informer and used to obtain a conviction of James Hoffa, the Teamsters' union leader, did not constitute an illegal search, because the informer was an invited guest; did not violate the RIGHT AGAINST SELF-INCRIMINATION, because compulsion was absent; and did not abridge the RIGHT TO COUNSEL, because the information did not breach the confidential relationship between petitioner and counsel. Hoffa's conviction for jury bribery was sustained.

LEONARD W. LEVY

HOKE v. UNITED STATES
227 U.S. 308 (1913)
CAMINETTI v. UNITED STATES
242 U.S. 470 (1917)

Opinions in CHAMPION V. AMES (1903) and HIPOLITE EGG CO. V. UNITED STATES (1911) laid the foundation for a unanimous decision sustaining the MANN ACT, which prohibited the interstate transportation of women for immoral purposes. Justice JOSEPH MCKENNA, generously construing the power over INTERSTATE COMMERCE, declared in *Hoke* that Congress might exercise means that "may have the quality of police regulations." He denied that the Mann Act violated the TENTH AMENDMENT by usurping the STATE POLICE POWER. In *Caminetti,* the Court held that transportation was illegal under the act, even if not accompanied by financial gain: "To say the contrary would shock the common understanding of what constitutes an immoral purpose." These cases helped establish a broad basis for the growth of the NATIONAL POLICE POWER.

DAVID GORDON

HOLDEN v. HARDY
169 U.S. 366 (1898)

Utah adopted a maximum hours law fixing an eight-hour day for miners. A mine owner, convicted for working his employees ten hours a day, claimed that the statute violated his FOURTEENTH AMENDMENT rights. For a 7–2 Supreme Court, Justice HENRY B. BROWN declared that the right to FREEDOM OF CONTRACT protected by SUBSTANTIVE DUE PROCESS of law is subject to legitimate POLICE POWER regulations intended to protect the public health. The Court sustained the statute as a reasonable exercise of the police power on the ground that mining is a dangerous occupation that requires an exception to freedom of contract. Brown realistically observed that employees are often induced by fear of discharge to obey management rules that might be detrimental to health. In such cases self-interest is an unsure guide, justifying legislative intervention. Had the Court adhered to this understanding, LOCHNER V. NEW YORK (1905) might have been stillborn.

LEONARD W. LEVY

HOLDING

The holding of a court is the *ratio decidendi* or the ground(s) upon which it bases its decision of a case. The holding, includes all the court's declarations of law necessary to the decision of the case; other pronouncements are OBITER DICTA. The holding in a case establishes a precedent and may be generalized into a DOCTRINE. The term may also be used more narrowly to signify the court's resolution of any particular legal issue or question of constitutional interpretation presented in a case.

DENNIS J. MAHONEY

HOLMES, OLIVER WENDELL, JR.
(1841–1935)

When he was appointed to the Supreme Court in 1902, at the age of sixty-one, he was best known to the general public as the son of a famous poet and man of letters; when he retired, thirty years later, he had been called "the greatest of our age in the domain of jurisprudence, and one of the greatest of the ages." Oliver Wendell Holmes's thirty years on the Supreme Court unquestionably made his reputation, and yet those years, given the aspirations of Holmes's earlier career, were years in which his mood as a judge can best be described as resignation. He was not able to achieve anything like what he thought he could achieve as a judge; regularly he confessed his inability to do anything other than ratify "what the crowd wants." He wryly suggested that on his tombstone should be inscribed "here lies the supple tool of power," and he allegedly told JOHN W. DAVIS that "if my country wants to go to hell, I am here to help it." For these expressions of resignation he was called "distinguished," "mature," and "wise," the "completely adult jurist." The constitutional jurisprudence of Holmes could be called a jurisprudence of detachment, indifference, or even despair; yet it was a jurisprudence in which contemporary commentators reveled.

Holmes's career hardly began with his appointment to the Court. He had previously written *The Common Law*, a comprehensive theoretical organization of private law subjects, taught briefly at Harvard Law School, and served for twenty years as a justice on the Massachusetts Supreme Judicial Court. Although he had not considered many constitutional cases as a state court judge, he had a distinctive philosophy of judging. There was little difficulty in the transition from the Massachusetts court to the Supreme Court; Holmes simply integrated a new set of cases with his preexistent philosophy. That philosophy's chief postulate was that judicial decisions were inescapably policy choices, and that a judge was better off if he did not make his choices appear too openly based on the "sovereign prerogative" of his power.

Arriving at that postulate had been an unexpected process for Holmes. He was convinced, at the time he wrote *The Common Law* (1881), that private law could be arranged in a "philosophically continuous series." His lectures on torts, criminal law, property, and contracts stressed the ability of those subjects to be ordered by general principles and the desirability of having judges ground their decisions in broad predictive rules rather than deferring to the more idiosyncratic and less predictable verdicts of juries. Holmes had accepted a judgeship in part because he believed that he could implement this conception of private law. Academic life was "half-life," he later said, and judging gave him an opportunity to "have a share in the practical struggle of life."

In practice, however, Holmes found that the law resisted being arranged in regular, predictable patterns. Too many factors operated to create dissonance: the need for court majorities to congeal on the scope and language of a decision; the insignificance of many cases, which were best decided by routine adherence to precedent; the very difficult and treacherous policy choices truly significant cases posed, fostering caution and compromise among judges. The result, for Holmes, was that legal DOCTRINE developed not as a general progression toward a philosophically continuous series but rather as an uneven clustering of decisions around opposing "poles" that represented alternative policy judgments. "Two widely divergent cases" suggested "a general distinction," which initially was "a clear one." But "as new cases cluster[ed] around the opposite poles, and beg[a]n to approach each other," the distinction became "more difficult to trace." Eventually an "arbitrary . . . mathematical line" was drawn, based on considerations of policy.

Thus judging was ultimately an exercise in making policy choices, but since the choices were often arbitrary and judges had "a general duty not to change but to work out the principles already sanctioned by the practice of the past," bold declarations of general principles were going to be few and far between. Indeed in many cases whose resolution he thought to turn on "questions of degree," or "nice considerations," or line drawing, Holmes attempted, as a state court judge, to avoid decision. He delegated "questions of degree" to juries where possible; he relied on precedents even where he felt that they had ceased to have a functional justification; he adhered to the findings of trial judges; he resorted to "technicalities" to "determine the precise place of division." And on those relatively few occasions when he was asked to consider the impact of a legislature's involvement, Holmes tended to defer to legislative solutions, especially in close cases. "Most differences," he said in one case, were "only one[s] of degree," and "difference of degree is one of the distinctions by which the right of the legislature to exercise the STATE POLICE POWER is determined." Deference to the legislature was another means of avoiding judicial policy choices.

Holmes thus brought a curious, if consistent, theory of judging with him to the Supreme Court. Although his original aim as a legal scholar had been the derivation of general guiding principles in all areas of law, as a judge he had concluded that principles were not derived in a logical and continuous but in a random and arbitrary fashion, and that in hard cases, where principles competed, policy considerations dictated the outcome. Judges should be sensitive to the fact that cases did involve policy choices, but they should exercise great caution in making them. Hard cases, turning on "questions of degree" or "nice considerations" should be delegated to other lawmaking bodies, such as the jury and the legislature, that were closer to the "instinctive preferences and inarticulate convictions" of the community. What started out as a theory of bold, activist judicial declarations of principle had ended as a theory of deference to lawmakers who were more "at liberty to decide with sole reference . . . to convictions of policy and right." The creative jurist of *The Common Law* had become the apostle of judicial self-restraint.

In his first month on the Supreme Court Holmes wrote to his longtime correspondent Sir Frederick Pollock that he was "absorbed" with the "variety and novelty of the questions." And indeed Holmes's docket was strikingly different from that he had encountered as a Massachusetts state judge: more federal issues, a greater diversity of issues, and far more cases involving the constitutionality of legislative acts. But the new sets of cases did not require Holmes to modify his theory of judging; they merely emphasized his inclination to defer hard policy choices to others. As a Massachusetts state judge Holmes had found only one act of the Massachusetts legislature constitutionally invalid; as a Supreme Court justice he was to continue that pattern. His first opinion, *Otis v. Parker* (1902), sustained a California statute prohibiting sales of stock shares on margin on the ground that although the statute undoubtedly restricted freedom of exchange, that "general proposition" did not "take us far." The question was one of degree: how far could the legislature restrict that freedom? Since the statute's ostensible purpose, to protect persons from being taken advantage of in stock transactions, was arguably rational, Holmes's role was to defer to the legislative judgments.

Otis v. Parker set a pattern for Holmes's decisions in cases testing the constitutionality of economic regulations. Rarely did he find that questions posed by statutes were not ones of "degree"; rarely did he fail to uphold the legislative judgment. He believed that the New York legislature could regulate the hours of bakers (LOCHNER V. NEW YORK, 1905) even though he thought that hours and wages laws merely "shift[ed] the burden to a different point of incidence." He supported PROHIBITION and antitrust legislation notwithstanding his beliefs that "legislation to make people better" was futile and that the SHERMAN ACT was "damned nonsense." His position, in short, was that "when a State legislature has declared that in its opinion policy requires a certain measure, its actions should not be disturbed by the courts . . . unless they clearly see that there is no fair reason for the law."

Deference for Holmes did not mean absolute passivity. He thought Congress and the states had gone too far in convicting dissidents in a number of war-related speech cases, including ABRAMS V. UNITED STATES (1919) (the case in which he proposed the CLEAR AND PRESENT DANGER test), GITLOW V. NEW YORK (1924), and UNITED STATES V. SCHWIMMER (1928). He invalidated a Pennsylvania statute that regulated mining operations without adequate compensation in *Pennsylvania Coal Company v. Mahon* (1922). He did not think that Congress could constitutionally allow the postmaster general to deny "suspicious" persons access to the mails, and said so in two cases, *Milwaukee Socialist Democratic Publishing Co. v. Burleson* (1920) and *Leach v. Carlile Postmaster* (1921). And he struck down a Texas statute denying blacks eligibility to vote in primary elections in NIXON V. HERNDON (1922), declaring that "states may do a good deal of classifying that it is difficult to believe rational, but there are limits."

Holmes was called, especially in the 1920s, the "Great Dissenter," and some of his dissenting opinions were memorable for the pithiness of their language. In *Lochner v. New York* (1905), Holmes protested against the artificiality of the FREEDOM OF CONTRACT argument used by the majority by saying that "the FOURTEENTH AMENDMENT does not enact Mr. Herbert Spencer's *Social Statics.*" In *Abrams* he said that "the best test of truth is the power of the thought to get itself accepted in the competition of the market," and that "every year . . . we have to wager our salvation upon some prophecy based on imperfect knowledge." And in *Olmstead v. United States* (1928), he decried the use of WIRETAPPING by federal agents: "I think it a less evil that some criminals should escape than that the government should play an ignoble part."

Each of these dissents was subsequently adopted as a majority position by a later Court. Freedom of contract was repudiated as a constitutional doctrine in WEST COAST HOTEL V. PARRISH (1937); Holmes's theory of free speech was ratified by the Court in such decisions as HERNDON V. LOWRY (1937) and YATES V. UNITED STATES (1957); and KATZ V. UNITED STATES (1967) and BERGER V. NEW YORK (1967) overruled the majority decision in *Olmstead.* Despite the eventual triumph of Holmes's position in these cases and despite the rhetorical force of his dissents, "Great Dissenter" is a misnomer by any standard other than a literary one. Holmes did not write an exceptionally large number of dissents, given his long service on the Court, and his positions were not often vindicated.

Holmes's dissents also gave him the reputation among commentators as being a "liberal" justice. But for every Holmes decision protecting CIVIL LIBERTIES one could find a decision restricting them. The same Justice who declared in *Abrams v. United States* (1919) that "we should be eternally vigilant against attempts to check the expression of opinions" held for the Court in BUCK V. BELL (1927) that a state could sterilize mental defectives without their knowing consent. "It is better for all the world, if instead of waiting to execute degenerate offspring for crime, or to let them starve for their imbecility, society can prevent those who are manifestly unfit from continuing their kind," Holmes argued. "Three generations of imbeciles are enough."

Holmes supported the constitutionality of laws prohibiting child labor, defended the right of dissidents to speak, and resisted government efforts to wiretap bootleggers. At the same time he upheld the compulsory teaching of English in public schools, supported the rights of landowners in child trespasser cases, and helped develop a line of decisions giving virtually no constitutional protection to ALIENS. For a time critics ignored these latter cases and followed the *New York Times* in calling Holmes "the chief liberal of the supreme bench for twenty-nine years," but recent commentary has asserted that Holmes was "largely indifferent" to civil liberties.

Holmes's constitutional thought, then, resists ideological characterization and is notable principally for its limited interpretation of the power of JUDICIAL REVIEW. How thus does one explain Holmes's continued stature? In an age where JUDICIAL ACTIVISM, especially on behalf of minority rights, is a commonplace phenomenon, Holmes's interpretation of his office appears outmoded in its circumscription. In an age where the idea of rights against the state has gained in prominence, Holmes's decisions appear to tolerate altogether too much power in legislative majorities. Only in the speech cases does Holmes seem to recognize that the contribution of dissident minorities can prevent a society's attitudes from becoming provincial and stultifying. Elsewhere Holmes's jurisprudence stands for the proposition that the state, as agent of the majority, can do what it likes until some other majority seizes power. That hardly seems a posture inclined to elicit much contemporary applause.

Yet Holmes's reputation remains, on all the modern polls, among the highest of those Justices who have served on the Supreme Court. It is not likely to change for three reasons. First, in an era that was anxious to perpetuate the illusion that judicial decision making was somehow different from other kinds of official decision making, since judges merely "found" or "declared" law, Holmes demonstrated that judging was inescapably an exercise in policymaking. This insight was a breath of fresh air in a stale jurisprudential climate. Against the ponderous intonations of other judges that they were "making no laws, deciding no policy, [and] never entering into the domain of public action," Holmes offered the theory that they were doing all those things. American jurisprudence was never the same again.

Second, Holmes, as a sitting judge, followed through the implications of his insight. If judging was inevitably an exercise in policy choices, if all legal questions eventually became "questions of degree," then there was much to be said for judges' avoiding the arbitrary choice. Other institutions existed whose mandate for representing current community sentiment seemed clearer than the judiciary's; judging could be seen as an art of avoiding decision in cases whose resolution appeared to be the arbitrary drawing of a line. In a jurisprudential climate that was adjusting to the shock of realizing that judges were making law, Holmes's theory of avoidance seemed to make a great deal of sense. Federal judges were not popularly elected officials; if they made the process of lawmaking synonymous with their arbitrary intuitions, the notion of popularly elected government seemed threatened. The wisdom in Holmes's approach to judging seemed so apparent that it took the WARREN COURT to displace it.

These first two contributions of Holmes, however, can be seen as having a historical dimension. To be sure, seeing judges as policymakers was a significant insight, but it is now a commonplace; judicial deference was undoubtedly an influential theory, but it has now been substantially qualified. The enduring quality of Holmes appears to rest on his having a first-class mind and in his unique manner of expression: his style. No judge has been so quotable as Holmes; no judge has come closer to making opinion writing a form of literature. Paradoxically, Holmes's style, which is notable for its capacity to engage the reader's emotions in a manner that transcends time and place, can be seen as a style produced out of indifference. The approach of Holmes to his work as a judge was that of a person more interested in completing his assigned tasks than in anything else. Holmes would be assigned opinions at a Saturday conference and seek to complete them by the following Tuesday; his opinions are notable for their brevity and their assertiveness. The celebrated epigrams in Holmes's opinions were rarely essential to the case; they were efforts to increase the emotional content of opinions whose legal analysis was often cryptic.

Holmes's style of writing was of a piece with his general attitude toward judging. Since judging was essentially an effort in accommodating competing policies, the outcome of a given case was relatively insignificant. Just where the line was drawn or where a given case located itself in a "cluster" of related cases insignificant. One might as well, as a judge, announce one's decision as starkly and vividly as one could. A sense of the delicacy and ultimate insignificance of the process of deciding a case, then, fostered a vivid, emotion-laden, and declarative style.

Thus the legacy of Holmes's constitutional opinions is an unusual one. As contributions to the ordinary mine run of legal doctrine, they are largely insignificant. Their positions are often outmoded, their analyses attenuated, their guidelines for future cases inadequate. One feels, somehow, that Holmes has seen the clash of competing principles at stake in a constitutional law case, but has not probed very far. Once he discovered what was at issue, he either avoided decision or argued for one resolution in a blunt, assertive, and arbitrary manner. One cannot take a Holmes precedent and spin out the resolution of companion cases; one cannot go to Holmes to find the substantive bottomings of an area of law. Holmes's opinions are like a charismatic musical performance: one may be inspired in the viewing but one cannot do much with one's impressions later.

As literary expressions, however, Holmes's opinions probably surpass those of any other Justice. While it begs questions and assumes difficulties away to say that "a policeman may have a constitutional right to talk politics, but he has no constitutional right to be a policeman," the vivid contrast catches one's imagination. While "three generations of imbeciles are enough" was a misstatement of the facts in *Buck v. Bell* and represents an attitude toward mentally retarded persons one might find callous, it engages us, for better or worse. In phrases like these Holmes will continue to speak to subsequent generations; his constitutional opinions, and consequently his constitutional thought, will thus endure. It is ironic that Holmes bequeathed us those vivid phrases because he felt that a more painstaking, balanced approach to judging was futile. He thought of judging, as he thought of life, as "a job," and he got on with it.

G. EDWARD WHITE

Bibliography

BURTON, DAVID 1980 *Oliver Wendell Holmes, Jr.* Boston: Twayne Publishers.

FRANKFURTER, FELIX 1938 *Mr. Justice Holmes and the Supreme Court.* Cambridge, Mass.: Harvard University Press.

HOWE, MARK DEWOLFE 1957 *Justice Oliver Wendell Holmes: The Shaping Years, 1841–1870.* Cambridge, Mass.: Harvard University Press.

_____ 1963 *Justice Oliver Wendell Holmes: The Proving Years, 1870–1882.* Cambridge, Mass.: Harvard University Press.

KONEFSKY, SAMUEL J. 1956 *The Legacy of Holmes and Brandeis: A Study in the Influence of Ideas.* New York: Macmillan.

LERNER, MAX 1943 *The Mind and Faith of Justice Holmes.* Boston: Little, Brown.

ROGAT, YOSEL 1963 Mr. Justice Holmes: A Dissenting Opinion. *Stanford Law Review* 15:3–44, 254–308.

WHITE, G. EDWARD 1971 The Rise and Fall of Justice Holmes. *University of Chicago Law Review* 39:51–77.

_____ 1982 The Integrity of Holmes' Jurisprudence. *Hofstra Law Review* 10:633–671.

HOLMES v. WALTON
(New Jersey, 1780)

Decided by the Supreme Court of New Jersey in 1780, this is the first alleged state precedent for JUDICIAL REVIEW. The case, which was unreported, is referred to in *State v. Parkhurst,* 4 Halsted 427, supposedly decided in 1802 but not reported until 1828, where the state court said that in *Holmes* a state act providing for trial by a six-man jury violated the state constitution. In fact, the act, which involved the seizure and forfeiture of goods traded with the enemy, provided for a TRIAL BY JURY. New Jersey employed six-man juries in cases of small amounts (under six pounds) from colonial times to 1844, twelve-man juries in all other cases. The property in *Holmes v. Walton* being valued at $27,000, Holmes had a right to a trial by a twelve-man jury. The trial judge having allowed him only a six-man jury, Holmes contended not that the seizure act was unconstitutional but that the trial judge denied him a twelve-man jury to which he was entitled under the seizure act as well as under the state constitution; the high court so held. The constitutionality of the seizure act was not at issue, and there was no opinion given in which the court discussed, even by OBITER DICTA, its power to void an act for UNCONSTITUTIONALITY. Soon after the decision of the case, which allowed Holmes a new trial by a jury of twelve members, disaffected citizens of the locality alleged in a petition to the state assembly that the high court of the state had held the seizure act unconstitutional. The legislature, however, supported the court by enacting in 1782 that in any suit exceeding six pounds trial by jury meant a jury of twelve. Somehow, a misleading view of the case originated in the 1780s and survived, making *Holmes v. Walton* a "precedent," however inauthentic, for judicial review.

LEONARD W. LEVY

HOME BUILDING & LOAN ASSOCIATION v. BLAISDELL
290 U.S. 398 (1934)

This was the most important CONTRACT CLAUSE case since CHARLES RIVER BRIDGE V. WARREN BRIDGE CO. (1837). The great Depression of the 1930s, by wiping out jobs and savings and savaging the economy, threatened homeowners, farmers, shopkeepers, and others with the loss of their property through foreclosures on mortgages. The states responded by enacting DEBTORS' RELIEF LEGISLATION that postponed the obligations of mortgagors to meet payments. Minnesota's statute authorized a state court, on application from a debtor, to exempt property from final foreclosure for no more than two years, during which time the creditor must be paid a reasonable rental value fixed by the court and the debtor might refinance the mortgage. The Supreme Court's precedents seemed to require a decision that the contract clause was violated by the statute, which operated retroactively on mortgages contracted prior to its enactment and delayed enforcement of the mortgagee's contractual rights.

By a 5–4 vote the Court sustained the statute in an opinion by Chief Justice CHARLES EVANS HUGHES. The prohibition of the contract clause, he declared, "is not an absolute one and is not to be read with literal exactness like a mathematical formula." In times of acute economic distress the states might employ their RESERVED POLICE POWER, "notwithstanding interference with contract," to prevent immediate enforcement of obligations by a temporary and conditional restraint, in order to safeguard the vital public interest in private ownership. As Justice GEORGE SUTHERLAND, for the dissenters, trenchantly observed, the POLICE POWER, whether reserved or inalienable, had never previously justified impairing the OBLIGATION OF CONTRACT between private parties. Hughes, however, distinguished precedents such as BRONSON V. KINZIE (1843) by saying that they had not, as here, provided for securing the mortgagee the rental value of the property during the extended period. Although the statute affected contracts, it was addressed to a legitimate end of the police power and employed reasonable means to achieve it. The restraint and realism that characterized this opinion and that in NEBBIA V. NEW YORK (1934) of the same term did not dominate the Court's opinions during the next two critical terms, when it confronted New Deal legislation. After *Blaisdell,* however, the contract clause lay almost dormant until the late 1970s.

LEONARD W. LEVY

HOMESTEAD ACT
12 Stat. 392 (1862)

The Homestead Act provided for distribution of public land to settlers who would live on the land and improve it. As enacted in 1862, the act provided for allocation of a quarter section (160 acres) to a homesteader who lived on it for five years and paid a ten dollar fee. The act was sponsored by Speaker of the House Galusha A. Grow (Republican of Pennsylvania), and its passage culminated more than a decade's efforts.

The act bespoke a national commitment to the farmer-freeholder as the prototypical American citizen. The system it established was designed, among other things, to solve the problem of SLAVERY IN THE TERRITORIES by insuring a permanent antislavery majority there; and, for that reason, earlier proposals for a homestead bill were supported by the Liberty and Free Soil parties. The homestead program populated the Midwest and plains with hundreds of thousands of independent farmers, and allowed rapid conversion of wilderness TERRITORIES into STATES.

The act was repealed in 1910, a victim of fraud and inefficiency, as well as of an antipathy during the Progressive era toward distribution of public land. In a little less than half a century, over 100 million acres had been distributed under the act.

DENNIS J. MAHONEY

HOMOSEXUALS' RIGHTS

See: Sexual Preference and the Constitution

HOOKER, THOMAS
(1586–1647)

To escape persecution for his Puritan beliefs, Thomas Hooker fled England in 1633 and settled in Newton, Massachusetts, as its Congregational minister. In 1636 he led most of his congregation to a new settlement at Hartford, thus becoming a founder of Connecticut.

A leader among Puritan clergy, Hooker wrote a major defense of New England Congregationalism and extended his theological convictions into politics. Adopting his flexible stand on formal church affiliation, Connecticut refused to limit the franchise to church members.

In 1639 Hooker's preference for explicit covenants probably prompted Connecticut's leaders to organize the colony's government by drawing up a SOCIAL COMPACT, regarded by some historians as the first written American CONSTITUTION, known as the FUNDAMENTAL ORDERS. This document mirrored Hooker's beliefs that civil government should be a covenant between citizens for the promotion of peace and unity; that political authority should reflect the free choice of the people; that rulers were responsible to those they ruled; that the people, as the source of government's existence, had the right not only to choose magistrates but specifically to limit their powers; and that magistrates should consult with the people on issues involving the common good and heed popular judgment in such matters.

THOMAS CURRY

Bibliography

MILLER, PERRY 1956 *Errand into the Wilderness.* Pages 16–47. Cambridge, Mass.: Harvard University Press.

HOOVER, HERBERT C.
(1874–1964)

Born in Iowa and trained as a mining engineer at Stanford University, Herbert Clark Hoover initially became involved in politics as chairman of the Commission for Relief in Belgium and of the United States Food Administration Board during World War I. After the war, President WOODROW WILSON made Hoover director of European economic relief, and in 1921 President WARREN G. HARDING appointed him secretary of commerce.

Hoover was elected President of the United States on the Republican ticket in 1928. Seven months after his inauguration, the stock market collapsed as the depression that had gripped Europe since the end of the war reached America as well. In the face of the economic crisis Hoover clung to his conservative constitutional principles. He advocated private, voluntary action to spur recovery and expanded relief programs at the state level. He resisted federal government intervention until the election year 1932, when he proposed the Reconstruction Finance Corporation.

Hoover's nominations to the Supreme Court were a mixed lot. He appointed former Justice CHARLES EVANS HUGHES to be Chief Justice in 1930. His nomination of conservative Judge John J. Parker of North Carolina to be an Associate Justice was narrowly rejected by the Senate, but two other appointments were confirmed: moderate OWEN J. ROBERTS of Pennsylvania in 1930 and liberal BENJAMIN N. CARDOZO of New York in 1932.

After FRANKLIN D. ROOSEVELT defeated him in the 1932 election, Hoover retired from public office, but remained influential within the Republican party. He was recalled to public service after World War II to direct food relief programs in Europe, and he served as chairman of two Commissions on the Organization of the Executive Branch. The Hoover Commission Reports of 1949 and 1955 led to greater efficiency in the executive branch, mostly through regrouping of functions and agencies.

DENNIS J. MAHONEY

Bibliography

NASH, GEORGE H. 1983 *The Life of Herbert Hoover.* New York: Norton.

HOOVER, J. EDGAR
(1895–1972)

From his graduation from George Washington University Law School in 1917 until his death in 1972, John Edgar Hoover was continuously employed by the United States Department of Justice. He started as a file reviewer, but in 1919 Hoover became special assistant to Attorney General A. MITCHELL PALMER, with oversight responsibility for the DEPORTATION cases arising out of the PALMER RAIDS. In 1921 Hoover was assigned to the department's Bureau of Investigations, and in 1924 he became its director.

Over the next decade, Hoover transformed his small bureau into a national police agency. As federal criminal law expanded, the bureau expanded with it, acquiring a reputation for professionalism, competence, and efficiency. By the time it was renamed the Federal Bureau of Investigation in 1935, the bureau had established a national fingerprint file, a crime laboratory, and a training academy. The FBI's dual mandate was to investigate violations of federal law and to serve as a domestic, civilian counterintelligence agency. The bureau's success in tracking down bootleggers, gangsters, kidnappers, and spies became legendary.

The FBI was largely Hoover's personal creation, and he ran it autocratically. Although formally supervised by the ATTORNEY GENERAL, Hoover operated with a great deal of independence, gained by tenure, public success, and, reputedly, maintenance of secret dossiers concerning his political superiors. Hoover used the FBI to conduct personal feuds, like that with MARTIN LUTHER KING, JR., and to publicize his own brand of anticommunism. In the end, his apparent indifference to CIVIL LIBERTIES compromised the very professionalism he had worked to instill in the FBI.

DENNIS J. MAHONEY

Bibliography

DE TOLEDANO, RALPH 1973 *J. Edgar Hoover: The Man in His Times.* New Rochelle, N.Y.: Arlington House.

H. P. HOOD & SONS v. UNITED STATES

See: *Wrightwood Dairy, United States v.*

HOSTILE AUDIENCE

Nothing is more antagonistic to the FREEDOM OF SPEECH than a mob shouting a speaker into silence. For state officials to suppress speech merely because the audience is offended by the speaker's message is a violation of the FIRST AMENDMENT. Although some lower courts have experimented with the notion of a heckler's First Amendment right, there is no place in our constitutional order for what HARRY KALVEN called the "heckler veto." The duty of the police, when the audience is hostile, is to protect the speaker so long as that is reasonably possible. Similarly, the potential hostility of an audience—even its potential violence—will not justify denying a license to meet or parade in a PUBLIC FORUM.

When police protection is inadequate, however, and audience hostility poses an immediate threat of violence, the police may constitutionally order a speaker to stop, even though the speech does not amount to INCITEMENT TO UNLAWFUL CONDUCT, and is otherwise protected by the First Amendment. The Supreme Court so held in FEINER V. NEW YORK (1951), a case involving no more than "some pushing, shoving and milling around" in an audience hostile to a speaker in a park. The principle retains vitality, although *Feiner* itself, on its facts, seems an insecure precedent.

The constitutionality of police action requiring someone to stop addressing a hostile audience depends on one form of the CLEAR AND PRESENT DANGER test: the police may not stop the speaker unless the threat of violence is immediate and police resources are inadequate to contain the threatened harm. Thus, if the speaker refuses to stop and is charged with BREACH OF THE PEACE, the court must look beyond the arresting officers' good faith—a point emphasized by the Supreme Court in *Feiner*—to the objective likelihood of violence. Appellate courts, too, in reviewing convictions in such cases, must closely examine lower courts' findings of fact. An important difference between *Feiner* and *Edwards v. South Carolina* (1963), where the Court reversed breach of peace convictions of civil rights demonstrators facing a hostile audience, lay in the *Edwards* Court's willingness to scrutinize the record and reject the state courts' findings of danger.

KENNETH L. KARST

Bibliography

KALVEN, HARRY, JR. 1965 *The Negro and the First Amendment.* Pages 139–145. Columbus: Ohio State University Press.

HOT PURSUIT

See: Exigent Circumstances Search

HOUSE COMMITTEE ON UN-AMERICAN ACTIVITIES

In 1938, because of a growing fear of Nazi and communist activity in the United States, conservative congressmen secured passage of a House Resolution creating a Special Committee on Un-American Activities (HUAC). Under publicity-conscious Texas congressman MARTIN DIES, the Committee set out to expose left-wing groups and individuals whom it considered security risks. After five renewals, by overwhelming votes, the group was made into an unprecedented standing committee of the House in 1945. From then until the mid-1950s, the Committee became a sounding board for ex-radicals, publicity seekers, and critics of the New Deal and the Truman administration. It identified the following tasks for itself: to expose and ferret out communists and their sympathizers in the federal government; to show how communists had won control over vital trade unions; and to investigate communist influences in the press, religious and educational organizations, and the movie industry. The sensational Alger Hiss-Whittaker Chambers hearings, in connection with turning over security information, and the resultant perjury conviction of Hiss, a former New Deal official, added to the Committee's prestige. By 1948, the Committee sponsored legislation against the Communist party, pushing the MUNDT-NIXON BILL.

The activities of HUAC, however, raised important constitutional questions. The Committee's constant probing into political behavior and belief led critics to charge that such forced exposure abridged FREEDOM OF SPEECH and association, and punished citizens for their opinions. Also questioned was the legitimacy of its "exposure for its own sake" approach, when action did not seem to relate to legitimate legislative purpose, and when legislative "trials" violated many aspects of DUE PROCESS including the right to be tried in a court under the protection of constitutional guarantees.

The Supreme Court ultimately dealt with both questions, with contradictory and changing results. In three cases (*Emspack v. United States,* 1955; *Quinn v. United States,* 1955; and WATKINS V. UNITED STATES, 1957) the Court narrowly interpreted the statutory authority for punishing recalcitrant witnesses, and questioned forced exposure of views and activities in light of the FIRST AMENDMENT. Facing sharp criticism, the Court retreated in the cases of BARENBLATT V. UNITED STATES (1958), *Wilkinson v. United States* (1961), and *Braden v. United States* (1961), only to move back again to a more critical position as the 1960s progressed—from 1961 to 1966 reversing almost every contempt conviction which came to it from the Committee. By mid-1966, conservative legislators were condemning the "unseemly spectacles" HUAC chronically elicited. Thus, in 1969, it was rechristened the Internal Security Committee, and although its procedures were modified somewhat in this new form, the committee was eventually abolished by the House in 1975.

PAUL L. MURPHY

Bibliography

GOODMAN, WALTER 1968 *The Committee: The Extraordinary Career of the House Committee on Un-American Activities.* New York: Farrar, Straus.

HOUSTON, CHARLES H. (1895–1950)

Charles H. Houston was the foremost black CIVIL RIGHTS lawyer before THURGOOD MARSHALL. He was a member of the faculty of Howard Law School and from 1932 to 1935 served as dean. He obtained accreditation and respect for the institution, which trained many civil rights lawyers. From 1935 to 1940 Houston was special counsel for the National Association for the Advancement of Colored People (NAACP). Although he returned to private practice thereafter, he remained active with the NAACP and other civil rights organizations. Marshall later called him "The First Mr. Civil Rights." Houston was of counsel in NIXON V. CONDON (1932), arguing against the white primary, and he assisted in the defense of the Scottsboro Boys. He argued and won MISSOURI EX REL. GAINES V. CANADA (1938), which forced the state to open its law school to black students. He also won from the Supreme Court decisions prohibiting discrimination against black railroad employees. Perhaps his most difficult and greatest victory came in HURD V. HODGE (1948), in which the Court accepted his arguments that the CIVIL RIGHTS ACT OF 1866 outlawed the judicial enforcement of RESTRICTIVE COVENANTS by the courts of the DISTRICT OF COLUMBIA, and that even in the absence of the congressional act, the enforcement of such covenants would violate the public policy of the United States.

LEONARD W. LEVY

Bibliography

MCNEIL, GENNA RAE 1982 *Charles Hamilton Houston and the Struggle for Civil Rights.* Philadelphia: University of Pennsylvania Press.

HOUSTON, EAST & WEST TEXAS RAILWAY CO. v. UNITED STATES (SHREVEPORT RATE CASE) 234 U.S. 342 (1914)

To relieve a competitive inequality in rail rates, the Interstate Commerce Commission (ICC) ordered the Texas Railroad Commission to raise intrastate rates to equal interstate rates. Shreveport, Louisiana, to east

Texas rates, set by the ICC, were higher than west Texas to east Texas rates, fixed by the states, thereby placing INTERSTATE COMMERCE at a competitive disadvantage. With only Justices HORACE LURTON and MAHLON PITNEY dissenting, Justice CHARLES EVANS HUGHES relied on the INTERSTATE COMMERCE ACT and the COMMERCE CLAUSE in upholding the ICC order. Hughes distinguished the MINNESOTA RATE CASES (1913) as neither involving an attempt at federal regulation nor adversely affecting or burdening interstate commerce. Emphasizing Congress's "complete and paramount" power over interstate commerce, he announced the SHREVEPORT DOCTRINE: "Wherever the interstate and intrastate transactions of carriers are so related that the government of the one involves the control of the other, it is Congress and not the state, that is entitled to prescribe the final and dominant rule."

DAVID GORDON

HOWARD, JACOB M.
(1805–1871)

Jacob Merritt Howard was an abolitionist, a champion of CIVIL RIGHTS, and a leading northern politician whose constitutional legacy derived from his advocacy of Radical Republicanism. Born and educated in New England, Howard moved to Detroit where, after admission to the bar, he began his political career as a Whig. In 1854 he helped found the Republican party and framed its resolutions.

In 1862 he became a United States senator, and for a decade he remained in the vanguard of the Radical Republican wing of his party. He advocated black VOTING RIGHTS, served influentially during the Civil War on both the Senate Judiciary Committee and the Committee on Military Affairs, and vigorously supported the FREEDMEN'S BUREAU ACT and the CIVIL RIGHTS ACT OF 1866. Howard was a coauthor of the THIRTEENTH AMENDMENT and, as a ranking Senate Republican on the powerful JOINT COMMITTEE ON RECONSTRUCTION, chaperoned the approval by the Senate of the FOURTEENTH AMENDMENT.

LEONARD W. LEVY

HOWE, MARK DEWOLFE
(1902–1966)

Mark DeWolfe Howe began his legal career as a clerk to Justice OLIVER WENDELL HOLMES, and throughout his life Holmes was the focus of much of Howe's most valuable scholarly work. While professor of law at Harvard Law School, Howe prepared definitive editions of Holmes's correspondence with Sir Frederick Pollock (1941) and HAROLD J. LASKI (1953), his Civil War diary and letters (1947), his *Speeches* (1962), and *The Common Law* (1963). Although Howe never lived to complete his biography of Holmes, the two volumes he did publish (1957, 1963) are unparalleled for their illumination of Holmes's intellectual life up to his appointment to the Massachusetts Supreme Judicial Court. A pioneer in the field of American legal history, Howe specialized in the history of freedom of religion. In his last published book, *The Garden and the Wilderness* (1965), Howe criticized the Supreme Court's reading of the history of religion in America, pointing out that the "wall of separation" between church and state was based as much on evangelical theory as Jeffersonian rationalism; Howe suggested that the Constitution recognized a *de facto* ESTABLISHMENT OF RELIGION in American society. An activist as well as a scholar, Howe worked tirelessly for the NAACP LEGAL DEFENSE & EDUCATIONAL FUND, both as a teacher and as a litigator.

RICHARD B. BERNSTEIN

HUDGENS v. NATIONAL LABOR RELATIONS BOARD
424 U.S. 507 (1976)

In terminating its experiment with extending MARSH V. ALABAMA (1946) to privately owned SHOPPING CENTERS, the Supreme Court, 7–2, announced in *Hudgens* that the refusal of owners to permit union picketing did not constitute STATE ACTION and thus did not violate the FIRST AMENDMENT, even though the private property was "open to the public." That vast shopping plazas, which are central features of American culture, are not required by the First Amendment to grant FREEDOM OF SPEECH is a highly significant feature of contemporary constitutional law.

MARTIN SHAPIRO

HUDSON v. PALMER

See: Prisoners' Rights

HUDSON AND GOODWIN, UNITED STATES v.

See: Federal Common Law

HUGHES, CHARLES EVANS
(1862–1948)

The only child of a Baptist minister and a strong-willed, doting mother who hoped their son would become a man of the cloth, Charles Evans Hughes compiled a record of public service unparalleled for its diversity and achievement by any other member of the Supreme Court with the exception of WILLIAM HOWARD TAFT. In addition to pursuing a lucrative career at the bar, Hughes taught law at Cornell, served as a two-term governor of New York, was secretary of state under two Presidents during the 1920s, and served as associate Justice and Chief Justice of the United States. By the narrowest of margins, he lost the electoral votes of California in 1916 and thus the presidency to the incumbent, WOODROW WILSON. Hughes was a man of imposing countenance and intellectual abilities, who left an indelible mark upon the nation's politics, diplomacy, and law.

First appointed to the Court as associate justice by President William Howard Taft, Hughes brought to the bench the social and intellectual outlook of many American progressives, those morally earnest men and women from the urban middle class who wished to purge the nation's politics of corruption, infuse the business world with greater efficiency and concern for the public welfare, and minister to the needs of the poor in the great cities. In an earlier era, such people had found an outlet for their moral energies in religion. By the turn of the twentieth century, they practiced a social gospel and undertook a "search for order" through secular careers in law, medicine, public administration, journalism, engineering, and social welfare.

"We are under a Constitution," Governor Hughes remarked shortly before his appointment to the bench, "but the Constitution is what the judges say it is, and the judiciary is the safeguard of our liberty and of our property under the Constitution." This statement reflected the ambivalence of many progressives about the nation's fundamental charter of government and its judicial expositers on the Supreme Court. On the one hand, Hughes and other progressives clearly recognized that constitutional decision-making was a subjective process, strongly influenced by the temper of the times and by the social biases and objectives of individual jurists. The Constitution, they believed, was flexible enough to accommodate the growing demands for reform that sprang from the manifold desires of businessmen, consumers, farmers, and industrial workers who wished to use government to promote economic security in an increasingly complex, interdependent capitalist economy. Like other progressives, Hughes saw government, both state and federal, as a positive instrument of human welfare that could discipline unruly economic forces, promote moral uplift, and guarantee domestic social peace by protecting the citizen from the worst vicissitudes of the marketplace.

At the same time, Hughes and other middle-class reformers had a morbid fear of socialism and resisted endowing government with excessive power over persons and property. They wanted social change under the rule of law, in conformity with American traditions of individualism, and directed by a disinterested elite of lawyers, administrators, and other experts of enlightened social progress.

By the time Hughes took his seat on the nation's highest court, the Justices had grappled inconclusively for almost five decades with the question of the reach of the constitutional power of the states and the national government to regulate economic activity. One group of Justices, influenced by the Jacksonian legacy of entrepreneurial individualism, equality, and STATES' RIGHTS, had combined an expansive reading of the FOURTEENTH AMENDMENT's DUE PROCESS clause and a narrow interpretation of the COMMERCE CLAUSE and the TAXING AND SPENDING POWER in order to restrict both state and federal regulation of private economic decision making. Another group of Justices, heirs to the radical Republican tradition of moral reform and positive government, had been more receptive to governmental efforts at ECONOMIC REGULATION and redistribution.

Hughes placed his considerable intellectual resources on the side of the economic nationalists and those who refused to read the due process clause as a mechanical limitation upon state regulation of economic affairs. In *Miller v. Wilson* (1915), for example, he wrote for a unanimous bench to sustain California's eight-hour law for women in selected occupations against a challenge that the law violated FREEDOM OF CONTRACT. The liberty protected by the due process clause, he noted, included freedom from arbitrary restraint, but not immunity from regulations designed to protect public health, morals, and welfare.

More significant, he joined the dissenters in COPPAGE V. KANSAS (1915), where six members of the Court, speaking through Justice MAHLON PITNEY, invalidated a Kansas law prohibiting YELLOW DOG CONTRACTS on the ground that the regulation deprived employers of their contractual liberty. Hughes endorsed the dissent by Justice WILLIAM R. DAY which argued that the law attempted only to protect the right of individual workers to join labor unions if they so pleased and represented a legitimate exercise of the STATE POLICE POWER, "not to require one man to employ another against his will, but to put limitations upon the sacrifice of rights which one may exact from another as a condition of employment."

Hughes's views on the federal commerce power were equally generous during this period. He wrote the two leading opinions of the era supporting the authority of Congress and the Interstate Commerce Commission (ICC) to regulate both interstate railroad rates and purely intrastate rates that undermined the efficiency of the nation's transportation network. In the MINNESOTA RATES CASES (1913) he upheld the particular exercise of rate-making by the state, although he and the majority affirmed that the power of Congress "could not be denied or thwarted by the commingling of interstate and intrastate operations" of the railroad. A year later, in the landmark Shreveport Case, HOUSTON, EAST & WEST TEXAS RAILWAY COMPANY V. UNITED STATES (1914), he spoke for all but two Justices in sustaining an order of the ICC that effectively required an increase in intrastate rates in order to bring them into line with those fixed by the commission for interstate carriers over the same territory. The power of Congress to regulate interstate commerce, he wrote, was "complete and paramount"; Congress could "prevent the common instrumentality of interstate and intrastate commercial intercourse from being used in their intrastate operations to the injury of interstate commerce."

Most progressives displayed little sympathy for the plight of either American blacks or the foreign immigrants who entered the country in large numbers during the decades before World War I. Hughes was a striking exception to the usual pattern of collaboration with the forces of racial and ethnic intolerance. He began to speak out in these years against various forms of oppression and bigotry and to lay the foundation for many of his subsequent opinions on CIVIL RIGHTS during the 1930s.

In *McCabe v. Atchison, Topeka & Santa Fe Railroad* (1914), Hughes led a five-Justice majority in striking down a state law that authorized intrastate railroads to provide dining and sleeping cars only for members of the white race. The state and the carriers argued that the statute was reasonable in light of the limited economic demand by black passengers for such services, a point of view that also appealed to Justice OLIVER WENDELL HOLMES. Hughes, however, flatly condemned the law as a violation of the Fourteenth Amendment's EQUAL PROTECTION clause. With support from all but one of the Justices, he also overturned, in *Truax v. Raich* (1915), an Arizona law that had limited the employment of ALIENS in the state's principal industries to twenty percent of all workers in firms with five or more employees. Discrimination against such inhabitants "because of their race or nationality," he declared, "clearly falls under the condemnation of the FUNDAMENTAL LAW."

His most impressive effort in this regard came in the famous debt peonage case, BAILEY V. ALABAMA (1911), where he both invalidated the state's draconian statute and gained a notable rhetorical victory over Justice Holmes. Under the Alabama law, as under similar ones in force throughout the South, a person's failure to perform a labor contract without just cause and without paying back money advanced was prima facie evidence of intent to defraud, punishable by fine or imprisonment. The accused, furthermore, could not rebut the presumption with testimony "as to his uncommunicated motives, purposes, or intention." Hughes condemned this "convenient instrument for . . . coercion" as a violation of both the THIRTEENTH AMENDMENT and the Anti-Peonage Act of 1867.

With a few exceptions, the progressives also displayed more concern for the suppression of crime than for the rights of the accused. The due process clause had seldom been invoked successfully against questionable methods of law enforcement and CRIMINAL PROCEDURE on the state level. In this field, too, Hughes attempted to break new ground that anticipated the jurisprudence of a later era. One case in point is FRANK V. MANGUM (1915), arising out of the notorious Leo Frank trial in Georgia. A young Jewish defendant had been convicted of murder and sentenced to death with a mob shouting outside the courtroom, "Hang the Jew, or we'll hang you." Frank and his lawyers had not been present during the reading of the verdict, because the trial judge could not guarantee their safety in the event of an acquittal.

Despite this evidence of intimidation, the Georgia Supreme Court upheld the conviction and sentence; a federal district judge refused Frank's petition for HABEAS CORPUS, which raised a host of due process challenges; and a majority of the Supreme Court affirmed that decision. Hughes joined a powerful dissent written by Holmes, which chastised the majority for its reasoning and called upon the Justices to "declare lynch law as little valid when practiced by a regularly drawn jury as when administered by one elected by a mob intent on death."

Hughes's initial appointment to the Court, following in the wake of his progressive achievements as governor of New York, had been received with almost unanimous acclaim. However, his nomination as Chief

Justice by President HERBERT HOOVER in 1930 sparked furious debate. Twenty-six senators, led by the redoubtable GEORGE NORRIS of Nebraska, voted against his confirmation. Many of them believed, as Norris did, that the former Justice's profitable law practice during the 1920s had turned him into a pliant tool of the "powerful combinations in the political and financial world" and therefore rendered him incapable of fairly deciding the "contests between organized wealth and the ordinary citizen." Events proved Norris to be half right.

Beginning in 1930, Hughes was called upon to pilot the Court through the years of social and economic crisis spawned by the financial collapse of 1929 and the Great Depression. These were the most turbulent years in the Court's history since the decade before the Civil War and the economic crisis of the 1890s—two earlier occasions when the Justices had attempted to hold back the tide of popular revolt against the status quo.

Under Hughes's leadership, the Court majority became aggressively liberal with respect to the protection of CIVIL LIBERTIES and civil rights, often building upon the doctrinal structure erected by the Chief Justice himself during the Progressive Era. In STROMBERG V. CALIFORNIA (1931), NEAR V. MINNESOTA (1931), and DEJONGE V. OREGON (1937) Hughes's distinguished opinions significantly enlarged the scope of FIRST AMENDMENT rights protected against state abridgment via the due process clause. He personally drove the first judicial nail into the coffin of the SEPARATE BUT EQUAL doctrine with his opinion in MISSOURI EX REL. GAINES V. CANADA (1938), holding that a state university's refusal to admit a qualified black resident to its law school constituted a denial of equal protection. He endorsed Justice GEORGE H. SUTHERLAND's opinion in the initial Scottsboro case, POWELL V. ALABAMA (1932), and wrote the second one, NORRIS V. ALABAMA (1935), himself. Both opinions tightened the Supreme Court's supervision over state criminal trials involving the poor and members of racial minorities.

Hughes contributed to Justice HARLAN F. STONE's famous fourth footnote in UNITED STATES V. CAROLENE PRODUCTS COMPANY (1938), where the latter suggested that the Court had a special role to play in defending PREFERRED FREEDOMS, including FREEDOM OF SPEECH, FREEDOM OF THE PRESS, and VOTING RIGHTS, from legislative abridgment and also to protect DISCRETE AND INSULAR MINORITIES from the tyranny of the majority. Under Hughes, finally, the Court broadened the reach of habeas corpus to attack constitutionally defective state criminal convictions, and greatly expanded the IN FORMA PAUPERIS docket which permitted INDIGENT defendants to seek Supreme Court review of their convictions. By any yardstick, Hughes as Chief Justice compiled a civil liberties record of impressive range and impact.

The Hughes who regularly cast his vote on the libertarian side in cases touching civil liberties and civil rights during the 1930s also voted in 1935 and 1936 against many of the social and economic reforms sponsored by the FRANKLIN D. ROOSEVELT administration and state governments in their efforts to cope with the economic crisis of the decade. It is this side of his performance as Chief Justice that has fueled the most controversy—and puzzlement, too, considering Hughes's toleration for many of the early anti-Depression nostrums of both the New Deal and the individual states. It was Hughes, after all, who wrote for the five-Justice majority in HOME BUILDING & LOAN ASSOCIATION V. BLAISDELL (1934), upholding a far-reaching mortgage moratorium law that many observers found to be in flat violation of the Constitution's CONTRACT CLAUSE. He also wrote for the narrow majority in the GOLD CLAUSE CASES, where the Justices sustained the New Deal's monetary experiments over the protests of Justice JAMES C. MCREYNOLDS who declared, "This is Nero at his worst. The Constitution is gone."

The Chief Justice sided as well with Justice OWEN J. ROBERTS's views in NEBBIA V. NEW YORK (1934), which expanded the sphere of business activities subject to state regulation, and he spoke out forcefully against the crabbed interpretation of the federal commerce power in RAILROAD RETIREMENT BOARD V. ALTON RAILROAD COMPANY (1935), where five Justices voted to strike down a mandatory pension plan for railway workers. In 1935 and 1936, however, Hughes began to vote more consistently with Roberts and the Court's four conservatives—Justices McReynolds, PIERCE BUTLER, WILLIS VAN DEVANTER, and Sutherland—against the New Deal and various state reform programs.

Six months later, in the aftermath of Roosevelt's crushing reelection victory and his threats to reorganize the federal judiciary, the Court reversed gears once again when a bare majority of the Justices—including Hughes and Roberts—sustained a minimum wage law in WEST COAST HOTEL COMPANY V. PARRISH (1937) and the New Deal's major labor law in the WAGNER ACT CASES (1937). Hughes wrote both landmark opinions, the first laying to rest "liberty of contract" and the second affording Congress ample latitude to regulate labor–management conflicts under the commerce clause.

Various explanations have been advanced since the 1930s to explain both Hughes's alignment with the conservatives and his eventual return to the progressive fold in 1937. Hughes justified his behavior during the first period by casting blame upon the New Deal's lawyers, who, he complained, wrote vague, unconstitutional statutes. This thesis has some credibility with respect to the controversial NATIONAL INDUSTRIAL RECOVERY ACT which the Court invalidated in SCHECHTER POULTRY CORPORATION V. UNITED STATES (1935), but none at all when one reflects upon the care with which very good lawyers wrote both the AGRICULTURAL ADJUSTMENT ACT and the Guffey Bituminous Coal Act. (See CARTER V. CARTER COAL CO.) Others have suggested that Hughes voted with Roberts and the four conservatives on several occasions in 1935 and 1936 in order to avoid narrow 5–4 decisions that might damage the Court's reputation for constitutional sagacity. But this hypothesis does not explain why he found 5–4 decisions in favor of the New Deal any less injurious to the Court in 1937.

A more plausible explanation may be that Hughes regarded many New Deal regulatory programs and some on the state level as dangerously radical, both to the inherited constitutional system and to the social order, because of their redistributive implications. Other old progressives also fought the New Deal for similar reasons after 1935. Those who resisted the leftward drift of the administration in 1935 hoped that the electorate would repudiate Roosevelt's course of action in the 1936 referendum, but Roosevelt's landslide victory left them with few alternatives but capitulation to the popular will. In bowing to the election returns, Hughes became the leader of the Court's progressive wing once again, salvaged the basic power of JUDICIAL REVIEW, and at the same time administered a fatal blow to the President's misconceived reorganization bill. It was a stunning triumph for the Chief Justice.

Hughes accomplished this feat without serious damage to his intellectual integrity. The Justice who wrote *Miller v. Wilson* in 1915 did not find it too difficult to sustain minimum wage legislation two decades later. And the ideas expressed in *NLRB v. Jones & Laughlin* (1937) had already been given initial shape in the *Minnesota Rates Cases* and the Shreveport Case. For a Justice as brilliant and as crafty as Hughes, leading the constitutional revolution in 1937 was as easy as resisting it a year before, but the latter course assured his place in history.

MICHAEL E. PARRISH

(SEE ALSO: *Constitutional History, 1933–1945.*)

Bibliography

FREUND, PAUL A. 1967 Charles Evan Hughes. *Harvard Law Review* 81:34–48.

HENDEL, SAMUEL 1951 *Charles Evans Hughes and the Supreme Court.* New York: Russell & Russell.

PUSEY, MERLO J. 1951 *Charles Evans Hughes.* 2 Vols. New York: Harper & Row.

HUGHES COURT
(1930–1941)

The years in which Chief Justice CHARLES EVANS HUGHES presided over the Supreme Court of the United States, 1930–1941, are notable for the skillful accomplishment of a revolution in CONSTITUTIONAL INTERPRETATION. The use of the DUE PROCESS clauses of the Fifth Amendment and FOURTEENTH AMENDMENT to protect FREEDOM OF CONTRACT and economic Darwinism against government regulation yielded to legislative supremacy and judicial self-restraint. The prevailing limits on the regulatory powers of Congress under the COMMERCE CLAUSE were swept away. The Hamiltonian view that Congress has power to spend money for any purpose associated with the general welfare was solidified by judicial approval. The Court acquiesced in the delegation of vast lawmaking power to administrative agencies. The groundwork was laid for expanding the constitutionally guaranteed FREEDOM OF SPEECH and freedom of the press.

Change was all about the Hughes Court. Of the eight Justices who flanked Hughes when he took his seat as Chief Justice, seven left the Court before he retired. The Court moved across the street from the cozy, old Senate Chamber in the Capitol to the gleaming white marble palace and ornate conference room used today. Profounder changes were occurring in the social, economic, and political conditions that give rise to constitutional litigation, that shape the briefs and arguments of counsel, and that the Court's decisions must address.

The preceding era had been marked by the rise to dominance of large-scale business and financial enterprise. Vast aggregations of men and women and material wealth were needed to develop America's resources, to harness the power unleashed by science and technology, and to capture the efficiencies of mass production for mass markets. Unlocking America's agricultural and industrial wealth made for higher standards of living and an extremely mobile society. With the gains had come corruption, hardships, injustices, and pressure for political action; but in the general prosperity of the 1920s the costs were too often ignored.

Yet the farmers were left behind and too much of the wealth was committed to speculation in corporate securities. The bursting of the latter bubble in November 1929 heralded an economic depression of unprecedented length and depth. Ninety percent of the market value of stock in industrial corporations was wiped out in three years. Twenty-five percent of the land in Mississippi was auctioned off in mortgage foreclosure sales. Factory payrolls were cut in half. One out of every four persons seeking employment was without work. The Depression destroyed people's faith in the industrial magnates and financiers, even in the ethic of individual self-reliance. The stability of American institutions seemed uncertain.

The election of FRANKLIN D. ROOSEVELT as President of the United States brought a new, more active political philosophy to government. Government, Roosevelt asserted, should seek to prevent the abuse of superior economic power, to temper the conflicts, and to work out the accommodations and adjustments that a simpler age had supposed could safely be left to individual ability and the free play of economic forces. Government should also meet the basic need for jobs and, in the case of those who could not work, for food, clothing, and shelter. For the most part these responsibilities must be met by the federal government, which alone was capable of dealing with an economy national in scope and complexity.

Roosevelt's "New Deal" not only provided money and jobs for the worst victims of the Depression; it enacted the legislation and established the government agencies upon which national economic policies would rest for at least half a century: the AGRICULTURAL ADJUSTMENT ACTS, the WAGNER NATIONAL LABOR RELATIONS ACT, the FAIR LABOR STANDARDS ACT, THE SOCIAL SECURITY ACT, and the SECURITIES AND EXCHANGE ACT.

JUDICIAL REVIEW permits those who lose battles in the executive and legislative branches to carry the war to the courts. Earlier in the century many courts, including the Supreme Court, had clung to the vision of small government, economic laissez-faire, and unbounded opportunity for self-reliant individuals. Judges had thus struck down as violations of the due process clauses of the Fifth and Fourteenth Amendments many measures now generally accepted as basic to a modern industrial and urban society: MAXIMUM HOURS AND MINIMUM WAGE LAWS, laws forbidding industrial homework, and laws protecting the organization of labor unions. The critical question for the Supreme Court in the Hughes era would be whether the Court would persevere or change the course of American constitutional law.

The response of Justices WILLIS VAN DEVANTER, JAMES C. MCREYNOLDS, GEORGE SUTHERLAND, and PIERCE BUTLER was predictable: they would vote to preserve the old regime of limited federal government and economic laissez-faire. Three Justices—LOUIS D. BRANDEIS, HARLAN F. STONE, and BENJAMIN N. CARDOZO—could be expected to eschew the use of judicial power to protect economic liberty, and might not condemn broader congressional interpretation of the commerce clause. The balance rested in the hands of Chief Justice HUGHES and Justice OWEN J. ROBERTS.

At first the Court challenged the New Deal. The National Recovery Administration sought to halt the downward spiral in wages and prices by stimulating the negotiation of industry-by-industry and market-by-market codes of "fair competition" fixing minimum prices and wages and outlawing "destructive" competitive practices. In SCHECHTER POULTRY CORPORATION V. UNITED STATES (1935) the Court held the underlying legislation unconstitutional. The major New Deal measure for dealing with the plight of the farmers was held unconstitutional in UNITED STATES V. BUTLER (1936) as "a statutory plan to regulate and control agricultural production, a matter beyond the powers delegated to the federal government." CARTER V. CARTER COAL COMPANY (1936) held that, because production was a purely local activity, Congress lacked power to legislate concerning the wages and hours of bituminous coal miners. In MOREHEAD V. NEW YORK EX REL. TIPALDO (1936) the four conservative Justices, joined by Justice Roberts, reaffirmed the 1923 decision in ADKINS V. CHILDREN'S MEMORIAL HOSPITAL invalidating a law fixing minimum wages for women. These opinions seemed to presage invalidation of such other fundamental New Deal measures as the National Labor Relations Act, a proposed federal wage and hour law, and even the Social Security Act.

President Roosevelt responded with strong criticism. The *Schechter* ruling, he said, was evidence that the Court was still living "in the horse and buggy age." On February 5, 1937, the President sent a special message to Congress urging enactment of a bill to create one new judgeship for every federal judge over the age of seventy who railed to retire. The message spoke of the heavy burden under which the courts—particularly the Supreme Court—were laboring, of the "delicate subject" of "aged or infirm judges," and of the need for "a constant infusion of new blood in the courts." No one doubted Roosevelt's true purpose. Six of the nine Supreme Court Justices were more than seventy years old. Six new Justices would ensure a majority ready to uphold the constitutionality of New Deal legislation. A month later the President addressed the nation more candidly, acknowledging that he hoped "to bring to the decision of social and economic problems younger men who have had personal experience and contact with modern facts and circumstances under which average men have to live and work."

Despite overwhelming popular support for New Deal legislation and despite the President's landslide reelection only a few months earlier, the Court-packing plan was defeated. The President's disingenuous explanation was vulnerable to factual criticism. Justice Brandeis, widely known as a progressive dissenter from his colleagues' conservative philosophy, joined Chief Justice Hughes in a letter to the Senate Judiciary Committee demonstrating that the Court was fully abreast of its docket and would be less efficient if converted into a body of fifteen Justices. Much of the political opposition came from conservative strongholds, but the current ran deeper. The American people had a well-nigh religious attachment to CONSTITUTIONALISM and the Supreme Court. They intuitively realized that packing the Court in order to reverse the course of its decisions would destroy its independence and erode the essence of constitutionalism. Yet no explanation is complete without recalling the contemporary quip: "A switch in time saves nine." The final defeat of the Court-packing plan came after a critical turning in the Court's own interpretation of constitutional limitations.

The shift first became manifest in WEST COAST HOTEL COMPANY v. PARRISH (1937), a 5–4 decision upholding the constitutionality of a state statute authorizing a board to set minimum wages for women. The Chief Justice's opinion overruled the *Adkins* case and markedly loosened the standards of SUBSTANTIVE DUE PROCESS that had previously constricted regulation of contractual relations. To the old STATE POLICE POWER doctrine confining the permissible objectives of government to health, safety, and morals, the Chief Justice added broadly the "welfare of the people" and "the interests of the community." Where the old opinions declared as an abstract truth that "The employer and the employee have equality of right and any legislation that disturbs the equality is an arbitrary interference with liberty of contract," the new majority more realistically asserted that a legislature may consider the "relatively weak bargaining power of women" and may "adopt measures to reduce the evils of the 'sweating system.'" There were also hints of greater judicial deference to legislative judgments: "regulation which is reasonable in relation to its subject and is adopted in the interests of the community is due process."

The *West Coast Hotel* case inaugurated a line of decisions sustaining every challenged economic regulation enacted by a state legislature or by the Congress. General minimum wage and maximum hour laws, price regulations, and labor relations acts—all were upheld. Even prior to Hughes's retirement, the trend was intensified by the normal replacement of all but one of the Justices who had sat with Hughes on his first day as Chief Justice. The philosophy of judicial self-restraint gradually became dominant on the Court, in the laws, and throughout the legal profession.

The troublesome problems of constitutional interpretation often call for striking a balance between the opposing ideals of democratic self-government and judicial particularization of majestic but general and undefined constitutional limitations. The philosophy of legislative supremacy and judicial self-restraint that came to dominate constitutional interpretation in the time of the Hughes Court was often asserted and widely accepted as broadly applicable to all constitutional adjudication except the enforcement of clear and specific commands. The Hughes Court thus set the stage for the central constitutional debate of the next major era in constitutional history. As claims to judicial protection of CIVIL LIBERTIES and CIVIL RIGHTS became the focus of attention, JUDICIAL ACTIVISM would be revived by substituting STRICT SCRUTINY for judicial deference in many areas of PREFERRED FREEDOMS and FUNDAMENTAL RIGHTS. Many of the new judicial activists would be liberals or progressives of the same stripe that had pressed for democratic self-government in the days when their political power confronted conservative dominance of the courts. But the opinions of the Hughes Court still mark the end of effective constitutional challenges to legislative regulation of economic activity.

The Hughes Court broke new ground in interpretation of the commerce clause only a few months after the minimum wage decision. In *National Labor Relations Board v. Jones & Laughlin Steel Corporation*

(1937) the Labor Board, under authority delegated by the Wagner Act, had ordered Jones & Laughlin to reinstate four employees discharged from production and maintenance jobs in a basic steel mill because of their union activity. Both Jones & Laughlin's anti-union activities and the order for reinstatement were beyond the reach of federal power as delimited by the old line between production and interstate movement. The lower court had so decided. Led by Chief Justice Hughes, a bare majority of the Supreme Court Justices reversed that decision. Rejecting the old conceptualism that had asked whether the regulated activity had a "legal or logical connection to interstate commerce," the Court appraised the relation by "a practical judgment drawn from experience." Congress could reasonably conclude that an employer's anti-union activities and refusal to bargain collectively might result in strikes, and that a strike at a basic steel mill drawing its raw materials from, and shipping its products to, many states might in fact affect the movement of INTERSTATE COMMERCE. (See WAGNER ACT CASES.)

The *Jones & Laughlin* opinion appeared to retain some judicially enforceable constitutional check upon the congressional power under the commerce clause: "Undoubtedly the scope of this power must be considered in the light of our dual system of government and may not be extended so far as to embrace effects upon interstate commerce so indirect and remote that to embrace them, in view of our complex society, would effectually obliterate the distinction between what is national and what is local and create a completely centralized government." But the check proved illusory. The quoted admonition, while operable as a political principle guiding congressional judgment, yields no rule of law capable of judicial administration. Once the distinctions between interstate movement and production and between "direct" and "indirect" effects upon interstate commerce are rejected, the number of links in the chain of cause and effect becomes irrelevant. Federal power would reach to the local machine shop that repaired the chain saws that cut the trees that yielded the pulp wood that yielded the pulp that made the paper bought by the publisher to print the newspaper that circulated in interstate commerce. The size of the particular establishment or transaction also became irrelevant, for the cumulative effect of many small local activities might have a major impact upon interstate commerce. The new judicial deference, moreover, called for leaving such questions to Congress.

A second doctrinal development accelerated the trend. The Fair Labor Standards Act of 1938 required employers to pay workers engaged in the production of goods for shipment in interstate commerce no less than a specified minimum wage. The act also forbade shipping in interstate commerce any goods produced by workers who had not received the minimum wage. Congress claimed the power to exclude from the pipeline of interstate commerce things that would, in its judgment, do harm in the receiving state. Goods produced at substandard wages and shipped in interstate commerce might depress wages paid in the receiving states, and also in other producing states. The theory had been applied as early as 1903 to uphold a congressional law forbidding the interstate shipment of lottery tickets, but in 1918, under the doctrine barring federal regulation of production, the Court had struck down an act of Congress barring the interstate shipment of goods made with child labor. Having rejected that doctrine in the Labor Board Cases, the Hughes Court readily upheld the constitutionality of the Fair Labor Standards Act upon the theory of the lottery cases. The direct prohibition against paying less than the specified minimum wage was also upheld as a necessary and proper means of preventing goods made under substandard conditions from moving in interstate commerce and doing harm in other states. Years later similar reasoning supported broader decisions upholding the power of Congress to regulate or prohibit the local possession or use of firearms and other articles that have moved in interstate commerce.

Much more than legal logic lay behind the Hughes Court's recognition of virtually unlimited congressional power under the commerce clause. The markets of major firms had become nationwide. A complex and interconnected national economy made widely separated localities interdependent. A century earlier layoffs at the iron foundry in Saugus, Massachusetts, would have had scant visible effect in other states. During the Great Depression no one could miss the fact that layoffs at the steel mills in Pittsburgh, Pennsylvania, reduced the demand for clothing and so caused more layoffs at the textile mills in Charlotte, North Carolina, and Fall River, Massachusetts. Even as the Hughes Court deliberated the Labor Board Cases, a strike at a General Motors automobile assembly plant in Michigan was injuring automobile sales agencies in cities and towns throughout the United States.

The states were incapable of dealing with many of the evils accompanying industrialization. Many states were smaller and less powerful than the giant public utilities and industrial corporations. Massachusetts might forbid the employment of child labor, or fix a minimum wage if the due process clause permitted, but the cost of such measures was the flight of Massachusetts industries to North Carolina or South Carolina. New York might seek to ensure the welfare of its dairy farmers by setting minimum prices that handlers should pay for milk, only to watch the handlers turn to Vermont farmers who could sell at lower prices. The commerce clause barred the states from erecting protective barriers against out-of-state competition.

A shift in intellectual mode was also important. The rise of LEGAL REALISM stimulated by publication of OLIVER WENDELL HOLMES's *The Common Law* in 1881 had made it increasingly difficult for courts to find guidance in such abstractions as the equality of right between employer and employee or in such rhetorical questions as "What possible legal or logical connection is there between an employee's membership in a labor organization and the carrying on of interstate commerce?" The harsh facts of the Depression made both impossible.

The proper division of regulatory activity between the nation and the states is and may always be a much debated question of constitutional dimension. Today the question is nonetheless almost exclusively political. The Hughes Court yielded the final word to Congress.

The enormous expansion of the federal establishment that began in the 1930s and continued for half a century finds a second constitutional source in the power that Article I, Section 8, grants to Congress: "to lay and collect taxes . . . and provide for the common defense and general welfare of the United States." Here, too, the key judicial precedents of the modern era are decisions of the Hughes Court.

The scope of the TAXING AND SPENDING POWER had been disputed from the beginning. Jeffersonian localists argued that the words "general welfare" encompassed only the purposes expressly and somewhat more specifically stated later in Article I. Spending for INTERNAL IMPROVEMENTS gradually became accepted practice in the political branches, but the Supreme Court had had no occasion to adjudicate the issue of constitutional power because no litigant could show that he or she had suffered the kind of particular injury that would sustain a cause of action.

The Roosevelt administration not only spent federal funds on an unprecedented scale in order to relieve unemployment; it also broke new ground in using subsidies to shape the conduct of both state governments and private persons. The Agricultural Adjustment Act of 1933 levied a tax upon processors in order to pay subsidies to farmers who would agree to reduce the acreage sown to crops. The aim was to stabilize the prices of agricultural commodities. Linking the subsidy payments to the processing tax gave the processors STANDING to challenge the tax on the ground that the payments exceeded the limits of the federal spending power. In *United States v. Butler* (1936) the Hughes Court held the act unconstitutional because conditioning the farmer's allotments upon the reduction of his planted acreage made the whole "a statutory plan to regulate and control agricultural production, a matter beyond the power delegated to the federal government."

The decision was a prime target of President Roosevelt's criticism. It aroused fears that the Hughes Court would also invalidate the Social Security Act, a key New Deal measure establishing systems of unemployment and old age and survivors insurance. The title of the act dealing with unemployment levied a federal payroll tax upon all employers of eight or more individuals but gave a credit of up to 90 percent of the federal tax for employer contributions to a state employment fund meeting federal standards specified in the act. Very few states had previously established unemployment insurance, but the act's combination of pressure and inducement proved effective. The combination was attacked as a coercive, unconstitutional invasion of the realm reserved exclusively to the states by the TENTH AMENDMENT, which, if generalized, would enable federal authorities to induce, if not indeed compel, state enactments for any purpose within the realm of state power, and generally to control state administration of state laws. In STEWARD MACHINE COMPANY V. DAVIS (1937) the five-Justice majority answered that offering a choice or even a temptation is not coercion. Spending to relieve the needs of the army of unemployed in a nationwide depression serves the general welfare, the majority continued; the spending power knows no other limitation.

In later decades congressional spending programs would grow in size, spreading from agriculture and social insurance to such areas as housing, highway construction, education, medical care, and local LAW ENFORCEMENT. Many FEDERAL GRANTS-IN-AID to both state and private institutions are conditioned upon observance of federal standards. The balance to be struck between federal standards and state autonomy is sharply debated, but in this area, as under the commerce clause, the question is now almost exclusively left to political discretion as a result of the decisions of the Hughes Court.

Questions concerning the DELEGATION OF POWER gave rise to the fourth major area of constitutional law shaped by the Hughes Court. Congress makes the laws, it is said; the executive carries out the laws; and the judiciary interprets the laws and resolves controversies between executive and legislative officials. Never quite true, this old and simple division of functions proved largely incompatible with the new role established for federal government by the Roosevelt administration. Much law, however denominated, would have to be made by executive departments or new administrative agencies authorized by Congress, such as the Securities and Exchange Commission and the Civil Aeronautics Board. Under the traditional division the new arrangements were subject to attack as unconstitutional attempts to delegate to other agencies part of the legislative power that Congress alone can exercise.

The flow of decisions in the Hughes Court upon this question paralleled the course taken under the due process, commerce, and spending clauses. At first the majority seemed disposed to resist the new political order as in PANAMA REFINING COMPANY V. RYAN (1935) and *Schechter Poultry Corporation v. United States* (1935). Later decisions, however, reversed the initial trend. UNITED STATES V. ROCK ROYAL COOPERATIVE, INC. (1939) is illustrative. The AGRICULTURAL MARKETING AGREEMENT ACT gave the secretary of agriculture broad authority to regulate the marketing of eight agricultural commodities, including milk, with a view to reestablishing the purchasing power of farmers at the level in a base period, usually 1909–1914. In the case of milk, however, if the secretary found the prices so determined to be unreasonable, he was authorized to fix producer prices at a level that would reflect pertinent economic conditions in local milk markets, provide an adequate supply of wholesome milk, and be in the public interest. The purported standards were numerous and broad enough to impose no significant limit upon the secretary's decisions. Nevertheless, the Court upheld the delegation. It was enough that Congress had limited the secretary's power to specified commodities, had specifically contemplated price regulation, and had provided standards by which the secretary's judgment was to be guided after hearing interested parties. The decision set the pattern for all subsequent legislative draftsmen and judicial determinations.

The contributions of the Hughes Court to the law of the FIRST AMENDMENT were less definitive than in the areas of the commerce clause, economic due process, the spending power, and delegation; but they were not less important. The Hughes Court infused the First Amendment with a new and broader vitality that still drives the expansion of the constitutional protection available to both individual speakers and institutional press.

Apart from the World War I prosecution of pacifists and socialists for speeches and pamphlets alleged to interfere with the production of munitions or conscription for the armed forces, federal law posed few threats to freedom of expression. State laws were more restrictive. The illiberal decisions of the 1920s sustaining the prosecution of leftists under state CRIMINAL SYNDICALISM LAWS assumed that the First Amendment's guarantees against congressional abridgment of freedom of expression are, by virtue of the Fourteenth Amendment, equally applicable to the states. These OBITER DICTA encouraged constitutional attack upon state statutes, municipal ordinances, and judge-made doctrines restricting political and religious expression. In this area Chief Justice Hughes and Justice Roberts quickly allied themselves with the three Justices of established liberal reputation.

Two early opinions highlight the protection that the First and Fourteenth Amendments afford the press against previous restraints. NEAR V. MINNESOTA (1931) was decided upon appeal from a state court's injunction forbidding further publication of *The Saturday Press,* a weekly newspaper, upon the ground that it was "largely devoted to malicious, scandalous and defamatory articles." The newspaper had charged Minneapolis officials with serious offenses in tolerating gambling, bootlegging, and racketeering; the articles were scurrilous and anti-Semitic in tone and content. The decree was authorized by a Minnesota statute. Minnesota had experienced a rash of similar scandal sheets, some of whose publishers were believed to use their journals for blackmail. In an opinion by Chief Justice Hughes, the Supreme Court held that the injunction against publication was an infringement upon the liberty of the press guaranteed by the Fourteenth Amendment regardless of whether the charges were true or false. For any wrong the publisher had committed or might commit, public and private redress might be available; but this PRIOR RESTRAINT was inconsistent with the constitutional liberty.

The law's strong set against previous restraints was underscored a few years later by GROSJEAN V. AMERICAN PRESS COMPANY (1936), where a review of history led the Hughes Court to conclude that the First and Fourteenth Amendments bar not only censorship but also taxes that single out the press and are thus calculated to limit the circulation of information.

The chief danger to freedom or expression by the poor, the unorthodox, and the unpopular lies in state statutes and municipal ordinances that give local authorities wide discretion in preserving the peace and public order. Such laws not only invite suppression of unorthodox ideas by discriminatory enforcement but they also encourage self-censorship in hope of avoiding official interference. The Hughes Court laid the foundations for current constitutional doctrines narrowing the opportunities for abuse.

LOVELL V. CITY OF GRIFFIN (1938) introduced the doctrine that a law requiring a license for the use of the streets or parks for the distribution of leaflets, speeches, parades, or other forms of expression must, explicitly or by prior judicial interpretation, confine the licensing authority to considerations of traffic management, crowd control, or other physical inconvenience or menace to the public. From there it was only a short step to holding in CANTWELL V. CONNECTICUT (1941) that a man may not be punished for words or a street DEMONSTRATION, however offensive to the audience, under a broad, general rubric that invites reprisal for the expression of unorthodox views instead of requiring a narrow judgment concerning the risk of immediate violence. THORNHILL V. ALABAMA (1941), once important for the ruling that peaceful PICKETING in a labor dispute is a form of expression protected by the First Amendment, also introduced the then novel and still controversial doctrine that an individual convicted under a law drawn so broadly as to cover both expression subject to regulation and constitutionally protected expression may challenge the constitutionality of the statute "on its face" even though his own conduct would not be constitutionally protected against punishment under narrower legislation. (See OVERBREADTH DOCTRINE.)

Supreme Court Justices and other constitutionalists still debate the theoretical question how far the First and Fourteenth Amendments secure individuals a right to some PUBLIC FORUM for the purposes of expression. The Hughes Court's decision in HAGUE V. CONGRESS OF INDUSTRIAL ORGANIZATIONS (1939) recognized such a right to the use of streets, parks, and like public places traditionally open for purposes of assembly, communication, and discussion of public questions: "Such use of the streets and public places has, from ancient times, been a part of the privileges, immunities, rights and liberties of citizens. The privilege . . . to use the streets and parks for communication of views on national questions may be regulated in the interest of all; . . . but must not in the guise of regulation be abridged or denied." On this ground *Schneider v. State* (1939) invalidated four city ordinances banning the use of the streets to hand out leaflets. Against this background later Justices would wrestle with the constitutional problems raised by restrictions upon house-to-house canvassing and the use of other government properties for the purpose of expression.

The Hughes Court presided over a revolution in constitutional interpretation. Many conservatives were convinced that in joining the liberal Justices, the Chief Justice and Justice Roberts unconscionably distorted the law to suit the winds of politics. Yet while the revolution is plain, the ground-breaking decisions did appreciably less violence than some reforming decisions of the later WARREN COURT and BURGER COURT to the ideal of a coherent, growing, yet continuing body of law binding the judges as well as the litigants. Doubtless the presence of two competing lines of authority in the Court's earlier decisions often made it easier for the Hughes Court to perform this part of the judicial function. Liberty of contract had never been absolute. The Court had previously sustained, in special contexts, the power of Congress to regulate local activities affecting interstate commerce. Acceptance of the Hughes Court's changes was also the easier because the Hughes Court was diminishing judicial interference with legislative innovations whereas the Warren and Burger Courts pressed far-reaching reforms without legislative support and sometimes against the will expressed by the people's elected representatives. That the old structure and powers of government should be shaped to industrialization, urbanization, and a national economy seemed more inevitable than that public schools should be integrated by busing, that prayer and Bible-reading should be banned from the public schools, or that abortion should be made a matter of personal choice. Yet even when the differences are acknowledged, much of the success of the Hughes Court in managing its revolution in constitutional interpretation seems attributable to the Chief Justice's belief in the value of a coherent, though changing, body of law, to his character, and to his talents combining the perception and sagacity drawn from an earlier, active political life with his extraordinary legal craftsmanship, earlier fine-honed as an Associate Justice.

ARCHIBALD COX

Bibliography

ALSOP, JOSEPH and CATLEDGE, TURNER 1938 *The 168 Days.* Garden City, N.Y.: Doubleday.

JACKSON, ROBERT H. 1941 *The Struggle for Judicial Supremacy.* New York: Knopf.

MURPHY, PAUL 1972 *The Constitution in Crisis Times 1918–1969* New York: Harper & Row.

PUSEY, MERLO J. 1951 *Charles Evans Hughes.* New York: Macmillan.

STERN, ROBERT L. 1946 The Commerce Clause and the National Economy, 1933–1946. *Harvard Law Review* 59:645–693.

SWINDLER, WILLIAM F. 1970 *Court and Constitution in the Twentieth Century,* Part I. Indianapolis: Bobbs-Merrill.

HUMPHREY, HUBERT H. (1911–1978)

Hubert Horatio Humphrey was the latest in a line of distinguished United States senators whose influence has exceeded that of many Presidents. He served as senator from Minnesota from 1948 to 1964 and from 1972 to his death, during which time he wrote over forty acts of Congress and coauthored considerably more than twice that many on subjects as diverse as children's nutrition, aid to education, nuclear disarmament, full employment, solar energy, and medicare. He led the anticommunist liberal wing of the Democratic party and cofounded its political organ, Americans for Democratic Action, whose constitution barred membership by communists and Fascists. In 1954 Humphrey wrote the COMMUNIST CONTROL ACT; his original version would have made it a crime to be a member of the party. He never spoke against Senator Joseph R. McCarthy in the Senate. Otherwise he was the quintessential liberal, involved in nearly every achievement and failure of American liberalism from the close of World War II until his untimely death. He believed that government existed to serve people, the more service to the larger number of people the better.

Humphrey's finest hours were devoted to CIVIL RIGHTS. In 1948 he became a national celebrity by leading a successful fight for a strong civil rights plank in his party's platform, provoking a walkout of intransigent Southerners who formed the Dixiecrat party. In 1964, when he was party whip, he was floor manager of the battle for the passage of the CIVIL RIGHTS ACT of that year.

As thirty-eighth vice-president, Humphrey was the most unflaggingly active of any in our history. When he was his party's nominee for President in 1968, he lost the election by half a million votes because his strong support of the VIETNAM WAR cost him the allegiance of antiwar voters, and because his civil rights record cost him southern votes that went to a third party candidate.

The pell-mell, all-directions-at-once character of the Great Society mirrored Humphrey as well as President LYNDON B. JOHNSON. Humphrey was not only an effective legislator. He was probably the gabbiest, most exuberant, open-hearted person in American public life.

LEONARD W. LEVY

Bibliography

SOLBERG, CARL 1984 *Hubert Humphrey: A Biography.* New York: Norton.

HUMPHREY'S EXECUTOR v. UNITED STATES 295 U.S. 602 (1935)

This decision probably more than any other contributed to President FRANKLIN D. ROOSEVELT'S animus against the Supreme Court. As Attorney General ROBERT H. JACKSON wrote, the opinion of the unanimous Court by Justice GEORGE SUTHERLAND gave the impression "that the President had flouted the Constitution, rather than that the Court had simply changed its mind within the past ten years." In MYERS V. UNITED STATES (1926) a 6–3 Court had sustained the removal power of the President in a case involving a postmaster. Sutherland had joined the opinion of the Court, including its OBITER DICTUM that the removal power extended even to members of independent REGULATORY COMMISSIONS. Roosevelt, relying on *Myers,* removed from the Federal Trade Commission (FTC) William Humphrey, who had been reappointed for a six-year term in 1931. The FEDERAL TRADE COMMISSION ACT provided for removal for cause, including inefficiency or malfeasance.

Humphrey was a blatantly probusiness, antiadministration official who thwarted the objectives of the FTC. After he died, his executor sued for Humphrey's back pay, raising the question whether a member of an administrative tribunal created by Congress to implement legislative policies can be removed as if he were a member of the executive department. Ruling against the removal power, Sutherland distinguished *Myers,* overruled the dictum, and failed to mention that Roosevelt had acted in good faith when he relied on *Myers.* Liberal Justices joined Sutherland for the reason given privately by Justice LOUIS D. BRANDEIS: if a Huey Long were President and the administration's argument prevailed, the commissions would become compliant agents of the executive.

Despite the Court's unanimity, its strict reliance

on a simplistic SEPARATION OF POWERS theory ignored the fact that the administrative agencies, however mixed their powers, were executive agencies and Congress acknowledged that fact. Moreover, had Roosevelt chosen to remove Humphrey for cause, the Court would not likely have challenged his judgment. The Court followed *Humphrey* in *Wiener v. United States* (1958), ruling that President DWIGHT D. EISENHOWER could not remove a member of a quasi-judicial agency without cause.

LEONARD W. LEVY

(SEE ALSO: *Appointing and Removal Power.*)

HUNT, WARD
(1810–1886)

Ward Hunt, a New York judge, was appointed to the Supreme Court by ULYSSES S. GRANT in late 1872; seven years later, although permanently incapacitated by a stroke, he refused to resign until Congress passed a special retirement act in 1882. His judicial contributions were largely unexceptional and insignificant. He consistently sided with the WAITE COURT majority in supporting bondholders' claims, upholding state regulation under traditional POLICE POWER doctrines, and denying claims for racial equality under the FOURTEENTH AMENDMENT.

Hunt also upheld claims of immunity from federal taxation for states or their instrumentalities. (See INTERGOVERNMENTAL IMMUNITY.) Earlier, in COLLECTOR V. DAY (1871), the Court had exempted state judges from the federal income tax. In one of his first opinions, Hunt treated municipally financed railroads as state agencies and as similarly exempt. "Their operation," he said in *United States v. Railroad Co.* (1873), "may be impeded and may be destroyed, if any interference is permitted." A few years later he dissented from the nationalistic holding in PENSACOLA TELEGRAPH CO. V. WESTERN UNION TELEGRAPH CO. (1877), in which the majority held that states could not interfere with telegraph lines established under federal law. Hunt, however, insisted that federal authority extended only to lands in the public domain.

Hunt usually followed his colleagues in ruling against claims advancing Negro rights. But in UNITED STATES V. REESE (1876) he alone dissented to support the constitutionality of the FORCE ACT (1870) which was designed to implement the FIFTEENTH AMENDMENT. Hunt interpreted the amendment as guaranteeing "the right to vote in its broadest terms" for all citizens, in all elections, state as well as federal. The majority had refused to sanction federal interference against acts of individual state officers who had refused on their own account to allow blacks to vote. For Hunt, it was obvious that such individual acts were tantamount to state action and subject to federal restraint. The word "state" in the Fifteenth Amendment, he maintained, included "the acts of all those who proceed under [a state's] . . . authority." The *Reese* decision reflected the growing national consensus for sectional reconciliation which inevitably meant abandonment of national protection for the freedmen's CIVIL RIGHTS. Hunt acknowledged this mood and he recognized that the majority's decision "brings to an impotent conclusion the vigorous amendments on the subject of slavery." Yet he silently acquiesced later that term in the further emasculation of the Force Act in UNITED STATES V. CRUIKSHANK (1876).

Hunt's fleeting concern for guaranteeing black suffrage did not extend to women. On circuit in 1873, he presided at the trial of Susan B. Anthony, who had voted in the 1872 presidential election in New York despite a state constitutional requirement limiting the franchise to men. Anthony claimed that the state denied her the PRIVILEGES AND IMMUNITIES guaranteed under the Fourteenth Amendment. Hunt flatly denied the argument. He invoked the reasoning of the recent SLAUGHTERHOUSE CASES (1873) and held that such regulations, however unjust, were under the absolute domain of the state. Hunt directed a guilty verdict, refused to poll the jury, and fined Anthony $100. The sentence was not enforced, and there was no APPEAL to the Supreme Court.

Hunt was a hard-working able craftsman during his brief career on the Court (1873–1882) but he had little apparent influence on his brethren or on constitutional law.

STANLEY I. KUTLER

Bibliography

FAIRMAN, CHARLES 1971 *Reconstruction and Reunion, 1864–1888.* Volume 6 of the *Oliver Wendell Holmes Devise History of the Supreme Court of the United States.* New York: Macmillan.

MAGRATH, C. PETER 1963 *Morrison R. Waite: The Triumph of Character.* New York: Macmillan.

HUNTER v. ERICKSON
393 U.S. 385 (1969)

In a perverse application of the EQUAL PROTECTION clause, an 8–1 Supreme Court struck down an amendment to the Akron, Ohio, city charter subjecting any council-passed OPEN HOUSING LAW to a REFERENDUM before it could take effect and requiring a referendum on an open housing law previously enacted.

Six Justices, speaking through BYRON R. WHITE, found in the referendum requirement an "explicitly racial classification," although they conceded that it drew "no distinctions among racial and religious groups." The majority argued that the charter amendment, by making open housing laws harder to enact, "disadvantaged those who would benefit" from such laws—and presumed that the potential beneficiaries were the members of ethnic and religious minorities. The FOURTEENTH AMENDMENT was held to protect minorities against barriers to enactment of favorable legislation.

Justice HUGO L. BLACK dissented, contending that referenda were part of the democratic political process and that advocates of particular types of legislation were not constitutionally disadvantaged merely because they might lose an election.

DENNIS J. MAHONEY

HURD v. HODGE

See: *Shelley v. Kraemer*

HURON PORTLAND CEMENT COMPANY v. DETROIT
362 U.S. 440 (1960)

In a case involving a major COMMERCE CLAUSE issue, a 7–2 Supreme Court sustained Detroit's Smoke Abatement Code. That city sued a Michigan manufacturer operating ships in INTERSTATE COMMERCE for violating its air pollution regulations. The manufacturer stressed its adherence to congressional regulations, claiming that Detroit could not impose stricter standards. Justice POTTER STEWART's opinion, devoted primarily to rejecting claims that federal laws had preempted the field, accorded a high priority to the STATE POLICE POWER. Exercise of that power must stand unless clearly discriminatory or violative of national uniformity, and nothing "suggest[s] the existence of any . . . competing or conflicting local regulations."

DAVID GORDON

HURTADO v. CALIFORNIA
110 U.S. 516 (1884)

DUE PROCESS OF LAW reached a watershed in *Hurtado.* For centuries due process had stood for a cluster of specific procedures associated especially with TRIAL BY JURY. Sir EDWARD COKE, for example, explicitly associated due process with INDICTMENT by GRAND JURY. The BILL OF RIGHTS enumerated many of the rights that the concept of due process spaciously accommodated. The FOURTEENTH AMENDMENT's due process clause was copied verbatim from the Fifth Amendment, where the same clause sat cheek-by-jowl with a number of specific guarantees that due process had embodied as a COMMON LAW concept. The framers of the Fifth Amendment had added the due process clause as an additional assurance, a rhetorical flourish, and a genuflection toward the traditions of MAGNA CARTA. In *Hurtado,* the Supreme Court began to whittle away at the conventional meanings of PROCEDURAL DUE PROCESS and did not pause until MOORE V. DEMPSEY (1923).

California tried and convicted Hurtado on an INFORMATION for murder, filed by his prosecutor. He claimed that because the state had denied him indictment by grand jury, it had violated the due process clause of the Fourteenth Amendment. The Court, sustaining the conviction, 7–1, rejected Hurtado's claim on the ground that "any legal proceeding" that protects "liberty and justice" is due process. Justice STANLEY MATTHEWS, for the Court, reasoned that the Constitution, having been framed for an undefined and expanding future, must recognize new procedures. To hold otherwise, he said, would render the Constitution "incapable of progress and improvement. It would be to stamp upon our jurisprudence the unchangeableness attributed to the Medes and the Persians. . . ." Matthews also argued that no part of the Constitution was superfluous; the fact that the Fifth Amendment included both a guarantee of grand jury proceedings in federal prosecutions and the guarantee of due process showed that the latter did not mean the former.

Justice JOHN MARSHALL HARLAN, dissenting, had history on his side when he found grand jury proceedings to be an indispensable requisite of due process, but whether history should have disposed of the question is a different issue. Harlan did not think that prosecuting individuals for their lives by information inaugurated a new era of progress in the constitutional law of CRIMINAL PROCEDURE. The Court's inexorable logic, he asserted, as if asserting the unthinkable, would lead to the conclusion that due process did not even guarantee the traditional trial by jury. Later cases justified his fears. (See MAXWELL v. DOW, 1900.)

LEONARD W. LEVY

HUTCHINSON, THOMAS (1711–1780)

Thomas Hutchinson, described by his biographer, Bernard Bailyn, as "the most distinguished, as well as the most loyal, colonial-born official of his time," was the leading exponent of "Tory" constitutional theory at the outbreak of the American Revolution. Hutchinson was not a political theorist, however, but a practical politician who turned to theory in order to justify his actions.

Hutchinson was the leader of the wealthy, interrelated clique that ruled Massachusetts in the eighteenth century. Although he was born in Boston, his loyalty was always to the ministry in England, and he defended his policies by appealing to the most extreme doctrines of royal and parliamentary supremacy. During his career he held every important office in the colony, and at one point (in 1763) he was simultaneously lieutenant governor, chief justice of the Supreme Court, president of the Council, and judge of probate.

In 1761 Hutchinson, as Chief Justice, presided over the PAXTON'S CASE, in which the Superior Court was asked to issue GENERAL WARRANTS to authorize searches by customs officials. He personally opposed the use of WRITS OF ASSISTANCE and as lieutenant governor had argued against their issuance on the governor's authority, but as a judge Hutchinson rejected the argument of JAMES OTIS that such writs were illegal under the COMMON LAW. It was sufficient that writs of assistance were valid in English law and that Parliament had, by statute, authorized their use in the colonies, and so the writs were issued.

Hutchinson became acting governor of Massachusetts in 1769 and governor in 1771. He was temperamentally unsuited for the position in so critical a time. When the policies he pursued became so unpopular that the Assembly would not appropriate money to pay his salary, Hutchinson secured for himself a special salary paid by the British crown. To insure that the courts would remain loyal to the British government he arranged that the judges' salaries, too, should be paid by the crown. These moves, which rendered the executive and judicial powers independent of the legislature and of the citizens, enraged public opinion.

Responding defiantly, Hutchinson summoned the General Court and, on January 6, 1773, delivered an address that spelled out his understanding of the principles of Anglo-American constitutionalism. The British Empire and Massachusetts's place in it, he argued, required the absolute and indivisible SOVEREIGNTY of the king-in-Parliament. The power of the British Parliament was unlimited and illimitable, but, since Parliament represented all British subjects, both in Britain and in the colonies, that power would necessarily be used benignly and humanely. As the American colonies were too weak to survive without British protection, the freedom of Americans depended upon their acceptance of absolute parliamentary authority. Hutchinson refused to concede the possibility that the General Court of Massachusetts exercised a separate legislative authority. "No line," he argued, "can be drawn between the supreme authority of Parliament and the total independence of the colonies."

If Hutchinson expected the address to quell criticism he was seriously mistaken. The effect was rather to enhance the standing of the most radical leaders of the opposition. The task of preparing the Assembly's response fell to SAMUEL ADAMS, the leader of the popular party and Hutchinson's chief rival. The Assembly adopted a resolution accepting, for argument's sake, Hutchinson's position that there could be no middle ground between absolute parliamentary authority and colonial autonomy. But the conclusion drawn was the opposite of Hutchinson's. The Assembly claimed that Massachusetts was a realm separate from Britain, sharing a common executive—the king—but with its own legislature. Only the General Court, and not Parliament, could legislate for Massachusetts.

Hutchinson was only reluctantly an enemy of his fellow colonists. He opposed many of the measures adopted by the British government, including the SUGAR ACT and the STAMP ACT. But Hutchinson's objections were prudential, not constitutional. He never doubted Parliament's right to legislate for the colonies, however disastrous the exercise of that right, or his own duty to obey and enforce such legislation.

After being forced in 1774 to flee to England, Hutchinson endured the six years until his death as a lonely pensioner of the crown. His career had a deep, if negative, influence on American constitutional thought: it was proof of the evils of plural officeholding and of an executive not dependent on the people's representatives for his pay. His outspoken insistence on the indivisibility of sovereignty helped to impel the formation of American theories of FEDERALISM.

DENNIS J. MAHONEY

Bibliography

BAILYN, BERNARD 1974 *The Ordeal of Thomas Hutchinson.* Cambridge, Mass.: Harvard University Press.

HUTCHINSON, THOMAS 1936 *History of the Colony of Massachusetts Bay.* Cambridge, Mass.: Harvard University Press.

HUTCHINSON v. PROXMIRE
443 U.S. 111 (1979)

This decision reaffirmed a line first drawn in GRAVEL V. UNITED STATES (1972) between official and unofficial communications by members of Congress. Senator William Proxmire gave one Dr. Hutchinson a "Golden Fleece" award for what Proxmire considered to be wasteful government-sponsored research conducted by Dr. Hutchinson. Proxmire publicized the award through a press release and a newsletter to constituents. Under the Supreme Court's interpretation of the SPEECH OR DEBATE CLAUSE, members of Congress are absolutely immune from suit only for legislative acts. In *Hutchinson,* the Court found that Proxmire's communications were not "essential to the deliberations of the Senate" and, therefore, were not legislative acts protected from libel actions by the speech or debate clause.

THEODORE EISENBERG

HYDE AMENDMENT

Beginning in 1976, Congress adopted a series of measures (amendments to appropriation bills, and JOINT RESOLUTIONS) prohibiting the use of any federal funds in the Medicaid program to pay for the costs of ABORTIONS. These provisions were known collectively as the "Hyde Amendment," after their original sponsor, Representative Henry J. Hyde of Illinois.

All versions of the amendment contained exceptions permitting federal funding of an abortion when the woman's pregnancy endangered her life. Some of them also permitted funding of abortions when pregnancies resulted from rape or incest. One version included still another exception when two physicians determined that "severe and long-lasting physical health damage to the mother would result" from a full-term pregnancy.

The Medicaid program was designed to provide federal financial assistance to states that reimbursed needy persons for medical treatment. Funds were provided for reimbursing the expenses of childbirth—at an average cost per recipient around nine times the cost of abortions. Some states continued to provide funds for needy women's abortions. In other states, the effect of the Hyde Amendment was to deny to poor women the financial assistance they needed to exercise the constitutional right recognized in ROE V. WADE (1973): to decide whether to terminate their pregnancies. Critics argued that the amendment was an unconstitutional WEALTH DISCRIMINATION, but the Supreme Court upheld its validity, 5–4, in HARRIS V. MCRAE (1980).

KENNETH L. KARST

(SEE ALSO: *Reproductive Autonomy.*)

Bibliography

PERRY, MICHAEL J. 1980 Why the Supreme Court Was Plainly Wrong in the Hyde Amendment Case: A Brief Comment on *Harris v. McRae. Stanford Law Review* 32:1113–1128.

HYLTON v. UNITED STATES
3 Dallas 171 (1796)

The first case in which the Supreme Court passed on the constitutionality of an act of Congress, *Hylton* stands for the principle that the only DIRECT TAXES are taxes on land and CAPITATION TAXES. The Constitution provides that no capitation "or other direct tax" be imposed except in proportion to the population of the states, but that "all duties, IMPOSTS and EXCISES" be levied uniformly, that is, at the same rate. Congress imposed a uniform tax of $16 on all carriages (horse-drawn coaches), despite protests that the tax should have been apportioned among the states according to the census. When Congress levied a direct tax it fixed the total amount of money it intended to raise, so that in a state with ten percent of the nation's population, the parties taxed (carriage-owners) would have paid ten percent of the total. Thus, if a tax on carriages were a direct tax, the amount raised in two states of equal population would be the same, but if one state had twice as many carriages as the other, the tax rate in that state would be twice as great. The contention in this case was that the carriage tax was unconstitutional because it was a direct tax uniformly levied.

The case seems to have been contrived to obtain a Court ruling on the constitutionality of Congress's tax program. To meet the requirement that federal JURISDICTION attached only if the amount in litigation came to $2,000, Hylton deposed that he owned 125 carriages for his private use, each of which was subject to a $16 tax; if he lost the case, however, his debt would be discharged by paying just $16. The United States paid his counsel, ALEXANDER HAMILTON, who defended the tax program he had sponsored as secretary of the treasury. Notwithstanding the farcical aspects of the case, its significance cannot be overestimated: if a tax on carriages were indirect and therefore could be uniform, Congress would have the utmost flexibility in determining its tax policies. As Justice SAMUEL CHASE said, "The great object of the Constitution was to give Congress a power to lay taxes adequate to the exigencies of government." Justice WILLIAM PATERSON, having been a member of the CONSTITUTIONAL CONVENTION OF 1787, explained why the rule of apportionment applied only to capitation and land taxes, making all other taxes indirect taxes. The judgment of the Court was unanimous.

LEONARD W. LEVY

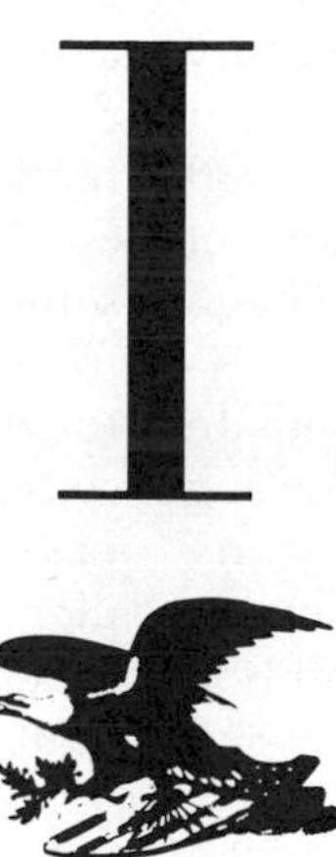

ILLEGITIMACY

The Anglo-American law of illegitimacy derives from two interrelated purposes of our institutional progenitors. First, imposing the legal disabilities of illegitimacy on a child was seen as a punishment of the parents for their sin. More importantly, the law of legitimacy supported a system of male control over economic resources. The chief effect of the principle of bastardy-as-punishment was to disable illegitimate children from making claims against their deceased fathers' estates. Similarly, formal marriage was the only basis for a woman's claim to inherit from the man who fathered her children. Thus the punishment was reserved for unmarried women and their children. Unmarried fathers, far from being punished, were strengthened in their power to control the transmission of wealth and status. As the Supreme Court began to recognize in two 1968 decisions, these themes are modern as well as medieval.

The cases were LEVY V. LOUISIANA and *Glona v. American Guarantee & Liability Insurance Co.* On EQUAL PROTECTION grounds, the Court invalidated provisions of Louisiana's wrongful death statute that allowed damages to a surviving child for the death of a parent, and vice versa, only in cases of legitimate parentage. From that time forward, most of the Court's decisions on illegitimacy have dealt with laws regulating inheritance by illegitimate children (especially from their fathers), and laws restricting the right to death damages or benefits in cases of illegitimacy. Both in their results and in their doctrinal explanations, these decisions have pursued a crooked path.

Much of the early doctrinal uncertainty surrounded the question of the appropriate STANDARD OF REVIEW. *Levy* and *Glona* purported to apply the RATIONAL BASIS standard, but in fact they represented a more demanding judicial scrutiny. There were good reasons for categorizing illegitimacy as a SUSPECT CLASSIFICATION that would demand STRICT SCRUTINY of the state's asserted justifications. As the Court has said more than once, it is "illogical and unjust" to burden innocent children because their parents have not married. The status of illegitimacy is out of the child's control. Illegitimates have suffered historic disadvantage. The status has been the centuries-old source of stigma; such legislative classifications are apt to be the result of habit, prejudice, and stereotype rather than serious attention to public needs. After a series of cases characterized by doctrinal instability, in *Mathews v. Lucas* (1976) the Court rejected the assimilation of illegitimacy to the suspect classifications category. The Court did remark, however, that its standard of review in such cases was "not a toothless one."

Part of the reason for the tortuous doctrinal path from *Levy* and *Glona* to *Mathews v. Lucas* was that the Justices were closely divided on the general issue of the Court's approach to illegitimacy as a legislative classification; in these circumstances, trifling factual distinctions tended to affect the decisions of cases. Even after *Mathews v. Lucas* this pattern continued, as TRIMBLE V. GORDON (1977) and LALLI V. LALLI (1978) illustrate—although the Court has identified a verbal formula for its standard of review: An illegitimacy classification must be "substantially related to a permissible state interest." As Justice LEWIS F. POWELL said for a plurality in *Lalli,* the Court's concern for the plight of illegitimates must be measured against a state's interest in "the just and orderly disposition of property at death." A seventeenth century probate lawyer would not be surprised to learn that the justice and order emerging from *Lalli* offered protection for a father's estate against the claims of illegitimate children, even though paternity had been established beyond question.

The Supreme Court has invoked its intermediate standard of review to invalidate state laws imposing severe time restrictions on suits to establish paternity and compel fathers to support children born outside marriage. But if *Lalli* validated an ancient tradition of domination through control over the transmission of wealth and status, *Parham v. Hughes* (1978), just four months later, validated the tradition of the illegitimacy relation as punishment for sin. An illegitimate child and his mother were killed in an automobile accident. State law would have allowed only the mother to sue for wrongful death damages, if she had survived. Given the mother's death, the father would have been entitled to bring the suit if he had formally legitimated the child. Although he had not undertaken formal legitimation proceedings, the father had signed the child's birth certificate, and had supported the child and visited him regularly; the child had taken the father's name. The Court upheld the state's denial of a right to sue, 6–3.

The state court in *Parham* had said the law was a means of "promoting a legitimate family unit" and "setting a standard of morality." The *Parham* dissenters, focusing on SEX DISCRIMINATION, faulted the state for doing its promoting and standard-setting selectively, along lines defined by gender. The decision also intruded seriously on the FREEDOM OF INTIMATE ASSOCIATION. The father–son relationship was complete in every sense but the formal one. Four members of the majority said it was all right, nevertheless, for the state to "express its 'condemnation of irresponsible liaisons beyond the bounds of marriage' " by denying the father the right to damages for the death of his son. In other words, the father should be ashamed of himself.

In *Glona,* the Court had rejected precisely this sort of reasoning. The fact that the legislature was "dealing with sin," the Court said, could not justify so arbitrary a discrimination as the denial of wrongful death damages. *Glona* had involved the claim of a mother, and mothers of illegitimate children have been the historic victims of a system of illegitimacy in a way that fathers have not. But *Parham* involved a man who not only sired a child but was a father to him. What had been protected in *Glona* was not merely the damages claim of a mother, but the status of the intimate relationship between a mother and her son. The *Parham* law's arbitrariness lay in its assumption that significant incidents of the parent-child relationship should be denied because of the absence of a formal marriage. Seen in this light, the law's discrimination demands some substantial justification for its invasion of the freedom of intimate association. *Glona* teaches that the required justification is not to be found in the state's wish to punish "sin." The Supreme Court plainly is not yet prepared to hold that the status of illegitimacy is itself constitutionally defective. When that day arrives, however, *Glona* will serve as a precedent.

KENNETH L. KARST

Bibliography

PERRY, MICHAEL J. 1979 Modern Equal Protection: A Conceptualization and Reappraisal. *Columbia Law Review* 79:1023–1084.

WALLACH, ALETA and TENOSO, PATRICIA 1974 A Vindication of the Rights of Unmarried Mothers and Their Children: An Analysis of the Institution of Illegitimacy, Equal Protection, and the Uniform Parentage Act. *University of Kansas Law Review* 23:23–90.

ILLINOIS v. GATES
462 U.S. 213 (1983)

This decision revived pre-WARREN COURT law of the FOURTH AMENDMENT concerning SEARCH WARRANTS issued on INFORMANTS' TIPS. Justice WILLIAM H. REHNQUIST for a six-member majority declared, "we . . . abandon the 'two pronged test' established by our decisions in *Aguilar* and *Spinelli.* In its place we reaffirm the totality of circumstances analysis that traditionally had informed PROBABLE CAUSE determination." In AGUILAR V. TEXAS (1962) the Court had developed a test to govern a magistrate's probable cause hearing to determine whether a warrant should issue. Although HEARSAY information (an informer's tip not reflecting the personal knowledge of the police) may underlie an officer's affadavit for a warrant, the officer must also explain his belief that the informant is trustworthy or that his information is reliable. SPINELLI V. UNITED STATES (1969) made the magistrate's hearing a mini-trial controlled by strict rules of EVIDENCE; the Court insisted on a degree of corroboration that proved the truthfulness of a tip apart from any evidence that might subsequently verify it.

In effect the Court had escalated the constitutional requirement of probable cause to reasonably certain cause in order to insure that a magistrate could evaluate all facts and allegations for himself. *Aguilar-Spinelli* meant that although the police secured a warrant based on a tip and their search uncovered evidence of crime, that evidence could be suppressed and a conviction set aside if a court later decided that the magistrate should not have issued the warrant. In *Illinois v. Gates* Rehnquist recalled that probable cause is founded on practical, nontechnical considerations and that magistrates should apply flexible standards based on all circumstances rather than on a rigid set of rules. Justice WILLIAM J. BRENNAN, dissenting, declared that the majority opinion reflected "an overly permissive attitude towards police practices" contrary to Fourth Amendment rights.

LEONARD W. LEVY

IMBLER v. PACHTMAN 424 U.S. 409 (1976)

Imbler established prosecutorial immunity from suit under SECTION 1983, TITLE 42, UNITED STATES CODE, for activities that are integral parts of the judicial process. *Imbler* left open the question whether prosecutors may be civilly liable for administrative or investigative activities. Justice LEWIS F. POWELL, writing for the Supreme Court, indicated in OBITER DICTUM that judges and prosecutors are subject to criminal prosecution for willful deprivations of constitutional rights.

THEODORE EISENBERG

IMMIGRATION

The ambivalence that characterizes today's national policies toward immigration had antecedents in the colonial era. Although the DECLARATION OF INDEPENDENCE complained that the king and Privy Council had tried "to prevent the population of these states," many of the colonies had resisted Roman Catholic immigration, and in 1776 some of them still resounded with expressions of nativist resentment against populations that were non-English. The nation is justly proud of its tradition as a refuge for the oppressed and persecuted. Yet American immigration policy, from colonial times to our own, has been dictated by the "native" majorities' perceptions of self-interest. The perceived need for settlers and workers hangs in precarious balance against the suspicions and hostilities that flow out of cultural differences. Congress decides how the balance shall be struck; in the field of immigration, constitutional law has placed few limits on governmental power.

For almost a century, Congress took little part in the regulation of immigration. Even the ALIEN AND SEDITION ACTS (1798), for all their spirit of partisan nativism, were not conceived as immigration restrictions. An early minimal state regulation of the immigration process survived challenge under the COMMERCE CLAUSE in MAYOR OF NEW YORK V. MILN (1837), but more severe state regulations were held invalid in the PASSENGER CASES (1849). Direct state limits on immigration were held unconstitutional in *Henderson v. New York* (1875), the same year in which Congress adopted the first direct national restriction, forbidding immigration by convicts and prostitutes.

By 1875, Congress's constitutional power to control immigration had come to be seen as one aspect of its power to regulate foreign commerce. Later, the Supreme Court articulated a more sweeping doctrine: the power of the national government to control FOREIGN AFFAIRS was inherent in the idea of nationhood and did not need explicit recognition in the Constitution. That doctrine eventually found its fullest expression in UNITED STATES V. CURTISS-WRIGHT EXPORT CORP. (1936), but it had surfaced half a century earlier in the context of immigration. In CHAE CHAN PING V. UNITED STATES (1889) the Court announced that if Congress "considers the presence of foreigners of a different race in this country, who will not assimilate with us, to be dangerous to its peace and security, . . . its determination is conclusive upon the judiciary." Having cast itself in an acquiescent role, the Court in *Nishimura Eiku v. United States* (1892) justified nearly absolute congressional power over immigration as "inherent in SOVEREIGNTY." An exceedingly inscrutable image of a national community now formally protected Congress's immigration decisions from effective constitutional challenge.

The law upheld in the *Chae Chan Ping* decision was the CHINESE EXCLUSION ACT of 1882. In the years since 1850, some 300,000 Chinese had come to the Pacific Coast, most of them responding to active recruitment of labor for mines and railroad construction in the American West. By the 1860s Chinese had come to compose about nine percent of California's population, and an anti-Chinese crusade was in full cry, fueled by racism and fear. After a long campaign, the Chinese Exclusion Act suspended immigration from China for ten years, made the Chinese ineligible for CITIZENSHIP—not even the strongest congressional supporters of unrestricted immigration could conceive of the Chinese as permanent members of the community—and imposed other restrictions on them.

Although the act was accompanied by unashamedly sinophobic rhetoric, it was ostensibly passed to protect citizen workers. So, too, was the federal legislation of 1882 that added new categories of prohibited immigrants—lunatics, idiots, and persons likely to become public charges—and went on to impose a head tax of fifty cents on each immigrant who entered the United States. Similar justifications were offered for the acts of 1885 and 1887, prohibiting payment for an immigrant's transportation to the United States in return for a promise of labor. This series of laws in the 1880s imposed the first severe restrictions on immigration in the nation's history.

The Supreme Court upheld the head tax, in the *Head Money Cases* (1884), on the basis of Congress's power to regulate foreign commerce—a theory broad enough to sustain the whole series of enactments. However, all the laws were ineffective by design. Congress left border inspections and collection of the head tax to state agencies, which largely ignored the laws. The contract labor laws exempted both skilled workers and domestics, along with foreigners residing temporarily in the country and "coincidentally" working here. The practical effect was to permit a continued disregard for the border and a deepening disrespect for the law, especially among Mexican laborers and the employers who recruited them.

From the 1880s on, a steady trickle of minor immigration restrictions issued from Congress. Paupers and polygamists were excluded, and then epileptics, professional beggars, and anarchists or persons believing in the violent overthrow of the government—the latter provisions a reaction to the assassination of President WILLIAM MCKINLEY. Not surprisingly, the next major immigration restrictions accompanied a new surge of nativism associated with a wave of immigration from eastern and southern Europe that began in the 1890s, encouraged by the demand for workers in a growing industrial economy. This nativist impulse was accelerated by World War I and reached a climax in the Red Scare of 1919–1920. Congress adopted a LITERACY TEST for immigrants in 1917, and in the early 1920s set in place a system of immigration quotas based on national origins. The quotas restricted the ethnic proportions of immigration to the ethnic proportions of the nation's population before 1890—that is, before the arrival of large numbers of eastern and southern Europeans. The quota system reflected some of the most respected "scientific" thought of the Progressive era; the racism that produced the Chinese Exclusion Act had broadened into Anglo-Saxonism, which extended its hostility and its assumptions of superiority beyond race to ethnicity.

The constitutionality of racial and ethnic restrictions on immigration was taken for granted in the 1920s. The *Chae Chan Ping* opinion had placed the whole matter outside the reach of substantive constitutional guarantees such as the EQUAL PROTECTION OF THE LAWS. To say the very least, however, this position is in tension with the Supreme Court's modern treatment of RACIAL DISCRIMINATION. Yet no recent decision has reexamined the premises of *Chae Chan Ping*, and the Court's opinions continue to refer, as in *Fiallo v. Bell* (1977), to "the limited scope of judicial inquiry in immigration litigation." Nonetheless, the modern constitutional climate in race cases seems to have contributed to the abandonment, in 1965, of the national origins quota system. In its place Congress has adopted a single worldwide annual ceiling on immigration, with a system of preferences designed to protect the interests of citizens and of aliens who are already documented residents.

The substantive problem of squaring the nation's constitutional commitment to equal protection with the tradition of judicial deference to Congress on immigration matters has a procedural counterpart. The *Nishimura Eiku* decision held that the DUE PROCESS clause of the Fifth Amendment imposed no limits on the power of Congress to govern procedures for entry into the United States. A few years later, in *Wong Wing v. United States* (1896), the Supreme Court did hold that due process forbade enforcement of the immigration laws by sentencing aliens to hard labor. In the modern era, *Landon v. Plascencia* (1982) has recognized due process rights of a resident alien who was seeking readmission after a short trip to Mexico. But such constitutional limitations are rare; the judicial protection of aliens in the exclusion process mainly has taken the form of interpretations of the immigration statutes.

A notable recent example is *Jean v. Nelson* (1985), in which the Court confronted the practice of long-term detention, without parole, of Haitian aliens who had been taken into custody as they attempted to enter the country without permission. The detention was challenged as unconstitutional discrimination based on race or national origin. Rather than decide that issue, the Court approved a REMAND of the case to determine whether immigration officials were observing the statutes and regulations, which, in the Court's interpretation, required individualized parole decisions without such discrimination. *Jean* appears to reflect an increasing judicial reluctance to keep the exclusion process unfettered by due process considerations. It also strongly suggests that if the Congress were to revive explicit racial exclusions, the PRECEDENT of *Chae Chan Ping* would not prevent judicial examination of their constitutionality.

The interpretation of the United States Constitution concerning immigration has always been influenced by widely shared attitudes concerning the constitution of American society. Today's issues of immigration policy focus on the use of "temporary" workers from other countries. Central to this theme is the story of Mexican labor migration. After 1882 Mexican and Japanese workers, along with immigrants from eastern and southern Europe, were recruited to help fill the void left by the exclusion of the Chinese. When Japanese immigration was effectively closed in 1907, employers in the Southwest intensified the recruitment of Mexicans. Assisted by statutory exemptions and waivers, many employers grew rich on the backs of immigrants who were poor and powerless. When poor whites competed for menial jobs, however—as after the crash of 1929—hundreds of thousands of Mexican workers were deported.

The pattern is repeated, from World War II through the 1942–1964 Bracero Program (admitting temporary workers) and beyond, in a cycle that has not yet ended: Mexican workers are recruited when they serve the needs of domestic employers, and expelled when their usefulness seems to decline. They fill jobs as needed, and at a low wage, but they are not to be allowed to burden local communities. The Bracero Program amounted to an official (but unacknowledged) program of undocumented Mexican migration. At a time when the Border Patrol might have made a real difference in curbing undocumented entry—and thus restricting American growers from employing undocumented workers—the agency's budget was cut. Since 1952, Congress has exempted employers from liability for employing undocumented workers.

The result of all these developments is that the cheapest labor in the United States has become almost exclusively the province of undocumented workers. An entrenched migratory culture now supplies workers from Mexico and other countries to fill low-paying and socially undesirable jobs. If recruitment has become unnecessary, effective enforcement of formal immigration law has become virtually impossible. Very large numbers of undocumented workers are here to stay—and, predictably, America's long-standing ambivalence toward immigration is translated into a paradox of constitutional law. On the one hand, government is to be given the widest powers to seek out and deport undocumented workers, including such far-reaching methods as BORDER SEARCHES and the factory sweeps approved in *Immigration and Naturalization Service v. Delgado* (1984). On the other hand, PLYLER V. DOE (1982), holding it unconstitutional for Texas to deny free public education to children of the undocumented, almost certainly rested on the premise that most of those children are going to remain part of the American community, whether or not Texas chooses to educate them. The *Plyler* decision is one of major potential importance for the definition of the boundaries of that community, and for the recognition and fulfillment of the national community's concrete responsibilities to all its members.

GERALD P. LÓPEZ
KENNETH L. KARST

Bibliography

GORDON, CHARLES AND ROSENFELD, HARRY N. 1985 *Immigration Law and Procedure,* Rev. ed. Vol. 1. New York: Matthew Bender.

LÓPEZ, GERALD P. 1981 Undocumented Mexican Migration: In Search of a Just Immigration Law and Policy. *UCLA Law Review* 28:615–714.

NOTE 1983 Developments in the Law—Immigration and the Rights of Aliens. *Harvard Law Review* 96:1286–1465.

IMMIGRATION AND NATURALIZATION SERVICE v. CHADHA
462 U.S. 919 (1983)

Immigration and Naturalization Service v. Chadha cast serious doubt on the use of the LEGISLATIVE VETO, a device by which Congress seeks to retain control over the use of DELEGATED POWERS. *Chadha* involved a provision in the IMMIGRATION AND NATIONALITY ACT that permitted either house of Congress, by resolution, to overturn orders of the attorney general suspending DEPORTATION of ALIENS.

The Supreme Court held, 7–2, that congressional review of such cases was legislative in character, and was therefore subject to the provisions of Article I requiring the concurrence of both houses and an opportunity for the President to exercise his VETO POWER before the resolution can have the force of law. The majority opinion, by Chief Justice WARREN E. BURGER, declared that the one-house legislative veto violated the constitutional principles of SEPARATION OF POWERS and BICAMERALISM.

Justice BYRON R. WHITE, dissenting, ascribed to

the decision much greater scope than did the majority. White asserted that the *Chadha* decision effectively invalidated every legislative veto provision in federal law. A majority in future cases, however, may choose not to apply the *Chadha* rationale to two-house legislative vetoes or to legislative vetoes of agency actions that are clearly legislative rather than executive or quasi-judicial. It would be curious indeed if administrative agencies promulgating regulations with the force of law were freed from congressional oversight by a Court intent on preserving the separation of powers and bicameralism.

DENNIS J. MAHONEY

IMMIGRATION AND NATURALIZATION SERVICE v. LOPEZ-MENDOZA

See: Deportation

IMMUNITY GRANT (SELF-INCRIMINATION)

"No person," the Fifth Amendment unequivocally states, "shall be . . . compelled in any criminal case to be a witness against himself. . . ." It does not add, "unless such person cannot be prosecuted or punished as a result of his testimony," and it does not refer to self-incrimination. Yet, if the government wants EVIDENCE concerning a crime, it can compel a witness to testify by granting immunity from prosecution. In law, such immunity means that the witness cannot incriminate himself and therefore has suffered no violation of his RIGHT AGAINST SELF-INCRIMINATION. The common sense of the matter is that to "incriminate" means to implicate criminally; in law, however, it means exposure to prosecution or penalties. The law indulges the fiction that when one receives a grant of immunity, removing him from criminal jeopardy, the right not to be a witness against oneself is not violated. If the witness cannot be prosecuted, the penalties do not exist for him, so that his testimony can be compelled without forcing him to incriminate himself or "be a witness against himself."

The first immunity statute in Anglo-American jurisprudence was probably the one enacted by Connecticut in 1698. That act specified that witnesses in criminal cases must give sworn evidence, on pain of punishment for refusal, "always provided that no person required to give testimonie as aforesaid shall be punished for what he doth confesse against himself when under oath." Similarly, an act that Parliament passed against gambling in 1710, which some colonies copied, guaranteed that gamblers who confessed their crimes and returned their winnings should be "acquitted, indemnified [immunized] and discharged from any further or other Punishment, Forfeiture, or Penalty which he or they may have incurred by the playing for or winning such Money. . . ." New York in 1758 obtained the king's pardon for certain ship captains in order to compel their testimony against the ships' owners. Although the pardons had eliminated the perils of the criminal law for the captains, they persisted in their claim that the law could not force them to declare anything that might incriminate them. A court fined them for contempt, on grounds that the recalcitrant captains no longer faced criminal jeopardy by giving evidence against themselves.

In modern language these colonial precedents illustrate grants of "transactional" immunity, an absolute guarantee that in return for evidence, the compelled person will not under any circumstances be prosecuted for the transaction or criminal episode concerning which he gives testimony. Absolute or transactional immunity was the price paid by the law for exacting information that would otherwise be actionable criminally. The paradox remained: one could be compelled to be a witness against oneself, but from the law's perspective the immunized witness would stand to the offense as if he had never committed it, or had received AMNESTY or a pardon despite having committed it.

Congress enacted its first immunity statute in 1857, granting freedom from prosecution for any acts or transactions to which a witness offered testimony in an investigation. Reacting against the immunity "baths" that enabled corrupt officials to escape from criminal liability by offering immunized testimony, Congress in 1862 supplanted the act of 1857 with one that offered only "use" immunity. Use immunity guarantees only that the compelled testimony will not be used in a criminal prosecution, but prosecution is possible if based on evidence independent from or unrelated to the compelled testimony. Under a grant of use immunity one might confess to a crime secure in the knowledge that his confession could not be used against him; however, if the prosecution had other evidence to prove his guilt, he might be prosecuted. By 1887 Congress extended the standard of use immunity from congressional investigations to all federal proceedings.

Until 1972 the Supreme Court demanded transactional rather than use immunity as the sole basis for displacing the Fifth Amendment right to remain silent. In COUNSELMAN V. HITCHCOCK (1892) the Court unanimously held unconstitutional a congressional act offering use immunity because use immunity was "not co-extensive with the constitutional provision." The compelled testimony might provide leads to evidence that the prosecution might not otherwise possess. To supplant the constitutional guarantee, an immunity statute must provide "complete protection" from all criminal perils; "in view of the constitutional provision, a statutory enactment, to be valid, must afford absolute immunity against future prosecution for the offense to which the question relates." Congress responded with a statute safeguarding against prosecution, forfeiture, or penalty for any transaction about which one might be compelled to testify. In BROWN V. WALKER (1896) the Court held that transactional immunity "operates as a pardon for the offense to which it relates," thus satisfying the constitutional guarantee. In effect the Court permitted what it had declared was impossible: congressional amendment of the Constitution. By a statute that served as a "substitute," Congress altered the guarantee that no one can be compelled to be a witness against himself criminally.

Until 1970 there were over fifty federal immunity statutes conforming with *Brown*'s transactional immunity standard, which the Court reendorsed in ULLMANN V. UNITED STATES (1956). When the Court scrapped its TWO SOVEREIGNTIES RULE in *Murphy v. Waterfront Commission* (1964), it held that absent an immunity grant, a state witness could not be compelled to testify unless his testimony "and its fruits" could not be used by the federal government. *Murphy* was a technical relaxation of the transactional immunity standard, as ALBERTSON V. SUBVERSIVE ACTIVITIES CONTROL BOARD (1965) proved, because a unanimous Court reconfirmed the transactional immunity standard.

Through the ORGANIZED CRIME CONTROL ACT of 1970, Congress made use immunity and derivative-use immunity the standard for all federal grants of immunity, and most states copied the new standard. No compelled testimony or its "fruits" (information directly or indirectly derived from such testimony) could be used against a witness criminally, except to prove perjury. In KASTIGAR V. UNITED STATES (1972) the Court relied on *Murphy*, ignored or distorted all other precedents, and upheld the narrow standard as coextensive with the Fifth Amendment, which it is not. One who relies on his right to remain silent forces the state to rely wholly on its own evidence to convict him. By remaining silent he gives the state no way to use his testimony, however indirectly. When he is compelled to be a witness against himself, his admissions assist the state's investigation against him. The burden of proving that the state's evidence derives from sources wholly independent of the compelled testimony lies upon the prosecution. But use immunity permits compulsion without removing criminality.

In *New Jersey v. Portash* (1979) the Court held that a defendant's immunized grand jury testimony could not be introduced to impeach his testimony at his trial. Whether the state may introduce immunized testimony to prove perjury has not been decided. In *Portash*, however, the Court conceded, "Testimony given in response to a grant of legislative immunity is the essence of coerced testimony." The essence of the Fifth Amendment's provision is that testimony against oneself cannot be coerced. Any grant of immunity that compels testimony compels one to be a witness against himself—except, of course, that it is "impossible," as the Court said in *Counselman*, for the constitutional guarantee to mean what it says.

LEONARD W. LEVY

Bibliography

LEVY, LEONARD W. 1974 *Against the Law: The Nixon Court and Criminal Justice.* Pages 165–187. New York: Harper & Row.

IMMUNITY OF GOVERNMENT OFFICIALS

See: Executive Immunity; Judicial Immunity; Legislative Immunity

IMPACT OF SUPREME COURT DECISIONS

The Supreme Court's decisions have regularly embroiled it in controversy. Its rulings have considerable impact. In its early years, the Court, over strenuous objection from the states, shaped our federal system and helped establish the national government's supremacy. The Court also had substantial effects on the economy, aiding in the creation of an American economic common market and providing opportunities for the private sector to develop. The Court's major effects on FEDERALISM and the economy subsided after the 1930s. However, its effect on CIVIL RIGHTS, visible earlier with respect to slavery and its emasculation of Reconstruction civil rights statutes, again became apparent as questions such as school DESEGREGATION came to the fore in the 1950s.

The Supreme Court's impact includes ways in which federal and state agencies and lower federal and state courts carry out the Court's decisions, but it also includes the ways in which the agencies and courts delay, circumvent, misunderstand, and erode them. It includes the response to decisions by different "populations"—those who explain or elaborate its rulings, those supposed to apply or implement them, those for whom the rulings are intended, and the general population. Because the Court, "the least dangerous branch," lacks the capacity to enforce its rulings directly, assistance from those at whom a ruling is directed or from others (legislatures, executive agencies, courts) is required. The Court is now recognized to be a political actor, but one must abandon the tacit assumption held by earlier scholars that Supreme Court decisions are self-executing and recognize that the law is what the judges say it is only after all others have had their say.

Impact and compliance are not identical but are related. Compliance, the process by which individuals accept a decision prior to its impact or effect, cannot occur unless a person knows of the ruling and is required to take or abstain from a certain action. Compliance means an individual's intentionally conforming behavior to the ruling's dictates, that is, doing what the decision commands because of the ruling. Because noncompliance, or refusal to obey, occurs relatively seldom despite the attention it receives, it is important to pay heed to implementation of decisions, the process by which they are put into effect. Short-run resistance may blend into longer-run obedience, as resulted in the aftermath of the REAPPORTIONMENT decisions.

Impact includes all effects, direct and indirect, resulting from a ruling of the Court, regardless of whether those affected knew about the decision; it includes the results of rulings permitting but not requiring the adoption of certain policies. When effects of a ruling indirectly induce behavior congruent with the ruling, that behavior is better viewed as impact than as compliance. Impact encompasses actions neither directly defiant nor clearly obedient, such as attempts at evasion coupled with technical obedience and efforts to anticipate the Court's decisions ("anticipatory compliance"). Impact also includes both short-term and long-run consequences of a decision, for example, massive resistance to school desegregation rulings and the rulings' arguable contribution to "white flight" to the suburbs. There will also be situations in which no response occurs, that is, where there is an absence of obvious impact.

The Supreme Court's effect on the President has generally been one of support and reinforcement. The Court has been least willing to overturn his acts in time of war, when presidential resistance to Court decisions would be most likely. Although limiting somewhat the President's authority to remove certain government employees, the Court, since the New Deal, has sustained DELEGATIONS OF POWER to the President and the executive branch and has generally been deferential to the REGULATORY COMMISSIONS since World War II. Confrontations between Court and President have been relatively infrequent; when the Court invalidates policies the President had espoused, for example, WIRETAPPING, it is not attacking the presidency as an institution. Presidents may have been reluctant to assist in enforcing the Court's decisions, but direct defiance is rare indeed. Both President HARRY S. TRUMAN and President RICHARD M. NIXON complied with orders when their actions (seizure of the steel mills and withholding of tapes) were ruled improper. In those situations, as with IMPOUNDMENT of appropriated funds, the Court insisted that the President follow the law as interpreted by the courts rather than determine for himself whether he should be subject to it; in the case of the STEEL SEIZURE, the Court insisted that he follow a course of action legislated by Congress.

The Court has had considerable impact on Congress's internal processes—its authority to exclude members, LEGISLATIVE INVESTIGATIONS, and the CONTEMPT POWER. Congressional reaction to the Court's decisions has been manifested in a number of ways. After the Court has engaged in statutory interpretation or, less frequently, has invalidated statutes for VAGUENESS, Congress has often rewritten or reenacted the laws to reestablish its "legislative intent," in effect establishing a continuing dialogue between Court and Congress. Congress has also shown negative reaction to the Court's ruling through proposals to eliminate APPELLATE JURISDICTION in particular classes of cases, for example, internal security, abortions, and school prayer, but these attempts have been less frequent and far less successful than those to rewrite statutes. Efforts to overturn the Court's rulings have also resulted in introduction of numerous proposals to amend the Constitution, but most such proposals die. Only a few—the ELEVENTH AMENDMENT, Civil War Amendments, SIXTEENTH AMENDMENT, and TWENTY-SIXTH AMENDMENT—have been both submitted and ratified.

The impact of the Supreme Court's decisions extends well beyond the other branches of the national government. Controversial Supreme Court rulings have affected public opinion and have produced divided editorial reaction on a wide range of decisions. Changes in the public's feelings of trust or confidence in the Court have paralleled changes in feeling about the presidency and Congress but generally have been somewhat more positive. Such ratings have changed rapidly, but shifts in the Court's doctrine on controversial topics (such as CRIMINAL PROCEDURE) in the direction of public opinion usually are not immediately reflected in changed public opinion ratings.

The public generally supports the Court's work. Those giving the Court general (or "diffuse") support, however, outnumber those giving the Court specific support (for particular rulings) by a large ratio. The proportion of the public that feels the Court may legitimately produce structural political change is quite small. Acquiescence in the Court's rulings, which helps produce compliance, has been more common than active approval of the decisions.

The public also has little information about the Court. Even many controversial decisions fail to penetrate the general public's consciousness. The greater the knowledge, however, the greater the *dis*approval, but those reporting negative views on specific cases outnumber those whose general view of the Court is negative. Those with negative views also tend to hold them more intensely, but seldom would most members of the public do more than write letters of protest; demonstrations and other overt protest are atypical. Negative views about the Court are usually accounted for by reactions to the few specific decisions that catch the attention of large proportions of the public. Those salient decisions change with considerable rapidity, shifting in the 1960s from civil rights and school prayer to criminal procedure.

The Supreme Court's impact on the states and local communities is varied. Effectuating many decisions involves little controversy, and implementation may be prompt and complete, particularly if actions of only a few public officials are necessary. Other rulings, such as those on school DESEGREGATION, school prayer, and criminal procedure, produce a disproportionate amount both of resistance or attempts to evade and of critical rhetoric—rhetoric at times not matched by reality. Despite claims that the warnings required by MIRANDA V. ARIZONA (1966) would have a negative impact on police work, suspects and defendants often talk to police after being "read their rights." However, even these criticized rulings have definite impacts, for example, more professional police work as a result of criminal procedure rulings. Although opponents of the rule that improperly seized evidence should be excluded (the EXCLUSIONARY RULE of MAPP V. OHIO, 1961) have claimed that the rule does not deter illegal seizures and is too costly because guilty defendants are set free, some studies have suggested that the rule might be having some of its intended effect. At least in some cities, few cases were dropped after motions to suppress evidence and a higher proportion of searches conducted after the rule was promulgated were constitutional.

If people are to comply with Supreme Court rulings or if the rulings are to have an impact, they must be communicated to those expected to implement or adhere to them. One cannot, however, assume that effective communication takes place. A ruling may have to be transmitted through several levels, at each of which distortion can be introduced, before reaching its ultimate audience. Lawyers may be accustomed to easy access to the Court's published opinions, but many others, such as police or school officials, often do not receive the opinions or have such direct access to them and must therefore rely on other means of communication through which to learn of them.

The mass media, with the exception of a few newspapers, provide only sketchy information about the Court's decisions. Specialized media, for example, trade publications, provide only erratic coverage even of decisions relevant to the groups for which they are published. Most newspapers and radio and television stations must rely on the wire services for information about Supreme Court rulings. Disproportionate nationwide emphasis is given to decisions the wire services emphasize, with little or no coverage given to other rulings. The media also have different patterns of coverage ("profiles"). Newspapers, for example, give more attention to postdecision events, while the wire services and television pay more attention to cases before they are decided. All the media, however, generally convey much information about immediate reaction to, or impact of, decisions instead of emphasizing the content of, or rationale for, the Court's rulings.

The lower courts do not constitute a bureaucratic structure through which decisions are fully communicated downward. Lawyers thus become particularly important in transmitting the Court's rulings, as they are in transmitting any law. Lower court judges who do not routinely follow the Court's decisions may find out about them only if lawyers arguing cases cite the decisions, which they do not always do accurately.

Lawyers, either individually or through their bar associations, do little to inform the general public about developments in the law. Some state attorneys general and local prosecutors undertake to inform state and local officials of recent rulings affecting their work. The failure of these officials to do so in most locations has led some local agencies, which can afford to do so, to hire their own lawyers, for example, police department "police legal advisers," to monitor the Court's rulings, provide appropriate information to the agency, and arrange for implementation.

Training programs—effective because they combine printed materials with oral presentation—can be particularly important in the transmission of rulings. They are especially necessary because the educational system has generally done little to educate students, later to be members of the general public, about the Court's functioning or its rulings. Training programs are, however, not available to all those expected to be cognizant or familiar with the Court's rulings. Many members of some important occupational groups such as the police do not receive adequate legal training about the Court's decisions. Even if initially well-trained, they are less likely to receive adequate follow-up through in-service training.

The impact of the Court's decisions is, of course, affected by far more than deficiencies and distortions in the lengthy, often convoluted process by which the decisions are communicated. Numerous other factors affect both the communication process, thus indirectly affecting impact, and impact itself. One is the legitimacy attributed to the Court and its work. If a particular audience, for example, the police during the WARREN COURT's "criminal procedure revolution," feels that the Court is not acting fairly or lacks appropriate information on which to base its decisions, that audience will heed the Court's word less carefully even when the opinions are fully communicated. Characteristics of the Court's rulings, such as their relative unanimity and relative clarity or ambiguity, are also important, as both unanimity and clarity are thought to produce greater compliance. In new and sensitive areas of policy such as civil rights and criminal procedure, the lower courts can exercise power over the Supreme Court by their resistance. Rulings by lower court judges applying and extending (or narrowing) the Court's decisions are particularly important in such situations and in those where gaps in doctrinal development—a result of case-by-case development of the law—leave unanswered questions. In many, perhaps most, areas of the law, however, lower court judges enforce Supreme Court rulings because those rulings are a matter of relative personal indifference for the judges, because they have been socialized to follow those rulings, and because they wish to avoid being reversed.

Whether someone follows up a decision, who that "someone" is, and how they act, also affect a decision's impact. Elites' support for a decision may be able to calm negative public reaction. The likelihood that desegregation would be accepted in either the short or long run was decreased because southern elites were not favorably disposed toward either the result of BROWN V. BOARD OF EDUCATION (1954) or the Court's opinion. Because most rulings of the Court are not self-enforcing, follow-up by government agencies is often crucial for effective implementation. Officials not committed to the values in the Court's rulings are less likely to be assiduous in their follow-up; thus the attitudes of individual decision makers, particularly those in key policymaking or enforcement positions, are of considerable importance.

The situation into which a Supreme Court ruling is "injected"—whether in a crisis or in normal times—also affects the ruling's impact. A local community's belief system and its past history both are part of that situation. So are community pressures on the individuals expected to carry out the Court's dictates. Often a wide variety of enforcement mechanisms must be used before compliance is achieved. Incentive systems in organizations can lead individuals either to follow the Court's rulings or to continue existing practices. Because organizations have considerable interest in maintaining such practices, externally imposed penalties may be insufficient to produce required change.

To overcome problems of communicating Supreme Court rulings so that they reach the appropriate audience might seem insuperable. The Court's rulings are, however, often complied with and do have widespread impact. Were it otherwise, we should not hear so much about the problems occurring in particularly sensitive areas of the law such as civil rights and CIVIL LIBERTIES. The difficulties in implementing the Court's decisions to achieve their greatest impact should remind us that, as an active policymaker, the Supreme Court faces many of the same problems faced by other policymaking institutions.

STEPHEN L. WASBY

Bibliography

BECKER, THEODORE L. and FEELEY, MALCOLM, EDS. 1973 *The Impact of Supreme Court Decisions: Empirical Studies*, 2nd ed. New York: Oxford University Press.

JOHNSON, CHARLES A. and CANON, BRADLEY C. 1984 *Judicial Policies: Implementation and Impact.* Washington D.C.: Congressional Quarterly Press.

KRISLOV, SAMUEL, ED. 1972 *Compliance and the Law: A Multidisciplinary Approach.* Beverly Hills, Calif.: Sage Publications.

WASBY, STEPHEN L. 1970 *The Impact of the United States Supreme Court: Some Perspectives.* Homewood, Ill.: Dorsey Press.

IMPEACHMENT

The English Parliament devised impeachment for the removal of ministers of the Crown, the House of Commons serving as prosecutor of charges that the House of Lords adjudged. This, ALEXANDER HAMILTON wrote, was the "model" of the American proceeding—the House of Representatives files and prosecutes charges and the Senate is the trial tribunal. The Framers of the Constitution also adopted the English grounds for removal, "TREASON, bribery, or other high crimes and MISDEMEANORS." They defined "treason" narrowly; "bribery" was a COMMON LAW term of familiar meaning; but the scope of "other high crimes and misdemeanors" remains a subject of continuing debate. Some would confine those terms to indictable crimes. At the other pole, Congressman GERALD FORD, in proposing the impeachment of Justice WILLIAM O. DOUGLAS in 1970, asserted that an impeachable offense is whatever the House, with the concurrence of the Senate, "considers [it] to be." The historical facts indicate, however, that an impeachable offense need not be indictable, but that such offenses have their limits, for which we must look to the English practice the terms expressed.

Advocates of the indictable crime interpretation point to the criminal terminology, for example, "high crimes and misdemeanors." Article III, section 2, of the Constitution provides, "The trial of all Crimes, except in cases of Impeachment, shall be by Jury"; Article II, section 2, confers a power to grant pardons "except in Cases of Impeachment," and pardons relieve from punishment for a crime. In England the House of Lords combined removal and punishment in the impeachment proceeding. But Article I, section 3, clause 7, made an important departure: "Judgment in cases of impeachment shall not extend further than to removal from office, and disqualification to hold and enjoy any [federal] office . . . but the party convicted shall nevertheless be liable and subject to INDICTMENT, trial, judgment and punishment, according to law." The separation of removal from criminal prosecution meant that political passions could no longer sweep an accused to his death, but that he would be tried by a jury of his peers.

In the North Carolina Ratification Convention, JAMES IREDELL explained that if the President "commits any misdemeanor in office, he is impeachable, removable from office. . . . If he commits any crime, he is punishable by the laws of his country," distinguishing an impeachable "misdemeanor" (which has a common law connotation of misconduct in office) from an indictable crime. Hamilton likewise distinguished between "removal from office" and "actual punishment in cases which admit of it," indicating that some impeachable offenses were not criminal. As will appear, some impeachable offenses were not and still are not punishable crimes; nor does the absence of fine and imprisonment, the customary criminal sanctions, comport with the view that impeachment is a criminal proceeding. The doctrine of DOUBLE JEOPARDY also conduces to this conclusion. Although double jeopardy at the framing of the Constitution referred to jeopardy of life, as the Fifth Amendment attests, Congress speedily made treason punishable by death. Impeachment for treason could not, therefore, be regarded as criminal without raising a bar to indictment. Such thinking was carried over to all impeachments by JAMES WILSON: because they "are founded on different principles . . . directed to different objects . . . the trial and punishment of an offense on impeachment, is no bar to a trial of the same offense at common law." Justice JOSEPH STORY deduced from the separation between removal and indictment that "a second trial for the same offense" would not be barred by double jeopardy. Thus double jeopardy requires impeachment to be read in noncriminal terms.

The Sixth Amendment furnishes further confirmation. Earlier Article III, section 2, clause 3, expressly exempted impeachment from the "Trial of all Crimes" by jury. With that exemption before them, the draftsmen of the Sixth Amendment required TRIAL BY JURY in "all criminal prosecutions," thereby canceling the former exception. Since the later Amendment controls, it must be concluded either that the Founders felt no need to exempt impeachment from the Sixth Amendment because they did not consider it a "criminal prosecution" or that jury trial is required if impeachment be in fact a "criminal" prosecution. The latter conclusion is inadmissible. Perhaps the use of criminal terminology is attributable to the fact that words like "offenses," "convict," and "high crimes" had been employed in the English impeachments, and the Framers, engaged in hammering out a charter of government that required major political compromises, could not pause to coin a fresh and different vocabulary for every detail.

Treason and bribery, in contradistinction to crimes against the individual such as murder and robbery, are crimes against the State—political crimes. James Wilson, a chief architect of the Constitution, observed that "impeachments are confined to political characters, to political crimes and misdemeanors." And Justice Story added that they are designed "to secure the state against gross official misdemeanors." By association with "treason, bribery," the phrase "other high crimes and misdemeanors" likewise may be deemed to refer to "political" offenses. "High crimes and misdemeanors" meant "and *high* misdemeanors," not as a matter of grammatical construction but of historical usage. "High misdemeanors" are first met in a 1386 impeachment, long before there was such a crime as a "misdemeanor." At that time FELONIES were coupled with TRESPASSES, private as distinguished from political offenses. It was not until well into the sixteenth century that "misdemeanors" replaced "trespasses" in the general criminal law; and in England "high misdemeanors" remained a term peculiar to impeachment and did not find its way into ordinary criminal law, as is true of American law but for a very few statutory "high misdemeanors." Explaining "high misdemeanors," Sir WILLIAM BLACKSTONE stated that the "first and principal is the *maladministration* of such high officers as are in the public trust and employment. This is usually punished by the method of parliamentary impeachment," which proceeded not under the common law but under the *lex parliamentaria,* the "laws and course of parliament."

Though this arguably left Parliament free to fashion political offenses ad hoc, the Framers took a more restricted view. English impeachments proceeded largely for neglect of duty, abuse of power, betrayal of trust, corruption; and early state constitutions likewise provided for removal for misconduct in office, maladministration, corruption. In the Convention there were proposals for removal upon malpractice, neglect of duty, betrayal of trust, corruption, malversation (misconduct in office). Throughout, the focus was on machinery for removal rather than punishment for misconduct. When the impeachment provision came to the floor of the Convention, it employed "treason or bribery." GEORGE MASON protested that the narrow definition of treason would not reach "many great and dangerous offenses," among them "attempts to subvert the Constitution," which lay at the root of the leading English precedent. He therefore suggested the addition of "maladministration," but Madison objected that "so vague a term will be equivalent to a tenure during the pleasure of the Senate," whereupon Mason substituted "other high crimes and misdemeanors." Some two weeks earlier RUFUS KING had identified treason "agst. particular States" as "high misdemeanors"; a week before, "high misdemeanor" had been replaced in the extradition provision because it had "a technical meaning too limited." These facts show, first, that "other high crimes and misdemeanors" referred to "high misdemeanors," and second, that the terms were chosen precisely because they were "limited and technical" and would not leave the accused at the "pleasure of the Senate." As with other common law terms employed by the Framers, they expected them to have the meaning ascribed to them under English practice.

Justice Story stated that for the meaning of "high crimes and misdemeanors" resort must be had "to parliamentary practice" or "the whole subject must be left to the arbitrary discretion of the Senate," a "despotism" "incompatible" with "the genius of our institutions," and, it may be added, with the legislative history of the provision. Were impeachment restricted to common law crimes it would founder because there are no FEDERAL COMMON LAW crimes; all federal crimes are creatures of statute. Early on Congress enacted statutes that made treason and bribery crimes; a few statutes made certain minor acts criminal "high misdemeanors." But no statute declared "abuse of power," "neglect of duty," or "subversion of the Constitution" to be criminal, yet the Founders unquestionably regarded these as impeachable offenses. Except for treason and bribery, the "silence of the statute book," said Story, would render the power of impeachment "a complete nullity" and enable the most serious offender to escape removal. It is preferable to regard such silence as a continuing construction by Congress that its impeachment powers are not dependent on a statutory proscription and definition of impeachable offenses, particularly because most of its impeachment proceedings have involved nonindictable offenses. In extrajudicial statements, Chief Justice WILLIAM HOWARD TAFT and Justice CHARLES EVANS HUGHES recognized that such offenses were embraced by "high crimes and misdemeanors."

Another much debated issue is whether impeachment constitutes the sole means for removal of judges. Long before there was mention of impeachment of Justices in the Convention, it conditioned judicial tenure on "GOOD BEHAVIOR." This wording was not, as has been urged, "used simply to describe a life term," but a technical phrase of established meaning: "as long as he shall behave himself well." Hamilton noted that "good behavior tenure" was a "defeasible tenure," copied from the British model. At common law an appointment conditioned on "good behavior" was forfeited on nonperformance of the condition, that is, it terminated on misbehavior. Given a lapse from "good behavior," WILLIAM MURRAY (Lord Mansfield) observed, there must be power to remove the officer lest the formula be impotent. The remedy, Blackstone wrote, was by writ of *scire facias* determinable by the judiciary. Attempts by the Crown to remove a couple of high court judges who enjoyed "good behavior" tenure, Sir John Walter, Chief Baron of the Exchequer, and Sir John Archer, a Justice of Common Pleas, met insistence on removal by *scire facias.* This view was endorsed by Chief Justice Holt, Lord Chancellor Erskine, the future Lord Justice Denman, William Holdsworth, and CHARLES MCILWAIN. When the Framers employed a common law term, they expected it would be given its accepted meaning, as is shown by their redefinition of treason to avoid historic excesses, by JOHN DICKINSON's caution that if EX POST FACTO were to be expanded beyond the Blackstonian association with criminal cases it "would require some further provision," and by assurances in the Virginia Ratification Convention that reference to "trial by jury" included all its attributes, including the right to challenge jurors.

The Framers conceived impeachment as a remedy for misconduct by the President, and throughout the Convention such was its almost exclusive focus. Hamilton explained that "the true light in which it ought to be regarded" is as "a bridle in the hands of the legislative body upon the executive servants of the government." Consequently the Framers placed the provision for impeachment of the President in Article II, the Executive article. Almost at the last minute they amplified it by the addition of the "Vice President, and all civil officers," suggesting it was to apply to officers of the Executive department. The interpretive canon that each provision of an instrument should, if possible, be given effect counsels recognition of judicial removal for breaches of "good behavior," particularly because the standards of "high crimes and misdemeanors" differ from those of "good behavior," so that to insist that impeachment is the sole means for removal of judges is to leave some judicial "misbehavior" beyond remedy.

A number of utterances may seem to require the exclusivity of impeachment; for example, Hamilton stated in THE FEDERALIST #79 that impeachment "is the only provision" for removal of judges found in the Constitution and "consistent with the necessary independence of judges." Yet he had said in *The Federalist* #78 that "the standard of good behavior" is an "excellent barrier . . . to the encroachments and oppression of the representative body"; independence from Congress, not from judges, was the aim. Hamilton recognized that the "standard of good behavior" created a "defeasible tenure," a tenure terminated by breach of "good behavior." So too, the debate in the First Congress respecting the President's power to remove his subordinates contains tangential references to the protection from removal (chiefly by the President) that "good behavior" tenure afforded judges. Removal of his subordinates by the President made a breach in the "exclusivity" of impeachment, notwithstanding the fact that they squarely fit within "all civil officers" of Article II. It is easier to recognize an "exception" from exclusivity for the forfeiture that was an established concomitant of "good behavior," thus giving effect to that separate provision, than to make an exception for Executive subordinates.

What the First Congress did do with respect to judges further undermines reliance upon such dicta. By the Act of 1790 it provided that upon conviction in court for bribery a judge shall "forever be disqualified to hold an office." Since the impeachment clause provides both for removal and disqualification upon impeachment and conviction, the Act represents a construction that the clause does not exclude other means of disqualification. As with "disqualification," so with "removal," for the two stand on a par in the impeachment clause. The action of the First Congress, whose constitutional constructions carry great weight, when it dealt with judges thus speaks against reliance upon passing remarks in a debate that did not involve their removal. The several remarks, moreover, do not meet the test laid down by Chief Justice JOHN MARSHALL, showing that had "this particular case been suggested"—that is, judicial removal of judges for "misbehavior"—"the language would have been so varied as to exclude it." Well aware of the perils posed to judges by "the gusts of faction which might prevail" in Congress, the Founders were little likely to jettison the time-honored nonpolitical removal trial of judges by the courts in favor of a factional proceeding in Congress. Impeachment could be reserved for the grave situation in which the judiciary neglects to cleanse its own house, exactly as impeachment remains available for removal of a wrong-doing subordinate or "favorite" whom the President fails to remove.

JAMES BRYCE observed that impeachment is so heavy a "piece of artillery" as to "be unfit for ordinary use." The Founders repeatedly stressed that impeachment was meant only for "great injuries"; like Solicitor General, later Lord Chancellor Somers, they were aware that "impeachment ought to be like Goliath's sword, kept in the temple, and used but on great occasions." Hamilton too referred in *The Federalist* #70 to the "awful discretion" of the impeachment tribunal to doom "to infamy the . . . most distinguished characters of the community." Such views do not square with the insistence that the wheels of the nation must grind to a halt so that Congress can oust a venal district judge. Congress is in fact reluctant to undertake the ouster of such judges even, said Senator William McAdoo, "in cases of flagrant misconduct," because an impeachment proceeding draws the Congress away for weeks from weightier tasks. That situation, he stated, constitutes "a standing invitation for judges to abuse their authority with impunity and without fear of removal." To insist that impeachment is the sole means of removal of judges is in practical effect to immunize grave misconduct. In the almost two hundred years since adoption of the Constitution hundreds of complaints have resulted in fifty-five investigations, followed in some cases by censure or resignation. But only nine judges have been impeached and only four convicted and removed.

Some regard the acquittal of Justice SAMUEL P. CHASE in 1805 as a triumph of justice over heated political partisanship. Others view his impeachment as a natural reaction to the gross partisanship of the Federalist judiciary, given to intemperate attacks upon the Republican opposition in harangues to the GRAND JURY, which might be regarded as an "abuse of power" for political ends. Of Chase's trial of James Callender for alleged violations of the ALIEN AND SEDITIONS ACTS, EDWARD S. CORWIN said that Chase came to the case "with the evident disposition to play the hanging judge," and there is evidence that he prejudged the case. Callendar was entitled under the canons of his time to a trial free of "the tyrannical partiality of judges," and Chase was under statutory oath to administer justice impartially. Most students of the era consider that conviction failed of a two-thirds vote because the inept, acid-tongued manager of the impeachment, JOHN RANDOLPH, had alienated many Republicans as well as Federalists.

The *cause célèbre* is the impeachment of President ANDREW JOHNSON in 1868, essentially, as Justice SAMUEL F. MILLER foresaw, "for standing in the way of certain political purposes of the majority in Congress," but ostensibly for discharging his secretary of war, EDWIN M. STANTON, whom Congress had attempted to rivet in place by the TENURE OF OFFICE ACT. Critics of Johnson have noted Stanton's "defective loyalty," his conferences with Republican leaders behind Johnson's back respecting measures that divided Congress from the President. Finally Johnson removed him, presenting the issue whether a President who considered a statute to be an unconstitutional invasion of his prerogative to remove a disloyal subordinate—Stanton himself had advised Johnson that the statute was unconstitutional—and who felt that it was his constitutional duty to exercise his independent judgment, was impeachable. Such differences were contemplated as part of the CHECKS AND BALANCES of the Constitution.

The tone of the proceedings was sounded in BENJAMIN BUTLER's opening statement: "You are bound by no law," "you are a law unto yourselves." THADDEUS STEVENS asserted that Johnson was "standing at bay, surrounded by a cordon of living men, each with the ax of an executioner uplifted for his just punishment." Stevens dared the Senators who had voted for the Tenure of Office Act four times now to vote for acquittal "on the ground of its UNCONSTITUTIONALITY," condemning backsliders to the "gibbet of everlasting obloquy." Senator CHARLES SUMNER dismissed "the quibbles of lawyers" in a trial that "is a battle with slavery." One of the impeachment articles charged that on his "Swing Around the Circle" before the 1866 elections, Johnson attempted to bring Congress into ridicule, disgrace, and contempt. But as Senator John Sherman pointed out, members of Congress themselves had resorted to grossly abusive epithets, so that Johnson was not to be blamed for responding in kind. FREEDOM OF SPEECH, Senator James Patterson cautioned, was not solely for Congress. Current revulsion against Johnson does not overcome the verdict of Samuel Eliot Morison and Eric McKitrick that the impeachment was a "disgraceful episode," "a great act of ill-directed passion." Johnson's conviction failed by one vote. Whatever his faults, Johnson was entitled to a FAIR TRIAL, and that, the record amply discloses, was denied to him. Had Johnson been convicted, a revisionist historian wrote, it would have established a precedent "for the removal of any President refusing persistently to cooperate with Congress."

The failure of that impeachment led another revisionist historian to prophesy in 1973 that impeachment would never again be employed to remove a President. Shortly thereafter the House Judiciary Committee instituted an investigation whether President RICHARD M. NIXON participated in the WATERGATE conspiracy to obstruct justice. Once more the proceedings evidenced that impeachments are swayed by political affiliations; with a few notable exceptions, a Republican phalanx opposed impeachment until the judicially compelled disclosure of the "White House tapes" revealed that Nixon was a participant in the conspiracy. When he learned as a result of that disclosure that he could not count on more than ten votes in the Senate, he resigned from the presidency. In accepting a pardon from his successor, President GERALD FORD stated, he acknowledged his guilt. Fortunate it was for America that the Founders provided "Goliath's sword" for "great occasions."

RAOUL BERGER

Bibliography

BERGER, RAOUL 1979 "Chilling Judicial Independence": A Judicial Scarecrow. *Cornell Law Quarterly* 64:822–854.

——— 1973 *Impeachment: The Constitutional Problems.* Pages 313–322. Cambridge, Mass.: Harvard University Press.

KAUFMAN, IRVING 1979 Chilling Judicial Independence. *Yale Law Journal* 88:681–716.

KURLAND, PHILIP 1974 Watergate, Impeachment and the Constitution. *Mississippi Law Review* 45:531–600.

IMPLIED CONSTITUTIONAL RIGHTS OF ACTION

One may seek judicial vindication of federal constitutional rights in at least three ways. Constitutional protections may be used as a shield against governmental misbehavior, as for example, when one relies on the Sixth Amendment guarantee of the RIGHT TO COUNSEL to contest a criminal prosecution. Second, one may rely on a constitutional right to enjoin allegedly unconstitutional behavior such as enforcement of an unconstitutional statute. Third, an aggrieved party may seek monetary compensation for past violations of constitutional rights. When invoked without express stautory authorization, the second and third techniques depend upon inferring the existence of implied rights of action to vindicate constitutional rights.

There is disagreement over whether, prior to EX PARTE YOUNG (1908), the offensive assertion of a federal right without a corresponding state-created right was sufficient to invoke a federal court's injunctive power. *Young,* which endorsed a federal INJUNCTION against enforcement of an allegedly unconstitutional state law, became the leading case to suggest that a federal cause of action for injunctive relief was implied merely from the existence of a constitutional right. This result has been a cornerstone of modern litigation contesting statutes and other government behavior. In later years, the Court interpreted SECTION 1983, TITLE 42, UNITED STATES CODE, to supply statutory support for both equitable and monetary relief in constitutional actions against state officials.

By 1971, in light of *Young* and section 1983, only the existence of implied damages actions against federal officials remained open to question. *Bell v. Hood* (1946) suggested that federal courts have JURISDICTION to consider whether alleged Fifth and FOURTH AMENDMENT violations by federal officials give rise to a cause of action for damages but it did not address the question of the cause of action's existence. In BIVENS V. SIX UNKNOWN NAMED AGENTS OF THE FEDERAL BUREAU OF NARCOTICS (1971), however, the Court held that an implied damages action exists for Fourth Amendment violations. DAVIS V. PASSMAN (1979) held that a damages action was implied in the EQUAL PROTECTION guarantee that has been found in the Fifth Amendment and constituted the Court's first extension of *Bivens* beyond Fourth Amendment claims. *Carlson v. Green* (1980), in which plaintiffs were allowed to bring an implied action under the Eighth Amendment, confirmed that *Bivens*-type actions are available under many constitutional provisions. Significantly, the Court has not held that such actions exist against state officials, a holding that would render superfluous much of its section 1983 jurisprudence.

Bivens, Davis, and *Carlson* suggested that Congress has an important role to play in determining the availability and scope of implied damages actions. The Court has left open the possibility of not inferring an implied damages action when defendants demonstrate "special factors counselling hesitation in the absence of affirmative action by Congress," or when, as in *Bush v. Lucas* (1983), Congress provides an effective alternative remedy. But *Davis* and *Carlson v. Green* indicated that the Court does not readily detect a congressional desire to foreclose *Bivens* actions. In *Davis,* Congress had declined to extend federal employment discrimination laws to preclude the behavior for which the Court inferred an implied private right of action. *Carlson* held that the existence of a remedy against the United States under the FEDERAL TORT CLAIMS ACT did not foreclose a *Bivens* action against individual officers alleged to have violated the Constitution.

THEODORE EISENBERG

Bibliography

DELLINGER, WALTER E. 1972 Of Rights and Remedies: The Constitution as a Sword. *Harvard Law Review* 85:1532–1564.

HART, HENRY M., JR. 1954 The Relations between State and Federal Law. *Columbia Law Review* 54:489–542.

IMPLIED POWERS

"Loose and irresponsible use of adjectives colors . . . much legal discussion. . . . 'Inherent' powers, 'implied' powers, 'incidental' powers are used, often interchangeably and without fixed ascertainable meanings." Justice ROBERT H. JACKSON's remark in YOUNGSTOWN SHEET & TUBE COMPANY V. SAWYER (1952) was correct. The vocabulary of "implied powers" is frequently used indiscriminately with other terms. It is associated with not less than six quite different usages.

The original use of "implied powers" was to contrast, rather than to explain, the powers that would vest in the United States. The national government would not automatically possess all the customary attributes of SOVEREIGNTY, but only those expressly provided. As to these, JAMES MADISON declared (in THE FEDERALIST #45): "The powers delegated by the proposed Constitution to the Federal Government, are few and defined. Those which are to remain in the State Governments are numerous and indefinite." Writing for a unanimous Supreme Court in 1804, Chief Justice JOHN MARSHALL, in *United States v. Fisher,* agreed that there were no implied-at-large national powers: "[I]t has been truly said, that under a constitution conferring specific powers, the power contended for must be granted, or it cannot be exercised." And more than a century later, Justice DAVID BREWER in *Kansas v. Colorado* (1907) confirmed the conventional wisdom: "[T]he proposition that there are legislative powers [not] expressed in the grant of powers, is in direct conflict with the doctrine that this is a government of ENUMERATED POWERS."

In this original sense, then, it may be said that the Constitution does not imply a government of general legislative, executive, and judicial powers; it establishes a government of limited, express, enumerated powers alone.

In 1936, in UNITED STATES V. CURTISS-WRIGHT EXPORT CORPORATION, Justice GEORGE SUTHERLAND, in an OBITER DICTUM for the Supreme Court, suggested that the national government need not rely upon any express power to sustain an assertion of executive authority prohibiting American companies from foreign trade which (in the President's view) might compromise the nation's neutral status at international law. Sutherland observed that the United States, as a nation within an international community of sovereign national states possessed "powers of external sovereignty" *apart* from any one or any combination of the Constitution's limited list of powers respecting foreign relations. Accordingly, Sutherland declared: "The broad statement that the federal government can exercise no powers except those specifically enumerated in the Constitution, and such implied powers as are necessary and proper to carry into effect the enumerated powers, is categorically true only in respect of our internal affairs." Such an extraconstitutional power may informally be described as one derived from the status of being a sovereign nation or as implied by the fact of national sovereignty.

The soundness of this view has been seriously questioned, however, and in fact its acceptance has not been necessary to the outcome of any case. Rather, its principal positive law use has been as a reference in support of very broad interpretations of the several provisions in the Constitution which expressly enumerate executive and congressional powers respecting FOREIGN AFFAIRS. It has also been relied upon to uphold extremely permissive DELEGATIONS OF POWER by Congress to permit the President to determine conditions of trade between American companies and foreign countries, or conditions of American travel and activity abroad.

Not inconsistent with the general view that any claim of implied-at-large national powers is precluded by the text and presuppositions of the Constitution, such specific powers as are conferred by the Constitution have been deemed to carry with them exceedingly wide-ranging implications. Partly this results merely from the doctrine of BROAD CONSTRUCTION that every specific grant of power is to be deferentially interpreted, rather than narrowly construed. For instance, the power vested in Congress to "regulate" commerce among the several states might have been interpreted quite narrowly, in keeping with the principal objectives of enabling Congress to provide for a nationwide free trade zone, as against the tendency of some states to enact discriminatory taxes, and other self-favoring economic barriers. Instead, the power was construed in no such qualified fashion. The power to regulate commerce among the several states is "the power to prescribe the rule by which such commerce shall be governed," which therefore includes the power to limit or to forbid outright such commerce among the states as Congress sees fit to disallow. The result has been that to this extent, the express power to regulate commerce among the states gives to Congress a limited NATIONAL POLICE POWER.

Beyond adopting an attitude of permissive construction respecting each enumerated power, however, the Supreme Court took an additional significant step. It accepted the view that acts of Congress not themselves direct exercises of conferred powers would be deemed authorized by the Constitution if they facilitated the exercise of one or more express powers. An act of Congress establishing a national bank under a corporate charter granted by Congress, vesting authority in its directors to set up branch banks with general banking prerogatives, may arguably facilitate borrowing on the credit of the United States, paying debts incurred by the United States, regulating some aspects of commerce among states, and serving as a place of deposit for funds to meet military payrolls. Each of these *uses* is itself identified as an express, enumerated power vested in Congress although the act establishing such an incorporated national bank may itself not be regarded as legislation that borrows money, pays debts, etc. Nevertheless, insofar as provision for such a bank might usefully serve as an instrument by means of which several expressly enumerated powers could be carried into execution, the Supreme Court unanimously concluded that the congressional power to furnish such a bank was "implied" "incidentally" in those enumerated powers. The opinion by Chief Justice Marshall in McCULLOCH v. MARYLAND (1819) is crowded with the repeated use of both terms. In tandem with the principle of generous construction, this view of "implied" incidental powers has had a profound influence in assuring to Congress an immense latitude of legislative discretion despite the conventional wisdom that the national government is one of specific, enumerated powers alone. Laws not probably within even a latitudinarian construction of specific grants of power, but nonetheless instrumentally relatable to such grants, are thus deemed to be adequately "implied" by those grants as incidents of grants.

A contemporary example is furnished by WICKARD v. FILBURN (1942). Though some of the "commerce" regulated by the act upheld in that case was not commerce at all (because it was not offered for trade, but was used solely for the farmer's personal consumption), and although the activity regulated was entirely local (growing and consuming wheat on one's own farm), insofar as the regulation of these local matters was nonetheless instrumentally relatable to an act fixing the volume of wheat permitted to be grown for purposes of interstate sale, the power to include local growing and consumption, as part of the larger regulation, was deemed to be implied by the express power to regulate commerce among the several states. The imaginative capacity of Congress to relate the aggregate interstate effects of local activity, thus bringing it within a uniform and integrated national economic policy, has made the principle of incidental implied power at least as important as the principle of broad construction in respect to enumerated national power. Indeed, the combination of the two doctrines has led Justice WILLIAM H. REHNQUIST, in HODEL v. VIRGINIA SURFACE MINING (1981), to suggest: "It is illuminating for purposes of reflection, if not for argument, to note that one of the greatest "fictions" of our federal system is that the Congress exercises only those powers delegated to it, while the remainder are reserved to the States or to the people. The manner in which this Court has construed the COMMERCE CLAUSE amply illustrates the extent of this fiction." However that may be, the notion that express powers imply an authority to undertake action instrumentally relatable to the use of those powers, albeit action not itself an exercise of any express power, has given to the national government a flexibility and discretion that it would not otherwise possess.

The bank case (*McCulloch*) and the wheat quota case (*Wickard*) are examples of implied powers incidental to *specific* enumerated powers. Each involved acts of Congress establishing an enterprise or furnishing a regulation instrumentally related to one or another express power. Different from this kind of "incidental implied power," but resting on much the same sort of constitutional justification, are implied powers common to each of the three branches of the national government. These powers, sometimes called INHERENT POWERS, are deemed to be implied as reasonably necessary to each department's capacity to discharge effectively its enumerated responsibilities. Because they are regarded as effecting that capacity generally (and not merely in respect to one or another specific enumerated power alone), however, they are generically implied, incidental powers.

A prominent example is the unenumerated (but implied) power of each house of Congress to hold legislative hearings, to subpoena witnesses, and otherwise to compel the submission of information thought useful in determining whether acts of Congress on particular subjects need to be adopted, repealed, or modified. The power to conduct LEGISLATIVE INVESTIGATIONS, nowhere expressly conferred, is deemed to be implied as a reasonable incident of the legislative function. Similarly, a power of federal courts to maintain order in adjudicative proceedings, independent of any act of Congress providing such a power (pursuant to the NECESSARY AND PROPER CLAUSE), rests on the same ground. And although never challenged, presumably the power of the Supreme Court to exclude all but its own members from its private conferences in which discussion is held and votes are taken on pending cases is an example.

A qualified power of EXECUTIVE PRIVILEGE, enabling the President to interdict discovery of advice, memoranda, and other internal executive communications is conceded by the Supreme Court to be implied as an incident of executive necessity and power. The principle common to these several examples was illustrated in a remark by ALEXANDER HAMILTON, in *The Federalist* #74, commenting briefly upon the express power vested in the President by Article II, authorizing the President to "require the opinion in writing of the principal officer in each of the executive departments upon any subject relating to the duties of their respective offices." As to this express provision, Hamilton suggested, "I consider [it] a mere redundancy in the plan; as the right for which it provides would result of itself from the office." And so, undoubtedly, it would, especially as the Supreme Court was subsequently to hold that the President has an implied power to dismiss any executive subordinate at will, though no express clause so provides, and the clause respecting appointment of such officers requires the consent of the Senate.

One may phrase the matter variously, as power "resulting" from the establishment of the executive, legislative, and judicial branches, or as powers "incidental" to their designated powers. The point is the same: instrumental powers deemed reasonably necessary generally to each department's independent capacity to exercise its express, vested powers are treated as generically implied by Articles I, II, and III.

As noted in *McCulloch* an act of Congress establishing a national bank in corporate form may be useful as a means of carrying into execution the several specific fiscal powers of the United States. Equally, a regulation of local commerce may be necessary to keep a regulation of INTERSTATE COMMERCE from frustration. In either case the Court has upheld such exercise of congressional power when instrumentally relatable to the exercise of an express, enumerated power. In neither case, however, is it necessary in fact to describe the power to adopt such instrumentally relatable laws as "implied" power. Rather, all such laws are themselves specifically and expressly authorized by an *enumerated* grant of enabling power vested in Congress: "Congress shall have power to make all laws necessary and proper to carry into execution the foregoing powers, and all other powers vested in the government of the United States or any officer or department thereof." This clause, located at the end of the enumerated powers of Congress in Article I, section 8, is known as the "necessary and proper" clause. Originally, in anticipation of its elasticizing effects, it was known as "the sweeping clause," vesting in Congress discretion to carry into effect its own enumerated powers, and those of the executive and judiciary as well, by means of its own choosing. Consistent with that background, and consistent also with the general doctrine of generous (or loose) construction, the sweeping clause has been construed by the Supreme Court very liberally: "necessary and proper" are regarded as synonymous with "reasonable." Thus, whatever acts of Congress may reasonably relate to a regulation of commerce among the several states are authorized by this clause. Likewise, whatever acts of Congress may reasonably relate to the conduct of the JUDICIAL POWER OF THE UNITED STATES, or the conduct of the executive powers (as described in Article II), as an aid to those departments to carry into execution the executive or judicial powers, are authorized by this clause.

Because of this interpretation of the sweeping clause, it is not clear why the Supreme Court developed the notion of incidental *implied* powers. From one point of view, the latter doctrine is both redundant, because it duplicates a power *already* provided in the Constitution, and illogical because insofar as there is a clause expressly providing for such an instrumental power vested in Congress, to speak of such a power as "implied" rather than as "express" makes little sense. Had there been no necessary and proper clause, the innovation of a doctrine of implied power, incidental to enumerated powers, might be rested on the felt necessity of rendering the national government equal to ultimate growth and needs of the nation. But insofar as the necessary and proper clause was itself construed to provide for such flexibility, no need remained to be filled by the additional innovation of "implied, incidental" power. The doctrine of generous construction (respecting the scope of enumerated power) and the necessary and proper clause (itself generously construed), would in combination grant a vast instrumental latitude to Congress in respect both to its own powers and to those of the executive and the judiciary.

One consequence of this partial redundancy is that there is no particular consistency in the pattern of Supreme Court decisions respecting unsuccessfully challenged acts of Congress. Sometimes they are sustained as but implied incidents of one or more enumerated substantive powers. And sometimes, as happened in *McCulloch,* they are sustained on both grounds at the same time.

Were it not for a related problem, the question whether an exertion of national power not within an express enumerated power (but nonetheless instrumentally relatable to such a power) properly rests on the necessary and proper clause, or instead merely represents an implied power instrumentally incidental to an express power, would be merely academic. But, unfortunately, it is not always so. The necessary and proper clause vests its power in Congress. It implies, by doing so, that if Congress believes it appropriate to facilitate the executive and judicial enumerated powers, it may do so by enacting legislation helpful, albeit not indispensable, to those departments. Merely "helpful" instrumental powers assertable by the executive or by the judiciary will depend, therefore, on whether Congress has, by law, acting pursuant to the necessary and proper clause, provided for them. Correspondingly, the absence of any such act of Congress providing for such incidental executive or judicial powers would be a sufficient basis for a successful challenge to any such unaided assertions of executive or judicial power.

On the other hand, if the mere enumeration of executive and judicial powers (in Articles II and III) are themselves deemed to imply incidentally helpful (but not indispensable) ancillary powers, then the absence of a supportive act of Congress is not fatal to such claims. Thus, in this instance, it does make a difference to resolve the relationship between the necessary and proper clause (addressed solely to what Congress may provide) and the doctrine of implied, incidental powers.

Interestingly, two centuries into the positive law history of the Constitution, this particular question has not been addressed by the Supreme Court. Rather, an uneasy accommodation has been made. Each department of government has been regarded by the Court as possessing a range of incidental powers implied by its express powers, and such assertions of authority have been generally upheld. Nonetheless, insofar as Congress has legislated affirmatively, and by statute has found that such an assertion of incidental executive (or judicial) authority is *not* necessary or proper, the tendency of the Supreme Court is to defer to the authoritative judgment of Congress and, correspondingly, rule against the assertion of "implied" incidental executive power.

The pragmatic accommodation of the doctrine of implied incidental powers and the necessary and proper clause, therefore, has been to treat Congress as *primus inter pares.* Each department of the national government has separate enumerated powers of its own, not subject to abridgment by either of the other two departments. In addition, each may assert implied incidental powers, instrumentally relatable to its enumerated powers albeit not literally within those enumerated powers as even generously construed. But a specific determination by Congress with respect to this latter class of powers is regarded as virtually conclusive of the subject. If the act of Congress confirms such power, it is virtually certain to be sustained. If the act of Congress either expressly or implicitly denies the appropriateness of such incidental executive or judicial power, then that determination also is likely to govern. The case best known for this view is *Youngstown Sheet & Tube Co. v. Sawyer.*

The Constitution enumerates express WAR POWERS and express powers enabling Congress to insure each state against domestic violence. Curiously, however, it has no express clauses directed to the internal security of the national government. Nevertheless, the authority to provide for laws punishing attempts of violent overthrow has been sustained as an implied power of self-preservation. Depending upon how deeply such laws may affect certain freedoms to criticize the government or to bring about fundamental changes in its composition by peaceful means, these acts of Congress may be vulnerable to challenge under the FIRST AMENDMENT or other provisions of the Constitution. Nevertheless, a considerable implied power of self-preservation is deemed to vest in Congress, essentially on the common-sense inference that its express enumerated powers imply a residual existence of the government possessing those powers and thus, of necessity, a power of self-preservation. The Sedition Act of 1798 (see ALIEN AND SEDITION ACTS) was sustained in the lower federal courts partly on this rationale.

Less frequently drawn into litigation, but presumably resting on similar grounds, is the implied power of Congress to provide for incidents of national status. The adoption of a national flag rests on no particular enumerated power. Rather, like other acts of Congress identifying symbols of national status, it is but an implied incident of an expressly established government—of the United States of America.

In sum, the phrase "implied powers" houses a half-dozen quite discrete meanings. They are bound together by but one common element, namely the obviousness of contrast with express powers. Beyond that, however, they speak to distinct (and not always completely reconcilable) propositions. One is an implied residual sovereign power of national self-preservation and the incidental power to adopt ordinary insignia of nationhood. In addition, there are implied powers peculiar to each of the three branches of the national government, incidental to the exercise of all enumerated powers expressly vested in each branch. Such generic implied powers apart, there are also implied cognate powers incidental to each expressly enumerated power, extending the reach of those enumerated powers even beyond what might otherwise be their scope under a doctrine of loose or generous construction. Then, too, although the usage seems inept in reference to an *enumerated* general enabling power, the necessary and proper clause of the Constitution has often been used to anchor the textual source of extensive, instrumental powers. And last, there is also the claim of implied, extraconstitutional power in respect to the external sovereign relations of the United States, standing over and apart from the several enumerations of power provided by the Constitution.

The solidness of the foundations respecting these several varieties of implied powers are not all of a piece, that is, quite plainly they are not all of equally convincing legitimacy. Rather, they but illustrate in still one more way how two centuries of history have operated to show what has followed from Chief Justice Marshall's observation that it is a Constitution we are expounding.

WILLIAM W. VAN ALSTYNE

Bibliography

GUNTHER, GERALD, ED. 1969 *John Marshall's Defense of McCulloch v. Maryland.* Stanford, Calif.: Stanford University Press.

HENKIN, LOUIS 1972 *Foreign Affairs and the Constitution.* St. Paul, Minn.: West Publishing Co.

VAN ALSTYNE, WILLIAM W. 1976 The Role of Congress in Determining Incidental Powers of the President and of the Federal Courts: The Horizontal Effect of the Sweeping Clause. *Law & Contemporary Problems* 1976:102–134.

IMPORT-EXPORT CLAUSE

The Constitution provides: "No State shall . . . lay any IMPOSTS or Duties on Imports or Exports, except what may be absolutely necessary for executing its inspection Laws." It also prohibits the federal government from placing any tax or duty on exports.

The limitation on state taxation of imports came before the Supreme Court in BROWN V. MARYLAND (1827). Chief Justice JOHN MARSHALL pointed out that the clear intention of the Framers was to prohibit the states from levying customs duties. Only Congress was to have this power. He recognized, however, that state power to raise revenues would be unduly restricted if goods that had come from another country could never be subject to taxation along with other goods within the state. He resolved the dilemma by holding that imported goods should be free from state taxation until they have been incorporated into the mass of property in the state. Such incorporation would take place when the importer sold the goods or when he took them out of the original package in which they were imported. Hence was born the ORIGINAL PACKAGE DOCTRINE, which survived as the measure for state taxation of imports until MICHELIN TIRE CORP. V. WAGES (1976).

In *Michelin* the Supreme Court held that the intention of the Framers was only to prevent the states from imposing special taxes on imports. Hence, it concluded that imported goods could, as soon as they came to rest in the taxing state, be subject to nondiscriminatory state property taxes.

The Supreme Court has long held that goods become exports—and thus free from either state or federal taxes—when they have actually commenced the journey to another country. Once the journey has commenced or they have been committed to a common carrier for transport abroad, they may not be taxed.

Application of the import-export clause to those businesses that transport or otherwise handle goods in FOREIGN COMMERCE has posed a separate problem. Recently the Court has held that nondiscriminatory taxes apportioned to cover only values within the taxing state may be imposed upon the instrumentalities of foreign commerce or the business of engaging in such commerce. Thus, in *Department of Revenue of Washington v. Association of Washington Stevedoring Companies* (1978), it upheld a Washington tax on the privilege of engaging in business activities measured by gross receipts as applied to a stevedoring company that confined its activities to the loading and unloading in Washington ports of ships engaged in foreign commerce.

In general, the rules governing state taxation of INTERSTATE COMMERCE now seem to apply to imports and exports.

EDWARD L. BARRETT, JR.

(SEE ALSO: *State Taxation of Commerce.*)

Bibliography

HELLERSTEIN, WALTER 1977 Michelin Tire Corp. v. Wages: Enhanced State Power to Tax Imports. *Supreme Court Review* 1977:99–123.

IMPOST

In its broadest sense the term "impost" refers to any tax or tribute levied by authority. By usage it has come to have the narrower meaning of a tax or duty imposed on imports. The Supreme Court has recently stated that "imposts and duties" as used in the Constitution "are essentially taxes on the commercial privilege of bringing goods into a country."

EDWARD L. BARRETT, JR.

(SEE ALSO: *Excise Taxes; Import-Export Clause; Michelin Tire Corp. v. Wages, 1976; State Taxation of Commerce.*)

IMPOUNDMENT OF FUNDS

Presidents from time to time, and especially beginning with the regime of FRANKLIN D. ROOSEVELT, have asserted a right not to execute the laws or parts thereof, by a decision to "impound" the funds provided by Congress for the effectuation of the law. In effect, this would be an exercise of an item VETO POWER. There is no warrant in the Constitution for the exercise of the power of impoundment. The history of the veto provision in the CONSTITUTIONAL CONVENTION OF 1787 makes clear that the Founders were wary of any veto authority, no less one that would allow the President to rewrite the laws of Congress to suit his predilections. Instead, the Constitution clearly requires that the President "take Care that the Laws be faithfully executed." Only if the provisions of Article II vesting the "executive power" are read to create implicit authority in the President to do as he pleases—what Arthur Schlesinger, Jr., calls a "plebiscitary" presidency—can the impoundment authority be deemed a constitutional one.

This is not to say that a President may not be authorized to exercise the impoundment power. But that authority must derive from legislation and not from the Constitution. Where Congress has mandated the expenditure of funds in support of a legislative program, the President has no choice but to effectuate Congress's will. But legislation may explicitly create discretion in the executive branch as to whether programs are to be carried out in whole or in part. And the courts have suggested that legislation may imply that such presidential power exists. Arguments have also been made that certain general statutes such as those ordering the executive to choose the most economic means of enforcement of the laws, or putting ceilings on the national debt, create a legislative warrant for presidential impoundment. There is little merit in the proposals that these statutes create a general statutory authority for the President to pick and choose among congressional programs.

The President has a veto power. If it is used successfully, the congressional program need not be effected for it is not the law. If the veto be used unsuccessfully, however, it is clear that Congress has mandated the program and it is Congress's will, not the President's, that makes the law of the land. Although there is no item veto, no restriction exists on the veto message explaining that the veto was invoked in response to a particular item in the legislation. If Congress overrides the veto, it will be clear that the portion found objectionable by the President was found desirable by the Congress.

After particularly egregious efforts by President RICHARD M. NIXON to throttle congressional legislation through "impoundment," the CONGRESSIONAL BUDGET AND IMPOUNDMENT CONTROL ACT was enacted (1974). This statute requires the President to inform Congress if he proposes to rescind or defer appropriations. There can be no rescission unless Congress acting through both houses concurs within forty-five days. A deferral can be invalidated by a resolution of disapproval by one house but is valid unless disapproved. The statute is thorny with constitutional issues, but both the legislators and the executive seem willing to accept it as an appropriate accommodation of their respective interests.

The question whether a President may refuse to enforce a law that he deems unconstitutional is not really an "impoundment" question. That issue was mooted but not resolved in the IMPEACHMENT and trial of President ANDREW JOHNSON. Clearly the President can challenge or refuse to defend in the courts any legislation he finds unconstitutional.

PHILIP B. KURLAND

Bibliography

FISHER, LOUIS 1972 *President and Congress: Power and Policy.* New York: Free Press.

GENERAL ACCOUNTING OFFICE 1977 *Review of the Impoundment Control Act of 1974.* Washington, D.C.: Government Printing Office.

INALIENABLE POLICE POWER

THOMAS COOLEY, writing on the STATE POLICE POWER in 1868, concluded that the CONTRACT CLAUSE did not permit a state "under pretense of regulation, [to] take from the CORPORATION any of the essential rights and privileges which the charter confers." Constitutional law changed quickly. In BOSTON BEER CO. V. MASSACHUSETTS (1878), when holding that the RESERVED POLICE POWER allowed a state to revoke the charter of a brewery company, the Supreme Court declared that even in the absence of a reserved power to revoke, the revocation would be valid: the legislature cannot contract away or otherwise alienate the sovereign power to protect the lives, health, safety, or morals of its citizens. A legislature can, however, alienate its tax powers, as NEW JERSEY v. WILSON (1812) and PIQUA BRANCH BANK v. KNOOP (1854) demonstrated. As the Court frequently explained, the tax power is a right of government that the contract clause does not protect; it protects property rights only. That distinction scarcely explains why the power of EMINENT DOMAIN, a government right, cannot be contracted away. Nevertheless, the inalienable police power proved to be an effective rationale for supporting a variety of regulatory legislation against contract clause claims.

In NORTHWESTERN FERTILIZING COMPANY v. HYDE PARK (1878) the Court upheld as a protection of public health an ordinance forcing the removal of a fertilizer plant. In STONE v. MISSISSIPPI (1880) the Court sustained a state act revoking the charter of a lottery company; the contract clause could not limit a power to protect public morality from gambling. Within a few years the Court upheld one state act revoking a monopoly of the slaughterhouse business and another establishing a commission to fix the rates of a railroad company whose charter expressly authorized it to fix its own rates. In the rate case, STONE v. FARMERS' LOAN AND TRUST COMPANY (1886), the fact that the state had not reserved a power to alter or amend the charter made the defeat of the contract clause claim seem kindred to a victory for the inalienable police power. The unreliability of the contract clause, especially in rate cases, led shortly to the acceptance of SUBSTANTIVE DUE PROCESS OF LAW to defeat the police power.

That the inalienable police power was not limited to cases of public health, safety, or morality is shown by the unanimous opinion in *Chicago and Alton Railroad v. Tranbarger* (1915), sustaining a state requirement that railroads construct roadbeds that prevent water damage to private property. Justice MAHLON PITNEY for the Court declared that all contract and property rights are held subject to the exercise of a police power that "is inalienable even by express grant" and is not limited by either the contract clause or the DUE PROCESS clause. Pitney added that the power embraced regulations promoting "public convenience or the GENERAL WELFARE and prosperity" as well as the "public health, morals, or safety." Protection of the "general welfare and prosperity" figured prominently in the Court's decision in HOME BUILDING AND LOAN ASSOCIATION v. BLAISDELL (1934). In that case the Court referred to the reserved police power but meant the inalienable police power.

LEONARD W. LEVY

Bibliography

WRIGHT, BENJAMIN F. 1938 *The Contract Clause of the Constitution.* Pages 195–213. Cambridge, Mass.: Harvard University Press.

INCITEMENT TO UNLAWFUL CONDUCT

Incitement to unlawful conduct raises a central and difficult issue about the proper boundaries of freedom of expression and of the FIRST AMENDMENT. Many of the Supreme Court's most important FREEDOM OF SPEECH decisions have involved some form of incitement. Though the term incitement sometimes refers to emotionally charged appeals to immediate action, the word is most often used to cover any urging that others commit illegal acts.

The basic problem about incitement is fairly simple, involving a tension between a criminal law perspective and a free speech perspective. Any society seeks to minimize the number of crimes that are committed. Some people commit crimes because others urge them to do so. Although the person who actually commits a crime may usually seem more to blame than someone who encourages him, on other occasions the inciter, because of greater authority, intelligence, or firmness of purpose, may actually be more responsible for what happens than the person who is the instrument of his designs. In any event, because the person who successfully urges another to commit a crime bears some responsibility and because effective restrictions on incitement are likely to reduce the amount of crime to some degree, sound reasons exist for punishing those who incite.

Anglo-American criminal law, like the law of other traditions, has reflected this view. In 1628, EDWARD COKE wrote that "all those that incite . . . any other" to commit a FELONY are guilty of a crime; and, at least by 1801, unsuccessful incitement was recognized as an offense in England. Modern American criminal law generally treats the successful inciter on a par with the person who performs the criminal act; the unsuccessful inciter is guilty of criminal solicitation, treated as a lesser crime than the one he has tried to incite.

From the free speech perspective, the problem of

incitement takes on a different appearance. A basic premise of a liberal society is that people should be allowed to express their views, especially their political views. Some important political views support illegal actions against actual or possible governments. Indeed, one aspect of the political tradition of the United States is that revolutionary overthrow of existing political authority is sometimes justified. Other views deem certain illegal acts justified even when the government is acceptable. Were all encouragements of illegal activity suppressed, an important slice of political and social opinions would be silenced. Further, in the practical administration of such suppression some opinions that did not quite amount to encouragement would be proceeded against and persons would be inhibited from saying things that could possibly be construed as encouragements to commit crimes. Thus, wide restrictions on incitement have been thought to imperil free expression, particularly when statutes penalizing incitement have been specifically directed to "subversive" political ideologies.

The tension between criminal law enforcement and freedom of expression is addressed by both legislatures and courts. Legislatures must initially decide what is a reasonable, and constitutionally permissible, accommodation of the conflicting values. When convictions are challenged, courts must decide whether the statutes that legislatures have adopted and their applications to particular situations pass constitutional muster.

Most states have statutes that make solicitation of a crime illegal. These laws are drawn to protect speech interests to a significant extent. To be convicted of solicitation, one must actually encourage the commission of a specific crime. Therefore, many kinds of statements, such as disinterested advice that committing a crime like draft evasion would be morally justified, approval of present lawbreaking in general, or urging people to prepare themselves for unspecified future revolutionary acts, are beyond the reach of ordinary solicitation statutes.

One convenient way to conceptualize the First Amendment problems about incitement is to ask whether any communications that do amount to ordinary criminal solicitation are constitutionally protected and whether other communications that encourage criminal acts but fall short of criminal solicitation lack constitutional protection.

All major Supreme Court cases on the subject have involved political expression of one kind or another and have arisen under statutes directed at specific kinds of speech. Some of the cases have involved CRIMINAL CONSPIRACY charges, but because the conspiracy has been to incite or advocate, the constitutionality of punishing communications has been the crucial issue. In SCHENCK V. UNITED STATES (1919) the Court sustained a conviction under the 1917 ESPIONAGE ACT, which made criminal attempts to obstruct enlistment. The leaflet that Schenck had helped to publish had urged young men to assert their rights to oppose the draft. Writing the majority opinion that found no constitutional bar to the conviction, Justice OLIVER WENDELL HOLMES penned the famous CLEAR AND PRESENT DANGER test: "The question in every case is whether the words used are used in such circumstances and are of such a nature as to create a clear and present danger that they will bring about the substantive evils that Congress has a right to prevent." Much was unclear about this test as originally formulated and as subsequently developed, but the results in *Schenck* and companion cases show that the Court then did not conceive the standard as providing great protection for speech. During the 1920s, while the majority of Justices ceased using the test, eloquent dissents by Holmes and LOUIS D. BRANDEIS forged it into a principle that was protective of speech, requiring a danger that was both substantial and close in time in order to justify suppressing communication. Even these later opinions, however, did not indicate with clarity whether the test applied to ordinary criminal solicitation or whether an intent to create a clear and present danger would be sufficient for criminal punishment.

During the 1920s, the majority of the Supreme Court was willing to affirm convictions for expression, so long as the expression fell within a statutory prohibition and the statutory prohibition was reasonable. Thus, in GITLOW V. NEW YORK (1925) the Court upheld a conviction under a criminal anarchy statute that forbade teaching the propriety of illegally overthrowing organized government. The Court concluded that the legislature could reasonably anticipate that speech of this type carried the danger of a "revolutionary spark" kindling a fire. The standard applied in *Gitlow* and similar cases would permit suppression of virtually any type of speech that a legislature might consider to create a danger of illegal activity, a category far broader than ordinary criminal solicitation.

In the 1930s the Supreme Court began to render decisions more protective of speech, and in HERNDON V. LOWRY (1937) the Court reversed a conviction for attempting to incite insurrection, when the evidence failed to show that the defendant, a Communist party organizer, had actually urged revolutionary violence.

The majority in *Herndon* referred to the clear and present danger test with approval. In a series of subsequent decisions, that test was employed as an all-purpose standard for First Amendment cases.

In 1951, the Supreme Court reviewed the convictions of eleven leading communists in DENNIS V. UNITED STATES. The defendants had violated the Smith Act by conspiring to advocate the forcible overthrow of the United States government. As in *Gitlow*, the expressions involved (typical communist rhetoric) fell short of inciting to any specific crime. The plurality opinion, representing the views of four Justices, accepted clear and present danger as the appropriate standard, but interpreted the test so that the gravity of the evil was discounted by its improbability. In practice, this formulation meant that if the evil were very great, such as overthrow of the government, communication creating a danger of that evil might be suppressed even though the evil would not occur in the near future and had only a small likelihood that it would ever occur. The dissenters and civil libertarian observers protested that this interpretation undermined the main point of "clear and present" danger. *Dennis* is now viewed by many as a regrettable product of unwarranted fears of successful communist subversion. In subsequent cases, the Court emphasized that the Smith Act reached only advocacy of illegal action, not advocacy of doctrine. In the years since *Dennis* only one conviction under the act has passed this stringent test.

The modern constitutional standard for incitement cases arose out of the conviction of a Ku Klux Klan leader for violating a broad CRIMINAL SYNDICALISM statute, not unlike the statute involved in *Gitlow*. Unsurprisingly, the Court said in BRANDENBURG V. OHIO (1969) that the broad statute was unconstitutional. But it went on to fashion a highly restrictive version of clear and present danger: that a state may not "forbid or proscribe advocacy of the use of force or of law violation except where such advocacy is directed to inciting or producing imminent lawless action and is likely to incite or produce such action." This test requires lawless action that is likely, imminent, and intended by the speaker. Only rarely could such a test possibly be met by speech that does not amount to criminal solicitation, and under this test both solicitation of crimes in the distant future and solicitation unlikely to be acted upon are constitutionally protected. In *Brandenburg*, however, the Court had directly in mind public advocacy; it is unlikely that this stringent test also applies to private solicitations of crime that are made for personal gain. The present law provides significant constitutional protection for political incitements, but how far beyond political speech this protection may extend remains uncertain.

KENT GREENAWALT

Bibliography

AMERICAN LAW INSTITUTE 1985 *Model Penal Code*, Section 5.02 and Commentary. St. Paul, Minn.: West Publishing Co.

GREENAWALT, KENT 1980 Speech and Crime. *American Bar Foundation Research Journal* 1980:647–785.

LINDE, HANS A. 1970 "Clear and Present Danger" Reexamined: Dissonance in the Brandenburg Concerto. *Stanford Law Review* 22:1163–1186.

INCOME TAX CASES

See: *Pollock v. Farmers Loan and Trust Company*

INCORPORATION DOCTRINE

According to the incorporation doctrine the FOURTEENTH AMENDMENT incorporates or absorbs the BILL OF RIGHTS, making its guarantees applicable to the states. Whether the Bill of Rights applied to the states, restricting their powers as it did those of the national government, was a question that arose in connection with the framing and ratification of the Fourteenth Amendment. Before 1868 nothing in the Constitution of the United States prevented a state from imprisoning religious heretics or political dissenters, or from abolishing TRIAL BY JURY, or from torturing suspects to extort confessions of guilt. The Bill of Rights limited only the United States, not the states. JAMES MADISON, who framed the amendments that became the Bill of Rights, had included one providing that "no State shall violate the equal rights of conscience, of the FREEDOM OF THE PRESS, or the trial by jury in criminal cases." The Senate defeated that proposal. History, therefore, was on the side of the Supreme Court when it unanimously decided in BARRON V. BALTIMORE (1833) that "the fifth amendment must be understood as restraining the power of the general government, not as applicable to the States," and said that the other amendments composing the Bill of Rights were equally inapplicable to the States.

Thus, a double standard existed in the nation. The Bill of Rights commanded the national government to refrain from enacting certain laws and to respect certain procedures, but it left the states free to do as they wished in relation to the same matters. State constitutions and COMMON LAW practices, rather than the Constitution of the United States, were the sources of restraints on the states with respect to the subjects of the Bill of Rights.

Whether the Fourteenth Amendment was intended to alter this situation is a matter on which the historical record is complex, confusing, and probably inconclusive. Even if history spoke with a loud, clear, and decisive voice, however, it ought not necessarily control judgment on the question whether the Supreme Court should interpret the amendment as incorporating the Bill of Rights. Whatever the framers of the Fourteenth intended, they did not possess ultimate wisdom as to the meaning of their words for subsequent generations. Moreover, the PRIVILEGES AND IMMUNITIES, due process, and EQUAL PROTECTION clauses of section 1 of the amendment are written in language that blocks fixed meanings. Its text must be read as revelations of general purposes that were to be achieved or as expressions of imperishable principles that are comprehensive in character. The principles and purposes, not their framers' original technical understanding, are what was intended to endure. We cannot avoid the influence of history but are not constitutionally obligated to obey history which is merely a guide. The task of CONSTITUTIONAL INTERPRETATION is one of statecraft: to read the text in the light of changing needs in accordance with the noblest ideals of a democratic society.

The Court has, in fact, proved to be adept at reading into the Constitution the policy values that meet its approval, and its freedom to do so is virtually legislative in scope. Regrettably in its first Fourteenth Amendment decision, in the SLAUGHTERHOUSE CASES (1873), the Court unnecessarily emasculated the privileges and immunities clause by ruling that it protected only the privileges and immunities of national CITIZENSHIP but not the privileges and immunities of state citizenship, which included "nearly every CIVIL RIGHT for the establishment and protection of which organized government is instituted." Among the rights deriving from state, not national, citizenship were those referred to by the Bill of Rights as well as other "fundamental" rights. Justice STEPHEN J. FIELD, dissenting, rightly said that the majority's interpretation had rendered the clause "a vain and idle enactment, which accomplished nothing. . . ." The privileges and immunities clause was central to the incorporation issue because to the extent that any of the framers of the amendment intended incorporation, they relied principally on that clause. Notwithstanding the amendment, *Barron v. Baltimore* remained controlling law. The Court simply opposed the revolution in the federal system which the amendment's text suggested. The privileges and immunities of national citizenship after *Slaughterhouse* were those that Congress or the Court could have protected, under the SUPREMACY CLAUSE, with or without the new amendment.

In HURTADO V. CALIFORNIA (1884) the Court initiated a long line of decisions that eroded the traditional procedures associated with due process of law. *Hurtado* was not an incorporation case, because the question it posed was not whether the Fourteenth Amendment incorporated the clause of the Fifth guaranteeing INDICTMENT by GRAND JURY but whether the concept of due process necessarily required indictment in a capital case. In cases arising after *Hurtado*, counsel argued that even if the concept of due process did not mean indictment, or freedom from CRUEL AND UNUSUAL PUNISHMENT, or trial by a twelve-member jury, or the RIGHT AGAINST SELF-INCRIMINATION, the provisions of the Bill of Rights applied to the states through the Fourteenth Amendment; that is, the amendment incorporated them either by the privileges and immunities clause, or by the due process clause's protection of "liberty." In *O'Neil v. Vermont* (1892), that argument was accepted for the first time by three Justices, dissenting; however, only one of them, JOHN MARSHALL HARLAN, steadfastly adhered to it in MAXWELL V. DOW (1900) and TWINING V. NEW JERSEY (1908), when all other Justices rejected it. Harlan, dissenting in *Patterson v. Colorado* (1907), stated "that the privilege of free speech and a free press belong to every citizen of the United States, constitute essential parts of every man's liberty, and are protected against violation by that clause of the Fourteenth Amendment forbidding a state to deprive any person of his liberty without due process of law." The Court casually adopted that view in OBITER DICTUM in GITLOW V. NEW YORK (1925).

Before *Gitlow* the Court had done a good deal of property-minded, not liberty-minded, incorporating. As early as *Hepburn v. Griswold* (1870), it had read the protection of the CONTRACT CLAUSE into the Fifth Amendment's due process clause as a limitation on the powers of Congress, a viewpoint repeated in the SINKING FUND CASES (1879). The Court in 1894 had incorporated the Fifth's JUST COMPENSATION clause into the Fourteenth's due process clause and in 1897 it had incorporated the same clause into the Fourteenth's equal protection clause. In the same decade the Court had accepted SUBSTANTIVE DUE PROCESS, incorporating within the Fourteenth a variety of doctrines that secured property, particularly corporate property, against "unreasonable" rate regulations and reformist labor legislation. By 1915, however, PROCEDURAL DUE PROCESS for persons accused of crime had so shriveled in meaning that Justice OLIVER WENDELL HOLMES, dissenting, was forced to say that "mob law does not become due process of law by securing the assent of a terrorized jury."

The word "liberty" in the due process clause had absorbed all FIRST AMENDMENT guarantees by the time of the decision in EVERSON V. BOARD OF EDUCATION (1947). Incorporation developed much more slowly in the field of criminal justice. POWELL V. ALABAMA (1932) applied to the states the SIXTH AMENDMENT'S RIGHT TO COUNSEL in capital cases, as a "necessary requisite of due process of law." The Court reached a watershed, however, in PALKO V. CONNECTICUT (1937), where it refused to incorporate the ban on DOUBLE JEOPARDY. Justice BENJAMIN N. CARDOZO sought to provide a "rationalizing principle" to explain the selective or piecemeal incorporation process. He repudiated the notion that the Fourteenth Amendment embraced the entire Bill of Rights, because the rights it guaranteed fell into two categories. Some were of such a nature that liberty and justice could not exist if they were sacrificed. These had been brought "within the Fourteenth Amendment by a process of absorption" because they were "of the very essence of a scheme of ORDERED LIBERTY." In short, they were "fundamental," like the concept of due process. Other rights, however, were not essential to a "fair and enlightened system of justice." First Amendment rights were "the indispensable condition" of nearly every other form of freedom, but jury trials, indictments, immunity against compulsory self-incrimination, and double jeopardy "might be lost, and justice still be done."

The difficulty with *Palko*'s rationalizing scheme was that it was subjective. It offered no principle explaining why some rights were fundamental or essential to ordered liberty and others were not; it measured all rights against some abstract or idealized system, rather than the Anglo-American accusatory system of criminal justice. Selective incorporation also completely lacked historical justification. And it was logically flawed. The Court read the substantive content of the First Amendment into the "liberty" of the due process clause, but that clause permitted the abridgment of liberty with due process of law. On the other hand, selective incorporation, as contrasted with total incorporation, allowed the Court to decide constitutional issues as they arose on a case-by-case basis, and allowed, too, the exclusion from the incorporation doctrine of some rights whose incorporation would wreak havoc in state systems of justice. Grand jury indictment for all felonies and trials by twelve-member juries in civil suits involving more than twenty dollars are among Bill of Rights guarantees that would have that result, if incorporated.

In ADAMSON V. CALIFORNIA (1947) a 5–4 Court rejected the total incorporation theory advanced by the dissenters led by Justice HUGO L. BLACK. Black lambasted the majority's due process standards as grossly subjective; he argued that only the Justices' personal idiosyncrasies could give content to "canons of decency" and "fundamental justice." Black believed that both history and objectivity required resort to the "specifics" of the Bill of Rights. Justices FRANK MURPHY and WILEY RUTLEDGE would have gone further. They accepted total incorporation but observed that due process might require invalidating some state practices "despite the absence of a specific provision in the Bill of Rights." Justice FELIX FRANKFURTER, replying to Black, denied the subjectivity charge and turned it against the dissenters. Murphy's total-incorporation-"plus" was subjective; total incorporation impractically fastened the entire Bill of Rights, with impedimenta, on the states along with the accretions each right had gathered in the United States courts. Selective incorporation on the basis of individual Justices' preferences meant "a merely subjective test" in determining which rights were in and which were out.

Frankfurter also made a logical point long familiar in constitutional jurisprudence. The due process clause of the Fourteenth, which was the vehicle for incorporation, having been copied from the identical clause of the Fifth, could not mean one thing in the latter and something very different in the former. The Fifth itself included a variety of clauses. To incorporate them into the Fourteenth would mean that those clauses of the Fifth and in the remainder of the Bill of Rights were redundant, or the due process clause, if signifying all the rest, was meaningless or superfluous. The answer to Frankfurter and to those still holding his view is historical, not logical. The history of due process shows that it did mean trial by jury and a cluster of traditional rights of accused persons that the Bill of Rights separately specified. Its framers were in many respects careless draftsmen. They enumerated particular rights associated with due process and then added the due process clause partly for political reasons and partly as a rhetorical flourish—a reinforced guarantee and a genuflection toward traditional usage going back to medieval reenactments of MAGNA CARTA.

Numerous cases of the 1950s showed that the majority's reliance on the concept of due process rather than the "specifics" of the Bill of Rights made for unpredictable and unconvincing results. For that reason the Court resumed selective incorporation in the 1960s, beginning with MAPP V. OHIO (1961) and ending with *Benton v. Maryland* (1969). The Warren Court's "revolution in criminal justice" applied against the states the rights of the Fourth through Eighth Amendments, excepting only indictment, twelve-member civil juries, and bail. IN RE WINSHIP (1970) even held that proof of crime beyond a REASONABLE DOUBT, though not a specific provision of the Bill of Rights, was essential to due process, and various decisions have suggested the Court's readiness to extend to the states the Eighth Amendment's provision against excessive bail.

The specifics of the Bill of Rights, however, have proved to offer only an illusion of objectivity, because its most important clauses, including all that have been incorporated, are inherently ambiguous. Indeed, the only truly specific clauses are the ones that have not been incorporated—indictment by grand jury and civil trials by twelve-member juries. The "specific" injunctions of the Bill of Rights do not exclude exceptions, nor are they self-defining. What is "an ESTABLISHMENT OF RELIGION" and what, given libels, pornography, and perjury, is "the freedom of speech" or "of the press"? These freedoms cannot be abridged, but what is an abridgment? Freedom of religion may not be prohibited; may freedom of religion be abridged by a regulation short of prohibition? What is an "UNREASONABLE" SEARCH, "PROBABLE" CAUSE, or "excessive" bail? What punishment is "cruel and unusual"? Is it really true that a person cannot be compelled to be a witness against himself in a criminal case and that the Sixth Amendment extends to "all" criminal prosecutions? What is a "criminal prosecution," a "SPEEDY TRIAL, or an "impartial" jury? Ambiguity cannot be strictly construed. Neutral principles and specifics turn out to be subjective or provoke subjectivity. Moreover, applying to the states the federal standard does not always turn out as expected. After DUNCAN V. LOUISIANA (1968) extended the trial by jury clause of the Sixth Amendment to the states, the Court decided that a criminal jury of less than twelve (but not less than six) would not violate the Fourteenth Amendment, nor would a non-unanimous jury decision. (See JURY SIZE.) Examples can be multiplied to show that the incorporation doctrine has scarcely diminished the need for judgment and that judgment tends to be personal in character.

On the whole, however, the Court has abolished the double standard by nationalizing the Bill of Rights. The results have been mixed. More than ever justice tends to travel on leaden feet. Swift and certain punishment has always been about as effective a deterrent to crime as our criminal justice system can provide, and the prolongation of the criminal process from arrest to final appeal, which is one result of the incorporation doctrine, adds to the congestion of prosecutorial caseloads and court dockets. However, the fundamental problem is the staggering rise in the number of crimes committed, not the decisions of the Court. Even when the police used truncheons to beat suspects into confessions and searched and seized almost at will, they did not reduce the crime rate. In the long run a democratic society is probably hurt more by lawless conduct on the part of law-enforcement agencies than by the impediments of the incorporation doctrine. In the First Amendment field, the incorporation doctrine has few critics, however vigorously particular First Amendment decisions may be criticized.

LEONARD W. LEVY

Bibliography

ABRAHAM, HENRY J. 1977 *Freedom and the Court,* 3rd ed. Pages 33–105. New York: Oxford University Press.

CORTNER, RICHARD C. 1981 *The Supreme Court and the Second Bill of Rights: The Fourteenth Amendment and the Nationalization of Civil Liberties.* Madison: University of Wisconsin Press.

FRIENDLY, HENRY J. 1967 *Benchmarks.* Pages 235–265. Chicago: University of Chicago Press.

HENKIN, LOUIS 1963 "Selective Incorporation" in the Fourteenth Amendment. *Yale Law Journal* 73:74–88.

NORTH, ARTHUR A. 1966 *The Supreme Court: Judicial Process and Judicial Politics.* Pages 65–133. New York: Appleton-Century-Crofts.

INCORPORATION OF TERRITORIES

Incorporation is the process of formally making a territory part of the United States. Even before the Constitution was written, the United States exercised SOVEREIGNTY over lands not part of any state; but those TERRITORIES were to be organized and prepared for statehood. In the late nineteenth century the United States began to acquire territory outside North America, most of which appeared unsuited for statehood. The Constitution contains no provision for governing a colonial empire, but Congress, under Article IV, section 3, made rules and regulations respecting overseas possessions and dependencies. In the INSULAR CASES (1901–1911) the Supreme Court formulated a DOCTRINE to define the constitutional status of the territories. Those which Congress, expressly or implicitly, intends to make part of the United States are deemed to be incorporated. The people of incorporated territories are United States citizens with all the rights guaranteed by the Constitution. Absent such congressional intent, territories are unincorporated. The residents of unincorporated territories enjoy protection of fundamental NATURAL RIGHTS but not of rights merely procedural or formal—although Congress may, at its discretion, extend United States CITIZENSHIP and full CIVIL RIGHTS to the people of unincorporated territories. There are currently no incorporated territories.

DENNIS J. MAHONEY

INDEPENDENT STATE GROUNDS

See: Adequate State Grounds

INDIANS

See: American Indians and the Constitution

INDICTMENT

An indictment is a formal written accusation charging an individual with a crime. An indictment is issued by a GRAND JURY when, in its view, there is PROBABLE CAUSE to believe that an individual has committed a crime.

Indictments generally arise in two ways. Most commonly, a prosecutor will submit a bill of indictment to the grand jury alleging specific criminal activity by an individual. If the grand jury believes the allegations, the grand jurors will endorse the bill of indictment with the words "a true bill" and thereby officially indict the accused individual. The grand jury can also decide that the accused should not be prosecuted, in which case the bill of indictment will be marked "no true bill" and be dismissed.

An indictment can also originate from a grand jury as a result of the grand jury's own information or as a result of an investigation conducted by a special or investigative grand jury. This type of indictment often arises in cases involving organized crime or political corruption after a secret, lengthy grand jury investigation.

Grand jurors need not be unanimous to indict. The federal grand jury, for example, consists of between sixteen and twenty-three persons, twelve of whom must concur to indict.

The indictment process had its origin in the English grand jury system. Indictments were designed, as the Supreme Court said in *Costello v. United States* (1956), to provide "a fair method for instituting criminal proceedings against persons believed to have committed crimes." Indictment by a grand jury was historically seen as a way of ensuring that citizens were protected against unfounded criminal prosecutions; however, there is now considerable debate as to whether indictment actually fulfills its protective function. Indictments are also designed to inform accused individuals of the charges against them so that they may adequately prepare their defense.

Under the Fifth Amendment an individual has a right to a grand jury indictment in all federal FELONY prosecutions. The Supreme Court, however, held in HURTADO V. CALIFORNIA (1884) that grand jury indictments are not constitutionally required in state criminal prosecutions. Nevertheless, some states, pursuant to their state constitutions, require grand jury indictments in all felony prosecutions.

One recurring question about indictments has been whether they can be based on EVIDENCE that would be inadmissible at trial. The Supreme Court held in CALANDRA V. UNITED STATES (1974) that "an indictment valid on its face is not subject to challenge on the ground that the grand jury acted on the basis of inadequate or incompetent evidence." Indictments can be based even on evidence obtained illegally, which must therefore be excluded at trial.

Furthermore, a grand jury indictment can be based on HEARSAY evidence and other types of evidence that would not be admissible at trial. These decisions rest on the historical view of the grand jury as being a lay body with broad investigative powers that should not be restrained by technical rules of evidence. In addition, the Supreme Court has observed that an indictment is only a formal charge, not an adjudication of guilt or innocence. "In a trial on the merits, defendants are entitled to a strict observance of all the rules designed to bring about a fair verdict," the Court said in *Costello,* so defendants are not prejudiced by indictments based on inadmissible evidence. The prosecutor, therefore, is permitted to find some admissible evidence to support the indictment between the time it comes from the grand jury and the time of trial.

CHARLES H. WHITEBREAD

Bibliography

FRANKEL, MARVIN E. 1977 *The Grand Jury: An Institution on Trial.* New York: Hill & Wang.

INDIGENT

An indigent is a person too poor to provide for certain basic needs. It would be unconstitutional for a state or the national government deliberately to deny benefits or impose burdens on the basis of a person's indigency. To this extent, today's law fulfills Justice ROBERT H. JACKSON's prescription, concurring in EDWARDS V. CALIFORNIA (1941): "The mere state of being without funds is a neutral fact—constitutionally an irrelevance, like race, creed, or color." In a market economy, however, indigency is anything but an irrelevance; unrelieved, it bars access to virtually everything money can buy. Unsurprisingly, therefore, the Supreme Court has found in the Constitution affirmative obligations on government to supply to indigents certain benefits that they cannot afford to buy for themselves. These obligations are few in number; the very idea of a market economy implies de facto WEALTH DISCRIMINATION in the sense of differential access to goods and services, and in no sense has the Court declared capitalism unconstitutional. (See FREEDOM OF CONTRACT.)

The first focus for the Court's egalitarian concerns for relieving the poor from consequences of their poverty was the criminal process. In cases such as GRIFFIN V. ILLINOIS (1956) and DOUGLAS V. CALIFORNIA (1963), one doctrinal vehicle was the EQUAL PROTECTION clause. But the goal of "equal justice for poor and rich, weak and powerful alike" contained no easily discernible place to stop, and it was always clear that the Court would not require the states to make unlimited funds available so that all accused persons could match the spending of the very rich on their criminal defense. The alternative to the equality principle was insistence on minimum standards of criminal justice for everyone, and the Court's post-1950 decisions tightening those standards—not merely in areas such as the RIGHT TO COUNSEL or the setting of BAIL but throughout the criminal process—can be seen in this egalitarian light, reflecting a recognition that the criminal justice system generally bears most heavily on the poor.

A similar approach, setting minimum standards of justice, had characterized the Court's treatment of claims by the poor to access to civil courts and administrative hearings. PROCEDURAL DUE PROCESS, not equal protection, provides the doctrinal foundation for this development. A concern for hardship to the poor surely played an important role in decisions such as BODDIE V. CONNECTICUT (1971) (access to divorce courts for persons unable to afford filing fees), *Sniadach v. Family Finance Corp.* (1969) (prior hearings prerequisite for prejudgment garnishment), and GOLDBERG V. KELLY (1970) (prior hearings prerequisite for termination of WELFARE BENEFITS). But just as the Court has stopped far short of a general principle of equal access to criminal justice, so it has refused to make equality the guiding principle for its decisions on access to civil justice; in LASSITER V. DEPARTMENT OF SOCIAL SERVICES (1981) the Court denied the existence of a right to state-appointed counsel in proceedings to terminate parental rights.

The one area where the equality principle has guided the Supreme Court's treatment of poverty is the electoral process. The development began with HARPER V. VIRGINIA STATE BOARD OF ELECTIONS (1966), which invalidated a POLL TAX as a condition on voting in a state election. Property qualifications to vote, too, were invalidated, except in the elections of special-purpose districts. Not only VOTING RIGHTS but also rights of access to the ballot were secured against financial barriers that would disqualify the poor.

The early 1970s marked a turning point in the constitutional protection of indigents against the consequences of their poverty. Since that time, the Court has drawn one line after another constricting the expansion of either equal protection or due process doctrines to impose on government further affirmative obligations to relieve the burdens of poverty—even when those burdens affect the quality of an indigent's relations with government itself.

KENNETH L. KARST

Bibliography

BRUDNO, BARBARA 1976 *Poverty, Inequality, and the Law.* St. Paul, Minn.: West Publishing Co.

INDIRECT TAXES

See: Direct and Indirect Taxes

INFAMY

Our legal system depends upon the reliability of a person's word—his oath as an officer, his promise as a contractor, his testimony as a witness. Under the COMMON LAW, conviction of certain crimes so diminished a person's credibility that he permanently forfeited certain of his CIVIL RIGHTS, his oath was of no legal value, and he was incompetent to testify in court. Infamy, as this is called, resulted from conviction of TREASON, FELONY, or a crime involving willful falsehood. The Fifth Amendment requires PRESENTMENT or INDICTMENT by a GRAND JURY before a person may be tried in federal court for an infamous crime.

In modern political rhetoric, the term "infamy" often means general harm done to a person's reputation, especially as a result of LEGISLATIVE INVESTIGATIONS or other governmental action.

DENNIS J. MAHONEY

INFLUENCE OF THE AMERICAN CONSTITUTION ABROAD

It can easily be argued that America's most important export has been the Constitution of the United States. It was the first single-document CONSTITUTION. It is the longest-lived. And in only two centuries, virtually every nation has come to accept the inevitability and value of having a constitution. This fact transcends differences of culture, history, and legal heritage. The United States Constitution is perceived as the fundamental point of reference, even by regimes whose philosophical outlook is antidemocratic. Furthermore, nearly every nation has accepted the "Philadelphia formula"—either internally or universally—as the means by which an effective constitution can best be produced.

The international impact of the U.S. Constitution is an ongoing reality: most of the world's constitutions have been written in the last forty years, and constitutions are rewritten and revised all the time. The Constitution of the United States continues to be the guiding pattern, and a wellspring of inspiration and innovation. The fundamental idea behind the U.S. Constitution was the belief that the people of a nation comprise the constituent power. The founders of this country, conceiving of the people as the sovereign, asserted that the people themselves could formulate and promulgate a constitution. The idea of a constitutional convention was the natural expression of this concept, for it literally embodied the SOVEREIGNTY of the people.

Universally influential also have been the American ratification and amending processes. For it was these that gave the U.S. Constitution—and all subsequent constitutions—the essential characteristic of permanence. Prior to the creation of such machinery, any law could be superseded by another law. Now it is no longer possible. A method had been created for public approbation of the work of the constitution-makers before the constitution could come into effect. And a method had been created for constitutional change to be effected by that public. Every constitution has since copied or been guided by those formulations. Indeed, the very nature of maintaining permanent written constitutions depends upon the creation of these political devices.

The federal structure—the essential product of the U.S. Constitution—innovated a means by which local and central power could be reconciled. The underlying assumption was that the citizenry, and not the government, is sovereign and is the source of derived power. Thus was established a basis for maintaining national unity, and it has been widely adapted.

Australia, Canada, West Germany, Switzerland, Yugoslavia, and, most recently, Nigeria boast of adherence to American concepts in the creation of their own federal structure and so to a lesser extent do Argentina, Brazil, Mexico, and Venezuela.

The United States was the first nation to have an elected head of state called a president. It was a constitutionally created president, described by HAROLD J. LASKI as "both more and less than a king; both more and less than a prime minister." Today more than half the world's nations have presidents as their chief executives, some with even more constitutional power than the American president (France, South Africa), many with only nominal ceremonial powers (India, Zimbabwe).

The American Constitution formalized the concepts required to make such a system work: the SEPARATION OF POWERS and the system of CHECKS AND BALANCES. The result balances leadership and minimizes abuse, encourages stability and obviates tyranny.

It is now universally understood—as it was by a vocal American citizenry that backed the BILL OF RIGHTS 200 years ago—that fundamental freedoms cannot be guaranteed merely by good intentions. The ratifiers of the U.S. Constitution taught that there could be no fundamental law of the land without a separate section listing individual rights. With the adoption of the Canadian Charter of Rights and Freedoms in 1982, the United Kingdom is the only major nation without a constitutional Bill of Rights, although such has been proposed. The belief that liberties require an explicit statement in order to assure their protection animates political endeavors and constitutionalism throughout the world today.

The sheer longevity of America's constitutional experiment illuminates with each passing year a great, yet hidden strength of the U.S. Constitution: It is a device for assuring national dialogue and conflict resolution. The legislative branch, the executive, and especially the judiciary are more than divisions of government. They are America's ongoing constitutional convention. And as much as anything, this aspect of their identities explains why the American constitutional model remains so attractive and thought-provoking at its bicentennial.

Any study of the international influence of the U.S. Constitution must take into account the fact that this influence is both historic and ongoing. And it should consider how American guidelines, practices, and innovations have been improved on by other nations. But more would be accomplished than just a study of the past. A new understanding would be achieved, of what is fundamental to the American Constitution and what is ephemeral, of what is exportable, and even universally applicable.

So pervasive has been the influence of the Constitution of the United States that most nations have followed its lead by adopting one-document constitutions of their own. Beginning in 1791 with Poland and France, the American concept of a constitution to create government speedily became the norm.

Although some nations are under martial rule or have a transitional government with their constitutions in suspension, all but the United Kingdom, New Zealand, and Israel are committed to the concept and principle of the one-document constitution and all have such a document in some stage of preparation or have one in place. Significantly, the act of constitutional suspension has become the most extreme political act of modern government. What makes this American-influenced constitutional universality so historically significant is its short duration on the world stage.

What has made the U.S. Constitution so admired and so imitated? It was not the establishment of a supreme LAW OF THE LAND; that was no innovation. Plato taught in *The Laws* that "some body of law should exist on a permanent basis, on a superior plane—neither subject to individual tyranny nor to raw majority democracy." Historian K. C. Wheare noted that "from the earliest times . . . people had thought it proper or necessary to write down in a document the fundamental principles upon which their government for the future should be established and conducted."

Nor was it the theory of LIMITED GOVERNMENT that intrigued foreign statesmen. Even the notions of establishing a republic or electing a president or the radical concept of POPULAR SOVEREIGNTY were already commonplace—at least in theory. The philosophers of the Enlightenment and their forebears all had written on such subjects and were familiar with each other's works. And there had already existed such governmental documents as the 1579 Act of Union of the United Provinces of the Netherlands, but until the American experience no one had thought of calling their documents "constitutions."

The written constitution is an American innovation. Its genesis can be traced to THOMAS HOOKER's FUNDAMENTAL ORDERS OF CONNECTICUT (1639) which was the first to create a state or governmental entity. This prefigured the state constitutions of Virginia and Pennsylvania, which in turn influenced the French Declaration of the Rights of Man. The U.S. Constitution, however, was the document that influenced and continues to influence foreign constitution-makers. For since that date nationhood was to be achieved via a constitution.

The primary reason for the great influence of the U.S. Constitution abroad is that it institutionalized government based on the sovereignty of the people. Americans also created the machinery to translate constitutional philosophy into constitutional reality. Their main device was the CONSTITUTIONAL CONVENTION or constituent assembly. This device has been the most significant and most followed precedent in constitutional development. For in this way a nation can be formed and gets its "supreme law of the land" (save in those instances where the former colonial power grants independence and bestows a constitution for independence). The constituent assembly institutionalized democracy. It legitimized revolution, enabling men to do what they had not yet been able to do peacefully and legally—to alter or abolish government and institute new governments deriving their authority from the consent of the governed.

By following the United States model, all constitution writers after 1787 could legitimize their revolutions, their independence, their nationhood. In his study of Latin American political institutions, Jacques Lambert wrote: "Here . . . was the worthy model of a constitution that repudiated monarchy and clearly proclaimed the principle of political freedom. . . . The Constitution of the United States lent authority the cloak of democratic respectability. A few countries very shortly adopted constitutions directly inspired by it—Venezuela in 1811, Mexico in 1824, the Central American Federation in 1825, and Argentina in 1826."

Just by being the first, the U.S. Constitution inevitably influenced constitutions abroad. It was the only available national model for the 1791 constitution-makers of Poland who copied its preamble and its impeachment provisions, and in their famous Article V provided Europe's first statement of popular sovereignty.

Another reason for the widespread influence of the United States Constitution abroad is that constitutions are largely written by lawyers, and lawyering normally involves the search for source and precedent. Lawyers have dominated the constituent assemblies and constitutional conventions abroad. The lawyer constitutionalists of America were also proselytizers. They shared the gospel so often proclaimed by THOMAS JEFFERSON. "We feel," he wrote, "that we are acting under obligations not confined to the limits of our own society. It is impossible not to be sensible that we are acting for all mankind."

This message has been well received, starting with France and the men who made the French Revolution. The fact that the constitution consisted of lawyers' ideas contributed to their ready transmittal. Lawyers were popular; the Dantons and Robespierres had sided with the people in their revolt against authority. Jacques Vincent de la Croix, a lawyer, offered a course on the Constitution of the United States at the Lycée de Paris, an institution of free higher education established in 1787. This pattern has continued. The lawyer has been the commoner charged with teaching constitutionalism and translating the needs and aspirations of the people into a legal document. Every constitutional lawyer in the world knows about the U.S. Constitution.

The lawyers who wrote the American constitutions also wrote about them. JOHN ADAMS, author of the MASSACHUSETTS CONSTITUTION and prime "inventor" of the concept of a constitutional convention, could not be in Philadelphia in 1787 as he was then envoy to England. But his *Defence of the Constitutions of Government of the United States of America* was one of the most influential works on constitutionalism, at home and abroad.

Even more influential was THE FEDERALIST, almost immediately translated into French, German, and Spanish to provide constitutional guidelines for a dozen or more nations in Europe and Latin America. Now translated into more than twenty languages, *The Federalist* is still taught in constitutional law classes abroad and new translations are still being published.

The records of the 1848 German constitutional assembly at Frankfurt contain references not only to the U.S. Constitution and *The Federalist* but also to the constitutional commentaries of Justice JOSEPH STORY and Chancellor JAMES KENT. Modern examples abound, with copious references in India's 1947 Constituent Assembly Debates, and, more recently, in the commentaries on the Nigerian Constitution of 1979.

The tradition of the American participant, counsel, or consultant in foreign constitution-making dates from the service of THOMAS PAINE as a member of the 1791 French constitutional assembly. Lawrence Ward Beer wrote of the American role in constitution-making in Asia: "A basic context for American influence has been the *consultation* of American experts on constitutionalism and law during the process of drawing up, applying, interpreting, or amending a national constitution. Concretely, the views of individual American judges and legal scholars have been solicited during visits by Asian constitutionalists to America; American legal literature (including judicial precedent) has been studied, and many Americans have been directly involved in Asian constitution-making."

And the tradition continues. Americans have influenced the writing of constitutions for nations throughout the world, including Liberia, China, Ethiopia, Nigeria, Zimbabwe, Bangladesh, and Peru. ALEXIS DE TOCQUEVILLE was the best known of the foreigners who came to study United States government and who returned home as advocates of the American system. His *Democracy in America*, published in French editions in 1835 and 1840, heightened interest in the United States constitutional system both in Europe and in Latin America.

But Tocqueville was preceded by scores of other Europeans who were attracted by the hope and promise of the new world, most notably Thaddeus Kosciusko, who was later to lead the struggle for democracy in Poland. And Tocqueville was followed by many thousands of scholars in law, government, history, and political science who likewise transported American constitutional ideology. Current manifestations of this development are apparent in the 1982 constitutions of Canada and Honduras and the 1983 constitution of El Salvador.

The United States, a great colonizer, has offered a solution to colonialism. As pointed out by Henry Steele Commager:

> No Old World nation had known what to do with colonies except to exploit them for the benefit of the mother country. The new United States was born the largest nation in the Western world and was, from the beginning and throughout the 19th century, a great colonizing power with a hinterland that stretched westward to the Mississippi and, eventually,

to the Pacific. [And thence beyond the mainland to Alaska and Hawaii.] By the simple device of transforming colonies into states, and admitting these states into the union on the basis of absolute equality with the original states, the Founding Fathers taught the world a lesson which it has learned only slowly and painfully down to our own day.

This constitutional concept has been studied and followed in France, Portugal, Spain, Yugoslavia, and the Soviet Union, to provide a few examples, but not always with successful results. Algeria is no longer part of Metropolitan France, but French Guiana, Guadeloupe, Martinique, Reunion, and Saint Pierre and Miquelon are. Angola is no longer an integral part of Portugal, but Madeira and the Azores are.

Another reason for the influence of the American Constitution abroad is rooted in military conquest. Although the influence of the Philadelphia experience had been felt in Baden, Bavaria, Frankfurt, and Württemberg before there was a unified Germany, a more general reception of American style constitutionalism attended the preparation of the post-World War II 1949 Basic Law of the Federal Republic. Similarly, the "MacArthur Constitution" influenced—to use an understatement of the greatest order—Japan's 1947 constitution.

Under United States military authority following the Spanish-American War, Cuba's 1901 constitution bears obvious American imprints. And so does the 1904 constitution of Panama, which in Article 136 gave the United States authority to intervene to establish "constitutional order." Haiti's 1918 constitution, putatively the work of then Assistant Secretary of the Navy FRANKLIN D. ROOSEVELT, was based on compromises between existing government forums and the ideologies of the American military forces which had occupied the country since 1915.

American influence was also significant in the preparation of the South Vietnam Constitution of 1967. The Vietnamese actually copied more from the United States model than was appropriate for a nation with a French legal tradition. (The preamble to the North Vietnamese Constitution had been taken directly from Lincoln's Gettysburg Address.)

Most pervasive has been the influence of the U.S. Constitution upon its former colony, the Republic of the Philippines. Under American sovereignty from 1896 until its independence in 1946, the Philippines were given a commonwealth constitution in 1935 which remained virtually unchanged until 1973. And on the eve of the American constitutional bicentennial there was a significant movement to call a new constitutional convention in Manila. A new constitutional structure will predictably once again follow the Philadelphia model.

ALBERT P. BLAUSTEIN

Bibliography

BEER, LAWRENCE W. 1979 *Constitutionalism in Asia: Asian Views of the American Influence.* Berkeley: University of California Press.

BLAUSTEIN, ALBERT P. 1984 The United States Constitution: A Model in Nation Building. *National Forum* 64:14–17.

BLAUSTEIN, ALBERT P. and FLANZ, GISBERT H., EDS. 1971 *Constitutions of the Countries of the World.* 20 Vols. looseleaf, updated quarterly. Dobbs Ferry, N.Y.: Oceana.

CAPPELLETTI, MAURO 1971 *Judicial Review in the Contemporary World.* Indianapolis: Bobbs-Merrill.

COMMAGER, HENRY STEELE 1977 *The Empire of Reason: How Europe Imagined and America Realized the Enlightenment.* Garden City, N.Y.: Anchor Press/Doubleday.

HAWGOOD, JOHN A. 1939 *Modern Constitutions Since 1787.* New York: Macmillan.

HENDERSON, DAN FENNO, ED. 1968 The Constitution of Japan: Its First Twenty Years, 1947–67. Seattle: University of Washington Press.

PALMER, R. R. 1959 *The Age of the Democratic Revolution: A Political History of Europe and America, 1760–1800.* 2 Vols. Princeton, N.J.: Princeton University Press.

STARCK, CHRISTIAN, ED. 1983 *Main Principles of the German Basic Law.* Baden-Baden: Nomos.

INFORMANT'S TIP

A police officer's own observations may not be required to establish PROBABLE CAUSE for an ARREST WARRANT or SEARCH WARRANT (or for an arrest without warrant). Probable cause may be established by an informant's tip, even if it is hearsay, if there is adequate basis to credit his word. The Supreme Court has, however, been troubled by the criteria necessary to determine an informant's truthfulness.

DRAPER V. UNITED STATES (1959) was the first case to hold that an informant's word, when corroborated, was sufficient to establish probable cause; the informant had previously proved reliable, and his story was later substantially verified by the officer's own observations. AGUILAR V. TEXAS (1964) established a "two-pronged" test, amplified in SPINELLI V. UNITED STATES (1969) and generally followed until 1983: the affidavit (or the officer's personal testimony) must make clear to the magistrate, first, some of the underlying circumstances from which the *informant* concluded that criminal activity was afoot (such as personal observation of the suspect's action), and second, some of the circumstances from which the *officer* concluded that the informant was telling the truth (for example, his previous record of reliability). Failure fully to satisfy either "prong" could be remedied by substituting highly detailed information (even of a nonsuspicious nature) demonstrating that the informant's statement was based neither on rumor nor on the suspect's bad reputation.

In ILLINOIS V. GATES (1983) the Court abandoned the *Aguilar-Spinelli* test in favor of a much looser "totality of the circumstances" approach, which would permit "a balanced assessment of the relative weight of all the various indicia of reliability." Thus, said the Court, the report of an informant who had previously been usually reliable would be acceptable even if it did not explain the basis of his knowledge.

The need to corroborate an informant's statement and demonstrate his reliability arises when the informant has a criminal past; his veracity is naturally suspect. The word of a law enforcement officer who provides information to another officer or that of an honest private citizen without ulterior motive requires no such corroboration according to the decision in *Ventresca v. United States* (1965). Uncorroborated anonymous tips to the police are worthless for establishing probable cause.

In order to prevent reprisals and maintain the future effectiveness of informants, the Court denied in MCCRAY V. ILLINOIS (1967) that a defendant has the right to demand the identity of a government informant at a suppression hearing on the question of probable cause. The accuracy of statements, including those of informants, in affidavits for warrants can be challenged at a hearing if the defendant offers proof that the affiant lied or acted with "reckless disregard for the truth" in statements pertinent to the establishment of probable cause. The warrant's legality will not be affected by an informant's misrepresentation, however, if the officer had no reason to doubt the truth of the informant's statement.

JACOB W. LANDYNSKI

Bibliography

LAFAVE, WAYNE R. 1978 *Search and Seizure: A Treatise on the Fourth Amendment.* Vol. 1:489–586. St. Paul, Minn.: West Publishing Co.

IN FORMA PAUPERIS

(Latin: "In the manner of a poor person.") To insure that ACCESS TO THE COURTS is not barred by inability to pay the costs of litigation, poor persons may have fees and some procedural requirements waived and counsel appointed at public expense. In the federal courts this privilege is granted by law to anyone swearing he is without means.

More than half the petitions received by the Supreme Court are filed *in forma pauperis,* often by prisoners seeking review of criminal convictions or of denials of HABEAS CORPUS petitions on constitutional grounds. Probably the most famous case to arise in this way was GIDEON V. WAINWRIGHT (1963).

DENNIS J. MAHONEY

INFORMATION

An information is a formal written accusation against a person for a criminal offense presented under oath by a public officer, usually a prosecutor. An information is used to charge an individual with criminal activity in cases where an INDICTMENT by a GRAND JURY is unnecessary or is waived by the accused. Like an indictment, the filing of an information results in the commencement of a formal prosecution. Thus, the information must be clear and specific in order to give adequate notice to the accused of the charges against him and permit him to prepare his defense.

Most states permit prosecution by information or indictment at the option of the prosecutor. In these states, it is rare for a prosecutor not to use an information because it is easier and less time-consuming than an indictment. Grand jury indictments will be used in these jurisdictions only when the prosecutor wants to use the investigative powers of the grand jury. In other states, indictments are required in all FELONY cases or in all capital cases. However, even in these states, informations are used in MISDEMEANOR cases and in felony cases where the accused has waived his right to a grand jury indictment.

In federal misdemeanor cases, prosecutors have the option under the FEDERAL RULES OF CRIMINAL PROCEDURE to proceed by indictment or information. In federal felony cases, accused individuals have the right to insist on prosecution by indictment, but this right can be waived in all but capital cases.

Most jurisdictions limit the prosecutor's discretion to file an information. Generally, the prosecutor cannot file an information unless the accused has had a preliminary hearing before a magistrate. This requirement is designed to weed out groundless charges, thereby relieving an accused of the burden of preparing a defense. However, the effectiveness of this limitation on prosecutorial abuse in filing informations is undercut in several ways. First, in most jurisdictions, a finding of no PROBABLE CAUSE by one magistrate at a preliminary hearing does not preclude presenting the case to another magistrate. Thus, a prosecutor can "shop around" for a magistrate who will find the requisite probable cause and enable the prosecutor to file an information.

In addition, in filing an information, the prosecutor is not always bound by the findings of the magistrate at the preliminary hearing. Some states permit the prosecutor to charge the accused in the information only with the crimes for which the magistrate decided there was probable cause. In other states, the information can charge the offense for which the accused was bound over at the preliminary hearing and any other offenses supported by the EVIDENCE at the preliminary hearing.

Another problem with using the preliminary hearing as a check on the prosecutor's decision to file an information is that the prosecutor often dominates the magistrate's hearing. Furthermore, in *Gerstein v. Pugh* (1975), the Supreme Court implied that the federal Constitution does not require a preliminary judicial hearing to determine whether there is probable cause for the prosecutor to file an information.

CHARLES H. WHITEBREAD

Bibliography

AMERICAN BAR ASSOCIATION, SECTION OF CRIMINAL JUSTICE 1977 *Policy on the Grand Jury.* Washington, D.C.: ABA Section of Criminal Justice.

INGERSOLL, JARED
(1749–1822)

Jared Ingersoll represented Pennsylvania at the CONSTITUTIONAL CONVENTION OF 1787 and signed the Constitution. Although reputed the best trial lawyer in Philadelphia, he was not a frequent speaker at the convention. He unenthusiastically described the plan proposed by the convention as "all things considered, most eligible."

DENNIS J. MAHONEY

INGRAHAM v. WRIGHT
430 U.S. 651 (1977)

Two Florida junior high school students, disciplined by severe paddling, sued school officials for damages and injunctive relief, claiming that the paddling constituted CRUEL AND UNUSUAL PUNISHMENT. They also claimed that they had been deprived of their right to a prior hearing in violation of their PROCEDURAL DUE PROCESS rights. The lower federal courts denied relief, and the Supreme Court affirmed, 5–4.

For the majority, Justice LEWIS F. POWELL, a former school board president, concluded that the guarantee against cruel and unusual punishment was limited to cases of punishment for criminal offenses and thus had no application to paddling as a means of school discipline. The openness of public schools provided a safeguard against abusive punishments of the kind that might be visited on prisoners. COMMON LAW restraints on the privilege of school officials to administer corporal punishment were sufficient to prevent excesses. As for due process, Powell conceded that the paddling had implicated a "liberty" interest, but he concluded that due process required no hearing, in view of the availability of common law remedies or damages.

For the dissenters, Justice BYRON R. WHITE argued that it was anomalous to conclude that some punishments are "cruel and unusual" when inflicted on convicts but raise no such problem when they are inflicted on children for breaches of school discipline. The relevant inquiry, White argued, was not the label of criminal punishment but the purpose to punish. While some spanking might be permissible in public schools, the majority was wrong in saying "that corporal punishment in the public schools, no matter how barbaric, inhumane, or severe, is never limited by the Eighth Amendment." Here the record showed not just spanking but severe beatings. Furthermore, the risk of erroneous punishment—a crucial aspect of the due process calculus established in MATHEWS V. ELDRIDGE (1976)—demanded at least some informal discussion between student and disciplinarian before paddling was administered. The common law damages remedy offered no redress for punishments mistakenly administered in good faith and obviously could not undo the infliction of pain.

Ingraham seems an unstable precedent. Constitutional law, following social practice, has increasingly insisted that children be treated as persons, as members of the community deserving of respect. (See CHILDREN'S RIGHTS.) The due process right to a hearing rests partly on the premise that the dignity of being heard, before the state takes away one's liberty or property, is one of the differences between being a participating citizen and being an object of administration. The *Ingraham* majority, unmoved by such concerns, reflected nostalgia for a day when children were seen and not heard.

KENNETH L. KARST

INHERENT POWERS

In theory the Constitution establishes the institutions of the national government and vests those institutions with their responsibilities. Such a government is one of delegated powers. Some of these powers are expressed, others are implied. But all powers of the government—expressed and implied—are delegated powers originating in deliberate acts of the sovereign people. This theory cannot successfully deny that the Constitution may in fact succumb to "necessity," or prove inadequate in contingencies beyond human foresight and control. Nor does it deny that the document's terms (like "due process" and "executive power") are open to construction in light of broader ideas and needs. It simply means that to be lawful, a move of the government must fall within a range permitted by arguable interpretations of constitutional language and tradition.

Constitutional theory can admit a notion of "inherent power" in a sense of IMPLIED POWER as in inherent powers of executive privilege and removal of certain administrative appointees. But constitutional theory cannot admit the doctrine of "inherent power" that finds governmental powers beyond those that have been delegated expressly or by implication on the argument that a government must have certain powers before it can be considered a real government. This strong sense of inherent power is the subject here.

A doctrine of inherent power is frequently asserted in connection with a right to national self-preservation, which, as an inherent power, would differ from implied powers, like an implied power of national defense. Looked upon as an implied but still delegated power, a power of national defense can be derived from such expressed constitutional provisions as authorizing Congress to raise, support, and govern military and naval forces, and to declare war. Questions about the scope of an implied power of national defense would have to be answered in ways that would retain its status as part of a greater whole. A constitutionally derived power of national defense would be consistent with the SEPARATION OF POWERS, individual rights, and other provisions, or arguable interpretations thereof. By contrast, inherent powers need not be consistent with other constitutional provisions; asserting them does not require the interpretive adjustments needed to make something fit into a greater whole. A power to suspend elections and declare a dictatorship during a foreign invasion might become a practical necessity, but it could not be considered an implied power of national defense because no plausible interpretation of the Constitution could make room for such a power.

Appeals to inherent power should be distinguished from appeals to HIGHER LAW to which the Constitution might be open. The latter provide arguments for interpreting the Constitution in certain ways. The former propose reasons that might justify violating or suspending the Constitution. Historically, the former usually invoke considerations of "necessity" or "self-preservation" as reasons for ignoring the separation of powers and the BILL OF RIGHTS. These considerations have surfaced in decisions to put innocent Americans in war-time concentration camps and to deny that the government has an obligation to treat ALIENS fairly. They have been used to rationalize congressional abdications of responsibility, especially in FOREIGN AFFAIRS. They therefore imply the supremacy of material safety over constitutional ideals and structures, even over the Constitution itself as a product of deliberative reason.

A strong doctrine of inherent power may have seemed necessary to constitutional theory as a way to circumvent artificially narrow conceptions of national power originating largely in a STATES' RIGHTS parochialism. But this is no longer the problem it used to be. Understanding national powers in terms of the broad ends to which they point—national defense, for example,—reduces the need for a doctrine of inherent power—unless precisely what is sought is justification for ignoring the Constitution.

SOTIRIOS A. BARBER

(SEE ALSO: *Constitutional Reason of State; Delegation of Power; Enumerated Powers; Necessary and Proper Clause; Tenth Amendment.*)

Bibliography

HENKIN, LOUIS 1972 *Foreign Affairs and the Constitution.* Mineola, N.Y.: Foundation Press.

LOFGREN, CHARLES A. 1973 United States v. Curtiss-Wright Export Corp.: An Historical Reassessment. *Yale Law Journal* 83:1–32.

INITIATIVE

Initiative is the practice by which legislation may be proposed and voted on directly by the people (rather than their representatives). Its adoption was an important element of the Progressive era political reform movement. Of some twenty states that now use the initiative all but Alaska adopted it before 1919. Initiative makes possible enactment of legislation that contravenes the class interest of politicians—such as tax reduction and limitation on public expenditure.

Restrictions on the initiative process, such as a requirement for an extraordinary majority to enact housing legislation, have been held to violate the EQUAL PROTECTION clause of the FOURTEENTH AMENDMENT when the Justices were convinced that the intent was to disadvantage racial minorities.

Although the people of a state may reserve a portion of the legislative power, they may not, by initiative, directly exercise powers (for example, RATIFICATION OF AMENDMENTS) conferred on the state legislatures by the federal Constitution.

DENNIS J. MAHONEY

INJUNCTION

In use long before the Constitution, the injunction in the twentieth century came to play one of its most important roles as the enforcer of constitutional and CIVIL RIGHTS. Precisely because it is effective, flexible, and open-ended, the injunction has drawn opposition, and constitutional cases have often included fierce battles over whether the injunction ought to be used as a remedy. These battles have resulted in some complex judicially imposed limitations on the use of injunctions in public law cases.

The injunction rests on a simple idea: that a court may order someone to perform or to cease some action. However simple the idea, it was not a usual feature of the earliest English COMMON LAW. Although it is inaccurate to say that early common law never commanded the performance of an action, by the sixteenth century its typical judgment simply decreed that A, having won the suit, was entitled to "take" some sum of money from B. If B did not cooperate, A could often gain the assistance of the sheriff, but B was subject to no direct order to do anything.

By contrast to the common law courts, the Court of Chancery administered a system of remedies that came to be called EQUITY, vindicated by an order directing someone to do or cease doing something. At an early stage only the imagination of the Chancellor, who presided over the court, limited the precise nature of such orders. Equity has never lost this tradition of flexibility and discretion, but as Chancery developed a sense of precedent, the occasions for such orders began to seem standardized. For example, a court might require a defendant to perform a trust, to convey land, to carry out a contract, or to pay money owed to a business partner. Some orders, typically those forbidding an action (for example, requiring a party to halt a lawsuit or to cease polluting a stream), came to be called injunctions, though the term "injunctive relief" is often used broadly to refer to direct judicial orders of many sorts. Such equitable remedies always remained relatively discretionary: Chancery would not, for example, enter an injunction in all cases; the litigant seeking such an order first had to convince that court that his remedy at law (*i.e.*, from the common law courts) would be "inadequate," a deceptively simple term that over five centuries has taken on some surprising baggage. Because of this requirement a litigant can have a valid legal right for which, however, he cannot obtain injunctive relief.

In America before the civil rights era the injunction saw its most controversial use in labor disputes in which courts, acting on the view that union organizing and strikes were either common law torts or violations of antitrust statutes, frequently enjoined strikes or PICKETING by workers. Such actions engendered great bitterness and led to Congress's withdrawing from federal courts JURISDICTION to enter an injunction in any labor dispute. (See NORRIS-LAGUARDIA ACT.) That withdrawal in turn has bolstered arguments in favor of occasional proposals to withdraw injunctive jurisdiction in other areas in which courts were enforcing unpopular decisions.

In the late twentieth century the injunction has had its most prominent career not as a remedy in tort, contract, and property disputes but as a vindicator of civil rights. That new role flowed largely from EX PARTE YOUNG (1908), which held that although SOVEREIGN IMMUNITY might bar a damage action against a state, it did not bar injunctive relief against a state official acting unconstitutionally. This development meant that even if there was no remedy for past unlawful action, an injunction could halt continuation of that activity. Until the birth of the modern civil rights damage action with MONROE V. PAPE (1961) and the CIVIL RIGHTS ACTS of the 1960s, the injunction served as a primary tool for the enforcement of civil and constitutional rights.

Because the injunction is open-ended, it has the potential for use in a wide variety of contexts. Not only can simple acts be required or forbidden but, more important, elaborate public institutions can be restructured. Probably the most noteworthy and certainly the most controversial use of injunctive relief came in the years following BROWN V. BOARD OF EDUCATION (1954) as the courts ordered school systems to end racial SEGREGATION. Drawing on their experience in complex antitrust and BANKRUPTCY cases, the courts employed the injunction as a tool for the reorganization of the schools. In the case of recalcitrant systems, such desegregation decrees sometimes called forth elaborate and detailed orders concerning the assignment of students and teachers, the curriculum, and other details of the schools' operation. Such orders often engendered resistance and involved the courts in the conduct of the schools over a number of years in particularly intractable cases. Courts have also ordered injunctive relief in INSTITUTIONAL LITIGATION involving PRISONERS' RIGHTS and the rights of mental patients.

Part of what makes the injunction such a powerful and controversial tool is the enforcement power that stands behind it. One disobeying an injunction is subject to CONTEMPT penalties—with the threat of indefinite imprisonment and mounting fines until one obeys the order. Perhaps because the injunction carries with it such a formidable arsenal for enforcement, the Supreme Court has enunciated a series of restrictions on the use of injunctive relief in favor of litigants wishing to challenge official action. Thus a federal court may abstain from deciding the constitutionality of a state practice until the state courts have had an opportunity to clarify the law or practice in question, as in *Railroad Commission of Texas v. Pullman Co.* (1941). Moreover, even if the law or practice is clear, a federal court should refrain from adjudicating the constitutionality of a state statute if the challenger of the statute will have an adequate opportunity to present that challenge in pending litigation to which the state is a party (YOUNGER V. HARRIS, 1971). Both the so-called *Pullman* and *Younger* ABSTENTION doctrines have complexities not hinted at in these summaries; they testify to the power of the injunction and its centrality in much modern constitutional litigation.

STEPHEN C. YEAZELL

Bibliography

FISS, OWEN 1978 *The Civil Rights Injunction.* Bloomington: Indiana University Press.

FRANKFURTER, FELIX and GREENE, NATHAN 1930 *The Labor Injunction.* New York: Macmillan.

IN PERSONAM

(Latin: "Against the person.") A legal action or case is *in personam* if it is directed against a particular individual to enforce an obligation. Cases in EQUITY proceed *in personam.*

DENNIS J. MAHONEY

IN RE

(Latin: "In the matter [of]. . . .") This is a way of titling a case that presents a question to be decided or an action to be taken in the absence of adversary parties.

DENNIS J. MAHONEY

IN RE . . .

See under name of party

IN REM

(Latin: "Against the thing.") A legal action or case is *in rem* if it undertakes to establish the title to or status of a thing with respect to all persons.

DENNIS J. MAHONEY

INSTITUTIONAL LITIGATION

"Institutional litigation" refers to cases in which the courts, responding to allegations that conditions in some institutions violate the Constitution or CIVIL RIGHTS statutes, become involved in supervising the institutions in question. Loosely used, the term might describe any number of lawsuits, ranging from an assertion of discriminatory employment practices in a CORPORATION to an attack by inmates on the conditions at a state prison. What such apparently diverse cases have in common is the possibility that if the plaintiffs convince the court that a violation of the law has occurred and if the institution proves recalcitrant in remedying the violation, the court may become involved in detailed supervision of the institution over long periods. Though details of such complex suits naturally vary widely, it is the combination of continuous judicial scrutiny and detailed substantive involvement that has characterized institutional litigation.

Laws such as those forbidding discrimination in employment apply to both public and private institutions. Many constitutional provisions, however, guarantee rights only against the government and most institutions to which individuals are involuntarily committed are run by the government. Consequently most of the institutions involved have been public: prisons, mental hospitals, school systems, and the like. Moreover, though the Constitution binds both state and federal courts, the latter tribunals have played the most active role in vindicating constitutional rights. The typical institutional case therefore has involved a federal district court supervising the conduct of a state institution, a setting that has raised constitutional concerns beyond those of the particular substantive law of the case.

From a wide perspective one can trace the roots of institutional litigation to earlier classes of cases: nineteenth-century EQUITY receiverships, bankruptcy reorganizations, antitrust decrees requiring the restructuring of a large industry, even to the efforts of fifteenth-century English chancellors to enforce the duties of trustees to establish and supervise the religious and charitable institutions endowed in a will. Modern institutional cases also have more recent origins in the efforts of the federal judiciary to desegregate schools in the 1950s and 1960s. Resistance to simple desegregation decrees forced federal courts to become involved in many details of local school administration. As some school boards adjusted their strategies for resistance, courts delved deeper into school board practices, to the point of displacing some traditional school board functions. In GRIFFIN v. SCHOOL BOARD OF PRINCE EDWARD COUNTY (1964) the Supreme Court even suggested that a federal court could order taxes imposed to raise funds to finance a public school system that officials had closed to avoid desegregation.

At about the same time courts were articulating other constitutional rights, including constitutional limitations on prison and mental hospital conditions. In cases such as *Wyatt v. Stickney* (1971) and *Holt v. Sarver* (1969) lower federal courts combined the procedural aggressiveness of the school desegregation cases with the newly developed constitutional rights, enforcing their decrees against recalcitrant officials with INJUNCTIONS backed by the force of the contempt power. In dozens of institutional cases in the 1970s these same forces triggered widespread court-ordered institutional reform that covered such details of institutional life as cell size, visiting hours, telephone privileges, hygiene, and disciplinary procedures.

Describing institutional litigation and tracing its origins are easier than isolating, much less resolving, the controversies that surround it. Nearly all the issues that arise in public discourse about a federal system and an independent judiciary eventually appear in some discussion of institutional litigation. Perhaps the most central of these issues are questions about the relationship of institutional litigation to (1) the nature of litigation; (2) the judicial capacity to run institutions; (3) the power of the purse; and (4) FEDERALISM.

Some view institutional cases as a form of litigation previously unknown to Anglo-American jurisprudence. In the contrasted traditional vision of litigation, a lawsuit involves two parties who present an isolatable set of facts to a court, which issues a JUDGMENT; the losing party complies with the court's decree, and judicial involvement with the case ends. To the extent that this statement of traditional litigation is accurate, institutional litigation involves a substantial departure. In institutional litigation the set of facts presented to the court often constitutes all of the physical, psychological, and social conditions within the institution. Such widespread allegations prevent the court from addressing any single dispute which, when resolved, will restore the parties to a proper relationship. In several institutional cases, no matter how many disputes the court resolves, additional issues arise with respect to implementation of and compliance with previous orders.

The frequency with which institutional litigation requires courts to address some aspect of institutional life highlights the second central issue—judicial capacity to supervise large public institutions. By training, judges are neither wardens nor hospital administrators. Some critics question whether judges should substitute their judgment about institutional life for that of professional administrators appointed by elected officials. Courts often try to compensate for their inexperience by appointing SPECIAL MASTERS and expert advisory panels and by seeking the views of the defendant administrators. But these tactics may raise further questions about institutional litigation's departure from traditional ideas about litigation. Yet, once a court has concluded that institutional life is constitutionally deficient because of the acts of the regular administrators, it is difficult for courts simply to defer to the judgment of those same persons found to be responsible for the unconstitutional conditions.

In many cases, however, institutional conditions are constitutionally deficient less because of the acts of administrators than because the state has allocated insufficient funds to institutional budgets. Even willing administrators experience difficulty in upgrading conditions at some institutions. A new prison building may be necessary or more staff may need to be hired. When institutional reform may be accomplished only through expenditures of substantial sums, a new issue arises: may courts order the allocation of public funds against the wishes of legislators who presumably reflect their constituents' wishes?

For many observers, this fiscal confrontation reveals the least palatable aspect of institutional litigation—the antimajoritarian judicial usurpation of legislative and executive authority. Courts, self-conscious about express allocative decision making, sometimes disavow authority to order funds raised to carry out institutional reform. And, despite *Griffin*'s OBITER DICTUM about imposing taxes, there is doubt about how far courts may and ought to go in ordering funds raised to satisfy their orders. Yet it is also a commonplace for courts to state that lack of funds is no excuse for failure to comply with the Constitution. Since any public law decision may have important fiscal effects, perhaps institutional cases have been unjustifiably isolated from the rest of the public litigation on this issue. Indeed, if one assumes that, put to the choice between releasing inmates and rectifying the conditions of their institutional confinement, the public and their elected officials would choose the latter, judicially decreed funding may be more in accord with the majority's wishes than any other course of action.

Ironically, institutional cases flourished during the 1970s, while the Supreme Court was emphasizing that federal courts should not interfere with traditional state or local functions. In RIZZO V. GOODE (1976) and O'SHEA V. LITTLETON (1974) the Court rejected systemic attacks on, respectively, a police department and a city's system of criminal justice. In YOUNGER V. HARRIS (1971) and its progeny the Court established prohibitions on federal court interference with state adjudicative proceedings. As a doctrinal matter, the issues in most institutional cases proved distinguishable from the issues in *Rizzo*, *O'Shea*, and *Younger*. Nevertheless the Court's federalism theme could have been viewed as requiring curtailment of judicial receptivity to institutional litigation. Yet during this period of growing deference to states, the lower federal courts, without Supreme Court disapproval, continued to hear and resolve institutional cases.

THEODORE EISENBERG
STEPHEN C. YEAZELL

Bibliography

CHAYES, ABRAM 1976 The Role of the Judge in Public Law Litigation. *Harvard Law Review* 89:1281–1316.

DIVER, COLIN S. 1979 The Judge as Political Powerbroker: Superintending Structural Change in Public Institutions. *Virginia Law Review* 65:43–106.

EISENBERG, THEODORE and YEAZELL, STEPHEN C. 1980 The Ordinary and the Extraordinary in Institutional Litigation. *Harvard Law Review* 93:465–517.

FISS, OWEN M. 1979 The Supreme Court 1978 Term, Foreword: The Forms of Justice. *Harvard Law Review* 93:1–58.

INSULAR CASES

Originally applied to three cases decided in 1901, the term "insular cases" has come to denominate a series of cases decided in the early twentieth century defining the place of overseas TERRITORIES in the American constitutional system. Following the acquisition of PUERTO RICO, the Philippines, Hawaii, and various other island possessions, the Supreme Court was called upon to decide whether, or to what extent, in William Jennings Bryan's phrase, "the Constitution follows the flag." From the insular cases emerged the DOCTRINE of INCORPORATION OF TERRITORIES.

The first three insular cases (*DeLima v. Bidwell, Dooley v. United States, Downes v. Bidwell*) were argued together and decided in 1901. They raised the question whether Puerto Rico was part of the United States within the meaning of the "uniformity clause" for purposes of levying customs duties. In *DeLima* and *Dooley*, the Court held that from the Treaty of Paris (1899), by which Spain ceded Puerto Rico to the United States, until the Foraker Act (1900), by which Congress organized the territorial government, the collection of duties on goods moving between the United States and Puerto Rico was unconstitutional. In the far more important *Downes* case, the court upheld collection of duties after passage of the Foraker Act. The apparent meaning of the three cases was that the constitutional status of overseas possessions is for Congress to determine, but constitutional protection is to be assumed in the absence of congressional action. The Justices divided into three schools of thought: four Justices, led by Chief Justice MELVILLE W. FULLER and Justice JOHN MARSHALL HARLAN, contended that the Constitution applied automatically and completely to any territory under United States SOVEREIGNTY; Justice HENRY B. BROWN, who wrote the lead opinion in all three cases, believed that Congress, under Article IV, section 3, enjoyed plenary power over the territories and could extend to them all, any part, or none of the Constitution, at its discretion; and four Justices, led by Justice EDWARD D. WHITE, argued that the Constitution applied fully to the territories only after positive action by the Congress to incorporate them into the United States.

In 1903 and 1904 the Court decided four cases dealing with CRIMINAL PROCEDURE in Hawaii, Puerto Rico, and the Philippines (*Hawaii v. Mankichi, Crowley v. United States, Kepner v. United States, Dorr v. United States*). The Court made a distinction between fundamental or NATURAL RIGHTS, which are constitutionally protected everywhere, and rights merely procedural or remedial, peculiar to Anglo-American jurisprudence, which do not apply in the territories—at least "until Congress shall see fit to incorporate the . . . territory into the United States." In the former category was protection against DOUBLE JEOPARDY; in the latter were INDICTMENT by GRAND JURY, TRIAL BY JURY, and JURY UNANIMITY. *Dorr* (1904) was the first case in which the incorporation of territories doctrine received the formal assent of a majority of the Court.

In the 1905 case of *Rasmussen v. United States*, the Court unanimously held the jury trial guarantee of the SIXTH AMENDMENT applicable to Alaska. White, writing for himself and six colleagues, demonstrated that Congress had explicitly incorporated Alaska into the United States and thus had brought its residents under complete constitutional protection. Harlan and Brown, in separate CONCURRING OPINIONS, each reiterated his original position on the Constitution and the territories.

In *Trono v. United States* (1905) and *Dowdell v. United States* (1911), the Court sustained Philippine criminal convictions obtained through indigenous procedures which would have violated the Sixth Amendment had the Philippines been incorporated territory. But in WEEMS V. UNITED STATES (1910), the Court ruled that since Congress had extended the protection against CRUEL AND UNUSUAL PUNISHMENT to the Philippines, the protection was identical to that enjoyed by mainlanders under the Eighth Amendment.

The most forceful and consistent opposition to the incorporation doctrine came from Justice Harlan. He argued that all of Congress's power flows from the Constitution, and therefore Congress is bound in its every action by that document's limitations and guarantees. The "occult" doctrine of the insular cases, he said, permitted Congress, contrary to the spirit and genius of the Constitution, to erect a colonial empire and exercise absolute dominion over dependent peoples.

In *Board of Public Utilities Commissioners v. Ynchausti* (1920), White, by then Chief Justice, was able to report the Court's unanimous acceptance of the incorporation of territories doctrine; and in *Balzac v. Porto Rico* (1922), Chief Justice WILLIAM HOWARD TAFT, for a unanimous Court, applied it as the settled law governing the status of territories.

DENNIS J. MAHONEY

Bibliography

BLOOM, JOHN PORTER, ED. 1973 *The American Territorial System.* Athens: Ohio University Press.

COUDERT, FREDERICK R. 1926 The Evolution of the Doctrine of Territorial Incorporation. *Columbia Law Review* 66:823–850.

FUSTER, JAIME B. 1974 Origins of the Doctrine of Territorial Incorporation and Its Implications Regarding the Power of the Commonwealth of Puerto Rico to Regulate Interstate Commerce. *Revista Juridica de la Universidad de Puerto Rico* 43:259–294.

SEMONCHE, JOHN E. 1978 *Charting the Future: The Supreme Court Responds to a Changing Society, 1890–1920.* Chaps 5 and 6. Westport, Conn.: Greenwood Press.

INTEGRATION

See: Desegregation; Segregation

INTEREST GROUP LITIGATION

Interest group litigation is sponsored by organizations whose attorneys typically are less interested in specific legal claims than in the constitutional principles that a litigation represents. In contrast, most court cases are pursued for the benefit of the parties directly involved.

In seeking their clients' immediate interests private attorneys sometimes invoke constitutional arguments, but these are incidental to the specific claims of the parties. A sponsored case, however, is often pursued in the name of a litigant even though it is initiated, financed, and supported by an organization seeking its own constitutional goals. Interest groups are particularly attracted to cases involving constitutional principles because the judicial decisions emerging from such cases are relatively insulated from subsequent attacks by legislators and other public officials.

It is arguable, of course, that group-supported litigation has always been in existence. For example, following the WAGNER (NATIONAL LABOR RELATIONS) ACT and other New Deal legislation, litigation was managed, or otherwise assisted, by labor unions, trade associations, stockholder groups, and other business interests. However, the social and economic ferment of the 1960s and 1970s brought interest group litigation into sharper focus. The CIVIL RIGHTS movement and the Vietnam conflict not only produced federal legislation but also stimulated new constitutional demands by litigious organizations representing women, welfare recipients, consumers, and persons resisting military service.

The strategies and tactics of interest group litigants

are heavily influenced by SOCIOLOGICAL JURISPRUDENCE and LEGAL REALISM. These philosophies hold that judges, especially Supreme Court Justices, decide controversial cases by choosing among conflicting goals and policies. Such judges do not reach results or write opinions merely by construing statutes, analogizing cases, or analyzing DOCTRINES. Instead, inquiries into judicial decision making have focused on the ways litigation is influenced by the timing of cases and the quality of the constitutional arguments reaching the appellate courts.

Prototypes of interest group litigation are the cases managed by the United States Department of Justice and similar state agencies. Their attorneys select the appropriate government cases to be appealed, and by confessing error or by compromising cases brought against the government, they seek to inhibit the establishment of unfavorable precedents. Also, a federal Legal Service Corporation, independent of the Department of Justice, has become one of the principal sources for funding and supporting litigation aimed at social and economic reform. Consumers, poor people, prisoners, and other low-resource persons have been represented by government-subsidized attorneys in suits against federal and state agencies and private organizations. Besides managing their own cases, government agencies promote private interest group litigation by reimbursing attorneys who participate and intervene for them in administrative proceedings and in court cases involving ADMINISTRATIVE LAW.

Although strategically less favorably situated than government attorneys, those representing private interest groups are also in a position to choose cases for APPEAL and to control the flow of argument in the higher courts. Unlike government litigation, however, the legal requirements for participation in private law suits sometimes prevent an organization from suing on its own, in behalf of its members, or for a similarly situated class of people. This problem has been partially alleviated by Supreme Court decisions liberalizing rules of legal STANDING to permit lawsuits by environmentalists, taxpayers, and other special interests.

Litigation activity by interest groups is visible in constitutional civil cases as well as in the criminal *cause célèbre.* In some of these cases attorneys representing factions of social movements vie for litigation sponsorship. The extensive publicity often connected with such cases, the constitutional issues perceived to be intertwined in the conflict, and the opportunities for fund-raising sometimes result in interest group controversies. For example, in several church–state cases attorneys representing different organizations have quarreled over the management of litigation. In the "Scottsboro" case, involving blacks accused of rape, attorneys representing civil rights organizations and those representing a communist-sponsored legal defense organization disagreed about the use of trial publicity.

Ideological differences among lawyers are occasionally reflected in varying conceptions of litigation strategy. Some attorneys emphasize the importance of a complete trial record raising all possible legal issues while others concentrate on the constitutional issues.

An alternative approach to a single TEST CASE is a litigation program aimed at accumulating a series of favorable decisions changing constitutional law. An incremental approach emphasizes narrow factual issues and specific claims, and groups with large legal staffs and cooperating attorneys are strategically positioned to conduct litigation in this way. Litigation programs of this kind have achieved changes in the constitutional doctrine governing racial SEGREGATION, CRIMINAL PROCEDURE, selective service, religion, and employment.

In politically tinged criminal cases the less provident and unpopular groups are not likely to use incremental litigation; they usually face immediate problems of securing relief for organization leaders and raising money for their causes. For example, in the 1950s when large numbers of cases involving congressional investigations of communism reached the Supreme Court, the lion's share was controlled by lawyers who depended on individual financial contributions to sustain their legal work.

When litigation is controlled by interest groups, constitutional issues are likely to be advanced and developed at the trial level. The "perfecting of a trial record" also gives the adversaries an opportunity to debate broader issues that are likely to be considered on appeal.

The development of a "good" trial record facilitates the preparation of appellate briefs interlaced with statistical and authoritative bibliographical references to social and economic facts supporting particular constitutional arguments. This technique was first used in the early-twentieth-century social legislation cases, and it has been used to illuminate fields ranging from racial equality to abortion. Similar forms of extralegal argument are found in complex court cases involving PUBLIC UTILITY REGULATION and other economic matters. (See BRANDEIS BRIEF.)

Besides expanding the scope of their arguments,

interest group attorneys have become increasingly adept at coordinating litigation by discouraging the appeal of inconsistent cases or those with less developed records. They have also been successful in getting publication of sympathetic views in legal, scholarly, and popular journals. Networks of attorneys and other observers have also emerged to monitor court decisions and keep central clearinghouses informed about promising court cases.

Sometimes the immediate concerns of the litigants may conflict with those of the sponsoring interest group. A litigant's claim may be compromised or settled. Legal issues advanced by the parties may be formulated so as to avoid the constitutional issues raised by the sponsor. Also, the trial and appellate preparation may be a labor of love, or the work-product of an attorney who jealously guards his professional prerogatives.

A failure to control a litigation does not necessarily mean that an interest group lacks influence. When the issues defined in court are narrow, or the litigant's attorney has failed to develop the case's constitutional implications, an interest group attorney can still participate as AMICUS CURIAE (friend of the court). Nowhere has this phenomenon been more visible than in the medical school admission case, REGENTS OF THE UNIVERSITY OF CALIFORNIA V. BAKKE (1978). In this case fifty-seven organizations submitted amicus curiae briefs to the Supreme Court. Although some interest group attorneys will refrain from submitting such briefs when a client's attorney adequately has argued the constitutional issues, the filing of such a brief does serve the political function of announcing the group's support for a constitutional argument. Amicus curiae participation usually requires the consent of both parties or the approval of the court, and the influence of either briefs or ORAL ARGUMENTS as amicus remains debatable.

Even though interest group litigation is growing, part of the increase is attributable to government legal services and private foundation philanthropy. If government support is curtailed and private foundations are subjected to closer tax scrutiny, individual contributions and voluntary legal services will be called upon to fill the gap. Such a decline in government support seems likely since some judges and political leaders have expressed concern about government-sponsored litigation directed against public officials. They also criticize lawyers who represent causes rather than clients and overburden the judicial process. Other factors affecting the growth of interest group litigation are the strictness of enforcement of traditional restrictions on the scope of law suits (see INSTITUTIONAL LITIGATION) and the rules governing the award of attorneys' fees to interest group attorneys.

Finally, no description of interest group litigation would be complete without noting that many highly publicized civil cases and "showcase" criminal trials as well as ordinary law cases are financed and carried forward without the participation of organized interest groups. The constitutional and policy arguments advanced by attorneys in these cases, in many instances, are just as likely to advance the development of legal and constitutional doctrine.

NATHAN HAKMAN

Bibliography

COUNCIL FOR PUBLIC INTEREST LAW 1976 *Balancing the Scales of Justice: Financing Public Interest Law in America.* Washington, D.C.: Council on Public Interest Law.

HAKMAN, NATHAN 1966 Lobbying the Supreme Court: An Appraisal of "Political Science Folklore." *Fordham Law Review* 35:15–50.

______ 1972 Political Trials in the Legal Order: A Political Scientist's Perspective. *Journal of Public Law* 21:73–126.

KIRCHHEIMER, OTTO 1961 *Political Justice: The Use of Legal Procedure for Political Ends.* Princeton, N.J.: Princeton University Press.

VOSE, CLEMENT E. 1972 *Constitutional Change: Amendment Politics and Supreme Court Litigation Since 1900.* Lexington, Mass.: D. C. Heath.

WEISBROD, BURTON A., HANDLER, JOEL F., and KOMESAR, NEIL K. 1978 *Public Interest Law: An Economical and Institutional Analysis.* Berkeley: University of California Press.

INTERGOVERNMENTAL IMMUNITY

Intergovernmental immunities are exemptions of the state and national governments from attempts to interfere with each other's governmental operations. Thus, one government may claim immunity from the other's regulations and taxes. Though immunity claims may invoke specific provisions such as the TENTH AMENDMENT, they reflect deeper assumptions about the institutional structure envisioned by the Constitution as a whole. Immunity problems originate in the tension between the nation's need to acknowledge the supremacy of federal policies while respecting a tradition of indestructible states. Governmental structures are not ends in themselves in constitutional theory; their ultimate status depends on their efficacy in securing what THE FEDERALIST #45 called "the solid happiness of the people." Implying ends, institutions also imply powers. (See NECESSARY AND PROPER CLAUSE.) Grant the supremacy of national powers over state powers, and the erosion of state institutions follows eventually despite talk of indestructible states. Conversely, protection for state institutions will eventually defeat national power in some respects, talk of federal supremacy notwithstanding. On balance, judicial resolutions of this tension have favored national supremacy.

Immunity claims usually occur in the areas of taxation, regulation, and litigation. Most of the latter involve state claims of immunity from suits by private parties in federal court under the ELEVENTH AMENDMENT. The amendment, however, does not extend immunity that would be considered inconsistent with the Constitution's general plan of government, including the principle of national supremacy. The amendment grants no immunity from suits by other states and the national government. It is not a barrier to Supreme Court review of state court decisions involving federal law. Nor does the amendment bar private plaintiffs seeking federal court injunctions to enforce Congress's CIVIL RIGHTS laws or federal constitutional rights. In *Parden v. Terminal Railway* (1964) the Court declined to exclude state-owned railroads from a congressional act authorizing employees' suits for negligence. The Court reasoned that the state had effectively waived immunity by engaging in activity subject to congressional regulation. Though later decisions gave this doctrine of "constructive waiver" a STATES' RIGHTS twist by requiring clear statements of congressional intent, the Court still assumes that Congress can lift state immunity as necessary for national objectives.

The doctrine that one government cannot tax the instrumentalities of the other is sometimes credited to the OBITER DICTUM in MCCULLOCH V. MARYLAND that power to tax is power to destroy. Chief Justice JOHN MARSHALL made this remark in the course of voiding a state tax on the Second Bank of the United States; he was not seeking to protect the states against Congress. But future Courts transformed Marshall's doctrine of federal immunity into a dual-federalist or states' rights doctrine of reciprocal immunity. In COLLECTOR V. DAY (1871) a Court grown fearful of Reconstruction voided a Civil War federal income tax on the salary of a Massachusetts judge, arguing that if immunity was necessary to preserve the federal government, the same held for the states. Laissez-faire Justices later expanded the immunity doctrine to protect both governments. Items held immune to state taxation included the income of lessees of federal oil lands, sales of gasoline to the national government, and royalties from a federal patent. Fewer decisions went against Congress, but the Court did void some federal taxes, including taxes on income from municipal bonds, profits of state oil leases, and motorcycle sales to a municipal police department.

This pattern of decision ended in the late 1930s as the HUGHES COURT began overruling the most important of the earlier decisions, including those conferring tax immunity on the incomes of governmental officials and contractors. Some tax immunity remains, however. On a theory that combines the principle of national supremacy with the argument that states' interests receive more representation in Congress than national interests receive in state legislatures, the modern Court recognizes a narrower tax immunity for the states than for the national government. Dicta identify state property, state revenues, and traditionally essential state activities as immune to federal taxation. These dicta did not prevent a recent decision upholding a federal registration on state police helicopters. As for federal tax immunity, Congress can confer it on federal contractors and others. Where Congress has not done so, the Court recognizes immunity from state taxation only when the tax legally falls on the federal government itself or its closely connected agencies and instrumentalities. This rule offers no protection to a federal government contractor even where, by contract, the economic impact of a state tax is passed on to the government. The Court continues to invalidate state taxes that discriminate against entities doing business with the federal government or that manifest hostility to federal policy.

Although the SUPREMACY CLAUSE protects federal officials and agencies from state attempts to control the performance of their duties, federal personnel are subject to state laws that do not conflict with federal policies. Indeed, under the federal Assimilative Crimes Act, state criminal law applies to persons on federal enclaves where Congress has not provided otherwise. Examples of state regulations held in conflict with federal policies include attempts to regulate liquor sales and milk prices on military bases and to inspect fertilizer distributed in a national soil conservation program. Until 1985 states were immune from direct federal attempts to interfere in the performance of "functions essential to [the states'] separate and independent existence." The Court failed to give a formula for identifying these essential functions, but they included decisions on where to locate a state capital and the hours and wages of certain state employees. (See NATIONAL LEAGUE OF CITIES V. USERY, 1976.) The Court permitted federal regulation of such "nonessential" state functions as state liquor, timber, and railroad operations and it declined to apply the *Usery* rationale against federal policies affecting state agencies in the areas of civil rights, environmental regulation, and energy policy. The Court overruled *Usery* in 1985 and all but eliminated direct regulatory immunity for the states. (See GARCIA V. SAN ANTONIO METROPOLITAN TRANSIT AUTHORITY, 1985.) Massive, though indirect, federal regulatory control of state policy continues through conditional FEDERAL GRANTS-IN-AID to the states. (See GENERAL WELFARE CLAUSE.)

SOTIRIOS A. BARBER

Bibliography

POWELL, THOMAS REED 1940 Intergovernmental Tax Immunities. *George Washington Law Review* 8:1213–1220.

TRIBE, LAURENCE H. 1978 *American Constitutional Law.* Pages 131–143. Mineola, N.Y.: Foundation Press.

INTERLOCUTORY

The term means temporary, not final, provisional. An interlocutory order is one entered by a court before it renders FINAL JUDGMENT—for example, a preliminary INJUNCTION, to preserve conditions during trial.

KENNETH L. KARST

INTERNAL COMMERCE

See: Intrastate Commerce

INTERNAL IMPROVEMENTS

"Internal Improvements" was the name given to large public works programs in the first half of the nineteenth century. State governments engaged in planning, subsidizing, building, and in some instances owning and operating roads, bridges, canals, and railroads. Most had ambitious programs. None was more successful than New York's Erie Canal. Completed in 1825, it had profound effects on American economic development.

Federal support for internal improvements commenced in 1806 when Congress appropriated money for construction of the Cumberland, or National, Road. The policy was not then a serious constitutional issue, although President THOMAS JEFFERSON, proposing a major program, called for a constitutional amendment to place it beyond cavil. It became a serious constitutional issue after the War of 1812. A federal program was advocated on several grounds: to bind the Union together, to lower the cost of transportation, to effect the "home market" of the AMERICAN SYSTEM. HENRY CLAY and others found constitutional warrant for federal assistance in the powers to establish post roads, to provide for the common defense and GENERAL WELFARE, and to regulate INTERSTATE COMMERCE. In 1817 Congress passed the Bonus Bill to create a permanent fund for internal improvements from the bonus paid by the Bank of the United States for its charter and future dividends on government-owned Bank stock. Surprisingly, President JAMES MADISON, in a return to STRICT CONSTRUCTION principles, vetoed the bill and called for an amendment. His successor, JAMES MONROE, at first took the same position. In 1822, however, he conceded the unlimited power of Congress to appropriate money for improvements of national character, though not to build or operate them. Two years later he approved the General Survey Bill, which offered substantial government assistance. Many projects, the greatest of which was the Chesapeake and Ohio Canal, were launched under federal auspices. The movement was then brought to a virtual halt by President ANDREW JACKSON's veto of the MAYSVILLE ROAD BILL in 1830. He, too, asserted strict construction principles and repeated the call, knowing it to be futile, for a constitutional amendment.

MERRILL D. PETERSON

Bibliography

GOODRICH, CARTER 1960 *Government Promotion of American Canals and Railroads, 1800–1890.* New York: Columbia University Press.

HARRISON, JOSEPH HOPSON 1954 The Internal Improvements Issue in the Politics of the Union, 1783–1825. Ph.D., diss., University of Virginia.

INTERNAL SECURITY ACT
64 Stat. 987 (1950)

The Internal Security Act, or McCarran Act, of 1950 was a massive and complex conglomeration of varied security measures as well as many features of the MUNDT-NIXON BILL and an Emergency Detention

Bill, which had been introduced, unsuccessfully, earlier in 1950. Passed over President HARRY S. TRUMAN's veto in September, shortly after the outbreak of hostilities in Korea, the measure went beyond the Truman loyalty program for government employees and attempted to limit the operation of subversive groups in all areas of American life. It also sought to shift the authority for security matters to congressional leadership.

The measure, the most severe since the SEDITION ACT of 1918, was composed of two parts. Title I, known as the Subversive Activities Control Act, required communist organizations to register with the attorney general and furnish complete membership lists and financial statements. Although membership and office holding in a communist organization was not, by the act, a crime, the measure did make it illegal knowingly to conspire to perform any act that would "substantially contribute" to the establishment of a totalitarian dictatorship in the United States. It also forbade employment of communists in defense plants and granting them passports. Finally it established a bipartisan SUBVERSIVE ACTIVITIES CONTROL BOARD to assist the attorney general in exposing subversive organizations. In ALBERTSON V. SUBVERSIVE ACTIVITIES CONTROL BOARD (1965), the Court held the compulsory registration provisions unconstitutional. (See MARCHETTI V. UNITED STATES, 1968.)

Title II provided that when the President declared an internal security emergency, the attorney general was to apprehend persons who were likely to engage in, or conspire with others to engage in, acts of espionage or sabotage and intern them "in such places of detention as may be prescribing by the Attorney General." Congress subsequently authorized funds for special camps for such purposes. (See PREVENTIVE DETENTION.) Other provisions denied entrance to the country to ALIENS who were members of communist organizations or who "advocate[d] the economic, international, and governmental doctrines of any other form of totalitarianism." Naturalized citizens joining communist organizations within five years of acquiring CITIZENSHIP were liable to have it revoked.

The courts subsequently held invalid the passport, registration, and employment sections of the act. Section 103, establishing detention centers for suspected subversives, was repealed in September 1971.

PAUL L. MURPHY

Bibliography

HARPER, ALAN 1969 *The Politics of Loyalty: The White House and the Communist Issue, 1946–1952.* Westport, Conn.: Greenwood Press.

INTERNATIONAL EMERGENCY ECONOMIC POWERS ACT
91 Stat. 1625 (1977)

This act grants the President limited economic powers "to deal with any unusual and extraordinary threat . . . to the national security, foreign policy, or economy of the United States" which arises "in whole or substantial part outside the United States" and which is declared by the President to constitute "a national emergency." The primary purpose of the act, however, was to restrict the Trading With the Enemy Act of 1917, under which the President had come to enjoy large discretionary power during times of declared emergency.

The 1977 act limits the authority created by declaration of a national emergency to an instant threat only and removes the President's authority to exercise during peacetime certain economic powers available in time of war. It also obligates the President to "consult" with Congress, if possible, prior to the declaration of a national emergency, to report on the circumstances said to necessitate the extraordinary measures, and to report to Congress every six months on the exercise of powers under the act.

Although the act permits the termination of a declared national emergency by concurrent resolution of Congress, the decision in IMMIGRATION AND NATURALIZATION SERVICE V. CHADHA (1983), declaring the use of the LEGISLATIVE VETO unconstitutional, places this restraint in doubt. In sum, however much Congress may have intended to restrict presidential EMERGENCY POWERS over international economic transactions, the actual extent of the change is uncertain.

BURNS H. WESTON

(SEE ALSO: *Dames & Moore v. Regan,* 1981; *Foreign Affairs; War Powers; War Powers Resolution.*)

Bibliography

HENKIN, LOUIS 1972 *Foreign Affairs and the Constitution.* Pages 118–123. Mineola, N.Y.: Foundation Press.

NOTE 1978 Presidential Emergency Powers Related to International Economic Transactions: Congressional Recognition of Customary Authority. *Vanderbilt Journal of Transnational Law,* 11:515–534.

INTERPOSITION

State governments have occasionally declared that acts of Congress are unconstitutional and have sought to "interpose" their authority between their citizens and the national government. This interposition has taken several forms, from refusals to cooperate with federal administration to the purported NULLIFICATION of federal acts, SECESSION, and even armed rebellion. JAMES MADISON and THOMAS JEFFERSON lent their prestige to the general notion of interposition when they wrote, respectively, the VIRGINIA AND KENTUCKY RESOLUTIONS in opposition to the ALIEN AND SEDITION ACTS of 1798. New England Federalists claimed powers of interposition in opposition to trade embargoes and the federal use of state militias during the War of 1812. Acting on the state sovereignty theory of JOHN C. CALHOUN in 1832, South Carolina declared two tariff acts "null, void, and no law." Antislavery legislatures enacted PERSONAL LIBERTY LAWS to obstruct federal fugitive slave laws. Long after the Civil War, southern legislatures attempted "massive resistance" to school DESEGREGATION. And in 1970 Massachusetts sought to prohibit the conscription of its citizens for the VIETNAM WAR.

Although these and other attempts express no single constitutional philosophy, interposition is usually associated with the theory that the sole basis of the Union is the written Constitution, not a common culture or other integrative forces; that the people who created the Constitution were members of separate and still sovereign states, not a national community; and that the Constitution is a mere contract among the states for establishing a general government with but few, well-defined objectives. From these premises it was supposed to follow that individual states could interpose to protect their reserved powers. To Calhoun and his followers in the 1830s interposition included nullifying federal laws and, in extreme cases, secession. The nullificationists cited the Virginia and Kentucky Resolutions and presented their position as consistent with the Constitution. Madison, then in his eighties, bitterly opposed and sought to disclaim paternity of any nullificationist theory. He insisted that his original version of interposition sanctioned no more than nonbinding state expression of constitutional opinion as steps toward arousing the public or amending the Constitution. This kind of interposition was fully consistent with national supremacy, the divisibility of sovereignty between nation and states, and a perpetual union. The nullificationists, said Madison, were asserting a RIGHT OF REVOLUTION, not a constitutional right.

Scholars point out that an extended constitutional debate would hardly have been necessary in the 1790s if all that Madison had then contemplated was a state's right to express and invite other states to express nonbinding opinions. But, Madison's candor aside, his final version of interposition need not have been toothless. The history of interposition shows that the states' role in the AMENDING PROCESS gives even the nonbinding opinions of a small number of states a special potential for awakening public interest in constitutional questions and undermining the perceived legitimacy of national policy. Practiced with sufficient regularity by enough states, the tamest kind of interposition might have had a strong influence on the pace and direction of constitutional change.

SOTIRIOS A. BARBER

(SEE ALSO: *Theories of the Union.*)

Bibliography

CORWIN, EDWARD S. 1912 National Power and State Interposition. *Michigan Law Review* 10:535–551.

KILPATRICK, JAMES JACKSON 1957 *The Sovereign States: Notes of a Citizen of Virginia.* Chicago: Henry Regnery Co.

INTERPRETIVISM

See: Constitutional Interpretation

INTERSTATE COMITY

See: Full Faith and Credit; Privileges and Immunities

INTERSTATE COMMERCE

The term "interstate commerce" does not appear in the Constitution. Nor do the few debates in the CONSTITUTIONAL CONVENTION OF 1787 over the wording of the COMMERCE CLAUSE offer much help in discerning what the Framers meant by granting Congress the power to regulate commerce "among the several states." The absence of expressed specific intent led WILLIAM W. CROSSKEY to examine contemporary usage and to theorize that the national power over commerce was intended to be virtually exclusive and to include not only interstate commerce but INTRASTATE COMMERCE as well. One of the Framers' intentions was to eliminate the destructive conflicts between contradictory state practices under the Confederation government. Chief Justice JOHN MARSHALL so assumed when he defined the term in GIBBONS V. OGDEN (1824), a case that has guided interpretation to this day. Interstate commerce, he wrote, is that "which concerns more states than one" and it even extends "to those internal concerns which affect the states generally." In the nineteenth century the clause was more often applied as a restriction on state powers than as a positive grant of national power, and as EDWARD S. CORWIN remarked, "the word 'commerce,' as designating the thing to be protected against State interference, long came to dominate the clause, while the potential word 'regulate' remained in the background." In HOUSTON, EAST & WEST TEXAS RAILWAY V. UNITED STATES (1914), the Court expanded the reach of congressional power by permitting federal regulation of purely intrastate commerce because, in the railroad case before it, the two were inextricably linked.

The scope of the commerce clause has encouraged the Court to devise a number of tests throughout its history to determine limits to the term, the best known of which is the STREAM OF COMMERCE DOCTRINE. (See also SELECTIVE EXCLUSIVENESS, EFFECTS ON COMMERCE, and SHREVEPORT DOCTRINE). The Supreme Court has thus held that "interstate commerce" means both movement that crosses state lines and movement that does not but that adversely affects interstate commerce. It includes tangible items as well as intangible ones. In *Gibbons,* Marshall defined it as "commercial intercourse," but even this expansive reading has been widened. *Caminetti v. United States* (1917) is only one of many cases in which the Court decided that no commercial motive need be present. Moreover, movement itself is not essential; in WICKARD V. FILBURN (1942), Justice ROBERT H. JACKSON disdained semantic formulas and declared that agricultural PRODUCTION affects interstate commerce. Such a broad view of the commerce power has allowed Congress to regulate not only traditional SUBJECTS OF COMMERCE but also criminal activity, professional sports, antitrust cases, and RACIAL DISCRIMINATION.

DAVID GORDON

Bibliography

STERN, ROBERT L. 1955 The Scope of the Phrase *Interstate Commerce. American Bar Association Journal* 41:823–826, 871–874.

INTERSTATE COMMERCE ACT
24 Stat. 379 (1887)

This act, which initiated federal authority in ECONOMIC REGULATION, created an administrative commission to wield federal power. Congress's approach, in Isaiah Sharfman's words, was "tentative and experimental" because doubts existed whether the government could so act. The legislation nevertheless marked a first attempt to organize an increasingly chaotic field.

Until the 1870s railroads had been free to expand and operate, essentially unregulated, yet encouraged by land grants and public subsidies. As speculation, rate discrimination, and other abuses increased, popular opinion grew correspondingly negative. State legislatures, especially in the Midwest, began setting maximum rail rates and establishing commissions to maintain their reasonableness. Although the Supreme Court sustained such regulation in the GRANGER CASES (1877), it soon retrenched and, in WABASH, ST. LOUIS & PACIFIC RAILWAY V. ILLINOIS (1886) the Court asserted the states' inability to regulate rates even partly interstate. The Court thus created a vacuum—the states could not regulate and Congress had not regulated.

Compromise legislation finally passed Congress in 1887, the outcome of over 150 bills in nearly twenty years. The act applied to "any common carrier or carriers engaged in the [interstate or foreign] transportation of passengers or property," and specifically exempted INTRASTATE COMMERCE. Reiterating the COMMON LAW, the act ordered all charges to be "reasonable and just." The act created the INTERSTATE COMMERCE COMMISSION (ICC), empowered it to set aside unjust rates, but neglected to give it the power to replace them with new ones. The ICC also had authority to investigate complaints; significantly, an individual need not demonstrate direct damage to file a complaint. Several sections forbade devices such as rebates, pooling, and LONG HAUL–SHORT HAUL DISCRIMINATION. The act also required publication of rate schedules, rendering the carriers liable for injuries sustained as a result of any violations. Courts were to consider ICC findings *prima facie* EVIDENCE but commission orders became effective immediately *only* if voluntarily obeyed. Carriers took advantage of this loophole to APPEAL virtually every order, leaving them free to disregard the ICC until a court sustained it. Demanding to hear cases *de novo,* the courts implicitly invited the carriers to withhold evidence from the ICC; courts reversed ICC orders regularly on both legal and policy grounds. As Sharfman noted, the commission's powers were thus "restricted in scope and feeble in effect." In 1897 the Supreme Court dealt the ICC two stunning blows. Even though the act had not expressly granted the ICC rate-setting authority, the commission had assumed the power. In INTERSTATE COMMERCE COMMISSION V. CINCINNATI, NEW ORLEANS & TEXAS PACIFIC RAILWAY, the

Court denied the commission this power. *ICC v. Alabama Midland Railway Co.* (1897) rendered the long haul–short haul clause a dead letter.

In part because of the judicial evisceration of the act, Congress amended it nearly a dozen times by 1925. Among the most important supplementary legislation were the ELKINS ACT, the HEPBURN ACT, and the MANN-ELKINS ACT. The Supreme Court endorsed Congress's efforts in several cases, culminating in INTERSTATE COMMERCE COMMISSION V. ILLINOIS CENTRAL RAILROAD (1910).

DAVID GORDON

Bibliography

HOOGENBOOM, ARI and OLIVE 1976 *A History of the ICC: From Panacea to Palliative.* New York: W. W. Norton.

SHARFMAN, ISAIAH L. 1931 *The Interstate Commerce Commission.* Vol. I. New York: Commonwealth Fund.

INTERSTATE COMMERCE COMMISSION

See: Regulatory Commissions

INTERSTATE COMMERCE COMMISSION v. ALABAMA MIDLAND RAILWAY COMPANY

See: *Interstate Commerce Commission v. Cincinnati, New Orleans & Texas Pacific Ry. Co.*

INTERSTATE COMMERCE COMMISSION v. CINCINNATI, NEW ORLEANS & TEXAS PACIFIC RAILWAY
167 U.S. 479 (1897)
INTERSTATE COMMERCE COMMISSION v. ALABAMA MIDLAND RAILWAY COMPANY
168 U.S. 144 (1897)

As one of Justice JOHN MARSHALL HARLAN's dissents in these cases declared, these decisions stripped the Interstate Commerce Commission (ICC) "of authority to do anything of an effective character." The ICC succeeded in only one APPEAL to the Supreme Court between 1897 and 1906. The INTERSTATE COMMERCE ACT required "reasonable and just" rates and, although it gave the commission the right to set aside unreasonable rates, it did not expressly grant them power to revise rates. The ICC had operated for a decade on the assumption that it had had such power; without it, the statute's injunction to provide reasonable rates could hardly be accomplished. In *ICC v. Cincinnati, New Orleans & Texas Pacific Railway* (1897) the Court majority insisted that if the act's framers had intended to grant them such powers, they "would have said so." The act provided no explicit authority, however, and the extent of the power militated against "such a grant . . . by mere implication." If the commission exercised such rate-making powers, it would have been making law and it had only the power to "execute and enforce, not to legislate." Such a quasi-legislative DELEGATION OF POWER could not yet secure approval from the Court; denied power to set rates, the commission now had only the right (of questionable use) to void unreasonable rates. Justice Harlan dissented from that decision as well as from Justice GEORGE SHIRAS's opinion in *ICC v. Alabama Midland Railway Company* (1897), decided a few months later. That case nearly destroyed the LONG HAUL–SHORT HAUL provision in the act as well as the commission's fact-finding authority. Despite unequivocal language declaring the ICC findings of fact to be conclusive and binding on courts, Shiras decided that the clause empowering CIRCUIT COURTS to hear appeals necessarily implied a right of the courts to reexamine all the facts; they could not overrule the commission in both law and fact. By not presenting all EVIDENCE until an appeal, the railroads could and soon did mock ICC orders. These decisions severely restricted the commission's usefulness; not until the HEPBURN ACT of 1906 and the MANN-ELKINS ACT of 1910 would Congress move to revive the commission.

DAVID GORDON

INTERSTATE COMMERCE COMMISSION v. ILLINOIS CENTRAL RAILROAD
215 U.S. 452 (1910)

The HEPBURN ACT of 1906 and a decision by the Supreme Court the following year began reviving the Interstate Commerce Commission (ICC) after a series of devastating decisions. The Court had denied the commission the power to revise rates in INTERSTATE COMMERCE COMMISSION V. CINCINNATI, NEW ORLE-

ANS & TEXAS PACIFIC RAILWAY (1897), and had struck hard at the provision of the INTERSTATE COMMERCE ACT outlawing LONG HAUL–SHORT HAUL DISCRIMINATION in *Interstate Commerce Commission v. Alabama Midland Railway Co.* (1897). The Court reversed ICC orders on both legal and policy grounds at an astonishing rate, and the commission spent nearly the first twenty years of its existence fighting Court-imposed obstacles.

The Interstate Commerce Act had declared that ICC findings were to be considered *prima facie* evidence but until 1907 the Court, in fact, reviewed all evidence *de novo,* thereby allowing the railroads to present previously withheld EVIDENCE on APPEAL. This practice discredited the commission and put the Court in the business of rate regulation. In *Illinois Central Railroad Company v. Interstate Commerce Commission* (1907), the Court declared that it would no longer reexamine the facts of a case on appeal; the commission was a responsible tribunal and its findings of fact would be accorded "probative force."

Because of the passage of the MANN-ELKINS ACT and a favorable 8–1 decision in *Interstate Commerce Commission v. Illinois Central Railroad,* 1910 was a good year for the ICC. In this case the Court indicated its willingness to support the commission, laying down its guidelines for the determination of the validity of ICC orders. The Justices expected to continue to review commission orders, but solely in reference to constitutional issues, statutory construction of "the scope of the delegated authority" under which the ICC issued the order, and the practical "substance" of the order. Nevertheless, the Court henceforth specifically refused "under the guise of exerting judicial power, [to] usurp merely administrative functions by setting aside a lawful administrative order upon our conception as to whether the administrative power has been wisely exercised. Power to make the order and not the mere expediency or wisdom of having made it is the question."

DAVID GORDON

INTERSTATE COMPACT

The Constitution, in Article I, section 10, recognizes the right of the states to enter into compacts and agreements with one another, but provides that the right shall not be exercised without the consent of Congress. In this respect, the Constitution continued the practice that had obtained under the ARTICLES OF CONFEDERATION. The right to enter into compacts and agreements is, as the Supreme Court said in *Hinderlider v. La Plata Company* (1938), the survival under the Constitution of "the age-old treaty-making power of independent sovereign nations."

Before 1921, most interstate compacts involved two (or at most three) states, and were either about boundaries or about boundary streams. One notable exception was the Chesapeake and Ohio Canal Compact (1825), involving Virginia, Maryland, Pennsylvania, and the District of Columbia, providing for joint incorporation of the canal company and mutual acceptance of legislation in its favor. Another was the Virginia-West Virginia Compact (1862) by which seceding Virginia agreed to the creation of West Virginia from part of its territory while the latter assumed part of the state debt.

The modern era of interstate compacts began with the New York Port Authority Compact (1921) and the Colorado River Compact (1923). The former created a single commission, jointly appointed by New York and New Jersey, to administer the Port of New York and the surrounding area. The latter was the first true multistate compact, allocating irrigation water among six states drained by the Colorado.

The success of these two agreements led politicians and scholars to see in interstate compacts a great potential for solving multistate problems without national legislation. FELIX FRANKFURTER and JAMES M. LANDIS, in an influential article published in 1925, advocated "imaginative adaptation" of the device to reach a multitude of subjects they deemed beyond the scope of congressional power under the Constitution, such as the generation and distribution of electricity. Buoyed by this public optimism, states proposed open-membership compacts on subjects such as WORKERS' COMPENSATION and child labor. Experience, however, demonstrated that interstate compacts were not a panacea for the ills of FEDERALISM, and, although the number negotiated steadily increased, after the 1930s compacts were confined to more narrowly interstate matters. This is true even of compacts to which all the states are parties, such as the Interstate Compact for Supervision of Parolees and Probationers.

Compacts between states are somewhat more binding than treaties between sovereign nations, because the states are subject to the CONTRACT CLAUSE, and, within the limits of the ELEVENTH AMENDMENT, the obligations imposed by interstate compacts are enforceable in federal courts.

On its face, the Constitution seems to require congressional consent to all interstate compacts and agreements. However, in *Virginia v. Tennessee* (1893) the Supreme Court held that a boundary agreement of 1802 had received Congress's consent through acquiescence because, although it never voted to approve the agreement, Congress followed its terms in such matters as establishing judicial districts. The court reasoned that only compacts touching on the powers of the national government or substantially affecting intergovernmental relationships within the federal system required explicit congressional approval. On the other hand, Congress may veto *any* compact or agreement, even if the states would have been fully competent to act in the absence of the compact.

When explicit approval is required, it may be given either before or after the compact is negotiated by the states. But the failure of Congress to enact a resolution of consent is not equivalent to a denial of consent: it may signify no more than that Congress believes its explicit consent to a particular compact is unnecessary.

DENNIS J. MAHONEY

Bibliography

FRANKFURTER, FELIX and LANDIS, JAMES M. 1925 "The Compact Clause of the Constitution—A Study in Interstate Adjustments." *Yale Law Journal* 34:685–729.

ZIMMERMANN, FREDERICK L. and WENDELL, MITCHELL 1951 *The Interstate Compact Since 1925.* Chicago: Council of State Governments.

——— 1976 *The Law and Use of Interstate Compacts.* Chicago: Council of State Governments.

INTIMATE ASSOCIATION

See: Freedom of Intimate Association

INTOLERABLE ACTS

See: First Continental Congress

INTRASTATE COMMERCE

The CONSTITUTIONAL CONVENTION OF 1787, by listing among Congress's enumerated powers the power to regulate commerce "among the several states" as well as with Indian tribes and foreign countries, appeared to reserve for regulation by each state its own domestic commerce. Indeed, notwithstanding Chief Justice JOHN MARSHALL's dictum that commerce does not stop at the state line but penetrates into the interior, for most of American constitutional history Congress respected and the Supreme Court enforced that division of power over commerce. After WICKARD V. FILBURN (1938), the distinction between intrastate and INTERSTATE COMMERCE effectively ceased to have any significance in constitutional law.

DAVID GORDON

INVALID ON ITS FACE

Legislation may be unconstitutional as applied to all, some, or none of the behavior it addresses. Usually, affected parties challenge a law's constitutionality only as applied to their own behavior. Occasionally, they claim a law is constitutionally invalid on its face—and therefore unenforceable against anyone, including them—because it would be unconstitutional ever to apply it. A penal law is invalid on its face, for example, when it so vaguely describes the conduct outlawed that it cannot give fair warning to anyone, or when every act the law prohibits is constitutionally protected. A challenge to such a law would present no STANDING problem. Sometimes, however, a litigant will assert that, regardless of whether a law is constitutional as applied to him it should be held invalid on its face because its coverage includes unconstitutional regulation of others.

Normally a federal court will deny standing to raise such a facial challenge when the law constitutionally regulates the would-be challenger, for the court perceives the claim as a request to go beyond the case before it. Responding to the request would require the court to decide what other situations the law governs—frequently an unresolved question of statutory interpretation—and then to decide whether some of the law's unapplied coverage would be unconstitutional. If the court should conclude that part of the law is invalid and part valid, it would have to decide whether the legislative framers would want the valid part to stand separately or the whole law to fall. Finally, if the law is constitutional as applied to the litigant, but would be unconstitutional in hypothetical application to others, the court may still have to decide whether to hold the law facially invalid despite a legislative desire to have the law's valid applications stand.

Formidable considerations militate against judicial rulings that laws are facially invalid. JUDICIAL REVIEW originates in the need to apply constitutional law to decide the case before the court, and a corollary principle requires courts to refrain from deciding hypothetical questions. When a court focuses only on the situation before it, it minimizes the need for unnecessary decisions of issues of both statutory and constitutional interpretation, and avoids considering other possible applications of the law in a factual vacuum. Finally, a conclusion of facial invalidity would prevent the valid enforcement of the law against a party whom the legislature intended to regulate. Normally, then, the Supreme Court denies a litigant STANDING to assert the unconstitutionality of legislation as it would be applied to others, except when the most compelling reasons are present.

The reason most often found compelling is the need to protect the freedom of expression of persons not before the court whom the law might inhibit. That was the rationale, for example, of THORNHILL V. ALABAMA (1940). Specifically, the FIRST AMENDMENT doctrines of OVERBREADTH and VAGUENESS sometimes permit one whose conduct the law constitutionally could reach to escape punishment, arguing that the law is invalid on its face because its seeming application to others discourages their protected expression. Intense controversy surrounds these facial challenges, however, largely because of differing perceptions of how inhibiting such laws really are. In areas involving other fundamental freedoms, such as the RIGHT TO TRAVEL, facial challenges have occasionally been successful, as in APTHEKER V. SECRETARY OF STATE (1964), again to protect persons who are never likely to be before a court from having their liberty circumscribed by the seeming applicability of an unconstitutional regulation.

A court will hold a law invalid on its face only in a case of necessity: where the law's very existence may affect the exercise of cherished liberties by nonparties lacking opportunity or willingness to challenge them, and where the inhibiting feature of the law cannot easily be cured by statutory interpretation. Absent such conditions federal courts will not, at the request of one whose behavior may constitutionally be regulated, decide how a law might apply and whether the law's potential application to other situations warrants holding it invalid on its face. The degree to which the Supreme Court permits facial challenges to legislation directly reflects the Justices' collective perception of the Court's institutional role in enforcing the Constitution. Narrow views of that role incline the Court to restrict facial challenges; a broader view commends it to entertain and encourage such a challenge in the interest of assuring the constitutional governance of society beyond the immediate case.

JONATHAN D. VARAT

INVASION OF PRIVACY

See: Right of Privacy

INVERSE CONDEMNATION

The course of action which a property owner may pursue against a governmental defendant to recover the JUST COMPENSATION guaranteed by the Fifth and FOURTEENTH AMENDMENTS when the defendant, without initiating an eminent domain proceeding, "takes" private property is called "inverse condemnation."

The elements of a compensable TAKING OF PROPERTY can occur under many different circumstances. An action to establish inverse condemnation is clearly proper when a governmental entity has destroyed, confiscated, or substantially abridged some right or privilege in the plaintiff's property or when the normal operation of governmental facilities results in a destructive interference with the use of the plaintiff's property by third persons, as by jet aircraft noise. Excessive regulation, resulting in an effective prohibition of substantially all use and value of the interest regulated, may also constitute a taking.

The most intractable issue in inverse condemnation litigation currently relates to regulatory takings. Although government may carry out many types of programs that adversely affect economic values without its actions constituting a taking, in some contexts POLICE POWER regulations may be so restrictive in character as to constitute a compensable taking, as in *Pennsylvania Coal Co. v. Mahon* (1922). However, no "set formula" has been developed for determining when a legislative measure has adversely affected property interests to that degree. The relative magnitude of the loss sustained by the property owner is relevant but not controlling. Factors suggestive of a taking, however, include the extent to which the government's actions have impaired legitimate investment-backed expectations of the owner and the fact that the regulation has resulted in an uncompensated acquisition of resources by the public entity. (See PENN CENTRAL TRANSPORTATION CO. V. NEW YORK CITY, 1978.) Factors often relied upon to negate a taking include the existence of widely shared compensating benefits resulting from the restrictions and the reflecting in the regulation of a rational legislative choice between mutually incompatible private interests.

Inverse condemnation jurisprudence is also complicated by uncertainty, so far not resolved by the Supreme Court, as to the scope of the relief available for regulatory takings. In many cases, for example, *Pennsylvania Coal Co.*, the taking rationale has been invoked to invalidate excessive regulatory action; in others, an award of monetary compensation has been granted. In *San Diego Gas & Electric Co. v. City of San Diego* (1981), four Justices, with a supporting dictum from a fifth, intimated that when a taking is enjoined, compensation for interim losses sustained by the property owner should be granted. And when overriding public interest so requires, governmental action that effects a taking may even be declared valid, subject to the payment of just compensation to those persons whose property has thereby been taken. (See DAMES & MOORE v. REGAN, 1981.)

Some commentators have argued, and a few courts have held, that the exclusive remedy for a regulatory taking is invalidation of the offending measure. These decisions generally reflect judicial reluctance to impose onerous burdens that could interfere with orderly fiscal planning by governmental agencies engaged in regulatory functions. They appear to be based on the questionable assumption that invalidation will necessarily be less disruptive to the achievement of public objectives than payment of compensation. As Justice WILLIAM J. BRENNAN suggested in *San Diego Gas & Electric Co.*, a more appropriate remedial posture would permit the governmental entity to choose whether to repeal the offensive regulation with payment of compensation for temporary losses or to retain it in force with payment of full compensation.

ARVO VAN ALSTYNE

Bibliography

MICHELMAN, FRANK I. 1967 Property, Utility, and Fairness: Commentaries on the Ethical Foundations of "Just Compensation Law." *Harvard Law Review* 80:1165–1258.

SAX, JOSEPH L. 1973 Takings and the Police Power. *Yale Law Journal* 74:36–76.

INVESTIGATIVE POWER

See: Legislative Investigations

INVIDIOUS DISCRIMINATION

Justice WILLIAM O. DOUGLAS led the Supreme Court's modern expansion of the guarantee of EQUAL PROTECTION OF THE LAWS. As early as 1942, in SKINNER v. OKLAHOMA, Douglas used the term "invidious discrimination" to differentiate state-imposed inequalities demanding strict judicial scrutiny from other discriminations (particularly economic regulations) that were valid so long as they had a RATIONAL BASIS. The word "invidious," which suggests a tendency to provoke envy or resentment, is an appropriate label for governmental discriminations imposing the stigma of caste, especially RACIAL DISCRIMINATIONS. Fittingly, Douglas used the same label in LEVY v. LOUISIANA (1968) to describe discrimination based on the status of ILLEGITIMACY.

In HARPER v. VIRGINIA STATE BOARD OF ELECTIONS (1966), Douglas termed "invidious" the state's use of a POLL TAX as a condition on voting. As a WEALTH DISCRIMINATION case, *Harper* fit the dictionary definition of "invidious." In another view, however, *Harper* required STRICT SCRUTINY because the state impaired the FUNDAMENTAL INTEREST in voting. In this perspective, "individious discrimination" broadens into a label for the Court's ultimate conclusion on the issue of an equal protection violation. For Justice Douglas, either use of the term was acceptable.

In more recent racial discrimination decisions, the Court has turned the dictionary meaning of "invidious" upside down, using it to denote not the tendency of a discrimination to provoke ill will, but the malevolent purpose of government officials. In WASHINGTON v. DAVIS (1976), for example, the Court held that a law's racially selective impact did not demand strict scrutiny, absent a showing of "invidious discriminatory purpose." The language of constitutional doctrine, like the language of diplomacy, stands ready to serve causes both fair and foul.

KENNETH L. KARST

Bibliography

KARST, KENNETH L. 1969 Invidious Discrimination: Justice Douglas and the Return of the "Natural-Law–Due-Process Formula." *UCLA Law Review* 16:716–750.

INVOLUNTARY SERVITUDE

See: Peonage; Slavery and the Constitution

IREDELL, JAMES (1751–1799)

James Iredell was one of the most active and important members of the United States Supreme Court during the 1790s. Although he was a strong nationalist and vigorous advocate of judicial power, he also was a political realist who understood, in a way that his contemporaries on the High Court did not, the widespread distrust of centralized government and an independent judiciary that existed in America following the American Revolution.

Iredell was the eldest son of a well-connected but financially troubled merchant from Bristol, England. When his father suffered a paralytic stroke, his mother's family, in 1768, arranged for him to become comptroller of the customs in Edenton, North Carolina. While performing his duties, Iredell studied law with Samuel Johnston, a leading member of the North Carolina bar, whose sister he married in 1773. Although he remained in the service of the king until the spring of 1776, his real sympathies were with the colonists, and after independence he became a firm supporter of the patriot cause. Following the break with England he served on a committee to revise old laws and draft new legislation to make government in North Carolina compatible with republicanism. He also helped create a judiciary system for the state, and reluctantly accepted an appointment as a Superior Court judge, a position from which he resigned after six months because he disliked riding circuit. In 1779 he was appointed attorney general of North Carolina.

In the sharp struggle that took place over the writing of a state constitution, Iredell sided with the more moderate and conservative Whigs who favored as few changes as possible from the old colonial form of government and wanted to see an independent judiciary, a strong executive, and property qualifications for voting. And in the political struggle of the 1780s, Iredell aligned himself with those who favored the enforcement of contracts, opposed debtor relief legislation, and defended the rights of Tories as protected by the Paris Peace Treaty of 1783. He denounced a number of laws adopted in the mid-1780s to confiscate Loyalist property, and in "An Address to the Public" in 1786 expressed his belief in the need for limitations upon the authority of the legislature: "I have no doubt but that the power of the Assembly is limited, and defined by the Constitution. It is the creature of the Constitution." Iredell further elaborated on how unbridled legislative authority could be checked in an August 26, 1787, letter to RICHARD DOBBS SPAIGHT, a delegate to the CONSTITUTIONAL CONVENTION, which contained one of the earliest and clearest theoretical expressions of the doctrine of JUDICIAL REVIEW: "I confess it has ever been my opinion that an act inconsistent with the Constitution was void; and that the judges consistently with their duties, could not carry it into effect. The Constitution appears to me to be a fundamental law, limiting the powers of the legislative, and with which every exercise of those powers must, necessarily, be compared."

Iredell was a warm proponent of the adoption of the United States Constitution in 1787–1788, even though the opposition to it was particularly intense in North Carolina. In fact, North Carolina at first refused to ratify the Constitution, and did not accept the new government until November 1789, eight months after it had begun operations. During the course of the debate over ratification Iredell published a pamphlet entitled "Answers to Mr. [George] Mason's Objections to the New Constitution," which attracted national attention. In February 1790, President GEORGE WASHINGTON, recognizing Iredell to be a firm friend of the central government, appointed him to the United States Supreme Court.

Although Iredell continually complained about the hardships entailed in riding circuit, he performed his duties conscientiously and participated in almost all the important cases of the 1790s. Despite the fact that his various decisions were knowledgeable in the law, intelligent, and forcefully presented, it is not easy to classify Iredell according to the political and intellectual currents of his day. To be sure, as a Federalist he supported ALEXANDER HAMILTON's financial program, JAY'S TREATY, and the ALIEN AND SEDITION ACTS. Moreover, his opinions in *Penhallow v. Doane's Administrators* (1795) and HYLTON V. UNITED STATES (1796) had strong nationalist implications, and in CALDER V. BULL (1798) he reiterated his belief in judicial review. He also argued in behalf of an independent judiciary by taking strong exception to an attempt by Congress to require the Justices of the United States Supreme Court to serve as pension commissioners. But Iredell's experiences with North Carolina politics made him not only aware of but also sensitive to the jealousy of the states for their rights and the popular hostility that existed toward the federal judiciary. He thus dissented when the Supreme Court ruled against the state of Georgia in a suit brought by a citizen of South Carolina in CHISHOLM V. GEORGIA (1793). Iredell argued that the decision would be viewed as a dangerous assault upon the sovereignty of the states. His fears were well founded, for the protests against the decision were so widespread and intense that the ELEVENTH AMENDMENT to the Constitution was quickly adopted to deny jurisdiction to the federal courts in suits brought against a state by the citizens of another state or by foreigners. He also dissented in WARE V HYLTON (1796) when the High Court declared invalid a Virginia statute of 1777 sequestering pre-Revolutionary debts of British creditors. Although ultimately upheld and enforced, the decision, as Iredell recognized, was the source of much popular dissatisfaction.

RICHARD E. ELLIS

Bibliography

GOEBEL, JULIUS, JR. 1971 *History of the United States Supreme Court: Antecedents and Beginnings to 1801.* New York: Macmillan.

MCREE, GRIFFITH J., ED. 1857 *Life and Correspondence of James Iredell.* New York: D. Appleton.

IRREBUTTABLE PRESUMPTION

Virtually any statutory classification can be seen as an irrebuttable presumption. A law forbidding automobile driving by anyone under sixteen may be described as a conclusive presumption that younger persons are unfit to drive—a presumption that is not universally true. The irrebuttable presumptions DOCTRINE was never applied to strike down an age classification, but its reasoning would have served: the law arguably denied PROCEDURAL DUE PROCESS by denying an individualized hearing on the fitness to drive of a person under sixteen. For a brief season in the mid-1970s, the Supreme Court was fond of this sort of analysis, but the infatuation soon ended.

The doctrine was foreshadowed in Chief Justice HARLAN FISKE STONE's concurrence in SKINNER V. OKLAHOMA (1942), which invalidated an Oklahoma law requiring the STERILIZATION of three-time felons. The Court rested on the EQUAL PROTECTION clause, but Stone argued that the law denied due process by denying a hearing on the inheritability of the defendant's criminal traits. He might have called the law an irrebuttable presumption of the inheritability of criminal traits of three-time felons. We can speculate that Stone thought the sterilization law was an irrational deprivation of liberty, but he was disinclined to revive SUBSTANTIVE DUE PROCESS so soon after the Court had tried to lay that doctrine to rest.

When, a generation later, the Court explicitly invoked the irrebuttable presumptions theory, one contributing factor surely was a similar wish to avoid resting decision on another theory. In the mid-1970s the Court was struggling with the question whether sex, like race, should be characterized as a SUSPECT CLASSIFICATION for purposes of equal protection analysis. (See FRONTIERO V. RICHARDSON, 1973.) In two cases, the Court avoided that issue by resorting to irrebuttable presumptions analysis. *Stanley v. Illinois* (1972) invalidated a law providing that the children of an unwed father became wards of the state upon the death of the mother. The law was attacked on SEX DISCRIMINATION grounds, but the Court escaped that issue, holding that the law violated due process by denying Stanley an individualized hearing on his fitness as a parent. Similarly, in CLEVELAND BOARD OF EDUCATION V. LAFLEUR (1974), a school board insisted that a pregnant teacher take maternity leave of several months before the expected birth of her child, and the Court avoided the sex discrimination issue by calling the law an irrebuttable presumption of unfitness to teach during the months of mandatory leave. The denial of a teacher's right to a hearing on her individual fitness was held to deny procedural due process.

The Court's strongest articulation of the irrebuttable presumptions doctrine came in VLANDIS V. KLINE (1973), which invalidated a state law conclusively presuming that a person who was a nonresident upon entering a state college remained a nonresident (for tuition purposes) throughout his college career. It violated due process to deny resident tuition rates on the basis of this presumption which was "not necessarily or universally true."

The irrebuttable presumptions doctrine was severely criticized both within and outside the Court. It was accurately seen as an equal protection or substantive due process doctrine in disguise, demanding the strictest sort of STRICT SCRUTINY of the necessity of legislative classifications. The Court plainly could not invalidate all classifications resting on factual assumptions "not necessarily or universally true." By 1975, the Court had had enough. In *Weinberger v. Salfi* (1975) the Court considered an antifraud provision of the SOCIAL SECURITY ACT allowing death benefits to a surviving spouse only when the couple had been married nine months before the decedent's death. A widow claimed benefits even though she had been married a shorter time, noting that her husband had died of a sudden, unexpected heart attack. The law was an excellent candidate for irrebuttable presumptions reasoning, but the Court blandly upheld it on grounds of administrative convenience. The whole doctrinal development had run its course in four terms of court.

KENNETH L. KARST

Bibliography

NOTE 1974 The Irrebuttable Presumption Doctrine in the Supreme Court. *Harvard Law Review* 87:1534–1556.

IRVIN v. DOWD
366 U.S. 717 (1961)

The Supreme Court ordered a new trial for a convicted mass murderer in Indiana on the ground that extensive pretrial coverage of the case by newspapers and radio had made it impossible for him to receive a FAIR TRIAL, even after one change of VENUE to a nearby county. In his opinion for the Court, Justice TOM C. CLARK noted that two-thirds of the jurors had been familiar with the facts of the case and believed Irvin to be guilty of the crimes. Justice FELIX FRANKFURTER used this occasion for one of his patented denunciations of overzealous reporting in criminal cases.

MICHAEL E. PARRISH

IRVINE v. CALIFORNIA
347 U.S. 128 (1954)

California police installed a listening device in a bedroom. Although this action violated fundamental constitutional principles protecting personal security, the Supreme Court held that under WOLF V. COLORADO (1949) the unconstitutionally obtained EVIDENCE could be used; the bedroom microphone did not sufficiently "shock the conscience," under ROCHIN V. CALIFORNIA (1952), to warrant exclusion.

HERMAN SCHWARTZ

ISLAND TREES BOARD OF EDUCATION v. PICO

See: *Board of Education v. Pico*